The Robert J. Wickenheiser Collection of

John Milton

at the University of South Carolina

Original drawing of John Milton, ca. 1730, by Jonathan Richardson the elder (1665–1745), with Richardson's stamp on right margin, sepia drawing of the blind Milton "from a model of Milton in clay. Coll[ection] of Mr. G. Vertue" (on the back). The engraver and antiquary George Vertue (1684–1756) also owned the drawing known as the Faithorne portrait, now at Princeton.

The
ROBERT J. WICKENHEISER COLLECTION
OF

John Milton

AT THE
UNIVERSITY OF SOUTH CAROLINA

*A Descriptive Account
with Illustrations*

ROBERT J. WICKENHEISER

THE UNIVERSITY OF SOUTH CAROLINA PRESS

*Published in Cooperation with the
Thomas Cooper Library, University of South Carolina*

© 2008 University of South Carolina

Published by the University of South Carolina Press
Columbia, SC 29208

www.sc.edu/uscpress

Manufactured in China

17 16 15 14 13 12 11 10 09 08   10 9 8 7 6 5 4 3 2 1

Library of Congress Cataloging-in-Publication Data

Wickenheiser, Robert J.
 The Robert J. Wickenheiser Collection of John Milton at the University of South Carolina : a descriptive account with illustrations / Robert J. Wickenheiser.
     p. cm.
 "Published in cooperation with the Thomas Cooper Library, University of South Carolina."
 Includes bibliographical references and index.
 ISBN 978-1-57003-723-8 (cloth : alk. paper)
 1. Milton, John, 1608–1674—Bibliography. 2. Thomas Cooper Library—Catalogs. I. Thomas Cooper Library. II. Title.
 Z8578.W63 2008
 [PR3581]
 016.821'4—dc22

2007048837

Permission to print the photograph of "Tablet for the God of Israel" by Robert Medley from Samson Agonistes (1979) has kindly been granted by The Robert Medley Estate.

Endpapers: Front view of the Wickenheiser Milton library

Photos by Carl V. Margeson
3rd Street Studio
Allegany, NY 14706

For Pat, who started me off and gave up much that this might be.
For Bob Taylor, without whom this collection would not be what it is today.
For Bill Richter, whose rare friendship means more than he will ever know.

Contents

Acknowledgments *ix*

Notes and Abbreviations *xiii*

    I. Introduction: The Collection and Its Origins *1*

   II. Descriptive Listing of Editions *33*

  III. Descriptive Listing of Miltoniana *679*

        A. Seventeenth-century Miltoniana *679*
        B. Eighteenth-century Miltoniana *692*
        C. Nineteenth-century Miltoniana (Selected) *708*
        D. Twentieth-century Miltoniana (Selected) *731*

  IV. John Milton in Select Anthologies (Chronologically Listed) *751*

   V. Original Drawings, Illustrations, Engravings, and Other *765*

  VI. John Martin (1789–1854) *793*

 VII. Ephemera and Objets d'Art *801*

VIII. Photographs of Additional Select Items *811*

Appendix: Recent Additions of Note *819*

Bibliography *821*

Index *827*

Acknowledgments

Milton has been the poet for all ages, evident in a collection such as this, which it has been my privilege to gather together, while simultaneously caring for and coming to know and cherish it as I have. This collection represents more than thirty-five years of collecting. It represents the many vacations my family did not have and the many dinners and niceties my wife gave up for a book or books. It represents the amazing support of two extraordinary friends, Robert H. Taylor and Michael Papantonio: Mike during my early and formative years of collecting and Bob Taylor, a very close friend and mentor, who befriended me and my family in untold ways and whose influence in collecting began at the outset and continues to endure. And it represents the support of bookdealers who have been very kind to me over the years and who have cared about ensuring that many of their most special Milton items found a home in this collection.

Without my bookseller friends, my Milton collection would most assuredly be far less extensive and far less inclusive than it is today, and I reiterate my gratitude to each of them again here for their many kindnesses to me through the years; they helped give the collection, and thereby this book, purpose and meaning in enormous ways. My gratitude for their catalogues is also reiterated in my "Notes and Abbreviations," for the education they gave me over the years and for the influence they had on me in providing background information for various Milton books here.

I am particularly grateful to Mike Papantonio, whose rare bookshop Seven Gables Bookshop in New York, was the first rare bookshop I ever visited. I made the visit with Bob Taylor, who invited me to join him on one of his regular excursions to Seven Gables and to meet Mike. The occasion will remain forever memorable to me. From that point on our friendship grew, and Mike made certain that all rare Milton editions and Miltoniana, as well as illustrated Milton editions, made their way to me and my rapidly growing collection.

Without Mike Papantonio, the foundation of my Milton collection would not have been laid as firmly as it was nor with as much breadth and scope had we not worked together as closely as we did over those early years. I hope that I have built well upon the foundation, and that in the continued expansion of the breadth and scope of the collection, I have expressed my gratitude to a dear friend and a giant in the bookworld of yesterday.

Without Bob Taylor's great friendship and support, my Milton collection simply would not be the collection it is today. His enthusiasm, as he would often say, grew from my own enthusiasm for discoveries of Milton I would make. Both Bob and Mike considered my enthusiasm for collecting Milton contagious, and my discoveries the result of serendipity. Before our friendship had formed the unique bond that developed between us, Bob never had any real interest in Milton, surprising as this was to me about someone so widely read; who had such a genuine love of literature; and who could quote virtually any poet, including Milton. Our friendship changed all of that.

My gratitude to Bob has been lifelong, for he taught me more about the love of literature than any teacher did or could; he taught me by example about the love of books and their importance in life and quality of living. My gratitude to Bob remains profound and is expressed, I sincerely hope, in the affection with which I have guided the collection's growth and led its direction to be available for future generations of scholars, students, and book enthusiasts. Bob kept his own great collection of English and American literature and manuscripts together, which he collected over more than fifty years, and it has been kept together at Princeton University for the use of scholars and students. While by no means anywhere near comparable to Bob's distinguished collection, I would like to believe that, among his many influences, he has influenced me to keep my collection together for purposes analogous to his.

I am tremendously grateful and very happy that my collection has found a wonderful home in Rare Books and Special Collections of the Thomas Cooper Library at the University of South Carolina, where it will be kept together as the collection it is, but far more importantly, where it will be available to scholars and students and from time to time to the public through exhibits. A number of individuals played a key role in this happening and though I thank several of them in my introduction, I want to reiterate my gratitude here:

Dr. Roy Flannagan, Scholar-in-Residence at the University of South Carolina at Beaufort after thirty-two years as Professor of English at Ohio University, visited my collection after lecturing at St. Bonaventure University when I was president there. He had the foresight to send the notice that my collection was available to Dr. Patrick Scott, Director of Rare Books and Special Collections and Professor of English, with a cover note supporting the collection and its importance. By pure happenstance, I received a copy of Patrick's email expressing interest, which resulted in our having a long preliminary conversation about the collection.

From the outset Dr. Scott strongly supported the university acquiring my Milton collection, as did Dean Paul Willis, Dean of Libraries, when he learned about the collection from Patrick Scott. Admittedly, timing was difficult, since not only was Paul Willis relatively new as Dean, but he faced a fund-raising deadline for the expansion of rare books and exhibit space in the Thomas Cooper Library. Nonetheless, he joined Patrick Scott in wanting to acquire the collection for the University, and I am most grateful to him for all that he did to help bring my collection to the Thomas Cooper Library.

President Andrew A. Sorensen also became a strong advocate of bringing the collection to the university. Yet he, too, like Dean Paul Willis, faced important university-wide fund-raising deadlines and priorities that demanded his attention. He was gracious in meeting with me and later in having lunch with my good friend William Richter and me. President Sorensen's support for the library acquiring my Milton collection never wavered, and I am truly grateful for that and doubly grateful for his recognition of the significance of the acquisition of the collection in the midst of many other demands made upon him and his time.

I am especially thankful to William L. Richter and the Richter Family Foundation for their generosity in enabling my collection to come to the University of South Carolina. Bill Richter makes things happen, and in this instance, as the close friend he is, he helped to make the seemingly impossible happen. A portion of the Milton collection will be housed in the room named for him in the new addition being built for the University's rare books and special collections. As I say in my introduction: It is an honor for me to be associated with Bill Richter in this special way in the years to come, for he is someone whom I have grown to know and respect as one of the kindest and gentlest of men, about whom there can be no superlatives. He is also that rare friend, warmly caring about matters large and small, and I shall always be profoundly grateful that our names will be linked together in such an extraordinary way, for such an extraordinary purpose: affording students, scholars, and visitors now and in years to come the opportunity to view and study Milton and other features of this collection in the William L. Richter Seminar Room.

I also want to express my deepest gratitude for Bill Richter's personal support and encouragement throughout this project; they have meant more to me than can ever be adequately expressed in words. His many kindnesses to countless others as well as to me have demonstrated again and again what true Franciscan values mean.

While the collection was still in the library my wife Pat and I had built for it in our home in Olean, New York, Dr. John Mulryan, Professor of English and distinguished Board of Trustees Professor at St. Bonaventure University, would regularly bring Milton scholars and other guests to see it. I want to thank him here for that, and also for using his considerable respect as a Miltonist to obtain invitations for me to join him in attending Milton seminars for select Milton scholars, and for a great deal more; I shall always be very grateful to him, one-time Bonaventure colleague and fellow University of Minnesota PhD graduate.

I am deeply grateful to Dr. John T. Shawcross, who has helped and guided me throughout the completion of this book in untold ways. Although "retired," he continues to lecture and write important books, attend seminars, give papers, participate in conferences, help individuals like me, and more. He has contributed substantively to my interest in descriptive bibliography and the important purpose it serves. During his review of my eighteenth-century holdings several years ago, he shared his insights and his vast knowledge about eighteenth-century Milton editions and Miltoniana with me in such a way as to make my descriptions of eighteenth-century editions and Miltoniana far better than they otherwise would have been. He has also answered questions freely and thoroughly about other books whenever I asked him for advice, and I always benefited by asking because of his boundless knowledge of Milton and of publications of Milton's works and about the poet through the centuries.

I want to thank Dr. Oleg Bychkov, Associate Professor at St. Bonaventure University, for kindly providing all of the Russian translations herein.

I owe special thanks to Patrick Scott who helped me in enormous ways. His support for the publication of this book has been strong from the outset; he demonstrated that support again and again whenever I called upon him for assistance. He helped to make this book better than it otherwise would have been and I am most grateful to him and always will be. I am also very grateful to two wonderful members of his staff: Elizabeth Sudduth, Head of Special Collections Processing and Services, for her ready response whenever I turned to her for help, which was often; she is a jewel in a very special place; and Jeffrey Makala, Assistant Librarian, for his gracious assistance in helping to obtain information I needed, never easy to find but always obtained by this wonderful and very dedicated young man.

A project as complex as this requires a team of experts to prepare it for publication. I was fortunate to have such a team in everyone at Scribe, Inc. I want especially to thank Stacy Claxton, Composition Assistant and director of this project, whose oversight helped to ensure everyone meeting deadlines in a relatively short time frame, always with an emphasis on quality. I want also to thank Yvette M. Chin, Composition Assistant, who worked meticulously through over 950 pages of my text. Her suggestions were invaluable, and her efforts more deeply appreciated than she will ever know; the book is far better because of her good work.

For bringing the package together I want to thank Curtis L. Clark, Director of the University of South Carolina Press. He has cared about publishing this book since we first talked about it, and I want to thank him and his colleagues at the press, particularly Pat Callahan, Design and Production Manager, for their dedicated efforts in bringing closure and in doing so in the best tradition of the University of South Carolina Press.

Someone special who deserves my heartfelt gratitude is my nephew, Donald A. Keller. For more than twenty-five years Don has been a highly recognized medical illustrator whose specialty is ocular surgery illustration. At my request he designed my bookplate for the collection, shown at the end of the introduction.

I would like to express particular gratitude to Carl V. Margeson, 3rd Street Photography Studio, Allegany, New York, for the wonderful photographs of the collection shown within this book. We worked together for more than three weeks, long days each, so that Carl could take over eight hundred photographs, from which the three hundred or so photographs in this book have been selected. Carl's professionalism as well as his patience were always present, and he never hesitated to take yet another picture if I requested it or one was needed, later working meticulously for long hours to ensure that the pictures were shown here in their highest quality. My thanks also to Kamrooz Sanii, MD, for the earlier photographs he took which were used in a variety of helpful ways.

I want to acknowledge and thank in a special way some very close friends and supporters of me and of the publication of this book. Their encouragement and support have meant a great deal to me and have helped to make this book a better publication than it would otherwise have been. Their friendship has meant more to me than I can possibly say and will continue to be invaluable to me in the years ahead. Some I have known since serving as president of Mount St. Mary's University, Maryland, from 1977 to 1993 and some since serving as president of St. Bonaventure University from 1994 to 2003; in each instance it has been my great blessing and good fortune to have our paths cross and friendship develop and continue through the years. I hope that this publication indicates a portion of the gratitude I feel and shall always feel toward these very dear friends.

> Priscilla Cunningham and Jay LickDyke
> Bettie and George Delaplaine
> Lynne and Joseph Horning
> Carole and Robert Jones
> Pat and Louis Magnano
> Kay and John Meisch
> Ilonka and Emile Nakhleh
> Kathleen and James O'Hara
> Jan and Peter O'Malley
> JoAnn and John Rooney
> Lynn and Michael Shane
> Fr. Francis Storms, OFM

I am also very grateful for the commitment and support of the University of South Carolina Libraries in helping to bring the collection to the University and in contributing to the publication of this book.

To thank my wife, Pat, for her constant support, understanding, and encouragement is far too little, but thank her I do, for without her this Milton collection would not exist, and as we have shared in everything else, so she shares in this collection. If collecting is an addiction, and most assuredly it is, then Pat began mine by taking me on jaunts to estate sales to find nineteenth-century editions of writers I was reading and studying while in graduate school. My addiction only grew from then on, with Pat feeding it by happily stopping at bookshops on any trip we took and always mapping routes with bookshops on trips, no matter how far out of the way the book shop might happen to be. We became one in collecting as we have become one in life together for forty years, and Pat has shared my joy in finding a rare Milton as much as I have. Together we are thrilled that the collection now belongs to the University of South Carolina and that it will be housed together in the new Rare Books and Special Collections Wing of the Thomas Cooper Library, for use by students and scholars and where the public will have an opportunity from time to time to view its varied holdings in various exhibits.

Notes and Abbreviations

Descriptive Terminology

Titles are given in full as they appear on the title page, including the publisher's imprint. Books are described fully with vital information and other special features provided; for example, format, number of pages, the edition of the book, if known (i.e., first, second, etc.), illustrations, decorations, facsimiles, large paper copy, and a description of the binding. An endeavor is made to identify first as well as later editions, when known. A "First edition?" with a question mark indicates that there is considerable probability that this is a first edition based on the number of editions in the collection and other contributing factors. The first or earliest edition contains information about later editions and references to other editions in the collection.

A title on the spine or cover that differs from the title of the book on the title page is given in parentheses: for example, ("Poems" or "Works") when the title is *Poetical Works*; or ("Milton") when the title is *Poems*; or ("Poetical Works") when the title is *Complete Poetical Works*.

Signatures are by no means easy to understand, especially in books in which signatures are not always indicated, as is often the case in the late nineteenth and twentieth centuries. Self-taught to recognize and understand the various book formats, with generous assistance along the way from friends who really do understand them—in particular John Shawcross, to whom I am especially indebted for giving so freely of his time—I have endeavored to be as accurate as possible in providing book formats, recognizing such nuances as octavo in fours or duodecimo in sixes, and even books that are sixteenmo and more rarely, eighteenmo. As this collection affords students interested in Milton an opportunity to study him as he was appreciated and printed through the ages, so too it allows for appropriate corrections to be made if and when called for in the format of a book as I might have seen it, or not seen it, as the case might be. I welcome corrections of any mistakes I might have made, knowing that I was taught sufficiently well to correct mistakes where I least expected them, leading me to make this caveat: when in doubt, check signatures yourself, and check them carefully.

The following are some of the more common signatures:

- Folio (2°): a very large, tall book, page size determined by folding the sheet two times
- Quarto (4to, 4°): a book essentially squarish in shape but varying in size, with page size determined by folding the sheet four times, roughly equivalent to a modern telephone directory

- Octavo (8vo, 8°): a book size most commonly known today; page size determined by folding the sheet eight times—roughly equivalent to a modern 6" x 9" trim size
- Duodecimo (12mo, 12°): also called a twelvemo; page size determined by folding the sheet twelve times; customarily a small size book—roughly equivalent to a modern 5 ½" by 8 ½" trim size.

The most useful reference for book terminology has long been John Carter's classic *ABC for Book Collectors*. This has been revised and expanded, with a new introduction by Nicolas Barker, and is available from Oak Knoll Press in New Castle, Delaware.

Bibliographic References

Reference to rareness and scarcity is premised on sources when available, on scholar friends like John Shawcross, on reliable booksellers, and on my own experience of thirty-five years of collecting Milton. If I have not seen an edition in a bookshop or in a catalogue or at auction, or one has not been offered to me since I started collecting Milton in the early 1970s, I feel fairly confident that that edition is scarce, even rare. The rarity of some editions is indicated by the relatively few copies that have been cataloged by libraries in one or other of the major online cataloging consortia, such as the Online Computer Library Center (OCLC) or the Research Library Information Network (RLIN).

In all seventeenth- and eighteenth-century editions and Miltoniana, reference is made consistently to K. A. Coleridge's *Descriptive Catalogue of the Milton Collection in the Alexander Turnbull Library* (Oxford: Published for the Alexander Turnbull Library, National Library of New Zealand, by Oxford University Press, 1980) because of the significance of this work and its scholarship in its presentation of seventeenth- and eighteenth-century Milton editions and Miltoniana in the Turnbull Library (WTu) in Wellington, New Zealand, through to 1975. (Cited as Coleridge; references are to numbers, not pages.)

Reference is also made consistently in the editions through to 1914 to *The Catalogue of the Kohler Collection of John Milton* (Dorking, Surrey: C. C. Kohler, 1993), which is an important catalogue for the inroads it makes with respect to nineteenth-century editions of Milton's works in particular as well as other important works by Milton in that collection. The Kohler collection ends in 1914; it also has no Miltoniana, and so no reference is made to Kohler in editions later than 1914 or throughout the Miltoniana listings. Kohler gives regular notice of an edition missing in the Milton holdings in the British Library, the Bodleian Library, and Cambridge University Library; these notices are cited here. (Cited as Kohler; references are to numbers, not pages.)

D. H. Stevens's *Reference Guide to Milton from 1800 to the Present Day* (Chicago: University of Chicago Press, 1930) is also referenced, although not consistently and without referencing items not listed by Stevens as with Coleridge and Kohler. As valuable a reference as Stevens is—and given that editions are bound to go unrecorded in as broad a period as his bibliography covers—there is no consistency in whether or not Stevens will comment on or critique an edition, even important editions, although contemporary reviews are frequently cited; more often than not, an edition is listed without comment, very often without format, and often without number of pages. My guiding principle for citing Stevens is the importance of commentary Stevens provides on a given edition, and then only for certain editions, depending on the continuing value of what Stevens comments on, the significance of the edition itself, the importance of the edition in relation to other editions and its impact on a period, or in helping to date or define the importance of still other editions at the time and from a passing perspective. (Cited as Stevens; references are to numbers, not pages.)

Reference is made on a regular basis to W. R. Parker's *Milton: A Biography* (Oxford: Clarendon Press, 1968) and to several vital bibliographical works by John T. Shawcross:

- *Milton: The Critical Heritage* (London: Routledge & Kegen Paul, 1970; New York: Barnes & Noble Inc., 1970)—cited as Shawcross, 1970; references are to pages.
- *Milton, 1732–1801: The Critical Heritage* (London: Routledge & Kegen Paul, 1972)—cited as Shawcross, 1972; references are to numbers, not pages.
- *Milton A Bibliography For the Years 1624–1700* (Binghamton, N.Y.: Medieval & Renaissance Texts and Studies, 1984)—cited as Shawcross, 1984; references are to numbers, not pages.
- *The Collection of the Works of John Milton And Miltoniana in the Margaret I. King Library University of Kentucky Compiled by John T. Shawcross With a Foreword by Thomas B. Stroup.* Occasional Paper No. 8. (Lexington: University of Kentucky Libraries, 1985)—cited as Shawcross, Kentucky; references are to numbers, not pages.
- "A Survey of Milton's Prose Works," appendix in Michael Lieb and John T. Shawcross, eds. *Achievements of the Left Hand: Essays on the Prose of John Milton* (Amherst: University of Massachusetts Press, 1974)—cited as Shawcross, 1974; references are to pages.

Other important bibliographies, reference works, and catalogues are also referenced regularly and as warranted. Their bibliographical information is provided in the bibliography.

While it is not my intention to make reference in my descriptive listings to important Milton collections in America, let me state here that important collections of Milton and Miltoniana are located at the University of Illinois (surely the most important collection in this country), Harvard University, the Newberry Library, the University of Kentucky, Indiana University, the New York Public Library, Yale University, Princeton University, the Morgan Library, and the Folger Shakespeare Library; also the Huntington Library, the Clark Library, the University of Michigan Library, and the Harry Ransom Library at the University of Texas. Along with the Turnbull Library in Wellington, New Zealand, there are also very important Milton and Miltoniana collections at the University of Western Ontario Library in London, Ontario, and at the Bibliothèque Nationale in Paris, along with the British Library, the Bodleian Library in Oxford, and the Cambridge University Library. It is also not my intent by any means to indicate rarity by location, or to indicate libraries in which a given copy of a rare edition of Milton is located. I intend only to locate a rare book with any consistency by way of reference to Coleridge and to Kohler; other references to location are provided very sparingly and only when known, and without any attempt on my part to try and identify additional locations. This is simply not an intent of mine, nor of this book, and I wish to offend no one by occasionally referring to a location, when certainly there are other locations among the great libraries in our country.

I have learned much from bookdealers over the years. My learning has come from being privileged to be part of lively conversations about books, especially among dealers in London and New York, many of whom were giants in their day as I discuss in my introduction; and it has come from catalogues that have arrived regularly in my mail over the past thirty-five years. I have leaned a great deal from these catalogues, and I have always been very grateful to receive them, even when I did not buy something from them. I also owe much to the catalogues and to the bookdealers who compiled them, for at times I have taken freely from them in providing background information for various Milton books here. In drawing freely from one bookdealer's catalogue or another's, I have discovered how knowledgeable and even scholarly many are, and in my eclectic reading over the years I have come to appreciate the range and scope of knowledge bookdealers bring to their catalogues. I am grateful to bookdealers for the useful and important information their catalogues provide, which I have at times freely incorporated into my descriptions here, giving credit whenever I am able. If I can no longer recall the source, I sincerely hope that my heartfelt expression of gratitude here and elsewhere will be accepted in the spirit in which it is given, with genuine gratitude to bookdealers for the privilege of being educated over many years in ways that have been truly unique. Their catalogues remain indeed a wonderfully pleasurable source of being exposed to and learning about riches that open doors to new glories in a world at once both old and new.

Finally, it is noteworthy to add that the collection is being made available online and kept up-to-date by Rare Books in The Thomas Cooper Library. Entries for individual items in the collection, along with other Milton items in the library's holdings, are available in the library's online catalogue at http://www.sc.edu/library/catalog. These entries include locations, as well as cross-references to the item numbers used in this catalogue and standard Milton bibliographies. The online catalogue is fully searchable within descriptions: by using the online catalogue's advanced search and limiting the search to items in Rare Books, it is possible easily to list items, for example, by a particular publisher, artist, illustrator, engraver, binder, or binding.

Abbreviations Used for Milton's Works

When used, the following abbreviations, in italics, represent Milton's works:

A (*Areopagitica*)
Ar (*Arcades*)
C (*Comus*)
CEP (*Complete English Poems*)
CP (*The Complete Poems*)
CPty (*Complete Poetry*)
CPW (*Complete Poetical Works*)
CPW of JM (*Complete Poetical Works of John Milton*)
CSP (*The Complete Shorter Poems*)
EMP (*English Minor Poems*)
EngP (*English Poems*)
EP (*Early Poems*)
HB (*History of Britain*)
IlP (*Il Penseroso*)
L (*Lycidas*)
L'A (*L'Allegro*)
LP (*Latin Poems*)
Misc (*Miscellanies*)
MP (*Minor Poems*)
NO (*Nativity Ode*)
O (*Odes*)
Of Ed (*Of Education*)
On S (*On Shakespeare*)
On U Carrier (*On the University Carrier*)
OP (*Other Poems*)
P (*Poems*)
PL (*Paradise Lost*)
PR (*Paradise Regained*)
Psm (*Psalms*)
PW (*Poetical Works*)
S (*Sonnets*)
SA (*Samson Agonistes*)
Trans (*Translations*)

I
Introduction

The Collection and Its Origins

Robert J. Wickenheiser, PhD, in his library

This is a book about a collection put together based on a deep-seated affection for the poet John Milton and a love of books. It is a descriptive bibliography of an extensive collection of Milton editions and Miltoniana gathered together over thirty-five years. My first focus was on illustrated works of Milton through the ages in order to understand what different ages and cultures saw in Milton as reflected in the eyes of their artists and illustrators, from the first illustrated edition of *Paradise Lost* to the present. Over time I endeavored to gather together as many editions of Milton published through the centuries as possible; therefore, books are described with respect to their look as well as their content, and some three hundred photographs have been provided to bring the collection as visually alive as possible.

A collection as large as this one has become over the years shows just how admired a poet Milton has been through the ages. For example, during the Romantic period in the early nineteenth century, perhaps more illustrated editions of Milton's works were published in different formats than of any other poet. Such a collection shows the ongoing excitement through the centuries that has made Milton one of the two most published English authors. A collection as diverse as this also shows how much of an icon Milton has become, seen in his appearance on medals as early as the eighteenth century and as recently as a 1984 Russian medal; on brass plaques of all sizes and ages; on variously dated nineteenth- and twentieth-century tobacco cards; on busts and statues of all sizes and kinds from all periods; and even on a 1920s cameo plaque.

The collection contains over 6,000 books and Milton-related items in total, with some 3,450 editions and some 800 Miltoniana from all centuries, including rarities in seventeenth- and eighteenth-century Miltoniana. While certainly not everything can be included for listing or even mentioned here, an endeavor has been made to provide a selective presentation that captures the essence of the collection in all of its dimensions. This book provides a full recording of all seventeenth- and eighteenth-century editions, along with the great majority of nineteenth-century editions, and all the important twentieth-century editions, including previously unrecorded editions from both periods, but especially from the nineteenth century.

All collections have a beginning; mine had two. I first began collecting while working on my master's degree and then my doctorate with Leonard Unger at the University of Minnesota from the fall of 1966—having previously been a Benedictine monk for four years in Assumption Abbey in Richardton, North Dakota—to the spring of 1970. Textbooks were expensive, and my wife, Pat, introduced me to local estate sales, where a writer's complete works could be had for a very modest cost and often in a fine binding. Since I was especially interested in poetry, regular jaunts to local estate sales produced great finds of my favorite seventeenth-century poets in nineteenth-century editions, usually complete, always reasonable, and more often than not, in attractive bindings that were in fine condition.

Soon our estate searches became something we looked forward to more than anything else. Although perennially broke (what graduate student is not!), we managed somehow to save a little for our regular estate sale visits; Pat, in search of any inexpensive treasure she might find for our apartment and future home, always kept an eye out for books that might interest me, often tempting me with books far removed from my current studies. Meanwhile, I hunted for books to buy according to three broadly defined principles: (1) they belonged to poets within "my canon" of poets, particularly George Herbert, on whose Latin poems I was doing my doctoral dissertation and whose Latin poems could not at the time be found complete except in a nineteenth-century edition I discovered at an estate sale; (2) they were affordable, or more preferably still, cheap; and (3) they touched my heart and just had to be bought, which made me realize that I was becoming addicted to books in a way I had never imagined possible.

I continued collecting in this manner through to my appointment to the faculty at Princeton University after completing my PhD in 1970. Several good things happened to me at Princeton to introduce me to a whole new world of collecting and the wonderful people in it. Soon after my arrival, a colleague of mine and I were asked by the department of English to represent the department at a dinner hosted by Mary Hyde (noted collector and scholar, widow of Donald Hyde, and later Viscountess Eccles) for the International Bibliophile Society at Four Oaks Farm in Somerville, New Jersey.

The setting could not have been more pleasant, nor the hostess more perfect. Fortunately I had had the pleasure of meeting Mary Hyde once before, after a gathering of the department's Council of Advisors on which she served. She welcomed everyone to her home with unequaled charm and invited all to visit the library and to view the rare treasures on display from the greatest Samuel Johnson collection in the world, now at Harvard in a room named after Donald and Mary Hyde.

We all wore name tags. Pat had dinner with someone whom she remembers fondly to this day as the remarkable self-described "ball bearing king" of Germany. I sought a familiar face but found none. I did, however, find someone who had "Princeton Library" written under his name, and I felt that this was as safe a person as I could possibly dine with; someone who would speak English and from whom I could learn something about much that was still very new to me at Princeton, while expecting little more of me than my views of the English department and the library. We sat together near large doors that opened to the patio and began having a lively conversation about books and collecting. The longer we talked and dined together, the more comfortable I felt in his presence and in opening up to him. Therefore, when he asked me what I collected, I readily answered, "seventeenth-century poets," failing to add, "in nineteenth-century editions." The evening progressed as one of those most memorable of memorable evenings; I introduced my new acquaintance, Bob, to my wife, Pat, and together we viewed the library and exhibits, which he knew very well and which he gladly told us about in such wonderful and enlightening detail. As the evening drew to a close, Bob invited me to visit his room in the Firestone Library. I told him I would be delighted to do so and to view his collection with him.

Only later as we were leaving Mary Hyde's did I learn that Bob was the distinguished collector whose remarkable collection of English and American literature was housed in the Robert H. Taylor Room in Firestone Library on campus; the acclaimed president of the Friends of the Princeton Library; the noted Grolier Club member who was then serving as president; and more. He was not merely "someone" from the library, as I had assumed from his name tag and an impression he cared little about correcting.

On our drive home, I told Pat about my collecting statement to Bob, and we both knew that I would have to clarify what I meant by it, lest he think I was in competition with him. When I next met Bob in the Taylor Room, after being overwhelmed by his collection, I clarified what I meant when I said that I collected seventeenth-century poets, having failed to add the qualification "in nineteenth-century editions." He then said he was very happy to hear this because he had gone home that evening uneasy that here was yet another collector he had to worry about bidding against for poets he too coveted for his collection.

For someone who had never seen a rare book until graduate school, and then only very sparingly, Bob's room was a veritable "Solomon's Mine" of rare books. Bob was enormously generous in showing his books to me and in allowing me to handle them freely, which I did with loving care. Over the next six years, he allowed me to teach in his room in the library and to show certain books to my students, who, like me before them, had never seen a rare or even an "old" book; often Bob would show his books to the students' and my own great delight. Bob and I went on to spend many hours in his room taping his remembrances of select books: where and when he got them; why he got them; how much he paid for them; what his relationship was with the bookdealers from whom he got his books and manuscripts; and anything else he cared to say about a given book. Bob even agreed to teach a seminar on his books in the Princeton Adult School, where I was president for a number of years and where I also enjoyed teaching a variety of courses, including one on Milton and the power of his poetry

Bob frequently invited me to join him on book trips to New York, and on these trips my collection had its second and most serious beginning. These full-day trips to New York centered around a visit to Michael Papantonio of Seven Gables Bookshop at 3 West Forty-sixth Street, a very close friend of Bob's and in a very short time my close friend as well. These trips allowed me to learn of a book world that can only be described as part of a great golden age, then still very much alive in collectors like Bob Taylor, Bradley Martin, Mary Hyde, Waller Barrett, and others, as well as in booksellers like Michael Papantonio and his colleagues John Kohn and John Brett-Smith at Seven Gables; John Fleming, formerly with the late Dr. A. S. W. Rosenbach; and many others, both in the United States and abroad, some of whom I would have the good fortune of meeting while forming my Milton collection. Many collectors, at one time or another, made their way to Seven Gables, and many were taken to lunch regularly at the nearby Miramar restaurant for priceless conversations about books, auctions, collectors, dealers, and how things had changed from days gone by.

Regular trips from Princeton to New York allowed me to learn much about collecting, collectors, and booksellers from Bob Taylor. I could have had no better mentor! Regular attendance at luncheons hosted by Mike Papantonio afforded me the opportunity to learn still more about these same topics from different perspectives and in the context of different times and settings. The neophyte was becoming more and more aware of why the collector collects and what it means to find just the right book, as well as what the bookseller means to the collector. The collector Bob had told me always to trust the bookseller and never to haggle over price; the dealer Mike showed me the merit in always following these principles; and both would be my sponsors to the New York Grolier Club in 1979. I have lived by those principles ever since, realizing only too well that without the bookseller, it is impossible to put together any kind of collection, much less one of distinction.

On one of our book trips to New York in early 1974, while Bob was still president of the Grolier Club, we stopped by the club because Bob had some business that needed his attention. He told me he knew I would be happily entertained with the present exhibition, and indeed I was very delighted with the exhibition entitled "John Milton: The Poet Illustrated," made up primarily of books in the Leonard B. Schlosser collection. Bob returned, apologizing for being away for well over an hour. He was surprised to see me still where he had left me: viewing John Martin's illustrations of *Paradise Lost*. Martin's illustrations had so captivated me that I had been unaware of how long Bob had been gone. Today Martin forms a collection unto himself within my Milton collection, deserving a section with photographs in this book. I told Bob that I had gotten no farther than Martin, near the very beginning of the exhibit, and together we viewed the rest of the exhibit. From that moment on, Bob influenced my growth as a collector in a way that was profound and lasting. It is truly amazing how important that day ultimately turned out to be.

When I first arrived at Princeton in the fall of 1970, Milton scholar Maurice Kelley invited me to serve as preceptor in his Milton course. Upon his retirement in 1972, I became the Milton lecturer at Princeton for several years until a known Milton scholar could be appointed. I very much enjoyed teaching Milton; I also enjoyed collecting him, and while I had "collected" Milton before that day at the Grolier Club with Bob Taylor, I knew then that I wanted to collect Milton in earnest. Seeing the Schlosser exhibition at the Grolier Club excited me about the prospect of collecting illustrated editions of Milton in order to see Milton as he was seen by the artists and illustrators through the ages. I wanted to see which of Milton's poems or lines in a poem inspired an artist enough to warrant being illustrated and why. And I wanted to see how the illustrations changed from period to period, century to century.

Fortunately Leonard Schlosser decided to make his collection available to others the following year; even more fortunately for me, he decided to sell his collection through Mike Papantonio with a published catalogue, which also had a supplement by Seven Gables. The books were all shelved together for viewing at Seven Gables. View them I did, trip after trip. Slowly, with the support of Bob and the understanding of Mike, I managed to acquire many books from the Schlosser collection—all of the illustrated editions and many of the finer and rarer books—which now form the nucleus of my collection. My purpose in collecting was defined by the exhibit, and the sale helped to solidify my resolve.

Four years after viewing the Schlosser exhibition at the Grolier Club, in 1978, totally unexpected by me, I was accepted into the The New York Grolier Club, with Bob Taylor and Mike Papantonio as my sponsors.

Going on at the same time as the Schlosser sale was the Hanrahan sale of his Milton collection. Perhaps his sale accounted for the Schlosser sale not moving any faster than it did, thereby allowing me time to purchase key items over a longer period of time than was originally anticipated by either Leonard Schlosser or Mike. I also managed to obtain some important items from the Hanrahan sale, and I only wish I could have acquired more from his collection, which was quite spectacular; however, I am grateful for the number of items I did absorb into my collection, including several fine Martin proof plates.

Maintaining my resolve to collect illustrated editions of Milton was difficult in many ways, but particularly financially. I never could have amassed such an extensive collection without the help of some very important people. Mike was always kind to me in ensuring the growth of my Milton collection by pricing books he found for me at prices I could afford and by allowing me to pay for books over a period of time. Pat kindly agreed that any additional money, earned by teaching in the Princeton Adult School and additional lecturing or saved from grants I received, could be used to buy books—not to mention money she made working overtime as a nurse at the Princeton Medical Center. At times, for that very special book, Bob lent his support or surprised me on my birthday or at Christmas.

From trips to New York with Bob, we moved on to trips abroad. The first trip abroad involved Bob, Pat, and me in Venice, then Florence, and finally London for book hunting. Bob wanted us to enjoy a portion of "the grand tour" with him as it was intended to be experienced and enjoyed in years gone by. Any book trip to London is centered around the June book fair, as was ours. Little did I know that this was to be the beginning of many more delightful June trips to London in search of books wherever they might be found: trips with Bob and Mike, until Mike died in 1979, and then with Bob and Alexander Wainwright, Associate University Librarian for Collection Development at Princeton University, until Bob died in 1985.

As with trips to New York, so with trips to London, the books I sought were essentially Milton; also Herbert because of my initial and ongoing commitment to him; and occasionally books that simply touched my heart and were reasonably priced, as was often the case at some of the out-of-the-way bookshops and antique markets or hypermarkets, as some were called. Books seemed plentiful; through Mike and Bob, I met dealers in the book world I would not otherwise have met, and I was able to obtain books I would otherwise never have been able to add to my collection. Visits to bookshops were visits with longtime friends and involved leisurely conversation about the current state of book affairs and friends, pending auctions, and "Oh! By the way, I happen to have something you might like to see. . . . " I learned much by listening to these conversations, sometimes browsing the stacks nearby at the same time. Frequently there were invitations to long lunches, where conversation continued, and sometimes invitations to drink hundred-year-old port at distinguished establishments such as the Garrick Club. Evenings were most often reserved for theatre, which I grew to love and anticipated with increasing enthusiasm from year to year.

Visits began by seeing Dudley Massey of Pickering & Chatto, who was an old friend of Bob's and Mike's, and who was generous with his time and in sharing his knowledge with me about books I took from his shelves at a rather rapid pace. Before long we became friends and a number of rarities in my collection today came from Dudley at prices I am well aware he reduced for me because of his long-standing friendship with Mike and Bob, perhaps even because of my enthusiasm for books and for Milton. Among the rarities and gems that Dudley generously helped to make a part of my Milton collection today is most notably the 1688 folio, first illustrated edition of *Paradise Lost* in contemporary black morocco (#607 in Chapter II), described in detail within the listings. I had long admired this book as it stood majestically above Dudley's desk. Each time I asked Dudley about it he simply stated that it was not for sale—who could blame him for not wanting to part with this magnificent book? In our June 1980 visit to London, shortly before Dudley died, he sent word from the hospital to the bookshop that the book was to be sold to me. Just another of many instances of the value of the bookdealer and the wisdom of placing one's trust in the dealer.

Other early visits to London included two of London's oldest bookselling establishments, Maggs Bros., at 50 Berkley Square, and Quaritch, at 5–8 Lower John Street, Golden Square. Both are bookshops that I would neve r have entered on my own and did not while on fellowships in England in 1969, 1971, and 1972. With Bob I discovered the wonder of these bookshops; the friendliness of everyone in them; and the remarkable books that grace their shelves.

At Maggs it was primarily Bryan Maggs with whom I had dealings, following Bob and Mike in this regard, since he was responsible for English literature. Bryan is also a highly regarded binder, and I admired several of his bindings firsthand on various of our visits to 50 Berkley Square. It would be impossible to mention here all of the truly splendid and remarkable books in my collection that have come from Maggs and now help to make the collection as distinctive as it is, such as the 1906 Lyceum Press edition of *Paradise Lost* (#1351 in Chapter II)—one of a few printed on vellum, bound in blue morocco by the Doves Bindery, described in detail within the listings—or the 1843 first edition of *Poetical Works* by Tilt and Bogue—with engravings by William Harvey, in two volumes, printed as a special set on India paper, bound in fine contemporary full blue morocco, reportedly one of only two such sets, described in detail within the listings (#1901 in Chapter II).

Because of Mike I often was allowed into places off limits to the general public, such as the basement of Maggs, where I would lose myself in rows of books while everyone sat and talked upstairs, forgetting that I was among "treasures" not yet intended for public viewing or sale. One such treasure found in the basement now in my collection and very rare (though how rare was unknown to me at the time) is *The Cabinet Of Genius* (London, Printed for C. Taylor, 1787–[90]) (#347 in Chapter II*)*. In volume 2 are two beautiful engravings for *L'Allegro*. Upon seeing these illustrations, I knew that I had to have this set, since everything about it was right: it was old (eighteenth century), bound in leather, in splendid condition, and it had two fine engraved illustrations for a poem by Milton; the set is described in detail within the listings. When I brought it upstairs along with several other Milton treasures I had found, Bryan readily parted with everything but this set, observing, "Now that's something rare! How did you find it?" But he knew it was going to a good home, and he even priced it accordingly. Without it, my collection would certainly not be what it is today. The special relationship with a bookseller once again! Bryan continued to provide me with superb and rare Milton editions and Miltoniana throughout the years.

At Quaritch Arthur Freeman, specialist in English literature, and Nicholas Poole-Wilson, specialist in continental literature, along with Joan Wintercorn and several other young colleagues, always welcomed us warmly. As with Maggs, it would be virtually impossible to mention all of the superb books that have come from Quaritch over the years that help to make this Milton collection as distinctive as it is. During visits to the shop accompanied by long lunches, I learned much about the book world past and present, and it was a rare pleasure for me to be a part of the these luncheons at that time, as it was to be a part of Mike's luncheons at the Miramar restaurant in New York. Much as I wanted to obtain books, I also wanted to listen and learn, for I realized only too well that this was a special time in my life as well as a special time in the world of books. I hoped to absorb as much as I could, while also buying as much as I could for my growing Milton collection. The rarities on the shelves of Quaritch, Maggs, or Pickering & Chatto were just that: rare. To let them get away would mean perhaps never seeing them or their kind again.

Arthur Freeman's knowledge was superior in a great many fields, not just in English literature—although this was his designated field of expertise at Quaritch. Listening to him and Bob in discussion was an experience from which one could only learn a great deal: from Arthur because of his vast reservoir of knowledge of a great many works, authors, and related topics; from Bob because of his lively intellect and love of books, which he not only collected but also read extensively, and from which he could readily quote at random. While listening, I would view the shelves, or review books I had already put aside or which Arthur had shown me. Many times Arthur lowered the price to help me add a very rare item to my collection, which he continued to do throughout the years. One such rarity is the 1727 octavo edition of *Paradise Lost* rebound quarto size in two volumes with copious annotations in the neat eighteenth-century hand of an educated reader or possible editor on the quarto leaves bound next to each octavo page and illustration (#623 in Chapter II). Another rarity from Quaritch—which I managed to persuade Nicholas Poole-Wilson to pass along to my collection literally as he was returning with it from the auction at which he had just acquired it—is the 1740 octavo edition of *Il Paradiso Perduto*, with splendid illustrations by the great Venetian artists, in original speckled paper over thin boards, in remarkable condition, about which Nicholas told me: "For every ten 1742 folio editions you see, scarce as that edition is, you see only one of this 1740 edition," described in detail within the listings (#639 in Chapter II). Nicholas was more than happy to see the set find its home in my collection. Being in the right place at the right time is every collector's dream and is clearly demonstrated here, but having a bookdealer who is responsive and with whom you have a relationship built upon respect comes first or else it makes little difference who you are or where you are at any given time.

With Mike there was no day off while he was with us in London. Auctions were still new experiences for me, and each Sotheby's auction was exciting as I watched bookdealers bid against one another with the various strategies each used to buy a book, most often for a client, sometimes for stock, depending on price. Sundays were entirely different. Since virtually everything was closed in London, a car and driver were engaged for well-planned journeys into the provinces to see dealers who welcomed us with open arms. I recall well very pleasant visits, often with lunches, with Charles Traylen in his bookshop in Guilford; with Arnold Muirhead in St. Albans; with Nigel Traylen when he was at Beeleigh Abbey outside London; and with John Manners when he headed Blackwell's Rare Books at Fyfield Manor in Abingdon—all with wonderful book-buying results for my collection, not to mention meeting new friends who were especially kind in welcoming me to the world of books.

And what a rich and exciting world this was. At Charles Traylen's Bookshop in Guilford, there always seemed to be books for me, since his stock included literature with editions from all periods, more often than not in attractive bindings, and with prices to match—just my choice of bookshops. On an early visit I managed to find not only several attractive editions of Milton in the open shelves, but in the vault I came across the first edition of *Paradise Lost*, with sixth title page, reasonably priced (#602 in Chapter II). I found Mike and Bob, and we all agreed that I had indeed made a rare find and that Mike should quickly conclude the purchase because of his relationship with Charles. In no time at all the purchase was completed, and upon my request the book was wrapped for my personally carrying it away. Such a find as this I was determined to carry home with me. The decision turned out to be the right one since shortly afterward, when we were all back in the States, Mike was notified that another buyer was claiming first right of purchase and wanted the book returned. When I asked Mike and Bob about what I should do, they said that I owned the book and was under no obligation to return it. I followed their advice, as I always did, grateful that I had carried the book home with me rather than leaving it to be posted.

Another of our Sunday excursions took us to Beeleigh Abbey just outside London, where we had the good fortune of discovering that Nigel Traylen, son of Charles Traylen, was then in charge of The Abbey's Rare Books. He kindly allowed us to view the books that still needed to be sorted. While I was madly dashing from one area to another searching for Milton and hoping for wonderful finds at reasonable prices, Pat kept urging me to look at a book she was sure was important. After continual prodding, I finally joined her, and there, at the bottom of a number of books, upside down in a red case was the 1792 French edition of *Le Pardis Perdu* with color illustrations by Jeano-Frédérick Schall (#775 in Chapter II). The volume is bound in a rich red morocco binding designed for Ferdinand-Louis-Phillipe, with the book label of J. R. Abbey, all described in detail within the listing. Pat gently and rightly reminds guests that I well might not have this great treasure were it not for her, and I always readily concur, smiling as I recall that very special day with her, Mike, and Bob, and our drive through the countryside of England to an abbey very different from the one to which I had once belonged.

Sometimes Mike and I would roam off on our own, to E. Joseph on Charring Cross Road, where I acquired some superb books in the back room because of Mike's presence, and to Cecil Court, a small courtyard filled with small bookshops, each with a specialty, although always worth dropping in for a look since one never knew what might be found regardless of the stated specialty. Mike wanted especially to visit H. M. Fletcher, who was a legend among booksellers, had been at 27 Cecil Court for many years, and had also been a long-time friend of Mike's. On one occasion in June 1977, Mike wanted to go to Fletcher's shop, the first small bookshop on the right as you entered Cecil Court from Charring Cross Road. I was particularly excited about joining Mike because when our trip began Mike had asked me what I had hoped to find this time, and without missing a beat I had answered: "the leaf from the 1632 Shakespeare folio with Milton's sonnet 'On Shakespeare.'" Both he and Bob laughed at my naiveté. I knew, though, that if I was ever going to find this leaf, it was most likely going to be at a place like Fletcher's, especially in his basement; and if anyone could get me into his basement, I knew Mike could.

Without saying anything, I asked for Mike's help in gaining entrance to Fletcher's basement. Long and narrow as the shop above it, and dimly lit, I made my way to a stack of loose leaves and started the slow search of going through the stack one leaf at a time. As I was nearing the end of the stack and after searching a long time I heard the dreaded call from Mike that it was time to go. I still had not found my prize. Nonetheless I said I would be right up, but frantically kept on looking in the hope that the page I wanted would still turn up. One more call from Mike and one more turn of a page, and unbelievably there it was: the second folio leaf with Milton's sonnet. I made my way back upstairs worried now that my labors might still be in vain. Finding it was one thing, owning it quite another. I showed Mike what I had found, and he laughed as I asked if he would intercede on my behalf. He did, and there was some friendly banter first with me as to how in the world I found it and then with Mike as to the price. Thank goodness he did. When it was finally priced, fairly modestly I thought, considering its rarity, Mike asked, "Now how in the world did you arrive at that figure?" to which Fletcher responded, "I counted up the words and charged per word." Mike looked at me and simply said, "Serendipity!" which he repeated to Bob when we regrouped later. For me, I recognized once again the value of trusting the bookseller—in this case, two booksellers. I also appreciated that if it was meant to be, then it would happen. The leaf is now housed in a fine casing made for it by Sangorski and Sutcliffe at Mike's insistence (#329 in Chapter II).

Bob and I would always visit H. D. (Dick) Lyon in Chelsea, who was Bob's friend from many years before and who immediately befriended me and was happy that I wanted to see his books. I loved the sight and feel of Dick's books, which were mostly in immaculate red or black morocco bindings from the seventeenth and eighteenth centuries and in fine condition; they often touched my heart for simply the beautiful books they were. Fortunately for me, when Dick found out that I collected illustrated Milton but had no continental editions, he took it upon himself to find me some of the finest continental illustrated editions, which are now an important part of my collection, all in superb condition—for example, the splendid 1742 illustrated folio edition of *Il Paradiso Perduto* with stunning engraved plates in an elegant binding (#643 in Chapter II), an enlarged edition of the rare two-volume octavo edition published in 1740 (identified above as the copy obtained from Nicholas Poole-Wilson).

As we walked from our hotel, we would occasionally pass by John Faustus on Jermyn Street. I prevailed upon Bob and Mike to stop in, although both insisted that I would find nothing. The several times we did make a stop, I found just the right Milton for my collection. Early on Bob and I would also go to Francis Edwards at 83 Marlybone High Street, no longer in existence. What an establishment it was, with a remarkable number and kind of antiquarian and modern books! On my several visits there, I found some fine copies of Milton editions and several other books for my other interests, regretting when it closed that I did not have the chance to search for more books among its shelves.

Several times Bob and I were invited to dinner at the homes of Bryan and Edna Maggs, Arthur and Viki Freeman, and Joan Wintercorn. Nothing is more pleasant when traveling than to be invited to a friend's home for dinner. Conversation flowed and focused on books, pending auctions, the future of book collecting, and great collectors, with one of the greatest in our midst. We were also invited to dinner with Ted Hofmann and his wife Sally in Otford,

Seven Oaks, Kent. Before dinner we visited Ted's bookshop in Otford, and then enjoyed a lovely dinner and evening in Ted's home, where I marveled at his own books. Ted was very generous and kind in responding to my interest in Milton, as well as my interest in Herbert, and he added a number of rarities to each collection—for example, a rare edition of Thomas Heywood's *The Hierarchie Of The Blessed Angells* (1635) in fine contemporary unlettered sheep (#19 in Seventeenth-century Miltoniana).

With Alex we would always visit Tony Rota at 30 Long Acre and Martyn Hamlyn (Peter Murray Hill) in Highgate. Once again both were longtime friends of both Bob and Alex. Tony Rota focused on modern literature, an area of interest to Bob for a long time and one in which his collection was very rich. Given his responsibility for the development of collections at Princeton, Alex always watched out for the best interests of Princeton's Rare Books and Special Collections, in particular the Morris L. Parrish Collection of Victorian Novels, of which he had been curator for many years. Martyn Hamlyn had long been a member of the book scene in London; he knew everyone and everyone knew him, particularly because of his association with what was formerly the book firm of Peter Murray Hill. I was very fortunate to meet both Tony and Peter, and through lunches and teas I learned about different periods of collecting and collectors from different perspectives. I also found some wonderful books for my collection—often different from those I found and bought elsewhere—at Martyn Hamlyn's, who prided himself on having antiquarian literature on subjects different from the norm, and at Tony Rota's where wonderful press books of every kind lined the shelves in the front on both sides and some antiquarian books could be found in various areas around the shop. The 1794 Richter illustrated edition of Milton's *Paradise Lost* with hand-colored plates (#780 in Chapter II), described in detail there, came from a visit to Tony Rota in June 1981.

I managed also to wander off on my own to visit and discover bookshops that had books that helped to broaden my collecting appetite to include Milton in all ages and editions, along with Miltoniana, and also Herbert as well as books in fine bindings that were remarkably reasonable in price. Visits for over a decade to these bookshops sometimes added very important and very stunning books to my ever-growing Milton collection, as well as my Herbert collection and my group of beautifully bound anthologies and select other books—a growing passion of mine commended and encouraged, as Bob and Mike stood in wonderment, during a purchase I made at the stall of Deval & Muir during a London Book Fair.

London Book Fairs were always kind to me, and every Book Fair has a special memory. One such occurred as Bob and I were turning the corner of a crowded area of stalls, the book fairs were always crowded, when suddenly out of nowhere Justin Schiller, noted dealer in children's literature, appeared, very excited with a document he was carrying rolled up in his hands. He told us he had with him a colored "Child's Writing Sheet Taken From Milton's *Paradise Lost*" dated "November 1801" with a vignette illustration in color for each book of *Paradise Lost* as border trim. My excitement was by now far greater than Justin's. As the expert, Justin also said that he had never seen such a child's writing sheet before and he knew of none for Milton; nor did he know of anyone else who did. He also said that this sheet came "from the personal collection of Percy Muir," from whose widow he had just then retrieved it. Needless to say, both Bob and I knew that this rare Milton item belonged in my collection. After some discussion with Justin, there was uniform agreement, and ever since that June 1982 Book Fair this unique item has been in my Milton collection (#4 in Chapter V).

A regular stop for me was Henry Sotheran on Sackville Street off Piccadilly, where I always found a number of nineteenth-century Milton editions in wonderful period bindings, sometimes beautifully bound sets. Many of these have now become very scarce and even rare. It was my good fortune to see them then and to be able to buy them at reasonable prices. Over the years I developed a close relationship with John Sprague at Sotheran, who always treated me kindly and kept me apprised of interesting and important Milton books that became available, and from whom I acquired some nineteenth-century editions of Milton in very fine

Victorian bindings of all kinds. A number of earlier editions are also in the collection because of John's kindness in notifying me of them because of my Milton collecting interests.

I returned several times to a bookseller friend, Basil Savage, from whom I had purchased a fairly large number of splendid books at very reasonable prices in the summers of 1971 and 1972 when I was in London on a grant each summer. By skipping lunch each day and eating only a very light supper, I managed to pool together a sum of funds that would allow me to go book hunting on Saturdays or to join with my colleague from Princeton, Bishop Hunt, to visit Basil Savage where we knew that we, and surely I, would find an astounding number of fine books to buy. Basil was Bishop's friend, and Bishop had introduced me to him in 1971. The books I bought from him are among some of the finest in the collection in terms of condition—for example, the three-volume 1806 illustrated edition "Printed for G. Kearsley" in London, described in full within the listing of editions (#1803 in Chapter II)—and some have turned out to among the scarcest editions of Milton in the early nineteenth century.

It was John Ruskin who wrote that "No book, I believe, is ever worth half as much to its reader as one that has been coveted for a year at a bookstall; and bought out of saved half-pence; and perhaps a day or two's fasting." I have always believed in fasting and saving for a book that I really want, and I was amazed at how much my fasting during the week allowed me to spend on books every Saturday during the summer months I was in London alone in the early 1970s. I readily admit though that having to "covet" a book "for a year" is a little too long for me, although there have been times when I have had to ask for a period in which to pay for a purchase. Fortunately, dealers have always been very kind in their responses, and I have always tried to complete the transaction in less than the agreed-upon amount of time.

Other stops included G. Heywood Hill on Curzon Street, who always had surprises among books that were reasonably priced and who was ready to help in any way he could. He allowed me into his basement to look for an early nineteenth-century annual, when I was fervently seeking to complete my Martin collection of annuals with his illustrations in them. Another stop was Harrington Bros. in the Chelsea Antique Market on Kings Road, who had a wide array of fine antiquarian books that always included Milton editions in single volumes and in sets. There I invariably found a great many of the most beautifully bound books in my collection—their Christmas cards through the years have been most welcome for harkening to the past by the warmth of the scenes on their covers and for the kindness in being remembered. I frequented all of the bookshops around the British Museum, including Boswell Books & Prints on Great Russell Street; the Museum Book Shop (across from the Ivanhoe Hotel); M. Ayers at 31 Museum Street, from whom I acquired some interesting illustrated editions; and Arthur Page at 29 Museum Street where in 1979 I bought, quite by chance, a lovely set of the 1810 edition of *Cowper's Milton* with frontispiece (sometimes missing) (#297 in Chapter II), at a price I thought quite high, not knowing how rare this set is until much later and having seen only one set for sale since then.

I would journey occasionally to Thorp's, first at 47 Holborn Viaduct, and then at St. Albans, where the stock was large and worth looking through with determination. I had plenty of the latter, and as a result a great many Milton items are now a part of my collection, which would not otherwise have been the case. I also regularly visited other shops I had come to know would have books of interest to me: in Cecil Court, where the bookstores were often plentiful and close by to one another, including Peter Stockham's Images, and next to it Frognal's, both with small but very interesting stock; the Green Knight Bookshop just a street up from Cecil Court in St. Martin's Lane where I often bought Milton editions in amazingly decorated cloth bindings, usually in mint condition, a shop I was sorry to see close; Monk Bretton Books on New Bond Street, with choice books among which I found a few.

I found London to be a booklover's paradise during my regular visits from 1971 to 1984, with antiquarian bookstores large and small located throughout the city and with small out-of-the-way shops filled with books for sale at reasonable prices. The only way to discover these latter shops was to walk the city and discover them. I did this while also going to antique markets, which always had bookstalls. Always I found desirable Milton books that apparently were either readily available or else had stood waiting for someone like me to come along and salvage them at very reasonable prices. At the antique market bookstalls I made some singular finds that I would not have found elsewhere. For example, from Bernard J. Shapero in Gray's Antique Market at 58 Davies Street, I acquired a remarkable extra-illustrated Milton filled with eighteenth- and early nineteenth-century illustration plates, portrait plates, and other Milton items; from Joseph Del Grosso at Bibliopola in Alfie's Antique Market at 13–25 Church Street in Marlybone, the transcription of *L'Allegro* by F. W. Mercer in 1927 with decorated borders in a vellum binding (#14 in Chapter V). Regular Provincial Book Fairs also had outstanding books at remarkably reasonable prices, and while some of the "high spots" in the collection usually came from the London Book Fairs, I found some of the special Miltons that are now in my collection at these provincial fairs.

On several occasions Bob joined me in visiting Marlborough Books at 35 Old Bond Street where Michael Brand was always a gracious host. A number of extraordinary items in my collection have come from Marlborough Books, but none perhaps more so than the original drawings by Henry Richter for the 1794 edition of Milton's *Poetical Works* edited by John Richter, Henry's father, who also engraved the plates for the edition. Nine of the original drawings were used, and three were unused. Several of the original drawings are shown here in Chapter V.

The 1970s was also the time for searching for Martin, a search that both Bob and Mike joined. Bob and I were fortunate to find a number of significant Martin items while in London, having let our bookdealer friends know how important this was to me and my growing Milton collection. The result was stupendous, really, based on the recommendation of a friend sending us to a friend, which is how the very rare Martin in parts (#889 in Chapter II) was obtained from Christopher Drake in conjunction with the London Book Fair in 1975. Pat, who was along with us, got even more excited than Bob and I did over our good fortune. Proof impressions of large and small plates for *Paradise Lost* came from the Weston Gallery, including the artist's prepublication proof before all letters of the small plate of *Eve Tempts Adam* (#897 in Chapter II), also in 1975. And an original pencil drawing by Martin for *Belshazzar's Feast—A Study* also came from Hazlitt, Gooden & Fox in 1976 (#2052 in Chapter II).

That same year, 1976, Mike found the very rare Imperial folio edition of Septimus Prowett's edition of *The Paradise Lost* with proof impressions of the twenty-four large mezzotint plates by John Martin, originally published in 1827 in only fifty copies (#894 in Chapter II). Bob Taylor had already added a gorgeous copy of the Imperial quarto edition with the twenty-four large mezzotint plates in 1974 (#895 in Chapter II). Again in 1976 Mike found a copy of the rare second Imperial quarto with proof impressions of the twenty-four small mezzotint plates (#897 in Chapter II); and in that same year Dick Lyon produced a fine, large paper copy of the Imperial octavo edition (#898 in Chapter II). Martin was becoming very complete, and as the listings show, later editions round out the Martin holdings with respect to Milton very soundly and very handsomely. The Martin section shows the completeness of Martin within the Milton collection by sample photographs of Martin Bible illustrations and illustrations in early annuals.

I remember all auctions and especially all visits to bookdealers with fondness, and I appreciate the absolute importance of every bookdealer and auction. Nonetheless, my Milton collection took on its special character and quality from the 1970s to the mid-1980s because of Bob Taylor and his support and care for the growth of my collection, as well as his great affection for my enthusiasm for Milton and book collecting, and my desire to form as distinctive a Milton collection as possible. Mike Papantonio cared about the same and so went out of his way to ensure that a great many books in the Schlosser collection found their way into my collection; he then went on to find a great many more important books to help expand the collection in substantive ways. My gratitude to each was long ago expressed, but I sincerely hope that the collection as it now stands is a further expression of my abiding gratitude.

When I became president of Mount St. Mary's College, Maryland, in July 1977 at age thirty-four, Bob and Mike joined many Princeton friends and colleagues to attend my inauguration in September. Toward the end of the day, they were among those invited to our home for dinner and a friendly get-together. Naturally I had worked hard to get my library ready for my special guests, and I had a very large room available for my books, all of which I had moved myself from Princeton with the help of a friend in order to ensure that they received the best care possible. We had purchased our new home in Carroll Valley, Pennsylvania, just across the Maryland border, and the original owner had used what was now my new library as a gambling room for friends, hence its large size and the presence of several indelible marks of where the heavy gambling tables had once stood on the carpet. Better that it was now a library, and I was delighted with the room because it afforded me the opportunity to place long shelving along the walls and to expand over the years. A book collector's dream! No gambler ever thought of that, I'm sure, and stories abounded about who had at one time or another gambled in that room.

When I brought Mike Papantonio into the room, now my library, and before I could give him any background about what it had been and why it was so large, Mike walked around, looked at the eight-row high shelves, looked at how far down the room the shelving extended on each side and behind my desk, turned to me and said, "Bob, you have put together a real collection, and this is quite a library." Coming from Mike this was high praise indeed. I reminded him, of course, of the large role he had played and that I looked forward to him continuing to play. He shared his enthusiasm about that. Unfortunately, too few years remained, although we managed to cram a great amount into a very short time.

For Bob Taylor our home in Carroll Valley was a wonderful place to visit, and he did so often. We had special rooms set aside for him so that he could remove himself from the noise of our children whenever he wanted; somehow, though, he never did. During his visits we would marvel at the growth of my library, and together we would review new additions to the Milton collection. Those were the only times I would stop to allow myself to be captivated by my library and its growth, when he and others who visited were amazed by it.

Trips to London continued and were very special because they occurred once a year for a two-week period and were focused almost solely on books, with the assurance of warm friends, good food, and great theatre in the evening. Moreover, London was certainly then a city of numerous booksellers and time-honored bookshops, with variety in kind and size, and with an increasing number of dealers in original prints and fine arts, including Christopher Powney, Andrew Edmonds, those mentioned above, and others to call upon from time to time.

In the meantime trips to New York were usually monthly occurrences and were always filled with surprises and excitement for me because they would include—in addition to the initial visit to Mike Papantonio at Seven Gables and friends who might be there—a visit to the New York Book Fair; attendance at a book auction at Sotheby's or occasionally Christie's; a visit to the Morgan Library, sometimes to see Charles Ryskamp, whom we also saw upon occasion at Princeton; a visit to the Grolier Club; or visits to other bookdealers. Because these were day trips, Pat could sometimes join us, and that made these trips all the more special.

After visiting Mike to see what treasures he had turned up since our last visit and after lunches at the Miramar restaurant with a variety of book friends who might have stopped by (often Bradley Martin, frequently Don Eddy, and sometimes others whose interests in books brought a fresh perspective to the discussion), we would visit other booksellers in the city. Unfortunately, as Bob often lamented, the number of booksellers in New York was no longer what it used to be, and I then learned what the past had to offer that no longer existed in New York at that time, from 1973 to 1985.

We sometimes visited Stephen Weissman at Ximenes (now in England), who welcomed us warmly. Steve's stock was always choice, ranging over a number of centuries in various fields.

While his Milton inventory was never large, what he had was worth having. Because of those visits I have a number of scarce items in my collection that I would not otherwise possess, including a fine copy of the scarce first book edition of *The Maiden & Married Life Of Mary Powell, Afterwards Mistress Milton* (1850) listed in full here with Nineteenth-century Miltoniana (#66). I also have some other fine works, the result of culling the shelves while listening and learning from Bob and Steve discussing a topic or reviewing a book or some item shown Bob by Steve.

More and more often as time went on we visited John Fleming—"formerly associated with Dr. A. S. W. Rosenbach," as his letterhead stated—at his magnificent establishment at 322 East 57th Street. For me these visits were most memorable for a number of reasons. First of all I was allowed to listen to the conversation of two of America's great book men, each with very different perspectives, as they shared their views about books, former dealers, friends, the present state of book collecting, collectors past and present, the influence of Dr. Rosenbach on book collecting, the future of book collecting, great auctions in the past forty years, and a great many other topics. Moreover, I was allowed to be a part of it all in a setting that can only be described as elegant, with enormously high ceilings, a long table in the center, very highly polished mahogany bookshelves along the sides, a large sitting alcove in one area with very tall windows, and elevated at one far end a dining area.

The visits with John Fleming were very special, and I know they were as special for Bob as they were for me, or else we would not have returned as frequently as we did. Over time I was invited to view the books on the shelves, which I had been very eager to do, and in the process I became a friend of John's who urged me to select books for my Milton collection and who eventually brought out books from the vault saying "this belongs in your collection," including a very fine copy of the 1670 *History of England*, first issue of the first edition, with a fine impression of the William Faithorne portrait frontispiece (#333 in Chapter II). On another occasion in mid-December 1980, as we were visiting, John went to the large walk-in vault and brought out a nice copy of the 1711 Tonson edition of *Paradise Lost*, the first octavo edition with the 1688 plates reduced (#616 in Chapter II). I expressed my enthusiasm over the copy, and John said that it was a Christmas gift for me. I was delighted with the little treasure, which, as I discovered later according to notes within, belonged to Joseph Addison. John wrote me shortly before Christmas: "Dear Bob, Here is the description of the Addison copy of Milton's *Paradise Lost*, which is more important than I had thought. However, if I'd known I'd still have given it to you as a gift. Study it well."

Through the kindness of Mike Papantonio, Bob Taylor and I were often invited to auctions at Sotheby Parke Bernet in New York. The three I remember most vividly are the Stockhausen sale in November 1974, the Borowitz sale in November 1977, and an auction about this same time in support of the Grolier Club. The Stockhausen sale was my very first auction, and I can remember the thrill of it as if it were yesterday, particularly since the Stockhausen collection of English and American literature was an important collection, and sales of this kind and quality of books were becoming rarer and rarer. I attended with great awe, watching dealers bid, expecting nothing, but simply grateful for the invitation to be in attendance with two wonderful friends who were introducing me to a world wholly new to me. As it turned out, my copy of the first edition of *Paradise Regain'd* (1671) came from the Stockhausen sale (#1528 in Chapter II).

The Borowitz sale was every bit as exciting, if not more so, with important books, including a first edition of *Paradise Lost* with first title page. I enjoyed the thrill of that auction enormously, again expecting nothing, and when there was a lull in the bidding on the *Paradise Lost* at a figure much lower than the estimate, to the surprise of Mike and Bob, who readily nodded to each other, there was great surprise among the three of us when the hammer was knocked down and the book sold to Mike for that low figure. Somehow, for some unknown reason, people had left the room or were concentrating on what was coming ahead, but no one except the three of us seemed to be focused on this fine copy of *Paradise Lost* (#598 in Chapter II). It was not long before the room was buzzing about the great bargain Mike had gotten, with questions about what in the world had happened. A number of offers were made for the book before we departed that evening, but Mike held on tight to his remarkable purchase, and I am very glad he did because the copy is in my collection today and has been ever since that memorable evening.

The Borowitz copy of *Paradise Lost* became the centerpiece of my Milton collection, taking its place beside other copies of the first edition with other important title pages I had been extremely fortunate to add to my collection because of the kindness of Bob and Mike: the second title page from the Seven Gables supplement in conjunction with the Schlosser sale in 1975; the fourth title page through Mike's efforts in 1976; the fifth from the Schlosser sale in 1975; and the sixth from Charles Traylen in Guilford while traveling with Mike and Bob in England in June 1977. All five first editions with different title pages are featured in a common photograph (#598 in Chapter II); each is described in detail among the listing of editions. The third title page has always eluded me, and I used to say in a joking way that someone would surely come along some day and say that this was the "first" title page, which would then cause the price to rise beyond the reach of all but a few. That happened in 1983, as I discuss at the beginning of the *Paradise Lost* listings.

Before leaving Princeton for my first presidency in mid-1977, it was my rare privilege to serve as guest editor of a double issue of *The Princeton University Library Chronicle* in honor of Bob Taylor's fiftieth anniversary as a collector. I endeavored to show both my admiration and affection for this remarkable man who quietly and single-handedly put together a universally admired collection of English and American literature with unmatched rarities over fifty years of collecting. I asked a select group of distinguished individuals who admired Bob and knew his collection to contribute essays on various perspectives of Bob's collection. Everyone I asked responded immediately that they would be honored to contribute an essay, and the contributors reads as a list of who's who as recognized scholars in their field as well as friends of Bob's. The publication stands as a tribute to a truly remarkable man, one of America's distinguished collectors, and an outstanding collection.

Bob and I used to share thoughts about how one never starts out with the intention of forming a collection, but rather, circumstances lead to what one day surprises the collector as much as others. In Bob's case, it was because there was no collected edition of Anthony Trollope available when he was a student, and so he was "reduced," as he would say, to buying first editions of his novels (usually the only editions available), remotely analogous, I would tell him, to my having to buy nineteenth-century editions of seventeenth-century poets in order to get hold of their entire works when I was in graduate school.

Besides buying books directly at a dealer's bookshop, many of my books have come from catalogues over the years, often catalogues from bookdealers I never met or who dealt primarily in catalogues. Some of my most choice and rarest items were also offered to me privately by dealers who wanted to ensure the right home for a given item or who supported my Milton collection and wanted me to have an opportunity to obtain something that they thought belonged in it—and more often than not they were right. Times have changed collecting in a number of ways, primarily because of the Internet, which allows one to order more quickly and one hopes more successfully. But the Internet has also brought about fewer catalogues, with Web sites and online listings taking their place.

But from the 1970s largely through the 1990s, the catalogues I received helped me broaden my Milton collection, educated me about collecting and in particular about collecting Milton, and broadened my education about a variety of subjects. They have also remained an invaluable resource. Often the catalogues have been beautifully printed, sometimes stunningly so, with photographs in color to show exactly why a given item was worth the price. Descriptions ranged from excellent to okay, depending on the purpose of the catalogue or listing. I lived for catalogues to arrive and devoted my free time to studying each catalogue, first with respect to Milton, then in relation to other interests. I disliked marking my catalogues, though I often did so, and would have preferred two catalogues—one for marking and one for keeping as a clean reference copy—along the lines of the old book collecting adage: always have three copies of a book, one for reading, one for keeping clean, and one for lending. Given the printing and postage costs to the bookseller, I have always been grateful to receive a catalogue, and I remain so today.

Throughout the 1970s catalogues as well as private offerings from R & J Balding in Edinburgh provided me a ready and constant source of important Milton books, particularly from the eighteenth and nineteenth centuries. I never knew what the "R & J Balding" stood for until I had occasion to meet the partners at a London Book Fair. I was given the explanation by one of them pointing to the bald head of the other, with the other doing the same to his partner, and the comment that the initials are those of each partner, which is the way in which the name was originally selected. Book people are decidedly creative.

Other catalogues, which helped to expand and give depth to a rapidly growing Milton collection while filling out the shelves and demanding new ones at our home in Carroll Valley, Pennsylvania, came at a steady pace from Deighton Bell in Cambridge; Spike Hughes in Innerleithen, Scotland; George's in Bristol; David Bickersteth in Royston; Adam Mills in Cambridge; Bow Windows Bookshop in Lewes; Grant & Shaw in Edinburgh; Henry Sotheran in London, with John Sprague continuing also to offer me some choice selections privately; Blackwell's, especially when John Manners ran the rare books department at Fyfield Manor and then Alan Grant, from both of whom I obtained some outstanding books; Lamesa Booksellers in Lamesa, Texas, with Asalie Price, privately offering me some wonderful books; Charles Agvent (Mertztown, Pennsylvania), who also continued to offer me some important books privately; Tom Taylor in Austin, Texas, who for a period of years added some exceptional books to my collection.

In the splendid catalogues of David Block at the Book Block in Cos Cob (Greenwich), Connecticut; Simon Finch Rare Books in London; Robin de Beaumont Antiquarian & Fine Books in London; Bauman Rare Books in New York and Philadelphia; Ursus Rare Books in New York; and Heritage Book Shop in Los Angeles—catalogues which are always a joy to receive—I have found some real prizes to add to my collection over the years. Likewise is the case of James Cummins Bookseller in New York, in whose wonderful catalogues I have not only found choice items, but from whom not so long ago, through the efforts of Jane Callahan who worked for him, I was offered a rare eighteenth-century theatre broadside announcing the performance of *Comus* (#66 in Eighteenth-century Miltoniana). Jane worked for Seven Gables when Bob Taylor and I were making our regular visits to the shop. Once again the Seven Gables–Mike Papantonio and Bob Taylor connection accounts for a rarity making its way into my Milton collection.

Catalogues continue also to arrive from old friends: exceptional ones from Maggs and Quaritch on special occasions, almost always with rare Milton items—for example, the catalogue from Quaritch in 1988 that contained the earliest complete manuscript of Milton's epic, transcribed in a fine hand by Katherine Howard between 1733 and 1735, now in my collection (#13 in Chapter V); superb catalogues from Marlborough Rare Books on a regular basis with rare and unusual offerings, sometimes Martin-related, from which I acquired several non-Milton items, always interesting with that uncommon and special something waiting to be discovered. My two good friends at MacNeil's in Charlotte, North Carolina, also helped add some very fine books to my collection in the 1980s, more often by the offering of a choice item than by catalogue, but by catalogues as well from time to time.

Other catalogues from friends who have helped to see my Milton collection grow to what it has become today and from whom I have consistently purchased various books and items through the years continue to arrive from Pickering & Chatto, Tony Rota, Martin Hamlyn (Peter Murray Hill), and Bernard J. Shapero in London; K Books in York; Stephen Weissman (Ximenes), now in Kempsford, England, no longer New York; and Kenneth Karmiole in Santa Monica. Peter M. Cresswell (Humber Books) in Barton-on-Humber in England has consistently and kindly sent me his catalogues on antiquarian theology through the years, affording me an opportunity to acquire editions of Milton that are both uncommon and rare, while searching for other books of interest. Likewise is the case of James Fenning in Dun Laoghaire, Ireland, whose catalogues have allowed me to add several very scarce editions to the collection. And more locally, the catalogues and private offerings of Thomas Cullen, Rockland Bookman in Cattaraugus, New York, have done the same.

Brilliant catalogues from art dealers, especially in England, also arrive regularly in my mail, and I have learned much from them even though I have purchased little of late. The catalogues from Campbell Fine Art virtually always contain prints for sale of illustrations of Milton and almost always fine mezzotint plates by John Martin for sale. Michael Campbell is among the most knowledgeable of Martin, and his catalogues have taught me a great deal about the artist; lately Michael has personally taught me much that has hitherto either been unknown or little regarded about Martin, and I am grateful to him for his kindness.

The increasingly spectacular catalogues of Phillip J. Pirages in McMinnville, Oregon, beckon one to expand and acquire exquisite medieval manuscripts, lovely fine bindings, and a great many other exciting treasures, and it takes strong will power, along with an empty pocketbook, to stay the course. I began with Phil Pirages way back in the very early 1980s when he was still in Ann Arbor, Michigan. I received a nondescript catalogue that contained the offering of a large grouping of Milton critical studies in very good to fine condition. I ordered the lot and have been buying from him ever since, acquiring some rare illustrated editions in very fine bindings and other important Milton items, along with an occasionally inexpensive manuscript leaf for each of my children and for friends. While he has moved on to sell very expensive items, deservedly so, he continues to keep a range of books very affordable to the collector of all interests and capacities. He has also remained loyal to my collecting interests and mindful always of my commitment to Milton, helping me obtain that special item otherwise beyond my reach.

Virtually from the outset of my collecting, I have received and bought from the catalogues of Howes Bookshop in Hastings, East Sussex, England. A great many of my books in virtually every respect—from single editions to large sets to Miltoniana to rare critical studies—have come from Howes. It would be hard to imagine my collection and indeed my collecting life without catalogues from Howes arriving on a regular basis. By reading through these catalogues throughout my thirty-five years of collecting, I have learned a great deal. Most of all, perhaps, in an ever-changing world, it is comforting to know that some things do not change. Very recently I received a catalogue that listed a rare 1804 edition of *Paradise Lost*. I say rare because I have never seen or heard of it before. I quickly e-mailed Miles Bartley, whom I have come to know through letters and e-mails as he has come to know me in a similar manner, and asked if the book was still available, and if so, could I buy it. In an almost immediate e-mail response, I was informed that the book was mine. I replied that I was delighted to add the book to my collection (#809 in Chapter II) and that Miles could not possibly know how many important books over the years Howes had contributed to my collection and how grateful I was, to which Miles responded: "It is always gratifying to know that our efforts to find and offer rare and unusual books are appreciated by, it often appears, 'fit audience though few'!"

Anyone who collects on the East Coast has undoubtedly made a stop when in Philadelphia at W. H. Allen, a notable and historic bookshop on the landscape of bookshops in America. Aisles were narrow, lighting was dim, but patience and persistence in looking produced great finds at very reasonable prices. Visits to the "rare books room" upstairs provided more generous lighting and space, again with great finds to be had if one took the time to look. I stopped there every chance I could from the mid-1970s to the late 1990s. It was a catalogue to the department of English at Princeton that first alerted me to the bookshop because in that catalogue was the extra-illustrated 1720 edition edited by Thomas Tickell now in the collection (#1763 in Chapter II), which I purchased with simply a call and a request for the book. It was sent on approval, no questions asked. I knew then that not only was this a bookshop I had to visit but that the owner must be quite an individual to be so trusting. Indeed Mr. Allen was all of that and more, and both he and his bookshop will be sorely missed by scholars, students, and collectors in years to come.

I did not get a chance to stop by Buddenbrooks in Boston very often, but when I did I always found something special for my Milton collection. Because of the New York Book Fairs I attended with Bob and Mike in the 1970s and Bob in the 1980s, however, several choice items in the collection have come from Buddenbrooks. In another city farther south, I developed a close relationship with Theresa Johanson at the Kelmscott Bookshop in Baltimore, a bookshop I would visit whenever I could, and when I did I always found something for my collection. More often than not, I would receive private offerings, sometimes with valued Milton scholar associations—for example, books that once belong to Don Cameron Allen. Mrs. Johanson now operates as Johanson Rare Books and continues occasionally to offer me fine and rare books.

Throughout at least the last twenty-five years of my collecting Milton I have had a special relationship with a bookstore I have never been in, but always thought I would visit someday, a bookstore that has helped contribute to the breadth and character of this collection in unique ways. The bookstore is Zubal Books in Cleveland, and the private offerings from Michael Zubal have ranged from editions I have not seen elsewhere to a recent offering of an item with more than Miltonic interest: "Paradise Lost: Or, The Great Dragon Cast Out . . . By Lucian Redivivus. 'Better to reign on earth than serve in heaven' . . . Boston, 1872" (#97 in Nineteenth-century Miltoniana).

Most recently several rare items have been kindly made available to me by Amanda Hall, formerly with Pickering & Chatto, in private offerings—most notably, perhaps, the rare 1755 three-volume French edition of *Le Paradis Perdu* translated and inscribed by Louis Racine, son of Jean Racine, the famed dramatist, and also the rare 1746 French translation of *Of Education* in *Lettres Sur L'Education Des Princes. Avec Une Lettre De Milton*, first edition thus, with an early nineteenth-century oil painting on the front cover (#682 and #548 in Chapter II).

I never cease to be amazed by the ways in which Milton books make their way into my collection. I was a subscriber to *Biblio*, which I wish had never discontinued publication. But nonetheless, in one issue a man named Don Bell wrote an article about beautiful books he had discovered, including one in a decorated blue cloth binding, with accompanying photograph, lamenting in the process that the subject of such a lovely book was the poetry of John Milton, which he wondered how anyone could possibly read, much less like. I decided to write him through the editor for two reasons: (1) to tell him that Milton's poetry is sheer beauty beyond compare and (2) to ask if the book was for sale considering how much disdain he expressed for Milton. To my surprise the editor passed my letter along, and to my further surprise Mr. Bell answered me within a very short time. I now have the book, and Don and I have become very good friends. It turns out that he is part French and part Canadian, with a French wife. He is a book scout and freelance writer, and he offered to scout for me. Because of his various trips to Europe and through his friends there, I now have books in translations that I very much doubt I would ever have had the opportunity to acquire were it not for Don Bell and if I had not written my letter to him through *Biblio*.

Since 1998 the Internet has played an increasingly important role in collecting. Web sites and search engines are important means for finding some books that have been elusive. Dealers are using the Internet more and more, as are collectors, and the online auction site eBay—which was not very well known when I bought my first Milton edition on it in 1999—has now become a valuable source for finding important books and editions (if one has the patience and perseverance to find precisely the right book when it appears, along with the capacity to avoid being drawn into the auction frenzy of buying something that is not really wanted).

For me, the Internet has afforded opportunities to add nineteenth-century American editions of Milton to my collection; to broaden the scope of editions and Miltoniana in the collection; to replace one copy with a better copy; and at times to secure a rare, unrecorded eighteenth-century edition, often in quite good condition, sometimes with a binding in need of repair, but fresh and clean internally. The Internet has also enabled me to search for Milton among dealers I have never known and then to become acquainted enough to be on their list when catalogues are sent out. This happened with Stuart Bennett in Mill Valley, California, from whom I subsequently obtained, among other things, an interesting small book published in Providence, Rhode Island, in 1813, called *True And Infernal Friendship, Or The Wisdom Of Eve. And The Character Of The Serpent, With the Situation, Joys, And Loss Of Paradise* (#80 in Nineteenth-century Miltoniana).

Through the years, and most consistently, I have acquired books for my Milton collection from G. W. Stuart, Jr., the Ravenstree Company in Yuma, Arizona. I first learned of Jerry from Mike Papantonio in the mid-1970s at about the time that I was acquiring items from the Schlosser and Hanrahan sales. After contacting Jerry by letter, I learned that he had recently sold several major Milton collections that he had put together to the University of Western Ontario; to the Margaret I. King Library at the University of Kentucky; and to the Turnbull Library in Wellington, New Zealand. Jerry kindly sent me copies of the short title lists of each sale. From that point on I received copies of his catalogues, which grew increasingly devoted to Milton, and by 1985 he began releasing annual Milton catalogues, which were as informative as they were attractive in appearance and in the Milton items each catalogue contained. Considering the several major Milton collections Jerry had already sold as collections, one could only marvel at the number of rare and important Milton items Jerry continued to discover for sale on a regular basis.

As time went by and we became close friends, having never met except over the phone, Jerry kindly alerted me to choice items about to appear in upcoming catalogues, and when finances were not always available, he allowed me to make payments over a reasonable period of time so that I could obtain several rarities, rather than lose one or more. In 2003 Jerry visited my library in Olean to see my Milton collection and the effect his years of advising me and passing along remarkable Milton books had on the collection. The effect was obvious, and while I was pleased to see that Jerry was delighted that books formerly his had found their right home, Pat and I were very appreciative of Jerry's visit and of his positive response to the collection and to the library.

Jerry's advice with respect to Milton has always been candid and virtually always been on the mark, whether in terms of buying or in terms of some aspect of Milton about which I might have asked his opinion and which then resulted in stimulating conversation. Jerry is a knowledgeable bookman, certainly; he is also as knowledgeable about Milton as almost anyone else I know. He has devoted a lifetime to selling Milton, something no one else has done, speaking of himself in a 2003 catalogue in the "Ravenstree" series as having "spent over 40 years working with Milton items" (Cat. 106, #1164). His catalogues are a testimony to his long-standing commitment to Milton, and they will serve as an invaluable resource for Miltonians and many others for years to come.

While my collection would certainly be a very distinctive one because of the influence of Bob Taylor and Mike Papantonio—and the exceptional purchases from Mike and from some major booksellers identified above along with ongoing purchases from many other booksellers also identified there—the collection would be decidedly less distinctive and without the breadth or the singular character it has today because of the many additions from Jerry Stuart throughout the years in important and rare seventeenth- and eighteenth-century editions and Miltoniana, almost always in very nice or fine condition. From rare early editions in prose to rare early and important Miltoniana, from rare eighteenth-century editions to rare early translations, from rare early eighteenth-century stage adaptations to rare eighteenth-century Handel adaptations with musical notation, the list goes on so that collectively the items from Jerry Stuart take the collection to another level altogether, complementing in a unique way the earlier rarities purchased in the 1970s and early 1980s.

I have been extremely fortunate in knowing booksellers who have been enthusiastic about books and in caring about their books finding the right home and going into the right collection. It goes without saying that selling books is how booksellers make a living, but for the genuine bookseller of old, a love of books, a knowledge of books, and a sharing of both that love and knowledge are what have made collecting books so very special for me and the basis for mutual trust and respect, not to mention lifelong friendships. Without the many booksellers it has been my good fortune to know and who have been so very kind to me over the years, this Milton collection would not exist. I am grateful to them all for that, as I am sure the many who will use this collection in the future will also be. It is my fond hope that booksellers like them will be available and as special to collectors in the years ahead so that book collecting will continue to be the source of joy, excitement, and enthusiasm for others that it has always been for me.

Collecting one author has been enormously rewarding and has given me experiences I never anticipated, taking me into fields I never expected: from publishers and bindings in different centuries to private press publications, to translations, to anthologies that include selections from Milton (often illustrated), thereby opening a remarkably interesting field for study, to publications for use as textbooks, yet another area for study—the list goes on.

While my emphasis began with a focus on illustrated editions, in a very short time that focus expanded to include early editions of Milton in order to get as close to Milton and the original as possible. Of course, I never passed up a nice copy of any attractive edition of Milton, and very often I was able to obtain such editions for very reasonable prices. Given my good fortune of getting off to a strong start in the early to the late 1970s—and my further good fortune of having two wonderful friends who supported my collecting interest enthusiastically—near the end of the 1970s I found myself believing that maybe I was in a position to collect as many editions of Milton through the ages as possible, particularly since I already then had many of the early editions.

I really did want to collect every edition of Milton (confidence is great in the young!), and set out to do that I did, since a great many of the early editions were already on my shelves. Not everyone will agree that a modern edition paperback belongs among rare books, and my own children cringed as they saw my library take on more and more modern books, whether paperback or not, which they did not like to see placed next to the more stately books of old and were happy to see move farther to the back by the purchase of more and more eighteenth- and nineteenth-century editions. Yet my principle had to remain adhered to or else it was meaningless. This meant including, for example, John Shawcross's 1963 edition of *The Complete English Poetry Of John Milton* and the revised edition in 1971. Of course, it is all the more special to a collector that each is a signed copy.

Important as the 1645 *Poems* and the 1667 to 1669 title pages of *Paradise Lost* and the 1688 first folio / first illustrated *Paradise Lost* editions are, if my collection was going to be as complete as I could possibly make it, then editions from every age had to be included in as complete a manner as possible. This meant translations (fortunately often illustrated) and included also Miltoniana and critical studies, and as with collecting one author, my principle of completeness through the ages in editions, Miltoniana, and critical studies brought me not only many "new" books but also many new experiences, while opening doors to new areas for me to explore.

Collecting is great fun, so long as you are collecting what you want to collect and how you want to collect it. It is also very rewarding in a great many ways. I remember the joy of collecting rocks as a young boy, and stamps, and of course baseball cards, which got thrown out like everyone else's. The important principle of collecting is that it should always bring enjoyment. To collect for future value should always be secondary, since no one knows what people will want from one generation to the next; that is the reason for collecting only what you want to collect, not for speculation. There's nothing more self-rewarding and fulfilling than collecting, and the results are invariably different in the long run than one might ever have thought possible or ever anticipated, as I hope this collection and my observations about it and how it has come together show.

Collecting is fun for the people you meet, the books you buy, and even the books you do not buy. One such occasion of pure fun, meeting of new people, and something that simply would not have happened were it not for the book world, occurred during our June 1983 trip. Bob Taylor and I were invited to spend an afternoon with Douglas Cleverdon at his home in Islington, and we were excited about meeting this author and renowned publisher of significant press books, notably in the 1920s and 1930s, but on into the 1970s as well; he was also freelance producer of some famed BBC radio broadcasts in the late 1930s and 1940s. The afternoon was filled with anecdote after anecdote, and Douglas Cleverdon was spellbinding in the telling. When he learned of my Milton interest, he told us of his BBC production in the late 1940s of *Comus* in glowing detail, and then moved on to do the same with regard to his BBC production of *Paradise Lost*—produced about the same time as *Comus*—in which Dylan Thomas played Satan and, our host added gleefully, had to be "held in check!" We left after several hours, delighted to have met such a remarkable man, far better for it, each with a signed presentation copy of a Private Press publication of his *Fifty Years* from the Private Library, 1978.

The rarity or scarcity and condition of a book is determined by a great many factors, even though it is commonly believed that a book has to be old in order to be rare or scarce. If a great many people want a book published in 1974, then its availability is limited, and it is most likely a scarce book. Such is the case, for example, with *Asimov's Annotated Paradise Lost* (Doubleday & Company, 1974). I believe the edition is very scarce, and when a copy becomes available it is immediately snatched up for a rather large sum because of its limited availability. Though I would very much like to think that the attraction is to Milton, clearly it is to Isaac Asimov. Circumstances beyond wanting simply what might appear to be a relatively recent edition of Milton, therefore, make this book both scarce and expensive, depending upon condition. One might also conclude that only a limited number of copies were printed of Asimov's edition, but there is no way to know this for certain, or at least none of which I am aware. It took me more than twenty years to obtain my copy in pristine condition, and I consider myself very fortunate to have such a fine copy, as does the under bidder in the auction in which I won my copy.

The longer one collects, the more comfortable one feels about identifying the scarcity of a book and in appreciating condition. I have learned, sometimes the hard way, that not all editions are scarce and that settling too quickly upon a copy that will turn up in better condition sometime in the relatively near future will simply result in having two or more copies of the same edition, or in foregoing the second, better copy, unless you can sell the poorer copy you already have. But if a book I bought in the 1970s or even the 1980s is one I have not seen since then, given my thirty-five years of focused collecting of Milton—or conversely, if I discover a book now that I have not seen during all that time—then I believe it is fair to conclude that the book is certainly scarce and perhaps even rare.

All collectors want every book in their collection to be in mint condition. The likelihood of this happening is impossible, and becomes even more impossible when the range of collecting is as broad as mine has been with an author like Milton. Sometimes, therefore, one simply has to settle for the best condition in which one can find a copy, because it may be the only copy one is likely to get. Rarity governs condition more than age. To find a scarce or rare book in fine condition is truly a great find and is rare enough in itself, although great books are often enough treasured by their owners and therefore their condition is protected through time. Some editions of Milton were acceptable to me in less than good or even fair condition simply because they could not be found in any other condition, even though I have always tried to obtain an edition in the best condition possible.

Condition governs the purchase of a book, with the sole exception of rarity. When I determined I wanted to collect as many different editions of Milton as possible, not just as many different illustrated editions, the condition of books in my collection changed rather dramatically. Rarity determines what a collector will buy for a collection, and if the only edition or copy available is in less than the accustomed quality of one's collection or than the accustomed quality one would like, almost invariably, quality gives way to rarity in the hope that a better copy will some day come along. In the case of absolute rarity, that seldom happens, and if it does, cost then often becomes a factor in the "star" and more sought-after books. I have been fortunate to obtain "star" items early on and then fortunate many times, particularly with nineteenth-century editions, to purchase fine copies of editions for very reasonable and sometimes even cheap prices to replace editions I purchased earlier in sometimes shabby condition, not knowing whether or not I would ever see these editions again.

Over time I learned that some copies were really too scarce or even rare to pass up, even though the condition was poor, and this is when the collector in me had to bow to the principles of my collection. I believe I made the right choice each time and that the collection is better for it. Should I ever see a better copy of these editions, I would readily acquire them to replace copies now in the collection; I am confident my successors will do the same.

There is no such thing as a duplicate! My wife laughs at this, but has come to understand it as she looks at the variances that only seeing books by the same publisher side by side can show with absolute clarity. And when variances fail, she recalls Bob Taylor and me discussing the importance of having three copies of a book: one to read, one to keep pure, and one to lend to a friend or to use for research.

Far more seriously, however, often books will look the same to someone not familiar with the publishing history of an author or with the nuances or important differences between books so that what appears to look alike or the same actually is not. Perhaps the most serious debate in this respect is that concerning the number of title pages and the "true first title page" to *Paradise Lost*, which has gone on since the nineteenth century, once counting as many as seven title pages, more recently calling the traditional third of six title pages the first title page. (See commentary at the beginning of the *Paradise Lost* listings.)

From a very different perspective, and considering more recent editions, the collection has a number of copies of the ca. 1898 edition of *Paradise Lost* published by H. M. Caldwell in New York. They demonstrate very clearly why collecting different copies of the same edition with variant title page plates, variant publisher's imprints, variant portraits, in variant formats, and in variant publisher's bindings has real merit in pointing out such notable differences and more; and yet each book maintains its own individuality and attractiveness. Much the same holds true with the collection's numerous copies of the 1899 edition of *Paradise Lost* published by Henry Altemus in Philadelphia; likewise with respect to the collection's numerous copies of the ca. 1898 edition of *Paradise Regained* published by H. M. Caldwell in New York and of the ca. 1899 edition of *Paradise Regained* and of *Poems* published by Henry Altemus in Philadelphia.

There are reasons, of course, for buying "multiple" copies or "second" copies, to be distinguished from "duplicate" copies. Most of the reasons are fairly obvious: to obtain a better copy than the one you already have, and every collector has done this, collectors of single authors, like me, perhaps more often than other collectors because of the range and extent a single author commands; to help date a book when it was published without a date; and on occasion to determine first and second issues, and again the collector of a single author will perhaps have more occasion to buy multiple copies for this reason than other collectors.

As with comfort level about scarcity and whether or not to purchase a book in less than desirable condition, so too with dating a book, the longer one collects, the more comfortable one feels about identifying the date of an undated book. The nineteenth century, especially the latter half, seems to me to be notorious for not dating its books, although this period is by no means alone in this practice. Reading a listing of books that has only "later nineteenth century" given as a means of dating becomes an impossible challenge when looking for major distinctions to be made between editions published, for example, by Gall & Inglis in the 1850s, 1860s, and 1870s. With experience, though I once would never have believed it, the date of a book can be narrowed with some accuracy.

Librarians have advantages. Collectors who emphasize a single author do as well, perhaps with an advantage even over librarians because they have multiple editions in their collections. Dating an undated edition involves using one's detective's instincts and skills. Sometimes it can be fun; other times it can be very frustrating. Did a publisher leave a date off because he was moving and preferred his new address to show in a future publication of a dated copy, and is such the case, for example, with the undated ca. 1844 Kearny edition of *Paradise Lost* with one address, while the dated 1844 Kearny edition has another address (#956 and #957 in Chapter II); likewise with the undated ca. 1839 Wells edition of *Paradise Lost*, followed by the dated 1840, 1841, and 1842 Wells editions of Milton's epic (#938, #946, and #952 in Chapter II)? These are just two mid-nineteenth American examples; there are a great many more. Collecting calls for using one's detective's instincts and abilities. Dating *Paradise Lost* "Printed At The Caxton Press, By Henry Fischer," n.d. (#878 and #879 in Chapter II) as ca. 1823 allows for detective work with satisfying results.

Buying variant copies for reasons other than dating, whether for variant frontispiece, variant publisher's imprint, variant binding, whatever the reason might be, certainly conforms to the principle that there is no such thing as a duplicate. Often these variant copies will contain a contemporary presentation inscription or a contemporary dated signature. These are not always to be treated as exact, of course, but they certainly help to date a publication, and often, especially in a collection as large as this, help to narrow the time frame in which a book was published, sometimes by the process of elimination, as for example, with a dated 1873 inscription on an undated edition by Frederick Warne & Co. which helped to date that book, which I had otherwise dated ca. 1880 based on an inscription in a copy I had acquired earlier. I could list a great many other such examples, including a number with dated inscriptions or signatures earlier than the dates given them in published sources; the listings do that.

Buying a second or third copy or occasionally more copies is not only important for all of the above reasons, but sometimes because the book is special, an extra-illustrated copy, which in my case absolutely belongs in my collection and is not a second copy at all. Such books used to be called "grangerized" copies, named after the person who first put together copies that took freely from other copies original illustrations and portraits to embellish the basic copy or edition. My collection has a number of such "grangerized" editions, all listed in some detail, including one for *Paradise Lost* in a large, thick folio (#723 in Chapter II) and another using the Imperial quarto edition of Septimus Prowett's first edition of *Paradise Lost* with John Martin's plates as the basis for adding other illustrations, portraits, and more (#896 in Chapter II).

Buying that additional copy or copies is by no means additional and certainly not a duplicate when it contains a fore-edge painting. My collection contains a number of beautiful fore-edge paintings, two of which remain with the collection, one is shown by photograph (#2097 in Chapter II); the others are shown by photograph in a special section of several fore-edge paintings and bindings (Chapter VIII), which for now remain with me, but may someday find their way back home again. Such purchases are always unique, and they are particularly special when they are related to the subject being collected, in this case illustrated Milton, as the fore-edges in the collection are, with the exception of one which is on an edition which I did not otherwise have in the collection and therefore had to obtain for that purpose rather than for the fore-edge painting.

Adding another copy or copies of an edition because of variant bindings has been something I have regularly done because of my attraction to fine bindings from the very beginning of my collecting. The various bindings in the collection along with the variant bindings on a given edition afford an opportunity to study bindings throughout the past four centuries. In the case of the variant bindings of the 1858 Routledge edition of *Comus* (#244 in Chapter II), for example, I have been particularly pleased to cover several important aspects of this edition of *Comus* at the same time. Adding an illustrated edition of one of Milton's shorter poems to the collection is always a real joy; to do so with an edition illustrated by various artists in a half dozen beautifully decorated cloth bindings of the period makes the addition all that more gratifying. To top it off, the additional copies help to identify two states (originally pointed out in the *Book Collector* [Winter 1964]: 500): a first state in which the female figures by F. R. Pickersgill, R.A., on pages 7, 71, and 79 are unclothed and a second state in which these same figures are fully clothed (#244 and #248 in Chapter II).

As if one needed more reasons, additional copies also provide, sometimes purely by surprise and sometimes by choice, interesting association, other times interesting presentation copies, and if fortunate enough, one or the other with an accompanying letter or letters, and even rarely corrected proof copy. In a collection as large as this, as one might well imagine, there are bound to be a large and diverse number of association and presentation copies. Some examples include:

- William Riley Parker's copy of *The Reason Of Church-Government Urg'd Against Prelaty*, 1641, the first of Milton's publications to bear his name. This was one of the last Milton books Mike Papantonio found for me (#2648 in Chapter II) and it was given to me as a birthday gift by Bob Taylor, who is godfather to our third child, Kristin, in 1978.

- John Evelyn's copy of *Pro Populo Anglicano*, 1651. Third edition with bookplate and with the press mark "Erato:51" in the hand of Evelyn on the title page. The beautiful copy of the 1688 *Paradise Lost* in contemporary black morocco, which I was so very happy to receive from Dudley Massey shortly before he died, not only came from a great bookdealer, but it once belonged to Graham Pollard, with his bookplate (#2568 in Chapter II).

- William Hog's *Paraphrasis Poetica*, published just two years later in 1690, the first William Hog translation and the first complete Latin version of each of Milton's three great poems, is a presentation copy, with a presentation inscription in Latin by Hog to the Marquess of Tweeddale, with his bookplate (#1759 in Chapter II).

- R. W. Chapman's copy of *The [Prose] Works Of Mr. John Milton.* (Printed in the Year MDCXCVII.) Of interest in this spurious first edition of the first collection of Milton's English prose works are the annotations by Chapman in pencil throughout, whose remarks are often caustic to the extreme: "Infamous scurrility, Milton was a downright blackguard . . ." (p. 175); "A specimen of Milton's base scurrility and diabolical malignity . . ." (p. 297); "A barefaced libel . . ." (p. 299); "A nasty idea from a dirty stinking Puritan . . ." (p. 298, #2754 in Chapter II).

- Jacobus Masenius's *Sarcotis* (1771) beautifully bound in rich red contemporary French morocco was William Hayley's copy, with ownership inscription. This new edition (first published in 1664) was occasioned by Lauder's infamous claim that Milton's *Paradise Lost* was largely constructed of plagiarisms of this and other modern Latin works, including Grotius's *Adamus Exul* and Hog's *Paraphrasis Poetica*. A later ownership inscription belongs to John Wordsworth, scholar and nephew to William Wordsworth the poet. While "Lauder" is sort of a "mini collection" unto himself, as one of the photos attempts to show (#39 in Eighteenth-century Miltoniana), his *Poetarum Scotorum Musae Sacrae* (Edinburgh, 1739), second issue of volume 1, with new title page and preliminary matter, is an inscribed presentation copy to Thomas Ogilvie.

- *The Works Of John Milton, Historical, Political, And Miscellaneous* (London, 1753), which belonged to Edward Gibbon, with his engraved armorial bookplate in each volume. There is also a presentation copy in original uncut boards of William Hayley's 1796 edition of *The Life Of Milton*, inscribed "From the Author" on the front pastedown. This is the second, much enlarged edition, but the first separate edition, having first appeared in volume

1 of the great three-volume 1794–97 Boydell-Nichols edition of Milton's *Poetical Works*, is also in the collection (#32 in Eighteenth-century Miltoniana).

- A fine copy of *Paradise Lost* ("Printed for John Wood at Milton's Head, Edinburgh," 1765) in contemporary calf is from the library of Siegfried Sassoon, with the poet's signature in purple ink on the fly-leaf and with his posthumous monograph book label (#714 in Chapter II). And then there is Edmund Blunden's copy of Todd's 1826 edition of his *Life of Milton*, signed on a front blank (#115 in Nineteenth-century Miltoniana).

- An 1826 three-volume Pickering edition of *Poetical Works*, the first Pickering edition, is a presentation copy, inscribed by the editor Joseph Parkes to Chandos Leigh on the half-title of volume 1, and restated at the top of the title page, volume 1, with a three-page handwritten letter from Parkes to Leigh, signed by Parkes, bound in at the beginning of volume 1. The Leigh bookplate is in each volume (#1841 in Chapter II).

- The Trevelyan Family Milton: *Poetical Works*, illustrated with engravings by J. M. W. Turner, published by William Tegg in London in 1848, in a fine Harrow School Prize Binding, having been presented to George Otto Trevelyan while at Harrow in 1848, with the later signature of G. M. Trevelyan, Hallington, 1928 (#1935 in Chapter II).

- The five-volume 1848–53 *Prose Works* published by Henry G. Bohn in London, signed by the Wordsworth scholar Ernest De Selincourt on the endpaper in each volume and dated 1899 in volume 1, with his neat shelf number in manuscript on verso of title page, most volumes with neat notes in the margins or on the rear endpaper in pencil or ink by De Selincourt (#2634 in Chapter II).

- An 1851 three-volume Pickering edition of the *Poetical Works*, the fifth Aldine edition, in a somewhat worn contemporary brown calf binding is a special association copy originally from the "College of New Jersey [at Princeton]. Library of the American Whig Society" (later Princeton University), with the college bookplate in each volume, covering the ticket of either the binder or bookseller in volume 1, with "at Princeton" written beneath the "College of New Jersey" on the bookplate in a neat hand in volume 1, with the signature of W. B. Parsons on the front blank of volume 1 and the stamp of the American Whig Society in each volume (#1956 in Chapter II).

- Frederick Thrupp's own copy of his illustrated edition of *Paradise Lost*, 1879, signed by the artist on a front blank (#1121 in Chapter II).

- Two copies of the first edition of *Poetical Works*, Edited By H. C. Beeching. Oxford At The Clarendon Press, 1900, in variant bindings, one neatly signed by John Walker Lucas with a two-page letter to Lucas laid in, dated 1948, signed by Douglas Bush, editor of the Oxford Standard Authors edition of Milton, dismissing Norman Douglas's view of Milton as a plagiarist of Salandra (#2445 in Chapter II); the second from the Library of George Charles Williamson, with his bookplate, and with a one-page hand-written letter from the editor, Beeching, to Williamson, dated "17 July 08" and signed at the bottom, tipped in on fly-leaf (#2446 in Chapter II).

- Already mentioned: the wonderful copy of the 1906 Lyceum Press edition of *Paradise Lost* printed on vellum, with extra set of progressive plates—by printing process, start to finish—bound in at end, in a lovely binding by the Doves Bindery; not mentioned is that laid in this copy are four hand-written letters by T. J. Cobden-Sanderson, cofounder of the Kelmscott Press, of the Doves Press and Doves Bindery, regarding a binding job he was then doing (#1351 in Chapter II).

- *Milton's Prosody* by Robert Bridges. Revised Final Edition. Oxford University Press, 1921, with presentation inscription by Bridges on prelim to John Masefield; as well as E. M. W. Tillyard's first American edition of *Milton* (New York: Dial Press, 1930), with a one-page hand-written letter laid in from Tillyard to Edward Le Comte regarding his (Le Comte's) article on the "two-handed engine" commending Le Comte for "clearing away so much rubbish," signed by Tillyard and dated "Nov. 13, 1950" (#12 in Twentieth-century Miltoniana).

- A fine copy of the 1925 edition of *Poems* handsomely printed at the Florence Press, with a preface by H. J. C. Grierson, and signed and dated by Grierson, "May 5, 1927"; and a very nice set of the 1931–40 Columbia University Press edition of *The Works of John Milton* in twenty-three volumes including the two-volume index, which formerly belonged to Don Cameron Allen, with his bookplate in each volume (#2763 in Chapter II).

- A presentation copy of the 1975 Columbia University Press *Variorum Commentary on The Poems Of John Milton[.] Volume Four[:] Paradise Regained* to James Hutton from the editor, Walter MacKellar; and a presentation copy from Edward Le Comte of the 1978 Norwood Editions of *Justa Edovardo King* "With Introduction, Translations and Notes by Edward Le Comte" (1978) (#1677 and #476, respectively, in Chapter II).

From purely a collector's perspective and as a longtime collector, I mention only three association copies, as difficult as it is to select three, but these are special for very different reasons.

- The former Heber/Crew copy of *The Situation of Paradise Found Out* (1683), a seventeenth-century "Miltonic Novel" in very nice condition formerly owned by two of the most highly regarded twentieth-century collectors; the book has the inscription of "James Boswell" on the front fly-leaf, which may or may not be an early form of the biographer's signature (#9 in Seventeenth-century Miltoniana). To have this copy is one thing, to have the former Heber/Crew copy is quite another.

- I have already mentioned the 1711 *Paradise Lost*, which John Fleming gave to me as a Christmas gift, the book having formerly belonged to Dr. Rosenbach, and which both he and "the Doctor" believed to have belonged to Joseph Addison, at the sale of whose library it was sold in May 1799 as Lot 43. There is no finer association than Dr. Rosenbach, John Fleming, and of course Addison with such a book as the 1711 *Paradise Lost*, not to mention being given the book while with Bob Taylor (#616 in Chapter II).

- Exquisite as the 1792 edition is, with color illustrations by Jeano-Frédéric Schall in a beautiful French straight-grained full red morocco (ca. 1830) binding with the monogram of Ferdinand-Louis-Phillipe (1810–42) eldest son of King Louis Phillipe, the copy formerly belonged to J. R. Abbey, with his bookplate (#775 in Chapter II). Abbey was known for his impeccable taste in fine bindings, as witnessed in this superb binding on the only English poem chosen to be printed by the French in the 1790s period during their great experiment in printing color illustrations. See sale catalogue of Major Abbey (Sotheby's, June 1967, no. 2029).

Another kind of association copy in my collection resulted from my good fortune in having key Milton scholars visit my library and kindly inscribe a copy of their book or books on my shelves, for example, John Steadman and John Shawcross—to whom it was my rare privilege to award honorary degrees on behalf of St. Bonaventure University—Joe Wittreich, Anthony Low, Jason Rosenblatt, and others, always with kind inscriptions, for example, Jason Rosenblatt's in a first edition of his *Torah And Law In Paradise Lost*: "For President Bob Wickenheiser—Miltonist and host extraordinaire—with affection, admiration, gratitude, and envy—From Jason" (1998).

John Mulryan, Bonaventure's remarkable Milton and Renaissance scholar, who has consistently invited scholars to speak on campus—many of whom have then visited my library—has kindly inscribed his own publications on my shelves as well. John Shawcross also kindly responded to my request for his signature in the Arion Press 2002 edition of *Paradise Lost*, for which he edited the text and supplied a "Note on the Text," with a signature and also the kind inscriptions laid within, in Latin: "For my friend and fellow Miltonian—Robert J. Wickenheiser in memoriam cum suae virtutis, tum mei ergo se studij. John T. Shawcross," and in English: "For Robert J. Wickenheiser, whose great interest in and collection of John Milton's works and Miltoniana have been so very meaningful to me. John T. Shawcross."

A unique association copy is the facsimile copy of the *Manuscript of Milton's Minor Poems Preserved in the Library of Trinity College Cambridge* (Cambridge: At the University Press, 1899), which Milton scholar Maurice Kelley gave to me in disbound folio leaves when he retired in 1972 and which bears the simple inscription on the fly-leaf in Maurice's hand: "From the Fellows of Trinity College Cambridge, To Maurice Kelley, To Robert Wickenheiser." Bob Taylor kindly had the folio leaves bound for me.

Associations are of many kinds with many meanings. One of my most special association copies, based on one of my fondest memories, is a small, nondescript book given to me by John Sparrow, warden of All Souls College, during a visit to him by Bob, Mike, and me. I had been looking everywhere for a copy of Thomas Balston's *John Martin, 1794–1854, Illustrator and Pamphleteer*, published by the Bibliographical Society in London in 1934. It is a slim book reprinted from "The Transactions Of The Bibliographical Society," pages 383–432, and everyone I asked told me that the book would be virtually impossible to find. Still I kept looking. When we arrived at the warden's lodging at All Souls College in Oxford, I was awestruck by his book collection and particularly by his vellum binding collection, which Mike told me was among the finest anywhere. I felt a twinge about what might happen in the course of the afternoon, having no idea what that meant.

John Sparrow was delightful as warden, as our host, and as a person. He told story after story, and as the conversation steered to Milton and Martin's illustrations, he mentioned his good friend Tom Balston. The opportunity was too good to let pass, and I asked him if he happened to know where I might find a copy of Balston's 1934 *Illustrator and Pamphleteer*—a listing of Martin's works and one I had been eagerly looking for and hoping to add to my collection. He responded with a perfectly straight face, "Somewhere among my books. It's a small book, as I recall." What a dilemma: to look for the book that I really wanted or to stay and join in this once-in-a-lifetime conversation among three book world giants! The number of books was daunting, but I was never so close to seeing a copy of this important little book by Balston. I decided that once again I would try to both search and listen; so straining to hear at times, I searched shelf after shelf, being told by the good warden that he did not think I would find it because he thought he no longer had it.

Just as the visit was ending and with my heart sinking, I spotted one last section of shelving, and I quickly dashed to it looking among those shelves somewhat frantically, and there it was: a slim quarto in original black cloth, edges untrimmed. I took it to John Sparrow, and he said he really could not believe it and that obviously it was meant to belong with me. I noted that it was a presentation copy to him from Balston, to which he responded that he would then also make it one to me, and so beneath Balston's inscription with signature and the date of 1934, he inscribed the book to me with his signature and the date of 1976. After that visit we became good friends. Book collecting always involves being in the right place at the right time. Certainly such was the case here, as with a great many other books in my collection. Mike and Bob left the warden's lodging also speaking of "serendipity once again!" but I reminded them how diligently I had been looking for this book, yet it made no difference to them, nor for that matter to me, as I smiled with treasure firmly in hand.

Collecting one author has opened the door to a variety of fields, and as space has allowed, each field or area is represented in this book within sections with norms defined at the beginning of the section. Editions are listed with descriptive listings in a section unto itself, with guidelines defined at the beginning of the section. Additional guidelines are provided in "Notes and Abbreviations." Included with editions are translations in a great many languages, often illustrated, but not always, and often the first edition, but again not always. Miltoniana for each century appear in a separate section, with sections for books from the seventeenth century to the twentieth.

Being introduced to press books was a whole new experience for me from the outset. Bob Taylor's interests never tended toward press books because he did not think they added anything to the canon of an author's work or to the text. Besides, they were, and still are, almost always relatively expensive, for understandable reasons, given the nature of their publication and the limited number of editions or issues. In Milton's case, however, press books provide a source for some of the most compelling illustrations of Milton's poetry in our century, not to mention also some of the most beautiful printings of Milton's editions. Press books are almost always rare, because they tend to be printed in a limited number. The higher the quality, the rarer the press book, and also the more expensive.

Press books are given full listings among editions, and they are present in the collection far more than I ever thought possible thirty-five years ago, in names both known and unknown. Here is a list of some, but by no means all of them: the Arion Press, the Ashendene Press, the Ashlar Press, the Astolat Press, the Ballantyne Press, the Blue Sky Press, Harry Lorin Binsse, the Clerk's Press, the Chiswick Press, the Cresset Press, the Daniel Press, the Doves Press, the Elston Press, the Eragny Press, the De La More Press, the Golden Cockerel Press, the Golden Hind Press, the Gregynog Press, Mason Hill Press, the Lyceum Press, John Henry Nash, the Nonesuch Press, the Old Bourne Press, the Pear Tree Press, Steward Taylor at his private press, the Trianon Press, Allan Wingate, and the Whittington Press.

When I started collecting Milton I cowered at being asked to define what is meant by a "press book," and in fact did, to a certain degree, during an early visit to Rota's when Tony and Bob had some matters to attend to and I was roaming the floor and had stopped to look at a great many thin books and items in protective wrappers on shelves behind locked glass doors and was asked: "Is there something you would like to see, sir?" At that point I was not sure how to answer the question, and during the lull in the conversation, the attending staff person inquired further, "a certain press book or printing?" I still was not sure of quite what to say, but my curiosity had been peaked by several earlier purchases from the Schlosser collection, and so I thought there must be more to be found. There certainly was, but not by simply asking for it, except for the very well-known, because seldom is the "it" one wants to ask for available or perhaps even known about until found or offered, as in the case of Milton's *On the Morning of Christ's Nativity. An Ode*. With a 'Note' by F. Mary Wilson Parsons. Printed by F[rank]. Steward Taylor at his Private Press; Xmas 1893, 43/50 copies, numbered and signed by the printer, which Alan Grant at Blackwell's Rare Books kindly offered me by letter with the notation that "we cannot trace another example of this (or any other) work from F. Steward Taylor's press anywhere" (#593 in Chapter II). The importance of the bookdealer friend becomes apparent once again.

One of my favorite stories regarding text, ironically enough, given Bob Taylor's belief about press books and text, has to do with the 1937 Nonesuch edition of *Comus*, illustrated by Mildred Farrar. I was fortunate enough to obtain E. H. Visiak's copy as a second copy, but by no means a "duplicate" copy, along with the uncorrected proofs of the introduction and the first thirty-three pages of the text, corrected in manuscript by Visiak (#278 in Chapter II). In his autobiography, quoted in *The History Of The Nonesuch*, Visiak writes: "I had taken for *The Mask Of Comus* the second edition text; Milton was alive.... and would have attended to the proofs. But there was one alteration ... which in the consensus of Miltonian critics was invalid. The first edition has 'frighted' [steeds], the second 'flighted.' I was prevailed upon to substitute 'flighted' in the proofs. I did them up, with a heavy mind; and, suddenly overcome with fatigue, lay down upon a couch, there sank into a state between sleeping and waking. With stunning suddenness a fierce whisper sounded in my ear, 'That word is "frighted!"' It virtually precipitated me off the couch, and I tore off the wrapping from the proofs, re-read the context, crossed out 'flighted,' and wrote 'stett.' I gratified my fancy later on, by entering in the margin, 'At Milton's demand.'"

From my Princeton teaching days, I had developed an interest in the anthology and what it shows about the reading interests and influences of a given age. When I managed to obtain a copy of the first anthology, published in 1762, with Milton selections in it, I proceeded to increase my collecting of anthologies through the ages with Milton selections in them, confident, as I still am, that this will make a great study or studies on the reading choices of a given age. The first anthology, serving also as a school book for the period, is *The Poetical Miscellany; Consisting Of Select Pieces From the Works of the following Poets, viz. Milton, Dryden, Pope, Addison, Gay, Parnel, Young, Thomson, Akenside, Philips, Gray, Watts, &c. For the Use of Schools*. London: Printed for T. Becket and P. A. De Hondt, at Tully's Head, in the Strand. MDCCLXII. First edition (#3 in Chapter IV). The book contains selections from Milton's poetry, as well as a great many items that have close connections with Milton, for example, John Philips's *The Splendid Shilling*. While the copy is a little worn, it is scarce, with several perceptive comments in a contemporary hand in the margins, especially in the Milton section.

This is an important work in helping to establish a new manner in which Milton (and other great poets and writers) were to be read and studied in years to come. The "anthology" was to become in the next two centuries an important means for passing on selectively the great writings of poets like Milton, with selections being the method by which students and those with leisure time were exposed to great writers. As time went on, especially before the age of radio and television, the anthology became a special way in which great writers were selectively passed on to new generations of readers, from one culture to another. At the same time, anthologies provided a way of focusing on the writings that attracted a given age to a great writer: they tell us much about how a great writer is viewed, how attitudes changed, and to which works (or selections from works) an age is attracted, or, for that matter, exposed, and how these attractions changed (or readers were influenced and thereby compelled to change) through the generations, particularly with respect, now, to a poet like Milton.

The collection's holdings in anthologies, both illustrated and nonillustrated, are rather extensive, some 375 items. Space limitations once again preclude listing them all. A section is devoted to providing a sample listing of anthologies, along with photographs of select bindings of some of the anthologies in which Milton appeared. Anthologies in which the focus is on the full printing of one of Milton's poems (not selections from Milton's poems) are listed under that poem in Chapter II.

As evident from earlier observations I have made about Bob Taylor and Mike Papantonio supporting my enthusiasm for John Martin and encouraging me to obtain whatever I could whenever Martin became available, it is certainly no surprise that Martin occupies a central place within my collection. In fact, because Bob and Mike did what each could to make Martin available to me and to help me discover exciting rare Martins on a regular basis early on in my collecting career, Martin is not only central to my Milton collection, but he is also a rather complete collection unto himself within the larger Milton collection. The John Martin collection might be sorted into three major parts: Martin's illustrations of Milton; Martin's illustrations of the Bible; and Martin's illustrations of works other than Milton and the Bible, primarily early annuals but also other poets and writers. Descriptive listings among the Milton listings describe the large number of editions of Milton illustrated by Martin in the collection, with a photograph of the various formats chosen by Septimus Prowett in which he first published *Paradise Lost*—in parts, Imperial folio, Imperial quarto, and Imperial octavo (#889 in

Chapter II). A separate section on Martin uses photographs to show Martin's "proof" plates for *Paradise Lost* and for the Bible and also to show Martin's illustrations of early literary annuals and of several bindings.

It should be noted that the collection is also strong in its holdings of William Blake and Gustave Doré, in terms of publications with illustrations by each as well as studies about each, particularly Blake. Space simply does not allow a section on each illustrator of Milton, but Doré is captured in some important holdings in the collection including Doré's first appearance in parts (#1077 in Chapter II) and a fine first edition folio binding (#1078 in Chapter II) along with photographs of these and various splendid decorated cloth bindings of the period as well as several illustrations. The holdings in Blake are represented in the milestone publications of Blake's illustrations in the twentieth century beginning with the 1906 Lyceum Press edition printing in color and for the first time the set of illustrations for *Paradise Lost* in the Boston Museum of Fine Arts, an edition that the collection has in several bindings: original boards (#1349 in Chapter II), unbound and wholly uncut (#1350 in Chapter II), and bound by the Doves bindery (#1351), down to the splendid 2004 Arion Press reproduction of Blake illustrations in the Huntington Library (#1525 in Chapter II), of which the collection proudly owns copy number 2.

A section is devoted to capturing originals in the collection with select photographs. Through the years I have been very fortunate to add various originals to the collection, including some original illustrations of Milton's poetry. There are, of course, the important drawings of Henry Richter discussed above as to my obtaining them from Marlborough Rare Books. The collection also includes two small watercolor paintings by Francis Hayman of scenes in *Paradise Lost*; an original pencil sketch by George Romney of *The Fall of the Rebel Angels*; twenty unattributed and undated original sketches (ca. 1800) in its original scrapbook, of which fourteen are of scenes in Milton's *Paradise Lost*; drawings for *Paradise Lost* and *Comus* by John Bell, who designed part of the Albert Memorial in London; an original series of designs from *The Story of Sabrina in the Comus of Milton* by Henry Howard, nineteenth-century history and portrait painter; original illustrations of scenes in *Comus* by F. R. Pickersgill, member of the Art Union and contributor to the 1858 illustrated edition of *Comus*; the ca. 1730 sepia drawing of the blind Milton by Jonathan Richardson the Elder, which graces this book as its frontispiece; and a small unattributed nineteenth-century oval portrait of Milton in oils in a pale green velvet mat inside a charming oval Victorian period walnut frame. There are also illuminated Milton texts, early and important engravings (by James Gilray, Henry Fuseli, and others), and several manuscript texts.

A section is devoted to capturing select ephemera and objets d'art in the collection with select photographs. That Milton has become something of an icon can be seen in the various Milton ephemera and objets d'art that have accrued to the collection over the years, including Milton tobacco, tea, valentine, and other illustrated cards with appropriate quotations from Milton's poems; stamps from Hungary and Russia; and advertisements large and small quoting Milton and sometimes providing a portrait of Milton. Among the objets d'art are various bronze medals commemorating Milton, beginning with the Dassier medal in the 1730s and the much larger J. S. Tanner medal in 1737, two different memorial medals in 1818, and the Russian medal in 1984; as well as busts, statues, and brass plaques of all sizes and ages, including a 1920s cameo plaque.

Scholarship has been remarkably strong throughout the twentieth century continuing on into the twenty-first century, and interest in Milton can be seen in the great many critical studies that have been published during this period. In addition to over 3,450 editions and 800 Miltoniana (some very important and rare, particularly from the seventeenth and eighteenth centuries), more than 1,400 works of critical study are a part of the collection. While they have been catalogued, there is no room here to identify, much less provide a descriptive listing of, the critical studies in the collection. Most are fine copies, a fair number are association copies, often presentation copies from the author; several were identified earlier in this text. Included are complete runs of *Milton Studies* and the *Milton Quarterly* from their inaugural issues through to the present.

Substantial reference works from the nineteenth and twentieth centuries are also a part of the collection. While they, too, have been catalogued, as with the critical studies, they cannot be listed here because of space constraints. The two together, however, along with important Miltoniana, provide a great deal of what a Milton scholar or student needs to complete his study of Milton, often within the confines of a single setting.

Sale catalogues are likewise an important part of the collection, as are exhibition catalogues as part of the collection's reference works. Over thirty-five years of collecting Milton has brought a great many catalogues to my home, many of which have contained Milton items, and some of which have been devoted wholly or in part to Milton. There are catalogues from nearly a hundred dealers and bookshops, both the well-known and the not-so-well known, extending from the 1970s through to 2005. Together they provide an important resource and valuable reference to Milton's works through several key decades at the end of the twentieth century, in the context of other books and authors being sold during this same period.

Photographs are used throughout the book to show the extensive range in the collection of editions from the seventeenth through the twentieth centuries to the present; of varying illustrations and of interesting and sometimes unique bindings during this same period; and of statuary, brass hangings, cigarette cards, and a variety of other items showing Milton as the icon he is.

The listings here are intended to provide a sort of one-stop resource with the range of information provided. With regard to nineteenth-century editions, particularly illustrated editions, I hope to excite by providing details for editions published in that century, many of which have not been recorded before and which are listed with full descriptions here for the first time. The twentieth century has produced great scholarly editions of Milton and splendid texts for use by students; all stand alongside truly remarkable publications, by private presses in particular, which can only be admired for their uniqueness of achievement in print and design and with illustrations. Many will surely bear the test of time, as editions before them have. Whatever service the listings here provide, I hope they and everything else in this book help to advance the enthusiasm for a great poet, described by Dryden in his famous epigram:

> Three Poets in three distant Ages born—
> Greece, Italy and England did adorn.
> The First in loftiness of thought Surpass'd;
> The Next in Majesty: in both the Last.
> The force of Nature could no further goe;
> To make a Third she joyn'd the Former two.

No one attempting to provide a descriptive list of editions in a collection of this size, indeed a selective description of a collection this size, could possibly not want his endeavors to serve as a basis upon which to build. This book is just a beginning, intended to introduce a collection with a great many studies waiting to be done about a poet of the ages, whom Dryden praised as England's Homer and Virgil.

The selections in this book show the range and quality of a Milton collection that is the result of thirty-five years of collecting. This is a collection for the Milton scholar and student. It is also a collection for those interested in publishers and bindings through the ages; for the lover of books in all their changing beauty, from the splendor of rich morocco bindings, to richly decorated cloth bindings, mesmerizing marbled paper bindings, art nouveau bindings, and much more. As the collection is for the scholar and student of Milton, so is this book; but as the collection reaches far beyond Milton per se, because Milton himself does, so does this book—for collecting Milton through the ages has involved collecting Milton in varying formats, from the very large to the very small, in varying styles and bindings, and with a remarkable variety of illustrations, reaching beyond the views of any one age at any one time.

As the collection provides the basis for countless exhibitions for a great variety of reasons, so I have tried to capture that spirit in the photographs of the collection within this book: always focused on Milton, of course, but showing Milton in books as the book itself has evolved through the ages, as illustrators of Milton have evolved in styles and in what they illustrate in Milton and how they illustrate their chosen topic, and in examples of how Milton has become an icon through the ages.

Milton continues to live, and while this collection runs from his first published poem on Shakespeare (by virtue of that leaf from the famous 1632 Shakespeare folio) on through to editions published with illustrations in 2005, I have every confidence that there will be good reason to add regularly and broadly to this collection in the years to come: both new publications as well as works that should already be in the collection but unfortunately are not.

My wife Pat and I are thrilled that the collection now belongs to the University of South Carolina and that it will be housed together in the new Special Collections and Rare Books wing of the Thomas Cooper Library to be completed in 2008. I admire the University and in particular President Andrew A. Sorensen for their continuing commitment to rare books and special collections, evident by the construction of a remarkable new facility to house the University's rare books and special collections, and I am truly grateful for the University's acquisition of my Milton collection and for the leadership role President Sorensen played in the acquisition, along with Paul A. Willis, Dean of Libraries, and Patrick Scott, Director of Special Collections and Professor of English Literature. I had long hoped to keep my Milton collection together so that students and scholars would have ready access to it and so that a public that wants to, may have occasion to view its varied holdings in various exhibits. The collection being owned by the University of South Carolina makes that all possible, and I could not be happier.

I am deeply humbled by the University's commitment to keep this collection together as the "Robert J. Wickenheiser Milton Collection" and to house portions of the collection in the room named for William L. Richter, who played a major role in the collection coming to the University. I have happily said before and do so again here: to be associated with Bill Richter in this special way and for years to come is a real honor for me. I have come to know and respect Bill Richter as a man who cares deeply about others, as one of the kindest and gentlest of men to whom commitment means something. I shall always be profoundly grateful that our names will be linked together in such an extraordinary way, for such an extraordinary purpose: to afford scholars, students, and visitors in years to come the opportunity to view and study Milton and other features of this collection in the William L. Richter Room.

I am confident that the collection will bring great acclaim to the University of South Carolina. Today's most eminent Milton scholar, John Shawcross, kindly wrote of the collection that he considers it "one of the major collections of materials related to John Milton, editions and studies and artworks, in the world." I mention this not for personal satisfaction, startled and most gratified as I was when I first read these words, but because John's statement in a longer letter about the collection provided, I am sure, one of the important reasons why the University acquired the collection, and it should remain an incentive, as undoubtedly it will, for the University and its Friends of Special Collections to continue to add to the collection so that it will be used and appreciated by countless future generations of students, faculty, and all who know that "books are not absolutely dead things, but do contain a potency of life in them to be as active as that soul was whose progeny they are . . . [for] a good book is the precious lifeblood of a master spirit embalmed and treasured up on purpose to a life beyond life" (*Areopagitica*).

Robert J. Wickenheiser
May 5, 2006

Donald A. Keller, a medical illustrator whose specialty has been ocular surgery illustration for more than twenty-five years, is nephew to the collector at whose request he designed the bookplate for the collection.

II
Descriptive Listing of Editions

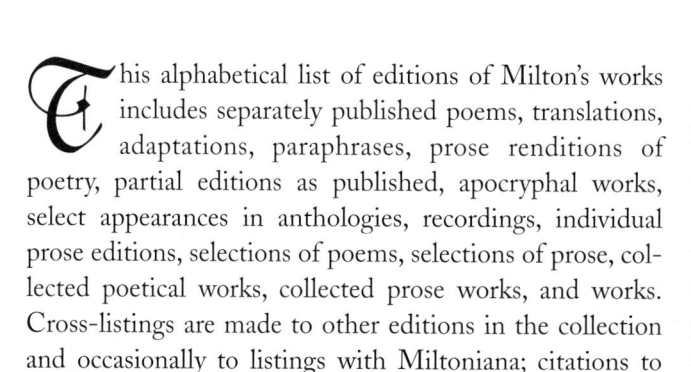

This alphabetical list of editions of Milton's works includes separately published poems, translations, adaptations, paraphrases, prose renditions of poetry, partial editions as published, apocryphal works, select appearances in anthologies, recordings, individual prose editions, selections of poems, selections of prose, collected poetical works, collected prose works, and works. Cross-listings are made to other editions in the collection and occasionally to listings with Miltoniana; citations to other editions are always to editions found in the collection.

Not all editions from among the 3,450 in the collection are included here. All seventeenth- and eighteenth-century editions are; likewise most nineteenth- and a great many twentieth-century editions are. With respect to the latter two centuries, first editions are always listed when known, others are listed in terms of importance and priority; reference to later editions is made in the first or earliest edition listed. Editions are listed chronologically in a given year up through 2005, where the collection ends. Illustrated editions precede nonillustrated editions, while editions printed in England appear before those printed in America. Translations appear before partial editions. Variant bindings are described, although the listing itself is provided in a shortened version from the first listing which provides full publishing details.

1. JOHN MILTON'S AN APOLOGY Against a Pamphlet Called A Modest Confutation of the Animadversions upon the Remonstrant against Smectymnus[.] Critical Edition by Milford C. Jochums[.] *University of Illinois Press, Urbana, 1950*. First edition thus. 4to, xii+255pp., half-title, title page in red and black, bibliography and index at the end, original red cloth, black cloth spine, spine lettered in gilt. "The facsimile text of the *Apology* presented in this edition is actual size" (p. 5). Fine.

Arcades

2. MILTON'S ARCADES AND COMUS With Introduction, Notes And Indexes By A. Wilson Verity, M.A. Sometime Scholar Of Trinity College, Cambridge. Edited For The Syndics Of The University Press[.] Pitt Press Series[.] *Cambridge: At The University Press[,] 1891. All rights reserved*. First edition thus. Slim 8vo, lxxvi+208+8pp., half-title, original blue cloth (a few notations in pencil, contemporary signature on fly-leaf), spine lettered in gilt with gilt emblem. Nice. Eight pages of advertisements at the end. Not in Kohler.

3. JOHN MILTON ARCADES With Introduction, Notes And Indexes Edited By A. W. Verity, M. A. Sometime Scholar Of Trinity College[.] *Cambridge: At The University Press[,] 1908*. Fourth edition thus. Slim 8vo, xxxi+28+[12]pp., half-title, original blue cloth, spine lettered in gilt. Fine. Twelve pages of advertisements at the end. First edition thus published in 1891 (copy preceding). Not in Kohler.

4. ARCADES BY JOHN MILTON[.] *Shaftesbury[:] At The High House Press[,] 1930.* Slim 8vo, 8pp., half-title, title page with typographic ornament in red, printed on handmade paper, original white paper spine, patterned blue paper over boards, edges untrimmed. Fine. No. 32 of 100 numbered copies.

4A. (Cross-listing) **ARCADES [In] FOUR POEMS BY JOHN MILTON[:] L'ALLEGRO[,] IL PENSEROSO[,] ARCADES[,] LYCIDAS[.]** With Wood-Engravings By Blair Hughes-Stanton[.] *[Newton, Wales:] The Gregynog Press[,] MCMXXXIII.* See *Four Poems*, 1933.

5. ARCADES A piece taken from "Poems of Mr. John Milton, both English and Latin, Compos'd at several times. Printed by his true Copies. London 1645." Afterword by John G. Demaray[.] *The King Library Press[,] Lexington[,] 1983.* Slim 8vo, [unpaginated, printing the poem on recto only]+[5]pp.+[colophon leaf], frontispiece illustration (first appearance of Gloria Thomas's line drawing of a dancing figure, traced from a Victor Hammer watercolor), original gray-green wrappers, repeating frontispiece illustration on front cover, enclosing original dark blue self-wrappers. "Printed on the Washington handpress of Joe Graves by Janice Miller with assistance from Norman Baylor," "Printing supervision by Joan Davis." Mint. No. 28 of 100 copies on Head paper.

Areopagitica

Milton's great work of prose, *Areopagitica*, stands as the most famous of all defenses of the freedom of the press. It is a mine of familiar quotations and rallying sentiments almost unparalleled in a short work of English literature: "Books are not absolutely dead things"; "As good almost kill a man as kill a good book"; "A good book is the lifeblood of a master spirit—embalmed & treasured up on purpose to a life beyond life"; "I cannot praise a fugitive and cloistered virtue"; "Opinion in good men is but knowledge in the making"; "Though all the winds of doctrine were let loose to play upon the earth . . . who ever knew Truth put to the worse, in a free and open encounter?"; "when God gave [man] reason, he gave him freedom to choose, for reason is but choosing," all present in the original pages here.

6. AREOPAGITICA; A SPEECH OF Mr. JOHN MILTON For the Liberty of VNLICENC'D PRINTING, To the PARLAMENT of ENGLAND. [Quotation in Greek from "Euripid. Hicetid" followed by poetic translation.] *LONDON, Printed in the Yeare, 1644.* First edition. Small 4to, 30pp.+[last 5 leaves of text lacking and supplied in xerox], decorative headpiece first page, double black border rule on title page, half blue morocco, marbled paper over boards (stain on title, a few top page numerals shaved, and the marginal gloss on B1 verso cropped, as usual), gilt rules on covers, gilt-decorated spine, raised bands, marbled endpapers, a.e.g. All of the previously stated sentiments are present in the original pages here. A second separate edition was not published until over a hundred years later in 1738 (following edition). According to Shawcross, "Printer unknown; may have been Augustine Mathewes." Rare. Pforzheimer 707; *Printing and the Mind of Man*, p. 133; Parker, p. 890; Wing M2092; Shawcross, 1984, 61; Shawcross, Kentucky, 14; Shawcross, 1974, pp. 304–8; Coleridge 4; Not in Kohler.

7. AREOPAGITICA: A Speech Of Mr. John Milton, For the Liberty of Unlicens'd Printing, To the Parliament of England. First Published in the Year 1644. With A Preface, by another Hand. [Quotation in Greek from "Euripid. Hicetid" followed by poetic translation.] *London: Printed for A. Millar, at Buchanan's-Head, over-against St. Clement's-Church, in the Strand. 1738. (Price One Shilling).* Second separate edition. 8vo, viii+58+[2]pp., preface, decorative head- and tailpieces and decorated initial letters, advertisement leaf at the end, modern paper wrappers, housed in a custom brown half morocco slipcase with gilt-stamped spine. Title a bit soiled and age-browned, otherwise a good copy, complete with advertisement leaf at end. James Thomson, author of *The Seasons*, provided the preface. The advertisement on the final leaf is for Milton's *Complete Collection* of 1738 (copy listed here), edited by Thomas Birch. Scarce. Coleridge 5; Not in Kohler.

8. AREOPAGITICA, 1780. [In] Blackburne, Francis. REMARKS ON JOHNSON'S LIFE OF MILTON. To Which Are Added, Milton's Tractate Of Education And Areopagitica. *London: MDCCLXXX.* First edition. 8vo, vi+369pp., contemporary quarter calf, boards (bit worn, spine chipped at top, hinges cracked, minor age spots), gilt rules on spine with decorations in blind, spine lettered in gilt: "Milton Of Education." Good copy in original state with early notation on preliminary blank: "Privately printed at the expense of Archdeacon Blackburne, without his name. Lowndes." After Blackburne's *Remarks* appear "The dates of the original editions of Milton's Prose Works" and then his "Poetical Works," followed by Blackburne's edition of *Of Education* and then his edition of *Areopagitica*, with "Preface by Mr Thomson" preceded by a reprinting of the 1644 title page. Coleridge discusses the printing of this work, suggesting that it might have appeared first in the appendix of Blackburne's *Memoirs of Thomas Hollis* (see copy with Eighteenth-century Miltoniana), published earlier in the same year, and was then printed, probably in a small number of copies and anonymously, separately with Milton's *Of Education* and *Areopagitica*, as here, later in the year. Shawcross indicates the opposite order of publication; Havens prefers the order given here and by Coleridge, who also indicates "additional materials . . . showing that both works were being printed at the same time." Rare. Shawcross, Kentucky, 435; Shawcross, 1972, pp. 311, 422; Havens, p. 31; Coleridge 6 (and see 283, Memoirs, for additional discussion); Not in Kohler.

9. AREOPAGITICA: A Speech To The Parliament Of England, For The Liberty Of Unlicensed Printing, By John Milton; With Prefatory Remarks, Copious Notes, And Excursive Illustrations, By T. Holt White, Esq. To which is subjoined, A Tract Sur La Liberté De La Presse, Imité De L'Anglois De Milton, Par Le Comte De Mirabeau. *London: Printed For R. Hunter, Successor To Mr. Johnson, No. 72, St. Paul's Churchyard, And Richard Steevens, Bell Yard, Temple Bar. 1819.* First edition thus. 8vo, [2]+lxxxi [verso blank]+311+[1]pp., half-title, glossary, separate half-title and title page for translation by Mirabeau, advertisement for White's *A Review of Johnson's Criticism on the Style of Milton's English Prose* on verso of last page of text (see extra-illustrated copy with Nineteenth-century Miltoniana), extensive footnotes, list of editions, contemporary half calf (neatly rebacked preserving original spine), marbled paper over boards with decorative gilt trim, gilt-decorated spine within the panels, thick raised bands with decorative gilt trim, red morocco label with gilt lettering and gilt rules, marbled endpapers and edges, bound by E. Pover, Chester, with his ticket. Nice copy, from the Library of Hugh, Second Duke of Westminster, with the Eaton Hall bookplate. For an original oval watercolor drawing of Thomas Holt White, see White's *Review of Johnson's Criticism on the Style of Milton's English Prose*, 1818, extra-illustrated edition, with Nineteenth-century Miltoniana. Stevens 1202; Kohler 489.

10. JOHN MILTON. AREOPAGITICA. [24 November] 1644. English Reprints. Preceded By Illustrative Documents. Carefully Edited By Edward Arber, Associate, King's College, London, F.R.G.S., &c. *London: Alex. Murray & Son, 30, Queen Square, W.C. Ent. Stat. Hall.] 1 January, 1868. [All Rights reserved.* First edition thus. Bound with **JOSEPH ADDISON. CRITICISM ON MILTON'S PARADISE LOST.** From 'The Spectator.' 31 December, 1711–3 May 1712. English Reprints. Carefully Edited By Edward Arber, Associate, King's College, London, F.R.G.S., &c. *London: Alex. Murray & Son, 30, Queen Square, W.C. 1 August, 1868. Ent. Stat. Hall.]* One Shilling. *[All Rights reserved.* First Arber edition. 2 volumes in one. 8vo, 80pp.,+152pp., title pages in red and black, decorative head- and tailpieces, decorated initial letters, facsimile reproduction of "An Order Of The Lords And Commons. . . For the Regulating of Printing . . . 1643"—that work preceding *A*—and of first edition title page of *Areopagitica* (1644), this order becoming that followed in later Arber editions, original quarter black morocco, red linen over boards (a bit rubbed at joints, foxing, some light pencil notations in a neat hand), spine lettered in gilt, bound Roxburghe style. Fine, with early name neatly inscribed on front blank. Kohler 491, listing *A* only.

11. Variant of Preceding. **JOHN MILTON. AREOPAGITICA** . . . *London: 5 Queen Square, Bloomsbury, W. C., Ent. Stat. Hall.] 1 January, 1868. [All Rights reserved.* First edition thus? 8vo, 80+15+[1]pp. (rest as preceding copy), original dark brown thick paper wrappers (worn, spine chipped, front joint barely holding, early owners' names [dated 1874 and 1879] on fly-leaf, marginal notes in ink in a fine hand), front cover lettered in gilt ("English Reprints" at the top, "John Milton Areopagitica 1644" at the center, and "Sixpence" at the bottom) with decorative black trim in the background, edges untrimmed. Despite being a little worn, a good copy with variant publisher's imprint on title page, in original wrappers, and with sixteen pages of advertisement bound in at the end. Not in Kohler.

12. Variant of Preceding. **AREOPAGITICA** [In] **ENGLISH REPRINTS.** Carefully Edited By Edward Arber, Associate, King's College, London, F.R.G.S., &c. John Milton. Areopagitica, 1644. Hugh Latimer. Ex-Bishop of Worcester. Sermon On The Ploughers, 1549. Stephen Gosson. The Schoole Of Abuse, 1579. A Short Apologie Of The Schoole Of Abuse, 1579. *London: Alex. Murray & Son, 30, Queen Square, W.C. Ent. Stat. Hall.] 1868. [All Rights reserved.* First edition thus. 8vo, 80pp.,+40pp., +80pp.,+7+[1]pp., half-title, general title page in red and black with advertisement for "English Reprints" on verso, title page in red and black for each of the three works, including: "**JOHN MILTON. AREOPAGITICA.** [24 November] 1644. English Reprints. Preceded By Illustrative Documents. Carefully Edited By Edward Arber, Associate, King's College, London, F.R.G.S., &c. *London: Alex. Murray & Son, 30, Queen Square, W.C. Ent. Stat. Hall.] 1 January, 1868. [All Rights reserved.*," (rest as preceding copies), original green cloth (bit rubbed, joints slightly cracked from within, early stamp "Private Library of R. P. Dow" on front and back endpapers), covers ruled in blind, spine lettered in gilt with small decorative gilt device, red endpapers, and red edges. Nice, with variant publisher's imprint on title page, in a variant publisher's binding, and with eight pages of advertisements bound in at the end. Not in Kohler.

13. Variant of Preceding. **JOHN MILTON. AREOPAGITICA** . . . *London, F.R.G.S., &c. London: 5 Queen Square, Bloomsbury, W.C. Ent. Stat. Hall.] 1 January, 1868. [All Rights reserved*. First edition thus. Similar to preceding editions but with variations in publisher's imprint (without "Alex. Murray & Son" and with a different address: "5" in place of "30"). Bound with **MILTON'S AREOPAGITICA. A COMMENTARY.** (Privately Printed.) First edition thus. Bound with **SIR PHILIP SIDNEY. AN APOLOGIE FOR POETRIE, 1595**. English Reprints. Carefully Edited By Edward Arber, Associate, King's College, London, F.R.G.S., &c. *London: 5 Queen Square, Bloomsbury, W.C. Ent. Stat. Hall.] 1 January, 1868. [All Rights reserved*. First edition thus. 3 volumes in one. Slim 8vo, 72pp.,+80pp.,+xvi+32pp., title pages for *Areopagitica* and Sidney's *Apologie* in red and black, with Sidney's *Apologie* appearing first in the volume, half-title for "A Commentary," which follows *A*, decorative head- and tailpieces, decorated initial letters, and facsimile reproductions as with first Arber edition listed here, original half black calf, marbled paper over boards (a little worn, joints cracked, label removed from front cover, small label removed from bottom of the spine, names removed from the top of flyleaf and each title page), red morocco label with gilt lettering and gilt rules on spine, raised bands with decorative gilt trim (faded). Despite the flaws, a good copy. Included after Milton's *A* is a "Commentary" by R. C. Jebb with an "Analysis" and extensive notes. Uncommon. Not in Kohler.

14. **JOHN MILTON. AREOPAGITICA.** [24 November] 1644. English Reprints. Preceded By Illustrative Documents. Carefully Edited By Edward Arber, Associate, King's College, London, F.R.G.S., &c. Large Paper Edition. *London: Alex. Murray & Son, 30, Queen Square, W.C. Ent. Stat. Hall.] 1 March 1869. [All Rights reserved*. Second edition thus, first issue. Slim 8vo, 80pp., title page in red and black, decorative head- and tailpieces, decorated initial letters, facsimile reproductions as with first Arber edition listed here, original thick dark brown paper wrappers (spine chipped at top and bottom, front joint slightly cracked, foxing at top of title page), front cover decorated in black and gold, edges untrimmed, partially unopened. Nice, with early dated signature in pencil on title page. Large paper copy. Uncommon. Not in Kohler.

15. Variant of Preceding. **JOHN MILTON. AREOPAGITICA.** [24 November] 1644. English Reprints. Preceded By Illustrative Documents. Carefully Edited By Edward Arber, Associate, King's College, London, F.R.G.S., &c. *London: 5 Queen Square, Bloomsbury, W.C. Ent. Stat. Hall.] 1 March 1869. [All Rights reserved*. Second edition thus, second issue, large paper copy. Bound with Hugh Latimer, **SERMON ON THE PLOUGHERS** . . . *London: Alex. Murray & Son, 1 March 1869*. Bound with Stephen Gosson, **THE SCHOOLE OF ABUSE** . . . *London: Alex. Murray, 1 March 1869*. Bound with Sir Philip Sidney, **AN APOLOGIE FOR POETRIE** . . . *London: Alex. Murray & Son, 1 March 1869*. Bound with Edward Webbe, **HIS TRAUILES, 1590** . . . *London: Alex. Murray & Son, 1 March 1869*. Bound with John Selden, **TABLE-TALK, 1689** . . . *London: Alex. Murray & Son, 1 March 1869*. Bound with Roger Ascham, **TOXOPHILUS, 1545**. *London: Alex Murray, 1 October, 1869*. Together, seven items in one volume. Thick, tall 8vo, 80pp.,+40pp.,+80pp., +72pp.,+40pp.,+120pp.,+168pp., title pages in red and black, contents, introduction, and notes for each work, with the addition of "Chronology" for all of the works except *Areopagitica*, decorative head- and tailpieces, decorated initial letters, and facsimile reproductions as with first Arber edition listed here, modern quarter calf, marbled paper over boards, gilt rules on spine with small decorative gilt pieces in the panels, red morocco label with gilt lettering and gilt rules, a.e.g. Most of the items are described as large paper copy. Very nice volume with variant publisher's imprint on title page of *Areopagitica* from that in preceding 1869 Arber edition. Uncommon. Not in Kohler.

16. **MILTON AREOPAGITICA** Edited With Introduction And Notes By John W. Hales, M.A., Professor of English Language and Literature at King's College, London; Formerly Fellow and Assistant Tutor of Christ's College, Cambridge; Barrister-at-Law of Lincoln's Inn; Editor of 'Longer English Poems'; Co-Editor of the 'London Series of English Classics,' &c. Third Edition, Revised[.] Clarendon Press Series. *Oxford[:] At The Clarendon Press[,] M DCCC LXXXII. [All rights reserved]*. Third edition thus, revised. 8vo, xlv+159pp., half-title, introductions to 1874, 1878, and 1882 editions, half-title for *A*, notes and index at end, original orange pebble cloth, blind rules on covers, spine lettered in gilt within gilt rules. Nice. First edition thus in 1866. Uncommon. Not in Kohler.

17. **AREOPAGITICA** [In] **FAMOUS PAMPHLETS[:]** Milton's Areopagitica[;] [Edward Sexby's] Killing No Murder[;] De Foe's Shortest Way With The Dissenters[;] Steele's Crisis[;] Whately's Historic Doubts Concerning Napoleon Buonaparte[;] Copleston's Advice To A Young Reviewer With An Introduction By Henry Morley[,] LL.D., Professor Of English Literature At University College, London[.] *London[:] George Routledge And Sons[,] Broadway, Ludgate Hill[;] New York: 9 Lafayette Place[,]*

1886. First edition thus. 8vo, 316+[4]pp., half-title before each work, original green cloth (used and stained), paper label (bit faded) lettered in black on spine, printed gray endpapers with advertisements, edges untrimmed. Four pages of advertisements bound in at the end.

18. AREOPAGITICA, Letter On Education, Sonnets, And Psalms. By John Milton. Cassell's National Library. *Cassell & Company, Limited: London, Paris, New York & Melbourne. 1888.* First edition thus. 16mo, [2]+192+[2]pp., half-title with advertisement for the series (including this edition) on verso, small medallion emblem on title page, original light brown cloth (a little used), front cover richly decorated in black and lettered in gilt and black, central floral decoration incorporating "Cassell's National Library" in black at the center, spine lettered in black, advertisements in black on back cover, advertisements on front and back pastedowns and endpapers with additional advertisements on verso of front and back endpapers. Decent copy of an uncommon edition with early and later book labels on front pastedown. Not in Kohler.

19. AREOPAGITICA A Speech Of Mr. John Milton For The Liberty Of Unlicensed Printing, To The Parliament Of England With An Introduction By James Russell Lowell[.] *New-York[:] The Grolier Club[.] MDCCCXC.* First edition thus. 8vo, lvii+189pp., half-title, engraved frontispiece portrait etched by G. Mercier after William Faithorne, introduction with half-title, facsimile reproduction of first edition title page of "*A*" (1644), decorative head- and tailpieces and decorated initial letters, original blue paper over boards (a bit rubbed, front joint slightly cracked, spine chipped at the top and missing two small pieces near the top), printed paper label on spine, edges untrimmed. Nice, with the bookplates of Robert Hoe and Leonard Schlosser. Loosely laid in is a folded signature of four leaves of the work printed on vellum, of which only three complete copies were printed. One of 325 copies on Holland paper. Not in Kohler.

20. AREOPAGITICA [In] SELECTIONS IN ENGLISH PROSE FROM ELIZABETH TO VICTORIA (1580–1880). Chosen And Arranged By James M. Garnett . . . *Boston, U.S.A.: Published By Ginn & Company. 1891.* First edition. 8vo, xi+701+[6]pp., original blue cloth (a bit worn), front cover and spine lettered in gilt. Six pages of "Advertisements" bound in at the end. Not in Kohler.

21. MILTON AREOPAGITICA Edited With Introduction And Notes By John W. Hales, M.A., Professor of English Language and Literature at King's College, London; Formerly Fellow and Assistant Tutor of Christ's College, Cambridge; Barrister-at-Law of Lincoln's Inn; Editor of 'Longer English Poems'; Co-Editor of the 'London Series of English Classics,' &c. Clarendon Press Series[.] *Oxford[:] At The Clarendon Press[,] M DCCC XCIV.* 8vo, xlv+159+8pp., half-title, original dark olive green sand grain cloth, blind rules on covers, spine lettered in gilt. Eight pages of advertisements bound in at the end. First edition thus in 1866. See copy of third, revised edition thus in 1882 listed here. Kohler 492, reporting "Not in the British Library. Not in the Bodleian Library. Not in Cambridge University Library."

22. JOHN MILTON[.] AREOPAGITICA[.] [24 November] 1644[.] Preceded By Illustrative Documents[.] Edited By Edward Arber[,] F.S.A., Etc. Late Examiner In English Language And Literature To The University Of London[.] English Reprints[.] *Westminster[:] A. Constable And Co. 1895.* Third edition thus by Constable. 8vo, 80pp., title page in red and black, facsimile reproduction of "An Order Of The Lords And Commons . . . For the Regulating of Printing . . . 1643"—that work preceding *A*—and of first edition title page of *Areopagitica* (1644), as with first Arber edition listed here, original green cloth (a bit rubbed, slight staining on both covers), front cover and spine lettered in gilt, edges untrimmed. First edition thus edited by Edward Arber published in 1868; second thus in 1869—both listed here. Not in Kohler.

23. Variant of this nicely printed edition with thirty pages of advertisements bound in at end. Not in Kohler.

24. AREOPAGITICA A Speech of Mr. John Milton For the Liberty of Unlicenc'd Printing to the Parlament [sic] of England[.] *London[,] Printed in the Yeare, 1644[.] New-York and London[:] G. P. Putnam's Sons[,] The Knickerbocker Press[.] n.d. [ca. 1895].* First edition thus? Slim 12mo, 134+[7]pp., half-title for "Ariel Booklets," engraved frontispiece portrait after the miniature by Faithorne, protective tissue guard with label in red, title page in red and black, contemporary crushed red calf (a bit worn along joints and extremities), decorative emblem in classical motif incorporating *A* at top of front cover, spine lettered in gilt, t.e.g., fore- and bottom edges untrimmed, white ribbon marker loosely laid in. Seven-page list of "Ariel Booklets" bound in at the end. Uncommon. Not in Kohler.

25. AREOPAGITICA & Other Tracts By John Milton[.] *MDCCCC · Published · By · J · M · Dent · And · Co: Aldine · House · London · W · C ·* First edition thus. 8vo, [i]+155pp., edited with notes by C. E. Vaughan, half-title in red and black ("The Temple Classics"), unsigned engraved frontispiece portrait within elaborate decorative frame, protective tissue guard, title page in red and black with elaborate decorative black border in art nouveau style, original blue calf over limp boards (spine ends a little worn), blind-stamped owl on front cover, spine lettered in gilt within decorative gilt trim, monument-style device printed in green on front pastedown containing Milton's name and dates along with his early prose works and dates, t.e.g., fore- and bottom edges untrimmed, red ribbon marker. Nice, with contemporary bookplate on front pastedown over Milton monument (see variant copy following for full monument). This small volume begins with an "Analysis Of The Order Of Parliament (June 14, 1643), Against Which The Areopagitica Was Directed," and follows with "Of Education," "Letter On Education," "Autobiographical Extracts" from several works, and "Notes" on each entry. Second edition thus was published in 1907; third thus in 1925—both listed here. Stevens 1245; Not in Kohler.

26. Variant of Preceding, original green calf over limp boards (spine a bit worn and spine ends a little chipped), t.e.g. Good, in a variant publisher's leather binding.

27. JOHN MILTON[.] AREOPAGITICA[.] [24 November] 1644[.] Preceded By Illustrative Documents[.] Edited By Edward Arber[,] F.S.A., Etc. Late Examiner In English Language And Literature To The University Of London[.] English Reprints[.] *Westminster[:] A. Constable And Co., Ltd. 1903.* 8vo, 80pp., facsimile reproductions and decorative head- and tailpieces and decorated initial letters as with first Arber edition listed here, notes, original green cloth, front cover lettered in blind, spine lettered in gilt, top and fore-edges untrimmed. Nice. First edition edited by Edward Arber published in 1868 (also listed here). Not in Kohler.

28. AREOPAGITICA. A Speech Of Mr. John Milton For The Liberty of Unlicenc'd Printing, To The Parlament [sic] of England. [Greek Quotation from Euripid. Hicetid. With English Translation] *[London: The Eragny Press; New York: John Lane. 1904.]* Small folio, 36+[1]pp.+[1] leaf (colophon and press mark), elaborate woodcut border on first page of text, delicate woodcut initial letters, woodcut device on final page, all designed by Lucien Pissarro and engraved on wood by Esther Pissarro, "Sold By The Eragny Press, London, And John Lane, New York" (colophon), original paper boards, "carnation cover printed in two colours," bookplate (spine darkened, binding a bit worn and soiled, fly-leaves discolored). Overall, an excellent copy of a beautifully designed and produced book. Presentation copy inscribed "To Miss Tisdall From E. L. Pissarro Jan 1. 1907" on fly-leaf. Laid in are two very attractive pieces of Eragny ephemera: a New Year's greeting from the Pissarro's on a 5 ½" × 2" stiff blue card printed in brown, and a finely printed three-page order form for the works of Milton, with an account of a bindery fire and the publication consequences. "Because 'the block used for the border page was only strong enough to print 160 copies,' this Eragny title has a smaller limitation than most other items from the press" (Phillip Pirages, Cat. 11, #444, 1986). The work was finished initially in October 1903, but a fire at the binder of Messrs. Leighton, Son & Hodge destroyed all but the printer's sample and forty unbound copies. A second issue (also listed here) was completed in March of 1904 in a printing of 160 copies (of which 134 were for sale). This is one of the few large format Eragny Press books and the only one to be printed in two columns. The paper used here is both splendid and shown to good advantage because of the book's remarkably wide margins. One of 134 copies (of 160 total). Forty unbound copies of an earlier issue, the remnants of the bindery fire, were also offered for sale. Taylor, *Art Nouveau Book*, pp. 121–22 (illus.); Franklin 207; Ransom, *Private Presses*, p. 263; Tompkinson 64; Kohler 494.

29. MILTON AREOPAGITICA Edited With Introduction And Notes By John W. Hales, M.A., [Etc.] Clarendon Press Series[.] New Edition. *Oxford[:] At The Clarendon Press[,] M DCCCC IV.* Fourth edition thus. 8vo, xlv+[1]+160+8pp., half-title, introductions to 1874, 1878, and 1882 editions, general index following notes, original dark olive green cloth (a bit rubbed), spine lettered in gilt with gilt rules and small seal of the press in gilt. Good. Eight pages of advertisements bound in at the end. Kohler 496, reporting "Not in the British Library. Not in the Bodleian Library. Not in Cambridge University Library."

30. MILTON'S AREOPAGITICA A Speech for the Liberty of Unlicensed Printing With Introduction And Notes by H. B. Cotterill, M.A., [Etc.] *London[:] Macmillan and Co., Limited[;] New York: The Macmillan Company[,] 1904[.] All rights reserved.* First edition thus. 8vo, xliii+118+[2]pp., half-title, "Chronological Summary" and index following notes, original red cloth (spine a little faded, former owner's signature and another's printed label on front pastedown and fly-leaf), front cover decorated in embossed blind with lettering in embossed blind at the top, spine lettered in gilt. Advertisement leaf bound in at the end. Not in Kohler.

31. AREOPAGITICA: A Speech Of Mr. John Milton For the Liberty of Unlicenc'd Printing, To The Parlament [sic] of England. [Greek Quotation from Euripid. Hicetid. With English Translation] *[Hammersmith: The Doves Press, 1907.]* 4to, 74pp.+colophon leaf, original limp vellum, spine lettered in gilt, edges untrimmed, bound at the Doves bindery. Lovely copy. Only 325 copies were printed; of these, 25 were on vellum and 300 were on paper, as this copy. Roderick Cave, *The Private Press*, p. 147; Stevens 1252; Ransom, *Private Presses*, p. 12; Not in Kohler.

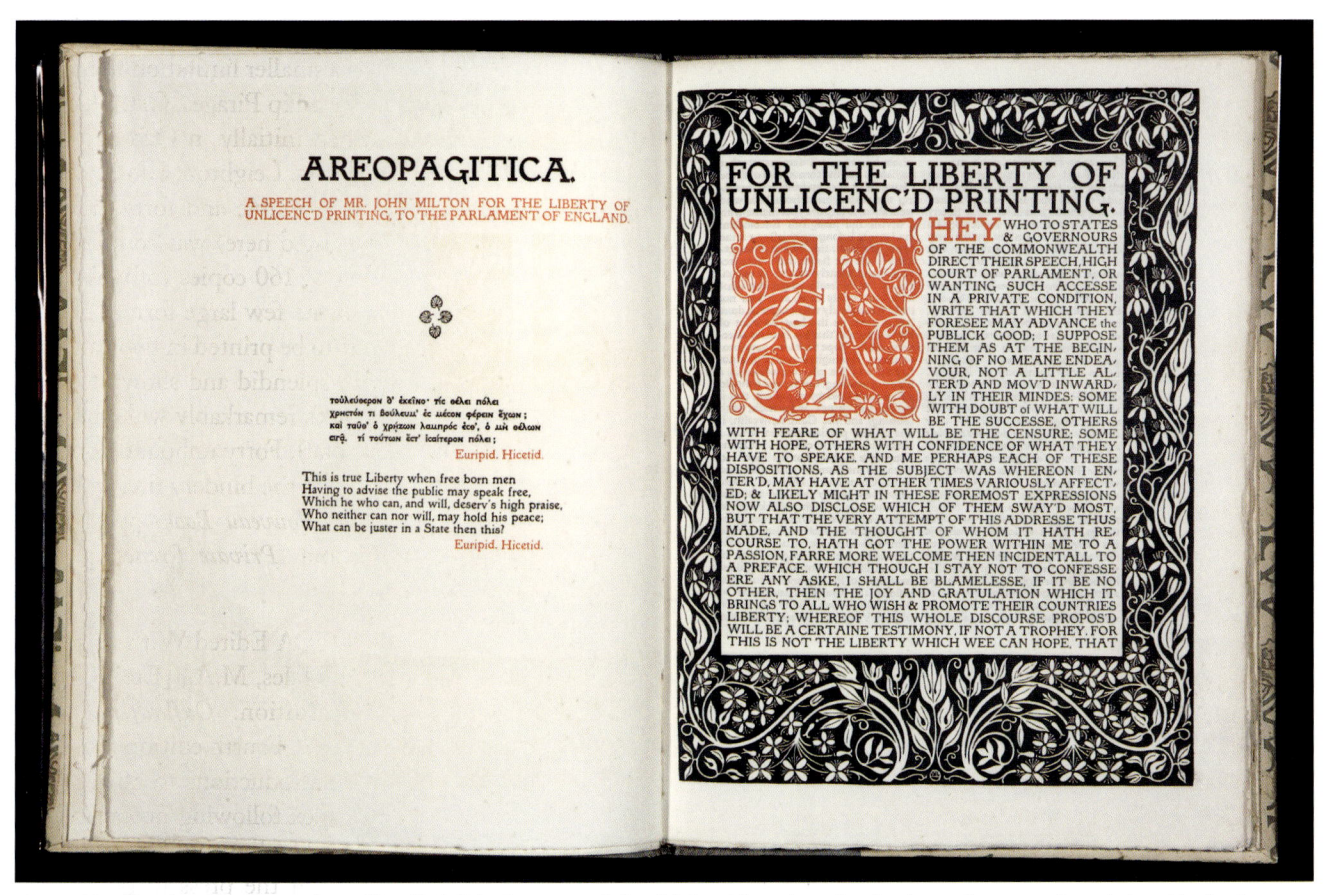

Areopagitica. [London: The Eragny Press; New York: John Lane. 1904]. Small folio, elaborate woodcut border on first page of text designed by Lucien Pissaro, engraved on wood by Esther Pissarro. Presentation copy. See #28.

32. AREOPAGITICA & Other Tracts By John Milton[.] MDCCCCVII · Published · By · J · M · Dent · And · Co: Aldine · House · London · W · C · Second edition thus. 12mo, [i]+155pp., edited with notes by C. E. Vaughan, half-title in red and black ("The Temple Classics), unsigned engraved frontispiece portrait within elaborate decorative frame, protective tissue guard, title page in red and black with elaborate decorative black border in art nouveau style, contents as with first edition listed here, original limp blue cloth (a bit rubbed, occasional marginal notes in a neat hand in ink with neat underlining in ink of famous passage, former owner's signature in ink on fly-leaf and again on back pastedown), blind-stamped owl on front cover, spine lettered in gilt within decorative gilt trim, monument-style device printed in green on front pastedown containing Milton's name and dates along with his early prose works and dates, t.e.g., fore- and bottom edges untrimmed, pink ribbon marker. A good copy. First edition thus published in 1900 (also listed here); third thus in 1925 (also listed here). Not in Kohler.

33. AREOPAGITICA [In] ESSAYS, CIVIL AND MORAL And THE NEW ATLANTIS By Francis Bacon[.] AREOPAGITICA And TRACTATE ON EDUCATION By John Milton[.] RELIGIO MEDICI By Sir Thomas Browne[.] With Introductions, Notes And Illustrations[.] *The Harvard Classics Edited By Charles W Eliot LL D "Dr Eliot's Five-Foot Shelf Of Books" P F Collier & Son[,] New York[,] (1909)*. First edition thus. 8vo, 347pp., frontispiece photograph of Browne, emblem in red on title page, half-title for each work, original blue cloth, spine lettered in gilt with small emblem of Harvard in white. A second edition thus was published in 1937 (also listed here). Not in Kohler.

34. AREOPAGITICA [In] THE WORLD'S GREATEST BOOKS. Joint Editors Arthur Mee[,] Editor and Founder of the Book of Knowledge[,] [And] J. A. Hammerton[,] Editor of Harmsworth's Universal Encyclopaedia. Vol. XX. Miscellaneous Literature[.] Index. *N.P.: Wm. H. Wise & Co. Copyright, MCMX[.] McKinlay, Stone & Mackenzie[.]* 8vo, vi+362pp., frontispiece portrait of Matthew Arnold, decorated title-page plate, index, original blue cloth, central device of several books within bookends in blind on front cover, gilt-decorated spine with gilt lettering. Not in Kohler.

35. AREOPAGITICA. Written by Mr. John Milton[.] Printed For Sydney Humphries[,] *Published By Adam And Charles Black[,] London[,] MCMXI.* Large 8vo, xxi+[i]+95pp., copyright page, "Special Note" page ("The whole of the profit derived from the sale of this book will be devoted to The London Library"), half-title, dedication page, crest at center of title page, original blue cloth (bit rubbed), gilt-ruled and gilt-lettered front cover and spine with elaborate crest in gilt at center of front cover, t.e.g., others untrimmed and partially unopened. Very nice. Printed by R. & R. Clark, Edinburgh, on handmade paper in a limited edition of 500 copies, from Blackburne's edition of 1780 (also listed here). "Unusually able editing" (Stevens). Stevens 1259; Kohler 497.

36. AREOPAGITICA & Other Tracts By John Milton[.] *MCMXXV • Published • By • J • M • Dent • & Sons • LD • Aldine • House • London • W • C[.]* Third edition thus. 12mo, [i]+155pp., edited with notes by C. E. Vaughan, half-title in red and black ("The Temple Classics") with small red emblem at the center, unsigned engraved frontispiece portrait of Milton within elaborate decorative frame, protective tissue guard, title page in red and black with elaborate decorative black border in art nouveau style, contents as with first edition, original blue pebble cloth, blind-stamped owl on front cover, spine lettered in gilt within decorative gilt trim, monument-style device printed in green on front pastedown containing Milton's name and dates along with his early prose works and dates, t.e. blue, fore- and bottom edges untrimmed. Mint. First edition thus published in 1900; reprinted in 1907—both editions listed here.

37. [AREOPAGITICA.] The Noel Douglas Replicas[:] John Milton • Areopagitica[.] [Facsimile Of The First Edition Of 1644 In The British Library.] *Noel Douglas 38 Great Ormond Street[,] London WC I[,] (1927).* Noel Douglas facsimile. Small 4to, [iii]+40pp., facsimile reproduction of first edition published in 1644 including title page, original blind-stamped parchment (bit age-darkened), spine lettered in red, edges untrimmed, partially unopened, bookplate on front pastedown. This facsimile reproduction was taken from the British Museum copy that Milton presented to Thomason and bears the manuscript corrections probably by Milton or authorized by him; it was "Made and printed in England by Percy Lund, Humphries & Co. Ltd. Bradford and London" (verso title page).

38. Variant of Preceding, identical in all respects, except in a variant original parchment binding without blind-stamping; the binding is clean and fresh with bright lettering on spine.

39. [AREOPAGITICA] THE ENGLISH REPLICAS[:] JOHN MILTON • AREOPAGITICA[.] . . . *Published By The Cambridge University Press In 1918[.] 1927[,] Payson & Clarke Ltd[.,] New York[.]* Payson & Clarke facsimile. Small 4to, [iv]+40pp., facsimile reproduction of first edition published in 1644 including title page, original boards (bit age-darkened with two slight circular marks at center of front cover), decorative blue trim incorporating title in blue within at center of front cover, spine lettered in blue, t.e. rough, fore- and bottom edges untrimmed. Good copy, fresh and clean within. This facsimile reproduction, like that of "The Noel Douglas Replicas" printed the same year (also listed here), was taken from the British Museum copy that Milton presented to Thomason and bears the manuscript corrections probably by Milton or authorized by him; it was "Made and printed in England by Percy Lund, Humphries & Co. Ltd. Bradford and London" (verso title page).

40. Variant of Preceding. Nice copy with the rare tipped in notice over the publisher's imprint: "This book is now published in the United States by Columbia University Press for the Facsimile Text Society[,] 2960 Broadway, New York, N.Y."

41. AREOPAGITICA AND OTHER PROSE WORKS OF JOHN MILTON. *London & Toronto[:] Published By J • M Dent & Sons Ltd & In New York By E • P • Dutton & Co[.,] (1927).* First edition thus, first issue. 8vo, xvii+306pp., half-title with advertisement for "Everyman Library" on verso (this edition being "No. 795"), frontispiece consisting of a quotation from Bacon with elaborate black border trim in art nouveau style, title page with similar elaborate black border trim in art nouveau style, "First Issue Of This Edition 1927" on verso of title page, "Made at the Temple Press Letchworth In Great Britain" at bottom of final page, original light orange cloth (stamp on fly-leaf), central emblem of the press in blind on front cover, spine lettered in gilt with decorative gilt trim at top and large decorative gilt device beneath the gilt lettering, decorated endpapers in art nouveau style, t.e. blue. Included are an "Introduction To The 'Areopagitica'" and *Of Education*; "Of Reformation In England"; *An Apology For Smectymnuus*; *The Ready And Easy Way*; *The Doctrine And Discipline Of Divorce*; "Meditations Upon Divine Justice And The Death Of King Charles The First"; and "Autobiographical Extracts."

42. Variant of Preceding. AREOPAGITICA AND OTHER PROSE WORKS[.] John Milton[.] *London: J. M. Dent & Sons Ltd.[;] New York: E. P. Dutton & Co. Inc.[,] (1927).* First edition thus, second issue. 8vo, xvii+306+16pp., half-title with advertisement for "Everyman Library" on verso, brief biographical statement about Milton on blank before title page, decorative emblem on title page, original dark orange cloth (spine slightly faded, name in ink on fly-leaf), central emblem in blind on front cover, spine lettered in gilt, lightly decorated endpapers, t.e. orange. Nice, with variant form of "First Published in this Edition 1927" on verso of title page, with variant half-title, variant title page and no frontispiece, in a variant publisher's binding, and with sixteen pages of advertisements for "Everyman's Library Edited By Ernest Rhys" (with its own title page) bound in at the end.

43. AREOPAGITICA AND OTHER PROSE WRITINGS BY JOHN MILTON Edited With An Introduction By William Haller[,] Associate Professor Of English In Columbia University[.] The Modern Readers' Series[.] *The Macmillan Company Publishers[,] New York[,] MCMXXVII.* First edition thus. 8vo, xvii+170+[3]pp., half-title with decorated frontispiece on verso, decorative border trim on title page, half-title for each for the works, "Notes" on each of the works, original bright blue cloth, front cover and spine lettered in gilt within decorative gilt piece, decorated endpapers, advertisement leaf bound in at the end. Very nice copy with armorial bookplate on front pastedown. Other works included are *Of Education*, *The Ready And Easy Way*, and "Autobiography," with selections.

44. AREOPAGITICA AND OTHER PROSE WRITINGS BY JOHN MILTON Edited With An Introduction By William Haller[.] *New York[:] The Book League Of America[,] 1929.* 8vo, xvii+170pp., half-title, "Special edition published by arrangement with The Macmillan Company" on verso of title page, half-title for various of the works, "Notes" on each of the works, original blue cloth, central emblem in gilt on front cover, spine lettered in gilt, fore-edge untrimmed, printed light gray publisher's wrappers (bit used) with "120 Standard Books" listed on front and back flaps. Very nice. This is a special publication by the Book League of America of the 1927 edition (first thus) by the Macmillan Company (also listed here).

45. AREOPAGITICA [In] ESSAYS, CIVIL AND MORAL And THE NEW ATLANTIS By Francis Bacon[.] AREOPAGITICA And TRACTATE ON EDUCATION By John Milton[.] RELIGIO MEDICI By Sir Thomas Browne[.] With Introductions and Notes[.] The Harvard Classics Edited By Charles W Eliot, LL. D. P. F. *Collier & Son Corporation[,] New York[,] (1937).* Second edition thus. 8vo, 332pp., half-title ("The Harvard Classics—Registered Edition"), frontispiece portrait of Sir Thomas Browne, half-title for various of the works, original green leather, decorative gilt border trim on front cover with central gilt seal of Harvard, spine ruled and lettered in gilt with gilt seal, raised bands, yellow endpapers. Fine. First edition thus published in 1909; second thus in 1937—both listed here; variously reprinted thereafter.

46. AREOPAGITICA John Milton[.] *The Caxton Press[,] Christchurch[, New Zealand,] (1941).* First edition thus. 8vo, [6]+55+[2]pp., half-title, central emblem in blue on title page, "Note on Areopagitica" and half-title before the essay, "Typographical Note" following, original blue cloth spine, marbled blue paper over boards (a bit rubbed, edges a bit worn, slight foxing). Printed in a limited edition of 150 copies.

47. AREOPAGITICA With A Critical Introduction, Notes and Comments And A Foreword By Prof. N. S. Takakhav, M.A., I.E.S. (Ret.). English Classics for Indian Students. John Milton. *Karnatak Publishing House[,] Bombay 2[,] 1942.* First edition thus. 8vo, ii[mispaginated "xii"]+ix+cvi+226pp., central emblem of the press on title page, 206-page "Introduction," original printed paper over boards (a bit rubbed, name on fly-leaf, several marginal notations in pencil).

48. JOHN MILTON AREOPAGITICA A Speech For The Liberty Of Unlicensed Printing To The Parliament Of England 1644[.] *Newly Imprinted In The Typography Department Of The Maidstone School Of Art And Crafts[,] MCMXLIV.* First edition thus. Tall, thin 8vo, 59pp., half-title, title page in red and black, "Analysis Of The Order Of Parliament (June 14, 1643) Against Which The Areopagitica Was Directed" with header in red and black, "Areopagitica" with initial letter ("T") in red, colophon at end: "This edition, designed and printed in the Typography Department of the Maidstone School of Art and Crafts, was produced under the direction of Charles L. Pickering, during the Principalship of A. S. Ryland and, later, Edward J. Morss . . . ," original orange cloth spine (slightly faded and rubbed), linen boards, orange label printed in black on front cover. Very nice, with a Reynolds Stone bookplate tipped on fly-leaf. Tipped on front blank and signed by Edward J. Morss, one of the principals in the publication of this edition, is a statement printed in red and black about the publication and the "happy coincidence" of the tercentenary anniversary of the publication of *Areopagitica* and the defense of liberty once again three centuries later. Privately printed in a small edition.

49. [AREOPAGITICA] JOHN MILTON REDE FUR DIE PRESSFREIHEIT UND GEGEN DIE ZENSUR *Deutsche Ubertragung von Hans Fleig[.] 1944[.] Verlag Ernst Ganzmann / Basel[.]* First edition thus. 8vo, 95pp., half-title preceded by page with small emblem at the center, "Erst Auflage" on verso of title page, "Geleitwort" ("Foreword") before the translation of "Areopagitica," with

"Anmerkungen Zur Rede" or "Notes to the Speech" at the end, original white boards, front cover lettered in maroon. Very nice.

50. JOHN MILTON AREOPAGITICA[.] *Published & Distributed By The Great Books Foundation[,] Chicago, Illinois[,] (1949)*. First edition thus, first issue. Slim 8vo, 65pp., emblem of the foundation at bottom right corner of title page, pamphlet (spine a bit sunned), original stiff gray paper wrappers, front cover lettered in brown with emblem of the foundation at bottom right corner. Part of "The Second Year Course" of "The Great Books Foundation Discussion Program," with a listing of the eighteen works included in the course, *A* being no. 11. Very nice. Part of a set of the eighteen works in the course, each in similarly nice condition (spines a bit sunned), preserved in original slipcase (a bit rubbed), broad side of the slipcase lettered in brown with emblem of the foundation in the center. The whole very well-preserved and in good condition.

51. JOHN MILTON AREOPAGITICA[.] *Published by Henry Regnery Company for The Great Books Foundation[,] Chicago, Illinois[,] (1949)*. First edition thus, second issue. Slim 8vo, 65pp., decorative piece at the center of title page, pamphlet, original stiff gray paper wrappers, front cover lettered in brown with central device in brown, major questions about *A* and commentary on the work printed in brown on inside front cover. Very nice.

52. AREOPAGITICA AND OF EDUCATION[.] John Milton[.] With Autobiographical Passages from Other Prose Works[.] Edited By George H. Sabine[,] Cornell University[.] *Appleton-Century-Crofts, Inc.[,] New York[,] (1951)*. First edition thus. Slim 8vo, xii+110pp., half-title, original printed stiff blue paper wrappers (a few underlinings in pencil), with advertisements for the series on inside front and back cover. Good copy of this Crofts Classics paperback.

53. AREOPAGITICA & Other Tracts By John Milton[.] *Boston[:] The Beacon Press, 1951*. First edition thus by the Beacon Press? 12mo, v+155pp., edited with notes by C. E. Vaughan, half-title ("Edited by Israel Gollancz") with emblem of the press in red at the center and with "Published In Great Britain By J. M. Dent And Sons Ltd. London" on verso, unsigned engraved frontispiece portrait within elaborate decorative frame, protective tissue guard, title page in red and black with elaborate decorative black border in art nouveau style, "Notes" at end, "Printed By Morrison And Gibb Ltd., London And Edinburgh" on verso of last page, original blue cloth over thin boards, owl stamped in blind relief at center of front cover, spine lettered in gilt with decorative gilt piece at the top and the bottom, a monument-style device with a list of Milton's early prose works and original dates printed in gold on front pastedown, t.e. blue, fore- and bottom edges untrimmed, partially unopened. A fine copy in printed rust publisher's wrappers lettered in white. Reminiscent of editions by Dent early in the century (see 1900, 1907, and 1925 editions listed here) with same content.

54. AREOPAGITICA[.] number 10 first year[.] *The Great Books Foundation[,] Chicago[,] (1955)*. First edition thus. Slim 8vo, 65+[1]pp., half-title before title page with brief biography of Milton on verso, half-title for *A*, paperback, printed red and black stiff paper wrappers. Nice. Bound with Shakespeare[.] *The Tragedy Of Macbeth*. Number 9 first year. *The Great Books Foundation[,] Chicago[,] (1955)*. Volumes 9 and 10 of ten-volume paperback set in original slipcase, the whole very well-preserved and in nice condition.

55. AREOPAGITICA [In] THE CAMBRIDGE TREASURY. VOLUME TWO: BURTON TO JOHNSON 1621–1781. *New York: Caedmon Publishers, (ca. 1965)*. 1 33 ⅓ rpm LP record. First edition thus. LP recording in original slipcase. Milton's *Areopagitica* is read in full since "the poetic passion of his pleading makes this pamphlet a monument of English literature." Caedmon TC1055.

56. [AREOPAGITICA] JOHN MILTON POUR LA LIBERTE DE LA PRESSE SANS AUTORISATION NI CENSURE AREOPAGITICA Traduit et préface par O. Lutaud[,] chargé de maîtrise de conférences à la Faculté des Lettres et Sciences humaines d'Orléans-Tours[.] *Aubier-Flammarion[,] (1969)*. 8vo, 248+[8]pp., general half-titles and title pages in English and in French, half-title for "Chronologie," half-title for 125-page "Introduction" by Lutaud in French, half-title before five-page "Bibliographie" in French, reproduction of 1644 title page, half-title in English and in French before Milton's treatise, paperback, original printed stiff paper wrappers, with a partial portrait of a middle-aged, long-haired Milton in red on left side of front cover with English title above in red, and with a partial portrait of the same middle-aged, long-haired Milton in black on right side of front cover with French title above in black, portrait repeated in miniature at top of back cover, with quotation "For Books are not absolutely dead things . . . " in English in red on left side and in French in black on right side below the portrait. Nice copy of this bilingual edition. Presentation copy inscribed by the editor with corrections on title page.

57. AREOPAGITICA AND OF EDUCATION By John Milton[.] Edited With introductions And Notes By

Michael Davis, M.A. Senior English Master at Marlborough College[.] *Macmillan, 1971.* 8vo in 16s, xv+131+[1]pp., half-title (with a listing of "English Classics—New Series" on verso), paperback, original printed stiff red paper wrappers lettered in black and white with a reproduction of a bust of Milton on front cover and a portion of the bust reproduced on back cover. Nice. Part of "English Classics. New Series" with the label "Macmillan's English Classics" on front cover. This edition first published in 1963.

58. JOHN MILTON. AREOPAGITICA. [24 November] 1644. Preceded By Illustrative Documents. Carefully Edited By Edward Arber, Associate, King's College, London, F.R.G.S., &c. *Albert Saifer[,] Philadelphia[,] 1972.* Slim 8vo, 80pp., reproduction of 1868 Edward Arber edition, including title page (although not in red and black as in original edition), facsimile reproduction of "An Order Of The Lords And Commons . . . For the Regulating of Printing . . . 1643"—that work preceding *A*—and of first edition title page of "*A*" (1644), original cream cloth, spine lettered in gilt. Very nice. Reprint edition of first edition thus by Edward Arber in 1868 (also listed here).

59. AREOPAGITICA[:] A Speech Of Mr John Milton For The Liberty Of Unlicensed Printing To The Parliament Of England. *[Printed At The Rampant Lions Press for Deighton, Bell & Company, 13 Trinity Street, Cambridge, 1973.]* 4to, xiv+[1]+49+[1]pp., edited, with an introduction and notes, by Isabel Rivers, half-title printed in red, title page printed in red and black in Palatino type and Monotype Palatino with initials in red in Grot R. throughout, introduction, half-title ("For The Liberty Of Unlicensed Printing"), "Notes" with half-title at the end, full dark olive green morocco, spine lettered in gilt within raised bands, t.e.g., others untrimmed, bound by John P. Gray and Son, Cambridge. Designed by Sebastian Carter, printed by him and Will Carter on mould-made paper by J. Barcham Green with the text set in two sizes: the larger type for Milton's main argument, the smaller type (in double column) for contemporary matters and historical analogies. Mint, in a buckram slipcase. "The aim of this edition, conceived by Sebastian Carter, is to present for the modern reader a text which separates what is of lasting value in Milton's work from what is ephemeral and merely polemical, in a format which will do it justice" (Introduction). Of the edition of 500 copies, this is one of 100 numbered deluxe copies bound in full morocco. Fitzwilliam Catalogue 53.

60. Variant of Preceding, original black buckram, tan morocco label with gilt lettering on spine, purple endpapers, t.e.g., others untrimmed, bound by Garp, Cambridge. A fine copy in a variant publisher's binding. No. 98 of 400 numbered regular copies. Fitzwilliam Catalogue 53.

61. AREOPAGITICA [In] JOHN MILTON[.] ZUR VERTEIDIGUNG DER FREIHEIT *Sozialphil-osophisce Traktate[.] 1987 Verlag Philipp Reclam jun. Leipzig.* First edition thus? 8vo, 308+[3]pp., half-title, facsimile reproduction of first edition title page before each work translated here (*Areopagitica, The Tenure of Kings, A Treatise Of Civil Power, The Readies & Easie Way*), notes, bibliography, and index, paperback, printed stiff paper wrappers, with illustration in black and white on front cover and a brief biography of Milton on back cover. Nice. Three pages of advertisements bound in at end. The translation is by Klaus Udo Szudra—Hrsg.

62. [AREOPAGITICA] [Reprint edition] *"This special edition of AREOPAGITICA By John Milton has been privately printed for the members of The Classics of Liberty Library[,] (1992)."* 8vo, lvii+189pp., decorative trim at top of reprint title page with "The Classics of Liberty Library Editorial Advisory Board" on verso, beginning then with reprint of original edition by the 1990 Grolier Club edition (also listed here), including half-title, title page, engraved frontispiece portrait etched by G. Mercier after Faithorne, introduction with half-title, facsimile reproduction of first edition title page of *A* (1644), decorative head- and tail-pieces and decorated initial letters, original half brown crushed morocco, brown silk, covers decorated with crossed gilt rules and decorative gilt device at the center, spine lettered in gilt with decorative gilt pieces at the top and bottom, raised bands within gilt rules, marbled endpapers, a.e.g., brown silk ribbon marker. Mint. Colophon page reads: "This special edition of Areopagitica By John Milton has been privately printed for the members of The Classics of Liberty Library by Arcata Graphics / Kingsport. . . . The volume has been quarter-bound in genuine leather by Arcata Graphics / Sherwood. Endleaves are a specially commissioned design of Richard J. Wolfe. . . . Cover stampings and design of the edition are by Daniel B. Bianchi and Selma Ordewer." Laid in: original advertisement card of "The Classics Of Liberty" (Delran, New Jersey) for *A* with a summary of Milton's argument and a description of the publication.

63. AREOPAGITICA[:] A Speech of Mr. John Milton for the Liberty of Unlicensed Printing, to the Parliament of England[.] London, Printed In The Year 1644[.] [Quotation from Euripides in Greek and English] *Bandanna Books • 1992 • Santa Barbara.* First edition thus, second printing. Slim 8vo, 44pp., "Second Printing" on verso of title page, half-title before text, paperback, original printed stiff paper wrappers with an unsigned sketch of Milton in black and white on front cover. Nice. A college edition, "with humanist editing by A. S. Ash" (front cover).

64. AREOPAGITICA[:] A Speech Of Mr John Milton For The Liberty Of Unlicensed Printing To The Parliament Of England. *London, 1644. Octavo Digital Edition (Standard) CD of Bridwell Library copy of John Milton['s] Areopagitica. [Palo Alto:] Octavo CD Digital Edition, 1998.* First edition thus. CD, including live text and commentary by Nicolas Barker. Every page and the binding photographed at very high resolution and presented on CD as Adobe PDF file with software to view, search, and print.

65. AREOPAGITICA AND OTHER POLITICAL WRITINGS OF JOHN MILTON[.] John Milton[:] Foreword by John Alvis[.] *Indianapolis[:] Liberty Fund[,] (1999).* First edition thus. 8vo, ix+463pp., half-title, unsigned frontispiece portrait of Milton, index, original three-quarter speckled gray buckram spine, tan buckram boards, front cover lettered in blind, spine lettered in gilt against a darker black background within gilt rules, patterned endpapers, black edges. Fine.

The collection also has this edition in its first paperback edition published the same year in fine brown stiff printed wrappers and with the same patterned endpapers.

66. THE ARTS OF EMPIRE, And Mysteries of State Discabineted. In Political and Polemical Aphorisms, grounded on Authority and Experience. And Illustrated with the Choicest Examples and Historical Observations. By the Ever-renowned Knight Sir Walter Raleigh, Published By John Milton Esq.; Quis Martem tunica tectum, Adamantina digne scripserit? *London, Printed by G. Croom, for Joseph Watts at the Angel in St. Paul's Church-yard, 1692.* Third edition, first issue. 8vo, [6]+238+[1]pp., double black rule around title page, two-page preface by Milton, nineteenth-century calf boards decorated in blind trim (rebacked with original spine laid down, a bit rubbed), thick raised bands, orange leather label near the top of the spine with title lettered in gilt, place and date lettered in gilt near the bottom, blue endpapers, speckled edges, small yellow book restorer's label tipped in at bottom of inside back cover. A nice copy of a rare book, complete with advertisement leaf at the end. "One of the curiosities of Milton bibliography," according to John Shawcross, is his edition of *The Cabinet-Council: Containing the Chief Arts of Empire, And Mysteries of State* (title given in brief here), which was first published in 1658 and again in 1661. Shawcross provides the details of this work, as well as the early publishing history. Coleridge 71a; Shawcross, 1974, pp. 330–32; Parker M1; Not in Kohler.

67. THE BEAUTIES OF MILTON, THOMSON, AND YOUNG: [Quotation from Thomson] *London. Printed for G. Kearsley, at No 46, Fleet Street.—1783. Price Half a Crown Sewed.* 12mo in 6s, xxiv+288pp., engraved title page with three vignette portraits of the poets (unattributed, with Milton at the center), dedication page, preface with a short life of each poet, Milton follows, half-title for Thomson and Young, new half calf antique style, old marbled boards, gilt rules on spine, original red morocco label with gilt lettering and decorative gilt trim, raised bands. A nice copy with early bookplate. Included are extensive poetical selections from Milton including: *L'A, IlP,* and *L*, complete, several of the sonnets, excerpts from *PR* and *SA*, as well as excerpts from *PL* and *C*, under special headings (for example, "Satan's Address to the Sun," "Description of Adam and Eve," "Hypocrisy," "Virtue and Evil," "Meditation and Beauty," "Philosophy"), identified in "Contents of Milton" and contained in "The Beauties Of Milton." Scarce. Not in Coleridge; Not in Kohler.

68. THE BEAUTIES OF MILTON, Consisting Of Selections From His Poetry And Prose. By Alfred Howard, Esq. *London: Printed By T. Davidson, For Thomas Tegg, No. 73, Cheapside; R. Griffin And Co. Glasgow; And J. Cumming, Dublin. n.d. [ca. 1833].* 12mo, iv+188pp., frontispiece portrait of Milton within an elaborate frame, "Engraved by W. T. Fry," "Published by Thos. Tegg. Cheapside." "London: Printed By Thomas Davison, Whitefriars" at bottom of last page," contemporary full blue calf (slight rubbing along joints and at corners), covers with richly tooled gilt border trim, decorative gilt trim on spine with red morocco labels, inner and outer dentelles finely tooled in gilt trim, a.e.g. A fine copy in a lovely Romantic binding with contemporary presentation inscription (dated 1833) on fly-leaf. Rare. Not in Kohler.

69. A BRIEF HISTORY OF MOSCOVIA And Of other less-known Countries lying eastward of Russia as far as Cathay Gather'd from the Writings of several Eyewitnesses by John Milton To which are added other curious documents, with an Introduction by Prince D. S. Mirsky[.] Illustrations by A. Brodovitch. *The Blackamore Press[,] 4 Moorgate • London • MCMXXIX.* First edition thus. Square 8vo, 120pp., half-title with an illustration in bronze coloring by A. Brodovitch, additional illustrations in black and white by Brodovitch, original tan buckram, gilt lettering on front cover and spine, t.e.g., others untrimmed, printed dark pink publisher's wrappers in a protective plastic cover. Fine, in original cardboard slipcase. Printed in a limited edition of 600 numbered copies by the Curwen Press (only the second overall) for the Blackamore Press.

70. [A BRIEF HISTORY OF MOSCOVIA] MILTON'S LITERARY CRAFTSMANSHIP. A STUDY OF A BRIEF HISTORY OF MOSCOVIA With An Edition Of The Text By Robert Ralston Cawley[.] *New York[:] Gordian Press, Inc.[,] 1965.* Second edition thus. 8vo, viii+[1]+103+[2]pp., half-title ("Princeton Studies In English Volume 24" on verso), printer's device on title page, facsimile reproduction of 1682 title page of *A Brief History Of Moscovia*, original blue cloth, spine lettered in gilt. A nice copy. Reprint of Cawley's first edition published in 1941.

71. THE CAMBRIDGE MANUSCRIPT OF JOHN MILTON[.] *Lycidas* and Some of the Other Poems Reproduced from the Collotype Facsimile[.] With A Biographical Note By Frank A. Patterson[.] *Published For The Facsimile Text Society By Columbia University Press[,] New York[.] M·CM·XXXIII.* First edition thus. 8vo, [iii]+[1]+[16]pp., half-title, "Biographical Note," sixteen leaves of facsimile reproduction, original printed cardboard wrappers. Volume 17 of *The Facsimile Text Society*. Nice.

72. Another copy of preceding. Presentation copy from Mark Van Doren with presentation inscription (dated "10/6/47") on fly-leaf.

A Common-Place Book of John Milton

73. A COMMON-PLACE BOOK OF JOHN MILTON. Reproduced By The AutoType Process From The Original Manuscript In The Possession Of Sir Frederick U. Graham, Bart. Of Netherby Hall, Co. Cumberland. With An Introduction By A. J. Horwood, Esq. Barrister-At-Law. Under The Direction Of The Royal Society Of Literature. *[London: Chiswick Press,] 1876. Only One Hundred Copies Printed For Private Subscription.* First edition. Large 4to, [iv]+[87]pp., introduction, "List Of Authors Cited By Milton In The Commonplace Book," eighty-seven leaves of photographically reproduced plates, original green cloth (covers a little marked, inner hinges strengthened), gilt lettering on front cover and spine, two early armorial bookplates on front pastedown. A very nice copy. Milton's original manuscript is here reproduced by a pioneering photofacsimile process referred to as the "Autotype Process." Only 100 copies were printed for private subscribers by Charles Whittingham at the Chiswick Press. Stevens 1232; Not in Kohler.

74. A COMMON-PLACE BOOK OF JOHN MILTON, And A Latin Essay And Latin Verses Presumed To Be By Milton. Edited, From The Original MSS. In The Possession Of Sir Frederick U. Graham, Bart., By Alfred J. Horwood, Of The Middle Temple, Barrister-At-Law. *[London:] Printed For The Camden Society. M.DCCC.LXXVI.* First edition. Small 4to, xx+69pp., page of the "Council of The Camden Society For The Year 1875–76" after title page, original reddish-brown cloth (a bit rubbed), covers ruled in blind with central gilt initials of the Camden Society on front cover, gilt-decorated spine with title in gilt, top edge rough. Presentation copy with presentation inscription from the editor to Willoughby on fly-leaf. Very nice. Scarce. Printed in a limited edition. Not in Kohler.

75. A COMMON-PLACE BOOK OF JOHN MILTON, And A Latin Essay And Latin Verses Presumed To Be By Milton. Edited, From The Original MSS. In The Possession Of Sir Frederick U. Graham, Bart., By Alfred J. Horwood, Of The Middle Temple, Barrister-At-Law. (Revised Edition). *[London:] Printed For The Camden Society. M.DCCC.LXXVII.* Second, revised edition. Small 4to, xxvi+68pp., page of the "Council of The Camden Society For The Year 1875–76" after title page, original reddish-brown cloth, covers ruled in blind with central gilt initials of the Camden Society on front cover, spine lettered in gilt within gilt-decorated design topped by a bright gilt star, t.e. rough. Fine, with bookplate of W. T. Marriott on front pastedown. Printed in a limited edition. Kohler 516.

Collections of Poetry and Prose

76. A COMPLETE COLLECTION OF THE HISTORICAL, POLITICAL, AND MISCELLANEOUS WORKS OF JOHN MILTON, BOTH ENGLISH AND LATIN WITH SOM PAPERS NEVER BEFORE PUBLISHED. In Three Volumes. To which is Prefix'd The Life of the Author. Containing, Besides the History of his Works, Several Extraordinary Characters of Men and Books, Sects, Parties, and Opinions. *Amsterdam [i.e., London], Finish'd in the Year M.DC.XC.VIII.* 3 volumes. First edition thus. Folio, 442pp.,+872pp. (continuous pagination with volume 1),+363pp., engraved frontispiece portrait of Faithorne, half-title on verso of portrait, general title page in red and black, volume 1; separate title pages for volumes 2 and 3, each in black and white, variously dated 1694 to 1698, with title page of volume 3 reading, "Joannis Miltoni Opera Omnia Latina . . . Amstelodami, Anno M.DC.XC.VIII," life of Milton by John Toland, volume 1, with separate title pages for several of the separate works in volumes 1 and 2, which give the English prose, while volume 3 gives the Latin prose; contemporary speckled calf, covers decorated in blind, gilt-ruled and lettered tan morocco labels (label chipped, volume 3), raised bands, gilt dentelles. Very good fresh set in fine contemporary state with early signature on fly-leaf. First complete edition of

Milton's prose; with first edition of John Toland's life in volume 1, also published separately the next year (see separate publication with Seventeenth-century Miltoniana); several letters are also published here for the first time. Wing M2087; Parker, pp. 1196–98; Coleridge 73; Shawcross, 1974, pp. 374–75, 340; Shawcross, 1984, 395; Shawcross, Kentucky, 122; Kohler 519.

77. A COMPLETE COLLECTION OF THE HISTORICAL, POLITICAL, AND MISCELLANEOUS WORKS OF JOHN MILTON: Correctly printed from the Original Editions. With An Historical and Critical Account Of The Life and Writings of the Author; Containing several Original Papers of His, Never before Published. In Two Volumes. *London: Printed for A. Millar, at Buchanan's Head, against St. Clement's Church in the Strand. M.DCC.XXXVIII.* 2 volumes. First Thomas Birch edition. Folio, [ii]+xcvii+628pp.,+[ii]+617+[24]pp. [unpaginated index], frontispiece portrait of Milton bust engraved by I. Richardson after G. Vertue, title page each volume in red and black, "Advertisement To The Reader," volume 1, "An Alphabetical Index Of The Principal Matters Contained in the Two Volumes" at the end of volume 2, original calf, gilt rules on covers and spines, red morocco label with gilt lettering and gilt rules, raised bands, early armorial bookplate on front pastedown in each volume, advertisement of "Books Printed for and Sold by A. Millar" on verso of last leaf, volume 2. Very fine set. The first edition of Milton's prose works after that in 1698 (preceding set); it was edited by Thomas Birch, whose editorial work here has been described as "indispensable" to the literary or historical student. It contains several hitherto uncollected pieces and is prefaced by a ninety-five-page life of Milton by Birch, which "employs the newly discovered Trinity MS. and various interviews with Milton's daughter Deborah and his granddaughter Elizabeth Foster" (Shawcross 1972). Volume 1 contains the English prose from 1641–69 along with Joseph Washington's translation of *A Defense of the People of England*; volume 2 prints the English prose from 1670–82 along with Edward Phillips's translations of *Letters of State* and the Latin prose, "including John Phillips's *Responsio*, and *Scriptum dom. Protectoris* (first attributed to Milton here)" (Shawcross 1974). A second revised edition was published in 1753 under the title *The Works Of John Milton, Historical, Political, And Miscellaneous* (see set under *Works*). Coleridge 74; Shawcross, 1972, 424; Shawcross, 1974, pp. 375, 340, 364; Shawcross, Kentucky, 221; Kohler 520.

78. THE COMPLETE ENGLISH POEMS OF JOHN MILTON[.] Edited and with Introductory Notes by John D. Jump, Reader in English Literature, University of Manchester, England[.] *Washington Square Press, Inc. • New York[.] (1964).* First edition thus. 8vo, xii+[1]+465+[1]pp., half-title (with brief biography of Milton, about "This Edition," and "About The Editor"), paperback (pages a little age-browned), with reproduction of Milton portrait at age twenty-one on front cover. Gift from Anthony Low.

79. [COMPLETE ENGLISH POEMS] THE ANNOTATED MILTON[.] COMPLETE ENGLISH POEMS with annotations lexical, syntactic, prosodic, and referential edited by Burton Raffel[.] *Bantam Books[,] New York[,] Toronto[,] London[,] Sydney[,] Auckland[:] A Bantam Classic[,] (1999).* First edition thus. 8vo, xxvi+[1]+686+[3]pp., leaf before title page with brief biography of Milton on recto and a list of Bantam Classics on verso, "Suggestions For Further Reading," paperback, original printed gold stiff paper wrappers with reproduction of an illustration by John Martin for *PL* in color on front cover. Nice, with several pages of advertisements for Bantam Classics bound in at the end. Intended for student use.

80. [COMPLETE ENGLISH POEMS] JOHN MILTON[.] COMPLETE ENGLISH POEMS, OF EDUCATION, AREOPAGITICA Edited by Gordon Campbell[,] Reader in English, University of Leicester[.] *J. M. Dent & Sons Ltd: London[,] Everyman's Library[,] (1990).* Fourth Everyman edition. 8vo, xxxiii+[1]+628pp., half-title, facsimile reproduction of first and second edition title pages, paperback (a bit rubbed), printed speckled black stiff paper wrappers with reproduction of *Spring or the Garden of Eden* by Nicolas Poussin in color on front cover. Included at the end are *Of Education*, an appendix with extracts from Edward Phillips's *The Life of Mr John Milton* (1694), *Areopagitica*, with facsimile reproduction of first edition title page as half-title, and an appendix with "The Licensing Order of 14 June 1643," followed by sections on "Milton And His Critics" and "Suggestions For Further Reading." According to Gordon Campbell in commentary: "This is the fourth Everyman Milton, and the second with which I have been associated. . . . The first Everyman Milton appeared in 1909, edited by W. H. D. Rouse. . . . The second Everyman Milton appeared in 1956 with a new text by B. A. Wright [see 1959 and 1976 editions under title of Poems]. . . . a third Everyman Milton was published in 1980 [under the title *John Milton The Complete Poems*, "With Introduction And Notes By Gordon Campbell," (also listed here)]. . . . Wright's text is now beyond all possibility of defence, and can no longer be used in good conscience by an editor. I have therefore prepared a fresh edition, the fourth Everyman Milton (p. xi). . . . This edition has been prepared primarily for students rather than for professional scholars" (p. xii). Nice copy.

81. [COMPLETE ENGLISH POEMS] JOHN MILTON[.] THE COMPLETE ENGLISH POEMS Edited and introduced by Gordon Campbell[.] *Everyman's Library[,] (1992)*. [No.] 97[.] 8vo, lxxi+620+[3]pp., half-title, "Published by David Campbell Publishers Ltd . . . London . . . Distributed by Random House" on verso of title page, original light brown cloth, black label with gilt lettering and decorative gilt rules and small gilt piece on spine, endpapers decorated with a reproduction of the emblem of the press in faint gold color, printed publisher's wrappers in red and black, gold ribbon marker. Contents as with 1990 Everyman's Library edition preceding. Fine, with three pages of "Titles In Everyman's Library" at the end.

82. Variant of Preceding with variant publisher's imprint: "Everyman's Library[,] Alfred A. Knopf[,] New York[,] Toronto" and variant statement on verso of title page: "This is a Borzoi Book Published By Alfred A. Knopf, Inc." in place of "Published by David Campbell Publishers Ltd . . . London . . . Distributed by Random House."

83. [COMPLETE ENGLISH POEMS] JOHN MILTON[.] COMPLETE ENGLISH POEMS, OF EDUCATION, AREOPAGITICA Edited by Gordon Campbell[,] University of Leicester[.] *Everyman[,] J. M. Dent • London[;] Charles E. Tuttle[,] Vermont[,] (1993)*. New edition, updated and reissued. 8vo, xliv+628pp., half-title with Everyman's emblem and motto with statement about Everyman's publishing goals on verso, paperback, with reproduction of *The Birth of Sin* by Henry Fuseli on front cover. Contents as with 1990 Everyman's Library edition listed here. Everyman's Library was founded in 1906; "In 1993, Everyman Paperback Classics were re-launched in an existing new format" (Fall 1995 Everyman Paperback Classics Catalogue). Fine copy.

84. THE COMPLETE ENGLISH POETRY OF JOHN MILTON (Excluding His Translations Of Psalms 80-88) Arranged In Chronological Order With An Introduction, Notes, Variants, And Literal Translations Of The Foreign Language Poems By John T. Shawcross. Anchor Books[.] *Doubleday & Company, Inc. Garden City, New York[.] 1963*. First edition thus by Doubleday Anchor Books; first Shawcross edition. 8vo, xv+[2]+574pp.+[5]pp., half-title, "First edition" on verso of title page along with "This edition has been especially prepared for Anchor Books and has never appeared before in book form," paperback, priced "$1.95" on front cover. Nice copy, signed by the editor on title page.

A reprint of this edition was published by New York University Press in 1963 in hardback and with a reproduction of the 1688 illustrations of *PL* (also listed here); a revised edition by Shawcross, under the title, *The Complete Poetry of John Milton*, was published by Anchor Books in 1971 (also listed here).

85. Variant of Preceding. Nice copy, dated 1963 on verso of title page, as with preceding copy, but without "First edition" on verso of title page, as with that copy, yet priced the same on front cover with the same Anchor number at top of front cover and at bottom of spine: "AC-2." Possibly first edition, second issue.

86. THE COMPLETE ENGLISH POETRY OF JOHN MILTON (Excluding His Translations Of Psalms 80–88) Arranged In Chronological Order With An Introduction, Notes, Variants, And Literal Translations Of The Foreign Language Poems By John T. Shawcross[.] *The Stuart Editions[.] [New York:] New York University Press[,] 1963[.]* First edition thus by New York University Press; second Shawcross edition. 8vo, xv+[1]+574pp., half-title ("The Stuart Editions" with advertisement for "The Stuart Editions J. Max Patrick, series editor" on verso), reproduction of frontispiece portrait after R. White with Dryden epigram originally printed as the frontispiece for Milton's *History of Britain*, 1670 (also listed here), reproductions of the twelve illustrations for the 1688 Tonson edition of *PL* (fine impressions of the reproductions) (see 1688 editions of *PL* with original illustrations listed here), original black cloth (a bit smoke-stained on outer edges), front cover decorated with gilt trim at bottom, spine lettered in gilt, printed publisher's wrappers (a little smoke-stained). Nice copy, fresh and clean within, signed by the editor on half-title.

"This book was first published in 1963 in the Doubleday Anchor Seventeenth-Century series [see copy here]" (verso of title page); a revised edition by Shawcross, under the title *The Complete Poetry of John Milton*, was published by Anchor Books in 1971 without reproduction of the 1688 illustrations (also listed here).

87. THE COMPLETE POEMS OF JOHN MILTON WRITTEN IN ENGLISH With Introduction, Notes And Illustrations[.] The Harvard Classics Edited By Charles W. Eliot LL D[.] *P. F. Collier & Son[,] New York[,] (1909)*. First edition thus. Large 8vo, 463pp., frontispiece portrait plate of Milton frontispiece portrait within decorative frame with "The Harvard Classics" scrolled at the top, protective tissue guard, central emblem of "The Harvard Classics" in red on title page, two-page (foldout) facsimile reproduction plate (full-size) of a page of the manuscript of *PL* in the Morgan Library, protective tissue guard with identification printed in red, a second facsimile reproduction plate "of a hitherto unpublished poem by John Milton, in the possession of the New York Public Library," protective tissue guard with identification printed in red, one additional plate of "Milton's Cottage, Chalfont St. Giles, from the garden," protective tissue guard with identification printed in red, original red cloth (spine ends a little worn, scratch on back cover), gilt lettering on spine ("The Harvard Classics" and "Charles W. Eliot" and "Complete Poems In English Milton"), with gilt seal of Harvard on front cover, t.e.g., others untrimmed and unopened. A good copy of the first Harvard Classics edition by Charles Eliot with four plates and with contemporary signature (dated 1909) on front blank. Major later reprints by Grolier Enterprises appeared in 1980 and 1988—both listed here. Not in Kohler.

88. Variant of Preceding, half-title deluxe printed in red and black ("The Harvard Classics Edition De Lvxe Limited Edition Of Which This Set Is No. 1256" [written in hand in red ink]) with elaborate border frame in black and gilt with Harvard crest in red at bottom, "Planned and Designed at the Collier Press" printed on last page, original green cloth (spine a bit faded, several library stamps with clean library pocket and due slip in back), central seal of Harvard in gilt and purple on front cover, spine lettered in gilt ("The Harvard Classics" "Complete Poems In English Milton") with small seal of Harvard in gilt and purple at the bottom, decorated endpapers, t.e.g., others untrimmed and unopened. Nice copy without frontispiece portrait but with an elaborate half-title, also thicker than the preceding copy (by about ¼"), in a variant publisher's binding, and with "Planned and Designed at the Collier Press" printed on last page (which does not appear in preceding copy). No. 1256 of a limited edition. Not in Kohler.

89. THE COMPLETE POEMS OF JOHN MILTON WRITTEN IN ENGLISH With Introduction, Notes And Illustrations[.] The Harvard Classics Edited By Charles W. Eliot LL D[.] "Dr. Eliot's Five-Foot Shelf Of Books." *P. F. Collier & Son[,] New York[,] (1909)*. First edition thus, variant edition. 8vo in 16s, 463pp., frontispiece plate of "Milton's Cottage, Chalfont St. Giles," original blue cloth, spine lettered in gilt ("The Harvard Classics"•"Complete Poems In English Milton") with the number "4" and a small seal of Harvard in white. Variant edition in a smaller octavo format with sixteen leaves to each signature and with variant title page, including the first appearance of "Dr. Eliot's Five-Foot Shelf Of Books" on title page. Good copy. Not in Kohler.

90. Variant of Preceding. THE COMPLETE POEMS OF JOHN MILTON With Introduction And Notes[.] Volume 4. The Harvard Classics. Edited By Charles W. Eliot LL D[.] *P. F. Collier & Son[,] New York[,] (1909)*. First edition thus, variant edition, as volume 4 of "The Harvard Classics • The Five Foot Shelf Book Of Books" (so labeled in gilt on spine). 8vo in 16s, 463pp., frontispiece plate of "Milton's Cottage, Chalfont St. Giles," original red cloth (spine worn at bottom), central gilt seal on front cover, spine lettered in gilt ("Harvard Classics • The Five Foot Shelf Book Of Books • Complete Poems In English Milton") with gilt rules and with "4" in gilt. Variant edition in a variant publisher's binding with several changes on title page: "Complete Poems Of John Milton" replaces "Complete Poems Of John Milton Written In English"—although "Complete Poems In English Milton" remains the title on the spine; "Illustrations" is dropped from "With Introduction And Notes," and "Volume 4" is added in place of "Dr. Eliot's Five-Foot Shelf Of Books." Reissued ca. 1969 (also listed here). Good copy. Not in Kohler.

The collection also has several other issues published in 1909 with minor variations in title page, variant bindings, and gilt lettering on the spines.

91. THE COMPLETE POEMS OF JOHN MILTON With Complete Notes by Thomas Newton, D.D., Bishop of Bristol[.] Illustrated By Gustave Dore And Others[.] *Crown Publishers[,] New York[,] 1936*. First edition thus. Thick 8vo, ix+[iv]+665pp., frontispiece illustration by Doré, other illustrations by Doré, Bida, Westall, Burney, Frost, Horsley, and others, "Life Of Milton" with a reproduction of "Milton [Age 62] From the original drawing by Vertue," Latin poems printed in small type and in double column at the end, original blue cloth (notes in ink on final blank), spine lettered in gilt with decorative gilt trim at top and bottom, printed publisher's wrappers (a bit rubbed) with Milton portrait on front cover. Nice copy.

92. THE COMPLETE POEMS OF JOHN MILTON With Complete Notes by Thomas Newton, D.D., Bishop of Bristol[.] Illustrated By Gustave Dore And Others[.] *Bonanza Books [A Division of Crown Publishers] • New York[,] (1936)*. First edition thus. 8vo, ix+[iv]+647+[18]pp., frontispiece illustration by Doré, other illustrations by Doré, Bida, Westall, Burney, Frost, Horsley, and others, Latin poems printed in double column at the end, original light blue cloth, spine lettered in black. Very good copy. Possibly a trade edition of a publication in a larger format by Crown Publishers in the same year (preceding copy).

93. THE COMPLETE POEMS OF JOHN MILTON With Introduction And Notes[.] Volume 4[.] The Harvard Classics Edited By Charles W. Eliot LL. *D. P. F. Collier & Son Corporation[,] New York[,] (1965)*. 8vo, 459pp., half-title ("The Harvard Classics Registered Edition • The Five-Foot Shelf of Books"), frontispiece reproduction of "Milton's Cottage, Chalfont St. Giles," original simulated red leather, seal in gilt within larger decorative gilt device at center of front cover with gilt rules and decorative corner pieces, spine lettered in gilt ("Complete Poems In English") against a black background within gilt rules and same decorative gilt device on front cover, gilt number "4" at the top, seal of the press in gilt near the bottom above gilt rules with "Edition Deluxe" in gilt at the bottom, marbled endpapers. Reprint of the first edition thus, variant edition, originally published in 1909 (also listed here). Fine copy.

94. THE COMPLETE POEMS OF JOHN MILTON With Introduction and Notes[.] The Harvard Classics Edited By Charles W. Eliot. LL.D. *P. F. Collier & Son Corporation[,] New York[,] [ca. 1969 reprint]*. 8vo, 459pp., half-title ("The Harvard Classics, Registered Edition," with seal) with frontispiece reproduction of "Milton's Cottage, Chalfont St. Giles" on verso, original dark green buckram, decorative gilt border trim on front cover with central gilt seal of Harvard, gilt lettering ("Milton Poems Deluxe Edition The Harvard Classics") and gilt rules on spine repeating the emblem in gilt. Very nice, in a handsome imitation morocco binding. A later reprint of the first edition thus, variant edition, originally published in 1909 (also listed here).

95. THE COMPLETE POEMS OF JOHN MILTON[.] The Harvard Classics Edited By Charles W. Eliot, LL.D. With Introductions and Notes[.] *Grolier Enterprises Corp. Danbury, Connecticut[,] (1980)*. 8vo, 459pp., half-title ("The Harvard Classics Registered Edition") with frontispiece portrait sketch of Milton dictating to his daughter by W. T. Mars on verso, original simulated brown leather (small stain on front external edges), front cover decorated in a gilt ruled pattern, decorative gilt corners, and small decorative gilt design at the center, spine lettered in gilt ("Milton Poems • The Harvard Classics Collector's Edition") with gilt rules and decorative gilt design at the center, decorated endpapers, t.e.g. Good copy in an attractive imitation leather binding with an uncommon frontispiece portrait sketch (possibly drawn especially for this edition). Reprint of the first edition thus published in 1909 (several copies listed here). This is a different edition from the following deluxe edition by Grolier Enterprises Corp.

96. THE COMPLETE POEMS OF JOHN MILTON Edited By Charles W. Eliot LL. D. With Introduction and Notes[.] The Harvard Classics[.] *Grolier Enterprises Corp. Danbury, Connecticut[,] (1980)*. 8vo, 459+[1]pp., half-title, elaborate decorative border in black on title page in manner of deluxe edition in 1909, original simulated crushed maroon leather, covers attractively decorated with gilt rules, decorative gilt corners with large gilt design at the center, spine lettered in gilt ("Milton Poems • The Harvard Classics"), raised bands within gilt rules, decorative gilt trim within the panels, marbled endpapers, a.e.g. Fine copy in a handsome imitation leather binding. "The Harvard Classics is published by Grolier Enterprises with text printed on fifty-five-pound Lockhaven paper specifically prepared for this edition by the Hammermill Paper Company. Printed and bound by R. R. Donnelley and Sons. End-leaf design is reproduced from an original marbled pattern created for this edition by Faith Harrison. Cover stampings and design by Daniel B. Bianchi and Selma Ordewer" (verso last page). Reprint of the first edition thus published in 1909 (several copies listed here). Another reprint by Grolier Enterprises was published in 1988 (also listed here).

97. THE COMPLETE POEMS OF JOHN MILTON With Introductions and Notes By Charles W. Eliot, LL.D. The Harvard Classic[.] *Grolier Enterprises Corp. Danbury, Connecticut[,] (1988)*. 8vo, 459pp., half-title, elaborate decorative border in black on title page in manner of deluxe edition in 1909, original simulated crushed maroon leather, covers attractively decorated in gilt with gilt rules, decorative gilt corners with large gilt design at the center, spine lettered in gilt ("Milton Poems • The Harvard Classics"), raised bands within gilt rules, decorative gilt trim within the panels, marbled endpapers, a.e.g. Fine copy in a handsome imitation leather binding. Reprint of the first edition thus published in 1909 (several copies listed here).

98. JOHN MILTON THE COMPLETE POEMS[.] Text Edited By B. A. Wright[.] Introduction And Notes By Gordon Campbell[,] Department of English, University of Leicester[.] *J M Dent & Sons Ltd[:] London[,] Melbourne[,] Toronto[;] E P Dutton & Co Inc[,] New York[,] (1980)*. Third Everyman edition; new edition. Thick 8vo, xxxiii+606pp., half-title. Facsimile reproduction of several first edition title pages, notes on all the poems, original brown cloth, spine lettered in gilt with small Everyman emblem in gilt at the bottom, printed orange publisher's wrappers (spine sun-faded) with *The Expulsion from the Garden of Eden* by Masaccio reproduced in color on front cover.

The first Everyman Milton was published in 1909 under the title *Poems*, edited by W. H. D. Rouse; the second in 1956 also under *Poems* with a new text by B. A. Wright (see 1959 and 1976 editions listed here); the third with text by Wright in 1980 under the title *Complete Poems* (also listed here); and the fourth Everyman Milton a fresh edition under the title *Complete English Poems*, with a new text by Gordon Campbell, in 1990 (listed here with commentary by Campbell about Wright's text).

99. JOHN MILTON THE COMPLETE POEMS[.] Text edited by B. A. Wright[.] Introduction and notes by Gordon Campbell[,] Department of English, University of Leicester[.] *Dent: London and Melbourne[.] Everyman's Library[.] (1986).* Thick 8vo, xxxiii+606pp., half-title, facsimile reproduction of several first edition title pages, paperback, original stiff paper wrappers with a reproduction of Masaccio's illustration of *The Expulsion* on front cover against a blue background. Fine.

100. JOHN MILTON THE COMPLETE POEMS edited with a preface and notes by John Leonard[.] *(London:) Penguin Books, (1998).* First edition thus. Thick 8vo, xxix+982+[12]pp., half-title, paperback, original stiff paper wrappers with reproduction of *Adam and Eve* by Peter Paul Rubens in color on front cover, vignette of Eve repeated in color at top of the spine. Fine.

101. JOHN MILTON COMPLETE POEMS AND MAJOR PROSE Edited by Merritt Y. Hughes[,] University of Wisconsin[.] Notes and Introductions by the Editor[.] *New York[:] Published by The Odyssey Press[,] (1957).* First edition thus. 8vo, xix+1059pp., double black rule on title page with "First Edition" on verso, various charts, facsimiles, and reproductions, including a reproduction of the Faithorne frontispiece portrait of Milton, prose printed in double column, appendix with "Some Early Lives of Milton," original black cloth spine, speckled blue cloth boards, spine lettered in gilt with gilt emblem of the press at bottom. Nice copy with signature on fly-leaf.

Became perhaps the most commonly used textbook in the latter half of the twentieth century, and the text of choice for students from its publication until the 1970s. The collection also has copies of the second and third editions, each of which was published later in 1957, attesting to the immediate popularity of the text; the contents are the same, and the bindings are those that become the hallmark of the edition throughout the years, very similar to that of the first edition: original black cloth spine, blue cloth boards, spine lettered in gilt with gilt emblem of the press at bottom. Both are nice copies. The edition was variously reprinted throughout the years, and the collection has several undated later editions, published ca. 1970 and as late as the twenty-second edition, all in the characteristic binding but the last with hardened blue paper boards; each in nice condition.

102. MILTON'S COMPLETE POEMS Printed together with new translations into English of his Italian, Latin, & Greek poems. Revised Edition. Edited by Frank Allen Patterson[,] Columbia University[.] *New York: Printed for F. S. Crofts & Co. and are to be sold at 41 Union Square West. 1934.* Third edition thus. 8vo, xlvi+439+94pp., half-title, original black cloth (some marginal notations in a neat hand in pen), title page emblem repeated in silver on upper right corner of front cover, spine lettered in silver. Good copy, without inclusion of any of Milton's prose as in Patterson's edition of *The Student's Milton* published the same time (several copies listed here). First edition thus published in 1930; second edition thus, revised, in 1933; revised edition in 1941 (also listed here).

103. MILTON'S COMPLETE POEMS Printed together with new translations into English of his Italian, Latin, & Greek poems[.] Revised Ed tion[sic][.] Edited by Frank Allen Patterson[,] Columbia University[.] *New York: Printed for F. S. Crofts & Co. and are to be sold at 101 Fifth Avenue. 1941.* 8vo, xlvi+439+94pp., half-title, original black cloth (a bit scuffed in places, some underlining in pencil), title page emblem repeated in silver on upper right corner of front cover, spine lettered in silver.

Complete Poetical Works

104. JOHN MILTON'S COMPLETE POETICAL WORKS Reproduced in Photographic Facsimile[.] A Critical Text Edition Compiled and Edited by Harris Francis Fletcher. *Urbana[:] The University of Illinois Press[,] 1943–48.* 4 volumes. First and only edition. 4to, [ii]+465pp.,+[i]+634pp.,+[i]+455pp.,+[i]+316pp., half-title each volume, photographic facsimile reproductions, half-titles for various of the poems, notes at bottom of page, "General Index" at the end of volume 4, original green cloth, seal of the university press in blind at the center of each front cover, spines lettered and ruled in gilt. Fine set. John Shawcross points out that "states of texts are observable by page comparisons." Printed in a limited edition of 550 copies. Huckabay 15; Shawcross, Kentucky II, 12.

Laid in: monograph reprint of J. Milton French's 1948 *Review* of this edition by Fletcher and the corrected typed copy of Milton French's *Review* of volumes III and IV, signed by French, together with page two of a typed cover letter on French's stationery, presumably to Maurice Kelley, signed "M." by Milton French above his typed name, along with several typed pages of a review and commentary (presumably by Maurice Kelley). Enclosures a gift from Maurice Kelley.

105. THE COMPLETE POETICAL WORKS OF JOHN MILTON: With Explanatory Notes, And A Life Of The Author, By The Rev. H. Stebbing, A.M. *London, Printed And Published By J. F. Dove, St. John's Square. n.d. [ca. 1830].* First edition thus. 12mo, xvi+548pp., frontispiece illustration engraved by Thomas Ranson after Thomas Uwins for *C*, protective tissue guard (a bit foxed), engraved and printed title pages, engraved title reading:

"The Poetical Works Of John Milton. With An Account Of His Life. London: Engraved For Dove's English Classics," illustration engraved by Ranson after T. Uwins for *PL* (*Satan, Sin, and Death*) on engraved title page, vignette illustration of a dove holding olive branch amidst clouds with Latin phrase "Perseverantia Et Amici" on printed title page, "Published By J. F. Dove, St. John's Square," at bottom of last page, contemporary green calf (a bit rubbed, especially at joints, some foxing), gilt rules with blind rules within and small corner pieces in blind on covers, gilt-decorated spine with remnants of a gilt-lettered red morocco label, marbled endpapers, and speckled edges. Nice copy with contemporary presentation inscription (dated 1830) on front blank. See similarities in the following edition for "Dove's English Classics." Not in Kohler.

106. Variant of Preceding, contemporary half green calf (a little worn at joints and corners), marbled paper over boards, gilt-lettered red leather label on spine with decorative gilt trim above and below, gilt rules at top and bottom of spine. Good copy in a variant, possible publisher's, binding.

107. THE COMPLETE POETICAL WORKS OF JOHN MILTON: With Explanatory Notes, And A Life Of The Author, By The Rev. H. Stebbing, A.M. To Which Is Prefixed, Dr. Channing's Essay On The Poetical Genius Of Milton. *London: Printed For Scott, Webster, And Geary, (Successors To Mr. Dove) 36, Charterhouse Square. n.d. [ca. 1835].* 12mo, iv+552pp., frontispiece illustration engraved by Ranson after Uwins for *C*, protective tissue guard (a little foxed), engraved and printed title pages, engraved title reading: "The Poetical Works Of John Milton. With An Account Of His Life. London: Engraved For Dove's English Classics," illustration engraved by Ranson after Uwins for *PL* (*Satan, Sin, and Death*) on engraved title page (both frontispiece and engraved title foxed), "London: Printed By A. Sweeting, 15, Bartlett's Buildings" on verso of printed title page and at the bottom of last page, original calf (worn, spine ends chipped), covers delicately decorated with gilt trim, spine decorated with gilt trim within the panels (faded), black leather label with gilt lettering, marbled endpapers and edges. Decent copy, with contemporary presentation inscription in ink in a neat hand (dated "Oct. 22d, 1837") on front blank. See similarities to ca. 1830 edition listed earlier and the same as dated 1839 edition following, with the same publisher's imprint on engraved and printed title pages. Scarce. Kohler 292, dating its copy "c. 1838" and reporting "Not in the British Library. Not in Cambridge University Library."

108. THE COMPLETE POETICAL WORKS OF JOHN MILTON: With Explanatory Notes, And A Life Of The Author, By The Rev. H. Stebbing, A.M. To Which Is Prefixed, Dr. Channing's Essay On The Poetical Genius Of Milton. *London: Scott, Webster, And Geary, 36, Charterhouse Square, 1839.* 12mo, iv+552pp., frontispiece illustration engraved by Ranson after Uwins for *C*, protective tissue guard, engraved and printed title pages, engraved title reading: "The Poetical Works Of John Milton. With An Account Of His Life. London: Engraved For The English Classics. Published By Scott, Webster & Geary," illustration engraved by Ranson after Uwins for *PL* (*Satan, Sin, and Death*) on engraved title page (both frontispiece and engraved title lightly foxed), "Printed By A. Sweeting, 15, Bartlett's Buildings" printed at the bottom of last page, original maroon pebble leather (rubbed along joints and extremities, lacking front fly-leaf), covers ruled in blind with a large emblem in blind at the center, spine lettered in gilt within elaborate decorative gilt trim, inner dentelles finely tooled in gilt, a.e.g. Nice copy with contemporary presentation inscription on verso of frontispiece illustration. See undated ca. 1835 edition preceding with variant publisher's imprint on printed and engraved title pages, the publisher on the printed title page the same as here. Uncommon. Not in Kohler.

109. THE COMPLETE POETICAL WORKS OF JOHN MILTON: With Explanatory Notes, And A Life Of The Author, By The Rev. H. Stebbing, A.M. To Which Is Prefixed, Dr. Channing's Essay On The Poetical Genius Of Milton. *New York: D. Appleton & Co., 200 Broadway[;] Philadelphia: Geo. S. Appleton, 148 Chestnut St. MDCCCXLIII.* First edition thus. Small 8vo, xvi+552+[4]pp., frontispiece portrait engraved by Thomas Illman and Edward Pilbrow after Faithorne, protective tissue guard, three illustration plates (unsigned, fine impressions) for *PL* (Book II), for *C*, and for *IIP*, each with protective tissue guard (some slight foxing on the first tissue guard which has affected the upper margin of the plate), double black border around the text, original brown ribbed cloth (a bit rubbed, small tear at top of spine repaired), covers decorated in embossed blind trim with central vignette of blind Milton dictating to his daughters in gilt on front cover, central device in blind on back cover, "Olton" and "Jenkins" stamped in small blind letters at the top within the blind rule and "Binders" and "N. York" stamped in small blind letters at the bottom within the blind rule on both covers, spine similarly decorated in blind with gilt lettering ("Milton's Poetical Works"), decorated endpapers. Four pages of advertisements bound in at the end. Very good copy in original publisher's binding with contemporary signature (dated 1845) and later signature. Stevens 147 (without reference to Philadelphia in the publisher's imprint); Not in Kohler.

See also 1844 (possible second edition thus), 1845, 1846, 1847, and 1850 illustrated editions of *The CPW of John Milton* listed here, published, as here, by D. Appleton of New York and Geo. S. Appleton of Philadelphia with six illustration plates, three more than here, the additional three after Turner; and see 1853, 1854, 1855, and 1856 illustrated editions of *The CPW of John Milton* listed here. Each, unlike here, published by Appleton of New York only, but each in the same small 8vo format as here with six illustration plates, three more than here, the additional three by Turner, with the 1855 and 1856 editions having different addresses in the publisher's imprint ("346 & 348 Broadway" in place of "200 Broadway"). See also 1851 illustrated edition of Milton's *PW* listed here published by Appleton of Philadelphia and New York (possible first thus) with reproductions of several illustrations after Martin.

110. THE COMPLETE POETICAL WORKS OF JOHN MILTON: With Explanatory Notes, And A Life Of The Author, By The Rev. H. Stebbing, A.M. To Which Is Prefixed, Dr. Channing's Essay On The Poetical Genius Of Milton. *New York: D. Appleton & Co., 200 Broadway[;] Philadelphia: Geo. S. Appleton, 148 Chestnut St. MDCCCXLIV.* Second edition thus? Small 8vo, xvi+552pp., frontispiece portrait engraved by Thomas Illman and Edward Pilbrow after Faithorne, protective tissue guard, six illustration plates (unsigned, fine impressions), each with protective tissue guard, double black border around text, original brown ribbed cloth (spine worn and reglued with portions missing, corners worn), covers decorated in embossed blind trim with central vignette of blind Milton dictating to his daughters in gilt on front cover, central urn in blind on back cover, "Olton" and "Jenkins" stamped in small blind letters at the top within the blind rule and "Binders" and "N. York" stamped in small blind letters at the bottom within the blind rule on both covers, spine decorated in gilt with gilt lettering ("Milton's Poetical Works"). Despite the worn spine, a good, tight copy. Not in Kohler.

The possible first edition thus was published in 1843 with only three illustrations, the three that, though unsigned, are Turneresque in style (also listed here with further editions by Appleton cited there). The pattern for illustrations is set with this edition, six illustration plates, unsigned, three of which, though unsigned, are by Turner: two for *PL* (Books VI and XII) and one for *L*; the other three are Turneresque in style: one each for *PL* (Book II), for *C*, and for *IlP*, and this pattern continues in the Appleton editions that follow.

111. Variant of Preceding, original red cloth (a little worn, some light inoffensive staining off and on throughout), covers decorated in embossed blind trim with central vignette of blind Milton dictating to his daughters in gilt on both covers, spine richly decorated in gilt with gilt lettering ("Milton's Poetical Works"), a.e.g. Nice copy in a variant publisher's binding in red cloth with central vignette in gilt on both covers, with gilt edges, and with a contemporary signature (dated 1845) on fly-leaf.

112. THE COMPLETE POETICAL WORKS OF JOHN MILTON: With Explanatory Notes, And A Life Of The Author, By The Rev. H. Stebbing, A.M. To Which Is Prefixed, Dr. Channing's Essay On The Poetical Genius Of Milton. *New York: D. Appleton & Co., 200 Broadway[;] Philadelphia: Geo. S. Appleton, 148 Chestnut St. MDCCCXLV.* Small 8vo, xvi+552pp., frontispiece portrait engraved by Thomas Illman and Edward Pilbrow after Faithorne, protective tissue guard, six unsigned illustration plates, as with 1844 edition preceding, each illustration with protective tissue guard, double black border around text, original dark green calf (bit rubbed, plates foxed), covers ruled in blind with various decorative gilt designs, spine lettered in gilt ("Milton's Poetical Works") with decorative gilt trim at top and bottom, thick raised bands with decorative gilt trim, outer dentelles finely tooled in gilt (faded), a.e.g. Nice copy with early name on front blank. The possible first edition thus was published in 1843 (also listed here with further editions by Appleton cited). Not in Kohler.

113. THE COMPLETE POETICAL WORKS OF JOHN MILTON: With Explanatory Notes, And A Life Of The Author, By The Rev. H. Stebbing, A.M. To Which Is Prefixed, Dr. Channing's Essay On The Poetical Genius Of Milton. *New York: D. Appleton & Co., 200 Broadway[;] Philadelphia: Geo. S. Appleton, 148 Chestnut St. MDCCCXLVI.* Small 8vo, xvi+552pp., frontispiece portrait engraved by Edward Illman and Thomas Pilbrow after Faithorne, protective tissue guard, six illustration plates (unsigned, fine impressions), each with protective tissue guard, double black border around text, original black calf (rubbed along joints and extremities, some light age-browning with occasional foxing), gilt rules on covers with central gilt urn within gilt laurel wreath, raised bands within gilt rules on spine with gilt lettering ("Milton's Poetical Works"), outer dentelles finely tooled in gilt (faded), a.e.g. Nice copy in a fine mid-nineteenth-century American publisher's calf binding and with fresh and clean impressions of the plates. The possible first edition thus was published in 1843 (also listed here with further editions by Appleton cited). Not in Kohler.

114. Variant of Preceding, original green cloth (two light stains at top of back cover, occasional foxing), covers decorated in embossed blind trim with central vignette of blind

Milton dictating to his daughters in gilt on front cover, spine richly decorated in gilt with gilt lettering ("Milton's Poetical Works"). Nice copy in a variant publisher's binding with early presentation inscription on fly-leaf.

115. THE COMPLETE POETICAL WORKS OF JOHN MILTON: With Explanatory Notes, And A Life Of The Author, By The Rev. H. Stebbing, A.M. To Which Is Prefixed, Dr. Channing's Essay On The Poetical Genius Of Milton. *New York: D. Appleton & Co., 200 Broadway[;] Philadelphia: Geo. S. Appleton, 148 Chestnut St. MDCCCXLVII.* Small 8vo, xvi+552pp., frontispiece portrait engraved by Illman and Pilbrow after Faithorne, protective tissue guard, six illustration plates (unsigned, fine impressions), as with 1844 edition listed here, each illustration with protective tissue guard, double black border around text, original light brown cloth (a bit rubbed, slight ink stain at upper right cover of front cover, early owner's decorative stamp at top of title page, early signature on fly-leaf), covers decorated in embossed blind trim with central vignette of blind Milton dictating to his daughters in gilt on front cover, spine richly decorated in gilt with gilt lettering ("Milton's Poetical Works"). Nice copy. The possible first edition thus was published in 1843 (also listed here with further editions by Appleton cited). Not in Kohler.

116. THE COMPLETE POETICAL WORKS OF JOHN MILTON. Together With A Life Of The Author. *New York: Published By Clark, Austin & Co. 205 Broadway. 1849.* 2 volumes in one. First edition thus? 12mo in 6s, 321+[1]pp.,+232pp., engraved frontispiece illustration after A. Dick for Book I of *PL* (of angels protecting Adam and Eve from Satan while they are sleeping), engraved and printed title pages, engraved title page ("The Poetical Works Of John Milton[.] New York[:] Clark, Austin & Co. 205 Broadway"), with unsigned vignette illustration of Satan rallying his troops for Book I of *PL* on engraved title, protective tissue guard, "Contents Of *PL*" page (which makes up all of volume 1), life by Elijah Fenton, "Contents" page of volume 2, half-title for *C* and *SA* (placed after *C* here), original red cloth (a little rubbed, corners worn, spine ends chipped, small inoffensive waterstain within bottom margin of first half of book diminishing until gone, foxing), covers decorated in embossed blind trim, spine richly decorated and lettered in gilt, contemporary signature on front blank. Scarce. Not in Kohler.

Also listed here are a possible second edition thus published in 1850; a possible third in 1851; and a possible fourth in 1852 with a variant edition with variant publisher's imprint published that same year. See virtually identical editions published in "Boston [by] Phillips, Sampson, And Company [and in] New York [by] James C.

Derby" with the same engraved frontispiece illustration by Dick and the same unsigned vignette illustration on engraved title page as here, in 1854 and in 1855—both listed here.

117. THE COMPLETE POETICAL WORKS OF JOHN MILTON: With Explanatory Notes, And A Life Of The Author, By The Rev. H. Stebbing, A.M. To Which Is Prefixed, Dr. Channing's Essay On The Poetical Genius Of Milton. *New York: D. Appleton & Co., 200 Broadway[;] Philadelphia: Geo. S. Appleton, 164 Chestnut St. MDCCCL.* Small 8vo, xvi+552pp., frontispiece portrait engraved by Illman and Pilbrow after Faithorne, protective tissue guard, six illustration plates (unsigned, fine impressions), as with 1844 edition listed here, each illustration with protective tissue guard, double black border around text, original olive green cloth (a little worn and faded, spine torn and reglued, spine ends chipped), covers decorated in embossed blind trim with central vignette of blind Milton dictating to his daughters in gilt on front cover, spine richly decorated in gilt with gilt lettering ("Milton's Poetical Works"), a.e.g. The possible first edition thus was published in 1843 with only three of the six illustrations here (also listed here with further editions by Appleton cited). Not in Kohler.

118. THE COMPLETE POETICAL WORKS OF JOHN MILTON. Together With A Life Of The Author. *New York: Published By Clark, Austin & Co. 205 Broadway. 1850.* 2 volumes in one. Second edition thus? 12mo in 6s, 321+[1]pp.,+232pp., engraved frontispiece illustration by A. Dick for Book I of *PL* (of angels protecting Adam and Eve from Satan while they are sleeping), engraved and printed title pages, engraved title page (reading "The Poetical Works Of John Milton[.] New York[:] Clark, Austin & Co. 205 Broadway"), with unsigned vignette illustration of Satan rallying his troops for Book I of *PL* on engraved title, protective tissue guard (a little foxed), "Contents Of Paradise Lost" page (which makes up all of volume 1), life of Milton by Fenton, volume 1, "Contents" page of volume 2, half-title for *C* and *SA* (placed after *C* here), original blue cloth (some foxing), covers decorated in blind relief with large central urn in gilt with small figure with a lyre at the bottom on front cover, spine richly decorated in gilt with gilt lettering, decorated endpapers, a.e.g. A very nice copy in a lovely publisher's binding. The possible first edition thus was published in 1849 (also listed here with further editions by Clark, Austin & Co. cited). Scarce. Not in Kohler.

119. THE COMPLETE POETICAL WORKS OF JOHN MILTON. Together With A Life Of The Author. *New York: Published By Clark, Austin & Co. 205 Broadway. 1851.* 2 volumes in one. Third edition thus? 12mo in 6s,

321+[1]pp.,+232pp., engraved frontispiece illustration by A. Dick and unsigned vignette illustration on engraved title (with publisher's imprint) as with first and second editions, likewise "Contents" for volumes 1 and 2, life by Fenton, and half-title for *C* and *SA*, original brown cloth (a bit rubbed, corners worn, spine ends chipped, with some foxing, ex-library with card and due date slip on back pastedown), covers decorated in blind relief with central harp in gilt with laurel draped over the top and books at the bottom on front cover, spine decorated in gilt and also lettered in gilt. A good copy in a nice publisher's binding. The possible first edition thus was published in 1849 (also listed here with further editions by Clark, Austin & Co. cited). Scarce. Not in Kohler.

120. THE COMPLETE POETICAL WORKS OF JOHN MILTON. Together With A Life Of The Author. *New York: Published By Clark, Austin & Co. 205 Broadway. 1852.* 2 volumes in one. Fourth edition thus? 12mo in 6s, 321+[1]pp.,+232pp., engraved frontispiece illustration by A. Dick and unsigned vignette illustration on engraved title (with publisher's imprint) as with first and second editions, likewise "Contents" for volumes 1 and 2, life by Fenton, and half-title for *C* and *SA*, original red cloth (a little worn, some foxing), covers richly decorated in gilt with central gilt device, spine decorated and lettered in gilt. The possible first edition thus was published in 1849 (also listed here with further editions by Clark, Austin & Co. cited). Not in Kohler.

121. Variant of Preceding. Original red cloth (a little worn, some foxing), covers elaborately decorated in embossed blind, spine richly decorated and lettered in gilt. Nice copy with variant publisher's imprint on title page: "Published By Clark, Austin & Smith, 3 Park Row And 3 Ann-Street. 1852," in an attractive variant publisher's binding with contemporary signature.

122. THE COMPLETE POETICAL WORKS OF JOHN MILTON: With Explanatory Notes, And A Life Of The Author, By The Rev. H. Stebbing, A.M. To Which Is Prefixed, Dr. Channing's Essay On The Poetical Genius Of Milton. *New York: D. Appleton & Co., 200 Broadway. 1853.* Small 8vo, xvi+ 552pp., frontispiece portrait engraved by Illman and Pilbrow after Faithorne, protective tissue guard, six illustration plates (unsigned, fine impressions), as with 1844 edition listed here, each illustration with protective tissue guard, double black border around text, original ribbed brown cloth (aged with some wear, light waterstaining at the very bottom of the plates), covers decorated in embossed blind trim, spine richly decorated in gilt with gilt lettering ("Milton's Poetical Works"). The possible first edition thus was published in 1843, unlike here by D. Appleton of New York and Geo. Appleton of Philadelphia, with only three of the six illustrations here (also listed with further editions by Appleton cited). Not in Kohler.

123. Variant of Preceding, original gilt and glazed to simulate maroon morocco (moderate wear to covers and spine, worn along edges, foxing), covers decorated in embossed blind trim, spine lettered in gilt ("Milton's Poetical Works") and richly ruled in thick gilt blocks with inner gilt rules and decorative gilt trim, red edges. Nice copy in a handsome variant publisher's glazed to simulate morocco binding.

124. THE COMPLETE POETICAL WORKS OF JOHN MILTON. With Life. Eight Engravings on Steel. *Edinburgh: Gall & Inglis, 38 North Bridge. n.d. [ca. 1854].* Small 8vo, xx+491pp., unsigned frontispiece illustration plate, engraved and printed title pages, with unsigned vignette illustration on engraved title, which bears the same publisher's imprint and address as the undated title page, six additional illustration plates (most unsigned, two after Ts. Brown) life of Milton with half-title, half-title for *PL*, black border line around text, original blue cloth (a bit worn, spine ends chipped, lacking fly-leaf), front cover richly decorated with an elaborate gilt border with large central urn in gilt, spine similarly richly decorated in gilt with gilt lettering, a.e.g. Not in Kohler.

Nice copy with the same address ("38 North Bridge") appearing on both the printed and engraved title pages. See undated ca. 1854 edition of *CPW* following with "Eight Engravings on Steel," with the same undated engraved title page as here ("Edinburgh: Gall & Inglis, 38 North Bridge"). See also undated ca. 1855 edition of *CPW* listed here by Gall & Inglis, with "Eight Engravings on Steel" and with the publisher's imprint ("Edinburgh, Gall & Inglis 6 George Street") the same on both the engraved and printed title pages; see, too, undated ca. 1862 edition of *CPW* listed here by Gall & Inglis, with "Eight Engravings on Steel" and with the publisher's imprint ("Edinburgh, Gall & Inglis 6 George Street") the same on both the engraved and printed title pages; and see ca. 1865 edition of *CPW* listed here by Gall & Inglis, with "Eight Engravings on Steel" and with a different publisher's imprint on the engraved title page ("Edinburgh, Gall & Inglis 38 North Bridge") from that on the printed title page ("Edinburgh: Gall & Inglis, 6 George Street").

125. Variant of Preceding, original full navy blue morocco (a bit rubbed along joints and extremities), covers richly decorated in gilt, with a thick gilt rule surrounding elaborate decorative gilt trim with large gilt device at the center, spine lettered in gilt and richly decorated within the panels, inner and outer dentelles finely tooled in gilt, a.e.g. A nice copy in a lovely variant publisher's navy blue morocco binding.

126. THE COMPLETE POETICAL WORKS OF JOHN MILTON. With Life. Eight Engravings on Steel. *London: Published By Thomas Holmes, Great Book Establishment, 76 St. Paul's Churchyard. n.d. [ca. 1854].* Small 8vo, xx+491pp., unsigned frontispiece illustration plate, engraved and printed title pages (with different publisher's imprints), with unsigned vignette illustration of *Eve Relating Her Dream to Adam* on engraved title, which bears the logo: "Edinburgh: Gall & Inglis, 38 North Bridge," undated, six additional illustration plates (most unsigned, two after Ts. Brown) life of Milton with half-title, half-title for *PL*, black border around text, original full green morocco (a bit worn along joints and extremities), elaborately gilt-decorated covers and spine, raised bands with decorative gilt trim, inner and outer dentelles finely tooled in gilt, a.e.g. A nice copy with plates that are fresh and clean and with contemporary presentation inscription (dated 1854) on fly-leaf. Not in Kohler (but see Kohler 338, with address of "70 St. Paul's Churchyard," dating its copy "ca. 1858").

See undated ca. 1854 edition of *CPW* preceding by Gall & Inglis with "Eight Engravings on Steel" published in Edinburgh with the same address ("38 North Bridge") appearing on both the printed and engraved title pages; see also other undated editions of *CPW* by Gall & Inglis in the ca. 1854 listing with the same undated publisher's imprint on the engraved title page as here.

127. THE COMPLETE POETICAL WORKS OF JOHN MILTON: With Explanatory Notes, And A Life Of The Author, By The Rev. H. Stebbing, A.M. To Which Is Prefixed, Dr. Channing's Essay On The Poetical Genius Of Milton. *New York: D. Appleton & Co., 200 Broadway. 1854.* Small 8vo, xvi+552pp., frontispiece portrait engraved by Illman and Pilbrow after Faithorne, six illustration plates (unsigned, fine impressions), as with 1844 edition listed here, each illustration with protective tissue guard, double black border around text, original brown calf over thick boards (rubbed along extremities, age-browning throughout), covers richly embossed in blind with Milton's name in gilt at the center, spine lettered in gilt ("Milton's Poetical Works"), raised bands with small decorative piece in blind within the panels, a.e.g. Nice copy in an attractive binding of the period. Not in Kohler.

The possible first edition thus was published in 1843, unlike here by D. Appleton of New York and Geo. Appleton of Philadelphia, in the same format as here, but with only three of the six illustrations here (also listed here with further editions by Appleton cited there).

128. THE COMPLETE POETICAL WORKS OF JOHN MILTON. Together With A Life Of The Author[.] *Boston: Phillips, Sampson, And Company. New York: James C. Derby[.] 1854.* 2 volumes in one. 12mo in 6s, 321pp.,+232pp., engraved frontispiece illustration by A. Dick for Book I of *PL* (of angels protecting Adam and Eve from Satan while they are sleeping), engraved and printed title pages, engraved title page (reading "The Poetical Works Of John Milton[.] Boston. Phillips, Sampson & Co."), with unsigned vignette illustration of Satan rallying his troops for Book I of *PL* on engraved title, protective tissue guard (both frontispiece and engraved title page a little foxed), "Contents Of Paradise Lost" (which makes up all of volume 1), life of Milton by Fenton, volume 1, "Contents" of volume 2, half-title for *C* and *SA* (placed after *C* here), original red cloth (occasional light foxing), covers elaborately decorated in embossed gilt with large embossed central gilt device, spine similarly decorated in embossed gilt with gilt lettering, a.e.g. A nice copy. Scarce. Kohler 329, describing its copy as "Octavo in 6s" and reporting "Not in the British Library. Not in the Bodleian Library. Not in Cambridge University Library."

The second edition thus with "New York: James C. Derby" in publisher's imprint was published in 1855 (several copies listed here). See also 1857 and 1858 editions without engraved frontispiece illustration and engraved title page and with only "Boston: Phillips, Sampson, And Company" in publisher's imprint on printed title page. See virtually identical edition published in New York "By Clark, Austin & Co.," with same engraved frontispiece illustration by A. Dick and same unsigned vignette illustration on engraved title page as here, and in 1849, 1850, 1851, and 1852—all listed here.

129. THE COMPLETE POETICAL WORKS OF JOHN MILTON. With Life. Eight Engravings on Steel. *Edinburgh, Gall & Inglis 6 George Street. n.d. [ca. 1855].* Small 8vo, xx+491pp., unsigned frontispiece illustration plate of *The Expulsion*, engraved and printed title pages, unsigned vignette illustration of *Eve Relating Her Dream to Adam* on engraved title, which bears the same publisher and address as that on title page, "Edinburgh, Gall & Inglis 6 George Street," undated, six additional illustration plates (most unsigned, two after Ts. Brown) black border line around text, original full green morocco (pen scribbling on blank endpapers, some age-spotting), elaborately gilt-decorated covers, spine richly decorated in gilt within the panels with gilt lettering ("Milton's Poetical Works"), raised bands, inner and outer dentelles finely tooled in gilt, a.e.g. Except for the scribbling on blank endpapers, a lovely copy in an elaborate Victorian publisher's morocco binding with the publisher's imprint the same on both the engraved and printed title pages: "Edinburgh, Gall & Inglis 6 George Street," and with a contemporary signature (dated "Feb. 17, 1860") on preliminary blank. Kohler 333.

See undated ca. 1854 edition of *CPW* by Gall & Inglis, with "Eight Engravings on Steel," as here, published in Edinburgh with the same address ("38 North Bridge") appearing on both the printed and engraved title pages; and see other Gall & Inglis editions of *CPW* cited there.

130. Variant of Preceding, original full navy blue morocco (a bit worn along joints and extremities), elaborately gilt-decorated covers, spine richly decorated in gilt within the panels with gilt lettering ("Milton's Poetical Works"), raised bands, inner and outer dentelles finely tooled in gilt, a.e.g. A very nice copy in an attractive variant publisher's morocco binding with the publisher's imprint the same on both the engraved and printed title pages: "Gall & Inglis, 6 George Street" (undated) and with a contemporary presentation inscription (dated "December 19th 1859") on fly-leaf. Kohler 333.

131. THE COMPLETE POETICAL WORKS OF JOHN MILTON. Together With A Life Of The Author[.] *Boston: Phillips, Sampson, And Company. New York: James C. Derby[.]* 1855. 2 volumes in one. 12mo in 6s, 321pp.,+232pp., engraved frontispiece illustration by A. Dick and unsigned vignette illustration on engraved title (with publisher's imprint: "Boston: Phillips, Sampson & Co.") as with 1854 edition, likewise "Contents" for volumes 1 and 2, life by Fenton, and half-title for *C* and *SA*, original blind-stamped brown cloth (frontispiece and title page foxed, joints split at top, spine ends chipped, one signature a bit loose, embrowning throughout), elaborately gilt-decorated spine with gilt lettering ("Milton's Poetical Works"), early signature in ink in a fine hand on fly-leaf and small bookshop label on front pastedown. Not in Kohler.

132. Variant of Preceding, original blind-stamped red cloth (foxing throughout, spine ends chipped, early names and stamps on front blanks), elaborately gilt-decorated spine with gilt lettering ("Milton's Poetical Works"). A decent copy in a variant publisher's binding. Not in Kohler.

133. THE COMPLETE POETICAL WORKS OF JOHN MILTON: With Explanatory Notes, And A Life Of The Author, By The Rev. H. Stebbing, A.M. To Which Is Prefixed, Dr. Channing's Essay On The Poetical Genius Of Milton[.] *New York: D. Appleton And Company, 346 & 348 Broadway. M.DCCC.LV.* Small 8vo, xvi+552pp., frontispiece portrait engraved by Illman and Pilbrow after Faithorne, protective tissue guard, "Memoir Of Milton's Life And Writings," "Dr. Channing's Essay On The Poetical Genius Of Milton," six illustration plates (unsigned, fine impressions), as with 1844 edition listed here, each illustration with protective tissue guard, double black border around text, original reddish-brown cloth (a bit rubbed at joints, spine a little faded), covers stamped in blind, spine lettered in gilt ("Milton's Poetical Works") with small shamrocks in gilt within the panels double ruled in gilt, brown endpapers. Nice copy with plates that are fresh and clean. The possible first edition thus was published in 1843, unlike here by D. Appleton of New York and Geo. Appleton of Philadelphia, with only three of the six illustrations here (also listed here with further editions by Appleton cited there). Not in Kohler.

134. THE COMPLETE POETICAL WORKS OF JOHN MILTON: With Explanatory Notes, And A Life Of The Author, By The Rev. H. Stebbing, A.M. To Which Is Prefixed, Dr. Channing's Essay On The Poetical Genius Of Milton[.] *New York: D. Appleton And Company, 346 & 348 Broadway. M.DCCC.LVI.* Small 8vo, xvi+552pp., frontispiece portrait engraved by Illman and Pilbrow after Faithorne, protective tissue guard, six illustration plates (unsigned, fine impressions), as with 1844 edition listed here, each illustration with protective tissue guard, double black border around text, original olive green cloth (a little rubbed, foxing, including the plates), covers stamped in embossed blind trim with Milton's name in blind at the center, spine lettered in gilt ("Milton's Poetical Works") with small shamrocks in gilt within the panels double ruled in gilt. See possible first edition thus in 1843 and other editions by Appleton cited there. Not in Kohler.

135. Variant of Preceding, original brown cloth (foxing), decorated as preceding. Nice copy in a variant publisher's binding.

136. THE COMPLETE POETICAL WORKS OF JOHN MILTON. Together With A Life Of The Author[.] *Boston: Phillips, Sampson, And Company.* 1857. 2 volumes in one. 12mo in 6s, 321+[1]pp., +232pp., engraved frontispiece portrait after J. J. McCarty "From a Miniature of the same size by Faithorne, Anno 1667 in the profession of William Falconer, Esq.," protective tissue guard, "Contents Of *PL*" (which makes up all of volume 1), life by Fenton, "Contents" of volume 2, half-title for *C* and *SA* (placed after *C* here), original red cloth (a little worn, frontispiece and title page foxed), covers decorated in embossed blind trim, spine richly decorated in gilt with gilt lettering, printed advertisements on endpapers. Not in Kohler.

See 1854 and 1855 editions listed here by Phillips, Sampson, and Company with engraved frontispiece illustration and engraved title page with vignette illustration, and with the addition of "New York: James C. Derby" in publisher's imprint on printed title page. See also 1858 edition listed here with only "Boston: Phillips, Sampson, And Company" in publisher's imprint as here, but without engraved frontispiece illustration as here or engraved title page. See, too, 1854, 1855, and 1857 illustrated editions of *PW* listed here published by Phillips, Sampson, and Company.

137. Variant of Preceding with printed title page as preceding and a title-page plate in color ("The Poetical Works of John Milton. Boston: Phillips, Sampson, & Company, 1857.") with a variety of multicolored flowers in a semicircle and at the center a harp intertwined with ivy, protective tissue guard, original blue cloth (a bit worn, bottom of spine chipped), covers ruled in blind with decorative emblem in blind at the center, spine lettered in gilt ("Milton's Poems") within elaborate decorative gilt frame, gray endpapers, a.e.g. A good copy in a variant publisher's binding with title-page plate in color and with color title page dated the same as the printed title page. See 1860 edition listed here for listing of editions with title-page plates in color in editions in the 1860s. Uncommon.

138. THE COMPLETE POETICAL WORKS OF JOHN MILTON. Together With A Life Of The Author[.] *Boston: Phillips, Sampson, And Company. 1858.* 2 volumes in one. 12mo in 6s, 321+[1]pp., +232pp., engraved frontispiece portrait after J. J. McCarty "From a Miniature of the same size by Faithorne, Anno 1667 in the profession of William Falconer, Esq.," protective tissue guard, "Contents Of Paradise Lost" (which makes up all of volume 1), life by Fenton, "Contents" of volume 2, half-title for *C* and *SA* (placed after *C* here), original red cloth (a bit rubbed, slight ink stain lower back cover, earlier ownership signature in pencil on title page), covers decorated in embossed blind trim, spine richly decorated in gilt with gilt lettering, printed advertisements on endpapers. Not in Kohler.

139. THE COMPLETE POETICAL WORKS OF JOHN MILTON Together With A Life Of The Author[.] *Boston: Crosby, Nichols, Lee & Company. 1860.* First edition thus. 2 volumes in one. 12mo in 6s, 321+[1]pp.,+232pp., color and printed title pages, title-page plate in color ("The Poetical Works of John Milton. Boston: 1860.") with a variety of multicolored flowers in a semicircle and at the center a harp intertwined with ivy, protective tissue guard, "Contents" at the outset of volume 1, life by Fenton, "Contents" at the outset of volume 2, original blue cloth (some slight wear, endpapers faded), covers ruled in blind with decorative emblem in blind at the center, spine lettered in gilt ("Milton's Poems") within elaborate decorative gilt frame, blue endpapers, a.e.g. Good copy of a scarce mid-nineteenth-century American edition with both color title-page plate and printed title page dated 1860. Scarce. Not in Kohler.

See variant edition following with color title page and printed title page dated differently from one another (1860/1861). The edition was printed a number of times throughout the decade in the same 12mo format by various publishers with the same engraved title-page plate in color (titled "The Poetical Works" and undated, with the colors not as bright and sharp as here, probably due to the repetitious printing), in a similar binding, and with the spine lettered "Milton's Poems" in gilt. See editions listed here: in 1863 published in Boston by Crosby and Nichols with color title page undated; in 1865 published in Boston by Crosby and Ainsworth and in New York by Oliver S. Felt with color title page undated; in 1869 published in Boston by Woolworth, Ainsworth & Co. and in New York by A. S. Barnes & Co. with color title page undated; and undated in ca. 1871 published in Boston by Crosby and Ainsworth and in New York by Oliver S. Felt with color title page undated. See, too, 1857 edition published in Boston by Phillips, Sampson, and Company with color title-page plate with a variety of multicolored flowers as here (also listed here); both color title-page plate and printed title page dated 1857.

140. Variant of Preceding. THE COMPLETE POETICAL WORKS OF JOHN MILTON Together With A Life Of The Author[.] *Boston: Crosby, Nichols, Lee & Company. 1861.* 2 volumes in one. 12mo in 6s, 321+[1]pp.,+232pp., color and printed title pages, title-page plate in color ("The Poetical Works of John Milton. Boston: Crosby, Nichols, Lee & Co. 1860.") with a variety of multicolored flowers in a semicircle and at the center a harp intertwined with ivy, (the colors on the engraved title being very crisp and sharp), protective tissue guard, "Contents" at the outset of volume 1, life by Fenton, "Contents" at the outset of volume 2, original blue cloth (a bit worn, small white stain on back cover, spine ends chipped, faded early presentation inscription on fly-leaf, later ownership stamp on front pastedown), covers ruled in blind with decorative emblem in blind at the center, spine lettered in gilt ("Milton's Poems") within elaborate decorative gilt frame, brown endpapers, a.e.g. Good copy of a mid-nineteenth-century American edition, both color title-page plate and printed title page dated differently from one another (1860/1861). Scarce.

141. THE COMPLETE POETICAL WORKS OF JOHN MILTON. With Life. Eight Engravings on Steel. *Edinburgh, Gall & Inglis 6 George Street. n.d. [ca. 1862].*

Small 8vo, xx+491pp., unsigned frontispiece illustration plate of *The Expulsion*, engraved and printed title pages, with unsigned vignette illustration of *Eve Relating Her Dream to Adam* on engraved title, which bears the same publisher and address as that on title page, "Edinburgh, Gall & Inglis 6 George Street," undated, six additional illustration plates (most unsigned, two after Ts. Brown), black border line around text, original green pebble grain cloth (bit rubbed), front cover richly decorated in embossed gilt with Milton's name in gilt at the center, back cover repeating in embossed blind the decorated gilt pattern on the front cover, spine richly decorated in gilt with gilt lettering ("Milton's Poetical Works"), a.e.g. A lovely copy in a richly decorated publisher's cloth binding with the publisher's imprint the same on both the engraved and printed title pages ("Edinburgh, Gall & Inglis 6 George Street"), and with a contemporary signature (dated 1863) on fly-leaf. See undated ca. 1854 edition of *CPW* by Gall & Inglis, with "Eight Engravings on Steel," as here, published in Edinburgh with the same address ("38 North Bridge") appearing on both the printed and engraved title pages; and see other Gall & Inglis editions of *CPW* cited there. Not in Kohler.

142. Variant of Preceding, original red pebble grain cloth (corners worn), front cover decorated with richly embossed border trim in gilt and a large gilt urn in the center, back cover repeating in embossed blind the decorated gilt pattern on the front cover, spine richly decorated in gilt with gilt lettering ("Milton's Poetical Works"), a.e.g. An attractive copy in a variant publisher's cloth binding with contemporary presentation inscription (dated 1862) on fly-leaf.

143. THE COMPLETE POETICAL WORKS OF JOHN MILTON Together With A Life Of The Author[.] *Boston: Crosby And Nichols. 1863.* 2 volumes in one. 12mo in 6s, 321+[1]pp.,+232pp., engraved and printed title pages, engraved title-page plate in color ("The Poetical Works of John Milton[.] Boston: Crosby & Nichols," n.d.) with a variety of multicolored flowers in a semicircle and at the center a harp intertwined with ivy, protective tissue guard, "Contents" at the outset of volume 1, life by Fenton, "Contents" at the outset of volume 2, original blue cloth (a bit rubbed, some very slight staining along outer edges of front and back blanks), covers ruled in blind with decorative emblem in blind at the center, spine lettered in gilt ("Milton's Poems") within elaborate decorative gilt frame, tan endpapers, a.e.g. Nice copy. See the edition published in Boston in 1860 by Crosby, Nichols, Lee & Company with both color title page and printed title page dated 1860 (also listed here with further editions cited). Scarce. Not in Kohler.

144. THE COMPLETE POETICAL WORKS OF JOHN MILTON. With Life Of The Author; And Dr. Channing's Essay On The Poetical Genius Of Milton. Eight Engravings On Steel. *Halifax: Milner And Sowerby; 1864.* First edition thus. Small 8vo, xx+537pp., half-title ("Milton's Complete Poetical Works"), frontispiece steel-engraved illustration plate of *Satan, Sin, and Death* after T. Brown (for Book II of *PL* with lines illustrated quoted beneath the illustration), engraved and printed title pages, with steel-engraved vignette illustration of Satan on his throne after T. Brown on engraved title-page plate (for Book II of *PL* with lines illustrated quoted beneath the illustration), engraved title reading: "Poetical Works of John Milton[,] Halifax[:] Milner And Sowerby," two additional steel-engraved illustration plates after T. Brown, one for Book IV of *PL* (of Adam and Eve in morning prayer) and one for Book IX of *PL* (of the temptation of Eve), four additional steel-engraved illustration plates (unsigned, with only "Banks & Sons, Edin." printed at the bottom of each plate): one for Book VIII of *PL* (of Adam naming the animals), one for Book XII of *PL* (of the expulsion), one for Book IV of *PR* (of Christ sitting "in calm and sinless peace" among "Infernal ghosts and hellish furies round!"), and one for *SA* (of Samson, hair shorn, with Delilah), with the lines illustrated quoted beneath each illustration, "Milner And Sowerby, Printers, Halifax" printed at bottom of last page, contemporary three-quarter calf, marbled paper over boards (slightly rubbed, plates a little foxed), spine decorated in a blind pattern within the panels, raised bands within gilt rules, maroon morocco label ruled in gilt with gilt lettering ("Poetical Works"), red speckled edges. Very nice, "Bound By Bemrost, Derby," with their stamp. Uncommon. Not in Kohler.

See other dated and undated editions published by Milner and Sowerby listed here: in Halifax in 1865 and 1867, and in London ca. 1867. The differences between the Halifax and London editions seem largely to be that "Eight Engravings On Steel" appears on the title page of the Halifax editions and not on the London editions, even though eight steel-engraved illustrations appear within the London editions (the same illustrations as appear in the Halifax editions) and the publisher's imprint of "Milner And Sowerby" with date appears in the Halifax editions while "Milner And Company, Paternoster Row" appears in the London editions without date. See also possible first edition thus of *PW* listed here published by Milner and Sowerby in 1853 and other editions by Milner and Sowerby cited there.

145. THE COMPLETE POETICAL WORKS OF JOHN MILTON. With Life. Eight Engravings on Steel. *Edinburgh: Gall & Inglis, 6 George Street. n.d. [ca. 1865].*

Small 8vo, xx+491pp., unsigned frontispiece illustration plate of *The Expulsion*, engraved and printed title pages, with unsigned vignette illustration of *Eve Relating Her Dream to Adam* on engraved title, which bears the publisher and address, "Edinburgh, Gall & Inglis 38 North Bridge," undated, six additional illustration plates (most unsigned, two after Ts. Brown) black border line around text, original full dark maroon morocco (joints a bit rubbed, plates lightly damp-stained along edges), elaborately gilt-decorated covers, spine similarly gilt-decorated with gilt lettering ("Milton's Poetical Works"), raised bands, inner and outer dentelles finely tooled in gilt, a.e.g. A very attractive copy in an elaborate Victorian publisher's morocco binding with a different publisher's imprint on the engraved title ("Edinburgh, Gall & Inglis 38 North Bridge") from that on the printed title page ("Edinburgh: Gall & Inglis, 6 George Street"). See undated ca. 1854 edition of *CPW* by Gall & Inglis, with "Eight Engravings on Steel," published in Edinburgh with the same address ("38 North Bridge") appearing on both the printed and engraved title pages; and see other Gall & Inglis editions of *CPW* cited there. Not in Kohler.

146. Variant of Preceding, original full red morocco (a bit worn along joints and at corners), covers delicately decorated in gilt, spine richly decorated in gilt within the panels with gilt lettering ("Milton's Poetical Works"), raised bands, inner dentelles finely tooled in gilt, a.e.g. A lovely copy in a variant original publisher's morocco binding with early presentation inscription on fly-leaf.

147. THE COMPLETE POETICAL WORKS OF JOHN MILTON. With Life Of The Author; And Dr. Channing's Essay On The Poetical Genius Of Milton. Eight Engravings On Steel. *Halifax: Milner And Sowerby; 1865.* Small 8vo, xx+537pp., half-title, frontispiece illustration, engraved and printed title pages, and illustrations as with preceding Halifax edition (dated 1864), "Milner And Sowerby, Printers, Halifax" printed at bottom of last page, contemporary three-quarter dark brown leather, marbled paper over boards (a little rubbed), spine delicately decorated in gilt within the panels, red morocco label with gilt rules and gilt lettering ("Poetical Works"), raised bands within gilt rules, marbled endpapers and edges. Very nice. The first edition by Milner and Sowerby was published in 1864 (also listed here with further editions by Milner and Sowerby cited). Uncommon. Not in Kohler.

148. THE COMPLETE POETICAL WORKS OF JOHN MILTON. With Life. Eight Engravings On Steel. *Boston: Gould & Lincoln, 59 Washington Street. n.d. [ca. 1865].* Small 8vo, xx+491pp., engraved and printed title pages, unsigned frontispiece illustration plate of *Raphael Recounting Story of Creation and Fall*, with unsigned vignette illustration of *Eve Relating Her Dream to Adam* on engraved title, which bears the same publisher as the printed title page ("Boston: Gould & Lincoln, 59 Washington Street," undated), six additional illustration plates—for *PL* (Books II, IX, and two for XII) and for *PR* (Book IV), and for *L'A*, black border around text, original blue cloth (very worn, spine missing, pages slightly age-darkened), covers decorated in blind with central urn in blind. Similar to Gall & Inglis editions published about this same time, ca. 1862 and ca. 1865 (several copies listed here) and ca. 1870s (also listed here). Scarce. Not in Kohler.

149. THE COMPLETE POETICAL WORKS OF JOHN MILTON Together With A Life Of The Author[.] *Boston: Crosby And Ainsworth. New York: Oliver S. Felt. 1865.* 2 volumes in one. 12mo in 6s, 321+[1]+pp.,+232pp. engraved and printed title pages, title-page plate in color ("The Poetical Works of John Milton[.] Boston: Crosby & Nichols." n.d.) with a variety of multicolored flowers in a semicircle and at the center a harp intertwined with ivy, protective tissue guard, "Contents" at the outset of volume 1, life by Fenton, "Contents" at the outset of volume 2, original blue cloth (a bit rubbed, spine chipped at top and bottom), covers ruled in blind with decorative emblem in blind at the center, spine lettered in gilt ("Milton's Poems") within elaborate decorative gilt frame, brown endpapers, a.e.g. Nice copy with same publisher's imprint on color title page and on printed title page. See the edition published in Boston in 1860 by Crosby, Nichols, Lee & Company with both engraved title-page plate in color and printed title page dated 1860 (also listed here with further editions cited). Not in Kohler.

150. THE COMPLETE POETICAL WORKS OF JOHN MILTON Together With A Life Of The Author[.] *Boston: Crosby And Ainsworth. New York: Oliver S. Felt. n.d. [ca. 1865].* 2 volumes in one. 12mo in 6s, 321+[1]pp., +232pp., frontispiece portrait engraved by J. J. McCarty "From a Miniature of the same size by Faithorne, Anno 1667, in the possession of William Falconer, Esq.," protective tissue guard, "Contents" at the outset of volume 1, life by Milton after Fenton, original green sand grain cloth (a bit worn, pages a little age-browned), spine lettered in gilt ("Milton's Poems" and "Cabinet Edition"). Variant from dated 1865 edition preceding, published, as here, by Crosby and Ainsworth in Boston, and by Oliver S. Felt in New York, as 2 volumes in one, with the same pagination, but in a smaller 12mo format and with a second undated title-page plate in multicolors. Decent copy of an uncommon edition. Kohler 355 dates its copy "[ca. 1865]," reporting "Not in Williamson. Not in the British Library.

Not in the Bodleian Library. Not in the Cambridge University Library."

151. THE COMPLETE POETICAL WORKS OF JOHN MILTON. With Life Of The Author; And Dr. Channing's Essay On The Poetical Genius Of Milton. Eight Engravings On Steel. *Halifax: Milner And Sowerby, 44 Patterson Row, And Halifax, Yorkshire. 1867*. Small 8vo, xx+537+[1]+14pp., half-title ("Milton's Complete Poetical Works"), frontispiece steel-engraved illustration plate of *Satan, Sin, and Death* after T. Brown (for Book II of *PL*, with lines illustrated quoted beneath the illustration), protective tissue guard, engraved title reading: "Poetical Works of John Milton[,] Halifax[:] Milner And Sowerby," additional steel-engraved illustration plates as with 1864 first edition published by Milner and Sowerby (also listed here), "Milner And Sowerby, Printers, Halifax" printed at bottom of last page, original blue pebble cloth (a bit worn, fly-leaf and half-title each missing a small portion at the top where name has been removed), covers decorated in embossed blind trim, spine elaborately decorated in gilt with gilt lettering ("Milton's Poetical Works"), a.e.g. Fourteen pages of advertisements for "A Catalogue Of Cheap Books, Published By Milner & Sowerby" bound in at the end. The first edition by Milner and Sowerby was published in 1864 (also listed here with further editions cited). Not in Kohler.

152. Variant of Preceding. **THE COMPLETE POETICAL WORKS OF JOHN MILTON.** With Life Of The Author; And Dr. Channing's Essay On The Poetical Genius Of Milton. *London: Milner And Sowerby, Patterson Row. n.d. [1867]*. As preceding, original green pebble cloth (lightly worn along joints, plates foxed), covers ruled in blind, with central embossed emblem in blind, spine decorated in black trim with gilt lettering ("Milton's Poetical Works") near the top and "London" at the bottom. A nice copy with variant title page (lacking reference to "Eight Engravings On Steel") with variant publisher's imprint: "London: Milner And Sowerby, Patterson Row," and undated, in a variant publisher's binding, with eighteen pages of advertisements for "Cheap Books Published By Milner & Sowerby, Paternoster Row, London" bound in at the end. Not in Kohler.

153. THE COMPLETE POETICAL WORKS OF JOHN MILTON. With Life Of The Author; And Dr. Channing's Essay On The Poetical Genius Of Milton. *London: Milner And Company, Paternoster Row. n.d. [ca. 1867]*. Small 8vo, xx+537+18pp., half-title ("Milton's Complete Poetical Works"), half-title, frontispiece illustration, engraved and printed title pages, and illustrations as with preceding dated and undated 1867 Milner editions, "Milner And Company, Printers, Halifax" printed at bottom of

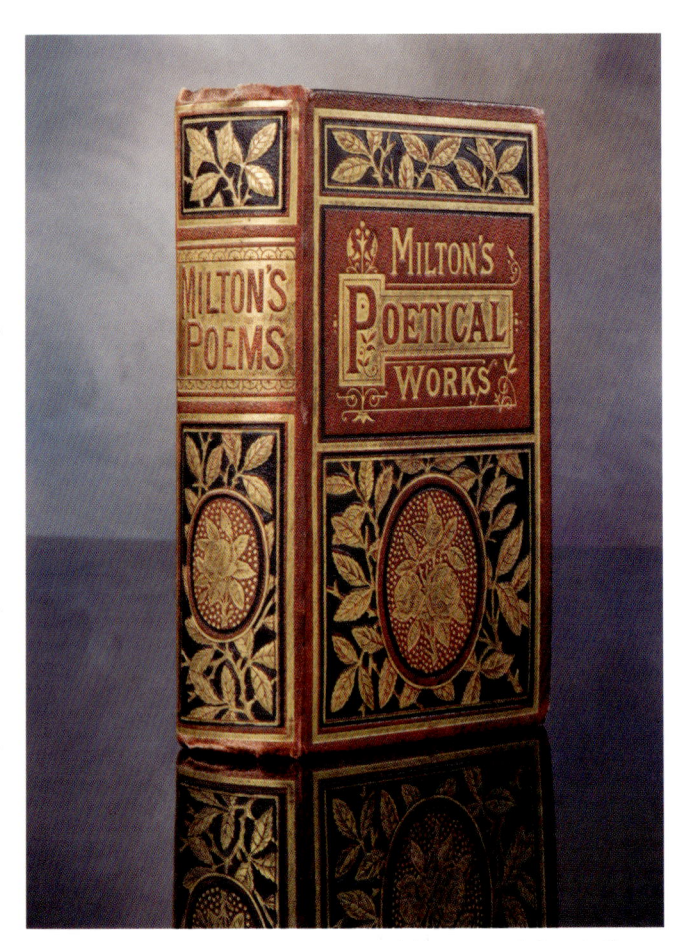

Complete Poetical Works. London: Milner and Company, n.d. [ca. 1867]. Original red pebble cloth, decorated in embossed black and gilt. See #153.

last page, original red pebble cloth (early name on fly-leaf), front cover richly decorated in black and gilt, with "Milton's Poetical Works" at the center, "Milton's" and "Works" in embossed gilt and "Poetical" in embossed red letters against a broad gilt band with a larger letter "P" decorated with gilt trim, all within a blocked red background; above at the top, is a small blocked section with embossed floral stems in gilt with red highlights against a black background, below, the bottom half is similarly decorated with embossed floral stems in gilt with red highlight against a black background, with an oval framing gilt-relief roses with pin-dot background in the middle, the spine is similarly decorated with a small blocked section at the top with embossed floral stems in gilt with red highlight against a black background, "Milton's Poems" lettered in embossed red letters against a bright, broad gilt band is near the center, and the bottom two-thirds is decorated in the same embossed floral stems in gilt with red highlight against a black background with an oval framing gilt-relief roses with pin-dot background in the middle, a.e.g., bookplate on front pastedown. A lovely copy in a rather stunning publisher's decorated cloth binding with eighteen paginated pages of advertisements for "Just Published" editions by Milner and Company bound in at the end (primarily for "Cheap Books" and "The Cottage Library," the latter including Milton's *PW*, see copies listed here). The first edition by Milner and Sowerby was published in 1864 (also listed here with further editions cited). Not in Kohler.

154. Variant of Preceding, original decorated green pebble cloth (a bit worn along joints and at corners, lacking front fly-leaf), front cover decorated in a black floral motif with a pictorial card (2" × 3 ½") decorated with a pink, blue, and green floral bouquet tipped into a recessed panel at the center with Milton's name in large embossed green letters set against a bright broad gilt band outlined in a black rule running diagonally across the top, spine lettered in gilt ("Milton's Poetical Works") near the top with a large floral vase in black and gilt near the bottom with decorative black trim at the top and bottom, back cover with thick embossed rules in blind. A nice copy, fresh and clean within, in an attractive variant publisher's binding with eighteen pages of paginated advertisements bound in at the end. Not in Kohler.

155. THE COMPLETE POETICAL WORKS OF JOHN MILTON Together With A Life Of The Author[.] *Boston: Woolworth, Ainsworth & Co. New York: A. S. Barnes & Co. 1869.* 2 volumes in one. 12mo in 6s, 321+[1]pp.,+v+232pp., engraved and printed title pages, engraved title-page plate in color ("The Poetical Works of John Milton[.] Boston: Woolworth, Ainsworth & Co." n.d.) with a variety of multicolored flowers in a semicircle and at the center a harp intertwined with ivy, (the engraved color plate being very crisp and clean with bright colors), protective tissue guard, "Contents" at the outset of volume 1, life by Fenton, "Contents" at the outset of volume 2, original blue cloth (a bit rubbed small white speck at top of front cover), covers ruled in blind with decorative emblem in blind at the center, spine lettered in gilt ("Milton's Poems") within elaborate decorative gilt frame, brown endpapers, a.e.g. A good copy, with contemporary signature in a neat hand. See 1860 edition published in Boston by Crosby, Nichols, Lee & Company with both title-page plate in color and printed title page dated 1860, citing further editions with title-page plates in color). Uncommon. Not in Kohler.

156. THE COMPLETE POETICAL WORKS OF JOHN MILTON Together With A Life Of The Author[.] *Boston: Crosby And Ainsworth. New York: Oliver S. Felt. n.d. [ca. 1871].* 2 volumes in one. 12mo in 6s, 321+[1]+pp.,+232pp., engraved and printed title pages, engraved title-page plate in color ("The Poetical Works of John Milton[.] Boston: Crosby & Ainsworth." n.d.) with a variety of multicolored flowers in a semicircle and at the center a harp intertwined with ivy, protective tissue guard, "Contents" at the outset of volume 1, life by Fenton, "Contents" at the outset of volume 2, original dark blue cloth (a bit worn, initial pages frayed, some foxing), covers ruled in blind with decorative emblem in blind at the center, spine lettered in gilt ("Milton's Poems") within elaborate decorative gilt frame, brown endpapers, a.e.g. A decent copy with contemporary presentation inscription as a Christmas gift (dated 1871) on front blank, and signature-style stamp of recipient on facing blank, and with variant publisher's imprint on engraved title page. See the edition published in Boston above in 1860 by Crosby, Nichols, Lee & Company, with both engraved title-page plate in color and printed title page dated 1860 (also listed here with further editions with title-page plates in color cited). Not in Kohler.

The collection also has a copy in original light blue cloth, a slightly variant publisher's binding. A nice copy with a brightly colored title-page plate.

157. THE COMPLETE WORKS, PROSE AND POETICAL, OF JOHN MILTON. With An Introduction By Robert Fletcher. *London: Chatto And Windus, Piccadilly. 1875.* 2 volumes in one. First edition thus? 4to in 8s, xliii+963+14+[1],+191+[1]pp., engraved frontispiece portrait plate of Milton engraved by W. C. Edwards after Vertue (fine impression), small central illustration device on title page, "An Introductory Review" by Robert Fletcher, volume 1, half-title for "Milton's Prose Works," "An Alphabetical Index Of Principal Matters" at end of volume 1, half-title for volume 2, *PW*, printed in double column, modern red cloth (a bit marked), spine lettered in gilt. Kohler 377, reporting "Not in the British Library. Not in the Bodleian Library. Not in Cambridge University Library."

158. THE COMPLETE POETICAL WORKS OF JOHN MILTON. Together With A Life Of The Author. *New York: Published By T. Y. Crowell, 744 Broadway. n.d. [ca. 1878].* 2 volumes in one. First edition thus by Crowell? 12mo in 6s, 321+231pp., life of Milton by Fenton, without separate title page for volume 2 but with half-title for *PR*, "Contents" page for volume 2, and separate pagination, original decorated green cloth (a little worn along joints and at ends of spine), front cover decorated with elaborate, embossed decorative black trim at the top and bottom and with "Milton's Poems" lettered in black at the center with decorated initial letter "P," spine similarly decorated with elaborate black trim at top and bottom with gilt lettering ("Milton's Poems") and a decorative gilt piece beneath at the center and gilt rules at top and bottom, back cover decorated in blind, dark green endpapers. A nice, tight copy with small early/contemporary bookplate from private library on front pastedown. Not in Kohler.

159. Variant of Preceding. A nice copy in an attractive variant publisher's binding with "Milton's Poems" lettered in gilt rather than black on the front cover, and with gilt edges rather than plain as in preceding copy, with contemporary presentation inscription (dated "Dec. 25, 1878") in a neat hand on front blank. Unlike the preceding copy, the last page of volume 2 (verso of p. 231) is not printed in this copy (leaving Psalm CXXXVI incomplete at the bottom of p. 231). See ca. 1885 Crowell edition listed here, similar to this edition, with printing completed on verso of p. 231.

160. THE COMPLETE POETICAL WORKS OF JOHN MILTON. Together With A Life Of The Author. *New York: Published By T. Y. Crowell, 744 Broadway. n.d. [ca. 1880].* 2 volumes in one. First edition thus by Crowell with illustrations. 12mo in 6s, 321+232pp., frontispiece illustration plate after engraving by Dalziel for *PL* (Book XII, *The Expulsion*), protective tissue guard, "Contents" page for volume 1, life of Milton by Fenton, half-title for each book of *PL*, without separate title page for volume 2 but with half-title for *PR*, "Contents" page for volume 2, and separate pagination, five additional illustration plates after engravings by Dalziel: for *PL*, Book IV (*Adam Sees Eve*, with lines quoted) and Book VIII (*Adam and Eve in Nature*, with appropriate lines quoted), for *SA* ("But Who is this? . . . Comes this way sailing / Like a stately ship?"), for *L'A* ("While the ploughman near at hand. . . ."), and for *On His Deceased Wife* (with appropriate lines quoted), red border around text, original decorated red cloth, front cover decorated in embossed black trim with a brightly decorated embossed black and gilt device with decorative gilt trim at the center incorporating the title "Milton's Poems" in embossed red letters in the foreground within a richly decorated broad gilt horizontal panel in front of an urn in gilt with long-stemmed flowers in gilt as a vertical backdrop outlined in decorative gilt trim, spine similarly decorated in embossed black and gilt with the title "Milton's Poems" in embossed red letters within two brightly decorated broad gilt bands at the top with floral motif in gilt similar to that on front cover, "T. Y. Crowell" in embossed red letters within a smaller decorated gilt band at the bottom, decorative trim in black and gilt at the top and bottom, green endpapers, bevelled edges, a.e.g. A fine copy in a stunning American publisher's decorated cloth binding, very crisp and clean within, with contemporary presentation inscription, "A Merry Christmas And A Happy New Year" (dated 1880) on front blank with small owner's stamp above and on title page. Not in Kohler.

See undated ca. 1878 nonillustrated edition and undated ca. 1883 illustrated edition listed here along with undated ca. 1885 nonillustrated and dated 1892 nonillustrated editions of Milton's *CPW* listed here, each published by Crowell; and see dated and undated illustrated editions of Milton's *PW* published by Crowell about this time, ca. 1883 and 1884—both listed here.

161. Variant of Preceding. Original decorated brown cloth (a bit rubbed), front cover richly decorated in embossed black and gilt floral trim with large bright gilt floral pattern at center incorporating Milton's name with decorated initial letter "M" in larger size, bevelled edges, spine similarly richly decorated in embossed black and gilt with the title ("Milton's Poems") incorporated within two thick bright gilt bands at the top and large embossed gilt and reddish-brown pattern beneath, with "T. Y. Crowell & Co." lettered in embossed brown within a gilt scroll at bottom, a.e.g. Fine copy with variant publisher's imprint ("Thomas Y. Crowell & Co., No. 13 Astor Place"), in a splendid variant publisher's binding, and with contemporary signature on front blank. Not in Kohler.

162. THE COMPLETE POETICAL WORKS OF JOHN MILTON. Together With A Life Of The Author. *New York: Thomas Y. Crowell & Co., No. 13 Astor Place. n.d. [ca. 1883].* 8vo, 562pp., frontispiece portrait plate of a young Milton after "E. Ronjat," protective tissue guard, four illustration plates after engravings by Dalziel: for *PL*, Book IV (*Adam Sees Eve*, with lines quoted), for Book VIII (*Adam and Eve in Nature*, with appropriate lines quoted), for *SA*, and for *Ad Leonoram Romae Canentem* (with appropriate lines quoted, plate with two stain marks along outer margins), red border around text, original decorated reddish-brown cloth (a bit rubbed, early signature on fly-leaf), front cover and spine elaborately decorated in embossed black and gilt, with large bright gilt emblem at top of front cover incorporating Milton's name, bevelled edges, decorative broad gilt panel at top of spine incorporating lettering in embossed reddish-brown ("Milton's Poems"), with "T. Y. Crowell & Co." lettered in gilt at bottom of spine, a.e.g. Not in Kohler.

163. THE COMPLETE POETICAL WORKS OF JOHN MILTON. Together With A Life Of The Author. New York: *Published By T. Y. Crowell, 744 Broadway. n.d. [ca. 1885].* 2 volumes in one. 12mo in 6s, 321+232pp., life of Milton by Fenton, half-title for each book of *PL* and for various of the poems, without separate title page for volume 2, but with half-title for *PR*, "Contents" page for volume 2, and separate pagination, original decorated red cloth (a bit rubbed, pages age-browned due to poor quality of the paper), front cover decorated in embossed black trim with decorative black trim at top and bottom, "Milton's Poems" lettered in embossed black letters at the top and a decorative harp in embossed black at the bottom left, spine decorated in embossed black and gilt with decorative black trim and gilt rules at top and bottom, an elaborately decorated gilt piece at the top incorporating "Milton's Poems" in embossed red letters with a decorative harp in embossed black at the center and gilt trim at the bottom incorporating "T. Y. Crowell" in embossed red letters within a small gilt band, dark green endpapers. A nice copy in an attractive American publisher's decorated cloth binding and with contemporary presentation inscription (dated 1885) on front blank. See ca. 1878 edition, similar internally to this edition, with the exception that this copy has the last page (p. 232) printed, thereby completing volume 2. Not in Kohler.

164. THE COMPLETE POETICAL WORKS OF JOHN MILTON With A Life Of The Poet And Notes On His Works By Thomas Newton, D.D. Bishop Of Bristol[.] Illustrated With Fifty Photogravures From Designs By Great Artists. India Proof Edition. *Philadelphia[:] Gebbie & Co., Publishers[,] 1890. Copyrighted. 2 volumes.* First edition thus. Large 8vo, xxxviii+322pp., +vii+[i]+322pp., half-title each volume ("India Proof Edition"), frontispiece photogravure portrait of Milton "From the original drawing by Vertue," with protective tissue guard, volume 1, title page in red and black each volume, fifty photogravure illustrations (extremely fine impressions), each labeled and printed on thick paper, each with protective tissue guard, with one illustration for *PR* as frontispiece for volume 2, "Publisher's Preface" and "The Life Of Milton, Abridged From Bishop Newton's Biography," volume 1, contemporary three-quarter crushed olive levant (spines evenly faded), marbled paper over boards, spines lettered ("Poetical Works Of Milton") and numbered in gilt, raised bands with decorative gilt trim, marbled endpapers, t.e.g., others untrimmed. Fine set, elegantly printed in a limited edition on India paper. India proof edition with striking impressions of the plates. "The features on which we claim that this excels all other editions—are the beauty of type, the excellence of the illustrations (artistic and technical), and the general style of the whole work. . . . so, on the whole, we believe we publish in this edition the best that has ever appeared of the poetical works of 'That mighty orb of song, The divine Milton' Wordsworth" (Publisher's Preface). Among the artists included are Martin, Flatters, Lemercier, Westall, Corti, Bevonville, Bida, Burney, Frost, Horsley, Landseer, and Fanfani. A second edition thus was published in four volumes in 1895 (see set listed here). Not in Kohler.

165. THE COMPLETE POETICAL WORKS OF JOHN MILTON With A Biographical Sketch By Nathan Haskell Dole[.] *New York[:] Thomas Y. Crowell Company Publishers[,] (1892).* First edition thus? 8vo, xxi+618pp., frontispiece portrait plate of a young, long-haired Milton "From a miniature by Faithorne, 1667," decorated tissue guard with identification of portrait printed on verso, copyright on verso of title-page plate dated 1892, "Introduction To Paradise Lost" with charts and spheres, original green cloth, front cover lettered in gilt ("Milton's Poems") within gilt trim with central gilt harp, spine lettered in gilt ("Milton's Poems") with decorative gilt trim, small bookstore label on front pastedown. Nice. See undated ca. 1880 illustrated edition of Milton's *CPW* published by Crowell and other editions by Crowell listed there. A second edition thus was published by Crowell in 1920 (also listed here). Not in Kohler.

166. Variant of Preceding, original soft brown leather (a bit worn along edges and spine), front cover lettered in gilt ("Milton's Poems") at the top with a large embossed emblem in blind beneath beautifully tooled in art nouveau style, marbled brown endpapers, t.e.g., others untrimmed. A good copy in a variant publisher's binding.

167. Variant of Preceding, original maroon leather over limp boards (spine a bit rubbed, lacking endpapers), front cover lettered in gilt ("Milton's Poems") at the top within rich decorative gilt box, spine lettered in gilt with rich decorative gilt trim above and below, pink pastedowns, t.e.g. A nice copy in a variant publisher's binding.

168. THE COMPLETE POETICAL WORKS OF JOHN MILTON With A Life Of The Poet And Notes On His Works By Thomas Newton, D.D. Bishop Of Bristol. Illustrated With Fifty Photogravures From Designs By Great Artists. Grand Edition De Luxe. *Philadelphia[:] The Gebbie Publishing Co., Ltd. 1895. 4 volumes.* Second edition thus. Large 8vo, 142pp.,+322pp.(continuous pagination, volumes 1 and 2),+vii+[i]+168pp.,+322pp.(continuous pagination, volumes 3 and 4), half-title each volume ("India Proof Edition"), frontispiece photogravure portrait of Milton "From the original drawing by Vertue," with protective tissue guard, volume 1, title page in red and black each volume, fifty photogravure illustrations (stunning impressions, with a "List Of Illustrations"), each labeled and printed on thick paper, each with protective tissue guard, "Publisher's Preface" and "The Life Of Milton, Abridged From Bishop Newton's Biography," volume 1, contemporary dark brown limp leather boards (worn along edges, front joint cracked, volume 1), front covers lettered in gilt ("The Complete Poetical Works Of Milton"), spines lettered in gilt "Poetical Works Of John Milton"), raised bands with gilt rules, marbled endpapers, a.e.g. Although the bindings show some wear, a fine set, elegantly printed, with striking impressions of the plates. Among the artists included are Martin, Flatters, Lemercier, Westall, Corti,

Bevonville, Bida, Burney, Frost, Horsley, Landseer, and Fanfani. The first edition thus was published in 1890 (see two-volume "India Proof Edition"). "Sixty copies of this book have been printed. Only fifty of them being for sale. This is Copy No. 4" (printed on half-title each volume, number hand-written in red ink). Not in Kohler.

169. THE COMPLETE POETICAL WORKS OF JOHN MILTON[.] *Cambridge Edition[.] Boston And New York[:] Houghton, Mifflin And Company[;] The Riverside Press, Cambridge[,] (1899).* First edition thus. 8vo, xxxiv+417pp., half-title ("The Cambridge Edition of the Poets Edited By Horace E. Scudder—Milton By William Vaughan Moody"), unsigned engraved frontispiece vignette portrait plate of Milton age twenty-one, protective tissue guard, engraved vignette of Chalfont St. Giles on title page, copyright 1899 on verso of title page, "Electrotyped And Printed By H. O. Houghton And Co. The Riverside Press Cambridge, Mass., U.S.A." on verso of last page, original deep red cloth (bit rubbed, pencil notes in a neat hand variously throughout), gilt rules on front cover with central decorative gilt device incorporating Milton's name in gilt, spine lettered in gilt ("Milton's Complete Poetical Works"), t.e.g., black endpapers. Good copy with contemporary signature in a neat hand on front blank. A "Student's Edition" was also published in 1899 (also listed here). A second edition thus was published in 1924 (also listed here). Stevens 243, "The criticism shows discriminating judgment of literary values but is occasionally wrong in its premises. . . . Issued under various dates." Kohler 428, reporting "Not in Williamson. Not in the Bodleian Library. Not in Cambridge University Library."

170. Variant of Preceding, original brown cloth, gilt rules on front cover with central decorative gilt device incorporating Milton's name in gilt, spine lettered in gilt, t.e.g. Fine copy, near mint, very crisp and clean within, with advertisement leaf before half-title, no reference to the press on verso of last page, in a variant publisher's binding.

171. Variant of Preceding, original blue cloth, gilt rules on front cover with central decorative gilt device incorporating Milton's name in gilt, spine lettered in gilt, t.e.g. Fine copy with variant half-title, with no reference to the press on verso of last page, and in a variant publisher's binding.

172. THE COMPLETE POETICAL WORKS OF JOHN MILTON[.] Student's Cambridge Edition[.] *Houghton Mifflin Company[,] Boston[,] New York[,] Chicago[,] The Riverside Press Cambridge[,] (1899).* First edition thus. 8vo, xxxiv+417pp., half-title ("The Cambridge Poets Student's Edition—Milton Edited by William Vaughan Moody") with advertisement for "The Cambridge Poets" on verso, unsigned engraved frontispiece vignette portrait plate of Milton age twenty-one, protective tissue guard, copyright date of 1899 on verso of title page, original dark green cloth (a bit rubbed, some notations and underlining in pencil, name on fly-leaf), central laurel wreath in blind incorporating Milton's name in blind on front cover, spine lettered in gilt ("Milton's Complete Poems"). Fine, tall copy. A second edition thus was published in 1924 (also listed here). Kohler 429, reporting "Not in Williamson. Not in the British Library. Not in the Bodleian Library. Not in Cambridge University Library."

173. THE COMPLETE POETICAL WORKS OF JOHN MILTON From The Edition Of The Rev. H. C. Beeching, M.A. The Oxford Miniature Edition[.] *London: Henry Frowde[,] Oxford University Press Warehouse Amen Corner, E.C. New York: 91 & 93 Fifth Avenue[,] 1900.* First edition thus. 16mo miniature, 1082pp., unsigned frontispiece portrait, protective tissue guard (front edge frayed), "Oxford: Horace Hart Printer To The University" on verso of title page and repeated on last page, facsimile reproduction of several first edition title pages, contemporary tree calf (front cover slightly warped, bottom of title page a little frayed), decorative gilt border trim on covers, spine richly gilt-decorated within the panels with gilt lettering ("Milton"), raised bands with decorative gilt trim, marbled endpapers, lightly marbled edges. Nice. A second edition thus was published in 1904 (also listed here). Scarce. Not in Kohler.

174. THE COMPLETE POETICAL WORKS OF JOHN MILTON From The Edition Of The Rev. H. C. Beeching, M.A. The Oxford Miniature Edition[.] *London: Henry Frowde[,] Oxford University Press Warehouse Amen Corner, E.C. New York: 91 & 93 Fifth Avenue[,] 1904.* Second edition thus? 16mo miniature, 1054pp., as first edition, original three-quarter brown calf, white paper over boards (a bit rubbed), spine lettered in gilt ("Milton"), raised bands, lightly marbled endpapers, t.e.g. A fine copy. The first edition thus was published in 1900 (preceding copy), and this edition is similar to that in virtually every respect except that it is printed anew, with changed title page, new pagination, and fewer pages. Kohler 448, reporting "Not in Williamson. Not in the British Library. Not in the Bodleian Library. Not in Cambridge University Library."

175. THE COMPLETE POETICAL WORKS OF JOHN MILTON Edited After The Original Texts By The Rev. H. C. Beeching, M.A. Oxford Edition[.] *London: Henry Frowde Oxford University Press, Amen Corner, E.C. New York: 29-35 West 32nd Street[;] Toronto: 25-27 Richmond Street West[;] Melbourne: Cathedral Buildings[,] 1908.*

8vo in 16s, xiii+[iii]+554pp., half-title, frontispiece portrait plate engraved by Emory Walker after Faithorne, protective tissue guard, facsimile reproductions of first edition title pages, "Oxford: Horace Hart, Printer To The University" repeated on last page, original brown diaper grain cloth, front cover ruled in blind with Milton's name in gilt at the center, spine lettered in gilt ("Milton's Poetical Works") with decorative gilt trim at top and bottom, brown endpapers, t.e.g., others untrimmed, partially unopened. Fine copy with small orange label of "J. Poole & Co., Educational Booksellers, 104 Charing Cross Road, London" tipped in at bottom of front pastedown. Laid in: advertisement leaf for "The Oxford Poets Uniform With This Volume." Uncommon. Kohler 455, reporting "Not in the British Library. Not in the Bodleian Library. Not in Cambridge University library."

176. THE COMPLETE POETICAL WORKS OF JOHN MILTON Edited After The Original Texts By The Rev. H. C. Beeching, M.A. *London: Henry Frowde Oxford University Press, Amen Corner, E.C. New York: 35 West 32nd Street[;] Toronto: 25-27 Richmond Street West[;] Melbourne: Cathedral Buildings[,] 1911.* 8vo in 16s, xiii+[iii]+554pp., half-title, frontispiece portrait plate engraved by Emory Walker after Faithorne, protective tissue guard, facsimile reproductions of first edition title pages, "Oxford: Horace Hart Printer To The University" on last page, contemporary full navy blue morocco, decorative gilt border trim on covers with central gilt seal on front cover, elaborately gilt-decorated spine, red morocco label with gilt lettering ("Milton's Poetical Works") and gilt trim, raised bands with decorative gilt trim, marbled endpapers and edges. Fine copy handsomely printed in a lovely Prize Binding with prize label tipped in on front pastedown. Not in Kohler.

177. THE COMPLETE POETICAL WORKS OF JOHN MILTON Edited After The Original Texts By H. C. Beeching, D.D. *London: Humphrey Milford Oxford University Press, Amen Corner, E.C. New York: 35 West 32nd Street[;] Toronto: 25-27 Richmond Street West[;] Melbourne: Cathedral Buildings[;] Bombay: Hornby Road[,] 1913.* 8vo in 16s, xiii+[iii]+554pp., half-title, frontispiece portrait plate engraved by Emory Walker after Faithorne, protective tissue guard, facsimile reproductions of first edition title pages, "Oxford: Horace Hart Printer To The University" on last page, three-quarter red morocco, red cloth, gilt rules on covers, gilt floral centers and single-line panels on spine, raised bands with decorative gilt trim, marbled endpapers, t.e.g. A fine copy, handsomely printed in a lovely binding with contemporary signature on fly-leaf. Not in Kohler.

178. THE COMPLETE POETICAL WORKS OF JOHN MILTON Edited After The Original Texts By The Rev. H. C. Beeching, D.D. Humphrey Milford *Oxford University Press[,] London[,] Edinburgh[,] Glasgow[,] Copenhagen[,] New York[,] Toronto[,] Melbourne[,] Cape Town[,] Bombay[,] Calcutta[,] Madras[,] Shanghai[,] Peking[,] 1921.* 8vo in 16s, xiii+[iii]+554pp., half-title, frontispiece portrait plate engraved by Emory Walker after Faithorne, protective tissue guard, facsimile reproductions of first edition title pages, contemporary tree calf (rubbed at joints), decorative gilt border trim on covers, elaborately gilt-decorated spine, red morocco label with gilt lettering ("Milton's Poetical Works") and decorative gilt trim, raised bands with decorative gilt trim, broad inner dentelles and outer dentelles finely tooled in gilt, marbled endpapers, a.e.g. Fine copy, handsomely printed, in a lovely binding with neat contemporary presentation inscription on front blank.

179. THE COMPLETE POETICAL WORKS OF JOHN MILTON With A Biographical Sketch By Nathan Haskell Dole*[.] New York[:] Thomas Y. Crowell Company Publishers[,] (1920).* Second edition thus. 8vo, xxi+627pp., frontispiece portrait plate of a young, long-haired Milton "From a miniature by Faithorne, 1667," protective tissue guard with identification of portrait printed on verso, decorated title-page plate printed in red and black with ornamental border trim in black, copyright on verso of title-page plate dated 1892 along with copyright renewal date of 1920, original green cloth (a few black marks on front cover), front cover lettered in gilt, spine lettered in gilt ("Milton's Poems") with decorative gilt trim, t.e.g. The first edition thus was published in 1892 (several copies listed here).

180. THE COMPLETE POETICAL WORKS OF JOHN MILTON[.] *Cambridge Edition[.] Boston And New York[:] Houghton Mifflin Company[;] The Riverside Press, Cambridge[,] (1924).* Second edition thus. 8vo, xxxiv+419pp., advertisement leaf for "The Cambridge Poets" before half-title, half-title ("The Cambridge Edition of the Poets—Milton Edited By William Vaughan Moody"), unsigned engraved frontispiece vignette portrait plate of Milton, age twenty-one, protective tissue guard, engraved vignette of Chalfont St. Giles on title page, copyright date of 1899 on verso of title page along with copyright renewal date of 1924, three-quarter crushed dark green morocco, contrasting light green cloth, gilt rules on covers, spine decorated in gilt within the panels with gilt lettering, raised bands with decorative gilt trim, t.e.g., dark green endpapers. Nice copy with contemporary presentation inscription on front blank. The first edition thus was published in 1899 (several copies listed here).

181. THE COMPLETE POETICAL WORKS OF JOHN MILTON*[.] Student's Cambridge Edition[.] Houghton*

Mifflin Company[,] Boston • New York • Chicago • Dallas • San Francisco[,] The Riverside Press Cambridge[,] (1924). Second edition thus. 8vo, xxxiv+419pp., half-title ("The Cambridge Poets Student's Edition—Milton Edited by William Vaughan Moody") with advertisement for "The Cambridge Poets" on verso, unsigned engraved frontispiece vignette portrait plate of Milton at age twenty-one, protective tissue guard, copyright date of 1899 on verso of title page along with copyright renewal date of 1924, original red cloth (early signature on fly-leaf), central laurel wreath in blind on front cover incorporating Milton's name in blind, spine lettered in gilt ("Milton's Complete Poems"), fore-edge untrimmed. Fine, tall copy. Possibly a large paper copy. The first edition thus was published in 1899 (also listed here). Stevens 258.

182. Variant of Preceding, original green cloth (marginal notations in a neat hand variously throughout), central laurel wreath in blind on front cover incorporating Milton's name in blind, spine lettered in gilt ("Milton's Complete Poems"). Good copy in a variant publisher's binding shorter than the preceding copy by ½".

183. THE COMPLETE POETICAL WORKS OF JOHN MILTON[.] A New Text Edited With Introduction And Notes By Harris Francis Fletcher[,] *The University Of Illinois*[.] *Houghton Mifflin Company[,] The Riverside Press Cambridge, (1941)*. First edition thus. Small 4to size (9 ¾" x 7 ¼"), x+[2]+574pp., half-title ("The New Cambridge Edition A Revision of the Cambridge Edition Edited by William Vaughn Moody"), frontispiece portrait plate reproducing portrait of Milton at age ten, "The Life and Times of John Milton" with additional plates with reproductions on both sides of Milton at ages twenty-one, "about" forty-eight, and sixty-two, original blue cloth (bookplate removed from fly-leaf), central gilt laurel wreath incorporating Milton's name on front cover, spine lettered in gilt, printed maroon publisher's wrappers (a little rubbed, slightly worn along top edge) with five shelves of books wrapping around from front to back, with large framed white label on front cover with title lettered in green and maroon with laurel leaves in green at the bottom within the label and a circular reproduction of Milton at age sixty-two in black and white at the top, both within and outside the label, "Cambridge Edition" lettered in white at the bottom of the front cover with a window looking out over snowy hills and leafless trees on back cover in the manner of the framed label on front cover, with a teal-colored inset listing "Other Volumes in the Cambridge Editions." A very nice copy in scarce original publisher's wrappers.

184. THE COMPLETE POETICAL WORKS OF JOHN MILTON Edited By Douglas Bush[,] Harvard University[.] *Houghton Mifflin Company • Boston[,] (1965)*. First edition thus. 8vo, xxxiii+[i]+570pp., half-title ("Cambridge Edition"), four plates reproducing six portraits of Milton, facsimile reproductions of first edition title pages, original blue cloth (four small specks on front cover), spine lettered in gilt with decorative gilt trim at top and bottom. Nice copy.

185. Variant of Preceding, original glazed green paper over boards (a few marginal notations in a neat hand), spine lettered in gilt with decorative gilt trim at top and bottom. A good copy in a variant publisher's binding.

186. THE COMPLETE POETICAL WORKS OF JOHN MILTON[.] *[New York and Paris:] Universal Classics. n.d. [ca. 1980]*. First edition thus? 8vo, xxxiv+316pp.+[31-page unpaginated index], half-title, double black border rule on title page, one thick and one thin, "Published by Leon Amiel, Publisher[,] New York • Paris" on verso of title page, original green buckram, initials of the press above intertwined branches of ivy in gilt at center of front cover, spine lettered in gilt ("Poetical Works Of John Milton") with gilt rules and with the initials of the press above intertwined branches of ivy repeated in gilt at the center in a very small version of that on front cover, printed publisher's wrappers (slightly used, two small tears at bottom of front cover), with portrait of Milton at center of front cover and smaller version of the portrait repeated on spine. Nice copy.

187. THE COMPLETE POETICAL WORKS OF MILTON AND YOUNG[.] *New Edition Illustrated[.] Blackwood's Universal Library Of Standard Authors. London[:] James Blackwood & Co., Lovell's Court[,] Paternoster Row[.] n.d. [ca. 1850]*. 8vo, 414pp., half-title ("Milton And Young"), unsigned frontispiece woodcut illustration portrait of Milton surrounded by four locales of importance during his life, four unsigned woodcut illustrations for Milton's poems: two for *PL* (Books V and XI), one for *SA*, and one for the sonnet "To The Nightingale," printed in double column, half-title for Young, with three illustration plates, original green crushed leather (possibly publisher's simulated leather) (endpapers foxed, early signature neatly written at top of Milton title page), spine lettered in gilt. Nice, with the portrait and illustrations on darker paper than the text. Scarce. Not in Kohler.

188. MILTON COMPLETE POETRY & SELECTED PROSE With English Metrical Translations of the Latin, Greek and Italian Poems[.] Edited By E. H. Visiak With a Foreword by Sir Arnold Wilson, M.P. *The Nonesuch Press. n.d. [March, 1938].* First edition thus. 8vo in 16s, xxvii+860pp., half-title, original dark blue cloth, spine lettered in gilt ("Milton") within decorative gilt trim, t.e. blue. A fine copy. Uncommon.

 A possible second edition thus was published in 1948 by the Nonesuch Press; a possible third edition thus was published in 1952 by the Nonesuch Library, and an undated edition with the addition of "London" and "New York: Random House Inc." in the publisher's imprint was published about this same time, ca. 1952; a possible fourth edition thus was published in 1964 by the Nonesuch Library—all listed here.

189. MILTON COMPLETE POETRY & SELECTED PROSE With English Metrical Translations of the Latin, Greek and Italian Poems[.] Edited By E. H. Visiak With a Foreword by Sir Arnold Wilson, M.P. *The Nonesuch Press[,] 1948.* Second edition thus. 8vo in 16s, xxvii+860pp., half-title, "First edition March 1938" on verso of title page, original blue cloth (spine a little faded), spine lettered in gilt ("Milton") within decorative gilt trim, t.e. blue. Very nice copy with prize label on fly-leaf.

190. MILTON COMPLETE POETRY & SELECTED PROSE With English Metrical Translations of the Latin, Greek and Italian Poems[.] Edited By E. H. Visiak With a Foreword by the late Sir Arnold Wilson. *The Nonesuch Library[,] 1952.* Third edition thus. 8vo in 16s, xxvii+860pp., half-title, original dark blue cloth, spine lettered in gilt ("Milton") within decorative gilt trim, t.e. blue, printed publisher's wrappers. A fine copy.

191. Variant of Preceding. MILTON COMPLETE POETRY & SELECTED PROSE With English Metrical Translations of the Latin, Greek and Italian Poems. Edited By E. H. Visiak With a Foreword by Sir Arnold Wilson, M.P. *London: The Nonesuch Press[;] New York: Random House Inc. n.d. [ca. 1952].* Variant edition with variant publisher. 8vo in 16s, xxvii+860pp., half-title, original black cloth, spine lettered in gilt ("John Milton Poetry Prose") within decorative gilt trim. A nice variant edition with variant publisher, with variant publisher's imprint, and in a variant publisher's binding.

192. MILTON COMPLETE POETRY & SELECTED PROSE With English Metrical Translations of the Latin, Greek and Italian Poems[.] Edited By E. H. Visiak With a Foreword by the late Sir Arnold Wilson. *The Nonesuch Library[,] 1964.* Fourth edition thus. 8vo in 16s, xxvii+860pp., half-title, original light blue cloth, spine lettered in gilt within decorative gilt trim, t.e. blue. A nice copy.

193. COMPLETE POETRY AND SELECTED PROSE OF JOHN MILTON[.] *The Modern Library • New York[,] (1942).* First edition by the Modern Library. 8vo, vi+756+[5]pp., half-title, original blue cloth (bit rubbed, name in ink on front endpapers, few marginalia notes), front cover and spine lettered in gilt ("Complete Poetry And Selected Prose") against a red background with small gilt figurine of the press, decorated endpapers, t.e. red. A nice copy with five pages of "A Complete List Of Titles In The Modern Library" bound in at the end.

194. COMPLETE POETRY AND SELECTED PROSE OF JOHN MILTON[.] *The Modern Library • New York[,] n.d. [ca. 1949].* Second Modern Library edition. 8vo, as the first edition, except in original red cloth with t.e. blue, published at the end of the decade in an undated ca. 1949 edition. A nice copy in publisher's wrappers (a bit used) with six pages of "A Complete List Of Titles In The Modern Library" bound in at the end. Uncommon.

195. COMPLETE POETRY AND SELECTED PROSE OF JOHN MILTON[.] *The Mayfair Edition[,] New York[,] n.d. [ca. 1949].* First edition thus? 8vo, xxiv+756pp., first appearance in print of introduction by Cleanth Brooks, "A Selected Bibliography" (with references up to 1948), contemporary three-quarter crushed red morocco, marbled paper over boards, gilt rules on covers, decorative gilt patterns with gilt lettering ("John Milton") on spine, raised bands with decorative gilt trim and within gilt rules, marbled endpapers, t.e.g. A nice copy, handsomely bound by Maurino with their stamp on front blank. This edition contains the first appearance of Cleanth Brooks's introduction as well as the first appearance of this "Selected Bibliography," both of which appeared about this same time in the 1950 Modern Library edition (possible third edition thus, also listed here). Uncommon.

196. COMPLETE POETRY AND SELECTED PROSE OF JOHN MILTON[.] Introduction by Cleanth Brooks[,] Professor Of English, Yale University[.] *The Modern Library • New York[,] (1950).* Third Modern Library edition? 8vo, xxiv+756pp., half-title, original red cloth, central black label with gilt lettering and gilt rule on front cover with small gilt figurine of the press at bottom, black label repeated on spine with gilt lettering ("Complete Poetry And Selected Prose"), gilt rule around label with small gilt figurine of the press at top, decorated endpapers with the emblem of the press at the center, t.e. blue, printed publisher's wrappers. Very nice copy in publisher's wrappers that are fresh and clean (with the price of $1.45 on inside front flap). This is the first appearance of Cleanth Brooks's introduction and this "Selected Bibliography" in a Modern Library edition.

197. Variant of Preceding with three pages of advertisements at the end, variant publisher's wrappers including variant price (with the price of $1.95 on inside front flap), and variant "List of Modern Library Books." Very nice copy. Laid in: erratum slip.

198. COMPLETE POETRY AND SELECTED PROSE OF JOHN MILTON[.] Introduction by Cleanth Brooks[,] Professor Of English, Yale University[.] *Modern Library College Editions[.] The Modern Library • New York[,] (1950).* Fourth Modern Library edition? First paperback edition. 8vo, xxiv+756pp., half-title, paperback (bit used, slight embrowning), blue trim with black lettering on front cover and spine. Decent copy with the signature of Milton scholar Maurice Kelley on front cover. Gift from Maurice Kelley.

199. Variant of Preceding, paperback, orange trim with black lettering on front cover and spine. A nice copy in a variant publisher's paperback binding. Fine copy.

200. COMPLETE POETRY AND SELECTED PROSE OF JOHN MILTON[.] Introduction by Cleanth Brooks[,] Gray Professor of Rhetoric, Yale University[.] *The Modern Library • New York[.] n.d. [ca. 1960].* 8vo, xxiv+756+[19]pp., half-title, original black cloth (name stamped on title page and on front edge), front cover lettered in blind, spine lettered in silver, decorated yellow endpapers. Nice. Nineteen-page listing of "Modern Library Giants," "Complete List Of Titles In The Modern Library," "Modern Library College Editions," and "Vintage Books" at the end. A later reprint of 1950 edition.

201. THE COMPLETE POETRY OF JOHN MILTON By John T. Shawcross[.] Revised Edition Arranged In Chronological Order With An Introduction, Notes, Variants, And Literal Translations Of The Foreign Language Poems[.] *Anchor Books[.] Doubleday & Company, Inc. Garden City, New York[,] (1971).* Revised edition. Thick 8vo, xviii+654pp., half-title, "Introduction to the Revised Edition," bibliography and index at end, paperback (bottom corners a little bent), printed stiff white paper wrappers with a reproduction in color of Fuseli's illustration of *The Expulsion* on front cover, "The Anchor Seventeenth-Century Series" at the top of the front cover, "Anchor" at bottom of the spine. Nice copy, signed by the editor on the title page. Gift from John Shawcross.

The following editions are also listed: the first edition thus published under the title *The Complete English Poetry of John Milton* by Doubleday Anchor Books in 1963 in paperback; a second edition thus by Doubleday Anchor Books also published in 1963; a reprint of the edition published under the same title by New York University Press in 1963 (the first edition thus by New York University Press, the second Shawcross edition) in hardback and with a reproduction of the 1688 illustrations for *PL*; a later reprint of the Doubleday Anchor Books published ca. 1965.

202. Variant of Preceding, printed stiff yellow paper wrappers with a reproduction in color of Fuseli's illustration of *The Expulsion* on front cover, black spine with white lettering with "The Anchor Literary Library" lettered in white against black along the spine edge of the front and back covers, "Anchor Press Doubleday" at bottom of the spine. Fine copy, signed by the editor on the title page, in a variant paperback binding. Perhaps a later reprint of the revised edition published in 1971 (preceding copy).

203. Variant of Preceding, printed stiff yellow paper wrappers with a reproduction in color of Fuseli's illustration of *The Expulsion* on front cover, black spine with white lettering, "Anchor Books" at bottom of the spine. Fine copy, signed by the editor on the title page. A later reprint of the revised edition published in 1971 (also listed here). Unlike the preceding copy, the lettering "The Anchor Literary Library" in white does not appear along the spine edge of the front and back covers. The price has also changed to "U.S. $10.95 / Canada $13.95" on the back cover of this copy.

204. THE COMPLETE POETRY OF JOHN MILTON By John T. Shawcross[.] Revised Edition Arranged In Chronological Order With An Introduction, Notes, Variants, And Literal Translations Of The Foreign Language Poems[.] *Anchor Books[.] Doubleday[,] New York[,] London[,] Toronto[,] Sydney[,] Auckland[,] [ca. 1994].* Revised edition. Thick 8vo, xviii+654pp., paperback, printed stiff light marbled gray paper wrappers with reproduction in color of Fuseli's illustration of *The Expulsion* on front cover, with lettering in black and light blue against a light green background as a marginal strip along outer edge of front cover, spine with similar lettering in black and light blue against a light green background with "Anchor Books" lettered in black at the bottom of the spine. Fine. Later reprint of the revised edition published in 1971 (copies preceding).

Complete Prose Works (1953–82)

205. COMPLETE PROSE WORKS OF JOHN MILTON[.] *New Haven: Yale University Press[;] London: Geoffrey Cuberlege: Oxford University Press[,] MCMLIII–MCMLXXXII. 8 volumes.* First edition thus of each volume. 8vo,xvi+[1]+1073pp.,+viii+[1]+840pp., vii+[1]+652pp.+xvi+[1]+686pp.,+xiv+[1]+1166pp.(continuous pagination as Part II of volume 4),+lx+467pp.+[index unpaginated with half-title],+xiv+[1]+876pp. (continuous pagination as Part II of volume 5)+[index unpaginated with half-title],+xxiv+[1]+863pp.,+xiii+[1]+547pp.,+xv+[1]+625pp., edited by Douglas Bush, Christopher Hill, Maurice Kelley, and others, under the general editorship of Don M. Wolfe, half-title each volume, facsimile reproductions of various title pages, "Index To Authors And Works" at the end of each volume, original blue cloth, spines lettered in gilt within dark blue piece ruled in gilt with gilt seal of the press at the bottom, printed publisher's wrappers (all but volume 4). An excellent set, virtually mint, with the revised edition of volume 7. Volumes 1 to 6 are from the library of Don M. Wolfe, a gift from Don Wolfe. Volume 6 (*De Doctrina*, edited by Maurice Kelley) is a presentation copy from Maurice Kelley, inscribed to me by Kelley on fly-leaf. With original Yale Press advertisement brochure and order form for volume 1 and for future volumes in the set, together with an advertisement for the set.

[together with]

206. [COMPLETE PROSE WORKS] ORIGINAL MATERIALS FROM DON WOLFE RELATED TO THE EIGHT-VOLUME YALE EDITION OF MILTON'S COMPLETE PROSE WORKS, of which Don Wolfe was general editor. Included are various original materials related to volumes 4, 5, and 6 (1950s–1970s): typed text with corrections in Don Wolfe's hand (copy of typed text of "Contemporaries at Work, January, 1650," chapter II of Don Wolfe's introduction to volume 4, part 1, with numerous corrections in Don's hand; copy of typed text of "Contemporaries at Work, January, 1651" [retitled "Milton among His Contemporaries, January, 1651"], chapter X of Wolfe's introduction to volume 4, part 1, with numerous corrections in Don's hand; marked copy of typed text of "The Ship of State: Needham As Spokesman February–April, 1651" for chapter VII of Wolfe's introduction to volume 4, part 1, with numerous corrections in Don's hand; clean typed copy of "The Life Of The Reverend Mr. Richard Baxter"); two notebooks having belonged to A. S. P. Woodhouse filled with notes in his hand (labeled "Milton Prose V Background" by Woodhouse on cover)—Woodhouse was originally designated the editor of volume 7, but he died before completion; marked copy and text for each of these volumes; correspondence regarding volume 5 and volume 7 (1974, first unrevised edition); Austin Woolrych's contents for his introduction to volume 7 (1974, first unrevised edition) marked with corrections in green; miscellaneous photos/photostats/xeroxes of Milton's prose works for these volumes together with additional photos/photostats/xeroxes of Milton's prose works used for the entire Yale Edition—in file folders neatly labeled by Don Wolfe. All in two folio-size protective fold-over boxes. Among some of Don's things that Mary Wolfe gave me in Princeton after Don died in April, 1976.

[together with]

207. [COMPLETE PROSE WORKS] ORIGINAL MATERIALS RELATED TO **PROSE PRELIMINARY TO PARADISE LOST** AND **PROSE PRELIMINARY TO SAMSON AGONISTES** (both edited by me) IN VOLUME 8 (1982) OF THE YALE EDITION OF MILTON'S COMPLETE PROSE WORKS, including copies of my original typed text for publication; letters from Maurice Kelley (general editor of the volume) to me and from me (copies) to him; corrected galley proofs (with corrections in Maurice's and my hands); and miscellaneous other related materials. All in a folio-size protective fold-over box.

208. COMPLETE PROSE WORKS OF JOHN MILTON[.] *Volume VII 1659-60[.] New Haven and London: Yale University Press[,]* MCMLXXIV. First, unrevised edition thus, recalled by the press and subsequently reedited and reprinted as a wholly new volume VII for the eight-volume *Complete Prose Works* (set preceding, 1853–1983). 8vo, xiii+[1]+538pp., edited by Robert W. Ayers, introduction by A. Woolrych, half-title, facsimile reproductions of various title pages, "Index To Authors And Works" at the end, original blue cloth, spine lettered in gilt within dark blue piece ruled in gilt with gilt seal of the press at the bottom, printed publisher's wrappers. Fine copy, virtually mint. Scarce.

209. JOHN MILTON COMPLETE SHORTER POEMS Edited By John Carey[.] *Longman[,] London and New York[,] (1971)*. First paperback edition thus. Thick 8vo, xx+531pp., half-title ("Longman Annotated English Poets General Editors: F. W. Bateson), "Preface" (dated 1966), paperback (a little used, several pencil markings), printed stiff paper wrappers with a black-and-white vignette sketch in abstract of Satan falling on front cover amidst lettering in blue and green. A good copy. The *CP* was first issued in one volume in the Longman Annotated English Poets Series in 1968; this edition of the *CSP* was first published separately in paperback in 1971 (copy also listed here); it was variously reprinted thereafter. A second edition thus was published in 1997 (also listed here).

210. JOHN MILTON COMPLETE SHORTER POEMS[.] Second Edition[.] Edited By John Carey[.] *Longman[,] London and New York[,] (1997).* Second edition thus. Thick 8vo, xxiv+523pp., half-title (with advertisement for the series on verso), "Preface to the First Edition" (dated 1966), "Preface to the Second Edition" (dated January 1996), bibliography and indexes at the end, original black buckram, spine lettered in silver, printed salmon publisher's wrappers with a reproduction of a detail from "The Blinding of Samson" (*Triumph of Dalila*) by Rembrandt on front cover. Fine copy. *The Complete Poems of Milton* first issued in one volume in the Longman Annotated English Poets Series in 1968. First edition of the *Complete Shorter Poems* first published separately in paperback in 1971 (also listed here). Fourth impression, with corrections 1981. This second edition published in hardback and paperback 1997 (both listed here) (verso of title page).

211. Variant of Preceding. **JOHN MILTON COMPLETE SHORTER POEMS**[.] Second Edition[.] Edited By John Carey[.] *Longman[,] London and New York[,] (1997).* Second edition thus. Thick 8vo, as preceding, except paperback, xxiv+523pp., paperback, printed stiff paper wrappers with a reproduction of a detail from "The Blinding of Samson" (*Triumph of Dalila*) by Rembrandt on front cover. Fine copy of this paperback edition.

Comus

211A. (Cross-listing) [COMUS] Putten, Hendrik Van Der. **COMVS**, Sive Phagesiposia Cimmeria Somnivm. *Excudebat Oxonii: Gulielmus Turner, impensis H. Curteyne, 1634.* Bound with **HISTORIAE INSVBRICAE LIBRI VI.** Oxonii: Gulielmus Turner, 1634. 2 volumes in one. 12mo, two title pages, index at end, contemporary calf (newly rebacked). The *Comvs*, a charming neo-Latin romance, first appeared in 1608, the year of Milton's birth. This edition is the first and only edition to appear in England and, as Parker notes (p. 792 notes), is a recognized source for Milton's *Comus*. Coleridge 42. See main listing with Seventeenth-century Miltoniana.

211B. (Cross-listing) [COMUS] Marino, Giambattista. **L'ADONE**, Poema Heroico Del C. Marino, Con gli Argomenti del Conte Sanvitale e l'allegorie di Don Lorenzo Scoto. Aggiuntovi La tavola delle cose notabili. Di nuovo ricorreto, e di figure ornatto. *In Amsterdam, nella Stamperia del S. D. Elsevier, Et in Parigi si vende Appresso Thomaso Jolly, Nel Palazzo. M. DC. LXXVIII.* 4 volumes. Small 8vo, engraved and printed title pages, volume 1, illustration after Sebastien Le Clerc on engraved title, central emblem on printed title page each volume, engraved illustration for each book, original vellum (a bit worn), each volume numbered by hand in ink on spine. *L'Adone*, a lavish allegorical epic poem written and published earlier in the seventeenth century, is a work which clearly influenced Milton, and Milton had a copy of it in his library. Boswell, in his *Milton's Library*, entry 961, remarks on the influence of *L'Adone* on Milton, providing particular inspiration for *Comus*. Rare. Parker, pp. 174–75. Willems, *Elzevier*, 1549; Boswell, *Milton's Library*, 961; Not in Coleridge; Not in Kohler. See main listing with Seventeenth-century Miltoniana.

Four Dalton Editions of *Comus* (1738)

212. COMUS, A MASK: (Now adapted to the Stage) As Alter'd from MILTON's Mask AT LUDLOW-CASTLE, Which was never represented But on Michaelmas-Day, 1634; BEFORE THE Right Honble. the Earl of Bridgewater, Lord President of WALES. The principal Performers were The Lord Brackly, Mr. Tho. Egerton, The Lady Alice Egerton. The Musick was composed By Mr. Henry Lawes, Who also represented the Attendant Spirit.—Quid vocis modulamen inane juvabit Verborum sensusque vacans numerique loquacis? MILTON. ad Patrem. *LONDON: Printed by J. HUGHS, near Lincoln's-Inn-Fields, For R. DODSLEY, at Tully's-Head, Pall-Mall. MDCCXXXVIII. (Price One Shilling.)* First Dalton edition. 8vo, 52pp., "Errata" leaf after title page with "Dramatis Personae" on verso, modern quarter morocco (bound without half-title, occasional light foxing), marbled paper over boards, spine lettered in gilt, raised band within gilt rules. A nice copy. Rare. Coleridge 226; Shawcross, Kentucky, 222; Not in Kohler.

This version of *Comus* was prepared by John Dalton and became the standard eighteenth-century acting edition. It proved enormously popular, and in this year of 1738, four editions were called for: this and the three editions following. This first Dalton edition is the rarest. "Despite the [title page] statement the music for the adaptation was by Thomas Arne, not the original music by Lawes" (Coleridge). Dalton's version was acted in 1750 as part of a benefit for Milton's granddaughter, Elizabeth, and published then again as a benefit for her; a *Prologue*, published separately in 1750, was written by Dr. Samuel Johnson and spoken by David Garrick. Dalton's adaptation abridges the text substantially and adds some songs, using words from *L'Allegro* and from other poems.

213. COMUS, A MASK: (Now adapted to the Stage) As Alter'd from MILTON's Mask AT LUDLOW-CASTLE, Which was never represented But on Michaelmas-Day,

1634; BEFORE THE Right Honble. the Earl of Bridgewater, Lord President of WALES . . . *[as with First edition]* . . . *The SECOND EDITION. LONDON: Printed by J. HUGHS, near Lincoln's-Inn-Fields, For R. DODSLEY, at Tully's-Head, Pall-Mall. MDCCXXXVIII. (Price One Shilling.)* Second Dalton edition. 8vo, 32 leaves, 61+[3]pp., half-title ["Comus, a Mask: (Now adapted to the Stage) As Alter'd from Milton's Mask, &c. (Price One Shilling.)"] "Dramatis Personae" page after prologue, epilogue at end, disbound, complete with half-title and final leaf (half-title has three stab-holes along inner edge). Nice copy. The second Dalton edition printed the *Prologue* and *Epilogue* for the first time. Rare. ESTC t031073; Not in Coleridge; Shawcross, Kentucky, 223; Kohler 232 (without reference to a half-title).

214. COMUS, A MASK: (Now adapted to the Stage) As Alter'd from MILTON's Mask AT LUDLOW-CASTLE, Which was never represented But on Michaelmas-Day, 1634; BEFORE THE Right Honble. the Earl of Bridgewater, Lord President of WALES . . . *[as with First edition]* . . . *The THIRD EDITION. LONDON: Printed by J. HUGHS, near Lincoln's-Inn-Fields, For R. DODSLEY, at Tully's-Head, Pall-Mall. MDCCXXXVIII. (Price One Shilling.)* Third Dalton edition. 8vo, 32 leaves, 61+[3]pp., half-title ["Comus, a Mask: (Now adapted to the Stage) As Alter'd from Milton's Mask, &c. (Price One Shilling.)"], "Dramatis Personae" page after prologue, epilogue at end, disbound, complete with half-title and final leaf (some light marginal browning). Nice copy, complete with half-title and final leaf. Not in Coleridge; Kohler 233 (without reference to a half-title), reporting "Not in Cambridge University Library"; Shawcross, Kentucky, 224.

215. COMUS, A MASK: (Now adapted to the Stage) As Alter'd from MILTON's Mask AT LUDLOW-CASTLE, Which was never represented But on Michaelmas-Day, 1634; BEFORE THE Right Honble. the Earl of Bridgewater, Lord President of WALES . . . [as with First edition] . . . —Of Forests, and Inchantements drear, Where more is meant than meets the Ear. Il Penseroso.—Quid vovis [sic] modulamen inane juvabit Verborum sensusque vacans numerique loquacis? MILTON. ad Patrem. *The FOURTH EDITION. LONDON: Printed by J. HUGHS, near Lincoln's-Inn-Fields, For R. DODSLEY, at Tully's-Head, Pall-Mall, and T. Cooper, in Pater-noster-Row. 1738. (Price One Shilling.)* Fourth Dalton edition (four were published in 1738, this being the fourth of these). 8vo, 32 leaves, 61+[3]pp., half-title ["Comus, a Mask: (Now adapted to the Stage) As Alter'd from Milton's Mask, &c. (Price One Shilling.)"], "Dramatis Personae" page after prologue, epilogue at end, disbound, complete with half-title and final leaf (very light watermarking to inner margin of half-title and title page, half-title a little soiled, slight age-darkening). All in all, a nice copy of this very scarce edition. Not in Coleridge; Kohler 234, reporting "Not in the British Library. Not in the Bodleian Library. Not in Cambridge University Library."

216. THE MUSICK IN THE MASQUE OF COMUS. Written by Milton. As it is performed at the Theatre-Royal in Drury-Lane. Composed by Mr. Arne. Opera Prima. *London. Printed for I. Walsh in Catharine Street in the Strand[.] n.d. [1738].* First edition. Folio, 47pp., twenty-four leaves of engraved music, old quarter morocco, marbled paper over boards (title page a bit soiled and trifle spotted with several minor mends to blank edges, final leaf backed, somewhat age-browned throughout), spine lettered in gilt, early armorial bookplate on front pastedown. A decent copy, and a "rather remarkable survival." The Masque was produced in March 1738, and ran for eleven nights. Thomas Arne (1710–78) was educated at Eton and gave up legal studies for music. He was the composer of "Rule Britannia." Dalton adapted Milton's original masque (preceding copies); its first performance was in this year of 1738, and it became the standard for the remainder of the eighteenth century. Arne's music is for this first Dalton presentation and includes the words for the performance. "We have never seen a copy of this" (G. W. Stuart, Jr., Ravenstree, Cat. 180, #3, 1996). Not in Coleridge; Not in Kohler; John Shawcross shared with me that "a copy is in the New York Public Library."

217. COMUS: A MASQUE. (Now adapted to the Stage) As alter'd from Milton's Masque At Ludlow-Castle, Which Never Represented but on Michaelmas-Day, 1634; Before the Right Honourable The Earl of Bridgewater, Lord President of Wales. The principal Performers were The Lord Brackly, Mr. Tho. Egerton, The Lady Alice Egerton. The Music was composed by Mr. Hen. Lawes, Who also represented the Attendant Spirit. *The Seventh Edition. London: Printed for R. Dodsley, at Tull's Head, Pall-Mall. M.DCC.XLIV.* 8vo, half-title, 60pp., "Dramatis Personae" page after prologue and epilogue, both prologue and epilogue appearing together at the beginning, later wrappers (a bit age-browned, slight tear on p. 31). A good copy of a scarce publication. Not in Coleridge; Kohler 236, reporting "Not in the British Library. Not in the Bodleian Library. Not in Cambridge University Library."

217A. (Cross-listing) [COMUS] A MASK PRESENTED AT LUDLOW-CASTLE, In The Year 1634. Before The

Earl of Bridgewater, then President of Wales. *Dublin: Printed by and for George Grierson, at the Two Bibles in Essex-Street, 1748.* First Irish edition. Bound with **PARADISE LOST** . . . Adorn'd With Sculptures. *Dublin: Printed by and for George Grierson, at the Two Bibles in Essex-Street, 1724.* Bound with **PARADISE REGAIN'D** . . . *Dublin: Printed by and for George Grierson, at the Two Bibles in Essex-Street, 1724.* First Irish edition. Bound with **SAMSON AGONISTES** . . . *Dublin: Printed by and for George Grierson, at the Two Bibles in Essex-Street, 1748.* First Irish edition. Bound with **POEMS UPON SEVERAL OCCASIONS.** Compos'd at several Times . . . *Dublin: Printed by and for George Grierson, at the Two Bibles in Essex-Street, 1748.* First Irish edition. 5 volumes bound in one. Stout 8vo, separate title page for each poem, contemporary calf. The very rare first Irish editions. Not in Coleridge; Coleridge 174a (citing an incomplete copy of *PL* and *PR*); Not in Kohler. See main listing under *PL*, 1724.

218. **COMUS: A MASK.** (Now adapted to the Stage) As Alter'd from Milton's Masque At Ludlow-Castle, Which Was First Represented on Michaelmas-day, 1634; Before the Right Honourable The Earl of Bridgewater, Lord President of Wales. The principal Performers were The Lord Brackly, Mr. Tho. Egerton, the Lady Alice Egerton. The Music was composed by Mr. Hen. Lawes, Who also represented the Attendant Spirit. *London: Printed for A. Millar, opposite to Katharine-Street, in the Strand. MDCCL.* 8vo, 58+[1]pp., half-title, advertisement leaf bound in at end (listing as the last item, #14, "A Complete Collection of the Historical, Political, and Miscellaneous Works of John Milton . . . By T. Birch . . . To which is added, A large Alphabetical Index, and a curious Head of the Author, engraved by Mr. Vertue, from a Drawing by Mr. Richardson. In Two Volume Folio. [see set listed here]," disbound. Fine copy, complete with half-title and advertisement leaf. This adaptation was acted in April 1750 in a benefit performance for Milton's granddaughter, Elizabeth, and published for her benefit. A separately published prologue was written for it by Samuel Johnson and spoken at the benefit by David Garrick. Rare. Coleridge 229; Not in Kohler.

218A. (Cross-listing) Two copper engravings by C. Taylor for **COMUS** (1791) [In] **PARADISE REGAIN'D** . . . **SAMSON AGONISTES: AND POEMS UPON SEVERAL OCCASIONS** . . . *Birmingham: Printed by John Baskerville For J. and R. Tonson in London. MDCCLVIII.* Together with **PARADISE LOST** . . . *Birmingham[:] Printed by John Baskerville for J. and R. Tonson in London. MDCCLVIII.* First Baskerville edition. Extra-illustrated, including, among others, two copper engravings by C. Taylor for *C:* of "Comus and Lady" and of "Sabrina & Lady," each "Publish'd June 1; 1791 by C. Taylor." See main listing under *PL*, 1858.

219. **COMUS, A MASQUE,** (Now adapted to the Stage) As alter'd from Milton's Masque At Ludlow-Castle, Which Was First represented, on Michaelmas-day 1634. Before the Right Honourable The Earl of Bridgewater, Lord President of Wales. The principal Performers were The Lord Brackly, Mr. Tho. Egerton, And the Lady Alice Egerton. The Music was composed by Mr. Hen. Lawes, Who also represented the Attendant Spirit. *Glasgow: Printed in the Year M,DCC,LVIII.* 12mo in 6s, 42pp., title page in red and black, disbound (slightly embrowned, especially bottom margins of pages 14–15). A very nice copy, complete with final blank. Rare. Not in Coleridge; Not in Kohler.

220. **COMUS: A MASQUE.** (Now adapted to the Stage) As Alter'd from Milton's Masque At Ludlow-Castle, Which was First Represented on Michaelmas-Day, 1634; Before the Right Honourable The Earl of Bridgewater, Lord President of Wales. The principal Performers were The Lord Brackly, Mr. Tho. Egerton, The Lady Alice Egerton. The Music was composed by Mr. Hen. Lawes, Who also represented the Attendant Spirit. *London: Printed for A. Millar, opposite to Katharine-Street, in the Strand. MDCCLIX.* 8vo, 58pp., bound with three other works of the period, contemporary calf (a bit rubbed along joints and extremities), covers decorated with finely tooled gilt borders and a decorative design in gilt at the center, spine elaborately decorated in gilt, black morocco label (partially missing) lettered and decorated in gilt, slightly raised bands with decorative gilt trim, outer dentelles trimmed in gilt, marbled endpapers, green silk ribbon marker, a.e.g. An attractive copy with contemporary armorial bookplate on front pastedown and the later armorial bookplate of J. R. Abbey on fly-leaf. Bound with *Comus* are three additional works of the period, identified briefly in a neat early, possibly contemporary, hand on front blank, given more fully here: (1) [Brome (Richard).] *The Jovial Crew. A Comic-Opera.* The Second Edition. *London: Printed for J. and R. Tonson, MDCCLX*; (2) [Thomson (James) and Mallet (David).] *Alfred: A Masque. London: Printed for A. Millar, M. DCC. LI,* a masque which is influenced strongly by *Comus*; and (3) Gay (John). *The Beggar's Opera.* The Sixth Edition: To which is Prefix'd the Overture in Score: And the Musick to each Song. *London: Printed for John Watts, MDCCXLIX.* The Gay has all the music including the eight pages of overture by Pepusch; the Thomson was first published in 1740 by Millar, with other editions between 1740 and 1751. Milton's *Comus,* according to G. W. Stuart, Jr. (Ravenstree, Cat. 184, #6, 2000), "is very rare." Not in Coleridge; Not in Kohler.

221. COMUS: A MASQUE. (Now adapted to the Stage) As Alter'd from Milton's Masque At Ludlow-Castle, Which was First Represented on Michaelmas-Day, 1634; Before the Right Honourable The Earl of Bridgewater. Lord President of Wales. The principal Performers were The Lord Brackly, Mr. Tho. Egerton, The Lady Alice Egerton. The Music was composed by Mr. Hen. Lawes, Who also represented the Attendant Spirit. *London: Printed for A. Millar, opposite to Katharine-Street, in the Strand. MDCCLX.* 8vo, 58pp., "Dramatis Personae" page after prologue and epilogue, both prologue and epilogue appearing together at the beginning, paper wrappers (waterstained), with early bookseller's printed description of a 1750 edition tipped in at bottom of title page. A fair copy of a scarce publication, complete with final blank. This adaptation by John Dalton was first published in 1738 (several copies listed here). Not in Coleridge; Not in Kohler.

222. COMUS: A MASQUE. (Now adapted to the Stage) As Alter'd from Milton's Masque At Ludlow-Castle, Which was First Represented on Michaelmas-Day, 1634; Before the Right Honourable The Earl of Bridgewater, Lord President of Wales. The principal Performers were The Lord Brackly, Mr. Tho. Egerton, The Lady Alice Egerton. The Music was composed by Mr. Hen. Lawes, Who also represented the Attendant Spirit. *London: Printed for A. Millar, opposite to Katharine-Street, in the Strand. MDCCLXII.* 8vo, 58pp., half-title, "Dramatis Personae" page after prologue and epilogue, both prologue and epilogue appearing together at the beginning, disbound. A very good copy, complete with half-title. This adaptation by John Dalton was first published in 1738 (several copies listed here). The present edition was the last published in his lifetime. Scarce. Coleridge 230; Kohler 237, reporting "Not in Cambridge University Library."

223. COMUS, A MASK. (Now adapted to the Stage) As Alter'd from Milton's Mask At Ludlow-Castle, Which was never represented But on Michaelmas-Day, 1634; Before The Rt. Hon. the Earl of Bridgewater, Lord President of Wales. The Principal Performers were The Lord Brackley, Mr. Tho. Egerton, The Lady Alice Egerton. The Music was composed By Mr. Henry Lawes, Who also represented the Attendant Spirit. The Third Edition, Corrected. To which is added, The Prologue and Epilogue.—Quid vocis modulamen inane juvabit Verborum sensusque vacans numerique loquacis? Milton. ad Patrem. *Dublin: Printed for G. and A. Ewing, and W. Smith, in Dame-street, G. Faulkner, on the Blina quay, and W. Whitesone, in Skinner-row, 1764.* Small 8vo, 63+[1]pp., "Dramatis Personae" page after prologue, epilogue at end, disbound (small waterstain at blank lower edges, slightly embrowned), lower edge untrimmed. An okay copy with early name and initials on title page. "In addition to the 1st and 2nd Dublin editions of 1738 and 1749 there was both a 'third' of 1764 . . . and one of 1766 . . . neither in WTu" (Coleridge, p. 299). Coleridge fails to take into account George Grierson's 1748 Dublin edition of Milton's *Mask* (also listed here). Scarce. Not in Coleridge; Not in Kohler.

224. COMUS: A MASQUE. Altered From Milton. As Performed At The Theatre-Royal In Covent-Garden. The Music Composed by Dr. Arne. *London: Printed for T. Lowndes; T. Caslon; S. Bladon; W. Nicoll; and T. Becket and Co. MDCCLXXII.* 8vo, [iv]+30pp., half-title ("Comus: A Masque. [Price One Shilling.]"), three-page "Advertisement," followed by a list of "Characters," stitched, possibly as issued (lacking wrappers, half-title dust-soiled). This alteration to two acts is to emphasize the dramatic, with the reasons given in the advertisement or preface by George Coleman. An unusually decent copy of this kind of program-publication complete with half-title. See 1738 first Dalton edition thus with Arne's music and Dalton's words for his adaptation of Milton's *Comus*. Rare. Not in Coleridge; Not in Kohler.

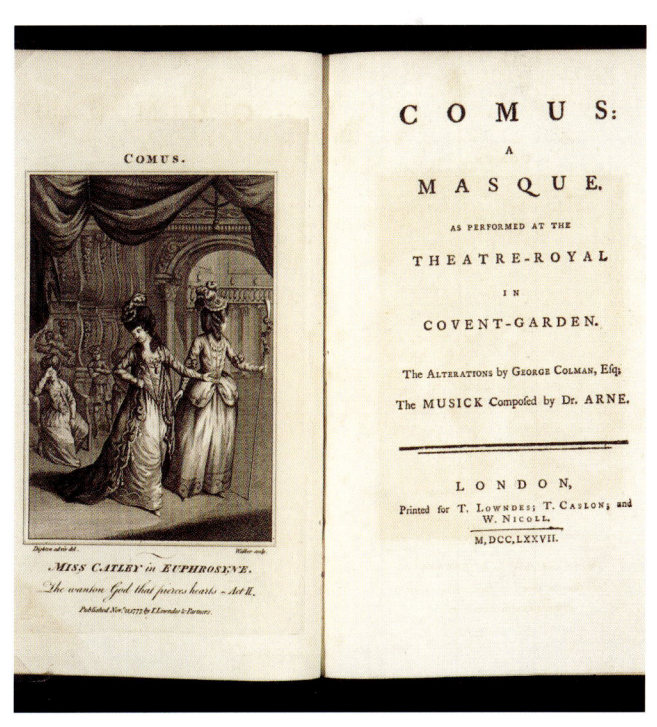

Comus: A Masque. As Performed At The Theatre-Royal In Covent-Garden. London, 1777. See #224.

225. COMUS, A MASQUE: As alter'd from Milton. Which was first represented at Ludlow-Castle, On Michaelmas-Day, 1634. The Music by Mr. Henry Lawes. The Fourth Edition.—Quid vocis modulamen inane juvabit Verborum sensusque vacans numerique loquacis? Milton. ad Patrem. *Dublin: Thomas M'Daniel, Meath-Street, MDCCLXXV.* 12mo, 58+[2]pp., disbound (title page browned, occasional mild soiling). A rare edition consisting of the adaptation by John Dalton, with "Prologue" leaf at the end. OCLC lists only two copies of this edition; Coleridge 232; Not in Kohler.

226. COMUS: A MASQUE. As originally adapted to the Stage, And altered from Milton. Distinguishing Also The Variations Of The Theatre, As Performed, In Two Acts, At the Theatre-Royal in Covent-Garden, Regulated from the Prompt-Book, By Permission of the Managers, By Mr. Wild, Prompter. Of Forests and Inchantements drear, Where more is meant than meets the ear. Il Penseroso.—Quid vocis modulamen inane juvabit Verborum sensusque vacans numerique loquacis? Milton. ad Patrem. Bell's Edition. *London: Printed for John Bell, near Exeter-Exchange, in the Strand. MDCCLXXVII.* 12mo, 44+[1]+[2]pp., engraved frontispiece illustration of *Miss Catley in the Character of Euphrosyne* ("Publish'd for Bell's British Theatre Feby. 26th. 1777," fine impression), engraved by J. Roberts after Thornthwaite, preface, "Dramatis Personae" page after prologue, epilogue at end followed by two pages of advertisements for "Books published by J. Bell" and final two blanks, disbound (lightly soiled, some age-browning). A good, complete copy. Coleridge points out this was issued in volume 9 of Bell's *British Theatre*, "but it was also sold separately." Also "some copies include a frontispiece," as here. Scarce. Coleridge 233; Not in Kohler.

227. COMUS: A MASQUE. As Performed At The Theatre-Royal In Covent-Garden. The Alterations by George Colman, Esq; The Musick Composed by Dr. Arne. *London: Printed for T. Lowndes; T. Caslon; and W. Nicoll. 1777.* 8vo, [iv]+30+[1]pp., half-title ("Comus: A Masque. [Price One Shilling.]"), engraved frontispiece illustration of *Miss Catley in the Character of Euphrosyne* ("Published Novr. 22, 1777, by T. Lowndes & Partners," fine impression), "Dighton ad viv del" and "Walker sculp.," three-page "Advertisement," followed by a list of "Characters" and final blank, disbound. A large, tall copy, complete. Rare. Not in Coleridge; Not in Kohler; John Shawcross told me a "Copy is owned by University of Michigan."

228. COMUS. A MASQUE. As it is Acted at the Theatres-Royal In Drury-Lane And Covent-Garden. Altered from Milton.—Quid vocis modulamen inane juvabit Verborum sensusque vacans numerique loquacis? Milton. ad Patrem. *London: Printed for and Sold by W. Oxlade, at Shakespeare's Head, Middle-Row, Holborn. M DCC LXXVII.* 12mo, 33pp., "Dramatis Personae" page after prologue and epilogue, both prologue and epilogue appearing together at the beginning, with small vignette illustration of an eagle tipped in at bottom of prologue page, small unsigned vignette illustration tipped in at bottom of last page of *Comus*. With **A DUKE AND NO DUKE. A FARCE** ... Written originally by Sir Aston Cokain ... *London ... MDCCLXXVI.* 40pp. With **THE REHEARSAL. A COMEDY** ... By George, late Duke Of Buckingham ... *London ... M DCC LXXVII.* 53pp. With **THE CONTRIVANCES. A BALLAD OPERA** ... By Harry Carey ... *London ... MDCCLXXVII.* 26pp. With **CHRONONHOTONTHOLOGOS: THE MOST TRAGICAL TRAGEDY** ... By Harry Carey ... *London ... M DCC LXXVII.* 26pp. With **DON QUIXOTE IN ENGLAND. A COMEDY** ... By Henry Fielding, Esq. *London ... MDCCLXXVII.* 48pp. Together six separate works, each with separate title page. Early one-half calf, marbled paper over boards (worn, covers detached), gilt-decorated spine (spine half missing), in a protective plastic cover. An okay copy with pencil notes on front pastedown and after the *Prologue* and with a table of "Contents" written out in a neat early (possibly contemporary) hand before title page. Rare. John Shawcross shared with me that "This is Colman's version," and that a "Copy is owned by University of Michigan." Not in Coleridge; Not in Kohler.

229. COMUS. A MASK. By John Milton. As Performed At the Theatre-Royal Covent-Garden. Regulated from the Prompt-Book, by permission of the Managers, By Mr. Wild Prompter. Characteristicks [of Comus, First Spirit, Second Spirit, Eld. Brother, Young. Brother, Lady, Euphrosyne, and Sabrina.] Bell's Characteristical Edition. *Edinburg: At the Apollo Press, by The Martins, for Bell, London, 1782.* 12mo, 37+[1]pp., engraved frontispiece illustration of *Miss Catley in the Character of Euphrosyne* ("Publish'd for Bell's British Theatre Feby. 26th. 1777," fine impression), engraved by J. Roberts after Thornthwaite, preface, "Dramatis Personae" at bottom of page after prologue, epilogue at end, disbound in cardboard wrappers. A nice copy. John Shawcross shared with me that "This is from *Bell's British Theatre* (1780), volume 9. I have used the copies owned by the University of Illinois and the University of Western Ontario libraries." Not in Coleridge; Not in Kohler.

229A. (Cross-listing) [COMUS] Marino, Giambattista. **L'ADONE** Poema Del Cavalier Marino Con gl' Argomenti, le Allegorie, e la Tavola delle cose notabili. *Londra. 1784.* 3 volumes. 12mo, engraved title page for each volume, with the same engraved illustration on each engraved title page, engraved illustration for each book (very fine impressions), protective homemade boards with black cloth spine. A fine set internally, fresh and crisp, with very fine impressions of the plates. A new edition of Marino's lavish allegorical epic poem, first published in the early part of the seventeenth century (see 1678 four-volume small 8vo edition, with fine engraved illustrations, with Seventeenth-century Miltoniana and cross-listed here). *L'Adone*, a lavish allegorical epic poem written and published earlier in the seventeenth century, is a work that clearly influenced Milton, and Milton had a copy of it in his library. Scarce. Parker, pp. 174–75; Willems, *Elsevier*, 1549; Boswell 961; Not in Coleridge. See main listing with Eighteenth-century Miltoniana.

230. COMUS; A MASQUE. As it is performed at the Theatres Royal in Drury Lane and Covent Garden. Composed by Dr. Arne, for the Voice, Harpsichord, And Violin. *London: Printed for Harrison & Co. No. 18, Paternoster Row. n.d. [1785]*. Oblong folio, 18pp., "Original Dramatis Personae," fifteen pages of musical notation, old boards (a bit worn, lightly embrowned, edges lightly worn), morocco spine label (worn) lettered in gilt. A good copy, engraved throughout. "We have never seen this in over thirty years— Of great rarity" (G. W. Stuart, Jr., Ravenstree, Cat. 179, #9, 1995). John Shawcross told me that there is a "Copy in Newberry Library." Not in Coleridge; Not in Kohler.

231. COMUS. A MASK. BY JOHN MILTON. Adapted For Theatrical Representation, As Performed First At The Theatre-Royal, Covent-Garden, In The Year 1744. Regulated From The Prompt-Book, By Permission of the Managers. "The Lines distinguished by inverted Commas are omitted in the Representation." *London: Printed for the Proprietors, under the Direction of John Bell, British Library, Strand, Bookseller to His Royal Highness the Prince of Wales. M D CC XCI*. Slim, large 8vo, 68pp., frontispiece illustration of *Miss Storace in Euphrosyne* ("D. Wilde ad viv del" "[J.] Thornthwaite Sculpt.," "London Printed for J. Bell British Library Strand, Jany. 31. 1791."), protective tissue guard, engraved and printed title pages, engraved title with vignette illustration engraved by Francesco Bartolozzi after E. F. Burney ("Printed for J. Bell British Library Strand London Sep. 20. 1790."), "Biographer To The World," "John Milton" "Comus," "Preface," "Prologue" followed by "Dramatis Personae," "Epilogue" at the end, later eighteenth-century quarter paper, marbled paper over boards (some slight foxing), labeled "Comic Opera 5" in ink on spine by an early hand, edges untrimmed, elaborate bookplate on front pastedown. Presentation copy on Whatman paper. A fine, large copy with wide margins. Laid in: a copy of another engraved title page (much smaller size) with vignette illustration engraved by Delattre after Burney ("Printed for J. Bell British Library Strand, London, Sep. 20. 1790."). The engravings do not appear in the 12mo edition of this year. The signature marks also differ from the 12mo edition. Coleridge 234a; Kohler 240, indicating a "Double frontispiece with an engraving by Thronthwaite ["Thornthwaite" in the engraving above] after De Wilde dated 31 Jan. 1791 and Delattre after E. F. Burney dated 20 Sept. 1790 [smaller engraved title page laid in copy here, rather than engraved title page, with vignette illustration engraved by Bartolozzi after E. F. Burney with the same date Kohler gives and which appears on engraved title laid in], Kohler reporting "Not in the Bodleian Library." Regarding the complex printing history of this edition, John Shawcross shared with me that "There were two 8vo editions (in 68 pp. and in 60 pp.) and three 12mo editions (two in 68 pp.—one from Dublin, and one in 48 pp. from Dublin)."

Comus, 1791. Frontispiece illustration and engraved title page dated 1790 with vignette illustration. See #231.

232. COMUS, A MASK Presented At Ludlow Castle 1634, Before The Earl Of Bridgewater, Then President Of Wales: By John Milton. With Notes Critical And Explanatory By Various Commentators, And With Preliminary Illustrations; To Which Is Added A Copy Of The Mask From A Manuscript Belonging To His Grace The Duke Of Bridgewater: By Henry John Todd, M.A. Chaplain To The Right Hon. The Earl Of Fife And The Lord Viscount Kilmorey And Minor Canon Of Canterbury. "The Harp Of Orpheus Was Not More Charming." Milton's Tractate of Education. *Canterbury: Printed by and for W. Bristow on the Parade: For Messrs. Rivingtons St. Paul's Church-yard, And W. Clarke New Bond-street, London; Messrs. Fletcher and Co. Oxford; and J. Deighton Cambridge. MDCCXCVIII.* Third separate edition. 8vo, xxi+[iii]+199pp., presentation leaf, preface, half-title to each part, numerous notes at bottom of the page, appendix ("No. I. Original Readings" and "No. 2. "Ashridge Manuscript"), followed by a more than six-page "Account Of Editions Of Comus; Either Separately, Or With Milton's Other Poetical Works," contemporary calf (rebacked preserving original spine), blind-decorated border trim on covers, spine decorated with gilt rules and small gilt harps within the panels, edges untrimmed. A fine, tall copy with early signature on fly-leaf and an early printed catalogue description of this volume tipped in on front pastedown. Apparently only the third separate edition of *C*, preceded by 1637 and 1747 editions. "A major edition of the poem, including a discussion of Ludlow Castle and the Bridgewater family, with remarks on Henry Lawes; an examination of the origin of *C*; a printing of the Ashridge MS. (now called the Bridgewater MS.), on permanent loan to the British Library; and a listing of editions of *C*" (Shawcross) with holography notes by Dunster. Scarce. Shawcross, Kentucky, 549; Coleridge 81; Not in Kohler.

In Exceptionally Well-Preserved Original Boards

233. COMUS, A MASK: Presented At Ludlow Castle 1634, Before The Earl Of Bridgewater, Then President Of Wales. By John Milton. To Which Are Added, L'Allegro And Il Penseroso, And Mr. Warton's Account Of The Origin Of Comus. The Harp Of Orpheus Was Not More Charming. Milton's Tractate of Education. *London: Printed By T. Bensley, Bolt Court, Fleet Street; For E. Harding, Pall Mall; And W. West, Paternoster Row. 1799.* First edition thus; fourth separate edition. 8vo, 124pp., half-title, unsigned frontispiece illustration plate of Ludlow Castle, three illustration plates engraved by R. H. Cromek after Thomas Stothard, one for *C*, one for *L'A*, and one for *IlP*, half-title for each of the poems, in exceptionally well-preserved original boards with the title written in ink on the spine in a neat contemporary hand, edges untrimmed and partially unopened. A remarkably fine copy, near mint. A scarce book and rare thus in exceptionally well-preserved original boards. Coleridge 82; Kohler 241, reporting "Not in Cambridge University Library."

This edition was edited by Henry Todd, although not mentioned on the title page, with his account of Ludlow Castle. Reportedly, only the fourth separate edition of *C*, preceded by 1637, 1747, and 1798 (also listed here).

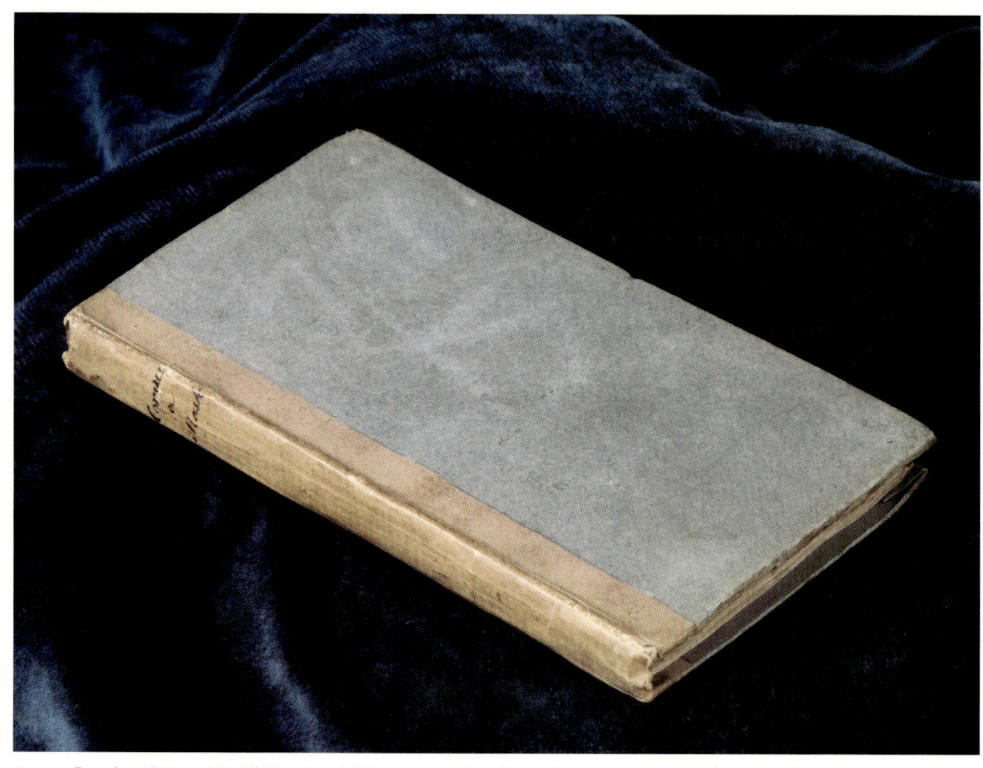

Comus, London: Printed By T. Bensley, 1799, in exceptionally well-preserved original boards. See #233.

234. IL COMO, FAVOLA BOSCHERECCIA DI GIOVANNI MILTON Rapresentata Nel Castello di Ludlow nel 1634 alla presenza del Conte di Bridgewater allora Presidente del paese di Galles, Tradotta Da Gaetano Polidori. *Londra 1802. Si Vende Presso Dulau In Soho Square; Gamu E Co. In Albemarle Street; E Didier E Tebbet No. 75 Saint James's Street.* First edition thus. Small 8vo, v+[iii]+63pp., "Prefazione," disbound. Nice, clean copy. This Italian translation, the first in Italian and the first by Polidori, is dedicated to the eccentric Eighth Earl of Bridgewater. A scarce work by G. Polidori, the father of John Polidori (author of *The Vampyre* and Byron's physician) and the grandfather of Christina, William Michael, and Dante Gabriel Rossetti. Also listed here: a second edition of Polidori's translation—equally rare—published in 1809, and a rare third edition from 1812. Polidori, a teacher of Italian in London, also translated *Lycidas, L'Allegro,* and *Il Penseroso* in 1814; he printed *Il Paradiso Perduto* in 1796. Both works are listed here. Not in Kohler.

Folio Scrapbook, Extra-Illustrated, ca. 1810

234A. (Cross-listing) **COMUS** [In] [**PARADISE LOST.** *(London:) Printed For The Proprietors, 1808.* Bound with **COMUS AND L'ALLEGRO AND IL PENSEROSO,** [n.d.]. Folio scrapbook, extra-illustrated [ca. 1810], paper watermarked 1794. Extra thick folio, in original binding, one-half calf, marbled paper over thick boards (rebacked). 8vo printed text of *PL* engraved title page, "Printed for the Proprietors" (dated 1808), with vignette illustration by Burney, and printed 16mo text of *C* and of *L'A* and *Il P* (edition unidentified), each page mounted on individual folio leaves, along with life and numerous illustrations and engraved portraits from the late eighteenth and early nineteenth centuries. See main listing under *PL*, 1808.

235. COMUS; A MASK, By John Milton. Presented At Ludlow Castle 1634, Before John, Earl Of Bridgewater, Then President Of Wales. Printed From The text Of The Rev. Henry John Todd, A.M. F.A.S. With Selected And Original Anecdotes And Annotations, Biographical, Explanatory, Critical and Dramatic. With Splendid Embellishments. *London: Printed by W. Clowes, Northumberland Court, Strand. Published By Mathews And Leigh, Strand[,] 1808.* First edition thus. 8vo, 89+[1]pp., half-title, numerous notes at bottom of the page, "The Beauties And The Faults Of Comus" at the end, disbound (half-title and title slightly embrowned, occasional foxing, possibly lacking frontispiece portrait and two plates), final blank present. "In *The Cabinet*, volume V. The 1798 edition, published at Canterbury, with additional notes from Warton and others. Both works contain unique materials on the background and circumstances of the first production, but the text variants are incomplete" (Stevens, without mention of frontispiece portrait or engraved plate, as in the Kohler copy). Scarce. Stevens 402; Kohler 243, indicating "Portrait frontispiece engraved by Woodman, Junr. after Faithorne 1670. Published Nov. 1st 1807 by Mathews & Leigh. Plate engraved by Evans from an original painting by Hudson in the possession of Ed. Quin esq. and published April 1st 1808 by Mathews & Leigh. Plate engraved by Evans after Lawrenson and published 1 July 1807 by Mathews & Leigh," citing "Williamson 74," and reporting "Not in Cambridge University."

236. MASQUE OF COMUS. By John Milton. Adapted For Theatrical Representation, As first performed at the Theatre-Royal, Covent-Garden, In The Year 1744. Regulated from the Prompt Books, By Permission of the Managers. With The Life Of The Author; By Dr. Johnson; And a Critique, By R. Cumberland, Esq. The Lines distinguished by Inverted Commas are omitted in the Representation. Cooke's Edition. Superbly Embellished. *London: Printed for C. Cooke, Paternoster Row, by Macdonald and Son, 46, Cloth-Fair, Smithfield, and sold by all the Booksellers in the United Kingdom. n.d. [1809].* [In] [**AN ANTHOLOGY OF BRITISH DRAMA.**] By Richard Cumberland. Cooke's Edition. *London: Printed for C. Cooke, Paternoster Row, by Macdonald and Son, and sold by all the Booksellers in the United Kingdom. [1806–9.]* Bound with **THE MOUNTAIN SYLPH!** A Romantic Grand Opera, In Two Acts. The Whole Of The Music Composed By John Barnett. *London, n.d. [1834].* 3 volumes. Stout 12mo, (each drama separately paginated—with *Comus* paginated as xlviii+[2]+37+[1]pp.), engraved frontispiece illustration for *Comus* of "Mrs. Storace as Euphrosyne [—] But the Nymph disdains to pine,[/]Who bathes the Wound in rosy Wine. [—] Printed for C. Cooke Jany. 23, 1809," life of Milton by Johnson, "Critique On Comus" by Cumberland; engraved illustrations, the contents of each volume written out in a neat early hand in ink on a preliminary blank, three-quarter calf (a little rubbed, scattered foxing throughout the set with some thumbing to the outer margins, including several pages of *Comus*, with several small pieces missing in the margins), plum pebble cloth sides, spines decorated with small decorative piece in blind within the panels, two gilt-lettered leather labels on each spine, raised bands decorated in blind, plum endpapers. A scarce collection and a scarce early nineteenth-century edition of *Comus*. Not in Kohler.

A collection of twenty-seven plays reprinted from the prompt books of the Covent-Garden and Drury-Lane theatres, most are preceded with a critique and a biography of the author by the dramatist, Richard Cumberland; biographies of Milton, Rowe, and Philips are by Samuel Johnson; most plays in the collection also have a critique by Cumberland. All but two of the plays contain an engraved frontispiece illustrating a character or scene from the work.

237. IL COMO FAVOLA BOSCHERECCIA DI GIOVANNI MILTON, Rapresentata Nel Castello Di Ludlow Nell' Anno MDCXXXIV, Alla Presenza Del Conte Di Bridgewater, Allora Presidente del Paese di Galles Tradotta In Italiano Da Gaetano Polidori Da Bientina. Seconda Edizione Migliorata, Corretta, e di Note corredata dal Traduttore. *Londra, Da' Torchj Di P. Da Ponte, 15, Poland Street. Per Didier et Tebbett, 75, St. James's Street. MDCCCIX.* Second edition of Polidori's translation. Tall 8vo, xiv+[ii]+87+[1]pp., dedication page, "Prefazione," contemporary full red morocco (rubbed along joints), elaborately gilt-decorated Regency style, princely coat of arms in gilt on front and back covers, richly gilt-decorated covers and spine, broad inner and outer dentelles finely tooled in gilt, pale blue watered silk doublures and endpapers, a.e.g., bookplates, blind-stamped coat of arms at top of title page, bound by Macnair, with his ticket on endpaper. Apparently a large and thick paper copy with an advertisement leaf for Polidori's other works at the end. This is the second edition of G. Polidori's translation into Italian. Polidori's own works were printed in a small number of copies and are apparently difficult to find. The first edition of Polidori's translation was published in 1802 (also listed here) and is very rare; this present edition may well be rarer; a third edition of Polidori's Italian translation—also rare—was published in 1812 (also listed here). Scarce. Not in Kohler.

238. IL COMO FAVOLA BOSCHERECCIA DI GIOVANNI MILTON, Rapresentata Nel Castello Di Ludlow Nell' Anno MDCXXXIV, Alla Presenza Del Conte Di Bridgewater, Presidente del Paese di Galles, Tradotta In Italiano Da Gaetano Polidori Da Bientina. Terza Edizione, Migliorata, e Coretta. *Parigi, da' Torchj di Firmin Didot, Tipographo Dell' Istituto Imperiale. MDCCCXII.* Third edition of Polidori's translation into Italian. 8vo, xi+[1]+80pp., dedication page, "Prefazione," original boards covered with speckled dark green paper (a bit rubbed), red paper label with gilt lettering and gilt rule on spine, edges untrimmed. Fine copy with small heraldic stamp in red at foot of title page and *ex libris* written in a neat early hand on front blank. Not in Kohler.

239. COMUS, MASQUE DE MILTON, Représenté Au Chateau De Ludlow, En 1634, Devant John Egerton,

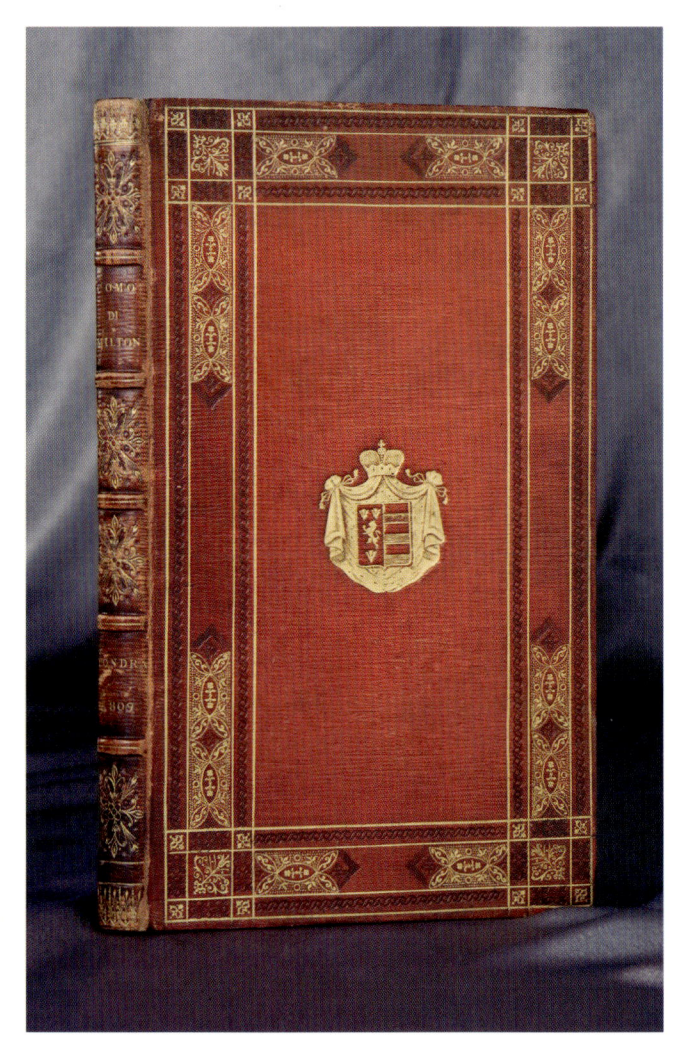

Il Como . . . Di Giovanni Milton, 1809, contemporary full red morocco, elaborately gilt-decorated Regency style, princely coat of arms in gilt on covers. Rare second edition of Polidori's translation into Italian. See #237.

Comte De Bridgewater, Lord Président du Pays de Galles. Traduction Littérale. *A Paris, De L'Imprimerie De P. Didot L'Aîné. 1812.* Very large 4to, xiii+[i]+85pp., Italian title page (**COMO, DRAMMA CON MASCHERE DI MILTON**, Rappresentato A Ludlow Castle, Nel 1634, In Presenza Di Giovanni Egerton, Conte Di Bridgewater, Lord Presidente, allora, di Galles. Traduzione Sostenuta Ad Litteram. *Parigi, Dai Torchi Di P. Didot Il Maggiore. 1812*) across from French title page, small red seal on each title page, the French and Italian translations of *Comus* are printed across from each other (French on the right, and Italian on the left), "Scrittori Intorno A Como" / "Critiques Sur Comus" at the end, with small red seal on each beginning page, contemporary pink boards (now quite faded and a little worn, some insect damage to blank endpapers and slight damage to outer blank edges of both the Italian and French title pages), black morocco label (chipped) with gilt lettering and gilt rules on spine.

Despite the flaws, a fine copy, printed on large and thick paper, possibly in a small edition. Not in Kohler.

240. MILTON'S COMUS: A MASQUE, In Two Acts, As Revived at The Theatre-Royal, Covent-Garden, Friday, April 28, 1815. The Original Music By Handel And Arne, With Some Additions By Bishop; The Overture By Cherubini. The Dances By Mr. Ware. *London: Printed For John Miller, 25, Bow-Street, Covent-Garden; And Sold In The Theatre. Printed by B. McMillan, Bow-Street, Covent-Garden. 1815. [Price Tenpence.]* 8vo, 29+[3]pp., "Advertisement," "Persons Represented," disbound (a bit foxed, small hole on title page without affecting any text), edges untrimmed. A good copy of this kind of program publication with three advertisement leaves for "New Dramatic Works, Published By John Miller" printed at the end. Scarce. Stevens 407; Not in Kohler.

241. COMUS, 1830. [In] THE GARLAND OF ENGLISH POETRY: CONSISTING OF AKENSIDE'S PLEASURES OF IMAGINATION; SOMERVILLE'S CHASE; DRYDEN'S PALAMON; MILTON'S COMUS; ETC. ETC. Embellished With Four Beautiful Engravings, from Drawings by Westall. *London: Printed For John Sharpe, Piccadilly. 1830.* First edition thus? 12mo in 6s, 107+108+108+108pp., engraved title page and half-title for each of the four works listed in the title, with vignette illustration on each engraved title (each dated 1825), contemporary three-quarter calf, marbled paper over boards (a little rubbed, joints a bit tender with slight crack along bottom third of front joint, each engraved title page and half-title foxed and slightly dirtied), spine decorated with four small gilt harps, each within gilt rules, black morocco label with gilt lettering and gilt rules, thick yellow endpapers (front endpaper reattached, lacking back endpaper), speckled red edges. Included are Milton's *C* and *SA*, with engraved title page for "Milton. Comus. Samson Agonistes," with decorative border trim and vignette illustration for *C* after R. Westall, engraved by W. Greatbatch, "Published Jan. 1, 1825, By John Sharpe, London." Uncommon. Not in Kohler.

242. COMUS, 1835. [In] THE REPUBLIC OF LETTERS; A REPUBLICATION OF STANDARD LITERATURE. Edited By Mrs. A. H. Nicholas. *Volume IV. New York: George Dearborn, Publisher. 1835.* 8vo in 16s, 402pp. (with individual pagination for each work), title page for each of the individual works, original three-quarter brown leather, marbled paper over boards (worn, joints cracked, age-browning), spine lettered in gilt with decorative gilt trim, marbled endpapers and edges. A good copy with early signature on front blank. *Comus* begins on page 157 with its own title page: "**COMUS; A MASK.** Presented At Ludlow Castle, 1634, Before The Earl Of Bridgewater, Then President Of Wales. By John Milton. *New York: George Dearborn, Publishers. 1835*"; it is printed in double column for thirteen pages with notes at the bottom of the page. Other works included are *Marriage; A Novel*; *The Life of Galileo*; *A Philosophical Enquiry into the Origin of our Ideas of The Sublime and Beautiful*; and *Lives of Eminent British Military Commanders*. Uncommon. Not in Kohler.

243. COMUS [In] THE BOOK OF CELEBRATED POEMS, Containing Forty-Three Of The Most popular Poems in the English Language Unabridged; Illustrated By Upwards Of Eighty Engravings From Drawings By C. W. Cope, Kenny Meadows, G. Dodgson, And J. Ferguson. *London: Samson Low And Son, 47, Ludgate Hill. 1854.* 8vo, viii+448pp., engraved and printed title pages, illustrations, original blue cloth, covers elaborately decorated in gilt and blind, spine richly decorated in gilt within the panels with gilt lettering, a.e.g., early bookplate. A nice copy in a handsome binding with contemporary presentation inscription (dated 1855) on fly-leaf. Included on pp. 85–122 is Milton's *C*, with half-title and with six vignette illustrations of scenes in *C*, by Kenny Meadows engraved by William Linton.

244. COMUS. A Mask. By John Milton. With Thirty Illustrations By Pickersgill, Corbould, Birket Foster, Harrison Weir, etc. Engraved By The Brothers Dalziel. *London: George Routledge & Co. Farringdon Street. New York: 18, Beekman Street. 1858.* First edition thus, first state. Small 4to, vii+[i]+90+[1]pp., half-title, frontispiece illustration and other illustrations by Pickersgill, Corbould, Foster, Weir, and others, engraved by the Dalziel brothers, original green pebble grain cloth (a bit rubbed at edges, spine a bit faded), thick outer edge of both covers ornately decorated in embossed gilt framing, darker green within trimmed in black with large central gilt device incorporating title, spine lettered and decorated in gilt, bevelled edges, a.e.g. A nice copy with several early and later inscriptions on fly-leaf. "There is an amusing item to be sought in Milton's Comus (Routledge, 1858), illustrated by Pickersgill and others. In otherwise identical copies, two states are to be distinguished. In one, the blocks on pp. 7, 71, and 79 are of typical Pickersgill figures, perhaps a trifle more luscious than usual; in the other the same females are well draped. It is needless to suggest which is the second state! The first is definitely rare" (White, p. 109). Based on state of the present copies in the collection (four in the first state and three in the second) and other copies formerly in the collection and available through the years, it would appear that both states are of about equal rarity. Stevens 418; Kohler 245; the latter two without mention of two states.

Illustration engraved by Dalziel in the first state (figure unclothed) from *Comus*. London: George Routledge & Co. and New York, 1858. See #244.

Illustration engraved by Dalziel in the second state (figure clothed) from *Comus*. London: George Routledge & Co. and New York, 1858. See #244.

Variant bindings of *Comus*, London and New York: George Routledge & Co., 1858. See #245–50.

245. Variant of Preceding. First edition thus, first state. Original brown pebble grain cloth (rubbed along edges), similarly decorated, bevelled edges, a.e.g. A good copy in a variant publisher's binding with the female figures by Pickersgill in the three illustrations on pp. 7, 71, and 79 unclothed. White, *English Illustration*, p. 109; Stevens 418; Kohler 245 (presumably the first state).

246. Variant of Preceding. First edition thus, first state. Original purple pebble grain cloth (joints a little rubbed, spine ends and corners a little worn), similarly decorated, bevelled edges, a.e.g. Decent copy in a variant publisher's binding with near-contemporary presentation inscription on fly-leaf, and with the female figures by Pickersgill in the three illustrations on pp. 7, 71, and 79 unclothed.

247. Variant of Preceding. First edition thus, first state. Original red pebble grain cloth (a little rubbed along joints, spine ends and corners a little worn), similarly decorated, bevelled edges, a.e.g. A good copy in a variant publisher's binding with contemporary signature on fly-leaf, and with the female figures by Pickersgill in the three illustrations on pp. 7, 71, and 79 unclothed.

248. Variant of Preceding. First edition thus, second state. Original pink pebble grain cloth (a bit worn, red mark on front cover, a few page edges fingered, lacks front endpaper), front cover decorated with variant gilt border trim on front cover without any black trim but with variant central gilt device incorporating title, back cover decorated in blind, bevelled edges, a.e.g. Decent copy in the second state with the unclothed female figures by Pickersgill in the three illustrations on pp. 7, 71, and 79 in the first state, clothed here in the second state, in a variant publisher's binding. See comments with first copy of first edition, first state listed here. White, *English Illustration*, p. 109.

249. Variant of Preceding. First edition thus, second state. Original brown pebble grain cloth (spine ends a little rubbed, corners a bit worn), covers decorated as with first copy here, bevelled edges, a.e.g. A nice copy in a variant publisher's binding with the female figures by Pickersgill in the three illustrations on pp. 7, 71, and 79 clothed.

250. Variant of Preceding. First edition thus, second state. Original red pebble grain cloth (rebacked and reinforced from within, a bit rubbed along bottom edges, occasional slight foxing), similarly decorated as pink pebble grain cloth binding above with variant gilt border trim on front cover, without any black trim and with variant central gilt device incorporating title, back cover decorated in blind, bevelled edges, reddish-brown endpapers, a.e.g. A good copy in a variant publisher's binding with the female figures by Pickersgill in the three illustrations on pp. 7, 71, and 79 clothed.

251. COMUS. By John Milton. With Prefatory And Explanatory Notes By The Rev. Henry R. Huckin, M.A. Head Master Of Repton School, England. English Classics. *New York: Clark & Maynard, Publishers, 771 Broadway. (1886)*. First edition thus. 8vo in 4s, 47pp., unsigned vignette portrait of a young Milton on title page, original printed cream wrappers (a little age-darkened), lettering in red on front cover similar to that on title page ("No. 29. English Classic Series With Explanatory Notes COMUS By John Milton. New York: Clark & Maynard Publishers, 771 Broadway. 1866"), decorative red border trim, advertisement in red on verso, listing of the series printed in red on both sides of back cover. Good copy. Uncommon. Not in Kohler.

See 1892 "Maynard & Co., Publishers" edition listed here of "*Comus*, English Classic Series.—No. 29. With Prefatory And Explanatory Notes By The Rev. Henry R. Huckin"; see also 1898 "Maynard, Merrill, & Co." edition listed here of "*Comus* English Classic Series.—No. 29., With Prefatory And Explanatory Notes By The Rev. Henry R. Huckin."

252. MILTON COMUS[.] *Clarendon Press Series*[.] *Oxford*[:] *At The Clarendon Press*[,] *M DCCC LXXXVIII*[.] *[All rights reserved]*. First edition thus? Slim 8vo, 53+[1]+[2]pp., two-page preface, notes at the end, original orange wrappers (a bit used, spine split, name on fly-leaf, chronology of major dates neatly written in pencil on end blank, two marginal notes in pencil), title page repeated on front cover with black border rule and small corner pieces, with "Price Sixpence" at the bottom, "London Henry Frowde" with the seal of the press and "Oxford University Press Warehouse Amen Corner, E.C." printed at the center of the back cover, advertisement leaf bound in at end. A good copy with contemporary name and address on fly-leaf. "The present edition of 'Comus' is taken from 'The English Poems of John Milton,' edited by R. G. Browne, M.A., for the Clarendon Press" (verso of title page). Scarce. Not in Kohler.

253. MILTON'S COMUS With Introduction And Notes By William Bell, M.A.[,] Professor Of Philosophy And Logic, Government College, Lahore[.] *London*[:] *Macmillan And Co*[.] *And New York*[,] *1890*[.] *[All rights reserved]* First edition thus? Slim 8vo, xx+117+[1]+[2]pp., original light gray cloth (a bit used, lacking front fly-leaf, a few pencil notes and markings), front cover and spine lettered in blue with small emblem in blue incorporating initials of the press in lower right corner of front cover, decorative device in blue incorporating initials of the press on back cover. Two advertisement leaves bound in at end. The edition was variously reprinted thereafter (see 1898 and 1899 editions listed here) on into the twentieth century. Uncommon. Not in Kohler.

254. COMUS. By John Milton. With Prefatory And Explanatory Notes By The Rev. Henry R. Huckin, M.A. Head Master Of Repton School, England. English Classic Series.—No. 29. *New York: Effingham Maynard & Co., Publishers, 771 Broadway And 67 & 69 Ninth Street. New Series, No. 15. February 22, 1892. Published Semi-weekly. Subscription Price $10. Entered at Post Office, New York, as Second-class Matter.* 8vo in 4s, 47pp., unsigned vignette portrait of a young Milton on title page, original printed light green wrappers, lettering on front cover similar to that on title page ("Maynard's English Classic Series With Explanatory Notes COMUS By John Milton. No. 29. New York: Effingham Maynard & Co., Publishers, 771 Broadway And 67 & 69 Ninth St.), a listing of the series printed on the inside of the front and back covers as well as on the back cover. A fine copy, well-preserved because of student's protective brown paper book cover in which it has been kept through the years. Early, possibly contemporary, student's name and address are written on the front cover of the protective wrapper. Uncommon. Not in Kohler.

255. MILTON COMUS Edited With Notes By Oliver Elton, B.A. Sometime Scholar Of Corpus Christi College, Oxford[.] Lecturer On English Literature At The Owens College (Victoria University), Manchester[.] *Oxford[:] At The Clarendon Press[,] 1898.* First edition thus. 8vo, 101+[1]+[2]pp., original printed orange wrappers (rubbed, spine chipped at top and bottom). Good. Advertisement leaf of "Clarendon Press Editions Of Milton" and "Tudor And Stuart Library 1906-7" bound in at end. Uncommon. Not in Kohler.

256. COMUS By John Milton With Introduction And Notes By Henry R. Huckin, M.A. Headmaster of Repton School, England[.] *New York[:] Maynard, Merrill, & Co. (1898) Maynard's English Classic Series.—No. 29[.] New Series, No. 72. June 29, 1898. Published semi-weekly. Subscription price $10. Entered at Post Office, New York, as Second-Class Matter.* 8vo in 4s, 47pp., frontispiece reproduction of portrait of Milton by D. Grosch on verso of title page, original printed light green wrappers (slight embrowning and a few slight stains on covers, notations in pencil at the beginning and at the end, with name in pencil on front cover), lettering on front cover similar to that on title page ("Maynard's English Classic Series With Explanatory Notes COMUS By John Milton. New York: Maynard, Merrill, & Co., 29, 31, and 33 East Nineteenth Street"), a listing of the series printed on the inside of the front and back covers as well as on the back cover. Good copy. Uncommon. Not in Kohler.

257. MILTON'S COMUS With Introduction And Notes By William Bell, M.A.[,] Inspector Of Schools, Lahore[.] *London[:] Macmillan And Co., Limited[;] New York: The Macmillan Company[,] 1898. All rights reserved[.]* Slim 8vo, xx+117+[1]+4pp., half-title with emblem incorporating initials of the press on verso, original light brown cloth (faded and aged), front cover and spine lettered in blue with small emblem in blue incorporating initials of the press in lower right corner of front cover, decorative device in blue incorporating initials of the press on back cover, bookplate on front pastedown. Four advertisement leaves for "Macmillan's English Classics" bound in at end. The possible first edition thus was published in 1890; it was variously reprinted thereafter in 1899—both editions listed here. Not in Kohler.

258. MILTON'S COMUS With Introduction And Notes By William Bell, M.A.[,] Inspector Of Schools, Lahore[.] *London[:] Macmillan And Co., Limited[;] New York: The Macmillan Company[,] 1899. All rights reserved[.]* Slim 8vo, xx+117+[1]+[2]pp., half-title, original cream cloth (a bit used and soiled), front cover and spine lettered in blue with small emblem in blue incorporating initials of the press in lower right corner of front cover, decorative device in blue incorporating initials of the press on back cover. Good copy. Advertisement leaf for "Macmillan's English Classics" bound in at end. The possible first edition thus was published in 1890 (also listed here). Not in Kohler.

259. MILTON'S COMUS, LYCIDAS AND OTHER POEMS And Matthew Arnold's Address On Milton Edited With Introduction And Notes By Andrew J. George, M.A. Department of English, High School, Newton, Mass. Editor Of "The Shorter Poems Of Milton," Byron's "Childe Harold," "From Chaucer To Arnold," Etc. *New York[:] The Macmillan Company[;] London: Macmillan & Co., Ltd.[,] 1899[.] [All rights reserved]* First edition thus. Small 8vo, xxxviii+178+[4]pp., half-title with advertisement for "Macmillan's Pocket English Classics . . . 16mo. Levanteen. 25c. each" (including this edition) on verso, frontispiece portrait plate with unsigned vignette portrait of Milton as a young man, copyright 1899 on verso of title page, original red cloth, small square in silver with silver lettering at left top of front cover, spine lettered in silver (faded). A nice copy with label, "With The Compliments Of The Publishers. Catalogue Price, The Macmillan Company, Tremont Building, Boston. List Price $.25[;] Introduction Price—21," tipped in on fly-leaf, partially unopened. Four pages of advertisements bound in at end. Not in Kohler.

While "16mo" is given as the size of the book in the advertisement notice on verso of half-title, the signatures conform to the traditional octavo format. The reference to "16mo" would seem to refer to the small size of the book: 5 ¾" × 4 ⅜". Later editions were published in 1902 (copy in the collection, a repeat of this edition, not listed); 1905 (see copy listed here with addition of frontispiece portrait plate reproducing Faithorne frontispiece portrait); 1906 (copy in the collection, a repeat of this edition, not listed); 1910 (copy in the collection, a repeat of this edition, not listed); and 1912 (see copy listed here, new edition edited with introduction and notes by Andrew George, and list of editions identified from there on reprinting the 1912 edition).

Signed Illustrated Edition with Hand-drawn Initial Letters

260. COMUS. A MASK. [*London: Essex House Press, MDCCCCI.*] Crown 8vo, [1]+47pp.+colophon leaf, first appearance of hand-colored wood block frontispiece illustration by Reginald Savage, printed on vellum in blue and black (stage directions printed in blue) with initial letters hand-drawn in red, including a large initial and one smaller initial in burnished gold, all by Florence Kingsford, the sketched press device on colophon page also hand-colored without attribution, protective tissue guards interleaved throughout, original natural vellum, blind-stamped design incorporating "SOVL IS FORM" on front cover, a design common to all volumes in the series, spine lettered in gilt, edges untrimmed. A fine copy in near mint condition. One of a series of "Great Poems," which C. R. Ashbee printed at the Essex House Press in small editions, all printed entirely on vellum, with charming hand-colored initials and at least one full-page woodcut, also hand-colored here by Reginald Savage and signed by him on colophon. No. 116 of 150 numbered copies on vellum. Stevens 438; Not in Kohler.

Hand-colored wood block frontispiece illustration by Reginald Savage from *Comus. A Mask*. [London: Essex House Press, MDCCCCI.] Crown 8vo, [1]+47pp.+colophon leaf, printed on vellum in black and blue. See #260.

261. COMUS[.] A MASKE BY JOHN MILTON. *[New Rochelle: The Elston Press, 1902.]* Tall 8vo, [ii]+29+[1]pp. +colophon leaf, half-title, elaborately decorated double-spread title page (without an illustration) in red and black with grapevine borders designed by Helen Marguerite O'Kane (wife of Clarke Conwell, proprietor of the Elston Press), printed in red and black in Caslon Old Style type on handmade paper, publisher's dark green cloth, spine lettered in gilt, t.e.g., others untrimmed. Very nice copy, "Printed From The Original Edition Of 1637" (colophon leaf). O'Kane's decorations are always praised for their high quality and for being an integral part of a book that is well-made and finely printed on excellent handmade paper. The influence of William Morris's Kelmscott Press is clear. The "elaborate full-page borders by O'Kane [are] touched by the Kelmscott effulgence and with pronounced elements of the sinuous and flowing lines of art nouveau" (Blumenthal, *The Printed Book in America*, p. 53, Plate 30). One of 160 copies. Stevens 439; Ransom, *Private Presses*, p. 9; Franklin, pp. 157–59; Cave, pp. 135–37; Not in Kohler.

Illuminated Edition, Signed by the Illuminator

262. COMUS BY JOHN MILTON Illuminated by [Enrico Monetti.] *George D. Sproul[,] MCMII.* 11 ¼" × 9", [56 unpaginated leaves], half-title with elaborate illuminated letter and floral decoration in various shades of red, blue, green, purple, brown, and gilt with printed colophon: "Saint Dunstan Edition . . . Illuminated By Enrico Monetti," signed by the illuminator, title page similarly elaborately illuminated with floral decoration in various shades of red, blue, green, purple, brown, and gilt, incorporating two dragons into the design, with printed title and elaborate illuminated initial letter and with printed publisher and illuminated initial letter, each page of text with five-line hand-painted and illuminated initial in various colors and gilt with leafy marginal embellishment extending the length of the inner and bottom margins (and usually forming a partial border at the top), printed on vellum on one side only, original linen-backed vellum covered boards (occasional trivial yellowing, which is typical of vellum, with very slight soiling at top of back cover), title in gilt on front cover, a.e.g. Superb copy of a lovely book with the bookplate of "Frank T. Hull, Printer" on front pastedown, in an excellent folding light gray cloth box, with black morocco label with gilt lettering and gilt rules on front cover. Both the elaborate half-title with colophon and the title page are illuminated in the manner of fifteenth-century books with elaborate marginal decoration. According to colophon on half-title: "Saint Dunstan Edition[.] Comus[.] It is guaranteed to subscribers that eighteen copies only of this edition have been made for sale in America, and twelve copies only for sale in Europe, and that no future edition will be issued; that it is printed from type and the type has been distributed; that this copy . . . has been specially illuminated throughout . . . and that no two copies are alike[.] Illuminated By Enrico Monetti." The unusual "St. Dunstan Edition" was part of an exceptionally beautiful series of famous works of literature produced around the turn of the century in strictly limited editions, all printed on vellum and each copy unique, with every page in some way illuminated by hand. One of only 30 total copies, printed on vellum on one side only, each copy unique in its illumination and signed by the illuminator. This copy is signed by Monetti on the colophon. Not in Kohler.

263. COMUS. "A Maske Presented at Ludlow Castle, 1634" By John Milton Reproduced in Facsimile from the First Edition of 1637 With an Introductory Note by Luther S. Livingston. *New York: Dodd, Mead & Company[,] 1903.* First edition thus. 4to, vii+[iii]+35pp., half-title, thirty-eight pages of facsimile reproductions, original green cloth, front cover and spine lettered in gilt, edges untrimmed. Nice copy. Facsimile reproduction of Milton's 1637 first edition *Comus*. This is #1 of Dodd and Mead's Facsimile Reprints of Rare Books, and "the Edition is limited to Five Hundred and Twenty Copies, of which Twenty are on Japan paper" (verso of half-title). Not in Kohler.

264. Variant of Preceding, original blue cloth, front cover and spine lettered in gilt, unopened. This appears to be one of the twenty copies printed on Japan paper. Nice copy. Not in Kohler.

265. MILTON'S COMUS, LYCIDAS AND OTHER POEMS And Matthew Arnold's Address On Milton Edited With Introduction And Notes By Andrew J. George, M.A. Department Of English, High School, Newton, Mass. Editor Of "The Shorter Poems Of Milton," Byron's "Childe Harold," "From Chaucer To Arnold," Etc. *New York[:] The Macmillan Company[;] London: Macmillan & Co., Ltd. 1905. All rights reserved[.]* Small 8vo, xxxviii+[1]+178+[4]pp., half-title with advertisement on verso, frontispiece portrait plate consisting of a reproduction of Faithorne frontispiece portrait, original red cloth (a little rubbed, name in ink on fly-leaf, notations in pencil on final blanks), front cover and spine lettered in white (faded). Four pages of advertisements bound in at the end. This edition introduces a change in frontispiece from earlier editions: from that of Milton as a young man to that of a reproduction of a Faithorne frontispiece portrait, used in all succeeding editions. The first edition thus was published in 1899 (also listed here with other editions and also a note regarding size of the book). Not in Kohler.

266. COMUS A MASQUE BY JOHN MILTON. *London[:] George Routledge & Sons, Limited[;] New York: E. P. Dutton & Co. n.d. (1906).* First edition thus. 8vo, 82+[2]pp., half-title ("The Photogravure and Colour Series") with advertisement for the series on verso, title page in red and black with central decorated black initial "R," a second decorated title page in black with central vignette illustration is dated "1634" in Roman numerals at the top ("Comvs A Maske By John Milton[.] Illustrated • By • Jessie • M • King[,] George • Rovtledge • And • Sons • Ltd. London: Broadway • Hovse • Lvdgate • Hill • E •"), eight photogravures and the first appearance of three half-tone illustrations by Jessie M. King—one of the photogravures as frontispiece, with protective tissue guard, and one of the half-tone illustrations on final page, decorated half-title following second title page, brief section commentaries, original half blue buckram, marbled paper over boards (a bit rubbed, plates foxed, as is common with this book), spine lettered in gilt, t.e. blue, others untrimmed. Very nice. (Dated according to *Milton Tercentenary*, 1908, Appendix, p. 152, #760; see following variant edition dated 1906 on title page, possibly a first trade edition.) Scarce. Not in Kohler.

267. Variant of Preceding. **COMUS A MASQUE BY JOHN MILTON.** *London[:] George Routledge & Sons, Limited[;] New York: E. P. Dutton & Co. n.d. (1906).* First edition thus. 8vo, 82+[2]pp., half-title ("The Photogravure and Colour Series") with advertisement for the series on verso (including this edition and *PL* illustrated by William Strang), title page in red and black with central decorated black initial "R," a second decorated title page in black with central vignette illustration is dated "1634" in Roman numerals at the top ("Comvs A Maske By John Milton[.] Illustrated • By • Jessie • M • King[,] George • Rovtledge • And • Sons • Ltd. London: Broadway • Hovse • Lvdgate • Hill • E •"), eight photogravures and the first appearance of three half-tone illustrations by Jessie M. King—one of the photogravures as frontispiece and one of the half-tone illustrations on final page, each with protective tissue guard, decorated half-title following second title page, "List Of Illustrations" (added to this edition), brief section commentaries, original red cloth (very worn because of mold damage sometime earlier—especially back cover—with boards a little warped, bit shaken), front cover and spine decorated with green trim and gilt ruling and lettered in gilt, with small figurine in gilt at bottom of front cover, t.e.g., others untrimmed. Despite the book cover having suffered badly from mold in the past, a very good and clean copy internally, with the binding cleaned up better than expected, in a protective plastic cover. See preceding copy, undated and the first edition thus. Gift from a bookdealer with the suggestion that this might best be thrown away as "hopelessly unsalvageable." Scarce. Not in Kohler.

Formerly Lewis Turco's Copy with His Signature

268. COMUS AND OTHER POEMS By John Milton[.] *Printed At The University Press, Cambridge & Published At The Cambridge University Press Warehouse, Fetter Lane, London, E.C. MCMVI.* Large 8vo, 84+[1]pp., half-title, large decorative engraving on title page in Renaissance style (not an illustration), printed on special paper, title pages reprinted for 1645 *Comus* and 1634 *Justa Edovardo King*, original quarter vellum paper spine (a bit rubbed and spine slightly chipped at top), light blue paper over boards (a bit faded, some shelf wear, corners bumped), printed vellum paper label ruled in black on front cover, t.e. rough, fore- and bottom edges untrimmed. The verso of the half-title reads: "Of this Edition, printed in the Cambridge type upon hand-made paper, two hundred & fifty copies have been printed, of which two hundred and twenty-five are for sale in England and America, & the type has been distributed," with "21 shillings, net" written in pencil within brackets at the end. Formerly Lewis Turco's copy, with his signature in ink, dated, with a third owner's small paper label bookplate. Kohler 482.

---

269. [COMUS] MILTON'S COMUS Being The Bridgewater Manuscript With Notes And A Short Family Memoir By The Lady Alix Egerton. *London[:] J. M. Dent & Sons Limited[,] 1910.* First edition thus. Large square 8vo, viii+99pp., half-title, title page in red and black, eight portraits in tinted photogravure (one as frontispiece), three facsimiles of the Bridgewater MS., protective tissue guards, original full vellum (a bit darkened, ties missing, occasional foxing), gilt-decorated covers and spine, spine lettered in gilt, t.e.g., others untrimmed, partially unopened. A good copy, fresh internally, with a contemporary presentation inscription in a neat hand on the front pastedown: "Sacharissa from the Scribe Christmas 1910." "Unusual material from the family papers and contemporary portraits; notes; some facts regarding variants" (Stevens). Scarce. Stevens 448; Not in Kohler.

270. COMUS, L'ALLEGRO[,] IL PENSEROSO AND LYCIDAS With Other Of Milton's Shorter Poems Edited

With Introduction And Notes By Clarence Griffin Child Ph.D., L.H.D., Professor Of English[,] The University Of Pennsylvania[.] The Scribner English Classics. *New York[:] Charles Scribner's Sons[,] 1910.* First edition thus. 8vo, xxx+163pp., half-title ("The Scribner English Classics") with a list of editions of "The Scribner English Classics" on verso, frontispiece portrait of "John Milton from an Engraving" (unsigned, although after Faithorne), substantive notes on each poem and an "Index To The Notes" at end, original red cloth (a bit dirtied, a few pages a little scuffed), front cover and spine lettered in black ("Milton's Shorter Poems"), with an emblem for "The Scribner English Classics" on front cover. Scarce. Not in Kohler.

271. MILTON COMUS Edited With Notes By Oliver Elton[,] Professor Of English Literature In The University Of Liverpool[.] *Oxford[:] At The Clarendon Press[,] 1911.* First edition thus. Together with **MILTON L'ALLEGRO** Edited, With Notes By Oliver Elton[,] B.A.[,] Sometime Scholar Of Corpus Christi College, Oxford Lecturer On English Literature At The Owens College (Victoria University), Manchester[.] *Oxford[:] At The Clarendon Press[,] 1893.* First edition thus. Together with **MILTON IL PENSEROSO** Edited, With Notes By Oliver Elton[,] B.A. Late Scholar Of Corpus Christi College, Oxford, Lecturer In English Literature At The Owens College, Manchester[.] *Oxford[:] At The Clarendon Press[,] 1897.* First edition thus. Together with **MILTON LYCIDAS** Edited, With Notes By Oliver Elton[,] M.A. Professor Of English Literature In The University Of Liverpool[.] *Oxford[:] At The Clarendon Press[,] 1910.* First edition thus. Together with **ARCADES** and **SONNETS**, each with half-title. 8vo, 101pp.,+16pp.,+16pp.,+24pp.,+[6]pp.,+26pp.,+8pp., half-title, four title pages with different dates, "Introduction," "Notes," and "Glossary" for each work, original purple cloth (early ownership name written in a fine hand on fly-leaf, several marginal notes in pencil in a neat hand in *Comus*), front cover lettered in white, spine lettered white. Nice copy. Eight pages of advertisements bound in at end. Not in Kohler.

272. MILTON'S COMUS, LYCIDAS AND OTHER POEMS And Matthew Arnold's Address On Milton Edited With Introduction And Notes By Samuel Edward Allen, A.M. Department Of English, Williams College[.] *New York[:] The Macmillan Company[,] 1912[.] All rights reserved.* First edition thus of Allen edition. Small 8vo, lxxvii+[1]+164+[4]pp., half-title with advertisement for "Macmillan's Pocket American and English Classics . . . 16mo. Cloth. 25c. each" on verso and on recto of next leaf (including this edition and *Milton's Paradise Lost, Books I and II*), frontispiece portrait plate reproducing a Faithorne frontispiece portrait, original olive green cloth (a little rubbed, spine a bit worn and faded), front cover elaborately decorated in dark blue with dark blue lettering, spine lettered in blue with initials of the press in blue at top and bottom, brown endpapers. A decent copy with contemporary presentation inscription on fly-leaf, and four pages of advertisements bound in at the end. Not in Kohler.

While "16mo" is given as the size of the book in the advertisement notice on verso of half-title, the signatures conform to the traditional octavo format. The reference to "16mo" would appear to refer, as with its predecessor in 1899, to the small size of the book: 5 ¾" × 4 ⅜". This edition replaces the 1899 first edition by Macmillan edited with introduction and notes by Andrew J. George, which was variously reprinted through the mid-1920s, with the Faithorne frontispiece portrait introduced in the 1905 edition (copy listed here).

273. MILTON'S COMUS, LYCIDAS AND OTHER POEMS . . . [as with preceding]. *New York[:] The Macmillan Company[,] 1912[.] All rights reserved.* First edition thus, second issue. Small 8vo, lxxvii+[1]+164+[4]pp., half-title with advertisement for "Macmillan's Pocket American and English Classics . . . 16mo. Cloth. 25c. each" on verso and on recto of next leaf, frontispiece portrait plate reproducing in vignette the Faithorne frontispiece portrait, original olive green cloth (spine worn, small spot on front cover, red spot on back cover), front cover elaborately decorated in dark blue with dark blue lettering, spine lettered in blue with initials of the press in blue at top and bottom, brown endpapers. A decent copy. Four pages of advertisements bound in at end. Scarce. Not in Kohler.

The first edition thus, first issue, was published in "March, 1912" (copy listed here, see note there regarding size of the book); a second issue was published in "September, 1912" (also listed here); it was variously reprinted thereafter.

Present in the collection are editions that followed in 1913 and 1914, each in original olive green publisher's cloth binding, and in 1916, 1919, 1921, 1924, and 1925, each in original brown publisher's cloth binding, all with four pages of advertisements bound in at the end.

Signed by Arthur Rackham

274. COMUS BY JOHN MILTON Illustrated By Arthur Rackham[.] *London: William Heinemann[;] New York: Doubleday Page & Co. n.d. (1921).* First Rackham edition. Very large 8vo, xviii+76pp., decorative piece in lower right corner of front blank, half-title, the first appearance of twenty-four full-page illustrations in color and thirty-seven line drawings in black and white within the text by

Arthur Rackham, each of the color illustrations tipped in on brown paper, each with protective tissue guard printing the poetic lines illustrated, decorative piece on title page, decorative head- and tailpieces, facsimile reproduction of first edition title page, original vellum spine, cream-colored boards (slightly rubbed and aged), gilt lettering on front cover and spine, elaborate gilt emblem on front cover, decorated blue endpapers, t.e.g., others untrimmed, partially unopened, endpapers by Rackham. A very good, tall copy, printed in Great Britain by the Cornwall Press Ltd., London (last page). No. 76 of 550 numbered copies, limited edition deluxe signed by Rackham on verso of half-title. Stevens 452; Latimore and Haskell, p. 54.

275. Variant of Preceding. **COMUS BY JOHN MILTON** Illustrated By Arthur Rackham[.] *London: William Heinemann[;] New York: Doubleday Page & Co. n.d. (1921)*. First Rackham trade edition. Very large 8vo, xviii+76pp., decorative piece in lower right corner of front blank with a list of "Books Illustrated By Arthur Rackham" on verso, half-title, the first appearance of twenty-four full-page illustrations in color and thirty-seven line drawings in black and white within the text by Arthur Rackham, each of the color illustrations tipped in on brown paper, each with protective tissue guard printing the poetic lines illustrated, decorative piece on title page, decorative head- and tailpieces, facsimile reproduction of first edition title page, original green cloth, central design/illustration in gilt on front cover, front cover and spine lettered in gilt, pictorial endpapers, t.e. green, fore- and bottom edges untrimmed. A very nice copy of this trade edition, printed in Great Britain by the Cornwall Press Ltd., London (on the last page) and bound in publisher's green cloth. Stevens 452; Latimore and Haskell, p. 54.

276. **COMUS: A MASK BY JOHN MILTON** With Eight Illustrations by William Blake Edited from the Edition of 1645 and the Autograph Manuscript With a Preface by Darrell Figgis. *London[:] Published for the Julian Editions by Ernest Benn Limited[,] 1926*. First edition thus. 4to, xxiii+35pp.+colophon leaf, half-title, the first appearance of these black-and-white illustration plates modeled after Blake, half-title before the poem, original black cloth, decorative gilt border trim on covers, spine lettered in gilt, t.e.g., others untrimmed, in publisher's black paper slipcase (worn). A very nice copy with "Review Copy" blind-stamped on colophon leaf. The illustrations are reproduced from the original watercolors in the Museum of Fine Arts, Boston. One of 300 copies "printed at the University Press Cambridge for the Julian Editions 1926" (colophon leaf). Stevens 454.

277. **COMUS A MASK BY JOHN MILTON** With A Frontispiece And The Six Characters In Costume Designed And Engraved On Wood by Blair Hughes-Stanton[.] *[Newton, Wales:] The Gregynog Press[,] MCMXXXI*. Small folio, [vi]+25+[1]pp.+colophon leaf, half-title with frontispiece illustration on verso and the first appearance of five additional full-page wood-engraved illustrations by Blair Hughes-Stanton, wood-engraved illustration on title page and another wood-engraved illustration on final page, facsimile reproduction of first edition title page, printed on Japan paper, special red brocade binding, decorated with dancing figures in black and gold, the brocade cloth repeated to provide thick endpapers, marked "created and bound by Hammoneau," t.e.g. A splendid copy in a vellum-covered, finely designed slipcase. "Blair Hughes-Stanton collaborated in the printing, designed and engraved the wood blocks. The book was set by hand and printed by Idris Jones" (colophon leaf). Not only a beautiful and finely made book, but a technically innovative one as well. Douglas Cleverdon observed in *The Dolphin: A Journal Of The Making Of Books* that the "remarkable series of wood engravings by Blair Hughes-Stanton . . . mark an entirely new technical development in modern English book illustration. By the use of the multiple tool (which engraves several parallel lines together), the engraver has achieved delicate effects of lightness and transparency that one would have thought impossible in this medium. . . . The result is brilliant. Nor is the success merely technical: the engravings are filled with grace and beauty." One of 25 copies in special brocade binding; no. 60 of 250 total copies. Harrop 19.

278. **JOHN MILTON HENRY LAWES THE MASK OF COMUS** The Poem, originally called 'A Mask Presented at Ludlow Castle, 1634, &c.' edited by E. H. Visiak[.] The Airs of the five Songs reprinted from the Composer's [Henry Lawes] autograph manuscript edited by Hubert J. Foss. With A Foreword by The Earl Of Ellesmere. Ornamented By M. R. H. Farrar[.] *Published by The Nonesuch Press, Bloomsbury[,] 1937*. Folio, xxiv+44pp.+colophon leaf, the first appearance of five full-page linocut illustrations printed in colors "from the artist's linoleum-cuts by the Curwen Press" (colophon leaf), large circular color illustration of Ludlow Castle at center of title page, and black-and-white ornamental initials, all after Mildred Farrar, text printed in Fell, eight pages of musical notation in Walpergen, types at the Oxford University by John Johnson, original simulated parchment boards embossed with a diagonal pattern and fleuron devices on

Comus, The Gregynog Press, 1931. Special red brocade binding, decorated with dancing figures in black and gold, the brocade cloth repeated to provide thick endpapers, marked "created and bound by Hammoneau." One of 25 copies in special brocade binding; no. 60 of 250 total copies. See #277.

covers, yapp edges, spine lettered in gilt, bound "by the Leighton-Straker Bookbinding Company" (colophon leaf), partially unopened. A very nice copy with large, elaborate bookplate on front pastedown. In publisher's paper-covered slipcase (faded, top chipped and reglued) with full-page color illustration tipped on side. An unusual Nonesuch publication, the largest format of any book of the press. This is the only book Farrar illustrated, and she is believed to have died in World War II. The book was designed by Harry Carter. The music was printed from types of the seventeenth century. Laid in: *The Nonesuch News* (Number One, September 1938). No. 492 of 950 numbered copies. Huckabay 216; Dreyfus 109.

[together with]

279. THE PROSPECTUS for this Nonesuch Press publication: **JOHN MILTON HENRY LAWES THE MASK OF COMUS** The Poem, originally called 'A Mask Presented at Ludlow Castle, 1634, &c.' edited by E. H. Visiak[.] The Airs of the five Songs reprinted from the Composer's [Henry Lawes] autograph manuscript edited by Hubert J. Foss. With A Foreword by The Earl Of Ellesmere. Ornamented By M. R. H. Farrar[.] *Published by The Nonesuch Press, Bloomsbury[,] 1938*. Folio, [4]pp., circular linocut illustration in color on title page, together with sample printed pages of text and music, original self wraps. Also included is a subscription form for Nonesuch members. A fine copy of the prospectus in original mailing envelope with large "Nonesuch Fellowship" mailing label and three canceled stamps (the envelope a bit frayed and worn along the edges). Rare.

Editor's Copy with Proof Sheets Corrected in Manuscript

280. Variant of Preceding **JOHN MILTON HENRY LAWES THE MASK OF COMUS** . . . edited by E. H. Visiak . . . [as preceding] . . . *Published by The Nonesuch Press, Bloomsbury[,] 1937*. First edition thus. Folio, xxiv+44pp.+colophon leaf, as preceding, original simulated parchment boards embossed with a diagonal pattern and fleuron devices on covers, yapp edges, spine lettered in gilt (spine a little darkened), bound "by the Leighton-Straker Bookbinding Company" (colophon leaf), edges untrimmed. From the library of the editor, E. H. Visiak,

Corrected folio proof copy by E. H. Visiak, editor of *John Milton Henry Lawes The Mask Of Comus The Poem* . . . Published by The Nonesuch Press, Bloomsbury, 1937, with the correction "flighted" crossed out in Visiak's hand and beneath it written, "At Milton's demand," with Visiak's initials. See #278.

with his signature and bookplate on front pastedown. Laid in: photograph of Visiak in black and white and two letters addressed to him from the Nonesuch Press, one signed by Francis Meynell. Also laid in are the uncorrected proofs of the introduction and the first thirty-three pages of the text, corrected in manuscript by Visiak. The proofs have been folded, and some pages have tears and ragged edges. Edition limited to 950 numbered copies, this one out of series. Huckabay 216; Dreyfus 109.

In his autobiography, quoted in *The History Of The Nonesuch*, Visiak writes, "I had taken for *The Mask Of Comus* the second edition text; Milton was alive. . . . and would have attended to the proofs. But there was one alteration . . . which in the consensus of Miltonian critics was invalid. The first edition has 'frighted' [steeds], the second 'flighted.' I was prevailed upon to substitute 'flighted' in the proofs. I did them up, with a heavy mind; and, suddenly overcome with fatigue, lay down upon a couch, there sank into a state between sleeping and waking. With stunning suddenness a fierce whisper sounded in my ear, 'That word is "frighted!"' It virtually precipitated me off the couch, and I tore off the wrapping from the proofs, re-read the context, crossed out 'flighted,' and wrote 'stett.' I gratified my fancy later on, by entering in the margin, 'At Milton's demand.'"

281. THE MASQUE OF COMUS The Poem By John Milton With A Preface By Mark Van Doren & The Airs By Henry Lawes With A Preface By Hubert Foss[.] Illustrated With Water-Colors By Edmund Dulac[.] *Printed For The Members Of The Limited Editions Club At The University Press[,] Cambridge[,] 1954.* First edition thus. Slim, tall 4to, [1]+57pp.+[1]+[14pp. of unpaginated musical notation],+colophon leaf, half-title with decorative piece in blue—a decorative piece repeated in blue variously throughout, frontispiece illustration plate and first appearance of five other illustration plates after watercolors by Edmund Dulac, title page in blue and black with a small central harp and laurel wreath, half-title before poems with decorative piece in blue, thirteen pages of musical notation, half-title before "The Airs Of The Songs By Henry Lawes With His Version Of The Words" with decorative piece in blue, original half vellum, marbled paper over boards, spine lettered in gilt, t.e.g., in publisher's slipcase, spine lettered in gilt, with original publisher's glassine dust wrappers. This is the final work done by Dulac, who died before he could sign the colophon. Reprinted in 1997 by the Easton Press (also listed here). Fine copy, near mint. No. 3 of 1,500 copies printed by Brooke Crutchley, printer of the University, Cambridge, England. Huckabay 265.

282. THE MASQUE OF COMUS The Poem By John Milton With A Preface By Mark Van Doren & The Airs By Henry Lawes With A Preface By Hubert Foss[.] Illustrated With Water-Colors By Edmund Dulac[.] *Printed For The Heritage Press At The University Press[,] Cambridge[,] n.d. [1954].* First edition thus. Large 8vo, [1]+57+[1]+[14]pp.+colophon leaf, half-title with decorative piece in blue—a decorative piece in blue repeated variously throughout, frontispiece illustration and five other illustrations after watercolors by Edmund Dulac, title page in blue and black with small central harp and laurel wreath, half-title before poems with decorative piece in blue, half-title before "The Airs Of The Songs By Henry Lawes With His Version Of The Words" with decorative piece in blue, original half black cloth, marbled paper over boards, spine lettered in gilt, t.e. blue. Fine copy, near mint, in publisher's slipcase, with original glassine dustwrapper. Laid in: Heritage Club newsletter on this edition. A reprint of the Limited Editions Club publication in 1954 (preceding copy), in which Dulac's illustrations for *Comus* first appeared.

283. **COMUS AND SOME SHORTER POEMS OF MILTON** Edited With An Introduction By E. M. W. Tillyard[,] Litt.D., Master of Jesus College, Cambridge[,] And With Noted By Phyllis B. Tillyard[,] M.A.[,] Girton College, Cambridge[.] *George G. Harrap & Co. Ltd[.] London[,] Toronto[,] Wellington[,] Sydney[,] (1955)*. Third edition thus. Small 8vo, 223pp., half-title ("Harrap's English Classics") with a list of available editions on verso, frontispiece illustration plate of "Apollo And Daphne by Tiepolo," small emblem of the press on title page, lengthy introduction, extensive notes on each poem at the end, original red cloth, front cover and spine lettered in black. First edition thus published in 1952; second thus in 1953.

284. **COMUS** A Masque with music by Henry Lawes. Together with **SAMSON AGONISTES** (Excerpts). Read by Barbara Jefford, Ian Holm, William Squire, Tony Church, Margaret Rawlings, Gary Watson. *London: Argo Record Company, Limited, (1968)*. 2 33 ⅓ rpm LP records. First edition thus. LP recording in original folding slipcase, with reproduction of Blake illustration in color on front cover. Laid in: descriptive page on the recording of *Comus: A Maske* and *Samson Agonistes* herein ("Printed by Graphis Press Limited"), and the text of **A MASK (COMUS)**. *London: Oxford University Press In Association With The British Council, 1967–68. (Z)RG 544/5*.

285. **COMUS** [In] **A MASKE AT LUDLOW**[:] Essays On Milton's Comus Edited by John S. Diekhoff With the Bridgewater Version of Comus[.] *The Press Of Case Western Reserve University[,] Cleveland[,] 1968*. First edition thus. 8vo, viii+[3]+280pp., original blue cloth, front cover and spine lettered in gilt with small gilt device on front cover. Included is "The Bridgewater *Comus*: Text of *A Maske*" with "The Airs of the Songs by Henry Lawes with His Version of the Words" with a reproduction of the musical notation, together with various essays on *Comus* and its text.

286. **JOHN MILTON A MASKE** The Earlier Versions Edited by S. E. Sprott[.] *[Toronto and Buffalo:] University Of Toronto Press, (1973)*. Oblong 8vo, 230pp., original orange cloth, front cover and spine lettered in black with a large decorative design in black on front cover, black endpapers.

287. **COMUS** [In] **THE TRANSCENDENTAL MASQUE**: An Essay on Milton's *Comus*. By Angus Fletcher. *Ithaca & London: Cornell University Press, 1971*.

First edition. 8vo, xiv+261pp., original brown cloth, spine lettered in gilt, printed publisher's wrappers. Included at the end, with half-title, are sixteen full-page color plates reproducing "Blake's Illustrations for *Comus* in Eight Scenes" from the "Two Series: From The Henry E. Huntington Library and Art Gallery, San Marino, California, And From The Museum of Fine Arts, Boston, Massachusetts."

288. **COMUS AND SOME SHORTER POEMS OF MILTON** Edited With An Introduction By E. M. W. Tillyard Litt.D., F.B.A. And With Notes By Phyllis B. Tillyard, M.A. Girton College, Cambridge[.] *Harrap[,] London[,] (1977)*. Small 8vo, 223pp., frontispiece illustration of *Comus*, "*Apollo And Daphne* after Tiepolo," illustrating lines 659–62, introduction, "Notes," and "Appendix" ("The Conception Of The Universe In The Seventeenth Century") at end, paperback, printed stiff paper wrappers with line drawing of Milton on front cover. The first edition thus was published in 1952; variously reprinted since then.

289. **MILTON COMUS AND OTHER POEMS** Edited By F. T. Prince. *[Oxford:] Oxford University Press, (1979)*. 8vo, xv+[1]+197pp., "Introduction," "Note On The Text," notes at bottom of page, "Commentary" on the poems at end, paperback, original printed stiff paper wrappers with large orange piece with black trim on front and back covers.

290. **COMUS**. BBC tape, 1980s. One cassette. A BBC production, recorded in the 1980s. In good condition. First performed at Ludlow Castle in 1633, the music was composed by Henry and William Lawes for the original production. In this adaptation by R. D. Smith, Ronald Pickup is Comus and Barbara Jefford the Lady. No. ECN100.

291. **MILTON'S COMUS: FAMILY PIECE**. By William B. Hunter, Jr. *Troy, N.Y.: The Whitston Publishing Company, Inc., 1983*. First edition. 8vo, half-title, portraits and a photograph of Ludlow Castle, original green cloth, front cover lettered in gilt, black label with gilt lettering and gilt trim on spine. A fine copy. Laid in: original advertisement brochure (four leaves, folded) and a copy of the review in *MQ*. With Hunter's perspective being that *C* was written to be staged, he concludes his study of *C* with a suggested text of the play and with stage directions as it may have been performed in 1634.

292. **COMUS** Adapted By Margaret Hodges From A Masque At Ludlow Castle By John Milton Illustrated By Trina Schart Hyman[.] *Holiday House • New York, (1996)*. First edition. Small, slim 4to, (32pp., unpaginated), half-title with illustration in color, frontispiece illustration in color blending into illustration in color on title page, illustrations in color throughout by Trina Schart Hyman, "Author's Note" at the end, original red cloth spine, speckled white paper over boards, front cover lettered in blind, spine lettered in gilt, purple endpapers, printed publisher's wrappers with illustration in color on front and back covers. Fine copy. Laid in: copies of quotations from several reviews.

293. THE MASQUE OF COMUS The Poem By John Milton With A Preface By Mark Van Doren & The Airs By Henry Lawes With A Preface By Hubert Foss[.] Illustrated With Water-Colors By Edmund Dulac[.] The Collector's Library of Famous Editions[.] Bound In Genuine Leather[.] *The Easton Press[,] Norwalk, Connecticut[,] (1997)*. First edition thus. Large 8vo, 57pp.+[1]+[13pp. of unpaginated musical notation], frontispiece illustration plate, half-title with decorative piece in blue—a decorative piece repeated in blue variously throughout, five additional illustration plates after watercolors by Edmund Dulac, title page in blue and black with laurel wreath in black around "Famous Editions" near the bottom, half-title before the poem with decorative piece in blue, half-title before "The Airs Of The Songs By Henry Lawes With His Version Of The Words" with decorative piece in blue, thirteen pages of musical notation, original dark green morocco, covers decorated in gilt with a design that is complementary to the illustrations by Dulac, spine lettered in gilt with three small gilt designs, raised bands within gilt rules, thick tan silk endpapers, light green silk ribbon marker, a.e.g. Fine copy, virtually mint. Laid in: "Notes From The Archives" for "The Collector's Library of Famous Editions[,] The Easton Press," a four-page fold-over discussing Milton, his life and poetry, Edmund Dulac and Dulac's illustrations for *Comus*, and the quality of this publication. A reprint of the edition first published for "The Members Of The Limited Editions Club" in 1954 (copy listed here), which included for the first time the illustrations by Edmund Dulac.

294. CONSIDERATIONS TOUCHING THE LIKELIEST MEANS TO REMOVE HIRELINGS OUT OF THE CHURCH. Wherein Is also discours'd of Tythes, Church-Fees, Church-Revenues; And Whether any Maintenance of Ministers can be settl'd by Law. The Author John Milton. *London: Reprinted in the Year 1723*. Tall 8vo, [iv]+48pp., half-title ("Milton On Church-Government"), new plain gray boards (half-title, title, and final leaf browned, half-title with small hole repaired). Very good copy, complete with half-title with near-contemporary signature (dated 1776) on verso. Rare. ESTC 1223M4 (reporting Not in Bodleian). Not in Coleridge; Not in Kohler.

295. CONSIDERATIONS TOUCHING THE LIKELIEST MEANS TO REMOVE HIRELINGS OUT OF THE CHURCH. Wherein Is also discours'd of Tythes, Church-Fees, Church-Revenues; And Whether any Maintenance of Ministers can be settled by Law. The Author John Milton. *The Third Edition. London Printed: Re-printed in the Year 1743*. 8vo, [iv]+50pp., disbound (slight waterstains and soiling, small mend to one blank edge, name on title page), pages uncut. Rare. Not in Coleridge; Not in Kohler.

296. CONSIDERATIONS TOUCHING THE LIKELIEST MEANS TO REMOVE HIRELINGS OUT OF THE CHURCH. Wherein Is Also Discoursed Of Tithes, Church-Fees, & Church-Revenues; And Whether Any Maintenance Of Ministers Can be Settled By Law. By John Milton, Author of "Paradise Lost," "Paradise Regained," &c. &c. *London: J. Cleave, 1, Shoe Lane, Fleet Street. W. Johnston, Printer, Lovell's Court, St. Paul's. (1834)*. 8vo, 47pp., stitched as issued (title a bit soiled and creased), entirely unopened. Good copy of a scarce edition. See 1770 Philadelphia edition listed here of *An Old Looking-Glass For The Laity And Clergy Of All Denominations . . . Being Considerations Touching The likeliest Means to remove Hirelings out of the Church of Christ*, the first work by Milton published in America. Not in Kohler.

297. COWPER'S MILTON, IN FOUR VOLUMES. [Quotation from Mansus] *Chichester: Printed by W. Mason, For J. Johnson, & Co. St. Paul's Church-Yard, London. 1810*. 4 volumes. First edition by William Cowper. 8vo, xxix+[1]+422pp.,+469pp.,432+[1]pp.,+399+[1]pp., frontispiece portrait engraved by A. Raimbach after Richard Smirke of Milton bust with an imprint of Cowper, found only in "certain copies" (Russell, p. 292), title page each volume, "Introductory Letter by Hayley To The Rev. Dr. Johnson, The Kinsman Of Cowper" (dated 1810), "Adam: A Sacred Drama, Translated From The Italian, Of Gio. Battista Andreini," volume 3, contemporary calf (rebacked), decorative gilt border trim on covers, spine lettered and numbered in gilt, raised bands. A nice set with the very rare frontispiece portrait. Rare. Russell, *William Cowper*, 291 (noting a frontispiece that occurs only "in certain copies," as in this one); Stevens 112; Wlliamson 202; Not in Kohler.

This is a reprint in four volumes of the 1794–97 Boydell edition of Milton's *PW* (see set below) edited by William Cowper and William Hayley with notes and additional material in the life by Hayley; this 1810 edition was supervised by Hayley, Cowper having died in 1800. Besides Milton's works, there also appear Cowper's translations of various of Milton's poems, and of Andreini's *Adamo*, one of Milton's source-books.

298. [COWPER'S MILTON] MILTON'S POETICAL WORKS, With Cowper's Translations, And Hayley's Life Of The Author. In Four Volumes. Contents [Of Each Volume Listed] *Chichester: Printed and sold for a Kinsman of Cowper, By W. Mason, Sold Also By T. Payne, Pall-Mall, London. 1811. 4 volumes.* Second edition by Cowper. 8vo, xxix+[1]+422pp.,+469pp.,+432+[1]pp.,+399+[1]pp., frontispiece portrait engraved by Raimbach after Richard Smirke of Milton bust with an imprint of Cowper, title page each volume, "Introductory Letter" by Hayley (dated 1810), "Adam: A Sacred Drama, Translated From The Italian, Of Gio. Battista Andreini," volume 3, contemporary diced calf (bit worn, especially at top and bottom of spines and at corners, joints cracked), covers ruled in gilt with finely tooled inner gilt border trim, spines lettered in gilt with decorations in blind and decorative gilt trim, inner dentelles tooled in gilt, marbled endpapers and edges. Rare. Wlliamson 202; Not in Kohler.

A reprint edition of the 1810 four-volume Cowper edition of Milton's *PW* (set preceding) edited by William Cowper and William Hayley; the 1810 edition was itself a reprint of the 1794–97 Boydell edition of Milton's *PW* (see set listed here) with notes and additional material in the life—it was supervised by Hayley, Cowper having died in 1800.

298A. (Cross-listing) **DE DOCTRINA CHRISTIANA** . . . 1825. See **A TREATISE ON CHRISTIAN DOCTRINE**, Compiled From The Holy Scriptures Alone; By John Milton. Translated From The Original By Charles R. Sumner . . . *Edinburgh. 1825*. First edition. Together with **JOANNIS MILTONI ANGLI DE DOCTRINA CHRISTIANA** . . . M.DCCC.XXV. First edition. Together, two volumes, the second volume being the Latin text. First edition of both the Latin original and the English translation of *De Doctrina*. Large 4to, contemporary calf. See main listing under *A Treatise On Christian Doctrine*, 1825. See also *A TREATISE ON CHRISTIAN DOCTRINE* for all editions of "De Doctrina Christiana" and of "On Christian Doctrine."

A Defence of the People of England

John Milton's *Pro Populo Anglicano Defensio*, 1651 (copies listed later), of which the following are translations, stands as the official reply of Parliament to the *Defensio Regia* of the continental scholar Salmasius (listed with Seventeenth-century Miltoniana), which was written in response to Milton's *Eikonoklastes* published in 1649 (also listed here) and in defence of the King, and which was having a serious effect upon public opinion on the continent. Milton relished the opportunity to confront such an eminent figure as Salmasius, whom he considered a worthy opponent, and he always thought this was his most important prose work. With the Restoration in 1660, *Pro Populo* and *Eikonoklastes* were ordered to be burnt by the common hangman.

299. **A DEFENCE OF THE PEOPLE OF ENGLAND**, By John Milton: In Answer to Salmasius's Defence of the King. *[Amsterdam:] Printed in the Year 1692*. First edition in English, first issue, of *Pro Populo Anglicano Defensio*. 8vo, [iv]+xxii+[1]+246+[1]pp., "To The English Reader," "The Author's Preface," "An Advertisement To The Reader" at the end, contemporary sheep (some age-browning along edges, spine defective, front joint broken and rehinged from inside). Complete with two initial blanks, blank following "The Author's Preface," and final advertisement leaf (noting it "very well worth Translating" this work "for the benefit of *English* Readers." The former W. A. White copy with his signature in pencil on fly-leaf. While Pforzheimer thought that the translator may have been Dugard, the publisher of the London first edition of *Pro Populo* (1651), Masson and Parker (and others since) believe the translation was made by Joseph Washington of the Middle Temple. John Shawcross suggests further that this edition was "Apparently published in London, perhaps by Nathaniel Rolls." A second issue (very rare) was printed in 1695 (following copy). Madan 15; Wing M2104; Grolier, *Wither to Prior*, 590; Pforzheimer 726; Shawcross, 1984, 359; Coleridge 55a; Kohler 503.

300. **A DEFENCE OF THE PEOPLE OF ENGLAND**. By John Milton. In Answer to Salmasius's Defence of the King. *Printed in the Year 1695*. First edition in English, second issue, of *Pro Populo Anglicano Defensio*, which first appeared in 1651 (several copies listed here). 8vo, [iv]+xxii+[1]+246+[1]pp., with blank following "The Author's Preface" and final advertisement leaf, contemporary speckled sheep (a bit worn, covers detached), red morocco label with gilt lettering on spine, raised bands. Internally fine, with blank following "The Author's Preface" and final advertisement leaf. "First edition in English of the important and highly controversial *Pro Populo Anglicano*, and the very rare second issue, with a 1695 cancel title page" (Quaritch, #73, Cat. 1091, 1988). While the first issue in 1692 (preceding copy) is considered a relatively common book, this 1695 reissue is "excessively rare" (Parker, locating ten copies, and placing the title jointly seventy-sixth among eighty-seven categories of rarity, pp. 1192, 1212). This copy has not been rehinged, "in its original binding, so that the cancellation itself is easily visible" (Quaritch). New Wing M2104 (locating seven copies, including a Copy in the British Library); Not in Coleridge (although referred to in Coleridge 55b); Shawcross, 1984, 372; Not in Kohler

300A. (Cross-listing) **A DEFENCE OF THE PEOPLE OF ENGLAND** [In] **THE RIGHTS OF NATIONS TO DEPOSE THEIR KINGS** . . . And A New And Abridged Translation of His Great Work, Called A Defence Of The People Of England . . . To Which Is Added Areopagitica . . . With Notes, An Original Memoir, And A Brief Review Of Milton's Prose Works. Second edition. By William Greatheed Lewis. *London: T. Dolby, n.d. [ca. 1821].* Second edition thus. Frontispiece portrait by P. Roberts dated 1821. Not in Kohler. See main listing under *Tenure of Kings*, ca. 1821.

301. [DEFENSIO SECUNDA] **JOANNIS MILTONI DEFENSIO SECUNDA PRO POPULO ANGLICANO**: Contra infamem Libellum anonymum, cujus Titulus, Regii sanguinis clamor adversus parricidas Anglicanos. Accessit Alexandri Morri Ecclesiastae, Sacrarumque litterarum Professoris Fides Publica, Contra calumnias Ioannis Miltoni Scurrae. *Hagae-Comitvm, Ex Typographia Adriani Vlacq. M.DC.LIV.* Bound with three other works by Milton: *Pro Populo*, 1654; *Ratio Constitutae*, 1654; and *Literae Pseudo-Senatus Anglicani*, 1676; and two other works: *Regii Sanguinis Clamor*, 1652, by Peter DuMolin, and *Fides Publica*, 1654, by Alexander More. 2 volumes. Comprising six works altogether, four by Milton. 12mo, [xv]+128pp., title page with printer's device, old half green morocco, marbled paper over boards (bit worn), spines lettered in gilt. Shawcross, 1984, 188; Coleridge 58c (admirably untangling the bibliographical complexities of the various printings and editions of Milton's *Defensio Secunda*); Not in Kohler.

A very good collection of historically related pamphlets with notes in an early hand on front pastedown of each volume. Milton's *Defensio Secunda*, one of Milton's more significant prose writings and a highly personal statement, is his reply to DuMolin's pamphlet, present here, which Milton thought was by Alexander More. Milton's response (the third variant printing here and the first to contain the addition of Alexander More's work) contains "fourteen pages of straight-forward autobiography . . . a personal record of striking significance" (Parker, pp. 435, 437), in which he is moved to write of himself, his life, his acceptance of his recent blindness, and his evaluation of the Commonwealth government of Oliver Cromwell. Each work in the collection is listed separately with appropriate commentary on that work. *Pro Populo, Ratio Constitutae,* and *Literae Pseudo-Senatus Anglicani* are listed alphabetically among Milton's works here; *Regii Sanguinis Clamor* by Peter DuMolin and *Fides Publica* by Alexander More are listed under their author's name with Seventeenth-century Miltoniana. *Fides Publica* is More's defense of himself against Milton's attack on him in *Defensio Secunda* and called for on Milton's title page, hence technically issued with Milton's work. Milton, like others, thought that More was also the author of *Regii Sanguinis Clamor Ad Coelum*, also present here, and written by Peter DuMolin. Alexander More, a French Presbyterian minister of Scottish descent, was a professor at Middleburg, and was believed to be the author of *Regii Sanguinis Clamor*, a venomous royalist pamphlet published in March 1652. In fact, Peter DuMolin was the author, but as he lived in England and was close to Milton, this was kept secret. Milton replied with his *Defensio Secunda*, which included a fierce attack on More's character, prompting the reply (*Fides Publica*) from More. More's defense of himself was in turn attacked by Milton in his *Pro Se Defensio*, which included an appendix attacking the *Supplementum*.

302. [DIVORCE] **THE DOCTRINE AND DISCIPLINE OF DIVORCE**; Restor'd to the good of both Sexes, From the Bondage of Canon Law, and other mistakes, to the true meaning of Scripture in the Law and Gospel compar'd. Wherein also are set down the bad consequences of abolishing or condemning of Sin, that which the Law of God allows, and Christ abolisht not. Now the second time Revis'd, and much Augmented, In Two Books: To the Parliament of England, with the Assembly. The Author J. M. [Quotation from Matth. 13.52] [Quotation from Prov. 18.13] *London: Imprinted In the Year 1645.* Second ("Unauthorized") edition. 4to, [vi]+78pp. Milton's first pamphlet on divorce, *The Doctrine and Discipline of Divorce*, was published in August 1643. It was written to further the general cause of liberty, as he considered that no one could enjoy real and substantial liberty in his work and worship if he were indissolubly tied to a wife who would not or could not be to him the helpmate intended by God. His interest in the subject was made more personal by the unsatisfactory nature of his marriage to Mary Powell, whom he married in 1642, when he was age thirty-three; she was seventeen and soon deserted him and returned to her parents. Milton was inspired by this catastrophe to develop arguments in favor of divorce on the grounds of incompatibility. Such a proposition was shocking to his contemporaries. He subsequently collected material for two further treatises on divorce, *Colasterion* and *Tetrachordon*, both published in March 1645. Wing is unclear on three distinct 1645 editions of *The Doctrine and Discipline of Divorce*; Parker knew there were three but admitted to only two. Wing M2110, M2111, or unrecorded; Parker's second "unauthorized" edition; Shawcross, 1974, p. 297; Coleridge 17; Not in Kohler.

[bound with]

303. TETRACHORDON, Expositions Upon The foure chiefe places in Scripture which treat of Mariage, or nullities in Mariage. On Gen.I.27.28. compar'd and explain'd by Gen.2.18.23.24. Deut.24.1.2. Matth.5.31.32. with Matth.19. from the 3d.v. to the 11th. I Cor.7. from the 10th to the 16th. Wherin the Doctrine and Discipline of Divorce, as was lately publish'd, is confirm'd by explanation of Scripture, by testimony of ancient Fathers, of civill lawes in the Primitive Church, of famousest Reformed Divines, And lastly, by an intended Act of the Parlament and Church of England in the last yeare of Edward the sixth. By the former Author J. M. [Quotation in Greek from Euripides] *London: Printed in the yeare 1645*. First edition. 4to, [vi]+98pp. Published shortly after his *Areopagitica*, this work extends far beyond its importance as Milton's final divorce tract, and actually extends, expands, and elaborates the various points raised in *Areopagitica*. The several philosophical truths made evident in *Areopagitica* are used in *Tetrachordon*, but with more clarification. In *Tetrachordon*, too, Milton's personal bitterness with respect to divorce appears to have diminished, but he is still an impassioned apostle of human liberty arguing: "The law is to tender the liberty and human dignity of them that live under the law." Later Milton was to justify his divorce tracts in a much-discussed passage in *Defensio Secunda* (1652), linking them as a matter of lofty principle with *Of Education* and *Areopagitica*: "Since . . . there are in all three varieties of liberty without which civilized life is scarcely possible, namely ecclesiastical liberty, domestic or personal liberty, and civil liberty, and since I had already written about the first, and while I saw that the magistrates were vigorously attending to the third, I took as my province the remaining one. . . . This too seemed to be concerned with three problems: the nature of marriage itself, the education of the children, and finally the existence of freedom to express oneself" (trans. Helen North). Wing M2184; Parker, p. 893; Coleridge 67; Shawcross, 1984, 72; Not in Kohler.

The two 4to volumes bound together, contemporary calf (newly rebacked period style, tiny pinhole worming to extreme lower blank gutter of last half of first title and first half of last title, a few small short tears to blank edge or two), spine lettered in gilt, raised bands. Large copies of both editions.

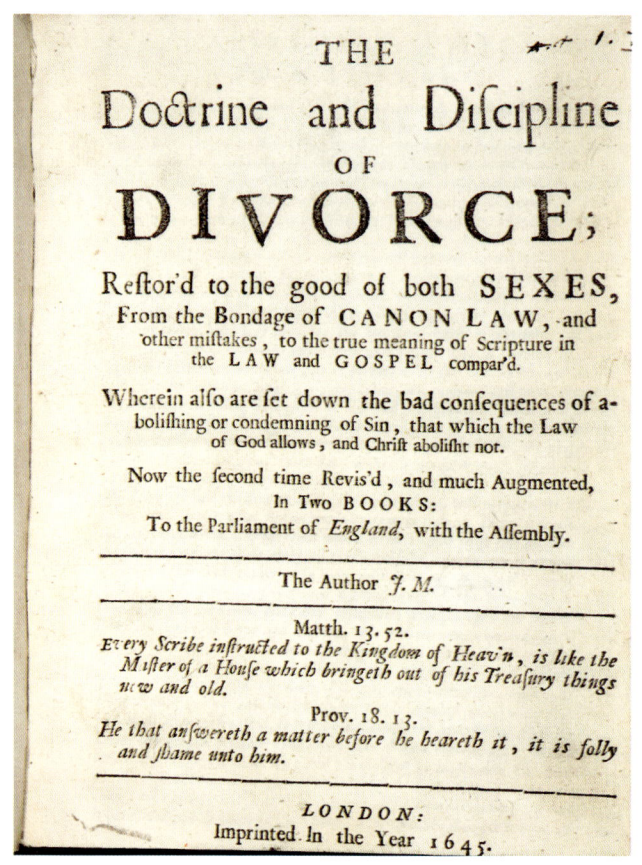

The Doctrine and Discipline Of Divorce. London, 1645. See # 302.

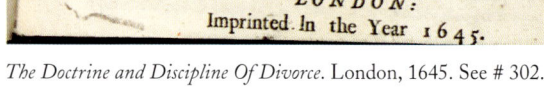

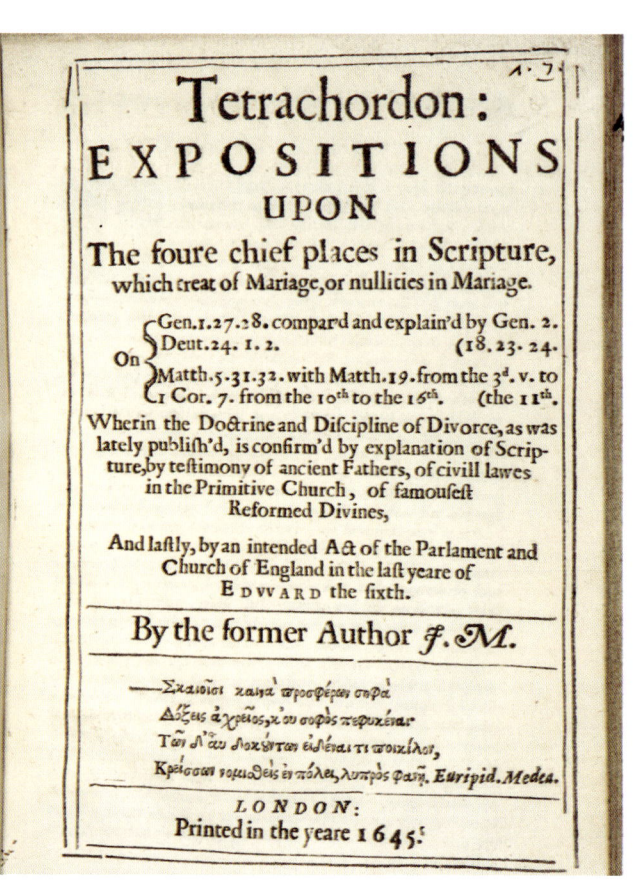

Tetrachordon, 1645. See #303.

304. MILTON'S DRAMATIC POEMS edited by Geoffrey & Margaret Bullough[.] *University of London[:] The Athlone Press[,] 1958.* First edition thus. 8vo, 224pp., half-title, lengthy introduction, facsimile reproduction of first edition title page of *Comus* and of *Samson Agonistes*, original cream-colored cloth (some notations and markings in pencil), blue lettering on front cover and spine with small device of the press in blue at bottom of spine. Nice copy.

305. MILTON'S DRAMATIC POEMS edited by Geoffrey & Margaret Bullough[.] *University of London[:] The Athlone Press[,] 1960.* Second edition thus. 8vo, 224pp., half-title, lengthy introduction, facsimile reproduction of first edition title page of *Comus* and of *Samson Agonistes*, original light green boards (a bit rubbed), white-and-black lettering on front cover and spine with small device of the press in black at bottom of spine. Nice copy.

306. MILTON'S EARLIER POEMS Including The Translations by William Cowper of those written in Latin and Italian. Cassell's National Library. *Cassell & Company, Limited: London, Paris, New York & Melbourne. 1886.* 16mo, 192pp., introduction by H[enry] M[orley], original white cloth (a bit rubbed, half-title pasted against front pastedown with printed advertisements showing through), front cover elaborately decorated and lettered in black, spine lettered in black, contemporary floral paper pasted over back cover (with a partial piece torn away at the center). A decent copy with contemporary inscription (dated 1887) on front pastedown and a contemporary floral Christmas card cut to fit pasted against the back pastedown with prize inscription (dated 1887). A possible second edition thus was published in 1892 (also listed here). Not in Kohler.

307. MILTON'S EARLIER POEMS Including The Translations by William Cowper of those written in Latin and Italian. Cassell's National Library. *Cassell & Company, Limited: London, Paris, & Melbourne. 1892.* 16mo, 190+4pp., half-title with "A Selection Of The Most Popular Volumes In Cassell's National Library" on verso, original blue cloth (a bit rubbed, slight waterstaining at the top corners and along front edge), front cover lettered in blind, spine lettered in gilt, small central emblem of "Cassell Standard Library" in blind on back cover. Good copy. Four pages of advertisements bound in at end. Uncommon. Not in Kohler.

308. MILTON EARLY POEMS[.] *[London: Vale Press, (1896).]* First edition thus. Large 8vo, ciiipp.+colophon leaf, frontispiece illustration (serving as title page), first appearance of decorated initial letters and decorations "designed and cut on the wood by Charles Ricketts under whose supervision the book has been printed by the Ballantyne Press [for the Vale Press]" (colophon), original cream linen cloth (spine a little faded), top edge rough cut, others untrimmed, bookplate of Leonard Schlosser. Nice. "This edition is limited to three hundred and ten copies of which three hundred are for sale" (Colophon). This was the second publication of the Vale Press. "Seen through the press by Charles Sturt" (Colophon). Stevens 295; Ransom, *Private Presses*, p. 1; Bland, p. 362; Kohler 231.

309. EARLY POEMS OF JOHN MILTON[.] Selected And Edited By Mercy A. Brann[,] English Department[,] Hartford Public High School[.] Illustrated By Isabel Bacheler[,] Art Department[,] Hartford Public High School[.] *New York[:] Henry Holt And Company[,] (1929).* First edition thus. 8vo, xi+235pp., half-title, frontispiece reproduction plate of the Onslow portrait of Milton at age twenty-one, preface (dated "August, 1928"), included in the biographical introductory remarks are a reproduction plate of the Janssen portrait of Milton at age ten and biographically related illustrations by Isabel Bacheler of "The Gate Of Christ's College," "King's College Chapel," "Milton's Rooms At Christ's College," "Horton Church," and "Milton's Cottage At Chalfont St. Giles," plus the first appearance of seventeen additional illustrations by Isabel Bacheler of the poems, decorative headpiece before each poem incorporating the title of that poem, notes and two appendices at end, original red cloth, front cover and spine lettered in gilt (gilt on spine a bit faded), decorated endpapers. Nice copy. Presentation copy from the artist with presentation inscription by Isabel Bacheler on title page.

The collection also has copies of the 1934 second, the 1935 third, and the 1940 fourth editions.

Eikonoklasthes

Being employed by the Council of State, Milton was given the task of refuting *Eikon Basilike*, or *King's Book*, allegedly written by the martyred Charles I (see copies with Seventeenth-century Miltoniana). This is Milton's first piece of official propaganda writing for the Commonwealth government. It brought a number of Royalist attacks on him, and because of this prose tract, Milton almost lost his head eleven years later at the Restoration. The book, together with his *Pro Populo Anglicano Defensio* (copy listed later), was ordered by the House of Commons on June 16, 1660, to be burnt by the common hangman.

310. EIKONOKLASTHES In Answer To a Book Intitl'd *EIKON BASILIKE*, The Portrature of his Sacred Majesty in his Solitudes and Sufferings. The Author I. M. [Quotation from Prov. 28. 1, 16, 17] [Quotation from Salust.

Conjurat. Catilin] *Published by Authority. London, Printed by Matthew Simmons, next dore to the gilded Lyon in Aldersgate street. 1649*. First edition. 4to, [10]+242pp., title page in red and black, preface, modern crushed brown morocco (large marginal waterstain to the first few leaves without affecting text, rebacked preserving original spine, new endpapers, lacking A1 as is quite usual), spine lettered in gilt, raised bands, broad inner dentelles richly tooled in gilt, outer dentelles ruled in gilt, a.e.g. Except for the slight waterstaining, a very good copy. Wing M2112; Pforzheimer 709; Grolier, *Wither to Prior*, 577; Shawcross, 1984, 78; Coleridge 18; Kohler 498.

311. EIKONOKLASTHES In Answer To a Book Intitl'd *EIKON BASILIKE*, The Portrature of his Sacred Majesty in his Solitudes and Sufferings. The Author I. M. [Quotation from Prov. 28. 1, 16, 17] [Quotation from Salust. Conjurat. Catilin] Publish'd now the second time, and much enlarg'd. London, *Printed by T.N. and are to be sold by Tho. Brewster and G. Moule at the three Bibles in Pauls Church-Yard near the West-end, 1650*. Second, revised edition. 4to, [12]+230pp., title page in red and black (with Milton's name filled out in ink in a neat early hand), preface, contemporary calf (spine worn and chipped at ends, joints broken and repaired, somewhat embrowned as usual, foxing, waterstains), with early signature of Joseph Bromehead, and later that of W. A. White, the noted collector, who observes in pencil on fly-leaf: "a decidely rare book Feb. 15, 1912." This edition, revised by Milton, carries manuscript corrections in some copies; this copy has those manuscript corrections as well as an anti-Milton note on the verso of the title, and a few further comments in that same hand in the text. "Very rare. This is the first copy we have catalogued for sale" (G. W. Stuart, Jr., Ravenstree, Cat. 163, #16, 1989). New Wing M2113; Parker 22; Shawcross, 1984, 87; Not in Coleridge; Not in Kohler.

312. EIKONOKLASTHES In Answer To a Book Intitul'd *EIKON BASILIKE*, The Portrature of his Sacred Majesty King Charles the First in his Solitudes and Sufferings. By John Milton. [Quotation from Prov. 28. 1, 16, 17] [Quotation from Salust. Conjurat. Catilin] *Amsterdam [i.e., London], Printed in the Year, 1690*. Third edition. 8vo, [12]+207+[1]pp., with the rare "Advertisement" leaf before title page, "Contents" as the last leaf, later calf (rebacked, age-browning throughout), new red morocco labels with gilt lettering and gilt rules. A good copy with bookplate of H. G. Fletcher, an earlier bookplate, and early signature. Laid in: a note by Michael Papantonio of Seven Gables bookshop from whom I obtained the copy in 1977 regarding the rarity of the "Advertisement" leaf, or "Anglesey Memorandum" as Grolier calls it, on verso of blank A1.

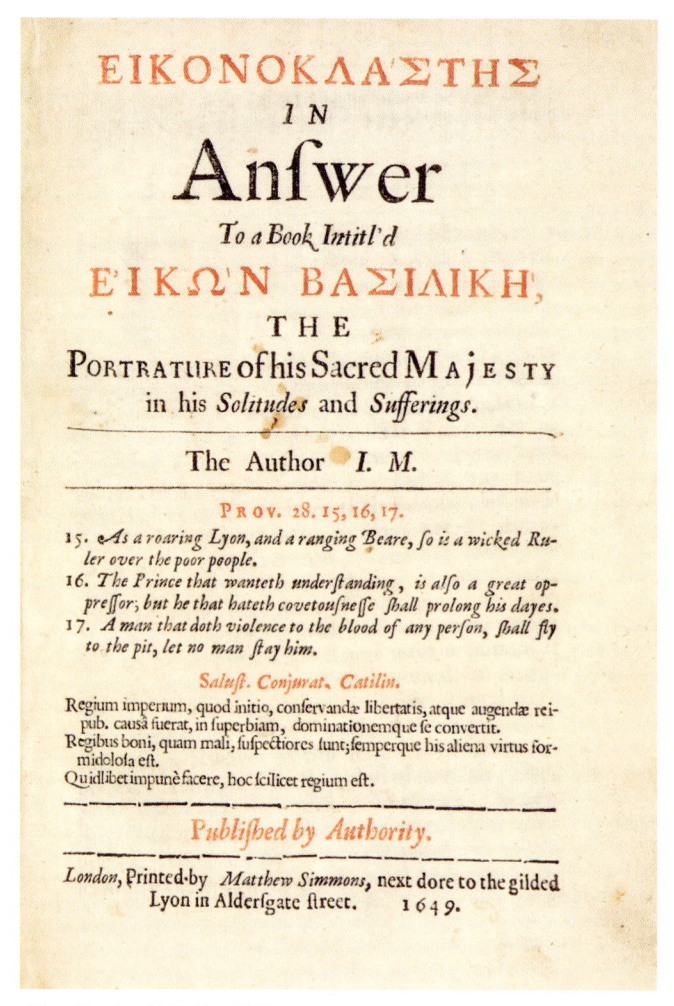

Eikonoklasthes, 1649. See #310.

The "Advertisement," separately printed by Anglesey, is critical to the entire authorship controversy of the *Eikon Basilike*, and it is the single cause of the eruption of the controversy. This third edition reprints the text of the first edition of 1649 (also listed here). There were two issues of a second edition in 1650 (see second issue preceding). The next separate edition of this book, with the exception of the Baron edition in 1756 (see copy following), was not issued until 1770. Rare. Wing M2115; Grolier, *Wither to Prior*, 579; Shawcross, 1984, 350; Coleridge 19; Kohler 499 (lacking "Anglesey Memorandum").

313. EIKONOKLASTHES. In Answer to a Book Intitled, Eikon Basilike, The Portrature of his Sacred Majesty in his Solitudes and Sufferings. By John Milton. Now first published from the Author's Second Edition, Printed in 1650. With Many Enlargements: By Richard Baron. With A Preface shewing the transcendent Excellency of Milton's Prose Works. To which is added An Original Letter to Milton, never before published. [Quotation from Dr. Akinside] *London: Printed for A. Millar, in the Strand.*

MDCCLVI. First edition by Richard Baron. 4to, vii+96pp., old half calf (rebacked in brown buckram, some age-browning), marbled paper over boards. A good copy with early dated signature on title page and with nineteenth-century bookplate of Sir Robert Walpole and another bookplate on front pastedown. Bound in: MS. transcript (possibly in an eighteenth-century hand) of "The Prayer of King Charles," from the 1686 *Works*. Coleridge 20; Shawcross, 1972, 424; Shawcross, 1974, p. 317; Kohler 500.

Friend of Thomas Hollis and follower of John Toland, Baron was a free-thinking republican who has been described as "an extremist as regards both religious & political liberty"; in 1753 he published a revised and expanded edition of Thomas Birch's 1738 collected edition of Milton's prose works (also listed here). The "Original Letter" he prints here is from John Wall, written in 1659 as the Commonwealth crumbled, on Liberty ("but it must be God's work, not Man's").

314. ENGLISH CLASSICS ABRIDGED; BEING SELECT WORKS OF ADDISON, POPE, AND MILTON, Adapted to the Perusal of Youth, of both Sexes At School. To Which Are Prefixed Observations on the Several Authors, Addressed To Parents and Preceptors. By J. Walker, Author of Elements of Elocution, Rhetorical Grammar, &c. [Latin quotation from Hor.] *London, Printed for G. G. J. and J. Robinson, Pater-noster Row. M DCC LXXXVI.* First edition. 8vo, xv+[1]+367pp., frontispiece portrait of John Walker, dedication, observations, contents, contemporary calf (a bit worn, minor age spots, front joint cracked, lacking label on spine), gilt rule on covers and at top and bottom of spine, raised bands with decorative gilt trim, small decorative pieces in bind within the panels, inner and outer dentelles ruled in gilt, marbled endpapers and edges, with the binder's ticket of the noted French émigré binder, the Comte de Caumont. A nice copy. Milton occupies the last third of the book, from pages 222 to 367; the selection is from *PL* with prose narrative summaries in between poetic selections from Milton's epic. For a discussion of the role of the anthology in selectively passing along the writings of great writers to new generations of readers, from one culture to another, see *The Poetical Miscellany* in "Selected Anthologies." John Shawcross has kindly indicated to me, "This [edition] is otherwise known only from its 1807 edition, 'The Second edition,' as owned by the British Library." See further comments by John Shawcross about the significance of this edition in *Milton Quarterly* 41, no. 1 (2007): 73. Very rare. Not in Coleridge; Not in Kohler.

English Minor Poems

315. ENGLISH MINOR POEMS[,] PARADISE LOST[,] SAMSON AGONISTES[,] AREOPAGITICA[.] By John Milton[.] *Encyclopaedia Britannica, Inc.[,] Chicago • London • Toronto[,] (1952).* First edition thus. Tall 8vo, vii+[3]+412pp., half-title, original light olive green cloth, spine decorated in gilt with gilt lettering against a dark maroon background with dark maroon trim at top and bottom edges, decorated endpapers with advertisements for the series "Great Books Of The Western World" (of which this is one). Nice.

316. Variant of Preceding, original light brown buckram, olive green labels on spine lettered and ruled in gilt with gilt rules at top and bottom of spine, decorated endpapers with advertisements for the series "Great Books Of The Western World." Nice copy in a variant publisher's binding.

317. ENGLISH MINOR POEMS[,] PARADISE LOST[,] SAMSON AGONISTES[,] AREOPAGITICA With Twenty-Seven Water-Color Drawings By William Blake[.] A Limited Edition[.] *The Franklin Library[,] Franklin Center, Pennsylvania[,] 1978.* 8vo, XXVII plates+504pp., half-title ("John Milton Works") with small decorative piece in blue, "Originally published by Encyclopaedia Britannica, in collaboration with The University of Chicago, under the direction of Doctor Robert Maynard Hutchins and Doctor Mortimer J. Adler" on verso of title page, half-title with small decorative piece in blue for "The water-color drawings of William Blake illustrating the works of John Milton From the collection of The Henry E. Huntington Library," illustration plates in color for *NO* (drawn ca. 1808), *C* (drawn ca. 1801), and *PL* (drawn ca. 1807), half-title with small decorative piece in blue for each section: *EMP*, *PL*, *SA*, and *A*, crushed brown morocco over thick boards, covers decorated with gilt rules and richly tooled wide gilt borders, spine equally richly decorated in gilt within the panels with gilt lettering ("Milton" in the top panel, "The Great Books" at the top, and "The Franklin Library" at the bottom), raised bands, gold silk endpapers, a.e.g., thick gold silk ribbon marker. A handsomely printed edition with fine reproductions of the water-color drawings by William Blake, in a splendid morocco binding. Printed in a limited edition, "This volume is published by the Franklin Library exclusively for subscribers to The 25th Anniversary Limited Edition of The Great Books Of The Western World" (blank before title page).

318. ENGLISH MINOR POEMS[,] PARADISE LOST[,] SAMSON AGONISTES[,] AREOPAGITICA[.] By John Milton[.] *William Benton, Publisher[.]*

Encyclopaedia Britannica, Inc.[,] Chicago • London • Toronto • Geneva • Sydney • Tokyo • Manila[,] (1980). Tall 8vo, vii+[1]+412pp., half-title, "Biographical Note," original black buckram spine, light olive green cloth, spine lettered in gilt against a tan background with gilt rules and small gilt seal, decorated endpapers with advertisements for the series "Great Books Of The Western World" (of which this is one). Nice copy. First edition thus published in 1952 (copy listed here).

English Poems

319. ENGLISH POEMS BY JOHN MILTON Edited With Life, Introduction, And Selected Notes By R. C. Browne, M.A. Associate Of King's College, London[.] *Volume I. Clarendon Press Series[.] Oxford[:] At The Clarendon Press[,] M DCCC LXX [All rights reserved].* Volume 1 Only (of 2 volumes). 8vo, lxxix+[1]+384pp., half-title, original reddish-brown pebble cloth (a little worn), "Clarendon Press Series" with emblem of the press stamped in blind at the center of each cover, spine lettered in gilt. This volume is inscribed in a neat hand in pencil to "J. H. Gilmore, From The Publishers 1870" on the fly-leaf, with printed book label at the top of front pastedown: "J. H. Gilmore. Working Library. Nov. 1876 [date written by hand], Number 306 [number written by hand], Value .75 [value written by hand]." Some marginal notations occur occasionally in pencil in a neat hand, especially in Book I. Stevens 190, citing 1866 edition, with note: "Life, Introduction, and notes that merited the many reprintings of this edition. The text is not important"; Not in Kohler.

320. ENGLISH POEMS BY JOHN MILTON Edited With Life, Introduction, And Selected Notes By R. C. Browne, M.A.[,] Associate Of King's College, London[.] Fourth Edition / New Edition, Revised[.] *Volume I. / Volume II. Clarendon Press Series[.] Oxford[:] At The Clarendon Press[,] M DCCC LXXVI And M DCCC LXXV [All rights reserved].* 2 volumes. Fourth edition thus, volume 1, and possibly third edition thus, volume 2. 8vo, lxxix+[1]+384pp.,+343+[1]pp., half-title each volume, separate title page each volume, original reddish-brown pebble cloth (a bit rubbed), spines lettered in gilt. Nice set with contemporary ownership signature (dated 1878) written in a neat hand in ink on fly-leaf of volume 1. Browne's edition was very popular and often revised and reprinted, and sets are frequently found together from different years; they were perhaps sold that way initially as well. Uncommon. Not in Kohler.

321. ENGLISH POEMS BY JOHN MILTON Edited With Life, Introduction, And Selected Notes By R. C. Browne, M.A.[,] Associate Of King's College, London[.] *Fourth Edition / New Edition, Revised[.] Volume I. / Volume II. Clarendon Press Series[.] Oxford[:] At The Clarendon Press[,] M DCCC LXXVIII And M DCCC LXXVII [All rights reserved].* 2 volumes. Fourth edition thus, volume 1, and third edition thus, revised, volume 2. 8vo, lxxix+[1]+384+16pp.,+343+[1]+16pp., half-title each volume, separate title page each volume, original maroon cloth (a little worn, a few underlinings in pencil), "Clarendon Press Series" with emblem of the press stamped in blind at center of each cover, spines lettered in gilt, early signature in ink on fly-leaf of each volume. Sixteen pages of advertisements bound in at end. Uncommon. Not in Kohler.

In the collection are also sets published at the Clarendon Press, 1880, fourth edition thus, revised; at the Clarendon Press, 1891; at the Clarendon Press, 1894 and 1892, revised edition; at the Clarendon Press, 1897 and 1894; and at the Clarendon Press, 1906 and 1902, revised edition.

322. ENGLISH POEMS BY JOHN MILTON Edited With Life, Introduction, And Selected Notes By R. C. Browne, M.A.[,] Associate Of King's College, London[.] New Edition[.] With The Etymological Notes Revised By Henry Bradley, M.A. *Oxford[:] At The Clarendon Press[,] (1923) & MDCCCII. 2 volumes, volume 2 dated MDCCCII.* Revised edition. 8vo, lxxix+384pp.,+343pp., half-title each volume, separate title page each volume, original brown cloth (used), with the bookplate and signature of Milton scholar Maurice Kelley along with numerous marginal notes throughout by Kelley—formerly his teaching copy. The first edition thus by Browne was published in 1866; volume 2 is the revised edition by Bradley. Gift from Maurice Kelley when he retired from teaching at Princeton in 1972.

323. THE ENGLISH POEMS OF JOHN MILTON From The Edition Of The Very Rev. H. C. Beeching, D.D. Dean of Norwich[.] *Henry Frowde[:] Oxford University Press[,] London, Edinburgh, Glasgow[,] New York[,] Toronto[,] Melbourne & Bombay[,] 1913.* First edition thus. 16mo, vii+488+8pp., half-title ("The World's Classics CLXXXII"), original light gray cloth (a bit age-darkened along edges and spine), spine decorated and lettered in gilt (faded). Eight pages of advertisements for "The World's Classics" (including Milton) bound in at the end. "Modernizes use of capitals and punctuation" (Stevens). Rather uncommon. Stevens 257; Not in Kohler.

"The World's Classics" edition became a very popular edition and was variously reprinted throughout the first half of the twentieth century: a second edition thus with eight pages of advertisements for "The World's Classics" bound in at the end, was published in 1921; a third, like the second, with eight pages of advertisements for "The World's Classics" bound in at the end, was published in 1923; a fourth in 1926; a fifth with sixteen pages of advertisements (with title page) for "The World's Classics" bound in at the end, in 1929; a sixth with sixteen pages of advertisements bound in at the end, in 1932; a seventh with sixteen pages of advertisements (with title page) for "The World's Classics" bound in at the end, in 1936. A copy of each edition is in the collection.

324. THE ENGLISH POEMS OF JOHN MILTON From The Edition Of H. C. Beeching Together With A Reader's Guide To Milton Compiled By Walter Skeat, M.A. *Oxford University Press[,] London: Humphrey Milford[,] (1940).* First Edition With A Reader's Guide To Milton Compiled By Walter Skeat. 16mo, vii+545+[1]+blank+16pp., half-title, seventy-six-page "Reader's Guide to Milton" with half-title at end, original blue cloth, covers ruled in blind relief with central emblem in blind relief on front cover, spine lettered in gilt, printed light blue publisher's wrappers (a bit frayed along edges) in a protective plastic cover, lettered in black and white on front cover with central seal in white and with white rules running from front to back cover, portrait of Milton and a brief biography on back flap. Sixteen pages of "A List Of The World's Classics Oxford University Press" bound in at the end with separate half-title.

325. THE ENGLISH POEMS OF JOHN MILTON From the edition of H. C. Beeching Together with an Introduction by Charles Williams And A Reader's Guide to Milton compiled by Walter Skeat, M. A., F. S. A. [Oxford:] Geoffrey Cumberlege *Oxford University Press[,] London[,] New York[,] Toronto[,] (1951).* 16mo, xx+543+[1]pp., half-title, original blue cloth, spine lettered in gilt, printed publisher's wrappers (frayed at bottom edge). "In 1940 a new edition was published with an introduction by Charles Williams and 'A Reader's Guide to Milton', compiled by Walter Skeat; reprinted in 1942, entirely reset in 1946, and reprinted in 1948 and 1951" (verso title page)—see preceding copy with "A Reader's Guide to Milton" by Walter Skeat but without an introduction by Charles Williams.

326. [ENGLISH POEMS] JOHN MILTON[:] ENGLISH POEMS[,] COMUS[.] *A Scolar Press Facsimile. The Scolar Press Limited[,] Menston, England[,] 1968.* First edition thus. 8vo, [8]+120+[3]pp., facsimile reproduction of 1645 *Poems* and 1645 *A Mask*, appendix reproducing a page from a copy in the British Museum, original printed green paper wrappers. Fine copy, near mint.

327. [EPISTOLARUM FAMILIARIUM LIBER UNUS] JOANNIS MILTONII ANGLI, EPISTOLARUM FAMILIARIUM LIBER UNUS: Quibus Accesserunt, Ejusdem, jam olim in Collegio Adolescentis, Prolusiones Quaedam Oratoriae. *Londini, Impensis Brabazoni Aylmeri sub Signo Trium Columbarum Via vulgo Cornhill dicta, An. Dom. 1674.* First edition. 8vo, 155+[3]pp., contemporary calf (newly rebacked period style), with early note on front blank and early armorial bookplate on front pastedown. A fine copy, complete with errata, ads, and first and last leaves blank and genuine. This rare work contains the first appearance in print of Milton's private letters as well as his earliest writing, the *Cambridge Prolusions*, written when he was a student. Wing M2117; Parker 56; Shawcross, 1974, pp. 345–47; Coleridge 23; Kohler 506.

328. THE ENGLISH SONNETS OF JOHN MILTON[.] Wood Engravings by Rachel Russell. *Chelsea[:] The Swan Press[,] MCMXXVI.* Slim 4to, [i]+XIX sonnets, one each to a page, +colophon page, half-title, wood-engraved border with decorative vignettes on title page by Rachel Russell, decorative vignette tailpieces also by Rachel Russell, one on each page at the end of the sonnet on that page, the repetitive vignettes being decorations not illustrations, printed in Baskerville type on Head's handmade paper, original quarter white cloth (free endpapers a bit browned), patterned paper over boards, printed paper label on spine, fore- and bottom edges untrimmed. A very nice copy. No. 80 of an edition limited to 100 copies.

329. AN EPITAPH ON THE ADMIRABLE DRAMATICKE POET, W. SHAKESPEARE. *[London, 1632].* Folio leaf, leaf A5 from the 1632 second folio of Shakespeare's works (some slight embrowning in the margins). First appearance in print of Milton's first poem. Nice copy, measuring 12 ½" × 8 ⅜", preserved in a handsome modern full red morocco binding by Sangorski and Sutcliff in a red buckram slipcase. Rare. Coleridge 75; Not in Kohler.

329A. (Cross-listing) **[EPITAPHIUM DAMONIS] [In] THE LYCIDAS AND EPITAPHIUM DAMONIS OF MILTON** Edited, With Notes And Introduction By C. S. Jerram, M. A. Trin. Coll. Oxon. [Quotation from Theoc. Idyll.] *London[:] Longmans, Green, And Co. 1874.* First edition thus. See main listing under *Lycidas*, 1874.

330. JOHN MILTON'S EPITAPHIUM DAMONIS Printed from the First Edition[.] With a new translation by Walter W. Skeat (e Coll. Christ.) In Memory Of Israel Gollancz[.] *Cambridge[:] At the University Press[,] 1933.* First edition thus. Slim 4to, 20+[2]pp., decorative border trim on title page, decorative head-trim, original printed wrappers reprinting title page on front cover (a

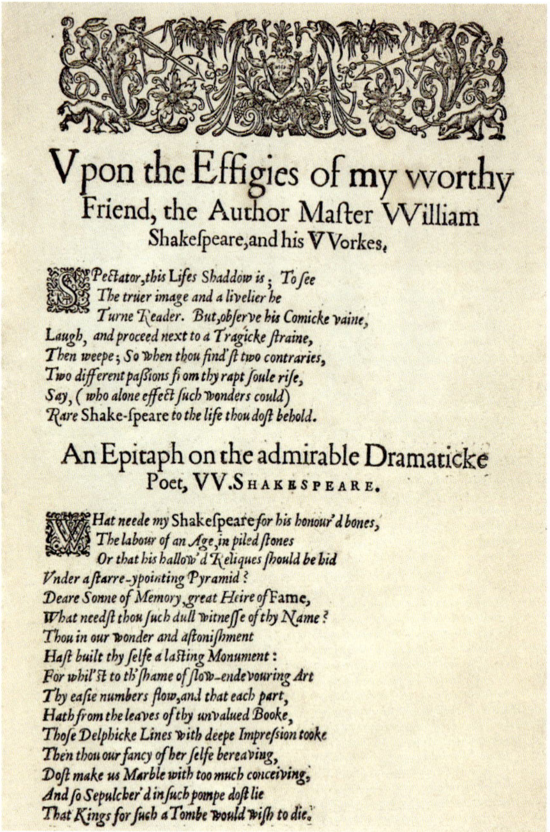

"On Shakespeare" (leaf from 1632 Shakespeare Folio). See #329.

Engraved frontispiece portrait and title page, *History of Britain*, 1670. See #333.

Page from *The Flowers Of Milton* [by Jane Elizabeth Giraud]. [Faversham, Kent: Printed by Day and Haghe for the Artist,] (1846). 4to, twenty-nine leaves, beautifully arranged and painted bouquets of flowers with verses from Milton printed below. See #331.

bit dust-soiled, slightly foxed), edges untrimmed. The first edition was not admitted to the canon until after 1926, and appeared in Pollard's old STC under "Damon." It is here reprinted with Skeat's English translation beneath. A foreword by A. W. Pollard explains the circumstances. Fine. NCBEL I, 1241.

331. THE FLOWERS OF MILTON [by Jane Elizabeth Giraud]. *[Faversham, Kent: Printed by Day and Haghe for the Artist,] (1846).* First and only edition. 4to, 29 leaves, title page hand-lettered in blue within hand-colored floral wreath, dedication page, beautifully arranged and painted bouquets of flowers with verses from Milton printed below, the flowers depicted being those mentioned in the verses, hand-colored lithograph plates and hand-colored floriated initial at the start of each verse by Jane Elizabeth Giraud with the flower (or plant) name in blue, protective tissue guards, original full green morocco (a little rubbed with some scuffing), gilt-decorated covers with gilt lettering on front cover, spine lettered in gilt, broad inner dentelles richly tooled in gilt, outer dentelles tooled in gilt (faded). A very pretty edition, privately printed in a limited edition. Nice copy of a scarce book. Not in Kohler.

332. FOUR POEMS BY JOHN MILTON[:] L'ALLEGRO[,] IL PENSEROSO[,] ARCADES[,] LYCIDAS[.] With Wood-Engravings By Blair Hughes-Stanton[.] *[Newton, Wales:] The Gregynog Press[,] MCMXXXIII.* Small folio, 33pp.+colophon leaf, first appearance of wood-engraved illustrations after Blair Hughes-Stanton, the text is that of Beeching's edition, original reddish-brown Hermitage calf (front cover partially sun-faded), blind-decorated, with the figure of Euphrosyne (after the title-page woodcut) in blind on front cover, spine and front cover lettered in black, large bookplate on front pastedown. This attractive binding "is one of the most successful to come from the [Gregynog] Press" (Harrop, p. 120). A very nice copy. One of 250 numbered copies. Huckabay 223.

The History of Britain

333. THE HISTORY OF BRITAIN, That part especially now call'd England. From the first Traditional Beginning, continu'd to the Norman Conqvest. Collected out of the antientest and best Authours thereof by John Milton. *London, Printed by J. M. for James Allestry, at the Rose and Crown in St. Paul's Church-Yard, M DC LXX.* First edition, first issue. 4to, 308+[53]+[1]pp., first appearance of engraved frontispiece portrait by Faithorne (fine impression), the portrait drawn especially for this work *ad vivum*, decorative head-trim, "An Index Of all the Chief Persons and Material Passages" at the end with "Errata" leaf following, contemporary calf (neatly rebacked preserving original black morocco label with gilt lettering), raised bands within gilt rules, armorial bookplate on front pastedown, speckled edges. A large, fresh copy in a brown cloth box with spine lettered in gilt. Scarce. Wing M2119; Grolier, *Wither to Prior,* 609; Pforzheimer 710; Coleridge 24a; Shawcross, 1984, 306; Shawcross, Kentucky, 52; Not in Kohler.

334. THE HISTORY OF BRITAIN, That part especially now called England. From The first Traditional Beginning, Continued to the Norman Conqvest. Collected out of the Antientest and best Authours thereof: By John Milton. *London, Printed by J. M. for Spencer Hickman, at the Rose in St. Paul's Church-Yard, MDCLXXI.* First edition, second issue. 4to, 308+[53]+[1]pp., engraved frontispiece portrait by Faithorne, decorative head-trim, "An Index Of all the Chief Persons and Material Passages" at the end with "Errata" leaf following, contemporary calf (spine chipped at top, new endpapers, some minor spotting), covers decorated in blind, gilt rules on spine with small decorative gilt pieces in the panels, red morocco label with gilt lettering and gilt rules, raised bands, bookplates on front pastedown and fly-leaf, contemporary signature on first page of text. Good copy with the rare engraved frontispiece portrait by Faithorne (seldom found with this edition) and with the

History of Britain, 1670, in contemporary calf binding. See #333.

errata leaf at end. Scarce thus. Wing M2120; Coleridge 24b; Shawcross, 1984, 307; Not in Kohler.

335. THE HISTORY OF BRITAIN, That Part especially now call'd England. From the first Traditional Beginning, Continu'd to the Norman Conqvest. Collected out of the Antientest and Best Authours thereof by John Milton. *London, Printed by J. M. for John Martyn at the Sign of the Bell in St. Paul's Church-Yard, MDCLXXVII.* Second edition, first issue. 8vo, 357+[58]pp., double black rule on title page, "An Index Of all the Chief Persons and Material Passages" at the end, contemporary calf (rebacked preserving original spine with new morocco label), gilt-decorated spine, red morocco label with gilt lettering and decorative gilt trim. Good, large copy with several early signatures on front pastedown and fly-leaf. Shawcross notes: "Printer was John Macock." Scarce. Wing M2121; Coleridge 25a; Shawcross, 1984, 323; Kohler 509 (indicating "[394]pp.").

336. THE HISTORY OF BRITAIN, That Part especially now call'd England. From the first Traditional Beginning, Continu'd to the Norman Conqvest. Collected out of the Antientest and Best Authours thereof by John Milton. *The Second Edition. London, Printed by J. M. for Mark Pardoe and are to be sold at the Black Raven over against Bedford-House, in the Strand. 1678.* Second edition, second issue. 8vo, 357+[59]pp., double black rule on title page, "An Index Of all the Chief Persons and Material Passages" at the end, nineteenth-century night-blue morocco, outer and inner gilt rules on covers with decorative gilt corner pieces, elaborately gilt-decorated spine with gilt lettering, raised bands with gilt rule, inner dentelles richly tooled in gilt, outer dentelles ruled in gilt, marbled endpapers, a.e.g. Fine copy with note about Milton as author of *PL* in a faint, early hand on title page, in an elegant nineteenth-century morocco binding, and with good margins. Scarce. Wing M2122; Coleridge 25b; Shawcross, 1984, 324; Not in Kohler.

337. THE HISTORY OF BRITAIN, That Part especially now call'd England. From the first Traditional Beginning, Continu'd to the Norman Conquest. Collected out of the Ancientest and Best Authors thereof, by John Milton. *London, Printed by R. E. for R. Scott, R. Chiswell, R. Bently, G. Sawbridge; and are to be Sold by A. Swall, and T. Child, in St. Paul's Church-yard. 1695.* Third edition. 8vo, 357+[58]pp., double black rule on title page, "An Index Of all the Chief Persons and Material Passages" at the end, contemporary calf (neatly rebacked preserving original red morocco label with gilt lettering and gilt rules, some slight age-browning), raised bands. Good copy from the library of the Marquess of Anglesey with the Paget arms in gilt on covers and a few early check marks and notations throughout. Scarce

copy of what is considered the rarest seventeenth-century printing of this work, complete with A1 (blank) before title. Wing M2124; Grolier, *Wither to Prior*, 611; Coleridge 26a; Shawcross, 1984, 374; Not in Kohler.

338. THE HISTORY OF BRITAIN, That Part Especially Now Called England; From The First Traditional Beginning, Continued To The Norman Conquest; Collected Out Of The Ancienest And Best Authours Thereof. By John Milton. *London: Printed For R. Wilks, 89, Chancery-Lane; And May Be Had Of All Booksellers. 1818.* Sixth separate edition with unabridged passages restored? Tall 8vo, xliii+400pp., edited by Francis Maseres, engraved frontispiece portrait of Milton "Engraved by Owen, from a Drawing by Vertue, in the Collection of Thos. Brand Hollis, Esq.," preface (dated 1818), life of Milton "By His Nephew Mr. Edward Philips," folding chronological chart, "An Index Of All The Chief Persons And Material Passages Contained In The Foregoing History" at the end, half-title for each of the additional works, original three-quarter calf, marbled paper over boards (a bit rubbed and worn, front joint cracked), spine lettered and ruled in gilt, early bookplate, with the full table of contents written out in pencil in a neat hand on verso of title page, bound by Blackwells with their ticket. A very interesting early nineteenth-century edition and apparently scarce, containing also *The Tenure of Kings*, *The Ready And Easy Way*, *The Present Means*, *A Letter to a Friend concerning the Ruptures of the Commonwealth* (1659), and *Brief Notes upon a late Sermon titled The Fear of God and the King; preached and since published, by Matthew Griffith*. This is the first and only edition by Francis Maseres, the noted literary figure. Williamson 125; Kohler 510, reporting "Not in the Bodleian Library. Not in Cambridge University Library."

339. [THE HISTORY OF BRITAIN] [In] BRITAIN UNDER TROJAN, ROMAN, SAXON RULE. By John Milton. ENGLAND UNDER RICHARD III. By Thomas More. THE REIGN OF HENRY VII. By Francis Bacon, Lord Verulam. Verbatim Reprint From Kennet's England, Ed. 1719. *London: Ward, Lock & Co. Warwick House, Dorset Buildings, Salisbury Square, E.C. n.d. [ca. 1895].* First edition thus? 8vo, 424+[18]pp., half-title, "Biographical Notices," notes at bottom of the page, "Index" at the end printed in double column, rebound in modern half green buckram, marbled green paper over boards (pages a bit age-browned, library stamps on title page and fore-edge with related materials, shelf-mark painted over on spine), spine lettered in gilt, new yellow endpapers. Eight page of advertisements bound in at end. Milton's "The History Of England" occupies the first third of the book. Scarce. Not in Kohler.

340. THE HISTORY OF BRITAIN[.] John Milton. A facsimile edition with a critical Introduction by Graham Parry[,] University of York[.] *Paul Watkins[,] Stamford, 1991.* First edition thus. 8vo, 48+357+[58 unpaginated Index]+[3]+11+[4]pp., half-title, facsimile reproduction of 1670 Faithorne frontispiece portrait of Milton, facsimile reproduction of the 1677 octavo edition (the second), including the title page, text, and "The Index" or "The Table," with a new forty-eight-page critical introduction, facsimile reproduction also, as appendix I, of the title page and of "*Mr John Miltons Character Of The Long Parliament And Assembly of Divines In MDCXLI.* London . . . 1681," with appendix II listing Milton's "possible subjects for British Tragedies while writing *The History of Britain*," original black cloth, spine lettered in gilt, printed black publisher's wrappers reproducing 1670 Faithorne frontispiece portrait of Milton on front cover. Fine, in mint condition. This reprint, the first as a separate book since 1818, is a facsimile of the second edition, the 1677 octavo edition (also listed here). "Issued in a limited edition of 500 copies only. This is copy number 398" (verso title page).

341. [ITALIAN POEMS] MILTON'S ITALIAN POEMS TRANSLATED, And Addressed To A Gentleman of Italy. By Dr. Langhorne. *London: Printed for T. Becket, the Corner of the Adelphi in the Strand. 1776. [Price One Shilling.]* First edition. 4to, [iii]+ix+[10]+16pp., disbound. Good copy. A rather uncommon effort of Langhorne's, addressed and with nineteen stanzas to a Signor Mozzi. Rare. Coleridge 89; NCBEL II, 667; Not in Kohler.

L'Allegro, Il Penseroso
"Set to Musick by Mr. Handel" (1741)

342. L'ALLEGRO, IL PENSEROSO, Ed Il Moderato. In Three Parts. Set to Musick by Mr. Handel. *London: Printed for J. and R. Tonson, 1741.* Second edition. Small 4to, 20pp., recent plain acid-free wraps, with John Dryden's *A Song for St. Cecilia's Day* (4 pp.) bound at rear. A very good copy in a custom reddish-brown quarter morocco, dark brown cloth folder, with spine lettered in gilt. Although the various parts are given (air, recitative, chorus), the work does not contain any printed musical notation. Beginning in 1739, Handel devoted one performance each year for the benefit of the Royal Society of Musicians, and always played the organ himself. "For 27 February 1740, he set to music an arrangement from Milton's *L'Allegro* and *Il Penseroso* made by a rich amateur, Charles Jennens, of Gopsall, Leicestershire, who added a third part, *Il Moderato*" (DNB). John Shawcross shared the following with me: "There were two editions in 1740, both by the Tonsons. One is in 20 pp., and this 1741 edition is a repeat of that; and the other is in 18 pp." NUC locates just two copies. Not in Coleridge; Not in Kohler.

343. L'ALLEGRO, IL PENSEROSO, Ed Il Moderato. The Words taken from Milton. Set to Musick by Mr. Handel. London. Printed for I. Walsh in Catherine Street in the Strand. Where may be had, Twelve Grand Concertos for Violins &c. in Seven Parts Compos'd by Mr. Handel[.] *n.d. [ca. 1741].* First edition, second issue. Folio, engraved title page, sixty-three pages of engraved music, disbound (light dust soiling and slight embrowning). A large, fine copy with early initials on title page and notation in an early hand on a small piece of paper tipped on verso of last page. Based on Milton's poem, Handel's adaptation was first performed in 1740 in Lincolns-Inn Fields Theatre in London; it consists of a series of lyrical cantatas, musical paintings of moods and sentiments (joy, moderation, pensiveness, melancholy), and evocations of nature, which might have influenced Haydn's *Seasons*. The score with words here is printed from engraved plates throughout, all the plates having previously been used in the first issue. In this edition for the first time all the pages are numbered consecutively at the top center, although the old pagination of the constituent parts also appears in its original places. The collection contains eighteen songs and a duet, including the second setting of "Or let ye merry Bells ring round." The librettist of Milton's poems was Handel's wealthy friend Charles Jennens. Handel's setting of Milton's *L'Allegro* and *Il Penseroso* was first published the previous year. John Shawcross shared with me: "There are other editions in 1741. One is from the Tonsons; one has no publisher; and one has no publisher but was apparently from Dublin. There is a separate reissue of [this edition] (and various other editions by Walsh, undated). The two issues are owned by the British Library, and looking at the two together indicates their differences in typography." Rare. Smith, *Handel*, p. 96, no. 13; Coleridge 244; Kohler 534.

344. L'ALLEGRO, IL PENSEROSO, Ed Il Moderato. By Milton. Set to Music by George Frederick Handel. With the After-pieces, St. Cecilia's Day, Musick of Bonduca, And Coronation Anthems. *London: Printed, by Assignment from the Heirs of Messrs. Tonson and Watts, for T. and W. Lowndes, No. 77, in Fleet-street. [Price Sixpence.] n.d. [ca. 1750s].* 8vo, 24pp. of text (without musical notation), disbound (slight foxing). Very good. Scarce. Not in Coleridge; Not in Kohler.

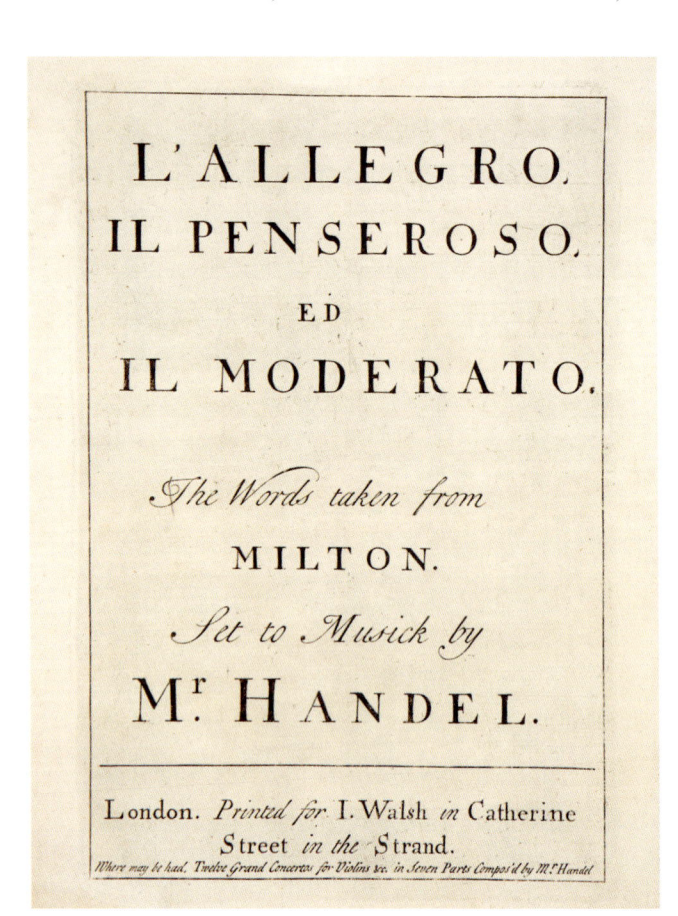

L'Allegro, Il Penseroso, Ed Il Moderato. The Words taken from Milton. Set to Musick by Mr. Handel. London. Printed for I. Walsh, ca. 1741. Folio, engraved title page, sixty-three pages of engraved music. See #343.

Rare 1752 First Edition of Simon Grynaeus's German Translation

344A. (Cross-listing) L'ALLEGRO AND IL PENSEROSO [In] JOHANN MILTONS WIEDER=ERO BERTES PARADIES, nebst desselben Samson, und einigen andern Gedichten, wie auch einer Lebens=Beschreibung Des Verfassers. Aus dem Englischen übersetst. *Basel, verlegts Johann Rudolf Imhof, 1752*. First edition thus. See main listing under *PR*, 1752.

❖

344B. (Cross-listing) L'ALLEGRO [In] HANDEL'S SONGS Selected from His Latest Oratorios For the Harpsichord, Voice, Hoboy or German Flute. The Instrumental Parts to the above Songs may be had Separate to Compleat them for Concerts. *London: Printed for I. Walsh, in Catherine Street, in the Strand, Of whom may be had, Compos'd by Mr[.] Handel. [Followed by a long list of "Oratorios," including "Samson" and "L'Allegro il Penseroso."] n.d. [ca. 1755]*. Oblong folio, 170pp., engraved title page and 168 pp. of engraved music, contemporary quarter calf, marbled paper over boards (worn, lightly embrowned). Milton's *Samson* is among the most popular in this collection, with ten selections; *L'A* is represented by six selections; the *Messiah* by one. Exceedingly rare collection. Not in Coleridge; Not in Kohler. See main listing under *SA*, ca. 1755.

345. L'ALLEGRO, ED IL PENSEROSO. *[London: Wenman, 1778.]* Single sheet (8 ½" × 5 ⅜"), printed on both sides, disbound (small hole affecting some text). Scarce. Not in Coleridge; Not in Kohler.

346. L'ALLEGRO, IL PENSEROSO, Ed Il Moderato. Composed by Mr. [George Friedrich] Handel, For The Voice, Harpsichord, And Violin; with the Choruses in Score. *London: Printed for Harrison & Co., No. 18, Paternoster Row. n.d. (1784)*. Oblong folio, engraved title page, sixty-three pages of engraved music, "Contents" on page 64, original quarter leather, marbled paper over boards (a bit rubbed, front joint cracked), gilt rules on spine (faded), central gilt-decorated and gilt-lettered red leather label on front cover. Good copy with early name on fly-leaf. The work, based on Milton's poems, complete with the additional songs and in vocal score, was arranged for Handel by his wealthy friend and librettist Charles Jennens. Handel's adaptation was first performed in 1740 in Lincolns-Inn Fields Theatre in London. William C. Smith, *Handel*, p. 96, no. 13; Not in Coleridge; Not in Kohler.

347. L'ALLEGRO [In] THE CABINET OF GENIUS containing Frontispieces and Characters adapted to the most Popular Poems, &c. with the Poems &c at large. *London, Printed for C. Taylor No. 10 near Castle Street, Holborn. 1787-[1790]*. 2 volumes. First edition. Small 4to, variously paginated with forty-five and fifty engravings, respectively, engraved title page each volume, engraved illustration plates (most impressions are in sepia), each illustration with accompanying text separately paginated, contemporary polished tree calf, gilt-decorated spine with decorative gilt pieces in the panels, red morocco title labels with decorative gilt trim, green morocco numbering labels with decorative gilt trim, raised bands, outer dentelles tooled in gilt. Very fine set, large paper copy with a possibly contemporary bookplate, early dated signature, and additional bookplate on fly-leaf. Included in volume 2 is Milton's poem, *L'A*, and two illustration plates "excudit C. Taylor" [i.e., Charles Taylor of Ongar, uncle of Ann and Jane Taylor] for the poem (very fine sepia impressions, engraved by W. Nutter) appearing before the poem, one plate titled "Morning," with the two lines illustrated printed beneath, the second plate titled "Evening," with the two lines illustrated printed beneath, each plate bearing the imprint: "London, Publish'd April 1, 1787 by C. Taylor No. 10 near

Castle Street, Holborn." The preliminary address ("To The Public") has a somewhat ambiguous paragraph (p. 3) on the Milton plates, which seems to suggest that they may also exist in a larger format (see following). The last paragraph (p. 4) suggests that proof impressions existed for special purchase (see following). The edition came out in monthly parts, each with two plates, finally reaching two volumes. This is the complete two-volume set with ninety-five total stipple-engraved plates (very fine sepia impressions) executed by Taylor and Ogborne mostly after designs by Samuel Shelley (1750–1808) and Robert Smirke (1752–1845). Charles Taylor and John Ogborne both were students of Bartolozzi, the great English master engraver; his influence on them is very discernible here. Besides Milton, the obvious classics of the time are included: Pope (*Autumn*; *Spring*; *Winter*; *Summer*), Gray (*Elegy*), Parnell (*The Hermit*), etc. Very rare, especially in such fine condition. "Over half of the copies listed by ESTC are defective, including both British Library copies, both Bodleian copies, and both Henry E. Huntington copies" (Ursus Rare Books, Catalogue 190, #47, 1997). ESTC T090563; Not in Kohler; John Shawcross reminded me that there is a "copy in University of Kentucky Library."

347A. (Cross-listing) Two large paper proof copper engravings on thick paper by C. Taylor for **L'ALLEGRO** (1787) [In] **PARADISE REGAIN'D . . . SAMSON AGONISTES: AND POEMS UPON SEVERAL OCCASIONS** . . . *Birmingham: Printed by John Baskerville For J. and R. Tonson in London. MDCCLVIII.* Together with **PARADISE LOST** . . . *Birmingham[:] Printed by John Baskerville for J. and R. Tonson in London. MDCCLVIII.* First Baskerville edition. Extra-illustrated, including, among others, two fine large paper proof copper engravings on thick paper by C. Taylor for *L'A*: of "Morning" and of "Evening," each "Publish'd April 1, 1787 by C. Taylor." See main listing under *PL*, 1858.

348. L'ALLEGRO[,] IL PENSEROSO, ed Il Moderato, The Words taken from Milton; The Musick Composed in the Year, 1739. By G. F. Handel. *[London: Samuel Arnold, n.d. (ca. 1795)]*. Folio, engraved title page, 148 pp. of engraved music with "Table of Contents" (upper portion repaired without affecting text) on page 149, modern burgundy polished sheep (some embrowning and minor foxing, small inoffensive stamps on title page, "Sons of Handel 1818" and the society of "Ancient Concerts 1937"), green labels lettered and ruled in gilt on spine, new endpapers. Overall, a fine copy. Handel's adaptation was first performed in 1740 in Lincolns-Inn Fields Theatre in London. The librettist of Milton's poems was Handel's wealthy friend Charles Jennens. Handel's setting of Milton's *L'A*

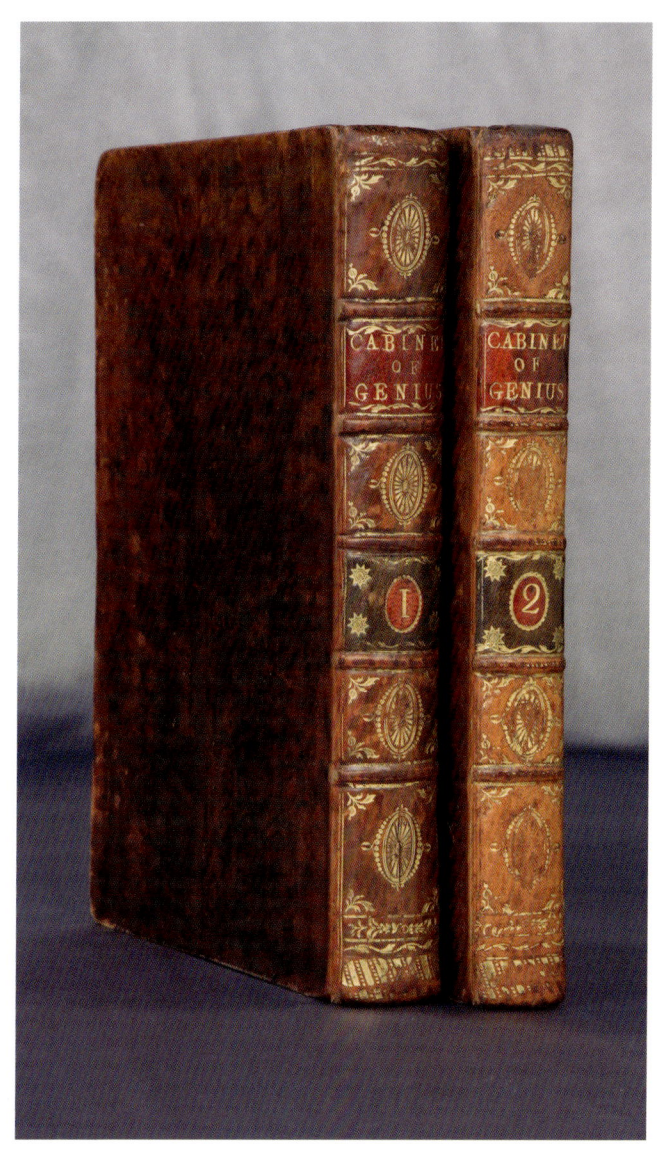

The Cabinet of Genius. London, Printed for C. Taylor, 1787–[90]. Small 4to with forty-five and fifty engravings, respectively, contemporary polished tree calf. Fine set, very large paper copy. Two engraved plates for *L'A* by C. Taylor with the poem appearing in volume 2. See #347.

and *IlP* was first published in 1740. "We have not handled this edition before. Rare" (G. W. Stuart, Jr., Ravenstree, Cat. 174, #1, 1992). Not in Coleridge; Not in Kohler; John Shawcross told me that there is a "copy in University of Illinois Library."

348A. (Cross-listing) **L'ALLEGRO AND IL PENSEROSO** [In] **COMUS, A MASK:** Presented At Ludlow Castle 1634, Before The Earl Of Bridgewater . . . To Which Are Added, L'Allegro And Il Penseroso . . . *London: Printed By T. Bensley, Bolt Court, Fleet Street; For E. Harding, Pall Mall; And W. West, Paternoster Row. 1799.* First edition thus. 8vo, three unsigned illustration plates engraved by R. H. Cromek after Thomas Stothard, one for *C*, one for *L'A*, and one for *IlP*, half-title for each of the poems, contemporary straight-grained full blue morocco. This edition was edited by Henry Todd, although not mentioned on the title page, with his account of Ludlow Castle. Coleridge 82; Kohler 241, reporting "Not in Cambridge University Library." See main listing under *Comus*, 1799.

348B. (Cross-listing) L'ALLEGRO AND IL PENSEROSO [In] [PARADISE LOST. *(London:) Printed For The Proprietors, 1808*. Bound with COMUS AND L'ALLEGRO AND IL PENSEROSO, [n.d.] Folio scrapbook, extra-illustrated [ca. 1810], paper watermarked 1794. The printed text of each poem is mounted on individual folio leaves, along with Milton's *Life* and numerous illustrations and engraved portraits from the late eighteenth and early nineteenth centuries. See main listing under *PL*, 1808.

348C. (Cross-listing) L'ALLEGRO AND IL PENSEROSO [In] IL LICIDA, L'ALLEGRO, ED IL PENSEROSO DI GIOVANNI MILTON. Tradotti Da Gaetano Polidori. *Londra... M DCCC XIV*. See main listing under *Il Licida*, 1814.

349. L'ALLEGRO [In] THE BOOK OF GEMS. The Poets And Artists Of Great Britain[.] Edited By S. C. Hall[.] *London[:] Saunders And Otley, Conduit Street[,] 1836. 3 volumes*. First edition. 8vo in 4s, xvi+304+[4]pp. (volume 1), half-title, central vignette on title page, vignette illustrations for many of the poems, protective tissue guards, "Clay, Printer, London" on the last page, four pages of facsimile reproductions of signatures of the poets at the end of the volume, including facsimile reproduction of the signature of Milton, contemporary full green morocco (slightly worn along joints, occasional light foxing), covers and spine ruled in gilt with large central gilt design, spine richly gilt-decorated in the panels with gilt lettering (*British Poets: Chaucer To Prior*), thick raised bands with decorative gilt trim, inner and outer dentelles ruled in gilt, a.e.g. Nice copy, as part of a nice set. Volume 1, *Chaucer to Prior*, contains several poetical selections from Milton (with a brief biographical headnote) with a vignette illustration engraved by W. Chevalier after D. M'Clise of "Euphrosyne" at the head of *L'A* complete. Among the other illustrations is John Martin's *Flight into Egypt*, for a poem by John Lydgate, engraved by E. Finden. Volume 3 (*Wordsworth To Bayly*) contains Martin's *Angels Appearing to Shepherds*, engraved by J. B. Willmore. Bohn issued a reprint in three volumes in 1844 (see 1848 reissue also listed here); then Bell & Daldy, Bohn's successors, brought out a one-volume reprint in 1866 in which the plates were retouched (also listed here); Fisher, Son and Co. published a two-volume edition with publisher's imprint of London and Paris in 1844 (also listed here).

350. L'ALLEGRO [In] THE BOOK OF GEMS. The Poets and Artists of Great Britain. By S. C. Hall. *Fisher, Son And Co. London & Paris. 1844*. 2 volumes. 8vo in 4s, xvi+304+[4]pp.,vi+302+[4]pp., half-title, vignette illustrations for many of the poems, protective tissue guards, four pages of facsimile reproductions of poets' signatures at the end of each volume, including facsimile reproductions of the signatures of Milton at end of volume 1, contemporary half blue calf (prelimaries foxed and small stain in margins of first few signatures, some foxing of contents), gilt rules on covers, spine elaborately decorated in gilt, red and brown morocco labels, marbled endpapers and edges, bookplate with shelf label on front pastedown of each volume. Fine set in very rich and attractive bindings of the period, "Bound by Maltby" neatly lettered on verso of flyleaf at the top. In the words of the bookseller who sold the set: "they look bonny sitting on a shelf!" Volume 1, *Chaucer to Prior*, contains several poetical selections from Milton (with a brief biographical headnote) with a vignette illustration engraved by W. Chevalier after D. M'Clise of "Euphrosyne" at the head of *L'A* complete. Among the other illustrations is John Martin's *Flight Into Egypt*, for a poem by Lydgate, engraved by E. Finden. Volume 2 is entitled *Pomfret To Bloomfield*. First edition published in three volumes in 1836 (set preceding).

351. L'ALLEGRO AND IL PENSEROSO, BY JOHN MILTON, With Thirty Illustrations Designed Expressly For The Art-Union Of London. 1848. First edition thus. 4to, Index+30pp.+30 first appearance of engraved illustration plates mostly by the Dalziel brothers, original half brown pebble calf (a little worn along joints and extremities), brown cloth (several slight stains), gilt rules on covers with central brown morocco label with gilt lettering and gilt trim on front cover, elaborately gilt-decorated spine, raised bands, bound by H. Hodge, Exeter, with his ticket. The artists include F. R. Pickersgill, E. H. Corbould, H. K. Browne "Phiz," and John Tenniel; many of the engravings are by the Dalziel Brothers. Good copy. Kohler 250, reporting "Not in Cambridge University Library."

352. L'ALLEGRO [In] THE BOOK OF GEMS. In 3 Vols. The Poets and Artists of Great Britain. [Edited by] S. C. Hall. *Henry G. Bohn, London. 1848*. Third edition. Volume 1 only, complete unto itself. 8vo in 4s, xvi+304+[4]pp., half-title, central vignette on title page, vignette illustrations for many of the poems, protective tissue guards, decorative tailpiece at the end of each volume (same as in the first edition in 1836 but without the appearance of "Clay, Printer, London" at the center), four pages of facsimile reproductions of signatures of the poets at the end of each volume, including facsimile reproduction of the signature of Milton at end of volume 1, contemporary full green morocco (a bit rubbed, joints weak), covers decorated with finely tooled wide borders and central emblem in gilt, spine decorated in gilt in the panels with gilt lettering (*British Poets: Chaucer To Prior*), raised bands with gilt trim (rubbed), inner and outer dentelles finely tooled in gilt, a.e.g. A good copy. Included are several poetical selections from Milton (with a brief biographical headnote) with a vignette illustration engraved by W. Chevalier after D. M'Clise of "Euphrosyne" at the head of *L'A* complete. As with the earlier editions, among the other illustrations is John Martin's *Flight Into Egypt*, for a poem by Lydgate, engraved by E. Finden. The first edition was published by Bohn in three volumes in 1836 (also listed here with further editions cited).

Large Quarto—Illustrations in Proof State

353. L'ALLEGRO By John Milton[.] Illustrated By The Etching Club. *London: Published For The Etching Club, By Joseph Cundell, 12, Old Bond Street. M DCCC XLIX.* First edition thus. Large 4to, [2]+[20]pp., title page in red and black, dedication page also in red and black, "L'Allegro" lettered in red at the center of the top of each page, twenty paginated leaves with etchings, each engraved leaf with guard sheet, contemporary full dark maroon morocco over thick boards (joints slightly rubbed), blind rules on covers, gilt lettering on front cover and spine, thick raised bands, a.e.g., bound by Hayday. A very fine copy of a sumptuous edition dedicated to the Queen and Prince Consort, handsomely printed on large, thick, cardlike paper, first appearance of these illustrations in proof state, each plate marked "Proof" in lower left corner. The artists include Townsend, Horsley, Redgrave, Cope, Greswick, Taylor, and Stonehouse; many of the engravings are by the Dalziel Brothers. According to Dick Lyon (London, 1978), from whom I obtained this lovely book: "Proof copy on large and thick paper. Very fine copy of one of the most beautiful mid-nineteenth-century illustrated books, rare in this state." Stevens 500; Kohler 251.

Folio—Illustrations in Proof State

354. Variant of Preceding. L'ALLEGRO By John Milton[.] Illustrated By The Etching Club. *London: Published For The Etching Club, By Joseph Cundell, 12, Old Bond Street. M DCCC XLIX.* First edition thus. Folio, [2]+20+[1]pp., pagination throughout unlike preceding copy, and also unlike that copy, this is one of a limited number of folio copies, title page in red and black, dedication page also in red and black, "L'Allegro" lettered in red at the center of the top of each page, twenty paginated leaves with etchings,

Illustration in "proof" state by H. J. Townsend of *L'Allegro* from the edition "Published For The Etching Club, By Joseph Cundell," 1849. First edition. From the 4to edition in the collection. See #353.

each engraved leaf with guard sheet, contemporary full red morocco (front joint broken, light foxing throughout), covers elaborately decorated with very wide intricately tooled gilt border trim, spine lettered in gilt, raised bands with gilt trim on each band and in-between the bands, inner and outer dentelles finely tooled in gilt, a.e.g. An impressive edition, dedicated to the Queen and Prince Consort, handsomely printed on extra large and thick paper, first appearance of illustrations in proof state (fine impressions), each plate marked "Proof" in lower left corner. The artists include Townsend, Horsley, Redgrave, Cope, Greswick, Taylor, and Stonehouse; many of the engravings are by the Dalziel brothers. Signatures (sometimes trimmed) appear in pencil in a neat hand in the lower right-hand corner identifying the artist or artists (in binder's hand or possibly Rauri McLean's hand), helpful in identifying those plates that are unsigned. A fine copy with advertisement leaf in red and black (foxed) bound in at end. Large paper copy. Rare in this state. From the library of Rauri McLean, with his bookplate and an earlier bookplate. Rauri McLean, *VBD*, p. 142; Not in Kohler.

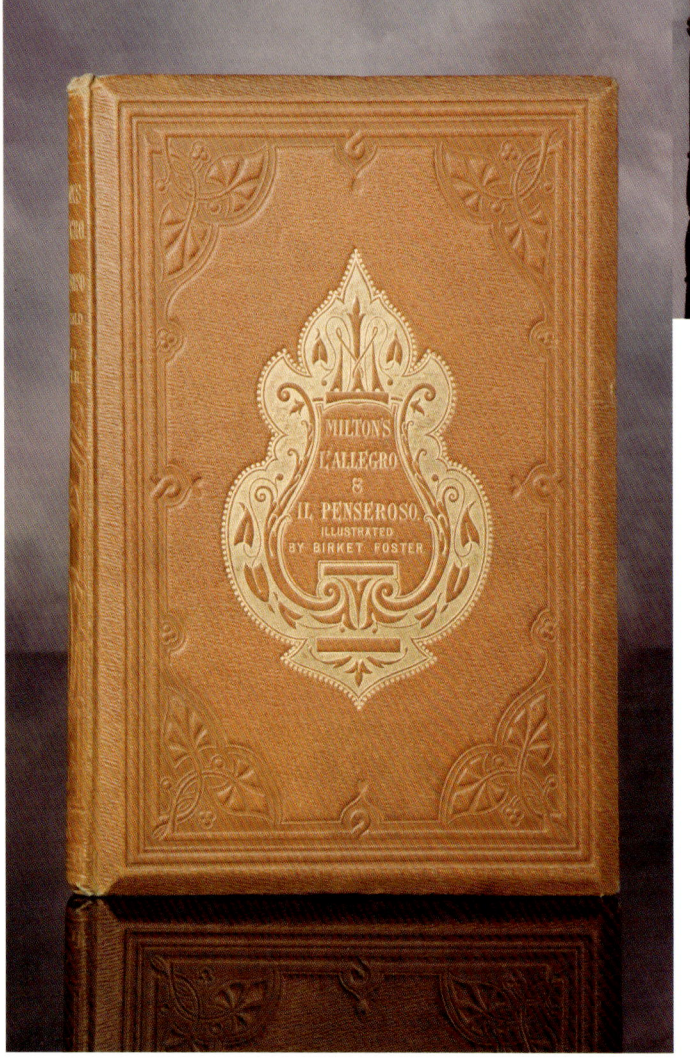

(above left) Illustration in "proof" state by H. J. Townsend of *L'Allegro* from the edition "Published For The Etching Club, By Joseph Cundell, 1849." First edition. (above) *L'Allegro*. Illustrated By The Etching Club. London: Published For The Etching Club, By Joseph Cundell, 1849. First edition thus. Large 4to, contemporary full dark maroon morocco over thick boards. Fine copy of a sumptuous edition handsomely printed with illustrations in proof state. See #354.

L'Allegro & Il Penseroso. London: David Bogue, 1855. First edition. Illustrated By Birket Foster, original plate-stamped ochre ribbed morocco grain cloth, covers elaborately decorated in blind with large central gilt ornament on front cover incorporating title in gilt; Bound by Leighton & Son, & Hodge, with their ticket. Nice, fresh copy. See #355.

355. [L'ALLEGRO AND IL PENSEROSO] MILTON'S L'ALLEGRO AND IL PENSEROSO. Illustrated With Etchings On Steel, By Birket Foster. *London: David Bogue, 86, Fleet Street. MDCCCLV.* First edition thus. 4to, twenty-four leaves of card printed on recto only, title page in red and black with engraved vignette portrait of a young, long-haired Milton, engraved by Birket Foster from the picture by Samuel Cooper, with twenty-nine additional etchings on steel on twenty-four pages by Birket Foster (some slight foxing), text, pagination, and title of poem in Caslon and printed in red throughout, thick tissue guards, original plate-stamped ochre ribbed morocco grain cloth, covers elaborately decorated in blind with bevelled edges, large central gilt ornament on front cover incorporating title in gilt, central ornament repeated in blind on back cover, spine similarly decorated in blind and lettered in gilt, yellow endpapers, a.e.g., bound by Leighton & Son, & Hodge, with their ticket. Nice, fresh copy with contemporary presentation inscription (dated 1856) on fly-leaf. The "very handsome edition" of the first of only four books to have etchings on steel by Birket Foster. It has "clearly been designed with taste, possibly by Joseph Cundall" and is unusual in that the etched illustrations appear not as separate plates but with the text overprinted on the same page. "The effect is superb. No name of printer is mentioned, but it was probably Clay. . . . The velvety blacks and the silvery middle-tones of the etchings are beyond anything that the wood engravers could achieve; their juxtaposition with the type is particularly effective, and makes the pages graphically exciting" (Rauri McLean, *VBD*, with full-page illustration, p. 163). Stevens 501; Rauri McLean, *VBD*, p. 162; Kohler 252.

Also in the collection and listed here are a second edition thus published by Kent & Co. in 1858; a third edition thus (by Kent & Co.) published in 1859; a fourth edition thus (by Kent & Co.) published in 1860; a fifth edition thus (first by Bohn) published in 1865; a sixth edition thus (first by Routledge) published in 1874.

356. [L'ALLEGRO AND IL PENSEROSO] MILTON'S L'ALLEGRO AND IL PENSEROSO. Illustrated With Etchings On Steel, By Birket Foster. *London: W. Kent & Co. (Late D. Bogue), 86, Fleet Street. MDCCCLVIII.* Second edition thus; first by Kent. 4to, twenty-four leaves of card printed on recto only, title page in red and black with engraved vignette portrait of a young, long-haired Milton, engraved by Birket Foster from the picture by Samuel Cooper, with twenty-nine additional etchings on steel on twenty-four pages by Birket Foster, text, pagination, and title of poem in Caslon and printed in red throughout, thick tissue guards, original plate-stamped brown grain cloth (slightly worn along edges, pages a bit loose), covers elaborately decorated in blind with bevelled edges, large central gilt ornament on front cover incorporating title in gilt, central ornament repeated in blind on back cover, spine similarly decorated in blind and lettered in gilt, a.e.g, bound by Leighton & Son, & Hodge, with their ticket. A good copy with early/contemporary presentation inscription on fly-leaf. Rauri McLean, *VBD*, pp. 162–63; Kohler 253, reporting "Not in the British Library. Not in the Bodleian Library. Not in Cambridge University Library."

357. [L'ALLEGRO AND IL PENSEROSO] MILTON'S L'ALLEGRO AND IL PENSEROSO. Illustrated With Etchings On Steel, By Birket Foster. *London: W. Kent & Co. (Late D. Bogue), 86, Fleet Street. MDCCCLIX.* Third edition thus; second by Kent. 4to, twenty-four leaves of card printed on recto only, title page in red and black with engraved vignette portrait of a young, long-haired Milton, engraved by Birket Foster from the picture by Samuel Cooper with twenty-nine additional etchings on steel on twenty-four pages by Birket Foster, text, pagination, and title of poem in Caslon and printed in red throughout, thick tissue guards, original purple ribbed cloth (faded, bit worn and soiled, loose in case due to deterioration of gutta percha binding, recently reglued), covers elaborately decorated in blind with bevelled edges, large central gilt ornament on front cover incorporating title in gilt, spine lettered in gilt with small decorative gilt trim, a.e.g., bound by Burns, with his ticket. A decent copy. Kohler 254, citing Williamson 221, and reporting "Not in the British Library. Not in the Bodleian Library. Not in Cambridge University Library."

358. L'ALLEGRO. By John Milton. *London: Sampson Low, Son & Co. 47, Ludgate Hill. MDCCCLIX.* First edition thus. Slim 8vo, [2]+21+[1]pp., unsigned vignette illustration on title page and other vignette illustrations engraved on wood after W. J. Linton, printed by Richard Clay on cardlike paper on recto only, interleaved with protective guards, original green grain cloth (bit rubbed, title page a little brittle along edge), covers elaborately decorated in blind with bevelled edges, central gilt ornament on front cover incorporating title in gilt, similar gilt ornament incorporating title in gilt on spine, a.e.g., bound by Bone & Son, with their ticket. Good copy with contemporary signature on fly-leaf. "The accompanying Illustrations, engraved on Wood by Mr. W. J. Linton, are copied, with permission, from the well-known edition of 'L'Allegro' published some ten years since by 'The Etching Club.' To secure the excellence of the impressions, only a limited number of the Etchings were printed" (prefatory note). Kohler 255.

359. Variant of Preceding, original blue grain cloth, covers elaborately decorated in blind with bevelled edges, central gilt ornament on front cover incorporating title, similar gilt ornament incorporating title in gilt on spine, a.e.g., bound by Bone & Son, with their ticket. Good copy in a variant publisher's binding with contemporary signature on fly-leaf. Kohler 255.

360. L'ALLEGRO By John Milton[.] *London: Samson Low, Marston, Low And Searle, Crown Buildings, 188, Fleet Street. n.d. [ca. 1859].* Second edition thus? Slim 8vo, 24pp., half-title, vignette illustration on title page and other unsigned vignette illustrations engraved on wood after W. J. Linton, printed by "R. Clay, Sons, And Taylor, Printers, London" (bottom of last page), original purple cloth (slightly rubbed), front cover elaborately decorated in black and gilt with central gilt device outlined in black incorporating the title, and with the additional lettering outlined in gilt ("The Choice Series" at the top, and "Straight Mine Eye Hath Caught New Pleasures" at the bottom), bevelled edges, spine lettered in black, a.e.g., bound by Burn & Co. with their ticket on back pastedown. A lovely copy with early bookplate on front pastedown. The possible first edition thus was published in the 1859 dated edition (also listed here). Kohler 256, indicating that "The British Library Catalogue gives '1859' as the date of this edition and W. J. Linton as the engraver," and reporting "Not in Cambridge University Library."

361. [L'ALLEGRO AND IL PENSEROSO] MILTON'S L'ALLEGRO AND IL PENSEROSO. Illustrated With Etchings On Steel, By Birket Foster. *London: W. Kent & Co. (Late D. Bogue), 86, Fleet Street. MDCCCLX.* Fourth edition thus; third by Kent. 4to, twenty-four leaves of card printed on recto only, title page in red and black with engraved vignette portrait of a young, long-haired Milton, engraved by Birket Foster from the picture by Samuel Cooper with twenty-nine additional etchings on steel on twenty-four pages by Birket Foster, text, pagination, and title of poem in Caslon and printed in red throughout, thick tissue guards (one missing a small portion of lower right corner), original plate-stamped ochre ribbed morocco grain cloth (spine age-darkened, a bit worn at corners and spine ends, some of the pages reglued), covers elaborately decorated in blind with bevelled edges, large central gilt ornament on front cover incorporating title in gilt, central ornament repeated in blind on back cover, spine similarly decorated in blind and lettered in gilt, yellow endpapers, a.e.g., bound by Leighton & Son, & Hodge, with their ticket. A fairly nice copy with contemporary prize inscription in a neat hand on front pastedown. The first edition thus was published by David Bogue in 1855 (also listed here with further editions cited). Kohler 257, reporting "Not in the British Library. Not in the Bodleian Library. Not in Cambridge University Library."

362. L'ALLEGRO. By John Milton[.] *New York: D. Appleton And Co. Broadway. n.d. [ca. 1860].* First edition thus? Slim 8vo, 21+[1]pp., vignette illustration on title page and other vignette illustrations after various artists (Townsend, Redgrave, Horsley, et al.), engraved on wood after W. J. Linton, printed on recto only, protective paper in between, "Printed by Richard Clay, Broadstreet Hill. London" (verso last page), original brown cloth (worn along spine, joints, and extremities), covers richly decorated in embossed blind trim with title in gilt within decorative gilt trim at the center, spine lettered in gilt (worn), raised bands, inner dentelles finely tooled in blind, decorated endpapers, a.e.g. Despite some wear, a nice copy with contemporary presentation inscription (dated 1860) in a neat hand on front blank. Laid in: presentation note in the same fine hand (dated 1860) along with a comparative chart of *L'A* and *IlP* in an early hand. Not in Kohler.

363. L'ALLEGRO AND IL PENSEROSO [In] GEMS FROM THE POETS, Illustrated. The Designs By F. A. Lydon. Printed In Colours From Wood Blocks. *London: Groombridge And Sons, 5, Paternoster-Row. M DCCC LX.* First edition. 4to, [iv]+62pp., engraved and printed title pages, engraved title decorated with circular vignette and lettered in gold, frontispiece illustration and twenty-seven full-page plates, all superbly printed in color from woodblocks by B. Fawcett from designs by F. A. Lydon, each printed on thin card, interleaved, original full dark green pebble morocco (a bit worn along extremities), elaborately gilt-decorated covers with central gilt urn on both covers, gilt-decorated spine within the panels with gilt lettering, raised bands, broad inner and outer dentelles finely tooled in gilt, blue endpapers, a.e.g. A handsome copy of one of the finest Lydon/Fawcett books. Included are poetical selections from Milton with two full-page illustrations after F. A. Lydon in color for *L'A* complete and two illustrations after Lydon in color for *IlP* complete. McLean, *VBD*, p. 204.

364. L'ALLEGRO [In] EARLY ENGLISH POEMS CHAUCER TO POPE. Chiefly Unabridged. Illustrated With Upwards Of One Hundred Engravings On Wood, From Drawings By Eminent Artists. *London: Sampson Low, Son & Co. 47, Ludgate Hill. 1863.* Small 4to, xii+308pp., half-title, illustrations, original red grain cloth, richly gilt-decorated covers and spine with central gilt device incorporating title in gilt on front cover, similar gilt device incorporating title in gilt on spine, a.e.g. A very attractive copy in an elaborately gilt-decorated publisher's (above) Illustration of " . . . how the hounds and horn / Cheerly rouse the slumbering morn" in *L'Allegro* "from a design by F. A. Lydon printed in colours from wood blocks" in *Gems From The Poets*, Illustrated. London: Groombridge And Sons, 1860. First edition. (right) Illustration of "Oft on a plat of rising ground / I hear the far-off curfew sound" in *Il Penseroso* by F. A. Lydon. Ibid. See #363.

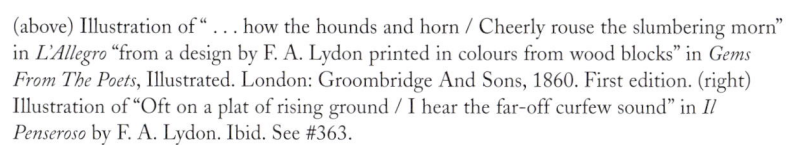

binding with contemporary presentation inscription in a neat hand on fly-leaf. Included is *L'A* complete with eleven illustrations by Cope, Townsend, Creswick, Redgrave, Horsley, Taylor, and Foster.

365. MILTON'S L'ALLEGRO AND IL PENSEROSO. Illustrated With Etchings On Steel, By Birket Foster. *London: Henry G. Bohn, York Street, Covent Garden. 1865.* Possible fifth edition thus; first by Bohn. 4to, twenty-four paginated leaves of card printed on recto only (a lighter weight card than that of the Bogue and Kent & Co. editions earlier), title page in red and black with engraved vignette portrait of a young, long-haired Milton, engraved by Birket Foster from the picture by Samuel Cooper at the top with twenty-nine additional etchings on steel by Birket Foster, text, title of poem, and pagination in Caslon and printed in red throughout, thick tissue guards, original plate-stamped red pebble cloth (worn at outer edge of lower front cover and spine ends, some slight foxing), covers decorated in blind with bevelled edges, large central gilt ornament on front cover incorporating title in gilt, spine lettered in gilt, a.e.g. Nice copy with a possibly contemporary handwritten bookplate on front cover together with a newspaper clipping with the portrait of Milton at age ten tipped in as part of the bookplate. The first edition with Foster's illustrations was published by David Bogue in 1855 (also listed here with further editions cited). Kohler 258, reporting "Not in the British Library. Not in Cambridge University Library."

366. L'ALLEGRO [In] GOLDEN LEAVES FROM THE WORKS OF THE POETS AND PAINTERS Edited By Robert Bell[,] Editor Of The Annotated Edition Of The English Poets[.] The Fourteenth to the Eighteenth Century[:] Geoffrey Chaucer To William Cowper[.] *London[:] Charles Griffin And Company, Stationers' Hall Court, Paternoster Row[,] 1865.* First edition? Small 4to, vii+[1]+240pp., frontispiece portrait of Robert Southey, title page in red and black, steel-engraved illustrations and wood-engraved ornaments (fine impressions), original tortoiseshell papier-mâché bevelled boards, brown morocco spine (rubbed, vertical repair to front pastedown, some foxing), gilt-decorated border trim on front cover with central gilt device incorporating title in gilt, elaborately gilt-decorated leather spine with gilt lettering within decorative gilt devices, decorated gilt star-patterned endpapers, a.e.g. A good copy in a fine papier-mâché binding of the period. Included are poetical selections from Milton with an illustration engraved by E. J. Portbury after H. Howard for *L'A* complete.

367. L'ALLEGRO [In] ROSES AND HOLLY: A Gift-Book For All The Year. With Original Illustrations By Gourlay Steell, R.S.A. R. Herdman, R.S.A. Clark Stanton, A. R.S.A. Samuel Bough, A. R.S.A. John MacWhirter. John Lawson. And Other Eminent Artists. Engraved By R. Paterson. *Edinburgh: William P. Nimmo. n.d. [ca. 1865].* First edition? 4to, xii+146+[2]pp., half-title, illustrations, original purple grain cloth with bevelled edges (a little rubbed, spine faded, some minor spotting), front cover and spine elaborately gilt-decorated with gilt-stamped framework borders of fleur-de-lis, holly, and dots, with central gilt design incorporating title on front cover, similar design incorporating title on spine, back cover decorated in blind, a.e.g. Good copy in an ornately decorated Victorian publisher's cloth binding. Included is *L'A* complete, as the only selection from Milton with an illustration engraved by R. Paterson after Clark Stanton and a decorative tailpiece. A possible second edition was published in a similar binding in a dated version in 1867 (also listed here).

368. L'ALLEGRO [In] THE BOOK OF GEMS. From The Poets And Artists of Great Britain. Edited By S. C. Hall, F.S.A. The Fourteenth To The Seventeenth Century. Geoffrey Chaucer To Dryden. *London: Bell And Daldy, 6, York Street, Covent Garden, And 186, Fleet Street. 1866.* Fourth edition; first edition thus by Bell and Daldy. 12mo, [xii]+304pp., half-title, fifty steel-engraved vignettes after J. Martin, C. S. Stanfield, J. M. W. Turner, and others, original imitation tortoiseshell papier-mâché (neatly rebacked preserving original spine, corners a bit chipped, little staining of a few leaves at end), gilt-decorated border trim on front cover with central gilt device incorporating title in gilt, elaborately gilt-decorated leather spine with gilt lettering within decorative gilt device, white silk endpapers, a.e.g. Nice copy in a very nice papier-mâché binding of the period. Included are poetical selections from Milton with a vignette illustration engraved by W. Chevalier after D. M'Clise of "Euphrosyne" at the head of *L'A* complete. Among the other illustrations is John Martin's *Flight into Egypt*. The first edition was published by Bohn in three volumes in 1836 (also listed here with further editions cited). One of the more unusual 1860s bindings. McLean, *VBD*, p. 109.

369. L'ALLEGRO [In] ROSES AND HOLLY: A Gift-Book For All The Year. With Original Illustrations By Gourlay Steell, R.S.A. R. Herdman, R.S.A. Clark Stanton, A. R.S.A. Samuel Bough, A. R.S.A. John MacWhirter. John Lawson. And Other Eminent Artists. Engraved By R. Paterson. *Edinburgh: William P. Nimmo. 1867.* Second edition? 4to, xii+146+[2]pp., half-title (with early name at top within a neatly scrolled design), original purple grain cloth with bevelled edges (a little worn), front cover and spine elaborately gilt-decorated with gilt-stamped framework borders, fleur-de-lis, holly, and dots, with central gilt design incorporating title on front cover, similar design incorporating title on spine, back cover decorated in blind, a.e.g. Good copy in an ornately decorated Victorian publisher's cloth binding bound by Hunter of Edinburgh with his ticket. Included is *L'A* complete, as the only selection from Milton, with an illustration engraved by R. Paterson after Clark Stanton and a decorative tailpiece. The possible first edition was published in a similar binding in an undated version, ca. 1865 (also listed here).

370. L'ALLEGRO [In] GEMS OF ENGLISH ART OF THIS CENTURY: Twenty-four Pictures From National Collections Printed In Colours By Leighton Brothers[.] With Illustrative Texts By Francis Turner Palgrave[,] Author Of "Essays On Art"[.] *George Routledge & Sons, London And New York[,] 1869.* First edition. 4to, viiii+144pp., half-title, frontispiece color illustration for *L'Allegro* "From A Painting By C. W. Cope, R.A.," twenty-four plates printed in colors in oil from woodblocks, protective tissue guards, vignette illustration at the bottom of last page, original bright blue pebble cloth (corners and spine ends rubbed, occasional foxing), front cover decorated in embossed black trim with bright gilt vertical bands on either side with various decorative pieces showing through in embossed blue, with a bright gilt horizontal band bearing the dark embossed lettering "English Art," with "Gems Of Modern" in decorated gilt lettering just above, spine decorated in gilt with title lettered in embossed blue within thick gilt bands, central emblem in blind on back cover, a.e.g., bookplate, bound by Burn & Co. with their ticket. A very lovely copy in a striking and well-preserved binding of the period with early inscription on half-title. Included is Milton's *L'A* complete with the frontispiece being an illustration for the poem from a painting by Cope with description and discussion of the painting on pp. 116–20. McLean, *VBD*, pp. 194, 221 (illus. in color, plate 125, but not of this binding).

371. L'ALLEGRO AND IL PENSEROSO [In] GEMS FROM THE POETS Illustrated from Original Designs By F. A. Lydon[.] [Quotation From Wordsworth] *London[:] Charles Griffin And Company[,] Stationer's Hall Court. n.d. [ca. 1870].* Royal 8vo, 61pp.+[29] plates, engraved and printed title pages, frontispiece illustration and engraved title and other illustrations in color printed from woodblocks by B. Fawcett from designs by F. A. Lydon, all printed on thin card, interleaved, with protective tissue guards (some foxed), printed title page in red and black, contemporary red cloth (neatly recovered preserving original covers and spine as well as original dark green endpapers, one plate damaged, engraved title page slightly frayed along front edge, new endpapers), elaborately gilt-decorated front cover with central gilt device incorporating title, back cover decorated in blind, gilt-decorated spine with gilt lettering, a.e.g. Included are poetical selections from Milton with two illustrations after F. A. Lydon in color for *L'A* complete and two illustrations after Lydon in (left) *Gems of English Art of This Century*. With Illustrative Texts by Francis Turner Palgrave. London and New York: George Routledge & Sons, 1869. First edition. 4to, original decorated bright blue cloth. (above) Included is Milton's *L'A* with frontispiece illustration for the poem from a painting by C. W. Cope. See #370.

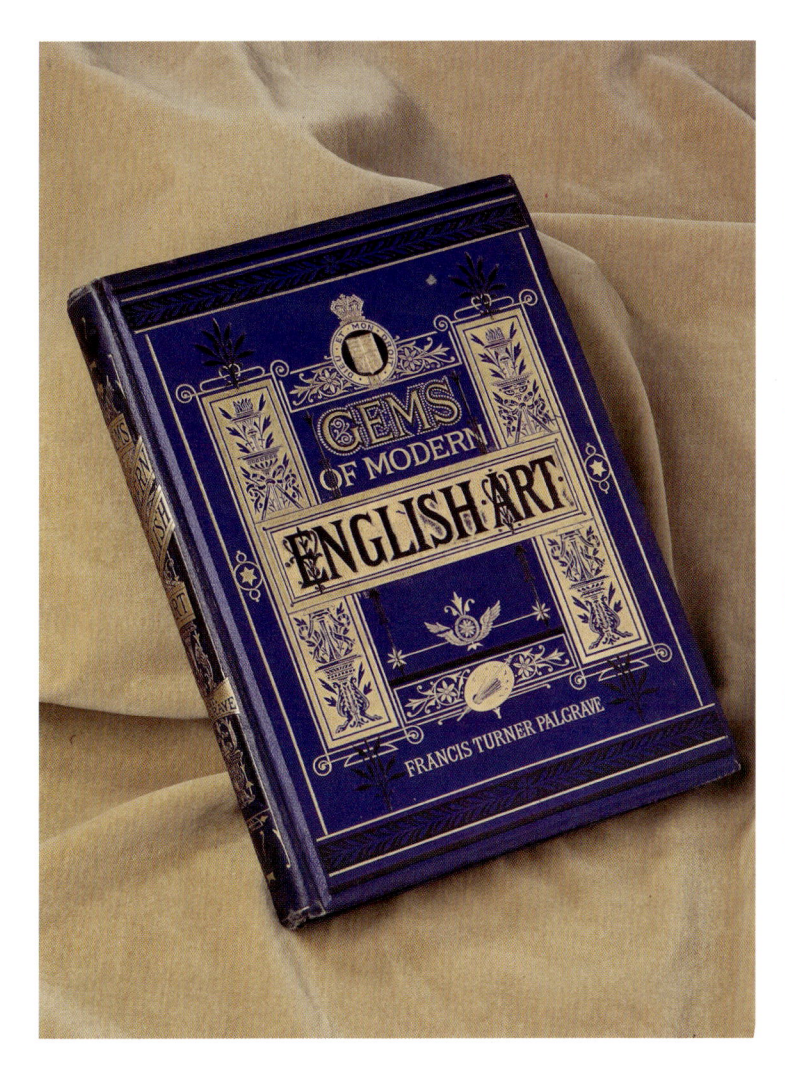

color for *IlP* complete. The first edition was published in 1860 (also listed here); see also 1885 edition listed here.

372. **MILTON'S L'ALLEGRO AND IL PENSEROSO** Illustrated With Etchings On Steel, By Birket Foster[.] *London And New York[:] George Routledge And Sons[,] 1874*. Sixth edition thus; first by Routledge. 8vo, twenty-four paginated leaves of thick card printed on recto only, title page in red and black with engraved vignette portrait of a young, long-haired Milton, engraved by Birket Foster from the picture by Samuel Cooper at the top with twenty-nine additional etchings on steel by Birket Foster, each with a protective tissue guard (several frayed along front edge), text, title of poem, and pagination in Caslon and printed in red throughout, original plate-stamped red cloth (a bit worn, some spotting, pages shaken and loose within), front cover elaborately decorated in black and gilt with bevelled edges, central gilt ornament on front cover with title in gilt at the top, spine decorated in black and lettered in gilt, a.e.g. While the binding is loose and a little worn, the text within is good. A decent copy with contemporary inscription on fly-leaf along with thirteen additional contemporary signatures. The first edition with Foster's illustrations was published by David Bogue in 1855 (also listed here with further editions cited). Not in Kohler.

373. **L'ALLEGRO, IL PENSEROSO, AND OTHER POEMS** By John Milton. Illustrated. *Boston: James R. Osgood And Company, Late Ticknor & Fields, and Fields, Osgood, & Co. 1877*. First edition thus? Small 8vo (miniature, measuring 3 ½" by 5"), 96pp., unsigned frontispiece illustration for *IlP*, small harp at center of title page, small circular illustration on verso, small unsigned vignette illustration on a full page before half-title with decorative trim for *L'A* with a small unsigned vignette illustration on verso, two full-page unsigned illustrations for *L'A*, small unsigned vignette illustration on a full page before half-title with decorative trim for *IlP* with a small unsigned vignette illustration on verso, additional full-page illustration for *IlP*, half-title with decorative trim for *NO* with a small unsigned vignette illustration on verso, half-title with decorative trim for *S* with a small unsigned vignette illustration on verso, decorative head- and tailpieces and decorated initial letters, "Cambridge: Printed by Welch, Bigelow, & Co." at the bottom of last page, endpapers lettered in red with a description of the "Vest-Pocket Series Of Standard and Popular Authors," a listing of the editions in the series and several statements commending the series, original decorated reddish-brown cloth (a bit rubbed), front cover decorated in black and lettered in gilt, central emblem in blind on back cover, spine decorated and lettered in black. A very nice copy of the "Vest-Pocket Series" edition of Milton. "The Vest-Pocket Series consists of volumes yet smaller than the 'Little Classics.' Their Lilliputian size, legible type, and flexible cloth binding make them peculiarly convenient for carrying on short journeys; and the excellence of their contents makes them desirable always and everywhere" (front pastedown). Scarce. Not in Kohler.

374. L'ALLEGRO (John Milton, 1608–1674.) Illustrated By The London Etching Club. [In] *Harper's New Monthly Magazine, 1877, Volume LVI, No. 335, pp. 705–17*. Illustrations by the London Etching Club in various sizes (fine impressions), disbound. In fine condition.

375. L'ALLEGRO By John Milton[.] *London: Samson Low, Marston, Low And Searle, Crown Buildings, 188, Fleet Street. n.d. [ca. 1878]*. First edition thus by Samson Low? Slim 8vo, 24pp., half-title, unsigned illustration on title page, other unsigned illustrations within the text in varying sizes, printed on thick cardlike paper on recto only, protective tissue guard between each page, small tailpiece on last page with "R. Clay, Sons, And Taylor, Printers, London" at bottom of page, original decorated red cloth (a little rubbed), front cover elaborately decorated in embossed black and gilt, "Milton's L'Allegro" lettered in embossed red letters within a large, bright gilt piece at the center surrounded by thick black and gilt borders, with "The Choice Series" lettered in embossed red letters within a smaller gilt piece at the top, and "Straight Mine Eye Hath Caught New Pleasures" within a similar smaller gilt piece at the bottom, spine lettered in black, a.e.g. Nice copy in a lovely publisher's binding with a contemporary presentation inscription (dated "Xmas/78") on fly-leaf. See undated ca. 1886 edition listed here (possible second thus), an identical edition in an identical binding (except in green cloth), with reference to "The Choice Series," published by "Cassell, Petter And Galpin" in New York. Not in Stevens, but Stevens 508 lists "L'Allegro. 'The Choice Series.' London: Sampson Low & Co., [1875]." Scarce. Not in Kohler.

376. L'ALLEGRO. By John Milton. Illustrated With Numerous Engravings. *Philadelphia: J. B. Lippincott Company[,] 715 And 717 Market Street. Bookseller's label ("The Burrows Bros. Co. Booksellers & Stationers[,] Cleveland, Ohio.") tipped in below (where date might have been printed). n.d. [ca. 1880]*. First edition thus? Small 4to, 40pp., half-title with unsigned illustration as frontispiece on verso, stamp of the press on verso of title page, half-title before two-page "List Of Illustrations," numerous unsigned illustrations, six full-page illustrations including frontispiece, the others within the text, decorative head- and tailpieces, original yellow boards (a bit aged, spine chipped), illustration in black at center of front cover with title and Milton's name also lettered in black. A nice copy. See undated ca. 1890 illustrated edition of *L'Allegro* by J. B. Lippincott Company listed here; that edition is slightly expanded, with forty-eight pages rather than forty pages, as here; and see undated ca. 1895 illustrated edition by J. B. Lippincott Company listed here, very similar to the edition here in a variant binding, in forty pages, as here. Scarce. Not in Kohler.

377. MILTON'S L'ALLEGRO AND IL PENSEROSO Edited By C. E. Brownrigg, M.A. The Junior School Milton. Magdalen College School, Oxford[.] *Blackies And Son Limited[,] 50 Old Bailey[,] London[,] Glasgow And Bombay[,] n.d. [ca. 1880]*. First edition thus? Slim 8vo, 32pp., "Milton's Life" preceding the poems, introductory remarks to each poem, "Notes" at the end, original printed pinkish colored wrappers, covers lettered in black (front cover: "Blackie's English Classics"), advertisements on back cover. Good copy. Not in Kohler.

378. L'ALLEGRO AND IL PENSEROSO. By John Milton. With Prefatory And Explanatory Notes. English School Classics. *New York: Clark & Maynard, Publishers[,] 734 Broadway. 1882*. First edition thus. Slim 8vo, 31pp., central circular vignette portrait of Milton as a romanticized figure on title page, advertisement on verso of title page, "Life Of Milton," "Critical Remarks On L'Allegro And Il Penseroso," notes at bottom of the page, original wrappers (a bit used, slight, inoffensive waterstain along top edge, small portion of lower right corner cut away on title page and first page of "Life Of Milton"), title page reprinted in red within decorative border trim on front cover, advertisement in red on inside of front cover and on inside and outside of back cover. Decent copy. Not in Kohler.

379. MILTON'S L'ALLEGRO AND IL PENSEROSO Illustrated With Etchings On Steel By Birket Foster[.] *London And New York[:] George Routledge And Sons[,] 1884*. 4to, twenty-four paginated leaves of card printed on recto only, engraved vignette portrait of a young, long-haired Milton, engraved by Birket Foster from the picture by Samuel Cooper, at the top of title page, twenty-nine additional etchings on steel by Birket Foster, each with protective tissue guard, original green cloth (a bit worn), front cover and spine lettered in gilt with vignette impression of

Milton in gilt at center of front cover, dark green endpapers, a.e.g. The first edition with Foster's illustrations was published by David Bogue in 1855 (also listed here with further editions cited). Not in Kohler.

380. **L'ALLEGRO, IL PENSEROSO, AND THE HYMN ON THE NATIVITY.** By John Milton. Illustrated. *Cassell & Company, Limited: London, Paris, New York & Melbourne. 1885. [All Rights Reserved.]* Slim 8vo, 57pp., title page in red and black, half-title for each poem with poem's title printed between two small decorative pieces, unsigned illustrations within the text for each poem, central decorative tailpiece on last leaf, original red cloth (a bit rubbed), elaborately decorated front cover with long green stems on the left side and with two shields, one in silver and one in red, and two swords at the bottom left-hand corner, large decorative gilt band across the top outlined in a black and red border with red and white scrolls within, wide black strip within narrower silver borders behind the decorative gilt band, narrow silver strip within very narrow black rules at the center, with gilt lettering ("L'Allegro And Il Penseroso By John Milton") above and below, without mention of *Hymn On The Nativity* being included, spine similarly lettered as the cover in gilt, a.e.g. A pretty copy in an attractive, colorful publisher's binding. Not in Kohler.

381. Variant of Preceding, original light blue cloth (a bit rubbed, several stains and some age-darkening on front cover), elaborately decorated as preceding copy, a.e.g. A pretty copy in an attractive, colorful variant publisher's binding. Not in Kohler.

382. Variant of Preceding, original sea green cloth (a bit worn at spine ends and corners with shelf wear along bottom edges), elaborately decorated maroon area on the left side of the front cover with a central sea green circle within in the manner of the sun with blazing heat waves, at the top is a tied bow outlined in gilt which flows down both sides, across the circle is titled "L'Allegro And Il Penseroso" in bright gilt surrounded by gilt and maroon rules, beneath "Illustrated" is lettered in maroon, at the bottom of the maroon area is Milton's name in full in embossed sea green letters within a shaped and very bright gilt background surrounded by maroon and sea green rules, the area outside the maroon area decorated in floral white trim, spine lettered "L'Allegro And Il Penseroso" in maroon letters (now faded), a.e.g. While this copy keeps *Hymn On The Nativity* without mention on the cover or spine, it is in its own attractive, colorful variant publisher's binding with sixteen pages of "Selections from Cassell & Company's Publications" bound in at the end. Not in Kohler.

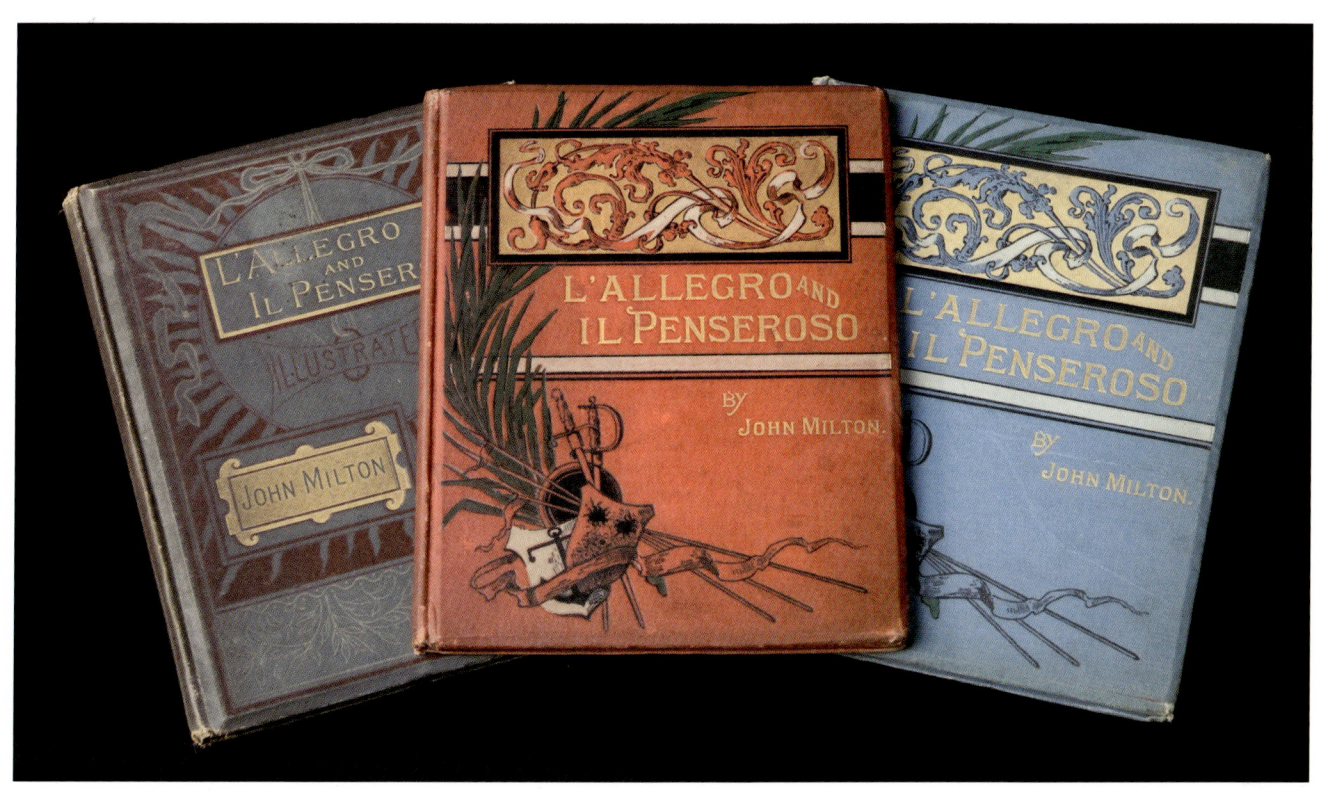

L'Allegro, Il Penseroso, And The Hymn On The Nativity. London, Paris, New York & Melbourne: Cassell & Company, 1885. Variant original decorated publisher's cloth bindings. See #380.

383. L'ALLEGRO AND IL PENSEROSO [In] GEMS FROM THE POETS Illustrated From Original Designs By F. A. Lydon[.] [Quotation from Wordsworth] *London: W. Swan Sonnenschein & Co., Paternoster Square[,] 1885.* Large 8vo, [ii]+34pp., engraved and printed title pages, engraved title in color, frontispiece illustration and other illustrations in color by F. A. Lydon, protective tissue guards, printed title in red and black, original green cloth with elaborate central gilt ornament on front cover incorporating title in gilt, black rules on front cover, spine lettered in gilt with two small decorative pieces in black, black endpapers, a.e.g. A very nice copy with small bookplate stamp on verso of frontispiece. Included are poetical selections from Milton with two illustrations after F. A. Lydon in color for *L'Allegro* complete and two illustrations after Lydon in color for *Il Penseroso* complete. The first edition was published in 1860 (also listed here); see also ca. 1870 edition.

384. L'ALLEGRO By John Milton[.] *Cassell, Petter And Galpin, 396, Broadway, New York. n.d. [ca. 1886].* Possibly second edition; first edition by Cassell, Petter and Galpin? Slim 8vo, 24pp., half-title, unsigned illustration on title page, unsigned illustrations within the text in varying sizes, printed on thick, cardlike paper on recto only, protective tissue guard between each page, small tailpiece on last page with "R. Clay, Sons, And Taylor, Printers, London" at bottom of page, original decorated green cloth (a bit rubbed, spine slightly chipped at bottom), front cover elaborately decorated in embossed black and gold, "Milton's L'Allegro" lettered in embossed green within a large, bright gilt piece at the center surrounded by thick black and gilt borders with "The Choice Series" lettered in embossed green within a smaller gilt piece at the top, and "Straight Mine Eye Hath Caught New Pleasures" within a similar smaller gilt piece at the bottom, spine lettered in black, a.e.g. Nice copy in a lovely publisher's binding with a contemporary signature (dated 1886) on fly-leaf. See undated ca. 1878 edition listed here, possible first thus, an identical edition in an identical binding (except in red cloth) with reference to "The Choice Series," published by "Samson Low, Marston, Low And Searle" in London. Scarce. Not in Kohler.

385. L'ALLEGRO. By John Milton. Illustrated With Numerous Engravings. *Philadelphia: J. B. Lippincott Company[,] 715 And 717 Market Street. n.d. [ca. 1890].* Small 4to, 48pp., half-title, unsigned frontispiece illustration, stamp of the press on verso of title page, half-title before two-page "List Of Illustrations," numerous unsigned illustrations, six full-page illustrations including frontispiece, the others within the text, decorative head- and tailpieces, original pink boards, indented with a pink cloth spine with gilt edging along the indented boards and around the edges of the boards, front board richly decorated with a large emblem at the top, with "L'Allegro" lettered in large red letters over a pink inset within a brilliant gilt backdrop with an embossed floriated pink ribbon intertwined around the inset and tied in a large bow in the front, and a black scroll at the bottom of the front cover with "By John Milton" in smaller red letters within the scroll and curled black lines running behind it, a.e.g. A very nice copy printed on thick paper in a lovely publisher's binding with contemporary presentation inscription (dated 1890) on fly-leaf. See earlier undated ca. 1880 illustrated edition by J. B. Lippincott Company, possible first thus; that edition was done in forty pages rather than forty-eight, as here; and see undated ca. 1895 illustrated edition by J. B. Lippincott Company listed here, very similar to the ca. 1880 edition and done also in forty pages rather than forty-eight, as here. Scarce. Not in Kohler.

386. MILTON'S L'ALLEGRO, IL PENSEROSO, ARCADES, LYCIDAS, SONNETS[,] ETC. With Introduction And Notes By W. Bell, M.A. Professor Of Philosophy And Logic, Government College, Lahore[.] *London[:] Macmillan And Co[.] And New York[,] 1891 [All rights reserved].* Third edition thus. 8vo, xv+183pp., design incorporating the initials of the press on front pastedown, original cream cloth (a bit used and dirtied, lacking fly-leaf), front cover and spine lettered in blue with small emblem in blue incorporating initials of the press in lower right corner of front cover, decorative device in blue incorporating initials of the press on back cover. A good copy. "First Edition, 1889. Reprinted, 1890 1891" (verso of title page). Not in Kohler.

387. L'ALLEGRO AND IL PENSEROSO. By John Milton. With Preparatory And Explanatory Notes. English Classic Series.—No. 2. *New York: Maynard, Merrill, & Co., 29, 31, And 33 East Nineteenth Street. New Series, No. 29. April 11, 1892. Published Semi-weekly. Subscription Price, $10. Entered at Post Office, New York, as Second-class Matter.* First edition thus. Slim 8vo, 31pp., unsigned vignette portrait of a young Milton on title page, a full-page reproduction of Milton portrait by D. Grosch on verso, original printed wrappers (a bit aged, early signature in pencil on title page and on back cover), front cover decorated with border trim and lettering in contrasting brown, called "Maynard's English Classic Series With Explanatory Notes," advertisements on inside front cover and on inside and outside of back cover. A decent copy. Not in Kohler.

388. Variant of Preceding, unsigned vignette portrait of a young Milton on title page, on verso an advertisement for a "A Complete Course In The Study Of English," original printed wrappers (top right corner bent on front cover), front cover decorated with border trim and lettering in contrasting brown, called "Maynard's English Classic Series With Explanatory Notes," advertisements on inside front cover and on inside and outside of back cover. A nice copy, fairly fresh for a publication of its kind, with several variants: an advertisement in place of portrait on verso of title page and variant advertisements on inside of front cover and inside and outside of back cover. Not in Kohler.

389. L'ALLEGRO, IL PENSEROSO, COMUS, AND LYCIDAS By John Milton[.] Eclectic English Classics[.] *New York • Cincinnati • Chicago[:] American Book Company[,] (1894).* First edition thus. Slim 8vo, 74+[6]pp., copyright "1894" on verso of title page, introduction, notes at the bottom of the page, original printed boards (rubbed), with advertisements on back cover. Six pages of advertisement at end. Good copy. The second edition thus was published by the American Book Company in 1911, edited by Philo Melvyn Buck, Jr., with a new introduction and a biography of Milton with "Suggested Questions And Topics For Discussion" and a "Bibliography" (also listed here). Not in Kohler.

390. Variant of Preceding, original printed tan boards (a bit rubbed) with advertisements printed on back cover. Six pages of advertisements at end. A nice copy with variant advertisements in a variant publisher's binding. Not in Kohler.

391. L'ALLEGRO & IL PENSEROSO OF JOHN MILTON With Drawings By William Hyde[.] *London: J. M. Dent & Co: Aldine House: 69 Gt. Eastern St. n.d. (1895).* First edition thus. Crown 8vo, 51pp., half-title, title page in red and black with decorative black border trim and large tree with leaves and roots, designed in art nouveau style by William Hyde, frontispiece photogravure, with poetic passage from *Il Penseroso* printed on protective tissue guard, introduction by T. Gregory Foster, dated "June, 1895," twelve additional photogravures by Walter Colls of paintings by William Hyde, printed on thick Abbey Mill paper, most with a protective tissue guard, original red bubble grain cloth (a bit rubbed), with central gilt-decorated border on front cover incorporating title in gilt, gilt-decorated spine, gilt floral pattern endpapers, t.e.g., others untrimmed. A nice copy with stunning photogravures of William Hyde's drawings for Milton's poems. Scarce. Not in Kohler.

392. L'ALLEGRO. By John Milton. Illustrated With Numerous Engravings. *Philadelphia: J. B. Lippincott Company[,] 715 And 717 Market Street. n.d. [ca. 1895].* Small 4to, 40pp., half-title with unsigned illustration as frontispiece on verso, stamp of the press on verso of title page, half-title before two-page "List Of Illustrations," numerous unsigned illustrations, six full page including frontispiece, the others within the text, decorative head- and tailpieces, original yellow boards (a bit aged, spine missing, endpapers spotted), large illustration in black at center of front cover with title and Milton's name also lettered in black. A nice copy with contemporary presentation inscription (dated 1895) on fly-leaf. See undated ca. 1880 illustrated edition by J. B. Lippincott Company (possible first thus), very similar to the edition here in a variant binding done in forty pages, as here; see also ca. 1890 illustrated edition of *L'A* by J. B. Lippincott Company in a slightly expanded version with forty-eight pages rather than forty pages, as here. Uncommon. Not in Kohler.

393. JOHN MILTON'S L'ALLEGRO, IL PENSEROSO, COMUS, AND LYCIDAS Edited With Notes And Introductions By William P. Trent, M.A. Professor Of English In The University Of The South[.] *Longmans' English Classics[.] New York[:] Longmans, Green, And Co. And London[,] 1895.* First edition thus. Slim 8vo, xviii+181+9+[9]pp., half-title, frontispiece portrait plate of Milton after D. Grosch, small emblem of the press on title page, copyright "1895" and "Trow Directory Printing And Bookbinding Company New York" on verso, "Preface" (dated 1895), original tan cloth (a bit rubbed, spine a little darkened), front cover lettered in reddish-brown with decorative reddish-brown border trim and small emblem of the press in reddish-brown at the center. Nice copy. Eighteen pages of advertisements bound in at the end. A variant edition, without frontispiece portrait, was published in 1897; it was variously reprinted thereafter. Not in Kohler.

394. L'ALLEGRO AND OTHER POEMS By John Milton Edited By Horace E. Scudder With Biographical Sketch[,] Introductions, And Notes[.] *Houghton, Mifflin And Company[,] Boston: 4 Park Street; New York: 85 Fifth Avenue[;] Chicago: 378-388 Wabash Avenue[,] The Riverside Press, Cambridge[,] (1895).* First edition thus. Slim 8vo, 96pp., emblem of the Riverside Press on title page, copyright "1895" on verso of title page, original printed stiff paper wrappers (a bit worn, marginal notations throughout in pencil), "Number 72 Issued Semi-Monthly January 16, 1895" on front cover), advertisements printed inside covers and on back cover. Not in Kohler.

395. L'ALLEGRO AND OTHER POEMS By John Milton Edited By Horace E. Scudder With Supplementary Notes For Careful Study, By Henry W. Boynton, M.A. The Riverside Literature Series. *Houghton Mifflin Company[,] Boston: 4 Park Street; New York: 85 Fifth Avenue[;] Chicago: 378-388 Wabash Avenue[,] The Riverside Press*

Cambridge[,] (1895). First edition thus. Slim 8vo, 108pp., emblem of the Riverside Press on title page, copyright "1895" on verso of title page, original green cloth (a bit rubbed, early name in pencil on fly-leaf), front cover and spine lettered in black with decorative classical pillars in black on front cover, central emblem with initials "RLS 72" in black on back cover. Not in Kohler.

396. L'ALLEGRO AND OTHER POEMS[.] PARADISE LOST BOOKS I - III By John Milton With A Biographical Sketch[,] Introductions, And Notes[.] The Riverside Literature Series*[.] Houghton Mifflin Company[,] Boston: 4 Park Street: New York: 85 Fifth Avenue[;] Chicago: 378-388 Wabash Avenue[.] The Riverside Press Cambridge[,] (1895/1896)*. First edition thus. Slim 8vo, 108pp.,+ 112pp., emblem of the Riverside Press on title page, copyright date of "1895 and 1896" on verso of title page, half-title before "Contents" page, original green cloth (well-used with marginal notations in a neat early hand, lacking front blank), front cover and spine lettered in contrasting darker green, central emblem with initials "RLS 72-94" in contrasting darker green on back cover. Bound in with half-title, separate pagination, and introduction: "**PARADISE LOST BOOKS I-III** By John Milton Edited, With Introduction And Notes, By William Vaughn Moody[.] The Riverside Literature Series[.]" Portrait of Milton as a young man tipped in on front pastedown and a reproduction of Mihaly Munkacsy's *Milton Dictating Paradise Lost* tipped in on verso of title page, marginalia in a neat contemporary hand, and several pages of summaries of the poems in a neat contemporary hand variously tipped in. A second edition was published in 1911 (also listed here). Not in Kohler.

397. Variant of Preceding. **L'ALLEGRO AND OTHER POEMS[.] PARADISE LOST BOOKS I - III** By John Milton With A Biographical Sketch[,] Introductions, And Notes[.] The Riverside Literature Series[.] *Houghton Mifflin Company[,] Boston: 4 Park Street: New York: 11 East Seventeenth Street[;] Chicago: 378-388 Wabash Avenue[.] The Riverside Press Cambridge[,] (1895/1896)*. First edition thus; variant issue. Slim 8vo, 108pp.,+112pp., emblem of the Riverside Press on title page, copyright date of "1895 and 1896" on verso of title page, half-title before "Contents" page, original brown cloth (a little used with a few marginal notations), front cover lettered in contrasting darker brown cloth with decorative contrasting darker brown border trim, spine lettered in contrasting darker brown with decorative trim at top and bottom, endpapers advertising Riverside editions. Bound in with half-title, separate pagination, and introduction: "**PARADISE LOST BOOK I–III** By John Milton With Introduction And Notes[.] The Riverside Literature Series[.]" Similar to preceding copy, but with a variant half-title for *PL*, variant address for New York in publisher's imprint on title page, in a variant publisher's binding.

398. L'ALLEGRO AND IL PENSEROSO. By John Milton. With Preparatory And Explanatory Notes. English Classic Series.—No. 2. *New York: Maynard, Merrill, & Co., 29, 31, And 33 East Nineteenth Street. New Series, No. 24, January 12, 1898. Published Semi-weekly. Subscription Price, $10. Entered at Post Office, New York, as Second-class Matter.* Slim 8vo, 31pp., unsigned vignette portrait of a young Milton on title page, with reproduction of Milton portrait after D. Grosch on verso, "Life of Milton," "Critical Remarks On L'Allegro And Il Penseroso," and "The Titles" precede the poems, notes at bottom of the page, "Examination Questions" at the end, original printed stiff paper wrappers (a bit rubbed), title page reprinted with decorative border trim in reddish-brown on front cover, called "Maynard's English Classic Series," advertisements on front and back endpapers and back cover. Nice. First edition thus published in 1892 (several copies listed here). Scarce. Not in Kohler.

399. [L'ALLEGRO] IL PENSEROSO. Engraved illustration after J. C. Horsley, engraved by E. Garner, measuring 8 ½" × 11 ½" (illustration measuring 6 ½" × 9"), with a glassine cover sheet that contains the passage illustrated printed in red ("Come, pensive nun . . ."). Taken from *Character Sketches of Romance, Fiction and the Drama*, published 1896–1902. In nice condition.

400. L'ALLEGRO, IL PENSEROSO[,] COMUS, AND LYCIDAS By John Milton Edited For School Use By Edward Everett Hale, Jr., Ph.D.[,] Professor Of Rhetoric In Union College[.] English Classics—Star Series[.] *Globe School Book Company[,] New York And Chicago[,] (1900)*. First edition thus. Slim 8vo, 1+140pp., frontispiece portrait plate after D. Grosch, small emblem of the press on title page, copyright 1900 and "Manhattan Press" on verso of title page, half-title for each poem, one illustration plate for *L'A*, two illustration plates for *IlP*, two illustration plates for *C*, one illustration plate for *L*, (all illustrations unsigned), original green cloth (a bit rubbed, spine a little faded, lacking front fly-leaf, first page of introduction torn and repaired with tape, a few light pencil markings and notations variously throughout), front cover decorated and lettered in contrasting dark green. Uncommon. Not in Kohler.

401. MILTON L'ALLEGRO, IL PENSEROSO[,] COMUS, LYCIDAS Edited With Introduction And Notes By Edward S. Parsons, M. A. Bemis Professor Of

English, Colorado College[.] [Quotation in Greek.] Number 7[.] *Benj. H. Sanborn & Co. Boston, U.S.A. (1900).* First edition thus. Small 8vo, 36+[2]+138+[1]pp., half-title ("The Cambridge Literature Series), unsigned frontispiece portrait of Milton at age sixty-two, protective tissue guard, copyright 1899 on verso of title page, preface (dated 1899), original crushed brown buckram (a few inoffensive markings here and there), front cover and spine lettered in white ("Milton's Minor Poems"). Nice copy with advertisement leaf bound in at the end. Not in Kohler.

402. MILTON'S L'ALLEGRO, IL PENSEROSO[,] COMUS[.] AND LYCIDAS Edited With Introduction And Notes By Tuley Francis Huntington, A.M. (Harvard) Litt.D. (Cornell College)[,] Author of "Elements Of English Composition[,]" "Elementary English Composition," Etc. Standard English Classics[.] *Ginn And Company[,] Boston • New York • Chicago • London, (1900).* First edition thus. Slim 8vo, li+130+[1]+[4]pp., frontispiece portrait plate "After an engraving by Faithorne," decorative border trim in black on title page with central decorative device incorporating "Standard English Classics," copyright "1900" and "The Athenaeum Press" on verso of title page, preface (dated 1899), original light green cloth (spine a bit rubbed, signatures in pencil and ink repeatedly on flyleaves, some notations in pencil throughout), black rule on front cover, front cover and spine lettered in black with decorative scroll incorporating "Standard English Classics" at top of front cover. Four pages of advertisement bound in at end. A second edition thus was published in 1901 (also listed here). Not in Kohler.

403. Variant of Preceding. MILTON'S L'ALLEGRO, IL PENSEROSO[,] COMUS[.] AND LYCIDAS Edited With Introduction And Notes By Tuley Francis Huntington, A.M. (Harvard) Litt.D. (Cornell College)[,] Author of "Elements Of English Composition[,]" "Elementary English Composition," Etc. Standard English Classics[.] *Ginn And Company[,] Boston • New York • Chicago • London • Atlanta • Dallas • Columbus • San Francisco, (1900).* First edition thus. Slim 8vo, li+130+[1]+[4]pp., as preceding. A nice copy with variant number of cities in publisher's imprint on title page, and variant number of advertisement pages at end (four compared to six). Not in Kohler.

404. Variant of Preceding. MILTON'S L'ALLEGRO, IL PENSEROSO[,] COMUS[.] AND LYCIDAS Edited by Tuley Francis Huntington, A.M., Litt.D. *Ginn And Company[.] (1900).* First edition thus (variant edition). Slim 8vo, li+130pp., frontispiece portrait plate "After an engraving by Faithorne," as preceding. A good copy with variant title page (without mentioning credentials for Huntington on title page with variant title page trim, with variant publisher's imprint—without place), without "The Athenaeum Press" on verso of title page, and without advertisement leaves at the end. Not in Kohler.

405. Variant of Preceding. MILTON'S L'ALLEGRO, IL PENSEROSO[,] COMUS[.] AND LYCIDAS Edited With Introduction And Notes By Tuley Francis Huntington, A.M. (Harvard) Litt.D. (Cornell College)[,] Author of "Elements Of English Composition[,]" "Elementary English Composition," Etc. Standard English Classics[.] *Ginn And Company[,] Boston • New York • Chicago • London • Atlanta • Dallas • Columbus • San Francisco[,] (1900).* First edition thus (variant edition). Slim 8vo, li+130pp., frontispiece portrait plate "After an engraving by Faithorne," as preceding. A nice copy with variant title page and publisher's imprint, with the bookplate of Milton scholar Maurice Kelley on front pastedown. Given to me by Maurice Kelley when he retired from Princeton in 1971. Kohler 474, without citing Huntington credentials on title page, otherwise the same, reporting "Not in Williamson. Not in the British Library. Not in Cambridge University Library."

406. Variant of Preceding. MILTON'S L'ALLEGRO, IL PENSEROSO[,] COMUS[.] AND LYCIDAS Edited With Introduction And Notes By Tuley Francis Huntington, A.M. (Harvard) Instructor In English In The Leland Stanford Junior University, Sometime Head of The Department OF English In The South Side High School, Milwaukee[.] Standard English Classics[.] *Ginn & Company[,] Boston • New York • Chicago • London, (1900).* First edition thus (variant issue). Slim 8vo, li+130+[1]+[4]pp., frontispiece portrait plate "After an engraving by Faithorne," as preceding, original dark greenish black cloth (markings in pencil and pen, especially on end-leaves), black rule with decorative black trim incorporating "Standard English Classics" on front cover, white lettering on front cover and spine. A good copy with variant title page (full information after Huntington, variant from that provided in other editions here, "Ginn & Company" instead of "Ginn And Company," and fewer cities), in a variant binding, with four pages of advertisement (with half-title) bound in at the end. Not in Kohler.

407. L'ALLEGRO, AND OTHER POEMS[.] John Milton[.] Ten Cent Pocket Series No. 317 Edited by E. Haldeman-Julius[.] *Haldeman-Julius Company[,] Girard, Kansas[.] n.d. [ca. 1900].* Slim 16mo, 64pp., pamphlet, original printed light blue wrappers. Nice copy with five-page listing of "Other Titles in Pocket Series" bound in at the end. See later, ca. 1920 edition, listed here. Scarce. Not in Kohler.

408. MILTON'S L'ALLEGRO, IL PENSEROSO[,] COMUS[.] AND LYCIDAS Edited With Introduction And Notes By Tuley Francis Huntington, A.M. (Harvard) Instructor In English In The Leland Stanford Junior University[,] Sometime Head Of The Department Of English In The South Side High School, Milwaukee[.] *Boston, U.S.A.[:] Ginn & Company, Publishers[,] The Athenaeum Press[,] 1901.* Second edition thus. Slim 8vo, li+130pp., frontispiece portrait plate "After an engraving by Faithorne," title page in red and black, preface (dated 1899), original light green cloth (a little rubbed with slight staining on front cover, a few underlinings, contemporary signature on fly-leaf, bottom portion of back blanks missing), contrasting dark green rule on front cover with dark green lettering ("Standard English Classics") and central decorative design in dark green, spine lettered in dark green. The first edition thus was published in 1900 (several copies listed here). Scarce. Not in Kohler.

409. L'ALLEGRO By John Milton Composed About 1632[.] With pictures by Maxfield Parrish. Small 4to, extracted from *The Century Magazine*, Christmas Number, LXIII, no. 2 (December 1901): 161–69, printed on glossy paper, title printed within decorative circular trim on verso of first illustration, decorative head- and tailpieces throughout, decorated initial letter at the beginning, four lithograph illustration plates in color by Maxfield Parrish, each plate measuring 6" × 9 ¼" overall, the image measuring 5" × 8", with the line or lines illustrated printed beneath. In fine condition. Not in Kohler.

410. L'ALLEGRO & IL PENSEROSO[.] John Milton[.] *The Blue Sky Press[,] Chicago[,] (1902).* First edition thus. 8vo, 42pp.+colophon page, half-title, title page in red and black with small decorative piece in red, half-title in red with decorative black trim for each poem, first appearance of illustrations after H. E. Townsend, one for each poem, decorated initial letters, title of poem printed in red in the margin of each page with initials in red, "A Note" by Thomas Wood Stevens at end with "A Note" printed in red in the margins, original boards, parchment spine (spine a bit darkened, boards a bit aged), decorated endpapers, edges untrimmed, partially unopened. A handsomely printed book. No. 54 of 100 copies printed on Japan vellum. Not in Kohler.

411. L'ALLEGRO AND IL PENSEROSO By John Milton[.] *[New Rochelle:] The Elston Press[,] 1903.* First edition thus. Small 4to, 31pp., title page in red and black with elaborate woodcut title border, first appearance of seventeen woodcut illustrations after designs by H. M. O'Kane, headpieces, decorated initial letters, printed in red and black by Clarke Conwell, original boards, linen spine, printed paper label, unopened. A fine copy. This is a fairly early example of one of the best American private presses of the period. Clarke Conwell was the printer, and the illustrations were by his wife Helen M. O'Kane. One of 160 copies. A scarce title. Not listed in Ransom, *Private Presses*; Not in Kohler.

411A. (Cross-listing) L'ALLEGRO AND IL PENSEROSO [In] LYCIDAS[,] L'ALLEGRO[,] IL PENSEROSO[,] AND THE ODE ON THE MORNING OF CHRIST'S NATIVITY[.] John Milton[.] *["This Volume Is Printed At The Chiswick Press, London, And Published By Alfred Bartlett, Cornhill, Boston" (colophon leaf).] n.d. [ca. 1903].* Possibly the first appearance of these illustrations and decorations by Robert Anning Bell, with the illustration in red for *L'A* and for *IlP*. Not in Kohler. See main listing under *Lycidas*, 1903.

411B. (Cross-listing) [L'ALLEGRO AND IL PENSEROSO] Byse, Fanny. MILTON ON THE CONTINENT: A Key To *L'Allegro* & *Il Penseroso*. With Several Illustrations, A Historical Chart, And An Original Portrait Of Galileo. By Mrs. Fanny Byse. *London: Elliot Stock, 1903.* First edition. Small 8vo, original wrappers. Presentation copy inscribed "From the Authoress London 1910." See main listing under *Byse* with Twentieth-century Miltoniana.

412. MILTON'S L'ALLEGRO, IL PENSEROSO[,] COMUS[.] AND LYCIDAS Edited With Introduction And Notes By Tuley Francis Huntington, A.M. (Harvard) Instructor In English In The Leland Stanford Junior University[,] Sometime Head Of The Department Of English In The South Side High School, Milwaukee[.] *Boston, U.S.A.[:] Ginn & Company, Publishers[,] The Athenaeum Press[,] 1904.* Third edition thus? Slim 8vo, li+130pp.+[6], frontispiece portrait plate "After an engraving by Faithorne," decorative border trim on title page, copyright date of "1900" on verso of title page, preface (dated 1899), introduction, half-title for *Comus* and for "Notes" at end, original blue cloth (a little worn with ink stain at bottom of front cover, endpapers heavily marked with notes and drawings, underlinings and marginal notations throughout), front cover lettered in yellow ("Standard English Classics") with yellow emblem at the center, spine lettered in faded yellow. The first edition thus was published in 1900 (several copies listed here); the second edition thus in 1901 (copy listed here). Not in Kohler.

413. [L'ALLEGRO] IL PENSEROSO[.] L'ALLEGRO AND ARCADES By John Milton[.] *London[:] At The De La More Press[,] 32 George Street Hanover Square W[.] 1907.* First edition thus. Slim 8vo, 30+[1]pp., half-title, title page in red and black, half-title before each poem, original red cloth (a bit rubbed), front cover elaborately decorated in gilt with central gilt emblem incorporating "De La More Booklets," spine lettered in gilt, a.e.g. A very nice copy. According to advertisement leaf for "The De La More Booklets" bound in at end: "In artistic Paper Covers, 6d. each net . . . Cloth gilt, 1/-net. In Moreen Binding, 1/6 each net. In Limp Lambskin, 2/6 each net." Included in the series are three Milton publications: "No. 4. Milton's 'Morning of Christ's Nativity'"; "No. 9. Milton's 'Lycidas'"; and "No. 24. Milton's 'Il Penseroso,' 'L'Allegro,' and 'Arcades.'" Not in Kohler.

414. JOHN MILTON'S L'ALLEGRO, IL PENSEROSO, COMUS, AND LYCIDAS[.] Edited With Notes And Introductions By William P. Trent, LL.D., D.C.L.[,] Professor Of English Literature In Columbia University[.] Longmans' English Classics. *New York[:] Longmans, Green, And Co. London, Bombay, And Calcutta[,] (1909).* Slim 8vo, x+181pp., original red cloth (a bit rubbed, pencil markings), front cover decorated and lettered in black, spine lettered in black. The first edition thus was published in 1897; it was variously reprinted thereafter. A variant edition with frontispiece portrait was published by Trent two years earlier in 1895 (copy listed here). Not in Kohler.

415. MILTON'S L'ALLEGRO, IL PENSEROSO, COMUS, AND LYCIDAS Edited By Philo Melvyn Buck . . . Eclectic English Classics[.] *New York • Cincinnati • Chicago[:] American Book Company[,] (1911).* Second edition thus. Slim 8vo, edited by Philo Melvyn Buck with a new introduction, notes at bottom of page (as in the first edition), and a new ten-page biography of "John Milton" with "Suggested Questions And Topics For Discussion" and a "Bibliography" at end, original brown cloth (slight wear, a few pencil marks throughout), lettered "Milton's Minor Poems" on front cover and spine. Twelve pages of advertisements bound in at end. Nice copy. The first edition thus was published by the American Book Company in 1894 without mention of an editor (several copies listed here). Kohler 486, reporting "Not in the British Library. Not in the Bodleian Library. Not in Cambridge University Library."

416. L'ALLEGRO AND OTHER POEMS[.] PARADISE LOST BOOKS I - III By John Milton With A Biographical Sketch[,] Introductions, And Notes[.] The Riverside Literature Series[.] *Boston[,] New York[,] Chicago[:] Houghton Mifflin Company[,] The Riverside Press Cambridge[,] (1911).* Second edition thus. Slim 8vo, 117+112pp., emblem of the Riverside Press on title page, half-title before the poems with "Contents" on verso, "Biographical Sketch," followed by the poems, "Notes For Careful Study" and "Suggestive Questions And Comments" at the end, original green cloth (a bit rubbed, lacking fly-leaf, with pencil notes on verso of back blank), front cover and spine lettered in contrasting darker green. Bound in, with half-title, separate pagination, and introduction: "**PARADISE LOST BOOK I-III** By John Milton Edited, With Introduction And Notes, By William Vaughn Moody[.] The Riverside Literature Series[.]" The first edition was published in 1895/1896 (copy listed here). Not in Kohler.

417. L'ALLEGRO AND IL PENSEROSO TOGETHER WITH THE SONNETS AND ODES By John Milton[.] Literary Gems[.] *New York and London[:] G. P. Putnam's Sons[,] The Knickerbocker Press. n.d. [1912].* First edition thus? Small 8vo (3 ½" × 4 ¾"), 133+[3]pp., half-title ("Literary Gems"), frontispiece illustration for *L'Allegro* signed "Maud Humphrey '12," protective tissue guard, title page in red and black, "Electrotyped, Printed, and Bound by The Knickerbocker Press, New York G. P. Putnam's Sons" on verso of title page, half-titles for *L'Allegro, Il Penseroso, Sonnets,* and *Odes,* decorative head- and tail-pieces throughout, original vellum cloth (a little worn), decorative gilt border trim on front cover with central emblem in gilt incorporating title and Milton's name, spine lettered in gilt and ruled in gilt at top and bottom, decorated endpapers, t.e.g., others untrimmed. A nice copy of an uncommon book in the series "Literary Gems." Three pages of advertisements for the series "Literary Gems" bound in at the end. Not in Kohler.

418. MILTON'S L'ALLEGRO, IL PENSEROSO, COMUS, AND LYCIDAS Edited By Martin W. Sampson[,] Professor Of English In Cornell University[.] *New York[:] Henry Holt And Company[,] (1912).* First edition thus. 8vo, xxxii+96pp., half-title ("English Readings for Schools"), frontispiece portrait of Milton at age twenty-one, introduction, "Descriptive Bibliography," half-title before the poems, sketch of Ludlow Castle before *C,* "Notes And Comment" (with half-title) at the end, original brown cloth (spine a bit rubbed along edges and ends, with a small crease at center), front cover and spine ruled and lettered in green, decorated endpapers. A possible second edition thus was published in 1930 (copy listed here), and a possible third edition thus in 1931 (copy listed here). Not in Kohler.

419. [MINOR POEMS] L'ALLEGRO[,] IL PENSEROSO[,] COMUS AND LYCIDAS By John Milton Edited for School Use By Edward Everett Hale, Jr., Ph.D.[,] Professor of English in Union College[.] English Classics—Star Series[.] *Yonkers-On-Hudson, New York[:] World Book Company[,] 1914.* First edition thus. Slim 8vo, 140pp., frontispiece portrait plate of Milton "After the painting by Faed, from the painting by Faithorne," elaborate decorative black border trim on title-page plate, with advertisement for the "English Classics—Star Series" on verso and copyright date of 1914, six unsigned illustration plates in black and white, with the lines being illustrated printed beneath each illustration, one for *L'A*, two for *IlP*, two for *C*, and one for *L*, half-title for each poem, original green cloth (a bit rubbed with small ink stain in lower corner of front cover, slight browning on frontispiece and title page from note paper folded within, pencil notations on endpapers and variously throughout), front cover lettered in black ("Milton Minor Poems"), with decorative blind border trim and central emblem in blind incorporating "English Classics Starr Series," spine also lettered in black ("Milton L'Allegro Hale"). Not in Kohler.

419A. (Cross-listing) [L'ALLEGRO] [In] **THE PAGEANT OF ENGLISH LITERATURE** Depicted By J. M. W. Turner, Daniel Maclise . . . Burne-Jones, etc. And Described By Edward Parrott . . . *London, Edinburgh, Dublin, And New York: Thomas Nelson And Sons, 1914*. First edition. Included are two chapters on Milton (Chapter XXIX, "Milton" and Chapter XXX, "*Paradise Lost*"). In the chapter entitled "Milton" is a reproduction in color of C. W. Cope's painting for *L'A*. See main listing under *Parrott* with Twentieth-century Miltoniana.

420. **L'ALLEGRO AND OTHER POEMS** John Milton[.] Ten Cent Pocket Series No. 317 Edited by E. Haldeman-Julius. *Haldeman-Julius Company[,] Girard, Kansas. n.d. [ca. 1920s]*. First edition thus. Small paperback, 3 ⅕" × 5", 64pp., original printed light gray wrappers (slightly faded along edges), front cover lettered in black. Nice copy with five-page listing of "Other Titles in Pocket Series" bound in at the end. See earlier, ca. 1900 edition. Scarce.

421. [L'ALLEGRO AND IL PENSEROSO] **MILTON'S L'ALLEGRO UND IL PENSEROSO**. *([Leipzig: Poeschel & Trepte for the members of the Gesellschaft der Bibliophilen, 1921], a reprint of the edition printed by Schwan, 1782, in "Manheim in der Schwanischen Buchhandlung MDCCLXXXII")*. Tall 8vo, 31pp.+colophon leaf, title page illustration and eight vignette illustrations, reproductions of the engravings done by Ferdinand Kobell for the original printing, English verse and German prose translation on facing pages, original publisher's paper boards (spine paper half gone), printed paper label on front cover. Except for the spine paper being partially gone, a fine copy of this facsimile reprint. Scarce.

422. L'ALLEGRO [In] **THE GOLDEN TREASURY** Of The Best Songs And Lyrical Poems In The English Language Selected And Arranged With Notes By Francis Turner Palgrave Fellow Of Exeter College Oxford[.] Illustrated By Eleanor Fortescue-Brickdale R. W. S. *Hodder And Stoughton Limited London[.] n.d. [ca. 1925]*. First London edition thus. Thick 8vo, xv+459pp., half-title, illustrations in color by Eleanor Fortescue-Brickdale, each tipped in on thick brown paper within gilt trim, each with protective tissue guard printing the poetic lines illustrated, original orange cloth (spine a bit faded), decorative vignette on upper corner front cover, lettering in black on front cover and spine with decoration on spine, t.e. yellow, "Index Of Writers" and "Index Of First Lines" at end. A very nice copy with contemporary inscription (dated "Xmas 1925") on fly-leaf. Included are poetical selections from Milton with an illustration by Eleanor Fortescue-Brickdale in color for *L'A* ("And the milkmaid singeth blithe," line 65).

423. L'ALLEGRO [In] **THE GOLDEN TREASURY** Of The Best Songs And Lyrical Poems In The English Language Selected And Arranged With Notes By Francis Turner Palgrave Fellow Of Exeter College Oxford[.] Illustrated By Eleanor Fortescue-Brickdale R. W. S. *New York: George H. Doran Company[,] n.d. [ca. 1925]*. First American edition thus. Thick 8vo, xv+459pp., half-title, illustrations in color by Eleanor Fortescue-Brickdale, each tipped in on thick brown paper within gilt trim, each with protective tissue guard printing the poetic lines illustrated, original half red cloth, bright orange and gilt marbled paper, spine lettered in gilt, t.e.g, others untrimmed, "Index Of Writers" and "Index Of First Lines" at end. Fine copy. Included are poetical selections from Milton with an illustration by Eleanor Fortescue-Brickdale in color for *L'A* ("And the milkmaid singeth blithe," line 65).

424. **L'ALLEGRO AND IL PENSEROSO** By John Milton[.] Illustrated By Peggy Norgate[.] *London[:] John Lane The Bodley Head Ltd.[,] (1927)*. First edition thus. Small 4to, 54+[1]pp., half-title ("The Helicon Series. III"), half-title each poem, frontispiece illustration and other illustrations (full-page and within the text) by Peggy Norgate, original black paper boards (some underlining and three marginal notations in a neat hand, name on front endpaper) with decorative trim in white at top and bottom of front cover and spine and lettering in white on front cover and spine, printed publisher's wrappers in red and black in a protective plastic cover, edges untrimmed. A nice copy, "Printed in Great Britain by R. & R. Clark, Limited, Edinburgh" (verso title page), apparently in a limited number.

424A. (Cross-listing) **L'ALLEGRO**. Transcribed By F. W. Mercer, 1927. Square 8vo, manuscript volume in which *L'Allegro* is written out in a fine script, with an elaborately hand-colored illuminated border on each page, handsomely bound in full vellum, spine lettered in gilt, a.e.g., silver clasp. See main listing under *Mercer* with *Editions*.

425. L'ALLEGRO AND IL PENSEROSO [In] MILTON'S L'ALLEGRO, IL PENSEROSO, COMUS, AND LYCIDAS Edited By Martin W. Sampson[,] Professor Of English In Cornell University[.] *New York[:] Henry Holt And Company[,] (1930)*. Second edition thus? 8vo, xxxii+96pp., half-title ("English Readings [sic, variant from first and third editions] General Editor Wilbur Lucius Cross"), frontispiece portrait of Milton at age twenty-one, introduction, "Descriptive Bibliography," half-title before the poems, sketch of Ludlow Castle before *Comus*, "Notes And Comment" (with half-title) at the end, original red cloth (a little used, small white speck on front cover, notes and sketches in green ink throughout), front cover and spine lettered in blind, decorated endpapers. The first edition thus was published in 1912 (copy listed here), the possible third edition thus in 1931 (copy also listed here).

426. L'ALLEGRO AND IL PENSEROSO [In] MILTON'S L'ALLEGRO, IL PENSEROSO, COMUS, AND LYCIDAS Edited By Martin W. Sampson[,] Professor Of English In Cornell University[.] *New York[:] Henry Holt And Company[,] (1931)*. Third edition thus? 8vo, xxxii+96pp., half-title ("English Readings for Schools General Editor Wilbur Lucius Cross"), frontispiece portrait of Milton at age twenty-one, [as second edition preceding], original red cloth (a bit rubbed, some staining at bottom half of front cover caused by something having been set on it, lacking front fly-leaf), front cover lettered in gilt, spine lettered in blind, decorated endpapers. A good copy.

427. MILTON'S L'ALLEGRO[.] *[Glen Head, N.Y.:] The Ashlar Press[,] 1932*. Slim 8vo, 9pp.+colophon leaf, half-title, woodblock illustration on title page after Rudolph Ruzicka, "L'Allegro" printed at the head of the poem, original white paper boards, spine lettered in gilt, edges untrimmed. Together with **MILTON'S IL PENSEROSO**[.] [Glen Head, N.Y.:] The Ashlar Press[,] 1932. Slim 8vo, 9pp.+colophon leaf, half-title, woodblock illustration on title page after Rudolph Ruzicka, "Il Penseroso" printed in white against black background at the head of the poem, original black paper boards, spine lettered in gilt, edges untrimmed and partially unopened. Together 2 volumes. A fine set in original slipcase covered with decorated paper in a patterned design with printed paper label in black and white on spine. "Of this edition of Milton's 'L'Allegro' / 'Il Penseroso', four hundred copies were made at The Ashlar Press, Glen Head, Long Island. The woodcut on the title page, by Rudolph Ruzicka, was printed from the original wood block" (colophon leaf at end of each volume). Rare.

427A. (Cross-listing) L'ALLEGRO AND IL PENSEROSO [In] FOUR POEMS BY JOHN MILTON[:] L'ALLEGRO[,] IL PENSEROSO[,] ARCADES[,] LYCIDAS[.] With Wood-Engravings By Blair Hughes-Stanton[.] *[Newton, Wales:] The Gregynog Press[,] MCMXXXIII*. One of 250 numbered copies. See main listing under *Four Poems*, 1933.

428. L'ALLEGRO AND IL PENSEROSO [In] MILTON[:] L'ALLEGRO, IL PENSEROSO ET SAMSON AGONISTES[.] Traduits, Avec Une Introduction, Par Floris Delattre, Professeur De Littérature Et Civilisation De La Renaissance Anglaise À La Sorbonne. *Fernand Aubier, Editions Montaigne, Paris[,] MCMXXXVII*. First edition thus. 8vo, xcii+[1]+151+x+[1]pp., half-title (with list of "Ouvrages Du Traducteur"), lengthy introduction (on the life, works, and style of Milton), reproduction of 1645 title page for *P* before *L'A*, reproduction of 1671 title page for *SA* before the poem, half-title before each poem, with the English text printed on the left side and the French translation on the right page, appendices at the end (consisting of several bibliographies of Milton studies), with the "Table" of Contents on the last leaf, original printed light orange stiff paper wrappers (half-title scissored off at the top right, some underlining in pen throughout the introduction with some notes in pencil on verso of last page, spine a little faded, pages a little age-browned), edges untrimmed, partially unopened. A good copy of this bilingual edition in original wraps that are quite clean, with a listing of "Aubier, Editions Montaigne" on the back cover. The introduction and the translation are by Florence Delattre.

429. [L'ALLEGRO AND IL PENSEROSO] JOHN MILTON'S L'ALLEGRO, IL PENSEROSO[,] COMUS, AND LYCIDAS Edited With Notes And Introduction By William P. Trent, LL.D., D.C.L. Professor Of English Literature In Columbia University*[.] Longmans, Green And Co.[,] New York[,] Chicago[,] Boston[,] Toronto[,] (1940)*. Small 8vo, x+181pp., half-title, front cover and spine lettered in gilt with large central emblem in blind on front cover. A fine copy, near mint. "First Edition August 1897" is printed on verso of title page, along with the reprint dates 1909 and 1940. A variant edition with frontispiece portrait was published in 1895. All three editions are listed here.

430. [L'ALLEGRO AND IL PENSEROSO] IL PENSEROSO[;] JOHN MILTON[;] LYCIDAS[;] 1608-1674[.] *London and Maidstone: L.C.C.Central School Of Arts & Crafts in exile at Saint Martin's School of ARTS, W. C.2 & Maidstone School Of Art & Crafts[,] 1943*. First edition thus. Slim 8vo, 19pp., title page in red and black, half-title for each poem, initial letters in red, colophon in red, original three quarter black leather, marbled paper over boards, front cover lettered in gilt. Colophon at end: "This edition was arranged and set in type by C. R. Adams in the Typography classes of the L.C.C. Central School of Arts and Crafts (evacuated to St. Martin's School of Art, W.C.2), during the Session 1940–41. Owing to the impossibility of completing printing, due to enemy action, the booklet has been printed at the K.E.C. Maidstone School of Art and Crafts during the Autumn Term, 1943. At both schools the work was supervised by Charles L. Pickering."

431. JOHN MILTON L'ALLEGRO IL PENSEROSO Illustrated By Bernard Meninsky[.] *Allan Wingate[,] London[,] MDMXLVII*. First edition thus. Tall 4to, 29pp.+ colophon leaf, half-title, first appearance of circular illustration in tinted blue on title page and other illustrations in tinted blue by Bernard Meninsky, half-title before each poem, "Printed by Spottiswoode Ballantyne & Co Ltd London & Colchester" and "Designed by Vincent Stuart" on colophon, original decorated stiff paper wrappers (a bit rubbed), with an illustration in outline form in red for *L'A* with black lettering on front cover and an illustration in red for *IlP* with black lettering on back cover, edges untrimmed. A nice copy.

432. L'ALLEGRO AND IL PENSEROSO [In] Van Sinderen, Adrian. BLAKE[:] THE MYSTIC GENIUS[.] *[Syracuse, N.Y.:] Syracuse University Press[,] 1949*. First edition thus. Square 8vo, 119pp.+colophon leaf, half-title, twenty-seven plates (one as frontispiece), twelve in full color, "Engraved and printed by The Beck Engraving Company[,] Designed by Lucia Howe" (colophon), original white buckram spine, decorated paper over boards, spine lettered in gilt, light gray endpapers. Very nice copy in publisher's slipcase with lettering in outline on front side. Blake's illustrations for *L'A* and *IlP* are reproduced in full color (twelve plates) and in black and white along with the text of Milton's companion poems. One of 1,100 copies. Bentley 2898.

433. [L'ALLEGRO AND IL PENSEROSO] JOHN MILTON L'ALLEGRO With The Paintings By William Blake Together With A Note Upon The Poems By W. P. Trent[.] *New York[:] The Limited Editions Club[,] 1954*. Together with **JOHN MILTON IL PENSEROSO** With The Paintings By William Blake Together With A Note Upon The Paintings By Chauncey Brewster Tinker[.] *New York[:] The Limited Editions Club[,] 1954*. First edition thus. Tall 8vo, 43pp.,+44pp.+colophon leaf, half-title for each poem, first appearance of twelve photogravure plates from the Blake originals in the Morgan Library, original green buckram, gilt lettering on each cover and spine, marbled endpapers over thick boards, with an extra set of the thick marbled endpapers bound between the poems, blue edges. Fine copy, near mint, in original glassine publisher's dust wrappers, in publisher's slipcase. Blake did one set of illustrations for *L'A* and *IlP* in 1817, published here for the first time. Printed dos-á-dos at the Thistle Press by Bruce Rogers, who also designed this book, in a limited edition of 1780 copies, of which this is number 605, with 280 copies printed for the Fellows of the John Pierpont Morgan Library.

434. JOHN MILTON L'ALLEGRO With The Paintings By William Blake Together With A Note Upon The Poems By W. P. Trent[.] *New York[:] The Heritage Press[,] n.d. (1954)*. Together with **JOHN MILTON IL PENSEROSO** With The Paintings By William Blake Together With A Note Upon The Paintings By Chauncey Brewster Tinker[.] *New York[:] The Heritage Press[,] n.d. (1954)*. First edition thus. Tall 8vo, 43pp.,+44pp., half-title for each poem, twelve illustrations after Blake reproduced, printed dos-á-dos, original quarter red buckram, marbled paper over boards, each cover with a small white label printed in black, spine lettered in gilt, marbled endpapers, with an extra set of the endpapers bound between the poems. A fine copy, near mint, in publisher's slipcase. A reprint of the Limited Editions Club publication in 1954 (preceding copy).

435. JOHN MILTON L'ALLEGRO AND IL PENSEROSO Edited by Elaine B. Safer [and] Thomas L. Erskine[,] University of Delaware[.] The Merrill Literary Casebook Series[:] Edward P. J. Corbett, Editor[.] *Charles E. Merrill Publishing Company[,] A Bell & Howell Company[,] Columbus, Ohio[,] 1970*. First edition thus. Slim 8vo, vi+146pp., footnotes at bottom of the page, excerpts from various Milton critics at the end, original printed stiff paper wrappers (a bit rubbed, name blacked out on title page). "These casebooks deal with literary works brief enough to be read at one sitting. They provide intensive study of one piece with different points of view" (back cover).

435A. (Cross-listing) L'ALLEGRO AND IL PENSEROSO Written out and illuminated by Florence Brooks. *[n.p.] 1971*. 8" × 10", 30pp., unbound. A fine modern calligraphic manuscript, written out on thirty pages of fine quality paper in black ink in a classic Arrighi Italic hand, with painted illumination in colors and raised gold, all by the renowned calligrapher Florence Brooks, unbound, colophon dated 1971. Very attractive. See main listing under Brooks, Florence, in Chapter V.

436. MILTON'S L'ALLEGRO AND IL PENSEROSO. Illustrated With Etchings On Steel, By Birket Foster.

London: The Scolar Press, 39 Great Russell Street, W.C.I[,] MDCCCLXXV. 8vo, [2]+24pp., half-title, title page in red and black with reproduction of vignette portrait of a young, long-haired Milton, engraved by Birket Foster from the picture by Samuel Cooper, reproduction of illustrations by Birket Foster, text reprinted in red with the etching in black on one side of each page, each page slip-sheeted with protective tissue guard, original cream buckram, etching reproduced in black line on front cover, gilt lettering on front cover and spine, brown endpapers, printed publisher's wrappers with an etching reproduced in black on front cover and another etching reproduced in black on back cover, covers and spine lettered in red. A fine copy. Facsimile reproduction by the the Scolar Press of the edition of 1860 printed in London and published by W. Kent & Co. (Late D. Bogue), (see original edition). The first edition with Birket Foster's illustrations was published in 1855 (copy listed here).

437. L'ALLEGRO. IL PENSEROSO. *Kettering, England, n.d. (1976).* First edition thus. Near miniature (4.5" × 6.3"), [18]pp., decorative head-trim, decorated initial letters, decorative tailpieces, original printed wrappers, with reproduction of Milton portrait at age twenty-one on blue front cover, brief biography of Milton with vignette portrait of Milton at age sixty-two on inside back cover. Fine copy.

438. [L'ALLEGRO] MILTON IL PENSEROSO Edited, With Notes By Oliver Elton, M.A. Professor Of English Literature In The University Of Liverpool[.] *[Norwood, Pa.:] Norwood Editions[,] 1976).* Reprint of 1891 edition published by the Clarendon Press, Oxford, as part of "Oxford Clarendon Series." Slim 8vo, 16pp., two title pages, one a reprint of original 1891 title page, original blue cloth, spine lettered in silver. Nice copy, stamped "Surplus, Library of Congress Duplicate" in red on fly-leaf. Printed in a limited edition of 100.

438A. (Cross-listing) L'ALLEGRO AND IL PENSEROSO [In] ON THE MORNING OF CHRIST'S NATIVITY & OTHER POEMS by John Milton with engravings by Brian Hanscomb[.] *London[:] The Folio Press[,] 1987.* See main listing under *On The Morning Of Christ's Nativity*, 1987.

439. L'ALLEGRO [In] THE LANGUAGE OF FLOWERS. Written By Gail Harvey[.] Designed By Liz Trovato[.] *Gramercy Books[.] New York • Avenel[, N.J.] (1995).* First edition. 8vo, 87+[1]pp., half-title, color illustrations throughout, "The Floral Dictionary" at end, original white cloth, spine lettered in dark green, dark green endpapers, printed publisher's wrappers with white printing against dark green background and floral reproduction in color on front and back cover. Fine copy. Included is a two-line quotation from *L'A* (lines 67–68) with a color illustration (in green and white) of the Hawthorn flower beneath.

Lament for Damon and Other Latin Poems

440. MILTON'S LAMENT FOR DAMON AND HIS OTHER LATIN POEMS Rendered Into English By Walter Skeat[,] Sometime Scholar Of Christ's College[.] With Preface And Introductions By E. H. Visiak[,] Author Of Milton Agonistes[.] *London[:] Oxford University Press[,] Humphrey Milford[,] 1935.* First edition thus. 8vo, vi+[1]+109+[1]pp., general half-title and half-title for each section, original blue cloth (a bit rubbed), front cover and spine lettered in gilt, fore- and bottom edges untrimmed. Nice copy with contemporary signature on fly-leaf.

441. [LATIN AND GREEK POEMS] A VARIORUM COMMENTARY ON THE POEMS OF JOHN MILTON[:] VOLUME ONE[:] THE LATIN AND GREEK POEMS DOUGLAS BUSH[;] THE ITALIAN POEMS J. E. SHAW AND A. BARTLETT GIAMATTI[.] *New York[:] Columbia University Press[,] 1970.* Volume 1 of the series, complete unto itself. First edition thus. 8vo, xi+389pp., half-title (with a list of "The Complete Series" on verso), half-title for various of the works, original blue buckram, spine lettered in gilt, printed dark blue publisher's wrappers (a bit worn at joints). Presentation copy inscribed on fly-leaf by Bart Giamatti to me when he was awarded an honorary degree, along with Frank Cashen, from Mount Saint Mary's College (M.D.) while I was president at May Commencement, 1989. Giamatti was the Commissioner of Baseball in the midst of the Pete Rose scandal at the time, nearing his decision and to meet with Rose in the week after receiving his degree at the Mount. Unfortunately, Bart died from cancer less than a year later. His loss was a profound one. Frank Cashen was then general manager of the New York Mets. Frank had been co-chair of the search committee that helped select me as president of the Mount in late 1976 when he was working his miracles as general manager of the Baltimore Orioles.

442. Variant of Preceding. A VARIORUM COMMENTARY ON THE POEMS OF JOHN MILTON[:] VOLUME ONE[:] THE LATIN AND GREEK POEMS DOUGLAS BUSH[;] THE ITALIAN POEMS J. E. SHAW AND A. BARTLETT GIAMATTI[.] *New York[:] Columbia University Press[,] (1970).* Volume 1 of the series, complete unto itself. Possible first edition thus (variant title page). 8vo, xi+389pp., half-title, (with a list of "The Complete Series" on verso), half-titles for various of the works, original blue buckram, spine lettered in gilt, printed publisher's light blue wrappers. A fine copy with a variant title page, with no date printed on title page, and with "First published 1970 by Columbia University Press, New York.... Printed in Great Britain" tipped at top of verso of title page.

443. LATIN AND ITALIAN POEMS OF MILTON TRANSLATED INTO ENGLISH VERSE, And A Fragment Of A Commentary On Paradise Lost, By The Late William Cowper, Esqr. With A Preface By The Editor, And Notes Of Various Authors. [Latin Quotation from Cicero] *Printed By J. Seagrave, Chichester, For J. Johnson, St. Paul's Church Yard, and R. H. Evans, Pall-Mall, London. 1808.* First edition. 4to, xxvii+328pp., first appearance of frontispiece illustration of Milton seated, surrounded by various references to his life and work, engraved by A. Raimbach after J. Flaxman (dated "March 29th. 1808"), and two other line-engraved illustration plates engraved by A. Raimbach after J. Flaxman (each dated "March 29th. 1808"), one plate for Elegy III and the other for Elegy IV, half-titles for various of the sections, recent one-half crushed brown morocco, blue marbled paper over boards, spine ruled and lettered in gilt, with decorative gilt devices in the panels, raised bands, new endpapers, edges untrimmed. A fresh, large paper copy of a scarce book. Stevens 1376; Kohler 226.

The translation is by Cowper, the whole edited by Hayley. This translation was Cowper's final great work. When his last decline overtook him, he was at work on the commentary, which is printed here as he left it. Cowper's is the first and apparently only edition to print the Latin poems in a different arrangement from that of 1673. Cowper and Hayley were the editors of the famous 1794–97 Boydell edition of Milton's *PW* (see set listed here).

444. THE LATIN AND ITALIAN POEMS OF MILTON. Translated Into English Verse, By Jacob George Strutt, Author Of The Rape Of Proserpine, And Other Translations From Claudian. *London: Published By J. Conder, 18, St. Paul's Church-Yard. 1816.* First edition thus. 8vo, viii+144+[22]pp., "Notes" at end with half-title, original boards (spine a little rubbed and chipped, light wear and soiling), original printed paper spine label (rubbed and age-darkened). A good copy of the first Strutt edition, very clean internally. Strutt explains in his preface that he had begun these translations before he knew of either Cowper's or Symmons's projected translations. He then notes that whereas both Cowper and Symmons had omitted poems that he considered significant, he resolved to present his complete translation of all the Latin and Italian poems. Rare. Not in Kohler.

445. LATIN AND ITALIAN POEMS [In] Levi, Peter. **EDEN RENEWED[:]** The Public and Private Life of John Milton[.] *St. Martin's Press • New York[,] (1997).* First edition. 8vo, xx+332pp., four illustration plates containing twelve illustrations of Milton and related Milton locations and personages, index at the end, original white paper over boards, spine lettered in red, red endpapers, printed black publisher's wrappers with illustration in color of Milton at age twenty-one on front cover and a reproduction in color of *Garden of Eden* by Roelandt Savery at bottom of front cover and at top of back cover. Fine copy. "Appendix One" contains "Translations of the Latin and Italian Poems of Milton by William Cowper"; "Appendix Two" contains "Selected entries from Flagellum Parliamentarium"—"an anonymous manuscript report on the Parliament of 1661 once attributed to Marvell, and surely written by an acquaintance of Milton."

446. MORE LATIN LYRICS FROM VIRGIL TO MILTON translated by Helen Waddell[.] Edited & with an Introduction by Dame Felicitas Corrigan[.] *W • W • Norton & Company Inc • New York[,] (1977).* First American edition. 8vo, 392pp., half-title, "Index To First Lines" and "Index Of Authors" at the end, original green cloth (ex-library copy with several stamps and shelf label on spine), spine lettered in gilt, printed dark green publisher's wrappers with sketch on front cover. Nice copy. Included are twenty-four pages of Latin poems by Milton with translations (pp. 337–61); among the selections is *Epitaphium Damonis*. The first edition was published in 1976 by Stanbrook Abbey.

447. THE LATIN POEMS OF JOHN MILTON Edited With An Introduction, An English Translation, And Notes, By Walter MacKellar[,] Instructor In English In New York University[.] Cornell Studies In English XV[.] *Published For Cornell University[.] New Haven: Yale University Press[;] London: Humphrey Milford[,] Oxford University Press[,] 1930.* First edition thus. 8vo, xii+382+[2]pp., half-title, copyright date of 1930 on verso of title page, half-title before preface, original printed wrappers (worn), advertisement leaf for "Cornell Studies In English" at end. Presentation copy from the editor to James Hutton with presentation inscription on fly-leaf.

448. JOHN MILTON LATIN WRITINGS[:] A SELECTION Edited And Translated By John K. Hale. *Van Corcum, Assen MRTS, Tempe, AZ[,] 1998.* First edition thus. 8vo, x+250pp., half-title with notice of "Bibliotheca Latinitatis Novae" on verso, preface dated 1998, reproduction of

"Frontispiece portrait of Milton, by William Faithorne for Milton's *History of Britain* (1670)" before introduction, forty-page introduction, English translation on facing page, bibliography and several indexes at end, original light blue cloth, front cover and spine lettered in silver. A fine copy.

❦

449. LETTERS OF STATE, Written by Mr. John Milton, To most of the Sovereign Princes and Republicks of Europe. From the Year 1649. Till the Year 1659. To which is added, An Account of his Life. Together with several of his Poems; And A Catalogue of his Works, never before Printed. *London: Printed in the Year, 1694.* First edition. Thick 12mo, [iv]+xlviii+[vi]+336pp., double black rule around title page, "To the Reader," "The Life Of Mr. Milton," "A Catalogue Of Mr. John Milton's Works," modern full calf period style over thick boards (new endpapers), black morocco label with gilt lettering and gilt rules on spine, raised bands, printed on thick paper. A fine, thick paper copy with early signature (dated 1815) on prelimary matter. This translation of *Literae Pseudo-Senatus Anglicani* (1676, see copies listed here) is by Milton's nephew and pupil, Edward Phillips, who also wrote the life of Milton prefixed to it and the account of Milton's writings. This copy has the first reading of "Six Verses" on page xxxv; later this was changed to the correct "Ten Verses." Among the first printings in this volume are three of Milton's sonnets: *To Cromwell*; *To Fairfax*; and *To Skinner*; also included here is Milton's sonnet *To Vane*, which first appeared in Sikes's *Life of Vane*, 1662 (see copy with Seventeenth-century Miltoniana). These four sonnets, which appear in the Trinity Manuscript, were not included in the 1673 edition of Milton's *Poems*, and thus Tonson did not include them in his subsequent editions of the *Poems* (1695, 1705, and 1707— see copies listed here), including them for the first time in his 1713 edition (see copy listed here). Rare thus. Wing M2126; Grolier, *Wither to Prior*, 621; Coleridge 34; Shawcross, 1984, 367; Shawcross, Kentucky, 106; Kohler 512.

Linguae

450. LINGUAE ROMANAE DICTIONARIUM LUCULENTUM NOVUM. A NEW DICTIONARY IN FIVE ALPHABETS ... The Whole Completed and Improved from the several Works of Stephens, Cooper, Gouldman, Holyoke, Dr. Littleton, *a Large Manuscript, in Three Volumes, of Mr. John Milton, &c* ... *Cambridge, Printed for W. Rawlins, et al, and the Executors of S. Leigh. M DC XC III (1693).* First edition. Stout quarto, unpaginated, contemporary paneled calf (worn, joints breaking, title is pinched in binding resulting in two short tears in inner margins, blank endpapers gone, embrowned, title and first several leaves waterstained, with light damp stain to lower outer corner of last section of the volume), raised bands. The title refers to Milton's "Large Manuscript, in Three Volumes." This was Milton's unpublished manuscript dictionary which was inherited by his nephew Edward Phillips. "Milton's manuscript, which has long since disappeared, might have told us something useful about his reading" (Parker, p. 1167). The only record we have is what Littleton has incorporated in this publication. "By no means a pretty copy, but the only one we have ever seen. The very rare first edition" (G. W. Stuart, Jr., Ravenstree, Cat. 170, #97, 1990). See 1703 edition, the fourth edition, following, complete with all the various tables including weights and measures, chronology, etc., as well as the frontispiece, the map, and the city plan of Old Rome. (See also Blount's *Glossographia: Or A Dictionary* ... 1681 with Seventeenth-century Miltoniana, which is based on Milton's dictionary here.) Wing L2565; Shawcross, 1984, 1363; Parker, pp. 656, 663, 1167; Not in Coleridge; Not in Kohler.

451. LINGUAE LATINE LIBER DICTIONARIUS QUADRIPARTITUS. Dr. Adam Littleton's Latin Dictionary, In Four Parts ... The Fourth Edition, Improved from the several Works of Stephens, Cooper, Holyoke, and *a Large Ms. in Three Volumes, of Mr. John Milton, &c* ... With Two Maps; one of Italy, another of Old Rome. *London: Printed for W. Rawlins, R. Chiswel, C. Harper, S. Sprint, F. Place, D. Midwinter, and T. Leigh. 1703.* Stout quarto, unpaginated, original reverse calf (now very worn with corners and edges of covers chipped, spine ends worn, joints breaking, bookplate removed from verso of title page, burn hole in leaf 2R3, removes several letters only, name at head of title). A good copy with the bookplate of Lord Herbert inside back cover, signed by him on the plate and in several other places including the front cover, blank endpapers with various early scribbles and names, complete with all the various tables including weights and measures, chronology, etc., as well as the engraved frontispiece, the map, and the city plan of Old Rome. See comments with first edition published in 1693 (copy listed here). Parker, p. 1167 (discussion of first edition preceding); Not in Coleridge; Not in Kohler.

Literae

452. LITERAE PSEUDO-SENATUS ANGLICANI, CROMWELLII, Reliquorumque Perduellium nomine ac jussu conscriptae A Joanne Miltono. *Impressae Anno 1676.* First edition. 12mo, [ii]+234pp., with the "Fruit" ornament on the title page, which distinguishes the true first edition from the close reprint of the same year (see copy listed here with the "Face" ornament), contemporary paneled calf (a bit rubbed), covers decorated in blind, red morocco label with gilt lettering and gilt rules, raised bands. An attractive copy in very good condition, with early armorial bookplate on front pastedown. The volume contains official correspondence written in Latin by Milton, in the years 1649–59, as Latin Secretary to the Council of State, to the various courts of Europe on behalf of Cromwell and the Commonwealth government. The letters were published surreptitiously after Milton's death; they were translated into English later, in 1694 (copy listed here), by Milton's nephew and pupil, Edward Phillips. The "Fruit" edition, as here, has printing errors that are corrected in a second edition, known as the "Face" edition (also listed here), sometimes called the "First Edition, Second Issue." The present edition was "Printed in Amsterdam by Peter and John Blaeu" (Shawcross); Coleridge adds that it has been shown (by Kelley 1960) that the edition was printed "possibly for Moses Pitt, a London bookseller known to have been planning such an edition." Scarce. Coleridge 29a; Wing M2128; Grolier, *Wither to Prior*, 619; Abbott 1156; NCBEL I, 1243; Parker, p. 1180; Shawcross, 1984, 321; Kohler 508.

453. Another Copy of **LITERAE PSEUDO-SENATUS ANGLICANI, CROMWELLII**, Reliquorumque Perduellium nomine ac jussu conscriptae A Joanne Miltono. *Impressae Anno 1676*. First edition. Bound with three other works by Milton: *Pro Populo*, 1654; *Defensio Secunda*, 1654; and *Ratio Constitutae*, 1654; and two other works: *Regii Sanguinis Clamor*, 1652, by Peter DuMolin, and *Fides Publica*, 1654, by Alexander More. 2 volumes. Comprising six works altogether, four by Milton. 12mo, [ii]+234pp., title page with the "Fruit" ornament, old half green morocco, marbled paper over boards (bit worn), spines lettered in gilt. A very good collection of historically related pamphlets with notes in an early hand on front pastedown of each volume. *Literae Pseudo-Senatus Anglicani* has the "Fruit" ornament on the title page, which distinguishes the true first edition from the close reprint of the same year (also listed here with the "Face" ornament). Each work in the collection is listed separately with appropriate commentary on that work. *Pro Populo*, *Ratio Constitutae*, and *Literae Pseudo-Senatus Anglicani* are listed alphabetically among Milton's works here; *Regii Sanguinis Clamor* by Peter DuMolin and *Fides Publica* by Alexander More are listed under their author's name with Seventeenth-century Miltoniana. Coleridge 29a; Wing M2218; Grolier, *Wither to Prior*, 619; Abbott 1156; NCBEL I, 1243; Parker, p. 1180; Shawcross, 1984, 321; Kohler 508.

454. **LITERAE PSEUDO-SENATUS ANGLICANI, CROMWELLII**, Reliquorumque Perduellium nomine ac jussu conscriptae A Joanne Miltono. *Impressae Anno 1676*. Second edition. 12mo, [ii]+234pp., with Medusa head or "Face" ornament on title page instead of fruit ornament (which distinguishes the true first edition—copy preceding—from the close reprint of the same year—present copy), eighteenth-century red morocco spine (bit rubbed along edges), marbled paper over boards, gilt rules on covers, spine lettered and decorated in gilt, marbled endpapers and edges. A very nice, tall, copy with the bookplate of Charles E. Dobell. The "Face" edition, as here, corrects the printing errors of the "Fruit" edition (first edition preceding). Sometimes this is called the "First Edition, Second Issue." The book was "Printed in Brussels by E. Fricx" (Shawcross). Scarce. Coleridge 30; Shawcross, 1984, 322; Shawcross, 1974, p. 348; Not in Kohler.

Lycidas

454A. (Cross-listing) **LYCIDAS** [In] **JOHANN MILTONS WIEDER=EROBERTES PARADIES**, nebst desselben Samson, und einigen andern Gedichten, wie auch einer Lebens=Beschreibung Des Verfassers. Aus dem Englischen übersetst. *Basel, verlegts Johann Rudolf Imhof, 1752*. First edition thus. See main listing under *PR*, 1752.

455. [LYCIDAS] **LICIDA DI GIOVANNI MILTON** Monodia Per La Morte Del Naufragato Edouardo King Tradotta Dall' Inglese Da T. J. Mathias[.] [Quotation from Theocrit. Idyl. 7] *Londra[:] Presso T. Becket[,] E[.] G. Porter[,] 81 Pall Mall[,] 1812*. First edition thus. 12mo, 55pp., half-title, dedication page, "Prefazione," half-title before translation, "Note," "Lycidas" in English with half-title, contemporary diced Russia (newly rebacked), decorative gilt border trim on covers, gilt rules on spine, red morocco label with gilt lettering and decorative gilt trim, blue endpapers, early armorial bookplate on front pastedown. The first Mathias edition and the first edition of *Lycidas* in Italian. Presentation copy with inscription "Dall' Autore" on title in Mathias's hand and an A.L.s. from him tipped in at the end, presenting this work to an unnamed correspondent. A very attractive, fresh copy. Dedicated to Gaetano Polidori, the father of Dr. John Polidori (author of *The Vampyre* and Byron's physician) and the grandfather of Christina, Dante Gabriel, and William Michael Rossetti; G. Polidori's translation of *Comus* into Italian was published in 1802; Poliodori also translated *Il Licida, L'Allegro, Ed Il Penseroso*, 1814; and Polidori printed *Il Paradiso Perduto* in 1796. All three editions are in the collection and listed here. Rare. Stevens 1435; Not in Kohler.

456. IL LICIDA, L'ALLEGRO, ED IL PENSEROSO DI GIOVANNI MILTON. Tradotti Da Gaetano Polidori. *Londra, Presso L'Autore No. 38, Great Pulteney Street, Golden Square. Dai Torchi Di Riccardo Ed Artur Taylor. M DCCC XIV.* First edition thus? 8vo, 60pp., general half-title, "Prefazione," half-title for *L'A* and for *IlP*, printer's device on title page and repeated at the bottom of last page, original polished speckled calf (spine a trifle faded), gilt rules on covers, spine lettered in gilt, marbled endpapers and edges, contemporary bookplate. A fine copy. Apparently the first Polidori translation. Rare. Not in Kohler.

457. [LYCIDAS] JUSTA EDOUARDO KING, Naufrago, Ab Amicis Moerentibus, Amoris . . . Canta-brigiae: Apud Thomam Buck, Et Rogerum Daniel, Celeberrimae Academiae Typographos. 1638. *Re-Impressum Dublinii: Apud R. Graisberry, Academiae Typographum. 1835.* First edition thus. Tall 8vo, 140pp., half-title, dedication page, title page for "Obsequies To The Memorie Of Mr. Edward King, Anno Dom. 1638. Printed By Th. Buck And R. Daniel, Printers To The Universitie Of Cambridge. 1638 Reprinted By R. Graisberry, At The University Press, Dublin. 1835," original red silk (worn, a bit faded, small ink stain on front cover, joints beginning to crack), printed paper label (quite rubbed) on spine. Presentation copy from the editor, W. J. Thornhill, with presentation inscription on fly-leaf. Scarce. Not in Kohler.

458. THE LYCIDAS AND EPITAPHIUM DAMONIS OF MILTON Edited, With Notes And Introduction (Including A Reprint Of The Rare Latin Version Of The *Lycidas* By William Hogg, 1694), By C. S. Jerram, M. A. Trin. Coll. Oxon. [Quotation from Theoc. Idyll] *London[:] Longmans, Green, And Co. 1874.* First edition thus. 8vo, xi+[3]+141pp., half-title, preface (dated 1874), copious notes for each poem at bottom of each page, two appendices at the end of *Lycidas* followed by "Translation Of Lycidas Into Latin Hexameters, By William Hogg, 1694," *Epitaphium Damonis* beginning on p. 110, with the translations by Symmons and Masson following the Latin poem at the end of the book, original brown cloth (slight waterstain lower right corner front cover), spine lettered in gilt with decorative gilt trim at top and bottom, brown endpapers. A good copy. "Extensive notes, etymologies" (Stevens). A second edition thus was published in 1881; a later edition in 1897 (also listed here). Stevens 272; Not in Kohler.

458A. (Cross-listing) **MILTON'S LYCIDAS.** Edited, With Notes By Homer B. Sprague . . . *Ginn And Company Boston • New York • Chicago • London • Atlanta • Dallas • Columbus • San Francisco[.] (1878).* First edition thus. Included with *L* are "Comments By Morley On The Poem," "Comments By R. C. Browne," "Chronology Of Incidents, Etc.," "Various Readings," and "Index Of Words Explained." Issued with his edition of "*Paradise Lost*, Books I and II," 1879; separately in later issues. See main listing under *PL*, 1879.

459. LYCIDAS [In] FIFTY PERFECT POEMS. Selected And Edited By Charles A. Dana And Rossiter Johnson. With Seventy Illustrations. *New York: D. Appleton And Company, 1, 3, And 5 Bond Street. 1883.* 4to, xii+203pp., title page in red and black (copyright dated 1882 on verso of title), preface, vignette illustrations, original brown silk (a bit rubbed), front cover and spine decorated and lettered in gilt, white silk endpapers, a.e.g. A very nice copy, handsomely printed on thick paper with striking illustrations. Included is Milton's *Lycidas* with four vignette illustrations surrounded by tinted borders by Walter Saterlee. The first edition was published in 1882.

460. LYCIDAS [In] FIFTY PERFECT POEMS. Selected And Edited By Charles A. Dana And Rossiter Johnson. With Seventy-Two Illustrations. *New York: D. Appleton And Company. MDCCCLXXXIV.* 4to, xii+203pp., frontispiece illustration, title page in red and black (copyright dated 1882 on verso of title), preface, vignette illustrations, original white silk (a bit worn, joints cracked, a bit soiled), front cover and spine decorated and lettered in gilt, white silk endpapers, a.e.g. A good copy, handsomely printed on thick paper, with striking illustrations (two more than in the first edition), in a protective plastic cover. Included is Milton's *Lycidas*, with four vignette illustrations surrounded by tinted borders by Walter Saterlee. The first edition was published in 1882.

460A. (Cross-listing) **LYCIDAS [In] L'ALLEGRO, IL PENSEROSO, COMUS, AND LYCIDAS** By John Milton[.] Eclectic English Classics[.] *New York • Cincinnati • Chicago[:] American Book Company[,] (1894).* First edition thus. Slim 8vo, original printed boards. The second edition thus was published by the American Book Company in 1911, edited by Philo Melvyn Buck, Jr., with a new introduction and a biography of Milton (copy listed here). Not in Kohler. See main listing under *L'Allegro*, 1894.

461. THE LYCIDAS AND EPITAPHIUM DAMONIS OF MILTON Edited, With Notes And Introduction (Including A Reprint Of The Rare Latin Version Of The *Lycidas* By William Hogg, 1694), By C. S. Jerram, M. A. Trin. Coll. Oxon. [Quotation from Theoc. Idyll] New Edition. *Longmans, Green, And Co.[,] 39 Paternoster Row[,] London[,] New York And Bombay[,] 1897.* 8vo, xiii+[1]+141+[4 blanks]+32pp., half-title, "Preface To The Second Edition" (dated 1881), "Preface To The First Edition" (dated 1874), contents page, copious notes for each poem at bottom of each page, two appendices at the end of *Lycidas* followed by "Translation Of Lycidas Into Latin Hexameters, By William Hogg, 1694," *Epitaphium Damonis* beginning on p. 110, with the translations by Symmons and Masson following the Latin poem at the end of the book, original brown cloth (a bit rubbed), spine lettered in gilt with decorative gilt trim at top and bottom, large bookplate on fly-leaf. A good copy with thirty-two pages of publications by "Messrs. Longmans, Green, & Co.'s" bound in at the end. The first edition thus was published in 1874 (copy listed here). Not in Kohler.

462. **LYCIDAS** By John Milton Edited By John Phelps Fruit, Ph.D. (Leipsic)[,] N. Long Professor Of English, Bethel College[,] Russellville, Kentucky[.] *Boston, U.S.A., And London[:] Ginn & Company, Publishers[,] The Athenaeum Press, 1897.* First edition thus. Slim 8vo, xvi+29+[2]pp., copyright date of 1897 on verso of title page with label for "Ginn & Company Publishers ... With the Compliments of The Athenaeum Press" tipped in at the top, introduction, notes at bottom of the page, appendix at the end, original maroon cloth (a bit rubbed), with title blocked in embossed letters at the top. A nice copy with two pages of advertisements bound in at the end. Not in Kohler.

462A. (Cross-listing) **LYCIDAS**. Manuscript. With Notes Collected And Arranged By H. P. Morrison. *Birmingham, 1897.* 4to, 240 leaves (numbered on recto only), manuscript volume by Hubert Peter Morrison, in which *Lycidas* is written out in a fine hand, with an introduction, followed by critical notes by various critics, on 240 leaves numbered on recto only, steel-engraved frontispiece of St. Michael's Mount, Cornwall, and manuscript map (on leaf 232), contemporary one-half green morocco, marbled paper over boards. An attractive manuscript item. See main listing with *Editions*.

463. **MILTON'S LYCIDAS** Edited By H. B. Cotterill, M.A. Sometime Assistant Master At Haileybury College[,] Editor Of Virgil, Aeneid I, Etc. With A Frontispiece[.] *London[:] Blackie & Son, Limited, 50 Old Bailey, E.C. Glasgow And Dublin[,] 1902.* First edition thus. Slim crown 8vo, 112pp., leaf listing "Blackie's Annotated English Texts" on each side, frontispiece "Facsimile (Reduced) Of A Page Of The Trinity College MS," "Preface" (dated 1902), original red cloth (spine very faded and slightly chipped at top and bottom, poem marked by some underlining in pencil, early name and place, Dublin, in ink in a neat hand on fly-leaf), small square emblem in blind on front cover incorporating "Blackie And Son Ltd," spine lettered in gilt. A good copy. Scarce. Not in Kohler.

464. **LYCIDAS** By John Milton With Illustrations By Gertrude Brodie[.] *John Lane: Publisher[,] London And New York[,] MCMIII.* First edition thus. Small square 8vo, 41+[3]+[2]pp., half-title ("Flowers of Parnassus-XVII Lycidas"), first appearance of frontispiece illustration and five other full-page illustrations by Gertrude Brodie plus a head- and tailpiece, "Wm. Clowes & Sons, Limited, Printers, London" on verso of title page, printed on high quality thick paper, original green cloth, central gilt device on front cover incorporating title, spine lettered in gilt with decorative gilt design at top and bottom, t.e.g., others untrimmed. A very nice copy of a scarce book with advertisement leaf for this series bound in at end. Not in Kohler.

465. **LYCIDAS[,] L'ALLEGRO[,] IL PENSEROSO[,] AND THE ODE ON THE MORNING OF CHRIST'S NATIVITY[.]** John Milton[.] *["This Volume Is Printed At The Chiswick Press, London, And Published By Alfred Bartlett, Cornhill, Boston" (colophon leaf).] n.d. [ca. 1903].* First edition thus. Small 8vo, 53pp.+colophon leaf, half-title in red and black ("Lycidas and Other Odes. By John Milton With Illustrations By R. Anning Bell"), with frontispiece illustration on verso with decorative border trim in art nouveau style, title page printed in red with decorative border trim in art nouveau style and with decorative illustration on verso, blank page before the poems with quarter-page illustration in upper left corner on verso, each poem with large illustration headpiece incorporating poem's title (title of poem printed in red, with an elaborate border frame in red for *L'A* and *IlP*), possibly the first appearance of full-page, half-page, and quarter-page illustrations and decorations by R. Anning Bell, original black cloth spine, light gray paper over boards (a bit rubbed, early name on fly-leaf), with central device in black on front cover incorporating title, Milton's name, and illustrator, spine lettered in gilt, t.e. rough, fore- and bottom edges untrimmed. A nice copy. Probably printed in a limited edition. Not in Kohler.

466. **LYCIDAS** By John Milton[.] *London[:] At The De La More Press[,] 298 Regent Street W[,] 1903.* First edition thus. Slim 8vo, 30pp., half-title, title page in red and black, printed on high quality paper, original suede leather over card covers (very slight wear on spine), two thin leather ties drawn through leather (ties themselves missing). A lovely edition with beautiful, clear type. Uncommon press edition apparently printed in a limited edition. Not in Kohler.

467. **LYCIDAS, SONNETS &C** By John Milton Edited With Introduction And Notes By W. Bell, M.A.[,] Professor of Philosophy and Logic, Government College, Lahore[.] *London[:] Macmillan and Co., Limited[;] New*

York: The Macmillan Company[,] 1905[.] All rights reserved[.] Slim 8vo, xv+183+4pp., half-title, "Glasgow: Printed At The University Press By Robert Maclehose And Co. Ltd." on verso of title page, original red cloth (a bit faded, contemporary owner's name and another name inside front cover, last contemporary owner's name stamped at bottom of title page, endpapers foxed), front cover lettered in blind with elaborate decoration in blind. Included is a selection of Milton's shorter poems, each with notes at the end. A nice copy with four pages of advertisements bound in at the end. The first edition was published in 1889; it was variously reprinted thereafter.

468. LYCIDAS, COMUS, L'ALLEGRO[,] IL PENSEROSO, AND OTHER POEMS By John Milton[.] Edited With An Introduction And Notes By Julian W. Abernethy, Ph.D., Principal Of The Berkeley Institute, Brooklyn, N.Y. *Merrill's English Texts[.] New York[:] Charles E. Merrill Co.[,] (1906).* First edition thus. 8vo, 198pp., frontispiece portrait plate of Milton at age twenty-one, "Publisher's Note" and copyright date of 1906 on verso of title page, unsigned preface, thirty-seven-page introduction, photograph of Ludlow Castle before *C*, original blue cloth (several underlinings in ink on one page in *IlP*), front cover ruled in contrasting darker blue with lettering in contrasting dark blue, spine lettered in similar contrasting dark blue. A nice copy. "[Merrill's English Texts] will include in complete editions those masterpieces of English Literature that are best adapted for the use of schools and colleges" ("Publisher's Note" on verso of title page). Not in Kohler.

469. Variant of Preceding. LYCIDAS, COMUS, L'ALLEGRO[,] IL PENSEROSO, AND OTHER POEMS By John Milton[.] Edited By Julian W. Abernethy, Ph.D., Principal Of The Berkeley Institute, Brooklyn, N.Y. Maynard's English Classic Series. No. 237-238. *New York[:] Maynard, Merrill, & Co.[,] 44-60 East Twenty-Third Street[,] (1906).* First edition thus, variant edition from the preceding with a variant title page and variant publisher's imprint, in a variant publisher's binding, original green cloth, contrasting dark green lettering on front cover and spine. Not in Kohler.

470. LYCIDAS By John Milton. With Four Original Etchings By Philip Evergood[.] *New York: 1929[,] Harry Lorin Binsse.* First edition thus. Slim folio, [1]+7pp. (illustrations unpaginated), half-title, engraved frontispiece illustration and first appearance of three additional illustrations by Philip Evergood, preface (dated 1929), original half vellum, marbled paper over boards, gilt lettering on front cover and spine, publisher's dust wrappers. "The text of this edition of *Lycidas* follows that of the edition of 1646" (Preface). A fine copy in virtually mint condition.

"This is one of the earliest and most important livres d'artiste done in the United States" (Thomas Boss, Cat. XIX, #189, 1994). "An important illustrated book, preceding Kurt Roesch's edition of Rilke's *Sonnets to Orpheus* by 15 years" (Black Sun Books, 1995 New York Book Fair List, #19). Lucy Lippard, *Graphic Work Of Philip Evergood*, 1966, p. 160. No. 39 of 60 copies.

470A. (Cross-listing) LYCIDAS [In] FOUR POEMS BY JOHN MILTON[:] L'ALLEGRO[,] IL PENSEROSO[,] ARCADES[,] LYCIDAS[.] With Wood-Engravings By Blair Hughes-Stanton[.] *[Newton, Wales:] The Gregynog Press[,] MCMXXXIII.* See main listing under *Four Poems*, 1933.

471. [LYCIDAS] JUSTA EDOVARDO KING Reproduced From The Original Edition, 1638, With An Introduction By Ernest C. Mossner[.] *Published For The Facsimile Text Society By Columbia University Press[,] New York: M·CM·XXXIX.* Facsimile reproduction. 8vo, xiv+[8]+36+25pp., half-title ("Justa Edovardo King Publication No. 45 Of The Facsimile Text Society"), introduction with list of "Contributors To The Edward King Memorial Volume," facsimile reproduction of first edition title page (1638), both Latin and English title pages, with decorative head- and tailpieces and decorated initial letters, original brown cloth, spine lettered in gilt. A fine copy. Given to me by Samuel Holt Monk.

472. LYCIDAS AND COMUS By John Milton With Introduction and Notes by W. Bell, M.A. Professor of Philosophy and Logic, Government College, Lahore. *London: Macmillan & Co[.,] Ltd[,] New York · St. Martin's Press[,] 1958.* 8vo, 117+[2]pp., original red cloth (a bit rubbed, earlier name and address written neatly in ink on front pastedown, some slight foxing throughout), front cover and spine lettered in black, with emblem in black at bottom of front cover of a knight on a horse and a rolling script beneath incorporating "Macmillan's English Classics." A good copy with advertisement leaf bound in at end. The first edition was published in 1899; it was variously reprinted thereafter.

473. MILTON'S LYCIDAS[:] THE TRADITION AND THE POEM Edited By C. A. Patrides[,] University of New York[.] Foreword by M. H. Abrams[,] Cornell University[.] *Holt, Rinehart and Winston[,] New York · Chicago · San Francisco · Toronto · London[,] (1961).* First edition thus. 8vo, x+246pp., copyright date of 1961 on verso of title page, the text of *L* with notes is printed along with *Epitaphium Damonis*, edited by H. W. Garrod and translated by Helen Waddell, paperback, original printed stiff green paper wrappers with a reproduction of Milton portrait at a young age with long hair on front cover. A very good copy.

474. MILTON'S LYCIDAS[:] THE TRADITION AND THE POEM Edited By C. A. Patrides[,] University of New York[.] Foreword by M. H. Abrams[,] Cornell University[.] *Holt, Rinehart and Winston[,] New York • Chicago • San Francisco • Toronto • London[,] (1965).* Third edition thus. 8vo, x+246pp., as preceding, paperback, original printed stiff green paper wrappers (a bit rubbed) with a reproduction of Milton portrait at a young age with long hair on front cover. A good copy, identical to 1961 first edition preceding in format and binding.

475. MILTON'S "LYCIDAS" EDITED TO SERVE AS AN INTRODUCTION TO CRITICISM[.] Scott Elledge[,] Professor of English[,] Cornell University[.] *Harper & Row, Publishers, New York & London[,] (1966).* First edition thus. 8vo, xxii+330pp., half-title, half-title for "The Poem" (which prints the text of 1638 along with "Textual Variations"), half-title for various of the sections: "The Tradition," "The Theory of the Monody," "Contemporary Elegies," "Justa Edovardo King," "John Milton," "England in 1637," "Commentary and Notes," and "Bibliographies," original blue cloth (half-title wrinkled), decorative gilt pieces (possibly laurel boughs) on lower right corner of front cover, spine lettered in gilt, endpapers reproducing *Lycidas* manuscript with corrections, printed publisher's wrappers (a bit darkened) with reproduction of the Onslow portrait of Milton at age twenty-one on front cover. A good copy, signed by the author on title page.

476. [LYCIDAS] JUSTA EDOVARDO KING A Facsimile Edition of the Memorial Volume in which Milton's "Lycidas" First Appeared, With Introduction, Translations, and Notes by Edward Le Comte[.] *Norwood Editions[,] 1978.* First edition thus. 8vo, viii+[viii]+36+25+72pp., dedication page ("To Douglas Bush"), introduction, facsimile reproduction of 1638 first edition title pages, both Latin and English, original blue buckram, spine lettered in gilt. A fine copy of this facsimile reproduction with translations and notes (with half-title). Presentation copy inscribed by Le Comte on fly-leaf: "For Lois Williams, with thanks for her helpful interest. Edward Le Comte."

477. MILTON'S LYCIDAS[:] THE TRADITION AND THE POEM[.] New and Revised Edition[.] Edited by C. A. Patrides[.] Foreword by M. H. Abrams[.] *University of Missouri Press[,] Columbia[, Mo.], 1983.* Revised edition. 8vo, xviii+370pp., half-title, "Foreword to the First Edition, by M. H. Abrams" (dated 1961), "Foreword to the Revised Edition, by M. H. Abrams" (dated 1983), original blue cloth, spine lettered in gilt. Very nice copy. Included is the text of the poem, *Lycidas*, with notes, *Epitaphium Damonis*, edited in Latin and translated into English, plus commentary essays. This edition is revised and enlarged from the first edition published in 1961 (copy listed here).

478. Variant of Preceding, as preceding, except this is in paperback, printed gold stiff paper wrappers with an illustration of *The Calling of the Apostles Peter and Andrew* (detail) by Duccio di Buoninsegna reproduced on front cover. Fine copy.

478A. (Cross-listing) LYCIDAS [In] ON THE MORNING OF CHRIST'S NATIVITY & OTHER POEMS by John Milton with engravings by Brian Hanscomb[.] *London[:] The Folio Press[,] 1987.* See main listing under *On The Morning Of Christ's Nativity*, 1987.

479. [LYCIDAS] [In] A BOUQUET OF FLOWERS By Barbara Milo Ohrbach[.] Sweet Thoughts, Recipes, and Gifts from the Garden with "The Language of Flowers[.]" *Clarkson N. Potter, Inc. / Publishers[,] New York[,] 1990.* First edition. Slim 8vo, [v]+56pp., decorated half-title as dedication page with floral trim in color, floral decorations and cherub in color on title page, full-page illustrations in color, color decorations throughout, original green cloth, emblem in blind on front cover, spine lettered in gilt, marbled endpapers, printed publisher's wrappers repeating title and floral decorations in color on front cover. A fine copy. The designs are by Justine Strasberg, the endpapers by Rita Singer. Included is a full-page color illustration after Justine Strasberg of a lady with floral decorations in her hair and on her dress, and with a line from *L* printed beneath: "Flowers that their gay wardrobe wear. John Milton," the whole within a decorative border trim in color. The full line in *Lycidas* reads: "Or Frost to Flowers, that their gay wardrobe wear" (line 47).

480. [LYCIDAS] JUSTA EDOVARDO KING with introduction, translation, and notes by Edward Le Comte[.] photographic reproduction courtesy of the Newberry Library[.] *Milton Quarterly, Volume Thirty Five, Number Three, October 2001.* Small 4to, 102pp. [pp. 125–225], sixty-six pages of facsimile reproductions, including the first edition title page (1638), both Latin and English title pages, and decorative head- and tailpieces and decorated initial letters, with "Translations" of "Obsequies For Edward King" following the facsimile reproductions, original printed stiff cream paper wrappers, with a reproduction of Faithorne's portrait of Milton and the imprint: "Blackwell Publishers" on the front cover. A "Special Issue" of *Milton Quarterly* reproducing the "Edward King Memorial Volume." Fine copy.

481. MILTON LYRICS. L'ALLEGRO, IL PENSEROSO, COMUS, AND LYCIDAS. Edited By Louise Manning Hodgkins, M.A. "Had Paradise Lost remained unwritten, the earlier lyrics of Milton would have ranked him above all his contemporaries in Lyric Poetry." Bayne. The Students' Series of English Classics. *Leach, Shewell, & Sanborn. Boston. New York. Chicago. (1893).* First edition thus. Slim, square 8vo, xii+102+[1]pp., advertisement leaf for "The Students' Series of English Classics," frontispiece portrait plate of a young, long-haired Milton, protective tissue guard, small emblem of the press on title page, copyright dated 1893 on verso of title page, "Preface" (dated "March 1893"), original light brown cloth, front cover lettered in decorative black lettering, spine lettered in black. A nice copy with contemporary signature on fly-leaf. While a similar edition edited by Louise Manning Hodgkins with the same preface was published in 1893 by a different publisher with a different frontispiece portrait in a smaller format (see following copies), no mention is made of that edition here. Not in Kohler.

482. MILTON LYRICS. L'ALLEGRO, IL PENSEROSO, COMUS, AND LYCIDAS. Edited By Louise Manning Hodgkins, M.A. "Had Paradise Lost remained unwritten, the earlier lyrics of Milton would have ranked him above all his contemporaries in Lyric Poetry." Bayne. The Students' Series of English Classics. *Sibley & Company[,] Boston [and] Chicago[,] (1893).* First edition thus. Bound with **MATTHEW ARNOLD'S SOHRAB AND RUSTUM** . . . Edited By Louise Manning Hodgkins, The Students' Series of English Classics. *Sibley & Company[,] Boston [and] Chicago[,] (1890).* First edition thus. 2 volumes in one.. Small 8vo, xii+102,+[4]+69+[1]pp., frontispiece portrait plate of Milton (reproduction of engraved frontispiece portrait by R. White with epigram by Dryden), small emblem of the press on title page, copyright dated 1893 on verso of title page, "Preface" (dated "March 1893"), separate title page for Matthew Arnold with frontispiece portrait plate of Arnold, original light green cloth (occasional pencil notations), front cover lettered in embossed contrasting darker green, spine lettered in contrasting darker green, with emblem of the press at bottom of front cover. A nice copy with advertisement leaf bound in at the end. See 1893 edition preceding edited by Louise Manning Hodgkins with the same preface, published by a different publisher ("Leach, Shewell, & Sanborn") with a different frontispiece portrait, in a variant publisher's binding, and in a larger format than that here. Not in Kohler.

483. THE LYRIC AND DRAMATIC POEMS OF JOHN MILTON[.] Edited, With An Introduction And Notes, By Martin W. Sampson[.] Professor of English in Indiana University[.] *New York[:] Henry Holt And Company[,] 1901.* First edition thus. 8vo, l+[1]+345+6pp., fifty-page preface, original cream cloth (bit used), front cover and spine lettered in red, front cover ruled in red with central red seal. Six pages of advertisements bound in at end. "Long introduction, notes, metrical apparatus" (Stevens). This edition was enlarged and revised by Sampson in 1925 under the title *Selections From John Milton* (copy listed here). Scarce. Stevens 313; Not in Kohler.

484. A MANIFESTO OF THE LORD PROTECTOR Of The Commonwealth of England, Scotland, Ireland, &c. Published by Consent and Advice of his Council. Wherein is shewn the Reasonableness of the Cause of this Republic against the Depredations of the Spaniards. Written in Latin by John Milton, and first printed in 1655, now translated into English. [Quotation from Britannia] To which is added, Britannia, a Poem; by Mr. Thomson, first published in 1727. *London: Printed for, and Sold by A. Millar, at Buchanan's Head, over against St. Clement's Church in the Strand. 1738.* (Price Six Pence.) Slim 8vo, 40pp., decorative head-trim and tailpiece, later maroon morocco spine (slightly rubbed at joints), maroon cloth (small hole on title page, some age-browning), spine lettered in gilt, marbled endpapers, t.e.g. A good copy of a scarce edition, neatly underlined and annotated in pencil in an earlier hand. First published in 1655, this *Manifesto* mentions Spanish cruelty toward English seamen and others in the Caribbean. Thomas Birch edited and translated this from the 1655 *Scriptum Dom Protectoris*, which Coleridge lists with other apocryphal works. According to G. W. Stuart, Jr., (Ravenstree) in his 1993 Milton Catalogue (Cat. 176, #106), "we understand that research establishing Milton's hand in this work is in progress." Coleridge 271 (note); Not in Kohler; see also *European Americana* 738/113.

485. THE MANUSCRIPT OF MILTON'S PARADISE LOST BOOK I Edited by Helen Darbishire[.] *Oxford[:] At The Clarendon Press[,] 1931.* First edition. Small 4to, xlvii+[40]+74pp., half-title, preface (dated 1931), "Errata" slip tipped in over "Contents" page, forty collotype reproductions of the manuscript in the Morgan Library with an introduction and commentary by Helen Darbishire, original black cloth, spine lettered in gilt with gilt emblem of the press at the bottom, unopened. A good copy with the bookplate of Leonard Schlosser. Scarce.

486. MAY MORNING [In] A MOSAIC BY THE ARTISTS' FUND SOCIETY OF PHILADELPHIA Edited By Harrison S. Morris[.] *[Philadelphia:] J. B. Lippincott Company[,] 1891.* First edition. Large 8vo, 135pp., half-title in decorated gilt, title page in red and black, illustrations in black and white and in various tints, printed on extra thick cardlike paper and perforated for easy removal and (one would assume) framing, original decorated white cloth, front cover elaborately decorated and lettered in gilt, burnished gilt, and silver, spine similarly decorated and lettered in gilt, burnished gilt, and silver, gold endpapers decorated in a small white floral pattern, t.e.g., others untrimmed. A very nice copy in a lovely binding of the period with neat contemporary presentation inscription (dated "Christmas, 1890") on front blank together with an uncanceled U.S. two-cent stamp of the period. Half-title for *The Return Of May Painted By E. B. Bensell*, with Milton's poem *May Morning* printed on verso, with a full-page reproduction in tinted blue of Bensell's depiction of Mirth, signed and dated 1889.

486A. **MILTON** edited by Maynard Mack. *Prentice-Hall, Inc. Englewood Cliffs, N.J. (1961)*. Second edition thus. See Poems, Milton, 1961.

487. **MILTON PAPERS** By David Harrison Stevens[,] Professor of English[,] The University of Chicago[.] *The University Of Chicago Press[,] Chicago • Illinois[,] (1927)*. First edition. Small 4to, ix+46pp., half-title preceded by leaf on "The Modern Philology Monographs Of The University Of Chicago," frontispiece plate reproducing "Transcript Of The Milton Deed To Property In Covent Garden," small emblem of the press on title page, second plate reproducing "A Sheet From The Lawes Autograph Setting Of Comus," blue cloth spine, original printed boards (two brown markings from previous tape strips on covers, library stamps with library due card in pocket on back fly-leaf), central emblem of the press on title page reprinted in blue on front cover with decorative border trim, printed paper label on spine with decorative blue trim, printed publisher's wrappers with decorative border trim on front cover (a bit worn with a few small pieces missing here and there) in a protective plastic cover. A good copy. Stevens 1813.

488. **MILTON'S PROLUSIO SCRIPT** By Hugh C. H. Candy[.] *London[:] The Bibliographical Society[,] 1934*. Slim 4to, 9+[2] leaves (paginated 331–39, first page and plates not paginated), decorated initial letter, facsimile reproduction plate "of an early Prolusio Script, found in the same box with the Commonplace Book," and two pages of facsimiles, pamphlet, original printed wrappers (a bit faded along spine), partially unopened. "Reprinted By The University Press, Oxford[,] From The Transactions Of The Bibliographical Society[,] The Library[,] Dec. 1934" (verso of title page). A good copy. Scarce.

Minor Poems

489. **THE MINOR POEMS OF JOHN MILTON**. Edited, With Notes, By William J. Rolfe, A.M., Litt.D., Formerly Head Master Of The High School, Cambridge, Mass. *New York: Harper & Brothers, Publishers, Franklin Square. 1887*. First edition thus. Slim 8vo, 229+[8]pp., frontispiece portrait of Milton as a young man, protective tissue guard, central seal of the press on title page, preface (dated 1887), half-title for several of the major sections and various of the poems, large decorative endpieces, original reddish-brown cloth (a bit rubbed, some occasional light pencil markings), front cover and spine lettered in gilt. Nice copy with contemporary name written on flyleaf. Ten pages of advertisements bound in at end. A variant edition thus was published by the "American Book Company" in the same year, 1887, (see copy following); a possible second edition thus by "Harper & Brothers, Publishers" was published in "New York And London" in 1899 (copy listed here). Scarce. Not in Kohler.

490. Variant of Preceding. **THE MINOR POEMS OF JOHN MILTON**. Edited, With Notes, By William J. Rolfe, A.M., Litt.D., Formerly Head Master Of The High School, Cambridge, Mass.[,] *New York • Cincinnati • Chicago[:] American Book Company[,] (1887)*. First edition thus, variant edition by variant publisher. Slim 8vo, 229+[8]pp., frontispiece portrait of Milton as a young man, central seal of the press on title page, preface (dated 1887), half-title for several of the major sections and various of the poems, large decorative endpieces, original red cloth (a bit worn along extremities, marginalia and underlining—rather heavy at times—with notes on front blanks), front cover and spine lettered in gilt. Eight pages of advertisements bound in at end. The first edition thus was published in the same year, 1887, in New York by "Harper & Brothers, Publishers" (preceding copy). Scarce. Not in Kohler.

491. **[MINOR POEMS] SELECT MINOR POEMS OF JOHN MILTON**. Hymn On The Nativity, L'Allegro, Il Penseroso, Comus, Lycidas. With Biography, Introductions, Notes, Etc. Edited By James E. Thomas, B.A. (Harvard), Master, Head of Department Of English In The Boys' English High School, Boston, Massachusetts[.] *Silver, Burdett And Company. New York . . . Boston . . . Chicago. (1895)*. First edition thus. Slim 8vo, 123pp., frontispiece portrait after D. Grosch, copyright date of 1985 on verso of title page, "Preface" (dated "August 1895"), original red cloth (front cover badly waterstained, unaffected internally), front cover and spine lettered in black, publisher's initials lettered in black on back cover. Not in Kohler.

492. Variant of Preceding, original olive green cloth (a bit rubbed, early name on fly-leaf, some marginal notations in pencil throughout), front cover lettered in contrasting dark green within decorative border trim in a classical motif on front cover, publisher's initials lettered in contrasting dark green on back cover. A nice copy without frontispiece portrait and in a variant publisher's binding. Not in Kohler.

493. THE MINOR POEMS OF JOHN MILTON Illustrated And Decorated By A. Garth Jones[.] *London[:] George Bell & Sons[,] 1898.* First edition thus. 8vo, xiv+[1]+206pp., half-title with advertisement on verso for "The Endymion Series" (of which this is one), frontispiece illustration with elaborate decorative border trim in red in art nouveau style, title page printed in black with similar elaborate decorative border trim in red in art nouveau style, "Prefatory Note" (dated 1898), first appearance of sixty-two vignette and full-page illustrations by Garth Jones in the art nouveau genre, "Chiswick Press:—Charles Whittingham And Co. Tooks Court, Chancery Lane, London" with emblem of the press on second last blank page, original decorated dark green cloth, front cover decorated with an illustration in a style similar to that of the illustrations within, in contrasting green with central figures in bright gilt and with Milton's name in bright gilt lettering, spine similarly decorated in contrasting green with gilt lettering, at the center of the back cover is an illustration of the press with the initial's of the press within and the initials "JM" on either side and "The Endymion Series" printed on top, decorated light blue endpapers in art nouveau style with the initials "JM" at the center, t.e.g., others untrimmed. An attractive book of the nineties. George Bell's file copy with Bell's stamp appearing several times on preliminary blanks. Gordon Ray comments on these "bold drawings" and on the "particular attractions" of the Endymion Series as a whole: "English commercial bookmaking of the period is here seen at its best" (*Illustrator*, pp. 182–84). See also John Russell Taylor, *Art Nouveau Book*, who also describes the series as having produced "among the best books of the era." A DeLuxe issue of 100 numbered copies only, printed on "Japanese vellum," was also published at the same time (also listed here). Kohler 472.

494. Variant of Preceding, original decorated light green cloth (a bit rubbed), front cover decorated with an illustration in a style similar to that of the illustrations within, in contrasting dark green with central figures in bronze and with Milton's name in bronze lettering (unlike the gilt on preceding binding), spine similarly decorated in contrasting dark green with bronze lettering (rather than gilt), decorated light blue endpapers art nouveau style with the initials "JM" at the center (a portion in black on front and back pastedowns, unlike preceding copy), at the center of the back cover an illustration of the press with the initial's of the press within and the initials "JM" on either side, t.e. rough, fore- and bottom edges untrimmed. A nice copy in a variant publisher's binding (in light green cloth, with bronze rather than gilt lettering, without printing "The Endymion Series" on back cover, modest variations in endpapers, t.e. rough rather than gilt), with contemporary name on front blank. Not in Kohler.

495. Variant of Preceding. THE MINOR POEMS OF JOHN MILTON Illustrated And Decorated By A. Garth Jones[.] *London[:] George Bell & Sons[,] 1898.* First edition thus. Tall 8vo, xiv+[1]+206pp., first half-title duplicating in deep blue and contrasting wine-red the front cover decoration/illustration on the original cloth binding of the regular issue (also listed here), second half-title—as with regular issue—with advertisement on verso for "The Endymion Series" (of which this is one), frontispiece illustration with elaborate decorative border trim in red in art nouveau style, title page printed in black with similar elaborate decorative border trim in red in art nouveau style, "Prefatory Note" (dated 1898), first appearance of sixty-two vignette and full-page illustrations after Garth Jones in the art nouveau genre, "Chiswick Press:—Charles Whittingham And Co. Tooks Court, Chancery Lane, London" with emblem of the press on second last blank page, long decoration in deep blue and contrasting sharp wine-red incorporating Milton's name and "G. Bell & Sons" in wine-red lettering on last blank, original hessian boards (spine a little darkened), spine lettered in black and red with emblem of the press in black at bottom, decorated endpapers art nouveau style, edges untrimmed. An excellent, large paper copy in very attractive fin-de-siècle art nouveau style book. Ray further observes that "it was evidently expected that [such a volume as the one here] "in [an] undecorated binding" [as hessian or burlap boards] "would be rebound in leather" (p. 182). On verso of the first half-title appears: "This edition, on Japanese vellum, is limited to One Hundred copies only" of which "This is No. 52" (number written in ink in hand). On front pastedown is an attractive bookplate—in a style similar to that of the illustrations—of T. Gilbert Jones cut in 1894 by A.O.J. (who may well be, one or both of them, related to the illustrator A. Garth Jones). Gordon Ray, *Illustrator And The Book In England*, pp. 182–84; John Russell Taylor, *Art Nouveau Book*; Not in Kohler.

496. [MINOR POEMS] FACSIMILE OF THE MANUSCRIPT OF MILTON'S MINOR POEMS Preserved in the Library of Trinity College Cambridge[.] *Cambridge At the University Press[,] 1899. All rights reserved[.]* First and only edition thus. Folio, 7pp. preliminary text, forty-seven leaves of photographic facsimiles of the original manuscript, with accompanying forty-seven leaves of letterpress transcriptions, edited by W. A. Wright with preface by Wright (dated 1899), half-title, modern brown morocco spine, marbled paper over boards, gilt rules and gilt lettering on spine, raised bands, pages reinforced, edges untrimmed (bound in 1974). A very good copy. Inscribed on fly-leaf to Milton scholar Maurice Kelley and from him to me: "From the Fellows of Trinity College Cambridge, To Maurice Kelley, To Robert Wickenheiser," Princeton, 1972. Facsimile reproduction. Laid in: possibly nineteenth-century facsimile pages of *PL* as a drama (fragile). Printed in a limited edition. Not in Kohler.

497. MINOR POEMS FROM JOHN MILTON[:] L'ALLEGRO[,] IL PENSEROSO[,] LYCIDAS[,] SONNETS[.] Excelsior 6¢ Classics*[.] D·H·Knowlton & Co Publishers[,] Farmington·Maine[.] n.d. [ca. 1899]*. Slim pamphlet, 32+[2]pp., frontispiece portrait plate of "Milton dictating *SA*," original pink wrappers stapled (a bit darkened, staples slightly rusted), front cover printed in green with decorated floral border trim in green and red, a listing of "School World Classics" printed on inside front cover, a listing of "Little People Classics" on inside back cover, and a listing of "Excelsior Six-Cent Classics" (of which this is one) on outside back cover, with additional advertisement leaf bound in at end. A good copy in a protective plastic folder. Not in Kohler.

498. THE MINOR POEMS OF JOHN MILTON. Edited, With Notes, By William J. Rolfe, A.M., Litt.D., Formerly Head Master Of The High School, Cambridge, Mass. *New York And London: Harper & Brothers, Publishers, 1899*. Second edition thus? Slim 8vo, 229+[8]pp., frontispiece portrait of Milton as a young man, "Copyright, 1887, by Harper & Brothers" on verso of title page along with a boxed list of "English Classics. Edited By Wm. J. Rolfe," half-titles for several of the major sections and various of the poems, large decorative endpieces, original reddish-brown cloth (a bit rubbed, a tiny white spot and tiny black mark on front cover), front cover and spine lettered in gilt. Nice copy with early ownership name and early bookplate on front pastedown and fly-leaf. Eight pages of advertisements bound in at the end. The first edition thus was published by Harper & Brothers in New York in 1887 (copy listed here). Not in Kohler.

499. [MINOR POEMS] SELECT MINOR POEMS OF JOHN MILTON[:] Hymn On The Nativity[,] L'Allegro[,] Il Penseroso[,] Comus[,] Lycidas[,] Sonnets[.] Edited, With Introduction, Notes, Etc., By Albert Perry Walker, M.A. *D. C. Heath & Co., Publishers[,] Boston[,] New York[,] Chicago[,] (1900)*. First edition thus. Small 8vo, x+[2]+186+[8]pp., frontispiece illustration plate and six additional illustration plates, with either the lines illustrated or identification printed beneath each illustration, plus one headpiece illustration, original cream cloth, title stamped in contrasting brown on front cover and spine. Very nice copy. The eight illustrations include one illustration plate for *IlP* (*Divinest Melancholy* after W. C. Thomas); three illustration plates for *C* (*The Lady in C* after J. D. Critenden—as frontispiece, *Circe* by J. H. Waterhouse, and *Ludlow Castle* after J. M. W. Turner), along with a fourth illustration, *The Education Of C* "From a Greek Vase"—as a headpiece illustration to the poem; one illustration plate for *L* (*Faun, Satyr, and Pan Pipes* after Harriet Hosmer); and one illustration plate for *NO* (*The 'Star-Led Wizards'* after J. Portaels). Not in Kohler.

Also in the collection and listed here: a second edition thus published in 1902; a possible third edition thus in 1908; a possible fourth edition thus in 1909; and a possible fifth edition thus in 1910. See also Walker's enlarged edition, *Milton's Select Poems* (1900), cross-listed here, in which the same illustration plates appear.

500. Variant of Preceding, in a binding identical to previous copy with six pages of advertisements (with half-title), bound in at end. Not in Kohler.

501. Variant of Preceding, original dark green cloth (a bit rubbed), title stamped in contrasting green on front cover and spine (bit darkened). The eight illustrations are as preceding. Very nice copy in a variant publisher's binding. Not in Kohler.

502. Variant of Preceding with preface dated 1900, whereas previously the preface had been undated. Not in Kohler.

503. [MINOR POEMS] Variant of Preceding. MILTON'S SELECT MINOR POEMS[:] Nativity Hymn, L'Allegro, Il Penseroso, Comus, Lycidas, Sonnets[.] Edited By Albert Perry Walker[.] Golden Key Series. *D. C. Heath And Company, Boston[,] New York[,] Chicago[,] Atlanta[,] San Francisco[,] Dallas[,] London[,] (1900)*. First edition thus. Small 8vo, x+[2]+186pp., frontispiece illustration plate, preface (undated), five additional illustration plates, with either the lines illustrated or identification printed beneath each illustration, plus one headpiece illustration, original crushed green cloth, title stamped in black with black trim on front cover, spine lettered in black with small decorative pieces. A very good copy with variant title ("Milton's Select Minor Poems" instead of "Select Minor Poems Of John Milton"), with variant publisher's imprint (other cities have been added), with undated preface, in a variant publisher's binding. The illustrations are identical to the preceding copies and other copies here. Kohler 475, indicating "Five unsigned plates by various artists (one double-sided)," and reporting "Not in the British Library. Not in the Bodleian Library. Not in Cambridge University Library."

504. MILTON'S MINOR POEMS With Sketch Of John Milton[.] The Lakeside Series of English Readings[.] *Chicago[:] Ainsworth & Company[,] 1900*. First edition thus. Slim 8vo, 75pp.,+[5 blank pages], unsigned frontispiece vignette sketch of Milton, original decorated stiff green paper wrappers (a bit used, front corners worn and repaired on inside), front cover lettered in red (title and publisher along with "No. 18 English Readings For High Schools. . . . Lakeside Series" at the top), contrasting dark green spine, publications of the "Lakeside Classics" listed on back cover. A fairly nice copy of this classroom edition. Scarce. Not in Kohler.

505. MILTON'S MINOR POEMS[:] L'Allegro, Il Penseroso, Comus, And Lycidas Edited For School Use By William Allan Neilson, M.A., Ph.D.[,] Instructor In English, Harvard University[.] The Lake English Classics[.] *Chicago[:] Scott, Foresman And Company[,] (1900)*. First edition thus. Small 8vo, 165pp., advertisement leaf for "The Lake English Classics" before title page, with "Scott, Foresman And Company Publishers . . . Chicago" at the bottom and "The Lake English Classics" on verso, copyright dated 1900 on verso of title page, original light blue cloth (a bit faded along edges), front cover lettered in embossed light blue within a broad black band at the top ("Milton's Minor Poems Neilson") and within a narrow black band at the bottom ("The Lake English Classics"), spine similarly lettered. Nice copy. A variant issue with the addition of "New York" in the publisher's imprint, was published the same year (see copy following). Also in the collection and listed here: a second edition thus published in 1903; a possible third in 1907; a possible fourth in 1908; and a revised edition thus in 1919. Not in Kohler.

506. Variant of Preceding, original blue cloth (a bit used, light pencil underlining with some marginalia in pencil throughout), front cover and spine lettered in black. A decent copy in a variant issue with the addition of "New York" in the publisher's imprint ("Chicago [and] New York"), and in a variant publisher's binding. Not in Kohler.

507. MINOR POEMS FROM JOHN MILTON[.] John Milton[,] L'Allegro[,] Il Penseroso[,] Lycidas[,] Sonnets[.] *D • H • Knowlton & Co[.] Publishers[,] Farmington • Maine. n.d. [ca. 1900]*. First edition thus? Slim 8vo, [1]+32+[2]pp., unsigned frontispiece portrait plate of "Milton dictating 'Samson Agonistes,'" life of Milton, notes at bottom of the page, original printed stiff brown paper wrappers with decorative floral border trim in contrasting brown and yellow on front cover, advertisement for "School World Classics" on inside front cover, for "Little People Classics" on inside back cover, for "Excelsior 5c. Classics" on back cover with advertisement plate bound in at the end. A nice copy, near mint, identified as an "Excelsior 5c Classics" on front cover, which also prints the title and a list of the contents within. Uncommon. Not in Kohler.

508. MILTON MINOR POEMS[:] L'Allegro[,] Arcades[,] On Shakespeare[,] Il Penseroso[,] On The Nativity[,] At A Solemn Music[,] Comus[,] Lycidas[,] Sonnets[.] With Introduction And Notes By Samuel Thurber[.] The Academy Classics[.] *Allyn And Bacon[,] Boston[,] New York[,] Chicago[,] (1901)*. First edition thus. Small 8vo, xxiv+[2]+129pp., unsigned frontispiece portrait plate of Milton, copyright date of 1901 and "Norwood Press" on verso of title page, original blue cloth (early name signed neatly on front pastedown), front cover and spine lettered in gilt. A fine copy, near mint. Kohler 476, reporting "Not in Williamson. Not in the British Library. Not in Cambridge University Library."

509. [MINOR POEMS] SELECT MINOR POEMS OF JOHN MILTON[:] Hymn On The Nativity[,] L'Allegro[,] Il Penseroso[,] Comus[,] Lycidas[,] Sonnets[.] Edited, With Introduction, Notes, Etc., By Albert Perry Walker, M.A. Master, And Teacher Of English And History In The English High School, Boston[.] *Boston, U.S.A.[:] D. C. Heath & Co., Publishers[,] 1902*. Second edition thus. Small 8vo, x+[2]+186+[8]pp., preface (dated 1900), five illustration plates plus one headpiece illustration, with either the lines illustrated or identification printed beneath each illustration, original red cloth (a bit worn, pencil markings on front pastedown, lacking frontispiece illustration plate and fly-leaf), title stamped in contrasting brownish red on front cover and spine. Six pages of advertisements bound in at end. The illustrations are identical to the *Select Minor Poems of John Milton*, 1900 (first edition thus listed here with further editions cited there). Not in Kohler.

510. MILTON'S MINOR POEMS[:] L'Allegro, Il Penseroso, Comus, And Lycidas Edited For School Use By William Allan Neilson, M.A., Ph.D.[,] Instructor In English, Harvard University[.] The Lake English Classics[.] *Chicago[:] Scott, Foresman And Company[,] (1903)*. Second edition thus. Small 8vo, 165pp., advertisement leaf for "The Lake English Classics" before title page, copyright dated 1900 on verso of title page, preface (dated "September, 1900"), original light blue cloth (a bit rubbed), front cover and spine lettered in silver in relief against a black backdrop ruled in silver. A good copy. The first edition thus, first issue, was published in 1900 with only Chicago in the publisher's imprint as here (also listed here with further editions cited). Not in Kohler.

511. MILTON'S MINOR POEMS With Introduction And Explanatory Notes[.] *Educational Publishing Company[,] Boston[,] New York[,] Chicago[,] San Francisco[,] (1903).* First edition thus. Small, square 8vo, 142+[2]pp., copyright dated 1903 on verso of title page, unsigned sketch of a youngish Milton before introduction, half-title for each work, notes at bottom of the page, original printed tan wrappers (worn, front cover detached, corners and edges of covers chipped, early names on front cover and title page), tan cloth spine, large laurel wreath in contrasting blue at center of front cover with lettering in dark blue ("Ten Cent Classics, volume IV, No. 14, May 15, 1901"), listing of "Ten Cent Classics" editions (including "Milton, *PL*. Book I. and II.") printed on inside of front cover and on inside and outside of back cover, with an advertisement leaf bound in at the end. A cheaply printed edition as a "Ten Cent Classics. (Texts that are Accurate and Authentic.)," "Entered at the Post Office, Boston, Mass., as second class matter[;] Published Semi-Monthly[.] Price, $2.40 per year[;] Single numbers, 10 cts." Uncommon. Not in Kohler.

512. MILTON'S MINOR POEMS Edited By Mary A. Jordan, A.M.[,] Professor Of English, Smith College[.] Gateway Series[.] *New York • Cincinnati • Chicago[:] American Book Company[,] (1904).* First edition thus. Small 8vo, 179+[13]pp., advertisement leaf before frontispiece plate and preceded by two blank pages, two-page frontispiece plate ("Facsimile Of Milton's Discarded MS. Lycidas, 142–151"), copyright date of 1904 on verso of title page, preface by the general editor of the Gateway Series, Henry Van Dyke, original dark red cloth (a bit rubbed), yellow border on front cover with title and small emblem in yellow, different emblem in yellow on back cover, spine lettered in yellow, thirteen pages of advertisements bound in at the end. A good copy, very clean within. Not in Kohler.

513. Variant of Preceding with a half-title, in a brighter red cloth binding than that of the preceding copy with different advertisements bound in at end. Not in Kohler.

514. MILTON'S MINOR POEMS With Sketch Of John Milton[.] The Lakeside Series of English Readings[.] *Chicago[:] Ainsworth & Company[,] 1904.* First edition thus? Slim 8vo, 8 [resuming on] 31 through 94pp., unsigned frontispiece portrait sketch of a young Milton within decorative trim, original green cloth (a bit rubbed, a few slight stains on covers, lower corner of frontispiece portrait bent, pencil notations on front pastedown and occasionally throughout), front cover lettered in white within white rules. A possible second edition thus was published in 1905 (see copy following). Uncommon. Not in Kohler.

515. MILTON'S MINOR POEMS With Sketch Of John Milton[.] The Lakeside Series of English Readings[.] *Chicago[:] Ainsworth & Company[,] 1905.* Second edition thus? Slim 8vo, 8 [resuming on] 31 through 94pp., unsigned frontispiece portrait sketch of a young Milton within decorative trim, original green cloth (a bit rubbed), front cover lettered in white within white rules. Good copy. The possible first edition thus was published in 1904 (copy listed here). Uncommon. Not in Kohler.

516. MILTON'S MINOR POEMS L'Allegro, Il Penseroso, Comus, And Lycidas[.] A Plan For Study With A Biographical Sketch[,] Suggestions To Teachers And Notes For Students[.] By Mary Devereux[,] Austin (Chicago) High School[.] *Chicago [:] A. Flanagan Company[,] (1905).* First edition thus. Slim 8vo, 181pp., "Copyright 1905" on verso of title page, original light blue cloth (a bit rubbed, spine a little faded, early names and notes on front and back blanks, numerous notes in a neat hand), front cover and spine lettered in black. Good copy. Uncommon. Not in Kohler.

517. MILTON'S MINOR POEMS With Introduction And Explanatory Notes By M. A. Eaton, B.A. *Educational Publishing Company[,] Boston[,] New York[,] Chicago[,] San Francisco[,] (1906).* First edition thus. Slim 8vo, 142pp., "Copyrighted 1906" on verso of title page, unsigned portrait sketch after "Contents" page and before introduction, original red cloth (a bit rubbed), front cover lettered in white within circular laurel trim at the top, spine lettered in white. A good copy. Not in Kohler.

518. Variant of Preceding, original wrappers lettered in blue, green cloth spine, large laurel wreath in blue with "Classic Library" in a scroll beneath, "Price, 15 Cents" in upper right corner, advertising for the Classic Library series on inside of front cover and on inside and outside of back cover. A nice copy in original publisher's wrappers. Not in Kohler.

519. MINOR POEMS By John Milton With Biographical Introduction by Hannaford Bennett[.] *London[:] John Long[,] 13 & 14 Norris Street, Haymarket[,] MCMVII.* First edition thus. Slim 8vo, 94pp., half-title ("John Longs Carlton Classics Minor Poems Edited by Hannaford Bennett"), with a listing of "John Long's Carlton Classics" on verso, original crushed blue leather (a little rubbed, spine chipped at top and bottom), small square emblem in gilt at the center of the front cover incorporating the initials of the publisher "JL" in blue, spine decorated and lettered in gilt, t.e.g. A good copy. Not in Kohler.

520. MILTON'S MINOR POEMS[:] L'Allegro, Il Penseroso, Comus, And Lycidas Edited For School Use By William Allan Neilson, M.A., Ph.D. Columbia University[.] The Lake English Classics[.] *Chicago[:] Scott, Foresman And Company[,] (1907)*. Third edition thus? Small 8vo, 165pp., advertisement leaf for "The Lake English Classics" before title page, original light blue cloth (a little used), front cover and spine lettered and ruled in in black. A good copy with early presentation inscription. The first edition thus, first issue, was published in 1900 with only Chicago in the publisher's imprint as here (also listed here with further editions cited). Not in Kohler.

521. [MINOR POEMS] SELECT MINOR POEMS OF JOHN MILTON[:] Hymn On The Nativity[,] L'Allegro[,] Il Penseroso[,] Comus[,] Lycidas[,] Sonnets[.] Edited, With Introduction, Notes, Etc., By Albert Perry Walker, M.A. Master, And Teacher Of English And History In The English High School, Boston[.] *Boston, U.S.A.[:] D. C. Heath & Co., Publishers[,] 1908*. Third edition thus? Small 8vo, x+[2]+186+[8]pp., frontispiece illustration plate and five additional illustration plates plus one headpiece illustration, with either the lines illustrated or identification printed beneath, original cream cloth (bit worn), title stamped in contrasting brown on front cover and spine. Good copy. Six pages of advertisements bound in at the end. Illustrations as with first edition thus in 1900 (see copies listed here with further editions cited). Not in Kohler.

522. MILTON'S MINOR POEMS[:] L'Allegro, Il Penseroso, Comus, And Lycidas[.] Edited For School Use By William Allan Neilson, M.A., Ph.D.[,] Columbia University[.] The Lake English Classics[.] *Chicago[:] Scott, Foresman And Company[,] 1908*. Fourth edition thus? Small 8vo, 165pp., advertisement leaf for "The Lake English Classics" before title page, original blue cloth (somewhat used, pencil markings, school stamp on front pastedown), front cover and spine lettered in black. Scarce. Not in Kohler.

523. [MINOR POEMS] SELECT MINOR POEMS OF JOHN MILTON[:] Hymn On The Nativity[,] L'Allegro[,] Il Penseroso[,] Comus[,] Lycidas[,] Sonnets[.] Edited, With Introduction, Notes, Etc., By Albert Perry Walker, M.A. Master, And Teacher Of English And History In The English High School, Boston[.] *Boston, U.S.A.[:] D. C. Heath & Co., Publishers[,] 1909*. Fourth edition thus? Small 8vo, x+[2]+186+[8]pp., frontispiece illustration plate and six additional illustration plates plus one headpiece illustration, with either the lines illustrated or identification printed beneath each illustration, original cream cloth (used and a bit soiled, front cover broken in the middle, pencil marking throughout), title stamped in contrasting brown on front cover and spine (dirtied). Six pages of advertisements (different from those in first edition) with half-title bound in at end. Illustrations as with first edition thus in 1900 (also listed here with further editions cited). Not in Kohler.

524. [MINOR POEMS] SELECT MINOR POEMS OF JOHN MILTON[:] Hymn On The Nativity[,] L'Allegro[,] Il Penseroso[,] Comus[,] Lycidas[,] Sonnets[.] Edited, With Introduction, Notes, Etc., By Albert Perry Walker, M.A. Master, And Teacher Of English And History In The English High School, Boston[.] *Boston, U.S.A.[:] D. C. Heath & Co., Publishers[,] 1910*. Fifth edition thus? Small 8vo, x+[2]+186+[8]pp., frontispiece illustration plate and six additional illustration plates plus one headpiece illustration, with either the lines illustrated or identification printed beneath each illustration, original cream cloth (bit aged, a few pencil markings), title stamped in contrasting brown on front cover and spine. Nice copy. Illustrations as with first edition thus in 1900 (copies listed here with further editions cited). Not in Kohler.

525. MILTON'S MINOR POEMS[:] L'ALLEGRO, IL PENSEROSO[,] COMUS, LYCIDAS By John Milton Edited with an Introduction and Notes by Cyrus Lauron Hooper of the Murray F. Tuley High School, Chicago[.] Thomas C. Blaisdell, Ph.D.[,] Professor of English Literature, Michigan State Agricultural College: Author of "Composition-Rhetoric" and "English in the Grades," and Co-Author of "Steps in English." Supervising Editor[.] The Excelsior Literature Series[.] *F. A. Owen Publishing Company, Dansville, N.Y.[,] (1910)*. First edition thus. Slim 8vo, 8+[2]pp., brief biography of Milton at the beginning, notes on each poem at the end, original gray wrappers, front cover lettered and decorated in black in art nouveau / art deco style ("Excelsior Literature Series No. 29"), advertisements printed on inside front and back covers and on back cover. Nice copy. Not in Kohler.

526. MINOR POEMS BY JOHN MILTON With Notes For Careful Study By Claude M. Fuess, Ph.D.[,] Instructor In English, Phillips Academy[,] Andover, Mass. And Suggestive Questions And Comments By Charles Swain Thomas, A.M.[,] Head Of The Department Of English[,] Newton High School[.] The Riverside Literature Series[.] *Boston[,] New York[,] Chicago[:] Houghton Mifflin Company[,] The Riverside Press Cambridge[,] (1914)*. Third edition thus. Slim 8vo, 126+[1]+[2]pp., frontispiece portrait plate (unsigned, reproduction of the Faithorne portrait, Milton looking out from the right side), original publisher's olive green cloth (slightly rubbed along extremities, spine ends a little worn, a few pencil markings, "Desk Copy" written in ink on fly-leaf), front cover lettered in black with Grecian pillars on either side in black holding up the lettering at the top ("Riverside Literature Series") while firmly set on a base in black at the bottom with the lettering within ("Houghton Mifflin Co."), spine lettered in black with small decorative pieces in black at the top and and bottom, central emblem with the series initials and number "RLS 72" in black on back cover. One leaf of advertisement bound in at the end. In surprisingly very good condition, perhaps because it was a "Desk Copy." The first edition thus was published in 1895; the second thus in 1911. Not in Kohler.

The collection also has a copy in original printed tan wrappers. Nice copy.

527. Variant of Preceding, a variant edition with the addition of "San Francisco" in the publisher's imprint ("Boston[,] New York[,] Chicago[,] San Francisco"), with a different frontispiece portrait (unsigned, Milton looking out from the left side), with a separate page for the "Table of Contents" instead of appearing on verso of title page, and in a variant publisher's binding (original publisher's dark green cloth).

The collection also has a copy of this variant edition in a variant binding (original publisher's light blue cloth). Nice copy.

528. Variant of Preceding, original printed light green wrappers (slightly rubbed, name on cover), title page repeated with elaborate ornamental trim in black on front cover, two pages of advertisements bound in at the end, advertisements for "Riverside Literature Series" printed on inside of covers and on back cover. Nice copy in original wrappers.

529. MILTON'S MINOR POEMS[:] L'Allegro, Il Penseroso, Comus, And Lycidas[.] Edited For School Use By William Allan Neilson[,] President Smith College[.] The Lake English Classics[.] Revised Edition With Helps To Study*[.] Scott, Foresman And Company[,] Chicago[,] Atlanta[,] New York[,] (1919)*. Revised edition. 8vo, 173pp., advertisement leaf for "The Lake English Classics" before title page, original light blue cloth (a bit rubbed, some marginal notations), front cover and spine lettered in black. A good copy with large bookplate on front pastedown. The first edition thus was published in 1900 with only Chicago in the publisher's imprint (copy listed here with further editions cited).

529A. (Cross-listing) [MINOR POEMS] MILTON'S POEMS 1645 Type-Facsimile[.] *Oxford[:] At the Clarendon Press[,] 1924*. See main listing under *Poems*, 1924.

530. MILTON'S MINOR POEMS With Introduction and Notes by M. A. Eaton, B.A. The Red Shield Classics. *Educational Publishing Company[,] Boston[,] New York[,] Chicago[,] 1925*. Slim 8vo, 142pp., unsigned portrait sketch after "Contents" page and before introduction, original green cloth spine, stiff brown wrappers (a bit used, front and back covers slightly stained along bottom edge), front cover lettered in black within scroll beneath laurel wreath. The first edition thus was published in 1906 (also listed here).

531. JOHN MILTON MINOR POEMS[.] The Noel Douglas Replicas[.] There Was A Second Edition Of This Book With Some Additions And Improvements In 1673 But It Was Not Like The First Edition Of 1645 Prepared For The Press By Milton And The Latter Has Been Chosen For Reproduction Here • The Second Half Of The Book Containing The Latin Poems Has Been Omitted • For A Final Text See Canon Beeching's Edition Of Milton Oxford 1900 • The Copy Reproduced Is That In The British Museum[.] *Noel Douglas[,] 38 Great Ormond Street[,] London WC I[,] (1926)*. First edition thus. Small 4to, [1]+[8]+120pp., "Made And Printed In England by Percy Lund, Humphries & Co. Ltd. Bradford And London" on verso of title page, facsimile reproduction of 1645 frontispiece portrait of Milton and 1645 title page, facsimile reproduction of 1645 edition of Milton's poems, original blind-stamped parchment, spine lettered in reddish-brown, edges untrimmed, partially unopened. A fine copy. Facsimile reproduction: Noel Douglas replicas. Edition limited to 250 copies.

532. Variant of Preceding. JOHN MILTON MINOR POEMS . . . *Noel Douglas[,] 38 Great Ormond Street[,] London WC I[,] (1926)*. First edition thus. Small 4to, [1]+[8]+120pp., as preceding, original parchment (covers a little darkened, spine missing), covers blind-stamped, edges untrimmed. Unlike the preceding, this one has a slip tipped in on title page over the publisher's imprint with the printed notation: "This Book Is Now Published In The United States By Columbia University Press For The Facsimile Text Society 2960 Broadway, New York, N.Y." Facsimile reproduction: Noel Douglas replicas. Edition limited to 250 copies—This copy published in the United States. Scarce.

533. MILTON'S MINOR POEMS With Introductions, Critical Comments, Explanatory Notes, And Questions For Class Study[.] Edited By Arthur Lee[,] Superintendent Of

Schools[,] Clinton[,] Missouri[.] *Lincoln[,] Chicago[,] Dallas[,] New York[:] The University Publishing Company[,] 1926.* First edition thus. Small 8vo, xxi+152pp., half-title, advertisement for the series on verso of title page, original blue cloth, front cover ruled and lettered in black, spine lettered in black. A fine copy.

534. JOHN MILTON MINOR POEMS[.] The English Replicas[.] There Was A Second Edition Of This Book With Some Additions And Improvements In 1673 But It Was Not Like The First Edition Of 1645 Prepared For The Press By Milton And The Latter Has Been Chosen For Reproduction Here • The Second Half Of The Book Containing The Latin Poems Has Been Omitted • For A Final Text See Canon Beeching's Edition Of Milton Oxford 1900 • The Copy Reproduced Is That In The British Museum[.] *1927 Payson & Clarke Ltd[,] New York.* First edition thus. Small 4to, [8]+120pp., facsimile reproduction of 1645 frontispiece portrait of Milton and 1645 title page, facsimile reproduction of 1645 edition of Milton's poems, original boards (small stamp on endpapers, paper clip remainder marks on front blanks), front cover lettered in blue within blue trimmed box, spine lettered in blue, edges untrimmed. A nice copy. Facsimile reproduction: the English Replicas—similar to the Noel Douglas replica edition published one year earlier in 1926 (also listed here). Printed in a limited edition.

535. MINOR POEMS John Milton Edited by S. E Allen[.] Revised by H. Y. Moffett[.] Illustrated by W. M. Berger[.] *[New York:] The Macmillan Company[,] (1930).* 2 volumes in one.. Second edition thus, revised with illustrations. 8vo, xliii+140pp., half-title ("New Pocket Classics"), first appearance of frontispiece illustration and other illustrations after W. M. Berger. Bound with MILTON [BY] THOMAS B. MACAULAY[.] ADDRESS ON MILTON [BY] MATTHEW ARNOLD[.] Edited By C. W. French[.] Revised By H. Y. Moffett[.] Illustrated By W. M. Berger[.] *[New York:] The Macmillan Company[,] (1930).* 8vo, xxxviii+125pp., first appearance of frontispiece portrait sketch of Milton by W. M. Berger, decorative black border trim in art nouveau style on title page, "Revised edition with illustrations published June, 1930" on verso of title page. Original red cloth (school stamp on front endpapers), small central emblem in gilt on front cover, central initials of the press in blind on back cover, spine lettered in gilt with small gilt decorative pieces, printed gray endpapers. Very nice. The illustrations designed for this edition are black and white line drawings (sometimes reminiscent of art nouveau style), with one illustration for *L'A*, one for *IlP*, one for *Arc*, six (including frontispiece) for *C*, and one for *L*. It is interesting to note that Milton's *NO* is not only *not* illustrated here, it isn't even included in this edition. The first edition thus of *MP* was published in 1912 without the illustrations; the third edition thus, a reprint of this second, revised edition with illustrations was published in "October, 1935" (also listed here), without the inclusion of Macaulay's *Milton* and Arnold's *Address*.

536. MILTON'S MINOR POEMS with Descriptive Poetry of the 18th, 19th and 20th Centuries[.] Edited by Kenneth W. Wright[,] Chairman English Department, DeWitt Clinton High School, New York[.] Noble's Comparative Classics[.] *Noble And Noble[,] 76 Fifth Avenue, New York[,] (1932).* First edition thus. 8vo, x+146pp., unsigned frontispiece sketch of Milton as a young man, decorative trim at top and bottom of title page with two small inverted triangles at the center, sketch of "Milton's Cottage" (signed "L.H.C.") in essay on "Milton's Life and Work," original dark green cloth (a bit rubbed, ex-library, with related library matter), front cover lettered in gold within an inverted triangle outlined in gold alongside contrasting green lettering within an inverted gold triangle as background, spine lettered in yellow. A good copy. Included with Milton's poems here are *The Borough* by George Crabbe under the heading "Descriptive Poetry Of The 18th Century School," *The Prelude* by William Wordsworth, under the heading "Descriptive Poetry Of The 19th Century," *The Great Lover* by Rupert Brooke and *Exiled* by Edna St. Vincent Millay under the heading "Descriptive Poetry Of The 20th Century." A second edition thus was published in 1934; a third edition thus (expanded by the inclusion of additional poems with study questions for the twentieth century) was published in 1935 (copy listed here).

537. MINOR POEMS John Milton Edited by S. E Allen[.] Revised by H. Y. Moffett[.] Illustrated by W. M. Berger[.] *[New York:] The Macmillan Company[,] (1935).* Third edition thus. 8vo, xlii+151pp., frontispiece illustration and other illustrations after W. M. Berger, decorative black border trim in art nouveau style on title page, original red cloth (a bit used), small central emblem in black on front cover, central initials of the press in blind on back cover, spine lettered in gilt, printed gray endpapers. A good copy. The illustrations are as with the 1930 second edition thus (also listed here). This reprint was published in "October, 1935" (verso of title page), without the inclusion of Macaulay's *Milton* and Arnold's *Address* as in the second edition thus and therefore without the frontispiece portrait sketch of Milton included there. The first edition thus was published in 1912 without the illustrations.

538. MILTON'S MINOR POEMS with Descriptive Poetry of the 18th, 19th and 20th Centuries[.] Edited by Kenneth W. Wright[,] Chairman English Department[,] DeWitt Clinton High School, New York[.] Noble's Comparative Classics[.] *Noble And Noble, Publishers, Inc. 100 Fifth Avenue[,] New York City[,] (1935).* Third edition thus. 8vo, xii+168pp., unsigned frontispiece sketch of Milton as a young man, decorative trim at top and bottom of title page with two small inverted triangles at the center, "Milton's Life And Work," with unsigned sketch of "Milton's Cottage," original green cloth, front cover lettered in embossed green and yellow within inverted triangles, spine lettered in yellow. A very nice copy. Among the "advantages claimed for the present volume" "is the opportunity furnished for the *comparative study* of descriptive poetry, by the inclusion of selections similar in appeal to the *companion poems*, from the eighteenth, nineteenth, and twentieth century schools of poetry" (Foreword). Expanded from the first edition published in 1932 (copy listed here) by the inclusion of additional poems with study questions for the twentieth century as noted there.

539. MILTON'S MINOR POEMS Compiled By Tom Peete Cross[,] Professor Of English And Comparative Literature, University Of Chicago[.] Illustrated By Marguerite Benjamin[.] *Ginn And Company[,] Boston • New York • Chicago • London • Atlanta • Dallas • Columbus • San Francisco[,] (1936).* First edition thus. 8vo, viii+130pp., first appearance of frontispiece illustration and other illustrations by Marguerite Benjamin, copyright dated 1936 along with "The Athenaeum Press" on verso of title page, original green cloth (a little rubbed), front cover lettered in contrasting dark green with decorative central device in dark green and gilt, spine lettered in gilt with small decorative gilt pieces and decorative gilt trim at top and bottom, unopened. A nice copy. The illustrations, designed for this edition, are black-and-white sketches of biographically related scenes as well as illustrations of the poems. Uncommon.

540. JOHN MILTON POEMS[.] L'Allegro[,] Il Penseroso[,] Comus • Lycidas[,] And The Complete Minor Poems[.] *The Peter Pauper Press • Mount Vernon[, N.Y.] n.d. [ca. 1950].* First edition thus? Tall, slim 8vo, 91pp.+ colophon leaf, medallion illustration/decoration in tinted blue on title page, additional medallion illustrations/decorations in tinted blue, all "from engravings of Greek Gems" and each symbolic in a general sort of way of the poem for which it appears as a headpiece, original boards covered with printed blue patterned paper, with a central vignette illustration in tinted blue on front cover and a central vignette illustration in tinted blue on back cover, spine printed in black with blue trim outline, t.e. blue. Fine copy in original slipcase with printed large paper label repeating title page with vignette illustration/decoration in tinted blue on one side. "The text of this edition follows that of Prof. David Masson. It has been set in the Baskerville Types and printed on a specially-made Peter Pauper Press paper. The decorations are from engravings of Greek Gems" (colophon).

541. MILTON'S MINOR POEMS[:] On The Morning Of Christ's Nativity[,] L'Allegro, Il Penseroso, Comus[,] Lycidas, Sonnets[.] Edited by W. J. Halliday, M.A., Ph.D. *Ginn And Company Ltd. 18 Bedford Row, London, W.C.I[,] (1958).* Small 8vo, xxvii+131pp., half-title, frontispiece portrait sketch of Milton (signed with the initials "AH") on verso of half-title, original green cloth over soft boards, front cover and spine lettered in gilt. A nice copy. The first edition thus was published in 1931.

542. JOHN MILTON MINOR POEMS edited by Ann Phillips, M.A.[,] Fellow Of Newnham College, Cambridge[.] *London[:] University Tutorial Press Ltd[,] Clifton House • Euston Road • N.W. I[,] (1966).* First edition thus. Slim 8vo, [1]+175pp., black device with initials of the press on title page, original red cloth, gilt lettering on front cover and spine with gilt device incorporating initials of the press on front cover. Fine copy.

543. [MINOR POEMS] A VARIORUM COMMENTARY ON THE POEMS OF JOHN MILTON[:] THE MINOR ENGLISH POEMS [Edited By] A. S. P. Woodhouse and Douglas Bush[.] [Volume Two, Parts One, Two, & Three.] *New York[:] Columbia University Press[,] 1972.* 3 volumes. [Called "Parts"—each "Part" a volume.] First edition thus. 8vo, xvii+338pp.,+xi+734pp.,+xi+1143pp., half-title each Part, title page each Part, original blue buckram, spines lettered in gilt. Fine set. Milton's "Minor English Poems" occupy "Volume Two" in "The Complete Series" of the "Variorum Commentary on the Poems of John Milton," and "Volume Two" in the "Series" consists of three "Parts" or volumes. A complete set, as here, is scarce, especially in such fine condition.

544. (Attribution) NOVA SOLYMA[.] THE IDEAL CITY; OR JERUSALEM REGAINED An Anonymous Romance Written [?By Samuel Gott] In The Time Of Charles I. Now First Drawn From Obscurity, And Attributed To The Illustrious John Milton[.] With Introduction, Translation, Literary Essays And A Bibliography By The Rev. Walter Begley[.] *New York[:] Charles Scribner's Sons Publisher's, Importers, And Booksellers[,] 743-745, Broadway[,] 1902.* 2 volumes. First and only translation of this apocryphal work by Milton; first American edition. 8vo, xxi+359pp.,+xi+414pp., half-title each volume, frontispiece facsimile plate reproducing title page of "Novae Solymae Libri Sex. Londini, Typis Joannis Legati. M DC XLVIII," volume 1, protective tissue guard, frontispiece facsimile plate reproducing p. 374 of "Liber Sextus," volume 2, protective tissue guard, separate title page each volume, additional facsimile plate reproducing p. 374 of "Novae Solymae," volume 2, bibliography and index at the end of volume 2, original half vellum, light brown cloth (a bit aged, notes in a neat hand on back end-pages of volume 1, library card pocket at end of volume 2, stamped "discarded"), spines lettered in gilt, with "By John Milton" added in black ink by a contemporary hand, t.e.g., others untrimmed. A good set with commemorative bookplate of the Free Public Library of Summit, New Jersey, on front pastedown of each volume. Originally reviewed in *National Review*, August 1904. See Coleridge 262 discussion of 1648 edition of *Novae Solymae*—Begley's "1902 translation [Begley's editions not in NUC] was the first place to suggest Milton as author. . . . Begley's argument is based principally upon a broad similarity of style, of educational ideas, and of ecclesiastical position. This attribution caused considerable debate but the question was cleared up by S. K. Jones in 1910"—(see Jones's article on "The Authorship of Nova Solyma" in *The Library*, July 1910, volume I, no. 3). This translation of *Nova Solyma* was published simultaneously in London (following set). Scarce. Stevens 2659 (see Stevens 2662, 2664–66, 2668–69, 2671); Not in Kohler.

545. (Attribution) **NOVA SOLYMA[.] THE IDEAL CITY; OR JERUSALEM REGAINED** An Anonymous Romance Written [?By Samuel Gott] In The Time Of Charles I. Now First Drawn From Obscurity, And Attributed To The Illustrious John Milton[.] With Introduction, Translation, Literary Essays And A Bibliography By The Rev. Walter Begley[.] *London[:] John Murray, Albemarle Street[,] 1902*. 2 volumes. First and only translation of this apocryphal work by Milton; first London edition. 8vo, xxi+359pp.,+xi+414pp., half-title each volume, frontispiece facsimile plate reproducing title page of "Novae Solymae Libri Sex. Londini, Typis Joannis Legati. M DC XLVIII," volume 1, protective tissue guard, frontispiece facsimile plate reproducing p. 374 of "Liber Sextus," volume 2, protective tissue guard, separate title page each volume, additional facsimile plate reproducing p. 374 of "Novae Solymae," volume 2, bibliography and index at the end of volume 2, original half vellum, light brown cloth, spines lettered in gilt, t.e.g., others untrimmed. A good set. See commentary and references with preceding set. This translation of *Nova Solyma* was published simultaneously in America (preceding set). Scarce. Not in Kohler.

546. ODES, PASTORALS, MASQUES[.] John Milton. Ode on the morning of Christ's nativity[,] The passion[,] Upon the circumcision[,] On time[,] At a solemn music[,] L'Allegro[,] Il Penseroso[,] Arcades[,] A Masque: Comus[,] Lycidas[.] Edited By David Aers . . . Peter Mendes . . . Winifred Maynard . . . Lorna Sage . . . John Broadbent . . . *[Cambridge:] Cambridge University Press[,] (1975)*. First edition thus. 8vo, xii+240pp., "Published by the Syndics of the Cambridge University Press. . . . Printed in Great Britain" (on verso of title page), bibliographical references, paperback, original printed stiff yellow paper wrappers with reproduction of Blake's *The Sun at His Eastern Gate* in the Morgan Library, illustrating *L'A* (1.60), on front cover. Very nice copy.

Of Education

547. OF EDUCATION, 1728. [In] Phillips, Jenkin Thomas. **A COMPENDIOUS WAY OF TEACHING ANTIENT AND MODERN LANGUAGES.** The Third Edition very much Enlarg'd By J. T. Philipps, Preceptor to his Royal Highness Prince William, Duke of Cumberland. *London: Printed for W. Meadows, at the Angel in Cornhill. 1728.* Two title pages, both are printed, the first with central engraved emblem (worn, somewhat dirtied, frayed at edges), the second title page reads: "A Compendious Way of Teaching Antient and Modern Language, Formerly Practiced by the Learned Tanaquil Faber; And Now With Little Alteration, successfully executed in London; With observations on the same Subject by several eminent Men, viz. Roger Ascham, Richard Carew, Mr. Milton, Mr. Lock. With An Account of the Education of the Dauphine, and of his Sons, the Dukes of Burgundy, Anjou, and Berry; with the Marchiness of Lambert's Letter to her Son. To which is added, An Essay on Rational Grammar. The Third Edition very much Enlarg'd By J. T. Philipps, Preceptor to his Royal Highness Prince William, Duke of Cumberland. London: Printed for W. Meadows, at the Angel in Cornhill. 1728." 8vo, 283+[2]pp., decorative head- and tailpieces, and decorated initial letters, contemporary blue paper over sheep, white paper spine (quite worn, waterstained at top and bottom of the first few leaves at each end, lacking front blanks). Except for some staining to the two title pages, really quite fresh internally. Scarce, with the two title pages seldom found together as in this copy. Milton's *Of Education* occupies pp. 110–30. This edition was first published in 1727, and Coleridge clarifies the distinction between these two editions, both of which are very rare. Coleridge 36b.

With an Early Nineteenth-century Oil Painting on the Front Cover—1746 French Edition

548. [OF EDUCATION] LETTRES SUR L'EDUCATION DES PRINCES. AVEC UNE LETTRE DE MILTON, Où il propose une nouvelle manière d'élever la Jeunesse d'Angleterre. [Quotation From Juvenal Sat. XIV] *A Edimbourg, Chez John Trueman, a l'Enseigne de Platon. M. DCC. XLVI.* First edition thus. 12mo in eights and fours, xciii+[iii]+176pp., early manuscript authorial attribution on title page, decorative head- and tailpieces with decorated initial letters, early nineteenth-century quarter morocco, marbled paper over boards, red morocco label on spine lettered in gilt, spine ruled in gilt with decorative gilt trim at top and bottom, front cover painted at the same date, in oils, depicting a little prince with his dog, marbled endpapers, blue speckled edges. Rare. Coleridge 40; ESTC T123898, listing six copies, with another issue adding three more; Shawcross, 1974, p. 302; Not in Kohler.

A charming and unusual binding with an early nineteenth-century oil painting on the front cover depicting a small boy who is presumably meant to be the prince of the book's subject matter. The prince has a northern European look about him, wearing a black tunic with a white ruff. The tunic is belted at the waist with a large buckle. He is also wearing a small blue hat and is carrying a bunch of flowers. There is a small white dog at his side and, in the background, a tree. The scene is framed within a gilt border.

Addressed to the Duke of Orleans, with a lengthy introduction discussing existing literature on the education of princes, the text comprises nine letters addressed to different people on various aspects of the subject. The final section is a translation of Milton's *Of Education* (pp. 136–76). "The translation and preface are by Jean Bernard LeBlanc (1707–81), an abbé who engaged in literary work, especially publicizing English thought" (Coleridge).

❈

548A. (Cross-listing) OF EDUCATION . . . 1748. [In] PARADISE LOST. The Eleventh Edition, Adorn'd With Sculptures. *Dublin: Printed by and for George Grierson, 1724.* First Irish edition. Bound with **PARADISE REGAIN'D** . . . *The Seventh Edition. Dublin: Printed by and for George Grierson, 1724.* First Irish edition. Bound with **SAMSON AGONISTES** . . . *Dublin: Printed by and for George Grierson, 1748.* First Irish edition. Bound with **POEMS UPON SEVERAL OCCASIONS.** *Dublin: Printed by and for George Grierson, 1748.* First Irish edition. Bound with A MASK, PRESENTED AT LUDLOW CASTLE . . . *Dublin: Printed by and for George Grierson, 1748.* First Irish edition. 5 volumes bound in one. See main listing under *PL*, 1724.

549. ESSAY ON EDUCATION. By John Milton, Author of Paradise Lost, &c. These are the Studies wherein our noble and our gentle Youth ought to bestow their Time, p. 14. *London: Printed, and sold by Charles Corbett in Fleet-Street; T. Trye in Holborn; and J. Jolliffe in St. James's Street. M.DCC.LI.* [Price Six-pence.] Large slender 8vo, [i]+ii+19pp., decorative printer's device on title page, dedication page, decorative headpieces and decorated initial letters, disbound (title and final leaf a bit dust-darkened, a few page numerals just shaved), stitched, long note in an eighteenth-century hand on verso of dedication page discussing this edition. Rare. Not in Coleridge; Not in Kohler.

549A. (Cross-listing) OF EDUCATION [In] Blackburne, Francis. REMARKS ON JOHNSON'S LIFE OF MILTON. To Which Are Added, Milton's Tractate Of Education And Areopagitica. *London: MDCCLXXX.* First edition. 8vo, contemporary quarter calf, spine lettered in gilt: "Milton Of Education." See main listing under *Areopagitica*, 1780.

550. MILTON'S PLAN OF EDUCATION, In His Letter To Hartlib, (Now Very Scarce); With The Plan Of The Edinburgh Academical Institution, Founded Thereon. *London: 1820.* 8vo, 36pp. (separately paginated, but also paginated 123 to 156), "Appendix," disbound. A very nice, clean copy. Gift from Arthur Freeman of Quaritch delivered by Bob Taylor in 1984, with a letter from Bob indicating he had been asked to pass this copy along to me as a "present" from Arthur. Scarce. Not in Kohler.

551. MILTON TRACTATE OF EDUCATION Edited With An Introduction And Notes By Edward F. Morris, M.A. Professor Of English Literature In The University Of Melbourne[.] *London[:] Macmillan And Co. And New York[,] 1895[.]* All rights reserved[.] First edition thus. Slim 8vo, xlv+50+4pp., half-title, preface dated "April 16, 1895," original buff cloth (a bit worn and faded, spine ends chipped), front cover and spine lettered in blue, with small circle incorporating "M&M Co." at lower right corner of front cover, decorative initials of the press in blue on back cover. A good copy with contemporary signature. Four pages of advertisements bound in at end. The first edition was published in "July 1895"—edition here dated "April 16, 1895" by virtue of its preface; it was reprinted in "September 1895" (see copy following). Uncommon. Not in Kohler.

552. [OF EDUCATION] MILTON TRACTATE OF EDUCATION Edited With An Introduction And Notes By Edward F. Morris, M.A. Professor Of English Literature In The University Of Melbourne[.] *London[:] Macmillan And Co. And New York[,] 1895[.]* All rights reserved[.] Second edition thus. Slim 8vo, xlv+50pp., half-title, original buff cloth (browned and soiled, H. M. stamp for public service on title page and again on first page of text), front cover and spine lettered in blue (spine darkened), with small circle incorporating "M&M Co." at lower right corner of front cover, decorative initials of the press in blue on back cover. The first edition thus was possibly published in "July 1895" (also listed here); it was reprinted in "September 1895" (verso of title page). Uncommon. Not in Kohler.

553. OF EDUCATION] TRACTATE OF EDUCATION By John Milton[.] Edited With An Introduction And Notes By Edward F. Morris, M.A. Professor Of English Literature In The University Of Melbourne[.] *Macmillan And Co., London[;] St. Martin's Street, London[,] 1918[.]* Slim 8vo, xlv+50pp., half-title with initials of the press on verso, 45-page introduction, notes at the end, original red cloth (spine and a portion of back cover sunfaded, former ownership signature on fly-leaf), front cover decorated in blind with black lettering, spine lettered in black. A good copy. The first edition thus was published in "July 1895" (also listed here); it was reprinted in "September 1895" (also listed here), 1903, 1911, and 1918 (also listed here).

554. [OF EDUCATION] MILTON ON EDUCATION[:] The Tractate Of Education With Supplementary Extracts From Other Writings Of Milton[.] Edited With An Introduction And Notes By Oliver Morley Ainsworth[,] Associate Professor Of English In Beloit College[.] Cornell Studies In English XII[.] *New Haven: Yale University Press[;] London: Humphrey Milford[;] Oxford University Press[,] MDCCCCXXVIII.* First edition thus. 8vo, xi+[1]+369+[1]pp., half-title, original printed gray paper wrappers (signature in a neat hand on half-title), title page with central seal of the press reprinted on front cover. Nice, clean copy. See copy of reprint edition by the Scholarly Press in 1970.

555. OF EDUCATION [In] LITERARY STUDIES FOR FRESHMAN COMPOSITION[.] Selected and Edited by Bernard L. Jefferson[,] Paul N. Landis[,] Arthur W. Secord[,] James E. Ernst[,] (University of Illinois)[.] *Thomas Nelson And Sons[,] New York[,] 1929.* First edition. 8vo, xi+717pp., half-title, original half blue cloth, marbled paper over boards, printed orange label on spine (a bit chipped), fore- and bottom edges untrimmed. Nice copy with ownership signature and stamp on fly-leaf and front pastedown. Included under the heading "Ideals And Standards" is Milton's *Of Education.*

556. [OF EDUCATION] JOHN MILTON VON DER ERZIEHUNG[.] Brief an [sic] Samuel Hartlib 1644. Deutsch und Englisch[.] *Verlag Maria Honeit Hamburg[,] (1946).* First edition thus. Slim 8vo, half-title, German translation followed by English text, original cardlike orange paper wrappers (a bit rubbed), front cover lettered in black. Scarce.

557. MILTON ON EDUCATION[:] The Tractate Of Education With Supplementary Extracts From Other Writings Of Milton[.] Edited With An Introduction And Notes By Oliver Morley Ainsworth[,] Associate Professor Of English In Beloit College[.] Cornell Studies In English XII[.] *New Haven: Yale University Press[;] London: Humphrey Milford[;] Oxford University Press[,] MDCCCCXXVIII[.] Republished 1970[,] Scholarly Press, 22929 Industrial Drive East[,] St. Clair Shores, Michigan 48080[.]* Reprint edition. 8vo, xi+[1]+369+[1]pp., half-title, original brown buckram, spine lettered and ruled in gilt. Fine copy, reprinting the first edition published in 1928 (copy listed here).

558. OF REFORMATION TOUCHING CHVRCH-DISCIPLINE IN ENGLAND: AND THE CAVSES THAT HITHERTO HAVE HINDRED IT. Two Bookes, Written to a Friend. *[London:] Printed, for Thomas Underhill, 1641.* First edition. 4to, [1]+90pp., decorative device on title page, decorative head- and tailpieces, decorated initial letters, disbound (lightly dust soiled, slight embrowning). A fine copy, complete with the rare errata leaf. "The first acknowledged prose work published by John Milton" (Shawcross, 1974, p. 292). Shawcross also points out that "Jefferson, in his commonplace book summarized and quoted from this pamphlet along with *Reason of Church-Government.*" The first edition of Milton's first prose work; it was preceded only by *On Shakespeare, Comus,* and *Lycidas* published in 1632, 1637, and 1638, respectively. Wing M2134; Parker, p. 847; Coleridge 42; Shawcross, 1984, 56; Shawcross, 1974, pp. 292–93; Kohler 487.

559. AN OLD LOOKING-GLASS FOR THE LAITY AND CLERGY OF ALL DENOMINATIONS, Who either give or receive Money under Pretence of the Gospel: Being Considerations Touching The likeliest Means to remove Hirelings out of the Church of Christ. Wherein are also discoursed of Tythes, Church-Fees, Church-Revenues, Christnings, Marriages, Burials, And

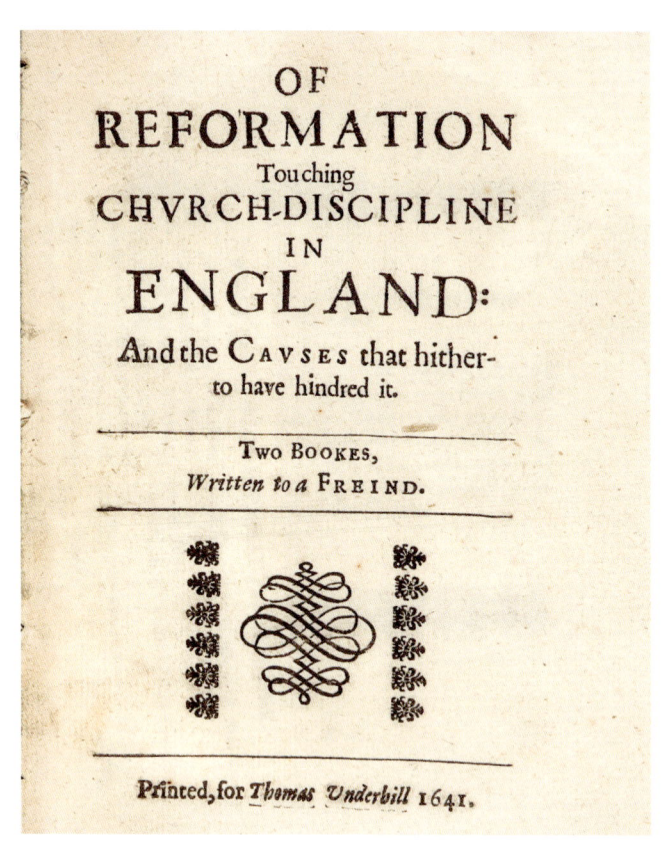

Of Reformation Touching Church-Discipline In England, 1641. See #558.

Whether any Maintenance of Gospel-Servants ought to be settled by Law. By John Milton, Author of Paradise Lost. With the Life of Milton: Also large Extracts from his Works, concerning Bishops. [Quotation from New Testament] [Quotation from Hickeringill] [Quotation from Milton] *Philadelphia: Printed for Robert Bell, and sold by J. Crukshank, and I. Collins, Printers in Third-Street. M,DCC,LXX.* 12mo in 6s, x+74pp., life of Milton, disbound (foxed). Despite the foxing (not uncommon to paper of this period), a decent copy. The first publication in America of any of Milton's works and the first edition under this title. The original English edition was entitled *Considerations Touching the Likeliest Means to Remove Hirelings Out Of The Church* (1659), itself a formidable rarity. An unassuming book for such a milestone: one of only eleven total eighteenth-century American editions of Milton's works. Of the eleven, the collection has eight: *PL*, 1777, and *PR, Samson, & Poems*, 1777, first American edition of each; *PR*, 1790, second American edition, and 1791, third American edition; *PL*, 1791, second American edition; *PW*, 1794, third American edition, and 1796, fourth American edition; and *An Old Looking Glass*, 1770, first American edition, volume here. As John Shawcross has kindly informed me, the other three are a different edition of *The Old Looking-Glass* published in New Haven in 1774; and two editions of *PW* from Philadelphia in 1791: one by Henry Taylor, which is a reissue of his *PL*, which is in the collection, and a different edition of the *PR* volume, not the one in the collection; and one by W. Woodhouse, which is a reissue of Taylor's *PW*. See 1723 and 1743 London editions of *Considerations Touching The Likeliest Means To Remove Hirelings Out of The Church*, two of a number of eighteenth-century editions, albeit rare editions, published in London and Dublin; see also 1834 London edition of *Considerations Touching The Likeliest Means To Remove Hirelings Out of The Church*, one of a number of nineteenth-century editions published in London and Dublin. Very rare. Evans 11745; Not in Coleridge; Not in Kohler.

560. ON ENGRAVED SCENES ILLUSTRATING OVID'S METAMORPHOSES [In] SOME NEWLY DISCOVERED STANZAS WRITTEN BY JOHN MILTON ON ENGRAVED SCENES ILLUSTRATING OVID'S METAMORPHOSES[.] This *Milton-Ovid Script* was written, ca. 1623; discovered, 1921; first printed, in *Notes and Queries*, 1922–23; and is now revised and reprinted, in one volume, with many additional notes by Hugh C. H. Candy[,] B.A., B.Sc. (Lond.)[,] Member of the Bibliographical Society[.] *London[:] Nisbet & Co. Ltd.[,] 22 Berners Street, W.1[,] (1924).* First edition. 8vo, 191pp., half-title, frontispiece portrait plate reproducing in black and white the portrait of Milton at age ten, small central emblem of the press on title page, additional black-and-white plates including several reproducing the stanzas, original linen spine (a bit soiled), green boards, printed paper label on front cover with a second printed paper label on spine, fore- and bottom edges untrimmed, bookplate. Presentation copy inscribed and dated by Candy on flyleaf. Scarce. Stevens 2673.

On the Morning of Christ's Nativity (Nativity Ode)

560A. (Cross-listing) **ON THE MORNING OF CHRIST'S NATIVITY [In] JOHANN MILTONS WIEDER=EROBERTES PARADIES,** nebst desselben Samson, und einigen andern Gedichten, wie auch einer Lebens=Beschreibung Des Verfassers. Aus dem Englischen übersetst. *Basel, verlegts Johann Rudolf Imhof, 1752.* See main listing under *PR*, 1752.

561. MILTON'S ODE ON THE MORNING OF CHRIST'S NATIVITY Illustrated By Eminent Artists[.] *London[:] James Nisbet And Co., Berners Street[,] 1868.* First edition thus. 8vo, 44pp., half-title, vignette portrait of Milton (age twenty-one) by W. J. Palmer on title page, eight full-page wood-engraved illustrations and numerous text illustrations engraved by W. J. Palmer from designs by

Lorenz Frolich, Albert Moore, William Small, Caroline Hullah, J. Jackson, C. J. Durham, and E. M. Wimperis, printed on recto only on thin cream cardlike paper, black border around text, decorated initial letters, original purple cloth (slightly rubbed, spine sunned, slight mark on back cover), covers elaborately decorated in blind, front cover and spine richly gilt-decorated, with central gilt emblem incorporating title on front cover, "Nisbet" appearing in gilt at bottom of spine, green endpapers (stained along edges), bevelled edges, a.e.g. A good copy in a fine publisher's binding. Of particular interest are the fine designs by Albert Moore, the painter, which represent his only examples of wood-engraved illustration. The designs of William Small are also very fine. As Robin de Beaumont informed me in his letter offering me the following copy in 1987, "there would appear to be confusion over the publisher and date of this book. Forrest Reid, p. 204, says Warne, [1867]. White, p. 135, gives Nisbet, 1867. The *English Catalogue of Books* says 'Nisbet, Nor. 1867'—so Nisbet 1868 is probably correct, and, indeed, my own copy [in blue and white] is so dated," as is the copy here. Becoming increasingly uncommon. McLean, *VBD*, p. 28, dating "Nisbet, 1867"; Kohler 264, with date of 1868.

562. Variant of Preceding. MILTON'S ODE ON THE MORNING OF CHRIST'S NATIVITY Illustrated By Eminent Artists[.] *London[:] James Nisbet And Co., Berners Street[,] n.d. [1868] (erased)*. First edition thus. 8vo, 44pp., half-title, vignette portrait of Milton (age twenty-one) by W. J. Palmer on title page, eight full-page wood-engraved illustrations and numerous text illustrations engraved by W. J. Palmer from designs by Lorenz Frolich, Albert Moore, William Small, Caroline Hullah, J. Jackson, C. J. Durham, and E. M. Wimperis, printed on recto only on thin cream cardlike paper, black border around text, decorated initial letters, original purple cloth, decorated exactly as preceding with "Nisbet" appearing in gilt at bottom of spine, green endpapers, bevelled edges, a.e.g. A very nice copy in a fine publisher's binding with early inscription on fly-leaf. A close inspection of the title page in this copy shows that the published date has carefully been erased. It would seem, as Robin de Beaumont further suggested in his letter to me offering me this book, that the book is dated 1868, as the preceding copy, and that the date was erased a few years before Nisbet sold the copyright to Warne in about 1872, when Warne proceeded to publish the book about that same time, adding Scribner of New York (copy listed here). Not in Kohler.

563. MILTON'S ODE ON THE MORNING OF CHRIST'S NATIVITY Illustrated By Eminent Artists[.] *London[:] Frederick Warne And Co.[,] Bedford Street, Covent Garden[;] New York: Scribner, Welford, And Armstrong[,] n.d. (ca. 1872)*. Second edition thus; first edition thus by Warne. 8vo, 44pp., as preceding (although variant publisher, in a variant binding), half-title, vignette portrait of Milton (age twenty-one) by W. J. Palmer on title page, eight full-page wood-engraved illustrations and numerous text illustrations engraved by W. J. Palmer from designs by Lorenz Frolich, Albert Moore, William Small, Caroline Hullah, J. Jackson, C. J. Durham, and E. M. Wimperis, printed on recto only on thin cream cardlike paper, black border around text, decorated initial letters, original blue cloth (a bit rubbed and scuffed), covers elaborately tooled in blind, front cover and spine richly decorated in gilt with central gilt emblem incorporating title on front cover, "Warne" appearing in gilt at bottom of spine, brown endpapers (stained along edges), bevelled edges, a.e.g., bookplate. Similar to preceding copies published by Nisbet in 1868, except published by Warne of London, to whom Nisbet sold the copyright sometime around 1872, with Scribner et al. of New York added to the publisher's imprint, whom Warne included in the new publication, and in a fine variant publisher's binding with contemporary signature (dated 1875) on preliminary blank. Scarce. Not in Kohler.

564. [ON THE MORNING OF CHRIST'S NATIVITY] [In] HARPER'S NEW MONTHLY MAGAZINE. No. CCCXXXI.—December, 1877.—Volume LVI. *Milton's Hymn On The Nativity*. 8vo size, 8pp., disbound, engraved illustrations, variously attributed (fine impressions), printed in doubled column, notes at bottom of page. Seven half-page illustrations, each titled: (1) *While the Heav'n-Born Child All Meanly Wrapt in the Rude Manger Lies*, signed "A.P."; (2) *When Such Music Sweet*, unsigned; (3) *And Leprous Sin Will Melt From Earthly Mould*, signed "Babbett"; (4) *The Old Dragon Under-Ground in Straiter Limits Bound*, signed "J. D. Davis"; (5) *A Voice of Weeping Heard and Loud Lament*, signed "G. Kruell"; (6) *The Flocking Shadows Pale*, signed "A.P."; and (7) *But See, The Virgin Blest Hath Laid Her Babe to Rest*, signed "A.P." Seven pages are devoted to Milton's *NO*; the eighth page begins "A Christmas Story" in prose. Fine copy.

565. [ON THE MORNING OF CHRIST'S NATIVITY] THE NATIVITY OF CHRIST[.] Milton[.] *London[:] Marcus Ward & Co Limited[;] Belfast & New York. n.d. [ca. 1888]*. Small 4to, [14pp.], title page lettered in gold and delicately decorated with three lilies in pink, yellow, and blue with long-leaved stems in gold and light blue at the center behind Milton's name lettered against a broad gold band within decorative light blue trim, illustrations in color with delicate floral trim at top and bottom of each

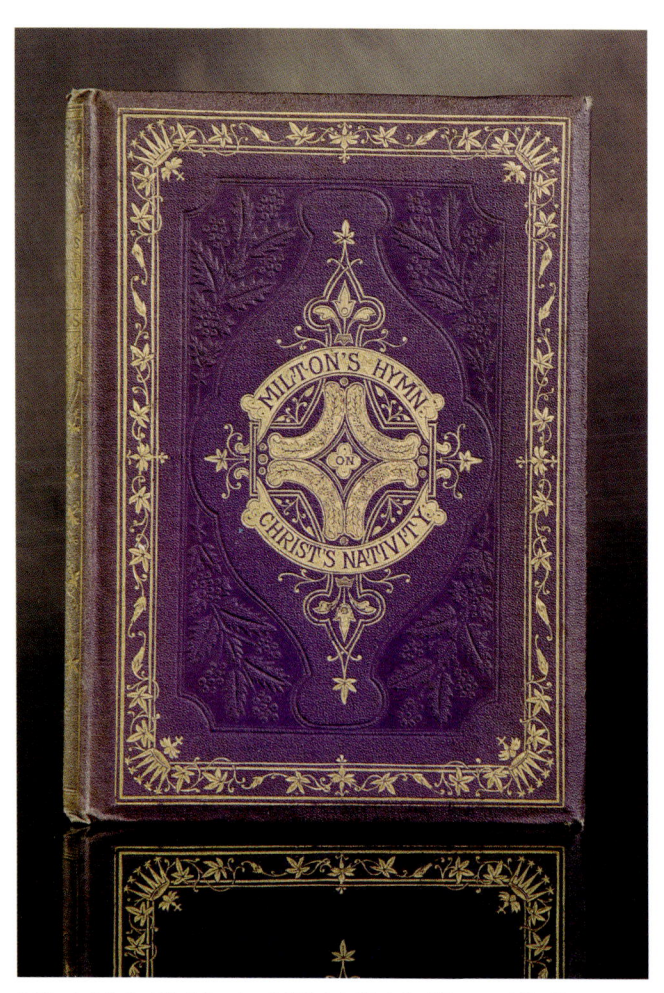

Milton's Ode On The Morning Of Christ's Nativity. Illustrated By Eminent Artists. London: James Nisbet, 1868. Original purple cloth (bit rubbed and scuffed), front cover and spine richly decorated in gilt. See ca. 1872 copy by Warne listed here. See #561.

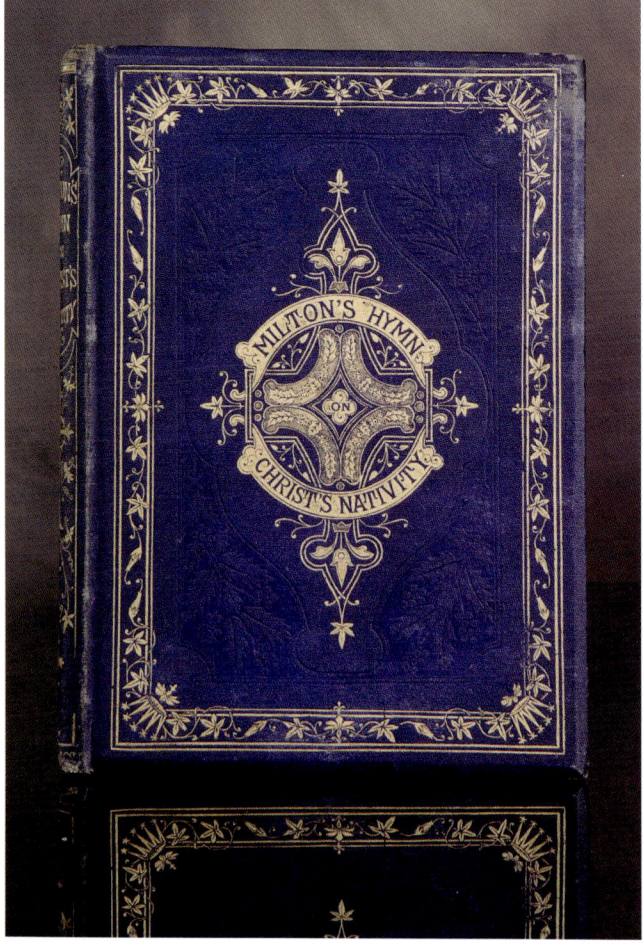

Milton's Ode On The Morning Of Christ's Nativity. Illustrated By Eminent Artists. London and New York: Frederick Warne, ca. 1872. Original blue cloth (bit rubbed and scuffed), front cover and spine richly decorated in gilt. See 1868 copy by Nisbet. See #563.

illustration, each illustration identified by title and museum, printed in sepia and gold throughout, with large initial letters in gold with delicate floral trim in light blue, yellow, and red interwoven through the initial letters on each page and the title within a gold scroll at the top of the first page of the poem, delicate emblem in gold incorporating letters of the press in gold on verso of last page, original crushed red morocco over padded boards (a bit rubbed, top and bottom of spine and corners a little worn), front cover lettered in embossed gilt ("The Nativity") within an embossed diagonal scroll over an embossed floral piece in gilt with Milton's name embossed in smaller letters below, name of the press embossed in blind within a small circle in lower right corner on back cover, gilt-decorated blue endpapers, a.e.g. A lovely copy with an early prize inscription (dated 1896) on front blank, with full-page illustrations of famous Madonna and Child paintings selected for Milton's poem from the Old Masters (mostly Raphael and Holbein), each illustration attractively printed in rich colors on the page opposite the text of the poem printed in sepia and gold throughout. Uncommon. Not in Kohler.

566. [ON THE MORNING OF CHRIST'S NATIVITY] [In] A CHRISTMAS TOKEN[.] *New York[:] The Holiday Publishing Company. n.d. [ca. 1880s]*. Square, slim 8vo, [3+13]pp., half-title, frontispiece decorated with holly, title page in color decorated with holly and angelic faces, printed in color throughout, most pages decorated with Christmas flowers, one page additionally decorated with angelic faces, original boards decorated with holly and angelic faces on front cover (worn, aged, pages loose, crudely rebacked some time ago with cloth tape), signatures on fly-leaf and half-title, in a protective plastic cover. Included are brief selections from Milton's *NO*, on the holly-decorated frontispiece and again on two additional undecorated pages. Although rather worn, this is a scarce copy of a popular late nineteenth-century American Christmas gift publication, and a good example of its kind.

567. [ON THE MORNING OF CHRIST'S NATIVITY] [In] A CHRISTMAS TOKEN[.] Cupples & Leon[,] New York[,] Published by permission of E. P. Dutton & Co. n.d. [ca. 1880s]. Tall, slim 8vo, [1+15]pp., title page in color decorated with holly and angelic faces, printed in color throughout on cardlike paper, most pages decorated with holly, several pages additionally decorated with angelic faces, one full-page illustration of angelic figures, last two pages decorated with holly and birds (robins)—second to last page also with bells and the last page also with a bird house, original boards lettered in gilt and decorated with holly and angelic faces on front cover. A fine copy. Included are brief selections from Milton's *NO*, one on a page decorated with angelic faces and two floral branches (each with green leaves and white buds) and again on three additional undecorated pages. Although similar to the preceding *Christmas Token* (with the same decorated cover), this is a different edition, and like the preceding this is scarce and a fine example of its kind.

568. MILTON'S ODE ON THE MORNING OF CHRIST'S NATIVITY, L'ALLEGRO, IL PENSEROSO AND LYCIDAS With Introduction, Notes And Indexes By A. Wilson Verity, M.A. Sometime Scholar Of Trinity College. Edited For The Syndics Of The University Press[.] *Cambridge: At The University Press. 1891 [All rights reserved.]* First edition thus. Slim 8vo, li+172+[2]+7pp., half-title, original blue cloth (a bit rubbed), spine lettered in gilt ("Lycidas And Other Poems") with small crescent of the press in gilt at the bottom. Nice copy. Eight pages of advertisements at the end. This edition was variously reprinted in 1898, 1904, 1905, and 1906 (copy in collection although not listed). Not in Kohler.

569. ON THE MORNING OF CHRIST'S NATIVITY[.] AN ODE, by John Milton With a 'Note' by F. Mary Wilson Parsons[.] *London: Printed by F[rank]. Steward Taylor At His Private Press; Xmas MDCCCXCIII.* 4to, 15pp., printed on Whatman's laid paper watermarked 1890, original azure morocco, front cover lettered in gilt, raised bands, t.e.g, others untrimmed. While fifty copies were printed, no other copies of this or any other work are traced anywhere by Blackwell's from F. Steward Taylor's press. This appears to be the first private press edition of Milton's *Nativity Ode*, which later became a Christmas favorite of many leading private presses. Very fine copy. No. 43 of 50 copies, numbered and signed by the printer on verso of half-title.

570. MILTON ODE ON THE MORNING OF CHRIST'S NATIVITY[.] *[Printed By H. Daniel: Oxford: Xmas: 1894.]* 12mo, 22pp.+[2] (including colophon with illustration on verso of last page), half-title before the poem, original printed gray wrappers (the spine a little sunned, extremities a bit frayed), edges untrimmed. A good copy of this scarce Daniel Press publication. No. 53 of 200 numbered copies printed by Mrs. Daniel. Kohler 265.

571. ON THE MORNING OF CHRIST'S NATIVITY [In] A BOOK OF CHRISTMAS VERSE Selected By H. C. Beeching: With Ten Designs By Walter Crane[.] *London: Methuen And Company[,] 36 Essex St. Strand: MDCCCXCV.* First edition. 8vo, xvi+174pp., half-title, title page in red and black with central vignette illustration, this along with five headpieces, first appearance of half-page illustrations and four full-page illustrations by Walter Crane, half-title for each of the sections, notes at end, original blue cloth, front cover and spine richly gilt-decorated with brilliant gilt design of "the Angels Announcing Christ's Birth to the Shepherds" on the front cover, t.e.g., others untrimmed. A very fine copy of a fine book with neat inscription (dated 1945) on fly-leaf. An important book and one that includes Milton's *Nativity Ode* complete with a full-page illustration by Walter Crane. Not in Kohler.

572. ON THE MORNING OF CHRIST'S NATIVITY [In] THE CENTURY MAGAZINE, Vol. LXI (December, 1900), No. 2, Christmas Number. MILTON'S ODE ON THE NATIVITY[.] *Copyright, 1900, By The Century Co. All Rights Reserved.* First edition thus. 4to, [15pp.] (from p. 163 to p. 177), unsigned central illustration of Madonna and Child in tinted green on title page, unsigned border illustration on next page, unsigned headpiece illustration in tinted green incorporating "The Hymn" within a scroll at the start of the hymn, two full-page illustrations in rich colors (signed "DuMond, 1900") following, unsigned border illustrations in tinted green on the next two pages, followed by a full-page illustration in rich colors (signed "DuMond, 1900") on verso, border illustration in rich colors (unsigned, but in the style of DuMond) on next page, text on following page with facing full-page illustration in rich colors (signed "DuMond, 1900"), unsigned border illustration in tinted green on next page, half-page illustration in black and white (signed "DuMond, 1900") incorporating text on following page, unsigned illustration in tinted green at bottom of the next page, concluding text on last page (with the start of the next article on verso), disbound, in a protective plastic cover. A fine copy, variously illustrated in tinted green, black and white, and dramatically rich colors. Scarce.

573. ODE: ON THE MORNING OF CHRIST'S NATIVITY By John Milton Prefaced By An Appreciation Taken In Part From The Works Of Henry Hallam[.] *Ralph Fletcher Seymour Publisher[,] Fine Arts Building[,]*

Chicago[,] Illinois[,] MDCCCCI. First edition thus. 8vo, [26 unpaginated leaves], half-title with decorative illustration, decorated frontispiece in red and black, title page in red and black with central decorative device, several headpieces, and the first appearance of full-page illustrations by Flesh Seymour, printed in red and black throughout, decorated initial letters, decorative tailpiece at end, original blue cloth spine, printed and decorated blue paper over boards (a bit rubbed), central gilt lettering with decorative corner pieces in contrasting dark blue on front cover with dark blue rule and dark blue lettering around edges, spine lettered in gilt, decorated endpapers with red corner pieces and central emblem and lettering in red, edges untrimmed, partially unopened. A very nice copy. One of 1,000 copies. Not in Kohler.

Richly Illumined Title Page, Initial Letters, and Margins

574. HYMN ON THE NIGHT OF CHRIST'S NATIVITY By John Milton[.] *Selected, printed, and published by The Book Lovers' Guild, Germantown, Philadelphia, A.D. MCMI.* First edition thus. Small 4to, 21+1pp., half-title, colophon page, title page with elaborately decorated hand-colored border in art nouveau style, title lettered within hand-colored gold border with small hand-colored emblem beneath the title, half-title for "The Poem" and "The Hymn" with a small hand-colored decorative piece beneath "The Hymn," elaborately decorated initial letters in art nouveau style, each hand-colored, with an elaborately decorated hand-colored margin in art nouveau style as part of the hand-colored decorated initial letter at the beginning of "The Poem" and at the beginning of "The Hymn," elaborately decorated hand-colored vertical border in art nouveau style across the center of the last page, original soft brown suede leather (with a small piece missing near the top of the outer edge of the front cover and some slight wear), front cover lettered in gilt within decorative gilt rules and gilt trim, white silk endpapers, a.e.g. A lovely copy. The title page, initial letters, and margins are richly "Illumined by K. McNabb" (attribution neatly hand-lettered beneath the printing on the colophon page after the half-title). "Three hundred and ten copies were printed" (colophon page, this copy being unnumbered). Not in Kohler.

575. HYMN ON THE MORNING OF CHRIST'S NATIVITY By John Milton[.] *[London: Old Bourne Press, n.d.] [1903].* Oblong 12mo, 27pp.+colophon, half-title in blue with decorative blue trim, small decorative flower in blue on verso of half-title, elaborate decorative border in blue in art nouveau style on title page, decorative woodcut borders and decorated initial letters throughout, printed in dark green and blue, printed in dark green and blue, original light blue linen spine, decoratively stamped cream boards with floral designs in red and green with title incorporated within elaborate device in green on front cover, decorated endpapers (slight browning), unopened and uncut. A near fine copy, "made into a book by W. Herbert Broome and James J. Guthrie at the Old Bourne Press for the Glory of God and all little children" (colophon). James Guthrie (1874–1952), a handpress enthusiast, founded the Pear Tree Press in Kent in 1899 with the sole intention of printing his own drawings. He was not dominated by typographic orthodoxy and developed his own personal style, in an art nouveau manner of flowing, coiling patterns of trees, clouds, and water. The Old Bourne Press was where Guthrie had some of his earlier books printed. One of 200 copies. Not in Kohler.

576. ODE ON THE MORNING OF CHRIST'S NATIVITY BY JOHN MILTON With An Introduction By Walter Taylor Field[.] *Paul Elder And Company[,] San Francisco And New York[,] (1907).* Slim square 4to, vii+[1]+17pp., unsigned frontispiece oval portrait of a young Milton, protective tissue guard, title page with double rule in red and central emblem in black with "The Abbey Classics" lettered in red at the center of the emblem, "Copyright, 1907, By Walter Taylor Field" on verso of title page, initial letters in red, original tan wrappers, front cover lettered in contrasting brown, edges untrimmed. Nice copy. Printed in a limited edition. Not in Kohler.

577. ON THE MORNING OF CHRIST'S NATIVITY AN ODE BY JOHN MILTON. *Imprinted At The Clerk's Press: Cleveland: Ohio –:– MDCCCCX.* Small, slim 4to (7" × 5 ¼"), 13pp.+colophon page with emblem of the press, decorative headpiece with smaller decorative piece beneath the title at the beginning of the poem, the same smaller decorative piece repeated at the end before the colophon page, original stitched printed stiff gray wrappers, front cover lettered in silver, edges untrimmed. "Done into Type by Charles C. Bubb, Clerk in Holy Orders, And Imprinted at his Press in the Parish of Grace Church in Cleveland, November seventeenth, mdcccx" (bottom p. 13). A nice copy of this scarce Clerk's Press publication. "This Edition consists of the following: Twenty-five Copies on Ruisdael Hand-made Paper[;] Two-hundred-and-fifty Copies on Alexandra Paper, This is Number 45." Ransom, *Private Presses*, p. 10; Not in Kohler.

578. ON THE MORNING OF CHRIST'S NATIVITY [In] A GOLDEN TREASURY OF SONGS AND

LYRICS[.] Frances Turner Palgrave[.] Pictures In Color Reproduced From Paintings By Maxfield Parrish[.] *New York[:] Duffield & Company[,] 1911.* First edition thus. 8vo, vi+373pp., half-title, frontispiece illustration in color and possibly the first appearance of seven additional illustrations in full color by Maxfield Parrish, protective tissue guards with text illustrated printed in red, half-title before the poems, original blue cloth (a little rubbed), color illustration lettered in gilt with gilt border tipped on front cover, spine lettered in gilt with decorative gilt trim at top and bottom, illustrated endpapers, fore- and bottom edges untrimmed. A good copy with near-contemporary signature on front blank. Included are several poetical selections from Milton with a color illustration of "the shepherds watching" by Maxfield Parrish for *NO* complete. Scarce.

579. ODE ON THE MORNING OF CHRIST'S NATIVITY By John Milton. *Published For The Medici Society LD. By Philip Lee Warner. London MDCCCCXV.* First edition thus. 8vo in 4s (opening lengthwise, 4 ½" × 6 ¼"), 37+[1]pp., original landscape green suede (a little worn and frayed along edges, typical of this kind of suede binding, bottom of spine slightly chipped), front cover lettered in gilt with emblem of three rings in gilt at bottom right-hand corner, lightly marbled endpapers, t.e.g., fore- and bottom edges untrimmed, white silk ribbon marker. "First printed as Memorabilia, Number iv, in the fourteen point Riccardi Fount, September MDCCCCXV. The badge on the cover has been designed by Mr. H. P. Horne after the well-known device—three rings—used by the early Medici" (verso title page). Colophon page at the end reads: "Here ends Memorabilia Number IV Imprinted In The Riccardi Press Fount By Chas. T. Jacobi, And Published For The Medici Society, LD. By Philip Lee Warner." A nice copy, "First printed as Memorabilia" "For The Medici Society." Undoubtedly printed in a very limited edition. Scarce.

580. ODE ON THE MORNING OF CHRIST'S NATIVITY *By John Milton. Published By The Medici Society LD. London In The Riccardi Fount MDMXV.* First edition thus, Variant Issue. 8vo in 4s (opening lengthwise, 4 ⅛" × 6"), 37+[1]pp., original linen spine, decorated paper over boards (a bit rubbed), printed paper label lettered in light green tipped on front cover. A nice copy, similar to the preceding issue, although a bit smaller with important variants: variant publisher's imprint on title page: "Published By" instead of "Published For" The Medici Society; without reference to "By Philip Lee Warner," with the addition of "In The Riccardi Fount," and with the year printed in a different roman numeral style; without notation on verso of title page; with publisher's imprint on front pastedown: "Toronto, Melbourne, and Bombay: Humphrey Milford, at the Oxford University Press"; without Colophon on verso of last page, and with "Memorabilia" printed on rear pastedown listing "Illustrated" editions available. Scarce.

581. HYMN OF CHRIST'S NATIVITY BY JOHN MILTON[.] *N.P. n.d. [ca. 1920s].* First edition thus. 4pp., 4to size, printed on recto only, without publication place, publisher, or date (the title page looks like a half-title rather than a title page), original lightly embossed light green stiff paper wrappers (slightly dust-soiled), tied with light green silk ribbon, with a card with an illustration in color of an angel with pale pink wings holding a wand with a star at the end in one hand and a small branch in the other, seated on a half moon, tipped in on front cover, edges of covers trimmed in the manner of "pinking shears" trimming. An attractive period piece, interestingly printed. The illustration on the front cover does not appear to be an illustration for Milton's poem but rather a period piece illustration; and while the branch held by the "angelic" figure looks to be just that, the blue above it might be a "sprig" or colorful "splash" of sorts. It might also be an attempt to provide the date "1929" (which is what it appears to look like under a magnifying glass, although without certainty of this).

582. ON THE MORNING OF CHRIST'S NATIVITY[.] Milton's Hymn With Illustrations By William Blake And A Note By Geoffrey Keynes, F.R.C.S. *Cambridge[:] At The University Press[,] 1923.* 4to, 32+[1]pp., half-title, title page in red and black with central device of the press in red, six Blake watercolor drawings in the Whitworth Institute Manchester reproduced here in black-and-white collotype for the first time in print, 1645 text also reproduced, printed on Bosinwerk paper, original linen spine, decorated blue paper over boards, t.e.g., edges untrimmed, original publisher's tissue. A very good copy in original publisher's wrappers printed in red and black with reproduction of a Blake illustration on front cover. Blake executed two sets of illustrations for *Ode on the Morning of Christ's Nativity*; one set in 1809, first published in 1981 (see edition by Whittington Press listed here); the other set in 1815, first published here.

583. ON THE MORNING OF CHRIST'S NATIVITY. *N. P.: (Arthur Rushmore), 1924.* Four folded leaves, 4to size, first appearance of woodcut illustration by Harry Cimino, printed on Japanese paper, edges untrimmed. Privately distributed as a Christmas greeting. Ode and verses I, V, and XXVII of the "Hymn" are printed. Scarce.

584. ON THE MORNING OF CHRIST'S NATIVITY By John Milton[.] *Haarlem[:] Joh. Enschedé En Zonen[,] Christmas[,] 1927.* Small slim 8vo, 14pp.,+colophon leaf, typography by J. Van Krimpen, original wrappers (front wrapper is slightly sunned), front cover lettered in black with central emblem in red, edges untrimmed, partially unopened. A very nice copy. "Van Krimpen's approach was literary, cultured, aristocratic, restrained, and elegant" (Blumenthal, *Art of the Printed Book: 1455–1955*). One of 150 copies of Milton's ode sent as a Christmas greeting to friends of the press with the foldover printed greeting enclosed.

585. HYMN ON THE MORNING OF CHRIST'S NATIVITY[.] John Milton[.] *Printed By St. John And Cicely Hornby For Their Friends[.] [Chelsea: Ashendene Press,] Christmas, 1928.* 4to, 13pp.+colophon leaf, the first appearance of this full-page wood-engraved illustration of the Madonna and Child after Noel Rooke, half-title before the poem, illuminated with red letter initials designed by Graily Hewitt, printed on French handmade paper, text printed in Ptolemy type, colophon with large device of the Ashendene Press, original printed blue wrappers, front wrapper lettered in black, edges untrimmed, in near mint condition, in a green cloth folding case with gilt lettering on spine. Issued as a Christmas keepsake. "This little Book has been printed to carry to our friends far & near our heartiest good wishes for a Merry Christmas and a Happy New Year 1928–1929" (colophon). Ashendene Bib., *Minor Pieces*, XII, p. 104. A fine copy of a scarce Ashendene Press publication, limited to 220 copies.

586. ON THE MORNING OF CHRIST'S NATIVITY. by John Milton[.] *[Pear Tree Press, Flansham, Bognor Regis, Sussex. 1930.]* Small 8vo, 4+26pp., half-title decorated with a tree in green, frontispiece woodcut illustration with slight decorative green border trim, title page elaborately decorated with slight decorative green border trim, first four pages printed in green, the next twenty-six pages print "The Hymn" in black with pagination in green and with a decorative headpiece in green, colophon printed in green, the first appearance of decorations and illustrations (frontispiece woodcut illustration, decorated half-title and title page, illustrated endpapers, and illustration on covers) after S. M. Thompson, who also set up and hand-printed the volume on hand-made paper, printed in Gothic type in black and green, original silver paper-covered boards with a printed design in black—the statues of three saints standing within three Gothic arches—with a white paper title label printed in green and black on front cover, illustrated endpapers printed in green showing the Madonna and Child surrounded by four praying angels, edges untrimmed. A fine, fresh copy (an insignificant pink spot appears on the outer corner of one page). This is the second publication of the Pear Tree Press's "Blackletter Series." No. 37 of 100 copies.

587. ON THE MORNING OF CHRIST'S NATIVITY[.] By John Milton[.] *Madison[,] N.J.[:] Published by The Golden Hind Press and to be sold at the sign of The Ship[.] Anno Dom. 1933.* 8vo, [2]+16pp.+colophon page, half-title with frontispiece on verso, frontispiece consisting of a facsimile of a Nativity print by Albrecht Dürer tipped in, protective tissue guard, title page printed in black with central ship in red, decorative headpieces, paper by Delight Rushmore, "set by hand in Garamond type by Edna and Arthur Rushmore" (colophon), original marbled paste-paper covered boards, printed paper label on spine. Nice. Presentation copy inscribed by the publisher to Arthur Swann on fly-leaf dated "Christmas 1933." No. 61 of 100 copies on Arches Paper in hand-set Gramond type. Huckabay 224; Not in Kohler.

588. ON THE MORNING OF CHRIST'S NATIVITY By John Milton. With A Wood Engraving By Alison McKenzie. *[Newton, Montgomeryshire:] Gregynog [Press,] MCMXXXVII.* Slim folio, 8pp.+colophon leaf, half-title with frontispiece illustration on verso—first appearance of a full-page wood-engraved illustration after Alison McKenzie, initial letters printed in blue, original fawn wrappers, blue stitching, blue lettering on front cover, edges untrimmed. An excellent copy. Christmas keepsake, printed on richly textured handmade paper. No. 5 of 250 copies. Harrop E-201.

589. ON THE MORNING OF CHRIST'S NATIVITY[.] John Milton[.] *[Washington, D.C., 1944.]* Square 8vo, [1]+[4]+colophon leaf, unsigned wood-engraved frontispiece illustration on verso of title page, original blue wrappers, stitched, paper label lettered in blue on front cover. A fine copy. Privately printed "Christmas Greetings, 1944[, from] Mickey, Peter and Lester Douglas" (colophon leaf). Scarce.

590. ON THE MORNING OF CHRIST'S NATIVITY AN ODE[.] John Milton[.] *[Pownal, Vt:] Mason Hill Press[,] MCMLXXV.* 4to, [8]+[1]pp.+colophon leaf, first appearance of woodcut frontispiece illustration by James Dignon, initial letters in blue by Mark Livingston, printed in blue and black, blue morocco spine with gilt rule on covers, marbled paper over boards, spine lettered in gilt, edges untrimmed. Fine copy. One of only thirty-five copies.

591. ON THE MORNING OF CHRIST'S NATIVITY[.] Milton's Hymn, with illustrations by William Blake and a note on the illustrations by Martin Butlin[,] Keeper of the British Collection, The Tate Gallery[.] *The Whittington Press & Angscot Productions, (1981).* Large 4to, xii+24pp.+colophon leaf, half-title, title page in red and black, first appearance of seven illustrations in color by Blake (one illustration a vignette portrait of Milton as headpiece), all mounted, printed in red and black in Caslon type on Barcham Green handmade paper, full green morocco goatskin, spine lettered in gilt, marbled endpapers, t.e.g., others untrimmed. Fine copy in original black cloth fold-over box with printed paper label on spine. In 1809, and again in 1815, Blake painted a series of six watercolor illustrations for Milton's Hymn. Neither of these sets has ever been reproduced in color before, although the 1815 set was reproduced for the first time in black and white in the Cambridge University Press 1923 edition (also listed here). The present illustrations are taken from the first and larger series painted for Rev. J. Thomas in 1809, now in the Whitworth Art Gallery, Manchester. The portrait of Milton is also by Blake and was commissioned for the frieze in William Haley's Sussex Library. No. 1 of 25 special copies bound in full Oasis Goatskin, with an additional set of the color plates laid in a pocket in the publisher's marbled paper board folder, with paper label on front cover. Limited edition of 350 total copies, 325 quarter-bound in vellum and buckram without the extra set of plates.

With four-page publisher's prepublication announcement/prospectus, with full-page color illustration tipped in. Accompanied by a pamphlet about the Whittington Press.

592. ON THE MORNING OF CHRIST'S NATIVITY [In] **A BOOK OF CHRISTMAS VERSE** Selected By H. C. Beeching With Ten Designs By Walter Crane[.] *Bonanza Books[,] New York[,] 1986.* 8vo, xv+174pp., half-title, central vignette illustration on title page, this along with five headpiece, half-page illustrations and four full-page illustrations by Walter Crane, original green buckram, spine lettered in silver, printed publisher's wrappers with illustration in color wrapping around both front and back covers. A fine copy, virtually mint. Included is Milton's *Nativity Ode* with a full-page illustration by Walter Crane. The first edition was published in London in 1895 (see copy listed here with *On The Morning Of Christ's Nativity*). This is a reproduction of the 1896 first American, second edition, published in New York by Dodd and Mead.

593. ON THE MORNING OF CHRIST'S NATIVITY & OTHER POEMS by John Milton with engravings by Brian Hanscomb[.] *London[:] The Folio Press[,] 1987.* First edition thus. Royal 8vo, 71pp., half-title, five tinted engravings by Brian Hanscomb, set in Caslon type and printed on "Zerkall Rough Antique Laid, acid-free, mould-made paper," "bound by Hunter & Foulis Ltd, Edinburgh with sides of Rackenmarmor Swedish hand-marbled paper and buckram spine and label" (verso title page), gray endpapers, t.e.g., fore-edge untrimmed, partially unopened. The buckram spine is orange, as is the gilt-ruled and gilt-lettered orange label on the front cover. Fine copy. Also included are *NO, L'A, IlP, L,* and *C*, each with a tinted vignette illustration by Brian Hanscomb on the half-title before each poem.

On the University Carrier

594. ON THE UNIVERSITY CARRIER - OR - OLD HOBSON [In] **POETS' WIT AND HUMOUR.** Selected By W. H. Wills. Illustrated With One Hundred Engravings from Drawings By Charles Bennet And George H. Thomas. *London: Joseph Cundall, 168, New Bond Street. n.d. [ca. 1860].* First edition? 8vo, [vi]+284pp., half-title within decorative trim, small illustration on title page, wood-engraved illustrations (full-page, headpiece, and vignette), decorated initial letters, original purple cloth (joints and corners lightly rubbed), front cover richly decorated in gilt and embossed blind stamping with title incorporated in gilt within an overall panel design at the center, back cover decorated in blind, spine similarly richly decorated in gilt with gilt lettering and decorative embossed blind-stamping, covers and spine decorated to an overall design by J. Leighton, a.e.g., bound by Leighton and Hodge, with their ticket. Designed by Joseph Cundall with his imprint on title. A lovely copy in an attractively bound book. Included is *Old Hobson* with a vignette illustration after Bennet/Thomas. Scarce. Ray, *VPB*, Illus., p. 14.

Original Letters and Papers of State

595. ORIGINAL LETTERS AND PAPERS OF STATE, Addressed to Oliver Cromwell; Concerning the Affairs of Great Britain. From the Year MDCXLIX to MDCLVIII. Found among the Political Collections Of Mr. John Milton. Now first Published from the Originals. By John Nickolls, Jun. Member of the Society of Antiquaries, London. *London: Printed by William Bowyer, And sold by John Whiston Bookseller, at Boyle's Head in Fleet-Street. M DCC XLIII.* First edition. Folio, iv+iv+164pp.+[8-page index, unpaginated], contemporary calf (rubbed, joints cracked), elaborately gilt-decorated spine, red morocco label with gilt lettering and decorative gilt trim, raised bands with decorative gilt trim (faded), marbled endpapers. Very nice copy with the bookplate and signature of the Earl of Cork and Orrery. Aware of the sensitive nature

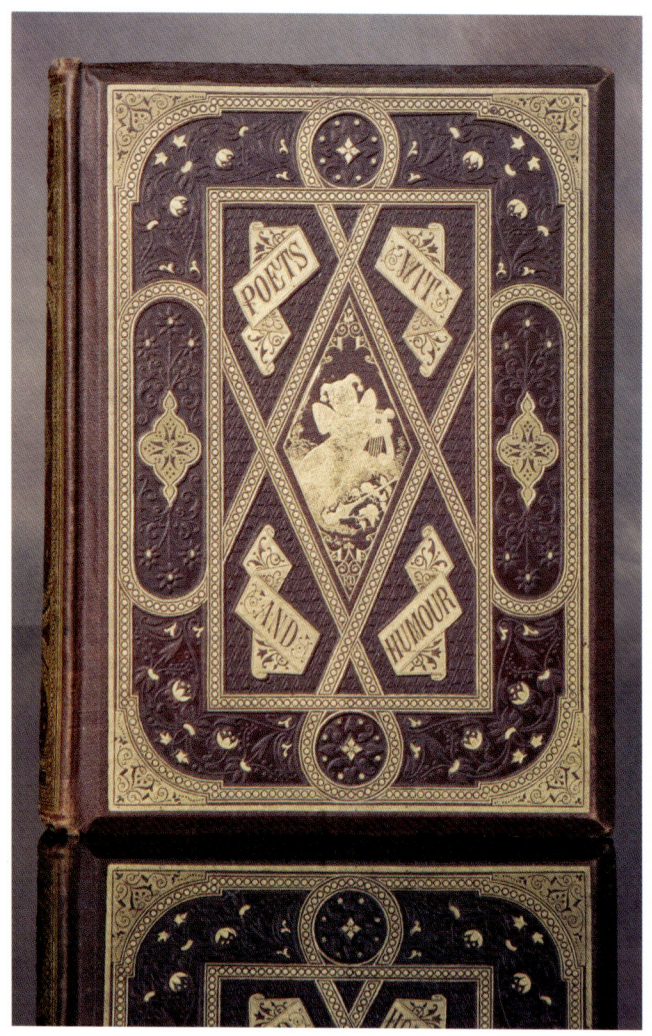

On The University Carrier OR *Old Hobson* [In] *Poet's Wit*. London: Joseph Cundall, n.d. [ca. 1860]. Original purple richly decorated in gilt to an overall design by J. Leighton, bound by Leighton and Hodge with their ticket. See #594.

of these papers, Milton entrusted them to his amanuensis, Thomas Ellwood. They remained unpublished for nearly a century until the noted antiquary Nickolls had them here printed for the first time. ESTC T056123 (noting copies in British Library and Liverpool University Library only in England); Coleridge 371; Not in Kohler.

596. ORIGINAL PAPERS ILLUSTRATIVE OF THE LIFE AND WRITINGS OF JOHN MILTON, Including Sixteen Letters Of State Written By Him, Now First Published From MSS. In The State Paper Office. With An Appendix Of Documents Relating To His Connection With The Powell Family. Collected And Edited, With The Permission Of The Master Of The Rolls, By W. Douglas Hamilton, Of H.M. State Paper Office, And University College, London, Author Of "Outlines Of The Constitutional History Of England," &. *Printed For The Camden Society. M.DCCC.L.IX.* [*The Author reserves the right of Translation.]* First edition. Square 8vo, viii+139pp., original green cloth (spine a little faded), large central emblem in blind on covers, spine decorated and lettered in gilt. Nice copy. Printed in a limited edition. Uncommon. Not in Kohler.

597. ORIGINAL PAPERS ILLUSTRATIVE OF THE LIFE AND WRITINGS OF JOHN MILTON, Including Sixteen Letters Of State Written By Him, Now First Published From MSS. In The State Paper Office. With An Appendix Of Documents Relating To His Connection With The Powell Family. Collected And Edited, With The Permission Of The Master Of The Rolls, By W. Douglas Hamilton, Of H.M. State Paper Office, And University College, London, Author Of "Outlines Of The Constitutional History Of England," &. *Printed For The Camden Society. M.DCCC.L.IX.* Reprinted with the permission of the Royal Historical Society[.] AMS Press[,] New York • London[,] (1968). First Ames edition. 8vo, viii+139pp., emblem on title page, "Series No. I, 75" on verso of title page, original blue cloth, spine lettered and ruled in gilt. A fine copy of this reprint edition of the 1859 first edition by the Camden Society (preceding copy).

Paradise Lost

597A. (Cross-listing) Andreini, Giovanni Batista. L'ADAMO SACRA RAPRESENTATIONE . . . *Milano: Geronimo Bordoni, 1617.* First edition, second issue. 4to, title page with engraved illustration, thirty-nine additional half- and full-page copperplate illustrations, signed with initials "C.B.," eighteenth-century calf (joints cracked, title lightly trimmed at edges and edges extended, some embrowning and minor soiling), decorative gilt border trim on covers, gilt-decorated red morocco spine, inner and outer dentelles gilt, green endpapers, a.e.g. Generally a clean and crisp copy with forty stunning baroque copperplate illustrations. Andreini was the son of Francesco and Isabella Andreini, the most famous actors of their day. He clearly was well situated to write what Leonardo Vinciana states is the most significant work of the seventeenth-century theatre. It is one of the earliest operas extant, and very likely was performed during Milton's continental tour. Voltaire remarks that Milton saw the opera performed in Milan and was inspired to write a tragedy. Milton did in fact begin work on what eventually became *Paradise Lost*, and a number of scholars commencing with Hayley have since demonstrated connections between *L'Adamo* and *Paradise Lost*. The first edition of *L'Adamo* was published in 1613. Rare. See main listing with Seventeenth-century Miltoniana.

Note to *Paradise Lost*, First Edition, 1667–69, and Its Title Pages

The publication of Milton's *Paradise Lost* between 1667 and 1669 has resulted in confusion of issues and title page states. For a period of time it was erroneously believed that there were seven, and even eight and nine title pages. It was finally agreed for a rather long period of time that Milton's epic was published with six different title pages: twice in 1667, twice in 1668 (with a second state to the first 1668 title page), and twice in 1669. The epic was published in ten books with important preliminary material added in the second of the 1668 title-page editions, or the first edition fourth title page, for the first time: "The Printer to the Reader" (here the six-line version), "The Argument" of each book, "The Verse" (Milton's celebrated defense of his choice of "English Heroic Verse without Rime"—blank iambic pentameter—for his lofty epic as stemming from Homer and Virgil), and a list of "Errata"; this fourth title-page edition was also the first to mention "S. Simmons," the owner of the copyright for Milton's poem and Milton's publisher.

In 1983, Hugh Amory set forth that the initial 1668 title, though the third to be set and printed, was the first to be actually supplied with the books as issued to the public (Hugh Amory, *Book Collector*, Spring 1983, pp. 41–66). For Amory and others, *Paradise Lost* was printed in 1667 and apparently published early in 1668. Amory argues that Simmons changed Milton's full name as it appeared on the 1667 title to the eponym on the 1668 title for reasons of political safety during the course of the press run and also dated the book a year ahead lest the new year arrive too soon. Reducing the author to "J.M." matches almost precisely the wording of the registry obtained by Simmons on August 20, 1667. Amory explains away copies in original condition that bear the 1667 titles as "remainders" of the first issue, pressed into service when the 1668 dated title pages with Milton's initials were exhausted, and when it seemed finally safe to print Milton's name in full with the book. As Arthur Freeman observes, "This last is an idea which has not gained universal credence." Freeman goes on to say that "Amory's first argument, that the initials-and-1668 title, matching the Stationer's Company entry, was first *intended* to serve the book and was the first which a reader would readily find in a London bookshop carries weight. It is certainly not likely that any concerted sale of the book with full-name-and-1667 titles took place before registry: before registry the book would not be copyright, nor properly licensed, and would be asking for serious trouble. Copies with the initials-and 1668-title, in its two slightly variant forms, may be best described, then, as the 'first authorized state' of the first issue of *Paradise Lost*"—referred to as Amory 1—(Arthur Freeman, *Quaritch Catalogue 1091*, 1988, No. 69; Freeman provides an expert analysis of Amory in lucid terms here and also in reexamining the publication of *Paradise Lost* and the order of issues between 1667 and 1669).

According to Amory, and Freeman concurring with Amory, the preliminary materials, including the "Arguments" of each book, were not printed until sometime in 1668, and they provide the principle changes of the second, third, and fourth issues (1668–69). The sheets of the epic as originally printed in 1667 were in 1668 bound up with the new fourteen-page preliminaries and issued with a fresh title page dated 1668 printing the author's name in full, thereby constituting the second issue of *Paradise Lost*, or Amory 2—formerly the "Fourth Title Page," representing—in the words of Arthur Freeman, "the first appearance of the completed work as it is known today" (Arthur Freeman, *Quaritch List 98/17*, Summer Acquisitions, 1998, no. 47; further discussion of the printed order of the issues is provided here).

At the time of this writing (Fall 2005), I have been alerted to a collection of essays, edited by Michael Lieb and John Shawcross, to be published by Duquesne University Press. One of the articles in the collection by Stephen B. Dobranski is a refutation of the order and date as argued by Amory. In an edition of the diplomatic text of the first issue, also edited by Michael Lieb and John Shawcross, to be published as companion to the above collection, John Shawcross has lengthy notes, titled "The First Edition of *Paradise Lost* (With Comment on the Second Edition and the Manuscript)." In the section subtitled "Issues of the First Edition" Shawcross indicates that the evidence of the title pages themselves refute Amory's argument, noting "that title pages 3, 3A, 4, 5, 6 all say 'The Author. . . .', following 'Paradise lost. A Poem in Ten Books.' with 3 omitting the period after Books'. The period after 'Books' is required by the syntax of 'The Author . . . ' and thus, in other words, 3 precedes 3A and 3A is united with 4, 5, 6 (which are dated 1668, 1669, 1669). In contrast are title pages 1 and 2 where no period is syntactically correct after 'Books': Paradise lost. A Poem Written in Ten Books By John Milton.' What happened with 3 was 'Books' without a period was followed from 2 but the next line on the title page was changed from 'By John Milton.' to 'The Author J.M.' / 'The Author John Milton.' necessitating a period after 'Books.' In other words, 3 is following 2 in error and that gets corrected in 3A." Seeing that not having a period after "Books" no longer made sense because of the change from "By John Milton." to "The Author J.M." / The Author John Milton." on title page "3", which was set following "2", the press was stopped and "3A" was set which has a period after "Books." "Being aware of this stop-press correction, the order of issuance is established: 1, 2, 3 and 3A, 4, 5, 6." As Shawcross points out, the title pages speak for themselves with respect to their order, an order as identified and defined pre-Amory and reasserted once again by Shawcross and also by Dobranski in his forthcoming article.

The companion volumes identified above were published in late fall 2007 under the titles *"Paradise Lost": A Poem Written in Ten Books, An Authoritative Text of the 1667 First Edition* for the first volume and *"Paradise Lost": A Poem Written in Ten Books, Essays on the 1667 First Edition* for the second.

PL, 1667–69: Five of six first editions, with five of the six title pages: 1667 (first title page, on far left), 1667 (second title page, showing at center), 1668 (fourth title page, second from left), 1669 (fifth title page, in contemporary calf), 1669 (sixth title page, on far right). See #598 and following.

598. PARADISE LOST. A Poem Written in Ten Books By JOHN MILTON. Licensed and Entred according to Order. *London[:] Printed, and are to be sold by Peter Parker under Creed Church neer Aldgate; And by Robert Boulter at the Turks Head in Bishopsgate-Street; And Matthias Walker, under St. Dunstons Church in Fleet-street, 1667.* First edition, first title page. Small 4to, decorative headpiece and decorated initial letter at the start of each book, Rivieré binding, full blue morocco, richly gilt-decorated covers and spine, with delicate gilt tooling depicting trees in various sizes on covers and spine, with central gilt-tooled panel incorporating title on front cover, panel repeated on back cover without title, inner and outer dentelles gilt-ruled, a.e.g. A fine copy with the bookplates of Matthew Chalmer Durfee Borden and David Borowitz. The former Borowitz copy, purchased at the Borowitz sale in 1977. Laid in: two-page handwritten letter from Luther Livingston to "Mr. Valentine, Rockefeller Institute Hospital," (dated March 29, 1913) about this copy, stating that "the book is genuine throughout and a good large copy." The tremendously difficult circumstances under which Milton produced his epic are legendary—he had been blinded by long years of service as secretary under Cromwell and was under political disfavor after the restoration of Charles II. The troubled printing history of the work carries with it its own difficulties. Samuel Simmons, purchaser of the copyright for the poem, whose name appears as publisher for the first time only on the fourth title page (also listed here), reluctantly agreed to print a small first edition of 1,300 to 1,500 copies, as he was assuming a heavy risk in sponsoring an epic poem for which no precedent in English publishing had been established. As payment for the first edition "Milton's contract provided for the payment of a second £5 to be paid after the sale of 1,300 copies and this was paid on 26 April 1669, 20 months after the copy was registered at Stationers' Hall, on 20 August 1667" (Coleridge). Rare. Parker, pp. 1108–16; Grolier, *Wither to Prior*, 599; Grolier, *Bibliographical Notes*, 33; Grolier, *One Hundred Books*, pp. 66–67; Coleridge 90a; Not in Kohler.

599. PARADISE LOST. A Poem Written in Ten Books By JOHN MILTON. Licensed and Entred according to Order. *London[:] Printed, and are to be sold by Peter Parker under Creed Church neer Aldgate; And by Robert Boulter at the Turks Head in Bishopsgate-Street; And Matthias Walker, under St. Dunstons Church in Fleet-street, 1667.* First edition, second title page, with Milton's name in small caps. Small 4to, decorative headpiece and decorated initial letter at the start of each book, Riviéré binding, full red morocco (head rule on title page cut away and rule on last leaf partially cut into, small repair to lower blank outer margin of title and small repairs to corners of a few leaves, small blank portion on Z1 filled in), richly gilt-decorated covers and spine, raised bands, inner and outer dentelles very delicately and finely tooled in gilt, a.e.g. A fine copy. Rare. Parker, pp. 1108–16; Grolier, *Wither to Prior*, 600; Coleridge 90b; Kohler 1.

600. PARADISE LOST. A Poem In Ten Books. The Author JOHN MILTON. *London, Printed by S. Simmons, and to be sold by S. Thomson at the Bishops-Head in Duck-lane, H. Mortlack at the White Hart in Westminster Hall, M. Walker under St. Dunstans Church in Fleet-street, and R. Boulter at the Turks-Head in Bishopsgate street, 1668.* First edition, fourth title page. Small 4to, decorative headpiece and decorated initial letter at the start of each book, Riviéré binding, full blue morocco, covers ruled in gilt with decorative gilt corner devices, elaborately gilt-decorated spine, raised bands, inner dentelles elaborately decorated in gilt, outer dentelles ruled in gilt, marbled endpapers, a.e.g. A fine copy with the bookplate of Haight (author of "I Want! I Want!"). This issue includes the first appearance of "The Printer to the Reader" (here the six-line version), "The Argument" of each book printed together at the beginning of the epic, "The Verse" (Milton's celebrated defense of his choice of "English Heroic Verse without Rime"—blank iambic pentameter—for his lofty epic as stemming from Homer and Virgil), and a list of "Errata"; its title page was also the first to mention the publisher Samuel Simmons (as "S. Simmons") and the first with an ornament composed of fleurs-de-lis replacing the words "Licensed and Entred according to Order." Rare. Parker, pp. 1108–16; Grolier, *Wither to Prior*, 602; Coleridge 90d; Shawcross, Kentucky, 47; Amory's "First Edition, Second Issue," Amory's "First Edition, Second Issue," Amory 2; Not in Kohler.

601. PARADISE LOST. A Poem In Ten Books. The Author JOHN MILTON. *London, Printed by S. Simmons, and are to be sold by T. Helder at the Angel in Little Brittain. 1669.* First edition, fifth title page. Small 4to, decorative headpiece and decorated initial letter at the start of each book, unlettered old sheep (a little worn, new free endpapers, some age-browning), in a half brown morocco, brown cloth box, with gilt-ruled spine, raised bands, and protective inner silk lining. A good copy. "The Printer to the Reader" appears here in four lines, not six, as in the fourth title-page issue; the six-line version also appears in some copies. Rare. *Tercentenary Catalogue*, p. 97 (illus.); Parker, pp. 1108–16; Grolier, *Wither to Prior*, 603; Coleridge 90e; Shawcross, Kentucky, 48; Amory's "First Edition, Third Issue," Amory 3; Not in Kohler.

602. PARADISE LOST. A Poem In Ten Books. The Author JOHN MILTON. *London, Printed by S. Simmons, and are to be sold by T. Helder at the Angel in Little Brittain, 1669.* First edition, sixth title page. Small 4to, decorative headpiece and decorated initial letter at the start of each book, full green morocco, covers ruled in gilt with decorative gilt corner devices, spine also ruled in gilt with the same decorative gilt devices in the panels, raised bands, inner and outer dentelles ruled in gilt, a.e.g. A fine copy. "The Printer to the Reader" no longer appears here as it does in the fifth and fourth title-page editions. In all six issues the text of Milton's poem—1,500 copies were printed according to the agreement—remained the same, only the title page and preliminaries were altered. Rare, considered to be even more scarce than the fourth and fifth issues. Parker, pp. 1108–16; Grolier, *Wither to Prior*, 604; Coleridge 90f; Amory's "First Edition, Fourth Issue," Amory 4; Kohler 3.

603. PARADISE LOST. A Poem In Twelve Books. The Author John Milton. The Second Edition Revised and Augmented by the same Author. *London: Printed by S. Simmons next door to the Golden Lion in Aldersgate-street, 1674.* Second and final lifetime edition; first octavo edition. 8vo, [v]+333pp., engraved frontispiece portrait by W. Dolle after Faithorne (first published in the 1670 *History*), decorated initial letter at the start of Book I, eighteenth-century paneled calf (a bit rubbed, lacking initial blank, a few ink scribblings on endpapers), with early signatures. On the whole, a fine, large copy. This important edition presents for the first time Milton's own final textual revisions as well as his rearrangement of the text from the original ten book form to the familiar, final twelve book form of the poem with the "Arguments" divided and placed at the beginning of each book. Milton created the twelve books by splitting Books VII and X into two, adding a few lines to the new openings; a total of fifteen additional lines were added, most as a result of the rearrangement of books. Commendatory verses by S. B. (Dr. Samuel Barlow?) in Latin and by Andrew Marvell in English also appear here for the first time. The definitive text. Only about 750 copies of the second edition were printed, so this edition is actually scarcer than the first. Rare. Wing M2144; Parker, pp. 1149; Grolier, *Wither to Prior*, 605; Shawcross, 1984, 318; Shawcross, 1970, pp. 26, 81–82; Coleridge 91a; Shawcross, Kentucky, 60; Kohler 4.

603A. (Cross-listing) [PARADISE LOST] Dryden, John. **THE STATE OF INNOCENCE AND FALL OF MAN: AN OPERA**. Written in Heroique Verse, And Dedicated to Her Royal Highness, The Dutchess. *London: T. N. for Henry Herringman . . . 1677*. First edition. 4to, new quarter morocco, marbled paper over boards, spine lettered in gilt. Very fresh internally. Dryden's opera represents the first major printed tribute to *PL*. Dryden obtained Milton's permission for this operatic version of *PL*; it was intended primarily as a tribute to the genius of Milton's epic. Wing D2372; MacDonald 81a; Not in Pforzheimer; Not in Kohler. See main listing with Seventeenth-century Miltoniana.

604. **PARADISE LOST**. A Poem In Twelve Books. The Author John Milton. The Third Edition. Revised and Augmented by the same Author. *London, Printed by S. Simmons next door to the Golden Lion in Aldersgate-street, 1678*. Third edition. 8vo, [viii]+331pp., two final blank leaves present, engraved frontispiece portrait by W. Dolle after Faithorne, contemporary calf (very neatly rebacked, new endpapers), gilt rules on spine, gilt-ruled and gilt-lettered red morocco label, raised bands. A very good, fresh copy. The two final blank leaves, Y7–8, are frequently lacking. This is the last edition published by Simmons, Milton's original printer, and is derived completely from the second edition of 1674. After its publication Simmons completed his payments for *PL* with a payment of £8 to Milton's widow and in 1681 transferred all his rights to Brabazon Aylmer for £25. Aylmer sold half his interests to Tonson in 1683, the other half to Richard Bentley, and they were responsible for the next edition of *PL*, the 1688 folio (several copies listed here). Scarce. Wing M2145; Parker, p. 1179; Grolier, *Wither to Prior*, 606; Williamson 49; Shawcross, 1984, 325; Coleridge 92; Kohler 5.

605. Another Copy of **PARADISE LOST**. A Poem In Twelve Books. The Author John Milton. The Third Edition. Revised and Augmented by the same Author. *London, Printed by S. Simmons next door to the Golden Lion in Aldersgate-street, 1678*. Third edition. 8vo, [viii]+331pp., as preceding copy, two final blank leaves present, contemporary paneled calf (front joint cracked, with inserted engraved frontispiece portrait after Dolle, defective at lower portion, trivial spotting, second final blank [Y8] restored at top fore corner), gilt rules and lettering on spine (bit faded), red morocco label, raised bands, bookplate. Capel Lofft's copy, overall in good state, with an interesting succession of ownership before and after him. Originally Charles Tryell's copy, with his purchase note and signature on front pastedown; then Capel Lofft's copy with his signature (dated "3 March 1797") on title page; more recently, in the library of Lord Vernon of Sudbury, Derbyshire, with his bookplate. Capel Lofft was the popular and eccentric eighteenth-century writer who in 1792 published "Milton's *Paradise Lost* . . . collated, the original system of orthography restored, the punctuation corrected and extended, with various readings, and notes chiefly rhythmical," of which only the first book was published (see presentation copy listed here). See references with preceding copy for third edition.

606. **PARADISUS AMISSA**, Poema Heroicum, Quod a Joanne Miltono Anglo Anglice scriptum in Decem Libros digestum est: Nunc autem a Viris quibusdam Natione eadem oriundis In Linguam Romanam Transfertur. Liber Primus. Imprim. Nov. 18. 1685. R. L'Estrange. *Londini: Impensis Thomae Dring, ad Insigne Occae in Vico Fleetstret dicto. MDCLXXXVI*. First edition thus. Small 4to, [vi]+32pp., mid-eighteenth-century calf-backed boards (rubbed and worn). A little dusty, but a very good, fresh copy. Bound with **SEVEN SERMONS** (1682–1746). First edition of the very rare Latin version of *PL*, Book I only, published in 1676; no more were published. The dedication to Sir Thomas Mompesson is signed "J.C.," but "little seems to be known of this rare book," says Parker, recording copies in nine libraries. New Wing adds two more (and fails to list one). By Parker's list of "surviving copies," this text ranks seventy-fourth (of eighty-seven). According to Parker (p. 661), early Latin translations of Milton's *PL* appeared as follows: (1) "J.C." (1686, *Paradisus Amissa*, Book I—edition here); (2) William Hogg (1690, *Paraphrasis Poetica*—see copy listed here); (3) "T.P." [Thomas Power] (1691); (4) Charles Blake (1694); (5) Michael Bold (1702, *Paradisus Amissa*, Book I,—see copy listed here); (6) Joseph Trapp (1741-44, *Paradisus Amissus*—see set listed here), and (7) William Dobson (1750-53, *Paradisus Amissus*—see set listed here). Scarce. New Wing M2155; Parker, p. 1186; Shawcross, 1984, 342; Not in Coleridge; Not in Kohler.

1688 First Folio Edition, First Illustrated Edition in Contemporary Black Morocco

607. PARADISE LOST. A Poem In Twelve Books. The Author John Milton. The Fourth Edition, Adorn'd with Sculptures. *London, Printed by Miles Flesher, for Jacob Tonson, at the Judge's-Head in Chancery-lane near Fleet-street. M DC LXXXVIII.* Fourth edition; first folio edition; first illustrated edition. Folio, [i]+343 (pagination goes to "250" and then "151" in Book IX, on to "196" in Book XI and then "297" on to "343")+[6]pp., first appearance of engraved frontispiece portrait after R. White (striking impression), with the first appearance of Dryden's famous epigram, twelve engraved illustrations, measuring 7 ⅜" × 11 ¼", one for each book of *PL*, eight after J. B. Medina (for Books III, V, VI, VII, VIII, IX, X, and XI, all but VIII signed), one after Bernard Lens (for Book IV, signed) and possibly three (for Books I, II, and XII, each unsigned) after Henry Aldrich, Dean of Christ Church, Oxford (first appearance of these illustrations, fine impressions), eleven engraved by M. Burghers (also Burg and Burgesse, assumed to be a single identity), one engraved by P. P. Bouche after Lens (for Book IV), list of subscribers (with Dryden included among them) at the end after Book XII, contemporary full black morocco, covers and spine very finely tooled in gilt, raised bands, a.e.g., with early signatures on verso of portrait. A handsome, tall, large paper copy, measuring 14 ½" × 9 ½", with nonconsecutive pagination from Book IX on, consistent with that identified by Coleridge, with plates that are fresh and crisp, in a splendid and well-preserved contemporary morocco binding with the bookplate of Graham Pollard. Rare thus, in such fine condition, with striking impressions of the plates, in a wonderful contemporary morocco binding, and formerly the copy of a great collector.

John Baptist Medina (ca. 1660–1710), who has been called "Kneller's equivalent in Scotland," was born in Brussels, trained under Francois Du Châtel, and "came to London in 1686 as a painter of history, landscapes and portraits. He seems to have spent most of his working life in Scotland where he was knighted in 1706. He died in 1710. Apart from his Milton illustrations, Medina's only known surviving work is in the field of portraiture" (Pointon, p. 1). For a full discussion of the illustrations and illustrators of the 1688 folio

PL, 1688, first folio edition, in contemporary black morocco binding.

PL, Bk. I, engraved illustration after J. B. Medina (possibly Henry Aldrich). *Satan Rising from the Flood*, 1688. From illustrations in the 1688 edition in the contemporary black morocco binding featured here. See #607.

PL, Bk. XII, engraved illustration after J. B. Medina (possibly Henry Aldrich). *The Expulsion*, 1688. From illustrations in the 1688 edition in the contemporary black morocco binding featured here. See #607.

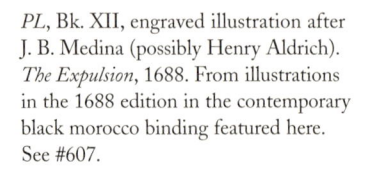

PL, Bk. IX, engraved illustration after J. B. Medina. *Satan in the Garden*, panoramic illustration, 1688. See #607.

edition of *PL*, see Boorsch, "The 1688 Paradise Lost and Dr. Aldrich," *Journal of the Metropolitan Museum* VI (1972): 133–50; see also Pointon, Chapter I, *Milton and English Art*, 1970; and see Mary D. Ravenhall, "Francis Atterbury and the First Illustrated Edition of *Paradise Lost*," *Milton Quarterly* 16, no. 2 (1982): 29–36.

Besides being the first folio edition of Milton and the first illustrated Milton edition, this is also the first subscription edition to be issued by Tonson and the book ranks also, in the words of Edward Hodnett, as "the earliest serious effort to illustrate an important work of English poetry" (*Five Centuries of English Book Illustration*, p. 63), therefore making it a most desirable book among collectors for reasons that go beyond Milton. "In publishing monumental editions of the works of classical authors, Tonson was following the example of his most significant precursors in the publishing business. In rescuing from obscurity or oblivion the masterpieces of English authors and publishing them with similar care, he was an innovator. His first and best triumph in this neglected field was the fourth edition of Milton's *PL*, which Tonson published with Bentley in 1688. . . . The 1688 edition, in the style of all of Tonson's more elaborate books, was distinguished by excellent paper, large, clear type, and ample margins" (Kathleen M. Lynch, *Jacob Tonson*, p. 128). While not the first example of publishing by subscription as a method of financing publication, it is one of the earliest examples, particularly for a work in English. Tonson followed this successful publication by subscription with many others, but when he had his portrait painted by Godfrey Kneller in 1717 for the Kitkat Club, he chose to have himself shown holding a copy of the 1688 *PL*. Since both Tonson and Bentley owned half the copyright, the edition was a joint venture, with each proprietor having a title page of his own (presumably for distribution to subscribers attracted by each), this being Tonson's title page, the title page following being Bentley's, and the third being a joint title page for the retail trade copy. Wing M2148; Grolier, *Wither to Prior*, 607; Hofer, *Baroque Book Illustration*, p. 63; Parker, pp. 1187–88; Boorsch, Pointon, Hodnett, and Lynch, as cited within the text; Coleridge 93b; Shawcross, 1984, 347; Shawcross, Kentucky, 88; Kohler 6.

1688 First Folio Edition, Second Variant Publisher's Imprint

608. Variant of Preceding. **PARADISE LOST** . . . *London, Printed by Miles Flesher, for Richard Bentley, at the Post-Office in Russell-street. M DC LXXXVIII.* Fourth edition, variant imprint; first folio edition; first illustrated edition. Folio, [i]+343(pagination goes to "250" and then "151" in Book IX, on to "196" in Book XI and then "297," on to "343")+[6]pp., first appearance of engraved frontispiece portrait after R. White, with the first appearance of Dryden's famous epigram, twelve engraved illustrations, measuring 7 ⅜" × 11 ¼", identified in preceding copy (first appearance of these illustrations, fine impressions), list of subscribers (with Dryden included among them) at the end after Book XII, contemporary calf (neatly rebacked), gilt-ruled and gilt-lettered red morocco label on spine, raised bands. A fine, tall, large paper copy, measuring 14 ¾" × 9 ½", with early signatures on verso of portrait. The nonconsecutive pagination sequence from Book IX on is consistent with that identified by Coleridge. A note on the front endpaper of a copy offered for sale by Buddenbrooks (Boston) at the New York Book Fair, 1989, stated: "Page 4 of this copy has the incorrect catchword 'That.' This is an extremely rare and unusual feature and I know of no other copies in which it appears. It points to the fact that the first page in this copy must be among the first batch that were printed." This copy has the same catchword "That"; the other two copies (preceding and following) do not. I see no mention of this in Coleridge. See commentary about the imprint, the illustrations and illustrators, and other commentary about this edition with preceding copy. Wing M2147; Suzanne Boorsch, "The 1688 Paradise Lost and Dr. Aldrich," *Metropolitan Museum Journal* 6 (1972): 133–50; Hofer, Lynch, Hodnett, and Pointon; Shawcross, 1984, 346; Coleridge 93a; Not in Kohler.

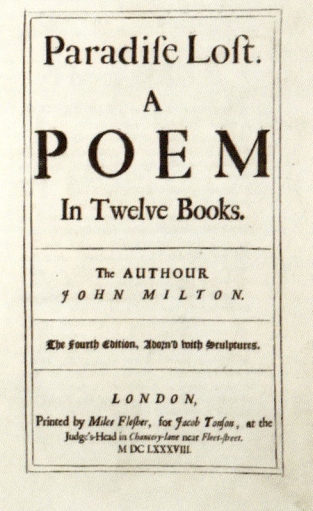

PL, The Fourth Edition, Adorn'd with Sculptures. London: Printed by Miles Flesher, for Jacob Tonson, 1688. With engraved frontispiece portrait by R. White (first appearance).

1688 First Folio Edition, Third Variant Publisher's Imprint

609. Variant of Preceding. **PARADISE LOST** . . . *London, Printed by Miles Flesher, for Richard Bently, at the Post-Office in Russell-street, and Jacob Tonson at the Judge's-Head in Chancery-lane near Fleet-street. M DC LXXXVIII.* Fourth edition, variant imprint; first folio edition (much smaller in size); first illustrated edition. Folio, [i]+343(pagination goes to "250" and then "151" in Book IX, on to "197" in Book XI and then "298," on to "343")+[6]pp., first appearance of engraved frontispiece portrait by R. White, with the first appearance of Dryden's famous epigram, twelve engraved illustrations, measuring 7 ⅜" × 11 ¼", identified in copy no. 1 (first appearance of these illustrations, fine impressions), list of subscribers (with Dryden included among them) at the end after Book XII, contemporary calf (worn, small mend to blank inner corner of frontispiece and title page, some slight waterstains throughout, short clean tear to first plate), gilt-lettered red morocco label on spine, raised bands. An okay, regular-sized folio copy of this variant imprint (much smaller than preceding two folio copies), with early inscriptions in ink on fly-leaf and title page. The erroneous pagination sequence here from Book IX on varies by one page number each way at the end in Book XI (197/196) and (298/297), as Coleridge says "Some copies print." This joint title page was presumably for the retail trade. Scarce, being the rarest of the three imprints. See commentary about the illustrations and illustrators (with references noted) and other commentary about this edition with copy no. 1 above. Wing M2146; Coleridge 93c; Shawcross, 1984, 345; Not in Kohler.

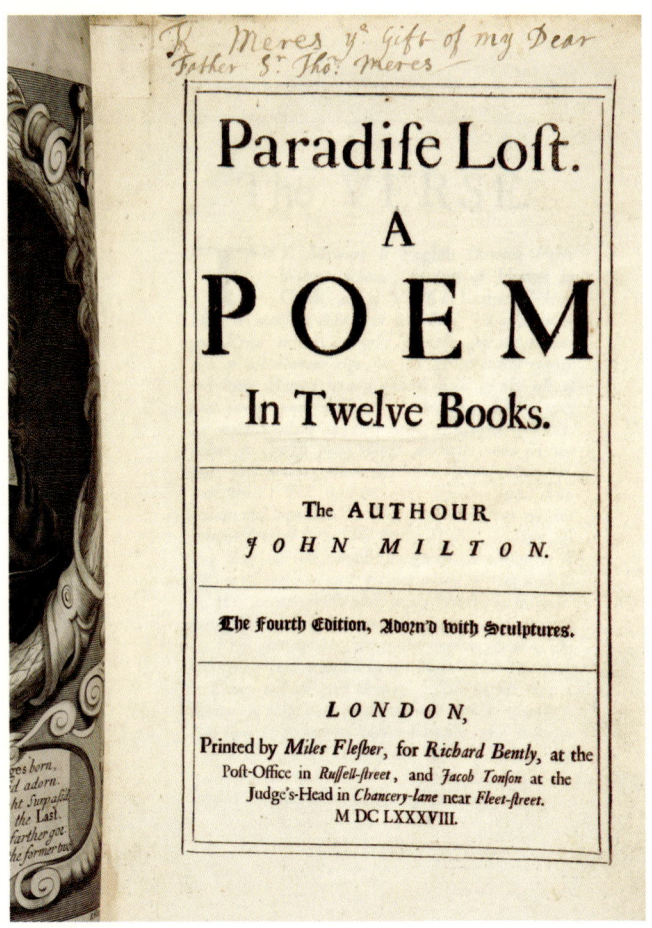

PL, The Fourth Edition, Adorn'd with Sculptures. London: Printed by Miles Flesher, for Richard Bently and for Jacob Tonson, 1688 (variant publisher's imprint). See #609.

610. PARADISE LOST. A Poem In Twelve Books. The Author John Milton. The Fifth Edition, Adorn'd with Sculptures. *London, Printed for Richard Bently in Covent-garden, and Jacob Tonson in Chancery-lane near Fleetstreet. MDCXCI.* Fifth edition. Folio, [i]+336pp., engraved frontispiece portrait by R. White (bound after title page), explanation leaf of "The Verse" bound at end, twelve engraved illustrations from 1688 edition, contemporary full vellum, gilt-decorated covers and spine, spine lettered in black, raised bands. A fine, tall copy with early names on title page and with fine impressions of the plates. Rare. Wing M2149 records two copies only in England: Trinity College and Cambridge; Williamson 53; Coleridge 94a; Parker, pp. 1190–91; Shawcross, Kentucky, 98; Shawcross, 1984, 357, reporting "Copy owned by University of Kentucky Library"; Kohler 7, reporting "Not in the British Library. Not in Cambridge University Library."

611. PARADISE LOST. A Poem In Twelve Books. The Author John Milton. The Fifth Edition, Adorn'd with Sculptures. *London, Printed for Jacob Tonson at the Judge's-Head in Chancery-Lane near Fleet-street. M DC XCII.* Alternate fifth edition. Folio, engraved frontispiece portrait by R. White, bound without the illustrations. Bound with **PARADISE REGAIN'D**. A Poem. In IV Books. To which is added Samson Agonistes. The Author John Milton. *London, Printed by R. E. and are to be sold by Randal Taylor near Stationers-Hall. M DC LXXXVIII.* Third edition; first folio edition. Bound with **SAMSON AGONISTES**, A Dramatick Poem. The Authour [sic] John Milton. Aristot. Poet. Cap 6...*London, Printed, and are to be Sold by Randal Taylor near Stationers-Hall, M DC LXXXVIII.* Third edition; first folio edition. Folio, [i]+336+66+[4]+57pp., separate title page and pagination for each work, contemporary paneled calf (a little worn, joints cracked), gilt-trimmed and gilt-lettered red morocco label on spine, raised bands. A good, tall copy, very fine internally. Tonson bought the second half of the copyright from Bentley in March 1691, prior to the 1691 edition and in time to publish this edition in 1692 with his name only on the title page. Wing M2150, M2154, M2177; Parker, pp. 1188–89, 1190–91; Coleridge 94b, 170; Shawcross, Kentucky, 98, reporting "Copy of *PL* owned by University of Kentucky Library"; *PL*—Shawcross, 1984, 362; *PL*—Not in Kohler; *PR* and *SA*—Kohler 179.

612. PARADISE LOST. A Poem In Twelve Books. The Author John Milton. The Fourth Edition, Adorn'd with Sculptures. *London: Printed by R. E. for Jacob Tonson, at the Judge's Head, near the Inner Temple Gate in Fleetstreet. M DC XCIII.* Second alternate fifth edition (despite being called "The Fourth Edition" on title page). Folio, separate title page for each work, separate pagination for each work, engraved frontispiece portrait by R. White, twelve engraved illustrations from 1688 folio (fine impressions). Bound with **PARADISE REGAIN'D**. A Poem. In IV Books. To which is added Samson Agonistes. The Author John Milton. *London, Printed by R. E. and are to be sold by Randal Taylor near Stationers-Hall. M DC LXXXVIII.* Third edition; first folio edition. Bound with **SAMSON AGONISTES**, A Dramatick Poem. The Authour John Milton. Aristot. Poet. Cap 6 . . . *London, Printed, and are to be Sold by Randal Taylor near Stationers-Hall, M DC LXXXVIII.* Third edition; first folio edition. Folio, [i]+336+66+[4]+57pp., separate title page and pagination for each work, contemporary full red morocco (neatly rebacked sometime preserving original spine), covers and spine finely tooled in gilt, black morocco label with gilt lettering and gilt rules, raised bands with decorative gilt trim, inner and outer dentelles finely tooled in gilt, a.e.g. Fine copy with early names and notations in an early hand on fly-leaf, additional notations in pencil on front pastedown. Regarding *PL*: "The 1693 TP is presumably an interim issue [before the publication of the 1695 *PW*, see copy listed here] to keep the market supplied with an up-to-date issue of *PL*" (Coleridge, note, p. 134). Parker calls this edition "excessively rare," accounting for three copies, including Illinois (Parker, p. 1191). *PL*—Not in Wing; Not in Coleridge; Shawcross, 1984, 363; *PR*—Wing M2154 and Coleridge 170; *PL*—Not in Kohler; *PR* and *SA*—Kohler 179.

612A. (Cross-listing) **PARADISE LOST** . . . The Sixth Edition, with Sculptures. To which is added, Explanatory NOTES upon each Book, and a TABLE to the POEM, never before Printed. *London: Printed by Tho. Hodgkin, for Jacob Tonson . . . M DC XCV.* Sixth edition; second illustrated edition. [In] **THE POETICAL WORKS OF MR. JOHN MILTON**. Containing, Paradise Lost, Paradise Regain'd, Samson Agonistes, and his Poems on several Occasions. Together With Explanatory NOTES on each Book of the PARADISE LOST, and a TABLE never before Printed. *London: Printed for Jacob Tonson, M DC XCV.* First complete collected edition. The "TABLE to the POEM" is first added in this 1695 edition. When reprinted in subsequent editions this *Table* is described as the "Index." "There are far fewer surviving copies of this

PL, 1691 edition in contemporary vellum binding, with portrait and plates. See #610.

important edition than one might expect" (Parker, p. 1194). Coleridge 214 (without general title page); Kohler 266; Shawcross, Kentucky, 110 ("While the edition appears to be the same as that of 1688, it has been reset and errors have been corrected"). See main listing under *PW*, 1695.

613. PARADISUS AMISSA, POEMA, PARADISE LOST. A Poem. Liber Primus. Book One. *London, Printed 1702*. First edition, first issue. 4to, 109pp., two title pages—one in Latin and one in English, Latin translation of Book I printed with the English text on opposite page, contemporary calf (minor embrowning, a few slight spots or stains, neatly rebacked period style), bookplate. A very nice copy inscribed on the English title page: "Ex dono Typographi" and on the Latin title page: "E librii Richardi" (surname illegible, and mainly erased). Foxon lists one of the two known variants of this translation by Matthew Bold; Coleridge describes both. Foxon B312 (variant); Coleridge 166a; Not in Kohler.

This is one of seven early Latin translations of Milton's *PL*, five of which are in the collection: (1) "J. C.," 1686, *Paradisus Amissa*, Book I—see copy listed here; (2) William Hog, 1690, *Paraphrasis Poetica*—see copy listed here; (3) "T[homas]. P[ower].," 1691; (4) Charles Blake, 1694; (5) Michael Bold, 1702, *Paradisus Amissa*, Book I,—edition here, 1736; (6) Joseph Trapp, 1741–44, *Paradisus Amissus*—see set listed here; and (7) William Dobson, 1750–53, *Paradisus Amissus*—see set listed here.

614. PARADISE LOST. A Poem, In Twelve Books. The Author John Milton. The Seventh Edition, Adorn'd with Sculptures. *London, Printed for Jacob Tonson, within Grays-Inn Gate next Grays-Inn Lane. 1705*. Seventh edition. Tall 8vo, [viii]+483+[9]pp., half-title ("The Poetical Works Of Mr. John Milton. In Two Volumes"), dedication page, engraved frontispiece portrait after Robert White rendition of Faithorne (fine impression), twelve engraved illustrations after 1688 plates (fine impressions), engraved by H. Eland, "A Table" at the end (first appeared in 1695 edition, see copy cross-listed here), contemporary calf (name removed from top of title page without affecting text, front cover rehinged from inside), paper label (worn), raised bands. Good copy, very clean and crisp internally, with half-title for "The Poetical Works Of Mr. John Milton. In Two Volumes." Companion volume to *PR*, 1705 (also listed here), together forming the *PW*. As Coleridge clarifies: "Some copies bind the 'Works' TP as a recto, others omit it. *PR&c* was issued in the same year to make the 2nd volume of the *PW*. The two volumes were sold together or separately, omitting the 'Works' TP in the latter case, though it is possible that sets have subsequently been broken. When either volume was out of print another edition would be printed, to be sold with the currently in print matching volume." See 1707 edition following with half-title ("The Poetical Works in Two Volumes") uniformly bound with *PR*, 1705. Rare. Williamson 47; Coleridge 95; Kohler 8.

615. PARADISE LOST. A Poem, In Twelve Books. The Author John Milton. The Eighth Edition, Adorn'd with Sculptures. *London, Printed for Jacob Tonson, within Grays-Inn Gate next Grays-Inn Lane. 1707*. Eighth edition. 8vo, [viii]+483+[9]pp., half-title ("The Poetical Works Of Mr. John Milton. In Two Volumes"), engraved frontispiece portrait after Robert White rendition of Faithorne (fine impression), twelve engraved illustrations after 1688 plates (fine impressions), engraved by H. Eland, "A Table" at the end, contemporary calf (expertly rebacked preserving original spine with fine new black morocco label lettered in gilt, raised bands, occasional light waterstaining, tiny wormhole at bottom just piercing the bottom edge of the plates), covers decorated in blind at the center, red speckled edges. A lovely copy, uniformly bound as volume 1 to *PR*, 1705 (also listed here), together forming the *PW*. See comments by Coleridge quoted with *PL*, 1705, regarding the sale of the volumes together as a set forming *PW* and as separates; as a set with either volume; when out of print, sold "with the currently in print matching volume," in this instance, a 1705 edition of *PR* with a 1707 edition of *PL*. Rare. Coleridge 185; Kohler 180.

Joseph Addison's Copy(?)

616. PARADISE LOST. A Poem, In Twelve Books. The Author John Milton. The Ninth Edition, Adorn'd with Sculptures. *London: Printed for Jacob Tonson, at Shakespear's Head, over-against Catherine Street in the Strand. MDCCXI*. Ninth edition; first 12mo edition. 12mo, [viii]+376+[42]pp., unsigned engraved frontispiece portrait, with Dryden epigram, twelve unsigned copper-engraved illustrations (1688 plates further reduced, very fine impressions), one for each book, dedication page, decorative headpieces, index at the end, contemporary calf (a bit rubbed), gilt rules on covers, delicately gilt-decorated spine (chipped at top and bottom), raised bands, red morocco label (chipped), marbled endpapers, armorial bookplate of James Ellsworth. An attractive early illustrated Milton, which Henry Todd says was the first edition to contain an index, but the index is in fact the table which the 1705 and 1707 editions reprinted from the 1695 edition of *PL* (several copies listed here). Becoming a scarce edition.

MS. note on fly-leaf reads: "This Book belong'd to Addison and was b-t at his sale May 1799." It was lot 43 in the "Catalogue of The . . . Library of Joseph Addison. . . . Sold by Auction by Leigh and Sotheby Covent Garden on Monday May 27, 1799 and four following days, . . ." where it fetched six pence. There is a further note on the back endpaper: "Addison's copy. Bought at the Sale of A. R. Pollock's library Jan. 28 to Feb. 2, 1889, by [Messrs?] Sotheby, London." Given the 1711 publication date of this volume, the notes relating the book to Addison within it, and Addison's involvement in writing for *The Spectator* during the years 1711–12 and his critique of *PL*, which appeared as "a series of seventeen papers . . . which appeared on Saturdays from 5 Jan. to 3 May 1712" (DNB), it is very likely that this book belonged to Addison. The volume formerly belonged to Dr. Rosenbach, and then John Fleming, who gave it to me during a visit to him at East 57th Street with Bob Taylor in December 1980. Not realizing the importance of his gift, John wrote me a follow-up letter to let me know that had he "known, I'd still have given it to you as a gift" (letter accompanies the book). A fine and rare association copy. Gift from John Fleming. Williamson 63; Coleridge 97; Kohler 10.

617. A possible variant in contemporary unlettered calf. Lovely copy, fresh and clean within. A curious copy, wider than other copies that have been at one time in the collection, with the sheets bulking to 1", normal copies bulking to ⅞", including preceding copy. Scarce.

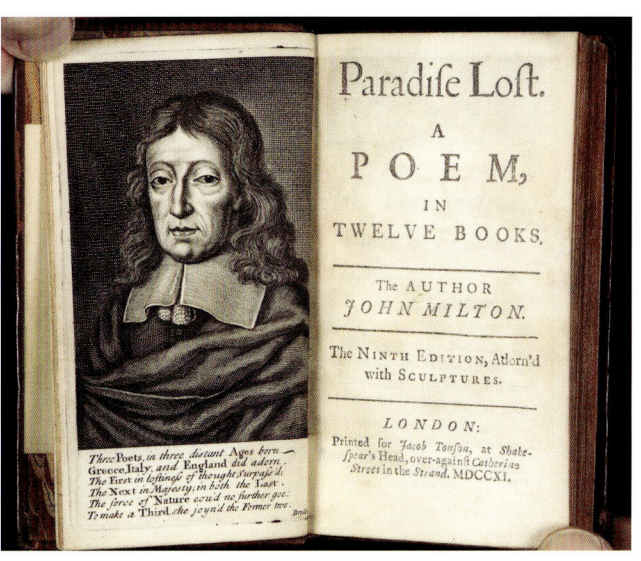

Engraved frontispiece portrait and title page, Tonson 1711 *PL*. First 12mo edition. See #616.

Reduced 1688 engraved plate, Bk. I, Tonson 1711 *PL* 12mo edition. See #616.

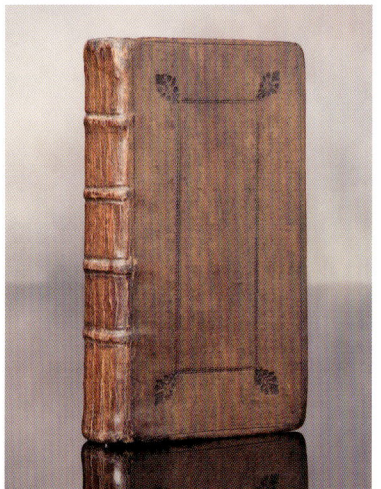

1711 Tonson edition of *PL*, contemporary calf. First 12mo edition, with 1688 plates reduced. Note in an early hand states: "This Book belong'd to Addison and was b-t at his sale May 1799." It was lot 43 of the "Catalogue of The . . . Library of Joseph Addison." See #616.

1711 *PL*, variant contemporary calf binding. Fine, tall copy. See #617.

618. PARADISE LOST. A Poem, In Twelve Books. The Author John Milton. The Tenth Edition, Adorn'd With Sculptures. *London: Printed for Jacob Tonson, at Shakespear's Head, over-against Katherine Street in the Strand. MDCCXIX.* Tenth edition; second of Tonson's 12mo editions. Stout 12mo, [viii]+315+[1]pp.,+[40]+[4]+148pp., unsigned engraved frontispiece portrait, with Dryden epigram, engraved illustrations (1688 plates further reduced), one for each book, decorative head- and tailpieces and decorated initial letters, at the end: an unpaginated forty-page index, a four-page listing of "Books Printed for Jacob Tonson" (listed by "Folio's," "Octavo & Duodecimo"—including "The Poetical Works of Mr. *John Milton* . . . Lately publish'd . . . in Neat Pocket Volumes"), and Addison's *Notes* (with its own title page: *Notes Upon The Twelve Books Of Paradise Lost.* Collected from the Spectator. Written by Mr. Addison. *London: Printed for Jacob Tonson, at Shakespear's Head, over-against Katherine Street in the Strand. MDCCXIX*), contemporary full red morocco (a bit rubbed, rebacked preserving original spine), gilt-decorated covers and spine, raised bands, inner and outer dentelles tooled in gilt, marbled endpapers, a.e.g. A fine, very tall copy with good impressions of the plates and with bookplates and early signature on verso of fly-leaf. First separate appearance of Addison's *Notes* (see copy of separate publication with Eighteenth-century Miltoniana) and first edition of *PL* to be accompanied by these notes. Williamson 63; Coleridge 98; Kohler 11, reporting "Not in Cambridge University Library."

618A. (Cross-listing) PARADISE LOST, 1720. Eleventh edition. [In] THE POETICAL WORKS OF MR. JOHN MILTON. *London: Printed for Jacob Tonson, at Shakespear's Head in the Strand. MDCCXX. 2 volumes.* First Tickell edition. Large 4to, edited by Thomas Tickell, engraved title page each volume, first appearance of engraved frontispiece portrait each volume after Vertue, first appearance of vignette illustration on engraved title page and other engraved head- and tailpiece illustrations after L. Cheron, engraved by C. van der Gucht et al., most of the tailpieces in elaborate baroque borders, decorated initial letters. The text of *PL* here is the eleventh edition without a separate title page. See main listing under *PW*, 1720.

618B. (Cross-listing) PARADISE LOST. MDCCXXI. [In] THE POETICAL WORKS OF MR. JOHN MILTON, In Two Volumes. Containing. I. Paradise Lost; with Notes, by the late Right Honourable Mr. Secretary Addison. II. Paradise Regained . . . Samson Agonistes. And Poems . . . With a Tractate of Education. Adorned with Cuts. *London: Printed, and are to be Sold by William Taylor at the Ship and Black-Swan, in Pater-Noster-Row. MDCCXXI.* Volume 1 of 2 volumes (volume 2 cited listed here). First edition thus by Taylor. 12mo, [viii]+315+[1]pp.,+[1]+[40]+[4]+148pp., unsigned engraved frontispiece portrait, with Dryden epigram, engraved illustrations (1688 plates further reduced), one for each book, decorative head- and tailpieces and decorated initial letters, at the end: an unpaginated forty-page index, a four-page listing of "Books Printed for Jacob Tonson," and Addison's *Notes* (with its own title page), contemporary calf. With the exception of the title page, this edition is published in identical format to that of the 1719 12mo Tonson edition (also listed here). See companion volume, as volume 2, listed here: "*Paradise Regain'd* . . . To which is added *Samson Agonistes.* And *Poems Upon Several Occasions.* With A Tractate Of Education. The Author John Milton. The Fifth Edition. Adorn'd with Cuts. *London*: Printed, and are to be Sold by W. Taylor, at the *Ship* and *Black-Swan*, in *Pater-Noster-Row.* 1721," which together with this volume forms a rare two-volume edition of Milton's *PW* published by William Taylor in 1721. Not in Coleridge; Not in Kohler. See main listing under *PW*, 1721.

619. PARADISE LOST. A Poem, In Twelve Books. The Author John Milton. The Eleventh Edition, Adorn'd With Sculptures. *Dublin: Printed by and for George Grierson, at the Two Bibles in Essex-Street, 1724.* Bound with **PARADISE REGAIN'D**. A Poem, In Four Books. The Author John Milton. The Seventh Edition. *Dublin: Printed by and for George Grierson, at the Two Bibles in Essex-Street, 1724.* 2 volumes in one. First Irish edition of each. 8vo, [xii]+315+61pp.+[24-page unpaginated index], first appearance of engraved frontispiece portrait after James Gwim, engraved and printed title pages for *PL*, engraved title in red and black with "Advertisement" on verso, separate title page in black for each poem, first appearance of twelve engraved folding plates for *PL* after J(ames). Gwim, decorative head- and tailpieces and decorated initial letters, index to *PL*, contemporary Irish full red morocco, decorative gilt border trim on covers, gilt-decorated spine, raised bands, gilt dentelles, a.e.g. A very fine copy with early bookplates, contemporary presentation signature, and later signatures. Laid in: a brief newspaper clipping (dated 1922) on Gwim. John Shawcross shared with me in 2000 that "The Grierson publications are confused, frequent, and variously combined. *PL* was issued separately in 1724; what you report is a reissue combined with *PR*. There is another reissue of *PL* and *PR*; and there are two other reissues of *PL* separately—all 1724. The number of editions of both poems is often erroneous as we move through the century." Rare. Coleridge 174a (indicating rarity—especially the two poems together); Not in Kohler.

II. Descriptive Listing of Editions   167

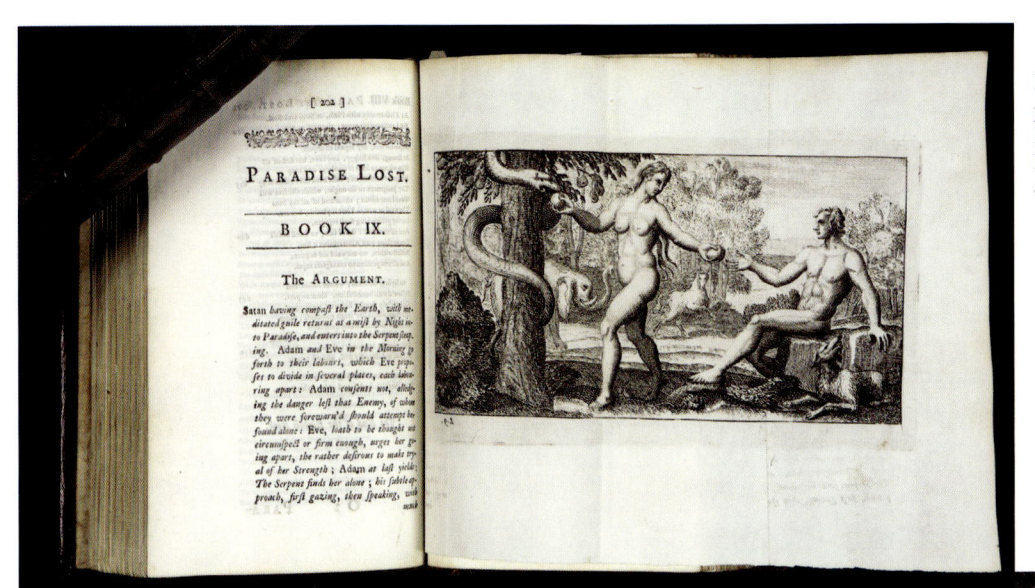

Engraved folding illustration plate after James Gwim of Eve tempting Adam, *PL*, Dublin, 1724. First Dublin edition. See #619.

Engraved folding illustration plate after James Gwim of *The Expulsion*, *PL*, Dublin, 1724. First Dublin editions. See #619.

620. Variant of Preceding. **PARADISE LOST.** A Poem, In Twelve Books. The Author John Milton. The Eleventh Edition, Adorn'd With Sculptures. *Dublin: Printed by and for George Grierson, at the Two Bibles in Essex-Street, 1724.* First Irish edition. Bound with **PARADISE REGAIN'D.** A Poems, In Four Books. The Author John Milton. The Seventh Edition. *Dublin: Printed by and for George Grierson, at the Two Bibles in Essex-Street, 1724.* First Irish edition. Bound with **SAMSON AGONISTES,** A Dramatick Poem. The Author John Milton. Aristot. Poet. Cap. 6...*Dublin: Printed by and for George Grierson, at the Two Bibles in Essex-Street, 1748.* First Irish edition. Bound with **POEMS UPON SEVERAL OCCASIONS.** Compos'd at several Times. By Mr. John Milton. [Quotation from Virgil] *Dublin: Printed by and for George Grierson, at the Two Bibles in Essex-Street, 1748.* First Irish edition. Bound with **A MASK, PRESENTED AT LUDLOW CASTLE . . .** *Dublin: Printed by and for George Grierson, at the Two Bibles in Essex-Street, 1748.* First Irish edition. 5 volumes bound in one. Stout 8vo, [vii]+315+ 61pp.,+[24-page unpaginated index]+196pp.[continuous pagination], first appearance of engraved frontispiece portrait after James Gwim, engraved and printed title pages for *PL*, engraved title in red and black with "Advertisement" on verso, separate title page in black for each poem, first appearance of twelve engraved folding plates for *PL* after J(ames). Gwim, decorative head- and tailpieces and decorated initial letters, index to *PL*, contemporary calf (front joint beginning to crack, name marked out on separate title page to *PL* and then on separate title page to *PR* causing a small hole in the latter and with date "1748" remaining on the former, a few plates shaved, minor worming to some blank edges), brown morocco label with decorative gilt trim and gilt lettering on spine, small decorative piece in gilt in the panels, raised bands. A very nice copy with early name on fly-leaf. Not all of Milton's poems are included in *P*; among those included are *L*, *L'A*, *IlP*, *Ar*, and *C*. Included at the end without separate title page is *Of Ed*, paginated 187 to 196, after "Finis" to *C* on page 182—indicating, as John Shawcross shared with me about this book that "the signatures indicate mispagination (which is not uncommon, of course)." Grierson clearly wished to present a complete collection of Milton's poetry and continued the signature sequence to the end, indicating to the binder how the separate parts were to be placed. "The separate parts themselves are most uncommon, and this is the first copy we have seen in 30 years with all the various components present and complete" (G. W. Stuart, Jr., Ravenstree, Cat. 174, #26, 1992). The very rare first Irish editions thus. Coleridge 174a (citing an incomplete copy); Not in Kohler.

621. **PARADISE LOST**. A Poem, In Twelve Books. The Author John Milton. The Twelfth Edition. To which is prefix'd An Account of his Life [by Fenton]. [Quotation from Homer] *London: Printed for Jacob Tonson in the Strand*. MDCCXXV. 12mo, xxviii+[viii]+350pp.+45-page unpaginated index [pp. 351–95, with the verso, 396, blank], engraved frontispiece portrait after Vertue, title page in red and black, life by Fenton (first appearance—although not attributed to him here), first appearance of engraved illustrations (after 1688 plates) by P. Fourdriner, one for each book, decorative head- and tailpieces and decorated initial letters, index, contemporary calf (rebacked preserving original spine, spine a bit chipped at top), covers finely tooled in blind, gilt-decorated spine, gilt-ruled red morocco label with gilt lettering, raised bands, gilt dentelles (bit faded), red speckled edges. A fine copy, very fresh internally, with early armorial bookplate and with early dated signature. Scarce. Coleridge 99; Kohler 12, reporting "Not in ESTC. ESTC lists only the 12mo edition. Not in the British Library. Not in the Bodleian. Not in the Cambridge University Library."

Besides providing the life of Milton, Fenton was also "editor of the text of this edition, [he] also edited the 1725 *PR&c*. He made several emendations in the text, not acceptable to modern editorial standards, and thereby provided precedent for Bentley's treatment in his 1732 edition [see copy listed here]. Fenton's life was frequently reprinted, with or without acknowledgment" (Coleridge). Uniformly bound with "*PR*, London: Printed for J. Tonson, in the *Strand*; and for M. Poulson. M.DCC.XXV," listed below. Scarce. Coleridge 99; Kohler 12, reporting "Not in ESTC. ESTC lists only the 12mo edition. Not in the British Library. Not in the Bodleian. Not in the Cambridge University Library."

622. **PARADISE LOST**. A Poem, In Twelve Books. The Author John Milton. The Thirteenth Edition. To which is prefix'd An Account of his Life . [Quotation from Homer] *London: Printed for Jacob Tonson in the Strand*. MDCCXXVII. 8vo, [ii]+xxv+[xi]+514[mispaginated "524"]pp.+[34-page unpaginated index], title page in red and black, engraved frontispiece illustration and other illustrations (after 1688 plates) by Fourdrinier (second appearance thus), one for each book, dedication with elaborate decorative headpiece and decorated initial letter, vignette portrait of Milton at the head of life of Milton by Fenton, with decorated initial letter, additional decorative head- and tailpieces, half-title for each book, early diced calf (rebacked, paper shelf labels on spines, some age-browning and foxing), decorative gilt border trim on covers, gilt rules on spines, black morocco labels, marbled endpapers. A nice copy. Second edition of Fenton's life, attributed here to Fenton for the first time. Scarce. Uniformly bound with *PR*, *London: Printed for Jacob Tonson in the Strand*, MDCCXXVII, listed here. Scarcer as a set. Coleridge 100; Kohler 13.

Special Copy Bound Quarto Size with Copious Notes in a Contemporary Hand

623. As preceding edition of **PARADISE LOST**, except this is a special copy. The edition is bound 4to, with each original printed octavo page and each octavo illustration bound in a special quarto volume next to its own leaf (quarto size), with numerous notes in English, Latin, Greek, and Hebrew in a neat contemporary (possibly an editor's) hand on the quarto leaves; the edition is bound in two volumes: volume I "Book I–VI" and volume II "Book VII–XII," each "With MS. Notes And Parallel Passages," as lettered in gilt on the spines. Each volume is bound in full red morocco over thick boards, with a small central gilt device on front covers, spines lettered in gilt, raised bands, marbled endpapers, bound by J. Leighton, with his stamp. A fine set with the armorial bookplate "E Libris Roberti Marchionis De Crewe" on front pastedown of each volume. An uncommon edition, rendered unique here in its design and intention, carefully put together, with copious notes and scholarly commentary in an original hand by an educated eighteenth-century reader or possible editor. While the annotator's identity remains unsettled, it may well be Thomas Edwards (1699–1757), the Shakespeare scholar. One of four receipts (for sums paid by Roger Warne), bound within volume I and used as scrap paper for further Milton annotations, is signed by Edwards. A copy of the 1727 edition with very brief marginal notes by him is at Princeton (see J. H. Hanford in *Princeton University Library Chronicle*, 23, 1962, 123–24), and Edwards's interest in annotating Milton (and his critique of Newton's edition) is also documented in his correspondence with Samuel Richardson, ed. Barbauld (1809). I am delighted that Dr. Patrick Scott has played a vital role in affirming the annotator as being very likely Thomas Edwards. See #23 in Chapter V with a photograph of a page of this heavily annotated edition.

❧

624. 'T PARADYS VERLOOREN. Heldendict In Tien Boeken. Door John Milton. Uyt het Engels in rymelooze Maat vertaald Door J: van Zanten, M.D. *Te Haarlem: By Geertruyd van Kessel, 1728.* First edition thus. 4to, [vi]+472pp., title page in red and black, decorated enlarged initial letters for each argument, original calf (joints cracked, covers slightly splayed), gilt-decorated spine, raised bands, outer dentelles tooled in gilt (faded), speckled edges. A large, fine copy, fresh and crisp internally. Milton's original ten-book version was used for this landmark translation by Van Zanten, the first edition in Dutch. The blank verse used for the translation virtually pioneers this verse form in the Dutch tongue. The "Inhoud" to each book includes verses signed "P. L." (Pieter Langendyk), "who had advised and encouraged Van Zanten" (Coleridge). See also the 1730 edition of this translation with the engraved title page; the first edition of this Dutch translation in rhyming verses by the playwright Lambertus Paludanus (pseudonym of Lambertus van der Broek); the first Dutch rhymed edition; and the first Dutch edition to use the twelve-book form; and see the rare 1735 edition listed here. Uncommon. Coleridge 155; Not in Kohler; Shawcross, Kentucky, 193.

624A. (Cross-listing) **[PARADISE LOST] HYMN OF ADAM AND EVE.** Out Of The Fifth Book Of Milton's *Paradise Lost* Set To Music By Mr. [Johann Ernst] Galliard. *[?London], 1728.* First edition. Small oblong 4to, engraved title page with splendid cartouche (very fine impression), thirty pages of engraved music, subscriber's list, original half calf, marbled paper over boards. Bound with four additional pieces of music (not related to Milton) from the period, each with its own title page. A very good copy with the lovely engraved title by Thomas Atkins after John Pine in exuberant Rococo style for the **HYMN OF ADAM AND EVE.** A second, undated issue appeared two years later ca. 1730 (see copy cross-listed here). Not in Coleridge, who lists only a scribal copy manuscript of 1739 and two later editions (Coleridge 239, 240, and 241); Not in Kohler; NUC lists two copies: at Harvard and at Princeton. John Shawcross shared with me that "There are a great many more editions of 'Hymn of Adam and Eve,' sometimes called 'The Morning Hymn of Adam and Eve.'" See main listing with Eighteenth-century Miltoniana.

625. LE PARADIS PERDU DE MILTON. Poème Héroïque. Traduit De L'Anglois. Avec les Remarques de M. Addisson. *A Paris, Chez Cailleau . . . Brunet . . . Bordelet . . . Henry . . . M. DCC. XXIX. Avec Approbation & Privilège du Roy.* 3 volumes. First edition thus, volumes 1 and 3; "Seconde édition, revue et corrigée," volume 2. 12mo, 24+cliv+228pp.,+324pp.,+304+[2]+[2]pp., half-title volumes 1 and 3, title page for each volume each with central decorative device (larger on volumes 1 and 3), "Seconde Edition, revue & corrigée" on title page of volume 2, Fenton's "Vie de Milton" and Addison's "Remarques," volume 1, decorative head- and tailpieces, decorated initial letters, notes at bottom of page, "Approbation," "Privilège Du Roy," and "Errata" at the end of volume 3, contemporary calf (a little scuffed, particularly volume 2, joints cracked, lower corner of front cover of volume 3 worn), gilt rules with decorative corner pieces on covers of volumes 1 and 3, elaborately gilt-decorated spines, red morocco labels with gilt lettering and decorative gilt trim, raised bands, inner dentelles of volumes 1 and 3 finely tooled in gilt, marbled endpapers, volumes 1 and 3 a.e.g, volume 2 with red edges. The translation here is in prose by N. F. Dupré de Saint-Maur, revised by C. J. Chéron de Boismorand; it was first translated into English and published in 1745 under the title *The State of Innocence: And Fall of Man. Described in Milton's Paradise Lost. Render'd into Prose* (also listed here). A second edition thus was published in Paris later the same year (set following). Rare. Not in Coleridge; Not in Kohler.

626. LE PARADIS PERDU DE MILTON. Poème Héroïque, Traduit De L'Anglois. Avec les Remarques de M. Addisson. Seconde Edition, revue & corrigée. *A Paris, Chez Cailleau . . . Brunet . . . Bordelet . . . Henry . . . M. DCC. XXIX. Avec Approbation & Privilège du Roy.* 3 volumes. Second edition, revised and corrected. 12mo, 24+cliv+235pp.,+324pp.,+306+[5]pp., separate title page each volume with central decorative device on each title page, Fenton's "Vie de Milton" and Addison's "Remarques," volume 1, decorative head- and tailpieces, decorated initial letters, notes at bottom of the page, "Approbation" and "Privilège Du Roy" on last three pages of volume 3, contemporary mottled calf, elaborately gilt-decorated spines within the panels, raised bands with decorative gilt trim, red morocco labels with gilt lettering and decorative gilt trim, outer dentelles finely tooled in gilt, marbled endpapers, speckled edges, red silk ribbon maker in each volume. The translation here is in prose by N. F. Dupré de Saint-Maur, revised by C. J. Chéron de Boismorand. A fine set with contemporary signature (dated 1736) on front blank. The first edition thus was published in Paris earlier the same year (set preceding). Rare. Not in Coleridge; Not in Kohler.

626A. (Cross-listing) **[PARADISE LOST] THE HYMN OF ADAM AND EVE,** Out of the Fifth Book of Milton's

Paradise Lost; Set to Musick by Mr. [John Ernst] Galliard. *London: Printed for I. Walsh, n.d. [ca. 1730].* First edition, second issue. Oblong 4to, engraved title page with splendid cartouche (very fine impression), thirty pages of engraved music, modern boards. A very clean and attractive copy with the lovely engraved title by Thomas Atkins after John Pine in exuberant Rococo style. Very rare. Not in Coleridge. See main listing with Eighteenth-century Miltoniana.

627. PARADISE LOST. A Poem, In Twelve Books. The Author John Milton. The Fourteenth Edition. To which is prefix'd An Account of his Life [by Fenton]. [Quotation from Homer] *London: Printed for Jacob Tonson in the Strand. MDCCXXX.* 12mo, xxviii+[viii]+350pp.+[45-page unpaginated index], engraved frontispiece illustration of Milton, Homer, and Virgil by Fourdrinier, with Dryden epigram, title page in red and black, engraved illustrations after 1688 plates by Fourdrinier, one for each book, decorative head- and tailpieces, decorated initial letters, half-title for each book, contemporary paneled calf, red morocco label on spine, raised bands. A fine copy, clean and fresh within, with contemporary armorial bookplate and early signatures on title page. Coleridge 101a; Not in Kohler.

628. HET PARADYS VERLOOREN. Geschetst Na 'T Engelsch Heldendicht van John Milton, Door L. P. *Te Amsteldam, By Evert Visscher, Boekverkooper in de Dirk van Hasseltsteeg, 1730.* First edition thus; second edition in Dutch. 8vo, [ii]+[vii]+[i]+[xi]+[i]+416pp., engraved and printed title pages, engraved title page after Jan Casper Philips with central vignette illustration depicting *Adam and Eve being Expelled by the Angel*, along with eleven border medallion scenes illustrating each book of the poem, engraved title dated 1729 and 1730, printed title dated 1730 with central decorative piece, decorative headpieces, decorated initial letters, contemporary full vellum, lettering on spine by an early hand. A very pleasant copy. An uncommon book and rarely found complete with the first issue of the engraved title page (later issues exist, with dates as late as 1742). First edition of this Dutch translation in rhyming verses by the playwright Lambertus Paludanus (pseudonym of Lambertus van der Broek); first Dutch rhymed edition; first Dutch edition to use the twelve-book form. The first Dutch translation, by Jacobus van Zanten, was published in 1728 (also listed here) without the engraved title page; see also rare 1735 edition listed here. Coleridge 156; Kohler 12, with 1730 "imprint date on the engraved title-page."

629. PARADISE LOST, A Poem, In Twelve Books: Written By John Milton. With an Account of the Author's Life. A new Edition, carefully corrected. [Greek quotation from Homer] *London[,] Printed For The Company, MDCCXXX.* 8vo, xx+300pp.+[22-page unpaginated index], general title page ("The Poetical Works Of John Milton: Volume 1. Containing, Paradise Lost. With Mr. Addison's Notes; And a new set of handsom cuts. London, Printed In The Year M. DCC. XXXI") in red and black with decorative device in black, separate title page for *PL* (as cited), volume 1, printed in red and black with large decorative device in black, engraved frontispiece portrait of Milton, a copy of the Faithorne portrait, signed "D. Coster sculpt." (first appearance, very fine impression), life of Milton, engraved illustrations (1688 plates reduced), one for each book, most unsigned, several signed D. Coster (first appearance), decorative head- and tailpieces, decorated initial letters, index at the end, early half red leather, marbled paper over boards (a bit rubbed, spine a little worn and chipped at top and bottom), front cover lettered with Milton's name in gilt, spine faintly lettered in gilt, raised bands. Nice copy with early armorial bookplate on front pastedown. Laid in: earlier handwritten description of the book. This edition of *PL*, printed in London "For The Company, 1730," appears separately (as here, in volume 1 only) as well as within a collection of Milton's *PW* (see sets listed here). Coleridge considers the edition "almost certainly a French piracy." Rare. Coleridge 102; Not in Kohler.

630. IL PARADISO PERDUTO POEMA INGLESE DEL SIGNOR MILTON Tradotto In Nostra Lingua Al Quale Si Premettono Osservazioni Sopra il Libro del Signor Voltaire che esamina l'Epica Poesia delle Nazioni Europee, Scritte Originalmente in Inglese, e in Londra stampate nel 1728. poi nella propria Lingua tradotte, Ed Al Marchese Scipione Maffei Dedicate Da Paolo Rolli. In Verona. *Per Alberto Tumermani Librajo nella Via delle Foggie Con Licenza De` Superiori M DCC XXX.* First edition thus. 8vo, [iv]+432pp., vignette illustration (non-Miltonic) engraved by Hylbrouck (I. Houbraken) after Balestra on title page, three-page dedication to "Al Nobilissimo Signor Marchese Scipione Maffei," "Osservazioni," "Vita Di Giovanni Milton," decorative head- and tailpieces, decorated initial letters, contemporary vellum (shelf-marks in an early hand on both sides of front free endpaper), light brown morocco label on spine with gilt lettering and decorative gilt trim, marbled pastedowns, speckled edges. A fine copy, handsomely printed and in an attractive contemporary binding, of the first Italian edition of *PL* printed in Italy; only Books I–VI are published in this edition The first edition in Italian precedes this edition by one year, being printed in London in 1729 (see second edition, first issue, of that edition in 1735 and the second edition, second issue, in 1736 listed here). The present edition includes a critical preface and a life of Milton. NUC lists four copies: Clark, Rochester, Harvard, and Minnesota;

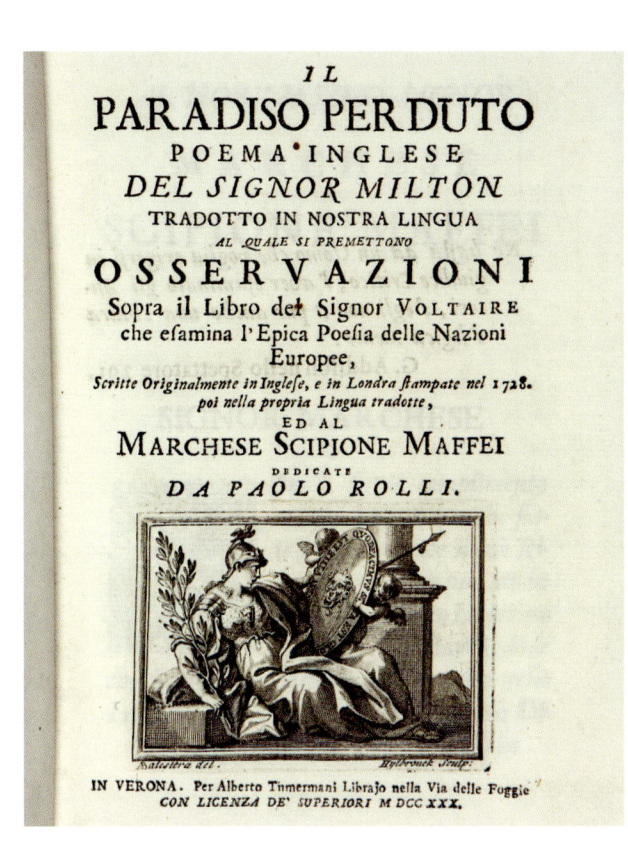

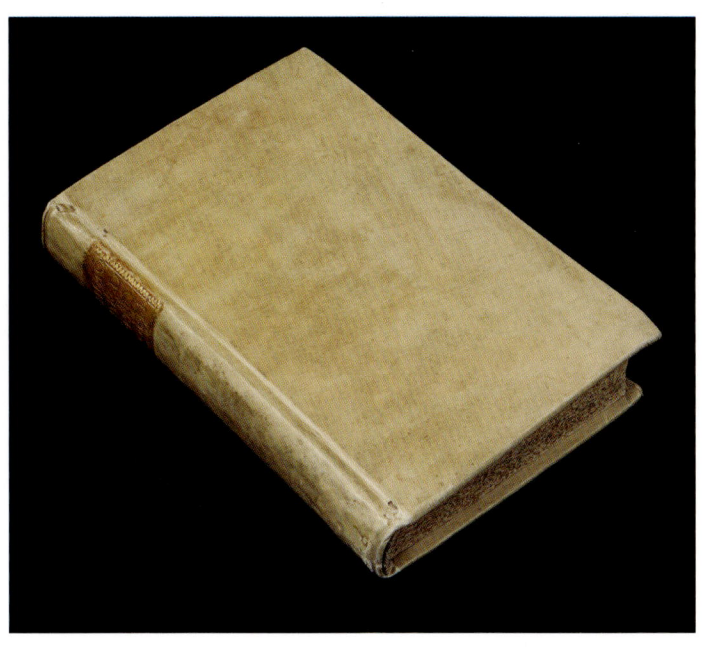

(left) Engraved title page, with elaborate vignette: *Il Paradiso Perduto . . . Dedicate Da Paolo Rolli*. Verona, 1730. First Italian edition of *PL*. (above) *Il Paradiso Perduto*, Verona, 1730, contemporary vellum binding. See #630.

John Shawcross shared with me that there is also a copy in the Huntington. Not in Coleridge; Not in Kohler.

631. MILTON'S PARADISE LOST. A New Edition, By Richard Bentley, D.D. *London: Printed for Jacob Tonson; and for John Poulson; and for J. Darby, A Bettesworth, and F. Clay, in Trust for Richard, James, and Bethel Wellington. MDCCXXXII.* First and only Bentley edition. 4to, [vii]+[ix]+399pp.+[17-page unpaginated index], half-title, two engraved portraits after Vertue (of Milton after Faithorne, and Milton age twenty-one, both very fine impressions), decorative center piece on title page, preface, arguments printed together at the beginning before Book I, notes at bottom of page, index, unlettered original calf (rubbed, joints slightly cracked), delicately blind-tooled border trim on each cover, raised bands, gilt dentelles. A fine copy with bookplate and signature of Sir John Trollope. Scarce. See Robert E. Bourdette, Jr., "'To Milton lending sense': Richard Bentley & *PL*," *Milton Quarterly* XIV, no. 2 (May 1980): 37–48; Michael M. Cohen and Robert E. Bourdette, Jr., "Richard Bentley's Edition of *PL* (1732): A Bibliography," *Milton Quarterly* XIV, no. 2 (May 1980): 49–54; Bartholomew & Clark, *Bentley*, 257; Coleridge 103; Shawcross, Kentucky, 205; Kohler 16.

An eccentric project by one of England's great classicists. Bentley proceeded "on the supposition that the blind poet had employed an amanuensis, who made numerous involuntary mistakes, and an editor, who not only did likewise, but also deliberately interpolated bad verses of his own" (DNB). A remarkable example of the application of classical scholarly principles to an English text. Bentley's annotations and emendations were also printed separately; they were variously critiqued, including by Edmond Miller (see copy with Eighteenth-century Miltoniana) and Zachary Pearce (see copy with Eighteenth-century Miltoniana). A reprint edition of Bentley's edition was published by Lubrecht & Cramer Ltd. in 1995 (also listed here).

631A. (Cross-listing) **PARADISE LOST, A POEM IN TWELVE BOOKS.** 1733–35. Folio, manuscript on paper, 282 pp. plus 7 pp. of significant additions (see listed here). Boughton near Chester, transcribed by Mrs. Katherine Howard between December 3, 1733, and May 17, 1735 (with additional notes dated August 22, 1753, and October 18–21, 1762), full contemporary paneled calf. Nice copy. This remarkable transcript of *PL* may be dismissed editorially, but it seems to be nonetheless the earliest complete manuscript of Milton's epic. A leisured lady, Katherine Howard (1672–1765) wrote out the whole of *PL* for her daughter. See main listing in this chapter.

632. PARADISE LOST. A Poem, In Twelve Books. The Author John Milton. The Fifteenth Edition. To which is prefix'd, An Account of his Life [by Fenton]. [Quotation from Homer] *Dublin: Printed by S. Powell in Crane-lane, For G. Risk, G. Ewing, and W. Smith, Booksellers in Dame's-street. MDCCXXXV.* 12mo, 365pp.+[18-page unpaginated

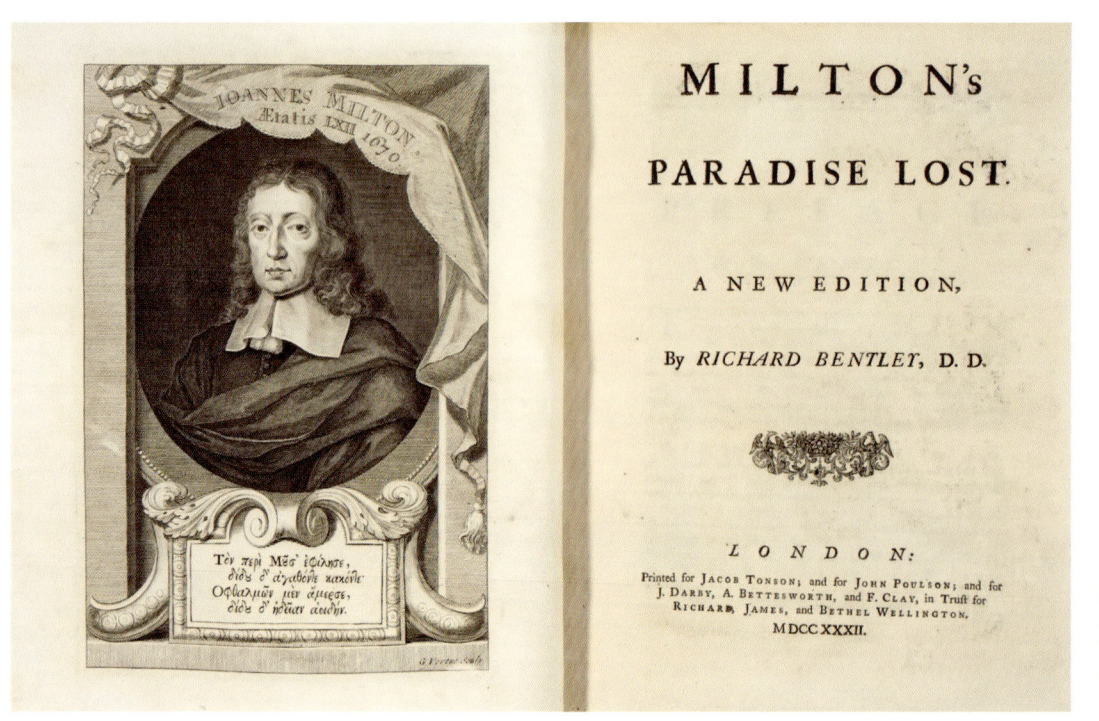

Engraved frontispiece and title page of *PL*. A New Edition By Richard Bentley. London, 1732. See #631.

index], engraved frontispiece illustration of Milton, Homer, and Virgil after "Phil Simms, Sculp" (loose, edges frayed, small tear at center), with Dryden's epigram, title page in red and black, additional illustrations (unsigned, crude recuttings of 1688 plates reduced), one for each book, half-title for each book, decorative headpiece and tailpieces, decorated initial letters, large decorative tailpiece at end of book, index, original calf (rubbed, endpapers lacking), orange label on spine, raised bands, with early (possibly contemporary) signature and inscription in a neat hand on verso of frontispiece. A nice copy. Rare. Not in Coleridge; Not in Kohler.

633. HET PARADYS VERLOOREN. Geschetst Na 'T Engelsch Heldendicht van John Milton, Door L. P. *Te Amsteldam, By Rudolf Brouwer, Boekverkooper bezyden de Beurs, over't Texelse Post Comptoir, A°. 1735.* 8vo, [xxiv]+416pp., title page in red, dedication page, "Voorbericht Aan Den Leezer," errata, life, a poem to Paludanus, decorated initial letters, original calf (a bit rubbed at joints and along edges), black morocco label on spine with gilt lettering and decorative gilt trim, raised bands, speckled edges. A fine copy. "Usually one comes across the 1730 edition of this translation [see preceding copy], or sometimes less frequently the 1742 reissue. Herman Scherpbier in his *Milton in Holland* remarks on the two editions of this work which apparently fall between the 1730 and 1742 editions, without giving dates and only referring to them as the 'second' and the 'third' editions. We have no record of this 1735 edition; we have not handled it in over 30 years; we find no bibliographical record for it and must assume that it is very rare indeed" (G. W. Stuart, Jr., Ravenstree, Cat. 178, #54, 1994). See the first Dutch translation by Jacobus van Zanten published in 1728 without the engraved title page; see also the 1730 edition above (the first edition of this Dutch translation in rhyming verses by the playwright Lambertus Paludanus [pseudonym of Lambertus van der Broek], the first Dutch rhymed edition, and the first Dutch edition to use the twelve-book form) with the engraved title page. Scarce. Not in Coleridge; Not in Kohler.

634. DEL PARADISO PERDUTO Poema Inglese Di Giovanni Milton Traduzzione Di Paolo Rolli Campagno Della Reale Societa In Londra L'Acclamato Nell'Accademia Degl'Intronati In Siena E Pastore Arcade In Roma. *Londra[:] Presso Carlo Bennet. M.DCC.XXXV.* First edition thus, first issue (of the full poem); second edition of this Italian translation of Books I–VI, and the first edition of this Italian translation of Books VII–XII. Folio, iv+[xxiv]+397+4pp., central device on title page, mezzotint portraits in sepia of Milton (as frontispiece); the dedicatee, Prince Friederich of Hanover (before the dedication); and the translator, Paolo Rolli (before Book I), after John Van der Gucht (first appearance of these portraits, very striking impressions), dedication and "Vita Di Giovanni Milton" before the poem, "Varie Lezzioni Et Emendazioni" at the end (for Books I–VI, as previously published in 1730, also listed here), decorative head- and tailpieces (some very elaborate) and decorated initial letters (variously decorated and some elaborate), original speckled calf (handsomely rebacked to match), spine lettered in gilt with a decorative device in gilt within each compartment, raised bands within gilt rules, red speckled edges. A fine copy of a very rare book with bookplates of the Milton Cottage Trust and an unidentified British peer. The publishing history of this translation began in 1729 with the publication of the first six books. Not until 1735 was the remainder of the work completed and published in the full twelve-book form with the inclusion of the engraved portraits (present edition). It subsequently was reissued the following year with the title dated 1736 (following copy). See 1730 Italian translation above published in Verona, the first Italian edition of *PL* printed in Italy. Coleridge 161b; Not in Kohler.

635. **DEL PARADISO PERDUTO** Poema Inglese Di Giovanni Milton Traduzzione Di Paolo Rolli Patrizio Tudertino Campagno Della Reale Societa In Londra Accademico Fiorentino L'Acclamato Nell'Accademia Degl'Intronati In Siena E Pastore Arcade In Roma. *Londra[:] Presso Carlo Bennet. M.DCC.XXXVI.* First edition thus, second issue (of the full poem); second edition of this Italian translation of Books I–VI, and the first edition of this Italian translation of Books VII–XII. Folio, iv+[xxiv]+397+4pp., central device on title page, mezzotint portraits in sepia of Milton, Rolli, and the dedicatee, Prince Friederich of Hanover, after John Van der Gucht (all three portraits bound at the beginning, very striking impressions), dedication and "Vita Di Giovanni Milton" before the poem, "Varie Lezzioni Et Emendazioni" at the end (for Books I–VI, as previously published in 1730, see copy above), decorative head- and tailpieces (some very elaborate) and decorated initial letters (variously decorated, some elaborate), original half calf, marbled paper over boards, gilt rules on covers, spine delicately tooled in gilt by compartments with gilt lettering, speckled edges. A very fine copy of a rare book with the bookplate of Leonard Schlosser. This is a reissue of the preceding edition, with a cancel title page. The publishing history of this translation is given in the copy. Coleridge 161c; Shawcross, Kentucky, 217; Not in Kohler.

636. **PARADISE LOST.** A Poem, In Twelve Books. The Author John Milton. The Fifteenth Edition. To which is prefix'd, An Account of his Life [by Fenton]. [Quotation from Homer] *London: Printed for J. and R. Tonson; and A. Ward, S. Birt, R. Chandler, J. Hutton, R. and B. Wellington, J. Brindley, J. Oswald, J. New. MDCCXXXVIII.* Small 8vo, xxviii+[x]+350pp.,+[45-page unpaginated index], engraved frontispiece illustration of Milton, Homer, and Virgil after Fourdrinier, with Dryden epigram, title page in red and black, copper-engraved illustrations (1688 plates reduced, unsigned), one for each book, life by Fenton followed by three-page postscript, half-title for each book, decorative head- and tailpieces, decorated initial letters, small decorative tailpiece at the end of the book, index, original calf (a bit rubbed, a little defective at head and foot of upper joint), gilt rules on spine (faded), red morocco label with gilt lettering and gilt rules, raised bands. A nice copy. Coleridge 104 (making no mention of the illustrations); Not in Kohler.

637. Variant of Preceding. **PARADISE LOST.** A Poem, In Twelve Books. The Author John Milton. The Fifteenth Edition. To which is prefix'd, An Account of his Life [by Fenton]. [Quotation from Homer] *London: Printed for J. and R. Tonson; and A. Ward, S. Birt, R. Chandler, J. Hutton, R. and B. Wellington, J. Brindley, J. Oswald, J. New. MDCCXXXVIII.* Small 8vo, xxviii+[x]+350pp.+[45-page unpaginated index]+144pp., engraved frontispiece illustration of Milton, Homer, and Virgil after Fourdrinier, with Dryden epigram, title page in red and black, unsigned copper-engraved illustrations (1688 plates reduced), one for each book, life by Fenton followed by three-page postscript, half-title for each book, decorative head- and tailpieces, decorated initial letters, small decorative tailpiece at end of book, index. Bound with **NOTES UPON THE TWELVE BOOKS OF PARADISE LOST.** Collected from the Spectator. Written by Mr. Addison. *London: Printed for J. and R. Tonson, at Shakespear's Head, over-against Catharine Street in the Strand. MDCCXXXVIII.* With separate title page, separate pagination (144 pp.), decorative head- and tailpieces, decorated initial letters, small decorative tailpiece at end of book. Original calf (a little rubbed, joints cracked, spine ends chipped), raised bands within gilt rules (faded). Nice copy, very fresh and clean within, with contemporary signature (dated 1742) on fly-leaf and several additional signatures or signature stamps on fly-leaf and front blank. "This is the first edition to list a substantial number of partners on the TP" (Coleridge). Coleridge 104 (making no mention of the illustrations; without Addison's Notes, referencing "some copies" having them with title page, as here); Not in Kohler.

638. **PARADISE LOST.** A Poem, In Twelve Books. John Milton, The Author. To which is prefix'd, An Account of his Life [by Fenton]. [Quotation from Homer] *London: Printed for a Company of Stationers. MDCCXXXIX.* 12mo in 6s, xvii+[vii]+317("307" misprinted as "730" and earlier "62" as "26")+[38-page unpaginated index]+143pp., engraved frontispiece illustration of Milton, Homer, and Virgil after Fourdrinier, with Dryden epigram, title page in red and black, double foldout frontispiece depicting Jacobus (James) Smith's rendering of the memorial of Milton in the Westminster Abbey Poet's Corner (the bust on the memorial was designed by H. Gravelot and executed by Michael Rysbrack), before life by Fenton, first appearance thus of engraved illustrations (after 1688 plates) by I. Lightbody, one for each book, decorative head- and tailpieces and decorated initial letters, index, Addison's *Notes*, with separate title page ("London, Printed for a Company of Stationers. n.d."), bound in at the end, contemporary mottled calf, gilt rules on covers, elaborately gilt-decorated spines, red morocco labels with gilt lettering and decorative gilt trim, outer dentelles tooled in blind. A lovely copy from the Kitley House Library with bastard armorial bookplate, fresh and clean throughout, with fine impressions of the plates and of the head- and tailpieces and decorated initial letters. Uniformly bound with *PR, London: Printed for J. & R. Tonson, R. Ware, J. Hodges, R. Wellington, R. Chandler, J. Brindley, R. Caldwell, and J. New. MDCCXLIII*, listed here. Generally reckoned to be a piracy by Robert Walker (details given in full by Coleridge). Companion volume with *PR, London: Printed for a Company of Stationers. MDCCXXXIX* (also listed here). Rare. Coleridge 105; Shawcross, Kentucky, 228; Not in Kohler.

639. IL PARADISO PERDUTO Poema Inglese Di Giovanni Milton Del quale non si erano publicati se non i primi sei Canti Tradotto in verso sciolto dal Signor Paolo Rolli Con la vita del Poeta e con le annotazioni sopra tutto il Poema Di G. Addison Aggiunte alcune Osservazioni critiche. *In Parigi [i.e., Verona/Venice]. MDCCXL. A spese di Giovanni Alberto Tumermani Librajo e Stampator Veronese. 2 volumes*. First edition thus. 12mo, [vi]+509+[8]pp.,+[v]+367pp., engraved title page each volume, each with central device, elaborate engraved decorative piece on first dedication page in each volume, first appearance of engraved frontispiece illustration (full-page, volume 1) and twelve additional engraved full-page illustrations by Zucchi, Tiepolo, and other Venetian artists, one for each book of *PL* (which occupies the whole of volume 1), each plate attributed, "Vita Di Giovanni Milton" with engraved headpiece portrait of a disheveled Milton by Zucchi in volume 2, followed by a translation of Addison's *Notes*, rather elaborate decorative head- and tailpieces in each volume with several decorated initial letters, contemporary speckled paper over thin boards, paper labels on spines lettered "Tomo I" and "Tomo II" in black ink in a neat contemporary hand, small bookplate in volume 1. A fine, tall set (possibly a large paper copy), well-preserved in original bindings, very fresh and clean internally, with extremely fine impressions of the plates. Not in Coleridge; Kohler 17, reporting "Not in the Bodleian Library. Not in Cambridge University Library."

Very rare and not as widely known as the 1742 folio edition (also listed here), which is sometimes referred to as being the first edition when it is actually the second, although the first folio edition with nine additional engraved illustrations for a total of twenty-two illustrations for *PL* (all but the frontispiece being head- and tailpiece illustrations); see also 1758 two-volume small 12mo edition listed here (a much smaller 12mo format than the present edition), bound as one volume with an engraved full-page portrait of a disheveled Milton by Antonio Baratti and with a reproduction of the same thirteen full-page engraved illustrations here, although unattributed; and see 1794 two-volume 12mo edition listed here (not as large as the present 12mo edition), with a reproduction of the same thirteen full-page engraved illustrations here, although unattributed, and with a reproduction of the full-page portrait of a disheveled Milton by Baratti in the 1758 two-volume small 12mo edition, although unattributed. John Shawcross shared the following with me: "Note that there was a 1744 edition of volume I followed by a 1757 edition of volume II; these lie behind the 1758 edition, which has two issues. volume I in 1744 and in 1758 have the same portrait and an illustration of inspiration from the Muses."

640. LE PARADIS PERDU DE MILTON. Poème Héroïque Traduit De L'Anglois. Avec les Remarques de M. Addisson. Nouvelle Edition. Augmentée du Paradis Reconquis, & de quelques autres Pièces de Poésie du même Auteur. *A La Haye, Chez M. G. Merville, Libraire. M.DCC.XL*. 3 parts in 2 volumes, with all three title pages. 12mo, 18+CII+328pp.,+233(misprinted "133")+170pp.,+308+[2]+154pp., title page each volume with a third title page for *Le Paradis Reconquis* ("Le Paradis Reconquis Traduit De L'Anglois De Milton. Avec Quelques Autres Pièces De Poésies. Nouvelle Edition. A La Haye, Chez M. G. Merville, Libraire. M.DCC.XL [1740]") in volume 2, decorative piece on each of the three title pages, Fenton's "Vie De Milton" (with separate pagination) and Addison's "Remarques" (with separate pagination) before *PL* in volume 1, "Le Paradis Reconquis De Milton" added at the end of volume 2 (with separate title page and separate pagination) and an "Argument" (not original to the poem) for each book, followed by *L, L'A, IlP*, and *NO* ("Su La Feste De Noël, Cantique de Milton"), with pagination continuing from *Le Paradis Reconquis* under the heading "Oeuvres De Milton," decorative headpiece trim and decorative tailpieces (some elaborate) throughout each volume, chipped at top and bottom, fly-leaf removed from second volume), spines decorated in gilt within the compartments, red morocco labels lettered in gilt with gilt rules. Good set. Milton's poems here are rendered into French prose: *PL* the prose translation by Nicholas Dupré de St. Maur, as revised by C. J. Chéron de Boismorand, first published in 1729 (see set listed here); the prose translation of *PR* and other poems by Père de Mareuil, first published in 1730 (also listed here); and the *Lettres critiques* by Bernard Routh. Rare. Not in Coleridge; Not in Kohler.

641. PARADISE LOST. A Poem, In Twelve Books. The Author John Milton. The Fourteenth Edition. To which is prefix'd An Account of his Life [by Fenton]. [Quotation from Homer] *London: Printed for J. and R. Tonson in the Strand. M DCC XLI.* 8vo, xxv+[xi]+514pp.+[34-page unpaginated index], engraved frontispiece illustration of Milton, Homer, and Virgil after Vertue, with Dryden epigram, title page in red and black, unsigned vignette portrait before life by Fenton, engraved illustrations (after 1688 plates) by Fourdrinier, one for each book, dedication, life by Fenton, postscript, index, rather elaborate decorative head- and tailpieces and decorated initial letters, contemporary calf (rebacked preserving original gilt-ruled and gilt-lettered red morocco labels), raised bands. A fine copy, very crisp and clean within. Large paper copy, printed on thick, high quality paper, with generous margins, and with splendid impressions of the plates. This is a "reset, line-for-line, reprint of the 1727 edition [see preceding copy]" (Coleridge). Uniformly bound with *PR*, 1742 (also listed here). Coleridge indicates that this edition "seems to have been issued uniform" with this edition of *PR*. Coleridge 106; Not in Williamson; Kohler 18, reporting "Not in Cambridge University Library."

642. JOHANNIS MILTONI PARADISUS AMISSUS, LATINE REDDITUS. Interprete Josepho Trapp, S.T.P. *Londoni: Typis J. Purser. Impensis L. Gilliver, sub Homeri capite, in Fleetstreet; J. Wood et C. Woodward, sub Columba, in Pater-noster-Row. MDCCXLI/MDCCXLIV. 2 volumes.* First edition. 4to (9" × 12"), [iv]+294+575pp. (continuous pagination in volume 2), decorative piece on title page, large decorative headpiece for the "Praefatio," decorated initial letter, smaller decorative tailpiece at end followed by "Errata" (with contemporary marginal notation in a neat hand in ink), large decorative headpiece at outset of each book, decorated initial letter, smaller decorative tailpiece at end of each book, "Errata" on last page of volume 2, contemporary calf (a little rubbed and worn, joints cracked, slight inoffensive waterstaining at the lower right margin of last few pages of volume 2), slight gilt rules on covers, spines elaborately decorated within the panels, red morocco lettering labels and black morocco numbering labels on spines, each label with decorative gilt trim, raised bands, new marbled endpapers. Nice set, handsomely printed on high quality paper. The translation into Latin is by Joseph Trap (1679–1747). This is one of seven early Latin translations of Milton's *PL*, of which the collection has five: (1) "J.C.," 1686, *Paradisus Amissa*, Book I—see preceding copy; (2) William Hogg, 1690, *Paraphrasis Poetica*—see preceding copy; (3) "T[homas]. P[ower].," 1691; (4) Charles Blake, 1694; (5) Michael Bold, 1702, *Paradisus Amissa*, Book I,—see preceding copy; (6) Joseph Trapp, 1741–44, *Paradisus Amissus*—edition here; and (7) William Dobson, 1750–53, *Paradisus Amissus*—see set listed here. Not in Coleridge; Shawcross, Kentucky, 238; Not in Kohler.

643. IL PARADISO PERDUTO Poema Inglese Di Giovanni Milton Del quale non si erano publicati se non i primi sei Canti Tradotto in verso sciolto dal Signor Paolo Rolli Con la vita del Poeta e con le annotazioni sopra tutto il Poema Di G. Addison Aggiunte alcune Osservazioni critiche. *In Parigi [possibly Verona/Venice]. MDCCXLII.* A spese di Giannalberto Tumermani Stamp. Veron. Con Licenza De' Superiori. Second edition thus; first folio edition. Folio, [vi]+143+96pp., engraved title page with elaborate central device, elaborate engraved headpiece on dedication page, first folio appearance of engraved frontispiece full-page illustrations and twenty-two additional engraved head- and tailpiece illustrations by Piazzetta, Zucchi, Balestra, Tiepolo, and other Venetian artists, one for each book of *PL* (head- and tailpiece illustrations for all but Books XI and XII—which have only headpiece illustrations), each plate signed, following the poem "Vita Di Giovanni Milton" with engraved headpiece portrait of a disheveled Milton after Zucchi, notes and Addison's observations, elaborate decorative head- and tailpieces with several decorated initial letters, printed in italics in double columns with decorative central divider running the full length of the columns, contemporary calf, covers elaborately tooled in blind with delicate gilt border roll, gilt-decorated spine with gilt floral devices, raised bands, marbled endpapers and edges, with the early bookplate of Saint-Yves d'Alveydre and a notation in ink (dated 1905) on verso of frontispiece. A splendid copy in a magnificent binding with superb impressions of the plates—nine of which are new with this edition. Particularly fine are the two engravings after original designs by Tiepolo, "The most brilliant and sought-after Italian painter of his period. His work sums up the splendours of Italian decorative painting" (Osborne). This edition is a typographical delight. It is printed on fine paper in Roman and Italic type. The elegant woodcut borders divide each page into two columns of text. See rare 1740 two-volume 12mo first edition thus, in which thirteen of the illustrations here and Zucchi's headpiece portrait of Milton first appeared; see also references to other editions cited there. John Shawcross shared with me: "I doubt that it was not published in Paris. Coleridge forgets that *PL* was under Interdict from the Papacy for all of Italy. On the other hand 'Parigi' may have been a ruse, of course, but there was a lot of publication in

Paris (as well as Amsterdam) to avoid confiscation of presses." Scarce, especially in such fine condition. Brunet III, 1731; Morazzoni 243 (and plates 142–43), discusses this book at some length; Lanckoronska 160 (and plate 45); Osborne, p. 1138; Not in Collins-Baker or in Pointon; Coleridge 162; Not in Kohler.

Engraved headpiece illustration after F. Zucchi of the Temptation of Eve, *Il Paradiso Perduto*, 1742. See #643.

Il Paradiso Perduto, Tradotto in verso sciolto Paolo Rolli. Paris, 1742. Folio, contemporary calf, covers elaborately tooled in blind, gilt-decorated spine. See #643.

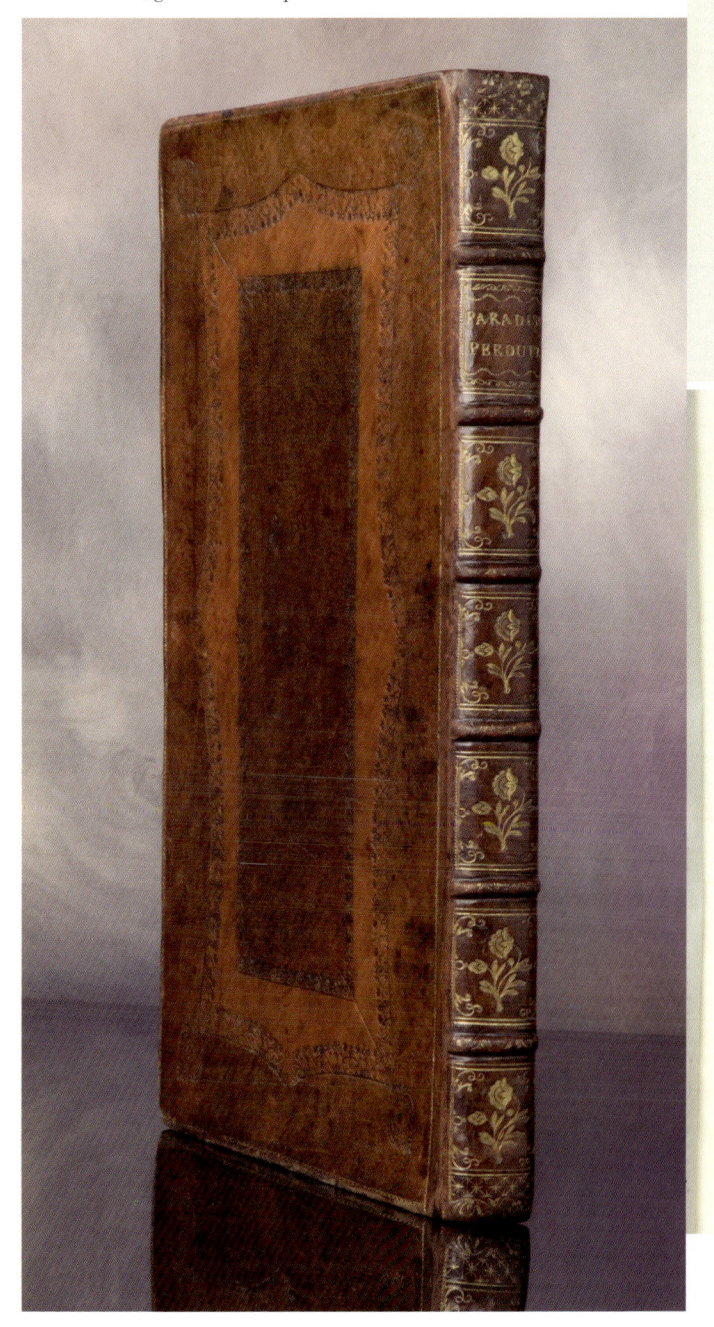

Engraved headpiece illustration of *The Expulsion*, engraved by F. Zucchi after Vitorio Bigeri, *Il Paradiso Perduto*, 1742. See #643.

644. LE PARADIS PERDU DE MILTON. Poème Héroïque, Traduit De L'Anglois. Avec les Remarques de M. Addisson. Nouvelle Edition; revue & corrigée. *A Paris, Chez Ganeau, rue Saint Jacques, vis-à-vis Saint Yves, à Saint Louis. M. DCC. XLIII. Avec Approbation & Privilège du Roy.* 3 volumes. 8vo, 24+cxlviii+[ii]+233pp.,+400pp.,+xvi+ 373+[3]pp., title page each volume with central decorative device on each title page, half-title, volume 3, Fenton's "Vie De Milton," Addison's "Remarques," "Avertissement" before *PL*, volume 1, volume 3 consisting of *PR*, with its own half-title and title page ("LE PARADIS RECONQUIS, Traduit De L'Anglois De Milton, Par le P. de Mareuil de la Compagnie de Jésus. Avec Six Lettres Critique Sur Le Paradis Perdu Et Reconquis. Par le P. R. de la Compagnie de Jésus. *A Paris, Chez Ganeau, rue Saint Jacques, vis-à-vis Saint Yves, à Saint Louis. M. DCC. XLIII*"), followed by "Preface" and "Arguments" (not original to the poem) for *Le Paradis Perdu Reconquis*, followed by *L* ("Lycidas, Idile de Milton"), *L'A, IIP*, and *NO* ("Sur La Feste De Noël") under the heading, "Oeuvres De Milton," followed by "A Vis Des Libraires Aux Lecteurs" and "Lettres Critiques Sur Le Paradis Perdu De Milton" with "Approbation" *Les Oeuvres de Milton*, dated "March 1730" and "Privilège Du Roy," dated "June 1730," on the last three pages of the volume, decorative head- and tailpieces (some elaborate), richly decorated initial letters, notes at bottom of the page, contemporary full red morocco, gilt rules on covers, richly gilt-decorated spines with gilt lettering, raised bands with decorative gilt trim, inner and outer dentelles finely tooled in gilt, marbled endpapers, a.e.g., red silk ribbon maker in each volume. Very fine set in a well-preserved contemporary French morocco binding. Milton's poems here are rendered into French prose: *PL* the prose translation by Nicholas Dupré de St. Maur, revised by C. J. Chéron de Boismorand, first published in 1729 (see set listed here); the prose translation of *PR* and other poems by Père de Mareuil, first published in 1730 (also listed here); and the *Lettres critiques* by Bernard Routh. Similar editions to the three-volume edition here were published in 1757 and 1758 (see sets listed here). Coleridge 178; Kohler 19, reporting "Not in Cambridge University Library."

645. PARADIS LOST. A Poem, In Twelve Books. The Author John Milton. A New Edition Corrected. To which is prefix'd An Account of his Life. *Printed in the Year M DCC XLIII.* 12mo in 6s, xxi+[viii]+344pp.+[36-page unpaginated index], "Advertisement Concerning This New Edition," dedication, life of Milton by Fenton, "postscript" and other prelimaries before *PL*, half-title for each book, index, original calf (a bit rubbed, some age-browning), delicately gilt-decorated spine in the panels, red morocco label with gilt lettering and gilt rules, raised bands, outer dentelles tooled in gilt, speckled edges. Very nice, with early signature and inscription. Scarce. Not in Coleridge; Not in Kohler.

646. [PARADIS LOST] THE STATE OF INNOCENCE: AND FALL OF MAN. DESCRIBED IN MILTON'S PARADIS LOST. Render'd into Prose. With Historical, Philosophical and Explanatory Notes. From the French of the Learned Raymond De St. Maur. By a Gentleman of Oxford. *London: Printed for T. Osborne, in Gray's-Inn, and J. Hildyard, at York. M D CCXLV.* First edition. 8vo, [ii]+436+[19]+[4]+[1 blank]+[7]pp., elaborate decorative head- and tailpieces, "Index" at the end, modern dark brown cloth with original calf covers and spine professionally laid over the cloth (uniformly age-tanned throughout), spine decorated in gilt within the panels with gilt lettering. A fine copy. Oras, pp. 173–96; Good, p. 181; Coleridge 254; Not in Kohler.

Discussion about the identity of the "Gentleman from Oxford" focuses on being either James Patterson or George Smith Green. Oras discusses the authorship at length and favors Patterson, concluding that Paterson reworked his "Complete Commentary," which had been published the year before (see copy with Eighteenth-century Miltoniana), into the "Historical, Philosophical and Explanatory Notes" here. Good more traditionally identifies the "Gentleman of Oxford" as George Smith Green. The very rare first edition of this version. The St. Maur edition referred to is the prose translation by Nicholas F. Dupré de Saint-Maur, first published in 1729 (also listed here).

647. PARADIS LOST. A Poem, In Twelve Books. The Author John Milton. *London: Printed for J. and R. Tonson and S. Draper, A. Ward, S. Birt, C. Hitch, B. Dod, J. Hutton, R. Wellington, J. Brindley, J. Oswald, and J. New. M DCC XLVI.* Thick 12mo, xxv+[xi]+378pp.,+[53-page unpaginated index], engraved frontispiece portrait after Faithorne, with Dryden epigram, volume 1, engraved illustrations (1688 plates further reduced, unsigned), one for each book, dedication with elaborate headpiece and decorated initial letter, life of Milton by Fenton with half-title printed between decorative trim, postscript and prelimaries before Book I in volume 1, index, volume 2, decorative head- and tailpieces (some very elaborate) and decorated initial letters (some very elaborate) throughout, contemporary calf (spine rubbed, joints cracked), gilt rules on covers (faded) raised bands. A good copy with early initials on fly-leaf. Coleridge 107a ("This issue not in WTu"); Williamson 62; Kohler 20, reporting "Not in ESTC. This is surely an error since the Bodleian holds a copy of this item. The ESTC lists a one volume 1747 instead. Not in the British Library. Not in Cambridge University Library."

This is the edition that was first published in 1746 in one volume. See commentary with 1746/1747 edition listed here, quoting Coleridge 107, which sorts out the bibliographical complexities of this edition, published in 1746 and again in 1747. John Shawcross shared the following with me about this edition: "One volume in 1746 (also Huntington copy); two volumes in 1746 and 1747 (also British Library copy); one volume in 1747 (reissue of one-volume edition in 1746; also Cambridge University Library); two volumes in 1747 (also University of Illinois)."

648. Variant, as preceding copy, except bound without the illustrations, contemporary diced calf (a bit worn, joints cracked, spine chipped), gilt rules on spine, new black morocco label with misleading title "Milton's Works," gilt dentelles. A nice copy with early signature on title page.

649. PARADISE LOST. A Poem, In Twelve Books. The Author John Milton. *London: Printed for J. and R. Tonson and S. Draper, A. Ward, S. Birt, C. Hitch, B. Dod, J. Hutton, R. Wellington, J. Brindley, J. Oswald, and J. New. M DCC XLVI.* 2 volumes. 12mo, xxv+[xi]+196pp.,+378pp.(continuous pagination from volume 1)+[53-page unpaginated index], engraved frontispiece portrait after Faithorne, with Dryden epigram, volume 1, engraved illustrations (1688 plates further reduced, unsigned), one for each book, dedication with elaborate headpiece and decorated initial letter, life of Milton by Fenton with half-title printed between decorative trim, postscript and preliminaries before Book I in volume 1, index, volume 2, decorative head- and tailpieces (some very elaborate) and decorated initial letters (some very elaborate) throughout, unlettered contemporary calf (a bit rubbed), raised bands, outer dentelles tooled in gilt (faded). A very nice set, clean and crisp within, with fine impressions of the plates and early (possibly contemporary) name in each volume. Uniformly bound with *PR* (imprint as here), MDCCXLVII, 2 volumes, listed here, with frontispiece illustration and decorative head- and tailpieces and decorated initial letters as here; a very nice set. Rare thus, together, as a set with *PR*. As John Shawcross indicated to me previously, a copy of this set is the British Library. See references cited with first issue of 1746 edition; additionally, see quotation from Coleridge with 1746/1747 edition following regarding the bibliographical complexities of the 1746 and 1747 editions and the endeavor to publish *PL* and *PR* in uniform 1747 issues. Coleridge 107a ("This issue not in WTu"); Kohler 21.

650. Variant of Preceding. **PARADISE LOST.** A Poem, In Twelve Books. The Author John Milton. *London: Printed for J. and R. Tonson and S. Draper, A. Ward, S. Birt, C. Hitch, B. Dod, J. Hutton, R. Wellington, J. Brindley, J. Oswald, and J. New. M DCC XLVI / M DCC XLVII.* 2 volumes. 12mo, xxv+[xi]+196pp.,+378pp.(continuous pagination from volume 1)+[53-page unpaginated index], as preceding copy (except for 1746/1747 title pages in volume 1 and 1747 title page in volume 2), engraved frontispiece portrait after Faithorne, with Dryden epigram, volume 1, with two title pages in volume 1, the first dated 1746 and the rare second title page, including "E. Wicksted" among the publishers, between "S, Birt" and "C, Hitch" (dated 1747), title page volume 2 also dated 1747 and including "E. Wicksted" among publishers, between ""S, Birt" and C, Hitch," as with second title page in volume 1, engraved illustrations (1688 plates further reduced, unsigned), one for each book, dedication with elaborate headpiece and decorated initial letter, life of Milton by Fenton with half-title printed between decorative trim, postscript and preliminaries before Book I in volume 1, index, volume 2, decorative head- and tailpieces (some very elaborate) and decorated initial letters (some very elaborate) throughout, contemporary calf (a bit rubbed, early names on preliminaries), gilt rules on covers, gilt rules on spines, red morocco labels with gilt lettering and gilt rules, raised bands. A neat set with two title pages in volume 1, one dated 1746 and the second dated 1747, and a separate title page in volume 2 dated 1747, the title pages dated 1747 each with near-contemporary presentation inscription, dated 1790, at the top. Coleridge 107a ("not in WTu"), 107b ("not in WTu"), and 107c; Not in Kohler.

According to Coleridge: "Both 1746 and 1747 are found in 1 volume and in 2 volumes. It would seem that the edition was first published in 1746 in 1 volume [see preceding copies]. Wicksted, who was named as a proprietor in the Chancery decision of 1739 [see 1739 edition of *PL*] was not included for some reason, but later that year he joined in and 2 new TP were printed, both introducing his name in the imprint. The first of these TP was probably the 1747 main TP, the other being the volume 2 TP. The divided volume, with the volume 2 TP, was probably on sale in 1746 but the division was intended to take effect in 1747, perhaps to provide a uniform issue with *PR* &c 1747." See John Shawcross's clarification cited with *PL*, 1746, regarding the publication of this edition in 1746 and 1747.

651. PARADISE LOST. A Poem, In Twelve Books. The Author John Milton. London: *Printed for* J. and R. Tonson *and* S. Draper, A. Ward, S. Birt, C. Hitch, B. Dod, J. Hutton, R. Wellington, J. Brindley, J. Oswald, *and* J. New. M DCC XLVII. 2 volumes. 12mo, xxv+[xi]+196pp., +378pp.(continuous pagination from volume 1)+[53-page unpaginated index], volume 2 title page as volume 1 (except for "Volume the Second" replacing "The Author John Milton"), engraved frontispiece portrait after Faithorne, with Dryden epigram, volume 1, engraved illustrations (1688 plates further reduced, unsigned), one for each book, dedication with elaborate headpiece and decorated initial letter, life of Milton by Fenton with half-title printed between decorative trim, postscript and preliminaries before Book I in volume 1, index at the end of volume 2, decorative head- and tailpieces (some very elaborate) and decorated initial letters (some very elaborate) throughout, contemporary calf (joints cracked, lettering labels gone from spines, name on endpaper, light wear, front fly-leaf gone from second volume), small decorative gilt piece within the panels on the spine, raised bands between gilt rules. A nice copy with fine impressions of the plates and with a title page in each volume dated 1747. See commentary from Coleridge 107 with preceding edition regarding the bibliographical complexities of the 1746 and 1747 editions, and also Shawcross's clarification with *PL*, 1746, about the publication of these editions. Rare ("we have had but once before," G. W. Stuart, Jr., Ravenstree, Cat. 182, #40, 1998). Coleridge 107c; Not in Kohler.

652. PARADISE LOST. A Poem In Twelve Books. The Author John Milton. Compared with the Authentic Editions, And Revised by John Hawkey, Editor of the Latin Classics. *Dublin: Printed by S. Powell, for the Editor, MDCCXLVII.* First Hawkey edition. Large 8vo, [1]+394+[6]pp., advertisement leaf, elaborate decorative headpiece for each book, six pages (unpaginated) of "The most remarkable Various Readings and Emendations," contemporary polished calf, finely tooled gilt-decorated spine, dentelles decorated in blind. A very attractive copy printed on large and thick paper with early bookplate. Hawkey's edition is praised for its textual accuracy. Bound uniformly with Hawkey edition of *PR*, Dublin: Printed by S. Powell, 1747, listed here, also praised for its textual accuracy. Scarce; Rarely found together, forming a very handsome set. Coleridge 108; Kohler 22.

653. LE PARADIS TERRESTRE, POEME IMITE' DE MILTON. Par Madame D. B. [Marie Ann DuBocage]*** Ouvrage enrichi de Figures en Taille-douce. *A Londres. M. DCC. XLVIII.* Tall 8vo, [1]+vi+121pp., engraved frontispiece illustration, "Pierre, Lu Del, Louise Le D. Sculp," vignette illustration after Durand on title page, headpiece illustrations, elaborate tailpiece devices, the head- and tailpieces are by Hubert Gravelot and Louise Le D.[oulceur] contemporary tree calf (rebacked), decorative gilt border trim on covers, gilt-ruled red morocco label on spine, raised bands, outer dentelles gilt-decorated (now very faint), marbled endpapers, bookplate. A very fine, possibly large paper copy. In a four-page introduction addressed to "Messieurs de l'Academie de Rouen," Madame DuBoccage explains her intentions in whittling down and making more accessible ("pour mon amusement") this "élégante" translation of Milton by M. Dupré de St. Maur. "J'ai voulu réduire en petit un grand & sublime tableau," she writes. The book contains the six "chants" of *Paradise Terrestre* in rhyming verse. It also includes DuBoccage's poem "A Milton" in French on p. 1. Several editions of this Miltonic imitation were published in 1748, and it is unclear which was the first. The second and third editions were published in 1754, and the fourth edition was published in 1755 (also listed here). DuBoccage's maiden name was "Friquet," and catalogue entries are sometimes found under this name. Scarce. Not in Coleridge; Not in Kohler; Shawcross, Kentucky, 262.

First Newton Variorum Edition of *Paradise Lost* with Rare Two-Leaf "Proposal For Printing By Subscription"

654. PARADISE LOST. A Poem, In Twelve Books. The Author John Milton. A New Edition, With Notes of various Authors, By Thomas Newton, D.D. *London: Printed for J. and R. Tonson and S. Draper in the Strand. M DCC XLIX.* 2 volumes, volume 2 reads simply: "London: Printed in the Year MDCCXLIX." First Newton edition; first variorum edition. Large 4to, [8]+[8]+lxi+[5]+16+[12]+459pp.,+444pp.+([132]-page unpaginated index and verbal index), engraved frontispiece portrait each volume, of Milton age sixty-two, first appearance of Vertue's version of Faithorne portrait with Greek verses beneath, volume 1, first appearance of Milton "Aetat. 21" by Vertue, volume 2, first appearance of engraved illustrations by Francis Hayman, engraved by S. F. Ravenet or C. Grignion (Books I, III, VII, and XII by Ravenet, the remainder by Grignion), title page each volume, dedication with elaborate decorative headpiece and decorated initial letter, dedication, preface, life of Milton, "A Critique upon the Paradise Lost. By Mr. Addison," "The List of the Subscribers," half-title for each book, notes at bottom of page, postscript, index, and verbal index at end of volume 2, rich contemporary calf binding over thick boards (some joints slightly cracked), covers ruled in gilt with Camperdon crest on front covers, intricately gilt-decorated spines, red morocco title labels, black morocco numbering labels, raised bands. A very handsome set with the bookplate of Leonard Schlosser. Laid in: the unusual and rare two-leaf "Proposal for Printing by Subscription" this work (in fine condition). Coleridge 110; Kohler 24.

PL, Book IX, engraved illustration after F. Hayman. *Eve Tempts Adam*, engraved by Grignion. See #654.

PL, Book XII, engraved illustration after F. Hayman. *The Expulsion*, S. F. Ravenet. See #654.

Hayman designed plates only for the 1749 edition. Hayman's designs were reworked by the engraver J. S. Müller and were variously reprinted thereafter into the nineteenth century. This is the first variorium to be published, and it became the standard text of the poems for the remainder of the century, continuing to be reprinted in various forms well into the nineteenth century. Uniformly bound with the first Newton *PR*, 1752, listed here, and with *The Works Of John Milton, Historical, Political, And Miscellaneous*, 1753, 2 volumes, the second Thomas Birch edition, listed here. Together, 5 volumes.

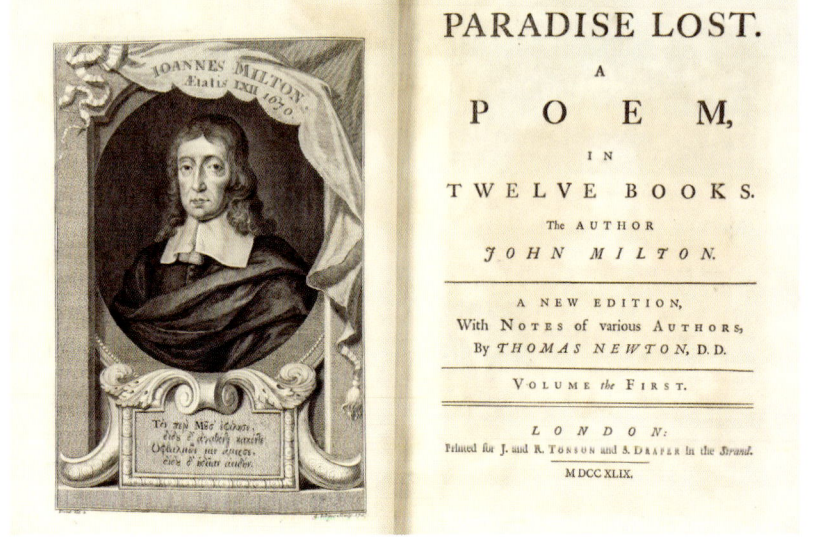

Engraved frontispiece portrait and title page of 1749 first Newton edition of *PL*. See #654.

655. LE PARADIS PERDU De Milton. Poème Héroïque. Traduit De L'Anglois. Avecles Remarques de M. Addisson. Tome Primier. *Paris, Chez Ganeau, rue S. Jacques, vis-à-vis S. Hyves, à S. Louis. M. DCC. XLIX. Avec Approbation & Privilège du Roi.* 12mo, cvi+283, small vignette illustration of the expulsion at the center of the title page, Fenton's "Vie de Milton," Addison's "Remarques," and "Avertissement" before *PL*, decorative head- and tailpieces, decorated initial letters, notes at bottom of page.

[together with]

656. LE PARADIS PERDU De Milton. Poème Héroïque. Traduit De L'Anglois. Avecles Remarques de M. Addisson. Tome Second. *A Paris, Chez Ganeau, rue S.*

Jacques, vis-à-vis S. Hyves, à S. Louis. M. DCC. XLIX. Avec Approbation & Privilège du Roi. Bound with **LE PARADIS RECONQUIS**, Traduit De L'Anglois, De Milton, Par le P. de Mareuil de la Compagnie de Jésus. Avec Six Lettres Critiques Sur Le Paradis Perdu Et Reconquis. Par le P. R. de la Compagnie de Jésus. *A Paris, Chez Ganeau, rue Saint Jacques, vis-à-vis Saint Yves, à Saint Louis. M. DCC. XLIX. Avec Approbation & Privilège du Roi.* 2 volumes in one. 12mo, 259pp.,+xii+229pp., same small vignette illustration of the expulsion at the center of volume 2 title page, separate title page volume 3 with small decorative piece at the center, "Avertissement," followed by "Preface" and "Arguments" (not original to the poem) for *Le Paradis Reconquis*, followed by *L* ("Lycidas, Idile de Milton"), *L'A, IlP*, and *NO* Aux Lecteurs" and "Lettres Critiques Sur Le Paradis Perdu De Milton," decorative head- and tailpieces, decorated initial letters, notes at bottom of page. 3 volumes bound in 2. Contemporary calf (a bit worn and scuffed, spine ends chipped volume 2, some age-browning, early name on back blanks, volume 2), spines richly decorated in gilt within the panels, maroon lettering and numbering labels in gilt, raised bands, marbled endpapers, red edges. Overall, a nice set. Milton's poems here are rendered into French prose: *PL* the prose translation by Nicholas Dupré de St. Maur, revised by C. J. Chéron de Boismorand, first published in 1729 (see set listed here); the prose translation of *PR* and other poems by Père de Mareuil, first published in 1730 (copy listed here); and the *Lettres critiques* by Bernard Routh. Scarce. Coleridge 179; Not in Kohler.

657. **PARADISE LOST**. A Poem, In Twelve Books. The Author John Milton. The Second [Newton] Edition. With Notes of various Authors, By Thomas Newton, D.D. *London: Printed for J. and R. Tonson and S. Draper, and for S. Birt, C. Hitch, J. Hodges, B. Dod, E. Wicksted, J. Oswald, J. Ward, J. Brindley, C. Corbet, and J. New. M DCC L.* 2 volumes, volume 2 has some changes in the list of names in the publisher list: "London: Printed for *J. and R. Tonson* and *S. Draper*; and for *S. Birt, T. Longman, C. Hitch, J. Hodges, B. Dod, E. Wicksted, J. Oswald, J. Ward, J. Brindley,* and *C. Corbet.* M DCC L. Second Newton variorum edition. 8vo, [10]+[11]+lxxxv+ [6]+[21]+510pp.,+456pp.+([218]-page unpaginated index and verbal index), engraved frontispiece portrait after Vertue, volume 1, engraved illustrations after Hayman (reduced), engraved for the first time by J. S. Müller, dedication, preface, life of Milton, Addison's "A Critique on the Paradise Lost," "The List of the Subscribers," volume 1, half-title for each book, notes at bottom of page, postscript, index, volume 2, decorative tailpieces, original calf (a bit rubbed, joints cracked), gilt-ruled red morocco labels with gilt lettering, raised bands, gilt dentelles (faded), uniformly bound, as volumes 1 and 2, with *PR*, 1753, listed here. A very good set with early signature on front blank. Included among the revisions and additions is a postscript discussing William Lauder, new to this edition. Also, Hayman designed plates only for the 1749 edition. Hayman's designs were reworked by the engraver J. S. Müller and were variously reprinted thereafter into the nineteenth century. In addition, Müller (ca. 1715–90) changed his name to John Miller after emigrating to England from Germany in 1744. Williamson 167; Coleridge 111; Kohler 25.

658. **PARADISE LOST**, A Poem, In Twelve Books. The Author John Milton. According To The Author's Last Edition, In The Year 1672 [sic!]. *Glasgow: Printed And Sold By R. & A. Foulis Printers To The University. M DCC L.* Second (possibly first) Foulis edition. 8vo, [xvi]+317+ [1]pp., complete with half-title and the rare advertisement leaf at the end, original calf, gilt-decorated spine, red morocco label with gilt lettering within gilt rules, raised bands. A fine copy with early armorial bookplate on verso of title page and advertisement leaf at end for "Books printed and sold by R. & A. Foulis." As with the 1667–69 issues of the first edition of *PL*, the arguments here are printed together before the poem rather than at the head of their respective books. See 1752 (third, possibly second) 12mo Foulis edition of *PL* listed here, where the incorrect date of "The Author's Last Edition, In The Year 1672" on title page here is corrected to 1674; see also 1761 and 1766 12mo Foulis editions of *PL* listed here, each two volumes in one, and each, as here, following the first edition of 1667–69 in printing the arguments together at the beginning of the poem; and see 1771 and 1776 12mo two-volume Foulis editions of *PL* listed here, without reference to "The Author's Last Edition" on title page, each edition, as here, printing the arguments together at the beginning of the poem, and each edition uniformly bound with a 1772 12mo two-volume Foulis edition of *PR, SA, and Poems.* According to Coleridge's commentary on this edition: "Robert Foulis seems to have first published *PL*, with other Milton poems, in 1747 (Gaskell 1964, No. 87 [p. 115], though he traced no copy). This 1750 edition is the 2nd from the Foulis press" (Coleridge 112, p. 154). John Shawcross shared the following with me: "As you know Gaskell is the only source for a first edition in 1747. There was an edition by the Foulises of *C, P, Of Ed, PR, SA* in 1747; it is a composite volume but they were not issued separately. Gaskell *assumes* that there must have been an edition of *PL* in the same year; and he may be right, but there is no known copy." As Coleridge observes about the 1771 12mo Foulis edition (also listed here): "Like the 1750 [8vo] Foulis edition this is one of a series of small reading editions published by the Foulis brothers" (Coleridge 133). Scarce. Gaskell, *Foulis*, 160; Coleridge 112; Not in Kohler.

659. PARADISUS AMISSUS. Poema Joannis Miltoni. Latine Redditum A Guilielmo Dobson, LL.B. *Oxonii, E Theatro Sheldoniano, MDCCL–MDCCLIII. 2 volumes.* First edition. 4to, [2]+304pp.,e+[1]+303pp., a profile forming a medallion vignette inscribed "Joannes Miltonus. Guls. Green Jun. delin. J. Wood sculp." appears on each title page, imprimatur on verso of volume 1 title page, volume 2 title page reading "Londini Typis Jacobi Bettenham. MDCCLIII (1753)," with the English text of *PL* appearing at the foot of each page, errata printed on verso of last page, volume 2, contemporary full crimson morocco (lower outer edges of front covers rather rubbed removing some of the surface), elaborately ornamental gilt border trim on covers, equally elaborately gilt-decorated spines, black morocco labels with gilt lettering and decorative gilt trim, raised bands, outer dentelles tooled in gilt, marbled endpapers, a.e.g. Handsome set, large paper copy with wide margins, handsomely printed, very clean and fresh throughout, with a fine provenance: The ownership inscription of Ballygarth Castle, County Meath, appears on the first page of the text of each volume, with further provenance note in the same hand on opposite page, "This copy was presented by the Revd. Edward Hales from the Library of his Father, author of Hale's chronology." William Hales (1747–1831) was incumbent of Killeshandra, County Cavan, 1788–1831. "This admirable translation was encouraged by Mr. Benson, who had erected in Westminster Abbey the monument to the poet" (Lowndes, p. 1560). This is one of seven early Latin translations of Milton's *PL*: (1) "J.C.," 1686, *Paradisus Amissa*, Book I—see preceding copy; (2) William Hogg, 1690, *Paraphrasis Poetica*—see preceding copy; (3) "T[homas]. P[ower].," 1691; (4) Charles Blake, 1694; (5) Michael Bold, 1702, *Paradisus Amissa*, Book I,—see preceding copy; (6) Joseph Trapp, 1741–44, *Paradisus Amissus*—see preceding copy; and (7) William Dobson, 1750–53, *Paradisus Amissus*—edition here. Williamson 147; Foxon D344–45; Coleridge 167; Shawcross, Kentucky, 275; Kohler 26.

660. PARADISE LOST. A Poem, In Twelve Books. The Author John Milton. *London: Printed for J. and R. Tonson and S. Draper; and for S. Birt, T. Longman, C. Hitch, J. Hodges, B. Dod, E. Wicksted, J. Oswald, J. Ward, J. Brindley, and C. Corbet. M DCC LI.* Large 12mo, xxviii+[10]+350pp.+[43-page unpaginated index], engraved frontispiece portrait after Vertue, engraved and printed title pages (printed title often lacking), engraved title closely resembling printed title but with different size type and different ordering of the names of the publishers ("London: *Printed for* J. & R. Tonson *and* S. Draper; T. Longman, S. Birt, E. Wicksted, C. Hitch, J. Hodges, B. Dodd, C. Corbet, J. Brindley, J. Oswald, *and* J. Ward. MDCCLI"), twelve illustration plates engraved by Miller after Hayman (reduced), life by Fenton, postscript, decorative head- and tailpieces, decorated initial letters, half-title for each book, index, contemporary speckled calf, gilt rules on covers, elaborately gilt-decorated spine with gilt lettering, outer dentelles finely tooled in gilt, marbled endpapers, red edges. A very nice copy, fresh and clean throughout, with fine impressions of the plates. Coleridge 113; Kohler 27, referencing Williamson 169, and reporting "Not in Cambridge University Library."

661. Variant of Preceding. PARADISE LOST . . . *M DCC LI.* Stout 12mo, xxviii+[10]+350pp.,+[43-page unpaginated index]+130pp., engraved frontispiece portrait after Vertue, engraved and printed title pages (engraved title often lacking), engraved title closely resembling printed title but with different size type and different ordering of the names of the publishers (see preceding copy), twelve illustration plates engraved by Miller after Hayman (reduced), life by Fenton, postscript, decorative head- and tailpieces, decorated initial letters, half-title for each book, index. Bound with **NOTES UPON THE**

Paradisus Amissus. Latine Redditum A Guilielmo Dobson. Oxonii, 1750–53. 2 volumes. First edition. 4to, contemporary full crimson morocco. See #659.

TWELVE BOOKS OF MILTON'S PARADISE LOST. Collected From The Spectator. Written By Mr. Addison. *London: Printed for a Company of Stationers*, with half-title. Contemporary polished calf (worn, front cover rehinged from inside, lacking last two blank leaves), gilt rules on covers, raised bands, early signatures on fly-leaf. Coleridge 113; Kohler 27.

662. MILTON'S PARADISE LOST. A Poem, In Twelve Books. With Notes, Etymological Critical, Classical, and Explanatory. Collected from Dr. *Bentley*; Dr. Pearce, the present Bishop of Bangor; *Richardson* and Son; *Addison*; *Patterson*; *Newton*, and other Authors; Intended as a Key to this Divine Poem; whereby Persons unacquainted with the Learned Languages, and Polite Literature, will be introduced into a familiar Acquaintance with the various Beauties and Excellencies of this Masterpiece of Heroic Poetry. Dedicated to the King. By John Marchant, Gent. Author of the Exposition of the Old and New Testament, &c. *London: Printed by R. Walker, in the birth Old Bailey.* M DCC LI. 2 volumes in one. First edition, first issue of both volumes. 12mo, 438pp.,+318pp.(for a total of 756pp., continuous pagination), separate title page for each volume, engraved frontispiece illustration of "The Three Poets" with Dryden's epigram, engraved by Lightbody, and engraved illustrations (1688 plates reduced, unsigned), one for each book and one folding plate of the Milton Memorial in Westminster Abbey, dedication to the King, preface, life of Milton by Fenton, postscript, decorative head- and tailpieces, notes at bottom of page, original sheep (a little worn, spine ends chipped, joints cracked, later front blank endpaper, some embrowning, light smudges, latter half wormed a bit in lower blank edge with worming barely touching the notes in several places as well as touching inner edge of the plates), raised bands, paper label on spine. The illustrations are a version of 1688 illustrations engraved by Lightbody. This edition is the subject of a lengthy discussion by Coleridge. "It is quite rare, and we have handled one other set in 25 years" (G. W. Stuart, Jr., Ravenstree, Cat. 156, #46, 1988). Coleridge 114a; Not in Kohler.

663. PARADISE LOST. A Poem, In Twelve Books. The Author John Milton. A New Edition, With Notes of various Authors, By Thomas Newton, D.D. *Dublin: Printed for John Exshaw, at the Bible on Cork-Hill, MDCCLI. 2 volumes.* First edition by John Exshaw in Dublin, and the first Dublin and first Irish edition of Newton's *PL*. 8vo, xlvi+[4]+22+[2]+[5]+[6]+372pp.,+474+18pp., unsigned engraved vignette portrait of Milton (age sixty-two, unsigned, somewhat after Faithorne) on each title page, engraved frontispiece portrait of Milton at age twenty-one with Dryden epigram engraved beneath inserted after the title page, volume 1, engraved vignette portrait from title page repeated in a larger form at the head of "The life of Milton," where attribution is given to T. Chambers, Addison's "Critique upon the Paradise Lost," "Names Of The Subscribers," dedication, preface, volume 1, half-title for each book, notes at bottom of page, index at end of volume 2, contemporary mottled calf (some joints cracked), gilt-decorated spines, red morocco lettering labels ("Milton's Poetical Works"), dark olive green numbering labels, raised bands, marbled endpapers, red edges. A fine set with early signature on each title page. Uniformly bound, as volumes 1 and 2, with *PR . . . Dublin: Exshaw, 1754*, 2 volumes (see set listed here), first edition by Exshaw in Dublin, and the first Dublin edition of Newton's *PR, &*, forming volumes 3 and 4 of a four-volume set of *Milton's PW* (so-labeled on spines); rare thus together. See rare variant following in which the order of the frontispiece portrait, dedication, life, Addison's critique, and preface in volume 1 differs from the order here. See 1773 Dublin edition of *PL* by Exshaw "Embellished With A Set of Engravings" listed here. Scarce. Not in Coleridge (although referred to in the entry for *PR* of 1754); Kohler 28 (without mention of the vignette portrait being repeated before life, reporting "Vignette on title pages" only, and "Not in Williamson. Not in the British Library. Not in the Bodleian Library").

664. Variant of the Preceding. PARADISE LOST . . . *Dublin: Printed for John Exshaw, at the Bible on Cork-Hill, MDCCLI. 2 volumes.* First edition by Exshaw in Dublin, and the first Dublin and first Irish edition of Newton's *Paradise Lost*. Unrecorded variant. 8vo, [2]+[5]+[6]+xlvi+[4]+22+[2]+372pp.,+474+18pp., unsigned engraved vignette portrait of Milton at age sixty-two (somewhat after Faithorne) on each title page, unsigned engraved frontispiece portrait of Milton at age twenty-one with the Dryden epigram engraved beneath, volume 1, dedication, preface, engraved vignette portrait from title page repeated in a larger form at the head of "The Life of Milton," where attribution is given to T. Chambers, Addison's "Critique upon the Paradise Lost," "Names Of The Subscribers," volume 1, half-title for each book, notes at bottom of page, index at end of volume 2, contemporary calf (minor wear, name on endpaper). A fine set of this unrecorded variant. The order in which the frontispiece portrait, dedication, life, Addison's critique, and preface appear in volume 1 differs from the order in the preceding set listed here. Besides these differences and more importantly, "This set of the rare first Irish publication of the famed Newton variorum is, we believe, unique in that the first volume has two different leaves signed A2. Both contain the opening leaf of the Dedicatory epistle to the Earl of Bath. One begins 'To The Right Honourable The Earl Of Bath' and occupies four lines preceding the text of the epistle; the other has the same wording but occupies only two lines prior to the text of the epistle. The leaf bearing the two-line heading reprints the text of the English printing, mentioning the copper plate illustrations. This leaf had to be canceled due to the fact that no illustrations ever appeared in this first Irish printing and we know of no other set that retains this leaf mentioning the non-existent illustrations. No bibliography records the existence of this leaf" (G. W. Stuart, Jr., Ravenstree, Cat. 181, #36, 1997). See comments by John Shawcross about the significance of this edition in *Milton Quarterly* 41, no. 1 (2007): 70. Not in Coleridge; Not in Kohler.

665. PARADISE LOST. A Poem, In Twelve Books. The Author John Milton. Adorned With Cuts. [Quotation from Homer] *Glasgow: Printed by Robert Urie, M DCC LII.* 8vo, 372pp.+[36-page unpaginated index], unsigned engraved frontispiece of Homer, Virgil, and Milton with Dryden epigram, first appearance thus of twelve engraved illustrations (reductions of 1688 plates) by R. Cooper, one for each book, life by Fenton, half-title for each book, index at the end, contemporary red speckled calf (a little rubbed, joints cracked, spine chipped at top and bottom), gilt rules on covers, elaborately gilt-decorated spine in the panels, red morocco label with gilt lettering within gilt rules, raised bands, marbled endpapers and edges, armorial bookplate. Nice copy. See small 12mo 1753 edition below "Printed by R. Urie" in "Glasgow" "For John Wood, Bookseller in Edinburgh" (a much smaller 12mo edition than the 8vo edition here), without any illustrations and without an index at the end. John Shawcross shared the following with me about this book: "The University of Western Ontario copy has a portrait from Faithorne by T. Phinn, sculp, with a legend around the oval and an illustration; below this is 'Vid. Lib. IX. Line 780 to 895.'" See one of the 1753 copies listed here, which has a frontispiece portrait like this. Scarce. Coleridge 115b; Kohler 29, reporting "Not in Williamson. Not in the British Library."

666. PARADISE LOST, A Poem In Twelve Books. The Author John Milton. According To The Author's Last Edition, In The Year 1674. *Glasgow, Printed And Sold By R. & A. Foulis Printers To The University.* M DCC LII. 2 volumes in one. Third (possibly second) Foulis edition. 12mo, [xii]+368pp.(179pp., volume 1)+[2]pp., half-title ("Paradise Lost"), volume 1, title page each volume, with the arguments printed together before the poem, original unlettered calf (sometime rebacked with original spine laid down, more recently provided with a kind of protective covering, slight embrowning, lacking endpapers), raised bands. Generally a very nice copy, complete with half-title, second title page, and the rare advertisement leaf at the end for "Books Printed and Sold by Robert & Andrew Foulis"; inscribed by Thomas Strafford in 1764 and subsequently Jane Strafford in 1812, with early signatures on half-title (recto and verso) and at top of first title page; with early inscription on verso of first title page; with notation at bottom of verso of "The Verse"; and with several early line identifications in a neat hand at the beginning of the poem. As with the 1667–69 printings of the first edition of *PL*, the arguments here are printed before the poem. Rare. Not in Coleridge; Not in Kohler.

See 1750 (possibly second, perhaps first) 8vo Foulis edition of *PL*, with the incorrect date of "The Author's Last Edition, In The Year 1672" on title page, corrected here to 1674, and commentary there; see also 1761 and 1766 12mo Foulis editions of *PL* listed here, each two volumes in one, and each, as here, printing the arguments together at the beginning of the poem; and see 1771 and 1776 12mo two-volume Foulis editions of *PL* listed here, without reference to "The Author's Last Edition" on title page, each edition, as here, printing the arguments together at the beginning of the poem, and each edition uniformly bound with a 1772 12mo two-volume Foulis edition of *PR, SA*, and *P*.

667. PARADISE LOST. A Poem, In Twelve Books. The Author John Milton. *London: Printed for J. and R. Tonson and S. Draper; And for S. Birt, T. Longman, C. Hitch, J. Hodges, B. Dod, E. Wicksted, J. Oswald, J. Ward, J. Brindley, and C. Corbet.* MDCCLIII. 12mo in 6s, xv+[8]+335pp., decorative device at center of title page, life of Milton, postscript, half-title for each book, contemporary calf (bit rubbed, joints weak), delicately gilt-decorated spine in the panels, red morocco label with gilt lettering and decorative gilt trim, outer dentelles gilt. Fine copy. See copy listed here with the rare frontispiece portrait for this edition. Coleridge notes that the text is Newton's version without his notes, apparently the only time this text was so published. Coleridge 116 (calling this 24mo); Kohler 30 (calling this "12mo in 6s"). John Shawcross shared with me that "Coleridge is wrong; it is 12mo in 6s (as Kohler has it)."

668. Variant of Preceding, contemporary calf (worn, joints cracked, lacking label on spine), gilt-decorated spine (faded), raised bands, gilt dentelles. A decent copy in a variant binding with early armorial bookplate on front pastedown, and contemporary signature on fly-leaf. Uniformly bound and issued with *PR*, 1753, listed here. While there is no general title page, the two volumes were designed to be issued together as the *PW*, although they were also issued separately. Coleridge cites the 1753 edition of *PR* as "the matching edition forming volume 2 of the Poetical works." Coleridge 116; Kohler 30.

669. Variant of Preceding, contemporary French marbled calf, spine richly decorated in gilt, raised bands with decorative gilt trim, gilt labels lettered in French, marbled endpapers and edges, light blue silk ribbon marker. A fine, thick, tall copy, possibly large paper, very fresh and clean throughout, paper very white with the appearance of being unread. Uniformly bound and issued with *PR*, 1753, listed here, the two volumes forming an edition of Milton's *PW*. Coleridge 116; Kohler 30.

670. Variant of Preceding. **PARADISE LOST**. A Poem, In Twelve Books. The Author John Milton. London: Printed for J. and R. Tonson and S. Draper; And for S. Birt, T. Longman, C. Hitch, J. Hodges, B. Dod, E. Wicksted, J. Oswald, J. Ward, J. Brindley, and C. Corbet. MDCCLIII. 12mo in 6s, xv+[8]+335pp., engraved frontispiece portrait (rather crudely done, with "GZ Sc 1756" printed beneath), decorative device at center of title page, life of Milton, postscript, half-title for each book, original French calf (somewhat aged, joints cracked, lacking label on spine), gilt-decorated spine with the panels, raised bands, marbled endpapers. Nice copy with the signature on front blank of "John Phillips, Sept 8, 175"[sic], with the rare frontispiece portrait, although the later date of 1756 beneath the portrait would seem to indicate that it was probably inserted, even though it appears to be an integral part of the edition. The frontispiece portrait, with "GZ Sc. 1756," appears in a 1754 illustrated edition of *PL* listed here, possibly an Irish or Scottish piracy with publisher's imprint: "London: Printed for T. Thompson, R. Damper, et al. MDCCLIV"; it also appears in an undated ca. 1756 illustrated edition of *PL* listed here "Printed for the Proprietors, and sold by all the Booksellers," n.d. and without place, by which the edition is dated. Coleridge 116 (calling this 24mo, not 12mo, and making no reference to a frontispiece portrait); Kohler 30 (correctly calling this "12mo in 6s," making no reference to a frontispiece portrait).

671. **PARADISE LOST**. A Poem, In Twelve Books. The Author John Milton. *Glasgow: Printed by R. Urie, For John Wood, Bookseller in Edinburgh, M DCC LIII*. 12mo, 351pp., "N.B. The text of this Poem is carefully compared with Dr. Newton's splendid edition in quarto" on verso of title page, contemporary calf (worn, front joint broken and front cover detached, spine chipped at top, library stamp on title page, age-browning), bookplate on front pastedown. See large 12mo 1752 edition "Printed by Robert Urie" in Glasgow (a much larger 12mo edition than the one here) with illustrations ("Adorned With Cuts"), without a statement about "Dr. Newton's splendid edition" on verso of title page, and with an index at the end. Rare. Not in Coleridge; Not in Kohler.

672. Variant of Preceding. **PARADISE LOST**. A Poem, In Twelve Books. The Author John Milton. *Glasgow: Printed by R. Urie, For John Wood, Bookseller in Edinburgh, M DCC LIII*. 12mo, 351pp., engraved frontispiece portrait from Faithorne by "T. Phinn, sculp," with a legend around the oval ("The Effigie of John Milton Author Of Paradise Lost"), and an illustration below this of Eve tempting Adam with "Vid. Lib. IX. Line 780 to 895," on verso of title page is "N.B. The text of this Poem . . . as preceding" contemporary calf (worn, front cover detached, spine chipped, back cover almost detached, age-browning, frontispiece edges chipped). While worn, this copy contains the rare frontispiece portrait of Milton with illustration. A copy of the 1752 edition "Printed by Robert Urie" and owned by the University of Western Ontario has this same frontispiece portrait, as told me by John Shawcross. Rare. Not in Coleridge; Not in Kohler.

673. **PARADISE LOST**. A Poem, In Twelve Books. The Author John Milton. *London: Printed for T. Thompson, R. Damper, L. Burch, H. Shorham, T. Clitch, B. Blossom, D. Lord, F. Fritchet, G. Townwold, J. Dwarf, J. Liblond, and W. Blanchard. M DCC LIV*. First edition thus? 12mo, [xiii]+328pp., engraved frontispiece portrait signed "GZ 1756," with Milton looking to his left, life by Fenton, first appearance thus of engraved illustrations (reduced 1688 plates) by T. Phinn and J. McLean, with some plates unsigned, one plate for each book, original calf (front cover rehinged from inside, lacking label), raised bands within gilt rules (faded) on spine. A good copy of a very rare edition with early signature on fly-leaf. Quite possibly an Irish or Scottish piracy. The frontispiece portrait with "GZ Sc. 1756" appears in a 1753 nonillustrated edition of *PL* listed here (probably inserted, although it appears to be an integral part of the edition); the frontispiece portrait also appears in an undated ca. 1756 illustrated edition of *PL* listed here "Printed for the Proprietors, and sold by all the Booksellers," n.d. and without place, by which this edition is dated. See the also very rare ca. 1761 and ca. 1765 editions listed here, each "Printed for J. Thomson and S. Dampier" (not "Damper" as here), each with plates as here, but each with different and variously identified frontispiece portraits: in ca. 1761, engraved frontispiece portrait by "A. Bell," with "Publish'd by Jo. Wood 1761" printed at the bottom, helping to date that edition, with Milton looking to his right, not his left, as here; in ca. 1765, engraved frontispiece portrait by "T. Phinn," "Published According to Act of Parliament," with Milton looking to his right, not his left, with a new title page printed in red and black. See comments by John Shawcross about the significance of this edition in *Milton Quarterly* 41, no. 1 (2007): 69–70. Scarce. Not in Coleridge; Not in Kohler.

674. MILTON'S PARADISE LOST, Or, The Fall Of Man: With Historical, Philosophical, Critical, And Explanatory Notes. From the Learned Raymond de St. Maur. Wherein The Technical Terms in the Arts and Sciences are explained; the original Signification of the Names of Men, Cities, Animals, &c. and from what Language derived, render'd easy and intelligible. Also The Mythological Fables of the Heathens, wherever referr'd to, historically related; difficult Passages cleared of their Obscurity; and the Whole reduced to the Standard of the English Idiom. In Twelve Books. Embellished with a great Number of Copper-Plates. *London: Printed for M. Cooper, Pater-noster-row; W. Reeve, Fleet-street; and C. Sympson, at the Bible-ware-house, Chancery-lane. MDCCLIV*. 8vo, 430+[18]pp., title page printed in red and black, twenty copper-engraved illustrations including frontispiece, with identifying biblical caption printed beneath each illustration, decorative head- and tailpieces, decorated initial letters, index, contemporary calf (newly rebacked), gilt rules on spine, red morocco label with gilt lettering, raised bands. A very nice, possibly large paper copy with contemporary dated signature. The plates are very striking and bear little relationship to the standard eighteenth-century illustrations for *PL*. Raymond de St. Maur's commentary originally appeared as *The State of Innocence and the Fall of Man* in 1745 (copy listed here). Another issue of this edition with a variant publisher was published in 1755 (copy listed here); the two-volume 1775 edition listed here with 1688 illustrations reduced and unsigned; and see the 1779 edition listed here with 1688 illustrations reduced by R. Cooper, an edition reprinted in 1784 (copy listed here); see, too, nonillustrated 1765 and 1770 editions listed here. Coleridge 255a; Not in Kohler.

675. PARADISE LOST. A Poem, In Twelve Books. The Author John Milton. The Third Edition, With Notes of various Authors, By Thomas Newton, D.D. *London: Printed for J. an*d *R. Tonson and S. Draper, S. Birt, T. Longman, C. Hitch, J. Hodges, B. Dod, E. Wicksted, J. Oswald, J. Ward, J. Brindley, and C. Corbet. M DCC LIV*. 2 volumes. Large 4to, [viii]+[viii]+lxix+[v]+[xvi]+491pp.,+460pp. +[116-page unpaginated index and verbal index], dedication with elaborate decorative headpiece and decorated initial letter, preface, life of Milton, "A Critique upon the Paradise Lost By Mr. Addison," title page each volume, half-title for each book, notes at bottom of page, one engraved illustration for Book VIII. See 1749 first Newton variorum edition of *PL*. Coleridge 117; Not in Kohler.

Together with **PARADISE REGAIN'D**. A Poem, In Four Books. To which is added **SAMSON AGONISTES**: And **POEMS UPON SEVERAL OCCASIONS**. The Author John Milton. A New Edition, With Notes of various Authors, By Thomas Newton, D.D. *London: Printed for J. and R. Tonson and S. Draper in the Strand. M DCC LII*. First Newton edition. Large 4to, [iv]+[ii]+690+[ii]pp., rebound without the portrait and the illustrations, preface, "The Table Of Contents," half-title for each book and for *SA*, *P*, *C*, and *Poemata*, notes at bottom of page, index. Coleridge 194; Shawcross, Kentucky, 285; Kohler 190.

Together, 3 volumes. Contemporary mottled calf (neatly rebacked preserving original gilt-ruled red morocco labels, corners neatly repaired, illustrations removed), decorative gilt border trim on covers, raised bands, marbled endpapers and edges. A very nice set, unfortunately with all but one of the illustrations removed.

676. PARADISE LOST, A Poem, In Twelve Books. The Last Edition. The Author John Milton. *at Paris, Printed for David, junior, Upon the Austins-friers-Key. M. DCC. LIV*. 2 volumes in one. First edition thus. 12mo, half-title each volume (full half-title, volume 1: "Paradise Lost, A Poem, In Twelve Books. The Last Edition." half-title, volume 2: "Paradise Lost. Tome Second."), xxv+[xi]+294pp.,+[2]+96pp.,+[64-page unpaginated index), dedication page, life of Milton by Fenton, Books I–IX, volume 1, "A Glossary" followed by the remaining three books of *PL*, volume 2, with an index at the end of volume 2, decorative head- and tailpieces in each volume, contemporary mottled calf (a bit rubbed, tiny nick at top edge of front cover), spine decorated in gilt within the panels, red morocco label lettered and ruled in gilt, raised bands, marbled endpapers, red edges. A nice copy of this attractive edition, with early owner's signature neatly written on half-title; also in the same neat early hand: quotation from Thomson praising Milton on verso of half-title, the poem's lines marked every five lines, and a correction to line 600 of Book IV (correcting "Silence accompagoy'd" to "Silence accompanied"). John Shawcross shared with me that "This is a French piracy by Ganeau"; it is identical to the edition listed here ("at Paris, Printed for Ganeau"), except for the publisher's imprint on title page and the poem, index, and glossary bound in natural order. Rare. Not in Coleridge; Not in Kohler.

677. PARADISE LOST. A Poem, In Twelve Books. The Last Edition. The Author John Milton. at Paris, *Printed for Durand, in Hay-street. M. DCC. LIV*. 2 volumes in one. First edition thus. 8vo in 4s and 8s, xxv+[xi]+294pp.,

+[2]+96pp.+[64-page unpaginated index), half-title each volume, dedication page, life of Milton by Fenton, with half-title, Books I–IX of *PL*, volume 1, Books X–XII followed by index, volume 2, decorative head- and tailpieces, contemporary calf (a little rubbed, front joint cracked, small piece missing at top of spine), spine decorated in gilt with small decorative gilt pieces, red leather label with gilt lettering and decorative gilt trim, marbled endpapers, red edges. Nice copy, fresh and clean throughout. Rare. Not in Coleridge; Not in Kohler.

678. PARADISE LOST. A Poem, In Twelve Books. The Last Edition. The Author John Milton. *at Paris, Printed for Ganeau, in Saint-Severin street. M. DCC. LIV.* 2 volumes in one. First edition thus. 8vo, xxv+[11]+294pp.,+[2]+96+[64]+76pp., half-title each volume (full half-title, volume 1: "Paradise Lost, A Poem, In Twelve Books. The Last Edition," half-title, volume 2: "Paradise Lost. Tome Second"), dedication page, life of Milton by Fenton, Books I–IX of *PL*, volume 1, Books X–XII followed by a sixty-four-page unpaginated index and a seventy-six-page "Glossary," volume 2, decorative head- and tailpieces in each volume, contemporary half calf, marbled paper over boards (a little worn, spine chipped at top and bottom, corners and edges worn), black leather label on spine with gilt lettering and decorative gilt trim, raised bands within gilt rules, lightly speckled edges. Good copy. With the exception of the publisher's imprint on title page and the poem, index, and glossary bound in natural order here, this edition is identical to the earlier edition ("at Paris, Printed for David, junior"), which John Shawcross told me "is a French piracy by Ganeau." Rare. Not in Coleridge; Not in Kohler.

679. JOHANN MILTONS VERLOHRNES PARADIES. Ein Episches Gedicht in zwolf Gesangen. Neu uberarbeitet, und durchgehends mit Anmerkungen von dem Uebersezer und verschiednen andern Verfassern. Erster/ZweiterBand, und vor diesem die critische Geschichte des Gedichtes. *Zurich, verlegts Conrad Orell und Compagnie, 1754.* 2 volumes in one. Thick 8vo, 304pp.,+312pp., title page each volume with decorated initial letters on each title page, decorative headpieces and decorated initial letters, contemporary three-quarter calf, marbled paper over boards (a bit worn, spine slightly cracked near the top and reglued, spine also a little chipped at the top), maroon morocco label with gilt lettering and gilt rules on spine, raised bands within decorative gilt trim, red edges. A nice copy with early (possibly contemporary) notations in ink in a very neat hand on back blank. The translation is by Johann Jakob Bodmer; Bodmer's translation into German was first published in 1732; and it provoked a considerable critical controversy (see Shawcross, 1972, p. 6; p. 424 for the 1732 edition). According to Coleridge, "Bodmer's translation was the second to be published in German, and the third to have been undertaken as far as is known. The first to appear was the 1682 version by Von Berge . . . which was apparently inspired by a translation by Theodor Haak (one of Milton's acquaintances) which remained in manuscript, incomplete" (Coleridge 159, re 1742 *PL* German translation). Scarce. Not in Coleridge; Not in Kohler.

680. PARADISE LOST. A Poem, In Twelve Books. The Author John Milton. The Fourth [Newton] Edition, With Notes of various Authors, By Thomas Newton, D.D. *London: Printed for J. and R. Tonson and S. Draper, and for S. Birt, M and T. Longman, C. Hitch, J. Hodges, B. Dod, E. Wicksted, J. Ward, J. Brindley, E. Dilly, and C. Corbet. M DCC LV.* 2 volumes. Volume 2 title page reads: **PARADISE LOST**. The Sixth [Newton] Edition . . . *London: Printed for J. and R. Tonson, B. Dodd, H. Woodfall, J. Rivington, R. Baldwin, T. Longman, L. Hawes, Clark and Collins, E. Dilly, T. Caslon, C. Corbet, T. Lownds, and Executors of J. Richardson. MDCCLXIII.* 8vo, [x]+[xi]+lxxxv+[vi]+[xxi]+510pp.,+463pp.+[185-page unpaginated index]+[1]pp., unsigned engraved frontispiece portrait, engraved illustrations after Hayman (reduced), half-title for each book, decorative tailpieces, notes at bottom of page, advertisement leaf of "Just Published A New Edition" of "The Poetical Works of John Milton" at the end of volume 2, contemporary calf (rebacked), spines lettered and numbered in gilt, black morocco labels, raised bands. Very nice set with a few marginal notations in pencil in a neat early hand throughout, with early signature on fly-leaf. Rare. Volume 1—Not in Coleridge; volume 2—Coleridge 125; Not in Kohler.

681. MILTON'S PARADISE LOST, Or, The Fall Of Man: With Historical, Philosophical, Critical, And Explanatory Notes. From the Learned Raymond de St. Maur. Wherein The Technical Terms in the Arts and Sciences are explained; the original Signification of the Names of Men, Cities, Animals, &c. and from what Language derived, render'd easy and intelligible. Also The Mythological Fables of the Heathens, wherever referr'd to, historically related; difficult Passages cleared of their Obscurity; and the Whole reduced to the Standard of the *English* Idiom. In Twelve Books. Embellished with a great Number of Copper-Plates. *London: Printed for H. Owen, White-Fryars, Fleet-street; and C. Sympson, at the Bible-ware-house, Chancery-lane. MDCCLV.* 8vo, 430+[18]pp., title page printed in red and black, twenty copper-engraved illustrations including frontispiece, with identifying biblical caption printed beneath each illustration, decorative head- and tailpieces, decorated initial letters, index, contemporary sheep (worn, leather gone from back cover, signature 3B mixed, lacking blank endpapers, spine cracked, ends chipped, joints cracked). All in all, an okay copy of a rare book with early date (1799) and signature on front pastedown. Rare. Coleridge 255b (with a discussion of the evolution of this text); Not in Kohler.

Raymond de St. Maur's commentary originally appeared as *The State of Innocence and the Fall of Man* in 1745 (also listed here). The present edition is another issue of the 1754 edition (also listed here), with changes on the title page, as Coleridge points out, "rendered easy" to "render'd easy" and a change in publisher's address from "London: Printed for M. Cooper, etc." to the one here, with the same striking plates which bear little relationship to the standard eighteenth-century illustrations for *PL*; see also two-volume 1775 edition listed here with 1688 illustrations reduced and unsigned, and see two-volume 1779 edition listed here with 1688 illustrations reduced and attributed to R. Cooper, this edition reprinted in 1784 (also listed here); see, too, nonillustrated 1765 and 1770 editions listed here.

Inscribed by the Translator Louis Racine

682. LE PARADIS PERDU DE MILTON. Traduction Nouvelle, Avec des Notes, la Vie de l'Auteur, un Discours sur son Poème, les Remarques d'Addisson; & à l'occasion de ces Remarques, un Discours sur le Poème Epique. Par M. Racine. *A Paris, Chez Desaint & Saillant, Libraires, rue S. Jean de Beauvais. M DCC LV. Avec Approbation Et Privilège Du Roy*. 3 volumes. First edition of this translation by Louis Racine. Small 8vo, cviii+450pp.,+456pp.,+233[i.e., 555]+[5]pp., title pages with elaborate central emblems for each volume, half-title before Book I of *PL*, volume 1, decorative head- and tailpieces and decorated initial letters, "Avertissement" leaf with moderate tailpiece, nineteen-page "Table Des Principales Matieres" (paginated as part of volume 3), two pages of "Errata" for each volume (unpaginated), and the "Approbation" and "Privilège Du Roi" (unpaginated) on the last three pages of the volume, contemporary polished calf (embrowning at the beginning and ending of each volume, spine slightly chipped at top of volumes 1 and 3), spines elaborately decorated in gilt within the compartments with a bee motif, red morocco lettering labels, green morocco numbering labels, outer dentelles ruled in gilt, marbled endpapers and edges, green silk ribbon marker in each volume. A charming set of Louis Racine's translation of *PL*, inscribed by the translator Racine to M. Abbeille on the title page of volume 1 (signature and inscription cropped) and bound in an attractive contemporary bee binding, "reliure à l'abeille." Louis Racine, the translator, was the son of Jean Racine, the famed dramatist (d. 1699). This is a different printing from the following set with small differences on the title pages, differences in printing and pagination, very different decorated initial letters and decorative head- and tailpieces, and major differences in volume 3, which does not include *PR* and several poems in prose translation, but in their place a "Table Des Principales Matieres," "Errata" for each volume, and the "Approbation" and "Privilège Du Roi." Rare. Coleridge 157; Kohler 31, reporting "Not in the Bodleian Library. Not in Cambridge University Library."

683. LE PARADIS PERDU DE MILTON. Traduction Nouvelle, Avec des Notes, la Vie de l'Auteur, un Discours sur son Poème, les Remarques d'Addisson[sic]; & à l'occasion de ces Remarques, un Discours sur le Poème Epique. Par M. Racine. *A Paris, Chez Desaint & Saillant, Libraires, rue St. Jean de Beauvais. M. DCC. LV. Avec Approbation Et Privilège Du Roi*. 3 volumes. First edition of this translation (by Racine) with variants. Small 8vo, lxxxiii+[1]+354pp.,+427pp.,+308+[2]+154pp.(124pp. for *PR*, pp. 125–35 for *L*, pp. 136–41 for *L'A*, pp. 142–50 for *IlP*, pp. 151–54 for *NO*), title page each volume with central emblem, half-title before Book I of *PL*, volume 1, Addison's "Remarques," with half-title followed by "Avertissement," "Avertissement" leaf with elaborate tailpiece before half-title for "Le Paradis Reconquis De Milton," with separate pagination and "Preface" and "Arguments" (not original to the poem) for *Le Paradis Perdu Reconquis*, followed by *L* ("Lycidas, Idile de Milton"), *L'A*, *IlP*, and *NO* ("Sur La Feste De Noël") under the heading, "Oeuvres De Milton," volume 3, decorative head- and tailpieces, decorated initial letters, notes at bottom of page, rebound in modern red buckram (first page of volume 2 torn away from verso of title page affecting bottom portion of text), spines lettered in gilt with gilt rules at top and bottom, new endpapers. A good set with penciled note on fly-leaf of volume 1: "dated 1754, '55 by BM." This is a different printing from the preceding set, with differences noted there. All early translations of Milton are scarce, but this set seems particularly rare. John Shawcross shared with me that "This edition is definitely unique: I have never seen a copy of the Racine in those signatures or paginations, nor one with *PR* and the short poems attached. I have made the appropriate changes/additions in my bibliography for both items." Not in Coleridge; Not in Kohler.

684. LE PARADIS TERRESTRE, POEME IMITE DE MILTON, Par Madame D. B. [Marie Ann DuBocage]***. Augmenté & corrigé par l'Auteur, & enrichi de Figures en taille-douce. *A Londres. M. DCC. LV.* Fourth edition. 8vo, vi+[ii]+122pp., engraved frontispiece portrait, "On l'admire au Parnasse, On l'adore à Cythere," vignette illustration after Durand on title page, engraved headpiece illustrations, tailpiece devices, decorated initial letters, later marbled wrappers, uncut throughout. The illustrations are by Tardieu after Loir. A scarce "Londres" printing of Madame du Bocage's popular imitation of Milton's *PL*, first published in 1748 (also listed here); two editions (the second and third) were published in 1754. DuBoccage's maiden name was "Friquet," and catalogue entries are sometimes found under this name. ESTC No. 023095 lists 4 copies only (Rice University, the National Library of Scotland, and Brotherton); Not in Coleridge; Not in Kohler.

685. PARADISE LOST. A Poem, In Twelve Books. The Author John Milton. *[?London:] Printed for the Proprietors, and sold by all the Booksellers, n.d. (ca. 1756).* 8vo, [vi]+[xiv]+[2]+370pp., engraved frontispiece portrait, signed "GZ Sc. 1756," "N.B. The text of this poem is carefully compared with Dr. Newton's splendid edition in quarto" is printed on verso of title page, twelve engraved illustrations (reduced copies of the 1688 designs, unsigned, surprisingly fresh), unlettered contemporary calf (front joint cracked, spine worn), raised bands, speckled edges, early signature on verso of frontispiece. A good copy. An unusual edition, dated from the engraved frontispiece portrait, as in the Turnbull copy cited by Coleridge. The frontispiece portrait, with "GZ Sc. 1756," appears in a 1753 nonillustrated edition of *PL* (probably inserted, although it appears to be an integral part of the edition); it also appears in a 1754 illustrated edition of *PL*, possibly an Irish or Scottish piracy with publisher's imprint: "London: Printed for T. Thompson, R. Damper, et al. MDCCLIV." Scarce. Coleridge 119; Kohler 32, referencing Williamson 170, and reporting "Not in Cambridge University Library."

686. PARADISE LOST. A Poem, In Twelve Books. The Author John Milton. The Fourth [Newton] Edition, With Notes of various Authors, By Thomas Newton, D.D. *London: Printed for C. Hitch and L. Hawes, J. Hodges, J. and R. Tonson, B. Dod, E. Wicksted, J. Ward, M and T. Longman, J. Richardson, J. Brindley, A. and C. Corbet, and E. Dilly. MDCCLVII. 2 volumes.* 8vo, [x]+[xi]+lxxxv+[vi]+[xxi]+510pp., 463pp.+[185-page unpaginated index and verbal index]+[1]pp., unsigned engraved frontispiece portrait, engraved illustrations after Hayman (reduced), half-title for each book, decorative tailpieces, notes at bottom of page, original calf (spine chipped at top, volume 2), gilt rules and central gilt arms on covers, gilt-decorated spine, red morocco labels with gilt lettering and decorative gilt trim, raised bands with decorative gilt trim (now faded), advertisement leaf of "Just Published A New Edition" of "The Poetical Works of John Milton," bookseller's ticket inside front cover, dated early signature on verso of portrait. A fine set with gilt stamp of Anglesey Arms and wax seal on front pastedown, volume 1. This is the first edition in which the Tonsons are not listed first among the publishing booksellers. Coleridge suggests this may be because of a recent change in the membership of the group that held the Milton copyright. Coleridge 120; Williamson 167; Kohler 33 reporting "Not in Cambridge University Library."

687. LE PARADIS PERDU De Milton, Poëme Héroïque, Traduit De L'Anglais; Avec les Remarques de M. Addisson. Nouvelle Edition, revue & corrigée. *A Paris, Chez Ganeau, rue S. Jacques, vis-à-vis Saint Yves, à S. Louis. M. DCC. LVII. Avec Approbation & Privilège Du Roi. 3 volumes.* 12mo, 24+cxlviii+233pp.,+400pp.,+xvi+373+[3]pp., title page each volume with central emblem on each title page, Fenton's "Vie De Milton," Addison's "Remarques," "Avertissement" before *PL*, volume 1, "Preface" and "Arguments" (not original to the poem) for *Le Paradis Reconquis*, followed by *L* ("Lycidas, Idile de Milton"), *L'A*, *IlP*, and *NO* ("Sur La Feste De Noël") under the heading, "Oeuvres De Milton," followed by "A Vis Des Libraires Aux Lecteurs" and "Lettres Critiques Sur Le Paradis Perdu De Milton" with "Approbation" *Les Oeuvres de Milton*, dated "March 1730" and "Privilège Du Roy," dated "June 1730," on the last three pages of the volume, volume 3 (with its own half-title and title page—"LE PARADIS RECONQUIS, Traduit De L'Anglais De Milton, Par le P. de Mareuil de la Compagnie de Jésus. Avec Six Lettres Critique Sur Le Paradis Perdu Et Reconquis. Par le P. R. de la Compagnie de Jésus. *A Paris, Chez Ganeau, rue Saint Jacques, vis-à-vis Saint Yves, à Saint Louis. M. DCC. XVII. Avec Approbation & Privilège du Roi.*"), decorative head- and tailpieces (some elaborate), richly decorated initial letters, notes at bottom of page, contemporary speckled French sheepskin (a bit scuffed along joints), red morocco labels with gilt lettering and gilt rules on spines, elaborate decorative trim within the panels, raised bands with decorative gilt trim, marbled endpapers, red edges. Nice set. Milton's poems here are rendered into French prose: *PL* the prose translation by Nicholas Dupré de St. Maur, revised by C. J. Chéron de Boismorand, first published in 1729 (see set listed here); the prose translation of *PR* and other poems by Père de Mareuil, first published in 1730 (also listed here); and the *Lettres critiques* by Bernard

Routh. Similar to the edition published in 1743 (see three-volume set preceding) and also in 1758 (see three-volume set listed here). Scarce. Not in Coleridge; Not in Kohler; Copy in Illinois.

688. IL PARADISO PERDUTO Poema Inglese Di Giovanni Milton Tradotto Dal Sig. Paolo Rolli Con le annotazioni Di G. Addison E alcune Osservazioni critiche. *In Parigi [i.e., Verona/Venice], MDCCLVIII. A spese di Bartolommeo Occhi. Librajo Veneto.* 2 volumes in one. Small, thick 12mo, 228pp., two title pages, each with elaborate decorative devices at center, full-page portrait of a disheveled Milton after Antonio Baratti after dedicatory remarks (dated 1730 and signed by Rolli) and before life, engraved frontispiece illustration and twelve additional engraved full-page illustrations after Piazzetta, Zucchi, Balestra, Tiepolo, and other Venetian artists, one for each book of *PL*, although the illustrations here are unsigned, separate title page for Addison's *Notes*, also dated MDCCLVIII, decorative head- and tailpieces with several decorated initial letters, contemporary full vellum (lower corner, volume 2, p. 205, torn with slight loss of text), red morocco label on spine with gilt lettering and gilt trim, speckled edges. Very nice copy with early signatures in Italian. Scarce. Not in Coleridge; Williamson 145; Kohler 35, reporting "Not in Cambridge University Library."

See 1740 two-volume 12mo edition (first thus—in a much larger 12mo format than the present edition) and 1742 folio edition (first folio, second thus, with nine additional engraved illustrations)—both listed here; see also the 1794 two-volume 12mo edition listed here (in a slightly larger 12mo format than the present edition), with, as here, the full-page portrait of a disheveled Milton by Baratti (although unsigned) and the same illustrations from the 1740 12mo first edition, as here, unsigned. The full-page portrait by Baratti does not appear in either the 1740 12mo edition or the 1742 folio edition, which have instead a headpiece illustration of a disheveled Milton by Zucchi. John Shawcross shared with me "that there was a 1744 edition of volume I followed by a 1757 edition of volume II; these lie behind the 1758 edition, which has two issues. Volume I in 1744 and in 1758 have the same portrait and an illustration of inspiration from the Muses."

689. LE PARADIS PERDU De Milton. Poème Héroïque. Traduit De L'Anglais. Avec les Remarques de M. Addisson. Nouvelle Edition, revue & corrigée. *A Paris, Chez Ganeau, rue Saint Jacques, vis-à-vis Saint Yves, à Saint Louis. M. DCC. LVIII. Avec Approbation & Privilège Du Roy.* 2 volumes. 12mo, 12+345pp.,+358+[1 blank]+vii+118pp., title page each volume with central emblem on each title page, Fenton's "Vie De Milton," Adison's "Remarques," "Avertissement" before *PL*, volume 1, at the end of volume 2 is *PR*, with separate title page ("**LE PARADIS RECONQUIS**, Traduit De L'Anglais, De Milton, Par le P. de Mareuil de la Compagnie de Jésus. *A Paris, Chez Ganeau, rue Saint Jacques, vis-a-vis Saint Yves, à Saint Louis. M. DCC. LVIII*") and separate pagination, with "Preface" and "Arguments" (not original to the poem), decorative head- and tailpieces, decorated initial letters, notes at bottom of the page, contemporary speckled French calf (a bit scuffed, age-browning, p. 3 of Addison's critique, volume 1, repaired without affecting any text), finely tooled gilt-decorated spines within the panels, gold labels decorated in gilt with lettering and numbers in gilt, raised bands with decorative gilt trim, red edges. Nice set with early signature on title pages. *PL* was rendered into French prose by Nicholas Dupré de St. Maur, revised by C. J. Chéron de Boismorand, first published in 1729 (see set listed here). *PR* was also rendered into French prose by P. de Mareuil, first published in 1730 (also listed here). Coleridge 176 (referring to *PR*, in volume 3, bound here at the end of volume 2); Not in Kohler.

690. LE PARADIS PERDU De Milton. Poème Héroïque, Traduit De L'Anglois. Avec les Remarques de M. Addisson. Nouvelle Edition, revue & corrigée. *A Paris, Chez Ganeau, rue Saint Jacques, vis-à-vis Saint Yves, à Saint Louis. M. DCC. LVIII. Avec Approbation & Privilège du Roi.* 3 volumes. (volume 3 dated 1857). 12mo, 12+345pp.,+358+vii+118pp.,+xvi+373+[3]pp., title page each volume with central emblem on each title page, half-title, volume 3, Fenton's "Vie De Milton," Addison's "Remarques," "Avertissement" before *PL*, volume 1, "Preface" and "Arguments" (not original to the poem) for *Le Paradis Reconquis* at the end of volume 2, volume 3 is dated 1757 (as in 1757 set listed here) with its own half-title and title page (see preceding 1757 title page), consisting of "Preface," *PR*, followed by *L*, *L'A*, *IlP*, and *NO* under the heading, "Oeuvres De Milton," and contents identified above, decorative head- and tailpieces (some elaborate), richly decorated initial letters, notes at bottom of page, contemporary speckled French calf (a bit rubbed, spine bottoms of volumes 1 and 3 slightly chipped, pages occasionally a little age-browned), spines elaborately decorated in gilt within the panels, red morocco labels lettered in gilt with decorative gilt trim, outer dentelles decorated in gilt trim, marbled endpapers, red edges. An attractive set in a fine French binding of the period, lacking 1858 volume 3, with an 1857 edition of volume 3 bound in its place. Milton's poems here are rendered into French prose: *PL* the prose translation by Nicholas Dupré de St. Maur, revised by C. J. Chéron de Boismorand, first published in 1729 (see set listed here); the prose translation of *PR* and other poems by Père de Mareuil, first published in 1730 (copy listed here); and the *Lettres critiques* by Bernard Routh. A similar edition to the edition here was published in 1743 (see three-volume set listed here) and also in 1757 (see three-volume set listed here). Scarce. Coleridge 176; Not in Kohler; Copy in Illinois.

1758 Octavo Baskerville Edition in Contemporary Morocco

691. PARADISE LOST. A Poem, In Twelve Books. The Author John Milton. From The Text Of Thomas Newton D.D. *Birmingham[:] Printed by John Baskerville for J. and R. Tonson in London. MDCCLVIII.* First Baskerville edition. 8vo, [iii]+[xviii]+lxix+416pp., preface, "Subscribers Names" (with Benj. Franklin listed among the subscribers), life of Milton (bound after half-title and preliminaries for *PL*), half-title for each book.

[together with]

692. PARADISE REGAIN'D. A Poem, In Four Books. To which is added SAMSON AGONISTES: And POEMS UPON SEVERAL OCCASIONS. The Author John Milton. From the Text of Thomas Newton, D.D. Birmingham: *Printed by John Baskerville For J. and R. Tonson in London. MDCCLVIII.* First Baskerville edition. 8vo, 390pp. half-title for each book of *PR* and for various of the poems. Together, 2 volumes. Contemporary full dark blue morocco (rebacked preserving original spines), decorative gilt border trim on covers, gilt-decorated spines, red morocco labels, raised bands, inner and outer dentelles tooled in gilt, marbled endpapers and edges, bookplate. A very nice set. The third product of the Baskerville Press, and one of its most attractive. Gaskell, *Baskerville*, 4a and 5a; Coleridge 121a, 201a; Kohler 34 and 196.

1758 Quarto Baskerville Edition in Contemporary Morocco

693. Variant of Preceding. PARADISE LOST . . . *Birmingham[:] Printed by John Baskerville for J. and R. Tonson in London. MDCCLVIII.* First Baskerville edition. 4to, [iii]+[xviii]+lxix+416pp., preface, "Subscribers Names" (with Benj. Franklin listed among the subscribers), half-title for each book.

[together with]

694. Variant of Preceding. PARADISE REGAIN'D . . . SAMSON AGONISTES: AND POEMS UPON SEVERAL OCCASIONS . . . *Birmingham: Printed by John Baskerville For J. and R. Tonson in London. MDCCLVIII.* First Baskerville edition. 4to, 390pp., life of Milton (bound here in volume 2, not 1), half-title for each book of *PR* and for various of the poems. Together, 2 volumes. The rare quarto issue, complete with the 1734 Richardson engraving of Milton bust (a blind Milton with laurel wreath, not always present, here a very fine impression) before title page, volume 2, the life of Milton (also not found in all copies), and "Subscriber's Names," contemporary full dark green morocco (a bit rubbed), gilt rules on covers, elaborately gilt-decorated spines in the panels, red morocco labels with gilt lettering and gilt rules, raised bands with decorative gilt trim (now faded), inner dentelles richly tooled in gilt, outer dentelles ruled in gilt, marbled endpapers, a.e.g., bookplate each volume. A very fine set. Rare. Gaskell, *Baskerville*, 4a, 5a; Coleridge 121a, 201a; Kohler 34, 196.

Extra-Illustrated with Two Original Watercolor Drawings by Francis Hayman

695. Variant of Preceding. PARADISE LOST . . . *Birmingham[:] Printed by John Baskerville for J. and R. Tonson in London. MDCCLVIII.* First Baskerville edition. 8vo, [iii]+[xviii]+lxix+416pp., preface, "Subscribers Names" (with Benj. Franklin listed among the subscribers), life of Milton, half-title for each book.

[together with]

696. Variant of Preceding. PARADISE REGAIN'D . . . SAMSON AGONISTES: AND POEMS UPON SEVERAL OCCASIONS . . . *Birmingham: Printed by John Baskerville For J. and R. Tonson in London. MDCCLVIII.* First Baskerville edition. 8vo, 390pp. half-title for each book of *PR* and for various of the poems. Together, 2 volumes. Full pebble blue morocco by Charles Lewis with triple gilt fillet borders (a bit rubbed along joints), gilt ruled spine bands, spines lettered in gilt, inner and outer dentelles ruled in gilt, marbled endpapers, t.e.g. Housed in a quarter blue morocco solander case by the Lakeside Press, spines lettered and numbered in gilt, raised bands with decorative gilt trim. A very impressive set, entirely uncut. Near fine. Not an illustrated edition, and illustrated only by virtue of illustrations added later. Gaskell, *Baskerville*, 4a, 5a; Coleridge 121a, 201a; Kohler 34, 196.

Following the original list of subscribers is a mounted autograph receipt for this publication made out to Charles Townsend and signed by the bookseller James Dodsley (Dodsley's autograph is apparently quite rare).

Extra-illustrated with (1) two original full-page watercolor paintings of Milton themes from Book I of *PL* by Francis Hayman, 1708–76: *Satan Rousing His Peers* and

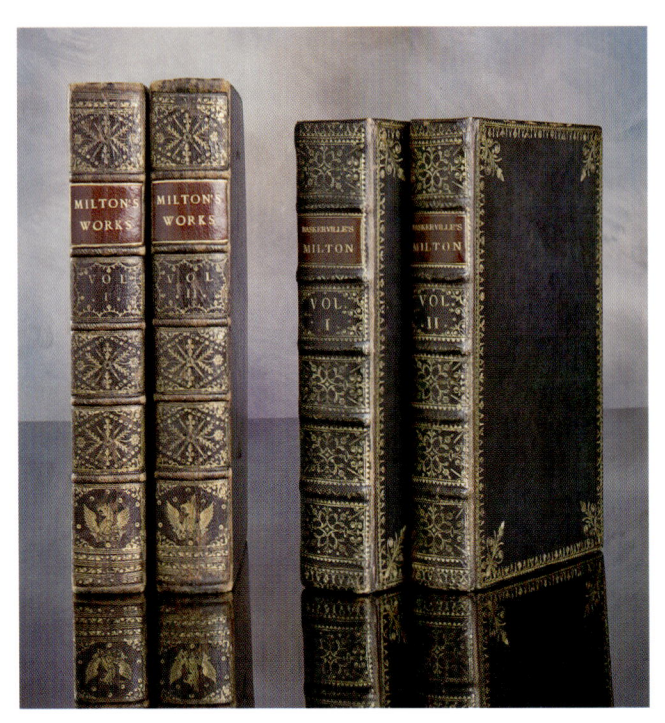

On right: 1758 first 8vo Baskerville edition of *PL* and *PR* in contemporary dark blue morocco; on left: rare 1758 first 4to Baskerville edition of *PL* and *PR*, with 1734 Richardson engraving of Milton bust, in contemporary dark green morocco. See #691, 692, 693, and 694.

1759 second Baskerville edition of *PL* and *PR*, small 4to edition, in mid-nineteenth-century claret calf binding, with distinctive provenance, from the Library of Chatsworth. See #698.

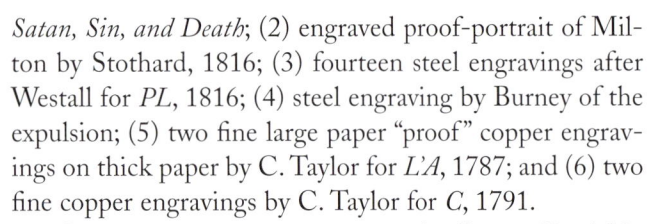

Satan, Sin, and Death; (2) engraved proof-portrait of Milton by Stothard, 1816; (3) fourteen steel engravings after Westall for *PL*, 1816; (4) steel engraving by Burney of the expulsion; (5) two fine large paper "proof" copper engravings on thick paper by C. Taylor for *L'A*, 1787; and (6) two fine copper engravings by C. Taylor for *C*, 1791.

Contemporary manuscript notes by George Daniel in 1835 explain how he put this splendid collection together. Later pencil note: "Bought by Dr. Addington at the Daniel Sale in 1864." Bookplate of George A. Armour, noted American book collector, on front pastedown of volume 1. Gilt inscription on box reads: "Ernest H. Wilkins [President of Oberlin]. Presented by Oberlin College Alumni Association of Chicago, March 7, 1946."

❧

697. **PARADISE LOST**. A Poem, In Twelve Books. The Author John Milton. From The Text Of Thomas Newton D.D. *Birmingham[:] Printed by John Baskerville for J. and R. Tonson in London. MDCCLIX*. Second Baskerville Milton. Small 4to, [v]+416pp., frontispiece portrait engraved by J. Miller, life of Milton (bound after half-title and preliminaries for *PL*), half-title for each book.

[together with]

698. **PARADISE REGAIN'D**. A Poem, In Four Books. To which is added **SAMSON AGONISTES**: And **POEMS UPON SEVERAL OCCASIONS**. The Author John Milton. From the Text of Thomas Newton, D.D. *Birmingham: Printed by John Baskerville For J. and R. Tonson in London. MDCCLIX*. Second Baskerville Milton. Small 4to, 390pp., "Table of Contents," title page in the first state, with "PSON" of "SAMPSON" erased and "SON" overprinted, half-title for each book of *PR* and for various of the poems. Together, 2 volumes. Mid-nineteenth-century claret calf (a few small scratches), covers finely tooled in gilt with border rules with small corner pieces and inner scrolled trim with decorative gilt pieces at the corners, richly gilt-decorated spines, raised bands with decorative gilt trim, inner and outer dentelles intricately tooled in gilt, marbled endpapers, a.e.g., bound by Birdsall, Northampton. A very handsome set from the Library of Chatsworth with a fine provenance identified by the inscriptions on preliminaries of each volume: "To my darling Child. Easter Day. Althorp 1856"; and beneath this inscription in volume 1 is a further explanatory inscription: "Sarah Spencer. This book was given to me by my dear devoted Governess H. J. Dunnett." Lady Sarah Spencer, the daughter of Frederick, Fourth Earl Spencer, was born in 1838. Gaskell, *Baskerville*, 6 and 7: "There are usually no plates [in *PL*], but occasionally a frontispiece [portrait, as here, is] . . . found." "Largest paper edition of Baskerville's Milton. The edition of 1759 was the second that Baskerville printed, but the only one to be issued wholly in quarto format. . . . [with] portrait in volume 1, described by Gaskell as 'occasionally found,' although invariably so in our experience" (Howe's, Cat. 240, #188, 1988). As John Shawcross reminded me about this set: "there are many cancels and thus various issues." Coleridge 122, 202; Kohler 36, 197, reporting "Not in the Bodleian Library. Not in Cambridge University Library."

699. JOHANN MILTONS VERLOHRNES PARADIES. Ein Episches Gedicht in zwolf Gesangen. Vierte verbesserte Auflage. *Zürich, ben Conrad und Comp. 1759.* 2 volumes in one ("2 Bande cplt. in 1 Bd."). First edition thus? 8vo, 336pp.,+319pp., title page for each volume, each title page with large decorated initial letter, decorative headpieces for several of the books, occasional modest tailpieces, original brown calf (a bit rubbed, labels on spine chipped, early name removed from top of front blank), spine elaborately gilt decorated within the panels, red and black morocco labels each with gilt lettering and gilt rules, raised bands, marbled endpapers and edges. Very nice copy of this German translation in prose. Rare. Not in Coleridge; Not in Kohler.

700. PARADISE LOST. A Poem, In Twelve Books. The Author John Milton. *London: Printed for C. Hitch and L. Hawes, J. and R. Tonson, B. Dod, J. Rivington, J. Ward, J. Richardson, S. Crowder and Co. T. Longman, E. Dilly, and A. and C. Corbet. MDCCLX.* 8vo, lxii+[ii]+350pp.+[44-page unpaginated index], frontispiece portrait engraved by J. Miller (not always present, with the lyre and laurel leaves and not Adam and Eve), twelve illustrations engraved by Miller after Hayman (reduced), life by Fenton, index, original calf (rebacked, slight embrowning), gilt rule on covers (faded), gilt rules on spine, black morocco label with gilt lettering, raised bands. Nice copy with contemporary signature (dated 1764) in attractive large script in ink on fly-leaf. Coleridge remarks that the frontispiece is frequently lacking and that "page x is sometimes blank" (printed in full in here). Uncommon. Coleridge 124; Kohler 37, referencing Williamson 147, and reporting "Not in the Bodleian Library."

701. DAS VERLOHRNE PARADIES, aus dem Englischen Johann Miltons in Reimfrene Berse ubersetzt, und mit eignen sowohl als andrer Anmerkungen begleitet von Friedrich Wilhelm Zacharia. Erster Theil. Mit Kupfern. *Altona, bey David Iversen, Konigl. privil. Buchh. in Holstein, 1760.* First edition thus. Together with **DAS VERLOHRNE PARADIES**, aus dem Englischen Johann Miltons in Reimfrene Berse ubersetzt, und mit eignen sowohl als andrer Anmerkungen begleitet von Friedrich Wilhelm Zacharia. Mit Kupfern. Zweyter Theil. Unter Konigl. Pohln. u. Churfl. Gachs. Privilegio. *Altona, bey David Iversen, Konigl. privil. Buchh. in Holstein, 1763.* First edition thus. 4to, [x]+266pp.,+[iv]+248pp., separate title page each volume, first appearance thus of engraved illustrations after Hayman engraved by Fritzsch (many plates unsigned), elaborately decorated head- and tailpieces, half-title for each book, notes at bottom of page, contemporary mottled calf, elaborately gilt-decorated spine in the panels, red morocco label with gilt lettering and gilt rules, raised bands, marbled endpapers and edges, bookplate of Leonard Schlosser. A fine copy with plates that are strikingly fresh and clean. A second edition of volume 1 was published in 1762 (also listed here). The translation is by F. W. Zacharia, the third publication in German, the second in verse. Von Berge's 1682 publication was the first, then the prose version by Bodmer in 1732, followed by this verse translation by Zacharia. Rare. Coleridge 160a and 160b; Not in Kohler.

702. PARADISE LOST. A Poem, In Twelve Books. The Author John Milton. From The Text Of Thomas Newton D.D. *Birmingham: Printed by John Baskerville, for J. and R. Tonson in London. MDCCLX.* Third and final Baskerville Milton. Large 8vo, [xix]+[v]+416pp., "Subscriber's Names," half-title for each book.

[together with]

703. PARADISE REGAIN'D. A Poem, In Four Books. To which is added **SAMSON AGONISTES**: And **POEMS UPON SEVERAL OCCASIONS**. The Author John Milton. From the Text of Thomas Newton, D.D. *Birmingham: Printed by John Baskerville For J. and R. Tonson in London. MDCCLX.* Third and final Baskerville Milton. Large 8vo, [ii]+lxii+390pp., half-title for each book of *PR* and for various of the poems. Together, 2 volumes. Contemporary tree calf (both volumes rebacked, preserving original spines, cor1ners repaired), decorative gilt border trim on covers, elaborately gilt-decorated spines, black morocco labels with gilt lettering and decorative gilt trim, inner and outer dentelles finely tooled in gilt, marbled endpapers. A nice set. Gaskell, *Baskerville*, 9, 10; Coleridge 123, 203; Kohler 38, 198.

704. PARADISE LOST, A Poem, In Twelve Books. The Author John Milton. According To The Author's Last Edition, In The Year 1674. *Glasgow: Printed And Sold By R. & A. Foulis Printers To The University[.] M.DCC.LXI.* 2 volumes in one. 12mo, [xii]+352+[4]pp., a second title page (volume II) before Book VII, contemporary calf (a bit worn, spine cracked with a small piece missing at bottom left, early ownership on each title page and endpapers and several times throughout), black morocco label (slightly defective) with gilt lettering and gilt rules on spine. Given its rarity, a nice copy with four pages advertising "Books printed by Robert and Andrew Foulis" bound in at end. As with the 1667–69 printings of the first edition of *PL*, the arguments are here printed together before the poem. Rare. Not in Coleridge; Not in Kohler.

See the 1750 (second, possibly first) 8vo Foulis edition of *PL* and commentary there, with the incorrect date of "The Author's Last Edition, In The Year 1672" on title page and with the arguments printed before the poem; see also the 1752 (third, possibly second) 12mo Foulis edition of *PL*, with the incorrect date "In The Year 1672" on title page of the 1750 8vo Foulis edition corrected to 1674, as here, and with the arguments printed together before the poem as here. The 1766 12mo Foulis edition of *PL* is also listed here, very similar to this edition, 2 volumes in one, with reference to "The Author's Last Edition" with correct date on title page and the arguments printed together before the poem. Finally the 1771 and 1776 12mo two-volume Foulis editions of *PL* are also listed here, without reference to "The Author's Last Edition" on title page, printing the arguments, as here, together at the beginning of the poem, each edition uniformly bound with a 1772 12mo two-volume Foulis edition of *PR, SA, and P*.

705. PARADISE LOST. A Poem, In Twelve Books. The Author John Milton. *London, Printed for J [sic] Thomson and S. Dampier in the Strand. n.d. [1761].* 12mo, [iv]+[viii]+[i]+324pp., engraved frontispiece portrait by "A. Bell," "Publish'd by Jo. Wood 1761" printed at the bottom, life by Fenton, engraved illustrations (reduced 1688 plates) by T. Phinn and J. McLean, with some plates unsigned, one plate for each book, original sheep (a bit worn, front cover detached, lacking back cover, light waterstaining along inside upper inner portion, age-browning throughout), raised bands within gilt rules on spine, red morocco label lettered in gilt. All in all, a decent copy of a very rare edition. Quite possibly an Irish or Scottish piracy. Rare. Not in Coleridge; Not in Kohler.

See also ca. 1765 edition listed here, which has a frontispiece portrait similar to the portrait here; it is signed "T. Phinn Sculpt" in lower right-hand corner and undated, with "Published According to Act of Parliament" printed in the center at the bottom. That edition appears to be a reprinting of this edition with a new impression of the frontispiece (although not as fresh a striking as here, yet consistent with the appearance of the plates within the edition), with a new title page printed in red and black, not the case here. See 1754 possible first edition thus, also very rare, "Printed for T. Thompson, R. Damper, et al" (not "Dampier" as here and in ca. 1765), with plates as here, but with a frontispiece portrait different from that here and identified differently: engraved frontispiece portrait signed "GZ 1756," with Milton looking to his left, not his right, as here and in the portrait by "T. Phinn," "Published According to Act of Parliament" ca. 1865. See comments about the portrait with the 1754 edition and its appearance in several editions of *PL*: 1753, 1754, and 1756 (each edition listed here).

706. DAS VERLOHRNE PARADIES, aus dem Englischen Johann Miltons in Reimfrene Berse ubersetzt, und mit eignen sowohl als andrer Anmerkungen begleitet von Friedrich Wilhelm Zacharia. Mit Kupfern. Zwente, durchaus verbesserte Ausgabe. / Zenter Theil. Unter Konigl. Pohln. u. Churfl. Gachs. Privilegio. Altona, bey David Iversen, Konigl. privil. *Buchh. in Holstein, 1762-63.* 2 volumes in one. Second edition of volume 1; first edition of volume 2. Small 4to, [x]+266pp.,+[iv]+248pp., first appearance thus of engraved frontispiece portrait after Fritzsch (fine impression), separate title page each volume, the first dated 1762, the second dated 1763, engraved illustrations after Hayman, engraved by Fritzsch (second appearance thus, many plates unsigned), elaborately decorated head- and tailpieces, half-title for each book, notes at bottom of page, contemporary mottled calf, elaborately gilt-decorated spine in the panels, red morocco label with gilt lettering and gilt rules, raised bands, marbled endpapers and edges, bookplate of Leonard Schlosser. A fine copy with plates that are strikingly fresh and clean. The translation is by F. W. Zacharia—the third publication in German, the second in verse. The first edition thus of volume 1 was published in 1760 (copy listed here). *Tercentenary Catalogue* 791; Coleridge 160b (volume 1) and 160a (volume 2); Kohler 40 ("Lacks frontispiece"), reporting "Not in the British Library. Not in the Bodleian Library."

707. PARADISE LOST. A Poem, In Twelve Books. The Author John Milton. The Sixth [Newton] Edition, With Notes of various Authors, By Thomas Newton, D.D. *London: Printed for J. and R. Tonson, B. Dodd, H. Woodfall, J. Rivington, R. Baldwin, T. Longman, L Hawes, Clark and Collins, E. Dilly, T. Caslon, C. Corbet, T. Lownds, and the Executors of J. Richardson. MD CC LXIII.* 2 volumes. 8vo,

[x]+[xi]+lxxxvi+[vi]+[xx]+510pp.,+463+[183-page unpaginated index / verbal index]+[1]pp., unsigned engraved frontispiece portrait, twelve engraved illustrations by J. Müller / Miller after Hayman (reduced), half-title for each book, decorative tailpieces, notes at bottom of page, advertisement leaf of "Lately Published, A New Edition" of "The Poetical Works of John Milton" at end of volume 2, contemporary polished calf, gilt rules on covers, gilt-decorated spines, red morocco title labels, black morocco numbering labels (black labels very worn), raised bands. A fine set, very fresh and clean throughout, with early signature and bookplate in each volume. Uniformly bound as volumes 1 and 2 with *PR, SA, P*, Hitch & Hawes et al., 1760, listed here. Coleridge 125; Kohler 41, referencing Williamson 148 and reporting "Not in Cambridge University Library."

708. PARADISE LOST. A Poem, In Twelve Books. The Author John Milton. Correctly Printed From The Text Of Thomas Newton, D.D. *[?London], M DCC LXIII.* 8vo, 332pp., original sheep (worn, spine chipped, lacking label, some age-browning and soiling), life by Fenton, gilt rules on spine (faded), early signature on fly-leaf. A passable copy of a very rare eighteenth-century edition, which could be a Scottish piracy, although neither place nor printer is given. Coleridge 126; Not in Kohler.

709. AN EXTRACT FROM MILTON'S PARADISE LOST. With Notes. *London: Printed by Henry Fenwick, MDCCLXIII.* First Wesley edition. 12mo in 6s, 322pp., "To The Reader," Notes on each book printed at the end of each book, decorative trim throughout, small decorative piece at end of each book, original sheep (extremities worn, joints cracked, spine ends and hinges chipped), with signature on end-leaf of "Mr. Rookes, Bath, 1780," and with his further note at the end of the introductory note: "NB When I purchased this book in the year 1780, it was then and there said that this Abstract or Extract was the Performance of John Wesley, A.M., the noted Methodist Preacher. W. R. Bath, March 17th 1780." "There was another edition in 1791 which is much more common" (Coleridge). Rare. "Not in ESTC or NUC, which record only the second edition of 1791" (Blackwell's, December "Advent" List, 1985). Green 222; Coleridge 152; Not in Kohler.

710. PARADISE LOST. A Poem, In Twelve Books. The Author John Milton. *London: Printed for L. Hawes, W. Clarke, and R. Collins, J. and R. Tonson, B. Dod, J. Rivington, R. Baldwin, J. Richardson, S. Crowder and Co. T. Longman, E. Dilly, C. Corbet, and T. Lownds. M DCC LXIV.* 12mo, lxxi+[1]+319pp.+[25-page unpaginated index]+[2]pp., frontispiece portrait engraved by J. Miller, twelve illustrations engraved by Miller (signed "J.M.") after Hayman (reduced), life by Newton, original calf (worn, joints cracked), gilt-decorated spine (defective at bottom), red morocco label (chipped), marbled endpapers, index, two pages of advertisement bound in at end. A fair copy, internally very nice. Coleridge 127; Kohler 41, reporting "Not in the Bodleian Library."

711. PARADISE LOST. A Poem, In Twelve Books. The Author John Milton. *London: Printed for J. Thomson and S. Dampier in the Strand. n.d. [ca. 1765].* 12mo, [iv]+[viii]+[i]+324pp., engraved frontispiece portrait by "T. Phinn," "Published According to Act of Parliament" printed at the bottom, title page in red and black, life by Fenton, engraved illustrations (reduced 1688 plates) by T. Phinn and J. McLean, with some plates unsigned, one plate for each book, original sheep (worn, lacking blank endpapers, age-browned, with a few erasures of notes throughout), raised bands within gilt rules on spine, red morocco label, ink notes in an early hand on pastedowns and on verso of portrait, early signatures. A decent copy of a very rare edition. Quite possibly an Irish or Scottish piracy. John Shawcross shared with me that "The portrait in the UK volume indicates that it was "Publish'd by Jo. Wood 1761." Rare. Not in Coleridge; Not in Kohler.

See 1761 edition, where frontispiece portrait is identified as "Publish'd by Jo. Wood 1761"; the portrait there is also identified as being "by A. Bell." The portrait here is signed "T. Phinn Sculpt" in lower right-hand corner and is also undated, with "Published According to Act of Parliament" printed in the center at the bottom. The edition appears to be a reprinting, with a new impression of the frontispiece (although not as fresh a striking as the earlier impression by Bell "Publish'd by Jo. Wood 1761," yet consistent with the appearance of the plates within this edition), with a new title page printed in red and black, not the case in the 1761 edition. See 1754 possible first edition thus, also very rare, "Printed for T. Thompson, R. Damper, et al" (not "Dampier" as here and in ca. 1761), with plates as here, but with a frontispiece portrait different from that here and identified differently: engraved frontispiece portrait signed "GZ 1756," with Milton looking to his left, not his right, as here and in the portrait by "A. Bell," "Publish'd by Jo. Wood 1761." See comments about the portrait with the 1754 edition and its appearance in several editions of *PL*: 1753, 1754, and 1756 (each edition listed here).

712. PARADISE LOST. A Poem, In Twelve Books. The Author John Milton. The Seventeenth Edition. To which is prefix'd, The Life of the Author, with an Account of his

Works and Controversies: together, with some particulars from that written by Dr. Newton. To this Edition is added, A Glossary, explaining the Antiquated and difficult Words used in this Work. *Dublin: Printed for W. and W. Smith, A. Ewing, and P. Wilson. M.DCC.LXV.* 12mo, lxvi+370pp. (pagination beginning at "p. 31"), unsigned engraved frontispiece of Milton, Homer, and Virgil with Dryden epigram, 1688 plates reduced (unsigned, fine impressions), rebound in modern three-quarter brown calf, marbled paper over thick boards, new marbled endpapers and new blanks. Very nice copy with fine impressions of the engravings. Rare. Not in Coleridge; Not in Kohler.

713. **PARADISE LOST.** A Poem, In Twelve Books. The Author John Milton. A New Edition. To which is added, Historical, Philosophical, and Explanatory Notes, Translated from the French of The learned Raymond de St. Maur. Together with Various critical Remarks and Observations from Mr. Addison, Dr. Warburton, Dr. Newton, Dr. Pearce, Dr. Bentley, Mr. Richardson, &c. *Edinburgh: Printed for John Wood, at Milton's Head, MDCCLXV.* 2 volumes in one. Large 12mo, xiii+[iii]+262pp.,+237pp.,+[22-page unpaginated index], title page each volume (volume 2 title page alters the critics' names), advertisement and life by Fenton, volume 1, half-title for Book VII after title page, volume 2, notes at bottom of page, contemporary calf (worn, especially the spine, lacking label), early name on front pastedown. Raymond de St. Maur's commentary originally appeared as *The State of Innocence and the Fall of Man* in 1745 (copy listed here). Scarce. Coleridge 128; Not in Kohler.

See also copy of the 1754 edition with striking illustrations (unsigned); see another issue of the 1754 edition in 1755 with a variant publisher with the same striking illustrations (unsigned); see also the two-volume 1775 edition listed here with 1688 illustrations reduced and unsigned and the two-volume 1779 edition listed here with 1688 illustrations reduced and attributed to R. Cooper, this edition reprinted in 1784 (copy listed here); see also the 1770 nonillustrated edition listed here, first edition thus for John Wood. See following one-volume edition of *PL* published this same year in Edinburgh for John Wood at Milton's Head.

714. **PARADISE LOST.** A Poem, In Twelve Books. The Author John Milton. A New Edition. To which is added, The Life of the Author, by E. Fenton; And, A Complete Index. *Edinburgh: Printed for John Wood, at Milton's Head, MDCCLXV.* 12mo, xiii+[iii]+304pp+[22-page unpaginated index], "N.B. To render this Edition of Paradise Lost as correct as possible, it has been compared with Dr. Newton's splendid Quarto Copy of Milton's Poetical Works" on verso of title page, life by Fenton, contemporary polished calf, gilt rules on spine, red morocco label with gilt lettering and decorative gilt trim, raised bands. A fine copy of this scarce eighteenth-century edition, from the library of Siegfried Sassoon (1886–1967), poet, signed in purple ink with his posthumous monograph book label. Printed at the end of the book: "Just published by John Wood, another edition of Paradise Lost, with Historical, Philosophical, and Explanatory Notes; Translated from the French of The learned Raymond de St. Maur. To which is added, Various critical Remarks and Observations, from Mr. Addison, Dr. Warburton, Dr. Newton, Dr. Pearce, Dr. Bentley, Mr. Richardson, &c." See preceding two-volume edition of *PL* published this same year in Edinburgh for John Wood, at Milton's Head, and referred to in statement at end of book here. John Shawcross shared with me that a "copy owned by the British Library" has "a frontispiece version of Haywood's three poets with the epigram, redrawn by R. C[ooper], who also did the illustrations." Rare. Not in Coleridge (referenced in 128); Not in Kohler.

715. **PARADISE LOST**, A Poem In Twelve Books. The Author John Milton. *Glasgow: Printed by James Knox, and sold at his Shop, near the head of the Salt-mercat [sic]. M DCC LXV.* 12mo, 318+[2]pp., original sheep (a little rubbed, joints cracked, spine chipped at bottom, early names and markings, rather heavy in places, on front and back blanks as well as on title page, small hole on title page resulting in the loss of the letter "m" in "Poem," small tear on front blank, edges of first few pages in the front and at the back a bit frayed), red morocco label (partially missing) with gilt lettering and gilt rules on spine, raised bands, small decorative gilt piece within the panels. Advertisement leaf bound in at end listing "Books Printed and Sold by James Knox." A very passable copy of a rare eighteenth-century edition. Not in Coleridge; Not in Kohler.

716. **LE PARADIS PERDU** De Milton, Poème Héroïque, Traduit De L'Anglois; Avec les Remarques de M. Addisson[sic]. Nouvelle Edition, revue & corrigée. *A Paris, Chez la Ve. Savoye, rue S. Jacques' a l'Esperance. M. DCC. LXV. Avec Approbation & Privilège du Roi.* 4 volumes 12mo, xxiv+280+[4]pp.,+310pp.,+231pp.,+375pp., half-title each volume, title page each volume with decorative border trim, small central decorative piece and double line above date on each title page, "Avis Du Libraire," Fenton's "Vie De Milton," Addison's "Remarques," "Avertissement" before *Paradise Lost*, volume 1, and four-page "Approbation" (dated "A Paris ce premier Decembre 1763") and "Privilege Du Roi" (dated "18 Janvier 1764," "20 Janvier 1764," and "25 Janvier 1764") at the end of volume 1, with "De l'Imprimerie de la Veuve Quillau" printed at bottom of last page, decorative head- and tailpieces (some rather elaborate), decorated initial letters (some rather elaborate), notes at bottom of page, "De l'Imprimerie de F. A. Quillau 1765" printed at bottom of last page of volume 4 (p. 375), contemporary speckled French calf (a bit rubbed, especially corners and edges, front joint of volume 1 slightly cracked, spines chipped at bottom of volumes 1 and 4), richly tooled gilt-decorated spines within the panels, red morocco lettering labels, green morocco numbering labels, each label lettered or numbered in gilt with gilt rules, marbled endpapers and edges. A nice set with early identification of the volume written in a neat hand in ink on front blank of volume 2. Included in volume 3 is *PR*, with half-title, "Preface," and "Argument" (not original to the poem) for each book, followed by "Oeuvres Diverses De Milton," with half-title, including *L*, *L'A*, *IlP*, and *NO* ("Cantique De Milton Sur La Fête De Noël"). Volume IV contains "Lettres Critiques Sur Le Paradis Perdu De Milton" and Addison's "Remarques" with half-title. Milton's poems here are rendered into French prose: *PL* the prose translation by Nicholas Dupré de St. Maur, revised by C. J. Chéron de Boismorand, first published in 1729 (see set listed here); the prose translation of *PR* and other poems by Père de Mareuil, first published in 1730 (copy listed here); and the *Lettres critiques* by Bernard Routh. Scarce. Not in Coleridge (although Coleridge 180 cites a similar four-volume edition with different publisher's imprint: "A Paris, Chez Ganeau, rue Saint-Severin, à S. Louis, & aux Armes de Dombes. M. DCC. LXV"); Not in Kohler (although Kohler 43 cites a similar four-volume edition with different publisher's imprint: "Paris: Chez la Ve. David, quai des Augustins, près le Pont S. Michel. 1765").

717. PARADISE LOST. A Poem, In Twelve Books. The Author John Milton. According To The Author's Last Edition, In The Year 1674. *Glasgow: Printed By Robert and Andrew Foulis, M.DCC.LXVI.* 2 volumes in one. 12mo, 352+[4]pp., half-title ("Paradise Lost," with quotation from Thompson on verso), contemporary roan (worn, joints cracked, some stains and age-browning, initial blanks fragile), gilt rules on spine, red leather label (deceptively labeled "Milton's Works"), raised bands. Given its rarity, a decent copy with contemporary signature on title page, dated 1800 presentation inscription on front blank, and later armorial bookplate. Four pages advertising "Books printed by Robert and Andrew Foulis" bound in at end. As with the 1667–69 printings of the first edition of *PL*, the arguments here are printed together before the poem. Rare. Not in Coleridge; Not in Kohler.

See also the 1750 (second, possibly first) 8vo Foulis edition of *PL* and commentary there, with the incorrect date of "The Author's Last Edition, In The Year 1672" on title page and with the arguments printed before the poem; see also the 1752 (third, possibly second) 12mo Foulis edition of *PL*, with the incorrect date "In The Year 1672" on title page of the 1750 8vo Foulis edition corrected to 1674, as here, and with the arguments printed together before the poem as here; see, too, 1761 12mo Foulis edition of *PL*, very similar to edition here, two volumes in one, with reference to "The Author's Last Edition" with correct date on title page and the arguments printed together before the poem; and see also the 1771 and 1776 12mo two-volume Foulis editions of *PL* listed here, without reference to "The Author's Last Edition" on title page, printing the arguments together at the beginning of the poem, as here, each uniformly bound with a 1772 12mo two-volume Foulis edition of *PR, SA,* and *P*.

718. PARADISE LOST. A Poem. In Twelve Books. The Author John Milton. With Notes Of Various Authors, By John Rice. *London: Printed for J. and R. Tonson, H. Woodfall, J. Rivington, R. Baldwin, T. Longman, L. Hawes, Clarke, and Collins, T. Caslon, C. Corbet, E. Dilly, T. Lownds, M. Richardson, and the Executors of B. Dod. MDCCLXVI.* Large 8vo, viii+488pp., preface, notes at bottom of page, contemporary speckled French calf (corners and ends of spine a bit worn), gilt-decorated spine with red morocco label and gilt lettering ("Paradies De Milton"), marbled endpapers, red edges. A fine, tall copy. Rice edited this edition for schools and general readers, surveying previous annotators like Bentley, who "so miserably mangled" the text, and Newton, "the best that has hitherto appeared." "Rice's footnotes are substantial and surprisingly free of the usual mass of classical and otherwise scholarly references. A most curious edition, unknown to Coleridge or to Parker. Rare" (G. W. Stuart, Jr., Ravenstree, Cat. 150, #68, 1987). Not in Coleridge; Not in Kohler; John Shawcross told me that the University of Michigan owns a copy.

719. MILTON'S PARADISE LOST. A Poem, in Twelve Books. With Prefatory Characters of the several Pieces; and the Life-of Milton. Sarah West. 1773. *Edinburgh: Printed by A. Donaldson, and sold at his Shops in London and Edinburgh. M DCC LXVII.* 12mo in 6s, lxxix+323+[19+1]pp., half-title within decorative border trim, decorative border trim on title page, engraved illustration plates after Thomas Phinn (for Books IV, VIII, IX, and XI of *PL*), unpaginated index at the end, later plain burgundy buckram (last three pages laid down for reinforcement), spine lettered in gilt, marbled edges. A very nice copy, fresh and clean within, with contemporary inscriptions on front blank and half-title, and nineteenth-century inscription on front blank, advertisement on verso of last page.

Rare copy of volume 1 only with "Life-of Milton. Sarah West. 1773" printed on title page. Not in Coleridge; Not in Kohler.

See also: *Milton's Poetical Works.* Volume I. Containing Paradise Lost . . . [With] Volume II. Containing Paradise Regain'd . . . Samson Agonistes; And Poems . . . *Edinburgh: Printed by A. Donaldson, and sold at his Shops in London and Edinburgh. M DCC LXVII.* 12mo in 6s, four engraved illustration plates after Thomas Phinn (for Books IV, VIII, IX, and XI of *PL*).

719A. (Cross-listing) [PARADISE LOST] Neander, L. B. [Neuman, Ludwig Bertrand.] LAPSUS PROTOPARENTUM EX POEMATA MILTONI CANTUS VI. Accedit Supplementum ad Lib. VI. Aeneid...*Vindobonae [Vienna]: Typis a Ghelenianis . . . MDCCLXVIII.* First and only edition. 8vo, engraved title with vignette portrait of Milton and elaborate border, quarter-page engraved illustration before each canto by T. Mansfeld and one full-page engraved illustration before supplement of *Aeneid* Book VI, also by T. Mansfeld, original tree sheep. Rare with fine impressions of the charming rococo illustrations to each canto. NUC locates only the copy at the University of Illinois; Not in Parker; Not in Brunet; and Not in Coleridge (although Turnbull has reportedly acquired a copy since); Kohler 44, reporting "Not in Williamson. Not in the British Library. Not in the Bodleian Library." See main listing with Eighteenth-century Miltoniana.

720. PARADISE LOST . . . The Seventh [Newton] Edition, With Notes of various Authors, By Thomas Newton . . . *London: Printed for J. Beecroft, W. Strahan, J. and F. Rivington . . . MDCCLXX.* 2 volumes. 8vo, [x]+[xi]+lxxxvi+[vi]+[xx]+510pp.,+463pp.+[185-page unpaginated index and verbal index]+[1]pp., frontispiece portrait after Vertue (engraved by J. Miller), volume 1, a second frontispiece portrait (unsigned, engraved by J. Miller), with unsigned vignette illustration of the expulsion beneath the portrait, volume 2, twelve illustrations engraved by J. Müller after Hayman (reduced), title page each volume, decorative tailpieces, volume 1, half-title for each book, notes at bottom of page, advertisements of "Lately Published, A New Edition" of "The Poetical Works of John Milton" at end of volume 2, contemporary polished calf, gilt rules on spines, red morocco labels. Fine set, clean and fresh internally, with early signature in each volume. Uniformly bound as volumes 1 and 2 with *PR, SA, P, Printed for J. and R. Tonson, T. Caslon, et al., 1766*, listed here. "The volume 2 Advertisements are the usual group, for a 3-vo. 4to and also for *PR&c* in 2 volumes. 8vo." (Coleridge). Coleridge 130 (and 206), the two editions were often combined and sold together; Not in Kohler.

721. PARADISE LOST. A Poem, In Twelve Books. The Author John Milton. *London: Printed for J. Beecroft, W. Strahan, J. and F. Rivington [and 27 others], MDCCLXX.* 12mo, lxxi+[i]+319pp.+[25-page unpaginated index]+2pp., frontispiece portrait engraved by J. Miller after Vertue, twelve illustrations engraved by J. Müller (signed "J.M.") after Francis Hayman (reduced), life of Milton, index, two advertisement leaves at the end, contemporary sheep (rebacked sometime ago, joints cracked, spine worn), red morocco label on spine with gilt lettering, raised bands. Despite the wear, a fairly good copy with bookplate and early signature on front blank. See the two-volume Newton edition also published by Beecroft et al., in 1770 (preceding copy). "This follows the 1764 12mo edition [see preceding copy]; it seems to be associated with the 1772 edition of *PR* [see copy listed here]. The advertisement is the usual one for 3 4to volumes of the *PW*, volume 3 available separately, and for the Works in 4 vols 8vo, also for *PL* and *PR* &c printed in 4to by Baskerville" (Coleridge). John Shawcross shared the following with me about this book: "This is a false imprint. It is a reissue of the 1772 edition, and it may be dated 1785." Coleridge 131; Kohler 45, referencing Williamson 97 and reporting "Not in the Bodleian Library. Not in Cambridge University Library."

722. PARADISE LOST, A Poem. The Author John Milton. *Glasgow: Printed By Robert And Andrew Foulis, Printers To The University, M.DCC.LXX.* First edition thus. Folio, [x]+466pp.+[10-page unpaginated index], unsigned engraved portrait on title page, advertisement leaf, subscriber's list, with the arguments printed together before the poem, printed in double column, index at the end, contemporary tree calf, decorative gilt border trim on covers, elegantly gilt-decorated spine, red morocco label, inner dentelles finely tooled in gilt, outer dentelles ruled in gilt, marbled endpapers. Large paper copy, measuring 15" tall as opposed to the regular paper copy measuring 12 ½" tall or less. A fine, handsome copy, beautifully printed with wide margins, fresh throughout, with the armorial bookplate of Methuen Castle. One of the superb Foulis editions; prints Newton's text without notes. "It is probably one of the most handsome editions of *PL* printed in the eighteenth century; it was the first Scottish subscription issue" (Coleridge). The subscriber's list includes David Hume and James Beattie. Gaskell, *Foulis*, 510; Blumenthal, *Art of the Printed Book*, p. 26, plate 79; Rothschild 2675; Coleridge 132; Kohler 46.

II. Descriptive Listing of Editions   199

Title page Foulis 1770 folio edition of *PL*. See #722.

1770 Foulis folio edition of *PL* in contemporary tree calf binding, gilt decorated. Fine copy. See #722.

Extra-Illustrated

723. Variant of Preceding. Folio, later half calf, marbled paper over boards (somewhat worn, newly rebacked, light inoffensive waterstains at upper edge), original red morocco labels on spine with gilt lettering and decorative gilt trim, raised bands. Letter tipped to endpaper acknowledging loan of this copy to the Old Glasgow Exhibition of 1894. A good copy, extra-illustrated with the addition of three engraved portraits of Milton in the front (ages ten, twenty-one, and sixty-two, each dated 1794) and twelve engraved plates after Westall (one for each book of *PL*), all mounted on stiff paper and variously dated 1794 and 1795, and taken from the Boydell edition of Milton. Large paper copy.

724. [PARADISE LOST] THE STATE OF INNOCENCE, AND FALL OF MAN, Described In Milton's *Paradise Lost*. Rendered Into Prose. With Historical, Philosophical, And Explanatory Notes. From the French of the Learned Raymond De St. Maur. By a Gentleman of Oxford. *Aberdeen: Printed and sold by John Boyle. MDCCLXX.* 8vo, iv+[iv]+428pp., preface, contents, notes at the bottom of the page, contemporary sheep (worn, joints cracked, spine ends chipped), gilt rules on spine (faded), black morocco label (chipped), with contemporary signature on fly-leaf. The first edition thus was published in 1745 (also listed here), which Coleridge suggests this edition "seems to follow quite closely" in content and structure. See 1754 Raymond de St. Maur edition (copy listed here) with striking illustrations (unsigned); see another issue of the 1754 edition in 1755 (copy listed here) with a variant publisher, with the same striking illustrations (unsigned); and see two-volume 1779 edition (copy listed here) with 1688 illustrations reduced by R. Cooper; this edition is reprinted in 1784 (copy listed here); see, too, 1765 nonillustrated edition (copy listed here). Coleridge 256; Not in Kohler.

725. Variant of Preceding. 8vo, unsigned engraved frontispiece portrait of Milton, modern quarter calf, marbled paper over boards (new endpapers), red morocco label with gilt lettering and gilt trim, raised bands. A nice copy, as preceding, except with an eighteenth-century frontispiece portrait bound in (which does not appear to be integral to the book). Coleridge 256 (without any mention of frontispiece portrait); Not in Kohler.

726. PARADISE LOST. A Poem. In Twelve Books. The Author John Milton. *Glasgow: Printed And Sold By R. & A. Foulis Printers To The University, M.DCC.LXXI. 2 volumes.* 12mo, [xii]+184pp.,+176pp., half-title ("Paradise Lost," with quotation from Thompson on verso), volume 1, title page each volume, arguments printed together before the poem as with 1667–69 printings of the first edition of *PL*, original calf, gilt rules on spines, red morocco labels with gilt lettering within gilt rules, raised bands. A very fine set. See 1750 (second, possibly first) 8vo Foulis edition of *PL* and commentary there and 1752 (third, possibly second) 12mo Foulis edition of *PL*, each with reference on title page to "According To The Author's Last Edition," absent here, with the arguments printed before the poem, as here; see also 1761 and 1766 12mo Foulis editions of *PL*, each two volumes in one, continuing "The Author's Last Edition" with correct date on title page and printing, as here, the arguments together at the beginning of the poem; and see very similar 1776 12mo two-volume Foulis edition of *PL* listed here, without reference to "The Author's Last Edition" on title page, printing the arguments together at the beginning of the poem, and uniformly bound with a 1772 12mo Foulis edition of *PR, SA, and Poems*. Gaskell 531; Coleridge 133; Not in Kohler.

Unlike the present edition, the 1776 edition has the dagger symbol preceding the signature marks, found in the 1776 Foulis edition of *PR, SA, and Poems*, and found also in the 1772 Foulis edition of *PR&c*. Uniformly bound with *PR, SA, and Poems*, Foulis, 1772, listed here. Rare. Not in Coleridge; Not in Kohler.

727. LE PARADIS PERDU DE MILTON, Poème Héroïque, Traduit De L'Anglois. Avec les Remarques de M. Addisson. Nouvelle Edition, Augmentée Du Paradis Reconquis & de quelques autres Pièces de Poésie du même Auteur. *A La Haye, Chez les Frères Van-Duren, Libraires. M. DCC. LXXI.* 12mo, [ii]+438+98pp., half-title, "Vie De Milton" and Addison's "Remarques" before *PL*, half-title for *PR*, with separate pagination, with "Preface" and "Arguments" (not original to the poem) for *Le Paradis Perdu Reconquis*, followed by L ("Lycidas, Idile de Milton"), *L'A*, *IlP*, and *NO* ("Sur La Feste De Noël") under the heading, "Oeuvres De Milton," decorative head- and tailpieces (some fairly elaborate), decorated initial letters, notes at bottom of page, contemporary speckled French calf (a bit rubbed, joints slightly cracked at bottom in front and back, spine slightly chipped at top and bottom), spine elaborately decorated in gilt within the panels, green morocco label lettered and ruled in gilt, red edges, green silk ribbon marker. Nice copy with early armorial bookplate on front pastedown and with an early (possibly contemporary) French presentation inscription in ink in a neat hand on front blank. Milton's poems here are rendered into

French prose: *PL* the prose translation by Nicholas Dupré de St. Maur, revised by C. J. Chéron de Boismorand, first published in 1729 (see set listed here); the prose translation of *PR* and other poems by Père de Mareuil, first published in 1730 (copy listed here). Not in Coleridge; Not in Kohler.

728. PARADISE LOST. A Poem. In Twelve Books. The Author John Milton. *London: Printed for R. Crowder, C. Ware, and T. Payne. M.DCC.LXXII.* First edition thus. Apparently a very rare separate issue. 12mo, 334pp., half-title, contemporary calf (a little worn, front joint cracked, early name on front pastedown, lacks front free endpaper), maroon morocco label with gilt lettering ("Paradise Lost") and gilt rules on spine, raised bands. A fairly good copy of a rare book. John Shawcross shared with me that this edition "was reissued with your [*PR*, 1772, listed here] in 1772 as 'Poetical Works,' copy owned by University of Western Ontario," which I have since acquired for the collection (see *PW*, 1772, copy listed here). The present edition of *PL* was apparently issued as a rare separate edition. As Shawcross further stated, "I have entered [your *PL*, 1772, copy here] in the bibliography [i.e., John's bibliographical publication of eighteenth-century editions] as apparently a separate issue just as [your *PR*, 1772, copy listed here] seems to be. I haven't found it separated anywhere else." Not in Coleridge (although Coleridge 134 makes reference to this edition, without having seen one); Not in Kohler.

729. PARADISE LOST. A Poem, In Twelve Books. The Author John Milton. A New Edition, With Notes of various Authors, By Thomas Newton, D.D. Embellished with a Set of Engravings. *Dublin: Printed by John Exshaw, in Dame-street. MDCCLXXIII.* 2 volumes. 8vo, [v]+[vi]+xlvi+372pp.,+474pp.+[18-page unpaginated index], unsigned engraved frontispiece portrait plate of Milton at age twenty-one with the Dryden epigram, volume 1, title page each volume with engraved vignette portrait of Milton (age sixty-two, unsigned, somewhat after Faithorne) on each title page, engraved illustration plates (unsigned, a powerful set, apparently not after Hayman/Miller), dedication, preface, life, with same vignette portrait by T. Chambers (fine impression), Addison's "A Critique on the Paradise Lost," half-title for each book, notes at bottom of page, index at end of volume 2, contemporary calf, elaborately gilt-decorated spine, red morocco title labels with gilt lettering within gilt rules, black morocco numbering labels with decorative gilt trim and gilt rules, raised bands with decorative gilt trim, outer dentelles tooled in gilt, marbled endpapers, speckled green edges. Very fine set with contemporary signature on front blank of volume

1. The first Dublin edition of Newton's *PL* and the first edition by John Exshaw was published without illustrations in 1751 (also listed here). Coleridge 135b; Kohler 48, referencing Williamson (which has neither the frontispiece nor the vignette portrait), and reporting "Not in the British Library. Not in the Bodleian Library."

730. Variant of Preceding. 2 volumes. 8vo, engraved vignette portrait of Milton (age sixty-two, unsigned, somewhat after Faithorne) on each title page, repeated again before life, volume 1, and attributed there to T. Chambers, unsigned engraved illustration plates (a powerful set, apparently not after Hayman/Miller), dedication, preface, life, with vignette portrait plate of Milton attributed to T. Chambers (fine impression), as preceding, contemporary polished calf (a few scuff marks), gilt-decorated border trim on all covers, elaborately gilt-decorated spines in the panels, red morocco lettering labels ("Newton's Milton") with decorative gilt trim, black morocco numbering labels with decorative gilt trim, outer dentelles tooled in gilt, marbled endpapers, light green edges. Uniformly bound as volumes 1 and 2, with *PR . . . Dublin. Exshaw, MDCCLIV*, 2 volumes (also listed here), the first Dublin printing of Newton's *PR* (with comparably striking illustrations after J. Dixon). A lovely set, clean and fresh throughout, with fine impressions of the plates, in contemporary polished calf, with an extra vignette portrait plate of Milton repeated before life, volume 1, and attributed there to T. Chambers.

731. PARADISE LOST. A Poem, In Twelve Books. The Author John Milton. Vol. I / Vol. II. *Edinburgh: Printed for A. Kincaid and W. Creech, and J. Balfour. M, DCC, LXXIII.* 2 volumes in one. 8vo, vi+182pp.,+173pp., general title page each volume ("The British Poets. Vol I / Vol. II. Edinburgh: Printed for A. Kincaid and W. Creech, and J. Balfour. M, DCC, LXXIII"), title page for *PL* each volume, original calf (a bit rubbed, joints cracked, spine chipped at top and bottom, label mostly gone), decorative gilt border trim on covers, gilt-decorated spine (a bit worn). A good copy of a scarce edition, complete with two title pages for each volume, with early armorial bookplate on front pastedown. John Shawcross shared the following with me about this edition: "These are the first two volumes in a set of four: volume 3 gives *PR*; volume 4 gives *Poems*. Copy owned by University of Illinois." Rare. Not in Coleridge; Not in Kohler.

732. [PARADISE LOST] THE FIRST SIX BOOKS OF MILTON'S PARADISE LOST, Rendered into Grammatical Construction; The Words of the Text being arranged, at the bottom of each Page, in the same natural

Order with the Conceptions of the mind; and the Ellipsis properly supplied, without any Alteration on the Diction of the Poem. With Notes Grammatical. Geographical, Historical, Critical, and Explanatory. To which are prefixed Remarks on Ellipsis and Transposition, exhibiting an early Method of construing, and reading with Judgment, either Prose or verse. Designed For the Use of our most eminent Schools, and of private Gentlemen and Ladies; and also of Foreigners of Distinction, who would read this admirable Poem with Understanding and Taste. By the late James Buchanan, Author of the British Grammar, a Regular English Syntax, &c. The Manuscript was left with Dr [sic] James Robertson, Professor of Hebrew, who has published it for the benefit of Mr [sic] Buchanan's Widow. *Edinburgh: Printed for A. Kincaid and W. Creech, and J. Balfour. M,DCC,LXXIII.* 8vo in 4s, 444pp., dedication page, advertisement serving as an introduction, original leather spine (worn), marbled paper boards (worn, front cover detached, title page foxed, early signature on front pastedown), red leather label with gilt-lettering and gilt trim on spine, raised bands. "This seems to be the first specimen of the text-book editions of Milton" (Coleridge). Rare. Coleridge 153; Not in Kohler.

732A. (Cross-listing) **PARADISE LOST**. A Poem, In Twelve Books. The Author John Milton. *London: Printed in the Year MDCCLXXIII.* Listed in appendix.

733. **LE PARADIS PERDU DE MILTON**, Poëme Héroïque, Traduit De L'Anglois. Avec les Remarques de M. Addisson. Nouvelle Edition, Augmentée Du Paradis Reconquis & de quelques autres Pièces de Poésie du même Auteur. *A La Haye, Chez les Frères Van-Duren, Libraires. M. DCC. LXXIV.* 12mo, 438+98pp., "Vie De Milton" and Addison's "Remarques" before *PL*, half-title for *PR* ("Le Paradis Reconquis De Milton"), with separate pagination, with "Preface" and "Arguments" (not original to the poem) for *Le Paradis Perdu Reconquis*, followed by *L* ("Lycidas, Idile de Milton"), *L'A*, *IlP*, and *NO* ("Sur La Feste De Noël") under the heading, "Oeuvres De Milton," decorative head- and tailpieces (some fairly elaborate), decorated initial letters, notes at bottom of page, original speckled sheep (a bit worn, joints cracked, spine rather rubbed and chipped at top and bottom), elaborately gilt-decorated spine, maroon morocco label (slightly chipped) lettered and ruled in gilt, marbled endpapers, red edges, green silk ribbon marker. Milton's poems here are rendered into French prose: *PL* the prose translation by Nicholas Dupré de St. Maur, revised by C. J. Chéron de Boismorand, first published in 1729 (see set listed here); the prose translation of *PR* and other poems by Père de Mareuil, first published in 1730 (copy listed here). John Shawcross shared with me "that there is a preliminary leaf (ii) which may be missing from your copy [it is!]. I have used the copy at Harvard; but I don't know where else it exists." Copy of the 1771 edition has it. Rare. Not in Coleridge; Not in Kohler.

734. **PARADISE LOST**. A Poem, In Twelve Books. The Author John Milton. The Eighth Edition, With Notes of various Authors, by Thomas Newton, D.D. Now Lord Bishop of Bristol. *London: Printed for J. Beecroft, W. Strahan, J. and F. Rivington, et al, M.DCC.LXXV.* 2 volumes. Large 4to, lxxiix+[iii]+[xvi]+491pp.,+460pp.+([116]-page unpaginated index and verbal index), engraved frontispiece portrait each volume, by Vertue, after the Onslow portrait, volume 1, after Faithorne, volume 2, engraved illustrations by Hayman, engraved by C. Grignion, title page each volume, dedication with elaborate decorative headpiece and decorated initial letter, half-title for each book, notes at bottom of page, index at the end of volume 2, contemporary mottled calf (neatly rebacked with original double maroon lettering pieces remounted, new endpapers), gilt rules on spine, raised bands. A handsome set, clean and fresh within, with striking impressions of the plates. The 1778 8vo edition of *PL* (copy listed here) is also called "The Eighth Edition" on the title page, "indicating a breakdown in the sequence, which was rather academic by this time, even though this is only the 8th edition of Newton's text and notes to be published by the approved successors of the Tonsons" (Coleridge). Newton's important edition was frequently reprinted and reissued into the nineteenth century (it was only superseded by Todd), though rarely in this handsome quarto format with Hayman's plates in full size. Uniformly bound with *PR*, *London: Printed for W. Strahan, J. F. and C. Rivington, et al., M DCC LXXVII*, listed here. Coleridge 137; Not in Kohler.

735. **PARADISE LOST**. A Poem, In Twelve Books. The Author John Milton. *London: Sold by J. Banners, W. Slackman, F. Rennington, W. Jones, T. Newton, and R. Bland. n.d. (ca. 1775).* Large 12mo, xviii+[i]+316pp., engraved frontispiece of Milton, Homer, and Virgil with Dryden epigram (although unsigned, a rendering of Vertue's three poets by Peter Larken), engraved illustrations (mainly after 1688 plates, somewhat crude imitations) after T. Phinn, J. McLean, and others (the plates are unsigned), one for each book, life by Fenton, small decorative endpieces, contemporary sheepskin (bit worn, joints cracked, spine chipped at top and bottom), gilt rules (faded) on spine, red leather label with gilt lettering and gilt rule, raised bands. A good copy with early signatures. See copies of 1754, 1761, and ca. 1765 editions (different publishers) with these same illustrations. Scarce. Not in Coleridge; Not in Kohler.

736. PARADISE LOST. A Poem, In Twelve Books. The Author John Milton. With Historical, Philosophical, and Explanatory Notes. Translated from the French of The learned Raymond de St. Maur. And Various critical Remarks and Observations, from Mr[sic] Addison, Dr[sic] Warburton, Dr[sic] Newton, Dr[sic] Pearce, Dr[sic] Bentley, Mr[sic] Richardson, and Mr[sic] Hume. A New Edition, adorn'd with Plates. Volume I / Volume II. *London: Printed for R. Bladon, T. Lawes, S. Crowder, C. Ware, and T. Payne. M DCC LXXV. 2 volumes.* 12mo, xiv+[ii]+231pp., +234pp.+[22 unpaginated index], half-title ("Paradise Lost, And Paradise Regain'd. In Two Volumes. [And With] Volume II.") and title page for each volume, unsigned engraved frontispiece portrait plate of Milton with inset at bottom of harp within laurel wreath with a small figure of a head at bottom of harp, advertisement dated 1775 and life by Fenton, volume 1, half-title for Book VIII at the start of volume 2 and for *PR* after *PL* and before index in volume 2, engraved illustration plates (after 1688 plates, unsigned, eight of twelve, lacking plates for Books IV, V, VII, and XI), misprint of "Book IX" for Book X in header on p. 69, volume 2, notes at bottom of page, original calf (joints, spines, and extremities a little worn, light embrowning, some worming to outer edges of first portion of volume 1 with slight loss to pages 13 through 25), red morocco labels with gilt lettering and gilt rules on each spine, raised bands within gilt rules. A very nice set with early signature in a neat hand in each volume. Raymond de St. Maur's commentary originally appeared as *The State of Innocence and the Fall of Man* in 1745 (copy listed here). See 1754 edition with striking illustrations (unsigned); see another issue of the 1754 edition in 1755 with a variant publisher with the same striking illustrations (unsigned); and see two-volume 1779 edition listed here with 1688 illustrations reduced, as here, and signed by R. Cooper, this edition reprinted in 1784 (copy listed here); see, too, copy of 1765 and of 1770 nonillustrated editions. "We have never seen another example of this edition, and ESTC On-line locates only the British Library and Inverness Public copies . . . and we do not locate an example in either the University of Western Ontario or University of Kentucky Milton collections" (G. W. Stuart, Jr., Ravenstree, Cat. 181, #47, 1997); Not in Coleridge; Not in Kohler.

The collection also has a variant of preceding. 2 volumes bound in one. 12mo in 6s, xiv+[ii]+231pp.,+234pp.+[22 unpaginated index], half-title and title page each volume, as preceding two volumes, with the engraved illustration plates as in that volume, lacking the same plates, contemporary calf (a little rubbed), brown leather label on spine double ruled in gilt with gilt lettering. A nice copy. Rare. Not in Coleridge; Not in Kohler.

737. PARADISE LOST [In] THE POETICAL WORKS OF JOHN MILTON. From The Text Of Dr. Newton, In Four Volumes. With The Life Of The Author, And A Critique On Paradise Lost, By Joseph Addison, Esq. *Edinburg[sic]: At The Apollo Press, By The Martins. Anno 1776.* Volumes 1 and 2 of four-volume set, complete unto themselves, bound as one volume. Bell's edition. 2 volumes in one. First edition thus. Stout 12mo, 240pp.,+ 228pp., engraved frontispiece portrait "From an Original in Ld. Chesterfield's Collection, by Cook," "Printed for John Bell near Exeter Exchange Strand London Novr. 12th. 1777," two engraved title pages for *PW* ("Bell's Edition, The Poets of Great Britain Complete From Chaucer to Churchill. Milton . . . Printed for John Bell near Exeter Exchange Strand London Novr. 20th. 1777"—second engraved title "Complete, From Chaucer to Churchill") and two printed title pages for *PL* ("Paradise Lost. A Poem. In Twelve Books. The Author John Milton. From The Text Of Dr. Newton, In Two Volumes. [Latin quotation] *Edinburg [sic]: At The Apollo Press, By The Martins. Anno 1776*"), each engraved title page with vignette illustration after J. H. Mortimer (for Book I and for Book VIII), each dated 1777, "From the Apollo Press, by the Martins, Sep. 3d, 1776" printed on last page, contemporary full red morocco, decorative border trim on covers, spine decorated in gilt, black morocco label with gilt lettering and decorative gilt trim, inner and outer dentelles tooled in gilt, marbled endpapers, a.e.g. A fine set. Coleridge 218; Kohler 268, reporting "Not in Cambridge University Library."

738. PARADISE LOST. A Poem. In Twelve Books. The Author John Milton. *Glasgow: Printed And Sold By R. & A. Foulis Printers To The University, M.DCC.LXXVI. 2 volumes.* 12mo, [xii]+184pp.,+176pp., dagger symbol preceding the signature marks, half-title ("Paradise Lost," with quotation from Thompson on verso), volume 1, title page each volume, arguments printed together before the poem as with 1667–69 printings of the first edition of *PL*, original calf (joints cracking), finely tooled gilt-decorated spines within the panels, red morocco lettering labels with gilt lettering ("Milton") and decorative gilt trim, green morocco numbering labels with gilt numbers and decorative gilt trim, raised bands with decorative gilt trim, outer dentelles finely tooled in gilt. A lovely set. Rare. Not in Coleridge; Not in Kohler.

See 1750 (second, possibly first) 8vo Foulis edition of *PL* and commentary there and 1752 (third, possibly second) 12mo Foulis edition of *PL*, each with reference on title page to "According To The Author's Last Edition," absent here, with the arguments printed before the poem, as here; see also 1761 and 1766 12mo Foulis editions of

PL, each two volumes in one, continuing "The Author's Last Edition" with correct date on title page and printing, as here, the arguments together at the beginning of the poem; and see very similar 1771 12mo two-volume Foulis edition of *PL*, without reference to "The Author's Last Edition" on title page, printing the arguments together at the beginning of the poem, and uniformly bound with a 12mo Foulis edition of *PR, SA, and Poems*. Unlike the 1771 edition, this edition has the dagger symbol preceding the signature marks, also found in the 1772 Foulis edition of *PR*, etc., uniformly bound with it. Uniformly bound with *PR, SA, and Poems*, Foulis, 1772, listed here, which also has dagger symbol preceding the signature marks.

739. PARADISE LOST. A Poem, In Twelve Books. The Author John Milton. *London: Printed For The Booksellers. M,DCC,LXXVII*. 12mo in 6s, [v]+[1]+280pp., Samuel Barrow's Latin poem, Andrew Marvell's poem, and "The Verse" precede Milton's epic, half-title for each book with "The Argument" on verso, original calf (some wear, joints cracked, front joint repaired, spine ends chipped). A decent copy of a very rare edition. An unusual edition with an even more unusual publisher's imprint, most likely a piracy. Rare. Unknown to John Shawcross; Not in Coleridge; Not in Kohler.

There are a number of piracy editions in the collection, ranging from the 1730 edition of *PL* "*Printed For The Company*," considered a French piracy (listed here), through to the 1792/1795/1796 editions of *PL* "Printed for A. Law., W. Millar, and R. Cater," considered possible Scottish piracies, listed here and a good many other piracies in-between, each identified when listed. There is also "*PR In Prose . . . Printed In The Year MDCCLXXI*," probably either a Scottish or Irish piracy, listed here, and *PW*, "*London, Printed In The Year M. DCC. XXI*," probably a French piracy, listed later. The number of piracy editions in a collection like this would indicate that these editions were common in the eighteenth century. Such printings point up two important things: there was a demand for cheap copies, clearly for reading rather than study (somewhat like the general public paperback audience for all kinds of books that may have easily fallen apart and were not preserved), and second, lack of copyright laws at this time clearly showed that such laws were needed to protect not only authors but also publishers, since the piracies certainly seem numerous and flagrant.

740. PARADISE LOST. A Poem, In Twelve Books. The Author John Milton. With the Life of Milton. By Thomas Newton, D.D. [Quotation from Thomson] *Philadelphia: Printed by Robert Bell, in Third-Street, MDCCLXXVII*. Volume 1 of 2 volumes. First American edition. 4to, 328pp., half-title with advertisement for "Modern Books Now Selling By Robert Bell" on verso, unsigned engraved frontispiece of Milton, Homer, and Virgil with Dryden epigram, the arguments for each book printed together before the first book after Marvell's poem, half-title for each book with the argument for the book printed on verso, printed on antique laid paper, contemporary sheepskin (worn, front joint cracked and reinforced from within, spine chipped at top and bottom, small piece of leather missing at top right corner of front cover, pages age-browned with some slight, inoffensive waterstaining here and there throughout including the bottom of frontispiece and title page, early name on title page, lacking free endpapers), raised bands. The engraved frontispiece portrait of Milton is "by [John] Norman [and] according to Hildeburn, is 'a very good specimen of John Norman's work;' [it is also] possibly the first portrait of Milton engraved on this continent" (Heritage Bookshop description on Bibliofind, 2000). A decent copy of volume 1, acquired separately. Rare. Evans 15443; Not in Coleridge; Not in Kohler.

[together with]

741. PARADISE REGAIN'D. A Poem, In Four Books. To which Are added **SAMSON AGONISTES**: And **POEMS ON SEVERAL OCCASIONS**. The Author John Milton. With The Life of the Author. By Thomas Newton. D.D. *Philadelphia: Printed and Sold by Robert Bell, in Third-Street, MDCCLXXVII*. Volume 2 of 2 volumes. First American edition. 4to, general half-title, 640pp. (continuous pagination from volume 1), reprint of "advertisement" "prefixed" "To the first edition of the author's poems printed in 1645" with "Contents Of The Second Volume" on verso, contemporary sheepskin (a little worn, front joint cracked at top and bottom, pages age-browned), half-title for "Poems On Several Occasions" followed by half-title for "The Twelfth Book Of Paradise Lost," half-title also for *PR*, *SA*, and *C*. Together two volumes, forming a complete set of Milton's English poems, with volume 1 containing the first eleven books of *PL*, while volume 2 begins with *PL*, Book XII, followed by the index and biography of Milton, on paging that continues from volume 1, pp. [331]–444, with signatures that are also continuous with volume 1, all three referred to on the "Contents" page of volume 2, continuing with *L'A, IlP, L, S, P*, and *PR, SA*, and *C*. A good copy, acquired separately. Not in Coleridge (211n); Not in Kohler.

Two of only eleven total eighteenth-century American editions of Milton's works. Of the eleven, the collection has eight: *PL*, 1777, and *PR, S, & P*, 1777, first American edition of each; *PR*, 1790, second American edition, and 1791, third American edition; *PL*, 1791, second American

II. Descriptive Listing of Editions   205

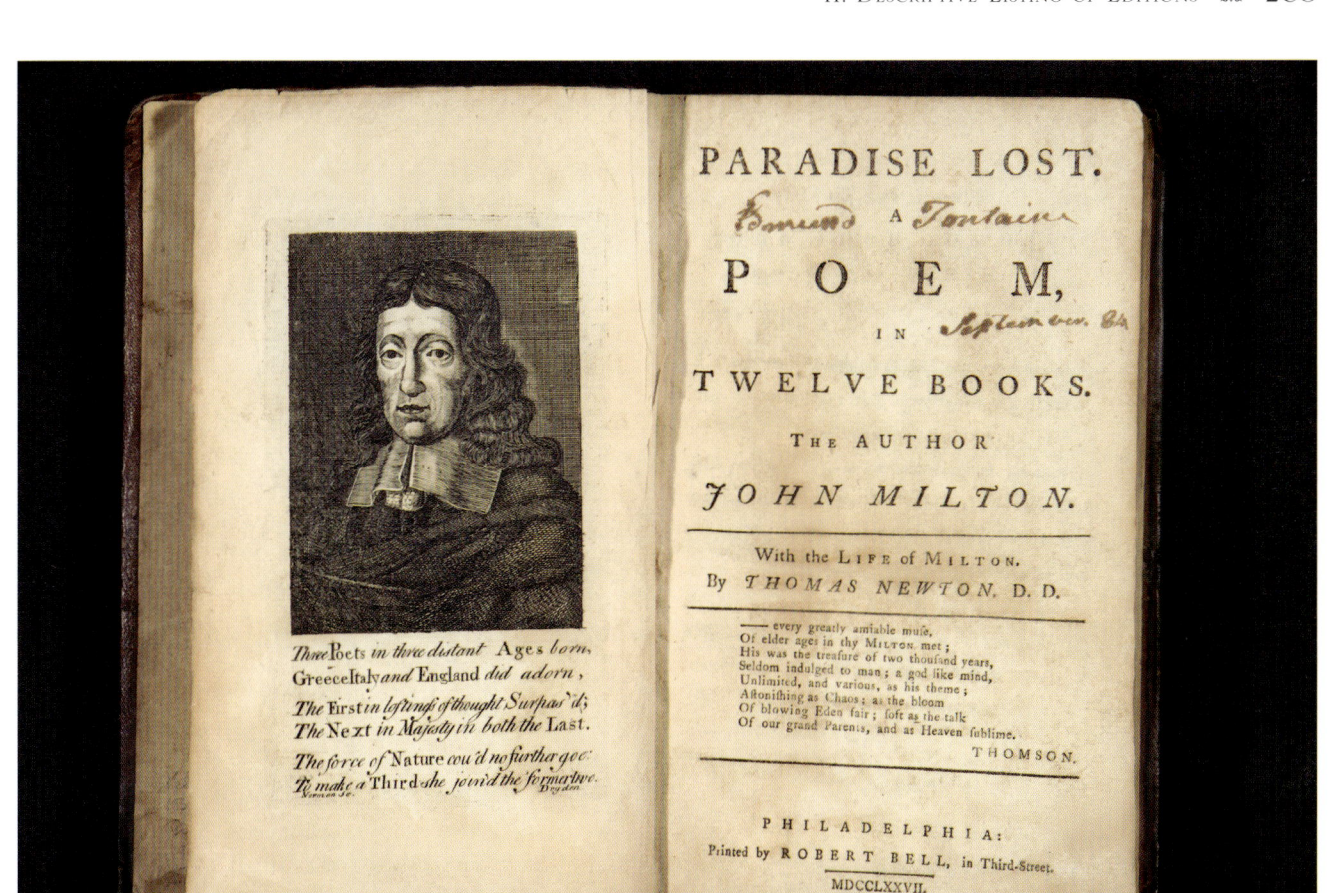

Frontispiece portrait and title page, *PL*, Philadelphia, 1777. First American edition. See #740.

Title page, *PR*, Philadelphia, 1777. First American edition. See #741.

edition; *PW*, 1794, third American edition, and 1796, fourth American edition; and *An Old Looking Glass*, 1770, first American edition. As John Shawcross has kindly informed me, the other three are a different edition of *The Old Looking-Glass* published in New Haven in 1774; and two editions of *PW* from Philadelphia in 1791: one by Henry Taylor, which is a reissue of his *PL*—which is in the collection—and a different edition of the *PR* volume—not the one in the collection; and one by W. Woodhouse, which is a reissue of Taylor's *PW*.

742. LE PARADIS PERDU DE MILTON, Poème Héroïque Traduit De L'Anglois. Avec les Remarques de M. Addisson. Nouvelle Edition, Augmentée Du Paradis Reconquis, & de quelques autres Pièces de Poésie du même Auteur. *A La Haye, Chez les Frères Van-Duren, Libraires. M. DCC. LXXVII.* 12mo, [ii]+438+98pp., half-title, "Vie De Milton" and Addison's "Remarques" before *PL*, half-title for *PR*, with separate pagination, with "Preface" and "Arguments" (not original to the poem) for *Le*

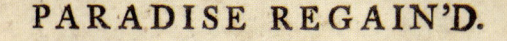

Paradis Perdu Reconquis, followed by *L* ("Lycidas, Idile de Milton"), *L'A*, *IlP*, and *NO* ("Sur La Feste De Noël") under the heading, "Oeuvres De Milton," decorative head- and tailpieces (some fairly elaborate), decorated initial letters, notes at bottom of page, original speckled sheep (a bit worn, spine chipped at top and bottom, last four signatures wormed at inner gutter), elaborately gilt-decorated spine within the panels, raised bands, outer dentelles ruled in gilt (very faded), marbled endpapers, red edges. A very respectable copy of a scarce edition. Milton's poems here are rendered into French prose: *PL* the prose translation by Nicholas Dupré de St. Maur, revised by C. J. Chéron de Boismorand, first published in 1729 (see set listed here); the prose translation of *PR* and other poems by Père de Mareuil, first published in 1730 (also listed here). Coleridge notes: "This omits the Lettres critiques by Bernard Routh but is otherwise the same collection as the 1743, 1749 and 1765 editions. . . . NUC has a series of editions (. . . dated 1767, 1771 [see copy here], 1774 [see copy here]) published by this firm, all with the same collation. This 1777 edition seems to be the last of the series." Coleridge 181; Not in Kohler.

743. **LE PARADIS PERDU DE MILTON**, Poème Héroïque Traduit De L'Anglois. Avec les Remarques de M. Addisson. A *Genève. M. DCC. LXXVII*. 3 volumes. Small 12mo, xx+237pp.,+297pp.,+328pp., half-title and title page each volume, each with small decorative piece at the center, frontispiece portrait signed "N. De Launay Sculp" and "Vie De Milton," volume 1, half-title for *PR*, with "Preface" and "Arguments" (not original to the poem) for *Le Paradis Reconquis* at end of volume 2, title page "Le Paradis Perdu" to volume 3 followed by "Oeuvres Diverses De Milton," including *L* ("Lycidas, Idylle de Milton"), *L'A*, *IlP*, and *NO* ("Sur La Fête De Noël"), along with the six letters, Addison's "Remarques" (with half-title), and "Approbation" and "Privilege Du Roi" at the end, decorative head- and tailpieces (some fairly elaborate), decorated initial letters, notes at bottom of page, original tree calf (minor wear, joints weak), decorative gilt border trim on covers with central signet arms in gilt on all covers, gilt-decorated spines, red morocco title labels, black morocco numbering labels with decorative gilt trim, outer dentelles tooled in gilt. A very pretty set with early inscriptions on half-titles. Milton's poems here are rendered into French prose: *PL* the prose translation by Nicholas Dupré de St. Maur, revised by C. J. Chéron de Boismorand, first published in 1729 (see set listed here); the prose translation of *PR* and other poems by Père de Mareuil, first published in 1730 (copy listed here); and the *Lettres critiques* by Bernard Routh. Scarce. Not in Coleridge; Kohler 49, reporting "Not in Williamson. Not in the Bodleian Library."

744. **PARADISE LOST**. A Poem, In Twelve Books. The Author John Milton. The Eighth Edition. With Notes of various Authors, By Thomas Newton, D.D. Now Lord Bishop of Bristol. *London: Printed for W. Strahan, J. and F. Rivington, L. Davis, B. White, T. Caslon, T. Longman, B. Law, J. Dodsley, E. and C. Dilly, G. Kearsly, E. Johnson, J. D. Cornish, T. Cadell, T. Lowndes, F. Newbury, T. Davies, J. Robson, T. Becket, G. Robinson, W. Nicoll, J. Knox, R. Baldwin, T. Evans, J. Bew, T. Beecroft, W. Otridge, and B. Collins, MDCCLXXVIII*. 2 volumes. 8vo, [10]+[11]+lxxxvi+[vi]+[xx]+510pp.,+463+(182-page unpaginated index and verbal index)+[1]pp., engraved frontispiece portrait each volume, after Vertue, after the Onslow portrait, volume 1, after Faithorne, volume 2, engraved illustrations after Hayman, engraved by I. S. Müller, title page each volume, half-title for each book, decorative tailpieces, notes at the bottom of each page, contemporary quarter calf, marbled paper over boards, gilt rules on spine, red morocco labels with gilt lettering and decorative gilt trim, raised bands. A very pleasing set with advertisement leaf of "Just Published A New Edition" of "The Poetical Works of John Milton" bound in at the end of volume 2. The final lifetime edition of Newton's extensive variorum edition. A one-volume 12mo edition was also published in the same year (see copy following). The 1775 quarto edition is also called "The Eighth Edition" on the title page (also listed here), "indicating a breakdown in the sequence, which was rather academic by this time, even though the 1775 4to edition is only the eighth edition of Newton's text and notes to be published by the approved successors of the Tonsons" (Coleridge, p. 182). Coleridge 138; Kohler 50, reporting "Not in Cambridge University Library."

745. **PARADISE LOST**. A Poem, In Twelve Books. The Author John Milton. *London: Printed for W. Strahan, J. F. and C. Rivington, L. Davis, B. White, T. Caslon, T. Longman, B. Law, J. Dodsley, E. and C. Dilly, G.Kearsly, E. Johnson, J. D. Cornish, T. Cadell, T. Lowndes, F. Newbery, T. Davies, J. Robson, T. Becket, G. Robinson, W. Nicoll, J. Knox, R. Baldwin, T. Evans, J. Bew, T. Beecroft, W. Otridge, and B. Collins, M.DCC.LXXVIII*. 12mo, lxxi+[i]+319pp.+[25-page unpaginated index]+[2]pp., engraved frontispiece portrait by T. Miller, engraved illustrations after Hayman (reproduced from reduced recuttings), engraved by T. Miller (signed "T.M."), life of Milton by Newton, small decorative tailpieces, index, contemporary calf (rubbed, front joint cracked, lacking front free endpaper), gilt rules on spine, outer dentelles tooled in gilt (faded), two advertisement leaves of "Lately Published, A New Edition" of "The Poetical Works of John Milton," of the Baskerville edition of Milton, and of two other publications bound in at end. A nice, thick copy with early signature (dated

1816), and presentation inscription from that signator (dated 1818) on verso of frontispiece. The final lifetime edition of Newton's extensive variorum edition. A two-volume octavo edition was also published in the same year (see set listed here). Williamson 97; Coleridge 139; Kohler 51, reporting "Not in the Bodleian Library. Not in Cambridge University Library."

746. **LE PARADIS PERDU**, Poeme De Milton, Traduit En Vers Francais Par M. Beaulaton. Le prix est de 6 liv. broche. *A Montargis, De l'Imprimerie CL. Lequatre, Imprimeur de la Ville & du College. M. DCC. LXXVIII. Avec Approbation & Privilège du Roi.* 2 volumes. Tall 8vo, xii+243pp.,+251+[4]pp., half-title and title page each volume, with small decorative emblem at the center of each title page, preface, volume 1, "Notes sur Le Paradis Perdu" and "Approbation" and "Privilege Du Roi" at end of volume 2, decorative headpieces, contemporary quarter calf, marbled paper over boards, gilt rules on spines, red lettering labels with decorative gilt trim, black numbering labels with decorative gilt trim (chipped, volume 2), edges untrimmed and partially unopened. Fine, tall set, possibly a large paper copy. See 1779 edition listed here, which reprints this verse translation. Rare. Not in Coleridge; Not in Kohler.

747. **LE PARADIS PERDU** De Milton, Poème Héroïque, Traduit De L'Anglois; Avec les Remarques de M. Addisson. Nouvelle Edition, revue & corrigée. *A Paris, Chez les Libraires Associés. M. DCC. LXXVIII. Avec Approbation, & Privilège du Roi.* 3 volumes. 12mo, xxiv+425pp.,+474pp.,+460+[3]pp., half-title and title page each volume, with black rule around each title page and decorative emblem at the center, "Vie De Milton," volume 1, half-title for *PR*, with "Preface" and "Arguments" (not original to the poem) for *Le Paradis Reconquis* at end of volume 2, title page "Le Paradis Perdu" to volume 3 followed by "Oeuvres Diverses De Milton," including *L* ("Lycidas, Idylle de Milton"), *L'A, IlP,* and *NO* ("Sur La Fête De Noël"), along with the six letters, Addison's "Remarques" (with half-title), and "Approbation" and "Privilege Du Roi" at the end, decorative head- and tailpieces (some fairly elaborate), decorated initial letters, notes at bottom of page, contemporary full mottled calf, decorative gilt trim with small decorative gilt pieces on spines, red morocco labels with gilt lettering and decorative gilt trim, outer dentelles ruled in gilt, marbled endpapers, speckled edges, red silk ribbon marker in each volume. A very fine set with the Salm-Krautheimische Schloss bookplate on front pastedown of each volume. Milton's poems here are rendered into French prose: *PL* the prose translation by Nicholas Dupré de St. Maur, revised by C. J. Chéron de Boismorand, first published in 1729 (see set listed here); the prose translation of *PR* and other poems by Père de Mareuil, first published in 1730 (also listed here); and the *Lettres critiques* by Bernard Routh. See 1882 three-volume edition listed here, virtually identical to edition here and equally rare. Not in Coleridge; Kohler 52, reporting "Not in the British Library. Not in the Bodleian Library. Not in Cambridge University Library."

748. **PARADISE LOST**. A Poem In Twelve Books. The Author John Milton. With Historical, Philosophical, and Explanatory Notes. Translated from the French of The learned Raymond de St. Maur. And Various critical Remarks and Observations, from Mr. Addison, Dr. Warburton, Dr. Newton, Dr. Pearce, Dr. Bentley, Mr. Richardson, and Mr. Hume. A new Edition, adorn'd with Plates. *London: Printed for R. Bladon, T. Lawes, S. Crowder, C. Ware, and T. Payne. M,DCC,LXXIX.* 2 volumes. 12mo, xiv+[ii]+231pp.,+232pp.+[28-page unpaginated index], unsigned engraved frontispiece of Homer, Virgil, and Milton with Dryden epigram, twelve engraved illustrations (reductions of 1688 illustrations) by R. Cooper, one for each book, title page for each volume, advertisement and life by Fenton, volume 1, index to *PL* at the end of volume 1, notes at bottom of page, half-title for Book VIII before title page in volume 2 along with half-title for *PR*, original sheep (joints slightly cracked, some minor spotting), gilt rules on spines, red morocco title labels lettered in gilt with decorative gilt trim, small black morocco numbering labels with decorative gilt trim. A nice set. Included is *PR*, although not mentioned on the title page. Raymond de St. Maur's commentary originally appeared as *The State of Innocence and the Fall of Man* in 1745 (copy listed here). See copy of 1752 12mo edition by R. Urie, first thus with Cooper's copies of the 1688 plates; see also copy of 1754 Raymond de St. Maur edition with striking illustrations (unsigned); see, too, another issue of the 1754 Raymond de St. Maur edition in 1755 with a variant publisher with the same striking illustrations (unsigned); see also two-volume 1775 set with unsigned 1688 illustrations reduced; and see 1765 and 1770 nonillustrated Raymond de St. Maur editions. "[The present] edition is almost certainly the same as John Wood's 1765 edition of *PL* [see copy here]," (Coleridge). See 1784 edition listed here. Scarce. Coleridge 175; Kohler 54, reporting "Not in Williamson. Not in the Bodleian Library. Not in Cambridge University Library."

749. **LE PARADIS PERDU**, Poeme De Milton, Traduit En Vers Francois [sic]. *A Paris, Chez J. - Fr. Bastien, Libraire, rue du Petit-Lion, Fauxbourg S. Germain. M. DCC. LXXIX. Avec Approbation & Privilège du Roi.* 2 volumes in one. 8vo, xii+243pp.,+251+[4]pp., half-title and title page each volume, with decorative emblem at the center of each title page, preface, volume 1, "Notes sur Le Paradis Perdu" and "Approbation" and "Privilege Du Roi" at end of volume 2, decorative headpieces, original marbleized polished sheep (spine with a few small worm punctures, slight one-inch break at head of front cover joint), decorative blind trim on covers, spines richly gilt within the panels, green morocco label with gilt lettering and gilt rules, raised bands with decorative gilt trim (a bit faded), outer dentelles ruled in gilt, marbled endpapers, red speckled edges. A lovely copy, beautifully printed and handsomely bound, reprinting the verse translation of the 1778 edition here. Rare. Not in Coleridge; Not in Kohler.

750. LE PARADIS PERDU DE MILTON, Poème Héroïque, Traduit De L'Anglois. Avec les Remarques de M. Addisson. Nouvelle Edition, Augmentée Du Paradis Reconquis; & de quelques autres Pièces de Poésie du même Auteur. *A Lyon, Chez J. M. Barret, Imprimeur-Libraire. M. DCC. LXXXI.* 12mo, 80+375pp.+107pp., "Vie De Milton" and Addison's "Remarques" before *PL*, half-title for *PR* ("Le Paradis Reconquis De Milton"), with new pagination, with "Preface" and "Arguments" (not original to the poem) for *Le Paradis Perdu Reconquis*, followed by *L* ("Lycidas, Idile de Milton"), *L'A*, *IlP*, and *NO* ("Sur La Feste De Noël") under the heading, "Oeuvres De Milton," decorative head- and tailpieces (some fairly elaborate), decorated initial letters, notes at bottom of page, page-and-a-half "Permission Simple" at the end, contemporary French speckled sheep, elaborately gilt-decorated spine in the panels, red morocco labels with gilt lettering within gilt rules, raised bands with decorative gilt trim (now faint), marbled endpapers and edges. A fine copy with contemporary signature on title page. Milton's poems here are rendered into French prose: *PL* the prose translation by Nicholas Dupré de St. Maur, revised by C. J. Chéron de Boismorand, first published in 1729 (see set listed here); the prose translation of *PR* and other poems by Père de Mareuil, first published in 1730 (also listed here). Rare. Not in Coleridge; Shawcross, Kentucky, 440; Not in Kohler.

751. PARADISE LOST A Poem In Twelve Books. By John Milton. With A Biographical And Critical Account of the Author and this [sic] Writings. *London: Printed for A. Millar, J. Wren, and J. Hodges. MDCCLXXXII.* 8vo, xviii+[ii]+283pp., original sheep (worn, front cover detached, lacking front endpapers, age-browning throughout), maroon morocco label (partially missing) lettered in gilt with gilt rules, raised bands within gilt rules. Scarce. Not in Coleridge; Not in Kohler.

752. LE PARADIS PERDU DE MILTON, Poème Héroïque, Traduit De L'Anglois; Avec les Remarques de M. Addisson. Nouvelle Edition, revue & corrigée. *A Paris, Chez les Libraires Associés. M. DCC. LXXXII.* Avec Approbation & Privilège du Roi. 3 volumes. 12mo, xxiv+425pp., +474pp.,+460+[3]pp., half-title and title page each volume with black rule around each title page and decorative emblem at the center, "Vie De Milton," volume 1, half-title for *PR* ("Le Paradis Reconquis De Milton, Avec Six Lettres Critiques Sur Le Paradis Perdu Et Reconquis"), with "Preface" and "Arguments" (not original to the poem) for *Le Paradis Reconquis* at end of volume 2, title page "Le Paradis Perdu" to volume 3 followed by "Oeuvres Diverses De Milton," including *L* ("Lycidas, Idylle de Milton"), *L'A*, *IlP*, and *NO* ("Sur La Fête De Noël") along with the six letters, Addison's "Remarques" with half-title, and "Approbation" and "Privilege Du Roi" at the end, decorative head- and tailpieces (some fairly elaborate), decorated initial letters, notes at bottom of page, original tree calf, intricately gilt-decorated spines with red title labels and blue number labels, green silk ribbon markers. A fine set. Milton's poems here are rendered into French prose: *PL* the prose translation by Nicholas Dupré de St. Maur, revised by C. J. Chéron de Boismorand, first published in 1729 (see set listed here); the prose translation of *PR* and other poems by Père de Mareuil, first published in 1730 (also listed here); and the *Lettres critiques* by Bernard Routh. Rare. Not in Coleridge; Not in Kohler.

753. JOHANN MILTONS VERLORNES PARADIES. Neue verbesserte Auflage. Erster Band / Zweiter Band. Mit Kaiserl. und Kurpfalzischen Privilegien. / Mit Kaiserlichem, Kurpfalzischen und Kursachsischen Privilegien. *Mannheim 1783.* 2 volumes. 8vo (4" × 6 ½" × 1" each volume), 272pp.,+272pp., small emblem of a person seated amidst books and manuscripts on title page, volume 1, repeated at the end of Book V, and small emblem of a farmer tilling the field in front of elaborate ruins on title page, volume 2, decorative headpieces, original boards, calf spine (a little rubbed, joints cracked, front cover just holding on volume 2, bottom corners of front and back covers, volume 1, worn, spines chipped at top and bottom with a small piece missing at the top of volume 2, slight age-browning), black morocco labels lettered in gilt within decorative gilt trim and gilt rules, raised bands within gilt rules, blue edges. Quite a nice set. Rare. Not in Coleridge; Shawcross, Kentucky, 448; Not in Kohler.

754. PARADISE LOST: A Poem, In Twelve Books. The Author John Milton. With Historical, Philosophical, and Explanatory Notes. Translated from the French of The learned Raymond de St. Maur. And Various Critical

Remarks and Observations, from Mr. Addison, Dr. Warburton, Dr. Newton, Dr. Pearce, Dr. Bentley, Mr. Richardson, and Mr. Hume. A New Edition. Volume I / II. *London: Printed for R. Bladon, T. Lawes, S. Crowder, C. Ware, and T. Payne. M,DCC,LXXXIV.* 2 volumes. 12mo in 6s, xiv+[ii]+231pp.,+232pp.+[20-page index], unsigned engraved frontispiece of Homer, Virgil, and Milton with Dryden epigram, twelve engraved illustrations (reductions of 1688 illustrations), signed by R. Cooper, one for each book, title page for each volume, advertisement (dated 1775) and life by Fenton, volume 1, index (to *PL*) at the end of volume 2, notes at bottom of page, half-title for Book VIII before title page in volume 2, half-title for *PR* at the end, original sheep (joints and corners rubbed), gilt-decorated spines, red morocco title labels lettered in gilt with decorative gilt rules, black morocco numbering labels. A very nice copy of this rare set with early armorial bookplate on both front and back pastedowns of each volume, front bookplates with later signature in a neat hand. Included is *PR*, although not mentioned on the title page. Rare. Not in Coleridge; Not in Kohler.

Raymond de St. Maur's commentary originally appeared as *The State of Innocence and the Fall of Man* in 1745 (copy listed here). See 1752 edition by R. Urie above, first thus, with the 1688 engraved illustrations reduced, signed by R. Cooper. See also 1775 edition above (first thus), which the present edition and a two-volume 1779 Raymond de St. Maur edition (also listed) with Cooper's illustrations signed by R. Cooper, as here, each reprint. Not in Coleridge; Not in Kohler.

755. [PARADISE LOST] COURS DE LANGUE ANGLOISE, A l'aide duquel on peut apprendre cette Langue chez soi, sans Maitre, & en deux ou trois mois de lecture. Par M. Luneau de Boisjermain. Tome I [And II]. *A Paris, Chez l'Auteur, rue Saint-Andre-des-Arts, près la rue Contrescarpe. 1784. 2 volumes.* First edition thus. 8vo in four's, xiv+[ii]+446pp.,+431(p. 106 goes to p. 109, p. 301 is repeated)+[2]pp., title page each volume with a different central emblem on each title page, "Avertissement De L'Auteur," half-title for "*Paradise Lost, Pardis Perdu*, A Poème. Un Poème," volume 1, half-title for volume 2, "Approbation" and "Privilege Du Roi" at end of volume 2, decorative head- and tailpieces, several of the tailpieces very elaborate, notes at bottom of page, contemporary French mottled calf (a bit rubbed, edges slightly bumped, tear on II YY4 just affecting text but with no loss), spines gilt in the compartments, lettered and numbered in gilt, marbled endpapers, all edges red. A very attractive set with the lavish (later) bookplate of Emil Blond and the book label of Jacques Pasques in each volume. A wonderful eighteenth-century edition of *PL* and the first appearance of this translation.

The English and French texts are printed together, line by line, with appropriate spacing so that the two run absolutely alongside. Furthermore a second and more fluent prose translation runs through both volumes in the form of footnotes. In his introduction, Boisjermain describes this manner of translation as more than an elucidation of the story of the poem but as a means to introduce readers to the beauty of the English language through the poem. He goes into great detail about his editorial choices and drifts into a brief but interesting discussion of the different demands of poetry in the two languages. The introduction is also used to some extent as self-justification, and he offers his own defense against many accusations leveled against him, both general and quoting specific instances. Scarce. Not in Coleridge; Not in Kohler.

756. PARADISE LOST. A Poem In Twelve Books. By John Milton. With A Biographical And Critical Account of the Author and his Writings. *London: Printed for J. Wren and W. Hodges. MDCCLXXXV.* 12mo, xviii+[i]+283pp., life of Milton by Fenton, original sheep (worn, joints cracked, lacking label on spine, age-browning, some signatures loose), gilt rules (faded) on spine. Fairly decent copy of a cheap edition with nineteenth-century initials (dated 1850) on fly-leaf. Rare. Not in Coleridge; Not in Kohler.

757. PARADISE LOST. A Poem. In Twelve Books. The Author John Milton. *London: Printed for R. Crowder, C. Ware, and T. Payne. MDCCLXXXV.* 12mo in 6s, half-title, xx+334pp., life of Milton by Fenton, original tree sheep (some age-browning, front joint cracked), red morocco label with gilt lettering and gilt rule on spine, raised bands. A nice copy, complete with half-title with nineteenth-century signature (dated 1814) on fly-leaf. Reprint of the first edition published in 1772 (copy listed here). Scarce. Coleridge 140; Not in Kohler.

758. PARADISE LOST. A Poem In Twelve Books. By John Milton. With A Biographical And Critical Account of the Author and his Writings. *Kilmarnock: Printed By J. Wilson, Bookseller, M,DCC,LXXXV.* 12mo in 6s, xviii+[i]+304pp. (continuous pagination), life of Milton by Fenton, original sheep (slightly worn, lacking blank endpapers, a little soiled, some age-darkening throughout), gilt rules on spine, red morocco label with gilt lettering and gilt rule, raised bands. An uncommon edition with contemporary signature and nineteenth-century signature on front pastedown. Printed by the printer of the Kilmarnock Burns (see 1789 edition listed here, printed by the same printer). Scarce. Not in Coleridge; Shawcross, Kentucky, 460; Kohler 58, reporting "Not in the Bodleian Library. Not in Cambridge University Library."

758A. (Cross-listing) [PARADISE LOST ABRIDGED] [In] **ENGLISH CLASSICS ABRIDGED; BEING SELECT WORKS OF ADDISON, POPE, AND MILTON,** Adapted to the Perusal of Youth, of both Sexes, At School. To Which Are Prefixed Observations on the Several Authors, Addressed To Parents and Preceptors. By J. Walker, Author of Elements of Elocution, Rhetorical Grammar, &c. [Latin Quotation from Hor.] *London, Printed for G. G. J. and J. Robinson, Paternoster Row. M DCC LXXXVI.* First edition. 8vo, xv+[1]+367pp., frontispiece portrait of John Walker, dedication, observations, contents, contemporary calf (a bit worn, minor age spots, front joint cracked, lacking label on spine), gilt rule on covers and at top and bottom of spine, raised bands with decorative gilt trim, small decorative pieces in blind within the panels, inner and outer dentelles ruled in gilt, marbled endpapers and edges, with the binder's ticket of the noted French émigré binder, the Comte de Caumont. A nice copy. Milton occupies the last third of the book, from pages 222 to 367; the selection is from *PL* with prose narrative summaries in between poetic selections from Milton's epic. See selections from Milton's poetry in eighteenth-century poetical miscellanies and in other anthologies in the Anthologies section. An important work for the vital role it played in advancing how great works and writers were to be read and studied for generations to come. Very rare. John Shawcross has kindly shared with me about this book that "it is otherwise known only from its 1807 edition, 'The Second Edition,' as owned by the British Library." Not in Coleridge; Not in Kohler. See main listing under *English Classics Abridged*, 1786, in *Anthologies*.

759. PARADISE LOST. A Poem In Twelve Books. The Author John Milton. From The Text Of Dr. Newton. In Two Volumes. [Quotation from Addison.] Vol. I. / [Quotation from Propert.] Vol. II. *London: Printed For John Bell, Bookseller To His Royal Highness The Prince Of Wales. 1788.* 2 volumes in one. 12mo in 6s, 234pp.,+213pp.(last page mispaginated "113"), engraved frontispiece portrait after H. Cook of a young Milton leaning on his right arm on several books, in a small circular frame with an ivy cluster above and Milton's name in large letters below, "From an Original in Ld. Chesterfield's Collection," with "London Printed for John Bell, British Library Strand, March 10th. 1785" printed below, volume 1, protective tissue guard, engraved and printed title pages for *PW* each volume, each engraved title page reads "Bell's Edition. The Poets of Great Britain Complete From Chaucer to Churchill," with vignette illustration of Satan after Mortimer for book I, line 223, engraved by Hall, volume 1, "Printed for John Bell near Exeter Exchange Strand London Novr. 20th. 1777" at the bottom, protective tissue guard, and vignette illustration of Eve after Mortimer for book VIII, line 44, engraved by Grignion, volume 2, "Printed for John Bell near Exeter Exchange Strand London Novr. 12th. 1777" at the bottom, protective tissue guard, each printed title page reads "The Poetical Works Of John Milton. From The Text Of Dr. Newton, In Four Volumes. With The Life Of The Author, And A Critique On Paradise Lost, By Joseph Addison, Esq. [Quotation from Dryden.] Vol. I. [No Quotation.] Vol. II. London: Printed Under The Direction Of J. Bell, British Library, Strand, Bookseller To His Royal Highness The Prince Of Wales," volume 1 printed title page dated 1788, volume 2 printed title page dated 1778, life of Milton followed by "Advertisement" and "A General Critique Upon The Paradise Lost. By Joseph Addison, Esq.," volume 1, contemporary calf (worn, joints cracked, covers nearly detached, spine chipped at top and bottom, lacking label). Despite the worn binding, a good copy, fine inside, with early signature in ink on fly-leaf and early shelf-mark in same ink on front pastedown. Scarce. See Coleridge 220; Not in Kohler.

Originally part of Bell's edition (Volumes 1–4, Bell's edition made up of some 200 or so total volumes), first published in 1776—see sets listed here, especially the 1776 four-volume Bell's edition of Milton's *PW* listed here (first edition thus), a choice set with a complete set of the engravings and all four portraits; see also 1779 four-volume set listed here (second edition thus); and see 1788 four-volume set listed here (with mispaginated "113" for p. 213 as last page in volume 2, as here).

760. MILTON'S PARADISE LOST ILLUSTRATED WITH TEXTS OF SCRIPTURE, By John Gillies, D.D. One Of The Ministers In Glasgow. [Quote from Book III] *London: Printed For J. F. And C. Rivington, L. Davis, et al, M.DCC.LXXXVIII.* First edition thus. 12mo, xxiii+[i]+384pp.+[21-page unpaginated index], dedication page, preface, life by Fenton, postscript, half-title for each book, notes at bottom of page, index at the end, original calf (a bit rubbed), decorative gilt rules with decorative gilt corner devices on covers, red morocco prize label at center of each cover, elaborately gilt-decorated spine, red morocco label with gilt lettering and decorative gilt trim, inner and outer dentelles tooled in gilt, marbled endpapers. A very nice copy with decoratively gilt-trimmed and gilt-lettered red morocco prize label on both covers bearing the inscription, "Merito Acquisitus December 1792," and with an ownership note by the prize recipient, "Thomas Barton's book Decr. 1792" on front blank. Gillies provides extensive footnotes referring to biblical sources. His work proved exceptionally popular, with two more editions in the next sixteen years, in 1793 (copy listed here), and 1804 (copy listed here). Scarce. Not in Coleridge; Kohler 59, reporting "Not in the Bodleian Library"; Shawcross, Kentucky, 483.

761. LE PARADIS PERDU De Milton; Traduction Nouvelle, Par M. Mosneron. Seconde Edition. Revue, corrigée et augmentée de plusieurs notes et d'un precis de la vie de l'auteur. Tome Premier/Second. *A Paris, De L'Imprimerie De Seguy-Thiboust. Chez Desenne, au Palais Royal, Onfroy, Quai des Augustins. M.DCC.LXXXVIII. Avec Approbation, Et Privilege Du Roi.* 2 volumes. Second edition thus. 8vo, xxxvi+340pp.,+303+[3]pp., half-title each volume, decorative headpieces (elaborate at head of Book I, volume 1, and at head of Book VII at the beginning of volume 2), notes at end of each volume, original stiff blue wrappers (spines a little faded, joints a bit cracked, spine slightly chipped at top of volume 1), title written lightly in ink in an early hand on front cover of each volume, hand-written paper label on spines, edges untrimmed. "Approbation" and "Privilège Général" (dated "16 April 1785. A Paris, le premier Decembre 1786. Signé, Cailleau, Adjoint") at the end of volume 2. A nice set. This translation entirely in prose by Jean-Baptiste Mosneron de Launay was first published in 1786; this second edition is considerably corrected and contains a life of Milton not found in the first edition. Rare. Rochedieu, p. 217; Not in Coleridge; Not in Kohler.

762. PARADISE LOST A Poem, In Twelve Books, By John Milton, With A Biographical And Critical Account Of The Author And His Writings. *Kilmarnock: Printed By J. Wilson. M,DCC,LXXXIX.* 8vo in 4s, 286pp., original sheep (very worn, front joint repaired, lacking front endpapers, age-browning throughout). An uncommon edition, printed by the printer of the Kilmarnock Burns (see copy of 1785 edition here by the same printer). Rare. John Shawcross told me that there is a "Copy in University of Illinois Library"; Not in Coleridge; Not in Kohler.

763. PARADISE LOST. A Poem In Twelve Books. By John Milton. With A Biographical And Critical Account of the Author and his Writings. *London: Printed for T. Vernor, J. Mathews, Ogilvie and Spears, J. Cuthel; J. Binns Leeds; Wilson and Spence, N. Frobisher, York; and W. Coke Leith. M,DCC,LXXXIX.* First edition thus? 12mo in 6s, xviii+[i]+300pp.(with pp. xv–xviii+[1] bound before last page [300]), life of Milton by Fenton, contemporary sheepskin (worn, small piece missing at bottom of spine, stain on back cover, foxing throughout, lacking front fly-leaf and back blanks), covers decorated in blind, with contemporary signature (dated 1790) on front blank. Rare. Not in Coleridge; Not in Kohler.

764. PARAISO PERDIDO, POEMA HEROICO DE J. MILTON; Traduzido Em Vulgar Pelo Padre José Amaro Da Silva, Presbitero Vimaranense. Com o Paraiso Retaurado, Poema do mesmo Author; Notas Historicas, Mythologicas, &c. de M. Racine: e as Observaçoes de M. Addisson sobre o Paraiso Perdido. Tomo II. *Lisboa, Na Typografia Rollandiana. 1789. Com licença da Real Meza da Commissao Geral sobre o Eccame, e Censura dos Livres.* volume 2 only. 8vo, 344pp., decorative head- and tailpieces, notes at bottom of page, contemporary calf (a little rubbed along joints and extremities), leather label on spine lettered and ruled in gilt, raised bands within double gilt rules, lightly speckled edges. A very nice copy, but of volume 2 only, with early (possibly contemporary) signature on front blank. Included in this volume are Books X to XII of *Paraiso Perdido*, *Observaçoes de M. Addisson sobre o Paraiso Perdido De Milton*, and ALSO *Paraiso Retaurado* complete, with "Arguments" (not original to the poem) and a decorative tailpiece at the end of each book. Rare. Not in Coleridge; Not in Kohler.

765. PARADISE LOST. A Poem, In Twelve Books. The Author John Milton. The Ninth Edition, With Notes of various Authors, By Thomas Newton, D.D. Late Lord Bishop of Bristol. In Two Volumes. Volume The First / The Second. *London: Printed for J. F. and C. Rivington, L. Davis, et al, M.DCC.XC.* 2 volumes. 8vo, [10]+[11]+lxxxvi+[vi]+[xx]+510pp.,+463pp.+([182]-page unpaginated index and verbal index)+[1]pp., engraved frontispiece portrait each volume, portrait unsigned, volume 1, with unsigned vignette illustration of the expulsion incorporated at the bottom, portrait after Vertue (dated 1750), volume 2, title page each volume, dedication, preface, life of Milton, Addison's "A Critique upon the Paradise Lost," volume 1, engraved illustration plates after Hayman, engraved by T. Müller, one for each book, half-title for each book, notes at bottom of each page, postscript, index, and advertisement leaf for books "Lately Published" (including *PR* and *PW*) at the end of volume 2, contemporary calf (a bit worn, joints cracked with covers rehinged from the inside), gilt-decorated spines (rubbed), black morocco numbering labels (lacking second label on volume 2 and both red morocco title labels). A respectable copy, fresh and clean internally, with early armorial bookplate on front pastedown in each volume. "This, actually the 10th [Newton] edition, is the last of the series which began with the 1749 4to [see sets here]. In 1801 Todd's edition of the *PW* in 6 volumes [see sets listed here] superseded Newton's work, although portions were used by subsequent editors" (Coleridge). Uncommon. Coleridge 141; Kohler 61, referencing Williamson 167, and reporting "Not in the Bodleian Library. Not in Cambridge University Library."

766. PARADISE LOST. A Poem, In Twelve Books. The Author John Milton. Printed From The Text Of Tonson's Correct Edition Of M.DCC.XI. *London: Printed For J. F. And C. Rivington, L. Davis, et al, M.DCC.XC.* 12mo, xxxv+345pp., frontispiece vignette portrait by T. Holloway, life of Milton by Fenton, postscript, half-title for each book, contemporary calf (a bit rubbed, joints weak), decorative gilt border trim on covers, gilt-decorated spine, inner dentelles finely tooled gilt, outer dentelles ruled in gilt, marbled endpapers, bookplate, bound by C. Kalthoeben, with his ticket on fly-leaf. A very pleasing copy with contemporary inscription (dated 1795) on front blank. Not in Coleridge; Not in Kohler.

767. PARADISE LOST: A Poem, In Twelve Books. By John Milton. With A Biographical And Critical Account of the Author and his Writings. *London: Printed For John Taylor. M.DCC.XC.* 16mo, xiv+[ii]+287pp., life of Milton by Fenton, without Barrow's Latin poem, original sheepskin (joints cracked), gilt rules on spine, red morocco label with gilt lettering and decorative gilt trim, speckled edges. A nice copy. Coleridge 142; Not in Kohler.

768. PARADISE LOST: A Poem, In Twelve Books. By John Milton. With A Biographical And Critical Account of the Author and his Writings. *London: Printed For Thomas Martin. M.DCC.XC.* 8vo, xiv+[2]+287pp., life of Milton by Fenton, without Barrow's Latin poem, original sheepskin (spine and joints cracked, spine ends chipped), gilt rules on spine with red morocco label with gilt lettering and decorative gilt trim. A good copy with early name of Rev. Arthur Brew on title page with his bookplate on front pastedown, and with dated nineteenth-century name on fly-leaf. This cheaply printed edition is quite likely a piracy. Very rare. Not in Coleridge (but see notes to Coleridge 142); Not in Kohler.

First Edition In Danish

769. [PARADISE LOST] DET TABTE PARADIIS. Et episk Digt af John Milton. Af der Engelske oversat ved Joh. Henr. Schønheyder. Medic Dr. og Prof. *Kiøbenhavn [Copenhagen], 1790. Trykt hos Johan Frederik Schultz, Hof- og Universitetsbogtrykker.* 2 volumes. First edition thus. 8vo, 300pp.,+604pp.(continuous pagination), half-title after title page, Addison's comments appear before each book, contemporary half sheep, marbled paper over boards (a bit rubbed, name cut from title page, volume 1, removing one letter, repaired), gilt-decorated spines (faded, labels missing). A nice set with early name on fly-leaf of each volume. The very rare first edition in Danish of Milton's *PL*. OCLC 6181548 records four additional copies: at California Berkeley, Luther College, Illinois, and Kentucky, with one further copy located at Yale; and NUC records another copy at Harvard; Not in Coleridge; Kohler 62.

770. PARADISE LOST: A Poem, In Twelve Books. By John Milton. With A Biographical And Critical Account Of The Author And His Writings. *Air: Printed By J. & P. Wilson. M,DCC,XCI.* 12mo in 6s, 288pp., life of Milton by Fenton, with Barrow's and Marvell's poems, recent green cloth (a bit rubbed, pages age-browned), spine lettered in gilt. All in all, a good copy of a scarce edition. Not in Coleridge; Kohler 64, reporting "Not in the British Library. Not in the Bodleian Library. Not in Cambridge University Library."

771. PARADISE LOST, A Poem, In Twelve Books. By John Milton. With A Biographical And Critical Account Of The Author And His Writings. *London: Printed For The Booksellers. M,DCC,XCI.* 12mo in 6s, 288pp., life of Milton by Fenton, with Barrow's and Marvell's poems, original calf (very rubbed with some wear), red leather label on spine lettered in gilt ("Milton"). A pleasant copy, clean internally, with the contemporary signature of "James Hamilton" on fly-leaf. This edition is identical to that from "Air: Printed By J. & P. Wilson" and to that from "London: Printed For Vernor & Hood" et al. in 1795; it is also very similar to the edition from "London Printed For John Taylor" in 1790 and to the edition from "London Printed For Thomas Martin" in 1790, and also to the edition from "London: Printed for A. Law, W. Millar, and R. Cater," in 1792—all listed here. John Shawcross kindly shared with me that while "James Hamilton is a common enough name," "It may be pertinent, that 'James Edward Hamilton' wrote 'A Short Treatise on Polygamy; or, the Marrying and Cohabiting with More than One Woman at the Same Time' from Dublin, Printed and Sold by the Boodsellers, 1786. The 'Boodsellers' is correct. There is a reference to Milton and his separation from his wife and his writing in defense of divorce on p. 14." Rare. Not in Coleridge; Not in Kohler.

772. PARADISE LOST: A Poem In Twelve Books, By John Milton. From The Text Of Doctor Newton. With The Life Of The Author. *Philadelphia: Printed And Sold By Henry Taylor. M.DCC.XCI.* Second American edition. 12mo, 316pp., half-title, life of Milton by Fenton, "Advertisement" (with narrative on Milton's changing ten books into twelve in the second edition and quotation of verses added at that time), original calf (very rubbed, age-browning throughout, several small tears, small bottom outer portion of back fly-leaf torn away), red morocco label (partially missing) with gilt lettering and decorative gilt trim, with rare half-title. All in all, a rather nice copy of an uncommon eighteenth-century American edition. One of only eleven total eighteenth-century American editions of Milton's works. Of the eleven, the collection has eight (see *PL*, 1777, here, for a listing of those in the collection and identification of the others). Not in Coleridge; Not in Kohler.

773. [PARADISE LOST] JOHANN MILTONS VERLORNES PARADIES. Neue verbesserte Auflage. Erster Band. Mit Kaiserl. und Kurpfalzischen Privilegien. *Mannheim, 1791.* Bound with [PARADISE REGAINED] DAS WIEDEREROBERTE PARADIES, DES JOHANN MILTON, nevst seiner Lebensveschreibung, und dramatischen Gedichten: Simson. Mit allerhochstem kaiserlichen Privilegio. *Mannheim, im Berlage ver Herausgeber der aulandischen schonen Geister 1791.* Bound with [SAMSON AGONISTES] SIMSON. Ein dramatisches Gedicht (half-title). 3 volumes in one. 8vo, xlv+272pp.,+272pp.,+ 208pp., separate title page for each volume of *PL* (volumes 1 and 2), life before Book I, separate title page for *PR* (volume 3), each title page with small central decorative design, half-title for *SA* (with both the half-title and the text of the poem misbound between *PL*, volume 1, and *PL*, volume 2), decorative headpieces, contemporary quarter polished black calf, marbled paper over boards (a bit rubbed, name cut from top of fly-leaf, a few minor stains or spots), gilt rules on spine with gilt lettering, speckled edges. A fine copy. "This exceedingly rare combination is the only one that we have seen. The British Library has the German *PR*, but not the *PL*; neither translation is in Coleridge" (G. W. Stuart, Jr., Ravenstree, Cat. 174, #55, 1992). About *PL* John Shawcross shared with me that "This is a reissue of 1783 [see copy here], otherwise unrecorded and not discovered in any German repository or such libraries as the British Library or Harvard University." Not in Coleridge; Not in Kohler.

774. PARADISE LOST, A Poem, In Twelve Books. By John Milton. With A Biographical And Critical Account of the Author and his Writings. *London: Printed for A. Law, W. Millar, and R. Cater. MDCCXCII.* 12mo, 299pp., unsigned engraved frontispiece portrait of a youngish Milton in circular form with ivy branches above and name printed below, life of Milton by Fenton, twelve engraved illustration plates derived from Hayman, one for each book, original sheep (spine a bit rubbed), gilt rules on spine, black morocco label with gilt lettering and gilt rules. A nice copy with contemporary signature (dated "Janu. the 2: [17]95") on fly-leaf and with fine impressions of the plates. This is possibly another Scottish piracy. See 1795 and 1796 editions listed here, with similar illustrations, unsigned. Scarce. Coleridge 143; Kohler 64, reporting "Not in Cambridge University Library."

Color Plates in Exquisite Morocco Binding for Ferdinand-Louis-Phillipe (With Book Label of J. R. Abbey)

775. LE PARADIS PERDU, Poeme Par Milton; Edition En Anglais Et En Francais Ornee de douze Estampes imprimees en couleur d'apres les Tableaux de M. Schall. *A Paris, Chez Defer De. Maisonneuve, rue du Foin S. Jacques, no. 11. 1792.* 2 volumes in one. First edition thus. 4to, viii+391pp.,+377pp., half-title each volume (half-title for volume 2 bound after title page for volume 2), title page each volume, "Vie De Milton" translated from Elijah Fenton's," volume 1, twelve color plates variously engraved after Jeano-Frédéric Schall (first appearance, three before all letters, the others with artists' names etched à la pointe), one for each book, half-title for each book, text in both English and French (verso English, recto French), the French a prose translation by N. F. Dupré de Saint-Maur, as revised by C. J. Chéron de Boismorand, first printed in 1729 (also listed here). French straight-grained full red morocco (ca. 1830), covers and spine elaborately tooled and richly decorated in gilt, a roll-tooled border enclosing a panel with large corner pieces, in the center of each cover is the monogram of Ferdinand-Louis-Phillipe (1810–42; eldest son of King Louis-Philippe), flat spine richly gilt in compartments, blue silk endpapers, a.e.g., in a red cloth box with green morocco labels on front cover and spine. An exquisite copy with the book label of J. R. Abbey, in fine condition. See sale catalogue of Major Abbey (Sotheby's, June 1967, No. 2029) and Cohen-de Ricci 708, where this copy, having formerly belonged to Abbey, is featured. Coleridge 158; Not in Kohler.

The plates here are noted for their early use of the fascinating color stipple process developed by Francis Bartolozzi, a process involving the tedious inking of each plate with the colors, so that the plate would be printed with one single pull. It was not only tedious but extremely expensive and apparently only five books were illustrated by this process (La Fontaine, Milton, Gessner, Florian, and Vade—Milton being the only English poet to be included), and those five were done in Paris at the height of the French Revolution. A landmark in French book illustration; a milestone in book arts; a sumptuous copy. The French color prints of the eighteenth century have long been prized by print collectors, thereby contributing all the more to the rarity of this book. Coleridge 158; Not in Kohler.

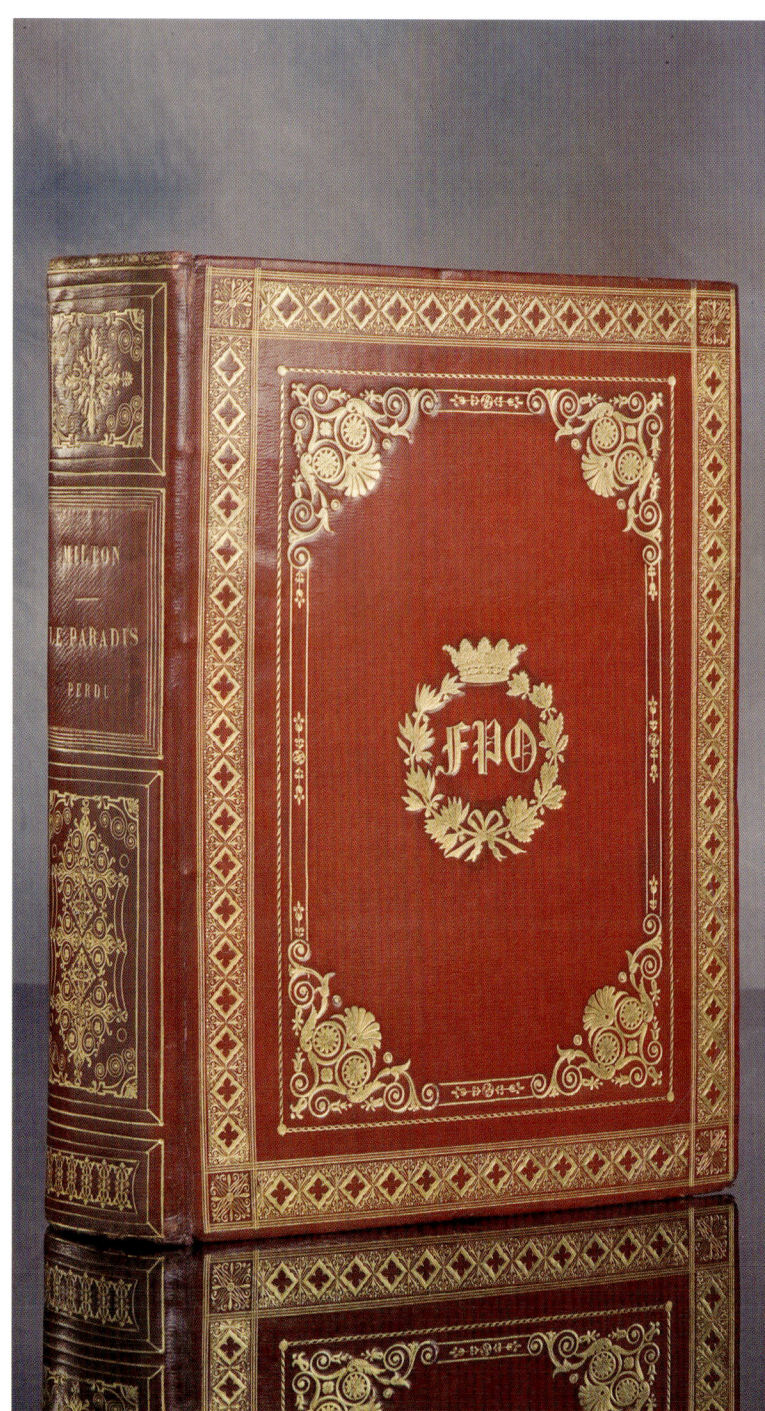

Le Paradis Perdu, Paris, 1792, with color illustrations by Jean-Frédéric Schall, in exquisite morocco binding (ca. 1830) for Ferdinand-Louis-Phillipe, formerly the Abbey copy. See #775.

Printed color illustration after Schall of Adam and Eve in the Garden, 1792 Paris edition. See #775.

Printed color illustration after Schall of *The Expulsion*, 1792 Paris edition. See #775.

Presentation Copy from Capel Lofft

776. PARADISE LOST: A Poem, In Twelve Books. The Author John Milton. Printed from the First and Second Editions collated. The Original System Of Orthography Restored; The Punctuation Corrected And Extended. With Various Readings: And Notes; Chiefly Rhythmical. By Capel Lofft. [Several Latin Quotations] *Bury St. Edmund's: Printed And Sold By J. Rackham, et al, M DCC XCII.* First edition thus. 4to, [ii]+lxii+[i]+[31]pp., advertisement, "Direction To The Binder," a lengthy preface of historical and critical interest, which includes a chart of "Editions of the Paradise Lost; either separately or with the other Poetical Works," followed by "Alterations In The Paradise Lost; As Specified In The Postscript To Fenton's Edition," "Appendix To The Preface," the arguments printed at the beginning before Book I, later calf, gilt rules on covers, also decorated with blind rules, gilt-decorated spine in the panels, red morocco label with gilt lettering and decorative gilt trim, inner dentelles finely tooled in gilt, outer dentelles ruled in gilt, marbled endpapers and edges. A fine copy. Presentation copy with presentation inscription from the author Capel Lofft to Rev. George Rogers on preliminary blank. Only Book I appears here, with a prefatory note that others would follow; Lofft published another, enlarged issue in 1793 with different title page, to include, according to that title page: "The First And Second Books." *Milton Tercentenary*, 1908, Addenda, p. 157, #800, lists "*PL.* Books I, II. Ed. Capel Lofft. Bury St. Edmunds, 1793." John Shawcross told me that there is a copy in the University of Illinois Library. There is also an edition (with different 'title') in 1793 as you note; copy [of that also] in the University of Illinois Library." See Capel Lofft's copy of the third edition of *PL* listed here. Rare. Coleridge 154a; Not in Kohler.

※

777. JOHANN MILTON'S VERLORNES PARADIES. Uebersetzt von Samuel Gottlieb Burde. Zwei Theile. *Berlin, 1793. bei Friedrich Bieweg, dem alteren.* First edition thus. 8vo, viii+304pp.,+xvi+327pp., engraved title-page plate with the possible first appearance of engraved vignette of *Adam and Eve in the Bower of Bliss* (fine impression) by D. Chock, engraved by "Zolt," half-title on thick paper, "Borrede," arguments for Books I to VII translated together in prose at the outset, printed title page for volume 2 (without vignette illustration), arguments for Books VIII to XII translated together in prose at the beginning, verse translation of the poem by Samuel Bürde (1753 to 1831), notes at bottom of page, original marbled paper over boards (a bit rubbed, spines slightly worn at top and bottom, corners bumped), light blue paper labels on spines with hand-written titles and gilt rules. A nice set with two early signatures on front pastedown and fly-leaf of each volume. Not in Coleridge; Kohler 65, reporting "Not in Coleridge. Not in the Bodleian Library. Not in Cambridge University Library."

778. MILTON'S PARADISE LOST ILLUSTRATED WITH TEXTS OF SCRIPTURE. By John Gillies, D.D. One Of The Ministers In Glasgow. [Quote from Book III] The Second Edition, With Additions. *London: Printed For B. White And Son, T. Longman, B. Law And Son, et al, M.DCC.XCIII.* Second Gillies edition. 12mo, xxxi+[i]+378+[1]pp.+[20-page unpaginated index], dedication page, preface, "Advertisement To The Second Edition," life by Fenton, postscript, half-title for each book, notes at bottom of page, index, contemporary tree calf (two scuff marks on front cover), richly gilt-decorated spine, red morocco label with gilt lettering and decorative gilt trim, outer dentelles tooled in gilt. A fine copy with contemporary signature (dated 1795) on fly-leaf along with a later signature. To his second edition Gillies added a new preface and a number of additional annotations to the extensive footnotes referring to biblical sources he had already included in his first edition, published in 1788 (also listed here). His work proved exceptionally popular, with two more editions in the next sixteen years, in 1793 and 1804—both listed here. Of those editions, Coleridge does not have the first and neither does the Bodleian, but Kohler has a copy; of the second edition, Coleridge has a copy, but Kohler does not; of the third edition, Coleridge has a copy, but Kohler does not. This collection has a copy of all three editions, each of which is rare. ESTC 936G5; Coleridge 144; Not in Kohler.

779. PARADISE LOST: A Poem, In Twelve Books. The Author John Milton. *London: Printed For J. And H. Richter, Great Newport-Street, By T. Spilsbury And Son, Snow-Hill. M.DCC.XCIV. 2 volumes.* First edition thus. Royal 4to, 493+[iv]pp.(plates paginated), separate title page each volume, first appearance of engraved frontispiece portrait plate by Richter, "Engraved from an Original by William Faithorne... Pubd. 13 June 1796 by I & H. Richter," elaborately printed dedication leaf with engraving of angels at the top, volume 1, first appearance of twelve stipple-engraved illustration plates and twelve circular vignette illustrations engraved by John Richter after drawings by his son, Henry Richter, one for each book, variously dated 1794, 1795, and 1796, half-title for each book, "A List Of The Subscribers" bound at the end of volume 2, contemporary full red morocco (front cover, volume 2, rehinged from the inside, joints rubbed, plates foxed), covers decorated in blind with richly tooled decorative gilt border trim, elaborately gilt-decorated spine, thick raised bands, each with lettering, inner and outer dentelles tooled in gilt (faded), marbled endpapers, a.e.g. A fine set in lovely contemporary red morocco (with the exception of the broken joints in volume 2 and the foxing, not uncommon). While the title page is dated 1794, the plates are dated 1796 and indicate this year as the actual publication date. Coleridge 145; Kohler 66, referencing Williamson, p. 10, and reporting "Not in the Bodleian Library."

Hand-colored Richter Plates

780. Variant of Preceding. 2 volumes in one. First edition thus. Royal 4to, 493pp. (plates paginated), first appearance of engraved frontispiece portrait plate by Richter, "Engraved from an Original by William Faithorne . . . Pubd. 13 June 1796 by I & H. Richter," elaborately printed dedication leaf with engraving of angels at the top, "A List Of The Subscribers," volume 1, first appearance of twelve stipple-engraved illustration plates and twelve circular vignette illustrations engraved by John Richter after drawings by his son, Henry Richter, one for each book, variously dated 1794, 1795, and 1796, except that in this copy the dedication page is beautifully hand-colored, as are most of the illustrations, half-title for each book, contemporary full dark navy blue morocco (a bit rubbed), decorative gilt border trim on covers, gilt rules with decoratively tooled corner gilt pieces on spine, slightly raised thick bands, inner and outer dentelles finely tooled in gilt, marbled endpapers and edges. A fine copy with plates beautifully hand-colored of the period, bound as two volumes with the "Subscribers" list at end of volume 1, in one, in a handsome variant morocco binding.

780A. (Cross-listing) Twelve original drawings by Henry Richter, one in watercolor, eleven in wash, of *PL*, of which nine were used for the plates in the preceding copies of *PL*, and three were rejected. The original drawings are each mounted and kept with a complete set of the stipple-engraved plates bound in original printed wrappers, edges untrimmed, all contained together in a red cloth fitted case. See main listing with *Editions*.

Engraved illustration after Henry Richter of Eve seeing herself in the water in the 1794 edition by Richter's father, John, who also engraved his son's illustrations. See #779.

Same Henry Richter illustration in another copy of the 1794 Richter edition: hand colored, as are most of the illustrations in this copy. See #780.

781. IL PARADISO PERDUTO Poema Inglese Di Giovanni Milton Tradotto dal Sig. Paolo Rolli Con Le Annotazioni Di G. Addison E alcune osservazioni critiche. *Venezia MDCCXCIV. Presso Andrea Santini Con Licenza de'Superiori. 2 volumes.* 12mo, 430pp.,+228pp., title page each volume, each with small central device, engraved frontispiece portrait of a disheveled Milton after Antonio Baratti (although unsigned), dedication, "Vita Di Giovanni Milton," volume 1, twelve engraved full-page illustrations by Piazzetta, Zucchi, Balestra, Tiepolo, and other Venetian artists, one for each book of PL (which occupies the whole of volume 1), the illustrations here, however, are unsigned although each contains plate number and page number, small decorative head- and tailpieces, small decorations around initial letters in volume 1, decorated initial letters in volume 2, the translation of Addison's *Notes* occupying all of volume 2, unlettered marbled paper over slight boards in original manner (with new endpapers). A very good set with small *ex libris* blind stamp at bottom of frontispiece portrait and title page, volume 1. Scarce. Williamson 145; Coleridge 163; Kohler 67, reporting "Not in the British Library. Not in Cambridge University Library."

See 1740 two-volume 12mo edition (first thus, in a larger 12mo format than the present edition) and 1742 folio edition (first folio, second thus, with nine additional engraved illustrations) here; see also 1758 two-volume small 12mo edition here (a smaller 12mo format than the present edition), in which the full-page portrait of a disheveled Milton by Baratti appears, with attribution, and in which the illustrations in the 1740 two-volume 12mo first edition are reproduced, as here, without attribution; see comments there about the portrait and related. The full-page portrait by Baratti does not appear in either the 1740 12mo edition or the 1742 folio edition, which have instead a headpiece illustration of a disheveled Milton by Zucchi.

782. IL PARADISO PERDUTO DI GIOVANNI MILTON Poema In Dodici Canti Tradotto Dall' Inglese In Verso Italiano Da Alessandro Pepoli Con Note. *Venezia[:] Dalla Tipografia Pepoliana[.] MDCCXCV.* 8vo, lxvi+[ii]+107+[i]pp., stipple-engraved frontispiece portrait engraved by Giacomo Zatta, "A' Lettori Il Traduttore," "Breve Saggio Preliminare," "Vita Compendiata Di Giovanni Milton Tratta Da Quella Del Vescovo Newton," one stipple-engraved illustration after Hayman also engraved by Zatta before half-title for Book I, original quarter calf, marbled paper over boards (slight inoffensive waterstaining along bottom of first third of pages). Book I only and that was all that was translated. A very nice copy with the bookplate of Leonard Schlosser. The "Verso Italiano" is actually in "Versi Sciolti," that is, in blank verse. John Shawcross shared the following with me about this book: "Although I knew through contemporary private letters that Pepoli had translated *PL*, I have not found a copy anywhere else." See comments by John Shawcross in *Milton Quarterly* 41, no. 1 (2007): 73. Very rare. Coleridge 146; Not in Kohler.

783. MILTON'S PARADISE LOST. *London: Published as the Act directs, Augt. 1, 1795, by T. Longman, B. Law, J. Dodsley, J. Johnson, C. Dilly, G. G. & J. Robinson, T. Cadell, R. Baldwin, J. Sewell, F. & C. Rivington, W. Golsmith, W. Lowndes, G. & T. Wilkie, W. Otridge & Son, J. Scatcherd, T. Payne, W. Bent, Vernor and Wood, G. Kearsley, J. Taylor; and E. Newbery.* First edition thus. 8vo, [i]+xlvi+382+[1]pp., frontispiece illustration plate of Adam and Eve in Eden by E. F. Burney engraved by T. Holloway (dated 1795), engraved title page, with vignette illustration by E. F. Burney engraved by P. Thomson for Book I of PL, ("Then with expanded wings he steers his flight," line 225), "Advertisement" leaf, life by Fenton, "Criticism On PL, By Samuel Johnson, LL.D." "Milton's Moral Character No Less Sublime Than His Poetical. From Mr. Hayley's Life of Milton," half-title for each book, vignette illustration of the expulsion by E. F. Burney engraved by Wm. Bromley at the end of Book XII, contemporary full straight-grained citron morocco, finely tooled gilt borders on covers, richly gilt-decorated spine, black morocco label with gilt lettering ("Milton's Poetical Works"), gilt numeral "I" within the panel, raised bands with gilt rules, inner dentelles finely tooled in gilt, outer dentelles ruled in gilt, blue endpapers, early armorial bookplate and bookplate of Leonard Schlosser on front pastedown. A splendid copy. This is the first appearance of these illustrations by Burney. Advertisement leaf at the end: "In The Press And Speedily will be published, Printed and Embellished uniformly with this volume, Paradise Regained, Samson Agonistes, And All The Other English Poem Of John Milton. With select Notes illustrative of difficult Passages." Uniformly bound with *PR*, T. Bensley, 1796, listed here. Coleridge 146; Kohler 68, reporting "Not in Cambridge University Library."

With Hand-colored Plates

784. Variant of the Preceding with an additional engraved title with the vignette illustration by Burney inserted within Book I and hand-colored, half-title for each book, vignette illustration of the expulsion by E. F. Burney engraved by Wm. Bromley at the end of Book XII, with an additional plate with Burney illustration inserted and hand-colored facing original plate, advertisement leaf as preceding, contemporary full straight-grained green morocco (lacking frontispiece), richly gilt-decorated border trim on covers, spine beautifully gilt-decorated in a pattern matching the trim on covers, inner dentelles finely tooled in gilt, outer dentelles ruled in gilt, marbled endpapers, a.e.g., thick red silk ribbon marker. A fine copy with early dated inscription on front blank, volume 1. This is a special volume, bound with a set of the plates that are beautifully hand-colored of the period. Uniformly bound with *PR*, T. Bensley, 1796, listed here, also bound with a set of the plates that are beautifully hand-colored of the period.

785. PARADISE LOST: A Poem, In Twelve Books. By John Milton. With A Biographical And Critical Account of the Author and his Writings. *London: Printed for A. Law, W. Miller, & R. Cater. MDCCXCV.* 12mo, 299pp., unsigned engraved frontispiece portrait of a youngish Milton in circular form with ivy branches above and name printed below, large decorative design at center of title page consisting of a lute, pipe, music, and sprays of flowers with arabesques beneath, life by Fenton, engraved illustration plates derived from the Hayman designs, one for each book, old sheepskin (neatly rebacked). A good copy. This is possibly another Scottish piracy. See 1792 and 1796 editions, both with similar, unsigned illustrations and both listed here. Scarce. Not in Coleridge; Not in Kohler.

Two sets of *PL* and *PR*, London, T. Longman et al., 1795–96, with engraved illustrations by E. F. Burney, second set with insertion of plates that are hand-colored. See #783.

Second copy of *PL*, London, T. Longman et al., 1795, with an additional Burney illustration plate hand-colored inserted facing original plate. See #784.

786. PARADISE LOST. A Poem, In Twelve Books. The Author John Milton. Printed From The Text Of Tonson's Correct Edition of 1711. A New Edition, With Notes And The Life Of The Author, In Three Volumes, By Thomas Newton, D.D. Late Lord Bishop Of Bristol, And Others. *London: Printed For The Proprietors. 1795. 3 volumes.* 12mo, ix+298pp.,+270pp.,+248pp., half-title and title page each volume (volume 3 consisting of the "Notes On The *PL*," with title accordingly), "Preface To The Pocket Edition. With The Notes Of Various Authors," signed "C.M." and dated "July 30th, 1795," Preface, life of Milton, "A Critique Upon The *PL* By Mr. Addison," volume 1, postscript and index at end of volume 2, contemporary tree calf (joints rubbed), decorative gilt border trim on covers, gilt-decorated spine, red morocco title labels, black morocco numbering labels, outer dentelles tooled in gilt (faded), marbled endpapers, speckled edges. A nice set with early armorial bookplate in each volume. The third volume incorporates notes by Newton, Bentley, Richardson, Hume, Addison, Warburton, Thyer, Pearce, Pope, and others. Scarce. Not in Coleridge; Not in Kohler.

787. PARADISE LOST: A Poem, In Twelve Books. By John Milton. With A Biographical And Critical Account Of The Author And His Writings. *London: Printed For Vernor & Hood; J. Dickson, J. Fairbairn, And Bell & Bradfute Edinburgh; J. & A. Duncan, and J. & M. Robertson, Glasgow; and J. & P. Wilson, Air. M,DCC,XCV.* 12mo in 6s, xvi+288pp., life of Milton by Fenton, contemporary speckled calf (bit rubbed), gilt rules on spine (faded), red morocco label with gilt lettering and decorative gilt trim. A nice copy. "Few copies of this edition have survived, for the only ones cited in the National Union Catalogue are in the New York Public Library and in Pittsburgh. British libraries seem not to own it. The New York copy has an almost completely mutilated title page. The copy in the Wickenheiser collection, however, is intact" (Shawcross, 2007, p. 70). Not in Coleridge; Not in Kohler.

788. PARADISE LOST. A Poem, In Twelve Books. The Author John Milton. Printed From The Text Of Tonson's Correct Edition Of M.DCC.XI. *London: Printed For T. Longman, B. Law, J. Dodsley, J. Johnson, C. Dilly, G. G. And J. Robinson, T. Cadell, R. Baldwin, J. Nichols, J. Sewell, F. And C. Rivington, S. Hayes, W. Lowndes, W. Otridge And Son, G. And T. Wilkie, J. Scatcherd, W. Goldsmith, Vernor And Hood, And E. Newbery. M.DCC.XCV (1795).* 12mo, xxxv+345pp., frontispiece portrait plate after T. Holloway ("Milton. From an Impression of a Seal of T. Simon, in the possession of the late Mr: Yeo. Published as the Act directs, 6 March 1795 by C. Dilly Poultry, & the rest of the Proprietors"), life by Fenton, half-title for each book, contemporary blue morocco (a bit rubbed with some light wear), gilt rules on covers with small decorative gilt pieces in the corners, spine lettered in gilt with gilt rules, raised bands with decorative gilt rule, inner dentelles tooled in gilt, corners of outer dentelles trimmed in gilt, marbled endpapers, a.e.g. A very nice copy in an attractive morocco binding of the period, bound by C. Kalthoeber with his ticket. John Shawcross told me that there is a "Copy in University of Illinois Library." Not in Coleridge; Not in Kohler.

789. [PARADISE LOST IN RUSSIAN—WITH RUSSIAN TITLE PAGE AND RUSSIAN TEXT] POTERI-ANNYJ RAI [PARADISE LOST] POEMA [POEM] IOANNA MILTONA [BY JOHN MILTON] perevedena s anglinskogo podlinnika [translated from the English original] s kartinami [with illustrations] tchast pervaia [Part One] s ukaznogo dozvoleniya [with permission, i.e., from the censor] *Moskva, v tipografii Selivanovskago i tovarishcha [Moscow, at the printers Selivanovsky and Comrade, i.e., work partner) 1795.* One volume only: volume 1 of 2 volumes. 8vo, 333pp., signatures "A" and "P" printed on light green paper (all else on white), original calf (worn, front joint cracked and attached by the chords, first few pages lose, including title page, some signatures sprung, small pieces missing at top and bottom of spine, occasional slight, inoffensive staining, library stamp on back pastedown), spine decorated in blind trim, red and black morocco labels (worn and chipped) with lettering in blind, decorated endpapers with a pattern repeating small white stars against a light maroon backdrop outlined in white. The prose translation begins: "Sing, o heavenly Muse, the transgression of the first man and his pernicious tasting of the forbidden fruit: the source whence both evil and death poured forth upon the earth, as well as the loss of Eden, until God-Man will come and restore for us this blessed dwelling. . . . " Scarce eighteenth-century Russian edition with notations in an early Russian hand in ink crossed out on back blank. Not in Coleridge; Not in Kohler.

790. PARADISE LOST: A Poem, In Twelve Books. By John Milton. With A Biographical And Critical Account of the Author and his Writings. *London: Printed for A. Law, W. Miller, & R. Cater. MDCCXCVI (1796).* 12mo, 299pp., unsigned engraved frontispiece portrait of a youngish Milton, large decorative design at center of title page consisting of a lute, pipe, music, and sprays of flowers, with "London" beneath within arabesques, life by Fenton, engraved illustration plates derived from the Hayman designs, one for each book, old sheep (rebacked with raised bands). A nice copy. The illustrations are derived from the Hayman designs. This is possibly another Scottish piracy.

See 1792 and 1795 editions here, each with similar illustrations, unsigned, the 1792 edition without any decorative design on title page, the 1795 edition with a design similar to that on title page here. Scarce. Coleridge 148; Not in Kohler.

791. PARADISE LOST By John Milton; With Notes, Selected from Newton and others, To which is prefixed The Life of the Author. With A Critical Dissertation On The Poetical Works Of Milton, and Observations on his Language and Versification, By Samuel Johnson, L.L.D. *London[:] Printed for T. Parsons, 21 Paternoster Row. 1796. 2 volumes*. First edition thus. Tall 8vo in 4s, iv+viii+lxxx+229pp.,+226+[25]pp., engraved title page with vignette portrait (somewhat after Faithorne) engraved by J. Roper, "Advertisement," "List Of Subscribers," life, "Dissertation On The Poetical Works Of Milton, With Observations On His Language And Versification, By Samuel Johnson, LL.D.," first appearance of engraved illustrations by R. Corbould and H. Singleton (very fine impressions), engraved by Saunders, Heath, and White, half-title for each book, with the rare second engraved title page with vignette portrait, volume 2, notes and index at the end of volume 2, contemporary calf (a bit rubbed, some slight foxing), decorative gilt border trim and gilt rules on covers with small decorative gilt piece at each corner, richly gilt-decorated spines, red morocco labels with gilt lettering and gilt rules, inner dentelles finely tooled in gilt, outer dentelles ruled in gilt, marbled endpapers, speckled edges. A very nice set. Scarce, especially with the second title page. Coleridge 147 (8vo, illustrating a title page for each volume, as with this set); Kohler 69, describing its copy as "Octavo in 4s . . . lack[ing] engraved title-page to volume 2," and reporting "Not in the Bodleian Library. Not in Cambridge University Library."

792. PARADISE LOST: A Poem, In Twelve Books. The Author John Milton. Correctly Printed From The Text Of Thomas Newton, D. D. *Belfast: Printed By William Magee. 1796*. 12mo, 328pp., dedication page, life by Fenton, contemporary sheep (joints cracked, upper blank tip of first half wormed without loss of any letter press, somewhat foxed due to poor quality of paper, lower outer corner a bit damp-stained), gilt rules on spine (faded), red morocco label with gilt lettering and decorative gilt trim. A respectable copy of a very rare edition. Not in Coleridge; Kohler 70, reporting Not in the Bodleian Library. Not in Cambridge University Library.

793. IL PARADISO PERDUTO Di Giovanni Milton, Tradotto In Verso Italiano Da Felice Mariottini. [Quotation From Dryden] Parte Prima. *Londra: Presso G. Polidori, E Co. No[.] 12, Cockspur-Street, Fronting Pall Mall. 1796. 2*

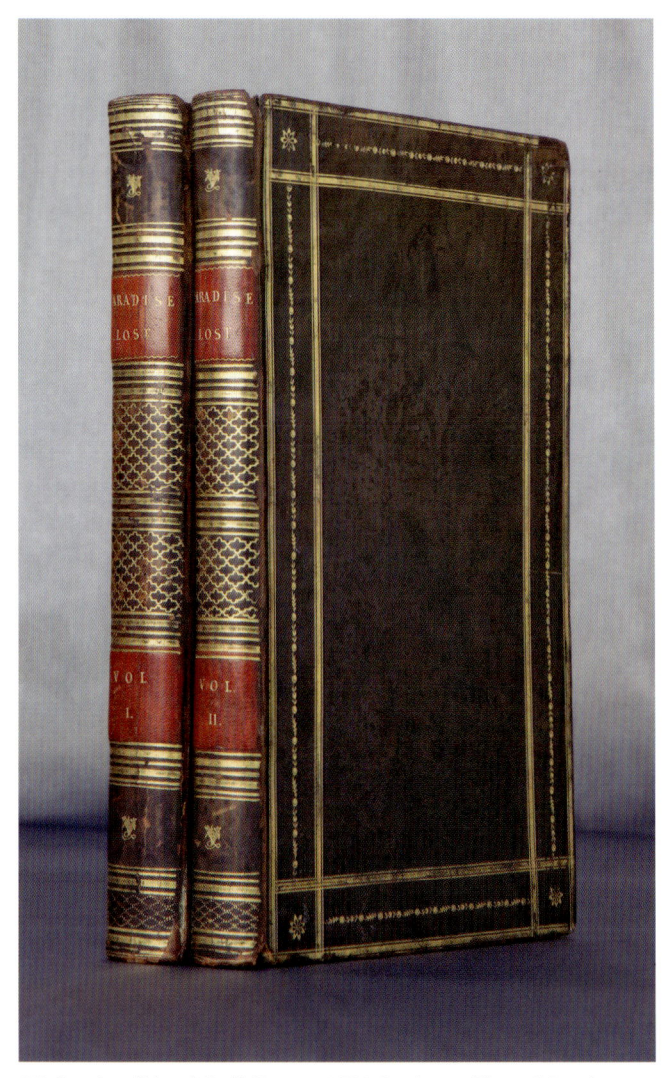

PL. London: Printed for T. Parsons, 1796. 2 volumes. First edition thus. Contemporary calf, gilt trim, red labels on spine, with engraved illustrations by R. Corbould and H. Singleton (first appearance). See #791.

parts in one. 8vo, xi+[i]+209pp.,+iv+208pp., engraved frontispiece portrait of Milton by Mariano Bovi with Dryden epigram, dedication page "Prefazione," contents, Part I, second printed title page for "Parte Seconda," dedication page "Prefazione," contents, Part II, contemporary three-quarter calf, marbled paper over boards, gilt-decorated spine, raised bands with decorative gilt trim, blue endpapers, marbled edges. A good copy with the bookplate of Leonard Schlosser and an early armorial bookplate. First complete edition translated by Mariottini. The printer, G. Polidori (a teacher of Italian in London), was the father of John Polidori (author of *The Vampyre* and Byron's physician) and the grandfather of Christina, William Michael, and Dante Gabriel Rossetti; G. Polidori also published a translation of *Comus* in 1802, with a second edition in 1809 and a third edition in 1812 —all listed here. Coleridge 164; Shawcross, Kentucky, 530; Not in Kohler.

794. PARADISE LOST: A Poem, In Twelve Books. By John Milton. With Notes Explaining some of the difficult Passages. *London: Printed For G. Whitfield, City-Road, And Sold At The Methodist Preaching-Houses, In Town And Country. 1798.* 18mo, 294pp., notes at the end of each book, original calf (worn, front cover detached, lacking back cover, some embrowning), gilt rules on spine, red morocco label with gilt lettering and gilt rules, fly-leaf loosely laid in with nineteenth-century presentation inscription. Coleridge suggests that "This edition seems to have been printed for the Methodist tract market." Rare. Not in NUC; Coleridge 149; Not in Kohler.

795. LE PARADIS PERDU DE MILTON, TRADUCTION NOUVELLE, AVEC DES NOTES. *A Paris, Chez J. Ch. Laveaux et Compagnie, Imprimeurs-Libraires, rue du faubourg Honoré, Maison ci-devant Beauveau. Moutardier, Libraire, quai des Augustius. An VIII. [i.e. 1799–1800].* 2 volumes in one. 8vo, viii+303pp.,+280pp., half-title each volume, title page each volume, "Notes" at end of each volume, original dark green straight-grained morocco (a bit rubbed, small shelf label with the number "193" in an early hand at top of spine), ribboned gilt border trim on covers with decorative gilt corner pieces, spine richly decorated with gilt trim and with red morocco gilt lettering and gilt numbering labels each with decorative gilt trim, speckled yellow edges. Fine copy, complete with both title pages and half-titles. The edition is in prose with no indication of the translator. Apparently rare. Not in Coleridge; Not in Kohler.

796. MILTON'S PARADISE LOST, with the Life Of The Author To which is prefixed the Celebrated Critique by Samuel Johnson LLD[.] *London[:] Printed by C. Whittingham Dean Street, Fetter Lane, for T. Heptinstall No. 304 Holborn. And Sold by H. D. Symonds Paternoster Row; T. H. Hookham Bond Street; T. T. Black Leadenhall Street; R. H. Wesley Strand; and all the principal Booksellers in England, Scotland, Ireland, & America. 1799 [i.e., 1800].* First edition thus. 8vo, xlix+371+[1]+[4]pp., engraved frontispiece portrait by Holl, "dated 1799 by T. Heptinstall Holborn," engraved title page with vignette illustration after Burney for Book X at the center, life by Evans, Johnson's criticism, twelve engraved illustration plates after Burney by various engravers (all "Published by Heptinstall" and dated between Aug. 19, 1799, and Jun 4, 1800), half-title for each book, advertisement leaf and list of subscribers bound in at end, original boards (a bit worn, trifle shaken, and a little age-darkened), wholly uncut. An exceptionally large copy in original boards, with splendid impressions of the plates, complete with original printed paper label on spine and with the ticket of Kerr & Richardson, Booksellers, Glasgow. A very fine copy. Rare thus. Coleridge 150; Kohler 72, referencing Williamson 154 and reporting "Not in the Bodleian Library. Not in Cambridge University Library."

797. PARADISE LOST. A Poem, In Twelve Books. By John Milton. With The Life Of The Author. *London: Printed By C. Whittingham, Dean Street, Fetter Lane, For T. Wills, No. 2, Stationers Court, Ludgate Street. 1800.* 12mo, 288pp., engraved frontispiece illustration for Book X (Eve tempting Adam), "Engrav'd by S. Springsguth," "London: Pubd. July 5 1892 by H D Symonds Paternoster Row," life by Fenton, contemporary full red morocco, delicate gilt floriated border trim on covers, gilt-decorated spine, inner and outer dentelles tooled in gilt, marbled endpapers, a.g.e. A very charming copy in a very well-preserved original binding, extra bright and clean, with a possibly contemporary inscription on front blank. Not in Kohler.

798. PARADISE LOST. A Poem, In Twelve Books. By John Milton. Printed From The Text Of Tonson's Correct Edition Of 1711. A New Edition, With Plates. *London: Printed For J. Johnson; G. And J. Robinson; W. J. And J. Richardson; R. Baldwin; Otridge And Son; J. Sewell; Longman And Rees; Vernor And Hood; F. and C. Rivington; T. Payne; J. Walker; J. Cuthell; W. Lowndes; J. Scatcherd; Cadell And Davies; G. Wilkie; Clarke And Son; Lackington, Allen And Co.; J. Taylor; J. Nunn; R. Lea; E. Jeffery; J. Mawman; Carpenter And Co.; T. Hurst; And J. Mathews; By C. Whittingham, Dean Street, Fetter Lane. 1801.* First edition thus. 12mo, iv+356pp., engraved frontispiece portrait after T.

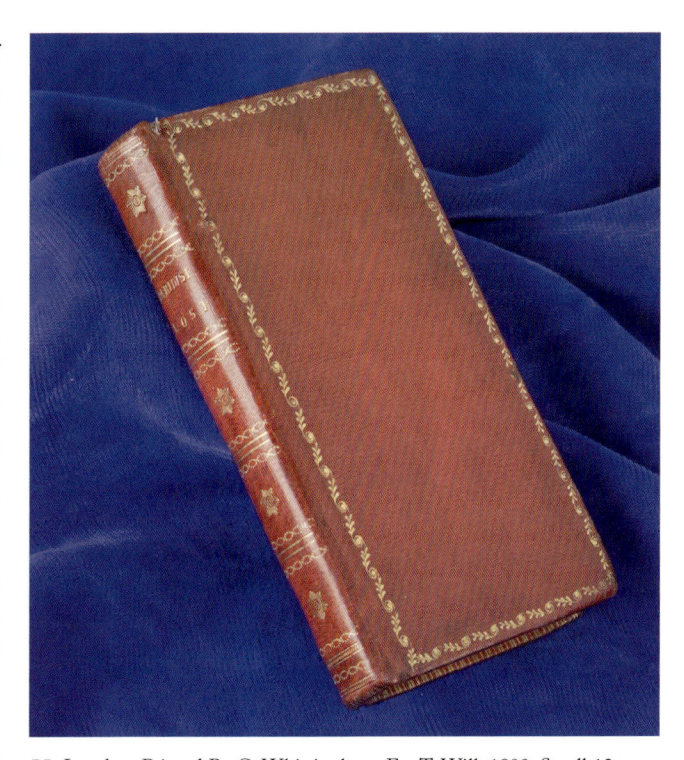

PL. London: Printed By C. Whittingham, For T. Will, 1800. Small 12mo, contemporary red morocco. Charming little Romantic volume. See #797.

Holloway, "From an Impression of a Seal of T. Simon in the possession of the late Mr. Yeo Published as the Act directs August 15, 1801 by J. Mawman Poultry, London and the rest of the Partners," first appearance of five engraved illustration plates after Howard and Thurston, one engraved by Cromek after Thurston, two engraved by Scott after Thurston, one engraved by Neagle after Howard, and one engraved by Warren after Thurston, contemporary calf (spine a bit rubbed and faded), gilt rule on covers, gilt-decorated spine, red morocco label with gilt lettering and gilt rules, outer dentelles tooled in gilt, marbled endpapers. A very good copy with the armorial bookplate of Ansty Hall. Kohler notes that "Pointon says that editions about 1805 appeared with Thurston illustrations, which this edition predates." The second edition thus with engraved illustrations after Thurston and Howard, was published by J. Johnson in 1805 (also listed here). The frontispiece portrait here appears in the 1804 edition of *PL* listed here with the same identification reprinted beneath and with the edition printed for many of the same booksellers or "Partners" as those who appear in the publisher's imprint here; that edition, unlike the present edition, is not illustrated. Uncommon. Kohler 73, referencing Williamson 211 and reporting "Not in the Bodleian Library. Not in Cambridge University Library."

799. PARADISE LOST, A Poem, In Twelve Books; By John Milton, With A Biographical And Critical Account Of The Author and his Writings. *Washington: Printed For Mathew Carey, Market-Street, Philadelphia. 1801.* 8vo, 289pp., original calf (rubbed, chipped at top of spine, some age-browning, first two signatures slightly sprung, proper correction of "deeps" to "deeds" made in a neat early hand in pencil on p. 23), gilt rules on spine (faded), black morocco label with gilt lettering and decorative gilt trim. A decent copy. Shaw & Shoemaker 933; Kohler 74, observing "Washington, Pennsylvania is about 28 miles from Pittsburgh and was a centre for printing in western Pennsylvania at the beginning of the nineteenth century," and reporting "Not in the British Library. Not in the Bodleian Library. Not in Cambridge University Library."

800. MILTON'S PARADISE LOST. A New Edition. Adorned With Plates. *London: Printed by T. Bensley, Bolt Court, Fleet Street; For F. J. Du Roveray. Sold By R. Dutton, B. Crosby And Co. E. Lloyd, And J. Bell. 1802. 2 volumes.* First edition thus. 8vo, [i]+264pp.,+250pp., frontispiece portrait "Engrav'd by Wm. Sharp, after an original miniature by Samuel Cooper: the ornaments by G. B. Cipriani And E. F. Burney. Published 1st July 1802, by F. J. Du Roveray, London," volume 1, with protective tissue guard, first appearance of twelve engraved illustration plates after Henry Fuseli and William Hamilton, engraved by various artists, six each volume with one as frontispiece, volume 2, title page each volume, half-title for each book, contemporary mottled calf (a bit rubbed, spines faded), elaborately gilt-decorated covers and spines, black morocco labels with gilt lettering and gilt rules, inner dentelles tooled in gilt, outer dentelles ruled in gilt, marbled endpapers, speckled edges, early signature. A very nice set, fresh and clean within, with plates that are very clean and crisp. Scarce. Kohler 76, referencing Williamson 222 and reporting "Not in Cambridge University Library."

801. PARADISE LOST. A Poem, In Twelve Books. By John Milton. With A Life Of The Author, And A Critique on the Poem. A New Edition. *London: Printed by T. Bensley, Bolt Court, Fleet Street, For J. Johnson, R. Baldwin, J. Sewell, J. Walker, Cuthell And Martin, J. Mathews, Ottridge And Son, R. Lea, J. Nunn, W. J. And J. Richardson, J. Scatchard, Longman And Rees, F. And C. Rivington, G. Wilkie, G. And J. Robinson, T. Payne, Clarke And Son, Cadell And Davies, Vernor And Hood, Lackington, Allen And Co., T. Hurst, E. Jeffery, And J. Mawman. 1802.* 8vo, xliii+420pp., engraved frontispiece portrait "Engraved by Holl," with protective tissue guard, engraved and printed title pages (the engraved title page "Published by J. Johnson, &c., 1802," in "London," being similar to the engraved title page for the 1799 T. Heptinstall, Burney-illustrated edition), with vignette illustration after Burney for Book X, "Engrav'd by Landseer & Neagle," on the engraved title page, the 1802 date being consistent with that on the printed title page, twelve engraved illustration plates after Burney, each with protective tissue guard, contemporary full red morocco (a bit rubbed with some scuff marks and darkening, front cover rehinged from inside), gilt-decorated covers, spine richly decorated within the compartments, raised bands (rubbed), inner dentelles ruled in gilt, outer dentelles trimmed in gilt at the corners, green endpapers, a.e.g. A good copy of the regular issue on regular paper with early signature of Capt. John Mackeson, on front blank. Kohler 75, referencing Williamson 154 and reporting "Not in the Bodleian Library."

802. Variant of Preceding, contemporary mottled calf (rubbed, front cover rehinged from the inside), decorative gilt border trim on covers, elaborately gilt-decorated spine within the panels, raised bands with outer dentelles delicately tooled in gilt, marbled endpapers and edges. A variant on thick paper, bulking to 1 ¾", which is half an inch thicker than regular paper examples, and measuring 5 ½" × 9" compared to 5" × 8" for regular paper examples, as preceding copy. Rare large and thick paper copy, clean and fresh internally.

(left) "Satan Starts at the Touch of Ithuriel's Spear" after Fuseli, Bk. IV, *PL*, Du Rouveray, 1802. Published with engraved illustrations by Fuseli and Hamilton (first appearance). (right) "Expulsion" after Fuseli, Bk. XII. Ibid. See #800.

803. PARADISE LOST. A Poem. In Twelve Books. By John Milton. Printed From The Text of Tonson's correct Edition of 1711. A New Edition, With Plates. *Dublin: Printed For P. Wogan, 23, Old-Bridge. 1802.* 12mo, xxiv+324pp., half-title, engraved frontispiece of Milton (a small side view within a circle) "From an Impression of a Seal of T. Simon in the possession of the late Mr. Yeo," life by Fenton, five stipple-engraved illustrations (unsigned, for Books II, line 546; IV, line 27; V, line 152; VI, line 643; and X, line 720, fine impressions), endpiece at the end of Book XII, original calf (joints repaired from within, Milton's dates written in pencil in an early hand beneath frontispiece portrait, title and name in pencil in an early hand on verso of portrait, occasional pencil markings and several notation in the margins, "the end . . ." written on last page in ink in an early hand, some worm-holing in the upper margin of the last few pages, later name in ink on front blank), spine ruled in gilt with red morocco label lettered and ruled in gilt. All in all, a very respectable copy of an uncommon edition. The illustrations are larger than vignettes but do not fill up the entire page, and each is angled at the corners; book and line reference are printed beneath each illustration. Scarce. Not in Kohler.

804. PARADISE LOST. A Poem, In Twelve Books. The Author John Milton. With his Life, and Historical, Philosophical, and Explanatory Notes, Translated from the French of The learned Raymond de St. Maur. And Various critical Remarks and Observations, from Mr. Addison, Dr. Warburton, Dr. Newton, Dr. Pearce, Dr. Bentley, Mr. Richardson, and Mr. Hume. A new Edition, adorned with three elegant Frontispieces. Volume I/II/III. *Vienna: Printed for R. Sammer Bookseller. M,DCCC,III. 3 volumes.* Sm. 8vo in 4s and 8s, xxv+[v]+231pp.,+214pp.,+210pp., engraved frontispiece illustration plate each volume (after Weinrauch for Book I, line 660 [Satan rallying his troops], volume 1; after Weinrauch for Book VI, line 864 [rebel angels being cast out of Heaven], volume 2; after Weinrauch for Book XII, line 637 [the expulsion], volume 3), half-title and title page each volume, advertisement and Fenton's life of Milton, volume 1, index and four pages of advertisements for "Books printed for R. Sammer, Bookseller at Vienna" at the end of volume 3, notes at the end of each volume, contemporary calf (some worming to volume 1, not affecting the text, some slight inoffensive waterstaining throughout), decorative gilt border trim on each cover, red morocco labels on spines with gilt lettering or numerals and decorative gilt trim (one of the six labels is missing), decorative gilt trim on spines with small decorative gilt pieces in the panels, outer dentelles ruled in gilt (faded), marbled endpapers, a.e.g. A nice set of this scarce continental printing of *PL* with an interesting selection of critical material, both translated from the French of St. Maur and taken directly from the English. Raymond de St. Maur's commentary originally appeared as *The State of Innocence and the Fall of Man* in 1745 (also listed here). Scarce. NUC records Princeton and Harvard copies only; Kohler 78, reporting "Not in the Bodleian Library."

See Coleridge 255a (where an enlightening discussion about the evolution of this text is provided). See 1754 edition listed with striking illustrations (unsigned) and editions cited there; see another issue of the 1754 edition listed in 1755 with a variant publisher, with the same striking illustrations (unsigned); see also two-volume 1775 edition listed with unsigned 1688 illustrations reduced; and see two-volume 1779 edition listed with 1688 illustrations reduced and attributed to R. Cooper, this edition reprinted in 1784 (also listed here); see, too, 1765 and 1770 nonillustrated editions each listed here.

805. **PARADISE LOST**. A Poem, In Twelve Books. By John Milton. Printed From The Text Of Tonson's Correct Edition Of 1711. A new edition in two parts. *Paris: Printed for Theophilus Barrois junior, Bookseller, Quay Voltaire, no. 5. 1803. 2 volumes.* Large 12mo, 186pp.,+175pp., title page each volume, contemporary quarter French calf, marbled paper over boards, gilt rules on spines, red morocco lettering labels with decorative gilt trim, black and light brown numbering labels with gilt trim, speckled edges. A choice set in original binding, well-preserved, and in fine condition. Not in Kohler.

806. Variant of Preceding. **PARADISE LOST**. A Poem, In Twelve Books. By John Milton. Printed From The Text Of Tonson's Correct Edition Of 1711. A new edition in two parts. *Paris: Printed for Theophilus Barrois junior, Bookseller, Quay Voltaire, no. 5. 1803. 2 volumes in one.* Large 12mo, 186pp.,+175pp., title page each volume, contemporary half green leather, green paper over boards (a bit rubbed, minor foxing throughout), spine lettered in gilt with decorative gilt rules and small decorative gilt pieces, marbled endpapers. A good copy. Not in Kohler.

807. **PARADISE LOST**; A Poem: In Twelve Books. By John Milton. A New Edition: With An Abridgment Of The Copious And Learned Notes Collected By Bishop Newton; Together With Additions, And A Life Of The Author, By The Rev. John Evans, A.M. In Two Volumes. Illustrated By Engravings. *London: Albion Press: Printed And Published By James Cundee, Ivy-Lane, Paternoster-Row. 1804. 2 volumes.* First edition thus. 12mo in 6s, xxxii+ 219pp.,+498pp.(continuous pagination), engraved frontispiece portrait of Milton (with a dove above), volume 1, "Ornamented & Engraved by J. Chapman, 1804," "Directions To The Binder," dedication page, "Advertisement By The Editor," "Sketch Of The Life And Writings Of John Milton, first appearance of twelve engraved illustration plates after W. M. Craig (one for each book, with one serving as frontispiece to volume 2), engraved by Mackenzie (each dated 1804), engraved tailpieces, descriptive narrative headnote each page, notes at bottom of page, contemporary polished calf, covers decorated with finely tooled border trim in blind, gilt-decorated spines, red labels with gilt lettering and decorative trim in blind and gilt rules, outer dentelles tooled in gilt, marbled edges. A choice set in a lovely and a very well-preserved Romantic binding with fine impressions of the plates and with a leaf of "Directions To The Binders," indicating where each plate should go and how the two volumes are to be divided. Six of Craig's illustrations were printed in octavo format, variously engraved, and dated 1812, in an edition of *PL & PR & SA* with "Life by The Rev. David M'Nicoll," "Printed By Nuttall, Fisher, And Dixon" in Liverpool, n.d. [1812] (also listed here). Craig's four illustrations for *PR* first appeared, unsigned, in 1806 editions by the Albion Press, "Printed And Published By James Cundee," in both octavo (several copies listed here) and duodecimo (also listed here). Rare. Kohler 80, calling its set "8vo," referencing Williamson 172 and reporting "Not in the Bodleian Library. Not in Cambridge University Library."

PL. London: Albion Press, 1804. 2 volumes. 12mo, contemporary polished calf, with twelve engraved illustration plates after Craig (first appearance). See #807.

808. PARADISE LOST. A Poem, In Twelve Books. The Author John Milton. Printed From The Text Of Tonson's Correct Edition Of 1711. *London: Printed by Bye and Law, Clerkenwell; For J. Johnson, R. Baldwin, W. J. And J. Richardson, F. And C. Rivington, Otridge And Son, W. Lowndes, Clarke And Sons, G. And J. Robinson, G. Wilkie, J. Walker, T. Payne, J. Mathews, R. Lea, J. Nunn, Cuthell And Martin, Cadell And Davies, Longman And Rees; Lackington, Allen, And Co.; E. Jeffery, Scatcherd And Letterman, J. Carpenter, T. Hurst, And J. Mawman. 1804.* 12mo in 6s, xxxv+345pp., engraved frontispiece portrait by T. Holloway, "From an Impression of a Seal of T. Simon in the possession of the late Mr. Yeo Published as the Act directs August 15, 1801 by J. Mawman Poultry, London and the rest of the Partners," life by Fenton, "Printed by Bye and Law, St. John's-Square" at bottom of last page, contemporary tree calf (a little rubbed), spine decorated in gilt, black leather label with gilt lettering, outer dentelles ruled in gilt (faded). A nice copy. The frontispiece portrait here first appeared, fittingly enough, in the 1801 edition of *PL* with the same identification printed beneath and with the edition printed for many of the same booksellers or "Partners" as those who appear in the publisher's imprint here (also listed here); that edition, unlike the present edition, is illustrated. Scarce. Kohler 79, referencing Williamson 211 and reporting "Not in the Bodleian Library. Not in Cambridge University Library."

809. PARADISE LOST: A Poem, In Twelve Books. By John Milton. To Which Is Prefixed The Life Of The Author. [Dryden Epigram] *Cupar=Fife: Printed And Sold By R. Tullis, Bookseller. 1804.* First edition thus. 12mo in 6s, xii+287pp., contemporary diced calf (bit rubbed at joints), gilt rules on covers, elaborately gilt-decorated spine, red morocco label with gilt lettering and gilt rules, inner and outer dentelles finely tooled in gilt, marbled endpapers, yellow edges. A very fine copy, attractively bound for "M: Greatrakes," whose name is blocked in gilt on front cover. A very scarce provincial printing of Milton's *PL*. Robert Tullis founded the Tullis Press in Cupar, Fife, in 1803, and this is one of his earliest imprints. The Tullis Press also issued Milton's *PW* in two volumes in 1804 (see set listed here), while issuing *PL* separately, as here, with a cancel title. *Nineteenth-century STC* locates a single copy of *PW* at Cambridge and a single copy of *PL* at the National Library of Scotland. Doughty 7a; Not in Kohler.

810. PARADISE LOST, A Poem, In Twelve Books. By John Milton. *Philadelphia: Printed For Benjamin Johnson, No. 31, And J. Johnson, No. 147, Market Street. William F. McLaughlin, Printer. 1804.* First edition thus. Nonodecimo, [ii]+318pp., engraved frontispiece portrait plate with oval portrait of Milton by W. Haines, half-title before each book, "Printed By W. F. McLaughlin, Fromberger's-Court" at bottom of last page, contemporary calf (worn, lacking front cover, spine chipped at top and bottom, some foxing throughout), spine ruled in gilt, red morocco label with gilt lettering and gilt trim on spine. I am indebted to John Shawcross for clarifying the signatures of this book (each with nine leaves) for me as something "that would have to be called a nonodecimo . . . word [to be found] in Tacitus' *Annales*, 13, 16." Also: "There are copies of this edition at the University of Illinois and Duke University libraries." Not in Kohler.

811. PARADISE LOST. A Poem, In Twelve Books. By John Milton. A New Edition. *London: Printed By R. Bassam, St. John's Street, West Smithfield, For T. Martin, No. 44, Gracechurch Street. 1804.* 12mo in 6s, 294pp., engraved frontispiece portrait of Milton, Homer, and Dante, engraved by Peter Larken, with Dryden epigram below, life by Fenton, contemporary three-quarter brown calf, marbled paper over boards (a little rubbed with a few scuff marks, some light foxing), spine lined in gilt, black morocco label with gilt lettering and gilt rules. A good copy. Rare.

812. MILTON'S PARADISE LOST, ILLUSTRATED WITH TEXTS OF SCRIPTURE, By John Gillies, D.D. One Of The Ministers In Glasgow. [Quotation from "B. III. 26."] The Third Edition, With Additions. *London: Printed by W. Flint, Old Bailey; For J. Johnson, R. Baldwin, W. J. And J. Richardson, F. And C. Rivington, Otridge And Son, W. Lowndes, Clarke And Sons, G. And J. Robinson, G. Wilkie, J. Walker, T. Payne, J. Mathews, R. Lea, J. Nunn, Cuthell And Martin, Cadell And Davies, Longman And Rees; Lackington, Allen, And Co.; E. Jeffery, Scatcherd And Letterman, J. Carpenter, T. Hurst, And J. Mawman. 1804.* Third Gillies edition. 12mo, xxxi+[i]+378+[1]pp.+[20 unpaginated index], dedication page, preface, "Advertisement To The Third Edition," life by Fenton, postscript, half-title for each book, notes at bottom of page, index, original red straight-grained morocco (slightly rubbed, especially at joints and extremities), covers decorated with elaborate gilt border trim, spine similarly decorated in gilt with decorative gilt pieces, gilt rules, and decorative gilt trim at top and bottom, marbled endpapers, inner and outer dentelles ruled in gilt, a.e.g. A fine copy with red morocco gilt bookplate inside front cover and with similar red morocco gilt bookplate inside rear cover stamped in gilt. Gillies provided extensive footnotes referring to biblical sources in his first edition published in 1788 (also listed here). His work proved exceptionally popular, with two more editions in the next sixteen years, in 1793 (copy listed here), in which Gillies added a new preface and a number of additional annotations, and 1804 (copy listed here). Rare. Not in Kohler.

813. LE PARADIS PERDU De Jean Milton, Traduit De L'Anglois. Seconde édition, revue & corrigée; précédée de la vie de J. Milton, et suivie de remarques, Par M. J. Mosneron, Membre du Corps Législatif. Anglais-François. *A Paris, Chez F. Louis, Libraire, rue de Savoie, No. 12. AN XIII – M.DCCC.IV. 2 volumes.* 12mo, xlvii+369pp., +402pp., half-title and title page each volume with emblem at the center, English verse and French translation in prose on facing pages, "remarques" on the poem in French at the end of volume 2, late nineteenth-century three-quarter crushed maroon morocco, red marbled paper over boards, gilt rules on each cover, spines elaborately decorated in gilt within the panels, red morocco label lettered and ruled in gilt, raised bands with decorative gilt trim, marbled endpapers, t.e.g., others untrimmed. A beautiful, tall set in exceptionally fine condition, in heavy cardboard slipcase (a bit rubbed along edges) covered in the same red marbled paper on the outside and contrasting marbled paper the same as the endpapers on the inside. Large paper copy. Rendered into a French prose version by M. J. Mosneron who also wrote a lengthy preface and comments on each book of *PL* in French. Scarce. Not in Kohler.

814. LE PARADIS PERDU, De Jean Milton, Traduit De L'Anglois. Seconde édition, revue & corrigée; précédée de la vie de J. Milton, et suivie de remarques, Par M. J. Mosneron, Membre Du Corps Législatif. *A Paris, Chez F. Louis, Libraire, rue de Savoie, No. 12. AN XIII — M.DCCC.IV.* Seconde édition, revue & corrigée. 12mo, xlvii+408pp. (variant edition from the preceding, with French translation only), half-title ("On trouve chez le même Libraire, L'édition originale, en anglois, I volume in-12, La traduction, avec le texte angloise en regard, précédée de la vie de Milton, et suivie de remarques, etc. par M. J. Mosneron, 2 volume in12." printed on verso), "Vie De Milton," half-title repeated before the poem, "remarques" on the poem in French at end, contemporary three-quarter mottled calf (a bit rubbed, spine chipped at top, corners bumped), spine decorated in gilt within the panels, red morocco label with gilt lettering and gilt rules, raised bands, lightly speckled edges. A nice copy. Scarce. Not in NUC; Not in Kohler.

815. PARADISE LOST. A Poem, In Twelve Books. By John Milton. Printed From The Text of Tonson's Correct Edition of 1711. A New Edition, With Plates[.] *London: Printed For J. Johnson; G. And J. Robinson; W. J. And J. Richardson; R. Baldwin; Otridge And Son; Ogilvy And Son; Longman, Hurst, Rees, Andorme; Vernor And Hood; F. And C. Rivington; T. Payne; J. Walker; J. Cuthell; W. Lowndes; J. Scatcherd; Cadell And Davies; G. Wilkie; Clarke And Sons; Lackington Allen And Co.; J. Taylor; J. Nunn; R. Lea; E. Jeffery; J. Mawman; James Carpenter; And J. Mathews. 1805.* Second edition thus. 8vo, xx+352pp., unsigned engraved frontispiece circular portrait, with protective tissue guard, "Printed By Biggs And Co. Crane-court, Fleet Street, London" (verso of title page), engraved illustration plates by John Thurston and Henry Howard, variously engraved by Cromek, Scott and Warren after Thurston and by Neagle after Howard, each with protective tissue guard, life of Milton by Fenton, postscript, half-title for each book, contemporary mottled calf (rubbed, rebacked in roan), gilt rules on covers, spine lettered in gilt, inner dentelles tooled in gilt, outer dentelles ruled in gilt, marbled endpapers, speckled edges, with dated early signature on title page. A good copy with fine impressions of the plates. The first appearance of these illustrations was published by J. Johnson in 1801, the first edition thus (copy listed here). Kohler 81, reporting "Not in Williamson. Not in the British Library. Not in the Bodleian Library. Not in Cambridge University Library."

816. Variant of Preceding, contemporary red morocco (a bit rubbed along joints and extremities), covers ruled in gilt, spine lettered and ruled in gilt, inner and outer dentelles ruled in gilt, marbled endpapers, a.e.g. A good copy in a variant binding of contemporary red morocco with early (possibly contemporary) notes in pencil on the endpapers and some scattered marginalia in a neat hand.

817. PARADISE LOST: A Poem, In Twelve Books. By John Milton. To Which Is Prefixed, The Life Of The Author. *Edinburgh: Printed For P. Cairns, College-Street, By D. Schaw And Son, Lawnmarket. 1805.* First edition thus. 12mo, 346pp., engraved and printed title pages, with large illustration for Book IV of Eve seeing her reflection by J. Burnett, engraved by R. Scott, on engraved title page, with "Vide Book IV. page 460" beneath the illustration and "Published by P. Cairns Edinburgh 1. Novr. 1805" at bottom of the page, contemporary three-quarter calf, marbled paper over boards (worn, front cover detached, back joint weak, lacking spine), early signature on front pastedown. Scarce. Not in Kohler.

818. PARADIS PERDU, Traduit Par Jacques DeLille. [In three volumes]. *A Paris, Ches Giguet Et Michaud, Imp.–Libraires, Rue Des Bons-Enfans, No. 6. 1805.—XIII. 3 volumes.* First edition thus. 8vo, 370pp.,+392pp.,+356pp., half-title for "Paradis Perdu, Traduit En Vers Français Par Jacques DeLille" with English title page with decorative piece at the center on verso ("Paradise Lost. The Author John Milton. Paris: Printed By Giguet And Michaud, Rue Des Bons-Enfans, No. 6. 1805.—XIII"), volume 1, engraved frontispiece illustration and separate title page in French each volume, with the same decorative piece at the center of each French title page as on the English title page, engraved frontispiece illustration plate with illustration by Monsiau [Monciau] for Book I (Satan rallying the troops, with lines quoted in French and "Book I" and page number cited below) engraved by Delignon between English and French title page, "Preface" by L. G. Michaud in French providing information about the translation history of Milton's *PL* in France, "Remarques D'Addisson," half-title for "Paradis Perdu, Livres I, II, III," with the English and French verse translations on facing pages following, and "Remarques" in French at the end of each book, volume 1, general half-title in volume 2 and again in volume 3 for "Oeuvres De Jacques DeLille" with half-title for "Paradise Lost. A Poem In Twelve Books. The Author John Milton" on verso, followed by half-title for "Paradis Perdu, Traduit En Vers Français Par Jacques DeLille" with English title page with decorative piece at the center on verso ("Paradise Lost. The Author John Milton. Paris: Printed By Giguet And Michaud, Rue Des Bons-Enfans, No. 6. 1805.—XIII"), engraved frontispiece illustration plate with illustration by Monsiau [Monciau] for Book V (Raphael counseling Adam and Eve, with lines quoted in French and "Book V" and page number cited below) engraved by T. Couche between English and French title page, half-title for "Paradis Perdu, Livres IV, V, VI, VII, VIII," with the English and French verse translations on facing pages following, and "Remarques" in French at the end of each book, volume 2, half-title for "Paradis Perdu, Traduit En Vers Français Par Jacques DeLille" with English title page with decorative piece at the center on verso ("Paradise Lost. The Author John Milton. Paris: Printed By Giguet And Michaud, Rue Des Bons-Enfans, No. 6. 1805.—XIII"), engraved frontispiece illustration plate with illustration by Monsiau [Monciau] for Book IX (Eve tempting Adam, with lines quoted in French and "Book IX" and page number cited below) engraved by Delvaux between English and French title page, half-title for "Paradis Perdu, Livres IX, X, XI, XII," with the English and French verse translations on facing pages following, and "Remarques" in French at the end of each book, volume 3, contemporary half green calf, marbled paper over boards (a bit rubbed, minor waterstains at front of volume 1 and end of volumes 2 and 3, some light foxing), gilt rules on covers, spines lettered in gilt with gilt rules at top and bottom, thick raised bands with decorative gilt trim, marbled edges. A very nice set with armorial bookplate of Thomas Davies Lloyd on front pastedown of each volume, with his signature in a neat hand on title page of each volume along with a marginal note in a neat hand (p. 126, volume 2). In addition to separate title pages in English and French, this edition has the text in each language on facing pages. A very nice copy of this translation by Jacques DeLille with variant engraved frontispiece illustration plates. Not in Kohler (but see Kohler 83, recording a set "12mo in 6s," with publisher and date on title page as here except for "no. 6. 1805—AN XIII" instead of "No. 6. 1805.—XIII," as here, and with variant frontispiece illustrations and other variants; and see Kohler 84, recording another edition as "Folio in 4s", with variant engraved frontispiece illustrations and other variants); Stevens 1447, reporting "in nine formats."

While Abbé Jacques Delille (1738–1813) was a noted member of the Academy and was selected by Charles Lamb to translate Lamb's verse on Hester (1803) into French, he is described in the *Oxford Companion to French Literature* as "a mediocre poet and an agreeable and lively talker, popular in his day, author of descriptive and didactic poems. . . . his translations [of Milton, Virgil, etc.] though elegant, fail to render the spirit of the original." See following octavo edition, similar to this set in a variant binding, and the quarto edition listed here, three volumes bound as one, with variant frontispiece illustration plates; besides being issued in octavo and quarto formats, the edition was also issued in duodecimo format; a two-volume 12mo edition of DeLille's translation was also published without the English text and without illustrations in 1805: "A Paris, Se Vend A Brunswick Chez Pluchart, A Leipzig Ches Besson" (see set listed here); and a three-volume 8vo edition of DeLille's translation was published without the English text and without illustrations in 1805: "A Paris, 1805.—AN XIII."

819. Variant of Preceding. **PARADIS PERDU**, Traduit Par Jacques DeLille. [In three volumes]. *A Paris, Ches Giguet Et Michaud, Imp.–Libraires, Rue Des Bons-Enfans, No. 6. 1805.—XIII. 3 volumes*. First edition thus. 8vo, 370pp.,+392pp.,+356pp., general half-title in each volume (not just volumes 2 and 3), "Oeuvres De Jacques DeLille" with half-title for "Paradise Lost. A Poem In Twelve Books. The Author John Milton" on verso, followed by half-title in each volume for "Paradis Perdu, Traduit En Vers Français Par Jacques DeLille" with English title page with decorative piece at the center on verso ("Paradise Lost. The Author John Milton. Paris: Printed By Giguet And Michaud, Rue Des Bons-Enfans, No. 6. 1805.—XIII"), engraved frontispiece illustration and separate title page in French each volume, with the same decorative piece at the center of each French title page as on the English title page, engraved frontispiece illustration plate with illustration for Book I by Monsiau [Monciau] (Satan rallying the troops, with lines quoted in French and "Book I" and page number cited below) engraved by Delignon between English and French title page, "Preface" by L. G. Michaud in French, "Remarques D'Addisson" in French, half-title for "Paradis Perdu, Livres I, II, III," with the English and French verse translations on facing pages following, and "Remarques" in French at the end of each book, volume 1, engraved frontispiece illustration plate with illustration for Book V by Monsiau [Monciau] (Raphael counseling Adam and Eve, with lines quoted in French and "Book V" and page number cited below) engraved by T. Couche between English and French title page, half-title for "Paradis Perdu, Livres IV, V, VI, VII, VIII," with the English and French verse translations on facing pages following, and "Remarques" in French at the end of each book, volume 2, engraved frontispiece illustration plate with illustration for Book IX by Monsiau [Monciau] (Eve tempting Adam, with lines quoted in French and "Book IX" and page number cited below) engraved by Delvaux between English and French title page, half-title for "Paradis Perdu, Livres IX, X, XI, XII," with the English and French verse translations on facing pages following, and "Remarques" in French at the end of each book, volume 3, contemporary polished calf, spines decorated with gilt trim and small decorative gilt piece, red morocco labels with gilt lettering and gilt numerals together with decorative gilt trim, blue marbled endpapers, lightly speckled edges. A fine set, very fresh and clean within, with striking impressions of the engraved frontispiece illustrations, with bookplates on front pastedown of each volume. In addition to separate title pages in English and French, this edition has the text in each language on facing pages. A splendid copy of this translation by Jacques DeLille (see comments about DeLille with preceding set), with variant engraved frontispiece illustration plates. See preceding octavo edition, similar to this set in a variant binding, and the quarto edition following, three volumes bound as one, with variant frontispiece illustration plates. Besides being issued in 8vo and 4to formats, the edition was also issued in 12mo format. See commentary with preceding set. Not in Kohler.

820. Variant of Preceding. **PARADIS PERDU**, Traduit Par Jacques DeLille. [In three volumes]. *A Paris, Ches Giguet Et Michaud, Imp.–Libraires, Rue Des Bons-Enfans, No. 6. 1805.–XIII.* 3 volumes in one. First edition thus. Large 4to (page size 10" × 13"), similar to preceding set (except for 4to size, variants in engraved frontispiece illustrations, and without half-title for "Oeuvres De Jacques DeLille"—present in preceding sets), 364pp.,+424pp., +388pp., half-title for "Paradis Perdu, Traduit En Vers Français Par Jacques DeLille" with English title page with decorative piece at the center on verso ("Paradise Lost. The Author John Milton. Paris: Printed By Giguet And Michaud, Rue Des Bons-Enfans, No. 6. 1805.—XIII"), volume 1, engraved frontispiece illustration and separate title page in French each volume, with the same decorative piece at the center of each French title page as on the English title page, engraved frontispiece illustration plate with illustration of the rebel angels being expelled from heaven by Monsiau [Monciau] engraved by L. Baquoy between English and French title page with protective tissue guard, "Preface" by L. G. Michaud in French, "Remarques D'Addisson" in French, half-title for "Paradis Perdu, Livres I, II, III," with the English and French verse translations on facing pages following, and "Remarques" in French at the end of each book, volume 1, half-title for "Paradis Perdu, Traduit En Vers Français Par Jacques DeLille" with English title page with decorative piece at the center on verso ("Paradise Lost. The Author John Milton. Paris: Printed By Giguet And Michaud, Rue Des Bons-Enfans, No. 6. 1805.—XIII"), volume 2, engraved frontispiece illustration plate with illustration of the expulsion by Le Barbier engraved by N. Thomas between English and French title page with protective tissue guard, half-title for "Paradis Perdu, Livres IV, V, VI, VII, VIII," with the English and French verse translations on facing pages following, and "Remarques" in French at the end of each book, volume 2, half-title for "Paradis Perdu, Traduit En Vers Français Par Jacques DeLille" with English title page with decorative piece at the center on verso ("Paradise Lost. The Author John Milton. Paris: Printed By Giguet And Michaud, Rue Des Bons-Enfans, No. 6. 1805.—XIII"), volume 3, engraved frontispiece illustration plate with illustration of the expulsion by Le Barbier engraved by N. Thomas between English and French title page with protective tissue guard, volume 3, same engraved illustration placed between volume 2 and repeated again before volume 3, half-title for "Paradis Perdu, Livres IX, X, XI, XII," with the English and French verse translations on facing pages following, and "Remarques" in French at the end of each book, contemporary dark maroon morocco over very thick boards (a bit rubbed, mispaginated "458" for "358," perhaps wanting half-titles), gilt rules on covers, with central diamond-shaped device in blind relief with gilt emblem in the center, spine heavily ruled in gilt with gilt lettering, thick raised bands, inner and outer dentelles richly tooled in gilt, a.e.g. A handsome copy of this three-volume quarto set bound as one large, thick, heavy tome in contemporary morocco. In addition to separate title pages in English and French, this edition has the text in each language on facing pages. A scarce copy of this edition of Jacques DeLille's translation, with variant engraved frontispiece illustration plates, and in 4to size. See comments about the translator DeLille with the first 8vo set listed here. Not in Kohler.

(left) *Paradis Perdu*, Paris, 1805. 3 volumes. 8vo, contemporary half green calf, marbled paper over boards. (center) *Paradis Perdu*, Paris, 1805. 3 volumes. Large 4to, bound as one large, thick, heavy tome in contemporary dark maroon morocco over very thick boards. (right) *Paradis Perdu*, Paris, 1805. 3 volumes. 8vo, contemporary polished calf. Each first edition thus. See #818, 820, and 819.

821. PARADIS PERDU, Traduit Par Jacques DeLille. Tome Premier / Tome Second. *A Paris, Se Vend A Brunswick Chez Pluchart, A Leipzig Ches Besson, 1805.* 2 volumes. 12mo, xlvi+275pp.,+315+4pp., half-title for "Oeuvres De Jacques Delille," volume 1, general half-title for "Paradis Perdu De J. Milton, Traduit En Vers Français" each volume, half-title (listing several other books of DeLille available on verso), volume 1, title page each volume, "Preface" by L. G. Michaud in French, "Remarques D'Addisson" in French, half-title for four books in volume 1 and half-title for eight books in volume 2, four-page "Catalogue" bound in at end of volume 2, original gray paper wrappers (some light foxing and minor dust soiling), printed paper labels on spines, edges uncut. The spine labels read: *Oeuvres De Jacques Delille*, with "Milton" written in ink on volume 1 label. A fine set of this translation by Jacques DeLille, in its original wrappers. "We have never seen this rare edition prior to this set; it is not in the British Library Catalogue [and] not in the National Union Catalogue" (G. W. Stuart, Jr., Ravenstree, Cat. 96, #108, 2001). Not in Kohler.

822. PARADIS PERDU, Traduit Par Jacques DeLille. [In three volumes]. *A Paris, 1805.—AN XIII.* 3 volumes in one. Small 8vo, xxiii+204pp.,+200pp.,+182pp., title page for each volume, preface by Michaud, followed by "Remarques D'Addisson Sur Le Paradis Perdu," half-title for each volume (listing the several books in the volume: three in volume 1, five in volume 2, and four in volume 3), "Remarques" at the end of each book, newly rebound in brown buckram and yellow cloth, new endpapers, silk green ribbon. The thirty-two-page preface by Michaud provides information about the translation history of Milton's *PL* in France. See commentary with early illustrated editions here with DeLille's translation published this same year, 1805. Not in Kohler.

823. PARADISE LOST A Poem In Twelve Books Written By John Milton. [Quotation in Greek from Homer's Odyssey] Vol. I./II. *Gotha[:] Printed For Steudel And Keil. 1805. 2 volumes.* 8vo, 332pp.,+211pp., title page for "English Library Authors In Verse. Vol I. Containing the first Part of Miltons Paradise lost. / Vol. II. Containing the second Part of Miltons Paradise lost and Paradise Regain'd. Gotha[:] Printed For Steudel And Keil. 1805" facing general title page in each volume, half-title for *PR* in volume 2, original boards (a bit rubbed, especially at joints, slight age-browning throughout), hand-printed label at the top of each spine (faded), speckled edges. A very nice set. Volume 1 contains the first ten books; volume 2 contains the last two books and *PR*. The arguments for each book of *PL* are not printed in this edition. Scarce. Kohler 82, reporting "Not in the British Library. Not in the Bodleian Library. Not in Cambridge University Library."

The collection also has a variant of preceding. 2 volumes bound in one. 8vo, 332pp.,+211pp., title pages as preceding, original marbled boards, two labels on spine. A nice copy, with some rubbing on spine and showing some wear at the corners and the top of the spine.

824. LE PARADIS PERDU [In] **PORTE-FEUILLE VOLE**, Contenant: 1. Le Paradis Perdu, poème en quatre chants; 2. Les Deguisemens De Vénus, tableaux imités du grée; 3. Les Galanteries De La Bible, sermon en vers. *A Paris, Ches A. G. Debray, Libraire, rue Saint-Honoré, vis-à-vis celle du Coq. Et chez Duprat-Duverger, Libraire, rue des Grands-Augustins, no. 24. 1805.* 12mo in 6s, 246pp., half-title and title page each volume, contemporary quarter sheep over bright pink boards (a bit rubbed), spine elaborately decorated in gilt by compartments with matching morocco label lettered in gilt, light blue endpapers. A lovely copy with *Le Paradis Perdu* as one of three pieces contained in the volume. Not in Kohler.

825. PARADISE LOST. A Poem, In Twelve Books. By John Milton. *London: Printed For Faulder; Vernor, Hood, And Sharpe; Kearsley; Ogilvy; Crosby; Lane And Newman; Ryan; Ebers; Higham And Wilson. 1806.* 12mo, 396pp., half-title ("Milton's Paradise Lost. volume 1.") before "The Verse," half-title before each book, three illustration plates by Thurston, engraved by Heath, for Book I (of Satan on his throne), for Book II ("Out of thy head I sprung"—of Sin, and for Book III (of Satan disguised as a cherub: "now a stripling cherub he appears . . . so well he feign'd"), contemporary tree calf (a little rubbed, extremities a bit worn, joints weak, lacking spine label, spine chipped at top and bottom), spine trimmed with gilt rules (faded) and small decorative gilt pieces, outer dentelles trimmed in gilt (very faded). A nice copy of a scarce edition. The reference to "volume 1" in the half-title would indicate that this volume was apparently issued with (or intended to be issued with) *PR* as volume 2, the two together serving as Milton's *PW*, each volume apparently being available for sale separately, following a custom initiated by Tonson early in the eighteenth century. Scarce. Not in Kohler.

826. PARADISE LOST, A Poem, In Twelve Books. By John Milton. With A Biographical And Critical Account Of The Author And His Writings. *Edinburgh: Printed By John Turnbull, Old Assembly Close, For William Anderson, Stirling, 1806.* 12mo in 6s, 288pp., life by Fenton, original half calf, marbled paper over boards (marbled paper worn, pages age-darkened with some occasional slight smudging, small piece missing on outer portion at top of pp. 265/266 with partial loss of text on p. 266, lacking front blanks), "Printed By John Turnbull, Old Assembly Close, Edinburgh" at bottom of last page. Scarce. Kohler 85, describing its copy as "8vo in 6s," and reporting "Not in the British Library. Not in the Bodleian Library. Not in Cambridge University Library."

827. PARADISE LOST, A Poem, In Twelve Books. By John Milton. *London[,] Published by W. Suttaby, & B. Crosby & Co. Stationer's Court; and C. Corrall, Charing Cross. 1806. C. Corrall Printer.* 12mo, viii+301+[1]+[10]+[2]pp., engraved title page in place of printed title page with a vignette illustration at the center (not for Milton) with the quotation from Thomas Gray's "Progress Of Poetry," engraved title with poet and lyre colored over in orange watercolor, contemporary tree calf (a little worn, spine slightly chipped, joints weak and beginning to crack at the top of front joint, lacking either a front blank or perhaps a frontispiece, poetic quotation written in pencil in a neat hand on engraved title page), covers ruled in gilt with decorative gilt border trim, spine trimmed in decorative gilt bands with small decorative gilt pieces in the panels, black morocco label with gilt lettering and decorative gilt trim, marbled endpapers. Although a bit aged, overall a nice copy of a scarce edition with a quotation from Gray "On Milton's Blindness" written in ink in a very neat early hand on verso of fly-leaf facing engraved title page. The engraved title page here for *PL* is the same engraved title page, with variations to the publisher's imprint ("Published by W. Suttaby . . . [variation within] . . . and C. Corrall, Charing Cross, 1804"), that appears in the 1805 edition of Milton's *PW* "Publish'd by W. Suttaby, Stationer's Court, Ludgate Street; and C. Corrall, Charing Cross" (copy listed here). Scarce. Not in Kohler.

828. PARADISE LOST, A Poem, In Twelve Books, By John Milton. To which is prefixed The Life Of The Author, And A Criticism On The Poem, By Dr. Johnson. [Quotation from Addison] *London: Printed For Thomas Tegg, No. 111, Cheapside. 1807.* 12mo in 6s, xiv+[2]+284pp., engraved oval frontispiece portrait, "Engraved by H. R. Cooke from a Miniature Painting in the Possession of Mr. Ascouth. Pub. by T. Tegg, Jan. 1 1807," tailpiece at the end of Bk. VIII, original decorated green paper boards (worn, spine partially missing, no blank endpapers—although none appears to be missing, small tear at top inner edge of frontispiece), front cover lettered in black at the center within decorative black trim, back cover similarly lettered in black (with an advertisement) at the center within decorative black trim, edges untrimmed. Despite the wear, an otherwise nice copy of a scarce edition. Not in Kohler.

829. LE PARADIS PERDU, De Milton. Traduction Nouvelle, Par Jacques-Barthelemy Salgues, Aucieu Professeur d'éloquence. *A Paris, Chez Leopold Collin, Libraire, rue Git-le-Coeur, No. 4. 1807.* 8vo, half-title, xxx+[2]+506pp., thirty-page preface, nineteenth-century quarter calf, marbled paper over boards (a bit rubbed), spine ruled in gilt with gilt lettering at the top and decorative gilt trim at bottom, marbled edges. A very nice copy. *PL* is translated into French prose here by Jacques-Barthelemy Salgues. Scarce. Not in Kohler.

830. PARADISE LOST. A Poem. In Twelve Books. By John Milton. Printed From The Text of Tonson's Correct Edition of 1711. A New Edition, With Plates. *London: Printed For J. Johnson; W. J. And J. Richardson; Otridge And Son; R. Baldwin; Vernor, Hood, And Sharpe; Cuthell And Martin; J. Walker; F. And C. Rivington; Scatcherd And Letterman; Wilkie And Robinson; J. Nunn; R. Lea; Longman, Hurst, Rees, And Orme; Cadell And Davies; T. Payne; W. Lowndes; Lackington, Allen And Co.; Clarke And Sons; J. Taylor; E. Jeffery; J. Mawman; Mathews And Leigh; J. Carpenter; And J. Booker; At The Union Printing Office, St. John's Square, by W. Wilson. 1808.* 8vo, xliii+372pp., half-title, frontispiece portrait "Engrav'd by Wm. Sharp, after an original miniature by Samuel Cooper: the ornaments by G. B. Cipriani And E. F. Burney. London: Publish'd by Vernor, Hood & Sharpe, Poultry, 1808," with vignette illustration of Eve tempting Adam beneath the portrait, engraved and printed title pages ("London. Printed for the Proprietors, 1808" at bottom of engraved title page), with vignette illustration by Burney for Book X on engraved title, "Life" by Fenton, "Criticism on *PL*" by Johnson, engraved illustration plates after Fuseli and Hamilton, one for each book, with three of Hamilton's illustrations engraved by Bartolozzi, half-title for each book, contemporary streaked calf (covers slightly chipped, joints rubbed, some browning of text, pp. 31–42 misbound between pp. 370–71 of text), decorative gilt border trim on covers, gilt-decorated spine, black morocco label with gilt lettering and gilt rules, outer dentelles ruled in gilt (faded), marbled endpapers and edges. A fine, large paper copy with plates that are especially clean and crisp, and with rare half-title (sometimes lacking). Williamson 224 (describing the frontispiece portrait at length on p. 18); Kohler 86.

831. PARADISE LOST. *(London:) Printed For The Proprietors, 1808.* Bound with **COMUS AND L'ALLEGRO AND IL PENSEROSO**, n.d. folio scrapbook, extra-illustrated [ca. 1810], paper watermarked 1794. Extra thick folio, in original binding, one-half calf, marbled paper over thick boards (rebacked), spine lettered in gilt with decorative black ornaments. 8vo text of *PL*, engraved title page, "Printed for the Proprietors" (dated 1808) with vignette illustration by Burney, and printed 16mo text of *C* and of *L'A* and *IlP* (edition unidentified), each page mounted on individual folio leaves, along with life and numerous engraved illustrations and engraved portraits from the late eighteenth and early nineteenth centuries. Aside from being interesting as an extra-illustrated folio scrapbook with illustrations put together with great care at the turn of the eighteenth to the nineteenth century, this is a truly valuable resource, hitherto unexplored. Not in Kohler.

832. PARADISE LOST: A Poem. In Twelve Books. By John Milton. *Philadelphia: Published By Johnson And Warner, No. 147, Market Street, 1808. Dickinson, Printer, Whitehall.* 12mo in 6s, engraved frontispiece portrait by W. Haines, one illustration engraved by C. Tiebout (dated 1804), contemporary speckled calf (a bit rubbed), gilt-decorated spine, red morocco label with gilt lettering and gilt trim, outer dentelles tooled in gilt (faded). A nice copy in a fine early American binding with contemporary signature (dated 1815) on fly-leaf. Scarce. Not in Kohler.

833. MILTON'S PARADISE LOST. A Poem. with Historical[,] Philosophical & Explanatory Notes, Translated from the French of the Learned Raymond de St. Maur and Various critical Remarks and Observations from Mr. Addison. Dr. Warburton. Dr. Newton. Dr. Pearce. Dr. Bentley. Mr. Richardson. and Mr. Hume. To which is prefixed Paradise Regained. [Vol. I & II] *Newcastle Upon Tyne. Printed & Sold by K. Anderson. 1809.* 2 volumes in one. 12mo in 6s, 606+[23 unpaginated index]+[1]pp., small, unsigned engraved circular frontispiece portrait in both volumes 1 and 2, undated engraved title page with vignette illustration of Eve giving the apple to Adam engraved by Lambert in both volumes 1 and 2, printed title page for *PR*, volume 2 (dated 1809), five unsigned engraved illustration plates (with book and line identification) for *PL*, volume 1, advertisement and life by Fenton, volume 1, notes at bottom of page, index at the end of volume 2, contemporary speckled calf (a bit rubbed, text occasionally fingered or smudged), spine ruled in gilt, red morocco label with gilt lettering and gilt trim, contemporary signature (dated 1811) in ink in a neat hand at the top of each engraved title page, bookplate with the same name (dated 1818) on front pastedown. Very nice copy with advertisement leaf bound in at end. The unsigned engraved illustration plates are for Book IV, line 27 (Satan seated on a rock), Book V, line 152 (Adam and Eve in morning prayer), Book VIII, line 484 (Eve being presented to Adam), Book IX, line 532 (the snake tempting Eve), and Book X, line 109 (Adam and Eve being judged by God). Raymond de St. Maur was first translated as *The State of*

Innocence and the Fall of Man with commentary in 1745 (see copy here and discussion there about authorship). See 1754 edition with striking unsigned illustrations; see another issue of the 1754 edition in 1755 with a variant publisher, with the same striking unsigned illustrations; see also two-volume 1775 edition with unsigned 1688 illustrations reduced; and see two-volume 1779 edition with 1688 illustrations reduced and attributed to R. Cooper, this edition reprinted in 1784; see, too, 1765 and 1770 nonillustrated editions—all listed here. Scarce. Kohler 87, with some variations, calling its volume "Octavo in 6s," indicating only one engraved title page, not two, as here, without reference to engraved illustration plates for *PL* as here, "with title-page for *PR*" on "Verso of T6," not the case here, and reporting "Not in Williamson. Problematical title-page but *PL* and *PR* appear to be complete. Not in the British Library. Not in the Bodleian Library. Not in Cambridge University Library."

834. PARADISE LOST. A Poem In Twelve Books. By John Milton. *(London: Printed For J. Bell, Gallery of Fine Arts, Southampton-Street, Strand. 1810.).* [In] **LA BELLE ASSEMBLEE OR, BELL'S COURT AND FASHIONABLE MAGAZINE, ADDRESSED PARTICULARLY TO THE LADIES**. Vol 1.—New Series. From January 1, To June 30, 1810. *London: Printed For J. Bell, Gallery of Fine Arts, Southampton-Street, Strand. 1810.* First edition thus? Slim 8vo in 4s, 110pp., engraved frontispiece portrait of Milton, "Engraved by R. Cooper," with the caption: "Milton. Engraven from an original Picture, for the 7th, being the supplemental Number to the New Series of La Belle Assemblée. Published July 1, 1810, by J. Bell, Southampton Street, Strand, London," printed in double column under the heading "Beauties Of The British Poets" at the top of each page together with "Milton.]" on one side after the pagination and "[Paradise Lost." on the other side, and with "No. 1" and "No. II.— N.S. Continued from the Poetical Part of No. I." to "No. VII.—N.S." at bottom of the page, "London: Printed by and for J. Bell, Southampton-street, Strand" near bottom of last page, disbound (with remnants of original leather spine, fore-edge of portrait slightly creased from having been folded for some time). This edition of *PL* was printed, without title page, as part of *La Belle Assemblée Or, Bell's Court And Fashionable Magazine, Addressed Particularly To The Ladies*, Vol. 1.—New Series. The engraved portrait of Milton appears to have been done for this issue of the magazine, while the magazine has an engraved title page consisting of pillars of Egyptian figures with additional decorative elements at the top and bottom. A nice copy of a scarce edition of Milton's *PL*. Not in Kohler.

835. PARADISE LOST, A Poem. In Twelve Books, By John Milton. To which is prefixed, The Life Of The Author. *London: Printed For Thomas Tegg, No. 111, Cheapside. 1812.* 12mo, vii+[1]+304pp., frontispiece illustration of *Adam and Eve in the Bower of Bliss*, "Engraved by Freeman, from a design by Vivares" ("London Published by Thomas Tegg, No.111 Cheapside March 2d.1812"), engraved and printed title pages, with vignette illustration of Eve tempting Adam by Vivares engraved by T. Freeman on engraved title, "Plummer and Brewis, Printers, Love Lane, Little Eastcheap" on verso of title page and repeated at bottom of last page, life by Fenton, contemporary calf (a bit worn, several pieces missing along inner joints, spine a bit chipped at bottom), covers decorated in a blind pattern with borders delicately tooled in gilt trim, spine elaborately decorated in gilt within the panels, raised bands with decorative gilt trim, red morocco label with gilt lettering and gilt rules, marbled edges. A nice copy with contemporary signature on front blank. Scarce. Not in Kohler.

See 1813 edition by Tegg listed here with engraved frontispiece illustration and engraved title page with vignette illustration as here; see also 1815 edition by Tegg listed here in the same format as here and as 1813 edition by Tegg, with the same title page and publisher's imprint as here, but with a different engraved frontispiece illustration from that here (of Eve discoursing with Adam, labeled simply "Milton" and unsigned, with publisher's imprint at the bottom identical to here, except for the date), and without engraved title page as here.

836. PARADISE LOST; A Poem, In Twelve Books. And Paradise Regain'd, In Four Books. Also Samson Agonistes, And Other Poems. By John Milton. A New Edition, Carefully collated with the best Authorities. To Which Is Prefixed, A Life Of The Author, By The Rev. David M'Nicoll. *Liverpool: Printed By Nuttall, Fisher, And Dixon, Duke-Street. Stereotype Edition. n.d. [1812].* First edition thus. 8vo in 4s, pagination continuing to p. 20, then with a jump in pagination, 33–428pp., engraved frontispiece portrait of Milton in a circular form with a crown of thorns amidst rays of sunlight overhead and foliage along both sides and bottom with snake and apple beneath the portrait, signed "R. Hicks," "Drawn by W. M. Craig Esqr. from a miniature by Cooper," "Publish'd by Nuttall, Fisher & Dixon. Liverpool. Mar. 30, 1812" at the bottom, protective tissue guard, eighteen-page "Life Of Milton. Compiled By The Rev. David M'Nicoll," seven engraved illustration plates after W. M. Craig, variously engraved by A. Warren, A. Smith, I. Romney, James, Bragg, and Pye (each dated 1812), each with "Publish'd by Nuttall, Fisher & Dixon. Liverpool" at the bottom of the plate, each with protective tissue guard, "A Glossary. Explaining the antiquated and difficult Words in Milton's poetical Works" at the end, contemporary tree calf (a bit rubbed, especially along extremities, joints tender but sound, plates a little foxed, early name in ink erased on title page), spine decorated and lettered in gilt. A pleasant copy. The "Other Poems" indicated on the title page include: *L'A, IlP* and *On The Death of a Fair Infant*. Craig's seven illustrations include six illustrations for *PL*: Book I (*Satan Rallying His Troops*, line 315); Book III (*The Transformation of Satan before Meeting Uriel*, line 645); Book V (*Raphael Counseling Adam and Eve*, line 391); Book VII (*Adam Beholds Eve*, line 481); Book IX (*The Temptation of Eve*, line 494, with slight staining at upper left corner partially affecting illustration); and Book XII (*The Expulsion*, line 637, with slight staining in upper margin without affecting illustration); and one illustration for *PR*: Book II (*The Temptation to "A Table Richly Spread,"* line 338, with slight staining in upper margin without affecting illustration). Craig's illustrations for *PL* first appeared in a 12mo two-volume edition published by the Albion Press in 1804 with twelve illustration plates engraved by Mackenzie (see set listed here); Craig's four illustrations for *PR* first appeared, unsigned, in 1806 editions by the Albion Press, in both octavo and duodecimo formats (both listed here). Here seven of Craig's illustrations are printed in an octavo format, variously engraved, and each dated 1812 for this edition. The edition was apparently published by subscription—the terminal glossary and the preliminary leaves comprise part 15 which explains the jump in pagination between the preliminaries and the beginning of the text proper at p. 33. An uncommon edition. Williamson 225 (see also 133); Not in Kohler (Kohler 89 describes an 1815 reissue of this edition).

See possible first London edition thus listed here ca. 1823; see also *PW* listed here in 1843, as here, with the same engraved frontispiece portrait (there dated 1843), same life by M'Nicoll, and same engraved illustration plates after Craig (there variously dated post-1835), and with the printed title page: "The Poetical Works . . . Fisher, Son, & Co. London Paris, And New York," undated.

837. PARADISE LOST A Poem In Twelve Books, By John Milton[.] *London, Published by Suttaby, Evance & Fox; & Crosby & Co. Stationers Court. 1812. Corrall Printer*. First edition thus? 12mo, viii+304+[1]+[8-page unpaginated index]+[2]pp., engraved title page, frontispiece illustration of Raphael counseling Adam and Eve "Drawn by W. Hamilton," engraved by R. Rhodes, "Published Jan. 1. 1812, by Suttaby & Co. London," engraved title page with vignette illustration of Adam telling Eve, "I descry / From yonder blazing cloud that veils the hill, / One of the Heavenly host" Book XI [lines 227–30] "Drawn by W. Hamilton," "Engraved by R. Rhodes," life by Fenton, half-title for each book, index at the end, contemporary calf (a little worn at joints and at corners, spine cracked at center, small slight inoffensive waterstain of sometime ago at top outer corner of frontispiece and engraved title), gilt-tooled border trim on covers, gilt-decorated spine with gilt lettering, marbled endpapers and edges. All in all, a decent copy of a very uncommon early nineteenth-century edition. A possible second edition was published in 1815 "by Suttaby, Evance & Fox, Stationers Court & Baldwin, Cradock & Joy," with the same frontispiece illustration and engraved title page. That edition, too, is very rare. See also 1821 edition of *PW* listed here "by Suttaby, Evance & Fox," which includes this edition of *PL* with index. Scarce. Not in Kohler.

838. PARADISE LOST, A Poem. In Twelve Books. By John Milton. To which is prefixed The Life Of The Author. *London: Printed For Thomas Tegg, No. 111, Cheapside. 1813.* 12mo in 6s, vii+[1]+304pp., frontispiece illustration of *The Bower of Bliss* "Engraved by Freeman from a design by Vivares ("London Published by Thomas Tegg No. 111 Cheapside March 2d.1813"), engraved and printed title pages, with vignette illustration of *The Temptation* by Vivares engraved by Freeman on engraved title, life by Fenton, contemporary polished calf (bit rubbed), gilt rule on covers, gilt-decorated spine, black leather label. An attractive copy with the bookplate of J. Moxon. See 1812 edition by Tegg with engraved frontispiece illustration and engraved title page with vignette illustration as here; see also 1815 edition by Tegg listed here in the same

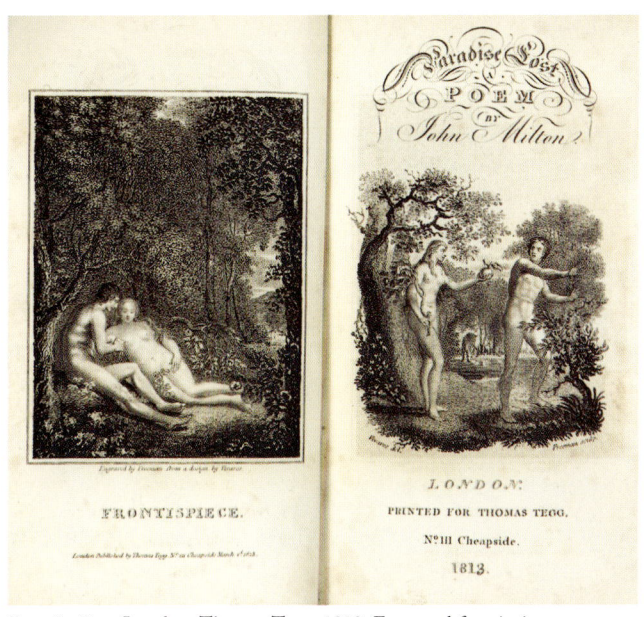

Paradise Lost. London: Thomas Tegg, 1813. Engraved frontispiece illustration by Vivares and engraved title page with vignette illustration by Vivares of Eve tempting Adam. See #838.

format as here, with the same title page and publisher's imprint, but with a different engraved frontispiece illustration from that here (of Eve discoursing with Adam, labeled simply "Milton" and unsigned, with publisher's imprint at the bottom identical to here, except for the date), and without engraved title page as here. Kohler 88, describing its copy as "Octavo in 6s," referencing engraved title page, but without reference to engraved frontispiece illustration, reporting "Not in the Bodleian Library. Not in Cambridge University Library."

839. PARADISE LOST: A Poem. In Twelve Books. By John Milton. With The Life Of The Author. *Baltimore, Published By Fielding Lucas Jun. And Joseph Cushing. T. & G. Palmer, printers. 1813.* 12mo, vi+[2]+314pp., frontispiece illustration by J. Thurston for *PL*, Book VI, engraved by "P. Maverick sc. Newark," with lines illustrated quoted beneath ("Published by F. Lucas Jr. & I. Cushing"), engraved title page ("Paradise Lost, A Poem, in Twelve Books; By John Milton. Baltimore[:] Published by F. Lucas Jr. & L. Cushing, 1813") with vignette illustration (not for Milton) engraved by "P. Maverick sc. Newark," with lines quoted and reference given: "Vide Gray's Progress of Poetry," life of Milton by Fenton, half-title for each book with argument on verso, index at the end, original tree calf (worn along joints and at corners with spine ends chipped, age-browning throughout with remnants of inoffensive waterstaining from sometime ago, library stamp on front and back blanks and on bottom edge), gilt border trim on covers, spine decorated in gilt with black label lettered in gilt, marbled endpapers. A decent copy of a scarce early nineteenth-century American edition of *PL* published in Baltimore. See 1818 edition of *PL* listed here published by "Cushing And Jewett. J. D. Toy, Printer" in Baltimore, with the same frontispiece illustration and the same engraved title page with vignette illustration for Gray as here. See also 1813 edition of *PW* listed here "Published by Fielding Lucas, Jun. And Joseph Cushing. T. & G. Palmer, printers," with engraved and printed title pages with the same vignette illustration for Gray on the engraved title page as here; and see 1818 edition of *PW* listed here "Published By Cushing & Jewett. J. D. Toy, Printer" in Baltimore, with the same frontispiece illustration and the same vignette illustration for Gray on engraved title pages as here, one engraved title dated 1813, the other 1818. Not in Kohler.

840. [PARADISE LOST] THE STATE OF INNOCENCE, AND THE FALL OF MAN, Described In Milton's Paradise Lost. Rendered Into Prose; With Historical, Philosophical, And Explanatory Notes. From The French Of The Learned R. De. St. Maur. By A Gentleman Of Oxford. *Trenton [New Jersey]: Published By William Robinson, And John C. Moore. William & David Robinson, Printers. 1813.* First American edition? 8vo in 4s, 450pp., frontispiece portrait by Seclesse, contemporary mottled sheep (rebacked in period style preserving original gilt-lettered red morocco label, some light age-browning throughout), decorative gilt trim on spine. A nice, possibly large paper copy with contemporary signature on fly-leaf. Apparently the first American edition of this prose version of *PL*, from the French of Nicolas François Dupré de Saint-Maur. The author of the "Notes" apparently is George Smith Green, and Shaw and Shoemaker enter the work under his name, although James Patterson has also received recognition as the author (see discussion with original listing). *The State of Innocence and the Fall of Man* originally appeared in 1745; the first edition of Nicholas F. Dupré de Saint-Maur's translation of *PL* into French prose was published in 1729. Both editions are listed here. Rare. Shaw & Shoemaker 28664 "recording only the American Antiquarian Society copy"; Not in Kohler.

841. MILTONS VERLORENES PARADIES. Ubersetzt von J[ohann]. F. Pries, Professor der Moral und Usthetik in Rostock. *Rostock und Leipsig. ben Stiller[,] 1813.* 8vo, lii+388+[1]pp., contents, "Milton's Leben, nach Johnson," half-title each book, original one-half calf, brown paper over boards (a bit worn, front joint slightly cracked, corners worn), gilt-lettered leather label on spine (label defective), decorative trim on spine, light blue endpapers (lacking back endpaper), red edges. A good copy. Rare. Not in Kohler.

841A. (Cross-listing) ["AN AMERICAN MILTON"] TRUE AND INFERNAL FRIENDSHIP, OR THE WISDOM OF EVE. AND THE CHARACTER OF THE SERPENT, WITH THE SITUATION, JOYS, AND LOSS OF PARADISE . . . *Providence, R.I. Printed By H. Mann And Co. For The Author. 1813.* First edition. 12mo, xx+[13]+176+[2]pp., contemporary roan-backed boards. First edition of a still-anonymous poem, extraordinary in that it treats what even in America at the time must have been regarded as the preeminently Miltonic subject. The anonymous author asserts two different kinds of friendship, exemplified in God's and Satan's treatment of Adam and Eve in the Garden of Eden, and along the way argues for the literal truth of earth's being "a *hollow globe*, containing a celestial region in its centre, and the same that is called Paradise . . . where *Adam* and *Eve* and the new *creation* were placed when created." Shaw and Shoemaker 29982. See main listing under *Milton: "An American Milton"* with Nineteenth-century Miltoniana.

842. PARADISE LOST A Poem In Twelve Books, By John Milton[.] *London, Published by Suttaby, Evance & Fox,*

Stationers Court & Baldwin, Cradock & Joy, Paternoster Row. 1815. Second edition thus? 12mo, viii+304+[1]+[8-page unpaginated index], engraved title page, frontispiece illustration of Raphael counseling Adam and Eve "Drawn by W. Hamilton," engraved by R. Rhodes, "Published Jan. 6. 1815, by Suttaby & Co. London," engraved title page with vignette illustration of Adam telling Eve "I descry / From yonder blazing cloud that veils the hill, / One of the Heavenly host" Book XI [lines 227–30] "Drawn by W. Hamilton," "Engraved by R. Rhodes," protective tissue guard, life by Fenton, half-title for each book, index at the end, contemporary calf (a bit rubbed, front cover detached, spine a little worn and slightly chipped at top and bottom, frontispiece and engraved title foxed), marbled endpapers and edges, green silk ribbon marker. All in all, a decent copy of a very uncommon early nineteenth-century edition with contemporary bookplate tipped in on front pastedown and a contemporary prize inscription written in ink in a neat hand on front blank. The possible first edition thus was published in 1812 "by Suttaby, Evance & Fox; & Crosby & Co. Stationers Court," with the same frontispiece illustration and engraved title page (also listed here). That edition, too, is very uncommon. Scarce. Not in Kohler.

843. PARADISE LOST, A Poem. In Twelve Books. By John Milton. To which is prefixed The Life Of The Author. *London: Printed For Thomas Tegg, No. 111, Cheapside. 1815.* 12mo in 6s, vii+[1]+304pp., engraved frontispiece illustration of Eve discoursing with Adam (labeled "Milton," unsigned, fine impression, "London Published by Thomas Tegg. No. 111. Cheapside. Oct. 26th, 1814" at the bottom), "Plummer and Brewis, Printers, Love Lane, Little Eastcheap" on verso of title page and repeated at the bottom of the last page, life by Fenton, original calf (worn, front joint cracked, slight embrowning throughout), black leather label with gilt lettering and decorative trim on spine. See 1812 and 1813 editions by Tegg in the same format as here and with the same title page and publisher's imprint as here, each with a different engraved frontispiece illustration from that here (of Adam and Eve in the Bower of Bliss, "Engraved by Freeman, from a design by Vivares"), with publisher's imprint at the bottom identical to here (except for the date), and each with engraved title page (not present here and not missing) with vignette illustration of the Temptation engraved by Freeman after Vivares. Scarce. Not in Kohler.

844. PARADISE LOST. By John Milton. Vol. I. / Vol. II. *Stockholm, Printed by Elmen & Granberg[,] 1815.* First edition thus. 2 volumes in one. 8vo in 4s, 362pp., half-title with decorative border trim each volume, statement in Swedish at center of leaf-like half-title with same decorative border trim at end of each volume, rebound in three-quarter orange pebble cloth, marbled paper over boards (spine a little faded), spine lettered in gilt with gilt rule at top and bottom. Nice. Possibly printed as a companion to the 1815 Stockholm *PL* in Swedish (following copy and variant). Rare. OCLC locates only one copy at Harvard.

First Edition in Swedish

845. DET FORLORADE PARADISET. Poem I Tolf Sanger, Af Milton. Ofversattning. *Stockholm, Tryckt hos Carl Delen, 1815.* First edition thus. 8vo, xi+[i]+452pp., "Foretal," "Poemets Amne" (repeated twice, before and after half-title, providing a brief summary of each book), notes at the end of each book, new half calf, marbled paper over boards, spine decorated with gilt rules and small decorative gilt pieces in the panels, red morocco label with gilt lettering and decorative gilt trim, raised bands, new endpapers, wholly untrimmed. A fine, large paper copy. The first edition in Swedish. The translation is by Johann Gabriel Oxenstierna, one of the leading Swedish poets of the early nineteenth century. Scarce. NUC records only three copies; Not in Kohler.

846. Variant of Preceding, contemporary red straight-grained morocco (manuscript inscription deleted from the title page), finely tooled decorative gilt border trim on covers, richly gilt-decorated spine, black morocco label with gilt lettering and decorative gilt trim, green endpapers, a.e.g., near-contemporary signature in a neat hand on front fly-leaf and again on front blank. A very attractive copy of this Swedish translation, in a variant binding, a handsome contemporary morocco binding on small paper. The first edition in Swedish. The translation is by Johann Gabriel Oxenstierna. Scarce.

847. PARADISE LOST, A Poem in Twelve Books. By John Milton. A New Edition. *Romsey. Printed for and sold by William Sharp[,] Church Street. 1816.* 8vo, xxxii+335pp., frontispiece portrait "Engraved by R. Page, from an Original Picture," engraved title page with vignette illustration engraved by David Read for Book X, line 351 (Adam cursing Eve after the fall), life by Fenton, "A Critique Upon The *PL*, By Joseph Addison, Esq.," half-title for each book with the argument printed on verso, "Printed By S. Jackson, Romsey, Hants" printed at bottom of the last page, contemporary marbled calf (a little worn, front cover detached, light foxing and soiling to first several leaves, small tear at bottom of engraved title, light worming to upper back cover), delicate gilt border trim on covers, spine lettered and ruled in gilt with small gilt designs between the gilt rules, marbled endpapers. A good copy of an edition probably printed in a limited edition. Scarce. Kohler 90, citing Williamson 240 and reporting "Not in the Bodleian Library. Not in Cambridge University Library."

848. PARADISE LOST[.] A Poem The Author John Milton. *London: Printed For John Sharpe, Piccadilly. 1816.* First edition thus? 8vo, xlviii+384pp., without printed title page ["**PARADISE LOST**. A Poem, In Twelve Books. The Author, John Milton. *London: Printed For John Sharpe, Piccadilly; By C. Whittingham, Chiswick. M DCCC XVII*"], only engraved title page, engraved frontispiece portrait plate "Engraved by Holl" ("Published by J. Mawman and the other Proprietors 1817"), possibly inserted from Mawman et al. edition (also listed here), engraved title page ("Paradise Lost A Poem The Author John Milton. London: Printed For John Sharpe, Piccadilly. 1816"), with vignette illustration of *Milton Composing Paradise Lost*, engraved by A. Raimbach after T. Stothard (labeled "Proofs" in lower right corner), dated 1816, vignette illustration by Westall for each book of *PL*, variously engraved, each plate dated "Aug. 24, 1816," engraved title with vignette illustration of *Milton's Reconciliation to His Wife*, engraved by E. Finden after R. Westall (dated 1816) bound near the end of Book X instead of at the beginning, half-title for each book, vignette illustration engraved by "Wm. Bromley" after E. F. Burney of the expulsion at the end of Book XII as endpiece, as in the 1817 Mawman et al. edition listed here, contemporary dark blue morocco (a bit rubbed at the joints and along extremities, plates foxed and some occasional light foxing throughout), richly gilt-decorated border trim with decorative corner pieces on covers, richly gilt-decorated spines with gilt lettering ("Poetical Works" "*PL* Vol. 1 / *PR* Vol. 2"), thick raised bands with decorative gilt trim, inner dentelles ruled in gilt, outer dentelles tooled in gilt at the corners, red endpapers, a.e.g., with the early armorial bookplate of "Samuel Parker, Esq." on front pastedown. A splendid copy of this beautifully printed edition of Milton's poems by Charles Whittingham at the Chiswick Press, handsomely bound in a lovely Romantic binding and nicely preserved through the years, with engraved plates dated 1816 (engraved title page labeled "Proofs"), the first appearance of these illustrations by Westall, and also a large paper copy of the illustrations. In this fine copy, the "Hull" engraved portrait of Milton from the Rivington, Mawman, et al. edition of the same time, 1817 (see copies of edition listed here), was used with a set of the newly engraved illustrations by Westall in 1816; the Bromley engraved vignette illustration of the expulsion after Burney from the same recently published edition of *PL* (see listed here) was also used as an endpiece for Book XII here (as there), providing an additional view of the expulsion to that of Westall's. Uniformly bound as a companion volume with *PR&c.*, *London: Printed For John Sharpe, Piccadilly, 1816*, listed here, together forming the *PW*. Scarce. Not in Kohler as such, but see Kohler 92 and 91.

849. PARADISE LOST. A Poem, In Twelve Books, By John Milton. A New Edition. *London: And Sold At Paris By Theophilus Barrois, Jun. Bookseller, No. 11. Quai Voltaire. 1816.* First edition thus? 12mo, 348pp., contemporary calf (worn along joints and extremities, some foxing), spine decorated with gilt rules and small gilt decorations, red leather label with gilt lettering and gilt rules, marbled endpapers. A nice copy of a scarce edition with near-contemporary owner's signature and date (1824) neatly written in ink at top of title page. See later Baudry editions: in 1833 (copy listed here) and in 1841 (copies of several different editions listed here). Scarce. Not in Kohler.

850. PARADISE LOST. A Poem. In Twelve Books. The Author, John Milton. *London: Printed For John Sharpe, Piccadilly, By C. Whittingham, Chiswick. M DCCC XVII. 2 volumes.* First edition thus. 12mo, 8pp. Life, *PL* unpaginated with line references only, Books I to VI, volume 1, Books VII to XII, volume 2, half-title each volume, engraved and printed title pages each volume, engraved title for volume 1: "**PARADISE LOST** A Poem The Author John Milton. *London: Printed For John Sharpe, Piccadilly. 1816,*" date in Arabic numerals, with engraved illustration of *Milton*

PL. London: John Sharpe, 1816. 2 volumes. With illustration plates by Westall & Stothard, contemporary dark blue morocco. Lovely Romantic binding, with first appearance of these plates. See #848.

Composing Paradise Lost, engraved by A Raimbach after T. Stothard, protective tissue guard, engraved title for volume 2: "**PARADISE LOST** . . . soon his heart relented / Towards her . . . Book X. L. 940. *London: Printed By John Sharpe, M D CCCXVI*," date in Roman numerals, with engraved illustration of *Milton's Reconciliation to His Wife*, engraved by E. Finden after R. Westall, protective tissue guard, life of Milton, volume 1, vignette illustration by Westall for each book of *PL*, variously engraved, each plate dated "Aug. 24, 1816," each with protective tissue guards, contemporary full straight-grained blue morocco (a bit rubbed at joints, plates slightly foxed), richly gilt-decorated border trim with decorative corner pieces on covers, gilt-decorated spines with gilt designs in the panels, raised bands with decorative gilt trim, inner and outer dentelles finely tooled in gilt. A pleasing set in a lovely Romantic binding with the first appearance of these vignette illustrations by Westall, and with binding instructions from the printer bound in at the end of volume 2: Dated "December 8, 1816. The Purchasers of this edition of *PL* are recommended to delay binding their copies a few months—the sheets having but just passed through the press, the type must necessarily for a short time be apt to set off; but if the books *must* be bound immediately, they are requested to give directions to the binder not to beat them:–careful pressing after folding, will, in addition to the hot-pressing they have previously had, answer every purpose." Further directions are given on where the plates are to be placed, with various sample title pages provided, including title pages for copies "sold without the Plates." Scarce. Kohler 92, reporting "Not in Cambridge University Library."

See 1821 Chiswick reissues listed here, one with 1816 plates and the other with plates dated 1822, and see 1825 Chiswick reissue listed here with plates dated 1822; and see 1825 Chiswick reissue with plates dated 1822; see also 1827 Chiswick reissue listed here, with the plates engraved by different engravers and dated 1827.

851. PARADISE LOST. By John Milton. To Which Are Prefixed, The Life Of The Author; And A Criticism On The Poem, By Samuel Johnson, LL.D. *London: Printed For F. C. And J. Rivington; J. Nichols And Son; G. Wilkie; J. Nunn; W. Clarke And Sons; Cadell And Davies; Carpenter And Son; Longman, Hurst, Rees, Orme, And Brown; Scatcherd And Letterman; Lackington And Co.; W. Lowndes; E. Jeffery; J. Otridge; R. Scholey; J. Mawman; John Richardson; Baldwin, Cradock, And Joy; Gale And Fenner; Walker And Edwards; G. Cowie And Co.; And R. Hunter. 1817.* 8vo, xlviii+384pp., engraved frontispiece portrait plate "Engraved by Holl" ("Published by J. Mawman and the other Proprietors 1817"), engraved and printed title pages, with vignette illustration "Engrav'd by Landseer & Neagle" after E. F. Burney of Adam and Eve after the fall (Book X, line 351: "Outstretch'd he lay . . . and oft curs'd his creation") on engraved title ("Published by J. Mawman and the other Proprietors 1817"), illustration plate of Adam and Eve "Engrav'd by Chas. Heath" after H. Corbould for Book IV, vignette illustration by E. F. Burney engraved by "Wm. Bromley" of the expulsion at end of Book XII as endpiece, half-title for each book, contemporary calf (rebacked with original spine laid down, corners repaired, new endpapers), covers with decorative border trim in blind within gilt rules, spine lettered in gilt with decorative gilt trim at top and bottom and variously throughout and with decorative pieces in blind within the panels, marbled endpapers. Uniformly bound as a companion volume with *PR&c.*, *London: Printed For F. C. And J. Rivington, J. Nichols And Son, et al., 1817* listed here, together forming the *PW*. Scarce. Kohler 91, making no reference to vignette illustration of the expulsion at the end of Book XII, and reporting "Not in Williamson."

852. Variant of Preceding. **PARADISE LOST** . . . *London: Printed For F. C. And J. Rivington; J. Nichols And Son; et al, 1817.* 8vo, xlviii+384pp., as preceding, with vignette illustration by E. F. Burney engraved by "Wm. Bromley" of the expulsion at end of Book XII as endpiece, half-title for each book, original boards, printed paper labels on spines, edges untrimmed. Large paper copy with early armorial bookplate of Robert Dalzell and the bookplate of Dudley Johnson. Uniformly bound with *PR*: Printed For F. C. And J. Rivington; J. Nichols And Son; et al., 1817, listed here, together forming the *PW*. Although the bindings are a bit worn and the plates foxed, this volume, and its companion volume, are nonetheless preserved in their original state, very large, in original boards, wholly uncut, and exceptionally fresh and clean within. Kohler 91, making no reference to vignette illustration of *The Expulsion* at end of Book XII.

853. PARADISE LOST: A Poem, In Twelve Books. The Author John Milton. With Notes, By Robert Hawker, D.D. Vicar Of Charles, Plymouth. *London: Printed by Paris & Myers, T, Took's Court, Chancery Lane; And Sold By Button & Son, Paternoster Row; Nisbet, Castle Street, Oxford Street; Williams & Co. Stationers' Court; Kent, 116, High Holborn; Ogle & Co. Holborn; Burton & Briggs, Leadenhall Street; and Cox, Borough:—Also by Ogle & Co. Edinburgh; M. Ogle, Glasgow; Nettleton & Son, Market Street—and Trego, Church Lane, Plymouth. 1817.* First edition thus. 8vo, l+[4]+414pp., half-title before the poem, notes at bottom of page, modern half dark brown leather, marbled paper over boards (some slight embrowning, including title page, occasional marks and foxing, new endpapers), red morocco label on spine with gilt lettering and gilt rules, raised bands within gilt rules, date in gilt at bottom of spine. Generally a very good copy. Scarce. Not in Kohler.

854. PARADISE LOST: A Poem, In Twelve Books. By John Milton. *Philadelphia: Published By Benjamin Warner, No. 147, Market Street. 1818. Griggs & Co. Printers.* 12mo, 356pp., frontispiece portrait by W. Haines, engraved and printed title pages with vignette illustration of *The Expulsion* by J. Yeager on engraved title ("Published by B. Warner Philad[elphi]a," undated), contemporary speckled calf (worn, front hinge barely holding, pp. 193–216 bound between pp. 240 and 241), decorative gilt border trim on covers, gilt-decorated spine with decorative gilt pieces in the panels, inner and outer dentelles tooled in gilt, marbled endpapers and edges. A good copy with contemporary bookplate on front pastedown. Gift from Mike Papantonio in 1975. Scarce. Not in Kohler.

855. PARADISE LOST: A Poem. In Twelve Books. By John Milton. With The Life Of The Author. *Baltimore: Published By Cushing And Jewett. J. D. Toy, Printer. 1818.* 12mo, 360pp., frontispiece illustration by J. Thurston for *PL*, Book VI, engraved by "P. Maverick sc. Newark," with lines illustrated quoted beneath ("Published by F. Lucas Jr. & I. Cushing"), with a clipped engraved portrait of Milton "Aged Forty-Two,—From The Original Drawing By Vertue" tipped in on verso, engraved and printed title pages, with vignette illustration (not for Milton) engraved by "P. Maverick sc. Newark," with lines quoted and reference given: "Vide Gray's Progress of Poetry," on engraved title ("Baltimore[:] Published By E. Lucas Jr. And I. Cushing, 1818"), life by Fenton, half-title for each book with argument on verso, rebound in brown cloth (pages a little age-browned, with frontispiece and title page slightly frayed along the edges), spine lettered in gilt, new endpapers. Generally a good copy with early Baltimore publisher's imprint. See 1813 edition of *PL* "Published by F. Lucas Jr. & L. Cushing" in Baltimore, with the same frontispiece illustration and the same engraved title page as here. See also 1813 edition of *PW* listed here "Published by Fielding Lucas, Jun. And Joseph Cushing. T. & G. Palmer, printers," with the same vignette illustration for Gray on engraved title pages as here; and see 1818 edition of *PW* listed here "Published By Cushing & Jewett. J. D. Toy, Printer" in Baltimore, with the same vignette illustration for Gray on engraved title pages as here, one engraved title dated 1813, the other 1818. Not in Kohler.

856. PARADISE LOST: A Poem, In Twelve Books. The Author John Milton. With Notes, By Robert Hawker, D.D. Vicar Of Charles, Plymouth. *London: Published By A. A. Paris, 53, Long Acre; Sold Also By Button & Son, Paternoster Row; Nisbet, Castle Street, Oxford Street; Williams & Co. Stationers' Court; Booth, Duke Street, Manchester Square; Ogle & Co. Holborn; Kent, 116, High Holborn; Burton & Briggs, Leadenhall Street; and Cox, Borough:—Also by Ogle & Co. Edinburgh; M. Ogle, Glasgow; Nettleton & Son, Market Street—and Trego, Church Lane, Plymouth. 1818.* First edition by Hawker. 8vo, l+[i]+414pp., half-title, preface dated 1817, life of Milton, postscript, preliminaries to the poem, half-title for each book, notes (some very extensive) at bottom of page, contemporary calf (rebacked preserving original spine and reinforced from the inside), gilt rules on covers, gilt-decorated spine with small gilt harp in each panel, black morocco labels lettered in gilt ("Hawker's Milton"), slightly raised bands, marbled endpapers and edges. A nice copy. The notes are judiciously chosen and noteworthy in content and commentary. See also 1820 edition listed here. Scarce. Not in Kohler.

857. PARADISE LOST: A Poem, In Twelve Books. The Author, John Milton. *Philadelphia: Published By Mitchell, Ames, And White. William Brown, Printer, Prune-street. 1818.* 12mo in 6s, vii+426pp., frontispiece portrait engraved by Westall after C. Tiebout, protective tissue guard, life of Milton, original calf (very worn, covers detached, spine missing), covers decorated with blind trim, lightly marbled edges. At the end, without mention on title page, is *SA* with half-title. Scarce. Not in Kohler.

858. PARADISE LOST, A Poem In Twelve Books; By J. Milton. With The Life Of The Author. *Lyons: Printed for W.[id]ow Buynand born Bruyset, no. 8, Plat-Street. 1818.* First edition thus. 12mo, 355pp., half-title, life of Milton by Fenton, original speckled French calf (a bit rubbed at joints and extremities), elaborately gilt-decorated spine, orange label with gilt lettering and decorative gilt trim, outer dentelles tooled in gilt. A very nice crisp copy in a fine contemporary French binding with contemporary signature on fly-leaf. The imprint is of particular interest, recording the book as published by the widow Buynand, born Bruyset. The Bruyset family was one of the leading bookselling families in Lyon; Jean-Marie Bruyset had died in 1817. Pickering & Chatto "suggest that the lady in question married one Jean François Anne Buynand des Echelles, a printer and writer, who had died in 1811, with his widow presumably continuing his publishing business" (Cat. 731, #173, 1995). A scarce Lyon printing of Milton's epic. Only one copy in NUC, Copy at Harvard; (I have seen one copy offered for sale since 1995); Kohler 93, reporting "Not in the British Library. Not in Cambridge University Library."

First Edition in Welsh

859. [PARADISE LOST] COLL GWYNFA, CYFIEI-THIAD GAN IDRISON. [Quotation from Cynddelw] *Llundain [London]: O Ail Argraffiad W. Marchant, et al, 1819*. First edition in Welsh. 8vo, xi+371pp., unsigned vignette illustration of *The Expulsion* on engraved title page, faintly hand-colored, dedication page, "Rhagfynegiad" with engraved vignette piece at end, labeled "Llundain, ar gyflawni triugain oed, sef Awst 7ed, 1819," Welsh glossary at end, original publisher's binding, quarter linen, boards (bit worn and soiled, title a bit embrowned), printed paper label (defective), edges untrimmed and partially unopened. The translator, William Owen Pughe, was a close friend of William Blake and one of the Twenty-four Elders appointed by Joanna Southcott, the religious fanatic. Robert Southey wrote of Pughe: "Poor Owen found everything he wished to find in the Bardic system, and there he found Blake's notions, and thus Blake and his wife were persuaded that his dreams were old patriarchal truths, long forgotten and now revealed." One may suppose that his translation of Milton into the Bardic tongue appealed to Blake. Uncommon. Kohler 93.

860. PARADISE LOST: A Poem, In Twelve Books. By John Milton. *Philadelphia: Published By Benjamin Warner, No. 171, Market Street. 1819. Griggs & Co. Printers*. 12mo, 356pp., engraved frontispiece portrait by W. Haines, engraved and printed title pages, with vignette illustration of the expulsion by J. Yeager on undated engraved title with the lines illustrated quoted beneath and with "Book XII" given after the lines along with "Published by B. Warner Philad[elphia]" printed at the bottom, half-title for each book, contemporary calf (a bit worn, front cover detached, back joint breaking, early name on title page), gilt-decorated spine (rubbed), black morocco label with gilt lettering and gilt rules. All in all, a decent copy of a scarce edition. Not in Kohler.

861. Variant of Preceding. This copy has the engraved frontispiece portrait by Haines, but unlike the preceding copy, it has a frontispiece illustration of Adam and Eve in hiding by Tiebout for Book X in place of an engraved title with vignette illustration of the expulsion by J. Yeager, with the lines illustrated quoted beneath and with "Paradise Lost. Book X." given after the lines, along with "Published by B. J. & R. Johnson 1804" printed at the bottom. Contemporary calf binding, albeit worn. Scarce. Not in Kohler.

862. PARADISE LOST [AND] SAMSON AGONISTES [In] THE WORKS OF THE BRITISH POETS. With Lives Of The Authors, By Ezekiel Sanford. Vol. VIII. Milton. *Philadelphia: Published By Mitchell, Ames, And White. William Brown, Printer. 1819*. Small 8vo, 426pp., frontispiece illustration of *Milton Composing Paradise Lost* by Westall, engraved by C. Tiebout, protective guard (foxed), half-title ("The Poetical Works Of John Milton, With A Life Of The Author, By Ezekiel Sanford"), contents, "Encomiums Upon Milton," half-title for each book of *PL* and for *SA*, contemporary calf (a little worn, some age-browning), spine lettered and decorated in gilt, corners of outer dentelles trimmed in gilt, marbled edges. Scarce copy of an early nineteenth-century American edition of Milton's poems that obviously ran to two volumes in the set, each volume complete unto itself, the other volume containing the life of Milton by Sanford and the remaining poetical works. Not in Kohler.

863. PARADISE LOST, A Poem. In Twelve Books. By John Milton. To which is prefixed, The Life Of The Author. *London. Printed For Thomas Tegg, No. 111, Cheapside. 1820*. 12mo, vii+[1]+304pp., frontispiece illustration by F. Bartolozzi of *Adam and Eve in the Bower of Bliss* "Engraved by S. Noble" ("London. Published by Thomas Tegg. No. 111. Cheapside. June.1.1817"), protective tissue

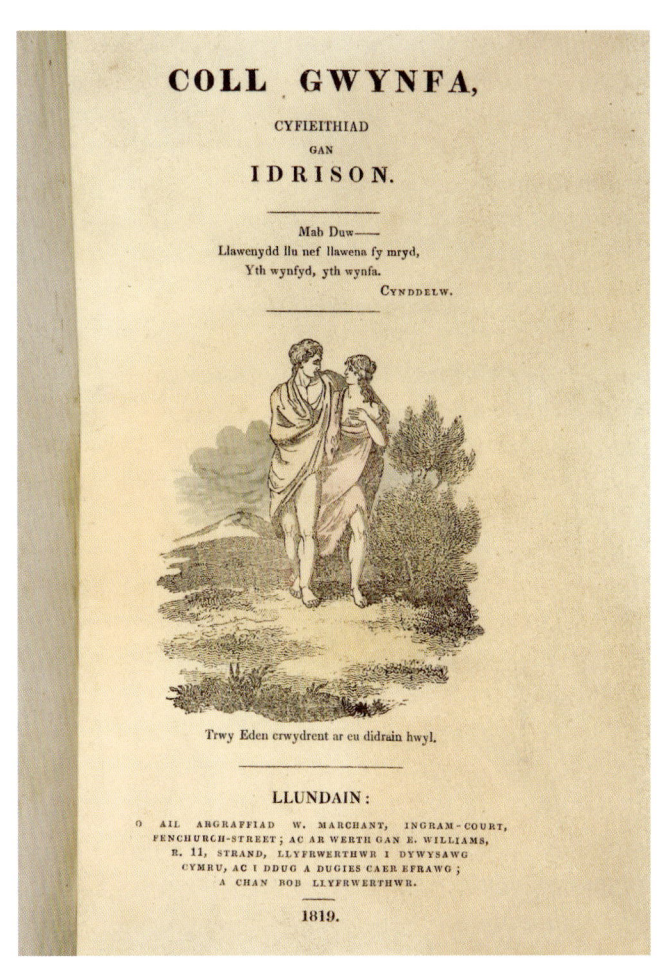

[Paradise Lost] Coll Gwynfa, Cyfieithiad Gan Idrison. London, 1819. First edition in Welsh. See #859.

guard, engraved and printed title pages, with vignette illustration by F. Bartolozzi of *Eve tempting Adam* "Engraved by S. Noble" on engraved title ("London. Printed for Thomas Tegg, 111. Cheapside. June 1st. 1817"), life by Fenton, original crushed calf over limp boards, gilt rules on covers, gilt lettering and gilt rules on spine, raised bands, a.e.g. Nice copy with elaborate armorial bookplate on front pastedown. Scarce. Not in Kohler.

864. PARADISE LOST, A Poem, In Twelve Books, By John Milton. *Boston: Published By Timothy Bedlington. 1820. Sylvester T. Goss, printer.* 12mo in 6s, viii+305pp.+[8-page unpaginated index], engraved and printed title pages, with vignette illustration by H. Hamilton of *The Judgment of Adam and Eve* "Engraved by D. Newcomb" on engraved title serving as frontispiece, life by Fenton, half-title for each book, index, contemporary full black morocco (slightly rubbed), decorative gilt border trim on covers, gilt-decorated spine, inner and outer dentelles finely tooled in gilt. A fine copy in an attractive contemporary American morocco binding. Not in Kohler.

865. Variant of Preceding, original half calf, marbled paper boards, gilt rules on spine with brown morocco label (chipped) with gilt lettering and gilt rules. A good copy, in original state, in a variant publisher's binding.

866. PARADISE LOST: A Poem, In Twelve Books. By John Milton. With Notes, Selected from the Writings of Addison, Warburton, Pearce, Newton, and various other Commentators. By Robert Hawker, D.D. *London: Printed by W. Myers, 21, Bedford Place, Commercial Road: And Sold By R. Baynes; Button & Son, Paternoster Row; et al, 1820.* 8vo, l+[iii]+414pp., half-title, 1817 preface reprinted, life of Milton, preliminaries to the poem, half-title for each book, notes at bottom of page (some extensive), contemporary diced calf (binding rubbed, spine a little faded), gilt rules on covers and spine, outer dentelles tooled in gilt, speckled edges. A good copy, complete with half-title, with early signature on title page. See 1818 edition here, fist edition by Hawker. Not in Kohler.

867. PARADISE LOST. A Poem, In Twelve Books. The Author, John Milton. *London: Printed For John Sharpe, Piccadilly; By C. Whittingham, Chiswick. M DCCC XXI.* 12mo, 8pp.+remainder unpaginated (lines given on each page in place of page number), engraved and printed title pages, first engraved title "**PARADISE LOST** A Poem The Author John Milton. *London: Printed For John Sharpe, Piccadilly. 1816*," date in Arabic numerals, with engraved illustration of *Milton Composing Paradise Lost*, engraved by A Raimbach after T. Stothard, protective tissue guard, the other engraved title "**PARADISE LOST** . . . soon his heart relented / Towards her . . . Book X. L. 940. *London: Printed By John Sharpe, M D CCCXVI,*" date in Roman numerals, with engraved illustration of *Milton's Reconciliation to His Wife* engraved by E. Finden after R. Westall at the outset of the life of Milton, vignette illustration by Westall for each book of *PL*, variously engraved, each plate dated "Aug. 24, 1816," contemporary full straight-grained red morocco, richly gilt-decorated border trim on covers with central gilt device, spines similarly richly gilt-decorated with gilt lettering, thick raised bands with decorative gilt trim, inner dentelles finely tooled in gilt, gray endpapers, a.e.g., early decorated bookplate on front pastedown. A very attractive copy, fresh and clean throughout, printed by the Chiswick press, bound in an elegant and well-preserved Romantic binding of the period. Uniformly bound as a companion volume with *PR & Poems, London: Printed For John Sharpe, M DCCC XIX*, listed here, together forming the *PW*. An 1821 reissue of the edition by Sharpe/Whittingham/Chiswick first published in 1817 (copy listed here), with a copy of the 1816 issue of the plates (first appearance). See also 1825 Chiswick reissue listed here, with plates dated 1822, and see 1827 Chiswick reissue listed here, with the plates engraved by different engravers and dated 1827. Kohler 97, reporting, "Not in Cambridge University Library."

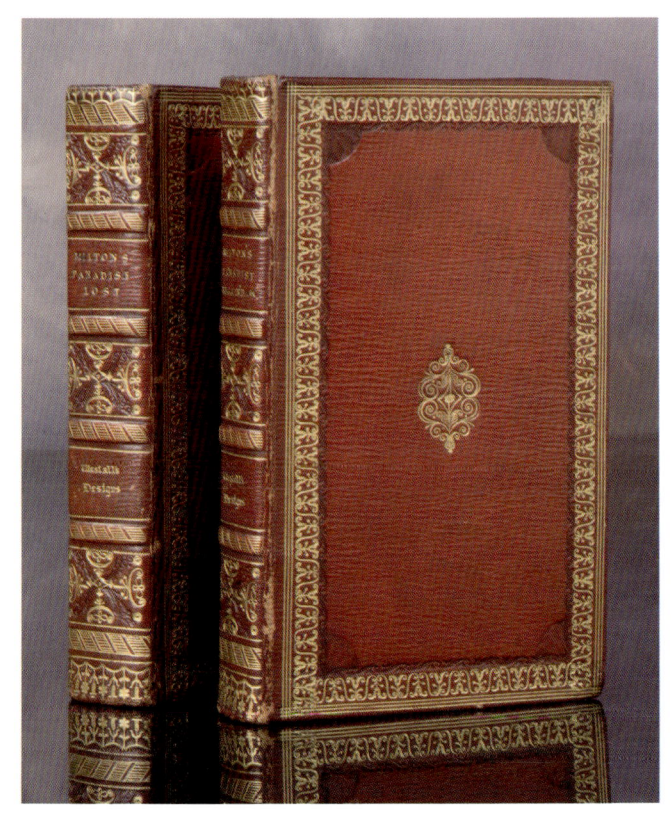

PL. London: Printed for John Sharpe by C. Whittingham, 1821. 12mo, with a copy of 1816 plates, contemporary full straight-grained red morocco. Uniformly bound as a companion volume with *PR & Poems*. See #867.

868. Variant of Preceding, the plates having been redone and dated "Jan. 1, 1822," and with a different engraver of the Stothard frontispiece: T. H. Robinson instead of Raimbach, contemporary calf (mild rubbing to the spine, the Finden engraving after Westall here bound in Book X), delicately gilt-tooled covers with complimentary delicate blind tooling surrounded by gilt rules, richly gilt-decorated spine, black morocco label with gilt lettering and gilt rules, thick raised bands with decorative gilt trim, inner and outer dentelles finely tooled in gilt, lightly marbled edges. An attractive copy, printed by the Chiswick press, in an attractive binding of the period. An 1821 reissue of the edition by Sharpe/Whittingham/Chiswick first published in 1817 (listed here) with the first appearance of 1816 Westall plates, those plates having been redone and dated "Jan. 1, 1822," here, and with a different engraver of the Stothard frontispiece. See also 1825 Chiswick reissue listed here, with a copy of the plates here dated 1822, and see 1827 Chiswick reissue listed here with the plates engraved by different engravers and dated 1827. Not in Kohler.

869. Variant of Preceding, contemporary maroon morocco (rubbed along joints and spine, engraved plates a little foxed, the Finden engraving after Westall here bound within life), covers decorated in embossed blind trim, spine decorated with embossed flowers within the panels, gilt lettering, wide embossed raised bands, inner and outer dentelles finely tooled in gilt, dark green endpapers, a.e.g. A nice copy, printed by the Chiswick press, in an attractive variant contemporary morocco binding, with the Stothard frontispiece engraved by Robinson instead of Raimbach, and with the plates redone and dated "Jan. 1, 1822." Not in Kohler.

870. PARADISE LOST, A Poem. In Twelve Books. By John Milton. To which is prefixed, The Life Of The Author. *London. Printed For Thomas Tegg, No. 111, Cheapside. 1821.* 12mo, vii+[i]+304pp., engraved title page with vignette illustration of Eve tempting Adam engraved by S. Noble after F. Bartolozzi, dated "London. Printed For Thomas Tegg, 111, Cheapside[,] June 1st, 1817," life by Fenton, contemporary full straight-grained deep green morocco (a bit rubbed along joints and extremities), rich decorative gilt border trim and slight gilt rules on covers, gilt-decorated spine with gilt lettering, thick raised bands with decorative gilt trim, inner and outer dentelles finely tooled in gilt, marbled endpapers, a.e.g. A lovely copy in a beautiful contemporary morocco binding with contemporary printed presentation label on front pastedown. See 1823 edition by Thomas Tegg listed here. Not in Kohler.

871. PARADISE LOST, By John Milton. To which are prefixed, The Life Of The Author, By Elijah Fenton; And A Criticism On The Poem, By Dr. Johnson. *London: Printed For John Bumpus, Holborn-Bars. 1821.* 8vo, xlviii+384pp., engraved frontispiece portrait "Engraved by Freeman from a Portrait in the Collection of the late C. Lamb" ("London, Published By John Bumpus, Holborn. 1822"), life by Fenton, "Criticism On Paradise Lost By Dr. Johnson," "Milton's Moral Character No Less Sublime Than His Poetical (From Mr. Hayley's Life Of Milton)," half-title for each book, contemporary three-quarter dark maroon calf (slightly rubbed at joints and corners), marbled paper over boards, gilt rules on spine, decorated in blind within the panels, raised bands with decorative gilt trim, marbled edges. A very nice copy. Kohler 95, reporting "Not in Williamson."

872. PARADISE LOST. In Twelve Books. With Other Poems. By John Milton. From The Text Of Thomas Newton, D.D.S.C. With The Life Of The Author. *London: Printed For John Bumpus, Holborn Bars[.] Sharpe, King Street; Samms, Pall Mall; et al, 1821.* 12mo in 6s, xxiii+300pp., frontispiece portrait "Engraved by Freeman" ("London. Published by John Bumpus. 1821"), life of Milton, with three poems from "Poems Upon Several Occasions" added at the end ("On The Death Of A Fair Infant Dying Of A Cough," "On Shakespeare, 1630," and "On Time"), contemporary full straight-grained purple morocco (a bit rubbed, top right corner torn from title page without affecting any text), finely tooled gilt borders on covers, richly gilt-decorated spine, raised bands with decorative gilt trim, inner and outer dentelles tooled in gilt, red endpapers, a.e.g., early bookplates, early signature on title page. A fine copy, beautifully bound in a lovely Romantic binding. Scarce. Kohler 96, but describing its copy with "Frontispiece engraved by Garner," and reporting "Not in the Bodleian Library. Not in Cambridge University Library."

873. [PARADISE LOST] JOHANN MILTON'S VERLORNES PARADIES. Neu übersetzt von Samuel Gottlieb Bürde. Esrter / Zwenter Theil. *Breslau, bei Johann Friedrich Korn, dem ditern. 1822. 2 volumes.* Small 8vo, xi+259pp.,+244pp., original marbled paper over boards in imitation of period calf (a bit rubbed along extremities), spines richly decorated with gilt trim, each with a light green label with gilt lettering, gilt number, and decorative gilt trim, brown silk ribbon marker each volume. A lovely set. "First published in Berlin, 1792; reprinted in 1826 [see copy listed here]" Stevens 1495; Not in Kohler.

874. [PARADISE LOST] Siddons, Sarah Kemble. **AN ABRIDGEMENT OF PARADISE LOST.** By Mrs.

[Sarah Kemble] Siddons. *London: John Murray, Albemarle-Street. 1822.* First edition, first issue of Mrs. Siddons's only book. 8vo, iv+190pp., prefatory remarks, contemporary three-quarter calf, marbled paper over boards, gilt rules on covers, gilt-decorated spine, black morocco label with gilt lettering and gilt rules, raised bands with decorative gilt trim. A fine copy. A second issue also appeared in 1822 with a changed title (see copy following). Scarce. Not in Kohler.

875. [PARADISE LOST] Siddons, Sarah Kemble. **THE STORY OF OUR FIRST PARENTS, SELECTED FROM MILTON'S PARADISE LOST: FOR THE USE OF YOUNG PERSONS**. By Mrs. [Sarah Kemble] Siddons. *London: John Murray, Albemarle-Street. 1822.* First edition, second issue of Mrs. Siddons's only book. 8vo, iv+190pp., prefatory remarks, contemporary diced maroon calf (rubbed along extremities, joints cracking, small inner portion at top of title page torn away without affecting any text, bookplate removed from front pastedown), rich decorative gilt border trim on covers, gilt-decorated spine, thick raised bands with decorative gilt trim, inner and outer dentelles finely tooled in gilt, marbled endpapers and edges. A very nice copy with contemporary signature (dated 1823) on title page. At some point during the publication of this work, the title was altered from that of the preceding issue to the present title, with the new title being pasted to the stub of the canceled title. The present title is also the basis for a pirated edition by Eliza Weaver Bradburn, published in New York in 1831, without a hint of Mrs. Siddons's authorship (copy listed here). Both issues are of about equal scarcity. Not in Kohler.

876. **PARADISE LOST**. A Poem In Twelve Books. By John Milton. *London: Published By Jones And Company, No. 3, Warwick Square. 1823.* First edition thus. Miniature (32 mo in 8s, measuring 3 ⅝" × 2 ¼"), xii+268pp., unsigned engraved frontispiece portrait within elaborate decorative frame, engraved and printed title pages (each dated 1823), with unsigned vignette illustration of *Satan Flying Toward Earth* on engraved title ("London, Published by Jones & Co. 3, Warwick Square. 1823"), "Glasgow: Andrew & John M. Duncan, Printers to the University" on verso of printed title page, life of Milton by Fenton, index, contemporary full straight-grained red morocco (engraved frontispiece and engraved title page somewhat foxed), covers framed with elaborate gilt and blind borders, gilt-decorated spine with large floral ornament in gilt within each gilt-ruled compartment, thick raised bands with decorative gilt trim, broad inner dentelles finely tooled in gilt, outer dentelles trimmed in gilt, marbled endpapers, a.e.g. A delightful miniature, in a charming contemporary morocco binding, in very fine, bright condition, with a possibly contemporary signature on front blank and later presentation inscription (dated 1873) with same family name on verso. Uniformly bound as a companion volume with *PR&c.*, *London: Published By Jones And Company, 1823*, copy listed here, together forming the *PW*. Scarce. Kohler 100, reporting "Not in Williamson. Not in the British Library. Not in the Bodleian Library. Not in Cambridge University Library"; Not in NSTC.

See following copy with rare half-title for "Works" and rare general title page for *PW*, dated 1823; see second edition thus listed here published in 1825, in a slightly taller copy with printed title page dated 1825 and engraved title dated 1824; see also 1832 edition listed here published by Jones & Company with engraved and printed title pages, engraved title dated 1824, printed title dated 1832.

877. Variant of Preceding. **PARADISE LOST**. A Poem In Twelve Books. By John Milton. London: Published By Jones And Company, No. 3, Warwick Square. 1823. First edition thus. Miniature (32 mo in 8s), xii+268pp., unsigned engraved frontispiece portrait within elaborate decorative frame (small portion of lower corner front edge torn away without affecting anything), engraved and printed title pages, engraved title dated 1824, printed title dated 1823 with unsigned vignette illustration of *Satan Flying Toward Earth* on engraved title ("*London, Published By Jones & Co. 3, Acton Place[,] Kingsland Road[,] 1824. University Edition*"), half-title for "Milton's Works," general title page for "**MILTON'S POETICAL WORKS**. In Two Volumes. Vol. 1. *London: Published By Jones And Company, No. 3, Warwick Square. 1823,*" with "*Glasgow: Andrew & John M. Duncan, Printers to the University*" on verso, title page for *PL*, with "*Glasgow: Andrew & John M. Duncan, Printers to the University*" on verso, life of Milton by Fenton, index, contemporary full red morocco (a little rubbed, engraved frontispiece and engraved title slightly worn and foxed, lacking final blank, slight foxing throughout, especially preliminaries, some underlining in a neat hand), decorative gilt border trim within gilt rules on covers, spine elaborately decorated and lettered in gilt, outer dentelles trimmed in gilt, marbled endpapers and edges, with "Clarissa T. Sill" lettered in gilt at center of front cover. A good copy of this miniature edition (3 ⅝" × 2 ¼") with rare half-title for "Works" and rare general title page for *PW*. Uniformly bound as a companion volume with *PR&c.*, *London: Published By Jones And Company, 1823*, copy listed here, together forming the *PW* in a presentation morocco binding. Scarce, especially with rare half-title for "Works" and rare general title page for *PW* (dated 1823), same as printed title page of *PL*. Not in Kohler (Kohler 100 making no reference to a half-title or general title page).

878. PARADISE LOST; A Poem, In Twelve Books. And Paradise Regain'd, In Four Books. Also Samson Agonistes, And Other Poems. By John Milton. A New Edition, Carefully Collated With The Best Authorities. To Which Is Prefixed, A Life Of The Author, By The Rev. David M'Nicoll. *London. Printed At The Caxton Press, By Henry Fisher, (Printer in Ordinary to His Majesty.) Published at 38, Newgate Street; and Sold by all Booksellers. n.d. [ca. 1823].* 8vo, pagination continuing to p. xxiv, then with a jump in pagination, 33–424pp., engraved frontispiece portrait of Milton in a circular form with a crown of thorns amidst rays of sunlight overhead and foliage along both sides and bottom with snake and apple beneath the portrait, signed "R. Hicks," "Drawn by W. M. Craig Esqr. from a miniature by Cooper," "Publish'd by Nuttall, Fisher & Dixon, Liverpool. Mar. 30, 1812" at the bottom, engraved and printed title pages, engraved full-page illustration of the expulsion (Eve holding onto Adam's arm with Archangel and burning sword behind them) and the crucifixion scene high on a mountain above by W. M Craig, engraved by E. Goodall on the engraved title page, with the title "Paradise Lost, And Regained, by John Milton" and "Published by Nuttall, Fisher & Co. Liverpool. Sept. 1815" at the bottom, emblem of the press at center of title page, "A Glossary Explaining the Antiquated and ifficult [sic] Words in Milton's poetical [sic] Works," at the end, seven engraved illustration plates after W. M. Craig, variously engraved by A. Warren, A. Smith, I. Romney, James, Bragg, and Pye, with the line illustrated quoted beneath each illustration along with "Published by Henry Fisher, Caxton, London, 1823," contemporary calf (a bit worn, front cover detached, spine chipped at top and bottom and missing a small piece near top front joint), red morocco label with gilt lettering and gilt trim within double gilt rules on spine. All in all, a decent copy of an uncommon edition with fine plates and with a near-contemporary signature on fly-leaf and a later signature on front pastedown. The "Other Poems" indicated on the title page include: *L'A, IlP* and *On The Death of a Fair Infant*. Williamson 225; Kohler 111, describing its copy: "Engraved title-page" dated 1825: "Frontispiece portrait engraved by Hicks 'drawn by W.M. Craig,'" dated 1823. Seven plates after Craig . . . dated 1823 and 1830," and reporting "Williamson 226. Not in the British Library. Not in the Bodleian Library. Not in Cambridge University Library."

In addition to the engraved title page illustration, the other illustrations by W. M. Craig include six illustrations for *PL*: Book I (*Satan Rallying His Troops*, line 315); Book III (*The Transformation of Satan before Meeting Uriel*, line 645); Book V (*Raphael Counseling Adam and Eve*, line 391); Book VII (*Adam Beholds Eve*, line 481); Book IX

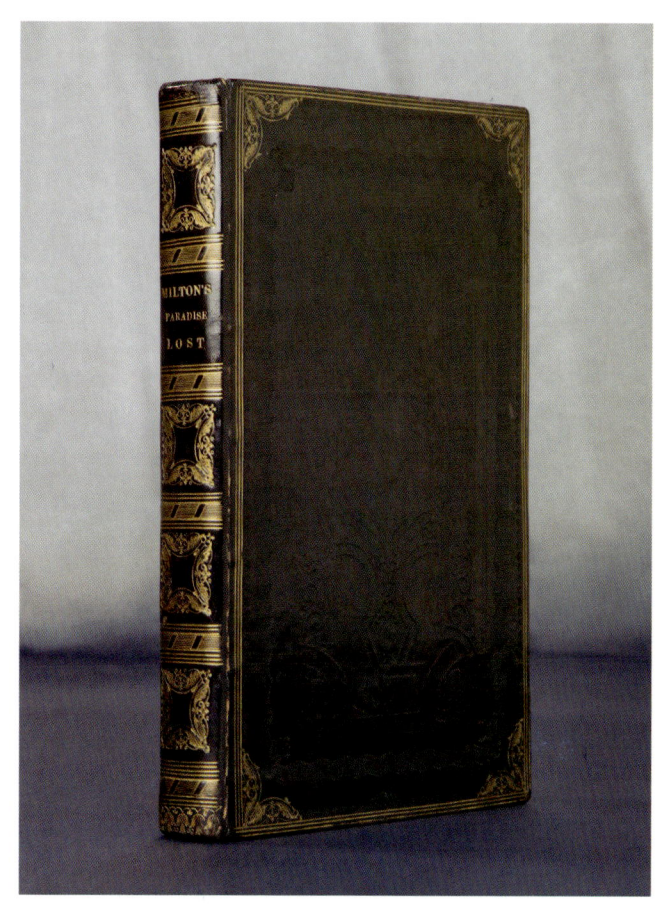

PL & PR & SA. Life Of The Author, By The Rev. David M'Nicoll. London. Printed At The Caxton Press, By Henry Fisher, n.d. [ca. 1823]. Contemporary highly polished black morocco, with seven octavo illustration plates after Craig. See #878.

(*The Temptation of Eve*, line 494); and Book XII (*The Expulsion*, line 637); and one illustration for *PR*: Book II (*The Temptation to "A Table Richly Spread,"* line 338). The first edition thus was published in Liverpool in 1812 by "Nuttall, Fisher, And Dixon," with life by David M'Nicoll and with seven of Craig's illustrations printed in an octavo format, variously engraved, and dated 1812 for the edition (see copy listed here and explanation regarding jump in pagination as a result of issuing by subscription); this repeats that edition and its particulars, with the addition of an engraved title page; possibly first London edition printed at the Caxton Press; see also *PW* listed ca. 1843, as here, with same engraved frontispiece portrait (there dated 1843), same engraved title page with same illustration (dated 1835), same life by M'Nicoll, and same engraved illustration plates after Craig (variously dated post 1835), but with the printed title page: "The Poetical Works . . . Fisher, Son, & Co. London Paris, And New York," undated. The present edition and the following are identical, with the exception of "Published by Henry Fisher, Caxton, London, 1823" appearing at the bottom of the frontispiece instead of "Publish'd by Nuttall, Fisher & Dixon, Liverpool. Mar. 30, 1812," as here.

Since each of the engraved plates in both copies here (this and the one following) is dated 1823 and contains the same publishing information, the publication date of this edition can safely be assumed to be ca. 1823 (not ca. 1830, as Kohler 111 dates its copy), with the engraved frontispiece portrait and the engraved title page selected from earlier printings and inserted before the undated printed title page. Kohler 111 is dated ca. 1830 apparently because of an illustration plate in it dated 1830; otherwise it is identical to the two copies here in content except for (1) the date of the engraved portrait (1825 compared to 1812 and 1823 in two copies here); (2) the date of the engraved title page (1825 compared to 1815 in both copies here); and (3) the dates of the seven engraved illustration plates (1823 and 1830 compared to 1823 consistently in both copies here).

879. Variant of Preceding. **PARADISE LOST** . . . *London. Printed At The Caxton Press, By Henry Fisher . . . n.d. [1823].* 8vo in 4s, as preceding copy—with differences noted below, engraved frontispiece portrait of Milton as preceding "Drawn by W. M. Craig Esqr. from a miniature by Cooper," "Published by Henry Fisher, Caxton, London, 1823" at the bottom, engraved and printed title pages, engraved full-page illustration on engraved title page, as preceding, "Published by Nuttall, Fisher & Co. Liverpool. Sept. 1815" at the bottom, emblem of the press at center of title page, seven engraved illustration plates after W. M. Craig, six for *PL* and one for *PR*, variously engraved, with the line illustrated quoted beneath each illustration along with "Published by Henry Fisher, Caxton, London, 1823," contemporary highly polished black morocco (a bit rubbed, plates foxed, some slight embrowning throughout), covers elaborately decorated in embossed blind tooling with gilt rules and decorative gilt corners, spine richly decorated in gilt within the compartments with gilt lettering, outer dentelles finely tooled in gilt, marbled endpapers and edges. A handsome copy of an uncommon edition, in a lovely Romantic binding. The first edition thus was published in Liverpool in 1812 by "Nuttall, Fisher, And Dixon," with life by David M'Nicoll (also listed here); this repeats that edition and its particulars, with the addition of an engraved title page; possibly first London edition printed at the Caxton Press. This copy and the preceding are identical, with the important exceptions of "Published by Henry Fisher, Caxton, London, 1823," appearing at the bottom of the frontispiece in place of "Publish'd by Nuttall, Fisher & Dixon, Liverpool. Mar. 30, 1812," and being in a handsome variant black morocco binding. Since each of the engraved plates in both copies here is dated 1823 with the same publishing information ("Published by Henry Fisher, Caxton, London, 1823,"), the date of this edition can safely be assumed to be ca. 1823 (not ca. 1830, as Kohler 111 dates its copy), with the engraved frontispiece portrait and the engraved title page selected from earlier printings and inserted before the undated printed title page. Williamson 226. Kohler 111 is dated ca. 1830 apparently because of an illustration plate in it dated 1830; otherwise it is identical to the two copies here in content except as noted above.

880. **O PARAISO PERDIDO**. Poema Epico, De Joao Milton, Traduzido Em Verso Portuguez Por Francisco Bento Maria Targini, Visconde De Sao Lourenco, Do Concelho De Sua Magestade Fide-lissima, E Do Da Sua Real Fazenda, Commendador Das Ordens Militares De Christo, E Da E Conceicao, Etc. Com As Reflexoens, E Notas Do Traductor. Cedite Romani Scriptores, Cedite Graii. Propert. *Pariz, Na Typographia De Firmino Didot, Impressor Do Rei, Rua Jacob, No 24. 1823. 2 volumes.* First edition thus. 8vo, xlii+[1]+402+[1]pp.,+427+[1]pp., half-title each volume, frontispiece illustration plate engraved by A. Massard after V. Adam (Adam and Eve being judged by God, without identification, fine impression of the plate), volume 1, with protective tissue guard, frontispiece illustration plate engraved by A. Massard after V. Adam (the expulsion, without identification, fine impression of the plate), volume 2, title page each volume, half-title for each book, small decorative piece at the end of each book, "Ode" printed in script type" and "Prologo Do Traductor" before Book I, volume 1, Dryden's epigram ("Three poets, in three distant ages born"—in both English and Portuguese) before Book VII at the beginning of volume 2, "Erratas" leaf at the end of each volume preceded by "Notas, E Reflexoens Do Traductor" and an "Index Dos Nomes Prorios" at the end of volume 2, contemporary tree calf (slight inoffensive waterstaining in lower margins of a few pages in volume 1), decorative border trim on each cover, gilt-decorated spines, black morocco labels with gilt lettering and decorative gilt trim, marbled endpapers (with the the initials "PB" wood-burnt on front pastedown, volume 1, and partially repeated on front pastedown, volume 2). A fine set. The first edition of this translation and the first publication of only the second Portuguese translation. Dedicated to the Marquez de Marialva with a dedicatory ode, presumably by Targini, who also includes a lengthy preface to his translation. A scarce Portuguese verse translation of *PL*, somewhat bizarrely published in Paris by Didot. Kohler 101, reporting "Not in the Bodleian Library."

881. PARADISE LOST, A Poem. In Twelve Books. By John Milton. To which is prefixed, The Life Of The Author. *London. Printed For Thomas Tegg, No. 11, Cheapside. 1823.* 12mo, vii+[i]+304pp., life by Fenton, early full red morocco (bit faded, trifle rubbed), rich decorative gilt border trim and gilt rules on covers, gilt-decorated spine, inner and outer dentelles tooled in gilt, marbled edges. A very nice copy with several leaves of MS in an early hand noting choice passages bound in at front. See 1821 edition by Thomas Tegg (copy listed here). Not in Kohler.

882. LE PARADIS PERDU De Milton, Avec des Notes, et les Remarques de M. Addisson [sic]; Traduit De L'Anglois, Par M. Dupré De Saint-Maur. Nouvelle Edition. *Avignon, Jean-Albert Fischer, Imprim.-Libraire. 1823.* 12mo, 357pp., half-title, slight decorative trim on title page, "Vie De Milton" before the poem, "Remarques De M. Addisson Sur Milton" bound in at end, slight decorative headpiece trim variously throughout, contemporary tree calf (a bit rubbed), spine decorated with gilt trim and decorative gilt pieces with red morocco label with gilt lettering within gilt rules, marbled edges. A very nice copy with a final leaf of labels for this and four other French works. Uncommon. Not in Kohler.

First Edition in Armenian

883. PARADISE LOST; A Poem In Twelve Books. By John Milton. [Title in Armenian]. [Translated into Armenian by Paschal Aucher.] *[Venice: Monaci Armeni di S. Lazzaro], 1824.* First edition in Armenian. 8vo, [2]+503pp., half-title, very small unsigned engraved illustration of Raphael counseling Adam and Eve (a fine engraving) at the center of title page, unsigned full-page engraved illustration of the bad angels being cast out of heaven (a fine engraving), at the beginning of the poem, very small unsigned engraved illustration of the expulsion (a fine engraving) at the end of Book XII as an endpiece, half-title before each book, notes at the end, contemporary full red morocco (a little worn and rubbed), decorative gilt border trim on covers, spine decorated in gilt with gilt lettering (rubbed), a.e.g. A good, sound copy with bookplate on front pastedown. Printed entirely in Armenian. See 1861 edition of *PL* printed, as here, entirely in Armenian. Rare. Not in Kohler.

❧

884. PARADISE LOST; A Poem In Twelve Books. By John Milton. A New Edition, With Notes, Critical And Explanatory, By John Williams, Esq. *London: Printed For G. And W. B. Whittaker, Ave-Maria Lane. 1824.* First edition

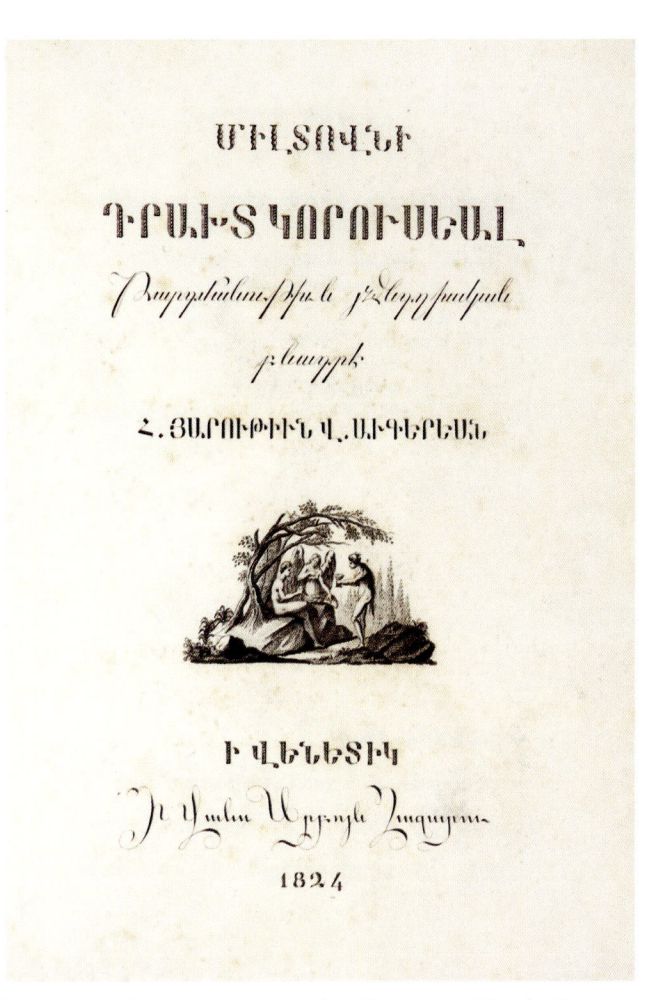

Title page for Armenian translation of *PL*. Venice, 1824. Translated into Armenian by Paschal Aucher. Very small engraved illustration of Raphael counseling Adam and Eve at the center of title page. See #883.

thus. 12mo, cxxxiii+[i]+437pp., advertisement, life of Milton, "Mr. Addison's Critique On *PL*," "Dr. Blair's Critique On *PL*," half-title for each book, contemporary full polished blue-green morocco (a bit rubbed at joints), gilt rules on covers and spines, red morocco labels with gilt lettering and gilt rules, thick raised bands with decorative gilt trim, inner and outer dentelles finely tooled in gilt, marbled endpapers and edges. A very nice copy with contemporary signature (dated 1835) on each title page. Uniformly bound with *PR, SA, P* (London: Printed For G. And W. B. Whittaker, 1824), copy listed here. Scarce. Not in Kohler.

885. PARADISE LOST. A Poem In Twelve Books. By John Milton. *London: Published By Jones And Company, No. 3, Warwick Square. 1825.* Second edition thus. 32mo in 8s (miniature), xii+268pp., unsigned engraved frontispiece portrait within elaborate decorative frame, engraved and printed title pages, engraved title dated 1824, printed title dated 1825, with unsigned vignette illustration of *Satan Flying Toward Earth* on engraved title ("London,

Published by Jones & Co. 3, Acton Place, Kingsland Road 1824. University Edition"), "Glasgow: Andrew & John M. Duncan, Printers to the University" on verso of printed title page, life of Milton by Fenton, index, contemporary full red morocco (some slight scuffing, joints a little rubbed), covers blind-tooled with gilt rules, gilt-decorated spine, black morocco label with gilt lettering ("Poems"), gilt Roman numeral (I), and gilt trim, marbled endpapers and edges. A fine miniature (3 ⅝" × 2 ¼"), in an attractive contemporary morocco binding. Uniformly bound as a companion volume with *PR&c.*, London: Published By Jones And Company, 1825, listed here, together forming the *PW*. The first edition thus was published in miniature edition in 1823 with engraved title page dated 1823 (see copies here, one with rare half-title for "Works" and also rare general title page for *PW*, dated 1823); see also 1832 edition listed here published by Jones & Company, with engraved and printed title pages, engraved title dated 1824, as here, printed title dated 1832. Scarce. Not in Kohler.

886. **PARADISE LOST**. A Poem, In Twelve Books. The Author, John Milton. *London: Printed For John Sharpe, Duke Street, Piccadilly; By C. And C. Whittingham, Chiswick. M DCCC XXV. [Printed title page in volume 2 has an abbreviated imprint: "London: Printed In The Year M DCCC XXV."] 2 volumes.* Slim 12mo, 8pp.+remainder unpaginated (lines given on each page at the top in place of page number), engraved and printed title pages each volume, engraved title for volume 1: "**PARADISE LOST** A Poem The Author John Milton. London: Printed For John Sharpe, Piccadilly. 1822," date in Arabic numerals, with engraved illustration of *Milton Composing Paradise Lost*, engraved by J. H. Robinson after T. Stothard, protective tissue guard, engraved title for volume 2: "**PARADISE LOST** . . . soon his heart relented / Towards her . . . Book X. L. 940. London: Printed By John Sharpe, M D CCCXXII," date in Roman numerals, with engraved illustration of *Milton's Reconciliation to His Wife*, engraved by E. Finden after R. Westall, protective tissue guard, life of Milton, volume 1, engraved vignette illustration after Richard Westall for each book of *PL*, variously engraved, each plate dated "Jan. 1. 1822," each with protective tissue guard, contemporary full blue morocco, delicately gilt-decorated covers and spines, thick raised bands with decorative gilt trim, spines lettered in gilt ("Milton's Poetical Works • *PL* • volume 1/2"), inner and outer dentelles finely tooled in gilt, marbled endpapers and edges. A fine set in a very lovely Romantic morocco binding. An 1825 reissue of the edition by Sharpe/Whittingham/Chiswick first published in 1817 (copy listed here) with the 1816 first appearance of the Westall plates, the plates here dated 1822—redone and dated 1822 with the 1821 reissue of the Chiswick edition (copy also listed here). See also 1827 Chiswick reissue with the plates engraved by different engravers and dated 1827. Uniformly bound as companion volumes with *PR* (copy listed here), and *Poems* (copy listed here), each: London: Published By John Sharpe, M DCCC XXIII, together forming a charming four-volume set of the *PW*. Kohler 103, reporting "Not in the Bodleian Library. Not in Cambridge University Library."

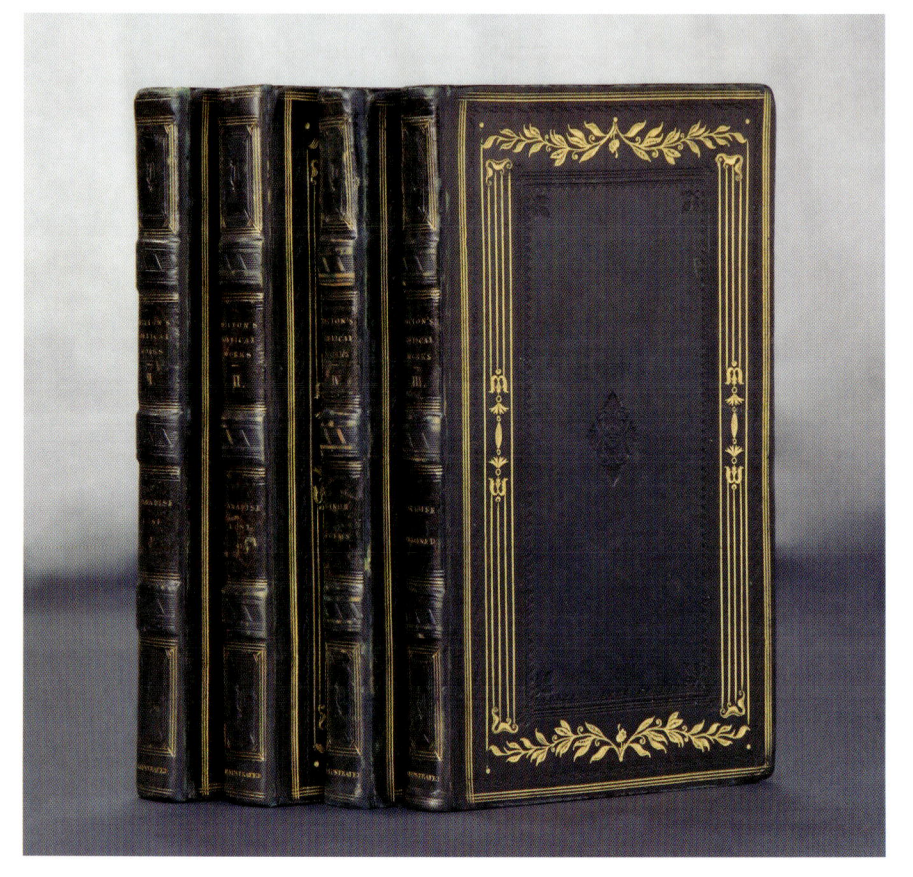

PL. London: Printed For John Sharpe, Piccadilly; By C. & C. Whittingham, Chiswick, 1825. 2 volumes. 12mo, with plates dated 1822, contemporary full blue morocco. Uniformly bound as a companion volume with *PR & Poems*, each with plates dated 1816 and each: London: Published By John Sharpe, 1823, each also shown here, together forming the *PW*, 4 volumes. See #886.

887. Variant of Preceding, contemporary calf Prize Binding (front cover volume 1 rehinged from inside), richly gilt-decorated covers and spines, red morocco labels lettered and decorated in gilt on spine, inner and outer dentelles finely tooled in gilt, marbled endpapers and edges, contemporary prize presentation inscription (dated 1832) on fly-leaf of each volume, with gilt initials "RNC" on all covers. A nice, tall set in a contemporary Prize Binding with prize inscription on fly-leaf. Kohler 103.

888. Variant of Preceding, contemporary full blue morocco (slightly rubbed, especially along extremities, some plates foxed), elaborately gilt-decorated borders on covers, similarly elaborately gilt-decorated spines, slightly thick raised bands with decorative gilt trim, inner and outer dentelles finely tooled in gilt, marbled endpapers and edges, bookseller's ticket each volume. A very nice tall set in a fine variant Romantic morocco binding with early armorial bookplate on front pastedown of each volume and contemporary family presentation inscription to John Mytton (dated 1828) on preliminary blank of each volume. Kohler 103.

John Martin—Twelve Original Parts, 1825–27

889. THE PARADISE LOST Of Milton With Illustrations, Designed And Engraved By John Martin. *London. Septimus Prowett, 1825-1827.* Twelve original parts. Imperial quarto, 218+[1 blank]+[5]pp., with the first appearance and first issue of twenty-four large mezzotint plates by John Martin, each engraving measuring 7 ¾" × 11 ⅛", each with "Designed & Engraved by J. Martin, Esq." half-title for each book, printer's emblem with "Thomas White, Johnson's Court, Fleet Street" at bottom of last page of Part XII, original printed blue paper wrappers, as issued (some parts a bit worn, as to be expected, some foxing, again as to be expected, minor restorations made to several issues), preliminaries for the published edition (see copies following) bound in at end of Part XII, including half-titles ("Milton's *PL.* volume I" and "Milton's *PL.* volume II"), title pages for volumes I and II ("**THE PARADISE LOST** Of Milton With Illustrations, Designed And Engraved By John Martin. *London. Septimus Prowett. M.DCCCC.XXVII*"), and dedication page. The first six parts appeared in 1825; five further parts appeared in 1826; the twelfth and last appeared in 1827; all in a very limited edition. A complete set in good condition (see #898). Very Rare. Balston, *Illustrator*, p. 389; Not in Kohler.

"The commission to illustrate *PL* must be among the most remarkable ever given by a publisher" (Balston, *Life*, p. 95). Martin was commissioned by the American publisher, Septimus Prowett, to produce twenty-four mezzotint illustrations of Milton's epic poem for £2,000, and "long before even the first part of the work had been published, a further commission of £1,500 for a smaller set of similar plates" was made (Balston, *Life*, p. 96). See commentary on the complicated publishing with folio and quarto editions listed here.

At the time of this commission, Martin was enormously popular in England. Part romantic, part neo-classic, part visionary, that popularity was founded largely on his prints. A skilled etcher, Martin experimented with mezzotint in the early 1820s—a printing process in which gray-scale images are screened through a patterned mesh. *PL* was his first ever undertaking in the medium ("one of the most sumptuous and complicated schemes ever undertaken by a publisher"—Balston, *Life*, p. 96). Through the mezzotint, Martin brought all of his creative genius to bear in illustrating *PL*, masterfully uniting brilliant highlights and starkly contrasting dark shadows and dense blacks to express his imagery in illustrations that are unique and never forgotten once seen. John Martin's mezzotint illustrations of *PL* are considered among the most powerful illustrations of Milton's epic.

890. PARADISE LOST. A Poem, In Twelve Books. By John Milton. Stereotyped By T. H. Carter & Co. *Boston: Published By T. Bedlington, No. 31, Washington-Street. 1826.* 12mo in 6s, 294pp., engraved frontispiece portrait by D. C. Johnston, protective tissue guard, engraved and printed title pages, engraved title dated 1826, printed title dated 1825, both frontispiece portrait and engraved title mounted on green card paper, contemporary half black calf, marbled paper over boards (a bit rubbed, spine chipped at top and bottom, foxing throughout), spine lettered in gilt with decorative gilt rules, speckled edges. A nice, tall copy of an early nineteenth-century American edition, in a contemporary binding bound by "W. M. G. Hathaway, Taunton, Mass.," with binder's label on front pastedown. The engraved portrait of Milton was one of D. C. Johnston's commercial jobs, and is a transcription of a portrait from an English source (Shaw & Shoemaker 21464). See 1831 edition listed here published by Langdon Coffin with engraved title page with publisher's imprint: "Boston. Published by T[.] Bedlington[,] No. 31, Washington St. 1826." Not in Kohler.

891. Variant of Preceding. Contemporary calf (a little rubbed, front joint split at the top, age-browning, tile page and several other pages frayed along the edges, with the last page frayed with slight loss of some text at the middle of the page), spine lettered in gilt with decorative gilt rules and two decorative gilt pieces. A decent copy in a contemporary American calf binding with "George E. Abbott" lettered in gilt on front cover (possibly a presentation binding) and other family member's names written in pencil on front blanks. Not in Kohler.

892. **JOHANN MILTON'S VERLORNES PARADIES** Neu übersetzt von Samuel Gottlieb Bürde. Erster / Zwienter Theil. *Wien, 1826. Gedructk und verlegt ben Chr. Fr. Schade.* 2 volumes in one. Small 8vo, 192pp.,+176pp., separate title page each volume, original marbled paper boards and spine (a bit rubbed), orange leather label lettered in gilt with decorative trim on spine. A good copy. Kohler 104, calling its copy "12mo in 8s," citing "verlegt bey . . . " (rather than "verlegt ben," as seems clearly to be the case in this copy and variant copy following), and reporting "Not in the Bodleian Library. Not in Cambridge University Library"; Stevens 1497, calling this a "Cheap printing of the 1822 edition" (also listed here).

893. Variant of Preceding, original marbled paper boards (some slight wear), black leather spine (a little worn, especially along joints and corners), spine lettered and numbered in gilt with gilt ruling and decorative gilt trim. A nice copy, generally very clean within, with two bookplates on front pastedown. Large paper copy, taller than the preceding copy by ½".

John Martin—Imperial Folio with Proof Impressions of the Plates

894. **THE PARADISE LOST** Of Milton With Illustrations, Designed And Engraved By John Martin. *London: Septimus Prowett, M.DCCC.XXVII.* 2 volumes. First edition folio by Martin. Imperial folio, 228pp.,+218pp., half-title and title page each volume, with proof impressions of the twenty-four large mezzotint plates by John Martin, each plate with "Proof" printed on lower right-hand corner, each engraving measuring 7 ¾" × 11 ⅛", half-title for each book, printer's emblem with "Thomas White, Johnson's Court, Fleet Street" at bottom of last page each volume, contemporary three-quarter blue morocco, pink paper over boards (a bit rubbed, some slight marginal foxing as usual, not affecting the plates), gilt seal of Greville Library on all covers, gilt-decorated spines, raised bands, thick black endpapers, a.e.g. A splendid set. Large paper copy, measuring 15 ¼" × 21 ¾". One of a limited edition of fifty copies of the imperial folio with proof impressions of the plates, "printed from the type as standing for the quarto edition [see following copies], with very large margins" (Balston, *Illustrator*, p. 391). Balston calls the work "one of the most sumptuous and complicated schemes ever undertaken by a publisher," and points out that this edition in the largest, folio format tended to be broken up for plates and "is now [1947] a very rare book." He locates only the copy "in the Royal Library at Windsor; but there is none in the British Museum or any of the great public libraries" (Balston, *Illustrator*, p. 97). Very rare. Kohler 106, reporting "Not in the British Library. Not in the Bodleian Library. Not in Cambridge University Library."

Martin's "apocalyptic steel-engraved mezzotints had many sources: the monumental buildings of London, the engravings of Piranesi, the many recently published volumes of eastern views, even incandescent gas, coalpit accidents, and Brunel's new Thames Tunnel" (Ray, *Illustrator*, p. 69). Martin mastered the process of the mezzotint and was the first to illustrate *PL* with illustrations in the mezzotint medium. See commentary on Martin in earlier twelve original parts edition and with copies following as well as at the head of the chapter on Martin. See William Feaver's full-length book study, *The Art of John Martin* (1975), and most recently, the comprehensive catalogue accompanying the remarkable exhibition in Spain: "John Martin, 1789–1854, Creation of Light: Prints and Drawings from the Michael J. Campbell Collection, 2006."

The catalogue of the same name as the exhibit contains undoubtedly the largest number of prints and drawing by Martin ever assembled together under the cover of one book. The hefty volume of 639 pp. includes stunning pictures with text in Spanish and in English. It will serve Martin aficionados very well for generations to come.

John Martin—Imperial Quarto with Twenty-four Large Mezzotint Plates

895. **THE PARADISE LOST** Of Milton With Illustrations, Designed And Engraved By John Martin. *London: Septimus Prowett, M.DCCC.XXVII.* 2 volumes. First edition quarto by Martin. Imperial quarto, 228pp.,+218pp., half-title and title page each volume, with dedication page, volume 1, with the twenty-four large plates by John Martin, each engraving measuring 7 ¾" × 11 ⅛", protective tissue guards, half-title for each book, printer's emblem with "Thomas White, Johnson's Court, Fleet Street" at bottom of last page each volume, contemporary full straight-grained blue morocco, richly gilt-decorated covers, gilt rules on spines, raised bands, inner and outer dentelles gilt-decorated, a.e.g. A splendid set, measuring overall about as Balston gives here, with contemporary signature (dated 1830) on title page, and with an additional early signature on half-title and a lengthy note on fly-leaf, volume 1. See commentary on Martin in earlier twelve original parts edition. See commentary with copy preceding and following. Balston Edition B (*Life*, p. 286, with the large plates

"Designed & Engraved by J. Martin, Esq." and "Printed by Chatfield & Coleman"). "The two chief editions were an Imperial Quarto 10 ⅞" × 15 ¼", with the larger plates [copy here], and an Imperial Octavo, with the smaller plates; see copies listed here. The same type was used for both, but for the Octavo edition some of the leading was removed to reduce its height, and the verse numbers were moved nearer to the verses to reduce its breadth" (Balston, *Illustrator*, p. 390).

The publication by Septimus Prowett of Milton's *PL* and John Martin's mezzotint illustrations of Milton's epic poem is complex: (1) first there is the publication in parts between 1825 and 1827 (see set listed here); during this same time the twenty-four plates in proof state, before letters, were also published and sold individually (see small plate thus for Book IX in chapter on John Martin); proof copies of the plates were also printed and sold during this same period of time (again, see "Proof" plates in chapter on John Martin); (2) in 1827 the imperial folio, with proof impressions of the twenty-four large plates, was published, limited to fifty copies (also listed here); (3) in 1827 an imperial quarto edition, with the twenty-four large plates, was also published (copy here); and (4) again in 1827 a second imperial quarto edition, with "proof" impressions of the twenty-four small plates, was published, limited to fifty copies (also listed here), "for which the same sheets were used as for the ordinary quarto edition" (Balston); and finally, (5) an imperial octavo edition, with the twenty-four small plates, was also published in 1827 (also listed here). These editions and the parts are captured together in the photo with entry 898. See Bland, *Hist. of Book Illus.*, pp. 191, 253; Ray, *Illustrator*, p. 69 (& Plate XXVII); Feaver, *Art of Martin*; Balston, *Life*, pp. 95–101, 286 and *Illustrator*, pp. 388–91, 410); Kohler 107, reporting "Not in the Bodleian Library. Not in Cambridge University Library."

The distinguishing feature of Martin's mezzotint illustration plates is that each of his mezzotint illustrations was designed and engraved by him and bears the identifying logo, "Designed & Engraved by J. Martin, Esq.," at the bottom of the plate. This is what makes these illustrations so brilliant, so starkly contrasting in dense blacks and bright whites, and so ultimately captivating to the viewer. Later impressions of the prints do not have the same rich quality of contrast or instantly memorable experience of once seen never forgotten. The publishing history continues, quoting Balston: "In 1833, the text was reset, in the same fount of type, and published by Charles Tilt with the smaller plates [see copy listed here and see also 1838 edition reissued by Tilt listed here, not recorded by Balston, and see 1836 edition of *PW* published by Childs with a set of Martin's smaller plates included]. Thereafter the plates, both of the text and the engravings, passed through various hands, Charles Whittingham's [see 1846 edition listed here—the first edition with the Martin plates published by Whittingham], Henry Washbourne's [see 1849 edition listed here—the first edition with the Martin plates published by Washbourne—and also the 1858 Washbourne edition listed here], and Samson Low's, and by 1866 at least seven more editions had been printed from them [see various other editions with Martin's plates listed here]. Ten years later there was a curious revival when Bickers & Son, then of Leicester Square, published the *PW of John Milton* with the twenty-four larger designs reproduced, much smaller, in permanent photography [with stunning photographic reproductions, in 1875 and in 1876, see editions listed here, the 1875 edition unrecorded by Balston]" (Balston, *Illustrator*, p. 391). The passing of the plates to Tilt, Whittingham, Washbourne, and Low, meant that these were the plates that were designed and engraved by Martin, and so they continue to bear at the bottom of each of plate: "Designed & Engraved by J. Martin, Esq."; the quality of the plates was also so much better than that of others.

896. Variant of Preceding. **THE PARADISE LOST** Of Milton With Illustrations, Designed And Engraved By John Martin. *London: Septimus Prowett, M.DCCC.XXVII.* 2 volumes in one. First edition quarto by Martin. Extra thick first imperial quarto, as preceding copy (except extra-illustrated [ca. late nineteenth century]), with the twenty-four large mezzotint plates by John Martin, some labeled "Printed by Chatfield & Co.," others labeled "Printed by J. Lahee," some unlabeled, each engraving measuring 7 ¾" × 11 ⅛", nineteenth-century full red morocco over very thick boards (a bit worn along joints and extremities), gilt-decorated covers and spine, raised bands, inner and outer dentelles tooled in gilt, marbled endpapers, a.e.g. Extra-illustrated [ca. late nineteenth century], with numerous eighteenth- and nineteenth-century Milton-related items, including engraved full-page, two-page, and vignette illustrations (by Westall, Stothard, Cipriani, Kirk, Doré, Blake, and others, including unsigned striking eighteenth-century illustrations), engraved frontispieces (by Sharpe and others), and engraved portraits (from Boydell's edition and others), each mounted on individual pages. A solid, very nice copy, the whole handsomely bound and indicative of someone's diligence and care in putting together a related and integral piece of collected illustrations on Milton's epic poem around the late 1860s or early 1870s, using the 1827 first edition Martin-illustrated *PL* (Balston Edition B) as a basis.

John Martin—Imperial Quarto (With Proof Impressions of the Small Plates)

897. Variant of Preceding. THE PARADISE LOST Of Milton With Illustrations, Designed And Engraved By John Martin. *London: Septimus Prowett, M.DCCC.XXVII. 2 volumes*. First edition quarto by Martin. Second imperial quarto, 228pp.,+218pp., half-title and title page each volume, with proof impressions of the twenty-four small mezzotint plates by John Martin, each plate with "Proof" printed on lower right-hand corner, each engraving measuring 5 ¾" × 8", protective tissue guards, half-title for each book, printer's emblem with "Thomas White, Johnson's Court, Fleet Street" at bottom of last page each volume, contemporary three-quarter calf, marbled paper over boards (some slight foxing, as usual, not affecting the plates), spine lettered in gilt with gilt numerals, thick raised bands, edges untrimmed. A very nice set, an inch taller than the preceding set and much thicker, with bookplates and an early photograph of Sydney Herbert's illustration of Satan and his legions tipped in on fly-leaf, volume 1. Balston Edition C, one of "fifty copies, with proof impressions of the smaller plates" (Balston, *Life*, p. 286). Not in Kohler.

John Martin—Imperial Octavo

898. THE PARADISE LOST Of Milton With Illustrations, Designed And Engraved By John Martin. *London: Septimus Prowett, M.DCCC.XXVII. 2 volumes*. First edition octavo by Martin. Imperial octavo, 228pp.,+218pp., half-title and title page each volume, with dedication page, volume 1, with the first appearance of twenty-four small mezzotint plates by John Martin (some foxing as usual with this edition, although far less than other copies I've seen), some labeled "Printed by Chatfield & Co.," others labeled "Printed by J. Lahee," some unlabeled, each engraving measuring 5 ¾" × 8", protective tissue guards, half-title for each book, printer's emblem with "Thomas White, Johnson's Court, Fleet Street" at bottom of last page each volume, contemporary three-quarter red morocco (rubbed at joints), marbled paper over boards, gilt rules on spine, raised bands with decorative gilt trim, marbled endpapers, a.e.g. Large paper copy. A fine, tall set with early (rather noteworthy) inscription tipped on front pastedown, volume 1, "Robert Palmer, Esq. a reminiscence of the late Rev. D. Pearson, November 17, 1856." Scarce. Balston Edition B. "The eighth plate of the small series is numbered 'Book

John Martin, *PL*: (clockwise from left) A complete set of Twelve Original Parts (1825–27, with twenty-four large plates); imperial 8vo (1827, with twenty-four small plates); imperial 4to (1827, with twenty-four large plates); imperial 4to (1827, with "Proof" impressions of the twenty-four small plates); imperial folio (1827, 1 of 50, with "Proof" impressions of the twenty-four large plates). See #889, 898, 895, 897, and 894.

3 line 301' by mistake for 'Book 3, line 501'" (Balston, *Illustrator*, p. 410). Not in Kohler.

See separate Martin Section with preliminary commentary and with photos (1) of a plate of *PL* in proof state, before letters and (2) of plates of *PL* in proof state; additionally (3) of an original pencil sketch and plates in proof state of the Bible; and (4) of Martin illustrations in several non-Milton publications.

❊

899. PARADISE LOST. A Poem, In Twelve Books. The Author, John Milton. *London: Printed For John Sharpe, Duke Street, Piccadilly. M DCCC XXVII.* Small 8vo, half-title, 8pp.+remainder unpaginated (lines given on each page in place of page number, plates unpaginated, with different engraver from those in the earlier editions), two engraved title pages, each dated 1827 (each date in Arabic numerals), first engraved title "MILTON'S PARADISE LOST. London: Printed By John Sharpe, Piccadilly. 1827," with engraved illustration of *Milton Composing Paradise Lost*, engraved by C. Rolls after T. Stothard, second engraved title "PARADISE LOST . . . soon his heart relented / Towards her . . . Book X. L.940. London: Printed By John Sharpe, 1827," with vignette illustration of *Milton's Reconciliation to His Wife*, engraved by C. Rolls after R. Westall, life of Milton, volume 1, vignette illustration engraved by Charles Rolls after R. Westall for each book of *PL*, each plate dated "May 1. 1827," contemporary scored calf, gilt rules on covers, gilt-decorated spine, brown leather label with gilt lettering ("Milton") and decorative gilt trim, marbled edges, bound by D. Dowsing, with his ticket. A very attractive copy of a scarce set in a charming and well-preserved binding of the period. Uniformly bound as a companion volume with *PR* (& *Poems*) (London: Printed For John Sharpe, M DCCC XXVII, copy listed here), with plates redone and dated 1827 as here, together forming a very scarce set of Milton's *PW*. Kohler 105, reporting "Not in the British Library. Not in the Bodleian Library. Not in Cambridge University Library."

An 1827 Chiswick reissue of the edition by Sharpe/Whittingham/Chiswick first published in 1817 (copy listed here), with the 1816 issue of the Westall plates (first appearance), with a reissue of the Westall plates, with a different engraver, Charles Rolls, from the various engravers of the 1816 plates, with a changed date of 1827, and a new printing of the publisher's imprint at bottom of the plate. See also 1821 Chiswick reissue (copies listed here), one with 1816 plates and the other with plates dated 1822, and see 1825 Chiswick reissue (copy listed here), with plates dated 1822.

900. Variant of Preceding, slightly thinner and taller, contemporary three-quarter crushed green calf (a little rubbed at joints and at extremities, some foxing), marbled paper, elaborately gilt-decorated spines with gilt lettering, raised bands with decorative gilt trim, marbled endpapers and edges. Large paper copy in a variant contemporary binding. A good copy. Uniformly bound as a companion volume with *PR* (London: Printed For John Sharpe, M DCCC XXIII, copy listed here).

901. IL PARADISO PERDUTO DI MILTON, Versione Italiana, Di Guido Sorelli, Fiorentino. *Londra: Presso Dulau E Co., 37, Soho Square. n.d. (1827).* Thick 12mo in 6s, viii+[i]+485pp., lithograph frontispiece portrait of the translator Guido Sorelli, with protective tissue guard, note before each book (unpaginated), contemporary full green morocco (slight wear, p. 303 repaired), covers and spine elegantly stamped in gilt and blind, thick raised bands with decorative gilt border trim, inner and outer dentelles finely tooled in gilt, marbled endpapers and edges. A fine copy with contemporary signature (dated 1827) on front blank. See 1832 Terza Edizione of Sorelli's translation (copy listed here). Scarce. Not in Kohler.

902. PARADISE LOST; A Poem, In Twelve Books, By John Milton. [Epigram on Milton by Dryden.] In Two Volumes. With The Life Of The Author. Vol. I/II. *Philadelphia: Published By J. Locken. 1828.* 2 volumes. Small 8vo in 8s and 4s, 197+176pp., engraved frontispiece portrait of Milton, signed "P. E. Hamm Sc.," within an elaborate frame hanging by a cord, with "John Milton" in large letters across the middle of the page and "Princeton, Published by D. A. Borrenstein, 1828," at the bottom of the page, volume 1, title page each volume, "Life Of The Author" by Fenton, volume 1, original linen spine, paper boards (foxing and slight age browning throughout), printed paper labels on spine (each label slightly chipped). A lovely set in original state with near-contemporary signature on front blank of each volume. Scarce. Not in Kohler.

First Icelandic Translation

903. [PARADISE LOST] ENS ENSKA SKALDS, J. MILTONS, PARADISAR MISSIR. A Islenzku Snuinn Af Pjodskaldi Islendinga, Joni Porlakssyni. *Kaupmannahofn: 1828.* First edition thus. 8vo, 12+408pp., half-title, introduction (dated 1828) followed by "Innihald Paradisar missirs," *PL* translated in double columns, notes at bottom of the page, contemporary quarter calf, blue marbled paper over boards, spine lettered in gilt with gilt monogram and blind-stamped in compartments with decorative gilt trim, uncut, multi-color silk ribbon marker. A fine copy in a distinctive contemporary binding of the first Icelandic translation of *PL* translated by Joni Porlakssyni, edited by Porgeir Gudmundsson and Porsteinn Helgason, and printed in Copenhagen. Stevens 1527; Not in Kohler.

904. PARADISE LOST. A Poem, In Twelve Books, By John Milton. [Dryden epigram on Milton] With The Life Of The Author. *London: Septimus Prowett. 1829.* 12mo in 6s, 332pp., life by Fenton, twelve small engraved mezzotint illustration plates after John Martin, each plate measuring 4 11/16" × 3 3/8" and each plate labeled "Designed & Engraved by J. Martin, Esqr." (two for Book I, with one as frontispiece, one for Book II, one for Book III, two for Book IV, two for Book V, one for Book IX, one for Book X, one for Book XI, and one for Book XII), all but frontispiece with protective tissue guard, half-title for each book, original paper boards (a bit worn, some minor staining, light foxing throughout), printed paper label (a little scuffed) on spine. A good copy with some plates more sharply printed than others. Martin's celebrated illustrations were first issued in twelve parts by Septimus Prowett between 1825 and 1827 (see set listed here); they were then published by Prowett in an edition of *PL*, in four different formats, in 1827 (see copies here with discussion there of Martin's illustrations and of subsequent editions). See copy of this edition following, without the illustrations by Martin. No mention of this edition by Prowett is made by Balston. Rare. Not in Kohler.

905. PARADISE LOST. A Poem, In Twelve Books, By John Milton. Three Poets in three distant ages born . . . [Dryden epigram on Milton] With The Life Of The Author. *London: Septimus Prowett. 1829.* 12mo in 6s, 332pp., half-title for each book, original green cloth (worn, covers detached), printed paper labels (chipped). See copy of this edition by Septimus Prowett preceding with twelve small illustration plates engraved by John Martin. No mention of this edition by Prowett is made by Balston. Rare. Not in Kohler.

906. PARADISE LOST: A Poem. In Twelve Books. By John Milton. With The Life Of The Author. *Philadelphia: Published By L. Johnson, No. 6 George Street. 1830.* 12mo, [1]+306pp., engraved frontispiece portrait of Milton, signed "P. E. Hamm Sc.," within an elaborate frame hanging by a chord with "John Milton" in large letters across the middle of the page and "Princeton, Published by D. A. Borrenstein, 1828," at the bottom of the page, life of Milton by Fenton, half-title for each book, contemporary calf (worn, spine chipped at top, joints cracked, slight embrowning throughout), spine decorated in gilt (faded), red leather label with gilt lettering and decorative gilt trim, early name on fly-leaf. The frontispiece portrait is the same as that in the edition by Locken published two years earlier in 1828 in edition. Uncommon. Not in Kohler.

907. PARADISE LOST; A Poem, In Twelve Books, By John Milton. [Dryden epigram on Milton] With The Life Of The Author. *New-York [sic]: S. & D. A. Forbes, Printers, No. 29 Gold Street. 1830.* 12mo, 316pp., frontispiece portrait of Milton by Illman and Pilbrow within an elaborate frame hanging by a cord (virtually identical to that by Hamm), engraved and printed title pages, engraved title printed against a dark background, life of Milton by Fenton, contemporary polished calf (a bit rubbed, some light age-spotting), spine lettered in gilt within gilt rules and two decorative gilt pieces. A nice copy with contemporary presentation inscription in a neat hand (dated 1831) on fly-leaf. Scarce. Not in Kohler.

908. PARADISE LOST: A Poem, In Twelve Books. By John Milton. *New York: Printed By J. H. Turney. 1831.* 12mo in 6s, 283pp., engraved and printed title pages, with vignette illustration of Adam and Eve repenting by R. Westall (engraved by A. B. Durand) on engraved title page with the lines illustrated quoted beneath the illustration, life of Milton by Fenton before *PL*, index at the end, contemporary calf (a bit worn, joints cracked, spine chipped at top and bottom, corners worn, age-browning throughout), spine elaborately decorated in gilt with gilt lettering. Although a bit worn, a good copy with a possibly contemporary signature in ink on front blank and other early signatures in pencil on front blanks and in ink on front pastedown. Scarce. Not in Kohler.

See 1832 edition of *PL* by Turney listed here with engraved frontispiece portrait and an engraved title page with a different vignette illustration on the engraved title from that here and bound with *PR* and the other poems also with engraved frontispiece portrait and an engraved title page with vignette illustration; see also 1832 edition of *PW* by Turney listed here, two volumes in one, with engraved title page for each volume of *PW*, each engraved title with a vignette illustration "Drawn by R. Westall, Engr'd by A. B. Durand."

909. PARADISE LOST. A Poem In Twelve Books. By John Milton[.] *New-York: Published By Solomon King, 148 Fulton-st. 1831.* 12mo in 6s, 283pp., frontispiece portrait by E. Prud'homme in an elaborate border frame, engraved and printed title pages, with unsigned vignette illustration on engraved title of Satan in flight (for Book I), life by Elijah Fenton, index at the end, original calf (rubbed, front cover partially loose, spine worn and chipped at top, some faint inoffensive watermarks at the inside top of last few pages). See companion edition listed here of *PR; And Other Poems*, published in the same year (1831) by Solomon King with same publisher's imprint as that here, one copy with frontispiece illustration of Madonna and Child after E. Prud'homme, a second copy with the same frontispiece portrait and engraved title page as here. Scarce. Not in Kohler.

910. PARADISE LOST. A Poem, In Twelve Books. By John Milton. Stereotyped By T. H. Carter & Co. *Boston: Published By Langdon Coffin. 1831.* 12mo in 6s, 234pp., engraved frontispiece portrait sketch of Milton (bottom half torn away), engraved and printed title pages, engraved title dated 1826 with publisher's imprint: "Boston. Published by T[.] Bedlington[,] No. 31, Washington St. 1826," contemporary calf (worn, front cover detached, pages badly age-browned), gilt-decorated spine, black morocco label with gilt lettering and decorative gilt trim. All in all, a fair copy of a scarce edition. The engraved frontispiece portrait of Milton is after D. C. Johnston as in 1825/1826 edition by Bedlington (several copies listed here). It was one of D. C. Johnston's commercial jobs and is a transcription of a portrait from an English source (Shaw & Shoemaker 21464). Scarce. Not in Kohler.

910A. (Cross-listing) PARADISE LOST. A Poem, In Twelve Books. By John Milton. Stereotyped By T. H. Carter & Co. *Amherst: Published By J. S. & C. Adams. 1831.* Listed in appendix.

911. [PARADISE LOST] Bradburn, Eliza Weaver. THE STORY OF PARADISE LOST, FOR CHILDREN. By Eliza Weaver Bradburn. *New York, Published By J. Emory And B. Waugh, For the Sunday School Union of the Methodist Episcopal Church, at the Conference Office, 14 Crosby-street. J. Collord, Printer. 1831.* First edition thus. Small 8vo, 112pp., original boards, roan spine (some slight, inoffensive waterstaining throughout), spine ruled and lettered in gilt (faded), bookplate of Leonard Schlosser on front pastedown. Despite minor flaws, a fine copy of a scarce book. This is the pirated edition of Mrs. Siddons's book, published in 1822, *An Abridgement Of Paradise Lost*, published also under the title *The Story Of Our First Parents Abridged From Milton's Paradise Lost, For The Use Of Young Persons* (see copy of each here). See undated ca. 1862 copy of Bradburn's edition listed here "Published By Carlton & Porter, Sunday-School Union, 200 Mulberry Street" in New York. Scarce. Not in Kohler.

912. PARADISE LOST. A Poem In Twelve Books. By John Milton[.] *New York: Printed And Published By J. H. Turney No. 133 East Broadway. 1832.* Bound with **PARADISE REGAINED; AND OTHER POEMS,** By John Milton. *New York: Printed And Published By J. H. Turney No. 133 East Broadway. 1832.* 2 volumes in one. 12mo in 6s, 283pp.,+215pp., engraved frontispiece portrait after E. Prud'homme, engraved and printed title pages for *PL*, with unsigned engraved vignette illustration on engraved title of Satan in flight (for Book I), Life of Milton by Fenton before *PL*, notes at bottom of page, index to *PL* at end of the poem, engraved frontispiece illustration after E. Prud'homme ("When that fatal wound shall be inflicted . . .") for *PR*, engraved and printed title pages for *PR*, with vignette illustration ("Crucifixion scene," unsigned) on engraved title for *PR*, half-titles for *C* and *SA*, in that order, following *PR*, contemporary sheep (covers and spine chafed with some wear, age-browning throughout). A good large paper copy with elaborate early (possibly contemporary) bookplate on front pastedown and early (possibly contemporary) signature in a neat hand in ink on front fly-leaf. See 1831 edition of *PL* by Turney listed here without a frontispiece portrait as here, with an engraved title page for *PL*, but with a different vignette illustration on the engraved title from that here and without being bound with *PR* and the other poems as here. See also 1832 edition of *PW* by Turney listed here, two volumes in one, with engraved title page for each volume, each engraved title with a vignette illustration "Drawn by R. Westall, Engr'd by A. B. Durand," and with engraved title page for *PR* "Drawn by R. Westall, Engr'd by A. B. Durand" and an engraved illustration for "Ode on the Nativity Drawn by R. Westall, Engr'd by Peter Maverick." Uncommon. Not in Kohler.

913. PARADISE LOST. A Poem In Twelve Books. By John Milton. *London: Published By Jones & Company, Temple Of The Muses, (Late Lackington's,) Finsbury Square. 1832.* 32mo in 8s (miniature, measuring 3 ⅝" × 2 ¼"), xii+268pp., unsigned engraved frontispiece portrait within elaborate decorative frame, engraved and printed title pages, engraved title dated 1824, printed title dated 1832, with unsigned vignette illustration of *Satan Flying Toward Earth* on engraved title ("London, Published by Jones & Co. 3, Acton Place, Kingsland Road 1824. University Edition"), life of Milton by Fenton, index at the end, contemporary maroon leather (a bit worn, frontispiece portrait and engraved title page slightly waterstained some time ago), covers decorated in blind, spine lettered and ruled in gilt. The first edition thus was published in 1823, with engraved title page dated 1823 (also listed here); the second edition thus was published in 1825 (also listed here), with engraved title page dated 1824, as here. Scarce. Not in Kohler.

914. LE PARADIS PERDU, Traduit En Vers Français, Par J. Delille. Tome Premier / Tome Second. *Paris. A. Hiard, Libraire-Editeur de la Bibliothèque des Amis des*

Lettres, Rue Saint-Jacques, No. 131. 1832. 2 volumes in one. 12mo in 6s, 229+207pp., half-title each volume, title page each volume with small emblem at the center of each title page, half red calf, marbled paper over boards, spine lettered in gilt with gilt rules and black bands in relief, marbled endpapers, red silk ribbon marker. A very nice copy in excellent condition with early armorial bookplate on front pastedown. See 1805 illustrated and nonillustrated editions here with first translation by Delille and with commentary about him there; see also 1834 illustrated and 1837 nonillustrated editions listed here, each with translation by Delille. Scarce. Not in Kohler.

915. IL PARADISO PERDUTO DI MILTON Riportato In Versi Italiani Da Guido Sorelli Da Firenze. Terza Edizione, Rivista, Corrètta E Toscanamente Accentuata. *Londra: Presso John Murray, Albemarle Street; E Dulau E Co. 37, Soho Square. 1832.* 2 parts in one. 8vo, xiv+227+228pp., dedication page, "Prefazione" dated "Londra, ai 20 Giugno, 1832. 201 Piccadilly," followed by "Sottoscrittori," half-title for "Paradiso Perduto. Seconda Parte," contemporary full black morocco (a little rubbed), gilt border rules with ornamental gilt design on covers, spine elaborately decorated in gilt within the panels, gilt lettering within gilt rules, raised bands with gilt rule, marbled endpapers, a.e.g. A lovely copy in an attractive morocco binding of the period. See ca. 1827 edition of Sorelli's translation here with a variant title page from that here. Scarce. Kohler 114, reporting "Not in the Bodleian Library. Not in Cambridge University Library."

915A. MILTON'S VERLOHRNES PARADIES in Deutschen Hexametern. Ubersetzer: Carl Friedrich von Rosenzweig, Konigl. Sachs. Leg. Rath. *Dresden und Leipzig, in Commission in der Arnoldischen Buchhandlung. 1832.* 4 volumes. First edition thus? Square 8vo, 123pp.,+ 134pp.,+115pp.,+124pp., title page each volume, variously colored endpapers (blue, pink, green, and white), variously colored paper over boards (white, blue, pink, and green), gilt numeral on the spine of each volume, a.e.g., with bookplate in each volume. A lovely set in original bindings and in original red morocco box with decorative gilt trim and gilt lettering. Not in Kohler.

Milton's Verlorhrnes Paradies in Deutschen Hexametern. Ubersetzer: Carl Friedrich von Rosenzweig, Konigl. Sachs. Leg. Rath. 1832. 4 volumes. Square 8vo, original bindings, variously colored paper over boards (white, blue, pink, and green), in original red morocco box. See #915A.

916. THE PARADISE LOST Of Milton With Illustrations By John Martin[.] *London[:] Charles Tilt[,] 1833[.]* Second edition thus; first edition by Tilt. 4to, [viii]+373pp. (plates unpaginated), "T. G. White And Co., Printers, Crane Court, Flcct Street" on verso of title page, with the twenty-four small mezzotint plates by John Martin (fine impressions), with the identifying logo, "Designed & Engraved by J. Martin, Esq.," at the center of each plate, each engraving measuring 5 ½" × 8", protective tissue guards, the arguments for each book printed together at outset before Book I followed by a "List Of The Engravings," contemporary full maroon morocco (a bit rubbed at extremities), covers delicately tooled in gilt, spine elaborately decorated and lettered in gilt, raised bands, inner and outer dentelles finely tooled in gilt, a.e.g., contemporary presentation inscription (dated 1836) on front blank. A very nice copy with very sharp impressions of the mezzotint illustrations by John Martin. Tilt reset the text for this, the second edition, in the same font of type as the first, using the smaller plates. Scarce. Not in Kohler.

Martin's celebrated illustrations were first issued in twelve parts by Septimus Prowett between 1825 and 1827 (see set listed here and commentary on Martin there); they were then published by Prowett in an edition of *PL*, in four different formats, in 1827 (see copies here with discussion of the different formats, Martin's illustrations, and of subsequent editions).

917. IL PARADISO PERDUTO Di Giovanni Milton Tradotto Da Lazaro Papi. Edizione V. Da Esso Riveduta. *Milano: A Spese Della Societa Editrice, 1833*. 12mo in 6s, xxiv+607+[1]pp., half-title, engraved frontispiece portrait by Gaet. Bonatti, engraved and printed title pages with vignette illustration of the expulsion engraved by Gaet. Bonatti after Derby on engraved title ("Milano, MDCC-CXXXIII" [1833]), with lines quoted beneath illustration, "Gli Editori," "Al Chiarissimo Signore Pier Angelo Guinigi," "Vita Di Milton," "Osservazioni Critiche Del Sig. Addisson [sic] Sul Paradiso Perduto," "Annotazioni" at the end of each book, original vellum spine, marbled paper over boards (bit rubbed), spine decorated in gilt with brown leather label with gilt lettering and gilt trim, yellow edges. A fine copy. Advertisement leaf bound in at end. Scarce. Kohler 116, reporting "Not in Williamson. Not in the British Library. Not in the Bodleian Library. Not in Cambridge University Library."

918. PARADISE LOST A Poem By John Milton. New Edition. Revised By J. W. Lake, And Embellished With A Portrait. *Paris, Baudry's European Library, Rue Du Coq, Near The Louvre. Sold Also By Théophile Barrois, Jun., Rue Richelieu; Truchy, Boulevard Des Italiens; Amyot, Rur De La Paix; Librairie Des Estrangers, Rue Neuve-Saint-Augustin; And French And English Library, Rue Vivienne. 1833*. 8vo, lviii+351+[1]pp., half-title, engraved frontispiece portrait by Maulet, protective tissue guard, emblem of the press on title page, "Life Of Milton. With Criticisms On His Works, By Dr. Johnson," "A General Critique Upon The Paradise Lost, By Joseph Addison, Esquire," "Advertisement," second half-title before Book I, "Contents" bound in at end, one-half brown calf, marbled paper over boards, gilt-decorated spine with gilt lettering, thick raised bands with decorative gilt trim, marbled endpapers and edges. A fine copy with near-contemporary foldover French prize citation (dated 1844) bound in before half-title. See other Baudry editions: in 1816 (also listed here) and in 1841 (see copies of several different editions listed here). Scarce. Kohler 115, without reference to second half-title, citing Williamson 259, and reporting "Not in the British Library. Not in the Bodleian Library. Not in Cambridge University Library."

919. LE PARADIS PERDU, Traduit En Vers Français, Par J. Delille. Tome Premier [Tome Second]. *Paris. Lebigre Frères, Libraires, Rue De La Harpe, No. 24. 1834*. 2 volumes. Small 12mo, 223pp.,+203pp., half-title each volume, title page each volume with thin decorative piece at the center of each title page, engraved frontispiece illustration plate to each volume and a further illustration plate in each volume, each illustration signed "Imprime par Dien," with the further signature that possibly reads "Tisco" on the two plates in volume 2 (the four illustrations consisting of

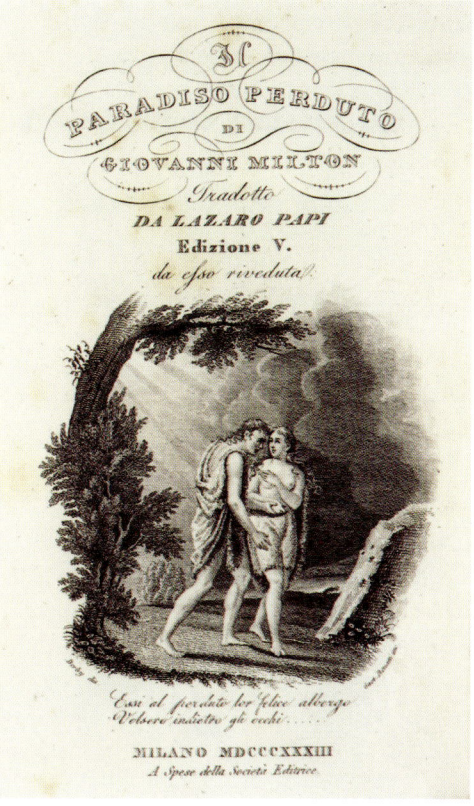

Il Paradiso Perduto. Tradotto Da Lazaro Papi. Milano, 1833. 12mo, engraved frontispiece portrait by "Gaet. Bonatti," title page with vignette illustration engraved by Gaet Bonatti after Derby. See #917.

Satan journeying to earth as frontispiece to volume 1, two angels with spears before Book I, Adam seeing Eve for the first time as frontispiece to volume 2, and Adam and Eve naming the animals before Book VIII), half-title with "Argument" on verso before each book, contemporary blue calf (plates slightly foxed, p. 207 cut close without affecting text), gilt rule on each front cover with the arms of the "College Royal de Henri IV" in elaborate gilt at the center, flat spines with plain central panel in gilt rules, each spine lettered and numbered in gilt, marbled endpapers, speckled edges, with Robert Garrison's bookplate on the front pastedown of each volume. A very attractive set of Delille's translation of *PL*, with interesting illustration plates. See 1805 illustrated and nonillustrated editions here with first translation by Delille, and comments about him there; see also 1837 nonillustrated edition listed here with Delille's translation. Scarce. NUC lists Harvard copy only; Not in Kohler.

920. PARADISE LOST A Poem In Twelve Books By John Milton. *London: William Pickering, 1835 and MDCCCXXVIII.* First Pickering edition. 16mo (miniature, 3 ½" × 2 ⅛"), viii+248pp., engraved frontispiece illustration of *Milton Dictating* engraved by Aug. Fox after Thomas Stothard, engraved and printed title pages, engraved title dated 1835 in Arabic ("William Pickering, Chancery Lane"), printed title dated MDCCCXXVIII in Roman numerals ("William Pickering" with "D. Sidney, Printer, Northumberland Street" on verso of title page), decorative headpiece, the "Arguments" printed together at the beginning before the poem, contemporary full red morocco (slightly worn), gilt-decorated covers and spine, raised bands, inner and outer dentelles finely tooled in gilt, a.e.g. Nice copy. This is one of Pickering's famed "Diamond Classics." Spielman 368; Keynes, *Pickering*, pp. 68 (describing the cloth as "red") and 79; Kohler 109, describing its copy as "24mo in 8s," "in the original tan linen texture cloth," with "Engraved title-page dated 1835," and reporting "Not in the British Library."

921. Variant of Preceding with half-title, original red silk, printed paper label on the spine. Very nice copy, larger than the preceding copy (nearly ½" taller and ⅛" wider), with half-title present. Not in Kohler.

922. Variant of Preceding. **PARADISE LOST** A Poem In Twelve Books By John Milton. *London: William Pickering, 1835.* First Pickering edition. Small 8vo / miniature (3 ½" high × 2 ½" wide—about the size of copy #1 here), viii+248pp., engraved frontispiece illustration of *Milton Dictating* engraved by Aug. Fox after Thomas Stothard, engraved and printed title pages, each dated 1835 in Arabic (engraved title: "William Pickering, Chancery Lane," printed title: "William Pickering"), decorative headpiece, the "Arguments" printed together at the beginning before the poem, original brown tan linen texture cloth (bit worn), original printed paper label (rubbed) on spine, edges untrimmed and partially unopened. Good copy. Variant edition with both engraved *and* printed title pages bearing the 1835 date in Arabic. "This variant is not in Keynes *Pickering*, though it clearly is one of Pickering's 'Diamond Classics.' Not in Keynes; rare" (G. W. Stuart, Jr., Ravenstree, Cat. 176, #54, 1993); Not in Kohler.

923. Variant of Preceding, maroon morocco (front hinge unobtrusively restored with near matching morocco, faint watermark to outer edges of frontispiece and engraved title), cover and spine elaborately tooled in gilt, spine lettered in gilt, raised bands with decorative gilt trim (rubbed), wide inner dentelles richly tooled in gilt, outer dentelles ruled in gilt, silk moire doublures with decorative gilt border trim, t.e.g. A very handsome copy, bound by Zaehnsdorf in 1894, with their stamp. Variant edition with both engraved and printed title pages bearing the 1835 date in Arabic, complete with half-title. Large paper copy (4 ½" × 3") in a splendid morocco binding. "This undescribed edition in the Pickering Diamond Classics is not in Keynes. Keynes makes no mention of any Diamond Classic being issued on Large Paper, yet this clearly is an example on Large Paper. Not in Keynes; rare" (G. W. Stuart, Jr., Ravenstree, Cat. 176, #55, 1993). Not in Kohler.

924. PARADISE LOST: A Poem In Twelve Books. By John Milton. With The Life Of The Author. *Exeter: Published By J. And B. Williams. 1835.* Small 8vo, 249pp., life of Milton by Fenton, original tan cloth, covers and spine decorated in blind with embossed berries and branches, paper label (a bit chipped) lettered and trimmed in black on spine. A nifty little copy in very nice condition with a contemporary signature (dated 1833) on fly-leaf. Kohler 117, describing its copy as "16mo in 8s" and reporting "Not in the British Library. Not in the Bodleian Library. Not in Cambridge University Library."

925. PARADISE LOST, A Poem In Twelve Books; By John Milton. *Paris And Lyons. B. Cormon And Blanc, Booksellers. Paris, 70, Mazarine Street; Lyons, 1, Roger Street; 3 Prefecture's Street. 1835.* 2 volumes in one. 12mo, 150+[2]pp.,+141pp., half-title each volume, separate title page each volume (title page for volume 2 with an altered publisher's imprint: "Paris And Lyons. B. Cormon And Blanc, Booksellers. Paris, 70, Mazarine Street; Lyons, 1, Roger Street. 1835"), original three-quarter calf, marbled paper over boards, spine lettered in gilt with gilt rules and several small decorative piece in gilt. A nice copy. Advertisement leaf ("Supplement Au Catalogue De Cormon Et Blanc, Libraires") at the end of volume 1. Scarce. Not in Kohler.

925A. (Cross-listing) **PARADISE LOST**: A Poem. The Author, John Milton. *London: Charles Tilt, Fleet Street: J. Menzies, Edinburgh: W. F. Wakeman, Dublin. MDCCCXXXVI.* 2 volumes. Listed in appendix.

926. **PARADISE LOST** By John Milton: To Which Is Prefixed, The Life Of The Author. *London: Printed For Thomas Tegg And Son, 73, Cheapside; Tegg, Wise, And Co., Dublin; And R. Griffin And Co., Glasgow. MDCCCXXXVI.* 12mo in 6s, xi+325pp., unsigned engraved title page with illustration of Adam and Eve being expelled from Eden by Michael and a cohort of angels (a few light smudges in the margins, small earlier inoffensive waterstain at the bottom), "London: Balne, Printer, Gracechurch Street" on verso of last page, original three-quarter green calf (a little worn along extremities and corners), marbled paper over boards (rubbed, a smudged contemporary signature on the first page of "The Life Of The Author," no printed title page, and none appears to be missing), spine richly decorated in embossed green and gilt, maroon morocco label (slightly chipped) with gilt lettering at top of spine. A nice copy. Uncommon. Not in Kohler.

927. **PARADISE LOST**. A Poem, In Twelve Books, By John Milton: With Explanatory Notes And A Life Of The Author. By The Rev. H. Stebbing, A. M. Stereotyped by J. A. James. *Philadelphia: James Kay, Jun. & Brother, 122 Chestnut St. Pittsburgh: John I. Kay & Co. 1836.* First edition thus. Small 8vo, xi+312pp., life by Stebbing, original calf (worn, joints cracked, spine ends chipped, some age-browning), black leather label lettered and ruled in gilt on spine. A decent copy of an uncommon edition with original owner's signature (dated 1838) on front blank. A possible second edition thus (in the same small 8vo format but with variant publisher's imprint) was published in 1839 (also listed here); later editions (with further variant publisher's imprints) were published in 1849 and 1853 (see copy of each listed here, with the 1853 edition in a very tall 8vo format compared to the others here). Scarce. Not in Kohler.

928. **LE PARADIS PERDU DE MILTON**. Traduction Nouvelle, Par M. De Chateaubriand. *Paris, Charles Gosselin Et Furne, Editeurs. M DCCC XXXVI. 2 volumes.* 8vo, xxviii+ 483+[3],+479pp., half-title and title page each volume, "Paris—Imprimerie De H. Fournier" on verso of each half-title, "Remarques" before the poem, half-title before Book I, and "Errata . . . Tome I" at the end, volume 1, half-title before Book VII and "Errata . . . Tome II" at the end, volume 2, English on left side of the page, with translated French by Chateaubriand facing on the right side, original plain blue wrappers (a little worn, preliminaries foxed, slight scattered foxing in both volumes, but not obtrusive), uncut. A good, tall set in original wrappers, understandably a bit worn, but amazingly intact given the bulk of the volumes and overall a remarkable survival thus. Stevens 1456; Not in Kohler.

Probably the second edition of Chateaubriand's great prose translation of Milton's epic, the first having appeared in 1831, often reprinted both separately and with his *Oeuvres Complètes*. The brilliant author of dozens of novels, essays, books of criticism and travel, Chateaubriand (who died in 1848) had already written a magisterial study of English literature with his *Essai sur la Litérature Anglaise* (see copy with Nineteenth-century Miltoniana), and here he announced his intention in his opening "Remarques" to produce not just another "traductione élégante" of Milton's epic, but something far more difficult: " . . . une traduction littérale dans toute la force du terme que j'ai entreprise, une traduction qu'un enfant et un poète pourront suivre sur le texte, ligne à ligne, mot à mot, comme un dictionnaire ouvert sous leurs yeux" (a literal translation that a child and a poet will be able to follow, line for line, word for word, like a dictionary open under their eyes). See undated ca. 1838 edition of *Le Paradis Perdu* listed here, "Illustré De Gravures Sur Acier[.] Oeuvres De Chateaubriand."

929. Variant of Preceding, contemporary three-quarter red leather, red marbled paper over boards (slight rubbing on back cover of each volume), gilt rules on covers, spines lettered in gilt with gilt rules, raised bands, marbled endpapers, t.e. red, fore- and bottom edges untrimmed, red and white silk ribbon markers. A very nice set, fresh and clean within, in an attractive variant binding; the typography and look of the books are superb. Stevens 1456; Not in Kohler.

930. **PARADISE LOST**, A Poem In Twelve Books. By John Milton. [Dryden epigram on Milton.] *Halifax: Hartley And Walker. 1837.* First edition thus? Small 8vo, 316pp., half-title, frontispiece illustration for Book VI (Satan being cast out of Heaven), signed "WHIMPER," contemporary half green morocco, green cloth (a bit worn, pages a little age-browned), spine lettered in gilt with gilt rules. A good copy with ownership signature of Lord Milner's mother, "Mary I. Cromie, 1839," on title page. Scarce. Not in Kohler.

930A. (Cross-listing) **PARADISE LOST**; With Explanatory Notes, And A Life Of The Author, By The Rev. H. Stebbing, A.M. *London: Scott, Webster And Geary, 36. Charterhouse Square. 1837.* Listed in *Appendix*.

931. **PARADISE LOST**. A Poem, In Twelve Books. By John Milton. Stereotyped By T. H. Carter & Co. *Boston: T. H. Carter.—Agent. 1837.* 12mo in 6s, 294pp., contemporary black leather spine, marbled paper over boards (worn, slight foxing throughout), spine lettered in gilt with gilt rules. A good copy. Not in Kohler.

932. PARADIS PERDU DE MILTON [Traduit En Vers Français, Par J. Delille, Quatrième Edition. *Paris, Firmin Didot Frères Et Cie. M DCCC XXXVII.*] [In] **OEUVRES DE J. DELILLE**. Avec Les Notes . . . Quatrième Edition. *Paris, Firmin Didot Frères Et Cie, Libraires-Editeurs, Imprimeurs De L'Institut De France, Rue Jacob, No 56, Lefèvre, Libraire Rue De L'Eperon, No 6. M DCCC XXXVII.* Thick 8vo, viii+914pp., half-title in French, engraved frontispiece portrait of Delille, central harp on title page, eight pages of biographical and literary notes about Delille by Madame Woillez, contemporary three-quarter red demi-basané/sheepskin, marbled paper over boards (a bit rubbed, corners slightly bumped, occasional foxing throughout—fairly heavy at the beginning of the volume), spine lettered in gilt with thick decorative gilt trim and smaller decorative gilt pieces, marbled endpapers, yellow edges lightly speckled in red. A good, thick copy. Abbé Jacques Delille's translation of *Paradise Lost* occupies pp. 637–826, with notes following the poem, from pp. 836–41. See 1805 illustrated and nonillustrated editions with first translation by Delille and with commentary about him there; see also 1832 and 1834 illustrated editions with Delille's translation. Scarce. Not in Kohler.

933. THE PARADISE LOST OF MILTON With Illustrations By John Martin[.] *London[:] Charles Tilt[,] 1838.* 4to, [6]+373+[2]pp., with the twenty-four small mezzotint plates by John Martin (fine impressions), each engraving measuring 5 ¾" × 8", the arguments for each book printed together at outset before Book I, early Victorian calf, covers nicely tooled in gilt with a floral emblem at each corner of covers, spine elaborately decorated and lettered in gilt, raised bands, inner and outer dentelles finely tooled in gilt, a.e.g., with early bookplate on front pastedown, "List Of The Engravings" bound in at end. A fine copy with very sharp impressions of the mezzotint illustrations by John Martin. Tilt published the "second" edition with Martin's plates, using the smaller plates, in 1833 (also listed here), of which this is a reissue. Martin's celebrated illustrations were first issued in twelve parts by Septimus Prowett between 1825 and 1827 (see set listed here); they were then published by Prowett in an edition of *PL* in four different formats in 1827 (see copies here with discussion of the different formats, Martin's illustrations, and of subsequent editions). Scarce. Not in Kohler.

934. LE PARADIS PERDU Illustré De Gravures Sur Acier[.] Oeuvres De Chateaubriand[.] *Paris[:] Arnauld De Vresse, Libraire-Editeur[,] 55, Rue De Rivoli, 55. n.d. [ca. 1838].* 12mo, 285+[2]pp., half-title ("Sèvres, Typ. L. Lefèvre" on verso), engraved frontispiece illustration ("Adam Et Eve Chassés Du Paradis" by Guilbert, "Hadengue Imp. r. du Faur S. G. 63. Paris," fine impression), protective tissue guard, edited by Arnauld de Vresse, "Table Des Matières" at the end, contemporary demi-chagrin/black pebble leather binding (a bit rubbed), covers ruled in blind relief, spine lettered in gilt within gilt rules, raised bands, small gilt ornaments within the panels, marbled endpapers. A very nice copy. The translation by Chateaubriand first appeared in a two-volume edition in 1831; see also the 1836 edition. Scarce. Not in Kohler.

935. PARADISE LOST, AND OTHER POEMS. By John Milton. In Two Volumes. Vol. I / Vol. II. *London: W. S. Orr And Co., Paternoster Row. MDCCCXXXIX.* Small 8vo (near miniature in size, 4 ¼" × 3 ⅜"), 200pp.,+216pp., unsigned frontispiece illustration each volume: "solemn council . . . At Pandemonium," volume I, protective tissue guard, temptation of Eve, volume II, protective tissue guard, engraved and printed title pages each volume, unsigned vignette portrait of middle-aged Milton on engraved title, volume I ("Paradise Lost; and other Poems, By John Milton. Vol. I. London: Wm. S. Orr & Co. Amen Corner, Paternoster Row, 1839"), unidentified and unsigned vignette illustration of lake with mountains in the background, volume II, ("Paradise Lost; and other Poems By John Milton. Vol. II. London: Wm. S. Orr & Co. Amen Corner, Paternoster Row, 1839"), "London: Bradbury And Evans, Printers, Whitefriars" on verso of each printed title page, half-title for each book of *PL* and for "Miscellaneous" poems at the end of volume II (poems including *L'A, IlP, L, C, Christmas Hymn* [so-titled], and several other shorter poems), "London: Bradbury And Evans, Printers To The Queen, Whitefriars" at bottom of last page, volume II, contemporary red pebble leather (a little worn along joints and corners, frontispieces and engraved titles a little foxed), decorated gilt urn at the center of each cover, spines lettered and numbered in gilt, raised bands, a.e.g. A nice set "Bound By Webb Liverpool" with his stamp in each volume. Scarce. Kohler 121, calling it "W.S. Orr & Co.'s Cabinet Edition," and reporting "Not in Williamson. Not in the British Library. Not in the Bodleian Library. Not in Cambridge University Library."

936. PARADISE LOST. A Poem, In Twelve Books, By John Milton: With Explanatory Notes And A Life Of The Author. By The Rev. H. Stebbing, A. M. Stereotyped by J. A. James. *Philadelphia: James Kay, Jun. & Brother, 122 Chestnut St[.] Pittsburgh: – C. H. Kay & Co. 1839.* Second edition thus? Small 8vo, x+312pp., "Memoir Of Milton's Life And Writings" by Stebbing, "Notes" at the end, contemporary roan (a little worn, occasional slight foxing), spine decorated and lettered in gilt. The possible first edition thus (with variant publisher's imprint from that here) was published in 1836 (also listed here with further editions cited). Not in Kohler.

937. Variant of Preceding, original decorated bright red cloth (rubbed at joints), covers ruled in blind trim and decorated with bright gilt design at the center, spine delicately trimmed in gilt with gilt lettering, a.e.g. A lovely copy in a very attractive variant publisher's binding with contemporary presentation (dated 1846) on fly-leaf. Not in Kohler.

938. PARADISE LOST. A Poem In Twelve Books. By John Milton*[.] New–York: Published By Charles Wells. n.d. [ca. 1839]*. First edition thus? 12mo in 6s, 283pp., life by Elijah Fenton, index at the end, contemporary black calf tooled in blind (worn, front joint cracked, top portion of spine missing). A good copy with contemporary signature (dated 1839) on fly-leaf, early bookseller's stamp on front blank, and a later ownership signature in pen on back blank. A possible second edition thus with frontispiece illustration was published in 1840; a possible third edition thus without frontispiece illustration was published in 1841; and a possible fourth edition thus without frontispiece illustration was published in 1842 —all listed here. Not in Kohler.

939. PARADISE LOST; A Poem, In Twelve Parts. By John Milton. A New Edition. *Boston: Weeks, Jordan & Company, 1839*. First edition thus? 12mo in 6s, 294pp., contemporary black leather spine, marbled paper over boards (a little rubbed, small piece missing at bottom left corner of front cover, some light inoffensive waterstaining along inner portion of back pages, light pencil notes on inside of front fly-leaf), spine lettered in gilt with gilt rules. A decent copy of an uncommon early nineteenth-century American edition. Not in Kohler.

940. MILTON'S PARADISE LOST: With Copious Notes, Explanatory & Critical, Partly Selected From The Various Commentators, & Partly Original: Also A Memoir Of His Life. By James Prendeville, B.A. Editor Of Livy, Etc. *London: Samuel Holdsworth, Amen Corner, Paternoster Row. 1840.* First edition thus. 8vo, xi+[i]+lxiii+[i]+452pp., dedication, "Editor's Preface," dated "December 24, 1839," half-title for each book, notes to each book and index printed in double column at the end of the volume, original calf (spine a little chaffed and slightly chipped at top, front joint cracked, light foxing to endpapers and title page), raised bands within gilt rules, black morocco label with gilt lettering on spine. A very good copy in a handsome contemporary full leather binding with bookplate on front pastedown and prize inscription (dated 1843) on fly-leaf. See second edition published in 1841 listed here. Scarce. Not in Kohler.

941. PARADISE LOST. A Poem In Twelve Books. By John Milton*[.] New–York. Charles Wells, 56 Gold-Street. 1840.* Second edition thus? 12mo in 6s, 283pp., unsigned engraved frontispiece illustration for Book I, life by Elijah Fenton, index at the end, contemporary black cloth (slightly worn, especially along spine, joints, and extremities, front joint weak and cracking, foxing throughout), covers elaborately tooled in blind with large central emblem in blind, spine elaborately tooled in blind and lettered in gilt with small urn in blind above the gilt lettering and larger urn with a figure on it in blind at the center, outer dentelles finely tooled in gilt. Although a bit worn, a good copy of a scarce edition. The possible first edition thus without frontispiece illustration as here was published in 1839 (copy listed here). Scarce. Not in Kohler.

942. PARADISE LOST. A Poem, In Twelve Books. By John Milton. Stereotyped By T. H. Carter & Co. *Boston: Weeks, Jordan, & Co. 1840.* 12mo in 6s, 294pp., half calf, marbled paper over boards (a bit worn, spine ends chipped), gilt rules on spine with gilt lettering, early (possibly contemporary) signature on fly-leaf. An agreeable, pocket-sized American edition of Milton's epic poem. The possible first edition thus appeared one year earlier in 1839 (copy listed here). Not in Kohler.

943. O PARA[D]ISO PERDIDO. Epopea De Joao Milton; vertida do original inglez para verso portuguez por Antonio Jose' De Lima Leitao . . . Genioi de Milton, sequirei teus voos Que nao me e dado emparelhar contigo. Contendo Os Seis Primeiros Cantos. *Lisboa: 1840. Typ. de J. M. R. e Castro Calcada de S. Joao Nepomuceno N.o[sic] 16. 2 volumes.* First edition of this translation. 8vo in 4s, [iv]+xv+[i]+249pp.,+[ii]+534+[1]pp., engraved frontispiece portrait of Milton by Sendin, dated "Lisboa, 1836," volume 1, engraved frontispiece portrait of the translator, dated "Lisboa, 1836," volume 2, dedication page, "Prefacio Do Traductor," "Vida De Joao Milton Escripta Por Eliab Fenton," "Nota sobre a Orthographia seguida nesta traduccao," "Argumento Geral Do Para[d]iso Perdid," "Erratas Do 1.0," volume 1, "Advertencia" and "Erratas Do 2.0" at the beginning of volume 2 and "Lista dos Assignantes at the end of volume 2, notes to each canto/book, contemporary black quarter roan, burgundy cloth boards (somewhat rubbed), gilt rules on spines with small decorative gilt devices, blue endpapers. First edition of this Portuguese verse translation with copious annotations to each canto. Scarce. NUC locates copies at Indiana and Harvard only; Kohler 122, reporting "Not in Williamson . . . Not in the Bodleian Library. Not in Cambridge University Library."

944. MILTON'S PARADISE LOST, With Variorum Notes Including Those Of Bp. Newton, Warburton, Warton, Jortin, Addison, Johnson, Todd, And Others. To Which Are Added Illustrations, And A Memoir Of The Life Of Milton, With Remarks On His Versification, Style, And Imitation Of The Ancient Classics. By James Prendeville, B.A. *London: Samuel Holdsworth, Amen Corner, Paternoster Row. 1841.* Second edition thus. 8vo, xi+[i]+lxiii+[i]+452pp., dedication, "Editor's Preface," erratum page, half-title for each book, notes to each book and index printed in double column at the end of the volume, original blue-green ribbed cloth, blind rules on covers, with central gilt device on front cover of Milton in relief enclosed in laurel wreath, angel decorations in gilt on spine, together with title incorporated within gilt globe, edges untrimmed. A fine copy in an attractive publisher's binding. See first edition published in 1840 here. Scarce. Not in Kohler.

945. MILTON'S PARADISE LOST: With Copious Notes, Explanatory And Critical, Partly Selected From Addison, Bentley, Bowle, Calmet, Callender, Dunster, Gillies, Greenwood, Hume, Heylin, Johnson, Jortin, Lord Monboddo, Newton, Pearce, Richardson, Stillingfleet, Thyer, Todd, Upton, Warburton, Warton, And Partly Original; Also A Memoir Of His Life By James Prendeville, B. A. Editor Of Livy, Etc. *Paris: Baudry's European Library, 3, Quai Malaquais, Near The Pont Des Arts, And Stassin And Xavier, 9, Rue Du Coq, Near The Louvre. Sold Also By Amyot, Rue De La Paix; Truchy, Boulevard Des Italiens; Girard Frères, Rue Richelieu; Leopold Michelsen, Leipzig; And By All The Principal Booksellers On The Continent. 1841.* 8vo, liv+383pp., vignette sketch of Milton ca. age sixty-two at center of title page, "Editor's Preface" (dated "London, December 24, 1839"), life of Milton, "Remarks On Paradise Lost," copious notes to each book at the bottom of each page, index printed in double column at the end, contemporary one half dark green morocco, marbled paper over boards (a little rubbed), gilt rules on covers, spine elaborately decorated in gilt at top and bottom with gilt lettering and gilt ducal emblem at the center, thick raised bands finely tooled in gilt, marbled endpapers and edges. A nice copy. See other Baudry editions: in 1816, in 1833, and in this same year, 1841, with parallel text in French and English —all listed here. Uncommon. Not in Kohler.

946. PARADISE LOST, A Poem In Twelve Books. By John Milton[.] *New–York: Charles Wells, 56 Gold-Street. 1841.* Third edition thus? 12mo in 6s, 283pp., life by Elijah Fenton, index at the end, contemporary brown cloth (a bit rubbed, spine chipped with a small piece missing at the bottom and reglued at the top, occasional embrowning throughout), large emblem elaborately tooled in blind at the center of each cover, spine lettered in gilt within decorative gilt trim. A good copy with contemporary ownership signature (dated 1843) in pencil in a neat hand at the top of the title page, notes neatly written in the same contemporary hand on a final blank. The possible first edition thus was published in 1839 (copy listed here with further reference to further editions by Charles Wells cited). Scarce. Not in Kohler.

947. PARADISE LOST. A Poem. In Twelve Books[.] By John Milton. A New Edition. *Boston: Published By E. Littlefield, 122 Washington Street. 1841.* 12mo in 6s, 294pp., original black leather spine, marbled paper over boards (joints worn and cracked, spine chipped at top and bottom, covers rubbed), spine lettered and ruled in gilt. A good copy of a scarce edition with early presentation inscription on fly-leaf. Not in Kohler.

948. PARADISE LOST. A Poem. In Twelve Books By John Milton. A New Edition. *Boston: Published By Lewis & Sampson. 122 Washington Street. 1841.* First edition thus? 12mo in 6s, 294pp., original half calf, marbled paper over boards (spine chipped at the top, slight inoffensive waterstaining along bottom portion of first half of book, foxing throughout), spine lettered in gilt with thick gilt lines. A decent copy with early presentation inscription in pencil on front pastedown and another name in ink on fly-leaf. A possible second edition thus was published in 1843 (copy listed here). Uncommon. Not in Kohler.

949. LE PARADIS PERDU DE J. MILTON. Traduit Par J. Mosneron. Cinquième Edition, Avec Le Texte En Regard. *Paris: Librairie Européenne De Baudry, 3, Quai Malaquais, Près Du Pont Des Arts, Et Stassin Et Xavier, 9, Rue Du Coq, Près Du Louvre. Se Trouve Aussi Chez Amyot, Rue De La Paix; Truchy, Boulevard Des Italiens; Girard Frères, Rue Richelieu; Leopold Michelsen, A. Leipzig; Et Chez Les Principaux Librairies Du Continent. 1841.* 8vo, 479pp., half-title ("Le Paradis Perdu, En Anglais Et En Français. Texte en Regard"), title page in English on verso with vignette sketch of Milton ca. age sixty-two at center of title page (same as in "Baudry's European Library" 1841 edition here), text page in French facing with decorative initials of the press at the center, half-title for "Paradise Lost. Le Paradis Perdu." following title page, French text on recto of each page, English text on verso, contemporary purple half calf, purple marbled paper over boards (a bit rubbed, especially the spine, occasional embrowning), spine lettered in gilt with gilt rules and decorative emblems in blind, marbled endpapers. Laid in: prize label in French (a little frayed and darkened along the top), dated 1863. A very nice copy. This translation by Jean-Baptiste Mosneron de Launay was first published in 1786; see also the 1788 second edition. See also "Baudry's European Library" edition in English published by Baudry in Paris in the same year, 1841, with the same publisher's address. Scarce. Not in Kohler.

950. LE PARADIS PERDU Par Milton, Traduction Nouvelle, Précédée D'une Notice, Par De Pongerville, Membre de l'Académie française. *Paris, Charpentier, Libraire-Editeure, 29, Rue De Seine. 1841.* 12mo in 6s, xvi+548pp., half-title (with listing of "Bibliothèque Charpentier. Ouvrages Publiés" on verso), "Sur Milton, Son Epoque Et Ses Ourvrages" prose translation of Milton's epic, book by book, original brown leather spine, marbled paper over boards (a little rubbed), marbled endpapers. A good, tight copy of Pongerville's prose translation of Milton's epic in original publisher's binding. See 1865 edition of Pongerville's translation of *PL* (copy listed here). Not in Kohler.

951. Variant of Preceding. LE PARADIS PERDU Par Milton, Traduction Nouvelle, Précédée D'une Notice, Par De Pongerville, Membre de l'Académie française. *Paris, Charpentier, Libraire-Editeure, 29, Rue De Seine. 1841.* 12mo in 6s, xvi+548pp. Not in Kohler. Bound with **VOYAGE: SENTIMENTAL . . . SUIVI DES LETTRES D'YORICK A ELIZA**, Par Sterne; Traduit de l'anglais Par M. Leon De Wailly, Et précédé du'une Notice sur la vie et les ouvrages de Sterne, Par Sir Walter Scott. *Paris, Charpentier, Libraire-Editeure, 29, Rue De Seine. 1841.* 8vo, xxiv+214+[2]pp., half-title (with listing of "Bibliothèque Charpentier. Ouvrages Publiés" on verso), "Table Du Volume" on last page. Three titles gathered under one binding with two title pages. Half black leather, pebbled black paper over boards (a bit rubbed, edges a little worn, some age-browning), spine lettered in gilt within gilt rules, raised bands with decorative gilt trim, gilt rules at top and bottom, marbled endpapers. Overall a nice copy.

952. PARADISE LOST, A Poem In Twelve Books. By John Milton[.] *New–York: Charles Wells, 56 Gold-Street. 1842.* Fourth edition thus? 12mo in 6s, 283pp., life by Elijah Fenton, index at the end, contemporary roan elaborately tooled in blind (a bit rubbed, front joint slight cracked at bottom, embrowning throughout, earlier ownership name and address blacked out on fly-leaf), spine elaborately tooled in blind and lettered in gilt. All in all, a nice copy with contemporary signature (dated 1843) on fly-leaf and front blank with a second later signature also on front blank. The possible first edition thus was published in 1839 (copy listed and other editions by Charles Wells cited there). Not in Kohler.

953. PARADISE LOST. A Poem. In Twelve Books By John Milton. A New Edition. *Boston: Published By Lewis & Sampson. 122 Washington Street. 1843.* Second edition thus? 12mo in 6s, 294pp., original brown silk cloth (a bit rubbed, spine ends slightly chipped, foxing throughout), covers decorated in blind trim, spine lettered in gilt between thick gilt lines with decorative blind trim, edges untrimmed. A nice, tall copy with early presentation inscription in pencil on front pastedown and another name in ink on fly-leaf. The possible first edition thus was published in 1841 (also listed here). Not in Kohler.

954. Variant of Preceding, original brown silk cloth (a bit rubbed, spine ends slightly chipped, foxing throughout, early name stamped on fly-leaf), covers decorated in blind trim, spine lettered in gilt between thick gilt lines with decorative blind trim, edges untrimmed. A nice, tall copy in a variant publisher's binding with early presentation inscription in pencil on front pastedown with variant blind trim on covers and spine, and taller than preceding copy by ¼".

955. PARADISE LOST. By John Milton. With Explanatory Notes By The Rev. Henry Stebbing, A.M. *New–York: D. Appleton & Co., 200 Broadway[;] Philadelphia: Geo. S. Appleton, 148 Chestnut-St[.] MDCCCXLIV.* First edition thus? 12mo, 296pp. (with pagination beginning at "p. 18" on verso of first page of Book I), unsigned engraved frontispiece illustration for Book II ("Caught in a fiery tempest . . . Each on his rock. . . . "), notes at bottom of page, contemporary brown silk cloth (a little worn, spine chipped at top and bottom, foxing throughout, tear across the bottom of pp. 121/122), covers finely tooled in embossed blind with border trim and central triangular emblem, spine richly decorated in gilt with gilt lettering, a.e.g. Good copy. The possible second, third, and fourth editions thus were published in 1845, 1846, and 1848 (see copy of each listed here), each with the same engraved frontispiece illustration as here; see also copy of 1850 (possible fifth thus) and copy of 1854 editions listed here, each with a different engraved frontispiece illustration from that here (of the expulsion); and see copy of 1857 edition listed here, with publisher's imprint of "New York: D. Appleton & Company" only, with the engraved frontispiece illustration of the expulsion; the pagination in each Appleton edition begins at "p. 18" on the verso of the first page of Book I as with the edition here. See also copy of 1851 edition listed here published by "D. Appleton & Co." in New York and "Geo. S. Appleton" in Philadelphia in octavo format with illustration plates after Martin and other editions cited there. Scarce. Not in Kohler.

956. PARADISE LOST: A Poem In Twelve Books. By John Milton. *New York: Published By Edward Kearny[,] 272 Pearl-Street. n.d. [ca. 1844].* First edition thus? 12mo in 6s, 283pp., life of Milton by Fenton, index at end, original brown diaper grain cloth (a little worn, pages age-browned), covers delicately tooled in blind, spine lettered in gilt within decorative gilt trim. A decent copy of a scarce edition with several signatures on front blanks and a large bookplate on front pastedown. See following dated edition of *PL* published by Edward Kearny about this same time with a different address from that here. Not in Kohler.

957. Variant of Preceding. **PARADISE LOST**: A Poem In Twelve Books. By John Milton. *New York: Published By Edward Kearny, 56 Gold-Street[,] 1844.* First edition thus? 12mo in 6s, 283pp., life of Milton by Fenton, index at end, original blue-green diaper grain cloth (some rubbing and occasional light foxing), covers delicately tooled in blind, spine decorated and lettered in gilt within decorative gilt trim. A nice copy. See preceding undated edition of *PL* published by Edward Kearny about this same time with a different address from that here. Kohler 127, reporting "Not in the British Library. Not in the Bodleian Library. Not in Cambridge University Library."

958. PARADISE LOST. By John Milton. With Explanatory Notes By The Rev. Henry Stebbing, A.M. *New-York: D. Appleton & Co., 200 Broadway[;] Philadelphia: Geo. S. Appleton, 148 Chestnut-St[.] MDCCCXLV.* Second edition thus? 12mo, 296pp. (with pagination beginning at "p. 18" on verso of first page of Book I), unsigned engraved frontispiece illustration for Book II ("Caught in a fiery tempest . . . Each on his rock. . . . "), protective tissue guard, notes at bottom of page, contemporary brown cloth (a bit rubbed, spine ends slightly chipped, frontispiece and title page foxed because of tissue guard, some slight embrowning throughout), covers finely tooled in embossed blind, spine richly decorated in gilt with gilt lettering. A nice copy with contemporary presentation inscription on front blank. The possible first edition thus was published in 1844 (also listed here with other editions cited); the pagination in each Appleton edition begins at "p. 18" on the verso of the first page of Book I as with the edition here. Scarce. Not in Kohler.

959. PARADISE LOST. A Poem. In Twelve Books By John Milton. A New Edition. *Boston: Published By Phillips & Sampson. 122 Washington Street. 1845.* First edition thus? 12mo in 6s, 294pp., original black leather spine (a bit rubbed, joints weak), marbled paper over boards (a little rubbed, extremities and corners worn, earlier signatures on front blank), spine lettered and ruled in gilt. A nice copy. Editions by Phillips & Sampson followed: in 1846 a possible second edition thus, in 1847 a possible third edition thus, and in 1848 a possible fourth edition thus (all listed here), each with the same publisher's imprint as here; other editions were published by Phillips & Sampson in 1849 ("Boston: Phillips, Sampson, & Co., 110 Washington Street," not in the collection), in 1850 ("Boston: Phillips, Sampson, & Co., 110 Washington Street," see copy listed here), 1852 (with same publisher's imprint as in 1850 edition, see copy listed here), and 1859 (with variant publisher's imprint from prior editions here: "Boston: Phillips, Sampson, & Co.," see copy listed here). See also editions of *PL* by Phillips & Sampson with frontispiece portrait with vignette illustration inset at the bottom, together with Young's *Night Thoughts*; variously published about this same time with various publisher's imprints: the possible first thus in 1847 ("Boston: Published By Phillips & Sampson, 110 Washington Street," also listed here with further editions cited). Uncommon. Not in Kohler.

960. THE PARADISE LOST OF JOHN MILTON With Illustrations By John Martin. *London: Charles Whittingham, 1846.* Large 4to, [6]+373+[1]pp., the arguments for each book printed together at outset before Book I, with proof impressions of most of the twenty-four small mezzotint plates by John Martin, those plates with "Proof" printed on lower right corner, all plates with the identifying logo, "Designed & Engraved by J. Martin, Esq.," at the center of the plate, each engraving measuring 5 ¾" × 8", thick protective tissue guards, original half black morocco, marbled paper (a trifle rubbed, foxing in the margins of some of the plates as usual, except for the last plate, which is fairly heavily foxed), gilt rules on covers, gilt lettering on spine with decorative gilt trim at top and bottom, raised bands with decorative gilt trim, marbled endpapers, a.e.g., "List Of The Engravings" bound in at end. An excellent copy with sharp impressions of the mezzotint illustrations by John Martin, most in proof state. Large paper copy of one of the most striking illustrated books of the nineteenth century (Ray, *Illustrator*, 69A) with contemporary presentation in ink at top of title page ("To Mrs. Rebecca Newton" in a neat hand) and with the same name in a comparably neat hand on a small piece of paper laid in. Martin's celebrated illustrations were first issued in twelve parts by Septimus Prowett between 1825 and 1827 (see set listed here with further commentary); they were then published by Prowett in an edition of *PL*, in four different formats, in 1827 (see copies listed here with discussion of the different formats, Martin's illustrations, and of subsequent editions). This is the first edition with the Martin plates published by Whittingham. Scarce. Not in Kohler.

961. PARADISE LOST. By John Milton. With Explanatory Notes By The Rev. Henry Stebbing, A. M. *New–York: D. Appleton & Co., 200 Broadway[;] Philadelphia: Geo. S. Appleton, 148 Chestnut-St[.] MDCCCXLVI.* Third edition thus? 12mo, 296pp. (with pagination beginning at "p. 18" on verso of first page of Book I), unsigned engraved frontispiece illustration for Book II ("Caught in a fiery tempest . . . Each on his rock. . . . "), protective tissue guard, notes at bottom of page, contemporary blue-green cloth (worn, lacking half the spine, foxing), covers decorated in blind, spine originally decorated in gilt, a.e.g. Despite the wear, a tight copy internally. The possible first edition thus was published in 1844 (see copy here and other references cited there); the pagination in each Appleton edition begins at "p. 18" on the verso of the first page of Book I as with the edition here. Not in Kohler.

962. PARADIS LOST. A Poem, In Twelv Bucs. Bi Jon Miltun. *Lundun: Publist Bi Izac Pitman, At The Fonetic Depo, 1, Cwenz Hed Pasej, Paturnostur Ro, And At The Fonetic Institushun, 5, Nelsun Plas, Bat. 1846.* First edition thus. 8vo, x+[unpaginated poem, with line references given on each page], dedication page, "Publisher's Preface," half-title before the poem, original green cloth, gilt lettering on spine, a.e.g. A very nice copy with early inscription in pen on fly-leaf. *Paradise Lost* is here published according to a phonetic alphabet, with a six-page publisher's preface explaining the raison d'être. Pitman's first complete book (apart from exercise and copy-books, etc.), printed in phonotype, a phonetic printing alphabet of forty letters. Spelling reform to ease the spread of popular education was one of Pitman's great enthusiasms, but it was found, after lengthy experiments, that the introduction of the necessary new types was an insurmountable obstacle, and the scheme was dropped. Kohler 128.

963. PARADISE LOST. A Poem. In Twelve Books. By John Milton. A New Edition. *Boston: Published By Phillips & Sampson. 122 Washington Street. 1846.* Second edition thus? 12mo in 6s, 294pp., original blind-stamped green cloth (a little worn, foxing throughout), spine lettered in gilt with gilt rules. The possible first edition thus by Phillips & Sampson was published in 1845 (also listed here with further editions cited). Scarce. Not in Kohler.

964. PARADISE LOST: A Poem, In Twelve Books, By John Milton; With A Life Of The Author, By The Rev. H. Stebbing, A, [sic] M. *Philadelphia: Uriah Hunt & Son, 44 North Fourth Street. 1846.* First edition thus? Small 8vo (5 ¼" × 3 ½"), 356 pp., black rule on title page, original brown leather spine, paper boards (a little worn), title page reprinted in black with decorative border trim on front cover (faded), advertisements on back cover (faded), spine ruled in gilt. Not in Kohler.

965. Variant of Preceding, original black calf, marbled boards (worn, rebacked with original spine laid down, front endpaper partially torn away, "Of The" rubbed out on title page), spine lettered in gilt with gilt rules. A good copy in a variant binding and much smaller size (near miniature) (4 ⅛" × 3") that much more cut down by the binder from the preceding copy. Not in Kohler.

966. PARADISE LOST: A Poem, In Twelve Books. By John Milton. With A Memoir Of The Author. Illustrated With Twelve Engravings. *Hartford: Published By S. Andrus & Son. MDCCCXLVII.* First edition thus? 12mo in 6s, 400pp., engraved frontispiece illustration of *Milton Dictating to His Daughters* engraved by "Lossing & Co." and ten additional illustrations after William Harvey (variously engraved by S. H. Clark, Maclees, Lossing, and unsigned), illustrations printed on slightly darker and thicker paper, half-title for each book with argument on verso, original black pebble morocco (worn along extremities and spine, joints cracked), with a rather brilliant gilt emblem of a cross within a crown of thorns amidst brilliant rays at the center of front cover and a different equally brilliant gilt emblem of a serpent wound around a flaming sword with apple on leaf amidst brilliant rays at the center of back cover, spine richly decorated in gilt with a depiction of Adam and Eve departing Eden in gilt at the top, and of a dove amidst brilliant rays in gilt at the bottom, with gilt lettering in the center (title and "Andrus' Illustrated Edition"), a.e.g. A good copy of a scarce mid-nineteenth-century American edition in a binding design similar to counterpart editions published earlier in the decade in London. Harvey's engravings include: (I) *Satan's Expulsion from Heaven*; (II) *Satan Presiding at the Infernal Council*; (III) *Garden of Eden*; (V) *Lucifer's First Act of Rebellion*; (VI) *Raphael in Conference with Adam*; (VII) *Urania*; (X) *Adam and Eve Hiding from the Presence of Their Maker*; (XI) *Effects of Adam's Fall on Creation*; (XI) *Cain and Abel* wrongly printed "IX" at top of corresponding page in all editions here; (XII) *Futurity Unfolded to Adam* labeled *Michael Unfolding Futurity to Adam* in 1847 and in 1851 editions. Of the "Twelve Engravings" called for on the title page, one engraving is not present in this edition: *Satan, Sin, and Death*. The plate would appear not to have been included; nor does it appear to be missing, since the binding is the original, with everything intact. Other editions of *PL* by S. Andrus & Son were published in 1849 and 1851 (see copy of each listed here), each with all twelve engravings, and in 1853 and 1856 (see copy of each listed here), each with the addition of an engraved frontispiece portrait plate after C. Burt and with all twelve engravings. Harvey's illustrations were first published in London by Tilt & Bogue in 1843 (see two-volume sets of *PW* listed here). The possible first edition of Milton's *PW* by Andrus & Son of Hartford with illustrations by Harvey (possibly the first appearance in America) was published in two volumes in 1847 (see set listed here). Scarce. Not in Kohler.

967. PARADISE LOST, A Poem, In Twelve Books. By John Milton. *Fitchburg, Mass. S. And C. Shepley. 1847*. First edition thus? Small 8vo, 220pp., engraved and printed title pages, engraved frontispiece portrait of Milton dictating to his daughters (unsigned, but after Stothard), protective tissue guards, undated engraved title page with vignette illustration of a woman in the foreground seated beside an urn with flowers and surrounded by a garden scene with a farming scene in the background consisting of man plowing behind a horse and plow with a home and trees farther in the background, original green cloth (a bit rubbed, some embrowning throughout), covers decorated in blind, central emblem in gilt on front cover, spine lettered and decorated in gilt, a.e.g. A good copy. The illustration appears to be added to embellish the edition of Milton's *PL* rather than to serve as an illustration for Milton's epic, as, e.g., with several editions by Leavitt & Allen. The possible second edition by Shepley was published in 1848 (copy listed here). Not in Kohler.

The collection also has a second copy in light blue cloth, with gilt spine, covers decorated only in blind, generally clean throughout, without a.e.g., and taller by ¼".

968. PARADISE LOST. In Twelve Parts. By John Milton. NIGHT THOUGHTS . . . By Edward Young. A New Edition. *Boston: Published By Phillips & Sampson, 110 Washington Street. 1847*. 2 volumes in one. First edition thus. 12mo in 6s, 294pp.,+288pp., frontispiece portrait of a robust Milton engraved by W. Hoogland after Samuel Cooper with a vignette illustration inset at the bottom consisting of Eve standing over Adam who is seated and clothed in a fig leaf, exhorting him with outstretched hand, protective tissue guard (bit age-browned), separate title page for Milton's *PL* and for Young's *Night Thoughts*, double black border around text, original reddish-brown cloth (a bit worn along extremities), elaborately gilt-decorated covers and spine with gilt lettering on spine, decorated endpapers, a.e.g. A good copy in an attractive (if a bit worn) publisher's binding.

Also in the collection and listed here: the second edition thus published in 1848; the third thus in 1849; the fourth thus in 1850 in which the publisher's imprint is changed from "Published By Phillips & Sampson" as it appears in the first three editions to "Phillips, Sampson, & Co."; later editions appear in 1851, 1852, and 1853 (each copy listed), and 1854 in which "New York: James C. Derby" appears on the title page for the first time, 1856 in which there is a different frontispiece portrait without vignette illustration inset at the bottom for the first time as well as the appearance of "New York: J. C. Derby" on the title page, 1857 in which the frontispiece portrait is that of the 1856 edition, but only "Boston: Phillips, Sampson, And Company" appear in the publisher's imprint; and 1859, with the frontispiece and publisher's imprint of the 1857 edition. See also separate editions of *PL* published by Phillips & Sampson without frontispiece portrait: the possible first edition thus in 1845 (also listed here with further editions cited). Not in Kohler.

969. PARADISE LOST. A Poem. In Twelve Books By John Milton. A New Edition. *Boston: Published By Phillips & Sampson. 122 Washington Street. 1847*. Third edition thus? 12mo in 6s, 294pp., original black leather spine (several small pieces missing at the top), marbled paper over boards (corners worn, earlier signatures on blanks), spine lettered and ruled in gilt. A good, tight copy. The possible first edition thus by Phillips & Sampson was published in 1845 (also listed here with further editions cited). Uncommon. Not in Kohler.

970. PARADISE LOST. By John Milton. With Explanatory Notes By The Rev. Henry Stebbing, A. M. *New–York: D. Appleton & Co., 200 Broadway[;] Philadelphia: Geo. S. Appleton, 148 Chestnut-St[.] MDCCCXLVIII*. 12mo, 296pp. (with pagination beginning at "p. 18" on verso of first page of Book I), unsigned engraved frontispiece illustration for Book II ("Caught in a fiery tempest . . . Each on his rock. . . . "), protective tissue guard, notes at the bottom of the page, contemporary dark green cloth (a little worn, top corner of back cover chewed, top of spine chipped, joints broken from within, lacking front fly-leaf), covers decorated in embossed blind trim, spine richly decorated in gilt with gilt lettering, a.e.g. A decent copy with early signature on verso of frontispiece and on back pastedown. The possible first edition thus was published in 1844 (also listed here with further editions cited; the pagination in each Appleton edition begins at "p. 18" on the verso of first page of Book I as here). Scarce. Not in Kohler.

971. PARADISE LOST. In Twelve Parts. By John Milton. NIGHT THOUGHTS . . . By Edward Young. A New Edition. *Boston: Published By Phillips & Sampson, 110 Washington Street. 1848*. 2 volumes in one. Second edition thus. 12mo in 6s, 294pp.,+288+[5]pp., frontispiece portrait of a robust Milton engraved by W. Hoogland after Samuel Cooper with a vignette illustration inset at the bottom consisting of Eve standing over Adam who is seated and clothed in a fig leaf, exhorting him with outstretched hand, with protective tissue guard (bit age-browned), separate title page for Milton's *PL* and for Young's *Night Thoughts*, double black border around text, original brown cloth (bit worn, spine ends chipped, slight foxing), elaborately gilt-decorated covers and spine with gilt lettering on spine, a.e.g. A fair copy with early signature in a neat hand (dated 1865) on fly-leaf. Five pages of advertisements bound in at the end. The possible first edition thus was published in 1847 (also listed here with further editions cited). Uncommon. Not in Kohler.

972. **PARADISE LOST**: A Poem, In Twelve Books, By John Milton; With A Life Of The Author, By The Rev. H. Stebbing, A, M. *New York: Leavitt & Allen. 379 Broadway. n.d. [ca. 1848]*. First edition thus? Bound with **PARADISE REGAINED, AND OTHER POEMS**. By John Milton. *New York: Leavitt & Allen. 379 Broadway. n.d. [ca. 1848]*. First edition thus by Leavitt? 2 volumes bound as one. Small 8vo (4 ¾" × 3 ½"), 356pp.,+190pp., engraved frontispiece illustration plate for Samuel Taylor Coleridge's "Fears in Solitude" (1798), engraved by Illman & Sons (a nature scene of a lady reclining beneath a large tree beside a lake with mountains in the background, with neither the poet, poem, or lines identified, although the lines illustrated are printed beneath the illustration), title page for each volume, contemporary blue pebble cloth (a little worn), central emblem in blind on each cover, spine lettered in gilt within decorative gilt trim ("Milton's Poetical Works," faded), a.e.g. A good copy. The illustration appears to be added to embellish the edition of Milton's poems, as with several other editions by Leavitt & Allen in the collection. *SA* and *C* are not included among the "Other Poems" in the second volume here, as with other editions published by Leavitt & Allen in the collection and referenced below. See copy of *PR* New York: Leavitt & Allen. 379 Broadway. n.d. [ca. 1848], below, as here. Not in Kohler.

See a second undated ca. 1848 edition following with same publisher's imprint as here, but a different edition (possible first edition thus) with different pagination (220 pp. compared to 356 pp. here), without frontispiece illustration, and a single volume. See also dated 1849 edition by "Leavitt & Company, 191 Broadway" (different publisher's imprint from that here) with an unsigned and untitled frontispiece illustration in color of Eve tempting Adam; and see a second dated 1849 edition by "Leavitt & Company, 191 Broadway" (different publisher's imprint from that here), without a frontispiece illustration.

See also other editions: several 1851 editions by "Leavitt & Company, 191 Broadway" (the same imprint for all 1851 editions) with variances between editions noted there, including a different frontispiece illustration in one copy and the appearance of "Leavitt's Cheap Edition"; 1852 edition by "Leavitt & Allen, 27 Dey Street"; several 1853 editions by "Leavitt & Allen, 27 Dey Street," variant editions with different numbers of pages and other variances noted there; 1856 edition, "Leavitt & Allen, 379 Broadway," with 220 pp.; undated ca. 1860s and undated ca. 1878 editions, "Leavitt & Allen Bros., No. 8 Howard Street," each bound with *PR, And Other Poems* as two volumes in one; and an undated ca. 1880s edition by "Leavitt & Allen Bros., No. 8 Howard Street," with a frontispiece portrait plate of Milton after C. Burt.

973. **PARADISE LOST**, A Poem, In Twelve Books. By John Milton. *New York: Leavitt & Allen. 379 Broadway. n.d. [ca. 1848]*. First edition thus by Leavitt? Small 8vo (4 ¾" × 3 ½"), 220 pp., contemporary gray cloth (a bit rubbed, two small chips near bottom of front joint, occasional foxing throughout, early names on front blank, some notations in pencil on front and back blanks), covers richly decorated in embossed blind floral trim, spine lettered in gilt and decorated in blind. A nice copy. Kohler 129, describing its copy "16mo. in 8s." and reporting "Not in the British Library. Not in the Bodleian Library. Not in Cambridge University Library."

974. **PARADISE LOST**. A Poem. In Twelve Books By John Milton. A New Edition. *Boston: Published By Phillips & Sampson. 122 Washington Street. 1848*. Fourth edition thus? 12mo in 6s, 294+[3]pp., original blind-stamped brown cloth (a little rubbed, sometime rebacked with original spine laid down, small tear at upper corner of fly-leaf repaired from backside, foxing throughout), spine lettered in gilt within thick gilt rules. A nice copy with contemporary signature in pencil on front blank. Three pages of advertisements bound in at end. The possible first edition thus by Phillips & Sampson was published in 1845 (also listed here with further editions cited). Not in Kohler.

975. **PARADISE LOST**, A Poem, In Twelve Books. By John Milton. *Fitchburg: Published By S. & C. Shepley, 1848*. Second edition thus? Small 8vo, 220pp., engraved frontispiece portrait of Milton dictating to his daughters (unsigned, but after Stothard), engraved and printed title pages, with vignette illustration on engraved title as with 1847 edition, original boards (front joint slightly split from the bottom up to about the halfway point, early owner's name lightly written on fly-leaf), title page with decorative black border trim reprinted on front cover, advertisement printed on back cover. A fine copy, virtually unused, except for occasional openings now and again, which account for the front joint being slightly split at the bottom. Called "School Edition" on front cover. The illustration appears to be more of a printer's decorative illustration than an illustration for Milton. The possible first edition by Shepley was published in 1847 (copy listed here). Not in Kohler.

976. THE PARADISE LOST OF JOHN MILTON, With Illustrations By John Martin. *London: Printed For Henry Washbourne, New Bridge Street. MDCCCXLIX.* 4to, [6]+373+[1]pp., the arguments for each book printed together at outset before Book I, with the twenty-four small mezzotint plates by John Martin, with the identifying logo, "Designed & Engraved by J. Martin, Esq.," at the center of each plate, each engraving measuring 5 ¾" × 8", three-quarter red morocco, red cloth, gilt rules on covers and spine with gilt lettering on spine, raised bands, "List Of The Engravings" bound in at end, bookplate. A fine copy with very sharp impressions of the mezzotint illustrations by John Martin. Martin's celebrated illustrations were first issued in twelve parts by Septimus Prowett between 1825 and 1827 (see set listed here); they were then published by Prowett in an edition of *PL*, in four different formats, in 1827 (see copies here with discussion of the different formats; of Martin's illustrations; and of subsequent editions). This is the first edition with the Martin plates published by Washbourne. Uncommon. Kohler 130, reporting "Not in the British Library. Not in the Bodleian Library. Not in Cambridge University Library."

977. PARADISE LOST: A Poem, In Twelve Books. By John Milton. With A Memoir Of The Author. Illustrated With Twelve Engravings. *Hartford: Published By S. Andrus & Son. MDCCCXLIX.* 12mo in 6s, 400+3+[2]pp., engraved frontispiece illustration of *Milton Dictating to His Daughters* engraved by "Lossing & Co." and eleven additional illustrations after Harvey (variously engraved by S. H. Clark, Maclees, Lossing, and unsigned), illustrations printed on slightly darker and thicker paper, half-title for each book with argument on verso, contemporary brown pebble calf (worn along joints and extremities and at corners, bottom of spine chipped), covers richly decorated in gilt, spine illustrated with a depiction of Adam and Eve departing Eden in gilt at the top and of a dove amidst brilliant rays in gilt at the bottom with gilt lettering in the center (title and "Andrus' Illustrated Edition"), a.e.g. A good copy of an uncommon edition. Harvey's engravings include the same eleven identified in the 1847 first Andrus edition listed here, plus the twelfth engraving: "Satan, Sin, & Death," (IV). See 1847 Andrus edition of *PL* (first thus, copy listed and other editions by Andrus cited there). Harvey's illustrations were first published in London by Tilt & Bogue in 1843 (see two-volume sets of *PW* here). The possible first edition of Milton's *PW* by Andrus & Son of Hartford with illustrations after Harvey (possible first appearance in America) was published in two volumes in 1847 (see set listed here). Scarce. Not in Kohler.

978. PARADISE LOST: A Poem, In Twelve Books. By John Milton. *New York: Published By Clark, Austin & Co. 205 Broadway. 1849.* First edition thus? 12mo in 6s, 283pp., engraved frontispiece illustration plate with vignette illustration (unsigned, for "Book III. L.667," with the lines quoted), engraved title-page plate (entitled "Milton's Poetical Works") with vignette illustration (unsigned, for "Book X. L.940," with the lines quoted), "The Life of John Milton" by Fenton, possibly the first appearance of illustration plates for Books II, IV, V, VIII, IX, X, XI, and XII (Books II, III, and X unsigned, Books IV, V, VIII, IX, XI, and XII signed "Anderson," the plates generally very clean and crisp), "Index To Paradise Lost" at the end, original light brown cloth (light wear, spine ends chipped, end blank missing, vignette illustrations on frontispiece plate and engraved title foxed, looking almost tinted in appearance), embossed covers, spine elaborately decorated in gilt with gilt lettering. Good copy of an uncommon mid-nineteenth-century American edition of *PL*, in a nice publisher's binding with contemporary presentation inscription on front blank. Uncommon. Not in Kohler.

See 1850 edition listed here of *PL* by Clark Austin & Co. (with same publisher's imprint as here), published together with *PR and Other Poems* with the same engraved frontispiece illustration plate and engraved title-page plate for "Milton's Poetical Works" as here but without the eight additional illustration plates here; and see variant 1850 edition listed here (with same publisher's imprint as here and other 1850 illustrated edition) with 321 pp. and a variant frontispiece illustration with variant illustration on engraved title page. See also nonillustrated editions listed here: in 1849, the same year as here and "Published By Clark, Austin & Co., 205 Broadway," identical to the edition here, except not illustrated and published as a "School Edition"; in 1850 ("Published By Clark, Austin & Co., 205 Broadway") similar to 1850 illustrated edition, except not illustrated; in ca. 1850 (published by "Clark, Austin & Smith, 3 Park Row And 3 Ann-Street"); in 1852 ("Published By Clark, Austin & Co., 205 Broadway"); in 1853 (two editions: one "Published By Clark, Austin & Co., 205 Broadway" dated "1851" on title page, the other published by "Clark, Austin & Smith, 3 Park Row And 3 Ann-Street" dated "1853" on title page, both with "Clark, Austin & Smith, 3 Park Row And 3 Ann-Street" dated "1853" on front cover); in 1855, in 1857, and in 1858, with "School Edition . . . New York: Clark, Austin & Smith, 3 Park Row And 3 Ann-Street" on front cover; see also undated ca. 1879 edition listed here published by "Clark and Maynard" with title page for Clark, Austin & Smith edition of *PL* repeated on front cover ("School Edition . . . New York: Clark, Austin & Smith, 3 Park Row And 3 Ann-Street")—all editions listed here.

979. PARADISE LOST. In Twelve Parts. By John Milton. **NIGHT THOUGHTS** . . . By Edward Young. A New Edition. *Boston: Published By Phillips & Sampson, 110 Washington Street. 1849.* 2 volumes in one. Third edition thus. 12mo in 6s, 294pp.,+288pp., frontispiece portrait of Milton engraved by W. Hoogland after Samuel Cooper with a vignette illustration inset at the bottom consisting of Eve standing over Adam who is seated and clothed in a fig leaf, exhorting him with outstretched hand, with protective tissue guard (slightly foxed), title page for Milton's *PL* with same title page repeated for Young's *Night Thoughts*, double black border around text, original red cloth (first title page a bit age-browned with corner bends in lower right corner), covers elaborately decorated in blind trim, with central device of harp and laurel in gilt on front cover, spine elaborately decorated in gilt with gilt lettering. Nice copy. Uncommon mid-nineteenth-century American edition. The first edition thus by Phillips & Sampson was published in 1847 (copy listed and other editions cited there). Not in Kohler.

980. PARADISE LOST, A Poem, In Twelve Books. By John Milton. *New York: Leavitt & Company, 191 Broadway, 1849.* Small 8vo (4 ⅝" × 3 ⅛"), 220pp., unsigned frontispiece illustration in color of Eve tempting Adam, life by Fenton, original brown cloth (a bit worn with spine chipped at lower front joint), covers decorated in blind with large bright central gilt decoration of poet's memorial tomb on front cover with a figure in gilt wrapped in laurel standing on tomb, the whole within a thick rounded bright gilt frame, same large bright gilt decoration on back cover with an urn with flowers replacing the figure on poet's memorial tomb and with doves in gilt above, the whole within a thick rounded bright gilt frame as on front cover, spine decorated and lettered in gilt, a.e.g., bookseller's label on front pastedown. An uncommon mid-nineteenth-century American edition with an interesting unsigned frontispiece illustration in color. The first edition thus by Leavitt & Allen was published ca. 1848 (copy listed and other editions by Leavitt & Allen cited there). Not in Kohler.

981. Variant of Preceding, original brown cloth (covers a bit soiled, early name in pencil on front fly-leaf, foxing), covers ruled in blind relief with "Leavitt's School Edition" stamped at the center within decorative blind trim, spine decorated in blind and lettered in gilt. A nice copy, tightly bound, without a frontispiece illustration in a variant publisher's binding with early bookseller's label on front pastedown. Not in Kohler.

982. Variant of Preceding, original olive green cloth (shadow of older waterstain inside bottom portion of first twenty-five pages), covers embossed in blind trim with large central bright gilt decoration (as on the back cover of the first copy) of urn with poet's memorial tomb and doves in gilt above, the whole within a thick rounded bright gilt frame, the gilt emblems crisp and bright, spine decorated in gilt with gilt lettering, a.e.g. A nice copy, tightly bound, without a frontispiece illustration in a fine attractive variant publisher's binding. Not in Kohler.

983. PARADISE LOST: A Poem, In Twelve Books. By John Milton. *New York: Published By Clark, Austin & Co. 205 Broadway. 1849.* 12mo in 6s, 283pp., "The Life of John Milton" by Fenton, "Index To *PL*" at the end, original maroon leather spine (small piece missing from top), printed paper boards (aged, corners worn, small piece missing in back), title reproduced on front cover, advertisement on back cover, gilt rules on spine. Labeled "School Edition" on front cover. Decent copy with early name in pencil on front blanks. The first edition by Clark Austin & Co. was also published with illustrations in the same year, 1849 (copy listed and other editions cited there). Not in Kohler.

984. PARADISE LOST: A Poem, In Twelve Books, By John Milton. With Explanatory Notes And A Life Of The Author. By The Rev. H. Stebbing, A.M. *Cincinnati: J. A. & U. P. James. Walnut Street, Between Fourth And Fifth, 1849.* First edition thus? Small 8vo in 4s and 8s, 287pp., contemporary light green cloth (a few slight foxing spots on edges), covers decorated in blind, spine richly decorated and lettered in gilt. A very nice copy of this pocket-size edition in excellent condition. Scarce. Not in Kohler.

985. PARADISE LOST. A Poem, In Twelve Books, By John Milton: With Explanatory Notes And A Life Of The Author. By The Rev. H. Stebbing, A. M. Stereotyped By J. A. James. *Philadelphia: Kay & Troutman, 193 Market Street. Pittsburgh:—C. H. Kay. 1849.* Small 8vo, x+312pp., life at the beginning, page of notes at the end, original calf (worn, joints cracked, spine chipped at top, early dated name on front blank with additional names in pencil on front and back blanks), black leather label lettered and ruled in gilt on spine. A decent copy of an uncommon edition. The possible first edition thus (with variant publisher's imprint from that here) was published in 1836 (copy listed and other editions cited there). Not in Kohler.

986. THE PARADISE LOST By John Milton. With Notes Explanatory And Critical. Edited By Rev. James Robert Boyd, Author of "Elements of Rhetoric," And "Eclectic Moral Philosophy." Milton, whose genius had angelic wings And fed on manna.—Cowper. *New York: Baker And Scribner. 1850*. First edition thus by Boyd. 8vo, 542pp., ten-page "Reasons For Preparing This American Edition" before Book I, six illustration plates, engraved by C. Burt after John Martin (reduced, plates included are for Books I, II, IV, VII, XI [as frontispiece], and XII), each with protective tissue guard, introductory and concluding remarks for each book, notes at bottom of page, "Concluding Observations," "The Life Of Milton A Great Epic Itself" (Gilfillan), "Strictures Upon Dr. Johnson's Criticism" (Sir E. Brydges) at end, original purple cloth (slightly rubbed), covers ruled in gilt with decorative gilt border trim and elaborate gilt corner pieces with central lettering in blind, spine elaborately decorated in gilt with gilt lettering, a.e.g. A fine copy with six attractive plates engraved by Burt after the stunning designs of John Martin in what appears to be a publisher's gift binding. First edition as edited with an introduction and copious commentary, by Rev. James Robert Boyd. Not in Kohler.

Rev. James Robert Boyd wrote treatises on rhetoric, literary criticism, and moral philosophy, which were widely used as textbooks during the late nineteenth century. His textbook here on Milton became enormously popular and was reprinted numerous times, not always with illustration plates after Martin: in 1851 and 1852, second and third Boyd editions, each published without illustration plates after Martin (each listed here); in 1853, "Published By A. S. Barnes & Co." in New York and by "H. W. Derby & Co." in Cincinnati in the same 8vo format as here with reduced illustration plates after Martin as here and with the addition of an index at the end; in 1854 and 1855 (copy of each in the collection, each a reprint of this edition, each not listed); in 1856, 1857, 1859 (copy of each in the collection, each a reprint of this edition, each not listed); in 1860; in 1862, 1864, 1865, 1866 (copy of each in the collection, each a reprint of this edition, each not listed); in 1868; in 1870; in 1872 revised edition; in 1873; and ca. 1888—all listed here.

987. PARADISE LOST: A Poem, In Twelve Books. By John Milton. *New York: Published By Clark, Austin & Co. 205 Broadway. 1850*. 12mo in 6s, 283pp., engraved frontispiece illustration plate with vignette illustration (unsigned, for "Book III. L.667," with the lines quoted), engraved title-page plate (entitled "Milton's Poetical Works") with vignette illustration (unsigned, for "Book X. L.940," with the lines quoted) on engraved title, "The Life of John Milton" by Fenton, "Index To Paradise Lost" at the end. Bound with **PARADISE REGAINED, AND OTHER POEMS** By John Milton. *New York: Published By Clark, Austin & Co. 205 Broadway. 1850*. 12mo in 6s, 215pp., "A Critique On *PR*," half-title for *C* and *SA*. 2 volumes in one. Original ribbed brown cloth (foxing throughout), covers ruled in blind with large emblem in blind at the center, spine richly decorated in gilt with gilt lettering ("Milton's Poetical Works"), small early bookseller's label tipped in at top of front pastedown. A fine copy. The first edition of *PL* by Clark Austin & Co was published in 1849 (copy listed and other editions cited there); see also copy of separate 1850 edition of *PR* listed here; and see copy of 1851 edition of *PW* listed here, which is like this copy with the same frontispiece illustration and engraved title page but with the printed title pages for *PL* and *PR* dated 1851 and 1850. Not in Kohler.

988. PARADISE LOST: A Poem, In Twelve Books. Together With A Life Of The Author. *New York: Published By Clark, Austin & Co. 205 Broadway. 1850*. Variant edition. 12mo in 6s, 321pp., engraved frontispiece illustration plate with vignette illustration (unsigned, for Book I, with reference cited), protective tissue guard, engraved title page (entitled "The Poetical Works Of John Milton") with vignette illustration (unsigned, for Book I, with reference cited), "The Life of John Milton" by Fenton, half-title for each book, original red pebble grain cloth (covers and edges rubbed with a few marks, ends of spine and corners worn, some scattered foxing), covers decorated in blind, spine richly decorated in gilt with gilt lettering, decorated endpapers. A decent copy with early presentation inscription on front blank and small contemporary bookstore label tipped on at top of front pastedown. This is a variant edition from the preceding, with a different title page, with a different number of pages, a different frontispiece illustration, a different vignette illustration on the engraved title page, and no index at the end. Uncommon. Kohler 131, calling its copy "Octavo" with, as here, "321 pp." and reporting "Not in the British Library. Not in the Bodleian Library. Not in Cambridge University Library."

989. PARADISE LOST. By John Milton. With Explanatory Notes By The Rev. Henry Stebbing, A.M. *New York: D. Appleton & Co., 200 Broadway[,] Philadelphia: Geo. S. Appleton, 164 Chestnut-St[.] M DCCC L*. Fifth edition thus? 12mo, 296pp. (with pagination beginning at p. 18 on verso of first page of Book I), engraved frontispiece illustration (the expulsion scene, unsigned, but after Turner), protective tissue guard, notes at the bottom of the page, contemporary olive green cloth (a little worn and stained, joints split, spine chipped at top and bottom, slight foxing throughout, early names on front endpapers), covers finely tooled in blind, spine decorated and lettered in gilt. The possible first edition thus was published in 1844 (also listed here with further editions cited; the pagination in each

Appleton edition begins at "p. 18" on the verso of the first page of Book I as here). Scarce. Not in Kohler.

990. PARADISE LOST. In Twelve Parts. By John Milton. NIGHT THOUGHTS . . . By Edward Young. A New Edition. *Boston: Phillips, Sampson, & Co., 110 Washington Street. 1850.* 2 volumes in one. Fourth edition thus. 12mo in 6s, 294pp.,+288+[6]pp., frontispiece portrait of Milton engraved by W. Hoogland after Samuel Cooper with a vignette illustration inset at the bottom consisting of Eve standing over Adam who is seated and clothed in a fig leaf, exhorting him with outstretched hand, with protective tissue guard (frontispiece and tissue guard very foxed), title page for Milton's *PL* and for Young's *Night Thoughts*, double black border around text, original red cloth (a little worn, back joint cracked, spine chipped at top and bottom), covers elaborately decorated in blind, with central gilt device of harp and laurel on front cover, spine elaborately decorated in gilt with gilt lettering, with early ownership stamp on front blank. Six pages of advertisements bound in at end. This edition is identical to earlier editions except for a change in the publisher's imprint: from "Published By Phillips & Sampson" to "Phillips, Sampson, & Co." The first edition thus by Phillips & Sampson was published in 1847 (copy listed and other editions cited there). Not in Kohler.

991. PARADISE LOST. A Poem. In Twelve Books By John Milton. A New Edition. *Boston: Phillips, Sampson, & Co., 110 Washington Street. 1850.* 12mo in 6s, 294pp., original half black calf, marbled paper over boards (bit rubbed, slight age-browning), spine lettered and ruled in gilt. A very nice copy with contemporary ownership signature on fly-leaf. The possible first edition thus by Phillips & Sampson was published in 1845 (copy listed and other editions cited there). Not in Kohler.

992. PARADISE LOST: By John Milton: To Which Is Prefixed The Life Of The Author, Together With Dr. Channing's Essay On The Poetical Genius of Milton. *Halifax: Printed And Published By William Milner, Cheapside. MDCCCL.* Small 8vo (5" × 3 ⅔"), xiv+239pp., half-title, "Chromo Lith." decorated title-page plate, with title "Milton's Paradise Lost" in gold, red, and blue within gold rule, the whole within a colorful decorative floral border in red and green within gold rule in the manner of medieval manuscript illumination with "Stott" printed in the bottom left-hand corner and "Chromo Lith" in bottom right-hand corner, printed title page, original red cloth (a bit rubbed, a few pages with spots of foxing), covers decorated in blind with a small bust of Milton on top of a book with laurel branch below and pen and quill beside at the center of front cover, spine lettered and decorated in gilt (faded), a.e.g. A nice copy with an attractive colorful "Chromo Lith." decorated title page. Uncommon. Not in Kohler.

993. PARADISE LOST A Poem In Twelve Books. By John Milton. *New York: Clark, Austin & Smith, 3 Park Row And 3 Ann-Street. n.d. [ca. 1850].* 12mo in 6s, 283pp., life of Milton by Fenton, index at the end, original dark brown leather spine (worn, small piece missing at bottom), tan paper over boards (both covers slightly stained and chipped, age-browning throughout with darker staining on inner edge of last portion of book), title page repeated on front cover, advertisements on back cover). Labeled "School Edition" on front cover. All in all, a decent copy of an uncommon book. The first edition by Clark Austin & Co. as a "School Edition" was published in 1849 (copy listed here); see also the illustrated edition published by Clark Austin & Co. in the same year, 1849 (copy listed and other editions cited there). Scarce. Not in Kohler.

994. PARADISE LOST: A Poem, In Twelve Books, By John Milton With Explanatory Notes And A Life Of The Author. By The Rev. H. Stebbing, A. M. *Cincinnati: Published By U. P. James, No. 167 Walnut Street. n.d. [ca. 1850].* First edition thus? Small 8vo (3 ½" × 5"), 287pp., original light brown paper boards reprinting title page on front cover and a list of "Choice Books" (of which this is one) on back cover, brown cloth spine. A lovely copy of this near-miniature edition. Scarce. Not in Kohler.

995. DAS VERLORENE PARADIES. Ein Gedicht in 12 Gesangen von John Milton. Deutsch von Adolf Böttger. *Leipzig, Druck und Berlag von Philip Reclam jun. n.d. [ca. 1850].* First edition thus? Small 8vo, 313+[21]pp., original maroon cloth (a bit rubbed, spine very faded), covers richly embossed in blind with large decorative gilt emblem finely trimmed in gilt at the center of front cover incorporating title in gilt lettering, spine decorated and lettered in gilt (faded), speckled edges. Translated into German verse by Adolf Böttger; "Proofed and Published by Philip Reclam jun." Uncommon. Not in Kohler.

996. PARADISE LOST, PARADISE REGAINED, AND OTHER POEMS, By John Milton. *Manchester: Printed And Published By Thomas Johnson, Livesey Street. 1851.* Small 8vo, 355pp.,+334pp., engraved frontispiece portrait plate ("Romney sculpt"), engraved title-page plate (entitled "Milton's Poetical Works") with vignette illustration of Raphael counseling Adam and Eve (unsigned, for Book V), "London: Engraved For The English Classics. Published By Thomas Johnson. Manchester" printed at the bottom, small unsigned vignette illustration at the head of each book. Bound with *PR* and other poems, without separate title page, although separately paginated, half-title for each book of *PR* with small unsigned vignette illustration at the head of each book, half-title for *SA* and for *C* with small unsigned vignette illustration at the head of each poem, half-title for several of the other poems, original brown ribbed silk cloth (bit rubbed, with unobtrusive small spot on each cover, lacking front fly-leaf, with early name written neatly on verso of frontispiece), covers intricately decorated in embossed blind trim, spine elaborately decorated in gilt with gilt lettering at top ("Milton's Poetical Works") and small vignette of an angel playing a harp at the center, top and fore-edges rough. A nice copy intended to serve as Milton's *PW* with appropriate half-title and with spine labeled accordingly, in an attractive publisher's binding, with interesting unsigned vignette illustrations. Not in Kohler.

997. PARADISE LOST. By John Milton. With Notes By Sir Egerton Brydges, Bart. [Quote from Thomson] Elegantly Illustrated With Designs By Martin. *Philadelphia: Geo. S. Appleton, 164 Chestnut Street. New York: D Appleton & Co., 200 Broadway. 1851.* First edition by Appleton with Martin plates. 8vo in 4s, 415pp., life of Milton, frontispiece illustration plate and six additional illustration plates by John Martin for *PL* (reduced plates for Books IV, V, two for IX, two for X, and XII), protective tissue guards (a bit foxed), original dedication leaf and original advertisement for 1835 edition, life of Milton, notes at bottom of the page, contemporary calf (front cover warped, joints cracked, slight foxing throughout, including plates), covers decorated with varying sized gilt borders and decorative gilt trim with indented panel at the center decorated with blind trim and a central harp, spine richly decorated in gilt within the panels and gilt lettering, a.e.g. Except for the warped cover and splitting joints, a nice copy in attractive contemporary American binding with a possibly contemporary inscription on fly-leaf. The possible first edition by Appleton was published in a 12mo format in 1844 (copy listed and other editions cited there); see also copy of 1851 8vo Appleton edition listed here without illustration plates after Martin, where pagination is the same as here. Scarce. Not in Kohler.

998. PARADISE LOST: A Poem, In Twelve Books. By John Milton. With A Memoir Of The Author. Illustrated With Twelve Engravings. *Hartford: Published By S. Andrus & Son. 1851.* 12mo in 6s, 400pp., engraved frontispiece illustration of *Milton Dictating to His Daughters* engraved by "Lossing & Co." and eleven additional illustrations by Harvey (variously engraved by S. H. Clark, Maclees, Lossing, and unsigned), half-title for each book with argument on verso, contemporary calf (a bit rubbed, spine slightly scuffed), black leather label with gilt lettering and gilt rules on spine (label slightly chipped), raised bands within gilt rules, outer dentelles finely tooled in gilt, marbled edges. A very nice copy in an attractive calf binding of the period. Harvey's engravings include the same as those included in the 1849 Andrus edition here. See 1847 Andrus edition of *PL* (copy listed and other editions cited there). Harvey's illustrations were first published in London by Tilt & Bogue in 1843 (see two-volume sets of *PW* here). The possible first edition of Milton's *PW* by Andrus & Son of Hartford with illustrations after Harvey (possible first appearance in America) was published in two volumes in 1847 (see set listed here). Uncommon. Not in Kohler.

999. PARADISE LOST. A Poem In Twelve Books. By John Milton. *New York: Published By Clark, Austin & Co. 205 Broadway. 1851.* 12mo in 6s, 283pp., engraved frontispiece illustration plate with vignette illustration (unsigned, for "Book III. L.667," with the lines quoted), engraved title-page plate (entitled "Milton's Poetical Works") with vignette illustration (unsigned, for "Book X. L.940," with the lines quoted), "The Life of John Milton" by Fenton, "Index To *PL*" at the end. Bound with **PARADISE REGAINED, AND OTHER POEMS** By John Milton. *New York: Published By Clark, Austin & Co. 205 Broadway. 1851.* 12mo, 215pp., contents, half-titles for *C* and *SA*. 2 volumes in one. Original ribbed green cloth (slight waterstaining first fifteen pages, including frontispiece and title page, light embrowning throughout), covers ruled in blind with large emblem in blind at the center, spine richly decorated in gilt with gilt lettering ("Milton's Poetical Works Complete"). The first edition thus by Clark Austin & Co was published in 1849 (also listed here with further editions cited). Uncommon. Not in Kohler.

1000. PARADISE LOST. In Twelve Parts. By John Milton. NIGHT THOUGHTS... By Edward Young. A New Edition. *Boston: Phillips, Sampson, & Co., 110 Washington Street. 1851.* 2 volumes in one. 12mo in 6s, 294pp.,+288pp., frontispiece portrait of a robust Milton engraved by W. Hoogland after Samuel Cooper with a vignette illustration inset at the bottom consisting of Eve standing over Adam who is seated and clothed in a fig leaf, exhorting him with outstretched hand, with protective tissue guard (a bit foxed), title page for Milton's *PL* and for Young's *Night Thoughts*, double black border around text, original dark maroon cloth (a bit worn, spine ends slightly chipped, frontispiece and title page a little foxed because of the protective tissue guard), elaborately gilt-decorated covers and spine with gilt lettering on spine, a.e.g. A nice copy with early signature in a neat hand on fly-leaf. The first edition thus by Phillips & Sampson was published in 1847 (also listed here with further editions cited). Not in Kohler.

1001. MILTON IL PARADISO PERDUTO POEMA [nella traduzione di Lazzaro Papi.] *Milano[:] Per Borroni e Scotti[,] 1851.* Small 8vo, 460pp., engraved frontispiece illustration of Raphael beholding Eve within an elaborate border trim with "?Sisco. dif" and "Ga. Bonatti. ?inc. ?acciajo" at bottom, engraved title page with engraved vignette illustration of the expulsion after "Gael. Bonatti inc," "Con notizie intorno alla vita di Milton e del Papi e con 'Osservazioni critiche sul "Paradiso Perduto" di Addisson,'" "Annotazioni" before each book, original paper wrappers (front wrapper detached and curled along edges, spine cracked, slight foxing throughout), with unsigned engraved illustration of Milton dictating to his daughter on front cover. A fairly nice copy with possibly contemporary/early name on front cover in a protective box. Scarce. Not in Kohler.

1002. PARADISE LOST, A Poem, In Twelve Books. By John Milton. *New York: Leavitt & Company, 191 Broadway, 1851.* Small 8vo (4 ⅝" × 3 ⅛"), 220pp., frontispiece illustration plate (of a young man with outspread arms on the shoulders of a wingéd angel in flight, unsigned), life of Milton by Fenton, original brown cloth (a little aged, small smudge on spine and on front cover), covers decorated in embossed trim with vignette in gilt at the center of a seated figure with open book and cupid above with arrow aimed directly at the seated figure, all within a gilt frame, spine elaborately decorated in gilt with gilt lettering, decorated endpapers, a.e.g. Decent copy of an uncommon edition with an unusual frontispiece illustration not present in the other editions published by Leavitt & Company this year or in other years. While the frontispiece illustration appears to be an illustration with a Miltonic theme, it nonetheless remains unidentified and unsigned, and therefore could simply be an illustration "of the period" used by the publisher to embellish the edition of Milton's poems, as with several other editions by Leavitt & Allen in the collection. The first edition thus by Leavitt & Allen was published 1848 (also listed here with further editions by Leavitt & Allen cited). Not in Kohler.

1003. Variant of Preceding. PARADISE LOST, A Poem, In Twelve Books. By John Milton. *New York: Leavitt & Company, 191 Broadway, 1851.* Small 8vo (4 ⅝" × 3 ⅛"), 220pp., unsigned frontispiece illustration plate not for Milton (of an elegantly dressed lady beside a large urn), original olive green cloth (a bit worn, some age-browning), covers decorated in embossed trim with vignette in gilt at the center of a seated figure with open book and cupid above with arrow aimed directly at the seated figure, all within a gilt frame, spine elaborately decorated in gilt with gilt lettering, decorated endpapers, a.e.g. Nice copy. Not in Kohler.

1004. Variant of Preceding. Variant edition ("Leavitt's Cheap Edition"). Small 8vo (4 ½" × 3 ½"), 356pp., contemporary light reddish-brown cloth (a bit rubbed, a little faded, spine slightly chipped at top and bottom, occasional foxing throughout with slight staining at the outer top edge of first few pages), covers ruled in blind with large decorative piece in blind at the center incorporating the lettering "Leavitt's Cheap Edition," spine decorated in blind and lettered in gilt. Rather nice copy of this variant thick pocket-size edition in a variant publisher's binding with early ownership signature in pencil on fly-leaf. Not in Kohler.

1005. Variant of Preceding, contemporary blue-green cloth (a little worn), covers ruled in blind with large decorative piece in blind at the center incorporating the lettering "Leavitt's Cheap Edition," spine decorated in blind and lettered in gilt. All in all, a nice copy of this variant pocket-size edition in a variant publisher's binding with early presentation inscription in pencil on front blank. Not in Kohler.

1006. Variant of Preceding. PARADISE LOST: A Poem, In Twelve Books, By John Milton; With A Life Of The Author, By The Rev. H. Stebbing, A, [sic] M. *New York: Leavitt & Company, 191 Broadway. 1851.* Together with **PARADISE REGAINED, AND OTHER POEMS.** By John Milton. *New-York: Leavitt & Company, 191 Broadway[,] 1851.* 2 volumes in one. Thick, small 8vo (5 ¼" × 3 ¾" × 1 ½" wide), 356pp.,+190pp., title page for each volume, black rule around text, original decorated red cloth, covers and spine richly decorated in embossed gilt figurines and floral gilt trim, including a lady seated and playing the harp within decorative gilt floral trim at the center of each cover and a young man seated and playing a horn in one corner and a young couple walking in the other corner at the bottom of each cover, with gilt lettering on spine ("Milton's Poetical Works"), a young lady standing and playing a harp at the bottom, and "Leavitts Cabinet Series" in embossed red within a gilt background at the bottom, a.e.g. A lovely copy in a beautiful and well-preserved variant publisher's decorated cloth binding with contemporary presentation inscription (dated 1855), and several additional early inscriptions on front blanks, including this notation in a neat hand at the top of fly-leaf: "The last book read by Aunt-Libbie, who died October 27 … 1873." While titled "Milton's Poetical Works" on the spine, *SA* and *C* are not included among the "Other Poems" in the second volume here, as in other editions by Leavitt & Company in the collection. A variant edition of "Leavitt's Cheap Edition." The first edition thus by Leavitt & Allen was published in 1848 (also listed here with further editions cited). Not in Kohler.

1007. PARADISE LOST, By John Milton; To Which Is Prefixed The Life Of The Author. *London: William Tegg And Co., 85, Queen Street, Cheapside. 1851.* First edition thus? 12mo in 6s, xi+[1]+325pp., original brown cloth (a bit rubbed, back joint cracked, spine chipped with a small piece missing at top right), covers decorated in embossed blind trim, spine lettered in gilt with decorative embossed blind trim, top and bottom edges untrimmed. A nice copy with early presentation inscription (dated 1886) on fly-leaf. Scarce. Not in Kohler.

1008. PARADISE LOST. By John Milton. With Notes By Sir Egerton Brydges, Bart. [Quotation From Thomson]. *Philadelphia: Geo. S. Appleton, 164 Chestnut Street. New York: D. Appleton & Co., 200 Broadway. 1851.* 8vo, 415pp., half-title, original dedication page to Wordsworth and Southey, "Advertisement To The Original Edition," life of Milton with appendix, introductory remarks to *Paradise Lost*, notes at the bottom of the page, black border around text, contemporary calf (a bit rubbed), gilt rules on spine, black leather label with gilt lettering and gilt rules. A nice copy. The possible first edition by Appleton was published in a 12mo format in 1844 (see copy listed here with other editions cited). See also copy of 1851 8vo Appleton edition with illustration plates after Martin; this is that edition published without the illustrations. Scarce. Not in Kohler.

1009. THE PARADISE LOST By John Milton. With Notes Explanatory And Critical. Edited By Rev. James Robert Boyd, Author Of "Elements Of Rhetoric," And "Eclectic Moral Philosophy." Milton, whose genius had angelic wings And fed on manna.—Cowper. *New York: Baker And Scribner. 1851.* Second edition by Boyd. 8vo in 4s, 542pp., content as with first edition in 1850, original green cloth (a little rubbed, slight age-browning, notes in an early hand on endpapers in a neat hand, some marginal notations in the same neat hand), covers decorated in blind with central emblem on each cover, spine decorated in blind and lettered in gilt. A nice copy. The first edition edited by Boyd was published in 1850 by "Baker And Scribner" in New York with reduced illustration plates after Martin (copy listed and other editions by Boyd cited there). Scarce. Not in Kohler.

1009A. (Cross-listing) PARADISE LOST. A Poem In Twelve Books. By John Milton. *New York: Published By Clark, Austin & Co., 205 Broadway. 1851.* 12mo in 6s, 283pp., life of Milton by Fenton before the poem, index at the end, original leather spine (worn), blue paper over boards (used), title page repeated on front cover, but with different publisher's imprint and date: "New York: Clark, Austin & Smith, 3 Park Row And 3 Ann-Street. *1853*," advertisements on back cover. Labeled "School Edition" on front cover. Scarce. Not in Kohler. See main listing under *PL*, 1853.

1010. PARADISE LOST. In Twelve Parts. By John Milton. NIGHT THOUGHTS . . . By Edward Young. A New Edition. *Boston: Phillips, Sampson, & Co., 110 Washington Street. 1852.* 2 volumes in one. 12mo, 294pp.,+288pp., frontispiece portrait of a robust Milton engraved by W. Hoogland after Samuel Cooper with a vignette illustration inset at the bottom consisting of Eve standing over Adam (who is seated and clothed in a fig leaf, exhorting him with outstretched hand), protective tissue guard, title page for Milton's *PL* and for Young's *Night Thoughts*, double border around text, original black cloth, richly gilt-decorated covers and spine, a.e.g. A most attractive copy in a fine mid-nineteenth-century American binding with elaborate gilt design on the covers and spine, in well-preserved condition, with neat contemporary signature (dated 1855) on fly-leaf. Uncommon, especially in such fine condition. The first edition by Phillips & Sampson was published in 1847 (also listed here with further editions cited). Not in Kohler.

1011. PARADISE LOST: A Poem, In Twelve Books. By John Milton. *Edinburgh: James Nichol. Glasgow: J. Griffin & Co. MDCCCLII.* First edition thus. 12mo in 6s, 337pp., frontispiece portrait of Milton engraved by J. T. Wedgwood after J. Thurston, "From a Picture by Dobson in Dr. Williams's Library. Edinburgh. James Nichol," half-title before the poem, original bright dark green pebble cloth (a bit rubbed, small chip on corner), covers ruled in blind relief, spine lettered in embossed green within elaborate gilt device at the top, circular piece in blind toward the bottom, t.e. rough. A good copy with near-contemporary signature in pencil on verso of frontispiece. Williamson 237; Kohler 132, reporting "Not in the British Library. Not in the Bodleian Library. Not in Cambridge University Library."

1012. Variant of Preceding, original olive green cloth (a bit rubbed with several spots, spine ends chipped, dated contemporary signature at top of title page), covers decorated in blind with elaborate border trim in blind, title and Milton's name in blind at the center with decorative floral trim in blind above and below, spine lettered in gilt within gilt rules at the top, several decorative pieces in blind, "Edin J. Nichols" in blind at the bottom. A good copy in a very interesting variant publisher's binding without frontispiece portrait, which appears not to have been bound in originally. Variant of Kohler 132.

1013. THE PARADISE LOST By John Milton. With Notes Explanatory And Critical[.] Edited By Rev. James R. Boyd, A.M. Author Of "Elements Of Rhetoric," And

"Eclectic Moral Philosophy." Milton, Whose Genius Had Angelic Wings, And Fed On Manna.—Cowper. *New York: Published by A. S. Barnes & Co.[;] Cincinnati:–H. W. Derby & Co. 1852.* Third edition by Boyd. 8vo, 552pp., content as with first edition in 1850, original red cloth with black cloth spine (worn, covers detached, top part of spine missing), decorated endpapers with advertisements. While the covers are worn, the book is internally very sound, with contemporary ownership signatures on front blanks. The first edition edited by Boyd was published in 1850 by "Baker And Scribner" in New York, with reduced illustration plates after Martin (also listed here with further editions by Boyd cited). Scarce. Not in Kohler.

1014. PARADISE LOST. A Poem. In Twelve Books By John Milton. A New Edition. *Boston: Phillips, Sampson, & Co., 110 Washington Street. 1852.* 12mo in 6s, 294+[8]pp., original half black calf, marbled paper over boards (worn, a small piece of marbled paper missing from front cover, small portion missing at top of the spine, some slight inoffensive waterstaining at the lower corners of several pages at the beginning and at the end), spine lettered and ruled in gilt. The possible first edition by Phillips & Sampson was published in 1845 (also listed here with further editions cited). Uncommon. Not in Kohler.

1015. PARADISE LOST, A Poem, In Twelve Books. By John Milton. *New–York: Published By Leavitt & Allen, 27 Dey Street. 1852.* Small 8vo (4 ½" × 3 ⅛"), 212pp., original dark brown cloth (a little worn, light waterstaining first dozen and last half dozen pages, possibly lacking the final 8pp.), covers ruled in blind with large decorative piece in blind at the center incorporating the lettering "Leavitt's Cheap Edition," spine decorated in blind and lettered in gilt. An incomplete pocket-size edition, published as a "Cheap Edition." The first edition by Leavitt & Company was published in 1848 (also listed here with further editions cited). Uncommon. Not in Kohler.

1016. PARADISE LOST. A Poem In Twelve Books. By John Milton. *New York: Published By Clark, Austin & Co. 205 Broadway. 1852.* 12mo in 6s, 283pp., life of Milton by Fenton, index at the end, original black leather spine (worn), blue paper over boards (worn, partially missing at the corners, slight age-browning, name stamped on flyleaf), title page repeated on front cover (darkened), advertisements on back cover. Labeled "School Edition" on front cover. All in all, a decent copy. The first edition by Clark Austin & Co. as a "School Edition" was published in 1849 (also listed here); see also the illustrated edition published by Clark Austin & Co. in the same year, 1849, (also listed here with further editions cited). Uncommon. Not in Kohler.

Signed by the Translator, D. Arnaldi

1017. A NEW EDITION OF MILTON'S PARADISE LOST With A New Translation Into Italian Poetry Verse By Verse By Domenico Arnaldi[.] Volume I / Volume II[.] *Genoa[:] Printed For Ponthenier[,] 1852.* PARADISO PERDUTO DI MILTON NUOVA EDIZIONE Con Una Nuova Traduzione In Poesia Italiana Verso A Verso Di Domenico Arnaldi[.] Volume I / Volume II[.] *Genoa[:] Stabilimento Tipografico Ponthenier[,] 1852.* 2 volumes. 8vo in 4s, [6]+cxli+301+[2]pp.,+412+[3]pp., half-title each volume, four-page address to "Reverendissima Monsignor Andrea Charvaz" in Italian before half-title and title page, volume 1, "Ad Lettore Italiano" before "Life of Milton, with Criticisms on his Works, by Dr. Johnson," "Critique . . . by Joseph Addisson [sic]," half-titles in English and Italian before the poem, with statement in Italian on verso of English half-title ("Having fulfilled all the conditions of law, the author means to enjoy the proceeds of this work, and denies as false all copies that do not belong to the company") signed in ink below by the translator, D. Arnaldi, volume 1, "Contents"/"Indice" at the end of each volume, original three-quarter black calf, marbled paper over boards (worn along joints and corners, ex-library with stamp on title pages, due date slip and pocket at back of volume 2, stamped "discarded" on top edge), spines lettered in gilt. Scarce. Not in Kohler.

1018. PARADISE LOST: A Poem, In Twelve Books. By John Milton. With A Memoir Of The Author. Illustrated With Twelve Engravings. *Hartford: Published By S. Andrus & Son. 1853.* 12mo in 6s, 400+[5]pp., engraved frontispiece illustration of *Milton Dictating to His Daughters* engraved by "Lossing & Co." after Harvey, engraved frontispiece portrait plate after C. Burt, eleven additional illustrations by Harvey (variously engraved by S. H. Clark, Maclees, Lossing, and unsigned), half-title for each book with argument on verso, original purple cloth (spine faded, foxing throughout), embossed covers with a large circular decorative device in gilt at center of front cover, spine richly decorated in gilt with a depiction of Adam and Eve departing Eden in gilt at the top, gilt lettering at the center (including "Andrus' Illustrated Edition"), and of a dove amidst brilliant rays in gilt at the bottom. A nice copy in an attractive publisher's cloth binding with a spine design similar to counterpart editions published earlier and later in London. Five pages of advertisements for "Books, Published And For Sale By Silas Andrus And Son" bound in at the end. Harvey's engravings include the same as those included in the 1849 and 1851 Andrus editions (copy of each edition listed here), with the appearance of the engraved frontispiece portrait plate by C. Burt added here (possibly for the first time) and included also in the 1853 edition (see copy listed here). See 1847 Andrus edition of *PL* (first thus listed here with further editions by Andrus cited there). Harvey's illustrations were first published in London by Tilt & Bogue in 1843 (see two-volume sets of *PW* listed here). The possible first edition of Milton's *PW* by Andrus & Son of Hartford with illustrations after Harvey (possibly the first appearance in America) was published in two volumes in 1847 (see sets listed here). Scarce. Not in Kohler.

1019. THE PARADISE LOST By John Milton With Notes Explanatory And Critical. Edited By Rev. James Robert Boyd, Author of "Elements of Rhetoric," And "Eclectic Moral Philosophy." Milton, whose genius had angelic wings And fed on manna.—Cowper. *New York: Published By A. S. Barnes & Co[.;] Cincinnati:—H. W. Derby & Co. 1853.* 8vo, 552pp., introductory material, notes, and six illustration plates engraved by Burt after John Martin, index at the end (possibly new with this edition), original blue cloth (a bit rubbed at top of spine, plate for Book XII badly foxed, as are protective tissue guards), covers ruled in gilt with decorative gilt corner pieces and with central decorative gilt device, spine lettered in gilt at the top within thick gilt rules with decorative gilt devices, decorative gilt trim at top and bottom, a.e.g., bookplate. A good copy. The first edition edited by Boyd was published in 1850 by "Baker And Scribner" in New York with reduced illustration plates after Martin (also listed here with further editions by Boyd cited). Scarce. Not in Kohler.

1020. PARADISE LOST. In Twelve Parts. By John Milton. **NIGHT THOUGHTS** . . . By Edward Young. A New Edition. *Boston: Phillips, Sampson, & Co., 110 Washington Street. 1853.* 2 volumes in one. 12mo in 6s, 294pp.,+288pp., frontispiece portrait of Milton engraved by W. Hoogland after Samuel Cooper with a vignette illustration inset at the bottom consisting of Eve standing over Adam, who is seated and clothed in a fig leaf, exhorting him with outstretched hand, protective tissue guard, title page for Milton's *PL* and for Young's *Night Thoughts*, double black border around text, original red silk cloth (a bit worn, spine chipped at top and bottom), small gilt emblem of lyre and laurel at center of front cover, spine elaborately decorated and lettered in gilt. A good copy with contemporary inscription (dated 1854) and bookplate. The first edition by Phillips & Sampson was published in 1847 (also listed here with further editions cited). Not in Kohler.

1021. Variant of Preceding, original brown silk cloth (a bit rubbed, two small white spots near bottom of spine), covers richly decorated in gilt with thick gilt border rules and corner trim and with a large elaborate decorative emblem in gilt at the center, spine similarly richly decorated in gilt with gilt lettering, a.e.g. A good copy in an attractive variant publisher's binding with a different gilt pattern on covers and spine and a contemporary presentation inscription (dated 1854) on fly-leaf.

1022. Variant of Preceding, original dark brown silk cloth (a bit worn, joints cracked, early owner's stamp lightly stamped on front blank and at top of title page), small gilt emblem of lyre and laurel at center of front cover, spine elaborately decorated and lettered in gilt. A good copy in a variant publisher's binding. Unlike the preceding copies, this one is much thicker, measuring 1 ¾", or well over ¼" thicker than either of the preceding copies.

1023. MILTON'S PARADISE LOST, With Notes, Critical And Explanatory, Selected And Original. For The Use Of Schools. By The Rev. J. R. Major, D.D. Head Master Of King's College School, London. [Quotation From Cowper] *London: B. Fellowes, Ludgate Street. MDCCCLIII.* First edition thus? 8vo, vii+[verso blank]+584pp., preface, half-title for each book, notes at bottom of page, "Index Of References To Classical Authors" at end, contemporary green calf (a bit rubbed), covers ruled in gilt with small decorative corner pieces and college coat of arms in gilt at the center, spine richly gilt-decorated within the panels, red morocco labels with gilt lettering and gilt rules, raised bands with decorative gilt trim, inner and outer dentelles decorated in gilt, marbled endpapers, a.e.g. A fine copy in an attractive Prize Binding. Scarce. Not in Kohler.

1024. PARADISE LOST: By John Milton. With Life and Notes By The Rev. Thomas Thomson. *London: Printed For Adam Scott, (Late Scott And Webster,) Charterhouse Square. 1853.* Small 8vo, xi+304pp. (pagination beginning at p. 6 after two unpaginated pages), frontispiece portrait ("From the Portrait by Cipriani") engraved by H. Meyer, protective tissue guard, "Glasgow: W. G. Blackie, And Co, Printers, Villafield" on verso of title page, life of Milton, notes at bottom of page, original drab green smooth silk (a little faded, occasional light foxing), covers decorated in embossed blind trim, spine lettered in gilt within a decorative gilt design. A very nice copy. Not in Kohler.

1025. Variant of Preceding, original dark green pebble cloth (front joint cracked from within, spine ends slightly chipped, diagonal waterstain from some time ago across the bottom of frontispiece portrait, top edge of fly-leaf torn away, occasional marginal notations in pencil), covers decorated in embossed blind trim, spine lettered in gilt within a decorative gilt design. A good copy with a near-contemporary signature at top of fly-leaf in a variant publisher's binding: dark green pebble cloth rather than drab green smooth silk, with variant blind trim on covers, and variant gilt trim on spine. Not in Kohler.

1026. THE PARADISE LOST By John Milton. With Notes Explanatory And Critical. Edited By Rev. James Robert Boyd, Author of "Elements of Rhetoric," And "Eclectic Moral Philosophy." Milton, whose genius had angelic wings And fed on manna.—Cowper. *New York: Published By A. S. Barnes & Co[.;] Cincinnati:—H. W. Derby & Co. 1853*. Large 8vo, 552pp., content as with first edition in 1850, index (added in 1853), original black cloth spine, red paper over boards (worn, front cover detached, spine missing, pages a little age-browned), covers decorated in blind, decorated endpapers with list of "A. S. Barnes & Company's" publications in the center, several dated contemporary signatures on front blank and fly-leaf. The first edition edited by Boyd was published in 1850 by "Baker And Scribner" in New York with reduced illustration plates after Martin (also listed here with further editions by Boyd cited). Scarce. Not in Kohler.

1027. PARADISE LOST: A Poem, In Twelve Books, By John Milton; With A Life Of The Author, By The Rev. H. Stebbing, A, [sic] M. *New York: Leavitt & Allen, 27 Dey-Street. 1853*. Bound with **PARADISE REGAINED, AND OTHER POEMS.** By John Milton. *New York: Leavitt & Allen, 27 Dey-Street. 1853*. 2 volumes in one. Small 8vo (6" × 4 ½"), 356pp.+190, engraved frontispiece illustration plate without reference to poet, poem, or lines illustrated (not for Milton, unsigned vignette of a man walking between two women alongside two horses against a pastoral background), protective tissue guard, "C. A. Alvord, Printer, 29 Gold-street" on verso of *PL* title page; *SA* and *C* not included among the "Other Poems," decorative floral border around text, original decorated reddish-brown cloth (a bit rubbed, corners bumped, spine faded, foxing throughout, including frontispiece and title page), covers richly decorated in a finely tooled gilt floral pattern in imitation of the floral border around the text with a thick circular gilt band at the center and an inner circular floral design with a similarly thick gilt band, spine similarly richly decorated in a finely tooled gilt floral pattern with a gilt floral vase at the center and gilt lettering ("Milton's Poetical Works") near the top, a.e.g. A good copy. Together Milton's *Poetical Works* (without the inclusion of *SA* and *C*, as with other editions by Leavitt & Allen). As with other editions published by Leavitt & Allen around this time, the frontispiece illustration here is not an illustration for Milton but rather an illustration from the period used by the printer to embellish this edition of Milton's poems. The first edition by Leavitt & Company was published in 1848 (also listed here with further editions cited). Not in Kohler.

1028. Variant of Preceding. PARADISE LOST: A Poem, In Twelve Books, By John Milton; With A Life Of The Author, By The Rev. H. Stebbing, A, [sic] M. *New York: Leavitt & Allen, 27 Dey-Street. n.d. [ca. 1853]*. Bound with **PARADISE REGAINED, AND OTHER POEMS.** By John Milton. *New York: Leavitt & Allen, 27 Dey-Street. 1853*. 2 volumes in one. Small 8vo (6" × 4 ½"), 356pp.+ 84pp., engraved frontispiece illustration plate (not for Milton, two young ladies: one listening with ear against a wall, the other seated holding a viola, engraved by R. S. Lauder after J. McRae), without reference to poet, poem, or lines illustrated, protective tissue guard, no other poems included among the "Other Poems," decorative floral border around text, original decorated reddish-brown cloth (a bit rubbed, corners bumped), covers richly decorated in a finely tooled gilt floral pattern in imitation of the floral border around the text with a thick circular gilt band at the center and an inner circular floral design with a similarly thick gilt band, spine similarly richly decorated in a finely tooled gilt floral pattern with a gilt floral vase at the center and gilt lettering ("Milton's Poetical Works") near the top, a.e.g. A nice copy. Milton's *PL* and *PR* together (without the inclusion of any other poems). Variances from the preceding edition include: undated title page for *PL* with no printer listed on verso of title; bound only with *PR* with no other poems included despite reference to "And Other Poems" on second title page; with an unsigned frontispiece illustration not for Milton and different from the frontispiece illustration in preceding edition and from frontispiece illustrations in other editions by Leavitt & Allen referenced here, but like them an illustration from the period used by the publisher to embellish the edition of Milton's poems. Not in Kohler.

1029. Variant of Preceding. PARADISE LOST: A Poem, In Twelve Books, By John Milton; With A Life Of The Author, By The Rev. John Stebbing, A, [sic] M. *New York: Leavitt & Allen, 27 Dey-Street. 1853*. Small 8vo (6" × 4 ½"), 356pp., engraved frontispiece illustration plate for William Cowper's "The Task" (ca. 1785), Book V ("The Winter Morning Walk," line 745f, engraved by Illman & Sons), protective tissue guard, decorative floral border around text, original decorated reddish-brown cloth (a bit rubbed, corners bumped, spine faded and a little chipped at bottom, prelims lightly foxed), covers richly decorated in a finely tooled gilt floral pattern in imitation of the floral border around the text with a thick circular gilt band at the center and an inner circular floral design with a similarly thick gilt band, spine similarly richly decorated in a finely tooled gilt floral pattern with a gilt floral vase at the center and gilt lettering near the top ("Milton's Poetical Works"—even though only *PL* is contained herein), a.e.g. A nice copy with an early (possibly contemporary) presentation inscription in ink on fly-leaf and an early sketch in pencil on front blank. Different from the preceding copies with a different frontispiece illustration and without being bound to "Paradise Regained And Other Poems." The frontispiece illustration here is not an illustration for Milton, but rather an illustration used by the publisher to embellish this edition of Milton's poems. Not in Kohler.

1030. **PARADISE LOST**, A Poem, In Twelve Books. By John Milton. *New York: Published By Leavitt & Allen, 27 Dey Street[,] 1853*. Small 8vo (4 ⅝" × 3 ⅛"), 220pp., life of Milton, original brown cloth (a bit rubbed, hole punctured in back cover affecting last third pages), covers decorated in embossed blind trim, spine decorated in blind and lettered in gilt. A good copy with contemporary presentation inscription written in ink in a neat hand on fly-leaf. This is a different edition from the three preceding 1853 editions by Leavitt & Allen with different pagination, without a frontispiece illustration, without decorative floral border around text, in a variant publisher's binding. Uncommon. Not in Kohler.

1031. Variant of Preceding, original light brown cloth, covers ruled in embossed blind with large decorative piece in blind in the center incorporating the lettering "Leavitt's Cheap Edition," spine decorated in a patterned design in blind and lettered in gilt. A fine copy of this pocket-size edition, in a variant binding, with contemporary signature on fly-leaf. Uncommon. Not in Kohler.

1032. **PARADISE LOST**. A Poem In Twelve Books. By John Milton. *New York: Clark, Austin & Smith, 3 Park Row And 3 Ann-Street. 1853*. 12mo in 6s, 283pp., life of Milton before the poem, index at the end, original black leather spine (worn), blue paper over boards (both covers water-stained, slight foxing throughout), title page repeated on front cover, advertisements on back cover. Labeled "School Edition" on front cover. All in all, a good copy with contemporary signature (dated 1853) in a neat hand in pencil on fly-leaf and notes in pencil in the same neat contemporary hand. The first edition by Clark Austin & Co. as a "School Edition" was published in 1849 (also listed here); see, too, the illustrated edition published by Clark Austin & Co. in the same year, 1849, (also listed here with further editions cited). Uncommon. Not in Kohler.

1033. Variant of Preceding. **PARADISE LOST**. A Poem In Twelve Books. By John Milton. *New York: Published By Clark, Austin & Co., 205 Broadway. 1851 [i.e., 1853]*. 12mo in 6s, 283pp., life of Milton by Fenton before the poem, index at the end, original leather spine (worn, joints cracked), blue paper over boards (used and a bit rubbed, pages slightly age-darkened), title page repeated on front cover, but with different publisher's imprint and date: "New York: Clark, Austin & Smith, 3 Park Row And 3 Ann-Street. *1853*," advertisements on back cover. Labeled "School Edition" on front cover. All in all, a fairly good, thick copy with early blind stamp on fly-leaf and early signature in pencil on front blank. Different from preceding edition with variant publisher's imprint and date (1851) on title page, with variant publisher's imprint and date (1853) on front cover, and 1" thick compared to ⅜". Not in Kohler.

1034. **PARADISE LOST**. A Poem, In Twelve Books, By John Milton: With Explanatory Notes And A Life Of The Author. By The Rev. H. Stebbing, A. M. Stereotyped By J. A. James. *Philadelphia: Troutman & Hayes, 193 Market Street. Pittsburgh-Kay & Co. 1853*. 8vo, x+312pp., life at the beginning, page of notes at the end, original green cloth (joints and edges rubbed, spine ends chipped, small stain on back cover), front cover ruled in gilt with angelic figure in gilt at the center within decorative gilt frame surrounded by decorative gilt trim, spine richly decorated and lettered in gilt, back cover stamped in blind with decoration on front cover, a.e.g. A very good copy. The possible first edition thus (with variant publisher's imprint from that here) was published in a smaller 8vo format from that here in 1836 (also listed here with further editions cited, each likewise in a smaller 8vo format from that here). Not in Kohler.

1035. **PARADISE LOST**. By John Milton. With Explanatory Notes By The Rev. Henry Stebbing, A. M. *New York: D. Appleton & Company, 346 & 348 Broadway. M.DCCC.LIV.* 12mo, 296pp. (pagination beginning at p. 18), engraved frontispiece illustration (the expulsion scene, unsigned, but after Turner), protective tissue guard, notes at bottom of page, contemporary brown cloth (a bit worn and faded, spine chipped at top and bottom, corners bumped, lacking front fly-leaf and both pastedowns, embrowning throughout), covers decorated in blind, spine decorated and lettered in gilt. Overall, a good copy of a scarce edition. The possible first edition thus with different frontispiece illustration was published in 1844 (also listed here with further editions cited); the pagination in each Appleton edition begins at "p. 18" on the verso of the first page of Book I as with the edition here. Not in Kohler.

1036. PARADISE LOST. In Twelve Parts. By John Milton. NIGHT THOUGHTS . . . To Which Is Added, The Force Of Religion. By Edward Young. A New Edition. *Boston: Phillips, Sampson, And Company[.] New York: James C. Derby. 1854.* 2 volumes in one. 12mo in 6s, 294pp.,+ 288pp., frontispiece portrait of Milton engraved by W. Hoogland after Samuel Cooper with a vignette illustration inset at the bottom consisting of Eve standing over Adam who is seated and clothed in a fig leaf, exhorting him with outstretched hand, protective tissue guard (foxed), title page for Milton's *PL* and for Young's *Night Thoughts*, double black border around text, original black cloth (spine slightly chipped at bottom), covers elaborately decorated in blind with central gilt device of harp and laurel on front cover, spine elaborately decorated in gilt with gilt lettering. A fine copy. The first edition by Phillips & Sampson was published in 1847 (also listed here with further editions cited). Not in Kohler.

1037. Variant of Preceding, engraved frontispiece portrait of Milton after A. Dick, original brown silk (occasional light foxing, a few pages slightly embrowned, earlier name in pencil on fly-leaf), covers richly decorated in embossed blind with a large emblem with elaborate trim and hanging tassels at the center, spine richly decorated in embossed gilt with the names of Milton and Young lettered in gilt near the top and a gilt emblem with hanging tassels in gilt at the center. A fine copy, largely fresh and clean within, with a variant frontispiece portrait of Milton from the preceding and other editions by Phillips, Sampson and Company prior to this edition. Uncommon. Not in Kohler.

1038. MILTON'S PARADISE LOST AND PARADISE REGAINED, With Explanatory Notes By The Rev. J. Edmondston. [Quote from Sir E. Brydges.] *T. Nelson And Sons, New York: London: And Edinburgh. MDCCCLIV.* First edition thus? Small 8vo, 468pp., black rule around title page, "Advertisement" (dated "June, 1854"), notes at bottom of page, original blue cloth (a bit rubbed), covers ruled in blind with embossed trim in blind at the top and bottom and a large embossed decorative piece in blind at the center, spine elaborately decorated in embossed blind trim with gilt lettering and modest decorative gilt trim, a.e.g. A fine copy with a lengthy near-contemporary presentation inscription in pen on fly-leaf. In the "Advertisement" the editor, Rev. Edmondston, states: "The notes appended to this edition of Milton's two chief poems have been partly selected from the voluminous collections that have been amassed by a succession of learned commentators, and partly written by the editor." The commentators identified as being among those included by Edmondston include Joseph Addison, William Cowper, Charles Dunster, John Hawkins, Bishop Thomas Newton, James Prendeville, Benjamin Stillingfleet, and Robert Thyer. Scarce. Not in Kohler.

1039. PARADISE LOST. A Poem, In Twelve Books, By John Milton: With Explanatory Notes And A Life Of The Author. By The Rev. H. Stebbing, A.M[.] Stereotyped By J. A. James. *Philadelphia: Hayes & Zell, Publishers, 193 Market Street. 1854.* First edition thus? Small 8vo, x+312pp., original black cloth (a bit rubbed), black leather spine (joints worn, small piece missing at bottom), spine decorated in blind and lettered in gilt. A good copy. See also 1856, 1857, and 1861 editions by Hayes & Zell listed here, the 1856 and 1857 editions in a larger octavo size than the present copy, the 1861 edition in the same size but with a variant publisher's imprint. Scarce. Not in Kohler.

1040. PARADISE LOST: By John Milton. To Which Is Prefixed, The Life Of The Author. *Philadelphia: John B. Perry, 198 Market Street. 1855.* First edition thus? Small 8vo (5 ⅛" × 3 ⅛"), x+270pp., engraved and printed title pages, engraved title for "Milton's Poetical Works. With his Life. John B. Perry. 198 Market St. Philad[elphi]a" with an unsigned vignette illustration of Satan (possibly after Westall) on engraved title, "Contents" (for *PW*) "Life Of The Author," original black leather spine, brown cloth (a little rubbed, slight stain at bottom of back cover, engraved title page slightly waterstained, modest staining on endpapers, early signatures in pencil on front pastedown and front blank), covers decorated with an embossed design in blind, spine lettered in gilt ("Perry's Edition" at the bottom), a.e.g. A nice copy. See Perry's 1855 edition of *PW* listed here; this is *PL* published separately with preliminary material from that edition without the portrait. Not in Kohler.

1041. THE PARADISE LOST By John Milton With Notes Explanatory And Critical. Edited By Rev. James Robert Boyd, Author of "Elements of Rhetoric," And "Eclectic Moral Philosophy." Milton, whose genius had angelic wings And fed on manna.—Cowper. *New York: Published By A. S. Barnes & Co[.;] Cincinnati:—H. W. Derby & Co. 1855.* 8vo, 552pp., content and six illustration plates engraved by Burt after John Martin as with first edition in 1850, index (added in 1853), original red cloth (spine ends chipped, plates foxed, several rather heavily, early name in pencil on front blank), covers ruled in blind with large central emblem in blind, spine lettered in gilt (faded), patterned endpapers with advertisements boxed at the center. A good copy of an uncommon edition. The first edition edited by Boyd was published in 1850 by "Baker And Scribner" in New York with reduced illustration plates after Martin (also listed here with further editions by Boyd cited). Scarce. Not in Kohler.

1042. MILTON LE PARADIS PERDU Traduction De Chateaubriand Précédé De Réflexions Sur La Vie Et Les Escrits De Milton Par Lamartine Et Enrichi De Vingt-Cinq Magnifiques Estampes Originales Gravées Au Burin Sur Acier. *Paris[:] Chez Bigot Et Voisvenel[,] Editeurs-Proprietaires[;] Chez Amable Rigaud[,] Libraire 50 Rue Sainte-Anne 50[;] Furne, Libraire-Editeur 45, Rue Saint-André-Des-Arts[;] A La Libraire Nouvelle[,] 45, Boulevard Des Italiens[;] Et Chez Tous Les Libraires De France Et De L'Etranger[,] 1855.* First edition thus. Folio, xxxi+157pp. (plates not included in pagination), half-title, first appearance of engraved frontispiece illustration and twenty-four other illustrations by Johan Jakob Flatters, Joseph The'odore Richomme, Lemercier, Melin, and Bernouville (very fine impressions with varying degrees of foxing along the margins without affecting the impression), engraved portraits of Alphonse de Lamartine, François-René de Chateaubriand, and Milton, "Reflexions Sur Milton" (dated "Mars 1855"), "Etude Historique Et Littéraire Sur Milton" printed in double column, "Arguments" for the books printed together at the beginning before Book I, splendid decorative head- and tailpieces, decorated initial letter each book, contemporary brown cloth (a little worn, front cover and spine detached but very repairable, spine frayed at top and bottom, back joint splitting near the top), front cover lettered in gilt at the center, spine decorated and lettered in gilt. A good copy of this amazingly illustrated book with splendid impressions of the original steel-engraved illustrations. Scarce. Stevens 1466; Not in Kohler.

The introduction is by Lamartine; the translation by Chateaubriand, which was first published in 1831 (see 1836 set listed here). See copy of the 1863 possibly second edition thus with prospectus (dated 1862) announcing the publication of this edition laid in listed here; see also a copy of the 1868 third edition thus also listed here; and see a copy of 1870 reproduction of these engraved illustrations listed here, bound without text, but with half-title and with title page dated 1870, each of the twenty-seven illustrations printed on high-quality paper as originally done in this 1855 edition, each beautifully hand-colored and mounted on cardlike paper and each identified; see also later editions: in 1882 (also listed here) and in 1891 (likewise listed here), with three illustrations "previously not published."

1043. PARADISE LOST. A Poem In Twelve Books. By John Milton. *New York: Clark, Austin & Smith, 3 Park Row And 3 Ann-Street. 1855.* 12mo in 6s, 283pp., life of Milton by Fenton, index at end, original pink paper boards (slightly aged, some age-browning), black leather spine (rubbed along joints with slight cracking at top and bottom of front joint), title page repeated on front cover within decorative trim, advertisements for books published by "Clark, Austin & Co." on back cover. Labeled "School Edition" on front cover. All in all, a nice copy. The collection also has another copy in a variant publisher's binding, original blue paper boards (bit aged and stained), black leather spine (worn), with different advertisement on back cover. Not in Kohler.

1044. DAS VERLORENE PARADIES. Das wiedergewonnene Paradies. von John Milton. Ubersetzt von Bernhard Schuhmann. *Stuttgart und Augsburg. J. G. Cotta'scher Berlag. 1855.* First edition thus? Thick 8vo, 466+[6]pp., +495pp., half-title before the poem. Bound with **LAIEN-EVANGELIUM**. Jamben von Friedrich von Sallet. *Leipsig, 1842. Berlag von Friedrich Boldmar.* Original ribbed green cloth spine, marbled paper over boards (a bit rubbed, joints with occasional slight cracks), spine ruled in gilt with gilt lettering within decorative gilt trim. A very nice copy with contemporary inscription in German (dated 1863) on flyleaf. *PL* is translated into German verse by Bernhard Schuhmann. Scarce. Not in Kohler.

1045. PARADISE LOST: A Poem, In Twelve Books. By John Milton. With A Memoir Of The Author. Illustrated With Twelve Engravings. *Hartford: Published By S. Andrus & Son. 1856.* 12mo, 400+[5]pp., engraved frontispiece illustration of *Milton Dictating to His Daughters* engraved by "Lossing & Co." after Harvey, engraved frontispiece portrait plate after C. Burt, eleven additional illustrations by Harvey (variously engraved by S. H. Clark, Maclees, Lossing, and unsigned), half-title for each book with argument on verso, original brown cloth (a little worn, spine ends chipped with a small piece missing, joints cracked), covers richly decorated with gilt floral design within thin and thick gilt rules, spine (albeit worn) richly decorated in gilt with a depiction of *Adam and Eve Departing Eden* in gilt at the top, gilt lettering at the center ("Andrus' Illustrated Edition"), and of a *Dove Amidst Brilliant Rays* in gilt at the bottom, a.e.g. A good copy in an attractive publisher's cloth binding with a spine design similar to counterpart editions published earlier and later in London. Five pages of advertisements for "Books, Published And For Sale By Silas Andrus And Son" bound in at the end. Scarce. Not in Kohler.

Harvey's engravings include the same as those included in the 1849 and 1851 Andrus editions listed here with the appearance of the engraved frontispiece portrait plate after C. Burt, possibly first included in the 1853 edition (also listed here). See 1847 Andrus edition of *PL* (first edition listed here with other editions by Andrus cited). Harvey's illustrations were first published in London by Tilt & Bogue in 1843 (see two-volume sets of *PW* listed here). The possible first edition of Milton's *PW* by Andrus & Son of Hartford with illustrations by Harvey (possibly its first appearance in America) was published in two volumes in 1847 (also listed here).

1046. PARADISE LOST. A Poem, In Twelve Books By John Milton: With Explanatory Notes And A Life Of The Author. By The Rev. H. Stebbing, A.M[.] Stereotyped By J. A. James. *Philadelphia: Hayes & Zell, Publishers. 193 Market Street. 1856.* 8vo, x+312pp. (last page wrongly printed "12"), original three-quarter brown calf, marbled paper over boards (worn, foxing throughout), spine lettered in gilt, raised bands. See 1854 possibly first edition by Hayes & Zell listed here in a much smaller octavo size than this edition; see also 1857 edition by Hayes & Zell listed here the same size as this edition; and see 1862 edition listed here in the same size as the 1854 edition but with a variant publisher's imprint. Scarce. Not in Kohler.

1047. PARADISE LOST, A Poem, In Twelve Books. By John Milton. *New York: Leavitt & Allen. 379 Broadway. 1856.* Small 8vo (near miniature: 4 ¾" × 3 ¼"), 220pp., original brown texture cloth (a little worn, small mark on back cover, occasional foxing throughout, early name on fly-leaf), covers richly decorated in embossed blind floral trim, spine decorated in blind and lettered in gilt. A good copy. The first edition by Leavitt & Allen was published in 1848 (listed here with further editions by Leavitt & Allen cited). Uncommon. Kohler 134, calling its copy "16mo in 8s" and reporting "Not in the British Library. Not in the Bodleian Library. Not in Cambridge University Library."

1048. PARADISE LOST. In Twelve Parts. By John Milton. **NIGHT THOUGHTS** . . . To Which Is Added, The Force Of Religion. By Edward Young. A New Edition. *Boston: Phillips, Sampson, And Company. New York: J. C. Derby. 1856.* 2 volumes in one. 12mo, 294pp.,+288pp., frontispiece portrait of Milton as a young man engraved by J. J. McCarty with protective tissue guard, title page for Milton's *PL* and for Young's *Night Thoughts*, double black border around text, original red cloth (similar to the possible second thus in 1849, a bit rubbed, spine slightly chipped at top and bottom), covers elaborately decorated in blind, spine elaborately decorated in gilt with gilt lettering. A good copy with dated contemporary signature on fly-leaf. An uncommon mid-nineteenth-century American edition in a nice publisher's binding. The first edition by Phillips & Sampson was published in 1847 (copy listed and other editions by Phillips & Sampson cited there). Not in Kohler.

1049. PARADISE LOST. By John Milton. With Explanatory Notes By The Rev. Henry Stebbing, A. M. *New York: D. Appleton & Company, 346 & 348 Broadway. M.DCCC.LVII.* 12mo, 296pp. (with pagination beginning at "p. 18" on verso of first page of Book I), engraved frontispiece illustration (the expulsion scene, unsigned, but after Turner), protective tissue guard, notes at bottom of page, contemporary brown cloth (a bit rubbed and faded, spine ends chipped, some inoffensive waterstaining at upper edge of pages near the end of the book), covers decorated in blind with central gilt illustration of Milton dictating to his daughters on front cover, spine decorated and lettered in gilt, blue endpapers. A nice copy. The possible first edition thus was published with a different frontispiece illustration in 1844 (also listed here with further editions cited); the pagination in each Appleton edition begins at "p. 18" on the verso of the first page of Book I as with the edition here. Scarce. Not in Kohler.

1050. PARADISE LOST. A Poem In Twelve Books. By John Milton. *New York: Clark, Austin & Smith, 3 Park Row And 3 Ann-Street. 1857.* 12mo, 283pp., life of Milton by Fenton, index at end, original boards (aged and worn, occasional foxing, early pencil doodling on front endpapers), black leather spine (worn), title page for this edition of *PL* repeated on front cover within decorative trim with advertisement on back cover. Labeled "School Edition" on front cover. The first edition by Clark Austin & Co was published in 1849 (also listed here with further editions cited). Uncommon. Not in Kohler.

1051. PARADISE LOST. A Poem, In Twelve Books By John Milton: With Explanatory Notes And A Life Of The Author. By The Rev. H. Stebbing, A.M. Stereotyped By J. A. James. *Philadelphia: Hayes & Zell, Publishers, 193 Market Street. 1857.* 8vo, x+312+[13]+16+[10]pp., original green cloth (a bit rubbed, occasional light foxing), covers decorated in blind, spine decorated and lettered in gilt. A good copy with 39 pp. of advertisements of "Hayes & Zell's School Publications" bound in at the end. See the 1854 possibly first edition by Hayes & Zell in a much smaller octavo size as here listed earlier; see also the 1856 edition by Hayes & Zell listed earlier, in the same size as that here and the 1862 edition listed later, and the same size as the 1854 edition, but with a variant publisher's imprint. Uncommon. Not in Kohler.

1052. PARADISE LOST. A Poem. In Twelve Books. By John Milton. A New Edition. *Boston: Phillips, Sampson, & Co., 1857.* Bound with **NIGHT THOUGHTS** . . . To Which Is Added, The Force Of Religion. By Edward Young. A New Edition. *Boston: Phillips, Sampson, And Company. 1857.* 2 volumes in one. 12mo in 6s, 294pp., +288pp., frontispiece portrait engraved by O. Pelton "From a Miniature of the same size by Faithorne, Anno 1667," double black border around title and text, original red cloth (a bit rubbed, covers a little waterstained, with waterstaining affecting the outer top edge of the pages, especially at the beginning and again for a few pages in the middle), separate title page for *Night Thoughts* by Edward Young, covers decorated in blind, spine decorated and lettered in gilt, endpapers printed with advertisements. A decent copy. The first edition by Phillips & Sampson was published in 1847 (also listed here with further editions cited). Not in Kohler.

1053. PARADIS LOST. In Twelve Parts. By John Milton. NIGHT THOUGHTS . . . To Which Is Added, The Force Of Religion. By Edward Young, D.D. A New Edition. *Boston: Phillips, Sampson, And Company. 1857.* 2 volumes in one. 12mo in 6s, 294pp.,+288pp., frontispiece portrait of Milton as a young man engraved by J. J. McCarty with protective tissue guard, title page for Milton's *PL* and for Young's *Night Thoughts*, double black border around text, original brown cloth (chipped on front and back covers, spine ends chipped, some age-browning), covers elaborately decorated in blind, spine elaborately decorated in gilt with gilt lettering, endpapers printed with advertisements. A good copy with dated contemporary signature in ink in a neat hand on fly-leaf and with some notations in ink in the same neat hand throughout. The first edition by Phillips & Sampson was published in 1847 (also listed here with further editions cited). Uncommon. Not in Kohler.

1054. LE PARADIS PERDU De Milton Traduction Nouvelle Par Paul Guérin[.] *Paris. Chez L. Hachette et Co Rue Pierre-Sarrazin, 44[.] Dijon. Chez Jules Dessaux Rue des Godrans, 28. 1857.* 8vo, 344pp., half-title, preface, note at the end, original printed wrappers (a bit frayed along edges, joints, and spine, wrappers slightly worn and age-darkened), title page reproduced on front cover with decorative border trim, edges untrimmed. A decent copy with personal library stamp in French on half-title. Uncommon. Not in Kohler.

1055. THE PARADISE LOST OF MILTON. With Illustrations By John Martin. *London: Printed For Henry Washbourne & Co., 25, Ivy Lane, Paternoster Row. MDCCCLVIII.* 4to, [viii]+373pp., the arguments for each book printed together at outset before Book I followed by a "List Of The Engravings," with the twenty-four small mezzotint plates by John Martin with the identifying logo, "Designed & Engraved by J. Martin, Esq.," at the center of each plate, each engraving measuring 5 ¾" × 8", contemporary full blue morocco, gilt rules on covers with inner border delicately tooled in blind, elegantly gilt-decorated spine, red morocco label with gilt lettering and gilt rules, raised bands with decorative gilt trim, outer dentelles tooled in gilt, marbled endpapers and edges. A very fine copy. Martin's distinctive illustrations were first issued in twelve parts by Septimus Prowett between 1825 and 1827 (see set listed here); they were then published by Prowett in an edition of *PL*, in four different formats, in 1827 (also listed here with further discussion of the different formats, subsequent editions, and Martin's illustrations). The first edition with plates published by Washbourne was published again in 1849 (second edition, copy listed here). Not in Kohler.

1056. PARADISE LOST. A Poem In Twelve Books. By John Milton. *New York: Clark, Austin & Smith, 3 Park Row And 3 Ann-Street. 1858.* 12mo in 6s, 283pp., life of Milton by Fenton, index at end, original boards (a bit rubbed), black leather spine (a bit rubbed, spine chipped at top and bottom), title page for this edition of *PL* repeated on front cover within decorative trim with advertisement on back cover. Labeled "School Edition" on front cover. A nice copy. The first edition by Clark Austin & Co was published in 1849 (also listed here with further editions cited). Not in Kohler.

1057. PARADISE LOST: A Poem. The Author, John Milton. *London: Groombridge And Sons, 5, Paternoster Row. MDCCCLIX.* 2 volumes in one. First edition thus? Small 8vo, 190pp.,+179pp., frontispiece illustration for Book I, line 330, after George Bonner, volume 1, title page each volume with decorative emblem incorporating initials of the press at the center, "London: Thomas Harrild, Printer Salisbury Square, Fleet Square" on verso of each title page, life of Milton by Fenton, volume 1, half-title for "Paradise Lost. Book I," "End Of Vol. I." on last page of Book VI followed by blank page, frontispiece illustration for Book IV, line 819, after Bonner, volume 2, half-title for "Paradise Lost. Book VII" with "Vol. II" printed in small letters in lower left corner, index at the end, black rule around text, original crushed green cloth over thick boards, covers richly decorated in blind with embossed outer rules with small decorative corner pieces and embossed patterns at the center, spine ruled and lettered in gilt, pink endpapers, a.e.g. An attractive copy, handsomely bound, in fine condition with early presentation inscription on fly-leaf. Scarce. Not in Kohler.

1058. LE PARADIS PERDU. Par M De Chateaubriand[.] Orné De Gravures[.] *Paris[:] Bernardin-Béchet, Libraire[,] 31, Quai Des Augustins[,] 1859.* 8vo, 456pp., engraved frontispiece illustration plate after "E Piaud" for Book XI ("L'archange Michel appraissant à Adam après son péché," with directions for where the plate is to be placed—"Livre XI. – p. 400."—the plate placed as frontispiece), "Remarques" before the poem, a second engraved illustration plate after "K. Girard" for Book I ("Bientôt les guerriers se meuvent en phalanges parfaites. Livre I. – Page 35."—with the plate located at p. 35), contemporary leather spine (worn, joints cracked, spine lacking a small piece at the top), marbled paper over boards (worn, corners and edges chipped, slight foxing here and there throughout, especially frontispiece and title page), speckled edges. Although the cover is rather scruffy, the text is clean. The translation by Chateaubriand (1768–1848) is printed here at the top of the page with Milton's poem printed in English at the bottom. Chateaubriand's translation first appeared in 1831 (see 1836 sets also listed here). Not in Kohler.

1059. PARADISE LOST. A Poem. In Twelve Books By John Milton. A New Edition. *Boston: Phillips, Sampson, & Co. 1859.* 12mo in 6s, 294pp., original half black calf, marbled paper over boards (a little worn, slight age-browning throughout, joints sprung at center), spine lettered and ruled in gilt. Although a little aged, a good copy with contemporary ownership signature on fly-leaf and notes on back blank. The possible first edition thus by Phillips & Sampson was published in 1845 (also listed here with further editions cited). Not in Kohler.

1060. PARADISE LOST. A Poem. In Twelve Books By John Milton[.] A New Edition. *Boston: Phillips, Sampson, & Co., 1859.* Bound with **NIGHT THOUGHTS** . . . To Which Is Added, The Force Of Religion. By Edward Young, D.D. A New Edition. *Boston: Phillips, Sampson, And Company. 1859.* 2 volumes in one. 12mo in 6s, 294pp.,+288pp., frontispiece portrait of Milton as a young man engraved by J. J. McCarty, title page for Milton's *PL* and for Young's *Night Thoughts*, double black border around text, original brown cloth (a little worn, spine ends chipped, bottom outer portion of first third of the book badly stained with lighter staining continuing along outer bottom edges throughout the book), covers elaborately decorated in blind, spine elaborately decorated in gilt with gilt lettering, endpapers printed with advertisements. The staining is unfortunate in a book that is uncommon, as this book is. The first edition by Phillips & Sampson was published in 1847 (also listed here with further editions cited). Not in Kohler.

1061. PARADISE LOST: A Poem. In Twelve Books, By John Milton. With A Life Of The Author, By The Rev. H. Stebbing, A.M. *New York: Leavitt & Allen Bros., No. 8 Howard Street. n.d. [ca. 1860s].* Bound with **PARADISE REGAINED, AND OTHER POEMS** By John Milton. *New York: Leavitt & Allen Bros., No. 8 Howard Street. n.d. [ca. 1860s].* 2 volumes in one. Small, thick 8vo (4 ½" × 3 ½" × ½" thick), 356pp.,+190pp., unsigned frontispiece illustration of a contemplative man out in nature, title page for each volume, original decorated reddish-brown cloth (worn, front joint split, a bit shaken internally, small piece missing upper right corner of fly-leaf), front cover and spine decorated in embossed blind trim outlined in black with Milton's name incorporated in embossed reddish-brown letters within a central gilt background extending sideways with a larger letter "M" within a decorated gilt shield, central urn device in blind on back cover, a.e.g. Although worn, a fair copy of a scarce mid-nineteenth-century American edition of most of Milton's poetical works, lacking most notably *SA* and *C*, which are not included among the "Other Poems" in the second volume here, as is the case with other editions by Leavitt & Allen in the late 1840s and early 1850s (see other editions listed here). The frontispiece illustration is probably an illustration "of the period" used by the publisher to embellish this edition of Milton's poem rather than an illustration for Milton. The first edition by Leavitt & Allen was published 1848 (also listed here with further editions by Leavitt & Allen cited). Uncommon. Not in Kohler.

1062. THE PARADISE LOST By John Milton. With Notes Explanatory And Critical. Edited By Rev. James R. Boyd, A.M. Author Of "Elements Of Rhetoric," "Eclectic Moral Philosophy," And Of An Improved Edition Of "Kames' Elements," Etc. Milton, Whose Genius Had Angelic Wings, And Fed On Manna.—Cowper. *New York: A. S. Barnes & Burr, 51 & 53 John-Street[,] 1860.* 8vo, 552pp., content and reduced illustration plates after Martin, including one as frontispiece, as with first edition, index (added in 1853) at the end, original red cloth (a little worn and soiled, spine ends chipped, plates foxed), covers decorated in blind, spine lettered in gilt. The first edition thus edited by Boyd was published in 1850 by "Baker And Scribner" in New York in a large 8vo format with reduced illustration plates after Martin (also listed here with further editions by Boyd cited). Scarce. Not in Kohler.

1062A. (Cross-listing) [PARADISE LOST.] Title page and text in Armenian. *Published in Venice, 1861.* Listed in appendix.

1062B. (Cross-listing) [PARADISE LOST] Sotheby, Samuel Leigh. RAMBLINGS IN THE ELUCIDATION OF THE AUTOGRAPH OF MILTON. *London: Printed For The Author By Thomas Richard, And Sold By All Booksellers, 1861.* First and only edition. 4to, [iii]+xxxviii+141+[1]+142a–142b,+143–263pp.+[10]leaves (index), two frontispiece photographs of Milton tipped in (early photographs taken specifically for this edition, with subscript identification by Leigh), the first of the bust of Milton at Trinity College, Cambridge, and the second of a drawing formerly in the possession of J. Richardson and Jacob Tonson, twenty-seven facsimile plates of various Milton manuscripts, signature and handwriting, original full green morocco (slightly rubbed at corners, some foxing), covers with contrasting recessed tan panels with pictorial designs in black by J. F. Rigaud and J. L. Tupper portraying scenes from *PL*, decorative gilt border trim and gilt rules on covers, spine attractively gilt in compartments, gilt-ruled raised bands, decorated endpapers with three progressive reductions of the cover illustrations printed on the pastedowns, t.e.g. A very nice copy in a splendid and well-preserved binding of the period. One of the more unusual 1860s bindings, executed by the accomplished John Wright. See main listing with Nineteenth-century Miltoniana.

1063. PARADISE LOST. A Poem. In Twelve Books By John Milton[.] A New Edition. *Boston: Crosby, Nichols, Lee & Company. 1861*. First edition thus? Large 12mo in 6s, 294pp., black cloth spine decorated in blind and lettered in gilt, original boards (used, spine chipped at top and bottom with small piece missing at bottom), title page essentially repeated on front cover (with address given without date beneath publisher: "117 Washington Street"), advertisements printed on back cover. Albeit a little used, nonetheless a good copy of a scarce mid-nineteenth-century American edition of Milton's *PL* with dated contemporary signature on front fly-leaf. The possible second edition thus was published by Crosby and Nichols in 1862; the possible third in 1863; the possible fourth in 1864—all listed here. Not in Kohler.

1064. PARADISE LOST. A Poem, In Twelve Books By John Milton. With Explanatory Notes And A Life Of The Author. By The Rev. H. Stebbing, A. M. Stereotyped by J. A. James. *Philadelphia: S. C. Hayes, 439 Market Street. T. Ellwood Zell, Publisher. 1861*. 8vo, x+312pp., notes on the last page, black leather spine (rubbed and worn at joints and corners), original brown silk cloth (a little worn, some soiling at the bottom of the first few pages, including title page, heavy spotting at the center for several pages, affecting the text a bit at the bottom of these pages, age-browning). A fair copy of an uncommon edition with contemporary/early ownership signature on front blank. See 1854 edition by Hayes & Zell (possible first edition) in same size octavo as here but with a variant publisher's imprint, see also 1856 and 1857 editions by Hayes & Zell in larger octavo size than here and with the same publisher's imprint as 1854 edition. Not in Kohler.

1065. PARADISE LOST. A Poem. In Twelve Books By John Milton[.] A New Edition. *Boston: Crosby, Nichols. 1862*. Second edition thus? 12mo in 6s, 294pp., original boards (used, spine ends chipped, pencil markings on endpapers and on title page where title is rewritten in a neat early hand in pencil) title page essentially repeated on front cover (with a modification in publisher and with address given without date beneath: "Crosby, Nichols, Lee & Co., 117 Washington Street"), advertisements printed on back cover, black cloth spine decorated in blind and lettered in gilt. See following copy, which is a reissue of this edition in a larger format with a number of differences. The possible first edition thus was published by Crosby and Nichols in 1861 (also listed here with further editions by Crosby cited). Not in Kohler.

1066. Variant of Preceding. PARADISE LOST. A Poem. In Twelve Books By John Milton[.] A New Edition. *Boston: Crosby, Nichols. 1862*. Second edition thus? Large 12mo in 6s, 288pp., steel-engraved frontispiece portrait of Milton after John J. McCarty "From a Miniature of the same size by Faithorne, Anno 1667. in the possession of William Faithorne, Esq.," protective tissue guard, double black border around the text. Bound with **THE COMPLAINT AND CONSOLATION; OR NIGHT THOUGHTS** . . . By Edward Young, D.D. A New Edition. *Boston: Crosby And Nichols. 1862*. 2 volumes in one. Large 12mo in 6s, 288pp., double black border around the text, original reddish-brown calf (worn, joints cracked, spine reglued, lacking bottom portion covered over by a piece of red leather for appearance sake, lacking last six pages of *PL*, which contain the ending of Book XII, but apparently bound as such, without any apparent loss of pages in the binding process itself), covers richly decorated in embossed gilt with large embossed gilt in the center, spine (albeit worn) lettered in gilt ("Milton • Young") with embossed gilt trim, a.e.g. This edition is a reissue of the preceding edition in a variant publisher's binding with a number of differences: (1) printed in a much larger format (possibly a large paper copy); (2) with an engraved frontispiece portrait of Milton; (3) with a double black border around the text; and (4) bound with Young's *Night Thoughts*.

1067. [PARADISE LOST] Bradburn, Eliza Weaver. **THE STORY OF PARADISE LOST, FOR CHILDREN**. By Eliza Weaver Bradburn. *New-York: Published By Carlton & Porter, Sunday-School Union, 200 Mulberry Street. n.d. [ca. 1862]*. Small 8vo, 119pp., original green cloth (a bit rubbed, first signature sprung), covers decorated in embossed blind, spine decorated and lettered in gilt (faded). A good copy of a scarce book with contemporary signature dated 1862 on front pastedown. See 1831 edition (first Bradburn edition, listed here) published in New York "By J. Emory And B. Waugh, For the Sunday School Union of the Methodist Episcopal Church, at the Conference Office, 14 Crosby-street. J. Collord, Printer." Bradburn's is the pirated edition of Mrs. Siddons's book, published in 1822: *An Abridgement Of Paradise Lost*, published also under the title *The Story Of Our First Parents Abridged From Milton's Paradise Lost, For The Use Of Young Persons* (both listed here). Scarce. Not in Kohler.

1068. MILTON'S PARADISE LOST. In Twelve Books. *London: Bell And Daldy, 186, Fleet Street. 1863.* First edition by Bell and Daldy. Small 8vo, [ii]+331+[2]pp., half-title with decorative trim, decorated initial letters and emblem of the press on title page, decorative head- and tailpieces, decorated initial letters, "Chiswick Press:— Whittingham And Wilkins, Tooks Court, Chancery Lane" on verso of last page, leather spine (worn, chipped at ends), red paper over boards (rubbed and worn along extremities, occasional foxing), spine lettered in gilt within decorative gilt trim, dark brown endpapers. A decent copy of an uncommon edition with large armorial bookplate on front pastedown and contemporary signature (dated 1865) and a later signature (dated 1896) on half-title. The decorative trim on the half-title and the decorated initial letters and emblem of the press on the title page are attractively hand-colored, the hand-coloring of the initial letters and decorative head- and tailpieces continues through Book VI and sporadically thereafter. Advertisement leaf bound in at the end. "This Edition of Milton's Poetical Works has been printed from the text of Mr. Keightley's Library Edition" (Preface). A possible second edition thus was published in 1865 (also listed here). Scarce. Not in Kohler.

1069. PARADISE LOST. A Poem. In Twelve Books By John Milton[.] A New Edition. *Boston: Crosby And Nichols. 1863.* Third edition thus? 12mo in 6s, 294pp., original boards (a bit rubbed, two slight inoffensive water stains at top of front cover), brown cloth spine finely decorated in blind embossed trim with gilt lettering, light pink paper over boards, title page essentially repeated on front cover (with address given without date beneath publisher: "117 Washington Street") with double black rule along outer edge, advertisements printed on back cover. A nice copy generally in very good condition with contemporary signature on front fly-leaf and later signatures on front and back blanks. The possible first edition thus was published by Crosby, Nichols, Lee & Company in Boston in 1861 (also listed here with further editions cited). Not in Kohler.

1071. MILTON'S PARADISE LOST. In Twelve Books. *New York: Frank H. Dodd, 506 Broadway. 1863.* First edition thus? Small 8vo, 331pp., half-title with decorative black trim, decorated initial letters with central decorative emblem in black on title page, decorative head- and tailpieces, decorated initial letters, contemporary brown pebble leather over thick boards (a bit rubbed, front joint weak, ex-library copy with shelf-mark in white on spine and pocket removed from back pastedown), covers decorated in embossed tooling in blind, spine lettered in gilt, raised bands, a.e.g. A nice copy with dated contemporary signature on fly-leaf. Very similar internally to small octavo edition by Bell & Daldy in 1863 (copy listed here). Not in Kohler.

1071. MILTON LE PARADIS PERDU Traduction De Chateaubriand Précédé De Réflexions Sur La Vie Et Les Escrits De Milton Par Lamartine Et Enrichi De Vingt-Cinq Magnifiques Estampes Originales Gravées Au Burin Sur Acier. *Paris[:] Amable Rigaud, Libraire-Editeur 50, Rue Sainte-Anne, 50[.] M.D.CCC.LXIII.* Second edition thus (first by Rigaud alone). Folio, xxx+157pp., half-title, engraved frontispiece illustration and twenty-four other illustrations by Flatters, Richomme, Lemercier, Melin, and Bernouville (superb impressions), engraved portraits of Milton, and of Lamartine and Chateaubriand, "Reflexions Sur Milton" (dated "Mars 1855"), "Etude Historique Et Littéraire Sur Milton" printed in double column, "Arguments" for the books printed together at the beginning before Book I, splendid decorative head- and tailpieces, decorated initial letter each book, contemporary three-quarter red calf, red cloth (a bit rubbed, some slight foxing without affecting any of the fine plates), raised bands delicately gilt-decorated, spine lettered in gilt, edges untrimmed. The introduction is by Lamartine; the translation by Chateaubriand, which was first published in 1831 (see 1836 sets listed here). Laid in: prospectus (dated 1862) announcing the publication of this edition. A nice copy of this amazingly illustrated book with stunning impressions of the steel-engraved illustrations. The first edition with these illustrations was published in 1855 (copy listed and other editions cited there, including 1870 edition, also listed here, with a listing of illustrations, each hand-colored). Scarce. Kohler 138, reporting "Not in Williamson. Not in the British Library. Not in the Bodleian Library. Not in Cambridge University Library."

1072. MILTON'S PARADISE LOST. Edited By The Rev. George Gilfillan. *New York: D. Appleton And Company, 443 & 445 Broadway. 1864.* First American edition thus? 8vo, 337pp., frontispiece portrait of Milton at age twenty-one by Cornelius Jansen engraved by W. C. Edwards, protective tissue guard, a second portrait plate of *Milton Dictating to His Daughters* after Romney, protective tissue guard, five illustration plates (four after Turner: *The Expulsion, Temptation on the Pinnacle, Temptation on the Mountain, Mustering of the Warrior Angels*; and one after Westall: *Satan*), several with protective tissue guard, contemporary brown calf (joints a bit rubbed), covers decorated in richly embossed trim with Milton's name in gilt at the center with decorated initial letter "M," spine lettered in gilt, raised bands (a bit rubbed), inner dentelles finely tooled in gilt, marbled endpapers, a.e.g. A very nice copy with fine impressions of the plates. Uncommon. Not in Kohler.

1073. PARADISE LOST. A Poem. In Twelve Books By John Milton[.] A New Edition. *Boston: Crosby And Nichols. 1864*. Fourth edition thus? 12mo in 6s, 294pp., original boards (a bit worn, early names on fly-leaf), title page essentially repeated on front cover, advertisements on back cover, dark brown cloth spine (partially missing in places) decorated in embossed blind trim, lettered in gilt. A decent copy of an uncommon mid-nineteenth-century American school book edition. The possible first edition was published by Crosby, Nichols, Lee & Company in Boston in 1861 (also listed here with further editions cited). Not in Kohler.

1074. LE PARADIS PERDU De Milton Traduction Lineaire, Metaphrastique Et Litterale Par Jean De Dieu Labor improbus omnia vincit. La Perte D'Eden. *Librairie De L. Hachette Et Ce Paris 77, Boulevard Saint-Germain. London 18, King William Street, Strand[.] 1864 Tous droits réservés*. First edition thus? 8vo, viii+479pp., half-title in French, prefatory remarks in French dated 1863, a second half-title in French before the poem, French translation in verse on verso with English text on recto, argument at the end of each book, brief "Notes" in French at the end followed by "Contents" in French and English, original brown cloth, brown calf spine (a little rubbed, top of spine and corners worn, foxing), covers ruled in blind with gilt laurel wreath surrounding "College S. Joseph Avignon" in gilt at center of front cover, spine lettered in gilt with decorative gilt pieces within the panels, marbled endpapers. Uncommon. Not in Kohler.

1075. MILTON'S PARADISE LOST. In Twelve Books. *London: Bell And Daldy, 186, Fleet Street. 1865*. Second edition by Bell and Daldy. 8vo, [iv]+331pp., half-title with decorative trim, frontispiece portrait plate by H. Robinson, protective tissue guard, decorated initial letters and emblem of the press on title page, decorative head- and tailpieces, decorated initial letters, "Chiswick Press:– Whittingham And Wilkins, Tooks Court, Chancery Lane" on verso of last page, original green cloth (a bit rubbed, slight staining on front cover), gilt rules on front cover with emblem of the press in gilt at the center, spine lettered in gilt with small emblem beneath title lettering and gilt rules at top and bottom, reddish-brown endpapers, t.e.g, other edges untrimmed. A nice copy with early signature on front pastedown. The possible first edition thus was published in 1863 (also listed here). Scarce. Not in Kohler.

1076. LE PARADIS PERDU De Milton Traduit Par De Pongerville De L'Académie Française[.] Nouvelle Edition, Revue Et Corrigée Précédé De Considérations Sur Milton, Son Epoque Et Ses Ouvrages Par Le Traducteur[.] *Paris[:] Charpentier, Libraire-Editeur[,] 28, Quai De L'Ecole[,] 1865*. 12mo in 6s, half-title, 356pp., contemporary half green calf, marbled paper over boards (a bit rubbed, some foxing throughout, former owner's stamp on title page), spine lettered in gilt, raised bands, marbled endpapers. A nice copy. The translation is in prose by Pongerville of the French Academy, and the arguments are printed together at the end. See 1841 edition of Pongerville's translation of *PL* (also listed here). Uncommon. Not in Kohler.

Gustave Doré—Twenty-five Original Parts (1865–66)

1077. MILTON'S PARADISE LOST, Illustrated By Gustave Doré. Edited, With Notes and a Life of Milton, By The Late Robert Vaughan, D.D. *Cassell, Petter, Galpin & Co. London, Paris & New York. [All Rights Reserved.] 1865-1866*. Twenty-five original parts. 4to, 329pp., first appearance and first issue of illustration plates by Gustave Doré (fine impressions), variously engraved, "Contents" and "List of Illustrations" at end of the last part (Part 25), original printed blue wrappers, as issued. A complete set, most in very fine condition, several a bit used, each with original price of "7 d." printed on front cover. "Initially, there was no parts edition for Doré's *Milton*. The first edition appears to be two different sizes (12" × 17" and 12" × 15"), but the 12" × 15" version is probably bound from the first parts edition a couple years later. But an 1871 catalogue lists a second parts edition as a 4to, yet I cannot find any copy before the 1880s smaller than 12" × 15". There are several 12" × 15" Cassell Doré titles, and all are listed as folios, not 4tos. So how can the 1871–72 Milton parts edition be called a 4to?" (Malan, *Doré*, p. 79). Rare. Not in Kohler.

Gustave Doré was born in Strasbourg in 1832. He received early employment as an illustrator for the newly formed journal *Le Journal Pour Rire* and found himself with the likes of Honoré Daumier and Paul Gavarni. He

II. Descriptive Listing of Editions   285

PL Illustrated By Gustave Doré. Cassell, Petter, Galpin & Co. London, Paris & New York. 1865–66. Twenty-five Original Parts. See #1077.

composed a vast number of illustrations for various magazines, and after his Bible illustrations of 1866, he was all the rage in England and the continent. "No other foreign illustrator and few native ones of the period so completely captured the English fancy" (Percy Muir, *VIB*, p. 227). Doré's wood engravings were found to complement perfectly Milton's text, one genius answering the Romantic grandeur in another. The first book edition with Doré's illustrations appeared about the same time as the parts (also listed here).

1078. MILTON'S PARADISE LOST. Illustrated By Gustave Doré. Edited, With Notes And A Life Of Milton, By Robert Vaughan, D.D. *London: Cassell, Petter, And Galpin, Ludgate Hill, E.C.; And 596, Broadway, New York. n.d. (1866)*. First edition thus. Thick folio (17 ½" × 12 ½"), lxii+329pp., title page in red and black with decorative initials "CPG" at center, illustration plates by Gustave Doré (first appearance in book form, fine impressions), variously

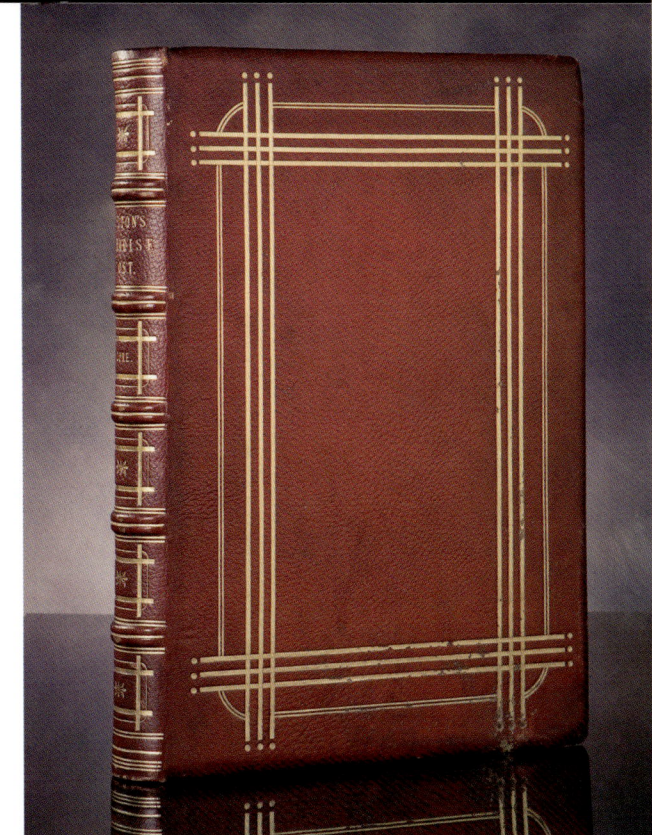

PL Illustrated By Gustave Doré. See #1078.

engraved, each with a protective tissue guard, "Contents," "Life of Milton," "Introduction," notes at bottom of page, contemporary full red morocco over thick boards, elaborately gilt-decorated covers and spine, raised bands, inner and outer dentelles finely tooled in gilt, marbled endpapers, bevelled edges, a.e.g., early armorial bookplate with medieval manuscript-style shield in gilt and color on front pastedown. This is an impressive edition of Doré's Milton with all the grandeur and skill for which Doré is known. The edition was part of an ambitious series in which Doré had planned to include the great masterpieces of literature (he intended to include thirty works in the series; he completed nine). A splendid copy in an elegant contemporary red morocco binding with fine impressions of the plates. "The earliest printing gives the addresses of the publisher [Cassell] in London and New York. It is superior to the later ones which do not" (Percy Muir, *VIB*, p. 243). Dated according to *Milton Tercentenary*, 1908, Appendix, p. 141, #541. Not in Kohler.

Doré's illustrations first appeared in twenty-five parts about this same time, 1865–66 (see complete set preceding). While Martin's illustrations never reached the masses in the same way Doré's did, Doré's illustrations carried with them something of the contrasting dark and light unique to Martin and united the Romantic imagination of the artist with the epic grandeur of the poet, making his illustrations among the most popular to be included in editions large and small for well over the next century. As with Martin, Doré's Bible illustrations were also very popular. At present, there appears to be the beginning of a well-deserved revival of interest in Doré's illustrations.

1079. PARADISE LOST. A Poem. In Twelve Books By John Milton[.] A New Edition. *Boston: Crosby And Ainsworth. New York: Oliver S. Felt. 1866.* First edition thus? 12mo in 6s, 294pp., original light brown cloth spine, printed pink paper over boards repeating title page in black on front cover, with advertisements on back cover (spine a bit rubbed and faded, slightly chipped at top, covers lightly stained, embrowning throughout). Despite some wear, a rather nice copy with a contemporary signature in pencil (dated 1870) on front blank and a small early bookshop label at the top of front pastedown. A possible second edition thus was published one year later in 1867, and a possible third edition in 1868 (where the publisher's imprint

Adam, Eve, and the snake after Gustave Doré, PL, Book IX, lines 784–85. *PL* Illustrated By Gustave Doré. Cassell, Petter, Galpin & Co. London, Paris & New York. n.d. (1866). See #1078.

Adam and Eve having been banished from Eden after Gustave Doré, *PL*, Book XII, line 645, ibid. See #1078.

reads "Oliver s.[sic] Felt")—both listed here. See also similar editions published by Crosby, Nichols, Lee & Company in Boston in 1861 (also listed here with other editions cited). Scarce. Not in Kohler.

1080. PARADISE LOST. A Poem. In Twelve Books By John Milton[.] A New Edition. *Boston: Crosby And Ainsworth. New York: Oliver S. Felt. 1867.* Second edition thus? 12mo in 6s, 294pp., original brown cloth spine, printed pink paper over boards repeating title page in black on front cover, with advertisements on back cover (a bit worn, large black ink spot on front cover spilling lightly over onto bottom of fore-edge, small circular stamp on back cover). All in all, a decent copy with a contemporary signature in pencil on front blank. The possible first edition thus was published one year earlier in 1866 (also listed here with further editions cited). Uncommon. Not in Kohler.

1081. PARADISE LOST. A Poem In Twelve Books. By John Milton. A New Edition With Explanatory Notes. *New York: Published By Hurd And Houghton. 459 Broome Street. 1867.* First edition thus? Small 8vo, 409pp., unsigned vignette sketch of Milton as a young poet at the center of the title page, copyright date of 1866 on verso of title page, "Advertisement" (dated July 1866), "Life of Milton," notes at bottom of page, index at the end, original reddish-brown sand grain cloth (joints a bit worn), central gilt piece on front cover incorporating title in reddish-brown relief within a bright gilt band above a small circular medallion in gilt incorporating "Riverside Classics" along with a decorative floral design in embossed reddish-brown, spine decorated and lettered in gilt, repeating title within decorative gilt trim and "Riverside Classics" within a smaller gilt band than that on the front cover. A good copy with a contemporary signature (dated 1867) in a neat hand in pencil on fly-leaf. See also the 1869 Riverside Press edition listed here published in Boston by "Houghton, Mifflin And Company" bearing the label "Riverside Classics" and other editions cited there. Uncommon. Kohler 140, reporting "Not in the British Library. Not in the Bodleian Library. Not in Cambridge University Library."

1082. DAS VERLORENE PARADIES. Episches Gedicht von John Milton. Uebersetzt von Karl Eitner. *Hildburghausen. Verlag des Bibliographischen Instituts. 1867.* First edition thus? 8vo, 338+[4]pp., general title page ("Bibliothek ausländischer Klassiker in deutscher Uebertragung. Milton's Verlorenes Paradies. Hildburghausen. Verlag des Bibliographischen Instituts. 1867") facing title page, "Milton's Leben und Werke," half-title before poetic translation, original blue-green pebble grain cloth, covers decorated with blind border trim, spine lettered in gilt with decorative gilt trim, marbled endpapers. A lovely copy of this verse translation by Karl Eitner. Four pages of advertisements ("Klassiker=Verlag des Bibliographischen Instituts" dated 1875) bound in at end. See also the 1890 edition of this German translation. Kohler 141, without advertisements at the end, reporting "Not in the British Library. Not in the Bodleian Library. Not in Cambridge University Library."

1083. PARADISE LOST: BOOK ONE [In] AN INTRODUCTION TO THE STUDY OF MILTON By Alex. Monfries, English Master, Montrose Academy. *Montrose[:] Alexander Rodgers, 62 High Street[.] 1867.* First edition thus. Small 8vo, ii+106pp., preface, notes at the bottom of page, original ribbed black cloth, covers decorated in blind. A nice copy. Book I only of *PL*, "With Questions On The Text For Home Study," "Notes, Containing Helps And Hints To The Answers," and an "Appendix, Containing Definitions And Tables For Parsing And Analysis." Not in Kohler.

1084. THE PARADISE LOST By John Milton. With Notes Explanatory And Critical. Edited By Prof. James R. Boyd, D.D., Author Of "Elements Of Rhetoric," "Eclectic Moral Philosophy," And Of An Improved Edition Of "Kames' Elements," Etc. Milton, Whose Genius Had Angelic Wings, And Fed On Manna.—Cowper. Revised Edition. *A. S. Barnes & Company, 751 Broadway, New York. n.d. [ca. 1868].* 8vo, 552pp., content and six illustration plates engraved by Burt after John Martin as in first edition, index (added in 1853), original green cloth (a bit rubbed), spine lettered in gilt with gilt rules at top and bottom, speckled edges. A nice copy. The first edition thus edited by Boyd was published in 1850 by "Baker And Scribner" in New York with reduced illustration plates after Martin (also listed here with further editions by Boyd cited). Not in Kohler.

1085. Variant of Preceding, in original brown cloth (a bit rubbed), spine lettered in gilt with gilt rules at top and bottom. A nice copy in a variant publisher's binding.

1086. MILTON LE PARADIS PERDU Traduction De Chateaubriand Précédé De Réflexions Sur La Vie Et Les Escrits De Milton Par Lamartine Et Enrichi De Vingt-Cinq Magnifiques Estampes Originales Gravées Au Burin Sur Acier. *Paris[:] Amable Rigaud, Libraire-Editeur 50, Rue Sainte-Anne, 50[.] M.D.CCC.LXVIII.* Possible third edition thus (second by Rigaud alone). Folio, xxvi+157pp., similar to 1863 edition thus listed earlier, half-title, engraved frontispiece illustration and twenty-four other illustrations by Flatters, Richomme, Lemercier, Melin, and Bernouville (very fine impressions), engraved portraits of

Milton, and of Lamartine and Chateaubriand, "Reflexions Sur Milton" (dated "Mars 1855"), "Etude Historique Et Littéraire Sur Milton" printed in double column, "Arguments" for the books printed together at the beginning before Book I, splendid decorative head- and tailpieces, decorated initial letter each book, one-half dark maroon morocco, marbled paper over boards (worn at corners, some slight foxing without affecting any of the fine plates), spine lettered in gilt with decorative gilt devices, raised bands, marbled endpapers. A good copy with brilliant impressions of the steel-engraved illustration plates and with presentation inscription in French tipped in on front blank. The introduction is by Lamartine; the translation by Chateaubriand, was first published in 1831 (see 1836 sets listed here). The first edition thus with these illustrations was published in 1855 (also listed here with further editions cited), including 1870 edition (listed here with a listing of illustrations, each hand-colored). Scarce. Not in Kohler.

1087. THE PARADISE LOST By John Milton. With Notes Explanatory And Critical Edited By Rev. James R. Boyd, A.M. Author Of "Elements Of Rhetoric," "Eclectic Moral Philosophy," And Of An Improved Edition Of "Kames' Elements," Etc. Milton, Whose Genius Had Angelic Wings, And Fed On Manna.—Cowper. *New York: A. S. Barnes & Co., 111 & 113 William Street, (Corner of John Street.) 1868.* 8vo, 552pp., "C.W. Benedict, Stereotyper, 201 Williams at NY" on verso of title page, remainder as with first edition in 1850, index (added in 1853), original boards (worn, spine missing, last page of index partially missing, some marginal notations in pencil throughout, pencil notes listed and crossed out on both sides of front blank), decorated title page printed in black on front cover under heading "National School Series" at the top with a small medallion illustration of a woman teaching several children at the center, advertisements printed on back cover. Fair copy of this "School and Academic Edition" in original binding. The first edition thus edited by Boyd was published in 1850 by "Baker And Scribner" in New York with reduced illustration plates after Martin (also listed here with further editions by Boyd cited). Uncommon. Not in Kohler.

1088. PARADISE LOST. A Poem. In Twelve Books By John Milton[.] A New Edition. *Boston: Crosby And Ainsworth. New York: Oliver s.[sic] Felt. 1868, [sic]* Third edition thus? 12mo in 6s, 294pp., index at the end, original black cloth spine, printed pink paper over boards repeating title page in black on front cover (a bit worn, with a few pencil marks on the first several pages of text, early name in pencil on back blank), with advertisements on back cover. Despite some age and wear, a rather nice copy with a large early bookplate on front blank. The publisher's imprint on the front cover here is not the imprint on the title page, but rather: "Boston: Woolworth, Ainsworth & Co. New York: A. S. Barnes & Co." The possible first edition thus was published in 1866; the possible second edition thus was published in 1867—both listed here. Scarce. Not in Kohler.

1089. PARADISE LOST, A Poem In Twelve Books, By John Milton. A New Edition With Explanatory Notes. *New York[:] Ivison, Phinney, Blakeman & Co. 1868.* First edition thus? 8vo, xiv+[2]+409pp., unsigned vignette sketch of a young Milton at center of title page, copyright date of 1866 on verso along with "Riverside, Cambridge: Stereotyped And Printed By H. O. Houghton And Company," "Advertisement" dated 1866, life of Milton, notes at bottom of page, index printed in double column at the end, original purple cloth spine (a bit rubbed), decorated green paper over boards (a little age-darkened with some slight rubbing, lacking front blank), front cover repeats title page within black rule including vignette sketch of a young Milton at the center, advertisements on back cover. A nice copy sharing many of the features of the 1867 "Riverside Press" edition. One year later, in 1869, a possible second edition thus was published. Both are listed here. Uncommon. Not in Kohler.

1090. EL PARAISO PERDIDO Poema Escrito En Ingles Por John Milton Con Notas De Addisson Saint-Maur Y Otros Traducida Al Gastellano Por D. Dionisio Sanjuan. Biblioteca La Ilustracion. *Barcelona. Casa Editorial La Ilustracion Calla De Mendizabal, Numero 4. 1868.* 8vo, 300+[3]pp., half-title, "Biografia De J. Milton," prose translation, "Indice" at the end, followed by advertisement leaf, original printed orange paper wrappers (aged with front corners turned up, foxing), advertisement on back cover, edges untrimmed. "Traduccion al castellano por D. Dionisio Zanjan. Barcelona. Imp. Luis Tasso. Edt. La Ilustracion." Scarce. Not in Kohler.

1091. PARADISE LOST A Poem In Twelve Books By John Milton[.] A New Edition. *Boston: Woolworth, Ainsworth & Co. New York: A. S. Barnes & Co. 1869.* First edition thus? 12mo in 6s, 294pp., original black cloth spine, printed pink paper over boards repeating title page in black on front cover (a bit rubbed, some occasional light foxing with some slight, inoffensive waterstaining on front cover and along bottom inner binding edge of last third of book and at bottom edge of back cover), with advertisements on back cover. Despite some slight aging and wear, a rather nice copy with early signature on fly-leaf. The publisher's imprint on the front cover here is the same as that on the title page; it is also the same as that on the cover of the 1868 Crosby-Ainsworth edition (copy listed here). See also the possible second edition thus published in Boston And Chicago in 1870 by Woolworth, Ainsworth & Co.; and see copies of similar editions published in Boston by Crosby and Ainsworth and in New York by Oliver S. Felt in 1867 and again in 1868 (copies listed here). Scarce. Not in Kohler.

1092. PARADISE LOST, A Poem In Twelve Books, By John Milton. A New Edition With Explanatory Notes. *New York: Ivison, Phinney, Blakeman & Co. 1869.* Second edition thus? 8vo, xiv+[ii]+409pp., unsigned vignette sketch of a young Milton on title page, copyright on verso of title page dated 1866, "Advertisement" (dated 1866, same as copyright date), notes at bottom of page, index, original black cloth spine, green paper over boards (a bit rubbed) with title page and vignette sketch of a young Milton (unsigned) reprinted on front cover, advertisements printed on back cover. A nice copy in rather well-preserved condition with contemporary signature (dated 1870) on fly-leaf. The possible first edition thus was published in 1868 (also listed here). Uncommon. Not in Kohler.

1093. PARADISE LOST A Poem In Twelve Books By John Milton[.] A New Edition, with Explanatory Notes[.] *Boston[:] Houghton, Mifflin And Company[,] The Riverside Press, Cambridge[,] (1869).* 8vo, xiv+[2]+409pp., unsigned vignette sketch of a young Milton on title page, copyright date of 1869 on verso, "Advertisement" dated 1866, life of Milton, notes at bottom of page, index printed in double column at the end, original decorated green cloth (a bit rubbed), front cover decorated in black trim with "Riverside Classics" and emblem of the press in bright embossed gilt against a black background outlined in gilt across the top and *PL* lettered in gilt in the center, spine lettered in embossed green against a bright gilt band within decorative black trim across the top with title lettered in gilt at the center along with "Edited By Torrey," with initials of the press within decorative black trim at the bottom, and gilt and black rules at the top and bottom, dark green endpapers. A very nice copy. See 1867 edition published by "Hurd and Houghton" in New York (possibly first edition thus), bearing the label "Riverside Classics." See 1879 and 1880 Riverside Press editions below published by "Houghton, Osgood And Company" in Boston; and see 1872 and 1875 Riverside Press editions below "Published By Hurd And Houghton. Cambridge" in New York. Not in Kohler.

The collection also has another copy in a variant binding: original decorated green cloth, decorated exactly as preceding copy with "Edited By Torrey" in gilt at the center of the spine.

1094. Variant of Preceding, in original contrasting green cloth (a little rubbed along extremities, names erased at top of title page), dark green spine lettered in small gilt letters with small gilt laurel wreath at the top, lighter green boards with contrasting darker green lettering (title at top and "The Riverside Classics" at bottom) and a long-stemmed flower and blossom that runs the length of the cover. A good copy in a narrower format, in a variant publisher's binding, with early art nouveau design.

1095. PARADISE LOST A Poem In Twelve Books By John Milton. *New York: Clark & Maynard, Publishers, No. 5 Barclay Street. 1869.* First edition thus? 12mo in 6s, 283pp., life of Milton by Fenton, index at end, original boards (worn and age-darkened, some age-browning, pp. 15/16 with a tear and the bottom portion of the page missing), black cloth spine (a bit rubbed, spine ends slightly chipped), title page repeated on front cover within decorative trim with "School Edition" at the top, advertisement on back cover (both covers worn and very faded). A fair copy. Scarce. Not in Kohler.

Also in the collection and listed here: a possible second edition thus published in 1872; an undated ca. 1879 edition published by "Clark and Maynard" with front cover ("School Edition . . . New York: Clark, Austin & Smith, 3 Park Row And 3 Ann-Street"); an undated ca. 1880 edition by "Clark & Maynard, Publishers 771 Broadway" with front cover ("School Edition . . . New York: Clark & Maynard, Publisher"); and an undated ca. 1885 edition by "Clark & Maynard, Publishers. No. 5 Barclay Street" (title page, as here) with front cover as here. See also editions published by Clark, Austin & Co., first thus in 1849 (also listed here with further editions cited, all similar to editions here and each, either labeled as or intended to serve as a "School Edition.")

1096. MILTON'S PARADISE LOST. Illustrated By Gustave Doré. Edited, With Notes And A Life Of Milton, By The Late Robert Vaughan, D.D. *Cassell, Petter, And Galpin, London And New York. n.d. [ca. 1870s].* Seventeen original parts. Imperial 4to, lxii+v-viii+329pp., through Part XIV, last three parts containing prelims (paginated differently) to the published edition ("Contents," "Life of Milton," "Introduction," and printed title page in red and black: "Milton's Paradise Lost. Illustrated By Gustave Doré. Edited, With Notes And A Life Of Milton, By Robert Vaughan, D.D. London: Cassell, Petter, And Galpin, Ludgate Hill, E.C.; And 596, Broadway, New York."), fifty illustration plates by Gustave Doré, variously engraved (fine impressions), each with protective tissue guard with printed passage for the illustration, notes at bottom of page, original printed light blue wrappers, stitched, as issued, advertisements on back covers. A complete set (a few showing some wear and slight foxing, some edges frayed a bit, two large tears on back cover of Part I repaired from within by special tape, occasional small tears to other covers). Most of the parts are in good to very good condition, with Parts XIV, XV, XVI, and XVII containing the prelims to the published edition. Bound in at end of Part I is a sixteen-page 8vo printed "List Of Works Published By Messrs. Cassell, Petter, & Galpin. London And New York" (including "Doré's Milton's Paradise Lost," "Doré Bible," and "Bunyan. The Pilgrim's Progress"). Printed on front cover of Part XVII: "Notice To Subscribers,—Milton's Paradise Lost is complete with this Part, and is published in One Volume complete at £2 10S., or morocco elegant, gilt edges, £6 6S . . . Subscribers who have not completed their Sets of Milton's Paradise Lost should give their Orders immediately for such Parts as they require." The first edition with Doré's illustrations of *PL* appeared in the mid-1860s (see 1865–66 set of parts and 1866 first book edition). Scarce. Not in Kohler.

1097. MILTON'S PARADISE LOST. Illustrated By Gustave Doré. Edited, With Notes And A Life Of Milton; By Robert Vaughan, D.D. *Cassell, Petter, & Galpin, London, Paris, And New York. n.d. [ca. 1870]*. Imperial 4to (14 ¾" × 12"), lxii+329+[4]pp., half-title, title page in red and black with decorative initials "CPG" at center, fifty illustration plates by Gustave Doré, variously engraved (fine impressions), each with protective tissue guard with printed passage for the illustration, "Contents," "Life of Milton," "Introduction," notes at bottom of page, original gilt-decorated red cloth (front cover lightly waterstained at lower right corner), front cover lettered in gilt with decorative border trim in black and gilt, spine lettered in gilt with three decorative gilt devices and with decorative trim in black and gilt at top and bottom, back cover decorated in blind, black endpapers, a.e.g. A very good, tall copy in an attractive binding of the period, with contemporary signature (dated 1870) on front blank, and with four pages of advertisements for "Selections From Messrs. Cassell Petter & Galpin's Publications" (including Doré's various illustrated editions) bound in at end. Not in Kohler (but see Kohler 142, citing "[ca. 1870]" edition, "Folio in 4s," and reporting "Not in Cambridge University Library").

1098. MILTON'S PARADISE LOST. Illustrated By Gustave Doré. Edited, With Notes And A Life Of Milton, By Robert Vaughan, D.D. *Cassell & Co., Limited: London, Paris, New York & Melbourne. [All Rights Reserved.] n.d. [ca. 1870]*. First edition thus. Imperial 4to (13 ½" × 11"—not as tall as preceding copy), lxii+329+8pp., title

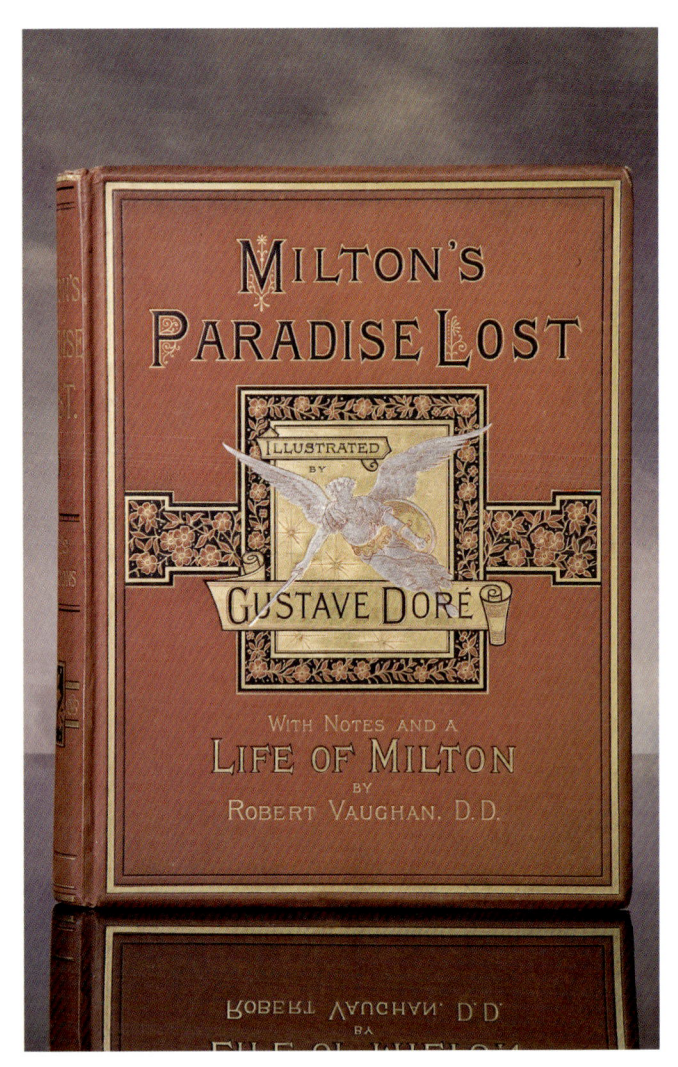

PL Illustrated By Gustave Doré. Cassell, Petter, Galpin & Co. London, Paris, New York & Melbourne. (ca. 1870). In original gilt-decorated cloth, a stunning publisher's binding. See #1098.

page in red and black with decorative device at center bottom, fifty illustration plates by Gustave Doré, variously engraved (fine impressions), each with protective tissue guard with printed passage for the illustration, "Contents," "Life of Milton," "Introduction," notes at bottom of page, original decorated reddish-brown cloth, front cover and spine elegantly decorated in gilt and black, back cover ruled in blind, with brilliant central gilt design on front cover featuring *The Destroying Angel* in bright silver, lettering in black incorporating "Illustrated by Gustave Doré," and outlined in floral decorations, a.e.g. A fine copy in a stunning publisher's binding with eight pages (paginated) of advertisements bound in at end ("A Classified Catalogue of Cassell & Company's Publications"). Not in Kohler.

1099. PARADISE LOST [In] THE DORE GALLERY. Containing Two Hundred And Fifty Beautiful Engravings,

Selected From The Doré Bible, Milton, Dante's Inferno, Dante's Purgatorio And Paradiso, Atala, La Fontaine, Fairy Realm, Don Quixote, Baron Munchausen, Croquemitaine, &c. &c. With Descriptive Letterpress, Memoir, and Essay, by Edmund Ollier, *Esq. New York: Cassell, Petter, & Galpin, 596 Broadway. n.d. [ca. 1870s].* Fifty original parts. First edition thus? 4to, unpaginated plates—five per part—each plate with protective tissue guard with printed passage for the illustration, last tissue guard numbered 250, fifty illustration plates by Gustave Doré, variously engraved (fine impressions), original printed blue wrappers, as issued with vignette portrait of Doré at the center, "Supplied To Subscribers Only," "Complete in Fifty Parts," with each part priced "One Dollar." A complete set, most of the parts in very good to fine condition (the first one showing some wear and some slight foxing) with half-title and title page in red and black supplied at the end of the last part, part 50. Scarce. Not in Kohler.

1100. PARADISE LOST [In] CASSELL'S DORE GALLERY: Containing Two Hundred and Fifty Beautiful Engravings, Selected From The Doré Bible, Milton . . . [As Preceding Copy.] *Cassell & Company, Limited: London, Paris & New York. n.d. [ca. 1870s].* 4to, xlix+152pp., half-title, title page in red and black, "Advertisement," "List Of Plates," "Memoir Of Gustave Doré," "Description Of The Plates," 250 plates including illustration plates of Gustave Doré's illustrations for *PL*, original full red morocco (rebacked preserving original spine), gilt-decorated cover and spine, a.e.g. A nice copy with early inscription in a neat hand on half-title.

1101. THE PARADISE LOST By John Milton. With Notes Explanatory And Critical Edited By Rev. James R. Boyd, A.M. Author Of "Elements Of Rhetoric," "Eclectic Moral Philosophy," And Of An Improved Edition Of "Kames' Elements," Etc. Milton, Whose Genius Had Angelic Wings, And Fed On Manna.—Cowper. *New York: A. S. Barnes & Co., 111 & 113 William Street, (Corner Of John Street.) 1870.* 8vo, 552pp., contents and six illustration plates engraved by Burt after John Martin as with first edition in 1850, index (added in 1853), original brown cloth (a bit rubbed, worn at corners, spine ends chipped), spine lettered in gilt. A good copy of this "School and Academic Edition." The first edition edited by Boyd was published in 1850 by "Baker And Scribner" in New York with reduced illustration plates after Martin (also listed here with further editions by Boyd cited). Boyd's edition became very popular over the next two decades, and most editions did not include the Martin plates. Uncommon. Not in Kohler.

Twenty-Seven Beautifully Hand-Colored Engraved Illustrations, Each Plate Finely Engraved and Mounted on Cardlike Paper

1102. [PARADISE LOST] MILTON LE PARADIS PERDU Traduction De Chateaubriand Précédé De Reflexions Sur La Vie Et Les Ecrits De Milton Par Lamartine Et Enrichi De Vingt-Sept Magnifiques Estampes Originales Gravées Au Burin Sur Acier. *Paris[:] Amable Rigaud, Libraire-Editeur[,] 50, Rue Sainte-Anne, 50[.] M.D.CCC.LXX.* Folio, [28 unpaginated leaves], half-title ("Paris.—Imprimé chez Jules Bonaventure, 55, quai des Grands-Augustins" on verso of half-title), twenty-seven hand-colored plates (fine impressions), without Milton's text or introductory text, modern red cloth, plates reinforced within the binding, maroon morocco label with gilt lettering and gilt rules on spine, new blank pages at beginning and end, marbled endpapers, t.e.g. The engraved illustrations in this volume were originally published in 1855 (also listed here) and comprise a total of twenty-seven beautiful engraved illustrations on high-quality paper, each hand-colored and mounted on cardlike paper. Beginning with hand-colored engravings of (1) a young Milton engraved by Sixdeniers ("Imp. F. Chardone aine, 30, r. Hautefille, Paris" at bottom); (2) Chateaubriand after Gaillard; and (3) Lamartine engraved by Pelée, the next fourteen hand-colored engraved illustrations are after Flatters and consist of the following: (1) untitled fall of the angels engraved by Delaistre ("Imp. F. Chardone aine, 30 r. Hautefille, Paris" at bottom); (2) *Raphael dans l'Air* engraved by Migneret; (3) *Satan à la Cour du Chaos* engraved by Allais; (4) *Satan et Belzébuth à la Découverte* engraved by Conquy; (5) *Satan Cotoyant les Murs du Ciel* engraved by Nyon; (6) *Le Conciliabule* engraved by Dien; (7) *La Chute des Anges* engraved by Gelée; (8) *Satan Blessé* engraved by Jouannin; (9) *Anges dans le Lac de Bitume* engraved by Bein; (10) *Satan Sorté du Couffre* engraved by Migneret; (11) *Satan Plongeant dans Le Styx* engraved by Darodes; (12) *Satan et Belzébuth se Consultent* engraved by Darodes; (13) *Les Forges* engraved by Audibrand; and (14) *Satan, la Mort, le Péché* engraved by Leroux. The next ten hand-colored engraved illustrations consist of the following: (1) *La Prière* after "Lemercier Pinxt Aubert AF," engraved by "Geille & Ch. Lalaisse Sculpt"; (2) *Le Réveil d'Eve* after "Melin Pinxt Aubert AF," engraved by "Pelle & Ch. Lalaisse Sculpt"; (3) *Eve Effeuillant des Roses* after "Lemercier Pinxt Aubert AF," engraved by "Pelle & Ch. Lalaisse Sculpt"; (4) *La Premier Baiser* after "Flatters Pinxt Aubert AF," engraved by "Caron Et Ch. Lalaisse Sculpt"; (5) *Eve se Mirant dans l'Eau* after "Richomme Pinxt," engraved by "St. Eve & Ch. Lalaisse Sculpt"; (6) *Eve Cueille la Pomme* after "Melin Pinxt," engraved by "St. Eve & Ch. Lalaisse Sculpt"; (7)) *Eve Donne la Pomme à Adam* after "Melin Pinxt Aubert AF," engraved by "Moret & Ch. Lalaisse Sculpt"; (8) *Adam Après le Péché* after "Flatters Pinxt," engraved by "Goulu Et Rensonnette Sc"; (9) *Le Pardon d'Adam* after "Melin Pinxt," engraved by "Pelle & Ch. Lalaisse Sculpt"; and (10) *Adam et Eve Chassés du Paradis* after "Bernouville Pinxt," engraved by "Pelle & Ch. Lalaisse Sculpt." A color print of *Satan, Sin, and Death* (5 ¼" × 7 ½") is tipped in on the blank leaf following the last engraved illustration plate. A unique gathering of hand-colored engraved illustrations without Milton's text. The first edition with these three engraved portraits and twenty-four engraved illustrations after Flatters, Richomme, Lemercier, Melin, and Bernouville was published in 1855 (see copy listed earlier with the full text of Milton's poem translated by Chateaubriand and an introduction by Lamartine); the second edition thus (first by Rigaud alone), with these same engraved illustrations and full text, was published in 1863 (also listed here), with original prospectus laid in; the third edition thus, with these same engraved illustrations and full text, was published in 1868 (also listed here); and see 1882 edition (also listed here). Scarce. Not in Kohler.

1103. PARADISE LOST A Poem. In Twelve Books By John Milton. A New Edition. *Boston And Chicago: Woolworth, Ainsworth & Co. 1870.* Second edition thus? 12mo in 6s, 294pp., original black cloth spine, printed pink paper over boards repeating title page in black on front cover (a bit worn, with a few pencil marks throughout) with advertisements on back cover, bookplate. Despite some age and wear, a rather nice copy. The first edition thus was published in 1869 (also listed here). See similar editions published in Boston by Crosby and Ainsworth and in New York by Oliver S. Felt in 1866 (also listed here with further editions cited). Scarce. Not in Kohler.

1104. THE PARADISE LOST By John Milton. With Notes Explanatory And Critical Edited By Rev. James R. Boyd . . . [as with 1870 edition preceding] *New York: A. S. Barnes & Co., 111 & 113 William Street, (Corner of John Street.) 1870.* 8vo, 552pp., contents as with first edition in 1850, index (added in 1853), leather spine (worn) lettered in gilt, original boards (worn, boards rubbed), decorated title page printed in black on front cover under heading "National School Series" at the top with a small medallion illustration of a woman teaching several children at the center, advertisements printed on back cover. A decent copy of this "School and Academic Edition" in original binding. The first edition thus edited by Boyd was published in 1850 by "Baker And Scribner" in New York with reduced illustration plates after Martin (also listed here with further editions by Boyd cited). Uncommon. Not in Kohler.

1105. PARADISE LOST A Poem. In Twelve Books By John Milton. A New Edition. *Boston: Nichols And Hall, No. 32 Bromfield Street. 1872.* First edition thus? 12mo in 6s, 294pp., original black cloth spine, printed pink paper over boards repeating title page in black (worn and faded, a bit age-browned, small tear in outer margin of p. 55 not affecting text), with advertisements on back cover. All in all, a decent copy. A possible second edition thus was published ca. 1878 (also listed here). Not in Kohler.

1106. PARADISE LOST, A Poem In Twelve Books, By John Milton. A New Edition With Explanatory Notes. *New York: Published By Hurd And Houghton. Cambridge: Riverside Press. 1872.* Small 8vo, xiv+[2]+409pp., vignette portrait sketch of a young Milton at center of title page, "Entered according to Act of Congress, in the year 1866" on verso of title page, "Advertisement" (dated 1866), "Life Of Milton," notes at bottom of page, "Index" at the end, original green pebble cloth (a little rubbed), central gilt piece on front cover incorporating title in green relief within a bright gilt band above a small circular medallion in gilt incorporating "Riverside Classics" along with a decorative floral design in embossed green, spine decorated and lettered in gilt, repeating title within decorative gilt trim and "Riverside Classics" within a smaller gilt band than that on the front cover. A nice copy. Scarce. Not in Kohler.

Also in the collection and listed here: 1867 edition (possible first edition thus) published, like here, by "Hurd and Houghton" in New York bearing the label "Riverside Classics" in a binding exactly like the binding here and 1869 Riverside Press edition published in Boston by "Houghton, Mifflin And Company" bearing the label "Riverside Classics" and other editions cited there.

1107. PARADISE LOST A Poem In Twelve Books. By John Milton. *New York: Clark & Maynard, Publishers. No. 5 Barclay Street. 1872.* Second edition thus? 12mo in 6s, 283pp., life of Milton by Fenton, index at end, original boards (somewhat worn, some page corners bent over and straightened out, numerous signatures and notations in pencil in a neat hand on front and back blanks), black cloth spine (spine ends slightly chipped), title page for Clark & Maynard, publishers edition of *PL* repeated on front cover within decorative trim ("School Edition . . . New York: Clark & Maynard, Publishers, 5 Barclay Street"), advertisement on back cover (worn and very faded). A fair copy.

The possible first edition thus by Clark & Maynard was published in 1869 (also listed here with further editions cited). Scarce. Not in Kohler.

1108. THE PARADISE LOST By John Milton. With Notes Explanatory And Critical[.] Edited By Rev. James R. Boyd, D.D . . . [as with 1870 edition listed here] Revised Edition. *A. S. Barnes & Company, New York And Chicago. 1872.* Revised edition. 8vo, 552pp., content as with first edition in 1850, index (added in 1853), original boards (rubbed, edges and corners worn), black leather spine (worn, joints cracked, spine chipped at top and bottom, early ownership stamps), title page within decorative border trim on front cover, advertisement for "Worman's Works" on back cover, spine lettered in gilt, advertisements on endpapers. Although a bit worn, still a fair copy in its original binding, in a protective plastic cover. The first edition thus edited by Boyd was published in 1850 by "Baker And Scribner" in New York with reduced illustration plates after Martin (also listed here with further editions by Boyd cited). This a revised edition published, as before, as a "School and Academic Edition" in the "National School Series" (so-labeled once again on front cover). Uncommon. Not in Kohler.

1109. SELECTIONS FROM "PARADISE LOST" A Poem, By John Milton, Translated Into The Manx Language By The Rev. Thomas Christian, Vicar Of Marown In 1796. [In] Manx Miscellanies volume 1. *Douglas, Isle Of Man Printed For The Manx Society[,] MDCCCLXXII.* Title page for **PARADISE LOST.** A Poem, By John Milton, Translated Into The Manks Language By The Rev. Mr. Thomas Christian, Of Ballakilley, KK. Marown. *Douglas: Printed By And For C. Briscoe. n.d. [1872].* 8vo, 120pp., original olive green pebble cloth, covers richly decorated in embossed blind trim, gilt seal at the center, different on each cover, spine lettered in gilt within decorative gilt trim, labeled "Manx Miscellanies Vol 1" sideways and "Vol. XX" in gilt at the top and "Manx Society MDCCCLXXII" at the bottom, contemporary armorial bookplate on front pastedown, unopened. A fine, fresh copy with selections from *PL*, without identification and without verse numbers, translated into Manx verse. Scarce. Not in Kohler.

There are several other short pieces in this volume, each with half-title: "The Emerald Vernicle Of The Vatican. By C. W. King, M.A., With Notes By 'Aspen.' With a Portrait of Our Saviour [tipped in] (see frontispiece)," protective tissue guard, twenty-four pages; "Ancient Portraitures Of Our Lord," fifteen pages; "The Seal Of Thomas, Bishop Of The Isle Of Man," with plate of the seal, seven pages; "Poetical Descriptions Of The Isle Of Man," twelve pages; and "The Diary of James VIIth Earl Of Derby," five pages; plus "The Manx Society For The Publication Of National Documents," fourteen pages.

1109A. (Cross-listing) **PARADISE LOST:** Or, The Great Dragon Cast Out; Being A Full, True And Particular Account Of The Great and Dreadful Bloodless Battle That Was Fought In The Celestial Regions About 6000 Years Ago. By Lucian Redivivus. "Better to *reign* on earth than *serve* in heaven." "Laugh at all things, / Great and small things." Lord Byron. – "L'univers perdu pour une pomme, / Et Dieu, pour le damner, créant le premier homme." *Boston: Published By Josiah P. Mendum, At The Office Of The Boston Investigator. 1872.* First edition thus. Small 8vo, 101pp., original green cloth. An irreverent parody of Milton's poem with copious notes filled with quotations from earlier commentators on Milton and from the Bible. A highly eccentric and yet very interesting work. Uncommon. See main listing under *Redivivus, Lucian* [pseud], with Nineteenth-century Miltoniana.

First Edition of This Spanish Prose Translation and First Spanish Edition with Doré's Illustrations

1110. EL PARAISO PERDIDO Por John Milton, Segun El Texto De Las Ediciones Mas Autorizadas[.] Nueva Traduccion Del Inglés, Anotada Y Precedida De La Vida Del Autor Por Don Cayetano Rosell, Ilustrada Por Gustavo Doré Con Cincuenta Magnificas Lamina Grabadas Sobre Boj[.] *Barcelona[:] Montaner Y Simon, Editores[,] Calle De Casanova, Numero 8[,] 1873.* First edition thus. Folio, liii+293+[2]pp., half-title with elaborate emblem on verso, fifty engraved plates after Gustave Doré (first appearance thus in a Spanish edition), "Vida De Juan Milton" before the poem, "Juicios Criticos Sobre El Paraiso Perdiodo De Milton," "El Paraiso Recobrado," and two indexes ("Indice" and "Pauta Cara La Colocacio De Las Laminas") at the end, notes at bottom of page, text within double black ruled border throughout, contemporary red morocco spine (some wear, especially along extremities), red cloth boards, red morocco label lettered in gilt with decorative gilt rules on spine, decorative gilt pieces within the panels, raised bands with decorative gilt trim (a little rubbed), decorated light green endpapers. A nice copy. Included at the end, without reference on title page, is Milton's *PR* ("*El Paraiso Recobrado* Traducido Por Enrique Leopoldo De Verneuill") This is the first edition of this Spanish prose translation and the first Spanish edition with Dore's illustrations. *PL* was first published in Spanish in 1812 in the translation by Juan de Escoiquiz; several other translations followed. The present prose translation of *PL* is by Cayetano Roseli; the prose translation of *PR*

(*El Paraiso Recobrado*, pp. 259–93) is by Enrique Leopoldo de Verneuill. See 1883 edition listed here of *El Paraiso Perdido* in verse translation by D. Juan Escoiquiz with Dore's illustrations; see also two-volume ca. 1890 edition listed here of *O Paraiso Perdido* in poetic translation by Antonio José de Lima Leitao, with Dore's illustrations. NUC records four copies: University of Illinois, Washington State University, University of California, and Harvard University. Not in Kohler, who records only an 8vo edition of 1873.

1111. THE PARADISE LOST By John Milton. With Notes Explanatory And Critical. Edited By Prof. James R. Boyd, D.D . . . [as with 1870 edition earlier.] Revised Edition. *A. S. Barnes & Company, New York And Chicago. 1873.* Revised edition. 8vo, 552pp., title page with advertisement for "Prof. James R. Boyd's Works" on verso, content as with first edition in 1850, index (added in 1853), original boards (a little rubbed, endpapers slightly age-spotted), black leather spine (a bit worn, front joint cracked, chipped at top and bottom), title page within decorative border trim on front cover, advertisement for "Worman's Works" on back cover, spine lettered in gilt, advertisements for various textbooks on endpapers. All in all, a nice copy. The first edition thus edited by Boyd was published in 1850 by "Baker And Scribner" in New York with reduced illustration plates after Martin (also listed here with further editions by Boyd cited). Uncommon. Not in Kohler.

1112. PARADISE LOST. In Ten Books. The Text exactly reproduced from the first edition of 1667. With an APPENDIX containing the Additions made in Later Issues and a Monograph on the Original Publication of the Poem. *London[:] Basil Montagu Pickering[,] 196 Piccadilly[,] 1873.* First edition thus. 4to, unpaginated, presentation page, half-title, Pickering imprint on title page, presentation page, appendix at end (with "I. Facsimile Of The Printer's Address To The Reader, The Argument To The Ten Books; Apology For The Verse, And Errata; II. A Monograph On The First Edition Of Paradise Lost"), colophon page at end with emblem incorporating "Chiswick Press," contemporary full rich red morocco (rebacked preserving original spine, a bit rubbed), triple gilt rules on covers with central gilt seal, back cover similarly decorated in blind, elaborately gilt-decorated spine within the panels, black morocco label with gilt lettering and gilt rules, raised bands, inner and outer dentelles delicately gilt-tooled, marbled endpapers, a.e.g. Facsimile reproduction of the first edition. A fine, large paper copy of this handsomely bound edition beautifully printed at the Chiswick Press. Printed presentation page from Oscar Browning, with written presentation inscription beneath dated 1875. Kohler 147.

1113. HET VERLOREN PARADIJS. Heldendicht In Twaalf Zangen. Door John Milton. In Nederduitsche Verzen Overgebracht Door Jan Jacob Lodewijk Ten Kate. Met Platen Van Gustave Doré. *Leiden, Albertus Willem Sijthoff. n.d. [ca. 1875].* First edition thus? 4to, xii+329pp., half-title, title page in red and black with emblem at the center, "Voorbericht" signed by "T.K.," twenty-eight full-page illustration plates after Gustave Doré, variously engraved, three-quarter yellow linen (occasional foxing), marbled paper over boards, front cover lettered in dark red, spine lettered in dark red with double dark red lines at top and bottom, yellow endpapers. A nice copy of this Dutch translation. While Doré's fifty plates are usually included, even in French, German, and Spanish translations, this Dutch translation, as Kohler observes, is complete with twenty-eight. Scarce. Kohler 149, reporting "Not in the British Library. Not in Cambridge University Library."

1114. PARADISE LOST: A Poem, In Twelve Books, By John Milton; With A Life Of The Author, By The Rev. H. Stebbing, A.M. *World Publishing House, 139 Eighth Street, New York. 1875.* Together with **PARADISE REGAINED**, And Other Poems By John Milton. *World Publishing House, 139 Eighth Street, New York. 1875.* 2 volumes in one. First edition thus? Thick, small 8vo, 356pp.,+ 190pp., engraved frontispiece portrait plate after C. Burt, protective tissue guard, volume 1, title page each volume, double black rule around text, original red cloth (a bit rubbed), front cover decorated with black harp at the center, thick black rules at top and bottom continuing on to spine, spine lettered in gilt ("Milton's Poetical Works") above a gilt circle incorporating "The World Edition" in gilt with the world's two spheres in gilt with decorative gilt trim within thick black rules at top and bottom, large floral piece in blind at center of back cover. A nice copy. Uncommon. Not in Kohler.

1115. PARADISE LOST. A Poem In Twelve Books, By John Milton. A New Edition With Explanatory Notes. *New York: Published By Hurd And Houghton. Cambridge: Riverside Press. 1875.* 8vo, xiv+[2]+409pp., vignette sketch of a young Milton at center of title page (copyright on verso dated 1866), "Advertisement" (dated 1866), "Index Of Well-Known Lines And Passages" and general "Index" at end, original reddish-brown cloth (worn, spine missing, pages age-browned, some loose within with frayed edges), decorative black trim on front cover with central gilt device incorporating title. See 1867 edition listed earlier, published by "Hurd and Houghton" in New York (possibly first edition thus), bearing the label "Riverside Classics"; see also 1869 Riverside Press edition listed earlier published in Boston by "Houghton, Mifflin And Company" bearing the label "Riverside Classics" and other editions cited there. Scarce. Not in Kohler.

1116. LE PARADIS PERDU Suivi De Essai Sur La Littérature Anglaise Par Chateaubriand[.] Nouvelle Edition Revue Avec Soin Sur Les Editions Originales[.] *Paris[:] Garnier Frères, Libraires – Editeurs[,] 6, Rue Des Saints-Pères, 6[.] 1876.* 8vo in 4s, xx+579+12pp., unsigned engraved frontispiece illustration for Book IV (*Raphael Counseling Adam and Eve*, lines quoted and page cited), half-title, "Remarques" before the prose translation of the poem, "Essai Sur La Littérature Anglois Et Considérations Sur Le Génie Des Temps, Des Hommes Et Des Révolutions" after the translation, with half-title, followed by "Avertissement" (sic), "Introduction," and lengthy "Essai," "Table" at the end, original printed wrappers (front cover a little frayed along front edge, front joint partially separated near the top, covers a bit age-darkened), title page printed on front cover within a black rule with decorative corner pieces, "Milton" neatly printed in ink at top of spine in an early hand and repeated at top of front cover in pencil, partially unopened. A nice copy with title page printed on front cover only, with twelve pages of advertisements, paginated, bound in at the end. The translation by Chateaubriand first appeared in a two-volume edition in 1831 (see 1836 set listed here). Uncommon. Not in Kohler.

1117. PARADISE LOST, As Originally Published By John Milton, Being A Facsimile Reproduction Of The First Edition. With An Introduction By David Masson, M.A., LL.D., Author Of The Life Of John Milton. *London: Elliot Stock, 62, Paternoster Row, E.C. 1877.* First edition thus. Small 4to, xviii+unpaginated, half-title with decorative pieces, decorative piece on title page, introduction by Masson (dated 1876) original imitation calf (a bit rubbed), spine lettered in gilt. A nice copy with several early bookplates and with early (possibly contemporary) notes in ink tipped in on half-title describing the book and where it was purchased. Facsimile reproduction of the first edition. Scarce. Not in Kohler.

1118. PARADISE LOST. A Poem. In Twelve Books By John Milton. A New Edition. *Boston: Nichols And Hall, No. 32 Bromfield Street. n.d. [ca. 1878].* Second edition thus? 12mo in 6s, 294pp., original printed pink paper over boards repeating title page in black (a bit worn), black cloth spine, advertisements of publications by Nichols and Hall on back cover. A decent copy with contemporary signature on front cover: "Mary F. Elger W.R.H.S. Class - '79," and the dates "Oct 16, 1878 - April 16, 1879 - 6 mos" in pencil in a contemporary hand on back blank. The possible first edition thus was published in 1872 (listed here). Uncommon. Not in Kohler.

1119. PARADISE LOST: A Poem. In Twelve Books, By John Milton: With A Life Of The Author, By The Rev. H. Stebbing, A.M. *New York: Leavitt & Allen Bros., No. 8 Howard Street. n.d. [ca. 1878].* Bound with **PARADISE REGAINED, AND OTHER POEMS** By John Milton. *New York: Leavitt & Allen Bros., No. 8 Howard Street. n.d. [ca. 1870s].* 2 volumes in one. 8vo, 356pp.,+190pp., engraved frontispiece illustration plate (after a "Painting by Beaume," engraved by O. Pelton, the scene unrelated to Milton: a young boy handing a cup to a young woman, presumably his mother, seated with a large pillow behind her with another young child with dog looking on, the scene set outside the home), protective tissue guard, title page for each volume, "Memoir Of Milton's Life And Writings," double black rule around the text, original decorated green cloth, front cover decorated in black and gilt trim with a broad gilt band across the top containing Milton's name in embossed letters, the letter "M" in a larger embossed green letter set off against a gilt shield backdrop, the remaining letters shaded in red, the whole surrounded by decorative gilt trim, the spine similarly decorated in black and gilt trim with the title ("Milton's Poems") in embossed green within a rolling gilt scroll at the top, "Leavitt & Allen Bros." in embossed letters within a gilt band in front of a decorative gilt piece at the bottom, a.e.g. A good copy with a contemporary signature (dated 1878) on fly-leaf. Not included among the "Other Poems" in the second volume here, as in other editions by Leavitt & Allen, are *Samson Agonistes* and *Comus*. The first edition by Leavitt & Allen was published in 1848 (also listed here with further editions by Leavitt & Allen cited). Uncommon. Not in Kohler.

1120. [PARADISE LOST] BOOKS I. AND II. OF MILTON'S PARADISE LOST, With Notes on the Analysis, and on the Scriptural and Classical Allusions, A Glossary Of Difficult Words. And A Life of Milton. By C. P. Mason, B. A., F.C.P., Fellow Of University College, London. Fifth Edition. Miller & Co.'s Educational Series. *Toronto: Adam Miller & Co., 1878.* Fifth edition. 8vo, 76pp., repeating pp. 17 & 18)+[several blank pages for note-taking],+70pp., "Preface," "Life of Milton," and "Examples Of The Analysis Of The Sentences" before Book I, notes at the end of each book, original gray cloth (cover worn and badly stained, top outer corner of back cover chewed away as with tip of outer corners of last few pages without affecting any text, spine chipped at the top with a small hole at the center, school stamp on front blanks), front cover decorated and lettered in black. Scarce. Not in Kohler.

The Artist's Own Copy, Signed

1121. PARADISE LOST By John Milton. Illustrated By Thirty-Eight Designs In Outline By Frederick Thrupp. Thirty-Four Of The Plates Engraved By The Artist And Four By F. Joubert. *London: Hardwicke And Bogue, 192, Piccadilly, W. 1879.* First and probably only edition thus. Oblong folio, unpaginated, half-title, "List Of Illustrations," two pages of prefatory remarks by Frederick Thrupp dated "January 1879," first appearance of thirty-eight line-engravings after Thrupp, original green cloth (a bit rubbed), covers decorated in blind, gilt lettering on front cover and spine. The artist's own copy, signed on front blank. Rare as an edition; special as the artist's own signed copy. Not in Kohler.

❈

1122. PARADISE LOST. A Poem In Twelve Books. By John Milton. *New York: Clark & Maynard, 5 Barclay Street. n.d. [ca. 1879].* 12mo in 6s, 283pp., life of Milton by Fenton, index at end, original boards (a little rubbed), black leather spine (worn, front joint cracked at bottom with a piece missing at bottom of spine, age-browning), title page for Clark, Austin & Smith edition of *PL* repeated on front cover within decorative trim ("School Edition . . . New York: Clark, Austin & Smith, 3 Park Row And 3 Ann-Street"), advertisement on back cover. Although a little worn, a good copy with contemporary presentation inscription (dated 1879) on fly-leaf. The possible first edition thus by Clark & Maynard was published in 1869 (also listed here with further editions cited). Uncommon. Not in Kohler.

1123. PARADISE LOST A Poem In Twelve Books By John Milton[.] A New Edition, with Explanatory Notes[.] *Boston[:] Houghton, Osgood And Company[,] The Riverside Press, Cambridge[,] (1879).* 8vo, xiv+[2]+409pp., vignette sketch of a young Milton at center of title page in red and black, "Entered according to Act of Congress, in the year 1872, by Hurd And Houghton" on verso of title page, "Advertisement" dated 1866, life of Milton, notes at bottom of page, index printed in double column at the end, original decorated green cloth (slight, inoffensive waterstaining along bottom corners of covers), front cover decorated in black trim with "Riverside Classics" and emblem of the press in bright embossed gilt against a black background outlined in gilt across the top and "Paradise Lost" lettered in gilt in the center, spine lettered in embossed green against a bright gilt band within decorative black trim across the top with title lettered in gilt at the center along with "Edited By Torrey," with initials of the press in gilt within decorative black trim at the bottom, and gilt and black rules at the top and bottom, gray endpapers. Except for the slight waterstaining, a very nice copy. See 1867 edition listed earlier published by "Hurd and Houghton" in New York (possible first edition thus), bearing the label "Riverside Classics"; see also 1869 Riverside Press edition listed earlier, published, like here, in Boston by "Houghton, Mifflin And Company" bearing the label "Riverside Classics" in a binding like here, and other editions cited there. Uncommon. Not in Kohler.

1124. PARADISE LOST. By John Milton. BOOK I. With Preparatory And Explanatory Notes. By E. F. Willoughby, M.D. English Classics. *New York: Maynard, Merrill, & Co., 43, 45, and 47 East Tenth Street. n.d. [ca. 1879].* First edition thus. Slim 8vo, 94pp., unsigned vignette portrait of a young, romanticised Milton on title page, preface dated 1879, original olive green cloth (some marginal notations and underlining in pencil), front cover lettered in black ("Paradise Lost Books I. By John Milton[.] Maynard's English Classic Series With Explanatory Notes . . . Mailing Price 30cts.") with decorative black border trim, advertisements printed in red on front and back endpapers, with additional advertisement leaf bound in at the end. Nice. Not in Kohler.

Editions were reprinted in 1885, 1887, 1889, 1889 (variant), and ca. 1900 (all listed here). The inclination to publish Books I and II only of *PL* became increasingly popular in the latter part of the nineteenth century, for similar reasons, one assumes, to those of the latter part of the twentieth century: to provide students and their teachers with a text of specific focus within Milton's epic with appropriate notes and critical commentary. With regard to the latter, Willoughby speaks to his refraining from citing "authorities" in the opening statement in his preface, conceding that "free use of the works of others" is of interest, but "I was led to this course [of not identifying authorities], not by any wish to ignore the labours of my predecessors, but by the example of the editor of the Clarendon Press Edition, who frequently attributes to Keightley, to whom he owes so much, remarks which I discovered in the writings of critics who wrote a hundred and fifty years ago."

1125. Variant of Preceding. PARADISE LOST. By John Milton. BOOK I. With Preparatory And Explanatory Notes. By E. F. Willoughby, M.D. English Classics. *New York: Maynard, Merrill, & Co., 43, 45, And 47 East Tenth Street. n.d. [1879].* First edition thus. Slim 8vo, 94+64+[2]pp., unsigned vignette portrait of a young Milton on title page, preface dated 1879, half-title for Book II

("With Notes, By Frances Storr"), separate pagination for Book II, original light gray cloth (a little used, some underlinings and marginal notations in pencil), front cover lettered in black ("Paradise Lost Books I–II. By John Milton[.] MAYNARD'S ENGLISH CLASSIC SERIES With Explanatory Notes . . . Mailing Price 40cts.") with decorative black border trim, advertisements printed in red on front and back endpapers, with additional advertisement leaf bound in at end. Decent copy with some important variances: (1) with Book II included, unlike preceding copy even though only Book I is referenced on title page; (2) with variant number of items listed in English Classics Series advertised on endpapers (184 compared to 166); (3) in a variant publisher's binding; and (4) with variant "Mailing Price" ("40cts." compared to "30cts."). See also the 1885 edition (listed later). Not in Kohler.

1126. Variant of Preceding. Slim 8vo, 94+64pp., frontispiece portrait of Milton after O. Grosch, preface dated 1879, as preceding, green cloth (cover a little age-darkened with some slight stains), front cover lettered in black ("Paradise Lost Books I–II. By John Milton[.] Maynard's English Classic Series With Explanatory Notes . . . Mailing Price 40cts.") with decorative black border trim, small book label on front fly-leaf. Good copy fresh and clean within with some important variances: (1) with frontispiece portrait instead of vignette portrait on title page; (2) with variant publisher's imprint (New York: Maynard, Merrill, & Co., 29, 31, And 33 East Nineteenth Street); (3) without advertisements on endpapers; and (4) in a variant publisher's binding. Not in Kohler.

1127. MILTON'S PARADISE LOST BOOKS I AND II With Introduction, Notes, And Diagrams By Homer B. Sprague, M. A. Ph.D. Formerly Headmaster Of The Girls' High School, Boston[.] *Ginn And Company Boston • New York • Chicago • London • Atlanta • Dallas • Columbus • San Francisco[.] (1879)*. First edition thus. Slim 8vo, xxxii+[2]+113pp.,+xiii+38pp., decorated title page, illustrative plate in black and white before dedication page ("Vertical Section, Showing [conjecturally] Milton's cosmography,—the Empyreal Heaven, our Starry Universe, Hell, and Chaos"), several textual diagrams depicting Milton's universe, two additional illustrative plates in black and white ("The Pantheon" and "Vertical Section: Realm Of Chaos And Night"), "Introduction" (with "Critical Comments" by Masson, Himes, Quarterly Review, DeQuincey, and Lowell), half-title for *PL* with "Suggestions To Teachers" on verso, index after Books I and II, notes at bottom of page, original green cloth (a bit worn, library stamp on front pastedown stamped "withdrawn"), central emblem of the press stamped on front cover, spine lettered in black (faded), notes, "Suggestions To Teachers," index. All in all, a good copy. Bound in at the end as a separate edition unto itself is *L* with its own title page and separate pagination (with copyright of 1878 on verso): **MILTON'S LYCIDAS**. Edited, With Notes By Homer B. Sprague . . . *Ginn And Company Boston • New York • Chicago • London • Atlanta • Dallas • Columbus • San Francisco[.] (1878)*. First edition thus. Included with *L* are "Comments By Morley On The Poem," "Comments By R. C. Browne," "Chronology Of Incidents, Etc.," "Various Readings," and "Index Of Words Explained." See also 1883 *PL* edition (possible second edition thus) and 1885 (possible third edition thus), 1888, 1889, 1894, 1895, and 1897 reprint editions—all listed here. Not in Kohler.

1128. MILTON'S PARADISE LOST Illustrated By Gustave Doré. Edited, With Notes And A Life Of Milton, By Robert Vaughan, D.D. *New York: Collier, 11, 13 And 15 Vandewater Street, n.d. [ca. 1880]*. First Collier edition? Imperial 4to, xlv+313pp., frontispiece illustration plate and other illustration plates after Gustave Doré, decorated initial letters on title page, life of Milton followed by introduction, notes at bottom of page, original stamped red cloth (a bit rubbed along the joints and at top and bottom of spine), front cover decorated with an illustration stamped in bright gilt and black, consisting of a fierce-looking angelic figure holding a crooked sword and a horn—both in gilt—incorporated along the front part of the letter "P" in gilt lettering "Paradise Lost" and a vignette scene of Eden in gilt within the open space of the letter "P," with artists brushes and palette beneath "Illustrated By Gustave Doré" in gilt lettering, spine elaborately decorated and lettered in black, a.e.g. A very good copy, with early bookplate on front pastedown, in an attractive, bright publisher's binding. Not in Kohler.

1129. DAS VERLORENE PARADIES von John Milton. Deutsch von Adolf Bottger. Mit 50 Vollbildern nach Originalen von Gustav Doré. Zweite Auflage. *Berlin: Neufeld & Henius, n.d. [ca. 1880]*. Large 4to, vi+342pp., "Biographische Skizze," fifty full-page engraved illustration plates after Gustave Doré, printed on one side only, floral decorated borders on each page in art nouveau style, original red cloth (spine a little faded), front cover and spine elaborately decorated in gilt in art nouveau style with gilt lettering, art nouveau decorated gold endpapers, decorated edges in art nouveau style. A fine copy in a stunning art nouveau binding, in fine condition, very clean and fresh within. The translation is by Adolph Bottger; the first German translated edition thus appeared in 1879—this is the second edition thus. Not in Kohler.

1130. Variant of Preceding, in an attractive art nouveau binding, similar to the preceding binding, except that the original red cloth is darker, with decorated gold endpapers different from the art nouveau decorated gold endpapers in the preceding copy, and with gilt edges instead of decorated edges in art nouveau style as in the preceding copy.

1131. PARADISE LOST [In] **CASSELL'S DORE GALLERY:** Containing Two Hundred and Fifty Beautiful Engravings, Selected From The Doré Bible, Milton, Dante's Inferno, Dante's Purgatorio And Paradiso, Atala, Fontaine, Fairy Realm, Don Quixote, Baron Munchausen, Croquemitaine, &c. &c. With Memoir of Doré, Critical Essay, And Description Letterpress, By Edmund Ollier. *Cassell & Company, Limited: London, Paris & New York. n.d. [ca. 1880].* 4to, xlvii+152pp. 250 full-page engravings, 250 plates including reproductions of Gustave Doré's illustrations for *PL*, "Advertisement," "List Of Plates," "Memoir Of Gustave Doré," "Cassell's Doré Gallery," "Description Of The Plates," decorative tailpieces and decorated initial letters, black border around text, original red pictorial cloth, front cover ruled in black with central illustration in black and brilliant gilt within brilliant gilt border with title at the top in gilt outlined in black, additional gilt lettering at the bottom, spine lettered in gilt with illustration in black and brilliant gilt, yellow endpapers. A fine, bright, crisp copy in a stunning publisher's binding.

1132. PARADISE LOST A Poem In Twelve Books By John Milton[.] A New Edition, with Explanatory Notes[.] *Boston[:] Houghton, Osgood And Company[,] The Riverside Press, Cambridge[,] 1880.* 8vo, xiv+[2]+409pp., vignette sketch of a young Milton at center of title page in red and black, "Entered according to Act of Congress, in the year 1866, by Hurd And Houghton" on verso of title page, "Advertisement" dated 1866, life of Milton, notes at bottom of page, index printed in double column at the end, original decorated reddish-brown cloth, front cover decorated in black trim with "Riverside Classics" and emblem of the press in bright embossed gilt against a black background outlined in gilt across the top and "Paradise Lost" lettered in gilt in the center, spine lettered in embossed reddish-brown against a bright gilt band within decorative black trim across the top with title lettered in gilt at the center along with "Edited By Torrey," with initials of the press in gilt within decorative black trim at the bottom, and gilt and black rules at the top and bottom, dark green endpapers. A beautiful copy in a bright and well-preserved publisher's binding with contemporary signature dated 1880. See 1867 edition, listed earlier, published by "Hurd and Houghton" in New York (possible first edition thus), bearing the label "Riverside Classics"; see also 1869 Riverside Press edition published, like here, in Boston by "Houghton, Mifflin And Company" bearing the label "Riverside Classics" and other editions cited there. Uncommon. Not in Kohler.

1133. PARADISE LOST. By John Milton. *New York: Hurst & Co., Publishers, 122 Nassau Street. n.d. [ca. 1880].* First edition thus? 8vo, 291+[2]pp., frontispiece portrait plate, "Argyle Press Printing And Bookbinding 24 & 26 Wooster St., N.Y." on verso of title page, original decorated light green cloth (some age-browning), front cover and spine decorated in black with embossed lettering against black backdrop on front cover and lettered in black and green against gilt backdrop on spine. Advertisement leaf bound in at end. Good copy in an attractive publisher's binding with "Arlington Edition" stamped on front cover. Not in Kohler.

See various undated nonillustrated editions of *PL* published by Hurst ca. 1895, one stamped "Arlington Edition" on front cover, but with variations from the edition here (including no address in publisher's imprint and no press citation on verso of title page). See also undated illustrated edition of *PL* published by "Hurst & Company Publishers" ca. 1900 (with frontispiece illustration) and undated nonillustrated edition of *PL* by "Hurst & Company" published about the same time, ca. 1900, in "The Companion Books" series by Hurst. See, too, illustrated and nonillustrated editions of Milton's *PW* published by Hurst about this same time, ca. 1880, and later, ca. 1905, and ca. 1907 (all editions listed here).

1134. PARADISE LOST: A Poem, In Twelve Books, By John Milton; With A Life Of The Author, By The Rev. H. Stebbing, A.M. *New York: Leavitt & Allen Bros., No. 8 Howard Street. n.d. [ca. 1880s].* Bound with **PARADISE REGAINED, AND OTHER POEMS** By John Milton. New York: Leavitt & Allen Bros., No. 8 Howard Street. n.d. [ca. 1880s]. 2 volumes in one. Small 8vo, 356pp., +190pp., frontispiece portrait plate of Milton after C. Burt, protective tissue guard, title page for each volume, double black rule around text, original decorated green cloth (a little used, spine chipped at top and bottom, name stamped on fly-leaf), front cover decorated in black and gilt with Milton's name incorporated in relief within a broad gilt band across the top of front cover, the letter "M" larger than the others set off against a gilt shield backdrop, spine similarly decorated in black and gilt trim with the title ("Milton's Poems") in embossed green within a rolling gilt scroll at the top, "Leavitt & Allen Bros." in embossed letters within a gilt band in front of a decorative gilt piece at the bottom, a.e.g. A good copy in an attractive American publisher's binding, without the inclusion of *SA* and *C*, as

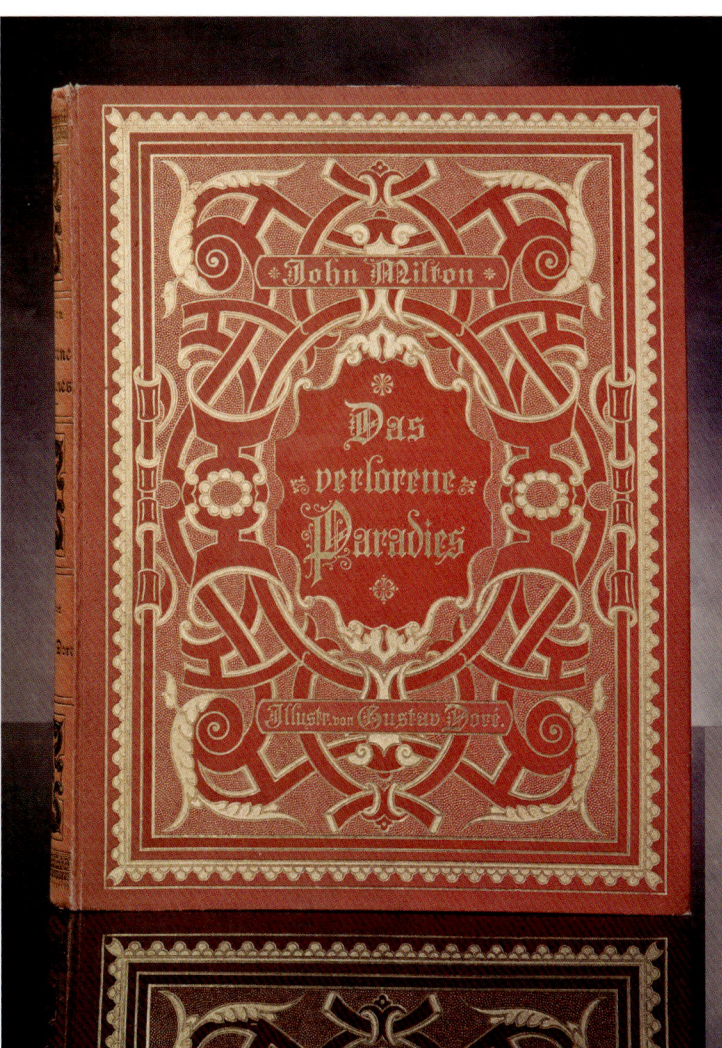

Das Verlorne Paradies. Deutsch von Adolf Bottger. Mit 50 Vollbildern nach Originalen von Gustav Doré. Zweite Auflage. Berlin: Neufeld & Henius, n.d. [ca. 1880]. Large 4to, original red cloth, front cover and spine elaborately decorated in gilt in art nouveau style. See #1129.

PL [In] Cassell's Doré Gallery: Cassell & Company, Limited: London, Paris & New York. n.d. [ca. 1880]. 4to, 250 plates including reproductions of Gustave Doré's illustrations for *PL*, original red pictorial cloth with letting and illustrations in brilliant gilt highlighted by black shadowing. A bright, crisp copy in a stunning publisher's binding. See #1131.

with other editions by Leavitt & Allen. See ca. 1878 Leavitt & Allen Bros. edition in a binding similar to the one here. The first edition thus by Leavitt & Allen was published ca. 1848 (also listed here with further editions by Leavitt & Allen cited). Uncommon. Not in Kohler.

1135. PARADISE LOST. A Poem In Twelve Books By John Milton. *New York: Clark & Maynard, Publishers 771 Broadway. n.d. [ca. 1880]*. 12mo in 6s, 283pp., life of Milton by Fenton, index at end, original boards (a little rubbed and worn, early ownership names on fly-leaf, some crossed out, underlinings in pencil throughout), black cloth spine (a bit worn), title page repeated on front cover with "School Edition" at the top, advertisements on back cover. Although a little worn, a decent copy. The possible first edition thus by Clark & Maynard was published with a different address ("No. 5 Barclay Street") in 1869 (also listed here with further editions cited). Scarce. Not in Kohler.

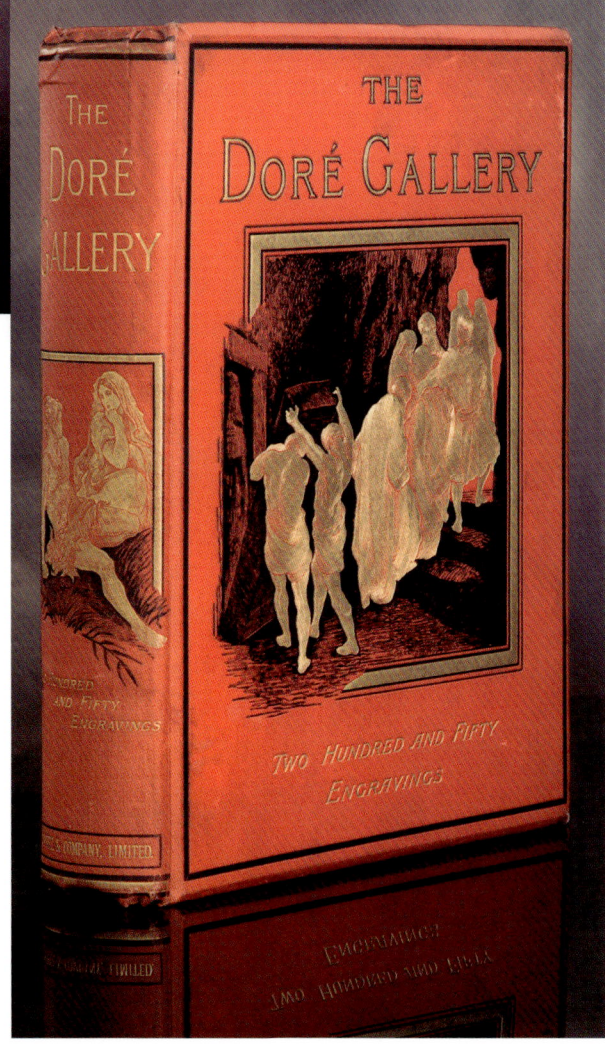

1136. MILTON'S PARADISE LOST. Illustrated By Gustave Doré. Edited, With Notes And A Life Of Milton, By Robert Vaughan, D.D. *Cassell, Petter, Galpin, & Co.: London, Paris & New York. 1882.* 4to, lxii+329pp., half-title, title page in red and black with decorative initials "CPG" at center, fifty illustration plates after Gustave Doré (fine impressions), each with protective tissue guard with printed passage for the illustration, "Contents," "Life of Milton," "Introduction," notes at bottom of page, contemporary three-quarter red morocco, red buckram, gilt rules on covers, elaborately gilt-decorated spine, raised bands, a.e.g. A fine copy. Kohler 154, reporting "Not in the British Library. Not in the Bodleian Library. Not in Cambridge University Library."

1137. PARADISE LOST: A Poem, In Twelve Books, By John Milton; With Memoir and Notes. Complete Edition. Illustrated. *New York: The American News Company, 39 And 41 Chambers Street. n.d. [ca. 1882].* First edition thus? 12mo, vii+[3]+292pp., frontispiece portrait plate reproducing Munkacsy's illustration of *Milton Dictating 'Paradise Lost' to His Daughters*, protective tissue guard (foxed), "Memoir Of John Milton," followed by "Contents" with decorative head- and tailpiece, nine unsigned illustration plates for *PL* (two for Book I, two for Book II, two for Book III, two for Book IV, one for Book V, one for Book VII, and one for Book XI) each with Milton's name, the lines illustrated along with the title of the poem, and the corresponding page printed beneath each illustration, notes at bottom of page, slight black rule around text, original decorated reddish-brown cloth (a bit rubbed), front cover richly decorated in embossed black and gilt trim with a wide border trim in black pattern design surrounding delicate gilt trim within, a large emblem at the bottom consisting of several books, laurel, an angelic figure seated reading a book, and an urn, with Milton's name in black lettering along a scroll at the center of the emblem, "Illustrated" lettered in gilt at the center of the cover, at the top a broad bright gilt band incorporating the title *PL* with thick black and gilt rules on either side decorated with floral trim in gilt with the figure of a head with laurel wreath in a bright gilt medallion at the center above the title, spine lettered in gilt with decorative gilt trim at the top and bottom, back cover decorated in blind, decorated green endpapers, a.e.g. A lovely copy in a bright, attractive publisher's binding. The illustrations are unsigned and circular, except the last one, which is square, though still like the others. The illustration for Satan in Book I is completely unlike the others (here and in other illustrated editions, except the decorated title-page plate of the ca. 1888 edition by the Henneberry Company) in character and design; it is elongated and dated "1878" in the lower right corner with the "8" partially missing and with the initials "PN" in larger size between "18" and "78." See copies of undated ca. 1882 and of undated ca. 1884 illustrated editions of *PW* published by the American News Company listed here, each of which uses several of the illustrations here; many of the illustrations in *PL* here also appear in the ca. 1884 edition of *PL* listed here, including the unique one with the initial "PN." Not in Kohler.

1138. MILTON LE PARADIS PERDU Traduction De Chateaubriand Précédé De Réflexions Sur La Vie Et Les Escrits De Milton Par Lamartine Et Enrichi De Vingt-Sept Magnifiques Estampes Originales Gravées Au Burin Sur Acier. *Paris[:] [Amable Rigaud, or] Gustave Guérin, Libraire-Editeur 26 Et 51, Rue Dé La Harpe, MD.CCC. LXXXII (1882).* Folio, xxvi+157pp., half-title (with "Paris – Imprimé chez Gauthier – Villars, 55, quai des Grands – Augustins." on verso), engraved frontispiece portrait of a young Milton after Sixdeniers, twenty-four illustrations after Flatters, Richomme, Lemercier, Melin, and Bernouville (very fine impressions), engraved portraits of Lamartine, and Chateaubriand, "Reflexions Sur Milton" (dated "Mars 1855"), "Etude Historique Et Littéraire Sur Milton" all, unlike the poem, printed in double column, "Arguments" for the books printed together at the beginning before Book I, splendid decorative head- and tailpieces, decorated initial letter each book, contemporary three-quarter red morocco, marbled paper over boards (a bit worn, joints slightly frayed at bottom of both covers, spine cracked at the center, first few pages—including frontispiece portrait and title page—loose, edges worn), spine lettered in gilt, slightly raised bands with decorative gilt trim, each raised band within slight decorative gilt trim, decorative gilt trim at the top and bottom, marbled endpapers, edges untrimmed. A good copy of this amazingly illustrated book with splendid impressions of the steel-engraved illustrations. Introduction by Lamartine, translation by Chateaubriand, which was first published in 1831 (see 1836 sets). The first edition thus was published in 1855 (also listed here with further editions cited, including 1870 edition with a listing of illustrations, each hand-colored). Uncommon. Not in Kohler.

1139. EL PARAISO PERDIDO poema escrito en inglés por John Milton traduccion en verso castellano De D. Juan Escoiquiz Gononigo de la Santa ingleia de Toledo Edicio Ilustrada Con Gran Numero De Vinetas Inspiradas Enlos Famosos Dibujos de Gustavo Doré[.] *Barcelona[:] Administracion: Nueva San Francisco, 11 y 13[,] 1883.* First edition thus? 8vo, 510+[2]pp., title page in red and black with elaborate border trim with a classical motif, "Imprenta y Litografia de los Sucesores de N. Ramirez y C.–Barcelona" on verso of title page, "Biographia" with decorative headpiece and decorated initial letter, "Prologo Del Traductor" illustrations after Gustave Doré within the text, elaborate headpiece and elaborately decorated initial letter at the outset of each book, slight tailpiece at the end of each book, "Notas De Addisson Al Paraiso Perdido" and "Notas Del Traductor [for each book]" at the end with the final leaf containing the "Indice" for the volume, original dark green cloth (a little rubbed, joints broken from within at title page, pages a bit age-darkened, small library stamp at bottom of title page), front cover decorated with embossed branch with leaves and snake wound throughout with bright embossed gilt medallion at the center containing the image of Milton in relief on one side and his name and dates of birth and death on verso shown below and with title in large letters in embossed gilt at the top, spine similarly decorated with the embossed impression of a snake wound from bottom to top and title in embossed green letters against a bright gilt block near the top, back cover with decorative border trim in black relief and with central medallion in black relief incorporating "Biblioteca Amena E Instructiva" in black lettering around the outside and containing an emblem in black within, elaborately decorated endpapers, green edges with repetitive floral motif in contrasting light yellow, floral decorated endpapers. A nice copy in a rather exceptional binding. Not in Kohler.

The verse translation by Juan de Escoiquiz of *PL* was first published in Spanish in 1812; several other translations followed. See 1873 folio edition here in prose translation by Cayetano Roseli, published in Barcelona by Montaner y Simon, the first Spanish edition with Doré's illustrations; see also two-volume ca. 1890 edition here of *O Paraiso Perdido* in poetic translation by Antonio José de Lima Leitao, with Doré's illustrations. The first edition with Doré's illustrations of *PL* appeared in the mid-1860s (see 1865–66 set of parts and 1866 first book edition here).

1140. THE PARADISE LOST By John Milton. With Notes Explanatory And Critical[.] Edited By Prof. James R. Boyd, D.D . . . [as with 1870 edition.] Revised Edition. *A. S. Barnes & Company, New York And Chicago. n.d. [ca. 1883].* 8vo, 552pp., content as with first edition in 1850, original light pink paper over boards (a bit rubbed), with decorated title page printed in black on front cover and advertisement for "National School Series" (of which this edition is one) printed in black on back cover, black leather spine (a bit rubbed) lettered in gilt. A nice copy of this "School and Academic Edition," well-preserved in its original binding. The first edition thus edited by Boyd was published in 1850 by "Baker And Scribner" in New York in a large 8vo format with reduced illustration plates after Martin (also listed here with further editions by Boyd cited). Not in Kohler.

1141. MILTON'S PARADISE LOST, BOOKS I. AND II. With Introduction, Notes, And Diagrams, By Homer B. Sprague, M.A., Ph.D., Head-Master Of The Girls' High School, Boston; And Formerly Principal Of The Adelphi Academy, Brooklyn, And Professor Of Rhetoric And English Literature In Cornell University. *Boston: Published By Ginn, Heath, & Co. 1883.* Second edition thus? Slim 8vo, xxxii+[2]+113pp.,+xiii+38pp.,+4pp., frontispiece plate in black and white, two additional illustrative plates in black and white, several textual diagrams depicting Milton's universe, and other introductory material as with 1979 first edition (given in full there), original green cloth (a bit worn, front fly-leaf lacking, top half of title page torn away from binding, pages age-browned, former ownership names, occasional pencil markings), front cover decorated in black trim near the top and bottom with black lettering in between, spine lettered in black. A fairly decent copy with four pages of advertisements bound in at the end. Bound in after **PARADISE LOST** as a separate edition unto itself is *L*, with its own title page and separate pagination: **MILTON'S LYCIDAS**. Edited, With Notes, By Homer B. Sprague . . . *Boston: Published By Ginn, Heath, & Co. 1883.* Second edition thus? As with the first edition (given in full there). The first edition thus was published in 1879 (also listed here with further editions cited). Not in Kohler.

1142. MILTON'S PARADISE LOST With Fifty Illustrations By Gustave Doré[.] *New York[:] John B. Alden, Publisher[.] 1884.* 4to, 118pp., title page printed in red and black, protective tissue guard, frontispiece illustration plate and forty-nine additional illustration plates after Gustave Doré, printed in double column, original green cloth (a bit worn at corners and spine ends), front cover elaborately decorated in embossed black trim with bright gilt lettering ("Doré Gallery") across the center, title within a large gilt medallion in bottom right corner, and vignette of a young Milton in gilt at the top, spine lettered in gilt ("Paradise Lost"), decorated endpapers, a.e.g. A good copy with dated contemporary signature on front blank. Not in Kohler.

1143. Variant of Preceding, in a variant publisher's binding: red cloth instead of green, decorated exactly as preceding copy, with same brilliant front cover.

1144. PARADISE LOST By John Milton[.] *New York: R. Worthington, 770 Broadway. 1884.* First edition thus by Worthington? 8vo, 291pp. (with pagination beginning at "16"), frontispiece illustration plate of *Adam Seeing Eve* (engraved by Dalziel) and one additional illustration plate of *Adam and Eve Naming the Animals* (engraved by Dalziel), red border around text, original decorated reddish-brown cloth (a bit rubbed, frayed along top edges and corners, spine a little age-darkened and very worn at the bottom on the right side), front cover elaborately decorated in embossed black and gilt lines and swirls in a floral and circular motif with central gilt emblem incorporating flowers, title incorporated in embossed lettering and gilt backdrop with floral motif, and a large decorated initial letter "P" at the top, spine decorated in embossed red, black, and gilt in a floral motif with reversed lettering against a gilt background toward the top, decorated endpapers, a.e.g. A decent copy of an uncommon edition. Scarce. Not in Kohler.

Also in the collection and listed here: a possible second edition thus published in 1886; a possible third edition thus in 1887 with a frontispiece illustration and two additional illustrations; a possible fifth edition thus in 1890 with, as here, a frontispiece illustration and one additional illustration, each edition, as here, with red border around text, but each with "A Memoir" on title page and a different publisher's imprint; a possible fourth edition thus, non-illustrated edition of *PL* published by Worthington about this same time (undated but ca. 1888), labeled "Franklin Edition" and "Illustrated" on front cover and spine, but without frontispiece illustration or any other illustrations and without red border around the text; and the 1884 illustrated edition of *PW* by Worthington with same publisher's imprint as that here.

1145. PARADISE LOST By John Milton[.] *Chicago And New York: Belford, Clarke & Company, Publishers. n.d. [ca. 1884].* First edition thus by Belford, Clark & Co.? 8vo, 291pp., illustration plate of *Adam and Eve Naming the Animals* (engraved by Dalziel), red border around text, "Trow's Printing And Bookbinding Company, New York" on verso of title page, original decorated blue cloth (worn, p. 27 has a small tear with a small piece missing without affecting any text, foxing throughout including the illustration plate, which is stained at the top and bottom edges), front cover ornately decorated in embossed floral design in blue, maroon, and black with title in embossed blue against a gilt background near the top, spine similarly lettered in embossed blue against a gilt background, decorated endpapers, a.e.g. A fair copy in an attractive (albeit somewhat used) publisher's binding, curiously ¼" thicker than the following variant copy. Not in Kohler.

1146. Variant of Preceding, frontispiece illustration of *Adam Seeing Eve* (engraved by Dalziel), protective tissue guard, and one additional illustration of *Adam and Eve Naming the Animals* (engraved by Dalziel), red border around text, "Trow's Printing And Bookbinding Company, New York" on verso of title page, original decorated dark red cloth (a bit rubbed, second plate waterstained along bottom right edge), front cover decorated in embossed black trim with small swirling patterns around the edges and a large embossed decorative piece at the center with a black background and with *PL* in bright gilt across the top, spine similarly decorated in embossed black trim with the figure of a scantily clad boy playing the flute at the center and the title in embossed red against a bright gilt background at the top and publisher's name in smaller embossed red against a bright gilt background at the bottom, decorated endpapers, a.e.g. A nice copy with early ownership name on front pastedown, in an attractive variant publisher's cloth binding, and with a second illustration plate. Not in Kohler.

1147. MILTON'S PARADISE LOST Illustrated By Gustave Doré. Edited, With Notes And A Life Of Milton, By Robert Vaughan, D.D. *Chicago And New York: Belford, Clark & Co., Publishers. 1885.* First edition thus by Belford, Clark & Co. with Doré plates? 4to, xlv+319pp. (plates unpaginated), frontispiece illustration and forty-nine additional illustration plates after Gustave Doré (fine impressions), decorated initial letters on title page, life of Milton, original stamped brown cloth (spine ends chipped), front cover decorated with an illustration stamped in gilt and black relief (the avenging angel from above in gilt holding a crooked sword, a brooding Satan below in brown and black seated on rocks encompassed in flames of gilt, tree trunks and branches in brown and black in the middle) with "Paradise Lost" in gilt in the center within a thick gilt border frame, additional gilt lettering at upper left and in lower right corners, spine similarly decorated with an illustration stamped in gilt and black (heavenly rays in gilt from the top, Satan in gilt, brown, and black at the bottom standing on rocks overlooking flames in gilt with raised arms brandishing a large club in his left hand) with lettering in gilt and black, decorated gold endpapers, a.e.g. A nice copy in an attractive publisher's binding. See undated ca. 1884 illustrated octavo edition by "Belford, Clarke & Company" [sic], with an illustration plate engraved by Dalziel. Not in Kohler.

1148. MILTON'S PARADISE LOST Illustrated By Gustave Doré[.] Introduction By Robert Vaughan, D.D. *New York[:] Cassell Publishing Company[,] 104 & 106 Fourth Avenue[.] n.d., [ca. 1885].* Large 8vo, 311pp., frontispiece illustration plate and forty-nine additional illustration plates after Gustave Doré, life of Milton followed by introduction, original stamped golden brown cloth (a bit rubbed), front cover decorated with an illustration stamped in bright gilt and black (an angelic figure with crooked sword and spear) incorporating title in gilt and black, spine decorated in black and lettered in blind. A nice copy in an attractive publisher's binding. Not in Kohler (although Kohler lists several other dated editions by Cassell & Company).

1149. Variant of Preceding, in original stamped reddish-brown cloth (a bit rubbed, endpapers a little foxed, pages a little age-browned), front cover decorated with an illustration stamped in bright gilt and black (an angelic figure with crooked sword and spear) incorporating title in gilt and black, spine decorated in black and lettered in blind. A good copy in an attractive variant publisher's binding.

1150. MILTON'S PARADISE LOST Illustrated By Gustave Doré. Edited, With Notes And A Life Of Milton, By Robert Vaughan, D.D. *New York: Pollard & Moss, 47 John Street. 1885*. 4to, xlv+313pp., frontispiece illustration plates with protective tissue guards, and other illustration plates by Gustave Doré, decorated initial letters on title page, life of Milton followed by introduction, original burgundy cloth richly decorated in black and gilt (some slight chaffing along top and bottom, corners worn, spine chipped at bottom, name written in ink and another stamped on fly-leaf), front cover decorated with an illustration stamped in bright gilt and black (a large angelic figure with crooked sword and outstretched arm standing on an orb with another smaller angel in shaded black flying above him and beneath him a snake in curled position in shaded black) incorporating title in bright gilt and black, spine decorated with an illustration stamped in bright gilt and black (*The Expulsion of Adam and Eve*) and lettered in gilt, decorated endpapers, a.e.g. A nice copy in an attractive (albeit a bit worn) publisher's binding. See copies of 1887 and 1889 editions by Pollard and Moss (each with some variations). Not in Kohler.

1151. PARADISE LOST By John Milton[.] *Syndicate Trading Company[,] New York[.] n.d. [ca. 1885]*. First edition thus? 8vo, 291pp. (pagination beginning at "16"), "Trow's Printing And Bookbinding Company, New York" on verso of title page, original decorated dark green cloth (pages age-darkened and a bit fragile because of the poor quality of paper used, name on fly-leaf), front cover decorated with leaves in relief against a black background with same decorative motif in a circular manner at the center and with the lettering "Gladstone Series" in two decorative scrolls at the top, spine similarly decorated with leaves in relief against a black background with bright gilt piece near the top incorporating title in embossed green with decorative embossed green trim at top and bottom edges of the gilt piece. An attractive publisher's binding. Not in Kohler.

1152. Variant of Preceding, original decorated brown cloth (pages age-darkened because of the poor quality of paper used), otherwise decorated as preceding copy. A good copy in an attractive variant publisher's binding, in brown rather than green cloth.

1153. PARADISE LOST. A Poem In Twelve Books. By John Milton. *New York: Clark & Maynard Publishers, No. 5 Barclay Street. n.d. [ca. 1885]*. 12mo in 6s, 283pp., life of Milton by Fenton, index at end, original boards (a little worn), black leather spine (a little worn, chipped at top and bottom, paper shelf label on spine), title page repeated on front cover within decorative trim (called "School Edition" at the top), advertisement on back cover. A fair copy with early signatures (dated 1895) on fly-leaf and label "Property Of The Town Of Kingston," bearing "Copyright, 1884, Knight, Adams Y Co." at the bottom on front pastedown with several borrower's names and dates listed on the label, the earliest dated 1890. The possible first edition thus by Clark & Maynard was published in 1869 (also listed here with further editions cited). Scarce. Not in Kohler.

1154. PARADISE LOST. By John Milton. Book I. With Preparatory And Explanatory Notes By E. F. Willoughby, M.D. English Classics. *New York: Clark & Maynard, Publishers, 771 Broadway. (1885)*. Slim 8vo, 94+64pp., unsigned vignette portrait of a young Milton on title page, original printed thin green boards (a little used, small stain on top edge of front pastedown, light inoffensive waterstaining at bottom of front and back edges without affecting text), title page reprinted with decorative border trim in black on front cover and dated 1885, advertisements printed in red on front and back endpapers and on back cover. The possible first edition by Willoughby was published ca. 1879 (also listed here). Uncommon. Not in Kohler.

1155. MILTON'S PARADISE LOST, BOOKS I. AND II. With Introduction, Notes, And Diagrams, By Homer B. Sprague, M.A., Ph.D., Head-Master Of The Girls' High School, Boston; And Formerly Principal Of The Adelphi Academy, Brooklyn, And Professor Of Rhetoric And English Literature In Cornell University. *Boston: Published By Ginn, Heath, & Co. 1885*. Third edition thus? Slim 8vo, xxxii+113pp.,+xiii+38pp.,+[4]pp., frontispiece plate in black and white, two additional illustrative plates in black and white, several textual diagrams depicting Milton's universe, and other introductory material as with 1979 first edition (given in full there), original green cloth (a bit rubbed), front cover decorated in black trim near the top and bottom with black lettering in between, spine lettered in black. A nice copy with contemporary ownership signature and note in pencil on fly-leaf and front pastedown, with four pages of advertisements bound in at the end. Bound in after **PARADISE LOST** as a separate edition unto itself is *Lycidas*, with its own title page and with separate pagination, as with the first edition (given in full there). The first edition thus was published in 1879 (also listed here with further editions cited). Not in Kohler.

1156. PARADISE LOST. By John Milton. With A Memoir. *New York: Worthington Co., 28 Lafayette Place, 1886.* Second edition thus? 8vo, xxiv+366pp. (with pagination beginning at p. 76), frontispiece illustration of the expulsion (engraved by Dalziel) and one additional illustration plate of *Adam and Eve Naming the Animals* (engraved by Dalziel), decorative piece on verso of title, notes at bottom of page, red border around text, original decorated gray cloth (slightly rubbed, spine ends chipped, slightly shaken from within, several page corners chipped or turned down), front cover decorated in embossed red and black lines and swirls in a floral and circular motif with the title *PL* incorporated in black lettering within a bright gilt band near the top and with a winged horse (pegasus) in red against a black background within a decorated circle of swirls and twirls in lower left corner, spine similarly elaborately decorated in embossed red, black, and gilt with floral motif at the center, the title ("Paradise Lost") lettered in black within a bright gilt band toward the top, and "Worthington Co" within a smaller gilt band at the bottom, decorated endpapers, a.e.g. A good copy in an attractive publisher's binding with contemporary presentation inscription in an elaborate hand on front blank. The possible first edition by Worthington was published in 1884 (also listed here with further editions cited). Not in Kohler.

1157. PARADISE LOST. By John Milton. With A Memoir. *New York: Worthington Co., 747 Broadway, 1887.* Third edition thus? 8vo, xxiv+366+[1]pp. (with pagination beginning at p. 76), frontispiece illustration of *The Expulsion* and two additional illustrations: *Adam Seeing Eve* and *Adam and Eve Naming the Animals*—all engraved by Dalziel—decorative piece on verso of title, unpaginated final page with decorative piece on front and verso, notes at bottom of page, red border around text, original decorated drab green cloth (a bit rubbed, spine a little faded and ends slightly chipped, light scuff marks on back cover), binding decorated as preceding. A good copy in an attractive publisher's binding with contemporary presentation inscription on front blank. Not in Kohler.

1158. MILTON'S PARADISE LOST With Fifty Full-Page Illustrations By Gustave Doré With Notes And A Life Of Milton By Robert Vaughan, D.D. *New York[:] Pollard & Moss[,] 47 John Street[.] 1887.* 4to, lv+401pp., frontispiece illustration plate with protective tissue guard, and forty-nine additional illustration plates after Gustave Doré, each with protective tissue guard, central emblem on title page, life of Milton followed by introduction, original green cloth richly decorated in black and gilt (some wear to covers and spine, slightly shaken from within, occasional light age-browning, earlier ownership identification in ink on verso of frontispiece), front cover decorated with an illustration stamped in bright gilt and black (a large angelic figure with crooked sword and outstretched arm standing on an orb with another smaller angel in shaded black flying above him and beneath him a snake in curled position in shaded black) incorporating title in bright gilt and black, spine decorated with an illustration stamped in bright gilt and black (*The Expulsion of Adam and Eve*) and lettered in gilt, decorated endpapers, a.e.g. A fairly nice copy albeit a bit aged. See 1885 edition and 1889 edition by Pollard and Moss (both listed here, each with some variations). Not in Kohler.

1159. PARADISE LOST. *London[:] George Routledge And Sons Broadway, Ludgate Hill[,] Glasgow And New York[.] 1887.* First edition thus? 16mo, 318+[1]pp., half-title, small emblem on title page, original three-quarter green cloth, marbled paper over boards, t.e.g., others untrimmed, advertisement leaf bound in at end. A fine copy printed at the "Ballantyne Press: Edinburgh And London." Large paper copy. See 1894 edition. Not in Kohler.

1160. Variant of Preceding. Original half red cloth, marbled paper over boards (a bit rubbed, spine a little darkened, early name stamped and written on fly-leaf), advertisement leaf bound in at end. Laid in: original advertisement for "Routledge's Pocket Library," including "1s. Red Cloth Back, Cut Edges (this copy); 1s. 6d. Green Cloth Back, Uncut Edges, Gilt Top, Cloth Corners" (preceding copy). A nice copy ½" shorter and ⅜" narrower, in a variant publisher's binding.

1161. [PARADISE LOST] THE POETICAL WORKS OF JOHN MILTON, With Biographical Notice By John Bradshaw, M.A., LL.D., Inspector Of Schools, Madras. Editor Of "An English Anthology," Etc. **PARADISE LOST.** *London: Walter Scott, 24 Warwick Lane, And Newcastle-On-Tyne. 1887.* First edition thus. Small 8vo, xxviii+339+[6]pp., advertisement leaf for the "Special Edition Of The Canterbury Poets" (including *PL*, No. 21) before title page, half-title for each book, red border around text, original three-quarter maroon cloth, light green paper over boards (a bit rubbed, spine slightly separated from within, p. 213 badly broken into several pieces that have been retaped together, but with portions of the page still missing), maroon spine and corner pieces decorated with a delicate gilt design, green paper boards decorated in a contrasting darker green design, spine lettered in gilt, decorated light blue endpapers, a.e.g. Good copy. Six pages of advertisements, partially unopened, bound in at the end. See undated ca. 1887 edition published in London and New York, with variations from the edition here; see also 1888 first edition "Canterbury Poets" edition of *PR* published by Walter Scott. Not in Kohler.

1162. Variant of Preceding. Original dark green cloth (a bit rubbed), front cover lettered in gilt, finely tooled decorative gilt trim along inner edge of front cover and extending through the spine to the inner edge of the back cover, spine lettered in gilt, corners rounded, green endpapers, a.e.g. A nice copy. Unlike preceding copy, this edition (1) does not have the advertisement leaf for the "Special Edition Of The Canterbury Poets" before the title page; (2) nor the six pages of advertisements for "The Canterbury Poets" bound in at the end; and (3) it is also in a variant publisher's binding.

1163. Variant of Preceding. Original dark green cloth (with a slight crease across the center of front cover, contemporary names in pencil on front and back endpapers), printed paper label (age-darkened) on spine, t.e. rough, fore- and bottom edges untrimmed. A good copy with variant half-title (with advertisement for *PR* as companion volume on verso), with variant edges, and with eight (instead of six) pages of advertisements bound in at the end.

1164. [PARADISE LOST] THE POETICAL WORKS OF JOHN MILTON, With Biographical Notice By John Bradshaw, M.A., LL.D., Inspector Of Schools, Madras. PARADISE LOST. *London: Walter Scott, Limited, Paternoster Square. New York: 3 East Fourteenth Street. n.d [ca. 1887]* Variant edition. Small 8vo, xxviii+339+[8]pp., half-title ("The Canterbury Poets" Edited By William Sharp"), life of Milton by Bradshaw with decorated initial letter, half-title for each book, "The Walter Scott Press, Newcastle-on-Tyne" at bottom of last page, contemporary green cloth (a bit rubbed), spine finely decorated in gilt with gilt lettering, bookplate of a Paris bookstore on front pastedown. A good copy with eight pages of advertisements for "The Canterbury Poets. Edited By William Sharp" (including this edition as well as for the "Life Of Milton. By Richard Garnet" [copy with Nineteenth-century Miltoniana]) bound in at the end. Not in Kohler.

1165. [PARADISE LOST] THE POETICAL WORKS OF JOHN MILTON, With Biographical Notice By John Bradshaw, M.A., LL.D., Inspector Of Schools, Madras. PARADISE LOST. *The Walter Scott Publishing Co., Ltd., London And Newcastle-On-Tyne. New York: 3 East 14th Street. n.d. (1887)*. Variant edition. Small 8vo, xxviii+339pp., half-title ("The Canterbury Poets" Edited By William Sharp"), contemporary black leather (worn, spine missing, front pages a little brittle and bent), covers decorated with a floral design in gilt, a.e.g. See dated 1887 edition published in London and preceding edition, each with variations from the edition here. Not in Kohler.

1166. PARADISE LOST. By John Milton. A New Edition. With Notes By Rev. John Mitford. *Philadelphia: Porter & Coates. n.d [ca. 1887]*. 8vo in 4s, 433+10pp., small emblem of the press on title page, notes at bottom of page, original floral decorated yellow cloth (a bit rubbed), front cover and spine handsomely decorated in embossed black trim incorporating the title "Paradise Lost" at the top of front cover and spine and "Alta Edition" on front cover, with a red silk ribbon marker. A nice copy in a lovely publisher's binding, with ten pages of advertisements bound in at the end. Despite "Illustrated" being stamped on the spine, there are no plates present, and none appear to be missing. Kohler 160, dating its copy "[ca. 1893]," without plates and noting that none "appear to be missing," reporting "Not in the British Library Not in the Bodleian Library. Not in Cambridge University Library."

1167. Variant of Preceding, in original floral decorated red cloth (a bit rubbed, spine ends and corners slightly worn), decorated as preceding copy, with red silk ribbon marker. A nice copy in an appealing variant publisher's binding, with variant advertisements bound in at the end. Despite "Illustrated" being stamped on the spine, there are no plates present and none appear to be missing. Kohler 160.

1168. Variant of Preceding, in original floral decorated light gray cloth (a bit rubbed, top corner of fly-leaf repaired, early names on fly-leaf), decorated as preceding copies, with "Illustrated" stamped on the spine, and with a red silk ribbon marker and the same ten pages of advertisements bound in at the end. A nice copy in a attractive variant publisher's binding. Kohler 160.

1169. Variant of Preceding, in original floral decorated purple cloth (a bit rubbed, back cover slightly stained, lacking front blank and red ribbon marker), decorated as preceding copies, with "Illustrated" stamped on the spine. A good copy in a fine variant publisher's binding. Kohler 160.

1170. PARADISE LOST. By John Milton. *Philadelphia[:] Published by Henry T. Coates & Co. n. d. [ca. 1887]*. First edition thus? 8vo in 4s, 433pp., title page lettered in green within a red border rule, the whole surrounded by a floral trim in green with a green flower in the center, notes at bottom of page, original green cloth, front cover with a bright red border rule, lettered in gilt, and with a large circular emblem in gilt and red at the center, spine lettered in gilt with two small red emblems, t.e.g., other edges untrimmed, red ribbon marker. A fine copy. Uncommon. Not in Kohler.

1171. PARADISE LOST. By John Milton. Book I. With Preparatory And Explanatory Notes. By E. F. Willoughby, M.D. English Classics. *New York: Clark & Maynard, Publishers, 771 Broadway. (1887)*. Slim 8vo, 94+64pp., unsigned vignette portrait of a young Milton on title page, half-title for Book II ("With Notes, By Frances Storr"), separate pagination for Book II, original printed thick red paper wrappers (a little worn), variation of title page including reference to "Books I–II" reproduced with decorative border trim in black on front cover and dated 1887, advertisements for "English Classic Series" printed in red on front and back endpapers, book advertisement on back cover. While Book I only is referenced on the title page, Books I and II are included in this text book intended for school use. The first edition thus, which also contained Book II with notes by Frances Storr, was published in 1879 (also listed here with further editions cited). Uncommon. Not in Kohler.

1172. MILTON'S PARADISE LOST Illustrated By Gustave Doré Edited By Henry C. Walsh, A.M., Editor of American Notes and Queries. Altemus' Edition. *Philadelphia[:] Henry Altemus[,] 507, 509, 511 And 513 Cherry Street[.] n.d. [ca. 1888]*. 4to, vi+319pp., frontispiece illustration and forty-nine additional illustration plates after Gustave Doré, life of Milton, original stamped blue cloth (a bit rubbed), front cover decorated with an illustration stamped in gilt and black (Adam—a distraught figure in gilt—being besieged by good and bad angels on either side—sketched in black) incorporating title in gilt and black above with a dragon-like serpent wrapped around the large "P" in "Paradise Lost" and with additional lettering in silver at the bottom, back cover decorated in blind, spine lettered in yellow with yellow rules and small yellow decorations in the panels, green endpapers, a.e.g. A nice copy in a striking publisher's binding with contemporary presentation inscription (dated 1888) on front blank. Kohler 158, in a very different binding, dates its copy "[ca. 1890]," reporting "Not in the British Library. Not in the Bodleian Library. Not in Cambridge University Library."

1173. Variant of Preceding, in original stamped golden brown cloth (a bit rubbed, some slight age-browning), decorated exactly as preceding, brown endpapers. A nice copy in an attractive variant publisher's binding.

1174. Variant of Preceding, in original stamped olive green cloth (a bit rubbed, minor wear to extremities, pages a little age-browned), decorated exactly as preceding, white endpapers. A very good copy in an attractive variant publisher's binding with a bright and clean illustration on front cover.

1175. Variant of Preceding, in original stamped silver / light gray cloth (spine ends, corners, and edges worn), dark green endpapers. A good, tight copy in an attractive variant publisher's binding.

1176. Variant of Preceding, in original white cloth spine with broad overlap, maroon cloth covers (a bit rubbed, slight inoffensive darkening at top and bottom of white cloth overlap), front cover cloth lettered in gilt, white cloth spine and broad overlap elaborately decorated in embossed gilt, spine lettered in gilt within decorative gilt trim, richly decorated endpapers, a.e.g. A nice copy, fresh and clean within, in a variant publisher's binding.

1177. MILTON'S PARADISE LOST Illustrated By Gustave Doré Edited By Henry C. Walsh, A.M., Editor of American Notes and Queries. *New York[:] John W. Lovell Company[,] 142, 144, 146, 148 And 150 Worth Street[,] And 3, 4, 5, And 6 Mission Place. n.d. [ca. 1888]*. First Lovell edition thus? 4to, vi+319pp., frontispiece illustration plate and forty-nine additional illustration plates after Gustave Doré, life of Milton, original stamped reddish-brown cloth (worn, front pages loose and frayed along edges, binding loose), front cover decorated with an illustration stamped in gilt and black, Adam—a distraught figure in gilt—being besieged by good and bad angels on either side—sketched in black, incorporating title in gilt and black above with a dragon-like serpent wrapped around the large "P" in "Paradise Lost" and with additional lettering in silver ("Illustrated By Gustave Doré") at the bottom, back cover decorated with a large emblem in blind at the center, spine lettered in gilt (faded) with gilt devices (faded) within double black rules, brown endpapers. A fair copy in an attractive (albeit a little worn) binding of the period. Uncommon. Not in Kohler.

1178. PARADISE LOST By John Milton[.] *New York[:] John W. Lovell Company[,] 150 Worth Street, Corner Mission Street. n.d. [ca. 1888]*. First Lovell edition thus? 8vo, 291pp. (beginning with p. 16), frontispiece illustration plate after an engraving by the Dalziel brothers for Book IV (*Adam Seeing Eve*, "'Till I espied thee...."), protective tissue guard, red border line around text, printed on thick paper, extra blank pages at beginning and end, original decorated green cloth, front cover elaborately decorated in black trim with broad embossed bright gilt trim outlining embossed green foliage against a black background across the top incorporating the title within a bright gilt scroll, beneath in the center in embossed green outlined in black against a black background is a large floral design, spine richly decorated in embossed bright gilt trim outlining embossed green foliage against a black background with title in gilt against a broad green background within decorative gilt trim near the top and "T. Y. Crowell & Co." in small gilt letters near the bottom, a.e.g. A fine copy in a lovely publisher's binding, in near mint condition. The book appears never to have been opened or read. While "John W. Lowell Company" appears as the publisher on the title page, interestingly enough, "T. Y. Crowell & Co." is printed in gilt letters on the spine. Not in Kohler.

John Lovell (1876–1932), born in Montreal, established his publishing firm in New York City in the late 1870s and 1880s for the purpose of reprinting cheap editions of British books. He started as a pirate with the intention of breaking the common courtesy of the trade and of the literary establishment. In 1881 he reorganized his business, calling it John W. Lovell Company, and the following year he introduced "Lovell's Library," a series of paperbacks priced at ten, twenty, or thirty cents. Lovell issued his books either in cloth or in paper. Publishing seven million cheap books a year, he became known as "Book-A-Day Lovell." In the early 1890s Lovell went bankrupt, and by 1900 he had completely disappeared from the annals of publishing.

1179. Variant of Preceding, with one additional illustration engraved by the Dalziel brothers for Book V (*Adam and Eve Naming the Animals*, without the lines quoted) as frontispiece, original light brown cloth (a bit rubbed along extremities and spine ends), decorated as preceding, a.e.g. A very good copy with one additional illustration, in an attractive variant publisher's binding. Again, while "John W. Lowell Company" appears as the publisher on the title page, "T. Y. Crowell & Co." appears in gilt near the bottom of the spine.

1180. Variant of Preceding, original decorated olive green cloth, front cover richly decorated in embossed orange, black, and gilt, six small circular medallions, three each along the inner and outer borders, each medallion containing an emblem associated with the arts, title in embossed olive green against a bright gilt background near the top, bright embossed orange background at the center with embossed black circle with lyre and long reed in lower right corner, spine similarly richly decorated in embossed orange, black, and gilt with title in embossed olive green against a bright gilt background near the top and "T. Y. Crowell & Co." in small gilt letters near the bottom, decorated endpapers, a.e.g. A nice, tall copy of a nineteenth-century American edition, with a variant publisher's imprint on title page ("New York[:] John W. Lovell Company[,] 150 Worth Street, Corner Mission Place"), and in an attractive variant publisher's binding. As with preceding, although "John W. Lowell Company" appears as the publisher on the title page, "T. Y. Crowell & Co." is printed in gilt letters on the spine. Not in Kohler.

1181. Variant of Preceding, with same publisher's imprint as preceding copy and frontispiece illustration as in first copy in original decorated dark green cloth (a bit rubbed along joints and at top and bottom of spine, early names on fly-leaf), decorated as preceding, a.e.g. A nice copy in an attractive variant publisher's binding. As with preceding copies, while "John W. Lowell Company" appears as the publisher on the title page, "T. Y. Crowell & Co." is printed in gilt letters on the spine. Not in Kohler.

1182. PARADISE LOST John Milton[.] *Chicago And New York[:] The Henneberry Company. n.d. [ca. 1888].* First edition thus by Henneberry Company? 8vo, 461pp., unsigned frontispiece portrait plate of a youngish Milton, protective tissue guard, title-page plate decorated in Greek Orthodox manner, in the character of the illustration for Book I of ca. 1882 edition by the American News Company with elaborate trim in varying styles, several crosses on either side, and a large figure of a praying angel at the center with "Paradise Lost" and Milton's name in red beneath, three illustration plates after engravings by the Dalziel brothers (for Books III ["Loud hosannas filled the eternal regions"], VI ["This greeting on thy impious crest receive"], IX ["Back to the thicket slunk the guilty serpent"]), original pink cloth, front cover richly decorated with fleurs-de-lis repeated in blind relief with a large cross outlined in black and decorated in black and gilt on the left side and with *PL* and Milton's name in small gilt letters within a delineated area in the lower right corner, spine similarly richly decorated with fleurs-de-lis repeated in blind relief with *PL* and Milton's name in gilt at the top and "The Henneberry Company" in small gilt letters at the bottom, t.e.g., red silk ribbon marker. A fine copy in a lovely publisher's binding, in near mint condition. The edition was reprinted in ca. 1895 (also listed here); undated nonillustrated editions were also published by "Donohue, Henneberry & Co." ca. 1895 (also listed here). Uncommon. Not in Kohler.

1183. PARADISE LOST BY JOHN MILTON[.] *New York[:] Frank F. Lovell And Company[,] 142 And 144 Worth Street. n.d. [ca. 1888].* 8vo, 291pp. (beginning with p. 16), "Trow's Printing And Bookbinding Company, New York" on verso of title page, original decorated brown cloth (front joint slightly cracked from within, pages age-browned and brittle as is common with paper from this period), front cover richly decorated in embossed black with a book at the center within the wings of a pegasus and with the Latin phrase ("Liber Atque Doce") at the bottom, spine similarly richly decorated in embossed black with title against a bright gilt band near the top and with "Aldine Edition" printed in black near the bottom and "Frank F. Lovell & Co." in smaller lettering against a black band at the bottom. A very nice copy in an attractive publisher's binding. Unlike the other Lovell editions, this edition is not illustrated. Uncommon. Not in Kohler.

1184. PARADISE LOST By John Milton[.] With A Memoir[.] *New York[:] Frederick A. Stokes & Brother[.] 1888.* First edition thus by Stokes? 12mo, xvi+224+[1]pp., title page in red and black reproducing in black at the center the emblem from the incunabula printing of *Ship of Fools* of a "scholar" poring over a book with a stack of folios around him, original half black cloth elaborately gilt-decorated, floral decorated paper over boards (a bit used), spine lettered and decorated in gilt, t.e.g. Despite some modest wear, a very nice copy in publisher's binding with advertisement leaf bound in at the end. See undated ca. 1895 edition published by "Frederick A. Stokes Company Publishers." Not in Kohler.

The emblem comes from Sebastian Brant, *Das Narrenshift* (Ship of Fools), a printed book (or incunabula) of the fifteenth century. It was a favorite of Bob Taylor's, and throughout the 1970s he would show the emblem on Brant's title page from among his books (rare though it was and remains) in his room in Firestone Library at Princeton University.

1185. Variant of Preceding, original half white cloth elaborately gilt-decorated, floral decorated paper over boards consisting of pink and white petals against a gold background (a bit rubbed at corners), spine lettered and decorated in gilt, t.e.g. A lovely copy in a variant publisher's binding, with advertisement leaf bound in at the end, and with early inscription on fly-leaf. Not in Kohler.

1186. PARADISE LOST. By John Milton[.] With A Memoir. *New York: Wm. L. Allison, Nos. 93 Chambers And 75 Reade Streets. n.d. [ca. 1888].* First edition thus? 8vo, 316pp., "Prepatory Memoir Of Milton," notes at bottom of the page, contemporary maroon cloth (a bit rubbed, spine a little faded), front cover decorated in blind with "Allison's Select Library" in embossed blind at the top, spine decorated in black and gilt with title in embossed lettering in reverse against a broad gilt band near the top. A nice copy of this inexpensively printed late nineteenth-century American edition of *PL*, in publisher's binding, with small early bookplate on front pastedown. Uncommon. Not in Kohler.

1187. PARADISE LOST. By John Milton. With A Memoir. *New York: Worthington Co, 747 Broadway. 1888.* Fourth edition thus? 8vo, 316pp., notes at bottom of page, original decorated reddish-brown cloth (spine ends chipped, pages age-browned and brittle because of the quality of paper used at the time), front cover decorated in embossed black lines and swirls with small angelic figure within laurel wreath holding a torch and book in lower left corner, "Franklin Edition" in large embossed reddish-brown letters within a black square in the center, "Illustrated" stamped at the bottom, delicately trimmed black border at top and bottom, spine similarly decorated in embossed black lines and swirls with *PL* in embossed reddish-brown letters within a broad gilt band near the top, "Franklin Edition" in embossed reddish-brown letters within a black square in the center, and "Illustrated" stamped below with "Worthington" in embossed reddish-brown letters within a black band at the bottom with decorative gilt trim at the top. A decent copy in an attractive publisher's binding. While labeled "Illustrated" on front cover and spine, there are no illustrations within, and none appear to be missing. The possible first edition by Worthington, an illustrated edition, was published in 1884 (also listed here with further editions cited). Not in Kohler.

1188. PARADISE LOST. By John Milton. With A Memoir. *New York: Worthington Co, 747 Broadway. n.d. [ca. 1888].* 8vo, 316pp., notes at bottom of page, original decorated orange cloth (a bit rubbed, library markings and stamps and related material, pages age-browned and brittle), front cover decorated in embossed black lines and swirls with small angelic figure within laurel wreath holding a torch and book in lower left corner, "Franklin Edition" in large embossed orange letters within a black square in the center and "Illustrated" stamped at the bottom, delicately trimmed black border at top and bottom, spine similarly decorated in embossed black lines and swirls with *PL* in embossed orange letters within a broad gilt band near the top, "Franklin Edition" in embossed orange letters within a black square in the center, and "Illustrated" stamped below with "Worthington" in embossed orange letters within a black band at the bottom with decorative gilt trim at the top, decorated endpapers. A good copy. Similar to preceding copy, except for being undated, thicker by about a ¼", and in an attractive variant publisher's binding with a contemporary presentation note (dated "Mar. 9. 1888.") laid in. While labeled "Illustrated" on front cover and spine, as with preceding copy, there are no illustrations within, and none appear to be missing. Not in Kohler.

1189. PARADISE LOST By John Milton In Twelve Books[.] *Chicago[:] Geo. M. Hill Company[,] 166-174 S. Clinton Street[,] n.d. [ca. 1888]*. First edition thus? Small 8vo, 423pp., original light brown cloth (a bit aged, spine ends chipped, pages a little brittle and age-darkened, with slight chipping on outer edge of title page), decorative red border trim on front cover with title lettered in silver, spine lettered in silver with small central decorative piece in silver. Despite some modest wear, a decent copy. Uncommon. Not in Kohler.

1190. MILTON'S PARADISE LOST, BOOKS I. AND II. With Introduction, Notes, And Diagrams, By Homer B. Sprague, M.A., Ph.D., Head-Master Of The Girls' High School, Boston; And Formerly Principal Of The Adelphi Academy, Brooklyn, And Professor Of Rhetoric And English Literature In Cornell University. *Boston: Published By Ginn & Company. 1888*. Slim 8vo, xxxii+[2]+113pp.,+xiii+38pp.,+[12]pp.[advertisements variously paginated], frontispiece plate in black and white, two additional illustrative plates in black and white, several textual diagrams depicting Milton's universe, and other introductory material as with 1979 first edition (given in full there), original green cloth (a bit rubbed, spine chipped at top and bottom, lacking fly-leaf), front cover decorated in black trim near the top and bottom with black lettering in between, spine lettered in black. A nice copy with twelve pages of advertisements bound in at the end. Bound in as a separate edition unto itself is *L*, with its own title page and with separate pagination: **MILTON'S LYCIDAS**. Edited, With Notes, By Homer B. Sprague . . . *Boston: Published By Ginn & Company. 1886*. The first edition thus was published in 1879 (also listed here with further editions cited). Not in Kohler.

1191. MILTON'S PARADISE LOST With Fifty Full-Page Illustrations By Gustave Doré[.] With Notes And A Life Of Milton By Robert Vaughan, D.D. *New York: Pollard & Moss, Publishers, 42 Park Place and 37 Barclay Street. 1889*. Small 4to, lv+[1]+401pp., frontispiece illustration plate and forty-nine additional illustration plates after Gustave Doré, small emblem in black at center of title page reproducing emblem from *Ship of Fools* of a "scholar" poring over a book with a stack of folios around him, life of Milton, notes at bottom of page, original green cloth (pages age-browned), front cover decorated with an illustration stamped in bright gilt and black (an angelic figure with crooked sword and outstretched arm standing on an orb with palm trees in embossed blue and shaded black behind him with an angel in embossed blue and shaded black flying above him, and beneath him a snake in embossed blue and shaded black in curled position) incorporating title in bright gilt and black, spine decorated with an illustration stamped in black (*The Expulsion of Adam and Eve*) and lettered in gilt, decorated endpapers, a.e.g. A nice, tight copy in an attractive publisher's binding, in unusually fine condition. See 1885 and 1887 editions (with some variations) by Pollard and Moss. Not in Kohler.

1192. PARADISE LOST. By John Milton. Cassell's National Library. *Cassell & Company, Limited: London, Paris, New York & Melbourne. 1889*. 2 volumes. First edition thus by Cassell. 16mo, [2]+192+[2]pp.,+[2]+192+[2]pp., half-title each volume (each half-title with "Cassell's National Library" listed on verso), title page each volume, emblem of the press on each title page, introduction by "H.[enry] M.[orley]," original decorated blue cloth, front covers decorated and lettered in black with title lettered in gilt against a black backdrop near the top, "Cassell's National Library" lettered in black within a decorative circular floral wreath, spines lettered in black, advertisements on back covers, endpapers consisting of printed advertisements. Advertisement leaf before half-title each volume; additional advertisement leaf at end of each volume. A nice set in fine original publisher's binding. A second edition by Cassell was published in 1891 and a later edition in 1904—both listed here. See also the first edition of *PR* by Cassell in 1889. Scarce. Kohler 156, reporting "Not in Cambridge University Library."

1193. MILTON LE PARADIS PERDU Traduit Par De Pongerville De L'Académie Française Nouvelle Edition Revue Et Corrigée Précédée De Considérations Sur Milton, Son Epoque Et Ses Ouvrages Par Le Traducteur[.] *Paris[:] Charpentier Et Cie, Editeurs 11, Rue De Grenelle, 11[.] 1889*. 12mo in 6s, 356pp., half-title, "Table Des Matieres" at the end, half black leather, marbled paper over boards (a bit rubbed, small blue stamp on title page), spine lettered in gilt with small decorative gilt pieces in the panels, raised bands, marbled endpapers, speckled edges. A nice copy with early signature in a neat hand on front blank. Uncommon. Not in Kohler.

1194. PARADISE LOST. By John Milton. BOOK I. With Preparatory And Explanatory Notes. By E. F. Willoughby, M.D. English Classics. *New York: Effingham Maynard & Co., Successors To Clark & Maynard, Publishers, 771 Broadway And 67 & 69 Ninth St. (1889)*. Slim 8vo, 94pp., unsigned vignette portrait of a young Milton on title page, original preface (dated 1879) reprinted, original printed boards (bit rubbed, few pencil markings), light blue cloth spine, variation of title page reproduced in contrasting colors of light blue, maroon, and white largely against light blue backdrop with elaborate decorative border trim on front cover and dated 1889, advertisements for "English Classic Series" printed in red on front and back endpapers and on back cover, red edges. Nice copy. The first edition thus, which also contained Book II with notes by Frances Storr, was published in 1879 (also listed here with further editions cited). Not in Kohler.

1195. Variant of Preceding. Bound together with **BOOK I**, as preceding, is **BOOK II**, with separate pagination, 64pp., and half-title for Book II ("With Notes, By Frances Storr"), original printed boards (a bit rubbed, small stain on outer edge of last few page), light blue cloth spine, variation of title page including reference to "Books I–II" reproduced in a variant style from preceding copy with elaborate decorative border trim in maroon and light blue on front cover and dated 1889, advertisements for "English Classic Series" printed in red on front and back endpapers and on back cover, red edges. Decent copy with early names on endpapers and title page. Not in Kohler.

1196. MILTON'S PARADISE LOST, BOOKS I. AND II. With Introduction, Notes, And Diagrams, By Homer B. Sprague, M.A., Ph.D., Headmaster Of The Girls' High School, Boston; And Formerly Principal Of The Adelphi Academy, Brooklyn, And Professor Of Rhetoric And English Literature In Cornell University. *Boston, U.S.A.: Published By Ginn & Company. 1889*. Slim 8vo, xxxii+113pp., +xiii+38pp.,+[30]pp., frontispiece plate in black and white, two additional illustrative plates in black and white, several textual diagrams depicting Milton's universe, and other introductory material as with 1979 first edition (given in full there), original green cloth (a bit rubbed, spine ends, lacking fly-leaf), front cover decorated in black trim near the top and bottom with black lettering in between, spine lettered in black. A good copy with thirty pages of advertisements with half-title bound in at the end. Bound in after **PARADISE LOST** as a separate edition unto itself is *L*, with its own title page and with separate pagination: **MILTON'S LYCIDAS**. Edited, With Notes, By Homer B. Sprague . . . *Boston, U.S.A.: Published By Ginn & Company. 1889*. The first edition thus was published in 1879 (also listed here with further editions cited). Not in Kohler.

1197. PARADISE LOST. By John Milton. With A Memoir. *New York: Worthington Co., 747 Broadway, 1890*. Fifth edition thus? 8vo, 316pp., frontispiece illustration and one additional illustration (unsigned), notes at bottom of page, red border around text, original decorated blue cloth (a bit rubbed), front cover decorated in embossed red and black lines and swirls in a floral and circular motif with the title incorporated in black lettering within a bright gilt band near the top and with a winged horse (pegasus) in red against a black background within a decorated circle of swirls and twirls in lower left corner, spine similarly elaborately decorated in embossed red, black, and gilt with floral motif at the center, the title lettered in black within a bright gilt band toward the top, and "Worthington Co" within a smaller gilt band at the bottom, decorated endpapers, a.e.g. A nice copy in a lovely publisher's binding. The possible first edition thus was published in 1884 (also listed here with further editions cited). Scarce. Not in Kohler.

1198. MILTON'S PARADISE LOST Illustrated By Gustave Doré. Edited, With Notes And A Life Of Milton, By Robert Vaughan, D.D. *New York: Collier, n.d. [ca. 1890]*. Second Collier edition? Imperial 4to, xlv+313pp., frontispiece illustration plate and forty-nine additional illustration plates after Gustave Doré, protective tissue guards, original green cloth, front cover decorated with an illustration stamped in bright gilt and black (a fierce-looking angelic figure holding a crooked sword incorporating along the front part of the letter "P" in gilt-lettered "Paradise Lost" a vignette scene of Eden in gilt within the open space of the letter "P" along with artists' brushes and palette beneath the lettering "Illustrated By Gustave Doré"), spine elaborately decorated and lettered in black. A very good copy in an attractive publisher's binding. See copy of the first Collier edition ca. 1880 with illustrations by Doré. Not in Kohler.

1199. MILTON'S PARADISE LOST Illustrated By Gustave Doré[.] Edited With Notes And A Life Of Milton By Robert Vaughan, D.D. *New York, London And Paris[:] Cassell & Company Limited[.] n.d., [ca. 1890]*. 4to, lxii+329pp., frontispiece illustration plate and forty-nine additional illustration plates after Gustave Doré, life of Milton followed by introduction, notes at bottom of page, original golden brown cloth (a bit rubbed, pages fragile with a few tears along edges in the front, slight inoffensive waterstaining to outer edges of last few pages), front cover decorated with an illustration in bright gilt and black (an angelic figure with crooked sword and spear) at the center incorporating title in gilt and black, spine decorated in black and lettered in gilt, decorated green endpapers, a.e.g. A good copy in an attractive publisher's binding. Not in Kohler.

1200. O PARAISO PERDIDO Poema Epico Em Doze Cantos[.] Em 2 Tomos[.] Biographia do poeta, analise do poema e notas por Xavier da Cunha[;] Traducao do Dr. Antonio José de Lima Leitao[;] Com ilustracoes de Gustave Doré[.] *Grafica E Editora Edigraf Limitada[,] Sao Paulo (Brazil), n.d. [ca. 1890]* 2 volumes. First edition thus. 4to, 203pp.,+397pp., half-title each volume, title page in red and black each volume, unsigned frontispiece portrait (etching), volume 1, half-title each volume with decorative trim, fifty illustration plates after Gustave Doré, "Quem E O Autor" "Que E O Poema" before the poem, volume 1, elaborate decorative headpieces, decorative tailpieces, decorated initial letters, printed in double column, "Indices" at the end of volume 2, original red cloth (a bit rubbed, slight, inoffensive white marking on back cover of volume 1), embossed pattern on covers with central embossed vignette of Milton on front cover of each volume and central embossed stamp ("Edicoes De Luxo") on back cover of each volume, spines lettered and elaborately decorated in gilt in a pattern consistent with that on the covers, richly marbled endpapers. A very attractive set. *PL* was first published in Spanish in 1812 in the verse translation by Juan de Escoiquiz; other translations followed. See 1873 edition of *El Paraiso Perdido* in prose translation by Cayetano Roseli, the first Spanish edition with Doré's illustrations; see also 1883 edition of *El Paraiso Perdido* in verse translation by D. Juan Escoiquiz, with Dore's illustrations. The present is a verse translation by Antonio Leitao. Not in Kohler.

1201. PARADISE LOST [In] **CASSELL'S DORE GALLERY**: Containing Two Hundred and Fifty Beautiful Engravings, Selected From The Doré Bible, Milton, Dante's Inferno, Dante's Purgatorio And Paradiso, Atala, Fontaine, Fairy Realm, Don Quixote, Baron Munchausen, Croquemitaine, &c. &c. With Memoir of Doré, Critical Essay, And Description Letterpress, By Edmund Ollier. *Cassell & Company, Limited: London, Paris, New York & Melbourne. n.d. [ca. 1890].* 4to, xlvii+152pp., half-title, title page in red and black, 250 plates including reproductions of Gustave Doré's illustrations for *PL*, "Advertisement," "List Of Plates," "Memoir Of Gustave Doré," "Cassell's Doré Gallery," "Description Of The Plates," decorative tailpieces and decorated initial letters, red border around text, contemporary one-half red morocco, red cloth (rubbed and with some wear, title page slightly soiled and a little light foxing or staining in places), spine ruled and lettered in gilt, raised bands with decorative gilt trim (rubbed), marbled endpapers, a.e.g. Not in Kohler.

1202. PARADISE LOST. By John Milton. **BOOK I.** With Preparatory And Explanatory Notes. By E. F. Willoughby, M.D. English Classics. *New York: Effingham Maynard & Co., Successors To Clark & Maynard, Publishers, 771 Broadway And 67 & 69 Ninth St. (1890).* Slim 8vo, 94+64pp., unsigned vignette portrait of a young Milton on title page, half-title for Book II ("With Notes, By Frances Storr"), separate pagination for Book II, original printed boards (a bit rubbed, light crayon marking on blank space at bottom of p. 8), variation of title page including reference to "Books I–II" reproduced in dark red brown on front cover, blue cloth spine (a little rubbed and darkened), advertisements printed in red on front and back endpapers and on back cover, red edges. While Book I only is referenced on the title page, Books I and II are included in this text book intended for school use. The first edition thus, which also contained Book II with notes by Frances Storr, was published in 1879 (also listed here with further editions cited). Not in Kohler.

1203. MILTON DAS VERLORENE PARADIES. Episches Gedicht. Aus dem Englischen von Karl Eitner. *Leipzig und Wien. Bibliographisches Institut.[.] n.d. [ca. 1890].* 8vo, 338pp., half-title, "Milton's Leben und Werke," half-title before poetic translation, original green cloth (a bit rubbed), decorative wide border trim in contrasting darker green on covers continuing through spine, spine additionally decorated in contrasting darker green trim with gilt lettering and gilt rules at top and bottom, red morocco label with gilt lettering and gilt rules, decorated endpapers, bluish green edges. A very nice copy of this verse translation by Karl Eitner. The possible first edition thus was published in 1867 (also listed here). Scarce. Kohler 159, reporting "Not in Cambridge University Library."

1204. Variant of Preceding, original three-quarter purple pebble cloth, purple plain cloth (a little spotted with a smudge on back cover), spine decorated in gilt, raised bands in-between gilt rules, small decorative gilt devices within the panels, gilt lettering, decorative gilt trim at top and bottom, richly decorated endpapers with the initials "JB" on front and back pastedowns with advertisements on front and back end-leaves, lightly marbled edges. A good copy with "Leipzig" only in the publisher's imprint, in a variant publisher's binding, and with eight pages of advertisements bound in at the end. Not in Kohler.

1205. DAS VERLORENE PARADIES von John Milton Uebersetzt von Friedrich Wilhelm Jachariä Mit einer Einleitung von Ludwig Proescholdt[.] Collection Spemann. *Stuttgart[:] Verlag von P. Spemann. n.d. [ca. 1890].* 8vo, 260+[2]pp. half-title, title in red on title page with an emblem near the bottom (incorporating the date 1873), original blue silk cloth (a bit rubbed, early name on half-title), front cover decorated with embossed rules on the outside and title at top and bottom with embossed decorative corner pieces and central circular emblem, the back cover is similarly decorated with embossed rules and trim and a central circular emblem different from that on the front cover, spine lettered in gilt and richly decorated in finely embossed trim, light green endpapers containing "Die englische Litteratur" printed in double column with a decorative border trim, back pastedown similar to the light green endpapers, advertising "Englische Classiker ver

Collection Spemann" (including this edition), front pastedown slightly darker than the light green endpapers, consisting of an elaborate printed bookplate as part of the publication allowing for the owner's name. Fine copy of this prose translation, in an attractive German binding of the period. Uncommon. Not in Kohler.

1206. LE PARADIS PERDU Suivi De Essai Sur La Littérature Angloise Par Chateaubriand[.] Nouvelle Edition[.] Revue Avec Soin Sur Les Editions Originales[.] *Paris[:] Garnier Frères, Editeurs 6, Rue Des Saints-Pères, 6[.] n.d. [ca. 1890].* 12mo, xx+579pp., general half-title, half-title for "Le Paradis Perdu," "Remarques" before prose translation of Milton's epic, half-title for "Essai Sur La Littérature Angloise Et Considérations Sur Le Génie Des Temps, Des Hommes Et Des Révolutions" (which occupies the second half of the book), "Table Le Paradis Perdu [&] Essai Sur La Littérature Angloise" at the end, contemporary half brown leather, marbled paper (a bit rubbed, pages a little age-browned around edges), purple ribbon marker. A good copy. Uncommon. Not in Kohler.

1207. MILTON LE PARADIS PERDU Traduction De Chateaubriand Précédé De Réflexions Sur La Vie Et Les Escrits De Milton Par Lamartine Et Enrichi De Trente Magnifiques Estampes Originales Sur Teinte Chine Dont Trois Inedits[.] *Paris[:] Gustave Guérin Et Cie, Libraires-Editeurs 22, Rue Des Boulangers, 22[,] M D CCC XCI (1891).* Folio, 157+xxvipp., half-title, twenty-seven illustrations by Flatters, Richomme, Lemercier, Melin, and Bernouville (fine impressions), engraved portraits of a young Milton by Sixdeniers, and of Lamartine and Chateaubriand, "Arguments" for the books printed together at the end of the poem, followed by "Reflexions Sur Milton" (dated "Mars 1855") and "Etude Historique Et Littéraire Sur Milton," all, unlike the poem, printed in double column, splendid decorative head- and tailpieces, decorated initial letter each book, contemporary half red demi-basané/sheepskin, marbled paper over boards (a little rubbed, edges worn, foxing), spine lettered in gilt with gilt rules and small decorative gilt devices within the panels, slightly raised bands, marbled endpapers. A good copy, "enhanced by 30 original china-tinted prints of which three are not previously published," according to the title page. The first edition with these portraits and twenty-seven of the illustrations was published in 1855 (also listed here). Scarce. Not in Kohler.

1208. PARADISE LOST. By John Milton. *Cassell's National Library. Cassell & Company, Limited: London, Paris & Melbourne. 1891.* 2 volumes. Second edition thus by Cassell? 16mo, 192+[4]pp., 192+[4]pp., half-title each volume (each half-title with "A Selection Of The Most Popular Volumes In Cassell's National Library" listed on verso), title page each volume, emblem of the press on each title page, introduction by "H.[enry] M.[orley]," original blue cloth, front covers ruled and lettered in blind, spine lettered in gilt, small initials of "Cassell & Co. Limited" in blind at center of each back cover. A nice set with four pages of advertisements for "Volumes Published in Cassell's Standard Library" bound in at the end of volume 1, and four pages of advertisements for "Selections From Cassell & Company's Publications" bound in at the end of volume 2. See possible first edition thus by Cassell in 1891. Uniformly bound with *PR & SA*, Cassell's National Library. *Cassell & Company, Limited: London, Paris & Melbourne. 1891.* Scarce. Not in Kohler.

1209. PARADISE LOST By John Milton With Introductions By David Masson, M.A., LL.D. Professor Of Rhetoric And English Literature In The Universit Of Edinburgh[.] Biographical Sketch By Nathan Haskell Dole[.] *New York[:] Thomas Y. Crowell Company Publishers[.] (1892).* First edition thus? 8vo, xiii+279pp., unsigned frontispiece portrait plate sketch of Milton at age sixty-two, decorated title-page plate printed in orange with decorative ornamental border trim in black, printed title page with copyright dated 1892 on verso, original red cloth, covers decorated in blind with small central emblem in blind on front cover, spine decorated with gilt trim at top and bottom and lettered in gilt. A good copy with early name on fly-leaf. Not in Kohler.

1210. PARADISE LOST A Poem in Twelve Books By John Milton[.] New American Edition[.] *Chicago[:] A. C. McClurg And Company[.] (1892).* First edition thus? 8vo, 352pp., half-title ("Lavrel Crowned Verse" along with title, printed within scroll-like forms intertwined with a laurel wreath), ("Laurel-Crowned Verse. Edited By Francis F. Browne" listed on verso with "Others to follow in the series. Each in 1 vol., 16mo, gilt top, $1.00"), title page in red and black with central emblem in red, three-quarter dark maroon, marbled paper over boards (a bit worn, front joint cracked, pages a bit age-browned, front blanks brittle and reinforced to strengthen, top corner of page 173/174 missing), marbled endpapers, t.e.g., fore-edge untrimmed Despite the flaws, a nice copy, bound by Ringer for A. C. McClurg and Company with his stamp. Scarce.

1211. MILTON'S PARADISE LOST, BOOKS V. AND VI. With Introduction, Notes, Glossary And Index By A. Wilson Verity, M.A. Sometime Scholar Of Trinity College. Edited For The Syndics Of The University Press[.] *Pitt Press Series[.] 1892 [All Rights reserved.]* First edition thus. Slim 8vo, lxixx+136+8pp., half-title preceded by advertisement page with excerpts from various sources commending Verity's edition, half-title for each book, "The Cosmology Of Paradise Lost," and "The Character Of Milton's Satan," "Glossary," and "Index" at the end, original green cloth (some wear, name and comment on fly-leaf), front cover and spine lettered in black with small crescent in black at bottom of front cover. A decent copy. Not in Kohler.

1212. PARADISE LOST BOOKS I. AND II. With Introduction, Notes, Glossary And Index By A. Wilson Verity, M. A. Sometime Scholar Of Trinity College. Edited For The Syndics Of The University Press[.] The Cambridge Milton for Schools. *Cambridge: At The University Press. 1893[.] [All Rights reserved.].* First edition thus. Small 8vo, lxxi+172+[2]+8pp., advertisement leaf for "The Cambridge Milton for Schools" general half-title, half-title before each book, "Appendix A. The Cosmology of Paradise Lost," "Appendix B. On The Character Of Milton's Satan," appendix C, D, and E on select lines of each book, "Appendix F. The Orders Of The Heavenly Beings," original olive green cloth (a bit worn, some pencil markings, contemporary ownership name on fly-leaf), front cover and spine lettered in black (spine a little faded) with the crest of the press on the front cover. Eight pages of advertisements bound in at the end. A second edition thus was published in 1894 (listed here); it was variously reprinted thereafter, including 1902 (copy in the collection, a repeat of this edition, not listed here), 1910 (copy in the collection, a repeat of this edition, not listed here), and the 1952, the "Third Edition, Revised and Re-set" (verso title page, see copy also listed here). Uncommon. Not in Kohler.

1213. PARADISE LOST, BOOKS I. AND II. Edited With Introduction And Notes By M. Macmillan . . . *London[:] Macmillan And Co. And New York[,] 1893. [All rights reserved]* Third edition thus. Slim 8vo, xxix+54pp.+[87pp. of unpaginated notes], half-title, original cream cloth (worn, spine chipped and defective, pencil markings throughout, slight embrowning), front cover and spine lettered in blue, initials for Macmillan And Co. in blue at the center of back cover, advertisement leaf bound in at end. The first edition thus was published in 1887; the second edition thus in 1891; the third edition thus in 1893 and again in 1899—both listed here. In 1900 a new edition was published by Macmillan as part of "The Macmillan Pocket Classics"; the edition was reprinted in 1923 and again in 1926—these also listed here. Not in Kohler.

1214. MILTON PARADISE LOST, BOOK II Edited By E. K. Chambers, B.A. Some Time Scholar Of Corpus Christi College, Oxford[.] *Oxford[:] At The Clarendon Press[,] 1893.* First edition thus. Slim 8vo, 118+[2]+8pp., half-title, original boards, green cloth spine (a little used, a few pencil markings, early name in a neat hand on fly-leaf), front cover lettered in black, back cover repeating the emblem and information on verso of half-title. Ten pages of advertisements bound n at the end. A good copy. Scarce. Not in Kohler.

1215. MILTON'S PARADISE LOST Illustrated By Gustave Doré[.] Edited With Notes And A Life Of Milton By Robert Vaughan D.D. Popular Edition[.] *Cassell And Company Limited[,] London[,] Paris & Melbourne[,] 1894. All Rights Reserved.* Large 8vo, lxviii+338+[16]pp., half-title, frontispiece illustration plate and forty-nine additional illustration plates after Gustave Doré, with protective tissue guard for frontispiece, title page in red and black with small emblem on verso, original blue cloth, front cover and spine finely decorated and lettered in gilt, black, and light green, decorated light green endpapers, back cover with central design consisting of black rules, a.e.g. Sixteen pages of "A Selected List Of Cassell & Company's Publications," with half-title, bound in at end. A bright, crisp copy in a lovely binding with Prize Label on front pastedown. Kohler 162, describing its copy in "original blue linen texture cloth" and reporting "Not in Cambridge University Library."

1216. PARADISE LOST By John Milton[.] *London[:] George Routledge & Sons, Limited[,] Broadway, Ludgate Hill. Manchester And New York[,] 1894.* 16mo, 318pp., half-title, central emblem on title page, "Ballantyne Press: Edinburgh And London" printed at bottom of last page, original red cloth spine (a bit rubbed, spine faded and ends chipped), marbled paper over boards (worn along extremities), black label with gilt lettering and rules on spine. A decent copy. See 1887 edition (possible first edition thus) listed earlier. Not in Kohler.

1217. PARADISE LOST By John Milton In Twelve Books[.] Salem Edition[.] *Boston And New York [:] Houghton, Mifflin And Company. The Riverside Press, Cambridge. 1894.* Small 8vo, 331+[10]pp., half-title, woodcut emblem of the press at center of title page, decorative head- and tailpieces, decorated initial letters, original decorated white cloth (soiled with small smudges on front cover and larger smudges on back cover, two small tears at top of half-title with a small tear and a missing piece along the side, pages age-darkened and a bit fragile because of the poor quality of paper, former ownership stamp on fly-leaf), front cover and spine decorated with small red decorative pieces, red lettering within decorative red trim on front cover and spine. Ten pages of advertisements bound in at end. A fairly good copy of an uncommon edition. Not in Kohler.

1218. PARADISE LOST By John Milton[.] With A Memoir[.] *New York [:] E. A. Lawson Company Publishers[.] n. d. [ca. 1894]* First edition thus? Small 8vo, 408pp., brief notes at the bottom of the page, original brown cloth (a bit rubbed, spine ends slightly chipped), front cover with decorative border trim in gilt (faded) and five decorative pieces in black and gilt, one in each corner and a slightly larger one in the center, similar decorative piece in black and gilt on spine with gilt lettering against a black background within gilt rules and decorative trim in black and gilt. A nice copy with contemporary signature (dated 1894) on fly-leaf. Scarce. Not in Kohler.

1219. IL PARADISO PERDUTO Poema Di Giovanni Milton Traduzione Del Cav. Andrea Maffei. *Torino: Unione Tipografico Editrice 33—Via Carlo Alberto—33[.] 1894.* 8vo, xxxix+383pp., half-title, decorative device on title page, decorated initial letters, contemporary half leather, marbled paper over boards, vellum corner tips, spine lettered and ruled in gilt, decorated endpapers, speckled edges. A fine copy in an attractive binding of the period. Uncommon. Not in Kohler.

1220. MILTON'S PARADISE LOST BOOKS I AND II With Introduction, Notes, And Diagrams By Homer B. Sprague, M. A. Ph.D. Formerly Headmaster Of The Girls' High School, Boston . . . *Boston, U.S.A.: Ginn And Company, Publishers. 1894.* Slim 8vo, xxxii+113pp.,+ xiii+38pp., frontispiece plate in black and white, two additional illustrative plates in black and white, several textual diagrams depicting Milton's universe, and other introductory material as with 1879 first edition (given in full there, as with title page), original olive green cloth (a little worn, marginalia in pencil, library stamps marked "withdrawn" with card pocket and due slip in back), front cover and spine lettered in black (*Paradise Lost* and *Lycidas*), advertisement leaves for various text books bound in at end. Bound in at end as a separate edition unto itself is L, with its own title page and separate pagination (with copyright of 1878 on verso): **MILTON'S LYCIDAS**. Edited, With Notes By Homer B. Sprague . . . *Boston, U.S.A.: Ginn And Company, Publishers. 1894.* The first edition thus by Sprague was published in 1879 (also listed here with further editions cited). Scarce. Not in Kohler.

1221. PARADISE LOST BOOKS I AND II. With Introduction, Notes, Glossary And Appendix By A. Wilson Verity, M. A. Sometime Scholar Of Trinity College; Editor Of 'The Pitt Press Shakespeare For Schools.' Edited For The Syndics Of The University Press[.] Second Edition. The Cambridge Milton for Schools. *Cambridge: At The University Press. 1894[.] [All Rights reserved.].* Second edition thus. Small 8vo, lxxi+174+[2]+8pp., advertisement leaf, half-title, "Note To First Edition" dated 1893, "Note To Second Edition" dated 1894, half-title before each book, various appendices at the end, original green cloth (a bit rubbed, some pencil markings), front cover and spine lettered in black (spine faded) with the crest of the press on the front cover. Eight pages of advertisement leaves bound in at the end. The first edition thus was published in 1893 (also listed here with further editions cited). Uncommon. Not in Kohler.

1222. PARADISE LOST BOOKS III. AND IV. With Introduction, Notes, Glossary And Indexes By A. Wilson Verity, M. A. Sometime Scholar Of Trinity College; Editor Of 'The Pitt Press Shakespeare For Schools.' Edited For The Syndics Of The University Press[.] The Cambridge Milton for Schools. *Cambridge: At The University Press. 1894 [All Rights reserved.].* First edition thus. Slim 8vo, lxxi+141+[3]+8pp., advertisement leaf, general half-title, half-title for each book, original green cloth (a little used), front cover and spine lettered in dark green with the crest of the press on the front cover. Eight pages of advertisement leaves bound in at the end. A decent copy with early bookplate and name in ink on label tipped in on front pastedown. A second edition thus was published one year later in 1895 (also listed here). Not in Kohler.

1223. PARADISE LOST By John Milton[.] *Chicago[:] W. B. Conkey Company[.] n.d. [ca. 1895].* First edition thus by Conkey? Small 8vo, 461pp., unsigned frontispiece portrait plate of Milton, title-page plate lettered in black and decorated in green in art nouveau style, three illustration plates after Doré, original white cloth (a bit rubbed), front cover decorated in a floral gilt design in art nouveau style with a small color photograph of two young girls walking tipped within a gilt frame on the right side at the middle of the front cover, spine decorated with a tall flower in green with green lettering above the open blossom, and with another blossom in green at the top. A nice copy in a lovely publisher's binding. Not in Kohler.

See undated nonillustrated editions published by "W. B. Conkey Company" about this same time (ca. 1895) in various attractive publisher's bindings. See also dated illustrated edition by "W. B. Conkey Company Publishers" published in 1900 and undated ca. 1900 illustrated edition by "W. B. Conkey Company Publishers," each with frontispiece portrait plate as here and also with three illustration plates. The W. B. Conkey Company was located in Hammond, Indiana, and was at one time the largest publishing company in North America, being the publisher of the first Sears & Roebuck Catalogue.

1224. PARADISE LOST John Milton[.] *Chicago And New York[.] The Henneberry Company[.] n.d. [ca. 1895].* 8vo,

461pp., unsigned frontispiece portrait plate of a youngish Milton, protective tissue guard, title-page plate elaborately decorated in a Russian motif with large crosses within an intricately detailed border trim in black and white, the whole page bordered by delicately detailed trim in black and white with a large angelic figure with folded hands in prayer at the center set against a striking contrasting patterned design in black and white with title and Milton's name in red toward the bottom of the page, three illustration plates after Doré, original brown cloth (a bit rubbed at corners and at top and bottom of spine), long narrow embossed decorative bright gilt band on front cover with title and Milton's name in gilt at the top and "New Century Edition" in gilt letters at the bottom, the whole outlined in gilt with the same long narrow embossed decorative bright gilt band repeated on the spine with title and Milton's name in larger gilt letters at the top and "The Henneberry Co. Chicago" in smaller gilt letters at the bottom. The possible first edition by Henneberry was published ca. 1888 in Chicago and New York (copy listed here) with three illustration plates after Doré and with the same striking title-page plate. Uncommon. Not in Kohler.

1225. PARADISE LOST By John Milton In Twelve Books[.] Salem Edition[.] *Boston And New York: Houghton, Mifflin And Company. The Riverside Press, Cambridge. 1895.* First edition thus? Small 8vo, 331+[blank]+[8]pp., half-title, emblem of the press on title page, decorative headpieces and decorated initial letters, original decorated cream cloth (a little age-darkened, pages age-browned), front cover and spine covered with small red decorative pieces in a patterned manner with "Milton's Paradise Lost" lettered in red within decorative red trim at the center, bookplate on front pastedown. A good copy of this small edition by the Riverside Press (possible first edition thus). Eight pages of advertisements bound in at the end. Not in Kohler.

1226. Variant of Preceding, in original decorated light green cloth (spine a bit rubbed, pages a little age-browned), front cover and spine covered with small red decorative pieces in a patterned manner and with "Milton's Paradise Lost" lettered in red within decorative red trim at the center. A good copy in a lovely variant publisher's binding. Eight pages of advertisements bound in at the end.

1227. PARADISE LOST By John Milton[.] *Chicago[:] M. A. Donohue & Co. n.d. [ca. 1895].* First edition by Donohue? Small 8vo, 423pp., unsigned frontispiece portrait plate of Milton tinted light green, tinted light green title-page plate lettered in contrasting dark green with decorative light green floral trim, original green cloth, front cover decorated with three columns of floral trim in black interspersed with three black lines, color photograph tipped in at the top with overlapping black lines and thick black sides with overlapping thin green lines, title lettered in black directly beneath the tipped in color photograph, spine similarly decorated and lettered in black. A nice copy in an appealing publisher's binding. See other undated editions published by Donohue about this same time, ca. 1895, in equally attractive bindings. Not in Kohler.

1228. Variant of Preceding, in an identical publisher's binding (slight staining at the bottom) with variant color photograph tipped in at the top.

1229. PARADISE LOST By John Milton[.] *Chicago[:] M. A. Donohue & Co. 407-429 Dearborn St. n.d. [ca. 1895].* Small 8vo, 423pp., unsigned frontispiece portrait plate of Milton tinted in burgundy, burgundy title-page plate also lettered in burgundy with decorative burgundy floral border trim, original soft padded burgundy leather (a bit rubbed along the edges and joints, spine a little faded), front cover lettered in gilt with a large decorative gilt piece beneath, spine lettered in gilt, a.e.g. A nice copy with variant tinted portrait plate, variant tinted title-page plate, and with variant publisher's imprint. Kohler 161, calling its copy "12mo," dating it "[ca. 1893]," making no mention of the portrait plate being tinted and making no mention of a title-page plate, in a variant binding ("Original 1/4-cream cloth, paper covered boards"), and reporting "Not in Williamson. Not in the British Library. Not in the Bodleian Library. Not in Cambridge University Library."

1230. Variant of Preceding, unsigned frontispiece portrait plate of Milton tinted light brown, light brown title-page plate lettered in contrasting dark brown with decorative dark brown floral border trim, original brown cloth (scuffed and a bit worn), front cover and spine decorated in dark blue and lettered in contrasting embossed brown. A fair copy with a variant tinted frontispiece portrait plate and variant tinted title-page plate, in a variant publisher's binding.

1231. PARADISE LOST Milton[.] *Chicago: M. A. Donohue & Co. 407-429 Dearborn St. n.d. [ca. 1895].* 8vo, 423pp., unsigned frontispiece portrait plate of Milton in black and white, decorated title-page plate printed in orange and black with elaborate ornamental black border frame with two angelic figures at the center, original soft crushed brown leather over padded boards (a bit rubbed, front endpaper and title page separated, slight tear at inner margin of title), front cover and spine lettered in gilt, decorated endpapers, a.e.g. A nice copy with variant title-page plate and in a larger octavo size than the other Donohue editions here. Not in Kohler.

1232. Variant of Preceding. **PARADISE LOST**[.] *Chicago: M. A. Donohue & Co[.] 407-429 Dearborn St. n.d. [ca. 1895]*. 8vo, 423pp., as preceding, original decorated light blue cloth (a bit aged), front cover decorated in art nouveau style with black and silver swirls surrounding a central figure of a lady on a balcony incorporating title in gilt at the top, spine similarly decorated in silver and black and lettered in gilt, decorated tan endpapers, t.e.g. A good copy with variant title page (in red and black instead of orange and black, without Milton's name appearing, and without a period after "Co"), in a charming variant publisher's binding.

1233. **PARADISE LOST** By John Milton In Twelve Books[.] *Chicago: Donohue Brothers, 407-429 Dearborn Street. n.d. [ca. 1895]*. Small 8vo, 423pp., original decorated white cloth (a bit rubbed and aged, some underlinings in pencil), spine and one-half of each cover decorated with small silver floral devices, remaining portion on each cover decorated in red and green floral trim, spine lettered in silver within silver rules. A good copy and an attractive (albeit a bit rubbed and aged) binding of the period, a smaller version once again, with another variant of the Donohue publisher's imprint. Scarce Donohue imprint. Not in Kohler.

1234. **PARADISE LOST** By John Milton In Twelve Books[.] *Chicago: Donohue, Henneberry & Co., 407-429 Dearborn Street. n.d. [ca. 1895]*. Small 8vo, 423pp., unsigned frontispiece portrait plate of Milton in tinted mauve, title-page plate printed in red and black, original floral cloth covers decorated in paisley colors with intricately designed pattern in silver over white cloth covering spine and almost one-half of each cover, spine lettered in silver, t.e.g., yellow ribbon marker. A fine copy, virtually mint, in the smaller version once again, in an attractive binding of the period, with another variant of the Donohue publisher's imprint. Not in Kohler.

1235. Variant of Preceding, original white cloth covering spine and almost one-half of each cover, decorated with intricately designed pattern in silver, spine lettered in silver ("Paradise Lost Milton"), floral cloth covers (corners a bit worn) decorated in paisley colors of pink, light blue, mauve, and green, t.e.g., blue ribbon marker. A fine copy, virtually mint, in an attractive and well-preserved variant publisher's binding, with a different floral design from that of the preceding copy and different lettering on spine, with contemporary presentation inscription (dated "Christmas 1902") in pencil on fly-leaf.

1236. **PARADISE LOST** By John Milton In Twelve Books[.] *Chicago. [sic] Donohue, Henneberry & Co. 407-429 Dearborn Street. n.d. [ca. 1895]*. Small 8vo, 423pp., original decorated drab green cloth (a bit rubbed, front joint weak from within, pages a little browned and fragile with age, early ownership names on fly-leaf), front cover decorated with large central circular device in silver incorporating title in silver with intertwining flowered branch in silver, spine similarly decorated and lettered in silver, bookplate on front pastedown. A fairly good copy with another variant of the Donohue title pages: with a variant title, and with a publisher's imprint (a period instead of a colon after Chicago, or else a misprint), with an attractive variant design in art nouveau style. Not in Kohler.

1237. Variant of Preceding, original decorated brown cloth (a bit used), front cover and spine decorated in attractive silver trim in art nouveau style with silver lettering as in preceding copy. A good copy in a variant publisher's binding with an attractive variant design in art nouveau style.

1238. **PARADISE LOST** By John Milton In Twelve Books[.] *Chicago: Donohue, Henneberry & Co. 407-425 Dearborn St. n.d. [ca. 1895]*. Small 8vo, 423pp., original decorated brown cloth (a little rubbed with several small spots on both covers, pages age-browned), silver border trim on front cover with title lettered in silver near the top and a decorative emblem in silver near the bottom, spine lettered in silver with decorative trim in silver at top and bottom and a large decorative piece in silver at the center, decorated light orange endpapers, bookplate. A decent copy in a nice publisher's binding without frontispiece portrait plate or title-page plate and with another variant of the Donohue publisher's imprint (a change in address).

1239. Variant of Preceding, in original decorated reddish-brown cloth (a bit rubbed, former owner's name stamped on front pastedown), silver border trim on front cover with title lettered in silver near the top and a decorative emblem in silver near the bottom, spine lettered in silver with decorative trim in silver at top and bottom and a large decorative piece in silver at the center, decorated light reddish-brown endpapers, stamp on front pastedown. A very good copy in a variant publisher's binding.

1240. Variant of Preceding, in original decorated reddish-brown cloth (front cover and spine a little chafed), front cover and spine decorated in striking silver with tall trees on either side of the cover, floral motif and wavy lines in art nouveau style in the center and bottom, lettering at the top, imitation thereof on the spine. Except for the chafing, a good, tight copy in a variant publisher's binding.

1241. Variant of Preceding, in original decorated red cloth (spine and extremities a little rubbed, former owner's name stamped on front pastedown), large silver design in art nouveau style on front cover with title at top, spine lettered in silver with silver trim. A good copy in another striking variant publisher's binding.

1242. Variant of Preceding. PARADISE LOST By John Milton In Twelve Books[.] *Chicago [sic] Donohue, Henneberry & Co. 407-425 Dearborn Street. n.d. [ca. 1895].* Small 8vo, 423pp., original light brown cloth (a bit rubbed, back cover lightly stained), front cover and spine decorated in striking silver decorative pieces in art nouveau style with silver lettering. A good copy with contemporary signature (dated "Jan. 22, 1899") on fly-leaf, with another variant of the Donohue publisher's imprints (neither a colon nor a period after Chicago, as in other imprints here, unless this is a misprint), in a variant publisher's binding, with an attractive variant design in art nouveau style. Not in Kohler.

1243. PARADISE LOST By John Milton[.] Chicago[:] W. B. Conkey Company[.] n.d. [ca. 1895]. 8vo, 461+[2]pp., unsigned frontispiece portrait plate of Milton, title-page plate decorated in black and green in art nouveau style, original light blue cloth (slightly rubbed), title in gilt on front cover surrounded with floral trim in white and green in the shape of a heart around title and with a gilt medallion at the top, spine lettered in gilt with small decorative gilt device incorporating lyre or harp and laurel, t.e.g. A very nice copy, fresh and clean throughout, in a lovely and rather well-preserved publisher's binding, with advertisement leaf bound in at the end. See undated illustrated edition listed earlier (possibly first edition thus) published by W. B. Conkey Company about this same time ca. 1895, in an attractive publisher's binding with three illustration plates after Doré, and other editions cited there. Not in Kohler.

1244. Variant of Preceding, unsigned frontispiece portrait plate of a young, long-haired Milton, title-page plate decorated in brown and green in art nouveau style, original decorated linen (a bit worn), lithograph light green floral paper with flowers in bright red and green tipped in on front cover within decorative floral trim in contrasting darker green, spine decorated and lettered in gilt, floral-decorated gold endpapers. A good copy with variant title-page plate, in an appealing variant publisher's binding, with advertisement leaf bound in at the end.

1245. Variant of Preceding, unsigned frontispiece portrait plate of Milton tipped in within red border, title-page plate decorated in black and green in art nouveau style, original crushed olive green calf (worn and faded, front joint cracked, spine ends chipped), front cover lettered in gilt with decorative gilt piece of leaves and branches in lower right corner, spine lettered in gilt, decorated green and white endpapers, a.e.g. While the binding is worn and spine faded, the copy is very fresh and clean internally, with frontispiece portrait plate of Milton tipped in (unlike any other copy here).

1246. PARADISE LOST By John Milton[.] *Chicago[:] W. B. Conkey Company[.] n.d. [ca. 1895].* First edition thus by Conkey? Small 8vo, 461+[2]pp., original decorated mauve cloth (spine edges and top of covers faded, lacking fly-leaf, pages age-browned), front cover decorated in art nouveau style with decorative black border trim and central floral piece in black with long green stems around it and title lettered in black above it, spine similarly decorated in black and green with black lettering. A good copy of an inexpensively printed edition by Conkey, in an attractive publisher's binding, similar to preceding copies, but small 8vo, without frontispiece portrait plate or title-page plate, with a plainly printed title page, and with advertisement leaf bound in at the end. Not in Kohler.

1247. PARADISE LOST By John Milton[.] *Chicago[:] Homewood Publishing Company Publishers[.] n.d. [ca. 1895].* 8vo, 461pp.+[2]pp., original red cloth (worn, lacks front fly-leaf and blank), gilt rule on front cover with title in gilt at center (faded), spine lettered in gilt (faded) with small decorative gilt emblem (faded), advertisement leaf bound in at the end, t.e.g. See undated ca. 1905 edition by Homewood Publishing Company Publishers with frontispiece portrait, title-page plate, and with contemporary presentation inscription. Not in Kohler.

1248. Variant of Preceding, in original decorated brown cloth (a bit worn, pages age-browned and fragile as happens with paper from that period), front cover lettered in black and elaborately decorated with a large central emblem in red and black and with a wide decorative border trim in black at the bottom and a narrow decorative border trim in red and black at the top, spine lettered in gilt (faded) and similarly decorated with a central emblem in red and black and with a wide decorative border trim in black at the bottom and a narrow decorative border trim in red and black at the top. A fairly good copy in an attractive variant binding.

1249. PARADISE LOST By John Milton With A Memoir. *New York: The Mershon Company Publishers[.] n.d. [ca. 1895].* Small 8vo, 358pp. (pagination beginning with p. 18, at the beginning of the poem, through p. 192, and then paginating 28 to 192, as with all other editions I have seen, with nothing appearing to be missing), original decorated brown cloth, front cover and spine decorated and lettered in contrasting darker brown trim. A nice copy with advertising label tipped in on front pastedown. Not in Kohler.

This same binding appears on a number of editions of Milton variously published about this same time: by the Mershon Publishing Company (see copies listed here) and by Chatterton-Peck (see copy of *PL* and also of *PR* listed later). See also undated ca. 1895 two-volumes-in-one edition published by "The F. M. Lupton Publishing Company" with "The Mershon Company Press, Rahway, N.J." printed on verso of each title page; see also undated ca. 1900 editions published by "The Mershon Company Rahway, N.J. [And] New York."

1250. Variant of Preceding, original decorated green cloth, front cover decorated with large classical design in art nouveau style at the center with title lettered in black above, spine similarly lettered and decorated in black in art nouveau style. A fine copy in an attractive variant publisher's binding. See undated ca. 1895 edition of *PR*, companion volume in identically decorated binding to that here.

1251. Variant of Preceding, in original green cloth (a little rubbed), front cover lettered in silver within an elaborate decorative border near the top in art nouveau style, spine lettered in silver. A fine copy in a lovely variant publisher's binding.

1252. Variant of Preceding, in original dark green cloth (a bit rubbed), front cover lettered in black and decorated in black trim in art nouveau style, spine lettered in black with similar decorative black trim. A nice copy in a variant publisher's binding. Not in Kohler.

1253. PARADISE LOST By John Milton[.] With A Memoir[.] *New York[:] Hurst And Company Publishers, n.d. [ca. 1895].* Small 8vo, 192pp. (pagination beginning at p. 18, as with other similar editions by Hurst here, with nothing appearing to be missing), unsigned frontispiece portrait plate (of a middle-aged, long-haired Milton), original decorated reddish-brown cloth, front cover and spine decorated in a floral motif in embossed red with title in black within contrasting red trim on front cover and in gilt on spine, "Hurst & Co" in black at bottom of spine. A lovely copy in a pretty publisher's binding decorated in art nouveau style. See undated ca. 1880 nonillustrated "Arlington Edition" of *PL* published by "Hurst & Co., Publishers" listed earlier (possible first edition thus) with frontispiece portrait, and other editions cited there. Not in Kohler.

1254. Variant of Preceding, in original decorated green cloth (a little rubbed and stained, earlier name and address stamped on fly-leaf), front cover and spine decorated in a floral motif in embossed blue and contrasting green, with title in black within contrasting green trim on front cover and in gilt on spine, "Hurst & Co" in black at bottom of spine. A good copy in a variant publisher's binding stamped in art nouveau style identical to the stamping on the binding on the preceding copy.

1255. Variant of Preceding, in original decorated light gray cloth (a little rubbed and stained), front cover and spine decorated in a floral motif in green and yellow with title in black at top of front cover and in gilt on spine, "Hurst & Co" in black at bottom of spine. A good copy in a variant publisher's binding attractively decorated in art nouveau style.

1256. Variant of Preceding, with frontispiece portrait plate reproducing an engraving of Milton by O. Grosch in green, title-page plate printed in red oval the remainder in green with two cherubs at the top, elaborate trim, and "Hurst & Company New York" within laurel wreath at the bottom, original decorated light gray cloth (a little rubbed and used), front cover and spine decorated in a floral motif with tall green floral stems with white blossoms within a delicate decorative reddish-brown border trim, title lettered in same at top of front cover, title and Milton's name lettered in gilt at top of spine, t.e.g. A good copy with variant frontispiece portrait plate, with variant title-page plate, in a lovely variant publisher's binding.

1257. PARADISE LOST. By John Milton. With A Memoir. *New York: Hurst & Company Publishers, n.d. [ca. 1895].* Variant edition. Small 8vo, 408pp., notes at bottom of page, original decorated black cloth, front cover and spine richly decorated in silver in art nouveau style with title in silver on front cover and spine, and with "Hurst & Co" in silver at bottom of spine. A fine copy in a lovely publisher's binding richly decorated in art nouveau style. Not in Kohler.

1258. Variant of Preceding, in original decorated green cloth (spine slightly sun-faded along with top portion of front cover), front cover lettered in white with oval floral picture in color tipped in at center and outlined in white, spine lettered in white (faded) with small laurel wreath in white at center and white rules at top and bottom. A nice copy in a charming variant publisher's binding.

1259. PARADISE LOST By John Milton[.] *New York[:] Hurst & Company Publishers, n.d. [ca. 1895].* Variant edition. Small 8vo, 408pp., frontispiece portrait plate reproducing an engraving of Milton by O. Grosch, notes at bottom of page, original decorated brown cloth (a little rubbed along joints, spine, and edges), front cover lettered in white ("Paradise Lost" and "Knickerbocker Classics"), with the sketch of an Edwardian lady in color on card like paper tipped along right side of the front cover, spine lettered in white. A nice copy of this "Knickerbocker Classics" edition in a delightful publisher's binding. See ca.

1907 edition of *PW* (without *PL*) published by Hurst in a binding similar to this one with "Knickerbocker Classics" lettered in small white letters at bottom of front cover and "Copyright, 1907 by Hurst & Co." in smaller white letters at the bottom of the picture (different from the one here). Not in Kohler.

1260. PARADISE LOST. By John Milton. *New York: Hurst & Company Publishers, n.d. [ca. 1895].* Variant edition. Small 8vo, 347pp. (pagination beginning at p. 18, as in other Hurst editions with 192pp., with nothing appearing to be missing), advertisement, original decorated purple cloth (a little rubbed and faded, spine a bit worn, pages age-browned and fragile, lacking fly-leaf), front cover decorated in black with central decoration incorporating "Arlington Edition," spine similarly decorated in black with small central emblem, gilt piece near top of spine within decorative black lines incorporating title in relief with "Hurst & Co" in black at bottom of spine. A good copy of this inexpensively produced publication of *PL* by Hurst, in an attractive publisher's binding in art nouveau style, with "Arlington Edition" stamped on front cover. See other editions by Hurst cited earlier. Not in Kohler.

1261. PARADISE LOST By John Milton With A Memoir[.] *New York[:] Frederick A. Stokes Company Publishers, n.d. [ca. 1895].* Slim 8vo, xvi+224pp., unsigned frontispiece portrait plate of a young, handsome Milton, medieval emblem of scholar behind a stack of folios at center of title page, original olive green cloth (spine a bit faded with a very slight staining near the top and at the very top of back cover), front cover decorated with a border line in red and a central wreath in silver incorporating title in red and decorated with floral trim in silver and red, spine lettered in silver with initials of the press in red at the bottom and a red line at top and bottom. A very nice, tall copy. A companion volume (although sold separately) with *PR*, 1895 (also listed here). See dated 1888 edition (possible first edition thus) of *PL* published by "Frederick A. Stokes & Brother." Uncommon. Not in Kohler.

1262. PARADISE LOST. By John Milton. *New York: The F. M. Lupton Publishing Company, Nos. 72-76 Walker Street. n.d. [ca. 1895].* 2 volumes in one. First edition thus by Lupton? Small 8vo, 192pp.,+192pp., half-title each volume, title page each volume, "The Mershon Company Press, Rahway, N.J." printed on verso of each title page, original light green cloth (a little worn, pages age-browned and somewhat brittle), front cover richly decorated in silver trim outlined in contrasting darker green with small floral pieces in silver and contrasting darker green with central dark green medallion trimmed in silver laurel with embossed lettering of *PL* within, spine decorated in contrasting darker green in a tall treelike manner with silver lettering. A decent copy in an attractive binding of the period. See undated ca. 1895 one-volume edition published by "The Mershon Company" in New York listed earlier here; see also undated ca. 1899 edition published by "The Mershon Company, Rahway, N.J." listed later here. Scarce. Not in Kohler.

1263. PARADISE LOST By John Milton With A Memoir[.] *Siegel-Cooper Co. New York [And] Chicago. n.d. [ca. 1895].* First edition thus by Siegel-Cooper? 8vo, 408pp., original decorated green cloth (a bit rubbed), front cover decorated in a floral motif in art nouveau style in contrasting darker green and red, spine lettered in gilt and similarly decorated in a floral motif in art nouveau style in contrasting darker green (spine a bit faded). A lovely copy in an attractive publisher's binding with contemporary signature (dated 1897) on fly-leaf. Uncommon. Not in Kohler.

1264. PARADISE LOST AND PARADISE REGAINED By John Milton With Biographical Sketch Of The Author[.] *New York[:] A. L. Burt, Publisher. n.d. [ca. 1895].* First edition thus by Burt? 8vo, xxv+[i]+312pp., frontispiece portrait plate reproducing an engraving of Milton by O. Grosch, protective tissue guard, "Sketch Of The Life Of John Milton," original red linen texture cloth (a bit rubbed, back cover marked, spine faded), spine lettered in gilt (*PL*) with decorative gilt trim at top and bottom. See undated editions listed later here of Milton's *PW* published by Burt in a similar manner to this edition about this same time (ca. 1895). Uncommon. Not in Kohler.

1265. DAS VERLORENE PARADIES. John Milton. Deutsch von Samuel Gottlieb Bürde. *Halle a. d. S. Druck und Verlag von Otto Hendel. n.d. [ca. 1895].* 8vo, 357+[3]pp., frontispiece portrait (signed "AM"), protective tissue guard, central emblem with initials of the press at center of title page, half-title for each book, decorative headpiece for each book, notes at bottom of page, original gray cloth (a bit rubbed, spine ends slightly chipped, early name written in a neat hand on front blank, with stamp of same owner on fly-leaf), front cover lettered in gilt with illustration of expelling angel holding crocked sword standing in front of Eden's plants with blazing sun above and serpent at top right, spine lettered in blind, decorated endpapers. A nice copy of the German translation in verse by Samuel Gottlieb Bürde with advertisement leaf bound in at the end. See Stevens 1515, which cites an 1894 two-volume edition; Not in Kohler.

1266. PARADISE LOST (ABRIDGED). Part I. By John Milton. Book I–The Rally Of The Fallen Angels In Hell. Book II–The Parliament Of Fiends. Book III–Man 'Twixt

God And Devil. Book IV–Satan In Paradise. Book V–The Story Of The Revolt In Heaven. Books VI.–XII. will appear in a subsequent Number. *The Masterpiece Library. London: "Review Of Reviews" Office*. Price One Penny. *n.d. [ca. 1895]*. First edition thus. Tall 16mo, 60+4pp., "Preface" on verso of title page, original printed orange wrappers (a bit rubbed and slightly age-darkened), "The Penny Poets. —X.," advertisements on inside of front cover and on inside and outside of back cover, with four additional pages of advertisements bound in at the end. A good copy of this "Penny Poets" publication.

[together with]

1267. PARADISE LOST (ABRIDGED). Part II. By John Milton. Book VI–The Overthrow Of The Rebel Angels. Book VII–The Story Of The Creation. Book VIII–The Nuptials In Eden. Book IX–The Temptation And The Fall. Book X–The Triumph Of Hell. Book XI–Exiled From Eden. Book XII–A Vision Of The Redemption. (Part I. of "Paradise Lost" was published as No. X of the Masterpiece Library.) *The Masterpiece Library. London: "Review Of Reviews" Office*. Price One Penny. Vol. IV. *n.d. [ca. 1895]*. First edition thus. Tall 16mo, 58+6pp., original printed orange wrappers (a bit rubbed and slightly age-darkened), "The Penny Poets. —X.," advertisements on inside of front cover and on inside and outside of back cover, with four additional pages of advertisements bound in at the end. A good copy of this "Penny Poets" publication. Together, two parts or booklets. A nice set. Uncommon. Not in Kohler.

1268. MILTON'S PARADISE LOST (BOOKS I. AND II.) Edited By Kate Stephens, A.M.[,] Editor Of "Johnson's Pope," "Stories From Old Chronicles," And Many English Classics[.] Eclectic English Classics[.] *New York • Cincinnati • Chicago: American Book Company[,] (1895)*. First edition thus. Slim 8vo, 90+6pp., unsigned frontispiece sketch of Milton as a young man, copyright date of 1895 on verso of title page, seventeen-page introduction ending with Dryden's epigram on Milton, notes at bottom of page, original brown cloth (some notations in pencil throughout and on back blank), front cover lettered in contrasting brown within decorative brown trim, central emblem of the press in contrasting brown on back cover, spine lettered in contrasting brown. A nice copy. Six pages of advertisements bound in at end. Similar to edition following, although this edition is much smaller in size, with the identification of the editor on the title page. Not in Kohler.

1269. Variant of Preceding. **PARADISE LOST (BOOKS I. AND II.)** By John Milton[.] Eclectic English Classics[.] *New York • Cincinnati • Chicago: American Book Company[,] (1895)*. First edition thus. Slim 8vo, 90+6pp., unsigned frontispiece sketch of Milton as a young man, copyright date of 1895 on verso of title page, seventeen-page introduction ending with Dryden's epigram on Milton, notes at bottom of page, original printed green boards (a bit rubbed), green cloth spine, title page repeated in decorated fashion on front cover, advertisement of the series printed on back cover, early name in a neat hand on fly-leaf. A nice copy in a variant publisher's binding, ¾" taller and ⅜" wider, with six pages of advertisements bound in at end, without identification of Kate Stephens as editor on title page. Not in Kohler.

The collection also has another copy in a variant publisher's binding: original printed tan boards (a little aged), tan cloth spine.

1270. MILTON'S PARADISE LOST, BOOKS I. AND II. With Introduction, Notes, And Diagrams, By Homer B. Sprague, M. A. Ph.D., Head-Master Of The Girls' High School, Boston ... *Boston, U.S.A.: Ginn & Company, Publishers. 1895*. Slim 8vo, xxxii+[2]+113pp.,+xiii+38+[8]pp., frontispiece plate in black and white, two additional illustrative plates in black and white, several textual diagrams depicting Milton's universe, and other introductory material as with 1879 first edition (given in full there), original olive green cloth (a little rubbed, slight waterstaining throughout), front cover and spine lettered in black ("Milton's Paradise Lost Books I & II & Lycidas"). Six pages of advertisements bound in at end. Bound in at end as a separate edition unto itself is *L*, with its own title page and separate pagination: **MILTON'S LYCIDAS**. Edited, With Notes By Homer B. Sprague ... *Boston, U.S.A.: Ginn & Company, Publishers. 1895*. As with first edition, also given in full there. The first edition thus was published in 1879 (also listed here with further editions cited). Not in Kohler.

1271. PARADISE LOST BOOKS III AND IV. With Introduction, Notes, Glossary And Indexes By A. Wilson Verity, M. A. Sometime Scholar Of Trinity College; Editor Of 'The Pitt Press Shakespeare For Schools.' Edited For The Syndics Of The University Press. Stereotyped Edition. The Cambridge Milton for Schools. *Cambridge: At The University Press. 1895 [All Rights reserved.]*. Second edition thus. Slim 8vo, lxviii+141+[3]+8+[2]pp., advertisement leaf, half-title, "Note" to first and second editions, each dated 1894, half-title before each book, original green cloth (bit rubbed), front cover and spine lettered in dark green with crest of the press on the front cover, advertisement leaf bound in at the end. A good copy with early signature on fly-leaf.

Twelve Etchings by Strang, Each Signed by the Artist

1272. PARADISE LOST By John Milton[.] A Series Of Twelve Illustrations Etched By William Strang[.] *New York[:] Edward Arnold[.] MDCCCXCVI*. First edition. Folio, first appearance of these unpaginated etchings, title page in red and black, frontispiece portrait mounted within thick matting paper with protective tissue guard, engraved with illustration of Milton playing on his viola surrounded by his daughters singing mounted within thick matting paper, and ten additional etchings by Strang, each mounted within thick matting paper, each labeled "London: John C. Nimmo, 1895," with text opposite on verso of printed argument for that book, argument printed for books not illustrated, "List of Illustrations Designed And Etched By W. Strang, And Printed By F. Goulding, London," original one-half red buckram, cream cloth, with large illustration in art nouveau style in black and cream in a slightly recessed panel with rich embossed black lettering on front cover, spine lettered in gilt, edges untrimmed. A very fine copy with the bookplate of Leonard Schlosser. 150 copies were issued, this being No. 124, printed "At the Ballantyne Press, Edinburgh," each of the twelve etchings signed by William Strang. Ray, *Illustrator*, pp. 168–69. Not in Kohler.

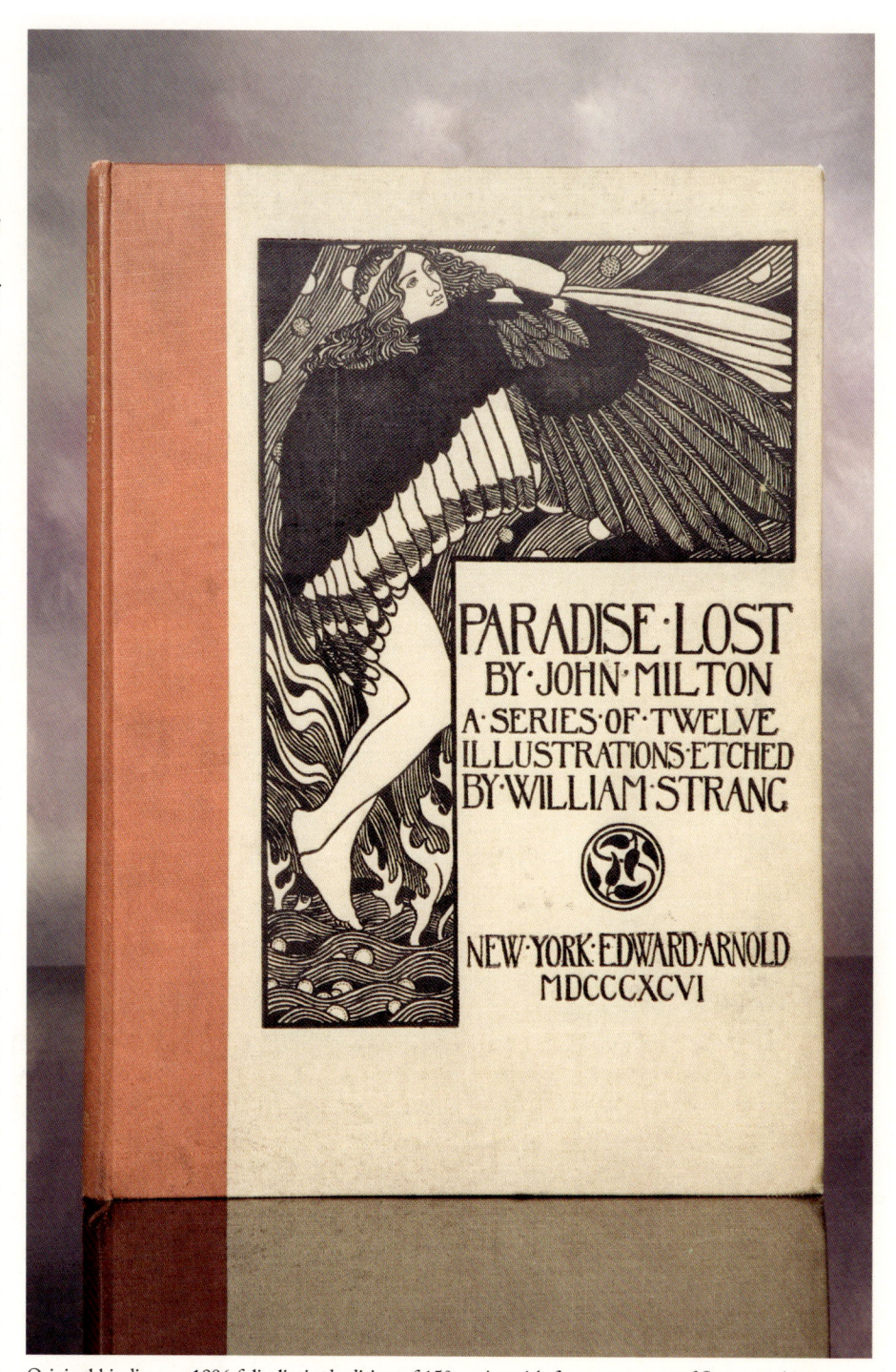

Original binding on 1896 folio limited edition of 150 copies with first appearance of Strang etchings, original one-half red buckram, cream cloth, with large illustration in art nouveau style in black and cream in a slightly recessed panel on front cover. See #1272.

A member of the Royal Academy and a respected and popular painter and graphic artist of his day, William Strang (1859–1921) chose to illustrate only ten of the twelve books of Milton's epic, omitting Books III and VI. The portrait of John Milton and the title page illustration, which Strang titled *Milton Playing to His Daughters*, complete Strang's work on the poem. See 1905 octavo edition with a reproduction of Strang's illustrations, the first printed appearance of Strang's illustrations; see also ca. 1973 tall 12mo edition with Strang's illustrations reproduced in a handsome publication "Distributed By Hebron Books"; see, too, 1984 Franklin Library limited edition with Strang's illustrations reproduced in another handsome format and one larger than the 1905 octavo edition—all listed here.

Satan Rising from the Burning Lake, etching by William Strang, signed by Strang, first published in folio in 1896 in a limited edition, one of 150 copies, with each etching signed by Strang. See #1272.

The Temptation of Eve, etching by William Strang, signed by Strang, first published in folio in 1896 in a limited edition, one of 150 copies, with each etching signed by Strang. See #1272.

1273. PARADISE LOST By John Milton With A Memoir[.] *New York[:] E. A. Lawson Company Publishers[.] n.d. [ca. 1896].* First edition thus? Small 8vo, 408pp., notes at bottom of page, original decorated light green cloth (a bit rubbed, lower right-hand portion of p. 223 torn away, including some text, small piece torn away from back endpaper), front cover decorated in art nouveau style, in contrasting dark green with seven small decorative pieces in red, spine lettered in gilt and decorated in contrasting green (spine a little faded). A good copy in a lovely publisher's binding similar to that on the ca. 1895 Sieger-Cooper edition listed earlier with contemporary signature (dated 1896) written in a neat hand on fly-leaf. Scarce. Not in Kohler.

1274. MILTON'S PARADISE LOST BOOKS I AND II. Edited With Introduction And Notes By Albert S. Cooke, Professor Of The English Language And Literature In Yale University[.] The Students' Series of English Classics. *Sibley & Company Boston Chicago[,] (1896).* First edition thus. Slim 8vo, ix+[3]+201+[2]pp., frontispiece portrait plate reproducing frontispiece portrait of Milton after White, "Copyright, 1896, By Leach, Shewell, & Sanborn" on verso of title page, original cream cloth (a bit rubbed), front cover and spine lettered in reddish-brown. A very nice copy with the signature of "James Hutton, Cornell University, 1923" on fly-leaf with a few underlinings and several marginal notations in ink by him. Scarce. Not in Kohler.

1275. MILTON'S PARADISE LOST BOOKS I AND II. Edited With Introduction And Notes By Albert S. Cooke, Professor Of The English Language And Literature In Yale University[.] The Students' Series Of English Classics. *Leach, Shewell, & Sanborn, Boston. New York. Chicago[.] (1896).* First edition thus. Slim 8vo, ix+[3]+201+[2]pp., similar to preceding copy (except for the publisher), "Copyright, 1896, By Leach, Shewell, & Sanborn" on verso of title page, original black cloth (a bit rubbed, possibly lacking fly-leaf and frontispiece), spine lettered in silver (a little faded). An okay copy of this variant publication. Scarce. Not in Kohler.

1276. PARADISE LOST BOOKS I - III By John Milton Edited, With Introduction And Notes[.] The Riverside Literature Series[.] *Houghton, Mifflin And Company[;] Boston: 4 Park Street; New York: 11 East Seventeenth Street[;] Chicago 158 Adams Street[.] The Riverside Press, Cambridge[,] (1896).* First edition thus. Slim 8vo, 112pp., emblem of the press on title page, copyright dated 1896 on verso of title page with "The Riverside Press . . . " at bottom of the page, pamphlet, original printed stiff gray wrappers (age-darkened, with a spot on front cover and one on back cover), title page reproduced in black within elaborate title-page design on front cover with publication information about the series ("Issued Semi-Monthly September to June[,] Number 94[,] March 18, 1896" at the top, and "Single Numbers Fifteen Cents[,] Double Numbers Thirty Cents[,] Trip Numbers Forty-Five Cents[,] Quadruple Numbers Fifty-Cents[,] Yearly Subscription $5.00" at the bottom), advertisements on verso of front cover and on both sides of back cover. A decent copy. Not in Kohler.

1277. PARADISE LOST BOOKS I - III By John Milton Edited, With Introduction And Notes, By William Vaughn Moody[.] The Riverside Literature Series[.] *Houghton, Mifflin And Company[;] Boston: 4 Park Street; New York: 85 Fifth Avenue[;] Chicago: 378-388 Wabash Avenue[.] The Riverside Press, Cambridge[,] (1896).* Slim 8vo, 112pp., emblem of the press on title page, copyright dated 1896 on verso of title page with "The Riverside Press . . . " at bottom of the page, pamphlet, original stiff gray wrappers (a little age-darkened, a few pencil markings, early name written in a neat hand at top title page and front cover), title page reproduced in black within elaborate title-page design on front cover, advertisements on verso front verso of front cover and on both sides of back cover. A good copy similar to preceding edition, but with identification of Moody as editor on title page, with a variant publisher's imprint, in a variant publisher's binding, with only "Number 94" at the top and only "Price, paper, 15 cents; linen, in one volume with No. 72, 40 cents" at the bottom," and with additional advertisements on back cover. Not in Kohler.

1278. Variant of Preceding. PARADISE LOST BOOKS I - III By John Milton Edited, With Introduction And Notes, By William Vaughn Moody[.] The Riverside Literature Series[.] *Boston[,] New York[,] Chicago[:] Houghton Mifflin Company[.] The Riverside Press Cambridge[,] (1896).* Slim 8vo, 112pp., with variant publisher's imprint and with different advertisements on back cover. Not in Kohler.

1279. Variant of Preceding. PARADISE LOST BOOKS I - III By John Milton Edited, With Introduction And Notes, By William Vaughn Moody[.] The Riverside Literature Series[.] *Boston[,] New York[,] Chicago[,] San Francisco[:] Houghton Mifflin Company[.] The Riverside Press Cambridge[,] (1896).* Slim 8vo, 112pp., with variant publisher's imprint, with only "Number 94" at the top of the front cover as the only information there, and with different advertisements on back cover (with the bottom half of the cover bare, unlike all of the other copies here). Not in Kohler.

1280. PARADISE LOST A Poem In Twelve Books By John Milton[.] *MDCCCXCVII • Published • By • J•M• Dent•And•Co: Aldine•House•London•E•C• (1897).* First edition by Dent. Small 8vo, xi+[1]+372pp., half-title ("The Temple Classics Edited by Israel Gollancz MA") with small red emblem at the center, unsigned frontispiece portrait of a young, long-haired Milton within circular decorative border trim with hanging device at the top, title page in red and black with wide decorative border trim in art nouveau style, half-title before the poem, glossary at the end, "Printed by T. and A. Constable, Printers to Her Majesty at the Edinburgh University Press" at bottom of last page, original olive green calf over limp boards (a little worn, small piece of calf missing at bottom of front cover), central emblem incorporating owl in gilt on front cover, spine lettered in gilt within decorative gilt trim, monument printed in green on front pastedown containing "John Milton" in large green letters at the top, "Born 1608 Died 1674" printed in small green letters beneath within a half laurel wreath in green, and beneath this on the monument itself is printed in green letters, "First Edition Published AD 1667," t.e.g, others untrimmed, red silk ribbon marker. A good copy. Uncommon. Not in Kohler.

Some confusion appears as to the first and third editions of *PL* published by Dent. Reference on the verso of the half-title of the 1897 and 1900 editions indicates the 1897 edition as the first edition and the 1899 edition as the second edition, with the 1900 edition making no reference to itself—each listed here. Reference on the verso of the half-title of the 1900, 1901, 1903, and 1904 editions list an 1898 edition (not in the collection) as the first edition, an alternate 1899 edition to the one in the collection as the second edition, the 1901 edition (also listed here) as the third edition, the 1903 edition as the fourth edition, and the 1904 edition (also listed here) as the fifth edition, with no reference to a 1900 edition. The 1898 Dent edition would, therefore, be an alternate first edition in this "new" series, while the 1900 Dent edition (also listed here) would be the third edition, with the 1901 Dent edition being an alternate third edition. In the 1897 Dent edition here and in all other Dent editions the following statement appears on the verso of the half-title before the poem: "This issue of Milton's *PL*, based on the text of Masson, has been edited by Mr. W. H. D. Rouse, M.A., formerly Fellow of Christ's College, Cambridge, who has revised the text, added the marginalia, and contributed the accompanying Glossarial Appendix of Proper Names and obsolete Words. I. G. November 8th (the day of Milton's death) 1897."

1281. MILTON'S PARADISE LOST, BOOKS I. AND II. With Introduction, Notes, And Diagrams By Homer B. Sprague, M. A. Ph.D., Headmaster Of The Girls' High School, Boston . . . *Boston, U.S.A.: Ginn & Company, Publishers. 1897.* Slim 8vo, xxxii+[2]+113pp.,+xiii+38+[8]pp., frontispiece plate in black and white, two additional illustrative plates in black and white, several textual diagrams depicting Milton's universe, and other introductory material as with 1979 first edition (given in full there as with title page), original olive green cloth (a little rubbed, spine chipped at top and bottom, slight inoffensive waterstaining throughout), front cover and spine lettered in black ("Milton's Paradise Lost Books I & II & Lycidas"), six pages of advertisements bound in at end. Bound in at end as a separate edition unto itself is *L*, with its own title page and separate pagination: **MILTON'S LYCIDAS**. Edited, With Notes By Homer B. Sprague . . . *Boston, U.S.A.: Ginn And Company, Publishers. 1897.* As with the first edition (given in full there). The first edition thus was published in 1879 (also listed here with further editions cited). Not in Kohler.

1282. [PARADISE LOST] SELECTIONS FROM PARADISE LOST Including Books I. And II. Entire, And Portions Of Books III., IV., VI., VII., And X. With Introduction, Suggestions For Study, And Glossary Edited By Albert Perry Walker, M.A. Teacher of English And History In The English High School, Boston. *Boston, U.S.A. D. C. Heath & Co., Publishers[.] 1897.* First edition. 8vo, xi+270+[1]pp., frontispiece illustration of "The Four Regions Of The Universe," several additional plates reproducing early maps, half-title before each book (with "The Argument" printed on verso of half-titles for Books I and II, and a brief summary by the editor printed on verso of half-titles for the other books), "Notes," "Glossary," and "Index" at the end, original burgundy cloth, front cover and spine lettered in black. A second edition was published in 1900; a possible third edition (with Books I and II only) was published in 1906 (also listed here). Not in Kohler.

1283. [PARADISE LOST] SELECTIONS FROM PARADISE LOST Including Books I. And II. Entire, And Portions Of Books III., IV., VI., VII., And X. With Introduction, Suggestions For Study, And Glossary Edited By Albert Perry Walker, M.A. *D. C. Heath & Co., Publishers[.] Boston[,] New York[,] Chicago[,] 1897.* First edition. 8vo, xiv+[2]+270pp., frontispiece portrait plate after "D. Grosch," illustrations of "The World (The Ptolemaic System)," "The Four Regions Of The Universe," several additional plates reproducing early maps as preceding, original green cloth (a bit rubbed, some marginal notations in pencil with pencil sketches on back blanks), front cover lettered in yellow within yellow rules, spine once lettered in yellow (now rubbed). Similar to preceding edition but in a slightly larger format, with frontispiece portrait plate, and with a number of other differences including a listing of "Works For Reference" before introduction. Not in Kohler.

1284. PARADISE LOST BOOKS I AND II Edited By Henry W. Boynton[.] The Academy Series Of English Classics[.] *Boston[:] Allyn And Bacon[.] (1897).* First edition. Slim 8vo, 124pp., copyright date of 1897 on verso of title page, preface dated "April, 1897," original brown cloth (a bit rubbed, outer edge of title page a bit frayed), front cover and spine ruled and lettered in dark brown. A good copy. A possible second edition was published in 1916 (also listed here). Gift from Milton scholar Anthony Low with his stamp. Not in Kohler.

The 1898 Caldwell Edition and Its Variants

Collectors believe "There is no such thing as a duplicate!" Looking at the following copies of the ca. 1898 Caldwell edition of *PL* together on a shelf or side by side shows very clearly why this statement is true and why collecting different copies of the same edition with variant title-page plates, variant publisher's imprints, variant portraits, in variant formats, and in variant publisher's bindings has real merit in pointing up such notable differences and more; and yet each book maintains its own individuality and attractiveness. The Caldwell Company published books from 1896 to 1914.

1285. PARADISE LOST[.] John Milton[.] *H·M· Caldwell Company[,] New York[.] n.d. [ca. 1898].* First edition thus by Caldwell. Small 8vo, 408pp., unsigned frontispiece illustration plate of *Raphael Conversing with Adam and Eve* (Book VII, line 537), title-page plate printed in red with elaborately decorative blue border trim in art nouveau style with an urn at the bottom on each side, and at the center at the top, the emblem of an open book within a laurel wreath with lighted flame above and scroll beneath containing the Latin inscription "Sapere Aude," four additional unsigned illustration plates: *Satan Rallying His Troops* (Book I, lines 314–15); *Satan* (Book IV, lines 985–86); *Eve amidst Fruits and Flowers* (Book VIII, line 44); and *The Expulsion* (Book XII, lines 641–42), notes at bottom of page, original avocado-green pebble cloth (a bit rubbed), front cover decorated with a lined gilt pattern in art nouveau style with central decorative gilt piece on each side and at the center the title page emblem in gilt of an open book within a laurel wreath with lighted flame above and scroll beneath containing the Latin inscription "Sapere Aude," spine decorated in a similarly lined gilt pattern in art nouveau style with gilt lettering, t.e.g., fore- and bottom edges untrimmed. A fine, tall copy in a beautiful publisher's binding with contemporary signature (dated 1900) on fly-leaf. This edition of *PL* by Caldwell and the similarly bound undated ca. 1898 edition of *PR* by Caldwell are companion volumes, that in blue cloth decorated in art nouveau style as here, together forming Milton's *PW*. See undated illustrated edition of *PL* published about this same time, ca. 1898, by Caldwell, with variant title-page plate and variant publisher's imprint adding "Boston" to "New York." Not in Kohler.

1286. Variant of Preceding, original decorated dark green cloth front cover and contrasting lighter green back cover (a bit rubbed), very large contrasting lighter green decorative piece at the center of front cover elaborately decorated in silver trim, the center lined in alternating light and dark green with silver lettering, the whole covered with small floral decorations in red and silver, the spine similarly decorated with contrasting light and dark green and elaborate silver decorative trim with silver lettering, with a contrasting lighter green central piece as on front cover elaborately decorated in silver trim, the whole covered with small floral decorations in red and silver. A fine copy in a lovely variant publisher's binding. Uniformly bound with an undated ca. 1898 illustrated edition of *PR* by Caldwell (also listed here), the two together forming Milton's *PW*, a lovely set in original publisher's bindings.

1287. Variant of Preceding, original half bright blue cloth overlapping front and back covers by one-half (bit worn along extremities), decorated in silver floral trim on front cover and spine, with silver lettering on spine, half cream paper boards, decorated in floral trim with blossoms in light blue and stems in gold. A nice copy without frontispiece portrait and in a variant publisher's binding. This edition of *PL* by Caldwell and the similarly bound undated ca. 1898 edition of *PR* by Caldwell are companion volumes, that in a half seafoam green cloth, together forming Milton's *PW*. Not in Kohler.

1288. Variant of Preceding, original brown limp leather (a trifle scuffed), oval photograph of lady and two cherubs tipped in within oval frame decorated in blind relief and gilt with similar lettering on front cover, marbled endpapers, t.e.g., bookplate. A very nice copy with a variant frontispiece portrait plate in elaborately decorated green frame (with signature and stamp dated 1903 on verso), with a variant title-page plate in decorative orange trim, in a lovely variant publisher's (possibly gift) binding.

1289. Variant of Preceding, original olive green cloth (spine chipped at top and worn at bottom) decorated in silver floral trim on front cover, spine and back cover, with silver lettering on spine and small title page emblem in silver with inscription "Sapere Aude" in the middle, half white silk cloth covers (worn at corners) decorated with vertical yellow blocks and winding floral trim in various paisley colors and yellow blossoms. A good copy in a smaller 8vo format (by ½") from the other Caldwell editions here (similar to the smaller Caldwell editions listed at the end), in a lovely (albeit bit used) variant publisher's binding.

1290. Variant of Preceding. **PARADISE LOST**[.] John Milton[.] *H•M•Caldwell Co., Publishers*[,] *New York And Boston*[.] n.d. [ca. 1898]. First edition thus by Caldwell? Small 8vo, 408pp., unsigned frontispiece illustration plate of *Raphael Conversing with Adam and Eve* (Book VII, line 537), title-page plate printed in red with decorative green apple tree as trim in art nouveau style, with the same four illustration plates identified in the first Caldwell edition, original decorated green cloth (a bit rubbed, spine slightly darkened), front cover elaborately decorated in gilt with a rich gilt design along either side, long-stemmed irises in green with blue blossoms in the center against contrasting darker green along the bottom and brilliant gilt at the top giving the effect of flowers in water beneath a bright gilt sky, spine similarly decorated with long-stemmed irises in green, contrasting greens and blue along the middle and bottom repeating the effect of flowers in water beneath a gilt sky (faded) with lettering in blind at the top. A nice copy with a different title-page plate from preceding copies, with "Boston" added to publisher's imprint, in a lovely variant publisher's binding. Uniformly bound with an undated ca. 1898 illustrated edition of *PR* by Caldwell (also listed here), the two together forming a collection of Milton's *PW*, a beautiful set in original publisher's bindings.

1291. Variant of Preceding, original decorated brown cloth (a bit rubbed, spine ends chipped), gilt rules on front cover with maroon crushed leather inlaid at center within gilt rules incorporating title in gilt at the top within gilt rules and with decorative gilt floral trim along bottom and sides, spine decorated with floral trim and lettered in faint yellow at the top, bookplate on front pastedown. A nice copy in an attractive variant publisher's binding. This edition of *PL* by Caldwell and the similarly bound undated ca. 1898 edition of *PR* by Caldwell are companion volumes, that in dark green cloth decorated as here, together form an appealing set of Milton's *PW*.

1292. Variant of Preceding, original light brown cloth (a bit rubbed, spine ends slightly worn), gilt rules on front cover with decorative scrolls in blind relief within the inner gilt rule and with central elaborate gilt trim incorporating "Superb Edition" with the initial letters "S" and "E" in decorative red against a gilt background, spine lettered in gilt and decorated with floral pieces in mauve and green, each within decorative gilt trim. A good copy with green apple tree trim title-page plate and "New York And Boston" in publisher's imprint, in a pleasing variant publisher's binding, in a smaller 8vo format (by ½") from the other Caldwell editions. Uniformly bound with an undated ca. 1898 illustrated edition of *PR* by Caldwell of the same size (also listed here), the two together forming a collection of Milton's *PW*. They were most likely published in these charming bindings, as with the two sets following, designed to be sold as a "gift" set.

1293. Variant of Preceding, original light blue cloth (spine a little rubbed and ends slightly worn), gilt rules on front cover with decorative scrolls in blind relief within the inner gilt rule and with central elaborate gilt trim incorporating "Superb Edition" with the initial letters "S" and "E" in decorative red against a gilt background, spine blocked in decorative gilt trim with gilt lettering against red and black labels (rubbed), each with decorative gilt trim. A nice copy with variant title-page plate (green border trim plate and "New York" only in publisher's imprint), in a variant publisher's binding, in the same smaller 8vo format (by ½" from the Caldwell editions), with contemporary ownership signature (dated 1898) on fly-leaf, and with bookplate on front pastedown. Uniformly bound with an undated ca. 1898 illustrated edition of *PR* by Caldwell of the same size (also listed here), the two together forming a collection of Milton's *PW*. They were most likely published in these lovely bindings, as with the two other sets here, and intended to be sold as a "gift" set.

1294. PARADISE LOST[.] John Milton[.] *H•M•Caldwell Company[,] New York[.] n.d. [ca. 1898]*. Variant edition by Caldwell. 2 volumes in one. Small 8vo, 182pp.,+192pp. (divided at Book VII), frontispiece illustration plate and four additional illustration plates identified in the first Caldwell edition, original olive green cloth, gilt rules on front cover with decorative scrolls in blind relief within the inner gilt rule and with central elaborate gilt trim incorporating "Superb Edition" with the initial letters "S" and "E" in decorative red against a gilt background, spine blocked in decorative gilt trim with gilt lettering and floral pieces in contrasting green and pink. A lovely copy with title-page plate (green border trim plate and "New York" only in publisher's imprint), in an attractive variant publisher's binding from the preceding, in the same smaller 8vo format (by ½" from the Caldwell editions), with small early bookseller's plate with gilt trim at top of front pastedown. The variances from the undated ca. 1898 editions preceding by H. M. Caldwell include: (1) perhaps most importantly, being divided into two books by pagination; (2) having no "Contents" page after the title page; (3) lacking "The Verse Of 'Paradise Lost.' From Milton's Own Edition, 1669" at the beginning of the poem; (4) having no notes at the bottom of the page; (5) pagination beginning at p. 18 instead of p. 6 as in other Caldwell editions here, although nothing appears to be missing; and (6) the appropriate book being given as the header on each page instead of "Paradise Lost" generically as in other Caldwell edition here. Uniformly bound with an undated ca. 1898 illustrated edition of *PR* by Caldwell of the same size (also listed here), the two together forming a collection of Milton's *PW*. They were most likely published in these appealing bindings, as with the two sets preceding, designed to be sold as a "gift" set. Not in Kohler.

1295. PARADISE LOST By John Milton[.] Illustrated[.] *Chicago[:] Montgomery Ward & Company Publishers[.] n.d. [ca. 1898]*. First edition thus? Small 8vo, 408pp., unsigned frontispiece illustration plate of *Raphael Conversing with Adam and Eve* (Book VII, line 537), title-page plate printed in red and blue with delicate ornamental pieces in blue in art nouveau style and with central device in red, four additional unsigned illustration plates: *Satan Rallying His Troops* (Book I, lines 314–15); *Satan* (Book IV, lines 985–86); *Eve Amidst Fruits and Flowers* (Book VIII, line 44); and *The Expulsion* (Book XII, lines 641–42), original light blue cloth (a bit rubbed), front cover and spine lettered in gilt and elaborately decorated in an embossed green and light blue floral motif against a very rich gilt background art nouveau style. A lovely copy in a charming binding of the period with contemporary signature (dated 1900) on fly-leaf. See illustrated editions of *PL* by Caldwell, published in New York about this same time, ca. 1898, with the same illustration plates as here. Not in Kohler.

1296. PARADISE LOST. By John Milton. A New Edition. With Notes By Rev. John Mitford. *Philadelphia: Henry T. Coates & Co. n.d. [ca. 1898].* First edition thus? 8vo in 4s, [2]+433+10pp., notes at bottom of page, original green cloth (joints cracked from within, some embrowning within), front cover and spine decorated in contrasting dark green swirls in art nouveau style, front cover lettered against a band of contrasting dark green at the center, spine lettered in gilt with "H.T. Coates & Co" in small letters in contrasting green at the bottom, ten pages of advertisements bound in at the end. A nice copy in an attractive publisher's binding with a contemporary signature dated "[18]98." Not in Kohler.

1297. Variant of Preceding, in original blue-green cloth, front cover decorated in an embossed black floral motif in art nouveau style with several small orange leaves scattered about, "Paradise Lost" lettered in large orange letters at the top and Milton's name in smaller orange letters at the bottom, a colored photograph (measuring 3" × 2 ⅛") of two young ladies of the period tipped in at the center outlined in a thick orange rule with an outer thin black rule, the cover blocked in a thick orange rule at top and bottom with a thinner black rule within, spine similarly decorated in an embossed black floral motif in art nouveau style with two small orange leaves in the center, title and Milton's name in gilt at the top with a thick orange rule with thinner black rule above and below, "Winston" lettered in orange letters at the bottom with a thick orange rule with thinner black rule below, with ten pages of advertisements bound in at the end. A lovely copy in very good condition, fresh and clean within, in a fine variant publisher's binding, with "Winston" at the bottom of the spine in place of "H.T. Coates & Co.," as in preceding copy.

1298. Variant of Preceding, identically decorated (some slight chafing at top corner of front corner, at top of spine, and slightly on back cover) with variant color photograph (measuring 3" × 2 ¼") of ships tipped in at the center outlined in a thick orange rule and with "Winston" at the bottom of the spine in place of "H.T. Coates & Co."

1299. PARADISE LOST A Poem In Twelve Books By John Milton With An Introduction And Notes On Its Structure And Meaning By John A. Himes[,] Professor Of English In Pennsylvania College[.] *New York • Cincinnati • Chicago[:] American Book Company[.] (1898).* First edition thus. 8vo, xxxii+482+[12]pp., half-title, copyright "1898 by Harper & Brothers" and "W.P.1" on verso of title page, six explanatory illustration plates—three of which depict Milton's universe and three of which are illustrations of mythological figures, extensive notes at the end, original green cloth, gilt lettering on front cover and spine, twelve pages of advertisement leaves (unpaginated) for various textbooks bound in at end. A good copy. Not in Kohler (but see Kohler 164, which list an edition with publisher's imprint: "New York And London: Harper & Brothers Publishers. 1898").

The collection also has two additional copies, in fine condition, each of which differs from this copy and from each other with variant identification numbers on verso of title page: "W.P.1" here; "W.P.3" on second copy; and "W.P.7" on third copy.

1300. PARADISE LOST BOOKS I. AND II. By John Milton. With Introduction and Notes. *Educational Publishing Company[.] Boston[,] New York[,] Chicago[, And] San Francisco[.] (1898).* Slim 8vo, xiv+101+[5]pp., copyright date 1898 on verso of title page, portrait plate of Milton as a young man, charts for the "Cosmology of *PL*," with a "Table of Deities," half-title for each book, original light brown cloth (bit darkened on spine and along top and foreedge of front cover), title in black against decorative red background in the shape of a shield at upper left corner of front cover, double black rules on front cover, spine lettered in black with black rules and modest decorative black trim at top and bottom. A good copy with five pages of advertisement leaves for "The Famous Ten Cent Classics" (see following) bound in at end. Scarce. Not in Kohler.

1301. Variant of Preceding as a "Ten Cent Classics" edition, contents as preceding, original printed tan wrappers (a bit used), blue cloth spine, front cover lettered in dark blue, including "Ten Cent Classics," "Vol. I. No. 12[,] August 15, 1898," "Published Semi-Monthly[,] Price, $2.40 per year[.] Single numbers, 20 cts.," advertisement leaves bound in at end, and advertisements printed on inside front and back covers and on the back cover. A decent copy with variation of introductory material, in original wrappers. Uncommon.

1302. MILTON'S PARADISE LOST BOOKS I AND II Edited For School Use By Frank Edgar Farley, Ph.D. Instructor In English, Syracuse University[.] *The Lake English Classics[.] Scott, Foresman And Company[,] Chicago [And] New York[,] (1898).* First edition. Slim 8vo, 160pp., advertisement leaf for "The Lake English Classics," before title page, seventy-four-page introduction, notes at bottom of page, glossary at the end, original light blue cloth (a bit rubbed, pencil markings and notations throughout), front cover and spine lettered in black. A second edition was published in 1899 (also listed here); it was reprinted in 1919 (also listed here). Uncommon. Not in Kohler.

The 1899 Altemus Edition and Its Variants

Looking at the following copies of the 1899 Altemus editions of *PL* together on a shelf or side by side demonstrates very clearly once again, as with the Caldwell editions listed earlier, why "there is no such thing as a duplicate!" and why collecting different copies of the same edition has real merit in pointing up notable differences, with each book maintaining its own individuality and attractiveness.

1303. PARADISE LOST[.] John Milton[.] *Philadelphia[:] Henry Altemus[.] n.d. [ca. 1899].* 2 volumes in one. First Altemus edition thus? Small 8vo, 192+192(beginning at p. 28 in volume 2)+16pp., half-title each volume, biographical leaf with brief life of Milton before half-title, introduction by Henry Marley, which first appeared in Cassell & Co.'s edition in 1889 (also listed here), volume 1, photographic title-page plate with classic motif, frontispiece illustration plate in color by W. H. Liston for Book V ("Copyright 1899, By Henry Altemus"), and title-page plate printed in red with decorative green trim in art nouveau style, volume 1, seven illustration plates (reduced reproductions of illustrations by Gustave Doré), original decorated olive green cloth (a bit worn, spine chipped at top, gilt faded), covers and spine decorated with large floral designs in contrasting greens with vertical gilt lines, front cover and spine lettered in gilt, endpapers decorated in light green swirls art nouveau style with letters of the press "HA" at the center. A decent copy in an attractive publisher's binding, with the apparently rare biographical leaf before half-title, volume 1, and with sixteen pages of advertisements for "Henry Altemus' Publications. Philadelphia, PA" bound in at the end. Kohler 165, noting that, as here, "Pagination for volume 2 begins on p. [28] but nothing appears to be missing," and reporting "Not in the British Library. Not in the Bodleian Library. Not in Cambridge University Library."

1304. Variant of Preceding, in original half white cloth, half white paper over boards, decorated in art nouveau style (a little used, especially spine, name on title page and on endpapers), half white cloth delicately decorated with floral designs in light green and gilt with gilt lettering on spine, white paper over boards decorated in small blue feathers with blue and gilt blossoms, endpapers decorated in light green swirls art nouveau style with letters of the press "HA" at the center. Despite the wear, a good copy in a variant publisher's binding, with different advertisement leaves for "Publications Of Henry Altemus Company Philadelphia[.] Altemus' Illustrated Vadecum Series" bound in at the end.

1305. Variant of Preceding, original half white cloth, patterned gold paper over boards (both white cloth and gold paper a little rubbed, spine a bit rubbed), white cloth portion of front cover and spine decorated in an embossed floral motif with long stems in green and large flowers in gilt, spine lettered in gilt, endpapers decorated in light green swirls art nouveau style with letters of the press "HA" at the center. A nice copy with an early presentation inscription in pencil on verso of fly-leaf, in an attractive variant publisher's binding, with sixteen advertisement leaves of "Henry Altemus' Publications. Philadelphia, PA." bound in at the end.

1306. Variant of Preceding, original blue cloth (a bit rubbed), front cover decorated with gilt border trim and a floral motif in art nouveau style with long-stem flowers in pink and maroon outlined in bright gilt with green leaves also outlined in gilt, spine lettered in gilt and similarly decorated with a floral motif in art nouveau style with long-stemmed flowers in maroon and green outlined in gilt, endpapers decorated in light green swirls art nouveau style with letters of the press "HA" at the center. A nice copy in a lovely variant publisher's binding, very fresh and clean, with sixteen pages advertising "Publications Of Henry Altemus Company[,] Philadelphia" bound in at the end.

Decorated cloth bindings on 1890s illustrated and nonillustrated Milton editions by the Henry Altemus Company and the Hurst Company—showing front covers.

1307. Variant of Preceding, original half white cloth (a little used, spine a bit worn) decorated with delicate floral designs in gilt and gilt lettering on spine, white paper over boards decorated in a tan floral pattern, endpapers decorated in light green swirls art nouveau style with letters of the press "HA" at the center. Overall, a good copy in original binding decorated in art nouveau style, with six (instead of seven) illustration plates, in an attractive variant publisher's binding, with sixteen pages of advertisements for "Publications Of Henry Altemus Company Philadelphia[.] Altemus' Illustrated Vadecum Series" bound in at end.

1308. Variant of Preceding, original dark blue cloth (a bit rubbed), color photograph tipped on front cover with slightly embossed gilt trim, thick gilt rules, and title lettered in gilt, spine decorated and lettered in gilt, endpapers decorated in light green swirls art nouveau style with letters of the press "HA" at the center. A fine copy in an attractive variant publisher's binding with twenty-four advertisement leaves for "Publications Of Henry Altemus Company Philadelphia[.] Altemus' Illustrated Vadecum Series" and several other series bound in at end.

1309. PARADISE LOST[.] John Milton[.] *Philadelphia[:] Henry Altemus[.] n.d. [ca. 1899]*. 2 volumes in one. Variant edition. Small 8vo, 192+192+36pp., half-title for volume 1, unsigned frontispiece illustration plate of *Satan* with elaborate decorative border trim in black, title-page plate printed in red with decorative green trim in art nouveau style, eleven-page introduction before the poem signed by Henry Marley, blank page before volume 2, followed by a second twenty-six-page introduction signed "H[enry].M[arley].," half-title for volume 2 before the poem, original decorated blue cloth (a bit rubbed), two color floral designs within wide strips against a white background on front cover, one on each side at the top, along with decorative gilt trim art nouveau style and the title lettered in gilt at the center, spine similarly gilt-decorated and lettered in gilt (a little faded). A nice copy. Variant edition in a lovely variant publisher's binding, without the reproduced Doré illustration plates, with a different frontispiece illustration plate, and with a greater number of advertisement pages—thirty-six pages of advertisements for "Publications Of Henry Altemus Company—Altemus' Illustrated Vademecum Series"—bound in at end. Not in Kohler.

1310. Variant of Preceding, original decorated light blue cloth (a bit rubbed), front cover delicately decorated with gilt trim with two narrow white cards each with a varied floral motif in color within gilt rules tipped in along either side and with gilt lettering ("Milton's Poems") blocked in gilt outline near the top, spine similarly gilt-decorated and lettered in gilt. A nice copy in a lovely variant publisher's binding, fresh and clean within, with thirty-six pages of advertisements bound in at end.

1311. Variant of Preceding, original decorated white cloth (a bit rubbed), front cover and spine decorated with gilt floral designs in art nouveau style with gilt lettering (front cover designs a little worn), t.e.g. A nice copy, slightly thicker than the other copies here, in an attractive (albeit slightly worn) variant publisher's binding, with thirty-six pages of advertisements bound in at end.

1312. Variant of Preceding, original decorated patterned green cloth (a bit rubbed, spine a little faded), printed paper label in red and black at bottom right-hand corner of front cover, printed paper label with black lettering, red lines, and small emblem of lion on spine (label slightly darkened and chipped). A decent copy, slightly thicker than the other copies here, as with preceding copy, in a scarce variant publisher's binding, with thirty-six pages of advertisements bound in at the end.

1313. Variant of Preceding. PARADISE LOST[.] John Milton[.] *Philadelphia[:] Henry Altemus Company[.] n.d. [ca. 1899]*. 2 volumes in one, each with an introduction. Small 8vo, 192+192+[36]pp., half-title for volume 1, unsigned frontispiece illustration plate of *Satan* (rich impression) with elaborate decorative border trim in black, title-page plate printed in red with decorative green trim in art nouveau style (rich impression), half-title for volume 2, introduction by Henry Marley, original decorated green cloth (a bit rubbed), front cover decorated in embossed gilt floral trim with occasional red coloring with a small (1 ½" × 2 ¼") color photograph of a tree tipped in within gilt rules near the bottom, spine lettered and decorated in gilt (a little faded). A nice copy with early inscription (dated 1910) on fly-leaf, with a variant publisher's imprint, with half-title for each volume, in a charming variant publisher's binding. Bound at the end: thirty-two advertisement leaves for "Publications Of Henry Altemus Company—Altemus' Illustrated Vademecum Series." Not in Kohler.

1314. Variant of Preceding. PARADISE LOST[.] John Milton[.] *Philadelphia[:] Henry Altemus Company[.] n.d. [ca. 1899]*. First edition thus? 2 volumes in one, each with an introduction. Small 8vo, 192+192+36pp., as preceding copy, half-title for volume 1, unsigned frontispiece illustration plate of *Satan* (rich impression) with elaborate decorative border trim in black, title-page plate printed in red with decorative green trim in art nouveau style (impression less good than in preceding copy), half-title for volume 2, original decorated green cloth (a bit rubbed), front cover decorated in embossed gilt floral trim (faded), with a small (1 ½" × 2 ¼") color photograph of a group of trees tipped in within gilt rules near the bottom, spine lettered and decorated in gilt (very faded). A nice copy in a pretty (albeit a bit rubbed) variant publisher's binding, with thirty-two advertisement leaves for "Publications Of Henry Altemus Company—Altemus' Illustrated Vademecum Series" bound in at end. Not in Kohler.

1315. [PARADISE LOST AND PARADISE REGAINED / POEMS IN RUSSIAN] in a new verse translation by O. N. Tchumina (with 50 large illustrations by artist G. Doré)[.] *Edition: A. Kaspari. St. Petersburg[,] Printing Company of the journal "Motherland," Ligovskaya Str., own house No.114[,] 1899*. First edition thus? Slim, tall 8vo (measuring 9" × 12 ¼"), ix+blank+156+[1]+blankpp., half-title, quarter-page unsigned portrait of Milton after Faithorne (fine impression) at the head of a four-page biographical section in an oval shape within decorative trim with name and dates below, illustrations by Doré, printed in double column throughout, decorative head- and tailpieces with decorated initial letters, index at the end, original printed wrappers (covers a bit age-browned, spine a little frayed, front joint slightly cracked at lower right corner), front cover richly decorated in black trim with an illustration of Adam and Eve seated at the center looking dejected beneath an apple tree, illustrator identified in Russian as "sketch by S. Isenberg," with title lettered above and a snake intertwined above that, advertisements on the back cover, edges untrimmed, partially unopened. A nice copy, entirely in Russian. Front cover reads across the top: "Monthly book" (on the left) "'Motherland'" (Rodina), Nov. 1899" (on the right), with "J. Milton" in large letters within the decorative trim beneath the intertwined snake at the center; "Paradise Lost and Regained" appear in very large letters above Adam and Eve, with "edition A. Kaspari St. Petersburg" lettered within the decorative trim below; and at the bottom is printed: "sketch by S. Isenberg" (at the left), "Printing Company of 'Motherland' (A. Kaspari)" (at the center), and "year 1899"(at the right). Rare.

[*PL And PR / Poems in Russian*] in a new verse translation by O. N. Tchumina (with fifty large illustrations by the artist G. Doré). St. Petersburg, 1899. Original printed wrappers, with illustration on front cover identified in Russian as "sketch by S. Isenberg." See #1315.

1316. PARADISE LOST[.] John Milton[.] *Philadelphia[:] Henry Altemus[.] n.d. [ca. 1899]*. 2 volumes in one. First edition thus? Small 8vo, 192+192(beginning at p. 28)+16pp., similar to first edition by Altemus listed here but without the frontispiece color plate or the Doré reproductions and without introduction to the second alternate illustrated edition, half-title each volume, title-page plate printed in red with decorative green trim in art nouveau style, original decorated blue cloth (bit rubbed), photograph in color tipped on front cover overlaid with decorative gilt trim, gilt rules, and title lettered in gilt, spine similarly decorated and lettered in gilt. A good copy in an attractive publisher's binding, as with the binding on the earlier sixth edition listed with twenty-six pages of advertisement leaves for "Publications Of Henry Altemus Company—Altemus' Illustrated Vademecum Series" bound in at end. Not in Kohler.

1317. PARADISE LOST A Poem In Twelve Books By John Milton[.] *MDCCCXCIX • Published • By • J•M• Dent•And•Co: Aldine•House•London•W•C• (1899)*. Second edition thus. Small 8vo, xi+[1]+372pp., half-title ("The Temple Classics Edited by Israel Gollancz MA") with small red emblem at the center ("First Edition, December 1897; Second Edition, April 1899" on verso—both editions listed here), unsigned frontispiece portrait of a young, long-haired Milton within circular decorative border trim with hanging device at the top, title page in red and black with wide decorative border trim in art nouveau style, protective tissue guard, half-title before the poem, glossary at the end, "Printed by T. and A. Constable, Printers to Her Majesty at the Edinburgh University Press" at the bottom of last page, original olive green calf over limp boards (a bit rubbed, spine faded and slightly chipped at ends), central emblem incorporating owl in gilt on front cover, spine lettered in gilt within decorative gilt trim, monument printed in green on front pastedown containing "John Milton" in large green letters at the top, "Born 1608 Died 1674" printed in small green letters beneath within a half laurel wreath in green and beneath this on the monument itself is printed in green letters, "First Edition Published AD 1667," t.e.g., red silk ribbon marker. A nice copy with large bookplate on fly-leaf. See 1897 first edition by Dent listed ealier and other editions cited there, along with clarification given regarding the early editions by Dent and the sorting out of the first, second, and third editions. Not in Kohler.

1318. MILTON'S PARADISE LOST, BOOKS I. AND II. Edited With Introduction And Notes By M. Macmillan . . . *London[:] Macmillan And Co., Limited[;] And New York[:] The Macmillan Company[,] 1899. All rights reserved[.]* Slim 8vo, xxix+54pp.+[87pp. of unpaginated notes], half-title, original cream cloth (worn, spine ends, slight embrowning, early name and notes in pencil on flyleaf), front cover and spine lettered in blue, initials for Macmillan and Co. in blue at the center of back cover. The first edition thus was published in 1887; the second edition thus in 1891; the third edition thus in 1893 (also listed here with further editions cited). Not in Kohler.

1319. MILTON: PARADISE LOST BOOKS [I–II] Edited by Alfred E. Ikin, B. Sc. (Hons.) Lond. LL.B. (Hons.) Lon., L.C.P. Brodie's Chosen English Texts[.] *London[:] James Brodie LTD., Denmark Place W.C.2[.] n.d. [ca. 1899].* 2 volumes in one. First edition thus. Slim 8vo, xiii+[i]+70pp.,+iv+66pp., title page each volume, vignette illustration with initials of the press at the center of each title page, "Printed At The Burlington Press, Foxton, Near Cambridge, England" printed at the bottom of the last printed page, original printed light gray wrappers (spine slightly faded), title pages (essentially the same) repeated in black within decorative black trim on front cover, spine lettered in black, advertisements for other Brodie texts printed on back cover. A nice copy in fine condition. The lengthy "Introduction" in volume I includes a "Life of Milton" and discussion of various aspects of Milton's epic poem. Uncommon. Not in Kohler.

1320. MILTON'S PARADISE LOST BOOKS I AND II Edited For School Use By Frank Edgar Farley, Ph.D. Instructor In English, Syracuse University[.] The Lake English Classics. *Chicago[:] Scott, Foresman And Company[.] 1899.* Second edition thus. Slim 8vo, 160pp., half-title with advertisements for "The Lake English Classics," seventy-four-page introduction, notes at bottom of page, original blue cloth (a bit rubbed), front cover and spine lettered against several black backdrops. A nice copy. The first edition thus was published the year before, in 1898 (also listed here); it was reprinted in 1919 (copy in the collection, a repeat of this edition, not listed here). Not in Kohler.

1321. MILTON'S PARADISE LOST Illustrated By Gustave Doré Introduction By Robert Vaughan, D.D. *Charles C. Thompson Co. Chicago, Ill. n.d. [ca. 1900].* Large 8vo, viii+311pp., frontispiece illustration and forty-nine additional illustration plates after Gustave Doré, original stamped red cloth (a bit rubbed), front cover decorated with an illustration stamped in gilt and black (two angelic figures in gilt with sword and spear flying over earth/mountains and water in search of or watching over) with title lettered in gilt at the top and "Illustrated By Gustave Doré" in silver at the bottom, spine decorated and lettered in black. A nice copy of this possible first edition by Thompson of Chicago. See 1901 dated edition by Thompson & Thomas of Chicago. Not in Kohler.

1322. Variant of Preceding, with a variant publisher's imprint on title page ("Thompson & Thomas[,] 334 Dearbon Street[,] Chicago"), in a variant publisher's binding (original publisher's stamped green cloth). The collection also has another copy with the same publisher's imprint as preceding, in a variant publisher's binding (original publisher's stamped bright red cloth, same as binding on dated copy).

1323. PARADISE LOST By John Milton[.] *Chicago[:] W. B. Conkey Company Publishers, (1900).* Small 8vo, 461+[3]pp., unsigned steel-engraved frontispiece portrait plate of a young, long haired Milton, with thick gilt border rule around the portrait, printed title-page plate elaborately decorated in floral trim in gilt in art nouveau style, "Copyright, 1900, by W. B. Conkey Company" on verso of title page, three illustration plates after Doré: for Book III: "Loud hosannas filled the eternal region," for Book VI: "This greeting on thy impious crest receive," and for Book IX: "Back to the thicket slunk the guilty serpent," (signed "J. Huyot"), original decorated white cloth (slightly used), front cover lettered and decorated in art nouveau style in embossed floral motif in light green with gilt accents, with a color photograph of a cottage in the distance in a pastoral setting within a purple floral motif tipped on the front cover near the edge within an embossed frame with a thick border in light green with gilt accents with a ribbon tied in a bow at the top, spine similarly lettered and decorated in art nouveau style in a floral motif in light green with gilt accents, t.e.g., with three pages of advertisements bound in at the end. An attractive copy with dated contemporary presentation inscription on fly-leaf. See undated ca. 1895 illustrated edition (possible first edition thus) published by

"W. B. Conkey Company" in a lovely publisher's binding with three illustration plates after Doré, and other editions by Conkey cited there. Uncommon. Not in Kohler.

1324. Variant of Preceding, original white cloth (front cover a little soiled), front cover decorated in a gilt floral motif with gilt lettering and with a color photograph of a young lady in Victorian dress and large floral hat tipped on the front cover near the edge within a broad gilt band with a ribbon in gilt tied in a bow at the top, spine similarly decorated in a gilt floral motif (a bit faded) with gilt lettering, t.e.g. A nice copy without a thick gilt border around frontispiece portrait, with variant title-page plate (printed title-page plate elaborately decorated in floral trim in green in art nouveau style), without copyright date on verso of title page, in a variant publisher's binding, with an advertisement leaf (instead of three pages) bound in at the end. Uncommon. Not in Kohler.

1325. PARADISE LOST By John Milton[.] *New York[:] Hurst & Company Publishers[.] n.d. [ca. 1900]*. 8vo, 408pp., frontispiece illustration plate depicting a pastoral scene in nature (a brook/river running through the woods), original decorated light gray cloth, front cover decorated in green and black, the green appearing to be a winding river beside a tree and beneath black leaves, with a photograph of two young girls in color tipped on the front cover at the center surrounded by thick black rules beneath "Paradise Lost" lettered in black within thick black rules at the top, spine (a little discolored) similarly decorated in green and black with black lettering, notes at bottom of page. A nice copy in a charming publisher's binding. See undated nonillustrated "Arlington Edition" of *PL* published by "Hurst & Co., Publishers" ca. 1880, with frontispiece portrait, and other editions by Hurst cited there. Not in Kohler.

1326. PARADISE LOST A Poem In Twelve Books By John Milton[.] *MDCCCC·Published·By·J·M· Dent·And·Co: Aldine·House·London·W·C· (1900)*. Third Dent edition. Small 8vo, xi+[1]+372pp., half-title ("The Temple Classics Edited by Israel Gollancz M.A.") with small red emblem at the center, "First Edition, March 1898[.] Second Edition, August 1899" on verso of general half-title, unsigned frontispiece portrait of a young, long-haired Milton within a circular decorative border trim with hanging device at the top, protective tissue guard, title page in red and black with wide decorative border trim in art nouveau style, half-title before the poem, glossary at the end, "Printed by T. and A. Constable, Printers to Her Majesty at the Edinburgh University Press" at the bottom of last page, original blue cloth over limp boards (a bit rubbed), central emblem incorporating owl in blind on front cover, spine lettered in gilt within decorative gilt trim, monument printed in green on front pastedown containing "John Milton" in large green letters at the top, "Born 1608 Died 1674" printed in small green letters beneath within a half laurel wreath in green, and beneath this on the monument itself is printed in green letters, "First Edition Published AD 1667," t.e.g, others untrimmed, red silk ribbon marker. A very nice copy. See 1897 first edition by Dent and other editions cited there, along with clarification given regarding the early editions by Dent and the sorting out of the first, second, and third editions. Not in Kohler.

1327. PARADISE LOST[.] *New York[:] Hurst & Company[.] The Companion Books[.] n.d. [ca. 1900]*. 8vo, 408pp., title page with decorative wide black border trim in art nouveau style, original orange limp leather (early name lightly written in pencil on fly-leaf and stamped in a small, unobtrusive stamp on title page and final blank, slight age-browning), central gilt seal ("The Companion Books") on front cover, spine lettered in gilt, lightly marbled endpapers, t.e. brown, printed publisher's wrappers (a bit worn and slightly chipped along edges, slightly age-browned) lettered: "Paradise Lost / John Milton / The Companion Books / 155 Volumes Ready / Additional Titles In Preparation / "Like Old Friends They / Wear Well" / Bound in Bookkraft Leather / New York." A nice copy of this special series published by Hurst with uncommon publisher's wrappers. Not in Kohler.

1328. PARADISE LOST By John Milton[.] *The Mershon Company[,] Rahway, N.J. [And] New York[.] n.d. [ca. 1900]*. Small 8vo, 192pp. (pagination beginning, as in the ca. 1895 edition by the Mershon Company, with p. 18, with nothing appearing to be missing), title-page plate with elaborate decorative frame in contrasting red incorporating a burning lamp on each side, a central device at the top, and a central device at the bottom with an angelic figure on each side holding up the corners of the border trim, original half cream cloth, decorated paper over boards (a bit worn at corners), cream cloth decorated in embossed gilt rules with decorative gilt pieces at top and bottom in art nouveau style, spine similarly decorated with gilt pieces in art nouveau style and with gilt lettering, paper over boards decorated in light pink and contrasting green floral pastel design, endpapers decorated in orange incorporating initials of the press. A nice copy in an attractive publisher's binding with contemporary presentation inscription (dated 1902) on front blank. See undated ca. 1895 two-volumes-in-one edition published by "The F. M. Lupton Publishing Company" with "The Mershon Company Press, Rahway, N.J." printed on verso of each title page. Not in Kohler.

1329. Variant of Preceding. Original half white cloth, purple floral cloth (a bit rubbed, light waterstaining at tip of lower right corner of first part of book), spine and portion of white on front cover elaborately decorated in gilt (faded), spine lettered in gilt (faded), decorated orange endpapers incorporating the initials "TMC" at the center, t.e.g. An interesting copy with a possibly rare frontispiece portrait plate, in a very attractive (albeit somewhat worn) variant publisher's binding, and with contemporary signature (dated "Christmas 1903") on front blank.

1330. Variant of Preceding. Original white silk over padded boards, front cover decorated with large floral arrangement in varying colors of purple, blue, and white against a gilt background with title in gilt at the top and Milton's name in gilt at the bottom, spine decorated and lettered in gilt, endpapers decorated in light green incorporating initials of the press. A fine copy, fresh and clean within with a variant title-page plate serving as frontispiece (colored floral plate with pansy in purple, with green stems and leaves against slightly yellow shaded background), in a lovely, well-preserved variant publisher's binding. Not in Kohler.

1331. PARADISE LOST By John Milton[.] *New York[:] The Prudential Book Co. n.d. [ca. 1900]*. First edition thus? Small 8vo, 192+[6]pp., advertisement leaf, title page with elaborate decorative border trim in black, original gray printed wrappers (a bit rubbed, small lower portion of spine and a small portion of corner of front cover missing), sketch of thatched roof house (possibly of Chalfont St. Giles) on front cover with elaborate decorative border trim in black. A good copy with six pages "To The Reader" explaining the purpose of the "Coupon System" for acquiring books bound in at the end. Uncommon. Not in Kohler.

1332. PARADISE LOST By John Milton[.] *Chatterton-Peck Company[,] New York, N. Y. n.d. [ca. 1900]*. First edition thus? Small 8vo, 192pp. (pagination beginning at "18," with nothing appearing to be missing), title page ruled in black with small decorative piece in black at the center, original decorative blue-green cloth (a little rubbed, spine faded), *PL* lettered in black at top of front cover with elaborate classical design in black in art nouveau design style below, spine similarly lettered and decorated in black in art nouveau style. A fairly nice copy of an uncommon edition, apparently published for convenience in pocketbook size. Companion volume to an edition by Chatterton-Peck of *PR* published about this same time ca. 1900 in a similar binding (also listed here). This identical binding appears on an edition of *PL* published about this same time ca. 1900 by the Mershon Company Publisher (also listed here). Scarce.

1333. PARADISE LOST. By John Milton. BOOK I. With Preparatory And Explanatory Notes By E. F. Willoughby, M.D. Maynard's English Classics. *New York: Charles E. Merrill Co. n.d. (ca. 1900)*. Slim 8vo, 94+64pp., unsigned frontispiece portrait of a young Milton, half-title for Book II ("With Notes, By Frances Storr"), separate pagination for Book II, original yellow cloth (spine a bit faded), front cover and spine lettered in black. While Book I only is referenced on the title page, Books I and II are included in this textbook intended for school use. Until this publication, editions were part of the "English Classic Series" and were published by Maynard, Merrill & Co. in 1879 (first edition thus), or successors to them: by Clark & Maynard in 1885, 1887, and 1890; by Effingham Maynard & Co., Successors To Clark & Maynard in 1889; and as part of "Maynard's English Classics" by Charles E. Merrill Co. Not in Kohler.

1334. MILTON'S PARADISE LOST BOOKS I. AND II. Edited With Notes And An Introduction By Edward Everett Hale, Jr., Ph. D.[,] Professor Of Rhetoric And Logic In Union College[.] *Longmans' English Classics[.] New York[:] Longmans, Green, And Co. London And Bombay[,] 1900*. Slim 8vo, lxxii+112+[8]pp., half-title, frontispiece portrait plate by D. Grosch, emblem of the press at center of title page, half-title before Books I and II, original light brown cloth (slight fading, a light mark on spine, a few pencil notations), front cover and spine lettered in reddish-brown, with central emblem of the press and decorative border trim also in reddish-brown. A very nice copy with a contemporary signature on fly-leaf. Eight pages of advertisements bound in at the end. "First Edition, July, 1896[;] Reprinted, August, 1897[,] February And July, 1898[,] January, 1900 [copy here]. Not in Kohler.

1335. MILTON'S PARADISE LOST Illustrated By Gustave Doré Introduction By Robert Vaughan, D.D. *Thompson & Thomas Chicago 1901*. Large 8vo, viii+311pp., frontispiece illustration and forty-nine additional illustration plates after Gustave Doré, original stamped green cloth (a bit aged), front cover decorated with an illustration stamped in gilt and black (two angelic figures in gilt with sword and spear flying over earth/mountains and water in search of or watching over) with gilt lettering, spine decorated and lettered in black, gray endpapers. Although a little aged, a good copy. See undated ca. 1900 edition (possibly first edition thus) by Thompson of Chicago. Not in Kohler.

1336. PARADISE LOST A Poem In Twelve Books By John Milton[.] *MDCCCCI·Published·By·J·M·Dent·And·Co: Aldine·House·London·W·C·*. Alternate third Dent edition. Small 8vo, xi+[1]+372pp., half-title ("The Temple Classics Edited by Israel Gollancz") with small red emblem at the center, unsigned frontispiece portrait of a young, long-haired Milton within circular decorative border trim with hanging device at the top, protective tissue guard, title page in red and black with wide decorative border trim in art nouveau style, half-title before the poem, glossary at the end, original blue cloth over limp boards (spine ends slightly rubbed, bottom of back cover slightly faded), central emblem incorporating owl in blind on front cover, spine lettered in gilt within decorative gilt trim, monument printed in green on front pastedown containing "John Milton" in large green letters at the top, "Born 1608 Died 1674" printed in small green letters beneath, within a half laurel wreath in green, and beneath this on the monument itself is printed in green letters, "First Edition Published AD 1667," t.e.g, others untrimmed, red silk ribbon marker. A very nice copy. See 1897 first edition by Dent and other editions cited there, along with clarification given regarding the early editions by Dent and the sorting out of the first, second, and third editions. Not in Kohler.

1337. PARADISE LOST A Poem in XII Books The Author John Milton[.] *The Doves Press No. 1 The Terrace Hammersmith[,] MDCCCCII.* 8vo, 387+[2]pp., preliminary material to *PL*, "Errata," half-title printed in red before the poem with the title and author printed in large type in red at the top of the page at the outset of the poem, the beginning initial of each book enlarged and printed in red or blue, each book identified in red in the margin of each page, original vellum binding (edges slightly embrowned), brown morocco label on spine with gilt lettering and gilt rules, "Printed by T. J. Cobden-Sanderson & Emory Walker at The Doves Press and finished 3 June 1902" (colophon). Printed and bound uniformly with *PR&c* (1905), also listed here. A lovely set from the Doves Press, a press founded by Cobden-Sanderson and Emory Walker, formerly of the Kelmscott Press, which has often been considered the best of them all and whose influence on the twentieth century was profound (Franklin, *Private Presses*). One of only 300 sets printed on paper; 25 copies were also printed on vellum. Ransom, *Selective Check Lists*, 5; Stevens 751; Kohler 166.

1338. MILTON'S PARADISE LOST Illustrated By Gustave Doré Edited With Notes And A Life Of Milton By Robert Vaughan, D.D. *Cassell And Company, Limited[.] London, Paris, New York & Melbourne. (1904–) MCMV. All Rights Reserved.* Eighteen original parts. Large 4to, lxii+[1]+329pp., through Part 15, last three parts containing prelims (paginated differently) to the 1905 published edition (also listed here), fifty illustration plates by Gustave Doré (fine impressions), life of Milton and notes by Robert Vaughan, original printed brown wrappers, as issued, with central vignette portrait of a young, romanticised Milton on all but the last part. A complete set (slightly rubbed, spines a bit faded, split to foot of spine on first part, sticker removed on first part). A nice set with extra title page bound in at the end, the "Concluding Part" (Part 18) and Parts 16 and 17 containing the preliminary leaves to the published edition: "Life of Milton," "Introduction," "The Verse," half-title, title page in red and black (dated "MCMV"), "Contents," and "List Of Illustrations." The set was published in eighteen monthly parts between September 1904 and May 1905. Kohler 170, making no mention of the extra title page in red and black dated "MCMV" and reporting "Not in the British Library. Not in Cambridge University Library."

1339. Variant of Preceding. A complete set. A particularly fine set, as preceding, with extra title page bound in at the end, the "Concluding Part" (Part 18) and Parts 16 and 17

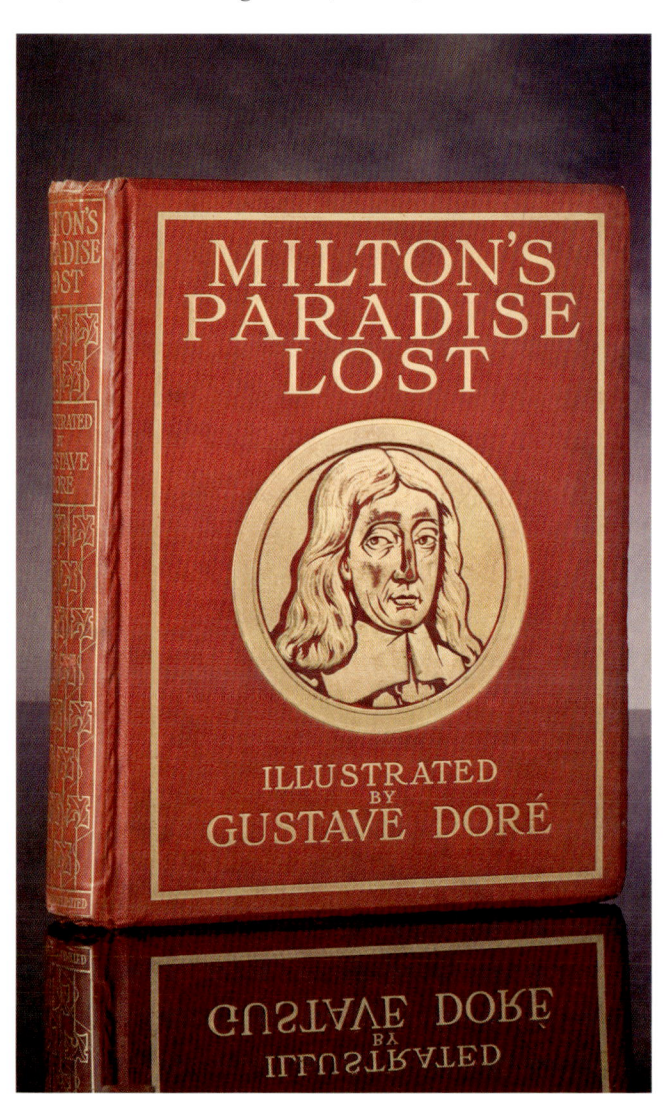

Milton's Paradise Lost Illustrated By Gustave Doré. London, Paris, New York & Melbourne. (1904-) MCMV. Thick 4to, original red cloth, large embossed central vignette portrait of Milton in rich gilt at center of front cover. See #1338.

containing the prelims to the published edition. The set was published in eighteen monthly parts between September 1904 and May 1905 and stored in original embossed red cloth folder/casing identical to the binding of the published edition shortly thereafter (also listed here): original publisher's red cloth casing (slight waterstaining some time ago to lower outer corners, some modest scuffing), thick gilt rule on front cover with embossed gilt lettering and with large embossed central vignette portrait of Milton in rich gilt, spine elaborately decorated in gilt with gilt-lettering, blind design at center of back cover. Binding identical to binding on previous copy. Kohler 170, making no mention of the extra title page and without original publisher's casing.

1340. PARADISE LOST By John Milton. With an Introduction by Henry Morley[.] *Cassell And Company, Limited[:] London, Paris, New York[,] And Melbourne. MCMIV. All Rights Reserved.* 2 volumes. 16mo, 192pp., 192pp., half-title each volume (each half-title with a listing of publications "In Cassell's National Library" on verso), frontispiece illustration plate by Doré each volume, title page each volume, original rose cloth (spines faded, contemporary and later names on fly-leaf of each volume), front covers ruled and lettered in white (including "Cassell & Co. Limited"), spines lettered in white with "36" and "37" at the bottom (number of each volume in the series, repeated at bottom of the frontispiece illustration). Good set. See possible first edition thus by Cassell, without Doré plates, in 1889, and also possible second edition thus by Cassell, likewise without Doré plates, in 1891. Scarce. Kohler 169, reporting "Not in Cambridge University Library."

1341. PARADISE LOST A Poem In Twelve Books By John Milton[.] MDCCCCIV•Published•By •J•M• Dent• And•Co: Aldine•House•London•W•C• *(1904).* Fifth edition thus. Small 8vo, xi+[1]+372pp., half-title ("The Temple Classics Edited by Israel Gollancz") with small red emblem at the center, unsigned frontispiece portrait of a young, long-haired Milton within circular decorative border trim with hanging device at the top, protective tissue guard, title page in red and black with wide decorative border trim in art nouveau style, half-title before the poem, glossary at the end, original blue cloth over limp boards, central emblem incorporating owl in blind on front cover, spine lettered in gilt within decorative gilt trim, monument printed in green on front pastedown containing Milton's name and dates at the top and within a half laurel wreath on the monument itself printed in green letters, "First Edition Published AD 1667," t.e.g, others untrimmed, red silk ribbon marker. A lovely copy with contemporary signature on fly-leaf. See 1897 first edition by Dent and other editions cited there, along with clarification given regarding the early editions by Dent and the sorting out of the first, second, and third editions. Not in Kohler.

1342. Variant of Preceding, original green leather over limp boards (a bit worn along edges, spine ends slightly chipped), rest as preceding. Despite some wear to extremities of the binding, a nice copy in a variant publisher's binding, with contemporary signature in ink in a neat hand, and later signature beneath on fly-leaf.

1343. PARADISE LOST BOOKS I AND II By John Milton Edited For High School Use By William I. Crane[,] Head Of The English Department[,] Steele High School, Dayton, Ohio[.] *New York[:] The Macmillan Company[;] London: Macmillan & Co., Ltd. 1904[.] All rights reserved[.]* Third edition thus. Small 8vo, l+[1]+125+[4]pp., half-title with a listing of "Macmillan's Pocket American and English Classics 16mo. Cloth. 25¢ each" on verso, frontispiece portrait plate reproducing an earlier frontispiece portrait with Dryden epigram, fifty-page introduction, three plates of "The Empyrean," five fullpage illustration maps, notes and index at the end, original red cloth (a bit rubbed, some pencil markings and notations), front cover lettered embossed in white within white rules, spine lettered in white (faded). A good copy with four pages of advertisements bound in at the end. The first edition of this popular series, Macmillan's Pocket Classics, was published in 1900 (copy not in the collection); it was reprinted in 1903, 1904 (copy here), 1910 (copy in the collection, a repeat of this edition, not listed), 1913 (copy in the collection, a repeat of this edition, not listed), 1914 (copy in the collection, a repeat of this edition, not listed), 1921 (copy in the collection, a repeat of this edition, not listed), 1923 (copy in the collection, a repeat of this edition, not listed), and 1926 (copy in the collection, a repeat of this edition, not listed). An earlier edition of the "Macmillan's English Classics" (including an edition of *PL, Books I. and II.*) was first published in 1887; it was reprinted in 1891 and again in 1893 (also listed here). Uncommon. Not in Kohler.

1344. MILTON'S PARADISE LOST Illustrated By Gustave Doré Edited With Notes And A Life Of Milton By Robert Vaughan, D.D. *Cassell And Company, Limited[.] London, Paris, New York & Melbourne. MCMV. All Rights Reserved.* Thick 4to, lxii+[i]+329pp., half-title, title page in red and black, frontispiece and forty-nine additional illustration plates after Gustave Doré, "Contents," "List Of Illustrations," "Introduction," "The Verse," followed by an undated second title page in black before Book I ("MILTON'S PARADISE LOST Illustrated By Gustave Doré Edited With Notes and a Life of Milton By Robert Vaughan, D.D. Cassell And Company, Limited[.] *London,*

1906 Lyceum Press edition of *Paradise Lost:* (left) in an elegant Doves binding; (center) as an unbound, wholly uncut copy; and (right) in original boards, quarter linen spine. See #1349.

Paris, New York & Melbourne[.] All Rights Reserved[.] n.d."), original red cloth, thick gilt rule on front cover with embossed gilt lettering and with large embossed central vignette portrait of Milton in rich gilt, spine elaborately decorated in gilt with gilt-lettering, blind design at center of back cover. A fine copy in a stunning and well-preserved publisher's binding. Also in the collection are companion volumes with a two-volume edition of Dante's *Inferno* (dated 1903) and *Purgatory and Paradise* (undated), each illustrated by Gustave Doré and each similarly elegantly bound with embossed central vignette portrait of Dante in rich gilt on the front cover. Kohler 172, making no mention of the second undated title page, in variant binding (see following).

1345. Variant of Preceding, original blue pebble cloth (slight rubbing along back spine joint), front cover lettered in blind relief with large blind embossed vignette portrait of Milton within a circular frame at the center, spine elaborately decorated in intricate blind pattern with bright gilt lettering. A very nice copy without the second title page in black before Book I, in an attractive variant publisher's binding. Kohler 172, in variant "1/2-green calf, pebble grain cloth" binding, reporting "Not in the Bodleian Library. Not in Cambridge University Library."

1346. PARADISE LOST By John Milton With Twelve Photogravures after Designs by William Strang. The Photogravure Series. *London[:] George Routledge And Sons, Limited[;] New York: E. P. Dutton And Co. 1905.* First edition thus. 8vo, 242pp., half-title, frontispiece portrait plate, engraved and printed title pages, with illustration on engraved title of Milton playing on his viola surrounded by his daughters singing, and ten additional illustration plates by William Strang (second appearance, first appearance thus), protective tissue guards, original light brown texture cloth, front cover decorated in contrasting browns with gilt trim and light green along inner and top edges with an illustration of the temptation reproduced in gilt at the bottom, spine decorated in gilt trim with gilt lettering and green trim on either side and with a flower in gilt with green petals at the bottom, t.e.g., fore-edge untrimmed. A very nice copy. Kohler 171.

This is the first appearance of Strang's illustrations in this printed format. A limited special folio edition, the first appearance of Strang's illustrations, with each etching illustration signed by the artist, was published in 1896; see also ca. 1973 tall 12mo edition with Strang's illustrations in a handsome publication "Distributed By Hebron Books; see, too, Franklin Library edition printed in a limited edition in

1984, with Strang's illustrations reproduced in an octavo format taller than here—all listed here.

1347. PARADISE LOST By John Milton[.] *Chicago[:] Homewood Publishing Company Publishers[.] n.d. [ca. 1905]*. 8vo, 461pp.+[3]pp., unsigned frontispiece portrait plate in tinted blue, title-page plate lettered in blue and decorated in art nouveau style with red and blue swirls and large and small floral blossoms, original light brown silk (edges and corners of front cover a bit rubbed, stamp on front and back fly-leaves), front board covered with glazed light green paper decorated with central floral bouquet in variant colors against a white background with floral trim in gold around the outside, spine richly decorated in gilt with gilt lettering, endpapers decorated in art nouveau style with a light green floral trim and central pegasus figure, with three pages of advertisements bound in at the end, t.e.g. A nice copy in an attractive publisher's binding with contemporary presentation inscription (dated "Christmas, 1905") on front cover. See undated ca. 1895 edition by Homewood Publishing Company Publishers, without frontispiece portrait or title-page plate. Uncommon. Not in Kohler.

1348. PARADISE LOST A Poem In Twelve Books By John Milton[.] *Methuen & Co. 36 Essex Street W. C. London, (1905)*. First edition thus. 8vo, xv+[5]+236+40pp., half-title with large emblem for "Methuen's Standard Library Arbor Scientia Edited By Sidney Lee" on verso, introductory remarks by Sidney Lee on Milton, original blue cloth (a bit rubbed, light foxing on beginning and final pages, signature on fly-leaf), spine lettered in gilt with large decorative gilt trim in art nouveau style, bottom edges untrimmed. A nice copy with "A Catalogue Of Books Published By Methuen And Company: London . . . September 1907" bound in at the end. Uncommon.

1349. PARADISE LOST By John Milton[.] Illustrations By William Blake[.] *Printed At The Lyceum Press, Liverpool, And Published By The Liverpool Booksellers' Co., Limited[.] 1906*. First edition thus. 4to, ix+397pp., title page in red and black, first appearance of twelve illustration plates in full color by William Blake, 4 ¾" × 5 ⅝", protective tissue guard for each illustration with the relevant lines being illustrated printed in black, "List of Illustrations," original boards, quarter linen spine (some inoffensive markings, end-leaves age-darkened), paper label on spine, fore- and bottom edges untrimmed, contemporary name neatly written on fly-leaf. Kohler 173.

The first printing in color of these illustrations of *PL* by Blake. Blake completed two sets of illustrations of *PL*: one set of twelve, with one illustration for each book, completed in 1807 and now in the Huntington Library, first published in this edition by the Lyceum Press. The other set of nine illustrations, completed in 1808 and now in the Boston Museum of Fine Arts, were first published in the 1940 edition by the Heritage Press (also listed here). The Huntington collection of Blake illustrations of *PL* was "printed at full scale in full color from the original works" by the Arion Press in 2004 "to accompany the edition of *PL* published in 2002 by The Arion Press" (also listed here with a separate list of prints), including the other much larger Blake drawing (also in the Huntington) with the same title as plate 2 in the 1807 series, *Satan, Sin, and Death: Satan Comes to the Gates of Hell*, probably executed in 1806.

1350. Variant of Preceding. A fine, unbound, wholly uncut copy in remarkable condition (despite some light dust-soiling). "The only copy we have seen thus" (G. W. Stuart, Jr., Ravenstree, Cat. 150, #88, 1987).

A Special Copy Printed on Vellum with Extra Set of Progressive Plates—By Printing Process, Start to Finish in a Special Binding by the Doves Bindery

1351. Variant of Preceding. 4to, ix+397pp., title page in red and black, first appearance of twelve illustration plates by William Blake in full color, 4 ¾" × 5 ⅝", protective tissue guard for each illustration with the lines being illustrated printed in black, "List of Illustrations," and an unpaginated series of plates illustrating the printing process from beginning to end, elegantly bound by the Doves Bindery in full blue morocco over thick boards, covers finely tooled in gilt rules with gilt pattern enclosing an oval-shaped gilt-decoration, spine lettered in gilt with similarly finely tooled oval-shaped gilt decoration within the panels, raised bands, broad inner dentelles finely gilt-tooled, outer dentelles ruled in gilt, a.e.g. A superb copy in fine condition. This is a special copy, one of a few only printed on vellum with an extra set of progressive plates by printing process, from start to finish bound in at the end, in a handsome morocco binding by the Doves Bindery.

Laid in: four hand-written letters by T. J. Cobden-Sanderson, co-founder together with Emory Walker, formerly of the Kelmscott Press, of the Doves Press and Doves Bindery, to a "Mr. Style" on Doves Bindery stationery, each two to four pages in length, written between November 1895 and April 1896, two signed with his full name, two with his initials only, concerning a special binding "job" (so-labeled in the letters), which Cobden-Sanderson was just then doing for style. Also included are neat (possibly early) transcriptions of each letter.

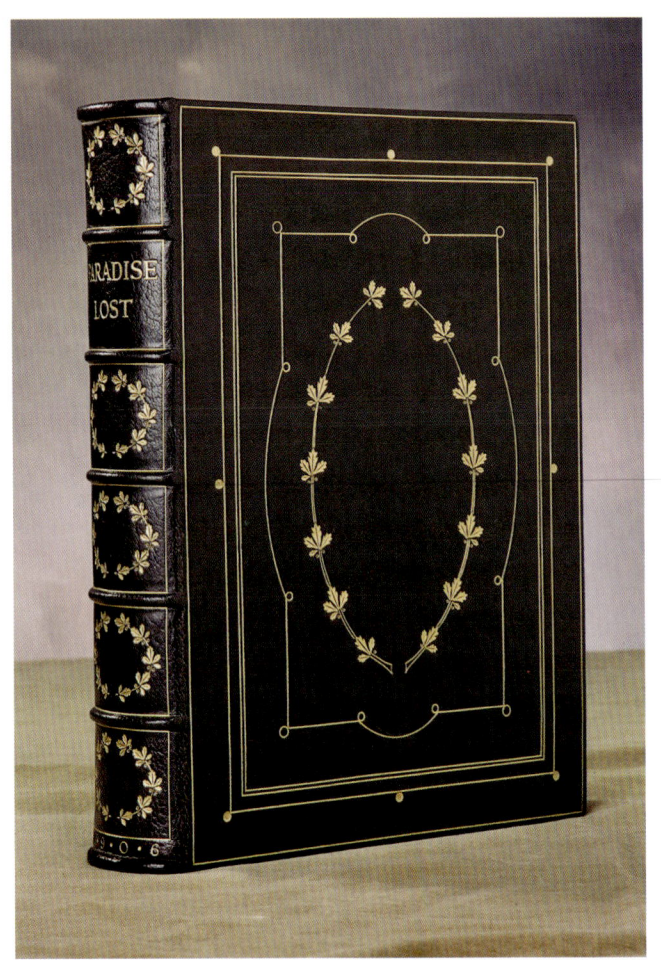

Paradise Lost Illustrations By William Blake. Printed At The Lyceum Press, Liverpool, 1906. 4to, first appearance of these illustrations by Blake in full color, elegantly bound by the Doves Bindery in full blue morocco over thick boards. One of a few copies printed on vellum. See #1351.

1352. PARADISE LOST Books I. And II. With Introduction and Explanatory Notes. *Educational Publishing Company[,] Boston[,] New York[,] Chicago[,] San Francisco[,] (1906).* First edition thus. Slim 8vo, 140+[4]pp., "Copyrighted 1906" on verso of title page, unsigned portrait sketch after "Contents" page and before introduction, half-title for Book II, notes at bottom of page, original wrappers lettered in blue, green cloth spine, large laurel wreath in blue with "Classic Library" in a scroll beneath, "Vol. 1 No. 10" in upper left corner, advertising for the Classic Library series on inside of front cover and on inside and outside of back cover. A nice copy in original publisher's wrappers. Not in Kohler.

1353. MILTON'S PARADISE LOST Books I. And II With Introduction, Notes, Etc. Edited By Albert Perry Walker, M.A. Master, And Teacher Of English And History In The English High School, Boston[.] *Boston, U.S.A. D. C. Heath & Co., Publishers[.] 1906.* Third edition thus. 8vo, vi+270pp. (continuous pagination), frontispiece portrait plate by "D. Grosch," illustrations of "The World (The Ptolemaic System)," "The Four Regions Of The Universe," several additional plates reproducing early maps, half-title before each book (with "The Argument" printed on verso), "Notes," "Glossary," and "Index" at the end, original yellow cloth (a bit worn, spine stained), front covered ruled and lettered in contrasting darker yellow. The first edition thus was published in 1897 under the title *Selections From Paradise Lost*, with additional "Portions of Books II, IV, VI, VII, And X" (also listed here); the second edition thus was published in 1900. Not in Kohler.

1354. MILTON'S PARADISE LOST Edited With Notes And A Life Of Milton By Robert Vaughan, D.D. Illustrated By Gustave Doré[.] *Cassell And Company, Limited[.] London, Paris, New York, Toronto And Melbourne MCMVII (1907) All Rights Reserved[.]* Tall 16mo, lxviii+[2]+268+4pp., half-title printed in red, frontispiece illustration plate by Doré, protective tissue plate, title page printed in red and black, twenty-three additional illustration plates by Doré, original orange cloth (a bit rubbed, front cover a little scuffed at bottom, spine slightly faded, ownership signature in pencil on fly-leaf), front cover lettered in gilt within decorative gilt trim, spine lettered in gilt with decorative gilt trim, small circular emblem at the center of front and back pastedowns, t.e.g., others untrimmed, small booksellers label at bottom of front pastedown. A nice copy of this "Dainty Pocket Edition," with four pages of advertisements of "Dainty Pocket Editions" bound in at the end, including this edition among the copies advertised. Not in Kohler.

1355. PARADISE LOST John Milton[.] *London: George G. Harrap & Co. LTD. 2-3 Portsmouth St. Kingsway And At Sydney[.] n.d. [ca. 1909].* First edition thus. 8vo, [ii]+322+[2]pp., half-title, with advertisement for "The Harrap Library" on verso of blank leaf preceding, frontispiece portrait line-drawing of a youngish Milton by Lionel Heath, title page with dark red circle beneath the title incorporating "Cogito Ergo Sum" in reverse white, "Printed at The Ballantyne Press Spottiswoode, Ballantyne & Co. Ltd. Colchester, London & Eton, England" on verso of title page at bottom, contents page listing each book of *PL* and page reference, quotation from Thomas Gray on verso, edited by Fred E. Bumby with "Editorial Note" dated "October 1909," original brown diced calf, gilt-decorated covers and spine, t.e.g., others untrimmed. A very nice copy printed at the Ballantyne Press on high-quality paper. Companion volume with *PR and MP* (with a different publisher's imprint: "London: George G. Harrap & Co. 9 Portsmouth St. Kingsway," ca. 1900) with preface by Bumby as here, but undated (whereas preface here is dated 1909), in an identical binding (also listed here). Not in Kohler.

1356. Variant of Preceding, original green morocco (a bit rubbed at corners and at top of joints), covers with double rule in blind and decorative corner trim in blind, large decorative circular gilt floral piece at the center of front cover, spine lettered in gilt with gilt rules and decorative gilt trim, t.e.g., others untrimmed, green silk ribbon marker, with contemporary inscription on fly-leaf signed by ten names. A lovely copy with a variant publisher's imprint ("London: George G. Harrap & Co. 15 York St. Covent Garden"), in a variant publisher's binding, with a different reference to "Printed By Ballantyne And Co. Limited Tavistock Street Covent Garden London" on verso of title page (rather than "Printed at The Ballantyne Press Spottiswoode, Ballantyne & Co. Ltd. Colchester, London & Eton, England"). Not in Kohler.

1357. PARADISE LOST John Milton[.] *New York: Dodge Publishing Company 220 East Twenty-Third St.[.] n.d. [ca. 1909]*. First edition thus. 8vo, [ii]+322+[2]pp., half-title (title at the top and "The Dodge Library" at the bottom), with advertisement for the "The Dodge Library" on verso of blank leaf preceding, frontispiece portrait line-drawing of a youngish Milton by Lionel Heath, title page with dark red circle beneath the title with white emblem in reverse white, contents page listing each book of *PL* and page reference, quotation from Thomas Gray on verso, edited by Fred E. Bumby with "Editorial Note" dated "October 1909," original red cloth (a bit age-darkened), gilt-decorated covers and spine with gilt lettering, fore- and bottom edges untrimmed, partially unopened. A nice copy. Similar to the editions published by Harrap about this same time (listed here). Companion volume with *PR and MP* (New York: Dodge Publishing Company 220 East Twenty-Third St., [ca. 1909]), in identical (although fresher) binding (also listed here). Not in Kohler.

1358. JOHN MILTON PARADISE LOST BOOKS V. AND VI. Edited By A. W. Verity[,] M.A. Sometime Scholar Of Trinity College[.] *Cambridge[:] At The University Press[,] 1910*. Small 8vo, lxxii+136pp., half-title ("Pitt Press Series"), "Note To First Edition," lengthy introduction, half-title before each book, "Notes" "Appendix A [On] The Cosmology of Paradise Lost," "Appendix B On The Character Of Milton's Satan," "Glossary," and "Index Of Words" at the end, original red paper over boards (a little faded, some occasional pencil underlinings), front cover and spine lettered in black. A good copy. The "First Edition [thus was published in] 1892 [copy listed here;] Reprinted 1898, 1901, 1905, 1907, [and] 1910 [copy here]," printed on verso of title page. Uncommon. Kohler 176, reporting "Not in the Bodleian Library. Not in Cambridge University Library."

1359. JOHN MILTON EL PARAISO PERDIDO Traduccion directa del ingles por M. J. Barroso Bonzon[.] Tercera Edicion[.] Ediciones Ibericas[.] *Apartado 8085 - Madrid, n.d. [ca. 1910]*. Small 8vo, 326+[2]pp., half-title, title page in red and black, "Indice" at the end with "Obras Varias" on verso, marbled endpapers, t.e. red, original soft red leatherette, front cover and spine lettered in black, printed publisher's wrappers lettered in red and black with advertisements for other publications on inside flaps and an illustration of *Eve Tempting Adam* reproduced in black and white on front cover. A nice copy. See ca. 1890 Spanish translation with references to other earlier Spanish translations. Not in Kohler.

1360. EL PARAISO PERDIDO Poema Escrito En Ingles Por John Milton Version Hecha Sobre La Traduccion De Don Juan Escoiquiz Canonigo de la Santa Iglesia de Toledo[.] Edicion ilustrada con 50 laminas del famoso dibujante Gustavo Dore[.] *Casa Editorial Maucci Gran medalla de oro en las Exposiciones de Viena de 1903, Madrid 1907, Budapest 1907, Londres 1913, Paris 1913 y gran premio en la de Buenos Aires 1910[,] Calle de Mallorca, 166.— Barcelona[.] n.d. [ca. 1913]*. 8vo, 558+18pp., half-title, unsigned frontispiece reproduction of Milton portrait as a young man in Puritanical garb with long curly hair, reproduction of illustrations by Gustave Doré, "Notas de Addisson" and "Notas De Escoiquiz" following the poem, with "Indice" at the end, elaborate decorative headpieces (one for each book, less elaborate for notes and index), original green cloth (front cover a little chafed, pages slightly age-browned), spine ruled and lettered in gilt, decorated endpapers. A good copy of this prose translation of Milton's *PL* with eighteen pages of advertisements bound in at the end. Uncommon. Not in Kohler.

1361. DET TABTE PARADISE John Milton Pa A Dansk Ved Uffe Birkedal[.] Andet Oplag[.] Glydendalske Boghandel – Nordisk Forlag – *Kjobenhavn Og Kristiania[.] MDCCCCXIV (1914)*. First edition thus. 8vo, xxiv+405pp., life, half-title followed by portrait plate of Milton as a young man with long hair before poem, notes at bottom of page, modern three-quarter Danish calf, marbled paper over boards (title page slightly foxed), spine lettered in gilt with slight gilt rules at top and bottom, raised bands. Bound in are the original printed stiff paper wrappers, with central vignette portrait of Milton as a young man with long hair on front cover (same portrait as on plate bound within) and central seal (possibly of the press) on back cover. A very nice copy. Not in Kohler.

1362. PARADISE LOST BOOKS I AND II Edited By Henry W. Boynton[.] *The Academy Classics. Allyn And Bacon Boston[,] New York[,] Chicago[.] (1916)*. Second edition thus? Slim 8vo, [i]+124pp., frontispiece illustration plate of "The blind Milton dictating *Paradise Lost* to his daughters from the painting of Munkacsy," original preface dated 1897, "Conclusion," notes to each book at the end, original black cloth (a bit rubbed along bottom edges, high school stamp on front pastedown), front cover and spine lettered in gilt. A nice copy. The first edition thus was published in 1897 (also listed here).

1363. JOHN MILTON PARADISE LOST BOOKS XI. AND XII. Edited By A. W. Verity, M.A.[,] Sometime Scholar Of Trinity College[.] *Cambridge[:] At The University Press[,] 1918*. Small 8vo, lxxii+106pp., half-title ("Pitt Press Series"), "Note To First Edition," lengthy introduction, half-title before each book, "Notes," "Glossary," and "Index" at the end, original red paper over boards, front cover and spine lettered in black. The "First Edition [thus was published in] 1892 [copy not in collection;] Reprinted 1912, 1917, 1918 [listed here]," printed on verso of title page. Uncommon.

1364. PARADISE LOST By John Milton With A Critical Introduction By James Holly Hanford[,] Graduate Professor of English, Western Reserve University[,] And An Additional Introductory Note By Frederick E. Bumby[,] University College, Nottingham[.] *Chelsea College Classics[.] New York[:] Robert M. McBride & Company[.] n.d. [ca. 1920]*. First edition thus. 8vo, [vi]+322+[1]pp., frontispiece portrait of Milton by Lionel Heath, small emblem of the press on title page, undated introduction by James Holly Hanford "Reprinted from the Encyclopedia Americana," "Editorial Note" by Frederick E. Bumby (dated "October 1909"), original burgundy cloth, spine lettered in gilt with decorative gilt device of the press at bottom, fore- and bottom edges untrimmed, partially unopened, original dust jacket (plain brown wrappers) with oval hole at the top to display title. A fine copy, mint. See dated 1936 edition of *PL* "Edited With Notes By James Holy Hanford" published by the Ronald Press Company (copy listed here). Scarce.

1365. PARADISE LOST By John Milton[.] Vol. I. *Miniature Dictionary Publishers, Inc., Sole agent, M. Minkus, 7 West 42nd Street, New York City. n.d. [ca. 1920]*. Volume 1 only [the only volume that may have been printed]. Miniature (1 ½" × 2"), 763+[1]+[4]pp., original brown leather over original thin red cloth, wrapped around with snap in front, opening oblong, gilt rule running along the edge, "Paradise Lost John Milton" lettered in gilt on front flap with a small decorative gilt piece on the snap and on either

Paradise Lost . . . Miniature Dictionary Publishers Inc., n.d.[ca.1920]. Volume 1 only [the only volume that may have been printed]. See #1365.

side of the snap, red edges. Present are Books I to VI, with a "Bibliography" (identified on last leaf as being continued "in Volume II") and three pages of advertisements for "other miniature books" bound in at the end, with statement on verso of last page: "Through the great success we have had with these very interesting and practical miniature editions we shall publish shortly other books of the world's best authors." A very nice copy of this miniature edition. Besides the two copies in the collection, I have had two others, and I have seen one other for sale, and in each case only volume 1 was present or offered without any suggestion of the existence of a volume 2, which leads one to conclude that perhaps volume 2 was never printed and that there is no volume 2. In any case, I have never seen a volume 2 during my thirty-five years of collecting Milton.

1366. Variant of Preceding. Volume 1 only [the only volume that may have been printed]. Miniature (1 ½" × 2"), original thin red cloth without any further covering (a bit rubbed, some corners bent), red edges. A good copy in a variant publisher's binding.

1367. MILTON[.] IL PARADISO PERDUTO Versione Di Lazaro Papi con Un Saggio Di T. B. Macaulay E La Biografia Del Traduttore per Atto Vannucci[.] *Istitvto Editoriale Italiano[,] Milano[.] n.d. [ca. 1920]*. 8vo, 432+[8]pp., half-title with illustration of a flame in black and white in art nouveau style at the center of the page, frontispiece illustration on verso in art nouveau style of open books on three different stands, each at different heights, signed "CD," lettered in blue letters beneath ("Gli Immortali E Altri Massimi Scrittori Raccolta Diretta Da Luigi Luzatti E Ferdinando Martini," with further black lettering at the bottom: "Serie I[,] Vol. XXV"), title page lettered in blue with a large sketch of the head of an eagle in black at the center, unsigned portrait of a long-haired youngish Milton engraved on thick paper (fine impression), protective tissue guard, decorative trim in light blue at top and bottom of each page, "Indice" at the end, followed by colophon leaf, with decorative endpiece in blue on recto of last page, original light gray cloth over thin boards, covers decorated with large embossed decorative piece in art nouveau at the center, front cover lettered in gilt, spine lettered and richly decorated in gilt, pictorial endpapers decorated with a depiction in art nouveau style of trees in dark olive green with a bright red flame in each tree, t.e. light gray. A fine copy of this early twentieth-century Italian verse translation of Milton's PL published in Milan in attractive art nouveau style.

1368. MILTON[.] PARADISE LOST Edited By A. W. Verity, M.A. Sometime Scholar of Trinity College. *Cambridge[:] At The University Press[,] 1921*. Second edition thus. Thick 8vo, lxxii+750pp., half-title, "Preface," "Introduction Life of Milton," "Notes," and "Glossary" at end, original green cloth, spine lettered in gilt with decorative gilt device at bottom and gilt rule at top and bottom, fore- and bottom edges untrimmed. A very nice copy. The first edition thus in one volume was published in 1910; this is the second edition "with some changes"; it was reissued in two volumes ("for the convenience of students") in 1929 (see volume 1, the text, listed here), and reprinted in 1934–36 (see set listed here).

1369. PARADISE LOST A Poem In Twelve Books By John Milton With An Introduction And Notes On Its Structure And Meaning By John A. Himes[,] Professor Of English In Pennsylvania College. *New York • Cincinnati • Chicago[:] American Book Company[,] (1926)*. Second edition. 8vo, xxxxii+482pp., half-title, original preface dated 1898, six explanatory illustration plates—three of which depict Milton's universe and three of which are illustrations of mythological figures, original dark green cloth, front cover and spine lettered in gilt. A very nice copy. Intended for school use, with extensive notes and an index to the notes. The first edition thus appeared in 1898 (also listed here).

1370. MILTON PARADISE LOST Edited By A. W. Verity, M.A. Vol. I Text / Vol. II Introduction, Notes, Etc. *Cambridge[:] At The University Press[,] 1929*. 2 volumes. Third edition thus. Thick 8vo, [1]+362pp.,+lxxii+750pp. (pagination continuing from volume 1), half-title and title page each volume, original green cloth (a bit rubbed, spines a little faded), spines lettered in gilt with university seal in gilt at bottom and gilt rules at top and bottom, fore- and bottom edges untrimmed. Each volume is very nice, with large, twentieth-century bookplates on front pastedowns. According to a "Note" at the beginning: "This edition is now issued in two volumes for the convenience of students. Volume I contains the text, founded on that of Masson's 'Globe' edition; Volume II the introduction, notes, appendix, glossary and indexes. A. W. V. July 1928." According to verso of title page: the "First Edition" thus "(in one volume") was published in 1910; it was "Reprinted, with some changes [in] 1921" (also listed here); it was "Re-issued, in two volumes [in] 1929, and reprinted in 1934–1936"—both sets listed here.

1371. [PARADISE LOST] MILTON AZ ELVESZETT PARADICSOM Forditotta Janosi Gusztav[.] Ravasz Laszlo Bevezetesevel[.] *Franklin-Tarsulat Kiadasa. n.d. [ca. 1930]*. First edition thus? 8vo, xxii+[i]+332pp.(misprinted "232" following upon a misprinting of the last several pages: pp. 230, 231, and 232, and then after p. 329), half-title, frontispiece portrait plate of Milton by "Franklin-T," introduction on Milton by Irta Ravasz Laszlo, half-title before the text, original purple cloth (spine a bit faded, lacking front blank, former ownership name written neatly in blue ink across first page of introduction), Milton's name in gilt at center of front cover, gilt-decorated spine with gilt lettering, thick brown endpapers. A nice copy of this Hungarian translation of Milton's epic into Hungarian verse. According to Don Bell, my book-scout friend from whom I obtained this copy, the page numbering mix-up at the end of the book "Must have been some mix-up in the prewar Hungarian printshop—anyway, it makes it a unique copy!" Uncommon.

1372. PARADISE LOST A Poem In Twelve Books The Author John Milton[.] *[London:] The Cresset Press[.] MDCCCCXXXI*. Large 4to, xii+442+[1]pp., half-title, first appearance of twelve engraved illustrations by D. Galanis, one for each book, text of the second edition, colophon on last leaf.

[together with]

1373. PARADISE REGAIN'D A Poem In Four Books The Author John Milton[.] *[London:] The Cresset Press[.] MDCCCCXXXI*. Large, slim 4to, 88+[1]pp., half-title, first appearance of four engraved illustrations by D. Galanis, one for each book, text of the first edition, colophon on last leaf. Together, 2 volumes, original cream buckram, gilt lettering on spine, edges untrimmed. A very fine set with sixteen full-page wood engravings and four engraved head- and tailpieces by D. Galanis, title page and woodcut initial letters designed by Anna Simons, printed on Batchelor handmade paper under the supervision of Bernard Newdigate. No. 147 of 195 numbered sets printed at the Shakespeare Head Press. Franklin, *Private Presses*, p. 148; Ransom, *Selective Check Lists*, p. 8, #22.

One of Ten Special Copies Printed on Vellum by Cresset Press and Bound in Full Morocco

1374. Variant of Preceding. **PARADISE LOST** A Poem In Twelve Books The Author John Milton[.] *[London:] The Cresset Press[.] MDCCCCXXXI*. Bound with **PARADISE REGAIN'D** A Poem In Four Books The Author John Milton[.] *[London:] The Cresset Press[.] MDCCCCXXXI*. 2 volumes in one. Thick, large 4to, xii+442+[1]pp.+88+[1]pp., half-title each volume, first appearance of sixteen full-page wood engravings and four engraved head-and tailpieces by D. Galanis, title page and woodcut initial letters designed by Anna Simons, printed at the Shakespeare Head Press under the supervision of Bernard Newdigate on vellum, handsomely bound in full brown morocco over heavy boards, covers and spine elaborately gilt-decorated, thick raised bands, inner and outer dentelles tooled in gilt, a.e.g. Housed in an equally handsome foldover protective box, half brown morocco and cream canvas over thick boards, with gilt-lettered spine and thick raised bands, green velvet lining inside. A splendid copy of one of the major publications of the period. No. 5 of only 10 copies printed on vellum and elegantly bound and housed. This special copy has been a part of the collection virtually from the beginning and will remain with the collector. Ransom, *Selective Check Lists*, p. 8, #22; Franklin, *Private Presses*, p. 148.

One of the sixteen full-page wood engravings by D. Galanis printed at the Shakespeare Head Press on vellum for the 1931 Cresset Press edition of *PL & PR* on vellum, one of 10 copies only [No. 5], this at the outset of Book IV: "him there they found / Squat like a Toad, close at the eare of Eve." See #1374.

PL [London:] The Cresset Press, 1931. [Bound With] *PR* [London:] The Cresset Press, 1931. 2 volumes in one. Thick, large 4to, handsomely bound in full brown morocco over heavy boards. One of 10 copies only [this No. 5] printed on vellum, elegantly bound and housed in a handsome foldover protective box. See #1374.

1374A. (Cross-listing) [PARADISE LOST] THE MANUSCRIPT OF MILTON'S PARADISE LOST BOOK I Edited by Helen Darbishire[.] *Oxford[:] At The Clarendon Press[,] 1931.* Forty collotype reproductions of the manuscript. See main listing under *Manuscript of Milton's Paradise Lost.*

1375. [JOHN MILTON'S PARADISE LOST Arranged And Edited By G. M. Davis, B.A. Formerly Senior English Mistress Cheltenham Ladies' College[.] *London[:] G. Bell & Sons, LTD, n.d. [ca. 1931].* Small 8vo, vii+139pp., half-title, double black border around title page, introduction, "Notes" and "Exercises" at the end, original blue cloth, front cover and spine lettered in black.

1376. PARADISE LOST, BOOKS I. AND II. By John Milton Edited With Introduction And Notes By M. Macmillan . . . *Macmillan And Co., Limited[,] St. Martin's Street, London[,] 1932.* Slim 8vo, xxix+54pp.+[87pp.—unpaginated—notes]+[3]+[2]pp., half-title, introduction, extensive notes and appendix ("Instances Of Figures Of Speech, Etc., In *PL*") after the text, original red cloth (a little rubbed, spine faded), front cover decorated in blind and lettered in black, spine lettered in black. A good copy with a leaf advertising "Macmillan's English Classics" bound in at end. The first edition thus was published in 1887; the second in 1891; the third in 1893 (also listed here).

1377. MILTON[.] PARADISE LOST Edited By A. W. Verity, M.A. Volume I Text / Volume II Introduction, Notes, Etc. *Cambridge[:] At The University Press[,] 1934-1936.* 2 volumes. Fourth edition thus. 8vo, 362+lxxii+750pp. (pagination beginning with p. 366 after Roman numeral pages in volume 2), half-title each volume, text in volume 1, "Preface," "Introduction[:] Life of Milton," "Notes," "Glossary," and "Indexes" in volume 2, original green cloth (volume 2 a bit rubbed), spines lettered in gilt with decorative emblem at bottom and gilt rules at top and bottom. A very nice set. The first edition thus was published in 1910; the second edition thus "with some changes" in 1921 (also listed here); it was reissued in two volumes ("for the convenience of students") in 1929 and reprinted in 1934–36—both sets listed here.

1378. JOHN MILTON PARADISE LOST[.] Edited by Merritt Y. Hughes[,] Associate Professor of English, University of California[.] *Doubleday, Doran & Company, Inc. Garden City[,] New York[.] (1935).* First edition thus. 8vo, lvi+412pp., half-title, frontispiece portrait plate reproducing Milton portrait by W. Dolle, emblem of the press on title page, "Chronology," "Introduction," "Bibliography," facsimile reproduction of (1674) second edition title page before poem, notes at bottom of page, original blue cloth (earlier owner's name on fly-leaf), gilt device with the initials "DD" on front cover, spine lettered in gilt with gilt trim. A very nice copy in a fresh and crisp publisher's binding, with original printed publisher's wrappers (frayed along edges with small pieces missing at top and bottom of spine), reproducing Milton portrait by Dolle in blue on front cover, with a listing of editions in "The Doubleday-Doran Series In Literature" on back cover. Reprint editions appeared variously after this publication (see copies following), with an index included in the second and subsequent editions.

1379. JOHN MILTON PARADISE LOST[.] Edited by Merritt Y. Hughes[,] Professor of English, University of Wisconsin[.] *Doubleday, Doran, & Company, Inc. Garden City[,] New York[.] n.d. (1935).* Second edition. 8vo, lvi+422pp., half-title, frontispiece portrait plate reproducing Milton portrait by Dolle, emblem of the press on title page, "Chronology," "Introduction," "Bibliography," facsimile reproduction of (1674) second edition title page before poem, notes at bottom of page, "Index" at the end, original blue cloth (spine worn), gilt device with the initials "DD" on front cover, spine lettered in gilt with gilt trim (faded). The index is new with this edition. An okay copy with bookplate and signature of Milton scholar Maurice Kelley.

1380. JOHN MILTON PARADISE LOST[.] Edited by Merritt Y. Hughes[,] Professor of English, University of Wisconsin[.] *The Odyssey Press, Inc., New York[.] (1935).* Sixth edition. 8vo, lvi+422pp., half-title, frontispiece portrait plate reproducing Milton portrait by Dolle, emblem (possibly of the press) on title page, "Chronology," "Introduction," "Bibliography," facsimile reproduction of (1674) second edition title page before poem, notes at bottom of page, "Index" at the end, original blue cloth (a bit worn), spine decorated and lettered in gilt. A fair copy with the signature of Milton scholar Maurice Kelley on fly-leaf. This is the first time that the "Odyssey Press Series In Literature" is referred to, replacing "Doubleday Doran Series In Literature."

1381. JOHN MILTON PARADISE LOST[.] Edited by Merritt Y. Hughes[,] Professor of English, University of Wisconsin[.] *The Odyssey Press, Inc., New York[.] (1935).* Tenth edition through thirtieth edition (lacking thirteenth, nineteenth, and twenty-ninth editions). Each as preceding. Twenty-second edition, with Odyssey Press review label ("This book is submitted for examination with a view to its adoption for class use") tipped in on front pastedown. Laid in: Odyssey Press card offering the book "for your consideration as a basic textbook for your classes."

Signed by the Artist-Illustrator

1382. PARADISE LOST AND PARADISE REGAIN'D By John Milton with an Introduction By William Rose Benét and Illustrations by Carlotta Petrina. *San Francisco: Printed for the Members of The Limited Editions Club by John Henry Nash[,] 1936.* First edition thus. Folio, xiii+441pp., first appearance of illustrations by Carlotta Petrina, half-title for *PR*, printed in Cloister Lightface type by John Henry Nash, original one-half linen cloth, decorated marbled paper over boards, printed paper label on spine with red line border, fore- and bottom edges untrimmed. A fine copy in publisher's slipcase (the case being rather worn). The Limited Editions Club was founded in 1929. One of a numbered edition of 1,500 copies, signed by the artist-illustrator.

1383. PARADISE LOST By John Milton Edited with Notes by James Holly Hanford[,] Western Reserve University[.] *New York[:] Thomas Nelson & Sons[,] 1936[.]* First edition thus. 8vo, [ii]+472pp. (pagination beginning with p. 167), half-title, notes at bottom of the page, original blue cloth (a little rubbed, some pencil notations throughout, former owner's name on pastedown), spine lettered in gilt. A good copy.

1384. PARADISE LOST A Poem By John Milton. *The Text Of The First Edition Prepared For Press By J. Isaacs And Printed At The Golden Cockerel Press [Waltham Saint Lawrence, England.] MDCCCXXXVII (1937).* First edition thus. Folio, 378+[2]pp., title page in red and black from a woodcut by Robert Gibbings, first appearance of thirty-eight wood-engraved illustrations by Mary Groom, type designed by Eric Gill, decorated half-title for each book, "The Verse And The Argument" added at the end with half-title, original one-half black morocco, marbled paper over boards, the marbled paper designed by Sydney Cockerell, spine lettered in gilt, raised bands, t.e.g., others untrimmed, bound by Zaehnsdorf. A very fine copy in original open fleece-lined, black cloth slipcase (worn). Groom's illustrations are considered some of the finest emanating from the Golden Cockerel Press, and in Pertelote 119 the press challenges: "We dare any expert printer to find fault with our presswork in this book." No. 17 of 200 numbered copies. Huckabay 150.

1385. PARADISE LOST By John Milton With The Illustrations By William Blake Printed In Color For The First Time And With Prefaces By Philip Hofer And John T. Winterich[.] *New York • The Heritage Press[,] (1940).* First edition thus. 8vo, xx+[6]+311+[1]pp., half-title, first appearance in full color of frontispiece illustration plate and eight other illustration plates by William Blake, half-title for *PL*, original silvery gray cloth, maroon morocco label with gilt lettering and gilt trim on front cover and again on spine, red speckled edges. A fine, tall copy (7 ½" × 10 ¼"), in publisher's maroon paper slipcase. Laid in: "The Heritage Club Sandglass," four-page foldover newsletter, number 12L, entitled "Let The Artist Starve!," "Issued Monthly To The Members Of The Heritage Club 595 Madison Avenue, New York 22," describing Blake's life and his illustrations of Milton's *PL*, Milton's life and poem, and this edition, including its type, paper, and binding. This is a different newsletter from that laid in the following edition from the Heritage Press. "The special contents of this edition are copyright 1940 by The Heritage Press for The George Macy Companies, Inc." (verso of title page). Blake completed two sets of illustrations of *PL*: one set of twelve, with one illustration for each book, completed in 1807 and now in the Huntington Library, first published in 1906 by the Lyceum Press (copies listed here). The other set of nine illustrations, completed in 1808 and now in the Boston Museum of Fine Arts, first published in this edition by the Heritage Press.

1386. Variant of Preceding, original cream brown cloth (a bit rubbed), red morocco label with gilt lettering and gilt trim on front cover, orange morocco label (a bit faded) with gilt lettering and gilt trim on spine, red speckled edges. A good, tall copy (7 ½" × 10 ½") in variant publisher's binding, in publisher's red paper slipcase (a bit worn), with a different statement on verso of title page from that in preceding edition: "The special contents of this edition are copyright 1940 by The Heritage Press." The first printing in color of these illustrations of *PL* by Blake.

1387. PARADISE LOST By John Milton With The Illustrations By William Blake Printed In Color For The First Time And With Prefaces By Philip Hofer And John T. Winterich[.] *New York • The Heritage Press[,] (1940).* First edition thus—club edition. 8vo, xx+[6]+311+[1]pp., half-title, frontispiece illustration plate and eight other illustration plates after William Blake in full color, original silvery gray cloth, red morocco label with gilt lettering and gilt trim on front cover and again on spine, red endpapers, plain white edges. A fine copy in a variant format, smaller than the preceding editions by about ¼", without the note on last page, and without the red speckled edges, as in the preceding edition, with variances in binding: red endpapers and t.e. red. Laid in: "The Heritage Club Sandglass," four-page foldover newsletter, number IIR:40, entitled "The Cosmic Imagination," "Issued Monthly To The Members

Of The Heritage Club Avon, Connecticut 06001," describing Blake's life and his illustrations for Milton's *PL*, Milton's life and poem, and this edition, including its type, paper, and binding. This is a different newsletter from that laid in the earlier edition entitled "Let The Artist Starve!" and issued for "Members Of The Heritage Club 595 Madison Avenue, New York 22."

1388. PARADISE LOST AND OTHER POEMS[.] John Milton. Edited, with Introduction by Maurice Kelley[.] *Published for the Classics Club by Walter J. Black • Roslyn, New York[.] n.d. (1943)*. First edition thus. 8vo, xx+386pp., half-title, initials of the Classics Club on title page, half-title for "John Milton," introduction, facsimile of "Song from *Comus* in Milton's own hand . . . Trinity College, Cambridge," original cream cloth, gilt-decorated small red insignia of the Classics Club on front cover, red label on spine with gilt lettering and decorative black and gilt trim, yellow endpapers, t.e. red. A very good, fresh copy, near mint.

1389. Variant of Preceding. A fine copy in near mint condition, in original brown dust wrappers.

1390. Variant of Preceding. A fine copy in original cellophane dust wrappers. Laid in: the "Classics Club Bulletin" regarding this edition of *PL*, a four-page foldover with a reproduction of Munkacsy's *The Blind Milton Dictating Paradise Lost to His Daughters*.

1391. WILLIAM BLAKE: PARADISE LOST. *New York, London: An American Studio Book, Published by Studio Publications, 1947*. First (and possibly only) edition thus. Folio, nine individual folio sheets (13 ¼" × 10 ½" on sheets measuring 17" × 13") reproducing in full color the illustrations by William Blake for *Paradise Lost*, in publisher's printed brown covering wrapper, with one of Blake's illustrations reproduced on front cover. Rendered by Albert Carman for American Studio Books with a foreword by Henry P. Rossiter, Curator of Prints, Museum of Fine Arts, Boston. A very nice copy. Scarce.

1392. JOHN MILTON PARADISE LOST BOOKS I. AND II. Edited By A. W. Verity[.] *Cambridge: At The University Press[,] 1947*. Small 8vo, lxxii+174pp., half-title ("Pitt Press Series"), half-title before each book, original red paper over boards (a bit rubbed), front cover and spine lettered in black. The first edition thus was published in 1893, the second thus in 1894; variously reprinted after that.

1393. PARADISE LOST[.] John Milton[.] *Published by Henry Regnery Company for The Great Books Foundation[,] Chicago, Illinois[,] (1949)*. First edition thus. 8vo, 314pp., decorative printer's device on title page, paperback, printed stiff paper wrappers (spine a bit age-browned, some age-browning throughout), front cover and spine printed in blue with "Great Books Foundation" printed in white within decorative blue piece on front cover, brief biography

Satan Watching Adam and Eve after Blake, Book IV, *PL*, (1808), *An American Studio Book*, New York and London, 1947. See #1391.

Temptation of Eve after Blake, Book IV, *PL*, 1808, ibid. See #1391.

Expulsion From Eden after Blake, Book IV, *PL*, 1808, ibid. See #1391.

of Milton printed in blue on inside front cover and carried over to inside back cover. A good copy.

1394. MILTON'S PARADISE LOST *Abridged & Edited By D. C. Somervell[,] MA[.] [London:] J. M. Dent & Sons Ltd[,] (1949).* 16mo, 192pp., half-title ("The Kings Treasuries Of Literature General Editor Sir A. T. Quiller Couch[.] London: J. M. Dent & Sons Ltd."), unsigned frontispiece portrait sketch of a youngish Milton with long curly hair surrounded by an elaborate border in art nouveau style with crown at the center at the top, title page with a similar elaborate border in art nouveau style with crown at the center at the top, "Made in Great Britain at The Temple Press, Letchworth, Herts[.] First published (in this edition) 1920[;] Last reprinted 1949" on verso of title page, decorative headpieces, commentary at the end, original green cloth (a bit rubbed, bottom half of outer edges of front and back covers deteriorated with loss of green cloth, spine ends a little worn, some markings in pencil with heavy marginal notations in pencil throughout Books I and II, earlier ownership names in pen on front endpapers), spine lettered in gilt with decorative gilt trim at top and bottom, small emblem of head at lower right corner of front cover, gold emblem on front endpapers, incorporating "This Book Belongs To" within the emblem on the front pastedown and "A Good Book Is The Precious Life-Blood Of A Master Spirit[,] Milton" within the emblem on the fly-leaf. Books I and II are provided complete, with the other books quoted from and summarized sometimes with reasons given for the quotation cited. First published in this edition in 1920; original edition by Dent first published in 1897 (also listed here with further editions cited, along with clarification given regarding the early editions by Dent and the sorting out of the first, second, and third editions). Uncommon.

1395. PARADISE LOST AND SELECTED POETRY AND PROSE[.] John Milton[.] Edited With An Introduction By Northrop Frye[.] *New York [And] Toronto: Rinehart & Co., Inc., (1951).* First edition thus. 8vo, xxxviii+601+[1]pp., half-title, "Chronological Table Of Events In Milton's Life," "Bibliographical Note," "Table Of Contents," half-title for various of the works including *PL*, "Selected Poetry And Sonnets," and "Selected Prose," paperback, printed green paper wrappers (a bit worn, pages age-browned), advertisement leaf at end. A fairly good copy of this first edition paperback edited with an introduction by Northrop Frye. The second edition thus was published in 1953; variously reprinted thereafter—all listed here.

1396. JOHN MILTON (1608-1674) PARADIS PERDU Introduction, traduction et notes de Pierre Messiaen[,] Agrege De L'Universite[,] Professeur A L'Institut Catholique De Paris[.] Tome I/II[.] Collection Bilingue Des Classiques Etrangers[.] *MCMLI & MCMLV Aubier, Editions Montaigne, Paris.* 2 volumes. First edition thus. 12mo, half-title and title page each volume, 293+[3]pp., +318+[2]pp., forty-nine-page introduction in French, volume 1, English and French texts printed side by side (English on verso and French on recto), half-title and reproduction of 1674 second edition title page before poem, volume 1, half-title before poem, volume 2, "Notes" and "Table Des Matieres" with colophon on verso at the end of each volume, original printed orange wrappers (a bit faded, volume 1), with a listing of "Litterature Anglaise" on the back, edges untrimmed. A nice set with bookplate in each volume. See companion volume, *Paradis Reconquis (Paradise Regained)*, published in 1955.

1397. JOHN MILTON PARADISE LOST BOOKS I. AND II. Edited By A. W. Verity[.] *Cambridge[:] At The University Press[,] 1952.* Third edition, revised and re-set. Small 8vo, lxxiv+172pp., half-title ("Pitt Press Series"), "Note To First Edition," "Note To Second Edition," and "Note To Third Edition," lengthy introduction, half-title before each book, "Notes," "Appendix," "Glossary," and "Index" at the end, original red paper over boards (occasional pencil markings), front cover and spine lettered in black. A nice copy. The first edition of this Pitt Press series edition edited by A. W. Verity was published by the Cambridge University Press in 1893 with the second edition in 1894 (both listed here); it was variously reprinted thereafter, including 1902 (copy in the collection, a repeat of this edition, not listed) and 1910 (copy in the collection, a repeat of this edition, not listed), this being the "Third Edition, Revised and Re-set" (verso of title page). Uncommon.

1398. PARADISE LOST AND SELECTED POETRY AND PROSE[.] John Milton[.] Edited With An Introduction By Northrop Frye[.] *New York [And] Toronto: Rinehart & Co., Inc., (1953).* Second edition thus. 8vo, xxxviii+601+[1]pp., half-title, "Chronological Table Of Events In Milton's Life," "Bibliographical Note," half-title for various of the works, paperback, printed green paper wrappers (a bit rubbed, name in ink inside of front cover). The first edition thus was published in 1951 (also listed here); variously reprinted thereafter (see copies listed here).

1399. PARADISE LOST [In] CLASSICS OF THE CHRISTIAN TRADITION: THE BIBLE [AND] JOHN MILTON. Edited By Dorothy Bethurum, Connecticut College [And] Randall Steward, Brown University[.] *Chicago[,] Atlanta[,] Dallas[,] New York [And] San Francisco: Scott, Foresman And Company[,] (1954).* First edition thus. Tall 8vo, [vi]+393pp., foreword, contents, half-title for each work, half-title and preface for Milton, original half black cloth, blue and white checkered paper over boards (slightly frayed at the corners), front cover and spine lettered in red, orange endpapers. A nice copy. Included are excerpts from the Bible and the whole of *PL*, with a critical introduction discussing Milton.

1400. JOHN MILTON PARADISE LOST BOOKS III. AND IV. Edited By A. W. Verity[.] *Cambridge: At The University Press[,] 1954*. Small 8vo, lxxii+141+[1]pp., half-title ("Pitt Press Series"), lengthy introduction, half-title before each book, "Notes," "Appendixes," "Glossary," and "Index" at the end, original red paper over boards (occasional pencil markings), front cover and spine lettered in black. A nice copy. The first edition of this Pitt Press series edition edited by A. W. Verity was published by the Cambridge University Press in 1894, with the second edition in 1895 (also listed here); it was variously reprinted thereafter: "1899, 1902, 1911, 1916, 1927, 1934, 1940, 1953, 1954" (verso of title page). Surprisingly uncommon.

1401. JOHN MILTON PARADISE LOST BOOKS VII. AND VIII. By The Late A. W. Verity[.] *Cambridge[:] At The University Press[,] 1954*. Third edition thus. Small 8vo, lxxii+106pp., half-title, lengthy introduction, half-title before each book, "Notes," "Appendixes," "Glossary," and "Index" at the end, original red paper over boards, front cover and spine lettered in black. A very nice copy. The "First Edition [thus was published in] 1895[;] Reprinted 1902, 1954 [copy here]" (verso of title page). Uncommon.

1402. PARADISE LOST. Milton[.] number 13 fourth year[.] *The Great Books Foundation Chicago[,] (1956)*. First edition thus. 8vo, 314pp., half-title with a brief bio of Milton on verso, paperback, original printed contrasting green paper wrappers (bit rubbed) with depiction of Satan climbing a cliff on front cover. "Reprinted from the edition of Houghton, Osgood, Riverside Press, Cambridge, 1888." Volume 7 of eight-volume paperback set (see following), no. 13 of 16 parts forming the "Fourth Year Course," the only part with a volume to itself.

1403. Variant of Preceding. Volume 7 of eight-volume paperback set here, No. 13 of 16 parts forming the "Fourth Year Course" for "The Great Books Foundation Chicago, 1956," the only part with a volume to itself, the eight-volume paperback set in its original box, the whole in generally good condition and rather well-preserved for this kind of publication.

1404. JOHN MILTON PARADISE LOST BOOKS IX. AND X. Edited By A. W. Verity[.] *Cambridge: At The University Press[,] 1956*. Small 8vo, lxxii+166+[1]pp., half-title, lengthy introduction, half-title before each book, "Notes," "Appendixes," "Glossary," and "Index" at the end, original red paper over boards, front cover and spine lettered in black. A very nice copy. The first edition of this Pitt Press Series edition edited by A. W. Verity was published by the Cambridge University Press in 1896; it was reprinted in "1913, 1918 (also listed here), 1935, 1937, 1952, 1956" (verso of title page). Uncommon.

1405. PARADISE LOST [BOOK I] By John Milton With Notes and Questions by Gordon H. Bailey[,] York Mills Collegiate Institute, North York[.] Authorized by the Minister of Education for Ontario[.] *The Macmillan Company of Canada Limited[,] Toronto[,] (1958)*. First edition thus. [In] **POEMS FOR UPPER SCHOOL 1958-59**[.] [Including] **PARADISE LOST . . . THE TITANIC** By E. J. Pratt...*The Macmillan Company of Canada Limited[,] Toronto[,] (1958)*. First edition thus. 8vo, 76pp., "Notes" on each poem at the end, original printed stiff gray paper wrappers (several ex-library stamps, one on title page, extensive notes and marginalia), front cover blocked in red with embossed lettering and with decorative red border trim.

1406. PARADISE LOST AND SELECTED POETRY AND PROSE[.] John Milton[.] Edited With An Introduction By Northrop Frye[.] *New York [And] Toronto: Rinehart & Co., Inc., (1958)*. 8vo, xxxviii+601+[1]pp., half-title, "Introduction" (dated "June, 1950"), "Chronological Table Of Events In Milton's Life," "Bibliographical Note," "Table Of Contents," half-title for various of the works, paperback, printed light green paper wrappers (a bit worn). The first edition thus was published in 1951; the second thus in 1953—both listed here; variously reprinted thereafter.

1407. PARADISE LOST. Read by Anthony Quayle. Directed by Howard O. Sackler. Book One, ll.1-end; Book Four, ll. 1-357, 358-588, 776-903, 917-end. *New York: Caedmon Publishers, (ca. 1958)*. 2 33 1/3 rpm LP records. First edition thus. LP recording in original folding slipcase, with reproduction of Matthew Leibowitz's illustration of *The Fall* and *The Expulsion from Paradise* in color on front cover. Records are near mint, as is the gatefold cover. Caedmon TC2008.

1408. PARADISE LOST AND SELECTED POETRY AND PROSE[.] John Milton[.] Edited With An Introduction By Northrop Frye[.] *Holt, Rinehart and Winston[,] New York[,] (1960)*. 8vo, xxxviii+601+[1]pp., half-title, "Introduction" (dated "June, 1950"), "Chronological Table Of Events In Milton's Life," "Bibliographical Note," "Table Of Contents," half-title for various of the works, paperback, printed light green paper wrappers. A good copy with former ownership signatures. The first edition thus was published in 1951; the second thus in 1953—both listed here; variously reprinted thereafter.

1409. JOHN MILTON EL PARAISO PERDIDO Traduccion del ingles por Dionisio San Juan Con un estudio biografico y critico por F. R. De Chateaubriand Notas de Addison, Saint-Maur y otros[.] *Coleccion Crisol Num. 187 (1960).* Cuarta edicion (on verso of title page). 16mo, 627pp., half-title, frontispiece portrait of a somewhat Spanish-looking Milton, signed "E. D.," "La Vida De Milton" with half-title, half-title before the poem, which is translated in prose, "Notas" at the end, original limp green leather (a bit rubbed at corners and at top and bottom of spine, pencil notations on back endpapers and occasionally throughout), central emblem in blind on covers with "Crisol" and emblem of the press from title page in blind beneath the emblem, spine lettered and decorated in silver, decorated green endpapers. A nice copy. See 1890 Spanish translation (copy listed here) with references to other earlier Spanish translations; see, too, copy of fifth edition in 1963.

1410. PARADISE LOST BOOKS IX AND X Edited With An Introduction And Notes By E. M. W. Tillyard[,] Litt.D., F.B.A. *George G. Harrap & Co. Ltd[.] London[,] Toronto[,] Wellington[,] Sydney[,] (1960).* First edition thus. 16mo, 172pp., half-title ("Harrap's English Classics"), small emblem of the press on title page, lengthy introduction, extensive notes on each book at the end, original orange cloth, front cover and spine lettered in blue. A nice copy.

1411. PARADISE LOST BOOKS I AND II Edited With An Introduction By E. M. W. Tillyard[,] Litt.D., F.B.A. formerly Master of Jesus College, Cambridge[,] And With Noted By Phyllis B. Tillyard[,] M.A.[,] Girton College, Cambridge[.] *George G. Harrap & Co. Ltd[.] London[,] Toronto[,] Wellington[,] Sydney[,] (1961).* Third edition thus. 16mo, 210+[1]pp., half-title ("Harrap's English Classics"), frontispiece illustration plate of "The 'Great Consult' Of The Devils by Doré," small emblem of the press on title page, lengthy introduction, extensive notes on each book at the end, followed by a leaf with a map of Palestine on recto and a map of Jerusalem on verso, original dark orange cloth (some underlinings in pencil), front cover and spine lettered in black. A nice copy. The first edition thus was published in 1956, the second in 1960, neither of which is in the collection.

1412. PARADISE LOST[,] SAMSON AGONISTES[,] LYCIDAS[.] John Milton[.] Newly Annotated and with a Biographical Introduction by Edward Le Comte[.] *A Mentor Classic Published By The New American Library[,] (December, 1961).* First edition thus. 8vo, 414+[2]pp., half-title, paperback, printed stiff paper wrappers (a bit rubbed, name in ink on half-title) with an illustration of three angels in color on front cover (signed "M. Glaser"), title different on front cover and spine ("Paradise Lost and other poems John Milton") from that on title page, advertisement leaf bound in at end. A very good copy which "presents a text in modern spelling (but the British rather than the American form of such words as *honour* and *theatre* is adhered to)." The second edition thus was published in 1964 (also listed here); the third edition thus in 1965 (copy in the collection, a repeat of this edition, not listed); the first Canadian edition in 1965 (also listed here); the fifth edition thus in 1965/1966 (copy in the collection, a repeat of this edition, not listed); and variously thereafter; a revised edition was published in 1981 (also listed here) and variously thereafter.

1413. Variant of Preceding, with gilt foil blind-stamped "A New Edition" tipped onto front cover.

1414. PARADISE LOST A Poem in Twelve Books[.] John Milton[.] A New Edition Edited by Merritt Y. Hughes[,] University of Wisconsin[.] *New York[:] Printed by The Odyssey Press[,] (1962).* First edition thus. 8vo, lx+324pp., "First Printing of New Edition" on verso of title page, preface, "A Chronology Of The Main Events In Milton's Life," bibliography, several textual illustrations (including Milton's Universe, Eden, and a facsimile of the second edition title page), notes at bottom of page, "The Life of Milton (1694) By Edward Phillips" reprinted at the end after the poem, paperback, printed charcoal gray stiff paper wrappers (name stamped on half-title). Good copy. Variously reprinted: ca. 1968 (possible second edition thus), ca. 1970, 1981, and 1998 editions (each listed here).

1415. PARADISE LOST BOOKS I AND II[.] Milton[.] Edited By F. T. Prince[.] *Oxford University Press[,] (1962).* First edition thus. 8vo, 205pp., half-title, introduction, commentary on each book, notes at bottom of page, several appendices, original blue patterned paper boards, front cover and spine lettered in blue. A nice copy. Prince's edition was reprinted in 1968, 1970, 1972, 1975, 1978 (twice), 1980, and 1986 (copy listed here).

1416. [PARADISE LOST] [In] THEODORE HAAK, F.R.S. (1605-1690) THE FIRST GERMAN TRANSLATOR OF PARADISE LOST By Pamela R. Barnett[.] *1962 Mouton & Co. • 'S-Gravenhage.* First edition thus. 8vo, 274pp., two title pages (the main one and another facing: "Anglica Germanica British Studies In Germanic

Languages And Literatures Edited By Leonard Forster[,] A. T. Hatto[,] E. L. Stahl[.] III[.] 1962 Mouton & Co. • 'S-Gravenhage"), portrait plate of Haak, two foldout copies of Haak's German translation with English lines translated and notes, foldout of Haak's family tree, original blue cloth, spine lettered in gilt, printed publisher's wrappers in a protective plastic cover. A nice copy. Scarce.

Included is an introduction and fifteen chapters on Haak, including a chapter on "The subsequent history of the manuscript *Verlustigtes Paradeiss* and Berge's printed version" and "A Critical discussion of *Das Verlustigte Paradeiss*," along with an appendix containing the first three books and fifty lines of Book IV (all that have been preserved) of Haak's verse translation, *Das Verlustigte Paradeiss*, followed by a bibliography and index. While only three books and fifty lines of Theodore Haak's translation have been preserved, Aubrey suggests that Haak translated "halfe" of *PL*. E. G. von Berge's translation of *PL* into German in 1682, *Das Verlustigte Paradeiss* (Zerbst, 1682), was "largely dependent upon Haak for his translation of at least the first three books" (Aubrey, p. 166), although Haak's translation was largely unknown (even to the eighteenth-century critics Gottsched and Bodmer) until the twentieth century. Haak's primary "motive in translating *PL* was quite simply to make the great English poem available in German form, not to contribute to the enrichment of his national literature" (p. 169).

1417. PARADISE LOST[,] PARADISE REGAINED[,] SAMSON AGONISTES[.] John Milton[.] With a New Introduction by Harold Bloom[.] *Collier Books[,] New York, N.Y. (1962).* First edition thus. 8vo, 350+[2]pp., title page printed across two pages with the seal of the press at bottom of left page, "First Collier Books Edition 1962" on verso of title page, paperback (a bit used, name in ink on fly-leaf), printed stiff paper wrappers with a reproduction of an unsigned illustration in brownish tint on front cover. A good copy with two pages of advertisements bound in at the end.

1418. PARADISE LOST AND SELECTED POETRY AND PROSE[.] John Milton[.] Edited With An Introduction By Northrop Frye[.] *Holt, Rinehart and Winston[,] New York[,] Chicago[,] San Francisco[,] Toronto[,] London[,] (1963).* 8vo, xxxviii+601+[1]pp., half-title, "Introduction" (dated "June, 1950"), half-title for various of the works, paperback, printed stiff paper wrappers with reproduction of a Blake illustration on front cover. A good copy (with either a variant orange spine or one quite faded) with signature of Milton scholar Maurice Kelley in pen on title page. The first edition thus was published in 1951; the second thus in 1953—both listed here.

1419. EL PARAISO PERDIDO Traduccion del ingles por Dionisio Sanjuan[,] Con un estudio biografico y critico por F. R. De Chateaubriand[,] Notas de Addison, Saint-Maur y otros[.] *Coleccion Crisol Num. 187[.] (1963).* Quinta edicion (verso of title page). 16mo, 627pp., half-title, frontispiece portrait ("Grabado por W. Faithorne Biblioteca Nacional • Paris"), small emblem of the press at bottom of title page ("Printed in Spain" on verso), "Notas" and "Indices" at the end, original limp green leather, lined design and emblem of the press in blind on covers, spine decorated in a lined design in silver with silver lettering, decorated green endpapers, printed publisher's wrappers with a sketch in outline of a fallen angel in green on front cover, green ribbon marker. A nice copy, printed entirely in Spanish, with a Spanish prose translation of *PL*. See copy of 1960 fourth edition listed here.

1420. PARADISE LOST BOOK IV[.] Edited With Introduction And Notes By M. Macmillan, B.A. (Oxon., D.Litt. *London[:] Macmillan & Co Ltd[,] New York • St. Martin's Press[,] 1963.* 8vo, half-title, xxxi+89+[4]pp., "Notes" and "Index" at the end, original red cloth (a few marginal notes in ink in a neat hand, additional notes in ink in the same neat hand on back pastedown, former owner's name in ink in the same neat hand on fly-leaf), front cover and spine lettered in black, with emblem in black incorporating "Macmillan's English Classics" in a scroll at bottom of front cover. A good copy with four pages of advertisements bound in at the end. "First Edition 1895[;] "Reprinted 1897, 1908, 1921, 1931, 1943, 1949, 1953, 1955, 1960, 1961, 1962, and 1963 [this copy]" (verso title page). Somehow I never managed to find or come across copies of the earlier editions.

1421. PARADISE LOST BOOKS I AND II[.] Edited with Introduction and Commentary by B. Rajan, M.A. PH.D. (Cantab) Sometime Fellow of Trinity College, Cambridge[;] Professor of English, Delhi University[.] *Asia Publishing House[,] New York[,] (1964).* First edition thus. 8vo, xliv+115pp., half-title ("Literary Perspectives No. 3"), notes at bottom of page, original blue cloth (slightly faded along upper edges and on spine), spine lettered in gilt. A good copy. Scarce.

1422. PARADISE LOST[,] SAMSON AGONISTES[,] LYCIDAS[.] John Milton[.] Newly Annotated and with a Biographical Introduction by Edward Le Comte[.] *A Mentor Classic Published By The New American Library[,] (April, 1964).* Second edition thus. 8vo, 414+[2]pp., half-title, paperback, printed stiff paper wrappers (a bit dirtied, name on half-title with inscription on verso) with an illustration of three angels in color on front cover (signed "M. Glaser"), title different on front cover and spine ("Paradise

Lost and other poems John Milton") from that on title page, advertisement leaf bound in at end. The first edition thus was published in 1961 (also listed here with further editions cited).

1423. PARADISE LOST By John Milton[.] *Dolphin Books[.] Doubleday & Company, Inc. Garden City, New York[.] n.d. [ca. 1965].* First edition thus. 8vo, 280pp., paperback, printed stiff paper wrappers (a bit rubbed) with an illustration of *Satan Burning in Hell* on front cover drawn for this edition by Colleen Browning. A good copy. Scarce.

1424. PARADISE LOST[,] SAMSON AGONISTES[,] LYCIDAS[.] John Milton[.] Newly Annotated and with a Biographical Introduction by Edward Le Comte[.] *A Mentor Classic Published by The New American Library Of Canada Limited, (1965).* First Canadian edition thus. 8vo, 414+[2]pp., half-title, paperback, printed stiff paper wrappers (a bit rubbed) with an illustration of three angels in color on front cover (signed "M. Glaser"), title different on front cover and spine ("Paradise Lost and other poems John Milton") from that on title page, advertisement leaf bound in at end. A good copy. "Mentor Books are published in Canada by The New American Library of Canada Limited[,] Toronto, Ontario[,] Printed In Canada[,] Cover Printed In U.S.A." (verso of title page). The first edition thus was published in 1961 (also listed here with further editions cited).

1425. JOHN MILTON (1604-1674) PARADIS PERDU Introduction, traduction et notes de Pierre Messiaen (Agrée De L'Université[,] Professeur A L'Institut Catholique De Paris[.] Collection Bilingue Des Classiques Etrangers[.] *Aubier, Editions Montaigne, Paris[,] (1965).* 2 volumes. First edition thus. 8vo, 293+[2],+318+[2]pp., half-title and title page each volume, original printed stiff orange and brown wrappers glazed over (a bit rubbed, occasional marginal notations in pencil), small reproduction of Milton at age sixty-two on front cover of each volume, edges untrimmed. A very good set with the English text appearing on the left and the French translation on the right. Uncommon.

1426. O PARAISO PERDIDO John Milton Traducao em prosa de Conceicao G. Sotto Maior[.] 50 ilustracoes de Gustave Doré[.] *(Rio de Janeiro, Brasil:) Edicoes De Ouro, (1966).* First edition thus. Small 8vo, 414+[2]pp., half-title, brief life of the poet with facsimile reproduction of first edition title page of *Paradise Lost*, illustration plates after Doré, unsigned illustration sketch within the text in the upper right-hand corner of each argument at the beginning of each book, original printed stiff paper wrappers (a bit used, former owners name in ink on title page), front cover lettered in red, purple, and black with a reproduction in color of "Chagall—Eva amaldicoada por Deus" at the bottom, reproduction of portrait of "John Milton por J. Richardson" in light blue within a red border on back cover, spine lettered in red and green. A good copy with advertisement leaf bound in at the end. Uncommon.

1427. JOHN MILTON FROM PARADISE LOST BOOKS 3 & 4 read by Tony Church[,] Michael Redgrave[,] Richard Johnson [and] Prunella Scales[.] *Argo Record Company Limited[,] 113 Fulham Road[,] London SW3, n.d. [ca. 1966].* First edition thus. LP recording in original printed wrapper within original printed slipcase, black-and-white reproduction of Blake illustration (*Satan Watches Adam and Eve*) on front cover, summary of Books III and IV with selections from Samuel Johnson, Samuel Taylor Coleridge, and T. S. Eliot on back cover. "Recorded in association with The British Council and Oxford University Press[;] directed by George Rylands" (back cover). Placed within: printed text of excepts read from Books III and IV, "London: Oxford University Press In Association With The British Council[,] 1966. This Selection British Council 1966. Printed In Great Britain." The record, slipcase (RG 463), and text within are all in very good condition (the record and text within appearing to be unused and near mint).

1428. PARADISE LOST[,] SAMSON AGONISTES[,] LYCIDAS[.] John Milton[.] Newly Annotated and with a Biographical Introduction by Edward Le Comte[.] *A Mentor Classic Published By The New American Library, New York And Toronto[;] The New English Library Limited, London[.] n.d. [ca. 1966].* Sixth edition thus. 8vo, 414+[2]pp., half-title, paperback, printed stiff paper wrappers (lower spine joint bumped) with an illustration of three angels in color on front cover (signed "M. Glaser"), title different on front cover and spine ("Paradise Lost and other poems John Milton") from that on title page, advertisement leaf bound in at the end. A nice copy. Gift from Milton scholar Anthony Low, with his stamp in blind on half-title. The first edition thus was published in 1961 (also listed here with further editions cited).

1429. PARADISE LOST[,] PARADISE REGAINED[,] SAMSON AGONISTES[.] John Milton[.] With A New Introduction By Harold Bloom[.] *Collier Books[,] New York[.] Collier-Macmillan LTD., London[.] (1967).* Fifth edition thus. 8vo, 350pp., half-title, paperback (a bit used, a few underlinings, some notations in ink in a neat hand on final blank), printed stiff paper wrappers with a reproduction of Satan being thrown out of heaven by Lynn Sweat in blue tint on front cover. The first edition thus was published in 1962 (also listed here with further editions cited).

1430. PARADISE LOST[,] SAMSON AGONISTES[,] LYCIDAS[.] John Milton[.] Newly Annotated and with a Biographical Introduction by Edward Le Comte*[.] A Mentor Classic Published By The New American Library, New York And Toronto[;] The New English Library Limited, London[.]* n.d. [ca. 1967]. Seventh edition thus. 8vo, 414+[2]pp., half-title, original boards (a bit rubbed, variant binding from preceding editions) with an unsigned illustration of three angels in color on front cover, title different on front cover and spine ("Paradise Lost and other poems John Milton") from that on title page, advertisement leaf (revised) bound in at the end. A nice copy. The first edition thus was published in 1961 (see copies listed here with further editions cited).

1431. PARADISE LOST 1667[.] John Milton[.] A Scolar Press Facsimile*[.] The Scolar Press Limited[.] Menston, England[.]* 1968. First Scolar edition, first state. 4to, printer's emblem of the Scolar Press on title page, "Note" between title page and first facsimile page, unpaginated facsimile reproduction, original green cloth, gilt emblem of the Scolar Press on front cover, spine lettered in gilt, printed publisher's wrappers reproducing an illustration by Blake on front cover (*The Downfall of the Rebel Angels*). A nice copy. Facsimile reproduction of the 4to first edition. John Shawcross shared with me that the "first state" is "easily recognized because it does not have the 'Note' on the copies used for replacement pages," but only information about the initial publication of *PL*, the variant title pages being "reproduced in an Appendix along with the new preliminary matter which Simmons added in 1668, perhaps to spur the lagging sales." Shawcross further shared that "there are textual differences which are not indicated" and that "Both volumes are incompetent since they do not identify the basic copy used (it is apparently a fifth title-page issue 1669), don't identify all the pages that are replaced, and some copy references are in error." Scarce.

1432. Variant of Preceding. PARADISE LOST 1667[.] John Milton[.] A Scolar Press Facsimile*[.] The Scolar Press Limited[.] Menston, England[.]* 1968. First Scolar edition, second state; first paperback edition thus. 4to, unpaginated facsimile reproduction, printer's emblem of the Scolar Press on title page, "Note" between title page and first facsimile page, unpaginated facsimile reproduction, paperback, original printed wrappers (a bit rubbed) reproducing an illustration by Blake on front cover (*The Downfall of the Rebel Angels*). A nice copy with my name and note given me by Earl Miner in 1972, and with Miner's bookplate.

Facsimile reproduction of the 4to first edition. Unlike the "first state" preceding, with "the "Note" on "lagging sales," the "Note" here identifies the copies used for replacement pages first and then adds the information in the "Note" in the "first state." John Shawcross further shared with me: "For textual differences, you might compare sig. Hlv (Book 2), which Scolar says is a substitute for BL copy 684.d.30 (issue 5). But in Edition 1 you'll see 'standerd' (line 986) and 'Havook' (line 1009), both States 1 and 2, but in Edition 2 you'll see 'Standerd' and 'Havock' (both State 3). The note says that the title page is a substitution from BL G.11558, which is a fifth issue (1669–1), but in the Appendix it gives the first title page as BL C.14.a.9. It says that Scolar's copy is a copy of the sixth title page, that is 1669–2. It also says in the note that 'the sheets of the poem—which are identical in all copies of the first edition, apart from the inevitable press corrections and minor alterations made within the impression—are to be found bound up with six different title pages. . . . ' Pretty obviously the 'identical' is very wrong; there are frequently two and three states of a page, which the 'apart . . . impression' does not adequately cover, and even more significant is the resetting of sigs. z (in Book 7) and Vv (in Book 10). The reset z and Vv were necessary for 1669–2 because sheets of those signatures had run out: the first printing appears in all issues except for 1669–2. Yet Scholar in both editions gives the first printing although it says it implies (by the title page notation) that their copy is 1669–2. It does not list these signatures as having replacements. There's something curious also for sigs. O1v and O3v. Both Scolars give State 1 for O1v but State 2 for O3v (no substitutions are indicated). That's possible because the various issues use different states inconsistently, but this is a strange case of mixture of states within a signature gathering. There is also a review of the Scolar in *Seventeenth-Century News*, but again it's to the second edition without any hint that there was a first edition."

1433. PARADISE LOST A Poem in Twelve Books[.] John Milton[.] A New Edition Edited by Merritt Y. Hughes[,] University of Wisconsin*[.] New York[:] Printed by The Odyssey Press[.]* n.d. [ca. 1968]. 8vo, lx+324pp., reproduction of Faithorne portrait, preface, bibliography, several textual illustrations (including Milton's universe, Eden, and a facsimile of the second edition title page), notes at bottom of page, "The Life of Milton (1694) By Edward Phillips" reprinted at the end after the poem, paperback, printed gray stiff paper wrappers. A good copy. The first edition thus was published in 1962 (also listed here); it was variously reprinted thereafter, including this edition here.

1434. PARADISE LOST AND PARADISE REGAINED[.] John Milton. *Airmont Publishing Company, Inc. 22 East 60th Street • New York 10022[.]* (1968). First edition thus. 8vo, 350+[2]pp., vignette sketch of a long-haired young

Milton at head of introduction by Frederic B. Tromly, notes by David Masson, paperback (a bit rubbed), printed stiff yellow and tan paper wrappers with an unsigned illustration in color of the *Fall of the Angels* on the front cover, advertisement leaf at end. A nice copy with "95¢" at the top of front cover. The collection also has a variant paperback in a variant publisher's binding with brown, rather than yellow, across the top, and the price of "$1.95," rather than "95¢."

1435. PARADISE LOST AND PARADISE REGAINED[.] John Milton[.] Edited By Christopher Ricks[.] The Signet Classic Poetry Series General Editor: John Hollander[.] *Published By The New American Library, New York And Toronto[;] The New English Library Limited, London[,] (February, 1968)*. First edition thus. 8vo, 396+[4]pp., "First Printing, February, 1968" on verso of title page, "Introduction," "Chronology," half-title for each poem, paperback, printed stiff paper wrappers (used copy with pencil markings), unidentified and unsigned photograph illustration on front cover, four pages of advertisement at end. A fair copy. See 1970 (copy in the collection, a repeat of this edition, not listed here), ca. 1975 (copy in the collection, a repeat of this edition, not listed), 1982, 1993, and ca. 1994 editions thus, the last three listed here and with revised bibliographies.

1436. Variant of Preceding. **PARADISE LOST AND PARADISE REGAINED[.]** John Milton. Edited By Christopher Ricks. The Signet Classic Poetry Series General Editor: John Hollander. *A Signet Classic from New American Library Times Mirror New York and Scarborough, Ontario[;] The New English Library Limited, London[,] (February, 1968)*. First edition thus with variant title page. 8vo, 396+[4]pp., paperback, printed stiff paper wrappers, unidentified and unsigned photograph illustration on front cover, four pages of advertisement at end. A nice copy.

1437. JOHN MILTON PARADISE LOST With a critical and biographical profile of the author by James H. Hanford, author of *John Milton, Englishman*[.] The World's Great Classics[.] *Grolier Enterprises Corp. Danbury, Connecticut[.] n.d. [ca. 1968]*. Together with **PARADISE REGAINED** (without reference on title page). First edition thus. 8vo, xxviii+443pp., half-title, title printed within thick black lines on title page with a vignette impression of a falling angel entirely in black at the center, small square emblem of the press with the letter "G" at the bottom of the page, "Set in Grolier Ultratype" (verso of title page), half-title for *PL*, half-title for *PR* (without mention on the title page), original imitation crushed maroon leather, emblem of crossed feather quills in gilt at lower corner of front cover, spine lettered in gilt with title ("Paradise Lost • Paradise Regained Milton") lettered in gilt against an imitation red leather background with broad gilt rules within narrower gilt lines in imitation of raised bands, emblem of crossed feather quills in gilt in lower panel, "Grolier" lettered in small gilt letters at the bottom, mauve endpapers, a.e.g. A fine, possibly large paper copy, handsomely printed, in an attractive imitation crushed maroon leather binding, virtually mint. The "critical and biographical profile of John Milton by James H. Hanford" is "Reprinted from The Encyclopedia Americana, 1968 copyright." Similar to the undated "Grolier Ultra Edition" listed here published about this time, ca. 1968, by "Grolier Incorporated" in New York and to the undated "Watts Ultratype Edition," likewise published about this time, ca. 1968, by "Franklin Watts, Inc. A Division Of Grolier Incorporated" also in New York (each edition, unlike here, making reference to *PR* on the title page). See statement regarding "Ultratype" on publisher's wrappers of the "Watts Ultratype Edition" listed here.

1438. Variant of Preceding, original cream buckram, front cover and spine lettered in silver ("Milton—Paradise Lost") against a red background repeating from the title page the figure of an angel falling in gilt at the center of the front cover, small square emblem of the press with the letter "G" in gilt at the bottom of the spine, mauve endpapers, a.e.g. A very finely printed edition, "set in Grolier ultratype," in a variant publisher's binding, near mint.

1439. PARADISE LOST • PARADISE REGAINED[.] John Milton[.] With a critical and biographical profile of the author by James H. Hanford, author of *John Milton, Englishman*[.] The World's Great Classics[.] *Grolier Incorporated[,] New York[,] n.d. [ca. 1968]*. First edition thus (variant issue). 8vo, xxviii+443pp., half-title ("The World's Great Classics"), emblem of crossed feather quills at top of title page, small triangular emblem of the press at the bottom of the page, "Set in Grolier Ultratype" on verso of title page, half title before each poem, original imitation crushed black leather, emblem of crossed feather quills in silver at lower corner of front cover, spine lettered in silver with titles ("Paradise Lost • Paradise Regained Milton") lettered in silver against a green backdrop with broad silver lines within narrower silver lines in imitation of raised bands, emblem of crossed feather quills in silver in lower panel, "Grolier" lettered in small silver letters at the bottom, green endpapers, t.e.g. A very nice copy in a handsome binding. Similar to the earlier undated "Grolier Ultra Edition" published about this time, ca. 1968, by "Grolier Enterprises Corp." in Danbury, Connecticut (making no reference to *Paradise Regained* on the title page) and to the undated "Watts Ultratype Edition," also published about this time, ca. 1968, by "Franklin Watts, Inc. A Division Of Grolier Incorporated." in New York (making reference to *PR* on the title page). See statement regarding "Ultratype" on publisher's wrappers of the "Watts Ultratype Edition."

1440. PARADISE LOST AND PARADISE RE-GAINED[.] John Milton[.] With a critical and biographical profile of John Milton by James H. Hanford, author of *John Milton, Englishman*[.] *A Watts Ultratype Edition*[.] *Franklin Watts, Inc. A Division Of Grolier Incorporated*[,] *575 Lexington Avenue*[,] *New York, New York 10022*[,] *n.d.* [ca. 1968]. First edition thus (variant issue). 8vo, xxviii+443pp., half-title with a list of "Watts Ultratype Editions" listed on verso, half-title before each poem, original black speckled gray cloth, front cover and spine lettered in black, printed publisher's wrappers in varying green colors lined in black and lettered in black and white, the publisher's wrappers (slightly rubbed) in a protective plastic cover. A very nice copy. The "critical and biographical profile of John Milton by James H. Hanford" is "Reprinted from The Encyclopedia Americana, 1968 copyright." Apparently the series of "Watts Ultratype Editions" began being published about this time (ca. 1968). According to the text on the inside of the front flap (where the original price is printed as "$5.95"): "The American College Dictionary defines the word 'ultra' as meaning 'going beyond what is usual or ordinary.' Research has proved that ULTRATYPE can be read faster, easier and with great comprehension. Each volume . . . contains an encyclopedic article about the author and his works. Each volume is library bound in buckram, especially reinforced for long and loving use, and is printed on specially made paper that will keep its color and flexibility for more than a century." Similar to the undated "Grolier Ultra Edition" listed earlier published about this time, ca. 1968, by "Grolier Enterprises Corp." in Danbury, Connecticut (making no reference to *PR* on the title page), and to the undated "Grolier Ultra Edition" listed earlier published about this time, ca. 1968, by "Grolier Incorporated" in New York (making reference to *PR* on the title page).

1441. PARADISE LOST[,] **SAMSON AGONISTES**[,] **LYCIDAS**[.] John Milton[.] Newly Annotated and with a Biographical Introduction by Edward Le Comte[.] *A Mentor Book from, New American Library Times Mirror New York and Scarborough, Ontario*[;] *The New English Library Limited, London*[,] *n.d.* [ca. 1968]. 8vo, 414+[2]pp., half-title, paperback, printed stiff paper wrappers (a bit rubbed, pages a little age-browned) with an illustration of three angels in color on front cover (signed "M. Glaser"), title different on front cover and spine ("Paradise Lost and other poems John Milton") from that on title page, advertisement leaf (revised) bound in at end. A fairly good copy. The first edition thus was published in 1961 (also listed here with further editions cited).

1442. PARADISE LOST[.] John Milton[.] Edited With An Introduction By William G. Madsen[,] Washington University[.] *Modern College Library Editions*[.] *New York*[:] *The Modern Library*[,] (1969). First edition thus. 8vo, xl+344pp., half-title, decorative leaves on title page with emblem of the press in lower right corner, chronology, bibliography, facsimile reproduction of second edition title page, decorative leaves on title page repeated as decorative head-trim at the outset of each book, notes at bottom of page, paperback, printed white and navy blue stiff paper wrappers. A nice copy. Gift from Milton scholar Maurice Kelley in 1971 when he and I were both teaching at Princeton University.

1443. Another copy, as preceding, although this copy belonged to Milton scolar Scott Elledge, signed by Elledge on half-title with marginal notes by Elledge—most in pencil, some in pen—and some underlinings by him throughout.

1444. PARADISE LOST BOOKS IX AND X[.] Milton[.] Edited By R. E. C. Houghton[,] Emeritus Fellow and Tutor of St. Peter's College, Oxford[.] *Oxford University Press*[,] *1969*. First edition thus. 8vo, 244pp., half-title, "Commentary" on each book, "Select Criticism," notes at bottom of page, paperback, printed stiff paper wrappers with orange center within black border on each cover. A nice copy.

1445. PARADISE LOST[,] **PARADISE REGAINED AND SAMSON AGONISTES**[.] John Milton. Introduction By Richard Eberhart. *Doubleday & Company, Inc. Garden City, New York*[,] (1969). First edition thus by Doubleday & Company. 8vo, 395pp., half-title, double black rule on title page, "Nelson Doubleday, Inc." on verso of title page, half-title repeated before introduction by Eberhart in which he bemoans that Milton has become confined to specialists and "is not an 'in' poet now," facsimile of the 1674 second edition title page of *PL* before the poem, facsimile of the 1671 first edition title page of *PR* before the poem, original blue cloth, spine lettered in gilt, decorated printed mauve publisher's wrappers (a bit rubbed). A very good copy.

1446. PARADISE LOST[,] **PARADISE REGAINED AND SAMSON AGONISTES**[.] John Milton. Introduction By Richard Eberhart. *International Collectors Library*[.] *Garden City, New York*[,] (1969). First edition thus, International Collectors Library. 8vo, a reproduction as part of "International Collectors Library," 395pp., half-title, double black rule on title page, "Nelson Doubleday, Inc." on verso of title page, half-title repeated before introduction by Eberhart (as in preceding copy), facsimile of the 1674 second edition title page of *PL* before the poem, facsimile of the 1671 first edition title page of *PR* before the poem, original imitation blue leather, front cover richly decorated in gilt with an elaborate gilt border and central gilt design, spine also richly decorated in gilt with gilt lettering, fore-edge untrimmed. An attractive copy.

1447. Variant of Preceding, brown crushed leather, gilt rules on front cover with decorative central gilt emblem, spine decorated and lettered in gilt, brown endpapers, t.e.g., fore-edge untrimmed. A lovely copy. Laid in: original brochure, printed in red and black, advertising this edition as part of "International Collectors Library," "a publishing program dedicated to the preservation of the immortal masterworks of the past . . . clothed in bindings truly worthy of their imperishable contents—in this instance, in what is called a 'replica' of 'The Marie Antoinette Binding.'"

1448. PARADISE LOST [In] POEMS IN ENGLISH With Illustrations By William Blake. John Milton[.] *1926 at the Nonesuch Press 16 Great James Street London[.] Republished, 1970 Scholarly Press, 22929 Industrial Drive East, St. Clair Shores Michigan 48080[.]* Reprint edition of Nonesuch 1926 edition (also listed here). 8vo, 359pp., decorative border trim on title page, illustrations by William Blake reproduced in black and white, "Notes on Blake's Illustrations To Paradise Lost by Geoffrey Keynes" at end, original green cloth, spine lettered in gilt, green endpapers. A fine copy.

1449. PARADISE LOST A Poem in Twelve Books[.] John Milton[.] A New Edition Edited by Merritt Y. Hughes[,] University of Wisconsin[.] *New York[:] Printed by The Odyssey Press[.] n.d. [ca. 1970].* 8vo, lx+324pp., "The Bayfordbury Portrait" of Milton "Traditionally Attributed To William Faithorne" as frontispiece, "A Chronology Of The Main Events In Milton's Life," bibliography, several textual illustrations (including Milton's universe, Eden, and a facsimile of the second edition title page), "The Life of Milton (1694) By Edward Phillips" reprinted at the end after the poem, paperback, printed red stiff paper wrappers with an unsigned illustration for *PL* (*Satan Cast out of Heaven*) reproduced on front cover. A fine copy. The first edition thus was published in 1962 (also listed here with further editions cited).

1450. PARADISE LOST AND SELECTED POETRY AND PROSE[.] John Milton[.] Edited With An Introduction By Northrop Frye[.] *Holt, Rinehart and Winston, Inc. New York • Chicago • San Francisco • Atlanta • Dallas • Montreal • Toronto • London • Sydney[.] n.d. [ca. 1970].* Tall 8vo, xxxviii+601+[1]pp., half-title, paperback, printed stiff paper wrappers (small puncture and small scratch on back cover) with an unsigned abstract illustration possibly of the archangel Michael on front cover. A nice copy fresh and clean throughout. The first edition thus was published in 1951 in a smaller 8vo format than the present edition (also listed here with further editions cited).

1451. PARADISE LOST[,] SAMSON AGONISTES[,] LYCIDAS[.] John Milton[.] Newly Annotated and with a Biographical Introduction by Edward Le Comte[.] *A Mentor Book from, New American Library[.] Times Mirror[.] New York and Scarborough, Ontario[:] The New English Library Limited, London[.] n.d. [ca. 1970].* 8vo, 414+[2]pp., half-title, paperback, printed stiff paper wrappers with orange trim at the top (variant binding from the earlier editions) and the price $1.25 with an illustration of three angels in color on front cover (signed "M. Glaser"), title different on front cover and spine ("Paradise Lost and other poems John Milton") from that on title page, advertisement leaf (revised) bound in at the end, yellow edges. A nice copy of this later reprint paperback edition. The first edition thus was published in 1961 (copy listed here with further editions cited).

1452. Variant of Preceding. Paperback, printed stiff paper wrappers with no color trim at the top (variant from the earlier bindings) and the price $2.25, with an advertisement leaf (revised) bound in at the end. A nice copy in a variant binding.

1453. PARADISE LOST AND OTHER POEMS[.] John Milton. Edited, with Introduction by Maurice Kelley[.] *Published for the Classics Club by Walter J. Black, Inc. • Roslyn, N.Y. (1971).* Second edition thus. 8vo, xx+386pp., half-title, initials of the Classics Club on title page, half-title for "John Milton," introduction, facsimile of "Song from *Comus*, in Milton's own hand . . . Trinity College, Cambridge," original cream cloth, gilt-decorated small red insignia of the Classics Club on front cover, red label on spine with gilt lettering and gilt rules and surrounded by black trim with decorative gilt trim, yellow endpapers, t.e. red. A fine copy. The first edition thus was published in 1943 (also listed here).

1454. MILTON'S PARADISE LOST[.] Screenplay for Cinema of the Mind by John Collier[.] *Alfred A. Knopf[,] New York[.] 1973.* First edition thus. Large 8vo, xiii+143+[1]pp., half-title, title page in black with white lettering and wood-engraved borders, "The Apology," decorative illustrative wood-engraved borders by Carol Iselin, half-title for *PL*, stage directions and scenic descriptions in white lettering on black paper interspersed throughout, original black cloth, spine lettered in gilt, printed publisher's wrappers in a protective plastic cover with an illustration of the expulsion in color wrapping around from the front cover to the back, cover design by R. Scudellari. A very nice copy. "The audacity of John Collier's 'screen-play' of Milton's great epic poem is matched only by its success: here is a startlingly alive, euphonious, and visual piece of work, an act of highest love. The extraordinary images of Milton's hideous and radiant monsters, of burning hell and glowing paradise, of archetypal human beings trapped in the pregnant situations of fable—all contribute to the realization of Collier's intention: not, presumptuously, to improve Milton, not even to dare to 'amplify' his work, but rather to celebrate him. The twentieth century here salutes the seventeenth; the master fantasist, Collier, uses the characteristic medium of our time to bring us closer to the greatest art of another epoch" (statement on front flap). The first edition thus was published simultaneously in paperback (following copy). Scarce.

1455. Variant of Preceding. MILTON'S PARADISE LOST[.] Screenplay for Cinema of the Mind by John Collier[.] *Alfred A. Knopf[,] New York[.] 1973*. First paperback edition thus. Large 8vo, xiii+143+[1]pp., half-title, title page in black with white lettering and wood-engraved borders, "The Apology," decorative illustrative wood-engraved borders by Carol Iselin, half-title for *PL*, paperback, stage directions and scenic descriptions in white lettering on black paper interspersed throughout, printed stiff paper wrappers (a bit rubbed) with an illustration of the expulsion in color wrapping around from the front cover to the back, cover design by R. Scudellari. A nice copy. The first edition thus was published simultaneously in hardback (preceding copy). Scarce.

1456. JOHN MILTON PARADISE LOST AND OTHER POEMS With an Introduction and Appreciation by David Thomson[.] Illustrations by William Strang[.] *Distributed by Heron Books. n.d. [ca. 1973]*. First edition thus by Heron Books. Tall 12mo, xiii+385+[2], half-title printed in red and black (with "Books That Have Change Man's Thinking" "A Collection distributed by Heron Books" printed on verso), frontispiece portrait of Milton after Faithorne, title page in red and black with small depiction of a heron as emblem of the press at the bottom, "Picture research by Andrew Lawson" on verso of title page, "Editor's Foreword," "Introduction," illustration after William Strang for Books I, II, IV, VII, IX, X, XI, and XII of *PL*, thirty-page "Appreciation by David Thomson" printed on tan paper with illustrations at the end, half crushed dark green calf, speckled gold imitation leather over slightly padded boards, front cover attractively decorated in gilt, spine richly decorated in gilt within the panels and lettered in gilt near the top, gold-patterned dark green endpapers, yellow silk ribbon marker. A fine copy with contemporary presentation inscription (dated 1973) on fly-leaf.

The "Appreciation by David Thomson" at the end is profusely illustrated with numerous reproductions of Milton portraits, title pages, personages, and places associated with Milton, including Milton at ages ten and twenty-one; the clay bust of Milton in Christ's College, Cambridge; *Milton Dictating to His Daughters* (after Munkacsy, without attribution); Ludlow Castle; the exterior of Milton's cottage at Chalfont St. Giles; the interior of Milton's cottage; Oliver Cromwell; Charles I; St. Giles's Church, Cripplegate; and much more. The illustrations by Strang first appeared in an edition of *PL* published in 1905 in London by George Routledge and Sons and in New York by E. P. Dutton and Co. (also listed here with further information about Strang). Among the "Other Poems" included are *PR*, *SA*, *C*, and *L*.

1457. PARADISE LOST: BOOKS IX-X[.] John Milton. Edited by J. Martin Evans. *Stanford University, California[.] [Quotation from W. H. Auden] Cambridge at the University Press[,] 1973*. First edition thus. 16mo, x+189pp., half-title, preface, "Topics" for each book, paperback, printed green stiff paper wrappers with a reproduction of Medina's illustration for Book IX on front cover. Very good copy. Part of "The Cambridge Milton for Schools and Colleges," a twelve-volume series published by the Cambridge University Press between 1972 and 1976 under the general editorship of John Broadbent.

1458. ASIMOV'S ANNOTATED PARADISE LOST[.] Text By John Milton[.] Notes By Isaac Asimov[.] *Doubleday & Company, Inc., Garden City, New York[,] 1974*. First edition thus. Thick 12mo, 761pp., half-title, with half-title repeated before poem, "Index Of Biblical Quotations" and an index of "General Information" at the end, original light gray cloth, spine lettered in gilt against a green background with additional lettering in green beneath and gilt at the bottom, green endpapers, fore-edge untrimmed, printed green publisher's wrappers in a protective plastic cover with an illustration of Adam and Eve on either side of a tree, done in a science fiction or embryonic style, the bodies facing away from each other in front of the tree ("Jacket By John Cayea"). A fine copy, virtually mint. Included at the end, with half-title, is *PR*. "Dr. Asimov manages to find every allusion that could possibly cause confusion. By merely turning the page confusion becomes clarity. *PL* is no longer unapproachable. With Isaac Asimov's guiding hand, a whole new audience can discover Milton and enjoy Paradise Lost as few ever thought it could be" (back inside flap of wrapper). Uncommon and highly sought after because of Asimov more than Milton.

1459. **PARADISE LOST; BOOKS VII-VIII[.]** John Milton. Edited by David Aers[,] University of East Anglia, Norwich[;] Mary Ann Radzinowicz[,] Girton College, Cambridge with additional material . . . [Quotation from Wallace Stevens] *Cambridge University Press[,] (1974).* First edition thus. 16mo, 146pp., half-title, preface, introduction to each book, "Appendix to Book VII," "Resources to Book VIII," paperback, printed blue stiff paper wrappers with a reproduction of details from "The angels of creation" by Edward Burne-Jones (from a stained-glass window) on front cover. A very good copy. Part of "The Cambridge Milton for Schools and Colleges," a six-volume series published by the Cambridge University Press between 1972 and 1976 under the general editorship of John Broadbent.

1460. **PARADISE LOST[:] AN AUTHORITATIVE TEXT[,] BACKGROUNDS AND SOURCES[,] CRITICISM[.]** John Milton[.] Edited by Scott Elledge[,] Cornell University[.] *A Norton Critical Edition[.] W • W • Norton & Company • Inc • New York[,] (1975).* First edition thus. 8vo, xxix+546pp., half-title with advertisement for "Norton Critical Editions" on verso, emblem of the press on title page, "First Edition" on verso of title page, "Preface," "Introduction," half-title for "The Text of Paradise Lost," "A Note on the Text," and "Backgrounds And Sources" after the poem following by "Norton Important Concepts And Topics In *PL*," "Criticism: Modern And Earlier" and a "Selected Bibliography," paperback, printed stiff blue paper wrappers with reproduction of *Adam and Eve* by Lucas Cranach (1526) on light blue front cover. A nice copy. The first London edition thus was published in the same year; a second edition thus, revised, was published in 1993—both copies listed here.

1461. **PARADISE LOST[:] AN AUTHORITATIVE TEXT[,] BACKGROUNDS AND SOURCES[,] CRITICISM[.]** John Milton[.] Edited by Scott Elledge[,] Cornell University[.] *A Norton Critical Edition[.] W • W • Norton & Company • Inc • New York • London[,] (1975).* First London edition thus. 8vo, xxix+546pp., contents as preceding, paperback, printed stiff purple blue paper wrappers with reproduction of *Adam and Eve* by Lucas Cranach (1526) on dark blue front cover. A nice copy. The first edition thus was published in New York earlier in the same year (preceding copy).

1462. **PARADISE LOST: BOOKS V-VI[.]** John Milton. Edited by Robert Hodge[,] University of East Anglia, Norwich[;] Isabel G. MacCaffrey[,] Harvard University[.] [Quotation from Wallace Stevens and William Blake.] *Cambridge University Press[,] Cambridge[,] London • New York • Melbourne[,] (1975).* First edition thus. 8vo, 159pp., half-title, paperback, printed pink stiff paper wrappers with a reproduction of a detail from *Fall of the Rebel Angels* by Pieter Bruegel the Elder (1562) on front cover. A very good copy. Laid in: book review notice. Part of "The Cambridge Milton for Schools and Colleges," a six-volume series published by the Cambridge University Press between 1972 and 1976 under the general editorship of John Broadbent.

1463. **PARADISE LOST** By John Milton[.] With The Illustrations By William Blake And With Prefaces By Philip Hofer And John T. Winterich[.] *The Heritage Press[,] Norwalk, Connecticut[,] 1976.* Large 8vo, xx+[4]+311pp., half-title, nine illustration plates after William Blake reproduced in color, original decorated blue cloth, blue leather label with gilt lettering and gilt trim on spine. A fine copy, near mint, in original publisher's slipcase (nice). Reprint of the first Heritage Press edition published in 1940 (also listed here). Laid in: "The Heritage Club Sandglass," discussing Milton, Blake's illustrations, and this edition.

1464. **PARADISE LOST** By John Milton[.] With The Illustrations By William Blake And With Prefaces By Philip Hofer and John T. Winterich. The 100 Greatest Books Ever Written. Collector's Edition Bound in Genuine Leather. *The Easton Press[,] Norwalk, Connecticut[,] (1976).* First edition thus. Large 8vo, xx+[4]+311pp., half-title, first appearance of frontispiece portrait of Milton in color after Robert J. Lee, half-title for *PL*, nine illustration plates after William Blake in full color, original crushed orange leather over thick boards, covers and spine gilt-decorated according to a pattern with emblem repeated in gilt on covers and spine, raised bands, spine lettered in gilt, orange silk endpapers, a.e.g. A fine, handsome copy in mint condition. "This Collector's Edition is published by advance reservation exclusively for subscribers to The Easton Press collection of *The 100 Greatest Books Ever Written*. The frontispiece portrait was specially commissioned for this edition and, like the other special contents, is copyright 1976 by The Easton Press" (verso title page). "The text of this edition was planned by the New York designer John Fass, who has created a format that alludes typographically to the book style of the seventeenth and eighteenth centuries. The typeface is fourteen-point Caslon, which is based upon the designs drawn by William Caslon in 1720; the large headings are typical of that period. . . . The binding is in a high-quality leather, drawn over heavy boards and spine hubs and stamped in leaf with a pattern drawn exclusively for this edition. It is further enhanced with moire endleaves, edges coated with leaf, and a ribbon marker" (from "The Publisher's Preface").

1465. PARADISE LOST[.] John Milton[.] *Buccaneer Books[,] Cutchogue, New York[.] n.d. (ca. 1976).* 16mo, 280pp., half-title, double black rule on title page, original red buckram, spine lettered in gilt. A fine copy of a simple edition that contains only the text of *PL* and none of the usual editorial inclusions (such as introduction, notes, and bibliography).

1466. Variant of Preceding, original maroon cloth, spine lettered in gilt. A fine copy in a variant publisher's binding.

1467. PARADISE LOST. John Milton. Edited By Richard Bentley (1732)[.] *1976 Georg Olms Verlag[,] Hildesheim • New York[.]* Reprint edition. 4to, [xx]+[1]+399pp.+[16 unpaginated index], half-title, engraved portrait by Vertue (one of the two portraits in original edition, placed here before Book I) with Bentley's notes at bottom of page, original red cloth, front cover lettered in gilt, spine lettered in gilt against a black label with gilt rules. A nice copy. Reproduction of 1732 Bentley 4to edition (original edition listed earlier), described as follows on verso of title page: "Note[:] The present slightly reduced facsimile is reproduced from a copy in the possession of the Library of the University of Bonn. Errors in foliation have been retained."

1468. PARADISE LOST: BOOKS XI-XII[.] John Milton. Edited by Michael Hollington[,] University of East Anglia, Norwich with Lawrence Wilkinson[.] [Quotations from William Carlos Williams and Edwin Muir] *Cambridge University Press[,] Cambridge[,] London • New York • Melbourne[,] (1976).* First edition thus. Slim 16mo, 115pp., "Preface to the Cambridge Milton," appendix, paperback, printed gray stiff paper wrappers with a reproduction of a detail from Jacopo della Quercia's the expulsion—marble relief sculpture in Bologna—on front cover. A fine copy. Part of "The Cambridge Milton for Schools and Colleges," a six-volume series published by the Cambridge University Press between 1972 and 1976 under the general editorship of John Broadbent.

1469. [PARADISE LOST: BOOKS I-IV] RADI OS 01-04 [By] Ronald Johnson[.] With An Afterword By Guy Davenport[.] *Sand Dollar / Berkeley / 1977. John Milton.* First edition. Slim tall 8vo, 99pp., unpaginated, 87pp. poem+12pp. afterword+colophon leaf, original stiff green wrappers (a bit rubbed), front cover and spine lettered in black, silver, and red, reworked text of Milton's poem in red and black on inside front and back cover. A nice copy. This poetic interpretation features a unique approach of finding poetic meter by splicing the epic into separate words and reforming the poem into a new form. As Guy Davenport states in his afterword: "The poem we are reading is still Milton's, but sifted. The spare scattering of words left on the page continues to make a coherent poem, Milton *imagistre*. (Wordsworth and Blake did the same thing to the poem, except that they filled up the spaces again with their own words.) Strange and wonderful things happen on these pages." According to colophon: "This First Edition designed and with a cover by George Mattingly; text facsimile is from the 1892 (Crowell) edition of Milton [copies listed here], printed winter 1976–77 by Braun-Brumfield Inc." The reason for the text facsimile being that of the 1892 Crowell edition is because that is the text the poet "picked off a Seattle bookshop shelf" one day ("A Note And A Dedication"). Most probably printed in a limited edition. Uncommon.

1469A. (Cross-listing) PARADISE LOST [In] ENGLISH MINOR POEMS[,] PARADISE LOST[,] SAMSON AGONISTES[,] AREOPAGITICA With Twenty-Seven Water-Color Drawings By William Blake[.] A Limited Edition[.] *The Franklin Library[,] Franklin Center, Pennsylvania[,] 1978.* 8vo, 504pp., half-title, illustration plates in color by Blake for *NO* (drawn ca. 1808), *C* (drawn ca. 1801), and *PL* (drawn ca. 1807), crushed brown morocco over thick boards, richly decorated in gilt, a.e.g. A handsome edition "published by the Franklin Library exclusively for subscribers to The 25th Anniversary Limited Edition of The Great Books Of The Western World." See main listing under *English Minor Poems*.

1470. PARADISE LOST. John Milton. With the illustrations of Gustave Doré. *The Franklin Library[,] Franklin Center, Pennsylvania[.] n.d. (1979).* First edition thus. 8vo, 338pp., half-title on verso of frontispiece printed in blue with decorative trim, frontispiece illustration and other illustration plates by Gustave Doré, title page printed in blue and black with decorative trim, "Special contents © 1979 Franklin Mint Corporation" on verso of title page, half-title for *PL* printed in blue between two angelic figures (one of an archangel with sword and the other of Satan being hurled from heaven), half-title for each book printed in blue with decorative trim, headers printed in blue throughout, first initial letter of each book in blue, half green morocco, green cloth, covers and spine decorated with large gilt pieces and decorative gilt rules, spine lettered in gilt, raised bands, marbled endpapers, a.e.g., green silk ribbon marker. A fine copy. Doré's illustrations of *PL* first appeared in the mid-1860s (see 1865–66 set of parts and 1866 first book edition listed here).

1471. Variant of Preceding, similar to preceding, but a variant issue in a variant binding, full blue morocco, richly gilt-decorated covers and spine, spine lettered in gilt, raised bands, decorated blue endpapers, a.e.g. A fine copy in a variant binding with variant statement on verso of title page: "Special contents copyright © 1979 The Franklin Library" together with a brief biography of Doré and reference to the illustrations for the first edition being used for reproduction here on verso of title page. "The engravings in this volume are reproduced from a deluxe folio edition of *Milton's Paradise Lost* published in London, Paris, and New York, by Cassell, Petter, Galpin and Company, 1866 [see copy listed here]," a note that also does not appear in the preceding edition.

1472. PARADISE LOST. John Milton. With engravings from an edition of 1688. A Limited Edition. *The Franklin Library[,] Franklin Center, Pennsylvania[,] 1981*. First edition thus. 8vo, 360pp., half-title in red with small decorative piece in black, title page in red and black with red and black rules, facsimile reproduction of the frontispiece portrait of Milton by Robert White of the Faithorne portrait and of the illustrations that appeared in the 1688 edition of *PL*, half-title for each book with each half-title printed in red with small decorative piece in black beneath the lettering and with red and black rules, arguments printed with red headings, red initials, page numbers and rules at the top throughout, original red morocco, covers and spine richly decorated in gilt, spine lettered in gilt, raised bands, red silk endpapers over thick paper, a.e.g., red ribbon marker. A lovely copy in an elegant binding, in mint condition, with fine reproductions of the 1688 illustrations (see copies listed here of original 1688 edition). "This limited edition of Paradise Lost is published exclusively for subscribers to The Franklin Library collection The 100 Greatest Books of All Time" (printed on page after half-title and before frontispiece).

[together with]

1473. NOTES FROM THE EDITORS[.] PARADISE LOST By John Milton[.] From the limited edition collection, The 100 Greatest Books of All Time[.] *The Franklin Library[.] 1981 Franklin Mint Corporation[.]* Small 8vo, twenty-two-page pamphlet with reproductions of (1) Munkacsy's painting of *Milton Dictating to His Daughters*; (2) a portrait of Milton "from a seventeenth-century painting by William Faithorne" in "The Bettmann Archive"; (3) Milton at age ten; (4) Milton meeting Galileo in 1638 (from "The Bettmann Archive"); and (5) Chalfont St. Giles, red section headings throughout, original red stiff paper wrappers, front cover printed in white and black. A fine copy of a pamphlet on Milton intended to accompany the Franklin Mint publication of *PL*. Scarce.

1474. PARADISE LOST A Poem in Twelve Books[.] John Milton[.] A New Edition Edited by Merritt Y. Hughes[,] University of Wisconsin[.] *New York[:] Printed by The Odyssey Press[.] n.d. (1981)*. 8vo, lx+324pp., "A Chronology Of The Main Events In Milton's Life," bibliography, several textual illustrations (including Milton's universe, Eden, and a facsimile of the second edition title page), "The Life of Milton (1694) By Edward Phillips" reprinted at the end after the poem, paperback, printed red stiff paper wrappers with an unsigned illustration of *Satan Cast out of Heaven* reproduced on front cover. A good copy. The first edition thus was published in 1962 (also listed here with further editions cited).

1475. PARADISE LOST: BOOKS III - IV[.] John Milton. Edited by Lois Potter[,] University of Leicester[,] John Broadbent[,] University of East Anglia, Norwich[.] [Quotations from Dante and T. S. Eliot.] *Cambridge University Press[,] Cambridge[,] London[,] New York[,] New Rochelle[,] Melbourne[, And] Sydney[,] (1981)*. 16mo, 136pp., paperback, printed olive green stiff paper wrappers with details of the statues of Adam (on front cover) and Eve (on back cover) by Tilman Riemenschneider in the Mainfrankishes Museum, Wurzburg. A fine copy. Part of "The Cambridge Milton for Schools and Colleges," a six-volume series published by the Cambridge University Press between 1972 and 1976 under the general editorship of John Broadbent.

1476. PARADISE LOST[,] SAMSON AGONISTES[,] LYCIDAS[.] John Milton[.] Newly Annotated and with a Biographical Introduction by Edward Le Comte[.] Revised and Updated Bibliography[.] *A Mentor Book New American Library Times Mirror[.] New York and Scarborough, Ontario[,] (1981)*. Revised edition thus. 8vo, 414+[2]pp., half-title, paperback (with name, some underlinings, and a few marginal notations in pen), printed stiff paper wrappers with an illustration of three angels in color on front cover (signed "M. Glaser"), title different on front cover and spine ("Paradise Lost and other poems By John Milton") from that on title page, advertisement leaf (revised) bound in at end listing "Signet Classic Mentor Books." The first edition thus was published in 1961 (also listed here with further editions cited).

1477. PARADISE LOST AND PARADISE REGAINED[.] John Milton[.] Edited By Christopher Ricks[.] Revised and Updated Bibliography[.] The Signet

Classic Poetry Series General Editor: John Hollander. *A Signet Classic from New American Library Times Mirror[,] New York and Scarborough, Ontario[,] (1982)*. Revised edition thus. 8vo, 396+[4]pp., paperback, printed stiff paper wrappers with the *Fall of the Rebellious Angels* by Pieter Bruegel reproduced in color on front and back covers. A fine copy. The first edition thus was published in 1968 (also listed here with further editions cited).

1478. Variant of Preceding. **PARADISE LOST AND PARADISE REGAINED[.]** John Milton[.] Edited By Christopher Ricks[.] Revised and Updated Bibliography[.] *A Signet Classic[.] New American Library[,] New York And Scarborough, Ontario[,] (1982)*. Revised edition thus. 8vo, 396+[4]pp., similar to preceding copy with variant title page. A fine copy.

1479. PARADISE LOST John Milton[.] A Prose Rendition by Robert A. Shepherd, Jr. Illustrated by Rodney Nevitt[.] *The Seabury Press • New York[,] (1983)*. First edition. 8vo, ix+166, "Contents" (with a prose summary of each book), illustration for each book after Rodney Nevitt, original half blue cloth, tan paper over boards, front cover and spine lettered in gilt. A nice copy. The "Contents" contain summaries (as in "Arguments") for each book. The illustrations by Rodney Nevitt are modern black-and-white renditions for each book and appear to be reflective of the illustrations by Carlotta Petrina and Mary Groom in the 1930s. Scarce.

1480. Variant of Preceding, paperback, original printed stiff paper wrappers with an illustration of the creation of Eve from Adam on front cover, a small picture of Robert A. Shepherd on the back cover. A nice copy in a variant publisher's binding. First paperback edition thus. Scarce.

Signed by the Artist

1481. JOHN MILTON'S PARADISE LOST synopsized and with illustrations by Terrance Lindall[.] *Rodney Graphics[.]. Copyright 1983 Terrance Lindall[.]* First edition. 8vo, 44pp., color illustration plate for each book by Terrance Lindall, each full color plate tipped in, original tan cloth, spine lettered in gilt, green endpapers, printed black publisher's wrappers with full color plate after Terrance Lindall tipped in at the center of front cover. A nice copy, signed by the artist before the first illustration plate, with color illustrations of Milton's epic, synopsized here by the artist. "Terrance Lindall's fanciful illustrations, in slides and on canvas, are bound to arouse response and provoke thought in the many persons interested in *PL* and its subjects, and in surreal illustration generally" (Professor Thomas Clayton, University of Minnesota Department of English, in a comment on preliminary blank). Probably printed in a limited edition.

1482. PARADISE LOST. John Milton. With the illustrations of Gustave Doré. The Oxford Library of the World's Great Books[.] *Oxford University Press[.] (1984)*. First edition thus. 8vo, [iii]+[iii]+[iii]+338pp., half-title printed in blue with decorative trim in black, frontispiece illustration and other full-page illustrations by Gustave Doré, title page printed in blue and black with decorative trim, "Introductory message copyright © 1984 Oxford University Press, New York" and "Special contents copyright © 1979 Franklin Library" on verso of title page, half-title for *PL* printed in blue between two angelic figures (one of an archangel with sword and the other of Satan being hurled from heaven), half-title for each book printed in blue with decorative trim in black (as with general half-title), headers printed in blue throughout, first initial letter of each book in blue, original full blue leather over thick boards, covers richly tooled in gilt with raised central emblem in blind on front cover, spine decorated in gilt within the panels with gilt lettering and decorative gilt trim at top and bottom, raised bands, marbled blue endpapers, a.e.g., thick silver ribbon marker. A fine copy. "This Special Edition of *PL* was prepared for subscribers to The Oxford Library of the World's Great Books" (blank before frontispiece illustration). "The Franklin Library has been selected by the Oxford University Press as publishers of The Oxford Library Of The World's Great Books" (verso of title page). Also included on verso of title page is a brief biography of Doré and a reference to the book used for reproducing Doré's illustrations: "The engravings in this volume are reproduced from a deluxe folio edition of *Milton's PL* published in London, Paris, and New York, by Cassell, Petter, Galpin and Company, 1866" (also listed here).

1483. PARADISE LOST By John Milton With The Illustrations Of William Strang[.] A Limited Edition[.] *The Franklin Library[,] Franklin Center, Pennsylvania[,] 1984*. First edition thus. 8vo, 334pp., half-title, leaf with brief biography of Milton (signed "The Editors"), publisher's note, reproduction of Strang's frontispiece portrait of Milton, title page printed in blue with reproduction of Strang's illustration of Milton and his daughters, "Contents" with list of "Illustrations" on verso, half-title for the poem repeated before the text, half-title printed in blue for each book, reproduction of Strang's ten additional illustrations for each book, except Books III and VI, contemporary crushed blue morocco, covers richly decorated with gilt border trim, spine richly decorated in gilt within the panels and lettered in gilt within decorative gilt trim, raised bands, thick silk blue endpapers, blue silk ribbon marker, a.e.g. A fine book, virtually mint, splendidly printed and handsomely bound. "The twelve etchings by William Strang which illustrate this Franklin Library edition of PL were reproduced from an edition printed by Ballantyne, Hanson & Co., at the Ballantyne Press, Edinburgh, 1896, and limited to 150 copies [each illustration signed by the artist, see copy listed here]." "This limited edition of PL is published exclusively for subscribers to The Collector's Library of The World's Best-Loved Books" (leaf before frontispiece portrait).

1484. JOHN MILTON DAS VERLORENE PARADIES Mit Illustrationen von John Martin[.] *Rütten & Loening[,] Berlin, (1984)*. First edition thus? 8vo, 421+[3]pp., half-title ("John Milton *Das verlorene Paradies*[,] Herausgegeben von Günther Klotz"), photographic reproductions of illustrations by John Martin, Klotz's "Nachwort," dated April 1983, "Anmerkungen" at the end, published by Günther Klotz, original olive green cloth, emblem in black on front cover, spine lettered in black with small emblem in gilt at the top and bottom, dark brown endpapers, printed brown publisher's wrappers (a bit rubbed with two scuffed places on back cover), lettering in black and gilt on front cover and spine with a reproduction of Martin illustration on front cover. A nice copy of the German translation in verse by Bernhard Schuhmann ("Titel der englischen Originalausgabe *PL*[,] Ubertragen von Bernhard Schuhmann [1855]") on verso of title page.

1485. PARADISE LOST: A Poem In Twelve Books. John Milton. *(SAPE: Printed in Spain, 1985)*. First edition thus. 8vo, 253+[3]pp., half-title ("The Library Of English And World Literature"), original blue imitation leather, front cover lettered in gilt with large central decorative device in gilt, spine lettered in gilt against imitation red leather background with gilt rules, raised bands, nicely decorated with gilt devices in the panels, marbled endpapers. A cheaply printed edition in a fine binding. A nice copy.

1486. JOHN MILTON FROM PARADISE LOST [Read by Michael Redgrave, Tony Church, Prunella Scales, and Michael Hordern.] *Newman Books-On-Cassette. 1985 Licensed from London Records Ltd. 2 Cassettes*. First edition thus. In original 8vo printed foldover case (some shelf wear, minor wear on front cover) with reproduction of Blake illustration of Satan in color on front cover. "Recorded in association with the British Council and the Oxford University Press . . . Directed by George Rylands" (inside foldover cover). "The extracts selected deliver the essence of Milton's vision" in *PL* (back cover). Total playing time: 2 hours, 29 minutes. Distributed by Newman Communications Corporation. See 1966 LP recording by Tony Church, Michael Redgrave, Richard Johnson and Prunella Scales, "recorded [by Argo Record Company Limited] in association with the British Council and the Oxford University Press . . . Directed by George Rylands."

1487. PARADISE LOST: A Poem In Twelve Books. John Milton. *(SAPE: Printed in Spain, 1986)*. Second SAPE edition. 8vo, 253+[3]pp., half-title ("The Book Lovers Library"), original blue imitation leather, front cover lettered in gilt with large central decorative device in gilt, red leather label on spine with gilt lettering and gilt rules, raised bands, nicely decorated with gilt devices in the panels, marbled endpapers. A fine copy. The first edition thus with half-title ("The Library Of English And World Literature"), was published in a similar format and binding in 1985 (also listed here).

1488. PARADISE LOST[.] John Milton[.] Edited By Alastair Fowler[.] *Longman [,] (1986)*. Thick 8vo, 650pp., half-title ("Longman Annotated English Poets"), printer's device on title page, paperback, printed white stiff paper wrappers (a bit used) with modern unsigned sketch in black of *Satan Falling* on front cover. A fairly good copy. First published as part of *The Complete Poems of Milton* in one volume by Longman in 1968 ("Longman Annotated English Poets Series"); *PL* first published separately in paperback with minor corrections in 1971; first American edition thus published under the title *Poems* by Longman and Norton in 1972 (also listed here); variously printed thereafter; published anew as the "Second Edition" with a new preface in 1998 (also listed here).

1489. PARADISE LOST BOOKS I AND II[.] Milton. Edited By F. T. Prince. *Oxford University Press, (1986)*. 8vo, 205pp., half-title, paperback, printed stiff paper wrappers with blue inset within black border on each cover. A fine copy. The first edition thus was published in 1962 (also listed here); it was variously reprinted.

1490. PARADISE LOST BOOKS IX AND X[.] Milton. Edited By R. E. C. Houghton. *Oxford University Press, (1986)*. 8vo, 244pp., half-title, paperback, printed stiff paper wrappers with orange inset within black border on each cover. A fine copy. The first edition thus was published in 1969; it was variously reprinted.

1491. PARADISE LOST BOOKS IX AND X[.] Milton. Edited With An Introduction And Notes By E. M. W. Tillyard Litt.D., F.B.A. *[London:] Nelson[,] (1986)*. 16mo, 172pp., half-title ("Harrap's English Classics" with advertisement on verso), paperback, printed gray stiff paper wrappers with reproduction of Milton portrait (age sixty-two) on front cover. A fine copy. First published by Harrap

Limited in 1960 (also listed here); reprinted fifteen times; seventeenth impression published by Thomas Nelson and Sons, Ltd., in 1986; printed and bound in Hong Kong.

1492. PARADISE LOST[.] John Milton[.] Edited By Alastair Fowler[.] *Longman[,] London and New York[,] (1987).* Thick 8vo, 650pp., half-title ("Longman Annotated English Poets"), printer's device on title page, paperback, printed stiff paper wrappers with reproduction of a detail from *The Fall of the Rebel Angels* (1562) by Pieter Bruegel on front cover. A fine copy. First published as part of *The Complete Poems of Milton* in one volume by Longman in 1968 ("Longman Annotated English Poets Series"); *PL* first published separately by Longman in paperback with minor corrections in 1971; first American edition thus published under the title *Poems* by Longman and Norton in 1972 (also listed here); variously printed thereafter (see 1986 edition); published anew as the "Second Edition" with a new preface in 1998 (also listed here).

1493. PARADISE LOST: BOOKS I - II[.] John Milton. Edited by John Broadbent . . . [Quotation from Edwin Muir] *Cambridge University Press[,] Cambridge, London, New York, New Rochelle, Melbourne, Sydney[,] (1987).* Slim 16mo, 149pp., half-title, paperback, printed stiff paper wrappers with reproduction of Blake's illustration of *Satan, Sin and Death* on front cover. A fine copy. The first edition thus was published in 1972. Part of "The Cambridge Milton for Schools and Colleges," a six-volume series published by the Cambridge University Press between 1972 and 1976 under the general editorship of John Broadbent.

1494. [PARADISE LOST] I, EVE. A Novel by Edward Le Comte. *New York: Atheneum, 1988.* First edition. Small 8vo, 134+[1]pp., half-title, slight decorative border trim on title page and on each of the four chapter half-title pages, illustrations by Mia Le Comte (one illustration for each of the four chapters), original dark green cloth spine, light green paper over boards, front cover lettered in blind, spine lettered in gilt, printed publisher's dark green wrappers in a protective plastic cover, with a color illustration of Eve by Mia Le Comte on front cover. A fine copy, near mint. "The elegant and enchanting story is a modern (and only slightly religious) version of the story of Adam and Eve and their offspring. . . . The Bible and Milton furnish the main inspiration . . ." (quoted from inside front flap). A variation of Milton and the Bible by a longtime Milton scholar. Laid in: review from *Milton Quarterly* 23, no. 1 (March 1989). Scarce.

1495. PARADISE LOST[.] John Milton[.] Edited With An Introduction By William G. Madsen[,] Washington University[.] *The Modern Library, New York(.) n.d (ca. 1988).* 8vo, xl+344pp., half-title, decorative leaves on title page, paperback, printed brown stiff paper wrappers. In near mint condition. The first edition thus was published in 1969 (also listed here); this is a later reprint.

1496. PARADISE LOST A Poem in Twelve Books[.] John Milton[.] A New Edition Edited by Merritt Y. Hughes[,] University of Wisconsin[.] *New York[:] Printed by The Odyssey Press[.] n.d. (1989).* 8vo, lx+324pp., "A Chronology Of The Main Events In Milton's Life," several textual illustrations (including Milton's universe, Eden, and a facsimile of the second edition title page), "The Life of Milton (1694) By Edward Phillips" reprinted at the end after the poem, paperback, printed red stiff paper wrappers with an unsigned illustration for *PL* (*Satan Cast out of Heaven*) reproduced on front cover. A good copy. The first edition thus was published in 1962 (also listed here with further editions cited).

1497. PARADISE LOST A Poem in Twelve Books By John Milton with an Introduction by John Wain and Illustrations by Ian Pollock[.] *London • The Folio Society • MCMXCI (1991).* First edition thus. Very large 8vo, xv+[1]+304pp., first appearance of frontispiece illustration in color with seventeen additional illustrations in color by Ian Pollock (one each for Books II, III, V, VII, VIII, X, and XII; two each for Books I, IV, VI, IX, and XI), "Bound by Butler & Tanner in full black buckram blocked with a design by the artist [on front cover]" (verso of title page), spine lettered in gilt, blue endpapers. A fine copy in original black buckram slipcase with gilt lettering on front cover. The text is that edited by William Aldis Wright originally published in the Cambridge University Press edition in 1903 (verso of title page). Folio Society publications are well-produced, nicely printed, well-illustrated, and in highly appropriate bindings; above all, they are aesthetically pleasing and a pleasure to read. See 2003 Folio Society edition with Blake illustrations listed here.

1498. PARADISE LOST[.] John Milton[.] Edited By Alastair Fowler[.] *Longman[,] London and New York[,] (1991).* Thick 8vo, 650pp., half-title ("Longman Annotated English Poets"), printer's device on title page, paperback, original printed light gray stiff paper wrappers with detail from *The Fall of the Rebel Angels* (1562) by Pieter Bruegel in color on front cover. A nice copy. First published as part of *The Complete Poems of Milton* in one volume by Longman in 1968 ("Longman Annotated English Poets Series"); *PL* first published separately in paperback with minor corrections in 1971; first American edition thus published under the title *Poems* by Longman and Norton in 1972 (see copy listed here); published anew as the "Second Edition" with a new preface in 1998 (also listed here).

1499. JOHN MILTON'S DRAMA OF PARADISE LOST [Edited By] Hugh M. Richmond[.] *Peter Lang[,] New York • San Francisco • Bern Frankfurt am Main • Paris • London[,] (1991).* First edition thus. Slim 8vo, [viii]+79+[1]pp., half-title, small printer's device on title page, "Table Of Contents," reproduction of Albrecht Dürer's *Kleine Passion* (1512), half-title repeated before introduction, textual note, "Milton's Epic In Dramatic Form," original cast list, paperback, original printed light green stiff paper wrappers with reproduction of Doré's illustration of *The Fall of the Rebel Angels* on front cover. A nice copy of "Paradise Lost[:] Milton's Epic In Dramatic Form As Performed in Wheeler Hall, U.C. Berkeley On 25 & 26 April, 1985" (title appearing before the "Cast List" and Milton's selected text. "This script of Milton's epic, *PL*, restores its original dramatic form, as first intended by Milton, by excerpting the key speeches from the great theatrical scenes that are its core" (back cover). Difficult to obtain, so apparently scarce.

1500. JOHN MILTON PARADISE LOST Edited by Roy Flannagan Ohio University[.] *Macmillan Publishing Company[,] New York[;] Maxwell Macmillan Canada[,] Toronto[;] Maxwell Macmillan International[,] New York[,] Oxford[,] Singapore[,] Sydney[,] (1993).* First edition thus by Macmillan. Large 8vo, vii+[iii]+686pp., half-title, "Foreword" by Roy Flannagan, reproduction of frontispiece portrait by R. White with Dryden epigram originally printed as the frontispiece for Milton's *History of Britain* (1670), a lengthy "*PL*: Introduction," containing sections on "The Epic Genre," "Milton's Theology And *PL*," "The Fable," "Rhetorical Strategies," "The Epic Poem And The Sister Arts, Architecture And Painting," "The Man And The Poem," "Critical Questions," "The Text Of *PL*," "Editions" (including a "Bibliography"), and a "Chronology," reproduction of the twelve illustrations for the 1688 Tonson edition of *PL* (one illustration for each book, without the original border to each illustration that had been cut off by the publisher, not the editor, in fitting the illustration to the page size), notes at bottom of page, index at the end, printed on high-quality glossy paper, original printed stiff paper wrappers, covers in light green with reproduction of Giovanni di Paolo's *The Creation of the World and the Expulsion from Paradise* in the Metropolitan Museum of Art on front cover. A fine copy. According to advertisement laid in: "Macmillan is proud to announce the first fully-annotated, original spelling edition of *PL* to be published in this century."

Flannagan indicated during a talk at St. Bonaventure University on April 14, 2000, that he began working on editing *PL* in 1992 for this edition of *PL* by Macmillan, once Simon & Schuster, a publishing company for which Flannagan had great respect and with which he had a very good working relationship, and that this edition had then appeared as an edition by Prentice Hall in the same year 1993 (see copy following) after Macmillan had been taken over by the "robber baron" Robert Maxwell (as Flannagan called him) and been passed on to Prentice Hall, an edition with which Flannagan subsequently had little to do or with which he had been allowed to do little, and an edition for which, as a result, he cared little. Much of the work for this 1993 Macmillan edition was incorporated into Flannagan's 1998 Riverside Milton (see copy under *Works*), an edition for which Flannagan expressed real pride with the hope that it might ultimately become the new Hughes, referring to the 1957 edition by Merritt Y. Hughes of *John Milton's Complete Poems And Major Prose* (see copy above), the long-standing text of choice.

1501. JOHN MILTON PARADISE LOST Edited by Roy Flannagan Ohio University[.] *Prentice Hall[,] Upper Saddle River, New Jersey 07458[,] (1993).* First edition thus by Prentice Hall. Large 8vo, vii+[iii]+686pp., half-title, "Foreword" by Roy Flannagan, reproduction of frontispiece portrait by R. White with Dryden epigram originally printed as the frontispiece for Milton's *History of Britain* (1670) a lengthy "*PL*: Introduction" as with 1993 Macmillan edition preceding, reproduction of the twelve illustrations for the 1688 Tonson edition of *PL* (one illustration for each book, without the original border to each illustration that had been cut off by the publisher, not the editor, in fitting the illustration to the page size), notes at bottom of page, index at the end, printed on high-quality glossy paper, original printed stiff paper wrappers, covers in light green with reproduction of Giovanni di Paolo's *The Creation of the World and the Expulsion from Paradise* in the Metropolitan Museum of Art on front cover. A fine copy, virtually a reprint by a new publisher of Flannagan's 1993 Macmillan edition (see preceding copy and comments by Flannagan about that edition and this 1993 reprint edition by Prentice Hall).

1502. PARADISE LOST[:] AN AUTHORITATIVE TEXT[,] BACKGROUNDS AND SOURCES[,] CRITICISM[.] John Milton[.] Second Edition[.] *Edited by Scott Elledge[,] Cornell University[.] A Norton Critical Edition[.] W • W • Norton & Company • New York • London[,] (1993).* Second edition thus, revised. 8vo, vii+[1]+688pp., half-title, emblem of the press on title page, preface, paperback, printed stiff paper wrappers (front cover slightly creased), front cover in purple with reproduction of *Adam and Eve* by Lucas Cranach (1526) in color at the center. A good copy. "The chief innovations in this second edition of the Norton Critical Edition of *PL* are the addition of a short, slightly revised version of a biography of Milton written by Milton's greatest biographer, David Masson; an abridgment of the first edition of Milton's *Doctrine and Discipline of Divorce*; five of Milton's sonnets; and several recent essays about *PL* whose presence increases the variety of critical approaches represented. To make room for all this, I deleted from the first edition an intrusive introduction, further abridged the selections from *Christian Doctrine*, and regretfully deleted several excellent critical essays simply because they seemed less likely to interest students and teachers today than they did seventeen years ago" (Preface). The first edition thus, first issue, was published in 1975 (also listed here); the first edition thus, second issue, was published in the same year and published simultaneously in New York and London (also listed here).

1503. [PARADISE LOST] JOHN MILTON DET TAPTE PARADIS I Norsk Gjendiktning Med Forord, Noter Og Efterord Av Arthur O. Sandved[.] Thorleif Dahls Kulturbibliotek[.] Forlagt Av H. Aschehoug & Co. *I Samarbeid Med Fondet For Thorleif Dahls Kulturbibliotek Og Det Norske Akademi For Sprog Og Litteratur[,] Oslo[,] 1993*. First edition thus? 8vo, 429pp., foreword, notes at the end, original blue cloth, orange cloth label with gilt lettering and gilt rules on spine with a small decorative gilt piece above and another below. A fine copy, printed entirely in Norwegian, with *PL* translated into Norwegian verse.

1504. PARADISE LOST AND PARADISE REGAINED[.] John Milton[.] Edited by Christopher Ricks[.] Revised and Updated Bibliography[.] The Signet Classic Poetry Series General Editor: John Hollander[.] *A Signet Classic[,] [ca. 1993]*. Revised edition thus. 8vo, 396+[4]pp., three pages of "Selected Bibliography," with the final page listing "Great Books" of "Signet" and "Mentor," paperback, printed stiff paper wrappers with the *Fall of the Rebellious Angels* by Pieter Bruegel reproduced in color on front and back covers. A fine copy. The first edition thus was published in 1968 (also listed here with further editions cited).

1505. PARADISE LOST The Novel by Joseph Lanzara Based upon the epic poem by John Milton With illustrations by Gustave Doré[.] *New Arts Library[,] New York[.] (1994)*. First edition. 8vo, 255pp., half-title, emblem of the press at the bottom of title page, six reproductions of Doré's illustrations (as frontispiece and for Books II, IV, VII, X, and XI), half-title for each book, decorated initial letter at the start of each book, original brown buckram, spine lettered in gilt, publisher's wrappers in a protective plastic cover, lettered in red and black with decorative blue trim on front cover and an oval reproduction in tinted blue within decorative black border trim of vignette illustration of *The Temptation of Eve* on back cover. A fine copy. "The definitive prose version of the world's greatest epic poem" (inside flap, back cover).

1506. JOHN MILTON PARADISE LOST Read by Anton Lesser, *Naxos AudioBooks Ltd., 1994*. First edition. 3 CDs, in original plastic case, with square booklet consisting of the poem as read by Lesser inserted within, 55pp., original wrappers with a reproduction of Blake's illustration of the temptation in color on front cover and a reproduction of the Faithorne portrait in black and white on back cover—the case insert repeating Blake's illustration on the front. Both the CDs and booklet are in fine condition. The booklet contains a brief assessment of the poem and an "Abridgement" of each book on the back of the front cover and on the first page. Milton's epic is read by Anton Lesser, "one of Britain's leading classical actors," "With Laura Paton (Eve) and Chris Larkin (summaries)"—quoted from back of CD case.

1507. JOHN MILTON PARADISE LOST Read by Anton Lesser, *Naxos AudioBooks Ltd., 1994*. First edition. Four tapes (one a "dummy" tape), similar to preceding copy except tapes instead of CDs, in original plastic case, with square booklet consisting of the poem as read by Lesser inserted within, 42pp., original wrappers with a reproduction of Blake's illustration of the temptation in color on front cover and a reproduction of the Faithorne portrait in black and white on inside of cover—the case insert repeating Blake's illustration on the front. Both the tapes and booklet are in fine condition. The booklet contains the text of the poem read by Anton Lesser, "With Laura Paton (Eve) and Chris Larkin (paraphrases)"—quoted from back of tape case.

1508. PARADISE LOST AND PARADISE REGAINED[.] John Milton[.] Edited by Christopher Ricks[.] Revised and Updated Bibliography[.] *The Signet Classic Poetry Series General Editor: John Hollander[.] A Signet Classic[,] [ca. 1994]*. Revised Edition Thus. 8vo, 396+[4]pp., paperback, printed stiff paper wrappers with the *Fall of the Rebellious Angels* by Pieter Bruegel reproduced in color on front and back covers. A fine copy. The first edition thus was published in 1968 (also listed here with further editions cited).

1509. JOHN MILTON'S PARADISE LOST[.] MAX Notes[.] Text by Corinna Siebert Ruth (M.A., California

State University-Fresno) Department of English Fresno Pacific College Fresno, California[.] Illustrations by Karen Pica[.] *[Piscataway, N.J.] Research & Education Association[,] (1995)*. First edition. 8vo, 136pp.+[2]pp., illustrations after Karen Pica for each book, paperback, original red and black stiff paper wrappers glazed over. A nice copy with two advertisement leaves bound in at the end. In addition to the detailed "summary" of each book, two illustrations are provided for each book by Karen Pica (except for Book VIII, which is nonillustrated, and Book XII, which has one illustration). An interesting concept, with very modern illustrations.

1510. PARADISE LOST[.] John Milton[.] *N.P. Powerline Publishing Co.) n.d (ca. 1995)*. First edition thus? 8vo, 280pp., half-title, double black rule on title page, original blue cloth (a bit rubbed), front cover and spine lettered in gilt. A nice copy. There is no indication as to why this edition was published.

1511. PARADISE LOST[,] SAMSON AGONISTES[,] LYCIDAS[.] John Milton[.] Newly Annotated and with a Biographical Introduction by Edward Le Comte[.] *Revised and Updated Bibliography[.] A Mentor Book[,] [ca. 1995]*. 8vo, 414+[2]pp., half-title, paperback, original printed stiff paper wrappers with an illustration of three angels in color on front cover (signed "M. Glaser"), title different on front cover and spine ("Paradise Lost and other poems By John Milton") from that on title page, advertisement leaf bound in at end. A fine copy. The first edition thus was published in 1961 (also listed here with further editions cited).

1512. PARADISE LOST BY JOHN MILTON*[.] (Los Angeles, Anaheim, Boston, Washington, D.C.: Cyber Classics, Inc., 1997)*. First edition thus. 8vo, xii+328pp., "List of Characters" and a "Synopsis" precede Milton's epic, paperback, original printed stiff paper wrappers with an unsigned sketch of a dove with an olive branch flying down to earth surrounded in chaos, the whole surrounded by rays of sunlight. A fine copy with software disk enclosed. According to information on the back cover: "Cyber Classics Provide The Most Comprehensive Guide To Required Reading By Putting The Latest Technology In Your Hands. Each Package Contains A Special Summary, The Original Text Of The Book, And In Addition, The Whole Book On Disk! Finally, Reading Has Entered The 21st Century."

1513. EL PARAISO PERDIDO John Milton[.] Edicion de Esteban Pujals[;] Traduccion de Esteban Pujals[.] Tercera Edicion*[.] Catedra[:] Letras Universales[,] (1998)*. 8vo, 509+[3]pp., half-title, "Introduccion," with commentary on Milton's life and works, including a half-page reproduction of Munkacsy's painting of *Milton Dictating to His Daughters*, and commentary on earlier translations and the present one, with a bibliography, half-title before the poem, three full-page illustrations: for Book II, of *Satan, Sin, and Death*, for Book VII, of *Adam Embracing Eve*, and for Book XII, of *The Expulsion*, paperback, original printed stiff white paper wrappers, decorative border trim on front cover with an illustration of Adam and Eve being expelled by Luciano Martin in the center. A fine copy, printed entirely in Spanish, with *PL* translated into Spanish verse. Advertisement leaf bound in at the end. The illustrations are very intriguing, with any attribution difficult to decipher.

1514. JOHN MILTON PARADISE LOST Edited By Alastair Fowler[.] Second Edition[.] *Longman[,] London and New York[,] (1998)*. Second edition thus. 8vo, xxiv+716pp., half-title ("Longman Annotated English Poets"), "Preface to the Second Edition" (dated August 1997), half-title before the poem, notes at bottom of page, "List of References" at the end, original black buckram, spine lettered in silver with small emblem of the press at the bottom, printed publisher's wrappers with *The Fall of the Titans* reproduced in color on front cover. A fine copy. First published as part of *The Complete Poems of Milton* in one volume by Longman in 1968 ("Longman Annotated English Poets Series"); *PL* first published separately in paperback with minor corrections in 1971; first American edition thus published under the title *Poems* by Longman and Norton in 1972 (also listed here); variously printed thereafter (see 1986 and 1987 editions); published anew as the "Second Edition" with a new preface in 1998 (copy here); a "Second Impression" was published in 1999 (also listed here).

1515. [PARADISE LOST JOHN MILTON—IN RUSSIAN WITH RUSSIAN TITLE PAGE AND RUSSIAN TEXT] JOHN MILTON • PARADISE LOST[.] *St.-Petersburg: Kristall, 1999*. First edition thus. Entirely in Russian, with other selections from Milton. 8vo in 16s, 607+[1]pp., half-title ("Library of World Literature) with frontispiece portrait of a young, long-haired Milton by "M. Epuscutta" [M. Yermolina] on verso, small decorative piece at center of title page, half-title with decorative trim before *PL*, four glossy illustration plates reproducing eight illustrations by Doré, title page decorative piece repeated as tailpiece throughout, half-title with decorative trim for *SA* and various of the *Poems*, contents at the end, original black imitation leather, front cover and spine richly ruled and lettered in gilt with light blue trim toward the bottom and a reproduction of Doré's illustration of a brooding Satan at center of front cover ruled in gilt. A fine copy. *PL* is translated by A. A. Steinberg; *SA* and *Poems* are translated by Yu. B. Korneev.

1516. JOHN MILTON PARADISE LOST Edited By Alastair Fowler[.] Second Edition[.] *Longman[,] London And New York[,] (1999)*. Second edition thus, second impression. 8vo, xxiv+716pp., half-title, small printer's device on title page, "From the Preface to the First Edition" (dated August 1966), "Preface to the Second Edition" (dated August 1997), "List of References" at the end, paperback, original printed stiff paper wrappers with *The Fall of the Titans* reproduced in color on front cover. A fine copy. First published as part of *The Complete Poems of Milton* in one volume by Longman in 1968 ("Longman Annotated English Poets Series"). "First edition of *PL* first published separately in 1971. This second edition published 1998. Second impression 1999" (verso title page).

1517. DAS VERLORENE PARADIES John Milton Aus Dem Englischen Ubertragen Und Heraugegeben Von Hans Heinrich Meier[.] Philipp Reclam Jun. *Stuttgart, (1999)*. 16mo, 467+[1]pp., original printed yellow stiff paper wrappers with a reproduction of illustration by Fuseli (1823) on front cover. A nice copy. The first edition thus was published in 1986.

1518. EL PARAISO PERDIDO John Milton[.] *Excel[,] San Jose[,] New York[,] London[,] Shanghai[,] (1999)*. First edition thus. 8vo, 254+[2]pp., emblem of the press (with the word "Alba" at the bottom) at the bottom of title page, paperback, original printed stiff paper wrappers with photographic reproduction of various apples in color (with a bite out of apple at the center) on front cover. A nice copy, printed entirely in Spanish, with advertisement leaf bound in at the end.

1519. [PARADISE LOST] Printed entirely in Japanese. 2 volumes., published in Japan, 1999 &1993. Small 8vo, 431+[17]pp.,+443+[5]pp., original decorated tan paper wrappers with stiff white publishers wrappers decorated in tan and red, with a small illustration of Satan on volume 1 and of the expulsion on volume 2. A fine set. The first edition thus was apparently published in 1981 (a date that appears in each volume, along with the dates given above).

1520. JOHN MILTON PARADISE LOST Edited with an Introduction and Notes by John Leonard[.] *Penguin Books, (2000)*. First edition thus. 8vo, lviii+453+[1]pp., half-title ("Penguin Classics," with brief biography of Milton), paperback, original printed stiff paper wrappers with a "detail from *The Fall of Satan and the Rebel Angels* By Jakob Swanenburgh" on front cover. A fine copy. The text and notes are a reissue of *PL* from Leonard's 1998 Penguin Books edition of John Milton *The Complete Poems* (also listed here) with a new introduction by Leonard.

1521. PARADISE LOST A Poem in Twelve Books By John Milton with a Preface by Peter Ackroyd an Introduction by John Wain and Illustrations by William Blake[.] *London • The Folio Society • MMIII*. First UK edition thus. Very large 8vo, 304pp., half-title, twelve full-page color illustration plates after William Blake, text set in hot-metal Monotype Bembo with Centaur display, Nigerian goatskin spine, Moire silk over boards, spine lettered in silver, initials of the Folio Society in silver within a silver circle at bottom of spine, dark green endpapers. A fine copy in original slipcase (also fine) covered in dark green paper (similar to the endpapers) with a reproduction of Blake's illustration of the temptation of Eve in full color tipped on one side. A splendid new folio edition of *PL* that brings together two of England's most powerful creative figures. See 1991 Folio Society edition with illustrations by Ian Pollock.

1522. JOHN MILTON PARADISE LOST I/II *(Madrid, Spain: Del Prado Publishers, 2003)*. 2 volumes. First edition. 16mo (miniature in size, 2 ⅝" × 2 ⅛"), 589pp.,+639pp., half-title ("The Miniature Classic Library") each volume, title page in red and black each volume, book and number in red, page number in red at bottom of page, index in red at the end of each volume, red simulated leather, volume 1 with cream lettering within green inset decorated in cream trim on front cover and spine; cream simulated leather, volume 2 with green lettering within white inset decorated in green trim on front cover and spine. Virtually mint.

1523. [PARADISE LOST] THE TALE OF PARADISE LOST Based on the poem By John Milton told as the story of the war in Heaven, the disobedience of Adam and Eve, and their exit from Eden into the world • retold by nancy willard and illustrated by jude daly. *New York[,] London[,] Toronto[,] Sydney[:] Atheneum Books for Young Readers. 2004*. First edition. Small 8vo, x+150pp., illustrations in color by Jude Daly, original green cloth, spine lettered in gilt, reddish-brown endpapers, printed publisher's wrappers with illustrations from within reprinted in color on front and back covers. Fine copy. "Newbery Award winner Nancy Willard retells Milton's astonishing poem in a prose adaptation that faithfully captures his vivid imagery and cinematic flourish" (inside front flap).

1524. PARADISE LOST A Poem In Twelve Books The Author John Milton Text edited by John T. Shawcross[.] Introduction by Helen Vendler[.] *Printed by Andrew Hoyem at The Arion Press[,] San Francisco[,] MMII*. Large 8vo (10" × 6 ⅞"), xxxiv+[i]+396+[1]pp., "Milton's Epic

Poem by Helen Vendler" before the poem, half-title for each book, "A Note on the Text by John T. Shawcross" and "Colophon by Andrew Hoyem" after the poem, full black linen over thick boards, round back spine, headbands, inset purple leather label lettered in gilt, fore- and bottom edges untrimmed. Mint, in original slipcase covered with the same black linen as the book, large fleur-de-lis in purple on each side, inset purple leather label on spine lettered in gilt as on spine of book. According to the prospectus, "Eventually, portions of the edition may be released with illustrations, and the artists and price for those copies will be announced at issue." Signed by John Shawcross on title page. With original prospectus published in 2002. This is the sixty-fourth publication of the Arion Press. No. 226 (number written in hand) of an edition "limited to 400 numbered copies for sale and 26 lettered copies for complimentary distribution to participants in the project" (colophon).

[together with]

1525. THIRTEEN WATERCOLOR DRAWINGS BY WILLIAM BLAKE ILLUSTRATING PARADISE LOST By John Milton[.] *The Arion Press[,] San Francisco[,] 2004.* The first facsimiles printed at full scale in full color from the original works in the collection of the Henry E. Huntington Library and Art Gallery, San Marino, California, with descriptions and commentaries by Robert N. Essick and John T. Shawcross to accompany the edition of *PL* published in 2002 by the Arion Press and text edited by John T. Shawcross and with an introduction by Helen Vendler. Sheet size is 22" × 17", smaller images range between 9 ¼" and 10 ⅛" vertical by 8 to 8 ⅛" horizontal, the larger image is 19 ½" × 15 ⅞", interleaving sheets between the prints "identify the following image and provide commentary on the iconography of the design and its relationship to the text, with citations and relevant excerpts from the poem; descriptions and interpretations of the drawings are by [Blake scholar Robert Essick]; additional material relating to *PL* is by [Milton scholar John Shawcross], who also chose the quotations" (Prospectus). Housed in a portfolio case (22 ¼" × 17 ⅛") covered in matching black linen with printed paper label on front cover. Mint. "This is the sixty-ninth publication of the Arion Press, supplementing the sixty-fourth, *PL* By John Milton. The edition is published on demand and is limited to no more than the edition of the book: 400 numbered copies for sale and 26 lettered copies for complimentary distribution." Copy 2 (number written in hand on the colophon).

"John Milton's *PL*, one of the monumental works of English literature, an epic poem of 10,565 lines, was published in a deluxe limited edition by the Arion Press in December 2002. Supplementing that publication in September 2004 is a portfolio of full-scale facsimiles of thirteen watercolor drawings by William Blake (1757–1827) depicting incidents in *PL*. These prints are exacting replicas of important works of art, suitable for exhibition by institutions or private display."

Blake completed two sets of illustrations of *PL*: the set here of twelve, with one illustration for each book, completed in 1807, first published by the Lyceum Press in 1906 (see copies listed here); the other set of nine illustrations, completed in 1808 and now in the Boston Museum of Fine Arts, first published in the 1940 edition by the Heritage Press (see copies listed here); the other much larger Blake drawing (also in the Huntington) with the same title as plate 2 in the 1807 series, "Satan, Sin, and Death: Satan Comes to the Gates of Hell," was probably executed in 1806 and is "printed at full scale in full color" here. The 1807 series of twelve drawings as illustrations of *PL* commissioned by Joseph Thomas was "not intended to be bound into a book, nor were engravings made from them" (Prospectus).

1526. JOHN MILTON PARADISE LOST Introduced by Philip Pullman[.] *Oxford University Press[,] (2005).* First edition. Large 8vo, [ii]+369+[5]pp., half-title in red, title page in red and black, title and book in red at the top throughout, illustrated by reproduction of the 1688 illustrations (see original 1688 editions listed here), one illustration for each book, original black cloth, spine lettered in gilt, red endpapers, printed black publisher's wrappers lettered in red and white with reproduction of illustration at bottom of front cover and repeated at top of back cover, red silk ribbon marker. A fine copy, printed on high-quality paper, signed on the title page by Philip Pullman, the novelist, whose enthusiasm for Milton as a poet is obvious in his introduction.

1527. MILTON'S PARADISE LOST[.] Illustrations By Gustave Doré[.] *[London:] Capella, (2005).* First edition thus. 4to, 384pp., half-title with frontispiece illustration on verso, forty-nine other illustration plates by Doré, "List Of Plates" at the end, original printed paper over thick boards in tones of gold at the top and black at the bottom, with color illustration by Doré reproduced on front cover with "Paradise Lost" in thick gilt letters, other lettering in bright gold, spine lettered in bright gold, illustration from front cover partially repeated on back cover with quotations in bright gold lettering against black background inset at the center. Newly reproduced engravings by Doré. As new. The first edition with Doré's illustrations of *PL* appeared in the mid-1860s (see 1865–66 set of parts and 1866 first book edition listed here).

II. Descriptive Listing of Editions   367

Nineteenth-century decorated cloth bindings on illustrated Milton editions—showing front covers.

Paradise Regain'd

Milton's friend and secretary Thomas Ellwood visited him in the Buckinghamshire cottage to which Milton had fled from plague-smitten London. In his *History Of The Life Of Thomas Ellwood*, 1714 (see copy with Eighteenth-century Miltoniana), Ellwood provides his account of being asked by Milton "How I liked it [*PL*], and what I thought of it" and responding, "Thou hast said much here of Paradise lost; but what has thou to say of Paradise found?' . . . [continuing] And when, afterwards, I went to wait on him . . . he showed me his second poem, called Paradise Regained, and in a pleasant tone said to me, 'This is owing to you, for you put it into my Head, by the Question you put to me at Chalfont; which before I had not thought of'" (pp. 233–34).

1528. PARADISE REGAIN'D. A Poem In IV Books. To which is added **SAMSON AGONISTES**. The Author John Milton. *London, Printed by J. M. for John Starkey at the Mitre in Fleetstreet, near Temple-Bar. MDCLXXI.* First edition, first issue. 8vo, 111+101+[2]pp., complete with the license leaf (dated July 2, 1670) before title page, with the misprint "loah" for "loth" (p. 67, line 2), and with the errata leaf in its earliest state at the end preceded by "Omissa" leaf, separate pagination and separate title page for "**SAMSON AGONISTES, A DRAMATIC POEM.** The Author John Milton. [Quotation from "Aristot. Poet. Cap. 6"] *London, Printed by J. M. for John Starkey at the Mitre in Fleetstreet, near Temple-Bar. MDCLXXI,*" decorative head-trim, contemporary calf (very neatly rebacked preserving original spine), lightly marbled edges, early signature (dated 1737) on fly-leaf and an earlier signature on verso of license leaf. A very fresh, tall copy with rare license leaf and rare errata leaf. Formerly the William Stockhausen copy. Wing M2152; Hayward 73; Grolier, *Wither to Prior*, 613; Coleridge 168; Shawcross, Kentucky, 41; Kohler 177 (making no mention of license leaf or errata leaf).

1529. PARADISE REGAIN'D. A Poem In IV Books. To which is added **SAMSON AGONISTES**. The Author John Milton. *London, Printed by J. M. for John Starkey at the Mitre in Fleetstreet, near Temple-Bar. MDCLXXI.* First edition, second issue. 8vo, 111+101+[2]pp., complete with the license leaf (dated July 2, 1670) before title page, with the correct reading "loth" (p. 67, line 2) and with the errata leaf in its earliest state at the end preceded by "Omissa" leaf, separate pagination and separate title page for "**SAMSON AGONISTES, A DRAMATIC POEM.** The Author John Milton. [Quotation from "Aristot. Poet. Cap. 6"] *London, Printed by J. M. for John Starkey at the Mitre in Fleetstreet, near Temple-Bar. MDCLXXI,*"

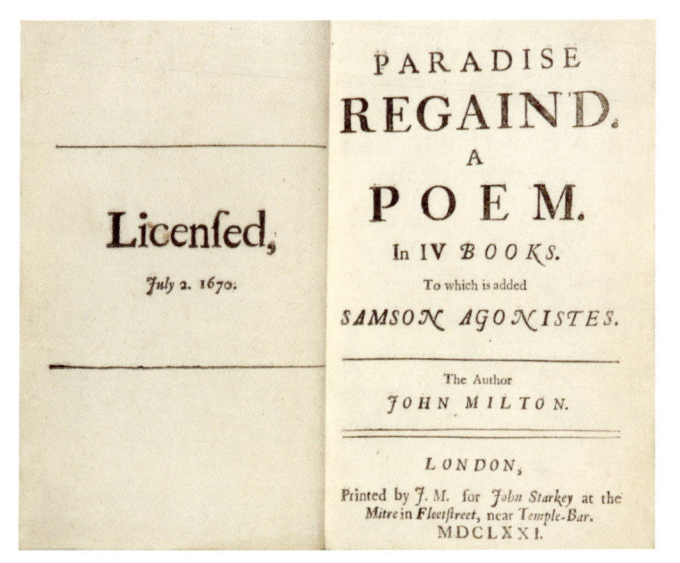

Paradise Regain'd . . . To which is added *Samson Agonistes.* London, 1671. See #1528.

decorative head-trim, nineteenth-century brown hard-grain morocco, spine lettered in gilt, raised bands, inner and outer dentelles ruled in gilt, a.e.g., bound by J. Clarke, with his stamp on front pastedown and with an early note in ink on back blank identifying the binder and dating the binding as 1855. A pleasing, tall copy with the correct reading "loth" and complete with both the rare license leaf and the rare errata leaf. Coleridge 168; Not in Kohler.

1530. PARADISE REGAIN'D. A Poem In IV Books. To which is added **SAMSON AGONISTES**. The Author John Milton. *London, Printed for John Starkey at the Mitre in Fleetstreet, near Temple-Bar. MDCLXXX.* Second edition. 8vo, 70+132+[4], complete with the license leaf and a second license leaf before title page, separate pagination and separate title page for "**SAMSON AGONISTES, A DRAMATIC POEM.** The Author John Milton. [Quotation from "Aristot. Poet. Cap. 6"] *London, Printed for John Starkey at the Mitre in Fleetstreet, near Temple-Bar. MDCLXXX (1680),*" decorative head-trim, later nineteenth-century calf (rebacked, first license leaf repaired), decorative gilt border trim on covers, gilt-decorated spine, red morocco labels, raised bands, marbled endpapers, a.e.g., with four pages advertising "A Catalogue Of Books Printed for John Starkey" bound in at end along with an extra advertisement leaf laid in. A fine, tall copy with the rare license leaf and a second license leaf and with the rare advertisements bound in at end. Wing M2153; Grolier, *Wither to Prior*, 613; Coleridge 169; Kohler 178 (mentioning "4 pages of advertisements at end," but making no mention of license leaf or separate title page for *SA*).

1530A. (Cross-listing) PARADISE REGAIN'D. A Poem. In IV Books. To which is added Samson Agonistes.

The Author John Milton. *London, Printed by R. E. and are to be sold by Randal Taylor near Stationers-Hall. M DC LXXXVIII.* Third edition; first folio edition. Bound with **SAMSON AGONISTES** . . . *London, Printed, and are to be Sold by Randal Taylor near Stationers-Hall, M DC LXXXVIII.* Third edition; first folio edition. Bound with **PARADISE LOST** . . . The Fifth Edition, Adorn'd with Sculptures. *London, Printed for Jacob Tonson at the Judge's-Head in Chancery-Lane near Fleet-street. M DC XCII.* Engraved frontispiece portrait by R. White, bound without the illustrations. Folio, separate title page for each work, contemporary paneled calf. A good, tall copy, very fine internally. Wing M2154, M2177, M2150; Parker, pp. 1188–89, 1190–91; Coleridge 170 (identifying the printer R. E. of this edition of *PR* as being Richard Everingham or Robert Everingham, both in business at the time, Robert being the more likely printer), 94b; Kohler 179 (bound with *PL*, 1691). See main listing under *PL*, 1692.

1531. **PARADISE REGAIN'D.** A Poem. In Four Books. To which is added **SAMSON AGONISTES. AND POEMS UPON SEVERAL OCCASIONS.** Compos'd at several Times. The Author John Milton. The Fourth Edition. *London, Printed for Jacob Tonson, within Grays-Inn Gate next Grays-Inn Lane. 1705.* Fourth edition; first edition thus. 8vo, 457+[4]pp., separate title page for "**SAMSON AGONISTES, A Dramatick Poem. The Author John Milton. Aristot. Poet. Cap. 6** . . . *London, Printed for Jacob Tonson, at Grays-Inn Gate next Grays-Inn Lane. 1705,*" and separate title page for "**POEMS UPON SEVERAL OCCASIONS.** Compos'd at several times. By Mr. John Milton. The Third Edition. *London, Printed for Jacob Tonson, at Grays-Inn Gate next Grays-Inn Lane. 1705,*" half-title for "Joannis Miltoni Londinensis Poemata. Quorum pleraque intra Annum Aetatis Vigesimum Conscripsit," "The Table" at the end, contemporary calf (spine a little worn, covers detached), covers decorated in blind, gilt-decorated spine (lacking label), raised bands, outer dentelles tooled in gilt (faded). Despite the detached covers and wear to the spine, a nice copy of this scarce edition nonetheless, very fresh and clean within. As Coleridge points out, this edition "was issued uniform with *PL* 1705 [copy also listed here] as vol. 2 of the *PW*; it seems to have been sold separately as well." See additional comments by Coleridge quoted with *PL*, 1705, regarding the sale of the volumes together as a set forming *PW* and as separates, as a set with either volume, when out of print, sold "with the currently in print matching volume." Coleridge also observes that this edition is noteworthy for its inclusion for the first time of both *SA* and the *MP*, combining to form the textual arrangement that became standard for virtually the next two centuries. The poems here are those of the 1673 edition, rearranged a bit. Companion volume to *PL*, 1705 (see rare copy listed here, which has the half-title: "The Poetical Works Of Mr. John Milton. In Two Volumes"), together forming the *PW*. Coleridge 185; Kohler 180.

1532. Variant of Preceding, contemporary calf (expertly rebacked preserving original spine with fine new black morocco label lettered in gilt, raised bands), covers decorated in blind at the center, red speckled edges. A lovely copy in a variant contemporary calf binding, uniformly bound as volume 2 to *PL*, 1707 (also listed here), which has the half-title: "The Poetical Works Of Mr. John Milton. In Two Volumes," together forming the *PW*. See comments by Coleridge quoted with *PL*, 1705, regarding the sale of the volumes together as a set forming *PW* and as separates, as a set with either volume, when out of print, sold "with the currently in print matching volume," in this instance, a 1707 edition of *PL* with a 1705 edition of *PR*. Coleridge 185; Kohler 180.

1533. **PARADISE REGAIN'D.** A Poem. In Four Books. To which is added **SAMSON AGONISTES. AND POEMS UPON SEVERAL OCCASIONS.** Compos'd at several Times. The Author John Milton. The Fifth Edition. *London, Printed for Jacob Tonson, within Grays-Inn Gate next Grays-Inn Lane. 1707.* 8vo, 457+[4]pp., separate title page for "**SAMSON AGONISTES, A Dramatick Poem. The Author John Milton. Aristot. Poet. Cap. 6** . . . *London, Printed for Jacob Tonson, within Grays-Inn Gate next Grays-Inn Lane. 1707,*" separate title page for "**POEMS UPON SEVERAL OCCASIONS.** Compos'd at several times. By Mr. John Milton. The Fourth Edition. *London, Printed for Jacob Tonson, within Grays-Inn Gate next Grays-Inn Lane. 1707,*" half-title for "Joannis Miltoni Londinensis Poemata. Quorum pleraque intra Annum Aetatis Vigesimum Conscripsit," "The Table" at the end, original paneled calf (a bit worn, front joint cracked, a little age-browned), gilt-decorated spine, outer dentelles tooled in gilt (faded). A good copy with early bookplate and contemporary note on fly-leaf about the purchase and cost of this book. Coleridge observes that "This is a line-for-line reprint of the 1705 edition. Like that it was issued uniform with *PL* of the same year, and was also presumably sold separately [as here]." Scarce. Coleridge 186; Kohler 181.

1534. **PARADISE REGAIN'D.** A Poem. In Four Books. To which is added **SAMSON AGONISTES. AND POEMS UPON SEVERAL OCCASIONS. WITH A TRACTATE OF EDUCATION.** The Author John Milton. The Fifth Edition. Adorn'd with Cuts. *London: Printed for J. Tonson, at Shakespeare's Head, over-against*

Catherine-Street in the Strand. 1713. First 12mo edition; first illustrated edition; first appearance thus of *Of Education*. 12mo, [v]+388pp., engraved frontispiece illustration for *PR* (unsigned—thought probably to be by J. B. Medina [Pointon, p. 16, although Wittreich disagrees, *Calm of Mind*, p. 310, as does John Shawcross], "The Table" (i.e., contents), one engraved illustration for each book of *PR* (by Nicholas Pigné, plate signed for Book I), separate title page for "**SAMSON AGONISTES**, A Dramatick Poem. The Author John Milton. Aristot. Poet. Cap. 6...*London, Printed in the Year 1713*," with engraved frontispiece illustration (by Nicholas Pigné), separate title page for "**POEMS, &C. UPON SEVERAL OCCASIONS**. In English and Latin, &c. Compos'd at several times. By Mr. John Milton. The Fifth Edition, with Additions. [Quotation from Virgil] *London, Printed in the Year 1713*," with reproduction of frontispiece portrait after W. Marshall's engraving in 1645 *Poems*, half-title for *C*, the *LP* ("Poemata"), and *Of Ed* ("A Small Tractate of Education, To Mr. Hartlib"), four additional engraved illustrations: one for *L'A* (by Pigné), one for *IlP* (unsigned), one for *On Shakespeare* (unsigned), and one for *On the University Carrier* (unsigned), decorative head- and tailpieces and decorated initial letters, original calf (a little rubbed, front joint cracked), gilt rules on covers and spine, red morocco label with gilt lettering and gilt rules, raised bands, final blanks covered by shorthand in an early hand, early signature on fly-leaf, bookseller's ticket on front pastedown. Folger duplicate, with duplicate stamp on back pastedown. A good copy with fine impressions of the plates. The four "political" sonnets (nos. 15, 16, 17, and 22)—*To Fairfax, To Cromwell, To Vane*, and *To Cyriack*—were printed together in the 1694 *Letters of State* (also listed here) and were not included in the 1673 edition of *Poems* (also listed here) and so Tonson did not include them in his subsequent editions of the *Poems* (1695, 1705, and 1707—see copies listed here), including them for the first time here, in his 1713 edition. The presence of the tractate *Of Ed* in the 1673 edition of *Poems* was the cause of its repeated incorporation in editions of the shorter poems in the eighteenth century, beginning with this edition by Tonson here. This edition, therefore, establishes the prototypical content for the balance of the eighteenth century, including for the first time *Of Ed*. Scarce. Coleridge 187a; Shawcross, Kentucky, 158; Kohler 182.

1535. Variant of Preceding, contemporary calf (joints cracked, a bit rubbed), gilt rules on covers, gilt-decorated spine, red morocco label (half missing), raised bands with decorative gilt trim, bound without the illustrations. A very nice, tall copy with early armorial bookplate. Coleridge 187a; Shawcross, Kentucky, 158; Kohler 182.

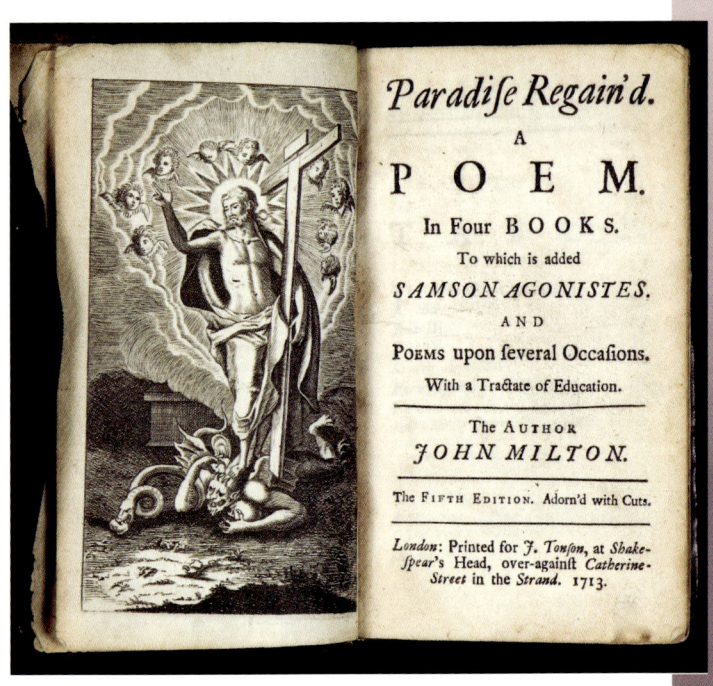

Engraved frontispiece illustration (unsigned) and title page, *PR*, 1713 Tonson 12mo edition. First 12mo *PR* edition. See #1534.

PR, 1713, contemporary calf. First 12mo edition. See #1534.

1536. PARADISE REGAIN'D. A Poem. In Four Books. To which is added SAMSON AGONISTES. AND POEMS UPON SEVERAL OCCASIONS. WITH A TRACTATE OF EDUCATION. The Author John Milton. The Fifth Edition. Adorn'd with Cuts. *London: Printed, and are to be Sold by W. Taylor, at the Ship and Black-Swan, in Pater-Noster-Row. 1721.* Second of Tonson's 12mo editions. 12mo, [v]+388pp., contents as with first edition (except reproduction of Marshall's engraving bound here within the poems), contemporary calf (joints cracked, spine ends chipped, a bit worn at corners), gilt rules on covers and spine, gilt-ruled red morocco label with gilt lettering, raised bands. A good copy of this reissue of the 1713 edition (also listed here). See rare companion volume: "*Paradise Lost . . . Adorned with Cuts. London: Printed, and are to be Sold by William Taylor at the Ship and Black-Swan, in Pater-Noster-Row. MDCCXXI*," which together with this volume forms a rare two-volume edition of Milton's *PW* published by William Taylor in 1721. [See listing under *PW*, 1721.] Coleridge references "this 1721 issue [of *PR*] with *PL* 1719" (also listed here) as "forming the *PW* published by Tonson in 2 v. 12mo," without reference to *PL* 1721 because the 1721 edition is unknown to Coleridge. Scarce. Williamson 41, 42; Coleridge 187b; Kohler 183, reporting "Not in the Bodleian Library. Not in Cambridge University Library."

1536A. (Cross-listing) PARADISE REGAIN'D. A Poems, In Four Books. The Author John Milton. The Seventh Edition. *Dublin: Printed by and for George Grierson, at the Two Bibles in Essex-Street, 1724.* Bound with PARADISE LOST. A Poem, In Twelve Books. The Author John Milton. The Eleventh Edition, Adorn'd With Sculptures. *Dublin: Printed by and for George Grierson, at the Two Bibles in Essex-Street, 1724.* 2 volumes bound in one. 8vo, [xii]+315+61pp.+[xxiv-page index], first appearance of engraved frontispiece portrait by James Gwim, engraved and printed title pages for *PL*, first appearance of twelve engraved folding plates for *PL* by J(ames). Gwim, index to *PL*, contemporary Irish full red morocco. Rare first Irish edition of each poem. Coleridge 174a (indicating rarity); Not in Kohler. See main listing under *PL*, 1724.

1537. PARADISE REGAIN'D. A Poem. In Four Books. To which is added SAMSON AGONISTES. AND POEMS UPON SEVERAL OCCASIONS. WITH A TRACTATE OF EDUCATION. The Author John Milton. The Sixth Edition, Corrected. *London: Printed for J. Tonson, at Shakespear's Head, over-against Catherine-Street in the Strand; and for M. Poulson. M.DCC.XXV.* 12mo, [v]+352pp., engraved frontispiece illustration (*The Baptism of Jesus*) for *PR* after Pigné by Fourdrinier, "The Table" (i.e., contents), half-title for *SA*, *C*, the *LP* ("Poemata"), and *Of Ed* ("A Small Tractate of Education, To Mr. Hartlib"), decorative head- and tailpieces and decorated initial letters, later eighteenth-century polished calf (front joint slightly cracked), covers ruled in blind, gilt-ruled and gilt-lettered red morocco label, raised bands. A fine copy with early signature and with the stamp "Fife Collection." Fenton edited this edition of *PR&c*, as he also edited the text of the 1725 edition of *PL* in which his *Life of Milton* first appeared. Coleridge distinguishes a first and second impression of this edition, the two impressions being identified by "some associated variants," including, for example, "errors: F8v-F9: Har./Hor. [error on F9]"; and O3-O3v: Foribus/Floribus" (error on O3). The present edition is the first impression, consistent with the variants identified by Coleridge. Coleridge 188 (first impression); Shawcross, Kentucky, 185; Not in Kohler.

1538. Variant of Preceding, contemporary calf (front joint cracked), covers finely tooled in blind, gilt-decorated spine, gilt-ruled red morocco label with gilt lettering, raised bands, outer dentelles in gilt (a bit faded). A fine copy in a variant contemporary binding, very fresh internally, with early armorial bookplate and early dated signature. This appears to be the second impression of this edition distinguished by Coleridge on the basis of "some associated variants": for example, "O3-O3v: Foribus/Floribus," correction ("Floribus") made in this copy. A number of other corrections, however, which Coleridge identifies as distinguishing the first from the second impression are not made here, for example, "F8v-F9: Har./Hor.; the error "Hor" on F9 remains here, rendering this edition something of an anomaly. Uniformly bound with *PL, London: Printed for Jacob Tonson in the Strand, MDCCV,* also listed here. Scarce. Coleridge 188 (second impression); Not in Kohler.

1539. PARADISE REGAIN'D: A Poem. In Four Books. To which is added SAMSON AGONISTES; AND POEMS UPON SEVERAL OCCASIONS. WITH A TRACTATE OF EDUCATION. The Author John Milton. The Seventh Edition, Corrected. *London: Printed for Jacob Tonson in the Strand, MDCCXXVII.* 8vo, [iv]+504pp., engraved frontispiece illustration (*The Baptism of Jesus*) for *PR* by Fourdrinier after Nicholas Pigné, title page in red and black, "The Table [of Contents]," separate title pages in red and black for *SA* and *Poems* (each dated 1727), half-title for *P* and *Of Ed*, decorative tailpieces, early diced calf (rebacked, paper shelf labels on spines, some age-browning and foxing), decorative gilt border trim on covers, gilt rules on spines, black morocco labels, marbled endpapers. A nice copy. Uniformly bound with *PL, London: Printed for Jacob Tonson in the Strand, MDCCXXVII,* also listed here. Scarce, but scarcer as a set. Coleridge 189; Kohler 184, reporting "Not in the Bodleian Library. Not in Cambridge University Library."

1540. PARADISE REGAIN'D: A Poem. In Four Books. To which is added **SAMSON AGONISTES; AND POEMS UPON SEVERAL OCCASIONS. WITH A TRACTATE OF EDUCATION.** The Author John Milton. The Seventh Edition, Corrected. *London: Printed for J. Tonson, at Shakespear's Head, over-against Catherine-Street in the Strand; and for Richard, James, And Bethel Wellington. M.DCC.XXX.* Small 8vo, [iv]+352pp., engraved frontispiece illustration (*The Baptism of Jesus*) for *PR* by Fourdrinier after Nicholas Pigné, "The Table" (i.e., contents), half-title with decorative black trim, for *SA*, *P*, *LP* ("Poemata"), and *Of Ed* ("A Small Tractate of Education, To Mr. Hartlib"), decorative head- and tailpieces and decorated initial letters, original French mottled calf (somewhat worn, spine ends chipped), gilt rules on covers and spine (faded), gilt-trimmed red morocco label with gilt lettering, raised bands. A good copy with early armorial bookplate of S. Peach on front pastedown. Scarce. Coleridge 190a; Kohler 184, reporting "Not in the Bodleian Library."

1541. LE PARADIS RECONQUIS TRADUIT DE L'ANGLOIS, DE MILTON, Avec Quelques Autres Pièces De Poésies. *A Paris, Chez Cailleau . . . Brunet Fils . . . Bordelet . . . Henry . . . M.DCC.XXX. Avec Approbation & Privilège du Roi.* First edition thus. 8vo, xix+[iii]+253+[1]pp., decorative piece on title page, "Preface" followed by "Approbation" and "Privilège Du Roi," "Argument" for each book of *PR*, decorative head and tailpieces, original calf (lightly worn), delicately gilt-decorated spine within the panels, raised bands, marbled endpapers, speckled edges. A nice copy with advertisement for new three-volume edition of *PL* on verso of last page. The first edition in French, which incorporates a number of Milton's separate poems, including *L* ("Lycidas, Idylle de Milton"), *L'A*, *IlP*, and *NO* ("Sur La Fête De Noël"). This translation into prose is by Père de Mareuil. The "Arguments" added to *PR* are not original to the poem. Together, *PR* with preface and arguments, along with the poems here, form the pattern of publication followed throughout the century. John Shawcross reminded me privately of "the French edition from La Haye (The Hague) by M. G. Mervile & J. Vander Kloot in 1730." Rare. In his 2000 *Ravenstree Milton Catalogue* (#99, Cat. 183), G. W. Stuart, Jr., states: "We have handled but one other example of this rare edition in over 35 years [my copy here, which I bought from Ravenstree in 1982]." Not in Coleridge; Not in Kohler.

1542. PARADISE REGAIN'D: A Poem. In Four Books. To which is added **SAMSON AGONISTES; AND POEMS UPON SEVERAL OCCASIONS. WITH A TRACTATE OF EDUCATION.** John Milton The Author. *London: Printed for a Company of Stationers. MDCCXXXIX.* 12mo in 6s, 274+[2]+143pp., title page in red and black, first appearance thus of engraved illustrations after N. Pigne for *PR* (Books 1, 2, and 4), each signed "I. Lightbody, sculpt," engraved frontispiece illustration after N. Pigne for *SA* signed "I. Lightbody, sculpt," and an engraved illustration for *IlP* signed "I. Lightbody, sculpt" (all after N. Pigné, each signed "I. Lightbody, sculpt," half-title for *SA*, *P*, and *Of Ed* ("A Small Tractate of Education, To Mr. Hartlib"), "The Contents" (i.e., table of contents) followed by Addison's *Notes* with separate title page ("Notes Upon The Twelve Books of Milton's Paradise Lost. Collected from the Spectator. Written by Mr. Addison. *London: Printed for a Company of Stationers. n.d.*"), decorative head- and tailpieces and decorated endpapers, contemporary mottled calf (somewhat worn), gilt rules on covers (faded), gilt-decorated spine, red morocco label with gilt lettering and decorative gilt trim, raised bands, early signatures. A good copy with early name written several times on title page. All engravings are in reverse of the 1713 plates that inspired them. Companion volume with *PL*, *London: Printed for a Company of Stationers. MDCCXXXIX* (also listed here). Rare. Not in Coleridge; Kohler 186, reporting "Not in Williamson . . . Not in the British Library. Not in Cambridge University Library," making no mention of the inclusion of Addison's *Notes*, citing a "Folding frontispiece portrait engraved by Jacobus Smith" (also in the University of Illinois' copy, according to John Shawcross, but not in the University of Kentucky's copy: Shawcross, Kentucky, 228).

1543. PARADISE REGAIN'D: A Poem. In Four Books. To which is added **SAMSON AGONISTES**; And **POEMS UPON SEVERAL OCCASIONS**. With a **TRACTATE OF EDUCATION.** The Author John Milton. The Eighth Edition Corrected. *London: Printed for J. & R. Tonson in the Strand. M DCC XLII.* 8vo, [iv]+504pp., engraved frontispiece illustration (*The Baptism of Jesus*) for *PR* by Fourdrinier (after Nicholas Pigné), title page in red and black, "The Table," separate title page for each work (each dated 1742), rather elaborate decorative head- and tailpieces and decorated initial letters, contemporary calf (rebacked preserving original gilt-ruled and gilt-lettered red morocco labels), raised bands. A fine copy, very crisp and clean within. Large paper copy, printed on thick, high-quality paper, with generous margins, and with splendid impressions of the plates. Uniformly bound with *PL*, 1741 (also listed here). Coleridge indicates that "This edition was apparently issued uniform" with that edition of *PL*. Coleridge 191; Kohler 187, reporting "Not in the Bodleian Library."

1544. PARADISE REGAIN'D. A Poem, In Four Books. To which is added **SAMSON AGONISTES**; And **POEMS UPON SEVERAL OCCASIONS**, With a **TRACTATE OF EDUCATION**. The Author John Milton. The Eighth Edition. *London: For J. & R. Tonson, R. Ware, J. Hodges, R. Wellington, R. Chandler, J. Brindley, R. Caldwell, and J. New. MDCCXLIII.* 12mo, [iv]+352pp., engraved frontispiece illustration (*The Baptism of Jesus*) for *PR* by Fourdrinier after Nicholas Pigné, title page in red and black, "The Table [of Contents]," half-title with decorative black trim, for *SA, P, C, LP* ("Poemata"), and *Of Ed* ("A Small Tractate of Education, To Mr. Hartlib"), decorative head- and tailpieces and decorated initial letters, new calf antique style (new endpapers, misleading green morocco label on spine with gilt lettering—"Milton Poems"—and gilt rules), raised bands. A good copy. Coleridge 192; Kohler 188, reporting "Not in Cambridge University Library."

1545. PARADISE REGAIN'D. A Poem, In Four Books. To which is added **SAMSON AGONISTES**; AND **POEMS UPON SEVERAL OCCASIONS**, WITH A **TRACTATE OF EDUCATION**. The Author John Milton. The Eighth Edition. *London: Printed for J. & R. Tonson, R. Ware, J. Hodges, R. Wellington, R. Chandler, J. Brindley, R. Caldwell, and J. New. MDCCXLIII.* 12mo, [v]+352pp., engraved frontispiece illustration (*The Baptism of Jesus*) for *PR* by Fourdrinier after Nicholas Pigné, title page in red and black, "The Table," half-title for *SA, P, Poemata,* and *Of Ed*, decorative head- and tailpieces and decorated initial letters (some very elaborate), contemporary mottled calf (one joint cracked), gilt rules on covers, elaborately gilt-decorated spines, red morocco labels with gilt lettering and decorative gilt trim, outer dentelles tooled in blind. A lovely copy from the Kitley House library with the bastard armorial bookplate, fresh and clean throughout, with fine impressions of the plates and of the head- and tailpieces and decorated initial letters. Uniformly bound with *PL, London: Printed for a Company of Stationers. MDCCXXXIX,* also listed here. Scarce. Coleridge 192; Kohler 188 reporting "Not in Cambridge University Library."

1546. PARADISE REGAIN'D. A Poem, In Four Books. To which is added **SAMSON AGONISTES**; And **POEMS UPON SEVERAL OCCASIONS**. With **A TRACTATE OF EDUCATION**. The Author John Milton. *London: Printed for J. and R. Tonson and S. Draper, R. Ware, J. Hodges, R. Wellington, C. Corbet, J. Brindley, R. Caldwell, and J. New. M DCC XLVII.* 2 volumes. 12mo, [iv]+163pp.,+387pp. (continuous pagination from volume 1), engraved frontispiece illustration (*The Baptism of Jesus*) for *PR* by Fourdrinier after Nicholas Pigné, half-title for *SA, P, C, LP,* and *Of Ed*, decorative head- and tailpieces (some very elaborate) and decorated initial letters (some likewise very elaborate) throughout, unlettered contemporary calf (a bit rubbed), raised bands, outer dentelles tooled in gilt (faded). A very nice set, clean and crisp within, with early (possibly contemporary) name in each volume. Uniformly bound with *PL,* (imprint as here), MDCCXLVI, 2 volumes, with the 1688 illustrations further reduced (fine impressions), and with decorative head- and tailpieces and decorated initial letters as here; a very nice set. Rare thus, together, as a set with *PL*. As I learned from John Shawcross, a copy of this set is in the British Library. See Coleridge's comments regarding the publication of *PL* and *PR* in uniform 1747 issues, with *PL,* 1746–47, also listed here. *PR* is scarce. Not in Coleridge; Kohler 189 (not as part of a set with PL) reporting "Not in Cambridge University Library."

1547. PARADISE REGAIN'D. A Poem, In Four Books. To which is added **SAMSON AGONISTES**; And **POEMS UPON SEVERAL OCCASIONS**. With A **TRACTATE OF EDUCATION**. The Author John Milton. The Ninth Edition. *Dublin: Printed on Irish Paper, For G. Risk, G. and A. Ewing, and W. Smith, Booksellers in Dame-street. M,DCC,XLVIII.* 12mo, 328+[4]pp., title page in red and black, half-titles for *SA, P, C,* and *LP*, contemporary calf (badly worn, bottom right corners of pp. 41–46 torn away without affecting any text, endpapers gone), raised bands. Bound in at the end is a four-page listing of "Books Printed for, and sold by G. Risk, G. and A. Ewing, and W. Smith, Booksellers in Dame-street." According to Coleridge: "This was issued together with *PL* of the same imprint"; Coleridge also indicates "A frontispiece copied [by S. Wheatley] from the Fourdrinier plate in the Tonson editions, showing Christ's baptism, is bound in" (lacking here, but present in University of Illinois copy). Scarce. Coleridge 193; Not in Kohler.

1548. PARADISE REGAIN'D. A Poem, In Four Books. *Dublin: Printed by George Grierson, Printer to the King's Most Excellent Majesty, at the King's-Arms and Two Bibles in Essex-Street, 1749.* 8vo, 61pp. (paginated from 3 to 61), title page in red and black with decorative fruit piece in black at the center, same decorative fruit piece repeated at end of last page, decorative head- and tailpieces and decorated initial letters, modern half dark brown leather, light orange cloth, printed paper label on front cover, new blanks and light orange endpapers. A fine copy. The first edition by Grierson was published in 1724 (also listed here) together with *PL* illustrated by James Gwim. Not in Coleridge; Not in Kohler.

[together with]

1548A. (Cross-listing) **POEMS UPON SEVERAL OCCASIONS** ... *Dublin: Printed by and for George Grierson,* *at the Two Bibles in Essex-Street, 1748.* First Irish edition. 8vo, 72pp. (paginated from 126 to 196), bound as *PR* and *SA*. A fine copy. Not in Coleridge; Not in Kohler. See main listing under *P*, 1748.

[together with]

1548B. (Cross-listing) **SAMSON AGONISTES** . . . *Dublin: Printed by and for George Grierson, at the Two Bibles in Essex-Street, 1748.* First Irish edition. 8vo, 58pp. (paginated from 66 to 121), bound as *PR* and *P*. A fine copy. Not in Coleridge; Not in Kohler. See main listing under *SA*, 1748.

Despite the editions being bound separately, Grierson clearly wished to present a complete and uniform collection of Milton's poetry, as indicated by the continuous pagination here of the separate parts (*PR*, *SA*, and *P*), from page 3 to page 196. John Shawcross likewise shared with me that "This was not issued separately. Libraries have sometimes listed their separated volumes as separate publications; this is incorrect. This reissue is the same as the 1748 edition (observe the signatures) except that the collection (*PR*) has a new title page dated 1749." The very rare first Irish editions of *SA* and *P*.

1548C. (Cross-listing) **LE PARADIS RECONQUIS**, Traduit De L'Anglois, De Milton, Par le P. de Mareuil de la Compagnie de Jésus. Avec Six Lettres Critiques Sur Le Paradis Perdu Et Reconquis. Par le P. R. de la Compagnie de Jésus. *A Paris, Chez Ganeau, rue Saint Jacques, vis-à-Saint Yves, à Saint Louis. M. DCC. XLIX. Avec Approbation & Privilège du Roi.* Coleridge 179; Not in Kohler. Bound with *Le Paradis Perdu*, 1749, also listed here.

First Newton Variorum Edition of *Paradise Regain'd*

1549. **PARADISE REGAIN'D.** A Poem, In Four Books. To which is added **SAMSON AGONISTES**: And **POEMS UPON SEVERAL OCCASIONS.** The Author John Milton. A New Edition, With Notes of various Authors, By Thomas Newton, D.D. *London: Printed for J. and R. Tonson and Draper in the Strand. M DCC LII.* First Newton edition; first variorum edition. Large 4to, [iv]+[ii]+690+[2]pp., first appearance of engraved frontispiece portrait of Milton "Aetat. 42" by Vertue from Richardson's drawing (dated 1751), first appearance of engraved illustrations by Hayman, preface and "Table of Contents," half-title for each book of *PR* and for various of the other works (including *SA*, *P*, *A Mask*, and *Poemata*), notes at bottom of page, "An index of the less common words," at the end, rich contemporary calf binding over thick boards (some joints slightly cracked), covers ruled in gilt with Camperdon crest on front covers, intricately gilt-decorated spines, red morocco title labels and black morocco numbering labels, raised bands. A very handsome copy. The index is to the "less common words" explained in the notes. First variorum to be published, it became the standard text of the poems for the remainder of the century, continuing to be reprinted in various forms well into the nineteenth century. Uniformly bound with first Newton variorum *PL*, 1749, also listed here. Coleridge 194; Shawcross, Kentucky, 285; Kohler 190.

1550. **PARADISE REGAINED.** A Poem In Four Books. With the other Poetical Works Of John Milton. Compared with the best Editions, And Revised by John Hawkey, Editor of the Latin Classics. *Dublin: Printed by S. Powell, for the Editor. M DCC LII.* First Hawkey edition. Large 8vo, 391pp., half-title for each of the separate works, elaborate decorative headpiece for each book of *PR*, other decorative headpieces, contemporary polished calf, finely tooled gilt-decorated spine, dentelles decorated in blind. A very attractive copy printed on large and thick paper, with early bookplate. As with Hawkey's edition of *PL*, Hawkey's edition of *PR&c.* is praised for its textual accuracy. Bound uniformly with Hawkey edition of *PL*, 1747, also listed here. Scarce; rarely found together, forming a very handsome set. See following copy of the first Hawkey edition of *PR*, 1752, with foldout illustration for *SA*. Coleridge 195; Kohler 192.

1551. Variant of Preceding, with unsigned engraved foldout illustration of multiple animals, figures engaged in various activities, an angel in the center, mounted horseman and a parade of others heading toward a castle in the distance placed before half-title for *SA*, brown cloth (crudely rebacked, broken in the middle, pages age-darkened, *ex libris* stamp). Rare. Unlike the regularly published edition (copy preceding), this copy contains an unsigned engraved foldout illustration for *SA*, which has been added.

Rare 1752 First Edition of Simon Grynaeus's German Translation

1552. [PARADISE REGAIN'D] JOHANN MILTONS WIEDER=EROBERTES PARADIES, nebst desselben Samson, und einigen andern Gedichten, wie auch einer Lebens=Beschreibung Des Verfassers. Aus dem Englischen übersetst. *Basel, verlegts Johann Rudolf Imhof, 1752.* First edition thus. 8vo, 48+344+[16]pp., title page in red and black, preface ("Vorbericht"), life of Milton ("Johann Miltons Leben"), half-title for *PR*, *SA*, *L*, *L'A*, *IlP*, and *NO*, contents and index at the end, decorative head- and tailpieces and decorated initial letters, some rather elaborate, select notes at bottom of page, contemporary calf (a bit rubbed along joints and spine), decorative delicate gilt border trim on each cover, spine decorated in gilt with gilt rules and small gilt pieces in the panels, black morocco label (chipped) with gilt lettering and gilt rules, raised bands. A nice copy with early/contemporary signature written unobtrusively on title page and another early/contemporary signature on front pastedown. "This is the extraordinarily rare first edition of Simon Grynaeus's German translation, and was not superseded until 1828. We have had but one other example in over thirty years" (G. W. Stuart, Jr., Ravenstree, Cat. 181, #63, 1997). Not in Coleridge; Not in Kohler.

1553. PARADISE REGAIN'D. A Poem, In Four Books. To which is added **SAMSON AGONISTES:** And **POEMS UPON SEVERAL OCCASIONS**. The Author John Milton. The Second [Newton] Edition. With Notes of various Authors, By Thomas Newton, D.D. *London: Printed for J. & R. Tonson and S. Draper; and for T. Longman, S. Birt, C. Hitch R. Ware, J. Hodges, C. Corbet, J. Brindley, and J. Ward. M DCC LIII.* 2 volumes. Second Newton edition; first octavo Newton edition. 8vo, [vi]+335pp.,+ [iv]+386+[4]pp., title page each volume, engraved frontispiece portrait of Milton at age twenty-one by Vertue, "Preface," "The Table of Contents," two engraved illustrations by Hayman (reduced) engraved by C. Grignion for Book I of *PR* and as frontispiece for *SA*, half-title for each book of *PR* and for *SA*, decorative endpieces, notes at bottom of page, volume 1, "The Table Of Contents," three engraved illustrations by Hayman (reduced) engraved by Grignion for *L'A*, *IlP*, and *C*, half-title for *P*, *C*, and *LP* ("Poemata"), notes at bottom of page, index, volume 2, original calf (a bit rubbed), gilt-ruled red morocco labels with gilt lettering, raised bands, outer dentelles tooled in gilt (faint), early signature and early armorial bookplate each volume. A very good set, uniformly bound as volumes 3 and 4 with *PL*, 1750, also listed here. Coleridge 196; Kohler 193, citing "Two plates" in volume 1 and "Two plates" (not three as here) in volume 2.

1554. PARADISE REGAIN'D. A Poem, In Four Books. To which is added **SAMSON AGONISTES:** And **POEMS UPON SEVERAL OCCASIONS**, With a **TRACTATE OF EDUCATION**. The Author John Milton. *London: Printed for J. and R. Tonson and S. Draper; And for T. and T. Longman, S. Birt, C. Hitch and L. Hawes, R. Ware, J. Hodges, C. Corbet, J. Brindley, and J. Ward.* *MDCCLIII.* 12mo in 6s, [3]+350pp., table of contents, half-title for each book of *PR*, *SA*, *P*, and *Of Ed*, decorative tailpiece at end, contemporary calf (a bit rubbed, front joint cracked, spine chipped at top), gilt rules on covers and spine, raised bands. A fine copy with early signature on flyleaf. While there is no general title page, this edition and *PL*, 1753, were issued together to form an edition of Milton's *PW*, although they were also issued separately, as here; the group of booksellers is slightly different from that in the 1753 *PL*. Coleridge 197b; Kohler 194, reporting "Not in the British Library. Not in Cambridge University Library."

1555. Variant of Preceding, contemporary calf (worn, joints cracked, third page of contents bound before first page), gilt-decorated spine (faded), raised bands, gilt dentelles. A decent copy in a variant binding, with early armorial bookplate on front pastedown, and contemporary signature on fly-leaf. Uniformly bound and issued with *PL*, 1753, also listed here. While there is no general title page, the two volumes together form an edition of Milton's *PW*; they were designed to be issued together as the *PW*, although they were also issued separately, as the preceding copy. Coleridge cites this 1753 edition of *PR* as "the matching edition forming vol. 2 of the Poetical works," with "a slightly different group of booksellers" from that in the 1753 *PL*. Coleridge 197b; Kohler 194.

1556. Variant of Preceding, contemporary French marbled calf, spine richly decorated in gilt within the panels, raised bands with decorative gilt trim, gilt labels lettered in French, marbled endpapers and edges, light blue silk ribbon marker. A fine, thick, tall copy, possibly large paper, very fresh and clean throughout, in a variant binding, paper very white with the appearance of being unread and in almost mint condition. Uniformly bound and issued with *PL*, 1753, also listed here, the two volumes forming an edition of Milton's *PW*.

Illustrations by J. Dixon (Apparently Unique)

1557. PARADISE REGAIN'D. A Poem, In Four Books. To which is added **SAMSON AGONISTES:** And **POEMS UPON SEVERAL OCCASIONS**. The Author John Milton. A New Edition, With Notes of various Authors, By Thomas Newton, D.D. *Dublin: Printed for John Exshaw, at the Bible in Dame-street. MDCCLIV.* 2 volumes. First edition by Exshaw in Dublin, and the first Dublin edition of Newton's *PR*, etc. 8vo, [5]+293pp.,+ [5]+318+[2]pp., engraved frontispiece portrait of Milton at age twenty-one with Dryden's epigram, volume 1, unsigned engraved vignette portrait of Milton at age sixty-two (somewhat after Faithorne) on each title page, repeated again before life in companion volume, *PL*, 1773, volume 1 (also listed here), and attributed there to T. Chambers, first appearance thus of engraved illustration for *PR* and for *SA* by J. Dixon, preface, table of contents, volume 2, notes at bottom of page, index at end of volume 2, contemporary polished calf (a few scuff marks, slight staining to lower right margin of *PR* illustration and to bottom margin of *SA* illustration without affecting the images), gilt-decorated border trim on all covers, elaborately gilt-decorated spines within the panels, red morocco lettering labels ("Newton's Milton") with decorative gilt trim, black morocco numbering labels with decorative gilt trim, outer dentelles tooled in gilt, marbled endpapers, light green edges. A lovely set, fresh throughout, with very striking impressions of the plates. Uniformly bound, as volumes 3 and 4 with *PL* . . . Dublin: Exshaw, 1773, 2 volumes (see set listed here). John Shawcross shared with me about the illustrations by Dixon: "I do not find the 'J. Dixon' in UK's 1754 *PR* or in the 1773 *PL*, which has the same title page medallions, Vertue's portrait, and Hayman/Grignion illustrations. Coleridge and Kohler do not mention Dixon; and there is no entry for him in Pointon or in Wittreich . . . The illustrations by J. Dixon . . . would appear to be unique. The only ones I've seen are without ascription, like your 1773 edition and like UK's copy of the 1754. I've not found any reference to Dixon's doing illustrations, as I remarked in my [previous] notes to you." See further comments by John Shawcross about the significance of this edition in *Milton Quarterly* 41, no. 1 (2007): 73. See 1754 Dublin edition of *PR* by Exshaw following without engraved illustrations after Dixon or frontispiece portrait of Milton at age twenty-one as here, but with unsigned engraved vignette portrait of Milton at age sixty-two (somewhat after Faithorne) on each title page, as here. Rare. Coleridge 198 (making no mention of the illustrations after Dixon, but mentioning the frontispiece portrait); Kohler 195 (without illustrations after Dixon and no mention of the frontispiece portrait), reporting "Not in Williamson. Not in the British Library. Not in the Bodleian Library."

1558. Variant of Preceding, contemporary mottled calf (some joints cracked), gilt-decorated spines, red morocco lettering labels ("Milton's Poetical Works"), dark olive green numbering labels, raised bands, marbled endpapers, red edges. A fine set with early signature on each title page. Uniformly bound, as volumes 3 and 4 with *PL* . . . Dublin: Exshaw, 1751, 2 volumes (see set listed here), first edition by Exshaw in Dublin, and the first Dublin and first Irish edition of Newton's *PL*, forming volumes 3 and 4 of a four-volume set of *Milton's PW* (so-labeled on spines); rare thus together. Unlike preceding set, this is without frontispiece portrait of Milton at age twenty-one with Dryden's epigram, though with the second unsigned portrait of Milton at age sixty-two, and without illustrations by Dixon. Scarce. Coleridge 198; Kohler 195, reporting "Not in Williamson. Not in the British Library. Not in the Bodleian Library."

❈

1559. PARADISE REGAIN'D. A Poem, In Four Books. To which is added **SAMSON AGONISTES**; And **POEMS UPON SEVERAL OCCASIONS**, With a **TRACTATE OF EDUCATION**. The Author John Milton. A new Edition Corrected. *Glasgow: Printed by R. Urie, for J. Wood, Bookseller in Edinburgh. M DCC LV.* 8vo, [ii]+315pp., engraved frontispiece portrait by T. Phinn, "The Contents," half-title for *SA*, *P*, *C*, *LP* ("Poemata"), and *Of Ed* ("A Tractate of Education; To Mr. Samuel Hartlib"), contemporary sheep (a bit worn, front cover detached). All in all, a good copy of an uncommon edition with rare engraved frontispiece portrait. Coleridge 199 (with no mention of frontispiece portrait); University of Illinois copy has frontispiece portrait; Not in Kohler.

1560. [PARADISE REGAIN'D] THE POETICAL WORKS OF MILTON. Volume II. Containing Paradise Regain'd, A Poem, In Four Books; Samson Agonistes; And Poems upon several occasions. With A Glossary; and, The Life of Milton. *Edinburgh: Printed by Sands, Murray, and Cochran. For A. Kincaid and A. Donaldson. MDCCLV.* Volume 2 only, complete unto itself and quite rare. Large 12mo in 6s, [2]+384pp., "Table of Contents" at the beginning and "A Glossary" and "The Life of Milton" at the end, contemporary calf (a bit rubbed, back spine joint slightly chipped from label to the top), gilt rules on cover, brown morocco label with gilt lettering and gilt rules (chipped on left side), number "2" printed in gilt on spine beneath the label, raised bands within gilt rules. A nice copy, fresh and clean within, volume 2 only: *PR* . . . *SA; And P*. According to Coleridge 118 (*PL* . . . Edinburgh: Printed by Sands, Murray, and Cochran. For A. Kincaid and A. Donaldson. MDCCLV): "Kincaid and Donaldson also published the *Poetical works* in 2 volumes in 1755 (NUCNM 0604324) and this is very probably a separate issue of vol. 1 of that edition. It may be compared with Donaldson's *Poetical Works* of 1762 [see copies listed here]. Not having seen any copy of the 1755 *Poetical Works* I describe the WTu copy as an edition of *PL* only." John Shawcross shared the following with me about this book: "I have not found Volume II of *The Poetical Works of Milton*, published in Edinburgh in 1755 anywhere else. I've added your copy [to my bibliography] and changed my annotation to Volume I. The copy of Volume I owned by the University of Kentucky has the first title page indicating that the edition is *The Poetical Works of Milton*; Coleridge's title page for *PL* is that copy's second title page. . . . Coleridge's statement that *PL* is 'very probably a separate issue of vol. 1' is incorrect." Rare. Not in Coleridge (although Coleridge 118 lists *PL . . . Edinburgh: Printed by Sands, Murray, and Cochran. For A. Kincaid and A. Donaldson. MDCCLV*, "as very probably a separate issue of vol. 1" of the 1755 set, referencing the 1755 set in the notes, quoted; while Coleridge 216 lists the 1762 Donaldson editions of the *PW*, also listed here); Not in Kohler.

1561. PARADISE REGAIN'D. A Poem, In Four Books. To which is added **SAMSON AGONISTES**; And **POEMS UPON SEVERAL OCCASIONS**; With a **TRACTATE OF EDUCATION**. The Author John Milton. *London: Printed for J. and R. Tonson; And for C. Hitch and L. Hawes, R. Ware, J. Hodges, J. Ward, M. and T. Longman, C. Corbet, J. Brindley, P. Davey and B. Law. MDCCLVI.* 12mo, [ii]+351pp., "The Table Of Contents," half-titles within decorative black trim for *SA*, *P*, *C*, the *LP* ("Poemata"), and *Of Ed* ("A Small Tractate of Education. To Mr. Hartlib"), decorative head- and tailpieces, original sheep (a bit rubbed at joints and edges), gilt rules on covers and spine, raised bands. A fine copy with contemporary signature (dated 1766) on fly-leaf. Coleridge 200; Not in Kohler.

1561A. (Cross-listing) PARADISE REGAIN'D. A Poem, In Four Books. To which is added **SAMSON AGONISTES**: And **POEMS UPON SEVERAL OCCASIONS**. The Author John Milton. From the Text of Thomas Newton, D.D. *Birmingham: Printed by John Baskerville For J. and R. Tonson in London. MDCCLVIII.* First Baskerville edition. 8vo, 390pp., half-title for each book of *PR* and for some of the poems.

[together with]

1561B. (Cross-listing) PARADISE LOST . . . *Birmingham[:] Printed by John Baskerville for J. and R. Tonson in London. MDCCLVIII.* First Baskerville edition. 8vo. Together, two volumes. Contemporary full dark blue morocco (rebacked preserving original spines). A very nice set. The third product of the Baskerville Press and one of its most attractive. See main listing under *PL*, 1758.

1561C. (Cross-listing) Variant of Preceding. PARADISE REGAIN'D . . . SAMSON AGONISTES: AND POEMS UPON SEVERAL OCCASIONS . . . *Birmingham: Printed by John Baskerville For J. and R. Tonson in London. MDCCLVIII.* First Baskerville edition. 4to, 390pp., life of Milton (bound here in volume 2, not 1), half-title for each book of *PR* and for some of the poems.

[together with]

1561D. (Cross-listing) Variant of Preceding. PARADISE LOST . . . *Birmingham[:] Printed by John Baskerville for J. and R. Tonson in London. MDCCLVIII.* First Baskerville edition. 4to. Together, two volumes. The rare quarto issue, complete with the 1734 Richardson engraving of Milton bust, a blind Milton with laurel wreath (not always present), before title page, volume 2, the life of Milton (also not found in all copies), volume 1, contemporary full green morocco. A very fine set. Rare. See main listing under *PL*, 1758.

1561E. (Cross-listing) PARADISE REGAIN'D. A Poem, In Four Books. To which is added **SAMSON AGONISTES**: And **POEMS UPON SEVERAL OCCASIONS**. The Author John Milton. From the Text of Thomas Newton, D.D. *Birmingham: Printed by John Baskerville For J. and R. Tonson in London. MDCCLIX.* Second Baskerville Milton. Small 4to, 390pp., "Table of Contents," title page in the first state, with "PSON" of "SAMPSON" erased and "SON" overprinted, half-title for each book of *PR* and for some of the poems.

[together with]

1561F. (Cross-listing) PARADISE LOST . . . *Birmingham[:] Printed by John Baskerville for J. and R. Tonson in London. MDCCLIX.* Second Baskerville Milton. Small 4to, [v]+416pp., engraved frontispiece portrait after J. Miller. Together, two volumes. Mid-nineteenth-century claret calf. A very handsome set from the Library of Chatsworth, with a fine provenance. Largest paper edition of Baskerville's Milton. See main listing under *PL*, 1759.

1561G. (Cross-listing) PARADISE REGAIN'D. A Poem, In Four Books. To which is added **SAMSON AGONISTES**: And **POEMS UPON SEVERAL OCCASIONS**. The Author John Milton. From the Text of Thomas Newton, D.D. *Birmingham: Printed by John Baskerville For J. and R. Tonson in London. MDCCLX.* Third and final Baskerville Milton. Large 8vo, [ii]+lxii+390pp., "Table Of Contents," life of Milton, half-title for each book of *PR* and for some of the poems.

[together with]

1561H. (Cross-listing) PARADISE LOST . . . *Birmingham: Printed by John Baskerville, for J. and R. Tonson in London. MDCCLX.* Third and final Baskerville Milton. Large 8vo, [xix]+[v]+416pp. Together, two volumes. Contemporary tree calf. A nice set. See main listing under *PL*, 1760.

1562. PARADISE REGAIN'D. A Poem, In Four Books. To which is added **SAMSON AGONISTES**: And

POEMS UPON SEVERAL OCCASIONS. The Author John Milton. The Third [Newton] Edition, With Notes of various Authors, By Thomas Newton, D.D. *London: Printed for C. Hitch and L. Hawes, J. and R. Tonson, J. Ward, S. Crowder and Co. T. Longman, A. and C. Corber [sic], B. Law and Co. and R. Ware. MDCCLX.* 2 volumes. 8vo, [vi]+335pp.,+[iv]+386+[4]pp., title page each volume, engraved frontispiece portrait of Milton at age twenty-one by Vertue, "Preface," "The Table of Contents," two engraved illustrations by Hayman (reduced) engraved by Grignion for Book I of *PR* and as frontispiece for *SA*, half-title for each book of *PR* and for *SA*, decorative endpieces, notes at bottom of page, volume 1, "The Table Of Contents," three engraved illustrations by Hayman (reduced) engraved by Grignion for *L'A, IlP*, and *C*, half-title for *P, C*, and *LP* ("Poemata"), notes at bottom of page, index, volume 2, contemporary polished calf, gilt rules on covers, gilt-decorated spines, red morocco title labels and black morocco numbering labels (the black labels chipped), raised bands. A fine set, very fresh and clean throughout, with early signature and bookplate in each volume, with advertisement leaf (for new 4to edition by Newton with Hayman plates) bound in at end of volume 2. Uniformly bound as volumes 3 and 4 with *PL*, J. and R. Tonson, B. Dodd, et al., 1763, also listed here. See 1752 4to edition also listed here, the first Newton edition. Coleridge 204; Not in Kohler.

1563. PARADISE REGAIN'D. A Poem. In Four Books. To which is added **SAMSON AGONISTES; AND POEMS UPON SEVERAL OCCASIONS. WITH A TRACTATE OF EDUCATION.** The Author John Milton. *London: Printed for C. Hitch and L. Hawes, J. and R. Tonson, J. Ward, S. Crowder and Co. T. Longman, P. Davey and B. Law, A. and C. Corbet, and R. Ware. MDCCLX.* Large 12mo, [iv]+359pp., engraved frontispiece illustration for *PR* and other engraved illustrations by Hayman (reduced) engraved by T. Müller, "The Table Of Contents," half-title for *SA, P,C, LP* ("Poemata"), and *Of Ed* ("A Small Tractate of Education. To Mr. Hartlib"), decorative head- and tailpieces, contemporary calf (spine worn, lacking label, ends chipped with small crack at center bottom half, inner middle marginal worming through last fifteen leaves barely touching text), gilt rules on covers, gilt-decorated spine (faded), marbled endpapers and edges. A good, large paper copy, very fresh and clean throughout with sharp impressions of the plates. Coleridge 204; Not in Kohler.

1564. PARADISE REGAIN'D. A Poem, In Four Books. To which is added **SAMSON AGONISTES; AND POEMS UPON SEVERAL OCCASIONS: WITH A TRACTATE OF EDUCATION.** The Author John Milton. *London: Printed by H. Fenwick, Cheapside. n.d. [ca. 1760].* 12mo, 240pp., original calf (a little worn, joints cracked, corners worn, spine chipped at top and bottom, lacking front fly-leaf), red leather label with gilt lettering and gilt trim on spine. All in all, a decent copy of a rare edition, fresh and clean within. Rare. Not in Coleridge (although Coleridge 152 records "An Extract From Milton's Paradise Lost. With Notes. London: Printed by Henry Fenwick. MDCCLXIII," see copy listed here); Not in Kohler.

1565. PARADISE REGAIN'D. A Poem, In Four Books. **SAMSON AGONISTES.** A Dramatic Poem. **COMUS.** A Mask. With **POEMS ON SEVERAL OCCASIONS.** And **A TRACTATE OF EDUCATION.** The Author John Milton. *London: Printed for T. Thompson, R. Damper, L. Burch, H. Shoram, T. Clitch, B. Blossom, D. Lord, F. Fritchet, G. Townwold, J. Dwarf, J. Liblond, and W. Blanchard. M DCC LXI.* 12mo in 6s, [ii]+62+58+38+94+17pp. (each work paginated separately), frontispiece portrait of Milton ("GB Sc. 1756") laid down on verso of endpaper causing a split between portrait and title, title page in red and black, separate title pages in black for *SA, C, P,* and *Of Ed*, each with abbreviated imprint: "*Printed In The Year M DCC LXI*," contemporary calf (a bit worn, lacking label on spine, pages uniformly age-browned), gilt rules on spine. A decent copy of a scarce edition with early ownership signature in a neat hand (dated 1823) on fly-leaf. John Shawcross shared the following with me: "Pirated edition . . . Kohler is correct; it is 12mo in 6s; but incorrect in that it is GB, not GV." Not in Coleridge; Kohler 199, citing "Portrait frontispiece engraved by G. V. and dated 1756," referencing "Williamson 170," and reporting "Not in the British Library. Not in the Bodleian Library. Not in Cambridge University Library."

1566. PARADISE REGAIN'D. A Poem, In Four Books. To which is added, **SAMSON AGONISTES; AND POEMS UPON SEVERAL OCCASIONS.** The Author John Milton. With A Glossary; and, The Life of Milton. *Edinburgh: Printed by A. Donaldson and J. Reid. For Alexander Donaldson. MDCCLXII.* 12mo in 6s, [ii]+387pp., "The Contents," contemporary calf (a little rubbed), gilt rules on spine, orange leather label with gilt lettering and gilt rules, raised bands. A nice, tall copy with early signature on title and fly-leaf. John Shawcross shared with me that it is important to "note that the poems [here] are rearranged by category, and, significantly, that various other items are added." Coleridge reports "Another issue, volume 2 only; title page" as here. After careful comparison with Coleridge and with volume 2 of the 1762 two-volume

Donaldson edition of *PW* and of a variant edition in the collection (both listed here), this is "Another issue" of volume 2, as identified by Coleridge. The volume 2 title page of the 1762 two-volume Donaldson edition of *PW* and variant reads: "The Poetical Works Of Milton. Volume II. Containing Paradise Regain'd, A Poem, In Four Books; Samson Agonistes; And Poems upon several occasions. With A Glossary; and, The Life of Milton. . . . [rest as above]. Rare. Coleridge 216a; Not in Kohler.

1567. PARADISE REGAIN'D. A Poem, In Four Books. To which is added **SAMSON AGONISTES; AND POEMS UPON SEVERAL OCCASIONS: WITH A TRACTATE OF EDUCATION.** The Author John Milton. *London: Printed for J. and R. Tonson, L. Hawes and Co., T. Caslon, T. Longman, B. Law, C. Corbet, T. Lownds and M. Richardson. MDCCLXV.* 12mo, [iv]+381+[2]pp., engraved frontispiece illustration for *PR* and other engraved illustrations by Hayman (reduced) engraved by T. Miller, "The Table Of Contents," half-title for *SA, P, C,* the *LP* ("Poemata"), and *Of Ed* ("A Small Tractate of Education. To Mr. Hartlib"), decorative head- and tailpieces, glossary, advertisement leaves, contemporary calf, red morocco label on spine with gilt lettering and decorative gilt trim, raised bands, red edges. A very fine copy with early dated signature on fly-leaf. This edition seems to have been sold uniform with *PL*, 1765 (also listed here); Coleridge 205; Kohler 200, reporting "Not in Cambridge University Library."

1569. PARADISE REGAIN'D. A Poem, In Four Books. To which is added **SAMSON AGONISTES: And POEMS UPON SEVERAL OCCASIONS.** The Author John Milton. With Notes of various Authors, By Thomas Newton, D.D. *London: Printed for J. and R. Tonson, T. Caslon, T. Longman, W. Johnston, R. Ware, C. Corbet, T. Lownds, W. Nicholl, and M. Richardson. MDCCLXVI.* 2 volumes. 8vo, [vi]+335pp.,+[iv]+386+[4]pp., title page each volume, engraved frontispiece portrait of Milton at age twenty-one by Vertue, "Preface," "The Table of Contents," two engraved illustrations by Hayman (reduced) engraved by Grignion for Book I of *PR* and as frontispiece for *SA*, half-title for each book of *PR* and for *SA*, decorative endpieces, notes at bottom of page, volume 1, "The Table Of Contents," three engraved illustrations by Hayman (reduced) engraved by Grignion for *L'A, IlP*, and *C*, half-title for *P, C,* and *LP* ("Poemata"), notes at bottom of page, index, volume 2, contemporary polished calf, gilt rules on spines, red morocco labels with gilt lettering and decorative gilt trim. A very fine set, clean and fresh internally, with early (possibly contemporary) notation on front pastedown in each volume. Uniformly bound as volumes 3 and 4 with *PL, Printed for J. Beecroft, W. Strahan, et al., 1770*, copy listed here. Coleridge 206; Kohler 201, reporting "Not in Cambridge University Library."

1570. [PARADISE REGAIN'D] THE RECOVERY OF MAN: OR, MILTON'S PARADISE REGAINED. In Prose. After The Manner Of The Archbishop of Cambray. To which is prefixed, The Life Of The Author. *Printed In The Year MDCCLXXI. Price Two Shillings.* Slim 12mo, 192pp., half-title with decorative black trim, contemporary unlettered sheep (somewhat worn, corners and spine ends chipped, joints breaking, light soiling), gilt rules on spine, raised bands. The life is based mainly on Fenton. This edition probably is either a Scottish or Irish piracy and is very rare. Coleridge 253; Not in Kohler.

1571. PARADISE REGAIN'D. A Poem. In Four Books. To which is added **SAMSON AGONISTES; AND POEMS UPON SEVERAL OCCASIONS. WITH A TRACTATE OF EDUCATION.** The Author John Milton. *London: Printed for J. Beecroft, W. Strahan, J. and F. Rivington, Hawes, Clarke and Collins, R. Horsfield, W. Johnston, B. White, T. Caslon, S. Crowder, T. Longman, C. Corbett, Z. Stuart, T. Cadell, G. Pearch, T. Lowndes, T. Davies, J. Robson, W. Nicoll, W. Flexney, S. Bladon, G. Robinson, and R. Baldwin. M DCC LXXII.* 12mo, [iv]+381+[2]pp., engraved frontispiece illustration for *PR* and other engraved illustrations by Hayman (reduced) engraved by T. Müller, "The Table Of Contents," half-title for *SA, P,C,* the *LP* ("Poemata"), and *Of Ed* ("A Small Tractate of Education. To Mr. Hartlib"), decorative head- and tailpieces, glossary, advertisement leaves ("Lately published, a New Edition" of "The Poetical Works of John Milton"), contemporary calf (front joint cracked), faint gilt rules on spine, red morocco label with gilt lettering and decorative gilt trim, raised bands. A fine copy. This edition of *PR* seems to be associated with the 12mo one-volume 1770 edition of *PL* (also listed here); see also 8vo one-volume 1785 edition. John Shawcross shared with me that "This is a reset reprint (reissue) of 1765 [an edition not in this collection] but with different proprietors." Coleridge 207; Kohler 202, reporting "Not in the British Library."

1572. PARADISE REGAIN'D. A Poem. In Four Books. The Author John Milton. *London: Printed for R. Crowder, C. Ware, and T. Payne. M DCC LXXII.* First edition thus. 12mo, 357pp., half-title for *SA, P,* and *C*, glossary at the end, contemporary calf (slightly worn, lacking endpapers, final page tipped on back cover as back pastedown thereby losing verso p. 357—last page of "Glossary" and of text [p. 358], age-browning, partial bookplate remaining from a bookplate tipped at top of front cover at an earlier time), red morocco label with gilt lettering on spine ("Milton's

Works") and number "2" below, small decorative gilt floral pieces in the panels, raised bands. A decent copy of a rare book. Although not so indicated on the title page, *SA*, *P*, and *C* are also included, each with its own half-title. John Shawcross shared with me that this edition "was reissued with your [*PL*, 1772, also listed here] in 1772 as 'Poetical Works,' copy owned by University of Western Ontario," since acquired for this collection (see *PW*, 1772, also listed here). Shawcross further stated that "I have entered this in the bibliography [i.e., John's forthcoming bibliographical publication of eighteenth-century editions] as apparently a separate issue just as [your *PL*, 1772, also listed here] seems to be. I haven't found it separated anywhere else." The description I had provided John Shawcross unfortunately failed to mention some important elements: the spine label and "2" in my description here, and also that upon much closer examination there appears the faint offprint of a general title page for "The Poetical Works" on the front pastedown. My apologies to John for my inadequate description: this copy is most likely not a separate issue, even though *PL* appears to be, as John has indicated. Rare. Not in Coleridge; Not in Kohler.

1573. PARADISE REGAIN'D. A Poem, In Four Books. To which is added **SAMSON AGONISTES**: And **POEMS UPON SEVERAL OCCASIONS, WITH A TRACTATE OF EDUCATION.** The Author John Milton. *Glasgow: Printed By Robert And Andrew Foulis, M.DCC.LXXII.* 2 volumes. 12mo, 182+[1]pp.,+[ii]+198+[2]pp., dagger symbol preceding the signature marks, half-title ("Paradise Regain'd, Samson Agonistes, And Poems Upon Several Occasions, According To Dr. Newton's Edition") each volume, title page each volume followed by "The Table of Contents," half-title for some of the poems, original calf, gilt rules on spines, red morocco labels with gilt lettering within gilt rules, raised bands. A very fine set with half-title for each volume. Advertisement leaf for "Books printed by Robert and Andrew Foulis In Small 12mo" (including this set—leaf printed on both sides) bound in at end of volume 2. Uniformly bound with *PL* (Foulis, 1771, 2 volumes) also listed here, which does not have the dagger symbol preceding the signature marks as here. Gaskell, *Foulis Press*, 548; Not in Coleridge; Not in Kohler.

1574. Variant of Preceding, original calf (joints cracking), finely tooled gilt-decorated spines within the panels, red morocco lettering labels with gilt lettering ("MILTON") and decorative gilt trim, black morocco numbering labels with gilt numbers and decorative gilt trim, raised bands with decorative gilt trim, outer dentelles finely tooled in gilt. A lovely set in an attractive contemporary variant binding, contents as preceding, with half-titles and advertisement leaf. Uniformly bound with *PL* (Foulis, 1776, 2 volumes) also listed here, which, as in the 1772 edition of *PR* here, has a dagger symbol preceding the signature marks. Gaskell, *Foulis Press*, 548; Not in Coleridge; Not in Kohler.

1575. PARADISE REGAIN'D. A Poem, In Four Books. To which is added **SAMSON AGONISTES**: And **POEMS UPON SEVERAL OCCASIONS.** The Author John Milton. A New Edition, With Notes of various Authors, By Thomas Newton, D.D. Now Lord Bishop of Bristol. *London: Printed for J. Beecroft, W. Strahan, J. and F. Rivington, Hawes, Clarke and Collins, R. Horsfield, W. Johnston, B. White, T. Caslon, S. Crowder, T. Longman, B. Law, C. Corbett, Z. Stuart, T. Cadell, T. Lowndes, T. Davies, J. Robson, W. Nicoll, W. Flexney, G. Robinson, J. Knox, and W. Otridge. M DCC LXXIII.* 2 volumes. 8vo, [vi]+335pp.,+[iv]+386+[4]pp., title page each volume (with numerous typographical differences on the title page of volume 2 and a different listing of the booksellers), engraved frontispiece portrait of Milton at age twenty-one by Vertue, "Preface," "The Table of Contents," two engraved illustrations by Hayman (reduced) engraved by Grignion for Book I of *PR* and as frontispiece for *SA*, half-title for each book of *PR* and for *SA*, decorative endpieces, notes at bottom of page, volume 1, "The Table Of Contents," three engraved illustrations by Hayman (reduced) engraved by Grignion for *L'A*, *IlP*, and *C*, half-title for *P*, *C*, and *LP* ("Poemata"), notes at bottom of page, index, volume 2, contemporary calf, gilt-decorated spine, red morocco title labels, black morocco numbering labels, raised bands. A very fine set with early signature on front blank and the bookplate of Leonard Schlosser. Coleridge 208; Kohler 203, reporting "Not in the Bodleian Library."

1576. PARADISE REGAIN'D. A Poem, In Four Books. To which is added **SAMSON AGONISTES**: And **POEMS UPON SEVERAL OCCASIONS.** The Author John Milton. A New Edition, With Notes of various Authors, By Thomas Newton, D.D. Now Lord Bishop of Bristol. *London: Printed for W. Strahan, J. F. and C. Rivington, et al., M DCC LXXVII.* Large 4to, [iv]+[ii]+690+[2]pp., engraved frontispiece portrait of Milton "Aetat. 42" after Vertue engraved by I. Richardson, engraved illustrations after Hayman, "The Table of Contents," half-title for each book of *PR* and for various of the other works, notes at bottom of page, index, contemporary mottled calf (neatly rebacked with original double maroon lettering pieces remounted, new endpapers), gilt rules on spine, raised bands. A handsome copy, clean and fresh within, with striking impressions of the plates. Newton's important edition was frequently reprinted and reissued into the nineteenth century; it was only superseded by Todd, though rarely in this handsome quarto format with Hayman's plates in full size. Coleridge points out, "This was a page-for-page reprint of the 1752" first Newton edition (also listed here), observing further that "As Todd's description suggests this was issued for uniform binding with the 1775 4to edition of *PL*," as here. Uniformly bound with *PL* (Eighth Newton edition. London: Printed for J. Beecroft et al., M.DCC.LXXV) also listed here. Coleridge 209; Kohler 190.

1577. PARADISE REGAIN'D. A Poem, In Four Books. SAMSON AGONISTES. A Dramatic Poem. COMUS. A Mask: With POEMS ON SEVERAL OCCASIONS. And A TRACTATE OF EDUCA-TION. The Author John Milton. *London: Sold by J. Banners, W. Slackman, F. Rennington, W. Jones, & T. Newton.* MDCCLXXVII. 12mo, [ii]+272pp., "The Contents," half-title for *SA, C, P*, the *LP* ("Poemata"), and *Of Ed* ("A Small Tractate of Education. To Mr. Hartlib"), decorative head- and tailpieces, contemporary calf (a bit worn, joints cracked, lacking spine label), gilt rules on spine (faded). All in all, a good, tall copy of a very scarce edition, which has the hallmark of a provincial printing. Rare. Not in Coleridge; Not in Kohler.

1577A. (Cross-listing) PARADISE REGAIN'D. A Poem, In Four Books. To which Are added SAMSON AGONISTES: And POEMS ON SEVERAL OCCASIONS. The Author John Milton. With The Life of the Author. By Thomas Newton. D.D. *Philadelphia: Printed and Sold by Robert Bell, in Third-Street,* MDCCLXXVII. Volume 2 of 2 volumes. First American edition. 4to, general half-title, 640pp. (continuous pagination from volume 1), reprint of "advertisement" "prefixed" "To the first edition of the author's poems printed in 1645" with "Contents Of The Second Volume" on verso, contemporary sheepskin (a little worn, front joint cracked at top and bottom, pages age-browned), half-title for "Poems On Several Occasions" followed by half-title for "The Twelfth Book Of Paradise Lost," half-title also for *PR, SA,* and *C*. A good copy. Together two volumes, forming a complete set of Milton's English poems, with volume 1 containing the first eleven books of *PL*, while volume 2 here begins with Book XII followed by the index and biography of Milton, on paging that continues from volume 1, pp. [331]–444, with signatures that are also continuous with volume 1, all three referred to on the "Contents" page of volume 2, continuing with *L'A, IlP, L, S, P,* and *PR, SA,* and *C*. Acquired separately. Rare. Not in Coleridge (211n); Not in Kohler.

[together with]

1577B. (Cross-listing) PARADISE LOST. A Poem, In Twelve Books. The Author John Milton. With the Life of Milton. By Thomas Newton, D.D. [Quotation from Thomson] *Philadelphia: Printed by Robert Bell, in Third-Street,* MDCCLXXVII. Volume 1 of 2 volumes. First American edition. 4to, 328pp., half-title, unsigned engraved frontispiece of Milton, Homer, and Virgil with Dryden epigram, arguments printed before the poem, contemporary sheepskin (worn). A decent copy of volume 1, which contains the first eleven books of *PL*. Acquired separately. Rare. See main listing under *PL*, 1777.

1578. PARADISE REGAIN'D. A Poem, In Four Books. The Author John Milton. *London: Printed for Toplis and Bunney, in Holborn; and J. Mozley, Gainsbrough.* M,DCC,LXXIX. 18mo, 108pp., unsigned engraved frontispiece illustration of the triumph of Jesus over Satan (fine impression), original calf (worn, front cover detached). Clean internally. This is a very rare edition with an apparently anonymous frontispiece illustration. As I learned from John Shawcross, later editions of *PR* with the same frontispiece illustration but somewhat different publisher's imprints include a 1786 edition (with publisher's imprint, "London Printed for W. Osborne and J. Griffin, in St. Paul's Church-Yard; and J. Mozley, Gainsbrough," copy also listed here) and a 1793 edition (with publisher's imprint, "London: Printed for Osborne and Griffin, and Mozley and Co. Gainsbrough"); these are simply reprints of this 1779 edition. This 1779 edition is the first in this series of editions; it is also, as Shawcross indicated to me, the first separate edition of *PR* he has found. Copy in the University of Illinois; Not recorded in Parker; Not in Coleridge; Not in Kohler.

1579. [PARADISE REGAIN'D, ETC.] DAS WIEDEREROBERTE PARADIES DES JOHANN MILTON, NEBST SEINER LEBENSBESCHREIBUNG, EINIGEN DRAMATISCHEN UND VERSCHIEDNEN KLEINERN GEDICHTEN. Mit allerhochstem kaiserlichen Privilegio. *Mannheim, im Verlage der Herausgeber der auslandischen schonen Geister [d. i. Anton von Kelein und J. C. Becke],* 1781. Second edition thus. 8vo, lxii+[ii]+302pp., decorative piece on title page (ornamental shell and foliage), life of Milton, half-title for each of the various works, decorative head- and tailpieces (several very large, others very small), original boards with light blue paper (partly missing on spine), later shelf label at top of spine. A nice copy with early signature on front pastedown. This collection includes prose translations of *PR, SA, C, L, L'A, IlP,* and poetic translations of several poems titled: "Un die Zeit" ("On Time"), "Ben einer fenerlichen Musik" ("At a Solemn Musick"), and "Auf den

Morgen der Geburt Christi" ("On the Morning of Christ's Nativity," without the Hymn). A sixty-two-page critical biography of Milton is also included. Coleridge notes that "This translation by Simon Grynaeus was first published in 1752 in Basel. It is in prose and [it] was not superseded until 1828. This is the 2nd edition of it recorded in NUC." Coleridge also notes that "The copy at WTu has a frontispiece showing a bust of Milton, resembling the Faithorne portrait." Coleridge 213; Shawcross, 1972, p. 7; Shawcross, Kentucky, 441, making no reference to a frontispiece, as Coleridge does; Kohler 204, also making no reference to a frontispiece and reporting "Not in the Bodleian Library. Not in Cambridge University Library." Uncommon.

1580. Variant of Preceding. **DAS WIEDEREROBERTE PARADIES DES JOHANN MILTON** . . . *Mannheim, im Verlage der Herausgeber der auslandischen schonen Geister [d. i. Anton von Kelein und J. C. Becke], 1781.* Second edition thus. 8vo, lxii+[ii]+302pp., frontispiece portrait of a bust of Milton on a pedestal with a snake intertwined with ivy and an apple in the front of the pedestal and "Milton's" name carved in the front of the base below and "E. Verhelst.sec.Mannheim" printed beneath the bust, decorative piece on title page (ornamental shell and foliage), life of Milton, half-title for each of the various works, decorative head- and tailpieces (several very large, others very small), original calf (worn), spine richly decorated in gilt with gilt lettering, decorated endpapers, red edges. Identical to the preceding copy in every respect, except that is has a frontispiece portrait of a bust of Milton and is in a variant contemporary binding. The image of Milton on the bust is eighteenth-century in appearance: an early middle-age man with rounded face and long dark hair in the style of the period *yet* overall continental in appearance. It is difficult to reconcile the frontispiece portrait here with the frontispiece described by Coleridge who notes that "The copy at WTu has a frontispiece showing a bust of Milton, resembling the Faithorne portrait," without mention of a snake intertwined with ivy or "E. Verhelst.sec.Mannheim" printed beneath the bust. Rare. Coleridge 213; Shawcross, 1972, p. 7; Kohler 204 (without frontispiece).

1581. **PARADISE REGAIN'D.** A Poem, In Four Books. To which is added **SAMSON AGONISTES, COMUS. A MASK:** And **POEMS UPON SEVERAL OCCASIONS,** With **A TRACTATE OF EDUCATION.** By John Milton. *London: Printed for A. Millar, and J. Hodges. MDCCLXXXIII.* 12mo, iv+272pp., unsigned engraved frontispiece illustration for *PR* engraved by Edward Malpas to his own design, small decorative device on title page, half-titles for *SA*, *C*, *P*, and *Of Ed* ("A Small Tractate of Education. To Mr. Hartlib"), decorative head- and tailpieces, contemporary sheep (quite worn, front joint broken and slightly chipped, printed on poor-quality paper with some foxing and embrowning), raised bands, early names on fly-leaf, in a protective plastic cover. Rare. Not in Coleridge; Shawcross, Kentucky, 449; Kohler 205, reporting "Not in the British Library. Not in the Bodleian Library. Not in Cambridge University Library."

1582. **PARADISE REGAIN'D.** A Poem, In Four Books. To which is added **SAMSON AGONISTES;** And **POEMS UPON SEVERAL OCCASIONS; WITH A TRACTATE OF EDUCATION.** The Author John Milton. *London: Printed for W. Strahan, J. F. and C. Rivington, R. Horsfield, B. White, T. Longman, B. Law, C. Corbett, T. Cadell, J. Robson, W. Flexney, G. Robinson, J. Knox, S. Bladon, T. Evans, W. Otridge, and W. Lowndes. M.DCC.LXXXV.* 12mo, [iv]+381+[2]pp., engraved frontispiece illustration for *PR* and other engraved illustrations after Hayman (reduced) engraved by T. Müller, "The Table Of Contents," half-title for *SA*, *P*, *C*, the *LP* ("Poemata"), and *Of Ed* ("A Small Tractate of Education. To Mr. Hartlib"), decorative head- and tailpieces, glossary, advertisement leaves ("Lately published, a New Edition" of "The Poetical Works of John Milton"), contemporary calf (rubbed, especially the spine), gilt-decorated rules on spine, red morocco label with gilt lettering and decorative gilt trim, outer dentelles finely tooled in gilt (faded). A nice copy with dated early signature-note on fly-leaf and earlier dated signature on back blank. See 12mo 1772 edition also listed here. See two-volume octavo edition by Strahan et al. following with variant title page (containing "A New Edition. With Notes of various Authors, By Thomas Newton, D.D. Now Lord Bishop of Bristol" and without reference to "With A Tractate of Education"); see also 12mo 1772 edition also listed here. Scarce. Not in Coleridge; Kohler 207, describing its copy as "Octavo in 12s" and reporting "Not in the British Library. Not in the Bodleian Library. Not in Cambridge University Library." John Shawcross informed me there is a "Copy in University of Illinois Library."

1583. **PARADISE REGAIN'D.** A Poem, In Four Books. To which is added **SAMSON AGONISTES:** And **POEMS UPON SEVERAL OCCASIONS.** The Author John Milton. A New Edition. With Notes of various Authors, By Thomas Newton, D.D. Now Lord Bishop of Bristol. *London: Printed for W. Strahan, J. F. and C. Rivington, R. Horsfield, B. White, T. Longman, B. Law, C. Corbett, T. Cadell, J. Robson, W. Flexney, G. Robinson, J. Knox, S. Bladon, T. Evans, W. Otridge, and W. Lowndes. MDCCLXXXV.* 2 volumes. 8vo, [vi]+335pp.,+[iv]+386+[4]pp., title page each volume, engraved frontispiece portrait of Milton at age twenty-one after Vertue, "Preface," "The Table of Contents," two engraved illustrations by Hayman (reduced) engraved by Grignion, for Book I of *PR* and as frontispiece for *SA*, half-title for each book of *PR* and for *SA*, decorative endpieces, notes at bottom of page, volume 1, "The Table Of Contents," three engraved illustrations by Hayman (reduced) engraved by Grignion for *L'A, IlP*, and *C*, half-title for *P, C*, and *LP* ("Poemata"), notes at bottom of page, index, volume 2, contemporary tree calf (joints cracked), decorative gilt trim on covers, gilt-decorated spines, red morocco title labels and black morocco numbering labels, outer dentelles tooled in gilt, marbled endpapers. A very nice set, fresh internally. See one-volume edition by Strahan et al. preceding with variant title page, with reference to "With A Tractate Of Education," lacking here, and without "A New Edition. With Notes of various Authors, By Thomas Newton, D.D. Now Lord Bishop of Bristol," present here. Scarce. Coleridge 210; Shawcross, Kentucky, 462; Kohler 206, reporting "Not in Cambridge University Library."

1584. PARADISE REGAIN'D. A Poem, In Four Books. The Author John Milton. *London: Printed For W. Osborne And J. Griffin, In St. Paul's Church-Yard; And J. Mozley, Gainsbrough, M DCC. LXXXVI.* 12mo, half-title, 108pp., engraved frontispiece illustration of the triumph of Jesus over Satan (fine impression), contemporary sheep (a bit worn, joints cracked, early name on front pastedown). A good copy, fresh and clean within. The frontispiece is a reprint of that which was first printed in the 1779 edition (also listed here with further commentary). Rare. Not in Coleridge; Not in Kohler.

1585. PARADISE REGAIN'D. A Poem, In Four Books. To which is added **SAMSON AGONISTES, COMUS. A MASK: And POEMS UPON SEVERAL OCCASIONS.** By John Milton. *London: Printed For J. Lackington, No. 46, Chiswell Street, Moorfields. M.DCC.LXXXVIII.* 8vo, iv+336pp., "The Contents," half-title within decorative black trim, for *SA, P, C*, and the *LP* ("Poemata"), glossary, contemporary tree sheep (a bit rubbed, front joint cracked, spine chipped at top and bottom, minor spotting), gilt-decorated spine (lacking label). See comments by John Shawcross about the significance of this edition in *Milton Quarterly* 41, no. 1 (2007): 69–70. Rare edition, published by one of the most famous eighteenth-century booksellers. Not in Coleridge; Not in Kohler.

1585A. (Cross-listing) **PARAISO RETAURADO** [In] **PARAISO PERDIDO, POEMA HEROICO DE J. MILTON**; Traduzido Em Vulgar Pelo Padre José Amaro Da Silva, Presbitero Vimaranense. Com o Paraiso Retaurado, Poema do mesmo Author; Notas Historicas, Mythologicas, &c. de M. Racine: e as Observaçoes de M. Addisson sobre o Paraiso Perdido. Tomo II. *Lisboa, Na Typografia Rollandiana. 1789. Com licença da Real Meza da Commissao Geral sobre o Eccame, e Censura dos Livres.* Volume 2 only. 8vo, 344pp., notes at bottom of page, contemporary calf. A very nice copy, but of volume 2 only. Included in this volume, however, is *Paraiso Retaurado*, complete with "Arguments" (not original to the poem) and a decorative tailpiece at the end of each book. Rare. Not in Coleridge; Not in Kohler. See main listing under *Paraiso Perdidi*, 1789.

1586. PARADISE REGAIN'D: A Poem In Four Books. By John Milton. From The Text Of Dr. Newton. [Quotation from Addison] *Philadelphia: Printed by W. Young, Bookseller, The Corner Of Second And Chestnut-Street. M,DCC,XC.* Second American edition. 12mo, 80+[4]pp., "Preface" with small decorative headpiece, original marbled paper wrappers (a bit aged, small library stamp inside back cover), some edges untrimmed, preserved in a red cloth case with folding inner protective wrappers. A large copy with four pages of advertisements: "Books' American Editions, Sold By William Young" (including *PL*). The first American edition of *PR* was published in 1777 (also listed here). Rare. Evans 22671; Not in Coleridge; Not in Kohler.

1587. PARADISE REGAIN'D: A Poem In Four Books. By John Milton. From The Text Of Doctor Newton. To Which Are Added, Poems on Several Occasions. *Philadelphia: Printed And Sold By Henry Taylor. M.DCC.XCI.* Third American edition. 12mo, 136pp., "Preface. [Extracted From Dr. Newton's Octavo Of 1773.]" with small decorative headpiece, half-title for each book of *PR*, half-title also for *P*, contemporary sheep (rubbed, front joint cracked, age-browning), gilt rules on spine (faded, lacking label). A good copy with early bookplate. Rare. Coleridge 211; Not in Kohler; John Shawcross also told me that there is a "copy in the Newberry Library."

1587A. (Cross-listing) [PARADISE REGAINED] DAS WIEDEREROBERTE PARADIES, DES JOHANN MILTON, nevst seiner Lebensveschreibung, und dramatischen Gedichten: Simson. Mit allerhochstem kaiserlichen Privilegio. *Mannheim, im Berlage ver Herausgeber der aulandischen schonen Geister 1791.* Bound with [PARADISE LOST] JOHANN MILTONS VERLORNES PARADIES. Neue verbesserte Auflage. Erster Band. Mit Kaiserl. und Kurpfalzischen Privilegien. *Mannheim, 1791.* Bound with [SAMSON AGONISTES] SIMSON. Ein dramatisches Gedicht (half-title). 3 volumes in one. 8vo, 272pp.,+xlv+272pp.,+208pp., separate title page for each volume of *PL* (volumes 1 and 2), life before Book I, separate title page for *PR* (volume 3), half-title for *SA*, decorative headpieces, contemporary quarter polished black calf, marbled paper over boards. Fine copy. "This exceedingly rare combination is the only one that we have seen. The British Library has the German *PR*, but not the *PL*; neither translation is in Coleridge" (G. W. Stuart, Jr., Ravenstree, Cat. 174, #55, 1992). Not in Coleridge; Not in Kohler. See main listing under *PL*, 1791.

1588. [PARADISE REGAIN'D] DET GIENVUNDNE PARADIIS eller Christi Fristelse i ørken. Et episk Digt af John Milton. Af det Engelske oversat ved Joh. Henr. Schønheyder. Meic. Dr. og Prof. *Kiøbenhavn 1792. Trykt hos Sebastian Popp.* First edition in Danish. 8vo, 116pp., contemporary half sheep, marbled paper over boards (a little rubbed), light olive green morocco label with gilt lettering and gilt rules on spine, slightly raised bands. A nice copy with a small engraving (classical in nature and not specifically related to Milton) tipped in on front pastedown. Translated by Johannes Henrich Schonheyder. This is the first and only known pre-1800 translation of *PR* into Danish; no subsequent editions or other translations into Danish are recorded. Rare. Coleridge 172; Kohler 208, reporting "Not in the Bodleian Library. Not in Cambridge University Library."

1589. PARADISE REGAIN'D: A Poem In Four Books. By John Milton. A New Edition, With Notes Of Various Authors, By Charles Dunster. [Greek Quotation from Plato] *London: Printed For T. Cadell, Jun. And W. Davies, (Successors To Mr. Cadell,) In The Strand. 1795.* First and only Dunster edition. 4to, [i]+[iv]+[ii]+280pp., bound without the engraved title page, but with the printed title page and dedication leaf as well as the large engraved folding map of paradise (map a trifle wrinkled), preface, half-title for each book, printed in double column, notes at bottom of page, contemporary tree calf (rebacked, covers repaired), gilt rules on spine, raised bands decorated in blind, black morocco label with gilt lettering and decorative trim in blind, outer dentelles tooled in gilt (faded), "Corrections And Supplemental Notes" with half-title at end. A large, fresh copy. "This is the first separate edition of *PR* with the range of editorial material to qualify as a variorum. A revised second edition was published in 1800. Dunster wrote the arguments to each book himself, as Milton had not provided any" (Coleridge). See 1977 Norwood Editions reprint also listed here. Rare. Coleridge 171; Kohler 209, reporting "Not in the Bodleian Library"; Shawcross, Kentucky, 522.

1590. MILTON'S PARADISE REGAINED; With Select Notes Subjoined: To Which Is Added A Complete Collection Of His Miscellaneous Poems, Both English And Latin. *London: Printed by T. Bensley; For T. Longman, B. Law, J. Johnson, C. Dilly, C. C. And J. Robinson, W. Richardson, W. Otridge And Son, R. Baldwin, F. And C. Rivington, J. Scatcherd, Ogilvy And Speare, W. Lowndes, G. And T. Wilkie, G. Kearsley, Vernor And Hood, T. Cadell, Junior, And W. Davies, And S. Hayes. 1796.* First edition thus. 8vo, [1]+428pp., engraved frontispiece illustration plate of *The Baptism of Jesus* for *PR*, dated 1796, and three additional engraved illustration plates by E. F. Burney (one for *SA*, one for *L'A*, and one for *IlP*) engraved by Fittler and Bromley, printed title page, preface, half-title for each book of *PR* and for some of the poems, contemporary full straight-grained citron morocco, finely tooled gilt borders on covers, richly gilt-decorated spine, black morocco label with gilt lettering ("Milton's Poetical Works"), gilt numeral "II" within the panel, raised bands with gilt rules, inner dentelles finely tooled in gilt, outer dentelles ruled in gilt, blue endpapers, early armorial bookplate and bookplate of Leonard Schlosser on front pastedown. A splendid copy. This is the first appearance of these illustrations by Burney. Uniformly bound with *PL* (T. Bensley, 1795) also listed here, with advertisement leaf at the end: "In The Press And Speedily will be published, Printed and Embellished uniformly with this volume, Paradise Regained, Samson Agonistes, And All The Other English Poem Of John Milton. With select Notes illustrative of difficult Passages." Coleridge 212; Not in Kohler.

With Hand-Colored Plates

1591. Variant of the Preceding, with four additional illustration plates after designs by E. F. Burney identical to those originally in the edition, each hand-colored of the period and appropriately placed: one of *The Baptism of Jesus* for *PR*, an illustration each for *SA*, for *L'A*, and for *IlP*, contemporary full straight-grained green morocco, richly gilt-decorated border trim on covers, spine beautifully gilt-decorated in a pattern matching the trim on covers, inner dentelles finely tooled in gilt, outer dentelles ruled in gilt, marbled endpapers, a.e.g., thick red silk ribbon marker. A fine copy. Uniformly bound with *PL* (T. Bensley, 1795) also listed here, also bound with plates that are beautifully hand-colored of the period.

1592. PARADISE REGAIN'D; A Poem: In Four Books. To Which Is Added **SAMSON AGONISTES**. By John Milton. A New Edition: With An Abridgment Of The Copious And Learned Notes Collected By Bishop Newton. Illustrated By Engravings. *[London:] Albion Press, Printed And Published By James Cundee, Ivy-Lane, Paternoster-Row.*

*1806. First edition thus. 8vo, 218pp., "Advertisement" leaf, first appearance of four engraved illustration plates for *PR* (unsigned, but after W. M. Craig), half-title for *SA*, with *L'A* and *IlP* included without mention on title page, notes at bottom of page, decorative tailpiece on last page, contemporary full red morocco, elaborate decorative gilt border trim on covers, gilt-decorated spine, raised bands with decorative gilt trim, inner dentelles finely tooled in gilt, outer dentelles ruled in gilt, brown endpapers, a.e.g. A fine copy, very fresh and clean within, in an attractive Romantic binding. Craig's illustrations for *PL* first appeared in a 12mo two-volume edition published by the Albion Press in 1804 with twelve illustration plates engraved by Mackenzie (set listed here). Not in Kohler.

1593. Variant of Preceding, contemporary mottled calf, decorative gilt border trim on covers, gilt-decorated spine, black morocco label lettered in gilt, outer dentelles tooled in gilt, marbled endpapers, early bookplate. A fine, large paper copy, in a variant binding, with plates that are very clean and crisp. Not in Kohler.

1594. Variant of Preceding, original half calf, original boards (slightly stained, lacking front blank, bookplate removed from front pastedown), gilt rules and small gilt decorative pieces on spine. A nice, large paper copy, in original boards. Not in Kohler.

1595. PARADISE REGAIN'D; A Poem: In Four Books. To Which Is Added **SAMSON AGONISTES**. By John Milton. A New Edition: With An Abridgment Of The Copious And Learned Notes Collected By Bishop Newton. Illustrated By Engravings. *[London:] Albion Press, Printed And Published By James Cundee, Ivy-Lane, Paternoster-Row. 1806.* First edition thus. Variant edition. Small 12mo in 6s, [ii]+205+[7]pp., first appearance of four engraved illustration plates for *PR* (unsigned, but after W. M. Craig, half-title for *SA*, notes at bottom of page, advertisement leaf bound before Book I, contemporary polished calf, decorative gilt border trim on covers, gilt-decorated spine with gilt lettering, marbled endpapers, speckled green edges. A nice copy, stamped "Fife Collection" on front blanks, with seven additional pages of advertisements bound in at end. This is a variant edition from the preceding: 12mo in 6s rather than octavo; much smaller, with less pages, and without *L'A* and *IlP* included. Seven additional pages of advertisements for "Books Published By James Cundee" (including editions of Milton) bound in at the end. Scarce. Kohler 211, with "1 p. of advertisements at end" and reporting "Not in the British Library. Not in the Bodleian Library. Not in Cambridge University Library."

1596. PARADISE REGAINED ETC. The Author John Milton. *London: Printed For John Sharpe, Piccadilly, 1816.* First edition, first issue. 2 volumes in one. 8vo, 432pp., engraved title with vignette illustration of *Milton Found Sleeping by an Italian Lady* by Richard Westall engraved by F. Engleheart with "Proofs" label in lower right corner, engraved illustration plates for *PR*, *SA*, and *C*, each with vignette illustration by Richard Westall, variously engraved, each plate dated "Aug. 24, 1816," half-title for each book of *PR*, *SA*, *P*, *Poemata*, and "Select Notes On The *PR*" at the end. Bound with **THE MINOR POEMS OF JOHN MILTON.** *London: Printed By John Sharp. MDCCCXVI.* Engraved title with vignette illustration of *Methought I Saw My Late Espoused Saint. Sonnet XXIII* by Richard Westall engraved by R. Rhodes with "Proofs" label in lower right corner, engraved illustration plates for *L*, *L'A*, *IlP*, *S* (with vignette illustration for *Sonnet X*), and *O* (with vignette illustration for *NO*), each with vignette illustration by Richard Westall, variously engraved, each plate dated "Aug. 24, 1816." Contemporary dark blue morocco (a bit rubbed at the joints and along extremities, plates foxed and some occasional foxing throughout), richly gilt-decorated border trim with decorative corner pieces on covers, richly gilt-decorated spines with gilt lettering ("Poetical Works" "*PL* Vol. 1 / *PR* Vol. 2"), thick raised bands with decorative gilt trim, inner dentelles ruled in gilt, outer dentelles tooled in gilt at the corners, red endpapers, a.e.g., with the early armorial bookplate of "Samuel Parker, Esq." on back pastedown. A splendid copy of this beautifully printed edition of Milton's poems by Charles Whittingham at the Chiswick Press, handsomely bound in a lovely Romantic binding and nicely preserved through the years, with engraved plates dated 1816 and engraved title pages for *PR* and *Poems* labeled "Proofs," the first appearance of these illustrations by Westall, and also a large paper copy of the illustrations. The engraved title page for *PR* is dated 1816 (Arabic numerals) and first appeared apparently without a printed title page here. Since the engraved plates are dated "Aug. 24, 1816," it would appear that the engraved title and plates were not published with a printed title page until the new year, 1817 (also listed here). Under this scenario, unless the copy here is a single put-together edition, both the 1816 and 1817 *PR* editions are first editions and can be distinguished as first and second issues. This volume uniformly bound as a companion volume with *PL* (London: Printed For John Sharpe, Piccadilly. 1816) listed here, together forming the *PW*. See 1819 and 1823 Chiswick reissues of *PR*, each with the 1816 issue of the plates, and also the 1827 Chiswick reissue, with new engravers of the plates dated 1827. Scarce. Not in Kohler.

1597. PARADISE REGAINED, By John Milton. With Select Notes Subjoined; To Which Is Added, A Complete Collection Of His Miscellaneous Poems, Both English And Latin. *London: Printed For F. C. And J. Rivington; J. Nichols And Son; G. Wilkie; J. Nunn; Cadell And Davies; Carpenter And Son; Scatcherd And Letterman; Longman, Hurst, Rees, Orme, And Brown; John Richardson; Lackington And Co.; W. Lowndes; Gale And Fenner; J. Otridge; W. Stewart; J. Mawman; Walker And Edwards; Baldwin, Cradock, And Joy; R. Hunter; And G. Cowie And Co. 1817.* 8vo, 432pp., half-title (with "Printed by S. Hamilton, Weybridge, Surrey" on verso), engraved frontispiece illustration plate of *The Baptism of Jesus* engraved by J. Fittler after E. F. Burney for *PR*, "Published by J. Mawman and the other Proprietors 1817," with one additional engraved illustration plate of *Samson and Delilah* by E. F. Burney engraved by J. Fittler ("Published by J. Mawman and the other Proprietors 1817"), half-title for each book of *PR*, for *SA, P, Poemata*, and for "Select Notes On Paradise Regained" contemporary calf (rebacked with original spine laid down, corners repaired, new endpapers), covers with decorative border trim in blind within gilt rules, spine lettered in gilt with decorative gilt trim at top and bottom and variously throughout and with decorative pieces in blind within the panels, marbled endpapers. Uniformly bound as a companion volume with *PL* (London: Printed For F. C. And J. Rivington, J. Nichols And Son, et al., 1817) also listed here. Scarce. Kohler 212, indicating "Frontispiece and one plate," and reporting "Not in the Bodleian Library. Not in Cambridge University Library."

1598. Variant of Preceding, with one engraved illustration plate by E. F. Burney of *Samson and Dalila* engraved by J. Fittler (foxed, "Published by J. Mawman and the other Proprietors 1817"), original boards, printed paper labels on spines, edges untrimmed. Large paper copy with early armorial bookplate of Robert Dalzell and the bookplate of Dudley Johnson. Uniformly bound with *PL* (Printed For F. C. And J. Rivington, J. Nichols And Son, et al., 1817), also listed here, together forming the *PW*. Although the binding is a bit worn and the plate foxed, this volume and its companion volume are nonetheless preserved in their original state—very large, in original boards, wholly uncut, and exceptionally fresh and clean within.

1599. PARADISE REGAINED, SAMSON AGONISTES, COMUS, AND ARCADES. The Author, John Milton. *London: Printed For John Sharpe, Piccadilly; By C. Whittingham, Chiswick. M DCCC XVII.* First edition, second issue. 12mo, [i]+*PR* unpaginated (with line numbers at top of each page)+64+39+7pp., half-title, engraved and printed title pages, engraved title: "PARADISE REGAINED ETC. The Author John Milton. London: Printed For John Sharpe, Piccadilly, 1816," with vignette illustration of *Milton Found Sleeping by an Italian Lady* by Richard Westall engraved by F. Engleheart, on engraved title with "Proofs" label in lower right corner, engraved illustration plates for *PR, SA,* and *C*, each with vignette illustration by Richard Westall, variously engraved, each plate dated "Aug. 24, 1816," half-title for *Arcades*, contemporary full straight-grained purple morocco (plates foxed), gilt rules with gilt corner decorations on covers, gilt-decorated spine, raised bands, inner and outer dentelles finely tooled in gilt, a.e.g. A fine tall, large paper copy, in a very attractive and well-preserved contemporary morocco binding, with the first appearance of these vignette illustrations with an 1817 printed title page. The engraved title page is dated 1816 (Arabic numerals) and first appeared apparently without a printed title page (also listed here). Since the engraved plates are dated "Aug. 24, 1816," it would appear that the engraved title and plates were not published with a printed title page until the new year, as here. Both the 1816 and 1817 *PR* editions are first editions and can be distinguished as first and second issues. See also 1819 and 1823 Chiswick reissues of *PR*, each with the 1816 issue of the plates, and also the 1827 Chiswick small 8vo reissue, with new engravers of the plates dated 1827. Kohler 213, reporting "Not in Cambridge University Library."

1600. Variant of the Preceding, contemporary polished calf (some foxing to the plates), gilt rules with small gilt corner decorations on covers, gilt-decorated spine with small gilt harps within the panels, green morocco labels lettered and ruled in green, raised bands with decorative gilt trim, inner and outer dentelles finely tooled in gilt, marbled endpapers and edges, brown silk ribbon marker. A fine tall, large paper copy, in an attractive and well-preserved variant binding of the period, with the first appearance of these vignette illustrations. This volume is uniformly bound with an edition of Milton's *Poems*, also published by John Sharpe at the Chiswick Press in 1817 (also listed here).

1601. PARADISE REGAINED, SAMSON AGONISTES, COMUS, AND ARCADES. The Author, John Milton. *London: Printed For John Sharpe, Piccadilly, By C. Whittingham, Chiswick, MDCCCXIX.* 12mo, [i]+*PR* unpaginated (with line numbers at top of each page in place of page numbers)+64+39+7pp., engraved title: "PARADISE REGAINED ETC. The Author John Milton. London: Printed For John Sharpe, Piccadilly, 1816," with vignette illustration of *Milton Found Sleeping by an Italian Lady* by Richard Westall engraved by F. Engleheart on

II. Descriptive Listing of Editions   387

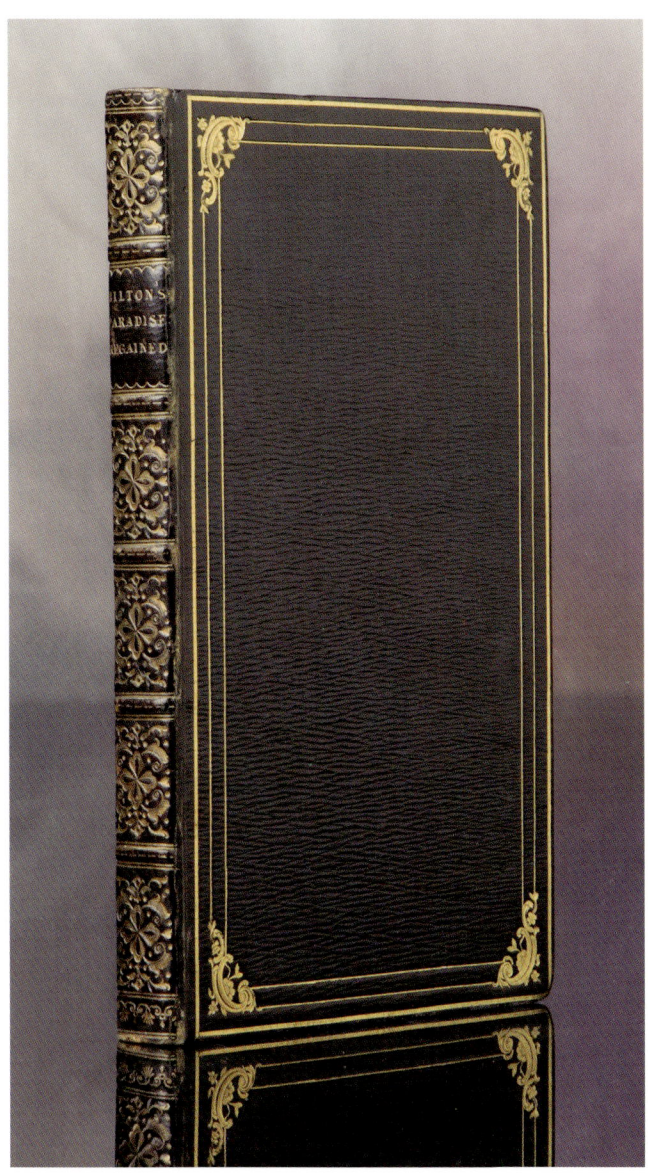

PR. London: Printed For John Sharpe, 1817. With a copy of 1816 plates, contemporary purple straight-grained morocco. Lovely Romantic binding. See #1599.

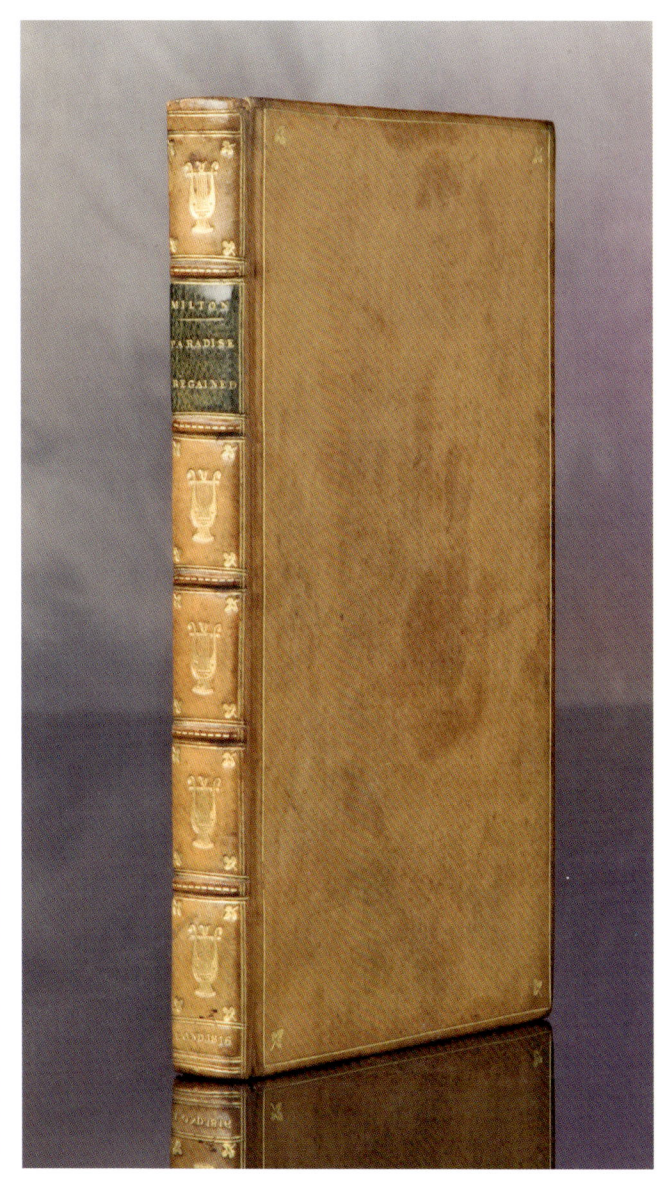

PR. London: Printed For John Sharpe, 1817. With a copy of 1816 plates, contemporary polished calf. Lovely Romantic binding. Uniformly bound with *Poems*, 1817. See #1600.

engraved title, engraved illustration plates for *PR*, *SA*, and *C*, each with vignette illustrations by Richard Westall, variously engraved, each plate dated "Aug. 24. 1816," half-title for *Arcades*, contemporary calf (somewhat worn, plates foxed, name on fly-leaf), covers ruled in gilt, spine decorated and lettered in gilt (faded), raised bands. An 1819 reissue of the edition by Sharpe/Whittingham/Chiswick first published in 1816/17 (listed here), each with the 1816 issue of the Westall plates (first appearance). See also 1823 Chiswick reissue listed here, with the 1816 issue of the plates, and also the 1827 Chiswick small 8vo reissue, with new engravers of the plates dated 1827. Not in Kohler (but see Kohler 214 following).

1602. Variant of the Preceding. **PARADISE REGAINED, SAMSON AGONISTES, COMUS, AND ARCADES**. The Author, John Milton. *London: Printed For John Sharpe, Piccadilly; By C. Whittingham, Chiswick. M DCCC XIX*. 12mo, [i]+*PR* unpaginated (with line numbers at top of each page in place of page numbers)+64+39+7pp., engraved title: "**PARADISE REGAINED ETC**. The Author John Milton. *London: Printed For John Sharpe, Piccadilly, 1816*," with vignette illustration of *Milton Found Sleeping by an Italian Lady* by Richard Westall engraved by F. Engleheart, engraved illustration plates for *PR*, *SA*, and *C*, each with vignette illustration by Richard Westall, variously engraved, each plate dated "Aug. 24. 1816," half-title for *Arcades*. Bound with **POEMS ON SEVERAL OCCASIONS**. Lycidas. L'Allegro. Il Penseroso. Sonnets. Odes. Miscellanies. Translations. Poemata. The Author, John Milton. *London: Printed In The Year MDCCCXIX*. 12mo, 188pp., engraved title page "**THE MINOR POEMS OF JOHN MILTON**. *London: Printed By John Sharp. MDCCCXVI*," with vignette illustration of *Methought I Saw My Late Espoused Saint. Sonnet XXIII* by Richard Westall engraved by R. Rhodes, engraved illustration plates for *L, L'A, IlP, S* (with vignette illustration for *Sonnet X*), and *O* (with vignette illustration for *NO*), each with vignette illustration by Richard Westall, variously engraved, each plate dated "Aug. 24. 1816," "Index To The Minor Poems" at the end. 2 volumes in one, contemporary full straight-grained red morocco, richly gilt-decorated border trim on covers with central gilt device, spines similarly richly gilt-decorated with gilt lettering, thick raised bands with decorative gilt trim, inner dentelles finely tooled in gilt, gray endpapers, a.e.g., early decorated bookplate on front pastedown. A very attractive copy, fresh and clean throughout, printed by the Chiswick press, bound in an elegant and well-preserved Romantic binding of the period. Uniformly bound as a companion volume with *PL* (London: Printed For John Sharpe, Piccadilly; By C. Whittingham, Chiswick. M DCCC XXI) listed here, together forming the *PW*. An 1819 reissue of the *PR* edition by Sharpe/Whittingham/Chiswick first published in 1816/17 (listed here), each with the 1816 issue of the Westall plates (first appearance). See 1823 Chiswick reissue listed here, with the 1816 issue of the plates, and also the 1827 Chiswick small 8vo reissue, with new engravers of the plates dated 1827. Kohler 214 reporting "Not in the British Library. Not in the Bodleian Library. Not in Cambridge University Library."

1603. **PARADISE REGAINED [AND OTHER [POEMS] [In] THE WORKS OF THE BRITISH POETS**. With Lives Of The Authors, By Ezekiel Sanford. Vol. VII. Milton. *Philadelphia: Published By Mitchell, Ames, And White. William Brown, Printer. 1819*. 12mo in 6s, engraved frontispiece illustration for Milton's *L'A* by Richard Westall engraved by C. Tiebout, half-title after title page: "The Poetical Works Of John Milton. With A Life Of The Author By Ezekiel Sanford," 135-page life of Milton followed by half-title for "Paradise Regained. In Four Parts. Vol. VII," and half-title for *C*, other poems without half-titles, contemporary marbled calf (heavily rubbed in places, front cover detached, back joints cracked, spine darkened, pages slightly age-browned), decorative gilt border trim on covers, spine decorated in gilt, black morocco labels (chipped) lettered in gilt with gilt rules, marbled endpapers and edges. A decent copy. Additional poems include *L, L'A, IlP, Arcades*, various "Sonnets," "Odes," including *NO*, "Miscellanies," and "Translations." While a single volume within a series of volumes devoted to "The Works Of The British Poets," this volume consists of poems by Milton that are complete unto themselves together with an extensive life of Milton by Ezekiel Sanford at the beginning of the volume and a frontispiece illustration for *L'A*. Not in Kohler.

1604. **PARADISE REGAINED, SAMSON AGONISTES, COMUS, ARCADES, LYCIDAS,** Etc. Etc. By John Milton. *Chiswick: Printed by C. Whittingham, College House. Sold by Thomas Tegg, Cheapside; R. Jennings, Poultry, London; And Richard Griffin And Co. Glasgow. 1823*. Small 8vo, iv+220pp., engraved and printed title pages for *PR* only, vignette illustration of the triumph of Jesus over Satan engraved by Thomas Ranson after Thomas Stothard for *PR* on engraved title (dated 1823) rebound in brown cloth (engraved title spotted), edges untrimmed. Scarce. Kohler 216, calling its copy "12mo in 8s," and reporting "Not in the British Library. Not in the Bodleian Library. Not in Cambridge University Library."

1605. **PARADISE REGAINED, SAMSON AGONISTES, COMUS, AND ARCADES**. The Author, John Milton. *London: Published By John Sharpe, Duke Street, Piccadilly. MD CCC XXIII*. Slim 12mo, [i]+*PR* unpaginated (with line numbers at top of each page in place of page numbers)+64+39+7pp., engraved title: "**PARADISE REGAINED ETC**. The Author John Milton. *London: Printed For John Sharpe, Piccadilly, 1816*," date in Arabic numerals, with vignette illustration of *Milton Found Sleeping by an Italian Lady* by Richard Westall engraved by F. Engleheart, engraved illustration plates for *PR, SA*, and *C*, each with vignette illustration by Richard Westall, variously engraved, each plate dated "Aug. 24. 1816," each plate with protective tissue guard, half-title for *Arcades*, contemporary full blue morocco, delicately gilt-decorated covers and spines, thick raised bands with decorative gilt trim, spines lettered in gilt ("MILTON'S POETICAL WORKS • PR• Vol. 3"), inner and outer dentelles finely tooled in gilt, marbled endpapers and edges. A fine copy in a very lovely Romantic morocco binding. Uniformly bound as a companion volume with *PL* (London: Printed For John Sharpe, M DCCC XXV, 2 volumes) also listed here and *Poems* (London: Printed In The Year M DCCC XXIII), together forming a charming four-volume set of the *PW*. An 1823 reissue of the edition by Sharpe/Whittingham/Chiswick first published in 1816/17 (listed here), each with the 1816 issue of the Westall plates (first appearance). See 1819 Chiswick reissue, with the 1816 issue of the plates, and also the 1827 Chiswick small 8vo reissue, with new engravings of the plates dated 1827. Not in Kohler.

1606. Variant of Preceding, **PARADISE REGAINED, SAMSON AGONISTES, COMUS, AND ARCADES.** The Author, John *Milton. London: Printed For John Sharpe, Duke Street, Piccadilly. M DCCC XXIII.* As preceding. Bound with **POEMS ON SEVERAL OCCASIONS.** Lycidas. L'Allegro. Il Penseroso. Sonnets. Odes. Miscellanies. Translations. Poemata. The Author, John Milton. *London: Printed In The Year M DCCC XXIII.* 12mo, 64+39+7pp.,+188pp., engraved title page "THE MINOR POEMS OF JOHN MILTON. *London: Printed By John Sharp. MDCCCXVI*," date in Roman numerals, with vignette illustration of *Methought I Saw My Late Espoused Saint. Sonnet XXIII*, by Richard Westall engraved by R. Rhodes, engraved illustration plates for *L, L'A, IlP, S* (with vignette illustration for *Sonnet X*), and *O* (with vignette illustration for *NO*), each with vignette illustration by Richard Westall, variously engraved, each plate dated "Aug. 24. 1816," "Index To The Minor Poems" at the end. 2 volumes in one, contemporary three-quarter crushed green calf (a little rubbed at joints and at extremities, some foxing), marbled paper, elaborately gilt-decorated spines with gilt lettering, raised bands with decorative gilt trim, marbled endpapers and edges. A good copy with *PR* and *Poems* bound as one, in a variant contemporary binding. Uniformly bound as a companion volume with *PL* (London: Printed For John Sharpe, M DCCC XXVII) listed here, together forming the *PW. PR*, as with *Poems*, is an 1823 reissue of the edition by Sharpe/Whittingham/Chiswick first published in 1816 (listed here), with the 1816 issue of the Westall plates (first appearance). See the 1819 Chiswick reissue, with the 1816 issue of the plates, and also the 1827 Chiswick small 8vo reissue, with new engravings of the plates dated 1827. Neither in Kohler.

1607. Variant of Preceding, with both half-titles (for "Paradise Regained, Etc.") and (for "Milton's Minor Poems"), contemporary crushed light brown morocco (a bit rubbed), richly gilt ornamental border trim on covers, spine elaborately gilt in the panels, thick raised bands with decorative gilt trim, inner and outer dentelles finely tooled in gilt, a.e.g. Large paper copy with rare both half-titles, in a variant binding, and a much taller copy, ¾" taller and ¼" wider, bound by Charles Hering, with his ticket. A handsome copy, attractively printed by Whittingham at the Chiswick Press and in an attractive binding by one of the best binders of the period. Not in Kohler.

1608. PARADISE REGAINED; And Other Poems. By John Milton. *London: Published By Jones & Company, No. 3, Warwick Square. 1823.* First edition thus. 32 mo in 8s (miniature), xvii+201pp., unsigned engraved frontispiece illustration of *Madonna and Child* within elaborate decorative frame for Book I of *PR*, engraved and printed title pages (each dated 1823) with unsigned vignette illustration of *Crucifixion* for *PR* on engraved title ("London, Published by Jones & Co. 3. Warwick Square. 1823"), "Glasgow: Andrew & John M. Duncan, Printers to the University" on verso of printed title page, contents, "A Critique On Paradise Regained," half-title for *C* and *SA*, contemporary full straight-grained red morocco (engraved frontispiece and engraved title page somewhat foxed), covers framed with elaborate gilt and blind borders, gilt-decorated spine with large floral ornament in gilt within each gilt-ruled compartment, thick raised bands with decorative gilt trim, broad inner dentelles finely tooled in gilt, outer dentelles trimmed in gilt, marbled endpapers, a.e.g. A delightful miniature (3 ⅝" × 2 ¼"), in a charming morocco binding of the period, in very fine, bright condition with a possibly contemporary signature on front blank and later presentation inscription (dated 1873) with same family name on verso. Uniformly bound as a companion volume with *PL* (London: Published By Jones And Company, 1823) also listed here, together forming the *PW*. See second edition thus published in 1825 (listed here), in a slightly taller copy with printed title page dated 1825 and engraved title dated 1823; see also 1834 edition of *PR* published by Jones & Company (listed here), without engraved title page. Scarce. Not in Kohler.

1609. Variant of Preceding, contemporary full red morocco (a little rubbed, lacking engraved frontispiece and title page, slight foxing throughout), decorative gilt border trim within gilt rules on covers, spine elaborately decorated and lettered in gilt, outer dentelles trimmed in gilt, marbled endpapers and edges with "Clarissa T. Sill" lettered in gilt at center of front cover. A decent copy of this miniature edition (3 ⅝" × 2 ¼"). Uniformly bound as a companion volume with a scarce edition of *PL* (London: Published By Jones And Company, 1823) also listed here, with rare half-title for "Works" and rare general title page for *PW* in *PL*, together forming the *PW* in a presentation morocco binding. Scarce. Not in Kohler.

1610. PARADISE REGAINED, AND MINOR POEMS. By John Milton. With Notes. *London: Printed For N. Hailes, Museum, Piccadilly; J. Bumpus, Holborn Bars; Andrews, New Bond Street; W. Charlton Wright, And J. Walker, Paternoster Row: And Griffin And Co., Glasgow. M.DCCC.XXIV* (1824). 12mo in 6s, frontispiece illustration after Stothard for *PR* ("London, John Bumpus, 1824"), original calf (joints cracked, spine chipped at top and bottom), covers tooled in blind with four small gilt floral decorations, gilt-decorated spine, inner and outer dentelles tooled in gilt, blue endpapers, marbled edges. A good copy. Scarce. Not in Kohler.

1611. PARADISE REGAINED; A Poem In Four Books. To Which Is Added **SAMSON AGONISTES**. And **POEMS ON SEVERAL OCCASIONS**. By John Milton. A New Edition, With Notes, Critical And Explanatory, By John Williams, Esq. *London: Printed For G. And W. B. Whittaker, Ave-Maria Lane. 1824.* First edition thus. 12mo, xx+414+[1]pp., contents, "Critique On Paradise Regained," "Critique on Samson Agonistes," half-title for each book of *PR*, *SA*, *P*, *C*, and *Poemata*, contemporary full polished blue-green morocco (a bit rubbed at joints), gilt rules on covers and spines, red morocco labels with gilt lettering and gilt rules, thick raised bands with decorative gilt trim, inner and outer dentelles finely tooled in gilt, marbled endpapers and edges. A very nice copy with contemporary signature (dated 1835) on each title page. Advertisement leaf of "Editions of the following Works, uniform with Milton's PW, are in the Press" bound in at end. Uniformly bound with *PL* (London: Printed For G. And W. B. Whittaker, 1824) also listed here. Scarce. Not in Kohler.

1612. PARADISE REGAINED; And Other Poems. By John Milton. *London: Published By Jones & Company, No. 3, Warwick Square. 1825.* Second edition thus. 32mo in 8s (miniature), xvii+201pp., unsigned engraved frontispiece illustration of *Madonna and Child* within elaborate decorative frame for Book I of *PR*, engraved and printed title pages with unsigned vignette illustration of *Crucifixion* for *PR* on engraved title ("London, Published by Jones & Co. 3. Warwick Square. University, [1823.] Edition"), "Glasgow: Andrew & John M. Duncan, Printers to the University" on verso of printed title page, contents, "A Critique On PR," half-titles for *C* and *SA*, contemporary full red morocco (some slight scuffing, joints a little rubbed), covers blind-tooled with gilt rules, gilt-decorated spine, black morocco label with gilt lettering ("POEMS"), gilt numeral (II), and gilt trim, marbled endpapers and edges. A fine miniature (3 ⅝" × 2 ¼"), in an attractive morocco binding of the period. Uniformly bound as a companion volume with *PL* (London: Published By Jones And Company, 1825) also listed here, together forming the *PW*. The first edition thus was published in 1823 (see copies listed here, one with engraved and printed title pages in each volume dated 1823, the other without engraved title page); see also 1834 edition of *PR*, published by Jones & Company without engraved title page and without illustration. Scarce. Not in Kohler.

1613. PARADISE REGAINED, SAMSON AGONISTES, COMUS, AND ARCADES. The Author, John Milton. *London: Printed For John Sharpe, Duke Street, Piccadilly. M DCCC XXVII.* Small 8vo, [1]+*PR* unpaginated (lines given on each page in place of page number), engraved title page "**MILTON'S PARADISE REGAINED.** London: Printed By John Sharpe, 1827" (date in Arabic numerals), with vignette illustration of *Milton Found Sleeping by an Italian Lady* by Richard Westall engraved by C. Rolls, engraved illustration plates for *PR*, *SA*, and *C*, variously engraved by engravers different from those who engraved the 1816 plates (each plate dated "July 1, 1827"), half-title for *Arcades*. Bound with **POEMS ON SEVERAL OCCASIONS**. Lycidas. L'Allegro. Il Penseroso. Sonnets. Odes. Miscellanies. Translations. Poemata. The Author, John Milton. *London: Printed In The Year M DCCC XXVII.* Small 8vo, 188pp., engraved title page "**THE MINOR POEMS OF JOHN MILTON**. London: Published By John Sharp. 1827" (date in Arabic numerals), with vignette illustration of *Methought I Saw My Late Espoused Saint. Sonnet XXIII* by Richard Westall engraved by C. Rolls, engraved illustration plates for *L*, *L'A*, *IlP*, *S* (with vignette illustration for *Sonnet X*), and *O* (with vignette illustration for *NO*), each with vignette illustration by Richard Westall, variously engraved by engravers different from those who engraved the 1816 plates, each plate dated "July 1, 1827," "Index To The Minor Poems" at the end. 2 volumes in one, contemporary scored calf, gilt rules on covers, gilt-decorated spine, brown leather label with gilt lettering ("Milton") and decorative gilt trim, marbled edges, bound by D. Dowsing, with his ticket. A very attractive copy in a charming and well-preserved binding of the period. This is an 1827 Chiswick reissue of the edition by Sharpe/Whittingham/Chiswick first published in 1816/17 (see copies listed here), each with the 1816 issue of the Westall plates (first appearance), with a reissue of the Westall plates, with different engravers: Charles Rolls instead of F. Engleheart for *L*; E. I. Portbury instead of Charles Heath for *L'A*; Charles Rolls instead of James Mitan for *IlP*; John Romney instead of Charles Heath for *S*; Charles Rolls instead of Edward Finden for *O*, and Charles Rolls for Engleheart and for Rhodes on the engraved title pages, with a changed date of 1827, and a new printing of the publisher's imprint at bottom of the plate. See also 1819 and 1823 Chiswick reissues, with the 1816 issue of the Westall plates. Uniformly bound as a companion volume with *PL* (London: Printed For John Sharpe, M DCCC XXVII) also listed here, with plates redone and dated 1827 as here, together forming a very scarce set of Milton's *PW*. *PR*—Kohler 467, reporting

"Not in the Bodleian Library. Not in Cambridge University Library"; *Poems*—Not in Kohler.

1614. Variant of Preceding, slightly thinner and taller, contemporary full green morocco (a bit rubbed at the joints), spine lettered in gilt (PR), slightly raised bands, yellow endpapers, a.e.g. A nice copy, fresh and clean within. Possibly a large paper copy in a variant contemporary morocco binding. *PR*—Kohler 467; *Poems*—Not in Kohler.

1615. PARADISE REGAINED; AND OTHER POEMS, By John Milton. *New York: Published By Solomon King, 148 Fulton-st. 1831.* First edition thus? 12mo in 6s, 215pp., frontispiece illustration of *Madonna and Child* by E. Prud'homme in an elaborate border frame, engraved and printed title pages, engraved title page for "Paradise Regained and other Poems By John Milton. New York[:] Published By S. King. 1831," with unsigned vignette illustration of the *Crucifixion* on engraved title, half-title for *C*—appearing here immediately after *PR*—and *SA*, original calf (worn, joints cracked, front cover detached, pages age-browned), outer dentelles tooled in gilt (now faded). See companion edition of *PL*, published in the same year by Solomon King with same publisher's imprint as that here and with the same frontispiece portrait and engraved title page as those found in following copy. Scarce. Not in Kohler.

1616. Variant of Preceding. **PARADISE REGAINED; AND OTHER POEMS,** By John Milton. *New York: Published By Solomon King, 148 Fulton-st. 1831.* First edition thus? 12mo in 6s, 215pp., frontispiece portrait of Milton by E. Prud'homme in an elaborate border frame, engraved and printed title pages, engraved title page for "Paradise Lost. New York. Published by S. King. 1831," with unsigned vignette illustration on engraved title of *Satan in Flight* ("Then with expanded wing he takes his flight"), half-title for *C*—appearing here immediately after *PR*—and *SA*, original calf (lacking front cover, spine edge chipped), brown morocco label with gilt lettering and gilt rules, pages slightly age-browned, early name on fly-leaf). Variant copy with different engraved frontispiece (portrait of Milton instead of an illustration) and different engraved title page (for *PL* rather than for *PR*). Scarce. Not in Kohler.

1617. PARADISE REGAINED; AND OTHER POEMS. By John Milton. *London: Published By Jones & Company, Temple Of The Muses, (Late Lackington's), Finsbury Square. 1834.* 32mo in 8s (miniature in size 3 ½" × 2 ¼"), xvii+201pp., original red silk (a bit rubbed), covers decorated in blind, gilt-decorated spine with gilt lettering, a.e.g., bound by W. H. Dalton, with his ticket. A fine copy with contemporary signature (dated 1849) on title page. See 1823 and 1825 editions published by Jones & Company, each with engraved and printed title pages. Scarce.

1618. PARADISE REGAINED; COMUS, A MASK; SAMSON AGONISTES, AND OTHER POEMS, By John Milton. *New–York: Published By Charles Wells. 1840.* First edition thus? 12mo, 215pp., contents, half-title for *C* and *SA*, contemporary black cloth (a little worn, slight waterstaining and embrowning throughout), central emblem in blind on covers, spine lettered in gilt within decorative gilt trim (a bit faded), slight bands. Although a bit worn, a good copy of a scarce edition. Scarce. Not in Kohler, (although Kohler 215 cites an undated edition "New York: Published By Charles Wells. n.d. [ca. 1822]," a date perhaps too early for the time frame in which Wells is publishing his other editions of Milton's works.

See 1839 edition (possible first edition thus), 1840 edition (possible second edition thus), 1841 edition (possible third edition thus), and 1842 edition (possible fourth edition thus) of *PL* published by Charles Wells ("New–York. Charles Wells"); and see dated illustrated 1839 edition (possible first edition thus) and dated illustrated 1840 edition (possible second edition thus) as well as undated illustrated ca. 1840 edition (possible first edition thus) of *PW* published by Charles Wells ("New–York. Charles Wells")—all listed here.

1619. PARADISE REGAINED, AND OTHER POEMS. By John Milton. *New York: Leavitt & Allen. 379 Broadway. n.d. [ca. 1848].* First edition thus by Leavitt? Small 8vo (4 ¾" × 3 ½"), 190pp., contemporary brown silk (worn, small pieces missing at top and bottom of spine, age-spotting), covers richly embossed, spine lettered in gilt with embossing. *SA* and *C* are not included among the "Other Poems," as with other editions published by Leavitt & Allen referenced in *PL*, 1848 (also listed here). A decent copy with early "Portland Oregon Stationer" stamp on fly-leaf. See copy bound with *PL* (New York: Leavitt & Allen. 379 Broadway. n.d. [ca. 1848]) also listed here. Not in Kohler.

1620. PARADISE REGAIN'D, And Other Poems By John Milton. *New York: Published By Clark, Austin & Co. 205 Broadway. 1850.* First edition thus? 12mo in 6s, 215pp., "A Critique On PR," half-title for *C* and *SA*, original brown cloth (spine ends a little chipped, corners worn, last three blanks torn out, occasional foxing), cover decorated in blind, spine decorated and lettered in gilt ("Milton's Paradise Regained"). A nice copy with contemporary presentation inscription, dated 1862, on fly-leaf. Editions of *PL* were published by Clark, Austin & Co. in 1849 and 1850 (see copy of each listed here); a copy of the 1850 edition was also bound with a copy of the 1850 edition of *PR&c*, as here; see, too, a copy of 1851 edition of *PW*, with the printed title pages for *PL* and *PR* dated 1851 and 1850, the latter a copy of the edition here. Not in Kohler.

1621. MILTON'S PARADISE REGAINED. AND OTHER POEMS. *London: Bell And Daldy, 186, Fleet Street, And Sampson Low, Son, And Co. 47, Ludgate Hill. 1862.* Small 8vo (5 ⅛" × 3 ¾"), vii+[i]+328pp., half-title, decorated letters and central emblem of the press on title page, decorated head- and tailpieces and decorated initial letters throughout, "Chiswick Press:—Whittingham And Wilkins, Tooks Court, Chancery Lane" printed at the bottom of the last page, original dark green cloth (early name neatly written on front blank), covers ruled in blind, spine lettered in gilt within decorative gilt trim near the top, gilt rules at top and bottom, brown endpapers, t.e.g., fore- and bottom edges untrimmed. A nice possibly large paper copy, "Bound By Bone And Son," with their ticket. See 1868 edition by Bell and Daldy, which prints one-half of this edition, everything through *C* (through p. 150), excluding the sonnets, psalms, *SA*, and Latin poems. Uncommon. Not in Kohler.

1622. MILTON'S PARADISE REGAINED. AND OTHER POEMS. *London: Bell And Daldy 186, Fleet Street. 1865.* Small 8vo, vii+[i]+328pp., decorated letters and central emblem of the press on title page, decorated head- and tailpieces and decorated initial letters throughout, contemporary full calf (a bit rubbed, spine slightly chipped at the top, lacking label on spine), gilt rules with small decorative corner pieces on the covers, spine decorated in gilt within the panels (gilt faded), raised bands, inner dentelles finely tooled in gilt, decorated endpapers, a.e.g. Not in Kohler.

1623. MILTON'S PARADISE REGAINED. AND OTHER POEMS. *London: Bell And Daldy, York Street, Covent Garden. 1868.* Small 8vo (5 ¼" × 3 ½"), [ii]+150pp., half-title, decorated letters and central emblem of the press on title page, decorated head- and tailpieces and decorated initial letters throughout, original light green cloth (some minor spotting on covers, top spine end chipped), spine lettered in gilt, decorative gilt trim at top and bottom, brown endpapers, red edges. "Other Poems" do not include Milton's sonnets, psalms, *SA*, and Latin poems. See 1862 edition by Bell and Daldy, which prints these poems, thereby doubling the size of the edition to 328 pp. Uncommon. Not in Kohler.

1624. PARADISE REGAINED A Poem In Four Books By John Milton Edited With Introduction And Notes By Charles S. Jerram, M.A. Trinity College, Oxford[,] Joint-Editor Of The Series: Editor Of Milton's 'Lycidas'[.] *London[:] Longmans, Green, And Co. 1877[.] All rights reserved[.]* First edition thus. Small 8vo, lii+193+[2]pp., half-title, two foldout maps in color at the end, original dark green cloth, front cover decorated and lettered in black (title and "London Series Of English Classics"), spine lettered in gilt with decorative emblem in black at the bottom and black rules at top and bottom, brown endpapers. A very nice copy with advertisement leaf bound in at the end. The second edition thus was published in 1894 (also listed here). Scarce. Not in Kohler.

1625. PARADISE REGAINED[,] SAMSON AGONISTES AND THE MINOR ENGLISH POEMS By John Milton[.] With Two Illustrations[.] The R. T. S. Library—Illustrated[.] *[London:] The Religious Tract Society[,] 56 Paternoster Row; 65 St. Paul's Churchyard And 164 Piccadilly[,] 1886[.]* 16mo, 192pp., frontispiece portrait of Milton at age twenty-one, half-title for *SA*, preceded by illustration of "Milton's House In The Barbican," original dark green cloth, front cover decorated in black trim with "The R.T.S. Library" and "Illustrated" lettered against a black backdrop at top and bottom, and with the title lettered against a bright gilt backdrop at the center with a large circular black trim in the background, spine lettered in black. A nice copy with dated contemporary signature on fly-leaf. Scarce. Not in Kohler.

1626. [PARADISE REGAINED] THE POETICAL WORKS OF JOHN MILTON. Edited By John Bradshaw, M.A., LL.D., Inspector Of Schools, Madras. Editor Of "An English Anthology," Etc. **PARADISE REGAINED. MINOR POEMS**. *London[:] Walter Scott, 24, Warwick Lane[;] New York: Thomas Whittaker[;] Toronto: W. J. Gage And Co. 1888.* First edition thus. Small 8vo, viii+315+[blank]+[4]pp., half-title ("The Canterbury Poets" Edited By William Sharp"), initial letter a decorated large red letter on title page, half-title for each book of *PR*, *SA*, and *P*, red rule around the text, contemporary light brown cloth (a bit rubbed, early dated signature and blind stamp on half-title), front cover decorated in black in floral trim with birds flying overhead, "The Canterbury Poets" lettered in black at the top and *PR* in embossed brown letters within a bright gilt band within decorative black trim at the bottom, spine similarly decorated in black trim with *PR* in embossed brown letters within a bright gilt band at the top and "Walter Scott" in black lettering at the bottom, dark brown endpapers, red edges. A nice copy with four pages of advertisements bound in at the end. A "Special

Edition" with frontispiece in photogravure was published ca. 1899 (also listed here). See both dated 1887 and undated ca. 1887 "Canterbury Poets" editions of *PL* published by Walter Scott (first edition thus). Scarce. Not in Kohler.

1627. PARADISE REGAINED. AND SAMSON AGONISTES. By John Milton. Cassell's National Library. *[Cassell & Company, Limited: London, Paris, New York & Melbourne. 1889.* First edition by Cassell. 16mo, 192+[4]pp., introduction by "H[enry]. M[orley].," half-title for *SA*, original white cloth (now quite browned, spine very darkened), covers ruled in red with red lettering (*PR*) on front cover, spine lettered in blind. A good copy, clean internally, with four pages of advertisements for publications "in Cassell's National Library" bound in at the end. Scarce. Kohler 219, reporting "Not in Cambridge University Library."

1628. PARADISE REGAINED. AND SAMSON AGONISTES. By John Milton. Cassell's National Library. *Cassell & Company, Limited: London, Paris & Melbourne. 1891.* Second edition by Cassell. 16mo, 192+[4]pp., half-title for "Paradise Regained, And Samson Agonistes" (with "A Selection Of The Most Popular Volumes In Cassell's National Library" listed on verso), introduction by "H.[enry] M.[orley]," half-title for *SA*, original blue cloth, front cover ruled and lettered in blind, spine lettered in gilt, small initials of "Cassell & Co. Limited" in blind at center of back cover. A nice copy with four pages of advertisements for "New Serial Publications" bound in at the end. Uniformly bound with *PL* (Cassell's National Library. Cassell & Company, Limited: London, Paris & Melbourne. 1891) also listed here. Scarce. Not in Kohler.

1629. PARADISE REGAINED A Poem In Four Books By John Milton Edited With Introduction And Notes By Charles S. Jerram, M.A. Trinity College, Oxford[,] Joint-Editor Of The Series: Editor Of Milton's 'Lycidas'[.] Eighth Edition[.] London[:] Longmans, Green, And Co. And New York: 15 East 16th Street[,] 1894[.] All rights reserved[.] Small 8vo, lii+193pp., half-title, two foldout maps in color at the end, original dark green cloth, front cover decorated and lettered in black (title and "London Series Of English Classics"), spine lettered in gilt with decorative emblem in black at the bottom and black rules at top and bottom, brown endpapers. A very nice copy. The first edition thus was published in 1877 (also listed here). Scarce. Not in Kohler.

1630. PARADISE REGAINED [AND SAMSON AGONISTES AND POEMS]. John Milton. *[No Place:] The F. M. Lupton Publishing Company, n.d. [ca. 1895].* First edition by Lupton? Small 8vo, iv+387pp., decorated half-title plate in blue and red with elaborate decorative border in blue and lettering in red ("The Daisy Series"), decorated title-page plate in blue and red with decorative border in red and lettering in blue, original decorated white cloth (somewhat soiled), front cover decorated with floral decorations in green and lettered in black, spine similarly decorated and lettered in gilt and black. Also included without mention on title page are *SA* and *MP*. Scarce. Not in Kohler.

1631. PARADISE REGAINED AND SAMSON AGONISTES By John Milton[.] *New York[:] The Mershon Company[,] Publishers[,] n.d. [ca. 1895].* First edition thus? Small 8vo, 192pp., introduction, original decorated light red cloth (spine a little faded, card removed on front pastedown and fly-leaf), classical design in black in art nouveau style at the center of the front cover with "Paradise Regained" lettered in black at the top, spine similarly lettered and decorated in black in art nouveau style. Without reference on the title page, *SA* is included at the end, with half-title. A nice copy. See undated ca. 1905 edition published by "The Mershon Company" in Rahway, New Jersey, and New York. See also undated ca. 1895 edition of *PL*, companion volume in identically decorated binding. See, too, undated ca. 1900 editions of *PL* and *PR* by Chatterton-Peck Company, each also in an identically decorated binding to that here. Not in Kohler.

1632. PARADISE REGAINED And Other Works By John Milton[.] *New York[:] Frederick A. Stokes Company Publishers, n.d. [ca. 1895].* First edition thus? Slim 8vo, iv+220pp., unsigned frontispiece portrait plate of a young, handsome Milton, emblem of scholar behind a stack of folios in black at center of title page, original olive green cloth (spine a bit faded with very slight staining near the top and bottom), front cover decorated with a border line in red and a central wreath in silver incorporating title in red and decorated with floral trim in silver and red, spine lettered in silver with initials of the press in red at the bottom and a red line at top and bottom. A very nice, tall copy. Companion volume (although sold separately) with *PL* (New York[:] Frederick A. Stokes Company Publishers, n.d. [ca. 1895]) also listed here. Uncommon. Not in Kohler.

1633. PARADISE REGAINED By John Milton[.] Illustrated[.] *Chicago[:] Montgomery Ward & Co. Publishers. n.d. [ca. 1898].* First edition thus? Small 8vo, 387pp., frontispiece portrait plate of Milton after Faithorne in tinted blue, title-page plate in red and blue, two unsigned illustration plates for *PR* (Books I and IV), notes at bottom of page, original decorated light brown cloth (a bit rubbed, some foxing and slight waterstaining throughout, including the plates), front cover decorated in a patterned floral motif in columns of contrasting dark brown with decorative silver trim and "La Belle Library" lettered in gilt against a contrasting dark brown background at the top, spine lettered in silver and similarly decorated in a patterned floral motif in a column of contrasting dark brown within decorative silver trim. An uncommon copy in an attractive publisher's binding of the period. See undated edition of *PL* published about this same time (ca. 1898) in Chicago by Montgomery Ward & Company Publishers. Not in Kohler.

1898 Caldwell Editions

Collectors believe "There is no such thing as a duplicate!" Looking at the following copies of the ca. 1898 edition of *PR* by H. M. Caldwell together on a shelf or side by side shows very clearly why this statement is true and why collecting different copies of the same edition has real merit in helping to recognize important and notable differences with regard to variant title-page plates, variant publisher's imprints, variant portraits, variant formats, variant publisher's bindings, and a great deal more; yet to the collector, each book maintains its own individuality and attractiveness. The Caldwell Company published books from 1896 to 1914.

1634. PARADISE REGAINED [AND SAMSON AGONISTES AND POEMS]. John Milton[.] *H·M· Caldwell Company New York. n.d. (ca. 1898)*. First edition thus by Caldwell? Small 8vo, 387pp., frontispiece portrait plate of Milton after Faithorne in tinted blue, title-page plate printed in red with elaborately decorative blue border trim in art nouveau style with an urn at the bottom on each side, and at the center at the top, the emblem of an open book within a laurel wreath with lighted flame above and scroll beneath containing the Latin inscription "Sapere Aude," "Contents" page, two unsigned illustration plates for *PR* ("Among the wild beasts" and "Satan, smitten with amazement fell"), notes at bottom of page, included are *SA* and *EP* (without mention on title page), original blue pebble cloth (a bit rubbed), front cover decorated with a lined gilt pattern in art nouveau style with central decorative gilt piece on each side and at the center the title page emblem in gilt of an open book within a laurel wreath with lighted flame above and scroll beneath containing the Latin inscription "Sapere Aude," spine decorated in a similar lined gilt pattern in art nouveau style with gilt lettering, t.e.g., fore- and bottom edges untrimmed. A fine, tall copy in an attractive publisher's binding with contemporary signature (dated 1900) on fly-leaf. This edition of *PR* by Caldwell and the similarly bound undated ca. 1898 edition of *PL* by Caldwell (also listed here) are companion volumes, that in green cloth decorated in art nouveau style as here, together forming Milton's *PW*. See undated illustrated edition of *PR* published about this same time (ca. 1898) by Caldwell, with variant title-page plate and variant publisher's imprint adding "Boston" to "New York." Not in Kohler.

1635. Variant of Preceding, original decorated dark green cloth front cover with contrasting lighter green back cover (a bit rubbed), very large contrasting lighter green decorative piece at the center of front cover elaborately decorated in silver trim, the center lined in alternating light and dark green with silver lettering, the whole covered with small floral decorations in red and silver, the spine similarly decorated with contrasting light and dark green and elaborate silver decorative trim with silver lettering. A nice copy in a lovely publisher's binding, with variant title-page plate (with elaborately decorative light maroon border trim in art nouveau style rather than blue), in an attractive variant publisher's binding. Uniformly bound with an undated ca. 1898 illustrated edition of *PL* by Caldwell (also listed here), the two together forming Milton's *PW*, a lovely set in original publisher's bindings.

1636. Variant of Preceding, decorative light maroon tile page plate, original half seafoam green cloth overlapping front and back covers by one-half (spine ends a bit rubbed), decorated in embossed silver floral trim on front cover and spine with silver lettering on spine, half light green paper over boards decorated with lilies of the valley. A nice copy in a lovely variant publisher's binding. This edition of *PR* by Caldwell and the similarly bound undated ca. 1898 edition of *PL* by Caldwell (also listed here) are companion volumes, that in a half bright blue cloth, together forming Milton's *PW*.

1637. Variant of Preceding, decorative light maroon tile page plate, original decorated green cloth, front cover elaborately decorated in gilt with a rich gilt design along either side, long-stemmed irises in green with light blue blossoms in the center against contrasting darker green along the bottom and brilliant gilt at the top giving the effect of flowers in water beneath a bright gilt sky, spine similarly decorated with long-stemmed irises in green, contrasting greens and white along the bottom repeating the effect of flowers in water beneath a bright gilt sky in the middle with gilt lettering at the top. A fine copy in a lovely variant publisher's binding. See undated ca. 1898 edition of *PR* by Caldwell with variant title-page plate and variant publisher's imprint ("Boston" added to "New York" only), in identical publisher's binding.

1638. Variant of Preceding, decorative light maroon tile page plate, original half white cloth (chipped at top), intricately decorated in silver floral trim on front cover and spine and back cover, spine lettered in silver, half light pink silk cloth (corners worn) decorated with brown stems, green leaves and white roses. A good copy in a smaller 8vo format (by ½") from the other Caldwell editions here (similar to the smaller Caldwell editions listed at the end), in a lovely (albeit bit used) variant publisher's binding. Intended to be sold as separates.

1639. Variant of the Preceding. **PARADISE REGAINED [AND SAMSON AGONISTES AND POEMS]**. John Milton[.] *H·M·Caldwell Co., Publishers New York And Boston. n.d. (ca. 1898)*. First edition thus by Caldwell? Small 8vo, 387pp., frontispiece portrait plate in tinted blue, title-page plate printed in red with decorative green apple tree as trim in art nouveau style, two unsigned illustration plates for *PR* ("Among the wild beasts" and "Satan, smitten with amazement fell"), included are *SA* and *EP* (without mention on title page), original decorated green cloth, front cover elaborately decorated in gilt with a rich gilt design along either side, long-stemmed irises in green with pink blossoms in the center against contrasting darker green along the bottom and brilliant gilt at the top giving the effect of flowers in water beneath a bright gilt sky, spine similarly decorated with long-stemmed irises in green, contrasting greens and white along the bottom repeating the effect of flowers in water beneath a bright gilt sky in the middle with gilt lettering at the top. A fine copy with a different title-page plate from preceding copies, with "Boston" added to publisher's imprint, in a stunning publisher's binding, in original printed light gray publisher's wrappers (a bit used and slightly frayed along edges), with a listing of "Caldwell's De Novo Library" printed on the back cover, of which this is no. 147. The binding has been well-preserved because of having been kept in the publisher's wrappers through the years. Uniformly bound with an undated ca. 1898 illustrated edition of *PL* by Caldwell (also listed here), the two together forming a collection of Milton's *PW*, a lovely set in original publisher's bindings. See also undated ca. 1898 edition of *PR* by Caldwell with variant title-page plate and variant publisher's imprint ("New York" only), in identical publisher's binding.

1640. Variant of Preceding, original decorated dark green cloth (a bit rubbed, "Contents" page and the second plate not bound in), gilt rules on front cover with maroon crushed leather inlaid at center within gilt rules incorporating title in gilt at the top within gilt rules and with decorative gilt floral trim along bottom and sides, spine decorated with floral trim and lettered in faint yellow at the top (faded). A nice copy in an attractive variant publisher's binding. This edition of *PR* by Caldwell and the similarly bound undated ca. 1898 edition of *PL* by Caldwell are companion volumes, that in brown cloth decorated as here, together forming Milton's *PW*. Not in Kohler.

1641. Variant of Preceding. **PARADISE REGAINED [AND SAMSON AGONISTES AND POEMS]**. John Milton[.] *H·M·Caldwell Co., Publishers New York And Boston. n.d. (ca. 1898)*. First edition thus by Caldwell? Small 8vo, 387pp., frontispiece portrait plate in tinted red with a wide and variously designed decorative green border frame in art nouveau style, title-page plate printed in red with decorative green apple tree as trim in art nouveau style, two unsigned illustration plates for *PR* ("Among the wild beasts" and "Satan, smitten with amazement fell"), notes at the bottom of the page, included are *SA* and *EP* (without mention on title page), original light brown cloth (a bit rubbed), half-circle color illustration of Calliope seated between two cherubs tipped in on front cover near the top, the color illustration surrounded by finely tooled gilt floral trim incorporating title at the bottom, spine similarly decorated in gilt with title lettered in gilt near the top (gilt a little faded). A very nice copy with a variant portrait plate (apparently one-of-a-kind), in a lovely variant publisher's binding. Not in Kohler.

1642. Variant of Preceding, original light brown cloth (a bit rubbed, spine ends slightly worn), gilt rules on front cover with decorative scrolls in blind relief within the inner gilt rule and with central elaborate gilt trim incorporating "Superb Edition" with the initial letters "S" and "E" in decorative red against a gilt background, spine lettered in gilt and decorated with floral pieces in mauve and green, each within decorative gilt trim. A good copy with maroon border trim plate and "New York" only in publisher's imprint, in a variant publisher's binding, in a smaller 8vo format (by ½") from the other Caldwell editions listed here. Uniformly bound with an undated ca. 1898 illustrated edition of *PL* by Caldwell of the same size (also listed here), the two together forming a collection of Milton's *PW*. They were most likely published in these charming bindings, as with the two sets following, designed to be sold as a "gift" set.

1643. Variant of Preceding, original blue cloth (spine a little rubbed and ends slightly worn, bookplate almost entirely removed from front pastedown), gilt rules on front cover with decorative scrolls in blind relief within the inner gilt rule and with central elaborate gilt trim incorporating "Superb Edition" with the initial letters "S" and "E" in decorative red against a gilt background, spine blocked in decorative gilt trim with gilt lettering and floral pieces in contrasting red and blue (a bit rubbed). A nice copy with variant title-page plate (blue border trim plate and "New York" only in publisher's imprint), in a smaller 8vo format (by ½") from the other Caldwell editions listed here. Uniformly bound with an undated ca. 1898 illustrated edition of *PL* by Caldwell of the same size (also listed here), the two together forming a collection of Milton's *PW*. They were most likely published in these lovely bindings, as with the two other sets here, intended to be sold as a "gift" set.

1644. Variant of Preceding, original olive green cloth, gilt rules on front cover with decorative scrolls in blind relief within the inner gilt rule and with central elaborate gilt trim incorporating "Superb Edition" with the initial letters "S" and "E" in decorative red against a gilt background, spine blocked in decorative gilt trim with gilt lettering and floral pieces in contrasting green and pink. A nice copy with variant title-page plate (maroon border trim plate and "New York" only in publisher's imprint), in an attractive variant publisher's binding, in the same smaller 8vo format (by ½") from the other Caldwell editions listed here, with small early bookseller's plate with gilt trim at top of front pastedown. Uniformly bound with an undated ca. 1898 variant illustrated edition of *PL* by Caldwell of the same size (also listed here), the two together forming a collection of Milton's *PW*. They were most likely published in these very appealing bindings, as with the two sets preceding, designed to be sold as a "gift" set.

There are several other editions in the collection that are not listed here. Among them is a lovely set with "New York and Boston" in the publisher's imprint. The title-page plate of *PL* of this set is also remarkable: it is printed in blue with elaborately decorative maroon border trim in art nouveau style; neither the design of the plate nor the plate itself appear in any other copy listed here.

1645. PARADISE REGAINED SAMSON AGONISTES & OTHER POEMS By John Milton[.] *MDCCCXCVIII (1898) • Published • By • J • M • Dent • And • Co: Aldine • House • London • E • C •* First edition by Dent. Small 8vo, 371+[1]pp., edited by W. H. D. Rouse, half-title in red and black ("The Temple Classics Edited by Israel Gollancz MA") with small red emblem at the center, engraved frontispiece portrait within elaborate decorative frame of Milton bust "From the Original at Christ's College Cambridge," protective tissue guard, title page in red and black with elaborate decorative black border in art nouveau style, half-titles for some of the poems, decorative tailpieces, "Glossary" at the end, original blue cloth over limp boards, blind-stamped owl on front cover, spine lettered in gilt within decorative gilt trim, monument printed in green on front pastedown containing Milton's name and dates and the titles of his main works and their publication dates, t.e.g., fore- and bottom edges untrimmed. A fine copy with contemporary signature (dated "99") on fly-leaf. "This issue of Milton's *PR*, and other poems, based on the text of Masson, with reference to the earliest editions in doubtful questions, has been edited by Mr. W. H. D. Rouse . . . who has revised the text, added the marginalia, and contributed the glossorial appendix of proper names and obsolete words. I. G. June 25th, 1898" (on verso of last printed page), with "Printed by T. and A. Constable, Printers to Her Majesty at the Edinburgh University Press" at the bottom of the page. See later editions of *PR, SA & OP* by Dent listed here: the 1899 second Dent edition; the 1903 third Dent edition; and the 1909 fourth Dent edition; and see also the 1897 first Dent edition of *PL* and other editions cited there. Not in Kohler.

1646. Variant of Preceding, original green limp calf (worn), blind-stamped owl on front cover, spine lettered in gilt within decorative gilt trim, monument printed in green on front pastedown (as preceding), t.e.g., fore- and bottom edges untrimmed. A decent copy in a variant publisher's binding.

1647. PARADISE REGAINED [AND SAMSON AGONISTES]. John Milton. *Philadelphia[:] Henry Altemus Company. n.d. (ca. 1899).* First edition thus by Altemus? Small 8vo, 192+[32]pp., half-title ("Paradise Regained, and Samson Agonistes"), unsigned frontispiece illustration plate for *PR* (*Henceforth Oracles Shall Cease*), title-page plate lettered in red with decorative green trim in art nouveau style, introduction by "H[enry]. M[orley].," which first appeared in Cassell's edition of *PR* in 1889 (also listed here), it also appeared in Mershon's undated ca. 1895 edition of *PR* (also listed here), as well as Chatterton-Peck's ca. 1889 edition (see copies listed here), included, without mention on title page is *SA*, with half-title, original decorated white cloth, front cover and spine lettered in gilt and decorated with flowers in green and gilt. A very nice copy in a lovely publisher's binding with sixteen pages of advertisement for "Publications Of Henry Altemus Company" bound in at end. The pattern of including *SA* without mention on title page, although mentioned on half-title, is maintained throughout all of the editions by Altemus here. Not in Kohler.

1648. Variant of Preceding, original decorated blue-green cloth (a bit rubbed, half-title and front blank with small tear at outer edge), front cover and spine decorated and lettered in gilt with a photograph of a tree in color tipped in within gilt borders on front cover. A nice copy in a lovely variant publisher's binding with sixteen pages of advertisement as preceding bound in at end.

1649. PARADISE REGAINED [AND SAMSON AGONISTES]. John Milton. *Philadelphia[:] Henry Altemus Company. n.d. (ca. 1899)*. First edition thus by Altemus? Small 8vo, 192pp., half-title ("PR, and SA"), unsigned frontispiece portrait plate of Milton as a young man ("Copyright 1899, By Henry Altemus"), title-page plate lettered in black with a red rule, included with half-title is *SA*, original decorated burgundy cloth (a bit rubbed, edges a bit worn), front cover and spine decorated and lettered in gilt with a photograph of an English farm scene in color tipped within gilt borders on front cover. A nice copy with ownership inscription in pencil on fly-leaf and front pastedown, in a lovely publisher's binding. Not in Kohler.

1650. Variant of Preceding. PARADISE REGAINED [AND SAMSON AGONISTES]. John Milton. *Philadelphia[:] Henry Altemus Company. n.d. (ca. 1899)*. First edition thus by Altemus? Small 8vo, 192pp., half-title ("PR, and SA"), engraved title-page plate, printed title-page plate lettered in red with decorative green trim in art nouveau style, included with half-title is *SA*, original decorated blue cloth (slightly rubbed at corners and spine ends), picture of leafless tree amidst snow tipped on front cover overridden by decorative gilt trim along with thick gilt rules and the title *PR* in large gilt letters near the top, spine delicately decorated with floral trim in gilt in art nouveau style (faded) and lettered in blind, endpapers elaborately decorated with green trim and the initials "HA" at the center. An attractive copy in a lovely publisher's binding, with contemporary presentation inscription on front blank, without frontispiece portrait plate, with variant printed title-page plate, in a variant publisher's binding. Not in Kohler.

1651. Variant of Preceding. PARADISE REGAINED [AND SAMSON AGONISTES]. John Milton. *Philadelphia[:] Henry Altemus. n.d. (ca. 1899)*. First edition thus by Altemus? Small 8vo, 192pp., half-title ("*PR*, and *SA*"), engraved title-page plate, unsigned frontispiece portrait plate of Milton as a young man ("Copyright 1899, By Henry Altemus"), printed title-page plate lettered in red with decorative green trim in art nouveau style, included with half-title is *SA*, original decorated yellow cloth (a bit rubbed at corners and spine ends), front cover decorated with floral stems and leaves in green and yellow against a gilt backdrop ruled in black, gilt border trim with "Paradise Regained" in large gilt letters at the top and "Milton" in smaller gilt letters at the bottom, spine delicately decorated with floral trim in black in art nouveau style and lettered in blind, endpapers elaborately decorated with green trim and the initials "HA" at the center. A nice copy in an attractive publisher's binding, with frontispiece portrait plate, with variant printed title-page plate, in a variant publisher's binding. Not in Kohler.

1652. Variant of Preceding, original decorated light reddish-brown cloth (a bit rubbed, slightly stained on spine and back cover), front cover decorated with floral stems and leaves in green and reddish-brown against a greenish gilt backdrop ruled in black, greenish gilt border trim with "Paradise Regained" in large greenish gilt letters at the top and "Milton" in smaller greenish gilt letters at the bottom, spine delicately decorated with floral trim in black in art nouveau style and lettered in blind, endpapers elaborately decorated with green trim and the initials "HA" at the center. All in all, a fair copy in a rather lovely variant publisher's binding, with eight pages of advertisements for "Publications Of Henry Altemus Company Philadelphia" bound in at the end.

1653. Variant of Preceding, original decorated deep teal cloth (a bit rubbed), art deco floral sprays in burgundy, pink, and gilt with decorative gilt floral stems and leaves, decorative gilt butterflies at the corners, decorative gilt trim along the edges, and title in gilt on front cover, spine similarly decorated with floral pieces in gilt and gilt lettering, endpapers elaborately decorated with green trim and the initials "HA" at the center. A nice copy in a lovely variant publisher's binding with sixteen (paginated) pages of advertisements for "Henry Altemus' Publications" (different from others already described) bound in at end.

1654. Variant of Preceding, original decorated turquoise cloth (a bit rubbed), art deco floral sprays in burgundy, pink, and gilt with decorative gilt floral stems and leaves, decorative gilt butterflies at the corners, decorative gilt trim along the edges, and title in gilt on front cover, spine similarly decorated with floral pieces in gilt and gilt lettering, endpapers elaborately decorated with green trim and the initials "HA" at the center. A nice copy in a lovely variant publisher's binding with sixteen pages of advertisements different from the preceding (fourteen pages paginated and two unpaginated) for "Henry Altemus' Publications" bound in at the end.

1655. Variant of Preceding, original decorated half white pebble cloth (rubbed along extremities and at corners, a bit soiled from use and age), the whole decorated in art nouveau style, with the picture of a lady in pink reading a book set against a circular motif in color tipped on right side of front cover along with a decorative floral design in gilt together with the title lettered in gilt on the left side, spine similarly delicately decorated with a floral design and the title lettered in gilt. An attractive copy in a lovely variant publisher's binding (albeit a bit worn), without the usual decorated Altemus endpapers with "HA" initials, with twenty-four pages (unpaginated) of advertisements for "Publications Of Henry Altemus Company Philadelphia" bound in at the end.

1656. PARADISE REGAINED[,] SAMSON AGONISTES[,] & OTHER POEMS By John Milton[.] *MDCCCXCIX • Published • By • J • M • Dent • And • Co: Aldine • House • London • W • C• (1899).* Second edition thus by Dent. 12mo, 371+[1]pp., edited by W. H. D. Rouse, half-title in red and black ("The Temple Classics Edited by Israel Gollancz MA") with small red emblem at the center ("First Edition, May 1898[;] Second Edition, April 1899" on verso of half-title), engraved frontispiece portrait within elaborate decorative frame of Milton bust "From the Original at Christ's College Cambridge," title page in red and black with elaborate decorative black border in art nouveau style, half-title for some of the poems, decorative tailpieces, "Glossary" at the end, original olive green limp calf (a bit rubbed along extremities, spine faded and chipped at ends), central emblem incorporating owl in gilt on front cover, spine lettered in gilt within decorative gilt trim, a monument style device printed in green on front pastedown (as with first edition by Dent), t.e.g., red silk ribbon marker. A nice copy with large bookplate on fly-leaf. Statement on verso of last printed page as with first edition by Dent. The first edition of *PR, SA & OP* by Dent was published in 1898 (also listed here with further editions cited). Scarce. Not in Kohler.

1657. PARADISE REGAINED AND MINOR POEMS [In] **THE POETICAL WORKS OF JOHN MILTON.** Edited By John Bradshaw, M.A. LL.D., Inspector Of Schools, Madras. **PARADISE REGAINED. MINOR POEMS.** *London: Walter Scott, Limited, Paternoster Square. New York: 3 East Fourteenth street. n.d. [ca. 1899].* Small 8vo, viii+315+[12]pp., advertisement leaf for "Special Edition of the Canterbury Poets: Square 8vo, Cloth, Gilt Top Elegant, Price 2s. Each Volume with a Frontispiece in Photogravure," unsigned engraved frontispiece portrait plate with "Swan Electric Engraving Co." at bottom of the impression (a young Milton), small circular engraving outlined in double black rule within a square frame outlined in a single black rule, large initial letter on title page, "Contents" page with a second contents listing of "Sonnets" immediately following, half-title for *PR, SA, P*, with "The Walter Scott Press, Newcastle-On-Tyne" printed at bottom of last page of poems (p. 315), included, without mention on title page is *SA*, with half-title, original delicately gilt-tooled three-quarter dark green cloth in contrasting gilt designs, light green gold-decorated paper over boards, spine lettered in gilt ("Paradise Regained"), light green gold-decorated endpapers identical to the gold decorated light green paper covering the boards, a.e.g. A very pleasing copy in a lovely art nouveau binding with twelve pages of advertisements for publications by "Walter Scott, Limited." Not in Kohler.

1658. PARADISE REGAINED By John Milton[.] *Chatterton-Peck Company[,] New York, N.Y. n.d. [ca. 1900].* First edition thus? Small 8vo, 192pp., frontispiece illustration plate in color of a large pansy after C. Klein, fifteen-page introduction by "H[enry]. M[orley].," original purple cloth (a little rubbed), front cover lettered in gilt at the top with a religious card in color consisting of a cross with floral trim (Easter lily) tipped at the center of the front cover beneath the gilt lettering, spine lettered in gilt, endpapers decorated in light green in art nouveau style with the initials "TMC" at the center, a.e.g. A nice copy. Without reference on the title page, *SA* is included at the end with half-title. The frontispiece illustration, though symbolic of spring and new life, is not really an illustration for *PR*. The introduction that appears here appeared also in the 1889 and 1891 editions by Cassell & Company of *PR* (see copy of each listed here); that introduction appears variously, including in the 1899 Altemus editions of *PR* (see copies listed here). Not in Kohler.

1659. PARADISE REGAINED By John Milton[.] *Chatterton-Peck Company[,] New York, N.Y. n.d. [ca. 1900].* Small 8vo, 192pp., introduction by Henry Morley, original decorated cream cloth (bit rubbed), "Paradise Regained" lettered in black at top of front cover with elaborate classical design in black in art nouveau style of other bindings like this, spine similarly lettered and decorated in black in art nouveau style. A nice copy. Without reference on the title page, *SA* is included at the end with half-title. Companion volume to an edition by Chatterton-Peck of *PL* published about this same time (ca. 1900) in a similar binding (also listed here). Not in Kohler.

1660. PARADISE REGAINED[,] SAMSON AGONISTES[,] & OTHER POEMS By John Milton[.] *MDCCCCIII • Published • By • J • M • Dent • And • Co: Aldine • House • London • W • C •* Third edition thus. Small 8vo, viii+371+[1]pp., edited by W. H. D. Rouse, half-title in red and black ("The Temple Classics Edited by Israel Gollancz MA") with small red emblem at the center, engraved frontispiece portrait within elaborate decorative frame of Milton bust "From the Original at Christ's College Cambridge," protective tissue guard, title page in red and black with elaborate decorative black border in art nouveau style, half-titles for some of the poems, decorative tailpieces, "Glossary" at the end, original blue cloth over limp boards, blind-stamped owl on front cover, spine lettered in gilt within decorative gilt trim, monument to Milton printed in green on front pastedown (as with first edition by Dent), t.e.g., fore- and bottom edges untrimmed, partially unopened. A lovely copy with contemporary signature on fly-leaf. Scarce. Not in Kohler.

1661. PARADISE REGAIN'D A Poem in IV Books To Which Are Added Samson Agonistes & Poems Both English and Latin Compos'd On Several Occasions The Author John Milton[.] *The Doves Press No. 1 The Terrace Hammersmith[,] MDCCCCV.* 8vo, 343+[1]pp., "Table Of Contents," half-title for each poem, opening line of *PR* in large type printed in red, beginning initials in red, each poem identified in red in the margin of each page, original vellum binding (edges slightly embrowned), brown morocco label on spine with gilt lettering and gilt rules, "Printed by T. J. Cobden-Sanderson & Emory Walker at The Doves Press, & finished June 1905" (colophon). Printed and bound uniformly with *PL*, 1902, by the Doves Press (also listed here). A lovely set from the Doves press, a press, founded by Cobden-Sanderson and Emory Walker, formerly of the Kelmscott Press, that has often been considered the best of them all and whose influence on the twentieth century was profound (Franklin, *Private Presses*). One of only 300 sets printed on paper; 25 copies were also printed on vellum. Ransom, *Private Presses*, p. 7; Stevens 1120; Kohler 221.

1662. PARADISE REGAINED AND SAMSON AGONISTES By John Milton[.] *Rahway, N.J. [And] New York[:] The Mershon Company[,] Publishers[,] n.d. [ca. 1905].* Small 8vo, 192pp., introduction, half-title for *SA*, original decorated light blue cloth (a little rubbed), *PR* lettered in silver at top left of front cover within an elaborate decorative silver border trim, spine lettered in silver. A nice copy with contemporary signature (dated 1906) on fly-leaf. See also the possible first edition thus published ca. 1895 by "The Mershon Company[,] Publishers" in New York (without reference to Rahway, New Jersey). Not in Kohler.

1663. PARADISE REGAINED AND MINOR POEMS John Milton[.] *London: George G. Harrap & Co. 9 Portsmouth St. Kingsway[.] n.d. [ca. 1909].* First edition thus. 8vo, [iv]+223+[1]pp., half-title with advertisement for the "The Harrap Library" on verso of blank leaf preceding, frontispiece portrait line-drawing by Lionel Heath after a drawing by Peter van der Plaas in the National Gallery, title page with central red emblem incorporating "Cogito Ergo Sum" in reverse white, "Printed By Ballantyne And Co. Limited Tavistock Street Covent Garden London" on verso of title page at bottom, undated "Editorial Note" by Fred E. Bumby, half-title for *PR* and *MP*, original brown diced calf, gilt-decorated covers and spine, t.e.g., others untrimmed. A very nice copy, printed at the Ballantyne Press on high-quality paper. Companion volume with *PL* (with a different publisher's imprint: "London: George G. Harrap & Co. LTD. 2-3 Portsmouth St. Kingsway And At Sydney," ca. 1909) with preface by Bumby as here, but dated 1909 (whereas preface here is undated), in an identical binding (also listed here). Not in Kohler.

1664. Variant of Preceding, original brown cloth, bright yellow label ruled in gilt near top of front cover with large decorative gilt design within incorporating "Cogito Ergo Sum" in gilt and title lettered in gilt above, similar yellow label on spine lettered and ruled in gilt, "Harrap & Co." lettered in gilt at bottom of spine, t.e.g., others untrimmed. A fine copy with wide margins, printed at the Ballantyne Press on high-quality paper, in a variant publisher's binding, with contemporary signature, dated "30. viii. XV. Bank House (?)Airderford 5/00." Not in Kohler.

1665. PARADISE REGAINED AND MINOR POEMS ••• John Milton[.] *New York[:] Dodge Publishing Company[,] 220 East Twenty-Third St. n.d. [ca. 1909].* First edition thus. 8vo, [iv]+224pp., half-title with advertisement for the "The Dodge Library" on verso of blank leaf preceding, frontispiece portrait line-drawing by Lionel Heath after a painting by Pieter Van der Plaas, in National Gallery, protective tissue guard, title page in black with small orange circle beneath the title near the top incorporating "Cogito Ergo Sum" in reverse white, "Printed By Ballantyne And Co. Limited Tavistock Street Covent Garden London" on verso of title page, original red cloth (spine a bit dulled, former owner's name on fly-leaf), front cover and spine lettered in gilt and stunningly decorated with a gilt pattern of roses and vines in art nouveau style, t.e.g, others untrimmed. A lovely copy in an attractive binding of the period with a frontispiece portrait sketch possibly done especially for this edition. Similar to the editions published by Harrap about this same time (see copies listed here). Companion volume with *PL* (New York: Dodge Publishing Company 220 East Twenty-Third St.) in identical binding (also listed here). Not in Kohler.

1666. PARADISE REGAINED SAMSON AGONISTES & OTHER POEMS By John Milton[.] *MCMIX (1909) • Published • By • J • M • Dent • And • Co: Arnie • House • London • W • C •* Fourth edition thus. 8vo, viii+371+[1]pp., edited by W. H. D. Rouse, half-title in red and black ("The Temple Classics Edited by Israel Gollancz MA") with small red emblem at the center, engraved frontispiece portrait within elaborate decorative frame of Milton bust "From the Original at Christ's College

Cambridge," protective tissue guard, title page in red and black with elaborate decorative black border in art nouveau style, half-titles for some of the poems, decorative tail-pieces, "Glossary" at the end, original blue cloth over limp boards (a bit rubbed), blind-stamped owl on front cover, spine lettered in gilt within decorative gilt trim, monument to Milton printed in green on front pastedown (as with first edition by Dent), t.e.g., fore- and bottom edges untrimmed. A nice copy with early signature on fly-leaf. The first edition of *PR, SA & OP* by Dent was published in 1898 (copy listed here with further editions cited). Not in Kohler.

1667. PARADISE REGAINED. John Milton. Decorated By Thomas Lowinsky. *London[:] The Fleuron[,] 1924.* First edition thus. Small 4to, [viii]+80pp., half-title, decorative piece at center of title page, first appearance of three full-page wood-engraved illustrations by Thomas Lowinsky, printed on handmade paper, with a number of elaborate decorative head- and tailpieces, original half blue cloth, blue paper over boards, printed publisher's wrappers, fore- and bottom edges untrimmed, partially unopened. A fine copy with an extra set of plates on Japan vellum in an envelope at the back. No. 302 of 350 numbered copies printed on handmade paper by Walter Lewis. Stevens 1121; Not in Kohler.

Thomas Lowinsky (1892–1947) was an active book illustrator and founder-member of the Double Crown Club, established in 1924 as a group interested in the art of the book. This was the third book Lowinsky illustrated. The Fleuron Society was formed by Holbrook Jackson, Francis Meynell, Bernard Newdigate, Stanley Morison, and Oliver Simon in 1922, "which Simon suggested should produce one book a year to demonstrate to collectors and others that books set by a machine could be quite as successful aesthetically as the work of the prewar private presses. The society did not flourish; indeed, it lasted for only two stormy meetings. But from these first discussions came [the well-known periodical] *The Fleuron* . . . Newdigate was to follow his own line at the Shakespeare Head Press, but it was Francis Meynell who was to follow the Fleuron Society's first ideas at his own press" (Cave, *Private Press*, pp. 162–63).

1668. [PARADISE REGAINED] MILTON PARADISE REGAINED Edited By L. C. Martin. *Oxford[:] At the Clarendon Press[,] 1925.* First edition thus. Slim 8vo in 4s, xx+[1]+51(paginated 451 to 502)+[18]pp., frontispiece reproduction of Faithorne portrait frontispiece, reproduction of title page of first edition of *PR* (1671) before the poem, "Notes" and appendices at the end, original green cloth, spine lettered in gilt. A fine copy, near mint.

1669. PARADISE REGAIN'D By John Milton Newly Edited With An Introduction And Commentary By E[.] H[.] Blakeney[.] [Quotation in Greek] *London • Eric Partridge LTD At The Scholartis Press • Museum Street • MDCCCCXXXII.* First edition thus. Royal 8vo, x+187pp., half-title, decorated initial letter on title page, dedication page in Latin, "Preface," "Introduction," half-title for the poem, decorated initial letter at the outset of each book, half-title for "Commentary" after the poem with "Corrigenda: Addenda" tipped in before, index at the end with emblem on verso of last page, original blue quarter cloth, white paper over boards, spine lettered in gilt, printed publisher's wrappers (a bit used) in a protective plastic cover. A nice copy. "This edition, printed by H. P. R. Finberg at the Alcuin Press, Campden, Gloucestershire, is limited to six hundred copies, of which 550 are for sale, and five copies printed on batchelor's Kelmscott handmade paper" (verso title page).

1670. PARADISE REGAINED THE MINOR POEMS AND SAMSON AGONISTES[.] John Milton. Complete and Arranged Chronologically[.] Edited By Merritt Y. Hughes[,] Professor of English, University of Wisconsin[.] *Doubleday, Doran & Company, Inc. Garden City[,] New York[.] (1937).* First edition thus. 8vo, lxiii+633pp., half-title ("The Doubleday—Doran Series In Literature[,] Robert Shafer[,] General Editor"), frontispiece portrait plate reproducing portrait of Milton "Aged 21 From the portrait at Nuneham," emblem of the press printed on title page, "Printed At The Country Life Press, Garden City, N.Y., U.S.A." and "First Edition" on verso of title page, chronology, introduction, bibliography, reproduction of 1645 *Poems* title page before the poems, notes at bottom of page, indexes at the end, original diced blue cloth, central gilt emblem on front cover, gilt-decorated spine with gilt lettering (faded). A nice copy with bookplate on front pastedown and dated contemporary signature on fly-leaf.

1671. PARADISE REGAINED THE MINOR POEMS AND SAMSON AGONISTES[.] John Milton. Complete and Arranged Chronologically[.] Edited By Merritt Y. Hughes[,] Professor of English, University of Wisconsin[.] *Doubleday, Doran & Company, Inc. Garden City[,] New York[.] (1937).* Second edition thus. 8vo, lxiii+633pp., half-title ("The Doubleday—Doran Series In Literature[,] Robert Shafer[,] General Editor"), frontispiece portrait plate reproducing portrait of Milton "Aged 21 From the portrait at Nuneham," emblem of the press printed on title page, "Printed At The Country Life Press, Garden City, N.Y., U.S.A." and "Second Edition" on verso of title page, chronology, introduction, bibliography, reproduction of 1645 *Poems* title page before the poems, notes at bottom of page, indexes at the end, original diced blue cloth, gilt emblem of the press on front cover, gilt-decorated spine with gilt lettering, printed publisher's wrappers (a bit used), front cover in red with reproduction of portrait of Milton at age twenty-one. A fine copy with early bookplate on fly-leaf.

The collection also includes the third, eighth, ninth, tenth, eleventh, twelfth, and later Doubleday-Doran Press Merritt Hughes editions, as here, original blue cloth, gilt-decorated spine with gilt lettering, generally in good or very good condition; the tenth edition with Odyssey Press card offering the book "for your consideration as a basic textbook for your classes" laid in; the twelfth with publisher's advertisement leaf for "The Odyssey Series In Literature" laid in.

1672. [PARADISE REGAINED] MILTON'S PARADISE REGAINED Edited by G. V. S. Mani. Rao Brothers (Regd.) *Guntur Copyright 1952.* First edition thus. Slim 8vo in 4s, [i]+xlxvii+120pp., introduction, notes, and appendix at end, original yellow cloth. A good copy. Scarce.

1673. [PARADISE REGAINED] JOHN MILTON LE PARADIS RECONQUIS. Etude Critique, Traduction Et Notes Par Jacques Blondel[,] Maitre de conferences a la Faculte des Lettres de Clermont-Ferrand[.] Collection Bilingue Des Classiques Etrangers*[.]. Aubier[,] Editions Montaigne, 13, Quai Conti, Paris[,] (1955).* First edition thus. 12mo, half-title, 270+[2]pp., 120-page introduction in French, reproduction of 1681 second edition title page before poem, English and French texts printed side by side (English on verso and French on recto), "Notes" and a brief "Bibliographie" in the back, "Table Des Matieres" with colophon on verso at the end, original printed orange wrappers with a listing of "Litterature Anglaise" on the back, in original protective glassine wrappers, edges untrimmed. A nice copy. See companion volume also listed here, *Paradis Perdu*, published in two volumes in 1951 and 1955.

1674. [PARADISE REGAINED] MILTON PARADISE REGAINED[:] Books I. II. III. IV. (excerpts) read by Ian 1671[.] A Scolar Press Facsimile[.] The Scolar P Holm[,] Denis McCarthy[,] John Neville[,] *Argo Record Company Limited[,] London[,] 1967.* 33 1/3 rpm LP Record, in original sleeve and original slipcase jacket "Printed by Graphis Press Limited" with reproduction of Blake illustration in black and white on front cover. A fine record, in fine original sleeve and fine original slipcase jacket. Laid in: libretto published in London by Oxford University Press "In Association With The British Council," 1967. Libretto also in fine condition.

1675. PARADISE REGAINED 1671[.] John Milton[.] Paradise Regained[,] Samson Agonistes[,] 1671[.] A Scolar Press Facsimile[.] *The Scolar Press Limited[.] Menston, England[,] 1968.* First Scholar Press edition thus. 8vo, unpaginated facsimile reproduction, printer's emblem of the Scolar Press on title page, original green cloth, gilt emblem of the Scolar Press on front cover, spine lettered in gilt. A good copy. Facsimile reproduction of the first edition.

1676. PARADISE REGAINED[,] SAMSON AGONISTES John Milton 1671[.] A Scolar Press Facsimile. *[Menston, England: The Scolar Press, 1973.]* Second Scolar Press edition thus. 8vo, 111+101+[2]pp., facsimile reproduction of the 1671 first edition, original gray cloth, spine lettered in gilt, printed green wrappers lettered in black and white with decorative black device on front cover. A nice copy.

1677. [PARADISE REGAINED] A VARIORUM COMMENTARY ON THE POEMS OF JOHN MILTON[.] VOLUME FOUR[:] PARADISE REGAINED [Edited By] Walter MacKellar[,] With a review of Studies of Style and Verse Form by Edward R. Weismiller. *New York[:] Columbia University Press[,] 1975.* First edition thus. 8vo, xxiv+379pp., half-title with advertisement for "The Complete Series" on verso, chronological table, introduction, index, original blue cloth, spine lettered in gilt, printed blue publisher's wrappers printed in white and black (spine a little faded). A fine copy. Presentation copy to Milton scholar James Hutton from the editor, Walter MacKellar, with presentation inscription on fly-leaf.

1678. Variant of Preceding. A VARIORUM COMMENTARY ON THE POEMS OF JOHN MILTON[.] VOLUME FOUR[:] PARADISE REGAINED [Edited By] Walter MacKellar[,] With a review of Studies of Style and Verse Form by Edward R. Weismiller. *London[:] Routledge & Kegan Paul. n.d [1975].* First London edition thus. 8vo, xxiv+379pp., half-title with advertisement for "The Complete Series" on verso, variation on verso of title page, chronological table, introduction, index, original blue cloth, spine lettered in gilt, printed blue publisher's wrappers printed in white and black. A fine copy.

1679. PARADISE REGAIN'D, A Poem, In Four Books, By John Milton. A New Edition, With Notes Of Various Authors, By Charles Dunster, M.A. [Greek Quotation from Plato] *Norwood Editions[,] 1977.* 4to, [i]+iv+[iv]+280pp., besides Norwood Editions title page consisting of a reprint of Dunster's 1795 title page with "Norwood Editions" and date added, Dunster's original title page is reproduced along with Dunster's edition including the large engraved folding map of paradise, which is reproduced on two pages, original black buckram, spine lettered in gilt. A very good copy with "Library of Congress Duplicate" stamped in red on fly-leaf. Reprint of the first Dunster edition published by T. Cadell in London in 1795 (also listed here), which was also the first separate edition of *PR*, with arguments to each book provided by Dunster because Milton had not provided any; a revised second edition by Dunster was published in 1800. Printed in a limited edition of 100 copies.

Hand-colored, Numbered, and Signed by the Artist

1680. [PARADISE REGAINED] THE TEMPTATION; FROM PARADISE REGAINED[.] John Milton[.] Illustrated by Sylvia Stokeld[.] *[Oxford:] Hanborough Parrot Press[,] 1988*. First edition thus. Royal 8vo, unpaginated [17pp.], half-title with hand-colored illustration, hand-colored frontispiece illustration and other hand-colored illustrations by Sylvia Stokeld (first appearance), "set in 16 pt Trump Mediaeval and printed on mould made paper," original white boards, large hand-colored illustration incorporating title on front cover, printed paper label on spine, endpapers decorated with hand-colored illustrations. A fine copy in mint condition. One of 85 numbered copies, this being one of the special copies, number IV of XXV copies (numbered in Roman numerals), hand-colored throughout and numbered and signed by the artist on colophon page at the end. The first publication under Dennis Hall's new imprint, successor to the Inky Parrot Press that he directed at Oxford Polytechnic.

Numbered and Signed by the Artist

1681. Variant of Preceding. THE TEMPTATION; FROM PARADISE REGAINED[.] John Milton[.] Illustrated by Sylvia Stokeld[.] *[Oxford:] Hanborough Parrot Press[,] 1988*. First edition thus. Royal 8vo, unpaginated [17pp.], half-title with illustration, first appearance of frontispiece illustration and other illustrations by Sylvia Stokeld, "set in 16 pt Trump Mediaeval and printed on mould made paper," original white boards, large illustration incorporating title on front cover, printed paper label on spine, gray endpapers decorated with illustrations. A fine copy in mint condition, variant of preceding copy in that this is one of the 60 copies in which the illustrations are not hand-colored and the endpapers are gray. One of 85 numbered copies (numbered in Arabic numbers), this being number 34, numbered and signed by the artist on colophon page at the end.

1682. [PARADISE REGAINED] JOHN MILTON PARADISE REGAINED ENTIRELY IN RUSSIAN] JOHN MILTON • PARADISE REGAINED • POEM[S.] Translated by Sergej Aleksandrovskij. *Moscow[:] Vremya, 2001*. First edition thus. Small 8vo, 188+189+[4]pp., unsigned portrait of Milton (somewhat after Faithorne) with reproduction of 1671 *PR/SA* first edition title page on verso, introduction by E.V. Vitkovskij, a second unsigned portrait of Milton dictating to his daughter (Russian style), reproductions of unsigned illustrations throughout (some after Doré), decorative head- and tailpieces, commentary before *PR* and notes at the end, commentary before the sonnets, contents at the end, original green cloth, front cover and spine lettered in gilt, black endpapers printed with poetic passages from *PR* in white, light green publisher's wrappers in half wrap style with gilt-stamped wording at the bottom and gilt-stamped emblem on the back, white silk ribbon marker. Sonnets translated by A.P. Prokopiev, with commentaries to the sonnets. Commentaries by A. Zinoviev before *PR* and before the sonnet. S.A. Aleksandrovskij's translation of *PR* is the first new Russian translation of Milton's brief epic in over one hundred years. A fine copy, entirely in Russian.

Nineteenth-century decorated cloth bindings on illustrated Milton editions—showing spines on several shelves.

Poems

1683. POEMS Of Mr. John Milton, Both English and Latin, Compos'd at several times. Printed by his true Copies. The Songs were set in Musick by Mr. Henry Lawes Gentleman of the Kings Chappel, and one of His Maiesties Private Musick. [Quotation from Virgil] *Printed and publish'd according to Order. London, Printed by Ruth Raworth for Humphrey Moseley, and are to be sold at the signe of the Princes Arms in S. Pauls Church-yard. 1645.* First edition, first issue. 8vo, [iv]+120+87pp., frontispiece portrait engraved by W. Marshall with Greek inscription "The Stationer To The Reader" beneath, separate title pages for *Comus* and the *Latin Poems* with decorative piece on each title page, decorative head- and tailpieces and decorated initial letters, modern full green morocco, gilt-decorated covers and spine, raised bands with decorative gilt rule, inner dentelles richly tooled in gilt outer dentelles ruled in gilt, a.e.g., bound by Francis Bedford, stored in half green morocco, marbled paper box, with brown morocco labels on spine lettered and ruled in gilt, and with raised bands, the box lined in yellow felt. A fine copy with the bookplate of Leonard Schlosser. There are two states of the last line in the imprint, one, as in the present copy, reading "S. Pauls Churchyard" and the other omitting the "S." Of the copies examined by Harris F. Fletcher, about two-thirds read "S. Pauls" and the remainder read "Pauls." This is the first published work to bear John Milton's full name on the title page. The book contains all of Milton's poems written up to this time. With the exception of the *Epitaph on Shakespeare*, *Comus*, and *Lycidas*, all of the poems make their first published appearance here. The collection was reprinted with an additional thirty-three poems in 1673 (copy following). The frontispiece is the earliest engraving from life and the earliest published portrait. "While Marshall the engraver was well-established as the best in London," as Coleridge points out, "the portrait is very poor," and Milton had a low opinion of it and of Marshall's skill—expressed in the Greek lines beneath the portrait ("my very friends [will] . . . laugh at the awkward imitation of the stupid artist"), which Marshall inserted, believing them to be complimentary. Rare. Wing M2160; Pforzheimer 722; Hayward 71; Grolier 572; Coleridge 84b; Kohler 222.

1684. POEMS, ETC. UPON SEVERAL OCCASIONS. By Mr. John Milton: Both English and Latin, &c. Composed at several times. With a small Tractate of Education To Mr. Hartlib. *London. Printed for Tho. Dring at the White Lion next Chancery Lane End, in Fleet-street. 1673.* Second edition, first issue. 8vo, [vi]+165+117+[5]pp., "The Table Of the English Poems" and "The Table Of the Latin Poems," "Errata" leaf, separate title page for the *Latin Poems* with decorative piece at the center, decorative head- and tailpieces and decorated initial letters, final advertisement leaves present ("A Catalogue of some Books printed for and sold by Tho. Dring at the Blew Anchor"), modern paneled calf (short tears in the lower inner and fore margins of the title page repaired, faint damp-staining to the top fore corners throughout and general slight embrowning), spine lettered in gilt (a bit faded), raised bands. Thirty-three additional poems are included in the second edition that do not appear in the first edition of 1645 (preceding copy). This prints all Milton's shorter poems, except the four "political" sonnets (nos. 15, 16, 17, and 22)—*To Fairfax*, *To Cromwell*, *To Vane*, and *To Cyriack*—which are printed together in the 1694 *Letters of State* (also listed here), and the fragmentary pieces in the prose works. The tractate *Of Education* is also included here in its second printing, having been first been published

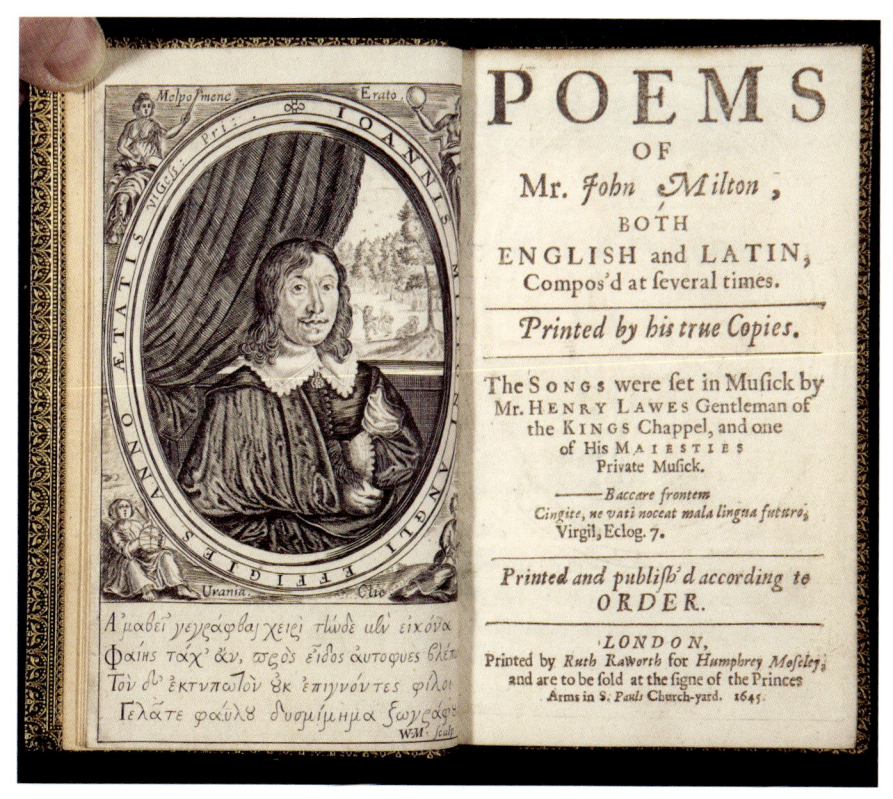

Engraved frontispiece portrait and title page, 1645 *Poems*. See #1683.

as a separate piece in 1644. "Its presence here was the cause of its repeated incorporation in the editions of the minor poems in the eighteenth century" (Coleridge). Two states of the imprint are known, one as here and another reading "At the Blew Anchor." There has been much discussion about the priority of these states, but no conclusive proof. Harrison Fletcher thinks there is no priority. The Pforzheimer catalogue, though, believes that the "White Lion" imprint is the earlier. Rare. Grolier, *Wither to Prior*, 573; Wing M2161; Pforzheimer 723; Coleridge 85a; Shawcross, Kentucky, 56; Kohler 223 ("at the Blew Anchor").

1684A. (Cross-listing) **POEMS UPON SEVERAL OCCASIONS**. Compos'd at several times. By Mr. John Milton. The Third Edition. *London: Printed for Jacob Tonson, at the Judge's Head, near the Inner Temple-Gate in Fleet-street, M DC XCV*. Third edition; first folio edition. [In] **THE POETICAL WORKS OF MR. JOHN MILTON**. Containing, Paradise Lost, Paradise Regain'd, *Samson Agonistes*, and his Poems on several Occasions. Together With Explanatory NOTES on each Book of the PARADISE LOST, and a TABLE never before Printed. *London: Printed for Jacob Tonson, at the Judge's Head near the Inner Temple-Gate in Fleet-street, M DC XC*. First complete collected edition. There are far fewer surviving copies of this important edition than one might expect" (Parker, p. 1194); Coleridge 214 (without general title page); Wing M2162; Kohler 266.; Shawcross, Kentucky, 110. See main listing under *PW*, 1695.

1685. **POEMS ON AFFAIRS OF STATE**: From The Time of *Oliver Cromwell*, to the Abdication of K. *James* the Second. Written by the *greatest Wits of the Age*. Viz. Duke of *Buckingham*, Earl of *Rochester*, Lord Bu———st, Sir *John Denham*, *Andrew Marvell*, Esq; Mr. *Milton*, Mr. *Dryden*, Mr. *Sprat*, Mr. *Waller*. Mr. *Ayloffe*, &c. With some Miscellany Poems by the same: Most whereof never before Printed. *Now carefully examined with the Originals, and Published without any Castration. Printed in the Year 1697*. 3 volumes in one. Stout 8vo, [vi]+267+[1]pp.,+[vi]+248+[1blank]pp.,+[v+1blank verso]+[6—with brackets for pagination, but unpaginated]+312pp., contemporary calf (sometime rebacked, a little worn, two pages with portions missing—one along the side and including some text, the other a small part of the lower corner without affecting any text, minor foxing), black morocco label with gilt lettering and gilt rules on spine, raised bands within gilt rules. A quite decent copy with early names on title page. "This edition is not the first; the first edition of *Poems on affairs of state* was [published] earlier the same year, without the *State poems* as a 2nd part . . . There were . . . further distinct collections in subsequent years, also reprinted several times. These later collections have no Milton references" (Coleridge). Rare. Wing P2719A, S5325A, P2722; Parker, pp. 860, 1101, 1203; Shawcross, 1984, 1542; Coleridge 388, 410.

1685A. (Cross-listing) **POEMS UPON SEVERAL OCCASIONS**. Compos'd at several times. By Mr. John Milton. The Third Edition. *London, Printed for Jacob Tonson, at Grays-Inn Gate next Grays-Inn Lane. 1705*. Alternate third edition. [In] **PARADISE REGAIN'D**. A Poem. In Four Books. To which is added **SAMSON AGONISTES. AND POEMS UPON SEVERAL OCCASIONS**. Compos'd at several Times. The Author John Milton. The Fourth Edition. *London, Printed for Jacob Tonson, within Grays-Inn Gate next Grays-Inn Lane. 1705*. 8vo, 457+[4]pp., separate title page for "**SAMSON AGONISTES** . . . London, Printed for *Jacob Tonson*, at *Grays-Inn Gate* next *Grays-Inn Lane*. 1705," separate title page for "**POEMS UPON SEVERAL OCCASIONS**. Compos'd at several times. By Mr. John Milton. The Third Edition. London, Printed for *Jacob Tonson*, at *Grays-Inn Gate* next *Grays-Inn Lane*. 1705," "The Table" (i.e., contents) at the end, contemporary calf. Companion volume to *PL*, illustrated seventh edition, 1705 (also listed here). Coleridge 185; Kohler 180 (without mention of separate title pages). See main listing under *PR*, 1705.

1685B. (Cross-listing) **POEMS UPON SEVERAL OCCASIONS**. Compos'd at several times. By Mr. John Milton. The Fourth Edition. *London, Printed for Jacob Tonson, within Grays-Inn Gate next Grays-Inn Lane. 1707* Fourth Edition. [In] **PARADISE REGAIN'D**. A Poem. In Four Books. To which is added **SAMSON AGONISTES. AND POEMS UPON SEVERAL OCCASIONS**. Compos'd at several Times. The Author John Milton. The Fifth Edition. *London, Printed for Jacob Tonson, within Grays-Inn Gate next Grays-Inn Lane. 1707*. 8vo, 457+[4]pp., separate title page for "**SAMSON AGONISTES** . . . London, Printed for *Jacob Tonson*, within *Grays-Inn* Gate next *Grays-Inn* Lane. 1707," separate title page for "**POEMS UPON SEVERAL OCCASIONS**." as cited, "The Table" (i.e., contents) at end, original paneled calf. Companion volume to *PL*, eighth edition, 1707 (copies listed here, one of which is bound without the illustrations). Coleridge 186; Kohler 181 (without mention of separate title pages). See main listing under *PR*, 1707.

1685C. (Cross-listing) **POEMS, &C. UPON SEVERAL OCCASIONS**. In English and Latin, &c. Compos'd at several times. By Mr. John Milton. The Fifth Edition, with Additions. [Quotation from Virgil] *London, Printed in the Year 1713*. Fifth edition; first 12mo edition. [In] **PARADISE REGAIN'D**. A Poem. In Four Books. To which is added SAMSON AGONISTES. AND POEMS UPON SEVERAL OCCASIONS. WITH A TRACTATE OF EDUCATION. The Author John Milton. The Fifth Edition. Adorn'd with Cuts. *London*: Printed for *J. Tonson*, at *Shakespeare's* Head, over-against *Catherine-Street* in the *Strand*. 1713. First 12mo edition; first illustrated edition; first appearance thus of *Of Ed*. 12mo, [v]+388pp., engraved frontispiece illustration, one engraved illustration for each book of *PR* (by Nicholas Pigné, plate signed for Book I), separate title page for "SAMSON AGONISTES, A Dramatick Poem. The Author John Milton. Aristot. Poet. Cap. 6 . . . London, Printed in the Year 1713," with engraved frontispiece illustration (by Nicholas Pigné), separate title page for "POEMS, &C. UPON SEVERAL OCCASIONS. In English and Latin, &c., " as cited, with reproduction of frontispiece portrait after W. Marshall's engraving in 1645 *Poems*, half-title for *C*, the *LP* ("Poemata"), and *Of Ed* ("A Small Tractate of Education, To Mr. Hartlib"), four additional engraved illustrations: one for *L'A* (by Pigné), one for *IlP* (unsigned), one for *On Shakespeare* (unsigned), and one for *On the University Carrier* (unsigned), decorative head- and tailpieces and decorated initial letters, original calf. The four sonnets—*To Fairfax, To Cromwell, To Vane,* and *To Cyriack*—were printed together in the 1694 *Letters of State* (copy listed here) and were not included in the 1673 edition of *Poems* (copy also listed here) and thus Tonson did not include them in his subsequent editions of the *Poems* (1695, 1705, and 1707—see copies, cross-listed), including them for the first time in this, his 1713 edition. The presence of the tractate *Of Education* in the 1673 edition of *Poems* was the cause of its repeated incorporation in editions of the minor poems in the eighteenth century, beginning with this 1713 edition by Tonson, which establishes the prototypical content for the balance of the eighteenth century, including for the first time *Of Education*. Scarce. Coleridge 187a; Kohler 182. See main listing under *PR*, 1713.

1686. POEMS UPON SEVERAL OCCASIONS. Compos'd at several Times. By Mr. John Milton. [Quotation from Virgil] *Dublin: Printed by and for George Grierson, at the Two Bibles in Essex-Street, 1748*. First Irish edition. 8vo, 72pp. (paginated from 126 to 196), decorative fruit piece on title page, separate title page for *Comus* with same decorative fruit piece on title page ("**A MASK PRESENTED AT LUDLOW-CASTLE**, In The Year 1634. Before The Earl of Bridgewater, then President of Wales. Dublin: Printed by and for George Grierson, at the Two Bibles in *Essex-Street*, 1748,") First Irish edition, same decorative fruit piece repeated at the end of last page, decorative head- and tailpieces and decorated initial letters, modern half dark brown leather, light orange cloth, printed paper label on front cover, new blanks and light orange endpapers. A fine copy. Not all of Milton's poems are included; among those included are *L, L'A, IlP, Ar,* and *C*. Included at the end without separate title page is *Of Ed*. Not in Coleridge; Not in Kohler.

[together with]

1686A. (Cross-listing) PARADISE REGAIN'D. A Poem, In Four Books. *Dublin: Printed by George Grierson, Printer to the King's Most Excellent Majesty, at the King's-Arms and Two Bibles in Essex-Street, 1749*. 8vo, 61pp. (paginated from 3 to 61), title page in red and black with decorative fruit piece in black at the center, bound as *SA*. A fine copy. Not in Coleridge; Not in Kohler. See main listing under *PR*, 1749.

[together with]

1686B. (Cross-listing) SAMSON AGONISTES, A Dramatick Poem. The Author John Milton. Aristot. Poet. Cap. 6 . . . *Dublin: Printed by and for George Grierson, at the Two Bibles in Essex-Street, 1748*. First Irish edition. 8vo, 58pp. (paginated from 66 to 121), decorative fruit piece on title page, bound as *PR* and *P*. A fine copy. Not in Coleridge; Not in Kohler. See main listing under *SA*, 1748.

Despite the editions being bound separately, Grierson clearly wished to present a complete and uniform collection of Milton's poetry, as indicated by the continuous pagination here of the separate parts (*PR*, *SA*, and *P*), from page 3 to page 196. John Shawcross likewise shared with me that "This was not issued separately. Libraries have sometimes listed their separated volumes as separate publications; this is incorrect. This reissue is the same as the 1748 edition (observe the signatures) except that the collection (*PR*) has a new title page dated 1749." The very rare first Irish editions of *PR*, *SA*, and *P*.

1687. [POEMS] THE POEMS OF MILTON. *[London: Printed By H. Hughs et al., M DCC LXXIX]*. 3 volumes. First edition thus. Small 8vo, iv+253+[1]pp., +241+[1]pp., +304pp., general title page each volume: "The Works Of The English Poets. With Prefaces, Biographical And Critical, By Samuel Johnson. Volume The First/Second/Third. London: Printed By H. Hughs et al., M DCC LXXIX," engraved frontispiece portrait by Bartolozzi, volume 1, half-title for *P* each volume, half-title for each book of *PL* and each book of *PR* and for some of the poems, "Contents" page at end of each volume, contemporary polished calf, elaborately gilt-decorated spines, double black morocco labels with gilt lettering and gilt rules, outer dentelles tooled in gilt, green ribbon markers. A very fine set from the first edition of Johnson's *Works of the English Poets*. Scarce. Not in Coleridge; Not in Kohler.

1688. POEMS UPON SEVERAL OCCASIONS, ENGLISH, ITALIAN, AND LATIN, With Translations, By John Milton. Viz. Lycidas, L'Allegro, Il Penseroso, Arcades, Comus, Odes, Sonnets, Miscellanies, English Psalms, Elegiarum Liber, Epigrammatum Liber, Sylvarum Liber. With Notes Critical And Explanatory, And Other Illustrations, By Thomas Warton, Fellow Of Trinity College And Late Professor Of Poetry At Oxford. *London, Printed for James Dodsley In Pall Mall. M DCC LXXX V.* First Warton edition. Stout 8vo, xxviii+620pp., edited by Thomas Warton, "Preface," "Contents," half-title for some of the poems, notes at bottom of page, contemporary speckled calf, gilt rules on spine, red morocco label with decorative gilt trim, outer dentelles tooled in gilt, blue edges, with a three-page listing of early editions of Milton's poetry at the end. A fine copy. The first and only lifetime Warton edition, which was recognized immediately as the best critical edition of Milton's poems ever produced. Its reputation extended far into this century, and as late as 1968 Parker quotes Warton and credits him with discovering vital facts about Milton and his work. A second, revised edition was published in 1791 (also listed here). Coleridge 86; Kohler 224.

1689. Variant of Preceding. POEMS UPON SEVERAL OCCASIONS, ENGLISH, ITALIAN, AND LATIN, With Translations, By John Milton. Viz. Lycidas, L'Allegro, Il Penseroso, Arcades, Comus, Odes, Sonnets, Miscellanies, English Psalms, Elegiarum Liber, Epigrammatum Liber, Sylvarum Liber. With Notes Critical And Explanatory, And Other Illustrations, By Thomas Warton, Fellow Of Trinity College And Late Professor Of Poetry At Oxford. *London, Printed for James Dodsley In Pall Mall. M DCC LXXX V.* 2 volumes. First Warton edition. 8vo, xxviii+304pp.,+620pp. (continuous pagination), edited by Thomas Warton, "Preface," "Contents," half-title for some of the poems, notes at bottom of page, contemporary speckled calf (joints weak), gilt rules on spine, red morocco title labels with decorative gilt trim, black morocco numbering labels with decorative gilt trim, marbled endpapers, red edges, with a three-page listing of early editions of Milton's poetry at the end. A fine set with the bookplate of Leonard Schlosser. Warton's fine critical edition bound into two volumes. Coleridge 86; Kohler 224.

1690. POEMS UPON SEVERAL OCCASIONS, ENGLISH, ITALIAN, AND LATIN, With Translations, By John Milton. Viz. Lycidas, L'Allegro, Il Penseroso, Arcades, Comus, Odes, Sonnets, Miscellanies, English Psalms, Elegiarum Liber, Epigrammatum Liber, Sylvarum Liber. With Notes Critical And Explanatory, And Other Illustrations, By Thomas Warton, B.D. Late Fellow Of Trinity College, Professor Of Poetry, And Camden Professor Of History, At Oxford. The Second Edition, With Many Alterations, And Large Additions. [Latin Quotation "Ad J. Rous"] *London, Printed for G. G. J. And J. Robinson, Pater-Noster Row. In Pall Mall. M DCC XCI.* Second Warton edition, revised. Large 8vo, xlvi+[1]+608pp., "Preface," "Appendix To The Preface. The Nuncupative Will of Milton. With Notes By The Editor," half-title for some of the poems, notes at bottom of page, "Appendix containing Remarks on the Greek Verses of Milton by Charles Burney," with its own half-title, along with a three-page listing of early editions of Milton's poetry at the end, contemporary calf (joints cracked), gilt rules on covers, black morocco labels with gilt lettering and decorative gilt trim. A fine copy with prize presentation inscription (dated 1805) on front pastedown and early signature (dated 1866) on fly-leaf. Warton had revised the text of this edition and among the additions are Charles Burney's noted remarks on Milton's Greek verses; Milton's will is among other important additions. The first Warton edition was published in 1785 (see copies listed here). Masson remarks that this is the best critical edition of Milton's minor works ever produced. Coleridge 87; Kohler 225.

1691. POEMS By John Milton, containing Extracts From Paradise Lost, Samson, L'Allegro, Il Penseroso, & Lycidas, With The Author's Life. *Published Oct. 31. 1800 by George Nicholson, Poughnill near Ludlow. Sold in London, by T. Conder, Bucklersbury: Champante, and Whitrow 4 Jewry street, Aldgate; R. Bickerstaff, 210 Strand; and by all other Booksellers.* 12mo in 6s, xxiv+103+[1]pp., vignette portrait of Milton by J. Chapman on title page, life of Milton, tailpiece illustration of a contemplative young man beneath a tree at the end, "Content" on verso of last page, contemporary calf (a little worn, especially along joints and at corners, joints a little weak), covers ruled in delicate blind trim with large embossed bright gilt emblem at the center, dark olive green morocco label with gilt lettering and gilt rules on spine, thick raised bands with decorative gilt trim and with thick gilt rule beneath, decorative gilt piece within the panels, marbled endpapers and edges. A nice copy with contemporary signature (dated 1829) on front blank. Not in Kohler.

1692. POEMS ON SEVERAL OCCASIONS. Lycidas. L'Allegro. Il Penseroso. Sonnets. Odes. Miscellanies. Translations. Poemata. The Author, John Milton. *London: Printed In The Year MDCCCXVII.* First edition thus. 12mo, 188pp., half-title ("Milton's Minor Poems"), engraved and printed title pages, engraved title "**THE MINOR POEMS** of John Milton. London: Published By John Sharpe. MDCCCXVI," with vignette illustration by Richard

Westall engraved by R. Rhodes, for the sonnet *Methought I Saw My Late Espoused Saint. Sonnet XXIII*, protective tissue guard, engraved illustration plates for *L*, *L'A*, *IlP*, *S* (with vignette illustration for *Sonnet X*), and *O* (with vignette illustration for *NO*), each with vignette illustration by Richard Westall, variously engraved, each plate dated "Aug. 24. 1816," each with protective tissue guard, "Index To The Minor Poems" at the end, contemporary full straight-grained red morocco, gilt rules on covers, spine lettered in gilt with decorative trim at top and bottom, raised bands within gilt rules, inner and outer dentelles ruled in gilt, red endpapers, a.e.g., bookplate. A very fine copy in a lovely Romantic binding with half-title present and with the first appearance of these vignette illustrations. See 1819 and 1823 Chiswick reissues here, with the 1816 issue of the plates, and also 1827 Chiswick small 8vo reissue, with new engravers of the plates dated 1827. Kohler 213, citing a two-volume edition of *PR* and *P*, each dated 1817, reporting "Not in Cambridge University Library."

1693. Variant of Preceding, contemporary polished calf (some foxing to the plates), gilt rules with small gilt corner decorations on covers, gilt-decorated spine with small gilt harps within the panels, green morocco labels lettered and ruled in green, raised bands with decorative gilt trim, inner and outer dentelles finely tooled in gilt, marbled endpapers and edges, brown silk ribbon marker. A fine copy in an attractive and well-preserved variant binding, with half-title present, and with the first appearance of these vignette illustrations. This volume is uniformly bound with an edition of Milton's *PR*, also published by John Sharpe at the Chiswick Press in 1817 (copy listed here).

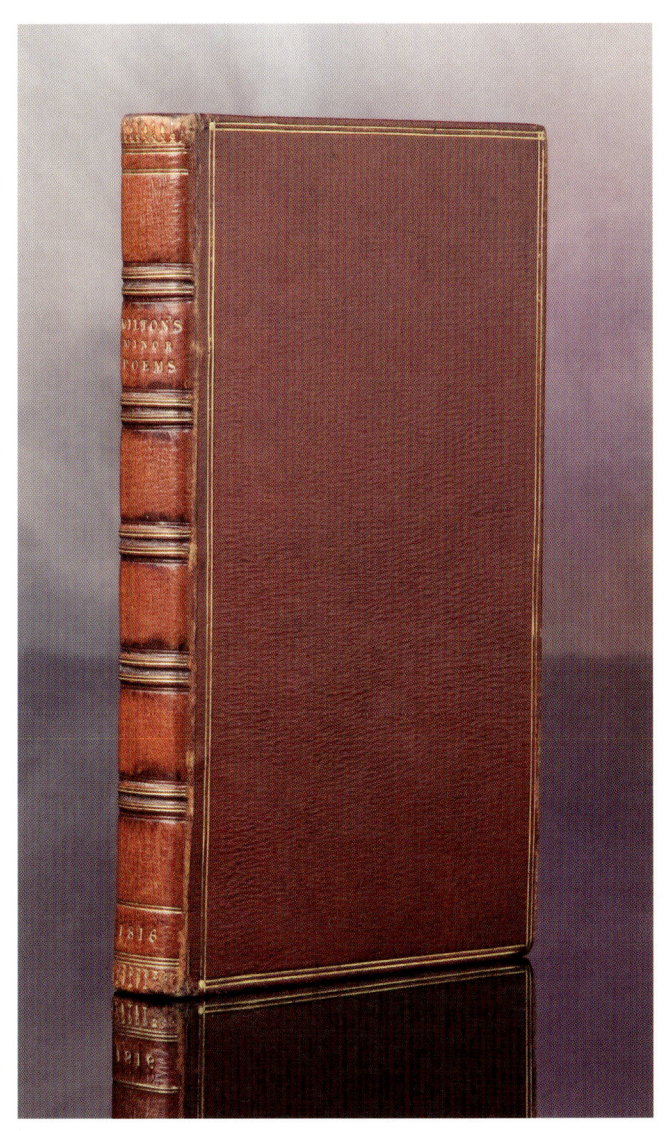

Poems. London, 1817. With a copy of 1816 plates, contemporary full straight-grained maroon morocco. Lovely Romantic binding. See #1692.

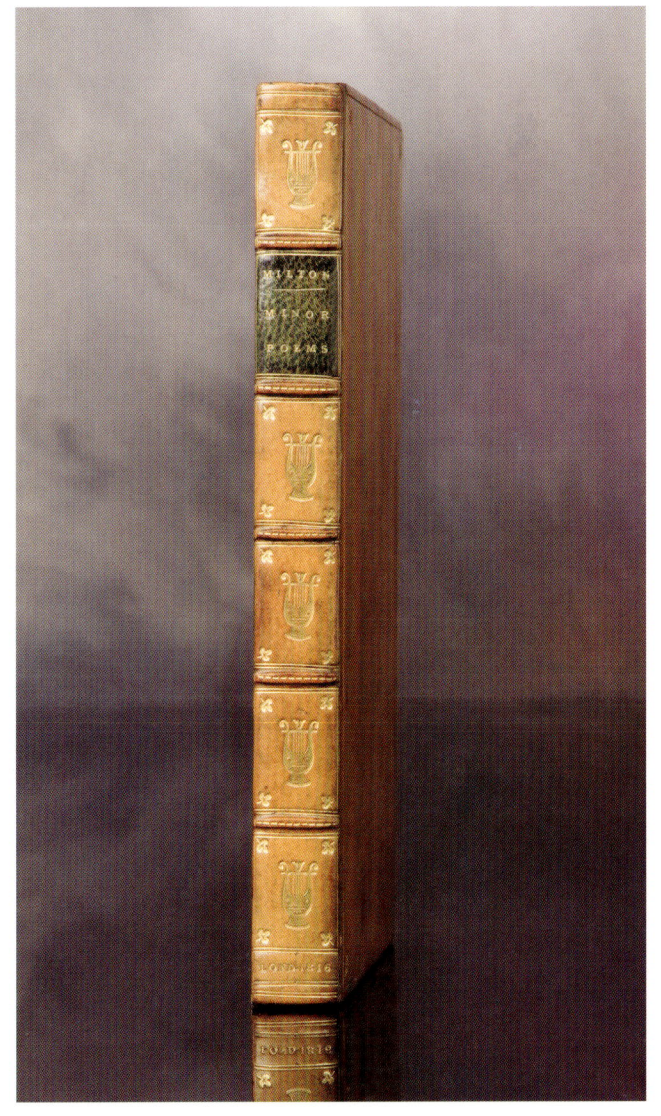

Poems. London, 1817. With a copy of 1816 plates, contemporary polished calf. Lovely Romantic binding. Uniformly bound with *PR*, 1817. See #1693.

1694. POEMS ON SEVERAL OCCASIONS. Lycidas. L'Allegro. Il Penseroso. Sonnets. Odes. Miscellanies. Translations. Poemata. The Author, John Milton. *London: Printed In The Year MDCCCXIX*. 12mo, 188pp., engraved and printed title pages, engraved title "THE MINOR POEMS of John Milton. London: Published By John Sharpe. MDCCCXVI," with vignette illustration by Richard Westall engraved by R. Rhodes, for the sonnet *Methought I Saw My Late Espoused Saint. Sonnet XXIII*, protective tissue guard, engraved illustration plates for *L, L'A, IlP, S* (with vignette illustration for *Sonnet X*), and *O* (with vignette illustration for *NO*), each with vignette illustration by Richard Westall, variously engraved, each plate dated "Aug. 24. 1816," "Index To The Minor Poems" at the end, contemporary full blue morocco (rubbed, joints weak, foxing), elaborate gilt border trim with inner gilt rules and decorative gilt corner pieces on covers, elaborately gilt-decorated spine in the panels, red morocco label with gilt lettering and gilt rules, raised bands, inner and outer dentelles finely tooled in gilt, marbled endpapers and edges, bookplate, with the card of Duncan Mcmillan, Ministry of Education, Cairo, laid in, inscribed and signed on verso. Although a bit worn, a good copy in a nice binding of the period, with interesting association. An 1819 reissue of the edition by Sharpe/Whittingham/Chiswick first published in 1817 (see copies listed here), with the 1816 issue of the plates (first appearance). See also 1823 Chiswick reissue, with the 1816 issue of the plates, and see 1827 Chiswick small 8vo reissue, with new engravers of the plates dated 1827. Kohler 214, citing a two-volume edition of *PR* and *P*, each dated 1819, reporting "Not in the British Library. Not in the Bodleian Library. Not in Cambridge University Library."

1695. Variant of Preceding, contemporary full black calf (plates a little foxed), covers decorated in embossed trim in the center with delicate gilt border trim, spine richly gilt decorated in the panels, two red morocco labels with gilt lettering and gilt rules, thick raised bands richly gilt decorated, inner and outer dentelles finely tooled in gilt, marbled endpapers and edges, with contemporary signature (dated 1825) on front blank. A charming copy in a lovely variant Romantic binding, beautifully preserved.

1696. THE POEMS OF JOHN MILTON. Vol. I/II/III. *Chiswick: From The Press Of C. Whittingham, College House. n.d. [1822].* Part of **THE BRITISH POETS**. Including Translations. In One Hundred Volumes. XVI/XVII/XVIII. Milton, Vol. I/II/III. *Chiswick: Printed by C. Whittingham, College House; For J. Carpenter, J. Booker, Rodwell And Martin, G. And W. B. Whittaker, R. Triphook, J. Ebers, Taylor And Hessey, R. Jennings, G. Cowie And Co. N. Hailes, J. Porter, B. E. LLoyd And Son, C. Smith, And C. Whittingham. 1822.* 3 volumes. 8vo, 269,+251,+252pp., half-title, general title page, and individual title page each volume, "Contents" page following the title page of each volume, half-title for *C* and *PR*, "The Life Of John Milton. By Dr. Johnson" in volume 1, "C. Whittingham, College House, Chiswick" printed at the bottom of the last page in each volume, three-quarter crushed blue morocco (spine and joints a little worn, corners a bit rubbed), marbled paper, covers ruled in gilt, maroon morocco lettering and numbering labels on spine, raised bands with delicate gilt trim, decorative gilt trim within the panels, marbled endpapers, t.e.g., others untrimmed, blue silk ribbon markers in each volume. A very nice set, printed on high-quality rag paper by the Chiswick Press, with early signed label (dated 1893) tipped in on front pastedown of each volume. Not in Kohler.

1697. POEMS ON SEVERAL OCCASIONS. Lycidas. L'Allegro. Il Penseroso. Sonnets. Odes. Miscellanies. Translations. Poemata. The Author, John Milton. *London: Printed In The Year M DCCC XXIII*. 12mo, 64+39+7pp., +188pp., engraved title page "THE MINOR POEMS OF JOHN MILTON. London: Printed By John Sharp. MDCCCXVI," date in Roman numerals, with vignette illustration of *Methought I Saw My Late Espoused Saint. Sonnet XXIII* by Richard Westall engraved by R. Rhodes, engraved illustration plates for *L, L'A, IlP, S* (with vignette illustration for *Sonnet X*), and *O* (with vignette illustration for *NO*), each with vignette illustration by Richard Westall, variously engraved, each plate dated "Aug. 24. 1816," each plate with protective tissue guard, "Index To The Minor Poems" at the end, contemporary full blue morocco, delicately gilt-decorated covers and spines, thick raised bands with decorative gilt trim, spines lettered in gilt ("Milton's Poetical Works • Poems• Vol. 4"), inner and outer dentelles finely tooled in gilt, marbled endpapers and edges. A fine copy in a very lovely Romantic morocco binding. Uniformly bound as a companion volume with *PL* (London: Printed For John Sharpe, M DCCC XXV) and *PR* (London: Published By John Sharpe, MD CCC XXIII), both listed here and together forming a charming four-volume set of the *PW*. An 1823 reissue of the edition by Sharpe/Whittingham/Chiswick first published in 1816 (also listed here), with the 1816 issue of the Westall plates (first appearance). See also 1819 Chiswick reissue, with the 1816 issue of the plates, and 1827 Chiswick small 8vo reissue, with new engravers of the plates dated 1827. Scarce. Not in Kohler.

1698. POEMS, 1824. [In] **THE BRITISH ANTHOLOGY; OR, POETICAL LIBRARY**. Milton. Parnell. Dryden. *London: Published by John Sharpe, Duke Street,*

Piccadilly. 1824. 8 volumes in 4 with Milton's poems appearing in volumes 1 and 2, and Milton and Dryden being the only seventeenth-century poets in the collection. First edition thus. 12mo in 6s, 108+36pp.,+36pp.,+108+36+36+36pp., volumes 1 and 2, advertisement leaf, engraved title pages for the individual works (some slight foxing), half-titles for the various works, contemporary full green morocco, blind rules on covers with central gilt harp, spine lettered in gilt within decorative gilt trim, inner dentelles finely tooled in gilt, a.e.g. A very fine set with contemporary presentation inscription, dated "Eton Col: July 24 1832," on front blank, volume 1. Among the poets represented is Milton, volumes 1 and 2 (titled "Milton, Parnell, Dryden"), half-title and engraved title page for "Milton. C, SA," with a vignette illustration by Richard Westall engraved by W. Greatbatch, for C on the engraved title, "Published Jan. 1, 1825, By John Sharpe. London," half-title for SA (without an illustration), half-title and a second engraved title page for "Milton. L'A, IlP," with a vignette illustration by Richard Westall engraved by W. Greatbatch, for IlP on the engraved title, "Published Septr. 1, 1824; By John Sharpe, London." Two parts in one, within volumes 1 and 2 of an eight-volume set bound in four volumes, with the second part also containing L, NO, and several of the S, although no mention of these poems appears on the engraved title. Not in Kohler.

1699. POEMS, 1824. [In] Variant of Preceding. THE BRITISH ANTHOLOGY; OR, POETICAL LIBRARY. Milton. Parnell. Dryden. *London: Published by John Sharpe, Duke Street, Piccadilly. 1824.* 6 volumes in 3, with Milton's poems appearing in volumes 1 and 2, and Milton and Dryden being the only seventeenth-century poets in the collection. First edition thus. 12mo, 108+36pp.,+36pp.,+108+36+36+36pp., volumes 1 and 2, as preceding set (although without volumes 7–8, "Warton, Johnson, Cooper, and Burns," as volume 4), advertisement leaf, engraved title pages for the individual works, half-titles for the various works, contemporary three-quarter red morocco, marbled paper over boards (a bit rubbed), spine lettered and numbered in gilt, raised bands, t.e.g. A very nice set with early armorial bookplate and signature on fly-leaf, volumes 1 and 2, and with engraved plates that are clean and fresh. Among the poets represented is Milton, volumes 1 and 2 (titled "Milton, Parnell, Dryden"), half-title and engraved title page for "Milton. C, SA," with a vignette illustration by Richard Westall engraved by W. Greatbatch, for C on the engraved title, "Published Jan. 1, 1825, By John Sharpe. London," half-title for S (without an illustration), half-title and a second engraved title page for "Milton. L'A, IlP," with a vignette illustration by Richard Westall engraved by W. Greatbatch for IlP on the engraved title with "Published Septr. 1, 1824; By John Sharpe, London." Two parts in one, within volumes 1 and 2 of a six-volume set bound in three volumes, with the second part also containing L, NO, and several of the S, although no mention of these poems appears on the engraved title. Not in Kohler.

1700. POEMS ON SEVERAL OCCASIONS. Lycidas. L'Allegro. Il Penseroso. Sonnets. Odes. Miscellanies. Translations. Poemata. The Author, John Milton. *London: Printed In The Year MDCCCXXVII.* Small 8vo, 188pp., engraved and printed title pages, engraved title "THE MINOR POEMS Of John Milton. London: Published By John Sharpe. 1827," with vignette illustration of *Methought I Saw My Late Espoused Saint. Sonnet XXIII* by Richard Westall engraved by C. Rolls, engraved illustration plates for L, L'A, IlP, S (with vignette illustration for S X), and O (with vignette illustration for NO), each with vignette illustration by Richard Westall, variously engraved, each plate dated "July 1. 1827," "Index To The Minor Poems" at the end, contemporary full black calf (slightly rubbed), delicately gilt-decorated covers, spine elaborately gilt-decorated in the panels, brown and black morocco labels with gilt lettering, raised bands with gilt rules, inner and outer dentelles richly tooled in gilt, marbled endpapers, a.e.g. A lovely copy, fresh and clean within, in an attractive binding of the period. An 1827 reissue of the edition by Sharpe/Whittingham/Chiswick first published in 1817, reprinted in a much smaller octavo format, with a reissue of the plates that first appeared in 1816 and that are dated 1827, with different engravers from those of the earlier plates: Charles Rolls instead of F. Engleheart for L; E. I Portbury instead of Charles Heath for L'A, Charles Rolls instead of James Mitan for IlP; John Romney instead of Charles Heath for S; and Charles Rolls instead of Edward Finden for O. Not in Kohler.

1701. Variant of Preceding, contemporary red cloth (a bit rubbed, some slight foxing of the plates), spine lettered in gilt within decorative gilt trim, edges untrimmed. A nice copy, fresh and clean within, with half-title, in a variant binding, taller than preceding copy, with a few early marginal notations in pencil in a very neat hand. Not in Kohler.

1702. POEMS OF JOHN MILTON. *New York: Leavitt & Company, 1851.* First edition thus. 8vo, 190pp., frontispiece illustration for L'A ("—the milkmaid singeth blithe, And the mower whets his scythe"), protective tissue guard, title page decorated with floral border trim continuing into an illustration of a lady reclined beside a brook reading a book at the top of the page, half-title for PR, double black border around text, original decorated red cloth (a little worn, spine chipped, corners bumped, some slight foxing), covers decorated with thick gilt border rules, decorative gilt trim within, central illustration of a young woman playing a lyre, spine decorated in gilt with gilt lettering, a.e.g. A good copy of a scarce mid-nineteenth-century American edition of Milton's *Poems*, with a brief contemporary inscription in a neat hand in pencil (dated 1852) on verso of frontispiece. Not in Kohler.

1703. POEMS, With Notes, By Thomas Keightley. [Quotation From Collins.] In Two Volumes. *London: Chapman And Hall, 193, Piccadilly. 1859.* 2 volumes. First Keightley edition. Royal 8vo, xv+454,+vi+486+[1]pp., half-title each volume, preface, volume 1, index at end of volume 2, notes at bottom of page, original purple cloth (a bit rubbed), blind rules on covers, spines lettered in gilt with gilt trim at top and bottom, t.e. rough, "Printed By John Edward Taylor, Little Queen Street, Lincoln's Inn Fields, London" (noted on final leaf bound into volume 2 here). A nice, tall set in publisher's binding. Uncommon edition by a useful nineteenth-century litterateur, praised especially for its "very good notes" (DNB). In 1855 Keightley published a biography of Milton—considered to be one of the significant biographies of Milton published in the nineteenth century (see copy with Nineteenth-century Miltoniana). Kohler 342.

1704. POEMS BY JOHN MILTON. Edited, With Life and Notes Critical and Philological, By John Merry Ross, University Of Glasgow, Senior Master Of English Literature In The High School Of Edinburgh. Nelson's School Series[.] *London: T. Nelson And Sons, Paternoster Row; Edinburgh; And New York. 1878.* 8vo, xxiv+279+[1]pp., elaborate headpiece incorporating "Nelson's School Series" at the top of title page, "Introductory Note" dated "August 1871," 129 pp. of "Notes" at the end with half-title, followed by "Glossary," original brown cloth (a bit rubbed, lacking front fly-leaf, slight spotting along edges, marginal notations in a neat hand continued in the same neat hand on back endpapers and on several note papers tipped in at the end), covers richly decorated in embossed blind borders with "Royal School Series" lettered in blind within a narrow scrolled banner at the top of the front cover above a large royal emblem in blind at the center and with Milton's name in large letters within embossed decorative trim at the bottom with "With Notes" in small letters below, spine lettered with Milton's name in embossed red letters against gilt background near the top with small gilt lettering and decorative gilt trim at top and bottom, fore- and bottom edges untrimmed. A nice copy with notes and annotations of a serious contemporary reader. Uncommon. Kohler 393, citing "279 pp." without reference to the preliminary "xxiv pp.," and reporting "Not in the British Library. Not in the Bodleian Library. Not in Cambridge University Library."

1705. MILTON'S POEMS[.] *Chicago: M. A. Donohue & Co. 407-429 Dearborn St. n. d. [ca. 1895].* First edition thus? 8vo, li+627pp., unsigned frontispiece portrait plate, protective tissue guard, decorated title-page plate printed in red with elaborate ornamental black border frame with two young angelic figures at the center, original decorated red cloth, front cover decorated in art nouveau style with black and silver swirls surrounding a central figure of a lady on a balcony incorporating title in gilt at the top, spine similarly decorated in silver and black and lettered in gilt, decorated green endpapers, t.e.g. A nice copy in a lovely publisher's binding. See Donohue editions of *PL* published about this same time (ca. 1895) with the same publisher's imprint, in bindings similarly decorated in art nouveau style—perhaps intended to serve as a companion volume. Not in Kohler.

1706. Variant of Preceding, original decorated olive green cloth (a bit rubbed, especially spine ends), front cover decorated in art nouveau style with black and silver swirls surrounding a central figure of a lady on a balcony incorporating title in gilt at the top, spine similarly decorated in silver and black and lettered in gilt, decorated green endpapers, t.e.g., near-contemporary inscription (dated 1905) on front blank. A lovely copy in an attractive variant publisher's binding.

1899 Altemus Editions

Looking at the following copies of the 1899 Altemus edition of Milton's *Poems* together on a shelf or side by side shows once again, as with the 1899 Altemus editions of *PL* and *PR* and the ca. 1898 Caldwell editions of *PL* and *PR*, why "there is no such thing as a duplicate!" and why collecting different copies of the same edition points up notable differences, while each book continues to maintain its own individuality and attractiveness.

1707. JOHN MILTON POEMS[.] *Philadelphia[:] Henry Altemus[.] n.d. [ca. 1899].* First edition thus by Altemus? 16mo, 192+[36]pp., unsigned frontispiece illustration plate for *L'A* (labeled "Frontispiece—Milton's Poems," with lines illustrated quoted beneath: "'Stretched Out All The Chimney's Length.' See page 150"), title-page plate printed in red with decorative green trim in art nouveau style, original decorated white cloth (a bit rubbed, back cover slightly stained), front cover elaborately decorated in a floral motif in green with gilt outline and small gilt pieces with gilt lettering ("Milton's Poems") blocked in gilt outline near the top, spine similarly elaborately decorated in a floral motif in green with gilt outline and with gilt lettering ("Milton's Poems") at the top and at the bottom ("Altemus"). A nice copy in an attractive publisher's binding with thirty-six unpaginated pages of advertisements for "Publications Of Henry Altemus Company" bound in at end. Not in Kohler.

1708. Variant of Preceding, original decorated light blue cloth (a bit rubbed, corners bent on last few pages), front cover delicately decorated with gilt trim with two narrow white cards each with a varied floral motif in color within gilt rules tipped in along either side near each other in the center with gilt lettering ("Milton's Poems") blocked in gilt outline near the top, spine decorated and lettered in gilt (faded) at the top ("Milton's Poems") and at the bottom ("Altemus"). A nice copy with early signature on fly-leaf, in a variant publisher's binding, with thirty-six unpaginated pages of advertisements for "Publications Of Henry Altemus Company" bound in at the end. Not in Kohler.

1709. Variant of Preceding, original decorated light blue cloth, scenic card with picture in color with gilt lettering ("Milton's Poems") at top tipped on front cover surrounded by patterned gilt trim in art nouveau style, spine lettered in gilt ("Milton's Poems") with similar patterned gilt trim in art nouveau style. A lovely copy in a charming variant publisher's binding with thirty-six unpaginated pages of advertisements for "Publications Of Henry Altemus Company" bound in at the end. Not in Kohler.

1710. JOHN MILTON POEMS[.] *Philadelphia[:] Henry Altemus[.] (1899)*. First edition thus by Altemus? 16mo, 192+[16]pp., half-title ("Milton's Earlier Poems"), engraved title-page plate ("Poems Milton"), frontispiece portrait plate (of Milton as a young man, unsigned, "Copyright 1899, by Henry Altemus"), printed title-page plate printed in red with decorative green trim in art nouveau style, original decorated blue cloth (a bit rubbed), scenic card with picture in color tipped on front cover surrounded by gilt trim with decorative gilt floral piece and gilt lettering, spine lettered in gilt with decorative floral piece in gilt and red, decorated endpapers. A nice copy, similar to editions preceding, except with a dated frontispiece portrait plate in place of an undated frontispiece illustration, in a lovely variant publisher's binding, with a variant number of advertisement pages: sixteen instead of thirty-six unpaginated pages of advertisements for "Publications Of Henry Altemus Company" bound in at the end. Not in Kohler.

1711. Variant of Preceding, original decorated green cloth (a bit rubbed), front cover and spine decorated with large floral bouquet of blossoms in white and maroon outlined in gilt and long stems in gilt, with title in gilt (gilt faded on spine), decorated endpapers with bookplate on front blank. A nice copy in a charming variant publisher's binding with sixteen unpaginated pages of advertisements for "Publications Of Henry Altemus Company" bound in at the end. Not in Kohler.

1712. Variant of Preceding. JOHN MILTON POEMS[.] *Philadelphia[:] Henry Altemus[.] n.d. (1899)*. First edition thus? 16mo, 192+[24]pp., half-title ("Milton's Earlier Poems"), unsigned frontispiece portrait plate of Milton as a young man ("Copyright 1899, by Henry Altemus"), printed title-page plate printed in red with decorative green trim in art nouveau style, original decorated white cloth (worn, slight waterstaining along outer bottom corner without affecting any text, gilt faded on front cover and spine), front cover decorated with Grecian column in gilt along inner edge with "Milton's Poems" incorporated at the top, together with floral arrangement in colors of green, white, and red, spine decorated with gilt piece running the length of the spine with gilt lettering at the top and bottom, t.e.g. A somewhat worn copy in a once lovely variant publisher's binding, without engraved title-page plate, with additional advertisement leaves: sixteen as in preceding copies, plus eight additional unpaginated pages advertising other "Publications by Altemus." Not in Kohler.

1713. POEMS By John Milton[.] *Henry Altemus Company[,] Philadelphia[.] (1899)*. Variant edition. 16mo, 192pp., half-title ("Milton's Earlier Poems"), title page lettered in red with decorative green trim in art nouveau style, original decorated green cloth (a little rubbed), front cover decorated in embossed gilt floral trim (gilt faded), spine lettered in gilt (gilt faded). A good copy of this variant edition, in a lovely variant publisher's binding decorated in art nouveau style. Not in Kohler.

1714. Variant of Preceding. JOHN MILTON POEMS[.] *Philadelphia[:] Henry Altemus[.] n.d. (1899)*. Variant edition. 16mo, 192pp., half-title ("Milton's Earlier Poems"), title page lettered in red with decorative green trim in art nouveau style, original decorated green cloth (a little rubbed), front cover richly decorated in embossed gilt floral trim incorporating title ("Milton's Poems") in gilt at the top, spine lettered in blind, fore- and bottom edges untrimmed. A nice copy of this variant edition, in an attractive variant publisher's binding decorated in art nouveau style, in rare original printed tan publisher's wrappers (a bit rubbed and faded, spine a little age-darkened), called "Altemus' Classic Series," with a listing of the series on the back, "Milton's Poems" being "No. 24" out of "32." Not in Kohler.

1715. THE POEMS OF JOHN MILTON. (Complete Edition.) *Chicago: M. A. Donohue & Co. 407-429 Dearborn St. n. d. [ca. 1900]*. 8vo, li+627pp., "Memoir Of Milton," original green cloth (a bit worn, library stamps marked "withdrawn," related library matter), spine lettered in gilt. An okay copy with contemporary signature (dated 1902) on front fly-leaf. Not in Kohler.

1716. THE POEMS OF JOHN MILTON[.] *London: Simpkin, Marshall, Hamilton, Kent & Co. Ltd. New York.[sic] Charles Scribner's Sons. n.d. [ca. 1901]*. First edition thus. 16mo, viii+526pp., half-title with Wordsworth's sonnet on Milton, frontispiece portrait sketch of Milton by Edmund Sullivan (full figure, Heathcliffean in nature), protective tissue guard, central emblem incorporating tree and serpent in black on title page, half-title for some of the poems, original light brown limp leather (a bit rubbed), large gilt device in the form of a tree on front cover with gilt lettering ("The Poems Of Milton") underneath, spine delicately gilt-decorated with gilt lettering (very faded, title at the top, "Simpkin" at the bottom), decorated endpapers in art nouveau style (tree, rising sun, dancing lady), t.e.g. An interesting turn-of-the-century edition of Milton's *P* with intriguing frontispiece portrait and decorated endpapers. Similar to edition also listed here by "George Newnes LTD" (which is dated 1901) in format, style, and binding. Not in Kohler.

1717. THE POEMS OF JOHN MILTON[.] *George Newnes LTD. Southampton Street W. C. London • MDCCCCI (1901)*. First edition thus. 16mo, viii+526pp., half-title with Wordsworth's sonnet on Milton, frontispiece portrait sketch of Milton by Edmund Sullivan (full figure, Heathcliffean in nature), protective tissue guard, central emblem incorporating tree and serpent in black on title page, half-title for *PL, PR, SA*, and *P*, "Printed by Ballantyne, Hanson & Co. Edinburgh & London" at bottom of last page, original light brown limp leather (a bit rubbed), gilt device in the form of a tree on front cover with gilt lettering (*MP*) underneath, spine decorated and lettered in gilt (title at the top, "Geo Newnes LTD" at the bottom), decorated endpapers in art nouveau style (tree, lady turned away beneath the tree, rising sun and another tree), t.e.g. A lovely copy. An interesting turn-of-the-century edition of Milton's *P* with same intriguing frontispiece portrait and decorated endpapers. Similar to undated edition listed here by "Simpkin and Scribner's Sons" in format, style, and binding. Not in Kohler.

1718. Variant of Preceding. THE POEMS OF JOHN MILTON[.] *"Imported By Charles Scriber's Sons New York" printed on a piece of paper tipped in over "George Newnes LTD. Southampton Street W. C. London • MDCCCCI" seen lightly showing through underneath*. 16mo, viii+526pp., half-title with Wordsworth's sonnet on Milton, frontispiece portrait sketch of Milton by Edmund Sullivan (full figure, Heathcliffean in nature), protective tissue guard, central emblem incorporating tree and serpent in black on title page, half-title for *PL, PR, SA*, and *P*, "Printed by Ballantyne, Hanson & Co. Edinburgh & London" at bottom of last page, original light brown limp leather (worn, covers detached), gilt device in the form of a tree on front cover with gilt lettering (*MP*) underneath, spine decorated and lettered in gilt (title at the top, "Geo Newnes LTD" at the bottom), decorated endpapers in art nouveau style (as preceding), bookplate on front pastedown, t.e.g., in a protective plastic cover. Uncommon. Not in Kohler.

1719. [POEMS OF] JOHN MILTON With An Introduction By Henry Newbolt[.] *Thomas Nelson & Sons Ltd[.] London & Edinburgh[.] n.d. [ca. 1901]*. First edition thus? 16mo, xiv+[1]+530pp., unsigned frontispiece portrait sketch of Milton (possibly drawn for this edition) within decorative border trim, same decorative border trim repeated on title page with decorated initial "N" as emblem of the press at the center, "Printed In Great Britain At The Press Of The Publishers" at bottom of last page, original blue cloth, spine lettered in gilt ("Poems Of Milton") with small decorative gilt piece, t.e. blue. A nice copy with an introduction by Henry Newbolt (English poet and man of letters, 1862–1938). "Scant biographical and political accounts. The lines are not numbered" (Stevens). Stevens 260; Not in Kohler.

1720. Variant of Preceding, original blue limp leather (a bit rubbed), Milton's name lettered in gilt on front cover, spine lettered in gilt ("Poems Of Milton," at the top, "Nelson" at the bottom) with long decorative design in gilt in art nouveau style at the center, marbled green endpapers, t.e.g., gold silk ribbon marker. A nice copy, very fresh and clean within, printed on Japan paper, with reference to publisher on verso of title page, in a variant publisher's binding.

1721. Variant of Preceding. [POEMS OF] JOHN MILTON With An Introduction By Henry Newbolt[.] *Thomas Nelson And Sons[.] New York[.] n.d. [ca. 1901]*. First American edition thus? 16mo, similar to preceding edition except for publisher's imprint with "New York" only here, xiv+[1]+530pp., unsigned frontispiece portrait sketch of Milton with decorative border trim, same decorative border trim repeated on title page with decorated initial "N" as emblem of the press at the center, "Printed In The United States Of America By The Berwick & Smith Co." at bottom of last page, original blue limp leather (a bit rubbed along joints, spine ends chipped), Milton's name lettered in gilt on front cover, spine lettered in gilt ("Poems Of Milton," "Nelson" at the bottom), with long decorative design in gilt in art nouveau style at the center, marbled green endpapers, t.e.g. A nice copy, very fresh and clean within, printed on Japan paper, with variant publisher's imprint, with an introduction by Henry Newbolt. Not in Kohler.

1722. [POEMS OF] JOHN MILTON With An Introduction by Sir Henry Newbolt[.] *Thomas Nelson and Sons Ltd. London[,] Edinburgh[,] New York[,] Toronto and Paris[.] n.d. [ca. 1901].* 16mo, xiv+[1]+530+[2]pp., half-title with unsigned frontispiece portrait sketch of Milton on verso, original light green cloth, spine lettered in gilt ("Poems Of Milton"). A good copy with an introduction by Henry Newbolt, with an advertisement page on verso of imprint page at the end. Similar to preceding editions, but without the decorative border trim around frontispiece portrait or on title page and with other variations on title page, including additional cities in publisher's imprint, with a half-title, and with advertisement page on verso of imprint page at the end. Uncommon. Not in Kohler.

1723. POEMS BY JOHN MILTON With An Introduction By Walter Raleigh[.] *The Gresham Publishing Company[,] 34 Southampton Street Strand London, (1905).* First edition thus. Small 8vo, xiii+231pp., half-title, frontispiece portrait "From a portrait in the Bruckmann Collection," title page in red and black, eight-page untitled "Introduction" by Walter Raleigh (dated "11th January, 1905"), titles printed in red throughout with occasional small decorative pieces in red, original green cloth (spine a little faded), small gilt emblem at center of front cover with Milton's name below, spine elaborately decorated in gilt repeating emblem on front cover, endpapers decorated in green vines with purple grapes in art nouveau style, t.e.g., others untrimmed and partially unopened. A nice copy that reprints the poems of the 1645 collection. Uncommon. Not in Kohler.

1724. POEMS BY JOHN MILTON With An Introduction By Walter Raleigh[,] Professor Of English Literature In The University Of Oxford[.] *Blackie • And • Son • Ld[.] • London. n.d. [ca. 1905].* First edition thus; variant from preceding. 12mo in 6s, xiii+231pp., half-title ("Red Letter Library"), unsigned frontispiece portrait sketch of a young Milton with elaborate decorative border trim in gold and black in art nouveau style, same elaborate decorative border trim in gold and black in art nouveau style repeated on title page, titles printed in red throughout with occasional small decorative pieces in red, eight-page untitled "Introduction" by Walter Raleigh (dated "11th January, 1905") original soft maroon leather over limp boards (a bit rubbed, spine slightly chipped at the top), bright gilt emblem at the center of front cover, spine lettered in gilt with decorative gilt piece at top and bottom, decorated light green endpapers in art nouveau style, t.e.g., partially unopened, white silk ribbon marker. A lovely copy with early signature (dated 1911) on fly-leaf. See following variant edition. Uncommon. Not in Kohler.

1725. MILTON POEMS Introduction By Walter Raleigh[.] *Blackie & Son Limited[.] London And Glasgow[.] n.d. [ca. 1905].* Variant edition. 12mo in 6s, xiii+231pp., frontispiece portrait plate of "John Milton" "From the painting by P. Van der Plaas in the national Portrait Gallery, London," double black rules on title page, "Blackie & Son Limited London, Glasgow" in publisher's imprint, "Printed in Great Britain by Blackie & Son, Ltd., Glasgow" at bottom on verso of title page, eight-page introduction by Walter Raleigh (dated "11th January, 1905"), half-title for "Translations," original blue cloth, spine lettered in gilt, original publisher's wrappers (a bit scuffed), in a protective plastic cover, lettered in blue, front cover lettered in blue and red with color vignette sketch of Milton holding a book while in the background is a sketch of the expulsion to the left of Milton and a sketch of the serpent wrapped around a tree to the right of Milton, signed "L M Brock" under Milton, an emblem of a tree and the title of the series, "The Wallet Library," are printed on the back cover, a listing of "The 'Wallet' Library" appears on the inside front flap (with "Printed in Great Britain 1/6 net" beneath), and a listing of "The Red Letter Poets" appears on the inside back flap, each series printed by "Blackie & Son LTD. London And Glasgow," t.e.g., gray endpapers. A nice copy of an uncommon edition in the series, "The Wallet Library." See preceding variant edition. Not in Kohler.

1726. MILTON'S POEMS 1645 Type-Facsimile[.] *Oxford[:] At the Clarendon Press[,] 1924.* First edition thus. 8vo, [iii]+[vii]+120+90pp., half-title, original limp vellum, spine lettered in black, unopened, "Notes" to the "English Poems" and "Latin Poems" at the end. Facsimile reproduction of the 1645 edition of Milton's *Poems*, with reproduction of frontispiece portrait, title page for *Poems*, and title page for *Joannis Miltoni Londinensis Poemata*, along with a reproduction of "Lycidas lines 23–35 Printer's correction of the original proof (1638)." A fine copy with the bookplate of Leonard Schlosser. One of "One Thousand Copies Printed on Linen-rag Paper" (verso of title page). Stevens 348.

1727. THE POEMS OF JOHN MILTON ENGLISH LATIN GREEK & ITALIAN Arranged In Chronological Order With A Preface By H. J. C. Grierson F. B. A. *At The Florence Press[.] London: Chatto & Windus[,] M•CM•XXV.*

2 volumes. First edition thus by the Florence Press. 8vo, xlii+375pp.,+xliv+371pp., half-title each volume, title page each volume with printer's pictorial device on each title page, "Printed In Great Britain At The Florence Press By R. & R. Clark Ltd. Edinburgh" on verso of each title page, preface each volume, half-titles for some of the poems, errata slip tipped in, volume 2, original one-half orange cloth, orange paper over boards, spines lettered in gilt, t.e.g, others untrimmed, printed orange publisher's wrappers (a bit used) in protective plastic covers. A fine set of a handsomely printed edition at the Florence Press by R. & R. Clark, Edinburgh, in original publisher's bindings, with publisher's wrappers, with the signature of H. J. C. Grierson (dated "May 5, 1927") on fly-leaf of volume 1. "The Shorter Poems[,] Paradise Regained[,] And Samson Agonistes" occupy volume 1, while "Paradise Lost" occupies volume 2. "The attempts to save only such archaic spellings as signify the older pronunciation and to punctuate logically are notable additions to the values of this edition arising from the editor's search for evidence on dates of composition. The prefatory matter is more marked by studious care for recent scholarship than appears in any other modern edition" (Stevens). Stevens 261.

1728. THE POEMS OF JOHN MILTON ENGLISH LATIN GREEK & ITALIAN Arranged In Chronological Order With A Preface By H. J. C. Grierson F. B. A. *Brentano's New York[.] n.d. (1925).* 2 volumes. First American edition thus by the Florence Press. 8vo, xlii+375pp.,+xliv+371pp., half-title each volume, title page each volume with "Printed In Great Britain At The Florence Press By R. & R. Clark Ltd. Edinburgh" on verso of each title page, preface each volume, half-titles for some of the poems, original red cloth, gilt rules on front covers with large central gilt laurel wreath surrounding title in gilt, gilt-decorated spines with gilt lettering, gilt rules, small gilt laurel wreath, and anchor device above "Brentano's" in gilt at the bottom, t.e.g., others untrimmed and partially unopened. A fine set, similar to the "London: Chatto & Windus" edition, but undated and printed for Brentano's in New York. Uncommon.

1729. JOHN MILTON POEMS IN ENGLISH WITH ILLUSTRATIONS BY WILLIAM BLAKE[.] Miscellaneous Poems[,] Paradise Regain'd & Samson Agonistes[.] *1926 at the Nonesuch Press[,] 16 Great James Street[,] London[.]* 2 volumes in one, as issued. 8vo, [i+vi]+283pp.,+[vii]+359pp., title page each volume (the second—for *PL*—as the first), each title page with typographic border printed in red and designed by Douglas Bliss, fifty-three plates reproducing Blake's illustrations in full color, printed on Oxford India paper with the illustrations on Japan vellum, original white vellum, spine lettered in gilt, edges untrimmed. Text by Canon Beeching, illustrations chosen and titled with notes by Geoffrey Keynes, under the direction of Francis Meynell, designed by Douglas Bliss. This is the special issue printed on Oxford India paper and bound in one volume. A nice copy of a scarce book, considered "The rarest and most desirable state of this fine edition" (Cummins, Cat #53, #227, 1997, statement made of another copy for sale). "The first volume reproduces 38 designs, including those illustrating *PR*, which had only once before been reproduced, a set of illustrations for *C*, for the *Hymn on the Morning of Christ's nativity*[sic], and twelve illustrations for *L'A* and *IlP* which were all reproduced for the first time . . . " (Dreyfus). Francis Meynell wrote of the book: "My favourite, I think, of Nonesuch publications." A limited two-volume edition was also published at the same time by the Nonesuch Press (set following). (See Nonesuch Press prospectus for this publication in *Nonesuch Books for Christmas 1925 and Spring 1926* with Twentieth-century Miltoniana.) One of 90 numbered sets (although this is unnumbered). Dreyfus 32.

1730. Variant of Preceding. **JOHN MILTON POEMS IN ENGLISH WITH ILLUSTRATIONS BY WILLIAM BLAKE[.]** Paradise Lost[.] *1926 at the Nonesuch Press[,] 16 Great James Street[,] London[.]* 2 volumes. 8vo, [i+vi]+283pp.,+[vii]+359pp., title page each volume (the second—for "Miscellaneous Poems[,] Paradise Regain'd & Samson Agonistes"—as the first), each title page with typographic border printed in red and designed by Douglas Bliss, fifty-three plates reproducing Blake's illustrations in full color, original quarter vellum, patterned boards, spines lettered in gilt, edges untrimmed. Text by Canon Beeching, illustrations chosen and titled with notes by Geoffrey Keynes, created under the direction of Francis Meynell, and designed by Douglas Bliss. A fine set of the regular Nonesuch Press edition. No. 235 of an edition limited to 1,450 copies.

1731. POEMS BY JOHN MILTON (Including "Paradise Lost," Books I. & II, "Comus," "Lycidas," Etc.) Bell's English Texts Edited By S. E. Winbolt, M.A. *London[:] G. Bell And Sons, Ltd. 1926.* Second edition. Small 8vo, 128pp., emblem of the press on title page, original green cardlike paper covers (spine faded, some marginal notations in pencil, early names on front pastedown), front cover decorated in a swirling pattern with black lettering, spine lettered in black, name and large emblem of the press on back cover. A decent copy. The first edition was published in 1913.

1732. POEMS OF JOHN MILTON Edited With An Introduction By Frank A Patterson[,] Associate Professor Of English In Columbia University[.] *The Macmillan*

Company Publishers[,] New York[,] MCMXXX (1930) The Modern Readers' Series.* First edition thus. 8vo, xix+468+[4]pp., half-title ("The Modern Readers' Series Ashley H. Thorndike, General Editor"), decorated frontispiece, title page with decorative border trim, half-title before the poems, half-titles for some of the poems, glossary at the end, original green cloth (worn, spine repaired with black library tape, library stamps and other markings, notations and underlinings in pencil throughout), with four pages of advertisements for "The Modern Readers' Series." A second edition thus was published in 1939 in "The Modern Readers' Series" (also listed here). Scarce. 1997.

1733. THE POEMS OF JOHN MILTON with Introduction and Notes by James Holly Hanford[,] Western Reserve University[.] *The Ronald Press Company[,] New York[,] (1936).* First edition thus. Small 8vo, lxxxviii+582pp., half-title ("A volume of a series in English, edited by Ernest Bernbaum"), half-title for *PL*, notes at bottom of page, appendix with "Study Topics" and bibliography, original blue cloth (a few pencil markings in Book IX), spine lettered in gilt with decorative gilt trim at top and bottom. A nice copy. The second edition thus was published in 1937 (see following copy); another edition, the eighth, appeared in 1946 (copy in the collection, a repeat of this edition, not listed); a revised edition in a larger 8vo format (called "The Second Edition" on title page) was published in 1953 (also listed here).

1734. THE POEMS OF JOHN MILTON with Introduction and Notes by James Holly Hanford[,] Western Reserve University[.] *New York[:] Thomas Nelson & Sons[,] 1937.* Second edition thus. Small 8vo, lxxxviii+582pp., half-title ("Nelson's English Series General Editor— Ernest Bernbaum"), half-title for *PL*, notes at bottom of page, appendix with "Study Topics" and bibliography, original blue cloth (a bit rubbed, numerous marginal notations in pencil in a fairly neat hand, pencil notations on fly-leaf), spine lettered in gilt with decorative gilt trim at top and bottom. A good copy. The first edition thus was published in 1936 (see preceding copy); a revised edition in a larger 8vo format (called "The Second Edition" on title page) was published in 1953 (also listed here).

1735. POEMS OF JOHN MILTON Edited With An Introduction By Frank A Patterson[,] Associate Professor Of English In Columbia University[.] *The Macmillan Company Publishers[,] New York[,] MCMXXXIX The Modern Readers' Series.* Second edition thus. 8vo, xix+468pp., half-title ("The Modern Readers' Series Ashley H. Thorndike, General Editor"), decorated frontispiece, title page with decorative border trim, half-title before the poems, half-titles for some of the poems, glossary at the end, original blue cloth (a bit rubbed, spine slightly faded), front cover and spine lettered in gilt within decorative gilt trim, decorated endpapers, glossary. A nice copy. The first edition thus was published in 1930 in "The Modern Readers' Series" (also listed here).

1736. POEMS OF MR. JOHN MILTON[.] The 1645 Edition with Essays In Analysis by Cleanth Brooks and John Edward Hardy[.] *New York[:] Harcourt, Brace and Company[,] 1951.* First edition thus. 8vo, xvi+[v]+353pp., preface, contents, "Chronology Of Events In Milton's Life, And The Life Of His Times, To 1645," facsimile of 1645 title page and "Stationer To The Reader," half-title to "Part One The Poems," half-title to "Part Two Essays in Analysis," half-title to "Appendixes," followed by "A Selective Bibliography" and "Index," original red cloth, spine lettered in gilt. A nice copy with bookplate on front pastedown.

1736A. (Cross-listing) Variant of Preceding. POEMS OF MR. JOHN MILTON[.] The 1645 Edition with Essays In Analysis by Cleanth Brooks and John Edward Hardy[.] *New York[:] Harcourt, Brace and Company[,] 1951 / London[:] Dennis Dobson, 1957.* First edition thus. See copy with 1957-printed label tipped in under *Poems Of Mr. John Milton*, 1957.

1737. THE POEMS OF JOHN MILTON Edited with Introduction and Notes by James Holly Hanford[.] Second edition[.] *The Ronald Press Company • New York[,] (1953).* Second edition thus. 8vo, x+615pp., brief biography by Hanford as half-title, preface new to this edition dated "Princeton, N.J. January, 1953," "Contents," "Life Of Milton" (with half-title), half-titles for various of the sections and poems with introduction for each, appendix with "Study Topics," bibliography, and index at end, notes at bottom of page, original dark blue cloth, front cover and spine lettered in gilt ("John Milton") within decorative gilt trim. A nice copy in original printed publisher's wrappers, also nice. The first edition thus was published in a smaller 8vo format in 1936; a second issue in a smaller 8vo format, was published in 1937—both listed here.

1738. Variant of Preceding, original light blue cloth, front cover and spine lettered in gilt ("John Milton") within decorative trim, printed publisher's wrappers (a bit age-darkened). A nice copy without the brief biography by Hanford as half-title, thinner than the preceding copy by ¼", in a variant publisher's binding (lighter blue); in original publisher's wrappers.

1739. MILTON: POEMS[.] Selected With An Introduction By L. D. Lerner[.] *Penguin Books[:] Melbourne • London • Baltimore[,] (1953).* First edition thus. 8vo, 316+[4]pp., half-title (with name in ink), paperback, printed stiff paper wrappers repeating a variation of the title page on front cover with decorative light green border trim on both covers. A good copy with four pages of advertisements bound in at the end. A second edition thus was published in 1971; a third edition thus, with a new introduction by David Daiches, was published in 1985 (see copies listed here).

1740. POEMS OF MR. JOHN MILTON[.] The 1645 Edition with Essays In Analysis by Cleanth Brooks and John Edward Hardy[.] *London[:] Dennis Dobson, 1957 / New York[:] Harcourt, Brace and Company[,] 1951.* First edition thus. 8vo, preface, contents, "Chronology Of Events In Milton's Life, And The Life Of His Times, To 1645," facsimile of 1645 title page and "Stationer To The Reader," half-title to "Part One The Poems," half-title to "Part Two Essays in Analysis," half-title to "Appendixes" followed by "A Selective Bibliography" and "Index," original red cloth, spine lettered in gilt, printed publisher's wrappers (a bit worn at top and bottom of spine) printed in green and white with reproduction of 1645 first edition title page on front cover, in a protective plastic cover. A nice copy with printed label "London[:] Dennis Dobson, 1957" tipped in over printed publisher's label "New York[:] Harcourt, Brace and Company[,] 1951" on title page.

1741. MILTON'S POEMS Edited, With Textual Introduction, By B. A. Wright, M.A., Professor of English Language and Literature in the University of Southampton[.] *London[:] J. M. Dent & Sons Ltd[;] New York[:] E. P. Dutton & Co[.] Inc[.,] (1959).* Second edition thus by Everyman? 8vo, xlii+479+4pp., half-title ("Everyman's Library 384 Poetry & Drama"), "Textual Introduction," half-title for "Miscellaneous Poems" with reproduction of 1645 and 1673 title pages of Milton's *P*, half-title for "A Mask" with reproduction of 1637 title page of *A Maske Presented A Ludlow Castle*, half-title for *PL* with reproduction of 1667 and 1674 title pages of *PL*, half-title for *PR* with reproduction of 1671 title page of *PR*, half-title for *SA* with reproduction of 1671 title page of *SA*, original green cloth (former ownership name in red ink on title page), spine lettered in gilt, decorated endpapers, printed publisher's wrappers. A nice copy with four pages of advertisements for "Everyman's Library" at the end.

The first Everyman Milton appeared in 1909, edited by W. H. D. Rouse; the second Everyman Milton appeared in 1956 under the title *Poems* with a new text by B. A. Wright (this 1959 edition being the second thus by Wright; and see 1976 reprint edition also under the title of *Poems, with a New Glossary*); the third Everyman Milton was published in 1980, edited by Gordon Campbell under the title *Complete Poems* with Wright's text supplemented by translations of the Latin, Greek and Italian poems, and by notes on all the poems (see 1986 and 1992 Everyman reprints of Wright's edition under title of *Complete Poems*); a fresh edition, the fourth Everyman Milton, was published in 1990, edited by Gordon Campbell under the title *Complete English Poems* (see 1992 edition).

1742. [POEMS] MILTON edited by Maynard Mack[,] Professor of English, and Fellow of Davenport College Yale University[.] Second University[.] Second Edition[.] English Masterpieces • An Anthology Of Imaginative Literature From Chaucer To T. S. Eliot • Under The General Editorship of Maynard Mack, Yale University[.] *Prentice-Hall, Inc. Englewood Cliffs, N. J. (1961).* Second edition thus. 8vo, 346pp., twenty-eight-page "Introduction," "Minor Poems," "Prose" (with only *Areopagitica*), "Major Poem," and "Appendix" (with selections from "Genesis" and "Judges" and "Bibliographical References"), paperback (a few minor underlinings, name in ink on title page), original printed stiff red and white wrappers. Nice copy. The first edition thus was published in 1950.

1743. MILTON: POEMS AND SELECTED PROSE Edited And With An Introduction By Marjorie Hope Nicolson[.] *Bantam Books / New York[,] (1962).* First edition thus. 8vo, vi+597+[3]pp., half-title with brief biographical note about Milton, frontispiece with symbol of "Bantam Classics," half-title before introduction, chronology, general bibliography, and editor's note, half-title for "I. Early Poems 1626–1640," half-title for "II. The Middle Years: Prose 1642–1654," half-title for "III. The Middle Years: Sonnets 1642–1658," half-title for "IV. The Major Poems 1667–1671," "Notes On The Sonnets," each section with "Editor's Note," "Glossary Of Proper Names," advertisement leaf for "Bantam Classics" bound in at end, paperback (a bit used, some notations in pencil) with reproduction in color of Munkacsy's painting, *Milton Dictating to His Daughters*, on front cover. A fair copy with my monastic stamp on half-title. The second edition thus was published in 1966, the third in 1969 (both listed here).

1744. MILTON [POEMS]. Selected, with an introduction and notes, by William G. Madsen. The Laurel Poetry Series. General Editor, Richard Wilbur. *[New York: Dell Publishing Co., 1964].* First edition thus. Small 8vo, 190+[2]pp., introduction, bibliography, and chronology at the beginning, notes and leaf listing "The Laurel Poetry Series" bound in at the end, paperback, printed stiff paper wrappers reproducing in tinted brown an illustration sketch of a seated, brooding Milton on front cover. A good copy.

1745. THE POEMS OF JOHN MILTON Edited By John Carey And Alastair Fowler[.] *Longmans[,] (1968).*

First edition thus. 8vo, xxii+1181pp., half-title ("Longmans' Annotated English Poets General Editor: F. W. Bateson"), printer's device on title page, preface, "Chronological Table of Milton's Life and Chief Publications," introductions to the poems, notes at the bottom of the page, reproduction plates of (1) Milton at age ten; (2) Milton at age twenty-one; (3) L—"From a facsimile of the Trinity manuscript"; (4) C—"From a facsimile of the Trinity manuscript"; (5) PL—"Pierpont Morgan manuscript"; (6) PL—"Pierpont Morgan manuscript"; (7) "Milton aged about 62 Engraving by William Faithorne. From HB 1670"; and (8) "Bust of Milton. Plaster cast of original in Christ College Cambridge, attributed to Edward Pierce," half-titles for various of the works, text illustrations of (1) "Title page of P, first edition, 1645"; (2) "Title page of P, second edition, 1673"; (3) "Title page of PL, first edition, 1667"; and (4) "Title page of PL, second edition, 1674," bibliography and index at the end, original gray cloth, printed publisher's wrappers with a reproduction of Milton at age twenty-one on front cover. A handsome copy with well-preserved dust jacket. A second edition thus was published in 1972 by Longmans and Norton (also listed here). Scarce.

1746. POEMS OF MR. JOHN MILTON[.] The 1645 Edition with Essays In Analysis by Cleanth Brooks and John Edward Hardy[.] *Gordian Press, Inc.[,] New York[,] 1968.* 8vo, xvi+[v]+353pp., preface, contents, "Chronology Of Events In Milton's Life, And The Life Of His Times, To 1645," facsimile of 1645 title page and "Stationer To The Reader," half-title to "Part One The Poems," half-title to "Part Two Essays in Analysis," original light blue-gray cloth, spine lettered in black, half-title to "Appendixes," followed by "A Selective Bibliography" and "Index." A fine copy in mint condition. A reprint of the 1951 first edition (see copies listed here).

1747. MILTON: POEMS AND SELECTED PROSE Edited And With An Introduction By Marjorie Hope Nicolson[.] *Bantam Books[.] Toronto / New York / London[,] (1969).* Third edition thus. 8vo, vi+597+[3]pp., half-title with brief biographical note about Milton, frontispiece with symbol of "Bantam Classics," as with first edition thus in 1966 (listed here), paperback with variant front cover, a reproduction of a sculpture of *Milton's Death Mask*. A good copy with advertisement leaf for "Bantam Classics" bound in at end.

1748. JOHN MILTON POEMS 1645[,] LYCIDAS 1638. A Scolar Press Facsimile. *The Scolar Press Limited[,] Menston, England[,] 1970.* First edition thus. 8vo, [viii]+120+90pp., emblem of the press on title page, original speckled black buckram spine, blue cloth, spine lettered in silver. Scolar Press facsimile reproduction of the 1645 edition of Milton's *Poems* with reproduction of frontispiece portrait, title page for *Poems*, and title page for *Joannis Miltoni Londinensis Poemata*. A fine copy.

1749. JOHN MILTON POEMS Reproduced in Facsimile from the Manuscript in Trinity College, Cambridge With a Transcript[.] *[Menston, England:] Scolar Press[,] 1970.* First edition thus. Slim 4to, 47+[2]+[5]pp., facsimile ("reprinted photographically") and transcript on alternate leaves, decorative border trim around title page, original crushed green morocco spine, light marbled green paper over boards, central medallion portrait of Milton in silver on front cover, spine lettered in silver ("Trinity Manuscript"). A fine copy with printer's label tipped in at bottom of front pastedown: "Edition Limited To 500 of which this is No. 112," the number written by hand in ink. A fine copy. A "Grammatype Facsimile" reproduction.

1750. Variant of Preceding. JOHN MILTON POEMS Reproduced in Facsimile from the Manuscript in Trinity College, Cambridge With a Transcript[.] *[Menston, England:] Scolar Press[,] 1970.* First edition thus. Slim 4to, 47+[2]+[5]pp., decorative border trim around title page, facsimile ("reprinted photographically") and transcript on alternate leaves, original dark brown leather antique style (slightly rubbed), covers gilt paneled with gilt lettering and central medallion portrait of Milton in gilt on front cover, t.e. brown. A fine copy in a variant binding. A "Grammatype Facsimile" reproduction. One of a limited number (although this is unnumbered).

1751. Variant of Preceding. JOHN MILTON POEMS Reproduced in Facsimile from the Manuscript in Trinity College, Cambridge With a Transcript[.] *[Menston, England:] Scolar Press[,] 1970.* First edition thus. Slim 4to, 47+[2]+[5]pp., facsimile ("reprinted photographically") and transcript on alternate leaves, decorative border trim around title page, original printed stiff orange wrappers with title page reprinted on front cover, in original glassine wrappers, in original card paper slipcase with mailing label and canceled "Postage Paid" label ("Olney Bucks. Great Britain") on front cover and with paper label on spine lettered in black calligraphy ("Milton: Poems • Trinity MS."). A fine copy in a variant binding. A "Grammatype Facsimile" reproduction. One of a limited number (although this is unnumbered).

1752. JOHN MILTON POEMS Reproduced in Facsimile from the Manuscript in Trinity College, Cambridge With a Transcript[.] *[Menston, England:] Scolar Press[,] 1972.* Slim 4to, 47+[2]+[5]pp., decorative border trim around title page, facsimile leaves ("reprinted photographically") and transcript on alternate leaves, original stiff pink paper wrappers (a bit faded, some minor scuffing and marks on front cover), title page with decorative border trim repeated on front cover. A good copy. A "Grammatype Facsimile" reproduction (verso front leaf). "The transcript of the MS. made by W. A. Wright in 1899 in his Facsimile of the Manuscript of Milton's Minor Poems [see copy listed here] has been reprinted with the following facsimile" (Preface). This sentence replaces "The remarkably accurate transcript of the MS. made by W. A. Wright in 1899 has been reprinted without alteration" in the preface of the 1970 edition (see preceding copies). Apparently printed in a limited number.

1753. THE POEMS OF JOHN MILTON Edited By John Carey And Alastair Fowler[.] *London[:] Longmans [And] Norton[,] (1972).* Second edition; first by Longmans & Norton. 8vo, xxii+1181pp., half-title ("Annotated English Poets General Editor: F. W. Bateson"), printer's device on title page, as with first edition in 1968 (also listed here), original gray cloth, printed publisher's wrappers with a reproduction of Milton at age twenty-one on front cover. A fine copy with fine dust jacket. The first edition was published in 1968 by Longmans only (also listed here); this is the first edition published by Longmans and Norton. Uncommon.

1754. POEMS 1645[,] LYCIDAS 1638. John Milton. A Scolar Press Facsimile. *[Menston, England: The Scolar Press, 1973.]* 8vo, [viii]+120+90pp., introductory note ("Reproduced [original size]"), original brown cloth, spine lettered in gilt, printed green publisher's wrappers. Scolar Press facsimile reproduction of the 1645 edition of Milton's *Poems*, with reproduction of frontispiece portrait, title page for *P*, and title page for *Joannis Miltoni Londinensis Poemata*. A fine copy. See also copy of 1970 Scolar Press facsimile edition.

1755. MILTON POEMS Edited, With Textual Introduction, By B. A. Wright[,] Formerly Professor of English Language and Literature in the University of Southampton[.] *Dent: London[.] Everyman's Library. Dutton: New York[,] n.d. (1976).* Small 8vo, xlii+501pp., half-title, emblem of the press on title page, "Textual Introduction," half-title for "Miscellaneous Poems" with reproduction of 1645 and 1673 title pages of Milton's *P*, half-title for "A Mask" with reproduction of 1637 title page of *A Maske Presented A Ludlow Castle*, half-title for *PL* with reproduction of 1667 and 1674 title pages of *PL*, half-title for *PR* with reproduction of 1671 title page of *PR*, half-title for *SA* with reproduction of 1671 title page of *SA*, original blue cloth, spine lettered in gilt, printed publisher's wrappers with vignette of *Milton's Death Mask* on front cover. Added at the end is a 200-page "Glossary By W. H. D. Rouse Revised and enlarged by Isobel Grundy." A very good copy. The first edition thus by Wright in the Everyman's Library series was published in 1956; the second thus was published in 1959 (see copy listed here for further information about Everyman).

1756. THE POEMS OF JOHN MILTON Edited By John Carey And Alastair Fowler[.] *Longman[,] London and New York[,] (1980).* Second edition thus with corrections. Thick 8vo, xxii+1181pp., half-title ("Longman Annotated English Poets General Editor: F. W. Bateson"), printer's device on title page, preface, "Chronological Table of Milton's Life and Chief Publications," corrections have been made to the text, otherwise as with first and second edition, original gray cloth, spine lettered in gilt, printed publisher's wrappers with a reproduction of Milton at age twenty-one on front cover, bibliography, index. A fine copy. The first edition thus was published in 1968 by Longman only; it was reissued and published with Norton in 1972—both listed here.

1757. POEMS. Selected By Laurence D. Lerner. Introduction By David Daiches. *London: Penguin Books, (1985).* Third edition thus with a new introduction by David Daiches. 8vo, 288pp., half-title with a brief sketch of Milton's life, introduction, chronological table, paperback, with the portrait of Milton at age twenty-one reproduced in color on front cover. A fine copy in mint condition. The first edition thus was published in 1953 (also listed here); the second edition thus in 1971; it is reprinted here with a new introduction (present copy).

1758. [MILTON POEMS[.] Everyman's Library Pocket Poets[.] *Alfred A. Knopf • New York • Toronto[,] (1996).* First edition thus. 8vo, 256pp., half-title, black rules on title page with small emblem of the press at the center, half-title for each of the selections, original red cloth, Milton's name in gilt within gilt rules on front cover, spine richly lettered in gilt against a black background within rich gilt rules, decorated endpapers, decorated red printed publisher's wrappers, front cover with Milton's name lettered in black within decorative gold trim and black and gold rules against a diagonal white background at the center and "Everyman's Library Pocket Poets" lettered in black against a gold background at the bottom, spine in white with decorative pieces in black and with Milton's name lettered in black against a gold background within black rules near the top and "Everyman's Library Pocket Poets" lettered in gold against a red background within gold rules at the bottom, red silk ribbon marker. A fine copy.

Poetical Works

Presentation Copy from William Hog

1759. [POETICAL WORKS] Hog, William. **PARAPHRASIS POETICA IN TRIA** Johannis Miltoni, Viri Clarissimi, Poemata, Viz. Paradisum Amissum, Paradisum Recuperatum, Et Samsonem Agonisten. Autore Gulielmo Hogaeo. *Londini: Typis Johannis Darby, Anno Domini MDCXC*. First edition. 8vo, xxxvi+510pp., title page in red and black, title page in black for each section ("Paradisum Amissum," "Paradisum Recuperatum," and "Samsonem Agonisten," each dated "Anno Domini MDCXC"), original calf (a bit rubbed, joints weak), paper labels on spine with title in ink in an early hand, raised bands, speckled edges. Presentation copy with presentation inscription in Latin from the translator William Hog to the Marquess of Tweeddale with his bookplate on fly-leaf. A very fine copy, printed on thick paper (bulking nearly 1 ¾", about ¾" thicker than usual), considerably rare thus. Wing H2362, M2158; Coleridge 184; neither noting the thick paper variant, although Parker (1189–90) mentions that the Lilly Library at Indiana University has a copy on thick paper; Shawcross, Kentucky, 94; Not in Kohler.

In his translation of *PL*, William Hog uses the original ten-book version with the arguments printed together preceding the poem; Hog's translations of *PL*, *PR*, and *SA* are the first Latin translation of Milton's three major poems. It was this work that William Lauder used so extensively in his notorious attempt to prove Milton a plagiarist. (See Lauder and commentary there with Eighteenth-century Miltoniana.) This is the first William Hog translation; it is the first complete Latin version of each of the three poems. According to Parker (p. 661), early Latin translations of Milton's *PL* appeared as follows: (1) "J.C." (1686, *Paradisus Amissa*, Book I—edition here); (2) William Hogg (1690, *Paraphrasis Poetica*—edition here); (3) "T.P." [Thomas Power] (1691); (4) Charles Blake (1694); (5) Matthew [Michael] Bold (1702, *Paradisus Amissa*, Book I,—see copy listed here); (6) Joseph Trapp (1741–44, *Paradisus Amissus*—see set listed here), and (7) William Dobson (1750–53, *Paradisus Amissus*—see set listed here).

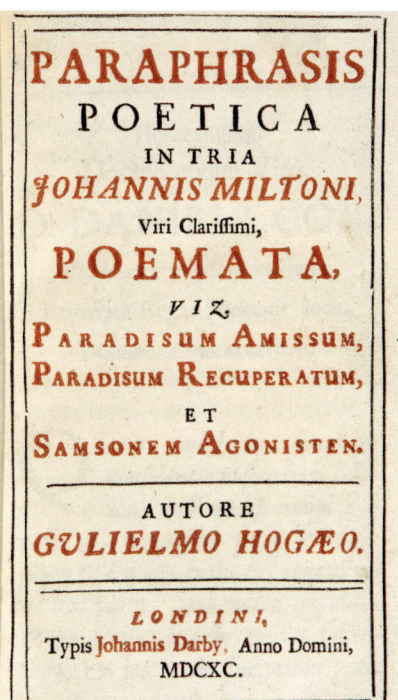

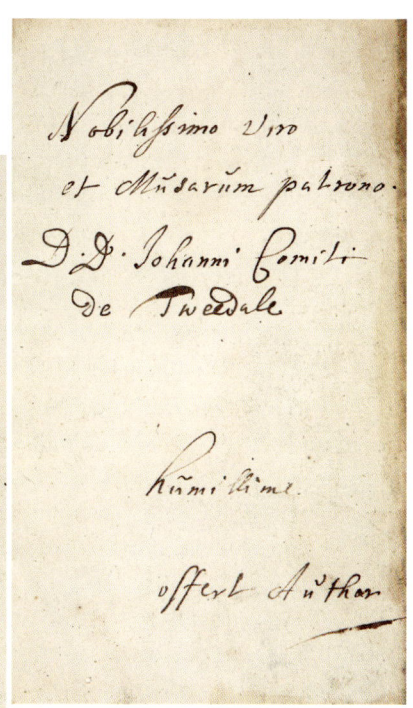

(left) *Paraphrasis Poetica*. William Hog, MDCXC. Rubricated title page. Presentation copy. (above) Presentation inscription from the translator on fly-leaf. See #1759.

1760. **THE POETICAL WORKS OF MR. JOHN MILTON**. Containing, Paradise Lost, Paradise Regain'd, *Samson Agonistes*, and his Poems on several Occasions. Together With Explanatory NOTES on each Book of the PARADISE LOST, and a TABLE never before Printed. *London: Printed for Jacob Tonson, at the Judge's Head near the Inner Temple-Gate in Fleet-street, M DC XCV*. Consisting of PARADISE LOST. A Poem In Twelve Books. The Authour [sic] John Milton. The Sixth Edition, with Sculptures. To which is added, Explanatory NOTES upon each Book, and a TABLE to the POEM, never before Printed. *London: Printed by Tho. Hodgkin, for Jacob Tonson, at the Judge's Head near the Inner Temple-Gate in Fleet-street, M DC XCV*. Sixth edition; second illustrated edition. Twelve engraved illustrations, one for each book of *PL*, as with 1688 edition (also listed here), most by J. B. Medina, one by B[ernard]. Lens (for Book IV) and one possibly by Dean Aldrich (for Book X) engraved by M. Burghers (also Burg and Burgesse, assumed to be a single identity). Bound with **PARADISE REGAIN'D**. A Poem. In IV Books. To which is added Samson Agonistes. The Author John Milton. *London, Printed by R. E. and are to be sold by Randal Taylor near Stationers-Hall. M DC LXXXVIII*. Third edition; first folio edition. Bound with **SAMSON**

AGONISTES, A Dramatick Poem. The Authour [sic] John Milton. Aristot. Poet. Cap 6 . . . *London, Printed, and are to be Sold by Randal Taylor near Stationers-Hall, M DC LXXXVIII.* Third edition; first folio edition. Bound with **POEMS UPON SEVERAL OCCASIONS.** Compos'd at several times. By Mr. John Milton. The Third Edition. *London: Printed for Jacob Tonson, at the Judge's Head, near the Inner Temple-Gate in Fleet-street, M DC XCV.* Third edition; first folio edition. Bound with **JOANNIS MILTONI LONDINENSIS POEMATA** (half-title). Bound with **ANNOTATIONS ON MILTON'S PARADISE LOST** . . . By P.[atrick] H.[ume] . . . *London: Printed for Jacob Tonson, at the Judge's Head near the Inner Temple-Gate in Fleet-street, M DC XCV.* First edition. Bound with **A TABLE** [i.e., index] Of the most remarkable parts of Milton's *Paradise Lost,* Under the Three Heads of *Descriptions, Similes,* and *Speeches.* First edition.

Together, the first collected edition of Milton's poetry. Folio, 343+[3]pp.,+66pp.,+57pp.,+[ii]+34pp.,+60pp.,+321+[3]pp., engraved frontispiece portrait by R. White with Dryden's epigram, general title page within two rules, separate title page for each of the works (except *Poemata,* half-title, and *A Table,* printed at top of *Index*), each title page with two rules, *P* and the Latin poems printed in double column, two copies of *A Table*—one bound immediately after *PL* before *PR,* the other bound at the end of the volume, eighteenth-century tree calf (joints a bit cracked, some foxing, *PR* title page slightly dirtied, slight tear at bottom of the page containing "The Verse" without affecting any text), spine decorated in gilt trim, red morocco label with decorative gilt-trim and gilt lettering. A very nice copy with fine impressions of the plates and with a passage "From Dr. Bentley's Preface" written in ink in a neat eighteenth-century hand on verso of "The Verse." Coleridge 214 (without general title page); Shawcross, Kentucky, 110; Kohler 266.

The *PL* in this volume is a close reprint of the first illustrated edition of 1688, with the 1688 plates, but *The Table of the most remarkable Parts of Milton's PL* is the first printing. When reprinted in subsequent editions this was described as the index. The 1695 edition of *PL* includes line numbers that are not present in the 1688 edition. The *Annotations on Milton's PL* by P[atrick] H[ume], here first published, ("P.H." identified as Patrick Hume in a neat contemporary hand in ink on title page), appeared separately as well (see copy with Seventeenth-century Miltoniana). Hume's *Annotations* is considered to be the first critical study of *PL.* It was used by all subsequent editors without acknowledgment right up to Todd and beyond. Parker comments that although each of Milton's poetical works herein has a separate title page, there does not seem to have been any separate publication on a significant scale. He notes the inclusion in a few copies (as this one) of the 1688 *PR* and 1688 *SA* (Parker, pp. 1194–95, note 176). Wing lists the component parts separately, and the volume is Wing M2163 comprising M2151, M2154, M2177, M2162, and H3663. "Tonson bought out his erstwhile partner in *PL* in 1691; Bentley probably had unsold stock of the 1688 edition which Tonson would wish to dispose of under his own name. . . . Tonson issued two collections in 1695, the parts of which are in large part the same, but with different arrangements" (Coleridge). Some contained 1688 editions of *PL* and of *PR* and *SA,* as here; "the second collection always contains the 1695 editions and is not always complete" (Coleridge).

1761. Variant of Preceding. [**THE POETICAL WORKS OF MR. JOHN MILTON.** Containing, Paradise Lost, Paradise Regain'd, *Samson* Agonistes, and his Poems on several Occasions. *London: Printed for Jacob Tonson, M DC XCV.*] First collected edition of Milton's poetry. [Without general title page.] Consisting of **PARADISE LOST.** A Poem In Twelve Books. The Authour [sic] John Milton. The Sixth Edition, with Sculptures. To which is added, Explanatory NOTES upon each book, and a TABLE to the POEM, never before Printed. *London: Printed by Tho. Hodgkin, for Jacob Tonson, at the Judge's Head near the Inner Temple-Gate in Fleet-street, M DC XCV.* Sixth edition; third illustrated edition; third folio edition. Twelve engraved illustrations, as identified in preceding. Bound with **PARADISE REGAIN'D.** A Poem. In IV.[sic] Books. To which is added Samson Agonistes. The Author John Milton. *London: Printed by R. E. and are to be sold by John Whitlock near Stationers-Hall. M DC XCV.* Fourth edition; second folio edition. Bound with **SAMSON AGONISTES,** A Dramatick Poem. The Authour [sic] John Milton. Aristot. Poet. Cap 6 . . . *London: Printed by R. E. and are to be sold by John Whitlock near Stationers-Hall. M DC XCV.* Fourth edition; second folio edition. Bound with **POEMS UPON SEVERAL OCCASIONS.** Compos'd at several times. By Mr. John Milton. The Third Edition. *London: Printed for Jacob Tonson at the Judge's Head, near the Inner-Temple-Gate in Fleet-street, 1695.* Third edition; first folio edition. Bound with **JOANNIS MILTONI LONDINENSIS POEMATA** (half-title).

Together comprising the **POETICAL WORKS,** the first collected edition of Milton's poetry, with each separate title page dated 1695. Folio, 343+[3]pp.,+66pp.,+57pp.,+[ii]+34pp.,+60pp., separate title page for each of the works (except *Poemata,* half-title, and *A Table,* printed at top of *Index* and bound here at the end of *PL*), each title page with a double black border, *P* and the *LP* printed in double column, contemporary paneled calf (rubbed), covers decorated in blind, red morocco label on spine with gilt rules and gilt lettering, raised bands. A nice copy, very fresh and clean within, with fine impressions of the plates. See Coleridge's comments regarding Tonson's purchase of *PL* in 1691 and the issue of two folio collections of Milton's *PW* in 1695. As John Shawcross observes with respect to the 1695 edition of *PL*, "While the edition appears to be the same as that of 1688, it has been reset and errors have been corrected" (Shawcross, Kentucky, 110). The 1695 edition of *PL* and of *PR* include line numbers that are not in the 1688 editions. Parker, 1194–95; Coleridge 214 (without general title page, as here); Shawcross, Kentucky, 111; Not in Kohler.

1762. THE POETICAL WORKS OF MR. JOHN MILTON. *London: Printed for Jacob Tonson, at Shakespear's Head in the Strand. MDCCXX.* 2 volumes. First Tickell edition. Large 4to, xiv+590+[11]pp.,+[ii]+527pp., edited by Thomas Tickell, engraved title page each volume, first appearance of engraved frontispiece portrait of Milton age sixty-six with Dryden epigram by G. Vertue each volume, vignette illustration on each engraved title page by Louis Chéron and engraved by G. van der Gucht of *Milton Inspired by the Muses*, volume 1, and *The Baptism of Jesus*, volume 2, engraved headpiece illustration occupying the upper portion of the beginning page of each book with large historiated initial letter, and with tailpiece illustrations, most of the tailpiece illustrations within elaborate baroque borders, one of the illustrations by James Thornhill and the others by Louis Chéron (first appearance), subscriber's list with half-title, volume 1, half-title for each book of *PL*, Addison's *Notes* (with its

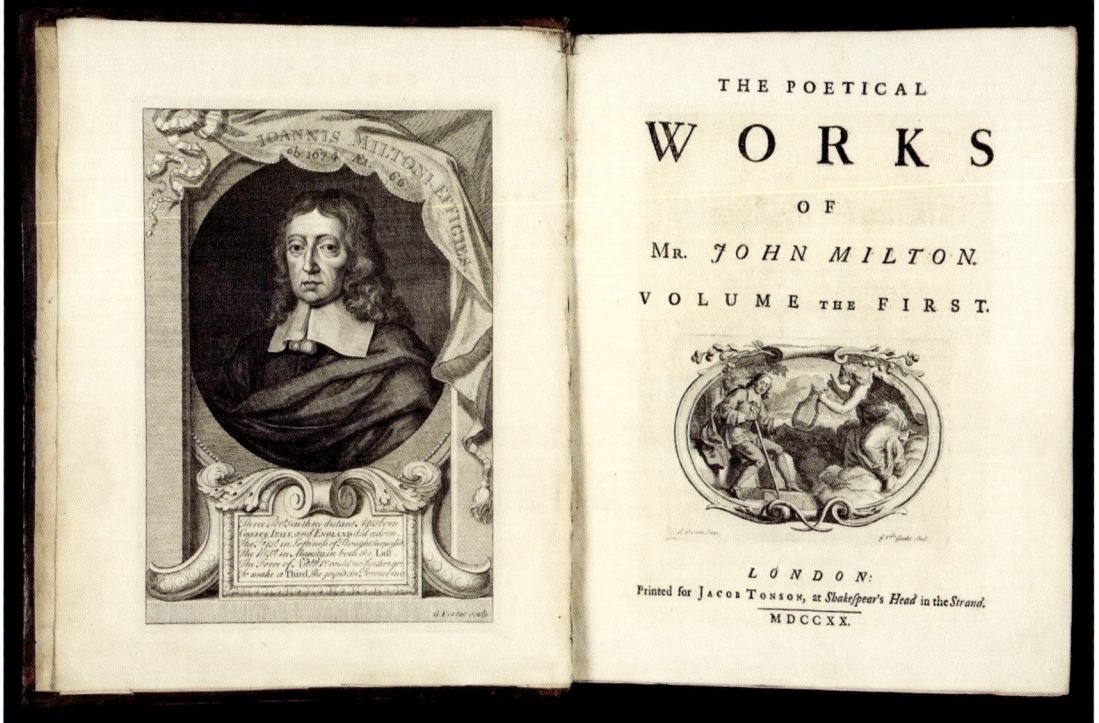

Engraved headpiece illustration of the Expulsion after L. Chéron, with historiated initial, in 1720 edition of *PW*. See #1762.

PW, London, Tonson, 1720. 2 volumes. First edition thus. Engraved frontispiece portrait and title page with vignette illustration after L. Chéron. See #1762.

own title page, with abbreviated imprint: "London: Printed in the Year MDCCXX") and index, volume 1, "Table of Contents" volume 2, title page for *SA*, *P*, and *C*, in volume 2 (each with abbreviated imprint: "London: Printed in the Year MDCCXX"), half-title for several of the separate works (including the *LP*, *Poemata*, and *Of Ed*), contemporary paneled calf (rebacked preserving original spine), covers decorated in blind, gilt-decorated spines, red morocco title labels, black morocco numbering labels, each with decorative gilt trim with date in gilt on black morocco label at bottom, raised bands. Each book of *PL* has a headpiece illustration, a decorated initial letter, and an endpiece illustration by Louis Chéron (one: *Satan Summons His Legions* by Sir James Thornhill engraved by G[erard]. van der Gucht or C. du Bosc.); each book of *PR* has a headpiece illustration, decorated initial letter, and endpiece illustration by Chéron engraved by G. van der Gucht or by Samuel Griberlin, Jr.; *SA* has a large headpiece illustration, decorated initial letter, and endpiece illustration by Chéron engraved by G. van der Gucht or by Samuel Griberlin, Jr.; *L*, the first poem printed among the *MP* has a headpiece illustration and a decorated initial letter by Chéron engraved by C. du Bosc. A handsome set with fine impressions of the plates, early armorial bookplate, and modern bookplate of Leonard Schlosser. The text of *PL* in volume 1 is the eleventh edition, without a separate title page. *Tercentenary Catalogue* 350; Williamson 54; Coleridge 215; Shawcross, Kentucky, 172; Kohler 267.

Extra-Illustrated

1763. Variant of Preceding. THE POETICAL WORKS OF MR. JOHN MILTON. *London: Printed for Jacob Tonson, at Shakespear's Head in the Strand. MDCCXX.* 2 volumes. First Tickell edition. Large 4to, xiv+590+[11]pp.,+[ii]+527pp., edited by Thomas Tickell, engraved frontispiece portrait of Milton age sixty-six with Dryden epigram each volume by G. Vertue (first appearance), as preceding copy within, nineteenth-century green paper over boards (a little worn, spines chipped, joints cracked), green speckled edges. The headpiece illustrations, decorated initials, and tailpiece illustrations are by Louis Chéron with one by Sir James Thornhill engraved by G[erard]. van der Gucht, C. du Bosc., Samuel Griberlin, Jr., or Louis Chéron. A good set with fine impressions of the plates. Extra-illustrated [ca. 1805]: with twelve engraved illustrations for *PL* by Hamilton and Fuseli from the 1801 edition of *PL* in which they first appeared (also listed here), each illustration mounted on its own page in volume 1. See references cited in preceding copy.

1764. THE POETICAL WORKS OF MR. JOHN MILTON, In Two Volumes. Containing. I. Paradise Lost; with Notes, by the late Right Honourable Mr. Secretary Addison. II. Paradise Regained: To which is added, Samson Agonistes. And Poems upon several Occasions. With a Tractate of Education. Adorned with Cuts. *London: Printed, and are to be Sold by William Taylor at the Ship and Black-Swan, in Pater-Noster-Row. MDCCXXI.* Volume 1 of 2 volumes (volume 2 preceding). First edition thus by Taylor. 12mo, [viii]+315+[1]pp.,+[1]+[40]+[4]+148pp., unsigned engraved frontispiece portrait with Dryden epigram, engraved illustrations (1688 plates further reduced), one for each book, decorative head- and tailpieces and decorated initial letters, at the end: an unpaginated forty-page index, a four-page listing of "Books Printed for Jacob Tonson" and Addison's *Notes* (with its own title page: *Notes Upon The Twelve Books Of PL*. Collected from the Spectator. Written by Mr. Addison. *London: Printed for Jacob Tonson, at Shakespear's Head, over-against Katherine Street in the Strand. MDCCXIX*), contemporary calf (a bit worn, joints cracked, spine slightly chipped at top), delicately tooled border trim in gilt on covers, Roman numeral "I" in gilt on spine, raised bands, speckled edges. With the exception of the title page, this edition is published in identical format to that of the 1719 12mo Tonson edition of *PL* (also listed here). See companion volume, as volume 2: "*Paradise Regain'd*. A Poem. In Four Books. To which is added *Samson Agonistes*. And *Poems Upon Several Occasions*. With A Tractate Of Education. The Author John Milton. The Fifth Edition. Adorn'd with Cuts. *London: Printed, and are to be Sold by W. Taylor, at the Ship and Black-Swan, in Pater-Noster-Row. 1721*," which together with this volume forms a rare two-volume edition of Milton's *PW* published by William Taylor in 1721. Rare. Not in Coleridge; Not in Kohler.

1765. THE POETICAL WORKS OF JOHN MILTON: Vol. 1. Containing, Paradise Lost. With Mr. Addison's Notes; And a new set of handsom [sic] cuts. *London, Printed In The Year M. DCC. XXXI.* Bound with **THE POETICAL WORKS OF JOHN MILTON: Vol. 2**. Containing, Paradise Regained, Samson Agonistes, And His Poems On Several Occasions, &c. A new Edition carefully corrected. *London, Printed In The Year M. DCC. XXXI.* 2 volumes in one. Small, thick 8vo, xx+[xxviii-page unpaginated index]+300pp.+136pp.,+iv+306pp., half-title each volume ("Milton's Poems, &c. Vol. I./II."), separate title page each volume, each printed in red and black with central decorative printer's device, separate title page for *PL*, volume 1, printed in red and black with large decorative device in black ("Paradise Lost, A Poem, In Twelve Books: Written By John Milton. With an Account of the Author's

Life. A New Edition, carefully corrected. [Greek quotation from Homer Odyss.] *London[,] Printed For The Company, MDCCXXX.*"), followed by life—with the rare first appearance of engraved portrait of Milton by D[avid]. Coster (very fine impression), postscript, and index (bound before *PL*), engraved illustrations (1688 plates reduced), one for each book of *PL*, most unsigned, several signed D[avid]. Coster (first appearance thus), separate title page in black for *Notes* by Addison (with abbreviated imprint: "London, Printed For The Company," n.d.), half-title for volume 2 followed by general title page for *PW* in red and black as preceding, "Table Of The Poems, &c." and engraved frontispiece illustration (*The Baptism of Jesus*) for *PR* signed D[avid]. Coster (first appearance, very fine impression), separate title page for *SA* and for *P* (each with abbreviated imprint: "London, Printed In The Year 1731"), half-titles for various of the works (including *C* and *Poemata*), *A Letter Concerning Education* is at the end, without half-title, decorative head- and tailpieces and decorated initial letters, original calf (a bit worn, some plates with lower blank edges reinforced, apparently at the time the volumes were bound), elaborately gilt-decorated spine, marbled edges. A good copy. John Shawcross shared with me that this edition is "Probably a French piracy"; and further: "There are two issues of Volume 1: one without the notes, the one with the notes alters the pages for the edition." The edition of **PARADISE LOST** . . . (London: Printed for the Company, 1730), which appears herein as well as separately (see copy listed here as volume 1 alone), is the sixteenth edition, printed for the Company in London (Moyles, p. 175). Rare. Not in Coleridge (*PL* is Coleridge 102); Not in Kohler.

The collection also has another set, bound as two volumes in which the engraved portrait of Milton serves as the frontispiece.

1766. THE POETICAL WORKS OF MILTON. Volume I. Containing Paradise Lost. A Poem, In Twelve Books. With A Critic upon the *Paradise Lost*, by Mr. Addison; and, A Preface. in which are inserted characters of the several pieces. *Edinburgh: Printed by Sands, Murray, and Cochran. For A. Kincaid and A. Donaldson. MDCCLV.* 12mo in 6s, cxv+321pp.[+20-page unpaginated index at the end], with general title page: "The Poetical Works Of Milton. With A Critic upon *Paradise Lost*, by Mr Addison; A Glossary, and an index; The Life of Milton; and, A Preface, in which are inserted characters of the several pieces. In Two Volumes. Edinburgh: Printed by Sands, Murray, and Cochran. For A. Kincaid and A. Donaldson. MDCCLV," and a second title page for volume 1, as cited, contemporary unlettered calf, raised bands. A very nice copy, fresh and clean within, complete with two title pages: the general title page and the title page to this volume. Found separately from volume 2 in 2005. Coleridge 118: "Kincaid and Donaldson also published the *Poetical works* in two volumes in 1755 and this is very probably a separate issue of vol. 1 of that edition. It may be compared with Donaldson's *Poetical works* of 1762 [see copies listed here]. Not having seen any copy of the 1755 *PW* I describe the WTu copy as an edition of *PL* only."

[together with]

1767. THE POETICAL WORKS OF MILTON. Volume II. Containing Paradise Regain'd, A Poem, In Four Books; Samson Agonistes; And Poems upon several occasions. With A Glossary; and, The Life of Milton. *Edinburgh: Printed by Sands, Murray, and Cochran. For A. Kincaid and A. Donaldson. MDCCLV.* Volume 2 only, complete unto itself. Large 12mo, [2]+384pp., "Table of Contents" at the beginning and "A Glossary" and "The Life of Milton" at the end, contemporary calf (a bit rubbed, back spine joint slightly chipped from label to the top), gilt rules on cover, brown morocco label with gilt lettering and gilt rules (chipped on left side), number "2" printed in gilt on spine beneath the label, raised bands within gilt rules. A nice copy, fresh and clean within, volume 2 only: *PR . . . SA; And P*. Found separately from volume 1 in 2000. As John Shawcross shared with me about this volume: "I have not found Volume II of *The Poetical Works of Milton*, published in Edinburgh in 1755 anywhere else. I've added your copy [to his bibliography, due to be published soon] and changed my annotation to Volume I. The copy of Volume I owned by the University of Kentucky has the first title page indicating that the edition is *The Poetical Works of Milton*; Coleridge's title page for *PL* is that copy's second title page . . . Coleridge's statement that *PL* is 'very probably a separate issue of Vol. 1' is incorrect." Rare. Not in Coleridge; Not in Kohler.

1768. THE POETICAL WORKS OF JOHN MILTON. With Notes of various Authors, By Thomas Newton, D.D. In Three Volumes. *London: Printed for J. and R. Tonson in the Strand. M DCC LXI.* 3 volumes. Fifth Newton edition. 4to, lxxix+[v]+[xvi]+491pp.,+460pp.+[116-page unpaginated index],+[vi]+690+[2]pp., engraved frontispiece portrait each volume, of Milton age sixty-two, Vertue's version of Faithorne portrait with Greek verses beneath, volume 1, of Milton "Aetat. 21" by Vertue, volume 2, of Milton "Aetat. 42" by Vertue, from Richardson's drawing, volume 3, separate title page (general title page as here) each volume, seventeen engraved illustrations by Francis Hayman, dedication, preface, life, and "A Critique upon the Paradise Lost. By Mr. Addison," volume 1, postscript, index, and verbal index at end of volume 2, *PL* occupying volumes 1 and 2, with half-title for each book of *PL*, preface, "The Table of Contents," and the remainder of the poems, volume 3, half-title for each book of *PR* and for various of the other works, "An index of the less common words," notes at bottom of page throughout the three volumes, contemporary calf (worn, joints weak with front joint of volume 3 broken, slight spotting and embrowning throughout), red morocco labels with gilt lettering and gilt trim on spines, raised bands. A good set with fine impressions of the plates. Scarce. Not in Coleridge; Not in Kohler.

Newton's very popular edition of *PL* with engraved illustrations by Hayman was first published in 1749 (see set listed here); *PR* and the remaining poems, also with engraved illustrations by Hayman, were first published in 1752 (also listed here). Volumes 1 and 2 here are a reissue of the 1749 edition, and volume 3 a reissue of the 1752, the three published together as *The Poetical Works*, each with the same general title page.

1769. THE POETICAL WORKS OF MILTON. In Two Volumes. Volume I. Containing Paradise Lost. A Poem, In Twelve Books. With A Preface, in which are inserted characters of the several pieces. *Edinburgh: Printed by A. Donaldson and J. Reid. For Alexander Donaldson. MDCCLXII.* Together with THE POETICAL WORKS OF MILTON. Volume II. Containing Paradise Regain'd, A Poem, In Four Books; Samson Agonistes; And Poems upon several occasions. With A Glossary; and, The Life of Milton. *Edinburgh: Printed by A. Donaldson and J. Reid. For Alexander Donaldson. MDCCLXII.* 2 volumes. First Donaldson edition, first issue. 12mo, xviii+324+[xvi]pp.,+[ii]+387pp., separate title page each volume, four engraved illustration plates after Tho. Phinn (clean impressions) for *PL*: Books IV (*Satan's First Sight of Adam and Eve*, bound here at the outset of Book III), VIII (*Adam's Discourse with Raphael*), IX (*Eve Tempting Adam*), and XI (*Michael Sets Forth in Vision for Adam Everything up to the Flood*), editor's preface before *PL* and unpaginated index at end of volume 1, "Table of Contents" at the beginning and "A Glossary" and "The Life of Milton" at the end of volume 2, contemporary calf (joints broken, front covers detached each volume, spine of volume 2 broken, small worm trail to blank lower corner of second volume), spines decorated in gilt within the panels, red morocco labels with gilt rules, raised bands. First issue of the first Donaldson edition. Rare. Coleridge 216a; Not in Kohler.

This is one of several editions published by Donaldson, all of which are rare, and all but one of which in the collection have a curious arrangement of plates, totaling no more than four plates in all, as here, sometimes three plates or one plate. In discussing the Donaldson printings Coleridge notes that some plates do occur, suggesting that happenstance appears to govern. See the following 1762 edition by Donaldson, also the first issue of the first Donaldson edition, a variant in two volumes, with one engraved illustration plate after Tho. Phinn for Book IV of *PL*; see also the first 1767 edition by Donaldson here in two volumes, without any illustration plates after Tho. Phinn; and see the second 1767 edition by Donaldson in two volumes, with three engraved illustration plates after Tho. Phinn, for Books IV, VIII, and XI of *PL*; see also the third 1767 edition in two volumes by Donaldson, with four engraved illustration plates after Tho. Phinn, for Books IV, VIII, IX, and XI of *PL*; and see 1772 edition here in two volumes by Donaldson, with frontispiece portrait after T. Phinn and with three engraved illustration plates after Tho. Phinn, for Books IV, VIII, and IX of *PL*. While happenstance may well govern the appearance of the plates in the Donaldson printings, the plates that do appear seem always to be for Books IV, VIII, IX, and XI of *PL*. See also the rare 1755 edition printed "For A. Kincaid and A. Donaldson." See, too, *PR*, 1762, above, another issue of volume 2 only, with its own title page.

1770. Variant of Preceding. THE POETICAL WORKS OF MILTON. In Two Volumes. Volume I. Containing Paradise Lost. A Poem, In Twelve Books. With A Preface, in which are inserted characters of the several pieces. *Edinburgh: Printed by A. Donaldson and J. Reid. For Alexander Donaldson. MDCCLXII.* Together with THE POETICAL WORKS OF MILTON. Volume II. Containing Paradise Regain'd, A Poem, In Four Books; Samson Agonistes; And Poems upon several occasions. With A Glossary; and, The Life of Milton. *Edinburgh: Printed by A. Donaldson and J. Reid. For Alexander Donaldson. MDCCLXII.* 2 volumes. First Donaldson edition, first issue. 12mo in 6s, xviii+324+[xvi]pp.,+[ii]+387pp., one engraved illustration plate after Tho. Phinn (clean impression) for Book IV of *PL*, "Editor's Preface" before *PL* and unpaginated index at end of volume 1 (with a page from the index misbound in "Editor's Preface"), "Table of Contents" at the beginning and "A Glossary" and "The Life of Milton" drawn from Newton's life with additions, at the end of volume 2, contemporary calf (some foxing), gilt rules on spines, red morocco labels, raised bands, gilt dentelles (faded). A nice set with one engraved illustration plate by Tho. Phinn rather than four, as in the preceding set. John Shawcross points out that "The poems are rearranged by category." Rare. Coleridge 216a; Shawcross, Kentucky, 354; Not in Kohler.

1771. THE POETICAL WORKS OF MILTON. With Prefatory Characters of the several Pieces; The Life of Milton; A Glossary, and an Index. In Two Volumes. *Edinburgh:*

Printed by A. Donaldson, and sold at his Shops in London and Edinburgh. M DCC LXVII. Together with **THE POETICAL WORKS OF MILTON.** Volume II. Containing Paradise Regain'd, A Poem, In Four Books; Samson Agonistes; And Poems upon several occasions: With A Glossary. *Edinburgh: Printed by A. Donaldson, and sold at his Shops in London and Edinburgh. M DCC LXVII.* 2 volumes. Volume 1 12mo in 6s; volume 2 8vo in 4s, lxxix+[1]+323pp.+[19-page unpaginated index]+[1]pp.,+iv+336pp., general title page, as cited, and individual title page, volume 1 ("Milton's Poetical Works. Volume I. Containing Paradise Lost. A Poem, In Twelve Books. With Prefatory Chacters of the several Pieces; and the Life of Milton. Edinburgh: Printed by A. Donaldson, and sold at his Shops in London and Edinburgh. M DCC LXVII."), decorative border trim around each title page, "Editor's Preface" and "Life of Milton" drawn from Newton's life, with additions, volume 1, "Table of Contents" at the beginning and "Glossary" at the end of volume 2, three engraved illustration plates after Thomas Phinn (for Books IV, VIII, and XI of *PL*), advertisement for "new Books . . . lately published, printed for A. Donaldson" on verso of last page, contemporary calf, not uniform (volume 1 lacks spine label, spine ends chipped; volume 2 a bit rubbed), volume 2 covers ruled in gilt, spine elaborately decorated in gilt with red morocco lettering and green morocco numbing labels, raised bands, outer dentelles tooled in gilt. The set is composed of two different volumes: volume 1 is smaller in size and 12mo in 6s, in rather plain calf; volume 2 is a bit larger, 8vo in 4s, and in very nice polished calf; it is very curious that one volume is 12mo and the other 8vo. This is one of several editions of *PW* published by Donaldson, all of which are rare and all of which have a curious arrangement of plates, totaling no more than four plates in all, sometimes three plates (as here) or one plate, and occasionally no plates at all. Rare. Not in Coleridge; Not in Kohler.

1772. MILTON'S POETICAL WORKS. Volume I. Containing Paradise Lost. A Poem, In Twelve Books. With Prefatory Characters of the several Pieces; and the Life of Milton. *Edinburgh: Printed by A. Donaldson, and sold at his Shops in London and Edinburgh. M DCC LXVII.* Together with **THE POETICAL WORKS OF MILTON.** Volume II. Containing Paradise Regain'd, A Poem, in Four Books; Samson Agonistes; And Poems upon several Occasions: With A Glossary. *Edinburgh: Printed by A. Donaldson, and sold at his Shops in London and Edinburgh. M DCC LXVII.* 12mo in 6s, lxxx+323pp.+[19-page unpaginated index]+[1],+iv+336pp., separate title page each volume, decorative border trim around each title page, "Editor's Preface" and "Life of Milton" drawn from Newton's life, with additions, volume 1, "Table of Contents" at the beginning and "Glossary" at the end of volume 2, four engraved illustration plates after Thomas Phinn (for Books IV, VIII, IX, and XI of *PL*), decorative trim at the head of major sections, before each book of *PL*, and before several of the major poems, half-titles with decorative trim for *PL* and some of the poems, small decorative tailpieces, advertisement for "new Books . . . lately published, printed for A. Donaldson" on verso of last page, contemporary polished calf (edges and corners of covers worn, newly rebacked in antique style to match, lacking the general title page for *The PW of Milton* in volume 1, the title page here being the second title page), spines lettered in gilt, raised bands within gilt rules. An attractive set with contemporary signature in a neat hand (dated 1775) on fly-leaf of each volume, with the Dorchester armorial bookplate on front pastedown of each volume. See the first of the 1762 Donaldson editions here for a listing of the four illustrations. Rare. "The ESTC on-line locates only three British copies plus a single copy in North America at Indiana" (G. W. Stuart, Jr., Ravenstree, Cat. 184, #92, 2000). Not in Coleridge; Not in Kohler.

1772A. See copy of volume 1 only: **MILTON'S PARADISE LOST.** A Poem, In Twelve Books. With Prefatory Characters of the several Pieces; and the Life-of Milton. Sarah West. 1773. *Edinburgh: Printed by A. Donaldson, and sold at his Shops in London and Edinburgh. M DCC LXVII.* 12mo in 6s, four engraved illustration plates after Thomas Phinn (as here), with "Life-of Milton. Sarah West. 1773" printed on the title page.

1773. **THE POETICAL WORKS OF MILTON.** With Prefatory Characters of the several Pieces; The Life of Milton; A Glossary, and an Index. In Two Volumes. *Edinburgh: Printed by A. Donaldson, and sold at his Shops in London and Edinburgh. M DCC LXVII.* 2 volumes. 8vo in 4s, lxxx+323pp.+[19-page unpaginated index]+[1],+iv+336pp., general title page, separate title page each volume ("Milton's Poetical Works. Volume I. Containing Paradise Lost. A Poem, In Twelve Books. With Prefatory Characters of the several Pieces; and the Life of Milton. Edinburgh: Printed by A. Donaldson, and sold at his Shops in London and Edinburgh. M DCC LXVII" and "The Poetical Works Of Milton. Volume II. Containing Paradise Regain'd, A Poem, in Four Books; Samson Agonistes; And Poems upon several Occasions: With A Glossary. Edinburgh: Printed by A. Donaldson, and sold at his Shops in London and Edinburgh. M DCC LXVII"), decorative border trim around each title page, "Editor's Preface" and "Life of Milton" by Toland, volume 1, "Table of Contents" at the beginning and "Glossary" at the end of volume 2, decorative trim at the head of major sections, before each book of *PL*, and before several of the major poems, half-titles with decorative trim for *PL* and some of the poems, small decorative tailpieces, advertisement for "new Books . . . lately published, printed for A. Donaldson" on verso of last page, contemporary calf (a bit worn, spine ends chipped, joints cracked, lightly embrowned, minor spotting or foxing), gilt rules on spine, red morocco lettering labels with gilt rules, black morocco numbering labels with gilt rules, raised bands, speckled edges. A nice set with advertisement leaf at the end of volume 1. This is one of several editions published by Donaldson, all of which are rare, and the only one in the collection without illustrations by Tho. Phinn. As John Shawcross points out this edition is a "reprint of Newton's edition." "A rare edition, which we have handled only once before in over thirty years" (G. W. Stuart, Jr., Ravenstree, Cat. 176, #85, 1993). Shawcross, Kentucky, 378; (the copy referred to in the Ravenstree quotation); Not in Coleridge; Not in Kohler.

1774. THE POETICAL WORKS OF MILTON. With Prefatory Characters of the several Pieces; The Life of Milton; A Glossary, and an Index. In Two Volumes. *Edinburgh: Printed by A. Donaldson, and sold at his Shops in London and Edinburgh. M DCC LXXII.* 2 volumes. 12mo, lxxx+323pp.+[19-page unpaginated index],+iv+336pp., general title page, volume 1, frontispiece portrait by T. Phinn, separate title page each volume ("Milton's Poetical Works. Volume First. Containing Paradise Lost; A Poem, In Twelve Books. With Prefatory Characters of the several Pieces; and the Life of Milton. Edinburgh: Printed by A. Donaldson, and sold at his Shops in London and Edinburgh. M. DCC. LXXVII" and "The Poetical Works Of Milton. Volume Second. Containing Paradise Regain'd, A Poem, in Four Books. Samson Agonistes; And Poems upon several Occasions: With A Glossary. Edinburgh: Printed by A. Donaldson, and sold at his Shops in London and Edinburgh. M. DCC. LXXII"), decorative border trim around each title page, "Editor's Preface" and "Life of Milton by Toland, volume 1, "Table of Contents" at the beginning and "Glossary" at the end of volume 2, three engraved illustration plates after Tho. Phinn, volume 1 (for Books IV, VIII, and IX of *PL*), decorative trim at the head of major sections before each book of *PL* and before several of the major poems, half-titles with decorative trim for *PL* and some of the poems, small decorative tailpieces, contemporary calf, spines lined in gilt, red morocco labels with gilt lettering and decorative gilt trim, outer dentelles trimmed in gilt (faded). A very fine set. This is one of several editions published by Donaldson, all of which are rare, and all of which have a curious arrangement of plates, usually totaling no more than four plates in all, and sometimes with no plates. See the first 1762 edition by Donaldson listed here which identifies the four illustrations along with the Donaldson editions in the collection and illustrations in each. "This [is a] very rare edition . . . we have not seen or handled a copy in over thirty years" (G. W. Stuart, Jr., Ravenstree, Cat. 179., #80, 1995). Not in Coleridge; Not in Kohler; copy in the University of Illinois.

1775. [POETICAL WORKS] PARADISE LOST. A Poem. In Twelve Books. The Author John Milton. *London: Printed for R. Crowder, C. Ware, and T. Payne. M.DCC.LXXII.* First edition thus. Volume 1 of 2 volumes, complete unto itself; issued as volume 1 with *PR*, 1772. 12mo in 6s, 334pp., general title page for *The Poetical Works of John Milton* ("THE POETICAL WORKS OF JOHN MILTON. In Two Volumes. With The Life of the Author, and a Glossary. Volume The First. London: Printed for R. Crowder, C. Ware, and T. Payne. M.DCC.LXXII"), separate title page for *PL* (as cited), contemporary calf (a bit rubbed, slight embrowning), black morocco label with gilt lettering and gilt rules on spine, raised bands, Roman numeral "I" in gilt. A nice copy with contemporary signature ("W. Dickie 2 Vols. Edinbr. 17th Ap. 1773") and other early (nineteenth century) signatures on fly-leaf, nice within. See John Shawcross's comments regarding the rarity of this edition as a separate issue with *PL*, 1772. The present edition was issued as volume 1 with general title page to form an edition of Milton's *PW* with *PR*, 1772, following, as volume 2, and as such is itself rare. Not in Coleridge; Not in Kohler.

[together with]

1776. [POETICAL WORKS] PARADISE REGAIN'D. A Poem. In Four Books. The Author John Milton. *London: Printed for R. Crowder, C. Ware, and T. Payne. M. DCC. LXXII. (1772).* First edition thus. Volume 2 of 2 volumes, complete unto itself; issued as volume 2 with *PL*, 1772. 12mo in 6s, 357pp., general title page for *The Poetical Works of John Milton* ("THE POETICAL WORKS OF JOHN MILTON. In Two Volumes. With The Life of the Author, and a Glossary. Volume The Second. London: Printed for R. Crowder, C. Ware, and T. Payne. M. DCC. LXXII"), separate title page for *PR* (as cited), "Contents," half-titles for *SA*, *P*, and *C*, glossary at the end, contemporary calf (worn, lacking front pastedown, spine ends chipped, lacking label on spine, early name [dated 1819] crossed out on front blank, other early names [dated 1819] written neatly in ink on general title page, small piece missing from lower corner of general title page without affecting any text), raised bands on spine, "2" in gilt. All in all, a rather decent copy of a scarce book, nice within. See related comments regarding this edition as a separate issue (with *PR*, 1772), which as such is very rare. The present edition was issued as volume 2 with general title page to form an edition of Milton's *PW* with *PL* (1772) as volume 1, and as such is itself rare; the two together are apparently rarer still. Each volume was acquired separately. Not in Coleridge; Not in Kohler.

1777. THE POETICAL WORKS OF JOHN MILTON. In Three Volumes. With The Life Of The Author, And A Glossary. *London: Printed for B. Long, and T. Pridden. M.DCC.LXXIII.* 3 volumes. Small 8vo in 4s, 264pp.,+293pp.,+277pp., half-title and title page each volume, with life and Books I through VIII of *PL* in volume 1, Books IX through XII of *PL* in volume 2, along with *PR* with half-title, and *SA* with half-title, *C*, *P*, and *Poemata* in volume 3 along with the glossary, original calf (worn with occasional scuffing, joints weak, spine ends chipped, two spine labels missing, front endpaper missing in volume 1, with early names and sketches on pastedowns and Milton's name written neatly in ink on front cover), raised bands within gilt bands. Despite cover wear, given its rarity, the set is overall quite decent and very fresh and clean within. Rare.

1778. THE POETICAL WORKS OF JOHN MILTON. From The Text Of Dr. Newton. In Four Volumes. With The Life Of The Author, And A Critique On Paradise Lost, By Joseph Addison, Esq. *Edinburg: At The Apollo Press, By The Martins. Anno 1776. Bell's Edition.* 4 volumes. First edition thus. 12mo in 6s, 240pp.,+228pp.,+216pp.,+216pp., engraved frontispiece portrait of a middle-aged Milton by I. Hall "Printed for John Bell near Exeter Exchange Strand London Mar. 1st, 1777," volumes 1 and 2, engraved frontispiece portrait of a young, pensive Milton "From an Original in Ld. Chesterfield Collection, Cook Sculp," "Printed for John Bell near Exeter Exchange Strand London Novr. 12th. 1777," volumes 3 and 4, engraved and two printed title pages each volume, each engraved title page reads: "Bell's Edition. The Poets of Great Britain Complete From Chaucer to Churchill," variously dated, "Novr. 20th. 1777," volume 1, "Novr. 12th. 1777," volume 2, and "Mar. 1st, 1777," volumes 3 and 4, with vignette illustration of Satan rising from the flames by Mortimer engraved by Hall on engraved title, volume 1, with a second engraved title page in volume 1 for the series "Bell's Edition. The Poets of Great Britain Complete From Chaucer to Churchill," dated "March 1st, 1777," with generic vignette illustration with Latin quotation, with vignette illustration of *Eve in the Garden* by Mortimer engraved by Grignion on engraved title, volume 2, with vignette illustration of *Samson* by Edwards engraved by Hall on engraved title, volume 3, with vignette illustration of *The Poet and His Muse* by Edwards engraved by Hall on

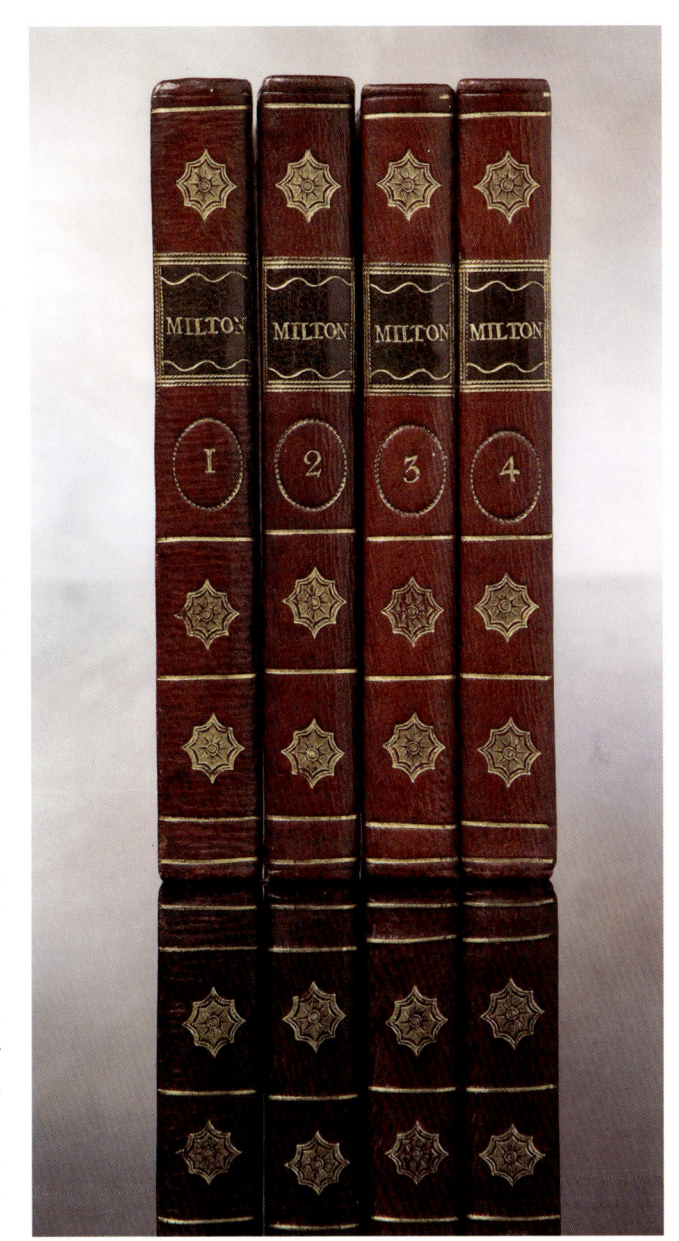

PW. Edinburg: At The Apollo Press, 1776. Bell's Edition. 4 volumes. First edition thus. Contemporary full red morocco. See #1778.

engraved title, volume 4, two printed title pages each volume, one for *PW*, the other for the contents of the given volume; the general printed title page in each volume reads: "The Poetical Works Of John Milton. From The Text Of Dr. Newton. In Four Volumes. With The Life Of The Author, And A Critique On Paradise Lost, By Joseph Addison, Esq. Vol. I/II/III/IV. Edinburgh: At The Apollo Press, By The Martins. Anno 1776; the printed title pages read: "Paradise Lost. A Poem In Twelve Books. The Author John Milton. From The Text Of Dr. Newton, In Two Volumes. [Latin quotation] Edinburg: At The Apollo Press, By The Martins. Anno 1776," Vols. 1 and 2; "Paradise Regain'd. A Poem In Four Books. Together with

Sams. Agonistes, Comus, L'Allegro, Il Penseroso, Arcades, Lycidas. The Author John Milton. From The Text Of Dr. Newton. Edinburg: At The Apollo Press, By The Martins. Anno 1776," volume 3; and "Poems Upon Several Occasions, Sonnets, Psalms, Elegies, Odes. &c. &c. &c. The Author John Milton. From The Test Of Dr. Newton. Edinburg: At The Apollo Press, By The Martins. Anno 1776," volume 4; life of Milton followed by "Advertisement" and "A General Critique Upon The Paradise Lost. By Joseph Addison, Esq.," volume 1, "Preface," volume 3, "A Glossary" and "Contents" at end of volume 4, contemporary full red morocco, gilt rules on covers and spines, green morocco labels with decorative gilt trim and gilt lettering on spines, outer dentelles tooled in gilt, marbled endpapers, a.e.g., small early bookplate on front pastedown of each volume. A choice set in a lovely contemporary red morocco binding, fresh and clean throughout, with a complete set of the engravings and all four portraits. Originally part of Bell's Edition (made up of some 200 or so total volumes). The second Bell edition was published in 1779 (also listed here). Coleridge 218; Kohler 268, reporting "Not in Cambridge University Library."

1779. Variant of Preceding. **THE POETICAL WORKS OF JOHN MILTON.** From The Text Of Dr. Newton. In Four Volumes. With The Life Of The Author, And A Critique On Paradise Lost, By Joseph Addison, Esq. *Edinburg: At The Apollo Press, By The Martins. Anno 1776. Belle's Edition.* 4 volumes bound uniformly in 2 volumes. 12mo in 6s, 240pp.,+228pp.,+216pp.,+216pp., engraved and two printed title pages each volume, each engraved title page reads: "Bell's Edition. The Poets of Great Britain Complete From Chaucer to Churchill," variously dated, "Novr. 20th. 1777," volume 1, "Novr. 12th. 1777," volume 2, "Novr. 20th. 1777," volume 3, and "Novr. 12th. 1777," volume 4, with vignette illustration of *Satan Rising from the Flames* by Mortimer engraved by Hall on engraved title, volume 1, with vignette illustration of *Eve in the Garden* by Mortimer engraved by Grignion on engraved title, volume 2, with vignette illustration of *Samson* by Edwards engraved by Hall on engraved title, volume 3, with vignette illustration of *The Poet and His Muse* by Edwards engraved by Hall on engraved title, volume 4; two printed title pages each volume, one for *PW*, the other for the contents of the given volume; the general printed title page in each volume reads: "The Poetical Works Of John Milton. From The Text Of Dr. Newton. In Four Volumes. With The Life Of The Author, And A Critique On Paradise Lost, By Joseph Addison, Esq. Vol. I/II/III/IV. [With a different publisher's imprint and date for each printed title page]: "Edinburg: At The Apollo Press, By The Martins. Anno 1776," volume 1, "London: Printed For, And Under the Direction Of, G. Cawthorn, British Library, Strand. 1799," volume 2, "London: Printed At The Apollo Press, By George Cawthorn, No. 132, Strand, Bookseller And Printer to Her Royal Highness The Princess Of Wales. 1802," volume 3, and "London: Printed Under The Direction Of J. Bell, British Library, Strand, Bookseller To His Royal Highness The Prince Of Wales. 1778," volume 4; the printed title pages read: "Paradise Lost. A Poem In Twelve Books. The Author John Milton. From The Text Of Dr. Newton, In Two Volumes. [Latin quotation] Edinburg: At The Apollo Press, By The Martins. Anno 1776," Vols. 1 and 2 (volume 2 with a different publisher's imprint and date: "London: Printed For, And Under the Direction Of, G. Cawthorn, British Library, Strand. 1799"), "Paradise Regain'd. A Poem In Four Books. Together with Samson Agonistes, Comus, L'Allegro, Il Penseroso, Arcades, Lycidas. The Author John Milton. From The Text Of Dr. Newton. London: Printed At The Apollo Press, By George Cawthorn, No. 132, Strand; Bookseller And Printer to Her Royal Highness The Princess Of Wales. 1802," volume 3, and "The Poetical Works of John Milton Containing Poems Upon Several Occasions. Sonnets, Psalms, Elegies, Odes. &c. &c. &c. [Quotation from Addison] London: Printed For John Bell, Bookseller To His Royal Highness The Prince Of Wales. 1788," volume 4, life of Milton followed by "Advertisement" and "A General Critique Upon The Paradise Lost By Joseph Addison, Esq.," volume 1, "Preface," volume 3, "A Glossary" and "Contents" at the end of volume 4, early tree calf (some age-browning in places), gilt-decorated rules on covers, elaborately gilt-decorated spines, black morocco labels with decorative gilt trim, outer dentelles tooled in gilt, speckled edges. A very nice set with a complete set of the engravings and one of the frontispiece portraits, also complete with engraved and two printed title pages (general and specific) for each volume, with dates that vary, some being later, thereby indicating that this set was bound ca. 1802. Originally part of Bell's edition. The second Bell edition was published in 1779 (also listed here). Coleridge 218; Kohler 268.

1780. **THE POETICAL WORKS OF JOHN MILTON.** From The Text Of Dr. Newton. In Four Volumes. With The Life Of The Author. And A Critique On Paradise Lost, By Joseph Addison, Esq. [Dryden Epigram.] *Edinburg: At The Apollo Press, By The Martins. Anno 1779.* 4 volumes. Second Bell edition? 12mo in 6s, 240pp.,+228pp.,+216pp.,+216pp., engraved frontispiece portrait "From an Original in Ld. Chesterfield Collection, Cook Sculp," "Printed for John Bell near Exeter Exchange Strand London Novr. 12th. 1777," volume 1, engraved and two printed title pages each volume, engraved title and one of the printed title pages for *PW*, each engraved title page: "Bell's Edition. The Poets of Great Britain Complete From Chaucer to Churchill," variously dated, "Novr. 20th. 1777," volume 1, "Novr. 12th. 1777," volume 2, and "Novr. 20th. 1777," volume 3, and "Novr. 12th. 1777," volume 4, with vignette illustration by Mortimer engraved by Hall on engraved title, volume 1, with vignette illustration by Mortimer engraved by Grignion on engraved title, volume 2, with vignette illustration by Mortimer engraved by Hall on engraved title, volume 3, with vignette illustration by Mortimer engraved by Grignion on engraved title, volume 4, the printed title pages in each volume dated 1779: "Paradise Lost. A Poem In Twelve Books. The Author John Milton. From The Text Of Dr. Newton, In Two Volumes. [Quotation from Addison] Edinburg[sic]: At The Apollo Press, By The Martins. Anno 1779," Vols. 1 and 2, "The Poetical Works Of John Milton. volume III. Containing Paradise Regain'd. A Poem In Four Books. Together with Samson Agonistes, Comus, L'Allegro, Il Penseroso, Arcades, Lycidas. [Quotation from Addison] Edinburg [sic]: At The Apollo Press, By The Martins. Anno 1779," volume 3, and "The Poetical Works Of John Milton. volume IV. Containing Poems Upon Several Occasions. Sonnets, Psalms, Elegies, Odes. &c. &c. &c. [Quotation from Addison] Edinburg: At The Apollo Press, By The Martins. Anno 1779," volume 4, life of Milton followed by "Advertisement" and "A General Critique Upon The Paradise Lost By Joseph Addison, Esq.," volume 1, "Preface," volume 3, "A Glossary" and "Contents" at end of volume 4, contemporary calf (a bit rubbed, two morocco gilt lettering pieces missing from spines), decorative gilt pieces on spines with decorative gilt trim, red and black morocco labels with decorative gilt trim, raised bands with decorative gilt trim, dentelles finely tooled in gilt. A very nice set with a complete set of the engraved and printed title pages, with the 1777 and 1779 imprints as is proper. Originally part of Bell's edition, first published in 1776 (see sets listed here). Rare. Coleridge 219; Not in Kohler.

1781. THE POETICAL WORKS OF JOHN MILTON. *London: Printed for A. Millar, and J. Hodges. MDCCLXXX.* 4 volumes. 12mo, 144pp.,+283pp.(continuous pagination with volume 1),+117pp.,+272pp.(continuous pagination with volume 3), copperplate engraved frontispiece portrait by Peter Larken of Virgil, Homer, and Milton with Dryden's epigram, volume 1, copperplate engraved frontispiece illustration for *PR*, "Malpas del et Sc.," volume 3, separate title page each volume, each with decorative piece, half-title for *SA*, *C*, *P*, and *Of Ed*, decorative head- and tailpieces, contemporary sheep (joints weak, spines chipped at top and bottom), gilt-decorated spines, red morocco title labels with decorative gilt rules, black morocco numbering labels with decorative gilt rules. A very nice set with several early signatures in ink neatly written on fly-leaf and front pastedown of each volume. See 1780 four-volume set printed, as here, in London "for A. Millar, and J. Hodges" and, as here, signed and paginated as two volumes, but a different edition, differently printed and with engraved Hayman illustration plates. Rare. Not in Coleridge; Not in Kohler; John Shawcross told me that there is a copy in the Newberry Library.

1782. THE POETICAL WORKS OF JOHN MILTON. *London: Printed for A. Millar, and J. Hodges. MDCCLXXX.* 4 volumes. 12mo, similar to preceding set (but a different edition), xviii+[ii]+162pp.,+313pp.(continuous pagination with volume 1),+iv+117pp.,+272pp.(continuous pagination with volume 3), copperplate engraved frontispiece portrait by Larken of Virgil, Homer, and Milton with Dryden's epigram, volume 1, engraved portrait plate by Vertue (slightly reduced and on thick cardlike paper) with two period signatures in ink in the same hand (dated 1758) on verso, before "The Life Of Milton," volume 1, engraved illustration plates by Hayman engraved by Müller (slightly reduced and on thicker paper as with portrait plate) inserted in volumes 1 and 2, one for each book of *PL*, engraved frontispiece illustration for *PR*, "Malpas del et Sc." (appropriate in size and manner to the volume), volume 3, separate title page each volume, each with decorative piece, half-titles for *SA*, *C*, *P*, and *Of Ed*, decorative head- and tailpieces, contemporary polished sheep (spines and extremities worn and rubbed, joints weak, volume 4 wormed at front affecting title and first dozen or so leaves), gilt-decorated spines, red and black labels (very worn or missing). The illustrations are the Hayman engravings, slightly reduced and probably added at the time of binding, as they are not mentioned on the title pages, are smaller than the leaves of the text, and are on thicker paper, with the exception of the illustration for *PR*. This curious set, although similar to the preceding set in being printed in London "for A. Millar, and J. Hodges," and, like it, signed and paginated as two volumes, is clearly a different edition, printed differently, with different pagination in volumes 1 and 2 (with volume 2 beginning on p. 163 as compared to p. 145 in volume 2 in the preceding set), differently printed half-titles in volumes 3 and 4, different head- and tailpieces throughout, and with engraved portrait after Vertue and engraved illustration plates after Hayman in volumes 1 and 2, although the portrait and plates would appear to have been inserted at the time of binding. Nothing new has been added, although the pagination and printing are entirely different, as indicated here, and as is readily evident when the two editions are put side by side. Rare. "We do not locate another copy, and we do not have a record of having seen or handled another copy in over thirty years" (G. W. Stuart, Jr., Ravenstree, Cat. 179, #81, 1995). John Shawcross shared with me about this set: "I have never seen [this edition], which I have now included in the bibliography with your descriptions. Thank you." Not in Coleridge; Not in Kohler.

1783. [POETICAL WORKS] THE WORKS OF THE ENGLISH POETS. With Prefaces, Biographical And Critical, By Samuel Johnson. Volume The First/Second. *Gottingen, Printed For I. C. Dieterich. MDCCLXXXIV.* 2 volumes. First edition thus? Small 8vo, 104+364+[1]pp., +[iv]+360pp., engraved frontispiece portrait of Johnson after Joshua Reynolds engraved by J. G. Sturm, separate title for *PL* ("THE POETICAL WORKS OF JOHN MILTON. Vol. I. Containing Paradise Lost. Gottingen, Printed For I. C. Dieterich. 1784"), preceded by an unsigned engraved frontispiece portrait of Milton engraved by J. G. Sturm (the portrait, like that of Johnson, is relatively small within a circular frame with laurel wreath across the top half, the framed portrait placed on a grooved block with Milton's name carved in it, the whole done in classical style), immediately following the title page for *PL* is a general half-title for "The Poems Of Milton. Volume I," half-title for each book of *PL*, "Contents Of The First Volume" at the end of volume 1, two separate title pages for volume 2: "THE POETICAL WORKS OF JOHN MILTON. Vol. II. Gottingen, Printed For I. C. Dieterich. 1784," as frontispiece facing the second title page, "THE WORKS OF THE ENGLISH POETS. With Prefaces, Biographical And Critical, By Samuel Johnson. Volume The Second. Gottingen, Printed For I. C. Dieterich. MDCCLXXXIV," "Contents Of The Second Volume" immediately following, half-title for each book of *PR*, followed by half-title for "Plans Of Paradise Lost, In The Form Of A Tragedy. From Milton's Manuscript," with additional half-titles for *SA*, *P*, *A Mask Presented At Ludlow-Castle*, and *Joannis Miltoni Londinensis Poemata*, contemporary three-quarter calf, marbled paper over boards (a bit rubbed, early signatures on fly-leaf of each volume), gilt-lettered leather labels with decorative gilt trim on spines, gilt rule at top and bottom of spines, raised bands within gilt rules, lightly speckled edges. A very nice set with title pages for Samuel Johnson's *Works Of The English Poets* and for *The PW Of John Milton*. Rare. Not in Coleridge; Not in Kohler.

1784. THE POETICAL WORKS OF JOHN MILTON. From The Text Of Dr. Newton, In Four Volumes. With The Life Of The Author. And A Critique On Paradise Lost, By Joseph Addison, Esq. [Dryden Epigram.] *London: Printed Under The Direction Of J. Bell, British Library, Strand, Bookseller To His Royal Highness The Prince Of Wales. 1788.* 4 volumes. 12mo in 6s, 234pp.,+213pp.(mispaginated "113"),+vi+209pp.(continuous pagination),+ 206pp., engraved frontispiece portrait "From an Original in Ld. Chesterfield Collection, Cook Sculp," "London Printed for John Bell, British Library Strand, March 10th. 1785," volume 1, with protective tissue guard, engraved and two printed title pages each volume, engraved title and one of the printed title pages for *PW*, each engraved title page: "Bell's Edition. The Poets of Great Britain Complete From Chaucer to Churchill," variously dated, "Novr. 20th, 1777," volume 1, "Novr. 12th. 1777," volume 2, "Novr. 20th, 1777," volume 3, and "Novr. 12th, 1777," volume 4, with vignette illustration by Mortimer engraved by Hall on engraved title, volume 1, with vignette illustration by Mortimer engraved by Grignion on engraved title, volume 2, with vignette illustration by Mortimer engraved by Hall on engraved title, volume 3, with vignette illustration by Mortimer engraved by Grignion on engraved title, volume 4, the other printed title pages: "Paradise Lost, A Poem In Twelve Books. The Author John Milton. From The Text Of Dr. Newton In Two Volumes. [Quotation from Addison] London: Printed For John Bell, Bookseller To His Royal Highness The Prince Of Wales. 1788," Vols. 1 and 2, "Paradise Regain'd. A Poem In Four Books. Together with Samson Agonistes, Comus, L'Allegro, Il Penseroso, Arcades, Lycidas. The Author John Milton. From The Test Of Dr. Newton. London: Printed For John Bell, Bookseller To His Royal Highness The Prince Of Wales. 1788," volume 3, and "The Poetical Works Of John Milton. Containing Poems Upon Several Occasions. Sonnets, Psalms, Elegies, Odes, &c. &c. &c. [Quotation from Addison] London: Printed For John Bell, Bookseller To His Royal Highness The Prince Of Wales. 1788," volume 4, life of Milton followed by "Advertisement" and "A General Critique Upon The Paradise Lost By Joseph Addison, Esq.," volume 1, "Preface," volume 3, "A Glossary" and "Contents" at end of volume 4, contemporary calf, gilt rules on spines, black morocco labels with gilt lettering and gilt rules, outer dentelles trimmed in gilt. A lovely set, choice, complete with all general titles, individual titles, and the frontispiece portrait in the first volume. Originally part of Bell's edition, first published in 1776 (see sets listed here). Rare. Coleridge 220; Not in Kohler.

1785. THE POETICAL WORKS OF MILTON. Containing Paradise Lost With Notes Critical And Historical; Paradise Regained, Samson Agonistes; And Poems upon several Occasions. Vol. 1. *London: Printed For The Booksellers. MDCCXC.* 1 volume only of two. 12mo in 6s, xv+ 375pp., life by Fenton, half-title for several of the books, original sheep (some wear, minor stains, short tears), red morocco label with gilt lettering and gilt rules on spine, additional gilt rules (faded) on spine, early signatures on endpapers. Given the rarity of this set, this volume carries with it an important association with the dated American bookplate on verso of title page: "This Book belongs to Joshua Thomas's Circulating Library, Opposite the Treasurer's Office, in Boston . . . 1793." This example contains the first eleven books of *PL*, plus the divisional title for Book XII on the proper final leaf. Rare ("We have had two complete sets of this edition in over thirty years" (G. W. Stuart, Jr., Ravenstree, Cat. 182, #98, 1998). Coleridge 221; Shawcross, Kentucky, 491 (complete set, calling it "Two volume sixmo edition"); Not in Kohler.

1786. THE POETICAL WORKS OF JOHN MILTON. Containing Paradise Lost[,] Paradise Regained, Samson Agonistis [sic], Comus, L'Allegro, Il Penseroso, Arcades, Lycedas [sic], Poems Upon Several Occasions, Sonnets, Psalms, Elegies, Odes, &c. &c. &c. To which is prefixed The Life Of The Author. [Dryden epigram.] *Edinburgh: Printed By Mundell And Son, Parliament Stairs. Anno 1792.* Large 8vo, 199pp., printed in double column, contemporary polished calf (rebacked), decorative gilt border trim on covers with central gilt seal on each cover, spine lettered in gilt, outer dentelles tooled in gilt. A fine, possibly large paper copy. It is important to note, as John Shawcross shared with me, that this "Volume was NOT published separately in 1792. This is part of the 1795 complete edition of *The Works of the Poets of Great Britain* by Robert Anderson. It is Volume 5. Other 'title page' dates for other poets give 1793, 1794, and 1795, in addition to 1792 dates." Not in Coleridge; Not in Kohler.

1787. THE POETICAL WORKS OF JOHN MILTON. With A Life Of The Author, By William Hayley. *London: Printed By W. Bulmer And Co., Shakespeare Printing-Office, For John And Josiah Boydell, And George Nicol; From the Types of W. Martin, 1794 97.* 3 volumes. First edition thus. Folio, 213pp.,+286pp.,+300pp., half-title each volume, separate title page each volume, first appearance of life by William Hayley, volume 1, three engraved portraits of Milton by Jansen and Vertue, engraved illustration of *Milton and His Daughters* by G. Romney, twenty-eight engraved illustration plates after R. Westall (first appearance) engraved by J. P. Simon, R. Earlom, L. Saebiavonetti, Thos. Kirk, J. Ogborne, B. Smith, M. Haughton, W. Leney, and C. Bestland, half-title for the various poems, contemporary full straight-grained blue morocco (a little rubbed, especially at extremities), richly gilt-decorated border trim on covers, spines trimmed in gilt with small decorative gilt pieces in the panels, raised bands within gilt rules, inner and outer dentelles finely tooled in gilt, a.e.g.

A very fine, large copy of *Bulmer's Milton*, a splendid production, which remains one of the major achievements of English book production, just a little over a hundred years after Tonson's monumental 1688 publication of *PL*, in an extremely handsome and well-preserved contemporary morocco binding. Westall later became Fuseli's partner in the 1802 Du Roveray edition of *PL* (also listed here). Russell 288; Coleridge 223; Kohler 269.

A magnificent edition. One of the major achievements of English typography, "generally acknowledged to be Bulmer's masterpiece" (Russell, 288). "Undeniably opulent . . . . These superb books must have occupied proud places in the stately libraries of eighteenth-century manor houses (Blumenthal, 31), considered subordinate by some only to the Boydell Shakespeare, which was being published at the same time. A "wonderful production—in simplicity of arrangement, in typography, and in presswork" (Updike, *Printing Types*, II, p. 145). The editors were William Cowper and William Hayley. Cowper had begun work on a separate edition of Milton's works for Joseph Johnson, at the same time as Hayley was preparing the present edition for Boydell. The two poets, who had admired one another (but until 1792 had never met), began to correspond, and then to cooperate. Eventually Johnson abandoned his edition, and a number of Cowper's translations from Milton were incorporated in Hayley's *Life*. The *Life* by Hayley printed here omits, for prudent reasons, passages dealing at greater length with Milton's political writings, Hayley's praise of *John Bradshaw, the regicide*, and his justification of rebellion under certain circumstances. These passages subsequently appeared in the separately printed *Life* of 1796 (see copy with Eighteenth-century Miltoniana). Cowper's interest seems to have been focused mostly on the Latin poems, and his translations were edited by Hayley and published with illustrations by Flaxman in 1808 (also listed here). The edition here was reprinted with additional material and notes in four volumes in 1810 (also listed here) under the supervision of Hayley, Cowper having died in 1800.

1788. THE POETICAL WORKS OF JOHN MILTON. From The Text Of Dr. Newton, In Two Volumes, With The Life Of The Author. And A Critique On Paradise Lost, By Joseph Addison, Esq. Adorned with elegant Copper-plates. Vol. I/II. [Dryden's Epigram.] *London: Printed And Sold By T. Wilkins, Aldermanbury. MDCCXCIV.* 2 volumes. First edition thus by Wilkins. 12mo in 6s, 312pp.,+ 578pp.(continuation pagination), engraved frontispiece portrait of Milton at age twenty-one "In the collection of the Rt. Honble Arthur Onslow Esqr.," engraved by B. Reading, "Wilkins's Edition Of The Poets Of Great Britain.," "Publish'd Augt. 24, 1793, as the Act directs, by

PW. London: Printed By W. Bulmer And Co., For John And Josiah Boydell, 1794–97. 3 volumes. Folio, contemporary full straight-grained blue morocco. Large copy of *Bulmer's Milton*, a splendid production, which remains one of the major achievements of English book production. See #1787.

J. Wilkins, Aldermanbury," volume 1, general title page each volume, separate title page for *PL* ("Paradise Lost, A Poem In Twelve Books. The Author John Milton. From The Text Of Dr. Newton. In Two Volumes. [Quotation from Addison] London: Printed By T. Wilkins, Aldermanbury. n.d.), volume 1, "The Life of Milton" followed by "Advertisement" and "A General Critique Upon The Paradise Lost By Joseph Addison Esq.," volume 1, engraved illustration for each book of *PL*, each illustration labeled "Wilkins's Poets" at the top, one attributed "E. Malpas sculpt.," several bearing the logo, "Published as the Act directs, Sept. 13/27/28, 1793, by T. Wilkins, No. 23, Aldermanbury," notes for each book of *PL* are printed immediately after each book, half-title for some of the poems, original sheep (a bit worn, joints weak), gilt rules on spines (faded), red morocco labels with gilt lettering and decorative gilt trim. A pleasant copy with early signature. "This is not a complete edition of the Poetical works; the only poems printed after 'Comus' . . . are 'Arcades', 'On May morning', 'On Shakespeare', the two Hobson poems, and the preliminaries to the Poemata" (Coleridge). Scarce. Copy in University of Illinois Library; Coleridge 222; Not in Kohler.

1789. THE POETICAL WORKS OF JOHN MILTON. From The Text Of Doctor Newton. With The Life Of The Author. In Two Parts. Vol. I / Vol. II. *Printed At Springfield, Massachusetts, By James R. Hutchins, For Ebenezer Larkin, Cornhill, And E. & S. Larkin, State-Street, Boston. MDCCXCIV (1794).* 2 volumes in one. Third American edition. 12mo in 6s, 314pp.(with "p.xxi" printed in error as "xxiii"),+76pp., general title page, with a second general title page before *PR* followed by a half-title for *PR*, life of Milton, original speckled calf (aged, with some embrowning within), gilt rules on spine (faded), red morocco label with gilt lettering and gilt rules. All in all, an okay copy of a scarce edition with library bookplate. Aside from being rare itself, this edition represents one of only eleven total eighteenth-century American editions of Milton's works. Of the eleven, the collection has eight: *PL*, 1777, and *PR, S, & P*, 1777, first American edition of each; *PR*, 1790, second American edition, and 1791, third American edition; *PL*, 1791, second American edition; *PW*, 1794, third American edition, and 1796, fourth American edition; and *An Old Looking Glass*, 1770, first American edition. As John Shawcross has kindly informed me, the other three are a different edition of *The Old Looking-Glass* published in New Haven in 1774; and two editions of *PW* from Philadelphia in 1791: one by Henry Taylor, which is a reissue of his PL and is in the collection, and a different edition of the *PR* volume, not the one in the collection; and one by W. Woodhouse, which is a reissue of Taylor's *PW*. Not in Coleridge; Not in Kohler.

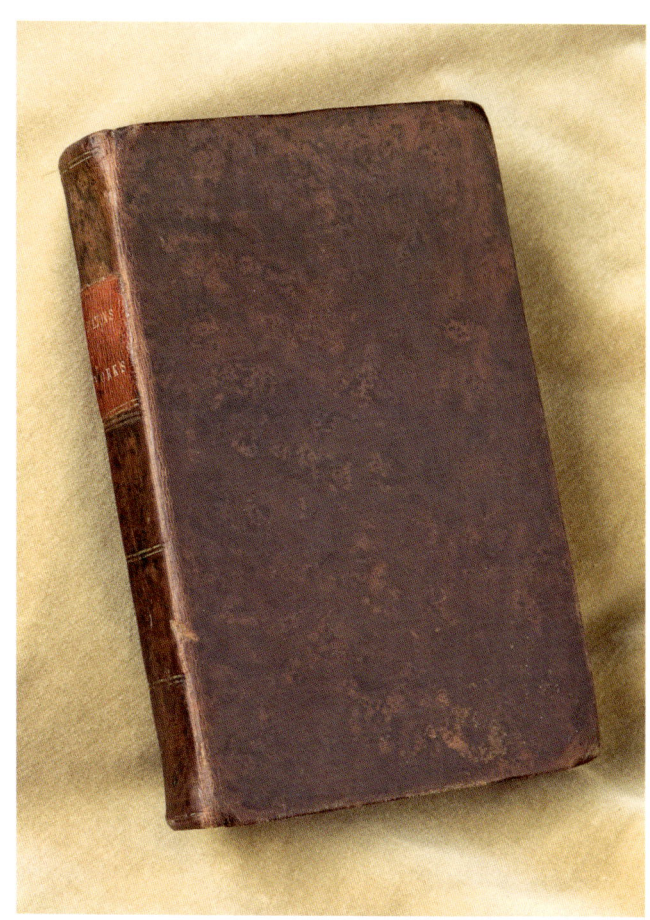

PW. Printed At Springfield, Massachusetts, By James R. Hutchins, 1794. Contemporary calf. See #1789.

1790. THE POETICAL WORKS OF JOHN MILTON. From The Text Of Dr. Newton. With The Life Of The Author. And A Critique On Paradise Lost, By Joseph Addison, Esq. Cooke's Edition. [Dryden's Epigram.] Embellished With Superb Engravings. *London: Printed for C. Cooke, No. 17, Paternoster-Row; And sold by all the Booksellers in Great Britain and Ireland. n.d. (1795/96).* 2 volumes. First edition thus. 12mo in 6s, 278pp.,+296pp., "The Life of John Milton" followed by "Advertisement" and "A General Critique Upon The Paradise Lost By Joseph Addison Esq.," volume 1, engraved and general printed title page each volume followed by half-title each volume, engraved frontispiece portrait plate "Engraved by W. Ridley from a drawing taken from a Bust in the possession of the Proprietor," labeled "Cooke's Edition Of Select Poets," "Printed for C. Cooke, 17, Paternoster Row, Janry. 23. 1796," volume 1, possible first appearance of engraved illustration plates by R. Corbould and T. Kirk variously dated 1795 and 1796, decorative endpieces, contemporary straight-grained calf (some occasional staining along inner margins affecting the inner edges of some plates, including frontispiece portrait and engraved title), gilt-decorated spines (faded), red morocco title labels with decorative gilt trim, black morocco numbering labels (missing, volume 1), outer dentelles tooled in gilt, speckled edges. A nice set. Coleridge 224; Not in Kohler.

1791. THE POETICAL WORKS OF JOHN MILTON. Consisting of Paradise Lost And Regained, And Poems on Several Occasions, From The Text Of Dr. Newton. With The Life Of The Author. *Boston: Printed By Joseph Bumstead. For E. Larkin, No. 47, Cornhill. 1796.* Fourth American edition. 8vo, 373+[ii]pp., original sheep (a bit worn, lacking blank endpapers, spine chipped at top, uniformly darkened leaves because of the heap paper used), gilt rules on spine, red morocco label with gilt lettering and gilt rule. A decent, tall copy in an appealing, inexpensive contemporary American binding with advertisement leaf for "American Editions" bound in at the end. Rare. Evans 30799. Not in Coleridge; Shawcross, Kentucky, 532; Kohler 270, reporting "Not in the British Library. Not in the Bodleian Library. Not in Cambridge University Library."

1792. THE POETICAL WORKS OF JOHN MILTON. From The Text Of Dr. Newton. To which are prefixed, The Life of the Author; A Criticism On His Works, By Dr. Johnson; And a Critique on Paradise Lost, by Joseph Addison, Esq. Cooke's Edition. Dryden's Epigram Embellished With Superb Engravings. *London: Printed for C. Cooke, No. 17, Paternoster-Row And sold by all the Booksellers in Great-Britain and Ireland. n.d. (1800).* Cooke's illustrated edition. 2 volumes. 12mo in 6s, 251pp.,+252pp., frontispiece portrait "Engraved by W. Ridley From a Drawing taken from a Bust in the possession of the Proprietor," labeled "Cooke's Edition Of Select Poets," volume 1, engraved title page with illustration by R. Corbould engraved by W. Hawkins for Book III of *PL*, illustration dated "February 13. 1800" (with "1800" written in ink in an early hand at bottom of page), general printed title page, volume 1, undated, printed title page for volume 1 undated, frontispiece illustration by T. Kirk engraved by W. Nutter for *MM*, dated "June 1, 1803," volume 2, engraved title page with illustration by R. Corbould engraved by W. Hawkins, for *IlP*, dated "Dec. 19 1800," general printed title page, volume 2, undated, printed title page for volume 2 undated, five illustration plates, volume 1: one engraved by W. Nutter after T. Kirk for Book I of *PL*, "Cooke's Edition of British Poets" dated 1795, a second engraved by W. Nutter after T. Kirk for Book V of *PL*, dated 1801, a third engraved by W. Ridley after T. Kirk for Book II of *PL*, "Cooke's Edition of British Poets," dated 1795, a fourth engraved by F. Strange after W. H. Brown for Book IV of *PL*, dated 1803, a fifth engraved by J. Weedinan after T. Kirk for Book I of *PL*, dated 1798, one illustration plate, volume 2: engraved by W. Ridley after T. Kirk for *L'A*, dated 1796, decorative tailpieces, "Glossary" and "Contents Of The Second Volume" bound in at end of volume 2, original boards, red paper spine (joints cracked, a bit aged), paper labels (chipped) on spines, edges untrimmed, each volume in a protective plastic cover. A good set in its original state with the bookplate of Clifford Bax and marginal notes in his hand. Scarce. See 1796 first "Cooke's Edition" listed earlier. Not in Kohler.

1793. THE POETICAL WORKS OF JOHN MILTON, From The Text Of Dr. Newton: With A Critical Essay By J. Aikin, M. D. *London: Printed For J. Johnson, et al, By H, Baldwin and Son, New Bridge-street, Blackfriars. 1801.* 4 volumes. First edition thus? Small 8vo, 257pp.,+245pp.,+259pp.,+iv+265pp., frontispiece portrait by R. H. Cromek, volume 1, thirty-nine-page "Essay On The Poetry Of Milton" by Aikin, volume 1, first appearance of illustrations by S. Rigaud (each dated 1801, each with protective tissue guard), six illustration plates for volume 1: one for each book of *PL*, six illustration plates for volume 2: one for each book of *PL*, five illustration plates for volume 3: four for *PR*, one for each book (Book III mislabeled "Paradise Lost" instead of "Paradise Regained"), and one for *SA*, three illustration plates for volume 4: one for *L'A*, one for *IlP*, and one for *C* (misbound in volume 4 among "Miltoni Poemata"), half-titles for each book of *PL* and for some of the poems, original blue morocco (very rubbed along spines and extremities, some foxing throughout), covers ruled in gilt, spines lettered in gilt with gilt rules, inner dentelles ruled in gilt, outer dentelles finely tooled in gilt, marbled endpapers, a.e.g., early bookplate of J. P. Sharp in each volume. A nice tall set (possibly a large paper copy), in original publisher's morocco binding, with fine impressions of the plates. See copy of second edition thus published in 1808. Not in Kohler.

1794. Variant of Preceding, contemporary diced calf, gilt rule on covers, elaborately gilt-decorated spines, red morocco labels, gilt dentelles, marbled endpapers and edges, bookplate each volume. A fine set in a variant contemporary Romantic binding, with fine impressions of the plates.

Extra-Illustrated

1795. THE POETICAL WORKS OF JOHN MILTON. In Six Volumes. With The Principal Notes Of Various Commentators. To Which Are Added Illustrations, With Some Account Of The Life Of Milton. By The Rev. Henry John Todd, M.A. [Latin Quotation from "Od. Ad J. Rous"] [Quotation from "Par. Lost] *London: Printed for J. Johnson, W. J. and J. Richardson, et al, and J. Mawman; By*

Bye and Law, St. John's-Square, Clerkenwell. M.DCC.I (1801). 6 volumes, plus index, dated 1809, as volume 7, bound uniformly. First Todd edition (including first edition of index). 8vo, [xiv]+[vi]+ccxv+303pp.,+504pp.,+494pp.,+xix+511pp.,+511pp.,+458pp.,+[405 unpaginated "Verbal Index], frontispiece portrait engraved by J. Baker after a drawing by T. Simpson from William Baker's painting by Faithorne, dedication page, preface, "Contents Of The Six Volumes," "The Life Of Milton," "List Of Editions," "Prolegomena, &c. " with half-title, volume 1, title page each volume, half-title for each book of *PL* and for various of the works, engraved plate, "Facsimile from the Original Drawing" of Queen Christina of Sweden in man's apparel engraved by T. Higham, for the Latin epigram, XIII. "Ad Christinam Suecorum Reginam, nomine Cromwelli," and "Glossorial Index," volume 6, engraved frontispiece portrait by T. Simpson engraved by J. Collyer, and "Verbal Index," volume 7, contemporary speckled calf (slightly rubbed, some joints weak, some foxing), ornately gilt-decorated spines, red morocco title labels with gilt lettering and gilt rules, black morocco numbering labels with decorative gilt trim, outer dentelles tooled in gilt, pink endpapers, bookplate each volume. The illustration depicting Queen Christina of Sweden is for the Latin epigram, XIII. "Ad Christinam Suecorum Reginam, nomine Cromwelli," thought to be by Marvell when he was assistant to Milston in the Latin Secretaryship, even though Newton had ascribed these lines to Milton. While not published as an illustrated edition, this set is extra-illustrated, having bound into it the plates for "Cooke's Edition Of Select British Poets," including portrait, volume 2, with illustrations by Kirke, Brown, and Corbould, variously dated 1795, 1796, 1798, 1800, 1801, and 1803. Pencil notation (sometimes cropped) on verso of each engraved plate gives binding directions as to where the plate is to be placed. A very nice set. Williamson 125.

1796. THE POETICAL WORKS OF JOHN MILTON. In Six Volumes. With The Principal Notes Of Various Commentators. To Which Are Added Illustrations, With Some Account Of The Life Of Milton. By The Rev. Henry John Todd, M.A. [Latin Quotation from "Od. Ad J. Rous"] [Quotation from "Par. Lost] *London: Printed for J. Johnson, W. J. and J. Richardson, et al, and J. Mawman; By Bye and Law, St. John's-Square, Clerkenwell. M.DCC.I (1801).* 6 volumes, plus index, dated 1809, as volume 7, bound uniformly. First Todd edition (including first edition of index). 8vo, [xiv]+[vi]+ccxv+303pp.,+504pp.,+494pp.,+xix+511pp.,+511pp.,+458pp.,+[405 unpaginated "Verbal Index], frontispiece portrait engraved by J. Baker after a drawing by T. Simpson from William Baker's painting by Faithorne, dedication page, preface, "Contents Of The Six Volumes," "The Life Of Milton," "List Of Editions," "Prolegomena, &c. " with half-title, volume 1, title page each volume, half-title for each book of *PL* and for various of the works, engraved plate, "Facsimile from the Original Drawing" of Queen Christina of Sweden in man's apparel engraved by T. Higham, for the Latin epigram, XIII. "Ad Christinam Suecorum Reginam, nomine Cromwelli," and "Glossorial Index," volume 6, engraved frontispiece portrait by T. Simpson engraved by J. Collyer, and "Verbal Index," volume 7, contemporary full red morocco (spines faded, most labels loose and laid inside the front cover available for reattachment), gilt-decorated spines, raised bands, a.e.g. A nice set. Volume 1 contains a valuable twenty-four-page "List of such Editions of Milton's *PW* as have hitherto been met with by the editor of these volumes." A second Todd edition, revised and expanded, was published in 1809; a third Todd edition was published in 1826; a fourth Todd edition—the last lifetime—in 1842; and a fifth and final Todd edition in 1852—all four sets are listed here. Williamson125; Stevens 102 (without index); Kohler 271 (without index), reporting "Not in Cambridge University Library."

1797. Variant of Preceding. **THE POETICAL WORKS OF JOHN MILTON.** In Six Volumes. With The Principal Notes Of Various Commentators. To Which Are Added Illustrations, With Some Account Of The Life Of Milton. By The Rev. Henry John Todd, M.A. [Latin Quotation from "Od. Ad J. Rous"] [Quotation from "Par. Lost] *London: Printed for J. Johnson, W. J. and J. Richardson, et al, and J. Mawman; By Bye and Law, St. John's-Square, Clerkenwell. M.DCC.I (1801). 6 volumes.* First Todd edition. 8vo, [xiv]+[vi]+ccxv+303pp.,+504pp.,+494pp.,+xix+511pp.,+511pp.,+458pp., frontispiece portrait engraved by J. Baker after a drawing by T. Simpson from William Baker's painting by Faithorne, dedication page, preface, "Contents Of The Six Volumes," "The Life Of Milton," "List Of Editions," "Prolegomena, &c. " with half-title, volume 1, title page each volume, half-title for each book of *PL* and for various of the works, engraved plate, "Facsimile from the Original Drawing" of Queen Christina of Sweden in man's apparel engraved by T. Higham for the Latin epigram XIII. "Ad Christinam Suecorum Reginam, nomine Cromwelli," and "Glossorial Index," volume 6, contemporary full Russia (joints slightly rubbed), gilt rules on covers and spines with decorative gilt devices on spines, inner and outer dentelles gilt, marbled endpapers, a.e.g. Large paper copy. A handsome set. References as with those listed at the end of the preceding copy.

PW. London, 1801. 6 volumes. First Todd edition. Contemporary full Russia. Large paper copy. See #1797.

1798. THE POETICAL WORKS OF JOHN MILTON. In Two Volumes. Containing Paradise Lost, Paradise Regained, Samson Agonistes, Comus, L'Allegro, Il Penseroso, Arcades, Lycidas, Poems Upon Several Occasions, Sonnets, Psalms, Elegies, Odes, &c. &c. &c. To Which Is Prefixed, The Life Of The Author. Dryden Epigram. *Cupar=Fife: Printed And Sold By R. Tullis, Bookseller. 1804.* 2 volumes. First edition thus. 12mo in 6s, xii+287pp.,+iv+275pp., contemporary polished tree calf (flyleaf, volume 1, frayed at edges), gilt rules on spines with gilt devices, green leather title labels, black leather numbering labels. A choice set in a very attractive binding of the period, with early signature of David Todd on title pages. A very scarce provincial printing of Milton's *PW*. The Tullis Press issued Milton's *PW* in two volumes in 1804, as here, and issued *PL* separately (also listed here) with a cancel title. Both *PW* and *PL* are among the earliest imprints of the Tullis Press founded by Robert Tullis Cupar, Fife, in 1803. Nineteenth-century STC locates a single copy of *PW* at Cambridge and a single copy of *PL* at the National Library of Scotland, but errs in calling for a "critique on the poem [by Samuel Johnson]." Doughty 7 and 7a; Not in Kohler.

1799. THE POETICAL WORKS OF JOHN MILTON, Paradise Lost, Paradise Regained, The Mask Of Comus, L'Allegro and Il Penseroso. Milton. *London. Publish'd by W. Suttaby, Stationer's Court, Ludgate Street; and C. Corrall, Charing Cross. 1805.* 2 volumes in one. First edition thus? 16mo, viii+301+[9]+[2]pp.,+xiv+95pp., engraved frontispiece illustration plate after J. Thurston engraved by A. Smith (for Book VI of *PL*, "a voice / From midst a golden cloud, thus mild was heard: / Servant of God, well done." "London, Printed for W. Suttaby, No. 2, Stationers Court [Successor to T. Wills] & C. Corrall, Charing Cross, 1804"), engraved title page for *PW* with oval portrait of Milton at the center "Engraved by Charles Grignion," engravd title-page plate for "Paradise Lost. A Poem, In Twelve Books By John Milton. London[:] Publish'd by W. Suttaby, No. 2, Stationer's Court, (successors to T Wills.) and C. Corrall, Charing Cross. 1804," with a vignette illustration at the center with the quotation, "Nor second he that rode sublime, / Upon the seraph wings of ecstasy. Vide Gray's Progress Of Poetry," engraved illustration plate after Craig engraved by Tye, for Book I of *PR* (with the lines quoted and "Page 3" cited with "Pubd. by W. Suttaby Stationer's Court, March 1, 1805" at the bottom), half-title for each book of *PL*, unpaginated nine-page index at the end of volume 1, separate title page for volume 2, half-title for *C* ("A Mask"), "Corrall, Printer, Charing Cross," at bottom of last page, contemporary brown calf (plates embrowned), spine richly decorated in gilt with thick gilt rules, red morocco label with gilt lettering ("Milton") and thick gilt rules. A very nice copy. The engraved title page here for *PL*, with vignette illustration and quotation "Vide Gray's Progress Of Poetry," appears as the title page, with variations to the publisher's imprint ("Published by W. Suttaby, & B. Crosby & Co. Stationer's Court; and C. Corrall, Charing Cross") in the 1806 edition of Milton's *PL* (also listed here). Scarce. Not in Kohler.

1800. THE POETICAL WORKS OF JOHN MILTON. Collated With The Best Editions: By Thomas Park, Esq. F.S.A. *London: Printed at the Stanhope Press, By Charles Whittingham, Union Buildings, Leather Lane; For John Sharpe, Opposite York-House, Piccadilly. 1805.* General title page in volume 3 and again in volume 4; title page for *PL* in volume 1 and again in volume 2: "**PARADISE LOST**: A Poem, In Twelve Books. The Author, John Milton. Collated With The Best Editions: By Thomas Park, Esq. F.S.A. London: Printed at the Stanhope Press, By Charles Whittingham, Union Buildings, Leather Lane; For John Sharpe, Opposite York-House, Piccadilly. 1805." 5 volumes. First edition thus. Small 8vo, 196pp.,+172+[1]pp.,+[i]+171pp.,+[vi]+168pp.,+7+166pp., half-title for each book of *PL* (volumes 1 and 2) and for *SA* and *C* (volume 3), copper-engraved illustration plate each volume (fine impression, inserted after the volume's title page): illustration plate engraved by P. W. Tomkins after Richard Westall for Book I, *PL*, volume 1, illustration plate engraved by P. W. Tomkins after Henry Fuseli for Book IV, *PL*, volume 1, illustration plate engraved by P. W. Tompkins after Henry Fuseli for Book IX, *PL*, volume 2, illustration plate engraved by P. W. Tomkins after Richard Westall for *L'A*, volume 3, illustration plate engraved by P. W. Tomkins after E. F. Burney for *MP*, volume 4 (although plate indicates "Vol. III"), illustration plate of "Milton composing *PL*" engraved by P. W. Tomkins after Richard Westall, volume 5, each plate "Published . . . by John Sharpe, Piccadilly" and dated 1805, each with protective tissue guard, original one-half red calf, marbled paper over boards (slightly rubbed), edges untrimmed. A very fine, tall set with early armorial bookplate in each volume. Volume 5 contains the "Prospectus for Sharpe's Cabinet Edition of the British Poets" (7 pp.) along with Addison's "Critique On Paradise Lost" (134 pp.) and Johnson's "Remarks on the Vindication of Milton" (32 pp.). See 1808 three-volume set, second edition thus, listed here, edited by Thomas Park, printed at the Stanhope Press by Charles Whittingham, with the same illustration plates by Fuseli and Westall printed in 1805 and published here for the first time. Rare. Stevens 105, referring to "The Works of the British Poets" and citing "2 vols. Illus."; Kohler 273, describing its copy as "12mo in 8s," "Four volumes in two," reporting "Not in the British Library. Not in the Bodleian Library. Not in Cambridge University Library."

1801. Variant of Preceding. THE POETICAL WORKS OF JOHN MILTON. Collated With The Best Editions: By Thomas Park, Esq. F.S.A. *London: Printed at the Stanhope Press, By Charles Whittingham, Union Buildings, Leather Lane; For John Sharpe, Opposite York-House, Piccadilly. 1805.* 4 volumes. First edition thus. Small 8vo, as preceding set except smaller in size, with the appearance of the general title page in each of the four volumes, without an illustration plate in each volume, and without volume 5, full contemporary speckled calf, gilt rules on covers, gilt-decorated spines, black morocco labels with gilt lettering and gilt trim, outer dentelles decorated in gilt, marbled endpapers. A fine set in an attractive binding of the period with bookplate in each volume. Rare. Not in Kohler.

1802. THE POETICAL WORKS OF JOHN MILTON, Complete in Two Volumes. *London: Publish'd by W. Suttaby, & B. Crosby & Co. Stationers Court; and C. Corrall, Charing Cross. 1806.* 2 volumes. First edition thus? 12mo, viii+301+[10]+[2]pp.,+xiv+[ii]+222+[2]pp., frontispiece illustration of *Satan* by Henry Fuseli engraved by Raimbach, "Publish'd by W. Suttaby Aug 1. 1806," volume 1, engraved title page each volume, engraved title, volume 2: "THE POETICAL WORKS OF JOHN MILTON, Complete In Two Volumes. London. Publish'd by W. Suttaby, & B. Crosby & Co. Stationer's Court; and C. Corrall, Charing Cross. 1806," vignette portrait of Milton (unsigned, "Engrav'd by Chapman") on engraved title, volume 1, frontispiece illustration of *The Lady in Comus* by T. Stothard engraved by F. Engleheart, "Publish'd by W. Suttaby Aug 1. 1806," volume 2, vignette illustration of *Samson* by Uwins engraved by F. Engleheart, on engraved title, volume 2, dated 1806, fourteen-page "Critique On The Paradise Regain'd" in volume 2, half-title for each book of *PL* and for various of the works, contemporary diced calf (rubbed at joints), gilt rules on covers, gilt-decorated spines by compartments, black morocco labels with gilt lettering (Milton) and decorative gilt trim, raised bands with decorative gilt trim, inner and outer dentelles finely tooled in gilt, marbled endpapers, a.e.g., ten-page index at the end of volume 1, advertisement leaf on editions published by "W. Suttaby, Stationers Court, and C. Corrall, 38, Charing Cross" each volume. A fine set with early signature on front blank. See possible second edition thus published in 1808 also listed here with a vignette illustration by Fuseli for *PL* on engraved title page, volume 1, in place of the vignette portrait of Milton here and with an eight-page index at the end of volume 1 instead of ten-page index here. Scarce. Williamson 173; Kohler 274, reporting "Not in Cambridge University Library."

1803. THE POETICAL WORKS OF JOHN MILTON. With A Preface, Biographical And Critical, By Samuel Johnson, LL. D. Re-edited, With New Biographical And Critical Matter, By J. Aikin, M.D. *London: Printed for G. Kearsley, Fleet-Street. 1806.* 3 volumes. 8vo, 337pp.,+[i]+310pp.,+[iv]+322pp., title page each volume, table of contents at the beginning of each volume, frontispiece portrait after Heath "From an original Painting," volume 1, illustrations engraved by Heath after J. Thurston: two for Book II and one for Book III of *PL*, volume 1, one for Book I of *PR*, volume 2, one for *L* and one for *IlP*, volume 3, half-title for each book of *PL*, each book of *PR*, *SA*, and some of the poems, life of Milton, volume 1, "T. Davison, White-Friars" printed on verso of last page, volume 1, "Thomas Davison, White-Friars" printed at the bottom of last page, volumes 2 and 3, contemporary full dark navy blue morocco (a bit rubbed, small chip at lower left spine, volume 1, occasional foxing, including the plates), elaborately gilt-decorated covers and spines, red morocco labels with gilt lettering and decorative gilt trim, raised bands with decorative gilt trim, inner and outer dentelles finely tooled in gilt, marbled endpapers and edges. A fine set in an attractive binding of the period with early signature (dated 1819) on fly-leaf. Scarce. Not in Kohler.

1804. Variant of Preceding, contemporary calf (worn, some chafing, front cover of volume 1 detached, top of volume 3 spine partially missing, some age-browning), spines lettered and decorated in gilt with a small decorative harp in gilt in one of the lower panels, marbled endpapers and edges. Although worn, a good copy of a scarce set. Even though there are two sets in the collection, the two sets differ: the set preceding is without half-title in each volume, present here, but with title page in each volume, lacking here, and without an advertisement leaf bound in at the end of each volume, present here. Not in Kohler.

PW. London: Kearsley, 1806, contemporary full dark navy blue morocco. 3 volumes. Frontispiece illustration each volume after J. Thurston. See #1803.

1805. THE POETICAL WORKS OF JOHN MILTON. With The Life Of The Author, By Samuel Johnson, LL.D. [Quotation from Thompson]. *London: Printed for Cadell and Davies, et al, and Samuel Bagster. 1807.* 4 volumes in 2. Small 12mo in 6s, 276+[1]pp.,+214pp.,+vi+203+[1]pp.,+[1]+207pp., frontispiece portrait by Cook "From an Original in Ld. Chesterfield's Collection," volume 1 (before "The Life Of John Milton"), engraved and printed title pages each volume, "The Poets of Great Britain," each engraved title page with an illustration by J. Mortimer, contemporary speckled calf (a little rubbed, joints cracked), gilt-decorated spines, red morocco title labels with gilt rules, black morocco numbering labels with gilt rules, outer dentelles tooled in gilt. A very nice set. Scarce. Not in Kohler.

1806. THE POETICAL WORKS OF JOHN MILTON, Complete In Two Volumes[.] *London. Published by W. Suttaby; Crosby & Co. Scatcherd & Letterman, and C. Corrall. 1808.* 2 volumes. Second edition thus? 12mo, viii+305+[8]+[2]pp.,+xiv+[2]+222+[2]pp., frontispiece illustration of *Satan* engraved by Raimbach after Henry Fuseli, "Publish'd by W. Suttaby Aug 1. 1806," volume 1, engraved title page each volume, engraved title, volume 2: "**THE POETICAL WORKS OF JOHN MILTON,** Complete In Two Volumes. *London. Publish'd by W. Suttaby, & B. Crosby & Co. Stationer's Court; and C. Corrall, Charing Cross. 1806,*" vignette illustration for Book I of *PL* engraved by A. Smith after Henry Fuseli on engraved title, volume 1, dated 1808, frontispiece illustration of *The Lady in Comus* engraved by F. Engleheart after T. Stothard, volume 2, dated 1806, vignette illustration of *Samson* engraved by F. Engleheart after Uwins on engraved title, volume 2, dated 1806 (someone having written an "8" over the "6" to make the title page date "1808"), fourteen-page "Critique On The Paradise Regain'd" in volume 2, half-title for each book of *PL* and for various of the works, original speckled calf (a little rubbed, joints weak), gilt rules on covers and spines, black morocco labels with gilt lettering and decorative gilt trim, eight-page index at the end of volume 1, advertisement leaf on editions published by "W. Suttaby, Stationers Court, and C. Corrall, 38, Charing Cross" each volume. A neat set with contemporary signature (dated 1810) and companion bookplate in each volume. See possible first edition thus published in 1806 also listed here with a vignette portrait of Milton on engraved title page, volume 1, in place of vignette illustration by Fuseli for *PL* here and with a ten-page index at the end of volume 1 instead of eight-page index here. Scarce. Not in Kohler.

1807. THE POETICAL WORKS OF JOHN MILTON; To which is prefixed The Life Of The Author. *London: Printed for J. Walker, et al, and J. Harris. 1808.* 12mo, xi+551pp., frontispiece illustration engraved by Rhodes after T. Uwins for Book XI of *PL*, engraved and printed title pages with vignette illustration engraved by Rhodes after T. Uwins for Book II of *PR* on engraved title, half-title for each book of *PL* and *PR* and for various of the works, original printed boards (a little worn, spine defective, covers barely holding), title page reproduced on front board, printed paper label on spine, edges untrimmed. All in all, a fair copy of a very scarce book in its original state, wholly uncut, with early signature (dated 1829) on front board. Not in Kohler.

1808. THE POETICAL WORKS OF JOHN MILTON. From The Text Of The Rev. Henry John Todd, M.A. With A Critical Essay, By J. Aikin, M.D. *London: Printed For J. Johnson, et al, and J. Harris. 1808.* 5 volumes. Second edition thus. 12mo in 6s, [i]+256pp.,+[i]+245pp.,+[i]+259pp.,+iv+265pp., frontispiece portrait by R. H. Cromek, "Published Jan 1. 1801 by Cadell & Davies," volume 1, title page for each of the four volumes, twenty engraved illustration plates by Rigaud (first appearance in 1801, see set listed here), half-title for each book of *PL* and *PR* and for various of the works, contemporary half calf, marbled paper over boards (a bit rubbed), gilt-decorated spines, red morocco title labels with gilt rules, green morocco numbering labels with gilt rules, early signature (dated 1824) on front pastedown of each volume. A very nice set with fine impressions of the plates bound together as volume 5, the volume bound uniformly with the other volumes. Scarce. Not in Kohler.

1809. THE POETICAL WORKS OF JOHN MILTON. Collated With The Best Editions: By Thomas Park, Esq. F.S.A. *London: Printed at the Stanhope Press, By Charles Whittingham, Union Buildings, Leather Lane; For John Sharpe, Opposite York-House, Piccadilly. 1808.* 6 volumes in 3. General title page each volume: **THE WORKS OF THE BRITISH POETS,** Collated With The Best Editions: By Thomas Park, F.S.A. *London: Printed For J. Sharpe, Opposite Albany, Piccadilly; And Sold By W. Suttaby, Stationers' Court, Ludgate Street. 1808.* Second edition thus. Small 8vo, 196+172pp.,+171+168pp.,+166+143pp., half-title each volume ("British Poets"), 2 volumes in one, volume 1, with general title page dated 1808 ("The Works Of The British Poets . . . Containing The First And Second Volumes Of Milton") and two title pages, each dated 1805—one title page each volume ("The Poetical Works," volume 1 and volume 2), volume 2, with general title page dated 1808 ("The Works Of The British Poets . . . Containing The Third And Fourth Volumes Of Milton") and two title pages, each dated 1805—one title page each volume ("The

Poetical Works," volume 3 and volume 4), volume 3, with general title page dated 1808 ("The Works Of The British Poets . . . Containing Addison's Critique, And Johnson's Remarks On Milton; And The Poems Of Sir John Denham") and individual title pages ("Critique On Paradise Lost, By The Right Hon. Joseph Addison. With Remarks On The Versification Of Milton, By Samuel Johnson, LL.D. London: Printed at the Stanhope Press . . . 1805" and "The Poetical Works Of John Denham . . . London: Printed at the Stanhope Press . . . 1807"), "Contents" page in each of the 6 volumes, half-title for each book of *PL* (volumes 1 and 2) and for *SA* and *C* (volume 3), illustration plates engraved by P. W. Tomkins after Richard Westall for Books IV and VI, *PL*, volume 1, illustration plate engraved by P. W. Tomkins after Henry Fuseli for Book IX, *PL*, volume 2, illustration plate engraved by P. W. Tomkins after Richard Westall for *L'A*, volume 3 (inserted here within *PR*), illustration plate engraved by P. W. Tomkins after E. F. Burney for *MP*, volume 4 (although plate indicates "Vol. III"), illustration plate of *Milton Composing PL* engraved by P. W. Tomkins after Richard Westall and illustration plate engraved by I. H. Wright after Richard Westall of *Friendship Against Love* by John Denham, volume 5, each plate "Published . . . by John Sharpe, Piccadilly" and each plate dated 1805 except the Denham plate (dated 1807), contemporary full diced calf (slightly rubbed along joints, volume 2 with very minor contemporary ink stains at the edges of several pages), gilt border rule on covers, spines decorated in gilt within the panels with small central gilt harp in each panel, double maroon morocco labels with gilt lettering and decorative gilt rules within slightly raised bands trimmed in blind on each spine, outer dentelles finely tooled in gilt. A very nice set with all the half-titles and title pages present, in an attractive binding very typical of the Regency period. The first appearance of these illustrations by Fuseli and Westall was in the 1805 edition printed by Charles Whittingham for John Sharpe at the Stanhope Press (see five-volume set, possible first edition thus, also listed here). Rare. Stevens 107; Not in Kohler.

1810. THE POETICAL WORKS OF JOHN MILTON, With Notes Of Various Authors. To Which Are Added Illustrations, And Some Account Of The Life And Writings Of Milton, By The Rev. Henry J. Todd, M.A.F.A.S. Rector Of Allhallows, Lombard-Street, &c. The Second Edition, With Considerable Additions, And With A Verbal Index To The Whole Of Milton's Poetry. In Seven Volumes. *London: Printed for J. Johnson; R. Baldwin; et al; and Mathews and Leigh: By Law and Gilbert, St. John's-Square, Clerkenwell. 1809.* 7 volumes. Second Todd edition. Large 8vo, xv+217pp.+[405 unpaginated "Verbal Index"],+xix+462pp.,+[i]+473pp.,+395pp.,+xix+503pp.,+[iii]+503pp.,+414+[1]pp.+[18 unpaginated "Glossarial Index"]+[6 unpaginated "Contents Of The Six Volumes"], frontispiece portrait plate engraved by J. Collyer after a drawing by T. Simpson from William Baker's painting by Faithorne, dedication page, preface, "Some Account Of The Life And Writing Of Milton," "List Of Editions," volume 1, separate title page each volume, half-title for each book of *PL* and for various of the works, unsigned engraved plate of Ludlow Castle before *C*, volume 6, engraved plate, "Facsimile from the Original Drawing" of Queen Christina of Sweden in man's apparel engraved by T. Higham for the Latin epigram in Book XII: "Ad Christinam Suecorum Reginam, nomine Cromwelli," volume 7, contemporary full straight-grained navy morocco, elaborate decorative gilt border trim and gilt rules on covers, gilt-decorated spines, raised bands, inner and outer dentelles finely tooled in gilt, pink endpapers, a.e.g. Large paper copy. A handsomely produced edition, printed on high-quality paper and splendidly bound by C. Hering, with his ticket on preliminary blank, inscribed "A Present from Lord Francis Spenser A.D. 1814" on second preliminary blank, with names of the May family and initials on title pages dated through 1888. This, the second and expanded Todd edition, incorporates the notes of Warton and others, and adds an index as volume 1—the only edition by Todd to include his massive verbal index or concordance to all of Milton's poetry, which necessitated the new seven-volume format; this second edition became the standard edition of the period, replacing Newton, and is the most handsome and formidable of the several edited by Todd. This edition is of particular significance not only for Todd's scholarly life of Milton but also for his bringing together for the first time the various critical commentaries and remarks on Milton, from David Hume and Joseph Addison through Dr. Samuel Johnson, Daniel Webb, and Thomas Birch to Charles Dunster and Robert Southey, among many others. Also, this is the sole edition to contain the extensive series of concordances with separate sections for English, Greek, Latin, and Italian words used by Milton in all his poetry. A limited number of copies of the index were printed with a distinct title page and sold separately (see copy of this scarce first separate edition of the index with Nineteenth-century Miltoniana). This 1809 revised edition was also reproduced by AMS Press Reproduction in 1970. The first Todd edition was published in 1801; the third Todd edition in 1826; the fourth Todd edition—the last lifetime—in 1842; and the fifth and final Todd edition in 1852—all five Todd sets listed here. Stevens 108; Williamson 150; Kohler 275, reporting "Not in the Bodleian Library."

PW. London, 1809. 7 volumes. Second Todd edition expanded, with index. Large 8vo, contemporary full straight-grained navy morocco. Large paper copy. See #1810.

1811. THE POETICAL WORKS OF JOHN MILTON. From The Text Of Doctor Newton. With The Life Of The Author. *New-York: Printed For Richard Scott By D. & G. Brucc. 1809.* First edition thus? 12mo in 6s, 345pp., life of Milton, half-title for *PL* and for "*PR*: With Other Poems," contemporary calf (a little worn, rubbed along joints and extremities, second signature sprung, age-browning throughout, with slight waterstaining along outer edges of first few pages), gilt rules on spine with black leather label with gilt lettering and gilt rules. A good copy with several contemporary signatures: one neatly written in ink on title page and repeated on fly-leaf along with another contemporary or early signature; a second contemporary signature neatly written in ink in capital letters (dated 1815) on inside back pastedown; a third neatly lettered in ink on front cover; with numerous marginal citations in ink and pencil in a neat, possibly contemporary or early hand throughout *PL* to scriptural sources. Scarce. Not in Kohler.

1812. THE POETICAL WORKS OF JOHN MILTON. With His Life By Samuel Johnson, LL.D. And Remarks By John Aikin. M.D. *London: Printed For John Sharpe, Piccadilly. 1810.* 3 volumes. 12mo in 6s, 337pp.,+310pp.,+[iv]+322pp., engraved title page each volume, each with vignette illustration after Stothard, variously engraved, "The Life Of Milton" volume 1, half-title for each book of *PL* and *PR* and for various of the works, contemporary diced calf (joints rubbed, some foxing, including the plates), gilt rules on covers, gilt-decorated spine with black morocco trim (chipped), gilt-ruled outer dentelles, marbled endpapers and edges. A nice set. Not in Kohler.

1813. THE POETICAL WORKS OF JOHN MILTON. Consisting Of Paradise Lost And Regained, And Poems On Several Occasions, From The Text Of Dr. Newton. With The Life Of The Author. *Brookfield: Printed By Isaiah Thomas, Jun. 1810. E. Merriam & Co. Printers.* 12mo in 6s, 348pp., original sheep (a bit worn, pages age-browned, a few pencil markings), gilt rules on spine (faded), black morocco label with gilt lettering and gilt rules. Nice copy of an early nineteenth-century American edition of Milton's *PW*. Not in Kohler.

1814. [POETICAL WORKS] [In] THE BRITISH POETS: With The Most Approved Translations Of The Greek And Roman Poets, With Dissertations, Notes, &c. The Text collated with the best Editions, By Thomas Park, Esq. F.S.A. Illustrated By A Series Of Engravings, By The Most Eminent Artists. In One Hundred Volumes. Vol[s]. XXIII [and XXIV] Containing The **POETICAL WORKS OF MILTON**. Vol. 1. Paradise Lost. Books I-VI. *London: Printed For J. Sharpe [By Charles Whittingham at the Stanhope Press]. 1810-1824.* Together 2 volumes, containing three volumes of Milton (together with *The PW Of William Collins*). Volume 1 (volumes 23 and 24) consists of *The PW Of William Collins . . . London: Printed at the Stanhope Press, By Charles Whittingham . . . For J. Sharpe . . . 1708* (sic, 1808) and Milton, volume 1, *PL*. Books I–VI, and,

Milton. Volume 2. *PL*. Books VII–XII. Volume 2 (volumes 25 and 26) consists of *PR* and "*Critique On PL*, By The Right Hon. Joseph Addison. With Remarks On The Versification Of Milton, By Samuel Johnson, LL.D. *London: Printed at the Stanhope Press, By Charles Whittingham, Union Buildings, Leather Lane; For John Sharpe, Opposite York House, Piccadilly. 1805*." 12mo in 6s, 64(misnumbered 54)+284pp.,+iv+220pp.,+166pp., title page for each of the three separate volumes of Milton's *PW*, for *Critique on PL*, and for *The PW Of William Collins*, half-title for *PL*, frontispiece illustration of *Milton Dictating* engraved by P. W. Tomkins after Richard Westall, volume 3, frontispiece illustration for Collins, volume 1, contemporary full red morocco, decorative gilt border trim on covers, spines decorated in gilt with gilt trim, corners of outer dentelles tooled in gilt, a.e.g. A lovely set in a very attractive Romantic red morocco binding. Not in Kohler.

1814A. (Cross-listing) [POETICAL WORKS] COWPER'S MILTON, IN FOUR VOLUMES. [Quotation from Mansus] *Chichester: Printed by W. Mason, For J. Johnson, & Co. St. Paul's Church-Yard, London. 1810.* 4 volumes. First edition thus. 8vo, frontispiece portrait engraved by Raimbach after Richard Smirke of Milton bust with an imprint of Cowper, found only in "certain copies," title page each volume, contemporary calf (rebacked). A nice set with the very rare frontispiece portrait. This is a reprint in four volumes of the 1794–97 Boydell edition of Milton's *PW* (set listed here) edited by William Cowper and William Hayley, with notes and additional material in the life by Hayley; this 1810 edition was supervised by Hayley, Cowper having died in 1800. Besides Milton's works, there also appear Cowper's translations of various of Milton poems and Andreini's *Adamo*, one of Milton's sourcebooks. Rare. Russell, *Cowper*, p. 291 (noting a frontispiece that occurs only "in certain copies," as in copy here); Stevens 112; Wlliamson 202; Not in Kohler. See main listing under Cowper, *Milton*, 1810.

1815. THE POETICAL WORKS OF JOHN MILTON; To which is prefixed The Life Of The Author. *London: Printed for J. Walker, et al, and J. Harris. 1811.* Thick 12mo, xi+551pp., frontispiece illustration for Book II of *PL* engraved by Rhodes after T. Uwins, undated, engraved and printed title pages with vignette illustration for Book II of *PR* engraved by Rhodes after Uwins on engraved title, undated, life by Fenton, half-title for each book of *PL* and *PR* and for various of the works, "Printed by S. Hamilton, Weybridge" at bottom of last page, contemporary tree calf (a bit rubbed, contemporary ownership signature [dated 1814] at top of title page in a neat hand), spine decorated in gilt with gilt lettering. A very nice copy, fresh and clean within, with contemporary presentation inscription in a neat hand (dated 1814) on front pastedown. Scarce. Kohler 276, describing its copy "16mo,"and reporting "Not in the British Library. Not in the Bodleian Library. Not in Cambridge University Library."

1815A. (Cross-listing) [POETICAL WORKS] MILTON'S POETICAL WORKS, With Cowper's Translations, And Hayley's Life Of The Author. In Four Volumes. Contents [Of Each Volume Listed] *Chichester: Printed and sold for a Kinsman of Cowper, By W. Mason, Sold Also By T. Payne, Pall-Mall, London. 1811.* 4 volumes. Second edition thus. 8vo, xxix+[1]+422pp.,+469pp.,+432+[1]pp.,+399+[1]pp., frontispiece portrait engraved by Raimbach after Richard Smirke of Milton bust with an imprint of Cowper, title page each volume, contemporary diced calf (a little worn). A good set of a rare edition. This is a reprint edition of the 1810 four-volume Cowper edition of Milton's *PW* (also listed here). Rare. Wlliamson 202; Not in Kohler. See main listing under Cowper, *Milton*, 1811.

1816. THE POETICAL WORKS OF JOHN MILTON. From The Text Of Doctor Newton. With A Critical Essay. By J. Aikin, M. D. Also, The Life Of The Author. Complete In One Volume. *Albany: Published By B. D. Packard, No. 51, State-Street. E. & E. Hosford, Printers. 1811.* First edition thus? 12mo in 6s, xxvi+484pp., "Contents," "Life," half-title for *PL, PR, SA, P,* and *C*, original calf (a bit worn, some embrowning throughout), leather label (cracked and partially defective) on spine lettered in gilt ("Milton's Works") with gilt rules (the gilt lettering and gilt rules faded). A good copy of an early nineteenth-century American edition in its original calf binding. Uncommon. Not in Kohler.

1817. THE POETICAL WORKS OF JOHN MILTON. With The Life Of The Author. In Two Volumes. Vol. I/II. *Baltimore, Published by Fielding Lucas, Jun. And Joseph Cushing. T. & G. Palmer, printers. 1813.* 2 volumes. 12mo, vi+[ii]316pp.,+249pp., engraved and printed title pages each volume, with vignette illustration (not for Milton) engraved by "P. Maverick sc. Newark," with lines quoted and reference given: "Vide Gray's Progress of Poetry," on engraved title in each volume, life of Milton by Fenton, half-title for each book of *PL* with argument on verso, index at the end of volume 1, half-title for each book of *PR, SA, C,* and *P* in volume 2, original calf (worn, front joint, volume 1, broken, label missing from volume 2, pages age-browned), red morocco label with gilt lettering and gilt rules on volume 1, gilt rules and volume numbers on spines. A decent copy of a scarce early nineteenth-century American edition of *PW* with a Baltimore publisher's imprint. Not in Kohler.

See 1818 edition of *PW* "Published By Cushing & Jewett. J. D. Toy, Printer" in Baltimore, with a frontispiece illustration and with the same engraved title page (dated 1813 and 1818, respectively) with the same vignette illustration for Gray as here. See also 1813 edition of *PL* "Published by F. Lucas Jr. & L. Cushing" in Baltimore, with the same frontispiece illustration and the same engraved title page with the same vignette illustration for Gray as here; and see 1818 edition of *PL* "Published by Fielding Lucas, Jun. And Joseph Cushing. T. & G. Palmer, printers," with the same frontispiece illustration and the same engraved title page with the same vignette illustration for Gray as here.

1818. THE POETICAL WORKS OF JOHN MILTON. With The Life Of The Author. In Three Volumes. Vol. 1. *New-York: Published By J. Forbes & Co. No. 78 Gold Street. 1815.* Volume 1 only of 3 volumes. 12mo, xi+[i]+206pp., frontispiece portrait by A. Anderson, half-title for each book, engraved illustration plates (for Books II, IV, and V after Anderson, attributed on plates IV and V, labeled "Forbes' Edit." at the top of each plate), ends with Books VII, contemporary calf (a little worn), red morocco label with gilt lettering and gilt rules on spine, additional gilt rules on spine. Scarce (and listed because of this). Not in Kohler.

1819. [POETICAL WORKS] Set of engraved plates, with engraved title page for each work marked "Proofs" or "Proof," including the engraved title page and engraved plate for each book of PARADISE LOST, title page marked "Proofs," *London: Printed For John Sharpe, Piccadilly, 1816,* with vignette portrait by T. Stothard of *Milton Composing PL* engraved by A. Raimbach; engraved plate for each book, each "Published By John Sharpe, Piccadilly, Aug. 24, 1816," each with vignette illustration by Richard Westall and variously engraved by Charles Heath, George Corbould, James Heath, William Finden, James Mitan, John Pye, and F. Engleheart. Together with the engraved title page for **PARADISE REGAINED** (London: Printed For John Sharpe, Piccadilly, 1816), marked "Proofs," with vignette illustration by Richard Westall engraved by F. Engleheart and one other engraved plate, "Published By John Sharpe, Piccadilly, Aug. 24, 1816," with vignette illustration by Richard Westall engraved by William Finden. Together with the engraved title page for **SAMSON AGONISTES** (Published By John Sharpe, Piccadilly, Aug. 24, 1816) with vignette illustration by Richard Westall engraved by John Romney. Together with the engraved title page for **THE MINOR POEMS** (London: Published By John Sharpe, 1816), marked "Proof," engraved plates with vignette illustrations all by Richard Westall, but variously engraved: one for *Methought I Saw* engraved by R. Rhodes; for *L'A* engraved by Charles Heath; for *IlP* engraved by James Mitan; for *C* engraved by Charles Heath; for *L* engraved by F. Engleheart; for *S* and for *SA* engraved by Charles Heath; and for *O* and for *NO* engraved by Edward Finden; each plate published "By John Sharpe, Piccadilly, Aug. 24, 1816." A complete set of the plates (first appearance of these vignette illustrations by Westall) with engraved title pages marked "Proofs" or "Proof," very tall (9 ¾" tall, 6 ¾" wide), untrimmed, preserved in homemade wrappers from a long time ago. Rare. Not in Kohler.

1820. THE POETICAL WORKS OF JOHN MILTON; To which is prefixed The Life Of The Author. *London: Printed for J. Walker; F. C. and J. Rivington; et al, and B. Reynolds: By S. Hamilton, Weybridge, Surrey. 1818.* Thick 12mo, xi+551pp., engraved frontispiece illustration for *IlP* engraved by C. Corbould after T. Uwins, protective tissue guard, engraved and printed title pages, with vignette illustration for *C* engraved by C. Corbould after T. Uwins on engraved title, ("London: Published by J. Walker & the other Proprietors, 1818,"), life of Milton by Fenton, half-title for each book of *PL* and for various of the works, contemporary polished calf (spine chipped at top and bottom, front joint cracked), decorative double gilt border trim on covers, spine elaborately decorated in gilt, black morocco label with gilt lettering and decorative gilt trim, corners of outer dentelles tooled in gilt, marbled endpapers and edges. A good copy with fine impressions of the plates. Not in Kohler.

1821. THE POETICAL WORKS OF JOHN MILTON. With The Life Of The Author. In Two Volumes. Vol. I/II. *Baltimore: Published By Cushing & Jewett. J. D. Toy, Printer. 1818.* 2 volumes. 12mo, 360pp.,+294pp., frontispiece illustration by J. Thurston for *PL*, Book VI engraved by "P. Maverick sc. Newark," with lines illustrated quoted beneath, "Published by F. Lucas Jr. & l. Cushing," volume 1, engraved and printed title pages each volume, with vignette illustration (not for Milton) engraved by "P. Maverick sc. Newark," with lines quoted and reference given: "Vide Gray's Progress of Poetry," on each engraved title page (dated 1813 in volume 1 and 1818 in volume 2), half-title for each book of *PL* with argument on verso, *PR*, *SA*, *C*, and *P*, original calf (worn, joints broken, initial pages embrowned, pp. 349–52 wrongly bound after title page, volume 1, bottom portion of front blanks, volume 2, torn away, early name signed on front blank of each volume), red leather label with gilt lettering on spines (mostly missing on volume 2). All in all, a decent copy of a scarce early nineteenth-century American edition of Milton's *PW* with a Baltimore publisher's imprint. The illustration for Gray,

Engraved illustration plate after Richard Westall of the temptation of Eve, dated 1816, together with a complete set of plates for Milton's *PW* (first appearance of these vignette illustrations by Westall and others), with engraved title pages marked "Proofs" or "Proof," untrimmed, in homemade wrappers. See #1819.

Engraved illustration plate after Richard Westall of the expulsion (among the same plates as the preceding). See #1819.

which had been used in the 1813 engraved title page for *PL* bound up in volume 1 here, also appears on the 1818 engraved title page for *PW* in volume 2 here. Scarce. Not in Kohler.

See 1813 edition of *PW* "Published by Fielding Lucas, Jun. And Joseph Cushing. T. & G. Palmer, printers," with the same engraved title page with the same vignette illustration for Gray as here. See also 1813 edition of *PL* "Published by F. Lucas Jr. & L. Cushing" in Baltimore, with a frontispiece illustration and with an engraved title page for *PL* with the same vignette illustration for Gray as here; and see 1818 edition of *PL* "Published by Fielding Lucas, Jun. And Joseph Cushing. T. & G. Palmer, printers," with a frontispiece illustration and with engraved and printed title pages for *PL*, with the same vignette illustration for Gray as here on the engraved title page.

1822. THE POETICAL WORKS OF JOHN MILTON; Complete In One Volume. *London. Published by Suttaby, Evance & Fox, Stationers Court, and Baldwin, Cradock & Joy, Paternoster Row. 1821. Corrall Printer.* 2 volumes in one. 12mo, viii+305+[8],+xiv+[2]+222+2pp., frontispiece illustration by H. Howard for *PL* (" . . . Moloch sceptred king, / Stood up; the strongest and the fiercest Spirit. Par. Lost, Book 2, pa. 28," "Published by Suttaby & Co. London, Oct. 1, 1821.") engraved by E. J. Portbury, engraved title page with vignette illustration by H. Howard for *PR*, ("Tempt not the Lord thy God. . . . Par. Regained. Book 4, pa. 34") engraved by E. J. Portbury, life of Milton by Fenton, half-title for *PL*, half-title for each book of *PL*, eight-page unpaginated index for *PL* after the poem followed by a fourteen-page unsigned "A Critique on The Paradise Regained" followed by "Contents" for the remainder of the volume, with *C* coming between *PR* and *SA* followed by *P*, half-title for *C* and for *SA*, contemporary dark green morocco (a little worn, front cover detached, spine missing a small piece at the top), gilt rules on covers, spine decorated in blind within the panels, red morocco label lettered in gilt with gilt rules, thick raised bands with decorative gilt trim, decorative gilt trim also at top and bottom of the spine, marbled endpapers and edges. A fairly good copy, fine internally, with an advertisement leaf for "Editions, in the same size, and on the same type . . . published by Suttaby, Evance, And Fox" bound in at the end. See 1812 edition of *PL* published, as here, by Suttaby, Evance & Fox. Kohler 278 observes correctly, I am sure, that "Although the title page says 'complete in one volume' this is clearly two volumes bound in one. There is [as here] no title-page present for volume 2," with separate pagination for each volume. Kohler also reports "Not in the British Library. Not in Cambridge University Library."

1823. THE POETICAL WORKS OF JOHN MILTON. With The Life Of The Author. In Two Volumes. *Philadelphia: Published By John Stevenson. Anderson & Meehan, printers. 1821.* 2 volumes. 12mo in 6s, xiii+267pp.,+282pp., engraved frontispiece illustration of *Milton Composing Paradise Lost with His Daughters* after "C. Tiebout Sc.," life of Milton by Fenton, engraved illustration for Book IX "Painted by H. Fuseli," engraved by "Kneass, Young & Co. Sc.," volume 1, title page each volume, half-title for each book of *PL* and for each book of *PR*, half-title for *SA* and for *P*, original calf (very worn, front cover of each volume missing, age-browning throughout). Similar to following set but without the additional engraved illustration for *L'A* as frontispiece in volume 2. Uncommon. Not in Kohler.

1824. Variant of Preceding. THE POETICAL WORKS OF JOHN MILTON. With The Life Of The Author. In Two Volumes. *Philadelphia: Published By John Stevenson. Anderson & Meehan, printers. 1821.* 2 volumes. 12mo in 6s, xiii+267pp.,+282pp., engraved frontispiece illustration of *Milton Composing Paradise Lost with His Daughters* after "C. Tiebout Sc.," life of Milton by Fenton, engraved illustration for Book IX after "Young & Kneass," volume 1, unsigned engraved illustration for *L'A* with lines quoted beneath, as frontispiece for volume 2, title page each volume, half-title for each book of *PL* and for each book of *PR*, half-title for *SA* and for *P*, original calf (worn, volume 1 rebacked with original spine laid down, front cover of volume 2 detached, slight waterstaining lower portion of first third of volume 1, age-browning). Unlike the preceding set, this set is taller by almost a ¼", has a frontispiece illustration for each volume (with illustration for *L'A* as frontispiece for volume 2), and a different form of attribution for the illustration for Book IX. Scarce. Not in Kohler.

1825. THE POETICAL WORKS OF JOHN MILTON; To which is prefixed The Life Of The Author. *London: Printed for F. C. and J. Rivington, et al. [31 additional named printers], and G. Cowie. By T. Davison, Whitefriars. 1822.* 12mo, xi+551pp., frontispiece illustration for Book XI of *PL* engraved by C. Warren after T. Uwins ("Printed for F. C. & I. Rivington and the other proprietors Septr. 1822"), protective tissue guard, engraved and printed title pages, with vignette illustration for Book II of *PR* engraved by C. Warren after T. Uwins on engraved title ("London Printed for F. C. & I. Rivington & the other proprietors Septr. 1822"), both illustrations engraved on steel plates as identified on each plate, half-title for each book of *PL* and *PR* and for various of the works, contemporary full green morocco, decorative gilt border trim on covers, covers elaborately tooled in blind, elaborately gilt-decorated spine, red morocco labels with gilt lettering and decorative gilt trim, raised bands within finely tooled gilt trim, inner and outer dentelles finely tooled in gilt, marbled endpapers and edges. A splendid copy in an attractive binding of the period. See 1832 edition listed here, with the same frontispiece illustration after T. Uwins and the same engraved title page with vignette illustration after T. Uwins, but a different publisher's imprint. Uncommon. Kohler 279, reporting "Not in the Bodleian Library."

1826. THE POETICAL WORKS OF JOHN MILTON; To which is prefixed The Life Of The Author. *London: Printed for T. and J. Allman; W. Baynes and Son[;] A. B. Dulau and Co.; et al; J. Anderson, jun. Edinburgh[;] M. Keene, and J. Cumming, Dublin. 1822.* First edition thus? 12mo, xii+480pp., engraved frontispiece illustration of the expulsion by R. Cooper engraved by W. Derby (fine impression), engraved and printed title pages, engraved illustration of Jesus "Queller of Satan" for *PR* by R. Cooper engraved by W. Derby, for *PR* ("Hail Son of the Most High heir of both worlds") on engraved title (fine impression, "London Printed for T. & J Allman. Princes Streets and the other Proprietors," printed at bottom of the page) emblem of the press on title page, half-titles for *PL*, *PR*, *SA*, and *C*, original boards (darkened and worn, occasional pieces missing), vellum spine, edges untrimmed. Despite its age and wear, a decent enough copy, well-preserved in its original state and original boards, with early signature in pencil (dated 1841) on fly-leaf. Scarce. Not in Kohler.

See 1824 edition listed here ("London: Printed For T. And J. Allman, Prince's Street, Hanover Square; And John Anderson, Jun. Edinburgh"); 1829 small 8vo edition listed here ("London: Printed For T. & J. Allman, 55, Great Queen Street, Lincoln's Inn Field; And G. Love & Co. Glasgow") with illustrations as here; and 1836 edition also listed here ("With Dr. Channing's Essay On The Poetical Genius Of Milton[.] London: T. Allman. 42, Holborn Hill").

1827. THE POETICAL WORKS OF JOHN MILTON. With The Life of the Author. In Three Volumes. *New-York: Published By R. & W. A. Bartow, 250 Pearl-St. And By W. A. Bartow, Richmond, (Vir.) Gray & Bunce, Printers.*

1822. 3 volumes. First edition thus. 12mo in 6s, 211pp.,+ 190pp.,+224pp., engraved and printed title pages each volume, frontispiece portrait "Engraved by Mr. Pekenino N.York 1821. New York Published by R. & W. A. Bartow 1822," life of Milton by Fenton, volume 1, vignette illustration ("Drawn by R. Westall, Engrd. A.B. Durand. New York, Published by R & W. A. Bartow 1822") for *PL* (Book III, with the lines illustrated printed beneath the illustration) on engraved title page bound as frontispiece, volume 2, vignette illustration ("Drawn by R. Westall, Engrd. by A.B. Durand. New York. Published by R. & W. Bartow, 1822") for *PL* (Book X, with the lines illustrated printed beneath the illustration) on engraved title page, volume 2, vignette illustration ("New York. Published by R. & W. A. Bartow. Drawn by R. Westall. Engrd. by Peter Maverick.") for *Ode on the Nativity* (with the lines illustrated printed beneath the illustration) on engraved title page bound as frontispiece, volume 3, half-title for each book of *PL*, each book of *PR*, *SA*, and *P*, original marbled calf (a little rubbed, joints weak, front covers detached on volumes 1 and 3, spine ends chipped volume 2, bottom portion of spine missing on volume 3, age-browning throughout), spines decorated in gilt, black morocco labels decorated and lettered in gilt. Although worn, a nice copy of a scarce set with contemporary presentation inscription (dated 1829) on front blank in each volume. Not in Kohler.

1828. THE POETICAL WORKS OF JOHN MILTON. *Paris: Published By Lefevre, Rue de L'Eperon, No. 6. M DCCC XXII.* 3 volumes. First edition thus. Small 8vo, xx+263+[1]pp.,+281+[1]pp.,+iv+308+[1]pp., half-title each volume ("The British Poets. With Biographical And Critical Prefaces By Sir John Byerley") with "Printed By P. Didot, Senior, Knight Of The Order Of St. Michael, And Printer To The King" on verso, title page each volume, "Contents" page at the end of each volume, original polished pale calf (a bit rubbed), covers decorated with blind trim within outer black border rule with small decorative gilt corner pieces, dark green morocco labels with gilt lettering and gilt rules on spines, raised band within gilt rules, decorative piece in blind within the panels, decorative gilt trim at top and bottom, inner dentelles finely tooled in gilt, outer dentelles ruled in gilt, marbled endpapers, a.e.g. A very handsome set bound by Baudry, with his ticket inside each front cover. Rare. Not in Kohler.

1829. THE POETICAL WORKS OF JOHN MILTON; Complete In One Volume. [Dryden epigram.] *London: Published By Jones & Company, No. 3, Warwick Square. 1823*. (Part of one-volume edition of "Jones's Cabinet Edition of Select British Poets, Vol. I Comprising The Works Of Milton, Cowper, Goldsmith, Thomson, Falconer, Akenside, Collins, Gray, & Somervile." Each section is individually paginated with its own independent title page and collation.) First edition thus. 12mo in 6s, vii+131pp.,+vi+114+[2]pp.,+20pp.,+iv+36pp.,+21pp.,+v+57pp.,+iv+14pp.,+vi+[1]+12pp.,+vi+21pp., small unsigned engraved frontispiece portrait of Milton within elaborate scrolled border trim, engraved and printed title pages, engraved title dated "May 1. 1825" at the bottom of the page, general engraved title page for "Jones's Cabinet Edition Of Select British Poets, Vol. 1. Comprising The Works Of Milton, Cowper, Goldsmith, Thomson, Falconer, Akenside, Collins, Gray & Somervile," with non-Miltonic vignette illustration after Corbould," "London, Printed for Jones & Co. 3. Acton Place, Kingsland Rd. University Edition. May 1. 1825," engraved title page for *PL* with unsigned vignette illustration of *Satan Taking His Flight*, "London: Published By Jones & Co.[,] 3, Warwick Square. 1823," protective tissue guard, engraved title page for "Paradise Regain'd and other Poems By John Milton," with unsigned vignette illustration of the Crucifixion scene, "London, Published By Jones & Co.[,] 3, Warwick Square. 1823" at bottom of page, protective tissue guard, printed in double column, original three-quarter calf (a bit rubbed), marbled paper over boards, gilt rules and gilt lettering on spine with small decorations in blind, raised bands. Milton's poetical works occupy the first third of the book with life by Fenton at the beginning and an index to *PL* at the end, each section thereafter is individually paginated with its own independent title page (except for Falconer) and collation, title pages variously dated 1823 and 1824, with frontispiece portrait for all but Falconer. A very nice copy with a four-line verse written in a contemporary hand on verso of Cowper title page. See variant edition following. A second edition thus was published in 1824; a third thus in 1825—both listed here. Scarce. Not in Kohler.

1830. Variant of Preceding. THE POETICAL WORKS OF JOHN MILTON; Complete In One Volume. [Dryden epigram.] *London: Published By Jones & Company, 3, Acton Place, Kingsland Road. 1823*. (Part of one-volume edition of "Jones's Cabinet Edition of Select British Poets, Vol. I Comprising The Works Of Milton, Cowper, Goldsmith, Thomson, Falconer, Akenside, Collins, Gray, & Somervile." Each section is individually paginated with its own independent title page and collation.) First edition thus. 12mo in 6s, vii+131pp.,+vi+114+[2]pp.,+20pp.,+iv+36pp.,+21pp.,+v+57pp.,+iv+14pp.,+vi+[1]+12pp.,+vi+21pp., unsigned engraved frontispiece portrait plate consisting of vignette portraits of Milton, Gray, Akenside, Goldsmith, and Thomson with Milton in the center, each portrait within elaborate decorative trim with lyre and laurel wreath at the bottom and floral trim beneath the whole ("London: Published by Jones & Co. March 20, 1824" at the bottom of the plate), protective tissue guard, printed in double column, original three-quarter calf (a bit rubbed), marbled paper over boards, gilt rules and gilt lettering on spine with small gilt decorations within the panels, raised bands with decorative gilt trim, marbled endpapers, t.e.g., others untrimmed. Very nice copy. Milton's poetical works occupy the first third of the book with life by Fenton at the beginning and an index to *PL* at the end, each section thereafter is individually paginated with its own independent title page and collation, title pages variously dated 1823 and 1824. While similar to the preceding edition, this edition differs substantially: with a different publisher's imprint on title page; and by not having (1) an engraved portrait of Milton; (2) a general engraved title page for the "Jones's Cabinet Edition Of Select British Poets;" (3) an engraved title page with vignette illustration for *PL*; and (4) an engraved title page with vignette illustration for *PR*. Scarce. Kohler 280, with publisher's address as here, describing its copy as "Octavo in 6s . . . Unsigned frontispiece portrait [presumably as with preceding copy]. General title-page dated 1824," and reporting "Not in Williamson. Not in the British Library. Not in the Bodleian Library. Not in Cambridge University Library."

1831. THE POETICAL WORKS OF JOHN MILTON. A New Edition. With The Life Of The Author, And Notes. In Two Volumes. Vol. I./II. *London: Printed For N. Hailes, Museum, Piccadilly; J. Bumpus, Holborn Bars; Andrews, New Bond Street; W. Charlton Wright, And J. Walker, Paternoster Row; And Griffin And Co., Glasgow. M.DCCC.XXIV.* 2 volumes. First edition thus? 12mo in 6s, xxiii+[i]+300pp.,vi+236pp., half-title each volume, frontispiece portrait of a middle-aged Milton "Engraved by Freeman" within an elaborate Victorian frame with "London. Published by John Bumpus, 1821" at the bottom, volume 1, unidentified frontispiece illustration labeled "Milton" after T. Stodhard engraved by R. Cooper with "London. John Bumpus, 1824" at the bottom, volume 2, title page each volume with same publisher's imprint dated 1824, "D. Cartwright, Printer, Bartholomew Close" on verso of each title page, "London: D. Cartwright, Printer, 91, Bartholomew Close" at bottom of last page each volume, contemporary crushed red morocco (a bit rubbed), covers delicately tooled with wide gilt borders, spines lettered and numbered in gilt, raised bands with gilt trim, richly decorated in gilt within the panels, inner and outer dentelles finely tooled in trim, charcoal gray endpapers, a.e.g. A fine set in rich contemporary red morocco, with large contemporary armorial bookplate on front pastedown of each volume. Scarce. Not in Kohler.

1832. THE POETICAL WORKS OF JOHN MILTON; To which is prefixed The Life Of The Author. *London: Printed For T. And J. Allman, Prince's Street, Hanover Square; And John Anderson, Jun. Edinburgh. 1824.* 12mo, xi+[1]+501pp., engraved frontispiece portrait "Engraved by Romney" "From an Impression of a Seal of T. Simon, in the possession of Mr. Yeo," engraved and printed title pages, unsigned engraved vignette illustration of *The Temptation of Eve* on engraved title with lines illustrated printed beneath, "London, Printed for T. & J Allman. Princes St. Hanover Sqe." printed at bottom of the page, emblem of the press on title page, half-titles for *PR*, *SA*, and *C*, "J. McGowan, Great Windmill Street" printed at bottom of last page, contemporary olive green morocco (a bit rubbed, light staining at outer front tips of frontispiece and engraved title), covers ruled in decorated inner blind trim and finely tooled outer gilt trim, spine richly decorated in gilt with a red morocco label lettered in gilt, inner and outer dentelles finely tooled in blind, marbled endpapers and edges. A handsome copy in a lovely Romantic morocco binding. See 1822 edition (possible first edition thus) listed here("London: Printed for T. and J. Allman" et al.) with further editions cited. Scarce. Not in Kohler.

1833. THE POETICAL WORKS OF JOHN MILTON, With Notes Of Various Authors, Principally from the Editions of Thomas Newton, D.D. Charles Dunster, M.A. And Thomas Warton, B.D. To Which Is Prefixed, Newton's Life Of Milton. By Edward Hawkins, M.A. Fellow Of Oriel College. *Oxford, Printed By W. Baxter, For J. Parker; And G. B. Whittaker, London. 1824.* 4 volumes. First edition thus. 8vo, 53+[1]+cxxxvi+[1]+430pp.,+620pp.,+vii+452pp.,+401pp., half-title each volume, folding "Fac Simile of part of Milton's Ode to Rouse from the Original in the Bodleian Library," volume 1, half-title for each book of *PL* and *PR* and for various of the works, copious notes at bottom of page, contemporary full Russia (a bit rubbed at joints, spines faded), covers ruled in gilt with decorative gilt border trim, spines decorated in gilt within the panels, raised bands, maroon morocco labels lettered and ruled in gilt, inner and outer dentelles trimmed in gilt, marbled endpapers and edges. A fine set with early presentation inscription (dated 1846) on front blank. Stevens 128.

1834. THE POETICAL WORKS OF JOHN MILTON; Complete In One Volume. [Dryden epigram.] *London: Published By Jones & Company, 3, Acton Place, Kingsland Road. 1824.* (Part of one-volume edition of "Jones's Cabinet Edition of Select British Poets: Volume I Comprising Milton, Cowper, Goldsmith, Thomson, Falconer, Akenside, Collins, Gray, and Somerville." Each section is individually paginated with its own independent title page and collation.) Second edition thus? 12mo in 6s, vii+131pp., +vi+114pp.,+[iv]+20pp.,+iv+36pp.,+[iv]+21pp.+v+[i]+56+[1]pp.,+iv+14pp.+vi+[i]+12pp.,+[1]+2+vi+21pp., engraved frontispiece portrait plate consisting of vignette portraits of Milton, Gray, Akenside, Goldsmith, and Thomson with Milton in the center, "London: Published by Jones & Co. March 20, 1824" at the bottom of the page, engraved and printed title pages, engraved title dated 1825, engraved title page for "Jones's Cabinet Edition Of Select British Poets, Comprising The Works Of Milton, Cowper, Goldsmith, Thomson, Falconer, Akenside, Collins, Gray & Somerville," "London, Printed for Jones & Co. 3, Acton Place, Kingsland Rd. University Edition. May 1, 1825" at the bottom of the page, with vignette illustration (not for Milton) after Corbould at center of engraved title, each section individually paginated with its own independent title page and collation, each title page dated 1825 (except Akenside, dated 1829), the title page for Milton's *PW* being the only one dated 1824, printed in double column, rebound in new black buckram (frontispiece and engraved title foxed), a.e.g. A good copy of an uncommon edition. Milton's poetical works occupy the first third of the book with the life by Fenton at the beginning and an index to *PL* at the end. Included before "The Chase By William Somerville" are two pages of advertisements for "Works Published By Jones And Company," advertising "The Drama, Or New British Theatre" (including Milton) and "To The Curious. The smallest and most beautiful Specimen of Miniature Publications ever printed; or The Diamond Poets" (including Milton in a collection of poets much like this one and individually in two volumes). The first edition thus was published in 1823 (see copy listed here with two engraved title pages for Milton, each with vignette illustration, and see variant copy of the first edition without engraved title pages); the third edition thus was published in 1825 (also listed here). Scarce. Kohler 282, reporting "Not in Williamson. Not in the British Library. Not in the Bodleian Library. Not in Cambridge University Library."

1835. [POETICAL WORKS] THE POETICAL WORKS OF JOHN MILTON; To which is prefixed the Life Of The Author. *London: Baynes and Son, Paternoster Row; Smith, Elder, and Co. Cornhill; J. Bain, Mews' Gate; William Mason, Pickett Street; T. Lester, Finsbury Place; J. Arnould, Spring Gardens; M. Iley, Somerset Street; R. Baynes, Paternoster Row; J. Hearne, Strand; J. F. Setchel, King Street; W. Booth, Duke Street; E. Wheatley, Leicester Square; R. Hoffman, Strand; H. Steel, Tower Hill; P. Write, Broad Street; H. Mozley, Derby; M. Keene, J. Cumming, C. P. Archer, and R. M. Tims, Dublin; and H. S. Baynes, Edinburgh. 1825.*

First edition thus? 12mo, iv+460pp., engraved frontispiece illustration plate for *Comus* (after Uwins engraved by Ranson), engraved and printed title pages with vignette illustration for *PL* (*Satan, Sin, and Death* after Uwins engraved by Ranson) on engraved title page, with publisher's imprint "For The Proprietors Of The English Classics" at the bottom of the engraved title, circular emblem at the center of the printed title page with crown at the top, crest at the center, and "Honi • Soit • Qui • Mal • Y • Pense" lettered around the crest, "Printed by J. F. Dove, St. John' Square" on verso of title page and at bottom of last page, contemporary diced calf (a little rubbed, library stamp on verso of title page, first few pages foxed and slightly embrowned, including frontispiece and engraved title page), orangish leather label on spine lettered and ruled in gilt, elaborately gilt decorated within the panels, slightly raised thick bands, marbled endpapers and edges. A nice copy. Scarce. Not in Kohler.

1836. THE POETICAL WORKS OF JOHN MILTON. With A Life Of The Author, By Elijah Fenton, And A Critique, By Samuel Johnson, LLD. In Two Volumes. *Glasgow: Printed By Robert Malcolm, Stanhope Press Office, Trongate. M.DCCC.XXV. (1825).* 2 volumes. First edition thus. 12mo in 6s, xx+304pp.,+317pp., half-title each volume, frontispiece portrait of Milton in a decorative frame "Engraved by Freeman," volume 1, engraved frontispiece illustration for Book XII of *PL* (*But Have I Now Seen Death*), "Garner fecit," volume 2, original boards, purple cloth spine (faded), printed paper labels, edges untrimmed. A very nice set, large paper copy, in original state. Not in Kohler.

1837. THE POETICAL WORKS OF JOHN MILTON; Complete In One Volume. [Dryden epigram.] *London: Published By Jones & Company[,] 3, Acton Place, Kingsland Road. 1825.* Third edition thus? 12mo in 6s, vii+131pp.,+vi+114pp.,+iv+20pp.,+iv+36pp.,+[iv]+21pp.,+2pp.,+v+[i]+56+[1]pp.,+2pp.,+iv+[i]+14pp.,+2pp.,+vi+[i]+12pp.,+2pp.,+vi+21pp.,+2pp., half-title ("[Jones's] Cabinet Poets"), printed in double column, contemporary calf (worn, lacking frontispiece plate with vignette portraits of the poets and engraved title page [see 1823 and 1824 editions listed here with both], front cover detached), covers ruled in gilt with thick decorated gilt border trim, spine originally decorated in gilt (now very worn), marbled endpapers and edges, with early ownership signature on title page and early bookplate on front pastedown. Milton's poetical works occupy the first third of the book with life by Fenton at the beginning and an index to *PL* at the end. Also included in the volume are (1) "Poems By William Cowper," (2) "The Poetical Works Of Oliver Goldsmith,"

(3) "The Seasons, A Poem, By James Thomson," (4) "The Shipwreck; A Poem, By William Falconer," (5) "The Poetical Works Of Mark Akenside," (6) "The Poetical Works Of William Collins," (7) "The Poetical Works Of Thomas Gray," and (8) "The Chase, And Other Poems, By William Somerville," each section individually paginated with its own independent title page and collation, each title page dated 1824, the title page for Milton being the only one dated 1825. Interspersed between several of the works is an advertisement page for "Works Published By Jones And Company, 3, Acton Place, Kingsland Road., London," advertising "The Drama, Or New British Theatre" (including Milton) and "To The Curious. The smallest and most beautiful Specimen of Miniature Publications ever printed; or The Diamond Poets" (including Milton in a collection of poets much like this one and individually in two volumes). See 1823 and 1824 (possible first and second Jones's Cabinet Poets) editions also listed here. Scarce. Not in Kohler.

1838. THE POETICAL WORKS OF JOHN MILTON. With Notes Of Various Authors. The Third Edition. With Other Illustrations; And With Some Account Of The Life And Writings Of Milton, Derived Principally From Documents in his Majesty's State-Paper Office, Now First Published. By The Rev. H. J. Todd, M.A.F.S.A. & R.S.L. Chaplain In Ordinary To His Majesty, And Rector Of Settrington, County Of York. In Six Volumes. *London: Printed For C. & J. Rivington, et al., And Saunders And Hodgson. 1826.* 6 volumes. Third Todd edition. 8vo, xxvii+[ii]+370+lxviipp.,+cxxxvi+535pp.,+527pp.,+501pp.,+xix+501pp.,+[iii]+517pp.,+[ii]+433pp.+[18 unpaginated "Glossarial Index"]+[6 unpaginated "Contents Of The Six Volumes"], frontispiece portrait plate engraved by T. A. Dean after a drawing by T. Simpson from William Baker's painting by Faithorne, dedication page, preface, "Some Account Of The Life And Writing Of Milton," "Appendix Containing An Inquiry Into The Origin Of Paradise Lost," facsimile plate (foxed), dated 1826, of Milton's signature and debt notice in his own hand in 1650, volume 1, separate title page each volume, half-title for each book of *PL* and for various of the works, unsigned engraved plate of Ludlow Castle before *C*, volume 5, engraved by T. Higham and dated 1826, engraved plate, "Fac-simile [sic] from the Original Drawing" of Queen Christina of Sweden in man's apparel, engraved by T. Higham, for the Latin epigram, XIII. "Ad Christinam Suecorum Reginam, nomine Cromwelli," "List Of Editions," and "Glossarial Index," volume 6, contemporary full blue morocco, covers and spines richly decorated in gilt, thick raised bands with decorative gilt trim, spines lettered in gilt, inner and outer dentelles finely tooled in gilt, a.e.g. A lovely set in a fine Regency binding, with early armorial bookplate on front pastedown of each volume. The first Todd edition was published in 1801; the second Todd edition, revised and expanded, in 1809; the fourth Todd edition—the last lifetime—in 1842; the fifth and final Todd edition in 1852—all listed here. The third Todd edition is a scarce set. Stevens 131; Williamson 152; Kohler 284, reporting "Not in Cambridge University Library."

1839. THE POETICAL WORKS OF JOHN MILTON. In Three Volumes. *London: William Pickering, Chancery Lane; Nattali And Combe, Tavistock Street; Talboys And Wheeler, Oxford. M.DCCC.XXVI.* 3 volumes. First Pickering edition. Small 8vo, lxviii+333pp.,+341pp.,+292pp., half-title each volume, printed title page each volume with central laurel wreath, "Thomas White, Printer, Johnson's Court. MDCCCXXV" with printer's device on verso of last page in volumes 1 and 2, index at the end of volume 3, original boards, printed paper labels on spines, edges untrimmed, contemporary signature (dated 1830) on flyleaf of each volume. A very fine set, possibly a large paper copy, in original boards, uncut, with original printed paper spine labels, with the Latin and Italian poems in William Cowper's translations, the life by Milton's nephew Edward Philips, and a substantial introduction by John Parkes (Keynes, *Pickering Check List*, p. 79). Stevens 130, indicating "text of Hawkey's (1757) Dublin edition"; Williamson 131; Kohler 283.

1840. Variant of Preceding, original publisher's crimson glazed muslin (spine chipped at top of volume 1), with original printer's paper spine labels, which differ from the original printed spine labels on preceding set, edges untrimmed, bound by Meehan, Bath, with his ticket. A nice set with bookplates (one belonging to Walter Blake) and several pasteins relating to Milton in volume 1. Possibly a large paper copy. "An attractive and uncommon edition" (Keynes, *Pickering Check List*, p. 79).

1841. Variant of Preceding, contemporary polished Russia (joints slightly cracked), gilt rules with finely tooled gilt corner pieces on covers, elaborately gilt-decorated spines, raised bands, inner and outer dentelles ruled in gilt, marbled endpapers, a.e.g. Presentation copy, inscribed by the editor Joseph Parkes to Chandos Leigh on half-title, volume 1, and restated at top of title page, volume 1, with a three-page hand-written letter from Parkes to Leigh, signed by Parkes, bound in at the beginning of volume 1. The Leigh bookplate is tipped in on front pastedown of each volume. A fine set with a very nice association.

1842. THE POETICAL WORKS OF JOHN MILTON, Printed From The Text Of Todd, Hawkins And Others;

450 ❦ THE ROBERT J. WICKENHEISER COLLECTION OF JOHN MILTON AT THE UNIVERSITY OF SOUTH CAROLINA

PW. London, 1826. 6 volumes. Third Todd Edition. 8vo, contemporary full blue morocco. A lovely set in a fine Regency binding. See #1838.

PW. London: William Pickering, 1826. 3 volumes. First Pickering edition. Small 8vo, contemporary polished Russia. Presentation copy, inscribed by the editor, Joseph Parkes, to Chandos Leigh, volume 1, with a three-page hand-written letter from Parkes to Leigh, signed by Parkes, bound in at the beginning of volume 1, with Leigh bookplate in each volume. See #1841.

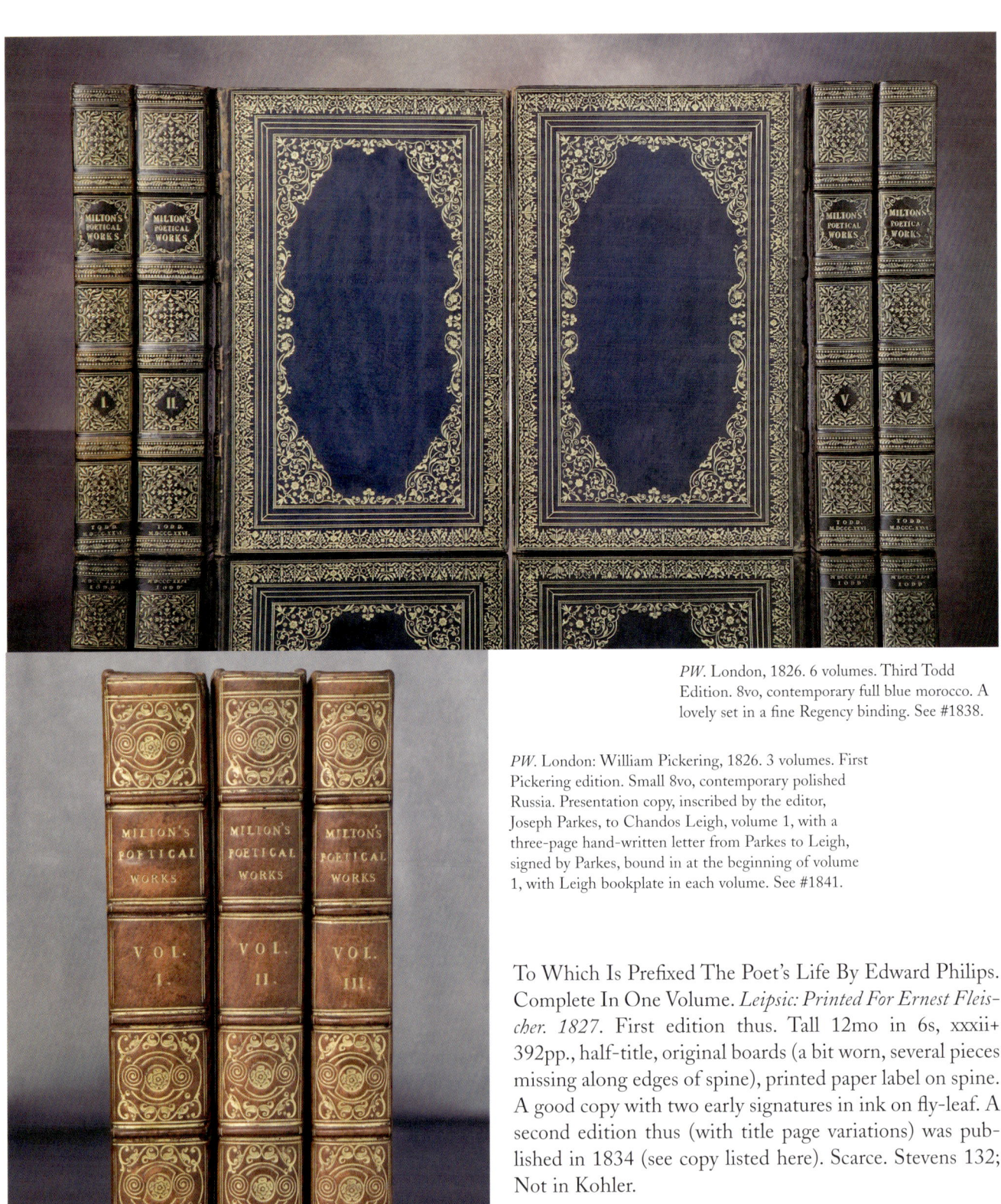

To Which Is Prefixed The Poet's Life By Edward Philips. Complete In One Volume. *Leipsic: Printed For Ernest Fleischer. 1827*. First edition thus. Tall 12mo in 6s, xxxii+ 392pp., half-title, original boards (a bit worn, several pieces missing along edges of spine), printed paper label on spine. A good copy with two early signatures in ink on fly-leaf. A second edition thus (with title page variations) was published in 1834 (see copy listed here). Scarce. Stevens 132; Not in Kohler.

1843. **THE POETICAL WORKS OF JOHN MILTON.** To Which Is Prefixed, The Life Of The Author. *London: Printed For Booksellers. 1829*. First edition thus? Small 8vo in 4s and 8s, xiii+488pp., unsigned engraved frontispiece illustration of *Adam and Eve in the Garden*, labeled "Milton" with "London. Published by Thomas Tegg. No. 111. Cheapside. Oct. 26, 1814" printed at the bottom, unsigned

"Biographical Preface," half-title for *PL*, *PR*, *SA*, and *C*, "G. Love & Co. Printers, Glasgow" at bottom of last page, original green cloth (a little worn, small white spot on front cover, occasional light foxing), paper label (a bit faded) on spine, edges untrimmed. All in all, a nice copy of an uncommon edition. Scarce. Not in Kohler.

1844. THE POETICAL WORKS OF JOHN MILTON, To Which Is Prefixed, The Life Of The Author. *London: Printed For T. & J. Allman, 55, Great Queen Street, Lincoln's Inn Field; And G. Love & Co. Glasgow. 1829.* Small 8vo in 4s and 8s, xiii+[3]+488pp., half-title with contemporary signature (dated 1831) on verso, unsigned engraved frontispiece illustration of *Adam and Eve in the Garden*, labeled "Milton" with "London. Published by Thomas Tegg. No. 111. Cheapside. Oct. 26, 1814" printed at the bottom, "Biographical Preface" (unsigned), half-title for *PL*, *PR*, *SA*, and *C*, "G. Love & Co. Printers, Glasgow" at bottom of last page, later white leather or kid (front cover and spine a bit soiled with page endings a little grubby in the beginning), spine lettered in gilt, raised bands, later blue marbled endpapers, small bookseller's label in burgundy and gold on front pastedown, t.e.g. All in all, a nice copy of an uncommon edition. See 1822 edition (possible first edition thus) listed here ("London: Printed for T. and J. Allman" et al., in 12mo and with different illustrations) with further editions cited. Scarce. Not in Kohler.

1845. THE POETICAL WORKS OF JOHN MILTON. *London: Engraved For The English Classics. Published By Thomas Johnson. Manchester. n.d. [ca. 1830].* 2 volumes in one. First edition thus? Small 8vo, [ii]+335pp.,+334pp., engraved frontispiece portrait by Romney, undated engraved title page with unsigned engraved illustration for *PL*, Book V (*Raphael Counseling Adam and Eve*), perhaps lacking printed title page, unsigned headpiece illustration with lines illustrated quoted beneath: for each book of *PL*, for each book of *PR*, for *SA*, for *C*, half-title for *PL*, each book of *PL*, each book of *PR*, *SA*, *C*, *L'A IlP*, *Ar*, *S*, *O*, *Misc.*, *Trans.*, "Psalms," "Elegies," and "Encomiums Upon Milton," original brown cloth (a bit rubbed, possibly lacking printed title page and perhaps even a title page for volume 2, occasional foxing throughout, including frontispiece and engraved title page), covers decorated in embossed trim in blind with small illustration in gilt (a little faded) at center of front cover (perhaps of Raphael seated), spine elaborately decorated in gilt with gilt lettering, a.e.g. A good copy of an uncommon edition. Scarce. Not in Kohler.

1846. THE POETICAL WORKS OF MILTON, YOUNG, GRAY, BEATTIE, AND COLLINS. Complete In One Volume. Stereotyped By J. Crissy And G. Goodman. *Philadelphia: John Grigg, No. 9. North Fourth Street. 1831.* First edition thus by Grigg. Thick 8vo, xxxii+170pp.,+viii+208pp.,+x+47pp.,+ix+23pp.,+iv+19pp., +[3]pp., frontispiece plate with vignette portrait of each poet engraved by J. B. Longacre (with Milton at the top), half-title for Milton and for each collection of poetical works with contents on verso, life of Milton and of each poet, printed in double column, contemporary full black morocco (joints and edges rubbed, foxing), elaborate decorative gilt border trim on covers, gilt-decorated spine, raised bands, inner and outer dentelles tooled in gilt, marbled endpapers, a.e.g. A very nice copy in a fine early nineteenth-century American binding, with three pages of advertisements bound in at the end. Scarce. Not in Kohler.

See other editions by Grigg in the collection: 1832 edition (second thus), and 1836 and 1839 editions; and see other editions by Grigg and Elliot in the collection: 1841 edition (possible first edition thus by Grigg and Elliot), 1843 edition and 1847 edition (perhaps the last edition by Grigg & Elliot, with two illustration plates for Milton, possibly the first time these plates were included in the edition); see also 1850 edition by "Lippincott, Grambo & Co., Successors To Grigg, Elliot & Co." with the same two illustration plates for Milton as in the 1847 edition and other editions by Lippincott, Grambo & Co.: in 1852, 1853, and 1854 (with two unsigned illustration plates bound within Milton); and other editions by Lippincott & Co.: in 1856 and 1857.

1847. THE POETICAL WORKS OF JOHN MILTON; To which is prefixed, The Life Of The Author. *London: Printed For Longman, Rees, Orme, Brown, And Green; T. Cadell; J. Richardson; R. Scholey; Baldwin And Cradock, J., G., And F. Rivington; A. K. Newman, And Co.; Wittaker, Treacher, And co.; T. Tegg; Sherwood And Co; J. Duncan; Simpkin And Marshall; J. Souter; W. Mason; Black, Young, And Young; Parkury, Allen, And Co.; Cowie And Co.; T. And Boosey; Poole And Edwards; And J. Nunn. 1832.* 12mo in 6s, xi+[1]+551pp., frontispiece illustration for Book XI of *PL* by T. Uwins engraved by C. Warren ("Printed for F. C. & I. Rivington and the other proprietors Septr. 1822"), engraved and printed title pages with vignette illustration for Book II of *PR* by T. Uwins engraved by C. Warren on engraved title ("London Printed for F. C. & I. Rivington & the other proprietors Septr. 1822"), both illustrations engraved on steel plates as identified on each plate, half-title for each book of *PL* and *PR* and for various of the works, contemporary full green morocco (a little rubbed along joints and extremities), gilt rules on covers, elaborately gilt-decorated spine, maroon morocco label with gilt lettering, thick raised bands within finely tooled decorative gilt trim, inner and outer dentelles finely tooled in gilt, marbled endpapers and edges. A handsome copy in an attractive morocco binding of the period. See 1822 edition with different publisher's imprint but the same frontispiece illustration after T. Uwins and the same engraved title page with vignette illustration after T. Uwins. Uncommon. Not in Kohler.

1848. MILTON'S POETICAL WORKS. *[New-York: Printed And Published By J. H. Turney No. 133 East Broadway. 1832].* 2 volumes in one. 12mo, 283pp.+[2 blanks]+215pp., engraved title page for each volume of *PW*, each engraved title page without publisher or date, each with a vignette illustration "Drawn by R. Westall, Engr'd by A. B. Durand," with the lines illustrated quoted beneath each illustration (for Book X, line 940, of Adam and Eve repenting, on the first engraved title page, and for Book III, line 667, "Brightest Seraph tell . . . ," on the second engraved title page), printed title page for "Paradise Lost. A Poem In Twelve Books. By John Milton. New-York: Printed And Published By J. H. Turney No. 133 East Broadway. 1832," a second printed title page for "Paradise Regained; And Other Poems, By John Milton. New-York: Printed And Published By J. H. Turney, 133 East Broadway. 1832," life of Milton by Fenton before *PL*, index to *PL*, volume 1, contents after printed title page for volume 2, followed by "A Critique On *PR*," with half-titles for *C* and *SA*, in that order following *PR*, contemporary calf (a little worn, lacking front endpaper, several early names on front blank and title page, library "Due Date" slip tipped on back fly-leaf, which is reinforced at the joint, slight foxing variously throughout), covers finely tooled in blind, spine lettered and elaborately decorated in gilt (now faded). All in all, a nice, tall copy. A different edition from the following edition, for reasons cited there. Uncommon. Not in Kohler.

See 1831 edition (possible first edition thus) of *PL* by Turney with the same illustration on the engraved title page as that here but without being bound with *PR* and the other poems as here; see also 1832 edition (possible second edition thus) of *PL* by Turney, a variant of this edition, with engraved frontispiece portrait and an engraved title page with a different illustration on the engraved title page from that here, bound with *PR* and the other poems as here, although, unlike here, with an engraved frontispiece portrait and a different vignette illustration on engraved title page.

1849. MILTON'S POETICAL WORKS., Consisting Of Paradise Lost, Paradise Regained, Mask Of Comus, Samson Agonistes, And Poems On Several Occasions, &c. &c. Together With The Life Of The Author. In Two Volumes.—Vol. One / Vol. Two. *New-York: Printed And Published By J. H. Turney, 133 East-Broadway. MDCCCXXXII.* 2 volumes in one. 12mo in 6s, 321pp.(engraved plates unpaginated),+[2 blanks]+232pp.(engraved plates unpaginated), printed title page for each volume of Milton's *PW*, engraved title page for each volume (both bound before volume 1), each engraved title with a vignette illustration "Drawn by R. Westall, Engr'd by A. B. Durand," with the lines illustrated quoted beneath each illustration (for Book X, line 940, of Adam and Eve repenting, on the first engraved title page, and for Book III, line 667, "Brightest Seraph tell . . . ," on the second engraved title page), frontispiece portrait "Engraved by M. Pekenino N.York" with "New York Published by J.H Turney, 1832" at bottom of the page, engraved illustration for *NO* by R. Westall engraved by Peter Maverick before printed title page for *PW*, volume 2, life of Milton by Fenton, volume 1, half-title for each book of *PL*, contents after printed title page for volume 2, with half-title for *C* and *SA*, in that order following *PR*, contemporary calf (worn, covers detached, spine cracked and partially missing at top and bottom, foxing), black leather label lettered and ruled in gilt on spine. Except for the binding (now very poor), a good copy within. A different edition from the preceding edition: published as *PW*: different pagination; lines unnumbered; half-title for each book of *PL*, no index to *PL* at the end of volume 1; no "Critique On *PR*" before the poem in volume 2; unlike the preceding edition, this edition does not have a printed title page for *PL* in volume 1 and for *PR* in volume 2, but rather a printed title page for *PW* in each volume; and along with the engraved title pages found in the preceding edition, this edition also includes a frontispiece portrait and an illustration before volume 2 that are not included in that edition. See 1831 edition of *PL* by Turney, with the same illustration on the engraved title page as that here; see also 1832 edition of *PL* by Turney, a variant of the preceding edition, with engraved frontispiece portrait different from that here and with a different illustration on the engraved title page from that here. Scarce. Not in Kohler.

1850. THE POETICAL WORKS OF JOHN MILTON[.] *London[:] William Pickering[,] 1832.* 3 volumes. Second Pickering edition; first Aldine edition. Small 8vo, xx+cxxxiv+[4]+[1]+153pp.,+372pp.,+iv+334pp., half-title ("The Aldine Edition Of The British Poets") for each volume, first appearance of engraved frontispiece portrait by H. Robinson, volume 1, dated "London, William Pickering, 1831," separate title page each volume with anchor emblem of the Pickering Press on each title page, twenty-page "Advertisement" by the editor John Mitford dated 1831, life of Milton by Mitford, followed by addenda and appendix, volume 1, half-title for some of the poems, anchor emblem of the Pickering Press on the last leaf of volume 3, printed by Charles Whittingham, original blue cloth, printed paper labels (worn) on spines, edges untrimmed. A nice set, large paper copy in original publisher's binding, from Pickering's distinguished Aldine series of British poets, edited by Mitford, with advertisement leaf for "Pickering's Aldine Poets" tipped in volume 1 (not always found). In 1832 Pickering began to use the familiar anchor and dolphin emblem employed by the Aldus family of Venetian printers in the sixteenth century, and he had the same purpose behind his work as did his Aldine predecessors: to provide the public with well-printed texts that were nevertheless obtainable even by a person of modest means. A short while before, in 1830, Pickering began publishing his famous "Aldine Poets" series, a project that covered more than twenty years and involved the production of fifty-three volumes, all well-printed and carefully edited by a reputable scholar. The prototype for this set was the first edition by Parkes in 1826, printed by Pickering; Aldine editions followed in 1832 (the first Aldine edition here, with the first appearance of Milton portrait after Robinson), then in 1834 (the second Aldine edition), in 1839 (the third Aldine edition), in 1845 (the fourth Aldine edition), in 1851 (the fifth Aldine edition), and in 1852 (the sixth and final Aldine edition)—all listed here. The 1832, 1845, and 1851 Aldine editions are the only editions to have the anchor emblem of the Pickering Press on the last leaf of volume 3. Williamson 10, commending the fine engraving of the 1831 frontispiece portrait; Stevens 133; Not in Kohler.

1851. THE POETICAL WORKS OF MILTON, YOUNG, GRAY, BEATTIE, AND COLLINS. Complete In One Volume. Stereotyped By J. Crissy And G. Goodman. *Philadelphia: John Grigg, No. 9. North Fourth Street. 1832.* Second edition thus by Grigg. Thick 8vo, [8]+xxxii+170pp.,+viii+208pp.,+x+47pp.,+ix+23pp.,+iv+19 pp., similar to 1831 edition (possible first edition thus) preceding, frontispiece plate with vignette portrait of each poet engraved by J. B. Longacre (with Milton at the top), protective tissue guard (foxed), half-title for Milton and for each collection of poetical works with contents on verso, life of Milton and of each poet, printed in double column, eight pages of "Valuable Works, Published By J. Grigg, Philadelphia" bound before title page, contemporary polished calf (bit worn, joints weak, some foxing), gilt rules on covers, gilt decorated spine, black leather labels with gilt lettering, outer dentelles trimmed in gilt at the corners, marbled endpapers and edges. Despite some age and wear, a good copy with bookplate on front pastedown. See 1831 first edition thus by Grigg listed here with further editions cited. Scarce. Not in Kohler.

1852. THE POETICAL WORKS OF JOHN MILTON: To Which Is Prefixed, A Biographical Sketch Of The Author, By Henry William Dewhurst, Esq., Surgeon; Professor of Anatomy and Zoology; Author of "The Natural History of the Order Cetacea," "A Dictionary of Anatomy," &c. ; and Fellow of several Learned Societies. Magnet Edition. *London: William Mark Clark, 19, Warwick Lane, Paternoster Row; And All Booksellers. 1833.* First edition thus? Small 8vo, xxiv+524pp., engraved frontispiece portrait of a long-haired middle-aged Milton within a decorative border frame with Milton's name beneath (the whole being 2 ¾" × 3 ¼", placed in the middle of the page), with "Engraved by W. T. Page for 'The Magnet Edition of British Poets' "Published by William Mark Clark. 1833" at the bottom of the page, "London: Printed by Thomas Foale, 2, Upper Southampton St., Pentonville" on verso of title page, dedication page (To Sir Arthur Brooke by H. W. Dewhurst), unsigned vignette illustration of the expulsion at the end of Book XII, "T. Foale, Printer, Upper Southampton Street, Pentonville" printed at the bottom of the last page, contemporary diced calf (very light waterstain at upper inner joint, traces of age wear and slight discoloration to the leather), gilt rules on covers, spine richly decorated in gilt within the compartments, thick black lines separating the compartments, Milton's name in gilt, decorative gilt trim at the top and bottom. A handsome copy with early signature (dated 1857) on front pastedown. Scarce. Not in Kohler.

1853. THE POETICAL WORKS OF JOHN MILTON. With A Life Of The Author. *Edinburgh: Thomas Nelson & Peter Brown. 1834.* First edition thus? 16mo, 228pp., unsigned engraved frontispiece portrait of a middle-aged Milton (the portrait measures 2" × 1 ¾" with a ¼" border trim, with contemporary library ownership and number above in ink), original three-quarter calf, marbled paper over boards (worn, signature sprung, some occasional embrowning), black morocco label with gilt lettering and gilt rules on spine, small decorative pieces in blind within the panels. All in all, a decent copy of an uncommon edition, with notes in a very neat early hand in ink on front and rear blanks and occasionally in margins throughout. Scarce. Not in Kohler.

1854. THE POETICAL WORKS OF JOHN MILTON. A New Edition, With Notes, And A Life Of The Author [By John Mitford]. *Boston: Hilliard, Gray And Company. 1834.* 2 volumes. First edition thus by Hilliard Gray and Company. 8vo in 4s, cxxix+[2]+371pp.,+ii+478pp., frontispiece portrait plate "Engraved by O. Pelton From a Miniature of the same size by Faithorne, Anno 1667, in the possession of William Falconer Esq. Boston Published by Hilliard Gray & Co.," volume 1, protective tissue guard, title page each volume, "Sonnet To Charles Lord Bishop Of Winchester On His Publication Of Milton De Doctrina" dated 1831 on leaf before original eighteen-page advertisement by John Mitford, and life of Milton by Mitford followed by addenda and an appendix, volume 1, half-title for some of the poems, notes at bottom of page, half brown leather, printed marbled paper over boards (rubbed along extremities, corners chipped, library stamp on each title page, library bookplate on front pastedown of each volume stamped "Withdrawn," shelf label on spine, "For Reference" label on front cover of each volume), spines lettered and ruled in gilt. A rather uncommon early American edition of Milton's *PW*. Scarce. Kohler 286, reporting "Not in Williamson. Not in the British Library. Not in the Bodleian Library. Not in Cambridge University Library."

See Stevens's note with 1834 third Pickering edition of Milton's *PW*, indicating that this is a reprint of the 1834 Pickering edition, as are the other editions of Milton's *PW* by Hilliard, Gray and Company here. The second edition by Hilliard, Gray and Company was published in 1836, the third in 1838; the fourth in 1839; the fifth in 1841—all listed here; and see 1845 two-volume edition of Milton's *PW* published by Little and Brown, a reprinting of this edition by Hilliard, Gray, and Company.

1855. THE POETICAL WORKS OF JOHN MILTON, Printed From The Text Of Todd, Hawkins And Others. A New Edition Complete In One Volume. With The Poet's Life By Edward Philips. *Leipsic: Printed For Ernest Fleischer. 1834.* Second edition thus. Tall 12mo (4 ¼" × 8 ¼"), xxxii+392pp., half-title, small emblem at center of title page, life by Edward Philips, contemporary three-quarter brown calf, marbled paper over boards (a bit rubbed, corners a little bumped), spine lettered in gilt with intricately tooled gilt trim at top and bottom, raised bands with decorative gilt trim. A very nice copy with inscription in pencil on fly-leaf: "Given to me in East Berlin by Dr. Elisabeth Richter-Heinrich. 1964. Denis Leigl." The first edition thus (with title page variation) was published in 1827 (also listed here). Scarce. Not in Kohler.

1856. THE POETICAL WORKS OF JOHN MILTON[.] *London[:] William Pickering[,] 1834-1835.* 3 volumes. Third Pickering edition; second Aldine edition. Small 8vo, xx+cxxxiv+[4]+153pp.,+372pp.,+334pp., edited by John Mitford with a life of Milton, half-titles ("The Aldine Edition Of The British Poets"), engraved frontispiece portrait by H. Robinson, volume 1, dated 1831, separate title page each volume with anchor emblem of the Pickering Press on each title page, volumes 1 and 2 title pages dated 1834, volume 3 title page dated 1835, life of Milton by Mitford followed by addenda and appendix, volume 1, half-title for some of the poems, notes to the text, printed by Charles Whittingham, contemporary maroon morocco (bit rubbed at joints, slight waterstaining bottom half of frontispiece, title page, and back endpapers of volume 1), spines lettered in gilt (a bit faded), raised bands (a bit rubbed), inner and outer dentelles finely tooled in gilt, a.e.g. A nice set with the bookplate of "Howard Anthony Pickering" and another early armorial bookplate in each volume. A nicely bound copy from Pickering's distinguished Aldine series of British poets. The first Aldine edition of Milton appeared in 1832 (with the first appearance of Milton's portrait after Robinson, dated 1831), see set listed here with further Aldine editions of Milton cited there; see also commentary provided with 1832 Aldine edition. This 1834 Aldine edition appears to be fairly uncommon; it is not listed by Keynes in his checklist of Pickering editions. Kohler 285, citing Williamson 76, which describes its set, as with Kohler's set, as having volume 1 title page dated 1839, volume 2 title page dated 1834, and volume 3 title page dated 1835, observing that "No Milton of any of these dates is listed in Keynes," and reporting "Not in the British Library." Stevens 137, observing, "Reprinted in Boston by Hilliard, Gray & Co., 1834, 1836, 1838, 1839, 1841" (see set by Hilliard, Gray & Co. listed here for reference to each of these editions in the collection).

1857. THE POETICAL WORKS OF JOHN MILTON. Edited By Sir Egerton Brydges, Bart. With Imaginative Illustrations By J. M. W. Turner, Esq., R.A. In Six Volumes. *London: John Macrone, St. James's Square, 1835.* 6 volumes. First edition thus. 8vo, 303pp.,+340pp.,+310pp.,+320pp.,+332pp.,+352pp., half-title ("The Poems Of John Milton") in volumes 1, 3, 4, and 6, substantial life of Milton comprising the whole of volume 1, engraved frontispiece portrait plate engraved by W. C. Edwards after Vertue and engraved illustration plate of *Mustering of the Warrior Angels* (*PL*, Book II) engraved by R. Brandard after J. M. W. Turner, volume 1, engraved frontispiece portrait plate engraved by W. C. Edwards after G. Romney and engraved illustration plate of *The Expulsion from Paradise* (*PL*, Book XII) after Turner (engraver unsigned), volume 2, engraved frontispiece illustration plate of Satan engraved by R. Graves after R. Westall and engraved illustration plate of *The Fall of the Rebel Angels* (*PL*, Book VI) engraved by E. Goodall after Turner, volume 3, engraved frontispiece portrait plate engraved by W. C. Edwards after Jansen and engraved illustration plate of *The Temptation on the Mountain* (*PR*, Book III) engraved by J. Cousen after Turner, volume 4, engraved frontispiece illustration

PW. Edited By Sir Egerton Brydges, Bart. With Imaginative Illustrations By J. M. W. Turner. London, 1835. 6 volumes, original publisher's green cloth. First edition thus, with first appearance of Turner's illustrations. [With] Separate twenty-three pages of advertisements for publications by Macrone, with title page for this edition, with vignette portrait of Milton on title. See #1857.

plate of *L'Allegro* (*L'A*) engraved by F. Bacon after R. Westall and engraved illustration plate of *Ludlow Castle—Rising of the Water Nymphs* (*C*) engraved by E. Goodall after Turner, volume 5, engraved frontispiece illustration plate of *St. Michael's Mount. Shipwreck of Lycidas* (*L*) engraved by W. Miller after Turner, volume 6, protective tissue guard between each set of plates, 16pp. of advertisements bound in at end of volume 1, "Notices" leaf with selected reviews bound in at end of volume 3, original publisher's green cloth, contemporary dated signature on flyleaf, volume 1. A fine set with the first appearance of the illustrations by J. M W. Turner. Uncommon in fine original publisher's cloth binding. Together with twenty-three pages of advertisements for present and forthcoming publications by Macrone, 8vo, with title page consisting of Brydges's 1835 six-volume edition here: *The Life And Poetical Works Of John Milton* with vignette portrait of Milton on title, along with other advertisements, disbound, edges untrimmed. Rather uncommon in such a fine original publisher's binding, as this set is; acquired from my bookseller friend Basil Savage in London in 1975; the advertisements were a gift from Michael Papantonio of Seven Gables Bookshop a short while later. Williamson 30 (observing that the portrait in volume 4 is not after Jansen, but would appear to be based on the Nuneham painting owned by Speaker Onslow); Bland, p. 249; Stevens 138; Kohler 287.

1858. THE POETICAL WORKS OF JOHN MILTON. In Two Volumes. Vol. I. / Vol. II. *London: Allan Bell And Co., Warwick Square; And H. Washbourne, Salisbury Square. MDCCCXXXVI.* 2 volumes. First edition thus? Small 8vo (miniature size: 4" × 2 ½"), 335pp.,+334pp., title page in red and black for each volume, decorated half-title for each book of *PL*, each book of *PR*, *SA*, and *C*, each half-title elaborately decorated in lightly tinted purple trim in a classical motif with "Illustrated British Classics" in a scroll at the top, three small figures within a circle above the scroll, and the date 1836 at the bottom, each decorated half-title followed by a vignette illustration in the same lightly tinted purple color of the half-title decoration at the top of the page immediately following with the lines illustrated quoted below, with unsigned vignette illustrations in lightly tinted purple for each book of *PL*, each book of *PR*, *SA*, and *C*, undecorated half-titles for *L*, *L'A*, *IlP*, *Ar*, *S*, *O*, *Misc.*, *Anno Aetatis XIX*, *Trans*, *Psalms*, *Elegies*, and *Encomiums Upon Milton*, original ribbed green cloth (a little rubbed), each cover decorated with a large emblem in gilt, spines similarly decorated with a gilt emblem incorporating volume number in gilt and gilt lettering ("Milton" with "British Authors" in smaller lettering in a scroll above), a.e.g. A nice set of an uncommon early nineteenth-century edition with vignette illustrations apparently designed for this edition in the "Illustrated

British Classics" / "British Authors" series. See 1837 two-volume edition here with title pages printed in red and black as here, but with half-titles undecorated and vignette illustrations untinted; see also 1840 two-volume edition here, bound as two volumes in one, with title pages printed in black only, and with half-titles undecorated and vignette illustrations untinted. Rare. Not in Kohler.

1859. THE POETICAL WORKS OF JOHN MILTON. *London: Frederick Westley And A. H. Davis. Stereotyped And Printed By J. R. And C. Childs. MDCCCXXXVI.* 8vo, 192pp., with the twenty-four small mezzotint plates designed and engraved by John Martin for *Paradise Lost* (a number of the plates have "J. Martin 1826" printed in white on the plate), printed in double column, contemporary half calf, marbled paper over boards (foxing, slight water staining at top of first third of book, inoffensive and without affecting the text), gilt-decorated spine, red morocco label, raised bands, marbled endpapers, a.e.g. Other than the slight staining and foxing, a very good copy of an uncommon edition, most likely with a set of Martin's small plates inserted during the binding process. Martin's celebrated illustrations for *PL* were first issued in twelve parts by Septimus Prowett between 1825 and 1827; they were published by Prowett in an edition of *PL*, in four different formats, in 1827; subsequently Charles Tilt published the "second" edition in 1833 (see also 1838 reissue by Tilt)—all listed here. Kohler 289, noting 192 pp., as here, but without the Martin plates and with a frontispiece portrait engraved by Edwards after Vertue; the Kohler copy is bound with *The Prose Works of John Milton*; With An Introductory Review, By Robert Fletcher. London: William Ball, 1838 (see copy of this edition of *The Prose Works* with prose editions listed here); Kohler also reports "Not in the British Library. Not in the Bodleian Library. Not in Cambridge University Library."

1860. THE POETICAL WORKS OF JOHN MILTON; With A Memoir; And Six Embellishments, By Fuseli, Westall, And Martin. *London: Edward Churton, 26, Holles Street. 1836.* First edition thus by Churton. 8vo in 4s, vii+[1]+527pp., half-title ("Churton's British Poets. First Series."), life of Milton, six illustration plates after Fuseli (one plate), Westall (two plates), and Martin (three plates), half-titles, nineteenth-century three-quarter brown morocco, marbled paper over boards (a bit rubbed), spine lettered in gilt, raised bands, marbled endpapers, t.e.g. A very nice copy, fresh and clean within. Laid in: some clippings from the *Times* and one other newspaper regarding a newly discovered poem by Milton; the poem is printed in the article and the date is July 28, 1868; also laid in is a hand-written note to William Dyce (whose copy this was, with name in pencil on verso of fly-leaf), neatly written in ink and dated "The Rectory, 8 Sun. of Trin—1847" (about the time of the binding). Scarce. Kohler 288, with frontispiece portraits, perhaps added, engraved by Edwards after Vertue and Jansen, reporting "Not in Williamson. Not in the British Library. Not in the Bodleian Library. Not in Cambridge University Library."

A second edition by Churton was published in 1838 (copy listed here), with "Six Embellishments" printed on title page; a third edition by Churton was published in 1840 (copy listed here), with the first appearance of "Seven Embellishments" printed on title page (referring to the portrait and six plates); a similar edition was first published by Chidley in 1841 (copy listed here) and again in 1842, 1845, 1846, and in 1847 (all listed here); a new edition was first published by Bohn in 1848 and again in 1852 and in 1855 (all listed here); see also edition by Robert John Bush in 1867 "Embellished With Engravings After Designs By Fuseli, Westall, And Martin" (also listed here).

1861. THE POETICAL WORKS OF JOHN MILTON: To Which Is Prefixed The Life Of The Author, Together With Dr. Channing's Essay On The Poetical Genius Of Milton[.] *London: T. Allman. 42, Holborn Hill. MDCCCXXXVI.* 12mo, xxiv+420pp., engraved frontispiece illustration of *Satan Rallying His Troops* within a delicately designed elaborate frame with "Page & Son Sculp." at the bottom just beneath the frame, engraved and printed title pages with an engraved vignette illustration of *Satan on the Burning Lake* on engraved title page, with publisher's imprint: "London. Thos. Allman. 42, Holborn Hill. 1836," all within a border rule, and "Page & Son, sc." at the bottom just beneath the border rule, "W. Lewis And Son, Printers, 91 Finch-lane, London" on verso of title page, life of Milton, Dr. Channing's Essay, half-title for *PR*, *SA*, and *C*, "Printed by W. Lewis, 21, Finch-lane, London" at bottom of last page, original green cloth (a bit rubbed, a little worn along back joint, a small spot on front cover, slight spotting on back cover, earlier name on front pastedown), spine elaborately decorated in gilt with title lettered in gilt and just beneath, also in gilt: "Price 4 & 6D," a.e.g. A nice copy, fresh and clean throughout. See 1822 edition (possible first edition thus) listed here ("London: Printed for T. and J. Allman" et al.) with further editions cited. Not in Kohler.

1862. Variant of Preceding, original brown cloth (a bit rubbed, back joint cracked), covers decorated in blind with large central emblem in blind, spine lettered in gilt, edges untrimmed. A tall, large paper copy, with variant printer's address on verso of title page: "W. Lewis, Printer, Finch-lane, London," untrimmed, in a variant publisher's binding. Not in Kohler.

1863. THE POETICAL WORKS OF MILTON, YOUNG, GRAY, BEATTIE, AND COLLINS. Complete In One Volume. Stereotyped By J. Crissy And G. Goodman. *Philadelphia: John Grigg, No. 9. North Fourth Street. 1836.* Third edition thus by Grigg? 8vo, [8]+xxxii+170pp.,+viii+208pp.,+x+ 47pp.,+ix+ 23pp.,+iv+19pp., similar to 1831 edition (possible first edition thus), frontispiece with vignette portrait of each poet engraved by J. B. Longacre (with Milton at the top), protective tissue guard (foxed), half-title for Milton and for each collection of poetical works with contents on verso, life of Milton and of each poet, printed in double column, eight pages of "Valuable Works, Published By J. Grigg, Philadelphia" bound before title page, contemporary brown calf (worn), gilt rules on covers, gilt-decorated spine (faded), black morocco labels, gilt dentelles (faded), marbled endpapers and edges. Though worn, an okay copy of a nicely printed early nineteenth-century American edition. See 1831 edition (first thus) by Grigg also listed here with further editions by Grigg; by Grigg and Elliot; and by their successors cited. Scarce. Not in Kohler.

1864. THE POETICAL WORKS OF JOHN MILTON. With Notes, And A Life Of The Author [By John Mitford]. A New Edition. *Boston: Hilliard, Gray, And Company. 1836.* Second edition thus. 2 volumes. 8vo in 4s, cxxix+[2]+371pp.,+ii+478pp., frontispiece portrait plate "Engraved by O. Pelton From a Miniature of the same size by Faithorne, Anno 1667, in the possession of William Falconer Esq.," volume 1, protective tissue guard, title page each volume with anchor emblem of the Pickering Press on each title page, "Freeman And Bolles, Washington Street" on verso of title page each volume, thirteen-page advertisement by John Mitford with the original date of 1831, and life of Milton by Mitford followed by addenda and an appendix, volume 1, half-title for some of the poems, notes at bottom of page, original lavender cloth with slightly raised floral decorations (a bit rubbed, some fading), spines lettered in gilt within gilt rules with anchor emblem of the Pickering Press in gilt at bottom of each spine, edges untrimmed. A very good set. A rather uncommon early nineteenth-century American edition of Milton's *PW*, especially in such fine condition. The first edition thus was published in 1834 (also listed here with further editions cited). Scarce. Not in Kohler.

1865. THE POETICAL WORKS OF JOHN MILTON. In Two Volumes. Vol. I. / Vol. II. *London: Allan Bell And Co., Warwick Square; T. Tegg And Son; And H. Washbourne [sic]. T. T. And H. Tegg, Dublin. MDCCCXXXVII.* 2 volumes. Small 8vo (miniature size: 4" × 2 ½"), 335pp.,+334pp., title page in red and black for each volume, small unsigned vignette illustration at the outset of each book of *PL* and each book of *PR*, and at the outset of *SA* and *C*, with the line illustrated quoted beneath, half-title for each book of *PL* and for various of the other poems, original embossed calf (worn, spine missing, volume 1, partially missing, volume 2, covers sometime reattached with library tape, early names in each volume), a.e.g. See 1836 two-volume edition listed here (possible first edition thus) with title pages in red and black, where half-titles are elaborately decorated in lightly tinted purple trim, and each vignette illustration is tinted in the same lightly tinted purple color of the half-titles; see also 1840 two-volume edition listed here, bound as two volumes in one, with title pages printed in black only, and, as here, with half-titles undecorated and vignette illustrations untinted. Scarce. Not in Kohler.

1866. THE POETICAL WORKS OF JOHN MILTON: To Which Is Prefixed, The Life Of The Author. *London: Printed For Thomas Tegg And Son, 73, Cheapside; B. Griffin And Co., Glasgow; T. T. And H. Tegg, Dublin; Also, J. And S. A. Tegg, Sydney And Hobart Town. MDCCCXXXVII.* First edition thus by Tegg; first Tegg illustrated edition? 12mo in 6s, xi+576pp., unsigned vignette illustration on title page, contemporary calf (a bit worn), gilt rules on covers, red morocco label with gilt lettering and gilt trim, raised bands with decorative gilt trim, outer dentelles tooled in gilt, marbled endpapers and edges. A good copy of a very scarce book. The vignette illustration depicts Michael and his angels expelling Adam and Eve from the Garden of Eden. The final several leaves include "Commendatory Verses On Milton" by various poets. Scarce. Kohler 291, describes its copy as "Octavo in 6s," reporting "Not in the British Library. Not in the Bodleian Library. Not in Cambridge University Library."

Other editions published by Tegg (with varying addresses) in the collection include: 1839 Tegg illustrated edition; 1840 Tegg nonillustrated edition; 1841 Tegg illustrated edition; 1842 Tegg illustrated edition; a second 1842 Tegg illustrated edition (Edited By Sir Egerton Brydges, Bart.) A New Edition, being the second Brydges/Turner edition; 1843 and 1844 Tegg illustrated editions; 1845 Tegg nonillustrated edition; 1846 Tegg illustrated edition; 1847 Tegg illustrated edition; 1848 Tegg illustrated edition, being the third Brydges/Turner edition; 1849 Tegg illustrated edition; 1851 Tegg nonillustrated edition; 1853 Tegg illustrated edition, being the fourth Brydges/Turner edition; 1855 Tegg illustrated edition; 1858 Tegg illustrated edition; and 1862 Tegg illustrated edition, being the fifth Brydges/Turner edition.

1867. THE POETICAL WORKS OF JOHN MILTON: To Which Is Prefixed, The Life Of The Author. *London: Printed For C. Daly. 14, Leicester Street, Leicester Square. 1836.* Small 8vo (miniature size, measuring 4 ¼" × 2 ¾"), x+479pp., unsigned engraved frontispiece portrait, engraved title page with lyre at the center and with publisher's imprint: "London. Charles Daly. 14, Leicester St Leicester Sq: 1837," three pages of "Commendatory Verses On Milton" at the end, original tan pebble cloth (a bit faded), spine decorated in gilt with gilt lettering, a.e.g. Nice little copy, very clean inside. See 1838 edition by Charles Daly ("Leicester Street, Leicester Square"); see, too, undated 1839 edition by Charles Daly ("19, Red Lion Square"), each with unsigned vignette illustration of Satan on engraved title page; see also undated ca. 1850 edition by Charles Daly listed here with other editions by Daly cited. Scarce. Kohler 290, describing its copy as "24mo in 8s" and reporting "Not in Williamson. Not in the British Library. Not in the Bodleian Library. Not in Cambridge University Library."

1868. THE POETICAL WORKS OF JOHN MILTON: To Which Is Prefixed The Life Of The Author. *London: Printed for Longman, Orme, and Co.; T. Cadell; Baldwin and Cradock; J. G. And F. Rivington; Newman and Co.; Whittaker and Co.; Sherwood and Co.; T. Tegg and Son; J. Duncan; Simpkin, Marshall, and Co.; J. Souter; Black and Armstrong; W. H. Allen and Co.; Cowie and Co.; W. Edwards; and J. Wacey. 1838.* 12mo, xi+[i]+551+[1]pp., frontispiece illustration plate for the line: ("He ended and the Arch Angel soon drew nigh," *PL*, Book XI), "Steel Plate" engraved by C. Warren after T. Uwins, engraved and printed title pages, with vignette illustration for *NO*, "Steel Plate" engraved by C. Warren after T. Uwins, on engraved title, "London[:] "Printed for J.G&F. Rivington & the other proprietors" at bottom of engraved title page, half-title for each book of *PL* and for some of the poems, "London: Printed by Manning and Mason, Ivy Lane, Paternoster Row" on verso of last page, contemporary polished green calf (a bit rubbed at joints), gilt rules on covers, gilt-decorated spine, red morocco label with gilt lettering, raised bands with decorative gilt trim, outer dentelles finely tooled in gilt, marbled endpapers and edges. A nice copy with contemporary inscription (dated 1848) on fly-leaf. Not in Kohler.

1869. THE POETICAL WORKS OF JOHN MILTON; With A Memoir: And Six Embellishments, By Fuseli, Westall, And Martin [And Turner]. *London: Edward Churton, 26, Holles Street. 1838.* Second edition thus by Churton? 8vo in 4s, vii+527pp., frontispiece portrait plate engraved by W. C. Edwards after Vertue with protective tissue guard, two additional portraits, portrait plate "Engraved By J. Cochran From A Miniature Painted By Mr. Samuel Cooper, Painter To Oliver Cromwell, And Originally In The Possession Of Milton's Daughter Deborah," with protective tissue guard, before "The Life Of John Milton," and portrait plate engraved by W. C. Edwards after Cornelius Jansen (Aet. XXI) together with portrait plate of *Milton Dictating to His Daughters* engraved by W. C. Edwards after G. Romney within the life, fifteen illustration plates (despite mention of "Six Embellishments" only on title page) after Fuseli (one plate), Westall (four plates), Martin (three plates), and Turner (seven plates), half-title for each book of *PL* and for some of the poems, original three-quarter red calf, marbled paper over boards (a bit rubbed, plates foxed), green morocco label with gilt lettering, gilt rules on spine, raised bands with decorative gilt trim, marbled edges. A nice copy, handsomely bound by "Birdsall Northampton," with their stamp. Extra-illustrated with portraits and with plates by Turner. The first edition thus was published by Churton in 1836 (also listed here with further editions cited). Scarce. Not in Kohler.

1870. THE POETICAL WORKS OF JOHN MILTON: To Which Is Prefixed, The Life Of The Author. *London: Printed For C. Daly, Leicester Street, Leicester Square. 1838.* Small 8vo (miniature in size, measuring 4" × 2 ¾"), x+479pp., unsigned frontispiece portrait plate, undated engraved title page with unsigned vignette illustration of Satan, simply titled *PL* beneath and with publisher's imprint ("London. Charles Daly. 14, Leicester St Leicester Sq. 1838"), half-title for *PL*, three pages of "Commendatory Verses On Milton" at the end, original three-quarter dark green leather (a little rubbed at the joints and corners), marbled paper over boards (slightly scuffed, occasional foxing), spine ruled and lettered in gilt within decorative gilt trim, small decorative pieces in blind within the panels, lightly marbled edges, small bookplate on front pastedown. A nice little copy that has survived in very good condition. See 1836 edition by Charles Daly listed here with further editions by Daly cited. Scarce. Not in Kohler.

1871. THE POETICAL WORKS OF JOHN MILTON. With Notes, And A Life Of The Author [By John Mitford]. A New Edition. *Boston: Hilliard, Gray, And Company. 1838.* Third edition thus. 2 volumes. 8vo in 4s, cxxix+[2]+371pp.,+ii+478pp., frontispiece portrait plate "Engraved by O. Pelton From a Miniature of the same size by Faithorne, Anno 1667, in the possession of William Falconer Esq.," volume 1, protective tissue guard with imprint of frontispiece portrait, title page each volume with anchor emblem of the Pickering Press on each title page, "Cambridge: Folson, Wells, And Thurston, Printers To The University" on verso of title page each volume, thirteen-page advertisement by John Mitford, with the original date of 1831, and life of Milton by Mitford followed by addenda and an appendix, volume 1, half-title for some of the poems, notes at bottom of page, original blue-green cloth, spines lettered in gilt within gilt rules with anchor emblem of the Pickering Press in gilt at bottom of each spine, edges untrimmed, the second volume wholly unopened. A very attractive set in original binding. The first edition thus was published in 1834 (also listed here with further editions cited). Uncommon. Not in Kohler.

1872. THE POETICAL WORKS OF JOHN MILTON: To Which Is Prefixed, The Life Of The Author. *London: Printed For Thomas Tegg, 73, Cheapside; Tegg And Co., Dublin; R. Griffin And Co., Glasgow; And J. And S. A. Tegg, Sydney And Hobart Town. MDCCCXXXIX.* Second edition by Tegg; second Tegg illustrated edition? Tall 12mo in 6s, xi+576pp., frontispiece portrait engraved by W. C. Edwards after George Vertue, portrait plate engraved by W. C. Edwards after Cornelius Jansen (Aet. XXI) inserted before life, along with portrait plate of *Milton Dictating to His Daughters* engraved by W. C. Edwards after G. Romney, seven illustration plates engraved by various engravers after J. M. W. Turner, two illustration plates engraved by R. Graves and by F. Bacon after R. Westall, each with protective tissue guard, contemporary full embossed maroon morocco (joints a bit rubbed, some foxing), covers decorated in gilt and ruled in blind, ornately gilt-decorated spine with gilt lettering, a.e.g. A very nice copy in a lovely binding of the period. The final several leaves include "Commendatory Verses On Milton" by various poets. See 1837 first illustrated edition by Tegg also listed here with further editions cited.. Scarce. Kohler 293, citing Williamson 135, "where there is no printer's imprint on this item," and reporting "Not in the British Library. Not in the Bodleian Library. Not in Cambridge University Library."

1873. THE POETICAL WORKS OF JOHN MILTON. Complete In One Volume. *New-York: Published By Charles Wells. 1839.* 2 volumes in one. First edition thus? Large 12mo in 6s, 283pp.,+215pp., unsigned engraved frontispiece portrait of Milton within elaborately decorative frame, engraved and printed title pages, unsigned vignette illustration of Satan on undated engraved title with the lines illustrated quoted beneath ("Then with expanded wings he takes his flight / Aloft incumbent on the dusky air"), life of Milton by Fenton, "Index To PL" at the end of the poem, volume 1, separate title page for *PR* ("PR; And Other Poems, By John Milton. New-York: Published By Charles Wells"—undated), followed by "Contents" and "A Critique On PR," half-title for *C* ("A Mask") and *SA*, volume 2, contemporary calf (a little worn, spine ends chipped, front cover detached, some embrowning, name in ink on title page and stamped on early blank), red morocco label with gilt lettering and gilt rules on spine, raised bands in between gilt rules, marbled endpapers and edges, in a protective plastic cover. Although the binding is worn, still a good copy of a scarce early nineteenth-century American edition. Not in Kohler.

See dated 1840 illustrated edition (possible second edition thus) by Wells also listed here, with the same frontispiece portrait and the same undated engraved title page as here; see also undated variant illustrated editions by Wells published about this same time (ca. 1840) one with the same frontispiece portrait and the same undated engraved title page as here. See, too, 1839 edition (possible first edition thus), 1840 edition (possible second edition thus), 1841 edition (possible third edition thus), and 1842 edition (possible fourth edition thus) of *PL* published by Charles Wells ("New–York. Charles Wells"); see also 1840 edition (possible first edition thus) of *PR, C, SA,* and *OP* published by Charles Wells ("New–York: Published By Charles Wells")—all listed here.

1874. MILTON'S POETICAL WORKS. With his Life. *London. Charles Daly. 19, Red Lion Square. [1839].* Small 8vo (miniature in size, 4" × 2 ½"), x+479pp., unsigned frontispiece portrait plate, undated engraved title page unsigned with vignette illustration of Satan (possibly after Westall), printed title page for *PL* with the same publisher's imprint as that on engraved title except for a colon after "London" and being dated 1839, three pages of "Commendatory Verses On Milton" at the end, original green ribbed cloth (light wear, small lighter stain on front cover, early dated signature in pencil on front pastedown), spine decorated and lettered in gilt, a.e.g. A nice copy of this charming miniature edition. See 1836 edition by Charles Daly listed here with further editions cited. Scarce. Not in Kohler (but see Kohler 310, dating its copy 1846: "London: Charles Daly. 19, Red Lion Square. [1846]," without mention of a dated title page for *PL* as here.)

1875. THE POETICAL WORKS OF JOHN MILTON[.] *London[:] William Pickering[,] 1839.* 3 volumes. Third Aldine edition. Small 8vo, cxxxiv+xx+153pp., +372pp.,+334pp., edited by John Mitford with a life of Milton, half-title ("The Aldine Edition Of The British

Poets") each volume, engraved frontispiece portrait by H. Robinson, dated "London, William Pickering, 1831," volume 1, separate title page each volume with anchor emblem of the Pickering Press on each title page, original "Advertisement" for the 1832 Aldine edition by John Mitford with original date of 1831, life of Milton by Mitford followed by addenda and appendix, volume 1, half-title for some of the poems, printed by Charles Whittingham, notes at bottom of page, contemporary green diced calf, gilt rules on covers, gilt-decorated spines, red morocco labels with gilt lettering, raised bands, outer dentelles finely tooled in gilt, marbled endpapers, a.e.g., with armorial bookplate of Viscount Falmouth. A very lovely set, clean and fresh internally, handsomely bound, from Pickering's distinguished Aldine series of British poets, a run of fifty-three different volumes, all well printed and well edited, begun in 1830 and continuing for two decades. The first Aldine edition of Milton appeared in 1832 (with the first appearance of Milton portrait after Robinson), see set listed here with further Aldine editions of Milton cited. The 1839 Aldine edition appears to be fairly uncommon; it is not listed by Keynes in his checklist of Pickering editions. Not in Kohler.

1876. THE POETICAL WORKS OF MILTON, YOUNG, GRAY, BEATTIE, AND COLLINS. Complete In One Volume. Stereotyped By J. Crissy And G. Goodman. *Philadelphia: John Grigg, No. 9. North Fourth Street. 1839.* Fourth edition thus? 8vo, [8]+xxxii+170pp.,+viii+208pp.,+x+47pp.,+ix+23pp.,+iv+19pp., similar to 1831 edition (possible first edition thus), frontispiece with vignette portrait of each poet engraved by J. B. Longacre (with Milton at the top), protective tissue guard (foxed), half-title for Milton and for each collection of poetical works with contents on verso, life of Milton and of each poet, printed in double column, eight pages of "Valuable Works, Published By J. Grigg, Philadelphia" bound before title page, original speckled calf (worn, some foxing, front blank torn), gilt rules on spine (faded), slight raised bands, leather label, gilt dentelles (faded), marbled endpapers and edges, early bookplate. Uncommon early nineteenth-century American edition of Milton's *PW*. See 1831 edition (first thus) by Grigg listed here with further editions by Grigg; by Grigg and Elliot; and by their successors. Not in Kohler.

1877. THE POETICAL WORKS OF JOHN MILTON. With Notes, And A Life Of The Author [By John Mitford]. A New Edition. *Boston: Hilliard, Gray, And Company. 1839.* 2 volumes. Fourth edition thus. 8vo, cxxix+[2]+371pp.,+ii+478pp., frontispiece portrait plate "Engraved by O. Pelton From a Miniature of the same size by Faithorne, Anno 1667, in the possession of William Falconer Esq.," volume 1, protective tissue guard (with imprint of frontispiece portrait), anchor emblem of the Pickering Press on each title page, "Cambridge: Folson, Wells, And Thurston, Printers To The University" on verso of title page each volume, twelve-page advertisement by John Mitford, dated 1831, and life of Milton by Mitford followed by addenda and an appendix, volume 1, half-title for some of the poems, notes at bottom of the page, rebound in brown buckram (new endpapers, foxing throughout), original maroon morocco labels with gilt lettering and gilt rules on spines. A good set with contemporary signature, "Jno. N. Washington, Yale '39." The first edition thus was published in 1834 (also listed here with further editions by Hilliard, Gray, and Company cited). Kohler 294, reporting that this edition is "Not in Williamson. Not in the British Library. Not in the Bodleian Library. Not in Cambridge University Library."

1878. THE POETICAL WORKS OF JOHN MILTON; With A Memoir; And Seven Embellishments, By Fuseli, Westall, And Martin. *London: Edward Churton, 26, Holles Street. 1840.* Third edition thus by Churton? 8vo in 4s, vii+[1]+527pp., engraved frontispiece portrait plate "Engraved By J. Cochran From A Miniature Painted By Mr. Samuel Cooper, Painter To Oliver Cromwell, And Originally In The Possession Of Milton's Daughter Deborah," six illustration plates after Fuseli (one plate), Westall (two plates), and Martin (three plates), protective tissue guard for frontispiece and each illustration, life of Milton, half-title for each book of *PL* and for some of the poems, contemporary full black morocco, gilt-decorated covers and spine, a.e.g. Presentation binding by B. West, St. James Walk, Clerkenwell, with his stamp and with presentation inscription (dated April 1840) on preliminary blank. A fine copy with early armorial bookplate and the bookplate of Leonard Schlosser. First appearance of "Seven Embellishments" on title page, which refers to the portrait and six plates. The first edition thus was published by Churton in 1836 (also listed here), with "Six Embellishments" printed on title page, and see other editions by Churton and by Chidley and by Bohn cited there. Kohler 296, referencing Williamson 218–21 and reporting "Not in Williamson. Not in the British Library. Not in the Bodleian Library. Not in Cambridge University Library."

1879. THE POETICAL WORKS OF JOHN MILTON In Two Volumes. Vol. I/II. *London: Allan Bell And Co., Warwick Square. MDCCCXL.* 2 volumes in one. Small, thick 8vo, (miniature size: 4" × 2 ½"), 335pp.,+332pp., title page each volume, small unsigned vignette illustration at the outset of each book of *PL* and *PR*, and at the outset of *SA* and *C*, with the line illustrated quoted beneath, half-title for each book of *PL* and *PR* and for the some of the poems, original calf (a bit worn, covers detached), covers decorated in gilt (faded), spine lettered and decorated in gilt (faded). See 1836 two-volume edition (possible first edition thus), with title pages printed in red and black, where half-titles are elaborately decorated in lightly tinted purple trim in a classical motif, and each vignette illustration is tinted in the same lightly tinted purple color of the half-titles; see also 1837 two-volume edition with title pages printed in red and black, but, as here, with half-titles undecorated and vignette illustrations untinted. Scarce. Not in Kohler.

1880. THE POETICAL WORKS OF JOHN MILTON. *[London:] Joseph Smith, 193, High Holborn, n.d. [ca. 1840].* 12mo, x+[ii]+501+[1]pp., unsigned engraved frontispiece portrait of a middle-aged Milton within a moderately elaborate frame, engraved title page with unsigned vignette illustration of the temptation of Eve with only the printer's address printed at the bottom of the page, "Biographical Preface" signed "Z," half-title for *PR*, *SA*, and *C*, original half calf, marbled boards (worn, frontispiece and engraved title loose at the bottom, frontispiece with a small inoffensive waterstain at bottom inside margin, engraved title a little embrowned), thick raised bands with gilt trim, maroon leather label lettered in gilt. The frontispiece portrait is from this period. A solid copy with later signature (dated 1855) on fly-leaf. Advertisement on verso of last page for "A Catalogue Of Books Published By J. Smith." Scarce. Not in Williamson. Kohler 298, without mentioning frontispiece portrait or engraved title with illustration, reporting "Not in the British Library. Not in the Bodleian Library. Not in Cambridge University Library."

1881. THE POETICAL WORKS OF JOHN MILTON. Complete In One Volume. *New-York: Charles Wells, 56, Gold-Street. 1840.* 2 volumes in one. Second edition thus? Large 12mo in 6s, 283pp.,+215pp., unsigned engraved frontispiece portrait of Milton within elaborately decorative frame, engraved and printed title pages, unsigned vignette illustration of Satan on engraved title, undated, with the lines illustrated quoted beneath ("Then with expanded wings he takes his flight / Aloft incumbent on the dusky air"), life of Milton by Fenton, "Index To PL" at the end of the poem, volume 1, separate title page for *PR* ("Paradise Regained; Comus, A Mask; Samson Agonistes, And Other Poems, By John Milton. New-York: Published By Charles Wells. 1840"), followed by "Contents" and "A Critique On PR," half-title for *C* ("A Mask") and *SA*, volume 2, modern half calf, marbled paper over boards, black label with pastedown. A good copy of a scarce early nineteenth-century American edition. See dated 1839 illustrated edition (possible first edition thus) by Wells also listed here, with the same frontispiece portrait and the same undated engraved title page as here, and other editions by Charles Wells cited there. Not in Kohler.

1882. THE POETICAL WORKS OF JOHN MILTON. Complete In One Volume. *New-York: Published By Charles Wells, 56 Gold-Street. n.d. [ca. 1840].* 2 volumes in one. Large 12mo in 6s, 283pp.,+215pp., unsigned engraved frontispiece portrait of Milton within elaborately decorative frame, engraved and printed title pages, unsigned vignette illustration of Satan on engraved title, undated, with the lines illustrated quoted beneath ("Then with expanded wings he takes his flight / Aloft incumbent on the dusky air"), life of Milton by Fenton, "Index To Paradise Lost" at the end of the poem, volume 1, separate title page for *PR* ("Paradise Regained; And Other Poems By John Milton. New-York: Published By Charles Wells"—undated), followed by "Contents" and "A Critique On PR," half-title for *C* ("A Mask") and *SA*, volume 2, contemporary black calf (worn and faded, joints cracked, name torn away from top of engraved title page, age-browning and foxing, early twentieth-century inscription on front blank), decorated in blind, spine lettered in gilt, lightly marbled edges. A decent copy. See dated 1839 illustrated edition (possible first edition thus) by Wells listed, with the same frontispiece portrait and the same undated engraved title page as here, and other editions by Charles Wells cited there. Not in Kohler.

1883. THE POETICAL WORKS OF JOHN MILTON. Complete In One Volume. *New-York: Published By Charles Wells. n.d. [ca. 1840].* 2 volumes in one. Large 12mo in 6s, 283pp.+[2],+215pp., engraved frontispiece illustration for *L'A* with lines illustrated quoted beneath and wrong page reference, engraved and printed title pages with unidentified and unsigned vignette illustration of a reclining figure under a tree and another figure in the background moving away on undated engraved title page, life of Milton by Fenton, "Index To PL" at the end of the poem, volume 1, separate title page for *PR* ("Paradise Regained; And Other Poems, By John Milton. New-York: Published By Charles Wells. n.d. [ca. 1840]), followed by "Contents" and "A Critique On *PR*," contemporary brown leather (a bit rubbed, slight foxing throughout), covers decorated with embossed impression of a cathedral in blind, spine lettered in gilt with a continuation of embossed impression of a cathedral in blind, a.e.g. A good copy of a scarce early nineteenth-century American edition. See dated 1839 illustrated edition (possible first edition thus) by Wells also listed here with further editions by Charles Wells cited. Scarce. Not in Kohler.

1884. MILTON'S POETICAL WORKS, Consisting Of Paradise Lost, Paradise Regained, Mask Of Comus, Samson Agonistes, And Poems On Several Occasions, &c. &c. Together With The Life Of The Author. Complete In One Volume. *New-York: Published By Charles Wells. n.d. [ca. 1840].* 2 volumes in one. 12mo in 6s, 321pp.,+[5]+232pp., engraved frontispiece illustration for Book I of *PL* engraved by A. Dirk (with "book" and "page" reference cited beneath illustration), engraved and printed title pages, with unsigned vignette illustration of Satan with "book" and "page" reference cited beneath illustration on engraved title page, undated, protective tissue guard, life of Milton by Fenton, half-title for each book of *PL*, blank page between volumes, "Contents" at the beginning of volume 2, half-title for *C* (following *PR*) and for *SA*, contemporary red pebble leather (foxing throughout, occasionally heavy), covers embossed in decorative blind trim with a gilt fleurs-de-lis in each corner and a large bright gilt design at the center consisting of a harp on a stand with intertwining ivy at the bottom, cupid with quiver pointing a finger on each side, and a peacock with fanned tail at the top, spine lettered in gilt, thick raised bands decorated in gilt trim, outer dentelles finely tooled in gilt, a.e.g. A nice copy in a splendid early nineteenth-century American leather binding. See dated 1839 illustrated edition (possible first edition thus) by Wells listed here with further editions by Charles Wells cited there. Scarce, especially in a such a fine binding as this. Not in Kohler.

1885. Variant of Preceding, with variant engraved frontispiece illustration (for *L'A* rather than for Book I of *PL*) in each instance with the lines illustrated printed beneath; with contemporary signature (dated 1840) at top of printed title page here; with variant engraved title page with variant vignette illustration: an unidentified and unsigned vignette illustration of a reclining figure under a tree and another figure in the background moving away on engraved title page, compared to *Satan Rallying His Troops* in Book I, each engraved title undated. Scarce. Not in Kohler.

1886. THE POETICAL WORKS OF JOHN MILTON; To Which Is Prefixed, The Life Of The Author. *London: Printed For Thomas Tegg, 73, Cheapside; MDCCCXL.* Third edition by Tegg? 12mo in 6s, xi+576pp., contemporary full red morocco (a bit rubbed at joints and edges, lacking front fly-leaf), gilt-decorated covers and spine, raised bands, a.e.g. A fine copy. The final several leaves include "Commentary Verses On Milton" by various poets. There are no illustrations here, unlike the other editions by Tegg, nor do any appear to be missing. It is unclear if this is the first edition published by Tegg purposefully without illustrations and without any portrait plates, or if this copy was simply bound without any illustrations. This is the first Tegg edition with the name of "Thomas Tegg" only in the publisher's imprint on title page: "Printed for Thomas Tegg, 73, Cheapside." See 1837 first illustrated edition by Tegg also listed here with further editions cited there. Not in Kohler.

1887. THE POETICAL WORKS OF JOHN MILTON. *London: Published By W. Smith, 113, Fleet Street; MDCCCXL.* 2 volumes in one. First edition thus 8vo, 79pp.,+vi+163pp.(continuous pagination), two general title pages, with "London: Bradbury And Evans, Printers, Whitefriars" on the verso of each title page and at the bottom of the last page, half-title for *PL* and *PR* and *OP*, printed in double column, double black rule around text. While bound within a collection of three other poems, interestingly, Milton's *PW* is broken into two distinct volumes here with a general title page for each, but with continuous pagination, "Contents" pages bound after second general title page. Scarce. Kohler 297, reporting "Not in British Library. Not in the Bodleian Library. Not in Cambridge University Library." This applies only to Milton's *Poetical Works*, not to the other works that happen to be bound with Milton's *PW*. In this case the text belongs here. Bound with **POEMS** By Samuel Rogers. *London: Edward Moxon, Dover Street. M.DCCC.XXXIX.* Bound with **ITALY**, A Poem, By Samuel Rogers. *London: Edward Moxon, Dover Street. MDCCCXL.* Bound with **FESTUS** A Poem By Philip James Bailey[.] *London[:] William Pickering 177 Piccadilly[,] 1848.* 8vo, 48pp.,+79pp.,+vi+163pp.(continuous pagination),+56pp.,+100pp.+[6]pp. of "Notices And Literary Opinions" regarding *Festus*, contemporary green calf (worn along joints and extremities, with a small piece missing at lower right corner of spine), decorative gilt border trim on covers, raised bands within gilt rules, dark maroon label with gilt lettering and decorative gilt trim, marbled endpapers, lightly marbled edges, early owner's stamp on front blank and bookplate on front pastedown.

1888. THE POETICAL WORKS OF JOHN MILTON; With A Memoir; And Seven Embellishments, By Fuseli, Westall, And Martin. *London: J. J. Chidley, 123, Aldersgate Street. 1841.* First edition by Chidley? 8vo in 4s, vii+[1]+527pp., engraved frontispiece portrait plate "Engraved By J. Cochran From A Miniature Painted By Mr. Sam Cooper, Painter To Oliver Cromwell, And Originally In The Possession Of Milton's Daughter Deborah," ("London: E. Churton, 26 Holles Street" printed at the bottom), life of Milton, six illustration plates after Fuseli (one plate), Westall (two plates), and Martin (three plates), half-title for *PL* and for each book, for *PR* and for each book and for some of the poems, "Woking: Printed And Stereotyped By B. Bensley, From Bolt Court, Fleet Street" printed at bottom of last page, contemporary three-quarter polished purple morocco (a bit worn, especially corners and spine, foxing), dark blue pebble cloth, spine lettered in gilt within double gilt rules. A good copy of a scarce edition. Kohler 302, citing Williamson 219 and reporting "Not in the British Library. Not in the Bodleian Library. Not in Cambridge University Library."

Also in the collection and listed here: the first edition thus, the basis for this edition published by Churton in 1836; a second edition by Churton published in 1838, both the first and second editions each with "Six Embellishments" printed on title page; a possible third edition by Churton published in 1840, with the first appearance of "Seven Embellishments" printed on title page, referring to the portrait and six plates; a possible second edition by Chidley published in 1842; a possible third edition by Chidley published in 1845; a possible fourth edition by Chidley published in 1846; and a possible fifth edition by Chidley published in 1847; similar editions were also published by Bohn in 1848, 1852, and 1855.

1889. THE POETICAL WORKS OF JOHN MILTON; To Which Is Prefixed, The Life Of The Author. *London: Printed for Thomas Tegg, 73, Cheapside. MDCCCXLI.* Fourth edition by Tegg? Tall 12mo in 6s, xi+576pp., frontispiece portrait engraved by W. C. Edwards after Vertue, portrait plate engraved by W. C. Edwards after Cornelius Jansen (Aet. XXI) inserted before life, along with portrait plate of *Milton Dictating to His Daughters* engraved by W. C. Edwards after G. Romney, seven illustration plates engraved by various engravers after J. M. W. Turner, two illustration plates engraved by B. Graves and by F. Bacon after R. Westall, contemporary full purple morocco, central gilt emblem on covers, gilt-decorated spine, a.e.g. A fine, tall copy with prize citation (dated 1841) tipped in on front pastedown. The final several leaves include "Commendatory Verses On Milton" by various poets. See 1837 first illustrated edition by Tegg also listed here with further editions cited. Not in Kohler.

1890. THE POETICAL WORKS OF JOHN MILTON. In Two Volumes. *London: William Smith, 113, Fleet Street. MDCCCXLI.* 2 volumes. 8vo, xxviii+273pp.,+vii+208pp., half-title each volume ("Smith's Souvenir Edition. Milton's Poems"), the possible first appearance of frontispiece illustration plate engraved by H. G. Watkins for *PL* (Book IX), volume 1, the possible first appearance of frontispiece illustration plate engraved by H. G. Watkins for *C*, volume 2, printer's device with initials "WS" on each title page, half-title for each book of *PL* and for some of the poems, contemporary black morocco (a bit rubbed at joints), covers elaborately decorated in gilt, spines finely tooled in gilt with gilt lettering and numbers, slight raised bands, a.e.g. A lovely set. Scarce. Kohler 299, reporting "Not in the Bodleian Library. Not in Cambridge University Library."

1891. THE POETICAL WORKS OF MILTON, YOUNG, GRAY, BEATTIE, AND COLLINS. Complete In One Volume. Stereotyped By J. Crissy And G. Goodman. *Philadelphia: Grigg & Elliot, No. 9 North Fourth Street. 1841.* Fifth edition thus; first edition thus by Grigg & Elliot. 8vo, [8]+xxxii+170pp.,+viii+208pp.,+x+47pp.,+ix+23pp.,+iv+19pp., similar to 1831 edition (first thus), frontispiece with vignette portrait of each poet engraved by J. B. Longacre (with Milton at the top), half-title for Milton and for each collection of poetical works with contents on verso, life of Milton and of each poet, printed in double column, original calf (bit rubbed, spine slightly chipped at top, occasional foxing), gilt rules on spine around slight raised bands, brown leather label with gilt lettering and gilt rules, marbled endpapers and edges. A very nice copy. See 1831 edition (first thus) by Grigg with further editions cited. Not in Kohler.

1892. THE POETICAL WORKS OF JOHN MILTON. With Notes, And A Life Of The Author [By John Mitford]. A New Edition. *Boston: Hilliard, Gray, And Company. 1841.* 2 volumes. Fifth edition thus. 8vo, cxxix+[2]+371pp.,+ii+478pp., frontispiece portrait plate "Engraved by O. Pelton From a Miniature of the same size by Faithorne, Anno 1667, in the possession of William Falconer Esq.," volume 1, protective tissue guard with imprint of frontispiece portrait, anchor emblem of the Pickering Press on each title page, "Cambridge: Folson, Wells, And Thurston, Printers To The University" on verso of title page each volume, twelve-page advertisement by John Mitford (dated 1831), and life of Milton by Mitford followed by addenda and an appendix, volume 1, half-title for some of the poems, notes at bottom of page, original brown cloth (a bit rubbed at extremities), covers decorated in blind, spines lettered in gilt within gilt rules with anchor emblem of the Pickering Press in gilt at bottom of each spine, edges rough trimmed and partially unopened. A splendid set in fine signed early American bindings, blind-stamped "B. Bradley Binder, Boston" on fly-leaf, volume 1, with contemporary signature (dated 1843) on front blank in each volume. The first edition thus was published in 1834 (also listed here with further editions by Hilliard, Gray, and Company cited). Not in Kohler.

1893. THE POETICAL WORKS OF JOHN MILTON; To Which Is Prefixed, The Life Of The Author. *London: Printed for Thomas Tegg, 73, Cheapside. MDCCCXLII.* Fifth edition by Tegg? Tall 12mo in 6s, xi+576pp., frontispiece portrait engraved by W. C. Edwards after Vertue, protective tissue guard, portrait plate engraved by W. C. Edwards after Cornelius Jansen (Aet. XXI) before life, protective tissue guard, along with portrait plate of *Milton Dictating to His Daughters* engraved by W. C. Edwards after G. Romney bound within life, protective tissue guard, seven illustration plates engraved by various engravers after J. M. W. Turner, two illustration plates engraved by B. Graves and by F. Bacon after R. Westall, each with protective tissue guard, each plate with slight foxing or waterstains, not affecting the illustration, contemporary full purple morocco (a bit rubbed), covers decorated with fine gilt tooling incorporating fine tooling in blind at the center, spine lettered in gilt with decorative gilt trim in the panels, outer dentelles tooled in gilt, a.e.g. An attractive copy. The final several leaves include "Commendatory Verses On Milton" by various poets. See 1837 first illustrated edition by Tegg also listed here with further editions cited. Kohler 300, reporting "Not in the British Library. Not in the Bodleian Library. Not in Cambridge University Library."

1894. THE POETICAL WORKS OF JOHN MILTON. Edited By Sir Egerton Brydges, Bart. [Quotation from Thomson] A New Edition. *London: Printed For Thomas Tegg, 73, Cheapside. MDCCCXLII.* Second Brydges/Turner illustrated edition; possible sixth edition by Tegg. 8vo, cvi+767pp., frontispiece portrait plate engraved by W. C. Edwards after Vertue (slightly waterstained inner top margin without affecting portrait), protective tissue guard, seven illustration plates engraved by various engravers after J. M. W. Turner (each with slight waterstains, not affecting the illustration), all but one of the illustrations with protective tissue guard, double black border around text, contemporary full red pebble calf (a bit rubbed, pages a bit weakened along edges), covers finely decorated in gilt, spine decorated in gilt within the panel and lettered in gilt, slightly raised thick bands with decorative gilt trim, outer dentelles tooled in gilt (faded), a.e.g. A very nice copy with "Advertisement to the Original [i.e., 1835] Edition" reprinted before life. Not in Kohler.

1895. Variant of Preceding, contemporary full black pebble calf (a bit rubbed), covers finely decorated in gilt, spine ruled in gilt within the panel and lettered in gilt, slightly raised bands, outer dentelles tooled in gilt (a bit faded), a.e.g. A very nice copy in a variant contemporary calf binding. Not in Kohler.

Extra-Illustrated

1896. Variant of Preceding. THE POETICAL WORKS OF JOHN MILTON. Edited By Sir Egerton Brydges, Bart. [Quotation from Thomson] A New Edition. *London: Printed For Thomas Tegg, 73, Cheapside. MDCCCXLII.* Second Brydges/Turner illustrated edition; possibly the sixth edition by Tegg. Stout 8vo, cvi+767pp., as preceding copies (except extra illustrated), half-title, frontispiece portrait plate engraved by W. Hoogland after a "Painting by Samuel Cooper" inserted, "Advertisement to the Original [1835] Edition" reprinted before life (see 1835 set also listed here), several engraved portraits inserted within life, seven illustration plates engraved by various engravers after J. M. W. Turner, numerous engraved illustration plates inserted, contemporary three-quarter black pebble calf, marbled paper over thick boards (a bit rubbed, front joint reinforced from within), raised bands, spine lettered in gilt and richly decorated in gilt within the panels, marbled endpapers, t.e.g., others untrimmed. A very nice copy. Extra-illustrated, with the additional engraved illustrations of Burney, Rigaud, and Fuseli carefully placed (with page notation to the binder in pencil), along with numerous miscellaneous engraved frontispiece portraits (depicting Milton in various styles and at various ages, mostly nineteenth-century publications, but some eighteenth-century engravings as well), each illustration and portrait plate mounted on an individual page and carefully inserted into this edition.

1897. THE POETICAL WORKS OF JOHN MILTON; With A Memoir; And Seven Embellishments, By Fuseli, Westall, And Martin. *London: J. J. Chidley, 123, Aldersgate Street. 1842.* Second edition by Chidley? 8vo, vii+[1]+527pp., engraved frontispiece portrait plate "Engraved By J. Cochran From A Miniature Painted By Mr. Sam Cooper, Painter To Oliver Cromwell, And Originally In The Possession Of Milton's Daughter Deborah," ("London: I. J. Chidley, 123, Aldersgate Street" printed at the bottom), life of Milton, six illustration plates after Fuseli (one plate), Westall (two plates), and Martin (three plates), half-title for *PL* and for each book, *PR* and for each book, and for some of the poems, "Woking: Printed And Stereotyped By B. Bensley, From Bolt Court, Fleet Street" at bottom of last page, contemporary full Russia (worn, frontispiece foxed, front cover rehinged from inside), covers stamped in blind with thick decorative gilt border trim, gilt-decorated spine (very worn and faded), raised bands, gilt dentelles, marbled endpapers and edges, early name on front blank. All in all, an okay copy of a scarce edition. The first edition by Chidley published in 1841 is listed and other editions by Chidley cited there. Williamson 155; Kohler 302, citing Williamson 219 and reporting "Not in the British Library. Not in the Bodleian Library. Not in Cambridge University Library."

1898. THE POETICAL WORKS OF JOHN MILTON, With Life By Stebbing & Essay By Channing. *London: Published By Scott, Webster & Geary, Charterhouse Square. 1842.* 12mo, iv+552pp., engraved title-page plate (foxed) with vignette illustration for *C* engraved by Ranson after T. Uwins, double black rules around text, contemporary full red morocco (a bit rubbed), covers elaborately tooled in gilt, spine decorated in gilt within the panels and lettered in gilt, a.e.g. A nice copy in a lovely binding of the period with contemporary signature on fly-leaf. See copy of 1846 edition "Printed For Adam Scott . . . (Charterhouse Square)" listed here. Scarce. Stevens 141; Not in Kohler.

1899. THE POETICAL WORKS OF JOHN MILTON. With Notes Of Various Authors; And With Some Account Of The Life And Writings Of Milton, Derived Principally From Original Documents In Her Majesty's State-Paper Office. By The Rev. Henry John Todd, M.A. Chaplain In Ordinary To Her Majesty, And Archdeacon Of Cleveland. Fourth Edition. In Four Volumes. *London: Rivingtons, Longman and Co., et al., And G. And J. Robinson, Liverpool. 1842.* 4 volumes. Fourth Todd edition. 8vo, xxviii+523pp.,+589pp.,+xxiii+431pp.,+viii+560pp., frontispiece portrait plate (foxed around edges) engraved by T. A. Dean after a drawing by T. Simpson from William Baker's painting by Faithorne, dated 1842, "Printed by A. Spottiswoode, New-Street-Square" on verso of title page, dedication page, "Advertisement To The Fourth Edition," dated 1842, preface, "Some Account Of The Life And Writing Of Milton," "Appendix Containing An Inquiry Into The Origin Of Paradise Lost," facsimile plate (foxed), dated 1826, of Milton's signature and debt notice in his own hand in 1650, volume 1, separate title page each volume, half-title for each book of *PL* and for some of the poems, unsigned engraved plate of Ludlow Castle before *C*, volume 4, engraved by T. Higham and dated 1842, engraved plate, "Fac-simile from the Original Drawing" of Christina Queen of Sweden in man's apparel engraved by T. Higham for the Latin epigram, XIII. "Ad Christinam Suecorum Reginam, nomine Cromwelli," dated 1842, "List Of Editions," and "Glossarial Index," volume 4, notes at bottom of page, contemporary full burgundy morocco (spines a little faded), double gilt rule on covers, spines lettered in gilt and decorated in gilt within the panels, raised bands, yellow endpapers, a.e.g. A very nice set in an attractive morocco binding of the period. The first Todd edition was published in 1801; the second Todd edition, revised and expanded, was published in 1809; the third Todd edition was expanded further and published in 1826—all Todd sets listed here. This, the fourth edition by Todd, is the last lifetime edition revised by Todd and contains some additional annotations, copious notes, and biographical material, along with critical comment on Lauder's interpolations. It was reprinted as a fifth edition in 1852 (also listed here). Uncommon. Stevens 144; Kohler 303, citing Williamson 152 and reporting "Not in the British Library. Not in the Bodleian Library. Not in Cambridge University Library."

1900. THE POETICAL WORKS OF JOHN MILTON. Containing Paradise Lost, Paradise Regained, Samson Agonistes, &c. With A Memoir Of The Author. [Quotations From Cowper.] *Fisher, Son, & Co. London, Paris, And New York. n.d. [1843].* 8vo in 4s, pagination continuing to p. xxiv, then a jump in pagination, 34–424 pp., engraved frontispiece portrait of Milton in a circular form with a crown of thorns amidst rays of sunlight overhead and foliage along both sides and bottom and with snake and apple beneath the portrait signed "Hicks," "Drawn by W. M. Craig Esqr. from a miniature by Cooper," "Fisher, Son, & Co. London, 1843" at the bottom, engraved and printed title pages, engraved full-page illustration of the expulsion (Eve holding onto Adam's arm with Archangel and burning sword behind them) and the crucifixion scene high on a mountain above by W. M Craig engraved by E. Goodall on the engraved title page, with the title "Paradise Lost, And Regained, By John Milton" and "Fisher, Son, & Co. London, 1835" at the bottom, printed title: "Poetical Works," as cited, eighteen-page "Life Of Milton. Compiled By The Rev. David M'Nicol" followed by "A Glossary Explaining the Antiquated and ifficult [sic] Words in Milton's poetical [sic] Works," with seven engraved illustration plates by W. M. Craig, variously engraved by A. Warren, A. Smith, I. Romney, James, Bragg, and Pye, each variously dated in the 1830s with the line illustrated quoted beneath each illustration along with "Fisher, Son, & Co. London," contemporary red morocco (a bit rubbed along joints and extremities, plates with slight waterstain marks at bottom edges from sometime ago without affecting image), decorative border trim in gilt on covers, spine richly decorated in gilt, maroon label with gilt lettering ("Milton's Works"), raised bands with gilt trim, a.e.g. A handsome copy of an uncommon edition with possibly contemporary signature on front pastedown. The "Other Poems" indicated on the title page include: *L'A, IlP*, and *On The Death of a Fair Infant*. In addition to the engraved title page illustration, there are seven additional illustrations after W. M. Craig, six illustrations for *PL*: Book I (*Satan Rallying His Troops*); Book III (*The Transformation of Satan before Meeting Uriel*); Book V (*Raphael Counseling Adam and Eve*); Book VII (*Adam Beholds Eve*); Book. IX (*The Temptation of Eve*); and Book XII (*The Expulsion*); and one illustration for *PR*: Book II (the temptation to "A table richly spread," wrongly bound here in *PL*, Book II). See first edition of *PL & PR & SA* published in Liverpool in 1812 by "Nuttall, Fisher, And Dixon," with life by David M'Nicoll and with seven of Craig's illustrations printed in an octavo format, variously engraved, and dated 1812 for the edition (also listed here with an explanation there regarding the jump in pagination as a result of issuing by subscription); this repeats that edition and its particulars, with a new date for the frontispiece portrait (there dated "Mar. 30, 1812" and signed "R. Hick"), with varying later dates for the engraved illustrations by Craig (each dated 1812 there). See also possible first London edition thus of *PL* (ca. 1823) with 1812 frontispiece portrait (one copy with 1823 date and printed at the Caxton Press), with engraved illustration plates after Craig (each dated 1823), and with an engraved title page (as here) with full-page illustration of the expulsion of Adam and Eve with the crucifixion scene high on a mountain above by Craig, with "Published by Nuttall, Fisher & Co. Liverpool. Sept. 1815" at the bottom. Scarce. Not in Kohler.

1901. THE POETICAL WORKS OF JOHN MILTON. With A Memoir, And Critical Remarks On His Genius And Writings, By James Montgomery; And One Hundred And Twenty Engravings By John Thompson, S. And T. Williams, O. Smith, J. Linton, &c. From Drawings By William Harvey. *London: Tilt And Bogue, Fleet Street. MDCCCXLIII.* 2 volumes. First illustrated Tilt edition. 8vo in 4s, lii+378pp.,+viii+341pp., half-title each volume ("Tilt's Illustrated Edition"), first appearance of illustrations by William Harvey, half-title for each book of *PL* and *PR* and for some of the poems, this being a special set, printed on India paper, bound in fine contemporary full blue morocco (a bit worn at joints, along raised bands and at spine ends, some spotting), delicately gilt-decorated covers and spines, raised bands, inner and outer dentelles finely tooled in gilt, marbled endpapers, red ribbon marker, gauffered gilt edges. Lowndes says only two copies of this special issue were printed: one for the publisher and one for the printer, neither of which was for sale, repeated to me when I obtained the set from Maggs in 1977. As one of those two special issues, this may perhaps be the publisher's copy since Ravenstree referred to another copy being the printer's copy for sale in its 1985 and 1986 Milton catalogues. A lovely set in very fine condition. Not in Kohler.

1902. THE POETICAL WORKS OF JOHN MILTON. With A Memoir, And Critical Remarks On His Genius And Writings, By James Montgomery; And One Hundred And Twenty Engravings By John Thompson, S. And T. Williams, O. Smith, J. Linton, &c. From Drawings By William Harvey. *London: Tilt And Bogue, Fleet Street. MDCCCXLIII.* 2 volumes. First illustrated Tilt edition. 8vo in 4s, lii+378pp.,+viii+341pp., half-title each volume ("Tilt's Illustrated Edition"), first appearance of illustrations by William Harvey, half-title for each book of *PL* and *PR* and for some of the poems, original publisher's maroon pebble morocco gilt-stamped (joints weak, a little worn along joints, with the stamp "Radlett Preparatory School" on front blank), a brilliant gilt emblem at the center of front covers and a different equally brilliant gilt emblem on back covers (the emblems—a serpent wound around a flaming sword with apple on a small branch with leaves, and a cross within a crown of thorns—are reversed from one volume cover to the other), gilt-decorated spines with a depiction of Adam and Eve departing Eden in bright gilt at the top of the spines and of a dove amidst brilliant rays in bright gilt at the bottom of the spines, a.e.g. A very nice set in original publisher's morocco binding. Stevens 145, reporting "Reprinted by Leavitt & Allen (New York) in 2 volumes, 1843, and by Harper & Bros. (New York) in 2 volumes [1847]. The basis of the Bohn edition"; Kohler 304.

1903. Variant of Preceding. 2 volumes. First illustrated Tilt edition. Original publisher's blue cloth, with a brilliant gilt emblem at the center of front covers and a different but equally brilliant gilt emblem on back covers (the emblems—a serpent wound around a flaming sword with apple on a small branch with leaves, and a cross within a crown of thorns—are reversed from one volume cover to the other), gilt-decorated spines with a depiction of Adam and Eve departing Eden in bright gilt at the top of the spines and of a dove amidst brilliant rays in bright gilt at the bottom of the spines, a.e.g. A nice, tall set in a fine variant publisher's binding. Kohler 304.

1904. Variant of Preceding. 2 volumes. First illustrated Tilt edition. Original publisher's blue-green morocco gilt-stamped (a little rubbed along extremities), with a brilliant gilt emblem at the center of front covers and a different equally brilliant gilt emblem on back covers (the emblems—a serpent wound around a flaming sword with apple on a small branch with leaves, and a cross within a crown of thorns—are reversed from one volume cover to the other), gilt-decorated spines with a depiction of Adam and Eve departing Eden in bright gilt at the top of the spines and of a dove amidst brilliant rays in bright gilt at

PW. With A Memoir, And Critical Remarks On His Genius And Writings, By James Montgomery; And One Hundred And Twenty Engravings From Drawings By William Harvey. London: Tilt And Bogue, 1843. First Tilt Illustrated Edition; first appearance of Harvey's illustrations. (right) Original publisher's maroon pebble morocco (a little worn), with a cross within a crown of thorns or a serpent wound around a flaming sword with apple on a small branch with leaves at the center of the covers, each in bright gilt—reversed from one volume cover to the other, and Adam and Eve leaving Eden depicted in bright gilt at the top of the spines and a dove amidst brilliant rays in bright gilt at the bottom. (left) Original publisher's blue cloth with the same emblems in bright gilt interchanged at the center and the same depictions in bright gilt on the spines. A nice tall set in fine publisher's binding. (center) A special set, printed on India paper, bound in fine contemporary full blue morocco. Lowndes reports only two such copies, one for the publisher and one for the printer, neither of which was for sale. Despite some wear on the spine, a lovely set. See #1902, 1903, and 1901.

the bottom of the spines, a.e.g. A very nice set in a fine variant publisher's morocco binding with contemporary signature in a neat hand dated 1844 on fly-leaf, volume 1. Kohler 304.

1905. THE POETICAL WORKS OF JOHN MILTON; To Which Is Prefixed The Life Of The Author. *London: Printed for Thomas Tegg, 73, Cheapside. MDCCCXLIII.* 12mo in 6s, xi+576pp., frontispiece portrait engraved by W. C. Edwards after Vertue, portrait plate engraved by W. C. Edwards after Cornelius Jansen (Aet. XXI) inserted before life, along with portrait plate of *Milton Dictating To His Daughters* engraved by W. C. Edwards after G. Romney, seven illustration plates engraved by various engravers after J. M. W. Turner, two illustration plates engraved by R. Graves and by F. Bacon after R. Westall, each with protective tissue guard, contemporary black morocco (a bit worn along edges and extremities), covers delicately tooled in gilt with central gilt urn, spine decorated in gilt by compartments and lettered in gilt, raised bands, outer dentelles finely tooled in gilt, a.e.g. Although a bit worn, a nice copy with early armorial bookplate on front pastedown and name on bookplate signed in ink on front blank. The final several leaves include "Commendatory Verses On Milton" by various poets. See 1837 first illustrated edition by Tegg and other editions by Tegg cited there. Scarce. Not in Kohler.

1906. MILTON'S POETICAL WORKS, Consisting of Paradise Lost, Paradise Regained, Mask Of Comus, Samson Agonistes, And Poems On Several Occasions, &c. &c. Together With The Life Of The Author. Complete In One Volume. *New York: Published By Edward Kearny, No. 56 Gold Street. 1843.* 2 volumes in one. 12mo in 6s,

321pp.,+232pp., unsigned frontispiece illustration plate for Book I of *PL*, protective tissue guard, engraved title page, undated, with an unsigned illustration for Book I of *PL* on engraved title, brief publisher's imprint, "New-York Edward Kearny. 56 Gold Street," at the bottom, printed title page for the entire volume, "Piercy & Reed Printers, 9 Spruce St., N.Y." on verso, "Contents" for each volume, life by Fenton, half-title for each book of *PL* and for some of the poems, notes at bottom of page, original three-quarter black leather, green cloth with floral pattern (leather worn, spine cracked, slight waterstaining at top of front cover, age-browning throughout), marbled endpapers, speckled edges. A good copy of a mid-nineteenth-century American edition. See undated ca. 1843 illustrated edition by Edward Kearny following and dated 1843 nonillustrated edition by Edward Kearny also listed here. Scarce. Not in Kohler.

1907. MILTON'S POETICAL WORKS, Consisting of Paradise Lost, Paradise Regained, Mask Of Comus, Samson Agonistes, And Poems On Several Occasions, &c. &c. Together With The Life Of The Author. Complete In One Volume. *New York: Published By Edward Kearny, No. 272 Pearl Street. n.d. [ca. 1843].* 2 volumes in one. 12mo in 6s, 321pp.,+232pp., unsigned frontispiece illustration plate for Book I of *PL*, protective tissue guard, undated engraved title page with an unsigned illustration for Book I of *PL* on engraved title, brief publisher's imprint, "New-York Edward Kearny." at the bottom, printed title page for the entire volume (completely blank on verso), "Contents" for each volume, life by Fenton, half-title for each book of *PL* and for some of the poems, notes at bottom of page, original light brown cloth (a bit rubbed with some wear at the corners, spine a little faded and slightly chipped at the top and bottom, occasional slight foxing), covers decorated in embossed trim, spine lettered and richly decorated in gilt, decorated endpapers. A good copy of a mid-nineteenth-century American edition. See dated 1843 illustrated edition by Edward Kearny preceding and dated 1843 nonillustrated edition by Edward Kearny. Scarce. Not in Kohler.

1908. THE POETICAL WORKS OF JOHN MILTON. Complete In One Volume. *New York: Edward Kearny, 56 Gold-St. 1843.* 12mo in 6s, 215pp., contemporary full green morocco (a little rubbed, especially along extremities, some age-browning), covers ruled in blind with elaborate central gilt harp, thick raised bands with decorative gilt trim, outer dentelles tooled in gilt (faded), marbled endpapers and lightly marbled edges. A nice copy in an attractive mid-nineteenth-century American binding. See dated 1843 and undated ca. 1843 illustrated editions by Edward Kearny also listed here. Scarce. Not in Kohler.

1909. THE POETICAL WORKS OF MILTON, YOUNG, GRAY, BEATTIE, AND COLLINS. Complete In One Volume. Stereotyped By J. Crissy And G. Goodman. P*hiladelphia: Grigg & Elliot, No. 9 North Fourth Street. 1843.* Sixth edition thus; second thus by Grigg and Elliot? 8vo, [8]+xxxii+170pp.,+viii+208pp.,+x+47pp.,+ix+23pp.,+iv+19pp., similar to 1831 edition (possible first edition thus), frontispiece with vignette portrait of each poet engraved by J. B. Longacre (with Milton at the top), half-title for Milton and for each collection of poetical works with contents on verso, life of Milton and of each poet, printed in double column, contemporary calf (worn, some foxing), gilt rules on spine, black leather label with gilt lettering, outer dentelles trimmed in gilt, marbled endpapers and edges. See 1831 edition (first thus) by Grigg and other editions by Grigg, by Grigg and Elliot, and by their successors cited there. Scarce. Not in Kohler.

1910. THE POETICAL WORKS OF JOHN MILTON. To Which Is Prefixed The Life Of The Author. *London: Printed for Thomas Tegg, 73, Cheapside. MDCCCXLIV.* 12mo in 6s, xi+576pp., frontispiece portrait engraved by W. C. Edwards after Vertue, portrait plate engraved by W. C. Edwards after Cornelius Jansen (Aet. XXI) inserted before life, along with portrait plate of *Milton Dictating to His Daughters* engraved by W. C. Edwards after G. Romney, seven illustration plates engraved by various engravers after J. M. W. Turner, two illustration plates engraved by R. Graves and by F. Bacon after R. Westall, each with protective tissue guard, contemporary black morocco (a bit rubbed, illustrations age-browned around edges), covers delicately tooled in gilt with central gilt urn, spine decorated in gilt by compartments and lettered in gilt, raised bands, outer dentelles tooled in gilt, a.e.g. A nice copy with early inscription on fly-leaf. The final several leaves include "Commendatory Verses On Milton" by various poets. See 1837 first illustrated edition by Tegg also listed here with further editions cited. Scarce. Kohler 305, describing its copy "Octavo in 6s," listing two portrait plates only, although not the portrait plate after Romney (as here and in other Tegg illustrated editions), and reporting "Not in the British Library. Not in the Bodleian Library. Not in Cambridge University Library."

1911. THE POETICAL WORKS OF JOHN MILTON. *Edinburgh: Published By Thomas Nelson, MDCCCXLIV.* 2 volumes in one. First edition thus. Small 8vo, xii+288pp.+228pp., half-title, frontispiece portrait (of a youngish Milton) engraved by T. Cowan after "Faithorn [sic]," engraved and printed title pages, with vignette illustration after A. Ritchie for Book X of *PL* (fine impression) on engraved title engraved by T. Cowan with lines illustrated printed beneath the illustration, half-title for *PR, SA,* and *C,* original light brown cloth (a bit rubbed, front joint cracked, spine ends chipped, marginal notes in pencil in a neat hand at the beginning of *PL*), covers decorated in blind, spine lettered and decorated in gilt, inner dentelles with gilt panels, encased in contemporary vellum with hand-painted illuminated borders in medieval style of colored flowers, leaves, and pointelles on front cover, the colors in pink, green, and light blue, spine similarly hand-painted with floral trim in the same colors, large floral piece similarly hand-painted in the same colors at the center of back cover. A nice copy with early bookplate on front pastedown, in a lovely nineteenth-century hand-painted vellum encasing with vellum ties. Scarce. Not in Kohler.

1912. THE POETICAL WORKS OF JOHN MILTON; With A Memoir: And Seven Embellishments, By Fuseli, Westall, And Martin. *London: J. J. Chidley, 123, Aldersgate Street. 1845.* Third edition by Chidley? 8vo, vii+527pp., engraved frontispiece portrait plate "Engraved By J. Cochran From A Miniature Painted By Mr. Sam Cooper, Painter To Oliver Cromwell, And Originally In The Possession Of Milton's Daughter Deborah," ("London. I. J.

(below) *PW.* Edinburgh: Published By Thomas Nelson, 1844. 2 volumes in one. First edition thus. Frontispiece portrait engraved by T. Cowan after "Faithorn [sic]," engraved title page with vignette illustration engraved by T. Cowan after A. Ritchie in lovely nineteenth-century hand-painted vellum encasing with vellum ties. (right) Previous edition encased in contemporary vellum with hand-painted illuminated borders in a medieval style of flowers, leaves, and gilt pointelles on front cover, in colors of pink, green, and light blue, spine similarly hand-painted with floral trim in the same colors, large floral piece similarly hand-painted in the same colors at the center of back cover, with vellum ties. See #1911.

Chidley, 123, Aldersgate Street" printed at the bottom), life of Milton, six illustration plates after Fuseli (one plate), Westall (two plates), and Martin (three plates), each with protective tissue guard, half-title for *PL* and for each book, *PR* and for each book, and for some of the poems, "J. Billing, Printer And Stereotyper, Woking, Surrey" printed on verso of title page and at bottom of last page, contemporary crushed red morocco (a little rubbed along extremities and corners, a dark spot at top of back cover, frontispiece lightly foxed, some light foxing in margins of several of the plates), covers ruled in gilt with delicate gilt tooling and a large emblem in blind at the center, spine richly decorated in gilt within the panels with gilt lettering and gilt rules within the bands, a.e.g. A nice copy in an attractive morocco binding of the period with a contemporary signature (dated 1845) on fly-leaf and a later bookplate on front pastedown. The possible first edition by Chidley was published in 1841 (also listed here with further editions cited). Uncommon. Kohler 308, reporting "Not in the British Library. Not in the Bodleian Library. Not in Cambridge University Library."

1913. THE POETICAL WORKS OF JOHN MILTON; To Which Is Prefixed, The Life Of The Author. *London: Printed for Thomas Tegg, 73, Cheapside. MDCCCXLV.* 12mo in 6s, xi+576pp., contemporary green morocco (a little rubbed, spine a little faded), covers decorated in gilt with central harp in gilt, spine lettered in gilt, raised bands, gilt rules within the panels, inner and outer dentelles finely tooled in gilt, decorated white endpapers, a.e.g. A nice copy with contemporary signature (dated 1846) on fly-leaf. See 1837 first illustrated edition by Tegg also listed here with further editions cited. Scarce. Not in Kohler (although Kohler 307 records this 1845 edition by Tegg as illustrated).

1914. THE POETICAL WORKS OF JOHN MILTON[.] *London[:] William Pickering[,] 1845.* 3 volumes. Fourth Aldine edition. Small 8vo, cxxxiv+[iv]+153pp.,+ 372pp.,+334+[1]pp., edited by John Mitford with a life of Milton, half-title each volume ("The Aldine Edition Of The British Poets"), engraved frontispiece portrait after H. Robinson, volume 1, dated "London, William Pickering, 1831," separate title page each volume with anchor emblem of the Pickering Press on each title page, original "Advertisement" for the 1832 Aldine edition by John Mitford with original date of 1831, life of Milton by Mitford followed by addenda and appendix, volume 1, half-title for some of the poems, anchor emblem of the Pickering Press on the last leaf of volume 3, printed by "C.[harles] Whittingham, Chiswick" at bottom of last page of volume 1, "London: Printed By C. Whittingham, Tooks Court" printed at bottom of last page of volumes 2 and 3, original brown calf (a little rubbed along joints and at extremities, ex-library stamped "Withdrawn"), covers ruled in blind with small decorative devices in blind at the corners, brown morocco labels on spines with gilt lettering and numerals, small decorations in blind in the panels, marbled endpapers, red edges. A good set, bookplate in each volume and presentation inscription (dated 1850) on front blank, volume 1. Though unaccountably not included in the Keynes bibliography, this is a handsomely bound copy from Pickering's distinguished Aldine series of British poets, a run of fifty-three different volumes, all well printed and well edited, begun in 1830 and continuing for two decades. The first Aldine edition of Milton appeared in 1832 (with the first appearance of Milton portrait plate after Robinson), see set listed here with further editions of Milton in the collection cited there. The 1832, 1845, and 1851 Aldine editions are the only editions to have the anchor emblem of the Pickering Press on the last leaf of volume 3. Not in Keynes; Williamson 76; Kohler 306, reporting "Not in the British Library. Not in the Bodleian Library. Not in Cambridge University Library."

1915. Variant of Preceding, contemporary polished green calf (spines faded, as always with green, to an even brown), decorative gilt border trim on covers, gilt-decorated spines in the panels with small gilt ornament in each panel and with gilt lettering, raised bands with decorative gilt trim, broad inner dentelles finely tooled in gilt, outer dentelles ruled in gilt, marbled endpapers, t.e.g. A fine set, large paper copy, ½" larger that the preceding set, in an attractive variant morocco binding by Sangorski and Sutcliffe (stamped on verso of front fly-leaf in each volume), with a large modern bookplate on the front pastedown of each volume, in a fleece-lined matching marbled paper slipcase. Not in Keynes; Kohler 306.

1916. THE POETICAL WORKS OF JOHN MILTON. With Notes, And A Life Of The Author [By John Mitford]. A New Edition. *Boston: Charles C. Little And James Brown. 1845.* 2 volumes. First edition by Little and Brown. 8vo, cxxix+[2]+371pp.,+ii+478pp., frontispiece portrait plate "Engraved by O. Pelton From a Miniature of the same size by Faithorne, Anno 1667, in the possession of William Falconer Esq.," volume 1, protective tissue guard, anchor emblem of the Pickering Press on each title page, "Cambridge: Metcalf And Company, Printers To The University" on verso of title page each volume, thirteen-page advertisement by John Mitford with the original date of 1831, and life of Milton by Mitford followed by addenda and an appendix, volume 1, half-titles for some of the poems, original brown silk (bit rubbed at corners), spines lettered in gilt within gilt rules, edges untrimmed, partially unopened. A fine, tall set, well-preserved in original mid-nineteenth-century American publisher's binding with contemporary signature in pencil (dated 1849) on flyleaf of each volume. A reprinting of the edition published by Hilliard, Gray, and Company, in Boston, the first edition thus published in 1834 (also listed here with further editions by Hilliard, Gray, and Company in the collection cited there); this edition appears to have been reprinted by D. Bixby in Lowell in 1848 (see two-volume edition also listed here). Uncommon. Stevens 150; Kohler 309, reporting "Not in Williamson. Not in the British Library. Not in the Bodleian Library. Not in Cambridge University Library."

1917. THE POETICAL WORKS OF JOHN MILTON: With Life and Notes By The Rev. Thomas Thomson. *London: Printed For Adam Scott, (Late Scott And Webster,) Charterhouse Square. 1846.* First edition thus? 12mo, viii+584pp., frontispiece portrait plate of Milton engraved by H. Meyer "From the Portrait by Cipriani," with protective tissue guard, engraved and printed title pages with vignette illustration after H. Meyer for *C* on engraved title, "London: Engraved for Scott's English Classics, 1846," half-titles for some of the poems, contemporary full red morocco (a bit rubbed), covers tooled in gilt with central gilt device within outline in blind, gilt-decorated spine in the panels with gilt lettering, a.e.g. A very nice copy in an attractive binding of the period with contemporary inscription (dated 1848) on front blank. A possible second edition thus was published in 1853 (also listed here) in a small 8vo format, unlike the 12mo format here, with printed title page dated 1853 and engraved title, as here, dated 1846. See also 1842 edition "Published By Scott, Webster & Geary, Charterhouse Square" (copy listed here). Scarce. Not in Kohler.

1918. THE POETICAL WORKS OF JOHN MILTON; With A Memoir: And Seven Embellishments, By Fuseli, Westall, And Martin. New Edition. *London: J. J. Chidley, 123, Aldersgate Street. 1846.* Fourth edition by Chidley? 8vo, vii+[1]+527pp., engraved frontispiece portrait plate "Engraved By J. Cochran From A Miniature Painted By Mr. Sam Cooper, Painter To Oliver Cromwell, And Originally In The Possession Of Milton's Daughter Deborah" ("with "London: I. J. Chidley, 123, Aldersgate Street" printed at the bottom), life of Milton, six illustration plates after Fuseli (one plate), Westall (two plates), and Martin (three plates), each with protective tissue guard, black border rule around text, half-title for *PL* and for each book, *PR* and for each book, and for some of the poems, black border rule around text, "Woking: Printed And Stereotyped By B. Bensley, From Bolt Court, Fleet Street." at bottom of last page, contemporary green cloth (some foxing), blind-stamped covers, spine elaborately decorated in gilt with scenes from *PL* and related emblems, edges untrimmed. A very good copy with the first appearance of "New Edition" on title page and the first appearance of a black border rule around text in an edition by Chidley. The first edition by Chidley was published in 1841 (copy listed and other editions by Chidley cited there). Scarce. Williamson 155; Not in Kohler.

1919. THE POETICAL WORKS OF JOHN MILTON; To Which Is Prefixed The Life Of The Author. *London: Printed for Thomas Tegg, 73, Cheapside. MDCCCXLVI.* 12mo in 6s, xi+576pp., frontispiece portrait engraved by W. C. Edwards after Vertue, portrait plate engraved by W. C. Edwards after Cornelius Jansen (Aet. XXI) inserted before life, along with portrait plate of *Milton Dictating to His Daughters* engraved by W. C. Edwards after G. Romney, seven illustration plates engraved by various engravers after J. M. W. Turner, two illustration plates engraved by R. Graves and by F. Bacon after R. Westall, each with protective tissue guard, contemporary full navy blue morocco (lacking a front blank), covers delicately tooled in gilt with central gilt harp, spine decorated in gilt by compartments and lettered in gilt, raised bands, inner and outer dentelles finely tooled in gilt, a.e.g. A very fine, tall copy. The final several leaves include "Commendatory Verses On Milton" by various poets. See 1837 first illustrated edition by Tegg also listed here with further editions cited. Scarce. Not in Kohler.

1920. MILTON'S POETISCHE WERKE. Deutsch von Adolf Böttger. Neue Ausgabe. *Leipzig, Hofzling'sche Buchhandlung. 1846.* 8vo, xiv+[2]+423+[1]pp., half-title with decorative border trim, engraved frontispiece portrait plate by Cochran after Cooper, "Verlag v. Franz Peter in Leipzig. Stich u. Druck v. Winkles & Lehmann in Leipzig" (printed in very small type beneath portrait), protective pink tissue guard, elaborate border trim with decorative corner pieces on title page, small emblem near the bottom of the title page, half-title with decorative border trim for "Biographische Skizze," half-title with decorative border trim for each book of *PL*, decorative border trim around text, "Leipzig, Druck von Friedrich Andra" on verso of last page, original marbled black paper over boards (a little rubbed, especially along joints and extremities, portrait slightly foxed, some slight foxing here and there), orange label lettered and ruled in gilt on spine, speckled blue edges. A nice copy in original boards. Kohler 311, referencing Williamson 220, and reporting "Not in the Bodleian Library. Not in Cambridge University Library."

1921. Variant of Preceding, original publisher's dark green cloth gilt-stamped (a bit rubbed), covers ruled in blind with a large decorative emblem in blind at the center of each cover, spine richly decorated in gilt with gilt lettering, marbled endpapers. A lovely copy, very tall, with variant title page (no emblem as in preceding edition), with clear protective tissue guard for frontispiece portrait (instead of pink as in preceding copy), in a variant publisher's binding, with near-contemporary signature dated 1857. Not in Kohler.

1922. THE POETICAL WORKS OF JOHN MILTON; With A Memoir: And Seven Embellishments, By Fuseli, Westall, And Martin. New Edition. *London: J. J. Chidley, 123, Aldersgate Street. 1847.* Fifth edition by Chidley? 8vo, vii+527pp., engraved frontispiece portrait plate "Engraved By J. Cochran From A Miniature Painted By Mr. Sam Cooper, Painter To Oliver Cromwell, And Originally In The Possession Of Milton's Daughter Deborah," ("London: I. J. Chidley, 123, Aldersgate Street" printed at the bottom), Life of Milton, six illustration plates after Fuseli (one plate), Westall (two plates), and Martin (three plates), each with protective tissue guard, black border rule around text, half-title for *PL* and for each book, *PR* and for each book, and for some of the poems, "J. Billing, Printer And Stereotyper, Woking, Surrey" printed on verso of title page and at bottom of last page, contemporary dark blue morocco, covers ruled in gilt with delicate gilt tooling as central border trim within a thin gilt rule, spine elaborately decorated in gilt within the panels with gilt lettering with gilt rules within the bands, a.e.g. A fine copy in an attractive morocco binding of the period with a contemporary signature, dated 1850. The first edition by Chidley was published in 1841 (also listed here with further editions cited). Not in Kohler.

1923. Variant of Preceding, original black cloth, blind-stamped covers, spine elaborately decorated in gilt with scenes from *Paradise Lost* and related emblems (a bit faded), edges untrimmed. A nice tall, large paper copy, ½" taller than the preceding copy in a splendid variant publisher's cloth binding. Not in Kohler.

1924. THE POETICAL WORKS OF JOHN MILTON; To Which Is Prefixed The Life Of The Author. *London: Printed For W. Tegg & Co., 73, Cheapside. Griffin & Co., Glasgow; And Cumming & Ferguson, Dublin. MDCCCXLVII..[sic]* 12mo in 6s, xi+576pp., frontispiece portrait engraved by W. C. Edwards after Vertue, portrait plate engraved by W. C. Edwards after Cornelius Jansen (Aet. XXI) inserted before life, along with portrait plate of *Milton Dictating to His Daughters* engraved by W. C. Edwards after G. Romney, seven illustration plates engraved by various engravers after J. M. W. Turner, two illustration plates engraved by R. Graves and by F. Bacon after R. Westall, each with protective tissue guard, contemporary full maroon morocco (slightly rubbed at joints, some foxing to the plates), covers delicately tooled in gilt with central gilt vase, spine decorated in gilt by compartments and lettered in gilt, raised bands, inner and outer dentelles finely tooled in gilt, a.e.g. A very fine copy with contemporary presentation inscription (dated 1847) on front blank. The final several leaves include "Commendatory Verses On Milton" by various poets. See 1837 first illustrated edition by Tegg also listed here with further editions cited. Scarce. Not in Kohler.

1925. THE POETICAL WORKS OF JOHN MILTON: With Explanatory Notes, and a Life of the Author, By The Rev. H. Stebbing, D.D. To Which Is Prefixed, Dr. Channing's Essay On The Poetical Genius Of Milton. *London: H. G. Bohn, York Street, Covent Garden. 1847.* First edition thus by Bohn? 12mo, iv+552pp., engraved and printed title pages with an engraved vignette illustration of *Satan, Sin, and Death* after T. Uwins engraved by Ranson on engraved title page ("The Poetical Works Of John Milton. With An Account Of His Life," with publisher's imprint, "London: Engraved for the English Classics"), notes at bottom of page, contemporary green calf (a little rubbed, covers scuffed, front joint slightly cracked), covers ruled in gilt with inner trim tooled in blind, spine delicately tooled in gilt within the panels, red morocco label lettered and ruled in gilt, raise bands trimmed in gilt, "Prize" lettered in capital letters in gilt at the bottom of spine, outer dentelles trimmed in gilt, marbled endpapers and edges. A nice copy with what would appear to be a contemporary presentation inscription in ink on verso of fly-leaf along with an inscription from "Hudson Bay Co. Victoria, B.C. to Mother Saturday – October. 27 – 1934 [with a quotation from Plato]" on protective tissue guard. A possible second edition by Bohn was published in 1849 (see copy listed here with a second engraved frontispiece illustration of *Satan, Sin, and Death* after H. Corbould engraved by C. Heath). Scarce. Not in Kohler.

1926. THE POETICAL WORKS OF JOHN MILTON. With A Memoir, And Critical Remarks On His Genius And Writings, By James Montgomery; And Thirty-Six Engravings, From Drawings By William Harvey. *Hartford: Published By S. Andrus & Son. MDCCCXLVII.* 2 volumes. First edition thus by Andrus & Son. 8vo, l+400pp.(pagination beginning at "18"),+369pp., frontispiece illustration of *Milton Dictating* engraved by "Lossing & Co," volume 1, initially engraved by "Thompson" in original publication of Harvey's illustrations, unsigned frontispiece illustration of

Milton *Mid books and papers in my study pent, If this be exile, sweet is banishment* engraved by "Clark," volume 2, full-page illustrations by William Harvey with in-text illustrations for *L'A* only (no in-text illustrations for *IlP* or other poems as in original publication of Harvey's illustrations), separate title page each volume, half-title for each book of *PL* and for each major poem, original publisher's gilt and glazed to simulate red morocco (a bit rubbed at joints and edges), a brilliant gilt emblem at the center of front covers and a different equally brilliant gilt emblem on back covers (the emblems—a cross within a crown of thorns on front covers, a serpent wound around a flaming sword with apple on a small branch with leaves on back covers), spines lettered in gilt (including "Andrus' Illustrated Edition" in small gilt letters at the center) and decorated in gilt with a depiction of Adam and Eve departing Eden in bright gilt at the top of the spines and of a dove amidst brilliant rays in bright gilt at the bottom of the spines, outer dentelles tooled in gilt, a.e.g. A fine set, very clean within, in a lovely mid-nineteenth-century American publisher's binding—a binding similar to that on one of the copies of the first edition with Harvey's illustrations by Tilt & Bogue in 1843 (also listed here). Scarce. Kohler 312, reporting "Not in the British Library. Not in the Bodleian Library. Not in Cambridge University Library."

Harvey's illustrations, which are not included in full here and which are, with the exception of *L'A*, reproduced as full-page illustrations rather than inclusive also of in-text illustrations as originally published, were first published in London by Tilt & Bogue in 1843 (see two-volume sets listed here). The second edition thus by Andrus & Son of Hartford with illustrations after Harvey was published in a similar sized 8vo format and binding as here in 1848 (see two-volume set listed here); the possible third edition by Andrus & Son in 1850 (see two-volume set listed here); and see 1853 and 1856 editions by Andrus & Son, two volumes in one, in larger sized 8vo formats, with illustrations after Harvey as here, and with an additional frontispiece portrait engraved by C. Burt in volume 1. The possible first edition of Milton's *PL* by Andrus & Son of Hartford with illustrations after Harvey was published in 1847 (also listed here).

1927. THE POETICAL WORKS OF JOHN MILTON. With A Memoir, And Critical Remarks On His Genius And Writings By James Montgomery; And One Hundred And Twenty Engravings From Drawings By William Harvey. In Two Volumes. Vol. I/II. *New York: Harper & Brothers, Publishers, 82 Cliff Street. n.d. [1847].* First edition thus by Harper & Brothers. 2 volumes. 8vo in 4s, 432pp.,+349pp., title page each volume, illustrations by William Harvey within the text as with first edition in 1843, half-title for each book of *PL* and *PR* and for some of the poems, original full dark green pebble morocco (a bit rubbed), covers delicately tooled in gilt with thick gilt rules with small depiction of Eve tempting Adam in gilt at the center of each cover, volume 1, and a small emblem of serpent wound around crucifix in gilt at the center of each cover, volume 2, spines similarly tooled in gilt with the same design within the panels and with gilt lettering and Roman numerals, slightly raised bands, inner and outer dentelles finely tooled in gilt, decorated endpapers, a.e.g. A lovely set in publisher's original gilt-stamped morocco, possibly a presentation binding, with name in gilt at bottom of front covers. This edition reprints Milton's text and Harvey's illustrations in full including decorated initial letters as in the first edition by Tilt & Bogue in 1843 (see two-volume sets listed here). Stevens 145; Not in Kohler.

1928. Variant of Preceding, original full maroon morocco (a bit rubbed), covers and spine identically tooled in gilt, decorated endpapers, a.e.g. A very nice set in an attractive variant publisher's original gilt-stamped morocco binding.

1929. Variant of Preceding, original red cloth (a bit rubbed), covers delicately tooled in blind in a pattern similar to that tooled in gilt in the preceding two copies, with finely tooled emblem of a fountain shooting water at three levels in gilt at the center of each cover, both volumes, emblem different from those on preceding copies, spines richly tooled and lettered in gilt, decorated endpapers, a.e.g. A lovely set in a variant publisher's cloth binding, variously decorated, with contemporary presentation inscription (dated "April 5th 1847") in a neat hand on front blank of each volume.

1930. THE POETICAL WORKS OF MILTON, YOUNG, GRAY, BEATTIE, AND COLLINS. Complete In One Volume. Stereotyped By J. Crissy And G. Goodman. *Philadelphia: Grigg & Elliot, No. 9 North Fourth Street. 1847.* 8vo, xxxii+170pp.,+viii+208pp.,+x+47pp.,+ix+23pp., +iv+19pp., frontispiece plate with vignette portrait of each poet engraved by J. B. Longacre (with Milton at the top), protective tissue guard, engraved illustration plates, protective tissue guard, half-title for Milton and for each collection of poetical works with contents on verso, life of Milton and of each poet, printed in double column, contemporary three-quarter black calf, dark red cloth (somewhat rubbed, spine ends chipped, corners worn, plates slightly foxed, some scattered foxing throughout), gilt rules on covers, spine lettered in gilt, raised bands between gilt rules, brown endpapers, speckled edges. Scarce nineteenth-century American edition of Milton's *PW*. Included are the poetical works of Milton with two engraved illustration plates (a bit foxed), one illustration for *Arcades*, entitled

PW. One Hundred And Twenty Engravings From Drawings By William Harvey. New York: Harper & Brothers. n.d. [ca. 1847] First edition thus by Harper & Brothers. 8vo, illustrations as with first edition by Tilt in 1843. (right) Publisher's original gilt-stamped dark green morocco, possibly a presentation binding, with name in gilt at bottom of front covers; gilt emblem at center of volume 1: small depiction of Eve tempting Adam; at center of volume 2: small emblem of serpent wound around Crucifix. (left) Original full maroon morocco, similarly decorated, with emblems at center reversed on volumes 1 and 2. (center) Original red cloth, covers delicately tooled in blind in the same pattern as that tooled in gilt in the other two copies; emblem at center of all covers: fountain shooting water at three levels. See #1927, 1928, and 1929.

Arcadia ("Drawn by C. R. Cockerell" and "Engd. on Steel by F. Kearny"), the other an untitled and unsigned illustration for *To a Virtuous Young Lady* (placed near Milton's sonnet). This edition is perhaps the last edition by Grigg & Elliot and possibly the first to have these plates included. See 1831 edition (first thus) by Grigg also listed here with further editions cited. Not in Kohler.

1931. THE POETICAL WORKS OF JOHN MILTON; With A Memoir; Embellished With Engravings After Designs By Fuseli, Westall, And Martin. *London: H. G. Bohn, York Street, Covent Garden. 1848.* 8vo, vii+527pp., engraved frontispiece portrait plate engraved by Cochran after a drawing by Cooper, illustration plates after Fuseli, Westall, and Martin, contemporary crushed maroon calf (rubbed at joints), gilt rules on covers with finely tooled inner border trim, elaborately gilt-decorated spine in the compartments with gilt lettering, raised bands with decorative gilt trim, inner dentelles tooled in blind, a.e.g. A nice copy with neat inscription to "Thomas Fowell Buxton . . . 1850," later Governor-General of West Australia, on front blank, along with two Buxton family bookplates (one armorial) on inside front pastedown. The first edition thus and the basis for this edition by Bohn was published by Churton in 1836 (also listed here with further editions by Churton and by Chidley in the collection cited). The possible first edition thus by Bohn was published in 1844 (also listed here with further editions cited). Not in Kohler.

1932. THE POETICAL WORKS OF JOHN MILTON; To Which Is Prefixed The Life Of The Author. *London: William Tegg And Co., 73 Cheapside. M.DCCC.XLVIII.* 12mo in 6s, xi+576pp., half-title, frontispiece portrait plate engraved by W. C. Edwards after Vertue, protective tissue guard, portrait plate engraved by W. C. Edwards after Jansen, at beginning of life, and portrait plate engraved by W. C. Edwards after Romney at end of life, nine engraved illustration plates: two after R. Westall and seven after Turner, contemporary blue polished calf (worn at joints and extremities and spine ends, joints tender, plates a little foxed), covers ruled in gilt, spine richly decorated in gilt with orange label lettered in gilt, raised bands with decorative gilt trim, outer dentelles finely tooled in gilt, marbled endpapers, a.e.g. A good copy with prize label tipped on front pastedown. Scarce. Not in Kohler (although Kohler 313 in reference to the next edition observes that "The British Library has a copy of the 12mo edition"; if that is in reference to this 12mo edition, it should be noted that this edition and the following, while similar, are different editions).

In Publisher's Original Morocco Gift Binding

1933. THE POETICAL WORKS OF JOHN MILTON. Edited By Sir Egerton Brydges, Bart. [Quotation from Thomson] Illustrated With Engravings From Drawings By J. M. W. Turner, R. A. A New Edition. *London: William Tegg & Co., Cheapside. MDCCCXLVIII.* Third Brydges/Turner illustrated edition. Thick 8vo, cvi+767pp., half-title, frontispiece portrait plate engraved by W. C. Edwards after Vertue, protective tissue guard (age-darkened), "To William Wordsworth And Robert Southey This Volume Is Appropriately Dedicated" on verso of title page, "Advertisement to the Original Edition" dated 1835, printed before contents, seven illustration plates engraved by various engravers after J. M. W. Turner, each with protective tissue guard (some age-darkening and slight foxing), double black border around text, original full dark maroon morocco (a bit rubbed), delicately gilt-tooled covers with narrow decorative border trim finely tooled in blind, elaborately gilt-decorated spines in the panels with gilt lettering, raised bands, inner and outer dentelles finely tooled in gilt, blue ribbon marker, a.e.g. A handsome copy in publisher's original morocco elaborately gilt gift binding, with an early bookplate on fly-leaf. Stevens 138, ref. 1848 ed.; Kohler 313, citing Williamson 135 and reporting "Not in the Bodleian Library. Not in Cambridge University Library," with the additional notation: that "The British Library has a copy of the 12mo edition"—copy preceding.

The illustrations by Turner first appeared in Brydges's 1835 six-volume edition of Milton's *PW*; the second Brydges/Turner illustrated edition was published by Tegg in 1842—both listed here; see 1837 first illustrated edition by Tegg (with vignette illustration on title page) also listed here with further editions cited.

1934. Variant of Preceding, contemporary calf (a bit worn), blind-stamped covers and spine, red morocco label with gilt lettering and decorative gilt trim, slightly raised thick bands with blind trim, inner and outer dentelles tooled in blind, marbled endpapers, red edges, blue ribbon marker, early armorial bookplate on front pastedown. A

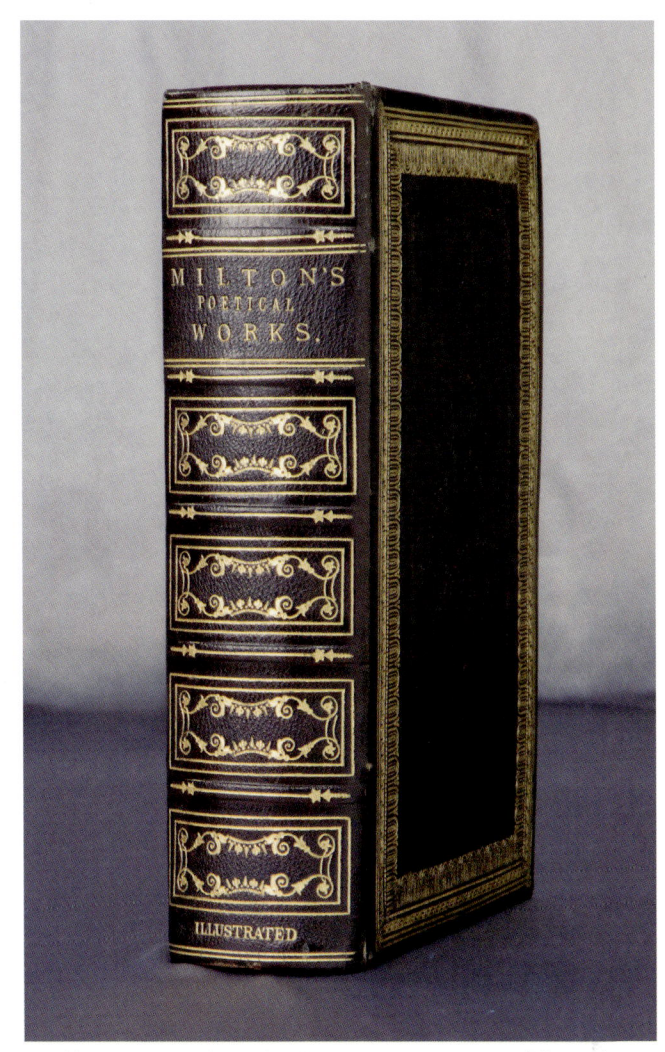

PW. Tegg, 1853, in a fine and well-preserved contemporary full straight-grained navy blue morocco, richly gilt decorated. See #1967.

good stout copy, very fresh and clean within, in publisher's original blind-tooled calf.

1935. Variant of Preceding, contemporary full blue polished calf (a bit rubbed), gilt rules on covers with central gilt arms on front cover, elaborately gilt-decorated spine within the panels, red morocco label with gilt lettering and decorative gilt trim, slightly raised thick bands with decorative gilt trim, inner dentelles tooled in blind, outer dentelles tooled in gilt (a bid faded), marbled endpapers, a.e.g. The Trevelyan family Milton, initially presented as a school prize to George Otto Trevelyan in 1848 while at Harrow, with school arms stamped in gilt on front cover and dated prize label tipped in on front pastedown; later ownership signature of G. M Trevelyan, Hallington, 1928. An attractive copy in a Harrow School Prize Binding, with a fine association.

1936. THE POETICAL WORKS OF JOHN MILTON. With A Memoir, And Critical Remarks On His Genius And Writings, By James Montgomery; And Thirty-Six Engravings, From Drawings By William Harvey. *Hartford: Published By S. Andrus & Son. MDCCCXLVIII.* 2 volumes. Second edition thus by Andrus & Son. 8vo, l+400pp.(pagination beginning at "18"),+369pp., frontispiece illustration of *Milton Dictating*, engraved by "Lossing & Co," volume 1, initially engraved by "Thompson" in original publication of Harvey's illustrations, frontispiece illustration of Milton *Mid books and papers in my study pent, If this be exile, sweet is banishment* engraved by "Clark," volume 2, full-page illustrations after William Harvey with in-text illustrations for *L'A* only (as in original publication of Harvey's illustrations), separate title page each volume, half-title for each book of *PL* and for each major poem, original red cloth (a bit rubbed at joints and corners, spines chipped at bottom of volume 1 and at bottom and top of volume 2), a rather brilliant gilt emblem at the center of front covers and a different equally brilliant gilt emblem on back covers (the emblems—a cross within a crown of thorns on front covers, a serpent wound around a flaming sword with apple on a small branch with leaves on back covers), spines lettered in gilt (title and "Andrus' Illustrated Edition" in small gilt letters at the center) and decorated in gilt with a depiction of Adam and Eve departing Eden in bright gilt at the top of the spines and of a dove amidst brilliant rays in bright gilt at the bottom of the spines, a.e.g. A nice set in a lovely mid-nineteenth-century American publisher's binding. Harvey's illustrations, which are not included in full here and which are, with the exception of *L'A*, reproduced as full-page illustrations rather than in-text illustrations as originally published, were first published in London by Tilt & Bogue in 1843 (see two-volume sets listed here). Scarce. Not in Kohler.

1937. THE POETICAL WORKS OF JOHN MILTON. A New Edition. With Notes, And A Life Of The Author, By John Mitford. *Lowell: D. Bixby And Company. 1848.* 2 volumes. First edition thus by Bixby. 8vo in 4s, cxxix+[2]+371pp.,+ii+478pp., frontispiece portrait plate "Engraved by O. Pelton From a Miniature of the same size by Faithorne, Anno 1667, in the possession of William Falconer Esq., Lowell: Published by Daniel Bixby & Co." protective tissue guard, volume 1, original twelve-page "Advertisement" by John Mitford dated 1831, and life of Milton by Mitford followed by addenda and an appendix, volume 1, half-titles for some of the poems, notes at bottom of page, original brown silk (ends of spines chipped, corners a bit rubbed), large urn in gilt at the center of each front cover with title in embossed arch above and Milton's name in embossed border below, decorative rules and corner pieces in blind, back covers similarly decorated in blind, spines lettered and numbered in gilt and decorated in blind, top edges rough, with the signature of Horace Davis in pen on each fly-leaf and in pencil on each title page. A nice set with a splendid association. This appears to be a reprint of 1845 Little and Brown edition (also listed here); see also two-volume 1849 edition (possible first edition thus), similar to the Bixby edition here, published by Baker in Lowell. Scarce. Stevens 153; Not in Kohler.

Horace Davis (March 16, 1831–July 12, 1916), manufacturer, congressman and prominent Californian, was born in Worcester, Massachusetts, the son of Governor Honest John Davis and Eliza (Bancroft) Davis. In 1849 he came to California in the Gold Rush and was involved in various business pursuits, one of which was the Golden Gate Flouring Mills of San Francisco. Elected to Congress in 1876, he served two terms and was quite active in the Chinese question. In 1888 he was elected president of the University of California. One of his major interests was the School of Mechanic Arts in San Francisco. His book collection was listed as one of the major private libraries in California in 1878.

1938. THE POETICAL WORKS OF JOHN MILTON; To Which Is Prefixed The Life Of The Author. *London: William Tegg And Co., Cheapside. M.DCCC.XLIX.* 12mo in 6s, xi+576pp., frontispiece portrait engraved by W. C. Edwards after Vertue, portrait plate engraved by W. C. Edwards after Cornelius Jansen (Aet. XXI) inserted before life, along with portrait plate of *Milton Dictating to His Daughters* engraved by W. C. Edwards after G. Romney, seven illustration plates engraved by various engravers after J. M. W. Turner, two illustration plates engraved by R. Graves and by F. Bacon after R. Westall, each with protective tissue guard, contemporary full red morocco, covers ruled in gilt with inner gilt rule and decorative trim pieces at the corners, spine decorated in gilt by compartments and lettered in gilt, raised bands with decorative gilt rule, inner and outer dentelles finely tooled in gilt, a.e.g. The final several leaves include "Commendatory Verses On Milton" by various poets. A very fine copy with contemporary inscription (dated 1851) on fly-leaf. See 1837 first illustrated edition by Tegg also listed here with further editions cited. Scarce. Not in Kohler.

1939. THE POETICAL WORKS OF JOHN MILTON: With Explanatory Notes, and a Life of the Author, By The Rev. H. Stebbing, D.D. To Which Is Prefixed, Dr. Channing's Essay On The Poetical Genius Of Milton. *London: H. G. Bohn, York Street, Covent Garden. 1849.* Second edition thus by Bohn. 12mo, iv+552pp., engraved frontispiece illustration of *Satan, Sin, and Death* after H. Corbould engraved by C. Heath, protective tissue guard, engraved and printed title pages with an engraved vignette illustration of *Satan, Sin, and Death* "before the gates," after T. Uwins engraved by Ranson, on engraved title page ("The Poetical Works Of John Milton. With An Account Of His Life," with publisher's imprint, "London: Engraved for the English Classics"), notes at bottom of page, contemporary red cloth (a bit rubbed and a little dirtied, joints slightly cracked, some foxing throughout, including frontispiece illustration and engraved and printed title pages), covers decorated in blind with a gilt harp at the center of the front cover, spine entirely covered over in gilt with a floral gilt pattern running throughout, the whole surrounded in red and gilt rules with the title embossed in gilt near the top within a red background, edges untrimmed. A nice copy. The possible first edition thus by Bohn of "the English Classics" was published in 1847 with only the illustration after T. Uwins (also listed here). Scarce. Not in Kohler.

1940. THE POETICAL WORKS OF JOHN MILTON. A New Edition. With Notes, And A Life Of The Author By John Mitford. *Lowell: William G. Baker. 1849.* 2 volumes. First edition thus by Baker? 8vo in 4s, cxxix+[2]+371pp.,+ii+478pp., frontispiece portrait plate "Engraved by O. Pelton From a Miniature of the same size by Faithorne, Anno 1667, in the possession of William Falconer Esq., Lowell: Published by Daniel Bixby & Co." protective tissue guard with imprint of frontispiece portrait, volume 1, original twelve-page "Advertisement" by John Mitford dated 1831, and life of Milton by Mitford followed by addenda and an appendix, volume 1, half-titles for some of the poems, notes at bottom of the page, original brown silk cloth (a bit frayed along edges and corners, ends of spines chipped, front cover of volume 2 broken, frontispiece portrait foxed, slight embrowning throughout), large urn in gilt at the center of each front cover with title in embossed arch above and Milton's name in embossed border below, decorative rules and corner pieces in blind, back covers similarly decorated in blind, spines lettered and numbered in gilt and decorated in blind, top edges rough, partially unopened. Despite the worn covers, a good set with early presentation inscription on front blank, volume 1. See two-volume 1848 edition (set listed here, possible first edition thus) published by Bixby in Lowell, similar to Baker edition here. Scarce. Kohler 315, with half-title for "Minor Poems" similarly misbound, reporting that this edition is "Not in Williamson. Not in the British Library. Not in the Bodleian Library. Not in Cambridge University Library."

1941. THE POETICAL WORKS OF JOHN MILTON; With A Memoir, And Essay On His Poetical Genius. By Dr. Channing; Together With Addison's Critique On The Paradise Lost. *London: Charles Daly, Greville Street, Hatton Garden. n.d. [ca. 1850].* 12mo, liv+450pp., unsigned engraved frontispiece portrait plate of a young Milton with protective tissue guard, undated engraved and printed title pages with unsigned steel-engraved vignette illustration for *L* on engraved title, protective tissue guard, original publisher's full red morocco (minor wear to extremities, minor embrowning), elaborately gilt-decorated covers with central device in gilt, elaborately gilt-decorated spine with gilt lettering, raised bands with decorative gilt trim, inner and outer dentelles finely tooled in gilt, a.e.g. A very pretty copy with contemporary signature (dated "July 16th/50") on fly-leaf along with two other early twentieth-century signatures, bound without the steel-engraved illustration plates in later undated editions published by Charles Daly. Uncommon. Not in Kohler.

See undated ca. 1850 edition by Daly following with unsigned vignette illustration for *L* on engraved title as here, with variations on printed title page (a period instead of a semi-colon after "Milton"; "Dr. Channing's Essay" instead of "With A Memoir, And Essay . . . By"; "Published By Charles Daly" instead of just "Charles Daly"; "17, Greville Street" instead of "Greville Street" without address in publisher's imprint) and with nineteen unsigned steel-engraved illustration plates not present here; see also third undated ca. 1850 edition by Daly, with unsigned vignette illustration for *L* on engraved title as here, with other variations on printed title page ("John Milton's Poetical Works"; "A Memoir, And Essay . . . By"; and printer's imprint on verso—not present here) and with sixteen unsigned steel-engraved illustration plates not present here; and see undated ca. 1862 edition by Daly with title page similar to the third undated ca. 1850 edition by Daly and with sixteen unsigned steel-engraved illustration plates not present here. Unlike the third undated ca. 1850 edition by Daly and the undated ca. 1862 edition by Daly, this undated edition, like the following undated ca. 1850 edition by Daly, has a different title ("The Poetical Works Of John Milton" compared to "John Milton's Poetical Works"), "p. liv" with "li" present (missing in the later editions), "p. 61" with the "6" present (missing in later editions), and "Lycidas" printed correctly in the headers here (misprinted as "Lucidas" in the later editions). See also 1836 nonillustrated miniature edition by Daly ("Leicester Street, Leicester Square") with unsigned frontispiece portrait; see, too, 1838 miniature edition by Daly ("Leicester Street, Leicester Square"), with unsigned frontispiece portrait and unsigned vignette illustration of Satan on engraved title page; and see [1839] miniature edition by Daly ("19, Red Lion Square") with unsigned frontispiece portrait and with unsigned vignette illustration of Satan on engraved title page; see also ca. 1867 edition with publisher's imprint "Charles Daly 19, Red Lion Square" on engraved title, with printed title page for PL with publisher's imprint as here: "Charles Daly, Greville Street, Hatton Garden," with unsigned vignette illustration of Satan on engraved title page.

1942. Variant of Preceding. **THE POETICAL WORKS OF JOHN MILTON.** With A Memoir, And Dr. Channing's Essay on his Poetical Genius; Together With Addison's Critique On The Paradise Lost. *London: Published By Charles Daly, 17, Greville Street, Hatton Garden. n.d. [ca. 1850].* 12mo in 6s, liv+450pp., unsigned engraved frontispiece portrait plate of a young Milton with protective tissue guard, undated engraved and printed title pages with unsigned steel-engraved vignette illustration for L on engraved title, protective tissue guard, nineteen unsigned steel-engraved illustration plates, each with protective tissue guard, contemporary full maroon morocco (a bit rubbed, foxing to prelims and plate borders), front cover and spine elaborately decorated in gilt, spine lettered in gilt, a.e.g. A nice copy in an attractive Victorian full morocco binding. Similar to preceding edition, but with variations on printed title page as noted there and with nineteen unsigned steel-engraved illustration plates (not present in that edition). See also other editions by Daly cited there. Uncommon. Not in Kohler.

1943. [POETICAL WORKS] **JOHN MILTON'S POETICAL WORKS:** A Memoir, And Essay On His Poetical Genius, By Dr. Channing: Together With Addison's Critique on the Paradise Lost. *London: Charles Daly, Greville Street, Hatton Garden. n.d. [ca. 1850].* 12mo in 6s, liv+449+[1]pp., unsigned engraved frontispiece portrait plate (of a young Milton), protective tissue guard, undated engraved and printed title pages, printer's imprint on verso of title page ("London: J. Davy And Sons, Printers, 137, Long Acre"), with unsigned steel-engraved vignette illustration for L on engraved title page and sixteen additional unsigned steel-engraved illustrations, each with protective tissue guard, original decorated blue cloth (some foxing, especially frontispiece and engraved title page), gilt-decorated covers and spine, a.e.g., bound by Weemys & Co., with their ticket. A good copy in an attractive publisher's cloth binding. See first undated ca. 1850 Charles Daly edition with further editions by Daly cited there. Uncommon. Kohler 316, citing "Hatton Gardens" on title page instead of "Hatton Garden," as here (and in the first and second undated ca. 1850 editions by Daly and undated ca. 1862 edition by Daly—both listed here), and also indicating "Octavo. In 6s" and reporting "Not in Williamson. Not in the Bodleian Library. Not in Cambridge University Library."

1944. **THE POETICAL WORKS OF JOHN MILTON.** With Life. [Quote from Thomson.] Complete Edition. *London: John Kendrick, Charlotte Row Mansion House. MDCCCL.* 8vo, xxx+658pp., half-title, unsigned frontispiece illustration plate of *Ascent of the Spirit* with protective tissue guard, other illustration plates include: *The Sorceress* after F. Corbaux (bound here in Book I of *PL*); *The Destruction of Babel* after H. C. Slous (bound here in Book XII, for Book II of *PL*); *March of the Israelites From Egypt* and *The Crucifixion* after John Martin (the first for Psalm CXXXVI and the second for Book III of *PL*); *The Destruction of Babel* after H. C. Slous (bound here in Book XII of *PL*); unidentified (within *L*) after Drummond; unidentified (*Such as hung on Hebe's cheek* ..., for *L'A*) after A. E. Chalon, protective tissue guard for each illustration, half-title for each book of *PL* and for some of the poems, half-title for each book of *PR* with "Argument" on verso (not original to the poem), triple black border around text, contemporary three-quarter blue morocco, brown cloth (rubbed at joints and corners), gilt seal of Graham College on front cover, gilt-decorated spine with small gilt devices in the panels, red morocco label with gilt lettering, raised bands with decorative gilt trim, marbled endpapers and edge. A nice copy in a lovely Prize Binding with blank prize label on front pastedown and contemporary presentation inscription (dated 1855) on verso of yellow front blank before half-title. See 1851 edition with the same address for Kendrick in publisher's imprint and different illustrations, and 1855 and 1859 editions, each with a different address for Kendrick in publisher's imprint and with illustrations identical to those in the 1851 edition—each edition listed here. Kohler 317, reporting "Not in the British Library. Not in the Bodleian Library. Not in Cambridge University Library."

1945. **THE POETICAL WORKS OF JOHN MILTON.** [Quote from Thomson.] *London: Thomas Nelson, Paternoster Row; And Edinburgh. MDCCCL.* First edition thus by Nelson? Small 8vo, xxxii+[ii]+639pp., advertisement leaf for a "List of Interesting Works, Published By Thomas Nelson," frontispiece portrait plate of a middle-aged Milton, the portrait in a circular form with decorative trim, the whole within a shaded background with Milton's name at the top and his dates beneath, "T. G. Flowers" at the bottom, protective tissue guard, engraved title-page plate ("T. Nelson, London & Edinburgh," n.d.) with an unsigned illustration of *The Judgment* for Book X of *PL* (in smaller form than the illustration plate for Book X in 1852 edition listed here), life of Milton, nine additional illustration plates, each image 3 ½" × 2 ⅛" on a 5 ⅛" × 3 ⅛" page with a decorative light blue border frame (each unsigned and possibly the first appearance of these illustrations), protective tissue guards, with the lines illustrated quoted beneath each illustration, double black rule around text, half-title for *PL, PR, SA, C*, original decorated green cloth (a bit rubbed, spine a little darkened), covers decorated in blind with central urn in gilt on front cover and in blind on back cover, spine lettered in gilt with decorative gilt trim at top and bottom and with the urn on the covers repeated in gilt at the center, a.e.g. A charming copy.

The illustration plates include an illustration of *Satan Summoning His Legions* for Book I of *PL*; an illustration of *The Judgment* for Book X of *PL* repeated from engraved title page; an illustration entitled *Satan Bound with Chains* for Book XII of *PL* ; an illustration entitled *Ancient Rome* for Book IV of *PR*; an illustration entitled *Ancient Rome* for Book IV of *PR*; an illustration entitled *Ruins of Athens* for Book IV of *PR*; an illustration entitled *Ruins of Athens* for Book IV of *PR* (after "W. H. Prior" engraved by "C. Measam"—the only plate with any identification); an illustration for *L*; an illustration for the sonnet *On The Religious Memory Of Mrs. Catherine Thomson, My Christian Friend, Deceased Dec. 16, 1646*; and an illustration entitled "The Waldenses" for the sonnet *On The Late Massacre In Piemont*.

A possible second edition thus was published by "T. Nelson and Sons" in 1852 (also listed here), without a frontispiece portrait or engraved title page but with the same illustrations as those here, identical in number and subject, and, like here, unsigned. A possible third edition was published by "T. Nelson And Sons" in 1853 (also listed here), without engraved title page, with the first appearance of "Complete Edition" on the title page, and with the appearance of six different illustrations (unsigned, possibly by T. G. Flowers) from the nine unsigned illustrations in the 1850 and 1852 editions, the latter illustrations also being larger than the earlier ones. Later editions by T. Nelson and Sons were published with variations in size, number of pages, illustrations, inclusion of photographs tipped in as frontispieces and on title pages, and head- and tailpieces: in 1855, 1858 (two variants), 1859, 1860, 1861, and 1862 (each listed here), similar to one another and to the 1850 edition here, with a frontispiece portrait of Milton (except for 1860 edition, portrait unsigned), with engraved and printed title pages (in all but the 1860 edition), with similar but not identical illustrations (unsigned, but after T. G. Flowers), and with half-titles as here; and 1856 edition published by "T. Nelson And Sons, London; Edinburgh; And New York," with engraved frontispiece portrait after Faithorne and vignette illustration after A. Ritchie on engraved title page; see also 1863 illustrated edition by "T. Nelson And Sons" (listed here) with elaborately decorated head- and tailpieces and elaborately decorated half-titles, and with each unsigned illustration in a decorative frame; see, too, editions by T. Nelson and Sons with illustrations after E. H. Corbould and John Gilbert in 1864 (possible first edition thus by T. Nelson and Sons), in 1866 (possible second edition thus), in 1867 (possible third edition thus), in 1868 (possible fourth edition thus), and in 1869 (possible fifth edition thus)—copy of each listed here; and see 1871, 1872, and 1874 editions by T. Nelson and Sons with reproductions of illustrations by Flowers and with new headpieces and half-titles—copy of each listed here. Scarce. Not in Kohler.

1946. THE POETICAL WORKS OF JOHN MILTON. With A Memoir, And Critical Remarks On His Genius And Writings, By James Montgomery; And Thirty-Six Engravings, From Drawings By William Harvey. *Hartford: Published By S. Andrus & Son. 1850.* 2 volumes. Third edition thus by Andrus & Son? 8vo, l+400pp.(pagination beginning at "19"),+369pp., frontispiece illustration of "*Milton Dictating,*" engraved by "Lossing & Co," volume 1, initially engraved by "Thompson" in original publication of Harvey's illustrations, unsigned frontispiece illustration of Milton *Mid books and papers in my study pent, If this be exile, sweet is banishment* engraved by "Clark," volume 2, full-page illustrations after William Harvey with in-text illustrations for *L'A* only (no in-text illustrations for *IlP* or other poems as in original publication of Harvey's illustrations), separate title page each volume, half-title for each book of *PL* and for each major poem, contemporary red pebble morocco (a bit rubbed at joints and edges), front covers elaborately tooled in gilt, spines decoratively lettered in gilt with a depiction of *Adam and Eve Departing Eden* in gilt at the top of the spines and of a *Dove Amidst Brilliant Rays* in gilt at the bottom of the spines, inner and outer dentelles finely tooled in gilt, a.e.g. A fine set in a lovely mid-nineteenth-century American morocco binding. See comments with first edition thus by Andrus & Son of Hartford in 1847 (see two-volume set also listed here with further editions cited). Scarce. Not in Kohler.

1947. THE POETICAL WORKS OF MILTON, YOUNG, GRAY, BEATTIE, AND COLLINS. Complete In One Volume. Stereotyped By J. Crissy And G. Goodman. *Philadelphia: Lippincott, Grambo & Co., Successors To Grigg, Elliot & Co., No. 14, North Fourth Street. 1850.* 8vo, xxxii+170pp.,+viii+208pp.,+x+47pp.,+ix+23pp.,+iv+19pp., frontispiece plate with vignette portrait of each poet engraved by J. B. Longacre (with Milton at the top), protective tissue guard (foxed), half-title for Milton and for each collection of poetical works with contents on verso, life of Milton and of each poet, printed in double column, engraved illustration plates (a bit foxed), protective tissue guards (foxed), original red cloth (worn, spine chipped at top, foxing), decorative central gilt emblem on front cover with decorative trim in blind, similar emblem repeated in blind on back cover, gilt-decorated spine with gilt lettering, a.e.g. Included are the poetical works of Milton with two engraved illustration plates (a bit foxed), one illustration for *Arcades*, entitled *Arcadia* ("Drawn by C. R. Cockerell" and "Engd. on Steel by F. Kearny"), the other illustration for *To A Virtuous Young Lady* (untitled and unsigned, but placed near Milton's sonnet). Scarce mid-nineteenth-century illustrated American edition of Milton's *PW*. Not in Kohler.

See 1831 edition (first thus) by Grigg listed and other editions cited there by Grigg and by Grigg and Elliot, including the 1847 edition (copy listed), perhaps the last edition thus by Grigg & Elliot, with two illustration plates for Milton, possibly the first time these plates were included in the edition; and see 1852, 1853, and 1854 editions by Lippincott, Grambo & Co. (copy of each listed), the 1854 edition with two unsigned illustration plates bound within Milton; see also 1856 and 1857 editions by Lippincott & Co. (copy of each listed), and 1882 edition by Lippincott, Grambo & Co. (copy listed).

1948. THE POETICAL WORKS OF JOHN MILTON; Complete In One Volume. [In] **CABINET EDITION OF THE BRITISH POETS.** In Four Volumes. Vol. I. Milton. Cowper. Goldsmith. Thomson. Falconer. Akenside. Collins. Gray. Somervile. *London: Jones And Co., Temple Of The Muses, Finsbury Square. n.d. [ca. 1850].* 8vo, vii+131pp. (for Milton), separate pagination for each of the poets, frontispiece consisting of vignette portraits of five of the poets in the collection within a floral frame with a vignette portrait of Milton at the center, separate title page for Milton's *PW*: "**THE POETICAL WORKS OF JOHN MILTON;** Complete In One Volume. Dryden Epigram. London: Published By Jones & Company, Temple Of The Muses, (Late Lackington's,) Finsbury Square. 1835," with engraved title page: "Cabinet Edition Of [?]Sacred British Poets, Comprising The Works Of Milton, Cowper, Goldsmith, Thomson, Falconer, Akenside, Collins, Gray & Somervile. London, MDCCCXLVII (1847)," with vignette illustration (not for Milton) on engraved title, "Drawn by Corbould" and "Engd. By Freeman," life of Milton by Fenton, "Index To Paradise Lost" at the end. Together with *The Works of Various Poets* (including Cowper, Goldsmith, Collins, Somerville, etc., each with separate title pate). Original red cloth (a bit worn, spine faded and chipped at the top), covers and spine decorated in blind, spine lettered in gilt, edges untrimmed, with early presentation inscription (dated 1862) on verso of frontispiece. A ca. 1850 reprint of the 1835 edition. Uncommon. Not in Kohler.

1949. THE POETICAL WORKS Of John Milton. **PARADISE LOST AND PARADISE REGAINED.** *Leipzig[:] Bernhard Tauchnitz[,] 1850.* First edition thus. Small 8vo, vi+358pp., original brown cloth (a bit rubbed), covers richly embossed in an attractive design, spine lettered and decorated in gilt, very lightly marbled edges, large bookplate (with a German shepherd dog and books) on front pastedown. A very nice copy in an attractive binding of the period. See 1920 reprint edition listed here. Kohler 318, identifying "Todd & Bowden 194b," stating that "The colophon is in the second state and so this is of a later date than 1850 but the exact date is unknown," and reporting "Not in Cambridge University Library."

1950. THE POETICAL WORKS OF JOHN MILTON. With Life. [Quote from Thomson] Complete Edition. *London: John Kendrick, Charlotte Row Mansion House. MDCCCLI.* 8vo, xxx+658pp., unsigned frontispiece illustration plate of *The Ascent of the Spirit*, seven additional illustration plates: (*Thus fame shall be achieved...*, for Book XI) engraved by E. Goodall after a painting by W. Linton (not in the 1850 copy listed here); *March of the Israelites from Egypt*, *The Crucifixion*, and *The Resurrection* after John Martin (all three for Book XII of *PL*); *The Destruction of Babel* after H. C. Slous (for Book XII of *PL*); *He must not float upon his watery bier...*, for *L* after C. Bentley (replacing an unidentified illustration for *L* after Drummond in the 1850 copy also listed here); unidentified (*Such as hung on Hebe's cheek...*, for *L'A*) after A. E. Chalon, protective tissue guard for each illustration, half-title for each book of *PL* and for some of the poems, half-title for each book of *PR* with "Argument" on verso (not original to the poem), triple black border around text, contemporary full dark maroon morocco (a little rubbed at joints), covers tooled in gilt with central gilt harp and gilt border rules, gilt-decorated spine in the panels with gilt lettering, raised bands (a bit rubbed), inner and outer dentelles finely tooled in gilt (outer dentelles faded), blue ribbon marker, a.e.g. A very nice copy in an attractive morocco binding of the period with contemporary inscription (dated 1852) on front blank. Scarce. Not in Kohler.

Similar to 1850 edition by Kendrick, except this edition has three illustrations by Martin instead of two, and besides adding the illustration plate after a painting by Linton, two illustration plates found in the 1850 copy are not found here: the unidentified illustration after Drummond and "The Sorceress" after F. Corbaux. See also 1855 and 1859 editions by Kendrick with illustrations identical to those here, but with a different publisher's address.

1951. [POETICAL WORKS] MILTON'S POETICAL WORKS. *New York[:] Clark, Austin & Co., 205 Broadway. n.d. (1851).* 2 volumes in one. 12mo in 6s, 283pp.,+215pp., unsigned engraved frontispiece illustration for *PL* (Book III, line 667), engraved title page for *PW* (as given) with unsigned vignette illustration for *PL* (Book X, line 940), two printed title pages, one for *PL* ("Paradise Lost. A Poem In Twelve Books. By John Milton. New York: Published By Clark, Austin & Co., 205 Broadway. 1851"), and one for ("Paradise Regained, And Other Poems By John Milton. New York: Published By Clark, Austin & Co., 205 Broadway. 1850"), index to *PL*, original green cloth (a bit rubbed, inoffensive staining to first twenty-five pages, including frontispiece and title pages), covers decorated with central decorative device in blind, spine decorated and lettered in gilt. A good copy of a scarce mid-nineteenth-century American edition. See copy of 1850 edition of *PL/PR* by Clark, Austin & Co. (listed here) with the same frontispiece illustration and engraved title page and with the same printed title pages, each printed title page dated 1850; see also copy of separate 1850 edition of *PR* (listed here). Not in Kohler.

1952. THE POETICAL WORKS OF JOHN MILTON. Edited by Sir Egerton Brydges, Bart. [Quote from Thomson.] Illustrated With Engravings, Designed By John Martin And J. W. M. Turner, R. A. *Philadelphia: Geo. S. Appleton, 164 Chestnut Street. New York: D Appleton & Co., 200 Broadway. MDCCCLI.* First edition thus by Appleton? Thick 8vo in 4s, 858pp., life of Milton, notes at bottom of page, illustrations by John Martin for *PL* (reduced plates included are those for Books IV, V, IX, and X) and one illustration for Book XII (while unsigned, Martin's Bible illustration of the "Expulsion" is used), each with protective tissue guard, original one-half calf, marbled paper over boards (worn, spine amateurishly repaired with blue tape, pages loose, a few pencil marginalia, some foxing on the plates, one plate chipped, library stamps marked "withdrawn," shelf label on spine, due-date card in pocket at back), in a protective plastic cover with leather around spine for appearance's sake. There is no explanation as to why illustrations by Turner are not included here or why none are included in the possible second edition thus (also listed here) published in 1852 by Appleton in New York (without Philadelphia in the publisher's imprint), which, like here, includes only plates by Martin, even though both Martin and Turner are mentioned on the title page. Scarce. Not in Kohler.

See also undated ca. 1860 and 1869 editions published by Appleton in New York (without Philadelphia in the publisher's imprint, each edition listed here), which appear to be reproductions of the edition of Milton's *PW* published by Phillips, Sampson, and Company in Boston in 1854 (also listed here), with the publisher's imprint of "Boston. Phillips, Sampson & Company" on the engraved title page and "New York: D. Appleton & Company" on the printed title page, with plates after Martin and Turner as well as after Westall and Romney. See, too, the following illustrated editions of Milton's *PW*—each edition also listed here: 1861 edition in a format similar to the 1860 and 1869 editions by Appleton with plates after Martin and Turner as well as Westall and Romney, published in Boston by Crosby, Nichols, Lee & Company; 1866 edition also in a format similar to the 1860 and 1869 editions by Appleton with plates after Martin and Turner as well as Westall and Romney, published in Boston by Crosby & Ainsworth and in New York by Oliver S. Felt; and 1868, 1869, and ca. 1872 editions in a format similar to the 1860 and 1869 editions by Appleton with plates after Martin and Turner as well as Westall and Romney, published in New York by W. I. Pooley. See, too, 1856 two-volume edition edited by Gilfillan and published by Appleton in New York with plates after Martin and Turner as well as Westall and Romney; and see 1859, 1861, 1868, and 1872 12mo editions published by "D. Appleton & Company" with reproductions of illustrations after Turner—each edition also listed here.

1953. Variant of Preceding, original green cloth (binding shows some wear), covers decorated in blind with a sketch of Milton in blind in the center, spine elaborately decorated in gilt with a large gilt harp near the bottom and a small figure of a lady playing the harp or lyre at the top, edges untrimmed. A decent copy in a variant publisher's binding, very tight and generally clean within, with a contemporary signature (dated 1852) on fly-leaf. With the exception of the frontispiece illustration, the engraved illustrations intended to accompany this edition of Milton, as with the preceding copy, seem not to have been included here; they do not seem to have been removed but rather appear not to have been originally bound within this copy. Not in Kohler.

1954. THE POETICAL WORKS OF JOHN MILTON; To Which Is Prefixed, The Life Of The Author. *London: William Tegg And Co., 85, Queen Street Cheapside. 1851.* 12mo in 6s, xi+576pp., contemporary polished calf (spine chipped at top, covers detached), gilt rules on covers with central gilt device on front cover, gilt-decorated spine repeating the gilt device on front cover in each panel, red morocco label with gilt lettering and gilt rules, raised bands with decorative gilt trim, outer dentelles tooled in gilt, marbled endpapers and edges. Prize Binding, with Harrow prize certificate fixed to front endpaper by a pin. Laid in: a possibly contemporary manuscript leaf regarding *PL* as a performance. A nice copy. See 1837 first illustrated edition by Tegg also listed here with further editions cited. Scarce. Not in Kohler.

1955. THE POETICAL WORKS OF JOHN MILTON[.] *London[:] William Pickering[,] 1851*. 3 volumes. Fifth Aldine edition. Small 8vo, cxxxiv+[iv]+[1]+153pp.,+372pp.,+334pp., edited by John Mitford with a life of Milton, half-title each volume ("The Aldine Edition Of The British Poets"), engraved frontispiece portrait by H. Robinson, volume 1, dated "London, William Pickering, 1831," separate title page each volume with anchor emblem of the Pickering Press on each title page, original "Advertisement" for the 1832 Aldine edition by John Mitford with original date of 1831, life of Milton by Mitford followed by addenda and appendix, volume 1, half-title for some of the poems, anchor emblem of the Pickering Press on the last leaf of volume 3, printed by Charles Whittingham, original dark green morocco bound by Hayday with his stamp on front pastedown (slightly rubbed, spines just very slightly faded toward olive green), covers with triple blind ruled border trim, spines lettered in gilt, raised bands, a.e.g. A very fine set in superb condition, the bindings still with their original brightness and with virtually no signs of use internally. In 1830 Pickering began publishing his famous "Aldine Poets" series, covering more than twenty years and producing a run of fifty-three different volumes, all well-printed and carefully edited. Pickering offered books from this 1851 series either in cloth at 5 shillings or in morocco by Hayday for 10 shillings, 6 pence per volume. See the first Aldine edition of Milton in 1832 listed here with further Aldine editions of Milton cited there. The 1832, 1845, and 1851 Aldine editions are the only editions to have the anchor emblem of the Pickering Press on the last leaf of volume 3. This, the fifth Aldine edition, is considered to be perhaps the scarcest of the five Pickering Aldine editions. Not in Kohler.

1956. Another copy of THE POETICAL WORKS OF JOHN MILTON[.] *London[:] William Pickering[,] 1851*. 3 volumes. Fifth Aldine edition. Small 8vo, as preceding, contemporary brown calf (worn, some age-browning, without half-titles), gilt rules on covers, gilt-decorated spines (leather labels mostly gone), marbled endpapers and edges, notes to the text. Though a somewhat worn set of this scarce Pickering edition, a special association copy from Pickering's distinguished Aldine series of British poets in a contemporary binding which comes from the "College of New Jersey [at Princeton]. Library of the American Whig Society," (later Princeton University) with the college bookplate in each volume, covering the ticket of either the binder or bookseller in volume 1, with "at Princeton" written beneath the "College of New Jersey" on the bookplate in a neat hand in volume 1, with the signature of W. B. Parsons on the front blank of volume 1 and the stamp of the American Whig Society in each volume.

1957. THE POETICAL WORKS OF JOHN MILTON. *Printed From The Original Editions With A Life Of The Author By The Rev. John Mitford[.] London[:] William Pickering[,] 1851*. 2 volumes. First edition thus. 8vo, ccii+270pp.,+xx+415pp., half-title each volume with decorative headpiece, frontispiece portrait "Engraved by W. Humphreys, from a Print by Faithorne," volume 1, title pages in red and black, each with central emblem of the Pickering Press in red and black, "Advertisement To The [Pickering] Edition Of 1851," folding genealogical table (as a multiple foldout), life of Milton, and folding (sideways) facsimile of "the Agreement between Milton and Mr. Symons" before appendix, with sketch of "The House at Chalfont St. Giles" bound before addenda, volume 1, decorative head- and tailpieces, decorated initial letters, half-title for some of the poems, handsomely printed by "C. Whittingham, Chiswick" with typographical figure of the press on last page of each volume, contemporary divinity-style brown calf (surface a bit scuffed, title page, volume 1, bears offprint of frontispiece), covers ruled in blind with small decorative corner pieces in blind, decorated in blind, marbled endpapers, red edges. A very good set, handsomely printed and handsomely bound, forming volumes 1 and 2 of Pickering's eight-volume 1851 edition of Milton's *Works* edited by Mitford (see set listed here), sold as separates. It is interesting to note that volume 1 contains *SA* and the *MP*, along with the preliminary material, while volume 2 contains *PL* and *PR*. Williamson 84l; Stevens 162; Not in Kohler.

1958. THE POETICAL WORKS OF JOHN MILTON. [Quote from Thomson] *London: T. Nelson And Sons, Paternoster Row; And Edinburgh. MDCCCLII*. Second edition thus by Nelson? Small 8vo, xxxii+[ii]+639pp., life of Milton, nine unsigned illustration plates, each with a decorative light blue border frame, each image 3 ½" × 2 ⅛" on a 5 ⅛" × 3 ⅛" page, protective tissue guard for all but one illustration, with the lines illustrated quoted beneath each illustration, double black rule around text, half-title for *PL*, *PR*, *SA*, and *C*, contemporary full red morocco (a bit rubbed), delicately gilt-decorated covers with central blind-stamped device, richly gilt-decorated spine within the panels with gilt lettering, slight raised bands, outer dentelles tooled in gilt, a.e.g. A fine copy in a lovely red morocco binding of the period with contemporary signature in a neat hand (dated 1856) on front blank. As with the 1850 (possible first) edition listed here, the illustration plates include an illustration of *Satan Summoning His Legions* for Book I of *PL*; an illustration of *The Judgment* for Book X of *PL*; an illustration entitled *Satan Bound with Chains* for Book XII of *PL*; an illustration entitled *Ancient Rome* for Book IV of *PR*; an illustration entitled *Ancient Rome* for Book IV of *PR*; an illustration entitled *Ruins of Athens* for Book IV of *PR* (after "W. H. Prior" engraved by "C. Measam"—the only plate with any identification); an illustration for *L*; an illustration for the sonnet *On The Religious Memory Of Mrs. Catherine Thomson, My Christian Friend, Deceased Dec. 16, 1646*; and an illustration entitled *The Waldenses* for the sonnet *On The Late Massacre In Piemont*. The illustrations in the 1850 edition by Nelson listed earlier are the same as those here in the 1852 edition, identical in number and subject, and, like here, are unsigned. The possible first edition thus by Nelson was published by "Thomas Nelson" in 1850 (also listed here with further editions cited). Uncommon. Not in Kohler.

1959. THE POETICAL WORKS OF JOHN MILTON; With A Memoir; Embellished With Engravings After Designs By Fuseli, Westall, And Martin. *London: H. G. Bohn, York Street, Covent Garden. 1852*. 8vo, vii+[1]+527pp., engraved frontispiece portrait plate engraved by Cochran after a drawing by Cooper, six illustration plates after Fuseli (one), Westall (two), and Martin (three), half-title for each book of *PL* and for some of the poems, contemporary diced calf (a bit rubbed), covers finely tooled in gilt with central gilt urn surrounded by decorative trim in blind, the whole surrounded by gilt rules, elaborately gilt-decorated spine in the compartments with gilt lettering, raised bands with decorative gilt trim, inner and outer dentelles elaborately tooled in gilt, a.e.g. A very fine copy with presentation prize inscription in a neat hand (dated 1853) on front blank. The first edition thus and the basis for this edition by Bohn was published by Churton in 1836 (also listed here with further editions by Churton and Chidley cited). See 1848 and 1855 editions by Bohn listed here. Stevens 164 (stating "Reprint of the edition of 1841" [by Bohn, see copy listed here]); Kohler 320, citing Williamson 218 and reporting "Not in the British Library. Not in the Bodleian Library. Not in Cambridge University Library."

1960. THE POETICAL WORKS OF JOHN MILTON. Edited by Sir Egerton Brydges, Bart. [Quote from Thomson] Illustrated With Engravings, Designed By John Martin And J. W. M. Turner, R. A. *New York: George S. Appleton. 1852*. Second edition thus by Appleton? Thick 8vo in 4s, 858pp. (first 110 pp. paginated in small Roman numerals, ending on page "cx"), frontispiece illustration of *The Creation* after Martin, life of Milton, six additional illustration plates after John Martin for *PL* (reduced plates include one for Book IV, two for Book V, two for Book IX, and two for Book X) and one illustration plate for Book XII (while unsigned, after Martin's Bible illustration of *The Expulsion*), each with protective tissue guard, original crushed red morocco (a little worn along extremities, spine worn and slightly chipped at top and bottom), covers with thick gilt rules in varying sizes, decorative gilt corners, and delicate gilt trim surrounding an indented panel at the center with central harp in blind, spine decorated in gilt within the gilt panels with gilt lettering, a.e.g. Despite the wear, a nice copy in an attractive contemporary morocco binding. There is no explanation as to why illustrations by Turner are not included here or why none were included in the possible first edition thus published in 1851 by Appleton, which, like here, includes only plates by Martin, even though both Martin and Turner are mentioned on the title page. See 1851 possible first edition thus by Appleton published in New York and Philadelphia with further editions cited there. Scarce. Not in Kohler.

1961. THE POETICAL WORKS OF JOHN MILTON. With A Memoir, And Critical Remarks On His Genius And Writings By James Montgomery; And Thirty-Six Engravings, From Drawings By William Harvey[.] Vol. I/II. *Hartford [Conn.]: Published By S. Andrus & Son. 1852*. 2 volumes. 8vo, l+400pp.(pagination beginning at "19"), +369+[4]pp., frontispiece illustration of *Milton Dictating* engraved by "Lossing & Co," volume 1, initially engraved by "Thompson" in original publication of Harvey's illustrations, unsigned frontispiece illustration of Milton *Mid books and papers in my study pent, / If this be exile, sweet is banishment* engraved by "Clark," volume 2, full-page illustrations after William Harvey with in-text illustrations for *L'A* only (no in-text illustrations for *IlP* or other poems as in original publication of Harvey's illustrations), separate title page each volume (each dated 1852), half-title for each book of *PL* and for each major poem, original blue cloth (a bit rubbed with some light discoloring at inside top of volume 1, spine ends slightly chipped), covers stamped in blind trim with a large bright gilt emblem at the center of each cover, spines lettered in gilt (including "Andrus' Illustrated Edition" in small gilt letters at the center) and decorated in gilt with a depiction of *Adam and Eve Departing Eden* in gilt at the top of the spines and of a *Dove Amidst Brilliant Rays* in gilt at the bottom of the spines. A nice copy of a mid-nineteenth-century American edition in original publisher's binding with four pages of advertisements bound in at the end. The first edition thus by Andrus & Son of Hartford with illustrations after Harvey was published in 1847 (see two-volume set listed here with further editions cited). Not in Kohler.

1962. Variant of Preceding, original black cloth (spine chipped at top, joints rubbed), blind-stamped covers with central gilt device incorporating lyre, elaborately gilt-decorated spine incorporating elaborately scrolled lettering in gilt. A good copy in a variant publisher's binding. Not in Kohler.

1963. THE POETICAL WORKS OF JOHN MILTON. With Notes Of Various Authors; And With Some Account Of The Life And writings Of Milton, Derived Principally From Original Documents In Her Majesty's State-Paper Office. By The Late Rev. Henry John Todd, M.A. Chaplain In Ordinary To Her Majesty, And Archdeacon Of Cleveland. Fifth Edition. In Four Volumes. *London: Rivingtons; Longman And Co; et al., And G. And J. Robinson, Liverpool. 1852.* 4 volumes. Fifth Todd edition, a reissue of the fourth and final Todd edition in 1842 (see set listed here). 8vo, xxviii+523pp.,+589pp.,+xxiii+431pp.,+viii+560pp., frontispiece portrait plate engraved by T. A. Dean after a drawing by T. Simpson from William Baker's painting by Faithorne, "Published by F. & J. Rivington, London, 1851," volume 1, with protective tissue guard, dedication page to the "Duke Of Bridgewater," "Advertisement To The Fourth Edition," dated 1842, preface, "Some Account Of The Life And Writing Of Milton," facsimile plate, dated 1826, of Milton's signature and on a 1650 debt notice in his own hand in 1650, volume 1, separate title page each volume, half-title for each book of *PL* and for some of the poems, unsigned engraved plate of Ludlow Castle before *C*, volume 4, engraved by T. Higham and dated 1842, engraved plate, "Fac-simile from the Original Drawing" of Queen Christina of Sweden in man's apparel, engraved by T. Higham for the Latin epigram, XIII. "Ad Christinam Suecorum Reginam, nomine Cromwelli," dated 1842, "List Of Editions," and "Glossarial Index," volume 4, contemporary polished calf, gilt rules on covers, elaborately gilt-decorated spines, maroon morocco title labels with gilt rules, green morocco numbering labels with gilt rules, inner dentelles tooled in blind, outer dentelles finely tooled in gilt, marbled endpapers and edges. A very fine set, clean and crisp throughout, with the armorial bookplate of Henry Cavendish in each volume. This is the final edition of the distinguished series of Todd editions that served as the standard text until supplanted by Masson's edition later in the century. The first Todd edition was published in 1801; the second Todd edition, revised and expanded, in 1809; the third Todd edition, further expanded, in 1826; the fourth Todd edition, last lifetime, in 1842—all Todd editions listed here. Williamson 152; Kohler 321, reporting "Not in the British Library. Not in the Bodleian Library. Not in Cambridge University Library."

1964. THE POETICAL WORKS OF JOHN MILTON[.] *London[:] William Pickering[,] 1852.* 3 volumes. Sixth Aldine edition? Small 8vo, xx+cxxxiv+[4]+153pp.,+372pp.,+334pp., edited by John Mitford with a life of Milton, engraved frontispiece portrait after H. Robinson (dated "London, William Pickering, 1831") with protective tissue guard, volume 1, separate title page each volume with anchor emblem of the Pickering Press on each title page, original "Advertisement" for the 1832 Aldine edition by John Mitford (with original date of 1831), life of Milton by Mitford followed by addenda and appendix, volume 1, half-title for some of the poems, notes at bottom of page, printed by Charles Whittingham at the Chiswick Press, contemporary full olive green morocco (a bit rubbed, joints worn, slight waterstain to lower portion of frontispiece), decorative gilt border trim on covers with inner rules in blind and gilt, elaborately gilt-decorated spines in the panels, two red morocco labels with gilt rules each volume, raised bands with decorative gilt trim, inner and outer dentelles finely tooled in gilt, marbled endpapers, a.e.g. A finely bound copy from Pickering's distinguished Aldine series of British poets, begun in 1830 and continuing for two decades. See the first Aldine edition of Milton listed in 1832 and other Aldine editions of Milton cited there. Not in Kohler.

1965. THE POETICAL WORKS OF JOHN MILTON. A New Edition. With Notes, And A Life Of The Author, By John Mitford. *Boston: Phillips, Sampson, And Company. 1852.* 2 volumes. 8vo in 4s, cxxix+[iii]+371pp.,+ii+478+[6]pp., frontispiece portrait engraved by O. Pelton "From a Miniature of the same size by Faithorne. Anno 1667 in the possession of William Falconer Esq., title page each volume, double black rule around text, original blind-embossed brown cloth (a bit rubbed, spine chipped at top and slightly nicked above title, volume 1, endpapers and frontispiece foxed), front covers lettered in blind, spines lettered in gilt. A fine, tall set. Possibly a large paper copy. Six pages of advertisements bound in at the end of volume 2. Uncommon. Not in Kohler.

Mitford is drawn upon from as early as the 1832 "Aldine Edition" through to the 1851 William Pickering two-volume edition of "The Poetical Works Of John

Milton. Printed From The Original Editions With A Life Of The Author By The Rev. John Mitford"—both listed here. See other editions by Phillips, Sampson, and Company in 1853 (published in Boston in two volumes, bound as two volumes in one, with frontispiece portrait, as here); in 1854 (published by Phillips, Sampson, and Company in Boston and by James C. Derby in New York in 2 volumes, with frontispiece portrait in volume 1 engraved by D. L. Glover of a young, long-haired Milton); and in 1856 (published by J. C. Derby in New York, by Phillips, Sampson & Co. in Boston, and by H. W. Derby in Cincinnati, in that order of appearance, with a frontispiece portrait of a young Milton, unsigned, and an engraved title page with an unsigned vignette illustration for *L*); and with illustrations in editions by Phillips, Sampson, and Company in 1854, 1855, 1857, and 1859—all editions listed here.

1966. THE POETICAL WORKS OF MILTON, YOUNG, GRAY, BEATTIE, AND COLLINS. Complete In One Volume. Stereotyped By J. Crissy And G. Goodman. *Philadelphia: Lippincott, Grambo & Co., Successor To Grigg, Elliott & Co., No. 14. North Fourth Street. 1852.* 8vo, xxxii+170pp.,+viii+208pp.,+x+47pp.,+ix+23pp.,+iv+19pp., engraved frontispiece illustration of a lady, protective tissue guard, life of Milton and of each poet, half-title for Milton and for each collection of poetical works, printed in double column, original brown calf (a little worn and chaffed, joints cracked, slight foxing throughout), maroon label on spine with gilt lettering and gilt rules. A good copy. Included are the poetical works of Milton. See 1850 edition by Lippincott, Grambo & Co. listed and editions by Grigg, and by Grigg and Elliot, and other editions by Lippincott, Grambo & Co., and by "Lippincott & Co., Successors To Grigg, Elliot & Co." cited there. Not in Kohler.

1967. THE POETICAL WORKS OF JOHN MILTON. Edited By Sir Egerton Brydges, Bart. [Quote From Thomson] Illustrated With Engravings From Drawings By J. M. W. Turner, R. A. A New Edition. *London: William Tegg & Co., 85, Queen Street, Cheapside. 1853.* Fourth Brydges/Turner edition. Thick 8vo, cvi+767pp., half-title with ("London: Bradbury And Evans, Printers, Whitefriars" on verso and printed again at bottom of last page), frontispiece portrait plate engraved by W. C. Edwards after Vertue, protective tissue guard, "To William Wordsworth And Robert Southey This Volume Is Appropriately Dedicated" printed on verso of title page, "Advertisement To The Original Edition" dated 1835, seven engraved illustration plates after Turner, each with protective tissue guard, double black border around text, contemporary full straight-grained navy blue morocco, covers finely tooled in wide gilt rules with central emblem in blind, elaborately gilt-decorated spine within the panels with gilt lettering, raised bands with delicate gilt trim, inner and outer dentelles finely tooled in gilt, blue ribbon marker, a.e.g. A splendid copy in a fine, well-preserved rich contemporary morocco binding. The illustrations by Turner first appeared in Brydges's 1835 six-volume edition of Milton's *PW* (also listed here). See 1837 first illustrated edition by Tegg also listed here with further editions cited. Stevens 138, ref. 1853 ed.; Kohler 325, referencing Williamson 135 and reporting "Not in the British Library. Not in the Bodleian Library. Not in Cambridge University Library."

1968. Variant of Preceding, contemporary full green morocco (rubbed at joints), covers elaborately tooled in gilt, elaborately gilt-decorated spine within the panels with gilt lettering, broad inner dentelles richly tooled in gilt, outer dentelles finely tooled in gilt, a.e.g. An attractive copy, handsomely bound by J. Wright, with his stamp, in a fine contemporary morocco binding. References to 1837 Tegg edition cited in preceding copy.

1969. THE POETICAL WORKS OF JOHN MILTON. With Life. [Quote From Thomson] Complete Edition. *London: T. Nelson And Sons, Paternoster Row; And Edinburgh. MDCCCLIII.* Third edition thus by Nelson? 8vo, xxx+523pp., unsigned engraved frontispiece portrait plate with protective tissue guard, life of Milton, six unsigned illustration plates (possible first appearance, with the frontispiece portrait and illustrations printed on paper different from that on which the text is printed, the texture being somewhat brownish in nature), all but one with a protective tissue guard, half-titles for *PL*, *PR*, *SA*, and *C*, contemporary full reddish-brown morocco (a bit rubbed at joints and along edges), ornately gilt-decorated covers with central diamond-shaped device in blind outlined in gilt rules, elaborately gilt-decorated spine within the panels with gilt lettering, raised bands (rubbed), inner dentelles finely tooled in gilt, a.e.g. A nice copy in an attractive morocco binding of the period, with the signature of T. E. Pollard on verso of fly-leaf. The illustrations (unsigned, but possibly by T. G. Flowers) include: *Adam and Eve among the Animals* for Book IV of *PL*; *Naming the Animals* for Book VIII of *PL*; *The Temptation of Eve* for Book IX of *PL*; *The Expulsion* for Book XII of *PL*; *The Baptism of Jesus* for Book I of *PR*; *The Temptation* for Book III of *PR*. Uncommon. Kohler 323.

See the possible first edition published by Nelson in 1850 (copy listed here) and the possible second edition by Nelson and Sons in 1852 (copy listed here) with unsigned illustrations different from those here. This is the first edition by Nelson and Sons with "Complete Edition" to appear on the title page and with these illustrations possibly after T. G. Flowers, each image measuring 5" × 3 ½" on a 6 ½" × 4" page compared to each image measuring 3 ½" × 2 ⅛" on a 5 ⅛" × 3 ⅛" page in the 1850 and 1852 Nelson editions. See the possible first edition thus by Nelson in 1850 listed and other editions by Nelson and Sons cited there.

1970. THE POETICAL WORKS OF JOHN MILTON. A New Edition, carefully Revised, From The Text Of Thomas Newton, D.D. To Which Is Prefixed A Biographical Notice. With Illustrations By William Harvey. *London: George Routledge And Co. Farringdon Street. 1853.* First edition thus. 8vo, xlvi+[ii]+570pp., frontispiece portrait plate of *Milton Dictating to His Daughters* engraved by the Dalziel brothers, black rule on title page, original preface by Theodore Alois Buckley (dated "London, 1853"), forty-six pages of biography as preliminary material, seven illustration plates engraved by the Dalziel brothers after William Harvey, notes at bottom of page, contemporary full polished red morocco (a little rubbed along extremities and corners, several marginal notations in pencil in a neat hand throughout *C*), covers ruled in gilt with small decorative corner pieces, spine elaborately decorated within the compartments, raised bands (slightly rubbed), olive green morocco label with gilt lettering and gilt rules, marbled endpapers and edges. A nice copy in an attractive contemporary morocco binding. Scarce. Kohler 324, reporting "Not in the British Library. Not in the Bodleian Library. Not in Cambridge University Library."

Harvey's illustrations were first published in London by Tilt & Bogue in 1843 (see two-volume sets listed); see also 1847 New York two-volume edition by Harper & Brothers (see set listed) with Harvey's illustrations in full as in the first edition by Tilt & Bogue (first appearance thus in America). See later editions thus by George Routledge and Co. in a similar smaller 8vo format, "With Illustrations By William Harvey," in 1854, 1855, 1857, 1858, 1860, 1862, 1863, 1864, 1865, 1866, 1867, and 1869 (see copy of each edition listed); see also undated illustrated editions by George Routledge and Sons, "With Illustrations By William Harvey" (sometimes five, sometimes seven), ca. 1872, ca. 1874 (two different editions), ca. 1875, ca. 1878 (with "Routledge's Red-Line Poets" on verso of title page with nine poets listed and also with "Routledge's Red-Line Poets" with twenty-five poets listed), ca. 1882, and ca. 1883 (see copy of each edition listed).

1971. THE POETICAL WORKS OF JOHN MILTON: With Life and Notes By The Rev. Thomas Thomson. *London: Printed For Adam Scott, Charterhouse Square. 1853.* Second edition thus? Small 8vo, viii+584pp., frontispiece portrait plate of Milton engraved by H. Meyer "From the Portrait by Cipriani," protective tissue guard, engraved and printed title page, engraved title dated 1846, with vignette illustration by H. Meyer for *C* on engraved title, "Glasgow: W. G. Blackie And Co., Printers, Villafield" on verso of printed title page, life of Milton, notes at bottom of page, contemporary maroon morocco (a bit worn along joints and edges, spine ends chipped with a small piece missing in lower right corner of spine, lacking front fly-leaf), covers decorated in blind, spine lettered in gilt and richly decorated in gilt within the compartments, raised bands, a.e.g. A good copy with early presentation inscription (dated "86"). The possible first edition thus was published in 1846 (also listed here) in a 12mo format, unlike the small 8vo format here, with printed and engraved title pages, each dated 1846. Scarce. Not in Kohler.

1972. THE POETICAL WORKS OF JOHN MILTON: To Which Is Prefixed The Life Of The Author, Together With Dr. Channing's Essay On The Poetical Genius Of *Milton. Halifax: Milner And Sowerby. 1853.* First edition thus? Small 8vo, xiv+[2]+431pp., engraved and printed title pages with unsigned vignette illustration of the judgment on engraved title page, "Life Of The Author" followed by "Dr. Channing's Essay," half-title for *PR*, *SA*, and *C*, original brown cloth (a little rubbed and scuffed, joints cracked), covers decorated in embossed blind, spine lettered in gilt within decorative gilt trim, edges untrimmed. All in all, a good copy of an uncommon edition called "The Cottage Library" on the spine. Scarce. Stevens 169; Not in Kohler.

A possible second edition thus by "Milner And Sowerby" was published in 1855; a possible third edition thus in 1856; a possible fourth edition thus in 1858—all listed here. See also first edition of *CPW* published by Milner and Sowerby in 1853 (possible first edition thus), copy listed and other editions by Milner and Sowerby cited there, including a ca. 1867 edition with eighteen pages of advertisements of "Just Published" editions by Milner and Company bound in at the end, with a listing of "The Cottage Library. Instructive & Entertaining Series. Royal 32mo–Coloured Cloth–Lettered–One Shilling Each."

1973. THE POETICAL WORKS OF JOHN MILTON. With A Memoir, And Critical Remarks On His Genius And Writings By James Montgomery; And Thirty-Six Engravings, From Drawings By William Harvey[.] *Hartford [Conn.]: Published By S. Andrus & Son. 1853.* 2 volumes in one. 8vo, l+400pp.(pagination beginning at "18"),+368pp., illustrations unpaginated, frontispiece illustration of *Milton Dictating* engraved by "Lossing & Co," volume

1, initially engraved by "Thompson" in original publication of Harvey's illustrations, with additional frontispiece portrait engraved by C. Burt, volume 1, a third unsigned frontispiece illustration of Milton *Mid books and papers in my study pent, If this be exile, sweet is banishment* engraved by "Clark" before title page of volume 2, full-page illustrations after William Harvey with in-text illustrations for *L'A* only (no in-text illustrations for *IlP* or other poems as in the original publication of Harvey's illustrations), separate title page each volume (each dated 1853), half-title for each book of *PL* and for each major poem, original brown cloth (a bit worn, spine chipped at top with small portion missing, joints rubbed), blind-stamped covers with central gilt device consisting of a lyre within a small decorative device, elaborately gilt-decorated spine incorporating vignette portrait of Milton in gilt at the center with a large female figure seated by large urn holding a book in gilt at the bottom and a bust and various artistic-related devices in gilt at the top with gilt lettering ("Milton's Works") above Milton's portrait. A good copy. Not in Kohler.

Harvey's illustrations, which are not included in full here with the exception of *L'A*, reproduced as full-page illustrations rather than in-text illustrations as originally published, were first published in London by Tilt & Bogue in 1843 (see two-volume sets listed here). The first edition thus by Andrus & Son of Hartford with illustrations after Harvey was published in a smaller sized 8vo format than here in 1847 (see two-volume set listed here with further editions cited).

1974. Variant of Preceding, original black morocco (a bit rubbed and worn along joints and extremities), covers elaborately decorated in floral gilt trim with large central emblem in gilt and thick gilt rules as borders, spine similarly elaborately decorated in floral gilt trim with large gilt lettering, a.e.g. A good, stout copy in original publisher's morocco binding. Not in Kohler.

1975. [POETICAL WORKS] WORKS. With Life, Critical Dissertation, and Explanatory Notes, By The Rev. George Gilfillan. *Edinburgh: James Nichol, 9 North Bank Street. London: James Nisbet And Co. M.DCCC.LIII.* 2 volumes. First Gilfillan edition. 8vo, xxviii+333pp.,+xxxvi+328pp., half-title each volume, half-titles for some of the poems, original blind-decorated green cloth (corners a bit rubbed), title lettered in gilt at top of the spine, emblem of lyre in gilt at the bottom, edges untrimmed. A very nice set in publisher's binding. Stevens 172; Kohler 327.

The possible second Gilfillan edition (possible first American edition) was published in 1854; the possible third Gilfillan edition (the first with text edited by Charles Cowden Clarke) was published in 1862; the possible fourth Gilfillan edition was published in 1866 (possibly the first with frontispiece portrait after J. Thurston engraved by J. T. Wedgwood)—all listed here; see also copies of two-volume 1868 and 1869 editions with text edited by Charles Cowden Clarke, the latter with frontispiece portrait after J. Thurston, published in Edinburgh by William P. Nimmo, and also copy of two-volumes-in-one ca. 1869 edition with text edited by Charles Cowden Clarke without frontispiece portrait after J. Thurston published in London, Paris, and New York by Cassell, Petter, & Galpin. The possible second American edition "With Life, Critical Dissertation, and Explanatory Notes, By The Rev. George Gilfillan" was published by D. Appleton & Co. with illustrations in 1856 (also listed here), made up of two volumes in one, with a general title page dated 1856, and a separate title page for each volume, each separate title dated 1854.

1976. THE POETICAL WORKS OF JOHN MILTON. With A Life, By Rev. John Mitford. In Three Volumes. *Boston: Little, Brown And Company. M.DCCC.LIII.* 3 volumes. First edition thus by Little, Brown and Company. Small 8vo, 4+xx+cxxxiv+[4]+[1]+153pp.,+372pp.,+334pp., four-page "Prospectus ... Of A New Edition Of The English Poets ... By Little, Brown, & Company," half-title ("The Poems Of Milton") each volume, engraved frontispiece portrait plate of Milton (unsigned, but after H. Robinson as in 1832 Pickering edition where the portrait is identified and dated "London, William Pickering, 1831"), volume 1, protective tissue guard (foxed), separate title page each volume, original "Advertisement" for the 1832 Aldine edition by John Mitford (with original date of 1831), life of Milton by Mitford followed by addenda and appendix, volume 1, half-title for some of the poems, notes at bottom of page, original green cloth (a little faded and aged, spines chipped at top), printed paper labels on spine (faded with two of the labels a little chipped), early bookplate on front pastedown of each volume. A nice set in rather well-preserved original mid-nineteenth-century American publisher's cloth binding, with advertisement leaves bound in at front of volume 1: "Prospectus Of A New Edition Of The English Poets, Now In Course Of Publication By Little, Brown, & Company ... edited by P. J. Child ... " (including this set of "Milton, 3 vols"). Scarce. Not in Kohler.

According to one of the "Notices" provided in the "Prospectus:" "It is a reprint of Pickering's Aldine edition, with Mitford's notes, and his life of the poet; and is in type, paper, and external appearance, an exact reproduction of the London copy with the advantage of greatly reduced price."—*New York Albion*. The first Aldine edition (with the first appearance of Milton portrait after Robinson) and second Pickering edition were published in 1832 (see set listed); Aldine editions followed as identified there. See also 1845 two-volume 8vo edition of Milton's *PW* published by Little and Brown (see set listed), a reprinting of an edition by Hilliard, Gray, and Company (similar in design and content to this Little and Brown edition here), first published in Boston in 1831 (see 1841 and 1845 sets each listed). The possible second edition thus by Little, Brown and Company with life by Mitford was published in 1854 (with the addition of "New York: Evans and Dickerson. Philadelphia: Lippincott, Grambo And Co." on title page); the possible third edition thus by Little, Brown and Company in 1856 (with the addition of "Shepard, Clark And Co. Cincinnati: Moore, Wilstach, Keys And Co." on title page); the possible fourth edition thus by Little, Brown and Company in 1859; the possible fifth edition thus by Little, Brown and Company, first with life by Masson, was published in 1864; the possible sixth edition thus by Little, Brown and Company, with life by Masson, was published in 1866—all listed here.

1977. THE POETICAL WORKS OF JOHN MILTON: With A Life of the Author; Preliminary Dissertations On Each Poem; Notes Critical And Explanatory; An Index To The Subjects Of Paradise Lost; And A Verbal Index to all the Poems. Edited By Charles Dexter Cleveland. [Quotation from Sir Egerton Brydges and Lord Erskine] *Philadelphia: Lippincott, Grambo & Co. 1853*. First edition thus. 12mo in 6s, 688pp., copyright date of 1853 on verso of title page, preface (dated 1853), half-title for some of the poems, notes at bottom of page, index to *PL* and verbal index to the whole at the end, original half green morocco (a bit rubbed, front joint cracked, joints rehinged on inside covers), marbled paper over boards, spine lettered in gilt, raised bands, marbled edges, bookplate. A good copy of a scarce edition of Milton's *PW*. A second edition thus was published in 1854; see also 1859 and 1865 editions—all listed here. Stevens 168; Not in Kohler.

1978. THE POETICAL WORKS OF JOHN MILTON. A New Edition. With Notes, And A Life Of The Author, By John Mitford. *Boston: Phillips, Sampson, And Company. 1853*. 2 volumes in one. 8vo in 4s, cxxix+[iii]+371pp.,+ii+478pp., frontispiece portrait engraved by O. Pelton "From a Miniature of the same size by Faithorne. Anno 1667 in the possession of William Falconer Esq." (a bit foxed in the margins), volume 1, title page each volume, double black rule around text, original brown calf (a little worn along edges and extremities), covers decorated with embossed floral trim with Milton's name lettered in gilt within a framed circular device at the center, raised bands, spine lettered in gilt, marbled endpapers, a.e.g, early bookplate. A good, tight copy. See two-volume edition by Mitford published in London by William Pickering in 1851 (set also listed here). See 1852 edition published by Phillips, Sampson, and Company in Boston in two volumes, with frontispiece portrait in volume 1 as here, listed and other editions by Phillips, Sampson, and Company cited there. Uncommon. Not in Kohler.

1979. THE POETICAL WORKS OF MILTON, YOUNG, GRAY, BEATTIE, AND COLLINS. Complete In One Volume. Stereotyped By J. Crissy And G. *Goodman. Philadelphia: Lippincott, Grambo & Co. 1853*. 8vo, xxxii+170pp.,+viii+208pp.,+x+47pp.,+ix+23pp.,+iv+19pp., engraved frontispiece illustration of a lady (mistakenly bound within the collection of Milton's poems), protective tissue guard, life of Milton and of each poet, half-title for Milton and for each collection of poetical works, printed in double column, original red cloth (a bit rubbed), decorative central emblem in blind on covers, spine lettered in gilt with gilt rule at top and bottom. A good copy. Included are the poetical works of Milton. See 1850 edition by Lippincott, Grambo & Co. listed here with further editions by Lippincott, Grambo & Co. cited there. Not in Kohler.

1980. THE POETICAL WORKS OF JOHN MILTON. Edited By Sir Egerton Brydges, Bart. [Quotation from Thomson] Illustrated With Engravings, Designe*]. Boston: Phillips, Sampson, And Company. 1854*. By John Martin And J. W. M. Turner, R.A. [One Also By Westall And One By Romney] First edition thus? 8vo in 4s, 858pp., frontispiece portrait "Engraved by O. Pelton" of a young, long-haired Milton "From a Miniature of the same size by Faithorne. Anno 1667, in the possession of William Falconer Esq." (frontispiece foxed), protective tissue guard, engraved and printed title pages with vignette illustration for *C* after Turner on engraved title (engraved title page foxed), reprinting of the original 1835 dedication page "To William Wordsworth And Robert Southey This Volume Is Appropriately Dedicated," "Advertisement To The Original Edition," dated 1835, "Life Of Milton," six engraved illustration plates, each with protective tissue guard, two engraved illustration plates after Martin for *PL* (Books VII and X), two engraved illustration plates after Turner—one for *PR* (Book III, *The Temptation on the Mountain*) and one for *C* (as vignette on engraved title page), and although not mentioned on the title page: one engraved illustration plate after Westall for *PL* (*Satan*, here bound within Book IV), and one illustration plate after Romney (*Milton Dictating To His Daughters*) engraved by D. L. Glover for *On His Blindness* (here bound with the poem), introductory remarks from the James Boyd edition for each book of *PL*, notes at bottom of page, black border around text, original brown silk (worn, joints rubbed, spine ends chipped, corners worn, some of the plates slightly foxed), covers elaborately decorated in gilt with a series of gilt rules and central Grecian figures and pillar in gilt with bust of Milton in gilt at the top, spine lettered in gilt with large figure of a woman playing a harp in gilt at the bottom and with a medallion portrait of Milton in gilt towards the top beneath the gilt lettering. Although worn, still a good copy of an uncommon edition, in an attractive mid-nineteenth-century American publisher's binding. Not in Kohler.

Boyd's edition of *PL* "With Notes Explanatory And Critical" first appeared in 1850 (also listed here); it was variously reprinted throughout the nineteenth century (see editions listed with 1850 edition of *PL*). See 1855 illustrated edition (possible second edition thus) with the addition of "New York: J[ames]. C. Darby" in publisher's imprint on title page, and 1857 (possible third edition thus) and 1859 (possible fourth edition thus) editions, each with publisher's imprint as here. See also two-volume non-illustrated editions of Milton's *PW* by Phillips, Sampson, and Company published in 1852, 1853, and 1854. See, too, editions of Milton's *PW* each in a format similar to here with identical illustrations: published by D. Appleton and Company in New York ca. 1860 and again in 1869; published by Crosby, Nichols, Lee & Company in Boston in 1861; published by Crosby and Nichols in Boston in 1864; published by Crosby & Ainsworth in Boston and by Oliver S. Felt in New York in 1866; published by W. I. Pooley in New York in 1868 and again in 1869; published by D. Appleton & Company in New York in 1869; and published by W. I. Pooley, Harper & Brothers' Building in New York ca. 1872—all listed here.

1981. Variant of Preceding, original publisher's gilt and glazed to simulate red morocco (covers a little rubbed, especially along extremities, front joint cracked, spine worn with several small portions missing at the top and a larger one at the bottom, some plates a little foxed, waterstain marks in outer margins of frontispiece portrait and engraved title page without affecting portrait or illustration), covers richly decorated in embossed gilt with large Grecian-style emblem at the center consisting of a Grecian pillar with two female figures at the bottom, two cherubic figures with wings toward the top, and a bust of Milton at the top, elaborate decorative floral trim at corners and across the bottom, several gilt border rules of varying thickness around the outside, spine similarly richly decorated in embossed gilt with a large female figure in gilt at the center of the spine crowned with laurel wreath playing a harp and seated on an elaborate gilt bench on a pedestal with floral vase alongside, an embossed vignette portrait of Milton in gilt within a decorative circular gilt frame above, and large gilt lettering ("Milton's Poetical Works") at the top, a.e.g. Although a little worn, a good copy in an attractive variant publisher's binding.

1982. THE POETICAL WORKS OF JOHN MILTON. A New Edition, carefully Revised, From The Text Of Thomas Newton, D.D. To Which Is Prefixed A Biographical Notice. With Illustrations By William Harvey. New Edition. *London: George Routledge And Co. Farringdon Street. New York: 18, Beekman Street. 1854.* Second edition thus by Routledge. 8vo, xlvi+570pp. (illustration plates unpaginated), frontispiece portrait plate of *Milton Dictating to his Daughters* engraved by the Dalziel brothers (bound here before Book I), black rule on title page, original preface by Theodore Alois Buckley (dated 1853), seven illustration plates engraved by the Dalziel brothers after William Harvey, notes at bottom of the page, contemporary full crushed brown morocco (a bit rubbed, especially the spine and along the joints and at the corners, lacking front fly-leaf, some slight staining at top of frontispiece, occasional slight embrowning throughout), blind rules on covers with intricately tooled emblem in blind at the center of each cover, spine lettered in gilt, raised bands within decorative trim in blind, small emblem in blind within the panels, decorative trim in blind at the bottom, marbled endpapers, gauffered gilt edges. Except for the rubbed spine, a very good copy of a scarce edition with dated contemporary inscription in pencil at top of title page. The first edition thus by George Routledge and Co. was published in 1853 (also listed here with further editions cited). Uncommon. Not in Kohler.

1983. THE POETICAL WORKS OF JOHN MILTON. A New Edition. With Notes, And A Life Of The Author, By John Mitford. Boston: Phillips, Sampson, And Company. *New York: James C. Derby. 1854.* 2 volumes. 8vo in 4s, cxxix+[iii]+371pp.,+ii+478pp., frontispiece portrait after D. L. Glover of a young, long-haired Milton (a little foxed because of the tissue guard), "Advertisement," volume 1, title page each volume, original publisher's blind-stamped green cloth (a bit rubbed, corners a little worn, three slight stains on front cover of volume 2, top ends of spines chipped), spines lettered in gilt with "British Poets" at the top above title, large anchor in gilt at the bottom, top edge gilt. Nice set. See 1852 edition (listed here) published by Phillips, Sampson, and Company in Boston in two volumes, with frontispiece portrait engraved by O. Pelton "From a Miniature of the same size by Faithorne. Anno 1667," and other editions by Phillips, Sampson, and Company cited there. Kohler 329, indicating an "engraved title page" as well as frontispiece portrait in volume 1 and lacking title page in volume 2, and reporting "Not in the British Library. Not in the Bodleian Library. Not in Cambridge University Library."

1984. THE POETICAL WORKS OF JOHN MILTON. With A Life, By Rev. John Mitford. In Three Volumes. *Boston: Little, Brown And Company. New York: Evans And Dickerson. Philadelphia: Lippincott, Grambo And Co. M.DCCC.LIV (1854).* 3 volumes. Second edition thus by Little, Brown and Company? Small 8vo, xx+cxxxiv+[4]+[1]+153pp.,+372pp.,+334pp., half-title ("The Poems Of Milton") each volume, engraved frontispiece portrait plate of Milton (unsigned, but by H. Robinson as in 1832 Pickering edition where the portrait is identified and dated "London, William Pickering, 1831,"), volume 1, protective tissue guard (foxed), separate title page each volume, original "Advertisement" for the 1832 Aldine edition by John Mitford with original date of 1831, life of Milton by Mitford followed by addenda and appendix, volume 1, half-title for some of the poems, notes at bottom of page, contemporary three-quarter calf, marbled paper over boards (a bit rubbed, labels missing or torn), gilt-decorated spines in the panels, slightly raised bands with decorative gilt trim, marbled endpapers and edges. A sturdy, handsome set in very good condition. The first edition thus by Little, Brown and Company with life by Mitford was published in 1853 (also listed here with further editions cited). Scarce. Not in Kohler.

1985. THE POETICAL WORKS OF JOHN MILTON. With Life, Critical Dissertation, and Explanatory Notes, By The Rev. George Gilfillan. *New York: D. Appleton & Co., Broadway. Edinburgh: James Nichol. M.DCCC.LIV (1854).* 2 volumes. First American edition thus; second Gilfillan edition? 8vo, xxviii+333pp.,+xxxvi+328pp., half-title and title page each volume, half-titles for some of the poems, original olive green cloth decorated in blind, spines lettered in gilt with gilt urn at bottom, edges untrimmed and partially unopened. A very nice set. The possible second American edition thus by Appleton "With Life, Critical Dissertation, and Explanatory Notes, By The Rev. George Gilfillan" was published with illustrations in 1856 (also listed here), made up of two volumes in one, with a general title page dated 1856, and a separate title page for each volume, each separate title page dated 1854 (as here), both general title page and separate title pages, unlike here, with "New York: D. Appleton & Co." as the only place and publisher listed. The first edition edited by Gilfillan was published in 1853 (listed here with other editions cited). Scarce. Kohler 330, reporting "Not in the British Library. Not in the Bodleian Library. Not in Cambridge University Library."

1986. THE POETICAL WORKS OF JOHN MILTON: With A Life of the Author; Preliminary Dissertations On Each Poem; Notes Critical And Explanatory; An Index To The Subjects Of Paradise Lost; And A Verbal Index to all the Poems. Edited By Charles Dexter Cleveland. [Quotation from Sir Egerton Brydges and Lord Erskine] *Philadelphia: Lippincott, Grambo & Co. 1854.* Second edition thus? 12mo in 6s, 688pp., copyright date of 1853 on verso of title page, original preface (dated 1853), half-title for some of the poems, notes at bottom of page, index to *PL* and verbal index to the whole at the end, original brown cloth (worn along extremities, spine ends chipped, lacking fly-leaf), covers decorated in blind trim, spine lettered in gilt. A fair copy of a scarce edition of Milton's *PW*, very clean within. The first edition thus was published in 1853; see also 1859 and 1865 editions—all listed here. Not in Kohler.

1987. THE POETICAL WORKS OF MILTON, YOUNG, GRAY, BEATTIE, AND COLLINS. Complete In One Volume. *Philadelphia: Lippincott, Grambo & Co. 1854.* 8vo, xxxii+170pp.,+viii+208pp.,+x+47pp.,+ix+23pp.,+iv+19pp., engraved frontispiece illustration of a lady after W. Brown for "Page 187" (Young's "The Revenge"), protective tissue guard, engraved color title-page plate ("The American Standard Edition Of The British Poets") with five vignette portraits of poets including Milton, printed title page, life of Milton and of each poet, half-title for Milton and for each collection of poetical works, two engraved illustration plates (unsigned, one bound within *C*, the other bound within *P*), one additional engraved illustration plate (unsigned, bound with Young), printed in double column, black rule around the end, advertisement leaf bound in at the end, contemporary calf over thick boards (a little rubbed, occasional slight foxing and staining, unfortunately reglued prior to my ownership with the body reglued too low to the spine), covers richly decorated in embossed blind, spine lettered in gilt, raised bands, small emblem in blind within the panels, brown endpapers, a.e.g. A good copy. Included are the poetical works of Milton. See 1850 edition by Lippincott, Grambo & Co. listed here with further editions cited. Not in Kohler.

1988. THE POETICAL WORKS OF JOHN MILTON; With A Memoir; Embellished With Engravings After Designs By Fuseli, Westall, And Martin. *London: H. G. Bohn, York Street, Covent Garden. 1855.* 8vo, vii+527pp., engraved frontispiece portrait plate engraved by Cochran after a drawing by Cooper, six illustration plates after Fuseli (one), Westall (two), and Martin (three), life of Milton, half-title for each book of *PL* and *PR* and for some of the poems, contemporary polished calf (a bit worn), gilt rules on covers with central gilt stamp of "Ashburton Free Grammar School 1855" on front cover, elaborately gilt-decorated spine in the compartments, red morocco label with gilt lettering and decorative gilt trim, raised bands with decorative gilt trim, inner dentelles tooled in blind, outer dentelles tooled in gilt, marbled endpapers and edges. A nice copy in a Prize Binding with contemporary signature (dated 1855) on front blank. The first edition thus and the basis for this edition by Bohn was published by Churton in 1836 (also listed here with further editions by Churton and Chidley cited). The possible first edition thus by Bohn was published in 1844 (also listed here with further editions cited). Not in Kohler.

1989. THE POETICAL WORKS OF JOHN MILTON. With Life. *T. Nelson And Sons, London; Edinburgh; And New York. MDCCCLV.* 8vo, xxx+[2]+523pp., unsigned engraved frontispiece portrait plate with protective tissue guard, engraved and printed title pages with vignette illustration after T. G. Flowers on engraved title, printed title page in red and black ruled in red with decorative device incorporating initials of the press at the center with "London" and "Edinburgh" printed on each side, six unsigned steel-engraved illustrations on thick paper, each with protective tissue guard, guard, life of Milton, half-title for *PL*, *PR*, *SA*, and *C*, contemporary full red morocco (some occasional foxing of the plates), attractively gilt-decorated border trim on covers with central blind-stamped device of an urn with floral arrangement, gilt-decorated spine in the panels with gilt lettering, raised bands, inner dentelles finely tooled in gilt, a.e.g. A very nice copy with first appearance of "Edinburgh And New York" on title page. Besides the vignette illustration by T. G. Flowers on the engraved title page of *Raphael Counseling Adam and Eve* for Book V of *PL*, the additional six steel-engraved illustrations (unsigned, but possibly by T. G. Flowers) on thick paper include: *Adam and Eve among the Animals* for Book IV of *PL*; *Naming the Animals* for Book VIII of *PL*; *The Temptation* for Book IX of *PL*; *The Expulsion* for Book XII of *PL*; *The Baptism of Jesus* for Book I of *PR*; and *The Temptation* for Book III of *PR*. See the possible first and second editions by Nelson and Sons published in 1850 and in 1852 with unsigned illustrations and different from those here—all listed here. See the possible first edition thus by "T. Nelson and Sons" in 1850 with further editions cited there. Kohler 331 reporting "Not in Williamson. Not in the Bodleian Library. Not in Cambridge University Library."

1990. THE POETICAL WORKS OF JOHN MILTON. To Which Is Prefixed, The Life Of The Author. *London: William Tegg And Co., 85, Queen Street Cheapside. 1855.* 12mo in 6s, xi+576pp., frontispiece portrait plate of Milton at age twenty-one engraved by W. C. Edwards after Cornelius Jansen, another portrait plate of *Milton Dictating to his Daughters* engraved by W. C. Edwards after G. Romney, inserted before "The Life Of The Author," five illustration plates after Westall and Turner (slight foxing on some plates), contemporary tan calf (a little rubbed along extremities, spine a bit worn), covers decorated with delicately tooled wide gilt borders within gilt rules with inner embossed trim in blind, spine elaborately gilt-decorated within the panels, raised bands with gilt trim, black morocco label (slightly chipped at the top) with gilt lettering and gilt rules, wide inner dentelles finely tooled in gilt, a.e.g. A nice copy with large bookplate of Baltimore book collector on front pastedown and blind embossed stamp of Newcastle On Tyne Bookseller on front blank. The final several leaves include "Commendatory Verses On Milton" by various poets. See 1837 first illustrated edition by Tegg, also listed here with further editions cited. Scarce. Not in Kohler.

1991. THE POETICAL WORKS OF JOHN MILTON. A New Edition, carefully Revised, From The Text Of Thomas Newton, D.D. To Which Is Prefixed A Biographical Notice. With Illustrations By William Harvey. Third Edition. *London: George Routledge And Co. Farringdon Street. New York: 18, Beekman Street. 1855.* Third edition thus by Routledge. 8vo, xlvi+[ii]+570pp., frontispiece portrait plate of *Milton Dictating to his Daughters* engraved by the Dalziel brothers, protective tissue guard, black rule on title page, original preface by Theodore Alois Buckley (dated 1853), seven illustration plates engraved by the Dalziel brothers after William Harvey, each with protective tissue guard, notes at bottom of page, contemporary full green morocco (a bit rubbed, front joint cracked), covers and spine elaborately tooled in blind relief, spine lettered in gilt, raised bands, marbled endpapers, gauffered gilt edges. A nice copy in an attractive Victorian binding with neat contemporary inscription (dated 1856) on front blank, another signature (dated 1919), and several early bookplates. The first edition thus by George Routledge and Co. was published in 1853 (also listed here with further editions cited). Uncommon. Not in Kohler.

1992. Variant of Preceding, original black pebble leather (joints and spine rubbed, plates foxed), covers and spine richly decorated in gilt with spine lettered in gilt, inner and outer dentelles finely tooled in gilt, a.e.g. A nice copy with contemporary family presentation inscription (dated 1856) on fly-leaf with accompanying note tracing family lineage, dated 1922. Not in Kohler.

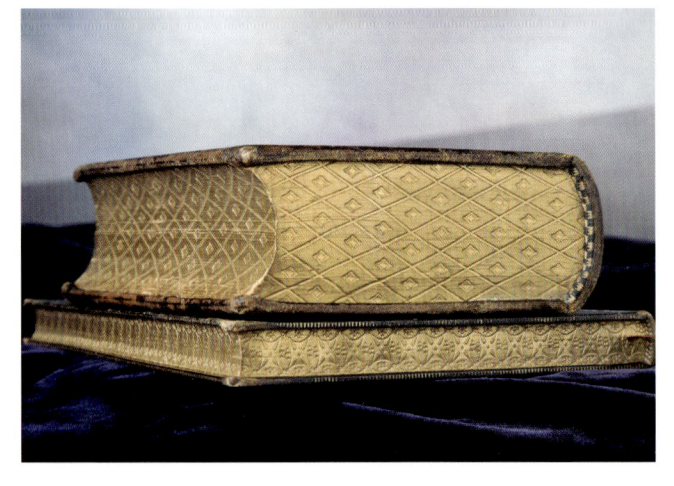

Examples of gauffered gilt edges.

1993. THE POETICAL WORKS OF JOHN MILTON. With Life. [Quote from Thomson.] Complete Edition. *London: John Kendrick, 27 Ludgate Street, St. Paul's; And 4 Charlotte Row, Mansion House. MDCCCLV.* 8vo, xxx+658pp., unsigned frontispiece illustration plate o*he Ascent of the Spirit*, seven additional illustration plates after W. Linton, John Martin, H. C. Slous, C. Bentley, and A. E. Chalon, protective tissue guard for each illustration, half-title for each book of *PL* and *PR* and for some of the poems, half-title for each book of *PR* with "Argument" on verso (not original to the poem), triple black border around text, half red leather (a little worn along joints and at the corners, first and last several pages heavily damp stained), marbled paper over boards, spine lettered in gilt. Despite the damp staining to the first and last few leaves (including frontispiece and title page), the remaining plates are clean and fresh. Uncommon. Not in Williamson; Kohler 332, reporting "Not in the Bodleian Library, Not in Cambridge University Library."

See 1850 edition (copy listed here) with different illustrations and a different address for Kendrick in publisher's imprint; see 1851 edition (copy listed here), with identical illustrations identified in detail there but with a different address for Kendrick in publisher's imprint, the same as that in the 1850 edition; the 1859 edition (copy listed here) has the same illustrations and address for Kendrick in publisher's imprint as here.

1994. THE POETICAL WORKS OF JOHN MILTON. Edited By Sir Egerton Brydges, Bart. [Quotation from Thomson] Illustrated With Engravings, Designed By John Martin And J. W. M. Turner, R.A. [One Also By Westall And One By Romney]. *Boston: Phillips, Sampson, And Company. New York: J[ames]. C. Derby. 1855.* Second edition thus? 8vo in 4s, 858pp., frontispiece portrait "Engraved by O. Pelton" of a young, long-haired Milton "From a Miniature of the same size by Faithorne. Anno 1667, in the possession of William Falconer Esq.," protective tissue guard, engraved and printed title pages with vignette illustration for *C* after Turner on engraved title (engraved title page foxed), reprinting of the original 1835 dedication page "To William Wordsworth And Robert Southey This Volume Is Appropriately Dedicated," "Advertisement To The Original Edition" dated 1835, "Life Of Milton," six engraved illustration plates, each with protective tissue guard, two engraved illustration plates after Martin for *PL* (Books VII and X), two engraved illustration plates after Turner—one for *PR* (Book III, *The Temptation on the Mountain*, here bound incorrectly into Book II of *PL*, but bound correctly in following copy and one for *C* (as vignette on engraved title page), and although not mentioned on the title page: one engraved illustration plate after Westall for *PL* (*Satan* here bound within Book IV) and one illustration plate after Romney (*Milton Dictating to His Daughters*) engraved by D. L. Glover for *On His Blindness* (here bound within life, but in following copy bound with the poem), introductory remarks from the James Boyd edition for each book of *PL*, notes at bottom of page, black border around text, original full brown calf over thick boards (slightly rubbed, plates a little foxed), covers elaborately decorated in thick blind relief with Milton's name in gilt at the center of each cover, spine lettered in gilt with small decorative pieces in blind within the panels, raised bands, marbled endpapers, a.e.g. A very nice copy in an attractive mid-nineteenth-century American publisher's binding. See 1854 edition (possible first edition thus) by Phillips, Sampson, and Company listed and other editions by Phillips, Sampson, and Company cited there. Not in Kohler.

1995. Variant of Preceding, original publisher's gilt and glazed to simulate black morocco (a little worn along edges and extremities, spine ends chipped, occasional heavy foxing to several pages in between pages that are otherwise very white and clean), covers richly decorated in embossed gilt with large Grecian-style emblem at the center consisting of a Grecian pillar with two female figures at the bottom, two cherubic figures with wings toward the top, and a bust of Milton at the top, elaborate decorative floral trim at corners and across the bottom, several gilt border rules of varying thickness around the outside, spine similarly richly decorated in embossed gilt with a large female figure in gilt at the center of the spine crowned with laurel wreath and playing a harp while seated on an elaborate gilt bench on a pedestal with floral vase alongside, an embossed vignette portrait of Milton in gilt within a decorative circular gilt frame above and large gilt lettering ("Milton's Complete Works") near the top with small gilt lettering ("Boston Edition Illustrated") at the bottom, the whole framed within a lattice-style Grecian hanging device in gilt, a.e.g. Although a little worn, a good copy in an attractive variant publisher's binding, with contemporary signature (dated 1855) on fly-leaf. Not in Kohler.

1996. THE POETICAL WORKS OF JOHN MILTON: To Which Is Prefixed The Life Of The Author, Together With Dr. Channing's Essay On The Poetical Genius Of Milton. *Halifax: Milner And Sowerby. 1855*. Second edition thus? Small 8vo, xiv+[2]+431+[4]pp., unsigned engraved frontispiece illustration of Adam being shown the flood (Book XI), engraved and printed title pages with unsigned vignette illustration of the judgment on engraved title page, "Life Of The Author" followed by "Dr. Channing's Essay," half-titles for *PR*, *SA*, and *C*, original blue cloth (a little rubbed and scuffed, joints slightly cracked, spine chipped at top and bottom, a small portion of bottom corner torn away from last page and first page of advertisement without affecting any text), covers decorated in blind with central vignette in gilt of a small bust of Milton on top of a book beside ink and quill, spine lettered and decorated in gilt with depiction of the expulsion in gilt, t.e. rough, fore- and bottom edges untrimmed. All in all, a good copy with four pages of advertisements bound in at the end. The possible first edition thus was published in 1853 (also listed here with further editions cited). Scarce. Not in Kohler.

1997. THE POETICAL WORKS OF JOHN MILTON: With Life and Notes. *Edinburgh: Oliver & Boyd, Tweeddale Court. n.d. [ca. 1855]*. First edition thus? 12mo in 6s, 539pp., unsigned engraved frontispiece portrait, contemporary brown calf (joints and edges rubbed, back joint cracking, corners worn), large gilt prize citation in Latin within laurel wreath at center of each cover, spine elaborately decorated in gilt within the panels, brown morocco label with gilt lettering and gilt rules, raised bands with decorative gilt tooling, marbled endpapers and edges. A pleasant copy in a nice Prize Binding, with contemporary prize plate from Edinburgh Academy (dated 1855) on front pastedown. Possibly dated as early as 1838 or thereabouts, the date inscribed in a copy for sale at a very expensive price on eBay in the summer of 2006. Kohler 351, dating its copy "[ca. 1863]" and reporting "Not in Williamson. Not in the British Library. Not in the Bodleian Library. Not in Cambridge University Library."

1998. Variant of Preceding. Original red cloth (few marks on covers, spine slightly faded), title blind-stamped within decorative device on covers, spine richly decorated in gilt with gilt lettering, a.e.g. A nice copy with contemporary signature (dated 1860) on fly-leaf along with a later signature, in a variant publisher's binding. Kohler 351, dating its copy "[ca. 1863]."

1999. MILTON'S POETICAL WORKS. With His Life. *Philad[elphi]a: John B. Perry, 198 Market St., [1855]*. Small thick 8vo (5 ¼" × 3 ½"), x+479pp., unsigned engraved frontispiece portrait, protective tissue guard, engraved title page, printed title page for "Paradise Lost: By John Milton. To Which Is Prefixed, The Life Of The Author, Philadelphia: John B. Perry, 198 Market St., 1855," with unsigned vignette illustration of Satan on engraved title page, "Contents," "Life Of The Author," original maroon pebble leather (a little rubbed with some light wear along extremities), covers and spine richly stamped in gilt, spine similarly decorated in gilt with large gilt lettering in the middle, and small gilt lettering at the bottom ("Perry's Edition"). A lovely little copy with contemporary signature (dated 1859) on front blank. Scarce. Not in Kohler.

2000. THE POETICAL WORKS OF JOHN MILTON[:] *Paradise Lost and Regained.* [Quotation from Thomson.] *T. Nelson And Sons, London; Edinburgh; And New York. MDCCCLVI*. Small 8vo, xxxii+443pp., half-title, engraved frontispiece portrait after Faithorne engraved by T. Cowan with protective tissue guard, engraved and printed title pages with vignette illustration after A. Ritchie engraved by T. Cowan on engraved title page, half-title for each poem, original blue cloth (joints a little worn, corners rubbed), covers decorated in blind, spine lettered in gilt ("Milton Paradise Lost & Regained") with an illustration of Michael casting Satan out of heaven in gilt beneath the lettering and double gilt lines at the top and bottom, a.e.g. A good copy with early signature on fly-leaf and early notation in pencil on front pastedown. While titled "The

Poetical Works of John Milton," this edition contains only the two poetical works identified on the printed title page: *PL* and *PR*. See the possible first edition by Nelson in 1850 also listed here with further editions cited. Scarce. Not in Kohler.

2001. THE POETICAL WORKS OF JOHN MILTON: To Which Is Prefixed The Life Of The Author, Together With Dr. Channing's Essay On The Poetical Genius Of Milton. *Halifax: Milner And Sowerby. 1856*. Third edition thus? Small 8vo, xiv+[2]+431pp., unsigned engraved frontispiece illustration of Adam being shown the flood (Book XI), engraved and printed title pages with unsigned vignette illustration of the judgment on engraved title page, "Life Of The Author" followed by "Dr. Channing's Essay," half-title for *PR*, *SA*, and *C*, original green cloth (a little rubbed and scuffed), covers decorated in blind, spine lettered in blind ("The Cottage Library") at the top and gilt, bookplate on front pastedown. A nice copy. The possible first edition thus was published in 1853 (also listed here with further editions cited). Scarce. Not in Kohler.

2002. JOHN MILTON'S POETICAL WORKS: A Memoir, And Essay On His Poetical Genius, By Dr. Channing. Together With, Addison's Critique on the Paradise Lost. *New York: J. C. Derby, 119 Nassau Street. Boston: Phillips, Sampson & Co. Cincinnati: H. W. Derby. 1856.* 12mo in 6s, liv+450pp., unsigned engraved frontispiece portrait plate of a young Milton with protective tissue guard, undated engraved and printed title pages, with unsigned engraved vignette illustration for *L* (with lines quoted beneath: "with incessant care / To tend the homely, slighted shepherd's trade") on engraved title with heading misspelled "Lucidas," original blue cloth (slight foxing to engraved frontispiece portrait and engraved title, binding a little rubbed, with some wear along extremities and at the corners), spine richly decorated in gilt with gilt lettering. A nice, tight copy in original publisher's binding. Similar to earlier editions by Charles Daly published in London, ca. 1850 and following editions (also listed here), with identical engraved frontispiece portrait and engraved title page, identical pagination, and with the same title and even the misprint "Lucidas" in some of the Daly editions, but without any of the illustrations beyond the engraved title page. For reference, see 1852 edition by Phillips, Sampson, and Company (possible first edition thus, copy listed and the other editions cited there), completely different from the edition here, with illustrations. Scarce. Not in Kohler.

2003. THE POETICAL WORKS OF JOHN MILTON. With Life, Critical Dissertation, and Explanatory Notes, By The Rev. George Gilfillan. Two Vols. In One. Beautifully Illustrated With Six Steel Engravings. *New York: D. Appleton And Company, 346 & 348 Broadway. 1856.* 2 volumes in one. Second American edition thus? Small 8vo, xxviii+333pp.,+xxxvi+328pp., engraved frontispiece portrait plate of Milton at age twenty-one, engraved by "W. C. Edwards after Cornelius Jansen," protective tissue guard, general title page dated 1856, separate title page for each volume, each title page dated 1854, ("THE POETICAL WORKS OF JOHN MILTON. With Life, Critical Dissertation, and Explanatory Notes, By The Rev. George Gilfillan. Vol. I / Vol II. *New York: D. Appleton & Co., Broadway. M.DCCC.LIV*"), "Life Of John Milton," with engraved illustration plate of *Milton Dictating to His Daughters* by G. Romney, engraved by W. C. Edwards, protective tissue guard, two engraved illustration plates for *PL*, one of Satan by R. Westall, engraved by R. Graves, the second of the expulsion by Turner, each with protective tissue guard, two engraved illustration plates after Turner for *PR* (for Books III and IV), each with protective tissue guard, half-title for some of the poems, contemporary full dark brown morocco over thick boards (a bit worn along extremities, joints cracked, rebacked with original spine laid down, foxing throughout, especially the plates and protective tissue guards), covers elaborately embossed with Milton's name in gilt at the center of each cover, spine lettered in gilt with small decorative pieces in blind within the panels, raised bands (rubbed), marbled endpapers, a.e.g. A good copy, which seems to have been repaired and treated kindly by a former owner. The first edition edited by Gilfillan was published in 1853 (also listed here with further editions cited). Uncommon. Not in Kohler.

2004. THE POETICAL WORKS OF JOHN MILTON. With A Memoir, And Critical Remarks On His Genius And Writings By James Montgomery; And Thirty-Six Engravings, From Drawings By William Harvey[.] *Hartford [Conn.]: Published By S. Andrus & Son. 1856.* 2 volumes in one. 8vo, l+400pp.(pagination beginning at "18"),+368pp., frontispiece illustration of *Milton Dictating*, engraved by "Lossing & Co," volume 1, initially engraved by "Thompson" in original publication of Harvey's illustrations, with additional frontispiece portrait engraved by C. Burt, volume 1, a third unsigned frontispiece illustration of Milton "Mid books and papers in my study pent, If this be exile, sweet is banishment," engraved by "Clark," before title page of volume 2, full-page illustrations after William Harvey with in-text illustrations for *L'A* only (no in-text illustrations for *IlP* or other poems as in original publication of Harvey's illustrations), separate title page each volume, second title page undated, half-title for each book of *PL* and for each major poem, double black rule around text, original decorated red cloth (a bit rubbed, rebacked with original spine laid down, hinges reinforced from the inside), covers decorated in blind with large central emblem in gilt, elaborately gilt-decorated spine incorporating vignette portrait of Milton in gilt at the center with classical figure (large female figure seated by large urn holding a book) in gilt at the bottom and a bust and various art-related devices in gilt at the top with gilt lettering ("Milton's Works") above Milton portrait, a.e.g. A nice copy in an attractive gilt-stamped publisher's binding. The first edition thus by Andrus & Son of Hartford with illustrations after Harvey was published in a smaller sized 8vo format than here in 1847 (two-volume set also listed here with further editions cited). Not in Kohler.

2005. Variant of Preceding, original publisher's mauve cloth (spine a little faded), covers decorated in blind with a small gilt emblem incorporating a harp in the center, elaborately gilt-decorated spine incorporating vignette portrait of Milton in gilt at the center with classical figure (large female figure seated by large urn holding a book) in gilt at the bottom and a bust and various art-related devices in gilt at the top with gilt lettering ("Milton's Works") above Milton portrait, a.e.g. A nice copy in a variant publisher's cloth binding. The collection also contains a copy in original full brown calf over thick boards. Not in Kohler.

2006. THE POETICAL WORKS OF JOHN MILTON. With A Life, By Rev. John Mitford. In Three Volumes. *Boston: Little, Brown And Company. Shepard, Clark And Co. Cincinnati: Moore, Wilstach, Keys And Co. M.DCCC.LVI.* 3 volumes. Third edition thus by Little, Brown and Company? Small 8vo, 4+xx+cxxxiv+[4]+[1]+153pp.,+372pp.,+334pp., half-title ("The Poems Of Milton") each volume, engraved frontispiece portrait plate of Milton (unsigned, but by H. Robinson as in 1832 Pickering edition, where the portrait is identified and dated "London, William Pickering, 1831"), volume 1, protective tissue guard, separate title page each volume, original "Advertisement" for the 1832 Aldine edition by John Mitford with original date of 1831, life of Milton by Mitford followed by addenda and appendix, volume 1, half-title for some of the poems, notes at bottom of page, original brown calf (worn with spines missing, frontispiece and title page, volume 1, foxed), early bookplate on front pastedown of each volume, marbled endpapers. The first edition thus by Little, Brown and Company with life by Mitford was published in 1853 (also listed here with further editions cited). Scarce. Not in Kohler.

2007. THE POETICAL WORKS OF MILTON, YOUNG, GRAY, BEATTIE, AND COLLINS. Complete In One Volume. *Philadelphia: J. B. Lippincott & Co. 1856.* 8vo, xxxii+170pp.,+viii+208pp.,+x+47pp.,+ix+23pp.,+iv+19pp., engraved frontispiece illustration of a lady, protective tissue guard, life of Milton and of each poet, half-title for Milton and for each collection of poetical works, printed in double column, original blue cloth (a bit rubbed), decorative central emblem of lady carrying a basket of fruit in gilt on covers, large Grecian-style illustration in gilt at bottom of spine with gilt lettering and decorative illustration trim in gilt at top. A good copy. See 1850 edition by Lippincott, Grambo & Co. listed here with further editions cited. Not in Kohler.

2008. THE POETICAL WORKS OF MILTON, YOUNG, GRAY, BEATTIE, AND COLLINS. Complete In One Volume. *Philadelphia: J. B. Lippincott & Co. 1857.* 8vo, xxxii+170pp.,+viii+208pp.,+x+47pp.,+ix+23pp.,+iv+19+[10]pp., engraved frontispiece illustration of a lady, protective tissue guard, life of Milton and of each poet, half-title for Milton and for each collection of poetical works, printed in double column, additional engraved illustration plate, protective tissue guard, rebound in quarter black buckram (plates foxed, library stamps with related library matter), paneled paper over boards, new endpapers, marbled edges. Ten pages of advertisements bound in at the end. See 1850 edition by Lippincott, Grambo & Co. listed here with further editions cited. Not in Kohler.

2009. THE POETICAL WORKS OF JOHN MILTON. Edited By Sir Egerton Brydges, Bart. [Quotation from Thomson] Illustrated With Engravings, Designed By John Martin And J. W. M. Turner, R.A. [One Also By Westall And One By Romney]. *Boston: Phillips, Sampson, And Company. 1857.* Third edition thus? 8vo in 4s, 858pp., frontispiece portrait "Engraved by O. Pelton" of a young, long-haired Milton "From a Miniature of the same size by Faithorne. Anno 1667, in the possession of William Falconer Esq.," protective tissue guard (foxed), engraved and printed title pages with vignette illustration for *C* by Turner on engraved title, reprinting of the original 1835 dedication page "To William Wordsworth And Robert Southey This Volume Is Appropriately Dedicated," "Advertisement To The Original Edition," dated 1835, "Life Of Milton," six engraved illustrations, each with protective tissue guard, two engraved illustration plates after Martin for *PL* (Books VII and X), two engraved illustration plates after Turner—one for *PR* (*The Temptation on the Mountain*, bound correctly here in Book III of *PR*) and one for *Comus* (vignette on engraved title page), and although not mentioned on the title page: one engraved illustration plate after Westall for *PL* (*Satan*, here bound within Book I), and one engraved illustration plate after Romney (*Milton Dictating to His Daughters*), engraved by D. L. Glover, for *On His Blindness* (here bound with the poem), introductory remarks from the James Boyd edition for each book of *PL*, notes at bottom of page, black border around text, original dark brown silk (slightly rubbed, spine ends a little chipped, joints a bit worn, frontispiece portrait and engraved title page a little foxed), spine lettered in gilt, edges untrimmed. A decent copy in original publisher's binding, wholly untrimmed. See 1854 edition (possible first edition thus) by Phillips, Sampson, and Company listed and other editions cited there. Not in Kohler.

2010. Variant of Preceding, original full brown calf over thick boards (slight foxing to engraved title page, bookplate removed from fly-leaf), covers elaborately decorated in thick blind relief with Milton's name in blind at the center, spine lettered in gilt with small decorative pieces in blind within the panels, raised bands, green endpapers, a.e.g. A nice copy with plates that are crisp and clear, in a variant publisher's binding, with contemporary signature in ink (dated 1860) on label tipped in on front pastedown and again on front blank. Laid in: a page listing in pencil the names and birth dates of contemporary family members. Not in Kohler.

2011. **THE POETICAL WORKS OF JOHN MILTON**. A New Edition, carefully Revised, From The Text Of Thomas Newton, D.D. To Which Is Prefixed A Biographical Notice. With Illustrations By William Harvey. Fourth Edition. *London: George Routledge And Co. Farringdon Street. New York: 18, Beekman Street. 1857.* Fourth edition thus by Routledge. 8vo, xlvi+[2]+570pp. (illustration plates unpaginated), frontispiece portrait plate of *Milton Dictating to His Daughters*, engraved by Dalziel, protective tissue guard, black rule on title page, original preface by Theodore Alois Buckley (dated 1853), seven illustration plates engraved by Dalziel after William Harvey, notes at bottom of page, contemporary full brown calf over thick boards (a bit rubbed at joints, corners, and spine ends, early name in ink, dated 1898, written on title page), covers richly decorated in embossed blind trim, spine similarly richly decorated in embossed blind trim within the panels with gilt lettering, raised bands, marbled endpapers, gauffered gilt edges. An attractive copy in a handsome leather binding of the period, bound by Edmands & Bemnants, with their stamp, possibly as a presentation binding, with name in gilt at bottom of front cover. The first edition thus by George Routledge and Co. was published in 1853 (also listed here with further editions by Routledge cited). Kohler 334, reporting "Not in the British Library. Not in the Bodleian Library. Not in Cambridge University Library."

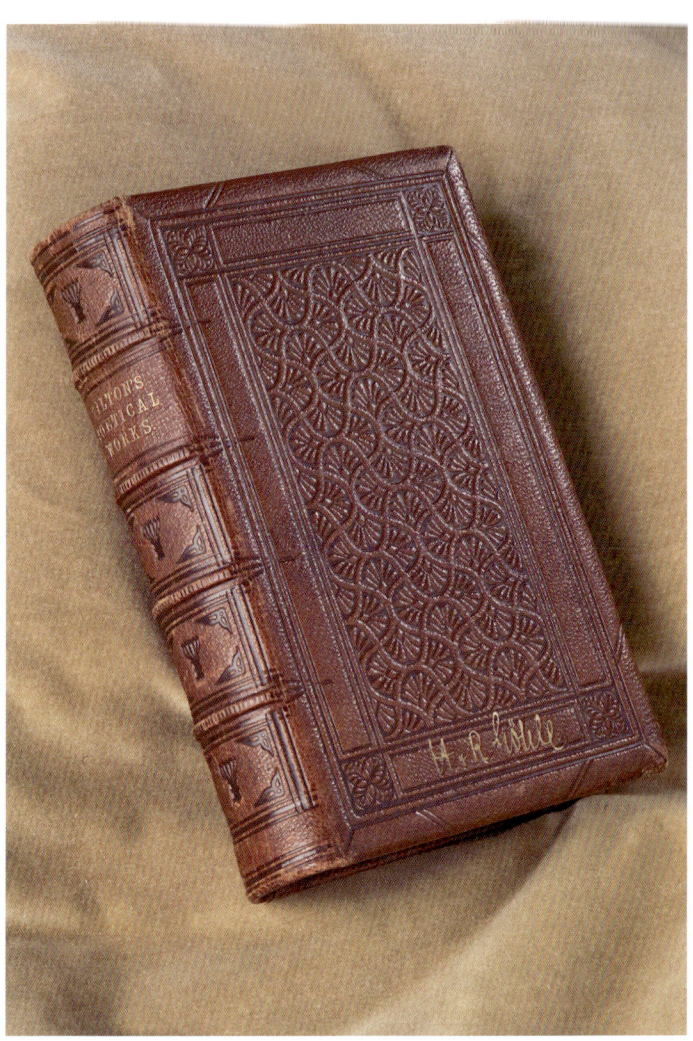

PW, With Illustrations By William Harvey. London: George Routledge And Co. [And] New York. 1857. Contemporary full brown calf over thick boards, covers richly decorated in embossed blind trim, gauffered gilt edges. Attractively bound by Edmands & Bemnants, with their stamp, possibly as a presentation binding, with name in gilt at bottom of front cover. See #2011.

2012. **THE POETICAL WORKS OF JOHN MILTON**. With Life. [Quotation from Thomson] Complete Edition. *T. Nelson And Sons, London: Edinburgh. And New York. MDCCCLVIII.* 8vo, xxx+[2]+523pp., unsigned engraved frontispiece portrait plate, engraved and printed title pages with vignette illustration by T. G. Flowers on engraved title, six unsigned steel-engraved illustrations printed on thick paper, life of Milton, half-title for *PL*, *PR*, *SA*, and *C*, contemporary full red morocco (a bit rubbed, slight dampstaining with back endpapers and back cover slightly waterstained, some underlining in pencil throughout life), elaborately embossed covers with Milton's name in gilt at the center of each cover, spine lettered in gilt, raised bands with decorative pieces in blind within the panels, brown endpapers, a.e.g. A good copy of an uncommon Milton edition. The illustrations here by T. G.

Flowers are identical to those in the 1855 edition by T. Nelson and Sons (copy listed and the illustrations given in detail there). See the possible first and possible second editions published by Nelson in 1850 (copy listed here) and by Nelson and Sons in 1852 (copy listed here), with unsigned illustrations different from those here. See the possible first edition thus by Nelson in 1850 (copy listed here and other editions cited there). Not in Kohler (although Kohler 339 records an edition of "*PW of John Milton. Paradise Lost and Regained.* London: T. Nelson and Sons, Paternoster Row; Edinburgh and New York. 1858," with 381pp., and with "Unsigned frontispiece portrait. Unsigned vignette on vignette title-page").

Extra-Illustrated

2013. Variant of Preceding, original decorated red cloth (a little rubbed), elaborately gilt-decorated front cover with central gilt urn, back cover similarly decorated in blind, elaborately gilt-decorated spine with gilt harp at top and central gilt device near bottom, a.e.g. A good copy in an attractive variant publisher's cloth binding. Besides the vignette illustration after T. G. Flowers on the engraved title page of *Raphael Counseling Adam and Eve* for Book V of *PL*, there are four (rather than six, as in preceding) additional steel-engraved illustrations (unsigned, but possibly by T. G. Flowers) on thick paper which include: *Adam and Eve among the Animals* for Book IV of *PL*; *The Temptation* for Book IX of *PL*; *The Expulsion* for Book XII of *PL*; and *The Temptation* for Book III of *PR*. Extra-illustrated with engraved illustrations after Hayman (eighteenth-century 8vo plates) for each book of *PL* (except Book V) bound in. Not in Kohler.

2014. THE POETICAL WORKS OF JOHN MILTON[:] *Paradise Lost and Regained.* [Quotation from Thomson.] *T. Nelson And Sons, London; Edinburgh; And New York. MDCCCLVIII.* Variant edition. Small 8vo, xxvii+443pp., half-title, unsigned frontispiece portrait plate of a middle-aged Milton, the portrait in a circular form with decorative trim, the whole within a shaded background with Milton's name at the top and his dates beneath, protective tissue guard, engraved and printed title pages with unsigned vignette illustration of the judgment of Adam and Eve on engraved title page, life of Milton, original brown cloth (a bit rubbed, trifle worn at top of front joint and at several corners), covers decorated in embossed blind trim with central device in gilt on front cover, spine illustrated and lettered in gilt with gilt lettering ("Milton" in larger letters at the top and "Paradise Lost & Regained" in very small letters at the bottom) and with a larger illustration of Michael casting Satan out of heaven in gilt in the middle and a smaller illustration of the judgment of Adam and Eve and the snake at the top. A nice copy and a variant edition from the preceding editions by T. Nelson and Son. While titled "The Poetical Works of John Milton," this edition contains only the two poetical works identified on the printed title page and spine: *PL* and *PR*, as with 1856 edition of *PW*. Unlike that edition, however, the frontispiece portrait here, although unsigned, is that of the 1850 edition (possible first edition thus) by Nelson, where the portrait is signed by T. G. Flowers; the engraved title page is also from the 1850 edition, where it is also unsigned and presumably by Flowers; there are no other illustrations in this edition. Both portrait and engraved title page here are very fresh and printed on very white plates. See copy of 1850 edition by Nelson, which includes more than *PL* and *PR*, and other editions cited there. Scarce. Not in Kohler.

2015. THE POETICAL WORKS OF JOHN MILTON. With Life. [Quotation from Thomson] Complete Edition. *London: C. H. Clarke, Paternoster Row. 1858.* 12mo in 6s, xv+[1]+544pp., unsigned engraved frontispiece portrait plate of a youngish Milton, engraved and printed title pages with unsigned vignette illustration of *Adam and Eve Naming the Animals* on engraved title, "List of Illustrations. Directions To The Binder," eight additional unsigned illustrations: four for *PL* (Books IV, VI, IX, and X), two for *PR* (Books I and IV), one for *L* and one for *C*, with elaborate decorative floral border trim surrounding each illustration, double black border around text, original red pebble cloth, covers decorated in blind with central gilt lettering within delicate gilt trim on front cover, intricately gilt-decorated spine with gilt lettering, a.e.g. A fine copy with "Addison's Critique Upon The Paradise Lost" in an appendix reprinting several Milton documents, and "Dr. Channing's Essay On The Poetical Genius Of Milton." An interesting mid-nineteenth-century edition in attractive publisher's cloth binding, with illustrations within elaborate decorative floral trim. Scarce. Not in Kohler.

2016. THE POETICAL WORKS OF JOHN MILTON. To Which Is Prefixed, The Life Of The Author. *London: William Tegg And Co., 85, Queen Street Cheapside. 1858.* 12mo in 6s, xi+576pp., frontispiece portrait plate engraved by W. C. Edwards after Vertue, with another portrait plate of Milton, age twenty-one, also engraved by W. C. Edwards after Cornelius Jansen inserted before life, portrait plate after Romney of *Milton Dictating to His Daughters* inserted within life, nine illustration plates after Westall and Turner, contemporary full purple morocco (a bit rubbed), gilt rules on covers with central gilt seal, elaborately gilt-decorated spine with small gilt emblem of a crown at the top and the initials "S & S" beneath, raised bands (rubbed), inner and outer dentelles finely tooled in gilt, a.e.g., bound by Nutt & Carbidge, with their stamp at bottom of front blank. A fine copy in a lovely Prize Binding, with prize inscription tipped in on front pastedown and early bookplate on verso of fly-leaf. See 1837 first illustrated edition by Tegg also listed here with further editions cited. Kohler 335, reporting "Not in the British Library. Not in the Bodleian Library. Not in Cambridge University Library" and "See Williamson 135 [and] Williamson 31."

2017. Variant of Preceding, contemporary full red morocco (a bit rubbed), covers decorated in blind relief with finely tooled gilt trim, finely gilt-decorated spine in the panels with gilt lettering (faded), raised bands (a bit rubbed), inner and outer dentelles tooled in gilt, a.e.g. A very nice copy in a variant contemporary morocco binding with several early signatures on fly-leaf. Kohler 335.

2018. THE POETICAL WORKS OF JOHN MILTON: To Which Is Prefixed The Life Of The Author, Together With Dr. Channing's Essay On The Poetical Genius Of Milton. *Halifax: Milner And Sowerby. 1858.* Fourth edition thus? Small 8vo, xiv+431pp., unsigned engraved frontispiece illustration of Adam being shown the flood (Book XI), half-title for *PR*, *SA*, and *C*, original red cloth (a little rubbed, spine ends chipped, joints broken from within), covers decorated in blind with central vignette in gilt of a small bust of Milton on top of a book beside ink and quill on front cover, spine lettered and decorated in gilt with depiction of the expulsion in gilt, t.e. rough, fore- and bottom edges untrimmed. A good copy. The possible first edition thus was published in 1853 (also listed here with further editions by Milner and Sowerby cited). Scarce. Not in Kohler.

2019. THE POETICAL WORKS OF JOHN MILTON. A New Edition, carefully Revised, From The Text Of Thomas Newton, D.D. To Which Is Prefixed A Biographical Notice. With Illustrations By William Harvey. New Edition. *London: George Routledge And Co. Farringdon Street. New York: 18, Beekman Street. 1858.* Fifth edition thus by Routledge. 8vo, xlvi+570pp., frontispiece portrait plate of *Milton Dictating to His Daughters*, engraved by Dalziel (bound before Book I), black rule on title page with first appearance of "New Edition" repeated before publisher's imprint, original preface by Theodore Alois Buckley (dated 1853) seven illustration plates engraved by Dalziel after William Harvey, notes at bottom of page, contemporary full maroon morocco (a bit rubbed at joints), blind rules on covers and spine, gilt lettering on spine, raised bands, decorated endpapers, a.e.g. A fine, possibly large paper copy, with early photograph of Chalfont St. Giles and a contemporary handwritten inscribed note in ink related thereto tipped in on front pastedown and fly-leaf respectively, with a prize inscription (dated 1859) on verso of fly-leaf, with the first appearance of "New Edition" repeated before publisher's imprint on title page. The first edition thus by George Routledge and Co. was published in 1853 (also listed here with further editions by Routledge cited). Kohler 336, reporting "Not in the Bodleian Library. Not in Cambridge University Library."

2020. Variant of Preceding, contemporary full brown morocco, richly gilt-decorated covers and spine, raised bands, inner and outer dentelles finely tooled in gilt, a.e.g. A very fine copy in an attractive, well-preserved variant contemporary morocco binding of the period. Kohler 336.

2021. THE POETICAL WORKS OF JOHN MILTON. With A Memoir, And Critical Remarks On His Genius And Writings. By James Montgomery; [Vol. I. / Vol. II.] *New York: Published By Leavitt & Allen, 379 Broadway. n.d. [ca. 1858].* First edition thus by Leavitt & Allen? 2 volumes in one. 8vo, xlix+[i]+[3]+400pp.(page numbering beginning with number "18"),+368pp.(page numbering beginning with number "10"), engraved frontispiece portrait plate after C. Burt (a little foxed), protective tissue guard, "Memoir," volume 1, second title page for volume 2 followed by "Contents Of Vol. II," illustrations (unsigned, but after Harvey) within the text for *L'A* with a vignette illustration at the beginning and another vignette illustration at the end of the poem and with vignette illustrations in the margins, half-title for each book of *PL* and *PR* and for some of the poems, original brown cloth (a bit rubbed, with some embrowning throughout and light, inoffensive waterstaining along bottom edge in the middle of the book, spine ends slightly chipped, early ownership name stamped and written several times on front blanks), covers decorated in embossed blind trim, spine delicately tooled in a gilt floral design with gilt lettering. A good copy in publisher's decorated cloth binding. See ca. 1858 illustrated edition (possible first thus, variant edition, copy listed following) "Published By Leavitt & Allen," without an address given in publisher's imprint. Not in Kohler (but see Kohler 345: "New York: Leavitt & Allen Bros., No. 8 Howard Street. n.d.," with a "Frontispiece engraved by A. H. Ritchie," rather than after C. Burt as here and in other editions following, dated "[ca. 1860]," without reference to any illustrations.)

See also undated ca. 1860 illustrated edition "Published [as here] By Leavitt & Allen, 379 Broadway," as two volumes in one in a much larger and thicker format than here, with engraved frontispiece portrait plate after Burt as here, engraved illustration plate of *Milton Dictating to His Daughters* after George Romney before "Memoir," three engraved illustration plates for *PL*, one engraved illustration plate for *PR*, an engraved illustration plate at the head of the section entitled "Odes," and illustrations (unsigned, but after Harvey) within the text for *L'A* as here, one of the two copies bearing a contemporary presentation inscription dated 1860 on front blank; and see a second undated ca. 1860 illustrated edition "Published By George A. Leavitt" as two volumes in one in a similar format and binding and with the same engraved Milton portraits and engraved illustration plates along with Harvey's illustrations (unsigned) for *L'A*, but with a different publisher's imprint (a simpler one without any street address). See, too, undated ca. 1870 illustrated edition, two volumes in one, with a contemporary signature (dated 1870) on front blank, which includes only the illustrations (after Harvey, but unsigned) for *L'A* and the engraved frontispiece portrait after C. Burt as here; see, too, undated ca. 1872 illustrated edition, two volumes in one, published by "Leavitt & Allen Bros. No. 8 Howard Street" (rather than by "Leavitt & Allen" as here, and with a different address), with a contemporary presentation inscription dated 1872 on front blank, with only the illustrations (after Harvey, but unsigned) for *L'A* and the engraved frontispiece portrait after C. Burt as here; see also undated ca. 1873 illustrated edition published by "Leavitt & Allen Bros." (rather than by "Leavitt & Allen" as here) as two volumes in one in a similar format and binding as the ca. 1860 editions but with a different address ("No. 8 Howard Street"), with a contemporary presentation inscription dated 1873 on front blank, and with several engraved illustration plates together with the illustrations (after Harvey, but unsigned) for *L'A* and the engraved frontispiece portrait after C. Burt as here; see, too, undated ca. 1875 illustrated edition published by "Leavitt & Allen Bros. No. 8 Howard Street," with a contemporary presentation inscription dated 1875 on front blank, in the same size format as here, with only the illustrations (after Harvey, but unsigned) for *L'A* and the engraved frontispiece portrait after C. Burt as here; and see undated ca. 1880 illustrated editions published by "Geo. A. Leavitt, Publisher" (rather than by "Leavitt & Allen" as here), each two volumes in one, each with the same address ("No. 8 Howard Street") as with the ca. 1870, ca. 1872, ca. 1873, and ca. 1875 editions, and each with the engraved frontispiece portrait after C. Burt, one with a contemporary presentation inscription dated 1880 on front blank, which includes only the illustrations (after Harvey, but unsigned) for *L'A*, the other with engraved illustrations similar to the illustrations in the ca. 1860 and ca. 1873 editions, one in a large format as here, the other in a small format.

2022. Variant of Preceding, original red cloth (a bit rubbed, with some embrowning throughout, spine a little faded), covers decorated in embossed blind trim with large central emblem in blind on front cover, spine delicately tooled in a gilt floral design with gilt lettering. A nice copy in a variant publisher's cloth binding, thicker than the preceding copy and other copies here, thicker by ¼", with a contemporary signature (dated "Decr. 25 1858") within decorative hand scroll on front blank. Not in Kohler.

2023. Variant of Preceding. THE POETICAL WORKS OF JOHN MILTON. With A Memoir, And Critical Remarks On His Genius And Writings. By James Montgomery; [Vol. I. / Vol. II.] *New York: Published By Leavitt & Allen. n.d. [ca. 1858].* 2 volumes in one. First edition thus by Leavitt & Allen; variant publisher's imprint? 8vo in 12s, xlix+[i]+[3]+400pp.(page numbering beginning with number "18"),+368pp.(page numbering beginning with number "10"), engraved frontispiece portrait plate after C. Burt (a little foxed), protective tissue guard (slightly foxed), "Memoir," volume 1, second title page for volume 2 followed by "Contents Of Vol. II," illustrations (unsigned, but after Harvey) within the text for *L'A* with a vignette illustration at the beginning and another vignette illustration at the end of the poem and with vignette illustrations in the margins, half-title for each book of *PL* and *PR* and for some of the poems, original green cloth (a bit rubbed with some embrowning throughout), covers decorated in embossed blind trim with large central emblem in blind on front cover, spine delicately tooled in a gilt floral design with gilt lettering. A nice copy in a variant publisher's decorated cloth binding, in fine condition, with variant publisher's address (without address in publisher's imprint on title page), with early signature on front fly-leaf and on back blank. Not in Kohler.

2024. Variant of Preceding. Original pink cloth (a bit rubbed, some embrowning, corners bumped, small ink blot at top of front cover), covers decorated in embossed blind trim with large central emblem in blind on front cover, spine delicately tooled in a gilt floral design with gilt lettering. A nice copy in a variant publisher's decorated cloth binding, with variant publisher's imprint of preceding. Not in Kohler.

2025. THE POETICAL WORKS OF JOHN MILTON. With A Memoir, And Critical Remarks On His Genius And Writings, By James Montgomery; And One Hundred And Twenty Engravings By John Thompson, S. & T. Williams, O. Smith, J. Linton, etc. From Drawings By

William Harvey. *London: W. Kent & Co. (Late D. Bogue), Fleet Street. MDCCCLIX.* 2 volumes. 8vo, lii+378pp.,+ viii+341pp., half-title ("Milton's Poetical Works. Bogue's Illustrated Edition.") and title page each volume, 120 engravings in the text after drawings by William Harvey, half-title for some of the poems, original blue cloth (very slightly rubbed at the joints), strikingly decorated in gilt and blind on the covers and spines with "Tilt's Illustrated Edition" lettered in gilt on each spine. A very fine, tall copy, perhaps a large paper copy, in a bright, clean publisher's binding, with extra wide margins, almost entirely unopened. A fine example of a handsome Victorian edition produced for the gift market, with armorial bookplate and neat (possibly contemporary) signature in each volume. Scarce. Kohler 340, reporting "Not in the British Library. Not in the Bodleian Library. Not in Cambridge University Library."

2026. THE POETICAL WORKS OF JOHN MILTON. With Life. [Quotation from Thomson] Complete Edition. *London: T. Nelson And Sons, Paternoster Row; Edinburgh; And New York. MDCCCLIX.* 8vo, xx[sic] for xxx+[2]+523pp., unsigned engraved frontispiece portrait plate, engraved and printed title pages with vignette illustration by T. G. Flowers on engraved title, six unsigned steel-engraved illustrations printed on thick paper, life of Milton, half-title for *PL*, *PR*, *SA*, and *C*, contemporary full red morocco (joints and edges a bit rubbed, front joint weak, spine slightly chipped at top, some foxing, including plates, early name erased some time ago on back of portrait leaving a small puncture near the top without affecting portrait itself), elaborately embossed covers with Milton's name in gilt at the center of each cover, spine lettered in gilt, raised bands with decorative pieces in blind within the panels, a.e.g. An attractive copy in a fine Victorian binding. The illustrations here by T. G. Flowers are identical to those in the 1855 edition by T. Nelson and Sons (copy listed and illustrations given in detail there). See the possible first and possible second editions published by Nelson in 1850 and by Nelson and Sons in 1852 (see copy of each listed), with unsigned illustrations different from those here. See the possible first edition thus by Nelson in 1850 (also listed here with further editions cited there). Kohler 331, reporting "Not in Williamson. Not in the British Library. Not in the Bodleian Library. Not in Cambridge University Library."

2027. Variant of Preceding, contemporary full green morocco (a bit rubbed, especially at spine ends and at the corners), covers elaborately decorated with gilt rules and decorative gilt corner pieces with embossed urn in blind at the center, spine lettered in gilt with decorative gilt pieces within the panels, raised bands with decorative gilt trim within gilt rules, a.e.g. An attractive copy in a fine Victorian Prize Binding with prize inscription in a neat hand (dated 1860) on front pastedown. Kohler 331.

2028. THE POETICAL WORKS OF JOHN MILTON. With Life. [Quotation from Thomson.] Complete Edition. *London: John Kendrick, 27 Ludgate Street, St. Paul's; And 4 Charlotte Row, Mansion House. MDCCCLIX.* 8vo, xxx+658pp., printed color floral dedication page, half-title, unsigned frontispiece illustration plate of *The Ascent of the Spirit*, seven additional illustration plates after W. Linton, John Martin, H. C. Slous, C. Bentley, and A. E. Chalon, protective tissue guard for each illustration, half-title for each book of *PL* and for some of the poems, half-title for each book of *PR* with "Argument" on verso (not original to the poem), triple black border around text, contemporary full rich brown pebble morocco (a bit rubbed along joints and at corners), brilliantly gilt-decorated covers and spine, raised bands, inner dentelles finely tooled in gilt, a.e.g. A very nice copy in a well-preserved morocco binding of the period with fine impression of the plates. See 1850 edition (copy listed here) with different illustrations and a different address for Kendrick in publisher's imprint; see 1851 edition (copy listed here) with identical illustrations identified in detail, but with a different address for Kendrick in publisher's imprint, the same as that in the 1850 edition; the 1855 edition (copy listed here) has the same illustrations and address for Kendrick in publisher's imprint as here. Not in Kohler.

2029. Variant of Preceding, printed color floral dedication page neatly inscribed and dated 1861 within, contemporary full green pebble morocco (a bit rubbed, joints tender), covers brilliantly decorated in gilt with thick gilt rules, spine lettered in gilt with decorative gilt trim within the panels, raised bands within slight gilt rules, inner dentelles finely tooled in gilt, a.e.g. A nice copy in a variant contemporary morocco binding. Not in Kohler.

2030. THE POETICAL WORKS OF JOHN MILTON. To Which Is Prefixed A Biography Of The Author, By His Nephew, Edward Philips. *New York: D. Appleton & Company, 346 & 348 Broadway. M DCCC LIX.* 12mo in 6s, 574pp., engraved frontispiece portrait plate of Milton engraved by "Illman & Pilbrow" after Faithorne, introduction, life by Edward Philips, six unsigned illustration plates (fine impressions), each with protective tissue guard, half-title for some of the poems, contents listed at the end original dark green cloth (a little rubbed along joints and extremities, spine ends chipped), covers decorated and lettered in blind, spine decorated and lettered in gilt (faded). A good copy. Three of the six illustrations, though

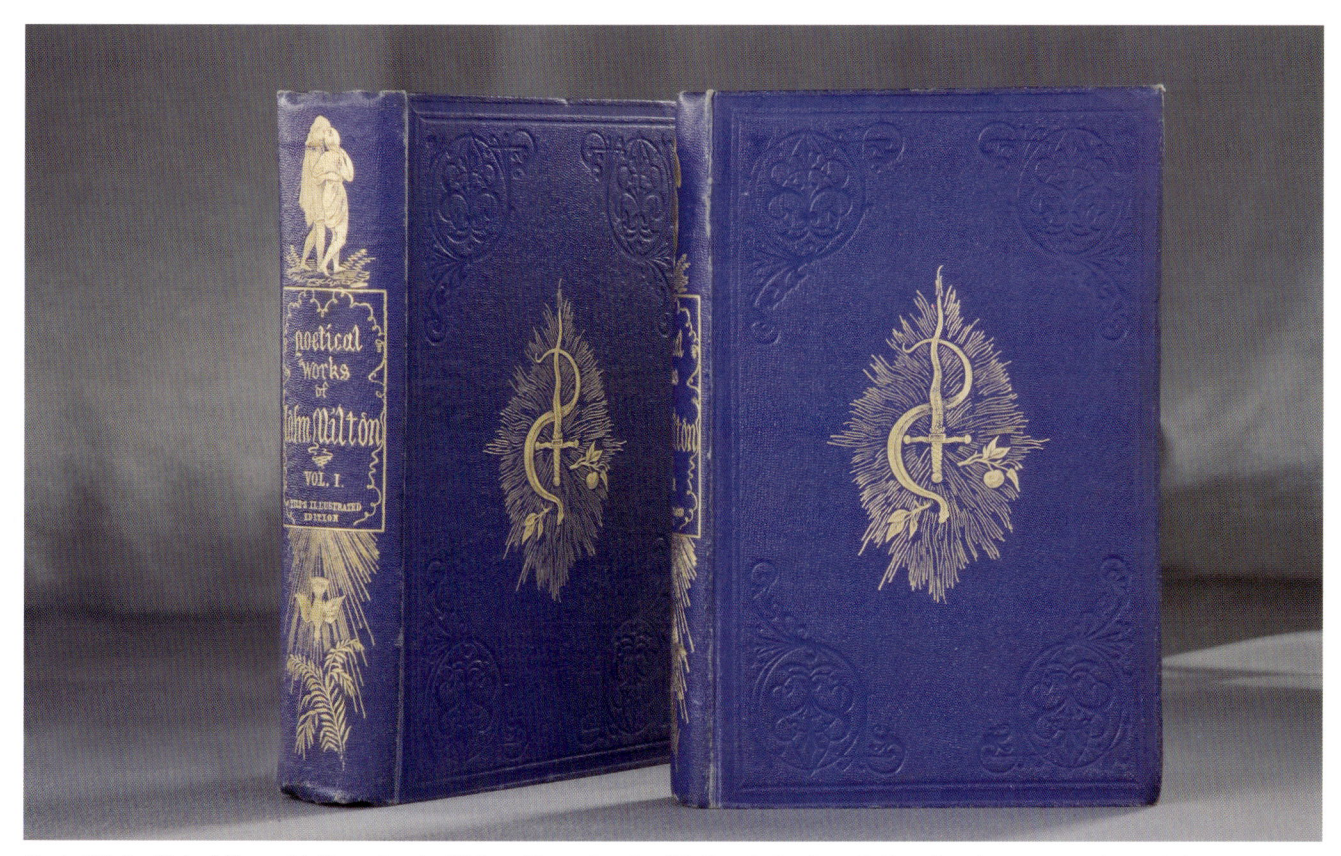

Poetical Works of John Milton with illustrations by William Harvey. London: W. Kent & Co. (Late D. Bogue), 1859. 8vo, original blue cloth, gilt emblems in the center and illustrations in gilt on the spine. See #2025.

Printed floral dedication page for personal dedication in *PW*, Kendrick, 1859. See #2028.

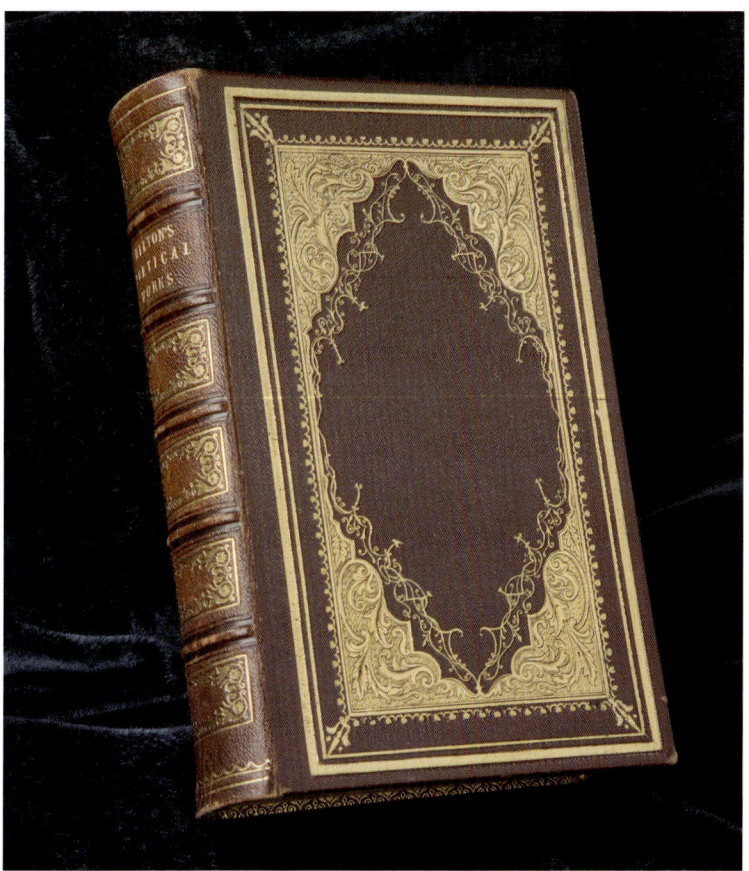

Rich brown morocco binding on *PW*, Kendrick, 1859. See #2028.

(left) Rich dark green morocco binding as with the copy of *PW*, Kendrick, 1859, with floral dedication page used for contemporary presentation inscription. (above) Printed floral dedication page for personal dedication filled in with dated contemporary written presentation in a neat hand, in another copy of *PW*, Kendrick, 1859. See #2029.

unsigned, are after Turner: two for *PL*, Books VI and XII, and for *L*; the other three are Turneresque in style: for *PL*, Book II, for *C*, and for *IlP*. Later editions by Appleton were published in 1861, 1864, 1868, and 1872 (copy of each listed here). See other illustrated editions by Appleton cited in 1851 edition (listed here). Not in Kohler.

2031. THE POETICAL WORKS OF JOHN MILTON. Edited By Sir Egerton Brydges, Bart. [Quotation from Thomson] Illustrated With Engravings, Designed By John Martin And J. W. M. Turner, R.A. [One Also By Westall And One By Romney]. *Boston: Phillips, Sampson, And Company. 1859.* Fourth edition thus? 8vo in 4s, 858pp., frontispiece portrait "Engraved by O. Pelton" of a young, long-haired Milton "From a Miniature of the same size by Faithorne. Anno 1667, in the possession of William Falconer Esq.," protective tissue guard (foxed), engraved and printed title pages with vignette illustration for *C* after Turner on engraved title, reprinting of the original 1835 dedication page "To William Wordsworth And Robert Southey," "Advertisement To The Original Edition" dated 1835, "Life Of Milton," six engraved illustrations, each with protective tissue guard, two engraved illustration plates after Martin for *PL* (Books VII and X), two engraved illustration plates after Turner—one for *PR* (*The Temptation on the Mountain*, bound correctly here in Book III of *PR*) and one for *C* (vignette on engraved title page), and although not mentioned on the title page: one engraved illustration plate after Westall for *PL* (*Satan*, here bound within Book IV), and one engraved illustration plate after Romney (*Milton Dictating To His Daughters*), engraved by D. L. Glover, for *On His Blindness* (here bound with the poem, plate and tissue badly foxed), introductory remarks from the James Boyd edition for each book of *PL*, notes at bottom of page, black border around text, original full brown calf over thick boards (slightly worn along joints and extremities, spine dry and cracked from age, occasional foxing, slight embrowning throughout), covers elaborately decorated in thick blind relief, spine lettered in gilt, raised bands, brown silk ribbon marker, a.e.g. A good copy. See 1854 edition (possible first edition thus) by Phillips, Sampson, and Company, copy listed and other editions cited there. Uncommon. Not in Kohler.

2032. THE POETICAL WORKS OF JOHN MILTON. With A Life, By Rev. John Mitford. In Three Volumes. *Boston: Little, Brown And Company. Shepard, Clark And Brown. M.DCCC.LIX.* 3 volumes. Fourth edition thus by Little, Brown and Company? Small 8vo, 4+cxxxiv+[4]+[1]+153pp.,+372pp.,+334pp., half-title ("The Poems Of Milton") each volume, engraved frontispiece portrait plate of Milton (unsigned, but after H. Robinson as in 1832 Pickering edition where the portrait is identified and dated "London, William Pickering, 1831"), volume 1, protective tissue guard, separate title page each volume, original "Advertisement" for the 1832 Aldine edition by John Mitford with original date of 1831, life of Milton by Mitford followed by addenda and appendix, volume 1, half-title for some of the poems, notes at bottom of page, original brown cloth (a little rubbed), covers ruled in blind with central device in blind, spines lettered in gilt. A very nice set, well-preserved in mid-nineteenth-century American publisher's binding with four-pages of advertisements bound in at front of volume 1. The first edition thus by Little, Brown and Company with life by Mitford was published in 1853 (see set listed here), a reprint, as here, of Pickering's Aldine edition, with Mitford's notes and his life of the poet (see 1853 Little, Brown and Company set also listed here with further editions cited). The first Aldine edition (with the first appearance of Milton portrait after Robinson) and second Pickering edition was published in 1832 (also listed here with further Aldine sets cited). Scarce. Not in Kohler.

2033. THE POETICAL WORKS OF JOHN MILTON: With A Life of the Author; Preliminary Dissertations On Each Poem; Notes Critical And Explanatory; An Index To The Subjects Of Paradise Lost; And A Verbal Index to all the Poems. Edited By Charles Dexter Cleveland. [Quotation from Lord Erskine.] *Philadelphia: J. B. Lippincott & Co. 1859[.]* 12mo in 6s, 688pp., copyright date of 1853 on verso of title page, preface (dated 1853), half-title for some of the poems, notes at bottom of page, index to *PL* and verbal index to the whole at the end, original brown cloth (corners worn, spine neatly repaired with library black tape, slight foxing throughout, early names on fly-leaf), raised bands, marbled edges, bookplate. A good copy of a scarce edition of Milton's *PW*. The second edition thus was published in 1854 (copy listed here), following upon the first edition in 1853 (Stevens 168); see also 1865 edition copy listed here. Not in Kohler.

2034. THE POETICAL WORKS OF JOHN MILTON. A New Edition, carefully Revised, From The Text Of Thomas Newton, D.D. With Illustrations By William Harvey. *London: Routledge, Warne, And Routledge, Farringdon Street. New York: 56, Walker Street. 1860.* Small 8vo, viii+570pp., frontispiece illustration of *Milton Dictating*, engraved by Dalziel, original preface by Theodore Alois Buckley (dated 1853), with eight pages of preliminary material rather than the forty-six pages in earlier editions by Routledge and without "To Which Is Prefixed A Biographical Notice" on title page as in earlier editions, seven illustrations plates from engravings by Dalziel after William Harvey, all but one with protective tissue guard, notes at bottom of the page, contemporary full green morocco (rubbed along joints and extremities), covers elaborately tooled in blind and black with central panel incorporating Milton's name in decorative gilt lettering, spine lettered in gilt, raised bands with small decorations in blind within the panels, a.e.g. A nice copy in an attractive Victorian morocco binding, the first Routledge edition without "To Which Is Prefixed A Biographical Notice" on title page and with only eight pages of preliminary material rather than the forty-six pages in earlier editions by Routledge, with contemporary prize citation (dated 1860) tipped in on front pastedown. The first edition thus by George Routledge and Co. was published in 1853 (also listed here with further editions cited). Kohler 344, reporting "Not in the British Library. Not in the Bodleian Library. Not in Cambridge University Library."

2035. Variant of Preceding, original decorated blue cloth (a bit used, spine ends chipped), front cover richly decorated in embossed red and black with decorative embossed red trim creating an angular design against a floral background with gold trim around the edge, "Milton" lettered at the top and "Illustrated" at the bottom, with the letters "GS" in orange over "R" in black over an embossed gold medallion at the center, spine similarly decorated in embossed black and gold with Milton's name in embossed red against a gold background at the top (slightly worn), back cover decorated in blind, brown endpapers, a.e.g. A decent copy in an attractive variant publisher's decorated cloth binding. Kohler 344.

2036. THE POETICAL WORKS OF JOHN MILTON. With Life. [Quotation from Thomson] Complete Edition. *London: T. Nelson And Sons, Paternoster Row; Edinburgh; And New York. MDCCCLX.* 8vo, xxx+[2]+523pp., six unsigned steel-engraved illustrations printed on thick paper, life of Milton, half-title for *PL*, *PR*, *SA*, and *C*, contemporary full red morocco (spine and extremities worn, front joint broken, spine slightly chipped at bottom, some age-browning), elaborately embossed covers with Milton's name in gilt at the center of each cover, spine lettered in gilt, raised bands with decorative pieces in blind within the panels, marbled endpapers, a.e.g., blue silk ribbon marker. A fair copy of a scarce Milton edition in an attractive (albeit somewhat worn) Victorian morocco binding, with illustrations that are bright and clear. The illustrations here by T. G. Flowers are identical to those in the 1855 edition by T. Nelson and Sons listed here in detail. See the possible first and possible second editions published by Nelson in 1850 (see copy listed here) and by Nelson and Sons in 1852 (see copy listed here), with unsigned illustrations different from those here. See the possible first edition thus by Nelson in 1850 and other editions cited there. Uncommon. Not in Kohler.

2037. THE POETICAL WORKS O JOHN MILTON. With A Memoir, And Critical Remarks On His Genius And Writings. By James Montgomery; Vol. I. / Vol. II. *New York: Published By George A. Leavitt. n.d. [ca. 1860].* 2 volumes in one. 8vo, xlix+[i]+[3]+400pp.(page numbering beginning with number "18"),+368pp.(page numbering beginning with number "10"), engraved frontispiece portrait plate after C. Burt, protective tissue guard (foxed), engraved illustration plate of *Milton Dictating to His Daughters* after George Romney before "Memoir," protective tissue guard (foxed), volume 1, second title page for volume 2 followed by "Contents Of Vol. II," three engraved illustration plates for *PL* (*Moloch*, unsigned, for Book II, a bit foxed; *Murmuring waters fall . . .*, unsigned, for Book IV, a bit foxed; *Death* engraved by Sartain after Jones, for Book X), one engraved illustration plate for *PR* (*The Fall of Jerusalem*, after Martin, inserted here in Book III), an engraved illustration plate (*Our Saviour* engraved by Burt after Delaroch) at the head of the section entitled "Odes," which begins with *On The Morning Of Christ's Nativity*, each engraved illustration plate with a protective tissue guard (each tissue guard foxed, some more heavily than others), illustrations (unsigned, but after Harvey) within the text for *L'A* with a vignette illustration at the beginning and another vignette illustration at the end of the poem and with vignette illustrations in the margins, half-title for each book of *PL* and *PR* and for some of the poems, double black border around text, contemporary full dark brown calf over thick boards (a bit worn along joints and extremities), covers elaborately embossed in blind with Milton's name in gilt at the center of each cover, spine lettered in gilt with small decorative pieces in blind within the panels, raised bands (rubbed), marbled endpapers, a.e.g. A good copy in an attractive (albeit a bit worn) richly embossed binding of the period. The possible first edition thus was published by Leavitt & Allen in 1858 (also listed here with further editions cited). Scarce. Not in Kohler.

2038. Variant of Preceding, contemporary full rich dark brown calf over thick boards (lightly rubbed along joints), covers richly embossed in blind with Milton's name in gilt at the center of each cover, spine lettered in gilt with small decorative pieces in blind within the panels, raised bands (lightly rubbed), marbled endpapers, a.e.g. A handsome copy with contents and illustrations as preceding copy but with a variant publisher's imprint (address added to publisher's imprint on title page: "New York: Published By Leavitt & Allen, 379 Broadway"), fresh and clean within, in a finely preserved embossed binding of the period with a contemporary presentation inscription dated "Jan 28th 1860" on front blank. Not in Kohler.

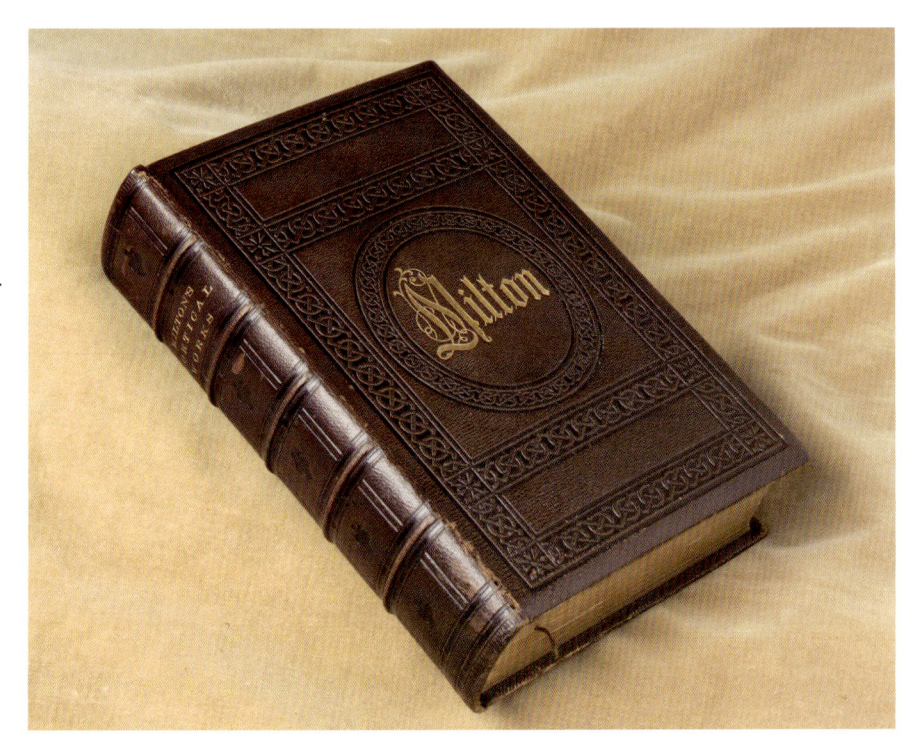

PW. New York: Leavitt & Allen. n.d. [ca. 1860]. 2 volumes in one. Contemporary full rich dark brown morocco over thick boards. See #2038.

2039. THE POETICAL WORKS OF JOHN MILTON. Edited By Sir Egerton Brydges, Bart. [Quotation from Thomson] Illustrated With Engravings, Designed By John Martin And J. W. M. Turner, R.A. [One Also By Westall And One By Romney]. *New York: D. Appleton And Company, 90, 92, & 94 Grand Street. n.d. [ca. 1860].* Thick 8vo in 4s, 858pp., frontispiece portrait "Engraved by O. Pelton" of a young, long-haired Milton "From a Miniature of the same size by Faithorne. Anno 1667, in the possession of William Falconer Esq.," protective tissue guard, engraved and printed title pages with vignette illustration for *C* after Turner on engraved title, engraved title page with "Boston. Phillips, Sampson & Company" as publisher, printed title page with "New York: D. Appleton And Company" as publisher, reprinting of the original 1835 dedication page "To William Wordsworth And Robert Southey," "Advertisement To The Original Edition" dated 1835, "Life Of Milton," six engraved illustration plates, each with protective tissue guard, two engraved illustration plates after Martin for *PL* (Books VII and X), two engraved illustration plates after Turner—one for *PR* (Book III, *The Temptation on the Mountain*) and one for *C* (as vignette on engraved title page), one engraved illustration plate after Westall for *PL* (Satan, here bound within Book IV), and one illustration plate after Romney (*Milton Dictating to His Daughters*), engraved by D. L. Glover, for *On His Blindness* (here bound right after the poem), unsigned introductory remarks from the James Boyd edition for each book of *PL*, notes at bottom of page, double black border around text, contemporary full rich brown calf over thick boards (slightly rubbed along joints and extremities, spine a little chafed), covers elaborately embossed in blind with Milton's name in gilt at the center of each cover, spine lettered in gilt, raised bands, broad inner dentelles widely tooled in gilt, richly marbled endpapers, a.e.g. A fine copy, very fresh and clean within, in a lovely embossed binding. See 1851 possible first edition thus of *PW* by Appleton published in New York and Philadelphia (also listed here with further editions by Appleton cited). Not in Kohler.

2040. THE POETICAL WORKS OF JOHN MILTON. With A Memoir, And Critical Remarks On His Genius And Writings. By James Montgomery; Vol. I. / Vol. II. *Boston: Lee And Shepard, Publishers; New York: Charles T. Dillingham. n.d. [ca. 1860].* 2 volumes in one. Large 12mo, l+[3]+400pp.(pagination number beginning with page number "18"),+368pp., engraved frontispiece portrait plate after C. Burt, protective tissue guard, second title page for volume 2 followed by "Contents Of Vol. II," unsigned engraved illustration plate of *Milton and His Daughter* (with what might be his wife speaking to the young child huddled against a standing "Milton," although the man hardly looks like Milton), at end of life, before Book I, two engraved illustration plates for *PL* (*Adam and Eve Driven out of Paradise* after Doré, bound in Book X, *The Deluge* after Doré, for Book XI), two engraved illustration plates for *PR* (*St. John the Baptist* after Doré for Book I, and *Christ and His Disciples* after Doré for Book IV), illustrations (unsigned, but after Harvey) within the text for *L'A* with a vignette illustration at the beginning and another vignette illustration at the end of the poem and with vignette illustrations in the margins, an engraved illustration plate (*Birth Of Christ* after Doré) for *On The Morning Of Christ's Nativity* at the beginning of *Odes*, an engraved illustration plate for *May Morning* after "W. Thomas," and an engraved illustration plate for *Defend the Poor and the Destitute* after "Geo F. Barnes," inserted in the *Translations*, intended for Psalm 82:3, which is translated: "Defend the poor and desolate," half-title for each book of *PL* and *PR* and for some of the poems, double black border around text, contemporary full dark brown morocco over thick boards (back joint broken, spine worn and chafed), covers elaborately embossed in blind, with Milton's name in large gilt letters at the top of each cover, with the letter "M" in a larger size decorated in floral trim recessed within a circular dark brown panel with decorative border trim, with an attractive image of Milton as a young man in embossed gilt at the center of each cover, spine lettered in gilt, raised bands (rubbed), wide inner dentelles finely tooled in gilt, marbled endpapers, a.e.g. Except for the worn spine and broken back joint, a decent copy in a fine binding of the period, with interesting prints that are fresh and clean. Similar in format to an illustrated edition by "Geo. A. Leavitt" and "D. Appleton And Company" about this same time, ca. 1860 (both listed here). Uncommon. Not in Kohler.

2041. THE POETICAL WORKS OF JOHN MILTON With A Memoir And Critical Remarks On His Genius And Writings By James Montgomery And One Hundred And Twenty Engravings By John Thompson, S. And T. Williams, O. Smith, J. Linton, Etc. From Drawings By William Harvey. New Edition. With An Index To Paradise Lost; Todd's Verbal Index To All The Poems; And A Variorum Selection Of Explanatory Notes By Henry G. Bohn. In Two Vols. *London: Henry G. Bohn, York Street, Covent Garden. 1861.* 2 volumes. 8vo, iv+liii+508,+lii+508pp., printed title page each volume, general title page, volume 2, printed here, engraved frontispiece portrait engraved by Cochran after Cooper, preface (dated "March 28th, 1861"), "Memoir Of John Milton, With Strictures On His Genius And Writings," illustrations variously engraved after William Harvey, half-title for each book,

"Notes to *PL*" and "Index Of Subjects *PL*" at end, volume 1, frontispiece facsimile of the sonnet *On Attaining Age 21*, protective tissue guard, "Contents Of Vol. II," illustrations variously engraved after William Harvey, half-title for some of the works, including "Todd's Verbal Index To Milton's Poetical Works. Revised And Enlarged," contemporary full polished red morocco, gilt rules on covers, gilt-decorated spines, black morocco title labels with decorative gilt trim, red morocco numbering labels with decorative gilt trim, outer dentelles finely tooled in gilt, marbled endpapers and edges. A charming set in a very attractive and well-preserved contemporary morocco binding, with early armorial bookplate on front pastedown of each volume and early presentation inscription in a neat hand (dated 1873) on front blank of each volume. "The present edition of Milton's Poetical Works is a repetition, with additions, of that originally published by Messrs. Tilt and Bogue, in 1843, and since by Messrs. Kent and Co." (Preface). Harvey's illustrations were first published in London by Tilt & Bogue in 1843 (see several sets listed here); see edition by Kent in 1859 in two volumes (see sets listed here). Separate title page each volume; in volume 1: "**PARADISE LOST**. A Poem. In Twelve Books. By John Milton. With A Memoir, And Critical Remarks On His Genius And Writings, By James Montgomery. Embellished With Numerous Engravings By John Thompson, S. And T. Williams, Orrin Smith, J. Linton, Etc. From Drawings By William Harvey. New Edition. With An Index And A Selection Of Explanatory Notes By Henry G. Bohn. London: Henry G. Bohn, York Street, Covent Garden. 1861." Separate title page in volume 2: "**PARADISE REGAINED, SAMSON AGONISTES, COMUS, ARCADES, AND OTHER POEMS** By John Milton. With A Memoir, And Critical Remarks On His Genius And Writings, By James Montgomery. Embellished With Numerous Engravings By John Thompson, S. And T. Williams, Orrin Smith, J. Linton, Etc. From Drawings By William Harvey. New Edition. To Which Is Added, An Index Verborum To The Whole Of Milton's Poems. London: Henry G. Bohn, York Street, Covent Garden. 1861," Scarce. Williamson 218; Kohler 346.

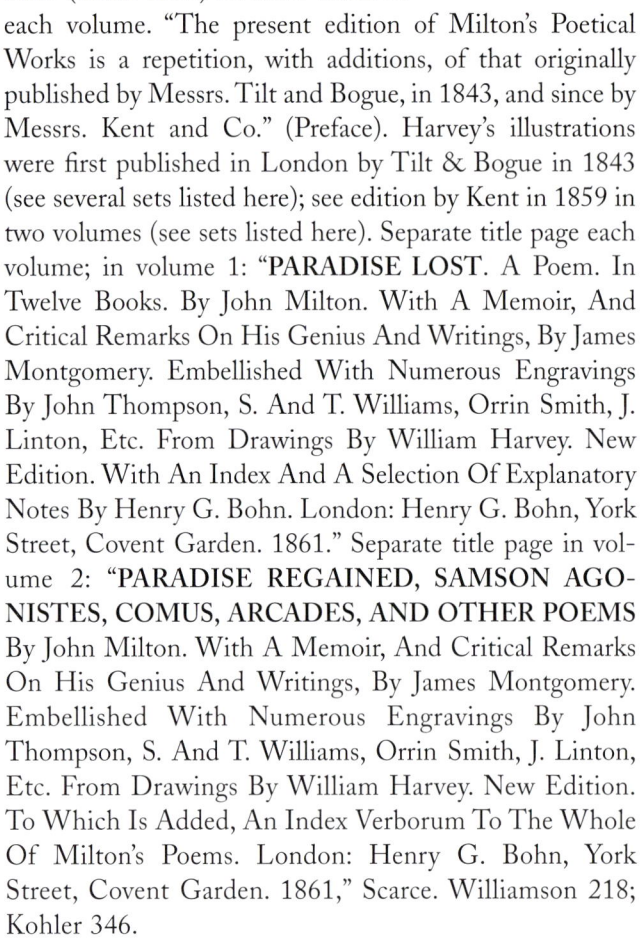

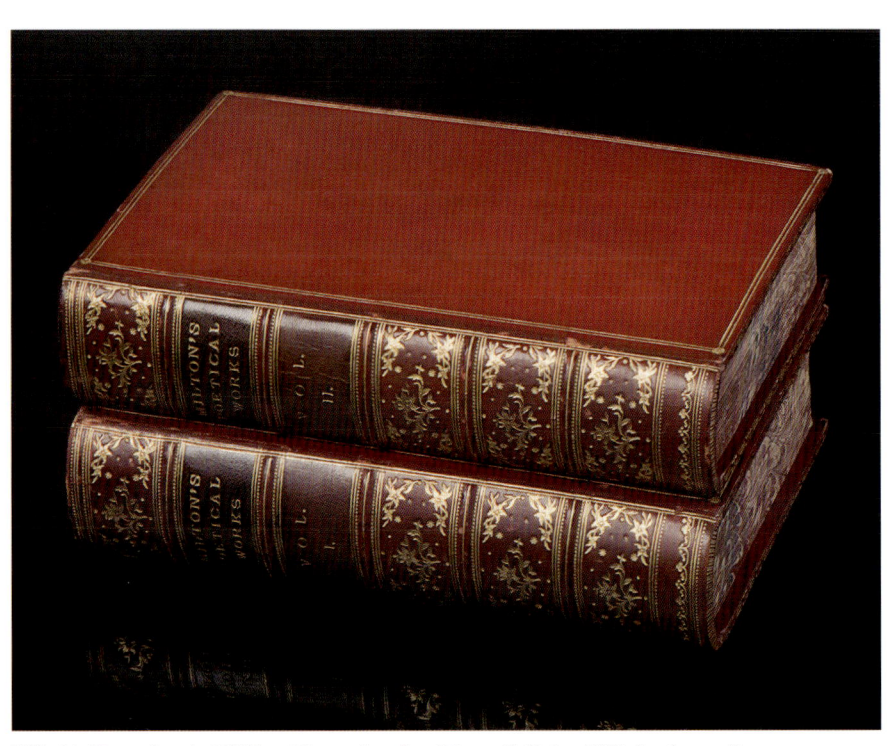

PW with illustrations by William Harvey. London: Henry G. Bohn, 1861. 2 volumes. 8vo, contemporary full polished red morocco. See #2041.

2042. THE POETICAL WORKS OF JOHN MILTON. With Life. [Quotation from Thomson] Complete Edition. *London: T. Nelson And Sons, Paternoster Row; Edinburgh; And New York. MDCCCLXI.* 8vo, xxx+[2]+523pp., unsigned engraved frontispiece portrait plate with protective tissue guard, engraved and printed title pages with vignette illustration by T. G. Flowers on engraved title, six unsigned steel-engraved illustrations printed on thick paper, all but one with a protective tissue guard, life of Milton, half-title for *PL*, *PR*, *SA*, and *C*, contemporary full dark green morocco (slightly rubbed, some plates slightly foxed, especially portrait and engraved title page), covers richly embossed in blind with Milton's name in gilt at the center of each cover, spine lettered in gilt, raised bands with decorative pieces in blind within the panels, marbled endpapers, a.e.g., blue silk ribbon marker. An attractive copy of a scarce Milton edition in a fine Victorian binding with contemporary ownership signature (dated 1862) on front blank. The illustrations here by T. G. Flowers are identical to those in the 1855 edition by T. Nelson and Sons also listed here in detail. See the possible first and possible second editions published by Nelson in 1850 and by Nelson and Sons in 1852 (see copy of each listed here), with unsigned illustrations different from those here. See the possible first edition thus by Nelson in 1850 with further editions cited. Uncommon. Not in Kohler.

2043. THE POETICAL WORKS OF JOHN MILTON. Edited By Sir Egerton Brydges, Bart. [Quotation from Thomson] Illustrated With Engravings, Designed By John Martin And J. W. M. Turner, R A [One Also By Westall And One By Romney]. *Boston: Crosby, Nichols, Lee & Company[,] 1861.* First edition thus by Crosby, Nichols, Lee & Company? Large 8vo in 4s, 858pp., frontispiece portrait "Engraved by O. Pelton" of a young, long-haired Milton "From a Miniature of the same size by Faithorne. Anno 1667, in the possession of William Falconer Esq.," protective tissue guard, engraved and printed title pages, engraved title with vignette illustration for *C* after Turner with publication imprint: "Boston. Phillips, Sampson & Company," original 1835 dedication page "To William Wordsworth And Robert Southey" reprinted after title page followed by a reprinting of the "Advertisement To The Original Edition" dated 1835, "Life Of Milton," six engraved illustration plates, each with protective tissue guard: two engraved illustration plates after Martin for *PL* (Books VII and X), two engraved illustration plates after Turner—one for *PR* (*The Temptation on the Mountain,* Book III) and one for *C* (as vignette on engraved title page), one engraved illustration plate after Westall for *PL* (*Satan,* Book IV), and one engraved illustration plate after Romney (*Milton Dictating to His Daughters*), engraved by D. L. Glover, for *On His Blindness* (bound with the poem), introductory remarks from the James Boyd edition for each book of *PL*, notes at bottom of page, black border around text, original stamped black cloth (joints worn, covers sometime reinforced internally and with black tape externally along joints), covers elaborately decorated in blind relief with central Grecian figures and pillar with bust of Milton at the top, spine lettered in gilt with large figure of a woman playing a harp in gilt at the bottom and with a medallion portrait of Milton in gilt toward the top beneath the gilt lettering. A decent copy in an attractive publisher's binding. See 1854 edition of Milton's *PW* by Phillips, Sampson, and Company (possible first edition thus) also listed here with further editions cited. Not in Kohler.

2044. Variant of Preceding, original three-quarter calf, marbled paper over boards (a little rubbed and worn, especially along extremities), maroon morocco presentation label with gilt rules and gilt lettering on front cover, black morocco label (cracked) with gilt lettering on spine, raised bands, marbled endpapers and edges. Nice copy, fresh and clean within, with clean plates, in a variant publisher's binding, with leather presentation label with gilt lettering and gilt rules at center of front cover. Not in Kohler.

2045. THE POETICAL WORKS OF JOHN MILTON. To Which Is Prefixed A Biography Of The Author, By His Nephew, Edward Philips. *New York: D. Appleton & Company, 443 & 445 Broadway. M DCCC LXI.* 12mo in 6s, 574pp., engraved frontispiece portrait plate of Milton engraved by "Illman & Pilbrow" after Faithorne, introduction, life by Edward Philips, six unsigned illustration plates (fine impressions), each with protective tissue guard, half-title for some of the poems, contents listed at the end, original brown leather (a bit heavily rubbed along joints and extremities, foxing throughout with the frontispiece and illustration plates more heavily foxed), covers richly embossed in blind relief with Milton's name in gilt at the center, spine lettered in gilt, small emblem in blind within the panels, raised bands, marbled endpapers, a.e.g. A nice copy with early bookplate on front pastedown and early presentation inscription in pencil on front blank. Three of the six illustrations, though unsigned, are after Turner: two for *PL*, Books VI and XII, and for *L*; the other three are Turneresque in style: for *PL*, Book II, for *C*, and for *IIP*. See 1859 edition also listed here with further editions cited. Not in Kohler.

2046. THE POETICAL WORKS OF JOHN MILTON. With Life. [Quotation from Thomson] Complete Edition. *London: T. Nelson And Sons, Paternoster Row; Edinburgh; And New York. MDCCCLXII.* 8vo, xxx+[2]+523pp., unsigned engraved frontispiece portrait plate with protective tissue guard, engraved and printed title pages with vignette illustration after T. G. Flowers on engraved title, six unsigned steel-engraved illustrations printed on thick paper, life of Milton, half-title for *PL*, *PR*, *SA*, and *C*, contemporary decorated blue cloth (a little worn, pages a bit brittle, with one page repaired some time ago with tape which has now darkened, some slight foxing, spine ends chipped), front cover and spine elaborately decorated in gilt incorporating title, a small figure of a dove, two crosses, one upside down and one right side up, each with a snake entwined around it, back cover similarly decorated in blind, spine elaborately decorated in gilt with gilt lettering and with a small crown above the lettering and a large tree with snake entwined around it beneath the lettering, a.e.g. A good copy in an attractive (albeit somewhat worn) Victorian binding. The illustrations here by T. G. Flowers are identical to those in the 1855 edition by T. Nelson and Sons also listed here in detail. See the possible first and possible second editions published by Nelson in 1850 and by Nelson and Sons in 1852 (see copy of each listed here), with unsigned illustrations different from those here. See the possible first edition thus by Nelson in 1850 and other editions cited there. Uncommon. Not in Kohler.

2047. THE POETICAL WORKS OF JOHN MILTON. Edited By Sir Egerton Brydges, Bart. [Quotation from Thomson] Illustrated With Engravings From Drawings By J. M. W. Turner, R.A. A New Edition. *London: William Tegg. MDCCCLXII.* Fifth Brydges/Turner edition. Thick 8vo, cvi+767pp., half-title, frontispiece portrait engraved by W. C. Edwards after Vertue, "To William Wordsworth And Robert Southey" on verso of title page, "Advertisement To The Original Edition," with the original date of 1835, life of Milton followed by appendix, seven illustration plates after Turner, protective tissue guards, notes to the poems at the bottom of each page, double black border around text, contemporary full polished red morocco, presentation binding, decorative blind border trim within gilt rules on covers with bright gilt seal of Christ's College at the center of the covers, spine elaborately gilt-decorated within the panels, raised bands with decorative gilt trim, green morocco label with decorative gilt trim and gilt lettering, marbled endpapers and edges. A lovely copy in a variant contemporary morocco binding, a well-preserved Prize Binding of the period from Christ's College—Milton's College two centuries earlier. The illustrations by Turner first appeared in Brydges's 1835 six-volume edition of Milton's *PW* (see set also listed here). See 1837 first illustrated edition by Tegg (with vignette illustration on title page) listed here with further editions by Tegg cited there. Williamson 135; Kohler 347, reporting "Not in the British Library. Not in the Bodleian Library. Not in Cambridge University Library."

2048. Variant of Preceding, original brown grained cloth (front joint cracked), central gilt urn on front cover, gilt lettering ruled in gilt on spine with decorative gilt device beneath, edges untrimmed. A good, stout, tall copy in a variant original binding, bound by Westleys of London with their ticket. Kohler 347.

2049. THE POETICAL WORKS OF JOHN MILTON. Edited By Sir Egerton Brydges, Bart. [Quotation from Thomson] Illustrated With Engravings From Drawings By J. M. W. Turner, R.A. A New Edition. *London: William Tegg. n.d. [ca. 1862 or ca. 1876].* Variant edition. Thick 8vo, cvi+767pp., frontispiece portrait engraved by W. C. Edwards after Vertue, "To William Wordsworth And Robert Southey This Volume Is Appropriately Dedicated" on verso of title page, "Advertisement To The Original Edition," with the original date of 1835, life of Milton followed by appendix, seven illustration plates after Turner, double black border around text, contemporary full coarse-grained black morocco (a bit rubbed along the joints), spine lettered in gilt, inner and outer dentelles gilt, marbled endpapers, a.e.g., notes to the poems at the bottom of each page. A very nice copy with presentation inscription from Sir John Fox tipped in on front pastedown. While similar to the dated 1862 edition by Tegg preceding, unlike that edition, this edition is undated and may perhaps be a later reprint as indicated by Kohler 383, which dates its copy "[1876]," quoting the title page as here, but without indicating "Quotation From Thomson," citing "767 pp. 1/2 title. Frontispiece portrait engraved by Edwards after Vertue. Seven plates after Turner," referencing Williamson 135, and reporting "Not in Cambridge University Library."

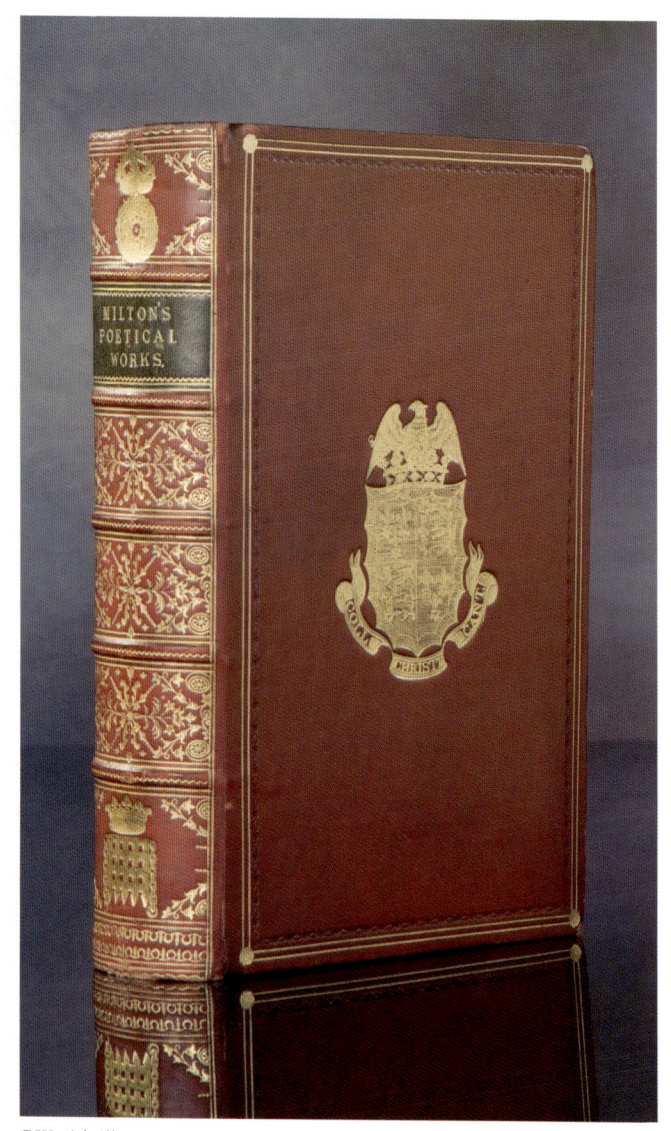

PW with illustrations by Turner. A New Edition. London: William Tegg, 1862. Contemporary full polished red morocco with bright gilt seal of Christ's College at the center of the covers. See #2047.

2050. Variant of Preceding, contemporary black pebble morocco blind stamped (a bit rubbed along joints), spine lettered in gilt, raised bands, broad inner dentelles elaborately tooled in gilt, marbled endpapers, a.e.g. A very nice

Gauffered edges on three sets of Milton's PW. (bottom) Special 1843 Tilt edition with illustrations by Harvey (first appearance) printed on India paper, bound in contemporary full blue morocco. (middle) 1854 edition by Routledge with illustrations by Harvey, contemporary full crushed brown morocco. (top) ca. 1862 edition by Charles Daly, contemporary full maroon morocco over thick boards. See #1901, 1982, and 2052.

copy in a variant contemporary morocco binding with early signature tipped in on front pastedown. Kohler 383.

2051. THE POETICAL WORKS OF JOHN MILTON. A New Edition, carefully Revised, From The Text Of Thomas Newton, D.D. To Which Is Prefixed A Biographical Notice. With Illustrations By William Harvey. New Edition. *London: Routledge, Warne, And Routledge, Farringdon Street. New York: 56, Walker Street. 1862.* 8vo, xlvi+[2]+570pp., frontispiece portrait plate of *Milton Dictating to His Daughters*, engraved by Dalziel, black rule on title page, original preface by Theodore Alois Buckley (dated 1853), "The Life Of Milton, Abridged From Bishop Newton," seven illustration plates engraved by Dalziel after William Harvey, notes at bottom of page, contemporary full brown pebble leather (bit rubbed along front joint), covers richly tooled in gilt borders with diamond-shaped decorative piece in gilt at the center, spine decorated in gilt within the panels with gilt lettering, inner and outer dentelles finely tooled in gilt, a.e.g. A lovely copy with the appearance for the first time of "To Which Is Prefixed A Biographical Notice" on the title page along with thirty-eight additional pages of biography as preliminary material and the inclusion of an additional illustration plate as the seventh plate—all repeated only in the 1867 possible tenth edition thus also listed here. The first edition thus by George Routledge and Co. was published in 1853 (also listed here with further editions by Routledge cited). Uncommon. Not in Kohler.

2052. [POETICAL WORKS] JOHN MILTON'S POETICAL WORKS: A Memoir, And Essay On His Poetical Genius, By Dr. Channing: Together With, Addison's Critique on the *Paradise Lost. London: Charles Daly, Greville Street, Hatton Garden. n.d. [ca. 1862].* 12mo in 6s, liv+449+[1]pp., unsigned engraved frontispiece portrait plate of a young Milton with protective tissue guard, engraved and printed title pages, both undated, with unsigned steel-engraved vignette illustration for *L* on engraved title page and sixteen additional unsigned steel-engraved illustrations (the plates properly placed consistent with page citation given on each plate), each with protective tissue guard, contemporary full maroon morocco over thick boards (a bit rubbed at joints), covers and spine elaborately tooled in blind, spine lettered in gilt, raised bands with small decorative pieces in blind in the panels, marbled endpapers, fine gauffered gilt edges, bookplate. A lovely, tall copy in an attractive binding of the period with fine impressions of the plates. "Lucidas" is misspelled in the header here, as it is in the second undated ca. 1850 edition, and "li" is missing from p. liv and "6" from p. 61. See first undated ca. 1850 edition by Charles Daly also listed here for discussion of related details and further editions by Daly cited there. Uncommon. Not in Kohler.

2053. THE POETICAL WORKS OF JOHN MILTON. With Life, Critical Dissertation, and Explanatory Notes, By The Rev. George Gilfillan. The Text Edited By Charles Cowden Clarke. In Two Volumes. *Edinburgh: James Nichol. London: James Nisbet And Co. Dublin: W. Robertson. Liverpool: G. Philip & Son. M.DCCC.LXII.* 2 volumes. 8vo, xxviii+333pp.,+xxxvi+328pp., half-title each volume ("Nichol's Library Edition Of The British Poets. In Forty-Two Vols. [Vols. XIV and XV: Milton's Poetical Works]," life of Milton, volume 1, "Critical Estimate Of The Genius And Poetical Works Of John Milton," volume 2, half-title for some of the poems, original maroon pebble cloth decorated in blind (some repair to spines), spines lettered in gilt, edges untrimmed. A good copy of an uncommon edition, fresh and clean within. The first edition edited by Gilfillan was published in 1853 (also listed here with further editions by Gilfillan cited). Scarce. Kohler 348, reporting "Not in the British Library. Not in the Bodleian Library. Not in Cambridge University Library."

2054. THE POETICAL WORKS OF JOHN MILTON Printed From The Original Editions With A Life Of The Author By A. Chalmers M.A. F.S.A. *London[:] Bickers And Son[,] 1 Leicester Square W. n.d. [ca. 1862].* 8vo, xxxi+687pp., half-title with decorative headpiece, frontispiece portrait engraved by "W. Humphreys, from a Print by Faithorne," title page in red and black with central emblem of the Chiswick Press, "Advertisement To The [Pickering] Edition Of 1851," life of Milton, decorative head- and tailpieces, decorated initial letters, half-title for some of the poems, handsomely "Printed By Whittingham And Wilkins, Tooks Court, Chancery Lane, Chiswick Press" with inverted triangular piece on page after *P* and again on last page of the volume, contemporary full blue morocco (joints and edges a little worn), elaborately decorated gilt border trim on covers, elaborately gilt-decorated spine in the panels with gilt lettering, raised bands (rubbed), inner and outer dentelles finely tooled in gilt (rubbed), marbled endpapers a.e.g. A nice copy, handsomely printed in a splendid contemporary morocco binding with early (1875) and later (1922) dated inscriptions on front blank. Similar to the 1851 Pickering edition, and as with that edition, volume 1 contains *SA* and the *MP*, along with the preliminary material, while volume 2 contains *PL* and *PR*. See Williamson 84; Not in Kohler, but see Kohler 349, which lists a very similar edition, with variations on title page: "Printed From The Original Editions" lacking; "M.A. F.S.A." missing after "Chalmers"; "W." missing after "1 Leicester Square"; with no reference to title page being in red and black; Kohler also indicates "699 pp."

2055. [POETICAL WORKS] MILTON'S POETISKA VERK. Det forlorade Paradiset ach Det Atervunna Paradiset. Ofversatta af Victor Emanuel Oman. *Upsala[:] Esaias Edquist. (1862).* Tall 8vo, xxvi+[2]+450pp., half-title, "Forord," "John Miltons Lefverne," half-title for *PL*, half-title for each book of *PL*, half-title for *PR*, notes at bottom of page, original purple cloth (top of front cover and spine faded), spine lettered in gilt, purple endpapers. A nice copy. While entitled Milton's *Poetiska Verk*, the edition consists of *PL* and *PR* only, translated into old Swedish by Victor Emanuel Oman. The language is apparently "old Swedish," with the spelling and typography also in old Swedish, and a Swede today might have real trouble reading it through. Scarce. Not in Kohler.

2056. THE POETICAL WORKS OF JOHN MILTON. A New Edition, carefully Revised, From The Text Of Thomas Newton, D.D. With Illustrations By William Harvey. New Edition. *London: Routledge, Warne, And Routledge, Farringdon Street. New York: 56, Walker Street. 1863.* 8vo, viii+570pp., frontispiece portrait plate of *Milton Dictating to His Daughters*, engraved by the Dalziel brothers, black rule on title page, original preface by Theodore Alois Buckley (dated 1853), seven illustration plates engraved by Dalziel after William Harvey, each with protective tissue guard, notes at bottom of page, original green cloth, elaborately blind-stamped covers and spine with large central gilt device incorporating Milton's name on front cover, elaborately gilt-decorated spine with gilt lettering, a.e.g. A fine copy in original cloth binding, fresh and clean within, with contemporary dated inscription on fly-leaf ("Nov 63"). The first edition thus by George Routledge and Co. was published in 1853 (also listed here with further editions by Routledge cited). Not in Kohler.

2057. Variant of Preceding, original reddish-brown morocco (spine rubbed and faded), elaborately embossed covers with a bright gilt band at center of front cover incorporating Milton's name, spine lettered in gilt, raised bands with decorative pieces in blind within the panels, marbled endpapers, a.e.g. A good copy in a variant binding, a rather lovely Victorian full morocco binding, fresh and clean within. Not in Kohler.

2058. Variant of Preceding, original full brown calf, covers richly decorated in gilt with elaborate gilt border trim and large central gilt device, spine lettered in gilt with decorative gilt trim at top and bottom and gilt devices within the panels, raised bands with decorative gilt trim within gilt rules, inner and outer dentelles finely tooled in gilt, a.e.g. A lovely copy in a splendid variant binding, well-preserved and fresh and clean within, with contemporary prize inscriptions on fly-leaf and on front pastedown. Not in Kohler.

2059. THE POETICAL WORKS OF JOHN MILTON. With Life. [Quotation from Thomson.] Complete Edition. *London: T. Nelson And Sons, Paternoster Row; Edinburgh; And New York. MDCCCLXIII (1863).* 8vo, xxx+[2]+523pp., unsigned steel-engraved frontispiece illustration of Satan, entitled "Paradise Lost," for Book I of *PL*, protective tissue guard, engraved and printed title pages with elaborately decorated initial letters and small medallion illustration depicting the judgment of Adam and Eve (unsigned) on engraved title, elaborate decorative trim at top of printed title page incorporating the small figure of an angel in the center, elaborate decorative headpiece on the "Contents" page and at the head of "Life Of Milton," six additional steel-engraved illustrations (all but one unsigned), each illustration within a decorative frame, each with protective tissue guard, elaborate headpiece at the beginning of each book of *PR*, sometimes illustrating a scene (I, depicting cross at center; II, depicting floral arrangement; III, depicting dove at center; IV, depicting crown at center), elaborately decorated half-titles for *PL, PR, SA,* and *C,* elaborate decorative headpieces for *L'A, IlP, Ar, L, P, S, Trans,* and *Psm,* elaborately decorated tailpieces throughout, contemporary full dark green morocco (a bit rubbed along extremities and raised bands, slight embrowning), elaborately embossed covers with Milton's name in gilt at the center of each cover, spine lettered in gilt, raised bands with decorative pieces in blind within the panels, brown endpapers, a.e.g., blue silk ribbon marker. An attractive copy of a scarce Milton edition, in a fine Victorian binding. In addition to the unsigned steel-engraved frontispiece illustration of Satan, within a decorative frame, entitled "Paradise Lost," for Book I of *PL* the six additional steel-engraved illustrations, each within a decorative frame, include: an illustration of Adam and Eve in morning prayer (unsigned) entitled "Paradise Lost," for Book V of *PL,* the judgment of Adam and Eve (unsigned), entitled "Paradise Lost," for Book X of *PL,* the expulsion of Adam and Eve (after Paterson), entitled "Paradise Lost," for Book XII of *PL,* an illustration of Christ (unsigned), entitled "Paradise Regained," for Book I of *PR,* an illustration of "Lycidas" (so-entitled, unsigned), and an illustration of "On The Late Massacre In Piemont" (so-entitled, unsigned). See the possible first and possible second editions published by Nelson in 1850 and by Nelson and Sons in 1852 (see copy of each listed here), with unsigned illustrations different from those here; see the possible third edition by Nelson and Sons in 1853 (also listed here), with illustrations unsigned (possibly by T. G. Flowers). See other editions by Nelson and Sons in the collection cited with the possible first edition thus by Nelson in 1850 (listed here). Not in Kohler.

2060. Variant of Preceding, contemporary full brown morocco (a little worn along extremities and raised bands), elaborately embossed covers with Milton's name in gilt at the center of each cover, spine lettered in gilt, raised bands with decorative pieces in blind within the panels, brown endpapers, a.e.g. A good copy in a variant contemporary morocco binding, fresh and clean within, with a contemporary presentation inscription on front blank. Not in Kohler.

2061. THE POETICAL WORKS OF JOHN MILTON Printed From The Original Editions With A Life Of The Author By The Rev. John Mitford[.] *London[:] Bickers And Bush[.] 1863.* 2 volumes. Second edition thus. 8vo, ccii+270pp.,+ix+[1]+417pp., half-title each volume, frontispiece portrait "Engraved by W. Humphreys, from a Print by Faithorne," volume 1, separate title page each volume, each in red and black, each with emblem of the Pickering Press, "Advertisement To The [Pickering] Edition Of 1851," folding genealogical table (as a multiple foldout), life of Milton, and folding (sideways) facsimile of "the Agreement between Milton and Mr. Symons" before appendix, with sketch of "The House at Chalfont St. Giles" bound before addenda, volume 1, decorative head- and tailpieces, decorated initial letters, half-title for some of the poems, handsomely printed by "C. Whittingham, Chiswick" with typographical figure of the press on last page of each volume, contemporary full red morocco (title page, volume 1, bears offprint of frontispiece), covers richly gilt-decorated with thick gilt border trim, spines lettered in gilt and richly gilt-decorated in the panels, raised bands, inner and outer dentelles finely tooled in gilt, a.e.g. A very attractive set, handsomely printed on good paper by Whittingham and Wilkins at the Chiswick Press; the first two volumes of an eight-volume edition of Milton's *Works,* published first by Pickering in 1851 and again by Bickers and Bush in 1863—both sets listed here. It is interesting to note that volume 1 contains *SA* and the *MP,* along with the preliminary material, while volume 2 contains *PL* and *PR.* Kohler 350, listing the eight-volume set of Milton's *Works* by Bickers and Bush, 1863.

2062. THE POETICAL WORKS OF JOHN MILTON. A New Edition. With Notes, And A Life Of The Author, By John Mitford. Vol. I / Vol. II. *Philadelphia: Willis P. Hazard, 724 Chesnut [sic] Street. 1863.* 2 volumes.

First edition thus? 8vo in 4s, cxxix+[3]+371pp.,+ii+478pp., title page each volume bearing "Riverside, Cambridge: Printed By H. O. Houghton And Company" on verso, half-title before *PL*, volume 1, half-title for *PL*, volume 2, with Books XI and XII following, half-title for *SA* and *C*, volume 2, notes at bottom of page, contemporary three-quarter green pebble morocco (joints and extremities a little worn), marbled paper over boards (a bit rubbed), spines lettered in gilt, raised bands, marbled endpapers and edges. A nice set. A possible second edition by Hazard was published in 1865 (see set listed here). Scarce. Not in Kohler.

2063. THE POETICAL WORKS OF JOHN MILTON. A New Edition, carefully Revised, From The Text Of Thomas Newton, D.D. To Which Is Prefixed A Biographical Notice. With Illustrations By William Harvey. New Edition. *London: Routledge, Warne, And Routledge, Farringdon Street. New York: 56, Walker Street. 1864.* 8vo, xlvi+[2]+570pp., frontispiece portrait plate of *Milton Dictating to His Daughters*, engraved by Dalziel, black rule on title page, "London: Savill And Edwards. Printers, Chandos Street" on verso of title page, original preface by Theodore Alois Buckley dated 1853, seven illustration plates engraved by Dalziel after William Harvey, each with protective tissue guard, half-title for *PL*, notes at bottom of page, contemporary crushed green morocco (worn along joints and at corners), covers ruled in gilt, spine lettered in gilt within gilt rules and decorative gilt trim, raised bands with decorative gilt trim, gilt rules within the panels, decorative gilt trim at top and bottom, inner and outer dentelles tooled in gilt, a.e.g. A nice copy in an attractive Victorian morocco binding with contemporary inscription on fly-leaf. The first edition thus by George Routledge and Co. was published in 1853 (also listed here with further editions by Routledge cited). Not in Kohler (although Kohler 353 records an 1864 Routledge edition with a different publisher's imprint than the one here: "London: Routledge, Warne, and Routledge, Broadway, Ludgate Hill; New York: 129, Grand Street. 1864," with "570 pp. Frontispiece and seven plates after Dalziel's engravings after Harvey").

2064. THE POETICAL WORKS OF JOHN MILTON. With Illustrations by E. H. Corbould and John Gilbert. [Quotation from Thomson.] *London: T. Nelson And Sons, Paternoster Row; Edinburgh; and New York. 1864.* First edition thus with illustrations by Corbould & Gilbert? 8vo, vi+528pp., frontispiece with an early photograph of Milton's tomb in St. Giles, Cripplegate, tipped in, engraved and printed title pages with an early photograph of Ludlow Castle mounted as vignette on undated engraved title, elaborate headpiece with angelic figure in the center at top of title page, decorative headpiece on the "Contents" page and at the head of "Life Of Milton," eight illustration plates after E. H. Corbould and John Gilbert, each with protective tissue guard, elaborate headpiece at the beginning of each book of *PL*, in some instances providing an illustration for the book, elaborate decorative headpieces for each book of *PR*, in some instances providing an illustration for the book, elaborate decorative headpieces for *SA, C, L'A, IlP, Ar, L P, S, Trans*, and *Psm*s, decorative half-titles for *PL, PR, SA*, and *C*, decorative tailpieces throughout, contemporary full brown calf (rubbed at joints, spine a bit faded), elaborately embossed covers with Milton's name in gilt at the center of each cover, spine lettered in gilt, raised bands with decorative pieces in blind within the panels, brown endpapers, a.e.g. The eight illustration plates after E. H. Corbould and John Gilbert include: *Satan on the Burning Lake* (Book I); *Michael and Gabriel Battling with Satan and His Angels* (Book VI); *The Temptation* (Book IX); *Adam and Eve [The Judgment]* (Book X); *The Expulsion* (Book XII); a depiction of Christ entitled "Paradise Regained" (Book I); an illustration for "Lycidas"; and one for "On The Late Massacre In Piemont." The elaborate headpiece at the beginning of each book of *PL* in some instances provide an illustration for the book: I, depicting the lamentation of Adam and Eve; II and X, same headpiece as on title page; III, depicting cross at center; IV, V, VIII, and XI each depicting floral arrangement; VI, depicting crown at center; VII, depicting dove at center; IX, Eve tempting Adam; XII, depicting the expulsion; at the beginning of each book of *PR*: I and III, depicting cross at center; II, depicting floral arrangement; III, depicting dove at center. Attractive copy in a fine Victorian binding. Stevens 188 ("Photographs of Milton's tomb in St. Giles and of Ludlow Castle; ten zinc etchings"); Kohler 352 (noting "nine plates" in its copy of this edition).

See 1866 edition by T. Nelson and Sons (possible second edition thus) listed with the same early photographs tipped in, with elaborately decorated half-title for some of the poems (different from those here and those in the 1867, 1868, and 1869 editions by T. Nelson and Sons listed later), with elaborately decorated tailpieces (different from those here and in the 1867, 1868, and 1869 editions by T. Nelson and Sons listed later), with 523 pp. instead of 528 pp. as here and in all other later editions by T. Nelson and Sons, and with the same eight illustration plates after E. H. Corbould and John Gilbert as here and as in the 1867, 1868, and 1869 editions by T. Nelson and Sons listed later, although unsigned and without identification on the title page as here and in each of the later editions. See also 1867 edition by T. Nelson and Sons (possible third edition thus) listed later with the same early photographs tipped in, with the same decorative half-titles as here for some of the poems, with the same number of pages as in the edition here, 528pp., and with illustration plates after E. H. Corbould and John Gilbert, so-identified, as here, on the title page—but with ten illustration plates instead of eight, as here and as in the 1866 and 1869 editions by T. Nelson and Sons; three of the illustration plates in the 1864 and 1866 Nelson editions do not appear in the 1867 Nelson edition: *Satan on the Burning Lake* (a different illustration plate from that similarly named as the second plate in the 1864 and 1866 Nelson editions), *Adam and Eve [The Judgment]*, and *Paradise Regained*, while five of the illustration plates in the 1867 Nelson edition do not appear in the 1864 and 1866 Nelson editions: *Milton Acts as Secretary to Oliver Cromwell*, *Satan on the Burning Lake* (a different illustration plate from that similarly named in the 1864 and 1866 Nelson editions), *Satan on His Throne*, *Adam and Eve—The Morning Hymn*, and *Raphael Discoursing with Adam and Eve*. The 1867 copy also has a fore-edge painting. See also 1868 edition by T. Nelson and Sons (possible fourth edition thus) listed without the early photographs tipped in, but with the same decorative half-titles as here for some of the poems, with the same number of pages in the edition as here, 528pp., and with the same eight illustration plates after E. H. Corbould and John Gilbert, so-identified, as here, on the title page. See, too, 1869 edition by T. Nelson and Sons (possible fifth edition thus) listed without the early photographs tipped in, but with the same decorative half-titles as here for some of the poems, with the same number of pages in the edition as here (528 pp.) and with the same eight illustration plates after E. H. Corbould and John Gilbert, so-identified, as here, on the title page. The 1869 copy also has a fore-edge painting. See the possible first and possible second editions published by Nelson in 1850 and by Nelson and Sons in 1852 (see copy of each listed here), with unsigned illustrations different from those here; see the possible third edition by Nelson and Sons in 1853 (see copy listed here), with illustrations unsigned (possibly by T. G. Flowers). See other editions by Nelson and Sons in the collection cited with the possible first edition thus by Nelson in 1850 (copy listed here).

2065. Variant of Preceding, original green sand cloth, (slightly rubbed lower left front corner and top back joint), front cover ruled in double gilt rules with gilt harps in each corner and Milton's name in embossed green in front of a gilt harp within a gilt medallion surrounded by decorative gilt trim at the center of front cover, back cover repeats front cover in blind, spine lettered in embossed green within bright gilt bands surrounded by decorative gilt trim, harp in blind at the center, brown endpapers, a.e.g. Very nice, virtually mint within, in an attractive variant publisher's cloth binding, with contemporary presentation inscription on front blank, bookplate on front pastedown. Kohler 352.

2066. THE POETICAL WORKS OF JOHN MILTON. Edited By Sir Egerton Brydges, Bart. [Quotation from Thomson] Illustrated With Engravings, Designed By John Martin And J. W. M. Turner, R A [One Also By Westall And One By Romney]. *Boston: Crosby And Nichols. 1864.* 8vo in 4s, 858pp., frontispiece portrait "Engraved by O. Pelton" of a young, long-haired Milton "From a Miniature of the same size by Faithorne. Anno 1667, in the possession of William Falconer Esq.," protective tissue guard, engraved and printed title pages with vignette illustration for *C* after Turner on engraved title with publication imprint: "Boston. Phillips, Sampson & Company," original 1835 dedication page "To William Wordsworth And Robert Southey" reprinted after title page followed by a reprinting of the "Advertisement To The Original Edition" dated 1835, "Life Of Milton," six engraved illustration plates, each with protective tissue guard: two engraved illustration plates after Martin for *PL* (Books VII and X), two engraved illustration plates after Turner—one for *PR* (*The Temptation on the Mountain*, Book III) and one for *C* (as vignette on engraved title page), one engraved illustration plate after Westall for *PL* (*Satan*, Book IV), and one engraved illustration plate after Romney (*Milton Dictating to His Daughters*), engraved by D. L. Glover, for *On His Blindness* (bound with the poem), introductory remarks from the James Boyd edition for each book of *PL*, notes at bottom of page, double black border rule around text, original calf boards (worn, spine missing, middle pages embrowned, plates foxed), marbled endpapers and edges. See 1854 edition of Milton's *PW* by Phillips, Sampson, and Company (possible first edition thus) listed and other editions cited there. Uncommon. Not in Kohler.

2067. THE POETICAL WORKS OF JOHN MILTON. To Which Is Prefixed A Biography Of The Author, By His Nephew, Edward Philips. *New York: D. Appleton & Company, 443 & 445 Broadway. M DCCC LXIV (1864).* Third edition thus? 12mo in 6s, 574pp., engraved frontispiece portrait plate of Milton engraved by "Illman & Pilbrow" after Faithorne, introduction, life by Edward Philips, five unsigned illustration plates (fine impressions), each with protective tissue guard, half-title for some of the poems, contents listed at the end, original brown cloth (a bit rubbed, spine faded, some light waterstaining to the plates), covers richly embossed in blind relief with Milton's name in blind at the center, spine decorated and lettered in gilt, green silk ribbon marker. A nice copy with small early bookplate on front pastedown. Three of the six illustrations, though unsigned, are after Turner: two for *PL*, Books VI and XII, and for *L*; the other three are Turneresque in style: for *PL*, Book II, for *C*, and for *IlP*. See 1859 edition listed here with further editions by Appleton cited. Uncommon. Not in Kohler.

2068. THE POETICAL WORKS OF JOHN MILTON. With A Life Of The Poet By David Masson. In Three Volumes. *Boston: Little, Brown And Company. M.DCCC. LXIV (1864).* 3 volumes. Fifth edition thus by Little, Brown and Company; first thus with life by Masson. Small 8vo, lxxvii+[4]+[1]+153pp.,+372pp.,+v+334pp., half-title ("The Poems Of Milton") each volume, engraved frontispiece portrait plate of Milton (unsigned, but after H. Robinson as in 1832 Pickering edition in which the portrait first appeared and where it is identified and dated "London, William Pickering, 1831"), volume 1, protective tissue guard, "Riverside, Cambridge: Stereotyped And Printed By Henry O. Houghton" printed on verso of title page, separate title page each volume, advertisement (first thus) on verso of contents, life of Milton by Masson, volume 1, half-title for some of the poems, notes at bottom of page, contemporary polished calf (rubbed at joints), elaborately gilt-decorated spines in the panels, maroon title labels with gilt rules, green morocco numbering labels with gilt rules, raised bands with decorative gilt trim, inner dentelles decorated in blind, outer dentelles tooled in gilt. Despite some wear, a fine set in a very nice Prize Binding of the period with central gilt seal within decorative gilt laurel leaves on covers and with contemporary prize citation (dated 1866) tipped in on front pastedown. According to the "Advertisement" on verso of contents: "The Life of Milton prefixed to this edition is from the pen of his latest biographer, Prof. David Masson, of London. The notes are those of the Rev. John Mitford. Before going to a new impression, occasion has been taken to correct a considerable number of errors, principally in the citations from the Greek, Latin, and Italian poets." The first Aldine and second Pickering edition was published in 1832 (see set listed, with a citing there of all Aldine editions of Milton, a copy of each of which is in the collection). The first edition thus by Little, Brown and Company with life by Mitford was published in 1853 (also listed here with further editions by Little, Brown, and Company cited). Scarce. Not in Kohler.

2069. THE POETICAL WORKS OF JOHN MILTON. A New Edition. With Notes, And A Life Of The Author, By John Mitford. Vol. I / Vol. II. *Philadelphia: Willis P. Hazard, 31 South Sixth Street. 1864.* 2 volumes. Second edition thus? 8vo in 4s, cxxix+[3]+371pp.,+ii+478pp., title page each volume, bearing "Cambridge: Printed By H. G. Houghton" on verso of each title page, "Advertisement" (by Mitford, dated 1831) and "Life of Milton," with "Addenda" and "Appendix," half-title before *PL*, volume 1, half-title for *PL*, volume 2, with Books XI and XII following, half-title for *SA* and *C*, volume 2, notes at bottom of page, finely printed on thick paper, contemporary three-quarter black morocco (a bit rubbed at joints), marbled dark green paper over boards, spines lettered in gilt ("Milton's Works" at the top, "Poems" and volume number in the middle) with decorative gilt trim within the panels, raised bands with gilt trim (faded), marbled endpapers, t.e.g. A very fine set. Large paper copy. The possible first edition by Hazard was published in 1863 (see set listed here). Uniformly bound with: *The Prose Works Of John Milton* (Philadelphia: Caxton Press Of C. Sherman, Son & Co. 1864. 2 volumes.), also listed here, together forming a handsome four-volume edition of Milton's *Works*. Scarce. Not in Kohler.

2070. THE POETICAL WORKS OF JOHN MILTON: With A Life Of The Author; Preliminary Dissertations On Each Poem; Notes Critical And Explanatory; An Index To The Subjects Of Paradise Lost; And a Verbal Index to all the Poems, By Charles Dexter Cleveland, Author Of The Compendiums Of English, American And Classical Literature. "It will not be too much to say, that . . . Milton's are the most worthy of profound study by all minds which would know the creativeness, the splendour, the learning, the eloquence, the wisdom, to which the human intellect can reach."—*Sir Egerton Brydges*. "That fervid Genius, which has cast a sort of shade upon all the other works of man."—*Lord Erskine. A. S. Barnes And Company, New York And Chicago. (1864).* First edition thus. 12mo in 6s, 688pp., advertisements for several text books on verso of title page with copyright date of 1864 at bottom, half-titles for several of the poems, original black cloth with black leather spine (a bit worn, joints cracked, spine ends slightly chipped), front cover ruled in blind with "Cleveland's Series" stamped in blind at center, spine lettered in gilt and decorated in embossed blind, speckled red edges. A decent copy of an uncommon edition with early signature (dated 1891) on fly-leaf. Scarce. Stevens 189 (mistakenly dating the edition "ca. 1865"; Not in Kohler.

2071. THE POETICAL WORKS OF JOHN MILTON. A New Edition, carefully Revised, From The Text Of Thomas Newton, D.D. With Illustrations By William Harvey. New Edition. *London: Routledge, Warne, And Routledge, Broadway, Ludgate Hill. New York: 129, Grand Street. 1865.* Small 8vo, viii+570pp. (illustration plates unpaginated), frontispiece portrait plate of *Milton Dictating to His Daughters*, engraved by Dalziel, black rule on title page, original preface by Theodore Alois Buckley dated 1853, seven illustration plates engraved by Dalziel after William Harvey, each with protective tissue guard, notes at bottom of the page, original decorated red cloth, front cover decorated with gilt medallions and devices of various sizes within decorative gilt border trim incorporating Milton's name in embossed red within gilt device at the center, spine similarly gilt-decorated with lettering in embossed red, a.e.g. A fine copy in lovely publisher's binding with the signature of Horace Radclyffe Dugmore (dated 1865) on fly-leaf. The first edition thus by George Routledge and Co. was published in 1853 (also listed here with further editions by Routledge cited). Not in Kohler.

2072. THE POETICAL WORKS OF JOHN MILTON. *Edinburgh: William P. Nimmo. 1865.* First edition thus? 8vo, xxxvii+[3]+454pp., unsigned engraved frontispiece portrait plate of a middle-aged Milton, engraved and printed title pages with vignette illustration (of the poet being inspired by heavenly choirs) after F. Borders on engraved title plate ("Edinburgh: William P. Nimmo," n.d. at the bottom), and with vignette illustration (of a young boy in a setting in nature with a cane laying beside him) signed with the initials "WS" on printed title, life of Milton by J. M. Ross, twelve illustration plates, most after F. Borders, some unsigned: four for *PL* (Books I, III, VI, XI), two for *PR* (Book I), one for *SA*, two for *C*, two for *L'A*, one for *IlP*, half-title for *PL, PR, SA, C, Ar, MP*, and *Poemata*, black border around text, contemporary polished maroon half calf, red grain cloth (cloth a little worn, some pages darkened, lacking last page, frontispiece and engraved title reinforced at inner edges), spine lettered in gilt, thick raised bands with finely tooled gilt trim, decorative pieces in blind within the panels, marbled endpapers, a.e.g. A good, solid copy with contemporary presentation inscription (dated 1867) on front blank. Other illustrated editions by Nimmo were published in 1869 (with half-title in color), 1872 (one with general half-title in variant colors and style, another with half-title in color), 1874 (with half-title in color), 1876, 1877 (with half-title in color), 1878, 1879 (with variant publisher's imprint: "Edinburgh[:] William P. Nimmo & Co."), 1881, 1883, 1887 (with variant publisher's imprint: "Edinburgh: W. P. Nimmo, Hay, & Mitchell"), ca. 1890, 1891 (with variant publisher's imprint: "Edinburgh: William P. Nimmo, Hay, & Mitchell")—all listed here. Only this edition by Nimmo has twelve illustrations, the others have eleven (with only one illustration for *L'A*) beyond the preliminary engraved material (portrait and engraved title page). Nonillustrated editions were also published by Nimmo: in two volumes in 1868, again in two volumes in 1869, in 1898, ca. 1900, and in 1901—all listed here. See also the undated ca. 1882 edition by John Walker & Company (copy listed here) published in London with the same unsigned frontispiece portrait of a middle-aged Milton, the same vignette illustration on the printed title page (signed with the initials "WS"), a life of Milton by J. M. Ross, and the same eleven illustration plates (most after F. Border, some unsigned) as in this edition by Nimmo. Scarce. Not in Kohler.

2073. THE POETICAL WORKS OF JOHN MILTON. Illustrated By F. Gilbert. *London: John Dicks, 313, Strand; And All Booksellers[.] n.d. [ca. 1865].* First edition thus? 12mo in 6s, 162+[ii]+[2]pp., engraved frontispiece illustration by F. Gilbert (signed with the initials "CF" and entitled "Frontispiece," consisting of three vignettes: a circular portrait of Milton as a young man above several books, a scroll, and a quill and ink bottle; the temptation of Eve; and the angel expelling; all three vignettes incorporating a large apple tree with serpent beneath), "Sketch Of The Life Of John Milton," "Contents" page at the end, printed in double column. Bound with **POETICAL WORKS OF WILLIAM COWPER.** Illustrated By F. Gilbert . . . *London: John Dicks, n.d.* Frontispiece illustration with inset vignette portrait of Cowper, "Contents" page at the end. 2 volumes in one. 8vo, v+162pp.,+ii+ 203+v+[1]pp., printed in double column, original half calf, marbled paper over boards, gilt-decorated spine, black morocco label, raised bands, marbled endpapers and edges, advertisement on last leaf. A very nice copy. See dated 1870 edition listed here with the same engraved frontispiece illustration. Not in Kohler.

2074. Variant of Preceding. THE POETICAL WORKS OF JOHN MILTON. Illustrated By F. Gilbert. *London: John Dicks, 313, Strand; And All Booksellers[.] n.d. [ca. 1865].* First edition thus? 8vo, 162+[ii]+[2]pp., engraved frontispiece illustration by F. Gilbert (signed with the initials "CF" and entitled "Frontispiece," consisting of three vignettes: a circular portrait of Milton as a young man above several books, a scroll, and a quill and ink bottle; the temptation of Eve; and the angel expelling; all three vignettes incorporating a large apple tree with serpent beneath), "Sketch Of The Life Of John Milton," "Contents" page at the end, printed in double column, original green cloth (a bit rubbed, slight foxing throughout), spine lettered in gilt. A good copy with four pages of "Advertisements" for publications by John Dicks bound in at end, in a variant publisher's binding. Not in Kohler.

2075. THE POETICAL WORKS OF JOHN MILTON With Explanatory Notes, Etc. Complete In Two Volumes. *New York[:] Thomas R. Knox & Co. Successors To James Miller[.] 813 Broadway[.] n.d. [ca. 1865].* 2 volumes in one. First edition thus? **[together with]** THE CHOICE PROSE WORKS OF JOHN MILTON[,] *New York[:]*

Thomas R. Knox & Co. Successors To James Miller[.] 813 Broadway[.] n.d. [ca. 1865]. First edition thus? Together, 3 volumes. 12mo in 6s, 408pp.,+387pp.,+viii+486pp., "Trow's Printing And Bookbinding Company, New York" on verso of title page of each volume, original blue cloth (a bit rubbed), spines lettered in gilt within gilt rules and with a small emblem in gilt of a harp within laurel wreath. A three-volume set with *Poetical Works* numbered 1 and 2 in gilt on spines. A nice set with early signature on fly-leaf of each volume. The prose volume is edited with a preface by Fayette Hurd (dated "July 12, 1865") and has elaborate decorative head- and tailpieces and decorated initial letters, with "A List Of Milton's Prose Works. Arranged In Chronological Order" and an "Index" at the end. Uncommon. Not in Kohler (neither the *Poetical Works* nor the *Choice Prose Works*).

2076. THE POETICAL WORKS OF JOHN MILTON: With A Life of the Author; Preliminary Dissertations On Each Poem; Notes Critical And Explanatory; An Index To The Subjects Of Paradise Lost; And A Verbal Index to all the Poems. [Quotation From Charles Dexter Cleveland, Sir Egerton Brydges And Lord Erskine.] *Philadelphia: Frederick Leypoldt. London: Sampson Low, Son & Marston. 1865.* 12mo in 6s, 688pp., half-title, title page in red and black, original half brown calf (somewhat worn), marbled paper over boards, spine originally decorated in gilt (now very faint), gilt-ruled black morocco labels with gilt lettering, raised bands, marbled endpapers and edges. A good copy. The first edition thus was published by Lippincott, Grambo, & Co., Philadelphia, in 1853; the second edition thus in 1854; and a later edition in 1859—all listed here. Scarce. Not in Kohler.

2077. THE POETICAL WORKS OF JOHN MILTON. A New Edition, carefully Revised, From The Text Of Thomas Newton, D.D. With Illustrations By William Harvey. *London: George Routledge And Sons, Broadway, Ludgate Hill. New York: 416, Broome Street. 1866.* 8vo, viii+570pp., frontispiece portrait plate of *Milton Dictating to His Daughters*, engraved by Dalziel, black rule on title page, original preface by Theodore Alois Buckley dated 1853, seven illustration plates engraved by Dalziel after William Harvey, each with protective tissue guard, notes at the bottom of the page, original decorated green cloth (a bit rubbed and shaken) front cover decorated with gilt medallions and devices of various sizes within decorative gilt border trim incorporating Milton's name in embossed green within gilt device at the center, spine similarly gilt-decorated with lettering in embossed gilt, a.e.g. A nice copy in a lovely publisher's binding with early signature in pencil (dated 1889) on fly-leaf. The first edition thus by George Routledge and Co. was published in 1853 (also listed here with further editions by Routledge cited). Uncommon. Kohler 357, reporting "Not in the British Library. Not in the Bodleian Library. Not in Cambridge University Library."

2078. THE POETICAL WORKS OF JOHN MILTON. [Quotation from Thomson.] *London: T. Nelson And Sons, Paternoster Row; Edinburgh; and New York. 1866.* Second edition thus by Nelson? 8vo, xxx+523pp., frontispiece with an early photograph of Milton's tomb in St. Giles, Cripplegate, tipped in, engraved and printed title pages with an early photograph of Ludlow Castle mounted as vignette on undated engraved title, elaborate headpiece with angelic figure in the center at top of title page, decorative headpiece on the "Contents" page and at the head of "Life Of Milton," eight illustration plates after E. H. Corbould and John Gilbert (without identification on the title page that the illustrations are after Corbould and Gilbert): *Satan on the Burning Lake* (Book II); *Michael and Gabriel Battling with Satan and His Angels* (Book VII); *The Temptation* (Book IX); *Adam and Eve [The Judgment]* (Book X); *The Expulsion* (bound here in Book I of *PR*); a depiction of Christ entitled "Paradise Regained" (Book I); an illustration for "Lycidas"; and one for "On The Late Massacre In Piemont," each with protective tissue guard, elaborate headpiece at the beginning of each book of *PL*, in some instances providing an illustration for the book (I, depicting the lamentation of Adam and Eve; II, same headpiece as on title page; III, depicting cross at center; IV, V & VIII, depicting floral arrangement; VI, depicting crown at center; VII, depicting dove at center; IX, Eve tempting Adam; X, same headpiece as on title page; XI, depicting the expulsion; XII, depicting the expulsion), elaborate headpiece at the beginning of each book of *PR*, in some instances providing an illustration for the book (I, depicting cross at center; II, depicting floral arrangement; III, depicting dove at center; IV, depicting crown at center), elaborate decorative headpieces for *SA, C, L'A, IlP, Ar, L, P, S, Trans,* and *Psm,* decorative half-titles for *PL, PR, SA,* and *C,* (each half-title with decorative centerpiece more detailed and elaborate than in the 1864, 1867, and 1869 editions by T. Nelson and Sons), elaborately decorated tailpieces throughout (different from those in 1864 and in 1867 editions by T. Nelson and Sons), contemporary full dark green calf (trifle rubbed at joints and along raised bands), elaborately embossed covers with Milton's name in gilt at the center of each cover, spine lettered in gilt, raised bands with decorative pieces in blind within the panels, brown endpapers, a.e.g. An attractive copy of a scarce Milton edition in a fine Victorian binding with contemporary presentation inscription on verso of frontispiece. See 1864 edition by T. Nelson and Sons (possible first edition thus) listed here with the same early photographs tipped in and with illustrations by E. H. Corbould and John Gilbert, with references to later editions by T. Nelson and Sons with illustrations by Corbould and Gilbert, and also to earlier editions with different illustrations (unsigned and by T. G. Flowers) in editions cited with the possible first edition thus by Nelson in 1850 (also listed here). Uncommon. Not in Kohler.

2079. MILTON'S POETICAL WORKS. With A Life Of The Author. [Quotation from Thomson.] *London: T. Nelson And Sons, Paternoster Row; Edinburgh; And New York. MDCCCLXVI (1866).* 8vo, xxiv+392pp., frontispiece illustration of Satan by T. Armstrong, decorative half-title for *PR*, decorative head- and tailpieces throughout, text ruled in black, contemporary green cloth (a bit rubbed), covers ruled in blind with decorative embossed corner pieces in blind and a central gilt shield with a small crown at the top incorporating the title in embossed green letters, two decorative gilt pieces on the spine, a large one near the top incorporating the title in embossed green letters, a small one near the bottom incorporating "With Life Of The Author" in embossed green letters with decorative gilt trim at the top and bottom. A nice copy with contemporary presentation inscription (dated 1871) on fly-leaf, and a biblical inscription in an early hand in ink on verso. See the possible first edition thus by Nelson in 1850 with further editions by Nelson and Sons in the collection cited. Scarce. Not in Kohler.

2080. THE POETICAL WORKS OF JOHN MILTON. Edited By Sir Egerton Brydges, Bart. [Quotation from Thomson] Illustrated With Engravings, Designed By John Martin And J. W. M. Turner, R.A. [One Also By Westall And One By Romney]. *Boston: Crosby & Ainsworth. New York: Oliver S. Felt. 1866.* First edition thus by Crosby & Ainsworth in Boston, and Felt in New York. 8vo in 4s, 858pp., frontispiece portrait "Engraved by O. Pelton" of a young, long-haired Milton "From a Miniature of the same size by Faithorne. Anno 1667, in the possession of William Falconer Esq.," protective tissue guard, engraved and printed title pages, reprinting of the original 1835 dedication page "To William Wordsworth And Robert Southey," "Advertisement To The Original Edition" dated 1835, "Life Of Milton," six engraved illustration plates, each with protective tissue guard: two engraved illustration plates after Martin for *PL* (Books VII and X), two engraved illustration plates after Turner—one for *PR* (*The Temptation on the Mountain*, Book III) and one for *C* (as vignette on engraved title page), one engraved illustration plate after Westall for *PL* (*Satan*, Book IV), and one engraved illustration plate after Romney (*Milton Dictating to His Daughters*), engraved by D. L. Glover, for *On His Blindness* (bound with the poem), introductory remarks from the James Boyd edition for each book of *PL*, notes at bottom of page, black border around text, original brown calf (worn, covers detached, lacking spine), marbled endpapers and edges, in a protective plastic cover. Although worn, clean inside with nice impressions of the plates. See 1854 edition of Milton's *PW* by Phillips, Sampson, and Company (possible first edition thus) also listed here with further editions cited. Not in Kohler.

2081. THE POETICAL WORKS OF JOHN MILTON. With Life, Critical Dissertation, and Explanatory Notes, By The Rev. George Gilfillan. The Text Edited By Charles Cowden Clarke. Two Vol. In One. *Edinburgh: James Nichol. London: James Nisbet And Co. Dublin: Geo. Herbert. Liverpool: G. Philip & Son. M.DCCC.LXVI (1866).* 2 volumes in one. Possibly the fourth Gilfillan edition; possible second edition thus (with text edited by Charles Cowden Clarke). Thick 8vo, xxviii+333pp.,+xxxvi+328pp., half-title for each volume bound within, frontispiece portrait engraved by J. T. Wedgwood after a drawing by Thurston after a picture by Dobson in Dr. Williams's library, volume 1, life of Milton, volume 1, "Critical Estimate Of The Genius And Poetical Works Of John Milton," volume 2, half-title for some of the poems, contemporary full brown morocco (a bit worn), covers and spine elaborately tooled in blind relief with Milton's name in gilt within central blind device on front cover, spine lettered in gilt, raised bands with small decorative pieces in the panels, a.e.g. A good copy in an attractive binding of the period. The first Gilfillan edition was published in 1853 (also listed here with further editions by Gilfillan cited). Scarce. Williamson 237; Not in Kohler.

2082. THE POETICAL WORKS OF JOHN MILTON. *London: Bell And Daldy[,] Fleet Street[,] 1866.* 3 volumes. First Bell and Daldy edition (dated). Small 8vo, xx+cxxxiv+[3]+[5]+153pp.,+[i]+372pp.,+vii+[1]+334pp., half-titles ("The Aldine Edition Of The British Poets"), frontispiece portrait by H. Robinson, volume 1, central emblem of the press consisting of bell and anchor on title page of each volume, original "Advertisement" for the 1832 Aldine edition by John Mitford with original date of 1831, life of Milton by Mitford followed by addenda and appendix, volume 1, half-title for some of the poems, contemporary black pebble morocco (a bit rubbed along joints, frontispiece a bit foxed), spines lettered in gilt, raised bands (bit rubbed), inner dentelles finely tooled in gilt, marbled endpapers, a.e.g. An attractive set in fine condition, printed at the Chiswick Press, in a handsome contemporary morocco binding. Kohler 356, reporting "Not in Cambridge University Library" and referencing Williamson 76.

A Bell and Daldy reissue (first thus) of the Aldine British Poets, published in an edition of fifty-two volumes. The Aldine British Poets edition of Milton was originally published by Pickering in 1832 (Milton set listed here, the prototype for which was the first Parkes edition of 1826, also printed by Pickering (sets listed here); Aldine editions followed in 1834 (second Aldine edition, set listed here), in 1839 (third Aldine edition, set listed here), in 1845 (fourth Aldine edition, set listed here), in 1851 (fifth Aldine edition, set listed here), and in 1852 (sixth Aldine edition, set listed here). After Pickering's death in 1854 "the rights of the Aldine Poets were acquired by Bell & Daldy, by whom their issue, with many volumes added, has been continued to the present time (1924)" (Keynes, *Pickering*, p. 28). An entirely new edition of Pickering's three-volume Aldine edition of Milton was published in two volumes in 1892 in London by "George Bell & Sons"; this set was reprinted in 1899 and again in 1908–9—all listed here.

2083. THE POETICAL WORKS OF JOHN MILTON. *London[:] Bell And Daldy York Street[,] Covent Garden. n.d. [ca. 1866].* 3 volumes. First Bell and Daldy edition (undated). Small 8vo, xx+cxxxiv+[5]+[1]+153pp.,+[i]+372pp.,+vii+[1]+334pp., half-title ("The Aldine Edition Of The British Poets") each volume, central emblem of the press consisting of bell and anchor on title page of each volume, original "Advertisement" for the 1832 Aldine edition by John Mitford with original date of 1831, life of Milton by Mitford followed by addenda and appendix, volume 1, half-title for some of the poems, original green cloth, covers attractively decorated in black trim incorporating Milton's name within a gilt device on front covers beneath "The Aldine Poets" in black lettering, the whole within a large, decorative black device at the center, Milton's name in gilt within similar gilt device and black trim on spines, edges untrimmed, handsomely printed by the Chiswick Press. Variant edition, with a different street location in publisher's imprint on undated title page and without a frontispiece portrait. A splendid set in a lovely, well-preserved publisher's cloth binding. Uncommon. Kohler 369, dating its copy in "Original green dot and line patterned cloth" "ca. 1872" and reporting "Not in the British Library. Not in the Bodleian Library. Not in Cambridge University Library."

2084. THE POETICAL WORKS OF JOHN MILTON. *London[:] Bell And Daldy[,] Fleet Street[,] 1866.* 3 volumes. First Bell and Daldy edition (Printed for the United States). Small 8vo, xx+cxxxiv+[3]+[1]+153pp.,+[i]+372pp.,+vii+334pp., half-titles ("The Aldinc Edition Of The British Poets"), frontispiece portrait by H. Robinson, volume 1, central emblem of the press consisting of bell and anchor on title page of each volume, original "Advertisement" for the 1832 Aldine edition by John Mitford with original date of 1831, life of Milton by Mitford followed by addenda and appendix, volume 1, half-title for some of the poems, original red cloth (worn, volume 1 spine amateurishly repaired from within with brown tape, other spines chipped, joints cracked, library stamps marked "withdrawn," very occasional marginal notes in a neat hand), original printed paper labels on spines, edges untrimmed, in protective plastic covers with red leather around volume 1 spine for appearance sake. Large paper copy. Scarce set, printed at the Chiswick Press, similar to preceding sets although in a crown octavo format and for sale in the United States: "No. 37 [of] 100 Copies [Printed] For The United States [of] 250 [Total] Copies." On a leaf before half-title, volume 1, printed two-thirds of the way up the page: "250 Copies Printed Before Stereotyping For Subscribers Only," and stamped just below in a circular stamp: "100 Copies For The United States," with "No." printed in the center and "37" handwritten in the blank space. Scarce. Not in Kohler.

2085. THE POETICAL WORKS OF JOHN MILTON. With A Life Of The Poet By David Masson. In Three Volumes. *Boston: Little, Brown And Company. M.DCCC.LXVI.* 3 volumes. Sixth edition thus by Little, Brown and Company? Small 8vo, lxxvii+[3]+[1]+153pp.,+[i]+372pp.,+v+334pp., half-title ("The Poems Of Milton") each volume, engraved frontispiece portrait plate of Milton (unsigned, but after H. Robinson as in 1832 Pickering edition where the portrait is identified and dated "London, William Pickering, 1831," the first appearance such), volume 1, protective tissue guard, "University Press: Welch, Bigelow, & Co., Cambridge" printed on verso of title page, separate title page each volume, advertisement (as in 1864 edition) on verso of contents, life of Milton by Mitford, volume 1, half-title for some of the poems, notes at bottom of page, contemporary crushed full red morocco, gilt rules on covers, spines intricately gilt-decorated within the panels and lettered in gilt, raised bands with decorative gilt trim, inner dentelles finely tooled in gilt, outer dentelles ruled in gilt, a.e.g., bookplate in each volume. A choice set of a mid-nineteenth-century American edition in a lovely contemporary morocco binding. The first edition thus by Little, Brown and Company with life by Mitford was published in 1853 (also listed here with further editions by Little, Brown, and Company cited), a reprint, as here, of

Pickering's Aldine edition, with Mitford's notes and his life of the poet. Scarce. Not in Kohler.

2086. THE POETICAL WORKS OF JOHN MILTON. A New Edition, carefully Revised, From The Text Of Thomas Newton, D.D. To Which Is Prefixed A Biographical Notice. With Illustrations By William Harvey. *London: George Routledge And Sons, Broadway, Ludgate Hill. New York: 416, Broome Street. 1867.* 8vo, xlvi+[2]+570pp., frontispiece portrait plate of *Milton Dictating to His Daughters*, engraved by Dalziel, original preface by Theodore Alois Buckley dated 1853, "The Life Of Milton, Abridged From Bishop Newton," seven illustration plates engraved by Dalziel after William Harvey, notes at bottom of page, original full red leather (a bit rubbed along joints and extremities, corners worn, spine faded, plates a little foxed), decorative gilt rules on covers, spine ruled and lettered in gilt with decorative gilt trim at top and bottom, raised bands with slight decorative gilt trim, inner and outer dentelles finely tooled in gilt, marbled endpapers, a.e.g. A nice copy in an attractive Victorian red morocco binding. The first edition thus by George Routledge and Co. was published in 1853 (also listed here with further editions by Routledge cited). Not in Kohler, although Kohler 360 cites an 1867 edition by George Routledge and Sons but without "To Which Is Prefixed A Biographical Notice" on title page as here, and with variant publisher's imprint, "The Broadway, Ludgate; New York" in publisher's imprint in place of "Broadway, Ludgate Hill. New York:" as here.

2087. Variant of Preceding, original full crushed green morocco (a little rubbed along joints and corners), covers ruled in blind with large decorative emblem in blind at the center of each cover and very small decorative corner pieces in blind, owner's name in gilt at the top of front cover, spine lettered in gilt, raised bands, small decorative emblems within the panels, inner dentelles finely tooled in gilt, marbled endpapers, a.e.g. A nice copy, fresh and clean throughout, in a variant original morocco binding, possibly a presentation binding, with name in gilt at top of front cover.

2088. Variant of Preceding, contemporary green pebble cloth (slight foxing to the plates, back cover waterstained), gilt rules on front cover with central medallion incorporating lyre, the whole surrounded by decorative black trim, gilt rules on spine with small decorative pieces and title lettered in gilt at the top and "Routledge" in gilt at the bottom, brown endpapers, a.e.g., "Bound By Wesleys & Co. London," with their ticket. A nice copy in a variant decorated cloth binding of the period.

Fore-edge Painting of the House of Commons

2089. THE POETICAL WORKS OF JOHN MILTON. With Illustrations by E. H. Corbould and John Gilbert. [Quotation from Thomson] *London: T. Nelson And Sons, Paternoster Row; Edinburgh; And New York. 1867.* Third edition thus by Nelson? 8vo, 528pp., frontispiece with an early photograph of Milton's tomb in St. Giles, Cripplegate, tipped in, engraved and printed title pages with an early photograph of Ludlow Castle mounted as vignette on undated engraved title, elaborate headpiece with angelic figure in the center at top of title page, decorative headpiece on the "Contents" page and at the head of "Life Of Milton," ten illustration plates after E. H. Corbould and John Gilbert, each with protective tissue guard, elaborate headpiece at the beginning of each book of *PL*, in some instances providing an illustration for the book, elaborate headpiece at the beginning of each book of *PR*, in some instances providing an illustration for the book, elaborate decorative headpieces for *SA, C, L'A, IlP, Ar, L P, S, Trans,* and *Psm*, decorative half-titles (as in the 1864 edition by T. Nelson and Sons) for *PL, PR, SA,* and *C*, decorative tailpieces throughout, contemporary full black calf (title page age-browned with some age-browning and foxing throughout), elaborately embossed covers with Milton's name in gilt at the center of each cover, spine lettered in gilt, raised bands with decorative pieces in blind within the panels, brown endpapers, a.e.g. A fine copy of a scarce Milton edition, in an attractive Victorian binding, with a splendid (possibly contemporary) fore-edge painting of the House of Commons. The ten illustrations include: *Milton Acts as Secretary to Oliver Cromwell* (not in the 1864, 1866, or 1869 editions by T. Nelson and Sons, bound here in life); *Satan on the Burning Lake* (different from the illustration plate similarly named in the 1864, 1866, and 1869 editions by T. Nelson and Sons, bound here in Book I); *Satan on His Throne* (not in the 1864, 1866, or 1869 editions by T. Nelson and Sons, bound here in Book II); *Adam and Eve—The Morning Hymn* (not in the 1864, 1866, or 1869 editions by T. Nelson and Sons, bound here in Book V); *Raphael Discoursing with Adam and Eve* (not in the 1864, 1866, or 1869 editions by T. Nelson and Sons, bound here in Book VI); *Michael and Gabriel Battling with Satan and His Angels* (bound here in Book VI); *The Temptation* (bound here in Book IX); *The Expulsion* (bound here in Book XII); an illustration for "Lycidas"; and one for "On The Late Massacre In Piemont." The elaborate headpiece at the beginning of each book of *PL*, in some instances providing an illustration for the book, include: I, depicting the lamentation of Adam and Eve; II, same headpiece as on title page; III, depicting cross at center; IV, V, VIII, & XI, depicting floral arrangement; VI, depicting crown at center; VII, depicting dove at center; IX, Eve tempting Adam; X, same headpiece as on title page; XII, depicting the expulsion. The elaborate headpiece at the beginning of each book of *PR*, in some instances providing an illustration for the book, include: I, depicting a cross at center; II, depicting a floral arrangement; III, depicting a dove at center; IV, depicting a crown at center. Uncommon. Not in Kohler.

See 1864 edition by T. Nelson and Sons (possible first edition thus) with the same early photographs tipped in on frontispiece and first title page and with illustrations by E. H. Corbould and John Gilbert (eight rather than the ten here), with references to later editions by T. Nelson and Sons with illustrations by Corbould and Gilbert, and also to earlier editions with different illustrations (unsigned and by T. G. Flowers) in editions cited with the possible first edition thus by Nelson in 1850 (copy listed here).

2090. [MILTON'S POETICAL WORKS. With His Life. *London: Charles Daly, 10, Red Lion Square. n.d. [ca. 1867].* Small 8vo (miniature size: 4 ½" × 3 ⅛"), x+479pp., unsigned engraved frontispiece portrait plate of a middle-aged Milton, engraved and printed title pages, engraved title for *PW* (London: Charles Daly. 19, Red Lion Square) with unsigned vignette illustration of Satan on engraved title page, printed title page for "*PL*: By John Milton. To Which Is Prefixed, The Life Of The Author. London: Charles Daly, Greville Street, Hatton Garden," original red cloth (spine half missing, an early signature sprung, several library stamps), covers decorated in blind, portion of spine remaining elaborately decorated in gilt. Except for the portion of the spine missing, a decent copy with contemporary presentation signature, "dated Oct '13 1867," at top of engraved title page. See earlier miniature editions by Daly: 1838 ("Leicester Street, Leicester Square") and 1839 ("19, Red Lion Square"); and see first undated ca. 1850 edition by Charles Daly with further editions by Daly cited. Uncommon. Not in Kohler.

2091. THE POETICAL WORKS OF JOHN MILTON; With A Memoir; Embellished With Engravings After Designs By Fuseli, Westall, And Martin. *London: Robert John Bush, 32, Charing Cross, S. W. 1867.* 8vo, vii+[1]+527pp., engraved frontispiece illustration of Satan after Westall, five additional plates after Fuseli, Westall, and Martin, original brown calf (joints rubbed, back joint cracked from within, spine ends and corners worn), decorative piece in blind at center of covers, spine lettered in gilt, raised bands, a.e.g. The first edition thus was published by Churton in 1836 (copy listed here), with "Six Embellishments" printed on title page, and see other editions by Churton and by Chidley and by Bohn cited there. Scarce. Kohler 361, with "Frontispiece portrait engraved by Cochran after Cooper," referencing Williamson 218 and reporting "Not in the British Library. Not in the Bodleian Library. Not in Cambridge University Library."

2092. THE POETICAL WORKS OF JOHN MILTON. With Illustrations by E. H. Corbould and John Gilbert. [Quotation from Thomson] *London: T. Nelson And Sons, Paternoster Row; Edinburgh; And New York. 1868.* Fourth edition thus by Nelson? Small 8vo, 528pp., unsigned engraved frontispiece portrait, elaborate headpiece with angelic figure in the center at top of title page, decorative headpiece on the "Contents" page and at the head of "Life Of Milton," eight illustration plates after E. H. Corbould and John Gilbert, elaborate headpiece at the beginning of each book of *PL*, in some instances providing an illustration for the book, elaborate headpiece at the beginning of each book of *PR*, in some instances providing an illustration for the book, elaborate decorative headpieces for *SA*, *C*, *L'A*, *IlP*, *Ar*, *L*, *P*, *S*, *Trans*, and *Psm*, elaborate decorative half-titles for *PL*, *PR*, *SA*, and *C*, decorative tailpieces throughout, elaborate headpiece at the beginning of each book of *PR*, in some instances providing an illustration for the book (I, depicting cross at center; II, depicting floral arrangement; III, depicting dove at center; IV, depicting crown at center), elaborate decorative headpieces for *SA*, *C*, *L'A*, *IlP*, *Ar*, *L*, *P*, *S*, *Trans*, and *Psm*, elaborate decorative half-titles (as in the 1864 and 1867 Nelson editions listed earlier) for *PL*, *PR*, *SA*, and *C*, decorative tailpieces throughout, contemporary full dark green morocco (rubbed at joints and corners, front joint broken and barely holding, some foxing), elaborately embossed covers with Milton's name in gilt at the center of each cover, spine lettered in gilt, raised bands with decorative pieces in blind within the panels, brown endpapers, a.e.g. The eight illustration plates after E. H. Corbould and John Gilbert are the same eight illustrations that appeared in the 1864 edition (listed earlier). An attractive copy of a scarce Milton edition in a fine Victorian binding (albeit a bit worn) with contemporary prize presentation inscription (dated 1869) on front blank. Uncommon. Not in Kohler.

See 1864 edition by T. Nelson and Sons (possible first edition thus, copy listed here) with early photograph tipped in on frontispiece and on first title page, with illustrations by E. H. Corbould and John Gilbert, as here, with reference to later editions by T. Nelson and Sons with illustrations by Corbould and Gilbert, and also to earlier editions with different illustrations (unsigned and by T. G.

Flowers) in editions cited with the possible first edition by Nelson in 1850 (copy listed here).

2093. THE POETICAL WORKS OF JOHN MILTON. Edited By Sir Egerton Brydges, Bart. [Quotation from Thomson] Illustrated With Engravings, Designed By John Martin And J. W. M. Turner, R.A. [One Also By Westall And One By Romney]. *New York: W. I. Pooley, 1868.* First edition thus by Pooley? 8vo in 4s. 858pp. (illustrations not included in the pagination), frontispiece portrait "Engraved by O. Pelton" of a young, long-haired Milton "From a Miniature of the same size by Faithorne. Anno 1667, in the possession of William Falconer Esq.," protective tissue guard, engraved and printed title pages with engraved illustration for *C* after Turner on engraved title, reprinting of the original 1835 dedication page "To William Wordsworth And Robert Southey," "Advertisement To The Original Edition" dated 1835, "Life Of Milton," six engraved illustration plates, each with protective tissue guard: two engraved illustration plates after Martin for *PL* (Books VII and X), two engraved illustration plates after Turner—one for *PR* (*The Temptation on the Mountain*, Book III) and one for *C* (as vignette on engraved title page), one engraved illustration plate after Westall for *PL* (*Satan*, Book IV), and one engraved illustration plate after Romney (*Milton Dictating to His Daughters*), engraved by D. L. Glover, for *On His Blindness* (bound with the poem), introductory remarks from the James Boyd edition for each book of *PL*, notes at bottom of page, double black rule around the text, original dark brown leather (rubbed along joints and extremities), covers elaborately decorated in thick blind relief with Milton's name in gilt at the center, spine lettered in gilt, raised bands decorated in blind relief (rubbed), broad inner dentelles finely tooled in gilt, marbled endpapers, a.e.g. A nice copy in an attractive American binding (albeit a bit rubbed) of the period. See 1854 edition by Phillips, Sampson, and Company (possible first edition thus) copy listed here with further editions cited. Uncommon. Not in Kohler.

2094. THE POETICAL WORKS OF JOHN MILTON. To Which Is Prefixed A Biography Of The Author, By His Nephew, Edward Philips. *New York: D. Appleton & Company, 90, 92, & 94 Grand St. 1868.* 12mo in 6s, 574pp., six unsigned illustration plates (fine impressions), each with a protective tissue guard, half-title for several of the major poems, "Contents" at the end, original green cloth (a bit rubbed), covers ruled in blind with central emblem of a globe in blind, spine lettered in gilt with decorative gilt trim in between and at the top and bottom with small globe in gilt at the center incorporating "Globe Edition." A nice copy. Three of the six illustrations, though unsigned, are after Turner: two for *PL* (Books VI and XII) and for *L*; the other three are Turneresque in style: for *PL* (Book II), for *C*, and for *IIP*. Laid in: advertisement leaf for "The Globe Edition Of The Poets" (including this edition): "Uniform in size, style, and price. Each volume beautifully printed in good, clear type, on fine tinted paper, and illustrated with numerous fine Steel Engravings." See 1859 edition with further editions by Appleton cited there. Not in Kohler.

2095. THE POETICAL WORKS OF JOHN MILTON. With Life, Critical Dissertation, and Explanatory Notes [By The Rev. George Gilfillan]. The Text Edited By Charles Cowden Clarke. In Two Volumes. *Edinburgh: William P. Nimmo. 1868.* 2 volumes. First edition thus? 8vo, xxviii+333pp.,+xxxvi+328pp., half-title and title page each volume, frontispiece portrait engraved by J. T. Wedgwood after a drawing by Thurston from a picture by Dobson in Dr. Williams's library, volume 1, half-title for some of the poems, original blue cloth (rubbed along extremities and corners), covers decorated in embossed blind with central gilt medallion on front covers (Milton seated, with "Poeta Nascitur Non Fit" framing the head), embossed blind stamping continues on the spines which are lettered in gilt within a rich gilt decoration at the top, additional gilt decoration at the bottom with decorative thick gilt rule at the top and bottom, brown endpapers, edges untrimmed. A very nice copy in a handsome publisher's binding with four pages of "Nimmo's Library Edition Of The British Poets. From Chaucer To Cowper" tipped in on fly-leaf, volume 1. Nimmo published a repeat of this two-volume edition in identical bindings in 1869 (set listed here). The first Gilfillan edition was published in 1853 (also listed here with further editions cited). In addition, Nimmo published illustrated editions (see copy of 1865 edition listed here with further editions cited, including 1869 edition following). Scarce. Not in Kohler.

2096. THE POETICAL WORKS OF JOHN MILTON. *Edinburgh: William P. Nimmo. n.d. [ca. 1869].* 8vo, xxxvii+455pp., unsigned engraved frontispiece portrait plate of a middle-aged Milton, protective tissue guard (foxed), half-title in color with pastel-like colors of red and green, gilt trim, and a large decorated initial letter "P" incorporating the figure of a woman in the same rich colors, engraved and printed title pages with vignette illustration (of the poet being inspired by heavenly choirs) after F. Borders on engraved title plate ("Edinburgh: William P. Nimmo." n.d. at the bottom), and with vignette illustration (of a young boy in a setting in nature with a cane laying beside him) signed with the initials "WS" on printed title, life of Milton by J. M. Ross, "Murray And Gibb, Edinburgh,

Printers To Her Majesty's Stationery Office" on verso of title page, eleven illustration plates, most after F. Borders, some unsigned: four for *PL* (Books I, III, VI, XI), two for *PR* (Book I), one for *SA*, two for *C*, one for *L'A*, one for *IlP*, half-title for *PL*, *PR*, *SA*, *C*, *Arc*, *MP*, and *Poemata*, black border around text, "Edinburgh: Murray And Gibb, Printers To Her Majesty's Stationery Office" printed at bottom of last page, contemporary shellacked bevelled wooden boards with the photographic image of a leaf pattern glazed over on each cover, the leaf pattern different for the front and the back boards, red leather spine (a bit worn), raised bands, gilt lettering, small decorative pieces in gilt within the panels, decorative gilt trim at top and bottom, inner dentelles finely tooled in gilt, a.e.g. A nice copy in a lovely contemporary papier-mâché binding. The possible first edition thus by Nimmo was published in 1865, illustrated (also listed here with further Nimmo editions, illustrated and nonillustrated, cited there). Only the 1865 edition has twelve illustrations, the others have eleven (with only one illustration for *L'A* instead of two, as in the 1865 edition). Scarce. Kohler 364, reporting "Not in Williamson. Not in the British Library. Not in the Bodleian Library. Not in Cambridge University Library."

Fore-edge Painting of Adam and Eve in the Garden

2097. THE POETICAL WORKS OF JOHN MILTON. With Illustrations by E. H. Corbould and John Gilbert. [Quotation from Thomson] *London: T. Nelson And Sons, Paternoster Row; Edinburgh; And New York, 1869.* Fifth edition thus by Nelson? 8vo, 528pp., unsigned engraved frontispiece portrait, elaborate headpiece with angelic figure in the center at top of title page, decorative headpiece on the "Contents" page and at the head of "Life Of Milton," eight illustration plates after E. H. Corbould and John Gilbert, elaborate headpiece at the beginning of each book of *PL*, in some instances providing an illustration for the book, elaborate headpiece at the beginning of each book of *PR*, in some instances providing an illustration for the book, elaborate decorative headpieces for *SA*, *C*, *L'A*, *IlP*, *Ar*, *L*, *P*, *S*, *Trans*, and *Psm*, elaborate decorative half-titles for *PL*, *PR*, *SA*, and *C*, decorative tailpieces throughout, contemporary full red calf (a bit rubbed, frontispiece and title page a little foxed), covers and spine elaborately tooled in gilt, raised bands, brown endpapers, a.e.g. A lovely copy in an elaborate Victorian binding, with a fine

(left) Contemporary shellacked bevelled wooden boards with the photographic image of a leaf pattern glazed over on each cover, the leaf pattern different for the front and the back boards, green morocco spine (*PW*, London: T. Nelson and Sons, Edinburgh and New York. 1874); (center) contemporary shellacked bevelled thick wooden boards with a large color picture of a pond and sunset pasted on front cover, green morocco spine (*PW*, London: George Routledge and Sons, n.d. [ca. 1878]); (right) contemporary shellacked bevelled wooden boards with the photographic image of a leaf pattern glazed over on each cover, the leaf pattern different for the front and the back boards, red leather spine (*PW*, Edinburgh: William P. Nimmo. n.d. [ca. 1869]). See #2184, 2272, and 2096.

II. Descriptive Listing of Editions 523

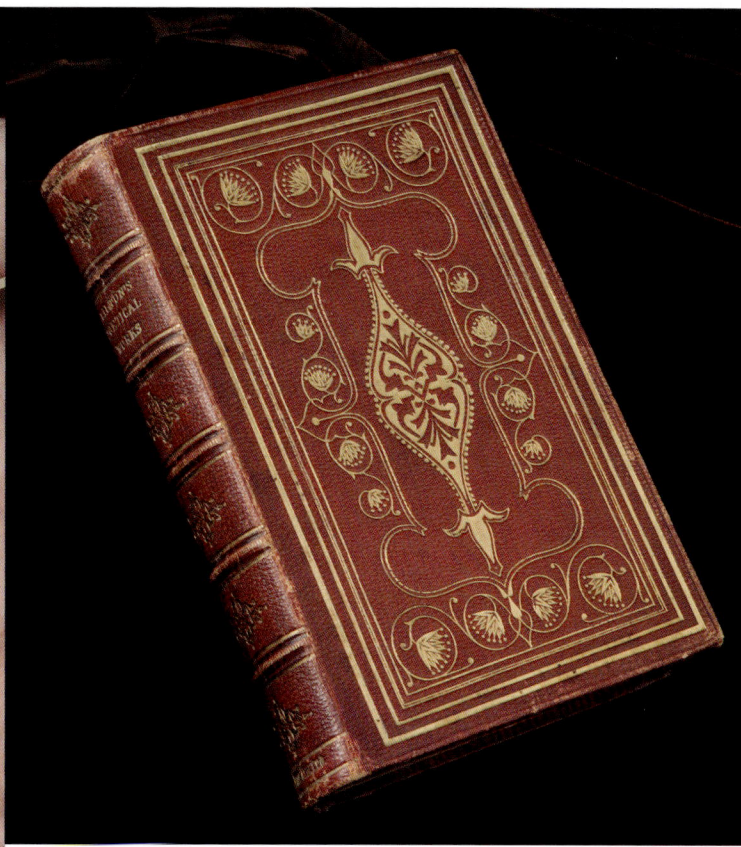

Fore-edge painting (probably early twentieth-century) of Adam and Eve in the Garden, along with apple, serpent, and also a leopard between them. On *PW*, With Illustrations by E. H. Corbould and John Gilbert. London: T. Nelson And Sons, And New York, 1869. See #2097.

fore-edge painting (probably early twentieth century) of Adam and Eve in the Garden of Eden, along with apple and serpent and curiously a leopard between them. The eight illustration plates after E. H. Corbould and John Gilbert are the same eight illustrations that appear in the 1864 edition. See 1864 edition by T. Nelson and Sons (possible first edition thus) listed with early photograph tipped in on frontispiece and first title page, with illustrations by E. H. Corbould and John Gilbert, as here, with reference to later editions by T. Nelson and Sons with illustrations by Corbould and Gilbert, and also to earlier editions with different illustrations (unsigned and by T. G. Flowers) in editions cited along with the possible first edition by Nelson in 1850 (copy listed here). Uncommon. Not in Kohler.

2098. THE POETICAL WORKS OF JOHN MILTON. A New Edition, carefully Revised, From The Text Of Thomas Newton, D.D. To Which Is Prefixed A Biographical Notice. With Illustrations By William Harvey. New Edition. *London: George Routledge And Sons, The Broadway, Ludgate. New York: 416, Broome Street. 1869.* 8vo, xlvi+[2]+570pp., frontispiece portrait plate of *Milton Dictating to His Daughters*, engraved by the Dalziel brothers, original preface by Theodore Alois Buckley dated 1853, "The Life Of Milton, Abridged From Bishop Newton," seven illustration plates engraved by the Dalziel brothers after William Harvey, half-title before the poem, notes at the bottom of page, original full red crushed morocco (a bit rubbed, especially along joints and corners), decorative gilt rules on covers with delicate gilt trim within and large gilt floral pattern at the center, spine ruled and lettered in gilt, inner dentelles finely tooled in gilt, a.e.g. A nice copy in an attractive Victorian red morocco binding with contemporary prize presentation (dated 1879) on front pastedown. The first edition thus by George Routledge and Co. was published in 1853 (also listed here with further editions by Routledge cited). Kohler 362, citing "six plates" instead of seven (as here) and reporting "Not in the British Library. Not in the Bodleian Library. Not in Cambridge University Library."

2099. THE POETICAL WORKS OF JOHN MILTON. Edited By Sir Egerton Brydges, Bart. [Quotation from Thomson] Illustrated With Engravings, Designed By John Martin And J. W. M. Turner, R.A. [One Also By Westall And One By Romney]. *New York: W. I. Pooley, 1869.* Second edition thus by Pooley? 8vo in 4s, 858pp., frontispiece portrait "Engraved by O. Pelton" of a young, long-haired Milton "From a Miniature of the same size by Faithorne. Anno 1667, in the possession of William Falconer Esq.," protective tissue guard, engraved and printed title pages with engraved illustration for *C* after Turner on engraved title, reprinting of the original 1835 dedication page "To William Wordsworth And Robert Southey," "Advertisement To The Original Edition" dated 1835, "Life Of Milton," six engraved illustration plates, each with protective tissue guard: two engraved illustration plates after Martin for *PL* (Books VII and X), two engraved illustration plates after Turner—one for *PR* (*The Temptation on the Mountain*, Book III) and one for *C* (as vignette on engraved title page), one engraved illustration plate after Westall for *PL* (*Satan*, Book IV), and one engraved illustration plate after Romney (*Milton Dictating to His Daughters*), engraved by D. L. Glover, for *On His Blindness* (bound with the poem), introductory remarks from the James Boyd edition for each book of *PL*, notes at bottom of page, double black border around text, original brown leather (a little worn, especially spine which has been reglued to the back, joints cracked, some foxing, especially the plates, which are foxed because of the protective tissue guards), black label with gilt lettering and gilt rules on spine, raised band in between gilt rules, outer dentelles tooled in gilt, marbled endpapers and edges. See 1854 edition by Phillips, Sampson, and Company (possible first edition thus, copy listed here and other editions cited there). Scarce. Not in Kohler.

2100. THE POETICAL WORKS OF JOHN MILTON. Edited By Sir Egerton Brydges, Bart. [Quotation from Thomson] Illustrated With Engravings, Designed By John Martin And J. W. M. Turner, R.A. [One Also By Westall And One By Romney]. *New York: D. Appleton & Company, 90, 92 & 94 Grand Street. 1869.* 8vo in 4s, 858pp., frontispiece portrait "Engraved by O. Pelton" of a young, long-haired Milton "From a Miniature of the same size by Faithorne. Anno 1667, in the possession of William Falconer Esq.," protective tissue guard, engraved and printed title pages with vignette illustration for *C* after Turner on engraved title, engraved title page with "Boston. Phillips, Sampson & Company" as publisher, printed title page with "New York: D. Appleton & Company" as publisher, reprinting of the original 1835 dedication page "To William Wordsworth And Robert Southey," "Advertisement To The Original Edition" dated 1835, "Life Of Milton," six engraved illustration plates, each with protective tissue guard, two engraved illustration plates after Martin for *PL* (Books VII and X), two engraved illustration plates after Turner—one for *PR* (Book III, *The Temptation on the Mountain*) and one for *C* (as vignette on engraved title page), one engraved illustration plate after Westall for *PL* (*Satan*, here bound within Book IV), and one illustration plate after Romney (*Milton Dictating to His Daughters*), engraved by D. L. Glover, for *On His Blindness* (bound here with the poem), introductory remarks from the James Boyd edition (unsigned) for each book of *PL*, notes at the bottom of the page, double black border around text, contemporary full rich brown morocco over thick boards (a bit rubbed, some slight scuffing, occasional light foxing, especially the plates and protective tissue guards), covers elaborately embossed with Milton's name in gilt at the center of each cover, spine lettered in gilt, raised bands, marbled endpapers, a.e.g. A nice copy in a fine embossed binding of the period. See 1851 edition by Appleton (possible first edition thus) also listed here with further editions by Appleton cited, and see 1854 edition by Phillips, Sampson, and Company (possible first edition thus) and other editions with the same plates and in a similar format cited there. Uncommon. Not in Kohler.

2101. THE POETICAL WORKS OF JOHN MILTON. With Life, Critical Dissertation, and Explanatory Notes [By The Rev. George Gilfillan]. The Text Edited By Charles Cowden Clarke. In Two Volumes. *Edinburgh: William P. Nimmo. 1869.* 2 volumes. 8vo, xxviii+333pp.,+ xxxvi+328pp., half-title and title page each volume, frontispiece portrait engraved by J. T. Wedgwood after a drawing by Thurston from a picture by Dobson in Dr. Williams's library, volume 1, half-title for some of the poems, original blue cloth (a bit rubbed, front blank missing), covers decorated in embossed blind with central gilt medallion on front covers (Milton seated, with "Poeta Nascitur Non Fit" framing the head), embossed blind-stamping continues on the spines, which are lettered in gilt within a rich gilt decoration at the top, additional gilt decoration at the bottom with decorative thick gilt rule at the top and bottom, brown endpapers, edges untrimmed. A handsome set with library stamp of "Farnborough Abbey Library" and several signatures on half-title, volume 1. Nimmo's possible first edition thus was published as here in two volumes in identical bindings in 1868 (see set listed here). The first Gilfillan edition was published in 1853 (also listed here with further editions cited). In addition, Nimmo published an illustrated edition the same year (also listed here) and various other illustrated editions (see copy of 1865 edition listed here with further editions, illustrated and nonillustrated cited). Scarce. Kohler 363, citing Williamson 237 and reporting "Not in the British Library. Not in the Bodleian Library. Not in Cambridge University Library."

2102. THE POETICAL WORKS OF JOHN MILTON. With Life, Critical Dissertation, and Explanatory Notes [By The Rev. George Gilfillan]. The Text Edited By Charles Cowden Clarke. In Two Volumes. *Cassell, Petter, & Galpin: London, Paris & New York. n.d. [ca. 1869]*. 2 volumes in one. 8vo, xxviii+333pp.,+xxxvi+328pp., two half-title, two title pages, contemporary three-quarter red morocco, red cloth, gilt rules on covers, gilt-decorated spine, raised bands with decorative gilt trim, marbled endpapers and edges. A very nice copy, finely printed, in a handsome binding of the period. The first Gilfillan edition was published in 1853 (see set also listed here with further editions cited). Scarce. Kohler 376, dating its copy "[1874]" describing it as "Octavo in 16s," and reporting "Not in Cambridge University Library."

2103. THE POETICAL WORKS OF JOHN MILTON. To Which Is Prefixed A Biography Of The Author, By His Nephew, Edward Philips. *New York: D. Appleton & Company, 90, 92 & 94 Grand St. 1869*. 12mo in 6s, 574pp., "Introduction," "The Life Of Milton, By His Nephew Edward Philips," half-title for *PR, SA, P, Poemata*, "Contents" at end, contemporary full blue morocco (a bit rubbed at joints and corners, light damp stain bottom half of covers and throughout text), gilt rules on covers, spine decorated in gilt within the panels and lettered in gilt, raised bands with decorated gilt trim, inner dentelles finely tooled in gilt, outer dentelles ruled in gilt, marbled endpapers, a.e.g. A fine copy, although one would wish the light damp staining away. See 1851 edition also listed here with further editions cited. Not in Kohler.

2104. Variant of Preceding, original printed paper wrappers (a bit worn, front cover detached and chipped at top right, spine a little frayed), front cover decorated in a patterned design in blue with a vignette portrait of Milton at the center with "Milton's Poetical Works" lettered in blue in a scroll across the top, and the "Price Fifty Cents" lettered in blue in a small banner above that, and "Complete With a Life of the Author" lettered in blue in a scroll beneath the portrait of Milton and "New York: D. Appleton & Co." lettered in blue in a small banner beneath that, spine lettered in black, advertising on back cover and on inside front cover. Despite the wear, a good copy in original publisher's wrappers, as issued. Scarce thus. Not in Kohler.

2105. MILTON'S POETISCHE VERKE. Deutsch von Adolf Böttger. Jünfte Auflage. *Leipzig, Druck und Verlag von Philipp Reclam jun. (1869)*. Small 8vo, xiv+494+[18]pp., half-title, dedication page dated 1869, "Biographische Skizze," half-title for some of the individual works, original red cloth, embossed decorative gilt border trim ruled in gilt on front cover with embossed central emblem in gilt incorporating Milton's name, spine decorated in a gilt pattern with Milton's name lettered in gilt toward the top, marbled edges. A fine copy in an attractive binding of the period with eighteen pages of advertisements bound in at the end. Not in Kohler.

Editions by Galls & Inglis

It is difficult to place a precise date on the following editions by Gall & Inglis, hence the large number of variants and broad range of dates. It is safe to say, I believe, that they were published in the 1870s.

2106. THE POETICAL WORKS OF JOHN MILTON. With Life. Engravings on Steel. Gall & Inglis. *Edinburgh: Bernard Terrace. London: 25 Paternoster Sqr. n.d. [ca. 1870s/1875]*. 8vo, xx+491pp. (with border trim on verso of final page), unsigned frontispiece illustration plate of *The Expulsion* (slight stain at top corner, not affecting anything), three additional unsigned illustration plates—for *PL* (Books VII and IX) and for *PR* (Book IV), decorative border trim around the text in alternating sepia and bluish green tint with varying background scenes, half-title for life of Milton, half-title for *PL*, original reddish-brown cloth (a bit worn, some slight age-browning and inoffensive damp staining throughout), front cover elaborately decorated in embossed black and gilt trim with decorative gilt scrolls incorporating the title in black lettering above and below a central recessed panel containing a varnished paper floral cutout, the recessed panel within an elaborate gilt device consisting of decorative gilt tooling and trim, the gilt scroll and elaborate gilt tooling around the central recessed panel over decorative black and brown trim with black lettering going round the recessed panel and beneath the gilt scrolls and printing "The Landscape Series Of Poets" in very small lettering with round gilt medallions at each corner, the two lower medallions containing impressions in gilt of William Shakespeare and Robert Burns, the two upper medallions containing impressions of what might be Westminster Cathedral (above Shakespeare) and a Scottish castle (above Burns), spine similarly elaborately decorated with various designs in embossed black and gilt with "Milton" lettered in embossed black within gilt background as with title, "Milton's Poetical Works," on front cover and with "The Landscape Series Of Poets" at the center in red within a gilt background, decorative gilt trim at the top and bottom incorporating "Gall & Inglis" in gilt on either side of a harp in gilt at the bottom and a small pastoral scene in gilt at the top, back cover decorated in embossed blind with central embossed harp, brown endpapers, a.e.g. A nice copy (albeit a bit worn), and a wonderful example of an elaborate Victorian book decoratively printed and bound in a lovely publisher's binding of the period—a variant binding from those of the following copies here. Kohler 379, dating a similar copy "[ca. 1875]."

See ca. 1870s edition of *PW* by Gall & Inglis with "Six Engravings on Steel" published in Edinburgh ("6 George Street") and London ("25 Paternoster Square")—with Edinburgh on the left and London on the right, as here; see ca. 1870s edition with "Six Engravings on Steel" published in Edinburgh ("Bernard Terrace") and London ("25 Paternoster Square")—with Edinburgh on the left and London on the right; see, too, ca. 1876–77 edition "With Six Engravings on Steel" published in Edinburgh (Bernard Terrace") and London ("25 Paternoster Square") with Edinburgh on the left and London on the right; see also ca. 1877 edition "With Six Engravings on Steel" published in London (25 Paternoster Square") and Edinburgh ("6 George Street)—with London on the left and Edinburgh on the right; and see ca. 1880 editions "with Six Engravings on Steel," one with the engravings and one without, both published in Edinburgh ("Bernard Terrace") and London ("25 Paternoster Sq.")—Edinburgh on the left and London on the right. See also undated ca. 1854 edition of *CPW* by Gall & Inglis, listing various later undated editions of *PW* by Gall & Inglis published in the 1870s and 1880s, with "Engravings on Steel" and with "Six Engravings on Steel" on the title page and with published in "Edinburgh (Bernard Terrace) and London (25 Paternoster Sqr.)"—with Edinburgh on the left and London on the right as here, and "London (25 Paternoster Square) and Edinburgh (6 George Street)"—with London on the left and Edinburgh on the right—all editions are listed here.

2107. Variant of Preceding, original decorated green cloth (a bit worn at spine ends and the corners, front joint slightly cracked from within, plate for Book VII repaired some time ago near the margin—without affecting the illustration—with tape which is now browning), front cover elaborately decorated in embossed black and gilt with decorative gilt scrolls incorporating the title in red lettering above and below a central recessed panel containing a varnished paper floral cutout, the recessed panel within

PW. Gall & Inglis, Edinburgh and London, ca. 1870s. Variant decorated cloth bindings. See #2106.

an elaborate gilt device consisting of varying decorative gilt tooling and trim, the gilt scrolls above and below connected to one another with black trim containing "The Landscape Series Of Poets" in black lettering with round gilt medallions at each corner, the two lower medallions containing impressions in gilt of Shakespeare and Burns, the two upper medallions containing impressions of what might be Westminster Cathedral (above Shakespeare) and a Scottish castle (above Burns), spine similarly elaborately decorated with various designs in embossed black and gilt with "Milton" lettered in embossed red within a gilt background within decorative gilt trim, with "Illustrated" beneath lettered in gilt and decorated with gilt trim, "The Landscape Series Of Poets" lettered in gilt at the center within gilt background, decorative black and gilt trim at top and bottom with "Gall & Inglis" in gilt on either side of a harp in gilt at the bottom and a small pastoral scene in gilt at the top, back cover decorated in embossed blind with central embossed harp, brown endpapers, a.e.g. Despite some wear, a charming edition of Milton's poetry in a variant Victorian publisher's binding.

2108. Variant of Preceding, original royal blue ribbed cloth (slightly rubbed, very small piece torn away from bottom right corner of first page of *PR* without affecting any text or border trim), front cover elaborately decorated in black and gilt with decorative gilt scrolls incorporating the title in red letters above and below a central varnished paper cutout centerpiece blocked in maroon, white, and gold of an angel with a harp in a recessed panel within an elaborate gilt device consisting of varying gilt tooling and trim, spine similarly elaborately decorated in black and gilt with Milton's name incorporated within a large, rich gilt device at the top and "The Landscape Series Of Poets" within a small circular gilt device toward the bottom with a gilt harp above and the initials "GI" in gilt within, decorative gilt trim at top and bottom incorporating "Gall & Inglis" at the bottom, back cover decorated in blind with central harp, brown endpapers, a.e.g., bookplate. A splendid copy with fine impressions of the illustrations and of the decorative border trim, and a wonderful example, in rather well-preserved condition, of an elaborate Victorian book decoratively printed and bound in a lovely publisher's binding—a variant binding from that of the preceding copies.

2109. Variant of Preceding, original ribbed green cloth (worn at corners, spine chipped at top and bottom, a little shaken within), front cover elaborately decorated in black and gilt with decorative gilt scrolls incorporating Milton's name in red relief above and the title in green relief below a central varnished paper cutout centerpiece blocked in black, white, and gold of an angel with a harp in a recessed panel within an elaborate gilt device consisting of varying gilt tooling and trim, spine similarly elaborately decorated in black and gilt with Milton's name incorporated within a bright broad gilt band at the top and "The Landscape Series Of Poets" within a small circular gilt device toward the bottom with a gilt harp above and the initials "GI" against a black background, decorative gilt trim at top and bottom incorporating "Gall & Inglis" at the bottom, back cover decorated in blind with central harp, brown endpapers, a.e.g. A good copy, albeit a little worn, in an attractive variant publisher's binding.

2110. Variant of Preceding, contemporary full blue morocco (a bit rubbed, especially along the joints and extremities), front cover richly decorated with double gilt rules and circular corner pieces surrounding thick indentations in blind with intricate central gilt scroll incorporating Milton's name in red relief on the top and title in green relief at the bottom, the whole appended to a delicately tooled gilt device on the left which scrolls upward and downward and then across with "Landscape" lettered in gilt at the top and "Edition of the Poets" lettered in gilt at the bottom, spine decorated with rich gilt devices in the panels, raised bands within delicate gilt tooling, back cover elaborately decorated in blind relief with large central oval device incorporating a small harp, brown endpapers, a.e.g. A very attractive copy in a variant contemporary morocco binding, a splendid and well-preserved Victorian binding, fresh and crisp within, with fine impressions of the illustrations and of the decorative border trim, and with a near-contemporary presentation birthday inscription written in ink in a neat hand on front blank. Among the editions included on the "List Of Gall & Inglis' *Landscape Edition of the Poets*" on verso of the final page is "Milton's Poetical Works, including the Sonnets, Psalms, Latin and Italian Translations." Kohler 379, with variations noted above, dating its copy ca. 1875, in "Original green morocco."

2111. Variant of Preceding, original decorated blue cloth (a bit rubbed, earlier owner's inscription and stamp on title page, dated "Christmas 1890"), front cover elaborately decorated in embossed red and gilt with Grecian design overall, Greek pillars along the sides, central altar at the bottom with small figurine in silver playing the harp standing atop the altar, large bright gilt piece with title and small decorative winged figures and other designs in embossed red across the top third, small silver medallion with Grecian figure in helmet at the center near the top, the medallion encompassed in red laurel wreath and attached to a decorative red border trim at the top and flowing red laurel down each side to the large bright gilt piece beneath, spine

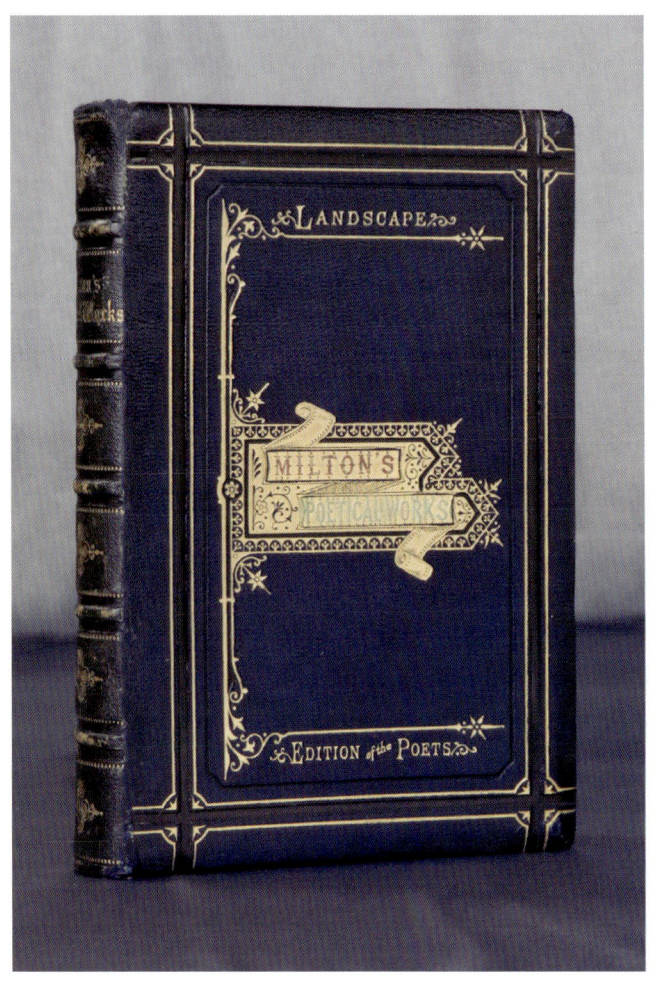

PW. Gall & Inglis, Edinburgh and London, ca. 1870s. "Landscape Edition of Poets." Blue morocco binding, gilt decorated. See #2110.

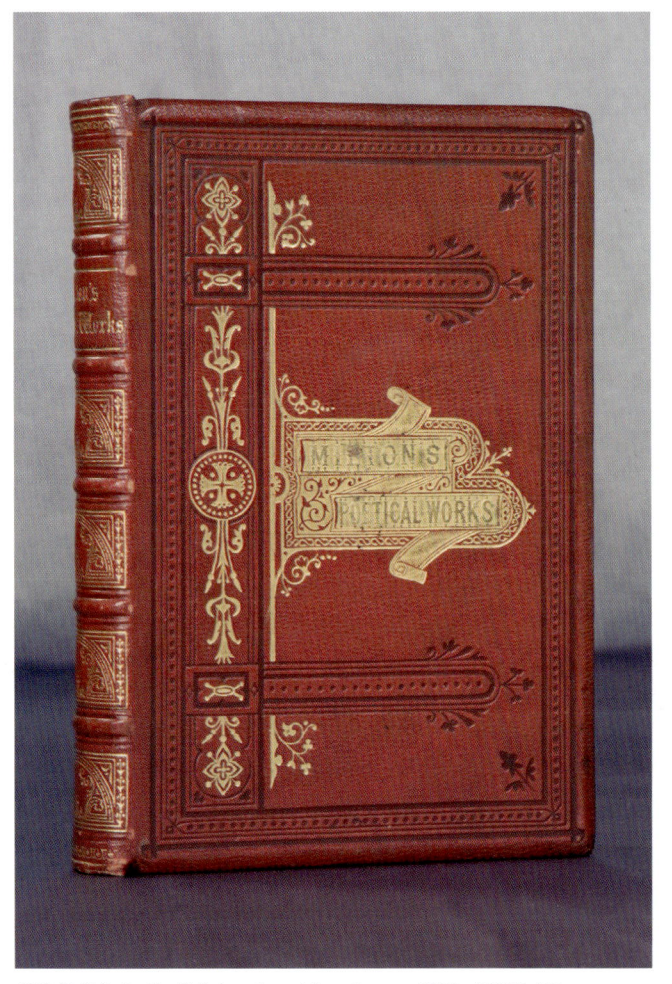

PW. Gall & Inglis, Edinburgh and London, ca. 1870s / 1876–77. "Landscape Edition of Poets." Red morocco binding, gilt decorated. Very pleasing example of the style that consciously imitated the illuminated books of the period, as with previous binding. See #2114.

similarly decorated in red and gilt with Milton's name incorporated in embossed red letters within decorative gilt device at the top, silver medallion repeated in a smaller form at the center, and the small figurine playing the harp from the front cover repeated at the bottom of the spine with "Gall & Inglis" incorporated in the base beneath, emblem in black at the center of the back cover, brown endpapers, a.e.g. A nice copy with variant border trim, no reference to "The Landscape Series Of Poets," in an attractive, well-preserved variant publisher's binding from those of the preceding copies, this binding rather distinctive in its own right. A variant of this binding is in the collection, in original decorated green cloth.

2112. Variant of Preceding, contemporary blue velvet covers over thick padded boards with blue cloth spine (showing some wear), large bronzed celluloid centerpiece on front cover incorporating Milton's name at center, decorated endpapers, a.e.g. A good copy with no reference to "The Landscape Series Of Poets," in an attractive (albeit a little worn) binding of the period, a nice example of an elaborate Victorian binding. Kohler 379, with slight variations noted above, dating its copy ca. 1875.

2113. THE POETICAL WORKS OF JOHN MILTON. With Life. Six Engravings on Steel. *Gall & Inglis. Edinburgh: Bernard Terrace. London: 25 Paternoster Sqr. n.d. [ca. 1870s/1876–77].* Variant edition. 8vo, xx+491pp., engraved and printed title pages with the printed title page reading *PW*, as printed, the engraved title page reading *CPW*, unsigned frontispiece illustration plate of the expulsion with unsigned vignette illustration of Eve relating her dream to Adam on engraved title, which bears the same publisher as the printed title page ("Edinburgh, Gall & Inglis. London," undated), four additional unsigned illustration plates—for *PL* (Books II, VII, and IX) and for *PR* (Book IV), red border around text, original decorated green cloth (a bit rubbed), front cover decorated in embossed black and gilt with large central white emblem incorporating angelic figure with lyre in gilt above Milton's name and a harp in gilt below Milton's name in gilt relief, the whole surrounded in decorative black and gilt trim, spine similarly decorated in embossed black and gilt with gilt emblem near the top incorporating Milton's name and the title in embossed green, a second gilt emblem below incorporating a Greek figure with decorative gilt trim at top and bottom, "Gall & Inglis" incorporated in the gilt trim at the bottom, a.e.g. Variant edition from preceding, with "Six Engravings On Steel" added to title page, a modified publisher's address, and with four additional illustration plates rather than three, in an attractive Victorian binding. Not in Kohler (see Kohler 379).

2114. THE POETICAL WORKS OF JOHN MILTON. With Life. Six Engravings on Steel. *Gall & Inglis. London: 25 Paternoster Square. Edinburgh: 6 George Street. n.d. [ca. 1870s/1876–77].* 8vo, xx+491pp., engraved and printed title pages, with the printed title page reading *PW*, as printed, the engraved title page reading *CPW*, unsigned frontispiece illustration plate of the expulsion with unsigned vignette illustration of Eve relating her dream to Adam on engraved title, which bears the same publisher as the printed title page ("Edinburgh, Gall & Inglis. London," undated), four additional unsigned illustration plates—for *PL* (Books II, VII, and IX) and for *PR* (Book IV), red border around text, contemporary full red morocco with intricate central gilt scroll incorporating Milton's name and the title in a greenish cast on the front cover, which is also ornamented in elaborate gilt and blind design, back cover decorated in similar blind design, spine prettily gilt in the panels with gilt lettering, raised bands, green endpapers, bevelled edges, a.e.g. Variant edition in a splendid and well-preserved Victorian binding. The binding is a very pleasing example of the style that consciously imitated the illuminated books of the period. (An anthology in the collection, *Gleanings From The Sacred Poets* [ca. 1875], containing Milton's *NO*, and *PW* [ca. 1880, listed in Chapter IV], is bound in identical, and similarly well-preserved binding.) Not in Kohler.

❦

2115. THE POETICAL WORKS OF JOHN MILTON. Edited, With A Critical Memoir, By William Michael Rossetti. With Full Page Illustrations. *Griffith, Farran, Okeden & Welsh, At The Sign Of The "Bible And Sun," West Corner Of St. Paul's Churchyard, London. n.d. [ca. 1870s].* 8vo, xx+460pp., engraved frontispiece portrait sketch of Milton (age ten) with protective tissue guard, six unsigned engraved illustration plates after Seccombe, four for *PL* (Books IV, VI, VIII, and XII), one for *C*, and one for *SA*, with the poem *C* coming between *PL* and *SA*, numerous elaborately decorated head- and tailpieces, red border around text, contemporary full crushed blue morocco (rather worn), Milton's name lettered in gilt on front cover and spine, a.e.g. A fair copy of an uncommon edition, with several marginal notations in early (possibly contemporary) hand. See similar undated ca. 1880 edition (copy listed here) published by "Griffith[,] Farran[,] Okeden & Welsh[,] Newbery House, London & Sydney, N.S.W." Scarce. Not in Kohler.

2116. THE POETICAL WORKS OF JOHN MILTON. Illustrated By F. Gilbert. *London: John Dicks, 313, Strand; And All Booksellers[,] 1870.* 8vo, v+162+ii+[2]pp., engraved frontispiece illustration after F. Gilbert (signed with the initials "CF" and entitled "Frontispiece," consisting of three vignettes: a circular portrait of Milton as a young man above several books, a scroll, and a quill and ink bottle; the temptation of Eve; and the angel expelling; all three vignettes incorporating a large apple tree with serpent beneath), "Sketch Of The Life Of John Milton" before the poems and "Contents" at the end, printed in double column, original green cloth (a bit rubbed, spine slightly chipped at top and bottom, slight foxing), covers ruled in blind, spine lettered in gilt, fore- and bottom edges untrimmed. A nice copy in publisher's cloth binding with advertisement leaf bound in at the end. Two variant copies: one in original printed tan wrappers (front cover detached and frayed along edges, spine almost gone, lacking back wrapper), front cover decorated with corner pieces and black border rules, with a circular portrait of Milton as a young man above several books, a scroll, and a quill and ink bottle at the center, lettered as the title page, with an additional publisher printed at the bottom, "Wm. W. Swayne, New York and Brooklyn," and "Price Sixpence" at the top; a second copy in original half brown calf, brown cloth. See undated (ca. 1865) edition (possible first edition thus) also listed here, with the same engraved frontispiece illustration. Stevens 1999, "cheaply printed"; Not in Kohler.

2117. THE POETICAL WORKS OF JOHN MILTON. With A Memoir, And Critical Remarks On His Genius And Writings. By James Montgomery; [Vol. I. / Vol. II.] *New York: Leavitt & Allen Bros., No. 8 Howard Street. n.d. [ca. 1870].* 2 volumes in one. 8vo, xlix+[i]+[3]+400pp.(page numbering beginning with number "18"),+368pp.(page numbering beginning with number "10"), engraved frontispiece portrait plate after C. Burt, protective tissue guard, volume 1, second title page for volume 2 followed by "Contents Of Vol. II," illustrations (unsigned, but after Harvey) within the text for *L'A* with a vignette illustration at the beginning and another vignette illustration at the end of the poem and with vignette illustrations in the margins, half-title for each book of *PL* and *PR* and for some of the poems, original green cloth, covers and spine richly decorated in black and gilt with decorative trim in black and gilt at the top and bottom, and Milton's name lettered in large embossed green letters within a large, bright gilt emblem ruled in black at the center, a.e.g. A fine copy in an attractive publisher's binding, fresh and clean within. The possible first edition thus was published by Leavitt & Allen in 1858 (also listed here with further editions by Leavitt & Allen in the collection cited there). Not in Kohler, but Kohler 345 dates its copy, "New York: Leavitt & Allen Bros., No. 8 Howard Street. n.d. [ca. 1860]," with a "Frontispiece engraved by A. H. Ritchie," rather than after C. Burt as here, with no reference to any illustrations.

2118. Variant of Preceding, original purple pebble cloth with decorative imitation binding strips in blind (spine faded), spine lettered in gilt with two decorative emblems in gilt, one incorporating "The World Edition," yellow endpapers with advertising for various publications, including "The World Edition" and this edition of Milton. Nice copy in a variant publisher's binding (similar to one on a copy of the ca. 1872 Leavitt & Allen Bros. editions listed here).

2119. THE POETICAL WORKS OF JOHN MILTON. *New York: Sheldon And Company, 498, And 500, Broadway. n.d. [ca. 1870s].* 8vo, xxxvii+455pp., unsigned engraved frontispiece, engraved and printed title pages with vignette illustration of a young poet and angels with their lyres and harps after Borders, nine illustration plates after Borders, contemporary reddish-brown morocco (rubbed along joints and at corners, pages age-browned and extremely fragile—breaking at the touch, the whole shaken and loose), covers richly embossed with gilt lettering at the top of the front cover and several small gilt decorations at the bottom, spine lettered in gilt, raised bands (rubbed), brown endpapers, a.e.g. An uncommon copy in an attractive late-nineteenth-century American binding, in the manner of the period, unfortunately shaken and very fragile within. Scarce. Not in Kohler.

2120. THE POETICAL WORKS OF JOHN MILTON. With Illustrations by E. H. Corbould and John Gilbert. [Quotation from Thomson] *London: T. Nelson And Sons, Paternoster Row; Edinburgh; And New York. 1871.* 8vo, 528pp., half-title, elaborate headpiece at top of title page (different from that in earlier editions by T. Nelson and Sons) with an angelic figure in the center within a circle incorporating the quotation from *PL*: "Brought Death Into The World And All Our Woe," decorative headpiece (different from that in earlier editions by T. Nelson and Sons) at the beginning of "Life Of Milton," seven steel-engraved illustration plates (unsigned, but reproductions of illustrations by T. G. Flowers), one following half-title and facing away from title page, several with protective tissue guards, elaborate headpieces (different from those in earlier editions by T. Nelson and Sons), in some instances serving as illustrations, elaborate decorative headpieces (different from those in earlier editions by T. Nelson and Sons) for *C, L'A IlP, Ar, L, P, S, Trans*, and *Psm*, half-title (undecorated as in earlier editions by T. Nelson and Sons) for *PL, PR, SA, C*, and some of the poems, decorative tailpieces throughout (similar to those in earlier editions by T. Nelson and Sons), contemporary decorated orange cloth (a bit worn and a little faded, spine chipped at top and bottom). front cover and spine elaborately decorated in black and gilt, Milton's name in embossed orange letters against a broad gilt band at center of front cover, small gilt medallion at top with harp within and another small gilt medallion at bottom with the initials "TNS" within, Milton's name in embossed orange letters against a broad gilt band at top of spine, small gilt medallion with harp within repeated against decorative black background at center of spine, "Nelson's Illustrated Poets" in embossed orange letters against a small gilt band at bottom of spine, brown endpapers, a.e.g. A good copy. Not in Kohler.

While the title page says "With Illustrations by E. H. Corbould and John Gilbert" (as in the editions by T. Nelson and Sons published in 1864, 1866, 1867, and 1869—all listed here), the steel-engraved illustration plates here are reproductions of illustrations by T. G. Flowers published in earlier editions by T. Nelson and Sons (see 1853, 1855, 1858, 1859, 1860, 1861, 1862 editions—all listed here). The seven unsigned steel-engraved illustrations include: *Adam and Eve among the Animals* for Book IV of *PL* (two plates: one plate bound within Book IV and a duplicate plate bound following the half-title, facing away from title page); *Naming the Animals* for Book VIII of *PL*; *The Temptation of Eve* for Book IX of *PL*; *The Expulsion* for Book XII of *PL*; *The Baptism of Jesus* for Book I of *PR*; and *The Temptation of Jesus* for Book III of *PR*. The elaborate headpieces, in some instances serving as illustrations, are unsigned and include one for each book of *PL*: Books I, IV, and X, same headpiece as on title page; Books II, VII, and XI depicting Sin and Death; Book III, depicting fruit at center with snake woven around headpiece; Books V and XII, depicting the head of an angel attired in a helmet between fiery swords; Book VI, depicting a fallen angel in armor; Book VIII, depicting fruit at center with snake woven around headpiece, the headpiece for Book III turned upside down; Book IX, depicting Eve in the garden holding the branch of a tree. The elaborate headpieces also include a headpiece for each book of *PR*: Book I, depicting Madonna and Child; Book II, depicting the face of Christ; Book III, depicting Christ in the Wilderness being tempted by Satan; Book IV, depicting three nails within a crown of thorns with a cherub at each end. There is also an elaborate illustration headpiece at the beginning of *SA*: depicting Samson's head lying in the lap of Delilah with several onlookers. This 1871 edition, like the 1872 and 1874 editions following, contains a mixture of elements from earlier editions published by T. Nelson and Sons, including reproductions of illustrations by T. Flowers, along with new elaborate illustrative headpieces (unsigned, perhaps by Corbould and Gilbert) and half-titles. See 1850 (possible first edition thus) by Nelson also listed here with further editions cited.

2121. THE POETICAL WORKS OF JOHN MILTON. Edited, With A Critical Memoir, By William Michael Rossetti. Illustrated By Thomas Seccombe. *London: E. Moxon, Son, & Co., Dover Street, And 1 Amen Corner, Paternoster Row. n.d. [ca. 1871].* First Moxon edition? 8vo, xx+460pp., engraved frontispiece portrait sketch of Milton (age ten) with protective tissue guard, engraved and printed title pages with vignette illustration by Thomas Seccombe for Milton's sonnet *On His Deceased Wife* on engraved title, "London[,] E. Moxon Son & Co. Dover Street" at the bottom, emblem of harp incorporating initials of the press with laurel branches beneath on title page, seven additional engraved illustration plates after Seccombe, four for *PL* (Books IV, VI, VIII, and XII), one for *C*, one for *SA*, and one for *On The Late Massacre In Piedmont*, numerous elaborately decorated head- and tailpieces, finely printed on thick paper by "Sanson & Co., Printers, Edinburgh" (bottom of last page), contemporary full crushed brown morocco (occasional slight foxing), delicately gilt-decorated covers with central gilt device, spine lettered in gilt, raised bands with gilt decorations and gilt rules in the panels, inner dentelles finely tooled in gilt, a.e.g. A fine copy in a lovely morocco binding of the period, with striking impressions of the engraved plates (possible first appearance of Seccombe illustrations) and of the decorative head- and tailpieces, printed on thick paper. See undated ca. 1878 edition of Milton's *PW* published by "Ward, Lock, & Co." as "Moxon's Popular Poets" with identification of illustrator on title page as here; a second undated illustrated edition was published by "Ward, Lock, Bowden And Co." ca. 1878 as "Moxon's Popular Poets," which does not identify the illustrator on the title page; see also undated nonillustrated edition published by "Ward, Lock, & Co." ca. 1878—all editions are listed here. Not in Kohler (but see Kohler 368, which dates its copy "[1871]," with title as here, but variant publisher's imprint: "London: E. Moxon, Son, & Company, 1 Amen Corner, Paternoster Row," "460pp. 1/2 title.").

2122. Variant of Preceding, later three-quarter red morocco, red cloth, gilt rules on covers, spine lettered in gilt with delicate gilt trim, thick raised bands, marbled endpapers, t.e.g. A very nice, tall copy with half-title, and with striking impressions of the engraved plates and the decorative head- and tailpieces, printed on thick paper.

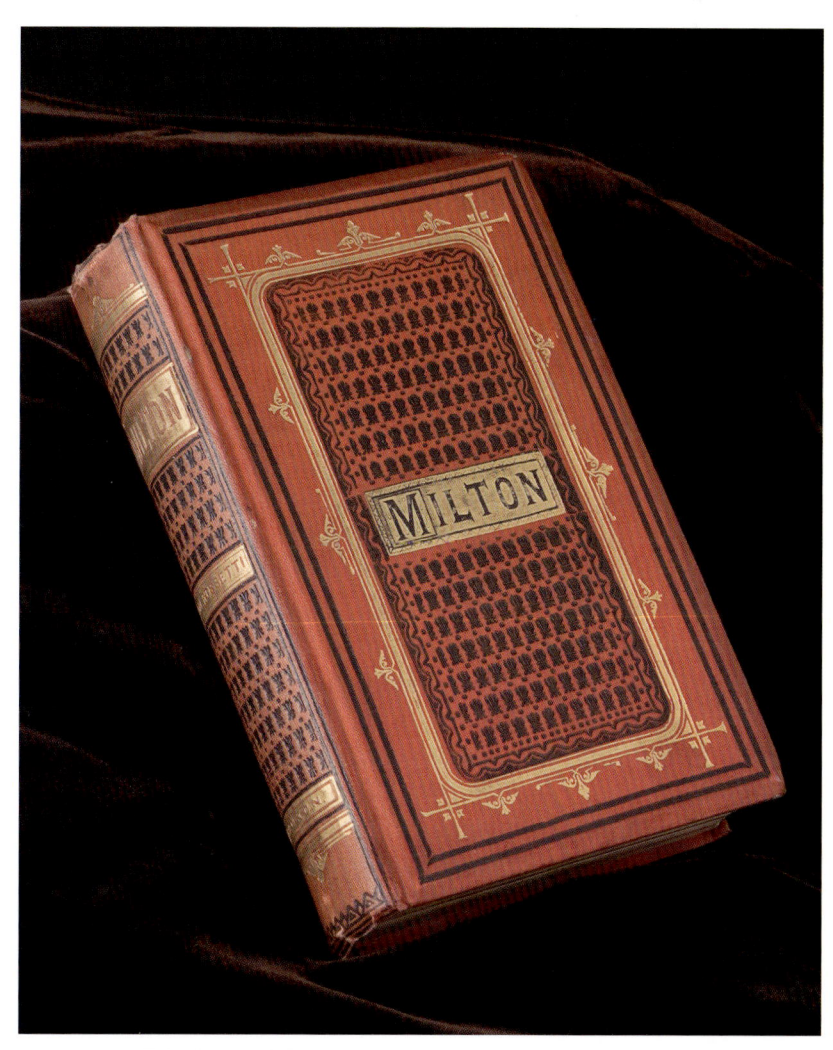

Poetical Works. Edited, With A Critical Memoir, By William Michael Rossetti. Illustrated By Thomas Seccombe. London: E. Moxon, Son. n.d. ca. 1871. Original decorated red cloth, richly decorated in black and gilt. See #2121.

2123. THE POETICAL WORKS OF JOHN MILTON. Edited, With A Critical Memoir, By William Michael Rossetti. Illustrated By Thomas Seccombe. *London: E. Moxon, Son, & Co., Dorset Buildings, Salisbury Square, E. C. n.d. [ca. 1871].* Alternate edition. 8vo, xx+460pp., engraved frontispiece portrait sketch of Milton (age ten), engraved and printed title pages with vignette illustration by Thomas Seccombe for Milton's sonnet *On His Deceased Wife* on engraved title, "London[,] E. Moxon Son & Co. Dover Street" at the bottom, emblem of harp incorporating initials of the press with laurel branches beneath on title page, six additional engraved illustration plates after Seccombe, four for *PL* (Books IV, VI, VIII, and XII), one for *C*, and one for *SA*, numerous elaborately decorated head- and tailpieces, original three-quarter green calf, green cloth (worn, a bit stained), gilt rules on covers, gilt-decorated spine, red morocco label with gilt lettering and gilt rules, raised bands with decorative gilt trim (now rather worn), marbled endpapers and edges, bookseller's ticket. A decent copy of an alternate edition with a different publisher's imprint on title page, with six instead of seven engraved illustration plates by Seccombe, in a smaller octavo format, in a publisher's binding, with contemporary presentation inscription (dated 1879) on front blank, and other later signatures, including the signature of Milton scholar A. E. Barker. Not in Kohler.

2124. Variant of Preceding, original decorated red cloth, front cover richly decorated in black and gilt with black rules around the edge, and a large patterned black design at the center within thick gilt rules surrounded by decorative gilt trim with Milton's name in embossed black letters at the center against a bright gilt background, spine similarly richly decorated in black and gilt with black rules around the edge and decorative trim at the bottom, and with a large patterned black design with decorative gilt trim at the top and bottom, with Milton's name in embossed red letters against a bright gilt background near the top of the patterned black design, W. M. Rossetti's name in embossed smaller red letters against a bright gilt background at the center of the patterned black design, and Moxon's name in embossed smaller red letters against a bright gilt background at the bottom, back cover decorated in embossed blind with the patterned design and Milton's name in the center, brown endpapers, a.e.g. Bound in at the end is an unpaginated thirty-two-page list of books published by Moxon, including "Moxon's Popular Poets. Edited by William Michael Rossetti" (with "Milton's Poetical Works" listed as No. 12, see copy listed here). A fine copy with half-title, with thirty-two pages of advertisements bound in at the end, in a variant publisher's binding, fresh and clean within, virtually mint.

2125. THE POETICAL WORKS OF JOHN MILTON. With Illustrations by E. H. Corbould and John Gilbert. [Quotation from Thomson.] *London: T. Nelson And Sons, Paternoster Row; Edinburgh; And New York. 1872.* 8vo, 528pp., half-title, half-title, engraved and printed title pages, steel-engraved frontispiece illustration (*Adam Naming the Animals*, *PL*, Book VIII), steel-engraved title-page plate, undated, with vignette illustration after T. G. Flowers for Book V of *PL* (*Raphael Counseling Adam and Eve*), elaborate headpiece at top of printed title page (as with 1871 edition listed here by T. Nelson and Sons and different from that in earlier editions by T. Nelson and Sons) with an angelic figure in the center within a circle incorporating the quotation from *PL*: "Brought Death Into The World And All Our Woe," five additional steel-engraved illustration plates (unsigned, but after T. G. Flowers), elaborate headpieces in some instances serving as illustrations for *C*, *L'A*, *IlP*, *Ar*, *L*, *P*, *S*, *Trans*, and *Psm* (as with 1871 edition by T. Nelson and Sons and different from those in earlier editions by T. Nelson and Sons), half-title (undecorated as in earlier editions by T. Nelson and Sons) for *PL*, *PR*, *SA*, *C*, and some of the poems, decorative tailpieces throughout (as with 1871 edition also listed here by T. Nelson and Sons and similar to those in earlier editions by T. Nelson and Sons), original decorated bright blue cloth (slightly rubbed along joints), front cover decorated in delicate black trim with small medallion in gilt at top and at bottom, one with small gilt harp within, the other with gilt initials of the press within, and with Milton's name in the center in embossed blue letters within a rich bright broad gilt band and decorative gilt trim, spine similarly decorated in black trim with Milton's name at the top in embossed blue letters within a rich bright broad gilt band with decorative gilt trim above and below, central medallion in gilt with small gilt harp as on front cover, and "Nelson's Illustrated Poets" at the bottom in embossed blue letters within a rich bright broad gilt band with decorative gilt trim below, back cover decorated in blind, brown endpapers, a.e.g. A fine copy in an attractive bright blue publisher's cloth binding, with plates that are clean and crisp, with contemporary prize inscription (dated 1872) on front blank. The binding was featured with a photograph in *Biblio* 2, no. 7 (July 1997): 53.

Unlike the following copies of this 1872 edition by T. Nelson and Sons, this copy has a half-title (lacking only in the third copy here) and seven (rather than six) illustration plates, with an additional illustration plate for Book IX of *PL*, as with the 1871 edition listed here. While the title page says "With Illustrations by E. H. Corbould and John Gilbert" (as in earlier editions by T. Nelson and Sons in 1864, 1866, 1867, and 1869), the steel-engraved illustration plates here are reproductions of illustrations by T. G. Flowers published in earlier editions by T. Nelson and Sons listed (see 1853, 1855, 1858, 1859, 1860, and 1861 editions). Besides the vignette illustration by T. G. Flowers on the engraved title page of *Raphael Counseling Adam and Eve* for Book V of *PL*, the six additional unsigned steel-engraved illustrations include: *Adam and Eve among the Animals* for Book IV of *PL*; *Naming the Animals* for Book VIII of *PL*; *The Temptation of Eve* for Book IX of *PL*; *The Expulsion* for Book XII of *PL*; *The Baptism of Jesus* for Book I of *PR*; and *The Temptation* for Book III of *PR*. The elaborate headpieces, in some instances serving as illustrations, are unsigned and are the same as in the 1871 edition (see listing). This 1872 edition, like the 1871 and 1874 editions listed, contains a mixture of elements from earlier editions published by T. Nelson and Sons, including reproductions of illustrations by T. Flowers, unsigned headpieces, and half-titles. See 1850 (possible first edition thus) by Nelson also listed here with further editions by Nelson and Sons in the collection cited. Not in Kohler.

2126. Variant of Preceding, with photographic reproductions on thick cards of illustrations by T. G. Flowers (not by "E. H. Corbould and John Gilbert," as stated on the title page), six illustrations rather than seven (without *The Temptation of Eve* for Book IX of *PL*), clean and crisp photographic plates with an overall clarity and sharpness as well as a tinted quality to them clearly delineating the illustration from the remainder of the card, in a variant publisher's cloth binding, original green cloth, decorated identically to the preceding copy in blue cloth. Not in Kohler.

2127. Variant of Preceding, original embossed calf (a bit rubbed at joints and corners, spine a little faded), elaborately embossed covers with Milton's name in gilt at the center of each cover, spine lettered in gilt, raised bands, brown endpapers, a.e.g. An attractive copy in a variant publisher's binding, a fine embossed calf binding, with photographic reproductions of illustrations, as in preceding copy, clean and crisp photographic plates, with a neat presentation inscription on front blank. Not in Kohler.

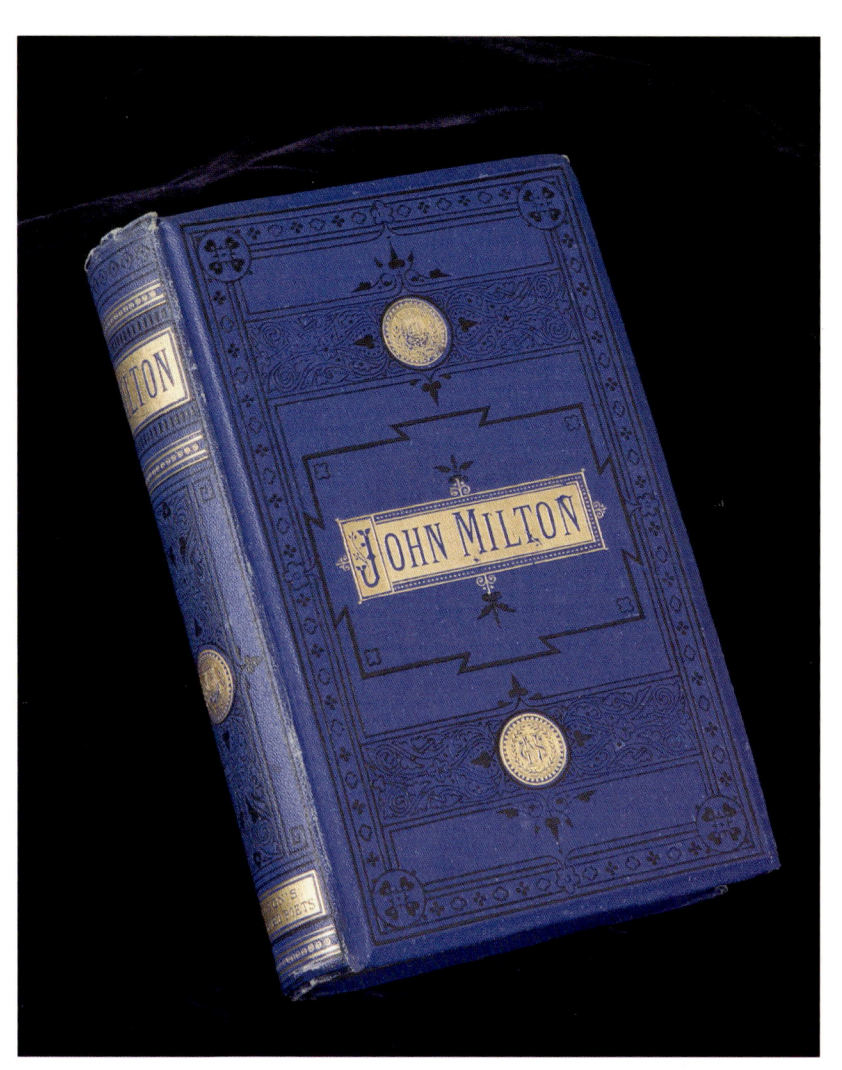

Poetical Works With Illustrations by E. H. Corbould and John Gilbert. London: T. Nelson and Sons, Edinburgh; And New York. 1872. Original decorated bright blue cloth. See #2126.

2128. THE POETICAL WORKS OF JOHN MILTON. *Edinburgh: William P. Nimmo, 1872.* Small 8vo, xxxvii+455+16pp., unsigned engraved frontispiece portrait plate of a middle-aged Milton, protective tissue guard, engraved and printed title pages with vignette illustration of the poet being inspired by heavenly choirs by F. Borders on engraved title plate ("Edinburgh: William P. Nimmo. London: Frederick Warne & Co." n.d.), vignette illustration of a young boy in a setting in nature with a cane laying beside him signed with the initials "WS" at center of printed title, life of Milton by J. M. Ross, eleven illustration plates, most by F. Borders, some unsigned: four for *PL* (Books I, III, VI, XI), two for *PR* (Book I), one for *SA*, two for *C*, one for *L'A*, one for *IlP*, half-title for *PL, PR, SA, C, Arc, MP,* and *Poemata*, black border around text, "Murray And Gibb, Edinburgh, Printers To Her Majesty's Stationery Office" at bottom of last page (p. 455), original green cloth (back cover slightly stained, some foxing), front cover finely decorated in black and gilt, spine similarly decorated in a splendid black and gilt design with gilt lettering, back cover stamped in blind, a.e.g., with small bookseller's ticket. Bound in at the end with its own title page: "Catalogue Of Popular And Standard Books Published By William P. Nimmo, Nimmo, Edinburgh, And Sold By All Booksellers. Edinburgh. 1872," including "Nimmo's Popular Edition Of The Works Of The Poets" "In fcap. 8vo, printed on toned paper, elegantly bound in cloth extra. . . . with a Portrait of the Author . . . and numerous full-page Illustrations" (with *Milton's Poetical Works* as No. VII). A nice copy in a lovely publisher's binding with contemporary signature (dated 1872) in a neat hand on verso of fly-leaf; the only copy of the four here with both engraved and printed title pages. The possible first edition thus by Nimmo was published in 1865, illustrated (also listed here with further Nimmo editions, illustrated and nonillustrated, cited there). Only the 1865 edition has twelve illustrations, the others have eleven (with only one illustration for *L'A* instead of two, as in the 1865 edition). Not in Kohler.

2129. Variant of Preceding, half-title ("Milton's Poetical Works") in color with pastel colors of red and green, with gilt trim, and a large decorated initial letter "P" incorporating the figure of a woman in the same rich colors, original decorated purple cloth (a little worn along extremities, without engraved title page), front cover decorated and lettered in gilt with an embossed image of fallen Satan at the center against black background within circular gilt trim, spine similarly decorated in gilt with Milton's name in embossed blue against a bright broad gilt band at the top, back cover ruled in blind with central emblem in blind, brown endpapers, a.e.g. "Bound By Marcus Ward & Co" with their ticket. Bound in at the end with its own title page dated 1872: sixteen-page "Catalogue Of Popular And Standard Books Published By William P. Nimmo, Edinburgh, And Sold By All Booksellers. Edinburgh. 1872." A nice copy with eleven illustrations as in first copy here, in a lovely variant decorated cloth binding, with half-title in color between frontispiece portrait and printed title page, the only copy of the four here with a half-title for the edition, and this in rich colors with a decorated letter "P." Not in Kohler.

2130. Variant of Preceding, half-title ("Nimmo's Popular Poets") in rich colors with wide border decorated in medieval style with intertwined vines in green, white, gold, and light blue against a red background outlined in black trim, toward the right side "Nimmo's" is lettered in light blue within a half circle above a smaller half circle filled with a gilt harp and a gilt laurel wreath against a red

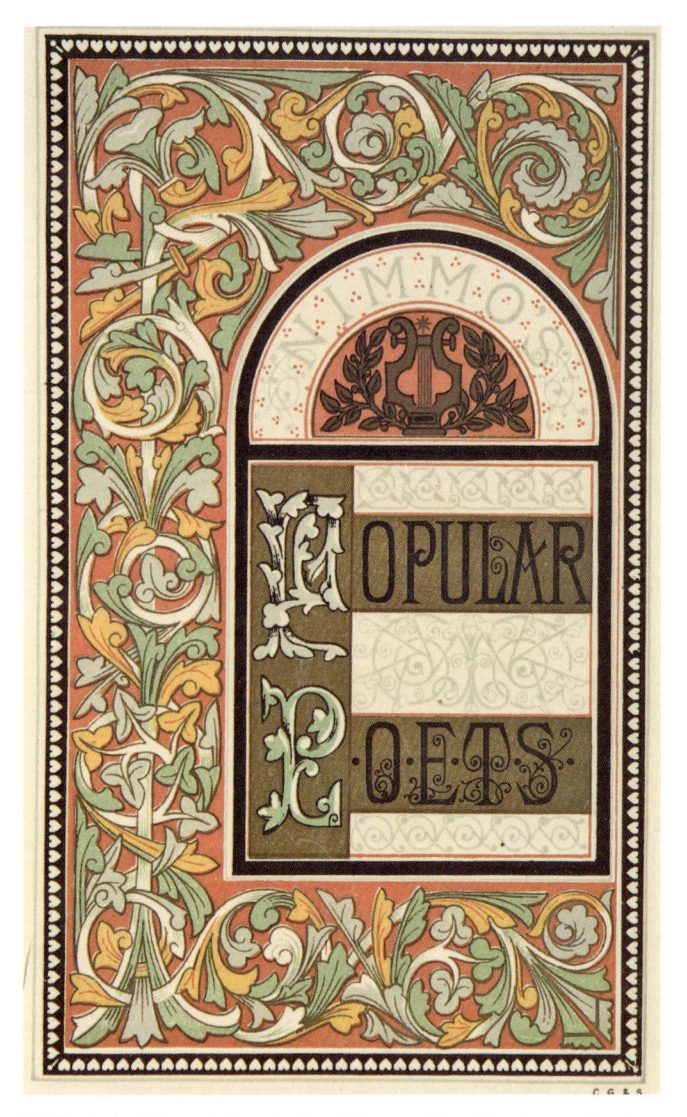

Half-title for "Nimmo's Popular Poets" decorated in rich colors medieval style, for *Poetical Works*. Edinburgh: William P. Nimmo, 1872. See #2130.

background, with "Popular" and "Poets" lettered below in embossed black against horizontal broad gilt bands with the letters "P" in decorated light blue against a vertical broad gilt band, the whole framed in a thick black border, original decorated green cloth (a little worn along joints and corners, spine ends rubbed, without engraved title page), front cover intricately decorated in black trim with gilt borders with a large decorated white curved piece of leather (a bit rubbed) tipped in near the center with Milton's name lettered in embossed gilt within a half circle above a smaller half circle filled with a gilt harp and a gilt laurel wreath against a red background, with "Poetical" and "Works" lettered below in embossed green and black against horizontal broad gilt bands with the letters "P" and "W" in decorated green and red letters against vertical green and red backgrounds, the whole framed in an inner black border and a thicker black outer border, spine decorated in black and gilt trim with Milton's name in embossed gilt letters against a bright gilt band near the top, a gilt harp and gilt laurel wreath each outlined in black at the center, a vignette portrait of Milton in gilt within a gilt border toward the bottom, "WP Nimmo" in embossed gilt letters against a smaller bright gilt band near the bottom, with decorative black trim at the top and bottom, brown endpapers, a.e.g. Despite modest wear, an attractive copy with contemporary signature, in a lovely variant publisher's cloth binding with the cover, half-title, and title page featuring sensational decorative schemes using gilt and decorative color patterning in medieval style, the (presumably) Scottish artist anticipating art nouveau in the decorative styling and patterning with general half-title in color between frontispiece portrait and printed title page, the only copy of the four here to have this scarce general half-title for "Nimmo's Popular Poets" in color, with sixteen pages of advertisements of "A Selection From Catalogue Of Popular and Standard Books Published By William P. Nimmo, Edinburgh" bound in at the end. Not in Kohler.

2131. Variant of Preceding. Contemporary full black morocco (a bit rubbed), covers and spine finely decorated in embossed blind trim, spine lettered in gilt, raised bands, brown endpapers, a.e.g. A very nice copy in an attractive variant divinity style morocco binding, with early signature in a neat hand on front blank, without printed title page, with six illustration plates instead of eleven, as in other copies here: two for *PL* (Books I and VI), one for *SA* (*different* from the one in the other Nimmo editions, unsigned, Samson chained, with a small boy, compared to Samson in battle by Borders), one for *C*, and two for *L'A*, with a different printer identified at bottom of last page ("Ballantyne And Company, Printers, Edinburgh") from that in other copies here, and without the sixteen-page "Catalogue" in the first copy and the sixteen pages of advertisements in the preceding copy. Not in Kohler.

2132. THE POETICAL WORKS OF JOHN MILTON[.] A New Edition, carefully Revised, From The Text Of Thomas Newton, D.D. To Which Is Prefixed A Biographical Notice. With Illustrations By William Harvey. *London: George Routledge And Sons, The Broadway, Ludgate. New York: 416, Broome Street. n.d. [ca. 1872]*. 8vo, xlvi+570pp., frontispiece illustration plate of *Milton Dictating* and seven additional illustration plates after William Harvey, engraved by Dalziel, "A New Edition, carefully Revised" in Gothic font on title page, "London: Savill, Edwards And Co., Printers, Chandos Street, Covent Garden" on verso of title page, original preface by Theodore Alois Buckley dated 1853, "The Life of Milton, Abridged From Bishop Newton," half-title for *PL*, notes at bottom

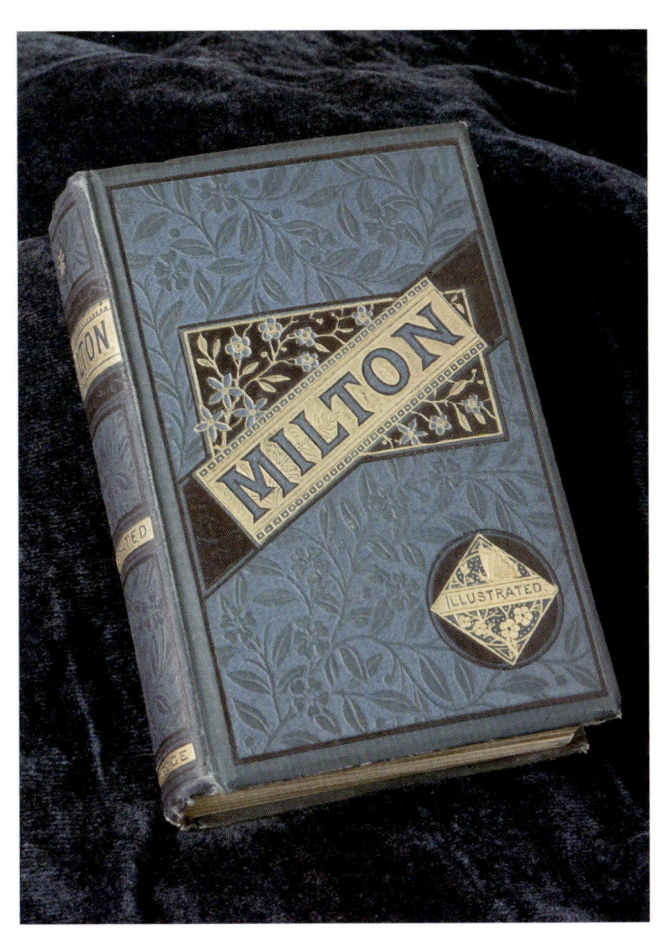

PW. With Illustrations By William Harvey. London: George Routledge and Sons. n.d. [ca. 1878]. Original decorated teal blue cloth. See #2132.

of page, contemporary full crushed maroon morocco (a bit rubbed at joints), covers and spine ruled in black and gilt, spine lettered in gilt, raised bands, inner dentelles finely tooled in gilt, marbled endpapers, a.e.g. A fine copy, handsomely bound. The first edition thus by George Routledge and Co. was published in 1853 (also listed here with further editions by Routledge cited). Uncommon. Not in Kohler (although Kohler 391 [see variant copies listed here] dates its copy "[ca. 1878]," with frontispiece and five plates, without "To Which Is Prefixed A Biographical Notice" on title page and with no mention of the preliminary xlvii pages or thirty-two-page "Life Of Milton, Abridged From Bishop Newton," with "The Broadway, Ludgate; New York: [sic]" in publisher's imprint).

2133. THE POETICAL WORKS OF JOHN MILTON. To Which Is Prefixed A Biography Of The Author, By His Nephew, Edward Philips. *New York: D. Appleton & Company, 549 & 551 Broadway, 1872*. 12mo in 6s, 574pp., six unsigned illustration plates, each with a protective tissue guard, half-title for several of the major poems, "Contents" at the end, original decorated red cloth (a bit rubbed, front cover and spine faded, thereby uniformly darkened, some occasional slight embrowning), front cover richly decorated in embossed black trim in a patterned style with two large triangular designs interconnecting at the center, each with embossed red trim and gilt fill, with Milton's name in large embossed green letters against a bright gilt background in the top triangle and "Illustrated" in large embossed green letters against a bright gilt background in the bottom triangle, with an embossed green floral pattern against a bright gilt circular pattern in between, with two smaller embossed circular patterns, each circled in a black thin line and containing an embossed four-leaf clover in gilt on either side, spine similarly decorated in embossed black and gilt with Milton's name in large embossed green letters against a bright gilt background near the top, "Illustrated" in smaller embossed green letters against a bright gilt background in the middle, and the embossed green floral pattern against a bright gilt circular pattern in oval form at the bottom, a.e.g. A nice, tight copy. Three of the six illustrations, though unsigned, are after Turner: two for *PL* (Books VI and XII), and for *L*; the other three are Turneresque in style: for *PL* (Book II), for *C*, and for *IlP*. See 1859 edition also listed here with further editions by Appleton cited. Not in Kohler.

2134. THE POETICAL WORKS OF JOHN MILTON. A New Edition, carefully Revised, From The Text Of Thomas Newton, D.D. With Illustrations By William Harvey. *Boston: Lee And Shepard, Publishers. New York: Lee, Shepard, And Dillingham. 1872*. First edition thus by Lee, Shepard and Dillingham? 8vo, viii+570pp., frontispiece illustration of *Milton Dictating* with protective tissue guard and other illustrations by William Harvey, "London: Savill, Edwards And Co., Printers, Chandos Street, Covent Garden" on verso of title page, original preface by Buckley (dated 1853) from first Routledge edition, original decorated green cloth, front cover richly decorated in embossed black, red, orange, and gilt with decorative gilt border with Milton's name in large embossed green letters within thick red rules across the top, decorative floral trim in black with blossoms in red with gilt outline on each side, embossed harp within a gilt medallion surrounded by gilt design at the center, and "Illustrated" in embossed green letters within thick red rules across the bottom, spine similarly richly decorated in embossed black and gilt incorporating Milton's name in large embossed red letters against a bright gilt background near the top, back cover decorated in blind, brown endpapers, a.e.g. A fine copy in a well-preserved and striking nineteenth-century American publisher's decorated binding, near mint. Not in Kohler.

The possible second edition by Lee, Shepard and Dillingham was published in 1873 (copy listed), without "London: Savill, Edwards And Co., Printers, Chandos Street, Covent Garden" on verso of title page, as here; the possible third edition in 1876 (copy listed). See 1879 edition by Lee and Shepard, and Dillingham, 2 volumes in one, with several illustrations after Harvey and others. This edition is similar to the editions published by George Routledge and Sons (see undated ca. 1872 editions ealier and ca. 1874 editions later, one copy in a binding almost identical to that here).

2135. Variant of Preceding, original decorated reddish-brown cloth (a bit rubbed, spine chipped at top and bottom, a little shaken within, slight waterstain on frontispiece plate), front cover elaborately decorated in embossed black, orange, blue, and gilt, incorporating harp in orange at center and Milton's name in red at the top and "Illustrated" in red at the bottom, spine similarly elaborately decorated in black and gilt, incorporating Milton's name in blue at the top, back cover decorated in blind, brown endpapers, a.e.g. A nice copy in an attractive variant publisher's decorated cloth binding. Not in Kohler.

2136. THE POETICAL WORKS OF JOHN MILTON. Edited By Sir Egerton Brydges, Bart. [Quotation from Thomson] Illustrated With Engravings, Designed By John Martin And J. W. M. Turner, R.A. [One Also By Westall And One By Romney]. *W. I. Pooley, Harper & Brothers' Building, New York. n.d. [ca. 1872]*. 8vo in 4s, 858pp., frontispiece portrait "Engraved by O. Pelton" of a young, long-haired Milton "From a Miniature of the same size by Faithorne. Anno 1667, in the possession of William Falconer Esq.," protective tissue guard, engraved and printed title pages, reprinting of the original 1835 dedication page "To William Wordsworth And Robert Southey," "Advertisement To The Original Edition" dated 1835, "Life Of Milton," six engraved illustration plates, each with protective tissue guard: two engraved illustration plates after Martin for *PL* (Books VII and X), two engraved illustration plates after Turner—one for *PR* (*The Temptation on the Mountain*, Book III) and one for *C* (as vignette on engraved title page), one engraved illustration plate after Westall for *PL* (*Satan*, Book IV), and one engraved illustration plate after Romney (*Milton Dictating to His Daughters*), engraved by D. L. Glover, for *On His Blindness* (bound here before "Life of Milton"), introductory remarks from the James Boyd edition for each book of *PL*, notes at bottom of page, double black border around text, original dark brown leather (rubbed along joints and extremities), covers elaborately decorated in thick blind relief with Milton's name in gilt at the center, spine lettered in gilt, raised bands decorated in blind relief (rubbed), small emblems in blind within the panels, broad inner dentelles finely tooled in gilt, marbled endpapers, a.e.g. A nice copy in an attractive American binding of the period, with contemporary date ("1874") on front blank, and with contemporary presentation stamped in gilt on front cover: "Mrs. John A. Riley from F. C. D. June 25th 1875." This is an undated reprint of the possible first edition thus by W. I. Pooley dated 1868, an edition as here in an identical binding, except for the date and without the addition of "Harper & Brothers' Building" added to publisher's imprint; see, too 1869 edition (possible second edition thus) by W. I. Pooley. See 1854 edition by Phillips, Sampson, and Company (possible first edition thus) also listed here with further editions cited. Uncommon. Not in Kohler.

2137. THE POETICAL WORKS OF JOHN MILTON. With A Memoir, And Critical Remarks On His Genius And Writings. By James Montgomery; [Vol. I. / Vol. II.] *New York: Leavitt & Allen Bros., No. 8 Howard Street. n.d. [ca. 1872].* 2 volumes in one. 8vo, xlix+[i]+[3]+400pp. (pagination number beginning with page number "18"), +368pp.(continuous pagination), engraved frontispiece portrait plate after C. Burt, protective tissue guard, illustrations (unsigned, but after Harvey) within the text for *L'A* with a vignette illustration at the beginning and another vignette illustration at the end of the poem and with vignette illustrations in the margins, half-title for each book of *PL*, a second undated title page followed by "Contents Of Vol. II" before *PR* and the remaining poems, half-title for each book of *PR* and for some of the poems, original decorated blue cloth (lightly rubbed along joints), front cover decorated in black and gilt with a small figure of a woman's head with laurel wreath in bright gilt in lower right corner, brilliant decorative gilt device at the center incorporating Milton's name in orange relief with the letter "M" in red and a larger size with bright gilt trim above and below, spine similarly decorated in black and gilt with bright gilt piece at the center incorporating Milton's name in blue relief, back cover decorated in blind, a.e.g. A fine copy in near mint condition with contemporary signature presentation inscription in pencil (dated "Christmas 1872") on front blank. The possible first edition thus was published by Leavitt & Allen in 1858 (also listed here with further editions by Leavitt & Allen cited). Not in Kohler, but Kohler 345 dates its copy "[ca. 1860]," with a "Frontispiece engraved by A. H. Ritchie," rather than by C. Burt as here, and without any reference to illustrations.

2138. Variant of Preceding, original red cloth (a bit rubbed, spine repaired), front cover decorated in black with Milton's name in embossed red against a black backdrop near the top, central emblem in blind on back cover, spine lettered in gilt with decorative black trim and with a gilt orb with the gilt lettering "The World Edition." A good copy in a variant publisher's binding (similar to one on a copy of the ca. 1870 Leavitt & Allen Bros. editions listed here), with early bookseller's label on front pastedown, and with contemporary presentation inscription (dated "December 25th 1875") on verso of frontispiece portrait. Not in Kohler.

2139. THE POETICAL WORKS OF JOHN MILTON. With Introductory Memoir[,] Notes, Bibliography[,] *Etc. London[:] Frederick Warne And Co. And New York[.] n.d. [ca. 1872].* 8vo, 607+[1]pp., central crescent on title page consisting of small laurel wings with a horseshoe at the center, half-title for *Samson Agonistes*, "Bibliography" at the end, "Printed By Morrison And Gibb Limited, Edinburgh" at bottom of last page, original light blue silk (a bit rubbed, slightly dirtied and a little worn at the top, final page age-browned), front cover decorated in a floral motif in bronze and white and yellow with gilt lettering at the center, spine similarly decorated in a floral motif in bronze and white and yellow with gilt lettering at the center, yellow endpapers. A decent copy in an interesting binding of the period with contemporary date, "Feb 21st, 1874," penciled on flyleaf. See other undated and dated illustrated and non-illustrated editions by Frederick Warne and Co. published in the 1870s, 1880s, and 1890s under the various series: "The 'Lansdowne' Poets," "The 'Arundel' Poets," "The 'Chandos' Poets," "The 'Imperial' Poets, "The 'Chandos' Classics," "The 'Albion' Edition," and the "Cabinet Poets." Not in Kohler.

2140. THE POETICAL WORKS OF JOHN MILTON. Reprinted From The Chandos Poets, With Memoir, Explanatory Notes. The "Chandos Classics." *London: Frederick Warne And Co., Bedford Street, Covent Garden. New York: Scribner, Welford And Armstrong. n.d. [ca. 1873].* 8vo, xxiv+581pp., frontispiece illustration plate after an engraving by Dalziel for "Ad Eandem"—the illustration titled *Milton Meeting Leonora Baroni at Cardinal Barberini's House*, protective tissue guard, small circular printer's device with lettering "F. Warne & Co. Bedford St. Covent Garden" on title page, "Woodfall And Kinder, Printers, Milford Lane, Strand, W.C." on verso of title page, seven additional illustration plates after engravings by Dalziel: four for *PL* (Books I, IV, VIII, and XII), one for *SA*, one for *On His Deceased Wife*, and one for *L'A*, half-title for *SA*, notes at bottom of page, original blue cloth (a bit used, spine ends slightly chipped, edges of front blank and frontispiece and title page frayed), front cover brilliantly decorated in gilt and black trim with gilt forming what looks like an "H" incorporating Milton's name in embossed blue in the crosspiece with a harp in gilt against a black backdrop at the bottom and a decorative gilt piece with black trim at the top, spine similarly decorated in bright gilt and black with harp in gilt against a black backdrop at the center beneath a bright gilt band incorporating Milton's name in embossed blue near the top, gilt rules with gilt blossoms at top and bottom, "F. Warne & Co." in embossed blue letters within a bright small gilt band at the bottom, back cover decorated in blind, blue endpapers, a.e.g. A decent copy of an interesting publisher's decorated cloth binding, with contemporary name and date ("Christmas 1873") neatly written on verso of frontispiece.

This type of book with its fine binding was published as a gift book during the late 1800s when reading was a major source of entertainment often in family or social settings around an evening fireplace. Such books were considered expensive and cultured gifts with which to entertain company and adorn the parlor bookshelf. This particular book was just such a gift with the recipient's name dated Christmas, 1873, in the front. A nice piece of literary history that also makes a nice copy of Milton's poems. For variants of this attractive Victorian publisher's cloth binding, similarly decorated and in very nice condition, see copy of ca. 1880 London Frederick Warne and Co. edition in decorated red cloth and copy of ca. 1880 New York Scribner, Welford and Armstrong edition in decorated blue cloth listed here, the latter with "Scribner & Co." at the bottom of the spine. Not in Kohler.

2141. THE POETICAL WORKS OF JOHN MILTON. With A Memoir, And Critical Remarks On His Genius And Writings. By James Montgomery; Vol. I. / Vol. II. *New York: Leavitt & Allen Bros., No. 8 Howard Street. n.d. [ca. 1873].* 2 volumes in one. 8vo, xlix+[i]+[3]+400pp.(page numbering beginning with number "18"),+368pp.(page numbering beginning with number "10"), engraved frontispiece portrait plate after C. Burt (foxed), protective tissue guard, engraved illustration plate of *Milton Dictating to His Daughters* after George Romney before "Memoir," with protective tissue guard (foxed), volume 1, second title page for volume 2 followed by "Contents Of Vol. II," three engraved illustration plates for *PL* (*Moloch*, unsigned, for Book II; *Murmuring waters fall . . .* , unsigned, for Book IV; *Death* engraved by Sartain after Jones, for Book X), an engraved illustration plate for *PR* (*The Fall of Jerusalem*, after Martin, inserted here in Book III), an engraved illustration plate (*Our Saviour* engraved by Burt after Delaroch) at the head of the section entitled "Odes," which begins with *On The Morning Of Christ's Nativity*, each engraved illustration plate with a protective tissue guard, illustrations (unsigned, but after Harvey) within the text for *L'A* with a vignette illustration at the beginning and another vignette illustration at the end of the poem and with vignette illustrations in the margins, half-title for each book of *PL* and *PR* and for some of the poems, double black border around text, contemporary full brown leather over thick boards (a little rubbed along joints and extremities), covers elaborately tooled in blind with Milton's name in gilt at the center of each cover, spine lettered in gilt and decorated in blind with small decorative piece in blind within the panels, marbled endpapers, a.e.g. A very nice copy, clean within, in a fine embossed binding of the period, with a contemporary presentation inscription in a rather elaborate hand (dated 1873) on front blank. The possible first edition thus by Leavitt & Allen was published in 1858 (also listed here with further editions cited). Not in Kohler (but see Kohler 345).

2142. Variant of Preceding, contemporary purple cloth, (a bit rubbed, spine faded, some foxing to plates and protective tissues guards), front cover decorated in embossed black with "Milton" lettered sideways at the center in embossed purple against a bright gilt background, with "The Works of" and "Illustrated" lettered sideways in embossed red against a black background above and below, back cover decorated in embossed blind trim, spine decorated in embossed black and gilt trim with "Milton" lettered in embossed purple against a bright gilt background occupying almost the entire spine, a.e.g. A very good copy with variant illustrations among those for *PL* (unidentified illustration of a boy with a fishing pole by a stream after H. Inman placed within Book II, *Moloch*, unsigned, placed within Book III, *The Fall of Troy* after Jones placed within Book VI), in a variant publisher's binding, with a contemporary signature (dated "Dec. 25th 1873") on front blank.

2143. Variant of Preceding, in a publisher's binding identical to preceding, very bright and solid, fresh and clean within, with variant illustrations among those for PL (illustration of *The Sea* after J. Wilson engraved by Welch & Walker placed within Book II, illustration of *The Soldier's Death Bed* after J. Wilson engraved by Welch & Walker placed within Book IV, illustration of *Death* after Jones engraved by Sartain placed within Book X).

2144. THE POETICAL WORKS OF JOHN MILTON. A New Edition, carefully Revised, From The Text Of Thomas Newton, D.D. With Illustrations By William Harvey. *Boston: Lee And Shepard, Publishers. New York: Lee, Shepard, And Dillingham. 1873.* Second edition thus by Lee, Shepard and Dillingham? 8vo, viii+570pp., frontispiece illustration of *Milton Dictating* with protective tissue guard, and other illustrations by William Harvey, original preface by Buckley (dated 1853) from first Routledge edition, original decorated blue cloth (a bit rubbed, spine ends slightly chipped, pages very age-browned), front cover richly decorated in embossed black and gilt with Milton's name in large embossed black letters within a broad gilt band across the top with a larger embossed capital letter "M" in gilt against a blue background, decorative floral trim in embossed blue within a broad gilt band along the side with a harp in embossed blue at the center and a small vase in embossed blue at the bottom, with "Illustrated" in embossed blue letters within a narrow bright gilt banner across the bottom, a small embossed shield in gilt at the center within black and gilt circular bands and decorative floral trim in gilt, all within a thick embossed black band surrounding a narrow inner gilt band, spine similarly richly decorated in embossed black and gilt, with Milton's name in embossed blue letters within a bright wide gilt band with decorative gilt trim near the top, "Illustrated" lettered in embossed blue letters within a bright embossed gilt band curved across the center, with an oil lamp in gilt surrounded by floral trim on either side in gilt directly above, "Lee & Shepard" lettered in embossed blue letters within a bright narrow embossed gilt band toward the bottom, the whole over an elliptical embossed thick gilt band with decorative gilt trim within and a thick outer black band running the length of the spine, with decorative embossed black and gilt trim at the top and bottom, back cover decorated in blind, brown endpapers, a.e.g. A good copy in an attractive publisher's decorated cloth binding, with stamp of same family name on title page and top of first page of text. Not in Kohler.

The possible first edition thus by Lee, Shepard and Dillingham was published in 1872 (also listed here with further editions cited), with "London: Savill, Edwards And Co., Printers, Chandos Street, Covent Garden" on verso of title page, which does not appear here. This edition is similar to the editions published by George Routledge and Sons (see 1853 first edition also listed here with further Routledge editions cited including undated ca. 1872 and ca. 1874 editions).

2145. THE POETICAL WORKS OF JOHN MILTON. Printed From The Original Editions With A Life Of The Author By The Rev. John Mitford[.] In Two Volumes[.] *London[:] Bickers And Son 1 Leicester Square W. n.d. [ca. 1873]*. 2 volumes. 8vo, ccii+270pp.,+ix+417pp., half-title each volume with decorative headpiece, frontiespiece portrait "Engraved by W. Humphreys, from a Print by Faithorne," volume 1, title pages in red and black, each with circular emblem of the press at the center, "Advertisement To The [Pickering] Edition Of 1851," folding genealogical table (as a multiple foldout), life of Milton, and facsimile of "the Agreement between Milton and Mr. Symons" folding (sideways) before appendix, with sketch of "The House at Chalfont St. Giles" bound before addenda, volume 1, decorative head- and tailpieces, decorated initial letters, half-title for some of the poems, handsomely "Printed By Whittingham And Wilkins, Tooks Court, Chancery Lane, Chiswick Press" with inverted triangular piece on last page of each volume, contemporary full vellum, gilt rules on covers, elaborately gilt-decorated spines, red morocco title labels, green morocco numbering labels (a bit faded), inner dentelles finely tooled in gilt, marbled endpapers, a.e.g., early bookplate on front pastedown. A very attractive set, handsomely printed by the Chiswick Press and very handsomely bound in full vellum by Mansell, with his stamp. Similar to the 1851 Pickering edition (see set listed here), and as with that edition, volume 1 contains *SA* and the *MP*, along with the preliminary material, while volume 2 contains *PL* and *PR*. Williamson 84; Kohler 373, dating its set "[ca. 1873]" and reporting "Not in the British Library. Not in the Bodleian Library. Not in Cambridge University Library."

2146. Variant of Preceding, contemporary full polished maroon morocco, gilt rules on covers with central gilt seal, gilt-decorated spines repeating in a smaller version the gilt seal on front covers, brown leather labels with gilt lettering and decorative gilt trim, raised bands with gilt rules, inner dentelles ruled in blind, outer dentelles ruled in gilt, marbled endpapers and edges. A very handsome set in a lovely Prize Binding, with prize citation (dated 1889) tipped in on front pastedown. Unlike the preceding copy, the frontispiece portrait in volume 1 of this set consists of an early photograph of the Vertue portrait engraved by W. H. Gardner tipped in. Kohler 373.

Extra-Illustrated

2147. Variant of Preceding. THE POETICAL WORKS OF JOHN MILTON. Printed From The Original Editions With A Life Of The Author By The Rev. John Mitford[.] In Two Volumes[.] *London[:] Bickers And Son 1 Leicester Square W. n.d. [ca. 1873]*. 2 volumes. 8vo, ccii+ 270pp.,+ix+ 417pp., half-title each volume with decorative headpiece, frontiespiece portrait of an early photograph of the Vertue portrait engraved by W. H. Gardner tipped in, volume 1, title pages in red and black, each with circular emblem of the press at the center, life, sketch of "The House at Chalfont St. Giles" bound before addenda, volume 1, decorative head- and tailpieces, decorated initial letters, half-title for some of the poems, handsomely "Printed By Whittingham And Wilkins, Tooks Court, Chancery Lane, Chiswick Press" with inverted triangular piece on last page of each volume, contemporary full polished calf (bound without the "Advertisement To The [Pickering] Edition Of 1851" and the facsimile of "the

Agreement between Milton and Mr. Symons" before addenda), gilt rules on covers, elaborately gilt-decorated spines in the panels, maroon title labels, blue morocco numbering labels, inner dentelles tooled in blind, outer dentelles tooled in gilt, marbled endpapers, a.e.g. A very fine set, beautifully bound in an extremely attractive and well-preserved polished calf binding, very fresh and clean internally. While not published as an illustrated edition, this set is extra-illustrated, having bound into it numerous early photographs of illustrations (by Westall and others, all unsigned), each photograph-illustration with book and poetic passage printed below tipped in on thick paper.

2148. THE POETICAL WORKS OF JOHN MILTON. With Illustrations by E. H. Corbould and John Gilbert. [Quotation from Thomson] *London: T. Nelson And Sons, Paternoster Row; Edinburgh; And New York. 1874.* 8vo, 528pp., photographic reproduction of an illustration for Book VIII of *PL*; (*Naming the Animals*, unsigned, possibly after T. G. Flowers) as frontispiece, photographic reproduction of a T. Nelson and Sons title-page plate, undated, with vignette illustration after T. G. Flowers for Book V of *PL* (*Raphael Counseling Adam and Eve*), elaborate headpiece at top of title page (same as that in 1871 and 1872 editions by T. Nelson and Sons also listed here) with an angelic figure in the center within a circle incorporating the quotation from *PL*: "Brought Death Into The World And All Our Woe," decorative headpiece (same as that in 1871 and 1872 editions by T. Nelson and Sons also listed here) at the beginning of "Life Of Milton," four additional photographic reproduction illustration plates (unsigned, but reproductions of illustrations by T. G. Flowers), each with a protective tissue guard, elaborate headpieces (same as those in 1871 and 1872 editions by T. Nelson and Sons also listed here), in some instances serving as illustrations, elaborate decorative headpieces (same as those in 1871 and 1872 editions by T. Nelson and Sons) for *C*, *L'A*, *IlP*, *Ar*, *L*, *P*, *S*, *Trans*, and *Psm*, half-title (undecorated as in earlier editions by T. Nelson and Sons) for *PL*, *PR*, *SA*, *C*, and some of the poems, decorative tailpieces throughout (similar to those in earlier editions by T. Nelson and Sons), contemporary shellacked bevelled wooden boards with the photographic image of a leaf pattern glazed over on each cover, the leaf pattern different for the front and the back boards (occasional foxing), joints reinforced within, gilt-decorated green morocco spine with small gilt pieces in the panels, gilt lettering, raised bands with decorative gilt trim (spine a bit rubbed), inner dentelles finely tooled in gilt, a.e.g., with a contemporary presentation inscription in a neat but somewhat elaborate hand (dated 1876) on fly-leaf. A fine copy with clean and crisp photographic plates, in an unusual Victorian binding, which appears to be the result of a silver printing-out process on thick wooden boards, with the photographic image captured on each cover being that of a simple, elegant silhouette of a leaf pattern—a similar binding to that of the 1872 edition by T. Nelson and Sons also listed here where the photographic image captured of a leaf pattern is likewise different for the front and the back boards.

While the title page says "With Illustrations by E. H. Corbould and John Gilbert" (as in the editions by T. Nelson and Sons published in 1864, 1866, 1867, and 1869—see copies listed), the illustration plates here are photographic reproductions of illustrations by T. G. Flowers published in earlier editions by T. Nelson and Sons (see 1853, 1855, 1858, 1859, 1860, 1861, and 1862 editions listed). Besides the photographic reproduction of the vignette illustration by T. G. Flowers on title-page plate of *Raphael Counseling Adam and Eve* for Book V of *PL*, and the photographic reproduction of an illustration for Book VIII of *PL*; (*Naming the Animals*, unsigned, but possibly by T. G. Flowers) as the frontispiece, the four additional photographic reproductions of illustrations (unsigned, but possibly by T. G. Flowers) include: *Adam and Eve among the Animals* for Book IV of *PL*; *The Expulsion* for Book XII of *PL*, *The Baptism of Jesus* for Book I of *PR*; and *The Temptation of Eve* for Book III of *PR*. The elaborate headpieces, in some instances serving as illustrations, are unsigned (perhaps by Corbould and Gilbert), and are the same as in the 1871 edition also listed here (new with that edition, see listing there). See 1850 (possible first edition) by Nelson listed here with further editions by Nelson and Sons in the collection cited there. Not in Kohler.

2149. THE POETICAL WORKS OF JOHN MILTON. William P. Nimmo. *London: 14 King William Street, Strand, And Edinburgh. 1874.* 8vo, xxxvii+[1]+440+16pp., unsigned engraved frontispiece portrait plate of a middle-aged Milton, half-title in rich colors ("Nimmo's Popular Poets") with wide border decorated medieval style with intertwined vines in green, white, gold, and light blue against a red background outlined in black trim, toward the right side "Nimmo's" is lettered in light blue within a half circle above a smaller half circle filled with a gilt harp and a gilt laurel wreath against a red background, with "Popular" and "Poets" lettered below in embossed black against horizontal broad gilt bands with the letters "P" in decorated light blue against a vertical broad gilt band, the whole framed in a thick black border, engraved and printed title pages, with vignette illustration (of the poet being inspired by heavenly choirs) by F. Borders on engraved title page ("William P. Nimmo. London And Edinburgh." n.d.), vignette illustration (of a young boy in a setting in nature with a cane laying beside him) signed with the initials "WS" on printed title, eleven illustration plates, most after F. Borders, some unsigned, life of Milton by J. M. Ross, eleven illustration plates, most after F. Borders, some unsigned: four for *PL* (Books I, III, VI, XI), two for *PR* (Book I), one for *SA*, two for *C*, one for *L'A*, one for *IlP*, half-title for *PL*, *PR*, *SA*, *C*, *Arc*, *MP*, and *Poemata*, black border around text, "Edinburgh: Printed By John Greig And Son" printed at bottom of last page, original decorated red cloth (worn, covers detached, pages age-browned), front cover intricately decorated in black trim with gilt borders with a large decorated white curved piece of leather tipped in near the center with "Milton's" name lettered in embossed gilt within the half circle above a smaller half circle filled with a gilt harp and a gilt laurel wreath against a red background, with "Poetical" and "Works" lettered below in embossed green and black letters against horizontal broad gilt bands with the letters "P" and "W" in decorated green and red letters against vertical green and red backgrounds, the whole framed in an inner black border and a thicker black outer border, spine decorated in black and gilt trim with Milton's name in embossed gilt letters against a bright gilt band near the top, a gilt harp outlined in black and a gilt laurel wreath at the center, a vignette illustration of a gilt figure holding lyre and staff within a circular gilt border toward the bottom, "WP Nimmo" in embossed blue letters within a bright gilt band near the bottom, and decorative black trim at the top and bottom, brown endpapers, a.e.g. Sixteen numbered pages of "A Selection From Catalogue Of Popular and Standard Books Published By William P. Nimmo, Edinburgh" bound in at end. Despite the wear, a decent copy with the cover, half-title, and title page featuring sensational decorative schemes using gilt and decorative color patterning in medieval style; the (presumably) Scottish artist anticipating art nouveau in the decorative styling and patterning. The possible first edition thus by Nimmo was published in 1865, illustrated (also listed here with further Nimmo editions cited). Only the 1865 edition has twelve illustrations, the others have eleven (with only one illustration for *L'A* instead of two, as in the 1865 edition). Not in Kohler.

2150. THE POETICAL WORKS OF JOHN MILTON. A New Edition, carefully Revised, From The Text Of Thomas Newton, D.D. With Illustrations By William Harvey. *London: George Routledge And Sons, The Broadway, Ludgate. New York: 416, Broome Street. n.d. [ca. 1874].* Small 8vo, viii+570pp. (illustration plates unpaginated), frontispiece portrait plate of *Milton Dictating to his Daughters*, engraved by Dalziel, protective tissue guard, black rule on title page with "A New Edition, carefully Revised" in Gothic font, "London: Savill, Edwards And Co., Printers, Chandos Street, Covent Garden" on verso of title page, original preface by Theodore Alois Buckley dated 1853, seven illustration plates engraved by Dalziel after William Harvey, notes at bottom of page, original decorated green cloth (a little rubbed), front cover richly decorated in embossed black and gilt with thick gilt borders incorporating Milton's name in large letters across the top, decorative floral trim and harp in embossed green on left side, initials of the publisher, "GR&S," within a gilt medallion surrounded by black and gilt at the center, and "Illustrated" in embossed green letters across the bottom, spine similarly richly decorated in embossed black and gilt incorporating Milton's name, "Illustrated," and "Routledge," back cover decorated in blind, brown endpapers, a.e.g. A nice copy in a lovely decorated Victorian publisher's cloth binding. The first edition thus by George Routledge and Co. was published in 1853 (also listed here with further editions by Routledge cited). Not in Kohler.

2151. Variant of Preceding, original decorated green cloth (a bit rubbed, a little shaken from within), front cover richly decorated in embossed black, red, orange, and gilt with decorative gilt border, with Milton's name in large embossed green letters within thick red rules across the top, decorative floral trim in black with blossoms in red with gilt outline on each side, embossed initials of the publisher, "GR&S," within a gilt medallion surrounded by gilt design at the center, and "Illustrated" in embossed green letters within thick red rules across the bottom, spine similarly richly decorated in embossed black and gilt incorporating Milton's name in large embossed red letters against a bright gilt background near the top, and "Illustrated" and "Routledge" in smaller embossed green letters at the middle and the bottom, back cover decorated in blind, brown endpapers, a.e.g. A nice copy in a lovely variant decorated publisher's cloth binding, with early inscription on fly-leaf. Not in Kohler.

2152. THE POETICAL WORKS OF JOHN MILTON[.] A New Edition, Carefully Revised From The Text Of Thomas Newton, D.D. With Illustrations By William Harvey[.] *London[:] George Routledge And Sons[,] The Broadway, Ludgate[;] New York: 416 Broome Street. n.d. [ca. 1874].* Variant edition. Slightly larger 8vo, viii+570pp., frontispiece illustration plate of Satan cast out of Heaven, protective tissue guard, and five additional illustration plates engraved by Dalziel after Harvey, "A New Edition, Carefully Revised From The Text Of Thomas Newton" in a clear, non-Gothic font on title page, "London: Savill, Edwards And Co., Printers, Chandos Street, Covent

Garden" on verso of title page, original preface by Theodore Alois Buckley dated 1853, notes at bottom of page, original decorated reddish-brown cloth (a bit rubbed, spine ends slightly chipped), covers and spine elaborately decorated in black and gilt with large gilt emblem at center of front cover, Milton's name in large letters above, and "Illustrated" in smaller letters beneath, back cover decorated in blind with central emblem in blind, spine similarly elaborately decorated in black and gilt with a large hawk with outspread wings at the top, Milton's name lettered beneath, "Illustrated" incorporated in the decorative design at the center, and "Routledge" at the bottom, a.e.g. A very nice copy in an attractive publisher's binding, with contemporary inscription by "Mary H. Blickensdufer" dated "Christmas 1874," on front pastedown. Variant edition from the preceding undated ca. 1874 edition by Routledge and Sons, in a slightly larger 8vo format, with a different frontispiece illustration, with variations on title page (including "Carefully Revised From The Text Of Thomas Newton" in a clear, non-Gothic font, and other minor variations), without a life of Milton, and without half-title for *PL*. The first edition thus by George Routledge and Co. was published in 1853 (also listed here with further editions by Routledge cited). Not in Kohler.

The collection also has a copy in an attractive variant decorated publisher's blue cloth binding, and a copy in an attractive variant decorated publisher's green cloth binding, both decorated as preceding binding.

2153. THE POETICAL WORKS OF JOHN MILTON: Edited, With Introductions, Notes, And An Essay On Milton's English, By David Masson, M.A., L.L.D., Professor Of Rhetoric And English Literature In The University Of Edinburgh. *London: Macmillan And Co. 1874. [All Rights reserved.]* 3 volumes. First edition thus. 8vo, cxxxii+[4]+456pp.,+viii+488pp.,+viii+555pp., unsigned frontispiece vignette portrait of Milton, age sixty-two, with "London Published by Macmillan & Co. 1874" printed at the bottom and four double-sided facsimiles, volume 1, protective tissue guard, preface written for this edition, unsigned frontispiece vignette portrait of Milton, age twenty-one, with "London Published by Macmillan & Co. 1874" printed at the bottom, volume 2, protective tissue guard, half-title for some of the poems, frontispiece vignette portrait of "Milton, Aetat. 10," "Engraved by Edwd. Radclyffe" "After a Photograph from the original picture, in the possession of Edgar Disney, Esqr., of the Hyde, Ingatestone, Essex" with "London Published by Macmillan & Co. 1874" printed at the bottom, volume 3, protective tissue guard, half-title for some of the sections, with "Notes" to the poems in the latter half of volume 3, "London: R. Clay, Sons, And Taylor, Printers, Bread Street Hill" printed at the bottom of the last page in each volume, original green linen texture cloth, decorative gilt border trim on front covers, with central vignette impression in gilt of the portrait of Milton after Faithorne, back covers stamped in blind, spines lettered in gilt with decorative gilt trim at top and bottom, edges untrimmed. A very fine set, "Bound By Burn & Co." with their ticket. The standard late Victorian annotated text of Milton's verse. Kohler 374.

Masson was a leading nineteenth-century Miltonist; he also edited Oliver Goldsmith and Thomas DeQuincey and wrote on the Romantics, and was a friend of Thomas and Jane Carlyle, William Makepeace Thackeray, and other leading literary figures of the period. A revised edition in a three-volume smaller octavo format (the first thus) was published in 1882; the second edition thus, enlarged, was published in 1890—both sets listed here. A relatively scarce set. Stevens 206, "Re-edited in 1890 [see set listed here]; text corrected, poems put in chronological order, and a memoir added at that time [actually added to the revision in 1882, see set also listed here, and quotation there from preface]."

2154. THE POETICAL WORKS OF JOHN MILTON: With Introductions And Notes By David Masson, M.A., LL.D., Professor Of Rhetoric And English Literature In The University Of Edinburgh. *London: Macmillan And Co. 1874. [The Right of Translation and Reproduction is reserved.]* 2 volumes. First edition thus. 8vo (Sometimes called "Dumpy 8vo," measuring 6 7/16" × 4 5/8"), lxxix+380pp.,+viii+480pp., half-title with "Golden Treasury Series" emblem on verso each volume, unsigned vignette portrait of Milton at age sixty-two on title page, volume 1, protective tissue guard, preface written for this edition dated "September 1874," "Memoir of Milton," "Introduction to Paradise Lost" with several charts, including one of the Ptolemaic universe, half-title for *PL* and "Notes to Paradise Lost" at end of volume 1, unsigned vignette portrait of Milton at age twenty-one on title page, volume 2, protective tissue guard, "Introduction to Paradise Regained," half-title for some of the poems, "Notes to the Minor Poems" at the end of volume 2, "R. Clay, Sons, And Taylor, Printers, Bread Street Hill" printed at the bottom of the last page in volume 2, original green linen texture cloth, decorative gilt border rules on front covers, with small central vignette impression in gilt of the head of Milton within a decorative circular gilt device, spines lettered in gilt with decorative thick gilt trim at top and bottom, edges untrimmed. A fine set in well-preserved condition, very clean and bright throughout, "Bound By Burn & Co." with their ticket. Having been printed in a limited edition, this attractive set is now rather scarce. Stevens 208; Kohler 375.

These attractive volumes in the Golden Treasury series were issued simultaneously with Masson's larger Cambridge Edition (preceding set), but with specially adapted introductions and notes, and also a specially written memoir. "The Text of the Poems in this edition will, it is hoped, be found very accurate, having been carefully prepared by the Editor for the larger Edition, called 'The Cambridge Edition,' which appears at the same time. The Introduction and Notes are an adaptation to the Golden Treasury size of the more extensive and minute editorial matter of the larger Edition. The prefixed Memoir has been written for the present Edition, with a view to make it, as one of the books of the Golden Treasury series, independently complete" (Preface).

2155. THE POETICAL WORKS OF JOHN MILTON. With A Memoir. Vol. I/II/III. *Boston: James R. Osgood And Company, Late Ticknor & Fields, And Fields, Osgood, & Co. 1874.* 3 volumes. First edition thus? Small 8vo, lxxvi+[ix]+153pp.,+372pp.,+372pp., half-title volume 1 and volume 3, title page each volume with small emblem incorporating the letters of the press near the bottom, half-title for some of the poems, original brown cloth (covers worn along extremities, volume 2 spine half missing, volume 3 spine missing a piece at the top and a small piece at the bottom), covers ruled in blind with central emblem in blind, spines lettered in gilt with small gilt shield (possibly of the press) at the bottom. A decent set, clean internally, each volume wrapped in a protective plastic cover. Advertisement on verso of "Contents" page volume 1: "The Life of Milton prefixed to this edition is from the pen of his latest biographer, Prof. David Masson, of London. The notes are those of the Rev. John Mitford. Before going to a new impression, occasion has been taken to correct a considerable number of errors, principally in the editions from the Greek, Latin, and Italian poets." A very uncommon set. Not in Kohler.

2156. THE POETICAL WORKS OF JOHN MILTON. Reprinted From The Chandos Poets. With Memoir, Explanatory Notes, &c. The "Chandos Classics." *London: Frederick Warne And Co., Bedford Street, Covent Garden. New York: Scribner, Welford And Armstrong.* n.d. [ca. 1874]. 8vo in 16s, xxiv+581+[1]+[2]pp., small circular emblem with "F. Warne Bedford St. Covent Garden" in the outer circle and the initials "FW & Co." in the inner circle at the center of the title page, "London: Printed By Woodfall And Kinder, Milford Lane, Strand, W.C." on verso of title page, "Prefatory Memoir Of Milton," notes at bottom of page, "Woodfall And Kinder, Printers, Milford Lane, Strand, London, W.C." printed at the bottom of last page (p. 581), original green cloth (a bit rubbed, spine a little worn at top and bottom), front cover decorated in black with black rules and inner black trim and a triangular emblem with the initials "FW C" at the center, back cover similarly decorated in blind, spine lettered in gilt with small decorative gilt trim and black rules at top and bottom. A decent copy with an advertisement leaf of publications by "Frederick Warne & Co., Publishers" bound in at the end, the contemporary ownership signature in a neat hand on the fly-leaf (dated "Feb 21st, 1874") and a small bookshelf label of the owner on the front pastedown. See other undated and dated illustrated and nonillustrated editions by Frederick Warne and Co. published in the 1870s, 1880s, and 1890s under the various series: "The 'Lansdowne' Poets," "The 'Arundel' Poets," "The 'Chandos' Poets," "The 'Imperial' Poets, "The 'Chandos' Classics," "The 'Albion' Edition," and the "Cabinet Poets." Kohler 385, dating its copy "[ca. 1876]."

With Contemporary Photographic Reproductions of Martin Plates (1875)

2157. THE POETICAL WORKS OF JOHN MILTON Printed From The Original Editions With A Life Of The Author By A. Chalmers M.A. F.S.A. With Twenty-Four Illustrations By John Martin[.] *London[:] Bickers And Son[,] 1 Leicester Square W. 1875.* First edition thus. Large 8vo, xxxi+687pp., half-title with decorative headpiece, frontispiece portrait engraved by W. Humphreys, from a Print by Faithorne," title page in red and black with central device of the Chiswick Press, on verso appears "Chiswick Press :— Printed By Whittingham And Wilkins, Tooks Court, Chancery Lane," "Advertisement To The [Pickering] Edition Of 1851," life of Milton, contemporary photographic reproductions of Martin's *PL* engravings (all very striking) within decorative borders with the appearance of lined matting, each photographic reproduction on thick paper, with appropriate lines and book reference printed beneath, and each measuring 4 ¾" × 3 ¼", decorative head- and tailpieces, decorated initial letters, half-title for some of the poems, handsomely "Printed By Whittingham And Wilkins, Tooks Court, Chancery Lane," identified beneath inverted decorative triangular piece incorporating "Chiswick Press" on last page of the volume, contemporary crushed maroon morocco (a bit rubbed, occasional foxing), covers decorated with gilt trim and gilt rules with decorative gilt corner pieces and a decorative gilt device in the center, gilt-decorated spines with decorative gilt devices in the panels, gilt lettering, and decorative gilt trim at top and bottom, raised bands with gilt rules (a bit rubbed) within decorative gilt trim on each side, inner and outer dentelles finely tooled in gilt, illustrations, in a handsome binding of the period. The order of the poems here maintains that of the first edition by Bickers and Son in 1851 (see one-volume editions and also two-volume editions also listed here), with *PL* and *PR* coming after *SA* and the earlier poems. Scarce. Not in Kohler.

John Martin's celebrated mezzotint illustrations for *PL* were first issued in twelve parts by Septimus Prowett between 1825 and 1827 (see sets listed here with further commentary); the plates were published by Prowett in an edition of *PL*, in four different formats, in 1827 (see copy of each format listed here with commentary regarding the subsequent publishing of Martin's plates by publishers to whom the engravings then passed). According to Balston, "And, finally, in 1876 Bickers & Son of Leicester Square published Chalmers's *PW of John Milton* with Martin's large series of *PL* engravings reproduced in small photographic prints" (Balston, *Life*, p. 258, referring to the 1876 edition following; see also Balston, *Illustrator*, p. 391). Balston makes no mention of the present 1875 octavo edition of Chalmers's *PW of John Milton* by Bickers & Son with photographic reproductions of Martin's *PL* engravings within decorative borders, the photographic reproductions being slightly smaller (4 ¾" × 3 ¼" compared to 5 ⅝" × 3 ⅞") than the photographic reproductions of Martin's *PL* engravings without decorative borders in the 1876 Chalmers edition identified by Balston.

❦

2158. THE POETICAL WORKS OF JOHN MILTON. With Life Of The Author, And An Appendix, Containing Addison's Critique Upon The Paradise Lost, And Dr. Channing's Essay On The Poetical Genius Of Milton. [Quote from Thomson.] Complete Edition, With Illustrations. *London: James Blackwood & Co., Lovell's Court, Paternoster Row. n.d. [ca. 1875].* First edition thus? 8vo, xvi+416pp., frontispiece portrait of a young, Romantic-influenced looking Milton, engraved and printed title pages, vignette illustration (unsigned, but after Westall, for *PL*, Book XI) on engraved title page, five additional illustrations (unsigned, for *PL*, Book X; for *L*, placed within Book XI; for *PR*, Book I; two for *PR*, Book IV), each within an elaborate floral frame with the lines illustrated printed below, original decorated blue cloth (a little worn, some spotting and age-browning throughout, ink marking on page 191 and on verso of plate preceding), front cover decorated in black trim with title lettered in large gilt lettering on an embossed orange color parallelogram ruled in a thick gilt border surrounded by very small gilt fleur-de-lis with gilt floral trim on either corner, a gilt flower at the center near the bottom, with three decorative floral straps which are carried over onto the spine which is similarly trimmed in black, with title lettered in gilt between thin gilt rules and gilt fleur-de-lis, with a decorative gilt device beneath the second gilt band, a.e.g. A decent copy of a rather uncommon edition, with contemporary signature (dated "5 Novr. 1875, Maryboro, Queensland, Australia") on front blank, in an attractive and unusual (albeit a little used) Victorian publisher's cloth binding, with very interesting unsigned illustrations. Scarce. Not in Kohler.

2159. THE POETICAL WORKS OF JOHN MILTON[.] A New Edition, Carefully Revised From The Text Of Thomas Newton, D.D. With Illustrations By William Harvey[.] *London[:] George Routledge And Sons[,] The Broadway, Ludgate[;] New York: 416 Broome Street. n.d. [ca. 1875].* Small 8vo, viii+570pp., frontispiece illustration plate of Satan cast out of Heaven and five additional illustration plates after William Harvey, engraved by Dalziel, "A New Edition, Carefully Revised From The Text Of Thomas Newton" in a clear, non-Gothic font on title page, "London: Savill, Edwards And Co., Printers, Chandos Street, Covent Garden" on verso of title page, original preface by Theodore Alois Buckley dated 1853, notes at bottom of page, original decorated blue cloth (a bit rubbed along joints and at corners, spine ends slightly chipped), front cover richly decorated in embossed black and gilt in a floral motif, with Milton's name in large embossed black letters at the center, a small harp at the top and a centralized floral motif at the bottom with "Illustrated" in semi-circular fashion above and a small shield at each corner at the bottom, spine similarly richly decorated in embossed black and gilt in a floral motif, with Milton's name in embossed red letters against a gilt background near the top, a small harp at the top, small shield in the center, "Illustrated" in small embossed red lettering beneath, and a floral motif at the bottom incorporating "Routledge" in small embossed red lettering, back cover decorated with floral border trim in blind, brown endpapers, a.e.g. A very nice copy in an attractive publisher's binding, with contemporary signature (dated "Dec. 1875") on back of frontispiece illustration. The first edition thus by George Routledge and Co. was published in 1853 (also listed here with further editions by Routledge cited). Not in Kohler (although Kohler 391 [cf. variant copies] dates its copy, "Routledge's Red-line Poets," "[ca. 1878]," with frontispiece and five plates, with "The Broadway, Ludgate; New York: [sic]" in publisher's imprint, and reporting "Not in the Bodleian Library. Not in Cambridge University Library").

2160. Variant copy in original decorated maroon cloth (a little worn, front joint cracked, back cover slightly scuffed and stained), decorated as preceding copy, a.e.g. A fairly good copy in an attractive variant publisher's binding, and

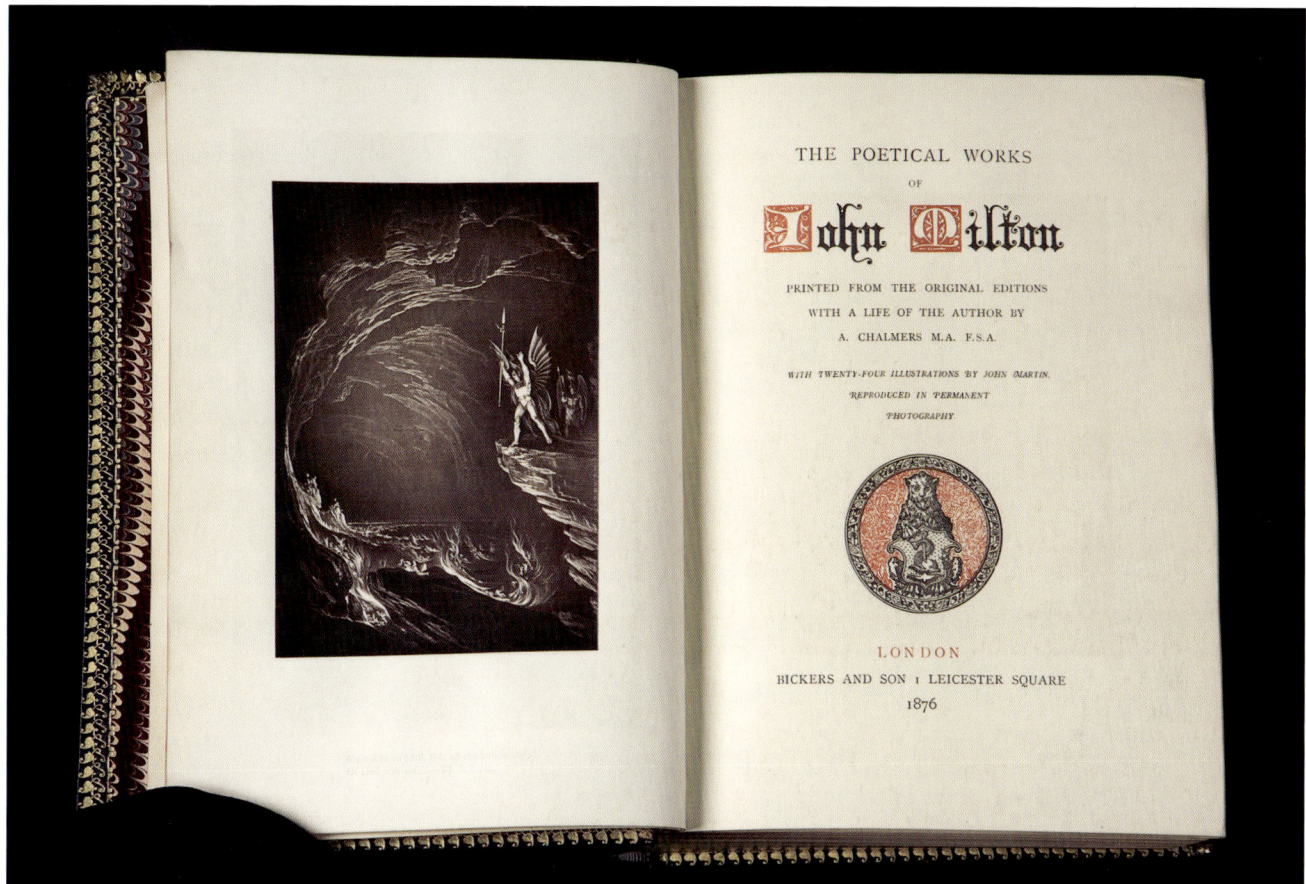

PW. With Twenty-Four Illustrations By John Martin, Reproduced In Permanent Photography. London: Bickers and Son, 1876. Large 8vo, contemporary full blue morocco over thick boards. Frontispiece photographic illustration and title page, and front view of binding. See #2167.

although showing its age, the ornately decorated cover still retains its original brilliance. Not in Kohler.

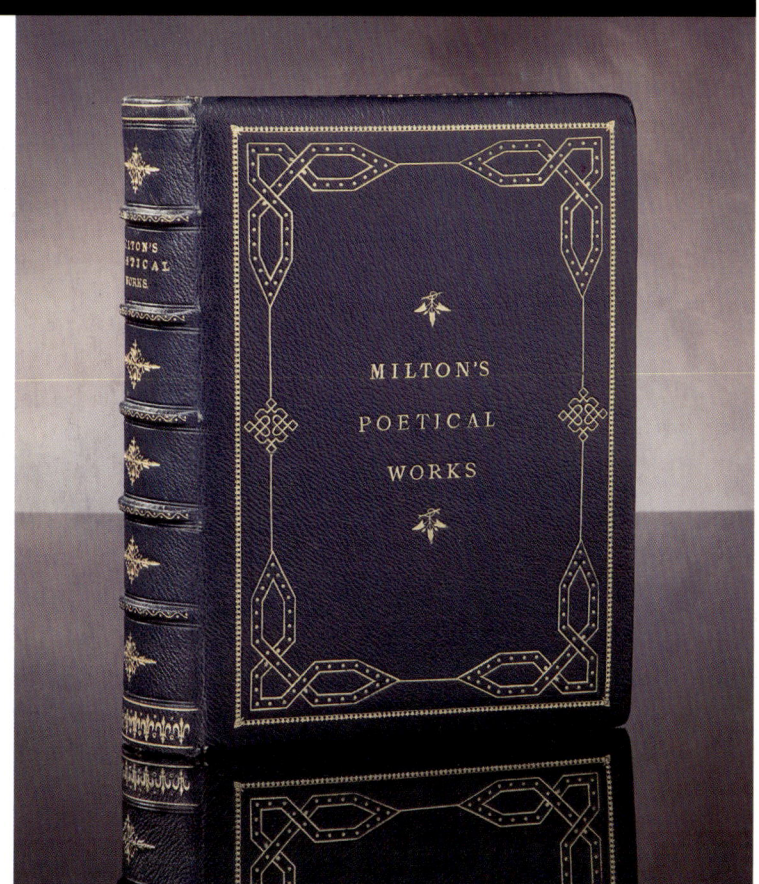

2161. THE POETICAL WORKS OF JOHN MILTON. With A Memoir, And Critical Remarks On His Genius And Writings By James Montgomery; Vol. I. / Vol. II. *New York: Leavitt & Allen Bros., No. 8 Howard Street. n.d. [ca. 1875]*. 2 volumes in one. 8vo, l+[3]+400pp. (page numbering beginning with number "18"), +368pp.(page numbering beginning with number "10"), engraved frontispiece portrait plate after C. Burt, protective tissue guard, illustrations (unsigned, but after Harvey) within the text for *L'Allegro* with a vignette illustration at the beginning and another vignette illustration at the end of the poem and with vignette illustrations in the margins, half-title for each book of *PL* and *PR* and for some of the poems, original red cloth (a little rubbed and worn at the corners and extremities, back joint broken from within, red reinforcement strips added sometime at top and bottom of spine in a manner that blends with the binding), front cover decorated with black trim and with Milton's name in large embossed red letters against a black backdrop, spine lettered in gilt (faded) and trimmed in black with the title in gilt at the top and "The World Edition" within a circle incorporating two hemispheres in gilt at the center, small bookseller's label tipped in at bottom of front pastedown. A decent copy in original binding, with contemporary presentation inscription (dated "Dec. 25th. 1875") on front blank. The possible first edition thus was published by Leavitt & Allen in 1858 (also listed here with further editions by Leavitt & Allen cited). Not in Kohler.

2162. THE POETICAL WORKS OF JOHN MILTON. A New Edition, With Notes, By Rev. John Mitford. [In Two Volumes.] *Philadelphia: Porter & Coates, 822 Chestnut Street. n.d. [ca. 1875].* First edition thus. 2 volumes in one. 4to, [ii]+371pp.,+478pp., title page for each volume, engraved frontispiece illustration of *Milton, Dictating His Paradise Lost to His Daughters* by "Decaisne Pinxt, H Dawe Sculpt," protective tissue guard, "Sonnet To Charles Lord Bishop Of Winchester On His Publication Of Milton De Doctrina Christiana" (dated "Nov. 1831"), engraved illustration plate for Book III of *PL* (unidentified—"Here walk'd the fiend at large in spacious field," line 430—and unsigned), protective tissue guard, engraved illustration plate of *Adam and Eve in the Garden* for *PL* (Book V), engraved by W. Radclyffe after I. Cristall, protective tissue guard, unsigned engraved illustration plate for *C*, protective tissue guard, and unsigned engraved illustration plate for *IlP*, protective tissue guard, double black rule around text, half-titles for *SA* and *C*, original reddish-brown cloth (a bit rubbed, especially at the corners and spine ends), decorative wide bands in gilt relief running from front cover to spine in imitation of a medieval binding with Milton's name lettered in decorative gilt relief at the center of the front cover, spine lettered in gilt, back cover decorated in blind in the same manner as front cover, green endpapers, a.e.g. A good copy with fine impressions of the illustration plates (possibly the first appearance of these). See undated [ca. 1887] Porter & Coates edition listed earlier, with the engraved frontispiece portrait as here, without "822 Chestnut Street" on title page as here, with three of the engraved illustration plates here, but without the engraved illustration for Book III of *PL* here. See also *PL* . . . A New Edition. With Notes By Rev. John Mitford. Philadelphia: Porter & Coates, n.d. [ca. 1887] listed earlier, called "Alta Edition" on front cover and stamped "Illustrated" on the spine, although the edition has no illustrations within. Kohler 381, making no reference to "822 Chestnut Street" being on the title page, as here, and reporting "Not in Williamson. Not in the British Library. Not in the Bodleian Library. Not in Cambridge University Library."

2163. Variant of Preceding, contemporary full brown calf over thick boards (a little rubbed along extremities, front joint cracked), covers elaborately embossed in blind with Milton's name in gilt at center of each cover, spine lettered in gilt and decorated in blind, raised bands, brown endpapers, a.e.g. A good copy in a variant contemporary embossed calf binding, very clean within. Kohler 381.

2164. THE POETICAL WORKS OF JOHN MILTON. With A Memoir, And Critical Remarks On His Genius And Writings. By James Montgomery; Vol. I. / Vol. II. *World Publishing House, 139 Eighth Street, New York. 1875.* 2 volumes in one. Large 12mo, 1+[3]+400pp.(pagination number beginning with page number "18"),+368pp., engraved frontispiece portrait plate after C. Burt, protective tissue guard (foxed), volume 1, second title page for volume 2 followed by "Contents Of Vol. II," three engraved illustration plates for *PL* (*Moloch*, unsigned, for Book II; an untitled and unsigned plate for Book VI, engraved by Sartain; *The Grave*, after Stothard, for Book X, engraved by Sartain), an engraved illustration plate for *SA* (*Deborah's Triumph*, after P. F. Rothermel, engraved by Sartain), illustrations (unsigned, but after Harvey) within the text for *L'A* with a vignette illustration at the beginning and another vignette illustration at the end of the poem and with vignette illustrations in the margins, an unidentified and unsigned engraved illustration plate among the sonnets with a protective tissue guard, half-title for each book of *PL* and *PR* and for some of the poems, double black border around the text, contemporary full brown calf over thick boards (a little rubbed along joints and extremities, with a few scuff marks), covers elaborately embossed in blind with Milton's name in gilt at center of each cover, spine lettered in gilt and decorated in blind, raised bands, marbled endpapers, a.e.g. A very nice copy, very clean within, in a fine embossed binding of the period, with contemporary signature (dated 1879) on front blank. Not in Kohler.

2165. THE POETICAL WORKS OF JOHN MILTON. William P. Nimmo. *London: 14 King William Street, Strand, And Edinburgh. 1876.* 8vo, xxxvii+[1]+440pp., unsigned engraved frontispiece portrait plate of a middle-aged Milton, engraved and printed title pages with vignette illustration (of the poet being inspired by heavenly choirs) by F. Borders on engraved title plate ("Edinburgh:

W. P: Nimmo." n.d.), vignette illustration (of a young boy in a setting in nature with a cane laying beside him) signed with the initials "WS" on printed title, "Printed by J. And J. Gray, Melbourne Place, Edinburgh" on verso of title page, eleven illustration plates, most after F. Borders, some unsigned, life of Milton by J. M. Ross, eleven illustration plates, most after F. Borders, some unsigned: four for *PL* (Books I, III, VI, XI), two for *PR* (Book I), one for *SA*, two for *C*, one for *L'A*, one for *IlP*, half-title for *PL*, *PR*, *SA*, *C*, *Arc*, *MP*, and *Poemata*, black border around text, printer not indicated at bottom of last page, original three-quarter red morocco, marbled paper over boards (a bit worn), gilt-decorated spine, marbled endpapers and edges. A nice copy. The possible first edition thus by Nimmo was published in 1865, illustrated (also listed here with further Nimmo editions cited). Only the 1865 edition has twelve illustrations, the others have eleven (with only one illustration for *L'A* instead of two, as in the 1865 edition). Kohler 382, reporting "Not in Williamson. Not in the British Library. Not in the Bodleian Library. Not in Cambridge University Library."

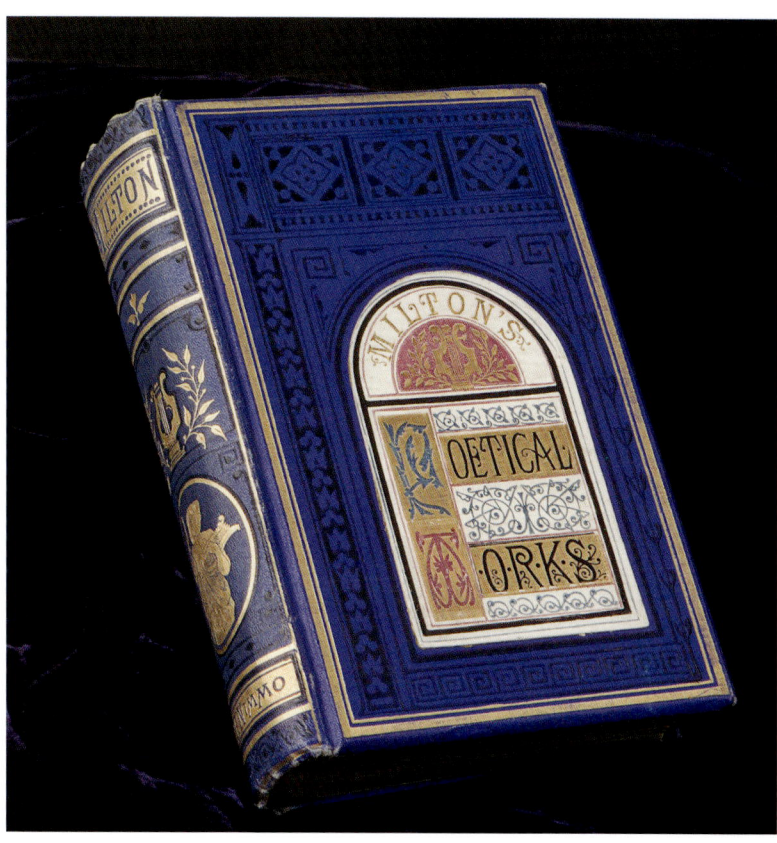

PW. William P. Nimmo. London and Edinburgh. 1876. 8vo, illustration plates, most after F. Borders, some unattributed, original decorated blue cloth. See #2165.

2166. Variant of Preceding. Original decorated blue cloth, front cover intricately decorated in black trim with gilt borders, with a large decorated white curved piece of leather tipped in near the center with "Milton's" name lettered in embossed gilt within the half circle above a smaller half circle filled with a gilt harp and a gilt laurel wreath against a maroon background, with "Poetical" and "Works" lettered below in embossed green and black letters against broad horizontal gilt bands surrounded by delicate light blue trim with the letters "P" and "W" in decorated embossed green and maroon letters against vertical gilt backgrounds, the whole framed in an inner black border and a thicker black outer border, spine decorated in black and gilt trim with Milton's name in embossed blue letters against a bright gilt band near the top, a gilt harp and gilt laurel wreath at the center, a vignette illustration of a gilt figure holding lyre and staff within a circular gilt border toward the bottom, "WP Nimmo" in embossed blue letters within a bright gilt band near the bottom outlined in gilt rules, and decorative black trim at the top and bottom, brown endpapers, a.e.g. Fine copy with later presentation inscription on fly-leaf and bookplate on front pastedown, in a lovely variant publisher's cloth binding, with sixteen numbered pages advertising "Books Published By William P. Nimmo" bound in at end. Kohler 382.

With Contemporary Photographic Reproductions of Martin Plates (1876)

2167. THE POETICAL WORKS OF JOHN MILTON Printed From The Original Editions With A Life Of The Author By A. Chalmers M.A. F.S.A. With Twenty-Four Illustrations By John Martin, Reproduced In Permanent Photography. *London[:] Bickers And Son[,] 1 Leicester Square[.] 1876*. Possible second edition thus (although Balston indicates that this is the first edition with photographic reproductions of Martin's *PL* engravings published by Bickers & Son). Large 8vo, xxxix+[1]+699pp., half-title with decorative trim, title page in red and black with central device of the Chiswick Press, on verso appears "Chiswick Press :— Printed By Whittingham And Wilkins, Tooks Court, Chancery Lane," life of Milton, contemporary photographic reproductions of Martin's *PL* engravings (all very striking) on thick paper, with appropriate lines and book reference printed beneath, each measuring 5 ⅝" × 3 ⅞", decorative head- and tailpieces, decorated initial letters, half-title for some of the poems, handsomely "Printed By Whittingham And Wilkins, Tooks Court, Chancery Lane," identified beneath inverted decorative triangular piece incorporating "Chiswick Press" at the bottom of the last page (p. 699), contemporary full blue morocco over thick boards, delicately gilt-decorated covers with central gilt lettering on front cover, spine lettered in gilt with decorative gilt devices within the panels, raised bands with decorative gilt trim, inner dentelles finely tooled in gilt, outer dentelles ruled in gilt, marbled endpapers, a.e.g., with early (possibly contemporary) bookplate on front pastedown. A splendid copy with rare early photographic reproductions of Martin's illustrations, handsomely bound in an elegant morocco binding of the period. Virtually mint. John Martin's celebrated mezzotint illustrations for *PL* were first issued in twelve parts by Septimus Prowett between 1825 and 1827 (also listed here with further commentary); the plates were published by Prowett in an edition of *PL*, in four different formats, in 1827 (see copy of each format listed here with commentary regarding the subsequent publishing of Martin's plates by publishers to whom the engravings then passed). According to Balston: "And, finally, in 1876 Bickers & Son of Leicester Square published Chalmers's *PW of John Milton* with Martin's large series of *PL* engravings reproduced in small photographic prints" (Balston, *Life*, p. 258, referring to the 1876 edition here; see also Balston, *Illustrator*, p. 391). Balston makes no mention of the 1875 edition of Chalmers's *PW of John Milton* by Bickers & Son with photographic reproductions of Martin's *PL* engravings (listed earlier), which, unlike here, are photographed within decorative borders, while these are not, and which are slightly smaller: 4 ¾" × 3 ¼" compared to 5 ⅝" × 3 ⅞"). The 1876 edition is overall also a much larger octavo edition. Scarce. Not in Kohler.

2168. THE POETICAL WORKS OF JOHN MILTON. Reprinted From The Best Editions. With Memoir, Explanatory and Glossorial Notes, &c. Portrait And Original Illustrations. The Chandos Poets. *London: Frederick Warne And Co., Bedford Street, Strand. New York: Scribner, Welford, And Armstrong. n.d. [ca. 1876].* Large square 8vo, xxiv+581pp., unsigned engraved frontispiece portrait of an early middle-aged Milton (with label "London: Frederick Warne & Co." at the bottom), title page in orange and black, twelve illustration plates after engravings by Dalziel: one for *NO*, one for *L'A*, six for *PL* (Books I, IV, V, VII, VIII, and XII), one for *PR* (Book I), one for *SA*, one for *On His Deceased Wife*, and one for *Latin Epigram VII* (the illustration titled *Milton Meeting Leonora Baroni at Cardinal Barberini's House*), tiny decorative tailpieces throughout, half-title for *SA*, notes at bottom of the page, orange border around text, "London[:] Printed By Woodfall And Kinder, Milford Lane Strand, W.C." on verso of last page (p. 581)—appears also on verso of title page, contemporary full crushed green morocco (a bit rubbed along joints, front joint just slightly cracked at top and bottom), covers double ruled in gilt, spine elaborately decorated in gilt within the panels, red morocco label lettered and ruled in gilt, gilt filleted raised bands, inner dentelles finely tooled in gilt, outer dentelles trimmed in gilt, marbled endpapers, a.e.g. A fine copy with contemporary presentation inscription (dated "Xmas 1876") on fly-leaf. See later publication of this edition published ca. 1887 (also listed here). Not in Kohler.

2168A. (Cross-listing) **THE POETICAL WORKS OF JOHN MILTON.** Edited By Sir Egerton Brydges, Bart. [Quotation from Thomson.] Illustrated With Engravings From Drawings By J. M. W. Turner, R.A. A New Edition. *London: William Tegg. n.d. [ca. 1876 or ca. 1862].* Variant edition. Thick 8vo, cvi+767pp., frontispiece portrait engraved by W. C. Edwards after Vertue, seven illustration plates after Turner, double black border around text, contemporary full coarse-grained black morocco. While similar to the 1862 dated edition by Tegg listed earlier, unlike that edition, this edition is undated and may perhaps be an 1870s reprint as indicated by Kohler 383, which dates its copy "[1876]," quoting the title page as here, but without indicating "Quotation From Thomson," citing "767 pp. 1/2 title. Frontispiece portrait engraved by Edwards after Vertue. Seven plates after Turner," referencing Williamson 135, and reporting "Not in Cambridge University Library." See main listing under *PW*, 1862.

2169. THE POETICAL WORKS OF JOHN MILTON Printed From The Original Editions With A Life Of The Author By A. Chalmers M.A. F.S.A. *London[:] Bickers And Son[,] 1 Leicester Square[,] n.d. [ca. 1876].* 8vo, xxxi+[1]+687pp., half-title with decorative trim, frontispiece portrait engraved by W. Humphreys, from a "Print by Faithorne," title page in red and black with central device of the Chiswick Press, "Advertisement To The [Pickering] Edition Of 1851," life of Milton, decorative head- and tailpieces, decorated initial letters, half-title for some of the poems, handsomely "Printed By Whittingham And Wilkins, Tooks Court, Chancery Lane," with inverted triangular piece on page after *Poems*) and again on last page of the volume, contemporary full green morocco (a bit rubbed), covers delicately tooled in gilt with decorative gilt border trim, gilt rules, inner gilt rule with decorative gilt corner pieces and central gilt decorative piece, spine similarly decorated in gilt with decorative gilt trim, small decorative gilt pieces in the panels, raised bands with gilt rules, inner and outer dentelles finely tooled in gilt, marbled endpapers, a.e.g. A fine copy, handsomely printed, in a splendid and well-preserved contemporary morocco binding, with early armorial bookplate on front pastedown, and prize inscription (dated 1876) on front blank. See dated 1876 Bickers and Sons edition listed earlier, illustrated with photographic reproductions of Martin's *PL* engravings; see also dated, nonillustrated, one-volume 1881 Bickers and Sons edition; see, too, undated, nonillustrated two-volume ca. 1873 / ca. 1862 / ca. 1851 edition listed earlier ("Printed From The Original Editions With A Life Of The Author By The Rev. John Mitford"), as well as undated, nonillustrated one-volume ca. 1851 / ca. 1862 edition listed earlier with "Printed By Whittingham And Wilkins, Tooks Court, Chancery Lane Chiswick Press" with inverted triangular piece on page after *Poems* and again on last page of the volume rather than "Printed By Whittingham And Wilkins, Tooks Court, Chancery Lane," as here. Not in Kohler.

2170. THE POETICAL WORKS OF JOHN MILTON. "But who is he, with modest looks, And clad in homely russet brown? He murmurs near the running brooks A music sweeter than their own." *London: Milner And Company Paternoster Row. n.d. [ca. 1876]*. Small 8vo, vi+503+[1]+2+[2]pp., unsigned frontispiece illustration in color for *PR*, half-title for *C*, original red cloth (rubbed, especially along edges and extremities), covers ruled in embossed blind trim, spine decorated in black and gilt with title in gilt near the top, a large flower in gilt outlined in black trim toward the bottom, and rich decorative trim in black and embossed red at top and bottom. Four pages of advertisements bound in at end. A fairly good copy in a nice publisher's decorated cloth binding, with contemporary signature (possibly dated 1876) on front pastedown. Not in Kohler.

2171. Variant of Preceding, original green cloth (a bit worn), covers ruled in embossed trim in blind, spine decorated with rich floral theme in gilt against a black background outlined in double light blue rules, with title lettered in gilt against a light blue background near the top. Four pages of advertisements bound in at end. A decent copy in a lovely variant publisher's binding. Not in Kohler.

2172. THE POETICAL WORKS OF JOHN MILTON[.] A New Edition, Carefully Revised From The Text Of Thomas Newton, D.D. With Illustrations By William Harvey[.] *Boston[:] Lee And Shepard, Publishers[;] New York[:] Lee, Shepard And Dillingham[,] 1876*. Third edition thus by Lee, Shepard and Dillingham? 8vo, viii+570pp., frontispiece illustration by William Harvey, protective tissue guard, "London: Savill, Edwards And Co., Printers, Chandos Street Covent Garden" on verso of title page, preface by Theodore Buckley dated 1853, five additional illustrations by Harvey, original reddish-brown cloth (a bit worn, some foxing), front cover and spine elaborately decorated in gilt and black incorporating Milton's name within central device on front cover, brown endpapers, a.e.g. A good copy in a lovely binding. The possible first edition thus by Lee, Shepard and Dillingham was published in 1872 (also listed here with further editions cited). This edition is similar to editions published by George Routledge and Sons (see undated ca. 1872 and ca. 1874 editions also listed here). Not in Kohler.

2173. Variant of Preceding, original green cloth (a bit worn with joint broken from within between frontispiece illustration and title page, some foxing), front cover and spine elaborately decorated in gilt and black incorporating Milton's name within central device on front cover, back cover decorated in blind, brown endpapers, a.e.g. A good copy in a lovely variant publisher's binding. Not in Kohler.

2174. THE POETICAL WORKS OF JOHN MILTON. William P. Nimmo[:] *London And Edinburgh[.] 1877*. 8vo, xxxvii+[1]+440pp., engraved half-title in multicolor ("Nimmo's Popular Poets") with colorful flowers and a bird in color against a circular gilt background in each corner, the whole against a black background surrounded by thick gilt and black rules with two thin rules rounded at the corners with outer gilt corner pieces and two thin gilt rules, unsigned engraved frontispiece portrait plate of a middle-aged Milton, engraved and printed title pages, with vignette illustration of the poet being inspired by heavenly choirs by F. Borders on engraved title plate ("William P. Nimmo. London And Edinburgh." n.d.), vignette illustration of a young boy in a setting in nature with a cane laying beside him signed with the initials "WS" on printed title, "Printed By J. And J. Gray, Melbourne Place, Edinburgh" printed on verso of title page, eleven illustration plates, most after F. Borders, some unsigned, life of Milton by J. M. Ross, half-title for *PL*, *PR*, *SA*, *C*, *Ar MP*, and *Poemata*, black border around text, original three-quarter black morocco, marbled paper over boards (a bit rubbed), gilt-decorated spine, red morocco label with gilt lettering, raised bands with gilt decorated trim, marbled endpapers and edges. A nice copy in original publisher's binding, with engraved half-title in multi-color ("Nimmo's Popular Poets"), with contemporary signature (dated 1879) on front blank. The possible first edition thus by Nimmo was published in 1865, illustrated (also listed here with further Nimmo editions, illustrated and nonillustrated, cited).

Kohler 386, reporting "Not in Williamson. Not in the British Library. Not in the Bodleian Library. Not in Cambridge University Library."

2175. THE POETICAL WORKS OF JOHN MILTON. Reprinted From The Chandos Poets. With Memoir, Explanatory Notes, &c. Portrait And Original Illustrations. The Lansdowne Poets. *London: Frederick Warne And Co., Bedford Street, Strand. New York: Scribner, Welford, And Armstrong[.] n.d. [ca. 1877].* 8vo, xxiv+581pp., unsigned frontispiece portrait of a middle-aged Milton, protective tissue guard (foxed), eight illustration plates after engravings by Dalziel: one for *NO*, four for *PL* (Books I, IV, VIII, and XII), one for *PR*, one for *SA*, and one for *On His Deceased Wife*, "Dalziel Brothers, Camden Press, London, N.W." on verso of last page, p. 581, notes at bottom of the page, contemporary dark blue morocco (a bit rubbed, especially the spine and at corners, occasional foxing, including frontispiece portrait and title page), covers decorated in blind, spine lettered in gilt, raised bands, marbled endpapers, a.e.g. A nice copy with contemporary presentation inscription (dated "Edinbr. 1rst Nov. 1877") on front blank. Uncommon. Not in Kohler (but see Kohler 385, very similar, not illustrated, which Kohler dates "[ca. 1876]").

2176. THE POETICAL WORKS OF JOHN MILTON. With Life. Six Engravings on Steel. *Gall & Inglis. London: 25 Paternoster Square. Edinburgh: 6 George Street. n.d. [ca. 1877].* 8vo, xx+491pp., engraved and printed title pages, with the printed title page reading *PW*, the engraved title page reading *CPW*, unsigned frontispiece illustration plate of *The Expulsion*, with unsigned vignette illustration of *Eve Relating Her Dream to Adam* on engraved title, which bears the same publisher as the printed title page ("Edinburgh, Gall & Inglis. London," undated), four additional unsigned illustration plates—for *PL* (Books II, VII, and IX) and for *PR* (Book IV), red border around text, contemporary decorated green cloth (a bit used, some minor foxing), front cover elaborately decorated in embossed black and gilt with large central crest-shaped emblem in white incorporating gilt urn and Milton's name in gilt relief, the whole surrounded in decorative gilt trim, spine similarly elaborately decorated in embossed black and gilt with gilt emblem near the top incorporating Milton's name in gilt relief and the title in embossed green letters, decorative gilt trim at the top and bottom, the bottom gilt trim incorporating "Gall & Inglis," back cover decorated in blind, a.e.g. A good copy in an attractive Victorian binding, with contemporary presentation inscription (dated 1877) on fly-leaf. See undated ca. 1870s / ca. 1875 edition published by Gall & Inglis in Edinburgh ("Bernard Terrace") and London ("25 Paternoster Sqr.") with only "Engravings on Steel" appearing on title page and with decorative border trim around text in alternating sepia and bluish green tint with varying background scenes above and other editions by Gall & Inglis cited there. Not in Kohler.

2177. THE POETICAL WORKS OF JOHN MILTON A New Edition, Carefully Revised From The Text Of Thomas Newton, D.D. With Illustrations By William Harvey[.] *London[:] George Routledge And Sons[,] The Broadway, Ludgate[;] New York: 416 Broome Street[.] n.d. [ca. 1878].* 8vo, viii+570pp. (illustrations not included in the pagination), frontispiece illustration plate for *C* and five additional illustration plates after William Harvey, engraved by Dalziel, "A New Edition, Carefully Revised From The Text Of Thomas Newton" in a clear, non-Gothic font on title page, "Routledge's Red-Line Poets" listed on verso of title page (the nine listings including Milton), original preface by Theodore Alois Buckley dated 1853, red border line around text with small decorative corner pieces, notes at bottom of the page, "Savill, Edwards and Co., Printers, Chandos Street, Covent Garden" at bottom of last page, original brown leather over thick boards (a bit worn), covers ruled in blind with decorative corner pieces in blind, large central oval shaped recessed panel on front cover containing a gold cutout with color floral arrangement (possibly hand painted) tipped in at the center, the recessed panel finely ruled and trimmed in gilt, "Milton" lettered in gilt above with delicate gilt decorative piece below, spine lettered in gilt, decorative gilt piece in the panels, raised bands, dark brown endpapers, a.e.g. Nice copy in a lovely binding of the period, with contemporary signature (dated "Dec 25–1878") and lengthy presentation inscription on front blank, with notes in a neat contemporary hand in ink on back blank. The first edition thus by George Routledge and Co. was published in 1853 (also listed here with further editions by Routledge cited). Kohler 391, dating its copy "[ca. 1878]" and reporting "Not in the Bodleian Library. Not in Cambridge University Library."

2178. Variant of Preceding, original decorated red cloth (a little worn at corners and along extremities), front cover elaborately decorated in black trim with a large bright gilt square emblem at the center incorporating floral trim in gilt with several gilt blossoms with red centers outlined in black with Milton's name in large embossed black letters outlined in red at the top and "Illustrated" in embossed red letters against a bright gilt band at the bottom, black floral trim surrounds the bright gilt square and at the top of the square is a bright gilt harp with a red star above and at the bottom a black vase with a bright gilt flower, spine similarly decorated in black and gilt with a small harp in black within double black rules at the center, with Milton's name in embossed red letters within a bright, wide gilt band at the top, and "Illustrated" and "Routledge" in progressively smaller embossed red letters within progressively smaller bright gilt bands, decorative black trim at the top and bottom with a bright gilt star at the top, back cover with floral arrangement in blind at the center, brown endpapers, a.e.g. A nice copy in an attractive variant publisher's binding. The edition here bears the same publisher's imprint as the preceding as well as the same printer's reference on the last page; it also has the same nine listings (including Milton) of "Routledge's Red-Line Poets" listed on verso of title page. See ca. 1883 Routledge and Sons edition with regard to each of these elements. Kohler 391.

2179. THE POETICAL WORKS OF JOHN MILTON: With Introductions By David Masson, M.A., L.L.D., Professor Of Rhetoric And English Literature In The University Of Edinburgh. The Globe Edition. *London: Macmillan And Co. 1877.* First globe edition by Macmillan. Smallish 8vo, xi+625+[1]pp., half-title (with emblem consisting of the letters of Macmillan and Co. on verso), "London: R. Clay, Sons, And Taylor, Printers" on verso of printed title page and on verso of last printed page (625), preface (dated "March 1877"), introductory material is from the "Golden Treasury" edition of 1874 (also listed here), with revisions, original three-quarter maroon calf (worn along joints, corners, and extremities, occasional foxing), marbled boards (a little rubbed with some fading), spine richly decorated in gilt within the panels, black label lettered in gilt (label defective), marbled endpapers and edges. A good copy of an increasingly difficult book to find, with contemporary presentation inscription on front blank. The second Globe edition was published in June, 1877; the third in 1878 (see copies listed here: one with illustrations inserted, the other the regular, nonillustrated, edition); the fourth in 1880 (copy listed here); it was variously reprinted thereafter in 1882, 1885, 1887, 1891, 1893, 1895, 1896, 1897, and 1899—all listed here, except for the 1896 edition; it was also variously reprinted in a moderate octavo format in the twentieth century: 1901, 1903, 1905, 1906, 1907, 1909, 1911, 1912, 1922, 1954, and 1961—all listed here, except for the 1905 edition. Scarce. Stevens 209; Not in Kohler.

2180. THE POETICAL WORKS OF JOHN MILTON: With Introductions By David Masson [as preceding.] The Globe Edition. *London: Macmillan And Co. 1878.* Third Globe edition by Macmillan (illustrations extra). Smallish 8vo, xi+ 625pp., half-title (with emblem consisting of the letters of Macmillan and Co. on verso), early photograph of a Milton bust mounted as frontispiece, engraved and printed title pages, with engraved title reading: "THE POETICAL WORKS OF JOHN MILTON. With Photographic Illustrations. London: R. & A. Suttaby, 2, Amen Corner. n.d.," engraved title in red and black with early photograph of Milton's home (Chalfont St. Giles) mounted as circular vignette illustration at the center, both frontispiece and engraved title page with gilt border trim, "London: R. Clay, Sons, And Taylor, Printers" on verso of printed title page, preface (dated "March 1877"), eleven unsigned additional early photographs as illustrations for Milton's works, several of John Martin's illustrations, each mounted on its own page, without identification of the lines illustrated or title of the poem printed with the illustration, gilt border around each photograph illustration, introductory material as with first edition in 1877, contemporary limp red morocco (spine a bit rubbed and slightly chipped at top and bottom, early presentation inscription on fly-leaf), gilt rules on covers with Milton's name in gilt on front cover, spine ruled in gilt with gilt lettering, raised bands, a.e.g. A nice copy of a scarce edition with interesting early photographs as illustrations. See undated edition of *PW* published by "R. & A. Suttaby, 2, Amen Corner" about this same time (ca. 1879, copy listed here) in London in a larger 8vo format, with the same photograph illustrations as here tipped in, although larger photographs than the ones here, with a red border line in place of the gilt border here, and with no printed title page, only the title page with the photograph of Milton's home mounted as a circular vignette illustration at the center; see, too, the undated edition of *PW* published by "R. & A. Suttaby, 2, Amen Corner" about this same time (ca. 1879, copy listed here), in London in a larger 8vo format, with different photographs tipped in; and see the undated ca. 1886 "Suttaby & Co." edition listed with illustrations after Dalziel. The Globe editions by Macmillan were published without illustrations; see the first Globe edition published in 1877 and other editions cited there. Kohler 387, reporting "Not in the British Library. Not in Cambridge University Library."

2181. THE POETICAL WORKS OF JOHN MILTON. William P. Nimmo[:] *London And Edinburgh[.] 1878.* 8vo, xxxvii+[3]+440+16pp., unsigned engraved frontispiece portrait plate of a middle-aged Milton, engraved and printed title pages with vignette illustration (of the poet being inspired by heavenly choirs) by F. Borders on engraved title plate ("William P. Nimmo, London And Edinburgh." n.d.), vignette illustration (of a young boy in a setting in nature with a cane laying beside him) signed with the initials "WS" on printed title, "Printed By J. And J. Gray, Melbourne Place, Edinburgh" on verso of title page, eleven illustration plates, most after F. Borders, some unsigned, life of Milton by J. M. Ross, half-titles for *PL*, *PR*, *SA*, *C*, *Ar*, *MP*, and *Poemata*, red border around text, original decorated green cloth (a bit worn, foxing throughout, occasionally very heavy), front cover elaborately decorated in black with a large central emblem in gilt and black, with central figure seated and playing a lute in gilt against a black background with a cherubic figure on either side in gilt against a black background with green trim, title lettered in gilt against a black background at the top, Milton's name in gilt against a black background at the bottom, spine similarly decorated in black and gilt, with same central figure (now standing) with lute in gilt against a black background within an emblem in black and gilt similar to that on front cover at the center, Milton's name in embossed green against a broad gilt band near the top, small gilt medallions with black border trim at top and bottom, the medallion at the top containing the title, the medallion at the bottom crossed through with "W.P. Nimmo" in embossed gilt against a small gilt band with black border trim, both medallions with decorative floral trim in gilt as with the decorative black background to the gilt figure at the center on the spine and on front cover, back covers ruled in blind with central emblem in blind, dark green endpapers, a.e.g. A good copy with sixteen numbered pages advertising "Books Published By William P. Nimmo" bound in at the end. The possible first edition by Nimmo was published in 1865 (also listed here with further editions by Nimmo cited). Scarce. Not in Kohler.

2182. THE POETICAL WORKS OF JOHN MILTON. Edited, With A Critical Memoir, By William Michael Rossetti. Illustrated By Thomas Seccombe. Moxon's Popular Poets. *London: Ward, Lock, & Co., Warwick House, Dorset Buildings, Salisbury Square, E. C. n.d. [ca. 1878]*. 8vo, xx+460pp., half-title, engraved frontispiece portrait sketch of Milton (age ten), protective tissue guard, engraved and printed title pages, with vignette illustration after Thomas Seccombe for Milton's sonnet *On His Deceased Wife* on engraved title, "London E. Moxon Son & Co. Dover Street" at bottom of page, printer's device (stack of books with printed sheet with the letters of the press) on title page, six additional engraved illustration plates after Seccombe, four for *PL* (Books IV, VI, VIII, and XII), one for *C*, and one for *SA*, numerous elaborately decorated head- and tailpieces (less than preceding editions), red border with decorative red corner piece around text, original green cloth, front cover and spine richly decorated in embossed black and gilt trim with Milton's name in large embossed green lettering against a broad bright gilt band at top of front cover with the title in large embossed green lettering against a broad bright gilt band at the bottom, with a large lovely gilt device at the center incorporating "Moxon's Popular Poets" in large embossed black lettering around the top within a gilt band and "Edited By W M Rossetti" in large embossed black lettering around the bottom within a gilt band, the whole surround by delicate gilt trim, with the figure of a lady wearing laurel wreath seated playing a harp surround by long-stemmed laurel vines and other floral trim, all in gilt against a black background, spine similarly richly decorated in black and gilt, with Milton's name in large embossed green lettering incorporated within a broad decorative gilt device at the top, large circular gilt device near the bottom incorporating "Moxon's Popular Poets" in embossed green lettering within a gilt band surrounded by gilt trim, with a harp with long-stemmed laurel vines in gilt at the center against a black background, "Ward Lock & Co." in small embossed green lettering within a small broad gilt band at the bottom, central emblem in blind on back cover, decorated endpapers (front fly-leaf partially removed). A very nice copy in a lovely Victorian binding. Bound in at the end is a twenty-two-page listing of "Ward, Lock & Co.'s" publications, including "Moxon's Popular Poets" (with "Milton's Poetical Works" as No. 12), "Ward & Lock's Standard Poets" (with "Milton's Poetical Works" as No. 4). See undated ca. 1871 edition (possible first edition thus, see copies listed here) published by E. Moxon, Son, & Co., illustrated by Thomas Seccombe with identification of illustrator cited, as here, on title page; see also undated editions of Milton's *PW* by Ward and Lock published about this same time with illustrations by Thomas Seccombe with and without identification of the illustrator cited on title page (copies listed here); and see an undated ca. 1878 edition (copy listed here) by "Ward, Lock, Bowden And Co." edited by W. M Rossetti called "Moxon's Popular Poets" as here. Kohler 389, dating its copy "[1878]," with "460pp. 1/2 title," and reporting "Not in Williamson. Not in the Bodleian Library. Not in Cambridge University Library."

2183. THE POETICAL WORKS OF JOHN MILTON. Edited, With A Critical Memoir, By William Michael Rossetti. With full Page Illustrations. *Ward, Lock, Bowden And Co., London: Warwick House, Salisbury Square, E.C., New York: Bond Street. Melbourne: St. James's Street. Sydney: York Street. n.d. [ca. 1878]*. 8vo, xx+460pp., half-title with decorative emblem on verso, frontispiece portrait plate of Milton at age ten, protective tissue guard, title page with decorative emblem on verso, two unsigned engraved illustration plates after Seccombe, one for *PL* (Book IV) and one for *C*, numerous elaborately decorated head- and tailpieces, red border with decorative corner devices around text, original decorated blue cloth (a little rubbed, especially at top and bottom of spine), front cover elaborately decorated in gilt and black, with Milton's name in gilt relief at the top inset against a black background within a gilt border outlined in decorative black rule and trim, the whole against small decorations in blind relief, with a brilliant gilt device at the left center consisting of two long horns in embossed gilt, delicate gilt swirls, and a central gilt device against black outline with "Moxon's Popular Poets" in a scroll within, and with "Edited By W M Rossetti" in gilt relief at the bottom inset against a black background within a double gilt border outlined in a decorative black rule and trim, the whole against small decorations in embossed blind relief, spine similarly decorated in black and gilt, with Milton's name lettered in embossed gilt at the top inset against a black background within gilt rules with small decorations (same as those in relief on front cover) in gilt and, with a brilliant gilt device at the center consisting of delicate gilt swirls and incorporating "Moxon's Popular Poets" in gilt lettering within a gilt laurel wreath at the center, and with "Ward Lock Bowden & Co" in gilt relief at the bottom inset against a black background within gilt rules with small decorations (same as those in relief on front cover) in gilt above and below, decorated light green endpapers, a.e.g. A good copy in an attractive binding of the period, with illustration plates that are crisp and clear. See editions cited in preceding copy. Not in Kohler.

2184. THE POETICAL WORKS OF JOHN MILTON. Edited, With A Critical Memoir, By William Michael Rossetti. Illustrated By Thomas Seccombe. *London: Moxon, Son, & Company, 1 Amen Corner, Paternoster Row: [sic] n.d. [ca. 1878].* 8vo, xx+460pp., half-title, engraved frontispiece portrait plate of Milton at age ten, protective tissue guard, title-page plate and printed title page with vignette illustration by Thomas Seccombe for Milton's sonnet *On His Deceased Wife* on title-page plate, "London E. Moxon Son & Co. Dover Street" at bottom of page, harp with printer's initials embedded within at center of title page, six additional illustration plates by Seccombe, four for *PL* (Books IV, VI, VIII, and XII), one for *C*, and one for *SA*, numerous decorated head- and tailpieces, original blue cloth (a little worn, especially along extremities and at corners, spine ends chipped, back cover spotted, front joint cracked from within, spine rubbed), front cover decorated in embossed black trim with a cherub in each corner and a large piece of round card paper in color and trimmed in gold tipped at the center with the figure of a lady wearing laurel wreath playing the lyre in the middle and Milton's name in larger embossed letters against gilt band rounded at the top, with "Moxon's-Popular-Poets" in embossed blue letters against a bright gilt band between the two cherubs at the top and "Edited-By-W-M-Rossetti" in embossed blue letters against a bright gilt band between the two cherubs at the bottom, spine decorated in embossed black trim with a walking figure of a lady at the center, Milton's name in very large embossed blue letters against a bright gilt band at the top and "Moxon Son & Co." in small embossed blue letters against a bright gilt band at the bottom, a.e.g. Despite the general wear, overall a decent copy of an uncommon edition, different from the other Moxon's Popular Poets" editions here, with a variant publisher's imprint, no red border around the text, and in an unusual and attractive variant publisher's binding. Not in Kohler.

2185. THE POETICAL WORKS OF JOHN MILTON. Edited With Notes, Explanatory And Philological, By John Bradshaw, M.A., LL.D. Senior Moderator, Trin. Coll., Dublin; Inspector Of Schools, And Fellow Of The University, Madras. *London: Wm. H. Allen & Co., 13 Waterloo Place, Publishers to the India Office. MDCCCLXXVIII [1878].* 2 volumes. First edition thus. 8vo, viii+405,+[i]+688pp., half-title each volume, half-title for some of the poems, decorative head- and tailpieces with decorated letters, black rule around text, "Index to the Notes" at the end of each volume, "Printed By William Blackwell And Sons." at the bottom of last page (p. 405), volume 1, and repeated again at the bottom of last page (p. 688), volume 2, original green cloth, front covers ruled in black with small decorative devices in black at corners and at the center top and bottom with a small decorative gilt device at the center, spines lettered in gilt with decorative gilt trim at top and bottom, green endpapers, unopened. A very nice set. Volume 1 contains *EP*, *C*, *S*, and *SA*, with extensive notes on each poem at the end of the volume; volume 2 contains *PL* and *PR*, with extensive notes on each poem at the end of the volume. A second edition appeared in 1885 (W. H. Allen and Co.). Scarce. Kohler 388.

2186. THE POETICAL WORKS OF JOHN MILTON: With Introductions By David Masson, M.A., L.L.D., Professor Of Rhetoric And English Literature In The University Of Edinburgh. The Globe Edition. *London: Macmillan And Co. 1878.* Third edition thus. 8vo, xi+625+[1]pp., half-title (with emblem consisting of the letters of Macmillan and Co. on verso), "London: R. Clay, Sons, And Taylor, Printers" on verso of printed title page, preface (dated "March 1877"), introductory material as with first edition, "London: R. Clay, Sons, And Taylor, Printers" on verso of last page (625), contemporary full rose-colored morocco (slightly rubbed along joints and at top and bottom of spine, with a slight waterstaining streak across top of front cover and a similarly slight waterstaining mark along bottom third of back cover, some slight foxing within), gilt rules with small decorative gilt corner pieces on covers, seal of "Halleybury College" embossed in gilt at the center of front cover, spine elaborately decorated in gilt within the panels, green morocco label lettered in gilt with gilt rules, raised bands with decorative gilt trim, inner and outer dentelles finely tooled in gilt, marbled endpapers and edges. Except for the slight waterstaining, a fine copy in a nice Prize Binding, with prize label tipped in on front pastedown. The first Globe edition was published in March 1877 (also listed here with further copies cited). Scarce. Not in Kohler.

2187. THE POETICAL WORKS OF JOHN MILTON. Reprinted From The Chandos Poets. With Memoir, Explanatory Notes, &c. The "Chandos Classics." *London: Frederick Warne And Co., Bedford Street, Strand. n.d. [ca. 1878].* 8vo, xxiv+581+[1]pp., printer's device with initials "FW & Co." on title page, "Camden Press: Dalziel Brothers, Engravers & Printers" within small circular printer's device on verso of title page, "Dalziel Brothers, Camden Press, N.W[sic]" on verso of last page (p. 581), original reddish-brown cloth (a bit rubbed, age-browned, name in ink on title page, small hole on upper corner of fly-leaf), front cover decorated and lettered in black, back cover stamped in blind repeating decoration on front cover, spine lettered against gilt trim with decorative black trim, blue endpapers with advertisements for publications by Warne And Co., for "The Lansdowne Poets" on front fly-leaf (including "Milton's Poetical Works" [see copies listed here]) and for "The Chandos Classics" on verso of front fly-leaf (including "Milton" as No. 15, [see copies listed here]), advertisement leaf for additional publications by Warne and Co. bound in at end, with advertisement for "The Chandos Poets" on verso (including "Milton's Poetical Works. With numerous Notes." [see copies listed here]). See other undated and dated illustrated and nonillustrated editions by Frederick Warne and Co. published in the 1870s, 1880s, and 1890s: "The 'Lansdowne' Poets," "The 'Arundel' Poets," "The 'Chandos' Poets," "The 'Imperial' Poets, "The 'Chandos' Classics," and "The 'Albion' Edition." Uncommon. Kohler 392, dating its copy "[ca. 1878]," reporting "Not in the British Library. Not in the Bodleian Library. Not in Cambridge University Library."

2188. THE POETICAL WORKS OF JOHN MILTON. *London: Ward, Lock, & Co., Warwick House, Dorset Buildings, Salisbury Square E. C. n.d. [ca. 1878].* 8vo, viii+460+[20]pp., half-title, emblem of the press at center of title page, decorative head- and tailpieces (which look like standard printer's devices rather than illustrations for Milton passages), original decorated blue cloth (spine a little faded, some age-browning), front cover richly decorated in embossed black and gilt with large, brilliant gilt emblem at the center incorporating Milton's name in black against a bright gilt background, back cover and spine decorated in blind. Bound in at end: twenty pages advertising "New Books and New Editions Published by Ward, Lock, and Co." A nice copy in an attractive Victorian publisher's binding. Kohler 389, dating its copy "[1878]" in a variant binding in "green sand grain cloth" similarly decorated in black and gilt (see following copy), citing "16pp. of advertisements at end" (instead of twenty pages as here and in following copy), and reporting "Not in the Bodleian Library."

2189. Variant of Preceding, original decorated green cloth (slight age-browning), front cover richly decorated in embossed black and gilt with large, brilliant gilt emblem at the center incorporating Milton's name in black against a bright gilt background, back cover decorated in blind, spine decorated in gilt within the panels with Milton's name in embossed green letters. A very nice copy in a variant publisher's binding with twenty pages of advertisements for "New Books and New Editions Published by Ward, Lock, and Co." bound in at the end. Kohler 389.

2190. THE POETICAL WORKS OF JOHN MILTON[.] *London[:] George Bell And Sons, York Street Covent Garden[,] 1886, 1878, and 1878.* 3 volumes. Volumes 2 and 3 dated 1878. First edition by Bell. Small 8vo, xx+cxxxiv+[3]+[5]+153+[1]+blank+[4]pp.,+[ii]+372+[4]pp.,+vii+[i]+334+[4]pp., half-title each volume ("The Aldine Edition Of The British Poets"), title page each volume, central emblem of the press on each title page (bell and anchor in volume 1, dated 1886, printer's device in volume 2 and 3, each volume dated 1878), "Chiswick Press:—C. Whittingham And Co., Tooks Court, Chancery Lane" on verso of title page of each volume and on verso of the last page in each volume, original "Advertisement" for the 1832 Aldine edition by John Mitford with original date of 1831, life of Milton by Mitford followed by addenda and appendix, volume 1, half-title for some of the poems, notes at the bottom of the page, original green cloth (occasionally a bit rubbed), covers attractively decorated in black trim incorporating Milton's name within central gilt device on front covers beneath "The Aldine Poets" in decorative black lettering, Milton's name in gilt within similar gilt device and black trim on spines, edges untrimmed, partially unopened. An attractive set, printed by Charles Whittingham at the Chiswick Press, in a lovely, well-preserved publisher's binding, each volume with four pages of advertisements for publications by "George Bell And Sons" bound in at the end, including an advertisement for "The Cheap edition Of The Aldine Poets" (listing "Milton.

With Memoir by the Rev. J. Mitford. 3 vols"). Laid in volume 1: contemporary light blue threefold brochure (5 ⅛" × 3 ⅝") advertising publications by George Bell & Sons for "Bohn's Libraries." The first edition thus by Bell and Daldy was published in 1866 (see set listed here), a reissue of Pickering's Aldine edition of the British Poets. The Aldine British Poets edition was originally published by Pickering in 1832 (see Milton sets listed here); four more Aldine editions of Milton followed through mid-century, as cited with the 1832 Aldine edition (copies of each are in the collection). After Pickering's death in 1854 "the rights of the Aldine Poets were acquired by Bell & Daldy, by whom their issue, with many volumes added, has been continued to the present time (1924)" (Keynes, *Pickering*, p. 28). An entirely new edition of Pickering's three-volume Aldine edition of Milton was published in two volumes in 1892 in London by "George Bell & Sons" (see set listed here). Uncommon. Neither 1878 or 1886 editions in Kohler.

2191. THE POETICAL WORKS OF JOHN MILTON. With Photographic Illustrations. *London: R. & A. Suttaby, 2, Amen Corner. n.d. [ca. 1879].* First edition thus? Square 8vo, xxiv+581pp., early photograph of a Milton bust mounted as frontispiece, title page in red and black with early photograph mounted as circular vignette illustration at the center, both frontispiece and title page with gilt border trim, ten additional early photographs of illustrations for Milton's works, unsigned, several of John Martin's illustrations, mounted as illustrations, each on its own page, *without* identification of the lines illustrated or title of the poem printed with the illustration, red border around text and around each photograph illustration, half-title for *SA* with small decorative piece at center of opposite page, "Bungay: Clay And Taylor, Printers" on verso of last page (581), contemporary full green morocco (a bit rubbed), gilt rules on covers with Milton's name in gilt on front cover, spine ruled in gilt with gilt lettering, raised bands, a.e.g. A good copy of a very interesting and scarce edition, with interesting early photographs as illustrations. While the printed text and general look of this edition appear to be the same as the following undated edition published by "R. & A. Suttaby, 2, Amen Corner" about this same time, ca. 1879, in London, unlike that edition, the early photographs mounted as illustrations in the edition here are photographs of illustrations for Milton's works, including several of Martin's illustrations, not photographs of nature and farming scenes as in the following Suttaby edition. See also dated 1878 edition of *PW* published by "R. & A. Suttaby, 2, Amen Corner" in London in a smaller 8vo format, with the same photograph illustrations as here tipped in, although smaller photographs than the ones here, with a gilt border line in place of the red border here, and with a printed title page, "The Globe Edition. London: Macmillan And Co. 1878"; See, too, undated ca. 1886 "Suttaby & Co." edition listed here with illustrations after Dalziel. Kohler 378, dating its copy "1875[?]," and describing it as having "581 pp. Tipped-in photograph frontispiece of bust of Milton. Vignette tipped in on title-page. Ten unsigned plates . . . Lack[ing] 1/2-title" (presumably the half-title here for *SA*, since no general half-title to the edition appears to be missing), and reporting "Not in the British Library. Not in Cambridge University Library."

2192. THE POETICAL WORKS OF JOHN MILTON. With Photographic Illustrations By Deswall Vaughan. *London: R. & A. Suttaby, 2, Amen Corner. n.d. [ca. 1879].* First edition thus? Square 8vo, xxiv+581pp., early unsigned photographic reproduction of a portrait of Milton at age sixty-two mounted as frontispiece, title page in red and black, with early photograph (not the same as in preceding copy) mounted as circular vignette illustration at the center, both frontispiece and title page with gilt border trim, eleven early photographs (several oval vignettes) by Deswall Vaughan, mostly of nature and farming scenes, mounted as illustrations, each on its own page, with the lines illustrated and the title of the poem cited beneath each illustration, printed in red, gilt border trim around each photograph illustration, red border around text, half-title for *Samson Agonistes* with small decorative piece at center of opposite page, "Bungay: Clay And Taylor, Printers" on verso of last page (581), with a "Publisher's Preface" for "an edition of Longfellow's Poems" (dated "London, October, 1879") bound in upside down at the end, contemporary full red straight-grained morocco, gilt rules on covers and spine, spine lettered in gilt, raised bands with decorative gilt trim, inner dentelles ruled and finely tooled in gilt, marbled endpapers, a.e.g., bound by R. & A. Suttaby, with their stamp on inner dentelles of front cover. A very fine copy of a scarce edition in a well-preserved contemporary binding, with contemporary armorial bookplate on front pastedown, and with interesting early photographs as illustrations. While the printed text and general look of this edition appear to be the same as the preceding undated edition published by "R. & A. Suttaby, 2, Amen Corner" about this same time, ca. 1879, in London, unlike that edition, the early photographs mounted as illustrations in the edition here are photographs of nature and farming scenes, not photographs of illustrations for Milton's works as in the preceding edition. See also dated 1878 edition of *PW* published by "R. & A. Suttaby, 2, Amen Corner" in London in a smaller 8vo format, with the same photograph illustrations as those in the preceding undated Suttaby edition, and with a printed title page, "The Globe Edition. London: Macmillan And Co. 1878"; See, too, undated ca. 1886 "Suttaby & Co." edition with illustrations after Dalziel. Scarce. OCLC (two locations: Texas HRC & Arizona) calls for seven mounted plates; not found in NUC or BLC. Not in Kohler.

2193. THE POETICAL WORKS OF JOHN MILTON,
With Photographic Illustrations. *London: Suttaby & Co., Amen Corner, St. Paul's. n.d. [ca. 1879].* First edition thus? Large, thick 8vo, xxiv+581pp., half-title with "Morrison & Gibb, Edinburgh. Printer's to Her Majesty's Stationery Office" on verso, early unsigned photograph of "Michael And Satan. Paradise Lost, Book 6" mounted as frontispiece illustration, title page in red and black with small circular early photograph of Milton (age sixty-two, unsigned) mounted at center, both frontispiece and title page with gilt border trim, with lettering on frontispiece in gold, five early unsigned photographs, mostly of nature and farming scenes, mounted as illustrations, each on its own page with the lines illustrated and the title of the poem cited beneath each illustration, printed in gold, gilt border trim around each photograph illustration, half-title for *SA* (without small decorative piece at center of opposite page, as in preceding copy), "Morrison & Gibb, Edinburgh. Printer's to Her Majesty's Stationery Office" on verso of last page (581), with a "Publisher's Preface" for "an edition of Longfellow's Poems" (dated "London, October, 1879") bound in upside down at the end, contemporary padded full green morocco (a bit rubbed at joints, some corners worn, spine faded to an even brown with ends rubbed), Milton's name lettered in gilt at the center of front cover and near the top of the spine, decorated endpapers, a.e.g. A nice copy of a scarce edition, with interesting early photographs as illustrations. Scarce. Not in Kohler.

This edition is similar to the preceding edition, perhaps a later edition, but with a number of notable differences: (1) this edition is printed in a smaller and thicker octavo format; (2) with a general half-title (while none appears to be missing in the preceding edition); (3) with a similar, although modified, publisher's imprinted on title page; (4) with an unsigned frontispiece illustration of a statue of Michael with spear uplifted standing over a downcast Satan [new to this edition]; (5) with the remaining five illustrations unsigned, although similar to the illustrations in the preceding edition, and also by Deswall Vaughan, with the lines illustrated and poem cited beneath each illustration lettered in gold, not red; (6) with no red border around the text as in preceding edition; (7) with "Morrison & Gibb, Edinburgh. Printer's to Her Majesty's Stationery Office" on verso of half-title and again on verso of last page rather than "Bungay: Clay And Taylor, Printers," as in preceding copy. See references cited in preceding edition.

2194. THE POETICAL WORKS OF JOHN MILTON.
With Memoir, Explanatory and Glossarial Notes, &c. Portrait and original Illustrations. The Lansdowne Poets. *London: R. & A. Suttaby, 2, Amen Corner. n.d. [ca. 1879].* First edition thus? 8vo, xxiv+581pp., unsigned engraved frontispiece portrait of an early middle-aged Milton (labeled "London: Frederick Warne & Co." at bottom), protective tissue guard, title page in red and black with a gold rule, seven illustration plates after engravings by Dalziel: one for *NO*, four for *PL* (Books I, IV, IX, and XII), one for *PR* (Book I), one for *SA*, one for *On His Deceased Wife*, half-title for *SA*, notes at bottom of the page, red border around text, "Dalziel Brothers, Camden Press, London, N. W." on verso of last page, contemporary tree calf (a bit rubbed, joints cracked), covers decorated with finely tooled border trim, black morocco label on spine lettered in gilt with gilt rules and gilt trim, raised bands ruled in gilt, elaborately gilt decorated within the panels, outer dentelles tooled in gilt, marbled endpapers and edges. A nice copy, bound by "Stedman, Godalming," with their stamp. Variant edition from the preceding editions, with similar or identical publisher's imprint. Not in Kohler.

2195. THE POETICAL WORKS OF JOHN MILTON.
Edinburgh[:] William P. Nimmo & Co. 1879. 8vo, xxxvii+[3]+440pp., unsigned engraved frontispiece portrait plate of a middle-aged Milton, protective tissue guard, engraved and printed title pages with vignette illustration (of the poet being inspired by heavenly choirs) by F. Borders on engraved title plate ("William P. Nimmo, London And Edinburgh." n.d.), vignette illustration (of a young boy in a setting in nature with a cane laying beside him) signed with the initials "WS" on printed title, "Printed By J. And J. Gray, Melbourne Place, Edinburgh" on verso of title page, eleven illustration plates, most after F. Borders, some unsigned, life of Milton by J. M. Ross, eleven illustration plates, most after F. Borders, some unsigned: four for *PL* (Books I, III, VI, XI), two for *PR* (Book I), one for *SA*, two for *C*, one for *L'A*, one for *IlP*, half-title for *PL*, *PR*, *SA*, *C*, *Arc*, *MP*, and *Poemata*, and *Poemata*, red border around text, printer not indicated at bottom of last page, original decorated reddish-brown cloth (spine ends and corners a little worn, light spotted waterstains on back cover), front cover richly decorated in black and gilt with outer gilt rules and gilt trim framed by a thick black rule on the inside and delicate gilt trim within that, and at the center a recessed panel in a clover shape with richly gilt-decorated lavender leather inlaid with Milton's name lettered in embossed red against a broad gilt panel at the center, the panel outlined in a thin gilt rule, a thick black rule, and decorative gilt trim, with decorative black trim outlining the inside of the cover, central device in blind on

back cover, bevelled edges, spine lettered in gilt and richly decorated in gilt within the panels, thick black rules with gilt trim in between in imitation of decorated raised bands, a.e.g., with a contemporary presentation inscription dated 1880. A nice copy in an attractive publisher's binding, with variant publisher's imprint from those in other editions by Nimmo identified here. The possible first edition thus by Nimmo was published in 1865, illustrated (also listed here with further Nimmo editions, illustrated and nonillustrated, cited there). Only the 1865 edition has twelve illustrations, the others have eleven (with only one illustration for *L'A* instead of two, as in the 1865 edition). Scarce. Not in Kohler.

2196. THE POETICAL WORKS OF JOHN MILTON. With A Memoir, And Critical Remarks On His Genius And Writings, By James Montgomery; [Vol. I./II.] *Boston: Lee And Shepard, Publishers; New York: Charles T. Dillingham. 1879.* 2 volumes in one. Large, thick 8vo, xlix+[iv]+400pp. (pagination number beginning with page number "18"),+368pp., engraved frontispiece portrait plate by C. Burt, protective tissue guard, separate title page for volume 2 followed by "Contents Of Vol. II," full-page illustrations, including *Milton and His Daughter* (unsigned) at the end of "Memoir," *Adam and Eve Driven out of Paradise* by Doré (bound in Book X), *The Deluge* by Doré (bound in Book XI), *St. John the Baptist* by Doré (bound in Book I of *PR*), *Christ and His Disciples* by Doré (bound in Book IV of *PR*), illustrations (unsigned, but by Harvey) within the text for *L'A* with a vignette illustration at the beginning and another vignette illustration at the end of the poem and with vignette illustrations in the margins, *Defend the Poor and Destitute* by Barnes (bound in "Translations"), *May Morning* (unsigned), *Birth of Christ* by Doré (bound before *NO*), half-title for each book of *PL* and *PR* and for some of the poems, half-title for each book of *PR* with argument on verso (not original to the poem), double black border around text, contemporary leather (worn, joints cracked, spine ends chipped), black morocco label (worn) on spine with gilt lettering and gilt rules, marbled endpapers and edges, with contemporary signature (dated "Christmas, 1882") on front blank. A fair copy, fresh and clean within. See 1872 (possible first edition thus), 1873 (possible second edition thus), and 1876 (possible third edition thus) editions by Lee, Shepard and Dillingham listed earlier with illustrations by Harvey. Scarce. Not in Kohler.

2197. THE POETICAL WORKS OF JOHN MILTON. With Memoir, Explanatory Notes, Etc. The "Imperial" Poets. *London: Frederick Warne And Co. And New York. n.d. [ca. 1880].* 8vo, xxvi+581pp., half-title with red border trim and with "Morrison And Gibb, Printers, Edinburgh" printed on verso with red border trim, unsigned early photograph of a young Milton with long, curly hair mounted as frontispiece, with the label "Portrait of Milton." printed in the center at the bottom along with "Foulton's Series" printed to the left and "Frontispiece" printed to the right, red border around photograph, protective tissue guard, decorative device at bottom center of title page, decorative device on verso, five additional unsigned early photographs of various scenes and settings mounted as illustrations, each on its own page, each labeled "Foulton's Series" with printed instructions as to where each photograph-illustration is to be placed and with the appropriate passage printed beneath the photograph-illustration, red border around each photograph-illustration, red border around text, half-title for *SA* with small decorative piece at center of opposite page, "Morrison And Gibb, Printers, Edinburgh" with red border trim on verso of last page (581), contemporary full polished blue morocco (some slight foxing), gilt rules on covers with central gilt emblem of Marlborough College (dated 1843) on front cover, elaborately gilt-decorated spine, red morocco label with gilt lettering and gilt trim, outer dentelles trimmed in gilt, marbled endpapers and edges. A very fine copy in a lovely Prize Binding, with early photographs mounted as illustrations. See dated 1896 ("The 'Imperial' Poets") edition published by Frederick Warne with the same photographs mounted as illustrations, each labeled "Foulton's Series" as here, but without printed instructions on each photograph-illustration as to where each is to be placed as here. Not in Kohler.

2198. THE POETICAL WORKS OF JOHN MILTON. Reprinted From The Chandos Poets. With Memoir, Explanatory Notes, &c. Portrait And Original Illustrations. The Lansdowne Poets. *London: Frederick Warne And Co., Bedford Street, Strand. n.d. [ca. 1880].* 8vo, xxiv+581pp., unsigned engraved frontispiece portrait of an early middle-aged Milton (labeled "London: Frederick Warne & Co." at bottom), protective tissue guard, printer's device with initials "FW & Co." in the form of a shield on title page, "Camden Press: Dalziel Brothers, Engravers & Printers" within small circular printer's device on verso of title page, red border trim, eight illustration plates after engravings by Dalziel: one for *L'A*, four for *PL* (Books I, IV, VIII, and XII), one for *SA*, one for *On His Deceased Wife*, and one for *Latin Epigram VII* ("Ad Eandem"—the illustration titled *Milton Meeting Leonora Baroni at Cardinal Barberini's House*), half-title for *SA*, red border around text, "Dalziel Brothers, Camden Press, N.W." printed on verso of last page, notes at bottom of page, contemporary full red morocco, covers tooled in blind, spine lettered in gilt, raised bands, inner dentelles finely tooled in gilt, marbled endpapers, a.e.g. A fine copy, crisp and fresh within, in a contemporary cardinal red morocco binding. Not in Kohler.

2199. Variant of Preceding, original full black pebble morocco (a bit rubbed along joints and edges), covers tooled in blind, spine lettered in gilt, raised bands, marbled endpapers, a.e.g. A very handsome copy in a variant publisher's black pebble morocco divinity-style binding; much thicker than the preceding copy, ¼" thicker; with no illustration for *L'A* or for "Ad Eandem" and in their place an illustration for *NO* and for *PR*, not present in preceding copy; and also without "N.W." appearing after "Camden Press" on verso of last page. Not in Kohler.

2200. Variant of Preceding, original decorated green cloth (a bit rubbed, corners worn), front cover elaborately decorated in embossed black and gilt trim, a bright gilt harp at the center, a rich gilt band with decorative gilt trim near the top incorporating Milton's name in embossed green letters against a broad bright gilt band with initials "JM" in gilt above, decorative gilt trim at the top and bottom with "The Lansdowne Poets" in black lettering beneath the decorative gilt trim at the top and "Notes, Life &C." in embossed green letters within a bright gilt scroll above the decorative gilt trim at the bottom, back cover with central device in blind with the number "13" blind-stamped in the center, spine similarly decorated in embossed black and gilt with small urn in gilt at the bottom and rich gilt panel within decorative gilt trim and thick gilt bands near the top incorporating Milton's name in embossed green letters, decorative gilt trim at top and bottom with "The Lansdowne Poets" in black lettering beneath the decorative gilt trim at top and "F. Warne & Co." in embossed green letters within a gilt band at the bottom, green endpapers, a.e.g. A nice copy in an attractive variant publisher's cloth binding, with advertisement leaf bound in at the end. Not in Kohler.

2201. Variant of Preceding, original decorated blue cloth (a bit rubbed, spine slightly darkened), front cover decorated in embossed black and gilt trim with a large, bright oval gilt piece at the center lined in gilt with floral insets outlined in black and gilt with Milton's name in large gilt outline against a horizontal blue panel surrounded by a thick gilt rule, the whole within decorative black trim at the sides and a small harp in gilt on each side at the top, "Notes, Life, &C." in embossed blue letters against a black backdrop at the bottom and "The Lansdowne Poets" lettered in black at the top, spine similarly decorated in embossed black and gilt trim with the same central decorative piece in black and gilt as appears in the middle of the front cover, in a smaller version, with gilt lettering, the back cover trimmed in blind with central device in blind with the number "13" blind-stamped in the center, brown endpapers, a.e.g. A nice copy in an attractive variant publisher's binding, with contemporary signature (dated 1880) on verso of portrait, and with two pages of advertisements for publications by "Frederick Warne And Co., Publishers" bound in at the end. Not in Kohler.

2202. Variant of Preceding, original decorated blue cloth (a bit rubbed, small piece of paper glued to corner of back cover), front cover decorated in embossed black and gilt trim with a large, bright oval gilt piece at the center lined in gilt with floral insets outlined in black and gilt and Milton's name in large gilt outline against a horizontal blue panel surrounded by a thick gilt rule, the whole within decorative black trim at the sides and a small harp in gilt on each side at the top, "Notes, Life, &C." in embossed blue letters against a black backdrop at the bottom and "The Lansdowne Poets" lettered in black at the top, spine similarly decorated in embossed black and gilt trim with the same central decorative piece in black and gilt as appears in the middle of the front cover, in a smaller version, with "Illustrated" in blind letters through the middle of the emblem, "Milton's" name lettered in gilt within double gilt rules above, "The Lansdowne Poets" lettered in gilt at the top, and "F. Warne & Co." lettered in gilt at the bottom, the back cover trimmed in blind with central device in blind with the number "13" blind-stamped in the center, brown endpapers, a.e.g. A nice copy in an attractive variant publisher's binding, without identity for the first time, of "Frederick Warne And Co." as printer at bottom of frontispiece portrait, but left unsigned; with variant publisher's imprint: with the addition of "New York: Scribner, Welford, And Armstrong," following "Bedford Street, Strand," with initials of the press "FW&Co." in a circular printer's device on title page; without identity of printer on verso of title page as in other copies here; and with early signature written in a neat hand on verso of frontispiece and two pages of advertisements for "Frederick Warne & Co., Publishers" bound in at the end. Not in Kohler.

The collection also has a number of other editions in variant publisher's bindings and with other variances: (1) in original decorated reddish-brown cloth, decorated exactly as the blue cloth preceding, with two pages of advertisements bound in at the end; (2) in original decorated green cloth, front cover decorated in embossed black and gilt trim, with a large, bright oval gilt piece at the center with Milton's name in large gilt outline against a horizontal green panel surrounded by a thick gilt rule, "Notes, Life, &C." in embossed green letters against a black backdrop at the bottom, and "The Lansdowne Poets" lettered in black at the top, decorated as the blue cloth binding above and, like that copy, with contemporary signature (dated 1880) on verso of portrait and two pages of advertisements bound in at the end; (3) in original decorated reddish-brown cloth, front cover elaborately decorated in black and gilt trim incorporating Milton's name in large outlined gilt letters at the center, with "The Lansdowne Poets" lettered in black at the top and "Notes, Life, &C." lettered in embossed reddish-brown letters against a black background at the bottom, spine similarly decorated in gilt and black with lettering in gilt and black with the number "13" blind-stamped in the center of the decorative blind piece on the back cover, brown endpapers, and two pages of advertisements bound in at the end, a.e.g.; and (4) in original navy blue pebble morocco, with no illustration for *L'A* or for "Ad Eandem" and in their place an illustration for *NO* and for *PR*, not present in most other editions here; "London, N.W." is also present after "Camden Press" on verso of last page, also not present in most other editions here.

2203. THE POETICAL WORKS OF JOHN MILTON. Reprinted From The Best Editions, With Memoir, Explanatory and Glossarial Notes, &c. Portrait And Original Illustrations. The Lansdowne Poets. *London: Frederick Warne And Co., Bedford Street, Strand. New York: Scribner, Welford, And Armstrong. n.d. [ca. 1880].* 8vo, xxiv+581+[2]pp., unsigned engraved frontispiece portrait of an early middle-aged Milton (with labeling "London: Frederick Warne & Co." at bottom), protective tissue guard, initials of the press "FW & Co." in a circular printer's device on title page, "London: Printed By Woodfall And Kinder, Milford Lane, Strand, W.C." on verso of title page and repeated on last page, eight illustration plates after engravings by Dalziel: one for *NO*, four for *PL* (Books I, IV, VIII, and XII), one for *PR*, one for *SA*, and one for *On His Deceased Wife*, notes at bottom of the page, original dark green cloth (a bit rubbed, some foxing), front cover elaborately decorated in gilt and black with angel playing a harp, a torch, Milton's name in gilt within decorative gilt border, and "The Lansdowne Poets" lettered in black at the top, spine similarly elaborately decorated in gilt and black, with gilt harp along with Milton's name in gilt at the center, "The Lansdowne Poets" in gilt at the top, and "F. Warne & Co." in gilt at the bottom, back cover ruled in blind with central device in blind, a.e.g. Bound in at end: an advertisement leaf advertising "The Chandos Library. A Series Of Standard Works In All Classes Of Literature" on recto and on verso. A nice copy in a rather well-preserved nineteenth-century publisher's gilt-stamped cloth binding, with a variant printer identification on verso of title page and on last page, without red border around text, and without an illustration for *L'Allegro* or for "Ad Eandem" and in their place an illustration for *NO* and for *PR*, a variant interchangeable pattern of illustrations commonly followed in "The Lansdowne Poets" editions by Frederick Warne and Co. Kohler 380, dating its copy "ca. 1875" and reporting "Not in Williamson. Not in the British Library. Not in the Bodleian Library. Not in Cambridge University Library."

2204. Variant of Preceding, original decorated green cloth (a little aged), front cover elaborately decorated in black and gilt, with central black and gilt decorative pieces incorporating Milton's name in embossed letters within a broad gilt band at the center and with "The Lansdowne Poets" lettered in black at the top and "With Explanatory Notes &C" lettered in black at the bottom, spine lettered in embossed green against a gilt background, back cover decorated in blind, a.e.g. Bound in at the end a leaf advertising "The Chandos Classics. A Series Of Standard Works In Poetry, Biography, &c. In large crown 8vo, price One Shilling each, stiff wrapper; or cloth gilt, 1s. 6d." (including Milton). A good copy in a variant publisher's decorated cloth binding, with several different illustrations: for *NO* instead of *L'A*, for Books V and VII instead of Books I and IV of *PL*, and for *PR* instead of "Ad Eandem." Not in Kohler.

2205. THE POETICAL WORKS OF JOHN MILTON. Reprinted From The Chandos Poets, With Memoir, Explanatory Notes, &c. With Illustrations. The "Chandos Classics." *London: Frederick Warne And Co. Bedford Street, Covent Garden. n.d. [ca. 1880].* 8vo, xxiv+581pp., frontispiece illustration plate after an engraving by Dalziel for *L'A*, protective tissue guard, small circular printer's device with lettering "F. Warne & Co. Bedford St. Covent Garden" on title page, nothing on verso of title page, seven additional illustration plates after engravings by Dalziel (as in the editions above): four for *PL* (Books I, IV, VIII, and XII), one for *SA*, one for *On His Deceased Wife*, and one for *Latin Epigram VII* ("Ad Eandem"—the illustration titled *Milton Meeting Leonora Baroni at Cardinal Barberini's House*, signed by Dalziel), half-title for *SA*, "Woodfall and Kinder, Printers, Milford Lane, Strand, London, W.C." at the bottom of last page, notes at bottom of page, original red cloth, front cover brilliantly decorated in gilt and black with gilt forming what looks like an "H" incorporating Milton's name in embossed red in the crosspiece with a harp in gilt against a black backdrop at the bottom and a decorative gilt piece with black trim at the top, spine similarly decorated in bright gilt and black with harp in gilt against a black backdrop at the center beneath a bright gilt band incorporating Milton's name in embossed red near the top, gilt rules with gilt blossoms at top and bottom, "F. Warne & Co." in embossed red letters within a bright small gilt band at the bottom, back cover decorated in blind, a.e.g. A fine copy, fresh and clean within, in a well-preserved Victorian publisher's decorated cloth binding. For variants of this attractive binding, similarly decorated, but in blue cloth, see ca. 1873 London Frederick Warne and Co . . . New York Scribner, Welford and Armstrong edition and ca. 1880 New York Scribner, Welford and Armstrong editions, both listed here, the latter with "Scribner & Co." at bottom of the spine. Not in Kohler.

2206. THE POETICAL WORKS OF JOHN MILTON. Reprinted From The Best Editions. With Memoir, Explanatory and Glossorial Notes, &c. Portrait And Original Illustrations. The Chandos Poets. *London: Frederick Warne And Co., Bedford Street, Strand. n.d. [ca. 1880].* Large square 8vo, xxiv+581+[2]pp., unsigned engraved frontispiece portrait of an early middle-aged Milton (labeled "London: Frederick Warne & Co." at bottom), title page in orange and black with central device incorporating the initials of the press, "FW & Co.," "Bungay: Clay And Taylor Printers" on verso of title page and of last page (p. 581), twelve illustration plates after engravings by Dalziel: one for *NO*, one for *L'A*, six for *PL* (Books I, IV, V, VII, VIII, and XII), one for *PR* (Book I), one for *SA*, one for *On His Deceased Wife*, and one for *Latin Epigram VII* ("Ad Eandem"—the illustration titled *Milton Meeting Leonora Baroni at Cardinal Barberini's House*), decorative tailpiece at the end of *PR*, half-title for *SA*, red border around text, notes at bottom of page, original decorated reddish-brown cloth (spine ends a little rubbed, lacking front fly-leaf), front cover richly decorated in black and gilt with vignette impression of Milton in gilt at the center within decorative gilt border trim with four small emblems in gilt at the center top and bottom and at the center on either side, spine richly decorated in black and gilt with decorative gilt emblems and gilt lettering, a.e.g. A lovely copy, very large, measuring 7 ½" × 5 ½", in a stunning gilt-stamped publisher's cloth binding, with the number "10" stamped in blind at the bottom of the front cover, and with an advertisement leaf for "The Chandos Poets" series of "New and Elegant Volumes of Standard Poetry" to be published by "Frederick Warne & Co., Publishers" bound in at the end. At the beginning of *PR* there is the notation in pencil in a neat hand at the top of the page: "Began to read this March 5th 1881." See other undated and dated illustrated and nonillustrated editions by Frederick Warne and Co. published in the 1870s, 1880s, and 1890s under the various series: "The 'Lansdowne' Poets," "The 'Arundel' Poets," "The 'Chandos' Poets," "The 'Chandos' Classics," "The 'Imperial' Poets," "The 'Albion' Edition," and the "Cabinet Poets." Not in Kohler.

2207. THE POETICAL WORKS OF JOHN MILTON. Reprinted From The Best Editions. With Memoir, Explanatory and Glossorial Notes, &c. Portrait And Original Illustrations. The Arundel Poets. *London: Frederick Warne And Co., Bedford Street, Strand. n.d. [ca. 1880].* Large square 8vo, xxiv+581pp., engraved frontispiece portrait (of a youngish looking middle-aged Milton, unsigned, with labeling "London: Frederick Warne & Co." at bottom), title page in orange and black with central device incorporating the initials of the press, "FW & Co.," twelve illustration plates after engravings by Dalziel (as in preceding edition by Frederick Warne & Co.), decorative tailpiece at the end of *PR*, half-title for *SA*, orange border around text, "Bungay: Clay And Taylor Printers" on verso of title page and of last page, notes at bottom of page, contemporary full red morocco (a bit rubbed at joints), elegantly blind-tooled covers with variously designed finely tooled gilt decorations, Milton's name in gilt on front cover with the letter "M" surrounded with a bold gilt background and delicate gilt trim, spine decorated in gilt and blind within the panels, raised bands (bit rubbed), inner and outer dentelles finely tooled in gilt, marbled endpapers, a.e.g. Possibly a large paper copy, measuring 8" × 5 ¾", or ½" taller and ¾" wider than other editions here by Frederick Warne and Co. A very handsome copy in a splendid contemporary morocco binding. Not in Kohler.

2208. THE POETICAL WORKS OF JOHN MILTON. Edited, With A Critical Memoir, By William Michael Rossetti. With full [sic] Page Illustrations. *Griffith[,] Farran[,] Okeden & Welsh[,] Newbery House, London & Sydney, N.S.W., n.d. [ca. 1880].* 8vo, xx+460pp., half-title, engraved frontispiece portrait sketch of Milton (age ten) with protective tissue guard, small emblem at center of title page, six unsigned engraved illustration plates after Seccombe, four for *PL* (Books IV, VI, VIII, and XII), one for *C*, and one for *SA*, with the poem *C* coming between *PL* and *SA*, numerous elaborately decorated head- and tailpieces, red border around text, contemporary full tree calf (a little rubbed along joints and extremities, joints tender), finely tooled gilt border trim on covers, spine elaborately decorated in gilt, green morocco label with gilt lettering and gilt rules, raised bands with decorative gilt trim, marbled endpapers and edges. A nice copy with late nineteenth-century signature. See similar undated ca. 1870s edition listed earlier published by "Griffith, Farran, Okeden & Welsh, At The Sign Of The "Bible And Sun," West Corner Of St. Paul's Churchyard, London." Scarce. Not in Kohler.

2209. THE POETICAL WORKS OF JOHN MILTON. With Life. Six Engravings on Steel. *Gall & Inglis. Edinburgh: Bernard Terrace. London: 25 Paternoster Sqr. n.d. [ca. 1880].* 8vo, xx+491pp., engraved and printed title pages, with the printed title page reading *PW*, the engraved title page reading *CPW*, unsigned frontispiece illustration plate of *The Expulsion*, with unsigned vignette illustration of *Eve Relating Her Dream to Adam* on engraved title, which bears the publisher "Edinburgh, Gall & Inglis. London," undated, with the appropriate passage cited beneath each illustration, additional unsigned illustration plates for *PL* (Books II, VII, and IX) and for *PR* (Book IV) with the appropriate passage cited beneath each illustration, life of Milton with half-title, half-title for *PL* after "Contents," red border around text, original decorated blue cloth (bit rubbed, occasional light spotted foxing in margins), front cover elaborately decorated in black and gilt, with brilliant central crest-shaped panel in white on front cover, with decorative gilt border trim and an urn in gilt at the center incorporating Milton's name in red relief within a red rule against a gilt backdrop, spine similarly elaborately decorated in black and gilt with the title ("Milton's Poetical Works") incorporated at a slant within a large gilt device at the top and Milton's name in red relief as on the front cover and "Poetical Works" in green relief, decorative gilt trim at the top and bottom, the bottom gilt trim incorporating "Gall & Inglis," back cover decorated in blind, a.e.g. A nice copy in a lovely Victorian publisher's cloth binding, with contemporary signature (dated "Christmas '77") on verso of frontispiece. See undated ca. 1870s / ca. 1875 edition listed earlier published by Gall & Inglis in Edinburgh ("Bernard Terrace") and London ("25 Paternoster Sqr") with only "Engravings on Steel" appearing on title page and with decorative border trim around the text in alternating sepia and bluish green tint with varying background scenes and other editions cited by Gall & Inglis cited there. Not in Kohler.

2210. Variant of Preceding, original green ribbed cloth (a bit rubbed along front joint and at spine ends, some foxing), front cover elaborately decorated in black and gilt, with brilliant central oval panel in white on front cover with decorative gilt border trim and a small angelic figure in gilt above and a small harp in gilt below Milton's name in red relief within a red rule against a gilt backdrop, the whole surrounded by gilt and black trim with a small figure playing the harp in gilt at the top, a small cherubic figure in gilt at the bottom, and a gilt harp on either side of the black and gilt trim at the bottom, spine similarly elaborately decorated in black and gilt with the title ("Milton's Poetical Works") incorporated within a large gilt device at the top and a small figure playing the harp incorporated within a large gilt device near the bottom, with decorative gilt trim at the top and bottom, the bottom gilt trim incorporating "Gall & Inglis," back cover decorated in blind, a.e.g. A very nice copy in an attractive variant publisher's decorated cloth binding. Not in Kohler.

2211. Variant of Preceding, original red cloth (a bit rubbed, tips of lower right-hand corners of two plates slightly waterstained), front cover elaborately decorated in embossed black and gilt with large central gilt device incorporating Milton's name with a small angelic figure in gilt above and a small harp and laurel leaf in gilt below, spine similarly elaborately decorated in black and gilt relief with the same gilt device as on the front cover incorporating Milton's name with decorative gilt trim at the top and at the bottom, back cover decorated in blind, a.e.g. A very nice copy in an attractive variant publisher's decorated cloth binding. Not in Kohler.

2212. THE POETICAL WORKS OF JOHN MILTON. Edited, With A Critical Memoir, By William Michael Rossetti. Illustrated By Thomas Seccombe. *London: Ward, Lock, & Co., Warwick House, Dorset Buildings, Salisbury Square, E.C. n.d. [ca. 1880].* Large square 8vo, xx+460pp., half title, early photograph of a portrait of Milton seated with right hand outstretched by "Vincent Brooks Day & Son" tipped in as frontispiece, protective tissue guard, printer's device (stack of books with printed sheet with the letters of the press) on title page, five engraved illustration plates after Seccombe, three for *PL* (Books IV, VI, and VIII), one for *C*, and one for *SA*, numerous elaborately decorated head- and tailpieces, red border with decorative corner devices around text, original half navy blue morocco, navy blue cloth (a little rubbed at joints and corners), gilt rules on covers, spine lettered in gilt with small decorative gilt devices in the panels, raised bands with decorative gilt trim (now rather faded), marbled endpapers, a.e.g. A good copy, possibly large paper copy, with prize inscription (dated 1884) on front blank. See undated ca. 1878 edition of Milton's *PW* (listed earlier) published by "Ward, Lock, & Co." as "Moxon's Popular Poets" with identification of illustrator on title page, as in undated ca. 1871 possible first Moxon edition and as here; a second undated illustrated edition was published by "Ward, Lock, Bowden And Co." ca. 1878 as "Moxon's Popular Poets" (also listed here), which does not identify the illustrator on the title page. See also copy of undated nonillustrated edition published by "Ward, Lock, & Co." ca. 1878 (listed earlier). Kohler 397, dating its copy "[1880]" and reporting "Not in Williamson. Not in the Bodleian Library. Not in Cambridge University Library."

2213. THE POETICAL WORKS OF JOHN MILTON. [Edited] By William Michael Rossetti. With full Page Illustrations. *London: Ward, Lock & Bowden, Limited, Warwick House, Salisbury Square, E.C., New York And Melbourne. n.d. [ca. 1880].* 8vo, xx+460pp., half-title, two unsigned engraved illustration plates after Seccombe, one for *PL* (Book IV) and one for *C*, numerous elaborately decorated head- and tailpieces, red border with decorative corner pieces around text, one-half navy blue morocco (a bit rubbed, spine a little faded), marbled paper over boards, red morocco label with gilt lettering on spine, decorative gilt pieces within the panels, raised bands with decorative gilt trim within gilt rules, decorative gilt trim at top and bottom, marbled endpapers and edges. A nice copy. The illustrations are by Thomas Seccombe, although they are not attributed to him on the title page here as in other undated editions of Milton's *PW* published by Ward and Lock about this time (see references cited in preceding copy). Uncommon. Not in Kohler (although see Kohler 396, with similar title and publisher's imprint: "The Poetical Works of John Milton. Edited by William Michael Rossetti. London, New York and Melbourne: Ward, Lock & Bowden, Limited, Warwick House, Salisbury Square, E.C. n.d. [ca. 1880] . . . 460pp.").

2214. THE POETICAL WORKS OF JOHN MILTON. Reprinted From The Chandos Poets, With Memoir, Explanatory Notes, &c. *New York: Scribner, Welford And Armstrong. n.d. [ca. 1880].* 8vo, xxiv+581+[2]pp., frontispiece illustration plate after an engraving by Dalziel for *NO*, protective tissue guard, small circular printer's device with lettering "F. Warne & Co. Bedford St. Covent Gar" on title page, nothing on verso of title page, seven additional illustration plates after engravings by Dalziel (as in the earlier editions): four for *PL* (Books I, IV, VIII, and XII), one for *PR*, one for *SA*, and one for *On His Deceased Wife*, half-title for *SA*, "London: Printed By Woodfall And Kinder, Milford Lane, Strand, W.C." on verso of last page, notes at bottom of page, original blue cloth (a bit used), front cover brilliantly decorated in gilt and black trim with gilt forming what looks like an "H" incorporating Milton's name in embossed blue in the crosspiece with a harp in gilt against a black backdrop at the bottom and a decorative gilt piece with black trim at the top, spine similarly decorated in bright gilt with harp in gilt against a black backdrop at the center beneath a bright gilt band incorporating Milton's name in embossed blue near the top, gilt rules with gilt blossoms at top and bottom, "Scribner & Co." in embossed blue letters within a bright small gilt band at the bottom, back cover decorated in blind, a.e.g. Bound in at the end: an advertisement leaf, advertising "The Chandos Library" on recto, and on verso "The Chandos Poets" (including "Milton's Poetical Works . . . Original Illustrations. Red-line border"). A nice copy in a rather well-preserved nineteenth-century American publisher's decorated binding. For variants of this attractive binding, see ca. 1873 London Frederick Warne and Co . . . New York Scribner, Welford and Armstrong edition in blue cloth and ca. 1880 London Frederick Warne and Co. edition in red cloth. Scarce. Not in Kohler.

2215. THE POETICAL WORKS OF JOHN MILTON. Reprinted From The Chandos Poets.[sic] With Memoir, Explanatory Notes, &c. Portrait And Original Illustrations. *Boston: Ira Bradley And Co., 162 Washington Street. n.d. [ca. 1880].* First edition thus by Ira Bradley Co.? 8vo, xxiv+581+[1]pp., unsigned engraved frontispiece portrait of an early middle-aged Milton (a bit foxed), protective tissue guard, eight illustration plates after engravings by Dalziel: one for *L'A*, four for *PL* (Books I, IV, VIII, and XII), one for *SA*, one for *On His Deceased Wife*, and one for *Latin Epigram VII* ("Ad Eandem"—the illustration titled *Milton Meeting Leonora Baroni at Cardinal Barberini's House*), half-title for *SA*, orange border around text, notes at bottom of page, original olive green cloth (bit rubbed along upper joints and at spine ends, some foxing), front cover elaborately decorated in embossed black trim with large embossed black floral design in the center and Milton's name in embossed olive green letters against a bright gilt band with floral trim at the top with the letter "M" in a larger size and outlined in gilt surrounded by decorative gilt floral pieces, spine decorated with a large bright gilt floral piece in the foreground and black floral stems in the background, with decorative black and gilt trim, with Milton's name in embossed olive green letters against a bright gilt band at the top and the initials "B & Co" in black letters within gilt trim at the bottom, a.e.g. Bound in at the end is an advertisement leaf for "Bradley's Red Line Edition of British Poets" (including "Milton, with memoir, notes, etc. . . . .[sic] 638 " [pages]"). One of "Bradley's Red Line Edition of British Poets." A good copy. See undated and dated illustrated editions by Frederick Warne and Co. published about this same time with the same engravings by Dalziel. Not in Kohler.

2216. Variant of Preceding, original green cloth decorated as preceding copy, without advertisement leaf bound in at the end. One of "Bradley's Red Line Edition of British Poets." A nice copy in an attractive variant publisher's decorated cloth binding. Not in Kohler.

2217. THE POETICAL WORKS OF JOHN MILTON. Reprinted From The Best Editions With Biographical Notice, Etc. *Chicago: Belford, Clarke & Co.[,] 1880.* First edition thus by Belford, Clarke & Co.? 8vo, iii+562pp., frontispiece illustration plate after an engraving by Dalziel for *SA*, protective tissue guard, three additional illustration plates after engravings by Dalziel: two for *PL* (Books IV and VIII) and one for *L'A*, red border around text, original decorated red cloth (a bit rubbed with some light wear along extremities and at top of spine, occasional slight staining on back, pages lightly age-browned), front cover richly decorated in embossed black and gilt, with embossed decorative black floral motif across the entire cover and Milton's name in large embossed red letters within a broad bright gilt band at the top within delicately tooled small black and gilt trim, all within a brighter gilt backdrop with embossed floral trim in red and black, with a self-contained larger decorated red letter "M" with delicately tooled black and gilt trim at the top and similarly delicately tooled black and gilt trim in a floral motif at the bottom, and at the center a bright gilt block in relief richly set off by two thin black rules with a large embossed flower in red with black trim running through it, spine similarly richly decorated in black and gilt with a floral motif in embossed red with black trim against a largely gilt backdrop, the flowers coming out of a vase in red and black near the bottom, with the title ("Milton's Poems") in large embossed red letters within two bright gilt bands at the top, each band within decorative black, red, and gilt trim, an embossed emblem at the center against a bright circular gilt background in relief set within a square red background heavily darkened and outlined in red set within a further triangular red background tooled and outlined in black, with decorative black, red, and gilt trim at the top and the bottom, decorated endpapers, a.e.g. See 1884 edition published by Belford, Clarke & Co. in Chicago and New York, as here, and with six illustration plates after Doré (the possible first edition thus by Belford, Clarke & Co. with Doré plates); see also 1886 edition published by Belford, Clarke & Co. in Chicago and New York with four illustration plates after Doré (the possible second edition thus by Belford, Clarke & Co. with Doré plates); and see 1888 edition published by Belford, Clarke & Co. in Chicago, New York, and San Francisco with six illustration plates after Doré (the possible third edition thus by Belford, Clarke & Co. with Doré plates)—all listed here. Uncommon. Not in Kohler.

2218. **THE POETICAL WORKS OF JOHN MILTON.** Reprinted From The Original Edition, And Containing Numerous Explanatory Notes. With Memoir By David Masson, M. A., LL. D., Author of "The Life And Times Of John Milton." The "Arundel Poets." The Arundel Print. *New York. (1880).* First edition thus by the Arundel Print? Small, thick 8vo, li+[i]+627pp., frontispiece illustration plate and twenty additional illustration plates after Gustave Doré, "Copyright, 1880, By The Arundel Print" on verso of title page, decorative head- and tailpieces, half-title for *SA*, notes at bottom of page, original three-quarter brown calf, marbled paper over boards, gilt-decorated spine, black leather label with gilt lettering and gilt rules, marbled endpapers and edges. A nice copy with contemporary signature (dated 1887) on front blank. A possible second edition thus by "The Arundel Print. New York," undated, was published ca. 1883, without a copyright date on verso of title page (also listed here). Another edition (with fewer illustration plates after Doré) was published in Boston by DeWolfe, Fiske & Company in 1884 (also listed here) with "Copyright, 1880, By The Arundel Print" on verso of title page as here. A similar edition was published in Chicago And New York by Belford, Clarke & Co. with "The 'Arundel Poets'" on title page as here, but with only several illustration plates after Doré, in 1884, 1886, and 1888—all listed here. Not in Kohler.

2219. Variant of Preceding. **THE POETICAL WORKS OF JOHN MILTON.** Reprinted From The Original Edition, And Containing Numerous Explanatory Notes. With Memoir By David Masson, M. A., LL. D., Author of "The Life And Times Of John Milton." The "Arundel Poets." The Arundel Print. *New York. (1880).* First edition thus (variant edition by the Arundel Print). Large thick 8vo, li+[i]+627pp., frontispiece illustration plate and twenty additional illustration plates by Gustave Doré, "Copyright, 1880, By The Arundel Print" on verso of title page, decorative head- and tailpieces, half-title for *SA*, double black border around text with small circular corner pieces, notes at bottom of page, original decorated yellow cloth (a bit rubbed, small tear at top of spine repaired, joints slightly shaken from within, small stamp of earlier owner's name on front pastedown), front cover and spine elaborately decorated in black and gilt, with decorative gilt patterns in black and gilt, with Milton's name in large outlined gilt lettering against a black backdrop at the top accented by a thick gilt border and a thick gilt band behind the letters within and by a floral trimmed larger letter "M" in black against a gilt background framed in gilt and black, "Illustrated" lettered in gilt at the center, spine similarly decorated in black and gilt with Milton's name and title at the top, small crest in gilt against a black backdrop at the center, and "Arundel Print" lettered in gilt at the bottom, decorated endpapers in a floral pattern, a.e.g. A handsome copy in a much larger octavo format than the preceding edition, measuring 9 ¼" × 7", or 1 ¾" taller and 1 ½" wider than the preceding edition, in a stunning publisher's binding. Not in Kohler.

2220. Variant of Preceding, original decorated red cloth (spine a bit faded), decorated exactly as the preceding copy in yellow cloth. A handsome copy in a very attractive variant publisher's cloth binding. Not in Kohler.

2221. THE POETICAL WORKS OF JOHN MILTON; With A Life Of The Author, By The Rev. H. Stebbing, A.M. *New York: Hurst & Co., Publishers, 122 Nassau Street. n.d. [ca. 1880].* First edition thus by Hurst? 8vo, xv+190pp., unsigned frontispiece portrait plate of Faithorne portrait with Dryden epigram, protective tissue guard, four illustration plates (unsigned—reproductions of illustrations by Doré) for *PL* (Book V, lines 12–13, *Adam Admiring Eve Sleeping*, placed here in Book VII; Book V, lines 468–70, *Raphael counseling Adam and Eve*, placed here in Book IX; Book IX, lines 74–5, *The Snake, Adam and Eve*, placed here in Book X; Book IX, lines 1121–23, *The Judgment*, placed here at the head of Book XII), and one unsigned illustration plate (Dorésque in nature) for *PR*, elaborate decorative red border trim around text, decorative tailpieces of different head sketches, small sketch of the head of a woman on verso of title page, original decorated reddish-brown cloth (a bit worn and a little shaken from within, pages somewhat fragile, library stamps marked "withdrawn," small shelf label on spine, due card in pocket at back), front cover and spine elaborately decorated in black and gilt incorporating Milton's name within bright gilt device at the top, brown endpapers, a.e.g. An early Hurst publication of Milton and a different edition from the others here, with different pagination and in a different publisher's binding from the others here. See other undated illustrated and nonillustrated editions of Milton's *PW* published by Hurst about this same time. Uncommon. Not in Kohler.

2222. THE POETICAL WORKS OF JOHN MILTON. With A Sketch Of His Life. *New York: Hurst & Co., Publishers, 122 Nassau Street. n.d. [ca. 1880].* First edition thus by Hurst? 8vo, 562pp., unsigned frontispiece portrait plate with Dryden epigram, protective tissue guard, "'Argyle Press,' Printing and Bookbinding, 24 & 26 Wooster St., N.Y." on verso of title page, four illustration plates (unsigned—reproductions of illustrations by Doré) for *PL* (Book V, lines 12–13, *Adam Admiring Eve Sleeping*, placed here in Book VII; Book V, lines 468–70, *Raphael Counseling Adam and Eve*, placed here in Book IX; Book IX, lines 74–5 *The Snake, Adam and Eve*, placed here in Book X; Book IX, lines 1121–23 *The Judgment*, placed here at the end of Book XII) and one unsigned illustration plate (Dorésque in nature) for *PR*, orange border around text, original crushed brown leather over padded boards (a bit rubbed, especially along spine), front cover and spine lettered in gilt, decorated endpapers, a.e.g. A very good copy of a late nineteenth-century illustrated American edition, in a nice American publisher's binding, with contemporary inscription (dated 1888) on first front blank and a later inscription on second front blank. See undated illustrated and nonillustrated editions of Milton's *PW* here published by Hurst ca. 1880, ca. 1881, ca. 1883, ca. 1895, ca. 1905, and ca. 1907. See also undated illustrated edition of *PL* published by Hurst ca. 1900 (with frontispiece illustration). Not in Kohler.

2223. Variant of Preceding, original decorated blue cloth, front cover decorated in embossed black and gilt with Milton's name incorporated within a bright gilt band framed in black and gilt rules at the top surrounded by laurel wreath in bright gilt with crossed torches in blue and other floral motif in bright gilt, spine similarly decorated in black and gilt with broad gilt band incorporating Milton's name at the top and with a smaller gilt band incorporating "Hurst & Co." at the bottom, just below Milton's name is winged pegasus within a small gilt circle inside a gilt square, decorated endpapers, a.e.g. A very nice copy in a variant publisher's cloth binding. Not in Kohler.

2224. Variant of Preceding, original decorated brown cloth, decorated as preceding copy. A nice copy in a variant publisher's cloth binding, with a decorative piece in place of "'Argyle Press,' Printing and Bookbinding, 24 & 26 Wooster St., N.Y." on verso of title page, and with early bookplate and shelf label on front pastedown. Not in Kohler.

2225. Variant of Preceding, original decorated red cloth (a bit rubbed, pages a little age-browned, spine slightly rubbed at top), decorated as preceding copies. A nice copy of a late nineteenth-century illustrated American edition, in a bright variant publisher's binding, without Dryden's epigram under the Milton frontispiece portrait as in all the other Hurst editions here. Not in Kohler.

2226. THE POETICAL WORKS OF JOHN MILTON. With A Memoir, And Critical Remarks On His Genius And Writings. By James Montgomery; Vol. I. / Vol. II. *New York: Geo. A. Leavitt, Publisher, No. 8 Howard Street. n.d. [ca. 1880].* 2 volumes in one. 8vo, xlix+[i]+[3]+400pp. (page numbering beginning with number "18"),+368pp. (page numbering beginning with number "10"), engraved frontispiece portrait plate after C. Burt, protective tissue guard, second title page for volume 2 followed by "Contents Of Vol. II," illustrations (unsigned, but after Harvey) within the text for *L'A* with a vignette illustration at the beginning and another vignette illustration at the end of the poem and with vignette illustrations in the margins, half-title for each book of *PL* and *PR* and for some of the poems, double black border around text, original orange pebble cloth (a bit used, spine ends rubbed), decorative straps in blind around covers and spine imitating straps on early bindings, spine lettered in gilt with title at the top, circle in the middle containing "The World Edition" with the two hemispheres of the world in gilt, and the initials of the press in gilt at the bottom, advertisements for various editions on endpapers. A fairly nice copy in publisher's cloth binding, fine internally, with contemporary signature (dated 1880) on verso of frontispiece and another later signature and ownership stamp on front blank. The possible first edition thus was published by Leavitt & Allen in 1858 (also listed here with further editions cited, including editions in the 1870s with reference to "The World Edition" on the binding). Not in Kohler.

2227. THE POETICAL WORKS OF JOHN MILTON. With A Memoir, And Critical Remarks On His Genius And Writings. By James Montgomery; Vol. I. / Vol. II. *New York: Geo. A. Leavitt, Publisher, No. 8 Howard Street. n.d. [ca. 1880 or ca. 1860].* 2 volumes in one. 8vo, xlix+[iv]+400pp.(pagination number beginning with page number "18"),+368pp., engraved frontispiece portrait plate after C. Burt, protective tissue guard, second title page for volume 2 followed by "Contents Of Vol. II," three engraved illustration plates: two for *PL* (*Moloch*, unsigned, for Book II and *Eleonora* for Book VI, "Designed & Engd. by A.H. Ritchie"), one engraved plate entitled *Death*, engraved by Sartain after Jones, inserted here within *SA*, each engraved illustration plate with a protective tissue guard, illustrations (unsigned, but after Harvey) within the text for *L'A* with a vignette illustration at the beginning and another vignette illustration at the end of the poem and with vignette illustrations in the margins, half-title for each book of *PL* and *PR* and for some of the poems, contemporary brown calf (very rubbed), covers elaborately decorated in embossed trim incorporating "Milton's Poetical Works" within a large gilt device at the center of front cover, spine similarly decorated in embossed trim with small gilt star within each panel, gilt lettering, and decorative gilt trim at the top and bottom, brown endpapers, a.e.g. A good copy of a scarce edition. Similar to the preceding edition by Leavitt, except in a much smaller format, approximately 2 ¼" shorter and 1 ½" narrower, without double black border around the text, and with several additional illustrations. The possible first edition thus by Leavitt & Allen was published in 1858 (also listed here with further editions cited). Not in Kohler.

2228. THE POETICAL WORKS OF JOHN MILTON. Reprinted From The Best Editions With Biographical Notice, Etc. *New York: John Wurtele Lovell, No. 24 Bond Street. n.d. [ca. 1880].* First edition thus by Lovell? 8vo, 562pp., engraved frontispiece portrait sketch of a young, romanticized looking Milton by "E. Ronjat," protective tissue guard, life of Milton, illustration plates after engravings by Dalziel, with lines quoted: two for *PL*, Book IV (*Adam Sees Eve*) and Book VIII (*Adam and Eve Naming the Animals*), one for *SA* ("But Who is this? . . . Comes this way"), one for *L'A* ("While the ploughman near at hand . . ."), and one for *Latin Epigram VII* ("Ad Eandem"—titled *Milton Meeting Leonora Baroni at Cardinal Barberini's House*), red border around text, original decorated reddish-brown cloth, front cover richly decorated in embossed black trim with a large, bright gilt decoration at the center incorporating a harp and Milton's name, spine similarly richly decorated in embossed black and gilt with bright gilt decoration at the top incorporating Milton's name, a bright gilt band in the center incorporating "Illustrated," a bright gilt urn toward the bottom, with "Lovell" incorporated within a decorative gilt band beneath, and decorated gilt trim at top and bottom, brown endpapers, a.e.g. A fine copy of a nineteenth-century illustrated American edition, in a lovely publisher's decorated cloth binding. Not in Williamson; Not in Kohler.

See undated ca. 1880 nonillustrated edition listed earlier published by Lovell with the same publisher's imprint as that of the Lovell edition here; and see dated 1881 illustrated edition (possible second edition thus) listed later published by Lovell with a different publisher's imprint from that of the Lovell edition here ("New York: John Wurtele Lovell, Publishers, 14, 16, 18, & 20 Astor Place") and without the lines printed for the second illustration for *PL* and with no title given for the illustration of *Milton Meeting Leonora Baroni*. See, too, undated ca. 1885 illustrated edition listed here published by Lovell in variant editions, both with a different publisher's imprint from here: one ("New York: John W. Lovell Company, 14 and 16 Vesey Street"), with same frontispiece portrait and the same illustrations with no title given for the illustration of *Milton Meeting Leonora Baroni* (bound before English sonnets XXI, "To Cyriac Skinner," and XXII, "To The Same"), the other a variant edition, with variant publisher's imprint ("New York[:] John W. Lovell Company[,] 150 Worth Street, Corner Mission Place"), with frontispiece illustration in place of frontispiece portrait and no other illustrations; see also undated ca. 1885 nonillustrated Lovell edition listed here, a reprint edition of the second variant ca. 1885 illustrated edition with the variant publisher's imprint ("New York[:] John W. Lovell Company[,] 150 Worth Street, Corner Mission Place"), without the frontispiece illustration; and see 1883 illustrated edition listed here published by D. Lothrop & Co. in Boston, and 1883 illustrated edition listed here published by J. B. Lippincott

& Co. in Philadelphia, each with the same frontispiece portrait by Ronjat and the same illustrations and in the same format as here.

John Lovell (1876–1932) was born in Montreal. In 1876 he established the firm of Lovell, Adam & Company in New York City for the purpose of reprinting cheap editions of British books. His partner was G. Mercer Adam, a fellow Canadian. Lovell first published at 24 Bond Street in 1878, later at 16 Astor Street, and then for a time from 1882 on at 14 Vesey Street. In 1888 he acquired the plates and stock of Munro Library. He moved to 142–150 Worth Street by 1891. In 1887 his partnership with G. Mercer Adam was dissolved, and Lovell began to publish on his own. Lovell started as a pirate caring nothing for the courtesy of the trade principle of the literary establishment. In 1881 he reorganized his business, calling it "John W. Lovell Company," and the following year he introduced "Lovell's Library," a series of paperbacks priced at ten, twenty, or thirty cents. Lovell issued his books either in cloth or in paper. Publishing seven million cheap books a year, he became known as "Book-A-Day Lovell." In 1890 Lovell's publishing activities culminated in the formation of the United States Book Company. Within three years, however, this firm went into bankruptcy, and by 1900 Lovell had completely disappeared from the annals of publishing. He died in 1932.

2229. Variant of the Preceding, original decorated blue cloth, decorated as preceding copy. A very nice copy of a nineteenth-century illustrated American edition, in an attractive variant publisher's decorated cloth binding. Not in Kohler.

2230. Variant of the Preceding, original decorated green cloth (spine a bit rubbed), decorated as preceding copies. A fine copy of a nineteenth-century illustrated American edition, in a lovely variant decorated publisher's cloth binding, very fresh and clean within. Not in Kohler.

2231. THE POETICAL WORKS OF JOHN MILTON. Reprinted From The Best Editions With Biographical Notice, Etc. *New York: Thomas Y. Crowell, No. 744 Broadway. n.d. [ca. 1880]*. First edition thus? 8vo, 562pp., engraved frontispiece portrait of a young, romanticized Milton by "E. Ronjat," protective tissue guard, life of Milton, five illustration plates after engravings by Dalziel, for *PL*, Book IV (*Adam Sees Eve*, with lines quoted) and Book VIII (*Adam and Eve Naming the Animals*, with appropriate lines quoted), for *SA* ("But Who is this? . . . Comes this way sailing / Like a stately ship?"), for *L'A* ("While the ploughman near at hand . . ."), and for *LE VII* ("Ad Eandem," "To The Same,"—*Milton Meeting Leonora Baroni at Cardinal Barberini's House*), red border around text, original decorated dark blue cloth (a bit rubbed, some slight scratches on front cover, spine ends slightly chipped corners a little worn), front cover decorated in embossed black trim with a brightly decorated embossed black and gilt device with decorative gilt trim at the center incorporating the title "Milton's Poems" in embossed blue letters in the foreground within a richly decorated broad gilt horizontal band in front of an urn in gilt with long-stemmed flowers in gilt as a vertical backdrop outlined in decorative gilt trim, spine similarly richly decorated in embossed black and gilt trim with the title "Milton's Poems" in embossed blue letters within two brightly decorated broad gilt bands at the top, with an urn in gilt with long-stemmed flowers in gilt similar to that on front cover, "T. Y. Crowell" in embossed blue letters within a smaller decorated gilt band at the bottom, decorative trim in black and gilt at the top and bottom, bevelled edges, green endpapers, a.e.g. A nice copy in an attractive publisher's cloth binding, with a contemporary ownership signature (dated "Nov. 1880") on front blank. Scarce. Not in Kohler.

See illustrated editions of Milton's *PW* published by Crowell—all listed here: undated ca. 1881 illustrated edition (with illustrations after engravings by Dalziel as here, with frontispiece portrait as here, and with same address in publisher's imprint as here, one with a contemporary inscription, 1880, and one in an exact binding as here); undated ca. 1883 illustrated edition (with illustrations after engravings by Dalziel as here, without frontispiece portrait as here, and with "No. 13 Astor Place" as address in publisher's imprint); dated 1884 illustrated editions (one with reproduction of Doré illustrations, another with illustrations after engravings by Dalziel); ca. 1886/1887 illustrated edition with illustrations after engravings by Dalziel as here; and 1892 illustrated editions (one, undated, with frontispiece illustration plate only after Doré and with contemporary signature dated 1893, one with copyright date of 1892, also with frontispiece illustration plate only after Doré, the other two with copyright date of 1892, one in a larger [crown/royal 8vo] format with numerous illustration plates [including photographic reproductions of several of Martin's illustrations—reduced] and the other an "Imperial Edition" with reproductions of Doré's illustrations for *PL*).

2232. Variant of Preceding, original green cloth, decorated exactly as preceding copy. A fine copy, near mint, in a variant publisher's decorated cloth binding. Not in Kohler.

2233. Variant of Preceding, original red cloth, decorated exactly as preceding copies. A fine copy in a variant publisher's decorated cloth binding. Not in Kohler.

2234. THE POETICAL WORKS OF JOHN MILTON: With Introductions By David Masson, M.A., L.L.D., Professor Of Rhetoric And English Literature In The University Of Edinburgh. The Globe Edition. *London: Macmillan And Co. 1880*. Fourth Globe edition by Macmillan. 8vo, xi+625+[2]+24pp., half-title (with emblem consisting of the letters of Macmillan and Co. on verso), "Preface" (dated 1877), "London: R. Clay, Sons, And Taylor, Printers" on verso of title page, "Contents," "Introduction to *PL*" with several diagrams and other introductory material as in the first editions, half-title for some of the sections and poems, "London: R. Clay, Sons, And Taylor, Printers" on verso of last page, original green cloth, covers ruled in blind with central emblem in blind (consisting of a vignette of Milton within lettering of "The Globe Edition") on front cover, spine lettered in gilt with small emblem in gilt at the bottom, brown endpapers, edges untrimmed. A nice copy in publisher's cloth binding, with early signature on half-title. Bound in at the end, one leaf of advertisement for "Macmillan's Globe Library" (including "Milton's Poetical Works") and twenty-four pages of advertisements for "Macmillan & Co.'s Catalogue of Works in Belles Lettres," including "Poetry, Fiction, etc." (with an edition of "Milton. By Mark Pattison" as part of "English Men Of Letters" series). The first Globe edition of Milton's *PW* was published in March 1877 (also listed here with further copies cited). Scarce. Kohler 395, making no mention of advertisement pages bound in at end, reporting "Not in the British Library. Not in the Bodleian Library. Not in Cambridge University Library."

2235. THE POETICAL WORKS OF JOHN MILTON. With Memoir, Explanatory Notes, Etc. The "Albion" Edition. *London: Thomas Yardley. n.d. [ca. 1880]*. 8vo, xxvi+581pp., half-title (with "Morrison And Gibb, Printers, Edinburgh" on verso), "Contents," "Prefatory Memory Of Milton," "Morrison And Gibb, Printers, Edinburgh" on verso of last page, contemporary polished back leather over padded boards, Milton's name lettered in gilt at top of front cover, "Milton's Poetical Works" lettered in gilt at top of spine, inner dentelles finely tooled in gilt, black and gold decorated endpapers, a.e.g. A fine copy, very fresh and clean within. Scarce. Not in Kohler.

2236. THE POETICAL WORKS OF JOHN MILTON. In Two Volumes. *London: W. Kent & Co., Paternoster Row. MDCCCLXXX (1880)*. 2 volumes. First edition thus. Small 8vo (miniature size, measuring 4 ½" × 3"), 320pp., +317pp., life of Milton, volume 1, original red cloth (a bit rubbed), spines lettered in gilt ("Milton's Poems"), a.e.g. A nice set with contemporary presentation inscription (dated 1880) on front blank. Kohler 399, describing its copy "16mo in 8s," and reporting "Not in Cambridge University Library."

2237. Variant of Preceding, original green cloth (a little worn, spines ends chipped, some scattered pencil notations), spines lettered in gilt ("Milton's Poems"), decorated endpapers, a.e.g., bookseller's stamp on fly-leaf. A decent set in a variant publisher's cloth binding. Kohler 399.

2238. THE POETICAL WORKS OF JOHN MILTON. With A Sketch Of His Life. *New York: American Book Exchange, Tribune Building. 1880*. First edition thus. 8vo, 562pp., original half brown calf (a bit rubbed), marbled paper over boards, gilt decorated spine with gilt lettering. A very nice, large paper copy, with contemporary signature (dated 1880) in a fine hand on front pastedown. A second edition thus was published in 1881 (also listed here). Not in Kohler.

2239. Variant of Preceding, original brown silk (a bit rubbed, pages a little age-browned), spine lettered in gilt, lightly decorated blue endpapers. A good copy in a variant publisher's binding, with contemporary presentation inscription (dated 1880) in a very neat hand (presented "for excellence in penmanship") on fly-leaf. Not in Kohler.

2240. THE POETICAL WORKS OF JOHN MILTON. Reprinted From The Best Editions With Biographical Notice, Etc. *New York: John Wurtele Lovell, No. 24 Bond Street. n.d. [ca. 1880]*. 8vo, 562pp., original decorated reddish-brown cloth (a bit rubbed, small white mark on spine, spine ends slightly chipped, early name on front blank), front cover richly decorated in embossed black, spine similarly richly decorated in embossed black with bright gilt decoration at the top incorporating Milton's name, brown endpapers. A nice copy in an attractive publisher's cloth binding. Milton's *PW* were possible first published by Lovell ca. 1880 (also listed here with further editions by Lovell cited). Not in Kohler.

2241. THE POETICAL WORKS OF JOHN MILTON. Reprinted From The Original Edition, And Containing Numerous Explanatory Notes. *New York: Hurst & Co., 122 Nassau Street. n.d. [ca. 1880]*. First edition thus by Hurst? 8vo, vii+627pp., notes at bottom of page, original green cloth (a bit rubbed), front cover ruled in black with large central device in black incorporating Milton's name, spine decorated and lettered in black and gilt with broad gilt band incorporating Milton's name at the top, a central harp in black, "Hurst & Co." lettered in gilt at the bottom, and decorative gilt trim at top and bottom, pink endpapers. A nice copy, called "Arlington Poets" on the spine. See possible first illustrated edition of Milton's *PW* by Hurst published about this same time ca. 1880 (see copy listed and other editions by Hurst cited there). Not in Kohler.

2242. THE POETICAL WORKS OF JOHN MILTON. With A Sketch Of His Life. *New York: Hurst & Co., Publishers, 122 Nassau Street. n.d. [ca. 1880].* First edition thus by Hurst? 8vo, 562pp., "Argyle Press,' Printing and Bookbinding, 24 & 26 Wooster St., N.Y." on verso of title page, original reddish-brown cloth (a bit rubbed, spine ends chipped, pages age-browned and very brittle, with some corners folded, but too fragile to unbend), front cover decorated in embossed black with "Arlington Edition" in embossed dark reddish-brown against a black background, spine similarly decorated in embossed black with broad gilt band incorporating Milton's name at the top and "Arlington Edition" in small black lettering near the center. A good copy in an attractive binding of the period, with contemporary bookplate on front pastedown and near-contemporary signature (dated 1888) on fly-leaf. It is unfortunate that this edition, like so many others of the period, was printed on poor quality paper which is becoming more and more brittle and fragile with age. Not in Kohler.

2243. THE POETICAL WORKS OF JOHN MILTON. With A Sketch Of His Life. *New York: Hurst & Company, Publishers. n.d. [ca. 1880].* First edition thus by Hurst? 8vo, similar to other undated nonillustrated editions by Hurst here, with variations, 562pp., unsigned frontispiece portrait (poor quality impression), original decorated blue cloth (a little worn, pages age-browned), red border around text, front cover decorated with white floral trim at the top, large circular decorative piece in blind at the center incorporating Milton's name in embossed blue lettering against a broad gilt band within decorative white trim with a torch that reaches to the top where a small flame in gilt appears in the middle of the white floral trim, spine similarly decorated with white floral trim at the top within decorative gilt trim, with Milton's name immediately beneath in embossed blue lettering against a broad gilt band surrounded by gilt trim, with a small laurel wreath in white at the center of the spine against a large decorative circular piece in blind, with "Hurst & Co." in embossed blue lettering against a small gilt band surrounded by gilt trim at the bottom, brown endpapers, a.e.g. Although a little worn, a good copy in a different kind of publisher's binding. Not in Kohler.

2244. THE POETICAL WORKS OF JOHN MILTON. With A Sketch Of His Life. *New York: Hurst & Co., Publishers, 122 Nassau Street. n.d. [ca. 1880].* First edition thus by Hurst? 8vo, 562pp., "Argyle Press,' Printing and Bookbinding, 24 & 26 Wooster St., N.Y." on verso of title page (as on verso of ca. 1880 illustrated editions by Hurst listed earlier), occasional small decorative pieces, half-title for some of the poems, original reddish-brown cloth (a bit rubbed, lacking front endpaper, pages age-browned), front cover ruled in black with central device in black and decorative corner pieces in black, spine elaborately decorated in black with broad gilt band incorporating Milton's name at the top and with a smaller gilt band incorporating "Hurst & Co." at the bottom, and "Illustrated" in blind at the center of spine, although there are no illustrations within. A good copy in a nice publisher's binding. Not in Kohler.

2245. THE POETICAL WORKS OF JOHN MILTON. With A Sketch Of His Life. *Butler Brothers, Incorporated, New York & Chicago, n.d. [ca. 1880].* First edition thus by Butler Brothers? 8vo, 562+[2]pp., unsigned frontispiece portrait of a long-haired middle-aged Milton, "Argyle Press, Printing And Bookbinding, 24 & 26 Wooster St., N. Y." on verso of title page, original decorated dark red cloth (a bit rubbed, spine slightly faded, age-browned throughout, lacking fly-leaf, early name on front blank), front cover richly decorated in embossed black floral design with a very large long-stemmed flower with varying sized petals against a black backdrop at the center, spine decorated in a patterned embossed black floral design with decorative embossed black trim at the top, Milton's name in embossed red lettering against a broad gilt background within a plain red area near the top, "Butler Bros." in smaller embossed red lettering against a black background in the form of a leaf at the bottom. A nice copy in an attractive publisher's binding of the period, with advertisement leaf (stiff cardlike page) bound in at the end advertising publications by "Butler Brothers, New York and Chicago" under the rubric: "You Can Own a Complete Library For $14.00," with "elegant Polished Maple Book Rack" on recto, and "the Department store – A Benefit to Mankind" with a lengthy statement on verso. Uncommon. Not in Kohler.

2246. THE POETICAL WORKS OF JOHN MILTON. *Edinburgh: William P. Nimmo & Co. 1881.* 8vo, xxxvii+[3]+440pp., unsigned engraved frontispiece portrait plate of a middle-aged Milton, engraved and printed title pages, with vignette illustration (of the poet being inspired by heavenly choirs) by F. Borders on engraved title plate ("Edinburgh: William P. Nimmo & Co. 1882."), protective tissue guard, vignette illustration (of a young boy in a setting in nature with a cane laying beside him) signed with the initials "WS" on printed title, life of Milton by J. M. Ross, eleven illustration plates, most after F. Borders, some unsigned: four for *PL* (Books I, III, VI, XI), two for *PR* (Book I), one for *SA*, two for *C*, one for *L'A*, one for *IlP*, half-title for *PL, PR, SA, C, Arc, MP,* and *Poemata*, red border around text, printer not indicated at bottom of last page, original three-quarter red leather, red pebble cloth (a little faded), spine lettered in gilt and richly gilt decorated within the panels, raised bands, marbled endpapers and edges. A nice copy, very fresh and clean within. The possible first edition thus by Nimmo was published in 1865, illustrated (also listed here with further Nimmo editions cited). Only the 1865 edition has twelve illustrations, the others have eleven (with only one illustration for *L'A* instead of two, as in the 1865 edition). Scarce. Kohler 401, reporting "Not in Williamson. Not in the British Library. Not in the Bodleian library. Not in Cambridge University Library."

2247. THE POETICAL WORKS OF JOHN MILTON. Reprinted From The Chandos Poets. With Memoir, Explanatory Notes, &c. Portrait And Original Illustrations. The Lansdowne Poets. *London: Frederick Warne And Co., Bedford Street, Strand. n.d. [ca. 1881].* 8vo, xxiv+581pp., engraved frontispiece portrait (of a youngish looking middle-aged Milton, unsigned, with labeling "London: Frederick Warne & Co." at bottom), protective tissue guard (foxed, with some foxing offset on frontispiece portrait and title page), printer's device with initials "FW & Co." on title page (a little different from devices on title pages of other editions here), "Camden Press: Dalziel Brothers, Engravers & Printers" within small circular printer's device on verso of title page, eight illustration plates after engravings by Dalziel: one for *L'A*, four for *PL* (Books I, IV, VIII, and XII), one for *SA*, one for *On His Deceased Wife*, and one for *Latin Epigram VII* ("Ad Eandem"—the illustration titled *Milton Meeting Leonora Baroni at Cardinal Barberini's House*), half-title for *SA*, red border around text, "Dalziel Brothers, Camden Press, N.W. [sic]" on verso of last page, notes at bottom of page, original one-half black morocco, black pebble cloth (some slight foxing and age-browning), covers ruled in gilt, brown leather label with gilt lettering and gilt rules on spine, spine decorated in gilt within the panels, raised bands finely tooled in gilt, marbled endpapers and edges. A good copy with contemporary presentation inscription in a neat hand (dated 1881) on front blank. See other dated and undated illustrated and nonillustrated editions by Frederick Warne and Co. in the collection published in the 1870s, 1880s, and 1890s under the various series: "The 'Lansdowne' Poets," "The 'Arundel' Poets," "The 'Chandos' Poets," "The 'Imperial' Poets, "The 'Chandos' Classics," "The 'Albion' Edition," and "The Cabinet Poets." Not in Kohler.

2248. Variation of Preceding, original three-quarter red morocco, red pebble cloth (bit rubbed, slight foxing), gilt rules on covers and spine, raised bands with decorative gilt lines, marbled endpapers and edges. A good copy in a variant publisher's binding. Not in Kohler.

2249. THE POETICAL WORKS OF JOHN MILTON. Reprinted From The Best Editions With Biographical Notice, Etc. *New York: Thomas Y. Crowell, No. 744 Broadway. n.d. [ca. 1881].* Second edition thus? 8vo, 562pp., engraved frontispiece portrait sketch of a young, romanticized looking Milton by "E. Ronjat," protective tissue guard, life of Milton, five illustration plates after engravings by Dalziel, for *PL*, Book IV (*Adam Sees Eve*, with lines quoted) and Book VIII (*Adam and Eve Naming the Animals*, with appropriate lines quoted), for *SA* ("But Who is this? . . . Comes this way"), for *L'A* ("While the ploughman near at hand . . ."), and for *Latin Epigram VII* ("Ad Eandem," "To The Same,"—*Milton Meeting Leonora Baroni at Cardinal Barberini's House*), red border around text, original decorated dark blue cloth, front cover richly decorated in embossed black and gilt with the title "Milton's Poems" incorporated in a brightly decorated embossed black and gilt device with decorative gilt trim at the center, spine similarly richly decorated in embossed black and gilt with the title "Milton's Poems" incorporated in a brightly decorated embossed gilt device with decorative gilt trim at the top, an attractive embossed black and gilt device similar to that on front cover at the center, "T. Y. Crowell" within decorative gilt trim at the bottom, and double gilt rules at the top and bottom, olive green endpapers, a.e.g. A fine copy in a lovely publisher's decorated cloth binding, clean, bright, and crisp, with contemporary gift inscription written in a fine hand on front endpaper dated "October 19, 1881," and with gift recipient's name gilt-stamped at bottom of front cover. The possible first edition of Milton's *PW* by Crowell was published ca. 1880 (also listed here with further editions by Crowell cited). Scarce. Not in Kohler.

2250. THE POETICAL WORKS OF JOHN MILTON. Reprinted From The Best Editions With Biographical Notice, Etc. *New York: John Wurtele Lovell, Publishers, 14, 16, 18, & 20 Astor Place. 1881.* Second edition thus? 8vo, 562pp., engraved frontispiece portrait sketch of a young, romanticized, Byronic-looking Milton by "E. Ronjat," protective tissue guard, life of Milton, illustration plates after engravings by Dalziel, two for *PL*, Book IV (*Adam Sees Eve*, with lines quoted) and Book VIII (*Adam and Eve Naming the Animals*, without identification or appropriate lines quoted), one for *SA* ("But Who is this? . . . Comes this way sailing / Like a stately ship?"), one for *L'A* ("While the ploughman near at hand . . ."), and one for *Latin Epigram VII* ("Ad Eandem," "To The Same," with the illustration titled: *Milton Meeting Leonora Baroni at*

Cardinal Barberini's House), red border around text, original decorated reddish-brown cloth (chafed along bottom and side of front cover, spine, and edges of back cover, spine ends a little chipped, joints broken from within), front cover decorated in embossed black trim with a large, bright square gilt emblem at the center trimmed in a black rule, incorporating a large harp with Milton's name in large letters and "Illustrated" in smaller letters, spine similarly decorated in embossed black trim with a bright gilt band near the top incorporating Milton's name, a smaller gilt band at the center incorporating "Illustrated," a large urn in gilt near the bottom, with a smaller gilt band beneath incorporating the publisher's name, "Lovell," brown endpapers, a.e.g. The possible first edition of Milton's *PW* by Lovell was published ca. 1880 (also listed here with further editions by Lovell cited) along with information about Lovell as publisher. Not in Williamson; Not in Kohler.

2251. THE POETICAL WORKS OF JOHN MILTON; With A Life Of The Author, By The Rev. H. Stebbing, A.M. *New York: Hurst & Co., Publishers, 122 Nassau Street. n.d. [ca. 1881].* 2 volumes in one. Small, squatty 8vo (4 ¾" × 3 ¼"), 356pp.,+190pp., unsigned frontispiece illustration of *Raphael Counseling Adam and Eve*, with lines illustrated quoted beneath, separate title page for second volume (*Paradise Regained And Other Poems By John Milton*), original green cloth (a bit rubbed, front joint slightly cracked from within, pp. 27–30 of volume 2 separated from the binding with the edges frayed), black rules and trim on front cover with small oval emblem of a seated male figure holding a lute in black at the center, back cover ruled in blind trim, spine lettered in embossed green letters ("Milton") against a bright gilt background, with "Cameo Poets" lettered in bright gilt above "Milton," decorative gilt trim at top and bottom of spine, and decorated letters of the press in bright gilt within a small book in bright gilt near the bottom of spine. A very nice copy of this "Cameo Poets" edition by Hurst, with contemporary signature (dated "Dec. 27, 1881") on fly-leaf. See following copy with a different frontispiece illustration. The possible first edition of Milton's *PW* by Hurst was published ca. 1880 (illustrated edition also listed here with further editions by Hurst cited). Not in Kohler.

2252. Variant of Preceding, unsigned frontispiece illustration of angels chasing Satan away from Adam and Eve sleeping, with lines illustrated quoted beneath, separate title page for second volume (*Paradise Regained And Other Poems By John Milton*), original green cloth (a little worn and slightly dirtied, front joint broken from within, with contents shaken from binding, lacking title page for volume 1), black rules and trim on front cover with small oval emblem of a seated male figure holding a lute in black at the center, back cover ruled in blind trim, spine lettered in embossed green letters ("Milton") against a bright gilt background, with "Cameo Poets" lettered in bright gilt above "Milton," decorative gilt trim at top and bottom of spine, and decorated letters of the press in bright gilt within a small book in bright gilt near the bottom of spine. While this copy is worn and lacks the title page to volume 1, it is of interest because of its variant frontispiece illustration which is different from that in the preceding copy. Not in Kohler.

2253. THE POETICAL WORKS OF JOHN MILTON Printed From The Original Editions With A Life Of The Author By A. Chalmers M.A. F.S.A. *London[:] Bickers And Son 1 Leicester Square[.] 1881.* 8vo, xxxv+[1]+699pp., half-title with decorative headpiece, frontispiece portrait after Faithorne, engraved by Humphreys, protective tissue guard, title page in red and black, with central printer's device, original "Advertisement To The Edition Of 1851" (see sets listed here), numerous elaborately decorated head- and tailpieces, decorated initial letters, handsomely printed by Charles Whittingham at the Chiswick Press, contemporary dark blue polished calf (slightly rubbed at joints and edges), gilt rules on covers, elaborately gilt-decorated spine, red morocco label with gilt lettering, raised bands with decorative gilt trim, inner dentelles tooled in blind, outer dentelles trimmed in gilt, marbled endpapers and edges. A fine copy in a very nice Prize Binding, with central gilt armorial seal of Sherborn School on covers and contemporary prize label (dated 1880) tipped in on front pastedown. A very attractive copy of an uncommon edition. Not in Kohler.

2254. THE POETICAL WORKS OF JOHN MILTON. With Life. Six Engravings on Steel. *Gall & Inglis. Edinburgh: Bernard Terrace. London: 25 Paternoster Sqr. n.d. [ca. 1881].* 8vo, xx+491pp., red border line around text, original decorated blue cloth (a bit worn, spine with number of chips and a piece missing at the top covered over with blue cloth for appearance sake), front cover finely decorated in black trim and design with the figure of an angel in bright gilt above an equally bright gilt device incorporating Milton's name in embossed blue lettering with decorative laurel leaf and lyre in bright gilt hanging beneath, spine similarly decorated with bright gilt device incorporating Milton's name in embossed blue lettering with decorative laurel leaf and Olympic flame in bright gilt hanging beneath and with decorative gilt trim at top and bottom of spine, back cover decorated in blind, red edges (with speckled blotches on front and bottom). Except for the chipped spine and blotched red edges, an otherwise nice copy in an attractive publisher's binding, with contemporary signature in ink (dated "Dec 25. 1881") on front fly-leaf, in a protective plastic cover. While "Six Engravings on Steel" is indicated on the title page, no illustration plates are included and none appear to be missing. See undated ca. 1870s / ca. 1875 edition listed here published by Gall & Inglis in Edinburgh ("Bernard Terrace") and London ("25 Paternoster Sqr") with only "Engravings on Steel" appearing on title page and with decorative border trim around the text in alternating sepia and bluish green tint with varying background scenes and other editions cited by Gall & Inglis cited there. Not in Kohler.

2255. THE POETICAL WORKS OF JOHN MILTON. With A Sketch Of His Life. *New York: American Book Exchange, Tribune Building. 1881.* Second edition thus. 8vo, 562pp., original brown cloth (a bit rubbed), spine lettered in gilt, light gray endpapers. A nice copy. The first edition thus was published in 1880 (also listed here). Not in Kohler.

2256. Variant of Preceding, original decorated dark green cloth (a bit rubbed, spine ends chipped), front cover decorated in embossed black and gilt with gilt lettering, back cover decorated in blind, spine similarly decorated in embossed black and gilt with gilt lettering. A nice copy in an attractive variant publisher's binding. Not in Kohler.

2257. THE POETICAL WORKS OF JOHN MILTON. *London: John Walker & Company, 96 Farringdon Street. E.C. n.d. [ca. 1882/1881].* First edition thus by John Walker & Company? 8vo, xxxvii+450pp., unsigned engraved frontispiece portrait plate of a middle-aged Milton, printed title page with vignette illustration (of a young boy in a setting in nature with a cane laying beside him) signed with the initials "WS," eleven illustration plates, seven by F. Borders, others unsigned, life of Milton by J. M. Ross, half-title for *PL*, *PR*, *SA*, *C*, *Ar*, and *MP*, red border around text, original green cloth (a bit rubbed, corners bumped and a little worn, spine ends chipped, title page loose, having sometime earlier been repaired by tape which has now become embrowned and brittle, resulting in a breaking away from the rest of the pages), front cover delicately tooled in black and gilt with a central recessed panel in a club shape with richly gilt-decorated white leather inlaid with Milton's name lettered in embossed red against a broad gilt panel at the center, the recessed panel trimmed in black and surrounded by a thin gilt line within a thicker black line all within intricately tooled gilt trim, decorative device in blind at the center of the back cover, spine lettered in gilt, with elaborate gilt decorations within the panels, each panel separated by a grouping of three very thin gilt lines, the middle one finely tooled between two thick black rules, the same three very thin gilt lines repeated at the top and bottom of the spine, a.e.g. A good copy in an attractive publisher's binding, with contemporary presentation label from a board of education (dated "December 22, 1882") on front pastedown. See earlier editions by William P. Nimmo upon which this edition by Walker is modeled: Nimmo was possible first published in Edinburgh in an illustrated edition in 1865 (also listed here with further Nimmo editions cited), with the unsigned frontispiece portrait as here of a middle-aged Milton, the vignette illustration as here on the printed title page (signed with the initials "WS"), the life of Milton by J. M. Ross, and the same eleven illustration plates (most after F. Borders, some unsigned) which appear in this edition by Walker. Not in Kohler.

2258. Variant of the Preceding, original decorated blue cloth (a bit rubbed), front cover delicately tooled in fine embossed black trim, with a large recessed panel in a diamond shape at the center, with a tipped in piece of white leather elaborately decorated overall in gilt with a vase and floral arrangement incorporating Milton's name across the center in large embossed letters in shaded red with the letter "M" in a larger embossed letter in shaded green, with gilt and black rules and delicate gilt trim surrounding the large recessed panel, spine decorated in black and gilt with lettering near the top in embossed blue ("Milton's Poems Illustrated") within gilt panels and decorative gilt trim, near the bottom a gilt urn sprouting floral boughs in black, and at the bottom the press ("John Walker & Co") lettered in embossed blue within a gilt band outlined in decorative gilt trim, decorative device in blind at the center of the back cover, a.e.g. A good copy in a lovely variant publisher's binding. See ca. 1882 edition by "George Routledge Sons" following in an identical binding, with "George Routledge" in place of "John Walker Co" at bottom of the spine. Not in Kohler.

The collection also has a variant of the preceding in red cloth binding (showing a little wear), identically decorated as the preceding except in red cloth with a tipped in piece of green leather. Not in Kohler.

2259. THE POETICAL WORKS OF JOHN MILTON A New Edition, Carefully Revised From The Text Of Thomas Newton, D.D. With Illustrations By William Harvey. *London[:] George Routledge And Sons[,] Broadway, Ludgate Hill[;] New York: 416, Broome Street[.] n.d. [ca. 1882].* 8vo, viii+570pp., frontispiece illustration plate of Satan cast out of Heaven, protective tissue guard, and five additional illustration plates after William Harvey, engraved by Dalziel, "A New Edition, Carefully Revised From The Text Of Thomas Newton" in a clear, non-Gothic font on title page, "Routledge's Red Line Poets" listed on verso of title page (the twenty-five listings including Milton), original preface by Theodore Alois Buckley dated 1853, red border line around text with small decorative corner pieces, notes at bottom of page, original decorated blue cloth (a little rubbed, spine ends slightly chipped, corners a bit frayed), front cover delicately tooled in fine embossed black trim with a large recessed panel in a diamond shape at the center, with a tipped in piece of white leather elaborately decorated overall in gilt with a vase and floral arrangement incorporating Milton's name across the center in large embossed letters in shaded red with the letter "M" in a larger embossed letter in shaded green, with gilt and black rules and delicate gilt trim surrounding the large recessed panel, spine decorated in black and gilt with lettering near the top in embossed blue ("Milton's Poems Illustrated") within gilt panels and decorative gilt trim, near the bottom a gilt urn sprouting floral boughs in black, and at the bottom the press ("Routledge") in embossed blue letters within a gilt band outlined in decorative gilt trim, decorative device in blind at the center of the back cover, a.e.g. A nice copy in an attractive publisher's binding, with contemporary presentation inscription (dated "Aug. 21 1882") on fly-leaf. The first edition of Milton's *PW* by George Routledge and Co. was published in 1853 (also listed here with further editions by Routledge cited). Not in Kohler.

2260. Variant of the Preceding, original decorated green cloth (a bit rubbed), front cover delicately tooled in fine embossed black trim, with a large recessed panel in a diamond shape at the center, with a tipped in piece of mauve leather elaborately decorated overall in gilt with a vase and floral arrangement incorporating Milton's name across the center in large embossed letters in shaded red with the letter "M" in a larger embossed letter in shaded green, the remainder decorated exactly as the preceding binding. A very nice copy in a lovely variant publisher's binding, with contemporary signature (dated "July 1. 1882") on front pastedown. Not in Kohler.

2261. THE POETICAL WORKS OF JOHN MILTON With Memoir and Notes. Complete Edition. Illustrated. *New York: The American News Company, 39 And 41 Chambers Street. n.d. [ca. 1882].* First edition thus by the American News Company? 12mo, xii+563pp., unsigned frontispiece illustration plate for *PR* ("Also it is written / Tempt not the Lord thy God," Book IV, lines 560–61), protective tissue guard, "Memoir Of John Milton," followed by "Contents," three unsigned illustration plates for *PL* (Book V, lines 93–94, "Thus Eve her night / related"; Book VII, lines 566–67, "Open, ye heavens your living doors: let in / The great Creator from His work returned"; and Book XII, lines 626-33, "The archangel stood— / —High in front advanced / The brandished sword of God"), two additional unsigned illustration plates for *PR* (Book I, line 303, "Full forty days He passed" and a second for Book IV, lines 593–95, "—Angelic choirs / Sung heavenly anthems of His victory / Over temptation and the temper proud"), each illustration is circular and printed beneath each is Milton's name, the lines illustrated along with the title of the poem and the corresponding page, red border with decorative corner pieces around the text, the same fine decorative piece in black on verso of title page, repeated at end of life and at the end of the book, notes at bottom of page, original decorated reddish-brown cloth, front cover elaborately decorated in embossed black floral trim, with a bright gilt band at the center incorporating Milton's name in embossed black letters with decorative trim in delicate red, the gilt band outlined in thick gilt rules and decorative black trim with a small gilt floral piece at each end and a larger gilt decorative piece above and below at the center, with a large floral bouquet in embossed bright gilt and contrasting black trim above the gilt band on the left end, and below in the lower left corner within embossed black floral trim a lyre, scroll, and quill, spine similarly decorated in embossed black trim with a bright broad gilt band near the top incorporating "Milton" in large letters, below that is "Illustrated" in embossed black letters, with a large harp in gilt just below the center and "Excelsior Edition" in embossed black letters near the bottom, decorative thick black and gilt bands with contrasting embossed green trim at the top and bottom, back cover decorated in blind trim, brown endpapers, a.e.g. A fine copy of a nineteenth-century illustrated American edition, in a lovely publisher's cloth binding, very nice within, with a long, contemporary presentation inscription in a neat hand (dated 1882) on front blank. Kohler 402, dating its copy "[ca. 1882]," with reference only to an "Unsigned frontispiece portrait" and no illustrations, and reporting "Not in Williamson. Not in the British Library. Not in the Bodleian Library. Not in Cambridge University Library."

See undated ca. 1884 12mo illustrated edition of Milton's *PW* (copy listed here) published by the American News Company with illustrations similar to those here, with different decorative pieces than those here, and called "Excelsior Edition" on the spine as here; see also undated ca. 1884 12mo illustrated edition of Milton's *PW* (copy listed here) published by the American News Company, a larger and more substantive edition than the other undated ca. 1884 edition and than the one here, with a contemporary signature (dated 1884) on fly-leaf, with a frontispiece portrait plate reproducing Munkacsy's illustration of

Milton Dictating 'PL' To His Daughters, and without "Excelsior Edition" on the spine as here and as on the other undated ca. 1884 edition. See, too, undated ca. 1882 12mo illustrated edition of *PL* (copy listed here) published by the American News, with a frontispiece portrait plate reproducing Munkacsy's illustration of *Milton Dictating 'PL' To His Daughters*, with the same three illustrations for *PL* as those here, including six additional illustrations similar in nature and one very different in nature and design from the others.

2262. Variant of Preceding, original decorated bright green cloth, decorated exactly as preceding copy. A lovely copy of this "Excelsior Edition," fresh and clean, in a bright, attractive variant publisher's binding, with a possibly contemporary presentation inscription in a neat hand on the front blank.

2263. Variant of Preceding, the same fine decorative piece in black on verso of title page and repeated at end of life (from among designs in other copies here), a smaller half decorative piece in black at the end of the book (different from the other two copies here, possibly new with this edition), original decorated bright blue cloth (a bit rubbed along extremities, spine slightly darkened, lacking front fly-leaf, early name on front blank), decorated exactly as preceding copies. A nice copy of this "Excelsior Edition," in an attractive variant publisher's binding.

2264. THE POETICAL WORKS OF JOHN MILTON: Edited, With Memoir, Introductions, Notes, And An Essay On Milton's English And Versification, By David Masson, M.A. LL.D., Professor Of Rhetoric And English Literature In The University Of Edinburgh. *London: Macmillan And Co. 1882.* 3 volumes. First edition thus (in a revised, smaller format). Small 8vo, lxixpp.,+[iii]+312pp.,+374,+vi+420pp., half-title each volume with the initials of the press on verso, unsigned engraved frontispiece portrait of a young middle-aged Milton, volume 1, protective tissue guard, engraved frontispiece portrait of a Milton at age ten, "Engraved by Edwd. Radclyffe", volume 2, protective tissue guard, unsigned engraved frontispiece portrait of Milton at age twenty-one, volume 3, protective tissue guard, title page each volume, preface (dated "Edinburgh: September 1882"), introduction, half-title for some of the poems, commentary and notes to each poem in volume 3, "Printed by R. & R. Clark, Edinburgh" at the bottom of the last page in each volume, original drab green cloth (light inoffensive staining along outer edge of covers from some time ago, light pencil notation at the end of volumes 1 and 2), gilt rules on front covers and spines, spines lettered in gilt, edges untrimmed, two elaborate bookplates in each volume, one on each front pastedown, the second ("The Cloisters") on each fly-leaf. A very nice, tall set in original publisher's cloth binding, wholly untrimmed. "The Golden Treasury Edition of Milton's Poetical Works having been for some time out of print, the present edition is substituted, as perhaps more conveniently intermediate in form between the Globe edition and the large Cambridge Edition. Certain other changes have been permitted by this change of form. The chronological arrangement of the Poems has been adopted, as having some advantages . . ." (Preface). Kohler 400, reporting "Not in Williamson."

2265. THE POETICAL WORKS OF JOHN MILTON: With Introductions By David Masson, M.A., L.L.D., Professor Of Rhetoric And English Literature In The University Of Edinburgh. The Globe Edition. *London: Macmillan And Co. 1882.* Fifth Globe edition by Macmillan. 8vo, xi+625+[2]+32pp., half-title with emblem consisting of the letters of Macmillan and Co. on verso, "Preface" (dated 1877), "Contents," "Introduction to *PL*" with several diagrams and other introductory material as in the first editions, half-title for some of the sections and poems, original green cloth, covers ruled in blind with central emblem in blind (consisting of a vignette of Milton within lettering "The Globe Edition") on front cover, spine lettered in gilt ("Milton's Poetical Works") with small emblem in gilt at the bottom, brown endpapers, edges untrimmed and partially unopened, bookplate. A nice copy. Bound in at end, one leaf of advertisements for "Macmillan's Globe Library" (including on verso, "Milton's Poetical Works. Edited, with introductions, by Professor Masson. *'In every way an admirable book.'* Pall Mall Gazette"), and thirty-two pages of advertisements for "Macmillan & Co.'s Catalogue of Works in Belles Lettres, including Poetry, Fiction, etc." (with several editions of Milton). The Globe edition of Milton's *PW* was first published in March 1877 (also listed here with further editions by Globe cited). Scarce. Not in Kohler.

2266. THE POETICAL WORKS OF MILTON, YOUNG, GRAY, BEATTIE AND COLLINS: Complete In One Volume. Illustrated. *Philadelphia: J. B. Lippincott & Co. 1882.* Large, thick 8vo, xxxiii+170pp.,+viii+208pp.,+x+47pp.,+ix+23pp.,+iv+19pp., frontispiece illustration for Gray, protective tissue guard, portrait of Gray, protective tissue guard, two additional illustrations for Gray, each with protective tissue guard, half-title and "Contents" page for each poet, printed in double column, notes at bottom of page, original decorated dark green cloth (a bit rubbed), front cover decorated with delicate small black patterns in contrasting green and black with large laurel wreath incorporating smaller harp and crossed torches in brilliant gilt at the center and with Milton's name in embossed green letters within a brilliant gilt background at the top and "Works" in embossed green letters within a brilliant gilt background at the bottom, back cover decorated in blind, spine similarly decorated with delicate black patterns in contrasting green and black with a harp and crossed torches in brilliant gilt at the center and "Milton's Works" in embossed green letters within a brilliant gilt background at the top and "J & B Lippincott & Co" in embossed green letters within a brilliant gilt background at the bottom, dark green endpapers, a.e.g. An attractive copy in a lovely publisher's binding of the period, in very nice condition. The first 203 pp. are devoted to "Milton's Works" with a life of Milton at the beginning. See 1850 edition by Lippincott, Grambo & Co. listed and other editions by Lippincott, Grambo & Co. cited there. See also 1883 illustrated edition of Milton's *PW* by Lippincott listed here. Uncommon. Not in Kohler.

2267. THE POETICAL WORKS OF JOHN MILTON. With Life. Engravings on Steel. *Gall & Inglis. Edinburgh: Bernard Terrace. London: 25 Paternoster Sqr. n.d. [ca. 1883].* 8vo, xx+491+[1]pp., unsigned frontispiece illustration plate of *The Expulsion*, three additional unsigned illustration plates —for *PL* (Books VII and IX) and for *PR* (Book IV), decorative border trim around the text in alternating sepia and bluish green tint with varying background scenes, original brown calf (a little worn, especially spine and along joints, endpapers and frontispiece slightly foxed), decorated in blind with various designs in blind relief, Milton's name scripted in black on front cover, spine also lettered in black, decorated endpapers (front endpaper chipped along edge), final leaf advertising "List Of Gall & Inglis' Landscape Edition of the Poets" (including "Milton's *PW*"). A fairly good copy with "Nov. 6th 1883" lightly penciled in a contemporary hand on front blank. Laid in: an extra set of the four plates in this edition (saved from another copy in very tattered condition). This is a reprint edition of the undated ca. 1870/1875 edition by Gall & Inglis in a slightly smaller octavo format (see copies listed here). See various undated editions of *PW* by Gall & Inglis published in the 1870s and 1880s, with "Engravings on Steel" and with "Six Engravings on Steel" on title page and with published in "London ("25 Paternoster Square") and Edinburgh (6 George Street)"—with London on the left and Edinburgh on the right as here, and with published in "Edinburgh (Bernard Terrace) and London (25 Paternoster Sqr.)"—with Edinburgh on the left and London on the right. Not in Kohler.

2268. THE POETICAL WORKS OF JOHN MILTON. *Edinburgh: William P. Nimmo & Co. 1883.* 8vo, xxxvii+[3]+440pp., unsigned engraved frontispiece portrait plate of a middle-aged Milton, engraved and printed title pages, with vignette illustration (of the poet being inspired by heavenly choirs) by F. Borders on engraved title plate ("Edinburgh: William P. Nimmo & Co. 1882."), protective tissue guard, vignette illustration (of a young boy in a setting in nature with a cane laying beside him) signed with the initials "WS" on printed title, life of Milton by J. M. Ross, eleven illustration plates, most after F. Borders, some unsigned: four for *PL* (Books I, III, VI, XI), two for *PR* (Book I), one for *SA*, two for *C*, one for *L'A*, one for *IlP*, half-title for *PL*, *PR*, *SA*, *C*, *Arc*, *MP*, and *Poemata*, red border around text, "Printed by Ballantyne, Hanson & Co., Edinburgh" printed at the bottom of the last page, three-quarter red leather, red pebble cloth (a little scuffed, ex-library, with various library markings and stamps, including "Withdrawn From Queens' College Library, Cambridge And Disposed Of"—what would Milton have thought of that!), spine lettered in gilt, raised bands delicately trimmed in gilt, floral decorations in gilt within the panels, marbled endpapers and edges. A decent copy. The possible first edition by Nimmo was published in 1865, illustrated (also listed here with further editions by Nimmo cited). Only the 1865 edition has twelve illustrations, the others have eleven (with only one illustration for *L'A* instead of two, as in the 1865 edition). Scarce. Not in Kohler.

2269. THE POETICAL WORKS OF JOHN MILTON. Reprinted From The Best Editions. With Memoir, Explanatory and Glossorial Notes, &c. Portrait And Original Illustrations. The Chandos Poets. *London: Frederick Warne And Co., Bedford Street, Strand. New York: Scribner, Welford, And Armstrong. n.d. [ca. 1883].* Large square 8vo, xxiv+581pp., engraved frontispiece portrait (of a youngish looking middle-aged Milton, unsigned, with labeling "London: Frederick Warne & Co." at bottom), title page in orange and black, twelve illustration plates after engravings by Dalziel: one for *NO*, one for *L'A*, six for *PL* (Books I, IV, V, VII, VIII, and XII), one for *PR* (Book I), one for *SA*, one for *On His Deceased Wife*, and one for *Latin Epigram VII* ("Ad Eandem"—the illustration titled *Milton Meeting Leonora Baroni at Cardinal Barberini's House*), decorative tailpiece at the end of *PR*, half-title for *SA*, orange border around text, "London: Printed By Woodfall And Kinder, Milford Lane, Strand. W.C." on verso of last page—appears also on verso of title page, notes at bottom of page, contemporary full maroon morocco, covers and spine decorated with blind rules, spine lettered in gilt, raised bands, inner dentelles finely tooled in gilt, a.e.g. A very nice copy with contemporary prize inscription (dated 1883) on front blank. Uncommon. Not in Kohler.

2270. THE POETICAL WORKS OF JOHN MILTON A New Edition, Carefully Revised From The Text Of Thomas Newton, D.D. With Illustrations By William Harvey. *London[:] George Routledge And Sons[,] Broadway, Ludgate Hill[;] New York: 416 Broome Street[.] n.d. [ca. 1883].* 8vo, viii+570pp., frontispiece illustration plate of Satan cast out of Heaven, protective tissue guard, and five additional illustration plates after William Harvey, engraved by Dalziel, "A New Edition, Carefully Revised From The Text Of Thomas Newton" in a clear, non-Gothic font on title page, "Routledge's Red Line Poets" listed on verso of title page (the twenty-five listings including Milton), "Printed By Ballantyne And Hanson London And Edinburgh" at bottom of last page, original blue-green cloth (a little rubbed), front cover decorated in embossed floral trim with a large horizontal recessed panel in black at the center outlined in gilt and black rules and filled with blue-green flowers outlined in gilt, diagonally across the panel is a bright gilt band with Milton's name lettered in large embossed blue-green letters with delicate gilt trim behind the first three letters, "Illustrated" is highlighted against a gilt background in the lower right corner, spine similarly decorated in embossed floral trim and embossed blue-green lettering with a floral blossom in gilt at the top, back cover decorated in embossed floral trim with "GRS" highlighted in embossed blue-green letters, a.e.g. A charming copy in a lovely publisher's binding. The first edition of Milton's *PW* by George Routledge and Co. was published in 1853 (also listed here with further editions by Routledge cited). Not in Kohler.

2271. Variant of Preceding. Original decorated green cloth (front cover and front endpapers waterstained along the outer edge and at the bottom corner, lower right corner of back cover also a little waterstained), front cover elaborately decorated in black trim with a large bright gilt square emblem at the center incorporating floral trim in gilt with several gilt blossoms with red centers outlined in black with Milton's name in large embossed black letters outlined in green at the top and "Illustrated" in embossed green letters against a bright gilt band at the bottom, black floral trim surrounds the bright gilt square and at the top of the square is a bright gilt harp with a green star and at the bottom a black vase with a bright gilt flower, spine similarly decorated in black and gilt, with a small harp in black within double black rules at the center, with Milton's name in embossed green letters within a bright, wide gilt band at the top, and "Illustrated" and "Routledge" in progressively smaller embossed green letters within progressively smaller bright gilt bands toward the bottom, decorative black trim at the top and bottom with a bright gilt star at the top, back cover with floral arrangement in black at the center, brown endpapers, a.e.g. Except for the waterstaining, an attractively bound copy with contemporary presentation inscription (dated "Dec. 25, 1883") on front blank. The edition here bears the same publisher's imprint as the preceding as well as the same printer's reference on the last page; it also has the same thickness and size. Like the ca. 1878 Routledge and Sons edition listed here, it has "Routledge's Red-Line Poets" listed on verso of title page (with nine listings, including Milton), not "Routledge's Red Line Poets" (with twenty-five listings, including Milton) as in the preceding edition. See ca. 1878 Routledge and Sons edition listed with regard to each of these elements. It is also in an attractive variant publisher's binding; the binding is exactly the same (except in green here) as the decorated red binding on one of the undated ca. 1878 editions. Not in Kohler.

2272. THE POETICAL WORKS OF JOHN MILTON A New Edition, Carefully Revised From The Text Of Thomas Newton, D.D. With Illustrations By William Harvey. *London[:] George Routledge And Sons[,] Broadway, Ludgate Hill[;] New York: 9 Lafayette Place[.] n.d. [ca. 1883].* Variant edition. 8vo, viii+570pp., frontispiece illustration plate of Satan cast out of Heaven, protective tissue guard, and five additional illustration plates after William Harvey, engraved by Dalziel, "A New Edition, Carefully Revised From The Text Of Thomas Newton" in a clear, non-Gothic font on title page, "Routledge's Red Line Poets" listed on verso of title page (the twenty-five listings including Milton), "Printed By Ballantyne, Hanson, And Co. Edinburgh And London" at bottom of last page, contemporary shellacked bevelled thick wooden boards with a large color picture of a pond and sunset pasted on front cover, with finely trimmed decorative gilt border, back cover is plain, green morocco spine (a little rubbed) with decorative gilt trim and a decorative gilt piece within the panels along with gilt lettering, raised bands (rubbed), inner dentelles finely tooled in gilt trim, lightly decorated patterned endpapers, a.e.g., purple ribbon marker. A very small chip near the top and another toward the bottom do not detract from this lovely copy with variant publisher's imprint, in an attractive Victorian papier-mâché binding. Rauri McLean describes a similarly bound edition of Milton: "Mauchline binding, the upper cover is chromolithographed paper stuck down over wood: the lower is plain wood. Both covers have been 'glazed' with shellac . . . Leather spine, all edges gilt. The Poetical Works of John Milton[.] John Walker, n.d. [1860s–70s]" (*VPB*, 1983, p. 73, with photograph) The first edition by George Routledge and Co. was published in 1853 (also listed here with further editions by Routledge cited). Not in Kohler.

2273. THE POETICAL WORKS OF JOHN MILTON. Reprinted From The Best Editions With Biographical Notice, Etc. *Philadelphia: J. B. Lippincott & Co., 1883.* First edition thus by Lippincott. 8vo, iii+[ii]+562pp., engraved frontispiece portrait sketch of a young Milton by "E. Ronjat," protective tissue guard, life, illustration plates after engravings by Dalziel, two for *PL*, Book IV (*Adam Sees Eve*, with lines quoted) and Book VIII (*Adam and Eve Naming the Animals*, without identification or appropriate lines quoted), one for *SA* ("But Who is this? . . . Comes this way sailing / Like a stately ship?"), one for *L'A* ("While the ploughman near at hand . . ."), and one for *Latin Epigram VII* ("Ad Eandem," without identification or appropriate lines quoted—the illustration titled in other editions: *Milton Meeting Leonora Baroni at Cardinal Barberini's House*), red border around text, original decorated green cloth (a bit rubbed), front cover elaborately decorated in embossed black and gilt, with Milton's name in gilt outline across the top within decorative gilt border trim with a small gilt flower within decorative floral trim above at the center, with fanned gilt piece with green trim growing larger off to the right side, large harp and floral trim in embossed black beneath Milton's name at the center of the front cover, spine similarly elaborately decorated in embossed black and gilt with bright gilt trim incorporating "Milton" in large letters across the top, with a bright gilt urn at the bottom with decorated black trim surrounding the urn, dark blue endpapers, a.e.g. A very nice copy of a nineteenth-century illustrated American edition in a lovely decorated publisher's cloth binding. Not in Kohler.

See 1882 nonillustrated edition by Lippincott (listed here). See also nonillustrated editions of Milton's *PW* published by Lippincott, Grambo & Co. in Philadelphia in 1853 (first edition thus), 1854, 1859, and 1865 (each edition listed here). See, too, undated ca. 1880 and dated 1881 illustrated editions published by Lovell and undated ca. 1885 illustrated edition (each edition listed here) published by Lovell (with slight variations), and see 1883 illustrated edition following published by D. Lothrop & Co. in Boston, each with the same frontispiece portrait by Ronjat and the same illustrations and in the same format as here.

2274. THE POETICAL WORKS OF JOHN MILTON. Reprinted From The Best Editions With Biographical Notice, Etc. *Boston: D. Lothrop & Co., 1883.* First edition thus by Lothrop. 8vo, 562pp. engraved frontispiece portrait sketch of a young Milton by "E. Ronjat," protective tissue guard, life, illustration plates after engravings by Dalziel, two for *PL*, Book IV (*Adam Sees Eve*, with lines quoted) and Book VIII (*Adam and Eve Naming the Animals*, without identification or appropriate lines quoted), one for *SA* ("But Who is this? . . . Comes this way sailing / Like a stately ship?"), one for *L'A* ("While the ploughman near at hand . . ."), and one for *Latin Epigram VII* ("Ad Eandem," without identification or appropriate lines quoted—the illustration titled in other editions: *Milton Meeting Leonora Baroni at Cardinal Barberini's House*), red border around text, original decorated grayish green cloth (a bit rubbed along extremities), front cover richly decorated in embossed black and gilt, with Milton's name with larger initial letter "M" in embossed light green letters against a large bright gilt background decorated in embossed floral trim near the top, with a shamrock in embossed light green within a bright gilt square at the center, spine similarly richly decorated in embossed black and gilt, with title in embossed light green within two bright broad gilt bands at the top, with a shamrock in embossed green tinted in black within a bright gilt circle within a black backdrop at the center and with "Lothrops" lettered in embossed light green within a gilt band at the bottom, lightly decorated endpapers, a.e.g. A fine copy of a nineteenth-century illustrated American edition, fresh and clean within, in an attractively decorated publisher's cloth binding. See undated edition following published by Lothrop and Company about this same time, ca. 1883, with circular illustrations after engravings by Dalziel different from those here. See undated ca. 1885 illustrated edition by Lovell in identical binding to the binding here (less fine condition) only "Lovell" in place of "Lothrop" at the bottom. Scarce. Not in Kohler.

2275. THE POETICAL WORKS OF JOHN MILTON With Memoir And Notes[.] Complete Edition[.] *Boston[:] D. Lothrop And Company[,] Franklin And Hawley Streets[,] n.d. [ca. 1883].* First edition thus by Lothrop? Variant edition. 8vo, xii+563+[1]pp., engraved frontispiece illustration plate with circular illustration after an engraving by Dalziel for *PL* (Christ as "The great Creator from His work returned"), protective tissue guard, life, two illustration plates with circular illustrations after engravings by Dalziel, one for *PL*, Book XII ("The Archangel stood . . . brandished sword of God") and one for *PR*, Book IV ("Angelic choirs Sung heavenly anthems of His victory Over temptation . . ."), notes at bottom of page, original green cloth (a bit rubbed, spine ends slightly chipped), front cover richly decorated in gilt with the initials "D L & Co" at the center, spine lettered in gilt with decorative gilt trim within the panels, t.e.g. A nice copy in attractive publisher's binding. See dated 1883 edition preceding published by Lothrop and Company, with illustrations after engravings by Dalziel different from those here. Uncommon. Not in Kohler.

2276. THE POETICAL WORKS OF JOHN MILTON. Reprinted From The Best Editions With Biographical Notice, Etc. *New York: Thomas Y. Crowell & Co., No. 13 Astor Place. n.d. [ca. 1883].* 8vo, 562pp., frontispiece illustration plate after an engraving by Dalziel for *PL* (*The Expulsion*, Book XII), protective tissue guard, decorative central device in black incorporating initials of the press on title page, five additional illustration plates after engravings by Dalziel, for *PL*, Book IV (*Adam Sees Eve*, with lines quoted) and Book VIII (*Adam and Eve Naming the Animals*, with appropriate lines quoted), for *SA* ("But Who is this? . . . Comes this way sailing / Like a stately ship?"), for *L'A* ("While the ploughman near at hand . . ."), and for *On His Deceased Wife* (with appropriate lines quoted), orange border around text, contemporary tree calf, brown leather spine (a bit rubbed, pages a bit age-darkened), decorative gilt border trim on covers, spine decorated in gilt (very faded), green morocco label with gilt lettering and gilt rules, slightly raised bands with decorative gilt trim, broad inner dentelles and outer dentelles finely tooled in gilt, decorated green endpapers, a.e.g. A fine copy, one of "Crowell's Red Line Poets" in "American Tree Calf Binding," as advertised in one of the advertisements bound in various other copies here. Milton's *PW* were possible first published by Crowell ca. 1880 (also listed here with further editions by Crowell cited). Kohler 412, dating its copy "[ca. 1888]" and reporting "Not in the British Library. Not in the Bodleian Library. Not in Cambridge University Library."

2277. Variant of Preceding, original decorated yellow cloth, front cover richly decorated in embossed black and gilt with a bright gilt emblem incorporating Milton's name within a thick bright gilt band with a larger decorated initial letter "M" at the beginning, gilt floral blossoms within embossed yellow leaves against a black background surround "Milton" in large letters at the top, in the middle is an embossed lyre in black, spine similarly richly decorated in embossed black and floral blossoms within embossed yellow leaves in the middle, three bright gilt flowers above "Thomas Y Crowell & Co." lettered in gilt at the bottom, a.e.g. A very nice copy, fresh and crisp, in a lovely decorated variant publisher's cloth binding, slightly thicker than the preceding copy.

2278. Variant of Preceding, original decorated brown cloth (a little rubbed with a few scuff marks on back cover), decorated exactly as preceding copy. A good copy in a lovely decorated variant publisher's cloth binding, as thick as the preceding copy, with contemporary inscription (dated "Christmas '83") on fly-leaf.

2279. Variant of Preceding, original decorated green cloth (spine ends a bit rubbed, several plates slightly waterstained at edges without affecting the illustration), decorated exactly as preceding copies, bookplate on front pastedown. A good copy in an attractively decorated variant publisher's cloth binding, as thick as preceding copy, with a neatly written contemporary inscription (dated "December 25, 1883") on fly-leaf.

2280. Variant of Preceding, original decorated reddish-brown cloth (a bit rubbed), decorated exactly as preceding copies. A fine copy in a lovely decorated variant publisher's cloth binding.

2281. Variant of Preceding, original decorated blue cloth (back cover a bit rubbed), decorated exactly as preceding copies. A nice copy in an attractively decorated variant publisher's cloth binding.

2282. Variant of Preceding, original embossed maroon calf over padded boards (a bit rubbed at joints and at top of spine), front cover and spine lettered in gilt, decorated green endpapers, a.e.g. A nice copy in a variant publisher's binding, slightly thinner than the preceding copy and the thinnest of all copies here, with eight pages of advertisement leaves bound in at end: for "Crowell's Red Line Poets" (including Milton), and for "Popular Poets: Crowell's Favorite Illustrated Edition[s]" (including Milton), and for additional editions by Crowell.

2283. THE POETICAL WORKS OF JOHN MILTON. Reprinted From The Best Editions With Biographical Notice, Etc. *New York: Hurst & Co., Publishers, 122 Nassau Street. n.d. [ca. 1883].* 8vo, xv+190pp., frontispiece illustration plate after an engraving by Dalziel for *PL* (*The Expulsion*, Book XII), protective tissue guard, decorative central device in black incorporating initials of the press on title page, five additional illustration plates after engravings by Dalziel, for *PL*, Book IV (*Adam Sees Eve*, with lines quoted) and Book VIII (*Adam and Eve Naming the Animals*, with appropriate lines quoted), for *SA* ("But Who is this? . . . Comes this way sailing / Like a stately ship?"), for *L'A* ("While the ploughman near at hand . . ."), and for *On His Deceased Wife* (with appropriate lines quoted), red border around text, original decorated green cloth (a bit rubbed along joints and extremities, spine ends slightly rubbed as well), front cover elaborately decorated in embossed black and gilt incorporating Milton's name in embossed green letters within bright gilt device with floral background near the top, in a plain green block beneath an embossed cherub figure playing a gilt harp with bright gilt floral pieces and bright gilt butterfly with floral stems and round backdrop in black contrast, along the inside a black inset with an embossed vase in green at the bottom with embossed long-stem flowers in green reaching up to a small harp in embossed black and gilt within a small bright gilt block at the side of Milton's name, spine similarly decorated in black and gilt, with Milton's name within a broad gilt band at the top, large floral decorations in gilt in the middle, "Hurst & Co." in gilt just below that, and contrasting flowers in black and gilt at the gilt with the title ("Milton's Poems") incorporated within two thick bright gilt bands at the top, with gilt bottom, a.e.g. A nice copy in an attractive American binding of the period, with contemporary presentation inscription (dated "Christmas 1883") on fly-leaf. The possible first edition of Milton's *PW* by Hurst was published ca. 1880 (illustrated edition also listed here with further editions by Hurst cited). Uncommon. Not in Kohler.

2284. **THE POETICAL WORKS OF JOHN MILTON.** Reprinted From The Original Edition, And Containing Numerous Explanatory Notes. With Memoir By David Masson, M. A., L.L. D., Author of "The Life And Times Of John Milton." The "Arundel Poets." The Arundel Print. *New York. n.d. [ca. 1883]*. Second edition thus? Thick 8vo, li+627pp., frontispiece illustration plate and twenty additional illustration plates after Gustave Doré, half-title for *SA*, notes at bottom of page, original decorated brown cloth (a bit rubbed), front cover decorated in black and gilt, with black rules at top and bottom, central illustration in brilliant gilt of three women (possibly the muses), one playing the harp, another writing, and the third thinking, the whole surrounded by decorative black trim, Milton's name in bright gilt at the top with decorative trim in black and bright gilt below, spine similarly decorated in black and gilt, with Milton's name in gilt at the top, decorative trim in black and bright gilt below, large emblem in black and gilt at the center, gilt lettering and black rules at the bottom, a.e.g. A nice copy in an attractive publisher's binding, fresh and bright, with contemporary signature (dated 1883) on front blank. The possible first edition thus by "The Arundel Print. New York," was published in 1880, with copyright date of 1880 on verso of title page (see copy listed here). Scarce. Not in Kohler.

2285. **THE POETICAL WORKS OF JOHN MILTON.** With A Sketch Of His Life. *New York: John B. Alden, Publisher, 1883.* First edition thus. 8vo, 562pp., original brown cloth (a bit rubbed, small tear on spine repaired), spine lettered in gilt ("Cyclopedia Of Poetry Milton"), light blue endpapers. A good copy. Not in Kohler.

2286. **THE POETICAL WORKS OF JOHN MILTON** Reprinted From The Best Editions With Biographical Notice, Etc. Illustrated By Gustave Doré[.] *New York[:] Thomas Y. Crowell & Co[,] (1884).* First edition thus (with Doré illustrations). Tall 8vo, 562pp., frontispiece illustration plate reproducing an illustration after Doré for *PL* ("A happy rural seat of various view"), protective tissue guard, copyright dated 1884 on verso of title page, "Sketch Of The Life Of John Milton" (unsigned, possibly by Nathan Haskell Dole, as in later editions by Crowell), illustration plates reproducing Doré's illustrations for *PL* (Books I: three illustration plates; II: one illustration plate; III: two illustration plates; IV: five illustration plates; V: one illustration plate; VI: two illustration plates; VII: one illustration plate; VIII: one illustration plate; IX: five illustration plates; X: no illustration plates; XI: one illustration plate; XII: one illustration plate), original light green cloth (bit worn at spine ends and corners), front cover richly decorated on the inside portion in embossed floral trim interwoven with green stems and leaves with orange blossoms against a black backdrop delineated by orange and black lines on either side of a dotted black area against a green background, the rest of the cover decorated in fine black trim with delicate orange blossoms with Milton's name in black letters against a large, bright gilt band near the top toward the right, delicately decorated in floral trim, the whole framed in a thin green rule, then a thinner gilt rule, and a still thinner green rule, followed by a successively thicker gilt rule and then a thick red rule, the spine similarly decorated with black trim, and a long, large gilt band at the center with Milton's name in black, framed in black rule, with three gilt blossoms over lined black rules at the top and bottom, and with thick gilt and black rules at the top and bottom, decorated light green endpapers, a.e.g. A lovely copy, handsomely printed, in an attractive American publisher's binding. The first edition with Doré's illustrations for *PL* appeared in the mid-1860s (see 1865–66 edition in parts and the 1866 first book edition, each listed here). Not in Kohler.

2287. **THE POETICAL WORKS OF JOHN MILTON** Reprinted From The Best Editions With Biographical Notice, Etc. Illustrated By Gustave Doré[.] *New York[:] Thomas Y. Crowell & Co., (1884).* First edition thus. 8vo, 562pp., frontispiece illustration plate reproducing an illustration after Doré for *PL* ("A happy rural seat of various view"), protective tissue guard, copyright dated 1884 on verso of title page, "Sketch Of The Life Of John Milton" (unsigned, possibly by Nathan Haskell Dole, as in later editions by Crowell), illustration plates reproducing Doré's illustrations for *PL* (Books I: three illustration plates; II: one illustration plate; III: two illustration plates; IV: five illustration plates; V: one illustration plate; VI: two illustration plates; VII: one illustration plate; VIII: one illustration plate; IX: five illustration plates; X: no illustration plates; XI: one illustration plate; XII: one illustration plate), original light green cloth (spine a bit darkened), decorative narrow maroon border rule on front cover with central white leather inlaid lettered in gilt with decorative trim in gilt and maroon, the whole within a decorative blind border trim in lighter green, spine decorated in gilt with gilt lettering, a.e.g. A lovely copy, handsomely printed on thick paper, in an attractive American publisher's binding. See undated ca. 1880 illustrated edition of Milton's *PW* by Crowell listed here with illustrations after engravings by Dalziel and other editions by Crowell cited there. Not in Kohler.

2288. THE POETICAL WORKS OF JOHN MILTON. Reprinted From The Best Editions With Biographical Notice, Etc. *New York: Thomas Y. Crowell & Co., No. 13 Astor Place. (1884)*. 8vo, iii+[ii]+562+[12]pp., frontispiece illustration plate after engraving by Dalziel for *PL* (*The Expulsion*, Book XII), protective tissue guard, decorative central device in black incorporating initials of the press on title page, copyright dated 1884 on verso of title page, five additional illustration plates after engravings by the Dalziel brothers, for *PL*, Book IV (*Adam Sees Eve*, with lines quoted) and Book VIII (*Adam and Eve Naming the Animals*, with appropriate lines quoted), for *SA* ("But Who is this? . . . Comes this way sailing / Like a stately ship?"), for *L'A* ("While the ploughman near at hand . . ."), and for *On His Deceased Wife* (with appropriate lines quoted), red border around text, original decorated brown cloth (slight rubbing at bottom of spine, several pages showing light offprint from earlier insertion of leaves), front cover decorated in black with bright gilt emblem incorporating Milton's name within a thick bright gilt panel with large decorated initial letter "M," spine decorated in black with the title ("Milton's Poems") incorporated within two thick bright gilt panels at the top, with gilt initials of Thomas Y Crowell & Co. at the bottom, and with double gilt rules at the very top and bottom, a.e.g. A very nice copy with contemporary inscription (dated "Christmas, 1889") in a neat hand on fly-leaf, and with twelve pages of advertisements for "Crowell's Poets" (including editions of Milton) bound in at the end. The possible first edition of Milton's *PW* by Crowell with illustration plates after engravings by Dalziel was published ca. 1880 (also listed here with further editions by Crowell cited). Kohler 412, dating its copy "[ca. 1888]" and reporting "Not in the British Library. Not in the Bodleian Library. Not in Cambridge University Library."

2288. Variant of Preceding, original decorated reddish-brown cloth (with some wear along extremities, spine ends slightly chipped), front cover richly decorated in black floral trim with a bright gilt emblem at the top incorporating Milton's name with a large decorated initial letter "M," spine similarly richly decorated in black and gilt floral trim with the title ("Milton's Poems") incorporated within two thick bright gilt bands at the top, with "Thomas Y Crowell & Co." lettered in gilt at the bottom, a.e.g. A nice copy in an attractively decorated variant publisher's cloth binding, with five pages of advertisement leaves for "Crowell's Red Line Poets" (including Milton), for "Popular Poets: Crowell's Favorite Illustrated Edition" (including Milton), and for additional editions by Crowell bound in at the end. "Copyright 1884 By T. Y. Crowell & Co." stamped in black at bottom of front cover. See other editions of Milton's *PW* published by Crowell in the collection as identified in preceding copy. Kohler 412, dating its copy "[ca. 1888]."

2290. Variant of Preceding, original decorated olive green cloth (two small white spots on front cover), front cover richly decorated in black and gilt floral trim with bright gilt emblem at the top incorporating Milton's name in embossed olive green letters with large decorated initial letter "M" at the beginning, spine similarly richly decorated in black and gilt floral trim with the title ("Milton's Poems") incorporated in embossed olive green letters within two thick gilt bands at the top, with "Thomas Y Crowell & Co." lettered in gilt at the bottom, with double black rules at top and bottom, a.e.g. Laid in: presentation label. A nice copy in an attractively decorated variant publisher's cloth binding, with five pages of advertisement leaves (as preceding) bound in at the end. Kohler 412, dating its copy "[ca. 1888]."

2291. THE POETICAL WORKS OF JOHN MILTON With Memoir and Notes. Complete Edition. Illustrated. *New York: The American News Company, 39 And 41 Chambers Street. n.d [ca. 1884]*. Large square 12mo (measuring 9" × 6 ¼" in relation to the much smaller 12mo editions following, or 1 ½" taller and 1 ½" wider), xii+563pp., frontispiece portrait plate reproducing Munkacsy's illustration of "Milton Dictating 'Paradise Lost' To His Daughters," protective tissue guard, pronounced red border with large decorative corner pieces on title page, decorative piece in black on verso of title page, "Memoir Of John Milton" with decorative piece in black at end (different from other decorative pieces), followed by "Contents," nine unsigned illustration plates for *PL*: two for Book I, one for Book II, two for Book III, one for Book IV, one for Book V, one for Book VII, and one for Book XI, two additional unsigned illustration plates for *PR*: one for Book I and one for Book IV, each illustration is circular, and printed beneath each is

Milton's name, the lines illustrated along with the title of the poem and the corresponding page, pronounced red border with large decorative corner pieces around text, decorative piece in black on verso of title page and a different decorative piece in black on verso of last page of life (as in other copies here), decorative piece in black at the end of the book (similar to designs in other editions by the American News Company, see undated ca. 1882 illustrated edition listed earlier and undated ca. 1884 illustrated edition listed later), decorative piece in black on verso of last page (different from designs in other editions by the American News Company), notes at bottom of page, original decorated orange cloth (rubbed along the joints and edges, a bit shaken within), front cover richly decorated in black with bright gilt trim, incorporating Milton's name across the front cover in large embossed black letters with decorative trim in red within a bright gilt band set against a dark black background, with a large central gilt urn with a floral arrangement in gilt that reaches to the top and surrounding the urn's base at the bottom are a lyre, the dramatic masks of tragedy and comedy, a sword unfolding into a manuscript, and the figure of a head in armored helmet, spine similarly elaborately decorated in black with bright gilt trim, incorporating Milton's name in large embossed red letters with decorative trim in red within a bright gilt band at the top with gilt-decorated black trim on either side, with a large figure of a woman's head (side view) on a pedestal in the middle with a small harp in gilt and black beneath surrounded by decorative gilt floral trim, decorative thick black and gilt bands at top and bottom, back cover decorated in blind, decorated endpapers, a.e.g. While the illustrations are unsigned, the illustration for Satan in Book I of *PL* is dated "1878" in the lower right corner with the "8" partially missing and with the initials "PN" in larger size between 18 and 78. This illustration and a number of others appear in the ca. 1882 edition of *PL* (also listed here). A large, handsome publication, substantive in size and quality, fresh and clean within, in a bright attractive binding of the period, with a contemporary signature (dated 1884) on fly-leaf. The possible first edition of Milton's *PW* by the American News Company was published ca. 1882 (also listed here with further editions by the American News cited). Uncommon. Not in Kohler.

2292. THE POETICAL WORKS OF JOHN MILTON With Memoir and Notes. Complete Edition. Illustrated. *New York: The American News Company, 39 And 41 Chambers Street. n.d. [ca. 1884].* 12mo, xii+563pp., unsigned frontispiece illustration plate for *PR* ("Also it is written / Tempt not the Lord thy God," Book IV, lines 560–61), protective tissue guard, "Memoir Of John Milton," followed by "Contents," three unsigned illustration plates for *PL* (Book V, lines 93–94, "Thus Eve her night / related"; Book VII, lines 566–67, "Open, ye heavens your living doors: let in / The great Creator from His work returned"; and Book XII, lines 626–33, "The archangel stood— / —High in front advanced / The brandished sword of God"), two additional unsigned illustration plates for *PR* (Book I, line 303, "Full forty days He passed" and a second for Book IV, lines 593–95, "—Angelic choirs / Sung heavenly anthems of His victory / Over temptation and the temper proud"), each illustration is circular and printed beneath each is Milton's name, the lines illustrated along with the title of the poem and the corresponding page, red border with decorative corner pieces around text, small decorative piece in black on verso of title page (from among designs in other editions by the American News Company), a larger decorative piece in black on verso of last page of life and repeated at the end of the book (possibly new with this edition, different from decorative pieces in earlier ca. 1882 edition by the American News Company also listed here), notes at bottom of page, original decorated olive green cloth (a bit rubbed), front cover elaborately decorated in embossed black floral trim, with a bright gilt band at the center incorporating Milton's name in embossed black letters outlined in gilt with decorative trim in olive green, the gilt band outlined in decorative black trim with a small gilt floral piece at each end and a larger gilt decorative piece above and below at the center, with a large floral bouquet in embossed black trim above the gilt band on the left end, and below in the lower left corner within embossed black floral trim a lyre, scroll, and quill, spine similarly decorated in embossed black trim, with a broad gilt band near the top incorporating "Milton" in large letters, the broad band outlined in decorative black trim on each side, with "Illustrated" lettered in black beneath, a large harp in embossed black just below the center, with "Excelsior Edition" lettered in black at the bottom, decorative black bands with contrasting embossed floral trim at the top and bottom of the spine, back cover decorated in blind trim, decorated light green endpapers, a.e.g. A good copy of a nineteenth-century illustrated American edition, in a lovely publisher's binding, nice within. The possible first edition of Milton's *PW* by the American News Company was published ca. 1882 (also listed here with further editions by the American News cited). Not in Kohler.

2293. Variant of Preceding, original decorated blue cloth, decorated exactly as preceding copy. A fine copy, fresh and clean, in an attractive variant late nineteenth-century American publisher's cloth binding, with bookplate and personal shelf label on front pastedown. Not in Kohler.

2294. Variant of Preceding, original decorated olive green cloth (spine and corners a bit rubbed, some age-browning), front cover decorated in embossed black floral trim with Milton's name in embossed gilt letters within bright decorative gilt trim across the top, spine similarly decorated in embossed black floral trim with Milton's name in embossed olive green letters within bright decorative gilt trim across the top at the same level as the front cover, with "Illustrated" lettered in black beneath Milton's name and "Excelsior Edition" in black at the bottom, decorated light orange endpapers, a.e.g. A nice copy, crisp and fresh, in an attractive variant late nineteenth-century American publisher's cloth binding. See the "Excelsior Publishing House" edition listed later with illustrations that are similar to those here, although less crisp, in an identical decorated cloth binding although a variant cloth color, also called "Excelsior Edition" at the bottom of the spine as here. Not in Kohler.

2295. Variant of Preceding, original decorated blue cloth (a bit rubbed, pages a little age-browned), decorated exactly as preceding copy. A good copy in an attractive variant publisher's cloth binding. See the "Excelsior Publishing House" edition following with illustrations that are similar to those here, although less crisp, in an identical decorated cloth binding, also called "Excelsior Edition" at the bottom of the spine as here. Not in Kohler.

2296. THE POETICAL WORKS OF JOHN MILTON With Memoir and Notes. Complete Edition. Illustrated. *New York: Excelsior Publishing House, 29 And 31 Beekman St. n.d. [ca. 1884]*. First edition thus? 8vo, xii+563+[1]pp., unsigned frontispiece illustration for *PL* (Book V, lines 93–94, "Thus Eve her night / related"), "Memoir Of John Milton," followed by "Contents," two additional unsigned illustrations for *PL* (Book VII, lines 566–67, "Open, ye heavens your living doors: let in / The great Creator from His work returned"; and Book XII, lines 626–33, "The archangel stood— / —High in front advanced / The brandished sword of God"), three unsigned illustrations for *PR* (one for Book I, line 303, "Full forty days He passed" and two for Book IV, lines 593–95 "—Angelic choirs / Sung heavenly anthems of His victory / Over temptation and the temper proud" and lines 560–61, "Also it is written / Tempt not the Lord thy God"), red border with decorative corner pieces around text, decorative piece in black on verso of title page, decorative piece in black on verso of last page of life and repeated at the end of the book, notes at bottom of page, original decorated orange cloth (a bit rubbed at corners and at top and bottom of spine, back cover a little marked), front cover decorated in embossed black floral trim with Milton's name in embossed gilt letters within bright decorative gilt trim across the top, spine similarly decorated in embossed black floral trim with Milton's name in embossed orange letters within broad gilt band and bright decorative gilt trim across the top at the same level as the front cover, with "Illustrated" lettered in black beneath Milton's name and "Excelsior Edition" in black at the bottom, decorated endpapers, a.e.g. A nice copy of a nineteenth-century illustrated American edition, in a lovely publisher's binding of the period. The illustrations, unsigned reproductions of illustrations which appeared earlier, are circular vignettes in black and white, with Milton's name, the lines illustrated, the title of the poem, and the corresponding page printed beneath each illustration. With the exception of a different publisher and illustrations that are less crisp, this edition is similar to the undated ca. 1884 illustrated edition listed here by "The American News Company" in an identical decorated cloth binding (also listed here). The publisher of this edition is "Excelsior Publishing House," and this edition, like the edition by "The American News Company" earlier, is identified as the "Excelsior Edition" at the bottom of the spine. Not in Kohler.

2297. Variant of Preceding, with identical illustrations (one of the illustrations for *PR* misbound in *SA*), original decorated blue cloth (a bit rubbed at corners and spine ends), decorated exactly as preceding copy. A nice copy in an attractive variant publisher's cloth binding. Not in Kohler.

2298. THE POETICAL WORKS OF JOHN MILTON. Reprinted From The Best Editions With Biographical Notice, Etc. *New York: R. Worthington, 770 Broadway. 1884*. First edition thus? 8vo, iii+562pp., frontispiece portrait plate of a young, romanticised Milton after C. Ronjat, protective tissue guard, five illustrate plates, two after engravings by Dalziel for *PL*: one for Book V (*Adam Sees Eve*, with appropriate lines quoted) and one for Book VIII (*Adam and Eve Naming the Animals*, without appropriate lines quoted), one after an engraving by Dalziel for *SA* (with appropriate lines quoted), one after an engraving by Dalziel for *L'A* ("While the ploughman near at hand...," with appropriate lines quoted), and one (unidentified and without appropriate lines quoted) for *Latin Epigram VII*: "Ad Eandem" (the illustration titled in other editions as *Milton Meeting Leonora Baroni at Cardinal Barberini's House*), red border around text, original decorated red cloth (spine a little faded and worn, chipped at top and bottom, edge of back cover a little worn and stained in two places, corners a bit frayed), front cover elaborately decorated in black and gilt with gilt piece at the center and Milton's name incorporated within gilt backdrop at the top, spine similarly decorated in black and gilt with title ("Milton's Poems") within gilt backdrop at the top (faded) and "Worthington" within gilt backdrop at the bottom (faded), decorated endpapers, a.e.g. Despite some wear, a good copy in an attractive nineteenth-century American publisher's binding, with contemporary presentation inscription in a neat hand (dated 1884) on front blank with red border. See 1886, 1887, and 1889 editions by Worthington, listed here, "Reprinted From The Chandos Poets" with similar illustrations, but with appropriate lines quoted beneath each illustration; see also undated and dated illustrated editions of Milton's *PW* by Frederick Warne and Co. with illustrations engraved by Dalziel published in the 1870s, 1880s, and 1890s under the various series: "The 'Lansdowne' Poets," "The 'Arundel' Poets," "The 'Chandos' Poets," "The 'Imperial' Poets, "The 'Chandos' Classics," "The 'Albion' Edition," and the "Cabinet Poets"; and see the 1884 illustrated edition of *PL* listed here by Worthington with same publisher's imprint as that here. Scarce. Not in Kohler.

2299. THE POETICAL WORKS OF JOHN MILTON Reprinted From The Original Edition, And Containing Numerous Explanatory Notes. With Memoir By David Masson, M.A., LL.D., Author of "The Life And Times Of John Milton." The "Arundel Poets." *Boston: DeWolfe, Fiske & Company, 365 Washington Street. 1884.* First edition thus by DeWolfe, Fiske & Company? 8vo, li+627pp., frontispiece illustration plate reproducing an illustration after Doré for *PL* ("Before the gates there sat"), "Copyright, 1880, By The Arundel Print" on verso of title page, "Memoir Of Milton," illustration plates reproducing Doré's illustrations for *PL* (for all but Books II and XII), slight decorative head- and tailpieces, notes at bottom of page, original decorated dark green cloth, front cover decorated in embossed floral design outlined in black against a maroon background with thick embossed decorative border trim near bottom and top, "Milton's Poems" lettered in embossed black within a bright, broad gilt band ruled in black and gilt at the top, "Illustrated" is similarly lettered in black within a smaller bright, broad gilt band near the bottom, spine similarly decorated in embossed floral relief outlined in black against a maroon background with decorative trim in embossed black, maroon, and gilt at top and bottom, Milton's name in large black letters within a bright, broad gilt band within embossed black, maroon, and gilt rules near the top, "Illustrated" (hyphenated) similarly lettered in black against a smaller bright, broad gilt band near the bottom, "DeWolfe, Fiske & Company" lettered in gilt at the bottom, a.e.g. A fine copy, fresh and crisp, in a lovely publisher's binding. The first edition thus (with more illustration plates after Doré than here) was published in 1880 (also listed here) with "The 'Arundel Poets.' The Arundel Print. New York" on title page and "Copyright, 1880 By The Arundel Print" as here on verso of title page; a possible second edition thus, undated, was published ca. 1883, without a copyright date on verso of title page (also listed here). A similar edition was published in Chicago and New York by Belford, Clarke & Co. with "The 'Arundel Poets'" on the title page and with the same pagination as here, but with only several illustration plates after Doré, in 1884, 1886, and 1888—all listed here. Not in Kohler.

2300. Variant of Preceding, original decorated light green cloth, decorated exactly as preceding copy. A very nice copy in a lovely variant cloth-colored publisher's binding, with contemporary prize inscription (dated Christmas 1888) on fly-leaf and accompanying note laid in. Not in Kohler.

2301. Variant of Preceding, original decorated brown cloth (some light rubbing), decorated exactly as preceding copy. A nice, tight copy, very fresh and crisp, near mint, within, in a lovely variant cloth-colored publisher's binding. Not in Kohler.

2302. THE POETICAL WORKS OF JOHN MILTON. Reprinted From The Original Edition, And Containing Numerous Explanatory Notes. With Memoir By David Masson, M.A., LL.D., Author Of "The Life And Times Of John Milton." Illustrated. The "Arundel Poets." *Chicago And New York: Belford, Clarke & Co.[,] 1884.* First edition thus by Belford, Clarke & Co. with Doré plates? 8vo, li+627pp., frontispiece illustration after Doré with protective tissue guard and five additional plates after Doré, half-title for *SA*, notes at bottom of page, "Printed And Bound By Donohue & Henneberry, Chicago" on verso of title page, original decorated gray cloth (a bit rubbed, some slight age-browning common to books of this period), front cover decorated in a floral motif of contrasting green and brown with decorative floral piece at the top incorporating a bright gilt band with Milton's name lettered in brown within, in the lower right corner a circular piece incorporating musical instruments and floral trim extending beyond it, spine similarly decorated in a floral motif of contrasting green and brown with decorative floral trim and bright gilt bands at top and bottom with "Milton's Poems" incorporated in brown lettering in the top bands, a brown flower in the square gilt band near the bottom, and "Belford, Clarke & Co" in the small gilt band at the bottom, decorated endpapers, a.e.g. A nice copy in an attractive publisher's binding of the period. See 1880 edition (possible first edition thus) by Belford, Clare & Co. listed here, with illustration plates after engravings by Dalziel. See 1886 and 1888 editions by Belford and Clark listed here with illustrations by Doré. Kohler 403, making no

PW by Gall & Inglis, ca. 1870s in contemporary blue velvet binding over thick padded boards with bronzed celluloid centerpiece on front cover [And] *Poetical Works* by E. & J. B. Young & Co., ca. 1885, in contemporary blue velvet covers with blue cloth spine, with large celluloid piece on front cover. See #2112 and 2304.

mention of "li" prefatory pages, with "2 pp. of advertisements at end," and reporting "Not in the British Library. Not in the Bodleian Library. Not in Cambridge University Library."

2303. Variant of Preceding, original decorated brown cloth (a little rubbed, age-browning), decorated exactly as preceding copy. A good copy in an attractive variant publisher's binding, with presentation inscription in a neat hand in pencil on a plate tipped in on front pastedown. Kohler 403.

2304. THE POETICAL WORKS OF JOHN MILTON Reprinted From The Original Edition, And Containing Numerous Explanatory Notes. With Memoir By David Masson, M.A., LL.D., Author of "The Life And Times Of John Milton." Illustrated. The "Arundel Poets." *E. & J. B. Young & Co., Cooper Union, Fourth Avenue, New York. n.d. [ca. 1885]*. 8vo, li+627pp., frontispiece illustration plate reproducing an illustration after Doré for *PL* ("Towards the coast of Earth beneath"), protective tissue guard, "Memoir Of Milton," six unsigned illustration plates reproducing Doré's illustrations for *PL* (for Books I, III—as frontispiece, IV, VI, VIII, and X), notes at bottom of page, contemporary blue velvet covers over thick padded boards, with blue cloth spine (a bit rubbed, pages a little age-browned), large celluloid piece on front cover of a bust of a classical woman with intertwining floral piece incorporating Milton's name near the top, marbled maroon endpapers, a.e.g. A good copy of a scarce edition, in an unusual binding of the period. Similar to editions by the Arundel Print in New York in 1880 and ca. 1883; by DeWolfe, Fiske & Company in Boston in 1884; and by Belford, Clarke & Co. in Chicago and New York in 1884, 1886, and 1888—all listed here. Not in Kohler.

2305. THE POETICAL WORKS OF JOHN MILTON. Edited, With A Critical Memoir, By William Michael Rossetti. With Full Page Illustrations. *Ward, Lock, And Co., London: Warwick House, Salisbury Square, E.C. New York: 10 Bond Street. n.d. [ca. 1885]*. 8vo, xx+460pp., engraved frontispiece portrait sketch of Milton (age ten) with protective tissue guard, engraved and printed title pages, with unsigned vignette illustration after Thomas Seccombe for Milton's sonnet *On His Deceased Wife* on engraved title, "London, Ward, Lock & Co." at the bottom, six additional unsigned engraved illustration plates after Seccombe, four for *PL* (Books IV, VI, VIII, and XII), one for *C*, and one for *SA*, numerous elaborately decorated head- and tailpieces, red border with decorative corner piece around text, original full red morocco, tooled in blind, spine lettered in gilt, raised bands, inner dentelles finely tooled in gilt, marbled endpapers, a.e.g. A fine copy in original morocco binding. The illustrations are by Thomas Seccombe, although they are not attributed to him on the title page here as in other undated editions of Milton's *PW* published by Ward and Lock about this time. See undated ca. 1871 Moxon edition of Milton's *PW* illustrated by Thomas Seccombe with identification of the illustrator on title page (see copy listed here); see also undated ca. 1880 "Moxon's Popular Poets" edition by Ward and Lock (see copy listed here). Not in Kohler.

2306. Variant of Preceding, contemporary full red morocco, delicately gilt-decorated covers and spine with gilt lettering on the spine, raised bands, broad inner dentelles elaborately tooled in gilt, marbled endpapers, a.e.g. A fine copy with half-title (not present in preceding copy), in a lovely variant contemporary morocco binding, very well preserved, with early undated presentation inscription in red ink (now faded) on front blank, later presentation inscription on verso. Not in Kohler.

2307. THE POETICAL WORKS OF JOHN MILTON. Edited, With A Critical Memoir, By William Michael Rossetti. With Full Page Illustrations. *Ward, Lock, And Co., London: Warwick House, Salisbury Square, E.C. New York: Bond Street. n.d. [ca. 1885].* 8vo, xx+460pp., half-title, engraved frontispiece portrait sketch of Milton (age ten) with protective tissue guard, engraved and printed title pages, with unsigned vignette illustration after Thomas Seccombe for Milton's sonnet *On His Deceased Wife* on engraved title, "London, Ward, Lock & Co." at the bottom, six additional unsigned engraved illustration plates after Seccombe, four for *PL* (Books IV, VI, VIII, and XII), one for *C*, and one for *SA*, numerous elaborately decorated head- and tailpieces, red border with decorative corner piece around text, original green pebble morocco (joints and corners a bit rubbed), gilt rule on covers, spine lettered in gilt, raised bands, small decorative gilt pieces within the panels, inner dentelles finely tooled in gilt, outer dentelles ruled in gilt at the corners, marbled endpapers, a.e.g. A fine copy, variant of the preceding, with variant publisher's imprint, in a variant publisher's morocco binding, with contemporary signature (dated 1887) on front blank. The illustrations are by Thomas Seccombe, although they are not attributed to him on the title page. See undated ca. 1885 nonillustrated edition by Ward, Lock, and Co. (copy listed here with same publisher's impression as here. Kohler 409, dating its copy "[ca. 1885]" and reporting "Not in Williamson. Not in the British Library. Not in the Bodleian Library. Not in Cambridge University Library."

2308. THE POETICAL WORKS OF JOHN MILTON. Reprinted From The Best Editions With Biographical Notice, Etc. *New York: John W. Lovell Company, 14 and 16 Vesey Street. n.d. [ca. 1885].* 8vo, 562pp., engraved frontispiece portrait sketch of a young Milton by "E. Ronjat," protective tissue guard, life of Milton, illustration plates after engravings by Dalziel, two for *PL*, Book IV (*Adam Sees Eve*, with lines quoted) and Book VIII (*Adam and Eve Naming the Animals*, without identification or appropriate lines quoted), one for *Samson Agonistes* ("But Who is this? . . . Comes this way"), one for *L'Allegro* ("While the ploughman near at hand . . ."), and one for *Latin Epigram VII* ("Ad Eandem," misplaced and without identification or appropriate lines quoted, bound here before English sonnets XXI, "To Cyriac Skinner," and XXII, "To The Same,"—the illustration titled in other editions: *Milton Meeting Leonora Baroni at Cardinal Barberini's House*), red border around text, original decorated olive green cloth (a bit rubbed), front cover richly decorated in embossed black floral trim stemming from an urn at the bottom, with Milton's name with larger initial letter "M" in embossed olive green letters against a large bright gilt background decorated in embossed olive green floral trim near the top, with a shamrock in embossed olive green shaded in black within a bright gilt square at the center, spine similarly richly decorated in embossed black and gilt, with title in embossed olive green within two bright broad gilt bands at the top, with a shamrock in embossed green tinted in black within a bright gilt circle within a black backdrop at the center and with "Lovell" lettered in embossed olive green within a gilt band at the bottom, a.e.g. A nice copy of a nineteenth-century illustrated American edition, in a lovely (even if a bit aged) decorated publisher's cloth binding. The possible first edition of Milton's *PW* by Lovell was published ca. 1880 (also listed here with further editions by Lovell cited along with information about Lovell as publisher). Not in Kohler.

2309. Variant of Preceding, original decorated red cloth, decorated exacted as preceding copy. A nice copy of a nineteenth-century illustrated American edition, in a fine variant publisher's cloth binding. This copy is bound without the illustration titled in some editions: *Milton Meeting Leonora Baroni at Cardinal Barberini's House*. Another copy in the collection, less good, has a contemporary signature (dated 1885) on front blank. Not in Kohler.

2310. Variant of Preceding, original decorated mauve cloth (a bit rubbed, small tear at top of first three pages: fly-leaf and first two blanks), front cover richly decorated in embossed tooling with Milton's name in embossed lettering across the top, with the letter "M" in larger size embossed in dark maroon within a light blue medallion, with a series of floral designs embossed in lighter maroon on light blue stems within dark maroon medallions set against a light blue background all intertwined with long-stemmed leaves woven throughout, delicately tooled in embossed dark maroon and light blue borders with small corner medallions each containing a floral design, the whole ruled in a thick and two thin light blue border rules, with another light blue border rule along the edge of the cover, the spine is similarly richly decorated in embossed floral tooling and designs with embossed lettering ("Milton's Poems" in larger lettering at the top and "Lovell" in smaller lettering at the bottom), decorated endpapers, red edges. A nice copy, fresh and tight, in an attractive variant publisher's binding. Not in Kohler.

2311. THE POETICAL WORKS OF JOHN MILTON. Reprinted From The Best Editions With Biographical Notice, Etc. *New York[:] John W. Lovell Company[,] 150 Worth Street, Corner Mission Place. n.d. [ca. 1885].* 8vo, 562pp., frontispiece illustration plate after engraving by Dalziel for *PL*, Book IV (*Adam Sees Eve*, with lines quoted), red border around text, original decorated bluish green cloth (a little rubbed, early name and notation in pencil on fly-leaf), front cover decorated in black and gilt, with decorative black trim and central emblem in black near the bottom and with the title in embossed bluish green against a gilt background surrounded by floral trim in gilt and bluish green against a black background near the top, spine similarly decorated in black and gilt with gilt lettering within decorative gilt trim near the top, a.e.g. A nice copy of a nineteenth-century American edition, in an attractive publisher's binding. Variant edition of the undated ca. 1885 illustrated edition by Lovell with a frontispiece illustration in place of frontispiece portrait, with no other illustrations, with red border around the text, and with a different publisher's imprint. The possible first edition of Milton's *PW* by Lovell was published ca. 1880 (also listed here with further editions by Lovell cited along with information about Lovell as publisher). Not in Kohler.

2312. THE POETICAL WORKS OF JOHN MILTON. Reprinted From The Best Editions With Biographical Notice, Etc. *New York[:] John W. Lovell Company[,] 150 Worth Street, Corner Mission Place. n.d. [ca. 1885].* 8vo, 562pp., red border around text, original embossed leaf motif on green calf over padded boards (a bit rubbed at joints and along extremities, uniformly faded to an almost even brown, early owner's name in blue pencil on fly-leaf), Milton's name lettered diagonally in gilt on front cover, a.e.g. A nice copy of a nineteenth-century American edition, in an attractive (albeit a bit rubbed) variant publisher's binding. Variant of the undated ca. 1885 illustrated edition by Lovell preceding, with the same publisher's imprint but without the frontispiece illustration. Uncommon. Not in Kohler.

2313. THE POETICAL WORKS OF JOHN MILTON. *London: Ward, Lock, & Co., Warwick House, Dorset Buildings, Salisbury Square, E.C. n.d [ca. 1885].* 8vo, viii+460pp., half-title, decorative head- and tailpieces, contemporary full green morocco (a bit rubbed), gilt rules on covers, spine richly gilt-decorated, red morocco label with gilt lettering and gilt trim, raised bands with decorative gilt trim (rubbed), marbled endpapers and edges. A fine copy in an attractive Prize Binding, with gilt seal of "Mill Hill School" on covers and prize label (dated 1885) on front pastedown. Unlike the other Ward Lock editions, this one does not have a red border with decorative corner device around text. Not in Kohler (although see undated ca. 1878 illustrated edition by Ward, Lock, & Co. listed earlier, in the "Moxon's Popular Poets" series, with same publisher's imprint as here, Kohler 389, dating its copy "[ca. 1878]."

2314. THE POETICAL WORKS OF JOHN MILTON. *Ward, Lock, & Co., London: Warwick House, Salisbury Square E. C. New York: Bond Street. n.d. [ca. 1885].* 8vo, viii+460+[12]pp., half-title, emblem of the press at center of title page, decorative head- and tailpieces, original decorated red cloth (spine a little faded), front cover richly decorated in embossed black lines with decorative red corner pieces against black backdrops, with Milton's name in embossed red letters at the center against a black backdrop with a decorative red circular piece against a black backdrop above and below, with "The People's Standard Library" in black letters at the top, spine decorated in embossed black trim with Milton's name in embossed red letters against a large gilt background at the top, with "The People's Standard Library" in gilt at the center, and "Ward Lock & Co" in small embossed red letters at the bottom. A very nice copy in an attractive publisher's binding, with twelve pages of advertisements bound in at the end. See undated ca. 1885 illustrated edition by Ward, Lock, and Co. listed later, with same publisher's imprint as here. Not in Kohler.

2315. THE POETICAL WORKS OF JOHN MILTON. Including The Latin Poems, And Translations from the Italian Poets. Edited By William Michael Rossetti. *Ward,*

Lock & Co., Limited, London And Melbourne. n.d. [ca. 1885]. 8vo, xx+460pp., half-title, frontispiece portrait after Vertue, engraved By W. C. Edwards, title page in red and black, contemporary full crushed green morocco over padded boards (front joint cracked, a bit worn along extremities, spine a little faded), central decorative letter "M" in gilt on front cover, Milton's name in gilt on spine, light green marbled endpapers, rounded edges, a.e.g. A good copy, fresh and clean within. Not in Kohler.

2316. THE POETICAL WORKS OF JOHN MILTON Edited, With Copious Notes And Notices, Critical And Explanatory. By William Michael Rossetti. *London: Croome & Co., 12, St. Bride Street Ludgate Circus, EC. n.d. [ca. 1885].* First edition thus by Croome? 8vo, viii+460+[12]pp., decorative head- and tailpieces, original decorated red cloth (a bit rubbed, spine slightly faded, front joint cracked from within, pages heavily age-browned), front cover decorated with floral trim in black, with Milton's name in embossed red letters against a bright gilt band near the top left within decorative black trim and black rules, and with "Poems" lettered in small black letters toward the bottom, spine similarly decorated with floral trim in black, with Milton's name in embossed red letters against a bright gilt band near the top, "Poems" in embossed red letters within a smaller gilt band in the middle and a larger band in black at the bottom, small decorative piece in black at the center of the back cover. A nice copy in an attractive publisher's binding, with an early ownership signature on fly-leaf. Scarce. Not in Kohler.

2317. THE POETICAL WORKS OF JOHN MILTON: With Introductions By David Masson, M.A., L.L.D., Professor Of Rhetoric And English Literature In The University Of Edinburgh. The Globe Edition. *London: Macmillan And Co. 1885.* Sixth Globe edition by Macmillan. 8vo, xi+625pp., half-title (with emblem consisting of the letters of Macmillan and Co. on verso), "Preface" (dated 1877), "Contents," "Introduction to *PL*" with several diagrams and other introductory material as in the first editions, half-title for some of the sections and poems, contemporary blue pebble morocco binding (a little rubbed at joints, spine a trifle faded), covers ruled in gilt with small gilt corners devices, spine richly gilt decorated within the panels, with Milton's name lettered in gilt, raised bands with decorative gilt trim, inner and outer dentelles finely tooled in trim, marbled endpapers, a.e.g. Handsomely bound by Mudie, with his stamp; and contemporary presentation inscription in a neat hand (dated 1888) on front blank. The Globe edition of Milton's *PW* was first published in March 1877 (also listed here with further editions by Globe cited). Scarce. Not in Kohler.

2318. THE POETICAL WORKS OF JOHN MILTON Printed From The Original Editions With A Life Of The Author By A. Chalmers M.A. F.S.A. With Twelve Illustrations By R. Westall R.A. *London[:] Bickers And Son I Leicester Square[,] 1886.* Royal 8vo, xxxix+[i]+699pp., early photograph of Milton portrait engraved by W. N. Gardiner after Vertue mounted as frontispiece, title page in red and black with central emblem of the Chiswick Press, early photographs of Westall illustrations mounted on thick paper, each on its own page, with line or lines being illustrated printed and identified beneath each photograph-illustration, decorative headpieces, decorated initial letters, printed by Charles Whittingham at the Chiswick Press, contemporary tree calf (neatly rebacked preserving original spine), decorative gilt border trim on covers, gilt-decorated spine, black morocco label with gilt lettering, raised bands with decorative gilt trim, inner dentelles finely tooled in gilt, outer dentelles gilt-decorated, marbled endpapers, a.e.g. A nice copy in a Prize Binding, with central gilt seal on front cover and with presentation inscription (dated 1890) on front blank. Not in Kohler (although Kohler 405, referencing Williamson 126, lists an edition similar to this with no illustrations).

2319. THE POETICAL WORKS OF JOHN MILTON. *London: Suttaby & Co., Amen Corner, St. Paul's. n.d. [ca. 1886].* First edition thus? 8vo, xxiv+581pp., engraved frontispiece portrait plate (of a youngish looking middle-aged Milton, unsigned), protective tissue guard, small crest at center of title page, eight illustration plates after engravings by Dalziel: one for *L'A*, four for *PL* (Books I, IV, VIII, and XII), one for *SA*, one for *On His Deceased Wife*, and one for *Latin Epigram VII* ("Ad Eandem"—the illustration titled *Milton Meeting Leonora Baroni at Cardinal Barberini's House*), half-title for *SA*, small decorative piece at center of verso of last page of *PR* across from the half-title, orange border around text, "Morrison And Gibb, Edinburgh, Printers To Her Majesty's Stationery Office. 710. 25xx. 31085. 707" on verso of last page (p. 581), notes at bottom of page, contemporary full red morocco over thin boards (slightly rubbed, preliminary leaves foxed), continuous gilt rule from to back cover, with small decorative corner piece in gilt at outside corners of each cover, "Milton" lettered in gilt at top of front cover, spine lettered in gilt, decorated light gray endpapers, a.e.g. A nice copy with contemporary ownership signature (dated 1886) on fly-leaf. The frontispiece portrait and illustrations after engravings by Dalziel here are exactly the same as those in the undated ca. 1880 "Lansdowne Poets" edition by Frederick Warne And Co., with "Camden Press: Dalziel Brothers, Engravers & Printers" on verso of last page (p. 581) (see copies listed earlier). See also undated ca. 1879 edition listed by "R. & A. Suttaby, 2, Amen Corner" (two copies, one with early photographs of illustrations for Milton's works, the other with early photographs by Deswall Vaughan, mostly of nature and farming scenes, mounted as illustrations). Scarce. Not in Kohler.

2320. THE POETICAL WORKS OF JOHN MILTON. Reprinted From The Original Edition, And Containing Numerous Explanatory Notes. With Memoir By David Masson, M.A., LL.D., Author Of "The Life And Times Of John Milton." Illustrated. The "Arundel Poets." *Chicago And New York: Belford, Clarke & Co. 1886.* 8vo, li+627pp., frontispiece illustration plate with protective tissue guard and three additional illustration plates after Doré, half-title for *SA*, notes at bottom of page, "Printed And Bound By Donohue & Henneberry, Chicago" on verso of title page, original decorated light blue cloth (a little worn, spine ends chipped, back cover scuffed, pages a little age-browned, p. xiii frayed around the edge), front cover decorated with swirls of embossed black with brown trim, with a large blue scroll toward the top incorporating Milton's name in black with a floral blossom in bright gilt above and one below, toward the lower right is a winged pegasus in blue against a black background with blue border trim, and at the bottom left "Poems" appears in black letters within a blue scroll, the whole set in front of a large brown panel framed by contrasting blue and black rules, spine similarly decorated in embossed black swirls with floral clusters in gilt, a bright brown background, and the figure of Pan playing his flute at the center, and embossed blue lettering against bright gilt backgrounds at the top ("Milton's Poems") and bottom ("Belford, Clarke & Co."), decorated endpapers, a.e.g. A good copy in an attractive (albeit bit used) publisher's binding of the period. The possible first edition of Milton's *PW* by Belford, Clarke & Co. with four illustration plates after Doré was published in 1884 (also listed here with further editions by Belford, Clarke & Co. cited). The first edition of Milton's *PW* by Belford, Clarke & Co. with four illustration plates after engravings by Dalziel, not Doré, was published in 1880 in Chicago (copy listed here). Uncommon. Stevens 225, without mentioning 1884 edition by Belford, Clarke, calling this "a cheap reprint of Masson"; Kohler 406, making no mention of "li" prefatory pages and reporting "Not in the British Library. Not in the Bodleian Library. Not in Cambridge University Library."

2321. Variant of Preceding. contents as preceding, except that there are six Doré illustration plates, two more than in the preceding copy, in a variant binding, original decorated brown cloth (a little rubbed, internally age-browned, with the paper fragile and showing signs of the poor quality paper used during this period), front cover and spine decorated in black trim in an embossed floral motif, with "Milton's Poems" lettered in large embossed brown letters within a very bright, large gilt band at the top of the front cover and the spine, and with "Household Edition" lettered in embossed small brown letters against a narrow black backdrop at the bottom of the front cover, attractively decorated endpapers. Interesting to note that the previous edition shows little of the poor quality of paper readily evident in this edition. It is also noteworthy that this edition was prepared as a "Household Edition," which is Not in Kohler.

2322. THE POETICAL WORKS OF JOHN MILTON. Reprinted From The Chandos Poets. With Memoir, Explanatory Notes, &c. Portrait And Original Illustrations. *New York: Worthington Company, 28 Lafayette Place. 1886.* 8vo, xxiv+581+[3]pp., frontispiece illustration plate after engraving by Dalziel for Book IV of *PL* (*Adam Sees Eve*, with appropriate lines quoted), protective tissue guard, decorative central device with harp in the center on verso of title page, three additional illustration plates after engravings by Dalziel for *PL* (Book I, *Fall of the Angels*, with appropriate lines quoted, Book VIII, *Adam and Eve Naming the Animals*, with appropriate lines quoted, and Book XII, *The Expulsion*, with appropriate lines quoted), decorative central device with harp in the center from verso of title page repeated on verso of the last page of *PR*, half-title for *SA*, red border around text, decorative floral piece on verso of last page, notes at bottom of page, original decorated gray cloth (a little worn), front cover elaborately decorated in embossed red and black lines and swirls in a floral and circular motif with Milton's name incorporated in black lettering within a bright gilt band near the top and a winged pegasus in red against a black background within decorated swirls in lower left corner, spine similarly elaborately decorated in embossed red, black, and gilt with a floral motif at the center, the title ("Milton's Poems") lettered in black within a bright gilt band at the top, and "Worthington Co" within a smaller gilt band at the bottom, decorated endpapers, a.e.g. Despite some wear, a nice copy in a rather lovely publisher's binding, with early name in pencil in a neat hand on front blank. The possible first edition of Milton's *PW* by Worthington was published in 1884 (also listed here with further editions by Worthington cited). Uncommon. Not in Kohler.

2323. THE POETICAL WORKS OF JOHN MILTON. With Memoir, Explanatory Notes, Etc. The "Albion" Edition. *London: Frederick Warne And Co., Bedford Street, Strand. n.d. [ca. 1886].* 8vo, xxiv+581pp., central crescent on title page consisting of small laurel wings with a horseshoe at the center, "Morrison & Gibb, Edinburgh, Printers to

Her Majesty's Stationery Office" on verso of title page and printed again on verso of last page, half-title for *SA*, notes at bottom of page, original three-quarter red morocco, marbled paper over boards (a little worn, covers detached), elaborately gilt-decorated spine, black morocco label with gilt lettering and gilt rules, raised bands with decorative gilt trim, marbled endpapers and edges. A decent copy with a beautifully decorated bird in freehand sketch in ink on fly-leaf with elaborate scrolling incorporating contemporary signature dated "10/4/86." See other undated and dated illustrated and nonillustrated editions in the collection by Frederick Warne and Co. published in the 1870s, 1880s, and 1890s under the series: "The 'Lansdowne' Poets," "The 'Arundel' Poets," "The 'Chandos' Poets," "The 'Imperial' Poets, "The 'Chandos' Classics," "The 'Albion' Edition," or the "Cabinet Poets." Kohler 404, dating its copy "[1884]" and reporting "Not in the British Library. Not in the Bodleian Library. Not in Cambridge University Library."

2324. Variant of Preceding, original brown cloth (a bit rubbed and scuffed) with central vignette depiction of Milton in gilt relief on front cover and "John Milton" signed in gilt below, spine lettered in gilt with gilt rules at top and bottom, brown endpapers. A nice copy in a variant publisher's binding, with advertisement leaf bound in at end, advertising "The Chandos Poets" on recto (including an edition of "Milton's Poetical Works") and "The Chandos Library" and "The Albion Poets" on verso. Kohler 404.

2325. THE POETICAL WORKS OF JOHN MILTON. Reprinted From The Best Editions With Biographical Notice, Etc. *New York: Thomas Y. Crowell & Co., No. 13 Astor Place. n.d. [ca. 1886/1887]*. 8vo, 562+[3]pp., frontispiece illustration plate after engraving by Dalziel for *PL* (*The Expulsion*, Book XII), protective tissue guard, decorative central device in black incorporating initials of the press on title page, five additional illustration plates after engravings by Dalziel, red border around text, original decorated yellow cloth (a bit rubbed, spine slightly chipped at top and bottom), front cover richly decorated in embossed black floral trim encompassing most of the cover with circular illustration in black of a mythical male figure seated holding a book riding a swan beneath an area near the top not covered with embossed black floral trim in which the title ("Milton's Poems") is lettered in gilt within gilt rules with decorative floral trim in bright gilt, spine similarly richly decorated in embossed black floral trim with the title ("Milton's Poems") incorporated within bright gilt bands at the top with floral trim and the small figure of a female behind a harp in gilt below, the initials of the press "TYC & Co" in bright gilt at the bottom, a.e.g. A fine copy, fresh and tight, in a lovely publisher's decorated cloth binding, with contemporary inscription (dated "Christmas 1886") on front blank. The possible first edition of Milton's *PW* by Crowell with illustration plates after engravings by Dalziel was published ca. 1880 (also listed here with further editions by Crowell cited). Kohler 412, dating its copy "[ca. 1888]" and reporting "Not in the British Library. Not in the Bodleian Library. Not in Cambridge University Library."

2326. Variant of Preceding, original decorated brown cloth (spine ends slightly rubbed), decorated as preceding copy. A fine copy, fresh and clean, in a lovely variant publisher's binding, with contemporary signature (dated "1887") on front blank, with five pages of advertisement leaves for "Crowell's Red Line Poets" (including Milton), for "Popular Poets: Crowell's Favorite Illustrated Edition" (including Milton), and for additional editions by Crowell bound in at the end. Kohler 412.

2327. Variant of Preceding, original decorated light brown cloth (frontispiece and title page embrowned because of protective tissue guard), decorated as preceding copies. A fine copy, near mint, in a variant publisher's binding, with contemporary presentation inscription dated "7-25-87" on fly-leaf, with five pages of advertisement leaves for "Crowell's Red Line Poets" (including Milton), for "Popular Poets: Crowell's Favorite Illustrated Edition" (including Milton), and for additional editions by Crowell bound in at the end. Kohler 412.

2328. THE POETICAL WORKS OF JOHN MILTON. Reprinted From The Best Editions. With Memoir, Explanatory And Glossorial Notes, &c. Original Illustrations And Steel Portrait. The Chandos Poets. *London: Frederick Warne And Co., Bedford Street, Strand. n.d. [ca. 1887]*. Large square 8vo, xxiv+581pp., unsigned engraved frontispiece portrait of an early middle-aged Milton (labeled "London: Frederick Warne & Co." at bottom), protective tissue guard, title page in red and black, twelve illustration plates after engravings by Dalziel: one for *NO*, one for *L'A*, six for *PL* (Books I, IV, V, VII, VIII, and XII), one for *PR* (Book I), one for *SA*, one for *On His Deceased Wife*, and one for *Latin Epigram VII* ("Ad Eandem"—the illustration titled *Milton Meeting Leonora Baroni at Cardinal Barberini's House*), half-title for *SA*, red border around text, "Camden Press: Dalziel Brothers, Engravers & Printers" within small circular printer's device on verso of last page—appears also on verso of title page, notes at bottom of page, original full red morocco (somewhat rubbed along joints, corners, and spine, frontispiece slightly foxed), covers and spine decorated with blind rules, spine lettered in gilt, raised bands, inner dentelles finely tooled in gilt, marbled endpapers, a.e.g. A good copy in original publisher's morocco binding, with contemporary presentation inscription (dated 1887) on verso of fly-leaf. See earlier publication of this edition published ca. 1876 (also listed here). Not in Kohler.

2329. Variant of Preceding, contemporary full tree calf, decorative gilt border trim on covers, elaborately gilt-decorated spine within the panels with gilt lettering, raised bands with decorative gilt trim, inner and outer dentelles finely tooled in gilt, marbled endpapers, a.e.g. A lovely copy in a variant, possibly publisher's, tree calf binding, with early Baltimore collector's bookplate on front pastedown. Not in Kohler.

2330. THE POETICAL WORKS OF JOHN MILTON. Reprinted From The Chandos Poets, With Memoir, Explanatory Notes, &c. Portrait And Original Illustrations. The Lansdowne Poets. *London: Frederick Warne And Co. And New York. n.d. [ca. 1887].* 8vo, xxiv+581+[3]pp., unsigned engraved frontispiece portrait of a youngish looking middle-aged Milton, protective tissue guard, small decorative device at center of title page, "Morrison & Gibb, Edinburgh, Printer's To Her Majesty's Stationery Office" on verso of title page, eight illustration plates after engravings by Dalziel: one for *L'A*, four for *PL* (Books I, IV, VIII, and XII), one for *SA*, one for *On His Deceased Wife*, and one for *Latin Epigram VII* ("Ad Eandem"—the illustration titled *Milton Meeting Leonora Baroni at Cardinal Barberini's House*), half-title for *SA*, red border around text, "Morrison And Gibb, Edinburgh, Printer's To Her Majesty's Stationery Office" on verso of last page, notes at bottom of page, original vellum (a bit rubbed), Milton's name lettered in gilt and red at top of front cover with decorative gilt trim at lower right corner, spine lettered in gilt, with small gilt emblem of the press at the bottom and gilt rules at top and bottom, t.e.g., others unopened. Bound in at the end: an advertisement leaf, advertising on recto: "Frederick Warne & Co.'s Series Of Classics, Poets, &c. The Arundel Poets" (including Milton) and on verso: "Frederick Warne & Co., Publishers, The Chandos Poets" (including Milton). A nice copy in a lovely Victorian publisher's binding, similar to preceding editions except for being printed in a larger octavo format; without the labeling of "London: Frederick Warne & Co." at bottom of frontispiece portrait; with a different device on title page and a different publisher's imprint: published in London and New York; with a different printer, "Morrison And Gibb," on verso of title page, repeated on verso of last page; without an illustration for *NO* or for *PR* and in their place an illustration for *L'A* and for "Ad Eandem," not present in preceding edition; and with several advertisement pages bound in at the end. Uncommon. Not in Kohler.

2331. THE POETICAL WORKS OF JOHN MILTON. *Edinburgh: W. P. Nimmo, Hay, & Mitchell, 1887.* Possible tenth edition thus with variant in publisher's imprint. 8vo, xxxvii+[3]+440pp., unsigned engraved frontispiece portrait plate of a middle-aged Milton, engraved and printed title pages, with vignette illustration (of the poet being inspired by heavenly choirs) after F. Borders on engraved title plate ("Edinburgh: William P. Nimmo & Co."), protective tissue guard, vignette illustration (of a young boy in a setting in nature with a cane laying beside him) signed with the initials "WS" on printed title, life of Milton by J. M. Ross, eleven illustration plates, most after F. Borders, some unsigned: four for *PL* (Books I, III, VI, XI), two for *PR* (Book I), one for *SA*, two for *C*, one for *L'A*, one for *IlP*, half-title for *PL, PR, SA, C, Arc, MP*, and *Poemata*, red border around text, "Printed by Ballantyne, Hanson & Co., Edinburgh" printed at the bottom of the last page, original padded green leather (worn), covers decorated with a broad border trim in blind, Milton's name written in gilt script at a slant on front cover, spine lettered in gilt, dark green endpapers, a.e.g. While the cover is worn, a decent copy, fresh and clean within, with variant publisher's imprint from other editions by Nimmo here (also listed here). The possible first edition thus by Nimmo was published in 1865, illustrated (also listed here with further Nimmo editions, illustrated and nonillustrated, cited). Only the 1865 edition has twelve illustrations, the others have eleven (with only one illustration for *L'A* instead of two, as in the 1865 edition). Uncommon. Kohler 407, reporting "Not in Williamson. Not in the British Library. Not in the Bodleian library. Not in Cambridge University Library."

2332. THE POETICAL WORKS OF JOHN MILTON. Reprinted From The Chandos Poets. With Memoir, Explanatory Notes, &c. Portrait And Original Illustrations. *New York: Worthington Co., 747 Broadway. 1887.* 8vo, xxiv+581+[3]pp., frontispiece illustration plate after engraving by Dalziel for Book IV of *PL* (*Adam Sees Eve*, with appropriate lines quoted), protective tissue guard, decorative central device with small cherubic face in the center on verso of title page, four additional illustration plates after engravings by Dalziel, one for *L'A* ("While the ploughman near at hand . . ."), two for *PL* (Book VIII, *Adam and Eve naming the animals*, with appropriate lines quoted, and Book XII, *The Expulsion*, with appropriate lines quoted), and one for *Latin Epigram VII* ("Ad Eandem"—the illustration titled *Milton Meeting Leonora Baroni at Cardinal Barberini's House*), decorative central tailpiece with angelic figure in the center at the end of *PR*, half-title for *SA*, red border around text, decorative tailpiece at the end of *PR* repeated on verso of last page, additional leaf with decorative central device (without angelic figure) on each side of the leaf, notes at bottom of page, original decorated red cloth (a bit worn, some pencil notations throughout), front cover elaborately decorated in embossed red and black lines and swirls in a floral and circular motif with Milton's name incorporated in black lettering within a bright gilt band near the top and a winged horse (pegasus) in red against a black background within decorated swirls and circle in lower left corner, spine similarly elaborately decorated in embossed red, black, and gilt with a floral motif at the center, the title ("Milton's Poems") lettered in black within a bright gilt band at the top, and "Worthington Co" within a smaller gilt band at the bottom, decorated endpapers, a.e.g. Despite some wear, a nice copy in a rather lovely nineteenth-century American publisher's binding. The possible first edition of Milton's *PW* by Worthington was published in 1884 (also listed here with further editions by Worthington cited); and see 1884 edition listed by Worthington with similar illustrations, but not "Reprinted From The Chandos Poets," as here. Not in Kohler.

2333. Variant of Preceding, original decorated yellow cloth (slightly rubbed), decorated exactly as preceding copy. A nice copy in a rather lovely variant publisher's cloth binding. Not in Kohler.

2334. THE POETICAL WORKS OF JOHN MILTON. A New Edition, With Notes, By Rev. John Mitford. [In Two Volumes.] *Philadelphia: Porter & Coates, n.d. [ca. 1887]*. 2 volumes in one. 4to, [ii]+371pp.,+478pp., title page for each volume, engraved frontispiece illustration of *Milton, Dictating His Paradise Lost to His Daughters*, "Decaisne Pinxt, H Dawe Sculpt," protective tissue guard, engraved illustration plate of *Adam and Eve in the Garden* for *PL* (Book V), engraved by W. Radclyffe after I. Cristall, protective tissue guard, unsigned engraved illustration plate for *C* ("Hail Foreign Wonder"), protective tissue guard, and unsigned engraved illustration plate for *IlP* ("Come, Pensive Nun, Devout and Pure"), protective tissue guard, double black border around text, half-title for *SA* and *C*, original decorated green cloth, front cover and spine elaborately decorated with floral trim in rich embossed gilt, red, and black, incorporating Milton's name in very large black letters, with decorated larger initial letter "M," at the top of front cover and "Illustrated" in smaller letters in gilt at the bottom, spine lettered in black and gilt, back cover ruled in blind, decorated light blue endpapers, a.e.g., with several bookplates of earlier collectors. A splendid copy, very well-preserved in an impressive publisher's binding, fresh and clean within, with fine impressions of the plates. The possible first edition by Porter & Coates was published ca. 1875 (also listed here with further editions cited). Not in Kohler (although see Kohler 381).

2335. Variant of Preceding, original decorated yellow cloth (a bit rubbed, slight tear at top of spine), decorated exactly as preceding copy. A handsome copy in a wonderful, equally well-preserved variant publisher's cloth binding, with small early pictorial bookplate on front pastedown. Not in Kohler.

2336. THE POETICAL WORKS OF JOHN MILTON. A New Edition, With Notes, By Rev. John Mitford. [In Two Volumes.] *Philadelphia: Porter & Coates, n.d. [ca. 1887]*. 2 volumes in one. 4to, [ii]+371pp.,+478pp., title page for each volume, engraved frontispiece portrait of *Milton, Dictating His Paradise Lost to His Daughters*, "Decaisne Pinxt, H Dawe Sculpt," protective tissue guard, original reddish-brown cloth (a bit worn along extremities and corners, spine ends slightly worn, joins cracked from within, age-browning along edges of pages), front cover richly decorated with embossed floral trim in varying sizes against a black background with orange blossoms across the top and bottom and along the inside, with Milton's name in large black letters near the top with the initial letter "M" larger than the other letters and decorated with floral trim, and "Illustrated" in smaller letters near the bottom, and with contrasting orange and black lines and occasional shades of gilt, spine similarly decorated in embossed floral trim with orange blossoms and orange and black trim, with title "Milton's Poetical Works" in embossed letters of varying sizes near the top, "New And Complete Edition" in blind at the center, and "Illustrated" in embossed letters near the bottom, dark brown endpapers. A good copy. While "Illustrated" appears on the front cover and spine, no illustrations are contained within and none is missing. Uncommon. Not in Kohler.

2337. THE POETICAL WORKS OF JOHN MILTON[.] *London[:] Kegan Paul, Trench & Co. MDCCCLXXXVII.* 2 volumes. Small 8vo, 317pp.,+ix+326+[1]pp., half-title each volume, title page each volume in red and black, with central emblem in black bearing the Latin inscription "Arbor Scientiae Arbor Vitae," contemporary full vellum, front covers and spines lettered in red and black, with title page emblem (possibly the seal of Chiswick Press) bearing the Latin inscription "Arbor Scientiae Arbor Vitae" repeated in black on front covers, t.e.g., fore- and bottom edges untrimmed. A very nice set, printed by R. & R. Clark, Edinburgh, in a fine Victorian publisher's vellum binding. See undated set later also printed by R. & R. Clark, Edinburgh, with the same number of pages in each volume as here, but published with a frontispiece in New York by White and Allen without publication date. Kohler 381, describing its set as "Bound by Burn in original vellum paper" and reporting "Not in Cambridge University Library."

2338. Variant of Preceding, original red cloth, front covers and spines lettered in gilt, with emblem of the press in gilt at lower right corner of each front cover, t.e. rough, fore- and bottom edges untrimmed, most of volume 2 unopened. A very nice set in a variant publisher's cloth binding, printed by R. & R. Clark, Edinburgh. Kohler 381.

2339. THE POETICAL WORKS OF JOHN MILTON[.] Empyreal Edition[.] *New York[:] White And Allen, n.d. [ca. 1887].* 2 volumes. Small 8vo, 317pp.,+ix+326+[1]pp., half-title each volume, frontispiece portrait plate of eighteenth-century Vertue portrait frontispiece, volume 1, title page each volume with central emblem of an embellished harp, "Printed by R. & R. Clark, Edinburgh" (so-indicated on last page of each volume), contemporary three-quarter green morocco (rubbed along joints and extremities), spine lettered in gilt with small gilt device within each panel, raised bands (a little rubbed), marbled endpapers, t.e.g. A nice set. Similar to preceding set also printed by R. & R. Clark, Edinburgh, with the same number of pages in each volume as in that set, although that set was published in London by Kegan Paul, Trench & Co. in 1887, and each volume is much thicker in size. Uncommon. Not in Kohler.

2340. THE POETICAL WORKS OF JOHN MILTON: With Introductions By David Masson, M.A., L.L.D., Professor Of Rhetoric And English Literature In The University Of Edinburgh. The Globe Edition. *London: Macmillan And Co. And New York. 1887. The Right of Translation and Reproduction is Reserved.* Small 8vo, xi+625pp., half-title (with emblem of the press consisting of the letters of Macmillan and Co. on verso), "Contents," "Introduction to *PL*" with several diagrams and other introductory material as in the first editions, half-title for some of the sections and poems, contemporary dark olive green morocco (spine a little faded), gilt rules on front cover with central gilt seal of St. Edmund's school, spine finely decorated in gilt within the panels, red morocco label with gilt lettering and decorative gilt trim, raised bands with delicate decorative gilt trim, inner and outer dentelles tooled in blind, marbled endpapers and edges, prize label (dated 1892) on front pastedown. A very good copy in an attractive Prize Binding. The Globe edition of Milton's *PW* was first published in March 1877 (also listed here with further editions by Globe cited). Scarce. Not in Kohler.

2341. THE POETICAL WORKS MILTON AND MARVELL With A Memoir of Each[.] Four Volumes In Two[.] Vol. I/II. *Boston[:] Houghton, Mifflin And Company[,] The Riverside Press, Cambridge[.] n.d. [ca. 1887].* 2 volumes. 8vo, lxxvii+[9]+317pp.,+ix+153+[1]pp.,+[2]+372pp.,+viii+334+liii+[i]+335pp., unsigned frontispiece portrait plate of Milton, protective tissue guard, volume I, title page each volume with small emblem of the press, half-title for *PL*, volume I, half-title for volume II ("The Poetical Works Of Milton And Marvell. Volume II"), unsigned frontispiece portrait plate of Marvell, protective tissue guard, volume II, half-title for volume II ("Poems On Several Occasions"), notes at bottom of page, three-quarter brown grained calf (a little scuffed), marbled paper (a bit rubbed), gilt rules on covers, spines lettered and numbered in gilt, raised bands, decorative gilt pieces and gilt rules within the panels, marbled endpapers and edges. A nice set with large bookplate on front pastedown of each volume and contemporary signature (dated 1887) on front blank of volume 1. Scarce. Not in Kohler.

2342. THE POETICAL WORKS OF JOHN MILTON. With Biographical Notice. Russell Edition. *New York: W. E. Russell, Publisher. n.d. [ca. 1887].* First edition thus. 8vo, iii+562pp., original green cloth (a little rubbed, several small spots on front cover, spine a bit scuffed, pages age-browned around all edges), printed paper label on spine (aged, with a few pieces missing), brown endpapers. A fair copy with contemporary signature in pencil (dated "87") on front blank. According to the "Publisher's Notice:" "Deeming a flashy binding inconsistent with dignified contents, as well as uncomplimentary to the public taste, I take pleasure in presenting to the public an edition which, by neatness, can absolve itself from the above charge, and which, by its low price, can at the same time come within the reach of *all* lovers of good literature. W.E.R." See undated reprint edition ca. 1890 also listed here. Scarce. Not in Kohler.

2343. THE POETICAL WORKS OF JOHN MILTON With Memoir, Etc. Family Edition. Fully Illustrated With New Wood Engravings. With Border By George Wharton Edwards. *New York[:] Frederick A. Stokes & Brother[,] 1888.* First edition thus by Stokes. Tall 8vo, xvi+224pp.+221pp. (*PR*, etc. paginated anew)+[1]+[2]pp., unsigned frontispiece portrait plate of Milton, protective tissue guard, border illustrations in varying tints throughout depicting scenes in *PL* (angel brandishing a fiery sword, Eve and Adam distraught after the judgment, and a figure, from shoulders up, observing from above right corner), illustration plates, including Munkacsy's *Blind Milton Dictating* (unsigned), Doré's illustrations for *PL* (Books I, III, IV, VI,

VII, IX, and XI), two unsigned illustration plates for *PR* (Books I and III), one unsigned illustration plate for *SA*, one illustration plate (unsigned, but after Cope) for *L'A*, one illustration plate (signed, but difficult to read) for *IlP*, and one unsigned illustration plate for *C*, original decorated blue cloth (spine ends and corners a bit rubbed), front cover decorated with leaves, branches, small circular devices, and ruled lines in embossed black and red, with portrait of Milton at age twenty-one against black background within circular device in lower right corner, and with Milton's name lettered in black within a bright broad gilt band at the top ruled in black and surrounded by a dotted reddish-brown border, spine similarly decorated in embossed black trim with Milton's name lettered horizontally in large embossed blue letters within a broad bright gilt band with three embossed blue rules on either side and with three bright gilt circular devices at the top and bottom each beneath a bright gilt rule, blue endpapers, a.e.g. A fine copy in a stunning publisher's binding, with advertisement leaf bound in at the end for Frederick A. Stokes & Brother's "'Family' Poets" series, including "Milton's CPW," with the notation: "The distinctive features of Frederick A. Stokes & Brother's edition of these volumes are New Illustrations, made by good artists especially for this edition; Beautifully Engraved Borders printed in soft tints on all the pages; Good Paper; Careful Presswork." Not in Kohler.

A possible second edition was published by Stokes in 1891 (copy listed here), with a variation in the publisher's imprint ("Frederick A. Stokes Company" in place of "Frederick A. Stokes & Brother," as here); see also nonillustrated 1891 edition (possible third edition thus) also listed here published by "Frederick A. Stokes Company," with the same title page and pagination, but without any illustrations. See, too, undated ca. 1891 illustrated edition also listed here published by "Frederick A. Stokes Company Publishers" (with further variant publisher's imprint and very intriguing unsigned illustrations); and see undated ca. 1895 nonillustrated edition also listed here published by "Frederick A. Stokes Company Publishers."

2344. Variant of Preceding, original decorated brown cloth (a bit rubbed at corners and spine ends), decorated exactly as preceding copy. An equally attractive copy in an equally attractive variant publisher's binding, with the end of Book III and the beginning of Book IV of *PL* reprinted and inserted—obviously accidentally—between the end of *PR* and the beginning of *SA*, from pp. 33 to 48, and with an advertisement leaf bound in at the end. Not in Kohler.

2345. THE POETICAL WORKS OF JOHN MILTON. Reprinted From The Original Edition, And Containing Numerous Explanatory Notes. With Memoir By David Masson, M.A., LL.D., Author Of "The Life And Times Of John Milton." Illustrated. The "Arundel Poets." *Chicago, New York And San Francisco: Belford, Clarke & Co. 1888.* 8vo, li+627pp., frontispiece illustration with protective tissue guard and five additional plates after Doré, half-title for *SA*, small decorative head- and tailpieces, notes at bottom of page, "Printed And Bound By Donohue & Henneberry, Chicago" on verso of title page, original decorated dark olive green cloth (a few scuff marks), front cover decorated with swirls of embossed black with brown trim, with a large blue scroll toward the top incorporating "Milton's" name in black with a floral blossom in bright gilt above and one below, toward the lower right is a winged horse (pegasus) in olive green against a black background with olive green border trim, and at the bottom left "Poems" appears in black within an olive green scroll, the whole set in front of an olive green panel framed by contrasting olive green and black rules, spine similarly decorated in embossed black swirls with floral clusters in gilt, a bright olive green background, and the figure of Pan playing his flute at the center, and embossed olive green lettering against bright gilt backgrounds at the top ("Milton's Poems") and bottom ("Belford, Clarke & Co."), decorated endpapers, a.e.g. A good copy in an attractive publisher's binding of the period. The possible first edition thus by Belford, Clarke & Co., with six illustration plates after Doré, as here, was published in Chicago and New York in 1884 (also listed here with further editions by Belford, Clarke & Co. cited); the possible first edition by Belford, Clarke & Co. was published in 1880 in Chicago (copy listed here) with four illustration plates after engravings by Dalziel, not Doré, as here. Kohler 411, making no mention of "li" prefatory pages and reporting "Not in the British Library. Not in the Bodleian Library. Not in Cambridge University Library."

2346. Variant of Preceding, original decorated blue cloth (a bit rubbed), decorated as preceding copy. A lovely copy in an attractive variant publisher's binding, with a contemporary presentation inscription (dated 1888) on front blank. Kohler 411.

2347. Variant of Preceding, original decorated reddish-brown cloth (spine a little darkened), decorated as preceding copies. A nice copy in an attractive variant publisher's binding. Kohler 411.

2348. THE POETICAL WORKS OF JOHN MILTON. With Memoir, Explanatory Notes, Etc. The "Albion" Edition. *London And New York: Frederick Warne And Co. 1888.* 8vo, xxiv+581pp., half-title with "Morrison and Gibb,

Edinburgh, Printer's to Her Majesty's Stationery Office" on verso and printed again at bottom of last page, emblem of the press (small laurel wings with a horseshoe) at the center of title page, half-title for *SA*, notes at bottom of page, contemporary full polished blue morocco (a bit rubbed), gilt rules on covers with small decorative corner pieces, elaborately gilt-decorated spine, red morocco label with gilt lettering and gilt rules, raised bands with decorative gilt trim, inner dentelles finely tooled in gilt, marbled endpapers, a.e.g. A fine copy in an attractive Prize Binding, with prize citation (dated "December 7th, 1888") tipped in on front pastedown. Kohler 410, reporting "Not in the British Library. Not in the Bodleian Library. Not in Cambridge University Library."

See dated editions listed following of the "Albion" edition in 1889; 1894; 1896 (each published by Frederick Warne and Co. in London and New York, as here); the 1896 edition with dated new preface; and see dated 1898 and 1899 and undated ca. 1907 editions of the "Albion" edition listed later, each published by Frederick Warne and Co. in London and New York, as here, and each with the addition of a frontispiece portrait and a reprint of the 1896 preface.

2349. THE POETICAL WORKS OF JOHN MILTON. With Memoir, Explanatory Notes, Etc. The "Chandos Classics," *London And New York: Frederick Warne And Co. 1888*. 8vo, xxiv+581pp., half-title with "Morrison and Gibb, Edinburgh, Printer's to Her Majesty's Stationery Office" on verso and printed again at bottom of last page, emblem of the press (small laurel wings with a horseshoe) at the center of the title page, half-title for *SA*, notes at bottom of the page, original red pebble cloth, red linen spine, (a bit rubbed, spine slightly chipped at bottom, several marginal notes in ink), red leather label with title lettered in gilt within gilt rules at top of spine, small leather label with publisher lettered in gilt within gilt rules at bottom of spine, black endpapers, t.e.g., fore-edge untrimmed. A nice copy in publisher's binding. Not in Kohler.

2350. THE POETICAL WORKS OF JOHN MILTON. With Memoir, Explanatory Notes, Etc. *London And New York: Frederick Warne & Co. n.d. [ca. 1888]*. 8vo, xxvi+581pp., half-title with "Morrison And Gibb, Printers, Edinburgh" on verso, emblem of the press (small laurel wings with a horseshoe) at the center of title page, half-title for *SA*, notes at bottom of page, contemporary decorated brown cloth (a bit rubbed, a little worn at corners, slightly frayed at top and bottom of spine), front cover and spine decorated with red- and green-leaved branches with Milton's name lettered in red outlined in black within black frame at the top and "Memoir, Notes &c." lettered in black within a decorative scroll in front of green branches in the lower right corner, "Cabinet Poets" stamped in blind within a decorative piece in blind on back cover, spine similarly decorated with red- and green-leaved branches, with Milton's name lettered in embossed brown within a large decorative gilt band at the top and "Warne & Co" in white at the bottom, yellow endpapers, yellow edges. A good copy in an colorful publisher's binding, with bookplate on front pastedown. While similar to "The 'Albion' edition" and "The 'Chandos Classics'" editions published by Frederick Warne and Co. in 1886, this edition is undated and is stamped "Cabinet Poets" on the back cover and has a variant publisher's imprint: "Frederick Warne & Co." compared to "Frederick Warne And Co." Not in Kohler.

2351. THE POETICAL WORKS OF JOHN MILTON With Introduction And Notes By Arthur Waugh[.] *London[:] George Routledge And Sons, Limited, New York[:] E. P. Dutton And Co[.] n.d. [ca. 1888]*. First edition thus by Dutton? 8vo, x+596pp., half-title, title page in red and black, "Biographical Introduction" and "Table of Contents" printed in double column, "Notes" and "Index" at the end also printed in double column, contemporary full polished royal blue morocco, gilt rules on covers with central gilt prize emblem and gilt lettering on front cover, richly gilt-decorated spine within the panels with gilt lettering, raised bands with decorative gilt trim, outer dentelles finely tooled in gilt, marbled endpapers and edges. A fine copy in an attractive Prize Binding, with prize citation tipped in on front pastedown. Not in Kohler.

2352. POETICAL WORKS OF JOHN MILTON. *London: Hyman A. Abrahams & Sons. n.d. [ca. 1888]* First edition thus? 8vo, 460pp., decorative head- and tailpieces, original red cloth (a bit rubbed), front cover and spine lettered in blind, decorative floral emblem in block form in blind at the center of front cover with a smaller emblem in blind at bottom right-hand corner, similar emblem in blind at bottom of spine with a smaller emblem in blind at the center, patterned endpapers, t.e.g. A good copy in publisher's cloth binding, with late nineteenth-century bookplate on front pastedown and contemporary presentation card laid in. Scarce. Not in Kohler.

2353. POETICAL WORKS OF JOHN MILTON. Reprinted From The Best Editions With Biographical Notice, Etc. *New York[:] American Publisher's Corporation[,] 310-318 Sixth Avenue, n.d. [ca. 1888]* First edition thus? 8vo, 562pp., original decorated green cloth (a bit rubbed), front cover and spine intricately decorated in black trim, spine lettered in gilt, t.e.g. A lovely copy in an attractive binding of the period, with late nineteenth-century bookplate on front pastedown and contemporary presentation card laid in. Scarce. Not in Kohler.

2354. THE POETICAL WORKS OF JOHN MILTON. With Memoir, Explanatory Notes, &c. Portrait And Original Illustrations. The "Lansdowne" Poets. *London And New York: Frederick Warne And Co. 1889.* 8vo, xxvi+581pp., half-title with "Morrison and Gibb, Edinburgh, Printer's to Her Majesty's Stationery Office" on verso and printed again at bottom of last page, engraved frontispiece portrait plate, emblem of the press (small laurel wings with a horseshoe) at the center of title page, decorative piece on verso of title page, eight illustration plates after engravings by Dalziel: one for *L'A*, four for *PL* (Books I, IV, VIII, and XII), one for *SA*, one for *On His Deceased Wife*, and one for *Latin Epigram VII* ("Ad Eandem"—the illustration titled *Milton Meeting Leonora Baroni at Cardinal Barberini's House*), decorative tailpiece at the end of *PR*, half-title for *SA*, notes at bottom of page, contemporary full red calf (joints, spine ends, and edges slightly frayed, corners worn), gilt rules on covers with Milton's name and decorative piece in gilt at top of front cover, spine lettered in gilt, a.e.g. A good copy with contemporary presentation inscription (dated "1890") on verso of portrait plate. See other undated and dated illustrated and nonillustrated editions by Frederick Warne and Co. published in the 1870s, 1880s, and 1890s under the various series: "The 'Lansdowne' Poets," "The 'Arundel' Poets," "The 'Chandos' Poets," "The 'Imperial' Poets, "The 'Chandos' Classics," "The 'Albion' Edition," and the "Cabinet Poets." Kohler 413, reporting "Not in the British Library. Not in the Bodleian Library. Not in Cambridge University Library."

2355. THE POETICAL WORKS OF JOHN MILTON. With Memoir, Explanatory Notes, &c. Portrait And Original Illustrations. The "Lansdowne" Poets. *London: Frederick Warne And Co. And New York. n. d. [ca. 1889].* 8vo, similar to preceding copy, xxiv+581pp., half-title with "Morrison And Gibb, Printers, Edinburgh" printed on verso, unsigned frontispiece portrait of an early middle-aged Milton (labeled "London: Frederick Warne & Co." at bottom), protective tissue guard, emblem of the press (small laurel wings with a horseshoe) at the center of title page, "Morrison And Gibb, Printers, Edinburgh" on verso of title page, eight illustration plates after engravings by Dalziel (illustrations as in preceding edition), half-title for *SA*, orange border around text, "Morrison And Gibb, Printers, Edinburgh" on verso of last page, notes at bottom of page, original blue cloth (bit rubbed at edges, some notations in pencil within), front cover elaborately decorated in gilt and black with bright gilt harp at the center and bright broad gilt bands with decorative gilt trim near the top incorporating Milton's name with "The Lansdowne Poets" in black lettering below and with decorative gilt trim at the top and bottom, spine similarly gilt-decorated with a bright gilt urn near the bottom and a bright broad gilt band with decorative gilt trim near the top incorporating "Milton" in large letters with "The Lansdowne Poets" in black lettering below and decorative gilt trim at top and bottom, back cover blind-stamped with central device in blind, a.e.g. A nice copy in a brilliant binding, very fresh and clean within, in a well-preserved Victorian publisher's decorated cloth binding, with the number "13" blind-stamped in the center of the device on the back cover. See copy of 1888 "Albion Edition" listed earlier published by Frederick Warne and Co. in London and New York, as here, and other editions cited there. Not in Kohler.

2356. THE POETICAL WORKS OF JOHN MILTON. Reprinted From The Chandos Poets. With Memoir, Explanatory Notes, &c. Portrait And Original Illustrations. *New York: Worthington Co., 747 Broadway. 1889.* 8vo, xxiv+581+[3]pp., frontispiece illustration plate after an engraving by Dalziel for Book I of *PL* (*Satan Addressing Cohorts*, with appropriate lines quoted), protective tissue guard, decorative central device with bee hive in the center on verso of title page, one additional illustration plate after an engraving by Dalziel for *PL* (Book VIII, *Adam and Eve Naming the Animals*, with appropriate lines quoted), decorative central tailpiece at the end of *PR*, half-title for *SA*, red border around text, decorative tailpiece at the end of *PR* repeated on verso of last page, additional leaf with decorative central device (without angelic figure) on each side of the leaf, notes at bottom of page, original decorated light red cloth (somewhat worn, small portion missing at bottom of p. 247 without affecting any text), front cover elaborately decorated in embossed red and black lines and swirls in a floral and circular motif with Milton's name incorporated in black lettering within a bright gilt band near the top and a winged horse (pegasus) in red against a black background within decorated swirls and circle in lower left corner, spine similarly elaborately decorated in embossed red, black, and gilt with a floral motif at the center, the title ("Milton's Poems") lettered in black within a bright gilt band at the top, and "Worthington Co" within a smaller gilt band at the bottom, decorated endpapers, a.e.g. Despite some wear, a nice copy in a rather lovely nineteenth-century American publisher's binding. The possible first edition of Milton's *PW* by Worthington was published in 1884 (also listed here with further editions by Worthington cited). Not in Kohler.

2357. THE POETICAL WORKS Of John Milton. In Two Volumes. Vol. I/II. *Cassell & Company, Limited: London, Paris, New York, & Melbourne. n.d. [ca. 1889].* 2 volumes. First edition thus? Slim 8vo (miniature size, measuring 4 ½" × 3"), 320+16pp.,+317+[3]+16pp., title page each volume, life of Milton, volume 1, "Contents" of volume 2, sixteen pages of advertisements at the end of each volume, original red French [or] Russia morocco, covers ruled in blind, spines ruled in blind and lettered in gilt, dark green endpapers, a.e.g. A nice set. In the sixteen pages of advertisement at the end, this set of Milton is included among the poets in "Cassell's Miniature Library Of The Poets. In half-cloth . . . in French [or] Russia Morocco." Scarce. Not in Kohler.

2358. THE POETICAL WORKS OF JOHN MILTON. With Memoir, Explanatory Notes, Etc. The "Albion" Edition. *London And New York: Frederick Warne And Co[.] 1889.* 8vo, xxvi+581pp., half-title with "Morrison and Gibb, Edinburgh, Printer's to Her Majesty's Stationery Office" on verso and printed again at center of last page, emblem of the press (small laurel wings with a horseshoe) at the center of title page, half-title for *SA*, notes at bottom of page, original green cloth (a bit rubbed), sketch of Milton in embossed gilt at center of front cover, with Milton's name in gilt lettered in script beneath, spine lettered in gilt, dark green endpapers, edges untrimmed. A nice copy in publisher's binding, with early stamp and presentation inscription in Latin on verso of fly-leaf. See other undated and dated illustrated and nonillustrated editions by Frederick Warne and Co. published in the 1870s, 1880s, and 1890s under the various series: "The 'Lansdowne' Poets," "The 'Arundel' Poets," "The 'Chandos' Poets," "The 'Imperial' Poets, "The 'Chandos' Classics," "The 'Albion' Edition," and the "Cabinet Poets." Kohler 415, reporting "Not in the British Library. Not in the Bodleian Library. Not in Cambridge University Library."

2359. THE POETICAL WORKS OF JOHN MILTON A New Edition, Carefully Revised, From The Text Of Thomas Newton, D.D. *London[:] George Routledge And Sons[,] Broadway, Ludgate Hill[;] New York: 416, Broome Street[.] n.d. [ca. 1889].* 8vo, viii+570pp., boxed listing of "Routledge's 'Excelsior' Series. Uniform with this volume" on verso of title page, original "Preface" by Theodore Alois Buckley (dated 1853), notes at bottom of page, "Printed By Ballantyne And Hanson[,] London And Edinburgh" printed at bottom of last page, original decorated reddish-brown cloth, covers decorated in embossed black trim with harp at the center, Milton's name in large black letters near the top, and "Excelsior Series" in smaller black letters at the very top, spine similarly decorated in embossed black trim with harp at the center, Milton's name in large black letters against a bright gilt background near the top, and "Excelsior Series" in decorative gilt lettering at the very top with "Routledge" lettered in embossed reddish-brown against a bright gilt background at the bottom. A fine copy, fresh and clean within, in an attractive publisher's binding. The first edition of Milton's *PW* by George Routledge and Co. was published in 1853 (also listed here with further editions by Routledge cited). Not in Kohler.

2360. Variant of Preceding, original decorated brown cloth, decorated exactly as preceding copy, light green endpapers advertising "Routledge's Excelsior Series" on the front endpapers and "Routledge's Standard Library" on the back endpapers. A fine copy, fresh and clean within, in an attractive variant publisher's binding, with advertisements printed on green endpapers. Not in Kohler.

2361. THE POETICAL WORKS OF JOHN MILTON. *Edinburgh: W. P. Nimmo, Hay, & Mitchell. n.d. [ca. 1890].* 8vo, xxxvii+[3]+440pp., unsigned engraved frontispiece portrait plate of a middle-aged Milton, engraved and printed title pages, with vignette illustration (of the poet being inspired by heavenly choirs) by F. Borders on engraved title plate ("Edinburgh: William P. Nimmo & Co."), protective tissue guard, vignette illustration (of a young boy in a setting in nature with a cane laying beside him) signed with the initials "WS" on printed title, life of Milton by J. M. Ross, eleven illustration plates, most after F. Borders, some unsigned: four for *PL* (Books I, III, VI, XI), two for *PR* (Book I), one for *SA*, two for *C*, one for *L'A*, one for *IlP*, half-title for *PL, PR, SA, C, Arc, MP*, and *Poemata*, red border around text, decorative pieces on verso of half-titles and at end of major poems, "Ballantyne Press: Edinburgh And London" printed at bottom of last page, full polished maroon morocco (a bit sun-faded along inner edge of front cover), double gilt rules with small gilt corner devices on each cover, circular prize seal ("Waterloo High School Honoris Causa") at the center of the front cover, gilt-lettered and gilt-decorated olive green morocco label on spine, raised bands with decorative gilt trim, richly gilt decorated within the panels, marbled endpapers and edges. A splendid copy, finely printed by the Ballantyne Press of Edinburgh and London, very fresh and clean within, in a handsome binding by Bickers & Son, with their stamp. The possible first edition thus by Nimmo was published in 1865, illustrated (also listed here with further Nimmo editions cited). Only the 1865 edition has twelve illustrations, the others have eleven (with only one illustration for *L'A* instead of two, as in the 1865 edition). Uncommon. Kohler 407, reporting "Not in Williamson. Not in the British Library. Not in the Bodleian library. Not in Cambridge University Library."

2362. THE POETICAL WORKS OF JOHN MILTON Edited With Memoir, Introductions, Notes, And An Essay On Milton's English And Versification By David Masson, M.A. LL.D. Professor Of Rhetoric And English Literature In The University Of Edinburgh[.] London[:] Macmillan And Co. And New York[.] 1890. All rights reserved. 3 volumes. Second edition thus, revised and enlarged. 8vo, xviii+536pp.,+vi+642+[2]pp.,+vi+618+[2]pp., half-title with decorative piece consisting of publisher's initials on verso each volume, frontispiece vignette portrait each volume (Milton age ten ["engraved by Edwd. Radclyffe"], age twenty-one [unsigned], and age sixty-two [unsigned]), protective tissue guard each volume, title page each volume, preface (dated 1890 and new to this edition), volume 1, half-title for some of the poems, original green cloth (a bit rubbed), spines lettered in gilt, edges untrimmed. A very nice set, fresh and clean within, with prize citation (dated 1896–97) tipped in on front pastedown, volume 1, and leaf advertising "Macmillan And Co.'s Publications" (including "The Life Of Milton . . . By David Masson" in six volumes, "Milton's Poetical Works. Edited . . . By Professor Masson. With Three Portraits engraved by Jeens. 3 volumes. Fcap. 8vo. 15s.," "Milton's Poetical works. Globe Edition. Edited . . . by Professor Masson. Globe 8vo. 3s. 6d.," and "Milton. By Mark Pattison" and "Milton. By the Rev. Stopford A. Brooke") at the end of volume 2, with the same advertisement leaf for "Macmillan And Co.'s Publications" bound in at the end of volume 3. The first edition thus by Masson was published in 1874 (see set listed here); a revised edition in a three-volume smaller octavo format (the first thus) was published in 1882 (see set listed here). Stevens 206; Kohler 416.

2363. THE POETICAL WORKS OF JOHN MILTON. Reprinted From The Chandos Poets. With Memoir, Explanatory Notes, &c. The "Chandos" Classics. *London: Frederick Warne And Co., Bedford Street, Strand. n.d. [ca. 1890].* 8vo, xxiv+581pp., central printer's device with initials "FW & Co." on title page, printed by the Dalziel Brothers at the Camden Press, with the seal of the press on verso of title page, half-title for SA, "Dalziel Brothers, Camden Press, London, NW" on verso of last page, original one-half red morocco, red marbled paper over boards (a bit rubbed), gilt-decorated spine, black morocco label with gilt lettering and gilt rules, raised bands with decorative gilt rule (rubbed), marbled endpapers and edges. A nice copy. See other undated and dated illustrated and nonillustrated editions by Frederick Warne and Co. published in the 1870s, 1880s, and 1890s under the various series: "The 'Lansdowne' Poets," "The 'Arundel' Poets," "The 'Chandos' Poets," "The 'Imperial' Poets, "The 'Chandos' Classics," "The 'Albion' Edition," and the "Cabinet Poets." Not in Kohler.

2364. THE POETICAL WORKS OF JOHN MILTON. With Memoir, Explanatory Notes, Etc. The "Albion" Edition. *London And New York: Frederick Warne And Co. 1890.* 8vo, xxvi+581pp., half-title with "Morrison And Gibb, Printers, Edinburgh" on verso and printed again on verso of last page, central emblem on title page consisting of small laurel wings with a horseshoe at the center, half-title for SA, notes at the bottom of the page, original brown cloth (slightly rubbed), small gilt sketch of Milton with his signature in gilt at center of front cover, spine lettered in gilt with gilt rules at top and bottom, dark green endpapers. A nice copy in publisher's binding. Not in Kohler.

2365. THE POETICAL WORKS OF JOHN MILTON. With Biographical Notice. Russell Edition. *New York: W. E. Russell, Publisher. n.d. [ca. 1890].* 8vo, 562pp., original green cloth (a bit worn, lacking blank before title page, pages a little age-browned), printed paper label on spine (worn and faded). A decent copy of this reprint edition, possible first published ca. 1887 (also listed here). Scarce. Not in Kohler.

2366. THE POETICAL WORKS OF JOHN MILTON. With Memoir, Explanatory Notes, &c. *London: Henry Frowde, Oxford University Press Warehouse, Amen Corner, E.C. 1890.* First edition thus? 8vo, xxvi+581pp., half-title (with "Morrison And Gibb, Printers, Edinburgh" on verso), red border around title page, notes at bottom of the page, "Morrison And Gibb, Printers, Edinburgh" on verso of last page, Victorian half brown morocco, marbled paper over boards, spine lettered in gilt, small decorative gilt piece in each panel, raised bands with decorative gilt trim, marbled endpapers, t.e.g, others untrimmed. A very nice copy. Uncommon. Not in Kohler.

2367. THE POETICAL WORKS OF JOHN MILTON. *Edinburgh: William P. Nimmo, Hay, & Mitchell[,] 1891.* 8vo, xxxvii+[3]+440pp., unsigned engraved frontispiece portrait plate of a middle-aged Milton, engraved and printed title pages, with vignette illustration (of the poet being inspired by heavenly choirs) by F. Borders on engraved title plate ("Edinburgh: W. P. Nimmo, Hay, & Mitchell." n.d.), protective tissue guard (foxed), vignette illustration (of a young boy in a setting in nature with a cane laying beside him) signed with the initials "WS" on printed title, "Ballantyne Press Ballantyne, Hanson And Co. Edinburgh And London" printed on verso of title page, Life of Milton by J. M. Ross, eleven illustration plates, most after F. Borders, some unsigned; four for PL

(Books I, III, VI, XI), two for *PR* (Book I), one for *SA*, two for *C*, one for *L'A*, one for *IlP*, half-title for *PL*, *PR*, *SA*, *C*, *Arc*, *MP*, and *Poemata*, red border around text, decorative pieces on verso of half-titles and at end of major poems, "Printed by Ballantyne, Hanson & Co., Edinburgh" at bottom of last page, original brown silk over padded boards (front joint repaired, two folds on frontispiece portrait plate), floral decoration in silver and gilt together with Milton's name in gilt on front cover, spine lettered in gilt with small harp in gilt at the bottom, a.e.g. A decent copy in publisher's binding, with neat presentation inscription on verso of frontispiece. The possible first edition thus by Nimmo was published in 1865, illustrated (also listed here with further Nimmo editions cited). Only the 1865 edition has twelve illustrations, the others have eleven (with only one illustration for *L'A* instead of two, as in the 1865 edition). Not in Kohler.

2368. Variant of Preceding, original decorated olive green cloth (bookplate removed from inside front pastedown), front cover decorated in embossed black, orange, and gilt with a tall flower with long green stems and three large orange blossoms all outlined in black within a bright bold vertical gilt background coming out of a small urn at the bottom in olive green and contrasting orange and bright gilt trim, decorative floral border in contrasting colors of orange blossoms and black stems at the top and bottom, two wide decorative bands in contrasting orange and black with Milton's name in embossed gilt at the top, spine repeats the decorations of the front cover, with "Milton's Poetical Works" lettered in embossed gilt at the top and "W. P. Nimmo, Hay, & Mitchell" in gilt at the bottom, olive green endpapers, a.e.g. A nice copy in an attractive variant publisher's binding, with near-contemporary presentation inscription on fly-leaf. Not in Kohler.

2369. Variant of Preceding, original decorated reddish-brown cloth (a bit rubbed), front cover decorated in embossed black and gilt trim with Milton's name lettered in embossed gilt at the center, a lyre in embossed black in lower right-hand corner, and a bright decorative gilt band with embossed floral piece in reddish-brown within thick gilt rules near the top with contrasting black trim along the side, spine similarly decorated in black and gilt with the decorative gilt piece at the top of the front cover repeated in the middle of the spine, "Milton's Poetical Works" lettered in gilt at the top and "W. P. Nimmo, Hay, & Mitchell" in gilt at the bottom, brown endpapers (small piece torn out of lower right-hand corner of fly-leaf), a.e.g. A very pleasing copy in a variant publisher's binding. Not in Kohler.

2370. **THE POETICAL WORKS OF JOHN MILTON.** Edited, With A Critical Memoir, By William Michael Rossetti. Illustrated By Thomas Seccombe. The "Grosvenor" Poets. *William Collins, Sons, & Co., Limited, London, Glasgow, And Edinburgh. n.d. [ca. 1891]*. 8vo, xx+460pp., half-title, frontispiece portrait of Milton at age ten, printer's emblem (orb with letters within and "Trade Mark" lettered on either side and an owl with outstretch wings on the top) on title page, six engraved illustration plates after Thomas Seccombe, four for *PL* (Books I, IV—two plates, V), one for *C*, and one for *SA*, numerous elaborately decorated head- and tailpieces, red border around text, contemporary padded crushed green calf (a bit rubbed), front cover and spine lettered in gilt, slightly raised bands, inner dentelles finely tooled in gilt, brown endpapers, a.e.g. A nice copy of a scarce edition, with contemporary prize citation (dated 1891) tipped in on front pastedown. Not in Kohler.

2371. **THE POETICAL WORKS OF JOHN MILTON** With Memoir, Etc. Family Edition. Fully Illustrated With New Wood Engravings. With Border By George Wharton Edwards. *New York[:] Frederick A. Stokes Company[,] MDCCCXCI*. Second edition thus? Tall 8vo, xvi+224pp.+221pp. (*PR*, etc. paginated anew)+[1]+[2]pp., unsigned frontispiece portrait plate of Milton, protective tissue guard, border illustrations in varying tints throughout depicting scenes in *PL* (angel brandishing a fiery sword, Eve and Adam distraught after the judgment, and a figure, from shoulders up, observing from above right corner), illustration plates, including Munkacsy's *Blind Milton Dictating* (unsigned), Doré's illustrations for *PL* (Books I, III, IV, VI, VII, IX, and XI), two unsigned illustration plates for *PR* (Books I and III), one unsigned illustration plate for *SA*, one illustration plate (unsigned, after Cope) for *L'A*, one illustration plate (signed, but difficult to read) for *IlP*, and one unsigned illustration plate for *C*, original decorated brown cloth (a little rubbed along edges and at the corners), front cover decorated with leaves, branches, small circular devices, and ruled lines in embossed black and red, with portrait of Milton at age twenty-one against black background within circular device in lower right corner, "Illustrated" lettered in black above the portrait, with Milton's name lettered in black within a bright broad gilt band at the top ruled in black and surrounded by a dotted reddish-brown border, spine similarly decorated in embossed black trim with Milton's name lettered horizontally in large embossed blue letters within a bright broad gilt band with three embossed blue rules on either side and with three bright gilt circular devices at the top and bottom each beneath a bright gilt rule, blue endpapers, a.e.g. A very good copy in a handsome publisher's binding, with advertisement leaf bound in at the end for Frederick A. Stokes & Brother's "'Family' Poets" series, as with first edition (see commentary there). Scarce. Not in Kohler.

The possible first edition thus was published by Stokes in 1888 (also listed here), with a variation in the publisher's imprint ("Frederick A. Stokes & Brother" in place of "Frederick A. Stokes Company," as here); see also nonillustrated 1891 edition listed here published by "Frederick A. Stokes Company," with the same title page and pagination as here, but in a much smaller octavo format with another variation in the publisher's imprint and without any illustrations. See, too, undated ca. 1891 8vo illustrated edition following published by "Frederick A. Stokes Company Publishers" (with yet another variant publisher's imprint, and with very intriguing unsigned illustrations); and see undated ca. 1895 nonillustrated edition published by "Frederick A. Stokes Company."

2372. THE POETICAL WORKS OF JOHN MILTON With Memoir, Etc. *New York[:] Frederick A. Stokes Company Publishers. n.d. [ca. 1891].* 8vo, xvi+224pp.+221pp. (*PR*, etc. paginated anew), unsigned frontispiece illustration plate and seven additional unsigned illustration plates for *PL* (Books II, III, IV, VI, as frontispiece, VII, IX, X, XI), two unsigned illustration plates for *PR* (Books I and II), two unsigned illustration plates for *SA*, one unsigned illustration plate for *L'A*, one unsigned illustration plate for *C*, one unsigned illustration plate for *L*, and one unsigned illustration plate for *Psm CXXXVI*, original decorated green cloth (a bit rubbed, small shelf label removed from spine, small book label and small green stamp on front pastedown, with small green stamp repeated on fly-leaf and on back pastedown), front cover elegantly decorated with finely tooled silver and gilt border trim at top and bottom, with a striking center piece design in similarly finely tooled silver and gilt incorporating Milton's name in large gilt letters within a raised broad white band decorated with silver trim, with silver and gilt rules outlining the cover, spine similarly decorated with finely tooled silver and gilt border trim at top and bottom, with two bands in designs repeated from the design of the centerpiece on front cover, and with gilt lettering ("Poems" and "Milton"), a.e.g. A handsome copy in a striking publisher's binding. The illustrations, while unsigned, are very captivating and virtually singular in character and manner; they are intriguing on several counts: as illustrations, for what they illustrate in Milton's poems, and for the style or design of the illustrations themselves. The possible first edition of Milton's *PW* by "Frederick A. Stokes & Brother" was published in 1888 (also listed here). Scarce. Not in Kohler.

2373. THE POETICAL WORKS OF JOHN MILTON With Memoir, Etc. Family Edition. Fully Illustrated With New Wood Engravings. With Border By George Wharton Edwards. *New York[:] Frederick A. Stokes Company[,] MDCCCXCI (1891).* 8vo, xvi+224pp.+221pp. (*PR*, etc. paginated anew), unsigned frontispiece portrait plate of Milton, reproducing at the center of the title page the emblem from the incunabula printing of *Ship of Fools* of a "scholar" poring over a book with a stack of folios around him, original half white cloth, decorated paper over boards (a bit worn at corners), half white cloth richly decorated in a gilt floral design with gilt lettering on spine, boards covered with white paper richly decorated with small pink rose buds with gilt floral stems, a.e.g. A lovely copy, fresh and clean, near mint, with small bookplate tipped in at top of front pastedown. While "Fully Illustrated With New Wood Engravings. With Border By George Wharton Edwards" appears on the title page, as in the first and second editions, unlike those editions, no illustrations or illustrated borders appear herein. The possible first edition of Milton's *PW* by "Frederick A. Stokes & Brother" was published in 1888 (also listed here with further editions by Stokes cited). Scarce. Not in Kohler.

2374. THE POETICAL WORKS OF JOHN MILTON. With Memoir, Explanatory Notes, Etc. The "Albion" Edition. *London And New York: Frederick Warne And Co. 1891.* 8vo, xxvi+581pp., half-title with "Morrison And Gibb, Printers, Edinburgh" on verso and printed again on verso of last page, emblem of the press (small laurel wings with a horseshoe) at the center of title page, half-title for *SA*, notes at bottom of page, original red cloth (spine a bit dirtied and chipped at top and bottom, front joint broken from within, ex-library with various library stamps and with library pocket holder on back endpaper and shelf label on spine), small gilt sketch of Milton with his signature in gilt at center of front cover, spine lettered in gilt with gilt rules at top and bottom. A fair copy. See other undated and dated illustrated and nonillustrated editions in the collection by Frederick Warne and Co. published in the 1870s, 1880s, and 1890s under the various series: "The 'Lansdowne' Poets," "The 'Arundel' Poets," "The 'Chandos' Poets," "The 'Imperial' Poets, "The 'Chandos' Classics," "The 'Albion' Edition," and the "Cabinet Poets." Not in Kohler (although Kohler cites several other editions by Warne and Co.).

2375. THE POETICAL WORKS OF JOHN MILTON[:] With Introductions By David Masson, M.A., L.L.D., Professor Of Rhetoric And English Literature In The University Of Edinburgh. The Globe Edition. *London: Macmillan And Co. And New York. 1891. The Right of*

Translation and Reproduction is Reserved. 8vo, xi+625pp., half-title with emblem consisting of the letters of Macmillan and Co. on verso, "Contents," "Introduction to *PL*" with several diagrams and other introductory material as in the first editions, half-title for some of the sections and poems, contemporary dark green cloth (a little used, pencil notations on half-title and title page and occasionally throughout), blind rules on front cover with small central embossed image in blind of Milton with "The Globe Edition" lettered above, spine lettered in gilt at the top with small gilt emblem of a globe at the bottom, dark green endpapers, edges untrimmed. The Globe edition of Milton's *PW* was first published in March 1877 (also listed here with further editions by Globe cited). Scarce. Not in Kohler.

2376. THE POETICAL WORKS OF JOHN MILTON With A Memoir And Critical Remarks On His Genius And Writings By James Montgomery And One Hundred And Twenty Engravings By John Thompson, S. And T. Williams, O. Smith, J. Linton, Etc. From Drawings By William Harvey. New Edition. With An Index To Paradise Lost; Todd's Verbal Index To All The Poems: And A Variorum Selection Of Explanatory Notes By Henry G. Bohn. In Two Vols. *London: George Bell & Sons, York St., Covent Garden, And New York. 1892.* 2 volumes. 8vo, iv+lii+508+[32]pp.,+viii+511+[32]pp., general title page and individual title page each volume, individual title page, volume 1, like general title cited is dated 1892, general and individual title pages, volume 2, dated 1900, "Preface" (by Bohn, dated 1861), "Index Of Subjects To Paradise Lost" at end of volume 1, "Contents" after title pages in volume 2 with "Todd's Verbal Index To Milton's Poetical Works. Revised And Enlarged" at the end of volume 2, illustrations variously engraved after William Harvey in both volumes 1 and 2, half-title for some of the works, original maroon diaper grain cloth (a bit rubbed), covers ruled in blind with central emblem in blind incorporating "Bohn's Libraries" on front covers, spines lettered in gilt with gilt rule at top and bottom and with gilt device of the press at the bottom consisting of a bell at the center and "Standard Library" lettered around with "Bohn's Libraries" in gilt at the bottom, t.e. rough, partially unopened. A fine set with thirty-two pages of advertisements for "An Alphabetical List Of Books Contained In Bohn's Libraries bound in at the end of each volume. Uniformly bound as volumes I and II of a seven-volume set, together with five volumes of "The Prose Works Of John Milton" listed here as volumes III, IV, V, VI, and VII (dated 1901–4). "This present edition of Milton's Poetical Works is a repetition, with additions, of that originally published by Messrs. Tilt and Bogue, in 1843 [see sets listed here], and since by Messrs Kent and Co. [see set listed in 1859]," (Preface). Scarce. Kohler 417, reporting "Not in the British Library. Not in the Bodleian Library. Not in Cambridge University Library."

2377. THE POETICAL WORKS OF JOHN MILTON. Reprinted From The Best Editions With Biographical Notice, Etc. *New York: Thomas Y. Crowell & Co., n.d. [ca. 1892].* 8vo, 562+[8]pp., frontispiece illustration plate reproducing an illustration by Doré for *PL* (Book III, *Satan Journeying to Earth*, with appropriate lines quoted), protective tissue guard, decorative printer's device in black on title page incorporating the publisher's initials "TYC," with no copyright date on verso of title page as in following copies, "Contents," "Sketch Of The Life Of John Milton," red border around text, original reddish-brown cloth (a bit rubbed, bookplate partially removed from front pastedown, spine ends slightly chipped, smudge on contents page), front cover lettered in gilt ("Milton's Poems"), with small decoration in gilt at bottom and with central gilt emblem with dancing angelic figurine in gilt within decorative square piece in black, spine lettered ("Milton's Poems") and decorated in gilt (faded), with central gilt harp, a.e.g. A good copy in a nice publisher's binding, with contemporary signature (dated 1893) on fly-leaf. Bound in at the end are eight pages of advertisements for publications by Crowell (including "Crowell's Poets Red Line Edition," listing Milton, and "Crowell's Poets Half Russia Edition," listing an edition of Milton in the series). Not in Kohler.

The possible first edition of Milton's *PW* by Crowell was published ca. 1880 (also listed here with further editions by Crowell cited). See also other editions of Milton's *PW* published by Crowell about the same time as this edition (1892), each with variations from the edition here and from each other: (1) one in a similar octavo size and with the same frontispiece illustration, but with significant differences including title page and publisher's imprint, with copyright date of 1892 on verso of title page, and with introduction and half-title before the various poetical works; (2) one an "Imperial Edition," in a slightly larger octavo format, with copyright date of 1892 on verso of title page, with reproductions of Doré's illustrations for *PL*, but with a different Doré illustration as frontispiece than here, with introduction and half-title before the various poetical works, and without "Contents" and red border around text; (3) one in a crown/royal octavo format, with title-page plate, with different publisher's imprint than here on title page, with copyright date of 1892 on verso of title page, with numerous illustration plates—none after Doré, with introduction and half-title before the various poetical works, and without red border around text; (4) one a

"Portrait Edition," with title-page plate, with different publisher's imprint than here on title page, with copyright date of 1892 on verso of title page, with reproductions of Doré's illustrations for *PL*, but with a portrait of Milton as frontispiece instead of a reproduction of Doré illustration, with introduction and half-title before the various poetical works, and without "Contents" and red border around text; (5) a two-volume edition, with the same publisher's imprint as here on title page, with copyright date of 1892 on verso of title page, and with numerous illustrations (including illustration plates after Doré for *PL*); (6) and one in a similar octavo size with the same title page and undated publisher's imprint and the same number of pages (562) although nonillustrated. See, too, 1892 nonillustrated editions published by Crowell of Milton's *PW*, each with title-page plate and each with copyright date of 1892.

2378. Variant of Preceding. **THE POETICAL WORKS OF JOHN MILTON** With Introductions By David Masson, M.A., LL.D. Professor Of Rhetoric And English Literature In The University Of Edinburgh[.] Biographical Sketch By Nathan Haskell Dole[.] *New York: 46 East 14th Street[;] Thomas Y. Crowell & Co. Boston: 100 Purchase Street[,] (1892)*. 8vo, xxi+618pp., frontispiece illustration plate reproducing an illustration by Doré for *PL* (Book III, *Satan Journeying to Earth*), protective tissue guard, copyright dated 1892 on verso of title page, half-title for *PL*, *PR*, *SA*, *MP*, and *P*, red border around text, original brown cloth, front cover elaborately decorated in black with decorative black border trim and with large circular emblem in brilliant gilt incorporating Milton's name at the center, spine lettered in gilt ("Milton's Poems") and richly decorated in gilt with three small decorative pieces in black and with decorative black trim at top and bottom, a.e.g. A fine copy with variant publisher's imprint, in an attractive and well-preserved variant publisher's binding, very fresh and crisp within, near mint. Not in Kohler.

2379. Variant of Preceding, original green cloth, decorated as preceding copy (a little worn). A fairly good copy in an attractive variant publisher's binding. Not in Kohler.

2380. **THE POETICAL WORKS OF JOHN MILTON** With Introductions By David Masson, M.A., LL.D. Professor Of Rhetoric And English Literature In The University Of Edinburgh[.] Biographical Sketch By Nathan Haskell Dole[.] *New York: 46 East 14th Street[,] Thomas Y. Crowell & Co. Boston: 100 Purchase Street[,] (1892)*. 8vo, xiii+618pp., frontispiece illustration plate reproducing an illustration by Doré for *PL* ("A happy rural seat of various view"), protective tissue guard, title page in orange and black, copyright dated 1892 on verso of title page, illustration plates reproducing Doré's illustrations for *PL* (Books I, II, III, IV, VI, IX, and XI), variously engraved, half-title for some of the poems, original dark green cloth (spine ends chipped, corners worn), decorative gilt border trim on front cover with gilt lettering at the center ("Milton's Poems"), spine lettered in gilt ("Milton's Poems" and labeled "Imperial Edition") with decorative gilt trim at top and bottom, a.e.g. A good copy, a bit larger and much thicker than the preceding edition. For references to other editions of Milton by Crowell see first ca. 1892 listing. Kohler 426, dating its copy, "[Imperial Edition]," "[ca. 1898]," with no reference to 1892 copyright date, and reporting "Not in the British Library. Not in the Bodleian Library. Not in Cambridge University Library."

2381. **THE POETICAL WORKS OF JOHN MILTON** With Introductions By David Masson, M.A., LL.D. Professor Of Rhetoric And English Literature In The University Of Edinburgh[.] Biographical Sketch By Nathan Haskell Dole[.] *New York[:] Thomas Y. Crowell & Co. Publishers[,] (1892)*. Crown/royal 8vo, xxii+[i]+618pp., frontispiece illustration plate (photogravure) reproducing Munkacsy's illustration of *Milton Dictating PL To His Daughters* (identified on "List Of Illustrations"), engraved and printed title pages, engraved title printed in orange with unsigned vignette portrait of a young, long-haired, romanticized Milton in the center, printed title with copyright dated 1892 on verso, numerous illustration plates, half-title for some of the poems, original green cloth (a bit rubbed), front cover decorated with an emblem of wings and a sword in brilliant gilt and white within decorative white border, spine similarly decorated and lettered in gilt, t.e.g., bookplate. A nice copy in a lovely publisher's decorated cloth binding. Included among the illustration plates are photographic reproductions of Martin's illustrations: six plates for *PL* (for Books I, III, IV, V, IX, and X); three plates for *PR* (Book I: *John the Baptist*, "From the painting by Andrea del Sarto"; Book II: *Mary, the Mother of Jesus*, "From the painting by Raphael"; and Book III: *The Temptation of Christ*, "From the painting by Scheffer"); one plate for *At A Vacation Exercise* ("Christ's College, Cambridge, From a photograph"); one plate for *NO* (*The Nativity*, "From the painting by Lerolle"); one plate for *The Passion* (*Jesus in Gethsemane*, "From the painting by Hofmann"); photographic reproduction of William Hyde's illustration for *Song on May Morning* ("Now The Bright Morning-Star, Day's Harbinger, Comes Dancing From The East"); photographic reproduction of William Hyde's illustration for *L'A* ("Where The Great Sun Begins His State"), photographic reproduction of William Hyde's illustration for *L* ("Under The Opening Eyelids Of The Morn We Drove Afield"), photographic reproduction of Oliver Cromwell portrait for *To The Lord General Cromwell* ("From the portrait by Sir Peter Lely"). For references to other editions of Milton by Crowell see first ca. 1892 listing. Uncommon. Not in Kohler.

2382. THE POETICAL WORKS OF JOHN MILTON With Introductions By David Masson, M.A., LL.D. Professor Of Rhetoric And English Literature In The University Of Edinburgh[.] Biographical Sketch By Nathan Haskell Dole[.] *New York: 46 East 14th Street[;] Thomas Y. Crowell & Co. Boston: 100 Purchase Street[,] (1892).* 8vo, xiii+618pp., unsigned frontispiece portrait plate of a young, long-haired Milton, protective tissue guard, title-page plate in orange and black with copyright dated 1892 on verso, half-title for *PL*, illustration plates by Doré for *PL* (three for Books IV and IX; two for Books. I, II, and III, V and VIII; one for Books VI, VII, X, and XI; none for Book XII), introductions followed by half-title for some of the poems, original olive green cloth (a little worn, spine ends chipped, slight inoffensive waterstaining along bottom portion of outer edge of first forty-eight pages), gilt border rule on front cover with vignette impression of Milton in gilt at center, spine lettered in gilt (labeled "Portrait Edition"), dark green endpapers, t.e.g., contemporary signature (dated 1895) on fly-leaf. Not in Kohler.

2383. THE POETICAL WORKS OF JOHN MILTON With Introductions By David Masson, M.A., LL.D. Professor Of Rhetoric And English Literature In The University Of Edinburgh[.] Biographical Sketch By Nathan Haskell Dole[.] *New York: 46 East 14th Street[;] Thomas Y. Crowell & Co. Boston: 100 Purchase Street[,] (1892).* 2 volumes. 8vo, xix+[3]+279pp.+618pp. (continuous pagination), unsigned frontispiece portrait plate of a young, long-haired Milton, volume 1, frontispiece plate reproducing *Cromwell's Visit to Milton* by David Neal, each with protective tissue guard, volume 2, title page in orange and black for each volume, each title page with protective tissue guard, with copyright dated 1892 on verso of title page, volume 1, "List Of Illustrations" in each volume, half-title for *PL*, and illustration plates after Doré for *PL* (three for Books IV and IX; two for Books. I, II, and III; one for Books VI, VII, VIII, and XII; none for Books V, X, and XI), volume 1, half-title for some of the poems, four illustration plates for *PR* (reproducing *John the Baptist* by A. del Sarto, *The Baptism of Christ* by Guido Reni, *Mary, the Mother of Christ* by Raphael, *Christ Tempted by Satan* by G. Cornicelius, *Temptation of Christ* by Ary Schefer), one illustration plate for *SA* (reproducing *Samson* by Guido Reni), illustration plate reproducing "Milton, Age 10 Years" before "General Introduction" to Minor Poems, illustration plates for *At A Vacation Exercise* ("Christ's College, Cambridge"), *NO* (reproducing *The Nativity* by H. Le Rolle), *The Passion* (reproducing *Jesus at Gethsemane* by H. Hofmann), *At A Solemn Music* ("The Chancel, Stratford Church"), *L'A* (reproducing *Hebe* by Schiavone), and *IlP* ("Interior of Ely Church"), with illustration plates reproducing *Milton* (at age twenty-one), *Cromwell* by Sir Peter Lely, and the *Blindness of Milton* by H. Munkacsy, volume 2, three-quarter brown calf (a bit rubbed), marbled paper over boards, spines decorated with gilt designs within each panel, gilt rules at the top and bottom, black morocco labels lettered in gilt with decorative gilt trim at top and bottom, raised bands each with a gilt rule, marbled endpapers, t.e.g. A fine set. For references to other editions of Milton by Crowell see first ca. 1892 listing. Not in Kohler.

2384. THE POETICAL WORKS OF JOHN MILTON. Reprinted From The Best Editions With Biographical Notice, Etc. *New York: Thomas Y. Crowell & Co., No. 13 Astor Place. n.d. [ca. 1892].* 8vo, 562, "Sketch Of The Life Of John Milton," original brown cloth (a bit rubbed, slight inoffensive staining at top of front cover, spine a little faded), front cover decorated with mauve floral blossoms outlined in gilt with gilt stems and leaves outlined in gilt on the left side, title in gilt at the top right side ("Milton's Poems"), spine similarly decorated in a floral motif, with gilt branches and green leaves outlined in gilt, gilt lettering ("Milton's Poems" in the middle and "TY Crowell & Co." at the bottom), a.e.g. Unlike the other nonillustrated dated 1892 Crowell editions which follow here, this edition by Crowell is undated; it also has fewer pages, 562 compared to 618. Although a different edition, it would nonetheless appear to be of the same period and similar to the undated illustrated ca. 1892 edition by Crowell, with a similar title page and the same number of pages (see first ca. 1892 listing and other editions by Crowell cited there). Not in Kohler.

2385. THE POETICAL WORKS OF JOHN MILTON With Introductions By David Masson, M.A., LL.D. Professor Of Rhetoric And English Literature In The University Of Edinburgh[.] Biographical Sketch By Nathan Haskell Dole[.] *New York: 46 East 14th Street[;] Thomas Y. Crowell & Co. Boston: 100 Purchase Street[,] (1892).* 8vo, xxi+618pp., unsigned frontispiece portrait plate sketch of Milton at age sixty-two, protective tissue guard, copyright dated 1892 on verso of title page, half-title for some of the poems, original brown cloth (tear on p. xiii), front cover elaborately decorated in black with decorative black border trim and with large central circular emblem in brilliant gilt incorporating Milton's name, spine lettered in gilt ("Milton's Poems") and richly decorated in gilt with three small decorative pieces in black and with decorative black trim at top and bottom, a.e.g. A nice copy, fresh and clean, in an attractive publisher's binding, similar to illustrated edition by Crowell with frontispiece illustration plate with Doré illustration in identical publisher's binding (also listed here). For references to other editions of Milton by Crowell see first ca. 1892 listing. Not in Kohler.

2386. THE POETICAL WORKS OF JOHN MILTON With Introductions By David Masson, M.A., LL.D. Professor Of Rhetoric And English Literature In The University Of Edinburgh[.] Biographical Sketch By Nathan Haskell Dole[.] *New York[:] Thomas Y. Crowell & Co. Publishers[,] (1892).* 8vo, xix+[1]+618pp., unsigned frontispiece portrait plate sketch of Milton at age sixty-two, protective tissue guard, decorated title-page plate printed in orange and black with ornamental border trim and central device in black, printed title page with copyright dated 1892 on verso, half-title for some of the poems, original half white cloth finely decorated in gilt floral decorations with gilt lettering on spine ("Milton's Poems"), white paper over boards finely decorated in colored floral patterns of mauve and green, (a bit rubbed, a little worn at corners, early name on fly-leaf), a.e.g. Despite some slight wear, a nice copy with a variant publisher's imprint, in a lovely variant publisher's binding.

2387. Variant of Preceding, red suede over padded boards (a bit rubbed in front cover), front cover and spine lettered in gilt ("Milton"), green marbled endpapers, a.e.g. A very nice copy in an unusual and attractive suede binding.

2388. Variant of Preceding, original light blue cloth spine, covers decorated in light green paper with patterned floral motif, at the center of the front cover a cottage scene in color on a thin card tipped in wrapped in a pink ribbon within decorative embossed gilt trim with several large pinkish white blossomed flowers, spine finely decorated and lettered in gilt. A fine copy in a lovely variant publisher's binding.

2389. Variant of Preceding, original light blue cloth spine, covers decorated in light green paper with patterned floral motif, at the center of the front cover a cottage scene in color on a thin card is tipped within decorative embossed gilt trim with several blue blossomed flowers, different from the preceding where the card is wrapped in a pink ribbon, spine finely decorated and lettered in gilt. A good copy (spine ends chipped, a bit worn along edges), in a lovely variant publisher's binding. Not in Kohler.

2390. Variant of Preceding, original decorated green cloth (a bit rubbed), front cover decorated in embossed floral motif with red petals and contrasting green vines with "Milton's Poems" lettered in gilt at the center, spine similarly decorated in a floral motif with red petals and contrasting green vines incorporating "Milton's Poems" lettered in gilt. A very nice copy in a lovely variant publisher's binding.

2391. Variant of Preceding. THE POETICAL WORKS OF JOHN MILTON With Introductions By David Masson, M.A., LL.D. Professor Of Rhetoric And English Literature In The University Of Edinburgh[.] Biographical Sketch By Nathan Haskell Dole[.] *New York: 46 East 14th Street[;] Thomas Y. Crowell & Co. Boston: 100 Purchase Street[,] (1892).* 8vo, xix+[1]+618pp., unsigned frontispiece portrait plate sketch of Milton at age sixty-two, protective tissue guard, decorated title-page plate printed in orange and black with ornamental border trim and central device in black, printed title page with copyright dated 1892 on verso, half-title for some of the poems, original red cloth, covers decorated in blind with central emblem of laurel leaves in blind on front cover incorporating the lettering, "Astor Edition," spine lettered in gilt with decorative gilt trim at top and bottom, decorated endpapers. A fine, fresh copy in a variant publisher's binding. Kohler 436, dating its copy, "[Astor Edition]" "[ca. 1900]" and reporting "Not in Williamson. Not in the British Library. Not in the Bodleian Library. Not in Cambridge University Library."

2392. Variant of Preceding, decorated title-page plate printed in orange and black with ornamental border trim and central urn with flowers in black, printed title page with copyright dated 1892 on verso, original red cloth (some marginal and textual markings in pen in Books I and II of *PL*, early name on fly-leaf), covers decorated in blind with central emblem of laurel leaves in blind on front cover incorporating the lettering, "Astor Edition," spine lettered in gilt with decorative gilt trim at top and bottom. A good copy with variant decorated title-page plate, in a publisher's binding, identifying this edition as the "Astor Edition" on the front cover. Kohler 436.

2393. Variant of Preceding, original green cloth (a bit rubbed, lacking front fly-leaf), black rules with decorative black corner devices and central gilt emblem on front cover, spine lettered in gilt, with central gilt emblem incorporating lettering "Gladstone Edition," t.e.g. A good copy in a variant publisher's binding, identifying this edition as the "Gladstone Edition" on the spine. Not in Kohler.

2394. Variant of Preceding, original red cloth (name in pencil on fly-leaf), black rules with decorative black corner devices and central gilt emblem on front cover, spine lettered in gilt with central gilt emblem incorporating lettering "Gladstone Edition," t.e.g. A nice, tight copy, fresh and clean within, in a variant publisher's binding, with "Gladstone Edition" on the spine, with variant title-page plate as in the "Astor Edition" with the same publisher's imprint as there: "New York[:] Thomas Y. Crowell & Co. Publishers," and also with the same printed page as in the Astor edition. Not in Kohler.

2395. Variant of Preceding, THE POETICAL WORKS OF JOHN MILTON With Introductions By David Masson, M.A., LL.D. Professor Of Rhetoric And English Literature In The University Of Edinburgh[.] Biographical Sketch By Nathan Haskell Dole[.] *New York: 46 East 14th Street[;] Thomas Y. Crowell & Co. Boston: 100 Purchase Street[,] (1892).* 8vo, xix+[1]+618pp., unsigned frontispiece portrait plate sketch of Milton at age sixty-two, protective tissue guard, printed title page with copyright dated 1892 on verso, half-title for some of the poems, original maroon leather over thick padded boards (rubbed, especially at top and bottom of spine), covers and spine decorated with embossed trim at the top, with Milton's name in gilt on front cover, decorated light green endpapers, a.e.g. A nice copy with variant publisher's imprint (identical to that in illustrated and nonillustrated editions listed earlier: "New York: 46 East 14th Street[;] Thomas Y. Crowell & Co. Boston: 100 Purchase Street"), in an attractive variant publisher's binding, without title-page plate as in other editions by Crowell here. Not in Kohler.

2396. Variant of Preceding, original dark red cloth (a bit rubbed, spine ends slightly worn, slight inoffensive waterstaining at outer bottom edge affecting nothing internally), spine lettered in gilt ("Milton's Poems" and "Standard Library Edition") with gilt rules, t.e.g. Laid in: advertisement leaf for "The Luxembourg Illustrated Library" published by Thomas Y. Crowell." A good copy in a variant publisher's binding identifying this edition as the "Standard Library Edition" on the spine, in a slightly taller octavo format than preceding Crowell editions, without title-page plate. Not in Kohler.

2397. Variant of Preceding, decorated title-page plate printed in orange with ornamental border trim and central device of an open book in black with the title "Poems Of John Milton" rather than "The Poetical Works Of John Milton" as on title-page plates of all other copies here published by Crowell, printed title page with copyright dated 1892 on verso, half-title for various of the poems, original green cloth (a bit smoke-stained, showing mostly on front cover), large bright decorative floral gilt piece at the center of the front cover with the title lettered in gilt above, spine elaborately decorated in gilt floral motif, with title lettered in gilt at the top and "T•Y•Crowell & Company" in gilt at the bottom, t.e.g. Despite the slight smoke-staining, a nice copy, in an attractive variant publisher's binding, in a Crown octavo format, with a near-contemporary presentation inscription, with a different vignette portrait plate (see similar vignette portrait plate of a young, long-haired, romanticized Milton in an 1892 *Complete Poetical Works* by Crowell in an earlier listing) with a different title and decorated title page plate. Not in Kohler.

2398. THE POETICAL WORKS OF JOHN MILTON With Introductions By David Masson, M.A., LL.D. Professor Of Rhetoric And English Literature In The University Of Edinburgh[.] Biographical Sketch By Nathan Haskell Dole. *New York: Thomas Y. Crowell & Co. Publishers, (1892).* Crown/royal 8vo, xix+[1]+618pp., unsigned frontispiece portrait plate sketch of a young, long-haired Milton, protective tissue guard, original green cloth (a bit smoke-stained, showing mostly on front cover, early signature on front pastedown), large bright decorative floral gilt piece at the center of the front cover with the title ("Milton's Poetical Works") lettered in gilt above, spine elaborately decorated in gilt floral motif, with "Milton's Poetical Works" lettered in gilt at the top and "T•Y•Crowell & Company" in gilt at the bottom, t.e.g. Despite the slight smoke-staining, a nice copy in an attractive variant publisher's binding, in a crown/royal octavo format, with a different vignette portrait plate (see similar vignette portrait plate of a young, long-haired, romanticized Milton in 1892 *CPW* by Crowell), with a different title and decorated title-page plate, with near-contemporary presentation inscription (dated 1900) on fly-leaf. Not in Kohler.

2399. THE POETICAL WORKS OF JOHN MILTON With Introductions By David Masson, M.A., LL.D. Professor Of Rhetoric And English Literature In The University Of Edinburgh[.] Biographical Sketch By Nathan Haskell Dole[.] *New York: 46 East 14th Street[;] Thomas Y. Crowell & Co. Boston: 100 Purchase Street[,] (1892).* 8vo, xix+[1]+618+[16]pp., copyright date of 1892 on verso of title page, half-title for some of the poems, original red cloth (spine a bit rubbed, especially at top and bottom), spine elaborately decorated with gilt trim at top and bottom with similar gilt device beneath gilt lettering ("Milton's Poems"), lightly marbled edges. A nice copy without frontispiece portrait plate, with variant publisher's imprint from the preceding, in publisher's binding, with contemporary signature (dated 1894) on fly-leaf and with a note in the same neat contemporary hand on verso of p. 337 (which is blank except for the note). Not in Kohler.

2400. THE POETICAL WORKS OF JOHN MILTON English and Latin Edited, With A Bibliographical Introduction, Life Of Milton, And An Analysis Of Addison's Criticism On Paradise Lost By John Bradshaw, M.A.,

LL.D. Editor Of The Poetical Works Of Gray, Chesterfield's Letters, And An English Anthology[.] In Two Volumes. *London[:] George Bell & Sons, York St., Covent Garden And New York[,] 1892.* 2 volumes. First edition thus. 8vo, lxiv+[1]+337pp.,+xvi+387pp., half-title each volume ("The Aldine Edition Of The British Poets"), frontispiece portrait plate after an engraving by H. Robinson, volume 1, protective tissue guard, separate title page each volume, symbol of the press on each title page, "Chiswick Press:—C. Whittingham And Co., Tooks Court, Chancery Lane" on verso of title page each volume, preface (dated "1st Dec., 1891"), "Analysis Of Addison's Criticism On Paradise Lost" (dated 1871), volume 1, "Prefatory Note: 'The Milton Window,' 'The Portraits Of Milton,' 'Milton's Cottage'" (dated 1891), volume 2, half-title for some of the poems and each book of *PL* and *PR*, original red cloth (a bit rubbed, spines slightly faded), spines lettered in gilt, fore- and bottom edges untrimmed, partially unopened, with early bookplate on front pastedown of each volume and with contemporary signature on fly-leaf of each volume. A very nice set in publisher's binding, printed at the Chiswick Press, with "Chiswick Press:—C. Whittingham And Co., Tooks Court, Chancery Lane" and the emblem of the press printed above it on the verso of the last page, volume 1, and the same listing of the press and publisher as in volume 1, without the emblem, printed at the bottom of the last page in volume 2. Stevens 236; Not in Kohler.

The Aldine British Poets edition of Milton was originally published by Pickering in 1832 (see set listed here with further references to other Aldine sets that followed—all within the collection). After Pickering's death in 1854, "the rights of the Aldine Poets were acquired by Bell & Daldy, by whom their issue, with many volumes added, has been continued to the present time (1924)" (Keynes, *Pickering*, p. 28). The 1892 edition here is an entirely new edition of Pickering's three-volume Aldine edition of Milton; this set was reprinted in 1899 and again in 1908–9—both sets listed here.

2401. THE POETICAL WORKS OF JOHN MILTON[.] *London[:] George Routledge And Sons[,] Limited[,] Broadway, Ludgate Hill[,] Manchester And New York[,] 1893.* 8vo, 448pp., half-title with a listing of "Routledge's British Poets" on verso (including Milton), engraved vignette of "Milton's Cottage, Chalfont, Bucks" on title page, frontispiece illustration plate engraved by Dalziel (after William Harvey, although unsigned) for Book I of *PL*, and five additional illustration plates engraved by Dalziel (after William Harvey, although unsigned): for Books X and XI of *PL*, for Book I of *PR*, for *SA*, and for *C*, red border around text, preface, notes at bottom of page, contemporary blue cloth (frontispiece and title page a little foxed), front cover ruled in gilt with central circular emblem of harp in gilt, back cover ruled in blind, spine lettered in gilt with gilt rules at top and bottom, brown endpapers, a.e.g. A nice copy with early inscription on half-title. The first edition of Milton's *PW* by George Routledge and Co. was published in 1853 (see copy listed here with further editions by Routledge and by Routledge and Sons cited there). See 1894 single volume edition by Routledge later, similar to the edition here, with illustrations as here, but with identification as being by Harvey on title page and in a much larger 8vo format than that here. Not in Kohler.

2402. THE POETICAL WORKS OF JOHN MILTON: Edited, With Memoir, Introductions, Notes, And An Essay On Milton's English And Versification, By David Masson, M.A., LL.D., Historiographer Royal For Scotland, Professor Of Rhetoric And English Literature In The University Of Edinburgh. *London: Macmillan And Co. And New York. 1893. All rights reserved.* 3 volumes. Small 8vo, x+lxix+312pp.,+374pp.,+[vi]+420pp., half-title each volume with decorative piece consisting of publisher's initials on verso, engraved frontispiece portrait plate each volume: Milton age sixty-two (unsigned), volume 1, Milton age twenty-one (unsigned), volume 2, Milton age ten ("Engraved by Edwd. Radclyffe" after Cipriani), volume 3, protective tissue guard for each portrait, half-title for some of the works, "Memoir of Milton," volume 1, "Introduction to *Paradise Lost*" with several diagrams, volume 2, "Introduction to *Paradise Regained*" and "Introduction to *Samson Agonistes*," volume 3, with notes to all three volumes at the end of volume 3, contemporary polished calf, covers decorated with gilt rules and small gilt corner pieces, spines elaborately decorated in gilt within the panels, red and olive green morocco labels with gilt lettering and decorative gilt trim on each spine, raised bands with decorative gilt trim, inner dentelles finely tooled in blind, outer dentelles decorated in gilt, marbled endpapers and marbled edges. A very lovely set in fine condition, bound by Worsfold, with their stamp, and with armorial bookplate on front blank in each volume. Uncommon. Kohler 419, reporting "Not in the British Library. Not in the Bodleian Library. Not in Cambridge University Library."

The first edition thus, based on Masson's earlier edition published in 1874, was published in 1882; it was reprinted in 1893 (set here), 1896, and 1903—all sets listed here. According to information printed on verso of each title page here: "First Edition 1874, 'Golden Treasury Series,' 2 volumes. (Pott 8vo)[;] Second Edition 1882, 3 volumes. (Foolscap 8vo)[;] Reprinted 1893 (Globe 8vo)."

2403. Another copy of THE POETICAL WORKS OF JOHN MILTON . . . *London: Macmillan And Co. And New York. 1893.* 3 volumes. Small 8vo, as preceding set, original red cloth. Kept in the collection because volumes 2 and 3 once belonged to famed Milton scholar and Princeton teacher Morris Croll, with numerous marginal notes in pencil in his hand (throughout *PL* in volume 2 and *SA* in volume 3) his bookplate on front pastedown of each of these volumes, and his signature on fly-leaf of each of these volumes dated 1895. Laid in volume 2: a leaf with notes in Croll's hand. Although brighter and in almost pristine condition, volume 1 has been added from another incomplete set in order to make this set complete.

2404. THE POETICAL WORKS OF JOHN MILTON[:] With Introductions By David Masson, M.A., L.L.D., Professor Of Rhetoric And English Literature In The University Of Edinburgh. The Globe Edition. *London: Macmillan And Co. And New York. 1893. The Right of Translation and Reproduction is Reserved.* 8vo, xi+625+[2]pp., half-title, original "Preface" (dated "March 1877"), "Contents," "Introduction to PL" with several diagrams and other introductory material as in the first editions, half-title for some of the sections and poems, "Richard Clay & Sons, Limited, London & Bengay" on verso of last page, original dark green cloth (small crack in front joint at the bottom, former owner's name written neatly at top of title page), small embossed hemispheres of the world in gilt within decorative gilt trim with the initials "MM" in each hemisphere at the center of front cover, spine lettered in gilt (title at the top, "The Globe Edition" and "Macmillan & Co." at the bottom), with gilt rules at the top and bottom continuing the blind rules on covers, edges untrimmed. A nice copy in clean publisher's binding, with two pages of advertisements for editions in "The Globe Library" (including this edition) bound in at the end. The Globe edition of Milton's *PW* was first published in March 1877 (also listed here with further editions by Globe cited). Kohler 418, reporting "Not in the British Library. Not in the Bodleian Library. Not in Cambridge University Library."

2405. THE POETICAL WORKS OF JOHN MILTON With Introductions By David Masson, M.A., LL.D., Professor Of Rhetoric And English Literature In The University Of Edinburgh[.] *London[:] Macmillan And Co. And New York[.] 1893.* 8vo, xi+625+[2]pp., half-title, "Richard Clay & Sons, Limited, London & Bengay" on verso of title page and repeated again on verso of last page, original "Preface" (dated "March 1877"), "Contents," "Introduction to *Paradise Lost*" with several diagrams, half-title for various poems and some of the sections, original dark green cloth (a bit rubbed, endpapers foxed, owners inscription and short notation in pencil on front endpapers, some marginalia and underling in pencil), central embossed vignette portrait of Milton in gilt on front cover and Milton's name in gilt at lower right-hand corner, spine lettered in gilt ("The Works Of Milton" at the top and "Macmillan & Co." at the bottom), t.e.g. A nice copy in a handsome original publisher's binding, with advertisement leaf for "New Uniform And Complete Editions Of The Poets" by Macmillan (including this edition of Milton) bound in at the end. Not in Kohler.

2406. THE POETICAL WORKS OF JOHN MILTON. With Memoir, Explanatory Notes, Etc. The "Albion" Edition. *London: Frederick Warne And Co. And New York. n.d. [ca. 1893].* 8vo, xxvi+581pp., half-title with "Morrison And Gibb, Printers, Edinburgh" on verso and printed again on verso of last page, emblem of the press (small laurel wings with a horseshoe) at the center of title page, half-title for *SA* preceded by small decorative piece on verso of last page of *PR* before half-title for *SA*, notes at bottom of page, contemporary full polished blue morocco (a bit rubbed along joints), delicately tooled decorative gilt border trim on covers, elaborately gilt-decorated spine, red morocco label with gilt lettering and decorative gilt rules and trim, raised bands with decorative gilt trim, inner dentelles tooled in blind, outer dentelles decorated in gilt, marbled endpapers and edges. A fine copy in an attractive contemporary morocco Prize Binding, with contemporary prize inscription in a fine hand (dated "Christmas 1893") on front blank. See other undated and dated illustrated and nonillustrated editions in the collection by Frederick Warne and Co. published in the 1870s, 1880s, and 1890s under the various series: "The 'Lansdowne' Poets," "The 'Arundel' Poets," "The 'Chandos' Poets," "The 'Imperial' Poets, "The 'Chandos' Classics," "The 'Albion' Edition," and the "Cabinet Poets." Not in Kohler.

2407. Variant of Preceding, original brown cloth (a bit rubbed), Milton's name lettered in gilt on front cover, spine lettered in gilt ("The Poetical Works Of Milton With Life, Notes, &c." at the top, "Albion Edition" in the middle, and "F. Warne & Co." at the bottom), with gilt rules at the top and the bottom, brown endpapers. A nice copy in original publisher's binding, with contemporary presentation inscription in a neat hand (dated 1894) on front blank. Not in Kohler.

2408. THE POETICAL WORKS OF JOHN MILTON With An Introduction By The Rev. Theodore Alois Buckley, M.A. Sir John Lubbock's Hundred Books. *London and New York[:] George Routledge And Sons Limited[.] n.d. [ca. 1893].* First edition thus. 8vo, 448pp., half-title, "Printed by Ballantyne, Hanson & Co. At the Ballantyne Press" on verso of title page, "Printed by Ballantyne, Hanson & Co. Edinburgh & London" at bottom of last page, original green linen texture cloth, spine lettered in gilt within gilt rules. A nice copy. Stevens 238, stating "T.A. Buckley nominal editor, but the brief footnotes are not critical"; Kohler 420, "[ca. 1893]," reporting "Not in Cambridge University Library."

2409. Variant of Preceding, original red pebble morocco (joints a bit rubbed), gilt rules on covers and spine, spine lettered in gilt, raised bands, marbled endpapers, a.e.g. A nice copy in an attractive Victorian publisher's full red morocco binding. Stevens 238; Kohler 420.

2410. THE POETICAL WORKS OF JOHN MILTON With Illustrations By W. Harvey[.] *London[:] George Routledge And Sons, Limited[,] Broadway, Ludgate Hill[.] Manchester And New York[.] 1894*. Large 8vo, 448pp., half-title with a listing of "Routledge's Popular Poets" on verso (including Milton), frontispiece portrait of *Milton Dictating* from an engraving by Dalziel (after William Harvey, although unsigned), vignette of "Milton's Cottage, Chalfont, Bucks" on title page, six illustration plates engraved by Dalziel after William Harvey: for Books I, X, and XI of *PL*, for Book I of *PR*, for *SA*, and for *C*, notes at bottom of page, "Printed by Ballantyne, Hanson & Co., Edinburgh and London" printed at bottom of last page, original decorated green cloth (spine a little faded), front cover elaborately decorated in embossed foliage with central gilt border trim incorporating Milton's name in gilt, spine elaborately decorated in embossed gilt foliage with gilt lettering, back cover with large central embossed decorative piece in blind, t.e.g., others untrimmed and partially unopened. A very nice copy in an attractive publisher's binding, with early inscription on fly-leaf. See 1893 single volume edition by Routledge, similar to the edition here, with illustrations as here, but without identification as being by Harvey as here and in a much smaller 8vo format than that here. See 1899 edition by Routledge, with a listing of "Routledge's Popular Poets" on verso of half-title as here, with illustrations after Harvey as here. The first edition of Milton's *PW* by George Routledge and Co. was published in 1853 (also listed here with further editions by Routledge and by Routledge and Sons cited). Kohler 421, reporting "Not in the British Library. Not in the Bodleian Library. Not in Cambridge University Library."

2411. THE POETICAL WORKS OF JOHN MILTON. With Memoir, Explanatory Notes, Etc. The "Albion" Edition. *London: Frederick Warne And Co. And New York. 1894*. 8vo, xxvi+581pp., half-title with "Morrison And Gibb, Printers, Edinburgh" on verso and printed again on verso of last page, central crescent on title page consisting of small laurel wings with a horseshoe at the center, half-title for *SA* preceded by small decorative piece on verso of last page of *PR*, notes at bottom of page, original red cloth (spine faded, covers a bit smudged), Milton's name lettered in gilt on front cover and spine, covers ruled in blind, gilt rules at top and bottom of spine, black endpapers. A good copy with contemporary prize label (dated 1896) on flyleaf. See copy of 1888 "Albion" edition published by Frederick Warne and Co. in London and New York, as here, and other editions cited there. Not in Kohler.

2412. Variant of Preceding, original three-quarter maroon morocco, marbled paper over boards (some foxing to the blank endpapers and to half-title), gilt rules on covers, gilt devices on spine in the panels, green morocco label with gilt lettering and gilt rules, raised bands (a bit rubbed), marbled endpapers and edges. A nice copy in a handsome variant publisher's binding. Not in Kohler.

2413. THE POETICAL WORKS OF JOHN MILTON Edited With Memoir, Introductions, Notes, And An Essay On Milton's English And Versification By David Masson, M.A., LL.D. Professor Of Rhetoric And English Literature In The University Of Edinburgh[.] *New York [:] Macmillan And Co. And London[.] 1894*. All rights reserved. 3 volumes 8vo, xviii+536pp.,+vi+642pp.,+vi+618pp., half-title with decorative piece consisting of publisher's initials on verso each volume, frontispiece vignette portrait each volume (Milton age ten ["engraved by Edwd. Radclyffe"], age twenty-one [unsigned], and age sixty-two [unsigned]), protective tissue guard each volume, title page each volume, preface (dated 1890), volume 1, half-title for some of the poems, original green cloth (a bit rubbed, slim white mark on back cover, volume 1, portrait plates slightly foxed, protective tissue guards a bit more so), spines lettered in gilt, t.e.g., other edges untrimmed. A nice set. The first edition thus by Masson was published in 1874; a revised edition in a three-volume smaller octavo format (the first thus) was published in 1882; the second edition thus, revised and enlarged, was published in 1890—all sets listed here. Not in Kohler.

2414. THE POETICAL WORKS OF JOHN MILTON. With Memoir, Explanatory Notes, etc. The "Grosvenor" Poets. *London & Glasgow: William Collins, Sons & Co., Limited. n.d. [ca. 1894]*. 8vo, xxvi+581pp., half-title (with small stamp "The Book Shop" in red) with "Morrison And Gibb, Printers, Edinburgh" printed on verso, frontispiece portrait (of a youngish looking middle-aged Milton, unsigned, with labeling "London: Frederick Warne & Co." at bottom), protective tissue guard, eight illustration plates after engravings by Dalziel: one for *L'A*, four for *PL* (Books

I, IV, VIII, and XII), one for *SA*, one for *On His Deceased Wife*, and one for *Latin Epigram VII* ("Ad Eandem"—the illustration titled *Milton Meeting Leonora Baroni at Cardinal Barberini's House*), decorative tailpiece at the end of *PR*, half-title for *SA*, red border around text, "Morrison And Gibb, Printers, Edinburgh" on verso of last page, notes at bottom of page, contemporary padded crushed red calf (spine ends slightly rubbed), Milton's name lettered in gilt on front cover, title lettered in gilt on spine, dark red endpapers, a.e.g. A nice copy with contemporary prize citation (dated 1895) tipped in on front pastedown. Not in Kohler.

2415. THE POETICAL WORKS OF JOHN MILTON: With Introductions By David Masson, M.A., L.L.D., Professor Of Rhetoric And English Literature In The University Of Edinburgh[.] The Globe Edition. *London: Macmillan And Co. And New York. 1895. The Right of Translation and Reproduction is Reserved.* 8vo, xi+625pp., half-title (with emblem consisting of the letters of Macmillan and Co. on verso), "Preface" (dated 1877), "Contents," "Introduction to *Paradise Lost*" with several diagrams, half-title for some of the poems and sections, "Printed by R. Clay & Son LD" on verso of title page, "Printed by Richard Clay & Son Limited, London & Bungay" on verso of last page, original dark green cloth, with central embossed vignette portrait of Milton in gilt on front cover and Milton's name in gilt in lower right-hand corner, spine lettered in gilt ("The Works Of Milton"), t.e.g., others untrimmed. A fine copy in publisher's cloth binding, with advertisement leaf bound in at the end. The Globe edition of Milton's *PW* was first published in March 1877 (also listed here with further editions by Globe cited). Not in Kohler.

2416. THE POETICAL WORKS OF JOHN MILTON. *Published By The Grand Colosseum Warehouse Co. (Founded by Mr. Walter Wilson in 1869.) General Offices And Wholesale Warehouses: 60 & 70, Jamaica Street, Glasgow. Branches in all the Principal Towns In Scotland. n.d. [ca. 1895].* First edition thus? 8vo, half-title (with listing of editions "Uniform with this Volume" on verso), viii+460pp., decorative head- and tailpieces, original bright red ribbed grain cloth (bit rubbed along joints, slight waterstain along inner top joint of front cover without affecting inside, modest staining of outer edges of last few pages), small emblem in blind at center of front cover and bottom of spine, front cover lettered in gilt ("Milton's Poems"), spine lettered in gilt ("Milton"), bevelled edges, t.e.g. A nice copy in publisher's cloth binding, with contemporary prize presentation inscription dated "July 1895" on fly-leaf. Kohler 433, dating its copy "ca. 1900" and reporting "Not in the British Library. Not in the Bodleian Library. Not in Cambridge University Library."

2417. Variant of Preceding, original green ribbed grain cloth, decorated as preceding copy. A nice copy in a variant publisher's binding, with large art nouveau bookplate on front pastedown. Kohler 433.

2418. THE POETICAL WORKS OF JOHN MILTON With Memoir and Notes. Complete Edition. Illustrated. *New York[:] New York Publishing Company, 26 City Hall Place, 1895.* 8vo, xii+563pp., notes at bottom of page, original three-quarter gold cloth (a little rubbed, some slight markings on spine, pages age-browned and rather brittle), marbled paper over boards, red morocco label lettered in gilt with decorative gilt trim and gilt rules on spine, slightly raised bands within gilt rules, small decorative gilt pieces within the panels, decorated endpapers, marbled edges. A good copy. Although "Illustrated" is printed on the title page, there are no illustrations included and none appear to be missing. Not in Kohler.

2419. Variant of Preceding, original maroon pebble calf (a little rubbed, pages a little age-browned), spine lettered in gilt ("Poetical Works Milton" at the top, "Empire Edition" in the middle), slightly raised bands, t.e.g. A good copy for an edition printed on the poor quality paper this is printed on, in original publisher's binding. Similar to preceding edition by New York Publishing Company, but with "Empire Edition" lettered in gilt on spine and without any reference to "Illustrated" on title page. Not in Kohler.

2420. Variant of Preceding, original maroon silk (a little rubbed, pages a little age-browned), central emblem in blind on front cover, spine lettered in gilt ("Poetical Works Milton" at the top, "Empire Edition" in the middle), slightly raised bands, t.e.g. A nice copy, fresh and tight, in a slightly variant publisher's binding, with contemporary signature (dated 1898) on fly-leaf. Not in Kohler.

2421. THE POETICAL WORKS OF JOHN MILTON With Memoir, Etc. Duodecimo Edition[.] *New York[:] Frederick A. Stokes Company Publishers[.] n. d. [ca. 1895].* 8vo, xvi+221+[1]pp., title page in red and black, reproducing in black at the center the emblem from the incunabula printing of *Ship of Fools* of a 'scholar' poring over a book with a stack of folios around him, "Prefatory Memoir Of Milton," original half white cloth elaborately decorated in a gilt pattern with "John Milton" in embossed gilt within a circle of gilt trim on front cover, half green silk decorated in a pattern of branches and leaves (somewhat worn), spine lettered in gilt ("Poems" at the top and "John Milton" at the bottom), with advertisement leaf bound in at the end, including an edition of Milton. Although a bit worn, still a fair copy in what was originally a very lovely publisher's binding, with contemporary presentation inscription (dated

"Oct. 3 / [18]95") on fly-leaf. See dated tall 8vo illustrated edition published by "Frederick A. Stokes & Brother" in 1888 (possible first edition thus, see copies listed here with further editions by Stokes cited). Not in Kohler.

2422. Variant of Preceding, original half white cloth elaborately decorated in a gilt pattern with "John Milton" in embossed gilt within a circle of gilt trim on front cover, half red silk decorated in contrasting light and dark red with a pattern of gilt decorations (a little worn, pages a bit age-darkened), spine lettered in gilt ("Poems" at the top and "John Milton" at the bottom), with advertisement leaf bound in at end, including an edition of Milton. Although a little worn, still a fair copy in a lovely variant publisher's binding, with contemporary presentation inscription (dated "April 17, 1900") on fly-leaf. Not in Kohler.

2423. THE POETICAL WORKS OF JOHN MILTON. *New York: A. L. Burt, Publisher. n.d. [ca. 1895].* (?)First edition thus (by Burt). 8vo, 562+[11]pp., "Sketch Of The Life Of John Milton," original blue linen texture cloth, spine lettered in gilt ("Milton's Poems") with bright decorative gilt trim at top and bottom, decorated endpapers, with advertisement leaves for "Burt's Home Library" bound in at end. A very fine copy in an attractive American publisher's binding. See undated edition of *PL* and *PR* published by Burt in a manner similar to this edition about this same time (ca. 1895). Not in Kohler.

2424. THE POETICAL WORKS OF JOHN MILTON With A Biographical Sketch Of The Author[.] New Revised Edition[.] *New York[:] A. L. Burt, Publisher. n.d. [ca. 1895].* Revised edition. 8vo, xxv+[i]+514pp., frontispiece portrait plate reproducing engraving of Milton by D. Grosch, protective tissue guard, "Sketch Of The Life Of John Milton," original green linen texture cloth (worn), decorative black border trim on front cover with central gilt emblem, spine lettered in gilt ("Milton's Poetical Works") with decorative gilt trim at top and bottom and with central gilt emblem repeated from front cover, t.e.g. An okay copy in publisher's cloth binding. Not in Kohler.

2425. THE POETICAL WORKS OF JOHN MILTON With A Biographical Sketch Of The Author[.] New Revised Edition[.] *[No Place—(?)New York:] A. L. Burt Company, Publishers, n.d. [ca. 1895].* 8vo, xxv+[i]+514pp., frontispiece portrait plate reproducing engraving of Milton by D. Grosch, protective tissue guard (title page darkened a bit because of tissue guard), "Sketch Of The Life Of John Milton," original red linen texture cloth (a few light underlinings and markings in pencil), spine lettered in gilt ("Milton's Poems" and "The Home Library") with gilt rules, t.e.g. A nice copy in a variant publisher's binding. Not in Kohler.

2426. Variant of Preceding, original limp brown suede leather, Milton's name in gilt at top of front cover, silk endpapers (slightly stained, back pastedowns cracked on inside), t.e.g. A nice copy with variant publisher's imprint (without place of publication given), in a variant publisher's binding. Not in Kohler.

2427. Variant of Preceding, in a well-preserved original binding of limp leather, a binding usually worn and often fragile, without place of publication given on title page, and with a variant frontispiece portrait plate reproducing an engraving of Milton seated by a table (unsigned, but after Faed), different from other editions by Burt here. A very nice copy. Not in Kohler.

2428. THE POETICAL WORKS OF JOHN MILTON With A Biographical Sketch Of The Author[.] New Revised Edition[.] *A. L. Burt Company, Publishers, 52-58 Duane Street, New York[.] n.d. [ca. 1895 / ca. 1900].* 8vo, xxv+[i]+514pp., frontispiece portrait plate reproducing engraving of Milton by D. Grosch, protective tissue guard, "Sketch Of The Life Of John Milton," original red linen texture cloth (faded), spine lettered in gilt ("Milton's Poems" and "The Home Library") with gilt rules, t.e.g. A good copy, fresh and clean within, with variant publisher's imprint, in a variant publisher's binding. Not in Kohler (although Kohler 435 cites an edition very similar to this, dating it "[ca. 1900]" and reporting "Not in Williamson. Not in the British Library. Not in the Bodleian Library. Not in Cambridge University Library").

2429. THE POETICAL WORKS OF JOHN MILTON With Introductory Memoir[,] Notes, Bibliography[,] Etc. The "Imperial" Poets. *London[:] Frederick Warne And Co. And New York[.] 1896.* 8vo, 607+[1]pp., half-title with red border trim and with decorative piece on verso with red border trim, early photograph of a young Milton with long, curly hair (unsigned) mounted as frontispiece, with the label "Portrait of Milton" printed in the center at the bottom along with "Foulton's Series" printed to the left, red border around photograph, protective tissue guard, decorative device at center of title page, decorative device on verso with red border trim, five additional early unsigned photographs of various scenes and settings mounted as illustrations, each on its own page, each labeled "Foulton's Series" with the appropriate passage cited beneath the photograph-illustration, red border around each photograph-illustration, red border around text, half-title for *SA*, two-page "Bibliography" at the end with "Printed By Morrison And Gibb, Limited, Edinburgh" at bottom of last page, contemporary tree calf, decorative gilt border trim on covers, with central gilt device on front cover, elaborately gilt-decorated spine, red morocco label with gilt lettering and decorative gilt trim, slightly raised bands with decorative gilt trim, broad inner dentelles finely tooled in blind, outer dentelles trimmed in gilt, marbled endpapers and edges, printed prize label (dated 1897) on front pastedown. A very fine copy in a lovely Prize Binding, with early photographs mounted as illustrations. See undated ca. 1880 illustrated edition of "The 'Imperial' Poets" listed earlier by Frederick Warne and Co. (one copy in a lovely prize binding as here, the other in fine polished calf) with the same photographs mounted as illustrations, each labeled "Foulton's Series" as here, but with printed instructions on each photograph-illustration as to where each is to be placed. Not in Kohler.

2430. THE POETICAL WORKS OF JOHN MILTON With Introductory Memoir[,] Notes, Biblio-graphy[,] Etc. The "Albion" Edition. *London[:] Frederick Warne And Co. And New York[.] 1896.* 8vo, 607+[1]pp., half-title, title page in red and black, emblem of the press (small laurel wings with a horseshoe) at the center of title page, above is "The 'Albion' Edition," new "Preface" (dated "April, 1896" and signed "L. Valentine"), half-title for *SA*, notes at bottom of page, "Bibliography" on last two pages with "Printed By Morrison And Gibb Limited, Edinburgh" at bottom of last page, original green cloth (a bit rubbed, pages slightly age-browned), covers ruled in blind at top and bottom, with Milton's name in gilt at center of front cover, spine lettered in gilt (title, "Albion Edition," and "F. Warne & Co.") with gilt rules at top and bottom, black endpapers. A good copy in publisher's binding, with contemporary signature on front blank. See copy of 1888 "Albion Edition" published by Frederick Warne and Co. in London and New York, as here, and other editions cited there. Stevens 241; Kohler 422.

2431. THE POETICAL WORKS OF JOHN MILTON With Introductory Memoir[,] Notes, Biblio-graphy[,] Etc. *London[:] Frederick Warne And Co. And New York[.] n.d. [ca. 1896].* 8vo, 607+[1]pp., half-title, title page in red and black, emblem of the press (small laurel wings with a horseshoe) at the center of title page, "Preface" (dated "April, 1896" and signed "L. Valentine"), half-title for *SA*, notes at bottom of page, "Bibliography" on last two pages with "Printed By Morrison And Gibb Limited, Edinburgh" at bottom of last page, original blue linen texture cloth (a bit rubbed, especially spine ends and corners, former owner's name in ink on title page), covers ruled in blind at top and bottom, with Milton's name in gilt at center of front cover, spine elaborately decorated and lettered in gilt with small laurel wreath in gilt at the top, title ("Milton's Poetical Works") in gilt just below, long-armed torch in gilt with long branches in gilt on either sided framed by gilt borders, with "F. Warne & Co." lettered in gilt at the bottom, decorated orange endpapers with "The Chandos Classics" lettered in white at the center. A good copy in publisher's binding, with contemporary signature on front blank. Kohler 434, dating its copy "[ca. 1900]" and reporting "Not in Williamson. Not in the British Library. Not in the Bodleian Library. Not in Cambridge University Library."

2432. THE POETICAL WORKS OF JOHN MILTON. With Memoir, Explanatory Notes, &c. *London: Frederick Warne And Co. And New York. n.d. [ca. 1896].* 8vo, xxvi+581pp., half-title with "Morrison And Gibb, Printers, Edinburgh" on verso and printed again on verso of last page, emblem of the press (small laurel wings with a horseshoe) at the center of title page, half-title for *SA*, notes at bottom of page, original maroon pebble leather over limp boards (a bit rubbed at corners and a top and bottom of spine), Milton's name scripted in large gilt letters at top left corner of front cover and similarly scripted in smaller gilt letters at top of spine, dark green endpapers, a.e.g. A lovely copy in a handsome publisher's binding, with contemporary signature (dated 1896) on half-title. Kohler 434, dating its copy "[ca. 1900]" and reporting "Not in Williamson. Not in the British Library. Not in the Bodleian Library. Not in Cambridge University Library."

2433. THE POETICAL WORKS OF JOHN MILTON: Edited, With Memoir, Introductions, Notes, And An Essay On Milton's English And Versification, By David Masson, M.A. LL.D., Historiographer Royal For Scotland, Professor Of Rhetoric And English Literature In the University Of Edinburgh. *London[:] Macmillan And Co., Ltd. New York: The Macmillan Co. 1896. All rights reserved.* 3 volumes. Small 8vo, x+lxix+312pp.,+[i]+374pp.,+[vi]+420pp., half-title each volume with decorative piece consisting of publisher's initials on verso of half-title in volume 3, frontispiece vignette portrait each volume (Milton age ten ["engraved by Edwd. Radclyffe"], age twenty-one [unsigned], and age sixty-two [unsigned]), separate title page each volume, preface (dated "Edinburgh: September 1882") and new to that edition) with a second preface (dated "Edinburgh: April 1893" and new to that edition), "Contents," "Memoir Of Milton," volume 1, various half-titles, "Printed by R. & R. Clark, Limited, Edinburgh" at the bottom of the last page in each volume, original red cloth (a little rubbed, some underlining and notes in pencil in a neat hand in volume 2), spines lettered in gilt with gilt rules at top and bottom, edges untrimmed. A nice, tall set in a publisher's cloth binding, with early signature on fly-leaf of each volume. The first edition thus, based on Masson's earlier three-volume edition published in 1874, was published in 1882; it was reprinted in 1893, 1896 (set here), and in 1903—all sets listed here. Williamson 33; Kohler 419, reporting "Not in the British Library. Not in the Bodleian Library. Not in Cambridge University Library."

2434. THE POETICAL WORKS OF JOHN MILTON With Introductions By David Masson, M.A., L.L.D. Professor Of Rhetoric And English Literature In the University Of Edinburgh[.] The Globe Edition. *London[:] Macmillan And Co., Limited[;] New York: The Macmillan Company[,] 1897.* 8vo, xi+625+[2]pp., half-title (with emblem consisting of the letters of Macmillan and Co. on verso), "Preface" (dated 1877), "Contents," "Introduction to *PL*" with several diagrams and other introductory material as in the first editions, half-title for some of the sections and poems, "Richard Clay & Sons, Limited, London & Bungay" printed on verso of last page, original green buckram, with central embossed vignette portrait of Milton in gilt on front cover and Milton's name in gilt at lower right-hand corner, spine lettered in gilt ("The Works Of Milton"), t.e.g. A fine copy in an attractive publisher's binding. Bound in at the end: two pages advertising "New Uniform And Complete Editions Of The Poets Large Crown 8vo [including Milton's Poetical Works With Introductions By Professor Masson], cloth gilt, $1.75. Bound in morocco, extra, $4.00." The Globe edition of Milton's *PW* was first published in March 1877 (also listed here with further editions by Globe cited). Scarce. Not in Kohler.

2435. MILTON'S POETICAL WORKS With Introduction by Arthur Waugh[.] *London and Glasgow[:] Collins' Clear-Type Press. n.d. [ca. 1898].* First edition thus? 8vo, x+596pp. (with Arabic pagination beginning at "3"), half-title (with "Printed in Great Britain" on verso), large tinted frontispiece portrait plate of Milton seated by a table with right outstretched "After Faed—Courtesy Rischgitz Studios," title-page plate elaborately decorated in art nouveau style signed "Garth Jones Norfolk," "Biographical Introduction" by Arthur Waugh printed in double column at the beginning, "Notes" and "Index of First Lines" at the end, original highly glazed crushed maroon morocco over limp boards (spine a little faded, earlier ownership signature and stamp on front blank), Milton's name in gilt on front cover, title lettered in gilt within decorative gilt trim at top of spine and "Collins" in gilt at the bottom, t.e. red. A lovely copy in an attractive possible publisher's morocco binding. See variant edition following; see also undated ca. 1903 illustrated edition published by Collins' Clear-Type Press "With Introduction and Notes by Arthur Waugh. With Four Black and White Illustrations." Stevens 232, if referring to this book, calling it "Illustrated," dates it "ca. 1890"; Not in Kohler.

2436. MILTON'S POETICAL WORKS With an Introduction by Arthur Waugh[.] *Collins[,] London & Glasgow. n.d. [ca. 1898].* Variant edition. 8vo, x+596pp. (with Arabic pagination beginning at "3"), half-title (with "Printed in Great Britain" on verso), frontispiece portrait plate of Milton seated by a table with hand reaching outward "After Faed—Courtesy Rischgitz Studios," small decoration on title page, "Biographical Introduction" by Arthur Waugh printed in double column at the beginning, "Notes" and "Index of First Lines" at the end, original crushed blue morocco over limp boards, gilt emblem (possibly of the press) on front cover, spine lettered in gilt (""Poetical Works Of Milton" at the top and "Collins" at the bottom), same gilt emblem from front cover repeated in smaller form, decorative gilt trim at top and bottom, light blue marbled endpapers, t.e.g., blue silk ribbon marker, contemporary bookplate (which has come loose from fly-leaf). A fine copy, virtually mint, in a lovely (possible publisher's morocco binding, in original blue card-paper slipcase (a little worn, joints reglued), with "British Made" lightly stamped in blind in the lower corner. A variant edition from the preceding, with variant publisher's imprint, with a variant frontispiece portrait plate, not tinted and with the image not as large and therefore not as imposing as in the preceding frontispiece, with no title-page plate, and in a variant publisher's binding. See also ca. 1903 Collins' Clear-Type Press illustrated edition cited in preceding copy. Stevens 232, if referring to this book, calling it "Illustrated," dates it "ca. 1890"; Not in Kohler.

2437. THE POETICAL WORKS OF JOHN MILTON. *Edinburgh[:] William P. Nimmo, Hay, & Mitchell[,] 1898.* 8vo, xxxvii+[iii]+440pp., unsigned engraved frontispiece portrait plate of a middle-aged Milton, engraved and printed title pages, with vignette illustration (of the poet being inspired by heavenly choirs) after F. Borders on engraved title plate ("Edinburgh: W. P. Nimmo, Hay, & Mitchell." n.d.), vignette illustration (of a young boy in a setting in nature with a cane laying beside him) signed with the initials "WS" on printed title, life of Milton by J. M. Ross, half-title for *PL*, *PR*, *SA*, *C*, *Ar* and *MP*, "Ballantyne Press: Edinburgh And London" printed at bottom of last page, original crushed maroon calf over padded boards (spine faded, joints broken from within, spine ends chipped), Milton's name lettered in gilt at top of front cover, spine lettered in gilt ("Milton's Poetical Works") above small decorative gilt trim, decorated gold endpapers, a.e.g. A nice copy. The possible first edition thus by

Nimmo was published in 1865, illustrated (also listed here with further Nimmo editions cited). Not in Kohler.

2438. THE POETICAL WORKS OF JOHN MILTON With Introductory Memoir[,] Notes, Biblio-graphy[,] Etc. The "Albion" Edition[.] *London[:] Frederick Warne And Co. And New York[,] 1898.* 8vo, 607+[1]pp., half-title, engraved frontispiece portrait plate (unsigned, of a long-haired, youngish Milton, labeled "F. Warne & Co." without date), protective tissue guard, title page in red and black with emblem of the press (small laurel wings with a horseshoe) at the center of title page, "Preface" (dated "April, 1896" and signed "L. Valentine"), half-title for *SA*, notes at bottom of page, "Bibliography" on last two pages with "Printed By Morrison And Gibb Limited, Edinburgh" at bottom of last page, original bright grained orange cloth (a bit rubbed, earlier ownership signature and list of owners on front blanks), front cover decorated in gilt and gold with Milton's name in gilt on a recessed piece of circular maroon leather within decorative gilt trim, spine trimmed in contrasting darker orange, decorated dark green endpapers, a.e.g. A nice copy in a publisher's binding reflective of the period. See copy of 1888 "Albion" edition published by Frederick Warne and Co. in London and New York, as here, and other editions cited there, the engraved frontispiece portrait new with this Albion edition. Kohler 423, reporting "Not in Williamson. Not in the British Library. Not in the Bodleian Library. Not in Cambridge University Library."

2439. Variant of Preceding, original crushed black leather over padded boards (a bit rubbed at top of spine and along corners), Milton's name in gilt at top of front cover, spine lettered in gilt, marbled endpapers, a.e.g. A nice copy in a handsome variant publisher's binding. Kohler 423.

2440. THE POETICAL WORKS OF JOHN MILTON With Introductory Memoir[,] Notes, Bibliography[,] Etc. *London[:] Frederick Warne And Co[.] And New York[,] n.d.[ca. 1899].* 8vo, 607+[1]pp., half-title, "Preface" (dated "April, 1896" and signed "L. Valentine"), half-title for *SA*, notes at bottom of page, "Bibliography" on last two pages with "Printed By Morrison And Gibb Limited, Edinburgh" at bottom of last page, original pink cloth (spine a bit faded, edges slightly waterstained sometime ago), front cover with Milton's name in large green letters outlined in gilt trim within a thick gilt rule at the top with a large green- and red-leaved branch behind it at the center and a partial orb in black relief behind it at the left, and at the bottom right corner "Memoir, Notes &c." lettered within a scroll shaded in green with a dark green-leaved branch behind it, spine lettered with Milton's name in embossed black letters within a bright, wide gilt band near the top with a green- and red-leaved branch behind, with "F. Warne & Co" in small gilt letters at the bottom, "Cabinet Poets" stamped in bind within a decorative circular device at the center of the back cover. A good copy in a pretty publisher's binding. Not in Kohler.

2441. THE POETICAL WORKS OF JOHN MILTON With Illustrations By W. Harvey[.] *London: George Routledge & Sons, Limited[,] Broadway House, Ludgate Hill, E.C. MDCCCXCIX (1899).* 8vo, 448pp., half-title with a listing of "Routledge's Popular Poets" on verso (including Milton), frontispiece portrait of *Milton Dictating* from an engraving by Dalziel after William Harvey, title page in red and black, illustration plates from engravings by Dalziel after William Harvey, original red cloth (spine a little soiled, early owner's name neatly written on fly-leaf), gilt lettering in lower corner of front cover ("Milton's Poetical Works"), spine lettered in gilt (title at the top, "Routledge" at the bottom), t.e.g., others untrimmed, "Printed by Ballantyne, Hanson & Co., Edinburgh and London" printed at bottom of last page. A good copy in a publisher's cloth binding. See 1894 edition by Routledge, with a listing of "Routledge's Popular Poets" on verso of half-title as here, with illustrations after Harvey as here. The first edition of Milton's *PW* by George Routledge and Co. was published in 1853 (also listed here with further editions by Routledge and by Routledge and Sons cited). Not in Kohler.

2442. THE POETICAL WORKS OF JOHN MILTON With Introductory Memoir[,] Notes, Bibliography[,] Etc. The "Albion" Edition[.] *London[:] Frederick Warne And Co. And New York[,] 1899.* 8vo, 607+[1]pp., half-title, unsigned engraved frontispiece portrait plate of a long-haired, youngish Milton (labeled "F. Warne & Co." without date), protective tissue guard with slight offprint, title page in red and black with emblem of the press (small laurel wings with a horseshoe) at the center, "Preface" (dated "April, 1896" and signed "L. Valentine"), half-title for *SA*, notes at bottom of page, "Bibliography" on last two pages with "Printed By Morrison And Gibb Limited, Edinburgh" at bottom of last page, contemporary tree calf (joints weak, spine a little rubbed, blank before half-title missing), covers decorated in finely tooled gilt trim, spine decorated in gilt trim (faded), maroon label with gilt lettering and decorative gilt trim, inner and outer dentelles finely tooled in gilt, marbled endpapers, a.e.g. A nice copy with early bookplate on front pastedown. See copy of 1888 "Albion" edition" published by Frederick Warne and Co. in London and New York, as here, and other editions cited there. Kohler 427, indicating "Frontispiece portrait engraved by

W. Holl," and reporting "Not in Williamson. Not in the British Library. Not in the Bodleian Library. Not in Cambridge University Library."

2443. THE POETICAL WORKS OF JOHN MILTON[.] English and Latin Edited, With A Bibliographical Introduction, Life Of Milton, And An Analysis Of Addison's Criticism On Paradise Lost By John Bradshaw, M.A. LL.D. Editor Of The Poetical Works Of Gray, Chesterfield's Letters, And An English Anthology[.] In Two Volumes. *London[:] George Bell & Sons[,] 1899.* 2 volumes. Second edition thus. 8vo, 8vo, lxiv+[1]+337pp.,+xvi+387pp., half-title each volume ("The Aldine Edition Of The British Poets"), frontispiece vignette portrait by H. Robinson, protective tissue guard, volume 1, emblem of the press on title page each volume, "Preface" (dated 1891), "Contents," "Introduction," "The Life And Writings Of Milton," "Analysis Of Addison's Criticism On *Paradise Lost*" (dated 1871), volume 1, "Prefatory Note: 'The Milton Window,' 'The Portraits Of Milton,' 'Milton's Cottage'" (dated 1891), volume 2, half-title for some of the poems and each book of *PL* and *PR*, "Chiswick Press:— Charles Whittingham And Co. Tooks Court, Chancery Lane, London" printed beneath the seal of the Chiswick Press on verso of last page, volume 1, "Chiswick Press:— C. Charles Whittingham And Co. Tooks Court, Chancery Lane." printed at bottom of last page, volume 2, original red cloth, spines lettered in gilt with title at the top ("Milton's Poetical Works" and volume number just below), "Bradshaw" lettered in gilt in the middle, emblem of the press in gilt near the bottom, and "Aldine Edition" lettered in gilt at the bottom, edges untrimmed, volume 2 unopened. A very nice set in publisher's cloth binding. Reprint of 1892 edition, which is a new edition of the Aldine Milton and continues on in that honorable tradition; the set is reprinted again in 1908–9—both sets listed here. Not in Kohler.

2444. [POETICAL WORKS] AN INTRODUCTION TO THE PROSE AND POETICAL WORKS OF JOHN MILTON Comprising all the Autobiographical Passages in his Works, the more Explicit Presentations of his Ideas of True Liberty[,] Comus, Lycidas, and Samson Agonistes With Notes and Forewords By Hiram Corson, L.L.D. Professor of English Literature in the Cornell University[.] *New York[:] The Macmillan Company[;] London: Macmillan & Co., Ltd. 1899. All rights reserved.* First edition thus. 8vo, xxxii+303+[2]pp., half-title with publisher's initials on verso, frontispiece portrait plate of Milton (of Faithorne portrait although unsigned), protective tissue guard, original blue cloth (signature and short-hand notes on fly-leaf), spine lettered in gilt with gilt rule at top and at bottom. A very nice copy with advertisement leaf for two other works by Corson bound in at end. Laid in: two-page letter (dated 1948) signed by Douglas Bush, editor of the Oxford Standard Authors edition of Milton. Not in Kohler.

2445. THE POETICAL WORKS OF JOHN MILTON Edited After The Original Texts By The Rev. H. C. Beeching, M.A., Balliol College, Oxford[,] Clark Lecturer At Trinity College, Cambridge[.] *Oxford[:] At The Clarendon Press[,] 1900.* First edition thus. Royal 8vo, xiii+[3]+554+[1]pp., half-title with "Henry Frowde, M.A. Publisher To The University Of Oxford," seal, and "London, Edinburgh, And New York" printed on verso, frontispiece facsimile plate "From The Autograph Manuscript Sent To Rous, And Preserved In The Bodleian Library Oxford," protective tissue guard, preface dated 1899 (new to this edition), facsimile reproductions of the title pages of the 1645 first and 1673 second editions of *P*, of the title pages of *Justa Edovardo King* (1638), of *C* (1637), of *Joannis Miltoni Londinensis Poemata* (1645), and of the 1667 first edition of *PL* and the 1671 first edition of *PR* and *SA*, a second facsimile plate of "From The Autograph Manuscript Of The Minor Poems Preserved In Trinity College Cambridge [*Comus*, 672–706]" with protective tissue guard, appendix, original blue cloth, central blind emblem on front cover, spine lettered in gilt with decorative gilt trim at top an bottom, fore- and bottom edges untrimmed. A nice copy in publisher's binding, with neat signature of John Walker Lucas on fly-leaf. Laid in: two-page typed letter to Lucas (dated 1948) signed by Douglas Bush, editor of the Oxford Standard Authors edition of Milton, dismissing Norman Douglas's view of Milton as a plagiarist of Salandra. Tipped-in on fly-leaf: one-page hand-written letter (dated "17 July 08") from the editor, H. C. Beeching. Kohler 431.

2446. Variant of Preceding, original reddish-brown cloth (small moisture stain at bottom of front cover), printed paper label (a bit worn and chipped) on spine. A very good copy in a variant publisher's binding, from the library of George Charles Williamson, with his bookplate, and with a one-page hand-written letter from the editor, Beeching, to Williamson, dated "17 July 08" and signed at the bottom, tipped in on fly-leaf. Kohler 431.

2447. THE POETICAL WORKS OF JOHN MILTON Edited After The Original Texts By The Rev. H. C. Beeching, M.A. Balliol College, Oxford[,] Clark Lecturer At Trinity College, Cambridge[.] *Oxford[:] At The Clarendon Press[,] 1900.* First edition thus; variant issue. 8vo, xiii+[3]+554pp., half-title with the seal of "Henry Frowde,

M.A. Publisher To The University Of Oxford" and "London, Edinburgh, And New York" printed on verso, frontispiece plate reproducing "Engraving after the Painting by Faithorne," protective tissue guard, preface dated 1899 (new to this edition, the same as in preceding edition), facsimile reproductions of the title pages of the 1645 first and 1673 second editions of *P*, of the title pages of *Justa Edovardo King* (1638), of *C* (1637), of *Joannis Miltoni Londinensis Poemata* (1645), and of the 1667 first edition of *PL* and the 1671 first edition of *PR* and *SA*, appendix, original tree calf (back joint cracked), decorative gilt border trim on covers, elaborately gilt-decorated spine within the panels, black morocco label with gilt lettering and gilt trim, raised bands with decorative gilt trim, inner and outer dentelles finely tooled in gilt, marbled endpapers, a.e.g. A nice copy of this variant issue: the main differences being the replacement of the frontispiece facsimile plate with a portrait plate and the dropping of the second facsimile plate; the size is also shorter than the preceding issue by 1 ¾". According to the preface here and in preceding copies: "This edition of Milton's Poetry is a reprint, as careful as Editor and Printers have been able to make it, from the earliest printed copies of the several poems." Kohler 432.

Beeching's text became the standard text for the next fifty years and was variously reprinted, including: 1904 (as a new edition thus, see reference, e.g., in 1946 and 1950 editions in which each state "This edition of Milton's Poems was first published in 1904"—perhaps because of the change in size, from 8vo here to 8vo in 16s); 1906; 1908 (copy listed here); 1910 (also listed here); 1912 (see copies listed here); 1914 (also listed here); 1916 (twice) (see copies listed here); 1919 (also listed here); 1922 (see copy listed here, apparently the first use of the traditional blue cloth with gilt emblem at center of front cover); 1925 (see copies listed here); 1928 (see copies listed here); 1930 (see copies listed here); 1932 (see copy listed here, in a larger format, still 8vo in 16s, with a newly engraved frontispiece reproducing a Faithorne frontispiece, and with the change to "H. C. Beeching" from "the Rev. H. C. Beeching, M.A." on title page); 1935 (see copies listed here); 1938 (when the Columbia edition of *Translations* and *A Reader's Guide by W. Skeat* were added), an edition which was then reprinted in 1941, 1944, 1946 (copy listed here), and 1950 (also listed here).

2448. Variant of Preceding, original black pebble leather over thin boards (a bit rubbed, joints weak, spine ends chipped, endpapers foxed), front cover and spine lettered in gilt, black endpapers, a.e.g. A nice copy in a variant publisher's binding, printed on India paper, making this issue half the size in width of the regular issue. Stevens 246: "Issued the same year on India paper with less leading of lines. No notes, but two collotypes of Milton's handwriting and nine facsimile title-pages are given." Not in Kohler.

2449. THE POETICAL WORKS OF JOHN MILTON. *Edinburgh[:] William P. Nimmo, Hay, & Mitchell[,] n.d. [ca. 1900].* 8vo, xxxvii+[iii]+440pp., unsigned engraved frontispiece portrait plate of a middle-aged Milton, engraved and printed title pages, with vignette illustration (of the poet being inspired by heavenly choirs) after F. Borders on engraved title-page plate ("Edinburgh: W. P. Nimmo, Hay, & Mitchell." n.d.), vignette illustration (of a young boy in a setting in nature with a cane laying beside him) signed with the initials "WS" on printed title, life of Milton by J. M. Ross, half-title for *PL, PR, SA, C, Ar* and *MP*, "Ballantyne Press: Edinburgh And London" printed at bottom of last page, original crushed maroon calf over padded boards (slight wear at spine ends and corners), Milton's name lettered in gilt at top of front cover, spine lettered in gilt ("Milton's Poetical Works"), decorated gold endpapers, a.e.g. A nice copy. The possible first edition by Nimmo was published in 1865 (also listed here with further Nimmo editions cited). Not in Kohler.

2450. THE POETICAL WORKS OF JOHN MILTON[.] *London[:] Society For Promoting Christian Knowledge, Northumberland Avenue, W. C. 1900.* First edition thus? Large 8vo, xv+[i]+422+[2]pp., engraved frontispiece portrait plate of Milton "After the portrait by Pieter Van der Plaas" (labeled "Lamerciergravure" and "Printed in Paris" at the bottom, fine impression), protective tissue guard, title page printed in red and black with elaborate decorative black border trim in art nouveau style on tan grained paper, elaborate decorative black headpieces in art nouveau style with red lettering before "Preface," "Contents" and *PL* (the headpiece before *PL* appearing at the outset of Book I being more elaborate in size than the other headpieces and incorporating "The Poetical Works Of John Milton"), small decorative red tailpieces, half-title for *PL, PR, SA, P, C,* and *LP*, "Plymouth: William Brendon And Son, Printers" on verso of last page, original reddish-brown cloth (a little worn, spine faded and ends chipped, frontispiece a little foxed, title page browned), central illustration within embossed thick gilt border frame on front cover, with classical motif of dancing figures in gilt against a black background, each figure identified in Greek letters (barely legible) on a scroll below, spine lettered in gilt at the top with a large classical figure in gilt playing the harp in the center and the letters of the press in gilt at the bottom, tan grained endpapers (similar to that of title page, with flyleaf repaired on verso), t.e.g., fore- and bottom edges untrimmed, partially unopened. A decent copy in publisher's binding, with prize label tipped on front pastedown.

Uncommon. Kohler 442, dating its copy "[ca. 1903]" and reporting "See Williamson 235 and 236. Not in the British Library. Not in the Bodleian Library. Not in Cambridge University Library."

2451. THE POETICAL WORKS OF JOHN MILTON[.] *London[:] Bliss Sands & Co[.] XII. Burleigh St. Strand W.C. n.d. [ca. 1900].* First edition thus? Large 8vo, xv+[i]+422+[2]+[8]pp., half-title printed in red and black within a decorative design in art nouveau style, half-title preceded by a listing of "The Apollo Poets Uniform With This Volume and already published" on verso of preceding page, engraved frontispiece portrait plate of Milton "After the portrait by Pieter Van der Plaas" (labeled "Lamerciergravure" and "Printed in Paris" at the bottom, fine impression), protective tissue guard, title page printed in red and black with elaborate decorative black border trim in art nouveau style, elaborate decorative black headpieces in art nouveau style with red lettering before "Preface," "Contents" and *PL*, small decorative red tailpieces, half-title for *PL*, *PR*, *SA*, *P*, *C*, and *LP*, "Plymouth: William Brendon And Son, Printers" on verso of last page, original red cloth (spine a little faded, bookplate removed from fly-leaf), central illustration within embossed thick gilt border frame on front cover, with classical motif of dancing figures in gilt against a dark blue background, each figure identified in small Greek letters on a scroll below, spine lettered in gilt at the top, with a large classical figure in gilt playing a harp in the center, and the name of the press ("Bliss, Sands & Co.") in gilt at the bottom, t.e.g., fore- and bottom edges untrimmed. Bound in at the end: eight pages of advertisements for publications by Bliss Sands & Co. A nice copy in publisher's binding, virtually identical to the edition preceding by the "Society For Promoting Christian Knowledge," except for the change in publisher, being undated, the addition of a half-title, and the inclusion of advertisement pages bound in at the end. Stevens 242, dating its copy "[1897]"; Kohler 444, dating its copy "[ca. 1903]" and reporting "See Williamson 235 and 236. Not in the British Library. Not in the Bodleian Library. Not in Cambridge University Library."

2452. THE POETICAL WORKS OF JOHN MILTON[.] *New York[:] Thomas Whittaker[,] 2 & 3, Bible House[.] n.d. [ca. 1900].* First edition thus? Large 8vo, xv+[i]+422+[2]pp., half-title printed in red and black with decorative design in art nouveau style, engraved frontispiece portrait plate of Milton "After the portrait by Pieter Van der Plaas" (labeled "Lamerciergravure" and "Printed in Paris" at the bottom, fine impression), protective tissue guard, title page printed in red and black with elaborate decorative black border trim in art nouveau style, elaborate decorative black headpieces in art nouveau style with red lettering before "Preface," "Contents" and *PL* (the headpiece before *PL* appearing at the outset of Book I being more elaborate in size than the other headpieces and incorporating "The Poetical Works Of John Milton"), small decorative red tailpieces, half-title for *PL*, *PR*, *SA*, *P*, *C*, and *LP*, "Plymouth: William Brendon And Son, Printers" on verso of last page, original red cloth (a little rubbed, joints cracked, front cover partially separated, spine a little faded), central illustration within embossed thick gilt border frame on front cover, with classical motif of dancing figures in gilt against a dark blue background, each figure identified in small Greek letters on a scroll below, spine lettered in gilt at the top, with a large classical figure in gilt playing a harp in the center, and the name of the press ("Whittaker") in gilt at the bottom, t.e.g., fore- and bottom edges untrimmed. Despite some flaws to the binding, a good copy in publisher's binding, virtually identical to the editions preceding by the "Society For Promoting Christian Knowledge" and "Bliss Sands & Co.," except for the change in publisher; being undated, like the Bliss Sands edition; having a half-title, which the "Society For Promoting Christian Knowledge" edition does not have and the "Bliss Sands" edition does, which this edition reprints using only the top half of the "Bliss Sands" edition half-title, dropping the bottom portion referencing the publisher. Not in Kohler.

2453. THE POETICAL WORKS OF JOHN MILTON Edited By Sir Egerton Brydges, Bart. [Quotation from Thomson] *New York: Hurst & Company, Publishers[.] n.d. [ca. 1900].* 8vo, vii+110-858pp., frontispiece portrait plate after D. Grosch, notes (sometimes copious) at bottom of the page, original blue cloth (worn, minor staining on front cover, a bit larger staining on back cover, shaken from within), Milton's name lettered in gilt on spine within gilt laurel wreath at the top, smaller laurel wreath in gilt in the middle. A decent copy in publisher's binding, interesting that its pagination begins at p. 111, as properly indicated on the "Contents" page. See copy of undated ca. 1880 illustrated edition of Milton's *PW* published by Hurst & Co. also listed here with further editions cited. Not in Kohler.

2454. Variant of Preceding, with frontispiece portrait plate reproducing in sepia a portrait of Milton (unsigned, but possibly after Faithorne), title-page plate with decorative border trim in green, notes (sometimes copious) at bottom of the page, original crushed black leather over padded boards (very worn, joints cracked, top of twenty or so pages slightly damaged without affecting any text), front cover lettered in gilt at the top between decorative floral pieces in gilt, floral piece in gilt repeated in lower right corner, spine lettered in gilt, decorated floral gilt white endpapers, rounded edges, a.e.g. As with preceding copy, pagination begins at p. 111; this copy, although worn, is very fresh and clean within, is in a variant publisher's binding, has a different and unsigned frontispiece portrait, and the inclusion of a title-page plate. Not in Kohler.

2454A. (Cross-listing) THE POETICAL WORKS OF JOHN MILTON With A Biographical Sketch Of The Author[.] New Revised Edition[.] *A. L. Burt Company, Publishers, 52-58 Duane Street, New York[.] n.d. [ca. 1900 / ca. 1895].* 8vo, xxv+[i]+514pp., frontispiece portrait plate reproducing engraving of Milton by D. Grosch, protective tissue guard, "Sketch Of The Life Of John Milton," original red cloth (a bit rubbed), spine lettered in gilt ("Milton's Poems" and "The Home Library") with gilt rules, t.e.g. A nice copy in publisher's binding. Not in Kohler. See main listing under *Poetical Works*, ca. 1895.

2455. THE POETICAL WORKS OF JOHN MILTON With Introductions By David Masson, M.A., L.L.D. Professor Of Rhetoric And English Literature In the University Of Edinburgh[.] *London[:] Macmillan And Co., Limited[;] New York: The Macmillan Company[,] 1901.* 8vo, xi+625pp., half-title with emblem consisting of the letters of Macmillan and Co. on verso, "Preface" (dated 1877), "Contents," "Introduction to PL" with several diagrams and other introductory material as in the first editions, half-title for some of the sections and poems, original green diaper grain cloth (a bit rubbed, spine chipped at bottom), with central embossed vignette portrait of Milton in gilt on front cover and Milton's name in gilt at lower right-hand corner, spine lettered in gilt ("The Works Of Milton"), t.e.g., others untrimmed A good copy with early presentation inscription on fly-leaf. The Globe edition of Milton's *PW* was first published in March 1877 (also listed here with further editions by Globe cited). Scarce. Kohler 437, with "2pp. of advertisements at end," reporting "Not in the British Library. Not in the Bodleian Library. Not in Cambridge University Library."

2456. [POETICAL WORKS] JOHN MILTON[.] With a Critical and Biographical Introduction by Brander Matthews, and a Frontispiece in Color by E. J. Cross[.] A Library of Poetical Literature In Thirty-Two Volumes[.] *The Co-Operative Publication Society[.] New York [and] London[.] n.d. [1902].* First edition thus? 8vo, v+514pp., frontispiece illustration plate in color of *Satan* after E. J. Cross (signed and dated 1902), protective tissue guard with illustrated passage printed in red ("Milton[:] Hell at last yawning received them whole."—"Paradise Lost"), title page lettered in maroon and decorated with rich Grecian style border in blue, decorated initial letter at the start of the brief "Sketch Of The Life Of John Milton" by Brander Matthews, original light blue linen texture cloth (a bit worn, especially along extremities, fading along edges and spine), spine lettered in gilt ("Poems Of Milton") within gilt rules. A good, tight copy. Similar to following edition, but a variant edition, with "A Library of Poetical Literature In Thirty-Two Volumes" on title page in place of "A Book Lover's Library Of Poetical Literature In Twenty-Five Volumes." Not in Kohler.

2457. [POETICAL WORKS] JOHN MILTON[.] With a Critical and Biographical Introduction by Brander Matthews, and a Frontispiece in Color by E. J. Cross[.] A Book Lover's Library Of Poetical Literature In Twenty-Five Volumes[.] *The Co-Operative Publication Society[.] New York [and] London[.] n.d. [1902].* Possible first edition thus (variant edition). 8vo, v+514pp., frontispiece illustration plate in color of *Satan* after E. J. Cross (signed and dated 1902), protective tissue guard with illustrated passage printed in red (quotation as preceding copy), title page decorated with rich Grecian style border in light green, decorated initial letter at the start of the brief "Sketch Of The Life Of John Milton" by Brander Matthews, original light green linen texture cloth (a bit rubbed, a little shaken from within, a few marginal notations for *L'A* in pencil in a neat hand, slight ink spot on outer bottom edge), front cover decorated in contrasting darker green interlocking straight- and curved-line design with a cream floral pattern, light blue spine lettered in gilt ("Poems Of Milton") above floral design in dark green and cream with same contrasting darker green interlocking straight lines at top and bottom. A good copy in an attractive art nouveau binding, with a different title page and a different series from that of preceding edition: "Book Lover's Library Of Poetical Literature In Twenty-Five Volumes" compared to "A Library of Poetical Literature In Thirty-Two Volumes." Kohler 466, dating its copy "[ca. 1914]," noting a "Coloured frontispiece by E. J. Cross," without reference to any date on the frontispiece, and reporting "Not in the British Library. Not in the Bodleian Library. Not in Cambridge University Library."

2458. THE POETICAL WORKS OF JOHN MILTON. With Introduction and Notes by Arthur Waugh. With Four Black and White Illustrations. *Collins' Clear-Type Press, London and Glasgow. n.d. [1903].* 8vo, x+596pp., half-title, frontispiece portrait plate of a young Milton in Puritanical garb with curly long hair parted in the middle, after A. A. Dixon (without attribution on the plate), title page in red and black, first appearance of three additional black-and-white illustration plates after A. A. Dixon (each illustration plate dated 1903), "Biographical Introduction" and

"Contents" at the beginning and "Notes" and "Index Of First Lines" at the end each printed in double column, *SA* appearing after *C* in the order of poetical works, contemporary three-quarter brown morocco, marbled paper over boards (a bit rubbed), gilt seal at center of front cover, spine lettered in gilt, raised bands (a bit rubbed), small decorative gilt devices in the panels, marbled endpapers and edges. A fine copy in a Prize Binding, with gilt seal on front cover and prize citation (dated 1905) tipped on front blank. The three black-and-white illustrations after Dixon are for *PL*: for Book I (*Satan Cast Out of Heaven*), Book II (*Satan Rallying His Troops*), and Book XII (*The Expulsion*), each with appropriate lines printed beneath. See following undated ca. 1903 illustrated editions of Milton's *PW* also published by Collins' Clear-Type Press in London and Glasgow, "With Introduction and Notes by Arthur Waugh," with the same frontispiece portrait as here (unsigned, but possibly after Dixon), and with the three black-and-white illustration plates after Dixon here along with additional illustration plates in black and white and in color after Dixon, C. J. Staniland, Herbert Cole, and unsigned. See also undated ca. 1903 illustrated edition of Milton's *PW* published by the Monarch Book Company in Chicago, listed later, "With Introduction and Notes by Arthur Waugh," with the same frontispiece portrait as here (unsigned, but possibly after Dixon), and with the three black-and-white illustration plates after Dixon here along with additional illustration plates in black and white and in color after Dixon, C. J. Staniland, Herbert Cole, and unsigned. See, too, undated ca. 1898 nonillustrated edition listed earlier of "*Milton's PW* With Introduction by Arthur Waugh. London and Glasgow[:] Collins' Clear-Type Press" and undated ca. 1898 nonillustrated edition listed earlier of "*Milton's PW* With an Introduction by Arthur Waugh[.] Collins[,] London & Glasgow." Stevens 232; Not in Kohler.

2459. THE POETICAL WORKS OF JOHN MILTON. With Introduction and Notes by Arthur Waugh. With Four Black and White *Illustrations. Collins' Clear-Type Press, London and Glasgow. n.d. [1903]*. Variant edition with additional illustration plates. 8vo, x+596pp., frontispiece portrait plate of a young Milton in Puritanical garb with curly long hair parted in the middle after A. A. Dixon (without attribution on the plate), half-title (placed here between the frontispiece portrait and title page), title page in red and black, eleven illustration plates in black and white and two in color (first appearance, six illustration plates after A. A. Dixon, each illustration plate after Dixon dated 1903, the other plates after C. J. Staniland, Herbert Cole, and unsigned, some dated 1903, the others undated), "Biographical Introduction" and "Contents" at the beginning and "Notes" and "Index Of First Lines" at the end each printed in double column, original crushed maroon leather over padded boards (very worn, the leather separating from the padding), front cover and spine lettered in gilt, in a protective plastic cover. The illustration plates include the same three black-and-white illustration plates after A. A. Dixon for *PL* in the preceding edition, each illustration plate signed and dated 1903: for Book I (*Satan Cast Out of Heaven*), Book II (*Satan Rallying His Troops*), and Book XII (*The Expulsion*), each with appropriate lines printed beneath. There are also three additional illustration plates after A. A. Dixon for *PL*, each illustration plate signed and dated 1903: for Book IV (discovery of Satan, "Squat like a toad, close at the ear of Eve"), Book VI (another illustration of Satan cast out of heaven, this plate in color), and Book IX (the temptation of Eve), each illustration with appropriate lines printed beneath; the black-and-white illustration plate for Book XI (Adam and Eve dejected) is unsigned, but in the manner of Dixon, with appropriate lines printed beneath. There are six additional illustration plates: two in black and white after C. J. Staniland for *PR*: Book I (the Baptism of Christ) and Book IV ("Satan smitten"), each plate signed by Staniland; two illustration plates for *SA*: one in color (of Samson between the pillars, bound here within *C*, unsigned [but possibly by Herbert Cole]), the second a black-and-white reproduction (of "Milton dictating SA," unsigned, "By permission of Henry Graves & Co."), *SA* appearing after *C* in the order of poetical works; one illustration plate in black and white for *L'A* (depicting a romantic pastoral scene, unsigned); and one illustration plate in black and white for the *NO* (a double page depiction of the nativity scene, unsigned, "By permission of Henry Graves & Co."), each illustration with appropriate lines printed beneath. Not in Kohler.

See following undated ca. 1903 illustrated edition of Milton's *PW* published, as here, by "Collins' Clear-Type Press, London and Glasgow," "With Introduction and Notes by Arthur Waugh," with the same frontispiece portrait as here (unsigned, but possibly after Dixon), and with the same illustration plates as here including the two additional illustration plates in color. See also undated ca. 1903 illustrated edition of Milton's *PW* published by The Monarch Book Company in Chicago, "With Introduction and Notes by Arthur Waugh," with the same frontispiece portrait as here (unsigned, but possibly after Dixon), and with the same illustration plates as here, except for a color illustration plate for *C* after Herbert Cole, signed and dated 1903, in place of the unsigned color illustration plate for *SA* bound here within *C*. See, too, preceding undated ca. 1903 illustrated edition of Milton's *PW* published, as here, by Collins' Clear-Type Press in London and Glasgow,

"With Introduction and Notes by Arthur Waugh," with the same frontispiece portrait as here (unsigned, but possibly after Dixon), with only three black-and-white illustration plates after Dixon, each signed and dated 1903 as here. See also undated ca. 1898 nonillustrated edition of "*Milton's PW* With Introduction by Arthur Waugh. London and Glasgow[:] Collins' Clear-Type Press" and undated ca. 1898 nonillustrated edition of "*Milton's PW* With an Introduction by Arthur Waugh[.] Collins[,] London & Glasgow."

2460. THE POETICAL WORKS OF JOHN MILTON. With Introduction and Notes by Arthur Waugh. With Numerous Illustrations. *Collins' Clear-Type Press, London and Glasgow. n.d. [ca. 1903].* Variant edition. 8vo, x+596pp., half-title, frontispiece portrait plate of a young Milton in Puritanical garb with curly long hair parted in the middle after A. A. Dixon (without attribution on the plate), title page in red and black, eleven illustration plates in black and white and four in color (first appearance, seven illustration plates after A. A. Dixon, each illustration plate after Dixon dated 1903, the other plates after C. J. Staniland, Herbert Cole, and unsigned, some dated 1903, the others undated), "Contents" at the beginning and "Notes" and "Index Of First Lines" at the end each printed in double column, original red cloth (a bit rubbed, slight darkening along edges of covers), front cover and spine lettered in gilt, black endpapers, t.e.g. A good copy in publisher's cloth binding. The illustration plates include seven after A. A. Dixon for *PL*, five in black and white and two in color, each illustration plate signed and dated 1903: for Book I (Satan cast out of heaven), Book II (Satan rallying his troops), Book IV (discovery of Satan "Squat like a toad, close at the ear of Eve"), Book VI (another illustration of Satan cast out of heaven, this plate in color), Book IX (the temptation of Eve), Book XI (Noah's Ark, this plate in color, unsigned, new with this edition), and Book XII (the expulsion), each illustration with appropriate lines printed beneath; the black-and-white illustration plate for Book XI (Adam and Eve dejected, bound here within Book III of *PR*) is unsigned, but in the manner of Dixon, with appropriate lines printed beneath. There are seven additional illustration plates: two illustration plates in black and white after C. J. Staniland for *PR*: for Book I (the baptism of Christ) and Book IV ("Satan smitten"), each plate signed by Staniland, with appropriate lines printed beneath; an illustration plate in color for *C* after Herbert Cole, signed and dated 1903, with appropriate lines printed beneath; two illustration plates for *SA*: one in color (of Samson between the pillars, unsigned [possibly by Herbert Cole]), the second a black-and-white reproduction (of "Milton dictating SA," unsigned, "By permission of Henry Graves & Co." bound here within Book I of *PR*), *SA* appearing after *C* in the order of poetical works; one unsigned illustration plate in black and white for *L'A* (depicting a romantic pastoral scene: cattle in the foreground amidst trees and standing in shallow water, more cattle grazing across the way, and a castle in the distance, bound here before Book X of *PL*); and one unsigned illustration plate in black and white for the *NO* (a double page depiction of the nativity scene, "By permission of Henry Graves & Co."), each illustration with appropriate lines printed beneath. Not in Kohler.

See following undated ca. 1903 illustrated edition of Milton's *PW* published by the Monarch Book Company in Chicago, "With Introduction and Notes by Arthur Waugh," with the same frontispiece portrait as here (unsigned, but possibly after Dixon), and with the same illustration plates as here, except for two less illustration plates in color. See also preceding undated ca. 1903 illustrated editions of Milton's *PW* published, as here, by Collins' Clear-Type Press in London and Glasgow, "With Introduction and Notes by Arthur Waugh," with the same frontispiece portrait as here (unsigned, but possibly after Dixon), one with only three black-and-white illustration plates after Dixon, each signed and dated 1903 as here, the other with the same illustration plates as here, except for two less illustration plates in color. See, too, undated ca. 1898 nonillustrated edition earlier of "*Milton's PW* With Introduction by Arthur Waugh. London and Glasgow[:] Collins' Clear-Type Press" and undated ca. 1898 nonillustrated edition earlier of "*Milton's PW* With an Introduction by Arthur Waugh[.] Collins[,] London & Glasgow."

2461. THE POETICAL WORKS OF JOHN MILTON. With Introduction and Notes by Arthur Waugh. With Numerous Illustrations. *The Monarch Book Company, Chicago, Illinois. n.d. [ca. 1903].* First edition thus. 8vo, x+596pp., half-title, frontispiece portrait plate of a young Milton in Puritanical garb with curly long hair parted in the middle after A. A. Dixon (without attribution on the plate), eleven illustration plates in black and white and two in color (first appearance, six illustration plates after A. A. Dixon, each illustration plate after Dixon dated 1903, the other plates after C. J. Staniland, Herbert Cole, and unsigned, some dated 1903, the others undated), "Contents" at the beginning and "Notes" and "Index Of First Lines" at the end each printed in double column, original maroon cloth (a bit rubbed), front cover and spine lettered in gilt, black endpapers, t.e.g. A nice, fresh copy in publisher's cloth binding. The illustration plates include six after A. A. Dixon for *PL*, five in black and white and one in color, each illustration plate signed and dated 1903: for Book I (Satan cast out of heaven), Book II (Satan rallying his troops), Book IV (discovery of Satan "Squat like a toad, close at the ear of Eve"), Book VI (another illustration of Satan cast out of heaven, this plate in color), Book IX (the temptation of Eve), and Book XII (the expulsion), each illustration with appropriate lines printed beneath; the black-and-white illustration plate for Book XI (Adam and Eve dejected) is unsigned, but in the manner of Dixon, with appropriate lines printed beneath. The remaining six illustration plates include two illustration plates in black and white after C. J. Staniland for *PR*: for Book I (the baptism of Christ) and Book IV ("Satan smitten"), each plate signed by Staniland, with appropriate lines printed beneath; an illustration plate in color for *C* after Herbert Cole, signed and dated 1903, with appropriate lines printed beneath; an illustration plate in black and white for *SA* (reproducing "Milton dictating SA," unsigned, "By permission of Henry Graves & Co."), *SA* appearing after *C* in the order of poetical works; an unsigned illustration plate in black and white for *L'A* depicting a romantic pastoral scene; and an unsigned illustration plate in black and white for the *NO* (a double page depiction of the nativity scene, "By permission of Henry Graves & Co."), each illustration with appropriate lines printed beneath. Not in Kohler.

See preceding undated ca. 1903 illustrated editions of Milton's *PW* published by Collins' Clear-Type Press in London and Glasgow, "With Introduction and Notes by Arthur Waugh," with the same frontispiece portrait as here (unsigned, but possibly after Dixon), and with the same illustration plates as here along with two additional illustration plates in color. See, too, undated ca. 1903 illustrated editions earlier of Milton's *PW* published by Collins' Clear-Type Press in London and Glasgow, "With Introduction and Notes by Arthur Waugh," with the same frontispiece portrait as here (unsigned, but possibly after Dixon), one with only three black-and-white illustration plates after Dixon, each signed and dated 1903, the other with the same illustration plates as here, except for an unsigned color illustration plate for *SA* bound within *C* in place of the color illustration plate here for *C* after Herbert Cole, signed and dated 1903. See also other undated ca. 1903 illustrated edition earlier of Milton's *PW* published by Collins' Clear-Type Press in London and Glasgow, "With Introduction and Notes by Arthur Waugh," with the same frontispiece portrait as here (unsigned, but possibly after Dixon), with only three black-and-white illustration plates after Dixon, each signed and dated 1903 as here.

2462. THE POETICAL WORKS OF JOHN MILTON: Edited, With Memoir, Introductions, Notes, And An Essay On Milton's English And Versification, By David Masson, M.A., LL.D., Historiographer Royal For Scotland, Professor Of Rhetoric And English Literature In the University Of Edinburgh. *London[:] Macmillan And Co., Limited[;] New York: The Macmillan Company[,] 1903[.] All rights reserved.* 3 volumes. Small 8vo, lxix+312pp.,+[ii]+374+[1]pp.,+[vi]+420pp., half-title each volume with decorative piece consisting of publisher's initials printed on verso, frontispiece vignette portrait each volume (Milton age ten ["engraved by Edwd. Radclyffe"], age twenty-one [unsigned], and age sixty-two [unsigned]), protective tissue guard each volume, separate title page each volume, preface (dated "Edinburgh: September 1882" and new to that edition) with a second preface (dated "Edinburgh: April 1893" and new to that edition), original red buckram (volume 1 slightly stained at top of front cover), spines lettered in gilt, edges untrimmed. A nice set with advertisement leaf (2 pp.) for "The Eversley Series" bound in at the end of volume 2 (including this three-volume edition of "The Poetical Works of John Milton"). The first edition thus, based on Masson's earlier edition published in 1874 (see set listed here), was published in 1882 (see set listed here); it was reprinted in 1893 and 1896 (see set of each listed here) and in 1903 (set here). Kohler 446, reporting "Not in Williamson. Not in the British Library. Not in the Bodleian Library. Not in Cambridge University Library."

2463. THE POETICAL WORKS OF JOHN MILTON With Introductions By David Masson, M.A., L.L.D. Professor Of Rhetoric And English Literature In the University Of Edinburgh[.] *London[:] Macmillan And Co., Limited[;] New York: The Macmillan Company[,] 1903.* 8vo, xi+625pp., half-title with emblem consisting of the letters of Macmillan and Co. on verso, "Preface" (dated 1877), "Contents," "Introduction to *PL*" with several diagrams and other introductory material as in the first editions, half-title for some of the sections and poems, original green cloth, with central gilt vignette portrait of Milton on front cover and Milton's name in gilt at lower right-hand corner, spine lettered in gilt "The Works Of Milton"), t.e.g., others untrimmed. A nice copy with contemporary signature (dated 1905) on fly-leaf. The Globe edition of Milton's *PW* was first published in March 1877 (also listed here with further editions by Globe cited). Kohler 445, reporting "Not in the British Library. Not in the Bodleian Library. Not in Cambridge University Library."

2464. THE POETICAL WORKS OF JOHN MILTON Edited with Critical Notes by William Aldis Wright, M.A. Hon. LL.D., D.C.L., Litt.D. Vice-Master Of Trinity College, Cambridge[.] *Cambridge: At The University Press. 1903.* First edition thus, 8vo, xxiv+607pp., half title with seal of the press and various addresses of the press on verso, preface (dated March 28, 1903), notes at the end, original blue linen texture cloth, spine lettered in gilt, printed publisher's wrappers (a bit rubbed). A very nice copy. Stevens 249, "The texts are based on manuscripts and the earliest editions. . . . Many anonymous conjectures are included"; Kohler 441.

2465. Variant of Preceding, original blue linen texture cloth, (a bit rubbed, early ownership signature on fly-leaf), central armorial emblem of the press in gilt on front cover, spine lettered in gilt ("The Poems Of John Milton"). A good copy printed on Oxford India paper, making this edition half the size in width of the previous issue, with variant spine label ("The Poems" as opposed to "The Poetical Works"). Stevens 249, "Issued in heavy and thin paper editions"; Not in Kohler.

2466. THE POETICAL WORKS OF JOHN MILTON[.] Etchings[,] Mezzotints[,] And Copper Engravings By William Hyde[.] [Guildford:] The Astolat Press[,] 34 Great Castle Street, W. MDCCCCIV. Large 4to, 194pp., half-title, title page in red and black with central device of the press in red, the text is that of Beeching and printed in double column, first appearance of fifteen illustration plates (one as frontispiece) after William Hyde, comprising seven mezzotints, six etchings, and two engravings, protective tissue guards, each printed with the poetic lines illustrated, with a "List Of The Plates," large wood-engraved head- and tailpieces and decorated initial letters, decorative device in red incorporating the name of the press on last page, original green linen texture cloth, gilt lettering on front cover and spine, t.e.g., others untrimmed. A very nice, tall copy in original binding. The illustrations are particularly striking—very much in the manner of Ricketts and post-Kelmscott, with numerous large wood-engraved initials decorated with foliage, and also with similar foliate book openings and tailpieces. Uncommon book, described by Ridler as "the magnum opus, and the most desirable item from this press." Ridler 8; Stevens 251; Kohler 451.

Numbered and Signed by the Artist William Hyde

2467. Variant of Preceding. THE POETICAL WORKS OF JOHN MILTON[.] Etchings[,] Mezzotints[,] And Copper Engravings By William Hyde[.] [Guildford:] The Astolat Press[,] 34 Great Castle Street, W. MDCCCCIV. Large 4to, internal as preceding, original muslin (binding a trifle soiled, with a small smudge at top corner of front cover), gilt lettering on front cover and spine, t.e.g., others untrimmed, early bookplate on front pastedown. Unlike the preceding copy, this is no. 12 of an unspecified number of copies, with number and signature in the artist's hand.

2468. THE POETICAL WORKS OF JOHN MILTON[.] In Two Vols. *London[:] Macmillan and Co. Limited[;] New York: The Macmillan Company[,] 1904.* 2 volumes. First edition thus. 8vo, xv+293+[2]pp.,+ix+288+[1]pp., edited by A. W. Pollard, half-title ("Library of English Classics—Milton") in red and black and title pages in red and black in each volume, "Bibliographical Note," volume 1, half-title for each of the major works, "Glasgow: Printed At The University Press By Robert Maclehose And Co." at the bottom of the last page of each volume, original red cloth (spines a bit faded), blind floral border trim at top and bottom of each front cover, spines lettered in gilt with decorative gilt borders at top and bottom, edges untrimmed, with advertisement leaf for "Macmillan's Library of English Classics" (including this set) bound in at the end of each volume. Macmillan's Library of English Classics, with a fifteen-page "Bibliographical Note" by Pollard (first appearance). A nice, tall set, printed on thick paper, in publisher's cloth binding. Stevens 252, "Masson's text, with some changes of capitalization and italic type"; Kohler 449.

2469. THE POETICAL WORKS OF JOHN MILTON Printed From The Original Editions With A Life Of The Author By A. Chalmers[,] M.A. F.S.A. *London[:] Bickers And Son 1 Leicester Square[,] 1904.* 8vo, xxxix+[1]+699pp., half-title with decorative headpiece, frontispiece portrait plate reproducing portrait "Engraved by W. Humphreys from a Painting by Faithorne," protective tissue guard, title page in red and black with central emblem of the Pickering Press, original "Advertisement To The [Pickering] Edition Of 1851," life of Milton, decorative head- and tailpieces, decorated initial letters, half-title for some of the poems, handsomely printed on good paper at "Chiswick Press :—[sic] C. Whittingham And Co., Tooks Court, Chancery Lane," contemporary dark blue polished calf, gilt rules and small decorative gilt corner devices on the covers, elaborately gilt-decorated spine with small gilt devices in the panels, raised bands with decorative gilt trim, inner dentelles tooled in blind, outer dentelles tooled in gilt, marbled endpapers and edges. A fine copy in a very attractive and well-preserved binding, with near-contemporary inscription in ink in a neat hand (dated 1910) on front blank. Not in Kohler.

First published by Bickers and Son with a life by Chalmers in an undated one-volume edition in the mid-nineteenth century, ca. 1851 or ca. 1862 (see copy listed here), similar to 1851 two-volume set by Pickering (see sets listed also listed here, originally two volumes of an eight-volume edition of Milton's *Works*), the Bickers and Son edition being a one-volume edition without folding genealogical table, facsimile, and appendix material, and with a life by Chalmers instead of by Mitford, although maintaining the order of the first 1851 edition (see sets listed here), with *PL* and *PR* coming last, not the case here.

2470. THE POETICAL WORKS OF JOHN MILTON Edited After The Original Texts By The Rev. H. C. Beeching, M.A. Oxford Complete Edition. Henry Frowde *[Oxford University Press.] London, Edinburgh, Glasgow, New York And Toronto[.] 1904.* 8vo in 16s, xiii+[3]+554pp., half-title, frontispiece reproduction plate of "Engraving after the Painting by Faithorne," protective tissue paper, "Oxford: Horace Hart Printer To The University" on verso of title page and recto of last page, preface (dated 1899), facsimile reproductions of the title pages of the 1645 first and 1673 second editions of *Poems*, of the title pages of *Justa Edovardo King* (1638), of *Comus* (1637), of *Joannis Miltoni Londinensis Poemata* (1645), and of the 1667 first edition of *Paradise Lost* and the 1671 first edition of *Paradise Regain'd* and *Samson Agonistes*, appendix, original blue cloth (a bit rubbed, spine a little faded, half-title slightly darkened—probably from a newspaper insert at one time), embossed trim in blue and black at top and bottom of front cover with Milton's name in gilt at the center, embossed circular emblem in blue and black at center of back cover. A good copy with early signature on fly-leaf. "Reprint of the 1900 edition" (Stevens); also listed here with further editions cited. Later editions refer to this 1904 edition as being the first edition thus; for example, the 1946 and 1950 editions each states "This edition of Milton's Poems was first published in 1904," making no reference to the 1900 edition, perhaps because of the change to a smaller octavo format, from an 8vo to an 8vo in 16s. See 1900 edition (first Oxford edition with text by Beeching) and the editions cited there. Stevens 250; Kohler 447, reporting "Not in Williamson."

2471. Variant of Preceding, original crushed red leather over limp boards (a little worn, especially at the corners and along the spine, which is missing small pieces at the top and bottom, name blanked out on front blank and on bottom edge), spine lettered in gilt with small decorative gilt pieces, t.e.g. Variant of preceding, printed on India paper, making this edition half the size in width of the regular issue edition, in a variant publisher's binding. Not in Kohler.

2472. THE POETICAL WORKS OF JOHN MILTON With Introductory Memoir[,] Notes, Bibliography[,] Etc. The "Albion" Edition[.] *London[:] Frederick Warne And Co. And New York[.] n.d. [ca. 1905].* 8vo in 16s, 607+[1]pp., half-title, unsigned engraved frontispiece portrait plate of a long-haired, youngish Milton (labeled "F. Warne & Co." without date), protective tissue guard, title page in orange and black with emblem of the press (small laurel wings with a horseshoe) at the center of title page, "Preface" (dated "April, 1896" and signed "L. Valentine"), half-title for *SA*, notes at bottom of page, "Bibliography" on last two pages with "Printed By Morrison And Gibb Limited, Edinburgh" at bottom of last page, original ribbed green silk cloth (a bit rubbed, endpapers, frontispiece, and title page foxed), Milton's name in gilt on front cover, spine lettered in gilt, t.e.g., fore- and bottom edges untrimmed. A nice copy with contemporary signature (dated "'05") on half-title. See copy of 1888 "Albion" edition published by Frederick Warne and Co. in London and New York, as here, and other editions cited there. Not in Kohler.

2473. Variant of Preceding, original crushed black leather over padded boards (a little worn at top and bottom of spine, frontispiece portrait slightly foxed due to the foxing on the protective tissue guard), gilt rules on covers, Milton's name lettered in gilt on front cover and spine, inner dentelles finely tooled in gilt, elaborately decorated gold endpapers, a.e.g. A good copy in a variant publisher's leather binding, with fine engraved bookplate on front pastedown and with contemporary presentation inscription (dated 1905) on verso of half-title. Not in Kohler.

Editions by Hurst & Company, ca. 1905

Of the following Hurst editions dated ca. 1905 here, some editions may well have been published earlier.

2474. THE POETICAL WORKS OF JOHN MILTON Reprinted From The Best Editions With Biographical Notice, Etc. *New York[:] Hurst & Company, Publishers[.] n.d. [ca. 1905].* 8vo, 562pp., frontispiece portrait plate reproducing engraving of Milton by D. Grosch, double black border around title page, "Sketch Of The Life Of John Milton," original white cloth richly swirled in brown twists over lightly padded boards (a bit rubbed, especially along spine), Milton's name lettered in gilt on front cover and spine, decorated light green endpapers, t.e.g. A good copy in an interesting turn-of-the century publisher's binding. The possible first edition of Milton's *PW* by Hurst was published ca. 1880 (see copy of illustrated edition and other illustrated and nonillustrated editions cited there). See also other undated nonillustrated editions by Hurst & Company published about this same time, ca. 1905 and ca. 1907. Not in Kohler.

2475. Variant of Preceding, original decorated half white cloth, white paper over boards (a bit worn), front cover card with color picture of a lady elegantly dressed tipped along the side, with gilt lettering ("Milton's Poems") near the top on the side and a small laurel wreath in gilt below, spine lettered in blind ("Milton") with a small laurel wreath in blind below. A decent copy in a lovely (albeit a bit used) variant publisher's binding, with a variant frontispiece color portrait plate of a long-haired Milton in bright, very rich colors (unsigned) within a pictorial frame. Not in Kohler.

2476. THE POETICAL WORKS OF JOHN MILTON Reprinted From The Best Editions With Biographical Notice, Etc. *New York[:] Hurst & Company Publishers[.] n.d. [ca. 1905]*. Small 8vo, 562pp., unsigned frontispiece illustration plate of a rural church and graveyard in a pastoral setting amidst trees, with cattle grazing in the foreground, double black rule around title page, "Sketch Of The Life Of John Milton," original decorated yellow cloth (a bit rubbed, small tear at bottom of title page), large card with color picture of two large yellow roses in bright color tipped across bottom third of front cover, with Milton's name lettered in gilt within decorative gilt trim at the top of the cover, Milton's name also lettered in gilt near the top of spine within double gilt lines above large decorative gilt piece, with decorative gilt trim at the top, "Hurst & Co." lettered in blind above decorative trim in blind at the bottom. A very attractive copy in a lovely publisher's binding. Not in Kohler.

2477. Variant of Preceding, original decorated red cloth (spine a little faded), large card with picture of two large roses in bright color, one red and one white, tipped across bottom third of front cover, with Milton's name lettered in gilt within decorative gilt trim at the top of the cover, rest decorated as preceding. A very attractive copy in a lovely variant publisher's binding, with a variant frontispiece portrait plate of Milton after D. Grosch, with undated, possibly contemporary, presentation inscription in a neat hand on fly-leaf. An attractive copy in a lovely variant publisher's binding. Not in Kohler.

2478. Variant of Preceding, original decorated green cloth, large card with picture of two large roses in bright color, one red and one white, tipped across bottom third of front cover (the card a bit chipped along side and bottom edges), with Milton's name lettered in gilt within decorative gilt trim at the top of the cover, rest decorated as preceding. An attractive copy in a lovely variant publisher's binding. Not in Kohler.

2479. Variant of Preceding, original decorated blue cloth (early name on fly-leaf), large card with picture of two large yellow roses in bright color with green stems tipped across bottom third of front cover, with Milton's name lettered in gilt within decorative gilt trim at the top of the cover, rest decorated as preceding. A fine copy in an attractive variant publisher's binding, fresh and bright. Not in Kohler.

2480. Variant of Preceding, with ornamental title-page plate elaborately decorated in pink with the title ("The Poetical Works of John Milton" printed in black at the center) and "Hurst & Co. New York" printed in the same color as the ornamental plate at the bottom, printed title page, original decorated limp leather (a bit rubbed, spine slightly chipped at top, pastedowns cracking), front cover hand-painted with large floral design in yellow, red, and green with hand-lettered title ("Milton's Poems") above, decorated silver gilt green endpapers, t.e.g. A nice copy in a lovely variant hand-decorated leatherette binding, with a variant title-page plate, with a contemporary presentation inscription (dated 1910) on fly-leaf. Not in Kohler.

2481. THE POETICAL WORKS OF JOHN MILTON With Introductions By David Masson, M.A., LL.D. Professor Of Rhetoric And English Literature In The University Of Edinburgh. The Globe Edition. *London[:] Macmillan And Co., Limited[;] New York: The Macmillan Company[,] 1906*. All rights reserved. 8vo, xi+625pp., half-title, "Preface" (dated 1877), "Contents," "Introduction to PL" with several diagrams and other introductory material as in the first editions, half-title for some of the sections and poems, original green cloth, front cover ruled in gilt with Milton's name lettered in gilt at center within double gilt rules, spine lettered in gilt ("The Works Of Milton"), t.e.g., others untrimmed. A fine copy. The Globe edition of Milton's *PW* was first published in March 1877 (also listed here with further editions by Globe cited). Not in Kohler.

2482. THE POETICAL WORKS OF JOHN MILTON Edited After The Original Texts By The Rev. H. C. Beeching, M.A. Oxford Complete Edition. Henry Frowde *[Oxford University Press.] London, Edinburgh, Glasgow, New York And Toronto[.] 1906*. 8vo in 16s, xiii+[3]+554pp., half-title (with "Oxford[:] Horace Hart, Printer To The University" on verso), frontispiece portrait plate reproducing Milton "From an Engraving after the Painting by Faithorne," small seal of the press at center of title page, original preface reprinted (dated 1899), facsimiles of original title pages (as with 1904 edition), appendix, original crushed green calf over padded boards (spine and corners a bit rubbed), front cover decorated with gilt rules and gilt lettering with two small decorative pieces in red and gilt with Milton's name lettered in gilt at the center with the initial letter "M" decorated in red and green within a gilt background, spine ruled and lettered in gilt ("Milton" at the top and "Oxford" at the bottom), with small decorative gilt devices in the panels, lightly marbled endpapers, a.e.g., green silk ribbon marker. A fine copy with contemporary signature, dated 1908 and 1909 on half-title, in an attractive publisher's binding. See 1904 and 1900 editions (see copy of each listed here). Kohler 452, reporting "Not in Williamson. Not in the British Library. Not in the Bodleian Library. Not in Cambridge University Library."

2483. Variant of Preceding, original red crushed calf over padded boards (spine faded), front cover decorated with small bright flowers in gilt with white blossoms and Milton's name lettered in gilt at the top, spine lettered in gilt, with gilt blossoms in the panels, marbled endpapers, red silk ribbon marker, a.e.g. A fine copy in a lovely variant publisher's binding. Kohler 452.

2484. Variant of Preceding, original red pebble calf over padded boards (spine faded), decorated embossed initials "JM" outlined in gilt at the center of the front cover, spine lettered in gilt, small decorative gilt pieces within the panels ruled in black, marbled endpapers, rounded corners, a.e.g., red silk ribbon marker. A fine copy in a lovely variant publisher's binding. Kohler 452.

2485. THE POETICAL WORKS OF JOHN MILTON With Introductions By David Masson, M.A., LL.D. Professor Of Rhetoric And English Literature In The University Of Edinburgh[.] The Globe Edition[.] *Macmillan And Co., Limited[;] St. Martin's Street, London[,] 1907*. 8vo in 16s, xi+625pp., half-title, emblem of the press (small laurel wings with a horseshoe) at the center of title page, "Preface" (dated 1877), "Contents," "Introduction to *PL*" with several diagrams and other introductory material as in the first editions, half-title for some of the sections and poems, original green cloth (a bit rubbed, a few marginal notations in pencil in the first several books of *PL*), front cover ruled in gilt with Milton's name lettered in gilt at center within double gilt rules, spine lettered in gilt ("The Works Of Milton"), t.e.g., others untrimmed and partially unopened. A nice copy. The Globe edition of Milton's *PW* was first published in March 1877 (also listed here with further editions by Globe cited). Not in Kohler.

2486. THE POETICAL WORKS OF JOHN MILTON With Introductory Memoir[,] Notes, Bibliography[,] Etc. The "Albion" Edition[.] *London[:] Frederick Warne And Co. And New York[.] n.d. [ca. 1907]*. 8vo, 607+[1]pp., half-title, unsigned engraved frontispiece portrait plate of a long-haired, youngish Milton (labeled "F. Warne & Co." without date), protective tissue guard, title page in orange and black with emblem of the press (small laurel wings with a horseshoe) at the center of the title page, "Preface" (dated "April, 1896" and signed "L. Valentine"), half-title for *SA*, notes at bottom of page, "Bibliography" on last two pages with "Printed By Morrison And Gibb Limited, Edinburgh" at bottom of last page, contemporary full polished navy morocco, decorative gilt border trim on covers with central prize seal in gilt on front cover, spine elaborately gilt-decorated in the panels with decorative gilt trim at top and bottom, red morocco label with gilt lettering and gilt rules, raised bands with decorative gilt trim, broad inner dentelles finely tooled in gilt, outer dentelles tooled in gilt, marbled endpapers and edges. A fine copy in a splendid Prize Binding, bound by "Allman & Son" with their stamp, with prize label (dated "December 1907") on front pastedown. See copy of 1888 "Albion" edition also listed here with further editions cited. Not in Kohler.

Of the following Hurst editions dated ca. 1907, some editions may well have been published earlier. While called the *PW*, they have in common the exclusion of *PL*—see note with first listing.

2487. THE POETICAL WORKS OF JOHN MILTON. With Explanatory Notes, Etc. *New York[:] Hurst & Company Publishers[.] n.d. [ca. 1907]*. Small 8vo, 387pp., frontispiece portrait plate after O. Grosch, original decorated reddish-brown pebble cloth (spine a little rubbed), front cover ruled and lettered in white ("Milton's Poems" and "Knickerbocker Classics"), with the sketch of an Edwardian lady in color on cardlike paper tipped along right side of the front cover (two small stains), with "Copyright, 1907, by Hurst & Co." printed in blue at the bottom of the picture, spine lettered in white (faded). A good copy of this "Knickerbocker Classics" edition, in an attractive publisher's binding, with contemporary presentation inscription (dated 1908) on fly-leaf. Included are Milton's poetical works with the exception of *PL*, published in a separate undated edition, ca. 1895 (also listed here), in a binding virtually identical to that here, identified as "Knickerbocker Classics," with a cardlike paper with sketch of a lady in color tipped along right side of front cover (as here) without copyright date or reference to Hurst & Co." on the card (as here). The possible first edition of Milton's *PW* by Hurst was published ca. 1880 in an edition very different from those here (see copy of illustrated edition listed here with further editions by Hurst cited). See also other undated nonillustrated editions by Hurst & Company published about this same time, ca. 1905 and ca. 1907. Not in Kohler.

2488. Variant of Preceding, original decorated black pebble cloth, front cover ruled and lettered in white ("Milton's Poems" and "Knickerbocker Classics"), with the sketch of an Edwardian lady in color (different from preceding) on cardlike paper tipped along right side of the front cover, with "Copyright, 1907, by Hurst & Co." printed in blue at the bottom of the picture, spine lettered in white (faded). A good copy of this "Knickerbocker Classics" edition, in an attractive variant publisher's binding. Not in Kohler.

2489. Variant of Preceding, original decorated limp leather (a bit fragile at joints as is customary for this kind of binding), front cover hand-painted with floral design in green, pink, and white with Milton's name in dark brown (perhaps wood-burned into the leather), decorated endpapers. A very nice copy with a variant frontispiece color portrait plate of a long-haired Milton in bright, very rich colors, in an attractive variant hand-decorated leatherette binding, with a contemporary presentation inscription (dated "Christmas, 1909") on verso of frontispiece portrait plate. Not in Kohler.

2490. Variant of Preceding, unsigned frontispiece illustration plate of an oasis-like setting in the Middle East, with camels alongside water and palm trees in the background, original reptile-like covering over padded boards, tan with central green coloring. A nice copy with variant frontispiece illustration plate, in an attractive variant publisher's binding. Not in Kohler.

2491. Variant of Preceding, frontispiece portrait plate after D. Grosch, original decorated limp leather, front cover hand-painted with floral design in colors of green, pink, and dark brown with Milton's name in dark brown (perhaps wood-burned into the leather), decorated endpapers. A very nice copy in an attractive variant hand-decorated leatherette binding. Not in Kohler.

2492. Variant of Preceding, unsigned frontispiece portrait plate reproducing Faithorne portrait, ornamental title-page plate elaborately decorated in pink, title in black at the center ("Milton's Poems"), "Hurst & Co. New York" in the same color as the ornamental plate at the bottom, printed title page, original decorated limp leather (pastedowns chipping away from leather, early signature on front blank), front cover hand-painted with floral design in colors of green, pink, and white with Milton's name in dark brown (perhaps wood-burned into the leather), decorated silver, gilt green endpapers. A very nice copy in an attractive variant hand-decorated leatherette binding, with a title-page plate. Not in Kohler.

2493. Variant of Preceding, original limp green leather over thin boards, spine richly decorated in gilt with gilt lettering at the top ("Milton's Poems"), decorated silver, gilt green endpapers, t.e.g., red ribbon marker. A lovely copy in a variant publisher's binding, fresh and clean. Not in Kohler.

2494. Variant of Preceding, original light gray cloth (a bit used, early ownership name on front cover), front cover lettered in embossed white with an oval floral piece in color tipped in at the center within surrounding embossed

Frontispiece color portrait of a long-haired Milton in bright, very rich colors, a variant from other frontispiece portraits of Milton in Hurst editions of Milton's *PW* published about this time, ca. 1907, in an attractive hand-decorated leatherette binding, with front cover hand-painted with floral design in green, pink, and white, with Milton's name in dark brown (perhaps wood-burned into the leather). See #2489.

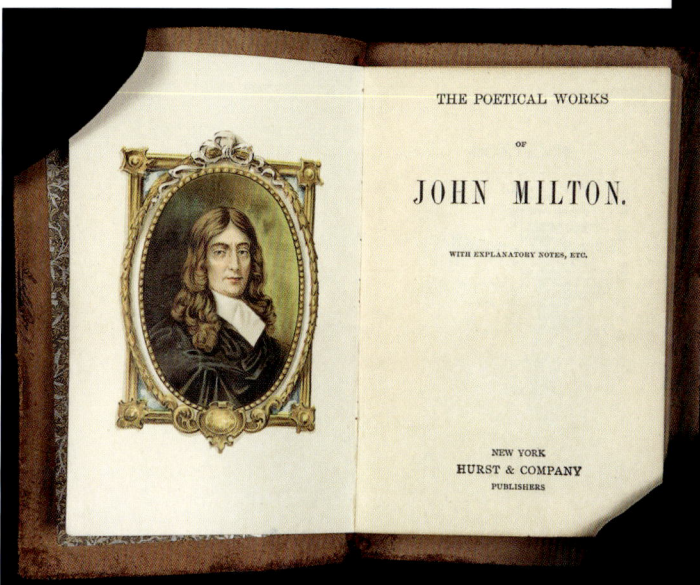

white-lined frame, spine lettered in white with small laurel wreath in white at the center. A decent copy in an attractive variant publisher's binding. Not in Kohler.

2495. THE POETICAL WORKS OF JOHN MILTON
With a Life of the Author and Illustrations[.] *Boston[:] R. H. Hinkley Company[,] (1908-09).* 4 volumes. 8vo, 284pp.,+251pp.,+274pp.,+247pp., half-title each volume, separate title page each volume each with decorative border trim in maroon, two portraits (Milton age twenty-one and sixty-two), first appearance of illustrations and ornaments in black by W. A. Dwiggins, each with elaborate decorative border trim in maroon, life of Milton by John Mitford, volume 1, half-title for some of the poems and for the life of Milton, attractively printed on handmade paper, handsomely bound in full dark brown pigskin over thick boards, covers elaborately tooled in embossed blind trim, raised bands with lettering in blind and decorations in blind within the panels, brown silk endpapers, t.e.g., others untrimmed. A splendid set in extremely fine condition, fresh and clean throughout, in a handsome binding, with colophon at the end of each volume: "Of This Hand-Made Paper Edition Of The Poetical Works Of John Milton, Five Hundred And Fifty Copies Were Printed By D. B. Updike, At The Merrymount Press Boston," the colophon printed in black together with a large decorative piece of the press and the set's number printed in red. The full-page illustrations by W. A. Dwiggins, each of which is a line drawing in black with the text illustrated printed in black beneath the illustration and the whole surrounded by an elaborate decorative border in maroon, include the following: in volume 1, two portraits of Milton ("From a portrait taken in his Twenty-first Year" and "From a Portrait taken in Later Life") and two illustrations for *SA*; in volume 2, an illustration (one each) for Books I, II, V, VI, and VII of *PL*; in volume 3, an illustration (one each) for Books VIII, IX, X, XI, and XII of *PL* and an illustration (one each) for Books I, II, III, and IV of *PR*; and in volume 4, an illustration for each of the following, *MP, C, NO, L'A,* and *On His Deceased Wife* (so-titled). Handmade paper edition; No. 43 of 555 copies. Not in Kohler.

PW. Boston: R. H. Hinkley Company, 1908–9. 4 volumes. 8vo, handsomely bound in full dark brown pigskin over thick boards, covers elaborately tooled in embossed blind. Illustrations and ornamental trim by W. A. Dwiggins. Five Hundred And Fifty Copies Were Printed By D. B. Updike, At The Merrymount Press Boston (colophon). See #2495.

2496. Variant of Preceding, handsomely bound in full crushed green morocco (joints and corners rubbed, pages are beginning to display age-browning), covers elaborately tooled in gilt, raised bands (some rubbed) with gilt lettering and decorations in gilt within the panels, marbled endpapers, wide inner dentelles tooled in gilt, t.e.g., others untrimmed, white silk ribbon markers. A handsome set, except this is a "Japan Vellum Edition," one of fifty-five copies, with colophon at the end of each volume: "Of This Japan Vellum Edition Of The Poetical Works Of John Milton, Fifty Copies Were Printed By D. B. Updike, At The Merrymount Press, Boston," the colophon printed in black together with a large decorative piece of the press printed in red and the set's number hand-lettered in red (No. 40 of 55 copies). Not in Kohler.

2497. THE POETICAL WORKS OF JOHN MILTON Edited After The Original Texts By The Rev. H. C. Beeching, M.A. Oxford Complete Edition. *Henry Frowde [Oxford University Press.] London, New York, Toronto, Melbourne[.] 1908.* 8vo in 16s, xiii+[3]+554pp., half-title, frontispiece reproduction plate of "Engraving after the Painting by Faithorne," preface (dated 1899), facsimiles of original title pages (as with 1904 edition), appendix, original red cloth (title page with a slight wrinkle), front cover decorated with embossed trim in blind at top and bottom with Milton's name in gilt near the top, spine lettered in gilt with decorative trim in blind at top and bottom. A good copy in an attractive publisher's binding. See 1904 and 1900 editions (copy of each listed earlier). Kohler 454, reporting "Not in the British Library. Not in the Bodleian Library. Not in Cambridge University Library."

2498. THE POETICAL WORKS OF JOHN MILTON English And Latin Edited, With A Bibliographical Introduction, Life Of Milton, And An Analysis Of Addison's Criticism Of Paradise Lost By John Bradshaw, M.A., L.L.D. Editor Of The Poetical Works Of Gray, Chesterfield's Letters, And An English Anthology. In Two Volumes. *London[:] George Bell And Sons[,] 1908-9.* 2 volumes. Volume one dated 1908; volume two dated 1909. Third edition thus. 8vo, lxiv+[1]+337pp.,+xvi+387pp., half-title each volume ("The Aldine Edition Of The British Poets"), frontispiece portrait plate after an engraving by H. Robinson, volume 1, protective tissue guard, emblem of the press on title page each volume, preliminary material as with 1892 and 1899 editions, half-title for some of the poems and each book of *PL* and *PR*, "Chiswick Press:—Charles Whittingham And Co. Tooks Court, Chancery Lane," printed at bottom of last page, volume 1, "Chiswick Press:—Charles Whittingham And Co. Tooks Court, Chancery Lane, London" printed beneath the seal of the Chiswick Press on verso of last page, volume 2, contemporary tree calf (a bit rubbed, joints tender), decorative gilt border trim on covers, spine decorated in gilt, red morocco labels with gilt lettering and decorative gilt trim, olive green morocco labels with volume number in gilt and decorative gilt trim, inner and outer dentelles finely tooled in gilt, marbled endpapers, t.e.g, others untrimmed. A lovely set, printed at the Chiswick Press. "New Edition, edited by Dr. Bradshaw, Published 1892 [see set listed here]. Reprinted 1899 [see set listed here], 1909 [copy here]" (verso of title page). The Aldine British Poets edition of Milton was originally published by Pickering in 1832 in three volumes (also listed here with further Aldine editions cited, all of which are in the collection). Bell continues on in the great Aldine tradition. Uncommon. Not in Kohler.

2499. THE POETICAL WORKS OF JOHN MILTON With Introductions By David Masson, M.A., LL.D. Professor Of Rhetoric And English Literature In The University Of Edinburgh. The Globe Edition. *Macmillan And Co., Limited[;] St. Martin's Street, London[.] 1909.* 8vo, xi+625pp., half-title (with emblem consisting of the letters of Macmillan and Co. on verso, with the addition of "Macmillan And Co., Limited" in London, New York, Toronto, etc.), "Preface" (dated 1877), "Contents," "Introduction to *PL*" with several diagrams and other introductory material as in the first editions, half-title for some of the sections and poems, original green cloth (slightly rubbed), front cover ruled in gilt with Milton's name lettered in gilt at the center within double gilt rules, spine lettered in gilt ("The Works Of Milton"), t.e.g., others untrimmed, partially unopened. A nice copy. The Globe edition of Milton's *PW* was first published in March 1877 (also listed here with further editions by Globe cited). Kohler 456, reporting "Not in the British Library. Not in the Bodleian Library. Not in Cambridge University Library."

2500. THE POETICAL WORKS OF JOHN MILTON[.] *London: Published by J•M•Dent•& Co. And In New York By E•P•Dutton & Co[.] n.d. [1909].* First edition thus. 8vo, xvi+554pp., half-title ("Everyman's Library Edited By Ernest Rhys . . . Milton's *Poetical Works* With Introduction By W. H. D. Rouse"), advertisement for Everyman's Library on verso, frontispiece (with quotation from Shelley) and title page decorated with elaborate border trim and decorated initial letter in art nouveau style, with vignette illustration on title page, "Bibliography," half-title for some of the poems, original green ribbed cloth, small emblem of the Press ("Dent Co.") in blind on front cover at the center, spine elaborately decorated in gilt floral design in art nouveau style with gilt lettering, light green endpapers decorated in art nouveau style. A nice copy with a nineteen-page glossary at the end. The Everyman's Library edition, first published in 1909, was reprinted in 1910 and 1912—all listed here; it was variously reprinted thereafter (see 1914, 1933, and 1937 editions, also listed here). Steven 254, dating its copy "[ca. 1909]"; Kohler 457, dating its copy "n.d. [1909]" and reporting "Not in Cambridge University Library."

2501. JOHN MILTONS POETISCHE WERKE. Vier Teile in einem Bande. Ubersetzt von Bernhard Schuhmann, Alexander Schmidt, Immanuel Schmidt und Hermann Ullrich. Herausgegeben mit biographisch-literarichen Einleitungen und vollstandigem Kommentar von Prof. Dr. Hermann Ullrich. Mit zwei Bildnissen des Dichters. *Leipzig. Max Hesses Verlag. (1909).* First edition thus. 8vo, 744+[1]pp., frontispiece portrait plate ("Milton im Ulter von 62 Jahren. Stich von W. C. Edwards nach Vertues Copie des Portrats von Faithorne"), small emblem of the press on title page, "Vorwort" dated 1909, additional portrait plate ("Milton im Ulter von 21 Jahren. Nach einer Miniatur im Besitze von Mr. A. E. Shipley, die wahrsscheinlich auf das verlorene Portrat von Onslow..."), half-title for each of the four parts, original dark green cloth (a bit rubbed along joints), front cover and spine intricately decorated with black tooling in relief in art nouveau style, red leather label with gilt lettering and decorative gilt trim on spine, central emblem in blind on back cover, dark green endpapers, t.e.g., green ribbon marker. A nice copy. Not in Kohler.

2502. Variant of Preceding, original light green cloth, front cover delicately decorated in black tooling in art nouveau style, central decorative device in similar art nouveau style in black tooling on back cover, spine similarly decorated in black tooling accentuated in gilt in art nouveau style with gilt lettering, green endpapers, green edges. A nice copy in a variant publisher's binding, with very different decorative tooling, with green edges, and with fifteen pages of advertisements bound in at the end. Not in Kohler.

2503. THE POETICAL WORKS OF JOHN MILTON: Edited, With Memoir, Introductions, Notes, And An Essay On Milton's English And Versification, By David Masson, M.A. LL.D., Historiographer Royal For Scotland, Professor Of Rhetoric And English Literature In the University Of Edinburgh. *Macmillan And Co., Limited[,] St. Martin's Street, London[.] 1910[.]* 3 volumes. Small 8vo, lxix+312pp.,+[ii]+374+[1]pp.,+[vi]+420pp., half-title each volume, frontispiece vignette portrait each volume (Milton age ten ["engraved by Edwd. Radclyffe"], age twenty-one ["engraved by Edwd. Radclyffe"], and age sixty-two [unsigned]), protective tissue guard each portrait, title page each volume, half-title for some of the poems, commentary and notes to each poem in volume 3, original red cloth, spines lettered in gilt, edges untrimmed, partially unopened. A very nice set with the bookplate of the Abbot of Farnborough tipped in on the front pastedown of each volume, with advertisement leaf (2 pp.) for "The Eversley Series" bound in at the end of volume 2 (including this edition). "First Edition 1874, 'The Golden Treasury Series,' 2 volumes [see set listed here;] Second Edition 1882, 3 volumes [see set listed here;] Reprinted 1893 (Globe 8vo), 1896, 1903, 1910 [each 3 volumes, see set of each listed]" (verso title page). Not in Kohler.

2504. THE POETICAL WORKS OF JOHN MILTON[.] *London: Published by J[.] M[.] Dent & Sons Ltd And In New York By E[.] P[.] Dutton & Co[.] (1910).* Second edition thus. 8vo, xvi+554pp., half-title ("Everyman's Library Edited By Ernest Rhys... Milton's *Poetical Works* With Introduction By W. H. D. Rouse"), advertisement for "The Publishers Of Everyman's Library" on verso, frontispiece (with quotation from Shelley) and title page decorated with elaborate border trim and decorated initial letter in art nouveau style, with vignette illustration on title page, "Bibliography," half-title for some of the poems, "Glossary" at the end, original red limp leather (slightly rubbed along extremities), decorative gilt piece on front cover incorporating gilt lettering, spine richly decorated in gilt with gilt lettering, t.e.g, red silk ribbon marker. A lovely copy. Not in Kohler.

2505. THE POETICAL WORKS OF JOHN MILTON Edited After The Original Texts By The Rev. H. C. Beeching, M.A. Oxford Edition. Henry Frowde[:] *Oxford University Press[.] London, New York, Toronto, Melbourne[.] 1910.* 8vo in 16s, xiii+[3]+554+[2]pp., half-title, frontispiece reproduction plate of "Engraving after the Painting by Faithorne," preface (dated 1899), facsimiles of original title pages (as with 1904 edition), appendix, original maroon cloth (a bit rubbed), covers decorated with blind trim, with Milton's name in gilt on front cover, spine lettered in gilt with decorative gilt trim at top and bottom. A nice copy with elaborate bookplate on front pastedown and early ownership signatures on fly-leaf. See 1904 and 1900 editions (copy of each listed here). Kohler 458, reporting "Not in the British Library. Not in the Bodleian Library. Not in Cambridge University Library."

2506. THE POETICAL WORKS OF JOHN MILTON With Introductions By David Masson, M.A., LL.D. Professor Of Rhetoric And English Literature In The University Of Edinburgh. The Globe Edition. *Macmillan And*

Co., Limited[;] St. Martin's Street, London[.] 1911. 8vo, xi+625pp., half-title, "Preface" (dated 1877), "Contents," "Introduction to *PL*" with several diagrams and other introductory material as in the first editions, half-title for some of the sections and poems, original green cloth (spine a little dirtied, a few pencil marks throughout), front cover ruled in gilt with Milton's name lettered in gilt at center within double gilt rules, spine lettered in gilt ("The Works Of Milton"), t.e.g., others untrimmed. A good copy. The Globe edition of Milton's *PW* was first published in March 1877 (also listed here with further editions by Globe cited). Kohler 461, reporting "Not in the British Library. Not in the Bodleian Library. Not in Cambridge University Library."

2507. THE POETICAL WORKS OF JOHN MILTON[.] *London: Published by J·M·Dent·& Sons·Ltd And In New York By E·P·Dutton & Co[.] (1912).* Third edition thus. 8vo, xvi+554pp., half-title ("Everyman's Library Edited By Ernest Rhys . . . Milton's *PW* With Introduction By W. H. D. Rouse"), advertisement for Everyman's Library (of which "This is No. 384") on verso, frontispiece (with quotation from Shelley) and title page decorated with elaborate border trim and decorated initial letter in art nouveau style, with vignette illustration on title page, "Bibliography," half-title for some of the poems, "Glossary" at the end, original green ribbed cloth (a bit used, several small slight stains on covers), small emblem of the press in blind at center of front cover, spine lettered in gilt, decorated endpapers in art nouveau style. Kohler 463, reporting "Not in the British Library. Not in the Bodleian Library. Not in Cambridge University Library."

2508. THE POETICAL WORKS OF JOHN MILTON Edited After The Original Texts By The Rev. H. C. Beeching, M.A. Oxford Edition. *Henry Frowde[,] Oxford University Press[,] London, New York, Toronto And Melbourne[.] 1912.* 8vo in 16s, xiii+[3]+554pp., half-title, frontispiece portrait plate reproducing "an engraving after the painting by Faithorne," central small seal of the press on title page, preface (dated 1899), facsimiles of original title pages (as with 1904 edition), appendix, original red cloth, decorative border trim in blind on covers with Milton's name in gilt on front cover, spine lettered in gilt with decorative gilt trim at top and bottom. A nice copy. Kohler 464, reporting "Not in the British Library. Not in the Bodleian Library. Not in Cambridge University Library."

2509. Variant of Preceding, original crushed green calf over padded boards, small decorative piece in gilt with red inlaid on front cover, with Milton's name lettered in gilt at the top, gilt rules and lettering and small decorative devices in gilt on spine, lightly marbled green endpapers,

a.e.g. A fine copy in an attractive variant publisher's binding. Kohler 464.

2510. THE POETICAL WORKS OF JOHN MILTON[.] *London: Published by J[.] M[.] Dent & Sons Ltd And In New York By E[.] P[.] Dutton & Co[.] (1914).* Fourth edition thus. 8vo, xvi+554pp., half-title ("Everyman's Library Edited By Ernest Rhys . . . Milton's *Poetical Works* With Introduction By W. H. D. Rouse"), advertisement for Everyman's Library (offering to send free list of publications) on verso, frontispiece (with quotation from Shelley) and title page decorated with elaborate border trim and decorated initial letter in art nouveau style, with vignette illustration on title page, "Bibliography," half-title for some of the poems, nineteen-page "Glossary" at the end, original light green cloth (a bit rubbed), central small emblem of the press in blind on front cover, spine lettered in gilt and richly decorated in gilt floral motif art nouveau style, decorated endpapers in art nouveau style. A good copy with early name written in a neat hand on verso of fly-leaf. The Everyman's Library edition was first published in 1909 (also listed here with further Everyman's Library editions cited). Not in Kohler.

2511. THE POETICAL WORKS OF JOHN MILTON Edited After The Original Texts By The Rev. H. C. Beeching, M.A. Oxford Edition. *Humphrey Milford[,] Oxford University Press[,] London, New York, Toronto And Melbourne[.] 1914.* 8vo in 16s, xiii+[3]+554pp., half-title, frontispiece portrait plate reproducing "an engraving after the painting by Faithorne," protective tissue guard, small seal of the press at center of title page, facsimiles of original title pages (as with 1904 edition), appendix, original red cloth (spine a bit faded, earlier ownership name in a neat hand on fly-leaf), decorative blind border trim on covers, Milton's name in gilt on front cover, gilt lettering on spine with decorative gilt trim at top and bottom. A very nice copy. Kohler 465, reporting "Not in the British Library. Not in the Bodleian Library. Not in Cambridge University Library."

2512. THE POETICAL WORKS OF JOHN MILTON Edited After The Original Texts By The Rev. H. C. Beeching, M.A. Oxford Edition. *Humphrey Milford[,] Oxford University Press[,] London[,] Edinburgh[,] Glasgow[,] New York[,] Toronto[,] Melbourne[,] Bombay[.] 1916.* 8vo in 16s, xiii+[3]+554pp., half-title, frontispiece portrait plate reproducing "an engraving after the painting by Faithorne," protective tissue guard (age-browned), central small seal of the press on title page, original preface dated 1899, facsimiles of original title pages (as with 1904 edition), appendix, original red cloth (spine a little faded, early name on fly-leaf), decorative blind border trim on covers, Milton's name in gilt on front cover, gilt lettering on spine with decorative gilt trim at top and bottom. A good copy. Not in Kohler (who lists nothing after 1914).

2513. Variant of Preceding, original polished maroon leather over limp boards (a bit rubbed along extremities, corners worn), decorative blind border rule on covers, Milton's name in gilt on front cover, spine lettered in gilt and richly decorated in gilt within the panel, raised bands within gilt rules, t.e.g. An attractive copy with early presentation inscription and book stationer's label on fly-leaf. A variant issue, printed on India paper, making this issue half the size in width of the regular issue, with a finely engraved frontispiece portrait rather than a portrait plate, handsomely bound in a fine leather binding.

2514. [THE POETICAL WORKS] THE SAVOY EDITION OF THE POETICAL WORKS OF JOHN MILTON With Introduction By Edmund Gosse[.] *London[:] Eyre & Spottiswoode (Bible Warehouse), Ltd. 33, Paternoster Row, E.C. Edinburgh And New York. n.d. [ca. 1917].* First edition thus? 8vo, xix+[1]+423+[1]pp., half-title in orange in black, frontispiece portrait plate reproducing an engraving after the painting by Faithorne (without so-identifying), title page in orange in black, half-title before each of the major poems, "Butler & Tanner, The Selwood Printing Works, Frome, And London" printed on verso of last page, original crushed maroon leather over padded boards (worn along the top and spine, joints cracked), central emblem on the front cover with the initials "JM" in rich gilt lettering surrounded by circular gilt trim with a finely tooled scroll in blind beneath, spine lettered in gilt, repeating the same "JM" initials in rich gilt lettering within a circular pattern in blind, attractively decoratively green floral silk endpapers, a.e.g. A good copy of a handsomely printed edition, called "Savoy Edition," in an attractive, albeit somewhat worn, binding, with a contemporary presentation inscription (dated 1917) on front blank.

2515. THE POETICAL WORKS OF JOHN MILTON Edited After The Original Texts By The Rev. H. C. Beeching, M.A. Oxford Edition. *Humphrey Milford[,] Oxford University Press[,] London[,] Edinburgh[,] Glasgow[,] New York[,] Toronto[,] Melbourne[,] Cape Town[,] Bombay[.] 1919.* 8vo, xiii+[3]+554pp., half-title, frontispiece portrait plate reproducing "an engraving after the painting by Faithorne," central small seal of the press on title page, facsimiles of original title pages (as with 1904 edition), appendix, original red cloth, decorative blind border trim on covers, Milton's name in gilt on front cover, gilt lettering on spine with decorative gilt trim at top and bottom. A nice copy.

2516. THE POETICAL WORKS Of John Milton. PARADISE LOST AND PARADISE REGAINED. *Leipzig[:] Bernhard Tauchnitz[,] 1850.* [In] COLLECTION OF BRITISH AUTHORS Tauchnitz Edition. Vol. 194. THE POETICAL WORKS Of John Milton. In One Volume. This volume has been reprinted in 1920[.] The usual quality of paper will again be used as soon as possible. Small 8vo, vi+358pp., original red ribbed cloth (pages a little age-browned, some underlining in pencil), central emblem in blind on front cover incorporating "Tauchnitz Edition," spine decorated in black trim with gilt lettering. A nice copy. The first edition thus was published in 1850 (see copy listed here). Uncommon.

2517. THE POETICAL WORKS OF JOHN MILTON With Introductions By David Masson, M.A., LL.D. Professor Of Rhetoric And English Literature In The University Of Edinburgh. The Globe Edition. *Macmillan And Co., Limited[;] St. Martin's Street, London[.] 1922.* 8vo, xi+625pp., half-title, "Preface" (dated 1877), "Contents," "Introduction to PL" with several diagrams and other introductory material as in the first editions, half-title for some of the sections and poems, original green cloth (spine ends rubbed, joints broken from within), with Milton's name in black within central box on front cover, spine lettered in gilt ("The Works Of Milton"). A decent copy with the signature of Milton scholar J. Holly Hanford on fly-leaf. The Globe edition of Milton's *PW* was first published in March 1877 (also listed here with further editions by Globe cited).

2518. THE POETICAL WORKS OF JOHN MILTON Edited After The Original Texts By The Rev. H. C. Beeching, M.A. Oxford Edition. *Humphrey Milford[,] Oxford University Press[,] London[,] Edinburgh[,] Glasgow[,] Copenhagen[,] New York[,] Toronto[,] Melbourne[,] Cape Town[,] Bombay[,] Calcutta[,] Madras[,] Shanghai[.] 1922.* 8vo in 16s, xiii+[3]+554pp., half-title, frontispiece portrait plate reproducing "an engraving after the painting by Faithorne," small seal of the press at center of title page, facsimiles of original title pages (as with 1904 edition), appendix, original blue cloth (slightly rubbed, spine ends a little chipped), central gilt emblem on front cover, spine lettered in gilt. A decent copy. Apparently the first use of the traditional blue cloth with gilt emblem at the center of the front cover. See 1904 and 1900 editions (each listed here).

2519. THE POETICAL WORKS OF JOHN MILTON Edited After The Original Texts By The Rev. H. C. Beeching, M.A. *Humphrey Milford[,] Oxford University Press[,] London[,] Edinburgh[,] Glasgow[,] Copenhagen[,] New York[,] Toronto[,] Melbourne[,] Cape Town[,] Bombay[,]*

Calcutta[,] Madras[,] Shanghai[.] 1925. 8vo, xiii+[3]+554pp., half-title, frontispiece portrait plate reproducing "an engraving after the painting by Faithorne," small seal of the press at center of title page (and the first time that "Oxford Edition" does not appear on title page), facsimiles of original title pages (as with 1904 edition), original blue cloth, central gilt emblem on front cover, spine lettered in gilt. A good copy.

2520. Variant of Preceding, original red leather over limp boards (spine chipped at bottom, lacking front fly-leaf), decorative border trim in blind on covers, spine decorated and lettered in gilt. A good copy in a variant publisher's binding.

2521. [POETICAL WORKS] MILTON OEUVRES CHOISIES Introduction, Traduction Et Notes Par Charles Cestre[,] Professeur `a l'Univerité de Paris. Les Cent Chefs-D'Oeuvre Etrangers. *Paris[:] La Renaissance Du Livre[,] 78, Boulevard Saint-Michel, 78[,] n.d. [ca. 1925].* 8vo, 203+[1]pp., half-title, frontispiece portrait plate of Milton ("d'aprés le tableau de Faithorne," unsigned), emblem of the press at the center of title page, "Introduction" (with a life of Milton and a critique of his works), "Note Bibliographique" and "Table Des Matieres" at the end, original blue paper wrappers (a bit faded along the edges and on spine), front cover and spine lettered in gilt within dark blue rule, edges untrimmed. A nice copy with contemporary signature (dated 1929) on fly-leaf. This edition is dated by virtue of the last listing in the bibliography, dated 1923. Included among the selections here are *L'A, C, L,* and two sonnets, each translated into French verse, *A* (selection), *PL* (selections translated into French prose, with summary of each book in French prose), *PR* (modest selections translated into French prose, with summary of each book in French prose), and *SA* (modest selections translated into French verse and prose, with remaining summaries in French). The translation, introduction, and bibliography are by Charles Cestre.

2522. THE POETICAL WORKS OF JOHN MILTON Edited after the Original Texts by the Rev. H. C. Beeching, M.A. *London[:] Oxford University Press[,] Humphrey Milford[,] 1928.* 8vo in 16s, xiii+[3]+554pp., half-title, frontispiece portrait plate reproducing "an engraving after the painting by Faithorne," original preface (dated 1899), facsimiles of original title pages (as with 1904 edition), appendix, original blue cloth, decorative blind border trim on covers, with central gilt device on front cover, spine lettered in gilt. A very good copy without, for the first time, the small seal of the press at the center of the title page and without additional place names beyond "London" in the publisher's imprint. See 1904 and 1900 editions (each listed here).

2523. Variant of Preceding, original red cloth, decorative blind border trim on covers, large decorative gilt device at center of front cover (variant from usual small device, as on front cover of preceding copy), and large gilt seal below, with "Distribute Cheerfully" on banner, spine lettered in gilt with decorative gilt trim at top and bottom. A very nice copy in a variant publisher's binding.

2524. Variant of Preceding, original maroon pebble leather, front cover and spine lettered in gilt, with Milton's name at the top and Oxford at the bottom of the spine, maroon endpapers, a.e.g. A fine copy in a variant publisher's binding, without frontispiece portrait, printed on India paper, making this edition half the size in width of the regular issue edition, with large bookplate on fly-leaf, virtually mint.

2525. THE POETICAL WORKS OF JOHN MILTON With Introductions By David Masson, M.A., LL.D. Professor Of Rhetoric And English Literature In The University Of Edinburgh[.] The Globe Edition[.] *Macmillan And Co., Limited[;] St. Martin's Street, London[,] 1929.* 8vo, xi+625pp., half-title, "Contents," "Introduction to *PL*" with several diagrams and other introductory material as in the first editions, half-title for some of the sections and poems, original green cloth (a little used, marginal notations in pencil throughout), spine lettered in gilt.

2526. THE POETICAL WORKS OF JOHN MILTON Edited after the Original Texts by the Rev. H. C. Beeching, M.A. *London[:] Oxford University Press[,] Humphrey Milford[,] 1930.* 8vo in 16s, xiii+[3]+554pp., half-title, frontispiece portrait plate reproducing "an engraving after the painting by Faithorne," facsimiles of original title pages (as with 1904 edition), appendix, "Printed In Great Britain At The University Press, Oxford By John Johnson, Printer To The University" printed on last page, original blue cloth, front cover ruled in blind with central gilt emblem, spine ruled in blind and lettered in gilt, t.e. blue. A good copy.

2527. Variant of Preceding, original red leather, covers ruled in blind, spine decorated and lettered in gilt, t.e.g. A fine copy in a variant publisher's binding, with a contemporary presentation inscription on fly-leaf.

2528. Variant of Preceding, original blue pebble leather (a bit worn at joints and corners and ends of spines), front cover ruled in gilt, spine lettered in gilt with gilt decorations by compartments, marbled endpapers, a.e.g. A nice copy in a variant publisher's binding.

2529. [POETICAL WORKS] MILTON POETRY & PROSE With Essays by Johnson[,] Hazlitt[,] Macaulay[,] With an Introduction by A. M. D. Hughes and Notes by various scholars. *Oxford At The Clarendon Press[,] (1930).* Second edition thus. Slim 8vo, xi+[1]+224+[2]pp., frontispiece portrait plate reproducing "an engraving after the painting by Faithorne," facsimile reproductions of several first edition title pages, notes at the end, original blue cloth (a bit rubbed, former owner's name neatly written in ink on fly-leaf), front cover lettered in gilt with decorative gilt piece, spine lettered in gilt (faded). A good copy with advertisement leaf for "The Clarendon Series Of English Literature" bound in at the end. The first edition thus was published in 1920.

2530. THE POETICAL WORKS OF JOHN MILTON Edited after the Original Texts by H. C. Beeching[.] *London[:] Oxford University Press[,] Humphrey Milford[,] 1932.* 8vo in 16s, xiii+[3]+554pp., half-title, engraved frontispiece reproducing a Faithorne frontispiece, engraved by Emory Walker, protective tissue guard, facsimiles of original title pages (as with 1904 edition), appendix, original blue cloth, front cover and spine lettered in gilt with decorative gilt trim beneath, t.e.g, others untrimmed. A very nice copy with an attractive (possibly contemporary) bookplate on front pastedown. This is a new printing of the Beeching edition, here in a special publication, possibly a large paper copy, certainly in a larger format than the previous editions since 1904 and than those following this edition, with reference, possibly for the first time, to "H. C. Beeching" rather than "the Rev. H. C. Beeching, M.A." on the title page, a reference which continues from this point on, and with an attractive newly engraved frontispiece reproducing a Faithorne frontispiece. See 1904 and 1900 editions (each listed here).

2531. THE POETICAL WORKS OF JOHN MILTON[.] *London & Toronto: Published By J. M. Dent & Sons Ltd & In New York By E. P. Dutton & Co. (1933).* 8vo, xvi+554+4pp., half-title with advertisement for Everyman's Library (of which "This is No. 384") on verso, frontispiece (with quotation from Shelley) and title page decorated with elaborate border trim and decorated initial letter in art nouveau style, with vignette illustration on title page, "Bibliography," half-title for some of the poems, nineteen-page "Glossary" at the end, original light green cloth (with a few notations in pencil in the first few pages), central small emblem of the press in blind on front cover, spine lettered in gilt, decorated endpapers in art nouveau style, four-page *raison d'être* of "Everyman's Library By Ernest Rhys" bound in at the end, printed publisher's wrappers. A very nice copy in fine condition, with original dust jacked in equally fine condition. The Everyman's Library edition was first published in 1909 (also listed here with further editions cited).

2532. Variant of Preceding, half-title with a brief biography of Milton on verso rather than the advertisement for Everyman's Library as in preceding copy which appears here on verso of front blank opposite half-title, original light green cloth (spine a little faded, early name on fly-leaf), small central emblem in blind on front cover (different from usual Dent emblem as on preceding copy and emblem used on Dent bindings from this point on), spine lettered in gilt, differently decorated endpapers, four-page *raison d'être* of "Everyman's Library By Ernest Rhys" followed by sixteen pages of advertisements for "Everyman's Library" (with its own title page) bound in at end, with early bookstore ticket tipped in on fly-leaf. A good copy, variant issue, without frontispiece, without title page in usual art nouveau style, and with various other differences in binding and endpapers (not in art nouveau style as usual and as in preceding copy).

2533. THE POETICAL WORKS OF JOHN MILTON Edited after the Original Texts by H. C. Beeching. *London[:] Oxford University Press[,] Humphrey Milford[,] 1935.* 8vo in 16s, xiii+[3]+554pp., half-title, frontispiece portrait plate reproducing "an engraving after the painting by Faithorne," facsimiles of original title pages (as with 1904 edition), appendix, original blue cloth, central small gilt seal on front cover, spine lettered in gilt. A fine copy in near mint condition.

2534. THE POETICAL WORKS OF JOHN MILTON Edited after the Original Texts by the Reverend H. C. Beeching, M.A.; including William Cowper's translations of the Latin and Italian poems[.] With an Introduction by Charles Grosvenor Osgood. Holmes Professor of Belles Lettres, Princeton University. *Oxford Standard Edition. New York[:] Oxford University Press[,] (1935).* First edition thus (with preface by Osgood). 8vo in 16s, xxxi+599pp., half-title, frontispiece portrait plate reproducing "an engraving after the painting by Faithorne," "Copyright, 1935" on verso of title page, facsimiles of original title pages (as with 1904 edition), original appendix followed (for the first time in this series of editions) by "Translations Of The Latin And Italian Poems Of Milton," original red cloth (a bit used), printed white label on spine. A good copy with first appearance of preface by Osgood and also of the "Translations." See 1904 and 1900 editions (each listed here).

2535. POETICAL WORKS[.] JOHN MILTON[.] *London: J. M. Dent & Sons Ltd.[;] New York: E. P. Dutton & Co.*

Inc. (1937). 8vo, xvi+554+4+[1]+16pp., advertisement for Everyman's Library (of which "This is No. 384") on verso of front blank, half-title ("Everyman's Library Edited By Ernest Rhys . . . Poetical Works Of John Milton[.] Introduction By W. H. D. Rouse") with a brief biography of Milton on verso, small decoration piece at top of title page, "Introduction" by W. H. D. Rouse, "Bibliography," "Contents," half-title for some of the poems, glossary at the end, original light green cloth, small emblem in blind at center of front cover (as with variant 1933 binding also listed here), spine lettered in gilt, decorated endpapers, four-page *raison d'être* of "Everyman's Library By Ernest Rhys" followed by a one-page blank and sixteen pages of advertisements for "Everyman's Library" (different from 1933 edition also listed here) bound in at end, printed publisher's wrappers (a bit rubbed). A nice copy.

2536. THE POETICAL WORKS OF JOHN MILTON Edited after the Original Texts by H. C. Beeching. New Edition with Translations of the Italian, Latin and Greek Poems from the Columbia University Edition and a Reader's Guide by W. Skeat. *Humphrey Milford[,] Oxford University Press[,] London[,] New York[,] Toronto[.] (1941).* 8vo in 16s, xiii+[3]+679pp., half-title, frontispiece portrait plate reproducing "an engraving after the painting by Faithorne," facsimiles of original title pages (as with 1904 edition), original appendix followed by "Appendix II Translations Of The Italian, Latin, And Greek Poems From the Columbia University Press Editions of Milton's Works" and "A Reader's Guide To Milton Compiled by W. Skeat Sometime Scholar of Christ's College," "Index Of First Lines," original blue cloth, central emblem in gilt on front cover, spine lettered in gilt, printed publisher's wrappers (a bit rubbed). A good copy with contemporary signature on fly-leaf, and with a seventy-page "Reader's Guide" by Skeat" added at the end (first appeared in the 1938 edition). See 1904 and 1900 editions (each listed here).

2537. POETICAL WORKS OF JOHN MILTON Edited after the Original Texts by H. C. Beeching[.] New Edition with Translations of the Italian, Latin and Greek Poems from the Columbia University Edition and a Reader's Guide by W. Skeat. *Humphrey Milford[,] Oxford University Press[,] London[,] New York[,] Toronto[.] (1944).* 8vo in 16s, xiii+[3]+679pp., half-title, facsimiles of original title pages (as with 1904 edition), original appendix followed by "Appendix II (as with earlier editions, see 1941 edition), original blue cloth, central emblem in gilt on front cover, spine lettered in gilt, original blue publisher's wrappers (a bit worn), front cover printed in black and white, with large seal in white at the center, a listing of "Oxford Editions Of Standard Authors" on the back cover. A fine copy with contemporary presentation inscription on fly-leaf.

2538. Variant of Preceding, original maroon leather over soft boards, covers ruled in blind, spine delicately decorated in a gilt pattern in art nouveau style with gilt lettering at the top, t.e.g., light green silk ribbon marker, another wide dark green silk ribbon marker laid in. A fine copy in a variant publisher's binding, without frontispiece portrait, printed on India paper, making this issue half the size in width of the other regular paper issue, with near-contemporary signature on fly-leaf.

2539. THE POETICAL WORKS OF JOHN MILTON Edited after the Original Texts by H. C. Beeching[.] New Edition with Translations of the Italian, Latin and Greek Poems from the Columbia University Edition and a Reader's Guide by W. Skeat. *Geoffrey Cumberlege[,] Oxford University Press[,] London, New York, Toronto[.] (1946).* 8vo in 16s, xiii+[3]+679pp., half-title, facsimiles of original title pages (as with 1904 edition), original appendix followed by "Appendix II (as with earlier editions, see 1941 edition), original blue cloth, central emblem in blind on front cover, spine lettered in gilt. A fine copy, near mint, with a seventy-page "Reader's Guide" by Skeat" added at the end (first appeared in the 1938 edition).

2540. THE POETICAL WORKS OF JOHN MILTON Edited after the Original Texts by H. C. Beeching[.] New Edition with Translations of the Italian, Latin and Greek Poems from the Columbia University Edition and a Reader's Guide by W. Skeat. *Geoffrey Cumberlege[,] Oxford University Press[,] London, New York, Toronto[.] (1950).* 8vo in 16s, xiii+[3]+679pp., half-title, facsimiles of original title pages (as with 1904 edition), original appendix followed by "Appendix II (as with earlier editions, see 1941 edition), original blue cloth (front cover a bit rubbed at bottom), central emblem in blind on front cover, spine lettered in gilt, t.e. blue. A nice copy, fresh and clean within, with a seventy-page "Reader's Guide" by Skeat" added at the end (first appeared in the 1938 edition). See 1904 and 1900 editions (each listed here).

2541. THE POETICAL WORKS OF JOHN MILTON Edited By Helen Darbishire[.] *Oxford[:] At The Clarendon Press[,] 1952-55[.]* 2 volumes: volume 1: *Paradise Lost*, dated 1952; volume 2: *Paradise Regain'd, Samson Agonistes[,] Poems Upon Several Occasions, Both English And Latin*, dated 1955. First edition thus. 8vo, xxxv+[3]+326pp., +xx+375pp., half-title each volume, decorative device of the press on each title page, facsimile reproduction of first two title pages of *PL* in volume 1, frontispiece plate reproducing "Trinity College Manuscript [–] Milton's holograph

L," volume 2, along with facsimile reproductions of first edition title pages in volume 2, "Preface," "Introduction" "Textual Commentary," and "Appendix I The Printing of '*PL*,'" "Appendix II Copies of '*PL*, First Edition, with corrected and uncorrected sheets," and four-page "Word-List," volume 1, "Preface," Introduction," "Textual Commentary," and "Appendix II The Printing of '*PR*,' '*SA*,' and '*P*' published in 1645 and 1673," volume 2, original blue buckram, central emblem in blind on each front cover, spines lettered in gilt with decorative gilt trim at top and bottom, fore- and bottom edges untrimmed. Milton scholar Bernard A. Wright's copy, with his signature on fly-leaf, volume 1, and numerous marginal notations in pencil in a neat hand (presumably Wright's) throughout the volume; volume 2 with publisher's wrappers in a protective plastic cover. A very nice set. Laid in volume 1: publication notification for "6 November 1952" "With Geoffrey Cumberlege's Compliments" with space for "Notes" on verso and a one and one-half page handwritten letter to "Professor Wright" from "A. Macdonald," dated "20th November 1952." Laid in volume 2: notice "With the Compliments of the Delegates of the Press[,] Clarendon Press Oxford." Scarce.

A second edition thus was published in 1962–67 (see set listed here). A one-volume edition of Milton's *PW*, including the Latin, Italian, and Greek poems, was edited by Helen Darbishire in 1958 (see copy listed here); that edition is a "Revised Edition" of the "Oxford Standard Authors"; a second edition thus of the one-volume "Revised Edition" of the "Oxford Standard Authors" was published in 1960 (copy listed here); a third edition thus of Darbishire's one-volume "Revised Edition" of the "Oxford Standard Authors" was published in 1961 (copy listed here), with a paperback edition also published that year (copy listed here).

2542. THE POETICAL WORKS OF JOHN MILTON With Introductions By David Masson, M.A., LL.D. *London[:] Macmillan & Co[.] Ltd[,] New York • St. Martin's Press[,] 1954.* 8vo, xi+625pp., half-title ("The Globe Edition"), original preface (dated 1877), "Contents," "Introduction to PL" with several diagrams, "Contents," "Introduction to *PL*" with several diagrams and other introductory material as in the first editions, half-title for some of the sections and poems, original green cloth, spine lettered in gilt with decorative gilt trim at top and bottom, printed publisher's wrappers in a protective plastic cover. A nice copy. The Globe edition of Milton's *PW* was first published in March 1877 (also listed here with further editions by Globe cited).

2543. [POETICAL WORKS] MILTON edited by Maynard Mack[,] Professor of English, and Fellow of Davenport College[,] Yale University[.] English Masterpieces • An Anthology Of Imaginative Literature From Chaucer To T. S. Eliot • Under The General Editorship Of Maynard Mack, Yale University[.] *New York • Prentice-Hall, Inc. (1955).* Fifth edition thus. 8vo, [3]+340pp., half-title with a listing of the volumes in the series on verso ("Volume Four • Milton"), introduction, half-titles for "Minor Poems" and "Major Poems," with a diagram of "Heaven or The Empyrean" on verso, notes at bottom of page, appendix reprinting the first three chapters of Genesis and chapters XIII to XVI of Judges, with "Bibliographical References" at end, original blue cloth, front cover and spine lettered in gilt. A good copy. The first edition thus was published in 1950, the second thus in 1951, the third thus and fourth thus in 1953.

2544. THE POETICAL WORKS OF JOHN MILTON Edited By Helen Darbishire With Translations of the Italian, Latin and Greek Poems from the Columbia University Edition[.] *London[:] Oxford University Press[,] New York[,] Toronto[.] 1958.* First edition thus. 8vo, xii+[3]+628pp., half-title, preface dated 1957, half-title for *PL*, facsimile reproductions of first edition title pages, "Appendix I Passages from the Trinity College Manuscript," "Appendix II Translations of the Italian, Latin and Greek Poems From The Columbia University Press Edition of Milton's Works," "Index of First Lines," original blue cloth, central emblem in blind on front cover, spine lettered in gilt ("The Poetical Works Of Milton"), t.e. blue, printed red publisher's wrappers (in a protective plastic cover)—on which is printed: "Revised Edition . . . Oxford Standard Authors." A fine copy.

Helen Darbishire edited a two-volume edition of Milton's *PW* in 1952 and 1955 (see set listed here); a second edition of this set was published in 1962–67 (see set listed later). The present one-volume edition (according to the front flap of the publisher's wrapper here) is a "new edition of Milton's *PW*, including the Latin, Italian, and Greek poems, [which] follows Helen Darbishire's Oxford English Text edition (Clarendon Press, 1952, 1955)"—also listed here; a second edition thus of this one-volume "Revised Edition" of the "Oxford Standard Authors" was published in 1960 (copy listed here); a third edition thus of Darbishire's one-volume revised edition of the Oxford Standard Authors was published in 1961 (copy listed here), with a paperback edition also published that year (copy listed here).

2545. THE POETICAL WORKS OF JOHN MILTON Edited By Helen Darbishire With Translations of the

Italian, Latin and Greek Poems from the Columbia University Edition[.] *London[:] Oxford University Press[,] New York[,] Toronto[.] (1960).* Second edition thus. 8vo, xii+[3]+628pp., half-title, original blue cloth, central emblem in blind on front cover, spine lettered in gilt ("The Poetical Works Of Milton"), t.e. light blue, printed tan publisher's wrappers (in a protective plastic cover) with central vignette of Milton sitting outside his home on front cover, the "Jacket engraving by Cecil Keeling," with the lettering "The Poems Of John Milton" on front cover and spine. A very good copy. The first edition thus was published in 1958 (also listed here with further editions cited).

2546. THE POETICAL WORKS OF JOHN MILTON Edited By Helen Darbishire With Translations of the Italian, Latin and Greek Poems from the Columbia University Edition[.] *London[:] Oxford University Press[,] New York[,] Toronto[.] (1961).* Third edition thus. 8vo, xii+[3]+628pp., half-title, original blue cloth (stamped withdrawn from Burlington County Library), spine lettered in gilt, printed blue publisher's wrappers (a bit worn—in a protective plastic cover) with central vignette of Milton sitting outside his home on front cover, the "Jacket engraving by Cecil Keeling," with the lettering "The Poems Of John Milton" on front cover and spine. A good copy.

2547. THE POETICAL WORKS OF JOHN MILTON Edited By Helen Darbishire With Translations of the Italian, Latin and Greek Poems from the Columbia University Edition[.] *London[:] Oxford University Press[,] New York[,] Toronto[.] (1961).* Fourth edition thus; first paperback edition. 8vo, xii+[3]+628pp., half-title, 1957 preface reprinted, half-title for *PL*, facsimile reproductions of first edition title pages, paperback, original red stiff paper wrappers (spine a little torn at the top), with central vignette of Milton sitting outside his home on front cover, the "Jacket engraving by Cecil Keeling," with the lettering "The Poems Of John Milton" on front cover and spine. Laid in: complimentary card: "This book goes to you at the suggestion of our representative: George B. Wingate Oxford University Press."

2548. THE POETICAL WORKS OF JOHN MILTON With Introductions By David Masson, M.A., L.L.D. *London[:] Macmillan & Co[.] Ltd[;] New York[:] St. Martin's Press[,] 1961.* 8vo, xi+625pp., half-title ("The Globe Edition"), "Preface" (dated 1877), "Contents," "Introduction to *PL*" with several diagrams and other introductory material as in the first editions, half-title for some of the sections and poems, original green cloth, spine lettered in gilt with decorative gilt trim. The Globe edition of Milton's *PW* was first published in March 1877 (also listed here with further editions by Globe cited).

II. DESCRIPTIVE LISTING OF EDITIONS 633

2549. THE POETICAL WORKS OF JOHN MILTON Edited By Helen Darbishire[.] *Oxford[:] At The Clarendon Press[,] (1962-67).* 2 volumes: volume 1: *Paradise Lost*, dated 1962–67; volume 2: *Paradise Regain'd, Samson Agonistes[,] Poems Upon Several Occasions, Both English And Latin,* dated 1966. Second edition thus. 8vo, xxxv+[3]+326pp.,+xx+375pp., half-title each volume, facsimile reproduction of first two title pages of *PL* in volume 1, frontispiece reproducing "Trinity College Manuscript [–] Milton's holograph *L*," volume 2, along with facsimile reproductions of first edition title pages in volume 2, original blue buckram, central emblem in blind on each front cover, spines lettered in gilt with decorative gilt trim at top and bottom. A very nice set. "Reprinted Lithographically In Great Britain At The University Press, Oxford[,] From Sheets Of The First Edition" (on verso of title page, volume 1); "Reprinted Lithographically In Great Britain At The University Press, Oxford[,] From Corrected Sheets Of The First Edition By Vivian Ridler[,] Printer To The University" (on verso of title page, volume 2). The first edition thus was published in 1952–55 (see set listed here).

2550. MILTON POETICAL WORKS Edited By Douglas Bush[.] *London[:] Oxford University Press[,] (1966).* First London edition thus. 8vo, xxxi+[1]+570pp., half-title, "Preface," "Contents," "Introduction," "Personal Passages," half-title for "The Complete Poetical Works of John Milton," introductions to some of the poems, facsimile reproductions of first edition title pages, notes at bottom of page, glossary and index at the end, original blue cloth (former owner's name in ink on fly-leaf), central emblem in blind on front cover, spine lettered in gilt, printed gold publisher's wrappers (a bit used, in a protective plastic cover) with black-and-white vignette of Milton seated in front of his cottage on front cover. A nice copy.

2551. MILTON POETICAL WORKS Edited By Douglas Bush[.] *London[:] Oxford University Press[,] (1967).* Second edition thus. 8vo, xxxi+[1]+570pp., as first edition preceding, original blue cloth (slightly waterstained along top edge of front cover), central emblem in blind on front cover, spine lettered in gilt, printed gold publisher's wrappers (a bit used, in a protective plastic cover) with black-and-white vignette of Milton seated in front of his cottage on front cover. A good copy.

2552. MILTON POETICAL WORKS Edited By Douglas Bush[.] *[Oxford:] Oxford University Press[;] London[:] Oxford[,] (1969).* First OUP paperback edition thus. 8vo, xxxi+[1]+570pp., half-title with Milton's birth and death dates on verso, "Preface," "Contents," "Introduction," "Personal Passages," half-title for "The Complete Poetical Works of John Milton," introductions to some of the poems, facsimile reproductions of first edition title pages, notes at bottom of page, glossary and index at the end, paperback, original printed stiff red paper wrappers (corners slightly creased, covers and edges a bit worn), with reproduction of Doré illustration on front cover. This edition was first published in London in the Oxford Standard Authors series by OUP in 1966 (copy listed here).

2553. THE POETICAL WORKS OF JOHN MILTON, With Notes Of Various Authors. To Which Are Added Illustrations, And Some Account Of The Life And Writings Of Milton, By The Rev. Henry J. Todd, M.A.F.A.S. Rector Of Allhallows, Lombard-Street, &c. The Second Edition, With Considerable Additions, And With A Verbal Index To The Whole Of Milton's Poetry. In Seven Volumes. *[London: Printed for J. Johnson; R. Baldwin; et al; and Mathews and Leigh: By Law and Gilbert, St. John's-Square, Clerkenwell. 1809.] AMS Press New York[,] (1970).* An AMS Press reproduction of the 1809 second enlarged Todd edition, which also added a complete index. Seven volumes (including volume 1 as the index, with life and Editions). Reproduction of the second (1809) Todd edition, enlarged. 8vo, xv+21+[1]+[405 unpaginated "Verbal Index"],+xix+462pp.,+[i]+473pp.,+395pp.,+xix+503pp.,+[iii]+503pp.,+414+[1]pp.+[18 unpaginated "Glossarial Index"]+[6 unpaginated "Contents Of The Six Volumes"], frontispiece portrait by T. Simpson, engraved by J. Collyer, volume 1, original blue cloth, spines lettered in gilt. A fine set, virtually mint. See fine copy of original 1809 second, revised and enlarged Todd edition listed here separately with further commentary. The first Todd edition appeared in 1801 (also listed herewith further Todd editions in the collection cited).

2554. [POETICAL WORKS] MILTON POETICAL WORKS Edited By Douglas Bush[.] *[Oxford:] Oxford University Press[;] London[:] Oxford[,] (1974).* Third OUP paperback edition thus. 8vo, xxxi+[1]+570pp., as with first OUP paperback edition listed earlier, paperback, original printed stiff red paper wrappers (slightly rubbed, shelf label on spine), with reproduction of Doré illustration on front cover. A nice copy. This edition was first published in London in the Oxford Standard Authors series by OUP in 1966(copy listed here); it was first issued as an OUP paperback in (copy listed here).

2555. [POETICAL WORKS] MILTON POETICAL WORKS Edited By Douglas Bush[.] *[Oxford:] Oxford University Press[,] (1979).* 8vo, xxxi+[1]+570pp., as with first edition listed earlier, original black cloth, central emblem in blind on front cover, spine lettered in gilt, printed publisher's wrappers. A fine copy in mint condition. This edition was first published in London in the Oxford Standard Authors series by Oxford University Press in 1966 (copy listed here).

2556. [POETICAL WORKS] MILTON ON DISK. 3 Original Mac disks containing the full text of *PL, PR, SA, L, C,* and the short poems and sonnets. *Clinton Corners, New York: Shakespeare On Disk, 1990.* First edition thus. In original folder, with original advertisement and "User Notes" laid in.

2557. [POETICAL WORKS]. JOHN MILTON Edited By Stephen Orgel And Jonathan Goldberg[.] *The Oxford Authors[.] Oxford [And] New York[:] Oxford University Press[,] 1991.* First edition thus. 8vo, xxxii+966pp., frontispiece reproduction of 1645 frontispiece portrait by William Marshall, "Introduction," "Acknowledgments," "Chronology," "Note on the Text," and "Letter to a Friend (ca. 1633)" at the beginning, "Notes," "Further Reading," and "Index" at the end, original blue cloth, spine lettered in gilt against red background with gilt rules, printed dark green publisher's wrappers in a protective plastic wrapper. A fine copy. This edition contains all of Milton's English and Italian poetry in chronological order ("arranged in accordance with the dates of publication") and most of his Latin and Greek verse. It also includes a generous sampling of Milton's prose works, in their entirety and important selections. Statement laid in: "Corrections And Apologies[.] Professor Orgel of Stanford University will send a list of corrections and errors found in the second printing of the Oxford Milton to anyone who writes to him directly. The corrections will be incorporated into the volume's third printing."

2558. [POETICAL WORKS] Variant of Preceding. First edition thus, paperback. As preceding, paperback, printed red stiff paper wrappers with reproduction in color of Milton at age twenty-one on front cover. A nice copy. The text is modernized, as all in the series are. "First published in 1991 in hardback [copy preceding] and simultaneously in a paperback edition [copy here]" (note on verso of title page).

2559. [POETICAL WORKS] JOHN MILTON[: A SELECTION OF HIS FINEST POEMS.] Edited By Jonathan Goldberg and Stephen Orgel[.] *The Oxford Poetry Library[.] Oxford [And] New York[:] Oxford University Press[,] [ca. 1994].* First edition thus in the Oxford Poetry Library. 8vo, xxvi+324pp., half-title advertisement, "Introduction," "Acknowledgments," "Chronology," and "Note on the Text," at the beginning, "Notes," "Further Reading," and "Index" at the end, paperback, printed red stiff paper wrappers with reproduction in of a small sketch of Milton at age twenty-one on front cover. A nice copy, reprinting selections from the edition first published in 1991 (also listed here).

2560. [POETICAL WORKS] JOHN MILTON Edited By Stephen Orgel And Jonathan Goldberg[.] *The Oxford Authors[.] Oxford [And] New York[:] Oxford University Press[,] [ca. 1994]*. Reprint edition, with corrections. 8vo, xxxii+966pp., as first edition, with corrections, paperback, printed red stiff paper wrappers with reproduction in of a small sketch of Milton at age twenty-one on front cover. A nice copy. First published in 1991 (also listed here).

2561. THE PORTABLE MILTON Edited, And With An Introduction, By Douglas Bush. *New York[:] The Viking Press[,] 1949*. First edition thus. 8vo, vii+693+[2]pp., half-title, decorative border trim on title page, with a twenty-six-page "Glossary Of Words And Proper Names" (with half-title) and two pages listing "Titles And Editors Of The Viking Portable Library (As of Spring, 1949)" at the end, original gray cloth, front cover and spine lettered in contrasting brown with brown lines on spine, printed publisher's wrappers (a bit frayed at top edge). Along with Milton's poetry are selections from his prose. A nice copy with the signature of Milton scholar Maurice Kelley on fly-leaf. A second edition thus, first paperback edition, was published by the Viking Press in 1955 (copy listed following).

2562. THE PORTABLE MILTON Edited, And With An Introduction, By Douglas Bush. *New York[:] The Viking Press[,] (1955)*. Second edition thus; first paperback edition. 8vo, vii+693pp., half-title, decorative border trim on title page, as preceding, paperback (a bit used, owner's name stamped on title page and elsewhere). A decent copy. Listed on the inside of the back cover are the "First 15 Viking Paperbound Portables" (including Milton).

The collection has two additional copies of "The Portable Milton, Edited, And With An Introduction, By Douglas Bush," published in paperback in New York by the Viking Press: in 1960 and in 1969.

2563. THE PORTABLE MILTON Edited, And With An Introduction, By Douglas Bush[.] *Penguin Books[,] (1985)*. 8vo, vii+693+[2]pp., contents as with the first edition, paperback, a two-page listing of "Some Volumes in The Viking Portable Library" printed at the end, paperback, cover design in color with inset vignette portrait of Milton at age twenty-one on front cover. A fine copy. *The Portable Milton* was first published by Penguin Books in 1976 (as a reprint of the Viking Press edition published in 1955, copy listed here) and by Viking / Penguin, Inc., in 1977 (again as a reprint of the Viking Press edition

published in 1955); it was variously reprinted thereafter, including an undated edition as here ca. 1991, a copy of which is in the collection.

2564. [PRIVATE CORRESPONDENCE] MILTON PRIVATE CORRESPONDENCE AND ACADEMIC EXERCISES Translated from the Latin by Phyllis B. Tillyard[,] Late Scholar of Girton College, Cambridge[;] Late Lecturer at Westfield and East London Colleges[.] With an Introduction & Commentary by E. M. W. Tillyard[,] University Lecturer in English[;] Late Fellow of Jesus College[,] Cambridge[.] *Cambridge[:] At The University Press[,] 1932*. First edition. 8vo, xxxix+143+[1]pp., half-title, seal of the press on title page, "Contents," "Preface," "Introduction," half-title before "Private Correspondence & Academic Exercises," "The Printer's Preface To The Reader," "Commentary" and "Textual Notes" at the end, original green cloth (spine a little faded), spine lettered in gilt with small gilt seal of the press at the bottom and decorative gilt trim at top and bottom. A nice copy with contemporary signature on fly-leaf. The whole of Milton's *Prolusions* and private correspondence in Latin has been translated, and Tillyard's introduction and commentary deals critically with both.

2564A. (Cross-listing) [PROLUSIO SCRIPT] MILTON'S PROLUSIO SCRIPT By Hugh C. H. Candy[.] *London[:] The Bibliographical Society[,] 1934*. Slim 4to, 9 leaves (paginated 331–39, first page and plate not paginated), decorated initial letter, facsimile reproduction plate "of an early Prolusio Script, found in the same box with the Commonplace Book," and two pages of facsimiles, pamphlet, original printed wrappers (a bit faded along spine), partially unopened. "Reprinted By The University Press, Oxford[,] From The Transactions Of The Bibliographical Society[,] The Library[,] Dec. 1934" (verso of title page). A good copy. Scarce. See main listing in Twentieth-century Miltoniana.

2565. PRO POPULO ADVERSUS TYRANNOS: Or The Sovereign Right And Power Of The People Over Tyrants, Clearly Stated and plainly Proved. With some Reflections on the late posture of Affairs. By a true Protestant Englishman, and Well-wisher to Posterity. *London, Printed in the Year, 1689*. Slim 4to, 27pp., new quarter morocco (title a little soiled and backed), gilt-decorated, with William Riley Parker's embossed stamp ("WRP MILTON LIBRARY") on title page along with signature of early owner, RI. Bacon, with Bacon's note that "This Book is for the most part taken out of Mr. Milton's Book intituled, The Tenure of Kings, and Magistrates. Printed in 1649," early armorial bookplate on front blank. Coleridge notes that "Parker 1942 was the first to identify that this is a freely abridged version of Milton's *Tenure of kings and magistrates*," 1649. It had been listed as an apocryphal writing of Milton's in the Columbia edition (XVIII, pp. 635–38). "Parker [further] suggests that James Tyrell may have been the editor." "The first and only Tyrell edition; the first edition in this form and the first edition under this title. It is a surprisingly scarce work, lacking in several major Milton collections" (G. W. Stuart, Jr., Ravenstree, Cat. 163, #87, 1989). Wing M 2164; Shawcross, 1974, p. 313; Coleridge 252; Not in Kohler.

Pro Populo Anglicano Defensio

2566. [PRO POPULO] JOANNIS MILTONI ANGLI PRO POPVLO ANGLICANO DEFENSIO Contra Claudii Anonymi, alias Salmasii Defensionem Regiam. *Londini, Typis Du Gardianis. Anno Domini 1651.* First edition, third issue. Small 4to, [i]+[xvii]+20pp., woodcut armorial shields on title page (first issue differs from second and third issues by use of circular woodcut device instead of rectangular), title page as A1 and the errata leaf as A2, decorative headpieces and decorated initial letters, old quarter cloth, marbled paper over boards (edges age-darkened, faint waterstain along edges toward end, single small wormhole at blank lower edge and one in blank gutter). The seventeen-page unpaginated "Praefatio" is lightly paginated in Roman numerals in an early hand. The Lowther copy with bibliographical note on front pastedown. Milton's *Pro Populo Anglicano Defensio* is important as being the official reply of the Parliament to the *Defensio Regia* of Salmasius (copy with Seventeenth-century Miltoniana), which was having a serious effect upon public opinion on the continent. The publication of *Eikonoklastes* by Milton in 1649 (copy listed here) was responded to by Salmasius (*Defensio Regia*) in defence of the King; Salmasius's treatise was in turn answered by Milton in *Pro Populo Anglicano*. There were a dozen editions of this popular work over two years: one dated 1650 (also listed here), and the remainder 1651 or 1652. "It has not unnaturally been assumed that the 1650 edition, a duodecimo . . . is the first. . . . But as the *Defensio* was not ordered to be printed till 23 December 1650, it cannot have been published before, at the earliest, the following January, and the 1650 imprint must therefore represent the old style of dating, under which the year did not officially begin till 25 March . . . " (Madan). This is the work which finally cost Milton his eyesight and which Warton characterized as "the best apology ever offered for bringing kings to the block." In 1660, all copies were ordered to be surrendered and, along with *Eikonoklasthes*, "to be burnt by the common hangman." "Third and probably only obtainable issue of the first edition" (G. W. Stuart, Jr., Ravenstree, Cat. 163, #88, 1989). Madan 1; Wing M2166; Grolier, *Wither to Prior*, 582; Shawcross, Kentucky, 22; Shawcross, 1974, pp. 319–27; Coleridge 44c; Kohler 501.

2567. [PRO POPULO] JOANNIS MILTONI ANGLI PRO POPVLO ANGLICANO DEFENSIO Contra Claudii Anonymi, alias Salmasii, Defensionem Regiam. Editio emendatior. *Londini, Typis Du-Gardianis. Anno Domini 1651.* Second edition, revised. Folio, 263pp., errata leaf before title, woodcut armorial shields on title page, decorative head- and tailpieces and decorated initial letters, contemporary calf (rebacked, new endpapers). A splendid copy of the rare revised second edition, very fresh internally, with the early bookplate of Thomas Fountayne (d. 1709), son of the Commonwealth judge, John Fountaine, commissioner along with Bradshaw and Tyrrell of the Broad Seal during the Commonwealth, and with later bookplate of F. J. P. Montague, direct descendent of Thomas Fountayne. On verso of errata leaf is the inscription: "Ex Dono Doctoris Nostri King 1670." See commentary with preceding copy. Madan 2; Wing M2167; Coleridge 45; Not in Kohler.

John Evelyn's Copy

2568. [PRO POPULO] JOANNIS MILTONI ANGLI DEFENSIO [SIC] PRO POPVLO ANGLICANO: [sic] Contra Claudii Anonimi [sic], alias Salmasii, Defensionem Regiam. *Londini, Typis Du Gardianis. Anno Domini 1651.* Third edition. 4to, [viii]+104+[6 unpaginated index]pp., large woodcut armorial shield on title page, "Praefatio," decorated initial letters, decorative tailpiece at end of text before index, "Index Rerum Memorabilium" at end, nineteenth-century polished calf (spine a bit faded and a little rubbed at top, some minor damp stains throughout lower edge), gilt rules with small gilt corner pieces on covers, black morocco label with gilt lettering and gilt rules, raised bands with decorative gilt trim within black trim and gilt rules, outer dentelles finely tooled in gilt, marbled endpapers and edges. A nice copy, bound by Kelly & Sons with their stamp. This edition has minor variations in the title from other editions: "Defensio" appears after "Angli" instead of after "Anglicano" and "Anonimi" is printed instead of "Anonymi." The John Evelyn copy with bookplate on front pastedown and with the press mark "Erato: 51" in the hand of John Evelyn on title page. Madan 3; Wing M2168; Coleridge 46; Not in Kohler.

2569. [PRO POPULO] JOANNIS MILTONI ANGLI PRO POPVLO ANGLICANO DEFENSIO, Contra Clavdii Anonymi, alias Salmasii, Defensionem Regiam[.] *Londini, Typis Dv Gardianis, Anno Domini 1650.* Fourth edition. 12mo, 244pp., device of Commonwealth arms on title page, decorative headpieces and decorated initial letters, contemporary full vellum, spine neatly lettered in ink by an early hand, bookplate. A very fine, fresh copy of the rare Madan 4, long thought to be the first edition. No. 1027 in The John Evelyn Catalogue—not in fact one of his books, but probably bought by one of his descendants, thus being in the John Evelyn Library before it was sold in 1977. There were a dozen editions of this popular work over two years: one dated 1650, and the remainder 1651 or 1652. "The '1650' edition was often thought to have been the first edition, until Madan's 1923 article [see comment quoted with 1651, first edition, third issue] . . . This edition was apparently printed by Theodorus ab Ackersdijck and Gisbertus à Zijll in Utrecht, for the ornaments are found in other works printed by them. . . . In the '1650' title page (b) the 'o' has been damaged. It would seem that the first title page had 1651 [since] the '1650' title page is always a cancel; presumably the first intention was to publish after March 25 but as copies were ready earlier the cancel title page was printed for the earlier date. It was the use of the old-style year which first suggested Utrecht as the place of publication; confirmation from the ornaments came later" (Coleridge, p. 61). Madan 4; Grolier, *Wither to Prior*, 580, 583; Coleridge 47b; Not in Kohler.

2570. [PRO POPULO] JOANNIS MILTONI ANGLI PRO POPVLO ANGLICANO DEFENSIO Contra Claudii Anonymi, alias Salmasii, Defensionem Regiam. *Londini, Typis Du-Gardianis, Anno Domini 1651.* Fifth edition. Bound with Salmasius, **DEFENSIO REGIA PRO CAROLO I**. *Ad Serenissimum Magnae Britanniae Regem Carolum II . . . Anno MDCXLIX (1649).* Sixth edition. 2 volumes in one. Thick 12mo, [18]+244pp.,+468pp., device of Commonwealth arms on title page, decorative headpieces and decorated initial letters, printer's device on Salmasius title page, contemporary full vellum (a bit rubbed), spine neatly lettered in ink by an early hand, early name on title page. A good copy with Latin notes and Latin poetry in an early hand on front blanks, and with an early printed description and an engraving of a charioteer tipped in on front pastedown. The publication of *Eikonoklastes* by Milton in 1649 (copy listed here) was responded to by Salmasius (*Defensio Regia*, copy listed with Seventeenth-century Miltoniana) in defence of the King; Salmasius's treatise was in turn answered by Milton in *Pro Populo Anglicano*. Madan 5 (the fifth edition, printed in Holland) of *Pro Populo* and Madan 6 (the sixth edition, printed in Holland) of *Defensio Regio*. Coleridge 48; Not in Kohler.

2571. [PRO POPULO] JOANNIS MILTONI ANGLI PRO POPVLO ANGLICANO DEFENSIO, Contra Clavdii Anonymi, alias Salmasii, Defensionem Regiam. Cum Indice. *Londini, Typis Dv Gardianis, Anno Domini 1651.* Sixth edition. 12mo, 260+[12]pp., device of Commonwealth arms on title page, decorative headpiece and decorated initial letter, unpaginated twelve-page "Index Rervm Memorabilivm" at end, decorative tailpiece on last page, contemporary full vellum (a bit soiled), red morocco label with gilt lettering and decorative gilt trim on spine. A good copy with early name on title page. Wing M2168b; Madan 6; Coleridge 49; Not in Kohler.

2572. [PRO POPULO] Another Copy of JOANNIS MILTONI ANGLI PRO POPVLO ANGLICANO DEFENSIO . . . *Londini, Typis Dv Gardianis, 1651.* Sixth edition. Bound with two other works: *Responsio Ad Apologiam*, 1651, and *Pro Rege*, 1651. 3 volumes in one. 12mo, as preceding copy, except bound with two other Milton-related works, newly rebound in marbled boards, printed green paper label on spine. Nice. Each work in the collection is listed separately with appropriate commentary on that work. *Responsio Ad Apologiam* is listed later, and *Pro Rege* is listed under Rowland, its author, with Seventeenth-century Miltoniana.

2573. [PRO POPULO] JOANNIS MILTONI ANGLI PRO POPVLO ANGLICANO DEFENSIO, Contra Clavdii Anonymi, alias Salmasii, Defensionem Regiam. *Londini, Typis Dv Gardianis, Anno Domini 1651.* Seventh edition. 12mo, 283pp., device of Commonwealth arms on title page, decorative headpieces and decorated initial letters, contemporary full vellum (age-darkened), spine faintly lettered in ink by an early hand, with an unsigned eighteenth-century engraved portrait of Milton (crowned with laurel wreath, closely cropped to fit this volume) tipped in as frontispiece. Madan 7; Coleridge 50; Not in Kohler.

2574. [PRO POPULO] JOANNIS MILTONI ANGLI PRO POPVLO ANGLICANO DEFENSIO Contra Claudii Anonymi, alias Salmasii, Defensionem Regiam. *Londini, Typis Du Gardianis. Anno Domini 1651.* Ninth edition. 12mo, [xxxviii]+330pp., device of Commonwealth arms on title page, early boards (joints and spine slightly chipped, later endpapers), paper label on spine lettered in ink in an early hand. A good copy. Madan 9 (who assigns this edition tentatively to J. Jansson of Amsterdam, who is known to have printed an edition); Coleridge 51; Not in Kohler.

2575. [PRO POPULO] Another Copy of JOANNIS MILTONI ANGLI PRO POPVLO ANGLICANO DEFENSIO . . . *Londini, Typis Du Gardianis. Anno Domini 1651.* Ninth edition. Bound with three other works by Milton: *Defensio Secunda* (1654); *Ratio Constitutae* (1654); and *Literae Pseudo-Senatus Anglicani* (1676); and two other works: *Regii Sanguinis Clamor* (1652) by Peter DuMolin, and *Fides Publica* (1654) by Alexander More. 2 volumes. Comprising six works altogether, four by Milton. 12mo, old half green morocco, marbled paper over boards (bit worn), spines lettered in gilt. A very good collection of historically related pamphlets, with notes in an early hand on front pastedown of each volume. Each work in the collection is listed separately with appropriate commentary on that work. *Defensio Secunda, Ratio Constitutae,* and *Literae Pseudo-Senatus Anglicani* are listed alphabetically among Milton's works here; *Regii Sanguinis Clamor* by Peter DuMolin and *Fides Publica* by Alexander More are listed under their author's name with Seventeenth-century Miltoniana. Madan 9; Coleridge 51; Not in Kohler.

2576. [PRO POPULO] JOANNIS MILTONI ANGLI PRO POPVLO ANGLICANO DEFENSIO, Contra Claudii Anonymi, alias Salmasii, Defensionem Regiam. *Londini, Typis Du Gardianis, Anno Domini, 1652.* Twelfth edition. 12mo, 192pp., device of Commonwealth arms on title page, decorative headpieces and decorated initial letters, contemporary calf (a bit rubbed, especially at joints, front joint a little cracked, title-page age-darkened with early name in ink, same early name in ink on front pastedown, small worm holes in blank margins), covers ruled in blind with early crest in gilt on front cover, raised bands. Despite some minor defects, a nice copy. There were a dozen editions of this popular work over two years: one dated 1650 and the remainder 1651 or 1652. This 1652 edition was probably printed at Antwerp, as was the 1651 Dutch edition to which it bears many similarities. The "1650" edition was often thought to have been the first edition, until Madan's 1923 article (see comment quoted with 1651, first edition, third issue). Madan 12; Wing M2169; Coleridge 52; Not in Kohler.

2577. [PRO POPULO] JOANNIS MILTONI ANGLI PRO POPVLO ANGLICANO DEFENSIO, Contra Claudii Anonymi, alias Salmasii, Defensionem Regiam. Cum Indice. *Londini. Typis Du Gardianis, Anno Domini 1652.* Thirteenth edition. Bound with Salmasius, **DEFENSIO REGIA PRO CAROLO I.** *Ad Serenissimum Magnae Britanniae Regem Carolum II . . . Anno MDCXLIX (1649).* Sixth edition. 2 volumes in one. Thick 12mo, 278+[12]pp., device of Commonwealth arms on title page, decorative headpiece and decorated initial letter, unpaginated twelve-page "Index Rervm Memorabilivm" at the end, decorative tailpiece on last page, coat of arms on Salmasius title page, contemporary calf (cover a bit rubbed, newly and finely rebacked antique style), covers decorated in blind, red morocco label on spine lettered in gilt. A nice copy. The Milton is Madan 13, and is rare; the Salmasius is also Madan 13. Wing M 2169A; Madan 13; Parker, p. 35; Coleridge 53; Kohler 502.

2578. [PRO POPULO] JOANNIS MILTONI ANGLI PRO POPULO ANGLICANO DEFENSIO SECUNDA . . . *Londini, Typis Neucomianis, 1654.* First edition. Bound with **JOANNIS MILTONI ANGLI PRO SE DEFENSIO** Contra Alexandrum Morum Ecclesiasten, Libelli famosi, cui titulus, Regii **SANGUINIS CLAMOR AD COELUM** . . . *Londini, Typis Neucomianis. 1655.* First edition. 2 volumes in one. 12mo, 173+[1]pp.,+204pp., title page for each work, decorated initial letters, errata at the end of each work, contemporary calf (newly and finely rebacked to match with raised bands). The very fine former Anthony William George Lowther copy. "*Defensio Secunda* is one of Milton's more significant prose works, in which he is moved to write of himself, his life, his acceptance of his recent blindness, his evaluation of the Commonwealth government of Cromwell, and in brief, to make of the *Defensio Secunda* a highly personal statement. The writing has a quiet impact that marks a particularly significant phase in Milton's development and gives promise of the mature masterpieces to come" (G. W. Stuart, Jr., Ravenstree, Cat. 156, #13, 1988). These two works together are clearly among the two most outstandingly personal works to flow from Milton's pen, and they reflect his most personal thoughts about subjects he cared most passionately. *Pro Populo* is also the first work Milton wrote after he had become completely blind. The very rare first edition of each. Wing M2171, M2172; Parker, pp. 1030, 1036; Shawcross, 1974, pp. 323–29; Coleridge 57, 59; Not in Kohler.

2578A. [PRO POPULO ANGLICANO DEFENSIO] See: **A DEFENCE OF THE PEOPLE OF ENGLAND,** By John Milton . . . *[Amsterdam:] Printed in the Year 1692.* First edition, first issue in English of *Pro Populo Anglicano Defensio.* See copy under *Defence Of The People Of England,* 1692.

2578B. [PRO POPULO ANGLICANO DEFENSIO] See: **A DEFENCE OF THE PEOPLE OF ENGLAND.** By John Milton . . . *Printed in the Year 1695.* First edition, second issue in English of *Pro Populo Anglicano Defensio.* See copy under *Defence Of The People Of England,* 1695.

Prose: Selections and Prose Works (Listed Alphabetically)

[For Individual Prose Works & Collections See Alphabetical Listing By Title]

2579. THE CHOICE PROSE WORKS OF JOHN MILTON[,] *New York[:] Thomas R. Knox & Co. Successors To James Miller[,] 813 Broadway[,] (ca. 1865).* First edition? 8vo, viii+486pp., "Trow's Printing And Bookbinding Company, New York" on verso of title page, edited with a preface by Fayette Hurd, preface dated "July 12, 1865," elaborate decorative head- and tailpieces, decorated initial letters, "A List Of Milton's Prose Works. Arranged In Chronological Order" and "Index" at the end, modern brown cloth (a little rubbed, slight staining on spine), spine lettered in gilt within double gilt rules, new endpapers. A very good copy, crisp and clean within. "The Prose Writings of Milton. . . . form the labors of his life, grand in thought and expression, as the poetic recreations of his earlier and later years are sublime and beautiful . . . It is the aim of this volume to present a selection from Milton's Prose Writings, comprising some of the author's best thoughts, and setting forth as clearly as possible Milton himself, showing impartially his merits and faults as a writer and as a man" (Preface). Scarce. Not in Kohler.

2579A. (Cross-listing) COMPLETE PROSE WORKS OF JOHN MILTON[.] *New Haven: Yale University Press[;] London: Geoffrey Cumberlege: Oxford University Press[,] MCMLIII–MCMLXXXII.* 8 volumes. First edition thus each volume. 8vo, edited by Douglas Bush, Christopher Hill, Maurice Kelley, and others, under the general editorship of Don M. Wolfe. See main listing under *Complete Prose Works*, 1953–82.

2580. ENGLISH PROSE WRITINGS OF JOHN MILTON Edited By Henry Morley, LL.D. *London[:] George Routledge And Sons[,] Broadway, Ludgate Hill[;] Glasgow, Manchester, And New York[.] 1889.* First edition thus. 8vo, 446+[2]pp., half-title for the Carisbrooke Library (of which this is volume 5), statement on "The Carisbrooke Library," introduction, half-title (by subject) for each of the various works, original green cloth, depiction of Carisbrooke Library in gilt on front cover, gilt lettering on front cover and spine, advertisement leaf bound in at end, bookplate of Earl Miner. Included is a selection of Milton's prose works, with a forty-eight-page introduction by Henry Morley. Gift from Earl Miner. Not in Kohler.

2581. (Prose) JOHN MILTON POLITICAL WRITINGS Edited By Martin Dzelzainis[,] Lecturer In English, Royal Holloway and Bedford New College, London[.] Translated By Claire Gruzelier. *Cambridge University Press[,] Cambridge[,] New York[,] Port Chester[,] Melbourne[,] Sydney[,] (1991).* First edition. 8vo, xxxiii+229+[1]pp., half-title (advertisement for "Cambridge Texts In The History Of Political Thought"), emblem of the press on title page, "Introduction," "Principal events in Milton's life," "Bibliographical note," facsimile reproduction of 1650 title page of *The Tenure Of Kings* and of 1658 title page of *Pro Populo Anglicano*, "Biographical notes," "Index of scriptural citations," "Index of subjects," "Index of proper names," original red cloth, black label with gilt lettering and gilt rules on spine, printed publisher's wrappers. A fine copy. Included are Milton's *The Tenure of Kings and Magistrates* and *A Defence of the People of England.*

2582. Variant of Preceding. JOHN MILTON POLITICAL WRITINGS Edited By Martin Dzelzainis . . . [As Preceding.] Translated By Claire Gruzelier. *Cambridge University Press[,] Cambridge[,] New York[,] Port Chester[,] Melbourne[,] Sydney[,] (1991).* First paperback edition. 8vo, xxxiii+229+[1]pp., as preceding, paperback, original printed stiff paper wrappers. A nice copy.

2583. JOHN MILTON SELECTED PROSE edited by C. A. Patrides[.] *Penguin Books[,] [Baltimore and Harmondsworth, Middlesex, England: Penguin Books,] (1974).* First edition thus. 8vo, 425+[6]pp., "To The Reader," "An Outline Of Milton's Life," "Introduction[:] Milton In The Seventeenth Century," half-title for each section, paperback, printed stiff paper wrappers with reproduction of Blake drawing for *Jerusalem* in color on front cover, orange spine, "Bibliography" followed by six advertisement leaves "About Penguins And Pelicans." A good copy. A second, revised edition thus was published in 1985 (copy following).

2584. JOHN MILTON SELECTED PROSE New and Revised Edition[.] Edited by C. A. Patrides[.] *University of Missouri Press[,] Columbia, 1985.* Second, revised edition thus. 8vo, 463pp., "To The Reader," "An Outline Of Milton's Life," "Introduction[:] Milton In The Seventeenth Century," half-title for each section, paperback, printed stiff paper wrappers, with Michelangelo's *Creation of the Sun, the Moon, and the Planets* from the Sistine Chapel reproduced in red on front cover, "Bibliography" at end. A fine copy. Laid in: original advertisement leaf for this revised edition of the first edition thus published in 1974 (also listed here).

2585. (Selections) JOHN MILTON[:] SELECTIONS, CHIEFLY AUTOBIOGRAPHICAL FROM THE PAMPHLETS AND LETTERS, WITH THE TRACTATE

ON EDUCATION AND AREOPAGITICA[.] Little Masterpieces Edited by Bliss Perry[.] *New York[:] Doubleday, Page & Company[,] 1901.* First edition thus. Small 8vo, xii+211pp., half-title ("Little Masterpieces"), unsigned engraved frontispiece portrait of Milton at age sixty-two (fine impression), protective tissue guard, engraved title page ruled in red with Milton's name in red, small rose emblem at the center, copyright 1901 on verso of title page, half-title (paginated) before each section or work, contemporary three-quarter dark green morocco, marbled dark green paper over boards, spine lettered in gilt with several small decorative floral pieces in gilt, marbled dark green endpapers, t.e.g., green silk ribbon marker. A fine copy. "In making this volume of selections, I have given the first place to four autobiographical passages, in which Milton tells his personal history, defends his purity of life and aim, comments nobly upon his blindness, and dedicates himself to the cause of Truth. Next comes a lofty description of perfect marriage, drawn from the 'The Doctrine and Discipline of Divorce.' For their political as well as religious interest I have reprinted the opening and closing pages of 'Reformation in England,' and have added the sketches of Bradshaw and Cromwell. The Letters of State which Milton dictated to foreign powers concerning the massacre of Protestants in Piedmont will be read with keen curiosity by all admirers of the sonnet. . . . Of Milton's personal letters I have chosen two, one relating to his blindness, the other to his peaceful old age. I have given in full the two best known of Milton's prose treatises, the tract 'On Education,' and the famous 'Areopagitica,' or plea for free speech. Brief preparatory notes accompany each selection in the volume" (Editor's Introduction). A second edition was published a year later in 1902 (also listed here). Not in Kohler.

2586. (Selections) JOHN MILTON[:] SELECTIONS, CHIEFLY AUTOBIOGRAPHICAL FROM THE PAMPHLETS AND LETTERS, WITH THE TRACTATE ON EDUCATION AND AREOPAGITICA[.] Little Masterpieces Edited by Bliss Perry[.] *New York[:] Doubleday, Page & Company[,] 1902.* Second edition thus. Small 8vo, xii+211pp., half-title ("Little Masterpieces"), preceded by a leaf engraved with a yellow bookplate ("The Pickering Edition deLuxe[,] The Number is 435 and the owner _____," with Pickering emblem in the center, the number hand-written in red ink, and the owner's line blank), unsigned engraved frontispiece portrait of Milton at age sixty-two (fine impression), protective tissue guard with a second thicker protective guard loosely laid in, engraved title page ruled in red with Milton's name in red, small rose emblem at the center, copyright 1901 on verso of title page, half-title (paginated) before each section or work, contemporary three-quarter dark green morocco (a bit rubbed along extremities, spine slightly chipped at top and bottom, corners chipped), marbled dark green paper over boards, spine lettered in gilt with several small decorative floral pieces in gilt, marbled dark green endpapers, t.e.g., green silk ribbon marker. A nice copy. "Brief preparatory notes accompany each selection in the volume" (Editor's Introduction). No. 435 of a limited edition. Not in Kohler.

2587. THE MILTON ANTHOLOGY SELECTED FROM THE PROSE WRITINGS[.] *New York[,] Henry Holt And Company[,] 1876[.]* 8vo, viii+486pp., 1865 copyright date on verso of title page, dedication leaf ("To John Greenleaf Whittier, This Edition Of Treasures From Milton's Prose Writings Is Dedicated By The publishers"), decorative head- and tailpieces and decorated initial letters, "A List Of Milton's Prose Works" and "Index" at the end, original brown cloth (a bit rubbed, spine a little chipped at the top and missing at the bottom, occasional pencil markings), covers and spine decorated with embossed trim in blind at the top and bottom, front cover lettered in gilt with laurel wreath in gilt at the center, spine lettered in gilt with initials of the press in gilt at the bottom, brown endpapers. A good copy with early signature. The "Preface," here signed "Fayette Hurd, July 12, 1865," appears in *The Choice Prose Works Of John Milton* (ca. 1865) possible first edition (see preceding copy where a large excerpt is quoted). Not in Kohler.

2588. MILTON'S PROSE Selected And Edited With An Introduction By Malcolm W. Wallace[,] Professor Of English Literature, University College, Toronto[.] *Humphrey Milford, Oxford University Press[,] London[,] Edinburgh[,] Glasgow[,] Copenhagen[,] New York[,] Toronto[,] Melbourne[,] Cape Town[,] Bombay[,] Calcutta[,] Madras[,] Shanghai[,] (1925).* First edition thus. 16mo, xxix+476+8pp., half-title ("The World's Classics CCXCIII"), central printer's device on title page, copyright date of 1925 on verso of title page along with brief biographical facts about Milton, half-title for each work reprinting title page and date of original publication, original green cloth, blind rules on covers, gilt-decorated spine with gilt lettering, eight pages of advertisements for "The World's Classics" (with separate title page) bound in at end. A good copy, including Milton's major works in prose, with introductions and notes. A second edition thus was published in 1931; a third edition thus in 1937—both editions listed here.

2589. Variant of Preceding, original blue buckram, blind rules on covers and spine, with central emblem in blind on front cover, spine lettered in gilt, t.e. blue, with contemporary signature (dated 1931) in a neat hand on fly-leaf. A nice copy in a variant publisher's binding, the binding which was to become traditionally used with the Oxford "Worlds Classics").

2590. (Prose) MILTON'S PROSE Selected And Edited With An Introduction By Malcolm W. Wallace[,] Professor Of English Literature, University College, Toronto[.] *Oxford University Press[,] London: Humphrey Milford[,] (1931).* Second edition thus. 16mo, xxix+476pp., half-title ("The World's Classics CCXCIII"), central printer's device for "The World's Classics" on title page, brief biographical facts about Milton on verso of title page, half-title for each work reprinting title page and date of original publication, original blue buckram (a bit rubbed, name on fly-leaf), blind rules on covers and spine, with central emblem in blind on front cover, spine lettered in gilt, t.e. blue. A nice copy. As with the first edition, Milton's major works in prose are included with introductions and notes.

2591. MILTON'S PROSE Selected And Edited With An Introduction By Malcolm W. Wallace[,] Professor Of English Literature, University College, Toronto[.] *Oxford University Press[,] London: Humphrey Milford[,] (1937).* Third edition thus. 16mo, xxix+476+16pp., half-title ("The World's Classics CCXCIII"), central printer's device for "The World's Classics" on title page, contents as with preceding, original blue buckram, blind rules on covers and spine, with central emblem in blind on front cover, spine lettered in gilt, t.e. blue, printed publisher's wrappers (a bit worn, top portion missing on front cover). A nice copy.

2592. MILTON'S PROSE Selected And Edited With An Introduction By Malcolm W. Wallace[,] Professor Emeritus, University College, Toronto[.] *London[:] Oxford University Press[,] (1959).* 16mo, xxix+476+16pp., half-title ("The World's Classics 203"), brief biographical facts about Milton on verso of title page, half-title for each work, original blue cloth, central emblem in blind on front cover, spine lettered in gilt, printed publisher's wrappers lettered in white and black. A nice copy.

2593. MILTON'S PROSE WRITINGS[.] Introduction By K[athleen]. M. Burton[.] *Dent: London[,] Everyman's Library[;] Dutton: New York[,] (1970).* 8vo, xv+367pp., half-title, introduction (dated 1958 and new with this edition), "Select Bibliography," index at the end, paperback (few scuff marks on bottom edge), original printed stiff paper wrappers with a sketch of Milton by Biro on front cover. Nice copy with a stamped price of "$1.95" on fly-leaf/half-title. The first edition thus in Everyman's Library was published in 1927; a revised edition was published in 1858; it was variously reprinted thereafter.

2594. MILTON'S PROSE WRITINGS[.] Introduction By K[athleen]. M. Burton[.] *Dent: London[,] Everyman's Library[;] Dutton: New York[,] (1974).* 8vo, xv+367pp., half-title, introduction (dated 1958 and new with this edition), "Select Bibliography," index at the end, paperback (a bit rubbed), original printed stiff paper wrappers with a sketch of Milton by Val Biro on front cover. A good copy with a sticker price of "$2.95" on back cover compared to printed price of 70p.

2595. THE POETRY OF MILTON'S PROSE; Selected From His Various Writings; With Notes, And An Introductory Essay [By Robert Carruthers]. [Quotation from Dryden] *London: Printed For Longman, Rees, Orme, Brown, And Green, Paternoster Row. 1827.* First edition. 12mo, lxvi+138pp., "Advertisement," "Contents," "Introductory Essay," half-title before the work itself, contemporary full polished calf (a bit rubbed, front joint cracked, some age-browning), central gilt arms of the Signet Library on covers, gilt rules on spine, red morocco label with gilt rules and gilt lettering, red speckled edges. A nice copy. Scarce. Kohler 523.

Probably best known as an editor and biographer of Alexander Pope, Carruthers published this volume anonymously very early in his literary career. The selection which he made from the prose works is interesting, but it is overshadowed by his fifty-eight-page "Introductory Essay." As editor, eventually, of Chambers's *Cyclopedia of English Literature* (listed in Chapter IV), Carruthers was presumably responsible for the lengthy section on Milton's prose in that anthology, which is treated separately from the commentary on the poetry.

2596. THE PROSE OF JOHN MILTON Selected and Edited from the Original Texts with Introductions, Notes, Translations, & Accounts of All of His Major Prose Writings[.] General Introduction by J. Max Patrick, Editor[.] *Anchor Books[,] Doubleday & Company, Inc. Garden City, New York[,] 1967.* First edition thus. 8vo, xxxv+[3]+675pp., half-title, introduction, general half-title before the works, half-title with foreword or introduction and copious notes for each work, general "Bibliography" at the end, paperback, original printed stiff paper wrapper (mark at top of front cover where price tag was removed). A very good copy, fresh and clean within.

2597. THE PROSE OF JOHN MILTON Selected and Edited from the Original Texts with Introductions, Notes, Translations, & Accounts of All of His Major Prose Writings[.] General Introduction by J. Max Patrick, Editor[.] The Stuart Editions[.] *New York: New York University Press[;] London: University of London Press, Limited[,] 1968.*

Second edition thus. 8vo, xxxv+[1]+675+[1]pp., half-title (with a listing of "The Stuart Editions . . . Already Published" on verso), introduction, general half-title before the works, half-title with foreword or introduction and copious notes for each work, general "Bibliography" at the end, original black cloth, decorative gilt trim at the bottom of front cover, spine lettered in gilt with small emblem of the press at bottom, printed publisher's wrappers (a bit rubbed and a little frayed along edges). Very good copy. "This book was first published in the Doubleday Anchor Seventeenth-Century Series" in 1967 (verso title page), copy preceding.

2598. PROSE OF MILTON: Selected And Edited, With An Introduction, By Richard Garnett, LL.D. *London: Walter Scott, LTD.[,] 24 Warwick Lane. n.d. [ca. 1894].* First edition thus? 8vo, xxii+[1]+256pp.+[16]pp., introduction (dated 1894), original blue cloth (spine faded, with very slight chipping beginning at top and bottom), printed paper label with red rule on spine (called "Camelot Series"), edges untrimmed, partially unopened. A nice copy with an early signature (dated 1905) on fly-leaf, and with sixteen pages of advertisements of publications by "The Scott Library" bound in at the end (with a listing of "Great Writers. A New Series Of Critical Biographies"—including Garnett's biography of Milton). Uncommon. Not in Kohler.

2599. PROSE OF MILTON: Selected and Edited, with an Introduction, by Richard Garnett, LL.D. *The Walter Scott Publishing Co., Ltd. London and Felling-on-Tyne[,] New York and Melbourne, n.d. [ca. 1894].* Second edition thus? 8vo, xxii+[1]+256pp., half-title ("The Scott Library"), undated introduction, original red cloth (a bit used, pages age-browned and slightly brittle as is common with some paper from this period), spine lettered in gilt (simply titled "Prose") with small emblem of the press in blind at the bottom. A good copy with an early signature on fly-leaf. See preceding edition published by Walter Scott, Ltd., in London, in which the introduction is dated 1894. The present edition with an expanded number of cities in the publisher's imprint would appear to have been published second. Uncommon. Not in Kohler.

2600. PROSE SELECTIONS Edited by Merritt Y. Hughes[,] Professor of English, University of Wisconsin[.] *New York: The Odyssey Press[,] New York[,] (1947).* First edition thus. 8vo, cxci+454pp., half-title ("Odyssey Series In Literature Robert Shafer, General Editor"), frontispiece facsimile of first edition title page of *Areopagitica*, "First Edition" on verso of title page, one additional facsimile, "Preface," "Chronology," "Introduction," "Bibliography," "Some Early Lives Of Milton," "Some Early Oratorical Performances," "Index" at the end, original blue cloth, spine lettered in gilt with gilt trim. Major selections from Milton's prose are included. A nice copy with signature on fly-leaf.

2601. PROSE SELECTIONS Edited by Merritt Y. Hughes[,] Professor of English, University of Wisconsin[.] *New York: The Odyssey Press[,] New York[,] (1947).* Second edition thus. 8vo, cxci+454pp., half-title, frontispiece facsimile of first edition title page of *Areopagitica*, "Second Edition" on verso of title page, one additional facsimile, as first edition preceding, original blue cloth (a bit rubbed), spine lettered in gilt with gilt trim. A nice copy.

2602. PROSE SELECTIONS Edited by Merritt Y. Hughes[,] Professor of English, University of Wisconsin[.] *New York: The Odyssey Press[,] New York[,] (1947).* Third edition thus. 8vo, cxci+454pp., as with the second edition, original blue cloth (a bit rubbed), spine lettered in gilt with gilt trim. A good copy with the signature of Gerald L. O'Grady on fly-leaf. O'Grady became a major film studies figure, founding the program at the State University at Buffalo, which is among the first such programs in the country.

2603. SELECT PROSE WORKS OF MILTON[.] Account Of His Own Studies. Apology For His Early Life And Writings. Tractate On Education. Areopagitica. Tenure of kings. [Vol. I.] Eikonoklastes. Divisions Of The Commonwealth. Delineation Of A Commonwealth. Mode of Establishing A Commonwealth. Familiar Letters. [Vol. II.] With Introductory Remarks and Notes By J. A. St. John. *London: Printed By The Proprietor; And Published By J. Hatchard And Son, Piccadilly; Oliver And Boyd, Edinburgh; And Cumming, Dublin. 1836.* 2 volumes. 8vo, lxxviii+[2]+329+[1]pp.,+xv+[1]+440pp., engraved frontispiece portrait of a disheveled Milton, engraved by T. Mollison, volume 1, engraved frontispiece portrait of "Cromwell in conference with Milton" (unsigned, or attribution removed), volume 2, "London: Printed By Joseph Rickerby, Sherbourn Lane" on verso of last page, volume 1, with a variation ("J. Rickerby, Printer, Sherbourn Lane") at bottom of last page, volume 2, half-titles for each of the various works, notes at bottom of page, contemporary blue polished calf (a bit rubbed at joints, slight chip missing at top of spine, volume 1, spine slightly worn at bottom of volume 2), gilt rules on covers, spines elaborately decorated in gilt within the panels with gilt lettering and numbering, raised bands with decorative gilt trim, wide inner dentelles finely tooled in gilt, corners of outer dentelles ruled in gilt, marbled endpapers, t.e.g. A fine set. Scarce. Kohler 525.

2604. (Selected prose) OF EDUCATION, AREOPAGITICA[,] THE COMMONWEALTH BY JOHN

MILTON With Early Biographies Of Milton[,] Introduction[,] And Notes Edited By Laura E. Lockwood[,] PH.D. Associate Professor Of The English Language[,] Wellesley College[.] The Riverside Literature Series[.] *London: George G. Harrap & Company[,] 2 & 3 Portsmouth Street, Kingsway, W.C. n.d. [ca. 1909].* First edition thus. Small 8vo, lxxxvi+205pp. "The Riverside Press Cambridge • Massachusetts U.S.A." on verso of title page, "Introduction," "Biographies Of Milton," notes at bottom of page, original green cloth, tall Grecian columns in black on either side of front cover with title lettered in black in the middle with "Riverside Literature Series" lettered in black at the top and "George G. Harrap & Co." lettered in black at the bottom, spine lettered in black (a bit rubbed), central device in black With "RLS 211" at center of back cover. Nice copy. See later editions of this publication by Laura Lockwood: in 1911, published by Houghton Mifflin Company, The Riverside Press, where "Selected Essays" appears on the title page of two of the editions of that year (see copies listed here), and in 1912 by "George G. Harrap & Company," where, like here, "Selected Essays" does not appear on the title page, nor does "The Riverside Literature Series" (although listed on title page here). Not in Kohler.

2605. (Selected prose) OF EDUCATION, AREOPAGITICA[,] THE COMMONWEALTH BY JOHN MILTON With Early Biographies Of Milton[,] Introduction, And Notes Edited By Laura E. Lockwood, PH.D. Associate Professor of the English Language, Wellesley College[.] The Riverside Literature Series[.] *Boston[,] New York[,] Chicago[:] Houghton Mifflin Company[;] The Riverside Press Cambridge[,] (1911).* Second edition thus; first edition thus by Houghton Mifflin. Small 8vo, lxxxvi+205+[5]pp., emblem of "The Riverside Press" on title page, copyright date of 1911 on verso of title page, "Introduction," "Biographies Of Milton," notes at bottom of page, original publisher's red cloth (spine faded), blind-stamped emblem of the press (different from that on title page here) on front cover, spine lettered in gilt with decorative gilt device, advertisements for "Literature Texts" by Houghton Mifflin bound in at the end. A good copy with the bookplate of Milton scholar Maurice Kelley signed by him (with some marginal notations and underlinings by him). Not in Kohler.

The possible first edition thus edited by Laura Lockwood was published in London in an undated ca. 1909 edition by Harrap & Company (see copy listed here). See also other editions published by Houghton Mifflin Company, The Riverside Press, later in 1911, with "Selected Essays" on title page, with "Riverside College Classics" in place of "The Riverside Literature Series," and with different cities in publisher's imprint (see copies listed here); and see edition published in 1912 by Harrap & Company (copy following) where, like here, "Selected Essays" does not appear on the title page, nor does "The Riverside Literature Series."

2606. (Selected prose) OF EDUCATION, AREOPAGITICA[,] THE COMMONWEALTH BY JOHN MILTON With Early Biographies Of Milton[,] Introduction[,] And Notes Edited By Laura E. Lockwood[,] PH.D. Associate Professor Of The English Language[,] Wellesley College[.] *London[:] George G. Harrap & Company[,] 9 Portsmouth Street Kingsway W.C. 1912.* Possible third edition thus; possibly second edition thus by Harrap & Company. Small 8vo, lxxxvi+205pp., central emblem on title page, "Introduction," "Biographies Of Milton," notes at bottom of page, "The Riverside Press Cambridge • Massachusetts U.S.A." on last page, original brown cloth (a bit rubbed, name in ink on fly-leaf, with some underlinings and a few marginal notes in ink), front cover and spine lettered in gilt, gilt rules at top and bottom of spine. A good copy. Not in Kohler.

The possible first edition thus of this publication by Laura Lockwood was published in London in an undated ca. 1909 edition by Harrap & Company (also listed here), where, like here, "Selected Essays" does not appear on the title page, but unlike here "The Riverside Literature Series" does. See also editions published by Houghton Mifflin Company, the Riverside Press, one year earlier in 1911—with different publisher's imprint, with either "The Riverside Literature Series" or "Riverside College Classics" and both with and without "Selected Essays" on title page (see copies listed here).

2607. (Selected prose) SELECTED ESSAYS[:] OF EDUCATION, AREOPAGITICA[,] THE COMMONWEALTH BY JOHN MILTON With Early Biographies Of Milton[,] Introduction, And Notes Edited By Laura E. Lockwood, PH.D. Associate Professor of the English Language, Wellesley College[.] Riverside College Classics[.] *Houghton Mifflin Company[;] Boston • New York • Chicago • Dallas • San Francisco[,] The Riverside Press Cambridge[,] (1911).* Second edition thus by Houghton Mifflin. Small 8vo, lxxxvi+205pp., emblem of the press on title page, copyright date of 1911 on verso of title page, "Introduction," "Biographies Of Milton," notes at bottom of page, original publisher's red cloth (slight staining on front cover, spine faded), blind-stamped emblem of the press (same as on title page) on front cover, spine lettered in gilt with decorative gilt device. A good copy with the bookplate of Milton scholar Maurice Kelley signed by him on front pastedown and again on fly-leaf (with some marginal notations and underlinings and extensive notations on back endpapers by him). Not in Kohler.

The possible first edition thus of this publication by Laura Lockwood was published in London in an undated edition, ca. 1909, by Harrap & Company (also listed here). See also the other edition published by Houghton Mifflin Company, The Riverside Press, earlier in 1911 (copy listed here)—without the inclusion of "Selected Essays" as here, with "The Riverside Literature Series" in place of "Riverside College Classics," with a different emblem of the press at center of title page, with fewer cities in publisher's imprint, and with advertisement leaves at the end; and see edition published in 1912 by Harrap & Company—where, unlike here, "Selected Essays" does not appear on the title page, but neither do "The Riverside Literature Series" or "Riverside College Classics" (also listed here).

2608. (Selected prose) Variant of Preceding, original publisher's red cloth, blind-stamped emblem of the press (same as on title page) on front cover, spine lettered in gilt with decorative gilt device. A very nice copy with fewer cities in publisher's imprint ("Boston[,] New York[,] Chicago[,] San Francisco"). Not in Kohler.

2609. SELECTED PROSE WRITINGS OF JOHN MILTON With An Introductory Essay By Ernest Meyers[.] *London[:] Kegan Paul, Trench & Co[.] MDCCCLXXXIIII [sic]*. First edition thus. Tall 8vo, xxx+[1]+258pp., half-title, title page in red and black with central seal of the Chiswick Press, half-title for each of the works, contemporary full crushed olive green morocco (spine faded to a rich brown), gilt rules on covers and spine, spine lettered in gilt with small decorative gilt devices in the panels (with incorrect date of "1888" in gilt at bottom of spine), raised bands with decorative gilt trim, broad inner dentelles richly tooled in gilt, outer dentelles ruled in gilt, marbled endpapers, t.e.g., others untrimmed. A very nice copy, handsomely "Bound By Ramage," with their stamp. The works include "Of Reformation in England (1641)"; "The Reason of Church Government (1641)"; "Animadversions (1641)"; "An Apology for Smectymnuus (1642)"; "The Doctrine and Discipline of Divorce [no date given]"; "Of Education (1644)"; "Areopagitica (1644)"; "The Tenure of Kings and Magistrates (1649)"; "Eikonoklastes (1649)"; "The Ready and Easy Way to Establish a Free Commonwealth (1660)." This is one of a limited large paper edition of 50 numbered copies, beautifully printed by the Chiswick Press on fine quality paper, with extremely generous margins. This is number 24, numbered and signed by the printer, Charles Whittingham of the Chiswick Press, on verso of blank facing half-title. Not in Kohler.

The second edition thus was published by D. Appleton and Company (the first thus by Appleton) in New York in 1884 (copy listed here); the third edition thus was published by Kegan Paul, Trench & Co. (the second thus by Kegan Paul) in London in 1888 (copy listed here); the possible fourth edition thus was published by D. Appleton and Company (the possible second thus by Appleton) in New York in 1896 (copy listed here); the possible fifth edition thus was published by D. Appleton and Company (the possible third thus by Appleton) in New York in 1898 (copy listed here).

2610. SELECTED PROSE WRITINGS OF JOHN MILTON With An Introductory Essay By Ernest Meyers[.] *New York[:] D. Appleton And Company[,] 1, 3, and 5 Bond Street[.] MDCCCLXXXIV*. Second edition thus (first thus by Appleton). Small 8vo, xxx+[1]+258pp., similar to preceding edition (except published by Appleton in New York), half-title, title page in red and black with central seal of the press, contents as with preceding, half-title for each of the works, contemporary full parchment (a bit soiled, especially the spine), front cover lettered in red with seal of the Chiswick Press in black in lower right corner, spine lettered in red and black, t.e.g., others untrimmed, partially unopened. A good copy in an attractive Victorian publisher's parchment binding. Uncommon. Not in Kohler.

2611. (Selected prose) **SELECTED PROSE WRITINGS OF JOHN MILTON** With An Introductory Essay By Ernest Meyers[.] *London[:] Kegan Paul, Trench & Co[.] MDCCCLXXXVIII*. Third edition thus; second thus by Kegan Paul, Trench & Co. Small 8vo, xxx+[1]+258pp., half-title, title page in red and black with central seal of the Chiswick Press, contents as with first edition, half-title for each of the works, contemporary full purple morocco (front cover detached), gilt rules and decorative gilt border trim on covers and spine, gilt lettering on front cover and spine, raised bands, broad inner and outer dentelles ruled in gilt, a.e.g. Except for the broken front joint, a very nice copy in an attractive morocco binding. Not in Kohler.

2612. Variant of Preceding, contemporary (possibly publisher) full parchment (a bit soiled), front cover lettered in red with seal of the Chiswick Press in black in lower right corner, spine lettered in red and black, t.e.g., others untrimmed. Nice copy in a variant original full parchment binding. Not in Kohler.

2613. SELECTED PROSE WRITINGS OF JOHN MILTON With An Introductory Essay By Ernest Meyers[.] *New York[:] D. Appleton And Company[,] 1896*. Possible fourth edition thus (possible second edition thus by D. Appleton and Company). Small 8vo, xxx+258pp., contents as with first edition, half-title, engraved frontispiece portrait plate after Faithorne, engraved by Illman and Pilbrow, protective tissue guard, small seal of the press at center of title page, half-title for each of the works, contemporary one-half red cloth, brown linen (a bit rubbed), spine lettered in gilt with decorative gilt trim at top and bottom and gilt emblem at the center, t.e. red, fore- and bottom edges untrimmed. A nice, tall copy (possibly a large paper copy) with the addition of a frontispiece portrait (a fine impression of the engraved frontispiece portrait of Milton after Faithorne). Uncommon. Not in Kohler.

2614. SELECTED PROSE WRITINGS OF JOHN MILTON With An Introductory Essay By Ernest Meyers[.] *New York[:] D. Appleton And Company[,] 1898.* Possible fifth edition thus (possible third edition by D. Appleton and Company). Small 8vo, xxx+[1]+258pp., half-title, frontispiece portrait plate (unsigned, "D. Appleton & Company" at the bottom), protective tissue guard, small seal of the press at center of title page, contents as with first edition, half-title for each of the works, contemporary three-quarter blue morocco, blue marbled paper over boards (rubbed along extremities, spine faded and chipped at top and bottom, decorated endpapers, t.e.g., others untrimmed and partially unopened. A good copy with the addition of a different frontispiece portrait (unsigned). Uncommon. Not in Kohler.

2615. (Selections) **A SELECTION FROM THE ENGLISH PROSE WORKS OF JOHN MILTON.** In Two Volumes. Vol. 1 / Vol. 2. *Boston: Published By Bowles And Dearborn, No. 72 Washington Street. 1826.* 2 volumes. First edition thus. 12mo, lxiv+296pp.,+vii+347pp., separate title page each volume, "Contents" each volume, lengthy "Preface," volume 1, original boards, printed paper labels on brown cloth spines (labels chipped and partially defective, minor age-browning), edges untrimmed and partially unopened. Presentation copy from the editor, with presentation inscription by the editor (Francis Jenks), "Charles Folsom. From the editor," on fly-leaf of each volume. Jenks has added an important sixty-page critical preface (dated "Boston, December 26th, 1826"). A very nice set in rather well-preserved original state. Scarce. Not in Kohler.

2616. SELECTIONS FROM THE PROSE AND POETRY OF JOHN MILTON Edited By James Holly Hanford, PH.D. Professor of English at the University of Michigan[.] *Riverside College Classics[.] Houghton Mifflin Company[,] Boston[,] New York[,] Chicago[,] San Francisco[,] The Riverside Press Cambridge, (1923).* First edition thus. Slim 8vo, vi+310pp., copyright date of 1923 on verso of title page, "Notes On The English Poems" at end, original red cloth (a bit rubbed, some light pencil markings and notations, name in ink on fly-leaf), central emblem of the press in blind on front cover, spine lettered in gilt. A good copy.

2617. Variant of Preceding. A nice copy with variant publisher's imprint (with the addition of Dallas to the list of cities), in a variant publisher's binding without emblem of the press in blind on front cover.

2618. SELECTIONS FROM THE PROSE WORKS OF JOHN MILTON With Critical Remarks And Elucidations. Edited By The Rev. James J. G. Graham, M.A., Oxon, Vicar Of Much Cowarne, Herefordshire. [Quotation from Milton] [Quotation from Keble] In One Volume. *London: Hurst And Blackett, Publishers, 13 Great Marlborough Street. 1870. The right of Translation is reserved.* First edition thus. 8vo, [i]+338+[1]pp., half-title, dedication page, preface (dated "February 1870"), original brown cloth (a bit rubbed), covers decorated in black, spine lettered in gilt with decorative gilt device beneath and with gilt trim at top and bottom, dark green endpapers, edges untrimmed. A good copy in a nice publisher's binding. Milton's works are "Arranged In Chronological Order." Presentation copy from the editor, with presentation inscription from the editor (dated 1882) on half-title. Not in Kohler.

2619. Variant of Preceding. A nice copy in a variant publisher's binding, original brown cloth, with a page entitled "Note" bound in at the end after appendix in which the editor's disagreements with Milton are expressed: "Believing, as the Editor does, in the Divine right of Bishops . . . he would gladly ignore, as much as possible in the following Extracts, Milton's hatred of Prelacy. . . . He was his own Bishop and Pope, and went wrong because he considered his own opinion orthodox and everybody else's heterodox. Ipse dixit—nay, ipsissimus . . . I John Milton have said it. . . ." Not in Kohler.

2620. SELECTIONS FROM THE WORKS OF TAYLOR[,] LATIMER[,] HALL[,] MILTON[,] BARROW[,] SOUTH[,] BROWN[,] FULLER AND BACON By Basil Montagu[,] Esq. M.A. Fourth Edition[.] *London[:] William Pickering[,] 1834.* Fourth edition. 8vo, xvi+340pp., Pickering device on title page, dedication page, "Preface To The First Edition" (1805), "Preface To The Second Edition" (1807), "Preface To The Third Edition" (1829), contemporary full red straight-grained morocco (a bit rubbed at joints and along edges), covers and spine finely decorated in gilt, spine lettered in gilt, inner dentelles finely tooled in gilt, a.e.g. A very nice copy of this Pickering edition with early bookplate. Uncommon. Not in Kohler.

2621. SELECTIONS FROM THE WORKS OF TAYLOR, LATIMER, HALL, MILTON, BARROW, SOUTH, BROWN, FULLER AND BACON. By Basil Montagu, Esq., M.A. First American From The Fifth London Edition. New Edition, Complete In One Volume. *New York: George P. Putnam, 155 Broadway. 1850.* First American From The Fifth London Edition. 8vo, xix+242pp., dedication page, "Preface To The First Edition" (1805), "Preface To The Second Edition" (1807), "Preface To The Third Edition" (1829), contemporary decorated dark blue cloth (a bit worn, portion from upper spine missing, slight inoffensive waterstaining throughout first third and bottom part of last portion of the book, ex-library with stamp and related library markings), covers and spine elaborately decorated in gilt, a.e.g., with contemporary signature (dated 1850) on fly-leaf. Uncommon. Not in Kohler.

2622. TREASURES FROM THE PROSE WRITINGS OF JOHN MILTON. [Quotation from Coleridge.] *Boston: Ticknor And Fields, 1866.* 8vo, 486pp., unsigned frontispiece portrait, small emblem of the press on title page, decorated head- and tailpieces and decorated initial letters, index at the end, "Cambridge: Stereotyped and Printed by Welch, Bigelow, & Co." at the bottom of the last page, original brown cloth (spine ends a little rubbed), covers ruled in blind, spine lettered in gilt, brown endpapers, red edges. A good copy with bookplate on front pastedown. Stevens 1223; Not in Kohler.

2623. THE PROSE WORKS OF JOHN MILTON; With A Life Of The Author, Interspersed With Translations And Critical Remarks, By Charles Symmons, D.D. Of Jesus College, Oxford. In Seven Volumes. *London: Printed by T. Bensley, Bolt Court, For J. Johnson; Nichols And Son; F. And C. Rivington; Otridge And Son; T. Payne; Ogilvy And Son; Cuthell And Martin; Vernor And Hood; R. Lea; J. Walker; Clarke And Son; J. Stockdale; Lackington And Co.; Longman And Co.; Cadell And Davies; J. Harding; R. H. Evans; J. Mawman; J. Hatchard; And Mathews And Leigh. 1806.* 7 volumes. First Symmons edition. Large 8vo, [i]+xliii+376pp.,+ii+472pp.,+[i]+494pp.,+ii+462pp.,+[i]+432pp.,+[i]+447pp.+[60-page unpaginated Index],+[1]+xi+[i]+566pp.,+[10-page unpaginated index], errata in volumes 1, 6, and 7, with volume 7 having an additional erratum at end, "An Alphabetical Index Of The Principal Matters Contained In The Six Volumes" at the end of volume 6, life of Milton occupies the whole of volume 7 with an "Index To The Life Of Milton" at the end, contemporary full Russia, decorative gilt borders and gilt rules on covers, with small decorative gilt corner pieces, finely gilt-decorated spines, raised bands with decorative gilt trim, inner dentelles tooled in gilt, outer dentelles ruled in gilt, marbled endpapers and edges. Large paper copy. An excellent set, rare thus, handsomely bound, with early armorial bookplate in each volume. Essentially preceded only by the three-volume edition, *Complete Collection* with Toland's life in 1698, and the two editions, each two volumes, by Thomas Birch: *A Complete Collection* in 1738 and *The Works* in 1753—each set listed here. Kohler 521.

Prose Works. London, 1806. 7 volumes. First Symmons edition. Large 8vo, contemporary full Russia. Large paper copy. See #2623.

2624. THE PROSE WORKS OF JOHN MILTON; Containing His Principal Political And Ecclesiastical Pieces, With New Translations, And An Introduction. By George Burnett, Late of Baliol College, Oxford. In Two Volumes. *London: Printed For John Miller, 72, Chancery Lane. 1809.* 2 volumes. First and only edition thus. 8vo, lxv+[iii]+449pp.,+[i]+623+[1]pp., half-title, volume 1, "W. People, Printer" (verso half-title and at bottom of last page each volume), separate title page each volume, dedication page, preface, introduction, half-titles for some of the works, original half blue paper boards, printed paper labels on spines, edges untrimmed and partially unopened, "Errors" printed after "Introduction, volume 1, "Errors" printed again at end of volume 2. A very nice set in rather well-preserved original state. Scarce. Kohler 522, reporting "Not in Cambridge University Library."

2625. THE PROSE WORKS OF JOHN MILTON; With An Introductory Review, By Robert Fletcher. *London: Westley And Davis, Stationers' Court. Stereotyped And Printed By J. R. And C. Childs, Bungay. MDCCCXXXIII.* First edition thus. Large 8vo, xliii+[i]+963pp.+[14-page index, unpaginated], frontispiece portrait plate of Milton after an engraving by W. C. Edwards, "Introductory Review," printed in double column, "An Alphabetical Index Of Principal Matters" at the end, contemporary three-quarter maroon leather (rebacked with red cloth preserving original printed paper label, new endpapers, corners and edges rubbed, foxing), printed paper label ("Prose Works Of John Milton With Portrait Price 25s.") on spine, edges untrimmed. A good copy. A second edition thus of *The Prose Works Of John Milton* was published in 1834 (see following copy), the third edition thus in 1835 (copy listed after that); the fourth edition thus in 1836 (copy listed here); the fifth edition thus in 1837 (copy listed with *Works*); the sixth edition thus in 1838 (copy listed here); the seventh edition thus in 1839 (copy listed with *Works*). Rare. Not in Kohler.

2626. THE PROSE WORKS OF JOHN MILTON; With An Introductory Review, By Robert Fletcher. *London: Westley And Davis, Stationers' Court. Stereotyped And Printed By J. R. And C. Childs, Bungay. MDCCCXXXIV.* Second edition thus. Large 8vo, xliii+[i]+963pp.+[14-page index, unpaginated], frontispiece portrait plate of Milton after an engraving by W. C. Edwards, "Introductory Review," printed in double column, "An Alphabetical Index Of Principal Matters" at the end, contemporary polished half calf (a little rubbed, foxing), elaborately gilt-decorated spine, red morocco label with gilt lettering and gilt rules, raised bands between gilt rules, marbled endpapers and edges. A very good copy with early armorial bookplate on front pastedown. Scarce. Referenced as 1834–35 in *Milton Tercentenary*, 1908, Appendix, p. 141; Kohler 524, reporting "Not in the British Library. Not in Cambridge University Library."

2627. THE PROSE WORKS OF JOHN MILTON; With An Introductory Review, By Robert Fletcher. *London: Westley And Davis, Stationers' Court. Stereotyped And Printed By J. R. And C. Childs. MDCCCXXXV.* Third edition thus. Large 8vo, xliii+[i]+963pp.+[14-page index, unpaginated], frontispiece portrait plate of Milton after an engraving by W. C. Edwards, protective tissue guard, as with first edition, original three-quarter calf, marbled paper over boards (slightly rubbed, frontispiece portrait and title page rather heavily foxed, much lighter foxing throughout), red morocco label on spine with gilt lettering and gilt rules, raised bands decorated with gilt rule trim. A very good copy. Scarce. Not in Kohler.

2628. THE PROSE WORKS OF JOHN MILTON; With An Introductory Review, By Robert Fletcher. *London: Westley And Davis, Stationers' Court. Stereotyped And Printed By J. R. And C. Childs. MDCCCXXXVI (1836).* Fourth edition thus. Large 8vo, xliii+[i]+963pp.+[14-page index, unpaginated], frontispiece portrait plate of Milton after an engraving by W. C. Edwards, as with first edition, contemporary full crushed black morocco over thick boards (a little rubbed at joints), gilt rules on covers and spine, spine lettered in gilt, raised bands with decorative gilt trim, marbled endpapers, t.e.g., others untrimmed, "An Alphabetical Index Of Principal Matters" at the end. A very good copy with the signature of James Hutton on front blank. A very good copy with early armorial bookplate on front pastedown. The first edition thus of *The Prose Works Of John Milton* was published in 1833 (also listed here with further copies in the collection cited). Scarce. Not in Kohler.

2629. THE PROSE WORKS OF JOHN MILTON; With An Introductory Review, By Robert Fletcher. *London: William Ball, Paternoster Row. Stereotyped And Printed By John Childs And Son. MDCCCXXXVIII.* Sixth edition thus. Large 8vo, xliii+[i]+963pp.,+[14]pp., frontispiece portrait plate of Milton after an engraving by W. C. Edwards, as with first edition, original green cloth (portrait foxed, spine a bit faded, joints cracked), covers blind-stamped, lettering in gilt within decorative gilt outline on spine, yellow endpapers, "An Alphabetical Index Of Principal Matters" at the end. A good copy. Presentation inscription from John Childs (dated 1840) on fly-leaf. Scarce. Kohler 527 Bound with *The Poetical Works of John Milton.* London: Frederick Westley and A. H. Davis . . .

1836 [also listed here], reporting "Not in the British Library. Not in Cambridge University Library."

2630. THE PROSE WORKS OF JOHN MILTON: With A Biographical Introduction, By Rufus Wilmot Griswold. [Quotation from Brydges] [Quotation from Wordsworth's Sonnet on Milton]. *Philadelphia: Herman Hooker, Publisher, No. 16 South Seventh Street. 1845.* 2 volumes. First edition thus? Large 12mo in 6s, xi+[i]+548,+550pp., separate title page each volume, "Biographical Introduction," volume 1, original blind-stamped brown silk (some slight staining on front cover of volume 1, spine ends chipped, slight foxing), decorative rules in blind on covers, spines lettered in gilt, anchor device (similar to Pickering anchor device) in gilt at bottom of spines. A nice large set with early signature (dated 1878) on fly-leaf. See possible second and possible third editions thus published in 1847 by different publishers in a virtually identical (though smaller) format and with a slightly different binding; see also possible fourth edition thus published in 1853. Uncommon. Kohler 528, reporting "Not in the British Library. Not in the Bodleian Library. Not in Cambridge University Library."

2631. Variant of Preceding, original rust brown cloth (spines a little faded, some minor foxing), decorative rules in blind on covers, spines lettered in gilt, anchor device (similar to Pickering anchor device) in gilt at bottom of spines, top edge rough, others untrimmed, partially unopened. A very nice large set in a variant publisher's binding, very tall, close to being a large paper copy, with contemporary signature (dated 1846) on fly-leaf. Uncommon. Kohler 528.

2632. THE PROSE WORKS OF JOHN MILTON: With A Biographical Introduction, By Rufus Wilmot Griswold. [Quotation from Brydges] [Quotation from Wordsworth's Sonnet on Milton]. *Philadelphia: John W. Moore, No. 193 Chestnut Street. 1847.* 2 volumes. Second edition thus? Large 12mo in 6s, xi+[i]+548,+550pp., separate title page each volume, "Biographical Introduction," volume 1, original blind-stamped brown silk (spines chipped at top and bottom, slight foxing), decorative designs in blind on covers and spines with gilt lettering on spines, yellow endpapers, bookplate. A good set with neat contemporary signature (dated 1848) on fly-leaf. Scarce.

The first edition thus was published by a different publisher in a virtually identical (though larger format and with a slightly different binding) in 1845 (see preceding copies); the possible third edition thus was published as here by Moore later in 1847 in the same size as here (see copy following); the possible fourth edition thus was published by Moore in 1853 (see copy listed here).

2633. THE PROSE WORKS OF JOHN MILTON: With A Biographical Introduction, By Rufus Wilmot Griswold. [Quotation from Brydges] [Quotation from Wordsworth's Sonnet on Milton]. *New York: Wiley And Putnam. Philadelphia: —John W. Moore. 1847.* 2 volumes. Third edition thus? Large 12mo in 6s, xi+[i]+548,+550pp., separate title page each volume, "Biographical Introduction," volume 1, original blind-stamped brown silk (spines chipped at top and bottom, foxing), decorative designs in blind on covers and spines with gilt lettering on spines, yellow endpapers, bookplate. A good set. Scarce. Not in Kohler.

2634. THE PROSE WORKS OF JOHN MILTON. With A Preface, Preliminary Remarks, And Notes, By J. A. St. John. *London: Henry G. Bohn, York Street, Covent Garden. 1848-1853.* 5 volumes. First edition thus. 8vo, xl+496+40pp.,+iv+548+40pp.,+iv+522pp.,+xxxvii+494pp.,+iv+522pp., half-title volume 1 ("Bohn's Standard Library"), separate title page each volume, volumes 1–3 dated 1848, volumes 4 and 5 dated 1853, engraved frontispiece portrait in each of the first three volumes (volume 1: a young Milton engraved by Cochran after Cooper; volume 2: "Cromwell in conference with Milton" (unsigned); volume 3: "Archbishop Laud," engraved by Read after Vandyke), each with protective tissue guard, original blind-stamped green cloth (volume 1), original blind-stamped blue cloth (volume 2), original blind-stamped bluish green cloth (volumes 3, 4, and 5), covers elaborately stamped in blind with gilt lettering on spines, edges untrimmed. Volumes 1–3 contain various of Milton's prose works; volumes 4 and 5 contain "A Treatise On Christian Doctrine, Compiled From The Holy Scriptures Alone. Translated From The Original By Charles R. Sumner . . . A New Edition, Revised and Corrected. London: Henry G. Bohn, York Street, Covent Garden. MDCCCLIII," together also with *The History Of Britain*, *The History of Moscovia*, and *Accedence Commenced Grammar* in volume 5. Yellow endpapers in volumes 1 and 2 with a very useful forty-page "Select Catalogue Of New Books At Reduced Prices Published Or Sold By Henry G. Bohn" bound in at the end of each volume; yellow endpapers in volume 3 with no advertisements; printed blue endpapers in volumes 4 and 5 with advertisements for "Bohn's Standard Library" printed in blue and with an extra advertisement leaf bound in at the end of each volume; forty-two-page index at the end of volume 5. Laid in (volume 1): a four-page "Prospectus Of Bohn's Standard Library." A handsome set of the principal mid-nineteenth-century edition of Milton's *Prose Works*, in original bindings, unusually excellent and bright and in uniformly very fine condition. All volumes are signed by the Wordsworth scholar Ernest De Selincourt on endpaper in each volume (dated 1899 in volume 1) with his neat shelf number in manuscript on verso of title; most volumes with neat notes in the margins or on rear endpaper in pencil or ink by De Selincourt. Williamson 218; Kohler 528.

2635. THE PROSE WORKS OF JOHN MILTON: With A Biographical Introduction, By Rufus Wilmot Griswold. [Quotation from Brydges] [Quotation from Wordsworth's Sonnet on Milton]. In Two Volumes. *Philadelphia: J. W. Moore, 193 Chestnut Street. 1853.* 2 volumes in one. Fourth edition thus? Large 12mo in 6s, xi+[i]+548,+550+[2]pp., separate title page each volume, "Biographical Introduction," volume 1, contemporary three-quarter calf, marbled paper over boards (bit rubbed, occasional slight foxing), spine lettered in gilt, raised bands. A good copy with advertisement leaf for "Valuable Books Published And For Sale By J. W. Moore" at the end. The first edition thus was published in 1845 (also listed here with further editions cited).

2636. THE PROSE WORKS OF JOHN MILTON: With A Biographical Introduction, By Rufus Wilmot Griswold. [Quotation from Brydges] [Wordsworth's Sonnet on Milton]. In Two Volumes. *Philadelphia: J. W. Moore, 193 Chestnut Street. 1856.* 2 volumes. Fifth edition thus? Large 12mo in 6s, xi+[i]+548,+550+[2]pp., separate title page each volume, "Biographical Introduction," volume 1, original brown silk cloth (a bit rubbed, corners worn, volume 1 spine a little faded, spines ends chipped), covers decorated in blind, spines lettered in gilt. A nice set with advertisement leaf for "Valuable Books Published And For Sale By J. W. Moore" at end of volume 2. The first edition thus was published in 1845 (also listed here with further editions cited). Not in Kohler.

2637. THE PROSE WORKS OF JOHN MILTON. [Quotation from Wordsworth] In Two Volumes. *Philadelphia: Caxton Press Of C. Sherman, Son & Co. 1864.* 2 volumes. First edition thus? Large 12mo in 6s, 548pp.,+ 550pp., title page each volume, notes at bottom of page, finely printed on thick paper, contemporary three-quarter black morocco (a bit rubbed at joints), marbled dark green paper over boards, spines lettered in gilt ("Milton's Works" at the top, "Prose" and volume number in the middle) with decorative gilt trim within the panels, raised bands with gilt trim (faded), marbled endpapers, t.e.g. A very nice set. Uniformly bound with: *The PW Of John Milton, Philadelphia: Willis P. Hazard, 31 South Sixth Street. 1864.* 2 volumes, together forming a handsome four-volume edition of Milton's *Works*. Scarce. Not in Kohler.

2638. PROSE WORKS OF JOHN MILTON, Author of "Paradise Lost," Etc. *New York: John B. Alden, Publisher. 1883.* 8vo, viii+486pp., "Preface" by Fayette Hurd, dated "July 12, 1865," decorative head- and tailpieces and decorated initial letters, index at the end, original reddish-brown cloth, front cover attractively decorated in black floral trim with title in gilt within decorative black and gilt trim near the top, spine similarly decorated in black and gilt with gilt lettering. A very nice copy. "It is the aim of this volume to present a selection from Milton's Prose Writings, comprising some of the author's best thoughts, and setting forth as clearly as possible Milton himself, showing impartially his merits and faults as a writer and as a man" (Preface). The "Preface" by Fayette Hurd also appears in *The Choice Prose Works Of John Milton*, ca. 1865, possible first edition (also listed here, where a larger excerpt is quoted). Not in Kohler.

2639. THE PROSE WORKS OF JOHN MILTON. Edited By J. A. St. John. [In Five Volumes] *London: George Bell & Sons, York St., Covent Garden, And New York. 1890-1895.* 5 volumes. 8vo, xl+496+40pp.,+iv+548+40pp.,+iv+ 522+[1]+40pp.,+xxxvii+494+40pp.,+iv+522+10+[2]pp., half-title volume 1 ("Bohn's Standard Library"), half-title, volume 2, separate title page each volume, variously dated (volume 1 dated 1893, volume 2 dated 1895, volume 3 dated 1890, volume 4 dated 1891, volume 5 dated 1894), engraved frontispiece portrait plate in volume 1: of a young Milton after Cooper, engraved by Cochran, in volume 2: "Cromwell in conference with Milton" (unsigned), and in volume 3: "William Laud, Archbishop Of Canterbury" engraved after "Vandyke," each with protective tissue guard, first three volumes containing various of Milton's prose works and labeled "Miscellanies" in gilt on the spines with Roman numerals "I," "II," and "III," the last two volumes containing "A Treatise On Christian Doctrine" (with title pages labeled "IV" and "V," the spines labeled "I" and "II" in gilt with title "Christian Doctrine" in gilt), with a forty-two-page "Index To The Principal Matters Contained In The Five Volumes" at the end of volume 5, original maroon diaper grain cloth (a bit rubbed, with contemporary ownership name in a fine hand on the flyleaf and title page of each volume), covers ruled in blind with central emblem in blind incorporating "Bohn's Libraries" on front covers, spines lettered in gilt with gilt rule at top and bottom and with gilt device of the press at the bottom consisting of a bell at the center and "Standard Library" lettered around with "Bohn's Libraries" in gilt at the bottom, t.e. rough. A very nice set with forty pages of "A Classified Catalogue Of Selected Works Including An Alphabetical List Of Bohn's Libraries Published By George Bell & Sons[.]" bound in at the end of volumes 1, 2, 3, and 4, each with separate title page dated 1896, and each list including editions of Milton; volume 5 has ten pages of "An Alphabetical List Of Books Contained In Bohn's Libraries. March, 1894," with half-title and including editions of Milton, with two additional pages of "The Aldine Edition Of The British Poets" (including the Aldine edition of Milton) bound in at the end. A handsome reissue of the principal mid-nineteenth-century edition of Milton's *Prose Works*, first published by Bohn in 1848–53 (see set listed here), in original bindings, very nice and in uniformly very fine condition. Scarce. Not in Kohler.

2640. THE PROSE WORKS OF JOHN MILTON. Edited By J. A. St. John. [In Five Volumes] *London: George Bell & Sons, York St., Covent Garden, And New York. Variously dated: 1901-1904.* 5 volumes. 8vo, xl+496+[32]pp.,+ iv+548+[32]pp.,+iv+522+[32]pp.,+xxxvii+494+[32]pp.,+ iv+522+[32]pp., half-title volume 1 ("Bohn's Standard Library"), separate title page each volume, variously dated (volume 1 dated 1904, volume 2 dated 1901, volume 3 dated 1904, volume 4 dated 1904, volume 5 dated 1901), engraved frontispiece portrait plate in volume 2: "Cromwell in conference with Milton" and in volume 3: "William Laud, Archbishop Of Canterbury" engraved after "Vandyke," each with protective tissue guard, first three volumes containing various of Milton's prose works and labeled "Miscellanies" in gilt on the spines with Roman numerals "I", "II," and "III," the last two volumes containing "A Treatise On Christian Doctrine" (with title pages labeled "IV" and "V," the spines labeled "I" and "II" in gilt with title "Christian Doctrine" in gilt), with a forty-two-page "Index To The Principal Matters Contained In The Five Volumes" at the end of volume 5, original maroon diaper grain cloth (a bit rubbed), covers ruled in blind with central emblem in blind incorporating "Bohn's Libraries" on front covers, spines lettered in gilt with gilt rule at top and bottom and with gilt device of the press at the bottom consisting of a bell at the center and "Standard Library" lettered around with "Bohn's Libraries" in gilt at the bottom, t.e. rough, partially unopened. A fine set with thirty-two pages of advertisements for "An Alphabetical List Of Books Contained In Bohn's Libraries" bound in at the end of each volume. Uniformly bound as volumes III, IV, V, VI, and VII of a seven-volume set, together with two volumes of "The Poetical Works Of John Milton" as Volumes I and II: "With A Memoir And Critical Remarks On His Genius And Writings By James Montgomery And One Hundred And Twenty Engravings . . . From Drawings By William Harvey. New Edition . . . London: George Bell & Sons, York St., Covent Garden, And New York. 1892 and 1900." A handsome reissue of the principal mid-nineteenth-century edition of Milton's *Prose Works*, first published by Bohn in 1848–53 (see set listed here), in original bindings, unusually excellent and bright and in uniformly very fine condition. Scarce. Kohler 533, dating its set "1904 (1901–1908)" and reporting "Not in the British Library. Not in the Bodleian Library. Not in Cambridge University Library."

2641. THE PROSE WORKS OF JOHN MILTON. Volume I. Eikonoklastes, The Tenure Of Kings And Magistrate. *Methuen & Co. 36 Essex Street W.C. London[.] 1905.* First edition thus. 8vo, x+174+[1 blank]+40pp., edited with a preface by Sidney Lee, half-title, frontispiece illustration for "Methuen's Standard Library, Edited By Sidney Lee," facsimile reproduction of title pages for *Eikonoklasthes* (1650) and for *The Tenure Of Kings* (1650), original blue cloth (bit rubbed), gilt-decorated spine with gilt lettering. A good copy with a forty-page listing of "A Catalogue Of Books Published By Methuen and Company" bound in at end. Although volume 1 only, *Eikonoklastes* and *The Tenure Of Kings* are complete herein. Not in Kohler.

2642. JOHN MILTON THE PROSE WORKS [Edited by] Thomas N. Corns[,] University of Wales. *Bangor[.] Twayne Publishers[,] An Imprint of Simon & Schuster Macmillan[,] New York[;] Prentice Hall International[,] London • Mexico City • New Delhi • Singapore • Sydney • Toronto, (1998).* First edition thus. 8vo, x+165+[1 blank]+1pp., half-title ("Twayne's English Authors Series, No. 546"), frontispiece portrait of Milton at age twenty-one, original maroon buckram, spine lettered in gilt. A fine copy in equally fine red publisher's wrappers with Milton's portrait (age twenty-one) in black on front cover.

2643. (Former attribution) **RATIO CONSTITUTAE** *Nuper Reipublicae Angliae, Scotiae, & Hiberniae,* Una cum Insulis aliisque locis ejus Ditioni subjectis, Penes D. Protectorem & Parlamentum. In qua [10 lines] Ex Anglico in Latinum versa. Hagae-Comitvm. *Typis Adriani Vlacq. 1654.* First edition. Bound with three other works by Milton: *Pro Populo* (1654) ninth edition; *Defensio Secunda* (1654); and *Literae Pseudo-Senatus Anglicani* (1676); and two other works: *Regii Sanguinis Clamor* (1652) by Peter DuMolin, and *Fides Publica* (1654) by Alexander More. 2 volumes. Comprising six works altogether, four by Milton. 12mo, 104pp., title page with printer's device, decorative headpieces and decorated initial letters, old half green morocco, marbled paper over boards (bit worn), spines lettered in gilt. A very good collection of historically related pamphlets, with notes in an early hand on front pastedown of each volume. Scarce. Shawcross, 1974, pp. 323–29; Coleridge 269 (is "Londini, Excudebat T. Newcomb.

1654," with "[9 lines]," 4to in size, with 62 pp., and with only a mention of this edition.

Ratio Constitutae is a translation into Latin of the new English Republic's constitution, once attributed to Milton because his office was responsible for translations, although there is no evidence that Milton himself did the translation. Each work in the collection here is listed separately with appropriate commentary on that work. *Defensio Secunda*, *Pro Populo*, and *Literae Pseudo-Senatus Anglicani* are listed alphabetically among Milton's works here; *Regii Sanguinis Clamor* by Peter DuMolin and *Fides Publica* by Alexander More are listed under their author's name with Seventeenth-century Miltoniana.

2644. READINGS FROM MILTON. Part I/II. *New York;[sic] Phillips & Hunt. Cincinnati;[sic] Walden & Stowe. 1883.* First edition thus. 2 volumes. 8vo (7 ⅛" × 4 ⅞"), 17pp., 20pp., original orange wrappers, each with printed title page on front cover, labeled "Home College Series" at the top, Part I being "Number Sixty-Three," Part II being "Number Sixty-Eight," decorative black border trim on front cover, statement about the series on inside of front cover signed by John H. Vincent and dated 1883, listing of the 100 items in the series on back cover. A nice set with Part I containing selections from Milton's early poems, and Part II containing selections from *PL* plus *NO*. Uncommon. Not in Kohler.

2645. READINGS FROM MILTON. With An Introduction By Bishop Henry White Warren, Counsellor C.L.S.C. Chautauqua Library . . . ..[sic]*Garnet Series. Boston: Chautauqua Press, 117 Franklin Street, 1886.* First edition thus. 8vo, xii+308pp., frontispiece sketch of a "Conjectural Diagram Of Milton's Cosmography. Vertical Section" with a description on facing page, both pages preceding title page, "Copyright, 1886, By Rand, Avery, & Co." on verso of title page, "Life Of John Milton" at the end, original red cloth (a bit rubbed), decorative black trim at top and bottom of front cover with gilt emblem incorporated in black trim at top, spine lettered in gilt. A nice copy of a late nineteenth-century selection of Milton's poems, including *Paradise Lost* (with introduction and with Books XI and XII summarized), *On The Morning Of Christ's Nativity*, *At A Solemn Music*, *Lycidas*, *L'Allegro*, *Il Penseroso*, [Four] *Sonnets*, and with "Life of John Milton." A second edition was published in 1890 (see copy following). Uncommon. Not in Kohler.

2646. READINGS FROM MILTON. With An Introduction By Bishop Henry White Warren, Counsellor [sic] C.L.S.C. Chautauqua Library. . . . [sic] *Garnet Series. New York: Chautauqua Press, 150 Fifth Avenue, 1890.* Second edition thus. 8vo, xii+308pp., frontispiece sketch of a "Conjectural Diagram Of Milton's Cosmography. Vertical Section" with a description on facing page, both pages preceding title page, "Copyright, 1886, By Rand, Avery & Co.—Copyright, 1890, By Educational Pub. Co." on verso of title page, "Life of John Milton" at the end, original red cloth (a bit rubbed, slight staining on front cover), front cover decorated with a genie-like looking lamp in silver within decorative black trim at the top, addition black trim at the bottom, spine lettered in gilt ("Readings From Milton, Garnet Series, Chautauqua Edition"). A good copy of a late nineteenth-century selection of Milton's poems, as in first edition preceding. Uncommon. Not in Kohler.

2647. A READY AND EASY WAY TO ESTABLISH A FREE COMMONWEALTH. The Author John Milton. [Greek Quotation from Soph. Antigone] [Latin Quotation from Machiavel] *London: Printed For J. Ridgway, No. 1, York-Street, St. James-Square. 1791.* Third edition. Small 4to, iv+44pp., originally a pamphlet, modern three-quarter black morocco, marbled paper over boards (with additional blank pages to give it size), gilt rules on covers, spine lettered in gilt, raised bands with gilt rules as trim, marbled endpapers, t.e.g. A very nice copy preserving original advertisement leaf after title page, with presentation inscription (dated 1940) on front blank, probably the date of the modern binding. Milton's *Readie And Easie Way* was first published in 1660, "aimed at influencing the Restoration settlement"; "it had no effect, but it did bring forth reaction" (Shawcross). The second edition was published separately in 1744, also "for J. Ridgway." Scarce. Not in Coleridge; Shawcross, 1974, p. 335–36; Not in Kohler.

2648. THE REASON OF CHURCH-GOVERNMENT URG'D AGAINST PRELATY By Mr. John Milton. In two Books. *London, Printed by E. G. for John Rothwell, and are to be sold at the Sunne in Pauls Church-yard. 1641.* First edition. 4to, 65+[1]pp., floral ornament on title, "Faults escap't in Printing are here corrected" on verso of last page, new half red morocco, red cloth (a few catchwords shaved, early name on title page), a.e.g. A good copy, having formerly belonged to W. R. Parker, with his initials stamped in blind on title and on A4. Milton's fourth anti-episcopal tract and the first of Milton's publications to bear his name. The work contains some revealing autobiographical passages, including Milton's belief in writing for "God's glory, by the honor and instruction of my country"; and "That what the [great poets of Athens, Rome and modern Italy] did for their country, I, in my proportion, with this over and above of being a Christian, might do for mine." Milton muses, though, "Time serves not now," over the great forms in which a poet may write: ranging from the "epic form" of which the poems of Homer, Virgil and Tasso are a "diffuse" model and "the book of Job a brief model; or whether the rules of Aristotle herein are strictly to be kept, or nature to be followed, which in them that know art, and use judgment is no transgression but an enriching of art; and lastly what king or knight before the conquest might be chosen in whom to lay the pattern of a Christian hero." Milton also emphasizes that the powers of the poet are equal to those of the pulpit: "These abilities [i.e., poetic powers], wheresoever they be found, are the inspired gift of God rarely bestowed, but yet to some . . . and are of power beside the office of a pulpit." Shawcross points out that the publication of this work "made no impact, as far as we know"; he also observes that "Jefferson, in his commonplace book summarized and quoted from [the] pamphlet [*Of Reformation Touching Church-Discipline*, see copy also listed here] along with *Reason of Church-Government*." Rare. Wing M2175; Parker, pp. 853–54; Coleridge 61; Shawcross, 1974, pp. 292–93, 294–95; Not in Kohler.

2649. [RESPONSIO AD APOLOGIAM] JOANNIS PHILIPPI ANGLI RESPONSIO AD APOLOGIAM ANONYMI cujusdam tenebrionis pro Rege & Populo Anglicano infantissimam. *Londini, Typis Dv-Gardianis. An.Dom. M.DC.LII.* Bound with two other works: *Pro Populo*, 1651, sixth edition, and *Pro Rege*, 1652. 3 volumes in one. 12mo, 112pp., device of Commonwealth arms on title page of *Responsio*, decorative headpiece and decorated initial letter, newly rebound in marbled boards, printed green paper label on spine. Nice. Scarce. Not in Wing; Willems 1671; Parker "G"; Shawcross 1974, pp. 323–29, 382–83; Shawcross, Kentucky, 26; Coleridge 62; Not in Kohler.

Each work in the collection is listed separately with appropriate commentary on that work. *Pro Rege* is Rowland's attack on Milton, answered here. It is listed under Rowland with Seventeenth-century Miltoniana. *Pro Populo* appears first in the binding; it is Madan 6; for discussion of this work, see *Pro Populo* listings. *Responsio Ad Apologiam* is a reply to John Rowland's attack on Milton (present in this collection) written by Milton's nephew under Milton's close supervision and involvement. "The *Responsio* was published as the work of John Phillips, and is normally so catalogued, but since 1694, it has customarily been included among Milton's works, on the basis of its inclusion by Edward Phillips in the list of Milton's writings that he published in his life. The consensus of opinion today is that John Phillips was deputed to write the work, Milton revised it and, in particular corrected the Latin. It was then published under Phillips's name" (Coleridge). This edition "is the first of the Continental reprints," after the "1st edition, published in London by Dugard," having

The Reason Of Church-government Urg'd against Prelaty. London, 1641. See #2648.

been printed "by Elzevir in Amsterdam" (Coleridge, who provides details of Milton's work, and clarifies the various editions).

2650. THE RIGHTS OF NATIONS TO DEPOSE THEIR KINGS And To Change Or Amend Their Systems Of Government; With A Vindication of the Killing of Tyrants: Being an Abridgment of Milton's celebrated Tract, Entitled, "The Tenure Of Kings And Magistrates." And a New and Abridged Translation of his great Work, Called "A Defence Of The People Of England, In Answer To Salmasius's Defence Of The King." To Which Is Added, **AREOPAGITICA**; Or, A Speech On The Liberty Of Unlicensed Printing. With Notes, An Original Memoir, And A Brief Review Of Milton's Prose Works. Second Edition. By William Greatheed Lewis. *London: Printed And Published Ay [sic] T. Dolby, At The Britannia-Press, 299, Strand. n.d. [ca. 1821]*. Second edition. 8vo, viii+223+[2]pp., engraved frontispiece portrait by P. Roberts, "Published By T. Dolby, 299, Strand, Oct. 1, 1821," dedication page, original half calf, marbled paper over boards (a bit rubbed, joints cracked), decorative gilt trim on spine, red leather label with "Milton" lettered in gilt. A good copy in a nice binding of the period, with advertisement leaf (cropped at top and bottom) bound in at the end advertising this edition with the notation that "In No. I. will be given a highly finished Portrait of the Divine Milton." Tipped-in on final blank is a newspaper clipping on "Milton's advice to his Countrymen." Scarce. Not in Kohler.

2650A. (Cross-listing) **THE RIVERSIDE MILTON** Edited By Roy Flannagan[,] *Ohio University[.] Houghton Mifflin Company[,] Boston New York[,] 1998*. First edition thus. See main listing under *Works*, 1998.

Samson Agonistes

2651. **SAMSON AN ORATORIO THE WORDS TAKEN FROM MILTON** Set to Musick by Mr. Handel. *London[:] Printed for I. Walsh in Catherine Street in the Strand, of whom may be had all Mr. Handel's Works. n.d. (1743)*. Second edition. Folio, 91pp., "A Table of Songs in the Oratorio call'd Samson" plus ninety pages of musical notation, modern quarter pigskin, marbled paper over boards (title lightly dust soiled, one leaf [pages 9–10] supplied from another slightly smaller copy laid in), red leather label with gilt lettering on spine. A nice copy. Adaptation by Handel. As I learned from John Shawcross, "There are two issues (or editions): one like yours in the British Library, and one with a license leaf in the William Andrews Clark Library." Very rare. Not in Coleridge; Not in Kohler.

2652. **SAMSON AN ORATORIO THE WORDS TAKEN FROM MILTON** Set to Musick by Mr. Handel. *London[:] Printed for I. Walsh in Catherine Street in the Strand, of whom may be had all Mr. Handel's Works. n.d. (1746)*. Folio, 91pp., "A Table of Songs in the Oratorio call'd Samson" plus ninety pages of musical notation, modern quarter pigskin, marbled paper over boards (minor embrowning, light dust soiling), red leather label with gilt lettering on spine. A nice copy. Adaptation by Handel. As with the 1743 second edition also listed here, a very rare edition. Smith, p. 135; Not in Coleridge; Not in Kohler.

2653. **SAMSON AGONISTES**, A Dramatick Poem. The Author John Milton. Aristot. Poet. Cap. 6 . . . *Dublin: Printed by and for George Grierson, at the Two Bibles in Essex-Street, 1748*. First Irish edition. 8vo, 58pp. (paginated from 66 to 121), decorative piece on title page, decorative head- and tailpieces and decorated initial letters, modern half dark brown leather, light orange cloth, printed paper label on front cover, new blanks and light orange endpapers. A fine copy. Not in Coleridge; Not in Kohler.

[together with]

2653A. (Cross-listing) **PARADISE REGAIN'D** . . . *Dublin, 1749*. 8vo, 61pp. (paginated from 3 to 61), bound as *SA* and *P*. A fine copy. Not in Coleridge; Not in Kohler. See main listing under *PR*, 1749.

[together with]

2653B. (Cross-listing) **POEMS UPON SEVERAL OCCASIONS** . . . *Dublin, 1748*. First Irish edition. 8vo, 72pp. (paginated from 126 to 196), decorative fruit piece on title page, bound as *SA* and *PR*. A fine copy. Not in Coleridge; Not in Kohler. See main listing under *P*, 1748.

Despite the editions being bound separately, Grierson clearly wished to present a complete and uniform collection of Milton's poetry, as indicated by the continuous pagination here of the separate parts (*PR*, *SA*, and *P*), from page 3 to page 196. John Shawcross likewise shared with me that "This was not issued separately. Libraries have sometimes listed their separated volumes as separate publications; this is incorrect. This reissue is the same as the 1748 edition (observe the signatures) except that the collection (*PR*) has a new title page dated 1749." The very rare first Irish editions of *SA* and *P*.

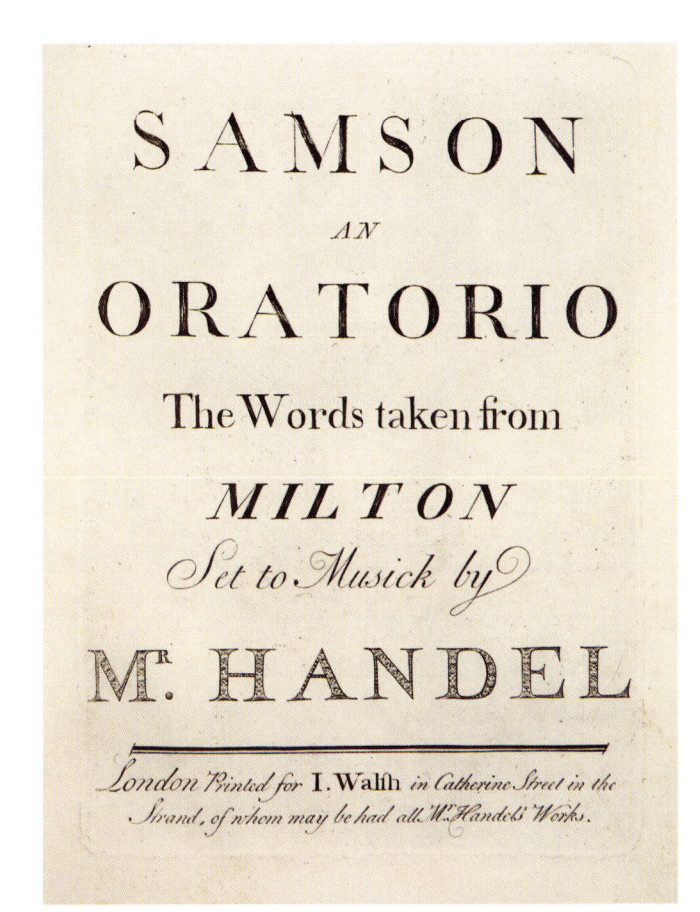

Samson An Oratorio The Words Taken From Milton Set to Musick by Mr. Handel. London, (1743). Second edition. Folio, ninety pages of musical notation. See #2651.

Rare 1752 First Edition of Simon Grynaeus's German Translation

2653C. (Cross-listing) SAMSON AGONISTES [In] JOHANN MILTONS WIEDER=EROBERTES PARADIES, nebst desselben Samson, und einigen andern Gedichten, wie auch einer Lebens=Beschreibung Des Verfassers. Aus dem Englischen übersetst. *Basel, verlegts Johann Rudolf Imhof, 1752.* First edition thus. 8vo, 244+[16]pp., *SA* is included among the other poems, each with half-title, select notes at bottom of page, index at the end, contemporary calf (a bit rubbed). The very rare first edition of Simon Gryanaeus's German translation. Not in Coleridge; Not in Kohler. See main listing under *PR*, 1752.

Rare 1755 Samson Libretto

2654. SAMSON: AN ORATORIO. *Printed in the Year 1755.* 8vo, 20pp., decorative device at center of title page, large decorative headpiece at the beginning, additional moderate decorative head- and tailpieces, modern quarto vellum, boards (early name on title trimmed a bit by binder, edges unevenly trimmed with light loss to fore-edge of leaf A6 affecting nearest letter to edge on about ten lines but not affecting legibility, spot of adhesion on final leaf results in most of the word "Thee" adhering to the end leaf and one other spot results in small paper tear touching on words but not affecting legibility). Overall a good copy of a very rare Milton edition. "We have not seen a copy of this rare libretto in our forty years of working with Milton Items" (G. W. Stuart, Jr., Ravenstree, Cat. 106, #1164, 2003). Very rare. Not in Coleridge; Not in Kohler.

Adaptations by Handel

2655. SAMSON [In] HANDEL'S SONGS Selected from His Latest Oratorios For the Harpsicord, Voice, Hoboy or German Flute. The Instrumental Parts to the above Songs may be had Separate to Compleat them for Concerts. London: Printed for I. Walsh, in Catherine Street, in the Strand, Of whom may be had, Compos'd by Mr[.] Handel . . . *n.d. [ca. 1755].* Adaptations by Handel. Oblong folio, 170pp., dedication page, "A Table of the Celebrated Songs from Mr[.] Handel's Oratorios contain'd in this Book," engraved title page and 168 pp. of engraved music, contemporary quarter calf, marbled paper over boards (worn, joints cracked, blank upper edge of title cut away presumably removing early owner's name, lightly embrowned), raised bands. Milton's *Samson* is among the most popular in this collection, with ten selections including the dazzling *Let the Bright Seraphims*; *L'Allegro* is represented by six selections; the *Messiah* by one, *Every Valley*. Considered a very rare collection. Not in Coleridge; Not in Kohler.

2656. SAMSON, AN ORATORIO, As it is Performed at the Theatre-Royal in Covent-Garden. Altered from the Sampson [sic] Agonistes of Milton. The Music Composed by George Frederick Handel, Esq. *London: Printed by J. Hardy, by Assignment of Mr. R. Tonson, and Sold by T. Lowndes in Fleet-street. n.d. (ca. 1768). [Price One Shilling.]* Adaptation by Handel. 4to, 23pp., central emblem on title page, decorative head- and tailpieces, disbound. A nice copy. Very rare ("we have not previously catalogued a copy of this," G. W. Stuart, Jr., Ravenstree, Cat. 156, #115, 1988); John Shawcross told me privately of a copy in the British Library; Not in Coleridge; Not in Kohler.

First Edition in Greek

2657. [SAMSON AGONISTES] SAMSON AGONISTES [in Greek] JOHANNIS MILTONI SAMSON AGONISTES Graeco Carmine Redditus Cum Versione Latina. A Georgio Henrico Glasse, A.M. Aedis Christi Nuper Alumno. [Quotation in Greek from Aeschylus] *Oxonii: A Typographeo Clarendoniano. M DCC LXXX VIII (1788).* First and only edition thus. 8vo, xl+266+[1]pp.,

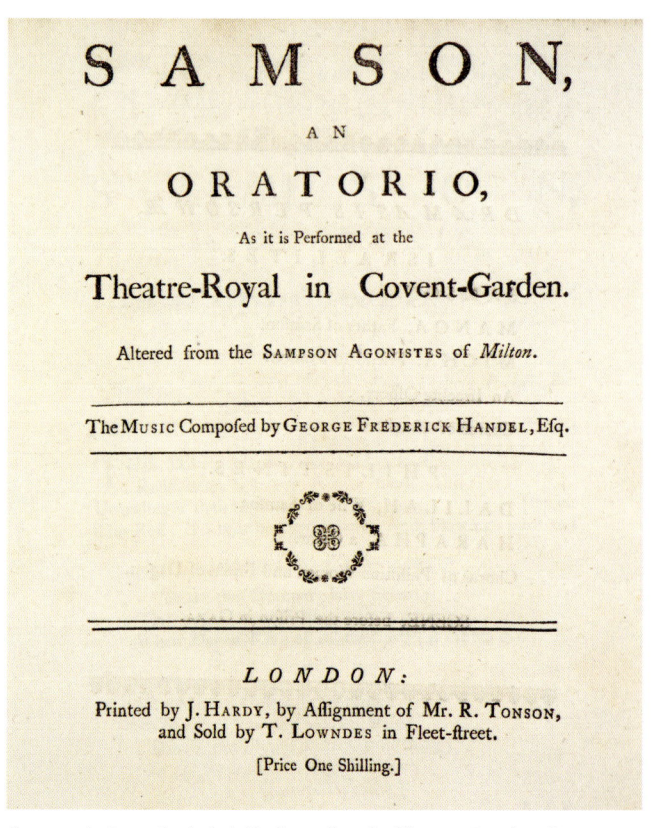

Samson, An Oratorio, As it is Performed at the Theatre-Royal in Covent-Garden. London, (ca. 1768). See #2656.

half-title (*SA* in Greek), dedication page in Latin after title page, Imprimatur on verso of dedication page, "Lectoris," "Praefatio" followed by *SA* in Greek, with a second half-title for *SA* before translation of the tragedy into Latin, "Errata" leaf at end, contemporary calf (a bit worn, joints cracked, front hinge repaired with a flexible glue), covers ruled in blind, decorated gilt trim on spine with gilt-lettered black morocco label, raised bands, inner dentelles ruled in gilt, marbled endpapers, early armorial bookplate of Frederick H. Glasse on front pastedown and early signature on verso of fly-leaf. A nice, large paper copy on thick paper, very fresh and clean within, with some occasional early marginal notations in pencil in a neat hand. "This is the second copy we have catalogued in over thirty years, and we suspect it was printed in a fairly small edition, with perhaps a few copies on larger and thicker paper. This present example is on thick paper, with very wide margins perhaps indicating large paper, which would tend to be borne out by the bookplate of a family member" (G. W. Stuart, Jr., Ravenstree, Cat. 181, #105, 1997). Some copies have an additional errata leaf, not present in this copy. Sole edition. Rare. Coleridge 173; Not in Kohler.

2657A. (Cross-listing) [SAMSON AGONISTES] SIMSON. Ein dramatisches Gedicht (half-title). Bound with [PARADISE LOST] JOHANN MILTONS VERLORNES PARADIES. Neue verbesserte Auflage. Erster Band. Mit Kaiserl. und Kurpfalzischen Privilegien. *Mannheim, 1791*. Bound with [PARADISE REGAINED] DAS WIEDEREROBERTE PARADIES, DES JOHANN MILTON, nevst seiner Lebensveschreibung, und dramatischen Gedichten: Simson. Mit allerhochstem kaiserlichen Privilegio. *Mannheim, im Berlage ver Herausgeber der aulandischen schonen Geister 1791*. 3 volumes in one. 8vo, half-title for *SA*. "This exceedingly rare combination is the only one that we have seen. The British Library has the German *PR*, but not the *PL*" (G. W. Stuart, Jr., Ravenstree, Cat. 174, #55, 1992). Not in Coleridge; Not in Kohler. See main listing under *PL*, 1791.

2658. SAMSON AGONISTES [In] DRAMATIC POEMS, SELECTED FROM THE CHOICEST WORKS OF MASON, MILTON & THOMSON, Viz. Elfrida, Caractacus, Samson Agonistes, Edward & Eleonora. *Baltimore—Printed By Warner & Hanna. 1804*. First edition thus? 12mo in 6s, 224pp., central device on title page, half-title for *SA* and for each of the other poems, three-quarter purple morocco, marbled paper over boards (bit rubbed at joints and edges, very slight age-browning), thick raised bands with gilt decorations, marbled endpapers. A very nice copy and one of the very early appearances of *SA* in America. Scarce. Not in Kohler.

2659. SAMSON AGONISTES: A DRAMATIC POEM. By John Milton. *New-York: George Dearborn, Publisher. 1836*. First edition thus? 8vo, 19pp. Bound with Three other contemporary works, each with a separate title page, *SA* being the second from the end, as the third of the four works, the whole volume bound as a library volume under the general title page: "*The Republic Of Letters; A Republication Of Standard Literature*. This Volume Contains, The History of the Russian Empire, under Peter the Great British Military Command-ers[sic]—Oliver Cromwell, John Duke of Marlborough, Charles Mordaunt, Earl of Peter-borough[sic]. Bubbles from the Brunnens of Nassau. Samson Agonistes; by Milton. The Rape of the Lock; by Alexander Pope. New-York: George Dearborn, Publisher. 1836." 8vo, 415pp. (258+88+[1]+19+7), modern blue library buckram (library stamp in red on fly-leaf, title page, edges, and end-leaves), spine lettered in gilt ("Samson Agonistes"). The edition of *SA* bound herein with its own title page is very rare. Not in Kohler.

2660. MILTON SAMSON AGONISTES Edited With Introduction And Notes By John Churton Collins[.] *Clarendon Press Series[.] Oxford[:] At The Clarendon Press[,] 1883*. First edition thus? Slim 8vo, 96pp., "London Henry Frowde Oxford University Press Warehouse 7 Paternoster Row" on verso of title page, introduction, reproduction in modern type of first edition 1671 title page, "Notes" at the end, original reddish-brown cloth (a bit rubbed, minor spot on front cover), front cover stamped in blind. A nice copy with a leaf advertising editions in the "Clarendon Press Series" (including an edition of Milton's Poems edited by Browne); signed by the Miltonist C. B. Wright on title page, with a handwritten note by Wright laid in. Tipped on front pastedown is a reproduction of portrait of Milton after Pieter van der Plaas. A possible second edition thus was published in 1893 (copy following); see also copies of editions in 1950 and 1957. Scarce. Not in Kohler.

2661. MILTON SAMSON AGONISTES Edited With Introduction And Notes By John Churton Collins[.] *Clarendon Press Series[.] Oxford[:] At The Clarendon Press[,] 1893*. Second edition thus? Slim 8vo, 94pp., introduction, reproduction in modern type of first edition 1671 title page, "Notes" at the end, original printed orange paper wrappers (used, a bit soiled, partially shaken, bottom half of spine missing), title page reprinted on front cover, "London Henry Frowde Oxford University Press Warehouse Amen Corner, E.C. [with seal of the press] New York Macmillan & Co., 112 Fourth Avenue" on back cover. Not in Kohler.

2662. SAMSON AGONISTES A Dramatic Poem By John Milton. *[New Rochelle, New York: Elston Press, 1904.]* 8vo, 65+colophon leaf, half-title in red and black, decorative headpieces for the preliminary prose and the "Argument," first page of text within decorated woodcut border, with a large initial "S" at the beginning, "decorations cut on wood from designs by H. M. O'Kane," printed in red and black throughout from the text of the 1671 first edition, original half linen, paper over boards, printed paper label on spine. The decorations are elaborately done. A very nice copy, handsomely printed by the Elston Press in a limited edition of 120 copies. Not in Kohler.

2663. MILTON'S SAMSON AGONISTES With Introduction, Notes, Glossary And Indexes By A. W. Verity, M.A. Sometime Scholar of Trinity College*[.] Cambridge[:] At The University Press[,] 1912.* Small 8vo, lxvi+[1]+170+[1]+8pp., half-title (Pitt Press Series), original blue cloth (a bit rubbed, lacking front free endpaper, some marginal notations in pencil), spine lettered in gilt with gilt seal of the press, early signature on title page. A good copy with advertisement leaves for "The Pitt Press Series" bound in at end. The first edition thus appeared in 1892; it was reprinted in 1897, 1901, 1910, 1912 (copy here), and variously thereafter. Not in Kohler (although Kohler 262 lists 1904 Verity edition and Kohler 263 lists 1910 Verity edition).

2664. SAMSON AGONISTES By John Milton With Notes By J. M. D. Meiklejohn, M.A.*[,]* Late Professor of Education in the University of St. Andrews. W. & R. *Chambers, Limited[,] 38 Soho Square, London, W. I; and Edinburgh[,] n.d. [ca. 1920s].* First edition. Slim 8vo, 80pp., original printed stiff reddish-brown paper wrappers (a bit used, several early names/labels, some pencil notations on inside back cover), title page reprinted on front cover. A nice copy. Not in Kohler, who lists no edition after 1914.

2665. JOHN MILTON DEN STAERKE SAMSON[.] Paa Dansk Ved Uffe Birkedal[.] *H. Chr. Bakkes Boghandel (Viggo A. Bang)[,] Kobenhavn[,] 1930.* First edition thus. Slim 8vo, 79pp., half-title, printed paper wrappers (a bit aged-browned), with central vignette of Milton in red on front cover, edges untrimmed. A nice copy. Scarce.

2666. SAMSON AGONISTES A Dramatic Poem By John Milton[.] [Quotation in Greek and Latin from Aristot. Poet. Cap.6] With Wood-Engravings By Robert Ashwin Maynard. *CMXXI (1931)[.] Printed by R. A. Maynard & H. W. Bray at the Raven Press[.] Harrow Weald[.]* 4to, 63pp.+colophon leaf, edited by H. C. Beeching, half-title, with central emblem of the Raven Press on title page, first appearance of ten large wood-engraved illustrations by Robert Ashwin Maynard, decorated initial letters, original vellum spine, black linen boards, gilt rules on covers, with gilt emblem of the Raven Press on front cover, spine lettered in gilt, t.e.g, others untrimmed, with the bookplate of Leonard Schlosser, in original brown paper slipcase (worn). A very fine copy, handsomely printed by the Raven Press on handmade paper and strikingly illustrated. "The text is that of the original edition of 1671" (colophon). The engraved illustrations are considered technically very fine and among the best that Maynard has produced. The edition was printed in a limited edition of 275 copies. Ridler 3; Huckabay 187.

2667. JOHN MILTON SIMSON DER KAMPFER Ubertragen von Professor Dr. Hermann Ulrich[.] Einfuhrung von Reinhold Schneider[.] *1947 Verlag Herder • Freiburg Im Breisgau [Herder & Co. Publishers • Freiburg In Breisgau.]* First edition thus. Tall, slim 8vo, vii+[1]+103+[1]pp., half-title ("Abendlandische Bucherei Herausgegeben von Reinhold Schneider") with English title on verso, German translation with English on facing page, original stiff paper wrappers with light blue marbled paper overlaid (a bit rubbed, spine and edges a little darkened), front cover lettered in black and red. A nice copy. Laid in: original German advertisement leaf for this and other editions in the series.

2668. MILTON'S SAMSON AGONISTES With Introduction, Notes, Glossary And Indexes By A. W. Verity[.] *Cambridge[:] At The University Press[,] 1949.* Small 8vo, lxvi+[1]+170+[1], half-title ("Pitt Press Series"), original red cloth (spine a bit faded), front cover and spine lettered in black. The first edition thus was published in 1892; it was variously reprinted (see 1912 copy listed earlier).

2669. JOHN MILTON SAMSON AGONISTES AND SHORTER POEMS Edited By A. E. Barker[,] Trinity College In The University Of Toronto[.] *Appleton-Century-Crofts, Inc. New York[,] (1950).* First edition thus. Slim 8vo, xii+114pp., half-title, "Principal Dates In The Life Of John Milton," notes at bottom of page, paperback, printed stiff blue paper wrappers (a bit rubbed), "Bibliography" to 1949 at the end, with advertisement for the series on inside front cover, including this edition, and advertisement for Crofts Classics editions of Shakespeare on back cover. A nice copy of this Crofts Classics paperback. Variously reprinted (see ca. 1964, ca. 1966, ca. 1968, and ca. 1975 editions listed here). Scarce.

2670. MILTON SAMSON AGONISTES Edited With Introduction And Notes By John Churton Collins[.] *Oxford[:] At The Clarendon Press[,] (1950).* Slim 8vo, 94pp., half-title, introduction, reproduction in type of first edition title page (1671), original green cloth, spine lettered in gilt, notes at the end. A nice copy. The first edition thus was published in 1883 (see copy listed here).

2671. MILTON SAMSON AGONISTES Edited With Introduction And Notes By John Churton Collins[.] *Oxford University Press[,] (1957)*. Slim 8vo, 94pp., half-title, original green cloth, spine lettered in gilt. A nice copy.

2672. JOHN MILTON SIMSON DER KAMPFER Ein dramatishes Gedicht*[.] Aufbau-Verlag Berlin[,] 1958*. First edition thus. Slim 8vo, 161+[3]pp., half-title, small emblem of the press on title page, thirty-two-page "Einleitung von Anselm Schlosser," original cream boards, front cover and spine lettered in red and black, light red edges, printed publisher's wrappers (a bit frayed along top edge). A very nice copy of this bilingual edition, with Milton's English text on verso and a German poetic translation on recto.

2673. JOHN MILTON SAMSON AGONISTES AND SHORTER POEMS Edited By A. E. Barker[,] University of Illinois[.] *New York[:] Appleton-Century-Crofts[;] Division of Meredith Publishing Company[.] n.d. [ca. 1964]*. Slim 8vo, xii+115pp., half-title, printed stiff blue paper wrappers with white lettering (bit rubbed), titled "Poems of John Milton" on spine, "Selected Bibliography," with advertisements for the series (updated) on inside front and back cover. A Crofts Classics paperback. The "Selected Bibliography" has been updated to 1964. A good copy of this inexpensive edition (priced $.50 on front cover). The first edition thus was published in 1950 (also listed here).

The collection also has a variant of the preceding, with a sticker price of $.65 tipped over original price of $.50.

2674. MILTON SAMSON AGONISTES Edited By F. T. Prince[.] *Oxford University Press, (1965)*. Fourth edition thus. Slim 8vo, 144pp., half-title, "Introduction," with "Notes," "Appendix A[:] On the Verse," "Appendix B[:] On the Style," and "Appendix C[:] The Chronology of Milton's Life," at end, original decorated paper over boards (a bit rubbed, name in ink on front pastedown, price label removed from fly-leaf). A good copy. The first edition was published in 1957; it was "reprinted lithographically in Great Britain at the University Press, Oxford[,] from corrected sheets of the first edition 1960, 1964, 1965" (verso title page).

2675. SAMSON AGONISTES By John Milton With Introduction And Notes By H. M. Percival, M.A.[,] Professor of English Literature, Presidency College, Calcutta[.] *London[:] Macmillan & Co[.,] Ltd[.] New York[:] St. Martin's Press[,] 1965*. Slim 8vo, xlvii+202pp., numerous notes at the end, original red cloth, front cover and spine lettered in black with emblem of a knight in armor above "Macmillan's English Classics" within a flowing scroll in black at bottom of front cover. A very nice copy. The first edition was published in 1890; it was variously reprinted thereafter.

2676. JOHN MILTON'S SAMSON AGONISTES The Poem and Materials for Analysis Selected And Edited By Ralph E. Hone[,] University Of Redlands[.] *Chandler Publishing Company[,] An Intext Publisher[.] Scranton, Pennsylvania 18515 (1966)*. First edition thus. 8vo, viii+[1]+284pp., half-title, frontispiece woodcut illustration in black and white (of Delilah cutting Samson's hair) by Hans Burgkmair, appendix consisting of "Suggested Topics for Study," "A Selected Bibliography," and a twenty-page section on "Documenting Your Research Paper," paperback, printed stiff paper wrappers with woodcut illustration by Burgkmair (of Delilah cutting Samson's hair) reproduced on front cover in tinted green and an enlarged detail of the illustration reproduced in black against an orange background on back cover, orange spine with white lettering, orange lettering on front cover. A fine copy.

2677. JOHN MILTON SAMSON AGONISTES AND SHORTER POEMS Edited By A. E. Barker[,] University of Illinois[.] *Appleton-Century-Crofts Educational Division New York Meredith Corporation[.] n.d. [ca. 1966]*. Slim 8vo, xii+115pp. (No. 751–22 verso title page), half-title, paperback, printed stiff yellow paper wrappers, with reproduction of Rubens's *Samson Seized by the Philistines* on front and back cover, "Selected Bibliography" at the end updated to 1964, as in the ca. 1964 edition. A Crofts Classics paperback, similar to ca. 1964 copy (listed earlier), in a taller format and variant binding, and without the advertisements for the series. A good copy of this inexpensive edition, priced .65 on front cover. The first edition thus was published in 1950 (also listed here).

2678. JOHN MILTON SAMSON AGONISTES AND THE SHORTER POEMS Edited by Isabel Gamble MacCaffrey[.] The Signet Classic Poetry Series[.] General Editor: John Hollander[.] *Published By The New American Library, New York And Toronto[;] The New English Library Limited, London[,] (1966)*. First edition thus. 8vo, xlix+216pp., half-title, "Introduction," "A General Note On The Text," "A Note On This Edition," paperback, printed stiff white paper wrappers, with decorative design in color on front cover. A nice copy of this "Signet Classic."

2679. JOHN MILTON SAMSON AGONISTES AND SHORTER POEMS Edited By A. E. Barker[,] University of Illinois[.] *AHM Publishing Corporation[,] Northbrook, Illinois 60062[.] n.d. [ca. 1968]*. Slim 8vo, xii+115pp. (No. 733 verso title page), half-title, "Introduction," paperback,

Tablet for the God of Israel. Illustration among others by Robert Medley for *SA*. [Published And Printed In Norwich 1979 (colophon leaf)]. Copy signed by the artist. No. 39 of 150. See #2681.

printed stiff yellow paper wrappers (a bit used) with reproduction of Rubens's *Samson Seized by the Philistines* on front and back cover, "Selected Bibliography" at the end. The "Selected Bibliography," updated to 1964, is the same as that included in the ca. 1964 Crofts Classics edition (copy listed here). A decent copy of this inexpensive edition. Possible first printing by AHM Publishing Corporation. The first edition as a Crofts Classics was published in 1950 (copy listed here).

2680. JOHN MILTON SAMSON AGONISTES, SONNETS, ETC. Edited by John Broadbent and Robert Hodge[,] University of East Anglia, Norwich[,] with translations of selected Latin and Italian poetry by Robert Hodge. [Italian Quotation from Guiseppe Ungaretti] *Cambridge University Press[,] Cambridge[,] London • New York • Melbourne[,] (1977)*. First edition thus. 8vo, xiv+235pp., half-title, paperback, printed stiff paper wrappers with reproduction of a detail from *Samson and Delilah* by Andrea Mantegna (ca. 1495) on front cover. A nice copy.

2681. SAMSON AGONISTES A Dramatic Poem By John Milton Illustrated By Robert Medley. *[Published And Printed In Norwich 1979 (colophon leaf)]*. Folio, unpaginated, title page with abstract illustration in color, first appearance of twenty-three lithograph illustrations in color and in black and white by Robert Medley, printed by Mell Clark in 12-point Caslon Antique, original light brown grayish canvas, front cover and spine lettered in blue, printed gray dust jacket lettered in blue in a protective plastic cover. A fine copy of this privately printed edition. Laid in: "Hand-List Of Illustrations"—which are stunningly abstract and which are described by the artist on the cover of the enclosed hand-list of explanations: "The illustrations, or images, are to be seen as an accompaniment to the unfolding of the drama. As far as the distribution of the text allows the illustrations are as closely allied to the particular line, or event, as possible." Number 39 of a limited edition of 150 copies, signed by the artist.

2682. SAMSON AGONISTES By John Milton[.] Edited With Introduction And Notes By Michael Davis. *[London:] Macmillan Education, (1987)*. Slim 8vo, xliii+[1]+162+[1]pp., half-title ("English Classics—New Series"), "Introduction The Life Of John Milton," "Time Chart," "The Story of Samson as told in the Book of Judges," facsimile reproduction of first edition title page (1771), "Critical Extracts," "Select Bibliography," notes on left side, text on right side, paperback, printed pink stiff paper wrappers with an unsigned portrait of Milton on front cover and a portion of the portrait on back cover. A fine copy. The first edition thus was published in 1968; variously reprinted thereafter.

2683. [SECOND DEFENCE] MILTON'S 'SECOND DEFENCE OF THE PEOPLE OF ENGLAND;' In Answer To An Infamous Anonymous Work, Entitled 'The Cry of the Royal Blood to Heaven against the English Parricides.' [Latin Quotation from "George." with English Translation] *N.P. n.d. [1816]*. 8vo, 199pp.,+28+27pp., engraved frontispiece portrait after I. Hopwood, dated "MDCCLXVII," original half plum pebble cloth, green paper boards (binding stained, portrait and final two pages remargined), edges untrimmed, bookplate. A good copy of a scarce book, containing Milton's *Second Defence* and two additional brief pieces. The portrait consists of a sketch of a bust of the blind Milton on a pedestal with another sketch of a portrait at the center of the pedestal. Translated by Francis Wrangham (1769–1842) forming part of his "Scraps," seven parts (dated 1816) of which, according to notation on title page in place of publisher and date, "only 50 copies [were] printed separately." Scarce. Not in Kohler.

Select Poems and Selections

2684. MILTON'S SELECT POEMS Edited By Albert Perry Walker, M.A. Master, And Teacher Of English And History In The English High School, Boston[.] Golden Key Series. *D. C. Heath And Company[,] Boston[,] New York[,] Chicago[,] Atlanta[,] San Francisco[,] Dallas[,] London[,] (1900)*. Second edition thus. Small 8vo, xiv+395pp., unsigned frontispiece portrait of Milton, decorative black border trim on title page, *Preface* dated 1900 (copyright on verso of title page dated 1897 and 1900), seven illustration plates plus one headpiece illustration with either the lines illustrated or identification printed beneath each illustration, five maps (including one in-text half-page illustration of "The World [Diagram of the Ptolemeic System]"), half-title for the various sections and selections of poems, bibliography, notes, glossary, and index at the end, original crushed green cloth (a bit rubbed, spine slightly darkened, several head notes in ink), covers and spine lettered in black. A good copy. The illustration plates are for *IlP* (one plate: *Divinest Melancholy* by W. C. Thomas); for *C* (three plates: *The Lady In C* by J. D. Critenden, *Circe* by J. H. Waterhouse, and *Ludlow Castle* by J. M. W. Turner, along with a fourth illustration, *The Education Of C* "From a Greek Vase"—as headpiece illustration); for *L* (one plate: *Faun, Satyr, and Pan Pipes* by Harriet Hosmer); and for *NO* (one plate: *The 'Star-Led Wizards'* by J. Portaels); with an illustration plate also in the preface of *The Four Regions of the Universe* by J. B. Poole. An interesting illustrated edition intended for classroom use, the purpose of which is stated in the preface: "Up to the present time it has been a somewhat general custom in American secondary schools to limit the study of Milton's works to the first two books of *PL* [increased here to include selections from other Books] . . . the opportunity [now] to undertake as careful and comprehensive a study of the work of the greatest English poet as is possible [by] pupils of secondary school age. It is such a comprehensive study that this book is designed to facilitate." The first edition thus was published in 1897. See also Walker's briefer edition, *Milton's Select Minor Poems* (1900), listed under *MP*, in which the same illustration plates appear; and see *Selections From The PW Of JM* (1909) also edited by Albert Perry Walker, in which the same preface and the same illustration plates also appear. Not in Kohler.

2685. [SELECTED LONGER POEMS] JOHN MILTON SELECTED LONGER POEMS AND PROSE Edited by Tony Davies[.] *Routledge[,] London And New York[,] (1992)*. First edition thus. 8vo, [ii]+342pp., paperback, printed light blue stiff paper wrappers with an unsigned illustration of the fall of the angels from Heaven in black and white on front cover, with lettering in black against yellow background. Included are selections from *PL* (Books I, II, IV, VII, IX, and XII) and from *The History of Britain*, with the whole of *SA*, with "Critical commentary," "Bibliography," and "Notes." A fine copy.

2686. SELECTED POEMS OF JOHN MILTON[:] L'ALLEGRO, IL PENSEROSO, COMUS, LYCIDAS Edited With An Introduction And Notes By Clara H. Whitmore, A.M. Teacher Of English In The Curtis High School[,] New York City[.] Standard Literature Series[.] *New York: Newson & Company, Publishers. n.d. [ca. 1900]*. First edition thus. Slim 8vo, 112+[4]pp., notes at bottom of page, original printed wrappers covered by narrow red cloth spine (bottom right corners of front cover and title page slight chipped, red cloth spine partially missing at bottom of front cover), front cover decorated and lettered in green ("Number 66 Standard Literature Series"), advertisements "For Critical Studies Of English In Grammar and High Schools on back cover (including this edition of "Milton's Minor Poems, No. 66"). A good copy with four pages of advertisements of editions in the "Standard Literature Series" bound in at the end. Not in Kohler.

2687. Variant of Preceding, original tan cloth (spine ends a bit rubbed, numerous marginal notations in a neat hand in pencil), front cover richly decorated and lettered in embossed green ("L'Allegro, Lycidas, Il Penseroso, Comus"), spine lettered in green ("S.L.S. Vol. 66. Milton's Minor Poems"). A good copy with an unsigned frontispiece portrait plate not in previous edition (of a middle-aged, long-haired Milton), in a variant publisher's binding, with four pages of advertisements of editions for "Standard Literature Series" bound in at the end. Not in Kohler.

2688. SELECTED POEMS OF JOHN MILTON with Introduction and Notes by James Holly Hanford[,] Western Reserve University[.] *New York[:] Thomas Nelson & Sons[,] 1936*. First edition thus. Small 8vo, lxxxviii+138pp., half-title, modest decorative border on title page, lengthy introduction, notes at bottom of page, original blue cloth (a bit rubbed, slight foxing throughout), front cover and spine lettered in gilt. A good copy. Scarce.

2689. SELECTED POEMS JOHN MILTON[.] Dover Thrift Editions[.] *Dover Publications, Inc.[,] New York[.] (1993)*. First edition thus. Slim 8vo, viii+[1]+113+[2]+[3]pp., "Note," "Contents," half-title before the poems, paperback, printed stiff paper wrappers with decorated front cover. A fine copy with three pages of advertisement for "Dover Thrift Editions" at end, running over to inside back cover. "This Dover edition, first published in 1993, is a new selection of unabridged poems reprinted from *The*

CP of JM, volume 4 of "The Harvard Classics," P. F. Collier & Son Company, New York, 1909 [see copy listed here]. The note, the footnotes and the alphabetical lists of titles and first lines have been prepared specially for the present edition" (verso title page).

2690. SELECTED POETRY JOHN MILTON[.] Edited with an Introduction and Notes by Jonathan Goldberg and Stephen Orgel[.] The World's Classics. *Oxford [And] New York[:] Oxford University Press[,] 1997.* First edition thus (as a "World's Classics paperback"). 8vo, xxvi+324+[2]pp., half-title with a brief biography of Milton and of each editor, "Introduction," Acknowledgements," "Chronology," and "Note on the Text," at the beginning, "Notes," "Further Reading," and "Index" at the end, paperback, printed red stiff paper wrappers with reproduction in color of Milton portrait at age twenty-one on front cover. A nice copy, reprinting selections from the edition of *PW* first published in 1991 in hardback and simultaneously in paperback (see copy of each listed here).

2691. [SELECTED SHORTER POEMS] JOHN MILTON SELECTED SHORTER POEMS AND PROSE WRITINGS Edited by Tony Davies. *Routledge • London And New York[,] (1988).* First edition thus. 8vo, viii+265pp., extensive commentary provided for each selection, "Glossary of classical names" at the end, paperback, printed light blue stiff paper wrappers with Blake's illustration of *The Brothers Driving out Comus* reproduced in black and white on front cover. A fine copy.

2692. A SELECTION FROM THE WORKS OF JOHN MILTON Arranged by Walter Fancutt[.] The Kingsgate Pocket Poets[.] *London[:] The Kingsgate Press[,] 4. Southampton Row W. C. 1[,]] (1947).* First edition thus. Slim miniature (measuring 4 ⅛" × 2 ¾"), 95+[1]pp., original crushed leather over limp boards, marbled endpapers and edges. A very nice copy with advertisement for other publications in the "The Kingsgate Pocket Poets" series on verso of last page, Milton being no. 7 of seven listed (the others: Shakespeare, Wordsworth, Browning, Tennyson, Shelley, and Keats).

2693. A SELECTION OF POEMS BY JOHN MILTON 1608-1674 exploring his pilgrimage of faith. Chosen And Introduced By Ruth Etchells. Poets And Prophets. *A Lion Book[,] Tring [Herts., England] • Batavia [Illinois] • Sidney[,] (1988).* First edition thus. Tall, slim 8vo, 48pp., half-title with "Milton's Poetry And Pamphlets in order of writing and publication" listed on verso, decorative red border trim on title page, printed in reddish-brown throughout, nine unsigned vignette illustrations and three decorations in red, notes at the end, printed in Italy, original gray cloth, small green decorations on covers, printed glazed green label incorporating title with central vignette illustration (of the tree of life with apples and serpent wrapped around it) in color tipped on front cover, green spine lettered in reverse, printed advertisement label on the series "Poets And Prophets" tipped on back cover, decorated endpapers. A fine copy. Besides the vignette illustration in color of the tree of life and serpent on the label on front cover, the illustrations include nine unsigned vignette illustrations in the text in red: a vignette illustration at the end of *Psalm 136*; a vignette illustration at the head of *Psalm 1*; a vignette illustration for *Sonnet XXII*; and six vignette illustrations (most reproductions of Doré illustrations) for *PL* (*The Enemy* [*Me Miserable*], Book IV, 108–13; *Glimpse of Creation Before the Fall*, Book IV, 724–35; *The Change* [depicting *Raphael Counseling Adam and Eve*], Book X, 1–14; *After The Fall* [depicting *The Serpent and Adam and Eve*], Book X, 710–25; *The Promise* [depicting *The Lament of Adam and Eve*], Book X, 315–23; *Into the World* [depicting a sunrise off in the distance rising over the ocean], Book XII, 641–49). Uncommon.

2694. [SELECTIONS] JOHN MILTON SELECTIONS FROM HIS WORKS AND TRIBUTES TO HIS GENIUS. [Arranged By Isaac Foot And Presented To Him By Nancy Astor(,) 1935.] *[Printed For Private Use By The Welsh Outlook Press, Newtown, Montgomeryshire, (1935).]* 8vo, 151pp., title page without publisher's imprint, half-title following title page, half-titles for "Poetry," "Prose," and "Tributes," "Chronological Table" and "Index" at the end, original purple cloth (slightly faded, bit rubbed at joints), spine lettered in gilt. A good copy. Presentation copy from the author, with inscription so noting on front blank. Printed in a limited edition. Scarce.

2695. SELECTIONS FROM JOHN MILTON Edited By Martin W. Sampson[,] Goldwin Smith Professor of English Literature in Cornell University[.] *F. S. Crofts & Co. New York[,] 1925.* First edition thus. 8vo, lvi+[1]+318pp., "Preface," "Introduction," "Dates In Milton's Life," "Notes," "Appendix," original half brown buckram, brown paper over boards (a bit rubbed, ex-library stamped "withdrawn," with other related library markings), spine lettered in gilt. Despite the library stamps, a good copy. According to the preface: "This volume is an enlargement and revision of the editor's *Lyric and Dramatic Poems of John Milton* (Henry Holt and company)" first published in 1901 (also listed here). Intended for classroom use, this edition consists primarily of poetical selections with notes; included also are brief selections from Milton's prose works, with notes. A second edition was published in 1930 (copy following).

2696. SELECTIONS FROM JOHN MILTON Edited By Martin W. Sampson[,] Goldwin Smith Professor of English Literature in Cornell University[.] *F. S. Crofts & Co. New York[,] 1930.* Second edition thus. 8vo, lvi+[1]+318pp., as with first edition preceding, original half brown buckram, brown paper over boards, spine lettered in gilt, bookplate. A fine copy.

2697. [SELECTIONS FROM THE POEMS OF JOHN MILTON. Translated by Jin Pao-Shu.] *?Tokyo, 1959.* First edition thus. Slim 8vo, [vi]+146pp., reproduction of unsigned vignette portrait of Milton as a young poet as frontispiece, Japanese ideogrammatic text with notes, pink cloth spine (a bit faded, ex-library, small label removed at bottom), printed paper over boards (a bit rubbed), front cover lettered in black (in Japanese) with elaborate decorations in gilt, spine lettered in black (in Japanese). A good copy.

2698. SELECTIONS FROM THE POETICAL WORKS OF JOHN MILTON With Introduction, Suggestions For Study, Notes, And Glossary Edited By Albert Perry Walker, M.A. Master, And Teacher Of English And History In The English High School, Boston[.] *Boston, U.S.A. D. C. Heath & Co., Publishers[,] 1909.* Small 8vo, xiv+[2]+[4]pp., unsigned frontispiece portrait plate of Milton, copyright on verso of title page dated 1897 and 1900, preface dated 1900, with half-title, illustration plate entitled *The Four Regions of the Universe* by J. B. Poole, four maps, and one in-text half-page illustration of *The World [Diagram of the Ptolemeic System]*, half-title for the various sections and selections of poems, including a half-title for "Minor Poems," followed by a general "Introduction To The Minor Poems," with an "Introduction" to each of the minor poems included, seven illustration plates plus one headpiece illustration for several of the minor poems, with either the lines illustrated or identification printed beneath each illustration, "Notes On The Minor Poems," "Glossary" to *PL*, index at the end, original dark red cloth (a bit used and marked, spine ends a little frayed), spine lettered in gilt. A good copy with early ownership signature on flyleaf and with an advertisement leaf (with half-title) at the end for "Heath's English Classics." The illustration plates (identified in an "Illustrations" list after the preface) are for *NO* (one plate: *The 'Star-Led Wizards'* by J. Portaels); for *IlP* (one plate: *Divinest Melancholy* by W. C. Thomas); for *C* (three plates: *The Lady In C* by J. D. Critenden, *Circe* by J. H. Waterhouse, and *Ludlow: 'The President's Castle'* by J. M. W. Turner, along with a fourth illustration, *The Education of C* "From a Greek Vase"—as headpiece illustration); and for *L* (one plate: *Faun, Satyr, and Pan Pipes* by Harriet Hosmer). An interesting illustrated edition intended for classroom use, the purpose of which is stated in the preface: "the opportunity [now] to undertake as careful and comprehensive a study of the work of the greatest English poet as is possible [by] pupils of secondary school age. It is such a comprehensive study that this book is designed to facilitate." The first edition thus was published in 1897. See also Walker's briefer edition, *Milton's Select Minor Poems* (1900), listed under *Minor Poems*, in which the same illustration plates appear; and see *Milton's Select Poems* (1900) also edited by Albert Perry Walker, in which the same preface and the same illustration plates also appear. Not in Kohler.

2699. A SERIES OF MAGNIFICENT ENGRAVINGS, To Illustrate The Various Folio Or Quarto Editions Of The Works Of Shakespeare And Milton; Or, Bound Up, To Form A Library Accompaniment To Any Of The Smaller Editions Of Those Authors. Price:£9: 9s. *London: Printed By J. Bartfield, Wardour-Street, for H. M'Lean, No. 8, Soho-Square. 1818.* Large folio (19 ¼" tall × 13" wide), fifty-one engraved plates after W. Sharpe, F. Bartolozzi, T. Stothard, W. Hamilton, H. Fuseli, and others, protective tissue guards, contemporary full straight-grained green morocco, wide gilt rules on covers surrounded by decorative border trim finely tooled in blind and gilt, spine elaborately decorated in gilt within the panels, raised bands, inner dentelles tooled in gilt, a.e.g. A very fine copy with early armorial bookplate on front pastedown. Of the fifty-one engraved plates (each a fine plate with a fine impression and a thick protective tissue guard), thirty-eight plates are for Shakespeare and thirteen plates are for Milton. The plates for Milton include (as identified in a fine hand reproduced at the top of the plate): (1) *Satan*, (2) *Pandemonium*, (3) *Sin and Death*, (4) *His Oblique Way*, (5) *Uriel and Satan*, (6) *Eve*, (7) *Faery Elves*, (8) *Adam and Eve*, (9) *The Gate of Heaven*, (10) *Adam and Eve and the Archangel Raphael*, (11) *Uriel*, (12) *Morning*, and (13) *The Morning Hymn*. Scarce. Not in Kohler.

Shorter Poems

2700. [SHORTER POEMS] MILTON'S SHORTER POEMS AND SONNETS Arranged in Chronological Order, And Edited, With Introduction And Notes, By Frederick Day Nichols, A.B. Associate In English, The University Of Chicago, In Charge Of English At The Morgan Park Academy, Morgan Park, Illinois. Twentieth Century Text-Books[.] *New York[:] D. Appleton And Company[,] (1899).* First edition thus. Small 8vo, x+153+[4]pp., half-title ("Twentieth Century Text-Books Edited By A. F. Nightingale," with a list of the editions in the series printed on verso, including this edition priced at 25¢), lengthy introduction, chronological table, notes at the bottom of the page and "Notes" at the end, original brown cloth (a bit used, heavy pencil notes on verso of fly-leaf), emblem incorporating "Twentieth Century Text-Books" on front cover, front cover and spine lettered in black. A fairly good copy with four pages of advertisement leaves of publications by D. Appleton Company bound in at the end. A second edition was published in 1904; later editions followed in 1910 and 1912—all listed here. Not in Kohler.

2701. [SHORTER POEMS] MILTON'S SHORTER POEMS AND SONNETS Arranged in Chronological Order, And Edited, With Introduction And Notes, By Frederick Day Nichols, A.B. Associate In English, The University Of Chicago, In Charge Of English At The Morgan Park Academy, Morgan Park, Illinois. Twentieth Century Text-Books[.] *New York[:] D. Appleton And Company[,] 1904*. Second edition thus? Small 8vo, x+153+[12]pp., half-title ("Twentieth Century Text-Books Edited By A. F. Nightingale"), introduction, chronological table, notes at bottom of page and "Notes" at the end, original brown cloth (a bit rubbed, a few marginal notations), emblem incorporating "Twentieth Century Text-Books" on front cover, front cover and spine lettered in black. A good copy with twelve pages of advertisement leaves of publications by D. Appleton Company bound in at the end. Not in Kohler.

2702. [SHORTER POEMS] MILTON'S SHORTER POEMS AND SONNETS Arranged In Chrono-logical Order, And Edited, With Introduction And Notes, By Frederick Day Nichols, A.B.[,] Associate In English, The University Of Chicago, In Charge Of English At The Morgan Park Academy, Morgan Park, Illinois[.] *New York[:] D. Appleton And Company[,] 1910*. Slim 8vo, x+153+[4]pp., half-title with advertisement for "Twentieth Century Texts In English" on verso, as with first edition in 1899, original brown cloth (a bit rubbed, a few pencil markings, contemporary name in ink [dated 1911] on fly-leaf), front cover lettered in black with "Twentieth Century Text-Books" printed within a decorative piece in black at the top, spine lettered in black, four pages of advertisements bound in at the end. A nice copy. Not in Kohler.

2703. [SHORTER POEMS] MILTON'S SHORTER POEMS AND SONNETS Arranged In Chrono-logical Order, And Edited, With Introduction And Notes, By Frederick Day Nichols, A.B.[,] Associate In English, The University Of Chicago, In Charge Of English At The Morgan Park Academy, Morgan Park, Illinois[.] *New York[:] D. Appleton And Company[,] 1912*. Slim 8vo, x+153+[4]pp., half-title with advertisement for "Twentieth Century Texts In English" on verso, as with first edition in 1899, original brown cloth, front cover lettered in black with "Twentieth Century Text-Books" printed within a decorative piece in black at the top, spine lettered in black, four pages of advertisements bound in at the end. A nice copy. Not in Kohler.

2704. A SHORTER MILTON Selected And Edited by F. J. Tickner, B.A. (Oxon.) *Thomas Nelson And Sons Ltd[,] London[,] Edinburgh[,] Paris[,] Melbourne[,] Toronto And New York[,] (1938)*. First edition thus. 8vo, 263pp., half-title, unsigned frontispiece portrait sketch, "First published in this Series, November 1938" on verso of title page, notes at bottom of the page, "Printed In Great Britain At The Press Of The Publishers" on verso of last page, original blue cloth (slightly waterstained around the edges sometime ago, early name), spine lettered in gilt, printed blue publisher's wrappers (a bit used, frayed along edges), with picture of Milton's home at Chalfont St. Giles in color on front cover and a small vignette of a tree with apples in color on the spine, t.e.g. A nice copy with bookseller's stamp on fly-leaf. "For those who feel that they must not neglect Milton, and are deterred by his length and learning, here he is *in parvo* to wit: '*PL*,' Books 1 and 2; '*PL*,' Selections from the remaining books; '*PR*," Selections; Miscellaneous Poems; Sonnets; '*C*,' A Mask; '*SA*'; Prose Works, Selections. The very necessary annotations appear throughout as footnotes" (inside front flap of publisher's wrappers). Scarce.

2705. THE SHORTER POEMS OF JOHN MILTON With Twelve Illustrations by Samuel Palmer[,] Painter & Etcher[.] *London[:] Published by Seeley & Company[,] Essex Street, Strand. 1889*. First edition. Folio, xx+124pp., half-title ("The Minor Poems of John Milton Illustrated by Samuel Palmer") in red and black, title page also in red and black, twelve photogravure illustration plates drawn and etched by Samuel Palmer (first appearance, striking impressions), original full vellum bound by Roger de Coverly, double fillet borders on covers and lettered within a somewhat scattered vignette frame, spine lettered in gilt, edges untrimmed, in a contemporary flowered cloth covering stitched to provide a protective covering for the book. A "stately" volume with illustrations which "rank with Palmer's best work" (Ray). Number 3 of 134 copies on large paper. Ray, *VPB*, 223; Not in Kohler.

See following regular edition. Some of the illustrations were begun by Palmer as early as 1854. He completed the series, considered to include some of his finest etchings, shortly before his death in 1881. They are reproduced here for the first time, together with a preface by his son, A. H. Palmer. The text is based on Warton's edition of the *Poems* (copy listed here), was edited by A. H. Palmer, and includes Samuel Palmer's own description for each of his illustrations.

[together with]

2706. Palmer, Samuel. THE COMPLETE ETCHINGS OF SAMUEL PALMER AND HIS ILLUSTRATIONS FOR VIRGIL AND MILTON. *Trianon Press, 1979-1990.* 107 etchings reproduced from Palmer's originals as he intended them, in 2 folio-size folders covered in yellow cloth. Originally intended for publication by the Trianon Press in 1979, the proposed volume never appeared, and the project was inherited by the Blake Trust. As stated in the 1990 advertisement in the *Book Collector*: "The plates are of considerable interest and provide in high-quality facsimile a complete record of Palmer's etchings together with facsimiles of significant states and of annotated proofs and drawings. Reproductions of watercolors and drawings related to the etchings, illustrations of Palmer's lifelong preoccupation with themes from Virgil and Milton, and a group of nine portraits of Palmer himself complete the collection." The original brochure in 1978 contained the following statement: "The etchings are reproduced with extreme accuracy by a combination of two-tone collotype with a third tone added from hand-bevelled copperplates. In addition Palmer's Illustrations for Virgil's *Eclogues* and for Milton's *Il Penseroso* and *Comus* etc. are reproduced for the first time as Palmer intended. They can be compared with the versions considerably altered by his son and published after Palmer's death."

2707. THE SHORTER POEMS OF JOHN MILTON With Twelve Illustrations by Samuel Palmer[,] Painter & Etcher[.] *London[:] Published by Seeley & Company[,] Essex Street, Strand. 1889.* First edition. 4to, xx+124pp., half-title ("The Minor Poems of John Milton Illustrated by Samuel Palmer") in red and black, title page also in red and black, twelve photogravure illustration plates drawn and etched by Samuel Palmer (first appearance, fine impressions), original blue cloth (a bit rubbed), front cover lettered in gilt ("The Minor Poems of John Milton") with central figure in gilt, spine lettered in gilt, edges untrimmed. Kohler 230 (describing a copy of the regular edition in "original blue sand grain cloth").

2708. THE SHORTER POEMS OF JOHN MILTON Including The Two Latin Elegies And Italian Sonnet To Diodati, And The Epitaphium Damonis Arranged In Chronological Order, With Preface, Introduction, And Notes By Andrew J. George, Department Of English, High School, Newton, Mass. Editor Of Wordsworth's "Prelude," "Select Poems Of Robert Burns," Tennyson's "Princess," Etc. *New York[:] The Macmillan Company[;] London: Macmillan & Co., Ltd. 1898.* First edition thus. 8vo, xxvi+299+[6]pp., half-title with initials of the Macmillan Company on verso, unsigned engraved frontispiece vignette portrait of Milton at age twenty-one, protective tissue guard, dedication page with dedication to David Masson "whose complete and scholarly works on Milton have won the admiration of all," notes, index, References, original red cloth, front cover and spine lettered in gilt, t.e.g., others untrimmed and partially unopened, bookplate. A nice copy with six pages of advertisements of books published by the Macmillan Company bound in at end. Not in Kohler.

2709. SHORTER POEMS OF JOHN MILTON With An Introduction By T. Cartwright, B.A. and a Portrait of Milton[.] *London: William Heinemann[,] 1908.* First edition thus. Small 8vo, xiv+[2]+79pp., half-title ("Favourite Classics: Shorter Poems of Milton") with list of "Heinemann's Favourite Classics" (including this edition) on verso, engraved frontispiece portrait of Milton after Pieter van der Plaas in the National Portrait Gallery, protective tissue guard, triple black rule on title page with large emblem at the center incorporating a Renaissance figure, half-title for each of the selections, ""Richard Clay & Sons, Limited, Bread Street Hill, E. C., And Bungay, Suffolk" on verso of last page, original soft red leather (a bit rubbed, lacking front fly-leaf), emblem of a tree in gilt at the center of front cover, spine lettered in gilt, t.e.g. A nice copy. Not in Kohler.

2710. SHORTER POEMS OF JOHN MILTON Selected And And Edited By Harold T. Eaton, A.M. Head of the Department of English[,] Brockton High School[,] Brockton, Massachusetts[.] *Lyons And Carnahan[,] Chicago [And] New York[,] (1928).* First edition thus. Slim 8vo, 136pp., reproduction of Munkacsy's *Milton and His Daughters* before "Life Of Milton," "Works Of John Milton," "Introduction To Poetry Study," "Simple Figures Of Speech," notes at bottom of page, with sections at the end on "Notes And Questions" and "Examination Questions" and "Building A Vocabulary," original black cloth, front cover decorated and lettered in orange, spine lettered in blind. A good copy of this edition of the "Stratford Classics" (so-identified on front cover).

2711. SHORTER POEMS OF JOHN MILTON Edited by B. A. Wright[,] Lecturer In English Literature In The University Of Glasgow[.] *Macmillan And Co., Limited[,] St. Martin's Street, London[,] 1938.* First edition thus. Small 8vo, xliv+210+[2]pp., half-title ("The Scholar's Library

General Editor:—Guy Boas, MA"), "Life And Introduction," "Chronology Of Milton's Life" "The Text," "Poems," "Introductions and Notes to Poems," "Appendix Milton's Cosmology," "Questions," original green cloth (a bit rubbed), small emblem in blind at center of front cover, spine lettered in gilt with emblem on the front cover repeated in gilt. A nice copy with two pages of advertisements for "The Scholar's Library" bound in at end. Presentation copy from the editor, with presentation inscription by the editor on fly-leaf and A.L.s. laid in. The letter from the editor (dated "25 July 1938") is to the same person in the presentation inscription. It is one page, written in a neat hand in ink on both sides and signed by the editor, B. A. Wright; in it, Wright speaks about his having "just been appointed to the Chair of English at Southampton" and the move there. The edition was reprinted in 1944, 1948, 1950 (listed here), 1959 (listed here), and 1961 (listed here).

2712. SHORTER POEMS OF JOHN MILTON Edited By B. A. Wright[,] Professor Of English Literature[,] University College, Southampton[.] *Macmillan And Co., Limited[,] St. Martin's Street, London[,] 1950.* Small 8vo, xliv+210+[2]pp., half-title ("The Scholar's Library), contents as with first edition in 1938 (copy preceding), original green cloth (spine faded), spine lettered in gilt and black. A good copy with two pages of advertisements for "The Scholar's Library" bound in at the end.

2713. [SHORTER POEMS] MILTON SHORTER POEMS[.] *The Decca Record Company Limited[.] Argo division[,] 115 Fulham Road London SW3[,] n.d. [ca. 1958].* First edition thus. LP recording in original slipcase, with reproduction of Milton "as a young man by an unknown artist and Milton engraving by G. Faithorne" in black, each in a large circle on red front cover of slipcase. Record is very good, and the cover is in nice condition. Record 3 of "The English Poets From Chaucer to Yeats recorded in association with The British Council and Oxford University Press directed by George Rylands." "Made in England" and "Printed by Robert Stace & Co. Ltd." Record No. PLP 1016. Poems read by Gary Watson, William Devlin, and William Squire. See recording of "Milton Shorter Poems" in 1968 by Argo Record Company Limited[,] very similar to the recording here.

2714. SHORTER POEMS OF JOHN MILTON Edited by B. A. Wright[,] Formerly Professor Of English[,] University of Southampton[.] *London[:] Macmillan & Co Ltd[,] New York • St. Martin's Press[,] 1959.* Small 8vo, xliv+209+[3]pp., half-title ("The Scholar's Library), contents as with first edition in 1938 (copy listed here), original green cloth, spine lettered in gilt with small figure of a head in gilt and triple gilt rules at top and bottom. A good copy with two pages of advertisements for "The Scholar's Library" bound in at end.

2715. SHORTER POEMS OF JOHN MILTON Edited by B. A. Wright[,] Formerly Professor Of English[,] University of Southampton[.] *London[:] Macmillan & Co Ltd[,] New York • St. Martin's Press[,] 1961.* Small 8vo, xliv+209+[3]pp., half-title ("The Scholar's Library"), contents as with first edition in 1938 (copy listed here), original green cloth, spine lettered in gilt with small figure of a head in gilt and triple gilt rules at top and bottom. A good copy with two pages of advertisements for "The Scholar's Library" bound in at end.

2716. [SHORTER POEMS] MILTON SHORTER POEMS[.] *The Argo Record Company Limited[,] 113 Fulham Road London SW3[,] n.d. [ca. 1968].* First edition thus. LP recording in original slipcase, with reproduction of Milton "as a young man by an unknown artist and Milton engraving by G. Faithorne" in black, each in a large circle on red front cover of slipcase. Record is in excellent condition, as is the slipcase. Record 3 of "The English Poets—A Major Recording Enterprise of works by "the major English poets from Chaucer to Yeats," with a complete text (8 pp.) of the contents, "recorded in association with The British Council and Oxford University Press directed by George Rylands." "Made in England" and "Printed by Graphis Press Limited." Record No. RG 433. Poems read by William Devlin, William Squire., and Gary Watson. See recording of "Milton Shorter Poems" in 1958 by Decca Record Company Limited[,] Argo division, very similar to the recording here.

2717. THE SHORTER POEMS OF JOHN MILTON Edited with an Introduction and Commentary by Dennis H. Burden[.] *Heinemann[,] London[,] (1970).* First edition thus. Slim 8vo, x+174pp., original tan cloth, spine lettered in gilt, printed orange publisher's wrappers lettered in black. A very nice presentation copy with presentation inscription from the editor to the president, inscribed and dated "1970" on fly-leaf, and with a hand-written one-page signed note from the editor to the President (dated 1970) laid in, observing that "The dust-jacket has a bad blunder on it about the sonnets," referring to the statement: "The editor normally follows the second printed edition of 1673, though he indicates where a poem was previously printed in the first edition of 1645, and includes four sonnets which appeared in the first edition but not in the second." Burden's letter goes on to say that "It [the bad blunder] arises partly out of an error in my own prose . . . but more importantly out of the publisher's not letting me look the jacket-blurb over beforehand."

2718. SPOKEN ARTS[:] TREASURY OF JOHN MILTON (1608-1674) Read by Robert Speaight and Robert Eddison[.] Presented by Arthur Luce Klein[.] *Spoken Arts, Inc., 95 Valley Road, New Rochelle, New York, n.d. [ca. 1958].* First edition thus. LP recording in original wrapper within original printed slipcase (library labels and stamps on front and on record label, stamp of record shop on back), large head sketch of Milton in black and white on front cover, biography of Milton and photographs of Speaight and of Eddison with biographies of each on back cover. Both the record and the slipcase, number 867 in the series, are in very good condition, the whole within a protective plastic cover. Selections of Milton's poetry are read.

Sonnets

2719. THE SONNETS OF SHAKSPEARE AND MILTON. *London: Edward Moxon, 64, New Bond Street. 1830.* First edition. 8vo, [iv]+[1]+186pp., "Bradbury And Evans Printers, Bouverie Street" (verso title page and repeated on last page), half-title for "Shakspeare's Sonnets" and for "Milton's Sonnets," original purple cloth (a little faded), printed paper label (rubbed and faded) on spine, edges untrimmed. A very nice copy with binder's ticket of W. Shaw in Manchester. One of Moxon's first imprints; he had begun his publishing career in April 1830, with Lamb's *Album Verses*. Scarce. Not in Kohler.

2720. THE SONNETS OF JOHN MILTON Edited by Mark Pattison[.] *London[:] Keegan Paul, Trench, & Co., I Paternoster Square[,] MDCCCLXXXIII (1883).* First edition thus. Small 8vo, 227pp., half-title, frontispiece photogravure of Vertue portrait of Milton frontispiece (striking impression), protective tissue guard, title page in red and black with central device of the press in black, half-title for "Introduction" and for some of the poems, "Index Of Names And Principal Words" at the end, Victorian publisher's parchment (a bit rubbed), "Printed by Ballantyne, Hanson & Co. Edinburgh and London" (printed on blank following index), front cover lettered in red with seal of the Ballantyne Press in black at lower right corner, spine lettered in red and black, t.e.g., others untrimmed and partially unopened, with label of Henry Sotheran tipped in on front pastedown, bound by Burn & Co with their ticket. A very nice, tall copy, fresh and clean within, with neat contemporary presentation inscription (dated 1884) on front blank. "Attempts a chronological arrangement. Analysis of the form and translations of Langhorne and Cowper included" (Stevens). Scarce. Stevens 628; Not in Kohler.

2721. THE SONNETS OF JOHN MILTON Edited By Mark Pattison[.] *New York[:] D. Appleton And Company[,] 1, 3, And 5 Bond Street[,] MDCCCLXXXIII (1883).* First edition thus. Small 8vo, 227pp., half-title, frontispiece photogravure of Vertue portrait of Milton frontispiece, title page in red and black with central device of the press in black, half-title for "Introduction" and for some of the poems, "Index Of Names And Principal Words" at end, original publisher's parchment (a little soiled, pages a bit age-browned), front cover lettered in red with seal of the press in black at lower right corner, spine lettered in red and black, t.e.g., others untrimmed. A good copy with contemporary ownership signature (dated 1883) neatly written on fly-leaf. The first edition thus printed by Appleton Press in New York, a reprint of the edition printed the same year in London by the Ballantyne Press (preceding copy), although a bit smaller in size; the possible second edition thus by Appleton was published in 1896 (also listed here). Not in Kohler.

2722. THE SONNETS OF JOHN MILTON Edited by Mark Pattison[.] *London[:] Keegan Paul, Trench, Trübner & Co. Ltd[,] MDCCCXCII (1892).* Small 8vo, 227pp., half-title, frontispiece photogravure of Vertue portrait of Milton frontispiece (striking impression), protective tissue guard, title page in red and black with central device of the press in black, half-title for "Introduction" and for some of the poems, "Index Of Names And Principal Words" at the end, with "Printed by Ballantyne, Hanson & Co. Edinburgh and London" on verso of last page, original red cloth (a little rubbed, former ownership signature and early date on fly-leaf), emblem of the press in gilt in lower right-hand corner of front cover, spine lettered in gilt, fore- and bottom edges untrimmed. A very nice copy, fresh and clean within, handsomely printed by the Ballantyne Press. Scarce. Not in Kohler.

2723. THE SONNETS OF JOHN MILTON Edited By Mark Pattison[.] *New York[:] D. Appleton And Company[,] 1896.* Small 8vo, xxx+258pp., half-title, engraved frontispiece plate of Vertue frontispiece portrait of Milton with Dryden epigram, protective tissue guard, small seal of the press at center of title page, half-title before introduction, half-title before sonnets, contemporary one-half red cloth, brown linen (a bit rubbed), spine lettered in gilt with decorative gilt trim at top and bottom and gilt emblem at the center, t.e. red, fore- and bottom edges untrimmed and partially unopened. A nice, tall copy (possibly large paper copy), with a fine engraved impression of the Vertue frontispiece portrait of Milton. The first edition thus by Appleton was published in 1883 (also listed here), a reprint of the edition printed the same year in London by the Ballantyne Press. Uncommon. Not in Kohler.

2724. THE SONNETS OF JOHN MILTON Edited By Mark Pattison[.] *New York[:] New Amster-dam Book Co. 1904.* First edition thus by New Amsterdam Book Co. Small 8vo, 227pp., half-title, frontispiece photogravure of Vertue portrait of Milton frontispiece, title page in red and black with central device of the press in black, half-title for "Introduction" and for some of the poems, "Index Of Names And Principal Words" at end, original white silk (a bit rubbed), front cover and spine lettered in gilt with large circular emblem swirling in purple with gold floral pieces within at the center of the front cover, t.e.g., others untrimmed. A lovely copy. The first edition thus printed by Amsterdam Book Co., a reprint of the edition first printed by the Ballantyne Press for Keegan Paul in London in 1883 (also listed here) and reprinted by Appleton Press in New York the same year (also listed here). Uncommon. Not in Kohler.

2725. MILTON'S SONNETS With Introductions, Notes, Glossary And Indexes By A. W. Verity, M.A. Sometime Scholar Of Trinity College; Editor Of 'The Pitt Press Shakespeare For Schools.' Stereotyped Edition[.] The Cambridge Milton for Schools[.] *Cambridge: At The University Press. 1898[.] [All Rights reserved.]* Second edition thus, with additions. 8vo, xxvii+78+8pp., half-title (with printing of the press's seal and locations on verso), preceded by an advertisement leaf for "The Cambridge Milton for Schools. Edited by A. W. Verity, M.A.," half-title repeated before the poems, with notes, appendix, and index at the end, followed by eight pages advertising "The Pitt Press Series," original olive green cloth (a bit rubbed), front cover lettered in black with small seal of the press in black at the bottom, spine lettered in black (faded). A good copy. The first edition thus was published in 1895. Not in Kohler.

2726. THE SONNETS OF MILTON With An Introduction & Notes By John S. Smart, M.A., D.Litt. Lecturer On English Literature In The University Of Glasgow. *Glasgow[:] Maclehose, Jackson And Co.[,] Publishers To The University[,] 1921.* First edition thus. 8vo, x+195pp., half-title, original blue cloth, spine lettered in gilt, edges untrimmed. A fine copy. Presentation copy from the editor, with presentation inscription on fly-leaf dated March 1, 1921. "Among the most valuable of recent works on Milton. Significant for its introductory study of the sonnet forms affecting Milton and for new biographical data that illuminate obscure points in the texts" (Stevens). Scarce. Stevens 634.

2726A. (Cross-listing) THE ENGLISH SONNETS OF JOHN MILTON[.] Wood Engravings by Rachel Russell. *Chelsea[:] The Swan Press[,] MCMXXVI.* Slim 4to, wood-engraved border with decorative vignettes on title page by Rachel Russell, decorative vignette tailpieces also by Rachel Russell, one on each page at the end of the sonnet on that page, printed in Baskerville type on Head's handmade paper. No. 80 of an edition limited to 100 copies. See main listing under *Sonnets*, 1926.

2727. THE SONNETS OF MR. JOHN MILTON, BOTH ENGLISH AND LATIN[.] *["Published by A. A. M. Stols, Maastricht, Holland:] The Halcyon Press[,] 1929.* First edition thus. Large 8vo, 28pp.+colophon leaf, designed with lovely typography and calligraphic initials by Jan van Krimpen, printed at Enschede, original full reddish-brown morocco (spine and joints a bit faded), spine lettered in gilt, raised bands, t.e.g., fore- and bottom edges untrimmed. Fine copy. Printed in a limited edition of 361 copies, this is one of thirty (hand-lettered "No. III") specially bound copies printed on Imperial Japanese paper, "of which XXVI to XXX are not for sale." For a regular copy, see following. Ransom 35.

2728. Variant of Preceding. THE SONNETS OF MR. JOHN MILTON, BOTH ENGLISH AND LATIN[.] *["Published by A. A. M. Stols, Maastricht, Holland:] The Halcyon Press[,] 1929.* First edition thus. Large 8vo, 28pp.+colophon leaf, designed with lovely typography and calligraphic initials by Jan van Krimpen, printed at Enschede, original black cloth (a bit rubbed, spine a little chipped at top and bottom and along edges), spine lettered in gilt, fore- and bottom edges untrimmed. A very good copy with label, "Property Of The Falcon Press Chicago" in red and black, on front pastedown. Printed in a limited edition of 361 copies, including thirty specially bound copies printed on Imperial Japanese paper, this is hand-lettered No. 80 of the 325 regular copies ("of which 301–325 are not for sale"). For a specially bound copy printed on Imperial Japanese paper, see preceding copy. Ransom 35.

2729. MILTON'S SONNETS. With Introductions, Notes, Glossary And Indexes By A. W. Verity, M.A. Sometime Scholar Of Trinity College; Editor Of 'The Pitt Press Shakespeare For Schools.' *Cambridge: At The University Press. 1933.* 8vo, xxxii+76pp., half-title ("Milton's Sonnets Pitt Press Series"), "Note" ("The Sketch of Milton's life is inserted in this volume as it illustrates some points that occur in the Sonnets"), original orange cloth (a bit faded and stained, slightly shaken), front cover and spine lettered in black. A good copy. "First Edition 1895[;] Reprinted 1898 1904 . . . 1933 (With additions and corrections from time to time)" (verso of title page).

2729A. (Cross-listing) SONNETS BY MILTON. Transcribed By F. W. Mercer. *(N.P. n.d.) [ca. 1939].* 6 ¾" × 9 ⅜", unpaginated, illuminated title page, illuminated initials and borders on each page, transcribed by F. W. Mercer, vellum spine, blue cloth over boards. A unique, hand-calligraphied and illuminated manuscript transcription of eighteen sonnets by Milton, with presentation inscription (dated 1939) on fly-leaf. See main listing in this chapter.

2730. THE SONNETS OF MILTON [Edited] By J. S. Smart[.] With A Preface By B. A. Wright[.] *Clarendon Press • Oxford[,] 1966*. 8vo, "Preface To This Reprint" by B. A. Wright, reproduction of 1921 first edition title page, "Appendix Of Documents And Authorities" and "General Index" at the end, paperback, printed blue stiff paper wrappers, with portrait of Milton (age twenty-one) on front cover. A nice copy. The first edition of Milton's sonnets by Smart was published in 1921 (copy listed here); this is a reprint of that edition and the first paperback edition thus.

2731. MILTON'S SONNETS Edited By E. A. J. Honigmann[,] Senior Lecturer In English In The University Of Glasgow[.] *MacMillan[,] London • Melbourne • Toronto[;] St. Martin's Press[,] New York[,] 1966*. First edition thus. 8vo, x+[1]+210pp., half-title, "Erratum" on verso of "Contents," half-title for each of the major sections with commentary on each sonnet, index at the end, original blue cloth, spine lettered in gilt, printed publisher's wrappers. A very nice copy with the signature of historian C[raig] R. Thompson on fly-leaf.

✤

2731A. (Cross-listing) Sotheby, Samuel Leigh. RAMBLINGS IN THE ELUCIDATION OF THE AUTOGRAPH OF MILTON. *London: Printed For The Author By Thomas Richard . . . 1861*. First and only edition. Folio, [iii]+xxxviii+141+[1]+142a+142b,+143-263pp.+[10]leaves (index), two frontispiece photographs of Milton tipped in (taken specifically for this edition, with subscript identification by Leigh), facsimiles of signatures and manuscripts, decorative initials at the outset of each section, appendix, contemporary full green morocco (slightly rubbed at corners, some foxing), covers with contrasting recessed tan panels with pictorial designs in black by Rigaud and J. L. Tupper portraying scenes from *PL*, decorative gilt border trim and gilt rules on covers, gilt-decorated spine by compartments, raised bands, decorated endpapers repeating in smaller version the illustrations on the recessed panels, t.e.g. A very nice copy in a splendid and well-preserved binding, with the bookplates of Herman Blum, Henry Wheatley, and George Wheatley, and the signature in pencil of W. S. Jackson on fly-leaf. The two frontispieces are very early photographs, one being of a bust of Milton and the other being of the Faithorne crayon drawing of Milton (now at Princeton University); both were photographed for the first time for this work. One of the more unusual 1860s bindings, executed by the accomplished John Wright. See main listing with Nineteenth-century Miltoniana.

Student's Editions of Milton

2732. A STUDENT'S EDITION OF MILTON Lu Peixian (Bei-Yei Loh) Vol. I: Texts / Vol. II: Life of Milton[,] Milton's Syntax[,] Notes to the Poems[.] *The Commercial Press[,] Beijing 1996[.]* 2 volumes. Second edition thus. 8vo, 2+490pp.,+465pp., original printed stiff purple paper wrappers, front covers lettered in English in black and white, spines lettered in Chinese. A nice set. Volume I contains the "Texts," and volume II contains Bei-Yei Loh's "Life of Milton," his essay on "Milton's Syntax," and his extensive "Notes to the Poems." The first edition thus was published in 1991 (which I tried to obtain throughout the 1990s, but to no avail; my various attempts to receive answers from either the publisher or editor/author were unsuccessful, and friends who visited China and went to the office of the publisher on my behalf invariably found the office closed). Ten years later, through the efforts of Professor Donald J. Swanz, of St. Bonaventure University, and my son, Kyle, working with Professor Swanz during one of his popular annual study trips to China, a copy of this second edition was obtained as a gift for me from Wang EnLin, Director of the International Student Center, Beijing Institute of Technology, to whom I remain very grateful.

2733. THE STUDENT'S MILTON Being the complete poems of John Milton with the greater part of his prose works, now printed in one volume, together with new translations into English of his Italian, Latin, and Greek poems[.] Edited by Frank Allen Patterson[,] Columbia University[.] *1930 New York: Printed for F. S. Crofts & Co. and are to be sold at 41 Union Square West*. First edition thus. 8vo, ix+1090+41pp., half-title, emblem of the press on title page, preface (dated 1930), half-title repeated before the poems, prose printed in double column, "Textual Notes" and "Glossary" at the end, original blue cloth (a bit used, marginalia in a neat hand throughout and on front endpapers), title page emblem repeated in gilt (faded) on upper right corner of front cover, spine lettered in gilt (faded). A fair copy. A second issue was published in 1931 (see copy following); a second edition thus, with a new preface, was published in 1933 (see copy listed here). See also Patterson's edition of *Milton's Complete Poems* first published in 1930, with a revised second edition thus in 1933 and a third edition thus in 1934 (see copy cross-listed). Scarce in any condition.

2734. THE STUDENT'S MILTON Being the complete poems of John Milton with the greater part of his prose works, now printed in one volume, together with new translations into English of his Italian, Latin, and Greek poems[.] Edited by Frank Allen Patterson[,] Columbia University[.] *New York: Printed for F. S. Crofts & Co. and are to be sold at 41 Union Square West. 1931.* First edition thus, Second Issue. 8vo, ix+1090+41pp., half-title, emblem of the press on title page, preface (dated 1930), half-title ("The Student's Milton") repeated before the poems, prose printed in double column, "Textual Notes" and "Glossary" at the end, original blue cloth, title page emblem repeated in gilt on upper right corner of front cover, spine lettered in gilt (faded), with gilt rule at top and bottom. A nice copy, very clean within, with contemporary signature (dated "Class '32") on front pastedown.

2735. THE STUDENT'S MILTON Being the complete poems of John Milton with the greater part of his prose works, now printed in one volume, together with new translations into English of his Italian, Latin, and Greek poems[.] Edited by Frank Allen Patterson[,] Columbia University[.] *Revised Edition. New York: Printed for F. S. Crofts & Co. and are to be sold at 41 Union Square West. 1933.* Revised edition. 8vo, liv+1170+119pp., half-title, emblem of the press on title page, "First Printing, July, 1930[,] Second Printing, August, 1931[,] Revised Edition, September, 1933[,]" on verso of title page, preface to the first edition (dated 1930) followed by "Preface To The Second Edition" (dated 1933)—as in following edition, "Introduction," "Biographies Of Milton," half-title ("Milton's Complete Poems") before the "Poems," prose printed in double column, "Textual Notes," "Glossary," "Notes On The Poetry," and "Notes On The Prose" at the end, original blue cloth, title page emblem repeated in gilt on upper right corner of front cover (faded), spine lettered in gilt. A good copy.

2736. THE STUDENT'S MILTON Being the complete poems of John Milton with the greater part of his prose works, now printed in one volume, together with new translations into English of his Italian, Latin, and Greek poems[.] Edited by Frank Allen Patterson. Revised Edition. *Appleton-Century-Crofts, Inc. New York[,] 1933.* Revised edition, second edition. 8vo, liv+1176+119pp., half-title, emblem of the press on title page, "Copyright, 1930, 1933" on verso of title page, preface to the first edition (dated 1930) followed by "Preface To The Second Edition" (dated 1933)—as in preceding edition, "Introduction," "Biographies Of Milton," half-title ("Milton's Complete Poems") before the "Poems," prose printed in double column, "Textual Notes," "Glossary," "Notes On The Poetry," and "Notes On The Prose" at the end, original blue cloth, title page emblem repeated in gilt on upper right corner of front cover, spine lettered in gilt. A nice copy.

2736A. (Cross-listing) [THE STUDENT'S MILTON] MILTON'S COMPLETE POEMS Printed together with new translations into English of his Italian, Latin, & Greek poems. Revised Edition. Edited by Frank Allen Patterson[,] Columbia University[.] *New York: Printed for F. S. Crofts & Co. and are to be sold at 41 Union Square West. 1934.* Third edition thus. 8vo, xlvi+439+ 94pp., emblem of the press on title page, half-title ("Milton's Complete Poems"), undated preface, "Introduction," "Biographies Of Milton," half-title ("Milton's Complete Poems") repeated before the "Poems," original black cloth. A good copy without inclusion of any of Milton's prose as in Patterson's edition of *The Student's Milton*. According to the preface: "The conveniences of modern book-making have enabled the publishers to print [this edition] separately from the *Student's Milton*." See main listing under *Complete Poems*, 1934.

2737. THE STUDENT'S MILTON Being the complete poems of John Milton with the greater part of his prose works, now printed in one volume, together with new translations into English of his Italian, Latin, and Greek poems[.] Edited by Frank Allen Patterson[,] Columbia University[.] Revised Edition[.] *New York: Printed for F. S. Crofts & Co. and are to be sold at 41 Union Square West. 1939.* 8vo, liv+1176+119pp., half-title, contents as with other editions of *The Student's Milton* here, original blue cloth (a bit rubbed, a few notes in pencil), title page emblem repeated in gilt on upper right corner of front cover, spine lettered in gilt. A good copy.

2738. THE STUDENT'S MILTON Being the complete poems of John Milton with the greater part of his prose works, now printed in one volume, together with new translations into English of his Italian, Latin, and Greek poems[.] Edited by Frank Allen Patterson[.] Revised Edition. *New York: Printed for F. S. Crofts & Co. and are to be sold at 101 Fifth Avenue. 1946.* 8vo, liv+1176+119pp., half-title, contents as with other editions of *The Student's Milton* here, original blue cloth (a bit worn, with a few marginal notations in pencil), title page emblem repeated in gilt on upper right corner of front cover, spine lettered in gilt, bookplate. A fair copy.

2739. THE STUDENT'S MILTON Being the complete poems of John Milton with the greater part of his prose works, now printed in one volume, together with new translations into English of his Italian, Latin, and Greek poems[.] Edited by Frank Allen Patterson. Revised Edition[.] *Appleton-Century-Crofts, Inc. New York (1961)*. 8vo, liv+1176+119pp., half-title, emblem of the press on title page, preface to the first edition (dated 1930) followed by "Preface To The Second Edition" (dated 1933), "Introduction," "Biographies Of Milton," half-title ("Milton's Complete Poems") before the "Poems," prose printed in double column, "Textual Notes," "Glossary," "Notes On The Poetry," and "Notes On The Prose" at the end, original blue cloth (a bit rubbed), spine lettered in gilt with gilt rule at top and bottom and with title page emblem repeated in gilt at center of spine. A good copy.

The Tenure of Kings and Magistrates

2740. THE TENURE OF KINGS AND MAGISTRATES: Proving, That it is Lawfull, and hath been held so through all Ages, for any, who have the Power, to call to account a Tyrant, or wicked King, and after due conviction, to depose, and put him to death; if the ordinary Magistrate have neglected, or deny'd to doe it. And that they, who of late so much blame Deposing, are the Men that did it to themselves. Published now the second time with some additions, and many Testimonies also added out of the best & learnedest among Protestant Divines asserting the position of this book. The Author, J.M. *London, Printed by Matthew Simmons, next doore to the Gil-/Lyon in Aldersgate Street, 1649*. First edition, second issue. 4to, 60pp., decorative headpiece, decorated initial letter, old calf rebacked (title dust-soiled), gilt rules on covers, gilt rules on spine, orange label with gilt lettering, raised bands, outer dentelles tooled in gilt (faded), marbled endpapers, armorial bookplate on front pastedown. A good copy of this rare edition. Wing M2182; Parker, p. 969; Shawcross, 1974, pp. 309–13; Coleridge 66; Not in Kohler.

Parker has discussed the three distinct issues of this work (p. 969) and has given a census of known copies. During 1649, the printer, Matthew Simmons, moved his shop. The first issue bears his February address "at the Gilded/Lyon." The second issue, which is this copy, bears the October address "next doore to the Gil-Lyon." Of the third issue, which is the rarest, Parker locates three copies. John Shawcross provides a full discussion of the three issues, and in particular of the second issue, disagreeing with Parker's view that the second issue was the result of "afterthoughts." Rather, Shawcross shows that "The reason for the second edition [or issue] of *The Tenure* seems to be that the supply had run out [of what Shawcross earlier in his discussion here had called "One of Milton's most significant prose works"]; the alterations and slight additions seem to have been made in an attempt to clarify; and the testimonies seem to have been added to forestall such comments as [Clement] Walker's that Milton would 'be tied to no obligation to God or man'" (1974, pp. 309, 312).

2740A. (Cross-listing) [THE TENURE OF KINGS] THE RIGHTS OF NATIONS TO DEPOSE THEIR KINGS And To Change Or Amend Their Systems Of Government . . . *London: Printed And Published Ay [sic] T. Dolby, At The Britannia-Press, 299, Strand. n.d. [ca. 1821]*. Second edition thus. See *Rights of Nations*, 1821.

2740B. (Cross-listing) THE TENURE OF KINGS [In] JOHN MILTON[.] ZUR VERTEIDIGUNG DER FREIHEIT Sozialphilosophisce Traktate[.] *1987 Verlag Philipp Reclam jun. Leipzig*. First edition thus. See *Areopagitica*, 1987.

※

2740C. TETRACHORDON, Expositions Upon The foure chiefe places in Scripture which treat of Mariage, or nullities in Mariage . . . By the former Author J. M. [Quotation in Greek from Euripides] *London: Printed in the yeare 1645*. First edition. 4to, [vi]+78pp. Published shortly after his *Areopagitica*, this work extends far beyond its importance as Milton's final divorce tract, and actually extends, expands, and elaborates the various points raised in *Areopagitica*. Bound with THE DOCTRINE AND DISCIPLINE OF DIVORCE; Restor'd to the good of both Sexes . . . Now the second time Revis'd, and much Augmented, In Two Books: To the Parliament of England, with the Assembly. The Author J. M . . . *London: Imprinted In the Year 1645*. Second ("Unauthorized") edition. See *Doctrine and Discipline of Divorce*, 1645.

To Echo

2741. TO ECHO [In] ENGLISH LYRICS FROM SPENSER TO MILTON[.] Illustrations By Robert Anning Bell And Introduction By John Dennis[.] *London[:] George Bell & Sons[,] York Street[,] Covent Garden[;] New York[,] 66 Fifth Avenue[.] MDCCCXCVIII*. First edition. 8vo, xv+222pp., half-title (with advertisement for "The Endymion Series" listing this edition as well as *Milton's Minor Poems* Illustrated by A. Garth Jones [copy listed here] on verso), frontispiece illustration with decorative red border classical style, similar decorative red border classical style on title page, possible first appearance of full-page and half-page headpiece illustrations by Robert Anning Bell, original decorated light green cloth (a bit rubbed, spine a little faded), front cover and spine decorated in dark green art nouveau style with central gilt lettering and decorative gilt piece at the top and at the bottom on front cover, back cover with central decorative device of the press in contrasting dark green and with "The Endymion Series" lettered in gilt above, spine lettered in gilt with decorative gilt device at top and at bottom, t.e.g., others untrimmed, illustrated endpapers with a design of lute-playing maidens stamped in gold. A good copy of a book printed and bound in the art nouveau style and manner of the period. Printed by Charles Whittingham and Company for the Chiswick Press. Included are a number of poetical selections from Milton, with a half-page headpiece illustration for *To Echo* by Robert Anning Bell. Scarce. Limited to 125 copies.

Hand-Colored Illustrations

2742. TO ECHO [In] Variant of Preceding. ENGLISH LYRICS FROM SPENSER TO MILTON[.] Illustrations By Robert Anning Bell And Introduction By John Dennis[.] *London[:] George Bell & Sons[,] York Street[,] Covent Garden[;] New York[,] 66 Fifth Avenue[.] MDCCCXCVIII (1898).* First edition. 8vo, as preceding copy, except that the illustrations by Bell are hand-colored by an anonymous artist. Included are a number of poetical selections from Milton, with a half-page headpiece illustration for *To Echo* by Robert Anning Bell, hand-colored.

2743. TO ECHO [In] ENGLISH LYRICS FROM SPENSER TO MILTON[.] Illustrations By Robert Anning Bell*[.] Bell & Hyman[,] London[,] (1979).* Reprint edition. 8vo, viii+222pp., contents as in original (preceding), original black cloth, spine letter and decorated in silver, printed publisher's wrappers. A nice copy. "Printed and bound [probably in a limited edition] in Great Britain by Redwood Burn Limited Trowbridge & Esher" (verso of title page).

2744. A TREATISE OF TRUE RELIGION, HERESY, SCHISM, TOLERATION, And What Best Means May Be Used Against The Growth Of Popery. By John Milton. To Which Is Prefixed A Preface On Milton's Religious Principles, And Unimpeachable Sincerity. By Thomas Burgess, D.D. F.R.S. F.A.S. P.R.S.L. Bishop Of Salisbury. Protestant Union. *London: F. And C. Rivington, Waterloo Place; And J. Hatchard And Son, Piccadilly. MDCCCXXVI.* First edition thus. 4to, xlix+56pp., half-title, dedication page, "Fac-simile [Plate] of Bishop Barringtons hand writing in his Ninety second Year," preface, postscript, half-title before Milton's work, original boards (joints a bit worn and cracked), printed paper label on spine (very faded), edges untrimmed, elaborate bookplate on front pastedown. Presentation copy with presentation inscription, "From the Author," on fly-leaf. First published in 1673. Not in Kohler.

A Treatise on Christian Doctrine

The publication of this work owed more to chance than to planning. Milton was working on it at the time of his death, and his amanuensis Daniel 'Syriack' Skinner, fearing persecution, sent the MS. to the Elzevirs to be printed. Nonetheless, an embargo was placed on the printing of so dangerous a work, and the MS was returned and thrown into a cupboard in the State Paper Office. Miraculously it escaped destruction, and a hundred and fifty years later it was discovered during a chance search. George IV expressed his pleasure, and it was therefore printed at the Cambridge University Press, with a new font of type cast expressly for the purpose. *De Doctrina* is the fullest exposition of Milton's metaphysics and of his reasoned opinions on questions of philosophy, ethics, and theology. It forms the codification of his beliefs, his thoughts on important doctrinal issues, and perhaps most importantly his thoughts on the relationship between man and God. Its effect is to show that although he is considered "the very genius of English Puritanism," Milton was also one of the first and greatest in the long line of English Liberals. The significance of *De Doctrina* in relation to *PL* has been debated from its discovery. In the twentieth century, Maurice Kelley set the bar, as it were, in his book, *This Great Argument* (1941, copy with criticism in the collection), by using "*De doctrina* as a gloss on *PL*" (p. ix), showing that an "intimate relationship exists between the prose treatise and the epic" (p. 72); Empson et al., however, deduce from *De Doctrina* that when Milton came to write *PL* he was no longer a Christian in the accepted sense. The appearance of Milton's work also occasioned the first of Macaulay's celebrated *Reviews* (see copy with Nineteenth-century Miltoniana). More recently, William B. Hunter and others, in *Visitation Unimplor'd* (1998), copy with criticism in the collection, challenge the acceptance of Milton's authorship of *De Doctrina* and invite reappraisal of Milton's religious thought. Barbara K. Lewalski responds definitively in support of Milton's authorship of *De Doctrina* in two places: first in her article, "Milton and *De Doctrina Christiana*," in *Milton Studies* (1998), copy with criticism in the collection, with some dozen or so reasons which support "evidence for Milton's authorship," "well beyond a reasonable doubt—to be in fact overwhelming" (p. 223), including a response to the British consortium regarding whether

Milton's manuscript is finished: "When Milton wrote the preface he was clearly ready to offer *De Doctrina Christiana* to the world, replete with its heterodoxies" (pp. 221–22); and then in her biography, *The Life of John Milton* (2000), pp. 415–17, copy with criticism in the collection.

2745. A TREATISE ON CHRISTIAN DOCTRINE, Compiled From The Holy Scriptures Alone; By John Milton. Translated From The Original By Charles R. Sumner, M.A. Librarian And Historiographer To His Majesty And Prebendary Of Canterbury. *Printed At The Cambridge University Press, By J. Smith, Printer to the University: For Charles Knight, Pall Mall East. Sold Also By Budd And Calkin, Booksellers n Ordinary To His Majesty, Pall Mall East; Ebers, Old Bond Street; Hurst And Robinson, Cheapside; Rivingtons, Waterloo Place, And St. Paul's Church-Yard; Booksellers Extraordinary To His Majesty; Hatchard And Son, Piccadilly; And Waugh And Innes, Edinburgh. 1825.* First edition. Together with **JOANNIS MILTONI ANGLI DE DOCTRINA CHRISTIANA** Libri Duo Posthumi, Quos Ex Schedis Manuscriptis Deprompsit, Et Typis Mandari Primus Curavit Carolus Ricardus Sumner, A.M. Bibliothecae Regiae Praefectus. Cantabrigiae, Typis Academicis Excudit Joannes Smith, Academiae Typographus. *Veneunt Londini Apud Knight; Budd Et Calkin; Ebers; Hurst Et Robinson; Rivington; Et Hatchard: Edinburgi Apud Waugh Et Innes. M.DCCC.XXV.* First edition. Together, 2 volumes, the second volume being the Latin text. First edition of both the Latin original and the English translation of *De Doctrina*. Large 4to, [1]+xlii+711pp.,+viii+544+[2]pp., two facsimile plates each volume of the opening of the *De Doctrina* manuscript and of an extract from the sonnets in the Trinity manuscript, one facsimile serving as frontispiece in each volume, three pages of "Addenda Et Corrigenda" at end of English volume, index at end of Latin volume followed by one-page "Addenda Et Corrigenda" with advertisement on verso, contemporary calf (a bit rubbed, neatly rebacked, small stamp of "University College London" at the foot of each title page and duplicate stamp on verso), gilt rules on covers, raised bands, black leather labels with gilt lettering and gilt trim, marbled endpapers and edges. A handsome set with the armorial bookplate of John Keats (1773–1852), headmaster of Eton, on front pastedown of each volume. 1931 Exhibition of Cambridge Books, 112; Williamson 175, 230; Kelley, *This Great Argument* (1941); Lewalski, *Milton Studies* (1998); Hunter, *Visitation Unimplor'd* (1998); Lewalski, *Life of John Milton* (2000); Coleridge 13; Kohler 513, 514.

2746. A TREATISE ON CHRISTIAN DOCTRINE, Compiled From The Holy Scriptures Alone; By John Milton. Translated From The Original By Charles R. Sumner, M.A. Librarian And Historiographer To His Majesty And Prebendary Of Canterbury. From The London Edition. *Boston. Published By Cummings, Hilliard, And Co.— Richardson And Lord—Charles Ewer—Crocker And Brewster—Timothy Bedlington—R. P. And C. Williams. 1825.* 2 volumes. First American edition, published the same year as the first English edition (preceding set). 8vo in 4s, lii+448pp.,+464pp., title page each volume, foldout facsimile each volume, modern black buckram (slight waterstaining along top outer edge of volume 2 without affecting any text), spine lettered in gilt. A nice set. Scarce. Not in Kohler.

2747. [TREATISE ON CHRISTIAN DOCTRINE] JOHN MILTON'S LAST THOUGHTS ON THE TRINITY. Extracted From His Posthumous Work Entitled "A Treatise On Christian Doctrine Compiled From The Holy Scriptures Alone." Lately Published By Royal Command. *London: Printed By Richard Taylor, Red Lion Court, Fleet Street; Sold By Rowland Hunter, St. Paul's Churchyard. 1828.* First edition thus. Slim 8vo, xii+96pp., preface, original three-quarter calf, blue marbled paper over boards (a bit rubbed at extremities), gilt rules on spine, gilt-ruled and gilt-lettered red morocco label, bound by J. Edmond, Aberdeen, with his ticket. A nice copy with armorial bookplate of the Earl of Kintore, and with five pages of advertisements bound in at end. Scarce. Not in Kohler.

2747A. (Cross-listing) [TREATISE ON CHRISTIAN DOCTRINE] EXTRACTS FROM THE PROSE WORKS OF JOHN MILTON, Containing The Whole Of His Writings On The Church Question. Now First Published Separately. *Edinburgh: William Tait, 78, Princes Street; Simpkin, Marshall, And Co., London; And John Cumming, Dublin. MDCCCXXXVI.* First edition. See *Prose: Extracts From*, 1836.

2748. [TREATISE ON CHRISTIAN DOCTRINE] EXTRACT FROM THE FIRST BOOK [In] *The Latter-Day Saints' Millennial Star. Vol. XVI, No. 21 (Saturday, May 27, 1854), "Price One Penny."* 8vo, 17pp. (pp. 321–36), printed in double column, disbound. In fine condition, pages clean and white. "Milton On Polygamy (From the First Book on 'Christian Doctrine.' Translated from the Latin, by Charles R. Sumner, D. D., Lord Bishop of Winchester)" occupies the first four pages.

2749. [A TREATISE ON CHRISTIAN DOCTRINE] MILTON ON THE SON OF GOD AND THE HOLY SPIRIT FROM HIS TREATISE ON CHRISTIAN DOCTRINE[.] With Introduction By Alexander Gordon, M.A. *London[:] British & Foreign Unitarian Association[,] Essex Hall, Essex Street, Strand W. C. 1908.* First edition thus. 8vo, xi+[1]+136+16pp., half-title, "Printed By Elsom And Co., Hull" (on verso of title page), introduction dated "30 October, 1908," original light blue cloth (spine a bit darkened), spine lettered in gilt with gilt rules at top and bottom. A good copy with sixteen pages of a "Catalogue of Publications Essex Hall . . . London[,] Books Of Liberal Religion," dated "January, 1909" bound in at the end. Laid in: a small notice, "With the Compliments of the Committee. British & Foreign Unitarian Association, Essex Hall . . . London," together with a stamp of the "British & Foreign Unitarian Association, Essex Hall, London" on front pastedown. Uncommon. Not in Kohler.

2750. TWENTY-SEVEN DRAWINGS, Being Illustrations (By William Blake) For *Paradise Lost, Comus,* And *The Bible*. *N.P.: Carl J. Smalley, Kansas, 1925*. First and only edition thus. Large slim 4to, one-page foreword, twenty-seven photo-lithograph plates of Blake's illustrations, original printed brown paper wrappers over boards, edges untrimmed. A nice copy. One of 1,050 copies printed.

2750A. (Cross-listing) VANE: SONNET ON [In] Sikes, George. LIFE AND DEATH OF VANE . . . *London . . . 1662*. First appearance of Milton's sonnet on Vane. Coleridge 83. See main listing with Seventeenth-century Miltoniana.

Works (Listed Chronologically)

2751. [WORKS] THE [PROSE] WORKS OF MR. JOHN MILTON. *[London:] Printed in the Year MDCXCVII*. The spurious first edition of the first collection of Milton's English prose works. Folio, [vi]+568pp., decorative device on title page, separate title pages for the following: (1) "The Doctrine and Discipline Of Divorce . . . In Two Books. To the Parliament of England, with the Assembly. The Author J. Milton . . . Printed in the Year MDCXCVII" (full page); (2) "Tetrachordon: Expositions Upon the Four chief Places in Scripture, Which Treat of Marriage, or Nullities in Marriage . . . Wherein the Doctrine and Discipline Of Divorce, As was lately Publish'd, is Confirm'd by Explanation of Scripture . . . The Author J. Milton . . . Printed in the Year MDCXCVII" (full page); (3) "Colasterion: A Reply To A Nameles Answer Against The Doctrine and Discipline of Divorce . . . The Author J. Milton" (half page); (4) "The Judgment Of Martin Bucer Concerning Divorce . . . Printed in the Year MDCXCVII" (full page); (5) "Of Reformation, Touching Church Discipline, In England . . . By the Author John Milton" (half page); (6) "The Reason Of Church-Government Urg'd Against Prelacy. The Author J. Milton. In Two Books. Printed in the Year MDCXCVII" (full page); (7) "A Treatise Of Civil Power In Ecclesiastical Causes . . . The Author J. Milton . . . Printed in the Year, MDCXCVII" (half page); (8) "Considerations Touching The likeliest Means to remove Hirelings out of the Church . . . The Author J. Milton . . . Printed in the Year, MDCXCVII (half-page), (9) "Of Prelatial Episcopacy . . . The Author J. Milton . . . Printed in the Year, MDCXCVII (half page), (10) Animadversions Upon The Remonstrants Defence Against Smectymnuus. The Author J. Milton . . . Printed in the Year, MDCXCVII (half page); (11) "An Apology Against A Pamphlet called a Modest Confutation of the Animadversions . . . The Author J. Milton . . . Printed in the Year, MDCXCVII (half page); (12) "The Ready and Easy Way To Establish A Free Commonwealth . . . The Author J. Milton . . . Printed in the Year, MDCXCVII" (half page); (13) "Areopagitica; A Speech Of Mr. John Milton For the Liberty of Unlicen'd Printing . . . Printed in the Year, MDCXCVII (1697)" (half page); (14) "The Tenure Of Kings And Magistrates . . . The Author J. Milton . . . Printed in the Year, MDCXCVII" (half page); (15) "Brief Notes Upon a Late Sermon . . . Wherein Many Notorious Writings of Scripture and other Falsities are observ'd by J. Milton" (half page); (16) "Of True Religion, Heresie, Schism, Toleration And what best Means may be us'd against the growth of Popery. The Author J. Milton" (half page); (17) "Eikonoklasthes . . . The Author J. Milton . . . Printed in the Year, MDCXCVII" (full page); (18) "Articles of Peace . . . The Author J. Milton" (half page), contemporary paneled calf (a little worn, front cover detached, name cut from top margin of title affecting ruled border), red morocco label with gilt lettering and decorative gilt trim and gilt rules, raised bands, red speckled edges. A tall copy, the text in remarkably fresh state. Formerly R. W. Chapman's copy, annotated throughout in pencil by Chapman, whose remarks are often caustic to the extreme, viz.: "Infamous scurrility, Milton was a downright blackguard . . . " (p. 175); "A specimen of Milton's base scurrility and diabolical malignity . . . " (p. 297); "A barefaced libel . . . " (p. 299); "A nasty idea from a dirty stinking Puritan . . . " (p. 298). Wing M2086; Parker, p. 82; Coleridge 72; Kohler 518;

2751A. (Cross-listing) [WORKS] COMPLETE COLLECTION OF THE HISTORICAL, POLITICAL, AND MISCELLANEOUS WORKS OF JOHN MILTON, BOTH ENGLISH AND LATIN WITH SOM [sic] PAPERS NEVER BEFORE PUBLISHED. In Three Volumes . . . *Amsterdam [i.e., London], Finish'd in the Year M.DC.XC.VIII*. 3 volumes. First edition thus. Folio, 442pp.,+872pp.(continuous pagination with volume 1),+

363pp., engraved frontispiece portrait by Faithorne, separate title page for volume 2 and for volume 3, each in black and white, variously dated 1694 to 1698, title page, volume 3: "Joannis Miltoni Opera Omnia Latina . . . Amstelodami, Anno M.DC.XC.VIII," life of Milton by John Toland (first edition). First complete edition of Milton's prose. See main listing under *A Complete Collection*, 1698.

2751B. (Cross-listing) [WORKS] A COMPLETE COLLECTION OF THE HISTORICAL, POLITICAL, AND MISCELLANEOUS WORKS OF JOHN MILTON: Correctly printed from the Original Editions. With An Historical and Critical Account Of The Life and Writings of the Author; Containing several Original Papers of His, Never before Published. In Two Volumes. *London: Printed for A. Millar, at Buchanan's Head, against St. Clement's Church in the Strand. M.DCC.XXXVIII.* 2 volumes. First Thomas Birch edition. Folio, [ii]+xcvii+628pp.,+[ii]+617pp.+[24 unpaginated index], frontispiece portrait of Milton bust engraved by I. Richardson after G. Vertue, title page each volume in red and black. This, the first edition of Milton's prose works after that of Toland in 1698 (see copy cross-listed preceding), was edited by Thomas Birch. It contains several hitherto uncollected pieces and is prefaced by a ninety-five-page life of Milton. See main listing under *A Complete Collection*, 1738.

2752. THE WORKS OF JOHN MILTON, HISTORICAL, POLITICAL, AND MISCELLANEOUS. Now more correctly printed from the Originals, than in any former Edition, and many Passages restored, which have been hitherto omitted. To which is prefixed, An Account Of His Life And Writings. In Two Volumes. *London: Printed for A. Millar, in the Strand. MDCCLIII.* 2 volumes. Second Thomas Birch edition, revised. 4to, [ii]+lxxviii+688pp.,+[ii]+710+[26]pp., frontispiece portrait of Milton bust engraved by I. Richardson after G. Vertue, volume 1, title page each volume in red and black (volume 1, "London: Printed for A. Millar, MDCCLIII"; volume 2, "London: Printed for W. Innys, J. Walthoe, J. and J. Bonwicke, S. Birt, D. Browne, T. and T. Longman, C. Hitch and L. Hawes, H. Whitridge, T. Osborne, and A. Millar. MDCCLIII"), "An Alphabetical Index Of The Principal Matters Contained in the Two Volumes" at end of volume 2, rich contemporary calf binding over thick boards (joints

1749 first Newton edition of *PL*, 2 volumes (first two volumes on the left); with 1752 first Newton edition of *PR* (volume in the middle); with 1753 second Thomas Birch edition of *Works Of John Milton, Historical, Political, And Miscellaneous*, 2 volumes (on the right). Together, 5 volumes, uniformly bound in contemporary calf over thick boards. A handsome set. See #654, #1549, and #2752.

slightly cracked), covers ruled in gilt with Camperdon crest on front covers, intricately gilt-decorated spines, red morocco title labels, black morocco numbering labels, raised bands. A very handsome set. Birch's first edition published in 1738 under the title *A Complete Collection Of The Historical, Political And Miscellaneous Works Of John Milton* (set cross-listed preceding) was revised for this 1753 edition by Richard Baron, who has been described as "an extremist as regards both religious & political liberty" and who was the scholarly protégé of Thomas Hollis. Uniformly bound with the two-volume first Newton *PL* (1749) listed earlier and the first Newton *PR* (1752) also listed earlier, together forming a very handsome five-volume set of Milton's *Works*. Not in Coleridge; Not in Kohler.

Edward Gibbon's Copy

2753. Another Copy of THE WORKS OF JOHN MILTON, HISTORICAL, POLITICAL, AND MISCELLANEOUS. [As Preceding.] In Two Volumes. *London: Printed for A. Millar, in the Strand. MDCCLIII*. 2 volumes. Second Thomas Birch edition, revised. 4to, [ii]+lxxviii+688pp.,+[ii]+710+[26]pp., frontispiece portrait of Milton bust engraved by I. Richardson after G. Vertue, volume 1, title page each volume in red and black, as preceding, "An Alphabetical Index" contents as in preceding copy, contemporary calf (rebacked preserving original spine), gilt rules on covers (faded), gilt-decorated spine by compartments, red morocco title labels, black morocco numbering labels, raised bands, red speckled edges. A fine set, very fresh internally. Edward Gibbon's copy, with his engraved armorial bookplate in each volume. Beckford bought the Gibbon's Library "to have something to read when I passed through Lausanne," where he kept the Gibbon's collection. Later Gibbons presented it intact to his physician Frederic Scholl. The books remained in Switzerland until the 1920s and were almost (though not quite) sold to Magdalen College, Oxford, after negotiations that went on through 1928–30; they were eventually consigned to auction in Bond Street by Southeby's, where in 1934 this set was bought by Lord Rothschild, who promptly inscribed it with his initials (dated 1934) on fly-leaf and gave it to a friend as a Christmas present. This set is recorded in Geoffrey Keyne's edition of Gibbon's Library Catalogue (Cape, 1940, p. 98), where it is noted as being Lot 152 in the Sotheby sale of December 1934.

2754. MILTON. I. PROSE WORKS. II. POETICAL WORKS. *London: William Ball, Paternoster Row. Stereotyped And Printed By J. R. And C. Childs. MDCCCXXXVII.* 2 volumes in one. Thick 8vo, xliii+[i]+963+14pp.,+192pp., frontispiece portrait plate of Milton after an engraving by W. C. Edwards (foxed), without separate title page for volume 1 (*Prose Works*), title page for volume 2: "THE POETICAL WORKS OF JOHN MILTON. *London: Frederick Westley And A. H. Davis. Stereotyped And Printed By J. R. And C. Childs. MDCCCXXXVI*", "Introductory Review" at the beginning of volume 1, "An Alphabetical Index Of Principal Matters" at the end of volume 1, printed in double column, contemporary leather (badly scuffed, joints weak, top portion of spine missing), labeled "Milton" on spine, marbled endpapers, red edges. Despite the defects in the binding, a good copy. Volume 1 is the fifth edition thus of Milton's *Prose Works*; volume 2 is another copy of Milton's *PW* listed earlier, but without the Martin plates in that copy. The two separate volumes are here bound together as Milton's *Works* with a frontispiece portrait of Milton and a general title page for the *Works*, dated MDCCCXXXVII. Scarce thus. The first edition thus of the *Prose Works* was published in 1833; the second edition thus in 1834; the third edition thus in 1835; the fourth edition thus in 1836; the sixth edition thus in 1838—all listed here. Scarce. Not in Kohler.

2755. MILTON. I. PROSE WORKS. II. POETICAL WORKS. *London: William Ball, Pater Noster Row. Stereotyped And Printed By John Childs And Son. MDCCCXXXIX.* 2 volumes in one. Thick 8vo, xliii+[i]+963+14pp.,+192pp., frontispiece portrait plate of Milton after an engraving by W. C. Edwards, protective tissue guard, title page for each volume, volume 1: "THE PROSE WORKS OF JOHN MILTON; With An Introductory Review, By Robert Fletcher. *London: William Ball, Pater Noster Row. Stereotyped And Printed By John Childs And Son. MDCCCXXXVIII*"; volume 2: "THE POETICAL WORKS OF JOHN MILTON. *London: Frederick Westley And A. H. Davis. Stereotyped And Printed By J. R. And C. Childs. MDCCCXXXVI*"; "Introductory Review" at the beginning of volume 1, "An Alphabetical Index Of Principal Matters" at the end of volume 1, printed in double column, contemporary black morocco (front cover detached and repaired with black tape), covers decorated in blind with central gilt laurel wreath, spine lettered in gilt ("Milton") and decorated in gilt in the panels, raised bands, inner dentelles finely tooled in gilt. A nice copy. Volume 1 is the seventh edition thus of Milton's *Prose Works*, volume 2 is another copy of Milton's *PW* listed earlier, without the Martin plates found in that copy. The two separate volumes are here bound together as Milton's *Works* with a frontispiece portrait of Milton and a general title page for the *Works*, dated MDCCCXXXIX. Uncommon thus. Kohler 527 (as here), reporting "Not in the Bodleian Library"; cross-listing Kohler 289, recording the *PW* (as here), cross-listing Kohler 527, and reporting for 289 "Not in the British Library. Not in the Bodleian Library. Not in the Cambridge University Library."

2756. MILTON. I. PROSE WORKS. II. POETICAL WORKS. *London: Henry G. Bohn, York Street, Covent Garden. MDCCCXLIV.* 2 volumes in one. First edition thus. Thick 8vo, xliii+[i]+963+14pp.,+191+[1]pp., frontispiece portrait plate of Milton "Engraved By W. C. Edwards, with "London Published by William Ball at the bottom of the page, "John Childs And Son Bungay" on verso of general title page, separate title page each volume: "THE PROSE WORKS OF JOHN MILTON; With An Introductory Review, By Robert Fletcher. *London: Henry G. Bohn, York Street, Covent Garden. MDCCCXLIV*"; "THE POETICAL WORKS OF JOHN MILTON. *London: Henry G. Bohn, York Street, Covent Garden. MDCCCXLIV*," introductory review, "An Alphabetical Index Of Principal Matters" to the prose works at end of volume 1, printed in double column, contemporary diced calf (some foxing), gilt rules on covers and spine, maroon morocco label with gilt lettering ("Milton's Works"), lightly marbled edges, name on front pastedown. A very good copy. The two separate volumes are here bound together as Milton's *Works* with a frontispiece portrait of Milton and a general title page for the *Works*, dated MDCCCXLIV. Not in Kohler.

2757. Variant of Preceding: Bound with 1838 William Ball edition of *Poetical Works*. **MILTON. I. PROSE WORKS. II. POETICAL WORKS.** *London: Henry G. Bohn, York Street, Covent Garden. MDCCCXLIV.* 2 volumes in one. Thick 8vo, xliii+[i]+963+14pp.,+191+[1]pp., frontispiece portrait plate of Milton after "Engraved By W. C. Edwards" (some foxing in the margins), with "Published by Westley and Davis, London" at the bottom of the page, protective tissue guard, title page each volume: "THE PROSE WORKS OF JOHN MILTON; With An Introductory Review, By Robert Fletcher. *London: Henry G. Bohn, York Street, Covent Garden. MDCCCXLIV*"; "THE POETICAL WORKS OF JOHN MILTON. *London: William Ball, Pater Noster Row. Stereotyped And Printed By John Childs And Son. MDCCCXXXVIII*"), introductory review, "An Alphabetical Index Of Principal Matters" to the prose works at end of volume 1, printed in double column, contemporary three-quarter calf, maroon cloth, black morocco labels with gilt lettering on spine (Milton's Works" in larger letters at the top and "F. A. Sondley" in small letters at the bottom), decorative gilt trim at top and bottom of spine, raised band with decorative gilt trim, red edges. A nice copy with book early label on front pastedown and early signature on fly-leaf. The two separate volumes are here bound together as Milton's *Works* with a frontispiece portrait of Milton and a general title page for the *Works*, dated MDCCCXLIV. Not in Kohler.

2758. THE WORKS OF JOHN MILTON IN VERSE AND PROSE Printed From The Original Editions With A Life Of The Author By The Rev. John Mitford[.] *London[:] William Pickering[,] 1851.* 8 volumes, being 2 volumes of poetry and 6 volumes of prose. First edition thus by Mitford. Royal 8vo, viii+ccii+270pp.,+xx+415pp.,+[i]+530pp.,+[i]+581pp.,+[i]+457pp.,+[i]+488pp.,+[i]+469pp., +[i]+569pp., half-title each volume with decorative headpiece, frontispiece portrait "Engraved by W. Humphreys, from a Print by Faithorne," volume 1, protective tissue guard, separate title page each volume in red and black, each with central emblem of the Pickering Press in red and black, "Advertisement," folding genealogical table (as a multiple foldout), life of Milton, and folding (sideways) facsimile of "the Agreement between Milton and Mr. Symons" before appendix, with sketch of "The House at Chalfont St. Giles" bound before addenda in volume 1, "Arguments" printed together before the poem *PL* in volume 2, decorative head- and tailpieces, decorated initial letters, half-title for some of the poems, index at end of volume 8, handsomely printed by "C. Whittingham, Chiswick" with typographical figure of the press on last page of each volume, contemporary full red morocco (a little worn at the joints and extremities), gilt-decorated covers and spine, raised bands, inner and outer dentelles finely tooled in gilt, marbled endpapers, a.e.g. A very nice set in a handsome contemporary red morocco binding with a contemporary inscription in a neat hand on front blank, volume 1: "John Duke Coleridge, on his birthday, Decr. 3, 1856. From his Father & Mother, Brothers—& Sisters—and his Wife with their most affectionate love." Laid in volume 1: MS. leaf, dated "Athenaeum, July 18, 1868," written on both sides in a fine contemporary hand, "Prof Henry Morley has had the good fortune to find an unpublished poem by John Milton," with the poem written out in full and a reference to its publication in the *Times*. It is worth noting that volume 1 contains *SA* and the *MP*, along with the preliminary material to this edition, while volume 2 contains *PL* and *PR*. An important edition, attractively printed in old face types on high-quality paper by Whittingham and Wilkins at the Chiswick Press, handsomely bound in a splendid contemporary morocco binding. Williamson 84; Keynes, p. 80; NCBEL I 464; Not in Kohler.

John Leng's Copy (1851), Noted Pioneer in Journalism and Politics

2759. Another Copy. THE WORKS OF JOHN MILTON IN VERSE AND PROSE Printed From The Original Editions With A Life Of The Author By The Rev. John Mitford[.] *London[:] William Pickering[,] 1851.* 8 volumes, being 2 volumes of poetry and 6 volumes of prose. First edition thus by Mitford. Royal 8vo, internally as with preceding, original blue linen (rubbed at edges, some foxing), printed paper labels on spine (a bit worn, a little darkened), edges untrimmed, with eight pages of advertisements ("Books Published By William Pickering") bound in at front of volume 1. An important edition, scarce in its own right and infrequently found in Pickering's original binding, attractively printed on high-quality paper by Whittingham and Wilkins at the Chiswick Press. Inscribed on verso of half-title: "Presented to Mr John Leng by the Proprietors of the *'Hull Advertiser'* newspaper in testimony of the diligence, fidelity and ability with which he discharged the duties of Reporter and Sub-Editor of that journal, and of his upright and honourable conduct in relation to them as proprietors for a period of more than four years. E. F. Collins & John Marling, sole proprietors. Hull June 30 1851." Such a eulogy from his first employers is entirely expected: Leng went on to fame as the radical proprietor of the *Dundee Advertiser* and as a notable pioneer in many aspects of both journalism and politics. The texts contain some ticking and sidelining in pencil, mainly marking up "liberal" or "radical" passages, including, of course, *Areopagitica*.

2760. THE WORKS OF JOHN MILTON IN VERSE AND PROSE Printed From The Original Editions With A Life Of The Author By The Rev. John Mitford[.] *William Pickering[,] London[;] Charles C. Little And James Brown[,] Boston, United States[,] 1851.* 8 volumes, being 2 volumes of poetry and 6 volumes of prose. First edition thus, published simultaneously in London and in Boston. Royal 8vo, viii+ccii+270pp.,+xx+415pp.,+[i]+530pp.,+[i]+581pp.,+[i]+457pp.,+[i]+488pp.,+[i]+469pp.,+[i]+569pp., similar to preceding sets, half-title each volume with decorative headpiece, frontispiece portrait "Engraved by W. Humphreys, from a Print by Faithorne," volume 1, protective tissue guard, separate title page each volume in red and black, each with central emblem of the Pickering Press in red and black, "Advertisement To The [Pickering] Edition Of 1851," folding genealogical table (as a multiple foldout), life of Milton, and folding (sideways) facsimile of "the Agreement between Milton and Mr. Symons" before appendix, with sketch of "The House at Chalfont St. Giles" bound before addenda in volume 1, "Arguments" printed together before the poem *PL* in volume 2, decorative head- and tailpieces, decorated initial letters, half-title for some of the poems, index at end of volume 8, attractively printed in old face types on high-quality paper by Whittingham and Wilkins at the Chiswick Press with typographical figure of the press on the last page of each volume, contemporary three-quarter tan calf, marbled paper over boards, gilt-lettered and gilt-ruled red and green morocco labels on spines, raised bands with gilt rules. A very nice set of a scarce edition. A reissue of the important and handsome Pickering edition published in London in 1851 (preceding sets) by Pickering in London and Little and Brown in Boston. Williamson 84; Keynes, p. 80; NCBEL I 464; Kohler 319.

2761. THE WORKS OF JOHN MILTON IN VERSE AND PROSE Printed From The Original Editions With A Life Of The Author By The Rev. John Mitford[.] *London[:] Bickers And Bush[,] 1863.* 8 volumes (being 2 volumes of poetry and 6 volumes of prose). Second edition thus after first Pickering edition in 1851. 8vo, viii+ccii+270pp.,+x+417pp.,+[i]+530pp.,+[i]+581pp.,+[i]+457pp.,+[i]+488pp.,+[i]+469pp.,+[i]+569pp., half-title each volume with decorative headpiece, frontispiece portrait "Engraved by W. Humphreys, from a Print by Faithorne," volume 1, protective tissue guard, separate title page each volume in red and black, each with central emblem of the Pickering Press in red and black, "Advertisement To The [Pickering] Edition Of 1851," folding genealogical table (as a multiple foldout), life of Milton, and folding (sideways) facsimile of "the Agreement between Milton and Mr. Symons" before appendix, with sketch of "The House at Chalfont St. Giles" bound before addenda in volume 1, "Arguments" each printed with the appropriate book of *PL* (unlike 1851 edition where the "Arguments" are printed together before the poem) in volume 2, decorative head- and tailpieces, decorated initial letters, half-title for some of the poems, index at end of volume 8, handsomely printed by "C. Whittingham, Chiswick" with typographical figure of the press on last page of each volume, contemporary polished calf (a bit rubbed, some joints weak), gilt rules on covers, gilt-decorated spines, red morocco labels with gilt lettering (some labels missing), marbled endpapers and edges. A very handsome set, attractively printed in old face types on high-quality paper by Whittingham and Wilkins at the Chiswick Press. A reissue of the handsome Pickering edition published in 1851 (sets also listed here), with the exception of printing the "Argument" with the appropriate book of *PL*. As with the 1851 Pickering edition, volume 1 contains *SA* and the *MP* along with the preliminary material to this edition, while volume 2 contains *PL* and *PR*. See Williamson 84; Kohler 350, reporting "Not in the British Library. Not in the Bodleian Library. The copy in Cambridge University Library is imperfect."

2762. THE WORKS OF JOHN MILTON IN VERSE AND PROSE Printed From The Original Editions With A Life Of The Author By The Rev. John Mitford[.] *Bickers And Son[,] London And Eton[,] 1867*. 8 volumes (being 2 volumes of poetry and 6 volumes of prose). Third edition thus after first Pickering edition in 1851. 8vo, viii+ccii+270pp.,+x+417pp.,+[i]+530pp.,+[i]+581pp.,+[i]+457pp.,+[i]+488pp.,+[i]+469pp.,+[i]+569pp., as with preceding, handsomely printed by "C. Whittingham [Chiswick], Tooks Court, Chancery Lane" with typographical figure of the press on last page of each volume, contemporary maroon morocco (front joint, volume 1, rubbed), gilt seal at center of all covers, spines lettered in gilt with small gilt seal at top and bottom, wide inner dentelles richly tooled in gilt, a.e.g. A very fine set, attractively printed on high-quality paper at the Chiswick Press and handsomely bound by Wiseman as a Trinity College Cambridge Prize Binding, with the college's arms in gilt on covers and spines and with prize label on front pastedown, volume 1, along with armorial bookplate of James Frederick Chance in each volume. Like the 1863 Bickers and Bush edition, this is a reissue of the splendid Pickering edition published in 1851, with the exception of the distribution of the arguments throughout *PL*. Not in Kohler.

2763. THE WORKS OF JOHN MILTON[.] *New York[:] Columbia University Press[,] 1931-1940*. 23 volumes, with the last two volumes comprising an index. First edition each volume. 8vo, half-title each volume, frontispiece portrait in color of Milton at age ten, volume 1, separate title page each volume with central device of the press in blue on each title page, facsimile reproductions and plates, half-title for some of the works, original brown buckram, blind border rule on all covers, with central embossed seal of the press on front covers, black leather labels with gilt lettering and gilt rules on spines of all volumes but index, orange leather labels with gilt lettering and gilt rules on spines of two volumes of the index. An excellent set, formerly having belonged to the Milton scholar Don Cameron Allen, with his bookplate in each volume. This edition was published under the general editorship of Frank A. Patterson, and it has served as a major resource throughout the twentieth century, being the only complete edition of Milton's works. The two-volume *An Index to the Columbia Edition of the Works of John Milton* by Patterson and French R. Fogle (New York: Columbia University Press, 1940) has been invaluable. 2,000 copies (of which this is one) were printed on rag paper for general sale; another 150 numbered copies were printed on handmade paper. Shawcross, Kentucky II, 10.

2763A. (Cross-listing) [WORKS] COMPLETE PROSE WORKS OF JOHN MILTON[.] *New Haven: Yale University Press[;] London: Geoffrey Cumberlege: Oxford University Press[,] MCMLIII-MCMLXXXII*. 8 volumes First edition thus each volume. 8vo, edited by Douglas Bush, Christopher Hill, Maurice Kelley, and others, under the general editorship of Don M. Wolfe. See *Complete Prose Works*, 1953–82.

2764. THE WORKS OF JOHN MILTON with an Introduction and Bibliography[.] *The Wordsworth Poetry Library[,] (1994)*. First edition thus. 8vo, ix+486pp., paperback, printed stiff paper wrappers with color reproduction of Milton portrait at age twenty-one on front cover. A nice copy. "Printed and bound in Great Britain by Mackays of Chatham plc, Chatham, Kent" (verso of title page). Included are Milton's shorter poems, *PL*, *PR*, and *SA*.

2765. [WORKS] THE RIVERSIDE MILTON Edited By Roy Flannagan[,] Ohio University[.] *Houghton Mifflin Company[,] Boston New York[,] 1998*. First edition thus. Large 8vo, xxxii+1213pp., "Preface" including "The Text of Milton's Works" by John Shawcross and excerpts from the "Early Lives" of Milton, reproduction of 1688 illustrations of *PL* (without the original border to each illustration, which had been cut off by the publisher, not the editor, in fitting the illustration to the page size, as Roy Flannagan shared with me), reproduction of title pages of each of the major works, substantive prose selections printed in double column, bibliography for each of the major works, "Chronology" at the beginning, "Index" at the end, notes at the bottom of the page, "printed on recycled paper," original orange colored boards with reproduction of *Samson and Delilah* from the National Gallery (London) in color on front cover and spine, lettering in white against a black background, the whole glazed over, "Chronology" of Milton's life and publications printed on endpapers. A fine copy. The edition is advertised by Houghton Mifflin Company as "The collected works, in prose and verse, of England's greatest epic poet . . . [which] now join those of Chaucer and Shakespeare in the definitive, one-volume Riverside series, the series of choice among students, teachers, and common readers everywhere." Included are all of Milton's poems and substantial selections from his prose. According to Flannagan in his prefatory remarks: "I have included most of the works included by Merritt Hughes, in an edition that has been the standard since 1957 [see copy of Hughes listed here], on the grounds that a modern edition should not fix what isn't broken." Flannagan's edition is considered by many to be "the most capacious edition—1,213 pp., many double-columned—bristling with information: early biographies; poems English and Latin; much prose" (Burton Raffel, *The Annotated Milton Complete English Poems*, p. 684).

2766. [WORKS] JOHN MILTON THE MAJOR WORKS Edited with an Introduction and Notes by Stephen Orgel and Jonathan Goldberg[.] Oxford World's Classics[.] *Oxford University Press[,] (2003)*. First edition thus (with revisions). 8vo, xxxii+966+10pp., frontispiece reproduction of the frontispiece "Engraving by William Marshall" for the 1645 *Poems*, notes and index at the end, paperback, printed stiff wrappers, color illustration of the *Fall of the Rebel Angels* by Andrea Commodi (1650–38), Uffizi Gallery, Florence" on the front cover. "First published 1991"; "First published, with revisions, as an Oxford World's Classics paperback 2003" on verso of title page (copy here). A nice copy.

2767. [WRITINGS] JOHN MILTON'S WRITINGS IN THE ANGLO-DUTCH NEGOTIATIONS, 1651-1654 by Leo Miller[.] *Duquesne University Press[,] Pittsburgh, Pennsylvania[,] (1992)*. First edition. 8vo, xxvi+341+[1]pp., half-title preceded by listing for "Duquesne Studies[:] Language And Literature Series [Volume Thirteen]," "Foreword," "A Note on Textual Readings," "A Brief Guide To The Manuscript Sources," "An Abstract in Place of a Preface," half-title for each of two parts, seventy-three-page facsimile reproduction of the 1652 *A Declaration* and the 1652 *Scriptum*, "Notes" and "Index [Part One Only]" at the end, black cloth spine, crushed silver buckram, covers lettered in black, spine lettered in silver with decorative silver rules, gray endpapers. A fine copy. "[T]he texts in this book . . . have not been known heretofore and thus did not exist in print in any form . . . [or] though known, were not available in print; . . . [or] have been available but in printed texts sometimes abbreviated or erroneous" (Foreword by Albert C. Labriola, General Editor, Language & Literature Series).

A selection of nineteenth-century miniature editions from the collection—showing spines on a shelf, with a miniature statue of Milton. Measuring 6" high, on a 3 ¾" wooden base, this bronze statue depicts a middle-aged, long-haired Milton, fully garbed in the dress of his day, facing straight ahead and holding onto his cloak in the front with his right hand, with his left arm outstretched and his left hand holding a rolled up scroll. Undated, from the nineteenth century.

III
Descriptive Listing of Miltoniana

A. Seventeenth-century Miltoniana

1. Andreini, Giovanni Batista. **L'ADAMO SACRA RAP-RESENTATIONE** Di Gio. Battista Andreini Fiorentino Alla M. Christ. Di Maria De Medici Reina Di Francia Dedicata. Con priuilegio. *Milano: Ad instanzo di Geronimo Bordoni libraro in Milano. 1617.* First edition, second issue. 4to, [xxiv]+177pp., title page with engraved illustration, thirty-nine additional half- and full-page copperplate illustrations, signed with initials "C. B.," eighteenth-century calf (joints slightly cracked, title lightly trimmed at edges and edges extended, some embrowning and minor soiling), decorative gilt border trim on covers, gilt-decorated red morocco spine, inner and outer dentelles gilt, green endpapers, a.e.g. Generally a clean and crisp copy, with forty stunning baroque copperplate illustrations. The first edition of *L'Adamo* was published in 1613. Rare. Shawcross, 1970, pp. 27–28 and no. 79; Not in Coleridge (although 428 refers to this issue and discussion occurs under Hayley, 327).

Andreini was the son of Francesco and Isabella Andreini, the most famous actors of their day. He clearly was well situated to write what Leonardo Vinciana states is the most significant work of the seventeenth-century theatre. It is one of the earliest operas extant and very likely was performed during Milton's continental tour. Voltaire remarks that Milton saw the opera performed in Milan and was inspired to write a tragedy (see Voltaire's *Essay Upon the Civil Wars of France . . . And Also Upon The Epick*

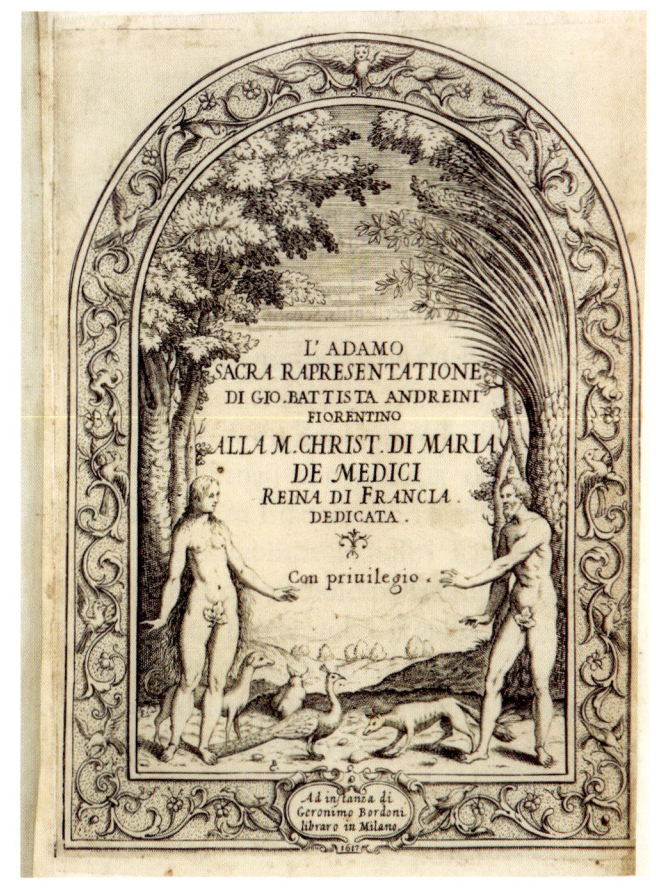

L'Adamo Sacra Rapresentatione, Giovanni Battista Andreini. Milano, 1617, engraved title page of a work that had a strong influence on Milton. See #1.

Poetry, 1728, with Eighteenth-century Miltoniana). Milton did in fact begin work on what eventually became *PL*, and a number of scholars commencing with Hayley have since demonstrated connections between *L'Adamo* and *PL*. Hayley's *Life of Milton* included reference to Voltaire's remarks on Andreini, with a summary of Andreini's work.

2. Blount, Sir Thomas Pope. **DE RE POETICA: OR, REMARKS UPON POETRY**. With Characters And Censures Of The Most Considerable Poets, Whether Ancient or Modern. Extracted out of the Best and Choicest Criticks. *London: Printed by Ric. Everingham, for R. Bently at the Post-house in Russet-street, in Covent-Garden. M DC XCIV*. First and only edition. 4to, [x]+248pp., new half calf antique style, marbled paper over boards (light waterstains, title a bit dust-soiled, minor age-browning), red morocco label with gilt trim and gilt lettering, gilt trim at top and bottom of spine, raised bands, red edges. Deals with various poetical forms in some detail and then reviews the greatest classical and the greatest English poets in alphabetical order, providing biographical and critical observations and commentary. Milton is mentioned variously throughout the 129-page preface; he is also provided pp. 135–38 in the biographical section. "Mr. Milton labour'd all he could, to free us from the troublesome Bondage of Rhyming, as he calls it; and by his Incomparable Poems of *PL* and *PR*, has given us a most perfect Example of Blank Verse." One of the earliest such bio-bibliographical dictionaries with essays and critical notes in English literature. Scarce. Wing B3347; Shawcross, 1970, p. 20; Coleridge 285.

3. Blount, Thomas. **GLOSSOGRAPHIA: OR A DICTIONARY INTERPRETING THE HARD WORDS** Of Whatsoever Language, now used in our refined English Tongue; With Etymologies, Definitions and Historical Observations on the same . . . Very usesfull for all such as desire to understand what they read. The Fifth Edition, with many Additions. By T. Blount, of the Inner-Temple, Esq; [Latin Erasm. Apoph.] *London: Printed by Tho. Newcomb, and to be sold by Tho. Flesher, at the Angel and Crown in St. Pauls Church-yard, 1681*. 8vo, [16]+712pp., printed in double column, original speckled calf (a bit rubbed), raised bands, marbled edges. A very fine copy with contemporary signature on fly-leaf. Based on Milton's manuscript dictionary (see 1693 first published edition, *Linguae Romanae Dictionarium*, in Chapter II). Uncommon. Wing B3338; Parker, p. 989; Gibson, *Bacon*, 288; Not in Coleridge.

4. Charles I. **EIKON BASILIKE** The Pourtraicture Of His Sacred Majesty In His Solitudes And Sufferings. [Rom. 8 and Latin Quotation.] *M. DC. XLVIII*. Bound

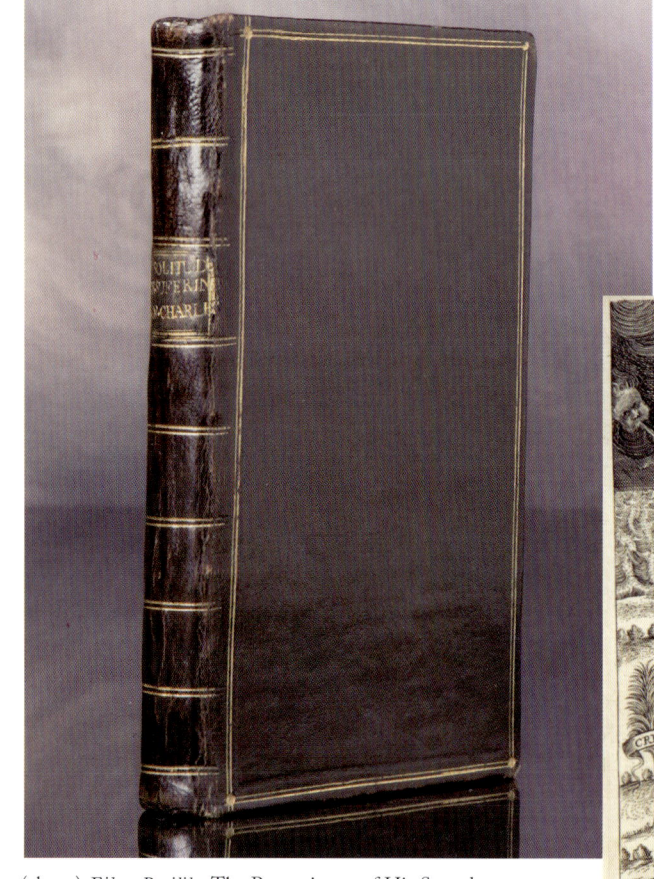

(above) *Eikon Basilike*. The Povrtraictvre of His Sacred Maiestie In His Solitudes And Sufferings. 1648 first edition, third issue, in fine contemporary black morocco binding.
(right) Engraved frontispiece portrait by Marshall, two-page plate of Charles kneeling in prayer. Fine impression. See #4.

with **RELIQUIAE SACRAE CAROLINAE**. The Works Of That Great Monarch And Glorious Martyr King Charles the Ist, both Civil and Sacred. With A Short View of the Life and Reign of that most blessed Prince from his Birth to his Buriall. [Latin Quotation from Tacitus.] *Hague, Printed by Sam: Browne, [1648].* 2 volumes in one. First edition of *Eikon Basilike*, second issue. No place or publisher is given. Small, thick 8vo, 355pp.,+[xii]+ 374pp., fine engraved frontispiece portrait by Marshall, two-page plate of Charles kneeling in prayer, explanation of the emblem and a second title page for "*Reliquiae Sacrae Carolinae*. Hague, Printed by Sam Browne," undated, preceding *Eikon Basilike* title page in red and black as is first title page for *Reliquiae Sacrae Carolinae*, bound here before *Eikon Basilike*, "Aditionall Prayers" and "Table of Contents" at the end, original calf (worn, back joint broken, some pages misbound near the end), in an early protective red velvet cloth covering. A good copy. "The reputed author was Charles I, but most of the text was written by his chaplain, John Gauden. The date is old style; that is, it was published in early 1649" (Shawcross). Milton attacked *Eikon Basilike* in his *Eikonoklastes* (see copy in Chapter II), which he prepared on the instructions of the Council of State because of the sympathy this work, *Eikon Basilike*, provoked for the executed king. Milton accused the King of plagiarizing prayers. Madan 1, second issue; Shawcross, Kentucky, 19; Shawcross, 1974, pp. 315–20; Coleridge 312a.

5. Charles I. **EIKON BASILIKE**. The Povrtraictvre of His Sacred Maiestie In His Solitudes And Sufferings. [Rom. 8 and Latin Quotation.] *M. DC. XLVIII.* First edition, third issue. No place or publisher is given. 8vo, [8]+269pp., fine engraved frontispiece portrait by Marshall, two-page plate of Charles kneeling in prayer, contemporary black morocco, gilt rules on covers and spine, gilt lettered green morocco label, a.e.g. A very fine copy. See Richard Perrinchief's life of Charles, *The Royal Martyr*, 1676, also listed here, designed to resemble an edition of the *Eikon Basilike*, complete with allegorical frontispiece. Madan 1, third issue; Wing E270; Coleridge 312b.

The collection also has a copy of Madan 26, issue 2.

Robert Southey's Copy?

6. Charles I. **EIKON BASILIKE**. The Pourtraicture Of His Sacred Majestie In His Solitudes And Sufferings. Rom. VIII. More than Conqueror, &c. [Latin quotation.] *London: Printed by R. Norton for Richard Royston, Bookseller to His most Sacred Majesty, M DC LXXXI.* 8vo, [10]+ 256pp., engraved frontispiece portrait of Charles kneeling by Marshall and one other engraved portrait of Charles, contemporary calf (recently rebacked), gilt rules on spine, red morocco label with gilt lettering. A very nice copy, with early armorial bookplate and early ownership note tipped in. Possibly Robert Southey's copy, with a pencil note on front pastedown: "Bought at Lairbeck Cottage Keswick after the death of Katherine Southey Augt. 1854. Marked with the initial 'S' of her father Robert Southey." Occasionally in the margins of the text there is an "S," although whether Southey marked his books in such a way is unclear. Madan 66; Coleridge 312b.

7. Charles I. **BASILIKE. THE WORKS OF KING CHARLES THE MARTYR**: With a Collection of Declarations, Treaties, and other Papers concerning the Differences Betwixt His said Majesty And His Two Houses of Parliament. With History of His Life; as also of His tryal and Martyrdome. The Second Edition. *London, Printed for Ric. Chiswell, at the Role and Crown in St. Paul's Church-Yard, MDC LXXXVII.* Second edition. Large 4to, 12+720+4pp., magnificent full-page engraved coat of arms as frontispiece, engraved and printed title pages, with splendid engraved title page consisting of monument to Charles (a portrait of Charles held by cherubs on a pedestal enshrined in a surrounding temple), three folding engravings (fine impressions), including the portrait of Charles kneeling in prayer (with the note "Place this figure before Eikon Basilike"), early full calf with some wear (rebacked sometime with older calf relaid, joints strengthened from within), raised bands, black label with gilt lettering. A very good copy, crisp and clean within, with large margins. Laid in: two early engraved illustrations (6 ¼" × 8", fine impressions) depicting "King Charles taking his last farewell of his Children the day before he was beheaded" and "King Charles beheaded at Whitehall on the 30. of Jany. 16 40."

8. [**CHURCH OF ENGLAND; BOOK OF COMMON PRAYER**] **A COPIE OF THE PROCEEDINGS** of some worthy and learned Divines, appointed by the Lords to meet at the Bishop of Lincolnes in Westminster: Touching Innovations in the Doctrine and Discipline of the Church of England, Together With Considerations upon the Common Prayer Book. *London, Printed 1641.* 4to, 10pp., disbound (title a bit dust-soiled with several markings). A good copy, from the Earl of Selbourne's library, with his shelf number. Rare. Wing C4103c, locating only the Union Theological Seminary copy.

9. [Coleraine, Henry Hare, Second Baron]. **THE SITUATION OF PARADISE FOUND OUT**: being an History of a late Pilgrimage unto the Holy Land. With a necessary Apparatus prefixt, giving light into the whole Design. I

have chosen the Way of Truth, Psal. 119. v.30. *London: Printed by J. C. and F. C. for S. Lowndes, over against Exeter-Exchange in the Strand, and H. Faithorne, and J. Kersey, at the Rose in St. Pauls Church-yard. 1683*. First and only edition. 8vo, [8]+243pp.+"Errata" page, old polished calf (without [A1], presumably blank, joints weak, a bit rubbed), gilt rules on covers and spine, spine lettered in gilt, marbled endpapers and edges. A very nice copy. The inscription "James Boswell" on the front fly-leaf may or may not be an early form of the biographer's signature. The former Richard Heber copy, with his stamp, and the former Robert Crew copy, with his bookplate. Curious allegorical novel in which various pilgrims, displeased with the world as it is, seek out the location of Paradise. In the preliminary "apparatus," Milton is quoted extensively. Nice association copy. Rare. New Wing C5064; Mish, *English Prose Fiction, 1600–1700*, p. 63; Not in Coleridge.

10. Cowley, Abraham. **POEMS**: Viz. I. Miscellanies. II. The Mistress, or, Love Verses. III. Pindarique Odes. And IV. Davideis, Or, A Sacred Poem Of The Troubles Of David . . . *London: Printed for Humphrey Moseley, at the Prince's Arms in St. Pauls Church yard, M.DC.LVI*. First collected edition. Tall 4to, [14]+"Errata"+41pp.,+80pp., +[4]+70pp.,+154pp.,+23pp., individual title page for *Pindarique Odes* and *Davideis*, each dated 1656, decorative headpieces and decorated initial letters, early three-quarter calf, marbled paper over boards, gilt rules on spine. A very nice copy with the bookplate of Everard Meynell. Cowley was a serious artist whose popularity may be judged by the large number of handsome editions of his works. Scarce. Wing C6683; Shawcross, 1970, pp. 133–35, 241 (quoting Dennis on Cowley and Milton).

11. Cowley, Abraham. **THE WORKS OF MR. ABRAHAM COWLEY** Consisting of Those which were formerly Printed: And Those which he Designed for the Press, Now Published out of the Author's Original Copies. To this Edition are added several Commendatory Copies of Verses on the Author, by Persons of Honour. As also a Table to the Whole Works, never before Printed. *London: Printed by J. M. for H. Herringman, and sold by Jos. Knight and Fra. Saunders, at the Sign of the Blue Anchor, in the Lower Walk of the New-Exchange. 1688*. Large 4to, [xlviii]+80pp.;+[iv]+70pp.;+154pp.;+148pp.,+[14]+161+[1]pp., engraved frontispiece portrait by Faithorne (fine impression), separate title page for *Davideis*, dated 1687, title page for *The Second Part Of The Works Of Mr. Abraham Cowley*, dated MDCLXXXIV, with engraved frontispiece of Cowley memorial after R. White (dated 1681), "Epilogus" appears at the end, contemporary paneled calf (a bit rubbed), covers decorated in blind, gilt-decorated spine, tan morocco label with gilt lettering, raised bands, gilt dentelles (a bit faded). A fine copy.

12. Dryden, John. **THE STATE OF INNOCENCE AND FALL OF MAN: AN OPERA.** Written in Heroique Verse, And Dedicated to Her Royal Highness, The Dutchess. By John Dryden, Servant to His Majesty. [Latin Quotation from Ovid's *Metamorphoses*.] *London: T. N. for Henry Herringman, at the Anchor in the Lower Walk of the New Exchange. 1677*. First edition. 4to, [xx]+45pp., new quarter morocco, marbled paper over boards (some margins a bit uneven), spine lettered in gilt with small gilt device at bottom. "On the whole, a large, decent, respectable copy of a play notoriously hard to find in earlier edition" (G. W. Stuart, Jr.), fresh internally. Wing D2372; MacDonald 81a; Not in Pforzheimer; Shawcross, 1972, pp. 23, 81–83; Shawcross, 1984, 754; Not in Coleridge.

John Dryden's opera represents the first major printed tribute to *PL*, which Dryden said in his preface was "undoubtedly one of the greatest, most noble and sublime poems which either this age or nation has produced." Dryden obtained Milton's permission for this operatic version of *PL*; it was intended primarily as a tribute to the genius of Milton's epic. The prefatory *Author's Apology* by Dryden is a significant early definition of the responsibilities of the literary critic, which closes: "I have only laid down, and that superficially enough, my present thoughts; and shall be glad to be taught better, by those who pretend to reform our Poetry." "The exceedingly rare first edition" and "one of the rarest and earliest tributes to Milton's genius" (G. W. Stuart, Jr., Ravenstree, Cat. 125, #156, 1985).

13. Dryden, John. **THE STATE OF INNOCENCE, AND FALL OF MAN: AN OPERA.** Written in Heroique Verse; And Dedicated to Her Royal Highness, The Dutchess. By John Dryden, Servant to His Majesty. [Latin Quotation from Ovid.] *London: Printed by H. H. for Henry Herringman, and are to be sold by Joseph Knight, and Francis Saunders, at the Anchor in the Lower Walk of the New Exchange. 1684*. Fourth edition. 4to, [xiv]+38pp., old half calf (a bit rubbed, title dust-soiled with a few minor spots, inner margin wrinkled with a few short tears, outer tip of lower blank removed and neatly restored, so that it is barely touching two letters, lacks advertisement leaf at end), spine lettered in gilt. All in all, an okay copy, fairly fresh internally, with earlier ownership signature on fly-leaf. Rare. Wing D2375; MacDonald 81e; Shawcross, 1984, 1039; Not in Coleridge.

14. Dryden, John. **THE STATE OF INNOCENCE, AND FALL OF MAN: AN OPERA.** Written in Heroique Verse; and Dedicated to Her Royal Highness The

Dutchess. By Mr. John Dryden. [Latin Quotation from Ovid.] *London: Printed for Henry Herringman, and are to be Sold by Abel Roper, at the Mitre near Temple-Barr, in Fleetstreet. 1692.* Seventh edition. 4to, [xii]+38+[1]pp., disbound, complete with the rare advertisement leaf at end. A very nice copy. Wing D2377; MacDonald 81g; Shawcross, 1984, 1320; Coleridge 236.

15. [DuMolin, (Peter)] REGII SANGUINIS CLAMOR AD COELUM ADVERSUS PARRICIDAS ANGLICANOS. *Hagae-Comitvn, Ex Typographia Adriani Vlacq. M.DC.LII.* First edition. Bound with four works by Milton—*Pro Populo*, 1654; *Defensio Secunda*, 1654; *Ratio Constitutae*, 1654, and *Literae Pseudo-Senatus Anglicani*, 1676, and one other work—*Fides Publica*, 1654, by Alexander More. 2 volumes comprising six works altogether, four by Milton. 12mo, [ii]+234pp., title page with printer's device, decorative headpieces and decorated initial letters, old half green morocco, marbled paper over boards (bit worn), spines lettered in gilt. A very good collection of historically related pamphlets, with notes in an early hand on front pastedown of each volume. Each work in the collection is listed separately with appropriate commentary on that work. *Pro Populo, Defensio Secunda, Ratio Constitutae,* and *Literae Pseudo-Senatus Anglicani* are listed alphabetically among Milton's works; *Fides Publica* by Alexander More is listed under More (also listed here separately). *Regii Sanguinis Clamor* is a "formidable attack on Milton's *Pro Populo Anglicano Defensio* [present here]" (Coleridge); it is also "the most brilliantly scathing rebuke [Milton] had ever received in print" (Parker). Coleridge 307 (describing this 12mo edition, but noting that "Vlacq published three editions simultaneously, one of them a quarto, and presumably the quarto is the first edition"); Parker, p. 421; Shawcross, 1974, pp. 323–29.

16. Eachard, John. THE GROUNDS & OCCASIONS OF THE CONTEMPT OF THE CLERGY And Religion Enquired into. In a Letter written to R. L. *London: Printed by W. Godbid for N. Brooke at the Angel in Cornhill. 1670.* First edition. 8vo, [iv]+131+[5]pp., central emblem on title page, new antique-style calf (title and last leaves a little soiled and frayed, hole in last few leaves not touching text), blind rules on covers, spine lettered in gilt. A good copy with five pages of advertisements at the end. Probably Eachard's most famous work, with numerous further editions before 1700 in which he comments wittily, for example, on Milton and divorce, boasting about Milton not being "any of those occasional writers that . . . being a little tormented with an ill chosen Wife, set forth the Doctrine of Divorce to be truly Evangelical" (A5). Scarce. Wing E50; Shawcross, 1974, p. 299; Coleridge 310.

17. Fletcher, Giles. CHRIST'S VICTORIE AND TRIUMPH IN HEAVEN AND EARTH, Over And After Death. [Latin Quotation.] The second Edition. *Cambridge: Printed for Francis Green, 1632.* Second edition. 4to, [xii]+84pp., central emblem on title page, decorative head- and tailpieces and decorated initial letters, modern three-quarter brown calf, brown cloth, (a bit rubbed at joints, new endpapers), spine decorated with gilt pieces within the panels, raised bands with decorative gilt trim, red morocco label with gilt lettering and gilt trim, marbled endpapers, a.e.g. A fine copy with early armorial bookplate and later bookplate. Originally published in 1610, *Christ's Victorie And Triumph* "is the chief monument of baroque devotional poetry between Robert Southwell and the young Milton. . . . who seems to have remembered Giles . . . even in the late and austere *PR*" (*English Literature in the Earlier Seventeenth Century*, pp. 86–87). Scarce. STC 11060; Not in Coleridge.

18. Fletcher, Phineas. THE PURPLE ISLAND, Or The Isle of Man: Together With Piscatorie Eclogs And Other Poeticall Miscellanies. By P. F. *Printed by the Printers to the Universitie of Cambridge. 1633.* First edition. 4to, xi+181pp.,130+[2]pp., title page in red and black within a decorative black border with central emblem, separate title page in black and white with central emblem for "Piscatorie Eclogs And Other Poeticall Miscellanies. By P. F. Printed by the Printers to the Universitie of Cambridge. 1633," original calf (rebacked, a bit rubbed), gilt rules on covers and spine, red morocco label with gilt lettering, bookplate. A fine copy, complete with rare leaf at the end containing the lines "To my deare friend, the Spencer of this age" by Francis Quarles. An elaborate allegorical description of the human body and of the virtues to which man is subject. The book was well-known to Milton, who was undoubtedly influenced by it in *PL*. Fletcher's Shakespearian and Spenserian imitations have never been without admirers of the highest order from Milton through James Joyce. According to Douglas Bush, "Fletcher may be called the Jacobean or Caroline Erasmus Darwin" (*English Literature in the Earlier Seventeenth Century*, p. 88). Rare. Hayward 65; Grolier, *Wither to Prior*, 101; Pforzheimer 376; STC 11082; Not in Coleridge.

19. Heywood, Thomas. THE HIERARCHIE OF THE BLESSED ANGELLS. Their Names, orders and Offices. The fall of Lucifer with his Angells Written by Tho. Heywood[.] [Latin phrase.] *London: Printed by Adam Islip 1635.* First and only edition. Folio, [viii]+622+[7]+[1]pp., engraved title after L. Cecill and nine full-page engraved plates, decorated headpieces and initial letters, with the imprimatur leaf and final blank, "A generall Table" and

"Errata" at the end, contemporary unlettered sheep (a few minor marks on the covers and one trifling defect to the spine), raised bands. A very fine copy, with contemporary (possibly early) signature at top of title page. The relationship between this ambitious poem with elaborate prose annotations and *PL* has never been sufficiently investigated, although the full-page passage on contemporary poets—Shakespeare, Jonson, Marlowe, and others—is well known, as is the history of Macbeth. There is no modern edition. Rare. STC 13327; Not in Grolier or Pforzheimer; Not in Coleridge.

20. [History: Civil War] (1) **A DIRECTORY FOR THE PUBLIQUE WORSHIP OF GOD THROUGHOUT THE THREE KINGDOMS OF ENGLAND, SCOTLAND, AND IRELAND.** Together with an Ordinance of Parliament for the taking away of the Book of Common Prayer: And For establishing and observing of this present Directory throughout the Kingdom of England, and Dominion of Wales. Die Jovis, 13. Martii, 1644. Ordered by the Lords and Commons assembled n Parliament, That this Ordinance and Directory bee forthwith Printed and Published: Joh: Brown, Cleric. Parliamentorum. H: Elsynge, Cler. Parl. D. Com. *London: Printed for Evan Tyler, Alexander Fifield, Ralph Smith, and John Field; And are to be sold at the Sign of the Bible in Cornhill, neer the Royall-Exchange. 1644.* Wing D. 544. (2) **A SUPPLY OF PRAYER FOR THE SHIPS OF THIS KINGDOME** That want Minister to Pray with them: Agreeable To The Directory Established by Parliament. Published by Authority. *London: Printed for John Field, & are to be sold at his house upon Addle-hill, n.d.* Wing S1619. (3) **C. R. BY THE KING. A PROCLAMATION** commanding the use of the Book of Common Prayer according to Law, notwithstanding the pretended Ordinances for the New Directory. *Printed at Oxford, by Leonard Lichfielde, Printer to the Universitie, 1645.* Broadside (foldout several times). Wing C2563. (4) [Hammond (Henry).] **A VIEW OF THE NEW DIRECTORY AND VINDICATION OF THE ANCIENT LITURGY OF THE CHURCH OF ENGLAND.** *Oxford: Printed at Oxford, by Leonard Lichfielde, Printer to the Universitie, 1645.* Wing H612. (5) Hammond (H.). [Greek Title], Or, **THE GROUNDS OF UNIFORMITY FROM 1. COR., 14.40.** Vindicated from Mr. Jeane's exceptions to One passage in the View of the Directory. By H. Hammond D.D. *London, Printed by J. G. for Richard Royston, at the Angel in Ivy-Lane, M.DC.LVII.* Wing H541. 4to, 40pp.;16pp.; broadside foldout; 112pp.; 24pp.; four tracts and one broadside bound in one volume, contemporary quarter calf, marbled paper over boards (spine a bit worn, joints weak), raised bands. No. 2 tract is in manuscript form and in a fine chancery hand, worthy of the Bickham whose armorial bookplate occurs twice in this volume. He is also responsible for a long relevant extract from Clarendon written on the fly-leaf. These tracts illustrate the fundamental religious differences between the King and the Roundheads. Hammond was Charles I's chaplain. Now "chiefly remembered by Keble's beautiful elegy; but in his own time, no man had a more beneficent influence on the religious literature of his age . . . [he] has been called 'the father of English Biblical criticism'" (W. H. Hutton, *CHEL*, vii, 147). Scarce.

21. Hume, Patrick. **ANNOTATIONS ON MILTON'S PARADISE LOST** Wherein The Texts of Sacred Writ, relating to the Poem, are Quoted; The Parallel Places and Imitations of the most Excellent Homer and Virgil, Cited and Compared; All the Obscure Parts render'd in Phrases more Familiar; The Old and Obsolete Words, with their Originals, Explain'd and made Easie to the English Reader. By P[atrick]. H[ume]. Philopoetus. Uni, cedit Miltonus, Homero Propter Mille annos. Juv. vii. 38. *London: Printed for Jacob Tonson, at the Judges Head near the Inner-Temple-Gate in Fleet-street, MDCXCV.* First edition. Folio, 321pp., double black border around title page, contemporary calf (a bit scuffed and rubbed at joints and corners), gilt rules on spine, black morocco label with gilt lettering, raised bands, gilt dentelles, speckled edges. A very fine copy, with the armorial bookplate of the Earl of Itchester. Supposed to accompany the sixth edition of *PL* (1695) but not always found with it (see copy in Chapter II). Hume is the first to attempt exhaustive annotations on the work of an English poet. Scarce. Wing H3663; Shawcross, 1972, 45; Not listed separately in Coleridge (see 214).

22. Johnson, Rev. Samuel. **JULIAN THE APOSTATE**: Being A Short Account Of His Life. The Sense of the Primitive about his succession. Together with A Comparison of Popery and Paganism. *London: Printed for Langley Curtis, on Lud-gate-hill. MDCLXXXII.* 8vo, xxix+[iii]+ 172pp., original calf (worn, joints cracked, endpapers and title page age-darkened), blind rules on covers, marbled edges. An okay copy with early signature and shelf-mark on fly-leaf and with the following comments in an early hand on title page: "a Libell against the Primitive Christians," and "a Truth against the Papists." Milton's *Defensio* is drawn upon in "The Preface to the Reader" (pp. iii–xxix). Wing J830; Shawcross, 1974, p. 326; Coleridge 335.

23. Leslie, Charles. **THE HISTORY OF SIN AND HERESIE.** Attempted From the First War that they Rais'd in Heaven: Through their various Successes and Progress upon Earth: To the final Victory over them, and their Eternal Condemnation in Hell. In Some Meditations Upon the Feast of St. Michael and all Angels. *London:*

Printed for H. Hindmarsh, at the Golden-Ball over against the Royal-Exchange, in Cornhil. 1698. First edition. 4to, vi+59+[1]pp., disbound (some age-browning). A decent copy with errata corrected in an early hand. Leslie discourses on the Bible, early to present, and Milton's *PL*, questioning what he considers to be Milton's unorthodox views as set forth in his epic poem. Rare. Parker, p. 1203; Wing L1135; Shawcross, 1970, p. 49; Not in Coleridge.

24. Mackenzie, Sir George. **JUS REGIUM**: Or, The Just and Solid Foundations of Monarchy In General; and more especially Of The Monarchy of Scotland: Maintain'd against Buchanan, Napthali, Dolman, Milton, &c. By Sir George Mackenzie, His Majesty's Advocate in Scotland. [Quotation from I Sam. 26, 27.] *London: Printed for Richard Chiswel, at the Rose and Crown in St. Paul's Churchyard. 1684.* First London edition. 8vo, iv+209+[1]+[4]pp., "Postscript" on final leaf, original sheep (a bit rubbed, new endpapers), raised bands, gilt dentelles (faded), speckled edges. A very fine copy with four pages of advertisements bound in at the end. Mackenzie was known as "Bloody Mackenzie" for his attitude as the King's Advocate in Scotland. He was as loyal to the King as he was anti-Milton. The first London edition was published the same year as the first Edinburgh edition. Scarce. Wing M164; Coleridge 361 (note).

25. Marino, Giambattista. **L'ADONE**, Poema Heroico Del C. Marino, Con gli Argomenti del Conte Sanvitale e l'allegorie di Don Lorenzo Scoto. Aggiuntovi La tavola delle cose notabili. Di nuovo ricorreto, e di figure ornatto. *In Amsterdam, nella Stamperia del S. D. Elsevier, Et in Parigi si vende Appresso Thomaso Jolly, Nel Palazzo. M. DC. LXXVIII.* 4 volumes. Small 8vo, (miniature size, 4 ⅛" × 2 ½"), 373pp.,+301pp.,+357pp.,+310pp.+[23-page unpaginated "tavola De Nomi Proprii"], engraved and printed title pages, volume 1, illustration after Le Clerc on engraved title, central emblem on printed title page each volume, engraved illustration for each book, original vellum (a bit aged and a little yellowed), each volume numbered by hand in ink on spine. A lavish allegorical epic poem, *L'Adone* was Marino's chief work and was written and published (1623) during his residence in Paris while under the protection of Louis XIII and Marie de Medici. It is a work that clearly influenced Milton, and Milton had a copy of it in his library. Boswell, in his *Milton's Library* (entry 961) remarks on the influence of *L'Adone* on Milton listing two articles on its particular inspiration for *Comus*. Rare. See 1784 three-volume 12mo edition in Eighteenth-century Miltoniana, with a new set of engraved illustrations. Parker, pp. 174–75. Willems, *Elzevier*, 1549; Boswell, *Milton's Library*, 961; Not in Coleridge.

26. More (Alexander). **FIDES PUBLICA**, *Contra calumnias Joannis Miltoni. Hagae-Comitvm, Ex Typographia Adriani Vlacq. M.DC.LIV.* First edition. Bound with four works by Milton—*Pro Populo*, 1654; *Defensio Secunda*, 1654; *Ratio Constitutae*, 1654, and *Literae Pseudo-Senatus Anglicani*, 1676, and one other work—*Regii Sanguinis Clamor*, 1652, by Peter DuMolin. 2 volumes comprising six works altogether, four by Milton. 12mo, 104pp., title page with printer's device, old half green morocco, marbled paper over boards (bit worn), spines lettered in gilt. Shawcross, 1974, pp. 323–29; Coleridge 365 (i–ii); Parker, pp. 453–59.

A very good collection of historically related pamphlets with notes in an early hand on front pastedown of each volume. Each work in the collection is listed separately with appropriate commentary on that work. *Defensio Secunda*, *Pro Populo*, and *Literae Pseudo-Senatus Anglicani* are listed alphabetically in Chapter II; *Regii Sanguinis Clamor* by Peter DuMolin is listed under DuMolin in this chapter. *Fides Publica* is More's defense of himself against Milton's attack on him in *Defensio Secunda* (present here) and called for on Milton's title page, hence technically issued with Milton's work. Milton, like others, thought that More was also the author of *Regii Sanguinis Clamor Ad Coelum* (also present here), and written by DuMolin. Alexander More, a French presbyterian minister of Scottish descent, was a professor at Middleburg and was believed to be the author of *Regii Sanguinis Clamor* (present here), a venomous royalist pamphlet published in March 1652. In fact Peter DuMolin was the author, but as he lived in England and was close to Milton, this was kept secret. Milton replied with his *Pro Populo Anglicano Defensio Secunda* (present here), which included a fierce attack on More's character, prompting this reply (*Fides Publica*) from More. More's defense of himself was in turn attacked by Milton in his *Pro Se Defensio*, which included an appendix attacking the *Supplementum*.

27. [Oxford University] **THE JUDGMENT AND DECREE OF THE UNIVERSITY OF OXFORD** Past in their Convocation July 21, 1683, Against certain Pernicious Books and Damnable Doctrines, Destructive to the Sacred Persons of Princes, their State and Government, and of all Humane Society. Rendred into English, and Published by Command. *[Oxford:] Printed at the Theater, 1683.* First edition. Folio, 9pp., large impression of classical building at center of title page, new quarter morocco, green cloth (several inner blank margins strengthened, title bit worn and soiled, fold mark on last leaf), spine lettered in gilt. This is the great decree by the University of Oxford ordering the burning of books by Thomas Hobbes, Richard Baxter, George Buchanan, the Fifth-Monarchy

Men, Milton (appearing on p. 3), and others. Rare. Wing 0891; Coleridge 374.

28. [Perrinchief, Richard] **THE ROYAL MARTYR**: Or, The Life And Death Of King Charles I. Romans 8. [Latin Quotation.] *London: Printed by J. M. for R. Royston, Bookseller to His most Sacred Majesty. 1676.* First edition. 8vo, [vi]+[i]+[iv]+311+[8]+[1]pp., engraved frontispiece portrait of Charles kneeling by R. White (fine impression), original calf (a bit worn, joints cracked, wormed throughout), gilt-decorated spine (faded), red morocco label with gilt lettering, raised bands, the contents and advertisement leaf bound in at the end. A good, tall copy with contemporary signature (dated 1686) repeated on endpapers and title page. "Perrinchief edited the works of Charles I, and attended Charles II as Chaplain. His work intentionally is designed to resemble an edition of the *Eikon Basilike*, complete with allegorical frontispiece. More than a popular biography, Perrinchief's work employs important primary and secondary sources for the life of Charles" (G. W. Stuart, Jr., Ravenstree, Cat. 150, #272, 1987). See copies of Charles I's *Eikon Basilike* described in this section. Wing P1601; Not in Coleridge (but mentioned 291).

29. Phillips, Edward. **THEATRUM POETARUM**, or a compleat Collection of the Poets, especially The most eminent, of all Ages. The Antients distinguish't from the Moderns in their several Alphabets. With some Observations and Reflections upon many of them, particularly those of our own Nation. Together with a Prefatory Discourse of the Poets and Poetry in Generall. By Edward Phillips. [Quotation in Greek from Hesiod.] *London: Printed for Charles Smith, at the Angel near the Inner Temple-Gate in Fleet-Street. Anno Dom. M. DC. LXXV.* First edition. 12mo, [xxx]+192+261+[2]pp., decorative headpieces and decorated initial letters, old sheep (rebacked, some age-browning), spine lettered in gilt, advertisements bound in at end. A sound copy, with some interesting scholia in an eighteenth-century hand along with some marginal notations. Written mainly by Milton's nephew, this work was certainly influenced by Milton; how strongly Milton influenced the work and how many were his contributions to it have been debated for several centuries, from Thomas Warton (see Warton in Chapter II) to William Godwin and Sir Egerton Brydges (see Godwin and Brydges with Nineteenth-century Miltoniana) on through Harrison Fletcher and William Riley Parker (both available in the collection, but neither listed here). Very rare. Wing P2075; Shawcross, 1970, p. 28; Coleridge 384; Not in Kohler.

Theatrum Poetarum is the first major gazetteer of English poets and dramatists, an extremely important biographical compilation, alphabetically arranged by first name. It is also the first reasoned attempt at a biography and bibliography, albeit modest, of Milton. The coverage of playwrights (for example, Shakespeare, "the glory of the English Stage," and Marlowe) and minor versifiers is impressive, and the supplement listing "Women among the Moderns eminent for Poetry" includes newcomers like Anne Bradstreet of Massachusetts Bay. Milton receives his comments on pp. 113–14 and is credited with having "reviv'd the Majesty and true Decorum of Heroic Poetry and Tragedy." Regarding his uncle's fame, Phillips says: "it will better become a person less related then my self, to deliver his judgement." William Winstanley's *Lives of the English Poets*, 1687 (copy listed here), is largely a plagiarism of Phillips. Egerton Brydges reworked the text of this first edition extensively in an edition he published in a limited number in 1800, which he then reworked extensively again and published in a second edition, once again in a limited number, in 1824 (see copy of each with Nineteenth-century Miltoniana).

30. Phillips, John. **A SATYR AGAINST HYPOCRITES**. *London: Printed for O. B. and R. H. 1680.* 4to, 25pp., new quarter green morocco, marbled paper over boards (some slight waterstaining, a few ink smudges on title page and p. 1), gilt trim on covers, spine lettered in gilt. This coarse satire was reprinted in 1710 as *Mr. Milton's Satyre against Hypocrites*, but it surely is by Milton's nephew. Scarce. Wing P2108; Not in Coleridge (which lists 1710 edition, #386).

31. Poole, Joshua. **THE ENGLISH PARNASSUS**: Or a Help to English Poesie. Containing a Collection of all the Rhythming Monosyllables, The choicest Epithets and Phrases. With some general Forms upon all Occasions, Subjects, and Themes, Alphabetically digested. By Josuhua Poole, M.A. Clare all Camb. Together with A short Institution to English Poesie, by way of Preface. *London, Printed for Henry Brome, Thomas Bassett, and John Wright. 1677.* Second edition. 8vo, [xxviii]+639pp., frontispiece woodcut illustration, title page in red and black, original calf (spine restored, some age-spotting, small worm hole at foot of title), spine decorated in gilt (now quite faded). A solid copy with early signatures and bookplate. The list of "The Books principally made use of in the compiling of this work" includes works of Chaucer, Jonson, Spenser, Sidney, and Milton (primarily extracts from the early poems). First published in 1657. Scarce. Wing P2815; Shawcross, 1970, p. 8; Coleridge 390 (note).

32. Putten, Hendrik Van Der. **COMVS**, Sive Phagesiposia Cimmeria Somnivm. *Excudebat Oxonii: Gulielmus Turner, impensis H. Curteyne, 1634.* Bound with his **HISTORIAE INSVBRICAE LIBRI VI**. *Oxonii: Gulielmus*

Turner, 1634. 2 volumes in one. 12mo, [xii]+[iv]+190pp., +[xxiv]+190+[31]pp.[unpaginated index], two title pages, decorative headpieces and decorated initial letters, contemporary calf (newly rebacked, minor age-spotting, some age-darkening), gilt-trimmed and gilt-lettered red morocco label. A decent copy with small library discard stamp on endpapers and early signatures and notes on first title page and endpapers. The *Comvs*, a prose allegory, was first published in 1608, the year of Milton's birth. This edition is the first to appear in England, and as Coleridge observes "is the only English printing." Parker notes (p. 792 notes) that it is a recognized source for Milton's *Comus*. Rare. STC 20516, 2051; Boswell 1197; Coleridge 442.

33. [Rowland, (John)]. **PRO REGE ET POPULO ANGLICANO APOLOGIA**, Contra Johannis Polypgragmatici, (alias Miltoni Angli) Defensionem destructivam, Regis & Populi Anglicani. *Antverpiae, Apud Hieronymum Verdussen, M.DC.LII.* Bound with two other works: *Joannis Philippi Angli Responsio Ad Apologiam Anonymi*, 1652, and *Pro Populo*, 1651, sixth edition. 3 volumes in one. 12mo, [xiv]+175pp., arms device on title page, newly rebound in marbled boards, printed green paper label on spine. Nice. Each work is discussed separately: *Responsio Ad Apologiam* and *Pro Populo* (which appears first in the binding here and is Madan 6) in Chapter II where both are listed. *Pro Rege* is Rowland's attack on Milton, answered here in *Responsio Ad Apologiam*. It was first published in 1651. Scarce. Shawcross, 1974, pp. 323–25; Coleridge 401 (notes, with discussion of the work and editions).

34. Saluste Du Bartas, Guillaume de Sieur. **BARTAS HIS DEUINE WEEKES & WORKES** Translated: & Dedicated To the Kings most excellent Maiestie by Iosvah Sylvester. *[London: Humphrey Lownes, 1605.]* Small 4to, [xxxiii]+blank+660+[2]pp.+[20-page unpaginated index]+[1]+blank+[3]+674-715pp., engraved title page, undated, separate printed title pages (ten) for the works included (each dated 1605, several with elaborate decorative pieces at the center), several full-page engravings, decorative headpiece trim and half-titles within decorative borders, elaborate decorative pieces and tailpieces variously throughout, decorated initial letters, "An Index Of The Hardest Words" at the end, contemporary calf (engraved title page skillfully repaired along upper outer edge and mounted for reinforcement, next leaf neatly repaired along the outer edge, several of the following pages slightly frayed along the edges, finely rebacked with new endpapers), gilt rule on covers with diamond gilt lozenge on each cover flanked by the letters "E. H." in gilt, new brown and green morocco labels on spine with bright gilt lettering and decorative gilt trim, thick raised bands. Mainly an excellent copy. This edition of Sylvester's translation of Du Bartas's works includes the seven days "of the first Weeke" and up to "The fourth Booke of the second Day, of the second Weeke"; also included, with separate title page, are "Fragments, and other small Workes of Bartas. With other Translations. By Iosvah Sylvester. 1605" (including "Jonas" and "Urania," among other works). STC 21649; Not in Coleridge (see 443, 1613 edition).

The great Elizabethan translation of Guillaume de Saluste Du Bartas, the French Protestant poet of the sixteenth century, whose scriptural epics were immensely popular all over northern Europe and England in the latter sixteenth and seventeenth centuries. Sir Philip Sidney and James I were among those who tried their hands at translating Du Bartas, but the adaptation into rhymed decasyllabic couplets by Joshua Sylvester at once eclipsed all rival versions. The subject is the story of the creation and enjoyed extraordinary popularity; it is known that this was a favorite book of Milton's at an early age and provided one of the sources for *PL*. Oddly enough the influence of Du Bartas on Milton seems to have been first suggested by William Lauder, whose other remarks on Milton's imitation of the moderns are wholly discredited. As Coleridge observes: "The extent of Sylvester's influence on seventeenth-century poetry to the Restoration is so considerable that it is difficult to know how much of the influence on Milton was direct and how much indirect" (p. 504). Early editions are uncommon and are handsomely printed.

35. Saluste Du Bartas, Guillaume de Sieur. **DU BARTAS HIS DEVINE WEEKS & WORKS** translated, & dedicated to the King's most excellent Majesty by Joshua Sylvester. *Printed at London by Humphrey Lownes, M.D.C.XI.* 2 volumes (formerly one volume). Third collected edition (and augmented). Small 4to, [xxvi]+420pp., +819pp.(continuous pagination from volume 1)+blank+[31-page unpaginated index]+blank+title+[xi]+blank+87pp.+blank+[6-page unpaginated index]+colophon leaf (dated 1611), engraved title page, full-page woodcut of the Garden of Eden, another of the Resurrection, separate printed title page for *Judith* (dated 1611), decorative head- and tailpieces, decorated initial letters, modern brown calf (title page and final leaf mounted, trimmed close), spine lettered in gilt. A good copy, clean and crisp within. The title page, engraved by J. Briot, has probably been taken from another work; the cartouches at the center and at the foot have been lightly colored yellow and titled by hand. According to Grolier 244, the present copy collates exactly as the Grolier copy, with the exception of the title page. This third edition is the most complete published at that time and includes for the first time the *Fourth Day*. *Judith* is also present in full.Grolier, *Wither to Prior*, 244; New STC 21651.

36. Saluste Du Bartas, Guillaume de Sieur. **DU BARTAS HIS DIVINE WEEKS & WORKS** with a Compleate Collection of all the other most delightfull Workes. Translated and written by yt famous Philomusus Josuah Sylvester Gent. *London: Printed by Humphray Lownes, 1621.* First folio edition, fifth edition; first complete collected edition. Thick folio, [xxviii]+1215pp., elaborately engraved title page by Renold or Reginold Elstracke with vignette illustrations around the border, separate printed title pages, decorative head- and tailpieces, decorated initial letters, contemporary calf over thick boards (a bit worn, neatly rebacked), faint gilt rules and decorative gilt corner devices with central gilt emblem on covers, red morocco label with gilt lettering and gilt rules, endpapers early printed pages (possibly considered incunabula). A very nice copy of the first complete collected edition, printing together Sylvester's final version of the *Divine Weekes* with original verse and translations from other poets, including "Micro-cosmo-graphia . . . or the Map of Man" from the Latin of Henry Smith, "Tobacco Battered," "Spectacles," and a number of other pieces. Also included here is "The History of Judith" translated from Du Bartas by Thomas Hudson (with a divisional title page dated 1620). Rare. STC 21653.

37. Saluste Du Bartas, Guillaume de Sieur. **DU BARTAS HIS DIVINE WEEKS & WORKS** With A Compleate Collectio~ of all the other most delightfull Workes Translated and written by yt famous Philomusus, Josuah Sylvester. *London: Printed by Robert Young, 1633.* Thick folio, [xxviii]+657pp., elaborately engraved title page by Elstracke with vignette illustrations around the border, separate printed title pages, decorative head- and tailpieces (very fine impressions), decorated initial letters, woodcut portrait on A5, woodcut illustration (very fine) on p. 637, contemporary polished calf (worn, joints cracked), blind rules on covers, red morocco label with gilt lettering and gilt rules, bookplate. A very nice copy with fine woodcuts. Not in Coleridge.

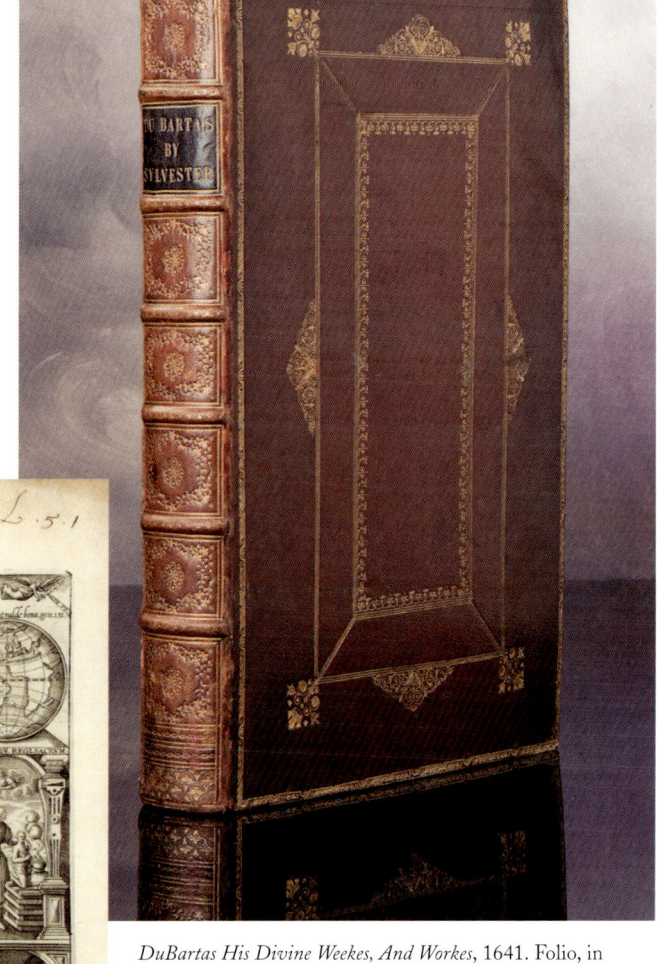

DuBartas His Divine Weekes, And Workes, 1641. Folio, in contemporary red morocco binding. See #38.

Engraved frontispiece portrait by Van Dalen, elaborately engraved title page by Elstracke with vignette illustrations around the border. See #38.

38. Saluste Du Bartas, Guillaume de Sieur. **DU BARTAS HIS DIVINE WEEKES, AND WORKES** with A Compleate Collectio~ of all the other most delightfull Workes Translated and Written by yt famous Philomusus, Josuah Sylvester, Gent. *London: Printed by Robert Young with Additions, 1641.* Folio, [xxviii]+670pp., engraved frontispiece portrait by Cornelis Van Dalen (fine impression), elaborately engraved title page by Elstracke with vignette illustrations around the border, printed title page with elaborate emblem at the center, additional vignette portrait A5, separate printed title pages, elaborate head- and tailpieces on virtually every page (very fine impressions), with the rare folding leaf *The Mysteries of Mysteries*, contemporary full red morocco, covers and spine finely decorated in gilt, black morocco label with gilt lettering, inner dentelles delicately gilt-decorated, outer dentelles ruled in gilt, splendid marbled endpapers, a.e.g., early signature on title page, bookplate. An elegant, large paper copy, measuring 13 9/16" × 8 5/8", in a superb and remarkably preserved binding of the period. Originally purchased by Dr. Rosenbach in the late 1930s and from his stock. Contains large amounts of new material not found in earlier editions. Rare in such a fine condition and with the folding leaf. Not in Coleridge.

39. Sandys, George. **CHRIST'S PASSION.** A Tragedy; With Annotations. By George Sandys, Author of the Paraphrase on the Psalmes, and Ovid's Metamorphosis, &c. The Second Edition, Illustrated with Sculptures. *London: Printed by J. R. for T. Basset, at the George near S. Dunstans Church in Fleetstreet. 1687.* Second edition. 8vo, [xii]+107+[5]pp., engraved frontispiece illustration and several additional engraved illustrations (nice impressions), original calf (worn, covers detached, lacking prelims). A decent copy with contemporary inscriptions in script inside front and back pastedowns and early signature (dated 1762) on title page. Sandys's translation of Grotius's work, the original of which was one of the works cited by William Lauder as being plagiarized by Milton. Rare. Wing G2093; Not in Coleridge.

40. Sandys, George. **A PARAPHRASE UPON THE PSALMS OF DAVID** And Upon The Hymnes Dispersed throughout The Old And New Testaments. By G. S. *London[:] At the Bell in St. Pauls Church-yard. MDXXXVI. Cum Privilegio Regia Majestatis.* First edition. 12mo, [xii]+271pp., contemporary calf (front joint rubbed), covers and spine ruled in blind. An excellent copy with early signatures on title page. Sandys served as treasurer for the English Company in Virginia, and after his return from America, he published the present volume of Carolingian verse. His couplets were admired from Dryden through Tennyson. Rare. Grolier, *Wither to Prior*, 783; STC 21724; Not in Coleridge.

41. Sandys, George. **A PARAPHRASE UPON THE DIVINE POEMS.** By George Sandys. *London, At the Bell in St. Pauls Church-yard, MDXXXVIII.* First edition thus. Tall 4to, [xx]+55pp.+blank;+title page+[x]+171pp.+blank;+15pp.,+blank;+33pp., central emblem on title page, half-title for *A Paraphrase Upon The Psalmes*, decorative headpieces, engraved musical notation, original unlettered calf (a bit rubbed at extremities, joints weak, half-title before *A Paraphrase Upon The Lamentations Of Jeremiah* three quarters missing), blind rules on covers, raised bands. A very nice copy in an attractive binding of the period. Only one portion of the entire volume appeared previously in print, *A Paraphrase Upon The Psalmes*, in 1636 (also listed here), and then it was without the music, here present, by Henry Lawes. The first edition thus of an outstanding monument of English poetry. Pforzheimer 852; Grolier, *Wither to Prior*, 784; STC 21725; Not in Coleridge.

42. Sandys, George. **A PARAPHRASE UPON THE DIVINE POEMS.** By George Sandys. *London: Printed for O.D., 1648.* 8vo, xxiv, 64pp., xii, 224pp., 18pp., 12pp., 27pp., decorative headpieces, engraved musical notation, contemporary black morocco (slightly rubbed, a few minor tears or paper faults, a little browning), covers and spine decorated with gilt rules and small decorative gilt devices, with the initials "EB" tooled in gilt on both covers, nineteenth-century red morocco label with gilt lettering and nineteenth-century endpapers, clasps (one thong missing), a.e.g. A very attractive copy with early bookplate. One portion of Sandys's *Paraphrase* was first published in 1636 (see preceding copy); the full work, with Lawe's music, was first published in 1638 (copy preceding). Scarce. Wing S674; Not in Coleridge.

43. [Sexby, Edward, and Silius Titus] **KILLING, NO MURDER.** With Some Additions Briefly Discourst In Three Questions Fit for Publick View; To deter and prevent Single Persons and Councils from Usurping Supream Power. By William Allen [pseud.] [Two Quotations from Chron.] *London, Printed MDCLIX.* 4to, disbound (bit aged and dust-soiled, several pages cut a little close affecting a few side notes, page numbers, and catchwords). All in all, a good copy. "Despite the 'London' on the title page, this was printed in Holland" (Coleridge). Sexby, a former colonel for Cromwell, turned against him and agitated for his death. This work is a plea for Cromwell's assassination, ironically dedicated to him. Sexby probably was aided by Titus, an ardent Royalist whom John Evelyn, in 1669, notes in his *Diary* as the author of this work. Sexby had this pamphlet printed in Holland and

shipped to England. Following it over from the continent, he was captured by Cromwell's soldiers and soon afterward died in prison. Parker calls this "one of the most highly inflammatory pamphlets of the whole period," noting that Milton could hardly have been pleased to find his arguments against Charles I here employed against Cromwell, along with "the dangerously respectful allusion to 'learned Milton.'" Scarce. Wing K474, T1311; Parker, p. 541; Coleridge 409 (note).

44. [Sikes, George] **THE LIFE AND DEATH OF SIR HENRY VANE, KT.** *[London:] Printed in the Year, 1662.* First edition. 4to, 162+[1]+pp., old quarter calf, marbled paper over boards (worn, lacking frontispiece portrait, covers detached, foxed), complete with final page: "Mistakes in Printing." Vane was executed as a regicide in 1662; he had led a distinguished career that had involved duties in the New England colonies. Milton knew him well, and Milton's *Sonnet on Vane* appears for the very first time in print on p. 93–94. The sonnet was not included in the 1673 *Poems* (see copy in Chapter II). Edward Phillips printed it in his life, prefixed to the 1694 *Letters of State* (see copy in Chapter II), without any indication of its having been previously published. Scarce. Wing S3780; Coleridge 83.

45. Symmons, Edward. **A VINDICATION OF KING CHARLES I.** Or A Loyal Subjects Duty. Manifested In Vindicating his Sovereign from those Aspersions cast upon Him by certain Persons, In a Scandalous Libel, Entituled, Kings Cabinet Opened: And Published (as they say) by Authority of Parliament. By Mr. Edward Symmons a Sequestred Divine. *Printed in the Year 1648. And now Republished for the Publick Good, By Richard Hollingworth, D.D. [Quotation from Psal. 89.] London, Printed by Tho. James, at the Printing-Press in Mincing-Lane. MDCXCIII.* 8vo, [xii]+ 384pp., original calf (joints cracked, a little age-browned), raised bands. A very respectable copy, fresh internally, with early signatures on front pastedown and fly-leaf. Republished by Hollingworth in his stirring the controversy surrounding the authorship of *Eikon Basilike*, which peaked anew with the publication shortly before in 1690, when a new edition of Milton's *Eikonoklastes* appeared (see copy in Chapter II). Scarce. Wing S6352; Not in Coleridge.

46. [Term Catalogues] Six Original **TERM CATALOGUES**, A Catalogue of Books Printed and Published at London in Michaelmas Term, 1670. [Series II], [Colophon:] Collected by Robert Clavel in Cross-keys Court in Little Britain, each including an advertisement for a work or works by Milton, each issue six to ten folio pages (formerly folded into fours with some leaves holed or splitting along the folds and with a very little loss in one or two cases), edges untrimmed, in a protective plastic cover. A very nice specimen of the genre. 1670–74. Folio. First edition each. Number 3 . . . Novemb. 22, 1670, advertises the first edition of *The History of Britain* and the first edition of *Paradise Regain'd* and *Samson Agonistes*. Numb. 9 . . . Easter Term, 1672, advertises *Artis Logicae Plenior Institutio*. Numb. 13 . . . Easter Term, 1673, advertises *Of True Religion*. Numb. 15 . . . Michaelmas Term, 1673, advertises second edition of *Poems*. Numb. 17 . . . Easter Term, 1674, advertises *Epistolarum familiarum liber*. Numb. 18 . . . Trinity Term, 1674, advertises second edition of *Paradise Lost* and the first edition of *The History of Muscovy*. During Milton's lifetime, eight issues of the *Term Catalogues* appeared containing advertisements for his works, of which six are in this collection. The *Term Catalogues* were a series of small folio broadsheets and pamphlets (rather like newspapers) published three times a year, in each of the law terms (hence the title), to advertise new books for sale. They were published from the late 1650s until the early eighteenth century. Edward Arber reprinted the whole series with indexes as part of his studies of the early book trade. A rather nice piece of contemporary Miltoniana. Rare. Not in Coleridge.

47. Toland (John). **AMYNTOR: OR, A DEFENCE OF MILTON'S LIFE.** Containing I. A general Apology for all Writings of that kind. II. A Catalogue of Books attributed in the Primitive Times to Jesus Christ, his Apostles and other eminent Persons . . . III. A Complete History of the Book, Entitul'd, Icon Basilike, proving Dr. Gauden, and not King Charles the First, to be the Author of it: With an Answer to all the Facts alledg'd by Mr. Wagstaf to the contrary; and to the Exceptions made against by Lord Anglesey's Memorandum, Dr. Walker's Book, or Mrs. Gauden's Narrative, which last Piece is now the first Time publish'd at large. [Quotation from Virgil.] *London, Printed, and are to be Sold by the Booksellers of London and Westminster. M.DC.XC.IX.* First edition. 8vo, [ii]+172pp., contemporary paneled calf (a little rubbed, joints cracked), cover's decorated in blind, hand-lettered label on spine, gilt dentelles (faded). A good copy, very clean and crisp internally. Toland defends certain key points he made in his *Life of Milton* (see copy listed here), particularly with respect to the authorship of *Eikon Basilike*, which Toland attributed to Charles's chaplain, John Gauden; Offspring Blackall led the dissent; Thomas Wagstaffe, Anthony Walker, and others carried on with the pamphlet wars. Wing T1760; Shawcross, 1970, p. 22; Shawcross, 1974, p. 319, states that it is the anonymous remarks by Offspring Blackall (see copy listed) that Toland attacks here; Coleridge 413.

47A. (Cross-listing) [Toland, John] Richardson, John. THE CANON OF THE NEW TESTAMENT VINDICATED: IN ANSWER TO THE OBJECTIONS OF J. T. IN HIS AMYNTOR. *London: . . . for Richard Sare, 1700.* First edition. Listing under *Richardson* with Eighteenth-century Miltoniana.

48. Toland (John). THE LIFE OF JOHN MILTON, Containing, besides the History of his Works, Several Extraordinary Characters of Men and Book, Sects, Parties, and Opinions. [Latin Quotations.] *London, Printed by John Darby in Bartholomew Close. M.DC.XC.IX.* First separate edition. 8vo, 165pp.+page listing "Errors" and "Amendments." Toland's *Life of Milton* was first prefixed to the Amsterdam edition of Milton's *Prose Works* published in 1698 (see copy in Chapter II). "This life copies to some extent from the life by Edward Phillips in the 1694 *Letters of State* [see copy in Chapter II] and it was often used by the eighteenth-century biographers, usually without acknowledgment" (Coleridge). Milton's first independent biographer carried on the controversies of his subject and created his own, primarily by attributing the authorship of *Eikon Basilike* to John Gauden. Offspring Blackall, Wagstaffe, Walker, and others could not let this pass without response and even censure. Toland, however, defended himself adequately in *Amyntor* (see copy preceding), and later scholarship has confirmed his claims. Rare. Wing T1766; Shawcross, 1970, pp. 21–22 and no. 50; Shawcross, 1974, p. 319; Coleridge 414.

[bound with]

49. REMARKS ON THE LIFE OF MR. MILTON, AS PUBLISHED BY J. T. WITH A CHARACTER OF THE AUTHOR AND HIS PARTY. In a Letter to a Member of Parliament. [Latin Quotation.] *London: Printed, and sold by J. Nutt near Stationers' Hall. Price One Shilling. 1699.* First edition. 8vo, [vi]+79pp. 2 volumes in one, contemporary paneled calf (sometime rebacked preserving original spine, with the date "1669" written in ink in an early hand at foot of *Life of Milton* title page), gilt-decorated panels on spine, later label with gilt lettering. All in all, a nice copy. Shawcross attributes this work to Offspring Blackall, and this is the work that Toland defends himself against in *Amyntor* (see copy preceding). The author of *Remarks* claims to respect Milton the poet while condemning the political views set forth by Toland in his *Life Of Milton*. Wing R933; Coleridge 395.

50. TRAGICUM THEATRUM ACTORUM, & CASUUM TRAGICORUM LONDINI, Publice celebratorum, Quibus Hiberniae Proregi, Episcopo Cantuariensi, ac tandem Regi ipsi, A liisque vita adempta, &c ad Anglicanam Metamorphosin via est aperta. *Amstelodami: Apud Jodocum Jansonium, Anno 1649.* First edition in Latin. Small 8vo, 320pp., engraved plates (fine impressions), original calf, gilt rules on covers with small gilt corner devices, red morocco label with gilt lettering and gilt rules, raised bands. All engraved plates are present, including the folding engraved plate of the execution of Charles I at Whitehall and also the frequently missing plate of Holland. An excellent copy with early bookplate on front pastedown and with early signature (dated 1732) on fly-leaf. First edition in Latin of *Engelandts Memoriae*, the work that continues on from where *Eikon Basilike* ended. Madan, *Eikon*, 114; Not in Coleridge.

51. Wheare, Degory. THE METHOD AND ORDER OF READING BOTH CIVIL AND ECCLESIASTICAL HISTORIES. In Which The most Excellent Historians are Reduced into the Order in which they are Successively to be Read; and the Judgments of Learned Men, concerning each of them, Subjoined. By Degoraeus Wheare, Camden Reader of History in Oxford. To which is Added, An Appendix concerning the Historians of Particular Nations, as well Ancient as Modern. By Nicholas Horseman. Made English and Enlarged By Edmund Bohun, Esq; Author of the Address to the Freemen and Freeholders. *London, Printed by M. Flesher, for Charles Brome, at the Gun at the West-end of St. Paul's Church-yard. 1685.* First edition in English. 8vo, [24]+[22]+362pp.+[a 12-page unpaginated index], license-leaf facing title page, new quarter calf, old boards (corners worn, title rather soiled with two small erasure holes mended touching a few letters, somewhat embrowned, scattered foxing, some thumbing, new endpapers), red morocco label with gilt lettering and gilt rules on spine, raised bands. A decent copy. In the lengthy section on the various histories of Britain and their authors is a brief discussion of Milton. Rare. Wing W1592; Coleridge 423.

52. Winstanley, William. THE LIVES OF THE MOST FAMOUS ENGLISH POETS, Or The Honor of Parnassus; In a Brief Essay Of The Works and Writings of above Two Hundred of them, from the Time of K. William the Conqueror, To the Reign of His Present Majesty King James II. [Latin Quotation.] Written by William Winstanley, Author of the English Worthies. Licensed, June 6, 1686. Rob. Midgley. *London, Printed by H. Clark for Samuel Manship at the Sign of the Black Bull in Cornhil, 1687.* First and only edition. 8vo, [xx]+[ii]+221pp., engraved frontispiece after F. H. Van Houe, "The Names of the Poets Mention'd in this Book" following "The Epistle to the Reader," nineteenth-century calf antique style (a few minor mends to blank edges), covers finely tooled in blind with gilt rules, gilt rules on spine with small gilt decorative devices, marbled endpapers, red edges. An excellent copy of a book "usually in wretched, worn, and badly patched condition" (G. W. Stuart, Jr.). Winstanley begins with Robert of Gloucester and Richard the Hermit and progresses to his contemporaries like John Dryden, William Wycherley, Elkunah Settle, etc. "[Winstanley] began his career as a barber, but put down his razor for a pen. One biographer notes that he retained his scissors, however, and his paste no doubt, for a goodly portion of this work is lifted from other authors, especially Edward Phillips' *Theatrum Poetarum*, 1675 [see copy preceding]" (G. W. Stuart, Jr., Ravenstree, Cat. 110, #180, 1984). The fate Winstanley predicted for Milton has been visited upon his own head, and as a result of his judgments, including that on Milton, Winstanley's own "Fame is gone out like a Candle in a Snuff, and his Memory will always stink." Scarce. Wing W3065; Shawcross, 1970, p. 22 and no. 36; Coleridge 424.

B. Eighteenth-century Miltoniana

1. Addison, Joseph. **NOTES UPON THE TWELVE BOOKS OF PARADISE LOST**. Collected from the Spectator. Written by Mr. Addison. *London: Printed for Jacob Tonson, at Shakespear's Head, over-against Katharine-Street in the Strand. MDCCXIX.* First separate edition. 12mo, 148pp., decorative headpiece and decorated initial letter, contemporary speckled calf (a bit scuffed, some slight foxing in the last two-thirds of the book), gilt rules on covers and spine, red morocco label with gilt lettering, raised bands. A fine copy with near-contemporary signature (dated 1736) on fly-leaf and with the bookplate of Leonard Schlosser. Scarce. ESTC T089182; Shawcross, 1970, p. 63; Coleridge 272.

Addison's *Notes On PL* first appeared in *The Spectator*, 1711; they were first published together with *PL* in the same year as this separate publication, 1719 (see copy of *PL* bound with Addison's *Notes* in Chapter II). The essays, when printed together, form a convincing and readable critique of Milton's great epic poem. They were "frequently reprinted as prefatory material in [later] editions of *PL*. They were also translated into various European languages and appear with translations of *PL* in those language" (Coleridge). "Without question Addison's [essays] have been reprinted more often than any other work on Milton, and they have been a major influence in forming opinion since their original publication" (Shawcross).

2. Addison, Joseph. **NOTES UPON THE TWELVE BOOKS OF PARADISE LOST**. Collected from the Spectator. Written by Mr. Addison. *London: Printed for a Company of Stationers, n.d. [ca.1750s].* 8vo, 143pp., decorative head- and tailpieces and decorated initial letters, original sheep (slightly worn, joints cracked, the outer edge of blank margin at end a trifle wormed), gilt rules on spine with small decorative gilt devices, raised bands, red morocco label with gilt lettering (defective). Generally a nice copy with elaborate bookplate and with contemporary signature on title page, with early note identifying where the book was purchased (dated "1751/2") on fly-leaf, and with a note in a later hand identifying the signature as that of "my great grandfather." Probably a piracy printed in either Scotland or Ireland. Scarce. Not in Coleridge.

3. Addison, Joseph. **CRITICISM AND NOTES UPON THE TWELVE BOOKS OF PARADISE LOST. WITH THE BEAUTIES OF THE POEM BY JOSEPH ADDISON, ESQ**; *London; Printed for B. Millar in the Strand and P. Dodsley in Pall-Mall. n.d. [ca. 1765].* Tall 12mo in 6s, 136pp., decorative headpiece, contemporary calf (front joint cracked, with small piece missing at top near spine), raised bands, black leather label with gilt lettering and decorative gilt trim. A nice copy with early book label on front pastedown and early signature with same name on fly-leaf. The imprint here is a fictitious one, utilizing the names of two of London's most prominent booksellers. Coleridge suggests that it might be a Scottish imprint (Coleridge 272 notes). Not in Coleridge.

4. Addison, Joseph. **NOTES UPON THE TWELVE BOOKS OF PARADISE LOST**. Collected from the Spectator. Written by Mr. Addison. To Which Is Prefixed A Critical And Biographical Account Of The Author and his Writings. *London: Sold by J. Thornton, R. Elliott, H. Crompton, and W. Richards. MDCCLXXIX.* 8vo, vii+[1]+150pp., unattributed engraved frontispiece portrait of Addison, short life of Addison, old calf (rebacked, rubbed). A nice copy with the rare frontispiece portrait, with contemporary signature (dated 1791) on fly-leaf.

5. Addison, Joseph. **MISCELLANEOUS WORKS, IN VERSE AND PROSE** Of the Late Right Honourable Joseph Addison, Esq; In Three Volumes. Consisting of such as were never before Printed in Twelves. With some Account of the Life and Writings of the Author, By Mr. Tickell. *London: Printed for Jacob Tonson in the Strand. MDCCXXVI.* 3 volumes. First edition. 12mo, xxv+[1]+267+[1]+[7]pp.,+321pp.,+328pp., decorative head- and tailpieces and decorated initial letters, title page each volume, title page for *Three Setts Of Medals Illustrated By the Ancients Poets* (dated 1726) with illustrations of the medals, half-title for various of the other works, "Contents" for each of the three volumes at the end of volume 1, contemporary paneled calf (spines a bit rubbed), covers decorated in blind, spines gilt-decorated, recent dark red leather labels, speckled edges. A very fine set with contemporary signature of Mary Roberts in each volume. Advertisements in each volume announce that "These Three Volumes, with the Tatlers, Spectators, Guardians, Freeholder, and Remarks on several Parts of Italy, compleat Mr. Addison's Works in Twelves"; it contains "Milton's Style imitated, in a Translation of a Story out of the Third Aeneid." First edition of this often reprinted collection. Not in Coleridge.

6. [Addison, Joseph.] **THE GUARDIAN.** *London, Printed By T. Gillet; For Messrs. Longman, Law, Johnson, Nichols, Dilly, Robinson, Richardson, Baldwin, Rivington, Otridge and Son, Hayes, Wilkie, W. Lowndes, Ogilvie and Son, J. Edwards, Vernor and Hood, Cadell and Davies, H. Lowndes, and Lee and Hurst. 1797.* 2 volumes. 8vo, iv+508pp.,+531pp., engraved illustration on each title page after Hayman, engraved by Grignion, "No. 17" in volume 1, "No. 167" in volume 2, index at the end of each volume, contemporary calf (a bit rubbed, joints cracked), black morocco labels lettered and numbered in gilt with gilt rules on spine (lettering label on volume 1 slightly chipped), spines decorated in gilt, outer dentelles tooled in gilt. A good set. Included is Addison's essay on "Milton's Description of Eve's treating an angel No. 138" in volume 2.

7. Addison, Joseph and Sir Richard Steele. **THE SPECTATOR.** *London: Printed for the Booksellers, MDCCXCIX.* 8 volumes. 12mo, 326[misprinted "324"]pp.,+336pp.,+312pp.,+290pp.,+296pp.,+308pp.,+316pp.,+282pp., engraved vignette illustration at the center of title page of each volume, contemporary calf (a little worn, joints cracked), decorative gilt rules on covers, spines decorated and lettered in gilt, outer dentelles tooled in gilt (rubbed), marbled endpapers. A rather nice set. Included are Addison's essays on Milton. The first collected edition, with the text revised, was published in 1712.

8. Addison, Joseph. **THE TATLER.** *London: Printed By Rivington, Marshall, And Bye; For Messrs. Rivington, Davis, Buckland, et al., 1789.* 4 volumes. 8vo, xvi+501+[1]+[14]pp., +[iv]+582+[14]pp.,+[iv]+536+[16]pp.,+vi[mispaginated "iv"]+585+[13]pp., title page each volume, each title page with illustration by Hayman engraved by Grignion (fine impression of each engraving), "General Advertisement," "Steele's Preface To the Original Octavo Edition, 1710" reprinted in volume 1, "Original Dedication" to each volume reprinted in each volume, unpaginated index at the end of each volume, contemporary tree calf (each volume rebacked), spines handsomely tooled in blind and gilt with maroon morocco title labels lettered and trimmed in gilt and green morocco numbering labels elaborately decorated in gilt, outer dentelles tooled in gilt (a bit rubbed), later marbled endpapers, yellow edges. A fine set.

9. Bayly, Anselm. **THE ALLIANCE OF MUSIC, POETRY AND ORATORY.** Under The Head Of Poetry Is Considered The Alliance And Nature Of The Epic And Dramatic Poem, As It Exists In the *Iliad, Aeneid* and *Paradise Lost*. *London: Printed for John Stockdale, Piccadilly, 1789.* First edition. 8vo iv+[2]+384pp., vignette illustration by Stothard on title page, contemporary half calf, marbled paper over boards (a bit rubbed, slight foxing, title and final leaf a little more heavily so), spine lettered in gilt with gilt rules, marbled endpapers and edges. A good copy with early bookplate. Rare. Not in Coleridge.

10. Blackburne, Francis, compiler. **MEMOIRS OF THOMAS HOLLIS, ESQ.** F.R. And A.S.S. Qviqve Svi Memores Alios Fecere Merendo. Virgil Aen. *London Printed MDCCLXXX.* 2 volumes. First edition. 4to, viii+839pp.[broken into two volumes at p. 506]+[1p. "Directions to the Bookbinder for Placing the Prints"]+[23-page unpaginated index], engraved frontispiece, engraved dedication leaf, engraved portrait of Hollis, thirty-three additional engraved plates (all fine impressions), many of them portraits of republicans or republican sympathizers, and including also five engraved portrait plates of Milton, and portraits of Edmund Ludlow, Andrew Marvell, John Locke, and a fine mezzotint of Sir Isaac Newton, engraved by Francesco Bartolozzi, Giovanni Battista Cipriani, James Basire, and others, original full calf (a few scuff marks), gilt rules on covers, spines richly decorated in gilt within the panels, thick raised bands with decorative gilt trim, black morocco lettering and numbering labels ruled in gilt, marbled endpapers and edges. An attractive copy of this extravagant production of the *Memoirs* of Thomas Hollis, compiled by Hollis's friend, Francis Blackburne, elegantly printed, with splendid engravings.

The five engraved portrait plates of Milton include: (1) Milton at age ten, "Drawn and etched MDCCLX by I. B. Cipriani a Tvscan from a picture painted by Cornelivs Johnson MDCXVIII now in the possession of Thomas Hollis"; (2) a bust of a blind Milton on a tall block and a vignette portrait toward the bottom; (3) Milton at twenty-one, "Drawn and etched MDCCLX by I. B. Cipriani a Tvscan at the desire of Thomas Hollis . . . from a pictvre in the collection of the Right Hon. Arthvr Onslow"; (4) a blind John Milton, "Drawn and etched MDCCLX by I. B.

Cipriani a Tvscan from a bvst in plaister modelled from the life now in the possession of Thomas Hollis"; (5) a portrait of Milton similar to the Faithorne portrait, "Drawn and etched MDCCLX by I. B. Cipriani a Tvscan at the desire of Thomas Hollis." Milton is discussed variously throughout the work along with Hollis's opinions and observations about Milton. At the beginning of the appendix, on p. 507, following the portrait of Milton at age twenty-one, Blackburne's *Remarks on Johnson's Life of Milton* begins, carrying through to p. 582, followed by "The dates of the original editions of Milton's Prose Works" and then his "Poetical Works" on pp. 583–84. Blackburne's *Remarks* was also published separately in 1780 together with Milton's *Of Education* and *Areopagitica* (see preceding cross-listed copy and discussion there about the publication of these two works).

Thomas Hollis (1720–74) was a wealthy recluse, with a fondness for seventeenth-century republican literature. He also edited among other works Toland's *Life of Milton* (see 1761 edition listed here bound with *Amyntor*, in a Hollis binding). He frequently presented to libraries, and to his friends, books specially bound and decorated with daggers, caps of liberty, and other republican symbols, and it was chiefly this that led to his being described as a republican, although he said of himself that he was "a true Whig." Scarce. Shawcross, 1972, 67; Coleridge 283.

10A. (Cross-listing) Blackburne, Francis. **REMARKS ON JOHNSON'S LIFE OF MILTON.** To Which Are Added, Milton's Tractate Of Education And Areopagitica. *London: MDCCLXXX.* First edition. 8vo, vi+369pp., contemporary quarter calf, boards (bit worn, hinges cracked, minor age spots), spine lettered in gilt: "Milton Of Education." Good copy in original state. Coleridge discusses the printing of this work, that it might have appeared first in the appendix of Blackburne's *Memoirs of Thomas Hollis* (copy following), published earlier in the same year, and was then printed, probably in a small number of copies and anonymously, separately with Milton's *Of Education* and *Areopagitica*, as here, later in the year. Shawcross indicates the opposite order of publication; Havens prefers the order given here and by Coleridge, who also indicates "additional materials ... showing that both works were being printed at the same time." Rare. Shawcross, Kentucky, 435; Shawcross, 1972, 311, 422; Havens, p. 31; Coleridge 6 (and see 283, *Memoirs*, for additional discussion). See main listing under *Areopagitica* in Chapter II.

11. Blackmore, Sir Richard. **A PARAPHRASE ON THE BOOK OF JOB**: As likewise on the Songs of Moses, Deborah, David: On Four Select Psalms: Some Chapters of Isaiah, And The Third Chapter of Habakkuk. By Sir Richard Blackmore, Kt. M. D. One of His Majesty's Physicians in Ordinary, and Fellow of the College of Physicians in London. *London: Printed for Awnsham and John Churchill, at the Black Swan in Pater-Noster-Row. 1700.* Small folio, [36]+291pp., contemporary paneled calf (rebacked, small piece torn from top corner of flyleaf), spine lettered and ruled in gilt, red morocco label, dentelles gilt (faded). A very nice copy. Wing B2641; Not in Coleridge.

12. Blair, Hugh. **LECTURES ON RHETORIC AND BELLES LETTRES** By Hugh Blair, D.D. One Of The Ministers Of The High Church, And Professor Of Rhetoric And Belles Lettre In The University, Of Edinburgh. In Two Volumes. *Dublin: Printed For Messrs. Colles, Moncrieffe, Gilbert, Walker, Exshaw, White And Byrne, M,DCC,LXXXIX.* 2 volumes. Second edition? 8vo, vi+[ii]+384pp.,+[2]+382+[26]pp., contemporary tree calf (worn, joints and spines cracked, age-browning throughout, slight tears on front blanks), index. A decent enough set with early signatures on front blanks and on each title page, and with early bookplate on front blank of each volume. Highly regarded for his sermons, this Scottish divine and professor of rhetoric was also highly respected for his lectures and writing on eighteenth-century aesthetics and rhetoric. Included in each volume here are discussions of and references to Milton. See 1805 edition of Blair's *An Abridgment Of Lectures On Rhetoric* with Nineteenth-century Miltoniana. The first edition was published in 4to size in 1783. Shawcross, 1972, 54; Not in Coleridge.

13. Blair, Hugh. **ESSAYS ON RHETORIC.** Abridged Chiefly From Doctor Blair's Lectures On That Science. Third American Edition, with Additions and Improvements. *Printed at Boston, by Samuel Etheridge, For Thomas and Andrews: Sold at their Bookstore; by Thomas, Andrews and Penniman, Albany; and by Thomas, Andrews and Butler, Baltimore. May, 1797.* Third American edition. 12mo in 6s, 249pp., contemporary calf (rebacked preserving original label, new endpapers, embrowning throughout), maroon morocco label lettered and ruled in gilt. A neatly repaired copy of this early edition of Blair, with contemporary signature in ink in a fine hand on verso of original end blank. Included are discussions of and references to Milton. Not in Coleridge.

14. Bourne, Vincent. **MISCELLANEOUS POEMS**: Consisting Of Originals and Translations. By Vincent Bourne, M.A. Formerly Fellow Of Trinity College, Cambridge, And Usher Of Westminster School. *London: Printed for W. Ginger, in College-Street, Westminster: And sold by J. Dodsley, in Pall-Mall; and E. Johnson, in Ave-Mary-Lane. MDCCLXXII.* First collected edition. 4to, xvi+[i]+352pp., contemporary calf (scuffed at bottom of

front cover, joints cracked), decorated gilt borders on covers (faded), gilt-decorated spine, marbled endpapers. An exceptionally large copy with early bookplate. *In Miltonum* occupies pp. 46–47. Scarce. Not in Coleridge.

15. [Charles I] MEMOIRS OF KING CHARLES I. And The Loyalists Who Suffered In his Cause; Chiefly Extracted From Lord Clarendon's History Of The Rebellion. Illustrated With Their Portraits, From Vandyke, etc. *London. Printed by R. Hindmarsh, Printer To His Royal Highness The Prince Of Wales, Old-Bailey, For I. Herbert, Bookseller And Publisher, No. 29, Great Russet-Street, Bloomsbury, 1795.* First edition thus. 4to, 54pp.+20 unpaginated engraved plates, engraved frontispiece portrait of Charles I and nineteen other engraved portraits on thick paper (fine impressions), original half calf, marbled paper over boards (worn, spine chipped at top, slight foxing). A good copy. Scarce. Not in Coleridge.

16. Cowley, Abraham. THE WORKS OF MR. ABRAHAM COWLEY: Consisting of Those which were formerly Printed: And Those which he Designed for the Press, Now Published out of the Author's Original Copies. With The Cutter of Coleman-street. The Ninth Edition. To which are added, some Verses by the Author, Never before Printed. *London: Printed for H. Herringman; and are to be Sold by Jacob Tonson within Grays-Inn-Gate next Grays-Inn-Lane, and Thomas Bennet at the Half-Moon in St. Paul's Church-yard. 1700.* Folio, [32]+94pp.;+[4]+56pp.[with some pages missing];+127pp.,+136(misprinted "129")pp.;+[4]+32pp.;+[4]pp., engraved frontispiece portrait by Faithorne (fine impressions), half-title for *Cutter of Coleman-street*, "The Table" at the end, contemporary paneled calf (a bit rubbed, back joint cracked, with some pages missing in "The Second Pindaric Ode of Pindar"), covers decorated in blind, gilt rules on spine with small gilt decorations in the compartments, red morocco label with gilt lettering and gilt rules, raised bands. A nice copy with early shelf marks and later bookplate on front pastedown. The first collected edition appeared in 1656 (see copy with Seventeenth-century Miltoniana). New Wing C6649; Not in Coleridge.

17. Defoe, Daniel. THE POLITICAL HISTORY OF THE DEVIL, As Well Ancient As Modern: In Two Parts. Part I. Containing a State of the Devil's Circumstances, and the various Turns of his Affairs, from his Expulsion out of Heaven, to the Creation of Man . . . Part II. Containing his more private Conduct, down to the present Times . . . *London: Printed for T. Warner, at the Black Boy in Pater-noster Row, 1726.* First edition. 8vo, [vi]+408pp., engraved frontispiece illustration, contemporary paneled calf (neatly rebacked, new endpapers, frontispiece a bit age-darkened around the edges with small tear to lower margin), covers decorated in blind, spine decorated in gilt. Generally a good copy. The first portion deals extensively with the concept of Satan as presented by Milton with direct quotations from *PL* used to illustrate Defoe's position. Rare. Moore, *Defoe*, p. 480; Not in Coleridge; Not in Kohler.

18. Dennis, John. THE GROUNDS OF CRITICISM IN POETRY. Contain'd In Some New Discoveries never made before, requisite for the Writing and Judging of Poems surely, Being A Preliminary to a larger Work design'd to be publish'd in Folio, and Entituled, A Criticism upon our most Celebrated English Poets Deceas'd. By Mr. Dennis. *London: Printed for Geo. Strahan at the Golden-Ball against the Exchange in Cornhill, and Bernard Lintott, at the Middle-Temple Gate, Fleet-street. 1704.* First edition. 8vo, [xliv]+127pp., half-title, double black border around title page, original paneled calf (front lower corner chipped, joints cracked), covers decorated in blind, spine decorated in gilt (faded), red morocco label with gilt lettering, raised bands. Very nice, the former Earl of Hopetoun copy, with his bookplate, fresh and clean internally, with rare half-title. "Dennis was the pioneer professional critic in the English language and his work, has in general, quite sound merits. He was admired—and quoted—by Dr. Johnson, and was one of the first highly vocal, critical admirers of Milton, whom he praises in considerable detail in this work. A very rare book, and a most important milestone in the history of English literary criticism" (G. W. Stuart, Jr., Ravenstree, Cat. 150, #196, 1987). Shawcross, 1970, no. 54 and p. 234; Not in Coleridge.

19. Dodd, [William]. A FAMILIAR EXPLANATION OF THE POETICAL WORKS OF MILTON. To which is prefixed Mr. Addison's Criticism on *Paradise Lost*. With a Preface By The Rev. Mr. Dodd. *London: Printed for J. and R. Tonson, in the Strand; and J. Newbery, in St. Paul's Church-Yard. MDCCLXII.* First and only edition. 8vo, vii+144pp.+[92-page unpaginated index]+[4]pp., edited by William Dodd (the forger), new three-quarter calf antique style, marbled paper over boards (some age darkening around the edges), red morocco label with gilt rules and gilt lettering, contemporary signature (dated 1789) and later signature (dated 1815) on front blank. A decent copy with four pages of advertisements ("Books Printed for J. Newbery") bound in at end. The former William Riley Parker copy, with his embossed WRP stamp on title page. The work encompasses Dodd's preface followed by the printing of Addison's *Critique* and then a substantial dictionary of the difficult words and terms used in *PL*, derivative of earlier writers. Rare. Roscoe, *Newbery*, A360; Coleridge 297.

20. Douglas, John. **MILTON VINDICATED** From the Charge of Plagiarism, Brought against him by Mr. Lauder, And Lauder himself convicted of several Forgeries and gross Impositions on the Public. In a Letter humbly addressed to the Right Honorable the Earl of Bath. By John Douglas, M.A. Rector of Eaton Constantine, Salop. [Latin Quotation from Virgil.] *London: Printed for A. Millar, opposite Catharine-Street, in the Strand. MDCCLI.* First edition. 8vo, 79pp., contemporary marbled paper wrappers (worn and a little frayed around the edges, title page a bit soiled). A good copy with contemporary inscription in a neat hand above armorial bookplate on front pastedown: "This Vindication of Milton in answer to Lauder by Doctor Douglas, Bishop of Salisbury, is uncommonly rare. I was many years in search of it until I obtained this from the Bishop himself. GM." Rare. Shawcross, 1972, 37; Coleridge 298.

See William Lauder's *Essay On Milton's Use And Imitation Of The Moderns, In His Paradise Lost*, 1750, first edition, first issue, with the *Preface* and *Postscript* by Dr. Johnson, as well as the first edition, second issue, with a *New Preface By The Booksellers* disclaiming Lauder's initial claims, and Lauder's *Charles I. Vindicated From the Charge of Plagiarism, Brought against him by Milton, And Milton himself convicted of Forgery*, 1754. See also Masenius's *Sarcotis*, 1756, 1757, and 1771 editions, and C. Falconer's *An Essay upon Milton's Imitations of the Ancients* (1741), and commentary provided with each. Lauder was exposed in the work here by John Douglas, Bishop of Salisbury, who proved that Lauder had taken the passages he cited as evidence of Milton's forgery from William Hog's Latin translation of Milton's epic, *Paraphrasis Poetica* (see copy in Chapter II), and not from the sources he (Lauder) claimed. This is the key work in the exposure of Lauder's fraud, and it called forth an apology, as well as a confession that was dictated by Samuel Johnson.

21. Ellwood, Thomas. **THE HISTORY OF THE LIFE OF THOMAS ELLWOOD** Or, an Account of his Birth, Education, &c. With Divers Observations on his Life and Manners when a Youth: And how he came to be Convinced of the Truth; with his many Sufferings and Services for the same, Also Several Other Remarkable Passages and Occurrences. Written by his own hand. To which is added A Supplement By J. W. [Heb. 11.2. Quoted.] *London: Printed and Sold by the Assigns of J. Sowle, in White Hart-Court in Gracious-Street, 1714.* First edition. 8vo, [30]+478+[2]+32pp., original paneled calf (a bit rubbed, front joint cracked, name clipped from top edge of leaf b6, with loss of several lines of index on verso, slight water-staining from some time ago at bottom margin of first third of book, minor spotting), covers finely tooled in blind, raised bands. Overall a decent copy with early signature (dated 1800) at top b2.

Thomas Ellwood (1639–1713) is perhaps best remembered as Milton's secretary, and this book provides his own account of his work with Milton; it also provides the well-known tale of Ellwood's response to Milton's asking him "How I liked it [*PL*], and what I thought of it" (p. 233): "Thou hast said much here of Paradise lost; but what has thou to say of Paradise found?" (p. 234) and Milton's equally well-known reply when he showed him *PR*: "This is owing to you, for you put it into my Head, by the Question you put to me at Chalfont; which before I had not thought of" (p. 234). Rare. Shawcross, 1970, pp. 223–24; Coleridge 314.

22. Ellwood, Thomas. **THE HISTORY OF THE LIFE OF THOMAS ELLWOOD** . . . Written by his own hand. To which is added A Supplement By J. W. [Heb. 11.2. Quoted.] The Second Edition. *London: Printed and Sold by the Assigns of J. Sowle, in White Hart-Court in Gracious-Street, 1714.* Second edition. 8vo, 466+[2]+32+[6]pp., disbound, but stitching and spine are intact (minor embrowning throughout). Internally a sound and decent copy of a scarce book, with six pages of "Books Printed and Sold at the Bible in George-Yard, Lombard-street" bound in at the end. Not in Coleridge (although Coleridge 314 references this edition). The collection also has the third edition in 1765 and fourth edition in 1791. Both are scarce. Neither is in Coleridge.

23. Ellwood, Thomas. **SACRED HISTORY: OR, THE HISTORICAL PART OF THE HOLY SCRIPTURES OF THE OLD TESTAMENT;** Gathered out from the other Parts thereof, and Digested (as near as well could be) into due Method, with respect to order of Time and Place. With some Observations, here and there, Tending to Illustrate some Passages therein. And a Table to the whole. By Thomas Ellwood. *London: Printed and Sold, by T. Sowle, in the White-hart-court, in Gracious-Street, M DCC V.* First edition. Bound with **SACRED HISTORY: OR, THE HISTORICAL PART OF THE HOLY SCRIPTURES OF THE NEW TESTAMENT;** Gathered out from the other Parts thereof, and Digested (as near as well could be) into due Method, with respect to order of Time and Place. With some Observations, here and there, Tending to Illustrate some Passages therein. And a Table to the whole. By Thomas Ellwood. *London: Printed and Sold, by T. Sowle, in the White-Hart-Court, in Gracious-Street, MDCCIX.* First edition. Very large 4to, [vi]+576pp.,+[17-page unpaginated "Table" or index];+[1]+VI+[iv]+iv+423+blank+viii+[8-page unpaginated "Table" or index]. Contemporary diced

Russia (neatly rebacked, preserving original spine, lacking final blank of first work and medial blank of second, some worming to lower margins of the first few leaves of 1705 edition and of a few other lower margins), covers blind-tooled in compartments with foliate borders, fleurons and acorns, two brass clasps, raised bands on spine, recent red leather label lettered in gilt. Fine copy in a handsome binding of the period. Not in Coleridge.

Ellwood figured prominently in the early history of the Quaker movement. His substantial *Sacred History* was the culmination of a lifetime's devotion to Quakerism and was reprinted four times. Ellwood was appointed reader to Milton in 1662 as the poet had wholly lost his sight by that time. His association with Milton was frequently interrupted, sometimes by illness, but more often by Ellwood's imprisonment for refusing to take oaths of allegiance and supremacy.

24. [Falconer, C. (?)] AN ESSAY UPON MILTON'S IMITATIONS OF THE ANCIENTS, IN HIS PARADISE LOST. WITH SOME OBSERVATIONS ON THE PARADISE REGAIN'D. *London: Printed in the Year 1741*. Slim 8vo, advertisement leaf preceding title, nineteenth-century half calf, marbled paper over boards, bound by David Ritchie, with his binder's ticket (light embrowning, advertisement leaf and title page with a few smudges and little heavier embrowning), some edges uncut. A nice copy. Variously attributed to C. Falconer (as Parker does), or Richard Meadowcourt (or Meadowcroft), or considered anonymous (as Shawcross does). It clearly provided Lauder with inspiration (see Lauder listed here and commentary there) as well as related works identified there. "It is of great rarity; this is only the second copy we have handled in over a quarter of a century" (G. W. Stuart, Jr., Ravenstree, Cat. 170, #117, 1990). Parker, p. 1292; Shawcross, 1972, pp. 26–27, no. 20; Not in Coleridge.

25. Fletcher, Phineas. **THE PURPLE ISLAND** Or The Isle Of Man. An Allegorical Poem. By Phineas Fletcher, Esteemed The Spenser Of His Age. To Which Is Added Christ's Victory And Triumph, A Poem, in Four Parts. By Giles Fletcher. Both written in the last Century. [Quotation from James Hervey.] A New Edition, Corrected & revised; with additional Notes by the Editor. *London: Printed by Frys & Couchman, Worship-Street, Upper-Moorfields: And Sold by J. Buckland, No. 57, Paternoster-Row; T. Wilkie, No. 71, St. Paul's Church-Yard; and J. Matthews, No. 18, in the Strand. M DCC LXXXIII*. First edition thus. 8vo, xvi+189pp.,+[1]+[1]+ix+[ii]+blank+75pp., "Preface To The New Edition Of The Purple Island," half-title and title page for "Christ's Victory And Triumph," later half calf, marbled paper over boards, red morocco label with gilt lettering and gilt trim, raised bands, edges untrimmed. A nice copy. The book was well known to Milton, who was undoubtedly influenced by it. The first edition appeared in 1610 (see 1633 edition with Seventeenth-century Miltoniana). Scarce. Not in Coleridge.

26. Galliard, Johann Ernst. [PARADISE LOST] **HYMN OF ADAM AND EVE**. Out Of The Fifth Book Of Milton's *Paradise Lost* Set To Music By Mr. [Johann Ernst] Galliard. *[London?], 1728*. First edition. Small oblong 4to, engraved title page with splendid cartouche (very fine impression), thirty pages of engraved music, subscribers' list, original half calf, marbled paper over boards. Bound with four additional pieces of music (not related to Milton) from the period, each with its own title page: (1) **PLAYING THE HARPSICHORD**, Spinnet or Piano-Forte, made easy by New Instructions [sic] . . . with choice Lessons selected from the most Eminent Masters, proper for Beginners . . . *Engraved and printed and Sold by Longman, Lukey and Co., [ca. 1775]*. First edition. Engraved frontispiece and title page, 36+[1] pages. British Union Catalogue of Early Music II, 791. International Inventory of Musical Sources notes that this contains music from Croix, Fisher, Handel, and Wagenseil. (2) Pleyl ([Ignas] J[oseph]). **1ST. BOOK OF TWELVE GERMAN DANCES** Adapted For The Piano Forte or Harpsichord. *London: Printed for R. Wornume, 1792*. First edition. Engraved title page, twelve pages. Not traced in British Union Catalogue; R. Benton, *Thematic Catalogue*, 601–2. (3) Hook (James). **TWELVE SONATINOS** for the Harpsichord or Piano-Forte for the use of Scholars. *London: Printed and Sold by C. and S. Thompson, [1776]*. Engraved title page and 24 additional engraved pages. British Union Catalogue I, 505. For fifty years Hook was organist at Vauxhall gardens, and a prolific composer of light music. (4) Wener (Francis). **SIX NEW MINUETS**, with three favourite Cotillons and figures, for Harp, Harpsichord, or Violin, Humbly Dedicated to the Nobility and Gentry Subscribers to Almacks Etc. *[ca. 1775]*. Engraved title page and thirteen engraved pages of music (final page laid down). British Union Catalogue II, 1068 citing only the imperfect copy in the British Library. Together some 119 pp. of engraved title pages and music. A very good copy with the lovely engraved title by Thomas Atkins after John Pine in exuberant Rococo style for the **HYMN OF ADAM AND EVE**. Very rare. A second issue, undated and folio size, appeared two years later ca. 1730 (see copy following). Not in Coleridge, who lists only a scribal copy manuscript of 1736 and two later editions (Coleridge 239, 240, 241). NUC lists two copies: at Harvard and at Princeton. John Shawcross shared the following with me: "I've used the copy owned by the William Andrews Clark Library. There are a great many more editions of 'Hymn of Adam and Eve,' sometimes called 'The Morning Hymn of Adam and Eve.'"

27. Galliard, Johann Ernst. [PARADISE LOST] THE HYMN OF ADAM AND EVE, Out of the Fifth Book of Milton's Paradise Lost; Set to Musick by Mr. [John Ernst] Galliard. *London: Printed for I. Walsh, n.d. [ca. 1730].* First edition, second issue. Oblong folio, engraved title page with splendid cartouche (very fine impression), thirty pages of engraved music, modern boards, calf spine label (inner blank edge of title a bit soiled), two early bookplates. A very clean and attractive copy with the lovely engraved title by Thomas Atkins after John Pine in exuberant Rococo style. Very rare. John Shawcross shared with me that although it says that Pine was the "Inv. & Sculp.," see 1730 issue, p. 30, "which identifies Thomas Atkins as the engraver." Not in Coleridge (see comment regarding Coleridge with preceding copy).

28. THE GENTLEMAN'S MAGAZINE . . . For March, 1779. 8vo, disbound, pp. 106–60. In fine condition. Contains "A Passage in Milton Illustrated" (p. 136).

29. THE GENTLEMAN'S MAGAZINE . . . For October, 1779. 8vo, disbound, pp. 474–520. In fine condition. Contains "Milton misrepresented by Dr. Johnson" (p. 492) and "The Anecdote of Milton being whipped examined" (p. 493).

30. THE GENTLEMAN'S MAGAZINE . . . For November, 1779. 8vo, disbound, pp. 522–68. In fine condition. Contains a "Short Character of Milton" (p. 558).

31. [Gildon, Charles] THE LAWS OF POETRY, As laid down by the Duke of Buckinghamshire In His Essay on Poetry, By the Earl of Roscommon in His Essay on Translated Verse, And by the Lord Lansdowne On Unnatural Flights in Poetry, Explain'd and Illustrated. *London: Printed for W. Hinchliffe, at Dryden's Head, under the Royal-Exchange; and J. Walthe, jun. over against the Royal-Exchange, in Cornhill. M DCC XXI.* 8vo, [xi]+[i]+351pp., half-title, title page in red and black, decorative head- and tailpieces, new three-quarter calf antique style, marbled paper over boards (lightly embrowned, minor foxing and a few light smudges, new endpapers), gilt rules and small decorative devices in gilt on spine, red morocco label with gilt lettering and decorative gilt trim. An attractive copy of this important milestone in the development of modern literary criticism, with sections on Shakespeare, Dryden, and Milton. Scarce. Shawcross 1970, p. 232; Not in Coleridge.

Original Boards Uncut, Inscribed "From the Author"

32. Hayley, William. THE LIFE OF MILTON, In Three Parts. To Which Are Added, Conjectures On The Origin Of Paradise Lost: With An Appendix. By William Hayley, Esq. [Quotations from Hesiod and Erasmus.] *London: Printed for T. Cadell, Junior, and W. Davies, (Successors To Mr. Cadell) in the Strand. M. DCC. XCVI.* "The Second edition, Considerably Enlarged"; first separate edition. 4to, xxiii+[1]+328pp., "Dedication To The Rev. Joseph Warton, D.D. &c," original boards (rubbed, neatly respined). A fine copy inscribed "From the Author" on the front pastedown. Strictly the second, heavily expanded, revised, and much enlarged edition, but the first separate edition. Hayley's *Life of Milton* first appeared in volume 1 of the great three-volume folio 1794–97 Boydell-Nichols edition of Milton's *PW* (see set in Chapter II). It remains the final major eighteenth-century biography of Milton and led directly to Hayley's meeting with Cowper and subsequent friendship with Blake. Hayley was the first to delve into the Italianate influences on Milton's poetry; one of the sections in the appendix contains large extracts from Andreini's *L'Adamo* (see copy with Seventeenth-century Miltoniana), with original Italian facing English translation. Hayley was also the first to question the accepted date of the composition of *SA*. Shawcross, 1972, 82, 83; Coleridge 327.

❦

33. Hayley, William. THE LIFE OF JOHN MILTON, With Conjectures On The Origin Of *Paradise Lost. Basil: Printed and sold by James Decker; Strasburgh: Sold by F. G. Levrault, 1799.* Third edition; second separate edition. 8vo, [1]+xxiv+362pp., half-title, original half calf, marbled paper over boards (a bit rubbed), spine trimmed in gilt with gilt lettering. A fine copy in well-preserved original binding. Scarce. Coleridge 327 (note).

34. Herbert, Sir Thomas, and others. MEMOIRS OF THE TWO LAST YEARS of the Reign of that unparallell'd Prince, of ever Blessed Memory, King Charles I. By Sir Tho. Herbert, Major Huntington, Col. Edw. Coke, and Mr. Hen. Firebrace. With the Character of that Blessed Martyr, By The Reverend Mr. John Diodati, Mr. Alexander Henderson, and the Author of the Princely Pelican. To which is added, The Death-Bed Repentance of Mr. Lenthal, Speaker of the Long-Parliament; Extracted out of a Letter written from Oxford, Sept. 1662. *London: Printed for Robert Clavell, at the Peacock, at the West-End of S. Paul's. MDCCII.* First edition. 8vo, vi+303+[1]pp., original calf (joints a little worn, light wear at corners and elsewhere), covers decorated in blind, spine elaborately decorated in gilt, red morocco label with gilt lettering, speckled edges. A fine copy, very fresh and crisp internally, printed on high-quality paper, with the Rolle family bookplate and with an early signature on title page. This reprints the rare tract, *The Princely Pelican* (1649), which was published as a defense of King Charles being the author of *Eikon Basilike*. Rare. Not in Coleridge.

34A. (Cross-listing) [Hollis, Thomas.] See Blackburne, Francis. MEMOIRS OF THOMAS HOLLIS, ESQ . . . *London Printed MDCCLXXX*. First edition. 2 volumes. 4to. Hollis's *Memoirs* were compiled by Francis Blackburne, with splendid engravings, including five of Milton.

35. Johnson, Samuel. THE LIVES OF THE MOST EMINENT ENGLISH POETS; With Critical Observations On Their Works. *London: Printed For C. Bathurst, et al, 1781*. First London edition. 8vo, vii+480pp.,+iii+471; +iii+462;+iii+503pp., engraved frontispiece portrait of Johnson, volume 1, contemporary calf (a bit rubbed), decorative gilt rules on spines, red morocco labels with gilt lettering and decorative gilt trim, gilt dentelles, marbled endpapers. The portrait of Johnson after Reynolds contains the publisher's imprint. A very clean fresh copy. Although the Dublin edition in 1779 is the first separate edition of the *Lives*, "the London edition is of greater authority" (Coleridge). Included is Johnson's *Life of Milton*, pp. 123–268, volume 1. Courtney & Smith, pp. 141–42; Shawcross, 1972, 64 (on Cowley and Milton), 65 (on Philips and Milton), 66 (substantial extracts from the life of Milton); Coleridge 336.

36. Jortin, John. TRACTS, PHILOLOGICAL, CRITICAL, AND MISCELLANEOUS By The Late Rev. John Jortin, D.D. Archdeacon Of London, Rector Of St. Dunstan In The East, And Vicar Of Kensington. Consisting Of Pieces, Many Before Published Separately, Several Annexed To The Works Of Learned Friends, And Others now First Printed From The Author's Manuscripts. *London: Printed by T. Bensley; For Benjamin White & Son, Fleet-Street, M.DCC.XC*. 2 volumes. First collected edition. 8vo, xxii+473pp.;+vii+blank+539+[1]pp., half-title and title page each volume, engraved frontispiece portrait, volume 1, original quarter calf, marbled paper over boards (front joint slightly cracked, volume 1), gilt numerals on spine, raised bands, edges untrimmed. A very fine set in original binding, with advertisement leaf at end of volume 2. This collection contains remarks on classical and modern authors, including the influential French writers Nicolas Boileau-Despréaux and Voltaire. Jortin's commentary on Spenser and Milton has long been highly regarded, provocative at times with respect to Milton—for example, his remark on *PR*: "This Poem has not met with the approbation that it deserves." Shawcross, 1972, 9; Not in Coleridge.

37. Lauder, William. AN ESSAY ON MILTON'S USE AND IMITATION OF THE MODERNS, IN HIS PARADISE LOST. Things Unattempted Yet In Prose Or Rhime. Milton. *London: Printed for J. Payne and J. Bouquet, In Pater-Noster-Row. MDCCL*. First edition, first issue. 8vo, [xxiv]+164pp.+[4]pp. Preface and postscript by Samuel Johnson, followed by a list of those taking "Subscriptions For The Relief Of [Milton's Grand-daughter]," contemporary calf (a bit rubbed, joints cracked), gilt rules on covers and spine, small decorative devices in gilt on spine, red morocco label with gilt lettering, speckled edges. A very nice copy with early ownership signature on flyleaf. Scarce. NUC locates just two copies of this first issue (although I've seen two others offered for sale). Courtney & Smith, p. 37; Shawcross, 1972, pp. 27–28 provides a clear overview of the Lauder plagiarism controversy; see also pp. 135–47, 171–98, including no. 35 and no. 26; Not in Coleridge.

William Lauder was a teacher and scholar whose entire adult life seemed dominated by failure and animosity. A man embittered by lack of advancement, he wrote this book in an attempt to discredit Milton and to thrust himself into the public consciousness. He fabricated evidence to prove his point that *PL* was largely plagiarized from the Latin poem *Sarcotis* by Jacobus Masenius or Jacopo Masenio (first published in 1664, see later editions listed here), from Hugo Grotius's Latin play, *Adamus Exul*, and Andrew Ramsay's *Poemata Sacra*. Lauder first published an article charging Milton with plagiarism in the *Gentleman's Magazine* in 1747. There followed four further articles as well as indignant rejoinders from Milton's defenders. In the present work, Lauder brings together for the first time his *Gentleman's Magazine* pieces, augmenting those pieces and claiming that Milton borrowed from no fewer than eighteen contemporaneous writers of Latin verse. The preface and the postscript were, innocently enough, written by Dr. Samuel Johnson, who thus lent his talents to this bizarre case. Lauder's claim caused a terrific furor, and still he continued with it, publishing yet another book that supposedly contained excerpts from the works Milton was to have plagiarized. It wasn't long before Lauder was discovered. When the Bishop of Salisbury exposed Lauder (see Douglas, *Milton Vindicated*, 1751, listed here) and ultimately proved that Lauder had taken the passages he cited, as evidence of Milton's forgery, from William Hog's Latin translation of Milton's epic, *Paraphrasis Poetica* (see copy in Chapter II), and not from the sources he (Lauder) claimed. Dr. Johnson recognized that his reputation was in question because of his participation in the publication of the present book (though he was entirely innocent of any knowledge of Lauder's fraud); Johnson therefore dictated a *Confession* and an *Apology*, which he forced Lauder to publish. A second issue (see copy following) was published with a *New Preface By The Booksellers* stating that the work (having been discovered to be fraudulent) was henceforth being published only out of historical interest. Though he tried desperately to retrieve his lost reputation, there was no hope, and Lauder eventually emigrated to Barbados, where he died (1771) in poverty after failing with a grammar school and then a huckster's shop. See also Masenius's *Sarcotis*, 1756, 1757, and 1771 editions listed here, and also C. Falconer's *An Essay upon Milton's Imitations of the Ancients*, 1741, and commentary provided with each.

38. Lauder, William. **AN ESSAY ON MILTON'S USE AND IMITATION OF THE MODERNS, IN HIS PARADISE LOST.** Things Unattempted Yet In Prose Or Rhime. Milton. *London: Printed for J. Payne and J. Bouquet, In Pater-Noster-Row. MDCCL.* First edition, second issue. 8vo, viii+[xx]+164+[4]pp., modern half calf antique style (minor spots, tiny mend to upper corner of title). A nice copy. This is the second issue of Lauder's publication accusing Milton of plagiarism with the *New Preface By The Booksellers* exposing and detailing the fraud perpetuated by Lauder, stating that "we now sell his book only as a curiosity of fraud and interpolation, which all ages of literature cannot parallel" (Preface). Scarce. Shawcross, 1972, 36; Coleridge 344.

39. [Lauder, William.] **KING CHARLES I. VINDICATED** From the Charge of Plagiarism, Brought against him by Milton, And Milton himself convicted of Forgery, and a gross Imposition on the Public. To the Whole is subjoined the Judgment of several Learned and Impartial Authors concerning Milton's Political Writings. [Quotations from Juvenal, Phaedrus, and Barlaeus.] *London: Printed for W. Owen, at Homer's Head, within Temple-Bar. MDCCLIV.* First edition? Slim 8vo, 64pp., original half calf, marbled paper over boards (worn, browning throughout), spine lettered in gilt (faded). An interesting copy with penned notation on fly-leaf: "John Dillon. 1853. Bought at Lord Macaulay's Sale." Scarce. Shawcross, 1972, p. 29; Shawcross, 1974, p. 320; Coleridge 345.

40. Lauder, William, editor. **POETARUM SCOTORUM MUSAE SACRAE:** Sive Quatuor Sacri Codicis Scriptorum, Davidis & Solomonis, Jobi & Jeremiae, Poetici Libri, Per totidem Scotos, Arct. Johnstonum & Jo. Kerrum, P. Adamsonum, & G. Hogaeum, Latino Carmine redditi: Quibus, ob argumenti similitudinem, adnectuntur alia, Scotorum itidem, opuscula sacra. [Latin Quotation.] *Edinburgi: Apud Tho. & Wal. Ruddimannos, M.DCC.XXXIX.* [WITH] **POETARUM SCOTORUM MUSAE SACRAE:** Sive Patricii Adamsoni, Sancti-Andreae in Scotia Archiepiscopi, Jobi, Threnorumque seu Lamentationum Jeremiae, ac Decalogi, Paraphrasis poetica. Gulielmi Hogaei, Jobi atque Ecclesiastis Solomonis, & duorum Mosis Canticorum, Paraphrasis poetica. Poeticum Duellum: seu G. Eglisemmii cum G. Buchanano pro dignitate Paraphraseos Psalmi CIV. Certamen. Cui adnectuntur ejusdem Psalmi aliae Parprases poeticae sex, Auctoribus totidem Scotis. Pars Altera. [Latin Quotation.] *Edinburgi: Apud Tho. & Wal. Ruddimannos, M.DCC.XXXIX.* 2 volumes. First edition of both volumes. 8vo, xiii+blank+lxxviii+208pp.,xxviii+520pp.(pagination continuing from volume 1), same engraved frontispiece portrait-illustration each volume, decorative headpieces and decorated initial letters, original speckled calf (a bit rubbed, hinges weak, first title page and first frontispiece a bit soiled), gilt rule on covers, delicately gilt-decorated spines, raised bands with gilt trim, marbled endpapers and edges (faint edges, volume 1), outer dentelles with gilt trim. Lovely copy of each volume, quite tall, fresh and clean internally. Lauder contributed an elaborate preface and a life of Arthur Johnston. The section by William Hog in these volumes may have given Lauder the idea of constructing a case for the false plagiarism charges against Milton. Case 425 (1a), 425 (2a); Shawcross, 1972, pp. 27–28; Not in Coleridge.

Inscribed Presentation Copy from Lauder to Thomas Ogilvie

41. Lauder, William, editor. **POETARUM SCOTORUM MUSAE SACRAE:** Sive Arcturi Jonstoni. Medici Regii, Psalmorum Davidicorum, Cantici Solomonis, & Canticorum Evangelicorum Paraphrasis Poetica. Joannis Kerri Cantici Solomonis Paphrasis gemina. Roberti Bodii a Trochoregia ad Christum Servatorem Hecatombe. [Latin Quotation.] *Edinburgi: Apud Tho. & Wal. Ruddimannos, M.DCC.XXXIX.* 8vo, same engraved frontispiece portrait-illustration as in preceding volumes, decorative headpieces and decorated initial letters, contemporary calf (worn, front cover almost detached), gilt rules and small gilt decorative pieces on spine (faded), raised bands, early bookplate. A reissue of volume 1 of the first edition (see preceding copy) with a new title and preliminary leaves. Presentation copy from Lauder to Thomas Ogilvie, inscribed in Latin on fly-leaf: "Doctissimo Viro, Thomae Ogilvaes, A.M. Scholae Aberbuthnotensis Moderatori, Hunc Librum, observantiae Testimonium, muneri mittit

(standing on left) Masenius, Jacobus, *Sarcotis*, 1761. Contemporary vellum. Superb copy, with the text printed in parallel, Latin on verso and Italian on recto, of the work first published in 1664 from which Milton was said to have plagiarized *PL*. See #45.

(standing second from left) Lauder, William. *An Essay On Milton's Use And Imitation Of The Moderns In His Paradise Lost*, 1750. First edition, second issue, with prefatory disclaimer. See #38.

(standing at center) Lauder, William. *Poetarum Scotorum Musae Sacrae*, Edinburgh, 1739. Reissue of volume 1, the first edition with a new title and prelims, contemporary calf. Presentation copy from Lauder to Thomas Ogilvie. See #41.

(standing, 2 volumes on right) Lauder, William. *Poetarum Scotorum Musae Sacrae*, 1739. 2 volumes. First edition of each volume, original speckled calf. See #40.

(title page showing on left) Lauder, William. *An Essay On Milton's Use And Imitation Of The Moderns In His Paradise Lost*, 1750. First edition, first issue. See #37.

(title page showing on right) Lauder, William. *King Charles I. Vindicated From the Charge of Plagiarism, Brought against him by Milton, And Milton himself convicted of Forgery*, 1754. See #39.

Eiusdem Editor, Guilielmus Lauderus." Lauder first developed his theories on Milton's plagiarism from his work on this edition. Not in Coleridge.

※

42. [Loveling, Benjamin.] **LATIN AND ENGLISH POEMS.** By A Gentleman of Trinity College, Oxford. [Latin Quotation from Horace.] *London: Printed for C. Bathurst, over-against St. Dunstan's Church in Fleet-street. M DCC XLI.* 8vo, [iii]+blank+[ii]+half-title+179[pagination beginning on p. 15],+blank+[4]pp., original calf (a bit rubbed, joints a little cracked, spine ends slightly chipped, some age-browning), gilt rules on spine. A rather attractive copy with contemporary signature on fly-leaf and front pastedown. Some of the more serious inclusions are either written in Miltonic style or are Miltonic imitations. First published in 1738. Scarce. Foxon, p. 432 (for comments on the 1738, first edition); Not in Coleridge.

43. Marino, Giambattista. **L'ADONE** Poema Del Cavalier Marino Con gl' Argomenti, le Allegorie, e la Tavola delle cose notabili. *Londra. 1784.* 3 volumes. 12mo, xxii+half-title+491pp.,+391+459pp., engraved title page for each volume, with the same engraved illustration on each engraved title page, engraved illustration for each book, decorative headpieces, protective homemade boards with black cloth spine. A nice set, generally fresh and crisp internally, with very fine impressions of the plates. A new edition of Marino's lavish allegorical epic poem, first published in 1623 (see later, 1678, four-volume 8vo edition, with fine engraved illustrations, with Seventeenth-century Miltoniana). *L'Adone* influenced Milton, and Milton had a copy of it in his library. Boswell, in his *Milton's Library*, remarks on the influence of *L'Adone* on Milton, listing two articles on its particular inspiration for *Comus*. All editions of *L'Adone* are Scarce. Parker, pp. 174–75; Willems, *Elzevier*, 1549; see Boswell, *Milton's Library*, 961; Not in Coleridge.

44. Masenius, Jacobus (Jakob Masen). **SARCOTIS. CARMEN.** Auctore Jacobo Masenio S. J. *Editio Altera Cura & studioi J. Dinouart. Coloniae Agrippinae, Et venit Parisiis Apud J. Barbou, Typographum-Bibliopolam, sub signo*

Ciconiarum, M DCC LVII. Bound with **LA SARCO-THEE.** *Poeme Tradut Du Latin Du. R.P. Masenius de la Compoagnie de Jesus. Par M. l'Abbe Dinouart. A Londres, Et se vend a Paris, Ches J. Barbou, rue S.. Jacques, aux Cigognes. M. DCC. LVII.* 2 parts in one, one Latin and the other French, each with its own title page. Large 12mo, 108pp.,+half-title+192+[4]pp., original calf (joints cracked, extremities worn), gilt-decorated spine, red morocco label with gilt lettering, raised bands, marbled endpapers, red edges. A nice copy. This new edition (like the 1769 and 1771 editions following), of the Latin poem *Sarcotis* by Masenius (first published in 1664), was occasioned by Lauder's infamous claim that Milton's *PL* was largely constructed of plagiarisms of this and other modern Latin works, including Hugo Grotius's *Adamus Exul*. See William Lauder's *An Essay On Milton's Use And Imitation Of The Moderns, In His Paradise Lost*, 1750, first edition, first issue and commentary there along with references. The French translation has an extensive commentary dealing with Milton, based on William Lauder's allegations of plagiarism by Milton. Rare. Brunet records only the 1771 edition (see copy listed here); Not in Parker; Not in Boswell; Not in Coleridge.

45. Masenius, Jacobus (Jakob Masen). **SARCOTEA POEMA DI JACOPO MASENIO** *Della Compagnia Di Gesu. Pubblicato la seconda volta in Colonia l'anno MDCLXI. otto anni avanti il Poema Di Giovanni Milton[.] Sopra il medesimo soggetto; ristampato in Parigi l'anno 1756. ed ora tradotto dall' Originale Latino in versi Italiani Da Giulio Trento[.] Con le Osservazioni sopra questo Poema, e sopra il Paradiso perduto del Milton, estratte dal Giornale Forestiero 1754. in due lettere scritte a P.P. Giornalisti di Trevoux. In Trevigi MDCCLXIX. Nella Stamperia Del Seminario. Con Licenza De Superiori.* First edition thus. 8vo, xxiv+292pp., with the text printed in parallel, Latin on verso and Italian on recto, the title page a cancel, contemporary vellum, label on spine lettered in gilt. A superb copy with the bookplate of the Marchionis Salsae. Scarce. NUC records three copies only, at the Newberry Library, Harvard, and Yale; Not in Coleridge.

William Hayley's Copy with Ownership Inscription

46. Masenius, Jacobus. **SARCOTIS, ET CAROLI V. IMP. PANEGYRIS. CARMINA**; Tum de Heroica Posei Tractatus, auctore Masenio. Adjecta est Lamentationum Jeremiae Paraphrasis, Auctore D. Grenan. *Londini; et venit Parisiis; apud J. Barbou, apud J. Barbou, via Mathurinensium. M DCC LXXI.* 8vo in 4s and 8s, [ii]+lxxii+269+[iii]pp., half-title, contemporary French red morocco, covers ruled in gilt, spine lettered in gilt and ruled in six compartments, each compartment with gilt fleurons in center and corners, blue endpapers, a.e.g. A fine copy in a lovely French morocco binding. In this edition the text of *Sarcotis* is prefaced by a French translation of Lauder's first attack, made in the pages of the 1747 *Gentleman's Magazine*. This edition also contains Masenius's prose treatise on epic poetry. William Hayley's copy, with his ownership inscription; afterward the Wordsworth/Hoare copy, with the later ownership inscription of John Wordsworth (scholar, nephew to William Wordsworth the poet), his collation mark on an end-leaf, and his inscription: "J Wordsworth dono dedit H. Hoare. Dec. 1825." Rare. Not in Parker; Not in Coleridge.

47. Mason, William. **MUSAEUS**: A Monody To The Memory of Mr. Pope, In Imitation of Milton's *Lycidas*. *London: Printed for R. Dodsley at Tully's Head in Pall-mall, and sold by M. Cooper at the Globe in Pater-noster-Row. 1747.* First edition of Mason's first publication. 4to, 22+[2]pp., half-title, engraved illustration on title page, modern quarter red morocco, red cloth, spine lettered in gilt. A very nice copy, complete with half-title and advertisement leaf at end. The vignette illustration on the title page is by Grignion after Hayman and depicts a grotto with Chaucer, Shakespeare, and Milton standing before Pope dying in his chair. Gaskell, *Mason*, p. 1; Foxon M126; Shawcross, 1972, 45; Not in Coleridge.

48. Mason, William. **POEMS.** *London: Printed for Robert Horsfield, at the Crown in Ludgate-Street; And sold by J. Dodsley in Pall-Mall, and C. Marsh at Charing-Cross. Also by W. Thurlbourn and J. Woodyer in Cambridge; W. Tesseyman in York; and W. Ward in Sheffield. MDCCLXIV.* First collected edition. 8vo, [ii]+318+[2]pp., dedication page, half-title ("Musaeus: A Monody To The Memory of Mr. Pope. In Imitation of Milton's *Lycidas*"), half-title for various of the poems, contents page at end, contemporary calf (a bit rubbed, joints weak), gilt rules on covers, spine decorated in gilt by compartments, red morocco label with gilt lettering, dentelles decorated in blind. A nice copy with contemporary signature (dated 1767) on front pastedown and with early bookplate. Shawcross, 1972, 49 (quoting extract, "Rise, hallow'd Milton!"); Not in Coleridge.

49. Mason, William. **POEMS** By William Mason, M.A. A New Edition. *York: Printed By A. Ward, And Sold By Robert Horsfield, No. XXII. In Ludgate-Street; J. Dodsley, In Pall-Mall; C.Marsh, At Charing-Cross, London; And W. Tesseyman,*

In The Minister-Yard, York. M.DCC.LXXI (1771). 8vo, [i]+29+[1]pp., dedication page, half-title for various of the poems, contents page at end, contemporary calf (worn, joints cracked, embrowning throughout, a bit heavy at beginning and end, edges slightly chipped on front blanks and title pages), brown ribbon marker. A fair copy with early signature on front blank. Earlier name on half-title for *Odes*, with several underlinings in a hand, and in *Elfrida* (p. 83) there is the marginal notation: "Miltons Lycidas."

49A. (Cross-listing) Meadowcourt. Richard. **AN ESSAY UPON MILTON'S IMITATIONS OF THE ANCIENTS** ... *London: Printed in the Year 1741*. Variously attributed to C. Falconer (as Parker does), or Richard Meadowcourt (or Meadowcroft), or considered anonymous (as Shawcross does). See also C. Falconer's *An Essay upon Milton's Imitations of the Ancients*, 1741, also listed here.

50. Meadowcourt, Richard. **A CRITICAL DISSERTATION. WITH NOTES ON MILTON'S PARADISE REGAIN'D**. By the Reverend Mr. Meadowcourt, Canon of Worcester. Latin Quotation. The Second Edition, Corrected. *London: Printed for A. Millar, opposite Catherine-Street in the Strand: And Sold by M. Cooper, at the Globe in Pater-noster-Row. 1748. (Price One Shilling.)* Second edition, corrected. 8vo, 49pp., disbound (slight foxing). A nice copy. Meadowcourt's *Critical Dissertation* first appeared in 1732, under the title *A Critique on Milton's PR*. Meadowcourt's study accorded Milton's "brief epic" "the honor of being the second work to be examined in a full study" (Shawcross). Rare. Shawcross, 1970, p. 17; Shawcross, 1972, 5; Not in Coleridge.

51. [Miller, Edmond.] **A FRIENDLY LETTER TO DR. BENTLEY**. Occasion'd by his New edition of Paradise Lost. By a Gentleman of Christ-Church College, Oxon. Latin Quotation from Virgil. The Second Edition. *London: Printed for J. Roberts, near the Oxford-Arms, in Warwick-Lane. M DCC XXXII*. Second edition. 8vo, 64pp., disbound, complete with half-title. A fine copy. "Half-humorous, half-serious commentary on Richard Bentley's eccentric edition of Milton's *PL* published in 1732 [see copy in Chapter II], which marked an extreme form of the principles of editorial interference; signed 'Semicolon' at the end" (Stephen Weissman, Ximenes, Occasional List No. 98, #209, 1993). The first edition was printed earlier the same year. A rare pamphlet. ESTC lists two copies, along with four complete copies of the first edition; Bartholomew, *Bentley*, 260; Not in Coleridge.

52. Neander, L. B. **LAPSUS PROTOPARENTUM EX POEMATA MILTONI CANTUS VI**. Accedit Supplementum ad Lib. VI. *Aeneid*. de Fatis Imperii Romano Germanici et Aug. *Gente Austriaca. Vindobonae [Vienna]: Typis a Ghelenianis MDCCLXXXIII*. First and possibly only edition. 8vo, [116pp., unpaginated], unatributed engraved title page with vignette portrait of Milton at the top and elaborate border, quarter-page illustration before each canto by J. Mansfeld and one full-page illustration also by J. Mansfeld for *Aeneid*, Book VI, before supplement, original tree sheep (a bit rubbed, spine ends and joints a bit wormed as well as first few signatures at upper inner edge, label missing), gilt-decorated spine, decorated endpapers, red edges. On the whole, a rather good copy of a very rare book, with fine impressions of the illustrations to each canto. An interesting Neo-Latin poem. Apparently very rare. NUC locates only the copy at the University of Illinois; Ravenstree offered a copy for sale in 1997 (Cat. 181, #161), where it is noted: "we locate examples at Harvard, Princeton, and University of Illinois and one other privately owned example [copy here]. This work has eluded the standard bibliographies." Not in Parker; Not in Brunet; and Not in Coleridge (although Turnbull has reportedly acquired a copy).

53. Neve, Philip. **CURSORY REMARKS ON SOME OF THE ANCIENT ENGLISH POETS, PARTICULARLY MILTON**. [Latin Quotation.] *London. M.DCC.LXXXIX*. First edition. Tall, slim 8vo, [iii]+blank+146pp., contemporary polished calf (rebacked preserving original spine), gilt rules on covers, elaborately gilt-decorated spine, red morocco label (defective) with gilt lettering, raised bands with gilt trim, inner and outer dentelles delicately decorated in gilt, marbled endpapers, a.e.g. Large paper copy. Very fine. Folger Library duplicate, with duplicate stamp inside back fly-leaf. W. Hazlitt's copy with early printed description of the book identifying it as having formerly belonged to Hazlitt on front blank. Neve's nineteen essays survey the greatest English poets from Chaucer to Spenser and Shakespeare, and from Jonson to Dryden, and "Particularly Milton," who receives the greatest amount of space: pp. 109–46. Rare. Privately printed in a limited edition of 200 copies, only a few of which are large paper copies. Shawcross, 1972, 76; Coleridge 369.

54. [Neve, Philip.] **A NARRATIVE OF THE DISINTERMENT OF MILTON'S COFFIN**, In The Parish-Church of St. Giles, Cripplegate, On Wednesday, 4th of August, 1790; And Of The Treatment Of The Corpse, During That, And The Following Day. The Second Edition, With Additions. [Latin Quotation from Tertull.] *London: Printed for T. and J. Egerton, Whitehall. MDCCXC*. Tall, slim 8vo, 50pp., half-title, paneled calf by Zaehnsdorf, rebacked preserving original spine, covers finely tooled in gilt, spine gilt-decorated, slightly raised bands, marbled endpapers, inner and outer dentelles delicately tooled in gilt, a.e.g. A fine copy with elaborated bookplate, and with an added engraved frontispiece of the blind Milton with laurel crown (after the Richardson sketch). Neve's gruesome treatise was completed August 14, 1790; this second edition contains a sixteen-page "Postscript" written several weeks later and dated September 8, 1790. "Evidence given by Neve and from other sources indicates that the corpse disinterred was not that of Milton" (Coleridge, p. 437). Very rare. Coleridge 370.

55. Newton, Thomas. **THE WORKS OF THE RIGHT REVEREND THOMAS NEWTON, D.D.** Late Lord Bishop of Bristol, And Dean of St. Paul's, London: With Some Account Of His Life, And Anecdotes of several of his Friends. Written By Himself. In Six Volumes. The Second Edition. *London: Printed For John, Francis, And Charles Rivington, No. 62, In St. Paul's Church-Yard. MDCCLXXXVII.* 6 volumes. 8vo, contemporary speckled calf (a bit worn, slight cracks in a few joints and on spines), gilt-decorated spines, black morocco labels with gilt lettering, speckled edges. A nice set. From the library of the Marquess of Anglesey with shelf mark. Newton is perhaps best remembered as the editor of Milton.

56. Paterson, James. **A COMPLETE COMMENTARY**, With Etymological, Explanatory, Critical, and Classical Notes On Milton's *Paradise Lost* Explaining 1. All the Hebrew, Chaldaic, Arabic, Syriac . . . 2. All the difficult Terms of Divinity, Philosophy, Mathematics, Astronomy . . . 3. All the fine Epithets, the Mythology (or Fables) of the Antients, all the Figures of Grammar and Rhetoric . . . [Latin Quotation from Tibull.] By James Paterson, M.A. And Philologist. *London: Printed by the Proprietor, R. Walker, in Fleet-Lane. MDCCXLIV.* First edition. 12mo in 6s, [ii]+512pp., title page in red and black, engraved frontispiece portrait of a disheveled Milton by N. Parr, contemporary calf (worn, front cover detached), spine decorated in gilt (faded), raised bands. The first extensive survey of its kind. Paterson based his research on the various commentaries which preceded him, drawing upon the work of Patrick Hume, John Richardson, Richard Bentley, Zachary Pearce, Joseph Addison, and others. Rare. Shawcross, 1972, 23; Coleridge 377 (making no mention of frontispiece portrait); Not in NCBEL.

57. [Pearce, Zachary.] **A REVIEW OF THE TEXT OF THE TWELVE BOOKS OF MILTON'S PARADISE LOST:** In which the Chief of Dr. Bentley's Emendations Are Consider'd; And several other Emendations and Observations are offer'd to the Public. *London: Printed for John Shuckburgh, at the Sun, near the Inner-Temple-Gate in Fleetstreet. M.DCC.XXXIII.* Second, revised edition. 8vo, vii+[i]+viii+400pp., central printer's device on title page, decorative head- and tailpieces and decorated initial letters, original calf (bit worn, joints cracked, label missing), gilt rules on covers, gilt-decorated spine, speckled edges. Nice copy with early armorial bookplate. Bentley's controversial edition of *PL*, which purported to improve upon Milton, was published in 1732. The critics responded immediately, and Pearce's work was among the first to appear. His *Review* was issued in three parts and then reissued with a new general title page. Pearce rightly critiques Bentley's edition (see copy in Chapter II) and disagrees with him rather extensively, albeit commending him in the Preface for giving "us some useful and judicious Remarks," and then adding, "many [of his] Emendations . . . may justly be call'd in question." Rare. Bartholomew, *Bentley*, 262; Shawcross, 1972, 7; Coleridge 378a.

58. Peck, Francis. **MEMOIRS OF THE LIFE AND ACTIONS OF OLIVER CROMWELL: AS DELIVERED IN THREE PANEGYRICS OF HIM, WRITTEN IN LATIN: THE FIRST, AS SAID, BY DON JUAN RODERIGUEZ . . . THE SECOND, AS AFFIRMED, BY A CERTAIN JESUIT . . . YET BOTH, IT IS THOUGHT, COMPOSED BY MR. JOHN MILTON (LATIN SECRETARY TO CROMWELL) AS WAS THE THIRD. WITH AN ENGLISH VERSION OF EACH.** The Whole illustrated with a large Historical Preface; many similar passages from the Paradise Lost & other Works of Mr. John Milton; & Notes from the best Historians. To all of which is added, A Collection of divers curious Historical Pieces relating to Cromwell & a great number of other remarkable persons (after the manner of Desiderata Curiosa Vol. I & II.) By Francis Peck, M.A. the Compiler of those Volumes, Adorned with the Heads of Essex, Fairfax, Hampden, Lady Falconberg, the Hand-Writing, Sign Manual, & medals of O. Cromwell. *London: Printed M, DCC, XL.* First edition. 4to, xii+47pp.,+ 130pp.,+[4]+113+[3]pp., engraved frontispiece portrait of Cromwell, general title page in red and black, dedication page with engraved half-page illustration and elaborately decorated initial letter at the beginning, additional title pages: one for each *Panegricus* and one for each *Panegyric Englished*, each title page with an engraving, and at the end *A Collection Of curious Historical Pieces relating to Cromwell & a great number of other remarkable persons . . .* by Francis Peck, with engraved frontispiece portrait of Peck, each title page dated 1740, and additional engraved portraits of Robert, Earl of Essex, Sir Thomas Fairfax, Johannes Hampden (foldout), and Lady Falconberg (on title page). Advertisement leaves and errata page at end, contemporary calf neatly rebacked (scuffed and a bit worn), raised bands, one blank endpaper detached with partial wax seal in upper corner. A wonderful Peck miscellany. The Third Panegyric is an extract from Milton's *Defensio Secunda* (see copy in Chapter II) translated by Peck. "The *Memoirs* were apparently intended for joint issue with the *New Memoirs* [see following copy], with which they are usually bound" (Coleridge). Scarce. Shawcross, 1974, p. 329, referring to the Third Panegyric; Coleridge 379.

59. Peck, Francis. NEW MEMOIRS OF THE LIFE AND POETICAL WORKS OF MR. JOHN MILTON: with I. An Examination of Milton's Stile: And, II. Explanatory & Critical Notes on divers Passages of Milton & Shakespeare: By the Editor. III. Baptistes: A Sacred Dramatic Poem, in Defence of Liberty; as, written in Latin, by Mr. George Buchanan; Translated into English, by Mr. John Milton; & first published in 1641. By Order Of The House Of Commons. IV. The Parallel, or Archbishop Laud & Cardinal Wolsey compared: a Vision, by Milton. V. The Legend of Sir Nicholas Throckmorton, Kt. Chief Butler of England, who died of poison, Anno 1570. an Historical Poem: By (his nephew) Sir Thomas Throckmorton, Kt. VI. Herod the Great: a Poem: By the Editor. VII. The Resurrection, a Poem in Imitation of Milton: by a Friend. And, VIII. A Discourse on the Harmony of the Spheres: by Milton. The Whole illustrated with proper Prefaces & Notes. *London, Printed 1740*. First and only edition. 4to, vi+[vi]+437+[1]pp.,+[iv]+57+[1]pp.,+[ii]+34pp.,+[ii]+7+[1]pp.,+[ii]+6pp., engraved frontispiece portrait of a young Milton with mustache by J. Faber, title page in red and black, engraved dedication page with vignette illustration and decorated initial letter, additional engraved plate with vignette of Milton by F. Tanner (bound as a second frontispiece here), subscriber's list, separate title page for *Baptistes: A Sacred Dramatic Poem, In Defence of Liberty* and for *Herod*, contemporary polished calf (rebacked preserving original red morocco label with gilt lettering), gilt rules on spine, outer dentelles decorated in gilt, speckled edges. A very nice copy with early signature on front pastedown. The title to *Herod*, apparently not in all copies, is present here. This is a noteworthy work, which Parker holds in high regard as a valuable early account of Milton ad one he cites on numerous occasions. "The critical notes on Milton and Shakespeare are remarkable, as being perhaps the first attempts made to illustrate their writings by extracts from contemporary writers, in accordance with the method subsequently followed by Steevens and Malone" (DNB). Shawcross, 1972, 18; Coleridge 380.

60. Philips, John. POEMS ON SEVERAL OCCASIONS. By Mr. John Philips, Student of Christ-Church, Oxon. The Third Edition. *London: Printed for J. Tonson, E. Curll, and T. Jauncy. M.DCC.XX. [Price Two Shillings and Six Pence.]* 12mo in 6s, 36pp.,+12pp.,+8pp.,+28pp.,+71pp.,+[1]pp., engraved frontispiece portrait of Philips, life of Phillips bound first in the volume before *Poems On Several Occasions*, separate title page for each work, *Life* (1720), *The Splendid Shilling* (1719), *Bleinheim* (1719), and *Cyder* (1720), with engraved frontispiece illustration and half-title for *Cyder*, printer's devices on *Poems*, *Splendid Shilling*, and *Bleinheim* title pages, decorative head- and tailpieces, and decorated initial letters, contemporary calf (a little rubbed, joints slightly cracked, several small defects on spine and at top of covers), gilt rules on covers and spine, with small gilt pieces on spine, black morocco label with gilt rules and gilt lettering, raised bands. A very nice copy. The individual poems were published earlier: *The Splendid Shilling* in 1702, without the author's consent, under the title "An imitation of Milton." It was published separately in 1705 as *The Splendid Shilling*. *Cyder* was first published in 1708, *Bleinheim* in 1705. As Coleridge observes with respect to Philips's *Poems*, "Reprints and reissues . . . appeared as *Poems, Poems on several occasions, Poems attempted in the style of Milton* and *Works* from time to time throughout the 18th century." Not in Coleridge (see 382 note).

61. Philips, John. POEMS ON SEVERAL OCCASIONS. Viz. An Ode to Henry Saint John, Esq; The Splendid Shilling. Blcinheim. Cyder. In Two Books. Six Pastorals, By Mr. John Philips, Student of Christ-Church, Oxon. To which is added, his Life, by Mr. George Sewell. *Dublin: Printed by S. Powell, for A. Bradley, at the Golden-Ball and Ring in Dame's-street, opposite Sycamore-Alley, MDCCXXX*. Slim 8vo, 144pp., engraved frontispiece portrait, decorative head- and tailpieces, and decorated initial letters, contemporary paneled calf (joints a bit rubbed), covers decorated in blind, black morocco label with gilt rules and gilt lettering, raised bands, speckled edges. A fine copy of this rather rare Dublin imprint, very fresh internally. The collection also has *Poems on several occasions*, 1728, and *Poems attempted in the style of Milton*, 1744, 1762, and 1776.

62. Philips, John. THE WHOLE WORKS OF MR. JOHN PHILIPS, Late Student of Christ-Church, Oxon. Viz. I. The Splendid Shilling: An Imitation of Milton. II. Blenheim: A Poem, inscrib'd to the Rt Honourable Robert Harley, Esq; II. Cyder: A Poem. In Two Books. IV. Ode ad Henricum St. John, Armig'. V. The same Translated by Mr. Newcomb. To which is prefixed his Life, By Mr. Sewell. *Loldon [sic]: Printed for Tonson in the Strand, and T. Jauncy at the Angel without Temple-Bar. M.DCC.XX*. 8vo, xxxixpp.,+60pp.(pagination beginning at p. 20),+89pp.,+13pp.,

engraved frontispiece portrait, half-title for *The Splendid Shilling* ("The Fourth Correct Edition"), for *Bleinheim* ("The Sixth Edition"), for *Cyder*, and for *An Ode*, with a frontispiece illustration for *Cyder*, contemporary paneled calf (slightly worn, front cover detached, back joint cracked), red morocco label (chipped) with gilt lettering, raised bands, gilt dentelles (faded). Formerly the Duke of Westminster's copy with his bookplate. A tall, fresh copy in a protective plastic cover, including at end the first edition of *Cyder* (1708) as is proper, with a fine impression of the engraved plate and a fine printing of the poem on high-quality paper. Notes in an early hand on fly-leaf; note with early names tipped in on back pastedown. Foxon 570; Coleridge 382 (note).

63. [Philo-Milton.] **MILTON'S SUBLIMITY ASSERTED**: In A Poem. Occasion'd by a late Celebrated Piece, Entituled, Cyder, a Poem; In Blank Verse, By Philo-Milton. [Latin Quotation from Virgil.] *London: Printed for W. Hawes, and Sold by J. Morphew near Stationer's-Hall, and Stephen Fletcher, Bookseller in Oxford. 1709.* First edition. 8vo, 30+[2]pp., disbound. A nice copy in fine condition, with advertisement leaf at end. As Coleridge observes: "Havens describes this with some justice as 'a curious and confused production' of an author whose 'sanity is open to question.'" Scarce. Foxon M267; Shawcross, 1970, p. 60; Havens, p. 100 (note); Coleridge 387.

64. Richardson, John. **THE CANON OF THE NEW TESTAMENT VINDICATED: IN ANSWER TO THE OBJECTIONS OF J. T. IN HIS AMYNTOR.** By John Richardson B. D[.] formerly Fellow of Emmanuel College in Cambridge. [Latin Quotation.] *London: Printed for Richard Sare, at Grays-Inn-Gate, in Holborn. 1700.* First edition. 8vo, [xx]+118+[1]pp., contemporary mottled sheep (a bit rubbed, spine ends chipped). A nice copy with early armorial bookplate, and with advertisement leaf bound in at the end. A reply to John Toland's account of Milton, which had just been published in 1699 (see copy with Seventeenth-century Miltoniana). Wing R1384; Shawcross, 1984, 1658; Not in Coleridge.

65. Richardson, J. and J. **EXPLANATORY NOTES AND REMARKS ON MILTON'S PARADISE LOST.** By J. Richardson, Father and Son. With the Life of the Author, and a Discourse on the Poem. By J. R. Sen. *London: Printed for James, John, and Paul Knapton at the Crown in Ludgate-street, near the West-End of St. Paul's. M.DCC.XXXIV.* First edition. Thick 8vo, clxxxii+546pp., etched frontispiece portrait of Milton based on the crayon sketch by Faithorne and engraved from a drawing by Richardson, Senior, original paneled calf (a bit rubbed), covers decorated in blind, paper label (lettering faded), raised bands, gilt dentelles. A very fine copy. The life is mostly by the father contributing hitherto unknown facts about Milton's life drawn from a variety of sources, including conversations with those whose ancestors had known Milton and his contemporaries; the commentary is "chiefly by him, although attributed to both father and son" (Coleridge). Richardson is positioned in the midst of a cluster of editors and commentators of the early 1730 to 1740 period, including Bentley, Pearce, and Peck. Scarce. Shawcross, 1972, 8; Coleridge 396.

66. [Theatre Broadside] Broadside for the **THEATRE IN THE BIGG-MARKET**, presenting by the Provincial players "The Celebrated Masque (written by Milton) call'd **COMUS**, With all the Original Music and Songs, composed by Dr. Arne, and as performed with universal Applause in London," followed by the farce *Barnaby Brittle: or the Fashionable Wife*, "Easter Monday, Being the 27th Instant." Dated from Newcastle: 1766-75. Folio size, 7 ½" × 12", slightly embrowned, some marginal wear, left margin

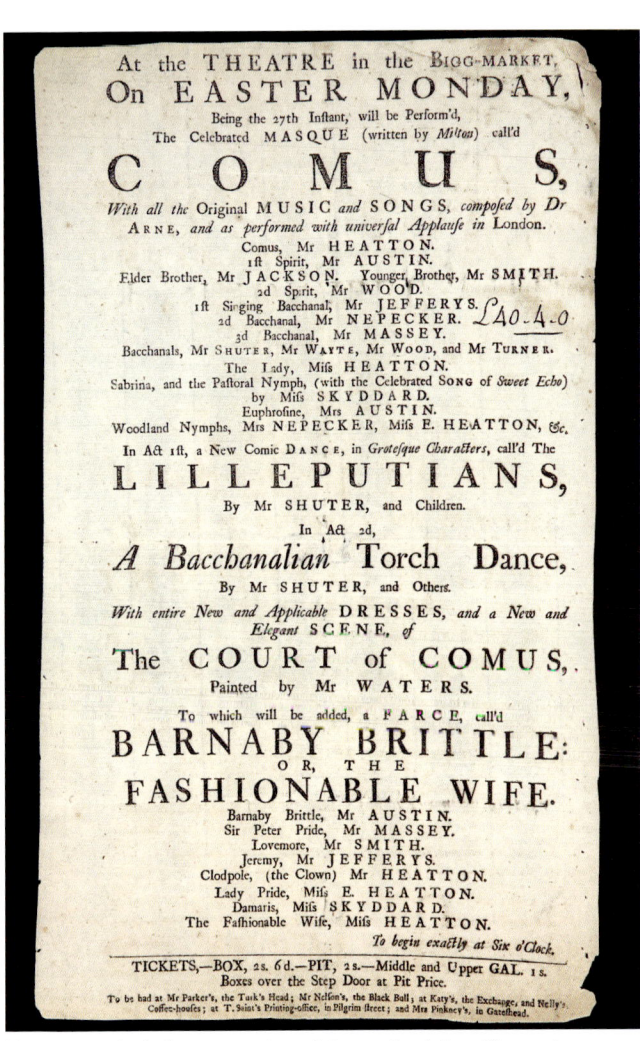

Theatre broadside for presentation of *Comus*, dated from Newcastle: 1766–75. See #66.

trimmed, otherwise a very good copy with a contemporary penned price noted on the main production. The itinerant playing company of Joseph Austin and Michael Heatton was a partnership that lasted from 1766 until 1775. Music and songs for the Masque were composed by Dr. Arne. The principal players in the Masque and the farce were Mr. Heatton, Mr. Austin, Mr. Jackson, Mr. Smith, Mr. Wood, Mr. Jefferys, Mr. Nepecker, Mr. Massey, Mr. Shuter, Mr. Wayte, Mr. Wood, Mr. Turner, Miss Heatton, Miss Skyddard, Mrs. Austin, Mrs. Nepecker, and Miss E. Heatton, with Mr. Shuter dancing. This included "a New and Elegant Scene, of The Court of Comus, Painted by Mr [sic] Waters." A nice example of a mid-eighteenth-century theatre broadside, in good condition. Rare.

67. Toland, John. **THE LIFE OF JOHN MILTON**; Containing, besides the history of his works, several extraordinary characters of men, and books, sects, parties, and opinions; With Amyntor; Or a defense of Milton's life: By John Toland. And Uarious Notes Now Added, [Latin Quotations] *London[:] Printed For John Darby MDCCLXI*. Second edition; first and only Hollis edition. 8vo, 259+[1]pp., bound by Matthewman for Thomas Hollis in red goatskin, tooled in gilt on the front cover with the palm branch, figure of Liberty, and olive branch emblems, and on the back cover with cock, Britannia, and owl sejant (Rothschild numbers 13, 1, 12, 10, 4 and 7a), spine in four compartments with the staff of Hermes in gilt at top and the wand of Aesculapius in gilt at the bottom (Rothschild 5 and 6), (trivial rubbing to extremities and slight dulling of the spine), olive green morocco labels with gilt lettering (lower label chipped), marbled endpapers and edges. An excellent copy, and a fine specimen of a characteristic Hollis binding, exemplifying nine of his seventeen emblematic tools, in an excellent state of preservation. Toland's *Life of Milton* and *Amyntor* were first published separately in 1699 (see copy of each with Seventeenth-century Miltoniana). This second edition, edited by Thomas Hollis, brings Toland's two works together and adds extensive notes. Hollis was a steadfast radical who supported the publication of a number of political works by seventeenth-century writers and then generously gave them to friends and libraries, sometimes as here, specially bound by Matthewman, decorated with appropriate emblematic tools designed by Cipriani, in what became known as Hollis bindings. This copy bears the armorial bookplate of James Frampton. Rothschild 2438–441 and p. 751; Coleridge 415.

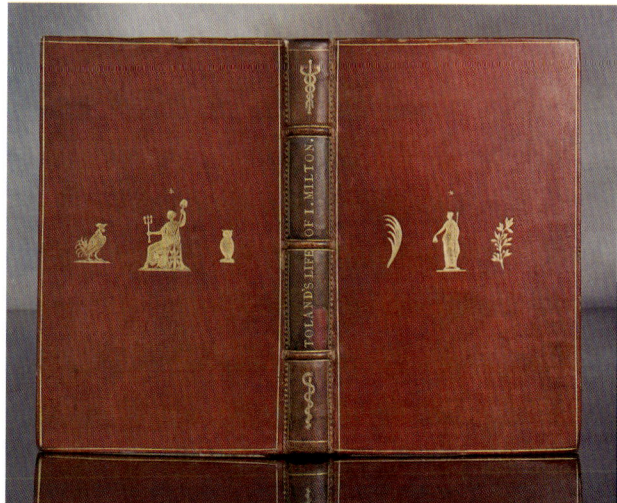

Toland's *Life of John Milton*, London, 1761. See #67.

Life of Milton (by Haley, open, by Toland in Hollis binding, and by Johnson, in contemporary calf). See #32, #67, and #35.

68. Upton, John. **CRITICAL OBSERVATIONS ON SHAKESPEARE**. By John Upton Prebendary of Rochester. [Latin Quotation from Horace.] *London: Printed for G. Hawkins, in Fleet-street. M,DCC,XLVI*. First edition. 8vo, [ii]+346+[16] [unpaginated index]+[2]pp., original calf (a bit rubbed, joints cracked, bookplate and front blank removed), gilt rules on covers, gilt-decorated spine, red morocco label with gilt lettering. A good copy. Upton writes not only of Shakespeare but also of Milton, holding both in the highest regard. He was against revisions of Shakespeare's texts, and he shared the same feelings about revising Milton's texts, and so was not favorable to Bentley's efforts with *PL* in 1732 (see copy in Chapter II). Scarce. Shawcross, 1972, pp. 17, 22; Not in Coleridge.

69. Voltaire. **AN ESSAY UPON THE CIVIL WARS OF FRANCE**, Extracted from curious Manuscripts. **AND ALSO UPON THE EPICK POETRY OF THE EUROPEAN NATIONS, FRO HOMER DOWN TO MILTON**. By Mr. de Voltaire. The Second Edition, corrected and revis'd by the Author. *London: Printed by Samuel Jallasson, in Prujean's Court, Old Baily; and sold by J. Roberts in Warwick Lane. M DCC XXVIII*. (Price stitched 1s. 6d.) Second edition, revised. Small 8vo, [vi]+130pp., disbound, red speckled edges. A nice copy. This as the first work by Voltaire to be translated into English, and Voltaire tells the story in it (and is thereby the source for it) that Milton, while traveling in Italy, saw Andreini's play *L'Adamo*, and "pierc'd through the Absurdity of that Performance to the hidden Majesty of the Subject, which being altogether unfit for the Stage, yet might be (for the Genius of Milton, and for his only) the Foundation of an Epick Poem." Rare. Shawcross, 1970, p. 79; Not in Coleridge.

70. Webb, Daniel. **REMARKS ON THE BEAUTIES OF POETRY**. By Daniel Webb, Esq; [Quotation from Essay on Criticism.] *London: Printed for R. and J. Dodsley, in Pall-Mall. MDCCLXII*. First and only edition. 8vo, 123pp., modern half calf, marbled paper over boards (apparently lacking a leaf before the title, either half-title or blank, vellum corners, green morocco label with gilt lettering, raised bands. A nice copy. While Webb is principally cited for his "extracts" here from Shakespeare, he is nonetheless very much a Miltonist, and the subject of a German monograph published at Hamburg, 1920. Most of the illustrative examples are taken from Shakespeare and Milton. Rare. NCBEL II, 44; Shawcross, 1972, p. 24 and no. 58; Not in Coleridge.

C. Nineteenth-century Miltoniana

The following have been selected from some three hundred nineteenth-century Miltoniana items in the collection. In addition to selections from what one might expect to find among "Miltoniana," I have included some school editions, almost always in first edition, as evidence of the desire to expose students at an early age to Milton's poetry and occasionally his prose. These school editions are not to be confused with anthologies from this same time frame, examples of which are given in a separate section. I have also included selections to show the value placed on historical and literary tradition.

1. Addison, Joseph. **CRITIQUE ON PARADISE LOST**, By The Right Hon. Joseph Addison. With Remarks On The Versification By Samuel Johnson. *London: Printed at the Stanhope Press By Charles Whittingham, Imopm Buildings, Leather Lane; For John Sharpe, Opposite York House, Piccadilly. 1805*. First edition thus? Small 8vo, 166+[1]pp., engraved frontispiece illustration of "Milton composing Paradise Lost" after Westall, engraved by P. W. Tomkins (fine impression), protective tissue guard, contemporary diced calf (a bit rubbed, corners worn, joints cracked), gilt rule on covers, gilt-decorated spine with gilt lettering, marbled endpapers and edges. A lovely copy with 1835 presentation inscription on front blank, and note from "The Proprietor of the British Poets" to "apprize his Subscribers of an alteration which has taken place" bound in at the end. Addison's *Criticism on Milton's Paradise Lost* was first published in 1719 (see copy with Eighteenth-century Miltoniana). Stevens 1835.

2. Addison, Joseph. **CRITICISM ON MILTON'S PARADISE LOST** From 'The Spectator.' 31 December, 1711–3 May, 1712. Carefully Edited By Edward Arber, Hon. Fellow Of King's College, London; F.S.A., Professor Of English Literature, Etc., The Mason Science College, Birmingham. English Reprints. *London: 36 Craven Park, Willesden, N.W. Ent. Stat. Hall.] 1 August, 1868. [All Rights reserved*. First Arber edition. Square 8vo, 152pp., title page in red and black, original printed thick paper wrapper (a bit aged, reinforced black cloth spine), front cover decorated in black with gilt lettering ("Large Paper Copy"), edges untrimmed. A nice copy.

3. Addison, Joseph. **CRITICISM ON PARADISE LOST**. Edited With Introduction And Notes By Albert S. Cook[,] Professor Of The English Language And Literature In Yale University. *Boston, U.S.A.: Published By Ginn &*

Company, 1892. First edition thus. 8vo, xxiv+200pp., original blue cloth, gilt lettering on front cover and spine. A nice copy. A second edition was published in 1926 (copy in the collection.)

4. Aikin, John. **LETTERS TO A YOUNG LADY ON A COURSE OF ENGLISH POETRY** By J. Aikin, M. D. [Quotation from Minstrel.] *London: Printed For J. Johnson, St. Paul's Church-Yard, By R. Taylor, Black-Horse-Court. 1804.* First edition. 12mo, xii+297+[1]+[2]pp., half-title, original boards (spine defective, front cover detached), edges untrimmed, advertisement leaf bound in at end. A fairly nice copy in original boards. Milton is the only poet who does not share a chapter with another poet, and he has two chapters to himself; another chapter is devoted to his imitators. See Aikin's four-volume 1801 edition of Milton's *PW* in Chapter II and the new issue in three volumes in 1806. Scarce.

5. Artman, Wm. and L. V. Hall. **BEAUTIES AND ACHIEVEMENTS OF THE BLIND.** By Wm. Artman And L. V. Hall. "E'en he who, sightless, wants his visual ray, / May by his touch alone award the day." *Auburn: Published For The Authors. 1857.* 12mo, 387pp., half-title, engraved frontispiece illustration, signed "N. Orr, N. Y.," protective tissue guard, copyright 1854 (verso of title page), original orange cloth (a little rubbed along extremities and at spine ends), covers decorated in embossed blind in a richly designed triangular pattern, spine decorated in gilt with gilt lettering, pink endpapers. A nice copy. There is a ten-page essay on Milton's blindness (pp. 43–52), including his sonnet: "Methought I saw," a selection from *PL*, and a poem which begins "I am old and blind," "lately discovered," as the authors say, "and published in the recent Oxford dictionary of Milton's works." The brief "Introduction" is by editors who were themselves blind. Uncommon.

6. THE AUTOGRAPHIC MIRROR. Inedited Autographs Of Illustrious And Distinguished Men Of Past And Present Times: Sovereigns, Statesmen, Warriors, Divines, Historians, Lawyers, Literary, Scientific, Artistic, And Theatrical Celebrities. *Lithographed By Vincent Brooks, Chandos St Charing Cross. Office: 13, Burleigh St. Strand, London, [ca. 1860].* 2 volumes in one. Folio, 132pp.+65+116+[4]pp., title page each volume, printed in English and French, numerous lithographs showing drawings, sketches, portraits, handwriting, manuscript pages, and a great deal more, with the lives of the lithograph entries in each volume (along side in volume 1, following in volume 2, hence the pagination difference), original three-quarter calf, marbled paper over boards (rebacked, some foxing, endpapers chipped along edges), gilt-lettered leather label with decorative gilt trim on front cover, spine lettered in gilt, marbled endpapers, a.e.g. Included in volume II is Milton's autograph (p. 141), with life (p. 53), and with translation of Latin autograph by Milton; translation in English and French.

7. Baldwin, James. **THE BOOK-LOVER.** A Guide to the Best Reading. By James Baldwin, Ph.D., Author Of "English Literature And Literary Criticism," Etc. Etc. [Quotation from Richard De Bury.] *Chicago: Jansen, McClurg, And Company, 1885.* First edition. 8vo, 201pp., decorative head- and tailpieces, decorated initial letters, contemporary one-half green levant, marbled paper over boards (some wear along joints and extremities), gilt rules on covers, spine lettered in gilt, raised bands with gilt decorations in the compartments, marbled endpapers, t.e.g., others untrimmed. Large paper copy. Included are several references to Milton. Extra-illustrated, with "the insertion of twenty-one portraits, two being very fine proofs, while some of the prints are rare." Included are three fine engravings of Milton: Westall's *Milton Composing Paradise Lost*, engraved by P. W. Tompkins, inserted as frontispiece here; Milton at age sixty-two, engraved by W. C. Edwards; and Milton at twenty-one, engraved by Edward Radclyffe. "Of this Edition only Three Hundred and Fifty Copies are printed, of which this is No. 347" (verso title page).

8. Barbauld, Anna Laetitia. **JOSEPH HOUGENDOBLER. THE FEMALE SPEAKER;** Or, Miscellaneous Pieces In Prose And Verse, Selected From The Best Writers, And Adapted to the use of Young Woman. By Anna Laetitia Barbauld. From the Last London Edition. *Boston: Wells And Lilly, 1824.* 12mo in 6s, x+387pp., contemporary calf (rubbed along joints, initial pages fragile, with bottom portion of title page missing, without affecting any text, age-browned throughout, top half of pp. 376–81 torn away). Intended for classroom use. "A taste for fine writing cannot be cultivated too early" (*Preface*). Included under the title *"Descriptive and Pathetic"* are several selections from Milton's *PL*: "Description of the First Air," "On the Marriage Tie," and "The First Housewife." Scarce.

9. Beers, Henry A. **AN OUTLINE SKETCH OF ENGLISH LITERATURE.** By Henry A. Beers. *New York: Chautauqua Press, C. L. S. C. Department, 805 Broadway, 1886.* First edition. 8vo, 294+[1]pp., original brown cloth (a bit rubbed), decorative floral pattern in contrasting darker brown in upper left corner of front cover with gilt circle incorporating letters of the press in bright gilt against a dark brown background with dark brown trim along top of cover, spine lettered in gilt. A nice copy with advertisement leaf bound in at the end. Included is a chapter devoted to Milton: "The Age Of Milton, 1608–1674."

10. Beers, Henry A. **FROM CHAUCER TO TENNYSON** With Twenty-Nine Portraits And Selections From Thirty Authors. By Henry A. Beers[,] Professor of English Literature in Yale University. Chautauqua Reading Circle Literature. *Flood And Vincent[,] The Chautauqua Century Press[,] Meadville, Penna[,] 105 Fifth Ave. New York[,] 1894.* First edition. 8vo, 313pp., frontispiece portrait of Shakespeare, emblem on title page, additional portraits, original light blue cloth (a bit rubbed), front cover decorated and lettered in black, spine lettered in gilt with decorative black trim, advertisement leaf for publications by "The Chautauqua Literary And Scientific Circle, Founded in 1878" bound before frontispiece. A very nice copy, well-preserved, in a lovely binding of the period. Included is a chapter on Milton (Chapter VI, "The Age Of Milton"), with a vignette portrait of a young, long-haired Milton.

11. [Bentley, Richard.] **BENTLEY.** By R. C. Jebb, M.A., LL.D. Edin., Knight Of The Order Of The Saviour, Professor Of Greek In The University Of Glasgow, Formerly Fellow Of Trinity College, Cambridge. *London: Macmillan And Co., 1882.* First edition. 8vo, 224+4pp., half-title ("English Men of Letters Edited By John Morley • Bentley," letters of the press in emblem at the bottom), original red cloth (spine a little rubbed), front cover and spine lettered in black, letters of the press in black at center of back cover, black and endpapers. A nice copy with four pages of advertisements bound in at the end. Bentley is one of England's great classicists who took on the eccentric project of editing and rewriting various lines in his 1732 edition of *PL* (see copy in Chapter II). Jebb's *Life* endeavors "to estimate [Bentley's] work, the character of his powers, and his place in scholarship" (*prefatory note*).

12. Bingham, Caleb. **THE COLUMBIAN ORATOR:** Containing A Variety Of Original And Selected Pieces, Together With Rules; Calculated To Improve Youth And Others In The Ornamental And Useful Art Of Eloquence. By Caleb Bingham, A. M. Author of the American Preceptor, Young Lady's Accidence, &c. [Quotation from Rollin.] Stereotype Edition. *Boston: Printed For Caleb Bingham And Co. And Sold at their Book-Store, No. 45 Cornhill. 1817.* 12mo in 6s, 300pp., contemporary calf (a bit rubbed, pages age-browned as usual, lacking front endpapers, very neatly rebacked sometime earlier with original spine laid down), gilt rules on spine with black leather label lettered and ruled in gilt. A handsome copy, quite tall, in a nice American binding of the period, with contemporary signature on title page. Included is a lengthy poetical selection from Milton: "*Christ triumphant over the apostate Angels.*" The copyright date on verso of title page is 1810. The collection also has another copy in a nice contemporary calf binding with the publisher's imprint, "Troy: Printed And Sold By William S. Parker, At The Troy Book-Store. 1821."

13. Birrell, Augustine. **OBITER DICTA.** Second Series. By Augustine Birrell[.] *London[:] Elliot Stock 62 Paternoster Row[,] 1887.* First edition. 12mo in 6s, ix+[iii]+289+[1]+[2]pp., half-title, with emblem of press on page facing and on verso of last page, original green cloth, gilt lettering on front cover and spine, with gilt emblem of the press in lower right corner of front cover, edges untrimmed. A very nice copy with early armorial bookplate. The first chapter is devoted to Milton, with a free reading of one who prides himself on "never [having] been inside the reading-room of the British Museum" (Preface). Birrell writes a charming essay in the last chapter on "Book-Buying," describing the climate of the day in a manner that might well remind one of the present: "Lower prices are not to be looked for. . . . Good finds grow scarer and scarcer. . . . Those days are over." Stevens 2172 (citing "Second Series," 1891).

14. Blair, Hugh. **AN ABRIDGMENT OF LECTURES ON RHETORIC.** Revised And Corrected. *Brookfield: Printed by E. Merriam & Co., October—1805.* 12mo in 6s, 295pp., contemporary calf (a bit worn, pages age-browned), black leather label (slightly chipped) with gilt lettering and gilt trim on spine. All in all, a fairly good copy with contemporary signature (dated 1809) on fly-leaf. Included are discussion of and references to Milton. The first edition was published in 1783. (See Blair's *Lectures On Rhetoric And Belles Lettre*, 1789, possible second edition, with Eighteenth-century Miltoniana and commentary there.)

15. Blair, Hugh. **DR. BLAIR'S LECTURES ON RHETORIC ABRIDGED.** With Questions. Dean's Stereotype Edition. *New-York: W. E. Dean, Printer & Publisher, 2 Ann Street. (1848).* First edition thus. 12mo in 6s, 268pp., copyright 1848 on verso of title page, contemporary calf (a bit rubbed), gilt rules on spine with black morocco label with gilt lettering and gilt rules. A nice copy. Included is a discussion of "Milton's Paradise Lost."

15A. (Cross-listing) Bradburn, Eliza Weaver. **THE STORY OF PARADISE LOST, FOR CHILDREN.** *New York: Published By J. Emory And B. Waugh, For the Sunday School Union of the Methodist Episcopal Church . . . 1831.* First edition thus. This is the pirated edition of Mrs. Siddons's book, 1822, *An Abridgement Of Paradise Lost* and *The Story Of Our First Parents Abridged From Milton's Paradise Lost, For The Use Of Young Persons* (see copies in Chapter II). Scarce. See main listing under *PL*, 1831, in Chapter II.

16. Bridges, Robert. **MILTON'S PROSODY[:]** An Examination Of The Rules Of The Blank Verse in Milton's later poems, with an Account of the Versification of *Samson Agonistes*, and general notes by Robert Bridges[.] *Oxford[:] At The Clarendon Press[,] 1893*. First edition. 4to, 80+[1]pp., half-title, original red cloth (faded), gilt lettering on front cover, t.e.g., others untrimmed. A tight, sturdy copy, printed on very good paper with the bookplate of the noted British architect Paul Waterhouse. First published several years earlier in a smaller, much shorter pamphlet, this greatly expanded edition is virtually a new work. One of 250 numbered copies on large paper. Stevens 2253; McKay 25.

A second edition, further enlarged and expanded under the title *Milton's Prosody And Classical Metres In English Verse*, was published in 1901 (copy with Twentieth-century Miltoniana), and a third edition was published in 1921 (copy with Twentieth-century Miltoniana, presentation from Bridges to John Masefield). Bridges's study clearly belongs among critical studies, but this distinction is not made in the nineteenth century and space precludes listing the sizable number of critical studies in the collection.

16A. (Cross-listing) [Brydges, Sir Egerton.] Phillips, Edward. **THEATRUM POETARUM ANGLICANORUM** . . . Now Enlarged By Additions To every Article From Subsequent Biographers And Critics [By Sir Egerton Brydges]. *Canterbury: Printed By Simmons and Kirb, 1800*. Second edition; first Brydges edition. See copy listed under Edward Phillips listed here. Brydges published a second edition in 1824 (in an edition limited to 100 copies—see copy of this second Brydges edition also listed under Edward Phillips) in which he builds upon his edition of 1800 and publishes for the first time his second volume, taking the period from the death of Queen Elizabeth I up to his own time.

17. [Bulwer-Litton (Sir Edward George).] **THE SIAMESE TWINS.** A Tale of the Times. To which is added, Milton, A Poem. By the Author of "Pelham," &c. &c. *London: Henry Colburn And Richard Bentley, New Burlington Street. MDCCCXXXI*. First edition. Large 12mo, xix+[iii]+360pp., engraved frontispiece illustration plate and five other engraved illustration plates after W. H. Brooke (Flaxmanesque in style), contemporary half calf, marbled paper over boards (a bit rubbed, front joint cracked, some slight foxing), central gilt seal of Signet Writers on covers, gilt rules on spine, red morocco label with gilt lettering, speckled edges. A nice copy. The poem *Milton*, with half-title, occupies the last part of the book (pp. 315–60); it is preceded by a two and one-half page "Advertisement To The Poem" (i.e., "Prefatory Remarks"), which begins: "A considerable part of this poem was written some years ago at College." The poem is intended as a sketch of the poet's life, prompted by the story "of the Italian lady seeing Milton asleep under a tree, and leaving some verses beside him, descriptive of her admiration of his beauty" ("Advertisement To The Poem"). This is the sole publication of *The Siamese Twins* (two editions only, both 1831). *Milton* has been reprinted in later collections albeit in a different format from its first appearance in this collection. Rare. Sadleir 443; Stevens 2621 (note).

18. Busby, Stanhope. **LECTURES ON ENGLISH POETRY, TO THE TIME OF MILTON.** By Stanhope Busby Esq. *London: Whittaker And Co. Ave-Maria Lane. 1837*. First edition. 12mo in 6s, vi+118pp., half-title for each section, "Notes" at the end, original blue cloth (inner joint broken), spine lettered in gilt. A nice copy. Included are Busby's "Lecture On English Poetry Before The Time Of Milton" and his "Lecture On The Poetry Of Milton, And Some of His Contemporaries." According to Stevens: "Good survey of the 'Miltonian era.'" Scarce. Stevens 1957.

19. [Butler's Series] **THE FIFTH READER.** Butler's Series. *Philadelphia: E. H. Butler & Co., (1883)*. First edition. 8vo, 384pp., frontispiece illustration, vignette illustration on title page, additional illustrations, original brown calf spine, brown cloth (several light spots on front cover), front cover lettered in black, spine decorated in blind and lettered in gilt. Designed for "pupils who have neither time nor opportunity to enter into an extended study of English and American literature" (Preface). A nice copy. Included are two selections from Milton's *PL*: "Eve's Account Of Her Creation" and "Expulsion From Paradise."

20. Cann, Miss Christian. **A SCRIPTURAL AND ALLEGORICAL GLOSSARY OF MILTON'S PARADISE LOST;** Dedicated, by permission, To The Honorable Lady Sutton. By Miss Christian Cann, Of Bromley, Middlesex. *London: Published For The Authoress, And Sold By Harvey And Darton, Gracechurch Street; Mr. Darton, Holborn Hill, And All The Respectable Booksellers In Town And Country. 1828. [Entered at Stationer's Hall.]* First edition. 8vo in 4s, xii+282+[1]pp., eight-page "List Of Subscribers," errata leaf at the end, original green cloth (several stain marks), spine lettered in gilt. Fine copy in publisher's binding, with contemporary signatures on flyleaf. Subscriber's list accounting for approximately 280 copies only. Rare. Stevens 779 (listing 1828 edition by C. and J. Rivington).

21. Channing, William Ellery. **REMARKS ON THE CHARACTER AND WRITINGS OF JOHN MILTON;** Occasioned By The Publication Of His Lately Discovered

'Treatise On Christian Doctrine.' From The Christian Examiner, Vol. III, No. 1 *Boston, Printed By Isaac R. Butts And Co. 1826.* Tall 8vo in 4s, 51pp., half-title, original printed wrappers (edges of wrappers a little frayed, spine chipped, a little foxed), front cover lettered in black. A nice, tall copy. Large paper copy. With the publication of this work, Channing established himself as the first great American critic of Milton; this was also one of the first substantial American essays on Milton and also the first serious critical work published on Milton's *De Doctrina Christiana* (see copy in Chapter II). This is the first separate publication and was occasioned by the publication of the recently discovered original manuscript of Milton's *De Doctrina Christiana*. Scarce. Not in Stevens (but Stevens 1282 cites 1896 reprint by Butts & Co., Boston, and references the earlier editions).

22. Channing, William Ellery. **REMARKS ON THE CHARACTER AND WRITINGS OF JOHN MILTON**; Occasioned By The Publication Of His Lately Discovered 'Treatise On Christian Doctrine.' Second Edition, Corrected. *Boston, Printed By Isaac R. Butts, And Co. 1826.* Second edition, corrected. 8vo in 4s, 48pp., disbound, contemporary signature on title page and repeated on first page. A nice copy. Scarce.

23. Channing, William Ellery. **REMARKS ON THE CHARACTER AND WRITINGS OF JOHN MILTON**; Occasioned By The Publication Of His Lately Discovered 'Treatise On Christian Doctrine.' By W. E. Channing, LL.D. Second Edition. *Boston, Printed:—London: Reprinted For Edward Rainford, 13 Red Lion Passage, Red Lion Square; Sold Also By R. Hunter, St. Paul's Church-Yard: And All Other Booksellers. 1828.* Second London edition. 8vo, 48pp., modern green calf spine, marbled boards. A nice copy. Scarce.

24. Channing, William Ellery. **REMARKS ON THE CHARACTER AND WRITINGS OF JOHN MILTON**; Occasioned By The Publication Of His Lately Discovered 'Treatise On Christian Doctrine.' By The Rev. Dr. Channing, Of Boston, North America. *Boston, Printed:—London: Reprinted For Edward Rainford, 13 Red Lion Passage, Red Lion Square; Sold Also By R. Hunter, St. Paul's Church-Yard: And All Other Booksellers. 1828.* Third edition. 8vo, 48pp., disbound. A good copy. "Literary Notices Of Dr. Channing's Publications" bound in after title page, with praise for Channing. Scarce.

The collection also has the following copies of Channing's works which contain his "Remarks on the Character and Writings of John Milton": *Discourses, Review And Miscellanies* (*Boston: Published By Gray And Bowen, 1830*), first collected edition; *The Works Of William E. Channing* (*Boston: American Unitarian Association, 1867*); and *The Works Of William E. Channing* (*Boston: American Unitarian Association, 1889*).

25. [Charles I] **CHARLES I**. By Sir John Skelton, K.C.B. *London, Paris, And Edinburgh: Goupil And Co., Jean Boussod, Manzi, Joyant & Co., Fine Art Publishers To Her Majesty. 1898.* Large 4to, 185pp.+colophon leaf, half-title, engraved frontispiece portrait in color, title page in red and black, numerous engraved illustrations (very fine impressions) several full-page color, contemporary full red morocco, elaborately gilt-decorated covers and spine, spine lettered in gilt, raised bands, inner and outer dentelles finely tooled in gilt, marbled endpapers, t.e.g., others untrimmed. An elegant copy in excellent condition with superb engravings. Printed and engraved by Jean Boussod, Manzi, Joyant, & Co., at Amieres-sur-Scine, near Paris, 1898. A miniature portrait of Milton by Alexander Cooper in the South Kensington Museum appears on p. 101. Companion volume to *Cromwell* (also listed here).

26. Charles I. **EIKON BASILIKE**. The Pourtraictvre of His Sacred Maiestie In His Solitudes And Sufferings. A Reprint Of The Edition Of 1648, And A Facsimile Of The Original Frontispiece, With An introduction Throwing Fresh Light Upon The Authorship Of The Work By Edward J. L. Scott, M.A., Oxon., Assistant Keeper of MSS., British Museum. *London: Elliot Stock, 62, Paternoster Row, E.C. 1880.* First edition thus. 8vo, xlii, [vi], 227pp., engraved folding plate of original frontispiece (fine impression), original blue cloth (a bit rubbed, ex-library copy with two modest stamps and light shelf mark on spine), front cover and spine lettered in gilt, fore- and bottom edges untrimmed. A nice copy. A reprint of the edition of 1648 (see copy with Seventeenth-century Miltoniana) with a lengthy preface by Edward Scott throwing fresh light on the authorship of the work. Inserted at the end of the preface is a printed mauve slip "announcing, that, while the present sheets were passing through the press, [discovery was made] in the Record Office [of] the original of the Second Prayer at the end of the Eikon (page 224) in the hand-writing of Charles I., of the date 1631."

27. Chateaubriand, Francois Rene De. **ESSAI SUR LA LITTERATURE ANGLAISE**. Et Consi-derations Sur Le Genie Des Hommes, Des Temps Et Des Revolutions, Par M. De Chateaubriand. *Paris: Furne Et Charles Gosselin, Editerus. M DCCC XXXVI.* 2 volumes. First edition. 8vo, 370+[1]pp.,+404+[1]pp., half-title and title page each volume, "Errata" leaf at the end of each volume, contemporary half red morocco, marbled paper over boards (slightly rubbed, joints cracked, minor foxing), raised bands within gilt rules on spines with gilt lettering, speckled edges. A

very nice set. Chateaubriand was a great admirer of Milton, speaking directly about him in his "Avertissement" (see reference quoted in English translation following), and he devotes nearly one quarter of his survey of English literature to Milton. See English translation following. His translation of *PL* into French in 1831 (see 1836 edition in Chapter II) was very popular and was variously reprinted thereafter. Scarce. NCBEL III, 100.

28. Chateaubriand, Francois Rene De. **SKETCHES OF ENGLISH LITERATURE**; With Consi-derations Of The Spirit Of The Times, Men, And Revolutions. By The Viscount De Chateaubriand. In Two Volumes. *London: Henry Colburn, 13, Great Marlborough Street. 1836.* 2 volumes. First edition. 8vo, viii+356pp.,+iv+361pp., half-title, volume 1, contemporary half diced calf (rubbed at extremities, occasional light foxing or spotting), marbled paper over boards, maroon morocco labels with gilt lettering and gilt rules on spines, speckled edges. A nice set of this translation of Chateaubriand's survey of English literature from the earliest times to the Lake Poets. Chateaubriand's admiration for Milton is expressed in his "Introduction:" "In this Review of English Literature I have treated at considerable length of Milton , , , I analyse his different works, I show that revolutions have approximated Milton to us; that he is become a man of our times, that he was as great a writer in prose as in verse; prose conferred celebrity on him during his life, poetry after his death; but the renown of the prose writer is lost in the glory of the poet" (p. vii). Scarce.

29. THE CHILDREN'S STORY BOOK OF GOOD AND GREAT MEN. *New York: James G. Gregory, n.d. [ca. 1865].* First edition? 8vo, 256pp., frontispiece illustration and other illustrations, original decorated blue cloth (some slight wear), covers decorated in blind with decorative emblem in gilt incorporating title on front cover, spine decorated and lettered in gilt. A good copy with contemporary presentation in a neat hand (dated 1865) on fly-leaf. Included as a brief chapter unto itself is a life of Milton written for children. It is uncommon to find the life of Milton contained in a "Story Book" for children. Scarce.

30. Coleridge, S. T. **SEVEN LECTURES ON SHAKESPEARE AND MILTON.** By The Late S. T. Coleridge. A List Of All The Ms. Emendations In Mr. Collier's Folio, 1632; And An Introductory Preface By J[ohn]. Payne Collier, Esq. *London: Chapman And Hall, 193, Piccadilly. 1856.* First edition. 8vo, cxx+275pp., half-title, original purple cloth (spine evenly faded and just a trifle rubbed), covers decorated in blind trim, spine lettered in gilt. A nice tall copy. "The erratic scholar John Payne Collier was at first accused of having fabricated the Coleridge notes, but he did in fact attend the lectures as a young man, and his notes are perfectly genuine, as his long preface here explains. The Shakespeare 'emendations,' however, from the so-called 'Perkins folio,' are quite another matter" (Stephen Weissman, Ximenes, Occasional List, No. 101, #40, 1993). Scarce. Stevens 2008; NCBEL III, 221, 1642.

31. THE COMMMON-PLACE BOOK OF LITERARY CURIOSITIES, Remarkable Customs, Historical And Domestic Anecdotes, And Etymological Scraps. By the Rev. Dr. Dryasdust, of York, Somewhile Preface-Writer To The Great Unknown. "With sweet variety your taste I'll please." *London: John Bumpus, 85, Newgate-Street. MDCCCXXV.* First edition. 12mo in 6s, hand-colored frontispiece illustration, three additional plates, contemporary half calf, marbled paper over boards (a bit rubbed), black leather label with gilt lettering. A nice copy. Included are several references to Milton.

32. [Copleston, Edward]. **ADVICE TO A YOUNG REVIEWER, WITH A SPECIMEN OF THE ART.** *Oxford: Sold By J. Parker, And J. Cooke; And By F. C. And J. Rivington, St. Paul's Curch-Yard, London. 1807.* First edition. 8vo, 17pp., disbound (title with several light brown stains, a few smudges, contemporary name at head of text, blank verso of last leaf with contemporary name, notes, and a small sketch). "Copleston's *Advice* is a marvelous piece of satire wherein he extorts the young reviewer to adhere to the fundamental principle of 'Write what will sell. . . . In particular, it will greatly lighten your labours to *follow* the public taste, instead of taking upon you to direct it.' The work closes with a substantial example, nine pages, of a mock review of Milton's *L'Allegro*. The exceedingly rare first edition of this noted satire" (G. W. Stuart, Jr., Ravenstree, Cat. 163, #129, 1989).

33. [Cromwell, Oliver] **CROMWELL. AN HISTORICAL NOVEL.** By Henry W. Herbert, Author Of "The Brothers," Etc. [Quotation from Rogers.] *Aberdeen: Published By George Clark And Son. Dublin:—J. M'Glashan, 21, D'Olier-Street. MDCCCXLVIII.* First edition? 12mo, 306+[4]pp., half-title, original blind-stamped dark green cloth, spine decorated and lettered in gilt, edges untrimmed. A very nice copy in a lovely publisher's binding, with a four-page "Catalogue Of New And Cheap Publications" bound in at the end.

34. [Cromwell, Oliver] **LIFE OF OLIVER CROMWELL;** or England's Great Protector. By Henry William Herbert. *Philadelphia: Porter & Coates, n.d. [ca. 1887].* 12mo, 447pp., frontispiece portrait sketch of Cromwell, dedication page "To The Public Of America" dated 1856, original yellow cloth, front cover and spine richly decorated in black trim, front cover with contrasting embossed yellow floral motif and embossed title in yellow letters against black background at the top, "Alta Edition" in the center, spine lettered in black against decorated gilt backdrop, black endpapers. A fine copy in a lovely publisher's binding, in virtually mint condition.

35. [Cromwell, Oliver] **OLIVER CROMWELL** By Samuel Rawson Gardiner, D,C.L., LL.D., Litt.D. *London, Paris, New York, Edinburgh: Goupil & Co., Jean Boussod, Manzi, Joyant & Co., Fine Art Publishers To The Queen. 1899.* Large 4to, 216pp.+colophon leaf (plates not included in pagination), half-title, engraved frontispiece portrait in color, title page in red and black, forty-five engraved illustrations (very fine impressions), including color frontispiece portrait and several additional full-page color engravings, contemporary full green morocco (slight foxing, some light earlier inoffensive waterstaining along bottom portion of first half of book), gilt rules on covers and spine, spine finely tooled in gilt by compartments, raised bands, inner dentelles ruled in gilt, t.e.g., others untrimmed. An elegant copy in excellent condition, with an extra title page bound in at the end. Included is a miniature portrait of Milton among a group of five miniatures in the collection of the Duke of Bucclech, at Montague House, London, appears on p. 141. Companion volume to *Charles I* (see copy listed earlier). No. 1403 of 1475 copies printed on fine paper.

36. Cyr, Ellen M. **CYR'S FIFTH READER.** By Ellen M. Cyr Author Of Cyr's Reads[.] *Boston: Ginn & Company, Publishers[,] The Athenaeum Press[,] 1899.* First edition. 8vo, frontispiece illustration and other illustrations, original decorated light brown cloth (spine a bit worn), front cover and spine lettered in contrasting darker brown. A good copy. Designed for classroom use. Included is a section on Milton with a biography, several poetical selections ("Death Of Samson" from *Samson Agonistes*, *Song On A May Morning*, and *On His Blindness*), and several illustrations (portrait and a reproduction of *Milton Dictating Paradise Lost* after Munkacsy).

37. Deverell, Robert. **ANDALUSIA**; Or, Notes, Tending To Show That The Yellow Fever Of The West Indies, And Of Andalusia in Spain, Was A Disease Well Known To The Ancients; And That They Assigned A Cause For It, And Used Effective Means For The Prevention And Cure Of It, Not Hitherto Attempted In Our Time. By Robert Deverell, Esq. M.P. January 19, 1805. [Greek Quotation from Thucydides.] [This Treatise Is Not Intended For Publication.] *London: Printed By S. Gosnell, Little Queen Street, Holborn. (1805).* First and only edition. 4to, 155+[3], half-title, folded map of Andalusia and a series of line drawings (as numbered plates) bound in at the end, original purple cloth (a bit faded), spine lettered in gilt within decorative gilt trim, speckled edges. A good copy, privately printed in a limited edition. Robert Deverell (1760–1841) was a "strange" man who privately published a variety of eccentric works. Here, he begins with Milton and moves backward to the ancients. The first fifty-seven pages treat *Comus* and *Lycidas*, in which, among other things, Deverell "shows" that "the scene of [*Comus*] lies in the province of Andalusia in Spain" (p. 5), as does the scene in *Lycidas* (p. 49). Rare.

Dictionaries

38. **THE NEW AMERICAN BIOGRAPHIC DICTIONARY**: Or, Memoirs Of Many Of The Most Eminent Persons That Have Ever Lived In This Or Any Other Nation: Including Divines, Philosophers, Lawyers, Physicians, Poets, Historians, Statesmen, Navigators, Warriors, and Extraordinary Women. By J. Kingston. "The Proper Study Of Mankind Is Man." Pope. By J. Kingston. *Baltimore: Printed For John Kingston, And sold at his Book and Stationary Store, 164, Market-Sreet. Warner and Hanna, Print. 1810.* First edition. 16mo, 303pp., engraved frontispiece portrait of George Washington, printed in double column, contemporary calf (a bit rubbed, age-browning), spine decorated in gilt with red morocco label lettered in gilt with gilt trim, outer dentelles tooled in gilt at top and bottom (now a bit faded). An attractive copy of this early nineteenth-century American book, with contemporary signature (dated 1809) on front blank. Included is a rather long (for the period and type of book this is) life of Milton, among the earliest such in America.

39. **A UNIVERSAL BIOGRAPHICAL DICTIONARY**, Containing The Lives Of The Most Celebrated Characters Of Every Age And Nation, Embracing Warriors, Heroes, Poets, Philosophers, Historians, Politicians, Statesmen, Lawyers, Physicians, Divines, Discoverers, Investors, And Generally, All Such Individuals, As From The Earliest Period Of History To The Present Time, Have Been Distinguished Among Mankind; To Which Is Added, A Dictionary Of The Principal Divinities And Heroes Of Grecian And Roman Mythology And A Biographical Dictionary Of Eminent Living Characters. *Printed For Subscribers[,] New-York. 1825.* First edition. 12mo, 444pp., engraved frontispiece consisting of vignette portraits, including a vignette portrait of Milton, printed in double column, contemporary tree calf (a bit rubbed, age-browning throughout, slight inoffensive waterstain from sometime ago inside bottom portion of first few leaves), spine

handsomely decorated in gilt with gilt lettering, yellow edges. A nice copy with early ownership signatures on front blank and fly-leaf. Included is a brief biography of Milton.

40. A DICTIONARY OF BIOGRAPHY. Comprising The Most Eminent Characters Of All Ages, Nations, And Professions By R. A. Davenport. Embellished With Numerous Portraits. [Quotation from Johnson.] *London: Printed For Thomas Tegg, 73, Cheapside; J. Cumming, Dublin: And R. Griffin And Co. Glasgow. 1831.* First edition. 12mo, 584pp., engraved vignette illustration on title page, engraved vignette sketches, printed in double column, contemporary three-quarter calf (some slight wear), red morocco label with gilt lettering and gilt rules on spine. A very good copy. Included is a brief biography of Milton with vignette sketch.

41. A DICTIONARY OF BIOGRAPHY; Comprising The Most Eminent Characters Of All Ages, Nations, And Professions By R. A. Davenport. First American Edition, With Numerous Additions, Corrections, And Improvements. And Illustrated By Two Hundred Fine Portraits, On Wood. *Exeter: Published By J. & B. Williams, 1836.* First American edition, expanded. 12mo, 527pp., engraved portrait of Washington on title page, additional engraved vignette sketches, printed in double column, original roan (back joint slightly cracked, a little faded, light, inoffensive waterstaining from sometime ago on the bottom fore-corner of the last few leaves), gilt-decorated spine with gilt lettering. A very good copy. Included is a brief biography of Milton, with vignette sketch. The first edition was published in London in 1831 (also listed here).

42. Dunster, Charles. **CONSIDERATIONS ON MILTON'S EARLY READING, AND THE PRIMA STAMINA OF HIS PARADISE LOST;** Together With Extracts From A Poet Of The Sixteenth Century. In A Letter To William Falconer, M.D. From Charles Dunster, M. A. *Printed By And For John Nichols, Red-Lion Passage, Fleet-Street, London; And Sold By R. H. Evans, (Successor To Mr. Edwards,) 26, Pall Mall; Robson, Bond-Street; Nicol, Pall Mall, Payne, Mews-Gate; Also By Bull, Meyler, And Bally, Bath; Deighton, Cambridge; Cooke, Oxford; Archer, Dublin; And Laying, Edinburgh. 1800.* First and only edition. 8vo, [2]+249+[1]pp., contemporary polished quarter sheep, marbled paper over boards (rubbed, joints broken). A good copy, fresh and clean internally, with numerous notes regarding Milton on front blanks, some quite possibly in Dunster's autograph, early bookplate of Signet Society on front pastedown and again on leaf preceding title, complete with errata and advertisement leaf at the end (of three editions by Dunster: an edition of *PR*, see copy in Chapter II; Philips's *Cider*, copy in collection; and a translation of Aristophanes's *Frogs*). Aside from the attention he pays Sylvester's Du Bartas and Milton, Dunster focuses mostly on Milton's short poems. Probably printed in a small number of copies. Rare. Coleridge 309; Shawcross, 1972, 89; Stevens 1817.

43. Edgeworth, Richard Lovell. **POETRY EXPLAINED FOR THE USE OF YOUNG PEOPLE.** By R. L. Edgeworth, Esq. *London: Printed For J. Johnson, 72, St. Paul's ChurchYard. 1802.* First edition. 12mo, xv+[1]+115+[1]pp., modern boards (a few minor smudges, slight embrowning), printed paper label on spine, edges untrimmed. A very attractive copy with advertisement leaf bound in at the end. As he says in his preface, "the following pages are addressed to those who have no literary prejudices." Richard Edgeworth wants to teach "children" the "pleasure" of poetry. While he considers six poems overall, he focuses primarily on Gray's *Elegy and* Milton's *L'Allegro* and *Il Penseroso*. Rare.

44. Edgeworth, Richard, and Maria Edgeworth. **READINGS ON POETRY.** *Boston: Published By Wells And Lilly. Sold by Van Winkle and Wiley, New York; and by M. Carey, Philadelphia, 1816.* First American edition. 12mo in 6s, 206+blank+[6]pp., original boards (a bit soiled, spine ends chipped, hinges cracked, minor age-darkening), edges untrimmed, partially unopened. A good copy with four pages of advertisements bound in at the end. "Adam's Morning Hymn" is discussed on pp. 104–29. Rare. Shaw & Shoemaker 37496.

45. Edmonds, Cyrus R. **JOHN MILTON: A BIOGRAPHY.** Especially Designed To Exhibit The Ecclesiastical Principle Of That Illustrious Man. By Cyrus R. Edmonds. [Quotation from Tacitus.] *London: Albert Cockshaw, 41, Ludgate Hill. And All Booksellers. 1851.* First edition. Small 8vo, viii+251pp., preface date 1851, original green cloth (a little worn, spine ends chipped, small circular shelf or book label on front cover, early pencil markings on fly-leaf), covers and spine decorated in embossed blind, spine lettered in gilt, edges untrimmed. Overall, a very decent copy. As a biography of Milton, Edmonds provides commentary on Milton's poems, with notice of observations by others, such as Johnson and Macaulay; he also provides extensive commentary on Milton's prose works. Uncommon. Stevens 1678.

46. Edmundson, George. **MILTON AND VONDEL:** A Curiosity of Literature. By George Edmundson, M.A. Late Fellow And Tutor Of Brasenose College, Oxford,

Vicar Of Northolt, Middlesex. "Suum cuique honorem." *London: Trübner & Co., Ludgate Hill. 1885. [All rights reserved.]* First edition. 8vo, vi+223pp., half-title, original blue cloth (front cover watermarked along front edge), printed paper label (a bit age-darkened) on spine, uncut and unopened. A good copy. Edmundson analyzes Joost van den Vondel's (1587–1679) four main plays: *Lucifer*, *Samson*, *Adam in Exile*, and *John the Messenger*, showing some clear parallels in Milton's works with excerpts from Vondel's plays. Stevens 838.

47. Fry, Alfred A., Esq. **A LECTURE ON THE WRITINGS, PROSE AND POETIC, AND THE CHARACTER, PUBLIC AND PERSONAL, OF JOHN MILTON,** Delivered At Several Metro-politan Literary Institutions, By Alfred A. Fry, Esq. Of Lincoln's Inn. [Several Quotations] *London: Henry Hooper, Pall Mall, East. 1838.* First edition. 8vo, 55pp., dedication page, disbound. A nice copy. Fry focuses on the greatness of Milton as poet and writer of prose, as statesman and "at once a politician and philosopher" (p. 53).

48. Garnett, Richard. **LIFE OF JOHN MILTON.** By Richard Garnett, LL.D. *London[:] Walter Scott, 24, Warwick Lane[,] 1890 (All rights reserved.).* First edition. 8vo, 197+xxxix+[10]pp., half-title ("Great Writers. Edited By Professor Eric S. Robertson, M.A."), index and bibliography at the end, original blue cloth, spine lettered in gilt, t.e.g., others untrimmed. A fine copy with ten pages of advertisements bound in at end. The "Bibliography" is "By John P. Anderson (British Museum)." Reproduced in 1970 (copy in collection). Stevens 1959.

49. Geffroy, Auguste. **ETUDE SUR LES PAMPHLETS POLITIQUES ET RELIGIEUX DE MILTON,** Par A. Geffroy, Docteur es-lettres, Professeur d'Histoire au Lycee Descartes, a Paris. Liberte de conscience. Reforme des Universites, Liberte de la Press. Divorce. Regicide. Contrat social. Rapports du spirituel et et du temporel. Salaire du clerge. Plan d'une constitution repulicaine. *Paris: Dezobry, E Magdeleine Et Cie, Libr.-Editeurs, Rue Des Macons-Sorbonne, 1. Stassin Et Xavier, 9, rue du Coq, pres le Louvre. 1848.* First edition. 8vo, [ii]+295pp., contemporary marbled boards, leather label with gilt lettering and gilt rules on spine. A fine copy. Presentation copy from the author, inscribed on the half-title. An early study of Milton's prose, with a detailed twenty-page bibliographical record of Milton's prose works and some related studies in the appendix. Stevens 1287; NCBEL I 1245.

50. Godwin, William. **LIVES OF EDWARD AND JOHN PHILIPS, NEPHEWS AND PUPILS OF MILTON.** Including Various Particulars Of The Literary And Political History Of Their Times. By William Godwin. To Which Are Added, I. Collections For The Life Of Milton. By John Aubrey, FRS. Printed From The Manuscript Cop In The Ashmolean Museum At Oxford. II. The Life Of Milton. By Edward Philips. Printed In The Year 1694. *London: Printed For Longman, Hurst, Rees, Orme, And Brown, Paternoster-Row: By S. Hamilton, Weybridge, Surrey. 1815.* First edition. 4to, xv+[errata]+410pp., frontispiece portrait of John Bradshaw, additional portraits, modern quarter morocco (preserving original red morocco label with gilt lettering, new endpapers, minor foxing), marbled paper over boards, gilt rules on covers and spine, with small decorative gilt devices on spine, marbled edges. A lovely, large copy. John and Edward Phillips "were nephews of Milton, were brought up under his roof, and in some measure adopted by him as his sons. Their history therefore affords us an advantage in studying his character, which it rarely happens for the admirers of a great genius or a poet to possess" (from Godwin's *Preface*). Scarce. Stevens 1656.

51. Gostwick, Joseph. **ENGLISH POETS.** Twelve Essays By Joseph Gostwick, Author of the Handbooks, "German Literature," and "American Literature," "German Poets," &c. &c. With Twelve Portraits. *London: Frederick Bruckmann, 17, Southampton St. Strand. 1876.* First English edition. 4to, 229+[1]+half-title, title page in red and black, with large central emblem, decorative head- and tailpieces and decorated initial letters, twelve early photographs tipped in on card thick paper before each poet's life, original reddish-brown cloth (a bit rubbed on back cover), front cover and spine elaborately decorated in embossed gilt and black, with large central gilt device incorporating *English Poets, Memoirs, Portraits* on front cover and spine, thick white silk endpapers, a.e.g. A fine copy with early photographs mounted on special paper, handsomely published at the Chiswick Press. Included is a chapter on Milton, with a photograph of Milton (twenty-one) by P. Kramer tipped in at the beginning. Other chapters, with mounted photographs, on Shakespeare, Addison, Pope, Goldsmith, Burns, Wordsworth, Scott, Byron, Shelley, and Tennyson. The collection also has the First American edition of *English Poets* published one year earlier in 1975 by the Chiswick Press for "D. Appleton And Co. New York" without date (copyright 1975), in the exact same binding and format.

52. Grandmaison, M.P. **CLASSICAL DESCRIPTIONS OF LOVE,** From The Most Celebrated Epic Poets: Homer, Ariosto. Tasso, Milton, Virgil, And Camoens. By M. P. Grandmaison. Translated From The French. *London: Printed For J. Blacklock. Royall-Exchange, by J. Swan and Son, 76, Fleet Street. 1809.* First edition in English. 8vo, v+[5]+224pp., engraved frontispiece illustration for Homer, five engraved illustrations, one for each of the other five poets, on recto of the five leaves before Canto I, original boards (rebacked, some minor age-browning), edges untrimmed. A good copy. Canto IV is devoted to a retelling of how Milton's Adam and Eve celebrated "the first hymeneal day" through a conversation between the two, with narrative supplied by the author along with critical commentary, and ending with "To the nuptial Bow'r I led her blushing like the morn," which is illustrated by Williams.

53. Hayens, Herbert, editor. WORLD FAMOUS AUTHORS. Edited by Herbert Hayens. Noble Lives Series. *London & Glasgow: Collins Clear Type Press, n.d. [ca. 1895].* 8vo, 224, half-title, frontispiece illustration in color and other illustrations in color, title page printed in color, black and white portraits, full red leather, decorative gilt border trim on covers, central gilt seal on front cover, spine elaborately decorated and lettered in gilt, raised bands with decorative gilt trim, outer dentelles finely tooled in gilt, red endpapers. A very nice copy in a Prize Binding, with undated prize citation tipped in on front pastedown. A chapter (pp. 169–92) is devoted to Milton, with a full-page portrait of a young Milton in black and white and with an unattributed illustration in color ("Scene from *PL* [Book XI]").

54. Hazlitt, William. LECTURES ON THE ENGLISH POETS Delivered at the Surrey Institution. By William Hazlitt. London: *Printed For Taylor And Hessey, 93, Fleet Street. 1818.* First edition. 8vo, errata+331pp., half-title (with advertisement notice on verso), contemporary three-quarter calf, marbled paper over boards (rebacked in pale mauve sprinkled sheep, minor foxing), gilt-ruled and gilt-lettered maroon morocco label. A good copy with armorial bookplate. Hazlitt's admiration for Milton is clearly expressed in his lecture "On Shakespeare and Milton" (Lecture III), and that admiration remains constant, as it does for Shakespeare, throughout his discussion of poets who follow. Stevens 1876; Keynes 33.

55. HOME PICTURES OF ENGLISH POETS, For Fireside And School-Room. *New York: D. Appleton And Company, 90, 92 & 94 Grand Street. 1869.* First edition. 12mo, 291+bland+[6]pp., copyright 1869 (verso title page), frontispiece illustration, preface by K. A. S. (dated 1868) numerous portraits and biographical illustrations, original half black buckram, black cloth (a bit worn at joints and on spine, some age-browning, occasional marginal notes in a neat hand), spine lettered in gilt, printed endpapers. A good copy with six pages of advertisements bound in at the end. "The writer . . . has attempted to interest the young student by making of each life a story as well as a lesson" (Preface). Included is a twenty-page biographical chapter on Milton, with a vignette portrait sketch of Milton and a vignette sketch of his cottage at Chalfont.

56. Hunter, Joseph. MILTON. A SHEAF OF GLEANINGS AFTER HIS BIOGRAPHERS AND ANNOTATORS. I. GENEALOGICAL INVESTIGATION. II. NOTES ON SOME OF HIS POEMS. By Joseph Hunter. *London: John Russell Smith, 4, Old Compton Street, Soho Square. MDCCCL.* First edition. 12mo, [i]+blank+72pp., contemporary purple cloth (front hinge and spine chipped), spine lettered in gilt. A good copy with several early notations in pencil in a neat hand, and with original wrappers (somewhat aged) laid down and bound in, with front wrap titled: "Mr. Hunter's Critical and Historical Tracts. No. III. Milton. June—1850," with two printer's devices. Among Hunter's genealogical investigations are findings regarding Milton's "Settlement In London," his first and second marriages, and his "Last London Residence." Hunter's "Notes on Some" of Milton's poems indicate a strong familiarity with Milton's poems and his editors and also an extensive knowledge of other poets, the Bible, and the classics. Scarce. Stevens 1677.

57. [Interviews] THE INTERVIEWS OF GREAT MEN: Their Influence On Civilization; From The Meeting Of Diogenes And Alexander, To The Final Interview Of Count Cavour And Victor Emanuel. Developing The Characteristics Of Men Who Influenced The Times In Which They Lived, And Showing Where Their Example Is Worthy Of Imitation. By The Author Of 'Heroines Of Our Time," Etc. [Quotation from Shakespeare.] *London: Darton And Co., 58, Holborn Hill. n.d. [ca. 1863].* First edition? 8vo, viii+312pp., frontispiece illustration and other illustrations throughout, contemporary red morocco (a bit rubbed along joints and extremities), spine elaborately decorated in gilt within the panels, olive green morocco label lettered and ruled in gilt, inner dentelles finely tooled in gilt, outer dentelles ruled in gilt, dark olive green endpapers, a.e.g. A lovely copy in a Prize Binding, with a prize inscription in a neat hand (dated 1863) on front blank. Included are two chapters on Milton: (1) "Milton's Interview with Galileo in the Prison of the Inquisition" (pp. 96–115), with an illustration after L. Stephenson, and (2) "Milton's Interview with the Duke of York" (pp. 116–29).

58. Ivimey, Joseph. JOHN MILTON: HIS LIFE AND TIMES, Religious And Political Opinions. With An Appendix, Containing Animadversions Upon Dr. Johnson's Life Of Milton, &c. &c. By Joseph Ivimey, Author Of The "History Of The English Baptists," &c. &c, [Quotations from Cooper and Hall.] *London: Published By Effingham Wilson, Royal Exchange. MDCCCXXXIII.* First

edition. 8vo, xvi+397pp., engraved frontispiece portrait of Milton after Faithorne, engraved by Cochran, original full diced blue morocco (scuff mark on front cover), gilt rules on covers, elaborately gilt-decorated spine by compartments, red morocco label with gilt lettering, raised bands, marbled endpapers and edges. A lovely copy with red leather prize label lettered in gilt (dated 1836) on front pastedown. An important biography of Milton. Scarce. Stevens 1666.

59. Keightley, Thomas. **AN ACCOUNT OF THE LIFE, OPINIONS, AND WRITINGS OF JOHN MILTON.** With An Introduction To *Paradise Lost*. By Thomas Keightley, Author Of 'Mythology Of Greece And Italy,' 'Fairy Mythology,' 'History Of England,' Etc. [Quotation from Dante.] *London: Chapman And Hall, 193, Piccadilly[,] 1855.* First edition. 8vo, xiv+[iv]+484pp., original red cloth (a bit used), covers blind-stamped, sea green endpapers, edges untrimmed, partially unopened. A nice copy with early signature (dated 1880) on title page. Part I is the Life. Part II consists of seven essays on Milton's religion, inspiration, and philosophy, and on his views on toleration, government, and education, and on his learning. Part III reviews each of Milton's published works, concluding with a hundred-page introduction to *PL*. Keightley's biography of Milton is one of the more significant biographies published in the nineteenth century. Keightley also edited a two-volume edition of Milton's *Poems* with extensive and useful notes in 1859 (see set in Chapter II). Scarce. Stevens 1688.

60. Lloyd, E. "Milton on his Blindness" [In] **CHRISTIAN LYRICS:** Chiefly Selected From Modern Authors. [Unidentified Quotation.] Angel with lute "From The Uffizi Palace." With Upwards Of One Hundred Engravings. *New York: Scribner, Welford, And Co. 1868.* Small 4to, 180+[4]pp., frontispiece illustration, red border on title page with black border within, numerous illustrations within text, decorative head- and tailpieces, with decorated initial letters, black border around text, original green calf over thick boards (a bit worn along extremities, front joint cracked, foxing), covers and spine richly decorated in finely embossed gilt trim and intricately decorated gilt design with gilt lettering, broad inner dentelles trimmed in gilt, marbled endpapers, a.e.g. A nice copy in a lovely binding of the period. Included is E. Lloyd's poem: *Milton on his Blindness* (pp. 39–40), with a vignette portrait of Milton (fine impression) after T. D. Scott above the title, with elaborately decorated initial letter, and with a vignette illustration by S. J. Crispin of four angels at the end of the poem, entitled "From angel lips I seem to hear the flow of soft and holy song."

61. Lovell, John E. **THE UNITED STATES SPEAKER:** A Copious Selection Of Exercises In Elocution; Consisting Of Prose, Poetry, And Dialogue: Drawn Chiefly From The Most Approved Writers Of Great Britain And America: Including A Variety Of Pieces Suitable For Very Young Speakers: Designed For The Use Of Colleges And Schools. By John E. Lovell, Formerly Instructor Of Elocution In the Mount Pleasant Classical Institution; Amherst, Mass. [Quotation from Quintilian.] Stereotype Edition, Revised And Improved[.] *New Haven: Published By S. Babcock. Sold By Hilliard, Gray, And Co. And Russell, Shattuck, And Co. Boston et al. 1836.* Second, revised edition. 12mo in 6s, xii+[vii]+504pp., frontispiece of oratorical gestures hand-colored, 1835 copyright on verso of title page, "Preface To The First Edition" dated 1833, and "Stereotype Edition" dated 1835, several pages of figures showing various gestures ("Oratorical," "Poetical," etc.), unlettered contemporary calf (somewhat worn and rubbed, age-browning). A good copy with near-contemporary signatures and markings on front and back pastedowns and fly-leaves. In the section, "Didactic And Rhetorical," are included three poetical selections from Milton's *PL*: "Moloch's Oration For War," "Speech Of Belial, Dissuading War," and "Meeting Of Satan And Death At The Gate Of Hell." Scarce.

62. Macaulay, Thomas Babington. **CRITICAL, HISTORICAL, AND MISCELLANEOUS ESSAYS.** By Lord Macaulay. With A Memoir And Index. In Six Volumes. *New York: Published By Hurd & Houghton; Cambridge: Riverside Press, 1871. (Copyright verso title page dated 1860.)* 6 volumes. 8vo, xxxv+543pp.,+496pp.,+[i]+495pp.,+[i]+426pp.,+[i]+539pp.,+[1]+490pp., half-title and title page each volume, original brown cloth (rubbed a bit along edges, spine ends a little chipped), covers decorated in blind, spines lettered in gilt with small crest of the press in gilt at the bottom, brown endpapers. A nice set. Included are Macaulay's essays on Milton: "A Conversation Between Mr. Abraham Cowley And Mr. John Milton Touching The Great Civil War" (which first appeared in *Knight's Quarterly Magazine*, August, 1824) and "Milton" (which first appeared in *Edinburgh Review*, August, 1825), both reprinted here in Volume I. Also included is Macaulay's essay on "Southey's Edition Of The *Pilgrim's Progress*" (which first appeared in *Edinburgh Review*, December 1830), here reprinted in Volume II, in which Macaulay calls the edition "eminently beautiful and splendid," but in which he expresses little liking for Martin's illustrations, going on to say that "He [Martin] should never have attempted to illustrate the *PL*. There can be no two manners more directly opposed to each other than the manner of his painting and the manner of Milton's poetry" (II, p. 151). On some things even the great ones get it wrong!

63. Macaulay, Thomas Babington. ESSAYS CRITICAL AND MISCELLANEOUS. By T. Babington Macaulay. *Philadelphia: Carey And Hart, Chestnut Street. Stereotyped By L. Johnson. MDCCCXLIII.* First edition thus. 12mo in 6s, iv+572pp., printed in double column, original orange boards, black cloth spine (foxing throughout), printed paper label on spine, early ownership signature. A nice copy. Included as the first essay here is Macaulay's *Milton*, which first appeared in the *Edinburgh Review* for August 1825 as a review of Sumner's translation of Milton's *De Doctrina Christiana* (see copy of *De Doctrina* in Chapter II), which had just appeared that year.

64. Macaulay, Thomas Babington. JOHN MILTON. AN ESSAY. With Biographical Sketches Of Milton And Macaulay, An Epitome Of The View Of The Best Known Critics Of Milton, And Explanatory Notes. Selected. Maynard's English Classics Series.–No. 102-103. *New York: Maynard, Merrill & Co., 29, 31, And 33 East Nineteenth Street, (1892).* First edition thus. Small 8vo, 81+[8]pp., frontispiece portrait of Macaulay, original gray cloth repeating title page on front cover, eight unpaginated leaves of advertisements bound in at end. A very fresh copy, almost mint, with school district stamp on front pastedown.

The collection also has a variant edition: with variant title page and variant publisher's imprint, variant number of advertisement leaves bound in at the end (here paginated), in a variant publisher's binding, with advertisements printed on endpapers, with the bookplate of Milton scholar Maurice Kelley on front pastedown.

In addition, the collection has a number of other editions of Macaulay's essay on Milton (listing only first editions here): *Essay On Milton And History*. School Edition. Reprinted From The Last London Edition. *Boston, [N. Publisher], 1876.* First thus; *An Essay On John Milton.* Eclectic English Classics. *New York, Cincinnati, Chicago: American Book Company, (1894).* First thus; *Macaulay's Essay On John Milton* Edited With Notes And An Introduction By James Greenleaf Croswell. Longmans' English Classics[.] *New York[:] Longmans, Green, And Co. And London[,] 1895.* First thus; *Essay On John Milton* Edited By William P. Trent. *Boston, New York, Chicago: Houghton, Mifflin And Company, The Riverside Press, Cambridge, 1896.* First thus; *Macaulay's Essay On Milton* Edited And Annotated By Charles Wallace French[.] *New York[:] The Macmillan Company[;] London: Macmillan & Co., LTD. 1898.* First thus; *Milton* With Notes By Margaret A. Eaton, A. B. *Boston, New York, Chicago, [And] San Francisco:* *Educational Publishing Company, (1899).* From the series "Ten Cent Classics," "Published Semi-Monthly" (as noted on front cover). First thus; *Macaulay's Essay On Milton And Addison.* Edited For School Use By Alphonso G. Newcomer. The Lake English Classics. Longmans' English Classics. *Chicago: Scott, Foresman And Company, 1899.* First thus; *Milton* With Notes By Margaret A. Eaton. *Boston, New York, Chicago, [And] San Francisco: Educational Publishing Company, (1899).* First thus.

65. M'Alpine, Frank. OUR ALBUM OF AUTHORS, A Cyclopedia Of Popular Literary People, By Frank M'Alpine, Editor Of "Treasures From The Poetic World," "Treasures From The Prose World" And "Popular Poetic Pearls." Sold Only by Subscription. *Philadelphia, Chicago, [And] Cincinnati: Elliott & Beezley, 1885.* First edition. Square 8vo, 4+416pp., engraved portrait plates, original red calf over thick boards (a little worn), front cover decorated in black with central gilt lettering, spine lettered in gilt and decorated in gilt in the panels with decorative gilt trim in imitation of raised bands, decorated endpapers, a.e.g. A good copy. Included is a biographical sketch of Milton and a discussion of his works with an unattributed engraved portrait of Milton at a young age. "'Our Album Of Authors' gathers into one volume a knowledge of the men and women who have made the standard literature of the world.... This volume will be valuable to those wishing to make up a library, as it gives a list of books published by standard authors and names each author's best works. It will be valuable to teachers for reference and study, because it not only gives extended sketches of the best authors, but it gives the critical estimation of each author's writings. It will be valuable to parents, because it carries their children into the society of good books..." (*Preface*).

The collection also has the second edition published in 1886, in a decorated publisher's cloth binding, virtually mint, the third edition published in 1887, and the fourth edition published in 1889. There are no changes between the editions, and perhaps the reprintings so close together are due to the copies being "Sold Only by Subscription," indicating that each edition was probably printed in a limited edition and demand exceeded availability by year's end.

66. [Manning, Anne.] THE MAIDEN AND MARRIED LIFE OF MARY POWELL, AFTERWARDS MISTRESS MILTON. *London: Printed for Hall, Virtue, & Co., n.d. (1850).* First edition. 8vo in 4s, 271pp.+[1]+[4]+16pp., wood-engraved frontispiece of "Milton's Arms" in red and black, title page in red and black, "London: Printed by Richard Clay" on verso of last page, double black border around text, original red cloth (a bit rubbed, spine ends a little chipped), covers decorated in blind, spine lettered in gilt, red endpapers, advertisements bound in at the end (as proper), bookplate. A good copy with twenty pages of advertisements (four unpaginated) bound in at the end. The popularity of this fictional journal of Milton's wife capitalized on the market for mock diaries along the lines of *Lady Willoughby's Diary* which had appeared in 1844 (see Chiswick Press edition under Willoughby). Printed in seventeenth-century style and a rather simplistic attempt at "ye olde Englishe" with a few references to seventeenth-century politics distinguish Mary Powell's adventures from what must have been both the chief dread—an unhappy marriage—and the chief aspiration—marriage to a famous man—of many nineteenth-century young ladies. Married young, after only a brief courtship, to a creditor of her father's, Mary is at first unable to adjust to life away from home and the austere temperament of her husband. A prolonged separation and a good bit of soul searching on both sides lead to a happy reconciliation of the couple. First published in *Sharpe's Magazine* in 1849, the work went through several editions, and in 1858 was provided with a sequel entitled *Deborah's Diary*. Scarce. Sadleir 1549; Stevens 2626 ("A clever fictitious diary built upon the statements of Phillips").

67. [Manning, Anne.] THE MAIDEN AND MARRIED LIFE OF MARY POWELL, AFTERWARDS MISTRESS MILTON. *Boston: Published At The Office Of The Living Age, By E. Littell & Co.; New York: Stringer & Townsend; Philadelphia: Getz & Buck, n.d. [1850].* First American edition. Large 8vo, 38+[8]pp., printed in double column, original printed wrappers (several stain marks on front cover, small piece at top of title page torn away without affecting any text), title page reprinted on front cover, edges untrimmed. A good copy with eight pages of publisher's advertisements bound in at the end. Scarce.

68. [Manning, Anne.] THE MAIDEN AND MARRIED LIFE OF MARY POWELL, AFTERWARDS MISTRESS MILTON. New Edition. *London: Printed for Arthur Hall, Virtue, & Co., n.d. [ca. 1860s].* 8vo in 4s, 271pp., frontispiece portrait of a young Milton (unattributed), title page in red and black, "London: Printed by Richard Clay" on verso of last page, double black border around text, contemporary full dark purple morocco (a bit rubbed), covers finely tooled in blind, spine lettered in gilt, raised bands, gauffered gilt edges. A handsome copy, reprinting the text of the first edition also listed here. The collection also has the fourth edition. Uncommon.

69. [Manning, Anne.] Variant of Preceding. THE MAIDEN AND MARRIED LIFE OF MARY POWELL, AFTERWARDS MISTRESS MILTON. *New York: Printed for M. W. Dodd, at 506, Broadway. n.d. [ca. 1870s].* Large 8vo, 271pp., title page in red and black with central emblem and double black border, "Cambridge: Press Of John Wilson And Sons" on verso, double black border around text, original three-quarter brown leather, marbled paper over boards (a bit rubbed, especially along extremities), spine decorated in gilt within the compartments (now faded), black morocco label with gilt lettering and decorative gilt trim, slightly raised bands, marbled endpapers and edges. A nice, large paper copy ("One hundred copies printed on large paper" printed on verso of title page, this copy unnumbered). Variant edition, printing the same number of pages as "Hall, Virtue & Co.," with identical text on each page, in variant publisher's binding. The collection has two additional editions by "M. W. Dodd, at 506, Broadway," undated, both small octavo, each with 271 pp., in variant publisher's bindings, one in original gilt-stamped green cloth, the other in original gilt-stamped brown cloth.

70. [Manning, Anne.] THE MAIDEN & MARRIED LIFE OF MARY POWELL (AFTERWARDS MISTRESS MILTON) And THE SEQUEL THERETO DEBORAH'S DIARY With An Introduction By The Rev. W. H. Hutton, B. D.[,] Fellow Of S. John's College, Oxford[.] And Twenty-Six Illustrations By John Jellicoe And Herbert Railton. *London[:] John C. Nimmo[;] New York: Charles Scribner's Sons[,] MDCCCXCVIII.* First edition thus. 8vo, xxxiv+358+[2]pp., frontispiece illustration plate and twenty-five additional illustration plates together with illustrations within the text after drawings by John Jellicoe and Herbert Railton (first appearance), title page in red and black, decorated initial letters, publisher's pictorial red cloth (slightly faded, trifle worn, inner joints cracked, spine sunned), front cover lettered and decorated in gilt with bright gilt illustration at the top, dark red endpapers, t.e.g., edges untrimmed. A nice copy with advertisement leaf bound in at the end. Uncommon. Stevens 2634 (referencing 1898 London edition).

71. Martyn, W. Carlos, Esq. LIFE AND TIMES OF JOHN MILTON. *Published By The American Tract Society, 150 Nassau-Street, New York. (1866).* First edition. 12mo, 307+3pp., engraved frontispiece oval portrait after Vertue, engraved by F. Halpin (portrait margins foxed, slight embrowning throughout), protective tissue guard (foxed), decorative piece with anchor at the center of title page, copyright 1866 on verso of title page, preface dated 1866, original purple cloth (spine slightly faded), vignette portrait of Milton embossed in gilt at center of front cover and embossed in blind at center of back cover, spine lettered in gilt within decorative gilt trim, brown endpapers, red edges. A nice copy with three pages of advertisements

bound in at the end. "No special claim to originality is made[, but instead, by drawing upon] existing and authentic data . . . to group in one volume those numerous and authentic historical, biographical, and anecdotal incidents which now lie scattered . . . and to present these from an American stand-point" (Preface). Stevens 2048.

72. Masson, David. THE LIFE OF JOHN MILTON: Narrated In Connexion With The Political, Ecclesiastical, And Literary History Of His Time. By David Masson, M.A., Professor Of English Literature In University College, London. Vols. 1-6: 1608-1674. *Cambridge: Macmillan And Co. And 23, Henrietta Street, Covent Garden, London. 1859-1880. [The Right of Translation is Reserved.]* 6 volumes. First edition. Thick 8vo, xiv+[ii]+778+foldout+24pp.,+xii+608pp.,+ix+729+[1]+[2]pp.,+xiii+642pp.,+xv+707pp.,+xix+840pp., half-title each volume, other volumes each have "London: Macmillan And Co." in publisher's imprint, engraved portrait of Milton age ten as frontispiece, volume 1, with additional engraved portrait of Milton at age twenty-one, each with protective tissue guard, folding facsimile of Milton's signatures at end of volume 1, engraved portrait of Milton age sixty-two (without identification), volume 6, protective tissue guard, original green pebble cloth (small library stamp on title pages and bottom edges, "Sold By Librarian" stamped on title pages, labels removed from spines with traces of marks), covers ruled in blind, spines lettered in gilt, edges rough trimmed, brown endpapers. Except for former library reminders, a very nice copy of this increasingly scarce set. Stevens 2024 ("Vol. I, greatly improved by revision, reissued in 1881"—as part of second edition, revised).

73. Masson, David. THE LIFE OF JOHN MILTON: Narrated In Connexion With The Political, Ecclesiastical, And Literary History Of His Time. By David Masson, M.A., LL.D., Professor Of Rhetoric And English Literature In The University Of Edinburgh. New And Revised Edition. Vols. 1-7: 1608-1674. *London: Macmillan And Co., 1881-1894. [The Right of Translation is Reserved.]* 7 volumes. Second edition, revised. 8vo, xxiii+[i]+834+foldout+[2]pp.,+xxii+608pp.,+x+729+[2]pp.,+xiii+642pp.,+xv+707pp.,+xix+840pp.,+[i]+242+[2]pp., half-title each volume, engraved portrait of Milton age ten as frontispiece, volume 1, with additional engraved portrait of Milton twenty-one, each with protective tissue guard, folding facsimile of Milton's signatures at end of volume 1, engraved portrait of Milton age sixty-two (without identification), volume 6, protective tissue guard, original green pebble cloth (a bit rubbed), covers ruled in blind, spines lettered in gilt, edges rough trimmed, dark green endpapers, bookplate in each volume. A fine set, including volume 7, index, sometimes missing. Uncommon. Stevens 2024 (comment and "Index added 1894").

74. Masson, David. THE THREE DEVILS: LUTHER'S, MILTON'S, AND GOETHE'S. WITH OTHER ESSAYS. By David Masson, M.A., LL.D., Professor of Rhetoric and English Literature in the University of Edinburgh. London: *Macmillan And Co. 1874. [The Right of Translation and Reproduction is Reserved.]* First edition. 8vo, [iv]+327+56pp., half-title with emblem of the press on verso, half-title for each section, original red cloth, spine lettered in gilt with a small emblem of the press in gilt at the bottom, black endpapers, t.e. rough. A nice copy with fifty-six pages of "Macmillan & Co.'s Catalogue of Works in Belles Lettres, March 1874" bound in at the end. Included are revised texts of five essays first published in 1856, including "The Three Devils: Luther's, Milton's, and Goethe's," and "Milton's Youth." At the end is a new piece, "How Literature May Illustrate History." Uncommon. Stevens 2078.

75. Mavor, William. THE BRITISH NEPOS: Consisting Of The Lives Of Illustrious Britons, Who Have Distinguished Themselves By Their Virtues, Talents, Or Remarkable Advancement In Life; With Incidental Practical Reflections. By William Mavor, LL.D. A New Edition, Improved And Enlarged, With Twenty-four Portraits. [Quotation from Virgil.] *London: Printed For Longman, Hurst, Rees, Orme, And Brown, Paternoster-Row; And To Be Had Of All Booksellers In Town And Country. 1820. (Price Five Shillings Bound.)* Second edition? 8vo, xi+[i]+455pp., preface to the first edition (dated 1798), "presenting to the public a new edition" (dedication page, dated "June 4, 1819"), engraved frontispiece illustration, additional engraved plates, contemporary tree calf (front joint broken), spine ruled in gilt. Except for the detached front cover, a very nice copy. Included is a ten-page life of Milton with a vignette portrait of the poet on an engraved plate consisting of five other vignette portraits. Intended "for the use of schools" (*Preface*). Scarce.

76. [McGuffey, Wm.] MCGUFFEY'S NEWLY REVISED ECLECTIC FOURTH READER: Containing Elegant Extracts In Prose And Poetry, With Rules For Reading, And Exercises In Articulation, Defining, Etc. Revised and Improved. By Wm. H. McGuffey, LL.D. Revised Electrotype Edition. Cincinnati: Sargent, Wilson & Hinkle. *New York: Clark & Maynard[,] (1853)*. 8vo in 4s and 8s, 322+[1]pp., advertisement on verso of title page, original half black leather, brown cloth (worn, lacking front blanks, top part of spine missing, spotting throughout), spine lettered in gilt. Designed for classroom use. Included

is one excerpt from Milton's *PL*: "Apostrophe To Light," with questions following.

77. [McGuffey, Wm.] MCGUFFEY'S NEWLY REVISED RHETORICAL GUIDE OR FIFTH READER: Of The Eclectic Series. Containing Elegant Extracts In Prose And Poetry: With Copious Rules And Rhetorical Exercises. Eclectic Educational Series. Revised and Improved. *Publishers: Winthrop B. Smith & Co. No. 137 Walnut Street., (1853).* 8vo in 4s and 8s, 480pp., advertisements on verso of title page, original half black leather, brown cloth (worn, spine ends chipped, foxing), spine lettered in gilt. While designed for classroom use, the book is solid and has no markings within. Included are three excerpts from Milton's *PL*: "Battle In Heaven"—with the admonition that "This lesson is adapted to the cultivation of a low tone"; "Satan, Sin, And Death"—with the direction that "The following lesson requires variety of tone"; and "Adam's Morning Hymn"—without admonition.

78. McGuffey, Wm. MCGUFFEY'S NEW SIXTH ECLECTIC READER: Exercises In Rhetorical Reading, With Introductory Rules And Examples . . . Stereotype Edition. *Cincinnati: Sargent, Wilson & Hinkle; Chicago: Cobb, Pritchard & Co.; New York: Clark & Maynard, (1867).* First edition thus. 8vo in 4s and 8s, original half black leather, brown cloth (very worn from age and use, front cover detached and repaired, spine chipped at top and bottom, age-browned), spine lettered in gilt. Designed for classroom use, "the first *Reader* appeared in 1836 and in its first seventy years sold some 122 million copies. After the Bible, it was the single most important influence on American education, culture, & morals in the 19th century" (Downs, 67). Included are two excerpts from Milton's *PL*: "Battle In Heaven"—with the admonition that "This lesson is adapted to the cultivation of a low tone; and "Satan, Sin, And Death"—with the direction that "The following lesson requires variety of tone." A brief biographical note, in which Milton is called "the acknowledged prince of British poets," precedes the first excerpt.

The collection also has a copy of the "Revised Edition" of *McGuffey's Sixth Eclectic Reader* published in 1879 with a brief biography of Milton and an excerpt from *SA*, along with John Dryden's epigram. This popular reader was reprinted in 1896, 1907, and 1921. A modern facsimile reproduction of the 1879 revised edition was published near the end of the twentieth century (copy in the collection).

79. Meyer, Jürgen Bona. MILTON'S PADAGOGISCHE SCHRIFTEN UND AUSSERUNGEN. Mit Einleitung und Unmerkungen herausgegeben von Dr. Jürgen Bona Meyer, Professor der Philosophie und Padagogik zu Bonn. *Langensalza, Druck und Verlag von Hermann Beyer & Sohne.* *1890.* First edition. Slim 8vo, xvi+64pp., half-title (with advertisement for the series on verso), original olive green cloth, front cover finely decorated in embossed black trim with black lettering at top and bottom with bright gilt lettering in the center, back cover ruled in blind, spine lettered in gilt, thick endpapers decorated in patterned green design. A fine copy in mint condition.

80. [Milton: "An American Milton"] TRUE AND INFERNAL FRIENDSHIP, OR THE WISDOM OF EVE. AND THE CHARACTER OF THE SERPENT, WITH THE SITUATION, JOYS, AND LOSS OF PARADISE. Herein view Truth and Constancy extoll'd, / And the Inconstant deep in grief involved. *Providence, R.I. Printed By H. Mann And Co. For The Author. 1813.* First edition. 12mo, xx+[13]+176+[2]pp., contemporary roan-backed boards (rubbed but sound, a few minor patches of foxing). A very good copy with early signature (dated 1852) on fly-leaf and early bookplate on front pastedown, complete with terminal errata leaf. First edition of a still-anonymous poem, extraordinary in that it treats what even in America at the time must have been regarded as the pre-eminently Miltonic subject without, apparently, any knowledge, and certainly without any acknowledgment, of *PL* other than a generic nod to its author: "Could I but sing as ancient *Homer* sung, / Or could I sing like *Milton, Pope,* or *Young* . . . ." In the preface, the author (speaking of himself in the third person) discusses the subject of the work, asserting two different kinds of friendship exemplified in God's and Satan's treatments of Adam and Eve in the Garden of Eden; the author is also said to believe literally that "the Earth is a *hollow globe,* containing a celestial region in its centre, and the same that is called Paradise . . . where *Adam* and *Eve* and the new *creation* were placed when created" (p. ix). Eve holds her own in rhyming couplets against Satan, as in "Freedom's our right and heaven has made us free, / And ought we now resign our right to thee?" But the couplet wears thin as does the author's misogyny in telling us ultimately at the end that the "vile Serpent" is female in gender, with the promise of "another work, (in stile like this,)" on man's "unhappy fate." Shaw & Shoemaker 29982.

81. MILTON'S MULBERRY TREE AND OTHER STORIES. Illustrated. *The Werner Company[,] New York[,] Akron, Ohio[,] Chicago[,] 1899.* First edition. 8vo, unpaginated, illustrations (full page and within the text), original cream cloth (small slight stain on spine), front cover lettered in green ("Milton's Mulberry Tree") with an illustration on the left side of the cover from top to bottom in green and contrasting darker green of a tall tree with a bench beneath it and a forest and sun rising in orange in the background. A fine copy of this collection of unattributed and unrelated group of seven stories. Included as the first story is "Milton's Mulberry Tree," with a full-page illustration entitled, "Tell Me Little Man Where You Saw The British Uniform," a sketch of "Milton At Nineteen— When At Cambridge" within the text, and a smaller illustration within the text near the end of the story entitled, "Milton's Mulberry Tree" (depicting the mulberry full grown). The story is about the mulberry tree Milton planted while at Cambridge, and that none of Milton's "associates could have imagined that this tree would be . . . so reverently cherished . . . for century after century . . . especially to the descendants . . . [of those who] had landed on Plymouth Rock, and, at the time when Milton was in Cambridge, were laying the foundations of civil and religious liberty in a New World" (ending of the story). Scarce.

See J. H. Wiffen's "To A Lady, With A Leaf Gathered From The Mulberry-Tree Planted By Milton In The Gardens Of Christ College, Cambridge" in *Forget Me Not* (1825) under *Wiffen* here.

81A. See: Redivivus, Lucian [pseud.] **PARADISE LOST**: Or, The Great Dragon Cast Out; Being A Full, True And Particular Account Of The Great and Dreadful Bloodless Battle That Was Fought In The Celestial Regions About 6000 Years Ago. *Boston: Published By Josiah P. Mendum, At The Office Of The Boston Investigator. 1872.* An irreverent parody of Milton's poem with copious notes filled with quotations from earlier commentators on Milton and from the Bible. See main listing under Redivivus.

82. Monroe, Lewis B. **THE SIXTH READER.** *Philadelphia: Cowperthwait & Co., (1872).* First edition. 8vo, 408pp., frontispiece illustration and other illustrations, decorative section headings, original half black calf, black cloth, front cover and spine lettered in gilt), brown endpapers. A good copy. Included is a poetical selection from *SA*, with brief biographical note of Milton. Uncommon.

83. [Murray, John]. **MODELS OF ENGLISH LITERATURE FOR THE USE OF COLLEGES AND ACADEMIES.** *Baltimore: Printed By John Murray, 146 Market Street. MDCCCXLII.* First edition. 12mo in 6s, 370pp., half-title, disbound (some age-browning). "In preparing the present volume for the use of English classes, our design has been to offer a selection free from every thing objectionable. . . . The lessons are arranged under different heads, *Narrative, Description*, etc., with *precepts* taken from . . . well known writers" (*Preface*). Included are several quotations from Milton under the headings *"Narrative," "Descriptive," and "Dialogues."* Scarce.

84. Murray, Lindley. **THE ENGLISH READER**: Or, Pieces In Prose And Poetry, Selected From The Best Writers. Designed To Assist Young Persons To Read With Propriety And Effect; To Improve Their Language And Sentiments; And To Inculcate Some Of The Most Important Principles Of Piety And Virtue. With A Few Preliminary Observations On The Principles Of Good Reading. By Lindley Murray, Author of an English Grammar, &c. *New York: Stereotyped By B. And J. Collins, n.d. [ca. 1810].* First edition. 12mo in 6s, 263pp., contemporary calf (a little worn, front joint broken, lacking front endpapers, pages age-browned), gilt rules on spine with black leather label with gilt lettering, marbled edges. All in all, a nice copy of an interesting early American reader designed for classroom use. Included are several poetical selections from Milton. In the lengthy introduction, the opening lines of *PL* are quoted and analyzed to "exemplify the superiour emphasis"; and later Milton is quoted to exemplify the caesura. Also included are three long excerpts from *PL*: "Discourse between Adam and Eve, retiring to rest"; "Adam's advice to Eve, to avoid temptation"; and "A morning hymn." Uncommon.

The collection also contains a number of other editions of *The English Reader* by Lindley Murray: "Boston: Printed & Published By Lincoln & Edmands, 1814"; "Albany: Printed And Sold By E. & E. Hosford, 1819"; "Philadelphia: Published By Edwin T. Scott, 1821"; "Baltimore: Published By Cushing & Jewett; Boston: And By Lincoln & Edmands, 1824," with the addition of the *Key* by Israel Alger; "Baltimore: Published By Cushing & Sons; Boston: And By Lincoln & Edmands, 1830"; "Philadelphia: Published By W. A Leary, 1848."

85. Murray, Lindley. **SEQUEL TO THE ENGLISH READER**: Or, Elegant Selections In Prose And Poetry . . . From The Third English Edition, Enlarged And Improved. *Poughkeepsie: Printed And Sold By P. Potter, Main Street. 1811.* Third English edition, enlarged and improved. 12mo in 6s, 292pp., contemporary calf (a bit rubbed, embrowning throughout, inoffensive staining from sometime ago at the top inside), gilt rules on spine with black morocco label lettered in gilt. A good copy with neat contemporary inscription (dated 1816) on fly-leaf. Included in the section, "Descriptive Pieces," is a selection from Milton's *PL* entitled "Night described"; the appendix contains a two-page life of Milton. "The 'English Reader' has been so favourably received by the public . . . it is presumed that [the present volume] forms a proper 'Sequel to the Reader,' and is calculated to improve, both in schools and in private families, the highest class of young readers" (*Introduction*). The collection also has two other editions: "Philadelphia: Published by Johnson and Warner, 1812" and "Philadelphia: Printed And Published By S. Probasco, 1831." Scarce.

86. OLD ENGLAND: A Pictorial Museum Of Regal, Ecclesiastical, Baronial, Municipal, And Popular Antiquities. *London: Charles Knight & Co., 1845.* 2 volumes. First edition. Large 4to, viii+392pp.,+vi+386pp., numerous engravings, many in color, original brown cloth (very worn, pages loose), sound internally. In a protective cover. From the library of J. B. Fairchild, with his signature on each flyleaf. Historical, literary, and related, with discussion of Milton, along with several reproductions of Milton portraits: "Milton at the age of Nineteen," "Portrait of Milton," "Milton and his Localities," "Milton, from a Miniature by Faithorne." "Knight's colour printing is best seen in two works of popular history, *Old England*, issued in ninety-six parts between 1844 and 1845, and *Old England's Worthies*, 1847 [see copy following]. . . . Knight's books were the first ever to offer printed colour plates to a wide and popular market. To our eyes, they have great subtlety and charm; but perhaps, for their intended market, they were not garish enough" (McLean, *VBD*, pp. 43–44).

87. OLD ENGLAND WORTHIES: A Gallery Of Portraits From Authentic Copies . . . Accompanied By Full And Original Biographies, With Illustrative Woodcuts And Twelve Splendid Illuminated Engravings. *London: Charles Cox, 1847.* First edition. Large 4to, 272pp., frontispiece illustration in color, numerous engravings, a number full-page color, original brown cloth (bit worn), covers blind-stamped, with central gilt device on front cover, spine lettered in gilt and decorated with gilt figures. A good copy. A section is devoted to Milton (pp. 146f), with vignette illustration (unattributed, but possibly by Knight) of *Adam and Eve Departing Eden* along with a full-page color engraving of Milton's *Monument in St. Giles Church, Cripplegate*. A brief biographical sketch of Milton appears in the index. See McLean's comment, preceding copy, on Knight's engravings.

88. Osgood, Lucius. **OSGOOD'S PROGRESSIVE FIFTH READER:** Embracing A System Of Instruction In The Principles Of Elocution, And Selections For Reading And Speaking From The Best English And American Authors. Designed For The Use of Academies and the highest Classes in Public and Private Schools. *Pittsburgh: Published By A. H. English & Co.[,] 98th Fourth Street[,] (1858).* First edition. 8vo, 480pp., original half black leather, black cloth (a bit worn along extremities), covers decorated in embossed blind trim, spine lettered in gilt, lightly marbled edges. A good copy. Designed for classroom use. Included are several poetical selections from Milton's *PL*: "Meloch's Speech in Favor of War," "Belial's Speech against War," "Meeting of Satan and Death," and "Hymn of Adam and Eve." Uncommon.

89. Painter, F. V. N. **INTRODUCTION TO ENGLISH LITERATURE** Including A Number Of Classics With Notes. *Sibley & Ducker[,] Boston [And] Chicago[,] (1894).* First edition. 8vo, viii+633+[2]pp., original green cloth, front cover and spine lettered in gilt, index. A nice copy with advertisement leaf bound in at the end. Preface begins: "This work is an attempt to solve the problem of teaching English literature." Included is a section on Milton, with *L'Allegro* and *Il Penseroso* printed and notes on each poem.

90. Pancoast, Henry S. **AN INTRODUCTION TO ENGLISH** *LITERATURE. New York: Henry Holt And Company, [1894?].* First edition. Small 8vo, xiii+[1]+556pp., half-title, frontispiece portrait of Shakespeare along with additional portraits, folding map of Elizabethan London in color, folding map of "Some Literary Landmarks In England" in color (with reference to two Milton localities), appendix (with tables of dates and events for each period, including Milton's), and index at the end, original red cloth (bit used, spine ends chipped), central blind crest on front cover, spine lettered in gilt. A fair copy of this textbook edition. Included is a chapter devoted to Milton, "The Puritan In Literature," with a reproduction of a portrait of Milton in his middle years and a detailed table of dates and events in the appendix. This popular textbook was followed by several editions: a second, revised edition in 1896, a third in 1902, and a third, enlarged, in 1907 (a copy of each of the latter two is in the collection with Twentieth-century Miltoniana).

91. Pattison, Mark. **MILTON.** By Mark Pattison, B.D. Rector Of Lincoln College, Oxford[.] *London: Macmillan And Co., 1879. The Right of Translation and Reproduction is Reserved.* First edition. 8vo, vi+[2]+220+4pp., half-title ("English Men of Letters Edited By John Morley • Milton," letters of the press in emblem at the bottom), a second half-title ("Milton") before the text after "Contents," original cream cloth, (a bit soiled, spine repaired), printed paper label (chipped), edges untrimmed, four pages of advertisement for other "English Men Of Letters Now publishing" bound in at the end. A good copy with the signature of James Hutton May, 1932, written in a neat hand beneath the name of "Harry Bompas Smith, April 28, 1880," written in an equally neat hand on fly-leaf. Uncommon. Stevens 2105.

92. Pattison, Mark. **MILTON.** By Mark Pattison, B.D. Rector Of Lincoln College, Oxford[.] *New York: Harper &*

Brothers, Publishers[,] Franklin Square[,] 1880. First American edition. 12mo in 6s, vi+215+[1]+[2]+4pp., half-title ("English Men of Letters Edited By John Morley"), small emblem on title page, original dark brown cloth, front cover and spine lettered in red, initials of the press in red on back cover, brown endpapers, bookplate. A nice copy with six pages of advertisement bound in at the end, one for "English Men Of Letters." Uncommon.

The collection also includes a number of other nineteenth-century editions of Pattison's *Milton*: "New York: Harper & Brothers, Publishers, n.d. (ca. 1882)." "London: Macmillan And Co., 1883"; "London: Macmillan And Co., 1885"; "New Edition. London and New York: Macmillan And Co., 1890"; "New York: Harper & Brothers, Publishers, Franklin Square. n.d. [ca. 1892]"; and "Macmillan And Co. And New York[,] 1895."

93. Phillips, Edward. **THEATRUM POETARUM ANGLICANORUM.** Containing The Names And Characters Of All The English Poets From The Reign Of Henry III To The Close Of The Reign Of Queen Elizabeth. By Edward Phillips, The Nephew Of Milton. First Published in 1675, And Now Enlarged By Additions To every Article From Subsequent Biographers And Critics [By Sir Egerton Brydges]. [Greek Quotation from Hesiod *Theog.*] *Canterbury: Printed By Simmons and Kirby, For J. White, Fleet-Street, London. 1800.* Second edition; first Brydges edition. 8vo, lxxix+blank+336+6 ("Contents")+[1]pp., half-title, contemporary calf (a bit worn, front joint cracked, back cover detached, some slight age-browning), Signet arms in gilt on covers, black morocco label (a little defective), raised bands, shelf label on front pastedown, advertisement leaf bound in at the end. A good copy of the first edition to appear since the original of 1675 (see copy with Seventeenth-century Miltoniana and commentary there). Apparently privately printed in a rather small number of copies. Rare. Stevens 1641; Not in Coleridge.

Brydges reworked the text extensively; selected only the English poets ("all that the compiler of the present work had occasion to select"); changed "the alphabetical order of their *christian* names. . . . into a chronological order, of which the advantage seems sufficiently obvious"; and added valuable notes. He also included a seventy-nine-page "Preface" after Phillips' Preface in which he provides background to the work; and in his six-page "Advertisement" at the beginning (from which the earlier quotations were taken), Brydges provides a brief life of Phillips and a review of Milton's hand in helping his nephew with this book, especially in writing the section on Shakespeare, citing two quotations from Warton.

94. Phillips, Edward. **THEATRUM POETARUM ANGLICANORUM**: Containing Brief Characters Of The English Poets, Down To The Year 1675. By Edward Phillips, The Nephew Of Milton. The Third Edition. Reprinted at the expence, and with the Notes, of Sir Egerton Brydges, Bart. etc. etc. *Geneva, From The Press Of Bonnant. 1824. (100 copies).* 2 volumes in one. Third edition; second Brydges edition. Tall 8vo, xlvi+[1 blank]+55+xxxiii+150+[8]pp., contemporary calf (a bit worn, front cover detached), gilt rules on covers, elaborately gilt-decorated spine within the panels, red morocco label lettered in gilt with decorative gilt trim, raised bands with decorative gilt trim, inner dentelles finely tooled in gilt, outer dentelles ruled in gilt, marbled endpapers, partly unopened, a.e.g. A nice copy, bound by F. Bedford with his stamp. Eight pages (unpaginated) of "Advertisement[s]" for "Works By The Editor Of This Reprint" bound in at the end. Brydges builds upon his edition of 1800 (copy preceding) and publishes for the first time his second volume, which takes up the rest of *Theatrum Poetarum Anglicanorum* covering the period from the death of Queen Elizabeth I up to his own time. Vol. II, or the "End Of Phillips's Characters," is found on p. 66; the remainder of this work consists of "Notes" by Brydges which provide valuable information, critical commentary, bibliographical information, lists of poets, and essays. As Brydges points out, "Of the Poets recorded by Phillips only six are included in Johnson's *Lives of the English Poets*: viz. Cowley, Milton, Denham, Waller, Sprat, and Dryden" (p. 67). Printed in an edition limited to 100 copies. Rare. Stevens 1661.

95. Pichot, Amedee. **LES POETES AMOUREUX** Episodes De La Vie Litteraire Par Amedee Pichot[,] Auteur de l'Histoire de Charles-Edouard, de la Chronique de Charles-Quint, du Dernier Roi d'Arles, etc.—Milton—Pope—Cowper—Chatterton—Canova[.] *Paris[:] Michel Levy Freres, Libraires-Editeurs[,] Rue Vivienne, 2 Bis[.] 1858[.] – Reproduction et traduction réservées –* First edition. 12mo, 321pp., half-title, contemporary one-half black leather, marbled paper over boards (a bit rubbed, joints slightly cracked), spine ruled in gilt with gilt lettering, marbled endpapers. A nice copy. The first chapter of 64 pp. is devoted to Milton.

96. Raub, Albert N. **THE NORMAL FIFTH READER.** *Philadelphia: Porter & Coates, (1878).* First edition thus. 8vo, 416pp., copyright and preface dated 1878, frontispiece portrait and other plates in black and white, original half maroon leather, brown cloth (a little worn, names, stamps, and doodles on endpapers), front cover lettered in black, spine lettered in gilt. An okay copy. Included is a poetical selection from *PL*: "*Morning Hymn of Adam and Eve*," and a brief biographical sketch. Uncommon, especially considering that it was designed for classroom use. The collection also has a variant edition, without the illustrations, in a variant publisher's binding.

97. Redivivus, Lucian [pseud.]. **PARADISE LOST**: Or, The Great Dragon Cast Out; Being A Full, True And Particular Account Of The Great and Dreadful Bloodless Battle That Was Fought In The Celestial Regions About 6000 Years Ago. By Lucian Redivivus. "Better to *reign* on earth than *serve* in heaven." "Laugh at al things, / Great and small things." Lord Byron. – "L'univers perdu pour une pomme, / Et Dieu, pour le damner, créant le premier homme." *Boston: Published By Josiah P. Mendum, At The Office Of The Boston Investigator. 1872*. First edition thus. Small 8vo, 101pp., original green cloth (a little rubbed, with stains on front cover), front cover lettered in gilt. Overall a good copy. An irreverent parody of Milton's poem with copious notes filled with quotations from earlier commentators on Milton and from the Bible. A highly eccentric and yet very interesting work. Uncommon.

98. Reed, Henry. **LECTURES ON ENGLISH LITERATURE**, From Chaucer to Tennyson. *Philadelphia: Parry & McMillan, Successors To A. Hart. Late Carey & Hart. 1855.* First edition. 12mo in 6s, 411pp., frontispiece portrait of Reed, copyright and preface dated 1855, original brown cloth (spine ends and corners worn), covers decorated in blind, spine lettered in gilt, with blind rules. A decent copy with early signature in pencil on fly-leaf. Included are two lectures on Milton.

99. Reed, Henry. **LECTURES ON THE BRITISH POETS**. In Two Volumes. *Philadelphia: Parry & McMillan, Successors To A. Hart. Late Carey & Hart. 1857.* 2 volumes. First edition. 8vo, 328pp.,+312+[14]pp., original brown cloth (a bit rubbed, spine ends chipped), covers decorated in blind, spines lettered in gilt. A nice set with fourteen pages of advertisements at the end of volume 2. Included is a lengthy lecture on "Milton"—on the man and his poetry (Lecture VI).

100. Rickard, Truman, and Hiram Orcutt. **CLASS BOOK OF PROSE AND POETRY**; Consisting Of Selections From The Best English And American Authors Designed As Exercises In Parsing; For The Use Of Common Schools And Academies. Revised and Enlarged Edition. *Boston: Published By Robert S. Davis & Co., Philadelphia: Keystone School And Church Furniture Co. New York: Baker, Pratt, & Co., 142 & 144 Grand Street. Chicago: Jansen, McClurg & Company. St. Louis: Gray, Baker, & Co. 1877.* Second, revised and enlarged edition. Slim 8vo, 144pp., original black cloth spine (a bit rubbed), printed green paper over boards repeating title page in black on front cover and advertisements on back cover (bit used, chipped at corners), marbled edges. A good copy, generally very fresh and clean inside. Designed for classroom use. Included are several poetical passages from Milton's *PL*: "Satan's Address to Beelzebub," the "Speech of Moloch," and "The Garden of Eden." The first edition was published in 1847. The collection has a copy of the 1850, second edition, "Boston: Published By Robert S. Davis," in original printed boards, well-used.

101. Ring, Max. **JOHN MILTON AND HIS TIMES**. An Historical Novel By Max Ring. Translated From The German, By F. Jordan. Complete In One Volume. With Illustrations by Gaston Fay. *New York: D. Appleton & Co., 90, 92 & 94 Grand Street. 1868.* First edition in English. 8vo, 308+4pp., wood-engraved frontispiece illustration and seven other wood-engraved illustrations by Gaston Fay, each with protective tissue guard, printed in double column, original dark green pebble cloth, blind rules on covers, spine lettered in gilt in-between decorative gilt pieces. A fine, tall copy with four pages of advertisements bound in at the end. The illustrations are biographical in nature and are not illustrations of any of Milton's poems. First published in German in 1857, this is the first edition in English, an American translation by F. Jordan. Scarce. Not in Hamilton (who had a number of other books illustrated by Fay). Stevens 2053.

The collection also has the second edition in English published by "John Heywood, Deanswood And Ridgefield, Manchester; I, Paternoster Buildings, London, 1889," with a frontispiece portrait of Milton engraved by Cochran after Cooper.

102. Rossetti, William Michael. **LIVES OF FAMOUS POETS**. A Companion Volume To The Series Moxon's Popular Poets. *London and New York: Ward, Lock, And Co., n.d. [ca. 1880s].* 8vo, xii+[1]+406+24pp. frontispiece portrait of Shakespeare, additional portraits and illustrations, red border around text, original decorated green cloth, front cover and spine elaborately decorated in black and gilt, with large gilt emblem incorporating "Moxon's Popular Poets" at center of front cover, decorated endpapers, a.e.g. A nice copy in an attractive publisher's binding, with contemporary signature (dated 1888) on fly-leaf. Included is a biographical chapter on Milton with a reproduction of Munkacsy's painting (although unattributed) of *Milton Dictating 'Paradise Lost'* (so-titled here).

103. Scott, William. **LESSONS IN ELOCUTION**; Or A Selection Of Pieces In Prose And Verse, For The Improvement Of Youth In Reading And Speaking By William Scott. To Which Are Prefixed Elements Of

Gesture, Illustrated By Four Plates; And Rules For Expressing With Propriety, The Various Passions, &c. Of The Mind. Also, An Appendix, Containing Lessons On A New Plan. From the last revised edition. *Concord, N. H.: Printed By Hill And Moore, And Sold By Them At The Franklin Bookstore, Sold also by all the principal booksellers. 1820.* 12mo in 6s, 384pp., contemporary calf (a little worn, spine chipped at top, lacking free endpapers, small tear at top right corner of title page without affecting any text, last page torn at lower right corner with loss of a few letters, pages age-browned). Scarce copy of an interesting early American reader designed for classroom use, with early signature (dated 1862) on back pastedown. Included are a number of poetical selections from Milton: in Section VIII ("In Reading"), "*L'Allegro*, or the Merry Man," "Adam and Eve's Morning Hymn," and "The Creation of the World"; in Part II, Section IV ("In Speaking"): "Moloch, the fallen Angel, to the Infernal Powers," and "Speech of Belial, advising Peace."

103A. (Cross-listing) Siddons, Sarah Kemble. **AN ABRIDGEMENT OF PARADISE LOST.** By Mrs. [Sarah Kemble] Siddons. *London: John Murray, 1822.* First edition, first issue of Mrs. Siddons's only book. See main listing under *PL* in Chapter II.

103B. (Cross-listing) Siddons, Sarah Kemble. **THE STORY OF OUR FIRST PARENTS,** Selected From Milton's *Paradise Lost,* For The Use Of Young Persons. *London: John Murray, 1822.* First edition, second issue. At some point during the publication of this work the title was altered from that of the preceding issue to the present title, with the new title being pasted to the stub of the canceled title. Both issues are of about equal scarcity. See main listing under *PL* in Chapter II.

104. Sotheby, Samuel Leigh. **RAMBLINGS IN THE ELUCIDATION OF THE AUTOGRAPH OF MILTON.** *London: Printed For The Author By Thomas Richard, And Sold By All Booksellers, 1861.* First and only edition. Large 4to, [iii]-xxxviii+141+[1]+142a-142b,+143-263pp.+[10]leaves (index), two frontispiece photographs of Milton tipped in (early photographs taken specifically for this edition, with subscript identification by Leigh), twenty-seven facsimile plates of various Milton manuscripts, signature and handwriting, decorated initial letters at the outset of each section, appendix, original full green morocco (slightly rubbed at corners, some foxing), covers with contrasting recessed tan panels with pictorial designs in black by Rigaud and J. L. Tupper portraying scenes from *PL*, decorative gilt border trim and gilt rules on covers, spine attractively gilt in compartments featuring large central lozenge of massed floral tools, floral and scrolling corner decoration, gilt-ruled raised bands, decorated endpapers with three progressive reductions of the cover illustrations printed on the pastedowns, t.e.g., others rough trimmed. A very nice copy in a splendid and well-preserved binding of

Sotheby's *Ramblings in the Elucidation of the Autograph of Milton.* London, 1861. First edition. Folio, original full green morocco, covers with contrasting recessed tan panels with pictorial designs in black by Rigaud and J. L. Tupper portraying scenes from *PL*. One of the more unusual 1860s bindings, executed by the accomplished John Wright. See #104.

the period, with the bookplates of Herman Blum, Henry Wheatley, and George Wheatley, and the signature in pencil of W. S. Jackson on fly-leaf. The two frontispieces are early photographs, one of a bust of Milton and the other of the Faithorne crayon drawing of Milton (now at Princeton University); both were photographed for the first time for this work. One of the more unusual 1860s bindings, executed by the accomplished John Wright. Probably produced in a small press run. Stevens 1693 (very modest commentary).

The book was put together by a descendant of the cofounder of the famous Sotheby auction house, who had acquired a wide knowledge of books and manuscripts as an auctioneer in the family business. Sotheby endeavors to identify Milton's amanuenses because he believed that a number of autograph documents supposedly penned by Milton himself were actually in the hand of others, dictated by Milton after he lost his sight. The book is at once "rambling" and a serious work filled with documentation. In the course of his work, Sotheby conveys much about Milton's life, his daughters, nephews, and friends.

105. Sotheby, Samuel Leigh. Variant of Preceding, in a variant binding (contemporary three-quarter morocco, marbled paper). Inserted at the front is a quantity of material related to the publication, including "Notice" of publication, a number of facsimile plates, including one of "the Handwriting of Milton," most are facsimiles of the Trinity MS. and a two-page autograph letter by Milton's biographer, Charles Symmons.

106. Spontini, Gasparo. **MILTON, OPERA** In un Atto e in Prosa dei Signori Jouy e Dieulafoy, Tradotta in versi Italiana da Luigi Balochi Posta In Musica Dedicata a Sua Maesta L'Imperatrice, Da Gaspare Spontini Maestro del Conservatorio di Napoli. Rappresentata per la prima volta sul Teatro dell'Opera Comica li 6 frimajo anno 13 (27, Novembre 1804) Prezzo 36th. le Parti Separate 30th. A Paris Chez Mlles Erard, Rue du Mail No. 37. Propriete des Editeurs. Enrege a la Bibliotheque Imle. *A Lyon, Chez Garnier, Place de la Comedie, No. 18. 529. n.d. [1804].* First edition. Large 4to, 209pp., engraved title page, engraved music, original speckled French calf (a little rubbed, without blank endpapers, a few small stamps throughout, initial publisher's catalogue lightly shaved at fore-edge), decorative gilt border trim on covers, gilt-decorated spine, red morocco label with gilt lettering, outer dentelles gilt. A fine, large copy. This is apparently the only known opera with Milton as its subject. Rare. Not in Parker; Not in Stevens.

107. Stockdale, Percival. **LECTURES ON THE TRULY EMINENT ENGLISH POETS**. By Percival Stockdale. [Quotation from Corregio.] In Two Volumes. *London, Printed By D. N. Shury, Berwick Street, Soho, For The Author: And Sold By Mess. Longman, Hurst, Rees, And Orme, Paternoster Row; And W. Clarke, New Bond Street. 1807.* 2 volumes. First edition. Tall 8vo, xi+607+16pp.,+656pp., frontispiece portrait of Percival Stockdale, volume 1, original light blue boards (spines chipped, some foxing), edges untrimmed and completely unopened, printed green paper labels (one defective). A nice set with eighteen pages of advertisements (dated March 1, 1807) bound in at the end. An eighteenth-century litterateur and personal friend of Johnson, Stockdale was seventy-one when this eccentric critique appeared. Excellent on Milton and on Johnson on Milton. Two full chapters are devoted to Milton. Scarce. Stevens 1849.

108. Symmons, Charles. **THE LIFE OF JOHN MILTON**. By Charles Symmons, D.D. Of Jesus College, Oxford. [Latin Quotations from Defen. secund. and from Dr. George.] *London: Printed By T. Bensley, Bolt Court, For J. Johnson; Nichols and Son; F. C. & J. Rivington; et al., 1806.* First edition. 8vo, xi+[i]+566pp.+[10-page index unpaginated], contemporary speckled calf (a little worn, joints cracked, first few leaves age-browned), decorative gilt border trim on covers, red morocco label with gilt lettering on spine, marbled endpapers. A good copy with early armorial bookplate. Published as part of Symmons's 1806 edition

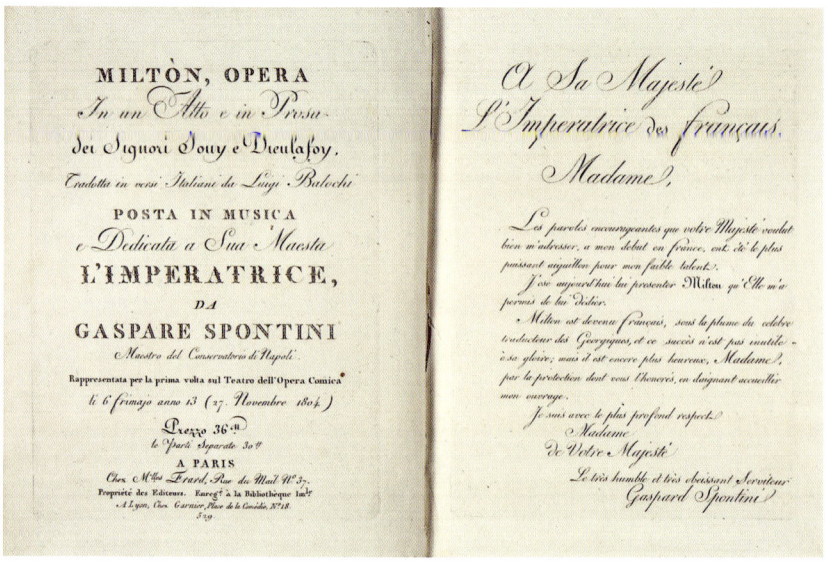

Spontini, Gasplaro. *Milton, Opera*. Tradotta in versi Italiana da Luigi Balochi Posta In Musica Dedicata a Sua Maesta L'Imperatrice. A Paris, chex Mlles Erard, n.d. (1804). First edition. Large 4to. The only opera known with Milton as its subject. See #106.

of *Milton's Prose Works* (see set in Chapter II). Uncommon. Stevens 1650.

109. Symmons, Charles. THE LIFE OF JOHN MILTON. By Charles Symmons, D.D. Of Jesus College, Oxford. Second Edition. [Latin Quotations from Defen. secund. and from Dr. George.] *London: Printed By T. Bensley, Bolt Court, Fleet-Street, For Nichols and Sons, F. C. & J. Rivington; et al., 1810*. Second edition; first separate edition (enlarged and revised). 8vo, 646pp.+[12-page unpaginated index], engraved frontispiece portrait sketch of Milton engraved by H. Meyer "from a Drawing by Mr. Cipriani in the Possession of the Rev. Dr. Disney" ("Published April 16. 1810, by T. Cadell and W. Davies Strand London"), contemporary diced calf (somewhat worn, spine chipped, especially at bottom, front cover reattached), covers decorated with gilt border trim, spine decorated in gilt within the panels, gilt lettering, thick raised bands decorated in gilt trim, marbled endpapers and edges. A good copy with early armorial bookplate. Symmons added an entirely new twenty-five-page preface to this edition. The edition contains a great deal of new material as well as a pointed attack on Hayley's reworking of Cowper's Milton in the 1808 *Latin and Italian Poems* (see copy in Chapter II), as well as the just-published 1810 edition of *PW* (see copy in Chapter II). Uncommon.

110. Taine, H. A. HISTORY OF ENGLISH LITERATURE Translated from the French by H. Van Laun[,] One of the Master at the Edinburgh Academy. *London: Chatto & Windus, Piccadilly[,] 1877*. 4 volumes. 8vo, xvi+433,+xi+477,+xiv+463,+xviii+476+40pp., half-title (with "New Edition Printed by R. & R. Clark, Edinburgh" on verso) each volume, ivy wreath on title page each volume, preface (dated 1773) volume 1, original red silk (a little worn, spines darkened and ends chipped), printed paper labels (darkened), edges untrimmed. A good set, very clean internally. Chapter VI, volume 2, is devoted to Milton.

111. Taine, H. A. HISTORY OF ENGLISH LITERATURE. By H. A. Taine, D.C.L. Translated From The French By H. Van Laun, One of the Master at the Edinburgh Academy. Complete In One Volume. *New York: Published By T. Y. Crowell, n.d. [ca. 1879]*. First edition thus. 8vo, 722pp., printed in double column, original reddish-brown cloth (a bit rubbed), front cover and spine lettered in gilt, dark green endpapers. A nice copy with contemporary signature (dated 1879) on front blank. Chapter VI, Book II, is devoted to Milton.

112. [Theatre Broadside] Broadside for the THEATRE ROYAL, COVENT-GARDEN. This present Saturday, April 15, 1815, with be acted (11th time) the Play of The Stranger. The Stranger acted by Mr. Kemble . . . After which, the Farce of Love, Law & Physick . . . Miss O'Neill Will Perform . . . On Thursday Juliet. And Mr. Kemble Will Perform On Monday, Brutus. On Wednesday, Macbeth. No Orders can be admitted . . . The Publick are respectfully informed that Milton's Masque of Comus, has been for a long time in preparation, and will be speedily produced—With every Novelty in the cast of Characters, the Scenery, Machinery, Decorations, &c. &c. Tall, single sheet, 12 ½" × 7", (small hole and slight tear at bottom left, not affecting text). A nice example of an early nineteenth-century theatre broadside, in very good condition. Scarce.

113. Todd, Rev. Henry John. SOME ACCOUNT OF THE LIFE AND WRITINGS OF JOHN MILTON. By The Rev. H. J. Todd, M.A. F.S.A. Rector Of Allhallows, Lombard-Street, &c. The Second Edition, With Additions, And With A Verbal Index To The Whole Of Milton's Poetry. *London: Printed for J. Johnson; R. Baldwin; et al.; and Mathews and Leigh: By Law and Gilbert, St. John's-Square, Clerkenwell. 1809*. Second edition, enlarged; first separate (stand-alone) edition. Large 8vo, vi+[ii]+217+[2]pp.[+403-page unpaginated index], half-title, engraved frontispiece portrait by T. Simpson after Faithorne, engraved by J. Collyer, half-title for "Verbal Index To The Poetry Of Milton," contemporary half white paper, marbled paper over boards (a bit rubbed and age-darkened, joints cracked, some occasional light foxing), printed paper labels, edges untrimmed. A nice copy. Scarce. Stevens 1850.

The first edition (without the *"Verbal Index"*) appeared in 1801 together with six-volume edition of Milton's *PW* edited by Todd (see sets in Chapter II); the second and expanded edition (present edition) adds the *"Verbal Index"* as volume 1 to the 1809 six-volume edition of Milton's *PW* edited by Todd (see sets in Chapter II). This edition is of particular significance not only for Todd's scholarly life of Milton but also for his bringing together for the first time the various critical commentaries and remarks on Milton, from Patrick Hume and Joseph Addison through Dr. Samuel Johnson, Daniel Webb, and Thomas Birch to Charles Dunster and Robert Southey, among many others. Also, this is the sole edition to contain the extensive series of concordances with separate sections for English, Greek, Latin, and Italian words used by Milton in all his poetry. The index was a massive undertaking and is still valuable today. A limited number of copies of the index were printed with a distinct title page, as here, and sold separately.

114. Todd, Rev. Henry John. Variant of Preceding. SOME ACCOUNT OF THE LIFE AND WRITINGS OF JOHN MILTON . . . The Second Edition, With

Additions, And With A Verbal Index To The Whole Of Milton's Poetry. *London: Printed for J. Johnson et al., 1809.* Second edition, enlarged; first separate edition. Tall 8vo, vi+[ii]+217pp., half-title, engraved frontispiece portrait by T. Simpson after Faithorne, engraved by J. Collyer, near-contemporary weave linen (some light wear with spine ends chipped, outer margins of frontispiece portrait and final few leaves a bit foxed), red morocco label with gilt lettering and gilt rules on spine, edges untrimmed. Large paper copy. A very good stout copy with text generally clean and crisp within, unusually tall, with wide margins, probably the large paper issue. While this is clearly one of the copies printed with a distinct title page and sold separately, this copy is without the verbal index to Milton's poetry referred to in the title, apparently often excluded from this stand-alone edition of the *Life*. Scarce.

115. Todd, Rev. Henry John. SOME ACCOUNT OF THE LIFE AND WRITINGS OF JOHN MILTON, Derived Principally From Documents in his Majesty's State-Paper Office. Now First Published. By The Rev. H. J. Todd, M.A. F.S.A. & R.S.L. Chaplain In Ordinary To His Majesty, And Rector Of Settrington, Country Of York. *London: Printed for C. And J. Rivington, et al., 1826.* Third edition. 8vo, vi+[ii]+370+lxvii+[1]pp., contemporary diced Russia (rebacked, edges repaired, some foxing, lacking frontispiece portrait), gilt rules on covers and spine, spine lettered in gilt, raised bands, marbled endpapers and edges. Edmund Blunden's copy with his signature on front blank. "Now First Published" on the title page refers to the many documents first included in this "third edition . . . greatly augmented with original documents illustrating the private and publick character of Milton, which have long been hidden . . . and till now have never been published" (Preface). Todd's "enlarged biography . . . in a separate volume" (Preface) is an important addition to his second edition in 1809. Scarce. Stevens 1663.

116. Watkins, John. CHARACTERISTIC ANECDOTES OF MEN OF LEARNING AND GENIUS, NATIVES OF GREAT-BRITAIN AND IRELAND, During The Last Three Centuries. Indicative Of Their Manners, Opinions, Habits, And Peculiarities, Interspersed With Reflections, And Historical And Literary Illustrations. By John Watkins, LL.D. *Albion Press: Printed For James Cundee, Ivy-Lane, Paternoster-Row, London. 1808.* First edition. 8vo, 552+10pp., preface (dated "London, December 1, 1807"), index at the end, rebound in brown imitation leather (several pages slightly embrowned, new endpapers), spine lettered in gilt. A nice copy. Among the various biographical sketches is a rather lengthy one of Milton (pp. 197–228). Other biographical sketches include Shakespeare, Addison, Swift, and Samuel Johnson (with a brief discussion of Milton herein).

Extra-Illustrated

117. White, T. Holt. A REVIEW OF JOHNSON'S CRITICISM ON THE STYLE OF MILTON'S ENGLISH PROSE; With Strictures On The Introduction Of Latin Idioms Into The English Language. By Thomas Holt White, Esq. [Greek Quotation.] [*London:*] *Printed For R. Hunter, Successor To Mr. Johnson, No. 72, St. Paul's Churchyard. 1818.* First edition. The original eighty-seven-page octavo first edition, with preface, notes, and "Excursive Illustrations" by White, including final advertisement leaf for the publication soon of *Areopagitica* by R. Hunter, inlaid to large folio size and extra-illustrated with portraits, prints, engravings, original drawings by Anna White including on oval watercolor of Thomas Holt White, copied by Anna White from the original by Smart, several full-page pencil portraits of Sir William Jones, of Richard Porson, and smaller ones of Sir Philip Sidney, Queen Elizabeth, and others, along with numerous engravings, including full-page eighteenth-century engravings of Milton and a miniature of him, engravings of Johnson, Addison and many more, all placed appropriately within the "Review" as named or discussed; bound Regency style in full hard-grained purple morocco (a bit scuffed, front joint repaired), gilt rules on covers with decorative gilt corner devices, spine decorated in gilt by compartments, raised bands, inner and outer dentelles ruled in gilt, a.e.g., armorial bookplate of Rashleigh Holt-White. Included are eleven portraits of Milton. A remarkable volume, assembled during the early part of the nineteenth century. See White's important edition of *Areopagitica* (1818) in Chapter II.

118. Wiffen, J. H., Esq. TO A LADY, WITH A LEAF GATHERED FROM THE MULBERRY-TREE PLANTED BY MILTON IN THE GARDENS OF CHRIST COLLEGE, CAMBRIDGE [In] FORGET ME NOT: A Christmas And New Year's Present for 1825. *London. Published by R. Ackermann[.]* 12mo, vii+[i]+303+[1]pp., engraved frontispiece illustration plate, and eleven additional engraved illustration plates, each with a protective tissue guard, contemporary full black morocco (a bit rubbed along joints and at spine ends), finely tooled wide decorative border trim in gilt on covers, spine lettered and decorated in gilt with a small gilt harp in each panel, wide raised bands with decorative gilt trim, inner and outer dentelles finely tooled in gilt, a.e.g. A lovely copy. See the story, *Milton's Mulberry Tree* also listed here under Milton.

119. [Willoughby]. SO MUCH OF THE DIARY OF LADY WILLOUGHBY AS RELATES TO HER DOMESTIC HISTORY, & to the Eventful Period of the Reign of Charles the First, the Protectorate, and the Restoration. *London: Longmans, Green, Reader, and Dyer, over against Warwick Lane, in the City of London. 1873.* 8vo, 287pp., half-title, double black border around text, decorative head- and tailpieces, decorated initials, contemporary full purple morocco (spine faded), large central gilt device on covers, spine lettered in gilt, raised bands, inner dentelles finely tooled in gilt, outer dentelles ruled in gilt, marbled endpapers, a.e.g. A lovely copy, handsomely printed by the Chiswick Press, in the style of the seventeenth century, as stated on the final leaf. The first edition of *Lady Willoughby's Diary*, written by Mrs. Hannah Mary Rathbone, appeared in 1844 and was followed in 1849–50 by Anne Manning's *The Maiden And Married Life Of Mary Powell, Afterwards Mistress Milton* (also listed here). Manning's book was a successful attempt to capitalize on the market for mock diaries along the lines of *Lady Willoughby's Diary*.

120. Wilson, James. BIOGRAPHY OF THE BLIND: Or, Lives Of Such As Have Distinguished Themselves As Poets, Philosophers, Artists, &c. By James Wilson, Who Has Been Blind From His Infancy. Third Edition. [Quotation Unidentified.] *Birmingham: Printed By J. W. Showell, 46, New-Street, And Sold Only By The Author. 1835.* Third edition. 12mo in 6s, xxv+[i]+300pp., original speckled brown paper over boards, printed paper label on spine (aged), Signet Society Writers bookplate on front pastedown. A good copy. A chapter is devoted to Milton (pp. 11–27). "The present edition is very much improved, and enlarged" ("Introduction" by Wilson). Scarce.

D. TWENTIETH-CENTURY MILTONIANA

The following have been selected to reflect the range of some 390 Twentieth-century Miltoniana holdings in the collection. In the twentieth century the line between "Miltoniana" and "Criticism" is very distinct. Occasionally selections chosen here blur that line primarily because critical study is not represented in this book, although it is strongly represented in the collection by more than 1,400 critical studies and an additional almost 100 important reference studies of Milton.

1. Ackroyd, Peter. MILTON IN AMERICA. *(London:) Sinclair-Stevenson, (1996).* First London edition. 8vo, 277pp., half-title, decorative headpieces, original orange cloth, spine lettered in black, brown endpapers, printed publisher's wrappers with reproduction in color of portrait sketch of Milton as a Native American by Dmitri Pavlenski on brown front cover. A fine copy. Contrary to a *New York Times* review by Tony Tanner that emphasizes that this novel is a "counterfactual" that is ultimately "pointless," the *Daily Mail* calls Ackroyd's work "Mesmerising, macabre and totally brilliant," and the *Observer* calls it "Gripping . . . a pungently vivid tale of London streets" (cited on back cover). The story is premised upon the following question: What if Milton (Cromwell's secretary) anticipated the king's return to London and had decided to flee England?

2. Ackroyd, Peter. MILTON IN AMERICA. *Nan A. Talese[,] Doubleday[,] New York[,] London[,] Toronto[,] Sydney[,] Auckland[,] (1997).* First American edition. 8vo, 307pp., half-title, black cloth spine, black paper boards, spine lettered in gilt, gold endpapers, fore-edge untrimmed, printed publisher's wrappers with reproduction in color of Blake engraving on front cover ("Jacket Design By Russell Gordon" noted on inside back flap). A fine copy.

3. Allen, B. Sprague. TIDES IN ENGLISH TASTE (1619-1800): A Background For The Study Of Literature. *Cambridge, Mass.: 1937. 2 volumes.* First edition. Royal 8vo, xxvii+269pp.,+282pp., half-title each volume, eighty plates, original blue cloth, spine lettered in gilt, t.e.g., others untrimmed, partially unopened, printed publisher's wrappers (spines faded). A fine set with several related items laid in: NYU Department of English invitation to honor Allen "on the occasion of the publication of his book *Tides In English Taste* . . . March 11, 1937"; advertisement leaf for Harvard University Press (including Allen's *Tides In English Taste*); two pages of typed notes on Allen's book (unsigned and unattributed); and the university newspaper obituary on Allen (dated March 22, 1935). Included in volume 2 is a discussion of Milton's "Garden of Eden" in *PL* (pp. 116–22), with two illustrations of *Eden*, one for *L'Adamo* and one by Rubens. Excellent survey of the changes in seventeenth- and eighteenth-century English taste. Uncommon.

4. Auslander, Joseph and Frank Ernest Hill. THE WINGED HORSE: The Story of the Poets and their Poetry . . . with decorations by Paul Honore and a bibliography by Theresa West Elmendorf. *Garden City, N.Y.: Doubleday, Doran & Company, Inc., 1927.* First edition. 8vo, xv+451pp., half-title, full-page and headpiece illustrations in black and white, original black cloth, front cover stamped with title and illustration of "The Winged Horse" in yellow, spine lettered in yellow with decorative emblem, illustrated green endpapers, t.e. yellow, others untrimmed. A very nice copy. Included is a chapter on Milton (Chapter XV: "Milton And His Angels"), with decorative vignette headpiece in black and white at outset of the chapter.

The collection also has two copies of the second edition published in 1928 in variant publisher's bindings, one virtually mint in fine publisher's wrappers, and a copy published in 1938, in similar publisher's binding, all three "Garden City, N.Y.: Doubleday, Doran & Company, Inc."

5. Beers, Henry A. **MILTON'S TERCENTENARY.** An address delivered before the Modern Language Club of Yale University on Milton's Three Hundredth Birthday. *New Haven[:] Yale University Press[,] 1910.* First edition. 8vo, 37pp., half-title, original boards, white cloth spine (bit dirtied), printed paper label on front cover, memorial prize bookplate on front pastedown, fore- and bottom edges untrimmed. A nice copy. Inscribed to "John Jay Chapman from his obliged friend and admirer Geo. Dudley Legmason" (dated 1920) with a long note regarding the memorial bookplate (apparently specially designed here) and Professor Beers. Scarce.

6. Belloc, Hilaire. **MILTON** By Hilaire Belloc[.] *Philadelphia[:] J. B. Lippincott Company[,] London[,] 1935.* First American edition. 8vo, 313pp., half-title (with a listing of "Books By Hilaire Belloc" on verso), frontispiece portrait plate of "John Milton By Jonathan Richardson," half-title for each chapter, "with 8 illustrations in doubleton and 12 maps," original red cloth, spine lettered in gilt, t.e. red, fore- and bottom edges untrimmed. A nice copy in printed gold publisher's wrappers (a bit worn), with portrait of Milton after Faithorne by Politzer in the center against a red background.

7. Blake, William. **MILTON, A POEM.** *This facsimile of Blake's MILTON a Poem is published by The Trianon Press for The William Blake Trust[,] London[,] 1967.* Demy 4to, fifty leaves reproducing in color facsimile the illustrations of Blake including ten full-page and eleven half-page plates+XVIIpp. (last page of Keynes's text hand-numbered in red)+[1 blank leaf]+[25 facsimile leaves, recto only), "Description And Bibliographical Statement" by Sir Geoffrey Keynes, full brown morocco (spine a little faded), spine lettered in gilt. A lovely copy in original slipcase, marbled paper over boards with brown morocco edge in front. One of twenty special copies of the Edition de Luxe of an edition limited to 400 copies, containing a series of progressive plates, collotype proofs, and an original guide sheet and stencil. With folded original prospectus offering the above edition de luxe for sale through Bernard Quaritch Ltd., ca. 1968. In fine condition.

8. [Blake, William] **WILLIAM BLAKE[:] MILTON A POEM** and the Final Illuminated Works: *The Ghost Of Abel On Homer's Poetry* [and] *On Virgil Laocoon* Edited with Introductions and Notes by Robert N. Essick and Joseph Viscomi[.] Blake's Illuminated Books Volume 5 General Editor David Bindman[.] *The William Blake Trust / Princeton University Press[,] (1993).* First edition thus. 4to, 286pp., half-title, sixty-three illustration plates, fifty-six in color and seven in black and white, half-title for "*Milton a Poem* The Text with commentary," plate-by-plate commentary, bibliography (as "Works Cited") at end, original brown cloth, spine lettered in gilt, tan endpapers, printed publisher's wrappers reproducing title page of *Milton* plate in color on front cover. A fine copy. This is the first-ever reproduction of the magnificent copy of *Milton* in the New York Public Library, presented here in full color and demonstrated by the editors as having been Blake's own copy. Blake's three final works in illuminated printing, *The Ghost of Abel*, *On Homer's Poetry* and *On Virgil*, and *Laocoon*, are also included in this volume, with illustrations in black and white.

9. Boas, Mrs. Frederick. **WITH MILTON AND THE CAVALIERS** By Mrs. Frederick Boas[,] Author Of 'English History For Children,' 'In Shakespeare's England[.]' *London: James Nisbet & Co., Limited, 21 Berners Street, 1904.* First edition. 8vo, viiii+336+8pp., half-title, frontispiece portrait plate of Milton "From the Painting by Van der Plaas in the National Portrait Gallery," protective tissue guard, additional portrait plates, original green cloth (a bit worn and faded with small waterstain at top outer corner of back cover), gilt lettering on front cover with central gilt medallion incorporating Milton vignette in gilt relief, spine lettered in gilt, t e g, others untrimmed. All in all, a good copy in an attractive publisher's binding. Included is a chapter on Milton, as well as chapters on Charles I and Cromwell, each with portrait. Stevens 2260.

The collection also has a copy of the second edition published in 1905 in "New York[:] James Pott And Company[;] London[:] James Nisbet & Co., Limited," in an identical binding in red cloth.

10. Bridges, Robert. **MILTON'S PROSODY** By Robert Bridges & **CLASSICAL METERS IN ENGLISH VERSE** by William Johnson Stone[.] *Oxford: [Henry Frowde], 1901.* Second edition, expanded. 8vo, vi+175pp., decorative border trim in black on title page, half-title for each work, indexes, original green cloth (spine a bit faded and a little rubbed at top and bottom), spine lettered in blind, edges untrimmed and partially unopened. A very nice copy with early ownership signature in a neat hand on fly-leaf. The first edition was published in 1893 in a limited edition of 250 copies (see copy with Nineteenth-century Miltoniana). As with that edition, this and the following certainly fall in the category of critical study, but space precludes listing the sizable number of critical studies in the collection. Scarce. Stevens 2256.

Presentation Copy from Robert Bridges to John Masefield

11. Bridges, Robert. **MILTON'S PROSODY WITH A CHAPTER ON ACCENTUAL VERSE & NOTES** by Robert Bridges[.] Revised Final Edition. *Oxford[: Humphrey Milford, Oxford University Press], 1921*. Third and final edition, revised. 8vo, viii+119pp., half-title, decorative border trim on title page with central decorative piece incorporating "Revised Final Edition," original blue cloth, central gilt device on front cover and spine, spine lettered in gilt, edges untrimmed, printed publisher's wrappers (bit aged and a little stained), in a protective plastic cover. Presentation copy to John Masefield with presentation inscription by Robert Bridges on front blank. A fine copy. Stevens 2267.

12. Brown, Eleanor Gertrude. **MILTON'S BLINDNESS** By Eleanor Gertrude Brown[.] *New York: Morningside Heights[,] Columbia University Press[,] 1934*. First edition. 8vo, vi+167+ [1]pp., half-title ("Columbia University Studies In English And Comparative Literature"), emblem of the press on title page, half-title for each of the four parts, bibliography and index at the end, original red cloth, blind emblem of the press at center of front cover, two black labels with gilt lettering and decorative gilt rules on spine. A nice copy. Laid in: printed card "With the Compliments of the Author." The definitive edition which studies the probable cause of Milton's blindness (glaucoma) and investigates all the autobiographical references to it, the blindness as reflected in his poetry, and the effects on his work. The collection also has a copy of the reprint edition published by Octagon Books, Inc., in 1968.

13. [Bush, Douglas.] **A MILTON EVENING IN HONOR OF DOUGLAS BUSH AND C. S. LEWIS**. *New York City: Modern Language Association, December 28, 1954*. Slim 8vo, 16pp., pamphlet, facsimile of Lewis's letter to the society, original printed stiff paper wrappers (some ballpoint marks on a few pages). In very good condition. Laid in: three contemporary letters from society officers (Wm. Hunter and Walter Bowman) and a list of Milton Society members 1954. A nice piece of Miltoniana. Scarce.

14. Byron, May. **A DAY WITH JOHN MILTON** By May Byron[.] *Hodder & Stoughton[,] n.d. [ca. 1915]*. First (and only) edition. Slim 8vo, unpaginated (twenty-six leaves, including four illustration plates), half-title with an unattributed sketch of Milton in black with lines illustrated by frontispiece printed on verso, frontispiece illustration plate in color plus four additional illustration plates in color, figure of an angel holding a sword in red on title page, original gray boards, unattributed portrait of Milton in color tipped in at center of front cover within dark maroon border frame ruled in gilt, with a figure of an angel holding a sword in dark maroon with gilt outline at top left and floral piece in dark maroon with gilt outline at top right, "Milton" lettered in black within gilt outline at the top and "*Days With The Poets*" similarly lettered at the bottom, initials of the press in gilt within laurel wreath in gilt at center of back cover. A nice copy in which the story of Milton's day is told from early rising to bedtime shortly after Marvell bids adieu, with Milton's own poetry quoted to define the poet's moods at various times. Included among the illustration plates in color, each signed "S. Meteyard," with the lines illustrated quoted on the leaf preceding, are the following: (1) *Paradise Lost*, Book XII "They, hand in hand . . . " (as frontispiece); (2) Vacation Exercise—" . . . for at thy birth / The Fairy ladies danced . . . "; (3) *Comus*—"Sabrina rises attended by water nymphs . . . "; (4) *Paradise Lost*, Book II—"Satan with less toil and now with ease . . . "; (5) *Il Penseroso*—"And may at last my weary age / Find out the peaceful hermitage . . . "

15. Byse, Fanny. **MILTON ON THE CONTINENT**: A Key To *L'Allegro* & *Il Penseroso*. With Several Illustrations, A Historical Chart, And An Original Portrait Of Galileo. By Mrs. Fanny Byse. *London: Elliot Stock, 62, Paternoster Row, E.C. Lausanne: Roussy's English Library[,] 1903*. First edition. Small 8vo, 77pp.+folding chart, frontispiece portrait of Galileo, several other illustrations, "Historical Chart of Milton's Contemporaries At The Time Of His Continental Tour, 1638–1639," original wrappers, gilt lettering on front cover and spine, edges untrimmed. Very nice presentation copy inscribed "From the Authoress London 1910." Scarce. Stevens 545.

The collection also has the Norwood Editions reprint published in 1976 and the Richard West reprint published in 1977, each without the illustrations and each in a limited edition of 100 copies.

16. Cecil, Lord David. **THE ENGLISH POETS**. With 12 Plates In Colour And 13 Illustrations In Black & White. *Published for Penns In The Rocks Press by William*

Collins Of London[,] 1941. First edition. Small 4to, 48pp., half-title, twelve plates in color and thirteen illustrations in color and in black and white, original printed light blue paper boards (a bit rubbed). A good copy. Included is a color plate of Milton (twenty-one) by Van der Gucht and a discussion of the poet (pp. 18–22). See also W. J. Turner's *Romance Of English Literature* (1944 edition) and *Impressions Of English Literature* (1947 edition), both of which reprint Cecil's *The English Poets*.

16A. (Cross-listing) Collins, John Churton. **MILTON.** [In] **POETS' COUNTRY** Edited By Andrew Lang. *London, 1907, pp. 116–26.* Stevens 2272. See main listing under *Lang*.

17. Cooke, John. **JOHN MILTON: 1608-1674.** By John Cooke, M.A. A Lecture, delivered in the Parochial Hall, St. Bartholomew's, Dublin, on the occasion of Milton's Tercentenary, December 9, 1908. *Dublin: Hodges, Figgis, & Co., Limited[,] Publishers To The University[,] (1909).* First edition. Small 8vo, 56pp., half-title, red initial letter, one-quarter white buckram, gray paper boards, title page in red and black, t.e.g. Presentation copy from the author with inscription (dated 1909) on fly-leaf. A very fine copy, nicely printed on high-quality paper by "Ballantyne, Hanson & Co. Edinburgh & London." Scarce. Stevens 2298.

18. Corkran, Alice. **THE POETS' CORNER OR HAUNTS AND HOMES OF THE POETS.** Illustrated by Allan Barraud, with Introduction by Fred E. Weatherly. *London: Ernest Nister: 24 St. Bride Street E.C. New York: E. P. Dutton & Co. 31 West Twenty Third Street. Printed by E. Nister at Nuremberg (Bavaria), n.d. (1900).* Square 8vo, [66pp. unpaginated], decorated half-title, illustrated frontispiece portrait of Shakespeare memorial and Holy Trinity Church, Stratford-on-Avon, decorated title page, numerous other illustrations, original decorated blue-green cloth, illustration of church window on front cover with gold banner incorporating title, spine lettered in black, a.e.g. A very nice copy with contemporary inscription (dated "Christmas, [19]00") on half-title. Included is a chapter on Milton, with a biographical sketch of the poet and two vignette illustrations (one of Chalfont, St. Giles, the other of the Bay of Naples). Scarce. Not in Stevens.

19. Crosby, H. Lamar. **THE VICE OF VERSES** and Other Slanderous Rhymes Concerning Famous Philosophers by H. Lamar Crosby, Jr. Professor of Philosophy, Emeritus[,] Hollins College[.] Illustrations by Joe Bascom. *The Ten-Thirty Press[,] New York[,] (1984).* First edition. 8vo, viii+87pp., illustrations, paperback. In good condition. Presentation copy inscribed on verso of front cover: "To Bob Taylor Regards from Lamar & Louise [Crosby], Jan. 1985." Included is a verse on *PL* with an illustration by Joe Bascom. The verse is described in the *preface*: "We know we can be argued down by Milton as he justifies God's ways to men . . . but what a joyful start we experience when, in the twelve light-verse lines of his own '*Paradise Lost*,' Crosby gets in his theologically disquieting plea for 'fair play' for poor Eve and, by implication, for 'the whole included race.' That's us!"

20. Cunliffe, J. W. **PICTURED STORY OF ENGLISH LITERATURE:** From Its Beginnings To The Present Day. Student's Edition. *D. Appleton-Century Company Incorporated[,] New York [And] London[,] (1933).* First edition. Large 8vo, xxxiii+[1]+436pp., frontispiece illustration of "British Museum Reading Room," numerous additional illustrations, original purple cloth, central emblem in blind on front cover, spine lettered in gilt, index. Included is a long section on Milton, with several full-page reproductions of Milton portraits and facsimiles of title pages.

21. Darbishire, Helen, editor. **THE EARLY LIVES OF MILTON** Edited with Introduction and Notes by Helen Darbishire[.] *London[:] Constable & Co[.] Ltd[,] 1932.* First edition. 8vo, lxi+353pp., half-title with a list of "Standard Literary Lives" on verso, frontispiece portrait plate reproducing frontispiece portrait of Milton to J. Richardson's *Explanatory Notes And Remarks On Milton's Paradise Lost* (see copy with Eighteenth-century Miltoniana), five additional plates reproducing various manuscripts connected to Milton, index at the end, original blue cloth, spine lettered in gilt. A nice copy in printed publisher's wrappers (a bit worn).

22. Drinkwater, John. **THE OUTLINE OF LITERATURE.** Edited By John Drinkwater[.] *London: George Newnes Limited[,] Southampton St. Strand W.C.2. n.d. [ca. 1930]. 2 volumes.* Large 8vo, 640pp. continuous (312pp., volume 1), frontispiece illustration in color each volume, title page lettered in blue, with decorative border trim in color, central emblem in color, illustrations throughout in color and in black and white, index at the end, original green cloth (a bit rubbed, spine of volume 1 a little faded), covers ruled in blind, front covers and spines lettered in gilt, red speckled edges. A nice set with early bookplate on front pastedown of each volume. In volume 1 is a chapter on Milton, with five illustration plates in black and white, including "*Samson Agonistes* From the painting by G. F. Watts" (full-page plate), "'Marvell's Last Meeting With Milton' By G. H. Boughton," and "Milton Dictating *SA* From a painting by J. C. Horsley" (full-page illustration).

The collection also has the three-volume edition "New York And London: G. P. Putnam's Sons, The Knickerbocker Press, (1926)," second edition.

23. French, J. Milton, Editor. **THE LIFE RECORDS OF JOHN MILTON.** Edited By J. Milton French. *Rutgers University Press[,] New Brunswick, New Jersey[,] 1949-1958. 5 volumes.* First edition each volume. Royal 8vo, x+[1]+446pp.,+vi+[1]+395pp.,+ii+[1]+470pp.,+[2]+482pp., +[viii]+[1]+518pp., half-title each volume, frontispiece portrait of Milton in each volume: at age ten, volume 1, at age twenty-one, volume 2, "From A Portrait Formerly Owned By Charles Lamb," volume 3, "Bayfordbury Portrait," volume 4, "Faithorne Portrait," volume 5, index at the end of each volume, original green buckram, spine lettered in gilt. A nice set, volumes 4 and 5 in printed publisher's wrappers (a bit rubbed), these volumes (together with an additional volume 3) belonged to Milton scholar Holly Hanford, inscribed to him on fly-leaf of volume 5 by Elva French and dated 1965. An invaluable resource.

24. Fuller, Edmund. **JOHN MILTON** By Edmund Fuller[.] Pictures by Robert Ball[.] *New York And London[:] Harper & Brothers Publishers(, 1944).* First edition. 8vo, 238pp., half-title, frontispiece illustration sketch of full-figured Milton and seven additional full-page illustrations by Robert Ball, a second half-title before "Chapter I," original cream cloth, Milton's initials in red on front cover, title in red on spine, publisher's wrappers in black and white with red lettering and an illustration on front cover. The wrappers are a bit worn, otherwise a nice copy with a presentation inscription written in ink by Fuller to a friend on fly-leaf, dated 1944. Written with a smooth, lively style, Fuller "one of America's foremost authors and critics brings to life for young people the passionate, fearless, fighting, brilliant man who was John Milton, against the rich and turbulent background of his times," front flap of dust jacket of second edition, a copy of which is also in the collection, published by "The Seabury Press[,] New York[,] (1967)." See *John Milton Clarion Voice of Freedom* by Flora Strousse (1962) a life of Milton also written for young people.

25. Garnett, Richard. **ENGLISH LITERATURE.** An Illustrated Record In Four Volumes. *London: William Heinemann; New York: The Macmillan Company, 1903. 4 volumes.* First edition. 4to, xv+368pp.,+xiv+389pp.,+xii+381pp.,+xii+462pp., color frontispiece each volume, numerous facsimiles and illustrations, some full-page color, original red buckram (a bit worn), gilt lettering on spine, gilt figure on covers, t.e.g., others untrimmed. Publisher's presentation copy with blind stamp "Presentation Copy" on title page, volume 1, and with "Review Presentation" slip tipped in before title page. Extra-illustrated, with various miscellaneous clippings, illustrations, and facsimiles inserted (some are just laid in). A very good set. Two major sections in volume 3, "From Milton To Johnson by Edmund Gosse," are devoted to Milton; included also are a number of facsimiles of portraits, title pages, and various Milton-related items along with a full-page color portrait after Faithorne as the frontispiece to volume 2.

26. Gosse, Edmund. **MODERN ENGLISH LITERATURE: A SHORT HISTORY.** New and Revised Edition With Seventy-two Plates. *London[:] William Heinemann, mcmv.* 8vo, x+[1]+420pp., half-title, frontispiece portrait of Chaucer, title page in red and black, numerous engraved portraits, original brown cloth (a bit rubbed, tear at top of spine), front cover decorated in black trim with red lettering, lettered in gilt and red with black trim, t.e.g., others untrimmed. A nice copy. Included is a section on Milton with a reproduction of a portrait engraved after Van der Plaas (p. 164). The first edition was published in 1897; this is a "New and Revised [Portrait] Edition."

27. Graves, Robert. **THE STORY OF MARIE POWELL, WIFE TO MR. MILTON** by Robert Graves With two halftone plates[.] *Cassell And Company Ltd. London, Toronto, Melbourne and Sydney[,] (1943).* First edition. Small 8vo in 16s, viii+372pp., half-title ("Wife To Mr. Milton," with other "Historical Novels By Robert Graves" printed on verso), frontispiece plate in black and white (map of "Oxford And Its Environs"), on verso of title page within a small emblem of book at the top ("Book Production War Economy Standard") and beneath ("This Book Is Produced In Complete Conformity With the Authorised Economy Standards") in the middle ("First published In Great Britain, 1943"), and at the bottom ("Printed in Great Britain by Wyman & Sons Limited, London, Reading and Fakenham F.143"), a second black-and-white plate of "John Milton As A Young Man[:] Supposed portrait by Daniel Mytens which has come into the possession of St. Paul's School" in which Milton has long flowing hair, original cream cloth, spine lettered in black. A nice copy. Scarce.

28. Graves, Robert. **WIFE TO MR. MILTON** The Story of Marie Powell by Robert Graves[.] *New York[:] Creative Age Press, Inc., (1944).* First American edition. 8vo (larger size than first edition 8vo), viii+380pp., half-title ("Wife To Mr. Milton," with other books "Also By Robert Graves" printed on verso), title page in red and black with "Wartime notice" printed on verso of title page at the top: "A Wartime Book. This Complete Edition is produced in full compliance with the Government's regulations for conserving paper and other essential materials," first appearance of "Copyright 1944 By Graves" printed immediately below, and "Designed By Herbert Cahn[,] Printed The United States Of America[,] American Book-Stratford Press, Inc., New York" printed at the bottom, original

blue cloth, front cover lettered in gilt, black label with gilt lettering and gilt trim on spine, printed map on endpapers, t.e. blue, printed publisher's wrappers with illustration of Chalfont St. Giles on front cover and photograph of Robert Graves on back cover (a bit used, slight wear along extremities). Nice copy, bookplate on fly-leaf, and with good publisher's wrappers. Uncommon.

29. Graves, Robert. **WIFE TO MR. MILTON**. The Story of Marie Powell. *New York: Creative Age Press, Inc., (1944)*. Second American edition. 8vo (same size as preceding, published without a half-title), viii+380pp., title page in red and black, with "Wartime Book" notice as in first American edition printed on verso of title page at the top, "Copyright, 1944, By Robert Graves" printed immediately below with "SECOND PRINTING" (in caps) printed immediately below that (as if added to verso of the first edition title page), other books "Also by Robert Graves" are listed in the middle, and "Designed By Herbert Cahn" (as with first edition) is printed at the bottom, binding as with first issue, without publisher's wrappers.

The collection also has the first Penguin Books edition published in 1954; a reprint of the second edition by "Octagon Books, A Division Of Farrar, Straus And Giroux" in 1979; and an "edition specially created in 1991 for Book-of-the-Month Club by arrangement with the Estate of Robert Graves."

30. Grierson, Sir Herbert. **THE ENGLISH BIBLE**. Sir Herbert Grierson With 8 Plates In Color And 21 Illustrations In Black & White[.] *William Collins Of London[,] MCMXXXXIII*. First edition. Slim 8vo, 47+[1]pp., half-title, color plates, illustrations in black and white, decorated initial letters, head- and tailpieces, original brown paper boards, front cover and spine lettered in white with central emblem in white on front cover, printed publisher's wrappers repeating front cover and spine (wrappers a bit worn and a little frayed at top, with small tear repaired). A nice copy. Included are references to and discussion of Milton (with reproduction of Vertue portrait), John Martin (with reproduction of illustration for *PL*), and Blake (with reproduction of an illustration in color). See also W. J. Turner's *Romance Of English Literature* (1944 edition) and *Impressions Of English Literature* (1947 edition), both of which reprint Grierson's *The English Bible*.

31. Halleck, Reuben Post. **HISTORY OF ENGLISH LITERATURE** By Reuben Post Halleck, M.A. (Yale). *American Book Company[,] New York[,] Cincinnati[,] Chicago[,] (1900)*. First edition. 8vo, 499pp., frontispiece illustration, "Literary Map Of England" in color, numerous textual illustrations in black and white, original blue cloth, spine lettered in blind, index. A nice copy. Included is a long section on Milton, with a brief review of his life, a discussion of the "Characteristics Of Milton's Poetry," and "Required" and suggested readings, along with several illustrations: including Milton at age ten, portrait of Milton as a young man, and a reproduction of *Milton Dictating Paradise Lost to his Daughters* [from the] Painting by Munkacsy."

32. Halleck, Reuben Post. **HALLECK'S NEW ENGLISH LITERATURE** By Reuben Post Halleck, M.A., LL.D. Author of "History Of English Literature[,] History Of American Literature[.]" *American Book Company[,] New York[,] Cincinnati[,] Chicago[,] (1913)*. First edition. 8vo, 647pp., frontispiece illustration in color ("The Fortune Theater During the Performance of an Elizabethan Play"), additional illustration in color ("Literary Map Of England"), numerous textual illustrations and facsimiles in black and white, original red cloth, spine lettered in gilt. A very good copy. Included is a the long section on Milton with a brief review of his life, a discussion of the "Characteristics Of Milton's Poetry," and "Suggested Readings With Questions And Suggestions," along with a number of illustrations including, "*Cromwell Dictating Dispatches to Milton* (From the painting by Ford Madox Brown)," "*Milton's Visit to Galileo in 1638* From the painting by T. Lessi," and a "Facsimile of Milton's Signature, 1663."

33. Hanford, James Holly. **JOHN MILTON, ENGLISHMAN**. James Holly Hanford. *Crown Publishers[,] New York[,] (1949)*. First edition. 8vo, xi+272pp., frontispiece reproduction of portrait after Faithorne, decorative border trim on title page, additional plates, including reproduction in black and white of "Milton, Age ten," reproductions in black and white of several Blake illustrations, reduced reproductions of several 1688 illustrations, index at the end, original green cloth, the initials "JM" in gilt on front cover, spine lettered in gilt, original printed green publisher's wrappers (a little worn) with small reproduction of Milton portrait at twenty-one on front cover. A nice copy with "Gimbels Book Store" label on top of inside back cover marked $3.75 and reduced to $1.75. "The book stands between factual narrative and interpretive criticism" (inside front flap). How many of us haven't grown to appreciate Milton all the more because of Hanford. His facts always informed and his "interpretive criticism" was always provocative, whether one agreed or disagreed with his interpretive approach.

The collection also has copies of two other editions: "New York: Crown Publishers, (1949). Bonanza Paperback," first paperback edition, with the plates; and "London: Victor Gollancz Ltd, 1950," second edition, first London Edition, without the illustrations.

34. Hayley, William. **THE LIFE OF MILTON.** (Second Edition, 1796). A Facsimile Reproduction With An Introduction By Joseph Anthony Wittreich, Jr. *Gainesville, Florida[:] Scholars' Facsimiles & Reprints[,] 1970.* 8vo (although Hayley's life was originally published in 4to), xiv+xxiii+328pp., half-title, original gray cloth, spine lettered in black. A nice copy. Facsimile reproduction. First reprint of Hayley's *Life of Milton* in its revised, second and first separate edition, originally published in 1796 (see original edition with Eighteenth-century Miltoniana and commentary there); the first edition was published in Boydell's 1794 edition of Milton's *PW* (see set in Chapter II). Wittreich's informative introduction discusses the significant changes between the first and second editions as well as the importance of Hayley's life.

The collection also has the Richard West facsimile reproduction published in 1978 in a limited edition of 100 copies.

Hand-Colored and in a Limited Number

35. Hubbard, Elbert. **LITTLE JOURNEYS TO THE HOMES OF ENGLISH AUTHORS.** Volume Six. New Series. *Written by Elbert Hubbard and done into a Printed Book by the Roycrofters at their Shop which is in East Aurora, Erie Co., New York, U.S.A., A.D. 1900.* First edition, 8vo, 148pp.+colophon leaf+leaf with emblem of the press, engraved frontispiece portrait of William Morris, protective tissue guard, decorated title page hand-colored in green, light blue, and orange with gilt border trim, "Copyright, 1899" on verso, following page printed in red identifying this as a limited edition, similarly decorated hand-colored initial letter and border trim on the first page of each chapter, decorated hand-colored initial letters throughout, half-title for each chapter, engraved portrait of each author, each with protective tissue guard, original green leather (now faded to a brown hue) over limp boards, brown leather labels with gilt lettering on front cover and spine, green silk pastedowns, t.e.g., others untrimmed. A lovely copy, handsomely printed on high-quality paper, the title page, initials, and ornaments having been designed by Samuel Warner and hand-colored. Included are chapters on William Morris, Robert Browning, Alfred Tennyson, Robert Burns, John Milton, and Samuel Johnson, each with a portrait; the portrait of Milton is of the poet seated in his sitting room (unsigned, but after Faed). While the copyright date of 1899 is given on verso of title page, the colophon leaf at the end gives the publishing date as MCM: "So here endeth the little journey to the home of John Milton, as written by Elbert Hubbard: the title page and initials being designed by Samuel Warner, the whole done into a printed book by the Roycrofters, at their shop, which is in East Aurora, Erie County, N.Y., in the month of May in the year MCM." "Of this edition there were printed and specially illumined but nine hundred and forty-seven copies" appears in red on the blank leaf following the title page (this copy not numbered). The chapter on Milton is rambling thoughts by Hubbard about Milton's early years, published numerous times in various formats over the next twenty years, of which the first issues are in the collection.

Hand-Colored and Signed by Hubbard

36. Hubbard, Elbert. **LITTLE JOURNEYS TO THE HOMES OF ENGLISH AUTHORS[:] JOHN MILTON.** *Done into print by the Roycrofters at the Roycroft Shop, which is in East Aurora, New York, U.S.A. (MCM).* First edition thus, first issue. 8vo, [6]+118pp. (pagination beginning at p. 97 and ending on p. 118)+[2]pp., engraved frontispiece portrait of Milton seated in his sitting room, protective tissue guard, decorated title page hand-colored in green, light green and orange with gilt border trim, "Copyright, 1899" on verso, following page printed in red identifying this as a limited edition and signed by Hubbard, followed by page with quotation from Book III of *PL*, half-title, hand-colored decorated initial letters, decorative head- and tailpieces, a second engraved illustration of Milton's cottage at Chalfont St. Giles, protective tissue guard, colophon leaf with advertisement for "Little Journeys to the Homes of English Authors" printed on verso, edges untrimmed, original suede leather over limp boards, leather labels on front cover with gilt lettering, brown silk endpapers, brown silk ribbon marker. A fine copy with large armorial bookplate on fly-leaf, handsomely printed "by the Roycrofters" on high-quality paper, the title page, initials, and ornaments having been designed by Samuel Warner and hand-colored. While the copyright date of 1899 is given on verso of title page, the colophon leaf at the end gives the publishing date as MCM, as with preceding copy. This edition is a reprint of the chapter on Milton in *Little Journeys To The Homes of English Authors* by Hubbard, published in the same year (preceding copy, also a special limited edition, hand-colored, as here). "Of this edition there were printed and illumined by hand but nine hundred and twenty-five copies. This book is Number 314," with "314" written in black ink and with the signature of Elbert Hubbard in black ink afterward (printed in red on the blank leaf following the title page).

37. Hubbard, Elbert. LITTLE JOURNEYS TO THE HOMES OF ENGLISH AUTHORS[:] JOHN MILTON. *East Aurora, New York: Done into print by the Roycrofters at the Roycroft Shop, (1900).* First edition thus, second issue. Crown 8vo, [4]+121pp. (pagination beginning at p. 99 and ending on p. 121)+[4]pp., engraved frontispiece portrait of Milton seated in his sitting room, decorated title page, half-title with Milton's name, decorated initial letters, decorative head- and tailpieces, original printed stitched wrappers, edges untrimmed, advertisement leaves bound in at end. A very nice copy, three advertisement leaves bound in at the end, and advertisement on inside front cover for *Little Journeys* now available as "booklets [which] will be stitched by hand with silk. A photogravure portrait on Japan Vellum will accompany each booklet as a frontispiece. The price of these booklets will be twenty-five cents each, or $3.00 for the year." Stevens 2222.

38. Hubbard, Elbert. LITTLE JOURNEYS TO THE HOMES OF ENGLISH AUTHORS: JOHN MILTON. *East Aurora, New York: The Roycroft Press, 1901.* Second edition thus. Crown 8vo, [4]+121pp. (pagination beginning at p. 99 and ending on p. 121)+colophon leaf and leaf with emblem of the press, engraved frontispiece portrait of Milton seated in his sitting room, protective tissue guard, decorated title page, half-title with Milton's name, decorated initial letters, decorative tailpieces, original boards, linen spine, printed paper label, edges untrimmed. A very fine copy.

39. Hulme, William H. TWO EARLY LIVES OF JOHN MILTON Edited by William H. Hulme[,] Professor of English[.] *Western Reserve University Bulletin[.] New Series Vol. XXVII[,] August, 1924[,] No. 8[.] Literary Section Supplement[.] Western Reserve Studies, Vol. No. 1, 8[.] Cleveland, O. (1924).* First edition. 8vo, 94pp., pamphlet, original brown wrappers, front cover lettered in black with central emblem of the University. A nice copy. Included are (1) *The Life Of John Milton* by John Toland (1698), and (2) *The Life Of John Milton* by Elijah Fenton (1725), "New Editions" by William H. Hulme."

40. Hutchinson, F. E. MILTON AND THE ENGLISH MIND by F. E. Hutchinson[,] D. Litt., F. B. A.[,] Sometime Fellow of All Souls College[,] Oxford[.] *Published by Hodder & Stoughton Limited for The English Universities Press At Saint Paul's House In The City Of London[,] (1946).* First edition. 16mo, xii+197pp., half-title ("Milton and the English Mind is one of the volumes in the Teach Yourself History Library Edited by A. L. Rowse"), with a list of "Volumes Ready Or In Preparation" on verso, frontispiece portrait plate with reproduction of Milton portrait on a bronze medallion, "A General Introduction to the Series" by A. L. Rowse, "Guide to Reading," two plates with Milton twenty-one and reproduction of first edition title pages, "Index" at the end, original light green cloth, spine lettered in black, t.e. blue. A nice copy, having formerly belonged to Milton scholar Bernard A. Wright, with printed light green publisher's wrappers (a little aged) with blue label and lettering on front cover and spine. This brief biography shows Milton "as not only among the greatest of our poets, but also a great and representative Englishman" (back cover). Laid in: an interesting letter (dated April 4, 1947) to Wright from the editor of *The Review Of English Studies*, John Butt.

The collection also has the two following editions: "New York[:] The Macmillan Company[,] (1948)," second edition, first American edition; and "Published by The English Universities Press At Saint Paul's House In The City Of London[,] (1950)," "Second Impression" (on verso of title page).

41. Jenks, Tudor. IN THE DAYS OF MILTON By Tudor Jenks[,] Author Of "In The Days Of Chaucer" And "In The Days Of Shakespeare[.]" Illustrated. *New York[:] A. S. Barnes & Company[,] MDCCCCV.* First edition. 16m0, x+306+[4]pp., half-title with advertisement on verso, unsigned frontispiece portrait plate of a youngish Milton and also facsimile reproduction plate of 1645 *Poems* frontispiece, original light brown cloth, front cover decorated in contrasting brown with red lettering within red trim at the top and lettering in contrasting darker brown at the bottom, spine lettered in red, appendix ("Chief Dates Relating To Milton's Life And Works"), and a second appendix consisting of "A Brief Bibliography For Young Students Of Milton," index. Very nice copy with contemporary signature (dated 1905) on front pastedown, and four pages of advertisements bound in at the end. Milton's life set against the spirit of his times. Stevens 2263.

42. Johnson, Samuel. PROLOGUE WRITTEN BY SAMUEL JOHNSON AND SPOKEN BY DAVID GARRICK AT A BENEFIT PERFORMANCE OF COMUS APRIL 1750 Reproduced in Type-Facsimile[.] *Oxford University Press[,] London: Humphrey Milford[,] 1925.* Small folio, eight leaves total, half-title with title printed between decorative trim (small piece missing at top without affecting text), decorative piece on title page, decorative headpieces and decorated letters, original blue cloth, printed paper label on front cover. A nice copy. "Facsimile Printed from type at the Clarendon Press 1925" (verso of facsimile title page). "Five hundred copies printed at the University Press Oxford, England" (verso of half-title). "The present reprint has been set up from a copy of the original in the possession of Professor R. W. Rogers, and the proof read with the British Museum copy" (separate leaf before "Postscript" at the end).

43. Johnson, Samuel. Variant of Preceding. Folio, fine within, original green cloth, spine lettered in gilt. A very nice copy, identical to preceding, except a large paper copy. "Facsimile Printed from type at the Clarendon Press 1925" (verso of facsimile title page). "Five hundred copies printed at the University Press Oxford, England" (verso of half-title).

44. Lang, Andrew, editor. **POETS' COUNTRY** Edited By Andrew Lang[.] Contributor Prof. J. Churton Collings, E. Harley Coleridge, W. J. Loftie, F.S.A., Michael Macmillan, Andrew Lang[.] With Fifty Illustrations In Colour By Francis S. Walker[.] *London: T. C. & E. C. Jack[,] 16 Henrietta Street, W. C. And Edinburgh[,] 1907.* First edition. 8vo, xiv+363pp., half-title, frontispiece illustration plate in color, additional illustrations in color throughout by Francis S. Walker, each with protective tissue guard with lettering in black identifying the illustration, laurel wreath in black at center of title page, original red cloth (spine ends and corners rubbed), front cover and spine decorated in floral motif in white, green, and gilt, with gilt lettering, t.e.g., others untrimmed. A very handsome copy of this elegant edition, in an attractive art nouveau binding of the period, beautifully illustrated with fifty color plates by Francis S. Walker. Included are chapters on the major poets from Shakespeare to Burns, with color illustrations of locations important to each poet. "The pictures in this book are of places associated with the poets either through their lives or scenes that are supposed to be sources of their inspiration" (artist's preface). The ten-page Milton chapter by John Churton Collins contains three illustration plates in color, each with protective tissue guard with lettering in black identifying the illustration: (1) "Chalfont St. Giles, Bucks[,] An English pastoral scene"; (2) "Milton's Cottage And Garden, Chalfont St. Giles"; and (3) "Interior Of Milton's Cottage." Stevens 2272 (note).

45. Leo, Brother. **ENGLISH LITERATURE.** A Survey And A Commentary. *Boston, New York, Chicago, etc.: Ginn And Company, (1928).* First edition. 8vo, frontispiece illustration in color, numerous illustrations in black and white, facsimiles, original blue cloth (checks and underlings variously throughout), front cover and spine lettered in blind. Designed for classroom use, with an introduction "To The Teacher" on how to use this book and "Suggestions For Reading." Included is a section on Milton, with several reproductions and facsimiles of title pages. The "Suggestions For Reading" contains a brief recommended bibliography for Milton.

46. Lincoln, Eleanor Terry. "JEAN DASSIER'S MILTON MEDAL: A FURTHER NOTE" [In] *The Princeton University Library Chronicle, Vol. XXXVII, No. 1 (Autumn, 1975), 24-29.* 8vo, journal, plates of medal belonging to Princeton, original printed stiff paper wrappers. In fine condition. See photograph of Dassier Milton medal in the collection.

47. Lindelof, U. **MILTON.** *Helsingfors[:] Holger Schildts Forlagsaktiebolag[,] (1920).* 8vo, 110pp., frontispiece portrait identified after Faithorne, portraits of Milton at age ten and twenty-one appear early in the text, original wrappers, with "Biografier, No. 9" and vignette portrait of Milton within decorative borders in black and blue trim on front cover, advertisement of the series on back cover, edges untrimmed, partially unopened. A nice copy of this biography of Milton in Swedish. Uncommon.

48. Long, William J. **OUTLINES OF ENGLISH AND AMERICAN LITERATURE.** An Introduction To The Chief Writers Of England And America, To The Books They Wrote, And To The Times In Which They Lived By William J. Long. [Quotation from Chaucer.] *Boston, New York, Chicago, etc.: Ginn And Company[,] (1917).* First edition. 8vo, xvii+557pp., frontispiece portrait of Shakespeare in color, additional illustrations in black and white, original red ribbed cloth, front cover and spine lettered in black with the lettering on the spine against a decorated orange background, index. A good copy. A chapter is devoted to Milton, with a vignette portrait of a young, long-haired Milton and vignette illustrations of Chalfont St. Giles and Ludlow Castle. Earlier, in 1909, Long published a "Textbook For Schools" entitled *English Literature*, a copy of which is in the collection.

49. Mabie, Hamilton W. **JOHN MILTON.** *[New York:] The Mentor [Association,] December 15 1915[,] Serial No. 97[,] Volume 3[,] Number 21[.]* Slim 4to, 11+[1]pp., fifteen vignette illustrations within the text (of Milton at various ages, Milton's homes, and other locales and persons associated with Milton's life), "The Magic of Milton" by T. B. Macaulay on verso of front cover, pamphlet, original printed wrappers (spine a bit cracked), with a portrait of Milton "From a Miniature by Faithorne" reproduced on front cover.

Accompanying the pamphlet, loosely laid in, and identified at the beginning of Mabie's article, are six "Mentor Gravures" in sepia tones: "John Milton At The Age Of Twelve By F. Newenham," "Bust Of Milton By Bacon," "Statue of Milton By Horace Montford," "Milton's Cottage," "Milton Dictating 'Paradise Lost' To His Daughters By M. Munkacsy" and "John Milton By P. Kramer." On the verso of each gravure is an essay, with decorated initial letter, "in The Mentor Reading Course," each essay "Prepared By The Editorial Staff Of The Mentor Association" (copyrighted 1915), beginning with "Boyhood And Youth" as "Monograph Number One in The Mentor Reading Course" on the verso of "John Milton At The Age Of Twelve, By F. Newenham," and proceeding with "Comus And Lycidas" as "Monograph Number Two in The Mentor Reading Course" on the verso of "John Milton, By P. Kramer"; "The Grand Tour" as "Monograph Number" on the verso of "Milton's Cottage, Chalfont, St. Giles, England"; "Marriage" as "Monograph Number Four" on the verso of "Statue of Milton, By Horace Montford—Outside Church Of St. Giles, Cripplegate, London, England"; "The Restoration" as "Monograph Number Five" on the verso of "Milton Dictating 'Paradise Lost' To His Daughters, By M. Munkacsy"; and "Last Years" as "Monograph Number Six in The Mentor Reading Course" on the verso of "Bust Of Milton, By Bacon—In Church Of St. Giles, Cripplegate, London, England." "The purpose of The Mentor Association is to give its members, in an interesting and attractive way, the information in various fields of knowledge which everybody wants to have. The information is imparted by interesting reading matter, prepared under the direction of leading authorities, and by beautiful pictures, produced by the most highly perfected modern processes. The Mentor is published twice a month" (inside back cover). Until 2005 this publication had apparently gone unrecorded. John Shawcross provides a splendid assessment and full identification of all items in the pamphlet in a recent article in *Milton Quarterly*, entitled "A 'New' Bibliographical Item and Its Accompanying Art Work," in *MQ*, vol. 39, no. 1 (2005): 45–48.

50. Macaulay, Rose. **MILTON** By Rose Macaulay[.] Great Lives[.] *Duckworth[,] 3 Henrietta Street[,] London W.C.2. (1934).* First edition, first issue. Slim 8vo, 141+1]pp., half-title (with list of "Other volumes" in the series "Great Lives" on verso), "First Published 1934" on verso of title page, bibliography on separate leaf at the end, printed "By The Camelot Press," original red cloth, spine lettered in gilt, fore-edge untrimmed. A fine, fresh copy, virtually mint, in original pink publisher's wrappers (a bit rubbed, spine a little sunned) with pegasus on front cover and printed price "2/-net."

51. Macaulay, Rose. **MILTON** By Rose Macaulay[.] Great Lives[.] *Duckworth[,] 3 Henrietta Street[,] London W.C.2. (1934).* First edition, second issue. Slim 8vo, 141+1]pp., half-title (with list of "Other volumes" in the series "Great Lives" on verso, ending with "No. 31. Newman"), "First Published January 1934 / Second Impression February 1934" on verso of title page, bibliography on separate leaf at the end, printed "By The Camelot Press," original red cloth, spine lettered in gilt. A nice, tall copy with penciled inscription, "Chalfont St. Giles, July, 1937," on fly-leaf, in original light green publisher's wrappers (a bit rubbed, spine a little dirtied and chipped at the top with a small tear off the backside) with Pegasus on front cover and printed price "2/- net."

The collection also has two other editions of Rose Macaulay's *Milton*: one published the following year "New York and London: Harper & Brothers Publishers, 1935," first American Edition; and the other published by "Collier Books[,] New York, N.Y.[,], (1962), First Collier Books Edition," paperback with reproduction of a long-haired young Milton on front cover.

52. Macy, John. **THE STORY OF THE WORLD'S LITERATURE**. By John Macy. Illustrated By Onorio Ruotolo. *Garden City, New York: Garden City Publishing Co., Inc., (1925).* First edition, possibly a regular issue. 8vo, xxiv+613pp., half-title with woodcut vignette illustration, frontispiece portrait sketch of Shakespeare, in this edition as a plate, preface dated "Christmas, 1924," additional portrait sketches and woodcut illustrations in black and white, original blue cloth, central emblem in blind on front cover, spine lettered in gilt, t.e. blue, others untrimmed. Included is a chapter on Milton, with a woodcut black-and-white illustration by Onorio Ruotolo of a snake wrapped around a tree with apples as decorated initial letter "M" at the outset of the chapter, (but without either the full-page portrait sketch of Milton when blind which first appeared—as a tinted plate—in the second issue [also listed here] or Ruotolo's full-page sketch of Milton which first appeared in the second edition, revised, published in 1932 [also listed here]), first appearance of an additional woodcut black-and-white illustration by Onorio Ruotolo of *Adam and Eve*.

53. Macy, John. **THE STORY OF THE WORLD'S LITERATURE**. By John Macy. Illustrated By Onorio Ruotolo. *Boni & Liveright: N.Y., (1925)* First edition, second issue. Crown 8vo, similar to preceding regular 8vo issue but in a larger format (7 ¼" × 10") and with tinted portrait plates added, xxiv+613pp., half-title with woodcut vignette illustration, frontispiece portrait sketch of Shakespeare, in this issue as a tinted plate, title page with elaborate decorative blue border, "First printing, October, 1925; Second printing, November, 1925" (verso title page), preface dated "Christmas, 1924," additional portrait sketches (in this edition all as tinted plates), woodcut illustrations in black and white, original blue cloth, central emblem in gilt on front cover with gilt lettering at the top, spine lettered in gilt, decorated gray endpapers, fore-edge

untrimmed. Large paper copy. Included is a chapter on Milton, as preceding, with the addition of a full-page portrait of Milton when blind—as a tinted plate (first appearance in this issue, unattributed and very different from Ruotolo's full-page portrait sketch of Milton which first appeared in the second edition, revised, published in 1932 [also listed here]).

54. Macy, John. THE STORY OF THE WORLD'S LITERATURE. By John Macy. Illustrated By Onorio Ruotolo. A Star Book. *Garden City, New York: Garden City Publishing Co., Inc., (1932).* Second edition, first issue. As first edition, except for the addition of full-page portrait sketches in place of full-page portraits, in original blue cloth. Milton's chapter is also the same, except for a full-page portrait sketch of Milton with sight by Ruotolo, dated "'32," (first appearance in this edition).

55. Macy, John. Another Copy of THE STORY OF THE WORLD'S LITERATURE. By John Macy. Illustrated By Onorio Ruotolo. *Garden City, New York: Garden City Publishing Co., Inc., (1932).* Second edition revised. Similar to preceding 8vo issue but in a larger format (identical to that of the first edition, second issue), without Ruotolo's portrait sketches and in their place the portrait plates which appear as tinted plates (they are not tinted here) in the 1925 first edition, second issue, in original red cloth. Large paper copy. Milton's chapter is the same, except for a full-page portrait of Milton when blind as an untinted plate (which first appeared as a tinted plate in the 1925 first edition, second issue—also listed here).

The collection also has three other editions: by "Liveright Publishing Corp., Liveright, N.Y., (1936)," third edition, revised; by "The World Publishing Company, Cleveland And New York, (1941)," fourth edition; and by "The World Publishing Company, Cleveland And New York, (1942)," fourth edition, revised.

56. Marsh, John Fitchett, editor. PAPERS CONNECTED WITH THE AFFAIRS OF MILTON AND HIS FAMILY. Edited By John Fitchett Marsh, From The Original Documents In His Possession. *Norwood Editions, 1977.* 4to, 46pp., title page of 1851 first edition reprinted, original blue cloth ("Library of Congress Duplicate" stamped in red on fly-leaf), spine lettered in gilt. A fine copy. Reprint of the 1851 first edition published for the Chetham Society. Printed in a limited edition of 100 copies.

57. Marshall, H. E. ENGLISH LITERATURE FOR BOYS AND GIRLS By H. E. Marshall[,] Author Of 'Our Island Story,' 'Scotland's Story[,]' 'Our Empire Story[.]' Illustrated with 20 Drawings in Colour By John R. Skelton. *New York[:] Frederick A. Stokes Company Publishers, (1909).* First edition. Large 8vo, half-title, xx+687pp., frontispiece illustration in color and nineteen additional full-page illustrations in color, original blue cloth, front cover and spine lettered in gilt, central brilliant red and gilt seal on front cover, decorative red and gilt device at top of spine, t.e.g., others untrimmed. A very nice copy in a fine binding of the period. Two chapters are devoted to Milton: "Milton—Sight And Growth" and "Milton—Darkness And Death," with a full-page color illustration of *Milton Sitting in His Garden at the Door of His House.*

58. Martin, John Rupert. THE PORTRAIT OF JOHN MILTON AT PRINCETON and its Place In Milton Iconography by John Rupert Martin. *Princeton: Princeton University Library, 1961.* First edition. Slim 4to, vi+34pp., half-title, twenty-four reproductions of Milton portraits in black and white, and a foldout color plate of the Faithorne portrait of Milton at Princeton at the end of the book, original orange buckram, central gilt emblem on front cover, brown label on spine lettered in gilt, dark brown endpapers, printed tan publisher's wrappers. A fine copy.

59. Masson, David. THE LIFE OF JOHN MILTON: Narrated In Connexion With The Political, Ecclesiastical, And Literary History Of His Time. New and revised edition. *Gloucester, Mass.: Peter Smith, 1965.* 7 volumes, including index. 8vo, frontispiece portrait each volume, modern orange cloth, spine lettered in gilt. A fine set. Reprint of Masson's *Life of Milton*, second edition, 1881–94 (see original set with Nineteenth-century Miltoniana); first published 1859–80 (see set with Nineteenth-century Miltoniana).

60. McDonnell, Michael F. J. A HISTORY OF ST. PAUL'S SCHOOL By Michael F. J. McDonnell Of The Inner Temple, Barrister-At-Law, Sometime Scholar Of St. John's College, Cambridge[.] With Forty-Eight Portraits And Other Illustrations. *London[:] Chapman And Hall, Ltd., 1909.* First edition. 8vo, xii+496pp., half-title, frontispiece portrait plate and other portrait and illustration plates in black and white, original black cloth (minor wear), central emblem in blind on front cover, spine lettered in blind, t.e.g., others untrimmed. A nice copy. Founded by John Colet, St. Paul's was Milton's school from his twelfth to sixteenth year, and he was the school's most famous pupil; while at the school Milton formed his friendship with Charles Diodati, immortalized in *Epitaphium Damonis.* Included are numerous references to and discussion of Milton and his works, with a portrait plate of Milton at age ten.

61. Mead, Lucia Ames. **MILTON'S ENGLAND**. Illustrated. *Boston: L. C. Page, 1903.* First edition. 8vo, 311pp., half-title, frontispiece portrait of Milton, "Photogravure from the engraving by T. Woolnoth of the miniature painted in 1667 by William Faithorne," protective tissue guard with identification of frontispiece printed in red on it, title page in red and black within black rules with small seal at the center, "Copyright, 1902" and "Published, September, 1902" on verso of title page, maps of "Milton's England" and of "Milton's London," thirty illustration plates, decorated initial letters, original gray cloth (slightly rubbed), gilt rules on front cover incorporating gilt lettering within gilt scrolls within further gilt rules with decorative gilt corner pieces and with elaborate central gilt emblem of shield and flags with small emblem and small crown each in gilt and white at the top, gilt rules and gilt lettering within decorative gilt trim on spine with gilt rules at top and bottom and repeating small emblem and small crown from front cover in gilt and white at the center, t.e.g., others untrimmed, bookplate. A fine copy. Stevens 2250.

The collection also has another copy in original red cloth, decorated exactly as preceding. A very nice copy in a lovely variant publisher's binding.

62. Miller, Leo. **MILTON'S PORTRAITS: AN IMPARTIAL INQUIRY INTO THEIR AUTHENTIC-ATION**. A special issue of *Milton Quarterly*, 1976. Slim 4to, journal, 39+[5]pp., four portrait plates, original printed stiff paper wrappers, with reproduction of Faithorne portrait in color on front cover and of Milton at age ten in color on back cover. A nice copy.

63. [Milton: Cottage] **MILTON'S COTTAGE[:] THE HISTORY OF A HOUSE** By D. G. Law[.] *Privately Printed and Published by Mrs. Law, Chalfont St. Giles, Obtained from Milton's Cottage, etc. n.d. [1960's].* Slim 8vo, 55pp., reproduction of a sketch of the cottage by T. Phillips "taken from the title page of Dunster's Edition of *PR*, published in 1779, and is, so far as I know, the earliest engraving of Milton's Cottage" (Preface), original green wrappers, front cover lettered in black. A nice copy.

64. [Milton: Milton] **GIANTS OF LITERATURE[:] MILTON**[.] *[Maidenhead, Berkshire, England:] Sampson Low, (1977).* First London edition. 4to, 136pp., half-title with small reproduction of illustration of Milton visiting Galileo with description below describing the event, reproduction of Doré's rendering of the fall of the angels as frontispiece with the illustration running over onto title page, numerous reproductions of illustrations for Milton's works and of paintings, personages, and historical events of Milton's period in color and black and white, including a two-page collection of "Milton's Contemporaries," also facsimile reproductions of various first edition title pages, original maroon buckram, front cover and spine lettered in gilt, printed light green publisher's wrappers, with a reproduction in color of an illustration by Blake in the center of front cover, and of Romney's Milton seated with a cape in the lower right corner, also a reproduction in color of Blake's illustration of the expulsion on back cover with quotation from Satan's soliloquy: " . . . The mind is its own place. . . . " A fine copy. This small quarto is a treasure trove of information about Milton, his age, his illustrators, his critics, and editions of his works, and is accompanied by numerous reproductions of important personages of Milton's time and of illustrations of Milton's poems. It is no longer an easy book to find. Scarce.

65. [Milton: Saint Giles Cripplegate] Clarke, H. Adams. **A HISTORY OF THE PARISH CHURCH OF ST. GILES**, With a Forward by the Rev. S. W. Hagger. *Published By H. Adams, Clarke, Pierscourt, Beaconsfield, Bucks, (1961).* 8vo, 97pp., four illustration plates, original green wrappers. A nice copy. St. Giles Cripplegate in London is the church where Milton is buried.

66. [Milton: Saint Giles Cripplegate] **SAINT GILES CRIPPLEGATE**. *[London: ca. 1970.]* Slim 4to, 8pp., photographs of interior, with color postcard of interior laid in, original red wrappers with illustration of early church on front and photograph of "architects' model of the Barbican development" on the back. A fine copy.

67. [Milton: Saint Giles Cripplegate] **SAINT GILES CRIPPLEGATE 900 YEARS 1090-1990**. *[London: 1990.]* Slim 4to, 20pp., numerous reproductions of portraits of people historically connected with the church, original wrappers with color illustration of the church in earlier times on front cover. A fine copy of this document celebrating the nine hundredth anniversary of St. Giles Cripplegate. Included is a reproduction of Milton portrait (at twenty-one), together with a brief biography of Milton. Also included with portraits and brief biographies are Sir Thomas Moore (who was born in the parish), Lancelot Andrews (the parish's most famous vicar), Ben Jonson (who lived for some years in the parish), Oliver Cromwell (who was married in the church), John Bunyan (who preached in the parish), and Daniel Defoe (who died in the parish); there are numerous others pictures of individuals and events with historical ties to the church.

67A. (Cross-listing) [Milton Tercentenary] See Beers, Henry A. **MILTON'S TERCENTENARY**. An address delivered before the Modern Language Club of Yale University on Milton's Three Hundredth Birthday. *New Haven[:] Yale University Press[,] 1910.*

68. [Milton Tercentenary] CATALOGUE OF AN EXHIBITION COMMEMORATIVE OF THE TERCENTENARY OF THE BIRTH OF JOHN MILTON 1608-1908 Including Original Editions Of His Poetical And Prose Works, Together With Three Hundred And Twenty-Seven Engraved Portraits. Held At The Grolier Club, December 3, 1908 To January 9, 1909. *[New York:] [The De Vinne Press], (1908)*. 8vo, 116pp., three hundred and twenty-seven engraved portraits, original printed wrappers (a bit age-darkened and lightly soiled, chipped at edges), front cover printed in red and black, uncut. A nice copy. Scarce.

69. [Milton Tercentenary] FACSIMILES OF AUTOGRAPHS AND DOCUMENTS IN THE BRITISH MUSEUM Published By Order Of The Trustees On The Occasion Of The Milton Tercentenary[.] *Sold At The British Museum[,] 1908[.] Price One Shilling: Single Plates, Threepence each [All rights reserved]*. First and only edition. 4to, 8 leaves, with facsimile and text on facing pages, facsimile on recto with descriptive text on verso, original stiff gray wrappers bound in (rear wrapper expertly repaired, "Kensington Public Libraries" in discreet small red stamp on title page and variously throughout), three-quarter crushed green morocco spine (worn), stippled green leather, Milton's name lettered in gilt on spine with gilt rules (faded), joints reinforced from within, large armorial bookplate of "The Royal Borough Kensington Public Library" tipped in on front pastedown. This large book was published on the occasion of the Milton Tercentenary in 1908, and contains facsimiles of "Milton's Commonplace Book," "Signatures Of John Milton, 1651 And 1655," Milton's Bible, "Sale Of The Copyright Of 'Paradise Lost.'" Uncommon. Stevens 2280.

70. [Milton: Tercentenary] JOHN MILTON AND CHALFONT ST. GILES by D. G. Law[.] *Published by Mrs. Law, Chalfont St. Giles[;] Printed by A. H. Partridge, Station Road, Gerrards Cross[,] n.d.* First edition. Slim 4to, 48pp., original blue wrappers, front cover printed in black: "John Milton And Chalfont St. Giles[.] A Tercentenary Publication." A nice copy with signature (dated "Chalfont St. Giles, May 1, 1969") on title page. Included are the following: "Part 1. Life Of John Milton. Part 2. The Great Plague Of London. Part 3. Milton And Thomas Ellwood. Part 4. Chalfont St. Giles."

71. [Milton: Tercentenary] THE JOHN RYLANDS LIBRARY MANCHESTER: CATALOGUE OF AN EXHIBITION OF ORIGINAL EDITIONS OF THE PRINCIPAL WORKS OF JOHN MILTON. ARRANGED IN CELEBRATION OF THE TERCENTENARY OF HIS BIRTH[.] *Printed By Order Of The Governors[,] December 9th, 1908*. Slim 8vo, 24pp., pamphlet, original printed wrappers (slight age-browning along edges). A very nice copy. Scarce.

72. [Milton: Tercentenary] MANSION HOUSE 9TH DECEMBER, 1908. (TERCENTENARY OF MILTON'S BIRTH) PROGRAMME OF MUSIC To be performed by the Students of the Guildhall School Of Music Under the personal direction of Dr. W. H. Cummings, F.S.A. Principal. The Right Honourable Sir George Wyatt Truscott, Lord Mayor. *[London, 1908.]* Royal 8vo, 17pp.+9 plates, frontispiece portrait of Milton at age ten, with other portraits interspersed, including portrait of Milton twenty-one, a second portrait of Milton at twenty-one "From a Miniature in the possession of Mr. Arthur E. Shipley," portrait of "Milton At The Age Of About 48 From the 'Woodcock' miniature in the collection of Dr. G. C. Williamson," reproduction of "The 'Bayfordbury' Portrait From an original crayon drawing, probably by W. Faithorne," reproduction of "The 'Hobart' Portrait From the painting by Faithorne," reproduction of "Milton At The Age Of 62 Engraving from life by William Faithorne, from Milton's 'History of England,' 1670," facsimiles of first edition title pages, original stiff wrappers printed in color to look like an old Cambridge calf binding. A very nice copy. Selections include *Ode: "At A Solemn Music"* (music by Sir Hubert Parry); *Madrigral: "Song On May Morning"* (music by Dr. W. H. Cummings); *Song With Chorus: "Haste Thee, Nymph"* (music by G. F. Handel, 1740); *Song: "Sweet Echo"* (music by Henry Lawes, 1634); *Song: "The Star That Bids The Shepherd Fold"* (music by Dr. T. A. Arne, 1738); *Song: "By Dimpled Brook"* (music by Dr. T. A. Arne, 1738); *Song: "Sometime Walking, Not Unseen"* (music by G. F. Handel, 1740); and a selection from *L'Allegro* at the outset. Also included are quotations from "Some Other Poets On Milton" praising Milton, and brief essays on *At A Solemn Music*, on *Comus*, on "The Authentic Portraits Of Milton," and on "The Mansion House." Scarce. Stevens 2635.

73. [Milton: Tercentenary] MASSACHUSETTS HISTORICAL SOCIETY[.] THE COMMEMORA-TION OF THE TERCENTENARY OF THE BIRTH OF JOHN MILTON, AT THE FIRST CHURCH IN BOSTON, ON DECEMBER NINTH, 1908. 4to, 31+[1]pp., half-title, portrait plate of Milton "At The Age Of Twenty-One From the portrait at Nuneham," with Dryden's epigram on verso, three-page "Order of Exercises" followed by three "Sonnets by Milton" and "Wordsworth's Sonnet On Milton," a long excerpt from *Areopagitica*, portrait plate of Milton "From the original portrait by Faithorne in the possession of Sir Robert H.

Hobart," reproduction of "Title-page of the first collective edition of Milton's Minor Poems, with the rare portrait by Marshall, 1645" on verso, additional facsimiles of first edition title pages, original gray wrappers ("Historical Society of North Dakota" stamped in light red on front cover and variously throughout), front cover lettered in black. A nice copy. Among the elements of the program were included the "Chorus from 'The Nativity,'" a "Reading [of sonnets]," "Hymn [from] Milton," and "'Choruses from 'Samson.'" Tennyson is also quoted, "God-gifted organ-voice of England, / Milton, a name to resound for ages" along with a quotation from Maurice: "It seems to me sometimes as if New England were a translation into prose of the thought that was working in Milton's mind from its early morning to its sunset." Other elements in the program are also printed, including the "Invocation," the four-page "Introduction By The President Of The Society" (C. F. Adams), the eleven-page main "Address By William Everett," and "Benediction." Scarce. Stevens 2307.

74. [Milton Tercentenary] MILTON TERCENTENARY. Catalogue Of Exhibits And Programme Of Entertainment. *Metropolitan Borough of Stoke Newington. Public Library. December 9th, 1908.* Small 4to, 55pp., frontispiece portrait plate, facsimiles of first edition title pages, original printed wrappers (bit worn, very lightly crumpled on corners, first few pages slightly stained). All in all, a good copy. Probably printed in a limited edition by Willis & Co, London. Scarce.

75. [Milton Tercentenary] MILTON TERCENTENARY: The Portraits, Prints, And Writings Of John Milton[.] [Edited By George C. Williamson With An Appendix And Index By C. Sayle.*] Exhibited at Christ's College, Cambridge[,] 1908.* First edition (June 12, 1908). 4to, engraved frontispiece "Photo mezzotint" of "John Milton. Aged 21 From the Portrait at Nuneham" (fine impression), and portrait plates of (1) Milton after Faithorne from Milton's *History of Britain,* 1670; (2) Milton after Faithorne "From the original work in the possession of Sir Robert H. Hobart"; (3) Milton "from the original portrait known as the Bayfordbury (or Tonson)"; (4) Milton after the "Portrait by Pieter van der Plaas in the National Portrait Gallery considered to represent John Milton"; (5) Milton after a "Miniature by Samuel Cooper . . . said to represent John Milton as a young man"; (6) Milton "when about 48. The Woodcock portrait"; (7) "The Clay bust of Milton, said to be the work of Pierce, now preserved in the Library of Christ's College, Cambridge"; (8) "Milton as a young man. The oil painting in the Hall of Christ's College, Cambridge"; (9) the "Engraving of John Milton by R. White, forming the Frontispiece to the 4th Edition of *PL*, folio, Tonson, 1688," in a two-page reproduction plate viewed sideways as a folio; numerous facsimile plates and reproductions, appendix (titled "Miltoniana" and listing both editions and Miltoniana) and index at the end, original half brown cloth, brown paper over boards, spine ruled and lettered in gilt, original wrappers (with "Under Revision" printed on upper right-hand corner) bound in. A very nice copy. Scarce. Stevens 1774 (under Williamson).

The collection also has the second edition issued "8 July 1908," one month after the first edition, and equally scarce, along with the reprint edition published by "Burt Franklin" as #215 of "Bibliography And Reference Series" in New York in 1968.

76. [Milton Tercentenary] [Lettered on front cover:] MILTON TERCENTENARY NUMBER *Christ's College Magazine, Michaelmas Term, 1908. Cambridge: Printed For The Editors At The University Press, Cambridge. Vol. XXIII. No. 68.* [Lettered on title page:] *Christ's College Magazine. Vol. XXIII. Cambridge: Michaelmas Term, 1908 and Lent And Easter Terms, 1909.* 8vo, 120pp., engraved frontispiece mezzotint of Milton (aged 21) from "The miniature of Milton which . . . belongs to Mr A. E. Shipley, and is No. 16 in the catalogue of the Milton exhibition" (also listed here), original printed tan wrappers (a bit frayed at corners, spine a little age darkened and chipped at top and bottom), edges untrimmed. A good copy. Included in this issue are various essays, including "Milton and his College," "The Milton Tercentenary Celebration" (including a two-page chart of seating arrangement at "Milton Tercentenary Dinner 10 July 1908"), "The Music in 'Comus'" (with musical notation), "The Milton Exhibition," and ten other essays. Laid in: an eight-page bibliographic listing, with addendum, of *Early Editions Of Milton's Works In Christ's College Library,* "Reprinted from the *Christ's College Magazine,* Vol. XXXIII, Michaelmas Term, 1921." Scarce. Stevens 2287.

77. [Milton Tercentenary] THE TERCENTENARY OF MILTON'S BIRTH[:] Inaugural Meeting At The Theatre, Burlington Gardens[,] Tuesday, December 8, 1908 (The Eve of the Tercentenary) Lines By George Meredith, O.M. Oration by Dr. A. W. Ward[,] Master Of Peter House, Cambridge; Fellow Of The British Academy[.] Summary Of Address On Milton And Music By Sir Frederick Bridge, M.V.O., M.A., Mus.D.[,],] Organist Of Westminster Abbey; King Edward Professor Of Music In The University Of London[.] The British Academy[.] [From the Proceedings of the British Academy, Vol. III] *London[:] Published for the British Academy By Henry Frowde, Oxford University Press[,] Amen Corner, E.C.*

(1908). Royal 8vo, 31pp., half-title, half-title for each of the individual sections, "Appendix Vocal Illustrations," original light gray wrappers, front and back covers lettered in black. A fine copy.

78. Minchin, Harry Christopher. **A LITTLE GALLERY OF ENGLISH POETS**[.] The Portraits Reproduced From Authentic Pictures, The Lives Written By Harry Christopher Minchin[.] [Quotation from Keats.] *Methuen & Co.*[,] *36 Essex Street W.C. London, (1904)*. First edition. Small 8vo, xiii+120pp. (twenty photogravures not included in the pagination), half-title, fine photogravure of each of the poets (lacking Jonson), each with protective tissue guard, original red cloth, front cover decorated in patterned gilt devices with gilt lettering at the top, spine similarly decorated and lettered in gilt. A lovely copy, attractively decorated in art nouveau style. Together with a splendid photogravure of Milton at twenty-one, a brief life of Milton is included (pp. 27–32) among the twenty other brief lives here, ranging from Chaucer to Browning. Scarce.

79. Mitton, G. E. **THE SCENERY OF LONDON** Painted By Herbert M. Marshall R.W.S. Described By G. E. Mitton[.] *Published By Adam & Charles Black • London • MCMV*. First edition. 8vo in 4s, xiii+223+[4]pp., frontispiece illustration in color and other full-page illustrations in color, each with protective tissue guard containing identification of the illustration, index, original decorated gray cloth, front cover and spine lettered in gilt, decorative design in pink, green, and brown on front cover and spine, t.e.g., others untrimmed. A very nice copy, handsomely printed with fine full-page color illustrations, with four pages of advertisements bound in at end. Included in the section entitled, "Great Men," is a chapter on Milton, with a full-page illustration in color of "St. Giles' Cripplegate, Milton's burial-place."

80. Neilson, William Allan, and Ashley Horace Thorndike. **A HISTORY OF ENGLISH LITERATURE**. *New York*[:] *The Macmillan Company, 1925*. Second edition? 8vo, half-title, frontispiece illustration in color, numerous illustrations throughout in black and white, original red cloth, front cover lettered in blind, spine lettered in gilt. Nice copy of this school text. Included is chapter on Milton, with a portrait sketch, several reproductions of title pages, and a chronological chart. First published in 1920.

81. O'Hara, J. D. **POETRY**. *Newsweek Books, New York, (1977)*. Second edition. Crown 8vo, 192pp. frontispiece illustration in color, additional plates in color and black and white, original red cloth, decorative gilt quill on front cover, spine lettered in gilt, color printed publisher's wrappers. A very good copy. Milton is discussed at length in chapter 4 ("In Praise of God, In Praise of Man"), with a full-page color plate at the head of this chapter reproducing Milton's study at Chalfont St. Giles ("filled with Milton memorabilia," including on a table in the foreground a bust of Milton and the open title page of Cresset Press 1931 edition of *PL*); other plates in black and white include first edition title page of *PL* and vignette portrait of Milton at twenty-one.

82. Osgood, Charles Grosvenor. **POETRY AS A MEANS OF GRACE**. *Princeton University Press*[,] *Princeton • mcmxli London: Humphrey Milford • Oxford University Press*. First edition. 8vo, 131pp., half-title, decorative border trim on title page with emblem of the University at the bottom, "Designed by Elmer Adler" (verso title page), original reddish-brown cloth, spine in contrasting brown cloth lettered in gilt and decorated in reddish-brown lines, gray endpapers. A nice copy in printed publisher's wrappers (bit frayed at edges). Included is a long chapter on Milton, entitled "Milton."

83. Osgood, Charles G. **THE VOICE OF ENGLAND**[.] A History of English Literature[.] *Harper & Brothers Publishers*[,] *New York and London, (1935)*. First edition. 8vo, xiii+[iii]+627pp., half-title, original red cloth (a bit rubbed, some underlining and check marks), front cover and spine lettered in gilt, fore- and bottom edges untrimmed. A good copy. Included is a long chapter on Milton, entitled "Milton," preceded by a chapter on "The Seventeenth Century."

The collection also has a copy of the second edition: "Harper & Brothers[,] New York, (1952), with the signature of Milton scholar Maurice Kelley on fly-leaf.

84. Otis, William Bradley, and Morriss H. Needleman. **A SURVEY-HISTORY OF ENGLISH LITERATURE**[[.] *New York*[:] *Barnes & Noble, Inc., 1938*. First edition. 8vo, xiv+670pp., original black cloth, front cover and spine lettered in gilt and lined in blind relief, original advertisement tipped on fly-leaf. A very nice copy. Included are two chapters on Milton: "The Age of Milton" and "The Age of Milton: John Milton." Among his "Suggested Merits" is the "Cosmic sweep of theme and sublimity of execution."

85. Parrott, Edward. **THE PAGEANT OF ENGLISH LITERATURE**. Depicted By J. M. W. Turner, Daniel Maclise, Sir John Millais, Briton Riviere[,] Sir Lawrence Alma-Tadema, Ford Madox Brown, E. M. Ward[,] J. W. Waterhouse, Sir James Linton, George H. Boughton[,] J. A. M'Neill Whisler, Sir E. J. Poynter, W. F. Yeames[,] Horace Vernet, Sir E. Burne-Jones, J. Doyle Penrose[,] Edgar Bundy, J. C. Dollman, Louis E. Fournier, Etc. And

Described By Edward Parrot, M.A., LL.D. Author of "The Pageant Of British History," Etc. *Thomas Nelson And Sons[,] London, Edinburgh, Dublin, And New York[,] 1914.* First edition. Crown 8vo, 480pp., frontispiece color illustration, additional full-page illustrations and portraits in color and in black and white, original blue cloth, front cover and spine ruled and lettered in gilt, t.e.g., illustrated endpapers. A very nice copy with prize label on front pastedown. Included are two chapters on Milton: Chapter XXIX—"John Milton"—with one full-page illustration in color, "*L'Allegro* (From the painting by C. W. Cope, R.A.)," and one full-page illustration in black and white, "*Circe, The Mother Of Comus.* (From the picture by Sir Edward Burne-Jones. Photo by F. Hollyer.)"; and Chapter XXX— "*Paradise Lost*"—with two full-page illustrations in color, "*Milton at Chalfont.* From the picture by A. L. Vernon)" and "*Milton dictating 'Samson Agonistes*'; (From the picture by J. C. Horsley)."

86. Parrott, Thomas Marc. **STUDIES OF A BOOK-LOVER.** *New York: James Pott & Company, 1904.* First edition (by Pott & Company). 8vo, ix+[3]+301pp., "Copyright, 1901 By The Booklovers Library"; "Copyright 1903, 1904 By The Library Publishing Co."; "Copyright, 1904 By James Pott & Co. First Impression September, 1904" (verso title page), half-title, frontispiece portrait of Matthew Arnold, original green cloth (spine a bit rubbed), front cover and spine lettered in gilt, with gilt lettering on front cover contained within a large blind floral design, fore- and bottom edges untrimmed. A good copy. Included is a chapter on Milton entitled "The Autobiography Of Milton," in which Parrott uses quotations from Milton's writings to depict his life. Parrott also states at one point that "I have sometimes thought that it would be a pleasant and not unprofitable task for a student of literature to go through the letters, essays and poems of Milton in detail, to pick out the autobiographical passages, and to arrange them in such an order that the poet might himself tell us the story of his inner and his outer life from boyhood till old age" (p. 128) Stevens 2257.

87. Pattison, Mark. **MILTON**[.] *Macmillan And Co., Limited[,] St. Martin's Street, London[,] 1909.* Bound with **CHAUCER** By Adolphus William Ward. *London[:] Macmillan And Co., Limited[;] New York: The Macmillan Company[,] 1907.* Bound with **SPENSER** By R. W. Church. *London[:] Macmillan And Co., Limited[;] New York: The Macmillan Company[,] 1906.* 3 volumes in one. 8vo, 207pp.,+188pp.,+227pp., half-titles, full contemporary blue morocco, gilt rules on covers, with central gilt seal on front cover, spine elaborately gilt-decorated, raised bands with gilt trim, outer dentelles gilt, marbled endpapers and edges. A fine copy in a splendid Prize Binding, with prize label (dated 1910) tipped in on front pastedown. *Milton* appears third here. First published in London in 1879 and in America in 1880 (see copy of each with Nineteenth-century Miltoniana).

The collection also has editions of Pattison's *Milton* by "A. L. Fowle[,] Publisher[,] New York, n.d. [ca. 1900]" in the series "Makers Of Literature," with frontispiece portrait, and continuing in "English Men Of Letter" by "Macmillan & Co., London, 1902."

88. Petti, Anthony G. **ENGLISH LITERARY HANDS FROM CHAUCER TO DRYDEN**[.] Anthony G. Petti[,] Professor of English at the University of Calgary[.] *[London:] Edward Arnold[,] (1977).* First edition. 8vo, ix+133, half-title, facsimile reproductions of handwriting on verso with related discussion and biography on recto, original green cloth (spine a bit faded, neat signature on fly-leaf), front cover elaborately lettered in blind, spine lettered in gilt. A nice copy. Included is a facsimile reproduction of Milton's handwriting, along with a discussion of the poet's handwriting. "More holograph material of Milton survives than of any other major English poet prior to the 18th century" (p. 59).

89. Piper, David. **THE IMAGE OF THE POET**[:] **BRITISH POETS AND THEIR PORTRAITS.** *Clarendon Press • Oxford[,] 1982.* First edition. 8vo, xxx+[ii]+ 219pp., half-title, numerous portrait reproductions throughout, original red cloth, spine lettered in large gilt letters with decorative gilt emblem at bottom, gray endpapers, printed publisher's wrappers. A fine copy. Included are five reproductions of Milton portraits with commentary: (1) Milton at age ten; (2) Milton at twenty-one (The "Onslow portrait," ca. 1629); (3) Milton bust in clay, unbaked; (4) frontispiece portrait from 1645 edition of poems; and (5) the Faithorne portrait, 1670. Later, in the chapter on Alexander Pope, several additional reproductions of Milton appear: (1) a reproduction of Jonathan Richardson's "Richardson and his son with an apparition of Milton"; (2) "Milton into Pope" by Jonathan Richardson, ca. 1734–35; (3) the Poets' Corner in Westminster Abbey; (4) "Shakespeare and Milton; Chelsea/Bow rococo porcelain figures, ca. 1760–70"; and (5) "Shakespeare and Milton. Neoclassic variations on the Chelsea/Bow figures."

90. Powell, Lawrence Clark. **YOU, JOHN MILTON** An Address By Lawrence Clark Powell At The Presentation Of The One Millionth Volume [*Areopagitica*] To The The University Of Oklahoma Library By Mrs. George P. Livermore January 14, 1966. *The Library University Of*

Oklahoma[,] Norman[,] (1966). Tall, slim pamphlet, 12pp., photograph of the presentation, original light green wrappers, title in black on front cover. The one millionth volume was a copy of *Areopagitica.* Powell's address is very appropriate to the occasion and to the significance of the book.

91. Powys, John Cowper. **ENJOYMENT OF LITERATURE.** *Simon And Schuster[,] New York • 1938.* First edition. 8vo, xxvii+522pp., title page with decorative green border, original cream cloth, central emblem in black with gilt initials on front cover, black label with gilt lettering on spine. A good copy with ownership signature and neat inscription on fly-leaf. Included is a chapter on Milton, with a reproduction of an unattributed portrait of Milton as a young man.

92. Rascoe, Burton. **TITANS OF LITERATURE** From Homer To The Present. Illustrated. *G. P. Putnam's Sons • 1932[.] New York And London.* First edition. 8vo, xiii+496pp., half-title, frontispiece illustration-portrait, additional portraits (none of Milton), original black cloth (a bit rubbed), gilt lettering on front cover and spine. A good copy. Included is a chapter on Milton, in which Rascoe expresses his utter disdain for Milton and Milton's poetry, contending: (1) "that *PL* and *PR* are horrible examples of what may occur when a man with a displeasing type of mind happens to be an expert versifying technician in what is loosely called the biblical style"; (2) that "Milton is lacking, in that epic, in common sense, in true loftiness of feeling, in kindness and generosity and give-and-take, and most all, he is thoroughly lacking in style, grand or common"; and (3) that "*PL* is one of the baldest plagiarisms in the history of literature."

93. Raymond, Dora Neill. **OLIVER'S SECRETARY[:] JOHN MILTON IN AN ERA OF REVOLT** By Dora Neill Raymond, Ph.D.[,] Professor Of History, Sweet Briar College, Sometime Jacob Schiff Fellow In Political Science, Columbia University[.] Illustrated. *Minton, Balch & Company[,] New York[,] 1932.* First edition. 8vo, xiv+341pp., half-title, frontispiece portrait of Milton "From the Portrait by William Dobson, Friend of Van Dyke," additional illustrations (*Milton in His Tenth Year, Title Page of Mercurius Politicus, Frontispiece of the Revolution of Time, The Burning of the Books, John Milton, Aetat 62*), half-title for each of the three major parts, "Footnotes" and index at the end, original red cloth, central black shield with red emblem within on front cover, black label on spine with red lettering within decorative black trim, fore- and bottom edges untrimmed. A fine copy in printed publisher's wrappers (a bit aged).

94. Rowlands, Walter. **AMONG THE GREAT MASTERS OF LITERATURE** Scenes in the Lives of Great Authors[.] Thirty-two Reproductions of Famous Paintings with Text by Walter Rowlands. *Boston: Dana Estes & Company Publishers, (1900).* First edition. 8vo, [vii]+225pp., half-title, frontispiece illustration, protective tissue guard with identification of illustration printed in red, title page in red and black with decorative black border trim and small central emblem, additional illustrations, each with protective tissue guard with identification of the illustration printed in red, original green cloth (spine and back cover a little rubbed), front cover elaborately decorated in gilt with Grecian pillars, laurel, ivy, open book, quill, and tassel, spine lettered in gilt, t.e.g., others untrimmed. A lovely copy, finely printed by the Colonial Press, Boston. One chapter is devoted to Milton with two illustrations: *Mr. Oliver Cromwell Of Ely Visits Mr. John Milton. From painting by David Neal.* and *Milton Dictating Paradise Lost to His Daughters. From painting by Michael Munkacsy.*

95. Saluste Du Bartas, Guillaume de Saluste, Sieur. **THE DIVINE WEEKS AND WORKS OF GUILLAUME DE SALUSTE SIEUR DU BARTAS** Translated by Joshua Sylvester[.] Edited with an Introduction and Commentary by Susan Sylvester. *[Oxford:] Oxford English Texts, 1979. 2 volumes.* 8vo, xvi+488pp.,+940pp.(pagination continuing from volume 1), half-title, frontispiece portrait plate of Joshua Sylvester, volume 1, of 1621 title page, volume 2, original blue buckram, spine lettered in gilt with gilt trim, original printed publisher's wrappers. A fine set. The subject is the story of the creation; it is known that this was a favorite book of Milton's at an early age and provided one of the sources for *PL.* See 1605 edition of Saluste Du Bartas *His Devine Weekes & Workes* and several other early seventeenth-century editions with Seventeenth-century Miltoniana and discussion there of the great popularity of this work. This is the first modern scholarly edition of one of the most popular works of the later Renaissance. STC 21653.

96. Sitwell, Edith. **THE ENGLISH ECCENTRICS** By Edith Sitwell[.] *Sephyr Books. The Continental Book Company AB[,] Stockholm/London, (1947).* First edition. 8vo, 332pp., half-title, original white wrappers beneath printed blue publisher's wrappers (spine ends chipped). The copyright is dated 1947 on verso of title page with the notation: "This edition must not be introduced into the British Empire or the U.S.A." In good condition. Included is a lengthy discussion of Milton (pp. 302–25).

97. Stevens, D. H. **MILTON PAPERS** By David Harrison Stevens[,] Professor of English The University of

Chicago[.] *The University of Chicago Press[,] Chicago · Illinois, (1927)*. First edition. Small 4to, ix+46pp., half-title preceded by leaf on "The Modern Philology Monographs Of The University Of Chicago," frontispiece plate reproducing "Transcript Of The Milton Deed To Property In Covent Garden," second plate reproducing "A Sheet From The Lawes Autograph Setting Of *Comus*," original printed boards, blue cloth spine, printed paper label on spine. A fine copy in original printed publisher's wrappers (a little age-browned, small piece missing at top and at bottom of spine). Scarce. Stevens 1813.

98. Strousse, Flora. **JOHN MILTON** · Clarion voice of freedom · Flora Strousse[,] Author of "The Friar and the Knight," etc. *The Vanguard Press, Inc. New York. (1962)*. First edition. 8vo, 283 pp., half-title, original dark orange cloth, spine lettered in gilt, gold endpapers, printed orange publisher's wrappers, with an illustration of a young boy with writing quill against a background of a burning London, a Civil War battle scene, and a sailing ship on front cover. A nice copy. "This is the first biography for young people of one of England's greatest poets" (statement on dust jacket). See *John Milton* by Edmund Fuller (1967) also listed here a book also written for young people.

99. Thomas, Edward. **FEMININE INFLUENCE ON THE POETS**. *London[:] Martin Secker, Number Five John Street[,] Adelphi[,] 1910*. First edition. 8vo, [iii]+352pp., half-title, engraved frontispiece illustration and three other engraved illustrations (very fine impressions), title page in blue and black, original blue cloth (spine faded), front cover lettered in black, spine lettered in gilt, t.e. blue, the others untrimmed, partially unopened. A very nice copy, handsomely printed by the Ballantyne Press. Included is a rather lengthy section on Milton, with quotations from his poems. Uncommon.

100. Toland (John). **THE LIFE OF JOHN MILTON ... WITH AMYNTOR; OR A DEFENSE OF MILTON'S LIFE.** By John Toland. And Various Notes Now Added ... *London Printed For John Darby MDCXCIX (1699). Printed For A. Millar In The Strand[.] MDCCLXI*. Reproduction edition, ca. 1970s. 8vo, 259pp., separate title page for *Amyntor* reproduced, original red buckram, spine lettered in gilt within gilt rules. A nice copy. A reproduction, without identification [ca. 1970s], of the second edition of Toland's *Life and Amyntor*, edited by Thomas Hollis and published together for the fist time in 1761 (the first Hollis edition). See copy of edition by Hollis of Toland's *Life and Amyntor* with Eighteenth-century Miltoniana; see copy of Toland's *Life of Milton* and his *Amyntor* first published separately in 1699 with Seventeenth-century Miltoniana.

101. Turner, W. J., editor. **ROMANCE OF ENGLISH LITERATURE**. Introduction by Kate O'Brien. Edited by W. J. Turner. With 48 plates in colour and 125 illustrations in black and white. *Hastings House Publishers[,] New York, (1944)*. First edition. 8vo, 324pp., half-title, full-page color plates, illustrations in black and white, decorated initial letters, original yellow cloth, spine lettered in gilt. A nice copy. Included are lengthy discussions of Milton in the section, "The Word Of God: Milton To Ruskin," in the chapter on "The English Bible" by Sir Herbert Grierson, and in the chapter on "The English Poets" by Lord David Cecil, with a reproduction of the Vertue frontispiece portrait of 1670, a facsimile of the *Lycidas* manuscript page, a full-page color reproduction of the portrait of Milton at twenty-one by Van der Gucht, and a reproduction of John Martin's illustration of *"The Appearance of Raphael to Adam and Eve."* Both Grierson's *The English Bible* and Cecil's *The English Poets* were published earlier as individual pamphlets, *The English Bible* in 1943 (see copy listed here under Grierson), and *The English Poets* in 1941 (see copy listed here under Cecil). See also *Impressions of English Literature*, which is a duplicate of this edition published a year later in 1945 under a new title and again in 1947 (see copy listed here).

102. Turner, W. J., editor. **IMPRESSIONS OF ENGLISH LITERATURE**. Introduction by Kate O'Brien. Edited by W. J. Turner. With 48 plates in colour and 125 illustrations in black and white. *Collins · 14 St. James's Place · London[,] MCMXLVII*. Third edition. Large 8vo, 324pp., half-title, full-page color plates, illustrations in black and white, decorated initial letters, original blue cloth (a bit rubbed), spine lettered in gilt, printed green publisher's wrappers (a little used, chipped at spine ends) decorated with two large flowers in contrasting gold and reddish-brown on front cover. A nice copy. Included are lengthy discussions of Milton with reproductions of portraits and illustrations as in *Romance of English Literature*, immediately preceding, of which this edition is a reproduction, under a new title, and published in London in 1946 and again in 1947.

103. Untermeyer, Louis. **LIVES OF THE POETS[:]** The Story Of One Thousand Years Of English And American Poetry by Louis Untermeyer[.] *Simon And Schuster[,] New York · 1959*. First edition. 8vo, x+757+[1]+pp., half-title, original black cloth, central gilt emblem on front cover, spine lettered in gilt, marbled green endpapers, t.e. blue, printed red publisher's wrappers. A very nice copy. A chapter, entitled "Blind Visionary," is devoted to Milton.

104. [Voltaire] **VOLTAIRE'S ESSAY ON MILTON** Edited By Desmond Flower[.] *Cambridge[:] Privately*

Printed[,], 1954. Slim 8vo, 29pp., half-title, frontispiece bust of Milton "in the Combination Room at Christ's College, Cambridge," foreword by Desmond Flower, printed on Whatman paper with types and ornaments made by Deberny & Peignot, original half light blue cloth, marbled paper over boards, spine decorated and lettered in gilt. A very fine copy. One of the few pieces written in English by Voltaire with "no edition of the original text . . . after that issued in Dublin in 1760" (foreword). "Printed and bound at the University Press, Cambridge, for presentation by the Printer to his friends in printing and publishing Christmas 1954" (colophon leaf at end). One of a limited edition of 400 copies. See copy of 1728 "Second Edition, corrected and revis'd by the Author," with Eighteenth-century Miltoniana.

105. Warner, Rex. **JOHN MILTON** with eight plates in photogravure[,] six illustrations in line[.] *Max Parrish[,] London[,] 1949.* First edition. Slim 8vo, 95pp., half-title ("Personal Portraits Edited by Patric Dickinson and Sheila Shannon"), decorative border trim on title page, eight plates in photogravure, six illustrations in line, original orange cloth, central emblem in gilt on front cover, spine lettered in gilt, printed publisher's wrappers with portrait of Milton from a 1747 engraving by George Vertue on front cover (spine and back cover of wrappers a little used). A nice copy.

106. Warner, Rex. **JOHN MILTON** with eight plates in photogravure[,] six illustrations in line[.] *Chanticleer Press[,] New York[,] 1950.* Second edition; first American edition. Slim 8vo, 95pp., half-title ("Personal Portraits Edited by Patric Dickinson and Sheila Shannon"), decorative border trim on title page, eight plates in photogravure, six illustrations in line, original orange cloth, central emblem in gilt on front cover, spine lettered in gilt, printed publisher's wrappers with portrait of Milton from a 1747 engraving by George Vertue on front cover. A fine copy.

107. Wedgwood, C. V. **MILTON AND HIS WORLD.** *London: Lutterworth Press, (1969).* First London edition. Slim 4to, 48pp., numerous portraits and illustrations, original black cloth, front cover and spine lettered in gilt, printed publisher's wrappers (slightly rubbed). A nice copy in near mint condition. Simultaneously published in New York, in original yellow cloth, a copy of which is also in the collection.

108. West, Paul. **SPORTING WITH AMARYLLIS.** *Woodstock, New York: The Overlook Press, (1996).* First edition. Slim 4to, 158pp., half-title, original black cloth spine, orange paper boards, printed publisher's wrappers with sensual illustration in color on front cover. A fine copy. "A novel by Paul West" about Milton as a sex maniac, which, according to a *New York Times* review by Tony Tanner (copy of review laid in) is "a pretentious, distasteful and futile book"; a "counterfactual" that is ultimately "pointless." An apt review about a book that has little, if any, merit in being published.

108A. (Cross-listing) Williamson, George C. **THE PORTRAITS, PRINTS, AND WRITINGS OF JOHN MILTON[.]** Milton Tercentenary[.] [Edited By George C. Williamson With An Appendix And Index By C. Sayle.] *Exhibited at Christ's College, Cambridge[,] 1908.* First edition (June 12, 1908). 4to. Stevens 1774. See main listing under Milton Tercentenary: Portraits, 1908, here.

109. Winterich, John T. **TWENTY-THREE BOOKS AND THE STORIES BEHIND THEM** By John T. Winterich[.] *1939[,] J. B. Lippincott Company[,] Philadelphia • New York • London • Toronto.* First edition. 8vo, [iv]+ 241pp., half-title, title page in red and black, frontispiece illustration, illustration for each chapter, original blue cloth, spine lettered in gilt, printed publisher's wrappers (aged). A very good copy with newspaper review and advertisement laid in. Chapter One is devoted to *Paradise Lost*, with a reproduction of the illustration *As Accurate as the Cherry-Tree Story* and a sketch of Milton dictating *PL* to his daughters by Mihaly Michael Munkacsy in the New York Public Library.

110. Wolfe, Don M. **MILTON AND HIS ENGLAND** By Don M. Wolfe[.] *Princeton, New Jersey[:] Princeton University Press • 1971.* First edition. Slim 4to, [xii+109+ 4pp.] unpaginated (with illustration numbered in place of pagination), half-title, illustrated title page, more than 150 illustrations, original orange cloth, spine lettered in gilt, printed publisher's wrappers, with reproduction of London at Milton's time on front cover and small vignette of Faithorne portrait in upper right corner. A fine copy.

IV

John Milton in Select Anthologies

(Chronologically Listed)

Space allows only a very few anthologies from among the 375 in the collection to be listed here. Some anthologies appear within the main listing because they contain illustrations for Milton's shorter poems, for example, the 1911 edition of Palgrave's Golden Treasury with Maxfield Parrish's illustrations of Milton's Ode on the Morning of Christ's Nativity, which is listed under the assumption that the primary emphasis in this instance, and in other similar instances, is on the poem, not the anthology.

See commentary on the role of the anthology with *The Poetical Miscellany. For the Use of Schools* (London: Printed for T. Becket and P. A. De Hondt, at Tully's Head, in the Strand. MDCCLXII).

A. (Cross-listing) **THE ENGLISH PARNASSUS**; Or a Help to English Poesie. Containing a Collection of all the Rhythming Monosyllables, The choicest Epithets and Phrases. With some general Forms upon all Occasions, Subjects, and Themes, Alphabetically digested . . . Together with A short Institution to English Poesie, by way of Preface. By Joshua Poole. *London: Printed for Henry Brome, Thomas Baffett, and John Wright, 1677.* Second edition. 8vo, [xxviii]+639pp., frontispiece woodcut illustration, title page in red and black, original calf (spine restored). "The Books principally made use of in the compiling of this work" include works of Chaucer, Jonson, Spenser, Burton, Sidney, Beaumont, and Milton. See main listing under *Poole* in Seventeenth-century Miltoniana.

1. A COLLECTION OF MORAL AND SACRED POEMS FROM THE MOST CELEBRATED ENGLISH AUTHORS. By John Wesley, M.A. Fellow of Lincoln-College, Oxford. *Bristol: Printed and sold by Felix Farley, et al, 1744.* 3 volumes. First edition. 8vo, vii+[1]+347,+373,+288+8+2+2pp., modern polished sheep (spine ends and joints rubbed, new endpapers, few brown spots), gilt rules and decorative gilt pieces on covers and spines, red and green leather labels. A good set with advertisement leaf and errata leaf bound in at the end of volume 3 after "Contents" pages. This significant poetical miscellany opens with Milton's *Morning Hymn* and his *Creation*; the majority of the poems are by John and Charles Wesley and their contemporaries. Very rare. Case 441 (1); Green 58.

2. A SELECT COLLECTION OF MODERN POEMS, Moral and Philosophical. By the most Eminent Hands. The Third Edition. [Quotations from Lucret.] *Glasgow: Printed for Robert Urie, MDCCLIX.* Third edition. 12mo in 6s, 207pp., contemporary polished calf (slight embrowning), gilt rules on covers, red morocco label with gilt lettering on spine, raised bands within gilt rules. A lovely copy. The collection opens with *C*, which is the most substantial work in the entire collection; *L, L'A, IlP, Song On May Morning*, and *A Sonnet to Cyriac Skinner* (No. 22) follow. Milton's poems occupy nearly a third of the entire volume. The second edition appeared in 1750. Very rare. Not in Case; Not in Coleridge; Not in Kohler.

3. THE POETICAL MISCELLANY; Consisting Of Select Pieces From the Works of the following Poets, viz. Milton, Dryden, Pope, Addison, Gay, Parnel, Young, Thomson, Akenside, Philips, Gray, Watts, &c. For the Use of Schools. *London: Printed for T. Becket and P. A. De Hondt, at Tully's Head, in the Strand. MDCCLXII.* First edition. 8vo, [vi]+340pp., decorative headpieces, contemporary sheep (worn, spine chipped, joints cracked), gilt rules on covers and spine (faded). A good copy with several contemporary signatures, some inoffensive underlinings throughout, and several perceptive comments in a contemporary hand in the margins, especially in the Milton section. Scarce. Not in Coleridge; Not in Kohler.

An important work in helping to establish a new manner in which Milton (and other great poets and writers) were to be read and studied in years to come. The "anthology" was to become in the next two centuries an important means for selectively passing on the great writings of poets like Milton. Students and those with leisure time were exposed to great writers through selections and excerpts. As time went on, especially before the age of radio and television, the anthology became a special way in which great writers could be passed on to new generations of readers, from one culture to another. At the same time, anthologies provided a way of focusing upon the writings that attracted a given age to a great writer; they tell us much about how a great writer is viewed, to which works (or selections from works) an age is attracted or exposed, and how these attractions changed (or how readers were influenced) through the generations, particularly with respect to a poet like Milton.

4. THE POETICAL MISCELLANY; Consisting Of Select Pieces From the Works of the following Poets, viz. Milton, Dryden, Pope, Addison, Gay, Parnel, Young, Thomson, Akenside, Philips, Gray, Wharton, &c. For the Use of Schools. The Second Edition. *London: Printed for T. Cadell, in the Strand. MDCCLXIX.* Second edition. 8vo, [viii]+310pp., half-title, decorative headpieces, contemporary calf (rubbed, rebacked), spine ruled and lettered in gilt with small gilt decorations, signature (dated 1786) of Charlotte, Countess of Leicester, on front blank, contemporary signature on title page, early armorial bookplate on front pastedown. A good copy. Scarce. John Shawcross told me privately of a copy in the University of Chicago Library; NCBEL II, 390; Not in Coleridge; Not in Kohler.

5. THE POETICAL MISCELLANY; Consisting Of Select Pieces From the Works of the following Poets, viz. Milton, Dryden, Pope, Addison, Gay, Parnel, Young, Thomson, Akenside, Philips, Gray, Wharton, Shakespeare, Goldsmith, Wilkie, &c. &c. For the Use of Schools. The Third Edition, with Improvements. *London: Printed for W. Strahan; and T. Cadell, in the Strand. 1778.* Third edition. 12mo, [viii]+332+[4]pp., half-title, decorative headpiece, original sheep (worn, joints broken, spine chipped), gilt-decorated spine, red morocco label, four pages of advertisements listing "Books Printed For T. Cadell, in the Strand" bound in at end. An okay copy, internally very nice, with contemporary signature "B. Bridges, 1779" on title and with bookplate of another member of the Bridges family (first name defaced). This collection of lyric poetry first appeared in 1762, then again in 1769—both listed here. Scarce. John Shawcross shared with me that "There is a third edition (and recorded on the title page) from Dublin in 1774." Not in Coleridge; Not in Kohler.

6. THE BEAUTIES OF THE POETS. Being A Collection Of Moral and Sacred Poetry, From the most eminent Authors. Compiled by the late Rev. Thomas Janes, Of Bristol. [Quotation from Tatler.] *London: Printed at the Cicero Press by and for Henry Fry, No. 5, Worship Street, Upper Moorfields. And sold by Scatcherd and Whitaker, Ave Maria Lane; W. Darton, White Lion Court, Birchin Lane, Cornhill; and in Bristol by Thomas Mills, in Wine Street. M.DCC.LXXXVIII.* 8vo, vii+[i]+ 316pp., subscriber's list, contemporary calf (worn, joints cracked, spine ends chipped, corners worn), gilt-decorated spine, gilt dentelles (faded). A good copy with early signature on front pastedown. The section on Milton occupies almost a tenth of the entire volume. John Shawcross shared with me that the first edition "was published [ca. 1777]; other editions were published in] 1790, 1792, and 1799." Besides the edition here, the collection also has an 1810 edition. Scarce. Not in Coleridge; Not in Kohler.

7. THE POETICAL MISCELLANY; Consisting Of Select Pieces From the Works of the following Poets, viz. Milton, Dryden, Pope, Addison, Gay, Parnel, Young, Thomson, Akenside, Philips, Gray, Wharton, Shakespeare, Goldsmith, Wilkie, &c. &c. For the Use of Schools. The Fourth Edition. *London: Printed for A. Strahan; and T. Cadell, in the Strand. 1789.* Fourth edition. 8vo, [viii]+332+[4]pp., half-title, decorative headpiece, original sheep (quite worn, joints cracked, spine chipped at top and bottom), gilt rules on spine, gilt dentelles. All in all, a decent copy of a very rare edition with four pages of advertisements listing "New Editions . . . printed for T. Cadell, in the Strand" bound in at end. This collection of lyric poetry first appeared in 1762; the second edition appeared in 1769; and the fourth in 1778—all listed here. Scarce. John Shawcross told me that there is a "Copy in Cambridge University Library"; Not in Coleridge; Not in Kohler.

8. **SPECIMENS OF THE EARLY ENGLISH POETS.** *London: Printed For Edwards, Pall-Mall. 1790.* First edition. 8vo, v+[3]+323pp., edited by George Ellis, original finely polished tree calf (front cover detached), ornately decorated gilt border trim on covers, gilt-decorated spine, black morocco label (defective), inner and outer dentelles finely tooled in gilt, marbled endpapers. A very nice copy with early book label in an early hand (dated 1802) tipped in on front pastedown. Included from Milton are *L'A* and *IlP*. The three-volume 1801 edition is also in the collection. Scarce. John Shawcross told me that "Kentucky has an extra-illustrated copy"; Not in Coleridge; Not in Kohler.

9. **THE AMERICAN ORATOR:** Or, Elegant Extracts in Prose and Poetry; Comprehending a Diversity of Oratorical Specimens, Of The Eloquence Of Popular Assemblies, Of The Bar, Of The Pulpit, &c. Principally intended for the Use Of Schools And Academies. To which are prefixed, A Dissertation On Oratorical Delivery And The Outlines Of Gesture. By Increase Cooke. *Sidney's Press, for Increase Cooke And Co. Book-Sellers, Church-Street, New Haven. 1811.* First edition. 12mo in 6s, 408pp., original sheep (joints and edges rubbed, age-browning throughout), gilt rules on spine (faded), red morocco label with gilt lettering, early names on endpapers. Among the many authors represented is Milton with a lengthy excerpt from *PL*: "Discourse between Adam and Eve retiring to rest" (pp. 367–70). Rare. Shaw & Shoemaker 22614.

10. **THE POETICAL REVIEW, OR SELECT SPECIMENS OF BRITISH POETRY,** Illustrated By Numerous And Elegant Critique, Etc. Extracted From The Best Review And Magazines In The Language, And From The Works Of The Most Celebrated Authors In English Literature. Edited By Henry Kelvey. [Quotation from Beattie.] *Sheffield: Printed For The Editor. MDCCCXXX.* First edition. 8vo, xvi+286pp., dedication page with quotation from Milton, preface dated "Sheffield, Dec. 27, 1830," original three-quarter calf, marbled paper over boards (very worn, spine partially torn at bottom and reglued, pages a little age-darkened, title page slightly frayed along edges, bottom portion of last page torn away, lacking endpapers, sketches of birds on front and back pastedowns), spine decorated in blind, black leather label lettered in gilt. Laid in: a contemporary note: "To Arthur S. Kimberley. This is a school book of your Grandfather Arthur Weale Bartletts when he attended boarding school at Black Heath England. F. S. Kimberley." Included is a large selection of Milton's poetry, from pp. 77–123, with critical commentary from various sources.

11. **STUDIES IN POETRY** Embracing Notices And Writings Of The Best Poets In The English Language, A Copious Selection Of Elegant Extracts, A Short Analysis Of Hebrew Poetry, And Translations From The Sacred Poets: Designed To Illustrate The Principle Of Rhetoric, And Teach Their Application To Poetry. By George B. Cheever. *Boston: Carter And Hendee, 1830.* First edition? 8vo, xvi+480pp. (pp. 361–72 are reprinted in place of pp. 445–56, which are lacking), engraved frontispiece illustration, original one-half black calf, marbled paper over boards (a bit rubbed, joints cracked, spine ends chipped, slight age-browning throughout), spine lettered and ruled in gilt with small decorative gilt devices. Included are poetical selections from Milton, in a section devoted to him with a brief biography at the outset of the section, along with Chaucer, Shakespeare, Dryden, Goldsmith, Cowper, Wordsworth, Coleridge, and others, and a selection of American poets.

12. **THE LONDON CARCANET.** Containing Select Passages From The Most Distinguished Writers. From The Second London Edition. *New-York: Charles H. Peabody, 129, Broadway. 1831.* First American edition. Small 8vo, 244+[7]pp., frontispiece illustration, engraved title page with central vignette illustration of an angelic figure, half-title, printed title page, "Preface" (dated 1830), "Index Of Authors," original printed orange paper boards (rubbed, with some wear and chipping, minor embrowning, some light spotting), front cover repeating title page in black, spine and back cover lettered in black, edges untrimmed, old historical society bookplate on front pastedown. A good copy with three pages of "extracts from English and American Journals of high repute" on the merits of this publication and three pages of advertisements. Primarily a collection of Romantic poets, although neither Keats nor Shelley are represented, with Shakespeare having two poems included and Milton four poems—the most representation outside the Romantics. Rare.

13. **SELECT WORKS OF THE BRITISH POETS** With Biographical and Critical Prefaces by Dr. Aikin. *Philadelphia: Published by Thomas Wardle, 1831.* First edition? 8vo, title page with engraved harp at center, printed in double column, contemporary full maroon morocco (bit rubbed along edges and corners), gilt rules on covers with central gilt harp, spine elaborately gilt-decorated in the panels, raised bands with gilt trim, inner and outer dentelles finely tooled in gilt, a.e.g. A lovely copy in a fine early American binding with contemporary presentation inscription on front blank. Included are extensive poetical selections from Milton, including *PL, PR, SA*, and select shorter poems, in a section devoted to him.

14. **POETICAL ANNUAL:** Being Selections From The English Poets: From Spenser To Beattie. *London: Scott,*

Webster, And Geary; And Thomas Wardle, Philadelphia. 1836. First edition? 8vo, x+406pp., steel-engraved frontispiece portrait of Goldsmith, engraved title page with steel-engraved vignette illustration, twenty-four steel-engraved illustrations, some as full-page plates and some as text vignettes, by Finden et al after pictures by H. Corbould, contemporary French romantic binding by Thierry "successeur de Petit-Simier" of forest-green morocco (slightly rubbed along joints), covers with central decorated lozenge within intricately gilt- and blind-tooled fancy borders, spine elaborately decorated in gilt with small decorative pieces in gilt within the panels, broad raised bands with delicately tooled decorative gilt trim, broad inner dentelles finely tooled in gilt, outer dentelles trimmed in gilt, marbled endpapers, t.e.g., others untrimmed. A splendid copy in an elegant French romantic binding of the period. Included are poetical selections from Milton's *Paradise Lost*, with an engraved vignette illustration (fine impression) of Eve tempting Adam, engraved by C. Heath after H. Corbould, and a full-page illustration (fine impression) of Satan meeting Sin and Death, engraved by C. Heath after H. Corbould. Uncommon. Faxon 1678.

15. CYCLOPAEDIA OF ENGLISH LITERATURE; Consisting Of A Series Of Specimens Of British Writers In Prose And Verse. Connected By A Historical And Critical Narrative. Edited By Robert Chambers. In Two Volumes. *Edinburgh: Published By William And Robert Chambers, 1843. 2 volumes*. First edition. Large 8vo, half-titles, preface (dated 1843), numerous illustrations, portraits, and facsimiles, double black border around text, contemporary three-quarter tan calf, marbled paper over boards, (rubbed at joints and corners), gilt rules on spines, brown morocco labels. A very good set. Included in volume 1 is a fourteen-page section on Milton (pp. 328–42), which contains selections from Milton's poems, with life and four biographical vignette illustrations (portrait, Ludlow Castle, Cottage at Chalfont, "Remains of Milton's House at Forest Hills, near Oxford; the scenery around which is described in *L'Allegro*"), and a vignette facsimile of "Milton's Second Receipt to Simmons." A vignette illustration of *Milton Dictating to His Daughters* appears at the outset of the section: "Fourth Period 1649 to 1689." Also included is a lengthy section of prose selections (pp. 396–401), which, together with the commentary, is probably by Robert Carruthers who helped to edit this work (see Carruthers's edition of *The Poetry Of Milton's Prose*, 1827, in Chapter II). "One of Chambers' most successful works, the last edition of which appeared nearly a century later. It was the first popular literary history of Britain, aiming to give extracts from all the principal authors, set in a biographical and critical framework. Much of the work was done by Robert Carruthers of Inverness, another tireless Scottish autodidact and a considerable author and editor in his own right" (Howe's, Cat. 260, #544, 1993). The first American edition of Chambers's *Cyclopaedia Of English Literature* was published in Boston "By Gould, Kendall, And Lincoln," a copy of which is in the collection. Scarce.

16. THE BOOK OF THE POETS. Illustrated With Forty Elegant Engravings On Steel, From Designs By Corbould, &c. With an Essay on English Poetry. *London: Darton & Co., Holborn Hill. n.d. (1850).* 8vo, xxxii+458pp., half-title ("The Book Of The Poets. Chaucer To Beattie") before the poems, frontispiece illustration, engraved and printed title pages, title page undated, illustration on engraved title with "London: Darton & Co. 1850" at bottom of illustration, engraved illustrations by Corbould and others, protective tissue guards, contemporary full black morocco, covers elaborately decorated in gilt with decorative gilt trim within gilt rules and with gilt design at the center, spines richly gilt-decorated in the panels, gilt rules at top and bottom, and gilt lettering, inner and outer dentelles richly decorated in gilt, a.e.g. A very nice copy with early signature on front blank and fine impressions of the plates. Included are poetical selections from Milton with one illustration engraved by T. Ranson after T. Uwins of the *Invitation of Comus to the Lady* in *Comus* and one illustration engraved by C. Heath after H. Corbould of *The Temptation of Adam by* Eve in *Paradise Lost*.

17. CHRISTMAS WITH THE POETS: A Collection Of Songs, Carols, And Descriptive Verses, Relating To The Festival Of Christmas, From The Anglo-Norman Period To The Present Time. Embellished With Fifty Tinted Illustrations By Birket Foster, And With Initial Letters And Other Ornaments. . . . *London: David Bogue, 86, Fleet Street, MDCCCLI.* First edition 8vo, x+[2]+189pp., engraved and printed title pages, engraved title elaborately styled with two vignette illustrations in color, decorated initial letters on title page with emblem of the press on verso, all illustrations after Birket Foster in tinted color, gilt rule and decorated border around the text, decorated initial letters and ornaments, original one-half red morocco, red cloth over thick boards (a bit worn), covers elaborately decorated with holly-style Christmas paper, glazed over, central gilt title on each cover, elaborately gilt-decorated spine with rich gilt lettering, a.e.g. A good copy, in an elaborate binding of the period. Included is Milton's *NO*, Milton's poem beginning here with the *Hymn*, with one vignette illustration in tinted color after Birket Foster.

"A notable gift book, which ... must have contributed considerably to the popular revival of the 'Old Christmas' atmosphere ... " (McLean, *VBD*, pp. 170, 176). The collection also has copies of the third edition in 1855, the fifth edition in 1864, and the sixth edition in 1872.

18. SELECTIONS FROM THE CHRISTIAN POETS, Ancient and Modern. *Seeleys. Fleet Street, And Hanover Street, London: MDCCCLI.* First edition? 12mo, xvi+431pp., half-title, engraved and printed title pages, the engraved title a color printed rustic title designed by Henry Noel Humphreys, with his initials, wood-engraved vignette illustrations and partial borders to each section, publisher's rose vertical rib cloth, decoratively blind-stamped borders, central urn with foliage in gilt on both covers, red morocco spine ornately gilt (slight rubbing to head of spine, sunning to edges and cloth hinges, ink mark on back cover, pale spotting), t.e.g., others untrimmed. A nice copy of an interesting book with dated contemporary presentation inscription on half-title. One of a few publisher's bindings of this period with cloth boards and morocco spine. An unusual Humphrey's item. Included are poetical selections from Milton. Uncommon.

19. GREAT TRUTHS BY GREAT AUTHORS, A Dictionary of Aids to Reflection, Quotations of Maxims, Metaphors, Counsels, Cautions, Aphorisms, Proverbs, &c &c From Writers of all Ages and both Hemispheres. *Philadelphia: Lippincott, Grambo & Co., 1853.* First edition. 12mo in 6s, viii+564pp., half-title, double black border around text, original bright blue cloth (front endpaper stained, partly torn, slight wear at top and bottom of spine and at the corners), covers decorated with gilt rules with a recessed oval in the center ruled in fine double gilt rules with an intricate gilt embossed emblem within, spine lettered in gilt within elaborate gilt trim, a.e.g. A fine copy, in a lovely binding of the period. Included are selections (both poetry and prose) from Milton. A copy of the second edition, published in 1858, is also in the collection.

20. SACRED POETS OF ENGLAND AND AMERICA, For Three Centuries. Edited by Rufus W. Griswold. Illustrated with Steel Engravings. *New York: Appleton & Co., 1857.* Thick 12mo in 6s, 552pp., frontispiece illustration and numerous other illustrations by Beidemann, Westall, and often unattributed, on thick paper, protective tissue guards, contemporary brown calf over thick boards, elaborately tooled in blind, gilt lettering on front cover and spine, raised bands. A very nice copy in a handsome binding with later presentation inscription. Included are poetical selections from Milton, with the vignette illustration for the *NO* appearing in the 1850, first edition (copy in the collection), placed several pages later here with Andrew Marvell. Virtually a reprinting of the 1850 edition (copy in the collection), with some slight variations in a virtually identical binding.

21. POETS OF ENGLAND AND AMERICA; Selections from the Best Authors of both Countries, Designed As A Companion To All Lovers Of Poetry. [Quotation from Wordsworth.] With Illustrations From Original Designs. *London: Hamilton, Adams & Co., Paternoster Row. Liverpool: Edward Howell, Church Street. MDCCCLX.* 8vo, xxxiv+472pp., frontispiece wood-engraved illustration of *L'Allegro*, engraved by F. Borders after S. L. Groves, and other wood-engraved illustrations, title page in red and black, a lengthy "Introductory Essay" on the merits of a "new Volume of Selections from the Poets, with references to Milton," original purple grained cloth (a bit rubbed, lacking front free endpaper, bookplate removed from front pastedown), elaborately gilt-decorated front cover and spine with central gilt device incorporating title, designed by WHR (W. Harry Rogers), back cover blind-stamped, a.e.g., bookseller's ticket. A nice copy, bound by Bone & Son, with their ticket. Included are a variety of poetical selections from Milton, including *L'Allegro* and *Il Penseroso*.

22. ENGLISH SACRED POETRY OF THE OLDEN TIME. Collected and Arranged By The Rev. L. B. White, M.A.[,] Rector of St. Mary Aldermary. *London: The Religious Tract Society, 56, Paternoster Row; 65, St. Paul's Churchyard; And 164, Piccadilly. 1864.* First edition. 8vo, xvi+190+[1]pp., full-page illustration plates with protective tissue guards, illustrations within text, decorative head- and tailpieces, black border around text, original purple cloth (a bit rubbed, spine a little faded), covers and spine elaborately decorated in gilt, with central gilt device incorporating title in gilt on both covers, small gilt medallions in the four corners identifying four poets with John Milton and George Herbert in opposite corners, gilt device incorporating title in gilt on spine, a.e.g. A fine copy, in an elegant publisher's binding. Included are poetical selections from Milton and a full-page engraved illustration of a blind *Milton And His Daughters* after C. Green for the sonnet *On His Blindness*. One of the more interesting books of the period with illustrations by Du Mauier, Green, North, Tenniel, Walker, and J. D. Watson. White, *English Illustration*, pp. 123–24.

23. Variant of Preceding, in a variant binding, original green cloth (a bit rubbed), identically decorated as preceding copy and identical in every way, except for the green cloth.

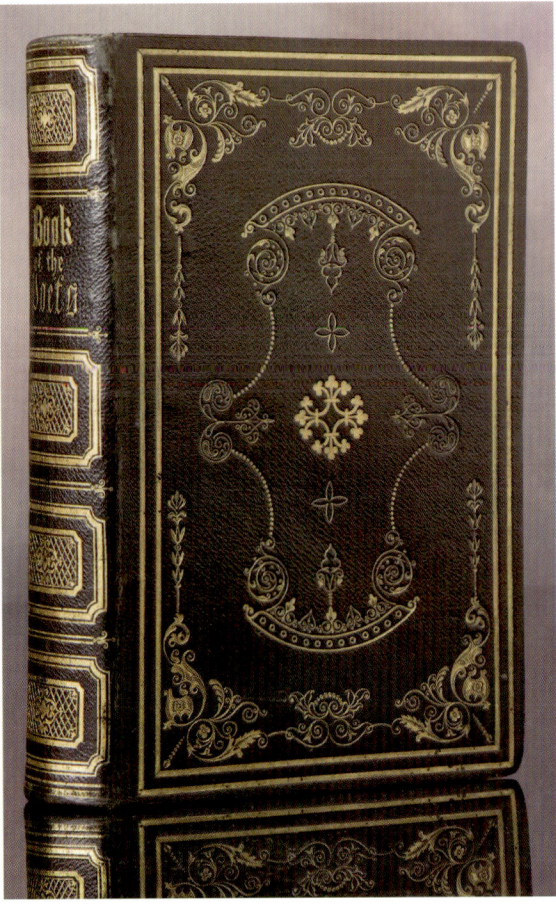

Early English Poems Chaucer To Pope. London: Sampson Low, Son & Co., 1863. Original red grain cloth, richly gilt-decorated covers and spine, with *L'A* illustrated by Cope and Townsend, Horsley, Birket Foster, and others. See #364 in Chapter II.

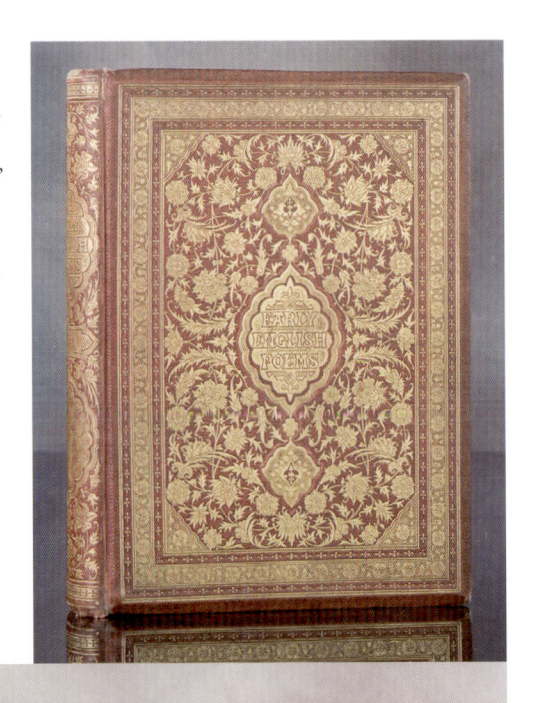

The Book of the Poets. London: Darton, 1850. Contemporary full black morocco, with covers and spine elaborately decorated in gilt with decorative gilt trim. One illustration for *C* and one for *PL*. See #16.

Golden Leaves: Chaucer To Cowper. Edited by Robert Bell. London: 1865. Small 4to. Original tortoiseshell papier-mâché beveled boards, richly gilt, brown morocco spine, with illustration for *L'A*. See #366 in Chapter II.

(top) *A Book Of Christmas Verse* Selected By H. C. Beeching: With Ten Designs By Walter Crane. London: Methuen And Company, 1895, original blue cloth, front cover and spine richly gilt-decorated with a brilliant gilt design. See #571 in Chapter II.

(bottom left) *English Sacred Poetry of the Olden Time*. London: The Religious Tract Society, 1864. Decorated original purple cloth, covers and spine elaborately decorated in gilt. See #22.

(bottom right) *English Sacred Poetry of the Olden Time* in a variant binding, original green cloth, identically decorated. See #23.

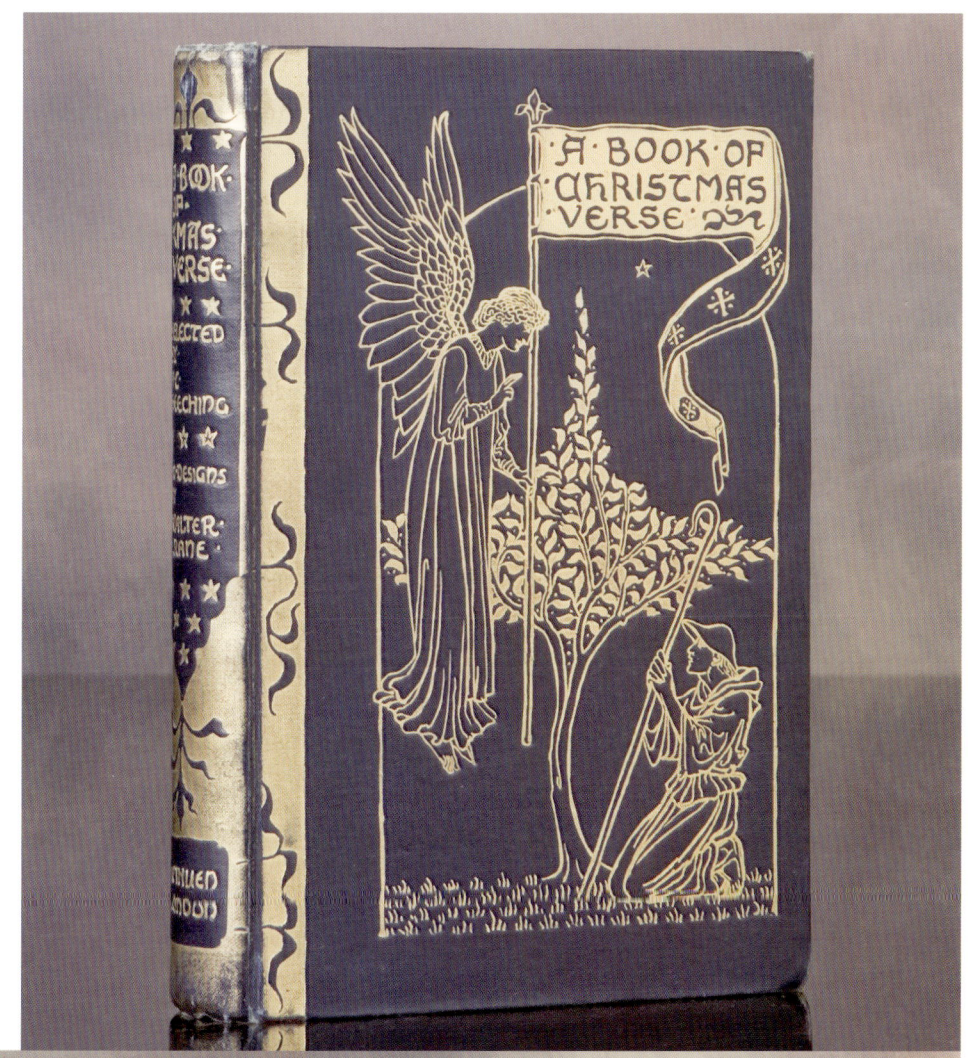

24. GLEANINGS FROM THE ENGLISH POETS, Chaucer To Tennyson, With Biographical Notices Of The Authors By Robert Inglis. Eight Engravings On Steel. Edinburgh: *Gall & Inglis, 6 George Street. London: Houlston & Wright, n.d. [ca. 1865]*. 8vo, xvi+544pp., engraved and printed title pages with vignette illustration on engraved title, engraved frontispiece illustration, and seven additional engraved illustrations, contemporary rich brown calf over thick boards (a bit rubbed), covers richly tooled in embossed blind over thick boards, spine similarly tooled in blind, front cover and spine lettered in gilt, raised bands, a.c.g., with contemporary inscription (dated 1865) on front blank. A lovely copy in a handsome binding. Included are poetical selections from Milton.

25. GEMS OF LITERATURE ELEGANT, RARE, AND SUGGESTIVE. [Quote from Alison] *Edinburgh: William P. Nimmo. 1866.* First edition. 8vo, 147pp., half-title, decorated title page in decorative black trim, printed title page in red and black with red border, "Schenck & McFarlane Printers Edinburgh" within decorated trim on verso of title page and with a decorative tailpiece on the last page, illustrations, decorative head- and tailpieces, decorated initial letters, red border around text, original reddish-brown cloth, front cover and spine richly decorated in gilt with gilt lettering, back cover decorated in blind, bevelled edges, a.e.g., "Bound by Leighton Son And Hodge," with their ticket on back pastedown. A fine copy, in a lovely publisher's binding. Included from Milton are two poems with illustrations and one prose passage with an illustration: (1) *On the Massacre at Piedmont* with an illustration at the bottom and along the right side; (2) *On His Blindness* with a vignette portrait of a blind Milton at the top and a decorative piece at the bottom; and (3) "A Book . . ." (from *Areopagitica*) with a vignette illustration at the bottom and a decorated initial letter at the beginning.

26. PEN AND PENCIL PICTURES FROM THE POETS. *Edinburgh: William P. Nimmo. 1866.* First edition? 4to, vii+150+[2]pp., half-title, vignette illustration on title page, engraved illustrations, decorated initial letters, decorative tailpieces, red border around text, original purple cloth with bevelled edges, elaborately gilt-decorated front cover and spine, back cover decorated in blind, title incorporated within central gilt device on front cover, repeated in blind on back cover, spine richly decorated in gilt with gilt lettering, a.e.g., advertisement leaf for publications by Nimmo bound in at end. A fine copy in a lovely binding of the period. Included are poetical selections from Milton, an illustration engraved by F. Borders after W. Small for *Il Penseroso*, and an illustration engraved by F. Borders after W. Small of "*The Baptism Of Jesus*" for *Paradise Regained*.

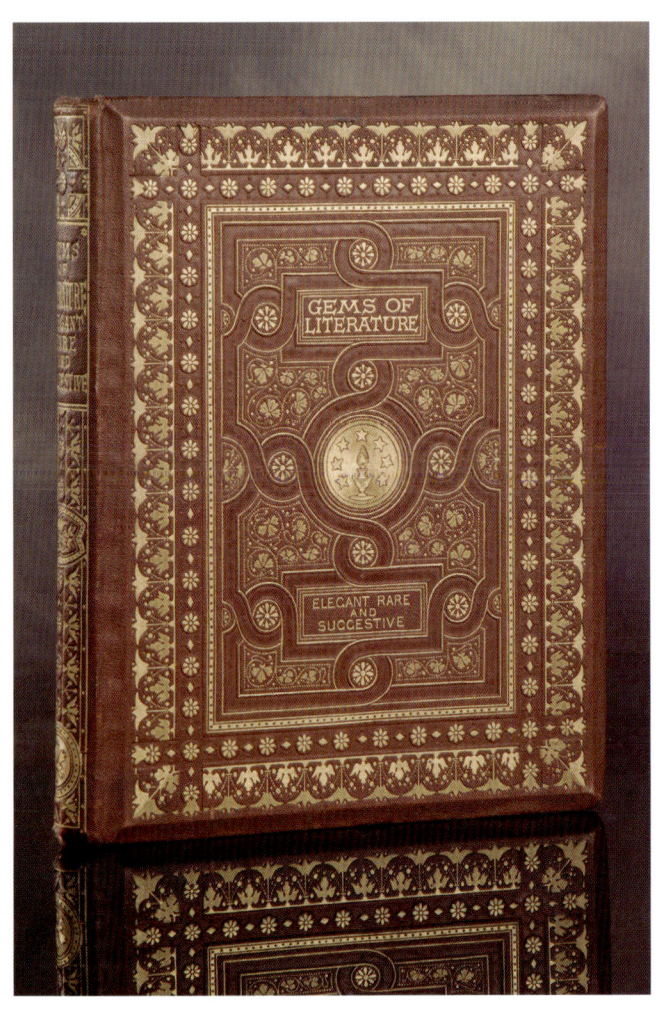

Gems of Literature. Edinburgh: William P. Nimmo, 1866. Decorated original reddish-brown cloth, front cover and spine richly decorated in gilt with gilt lettering, beveled edges. See #25.

27. ART AND SONG[:] A Series Of Original Highly Finished Steel Engravings From Masterpieces Of Art Of The Nineteenth Century Accompanied By A Selection Of The Choicest Poems In The English Language Edited By Robert Bell[.] *London[:] Bell and Daldy 6 York Street Covent Garden And 186 Fleet Street[,] 1867.* Second edition; first edition thus in 4to format. 4to, xiv+[2]+180pp., half-title with decorative trim, engraved frontispiece illustration and other engraved illustrations after designs by John Martin, Thomas Stothard, J. M. W. Turner, and others (very fine impressions), protective tissue guards, emblem of the press (an anchor and bell) on title page, decorated initial letters, contemporary full red crushed leather over thick boards (a few scuff marks, several pages loose, some minor spotting to some preliminary leaves), covers and spine richly decorated in gilt, with central gilt device incorporating title on both covers, raised bands, a.e.g. A splendid copy, in a handsome binding of the period. The quality of the steel engravings is remarkably good, and the whole is handsomely printed by the Chiswick Press of Whittingham and Wilkins. The edition was surely a choice gift book for special occasions. Included are poetical selections from Milton with one vignette illustration by John Martin for *May Morning*, engraved by J. Cousin, and one vignette illustration by J. M. Wright of *Guardian Angels* for *PL*, with four additional illustrations by Martin (none for Milton). The first edition was published in octavo format in 1836 (a copy of which is in the collection); a folio edition was also published in 1867 (a large paper copy of which is in the collection, in a special edition with the engraved vignette illustrations printed on thick India paper); the first American edition of this popular illustrated anthology was published in 1868 (a copy of which is in the collection); and a reissue of this 1867 edition appeared in 1892 (a copy of which is also in the collection). Scarce thus with illustrations printed on thick India paper.

28. PEARLS FROM THE POETS. Specimens Of The Works Of Celebrated Writers. Selected, With Biographical Notes, By H. W. Dulcken, With A Preface By The Rev. Thomas Dale . . . *London: Ward, Lock, And Tyler, n.d. (ca. 1869).* First edition. Small 4to, 220pp., half-title, engraved frontispiece illustration and other engraved illustrations, floriated initials, decorated borders of typographic ornaments around text, original red cloth, broad gilt ornamental border trim on front cover with inner black rule highlighted by red dots, with central diamond-shaped panel in green incorporating title surrounded by decorative gilt trim, repeated in blind on back cover, a.e.g. A lovely copy in a pleasant binding of the period with an elaborate contemporary signature (dated 1869) on fly-leaf. Unusual in that most of the illustrations are borrowed from German sources with two signed by Kretschmer. Included are poetical selections from Milton with an illustration (unattributed) for *Il Penseroso* and an illustration (unattributed) for *May Morning*.

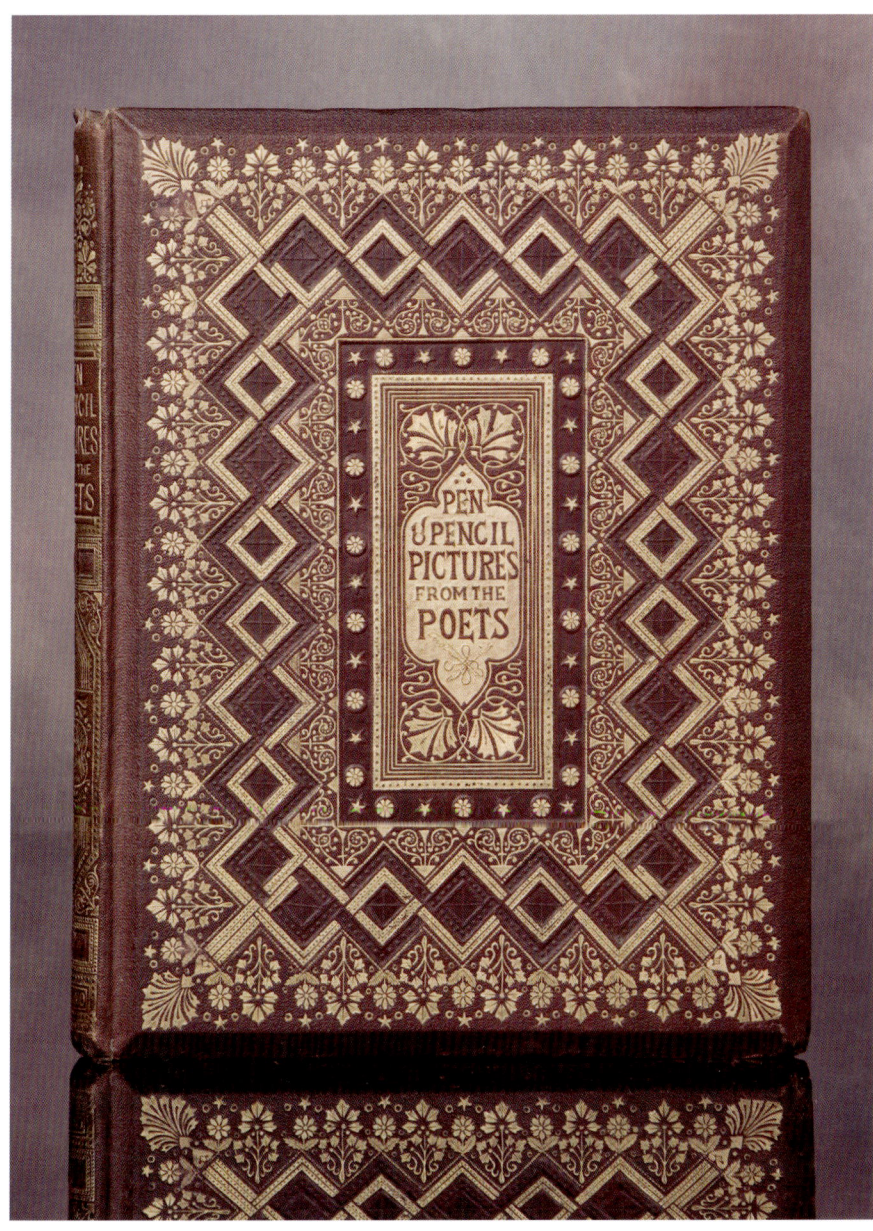

Pen & Pencil Pictures From The Poets. Edinburgh: Nimmo, 1866. Original purple cloth with beveled edges, elaborately gilt-decorated front cover and spine, with an illustration for *IlP* and for *PR*. See #26.

29. Variant of Preceding, in a variant binding, original green cloth (bit worn at ends of spine and at corners), decorated pretty much as preceding copy, except that the central diamond-shaped panel incorporating the title is purple and surrounding the panel, unlike the preceding copy, there are black designs arranged in a decorative pattern. A lovely copy with a colorful contemporary Victorian Christmas card tipped in on front pastedown in an attractive variant binding with a slightly variant design.

30. A NEW LIBRARY OF POETRY AND SONG Edited By William Cullen Bryant[.] Illustrated With Steel Portraits, Wood Engravings By English And American

Art And Song. London: Bell & Daldy, 1867. 4to, contemporary full red crushed leather over thick boards, covers and spine richly decorated in gilt, with vignette illustration by John Martin for *May Morning* and by J. M. Wright for *PL*. See #27.

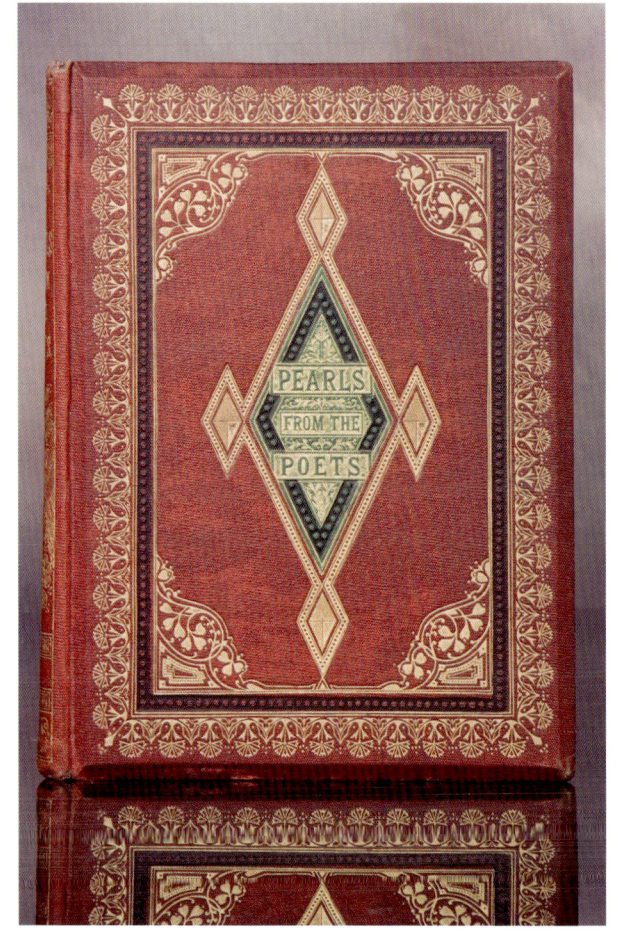

Pearls From The Poets. London: Ward, Lock, & Tyler, n.d. (ca. 1869). Decorated original red cloth binding, with an illustration for *IlP* and another for *May Morning*. See #28.

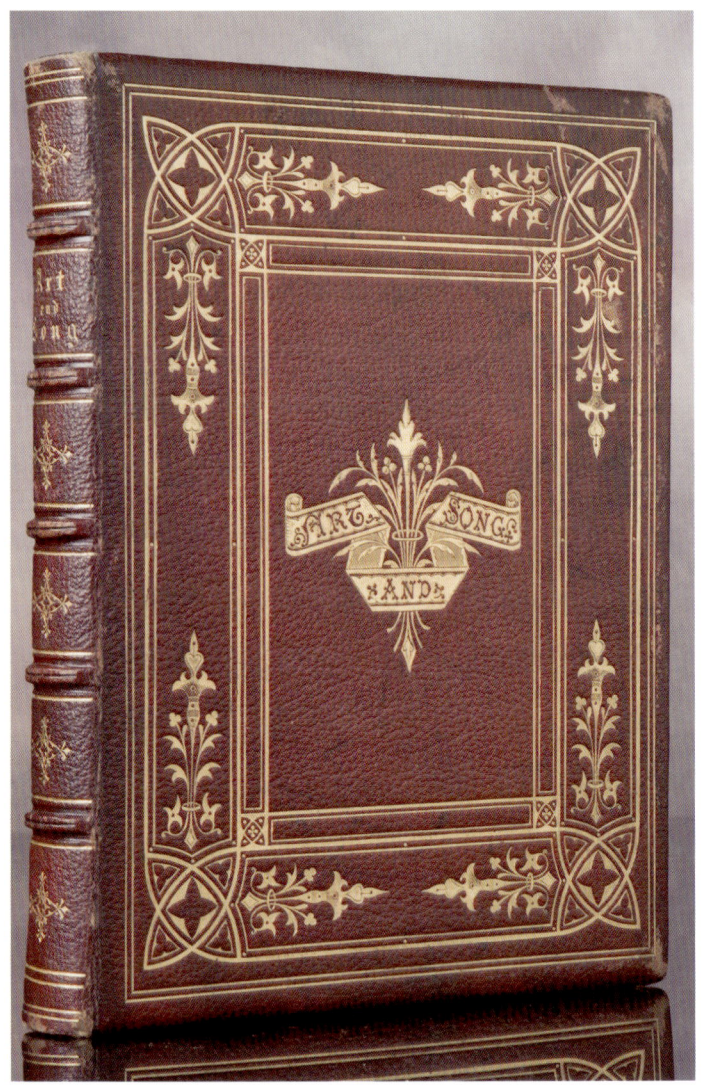

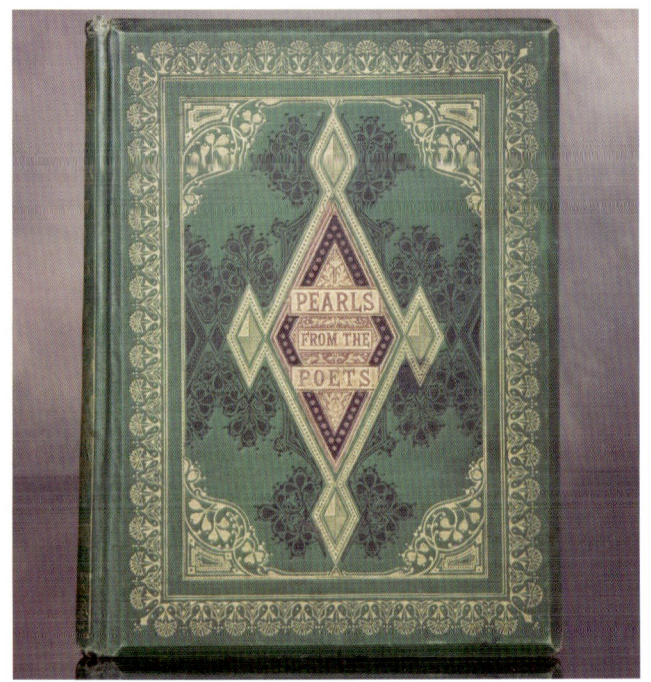

Pearls From The Poets in a variant binding. Decorated original green cloth binding, with identical illustrations. See #29.

Artists, Silhouette Titles, Manuscript Fac-Similes, Etc., Etc. *New York[:] J. B. Ford And Company[,] (1876).* 2 volumes. Revised edition. 4to, xxx+[6]+452pp.,+934pp. (continuous pagination), engraved frontispiece portrait each volume, each with protective tissue guard, separate title page each volume, each title page in red and black, illustrations, portraits, facsimiles, all on thick paper (fine impressions), protective tissue guards, decorated half-title for each section, original three-quarter brown morocco, brown leather (a little rubbed at joints and corners), gilt rules on covers with central ornamental harpsichord in black and gilt on front cover incorporating title and William Cullen Bryant's name in gilt, spine lettered in gilt with small gilt decorations in the panels and with decorative gilt trim at top and bottom, raised bands, white silk endpapers, a.e.g. A very fine set in a handsome binding of the period. Originally published as *A Library of Poetry and Song* in 1870 (the collection has the 1872, and 1873 editions as well as the 1878 revised edition), the present, extensively revised edition "with Mr. Bryant's active co-operation . . . has undergone an entire reconstruction, both as to matter and form . . . with the aim of gathering . . . the largest practicable compilation of the best Poems of the English language, making it as nearly as possible the choicest and most complete general collection of Poetry yet published" (Publisher's Preface). Included are poetical selections from Milton in both volumes, together with a full-page engraved vignette portrait (very fine impression) after J. S. King, volume 1, (added here), and a full-page illustration after A. Bobbett for *Milton On His Blindness*, volume 1, (an illustration that also appears, but as unattributed, in the earlier edition, *A Library of Poetry And Song*). This edition and its predecessor were very popular, and numerous editions were published well into the twentieth century.

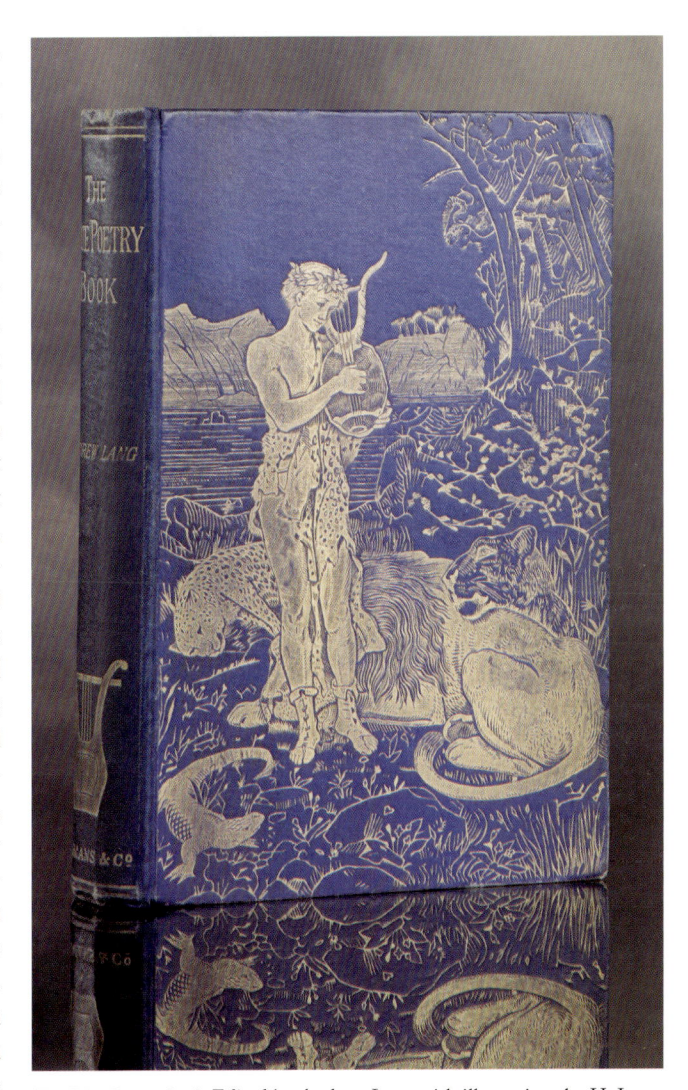

The Blue Poetry Book. Edited by Andrew Lang with illustrations by H. J. Ford and Lancelot Speed. London and New York: 1891. Original blue cloth with front cover strikingly decorated with a large illustration in gilt. Illustrations for *L'A, Il/P, L,* and *NO.* See #33.

31. A THOUSAND AND ONE GEMS OF ENGLISH POETRY. Selected And Arranged By Charles Mackay, LL.D. Illustrated By J. E. Millais, R.A., Sir John Gilbert, R.A., John Tenniel, Birket Foster, And Others. *London: George Routledge And Sons, The Broadway, Ludgate. New York: 416 Broome Street. 1878.* Second edition, revised? Thick 8vo, iv+538pp., frontispiece illustration and other wood-engraved illustrations, central vignette of harp within laurel wreath on title page, introduction from the first edition reprinted (dated 1867), printed in double column, index at the end, contemporary full red morocco (slightly rubbed, lacking front free endpaper), richly gilt-decorated covers and spine incorporating title, raised bands, broad inner dentelles finely tooled in gilt, a.e.g. A very nice copy in an handsome morocco binding of the period. Included are various poetical selections from Milton with a wood-engraved illustration engraved by Dalziel Brothers after Sir John Gilbert for *L'Allegro* ("Haste thee, Nymph"). The first edition was published ca. 1867 (two copies of which are in the collection) with illustrations by Millais, Gilbert, and Foster only; an edition also appeared in 1904 (a copy of which is in the collection), a reissue by Routledge of London with the Gilbert illustration for *L'Allegro* as the only illustration for the edition (included as the frontispiece).

32. SACRED GEMS FROM THE ENGLISH POETS: CHAUCER TO TENNYSON. With Biographical Notices Of The Authors. Illustrated. *New York: The American News Company, n.d. [ca. 1887/89].* 8vo, xvii+411pp., frontispiece illustration with protective tissue guard, original green cloth, front cover and spine elaborately decorated in black with title *Sacred Gems* against bright gilt background on spine. A fine copy in a lovely publisher's binding with neat contemporary presentation inscription (dated 1889) on front blank. Similar to possible first edition in 1887 (copy also in the collection). Included are poetical selections from Milton (none illustrated).

33. THE BLUE POETRY BOOK. Edited By Andrew Lang With Numerous Illustrations By H. J. Ford And Lancelot Speed. *London [And] New York: Longmans, Green, And Co., 1891.* First edition. 8vo, half-title (with advertisement for two "Blue Fairy Books"), frontispiece illustration, full-page and in-text illustrations, original blue cloth (bit rubbed along back joint and at corners, name in a neat hand on half-title), front cover strikingly decorated with a large illustration in gilt of the poet with lyre among the animals, spine lettered in gilt with gilt harp at the bottom, blue endpapers, a.e.g. An attractive copy in a lovely binding of the period. The book is "intended for lads and lassies" and "the purpose of this book is to put before children, and young people, poems which are good in themselves" (Introduction). Included are four poems by Milton, all illustrated: *L'Allegro* (two illustrations by Speed), *Il Penseroso* (two illustrations by Ford), *Lycidas* (three illustrations by Ford), and *Nativity Ode* (two illustrations by Speed).

34. ENGLISH LYRICS FROM SPENSER TO MILTON[.] Illustrations By Robert Anning Bell And Introduction By John Dennis[.] *London[:] George Bell & Sons[,] York Street[,] Covent Garden[;] New York[,] 66 Fifth Avenue[.] MDCCCXCVIII.* First edition. 8vo, xv+222pp., half-title (with advertisement for "The Endymion Series" listing this edition as well as *Milton's Minor Poems* illustrated by A. Garth Jones [copy in Chapter II] on verso), frontispiece illustration with decorative red border classical style, similar decorative red border classical style on title page, full-page and half-page headpiece illustrations by Robert Anning Bell, original decorated light green cloth (a bit rubbed with slight wrinkles at top center of front cover, spine a little faded), front cover and spine decorated in dark green art nouveau style with central gilt lettering and decorative gilt piece at the top and bottom on front cover, back cover with central decorative device of the press in contrasting dark green and with "The Endymion Series" lettered in gilt above, spine lettered in gilt with decorative gilt device at the top and bottom, t.e.g., others untrimmed, illustrated endpapers with a design of maidens playing a lute stamped in gold. A good copy of a book printed and bound in the art nouveau style and manner of the period.

English Lyrics from Spenser to Milton. Illustrations by Robert Anning Bell and Introduction by John Dennis. London: George Bell & Sons, 1898. Two copies with illustrations by Bell, one hand-colored by an anonymous artist. The two copies are shown here side by side with the hand-colored head-piece illustration accompanying Milton's poem "To Echo" on the right side. See #34 and 35

Printed by Charles Whittingham and Company for the Chiswick Press. Included are a number of poetical selections from Milton with a half-page headpiece illustration accompanying *To Echo* by Robert Anning Bell. Limited to 125 copies.

35. Variant of Preceding, binding very nice, with the illustrations by Bell hand-colored by an anonymous artist.

36. GOLDEN THOUGHTS From the Great Writers. A Volume of Selected Devotional Poems and Extracts Arranged by Alfred J. Fuller. *London: Ernest Nister; New York: E. P. Dutton & Co., Printed in Bavaria, n.d. [c. 1899].* 8vo, 192pp., decorated half-title, frontispiece illustration in color, numerous additional illustrations (full-page and within text, a number of full-page in color), decorations, and decorative head and tailpieces in black and white, decorated initial letters, black border around text, original green cloth (slight smudges on front cover), an elaborate design of a large flower in art nouveau style on the entire front cover with multiple stems and leaves in contrasting darker green with reddish-brown petals showing their pistils in gilt and with several dragonflies in gilt with darker green wings, and with the title in large gilt lettering at the top, spine similarly decorated and with gilt lettering, a.e.g. A nice copy. Included are numerous selections from Milton (some brief and others less so) variously titled and several with decorations/illustrations, including the following: *Care*, *Mercy*, *Morning*, and *Praise*. At the end a very brief biography of Milton is provided among similar biographies of the other poets featured in the collection.

37. Variant of Preceding, original reddish-brown cloth (a little rubbed along joints, corners a bit worn), front cover decorated as preceding copy with same emblem in green and contrasting reddish-brown with gilt highlight. A nice copy, in art nouveau style, in a variant publisher's binding.

38. ENGLISH POETRY FOR THE YOUNG. Compiled And Edited By S. E. Winbolt. *London, Glasgow, And Bombay: Blackie And Son Limited, n.d. (1904).* First edition. 8vo, 248+16pp., frontispiece illustration in color, original decorated blue cloth, front cover and spine decorated in orange and yellow in art nouveau style with blue lettering. A nice copy with advertisement leaf bound in before frontispiece for "Blackie's Crown Library" "for boys and girls" and sixteen pages of advertisements bound in at the end. While Milton is usually not included in anthologies for the young that are not school texts, there is a selection from Milton's *L'Allegro* under the heading "The Cheerful Man."

39. THE GOLDEN TREASURY OF POETRY AND SONG. A Complete Fireside Cyclopedia Of The Best Verse In The English Language. Over Thirteen Hundred Complete Poems By Nearly Two Hundred Noted Authors Comprising The Best Poems of the Most Famous Writers for Four Centuries, English And American . . . with Author and Subject Index and Explanatory Notes. Compiled And Edited By Henry T. Coates. Profusely Illustrated With Special, Duograph Engravings And Portraits. *Chicago, Ill.: A.B. Kuhlman Company, (1905).* Square 8vo, frontispiece illustration with illustration also on verso, title page in red and black, additional illustrations, printed in double column, original green cloth (a bit rubbed), covers decoratively stamped with an illustration and floral trim in dark green and pink with gilt lettering incorporating title, decorated endpapers. This is an example of a "salesman's sampler," with only a sampling of the full edition printed herein. A very nice copy, in an attractive binding of the period with a number of leaves for note-taking bound in at the end and, before these leaves, an advertisement leaf and a page containing "Estimates and Opinions of Great Reviews" praising this edition. The "Index of Authors" is printed in full, indicating that the full volume contains 815 pp. One of the plates includes a vignette portrait of Milton at the top, with the section heading, "The Great Poets of England," and the subheading, "Old Masters Of English Verse: Men whose lines have stood the test of time." With Milton are vignette portraits of Chaucer, Jonson, Pope, and Spenser. Milton's poetical selections from Milton's minor poems are arranged according to subjects.

40. THE GOLDEN TREASURY Of The Best Songs And Lyrical Poems In The English Language Selected And Arranged With Notes By Francis Turner Palgrave. Illustrated In Colour And Line By Robert Anning Bell. *London: J. M. Dent; New York: E. P. Dutton, 1907.* First edition thus. Large, thick 8vo, xvi+366+[2]pp., half-title, title page in red and black with protective tissue guard, frontispiece illustration and other illustrations in color by Robert Anning Bell, each tipped in on thick brown paper, introduction by Edward Hutton, head- and tailpiece illustrations in black and white, index at the end followed by illustrated "Finis" page with "Printed By Turnbull And Spears, Edinburgh" on verso, original full vellum, central gilt device on front cover incorporating title in gilt, gilt-decorated spine with gilt lettering, t.e.g., others untrimmed, green decorated endpapers. A lovely copy. Included are poetical selections from Milton with one full-page illustration in color for *Nativity Ode*, one full-page illustration in color for *Lycidas* as well as a headpiece illustration in black and white, one full-page illustration in color for *L'Allegro*, and two full-page illustrations in color for *Il Penseroso*. Several variant editions/issues (without illustrations tipped in, one dated 1907 and the other undated) are in the collection. This edition was also reprinted by Lamboll House in 1986 (copies of which are in the collection).

41. THE VISTA OF ENGLISH VERSE. Compiled By Henry S. Pancoast. Reprinted From "Standard English Poems," With Additional Selections. *New York: Henry Holt And Company, 1911*. First edition. Small 8vo, xiv+[1]+654pp., half-title before the poems, original red cloth (a bit rubbed at top of front joint), front cover richly decorated in gilt with illustration of a ship sailing past a castle and with gilt lettering, back cover ruled in gilt with abstract decorations of clouds in gilt at the top and small gilt emblem of an owl at the bottom, spine ruled in gilt with small illustration of the sailing ship in gilt and with gilt lettering, endpapers decorated with long rows of busts of the poets beginning with Shakespeare, Spenser, and Milton, a.e.g. A lovely copy in an attractive binding small enough for carrying along when traveling. Included are a number of selections from Milton. This is an expanded version of *Standard English Poems* for students published in 1899, designed so that "the reader may travel down the broad highway of English poetry" (Preface).

42. GREAT NAMES Being an Anthology of English & American Literature from Chaucer to Francis Thompson With Introductions by Various Hands & Drawings by J. F. Horrabin after Original Portraits[.] The Whole Edited by Walter J. Turner for The Nonesuch Press & here First Published by Special Arrangement[.] Lincoln Mac Veagh[.] *New York: The Dial Press: MCMXXVI*. First edition. Large 8vo, xi+282pp., preface, decorative border trim on title page with central emblem, original sketch for each poet included, original blue cloth, front cover and spine lettered in gilt with emblem on title page repeated in gilt on front cover. A fine copy in original printed publisher's wrappers (a little worn and age-browned) repeating title page on front cover, in a protective plastic cover. "This anthology, I venture to say has features that make it unique. The selection from each author is prefaced with an introduction written by a living writer of distinction and is decorated with a drawing by Mr. J. F. Horrabin after an original portrait of the author" (Preface). Included are poetical selections from Milton with a brief introduction by Lascelles Abercrombic and a sketch of Milton by Horrabin.

43. MASTER POEMS OF THE ENGLISH LANGUAGE Over one hundred poems together with Introductions by leading poets and critics of the English-speaking world[.] Edited by Oscar Williams[.] *Trident Press[,] New York[,] 1966*. First edition. Thick 8vo, xvi+1071+[1]pp., half-title, portrait of each poet, original black cloth, spine lettered in gilt, orange endpapers. A very nice copy. Williams, who died in 1964 and did not live to see this book published, conceived the book "as serving a dual purpose . . . to select a small number of English and American poems that could be called true masterpieces, poems that 'breathe fire and are filled with heady, intoxicating wine,' and to combine these highly select poems with 'gems of the critical art.' Each introductory essay was to be by a prominent poet or critic and with few exceptions was to be commissioned especially for the book" (Preface). Included are a portrait of Milton and several poetical selections with critical commentary: *Nativity Ode* by Jackson Matthews, *Lycidas* by Robert P. Adams, and *L'Allegro And Il Penseroso* by Richard Wilbur.

44. THE OXFORD LIBRARY OF ENGLISH POETRY Chosen and Edited by John Wain[.] *Oxford University Press, (1986). 3 volumes*. First edition, second issue. 8vo, xx+443pp.,+xiii+511pp.,+xvi+476pp., half-title and title page each volume, contemporary one-quarter blue bonded leather, blue milskin, decorative gilt border trim on covers and spine, in original decorated blue card paper box. A fine set. "The object of this collection is to provide a representative sample of the main course of English poetry during the last four centuries," to present in these volumes "a good showcase of what English poetry, from the Renaissance to the recent, has to offer" (Introduction). Milton is represented in volume 1 by *On the University Carrier*, *Lycidas*, five "Sonnets," and selections from *A Mask* (*Comus*), from *Paradise Lost*, and from *Samson Agonistes*. The edition first appeared earlier in 1986.

V

ORIGINAL DRAWINGS, ILLUSTRATIONS, ENGRAVINGS, AND OTHER

1. Artist Unkown (ca. 1800). Twenty original, unattributed, and undated illustrations drawn at the turn of the eighteenth century, having remained intact within original stiff purple wrappers of the period (now a little faded), attached by ribbon ties at the spine and with a ribbon tie for closure, measuring 10 ¾" × 9 ⅛". The sketches are mostly in pencil, several in pen, of varying sizes (most are approximately 8" × 7", several are much smaller, 4 ½" × 2 ½"), and mounted on all but the last few leaves. Of the twenty original illustration sketches, fourteen are of scenes in Milton's *PL*, each labeled, including *Adam's First Sight of Eve, Satan Alighted in Paradise, The Mattens Supplication, With Him Fled the Shades of Night, The Temptation*, and others, each with appropriate lines quoted. While the artist is unknown, two illustration are clearly signed "JP." Also included are an illustration of "The Bard" in color and an illustration for Homer. Included here are four sketches of scenes in *PL*.

2. Bell, John. A group of nine original drawings by John Bell, varying in size and quality, eight in pen and ink and one in colored texture, seven of which are definitely Miltonic and the other two possibly related—five certainly for *Paradise Lost* and two for *Comus*. Ranging in size from 6" × 7 ½" to 12 ½" × 12 ½". Circa 1850s–1860s. Principally a sculptor who designed part of the Albert Memorial in London, Bell also made a large number of prints with which his drawings here may be connected. Apparently these drawings, reminiscent of John Flaxman's line engravings in style, were never published. Included here are three drawings.

3. Brooks, Florence. L'ALLEGRO AND IL PENSEROSO Written out and illuminated by Florence Brooks. [n.p.] 1971. 8" × 10", 30pp., unbound. A modern calligraphic manuscript, written out in black ink on fine quality paper in a classic Arrighi Italic hand with decorative blue trim, the initial letter of each poem with painted illumination in colors and raised gold, as in *Il Penseroso*, shown here.

4. CHILD'S WRITING SHEET WITH MILTON'S PARADISE LOST AS ITS SUBJECT. Dated November 9, 1801. 14 ½" × 18 ⅝", in color, with unsigned vignette illustration for each book of *PL* as border trim. From the personal collection of Percy Muir. Fine, virtually mint condition. Very rare not only in itself but in the subject it treats. One might conjecture that this was certainly no ordinary writing sheet, given its subject matter, but one intended for a child of parents of the upper class or perhaps a private tutor; its preservation would indicate the respect it was given.

(clockwise from left) Original pencil sketch of *The Mattens Supplication* (7" × 6"), ca. 1800, artist unknown. Original pencil sketch of *Adam's First Sight of Eve and of Eve Seeing Herself in the Water* (8" × 7"), ca. 1800, artist unknown. Original pencil sketch of *With Him Fled the Shades of Night* (6 ¾" × 6 ⅝"), ca. 1800, artist unknown. Original pencil sketch of *The Temptation* (8" × 7 ⅝"), ca. 1800, artist unknown. See #1.

Original drawing in pen and ink by John Bell of Satan and his cohorts being cast out of Heaven (8 ¼" × 8 ½"). One of nine original drawings by Bell, ca. 1850–60, seven for *PL* and two for *Comus*.

Drawing in pen and ink, rather rich in texture, of *Comus and His Rabble Rout* (11 ½" × 8 ¼"). One of nine original drawings by Bell, ca. 1850–60, seven for *PL* and two for *Comus*.

ENCE loathèd
Melancholy,
Of Cerberus, and blackest midnight born,
In Stygian Cave forlorn
'Mongst horrid shapes, & shreiks, & sights unholy,
Find out som uncouth cell,
Where brooding darknes spreads his jalous wings,
And the night-raven sings;
There under Ebon shades, and low-brow'd Rocks,
As ragged as thy Locks,
In dark Cimmerian desert ever dwell.

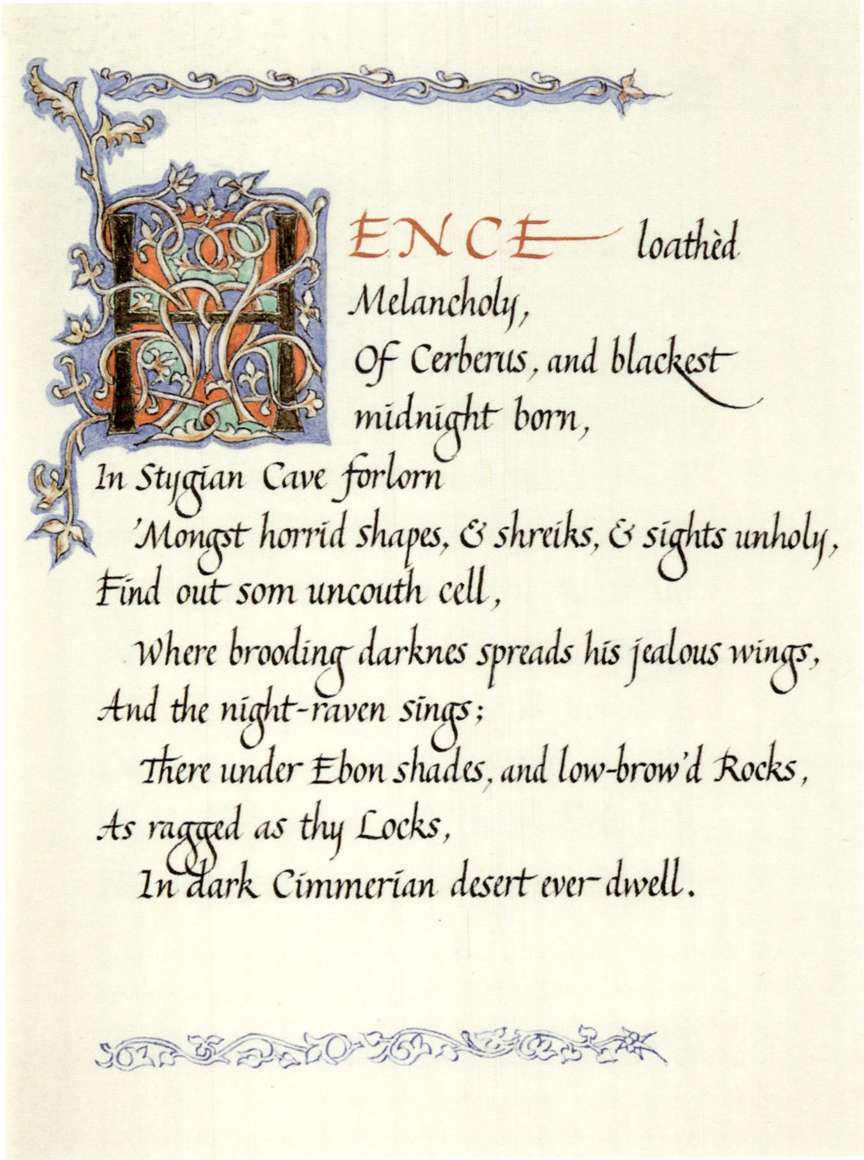

L'Allegro and Il Penseroso written out and illuminated by Florence Brooks. See #3.

Original drawing in pencil by John Bell with textured coloring, very rich in character, possibly of "Adam Being Visited By Raphael" (12 ½" × 12 ½"), in a striking rendering of this scene in *PL*. A very large drawing, ca. 1850–60.

Child's writing sheet taken from Milton's *Paradise Lost*. Dated November 9, 1801. 14 ½" × 18 ⅝", in color, with vignette illustration for each book of *PL* as border trim. From the personal collection of Percy Muir. Fine. Very rare. See #4.

5. Fuseli, Henry. *The Dream of Eve*. "Painted by H. Fuseli R. A. Engraved by M. Haughton & Publish'd as the Act directs Jany. 25th 1804, No 13 Berners Street London. Aquatint by F. C. Lewis." Fine etching and aquatint, 28" × 23", platemark 580 cm. × 494 cm., printed in dark brown, on paper watermarked Whatman, 1801, illustrating Book V, lines 86–91. See comments by John Shawcross about the significance of this and the following three Fuseli engravings in *Milton Quarterly* 41, no. 1 (2007): 71.

6. Fuseli, Henry. *The Dismission of Adam and Eve from Paradise*. "H. Fuseli R. A. Pinxt. Moses Haughton Sculpt. and Published by them as the Act directs July 20th 1805 Royal Academy, London." Fine etching and stipple engraving, 28" × 23", platemark 591 cm. × 456 cm., printed in dark brown, on paper watermarked Whatman, 1801, illustrating Book XII, lines 640–45.

7. Fuseli, Henry. *Adam Resolved To Share The Fate Of Eve*. "Henry Fuseli R. A. Pinxt. Moses Haughton Sculpt and Published by them as the Act directs Jany. 20, 1806 Somerset House, Strand, London." Fine etching and stipple engraving, 28" × 23", platemark 577 cm. × 473 cm., printed in dark brown, illustrating Book IX, lines 953–58.

8. Fuseli, Henry. *The Spirit of Plato*. "London Publish'd 1st Decr 1824 by H. Gibbs, Great Newport Street." Fine etching and stipple engraving, 28" × 23", platemark 476 cm. × 552 cm., printed in black. The title is followed by four lines of verses from *Il Penseroso*, which this illustration depicts. This appears to be an undescribed reprint with Gibbs's address; there is another impression in the British Museum with "Haughton's" and "Fuseli's" names but that impression has had the imprint cut off.

9. Gillray, James. *Sin, Death, and the Devil. Vide Milton*. "Pubd June 9th 1792. by H: Humphrey." Fine etching and engraving, 15 ¾" × 12 ½", with publisher's coloring. A satire on the struggle between William Pitt and Edward Thurlow (the Lord Chancellor) travestied as the scene on *Satan, Sin, and Death* in *PL*, almost certainly based on the Rowlandson print (also listed here) after William Hogarth's painting, published eight days earlier. Thurlow as Satan, Queen Charlotte as Sin, Pitt as Death, Cerberus with the heads of Henry Dundas, William Grenville, and Sir Richard Richards. It seems probable that the incentive to this print was primarily exasperation at Johnson's scheme (1790) for an edition of Milton similar to John Boydell's Shakespeare, for which Fuseli was to paint a series of pictures; one of these was *Satan, Sin, and Death*. It is considered one of the most outrageous caricatures of all time. It is certainly one of Gillray's rarest, a parody of Fuseli and Hogarth. See comments by John Shawcross about the significance of this engraving in *Milton Quarterly* 41, no. 1 (2007): 70.

See #9.

Fuseli, Henry (1741–1825)

Among the painters invited to contribute to the Boydell three-volume folio publication of *The Poetical Works of John Milton. With a Life of the Author*, by William Haley, which appeared in 1794, 1795, and 1796 was Henry Fuseli, a native of Switzerland. A copy of this set is in the collection (see #1787 in Chapter II). Fuseli copied Boydell's lead, who had established the Shakespeare Gallery in 1792, by beginning to organize a Milton Gallery in the same year with only his work on exhibit. It opened in 1799, and as John Shawcross observes, citing its catalogue documents, "There were twenty-one paintings for *Paradise Lost*, one for *Paradise Regain'd* and the *Nativity Ode*, three for *L'Allegro*, two for *Il Penseroso*, two for *Comus*, one for *Lycidas*, and three biographical subjects. . . . The original paintings will be found in various places, such as the Belfast Museum, the Auckland City Art Gallery, Die Sammlung Bollag in Zürich, but there are also a number that have never been located or have been destroyed. In the Wickenheiser Collection are three very important engravings by Moses Haughton in 1804, 1806, and 1805. . . . It is only through copies such as these etched by Haughton that we know what these paintings were. Fuseli continued his interest in Milton, and in this collection is 'The Spirit of Plato' with quotation of *Il Penseroso* engraved by Haughton and published in London in 1824. Fuseli was 'One of the greatest imaginations of his age and one of the leading forces behind the romantic movement,' in the words of Joseph Wittreich. Johann Wolfgang von Goethe's imperceptive dismissal of Fuseli arose from his 'addressing himself to the imagination in the same way that the poet does.' Attuned to Fuseli's achievements, William Blake lamented that his country 'must advance two centuries in civilisation before it can appreciate'" Fuseli. (Comments by John Shawcross about the importance of each engraving by Moses Haughton here appear in *Milton Quarterly* 41, no. 1 [2007]: 71).

The Spirit of Plato. "London Publish'd 1st Decr 1824 by H. Gibbs, Great Newport Street." Fine etching and stipple engraving, 28" × 23", platemark 476 cm. × 552 cm., printed in black. The title is followed by four lines of verses from *Il Penseroso*, which this illustration depicts. This appears to be an undescribed reprint with Gibbs's address; there is another impression in the British Museum with "Haughton's" and "Fuseli's" names but that impression has had the imprint cut off.

The Dream of Eve. "Painted by H. Fuseli R. A. Engraved by M. Haughton & Publish'd as the Act directs Jany. 25th 1804, No 13 Berners Street London. Aquatint by F. C. Lewis." Fine etching and aquatint, 28" × 23", platemark 580 cm. × 494 cm., printed in dark brown, on paper watermarked Whatman, 1801, illustrating Book V, lines 86–91.

The Dismission of Adam and Eve from Paradise. "H. Fuseli R. A. Pinxt. Moses Haughton Sculpt. and Published by them as the Act directs July 20th 1805 Royal Academy, London." Fine etching and stipple engraving, 28" × 23", platemark 591 cm. × 456 cm., printed in dark brown, on paper watermarked Whatman, 1801, illustrating Book XII, lines 640–45.

Adam Resolved to Share the Fate of Eve. "Henry Fuseli R. A. Pinxt. Moses Haughton Sculpt and Published by them as the Act directs Jany. 20, 1806 Somerset House, Strand, London." Fine etching and stipple engraving, 28" × 23", platemark 577 cm. × 473 cm., printed in dark brown, illustrating Book IX, lines 953–58.

10. **Hayman, Francis**. Original watercolor painting by Francis Hayman of *Satan, Sin, and Death* (6 ⅝" × 3 ¾" on a 9 ¼" × 5 ¾" page), apparently never having been published.

11. **Hayman, Francis**. A second original watercolor painting by Francis Hayman of *Satan Rallying His Cohorts* (6 ⅝" × 3 ¾" on a 9 ¼" × 5 ¾" page), apparently never having been published.

12. **Howard, Henry**. Eight original drawings in ink done for **THE STORY OF SABRINA IN THE COMUS OF MILTON**, with original vignette title page. London, paper watermarked J. Watman, 1816, bound in an album 18 ¼" × 11 ¾", original diced russia, gilt decorated. Fine. Henry Howard, history and portrait painter, won both the silver and gold medals of the Royal Academy Schools, becoming an academician in 1808. He went to Italy in 1791 and came under the influence of Flaxman in Rome. Subsequent work for the Society of Dilettante publications strengthened his neoclassical leanings. From 1795 onward he was producing paintings to illustrate the works of Milton, including *Sabrina* in 1805, now in the Victoria and Albert Museum. This was the first of a series of pictures illustrating *Comus*, which Howard worked on for the rest of his life. His drawings are considered his finest achievement. The present series represents a theme that was always nearest to his heart and was produced at a time when he was at the height of his powers. Two selections are presented here with the verses illustrated quoted beneath the illustration.

See #10.

See #11.

WHO PITEOUS OF HER WOES REAR'D HER LANK HEAD
AND GAVE HER TO HIS DAUGHTERS TO IMBATHE
IN NECTAR'D LAVERS STREW'D WITH ASPHODIL,

AND THROUGH THE PORCH AND INLET OF EACH SENSE
DROPT IN AMBROSIAL OYLS TILL SHE REVIV'D,
AND UNDERWENT A QUICK IMMORTAL CHANGE,

See #12.

13. **Howard, Mrs. Katherine**. PARADISE LOST, A POEM IN TWELVE BOOKS. Boughton, nr. Chester, 1733–35. Folio, 282pp.,+7pp. of significant diary additions, full contemporary paneled calf (a little rubbed, front joint cracked), covers decorated with gilt rules and inner floral corner pieces. In very good condition. As Arthur Freeman says, "This remarkable transcript of *PL* may be dismissed (editorially) as no more than evidence of obsessional copying, but it seems to be, nonetheless, the earliest complete manuscript of Milton's epic" (Quaritch, Cat. 1091, #71, 1988); transcribed by Mrs. Katherine Howard, between December 3, 1733, and May 17, 1735, for her daughter "to read often when I am gone." The source of her version is certainly a late seventeenth- or early eighteenth-century printed text, for the "Arguments" are placed at the beginning of each book, and Milton's note on "The Verse" is at the beginning of the poem. She writes in a neat hand and several times dates her progress.

Mrs. Howard was herself a woman of considerable contemporary reputation. As a young lady, she was twice painted by Sir Godfrey Kneller, and, at the age of eleven, she danced with the doomed pretender, James Scott, Duke of Monmouth, who told her she would one day be "the finest dancer in England." Her marriage to Captain James Howard (1698) took her to London and the court of William III who expanded the compliment to include all of "Europe." Along with receiving compliments at the court of William, she was a figure of some literary fun, including being the subject of at least one verse-satire in 1729. (Freeman points out that "Her journal or commonplace book was edited by G. P. Crawfurd in the *Journal of the Chester Archaeological Society*, XXVIII [1928], pp. 5–96"; and "For the diaries see Matthews, *British Diaries*, p. 67").

Sample pages from Mrs. Howard's transcript of *PL*. See #13.

14. Mercer, F. W. L'ALLEGRO. Transcribed By F. W. Mercer, 1927. Square 8vo, manuscript volume in which *L'Allegro* is written out in a fine script, with an elaborately hand-colored illuminated border on each page, handsomely bound in full vellum with silver clasp.

15. Mercer, F. W. SONNETS BY MILTON. Transcribed By F. W. Mercer. *(n.p., n.d.) [ca. 1939]*. 6 ¾" × 9 ⅝", unpaginated illuminated title page, followed by illuminated initials and borders on each page of manuscript transcription of eighteen sonnets, bound in Riviéré binding, vellum spine, blue cloth boards.

16. Portrait of John Milton. Engraved frontispiece portrait of Milton at age sixty-two after George Vertue, 1725. 14 ½" × 9" (overall engraving size: 11 ¾" × 15 ¾"), "Illustrissimo Dno. Dno. Algernon Comite de Hertford Dno. Percy &c. &c. Obsequentissime D.D.D. G. Vertue," with Milton's name and dates in Latin above and Dryden's epigram below. A fine, large, striking impression of this engraving, very fresh and clean, virtually mint. Vertue's portrait was incorporated in volume 1 of Boydell's great three-volume edition of Milton's *Poetical Works*, without Milton's name and dates at the top of the portrait or Dryden's epigram beneath, and with a smaller impression of the engraved image of Milton; it was engraved for the Boydell edition by "W N Gardinar. . . . From the Original Drawing by Vertue in the Collection of Tho. Brand Hollis Esq. . . . Publish'd June 4, 1794 by John & Josiah Boydell & Geo. Nicol."

17. Portrait of John Milton. Engraved portrait of John Milton at age twenty-one, "In the Collection of the Right Hon: Arthur Onslow Esqr. Speaker of the House of Commons. Impensis I. & P. Knapton Londini. 1741," printed at the bottom of the engraving, and "J. Houbraken sculps. Amst. 1741." printed in smaller type in the right corner above it. The image size is 14 ¼" × 9"; the paper size is 16" × 10 ¼". Engraved by the Dutchman Jacobus Houbraken ca. 1741, this is a fine engraved portrait of Milton as a young man and has become well-known through the ages as the "Onslow Portrait."

See #14.

See #15.

18. Portrait of John Milton. Engraved portrait of John Milton. "In the Collection of the Rt. Hon.ble Arthur Onslow Esqr: Publish'd as the Act directs, May 28 1785. Goldar sculpt. London: Engrav'd for Harrison's Editions of Rapin." Copperplate engraving on laid paper, measuring 15" × 9 ¼" (with the engraving itself measuring 7 ⅝" × 6 ⅜").

19. Portrait of John Milton. Oval portrait of Milton in oils. Unsigned, ca. 1850s. 6" × 3 ½", in pale green velvet mat inside a charming oval Victorian walnut frame with gilt inner band. This attractive oil portrait belongs to the Faithorne-Vertue likenesses of Milton.

20. Portrait of John Milton. 14" × 18 ¾" reproduction, ca. late nineteenth / early twentieth century, of the portrait of Milton at age ten in color by the famed portrait artist Cornelius Janssen (dated 1618) on a kind of cardboard, the original portrait originally in the collection of Mr. J. Passmore Edwards and now in the Morgan Library, in a gilt-trimmed wood frame. In very good condition. Gift from Milton scholar Maurice Kelley when he retired from Princeton University in 1972. Maurice told me that he had been given this framed color reproduction from Robert Cawley when he retired, and he was passing it along to me, and it has been with me ever since.

21. Monetti, Enrico. COMUS BY JOHN MILTON. Illuminated by [Enrico Monetti.] *George D. Sproul[,] MCMII*. 11 ¼" × 9", [56 unpaginated leaves]. Saint Dunstan edition. One of thirty copies printed on vellum on one side only, each leaf 11 ¼" × 9", each copy unique in its illumination and signed by the illuminator, Enrico Monetti. Title page shown here.

22. Morrison, H. P. LYCIDAS. Manuscript. With Notes Collected And Arranged By H. P. Morrison. *Birmingham, 1897*. Manuscript volume by Hubert Peter Morrison in which *Lycidas* is written out in a fine hand on excellent quality paper, with an introduction, followed by critical notes by various critics, on 240 leaves numbered on recto only, with a number of blanks incorporated, steel-engraved frontispiece of St. Michael's Mount, Cornwall, and manuscript map (on leaf 232), contemporary half green morocco, marbled paper over boards, gilt rules on covers and spine, raised bands, marbled end-papers, by Riviéré, with Morrison's card tipped in (on leaf 2). Very attractive.

23. PARADISE LOST. *London: Printed for Jacob Tonson in the Strand. MDCCXXVII*. The edition is bound in two 4to volumes, with each original printed octavo page and each octavo illustration bound in a special quarto volume next to its own leaf (quarto size), with numerous notes in English, Latin, Greek, and Hebrew in a neat contemporary hand on the quarto leaves. An uncommon edition, rendered unique here in its design and intention, carefully put together, with copious notes and scholarly commentary in an original hand by an educated eighteenth-century reader or possible editor. See #623 in Chapter II for comment on probable annotator.

24. Pickersgill, F. R. Original pen sketch of *The Lady Sleeping* in *Comus*, watched over by the attendant spirit. The drawing dates from ca. 1840–ca. 1860, is quite large (23 ½" × 18"), and apparently was never published.

25. Richardson, Jonathan, The Elder. Original drawing of John Milton, ca. 1730, by Jonathan Richardson the elder (1665–1745), with Richardson's stamp on right margin, sepia drawing of the blind Milton "from a model of Milton in clay. Coll[ection] of Mr. G. Vertue" (on the back). The engraver and antiquary George Vertue (1684–1756) also owned the drawing known as the Faithorne portrait, now at Princeton.

26. Richter, Henry J. Engravings from PARADISE LOST. *London, 1794*. 4to. A complete set of the stipple-engraved plates, engraved by John Richter after drawings by his son, Henry J. Richter, for the 1794 edition (first appearance, see copies with Chapter II), bound in their original printed wrappers, edges untrimmed.

[together with]

27. Richter, Henry J. Twelve original drawings by Henry Richter, one in watercolor, eleven in wash, of scenes in *PL*, of which nine were used for the plates in the 1794 edition and three were rejected. The original drawings are each mounted and contained together with the set of engraved plates in a red cloth fitted case. Richter was a pupil of Thomas Stothard and a friend of William Blake. John Richter was not only the engraver of his son's drawings for the 1794 edition, but the editor of the edition as well. Four selections of Richter's drawings appear here: two of his drawings that were rejected and two that were not.

See #16.

ßsee #17.

See #19.

See #18.

See #20.

page 44

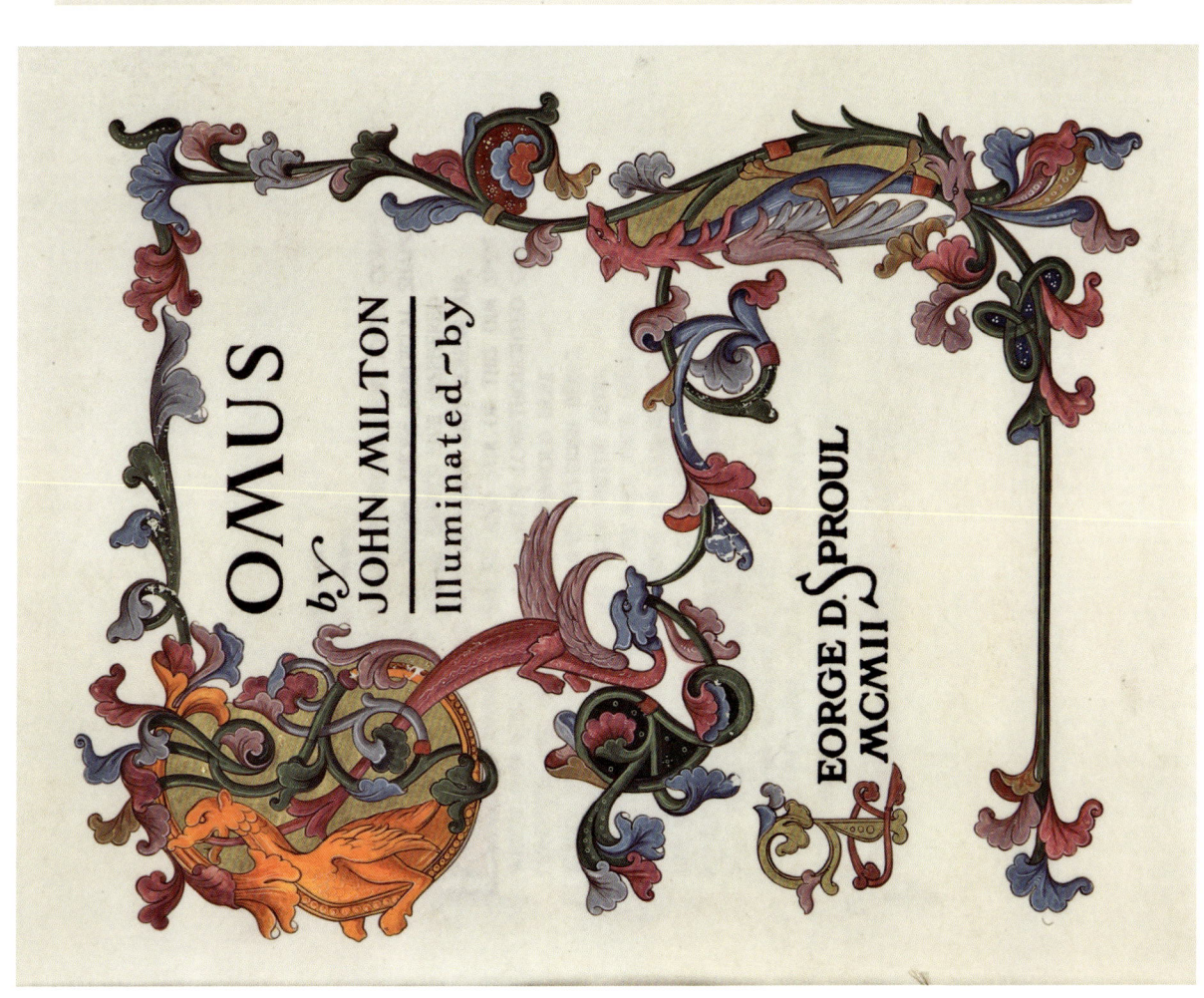

Lycidas.

In this Monody the Author bewails a learned Friend, unfortunately drowned in his passage from Chester on the Irish Seas, 1637; and, by occasion, foretells the ruin of our corrupted clergy, then in their height.

Yet once more, O ye laurels, and once more
Ye myrtles brown, with ivy never sere,
I come to pluck your berries harsh and crude,
And with forced fingers rude
Shatter your leaves before the mellowing year.
Bitter constraint and sad occasion dear
Compels me to disturb your season due;
For Lycidas is dead, dead ere his prime,
Young Lycidas, and hath not left his peer.

See #22.

COMUS by JOHN MILTON
Illuminated by
GEORGE D. SPROUL
MCMII

See #21.

See #23.

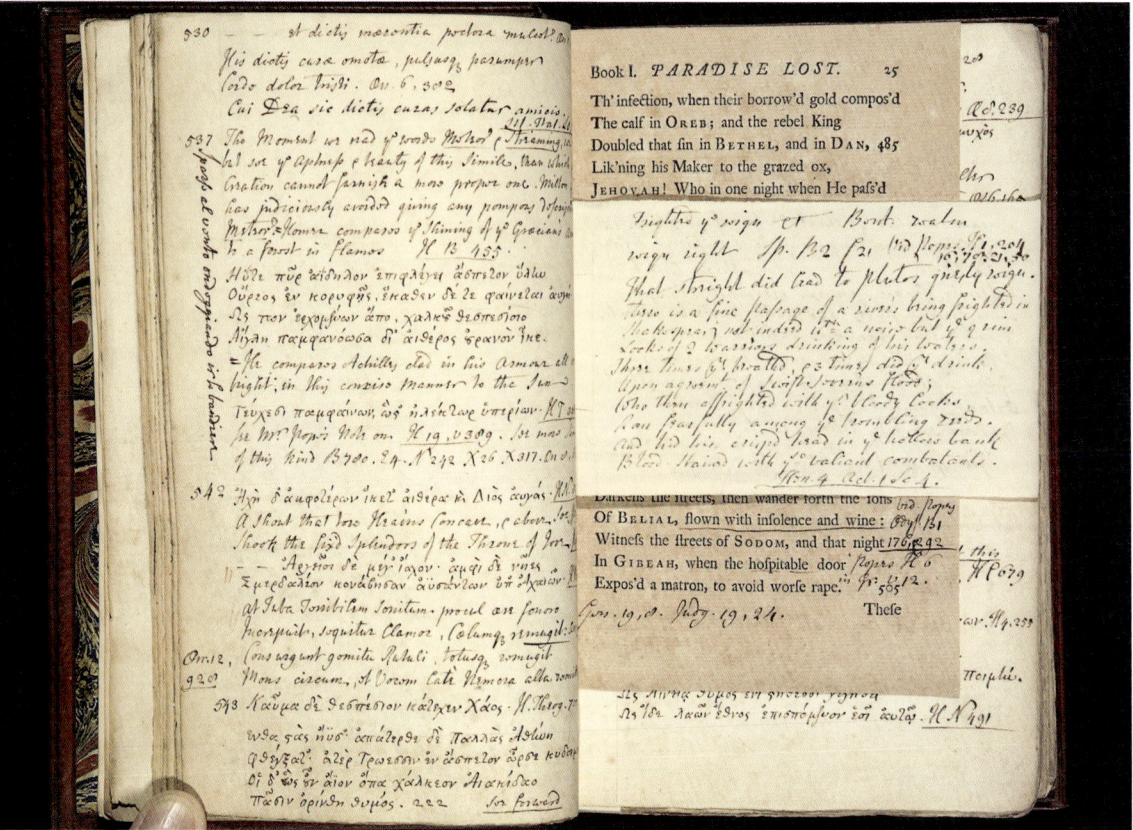

See #24.

(above) Original drawing by F. R. Pickersgill for *Comus*, one of four original drawings by Pickersgill for *Comus* (each, as here, 8" × 10"), including title page ("Compositions From Milton's Comus") ca. 1840–ca. 1860. The drawings are imaginative and Flaxmanesque and reflective of the illustrations Pickersgill contributed to the 1858 edition of *Comus*, which also includes illustrations by R. Corbould, Birket Foster, and others, all engraved by the Dalziel Brothers (see copies in Chapter II). Apparently none of the four was ever published. See #24.
(below) Original drawing by F. R. Pickersgill for *Comus*, one of four original drawings by Pickersgill for *Comus* (each 8" × 10"), including title page ("Compositions From Milton's Comus"), ca. 1840–ca. 1860. Apparently never published. See #24.

Twelve Original Drawings by Henry Richter

These drawings include one in watercolor, eleven in wash, of scenes in *PL*, of which nine were used for the plates in the 1794 edition and three were rejected. The original drawings are each mounted and contained together with the set of engraved plates in a red cloth fitted case. Richter was a pupil of Stothard and a friend of Blake. John Richter was not only the engraver of his son's drawings for the 1794 edition, but the editor of the edition as well. Four selections of Richter's drawings appear here: two of his drawings that were rejected and two that were not.

Adam & Eve at morning prayer (not used in the 1794 edition).

Adam & Eve in the bower of bliss (not used in the 1794 edition).

Watercolor drawing of the temptation of Eve (used for the plate in Book IX).

The expulsion of Adam and Eve from Eden (used for the plate in Book XII).

See #28.

See #29.

SATAN, SIN AND DEATH.
From Milton's Paradise Lost Book the 2.
The original Picture by Hogarth is in the Possession of M.r Garrick.

28. Romney, George. Original pencil sketch of **THE FALL OF THE REBEL ANGELS**, *PL*, Book I, lines 42–49, 5 ½" × 9 ¼", ca. 1790s, a composition which is dominated by the large figure of Satan on the right; another study of Satan is added in the top right-hand corner. This sketch remains with the collector.

29. Rowlandson, Thomas. **SATAN, SIN AND DEATH.** "Pubd 1 June 1792 by J. Thane. Etching by Thomas Rowlandson," 15" × 12 ½", engraved by J. Ogborne after William Hogarth (1697–1764), printed in dark sepia, for *PL*, Book II. See the satiric parody of this scene and print by James Gillray (also listed here) published eight days later.

30. Turner, J. M. W. **PARADISE LOST**, Book XII, lines 641–49 (*The Expulsion from Paradise*): large plate measuring 5 ½" × 8". "Engraver's Large Paper Proof Before All Letters By Turner, line engraving by E. Goodall." Engraver's proof before publication, prior to Rawlinson's first state, printed on fine white India paper, applied to original warm white wove backing sheet, with full margins.

The later lettered version of this engraving was issued in John Macrone's edition of *The Poetical Works of John Milton*, edited by Sir Egerton Brydges and published in 1835 (listed in Chapter II). "Fine proofs, such as this, are now rare" (Campbell Fine Art, Cat. 4, #162, London, 1993).

31. Westall, Richard, R. A. **MILTON COMPOSING PARADISE LOST.** Drawn & Engraved by R. Westall, R.A., n.d. [ca. 1810]. Hand-colored aquatint, 22 ½" × 28 ½", titled and signed in the plate. A very fine impression with exceptional hand-coloring, almost certainly by Westall himself (as stated by Christopher Mendez, London, in 1985, from whom I acquired the aquatint), the borders of the print washed in gray, slightly obliterating the engraved title and signature, laid down on several sheets of paper to make a cardlike support (the top left corner broken off).

See #30.

See #31.

VI

John Martin (1789–1854)

Early in 1823 John Martin was commissioned by the American publisher Septimus Prowett to produce twenty-four mezzotint illustrations of *Paradise Lost* for £2,000. "The commission to illustrate *Paradise Lost* must be among the most remarkable ever given by a publisher" and "long before even the first part of the work had been published, a further commission of £1,500 for a smaller set of similar plates" was made (Balston, *Life*, pp. 95–96).

The editions of *PL* by Septimus Prowett in which Martin's striking illustrations appeared have a publishing complexity of their own, and each edition is described in full here in Chapter II. Martin's illustrations first appeared in parts issued between 1825–27 with a large set of the plates; then in 1827 in a variety of formats with various sizes and states of the plates: in an Imperial folio limited to fifty copies with "Proof" impressions of the large plates; in an Imperial quarto with the large plates; in an Imperial quarto limited to fifty copies with "Proof" impressions of the small plates; and in an Imperial octavo with the small plates. These editions are all in the collection and appear together (see #7539 in Chapter II). The collection has extensive holdings in successive editions with Martin's illustrations throughout the century, and these later editions are also described in Chapter II, with a photograph of the frontispiece illustration and title page of the 1876 photographic edition by Bickers and Son (see #2157 in Chapter II) as well as of the rich contemporary blue morocco binding over thick boards for this edition (see #2157 in Chapter II).

Martin's mezzotint illustrations are spectacular and stunning, starkly contrasting bright whites and dense blacks, giving shape and form to scenes of vastness in Milton's epic totally enthralling to the viewer. Martin's powerful vision gives scope and definition to the caverns of Hell, the void of Chaos, the daunting size of Pandemonium, and the sweeping beauty of the plains of Heaven—captured in such riveting mezzotints as *Pandemonium, The Creation of Light, Heaven—The Rivers of Bliss*, and *The Bridge over Chaos*.

Mezzotint is a printing process in which gray-scale images are screened through a patterned mesh; in which soft steel rather than copper plates are used, and the engravings are produced by being designed directly on the plates, without the aid of preparatory sketches. Martin mastered the process of the mezzotint and was the first to illustrate *PL* with illustrations in the mezzotint medium. Through the mezzotint Martin brought all of his creative genius to bear in illustrating *PL*, masterfully uniting brilliant highlights and starkly contrasting dark shadows and dense blacks to express his imagery in illustrations that are unique and never forgotten once seen. His mezzotint illustrations of *PL* are considered among the most powerful illustrations of Milton's epic.

Before Martin's mezzotint illustrations appeared in book editions, they appeared in "proof state before letters" and also in "proof" state. These plates were sold as single plates before the editions were ready for publication. Photographs of five plates are shown here, all rare, some more than others.

Next appear photographs of an original pencil sketch by Martin and of plates in proof state of the Bible, followed by photographs of two color lithographs (unusual for Martin) for a poem-turned-annual and of a rare proof impression on India paper for a popular annual of the day.

All of the editions with Martin's plates remain with the collection. The plates and pencil sketch here remain with the collector as do the annuals below.

Paradise Lost

Eve Tempts Adam, Book IX, lines 995–97. Small mezzotint plate, 5 ⅝" × 8", in proof state before letters, 1825–26. Very rare.

Satan 'With Head-Up-Lift Above the Wave,' Book I, lines 192–94. "Designed & Engraved by J. Martin Esq. Printed by Chatfield & Co. London: Published by Septimus Prowett, 1825." Large mezzotint plate, 7 ⅞" × 11 ¼", slight foxing, proof impression with "Proof" printed on lower right-hand corner. Scarce.

VI. JOHN MARTIN (1789–1854)   795

Satan Starting from the Touch of Ithuriel's Spear, Book IV, lines 308–10. "Designed & Engraved by J. Martin Esq. Printed by Chatfield & Co. London: Published by Septimus Prowett, 1825." Large mezzotint plate, 7 ½" × 11", proof impression with "Proof" printed on lower right-hand corner. Scarce.

Adam and Eve See Raphael Approaching, Book V, line 813. "Designed & Engraved by J. Martin Esq. Published 1825 by Septimus Prowett." Large mezzotint plate, 7 ½" × 10 ⅞", proof impression with "Proof" printed on lower right-hand corner. Scarce.

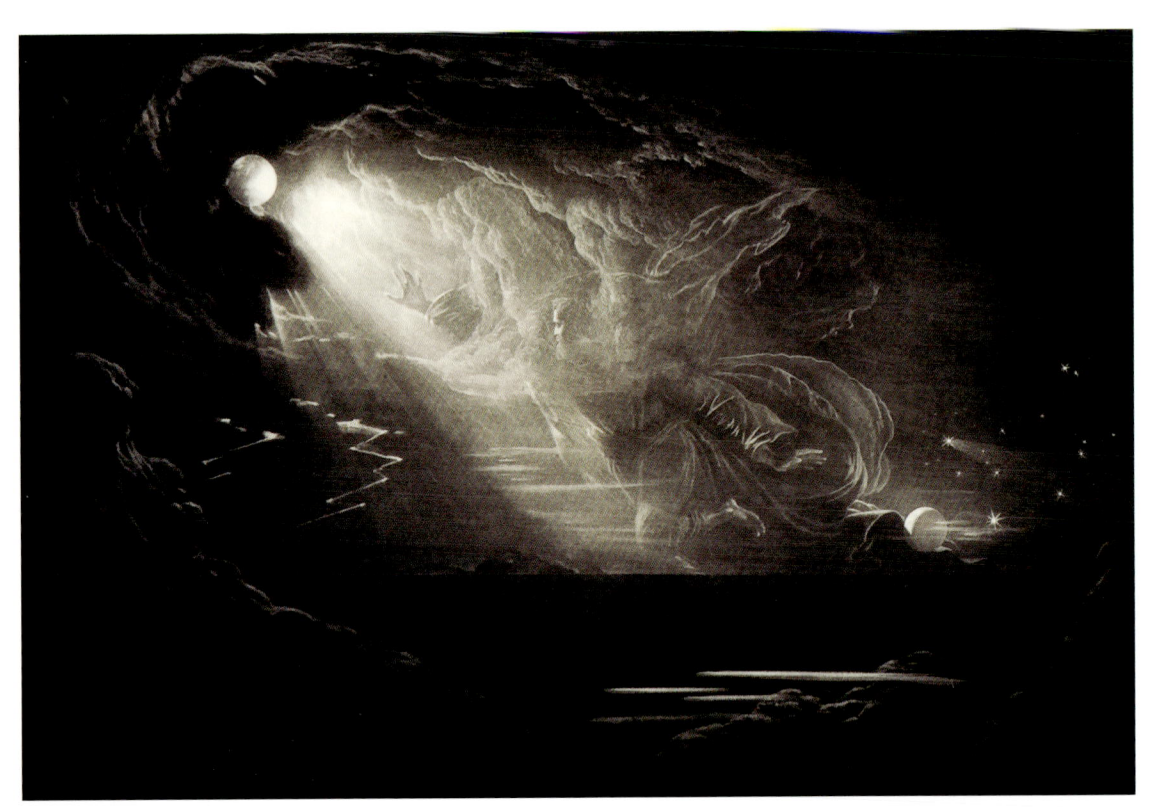

The Creation of Light, Book VII, lines 339–40. "Designed & Engraved by J. Martin Esq. Published 1825 by Septimus Prowett." Large mezzotint plate, 7 ½" × 10 ⅞", proof impression with "Proof" printed on lower right-hand corner. Scarce.

The Expulsion of Adam and Eve from Eden, Book IX, lines 641–49. "Designed & Engraved by J. Martin Esq. Printed by J. Lahee. Published by Septimus Prowett, 1827." Large mezzotint plate, 7 9/16" × 10 13/16" (slight foxing), proof impression with "Proof" printed on lower right-hand corner. Scarce.

The Bible

Belshazzar's Feast—A Study. Original pencil drawing by John Martin, 6 ¼" × 9" (15.8 cm. × 22.8 cm.). Presumably a working study for the mezzotint (7 ½" × 11 ½") published as plate 18 in Martin's *Illustrations of the Bible*, London, 1835.

The Fall of Man. "Designed and Engraved by John Martin. London: Published March 21st 1831 by John Martin." Large mezzotint plate, 14" × 18", proof impression by John Martin for his *Illustrations of the Bible*, 1835.

Adam and Eve Hearing the Judgment of the Almighty. "Designed and Engraved by John Martin. London: Published May 23rd 1831 by John Martin." Large mezzotint plate, 14" × 18", proof impression by John Martin for his *Illustrations of the Bible*, 1835.

The Sacred Annual: Being the Messiah by Robert Montgomery (1834)

The Temptation by Martin, one of the twelve lithographs "Coloured Under The Direction Of Charles Simpson" and tipped on stiff paper, with protective tissue guard, each lithograph inserted within *The Sacred Annual: Being The Messiah By Robert Montgomery. London: John Turrill, 1834. The Messiah*, 6,000 lines long, was published in 1832, and Montgomery's "publisher, John Turrill, decided to profit from the current vogue by issuing it as *The Sacred Annual for 1834*. For this purpose he took some sheets of the second edition, printed cancels of the first six pages, and inserted twelve lithographs, hand-colored 'under the direction of Charles Simpson,' . . . The volume was 'superbly bound in embossed violet-coloured velvet, with an antique Mosaic Gold Clasp.'" Martin contributed three pictures: *The Temptation* as frontispiece, *The Sermon on the Mount*, and *The Remorse of Judas*.

Hand-colored lithographs by Martin of *The Remorse of Judas* (left) and *The Temptation* (right).

Engraver's Proofs for Early Nineteenth-century Annuals

In Search of the Waters of Oblivion. Engraver's proof on India paper of illustration "Painted by J. Martin," "Engraved by E. J. Roberts," "Printed by McQueen" in "London, Oct. 1827." Published for the Proprietor by R. Jennings, Poultry" for *The Keepsake for 1828*, there entitled *Sadak*. This engraver's proof is bound with other engravers' proofs of engravings after Joseph Mallord William Turner, Thomas Stothard, Edwin Landseer, and other prominent painters on India paper for *The Keepsake for 1828* and *1829* and *The Anniversary* and *Gem for 1829* in a volume that formerly belonged to William Beckford, author of *Vathek*.

VII
Ephemera and Objets d'Art

Objets d'Art

Brass Plaques

Portrait of John Milton on Brass Plaque. A rectangular brass plaque depicting a portrait bust of Milton as a younger man in relief looking toward his left; of the poet and the struggles he has known in a lifetime, with blinded eyes and very long hair and with a long cloak thrown over his shoulders. At the bottom of the plaque, measuring 15 ¾" × 11 ¾", on a strip of different style brass is the name "Milton" in the center with a star at each end. Milton's image occupies most of the plaque. Undated, but from the nineteenth century. In very nice condition.

Portrait of John Milton on Brass Plaque. A round brass plaque depicting a portrait bust of Milton as a young man in relief facing right, in a simple collar with long flowing hair, set off against a smooth background with "Milton" and "1608 • 1674" framing the head, Milton's image measuring six inches, surrounded at an elevated level by an elaborate three-inch border, very detailed with flourishes and decorative pieces in relief, the whole brass plaque measuring 17 ½" in diameter. Undated, but from the nineteenth century. In very nice condition.

Milton's portrait on rectangular brass plaque.

Milton's portrait on round brass plaque.

Portrait of John Milton on Brass Plaque. A large round brass plaque depicting a portrait bust of Milton as a handsome young man in relief looking toward his right, in falling collar and with long flowing hair, and with "John" and "Milton" framing the head, the portrait area measuring over thirteen inches in diameter framed with embossed and hammered classical moldings, with heavy laurel wreath and finely detailed beading, the whole brass plaque measuring over twenty-four inches in diameter, with relief in excess of three inches. This large English brass medallion has been professionally polished and lacquered sometime in the last twenty-five years, with much of the original patina left in the deeply embossed areas to highlight the rich details. Undated but from the nineteenth century. In fine condition.

John Milton Portrait—Cameo Plaque. Cameo plaque of John Milton, ca. 1920s. The cameo depicts a portrait bust of Milton as the blind poet—a middle-aged man in relief turned slightly to the left, with long hair, in a simple collar, and with a gentle face. The cameo is in early vintage plastic (possibly Bakelite) and is formed from layers, measuring 1 ½" × 1".

Milton's portrait on large round brass plaque.

Milton's portrait on cameo plaque.

Cast-Iron Plaques

Illustration on Cast-Iron Plaque. Large cast-iron plaque coated in bronze from the late nineteenth century with an illustration of a standing "Raphael Counseling Adam And Eve" seated under foliage, with "Paradise Lost" lettered beneath, and bolt-like impressions around the border as if taken from a door or some other fixture, measuring 11 ¼" across, with the illustration measuring approximately 10" and the border 1 ¼", and weighing 6 ½ pounds. Slight oxidization as well as the appearance of a bronze coating to the edge of the plaque indicates the bronzed-over feature of the plaque; the base metal appears to be cast iron because of its weight and other characteristics evident from the backside. There is no readily apparent evidence of where this plaque is from, when it was done, or for what purpose it was intended.

Illustration on Cast-Iron Plaque. Cast-iron plaque coated in bronze from the late nineteenth century with an illustration of a standing *Raphael Counseling Adam and Eve* seated under foliage, measuring 9 ¼" across, and weighing approximately five pounds. Identical to the preceding cast-iron plaque, although without the additional border and identification of "Paradise Lost" lettered beneath the illustration within that border and also without the bolt-like impressions within the border. Like that plaque, however, the illustration is in well-defined relief and generally impressive overall. Unlike the previous cast-iron plaque, this piece is very bright, with the appearance of a bright gilt coating recently applied.

The similar cast iron plaques, each with the illustration of Raphael Counseling Adam And Eve seated under foliage.

Busts and Statues

Bust of John Milton. Large white plaster bust of the blind Milton at age sixty-two with long flowing hair, on a slight pedestal, overall 28" high × 20" wide. Influenced by the Michael Rysbrack bust on the Milton monument in Westminster Abbey, the bust dates from the ninteenth century and presents a fine visage of the poet. Despite a few chips on the cloak, the bust is in very good condition.

John Milton: Pewter Statue. Measuring twelve inches high with a three-inch ringed pedestal, the statue depicts a young, long-haired Milton turned sideways and gazing upward, dressed in a cloak, with his right arm outstretched and his hand curved upward; beside his right leg are two large volumes. Milton's name appears on the base as part of the statue; the pedestal is made of bell or pot metal. Undated, but from the nineteenth century.

John Milton: Porcelain Statue. Statue, ca. nineteenth century. Measuring 14 ¼" high, this heavy parian porcelain (or bisque china) statue of Milton depicts a young, long-haired Milton standing, gazing downward, dressed in a cloak, holding a scroll in his left hand and leaning with his left elbow on top of several books on a pedestal measuring 6 ¼" high; both Milton and the pedestal are on top of a two-inch terraced base. Fine. Parian porcelain was developed in the 1840s as a substitute for white marble in decorative pieces.

Milton pewter statue.

Large bust of Milton.

Milton heavy parian porcelain (or bisque china) statue.

Memorial Medals

Memorial Medal of John Milton. Large copper memorial medal to John Milton 1737 by J. S. Tanner, measuring fifty-two millimeters in diameter. The front of the medal depicts Milton as a portrait bust in relief facing right, with long hair, in falling collar, coat, and mantle. The legend "IOHANNES MILTONUS" frames the head.

The reverse side bears the inscription: "E MARMORE IN ECCLESIA SANCTI PETRI APUD WESTMONASTERIUM ERECTORE GULIELMO BENSONO ARM: ANNO SALUTIS HUMANAE M DCC XXXVII. RYSBRACHIUS SCULPSIT." William Benson, who had employed Michael Rysbrack to erect the monument to the memory of Milton in 1737, which now exists in Westminster Abbey, also engaged Tanner to engrave this medal. In fine condition.

Memorial Medal of John Milton. Copper memorial medal to John Milton 1730s by Jean Dassier, measuring forty-two millimeters in diameter (Raymond Waddington says forty-one millimeters). The front of the medal depicts Milton as a portrait bust in relief looking toward his left, after the White portrait, "wearing a doublet with a mantle over his right shoulder" (Waddington). The legend "IOANNES MILTON" frames the head.

The reverse side depicts Adam and Eve beneath the tree, with the serpent in its branches. Adam is seated with his head bowed resting on one hand; Eve stands beside him tending to (perhaps even consoling) Adam, with her left arm behind his head and over his shoulder. In the left background, wolves attack sheep, and birds of prey attack smaller birds; to the right, "demons invade the garden with flaming torches" (Eleanor Lincoln) or "Furies enter Paradise"; in the sky above them lightning flashes signal the distempered climate" (Waddington). On a scroll above the scene is the legend "DIRA DULCE CANIT ALTER HOMERUS" ("Another Homer sweetly sings of dire events"); at the bottom are the initials "I. D.," one of Dassier's usual signatures.

A fine copy of this medal.

Memorial Medal of John Milton. Bronze memorial medal to John Milton, 1818, measuring forty-one millimeters in diameter. The front side depicts Milton as a portrait bust in relief facing left, as a younger man with long hair, with ruff around his neck, and thickly corded shoulder. The legend "IOHANNES MILTON" frames the head. Beneath the shoulder in small letters: "VIVIER F."

The reverse side bears the inscription: "NATUS LONDINI IN ANGLIA AN. M.DC.VIII. OBIIT AN. M.DC.LXXI. [sic] SERIES NUMISMATICA UNIVERSALIS VIRORUM ILLUSTRIUM. M.DCCC. XVIII. DURAND EDIDIT." The medal would seem to have been intended as one of a series of "Illustrious Men," most likely done in a limited number. The origin is probably continental and very likely France. A fine copy of this medal.

Memorial Medal of John Milton. Variant bronze memorial medal to John Milton, 1818, measuring forty-one millimeters in diameter. The front side depicts Milton as a portrait bust in relief facing left, as a younger man but in a different image from that on the preceding medal, a less youthful face with a longer nose, with longer hair, without the ruff around his neck, and very plainly garbed. The legend "IOHANNES MILTON" frames the head. On the lower rim is engraved "MONACHII."

The reverse side bears the same inscription as the preceding medal: "NATUS LONDINI IN ANGLIA AN. M.DC.VIII. OBIIT AN. M.DC.LXXI. [sic] SERIES NUMISMATICA UNIVERSALIS

VIRORUM ILLUSTRIUM. M.DCCC. XVIII. DURAND EDIDIT." Like that medal, this would seem to have been intended as one of a series of "Illustrious Men," most likely done in a limited number. The origin of this medal is perhaps not continental as with the previous medal; possibly English by its look and character. As the British numismatist who sold me this medal said, "it has an exquisite patina that only comes with maturity of a piece."

[Milton Memorial Medal] A large Russian bronze memorial medal to John Milton, 1984, measuring fifty-nine millimeters in diameter and quite heavy. The front side depicts Milton's profile at age twenty-one in relief looking toward his left in striking Russian style, with long flowing hair, and holding a quill. Milton's dates in arabic and his name in Russian frame the head.

On the reverse side in relief is a poem, in Russian, dedicated to Milton by the Russian poet Pushkin, the whole engraved over an apple tree. A beautiful bronze medal designed by the Russian artist M. Romanovskaya and minted in the Leningrad, St. Petersburg, Mint, in 1984.

As new.

Ephemera

John Milton: Advertisement. 1916 magazine advertisement for the American Telephone and Telegraph Company. At the top of the ad is a reproduction of Michael (Mihaly) Munkacsy's painting of *Blind Milton Dictating to His Daughters*. The ad is titled "The Vision of the Blind" and begins with a quotation of the end of Milton's sonnet "On His Blindness": "Thousands at his bidding speed, And post o'er land and ocean without rest; They also serve who only stand and wait." The ad itself reads: "Was the spirit of prophecy upon John Milton when, more than two hundred and fifty years ago, he dictated those words to his daughter? Did the 'blind poet' have a vision of the millions of telephone messages speeding instantly over hundreds and thousands of miles of wire spanning the continent? 'They also serve who only stand and wait.' The Bell Telephone is your servant even while it 'only stands and waits.' The whole system is always prepared and ready for your instant command . . . American Telephone And Telegraph Company And Associated Companies[.] One Policy[.] One System[.] Universal Service[.]"

John Milton: Advertisement. Original advertisement/print published by the "Container Corporation of America," 1976, with quotation from *Of Education* at the top: "I call, therefore, a complete and generous education . . . ," and reproduction of Milton portrait at the bottom. The overall print measures 10 ½" × 14", the design within consisting of two wide black bands with jagged edges (3 ½" × 7" each) with a narrow white space (1 ½") in between (the overall design measuring 7" × 7 ½") with large white margins, the text of Milton and portrait printed on a narrow bright red strip (1 ½") running the length of the two black bands and through the white space in between (totaling 7 ½"), with Milton's text printed in black and his portrait (after Faithorne) below, Milton's name printed in white above his portrait and "ON THE PURPOSE OF EDUCATION" printed in white below his portrait. The design is signed in white script by "Burlin" in the lower left-hand corner.

John Milton: Advertisement. Original advertisement/print published by the "Container Corporation of America," 1976, with quotation from *Areopagitica*: "Where there is much desire to learn, there of necessity will be much arguing, much writing, many opinions; for opinion in good men is but knowledge in the making" (*Areopagitica*, 1644). The quotation appears under the heading "John Milton on opinion and knowledge" alongside a portrait sketch of Milton seated in a chair with armrests holding an open book on his knee with his left hand while his right hand is crossed over his heart. The portrait in black and yellow is by the "Artist: Charles Pickard," printed below, and measures 3 ¾" × 11". The advertisement measures 14" × 10 ¾".

VII. Ephemera and Objets d'Art ❧ 807

John Milton: Collage. Collage primarily of tobacco, cigarette, tea, and playing cards from England, France, Germany, Cuba, and the United States with a "Pepsin Gum Cello Pinback" (very small round button pin with Milton's image in color) near the center, dating from the late nineteenth century to the 1960s.

Postcards and Miniature

***Il Penseroso* Illustrated**. Postcard depicting in rich colors a small stone church amidst heavy foliage within a stone wall, with a shepherd and his dog and sheep passing by with farm buildings in the distance, the whole within an imprint of a leaf shape outlined in white against the deep gold color of the card, with four lines quoted from *Il Penseroso* outlined in white at the bottom: "The high embower'd roof / With antique pillars massy proof / The storied windows richly dight / Casting a dim religious light.—Milton" (lines 56–59). The postcard, measuring 3 ½" × 5 ½", is postmarked 1909 with a one-cent stamp.

A collage of four cards and a miniature from the late nineteenth and early twentieth centuries with quotations from Milton: a quotation from *Arcades* illustrated on a Valentine card, ca. 1900; a quotation from *PL* illustrated on a postcard dated 1905 and from *Il Penseroso* on another card postmarked 1909; a postcard with a nativity scene called "The Milton Postcard," dated 1913, but without a quotation from Milton; and a miniature book of *Rules* with a poetic quotation on each day of the week, published ca. 1890 in Germany, with Milton quoted on two days, Friday and Saturday.

***Paradise Lost* Illustrated**. "O fairest of creation, last and best!" (from *PL*, Book IX, line 896) on a postcard with an unsigned color illustration on front side showing "a fantasy scene of an angelic baby's breath brushing the lips of a lovely sleeping lady," with caption from *Paradise Lost* beneath, identified only as "Milton." Labeled postcard number 516 "Copyright, 1905, by U. Co. N.Y.," measuring 3 ½" × 5 ½", postmarked 1908, with a one-cent stamp.

***Arcades* and *Samson Agonistes* Quoted**. Valentine postcard with an embossed illustration in color on the front side of a young girl on the far left looking at two young boys and a young girl on the far right with the wording "To My True Love" within a heart-shaped red ribbon below and two lines from *Arcades* (lines 12–13) also below with the letter "L" enlarged in embossed white over a gold background similar to the gold background behind the illustration within an embossed white border: "Less than half we find exprest, / Envy bid conceal the rest. Milton" (*Samson Agonistes*, lines 271–72) Chicago[:] Allied Printing, n.d. [ca. 1900]. Valentine No. 1012. Unused.

"The Milton Postcard." Postcard with a picture in rich colors of the infant child in a manger surrounded by nature and a mule and cow in the background in a plasticized manner on front side, with a Christmas message quoted beneath: "When the Earth is rapt in slumber, / Slowly wakes the Christmas dawn, / Bringing tidings of great gladness / Unto us a son is born." The message is not from Milton. The postcard, dated 1913 and measuring 3 ½" × 5 ½", is labeled "The Milton Postcard" in red at the top on the verso or writing side of the card with a very small vignette portrait of Milton in red in the middle of the label and with "Trade Mark" printed above the portrait and "Milton" beneath. The card is British, postmarked "Brixton. S.W. 24 Dec 13," with a canceled "HALFPENNY" stamp from the period. It is certainly most curious that Milton's *Ode on the Morning of Christ's Nativity* is not quoted on this "Milton" postcard.

John Milton: Poetic Quotations. *Rules. Poetic Quotations For Each Day. Printed at the Works in Munich (Germany)[.] Trademark Registered The Art Lithographic Publishing Co[.] New York[,] London[,] Munich[,] Berlin. n.d. [ca. 1890].* Miniature (measuring 2 ½" × 3 ½"), 7pp. Given the miniature size of this publication, all quotations are of necessity very brief. Milton is quoted for two days, Friday and Saturday: "Who best bear his mild yoke they serve him best" and "They also serve who only stand and wait."

Postage Stamps

John Milton: Hungarian Stamp. A large stamp within a white border (2 7/16" × 2 ¼"), the whole within a gray frame, lettered "Amphilex 67" at the top and "F.I.P. Kongresszus Amsterdam" at the bottom. The stamp reproduces in bright color a painting of Milton seated by a table dictating to his daughters, with one writing at a desk in front of him, the other two listening beside and behind him, labeled "Orlai Petrics Soma: Milton" underneath with "10 ft Magyar Posta" at the bottom. Twentieth century. In mint condition. With "Matching Souvenir Sheet With Perforation" with identical image and also in mint condition. Hungary used to issue every stamp in two varieties: perforated and non-perforated.

John Milton: Russian Stamp. A forty-kopek stamp issued by the USSR in 1958 to commemorate the 350th anniversary of Milton's birth. Measuring 1 ⅜" × 1", the design in sepia monochrome is by V. V. Zavjalov with Milton's name below his image in Cyrillic characters; the inscription above translates as "The Great English Poet."

VIII

Photographs of Additional Select Items

Photographs in this section are of bindings and fore-edge paintings on books that have been a part of the collection virtually from the beginning and will remain with the collector, perhaps someday to be reunited with the collection once again. A copy of each edition here is in the collection, otherwise anything missing from this group would have remained with the collection.

Bindings

PARADISE LOST. A Poem, In Twelve Books. The Author John Milton, A New Edition, With Notes of various Authors, By Thomas Newton, D.D. London: Printed for J. and R. Tonson and S. Draper in the Strand. M DCC XLIX. 2 volumes. First Newton edition. Large 4to, engraved frontispiece portrait by Vertue after the Onslow portrait, volume 1, after Faithorne, volume 2, engraved illustrations by Hayman. See #654 in Chapter II for a full description of this edition. Eighteenth-century full rich maroon morocco, with the arms of Mancini-Nivernois stamped in gilt on all covers, with gilt rules, ornately gilt-decorated spines in the panels, black morocco title and numbering labels, raised bands with decorative gilt trim, inner dentelles finely tooled in gilt, elaborately decorated green silk end-papers, a.e.g. An elegant set in remarkable condition with a fine provenance, from the collections of Robert Schumann and A. S. W. Rosenbach, with his "R" paper label tipped in on front blank. From John Fleming. See De Ricci and Cohen 708, where this set is described.

PARADISE LOST. *London: Printed for J. and R. Tonson and S. Draper, 1749.* Volume 1 of the first Newton variorum edition. Large 4to, contemporary full red morocco, covers richly decorated in gilt with gilt decoration in the center, spine richly decorated in gilt by compartments alternating red and black morocco labels with gilt lettering and numeral, raised bands with decorative gilt trim, inner dentelles finely tooled in gilt, marbled endpapers, a.e.g. A splendid copy in a well-preserved contemporary presentation binding. Presentation copy from the dedicatee, inscribed on front blank: "The Gift of the Right Honourable The Earl of Bath to Henry Tolcher." The earl contributed the copper plates for the volumes and presumably was supplied with a number of copies. While the volume became separated from volume 2 through the centuries, the association of the volume and its handsome binding nonetheless give it merit of its own. From Michael Papantonio.

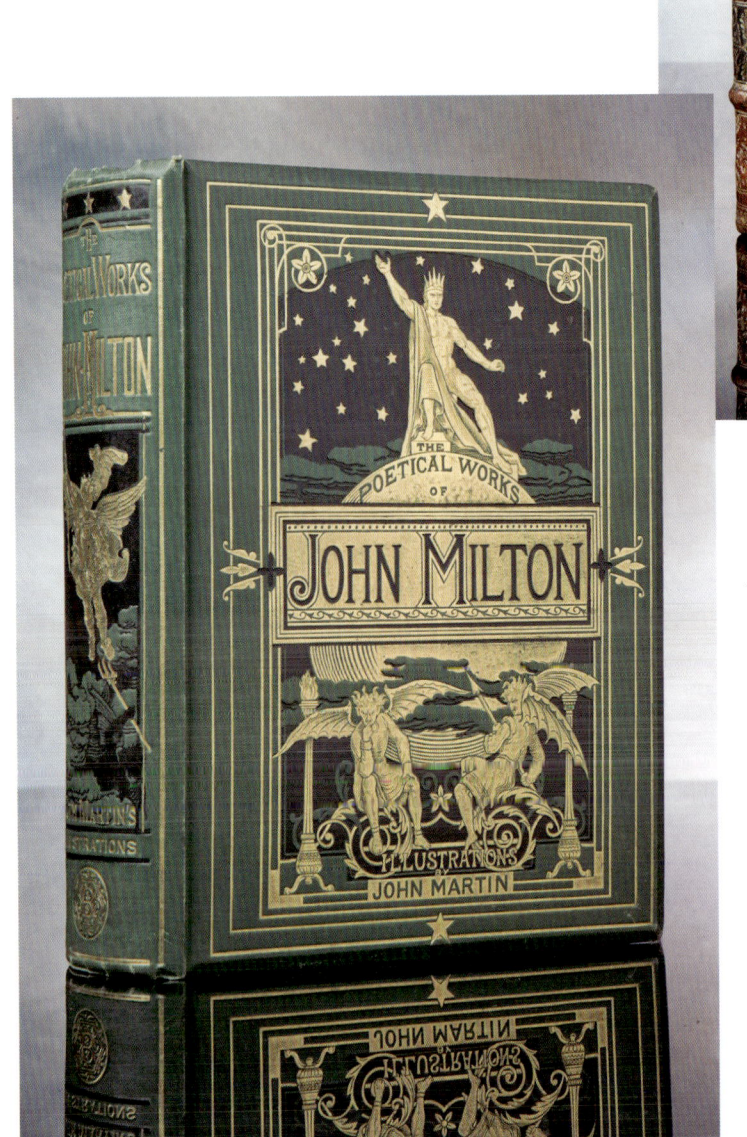

THE POETICAL WORKS OF JOHN MILTON Printed From The Original Editions With A Life Of The Author By A. Chalmers M.A. F.S.A. With Twenty-Four Illustrations By John Martin, Reproduced In Permanent Photography. *London[:] Bickers And Son[,] 1 Leicester Square[.] 1876.* Thick 8vo, original green cloth, front cover and spine elegantly decorated in gilt and black incorporating title within an illustration of Satan addressing his cohorts on the front cover and of Michael casting out the fallen angels on the spine, back cover decorated in blind, a.e.g.

PARADISE REGAINED. John Milton. Decorated By Thomas Lowinsky. *London[:] The Fleuron[,] 1924*. First edition. Small 4to, three full-page wood-engraved illustrations by Thomas Lowinsky, with a number of elaborate decorative head- and tailpieces, printed on handmade paper, full brown morocco, richly decorated in gilt and inlaid red, blue, black, and green morocco, wide turn-ins finely tooled in gilt, patterned thick green silk endpapers, gauffered gilt top edge, fore- and bottom edges untrimmed. Bound by A. Genova, Venice. With an extra set of plates on Japan vellum in an envelope at the back. No. 87 of 350 numbered copies.

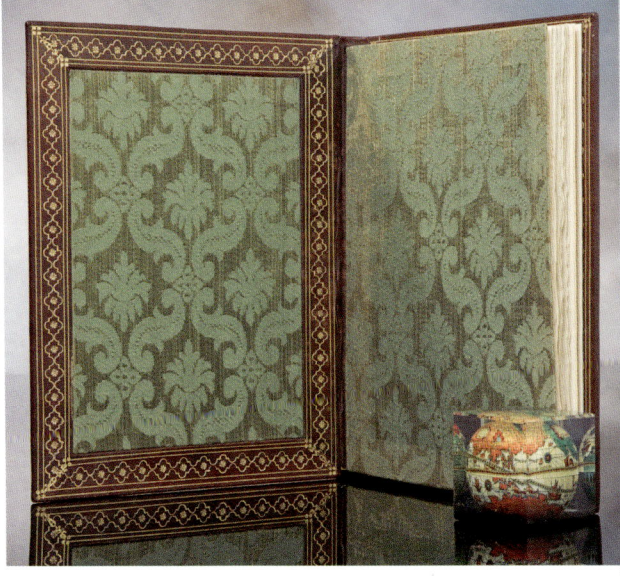

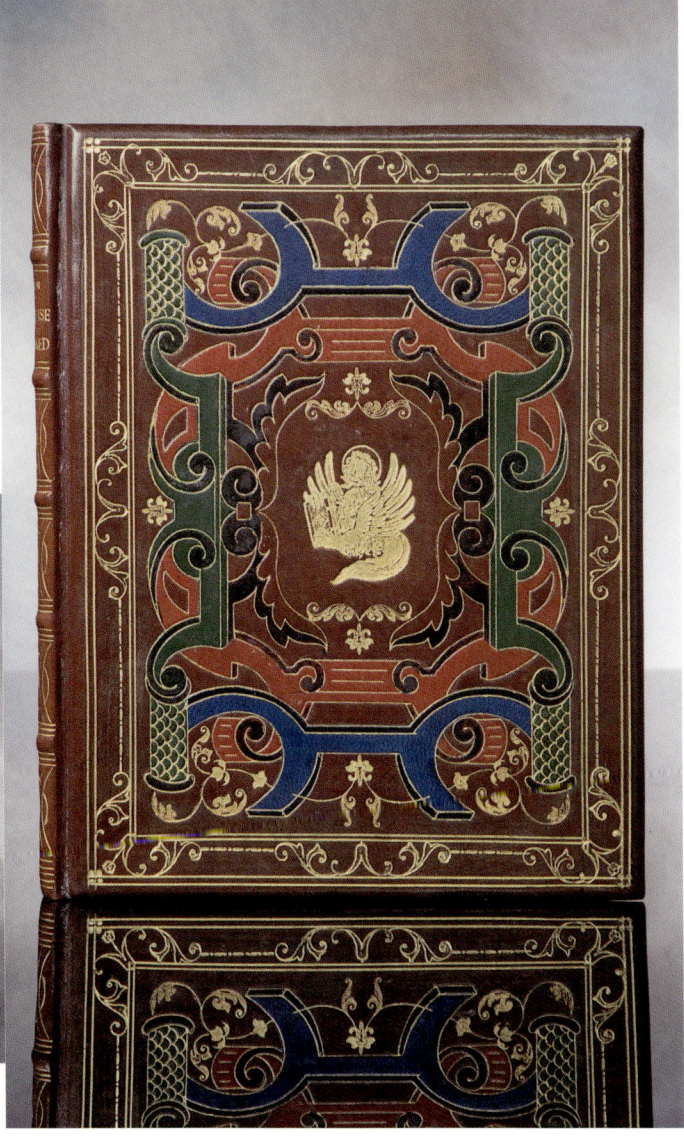

Belloc, Hilaire. **MILTON**. With A Frontispiece. *London, Toronto, Melbourne, and Sydney: Cassell And Company Ltd., (1935)*. Cosway binding. First edition. 8vo, full blue morocco, delicately gilt-decorated, with a miniature watercolor portrait of Milton as a young man on vellum inset under glass at the center of the front cover with two gilt rules encircling it, spine gilt-tooled to match the covers with slightly gilt-decorated raised bands, wide morocco turn-ins with gilt corner pieces, a.e.g., bound by Bayntun Rivieré. Extra-illustrated with the inclusion of twelve portrait plates in addition to the frontispiece portrait of Milton; among the portrait plates of figures associated with Milton is one of John Martin (see following page).

In a recent catalogue, Phillip J. Pirages provides a succinct origin of the term "Cosway binding": "The 'Cosway' style of binding, with painted miniatures inlaid in handsome morocco, apparently originated with the London bookselling firm of Henry Sotheran about 1909, the year G. C. Williamson's book entitled 'Richard Cosway' was remaindered by Sotheran and presumably given this special decorative treatment. The name 'Cosway' then was used to describe any book so treated whoever its author. The earliest Cosway bindings were executed by Miss C. B. Currie, usually from designs by J. H. Stonehouse. She worked for Sotheran for some 30 years, until her death" (Catalogue 52, #313, 2006). See also Howard M. Nixon, *Five Centuries of English Bookbinding* (London: Scolar Press, 1978), 100.

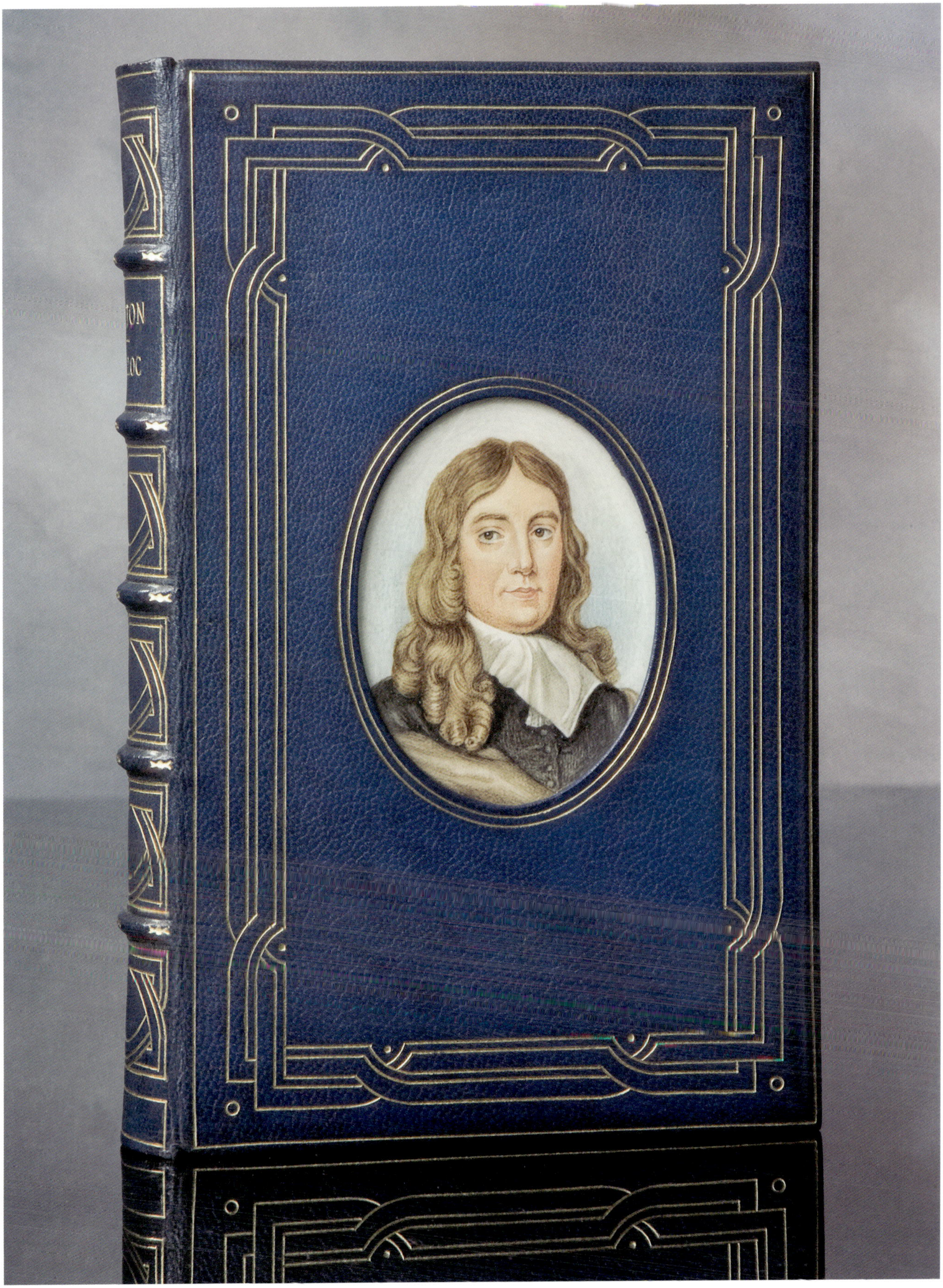

Fore-edge Paintings

A fore-edge painting takes it name from appearing literally on the fore-edge of a book. It is painted such that it is visible only by bending the pages of the book in a fanned or curved manner—very carefully so as not to damage the book—in order to see the painting. Some paintings lend themselves very easily to being opened and seen; others do not. Once closed, the painting on the fore-edge of the book disappears and is no longer visible, leaving only the gilt edge showing along with the top and bottom gilt edges. If the painting is shown a great deal, then its hidden appearance might be compromised when the book is closed.

All kinds of paintings appear as fore-edge paintings on all kinds of books. It is especially exciting to someone who does not collect fore-edge paintings *per se* to find a fore-edge painting on a book related to the main focus of the collection. It is even more exciting to find the fore-edge painting to be contemporary or very nearly contemporary to the publication of the book, and in my case, it has been particularly thrilling to find an occasional fore-edge illustration on an illustrated edition of Milton. It is also a treasured find to discover a fore-edge painting that treats the subject within the book or its author, and several fore-edge paintings illustrate scenes central to Milton's *Paradise Lost* as well as the poet and his homes. All fore-edge paintings here appear on editions that are in the collection and so only very brief identification of the book is cited.

MILTON'S PARADISE LOST, with the Life Of The Author To which is prefixed the Celebrated Critique by Samuel Johnson LLD[.] *London[:] Printed by C. Whittingham Dean Street, Fetter Lane, for T. Heptinstall. . . . 1799.* 8vo, with contemporary or near-contemporary fore-edge painting of the expulsion of Adam and Eve.

Another copy, with contemporary or near-contemporary fore-edge painting of the temptation of Eve.

PARADISE LOST... With A Life Of The Author, And A Critique on the Poem. A New Edition. *London: Printed by T. Bensley... for J. Johnson, et al., 1802.* 8vo, with contemporary or near-contemporary fore-edge painting consisting of three compartments: one at the left showing in miniature Milton's home in Westminster, one in the center depicting in miniature a portrait of Milton (age sixty-two), and one at the right showing in miniature Milton's burial place at St. Giles Cripplegate.

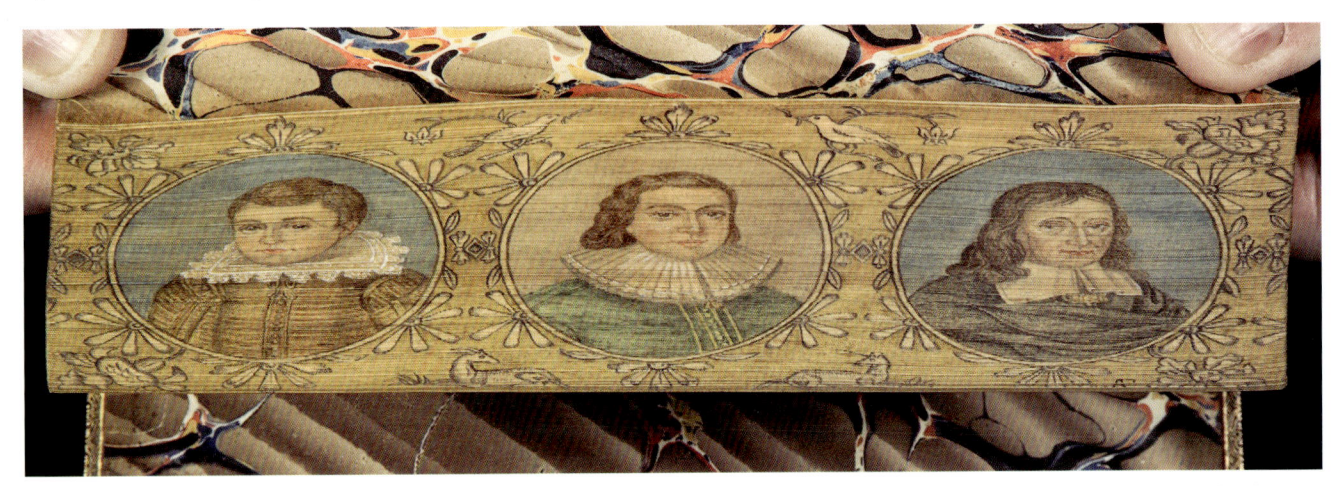

Symmons, Charles. **THE LIFE OF JOHN MILTON**. Third Edition. *London: Printed for G. And W. B. Whittaker... 1822.* 8vo, with contemporary or near-contemporary fore-edge painting depicting three portraits of Milton at ages ten, twenty-one, and sixty-two on a background design adapted from an unfinished tapestry saved from the Great Fire of 1666 in a house at Cheapside.

POETICAL WORKS. To Which Is Prefixed The Life Of The Author. *London: William Tegg And Co., 1849.* 8vo, with contemporary or near-contemporary fore-edge painting of Milton's home at Chalfont St. Giles.

VIII. Photographs of Additional Select Items 817

POETICAL WORKS. With A Memoir. And Critical Remarks On His Genius And Writings, By James Montgomery: And One-Hundred And Twenty Engravings . . . From Drawings By William Harvey. *London: W. Kent & Co. (Late D. Bogue), Fleet Street, 1859*. 2 volumes. 8vo, with a fore-edge painting on each volume: on volume 1, an angel protecting Adam and Eve from Satan while they sleep; on volume 2, Satan rebuffed by Gabriel.

Appendix: Recent Additions of Note

The following editions were selected for inclusion here from among those added to the collection after the text of this book was sent to the publisher and before publication. Their rarity and importance make them sufficiently important to add here. Reference to each is made in the main listing.

1. PARADISE LOST. A Poem, In Twelve Books. The Author John Milton. *London. Printed In the Year MDCCLXXIII.* 12mo in 6s, 295pp., printer's device at center of title page, life by Fenton, original calf (a little worn, small tear at outer edge of title page, lacking front blank), black leather label lettered and ruled in gilt on spine, raised bands. A decent copy with dated contemporary signature at the top of title page and the signature repeated on verso. On the fly-leaf of the copy in the Turnbull Library, there is a note: "This is a rare edition and is unmentioned by any bibliographers. There is no copy in the British Museum. The edition is interesting owing to a misprint in the first line of the poem which reads 'of man's first obedience,' &c." Rare. Coleridge 136b; Not in Kohler.

2. PARADISE LOST. A Poem, In Twelve Books. By John Milton. Stereotyped By T. H. Carter & Co. *Amherst: Published By J. S. & C. Adams. 1831.* 12mo in 6s, 294pp., original marbled calf (joints rubbed with cracking at the top of the front joint, some wear, pages age-browned), border trim in gilt on covers, spine decorated in gilt with red leather label lettered in gilt with gilt trim. A decent copy with early signature and stamp. Scarce. Not in Kohler.

3. PARADISE LOST: A Poem. The Author, John Milton. Vol. I/II. *London: Charles Tilt, Fleet Street; J. Menzies, Edinburgh; W. F. Wakeman, Dublin. MDCCCXXXVI.* 2 volumes. Small 8vo (2 ¾" x 4 ¼"), 190+2pp.,+179+4pp., half-title ("Tilt's Miniature Classical Library") each volume, frontispiece illustration each volume, "Awake, arise, or be forever fall'n!" (Book I, line 330), Vol. 1, and "So started up in his own shape the Fiend" (Book IV, line 814), Vol. 2, each illustration engraved by George W. Bonner, life by Elijah Fenton, half-title for each book with the Argument on verso, original leather (a little worn along extremities, front cover virtually detached, Vol. 1, stain at the top outer corner of each frontispiece plate without affecting the illustration), a.e.g. A good set, with early signature in each volume, and with advertisements bound in at the end of each volume. Scarce. OCLC lists only one copy in the United States; Not in Kohler.

4. PARADISE LOST; By John Milton: With Explanatory Notes, And A Life Of The Author, By The Rev. H. Stebbing, A.M. *London: Scott, Webster And Geary, 36. Charterhouse Square. 1837.* 12mo, 296+2pp., engraved frontispiece illustration of *Satan Meeting Sin and Death* engraved by C. Heath after H. Corbould, protective tissue guard, original brown pebble cloth, embossed design on covers, spine decorated in gilt with gilt lettering, a.e.g. A lovely copy of this rare edition in splendid condition, with dated contemporary signature on fly-leaf, and bookplate on front pastedown. Not in Kohler.

5. [PARADISE LOST.] Title page and text in Armenian. *Published in Venice, 1861.* 8vo (5 ½" × 8 ¾"), 273pp., engraved and printed title pages, frontispiece portrait of Milton after Bosselman (Paris), dedication page to Queen Victoria—the only page translated into English: "This Metrical Version Of Milton's Paradise Lost Into The Ancient Language Of Armenia Is, With Permission,

Respectfully Dedicated, . . . " with an engraved portrait of a young Victoria by Sir Wm. Ross facing the English text, additional engraved illustration of *Raphael Counseling Adam and Eve* after G. Staal, engraved by Fd. Delannoy (fine, clean engraving of an interesting illustration), original brown leather spine, brown marbled paper (some foxing, a bit heavy on the engraving of Victoria, small personal shelf label at bottom of spine, later signature on front pastedown, edges worn). Overall, a good copy. See 1824 edition of *PL* listed above, first edition in Armenian, and as here printed entirely in Armenian. Rare. Not in Kohler.

BIBLIOGRAPHY

Amory, Hugh. "Thing Unattempted Yet. A Bibliography of the First Edition of *Paradise Lost*." *The Book Collector* 32 (1983): 41–66.

Aubrey, John. *Aubrey's Brief Lives*. Edited from the original manuscripts and with a life of John Aubrey by Oliver Lawson Dick. Ann Arbor: University of Michigan Press, 1957.

Balston, Thomas. *John Martin 1789–1854: His Life and Works*. London: Duckworth, 1947. [Cited as Balston, *Life*]

———. *John Martin 1789–1854, Illustrator and Pamphleteer*. London: The Bibliographical Society, 1934. [Cited as Balston, *Illustrator*]

Bartholomew, A. T. *Richard Bentley, D.D.: A Bibliography of His Works and of All the Literature Called Forth by His Acts or His Writings*. With an introduction and chronological table by J. W. Clark. Cambridge: Bowes & Bowes, 1908. [Cited as Bentley]

Bland, David. *A History of Book Illustration: The Illuminated Manuscript and the Printed Book*. London: Faber and Faber, 1958.

Blumenthal, Joseph. *Art of the Printed Book 1455–1955. Masterpieces of Typography through Five Centuries from the Collections of the Pierpont Morgan Library*. New York: Pierpont Morgan Library, 1973.

———. *The Printed Book in America*. Boston: David R. Godine, 1977.

Boorsch, Suzanne. "The 1688 *Paradise Lost* and Dr. Aldrich." *Metropolitan Museum Journal* 6 (1972): 133–50.

Boswell, Jackson C. *Milton's Library*. New York and London: Garland Publishing, 1975.

Brunet, Jacques-Charles. *Manuel du libraire et de l'amateur de livres, contenant 1 un nouveau dictionnaire bibliographique . . . 2 une table en forme de catalogue raisonné . . . 5e éd. originale entièrement refondue et augmentée d'un tiers par l'auteur . . .* Paris: G.-P. Maisonneuve & Larose, 1965–66. [Cited as Brunet III]

Bush, Douglas. *English Literature in the Earlier Seventeenth Century, 1600–1660*. Oxford: Clarendon Press, 1948.

Campbell, Michael J. *John Martin, 1789–1854. Creation of Light: Prints and Drawings from the Campbell Collection*. Bancaja: Calcografia Nacional, Real Academia De Bellas Artes De San Fernando, Ayuntamiento De Madrid, Museo De Bellas Artes De Bilbao. Valencia, Madrid y Bilbao, 2006.

Carter, John, and Nicolas Barker. *ABC for Book Collectors*. 8th ed. With corrections, additions, and an introduction by Nicolas Barker. New Castle, Del.: Oak Knoll Press, 2004.

Carter, John, and Percy H. Muir, eds. *Printing and the Mind of Man: A Descriptive Catalogue Illustrating the Impact of Print on the Evolution of Western Civilisation*. London: Cassell; New York: Holt, Rinehart and Winston, 1967.

Case, Arthur E. *A Bibliography of English Poetical Miscellanies, 1521–1750*. Oxford: Bibliographical Society, 1935.

Cave, Roderick. *The Private Press*. 2nd ed. Revised and enlarged. New York: Watson-Guptill, 1971.

Coleridge, K. A., comp. *A Descriptive Catalogue of the Milton Collection in the Alexander Turnbull Library, Wellington, New Zealand Describing works printed before 1801 held in the Library at December 1975*.

Oxford: Published for the Alexander Turnbull Library, National Library of New Zealand, by Oxford University Press, 1980. [Cited as Coleridge; references are to numbers, not pages]

Collins-Baker, C. H. "Some Illustrators of Milton's *Paradise Lost*, 1688–1850." *The Library* 5, no. 3 (1948): 1–21, 101–54.

Courtney, William Prideaux, and David Nichol Smith. *A Bibliography of Samuel Johnson*. Oxford: Oxford University Press, 1968.

Croft, Sir William. "The Achievement of Bulmer and Bensley." *Signature*. New Series 16 (1952): 3–28. Includes "Handlist of Books Printed by Bulmer," 11–28.

A Descriptive Bibliography of the Books Printed at the Ashendene Press MDCCCXCV–MCMXXXV. San Francisco: Alan Wolfsy Fine Arts, 1976. [Cited as Ashendene Bib.]

De Ricci, Seymour, and Henri Cohen. *Guide de l'amateur de livres à gravures du XVIII siècle*. Sixth ed. Revised by Seymour De Ricci. Paris: Rouquette, 1912.

Doughty, D. W. (Dennis William). *The Tullis Press: Cupar, 1803-1849*. Dundee, U.K.: Abertay Historical Society Publication No. 12, 1967.

Downs, Robert B. *Books That Changed America*. New York: Macmillan, 1970.

Dreyfus, John, David McKitterick, and Simon Rendall. *A History of the Nonesuch Press. A Descriptive Catalogue*. London: Nonesuch Press, 1981.

Evans, Charles. *American Bibliography: A Chronological Dictionary of All Books, Pamphlets, and Periodical Publications Printed in the United States from the Genesis of Printing in 1639 Down to and Including the Year 1820*. 14 vols. Chicago: Charles Evans, 1903–59.

Faxon, Frederick W. *Literary Annuals and Gift Books: A Bibliography, 1823–1903*. Reprinted with supplementary essays by Eleanore Jamieson and Iain Bain. Pinner, U.K.: Private Libraries Association, 1973.

Feaver, William. *The Art of John Martin*. Oxford: Clarendon Press, 1975.

Fitzwilliam Museum. *The Rampant Lions Press: A Printing Workshop Through Five Decades*. Catalogue of an exhibition at the Fitzwilliam Museum, Cambridge, May 11–June 27, 1982. Edited by Sebastian and Will Carter. Cambridge: Rampant Lions Press, 1982. [Cited as Fitzwilliam Catalogue]

Foxon, David F. *English Verse, 1701–1750: A Catalogue of Separately Printed Poems with Notes of Contemporary Collected Editions*. 2 vols. Cambridge: Cambridge University Press, 1976.

Freeman, Arthur. "Commentary on the Title Pages of *Paradise Lost*." *Quaritch Catalogue* 1091 (1988): no. 69, and *Quaritch List* 98/17 (Summer Acquisitions, 1998): no. 47.

Franklin, Colin. *The Private Presses*. Chester Springs, PA: Dufour Editions, 1969.

Gaskell, Philip. *A Bibliography of the Foulis Press*. London: Rupert Hart-Davis, 1964.

———. *John Baskerville. A Bibliography*. Reprinted with additions and corrections. Chicheley, U.K.: Paul P. B. Minet, 1973.

———. *The First Editions of William Mason*. Cambridge: Bowes and Bowes, 1951.

Good, John Walter. *Studies in the Milton Tradition*. University of Illinois Studies in Language and Literature I, nos. 3–4. Urbana: University of Illinois Press, 1915.

Green, Richard. *The Works of John and Charles Wesley*. London: C. H. Kelly, 1896.

Grolier Club. *Bibliographical Notes on One Hundred Books Famous in English Compiled by Henry W. Kent*. New York: Grolier Club, 1903. [Cited as Grolier, *Bibliographical Notes*]

———. *Catalogue of Original and Early Editions of Some of the Poetical and Prose Works of English Writers from Wither to Prior, with Collations, Notes, and More than Two Hundred Facsimiles of Title-pages and Frontispieces. In Three Volumes*. New York: Imprinted for the Grolier Club, 1905. [Cited as Grolier, *Wither to Prior*]

———. *One Hundred Books Famous in English Literature with Facsimiles of the Title-pages and an Introduction by George E. Woodberry*. New York: Grolier Club, 1902. [Cited as Grolier, *One Hundred Books*]

Hamilton, Sinclair. *Early American Book Illustrators and Wood Engravers, 1670–1870: A Catalogue of a Collection of American Books, Illustrated for the Most Part with Woodcuts and Wood Engravings, in the Princeton Library. With An Introductory Sketch of the Development of Early American Book Illustration by Sinclair Hamilton. With a Foreword by Frank Weitenkampf*. 2 vols. Princeton, N.J.: Princeton University Press, 1968.

Hammelmann, Hanns. *Book Illustrators in Eighteenth-century England*. Edited and completed by T. S. R. Boase. New Haven, Conn.: Printed for the Paul Mellon Centre for Studies in British Art (London) by Yale University Press, 1975.

Hanford, James Holly. "Milton among the Book Collectors." *The Newberry Library Bulletin* IV, no. 4 (1956): 97–109.

Harrop, D. *A History of the Gregynog Press*. Pinner, U.K.: Private Libraries Association, 1980.

Havens, Raymond Dexter. *The Influence of Milton on English Poetry*. Cambridge, Mass.: Harvard University Press; London: Humphrey Milford, Oxford University Press, 1922.

Hayley, William. *The Life of Milton, in Three Parts. To Which Are Added, Conjectures on the Origin of Paradise Lost: With an Appendix*. London: Printed for T. Cadell, Junior, and W. Davies (Successors To Mr. Cadell) in the Strand, 1796.

Hayward, John. *English Poetry, A Catalogue of First and Early Editions of the English Poets from Chaucer to the Present Day*. London: National Book League, 1947.

———. *English Poetry, An Illustrated Catalogue of First and Early Editions Exhibited in 1947 at 7 Albemarle Street, London*. Compiled and revised by John Hayward. Cambridge: Cambridge University Press for the National Book League, 1950. [First done in wrapper form to accompany the exhibition (preceding), this volume contains the plates and a section of additions and corrections.]

Hildeburn, Charles Swift Riché. *A Century of Printing: The Issues of the Press in Pennsylvania, 1685–1784*. 4 vols. New York: Burt Franklin, 1968.

Hodnett, Edward. *Five Centuries of English Book Illustration*. Aldershot, U.K.: Scolar Press, 1988.

Hofer, Philip. *Baroque Book Illustration*. Cambridge, Mass.: Harvard University Press, 1951.

Huckabay, Calvin, comp. *John Milton: A Bibliographical Supplement, 1929–1957*. Duquesne Studies Philological Series. Pittsburgh: Duquesne University Press, 1960; Louvain: Editions E. Nauwelaerts, 1960; revised edition: 1929–68. Pittsburgh: Duquesne University Press, 1969.

Huckabay, Calvin, comp., and Paul J. Klemp, ed. *John Milton: An Annotated Bibliography, 1968–1988*. Pittsburgh: Duquesne University Press, 1996.

Hunter, William B. *Visitation Unimplor'd: Milton and the Authorship of* De Doctrina Christiana. Pittsburgh: Duquesne University Press, 1998.

Hutton, W. H. "Caroline Divines." In *Cambridge History of English Literature 7: Cavalier and Puritan, 1600–1660*, edited by A. W. Ward and R. A. Waller. Cambridge: Cambridge University Press, 1920.

Jaggard, William. *Shakespeare Bibliography: A Dictionary of Every Known Issue of the Writings of Our National Poet and of Recorded Opinion Thereon in the English Language*. Stratford-on-Avon, U.K.: Shakespeare Press, 1911.

Johnstone, Christopher. *John Martin*. London: Academy Editions, 1974.

Jones, S. K. "The Authorship of Nova Solyma." *The Library* 3, no. 1 (1910): 225–38.

Kelley, Maurice. *This Great Argument A Study of Milton's* De Doctrina Christiana *as a Gloss upon Paradise Lost*. Princeton, N.J.: Princeton University Press; London: Humphrey Milford, Oxford University Press, 1941.

Keynes, Geoffrey. *William Pickering Publisher. A Memoir & A Hand-list of His Editions*. London: Galahad Press, 1969.

Kohler, C. C. *Catalogue of the Kohler Collection of 550 Different Editions of the Writings of John Milton Published Between 1641 and 1914*. With a foreword by Christopher Hill. Dorking Surrey: C. C. Kohler, 1993. [Cited as Kohler; references are to numbers, not pages]

Lanckoronska, Maria Grafin. *Die Venezianische Buchgraphik des XVIII. Jahrhunderts*. Hamburg: Maximilian-Gesellschaft, 1950.

Latimore, Sara Briggs, and Grace Clark Haskell. *Arthur Rackham, A Bibliography*. Los Angeles: Suttonhouse, 1936. Reprint by New York: Burt Franklin, 1970.

Lewalski, Barbara K. *The Life of John Milton: A Critical Biography*. Oxford: Blackwell Publishers, 2000.

———. "Milton and De Doctrina Christiana: Evidence of Authorship," *Milton Studies* 36 (1998): 203–28.

Lincoln, Eleanor Terry. "Jean Dassier's Milton Medal: A Further Note." *Milton Quarterly* 37, no. 1 (1975): 24–28.

Lippard, Lucy R. *Graphic Work of Philip Evergood*. New York: Crown Publishers, 1966.

Lowndes, William T. *The Bibliographer's Manual of English Literature*. New edition, revised, corrected and enlarged by Henry G. Bohn. 4 vols. London: George Bell, 1858–64.

Lynch, Kathleen M. *Jacob Tonson: Kit-Cat Publisher*. Knoxville: Tennessee University Press, 1971.

MacDonald, Hugh. *John Dryden: A Bibliography of Early Editions and of Drydeniana*. Oxford: Clarendon Press, 1939.

Madan, Francis F. "Milton, Salmasius and Dugard." *The Library* 4, no. 4 (1923): 119–45; reprinted: *Milton, Salmasius and Dugard (with Facsimiles)*. London: Oxford University Press, 1923.

———. *A New Bibliography of the Eikon Basilike of King Charles the First, with a Note on the Authorship*. Oxford Bibliographical Society Publications, New Series. Vol. 3. London: Bernard Quaritch, 1950. [Cited as Madan, *Eikon*]

———. "A Revised Bibliography of Salmasius's 'Defensio Regia' and Milton's 'Pro Populo Anglicano Defensio.'" *The Library* 5, no. 9 (1954): 101–21.

Malan, Dan. *Gustave Doré: Adrift on Dreams of Splendour*. St Louis: Malan Classical Enterprises, 1995.

Masson, David. *The Life of John Milton: Narrated in Connexion with the Political, Ecclesiastical, and Literary History of His Time*. New and revised edition. 7 vols. London: Macmillan and Co., 1881–94.

McKay, George L. *Bibliography of Robert Bridges*. New York: Columbia University Press, 1933.

McLean, Rauri. *Victorian Book Design and Colour Printing*. London: Faber & Faber, 1972. [Cited as McLean, *VBD*]

———. *Victorian Publisher's Book-bindings in Cloth and Leather*. London: Gordon Fraser, 1974. [Cited as McLean, *VPB in C&L*]

———. *Victorian Publisher's Book-bindings in Paper*. Berkeley and Los Angeles: University of California Press, 1983. [Cited as McLean, *VPB in P*]

Mish, Charles C. *English Prose Fiction, 1600–1700: A Chronological Checklist*. Charlottesville: Bibliographical Society of Virginia at the University of Virginia, 1967.

Moore, John Robert. *A Checklist of the Writings of Daniel Defoe*. 2nd ed. Hamden: Archon Books, 1971.

Morazzoni, G. *Il Libro Illustrato Veneziano del Settecento*. Milano: Ulrico Hoepli, 1948.

Moyles, R. G. *The Text of Paradise Lost: A Study in Editorial Procedure*. Toronto, Buffalo, London: University of Toronto Press, 1985.

Muir, Percy. *Victorian Illustrated Books*. London: Portman Books, 1985; rev. ed.; first by Batsford, 1971. [Cited as Muir, *VIB*]

The National Union Catalog, Pre-1956 Imprints. London: Mansell; Chicago: American Library Association, 1975. Supplemented by *National Union Catalog*. Washington, D.C., 1958–. [Cited as NUC]

The New Cambridge Bibliography of English Literature. Edited by George Watson and I. R. Willison. 2 vols. Cambridge: Cambridge University Press, 1971–74. [Cited as NCBEL I and II]

Nixon, Howard M. *Five Centuries of English Bookbinding*. London: Scolar Press, 1978.

Oras, Ants. *Milton's Editors and Commentators from Patrick Hume to Henry John Todd (1659–1801: A Study in Critical Views and Methods)*. Tartu, Estonia: University of Tartu; London: Humphrey Milford, Oxford University Press, 1931.

Osborne, Harold, ed. *The Oxford Companion to Art*. Oxford and New York: Oxford University Press, 1970.

Parker, William Riley. *Milton: A Biography*. 2 vols. Oxford: Clarendon Press, 1968.

Pendered, Mary L. *John Martin, Painter: His Life and Times with 20 Illustrations and a Folding Map*. London: Hurst & Blackett, 1923.

Pertelote, A Sequel to Chanticleer, Being a Bibliography of the Golden Cockerel Press, October 1936–1943 April. London: Golden Cockerel Press, 1943.

Pforzheimer, Carl H. *The Carl H. Pforzheimer Catalogue English Literature, 1475–1700*. Edited by W. A. Jackson. New Castle, Del., and Los Angeles: Oak Knoll & Heritage, 1997.

Pointon, Marcia R. *Milton and English Art*. Toronto: University of Toronto Press, 1970.

Raffel, Burton, ed. *The Annotated Milton Complete English Poems with Annotations Lexical, Syntactic, Prosodic, and Referential*. New York: Bantam, 1999.

Ransom, Will. *Private Presses and Their Books*. New York: R. R. Bowker, 1929. [Cited as Ransom, *Private Presses*]

———. *Selective Check Lists of Press Books*. 5 vols. New York: Philip C. Duschines, 1945–47. [Cited as Ransom, *Selective Check Lists*]

Ravenhall, Mary D. "Francis Atterbury and the First Illustrated Edition of *Paradise Lost*." *Milton Quarterly* 16, no. 2 (1982): 29–36.

Ray, Gordon N. *The Illustrator and the Book in England from 1790 to 1914*. New York: The Pierpont Morgan Library; Oxford: Oxford University Press, 1976. [Cited as Ray, *Illustrator*]

———. *Victorian Publisher's Book-Bindings in Cloth and Leather*. London: Gordon Fraser, 1974. [Cited as Ray, *VPB*]

Reid, Forrest. *Illustrators of the Eighteen Sixties: An Illustrated Survey of the Work of 58 British Artists.* New York: Dover, 1975. Reprint of work originally published in 1928 by Faber & Gwyer, London, under the title: *Illustrators of the Sixties.*

Ridler, William. *British Modern Press Books. A Descriptive Check List of Unrecorded Items.* London: Covent Garden Press, 1971.

Rochedieu, Charles Alfred Emmauel. *Bibliography of French Translations of English Works, 1700–1800.* Chicago: University of Chicago Press, 1948.

Roscoe, Sydney. *John Newbery and His Successors, 1740–1814: A Bibliography.* Wormley, Hertfordshire, England: Five Owls Press, 1973.

Rothschild, Nathaniel Mayer Victor, Baron. *The Rothschild Library: A Catalogue of the Collection of Eighteenth-Century Printed Books and Manuscripts Formed by Lord Rothschild.* London: Dawsons of Pall Mall, 1969.

Russell, Norma. *A Bibliography of William Cowper to 1837.* Oxford: Oxford Bibliographical Society, with Clarendon Press, 1963.

Sadleir, Michael. *XIX Century Fiction: A Bibliographical Record.* 2 vols. London, 1951; reprinted New York: Cooper Square Publishers, 1969.

Schiff, Gert. *Johann Heinrich Füsslis Milton-Galerie. Schweizerisches Institut Für Kunstwissenschaft Zürich.* Schriften Nr. 5. Zürich/Stuttgart: Fretz & Wasmuth Verlag, 1963.

Seznec, Jean. *John Martin en France.* London: Faber and Faber, 1964.

Shaw, Ralph R., and Richard H. Shoemaker. *American Bibliography. A Preliminary Checklist. 1801–1832.* 37 vols. New York: Scarecrow Press Inc., 1958.

Shawcross, John T., ed. *The Collection of the Works of John Milton and Miltoniana in the Margaret I. King Library University of Kentucky Compiled by John T. Shawcross with a Foreword by Thomas B. Stroup.* Occasional Paper No. 8. Lexington: University of Kentucky Libraries, 1985. [Cited as Shawcross, Kentucky; references are to numbers, not pages]

———, ed. *Milton: The Critical Heritage.* London: Routledge & Kegan Paul, 1970; New York: Barnes & Noble, 1970. [Cited as Shawcross, 1970, with page reference]

———, ed. *Milton, 1732–1801: The Critical Heritage.* London and Boston: Routledge & Kegan Paul, 1972. [Cited as Shawcross, 1972; references are to numbers, not pages]

———. "A Survey of Milton's Prose Works," Appendix to *Achievements of the Left Hand: Essays on the Prose of John Milton*, edited by Michael Lieb and John T. Shawcross, 291–391. Amherst: University of Massachusetts Press, 1974. [Cited as Shawcross, 1974, with page reference]

———, comp. *Milton A Bibliography for the Years 1624-1700.* Binghamton, N.Y.: Medieval and Renaissance Texts and Studies, 1984. [Cited as Shawcross, 1984; references are to numbers, not pages]

———. "The Robert J. Wickenheiser Collection of John Milton." *Milton Quarterly* 41, no. 1 (2007): 69–73.

Smith, William C. *Handel, A Descriptive Catalogue of Early Editions.* 2nd ed. Revised with supplement. London: Sassell, 1960.

Sommervogel, Carlos, and Aloys de Backer. *Bibliotheque de la compagnie de Jésus. Bruxelles, 1890–1916.* 9 vols. Reprint Mansfield Centre, CT: Maurizio Martino, 1999.

Spielmann, Percy Edwin. *Catalogue of the Library of Miniature Books Collected by Percy Edwin Spielmann.* London: Edward Arnold, 1961.

A Short-title Catalogue of Books Printed in England, Scotland, & Ireland and English Books Printed Abroad, 1475–1640. Compiled by Alfred W. Pollard and G. R. Redgrave. London: Bibliographical Society, 1926. [Cited as STC]

A Short-title Catalogue of Books Printed in England, Scotland, & Ireland and of English Books Printed Abroad, 1475–1640. 2nd ed. Compiled by Alfred W. Pollard and G. R. Redgrave. Revised and enlarged, begun by W. A. Jackson and F. S. Ferguson, completed by Katharine F. Pantzer. 2 vols. London: Bibliographical Society, 1976. [Cited as New STC]

Stevens, David Harrison. *Reference Guide to Milton from 1800 to the Present Day.* Chicago: University of Chicago Press, 1930. [Cited as Stevens; references are to numbers, not pages]

Taylor, John Russell. *The Art Nouveau Book in Britain.* London: Methuen, 1966.

Todd, William B., and Ann Bowden. *Tauchnitz International Editions in English, 1841–1955. A Bibliographical History.* New York: Bibliographical Society of America, 1988.

Tompkinson, G. S. *A Select Bibliography of the Principal Modern Presses Public and Private in Great Britain and Ireland*. London: First Edition Club, 1928.

Twitchell, James B. *Romantic Horizons. Aspects of the Sublime in English Poetry and Painting, 1770–1850*. Columbia: University of Missouri Press, 1983.

Updike, Daniel Berkeley. *Printing Types: Their History, Forms, and Use*. 2 vols. Cambridge, Mass.: Harvard University Press, 1922.

Waddington, Raymond B. "The Iconography of Jean Dassier's Milton Medal," *Milton Quarterly* 19, no. 4 (1985): 92–96.

Ward, A. W., and A. R. Waller. *Cambridge History of English Literature 7: Cavalier and Puritan, 1600–1660*. Cambridge: Cambridge University Press, 1920. [Cited as *CHEL*]

[White, Gleeson.] *A Catalogue of Books from the Library of the Late Gleeson White*. London: A Lionel Isaacs, 1899.

———. *English Illustration: The Sixties, 1855–1870*. London: Constable, 1906.

Willems, Alphonse C. J. *Les Elzevier: histoire et annales typographiques*. Bruxelles: G. A. van Trigt, 1880.

Williamson, George C. *Milton Tercentenary. The Portraits, Prints and Writings of John Milton*. Exhibited at Christ's College, Cambridge, 1908. With an appendix and index by C. Sayle. Cambridge: Printed by J. Clay at the University Press, 1908. [Cited as Williamson; reference is to numbers, not pages]

Wing, Donald Goddard, comp. *Short Title Catalogue of Books Printed in England, Scotland, Ireland, Wales and British America and of English Books Printed in Other Countries 1641–1700*. New York: Printed for the Index Society by Columbia University Press, 1945; revised and edited by John J. Morrison and Carolyn W. Nelson, editors, and Matthew Seccombe, assistant editor. 3 vols. New York: Modern Language Association of America, 1982–98.

Wittreich, Joseph Anthony, Jr., ed. *Calm of Mind: Tercentenary Essays on Paradise Regained and Samson Agonistes in Honor of John S. Diekhoff*. Cleveland and London: Case Western Reserve University, 1971.

Wegelin, Oscar. *Early American Poetry 1800–1820 with an Appendix Containing the Titles of Volumes and Broadsides Issued During the 17th and 18th Centuries, which Were Omitted in the Volume Containing the Years 1650–1799*. New York: Oscar Wegelin, 1907.

Index

In a work of this nature and magnitude, it is impossible to account fully for every detail. Instead, this index can merely serve as a guide into the vast variety and scale of the collection. Included are the most significant individuals (publishers, illustrators, and authors), the most significant works by John Milton, and certain features that may be of interest to scholars using the collection. Because of the changing nature of publishing companies over the centuries, most publishers are listed either under the most commonly recognized form of their corporate name or under the personal name of the individual publisher.

Unless indicated by *p.* or *pp.*, most entries give reference to both the chapter and the entry number in which the subject in question appears. For example, an important reference to Joseph Addison can be found at entry "III.B.19," or chapter 3, section B (in this case, Eighteenth-century Miltoniana), entry number 19.

Addison, Joseph, II.10, 314, 616–18, 625–26, 629, 637–40, 643–44, 654–57, 661–64, 675, 683, 687–90, 713–14, 716, 727, 729–30, 733, 736–37, 742–43, 747–48, 750, 752, 754, 759, 765, 769, 781, 786, 804, 828, 833, 847, 866, 884, 918, 944–45, 1038, 1409, 1419, 1542, 1586, 1762–68, 1778–80, 1784, 1788, 1790, 1792, 1800, 1809–10, 1814, 1941–43, 2002, 2015–52, 2158, 2400, 2443, 2498; III.B.1–8, 19, 56; III.C.1–3, 51, 116; IV.3–5, 7; pp. 13, 25
Albion Press, II.807, 836, 1592–95, 2237, 2323–24, 2348, 2358, 2363–64, 2374, 2406–7, 2411–12, 2430, 2438, 2442, 2472–73, 2486; III.C.116
Alcuin Press, II.1669
Aldine Publishing Company, II.25–26, 32, 36, 391, 1183, 1280, 1317, 1326, 1336, 1341, 1645, 1656, 1660, 1850, 1856, 1875, 1914–15, 1955–56, 1964, 1976, 1984, 2006, 2032, 2068, 2082–85, 2190, 2400, 2443, 2498, 2639
Aldrich, Henry, II.607–9, 1760; p. 160

Allman, T. and J., II.1826, 1832, 1844, 1861, 2486
Allyn and Bacon, II.508, 1284, 1362
Altemus, Henry, II.1172–76, 1303–14, 1316, 1647–55, 1658, 1707–14
Andreini, Giovanni Batista, II.297–98; III.A.1; III.B.32, 69
Andrus, Silus, II.966, 977, 998, 1018, 1045, 1926, 1936, 1946, 1961–62, 1973–74, 2004–5
Appleton, D., II.52, 109–15, 117, 122–23, 127, 133–35, 362, 459–60, 955, 958, 961, 970, 989, 997, 1008, 1035, 1049, 1072, 1952–53, 1960, 1985, 2003, 2030, 2039–40, 2045, 2067, 2094, 2100, 2103–4, 2133, 2609–10, 2613–14, 2669, 2673, 2677, 2700–2703, 2721–24, 2736, 2739; III.C.51, 55, 101; III.D.20; IV.20
Arber, Edward, II.10–15, 22–23, 27, 58; III.A.46; III.C.2
Arcades, II.2–5, 271, 332, 386, 412–13, 508, 546, 620, 1599, 1601–6, 1613, 1688–90, 1778–80, 1784, 1786, 1788, 1798, 1845, 1858, 1930, 1947, 2041, 2059, 2064, 2072, 2078, 2089, 2092, 2097, 2120, 2125, 2148, 2174, 2181, 2257, 2437, 2449
Areopagitica
    seventeenth-century, II.6–7
    eighteenth-century, II.8
    nineteenth-century, II.9–26
    twentieth-century, II.27–65
    other appearances, II.80, 83, 301, 303, 315, 317–18, 620, 1686, 1742, 1845, 1858, 2059, 2064, 2072, 2078, 2089, 2092, 2097, 2119, 2125, 2148, 2173, 2181, 2257, 2437, 2449, 2521, 2585–86, 2600–2601, 2603–07, 2609, 2650, 2751, 2759; III.C.117; III.D.73, 90; IV.25; p. 806
Argo Records, II.284, 1427, 1486, 1674, 2713, 2716
Arion Press, II.1349–51, 1385–86, 1524–25
Arts of Empire, The, II.66
Ashendene Press, II.585
Ashlar Press, II.427
Asimov, Isaac, II.1458; p. 20
association copy, II.616, 696, 1694, 1785, 1841, 1935, 1937, 1956; III.A.9

Astolat Press, II.2466–67
Athenaeum Press, II.402, 404, 408, 412, 462, 539, 2758; III.C.36
Athlone Press, The, II.304–5
attributed to Milton, II.544–45, 548, 2643
Auden, W. H., II.1457
Aylmer, Brabazon, II.327, 604

Balestra, Antonio, II.630, 643, 688, 781
Ballantyne Press, II.308, 431, 1159–60, 1216, 1272, 1355–56, 1483, 1663–65, 1717–18, 2131, 2268, 2270–72, 2331, 2359–61, 2367–69, 2408–10, 2437, 2441, 2449, 2720–24; III.D.17, 99
Barrow, Samuel II.739, 770–71, 2620–21
Baskerville, John, II.218, 347, 691–98, 702–3, 721, 745
Baudry's European Library, II.918, 945, 949, 1828
Baynes, R. and W., II.866, 1826, 1835
Beacon Press, II.53
Beattie, James, II.722, 1846, 1851, 1863, 1876, 1891, 1909, 1930, 1947, 1966, 1979, 1987, 2007–8, 2266; IV.10, 14, 16
Bell, Allan, II.1858, 1865, 1879
Bell, George, II.493–95, 1375, 1731, 2376, 2400, 2443, 2498, 2639–40, 2741–43
Bell, John, II.226, 231, 737, 759, 800, 834, 1778–80, 1784
Bell, Robert Anning, II.465, 2741–43; IV.34–35, 40
Bell & Daldy, II.349, 368, 1069, 1075, 1621–23, 2082–84, 2190, 2400; IV.27
Bell & Hyman. *See* Bell, George
Belloc, Hillaire, III.D.6
Bentley, Richard, II.604–5, 607–9, 611, 621, 631, 662, 713–14, 718, 736, 748, 754, 786, 804, 833, 945, 1467, 1760–61; III.B.51, 56–57, 65, 68; III.C.11, 17
Bernouville, II.1042, 1071, 1086, 1102, 1138, 1207
Bida, II.91–92, 164, 168
Binsse, Harry Lorin, II.470
Birch, Thomas, II.77, 218, 313, 484, 1810, 2623, 2751–53; III.C.113
Biro, II.2593–94
Bixby, Daniel, II.1916, 1937, 1940
Blackies and Son, Ltd., II.377
Blackwood, James, II.107, 2158
Blake, William, II.276, 284, 287, 317, 432–34, 546, 582, 591, 859, 896, 1349–51, 1385–87, 1391, 1418, 1427, 1431–32, 1448, 1462–64, 1469, 1486, 1493, 1497, 1506–7, 1521, 1525, 1674, 1729–30, 1840–41, 2583, 2691, 2706, 2750; III.B.32; III.D.2, 7–8, 30, 33, 64; pp. 29, 771
Bloom, Harold, II.1417, 1429
Blue Sky Press, II.410
Bogue, David. *See* Tilt & Bogue
Bohn, Henry G., II.349, 352, 365, 368, 1878, 1902, 1925, 1931, 1939, 1959, 1988, 2041, 2091, 2190, 2376, 2634, 2639–40, 2756–57
Book League of America, The, II.44
bookplate, II.9, 19, 25, 28, 37, 43, 48, 67, 73, 75, 77, 153, 158, 216, 220, 231, 237, 243, 257, 262, 268, 278, 280, 308, 312–13, 322, 327, 332–34, 338, 347, 350, 354, 360, 365, 370, 383, 405, 451–52, 454–56, 461, 485, 495, 498, 529, 544, 560, 563, 595, 598, 600, 605, 607, 613, 616, 618–19, 621, 623, 627, 629, 631, 634–35, 638–39, 643, 652–54, 658, 665, 668, 671, 692, 694, 701, 706–7, 717, 721–22, 727, 731, 747, 754–55, 765–66, 768, 782–83, 786, 793, 798, 812, 818–19, 833, 838, 842, 848, 852, 854, 863, 867, 872, 875, 883, 888, 893, 897, 911–12, 914, 919, 933, 940, 956, 976, 1019–20, 1069, 1078, 1088, 1103, 1109, 1117, 1128, 1164, 1186, 1205, 1222, 1225, 1236, 1238, 1272, 1288, 1291, 1293, 1317, 1370, 1379, 1396, 1432, 1533, 1535, 1538, 1540, 1545, 1550, 1553, 1555, 1562, 1572, 1575, 1587, 1590, 1593, 1596, 1598, 1602, 1643, 1656, 1670–71, 1683, 1689, 1692, 1694, 1699, 1711, 1718, 1726, 1736, 1759, 1762, 1772, 1778, 1785, 1789, 1792–95, 1800–1801, 1806, 1831, 1837–38, 1840–41, 1851, 1854, 1856, 1870, 1875–76, 1879, 1887, 1905, 1911–12, 1914–15, 1931, 1933–34, 1949, 1956, 1963, 1976–78, 1990–91, 2001, 2006, 2016, 2025, 2033, 2041, 2045, 2052, 2065, 2067, 2085, 2108, 2145, 2166–67, 2169, 2192, 2224, 2242, 2264–65, 2279, 2293, 2329, 2334–35, 2341, 2350, 2352–53, 2368, 2373, 2377, 2381, 2400, 2402–3, 2417, 2436, 2442, 2446–67, 2473, 2503, 2505, 2524, 2530, 2565–69, 2580, 2586, 2605, 2607, 2620, 2622–23, 2626, 2628, 2632–33, 2657, 2666, 2683, 2696, 2699, 2708, 2738, 2740, 2745, 2747, 2753, 2762–63; III.A.6, 9–10, 17–18, 20–21, 31, 37–38, 42, 50; III.B.1–2, 9, 12, 14, 16, 18, 20, 27, 34, 41, 45, 48, 54, 57, 62, 64, 67, 68; III.C.13, 16, 42, 54, 66, 73, 80, 92, 104, 108–9, 120; III.D.5, 22, 28, 36, 61, 69; IV.4–5, 12, 21; p. 32
Borden, Matthew Chaloner Durfee, II.598
Borowitz, David, II.598; pp. 13–14
Borrenstein, D. A., II.902, 906
Boyd, James Robert, II.986, 1009, 1013, 1019, 1026, 1041, 1062, 1084–85, 1087, 1101, 1104, 1108, 1111, 1140, 1980, 1994–95, 1997–98, 2009–10, 2031, 2039, 2043–44, 2066, 2080, 2093, 2099–2100, 2136
Boydell, John and Josiah, II.297–98, 723, 896, 1787; III.B.32; III.D.34
Bridgewater Manuscript, II.212–15, 217–23, 232–35, 237–39, 242, 269, 285, 1686, 1963
Brief History of Moscovia, II.69–70, 2634
broadside, III.A.20; III.B.66; III.C.112
Brooks, Cleanth, II.195–98, 200, 1736, 1740, 1746
Bruegel, Hans Pieter, II.1462, 1477–78, 1492, 1498, 1504, 1508
Brydges, Sir Egerton, II.986, 997, 1008, 1038, 1857, 1866, 1894–96, 1933–35, 1952–53, 1960, 1967–68, 1977, 1980–81, 1986, 1994–95, 2009, 2031, 2039, 2043–44, 2047–50, 2066, 2070, 2076, 2080, 2093, 2099–2100, 2136, 2453–54, 2630–33, 2635–36; III.A.29; III.C.93–94; p. 791
Buoninsegna, Duccio di, II.478
Burgkmair, Hans, II.2676
Burnett, J., II.817
Burney, E. F., II.91–92, 164, 168, 231, 234, 696, 783–84, 796, 800–802, 830–31, 848, 851–52, 1590–94, 1597–98, 1800–1801, 1809, 1896

Cadell, T., II.744–45, 783, 788, 1571, 1575, 1582–83, 1589–90, 1679, 1847, 1868; III.B.31; III.C.109; IV.4–5, 7. *See also* Cadell and Davies
Cadell and Davies, II.798, 801, 808, 812, 815, 830, 851, 1597, 1805, 1808, 2623; II.B.6
Caedmon Press, II.55, 1407
Caldwell, H. M., II.638, 1285–94, 1544–46, 1634–44
Cambridge Manuscript, II.71–72
Carlyle, Thomas, II.2153
Carruthers, Robert, II.2595; IV.15
Carter, Sebastian, II.59–60
Cassell & Company, II.18, 306–7, 375, 380–82, 384, 1077–78, 1096–1100, 1131, 1136, 1148–49, 1192, 1199, 1201, 1208, 1215, 1303, 1338–40, 1344–45, 1354, 1471, 1482, 1627–28, 1647–48, 1658, 2102, 2357; III.D.27
Caxton, Press, II.46, 878–79, 1900, 2069, 2637
Chatfield & Coleman, II.895–98
Chatterton-Peck, II.1332, 1631, 1647–48, 1658–59
Chatto & Windus, II.157, 858, 1727; III.C.110. *See also* Pickering, William
Chaucer, Geoffrey, II.259, 265, 349–52, 364, 366, 368, 737, 759, 1742, 1778–80, 1784, 2095, 2543, 2713, 2716, 2765; III.A.31; III.B.47, 53; III.C.10, 98; III.D.26, 41, 48, 78, 87–88; IV.11, 16, 24, 32, 39, 42
Chéron, Louis, II.1762–63
Chéron de Boismorand, C. J., II.625–26, 640, 644, 656, 687, 689–90, 716, 727, 733, 742–43, 747, 750, 752, 775
Chidley, J. J., II.1888, 1897, 1912, 1918, 1922
Childs, J. R. and C., II.1859, 2625–29, 2754–57
Chiswick Press, II.73, 465, 493, 495, 848, 850, 867–69, 886–88, 1069, 1075, 1112, 1596, 1599–1607, 1613–14, 1621, 1692–97, 1700–1701, 1914–15, 1957, 1964, 2054, 2061, 2082–84, 2145–47, 2157, 2167, 2169, 2190, 2253, 2318, 2337–38, 2400, 2443, 2469, 2498, 2609–12, 2741, 2758–62; III.C.51, 66, 119; IV.27, 34–35
Chock, D., II.777
Christian Doctrine, A Treatise on. See De Doctrina Christiana
Churton, Edward, II.1860, 1869, 1878, 1888, 1931, 1959, 1988
Cimino, Harry, II.583
Cipriani, G. B., II.800, 830–31, 896, 1024–25, 1917, 1971, 2402–3; III.B.10, 67; III.C.109
Clarendon Press, II.16, 21, 29, 252, 255, 271, 319–22, 438, 485, 1214, 1668, 1726, 2445, 2447, 2529, 2541, 2544, 2549, 2657, 2660–61, 2670, 2730; III.A.20; III.B.15; III.C.16; III.D.42–43, 89
Clark, Austin, & Co., II.116, 118–21, 128, 978, 983, 987–88, 999, 1016, 1620, 1951
Clark, Austin & Smith, II.993, 1032–33, 1043, 1050, 1056
Clark & Maynard, II.251, 378, 1095, 1107, 1122, 1135, 1153–54, 1171, 1194, 1202, 1333; III.C.76, 78
Clerk's Press, The, II.577
Colasterion, II.302, 2751
Cole, Herbert, II.2458–61
Coleman, George, II.224, 895

Collier, P. F., II.33, 45, 87–90, 93–94, 1128, 1198, 1417, 1429, 1454–55, 2689
Commodi, Andrea, II.2766
Common-Place Book of John Milton, A, II.73–75
Comus, II.212–293
    eighteenth-century, II.212–233
    nineteenth-century, II.234–259
    twentieth-century, II.260–293
    other appearances, II.2, 67, 105, 107–11, 116, 118–19, 120, 128, 131–32, 136, 138, 304–5, 317, 326, 348–49, 389, 393, 400–406, 408, 412, 414–15, 418–19, 425–26, 429, 455, 468–69, 472, 481–82, 487–88, 491, 499, 503, 505, 508–10, 516, 520–25, 529, 535, 540–41, 546, 558, 593, 620, 657, 658, 660, 675, 680, 686, 696, 700, 707, 710, 741, 793, 831, 912, 935, 972, 987, 996, 999, 1006, 1027, 1061, 1119, 1134, 1388, 1453, 1456, 1469, 1534, 1537, 1544, 1546–47, 1553, 1559–63, 1565, 1567, 1569, 1571–72, 1575, 1577, 1579, 1581–85, 1596, 1599, 1601–6, 1608, 1611–21, 1683, 1686, 1688–90, 1696, 1698–99, 1729–31, 1745, 1762, 1764–65, 1776–82, 1784, 1786, 1788, 1793–94, 1798–1800, 1802, 1806, 1809–10, 1816–17, 1819–22, 1826, 1832, 1835, 1838, 1843–46, 1848–49, 1857–58, 1861, 1865, 1873, 1879–82, 1884–85, 1890, 1898–99, 1906–7, 1911, 1917, 1945, 1958, 1963, 1969–72, 1980, 1987, 1989, 1994, 1996, 2001, 2009, 2012, 2015, 2018, 2026, 2030–31, 2036, 2039, 2041–46, 2059, 2062, 2064–67, 2069, 2072, 2078, 2080, 2089, 2092–94, 2096–97, 2099–2100, 2113, 2119–31, 2133, 2136, 2148–49, 2162, 2165, 2169–2170, 2173–74, 2177, 2181–85, 2195, 2208, 2212–13, 2246, 2257, 2268, 2305–7, 2331, 2334, 2343, 2361, 2367, 2370–72, 2401, 2410, 2437, 2444–52, 2458–61, 2470, 2495–96, 2521, 2556, 2684, 2686–87, 2691, 2698, 2706, 2750; III.A.25, 32; III.B.43, 66; III.C.37, 112; III.D.14, 42, 72, 76, 85, 97; IV.16, 44; pp. 15, 20, 23, 27, 29, 765, 767, 771, 775, 779, 783, 785
Conkey, W. B., II.1223, 1243–46, 1323–24
Considerations Touching the Likeliest Means To Remove Hirelings out of the Church (aka An Old Looking-Glass), II.294–96, 559, 2751; p. 23
Cooper, R., II.665, 748, 754, 834, 836, 878–79, 1036–37, 1826, 1831
Cooper, Samuel, II.355–57, 361, 365, 372, 379, 436, 450, 451, 800, 830, 968, 971, 979, 990, 1000, 1010, 1020–21, 1869, 1878, 1888, 1896, 1897, 1900, 1912, 1918, 1920, 1922, 1931, 1959, 1988, 2041, 2091, 2634, 2639; III.C.101; III.D.75
Cope, C. W., II.243, 353–54, 364, 370, 419, 2343, 2371; III.D.85
Corbould, E. H., II.244, 351, 851, 1829, 1834, 1925, 1939, 1945, 1948, 2064, 2078, 2089, 2092, 2097, 2120, 2125–27, 2148; IV.14, 16
Corbould, R., II.791, 1790, 1792, 1795
Cosway binding, p. 813

Cowper, William, II.297–98, 306–7, 366, 443–45, 986, 1009, 1013, 1019, 1023, 1026–29, 1038, 1041, 1061–62, 1084–85, 1087, 1101, 1787, 1829–30, 1834, 1837, 1839–1841, 1900, 1948, 2073–74, 2095, 2534, 2720; III.B.32; III.C.82, 95, 109; III.D.91; IV.11
Craig, W. M., II.807, 836, 878–79, 1592–95, 1799, 1900
Crane, Walter, II.571, 592, 632, 815, 916
Cresset Press, The, II.1372–74; III.D.81
Cromwell, Oliver, II.301, 449, 452–54, 595, 598, 1456, 1534–35, 1684–85, 1795–97, 1810, 1838, 1869, 1878–88, 1897, 1899, 1912, 1918, 1922, 1963, 2064, 2089, 2381, 2383, 2578, 2585, 2603, 2634, 2639–40, 2659; III.A.43; III.B.58; III.C.25, 33–35; III.D.1, 9, 32, 67, 94
Crosby, B., II.800, 825, 827, 837, 842, 1079–80, 1802, 1806
Crosby, Nichols, Lee & Company, II.139–40, 1063, 2043
Crosby and Ainsworth, II.149–50, 156, 1079–80, 1088, 2080
Crosby and Nichols, II.143, 1065–66, 1069, 1073, 2066
Crowder, S. and R., II.700, 710, 728, 748, 754, 757, 1562–63, 1571–72, 1575, 1775–76
Crowell, Thomas Y., II.158–63, 165–67, 179, 1178–81, 1209, 1469, 2231–33, 2249, 2276–82, 2286–90, 2325–27, 2377–99; III.C.111
Crown Publishers, II.91–92; III.D.33
Curwen Press, II.69, 278

Dalton, John, II.212–16, 221–22, 224–25
Daly, Charles, II.1867, 1870, 1874, 1941–43, 2002, 2052, 2090
Dalziel, Brothers II.160–62, 244–50, 351, 353–54, 1144–47, 1156–57, 1178–82, 1970, 1982, 1991–92, 2011, 2019–20, 2034–35, 2051, 2056–58, 2063, 2071, 2077, 2086–88, 2098, 2132, 2140, 2150–52, 2159–60, 2168, 2175, 2177–78, 2180, 2187, 2191–92, 2194, 2198–2207, 2214–17, 2228, 2231–33, 2247–50, 2259–60, 2269–83, 2287–90, 2298, 2302–3, 2311, 2319–22, 2325–30, 2332–33, 2345–47, 2354–56, 2363, 2401, 2410, 2414, 2441; IV.31
Daniel Press, The, II.570
Davies, W. See Cadell and Davies
Dearborn, George, II.242, 2615, 2659
De Doctrina Christiana, II.205, 2634, 2639–40, 2745–49; III.C.21–24, 63
Defence of the People of England, II.77, 299–300, 2566–78; p. 23. See also *Second Defence of the People of England*
Defensio Secunda Pro Populo Anglicano. See *Second Defence of the People of England*
Defoe, Daniel, III.B.17; III.C.67
Deighton, Bell & Company, II.59–60, 232
De La More Press, II.413
Delaroch, II.2037–38, 2141–43
Dent, J. M., II.25, 32, 36, 41–42, 53, 80, 83, 98–99, 269, 391, 1280, 1317, 1326, 1336, 1341, 1394, 1645–46, 1656, 1660, 1666, 1741, 1755, 2500, 2504, 2507, 2510, 2531–32, 2535, 2593–94; IV.40
DeWolfe, Fiske & Company, II.2299–2301, 2304

Dignon, James, II.590
Dixon, J., II.1557–58, 1900
Doctrine and Discipline of Divorce, II.302
Dodd & Mead Company, II.263–64, 592, 660–61, 680, 707
Dolle, W., II.603–5, 1378–80
Doran, George H., II.423, 1377–80, 1670–71; III.D.4
Doré, Gustav, II.91–92, 896, 1077–78, 1096–1110, 1113, 1128–31, 1136, 1139, 1142, 1147–50, 1158, 1172–77, 1191, 1198–1201, 1215, 1223–24, 1243–45, 1303–16, 1321–24, 1335, 1338–40, 1344–45, 1354, 1360, 1411, 1426, 1470–71, 1482, 1499, 1505, 1515, 1527, 1682, 2040, 2196, 2217–25, 2284, 2286–87, 2299–2304, 2320–21, 2343–47, 2371, 2377–80, 2382–83, 2385, 2552, 2554, 2693; III.D.64; p. 29
Doubleday, II.84, 86, 201–2, 204, 274–75, 1377, 1379–80, 1423, 1445–46, 1458, 1669–70, 2585–86, 2596–97; III.D.2, 4
Douglas, Noel, II.37, 39, 184, 205, 277, 441–42, 476, 531–32, 534, 543, 589, 596–97, 1109, 1729–30, 2444–45, 2531, 2550, 2552, 2554–55, 2561–63; III.A.18; III.B.20; III.D.13
Doves Bindery, II.31, 1351; pp. 6, 24, 29
Dryden, John, II.86, 241, 342, 368, 482, 607–9, 616–18, 627, 632, 636–38, 641, 647–51, 662–65, 712, 729–30, 735, 740, 748, 754, 759, 793, 809, 811, 880, 902, 904–5, 907, 930, 1268–69, 1343, 1500–1501, 1557–58, 1685, 1698–99, 1760–64, 1780–82, 1784, 1786, 1788, 1790, 1792, 1798, 1829–30, 1834, 1837, 1948, 2221–22, 2225, 2595, 2723; III.A.12–15, 40, 52; III.B.31, 53; III.C.78, 94; III.D.73, 88; IV.3–7, 11
Dulac, Edmund, II.281–82, 293
DuMolin, Peter, II.301, 453, 2575, 2643; III.A.15, 26
Dunster, Charles, II.232, 945, 1038, 1589, 1679, 1810, 1833; III.C.42; III.D.63
Dürer, Albrecht, II.587, 1499
Dutton, E. P., II.41–42, 98, 266–67, 567, 800, 1346, 1741, 1755, 2351, 2500, 2504, 2507, 2510, 2531, 2535, 2593–94; III.D.18; IV.36, 40

Easton Press, II.281, 1464
Eikonoklastes, II.299, 310–13, 2566, 2570, 2603, 2641, 2751; III.A.4, 45
Ellwood, Thomas, II.595, 1064, 1527–28; III.B.21–23; III.D.70
Elsevier, S. D., III.A.25
Elston Press, II.261, 411, 2662
Epistolarum Familiarium Liber Unis, II.327
Epitaph on Shakespeare, II.329, 508, 558, 872, 1534, 1788
Eragny, Press, II.28
Etching Club, The, II.353–54, 358–59, 374
Evergood, Philip, II.470
Everyman's Library, II.41–42, 80–83, 98–99, 1741, 1755, 1758, 2500, 2504, 2507, 2510, 2531–32, 2535, 2593–94
Exshaw, John, II.663–64, 729–30, 1557–58; III.B.12
extra-illustrated, II.695–96, 723, 831, 896, 1763, 1795, 1869, 1896, 2013, 2147; III.C.7, 117; III.D.25; IV.8

facsimile, II.1, 10–15, 19, 22–23, 27, 37–40, 58, 61–62, 70–73, 80, 87–88, 98–99, 101, 104, 173–78, 184–85, 205–8, 263–64, 269, 274–75, 277, 304–5, 326, 340, 349–50, 352, 421, 436, 463, 471, 476, 480, 488, 496, 512–13, 531–32, 534, 544–45, 587, 1112, 1117, 1377–80, 1388–90, 1414, 1426, 1431–33, 1442–43, 1445–47, 1449, 1453, 1467, 1469, 1472–74, 1496, 1525, 1674–76, 1726, 1736, 1740, 1745–46, 1748–52, 1754, 1795–97, 1810, 1838, 1899, 1957, 1963, 2041, 2061, 2145–47, 2153, 2445–48, 2470–71, 2482–84, 2497, 2505, 2508–9, 2511–13, 2515, 2518–20, 2522–24, 2526–30, 2533–34, 2536–41, 2544, 2547, 2549–52, 2581–82, 2600–2601, 2641–42, 2682, 2706, 2745–46, 2758, 2760–61, 2763, 2767; III.C.26, 72–73, 104–5; III.D.7, 13, 20, 25, 32, 34, 41–43, 45, 64, 69, 72–75, 88, 101; IV.15, 30
Facsimile Text Society, The, II.40, 71–72, 471, 532
Faed, II.419, 2427, 2435–36; III.D.35
Faithorne, William, II.19, 24, 62, 76, 101, 109–15, 117, 122–23, 127, 133–38, 150, 165–67, 175–79, 235, 259, 265, 270, 272–73, 333–34, 340, 402–6, 408, 412, 419, 448, 480, 526–28, 603–5, 614–15, 629, 631, 647–51, 654, 663–65, 672, 729–30, 734, 744, 779–80, 791, 1052, 1066, 1315, 1419, 1433, 1449, 1456, 1472–73, 1506–8, 1557–58, 1579–80, 1633–34, 1668, 1682, 1745, 1768, 1795–97, 1810, 1838, 1854, 1864, 1871, 1877, 1892, 1899, 1916, 1937, 1940, 1945, 1957, 1963, 1965, 1978, 1980, 1983, 1994, 2000, 2009, 2030–31, 2039, 2043–45, 2054, 2061, 2066–67, 2080, 2093, 2099–2100, 2136, 2145–47, 2153, 2157, 2169, 2221, 2253, 2444, 2447–48, 2454, 2469–70, 2482–84, 2492, 2497, 2501–2, 2505–6, 2508–9, 2511–15, 2518–24, 2526–30, 2533–36, 2610, 2713, 2716, 2731, 2758–61; III.A.11; III.B.10, 16, 65; III.C.58, 86, 104, 113–14; III.D.6, 23, 25, 33, 47–49, 58, 61–62, 72–73, 75, 89, 110; pp. 13, 779, 806, 811
Falconer, C., III.B.24, III.C.42
Falconer, William, II.136–138, 150, 1829–1830, 1834, 1837, 1854, 1864, 1871, 1877, 1892, 1916, 1937, 1940, 1948, 1965, 1978, 1980, 1994, 2009–10, 2031, 2039, 2043–44, 2066, 2080, 2093, 2099–2100, 2136
Fanfani, Henry, II.164, 168
Farrar, Mildred, II.278–80; p. 27
Felt, Oliver, II.149–50, 156, 1079–80, 1088, 2080
Flannagan, Roy, II.1500–1501, 2765
Flaxman, J., II.443; III.C.17
Fleuron Society, The, II.1667
Flowers, T. G., II.1945, 1969, 1989, 2012–14, 2026–27, 2036, 2042, 2046, 2059–60, 2064–65, 2078, 2097, 2120, 2125–27, 2148
Folio Press, The, II.593
fore-edge painting, II.2089, 2097; pp. 22, 811, 815–17
Foster, Birket, II.244–50, 355–57, 361, 364–65, 372, 379, 436; IV.17, 31
Foulis, Robert and Andrew, II.593, 658, 666, 704, 717, 722–23, 726, 738, 1568, 1573–74
Fourdrinier, P., II.622–23, 627, 636–38, 641, 1537–40, 1543–47

Freeman, Arthur, II.550, 597n; pp. 6, 155, 777
Frye, Northrup, II.1395, 1398, 1406, 1408, 1418, 1450
Fuseli, Henry, II.83, 201–4, 800, 830, 1517, 1763, 1787, 1800–1802, 1806, 1809, 1823–24, 1860, 1869, 1878, 1888, 1896–97, 1912, 1918, 1922–23, 1931, 1959, 1988, 2091, 2699; pp. 29, 770–74

Galliard, Johann Ernst, III.B.26–27
Gall & Inglis, II.124–26, 129–30, 141–42, 145–46, 148, 2106–14, 2176, 2209–11, 2254, 2267; IV.24
Gebbie Publishing Company, II.164, 168
Gibbon, Edward, II.2753
Gillies, John, II.760, 778, 812, 945
Ginn, Heath, & Co., II.1141, 1155
Ginn & Company, II.20, 402–6, 408, 412, 462, 539, 541, 1127, 1141, 1155, 1190, 1196, 1220, 1270, 1281; III.C.3, 36; III.D.45, 48
Globe Edition, II.2094, 2179–80, 2186, 2191–92, 2234, 2264–65, 2317, 2340, 2362, 2375, 2404, 2415, 2434, 2481, 2485, 2499, 2506, 2517, 2525, 2542, 2549. *See also* Macmillan Company
Golden Cockerel Press, II.1384
Golden Hind Press, II.587
Gordian Press, II.70, 1746
Gott, Samuel, II.544–45
Graves, Robert, III.D.27–29
Gray, Thomas, II.347, 827, 839, 855, 1355–57, 1799, 1817, 1821, 1829–30, 1834, 1837, 1948, 2266, 2400, 2443, 2498; III.C.44; IV.3–5, 7
Great Books Foundation, The, II.30–51, 54, 1393, 1402–3
Gregynog Press, II.277, 332
Greig, John, II.2149
Grierson, George, II.223, 619, 620, 1548, 1686, 1727–28, 2653; III.D.30, 101
Grigg, John, II.854, 860–61, 1846, 1851, 1863, 1876, 1891, 1909, 1930, 1947, 1966
Grolier Club, The, II.19, 62, 95–97, 1437–40; III.A.35; III.D.68; pp. 4, 12, 13
Groom, Mary II.1384, 1479–80
Grosch, D., II.256, 387–88, 393, 398, 400, 491–92, 1283, 1334, 1353, 2424–28, 2453–54, 2474–75, 2477–80, 2487
Grosch, O., II.1126, 1256, 1259, 1264, 2487–94
Gucht, Gerard van der, II.1762–63; III.D.16, 101
Gucht, John van der, II.634–35
Gwim, James, II.619–620, 1548

Halcyon Press, II.2727–28
Hamm, P. E., II.902, 906–907
Hardwick and Bogue. *See* Tilt & Bogue
Harper & Row, II.475, 489–90, 498, 1299, 1902, 1927–29; III.C.92; III.D.24, 83
Harrap, George G., II.283, 288, 1355–56, 1410–11, 1491, 1663–65, 2604, 2606
Harvey, William, II.966, 977, 998, 1018, 1045, 1901–4, 1926–29, 1936, 1946, 1961–62, 1970, 1973–74, 1982,

Harvey, William (*continued*)
    1991–92, 2004–5, 2011, 2019–25, 2034–35, 2037–38, 2040–41, 2051–52, 2056–58, 2063, 2071, 2077, 2086–88, 2098, 2117–18, 2132, 2134–35, 2137–38, 2141–44, 2150–52, 2159–61, 2164, 2172–73, 2177–78, 2196, 2226–30, 2259–60, 2270–72, 2376, 2401, 2410, 2441, 2640; pp. 6, 23, 817
Hatchard, J., II.2603, 2623, 2745
Hawkey, John, II.652, 1550–51, 1839–41
Hayman, Francis, II.654, 657, 660–61, 680, 686, 695–96, 700–701, 706–7, 710, 720–21, 728–30, 734, 744–45, 765, 774, 782, 785, 790, 1549, 1553, 1557–58, 1562–63, 1567, 1569, 1571, 1575–76, 1582–83, 1768, 1781–82, 2013; III.B.6, 8, 47; pp. 29, 775, 811
Hazlitt, William, II.2529; III.B.53; III.C.54
Heath, D. C., II.499, 503, 509, 521, 523–24, 674, 681, 1282–83, 1353, 2684, 2698; IV.10, 14, 16
Herbert, George, IV.22
Heritage Press, The, II.282, 434, 1385–87, 1463
Hilliard, Gray and Company, II.1854, 1856, 1864, 1871, 1877, 1892, 1916, 2746; III.C.61
History of Britain, The, II.333–40, 2634, 2685; p. 13
Holbein, II.565
Holt, Henry, II.309, 418, 425–26, 473–74, 483, 1408, 1418, 1450, 2587, 2695; III.C.90; IV.41
Horsley, J. C., II.91–92, 164, 168, 353–54, 362, 364, 399; III.D.22, 85
Hosmer, Harriet, II.499, 2684, 2698
Houghton Mifflin Company, II.169–72, 180–85, 395–97, 416, 526–28, 1081, 1089, 1093–94, 1106, 1115, 1123, 1132, 1217, 1225–26, 1276–79, 1402–3, 2062, 2068–69, 2341, 2604–5, 2607, 2616–17, 2765; III.C.62. *See also* Osgood, James R.
Hullah, Caroline, II.561–63
Hume, David, II.722
Hume, Patrick, II.736, 748, 754, 786, 804, 833, 945, 1760–61, 1810; III.A.21; III.B.56
Hurst & Co., II.798, 801–2, 808, 812, 815–16, 830, 851–52, 1133, 1259–60, 1325, 1327, 1597–98, 2221–25, 2241–44, 2251–52, 2283, 2453–54, 2474, 2476–80, 2487–94, 2618–19, 2745; III.B.6; III.C.50, 75, 107
Hyde, Donald and Mary, 2–3
Hyde, William, II.391, 2381, 2466–67

Il Penseroso, II.67, 215, 226, 233–34, 270–71, 332, 342–439, 455–56, 468–70, 481–82, 491, 497, 499, 503, 505, 507–10, 516, 520–25, 529, 535, 540–41, 546, 568, 593, 620, 640, 644, 656, 683, 687, 690, 716, 727, 741–43, 747, 750–52, 831, 836, 878, 935, 1534, 1541–42, 1552–53, 1562, 1569, 1575, 1579, 1583, 1590–96, 1601–3, 1606–7, 1613–14, 1686, 1688–94, 1697–1701, 1729–30, 1778–80, 1784, 1786, 1792–94, 1798–99, 1803–4, 1819–20, 1845, 1858, 1900, 1926, 1946, 1961–62, 1973, 2004–5, 2030, 2045, 2059, 2064, 2067, 2072, 2078, 2089, 2092, 2094, 2096–97, 2120, 2125, 2128, 2133, 2148–49, 2162, 2165–66, 2195, 2246, 2268, 2331, 2334–35, 2343, 2361, 2367–68, 2371, 2383, 2645, 2684, 2686–87, 2698, 2706; pp. 765, 768, 770, 771, 808
Inglis. *See* Gall & Inglis
Ivison, Phinney, Blakeman & Co., II.1089, 1092

Jansen, Cornelius, II.1072, 1787, 1857, 1860, 1869, 1872, 1889, 1893, 1905, 1910, 1919, 1924, 1932, 1938, 1990, 2003, 2016–17
Johnson, Samuel, II.8–9, 214, 218, 236, 297, 783, 791, 796, 828, 841, 851–52, 871, 918, 944, 945, 986, 1017, 1268–69, 1687, 1696, 1699, 1783, 1792, 1798, 1800–1801, 1803–5, 1809–10, 1812, 1814, 1836, 2529; III.A.22; III.B.10, 18, 20, 29, 35, 37; III.C.1, 40, 45, 58, 94, 107, 113, 116–17; III.D.25, 35, 42–43; pp. 2, 770, 815
Jonson, Ben, III.A.19, 31; III.B.53; III.D.67, 78; IV.39

Keats, John, II.2692; III.D.78
Keegan Paul, II.2720, 2722, 2724
Keightley, Thomas, II.1069, 1124–26, 1703; III.C.59
Kelley, Maurice, II.104, 198, 205–7, 322, 405, 452, 496, 1379, 1380, 1388–90, 1418, 1442, 1453, 2561, 2605, 2607, 2745; III.D.83; pp. 4, 26, 779
Kelmscott Press, II.261, 1337, 1661, 1669; p. 24
Kent, W., II.356, 361, 365, 2025, 2041, 2236, 2376
Knickerbocker Press, II.24, 417, 1259, 2487–89; III.D.22
Knopf, Alfred A., II.82, 1454–55, 1758

laid in, II.19, 24, 28, 62, 104, 175, 197, 231, 278, 280, 282, 284, 291–93, 312, 362, 496, 591, 598, 619, 629, 654, 794, 949, 960, 1042, 1068, 1071, 1102, 1160, 1188, 1351, 1381, 1385, 1387, 1390, 1447, 1462–63, 1494, 1500, 1530, 1671, 1674, 1694, 1712, 1860, 1954, 2010, 2094, 2190, 2267, 2290, 2300, 2352–53, 2396, 2403, 2444–45, 2538, 2541, 2547, 2556–57, 2584, 2586, 2634, 2651, 2660, 2667, 2681, 2711, 2717, 2749, 2758; III.A.7; III.D.3, 12, 13, 25, 40, 49, 66, 76, 108–9; IV.10
L'Allegro, II.67, 148, 160, 233, 270–71, 332, 342–439, 456, 464, 468–470, 481–82, 491, 497, 499, 503, 505, 507–10, 516, 520–25, 529, 535, 540–41, 546, 568, 593, 620, 640, 644, 656, 683, 687, 690, 696, 716, 727, 732, 741–43, 747, 750, 752, 831, 836, 878, 935, 1534, 1541, 1552–53, 1562, 1569, 1575, 1577, 1579, 1583, 1590–96, 1602–3, 1606, 1613, 1686, 1688–1692, 1694, 1697–1702, 1707, 1729–30, 1778–80, 1786, 1792–93, 1798–1800, 1809, 1819, 1823–25, 1845, 1857–58, 1882–85, 1900, 1926, 1936, 1944, 1946, 1950, 1961, 1972–73, 2004, 2021–24, 2037, 2040, 2059, 2064, 2072, 2078, 2089, 2092, 2096–97, 2117, 2119–20, 2125, 2128–31, 2136–37, 2140–41, 2148–49, 2164–66, 2168, 2195–96, 2198–2206, 2215–17, 2226–31, 2246–50, 2268–69, 2272–74, 2276, 2283, 2287–88, 2298, 2308, 2319, 2328–32, 2343, 2354, 2361, 2367–69, 2371–72, 2381, 2383, 2414, 2457, 2459, 2460–61, 2495–97, 2521, 2645; III.D.15; pp. 6, 11, 765, 768, 771, 778

Lament for Damon, II.330, 440, 446, 448, 458, 461, 473, 477–78, 2708; III.D.60
Latin Epigram VII/Ad Eandem, II.2168, 2198–2202, 2205–6, 2215–16, 2228–30, 2247–50, 2269, 2273–74, 2298, 2308–10, 2319, 2328–30, 2332–33, 2354, 2414
Lauder, William, II.657, 1759, 1899; III.A.34, 39; III.B.20, 24, 37–41, 44, 46; p. 23
Leavitt, George A., II.972–73, 980–82, 1002–6, 1015, 1027–31, 1047, 1061, 1119, 1134, 1619, 1702, 1902, 2021–24, 2037–38, 2040, 2117–18, 2137–38, 2141–43, 2161, 2226–27
Leighton and Hodge, II.28, 278–80, 355–56, 361, 370, 594, 623; IV.25
Lens, Bernard, II.607–9, 1760–61
Liberty Fund, II.65
Lightbody, I., II.638, 662, 1542
Limited Editions Club, The, II.281–82, 293, 433–34, 1382
Lippincott, J. B., II.376, 385, 392, 486, 1947, 1966, 1977, 1979, 1984, 1986–87, 2007–8, 2033, 2076, 2266, 2273; III.D.6, 109; IV.19
Little, Brown and Company, II.1976, 1984, 2006, 2032, 2068, 2085
Lofft, Capel, II.605, 776
Longmans, II.393, 414, 429, 458, 461, 1334, 1624, 1629, 1745, 1753; III.C.64, 119; IV.33
Lovell, Frank F., II.1183
Lovell, John W., II.1177–81, 2228–30, 2240, 2250, 2274, 2308–12
Low, Anthony, II.78, 1284, 1428
Low, Samson, II.243, 360, 375
Lyceum, II.1349–51, 1385
Lycidas
    nineteenth-century, II.455–462
    twentieth-century, II.463–480
    other appearances, II.67, 71, 110–11, 234, 259, 265, 270–73, 332, 386, 389, 393, 400–408, 412–15, 418–19, 425–26, 429–30, 481–82, 491–92, 497, 499–503, 505, 507–10, 512, 516, 520–25, 529, 535, 540–41, 546, 558, 568, 593, 620, 640, 644, 656, 680, 683, 686–87, 690–700, 707, 710, 716, 727, 732, 741–43, 747, 750, 752, 935, 1127, 1141, 1155, 1190, 1196, 1220, 1270, 1281, 1412, 1422, 1424, 1428, 1430, 1441, 1451, 1456, 1476, 1511, 1541, 1552–53, 1562, 1577, 1579–80, 1596, 1602–4, 1606–7, 1613–14, 1624, 1629, 1683, 1686, 1688–95, 1697–1701, 1726, 1731, 1745, 1748, 1754, 1762–63, 1778–80, 1784, 1798, 1803–4, 1819, 1857–58, 1941–45, 1950, 1958, 1965, 2002, 2015, 2030, 2045, 2052, 2059, 2064, 2067, 2078, 2089, 2092, 2094, 2097, 2119–20, 2125, 2133, 2148, 2158, 2372, 2381, 2444, 2521, 2541, 2549, 2556, 2645, 2684, 2686, 2687, 2698; III.A.47–49; III.B.37; III.C.101; III.D.38; IV.33, 40, 43–44; pp. 771, 779
Lydgate, John, II.349–50, 352

Macaulay, Thomas Babington, II.1367, 2529, 2745; III.B.39; III.C.45, 62–64; III.D.49
Macmillan Company, II.30, 43–44, 57, 253, 257–59, 265, 272–73, 386, 467, 472, 535, 537, 551–53, 1213, 1318, 1343, 1376, 1405, 1420, 1429, 1500, 1732, 1735, 2153–54, 2179–80, 2186, 2191–92, 2234, 2264–65, 2317, 2340, 2362, 2375, 2402–5, 2413, 2415, 2433–34, 2444, 2455, 2462–63, 2468, 2481, 2485, 2499, 2503, 2506, 2517, 2525, 2542, 2547, 2642, 2661, 2675, 2682, 2708, 2711–12, 2714–15; III.D.25, 40, 80, 87. *See also* Globe Edition
Maggs, Brian, II.1901; pp. 5–6, 8, 15
Manifesto of the Lord Protector, A, II.484
Mantegna, Andrea, II.2680
map, II.450–51, 462, 1282–83, 1343, 1353, 1411, 1589, 1624, 1629, 1679, 2245, 2684, 2698; III.A.36; III.C.37, 90; III.D.6, 27–28, 31–32, 61
Mareuil, Pere de, II.640, 644, 656, 687, 689–90, 716, 727, 742–43, 747, 750, 752, 1541
Marino, Giambattista, III.A.25; III.B.43
Marlowe, Christopher, III.A.19, 29
Mars, W. T., II.95
Martin, John, II.79, 164, 168, 349–50, 352, 368, 889, 894–98, 904–5, 916, 933, 955, 960, 976, 986, 997, 1008–9, 1013, 1019, 1026, 1041, 1055, 1062, 1084–85, 1087, 1101, 1104, 1108, 1111, 1484, 1859–60, 1869, 1878, 1888, 1897, 1912, 1918, 1922–23, 1931, 1944, 1950, 1952–53, 1959–60, 1980–81, 1988, 1993–95, 2009–10, 2028–29, 2031, 2037–39, 2043–44, 2066, 2080, 2091, 2093, 2099–2100, 2136, 2141–43, 2157, 2167, 2169, 2180, 2191, 2381; III.C.62; III.D.30, 101; IV.27; pp. 4, 10, 11, 15, 16, 22, 26, 28–29, 793–800, 812, 813
Marvell, Andrew, II.445, 603, 739–40, 770–71, 1685, 1795, 2341; III.B.10; III.D.14, 22; IV.20
Masaccio, Tomaso, II.98–99
Mason Hill Press, II.590
Mathews and Leigh, II.1810, 2553
Maynard, Merrill & Company, II.256, 387–88, 398, 468–69, 1124–26, 1333
Mead, Edward S., II.263–64, 592. *See also* Dodd, Mead & Company
Medina, Jean Baptist, II.607–9, 1457, 1534, 1760–61
Merrill, Charles E. *See* Maynard, Merrill & Company
Merrymount Press, The, II.2495–96
Mershon Company Publishers, II.1249–52
Metcalf and Company, II.1916
Methuen and Company, II.571, 1348, 2641; III.D.78
Methuen Castle, II.722
Millar, A., II.7, 77, 218, 220–22, 313, 484, 751, 1581, 1781–82, 2751–53; III.B.20, 50; III.D.100
Miller, J. S., II.654, 657, 660–61, 697, 700, 707, 710, 720–21, 729–30, 744, 1782
Milner and Sowerby, II.144, 147, 151–54, 992, 1972, 1996, 2001, 2018, 2170–71
Milton, John, ephemera, pp. 778–82, 792, 801–10, 816
Milton papers, II.487; III.D.97

Monetti, Enrico, II.262; p. 795
Moore, Albert, II.561–63
More, Alexander, II.301, 453, 2575, 2643; III.A.15, 20, 26
Morris, William. *See* Kelmscott Press
Moxon, Edward., II.1887, 2121–24, 2182–84, 2212, 2305–6, 2313, 2719; III.C.102
Müller, J. S., II.654, 657, 707, 720, 1782
Munkacsy, Mihaly, II.396–97, 1137, 1362, 1390, 1456, 1473, 1513, 1743, 2291, 2343, 2371, 2381, 2383, 2710; III.C.36, 102; III.D.31, 49, 94, 109
Murray, Alex and John, II.10–15, 545, 874–75, 915, 1560, 1766, 1767, 2096, 2128; III.C.83

Nash, John Henry, II.1382
Naxos AudioBooks, Ltd., II.1506–7
Nelson, Thomas, II.419, 555, 1038, 1383, 1445–47, 1491, 1704, 1719–22, 1734, 1853, 1911, 1945, 1958, 1969, 1989, 2000, 2012–14, 2026–27, 2036, 2042, 2046, 2059–60, 2064–65, 2078–79, 2089, 2092, 2097, 2120, 2125–27, 2148, 2688, 2704; III.D.85
Newnes, George, II.1716–18; III.D.22
Newton, Thomas, II.91–92, 164, 168, 654, 657, 662–64, 667–72, 675, 680, 685–86, 691–98, 702–3, 706–8, 710–14, 718, 720–23, 729–30, 734–37, 740–41, 744–45, 748, 754, 759, 765, 772, 782, 786, 791–92, 804, 807, 833, 866, 872, 944–45, 960, 1038, 1549, 1553, 1557–58, 1562, 1569, 1573–77, 1582–83, 1586–87, 1592–95, 1768, 1770–73, 1778–80, 1784, 1788–95, 1810–11, 1813, 1816, 1833, 1970, 1982, 1991–92, 2011, 2019–20, 2034–35, 2051–52, 2056–58, 2063, 2071, 2077, 2086–88, 2098, 2132, 2134–35, 2144, 2150–52, 2159–60, 2172–73, 2177–78, 2259–60, 2270–72, 2359–60; III.B.55; p. 811
Nichols, John, II.788, 851–52, 1012, 1597–98, 2623; III.B.6, 32; III.C.42, 108–9. *See also* Crosby and Nichols; Crosby, Nichols, Lee & Company
Nichols and Hall, II.1105, 1118
Nimmo, William P., II.367, 369, 2072, 2095–96, 2101, 2128–31, 2149, 2165–66, 2174, 2181, 2195, 2246, 2257–58, 2268, 2331, 2361, 2367–69, 2437, 2449; IV.25–26
Nisbet, James, II.560–63, 853, 856, 1975, 2053, 2081; III.D.9
Nonesuch Press, The, II.188–192, 278–80, 1448, 1729–30; IV.42; p. 27
Norton, W. W. II.446, 1460–61, 1502, 1753; III.A.6
Nova Solyma, II.544–45
Nuttall, Fisher & Dixon, II.836, 878, 1900
Nutt & Carbidge, II.2016

Of Education, II.8, 25, 41, 43, 52, 57, 80, 83, 232–33, 544, 547–48, 550–57, 1405, 1534, 1536–37, 1539, 1540, 1542–47, 1554, 1559, 1561, 1563–64, 1567–68, 1571, 1573, 1577, 1581–83, 1684–85, 1694, 1764, 2257, 2604–7, 2609, 2664
O'Kane, H. M., II.2662
Old Bourne Press, II.575

On May Morning, II.486, 2040, 2196, 2381; III.C.36; III.D.72; IV.2, 27–29
Onslow, Arthur, II.309, 475, 734, 744, 1788, 1857, 2501–2; III.D.89
On the Morning of Christ's Nativity, II.317, 372–73, 380–82, 413, 491–92, 499, 503, 508–9, 521, 523–24, 535, 541, 546, 560–593, 640, 644, 656, 683, 687, 690, 716, 727, 732, 742–43, 747, 750, 752, 912, 1469, 1541, 1552, 1579–80, 1596, 1602–3, 1606–7, 1613, 1692–95, 1697–1700, 1729, 1819, 1827, 1849, 1868, 2037–38, 2040–41, 2114, 2141, 2168, 2175, 2194, 2196, 2199–2204, 2206, 2214, 2269, 2328–30, 2381, 2383, 2459–61, 2495–96, 2644–45, 2684, 2698; III.D.73; IV.33, 40, 43; pp. 27, 771
On the University Carrier (Old Hobson), II.594
Original Letters and Papers of State, II.595–96
Osgood, James R., II.1093–94, 1123, 1132, 1402–3, 2155. *See also* Houghton Mifflin Company
Oxford University Press, II.173–78, 205–8, 252, 289, 323–25, 440, 447, 554, 557, 580, 1415, 1444, 1482, 1486, 1489–90, 1526, 2366, 2470, 2482–84, 2497, 2505, 2508–9, 2511–13, 2515, 2518–20, 2522–24, 2526–30, 2533–34, 2536–40, 2544–47, 2550–52, 2554–55, 2557–60, 2579, 2588–92, 2660–61, 2671, 2674, 2690, 2763, 2766; IV.D.11, 42, 77, 82

Papantonio, Mike, II.312, 854, 1857; pp. 3–9, 11–14, 17–18, 23, 26, 28, 812
papers and letters, II.302, 327, 487, 488, 595–97, 2564, 2767
Paradise Lost
    seventeenth-century, II.598–612
    eighteenth-century, II.613–796
    nineteenth-century, II.797–1320
    twentieth-century, II.1321–1527
    other appearances, II.10, 67, 79, 84, 86–87, 105, 107–10, 116, 118, 124, 126, 128, 138, 144, 148, 151, 160, 162–63, 165, 187, 201, 207, 267, 272, 296, 314–15, 317–18, 336, 396, 397, 416, 443, 481–82, 485, 496, 549, 559, 1528, 1531, 1533, 1536–39, 1541–43, 1545, 1546–50, 1553–62, 1564, 1567, 1569, 1571–73, 1576–77, 1586–87, 1590, 1592, 1596–97, 1598, 1602, 1605–9, 1611–13, 1615–16, 1618–20, 1625, 1628, 1631–36, 1639–40, 1642–44, 1659, 1661, 1663, 1665, 1687, 1691, 1697, 1705–6, 1717–18, 1727, 1729–31, 1733–34, 1741, 1745, 1755, 1759–80, 1782–1800, 1802–3, 1806–30, 1833–36, 1838, 1843–45, 1847–49, 1857–59, 1865, 1868–70, 1873–74, 1878–79, 1882, 1884–85, 1887–88, 1890, 1897, 1899–1902, 1906–7, 1911–12, 1918, 1920, 1922–23, 1926–27, 1936, 1941–46, 1948–52, 1954, 1957–61, 1963, 1969, 1972, 1977, 1980, 1986, 1988–89, 1993–94, 1999–2000, 2002–4, 2009, 2012–15, 2021, 2023, 2026, 2028, 2030–31, 2033, 2036–37, 2039–43, 2045–46, 2052, 2054–55, 2059, 2061–64, 2066–67, 2069–70, 2072, 2076, 2078, 2080, 2089–90, 2092–94, 2096–97, 2099–2100, 2106, 2113–15, 2117, 2119, 2121, 2123, 2125–26, 2128, 2131–33, 2136–37, 2140–41, 2145,

2148–49, 2152, 2154, 2157–58, 2161–62, 2164–65, 2167–69, 2173, 2175–76, 2181–85, 2193–96, 2198, 2203–6, 2208–9, 2212–15, 2217, 2221–22, 2226–28, 2231, 2234, 2246–47, 2249–50, 2257, 2260, 2267–69, 2272, 2274–76, 2283, 2286–87, 2291–92, 2296, 2298–99, 2304–5, 2307, 2311, 2317, 2319, 2322, 2325, 2328, 2330–32, 2334, 2336, 2341, 2343–44, 2354, 2356, 2361, 2367, 2370–72, 2375–78, 2380–83, 2392, 2400–2403, 2405, 2410, 2414–15, 2423, 2437, 2443, 2445, 2447, 2449–52, 2456, 2458–61, 2469, 2470, 2485–87, 2495, 2498, 2516, 2521, 2541, 2544, 2547, 2549, 2556, 2638, 2644–45, 2684–85, 2693, 2698, 2731, 2745, 2750, 2752, 2758–62, 2764–65; III.A.1, 2, 12, 18–19, 21, 23, 34, 46; III.B.1–4, 9, 17, 19, 21, 24, 26, 27, 31, 33, 37–38, 44–45, 51, 56–58, 65, 68; III.C.1–3, 5, 7–8, 11, 15, 19–20, 27, 36, 42, 53, 59, 61–62, 75, 78, 80, 84–85, 88, 96–97, 100, 102–3; III.D.3, 14, 19, 21, 30–31, 36, 69, 75, 81, 85, 92, 94–95, 109; IV.14, 16, 44; pp. 5–9, 11, 13, 17, 19–25, 28–29, 765–68, 769, 771, 773–74, 777, 784, 791, 793–96, 802, 809, 811–13, 815–16, 819–20

Paradise Regain'd
    seventeenth-century, II.1528–30
    eighteenth-century, II.1531–91
    nineteenth-century, II.1592–1659
    twentieth-century, II.1660–82
    other appearances, II.67, 144, 148, 158–64, 296, 611–12, 619–20, 640, 644–50, 675, 683, 687, 689–98, 703, 716, 727, 733, 736, 741–43, 747–48, 752, 754, 773, 784, 820, 853, 856, 878–79, 912, 973, 997, 996, 999, 1006, 1027–29, 1038, 1061, 1110, 1114, 1119, 1134, 1264, 1315, 1373–74, 1382, 1396, 1417, 1429, 1434–40, 1445–77, 1456, 1458, 1478, 1504, 1508, 1682, 1684, 1687, 1696, 1702, 1717–18, 1727, 1729–30, 1760–65, 1767–86, 1789, 1793, 1798–99, 1802–9, 1811–17, 1819, 1821–27, 1829–30, 1843–45, 1847–49, 1861–62, 1865, 1873, 1879–85, 1897, 1900–1903, 1906–7, 1911, 1944–45, 1949–51, 1957–58, 1969, 1972, 1980, 1988–89, 1993–96, 2000–2004, 2009–15, 2018, 2021, 2023–24, 2026–28, 2031, 2036–43, 2059–62, 2064, 2066, 2072, 2078–80, 2089, 2092–93, 2096–2097, 2099–2100, 2103, 2106–8, 2113–14, 2117, 2120, 2125, 2128, 2136–37, 2141–42, 2145–46, 2148–49, 2157–2158, 2161, 2164–66, 2168, 2170–71, 2174–76, 2181, 2185, 2194–96, 2198–99, 2201–2207, 2209, 2214, 2221–23, 2226–27, 2246, 2154, 2251, 2252, 2402, 2257, 2261, 2267–67, 2275, 2291–92, 2296–97, 2319, 2322, 2328, 2330–32, 2343–44, 2354, 2356, 2361, 2367–35, 2371–73, 2377–78, 2381, 2383, 2400–2401, 2406, 2410–11, 2414, 2423, 2437, 2443–52, 2459–61, 2459–60, 2470, 2498, 2516, 2521, 2541, 2549, 2556, 2657, 2758–59, 2761, 2764; III.A.46, 2, 17; III.B.24, 50, 21, 36, 50; III.C.42; III.D.63, 92; IV.26; p. 771

Parrish, Maxfield, II.409, 578; III.D.105

Payson & Clarke, II.39–40, 534, 815, 830, 851, 1145, 1147, 1529, 1571, 1575, 2015, 2053, 2081, 2095, 2101–2, 2217–18, 2299, 2302, 2304, 2320, 2345, 2623; III.C.107; III.D.65
Pear Tree Press, II.575, 586
Penguin Books, II.100, 1520, 1739, 1757, 2563, 2583; III.D.29
People Of England, II.77, 299, 300, 2581, 2650, 2683
Peter Pauper Press, II.540
Philips, Edward, II.236, 338, 1839–42, 1855, 2030, 2045, 2067, 2094, 2103–4, 2133; III.C.42, 50; IV.3–5, 7
Philips, Jan Casper, II.628
Philips, John, III.B.60–62
Phinn, Thomas, II.665, 672–73, 705, 711, 719, 735, 1089, 1092, 1559, 1769–74
Piazzetta, Giovanni Battista, II.643, 688, 781
Pickering, William, II.858, 920–23, 1839–41, 1850, 1856, 1864, 1871, 1875, 1877, 1887, 1892, 1914–16, 1955–57, 1964, 1976, 1978, 1984, 2006, 2032, 2054, 2061, 2068, 2145–47, 2157, 2169, 2190, 2469, 2586, 2620, 2630–31, 2758–62; pp. 5, 2
Pickersgill, F. R., II.244–50, 351; pp. 23, 29, 779, 785
Pigné, Nicholas, II.1534, 1537, 1539–40, 1542–46
piracy, II.629, 638, 670, 673, 676, 678, 685, 705, 708, 711, 739, 768, 774, 785, 790, 1570, 1765; III.B.2
Plaas, Peter van der, II.1663–65, 1725, 2450–52, 2660, 2709; III.D.9, 26
poetry and prose, collections of, II.67–68, 76–211, 297–98, 304–9, 314–26, 328, 331–32, 341, 489, 546, 1683, 2561, 2579–2644, 2684–99, 2700, 2701, 2732–39, 2751–66; pp. 6, 11, 24, 812, 816, 817
Poole, Joshua, II.175, 1847, 2093, 2099, 2684, 2698; III.A.31
Pope, Alexander, II.314, 346–47, 364, 786, 2595, 2659; III.B.47, 48; III.C.38, 51, 80, 95; III.D.89; IV.3–5, 7, 39
Portaels, J., II.499–502, 2684, 2698
Powell, Mary, II.302, 596–97; III.C.65–70, 119; III.D.27–29
Prentice Hall, II.1501, 1742, 2543, 2642
presentation copy, II.28, 56, 72, 74, 205, 231, 309, 411, 441, 447, 455, 457, 476, 560, 587, 776, 1677, 1759, 1841, 2615, 2618, 2694, 2711, 2717, 2726; III.B.41; III.C.49; III.D.11, 15, 17, 19, 25
Pro Populo Anglicano Defensio. See *Defence of the People of England*
Prowett, Septimus, II.889, 894–98, 904–5, 916, 933, 960, 976, 1055, 1859, 2157, 2167; pp. 11, 22, 28, 793, 795–96
Putnam, G. P., II.24, 417, 2621, 2633; III.D.22, 92

Quaritch Books, II.300, 550; III.D.7; pp. 5–6, 15
Quercia, Jacopo della, II.1468

Rackham, Arthur, II.274–75
Rampant Lions Press, II.59
Random House, II.81–82, 191
Redgrave, G. R., II.353–54, 362, 364
Rembrandt, II.210–11
Richter, Henry, and J., II.779–80; pp. 29, 779, 786–90

Riemenschneider, Tilman, II.1475
Rigaud, Amable, II.1042, 1068, 1086, 1102, 1138
Rigaurd, S., II.1793, 1808, 1896; III.C.104
Riverside Press, II.169–72, 180–83, 394–97, 416, 526–28, 1081, 1089, 1093–94, 1106, 1115, 1123, 1132, 1217, 1225–26, 1276–79, 1402–3, 2062, 2068, 2341, 2604–8, 2616–17, 2765; III.C.62
Riviéré binding, II.598–600; p. 813
Romney, George, II.1787, 1857, 1869, 1872, 1889, 1893, 1905, 1910, 1919, 1924, 1932, 1938, 1980, 1990, 1994, 2037; p. 791
Romney, John, II.836, 878–79, 996, 1072, 1613–14, 1700–1701, 1819, 1832, 1845, 1900, 2003–4, 2009–10, 2016–17, 2031, 2039, 2043, 2066, 2080, 2093, 2099–2100, 2136, 2141; III.D.64
Rossetti, Dante Gabriel, II.234, 455, 793
Rossetti, William Michael, II., 2115, 2121, 2123–24, 2182–84, 2208, 2212–13, 2305, 2307, 2315–16, 2370; III.C.102
Routledge, George, II.17, 244–50, 266–67, 370, 372, 1159–60, 1216, 1346, 1678, 1970, 1982, 1991–92, 2011, 2019–20, 2034–35, 2051, 2056–58, 2063, 2071, 2077, 2086–88, 2098, 2132, 2150–52, 2159–60, 2177–78, 2258–60, 2270–72, 2351, 2359–60, 2401, 2408–10, 2441, 2580, 2685, 2691; IV.31
Rubens, Peter Paul, II.100, 2677, 2679; III.D.3
Ruzicka, Rudolph, II.427
Rysbrack, Michael, II.638; p. 803, 804

St. Martin's Press, II.445, 472, 1420, 2542, 2548, 2675, 2714–15, 2731
Salmasius, II.299–300, 2566, 2570, 2577, 2650
Samson Agonistes, II.67, 116, 118–21, 128, 131–32, 136–38, 144, 160–62, 187, 207, 241, 284, 304–5, 315–18, 428, 611–12, 620, 658, 675, 692–98, 703, 707, 720, 741, 773, 836, 857, 862, 878–79, 912, 987, 996, 999, 1412–13, 1417, 1422, 1424, 1428–30, 1441, 1445–47, 1451–52, 1456, 1476, 1511, 1515, 1528–40, 1542–69, 1571–77, 1579–85, 1587–1609, 1611–16, 1618–21, 1625–28, 1630–31, 1634–64, 1666, 1669–70, 1675–76, 1682, 1717–18, 1727, 1729–30, 1741, 1755, 1759–85, 1793–94, 1798, 1800–1801, 1803–4, 1809, 1816–17, 1819, 1821–24, 1826–27, 1832, 1843–45, 1848–49, 1858, 1861–62, 1865, 1873, 1879–82, 1884–85, 1900, 1906–7, 1911, 1945, 1957–58, 1969, 1972, 1989, 1996, 2001, 2012–13, 2018, 2026–27, 2036, 2041–42, 2046, 2054, 2059–62, 2064–65, 2069, 2072, 2078, 2089, 2092, 2096–97, 2103–4, 2115, 2121–31, 2139–40, 2145–49, 2157, 2162–66, 2168, 2175, 2181–82, 2184–85, 2191–95, 2197–2208, 2212, 2214–20, 2227–32, 2246–50, 2257–58, 2268–69, 2273–74, 2276, 2283–84, 2296–98, 2302–3, 2305, 2307–10, 2319–34, 2328–34, 2343–50, 2354–56, 2358, 2361, 2363–64, 2367–72, 2374, 2377–79, 2383, 2401–3, 2406–7, 2410–12, 2414, 2429–32, 2437–40, 2442–52, 2458–61, 2470–72, 2486, 2495–96, 2521, 2541, 2549, 2556, 2653–82, 2685, 2758, 2761, 2764; III.A.46; III.C.16, 36, 78, 82; III.D.22, 85; IV.44; p. 809

Sarto, Andrea del, II.2381, 2383
Sassoon, Siegfried, II.714; p. 26
Savage, Reginald, II.260
Savery, Roelandt, II.445
Schiavone, II.2383
Schlosser, Leonard, II.19, 308, 485, 635, 654, 701, 706, 782–83, 793, 911, 1272, 1575, 1590, 1683, 1689, 1726, 1762, 1878, 2666; III.B.1; pp. 4, 11
Scolar Press, II.326, 436, 1431–32, 1674–76, 1748–52, 1754
Scott, Foresman and Company, II.505–6, 510, 520, 522, 529, 1302, 1320, 1399
Scribner, Charles, II.270, 544, 562–63, 986, 1009, 1716–18, 2140, 2156, 2168, 2175, 2202–5, 2214, 2269; III.C.60, 70
Seabury Press, II.1479; III.D.24
Seccombe, Thomas, II.2115, 2121–24, 2182–84, 2208, 2212–13, 2305–7, 2370
Second Defence of the People of England, II.301, 2683. See also *Defence of the People of England*
Shakespeare, William, II.54, 220, 329, 508, 558, 872, 1221–22, 1271, 1373–74, 1534, 1683, 1787–88, 2106–7, 2556, 2669, 2692, 2699, 2725, 2729, 2765; III.A.19; III.B.31, 47, 53, 59, 68, 70; III.C.10, 30, 51, 54, 57, 90, 102, 116; III.D.9, 18, 41, 44, 48, 52–53, 89; IV.5, 7, 11–12, 41; p. 8
Sharpe, John, II.241, 825, 830, 848, 850, 867–69, 872, 886–88, 896, 899–900, 1596, 1599–1602, 1605–7, 1613–14, 1692–95, 1697–1701, 1800–1801, 1809, 1812, 1814, 1819; III.C.1, 66
Sharpe, W., II.2699
Shawcross, John T., II.5, 8, 66, 84–86, 104, 201–4, 216, 227–31, 232, 299, 314, 335, 342, 558, 559, 619, 620, 625, 630, 639, 643, 647, 649, 650, 658, 665, 667, 676, 678, 683, 688, 698, 711, 714, 721, 728, 731, 733, 741, 758, 771, 773, 782, 810, 1431, 1432, 1524–25, 1541, 1557, 1560, 1565, 1572, 1578, 1761, 1765, 1767, 1770, 1773, 1782, 1786, 1789, 2651, 2656, 2740, 2765; III.A.49; III.B.26–27; pp. 19, 25–26, 31, 155–56, 771
Shelley, Percy Blysse, II.2504, 2507, 2510, 2531, 2692; III.C.51
Shelley, Samuel, II.347
Shepard, Clark and Co., II.2006, 2032, 2040, 2134–35, 2144, 2172–73, 2196
Shepley, S. and C., II.967, 975
Sibley & Company, II.482, 1274; III.C.89
Sidney, Sir Philip, II.13, 15, 920, 1348, 2641, 2693; III.A.31; III.C.117; IV.9
signatures, II.2, 14, 30, 32, 76, 87, 101, 109, 111, 115, 116, 121, 129, 131, 138, 141, 155–56, 161–62, 169, 177, 181, 187, 198, 232, 242, 247, 268, 280, 294, 299, 311–13, 320–22, 334–35, 347, 349–50, 352, 354, 358–59, 372, 384, 387, 402, 408, 440, 449, 481, 551–55, 563, 566, 578, 595, 603, 605, 607–8, 618–19, 621, 626, 627, 631–32, 637, 645, 648, 657, 661, 663, 666, 668, 670, 673, 674, 676, 680–83, 685–86, 688–89, 700, 707–9, 711, 717, 720, 721, 724, 729, 732, 735, 742, 745, 750, 754, 757–59, 763–64, 771, 774, 777–78, 800–801, 815, 817–18, 832, 833, 835, 840, 846, 849, 858, 866, 872, 875–76, 878, 884, 895, 901–2, 908,

912, 919, 924, 926–27, 930, 938, 942, 946, 952, 956, 959, 969–71, 974, 991, 1000, 1004, 1010–13, 1025–26, 1031–33, 1040, 1048, 1053, 1059, 1063–64, 1067, 1069–71, 1075, 1079–81, 1091–92, 1097, 1107, 1118–19, 1132, 1142, 1153, 1155, 1193, 1218, 1242, 1261, 1263, 1271, 1273–74, 1285, 1288, 1293, 1295, 1296, 1329, 1334, 1341, 1342, 1348, 1354, 1379–80, 1408, 1418, 1528, 1534, 1537–38, 1542, 1552–55, 1558, 1561–62, 1565, 1566–67, 1575, 1579, 1582, 1608, 1611, 1617, 1625–26, 1634, 1645, 1660, 1662, 1664, 1666, 1670, 1690–91, 1695, 1699, 1708, 1715, 1724, 1727, 1772, 1775, 1781–83, 1785, 1788, 1798, 1802–3, 1806–8, 1811, 1815, 1826, 1837–39, 1842, 1844, 1852–53, 1857, 1874, 1877, 1880, 1885, 1892, 1898, 1899–1900, 1904, 1912–13, 1916, 1921–22, 1935, 1937, 1941, 1953, 1956, 1958, 1963, 1969, 1988, 1991, 1995, 1998–2000, 2010, 2017, 2022–23, 2025, 2042, 2050, 2070–71, 2075, 2077, 2090, 2101, 2123, 2128, 2130–31, 2137, 2142, 2156, 2158–59, 2164, 2170, 2174, 2177, 2196, 2201–2, 2208–9, 2218, 2226, 2231, 2234, 2238, 2242, 2251, 2254, 2260, 2284, 2291, 2307, 2309, 2316, 2319, 2323, 2326, 2341–42, 2364, 2374, 2377, 2382, 2398–2400, 2403, 2419, 2430–33, 2435, 2438, 2444–45, 2463, 2465, 2467, 2470, 2472, 2482, 2492, 2505, 2517, 2521, 2536, 2538, 2541, 2561, 2564–65, 2587, 2589, 2598–2600, 2602, 2621, 2628, 2630–32, 2631, 2632, 2657, 2663, 2698, 2721–22, 2731, 2734, 2757; III.A.3, 9, 13, 19, 22, 28, 31–32, 38–40, 45, 50; III.B.1–5, 12–13, 19, 21, 34, 37, 42, 48–49, 52, 59, III.C.12, 14, 20, 22, 38, 39, 50, 61, 69, 71–73, 80, 86, 91, 98, 102–4, 111, 113; III.D.10, 32, 36, 41, 69, 70, 83, 88, 91; IV.3–6, 16, 28

Silver, Burdett and Company, II.491–92
Simmons, Samuel, II.598, 598n, 600–605, 1431, 2740; III.C.93; IV.15
Simpkin and Marshall, II.1716, 1847, 1868
Smirke, Richard, II.297–98, 347
Sotheby's, II.775, 2753
Sowerby. *See* Milner and Sowerby
Sproul, George D., II.262
Stanhope, Busby, III.C.18
Stanhope Press, The, II.1800–1801, 1809, 1814, 1836; III.C.1
Sterne, Lawrence, II.951
Stevens, Wallace, II.1459, 1462
Stockhausen, William, II.1528; p. 13
Stonhouse, II.353–54
Stothard, Thomas, II.233, 696, 848, 850, 867–69, 886–88, 896–97, 899–900, 920–23, 967, 975, 1604, 1610, 1802, 1806, 1812, 1819, 2164, 2699; III.B.9; IV.27
Strang, William, II.267, 1272, 1346, 1456, 1469, 1483
Swan Press, The, II.328, 2726
Symmons, Charles, II.444, 458, 461, 2623; III.A.45; III.C.105, 108–9; p. 13
Symmons, Edward, III.A.45

Tasso, Torquato, II.2648; III.C.52
Taylor, F. Steward, II.569
Taylor, Robert H., pp. 3–9, 11–14, 17–18, 20–21, 26, 28
Tegg, Thomas and William, II.68, 828, 835, 838, 843, 863, 870, 881, 926, 1007, 1604, 1843–44, 1847, 1865–66, 1868, 1872, 1886, 1889, 1893, 1894–96, 1905, 1910, 1913, 1919, 1924, 1932–35, 1938, 1954, 1967–68, 1990, 2016–17, 2047–50, 2049; III.C.40; p. 24
Tenniel, John, II.351; IV.22–24, 31
Tennyson, Alfred Lord, II.2692, 2708; III.A.40; III.C.10, 51, 98; III.D.35, 73; IV.24, 32
tercentenary, II.48; III.D.5, 17, 68–77
Tetrachordon, II.302–3, 2751
Thackeray, William Makepeace, II.2153
Thistle Press, The, II.433
Thomas, W. C., II.499–503, 2684, 2698
Thornhill, James, II.1762–63
Thornhill, W. J., II.457
Thornthwaite, II.226, 229, 231
Thurston, John, II.798, 815–16, 825, 839, 855, 1011–12, 1799, 1803–4, 1821, 1871, 1877, 1892, 1975, 2081, 2095, 2101
Tickell, Thomas, II.1762–63; III.B.5; p. 16
Ticknor & Fields, II.373, 2155, 2622
Tiepolo, II.283, 288, 639, 643, 688, 781
Tilt, Charles. *See* Tilt & Bogue
Tilt & Bogue, II.355–57, 361, 436, 895, 916, 933, 966, 977, 998, 1018, 1121, 1859, 1901–4, 1926–29, 2025, 2041, 2376; IV.17; p. 6, 835
Todd, Henry John, II.232–33, 235, 616, 734, 765, 944–45, 1774, 1780, 61, 1795, 98, 1808, 1810, 1830, 1842, 1855, 1899, 1949, 1963, 2041, 2376, 2553; III.C.113–15
To Echo, II.2741–43; III.D.72; IV.34–35
Toland, John, II.76, 313, 1773–74, 2623, 2751; III.A.47–49; III.B.10, 64, 67; III.D.39, 100
Tonson, Jacob and R., II.86, 220, 342–44, 449, 604–5, 607–12, 61–18, 621–23, 627, 631, 636–38, 641, 647–51, 654, 657, 660–61, 667–70, 675, 680, 686, 691–98, 700, 702–3, 707, 710, 718, 720, 734, 744, 766, 786, 788, 798, 803, 805–6, 808, 815–16, 825, 830, 1500–1501, 1531–40, 1543–47, 1549, 1553–56, 1561–63, 1567, 1569, 1760–64, 1768, 1787; III.A.21; III.B.1, 5, 16, 19, 60, 62; III.D.75; pp. 13, 812
Townsend, H. J., II.353–54, 362, 364, 410
translations
  Armenian
    Paradise Lost, II.883; pp. 819
  Danish
    Paradise Lost, II.769, 1361
    Paradise Regained, II.1588
  Dutch
    Paradise Lost, II.624, 628, 633, 1113
  French
    Areopagitica, II.56
    collections, II.314, 653, 2763
    Comus, II.239
    L'Allegro/Il Penseroso, II.428
    Miltoniana, III.B.44; III.C.6, 27, 52, 110–11

translations, French (*continued*)
>*Of Education*, II.548
>*Paradise Lost*, II.640, 656, 687, 689–90, 716, 727, 742–43, 747, 749–50, 752, 755, 775, 813–14, 818–21, 829, 882, 928, 932, 949, 1054, 1074, 1076, 1086, 1396, 1425
>*Paradise Regained*, II.1541, 1673

German
>collections, II.1416
>*L'Allegro/Il Penseroso*, II.421
>*Of Education*, II.556
>*Paradise Lost*, II.679, 699, 701, 706, 773, 995, 1044, 1082, 1129, 1205, 1265, 1484
>*Paradise Regained*, II.1552
>*Samson Agonistes*, II.2667, 2672

Greek
>*Paradise Lost*, II.623
>poems, II.102–3, 188–92, 441–42, 1690, 1727–28, 1741, 1810, 2536–38, 2539–40, 2544–47, 2557, 2733–39
>*Samson Agonistes*, II.2657

Hungarian
>*Paradise Lost*, II.371

Icelandic
>*Paradise Lost*, II.903

Italian
>*Comus*, II.234, 237–39
>*Lycidas*, II.455
>*Paradise Lost*, II.630, 634–35, 643, 688, 782, 793, 901, 915, 1017, 1367
>poems, II.102–3, 188–92, 306–7, 341, 441–45, 1688–90, 1727–28, 1741, 1810, 1839–41, 2315, 2534, 2536–40, 2544–47, 2557–58, 2680, 2708, 2733–39

Japanese
>*Paradise Lost*, II.1519
>poems, II.2697

Latin
>*Arcades*, II.5
>collections, II.74–77, 91–92, 102–3, 188–92, 306–7, 440–48, 484, 531–32, 534, 1534, 1683–85, 1688–90, 1726–28, 1759–61, 1787, 1810, 1839–41, 2315, 2400, 2443, 2498, 2534, 2536–41, 2544–47, 2549, 2557–58, 2564, 2570–78, 2643, 2708, 2727–28, 2733–39, 2765
>*De Doctrina Christiana*, II.2745, 2748
>*Linguae*, II.450–51
>*Literae*, II.452–54
>*Lycidas*, II.458, 461, 471, 476–78, 480
>*Paradise Lost*, II.603, 606, 613, 623, 642, 659,
>*Paradise Regained*, II.1590, 1597, 1661
>*Samson Agonistes*, II.2657, 2680

Manx
>*Paradise Lost*, II.1109

Norwegian
>*Paradise Lost*, II.1503

Phonetic
>*Paradise Lost*, II.962

Portugese
>*Paradise Lost*, II.1200

Russian
>*Paradise Lost*, II.789, 1315, 1515
>*Paradise Regained*, II.1315, 1682

Spanish
>*Paradise Lost*, II.1110, 1139, 1359, 1409, 1419, 1513, 1518

Swedish
>*Paradise Lost*, II.844–46, 2055
>*Paradise Regained*, II.2055

Welsh
>*Paradise Lost*, II.859

Trianon Press, II.2706; III.D.7
Trinity Manuscript, II.77, 449, 463, 496, 1745, 1749–52, 2445, 2541, 2544, 2549, 2745; III.C.105
Troutman & Hayes, II.985, 1034
Turner, J. M. W., II.109–11, 368, 419, 499–502, 989, 1035, 1049, 1072, 1857, 1865, 1869, 1872, 1889, 1893–96, 1905, 1909, 1919, 1924, 1932–35, 1938, 1952–53, 1960, 1967–68, 1980–81, 1990, 1994–95, 2003, 2009–10, 2016–17, 2030–31, 2039, 2043–45, 2047–50, 2066–67, 2080, 2093–94, 2099–2100, 2133, 2136, 2168, 2684, 2698; III.D.85; IV.27; p. 791
Tuttle, Charles E., II.83

Unger, Leonard, p. 2
Uwins, Thomas, II.105–8, 1802, 1806–7, 1815, 1821, 1825, 1835, 1847, 1868, 1898, 1925, 1939; IV.16

van der Gucht, Gerard. *See* Gucht, Gerard van der
van der Gucht, John. *See* Gucht, John van der
van der Plaas, Peter. *See* Plaas, Peter van der
Vertue, George, II.77, 91, 157, 164, 168, 218, 338, 621, 631, 641, 654, 657, 660–61, 720–21, 734, 735, 744, 765, 855, 1467, 1549, 1553, 1557–58, 1562, 1569, 1575–76, 1583, 1762–63, 1768, 1782, 1787, 1857, 1859–60, 1869, 1872, 1889, 1893–96, 1905, 1910, 1919, 1924, 1932–35, 1938, 1967–68, 2016–17, 2047–50, 2146–47, 2315, 2318, 2339, 2501–2, 2720–24, 2752–53; III.C.71; III.D.30, 101, 105, 106
Visiak, E. H., II.188–92, 278–80, 440; p. 27
Vivares, II.835, 838, 843
Voltaire, II.630, 805, 806, 849; III.A.1; III.B.36, 69; III.D.104

Walker, John, II.314, 2072, 2257–58, 2272
Walpole, Henry, II.313
Ward, Lock & Co., II.339, 565
Warne, Frederick, II.561–63, 2034–35, 2051, 2056–58, 2063, 2071, 2128–29, 2139–40, 2156, 2168, 2175, 2187, 2194, 2197, 2198, 2200–7, 2214–16, 2247–48, 2269, 2298, 2319,

2323–34, 2328–30, 2348–50, 2354–55, 2358, 2363–64, 2374, 2406–7, 2411–12, 2414, 2429–32, 2438–40, 2442, 2472–73, 2486; p. 22

Warton, Thomas, II.233, 235, 944–45, 1688–90, 1699, 1810, 1833, 2566, 2705; III.A.29; III.B.31; III.C.93

Washbourne, Henry, II.895, 976, 1055, 1858, 1865

Waterhouse, J. H., II.499–502, 2684, 2698

Wesley, Charles and John, II.709; IV.1

Westall, Richard, II.91–92, 164, 168, 241, 696, 723, 848, 850, 857, 862, 867–69, 886–88, 896–97, 899–900, 908, 912, 1040, 1072, 1596, 1599–1603, 1605–7, 1613–14, 1692–1701, 1787, 1800–1801, 1809, 1814, 1819, 1827, 1848–49, 1857, 1860, 1869, 1872, 1874, 1878, 1888–89, 1893, 1897, 1905, 1910, 1912, 1918–19, 1922–24, 1931–32, 1938, 1952–53, 1959, 1980–81, 1988, 1990, 1994–95, 2003, 2009–10, 2016–17, 2031, 2039, 2043–44, 2066, 2080, 2091, 2093, 2099, 2100, 2136, 2147, 2158, 2318; III.C.1, 7; IV.20; pp. 791–92

White, Thomas Holt, II.9; III.C.117

Whittingham, Charles. *See* Chiswick Press

Whittington Press, II.582, 591

Wimperis, E. M., II.561–63

Windus. *See* Chatto & Windus

Wingate, Allan, II.431

Wolfe, Don M., II.205–6; III.D.110

Wolfe, Richard J., II.62

Woolworth, Ainsworth & Co., II.139–40, 155, 1088, 1091, 1103

Wordsworth, William, II.164, 349, 371, 383, 536, 1008, 1469, 1716–18, 1933, 1967, 1980, 1994, 2009, 2031, 2039, 2043, 2047–49, 2066, 2080, 2093, 2099–2100, 2136, 2630–37, 2692, 2708, 2764; III.B.46; III.C.51; III.D.73; IV.11, 21

Yale University Press, II.205–8, 447, 554, 557, 2763; III.D.5

Zaehnsdorf binding, II.923, 1384; III.B.54